The River Cottage

Mushroom Handbook

The River Cottage Mushroom Handbook

by John Wright

introduced by
Hugh Fearnley-Whittingstall

www.rivercottage.net

BLOOMSBURY
LONDON · NEW DELHI · NEW YORK · SYDNEY

to my Mother

First published in Great Britain 2007
This paperback edition published 2012

Text © 2007 by John Wright
Mushroom photography © 2007 by John Wright
Recipe photography © 2007 by Colin Campbell
Additional photography © 2007 by Alan Outen, Gordon Dickson,
Alan Hills, Bryan Edwards and Marie Derome

The moral right of the author has been asserted.

Bloomsbury Publishing Plc, 50 Bedford Square, London WC1B 3DP
Bloomsbury Publishing, London, New Delhi, New York and Sydney

A CIP catalogue record for this book is available from the British Library.

ISBN 978 1 4088 3605 7
10 9 8 7 6 5 4 3 2 1

Designed by willwebb.co.uk
Printed in China by C&C Offset Printing Co., Ltd.

All papers used by Bloomsbury Publishing are natural, recyclable products made from wood grown in well-managed forests. The manufacturing processes conform to the environmental regulations of the country of origin.

www.bloomsbury.com/rivercottage

While every effort has been made to ensure the accuracy of the information contained in this book, in no circumstances can the publisher or the author accept any legal responsibility or liability for any loss or damage (including damage to property and/or personal injury) arising from any error in or omission from the information contained in this book, or from the failure of the reader to properly and accurately follow any instructions contained in the book.

Contents

Starting Out	8
Edible Species	40
Poisonous Species	136
Recipes	180
The End	246

Mushroom hunting can be a perilous pursuit for the unwary and I have walked a narrow path in this book between gently encouraging you, dear reader, and frightening you to death.

I would like to say that this is the only book on mushrooms you will ever need, but I would be lying. I regularly consult over 50 books and, while you may not need to go to such anorak-y extremes, I do recommend that you buy at least one more identification guide.

And before you go any further, it is essential that you read the advice on p.45.

It's a thrill to introduce the first of the River Cottage Handbooks, in which we intend to explore some of the more specialised areas of our approach to food (and indeed to life), to share our passion for them, and generally show you the ropes. In mushrooms, I believe we could not have chosen a better subject to start the series. And in John Wright, I am certain that we could not have found a better man to write it.

The first time I went out foraging with John we had our sights set on one of the greatest fungal prizes of them all: the Summer Truffle. I had never found one – and didn't seriously expect to. But John was full of confidence. He knew there were Truffles to be rustled at his secret location – and he insisted on blindfolding me on the way there. (Luckily he was driving.)

At John's suggestion, we had recruited a third party to the hunt. She was known to have an instinctive nose for a Truffle, and I had done my best to hone her skills beforehand. John had given me a phial of a chemical called dimethyl sulphide – the synthesised version of the natural Truffle smell – and I had successfully trained her to find and dig up potatoes steeped in this pungent elixir. The only problem was that she would insist on eating them. 'She' was my resident breeding saddleback sow, Delia.

When we arrived, Delia was released into the undergrowth. She clearly found the whole experience thrilling. Right from the start she was snuffling up little treats from the forest floor. For all I could tell, she might have eaten ten truffles in the first half hour. John made a couple of valiant attempts to get between her snout and whatever morsel seemed to be exciting it; on one occasion he rescued an acorn, on another a small stone.

Finally, after a good couple of hours, John intervened in a particularly focused bout of Delia's nose-digging, and scrabbled a slightly muddy lump from the ground. As he brushed the earth from its stippled black surface he said, in a cautious, almost disbelieving voice: 'It's a Truffle. It really is … a Truffle.' We ate it right there and then in the woods – grated onto eggs scrambled over a camping stove. And Delia also managed to get her nose in the pan.

It was the beginning of a journey, and a friendship based around foraging, that has led meanderingly to this book. Of course mycologically speaking we are leagues apart – John is one of Britain's foremost mushroom experts, whereas I'm just a happy-go-lucky enthusiast, keen to find and eat as many species as possible, ideally without poisoning myself. But that is rather the point. This is the mushroom book I have been waiting for – the one that has been missing from my life.

Some years back I mentioned to John that, much as I enjoyed some of the existing literature on mushrooms (Roger Phillips for his taxonomic details, Jane Grigson for her gastronomic inspiration), there wasn't really a book that I felt hit the right note for those starting out on the mushroom adventure – or indeed for those who, like me, already loved mushroom hunting but wanted to consolidate their somewhat random knowledge and patchy experience. What I wanted to know (without becoming a fully fledged fungus academic) was how to be a better mushroom hunter, and how to enjoy my mushrooms more. Did he know of a book that could help me? 'Probably not,' he said. Then he added, with a twinkle, 'Perhaps I'll just have to write one.'

In the meantime, I realised, the best way for me to achieve my goal was simply to spend more time looking for mushrooms with John. He is a great person to forage with, generous with his vast knowledge (but never excessively so). He has a gift for capturing the charms or quirks of a species, and its place in the great scheme of things (I've always loved John's 'fact' that a Morel is as far from a Cep in the chain of life as a Christmas tree is from a cabbage). In explaining mushrooms, he never dissipates their mystery, but instead celebrates their sheer fabulousness – in the true sense of the word.

A couple of years back I asked John if he would like to host some mushroom foraging days for us at River Cottage HQ. And I have discovered that it isn't just me who finds his take on mushrooms so engaging. After their day with John, our guests leave us feeling charged with the confidence to go forth and forage on their own.

When the opportunity to make a River Cottage mushroom book came along, of course I wanted John to write it. I wondered, though, if it was too much to hope that the same wit and sparkle that he shows when leading a forage would find its way onto the page. I needn't have worried. One shouldn't expect to laugh out loud when reading about mushrooms – but I promise you will. John may take the fear out of fungus, but never the fun.

Hugh Fearnley-Whittingstall, Dorset, June 2007

Starting Out

What are mushrooms and toadstools?

'Venomous and muthering', 'evil ferment', 'poysonous damp weeds'. Few people of the past had a good word to say about fungi and, until the early eighteenth century, no one had the faintest idea what these 'earthie excrescences' actually were, though this did not stop people making something up. Fitting uncomfortably into the more familiar world of plants and animals, these mysterious agents of putrescence, decay and sometimes death have always been treated with great suspicion. But, practical people as they had to be, the ancients sensibly classified the fungi into two important groups: the 'esculenti' and the 'perniciosi'. This attitude, shared by this present book, was neatly expressed in the sixteenth-century *Grete Herball*, where we find the best known of all fungal quotations:

> 'Fungi ben mussheroms; there be two manners of them, one maner is deedley and slayeth them that eateth them and be called tode stoles, and the other doeth not.'

These pretty words go most of the way to answering the question I am asked most often after 'Can I eat it?' – 'What is the difference between a mushroom and a toadstool?' I think that the simplest differentiation is this:

> 'A toadstool has a cap and a stem and you can't eat it, a mushroom has a cap and a stem and you can.' Slayeth and doeth not.

Much has been written about the derivation and meaning of the words 'mushroom' and 'toadstool' and little agreed upon. 'Mushroom' is from the Old French 'mousseron', itself derived from 'mousse', which means 'moss' and is probably a reference to the soft texture of most fungi. The word 'toadstool' is very likely no more than it seems; the 'toad' part reflecting a perception of that animal's poisonous nature and the 'stool' a simple reference to shape. 'Toadstool' has sometimes, as above, been rendered as 'tode stole' with 'tode' being the German word for death. Whichever derivation one accepts, it is clear that 'toadstool' is a pejorative term, while 'mushroom' is not. There is a narrower definition that is very useful, though it can contradict the first one:

> 'A mushroom is a member of the genus *Agaricus*.'

The genus *Agaricus* includes *A. bisporus*, *A. campestris*, *A. arvensis* and *A. silvicola*, the Cultivated, Field, Horse and Wood Mushroom respectively, so you can see the sense of it. Indeed, the term 'the true mushrooms' is often used for *Agaricus* species.

The contradiction exists because there is also *A. xanthodermus*, the Yellow Stainer, which is poisonous. A pity, really. One last word on etymology: the word 'fungus' is derived from 'spoggos', which is Greek for sponge. By this time, most of my enquirers have regretted their question.

While there will always be more to learn, the essential nature of fungi has now been firmly established. Their inexplicable ability to appear suddenly in the same spot year after year, without apparent roots and sometimes in those mysterious rings, is now all explained. Mushrooms and toadstools – and most of the many other fungal forms one sees in the woods and fields – are not organisms. They are organs. The bulk of the organism is underground (or within some other sub-stratum, such as wood) and takes the form of microscopically thin (about a tenth of the diameter of a human hair) fibres called hyphae. These form a largely invisible, but nevertheless huge, cotton wool-like mass called a mycelium. Our mushrooms and toadstools are, quite simply, the reproductive organs, the fruit bodies, of this larger organism; their sole purpose is to produce and disperse spores. Billions of them.

So now we understand that mushrooms and toadstools grow quickly because all of their raw materials are ready and waiting in the mycelium, and they grow in the same place year after year because that is where the actual organism is situated. Mushrooms and toadstools do have the equivalent of roots, but they are usually too thin to see and they sometimes form rings because the mycelium from which they spring grows outwards from a central point and dies off in the middle. No lightning, no dragons, no pixies.

Early writers were correct in their assessment that fungi fitted poorly into the world of plants and animals. Fungi are neither. They inhabit their own great kingdom – Kingdom Fungi – which now sits alongside the other great kingdoms – Plantae, Animalia, and two or three more.

Organisms belong to their particular kingdom simply because their parents did, and not because they have certain characteristics (in the same way that dolphins still wouldn't be fish even if they looked twice as fishy as they do). Nevertheless, fungi do have certain properties which, taken together, distinguish them from members of the other kingdoms. Their cells are, in fact, the hyphae mentioned above and, unlike most plant and animal cells, need many nuclei scattered along their length to control the various cell functions. The cell walls are made not from cellulose as in plants, or proteins as in animals, but of chitin, a material more familiar as the crunchy bit of cockroaches. Their most important property viewed from an ecological viewpoint is an inability, shared with all animals and a very few plants, to make their own food. They either externally digest organic matter and absorb the resulting simple, soluble soup through their cell walls, or are provided for by plants with which they have formed a symbiotic relationship.

As with plants and animals, fungi are divided up into family groups. Of the major divisions of the fungi there are two that interest the mushroom hunter – the *Ascomycota* and the *Basidiomycota*. The former contains species as diverse as Truffles and Morels; the latter contains most of the rest of the species in this book. They are sometimes more approachably called the 'spore shooters' and the 'spore droppers'. These names are references to the hugely complex microscopic mechanisms by which the spores are formed and released.

Brian Spooner and Peter Roberts in their highly readable book *Fungi* point out that there is a lot more going on behind the scenes than the average mushroom hunter can imagine. I do hope that some of the excitement and wonder of mycology rubs off on you as you search for your supper.

How to collect fungi

There is a pure and all-consuming joy that comes from foraging for one's own food, a joy where other worries are forgotten in the single-minded pursuit of a quarry. Foraging is a deep instinct that has been shared by all our ancestors right back to that famous protozoan we can all call Grandmother and we are the poorer when we ignore it. Nevertheless, as with most joys, there are a few practical issues that need to be considered. Most of the rest of the book deals with that most practical issue of how not to poison yourself; this chapter considers all the others.

Mushroom hunting and the law

The laws governing the activities of us simple foragers are surprisingly complicated and not entirely settled.

The 1981 Wildlife and Countryside Act, which is often quoted when the legality of picking mushrooms is discussed, is steadfastly irresolute and vague on the whole matter and of almost no help at all. There is, however, a general acceptance in common law, enshrined in the 1968 Theft Act, that a person may collect the 'four Fs' – Fruit, Flowers, Foliage and Fungi – as long as these are growing wild and are collected for personal use. This right applies everywhere, even on private land, but there are exceptions and caveats:

   i. In some places there are bylaws that prohibit or restrict picking. If this is the case, there should be a notice to that effect.
  ii. It appears to be illegal to collect plants or any part of a plant (which would include blackberries!) from 'Right to Roam' land, but whether this includes fungi is unclear.
 iii. A question of legality hangs over collecting from 'sites of special scientific interest' (SSSIs), though it is unlikely that picking a few common mushrooms from such sites will land you in trouble.

If you are collecting commercially, even on a very small scale, you must ask permission from the landowner. If you don't, then you will be stealing.

While you might be allowed to pick fungi at a particular location, you might not be allowed to be there to do it; you could be trespassing. The law of trespass (England and Wales only; there is no Scottish law of trespass) says that if you go onto land that does not belong to you without the permission of the owner and if your action is not covered under legislation such as 'Right to Roam' or 'Rights of Way', then you are trespassing. (Incidentally, despite all those

'Trespassers will be Prosecuted' signs, you cannot be prosecuted – though you could, in principle, be sued.) If the landowner asks you to leave, you must do so immediately by the quickest route. It is an interesting fact that the landowner is not entitled to claim any mushrooms you might have picked from his land, though having established yourself so firmly on the moral lowground it would be an inopportune moment to argue the matter!

Many of the places you are likely to go to pick mushrooms, such as Forestry Commission or local authority land, are places where public access may be permitted, but it is just that – permission, not a right. Some organisations and authorities impose a limit on the amount you can collect per visit as part of a 'code of conduct'. This is usually one and a half kilograms and seems generous enough to me.

Britain has so far avoided most of the closed seasons, licences and quotas that have been introduced in mainland Europe, but as the popularity of mushroom hunting increases, it is unlikely that we will escape them for much longer.

To sum up: Don't trespass to pick fungi and, if in doubt, ask permission.

Mushroom hunting and conservation

While a casual consideration of the matter would suggest that pulling a mushroom out of the ground is as destructive as pulling a plant out of the ground, in fact, it is not. When you pull up a plant that is the end of it, but when you pull up a mushroom all you are doing is removing a reproductive organ. Eye-watering, yes; fatal, no. The main part of the organism, the cotton wool-like mycelium, is underground or within the log on which the mushroom is growing, and picking a mushroom is more like picking an apple off a tree – pick all the crab apples you want and the tree remains. Of course, you may affect the long-term reproductive success of the organism concerned, but consider how much crab apple jelly you would have to make before crab apple trees went into decline! What you cannot do by picking a mushroom is damage the fungus itself.

Does this mean that we can pick as many mushrooms as we like without damaging their viability? Well, maybe it does. It is probably only in mushrooming hotspots, where every single mushroom is picked shortly after it takes the unwise decision to pop its head out of the ground, that there is a real threat to the long-term survival of popular species, and then only locally. Furthermore, by the time mushrooms are found, they have usually produced billions of spores and, despite the best efforts of mushroom hunters, many more mushrooms go undiscovered than find their way into the kitchen.

Research in this area is extremely difficult and while many conservation bodies, zealous in the defence of their patch, point to over-picking as a cause of any perceived decline in mushroom populations, actual hard evidence is completely lacking. Few people would deny that there has been a decline, but some of this may have been caused by pollution and most, perhaps nearly all, has been caused by habitat loss. The loss of meadow and pasture, of ancient woodland and heath, has put great pressure on many species and impoverished us all. The conservation and creation of wildlife habitats will do far more for fungi than any amount of self-denial by foragers looking for their dinner.

Having argued forcefully that picking mushrooms does no damage, I am now going to beat a small retreat. Fungi expend enormous resources in producing their fruit bodies (mushrooms) and do so for a reason. On this basis I take the entirely unscientific view that, despite any lack of evidence that extensive picking is damaging, one should err on the side of caution and exercise some restraint. For each of the edible species described in this book I give some indication as to how common they are and sometimes indicate how much of this restraint should be employed.

There are four fungi that are considered to be so endangered that they are specifically protected under the 1981 Wildlife and Countryside Act and it is illegal to pick them. They are the beautiful yellow and purple Royal Bolete (*Boletus regius*), a frankly rather dull bracket fungus called *Buglossoporus pulvinus*, and a 'Puffball on a stick' known as the Sandy Stiltball (*Battaraea phalloides*). It is an extraordinary if inconsequential fact that the fourth member of the select quartet, the Lion's Mane Fungus (*Hericium erinaceus*), while still rare in the wild is now cultivated and can be bought in delicatessens. It is rather like setting up a panda farm and selling panda-burgers.

If you need further persuasion, here are a few other reasons for leaving at least some of the edible mushrooms you find where they are:

Picking only 'middle aged' mushrooms has some advantages – the youngsters have not usually acquired their full flavour (or size) and have not had chance to produce any spores at all, and the oldies, while past their culinary best, are producing spores by the billion.

Maggots do nothing to endear themselves to the mushroom hunter, but then the reverse is also true. Fungi play an extremely important role in supporting a huge variety of insect larvae and other organisms, many of them specially adapted to take advantage of these ephemeral habitats. The wholesale removal of fruit bodies can seriously affect these invertebrate populations.

Forests that have been scoured clean by bands of mushroom hunters have a distinctively barren look to them, so do leave some for others to enjoy.

The mushroom hunter's toolkit

This is a small and simple affair, consisting, at its most basic, of a basket, a knife and a determined expression. For those who want to take more, this is what I recommend:

A basket: it does not matter which sort. The notion that using one with an open weave allows spores to be scattered through the forest as you walk is fanciful in the extreme.

Plastic containers: to protect the more delicate species and in which to quarantine those as yet unnamed specimens which must always be kept away from your known edible finds. Plastic bags are completely useless, by the way, as the mushrooms sweat and become squashed. If your intellectual curiosity is roused by any of the species of tiny fungi that abound alongside their larger, edible cousins, then one of those compartmented boxes beloved of fishermen is ideal for transporting them back home in good condition.

A knife: for cutting mushrooms from trees (a perilous occupation, as I know to my cost) and for digging mushrooms out of the ground. If you want to look really professional, you can buy special knives that have a little cleaning brush on the end.

A hand lens: one of the folding 'loupe' variety is invaluable for looking at some of the finer identifying characteristics on your mushroom finds. It also instantly gives you an authoritative air when you hang it on a cord around your neck.

A notebook or a digital camera: to record the habitat in which the mushroom was found. Habitat is often an important clue in identification – some mushrooms are only found in pine woods, some only in beech woods, and so on.

A good field guide: the one you are holding should serve you well though you can never have too many. I have over 50 books that I use to identify my finds and they are getting very heavy to carry around. There are another 40 or so on my Christmas list. The main reason for actually taking a book with you is to prevent the heart-rending dilemma that comes when you find a huge patch of very promising-looking fungi and don't know whether to pick them or not.

A hat: as well as keeping the rain off, a hat will help protect your head from brambles and low branches, shield your eyes so that you can spot mushrooms lurking on a dark forest floor and, *in extremis*, act as an emergency mushroom basket.

When to look

While flowering plants produce their fruit and flowers to a timetable that seldom varies by more than a couple of weeks, fungi have a more independent spirit and take delight in appearing almost at random during the year and sometimes not at all. However, despite the vagaries of many species, there is undoubtedly a mushroom season and that, of course, is in the autumn.

The start of the season is ultimately a matter of rainfall; if August and September are dry, the season will be delayed. The end of the season occurs with the first hard frost, though a mild spell after this may revive mushroom hunting fortunes for a while. Of course, the climate is not the same everywhere and there will be considerable variation between one part of the country and another.

Sometimes we have a lovely wet, cool summer (I will sulk all the way through a hot August) and then the mushrooms come up from June to November. In a mild winter, mushrooms can be found until January. Occasionally, we have both, though there is a limit to how many fruit bodies a fungal mycelium can produce in one year.

In addition to the autumn, there is a distinct spring season when two notable mushrooms can be found: St George's Mushrooms and Morels. There are also several species that like the summer months: many of the Boletes, some *Agaricus* species, and Giant Puffballs. Even during autumn itself, some succession is discernible with species such as Blewits, Waxcaps and Velvet Shanks coming late in the year, giving us welcome continuation and variety.

Where to look

The rudest question you can ask a mushroom hunter is, 'Where did you find those?', but I am in a generous mood and prepared to pass on a few tips.

Very broadly there are two types of places worth looking – grassland and woodland. Apart from those rare lucky days when your basket fills with woodland Ceps and Chanterelles, it is in grassland that the big feasts are found. A good Field Mushroom field or Parasol patch can yield mushrooms by the tens of kilograms. I once found about 35kg of Giant Puffballs in a single field, and I remember on one glorious day standing on a hillside where the Parasols were beyond counting.

Grassland tends to come in varying grades according to, among other things such as acidity, how long it has been left undisturbed. Field Mushrooms can appear in quite young grassland while the wonderful Waxcaps, which take much longer to become established, are familiar in very old grassland. Grassland species are nearly always saprotrophs (they live on dead organic matter). As they grow outwards, they often enrich or impoverish the grass, producing distinctive rings. These give a clue to the presence of the mycelium even before the mushrooms appear in the familiar fairy ring pattern. Rings of dark grass can often be seen from across a valley and you can make a mental note of them for later exploration. Sometimes fairy rings are complete, with mushrooms all the way round; more often they are partial and mushrooms appear only on fragmentary arcs of the original ring.

Grass that has grazing animals on it is far richer in fungi than are hay meadows. The best demonstration of this is the Field Mushroom, which has a strong preference for fields where horses are kept. Mushrooms do not like to fight their way through tall grass, so intensively grazed land is nearly always the best. Grass that is a beautiful lush green has probably been 'improved' with nitrates and phosphates and is unlikely to be a happy home for many fungi.

While grassland provides us with delicious mushrooms in abundance, the real gourmet fungi – the ones you pay a lot for in restaurants – come from the woods. Ceps, Chanterelles, Horns of Plenty, Morels and Truffles are all woodland species. It is also true to say that there are more woodland fungi, edible or not, than grassland fungi; two-thirds of the mushrooms in this book are found in woods.

Because many fungi can only grow near certain tree species with which they can form a symbiotic relationship, it is possible to approach a patch of forest with an educated optimism about what you might hope to find.

Beech and oak jointly lead the field in having the largest number of fungal species found near them. Over 2,000 fungal species have been found in association with, or at least in close proximity to, both these trees. Next come birch and pine with 1,600 species each. Many other types of tree are associated with fungi, but the fact that some are not explains why ash and sycamore woods prove to be such poor hunting grounds. The worst large tree for finding fungi of any description is the yew.

How, or indeed if, the wood is managed has a strong bearing on its ability to produce fungi. Fungal fruiting bodies do not like competition, and undergrowth is a major limiting factor; anything that reduces it, such as physical intervention, the encouragement of a heavy forest canopy or the introduction of grazing, will open out the forest and allow the fungi to establish a foothold. On the other hand, over-tidy foresters who habitually remove fallen trees deprive us of fungi such as Oyster Mushrooms that depend on this dead wood for their livelihood.

So, there you are, standing in the middle of a nice open piece of beech woodland expecting to be surrounded by mushrooms. Except that the mushrooms are mysteriously absent. The depths of a seemingly perfect wood are often almost devoid of fungi. The problem is not that the fungal mycelium from which the mushrooms grow is unhappy here, but that it is *too* happy. Life is easy, so why bother to expend any energy on an ungrateful future generation? It is only when the mycelium runs out of food or is otherwise threatened that it gives any thought to the morrow and decides to reproduce. This is the 'car park' effect. Experienced mushroom hunters seldom set off straight away into the depths of a wood but hang around the edge of the tarmac. Fungal mycelia cannot eat car parks and they'll start to panic; it is then that they produce their fruiting bodies. Of course, it is not just car parks that have this effect; so do any other places where there is a change from one environment to another – wood margins, paths, soil change, different vegetation, earth banks. Life on the edge.

It is obvious that the countryside is where most wild mushrooms will be found, but the city dweller does not always have to travel so far. Many mushrooms are quite at home in odd corners of the urban environment: parks and gardens, road verges and, my particular favourite, cemeteries, can all be very productive. Certain species of Morel are the best-known of the metropolitan mushrooms, having acquired pieds-à-terre in the forest bark mulch that covers so many domestic and municipal flowerbeds. Shaggy Inkcaps are found much more frequently on road verges than in fields, and there is one species, a close relative of the cultivated mushroom, called the Pavement Mushroom (*Agaricus bitorquis*), which effortlessly punches its way through tarmac leaving neat round holes.

A certain amount of extra caution is required when picking mushrooms in town because of the increased risk of pollution, both airborne and from soil residues (and, we must never forget, dogborne). Mushrooms are well known for their ability to concentrate heavy metals, though the risk from this unfortunate talent has reduced considerably since the removal of lead from petrol. But you do need your wits about you. I once picked a nice collection of Fairy Ring Champignons from a park in Stockholm only to realise, just in time, that the barely perceptible fine white powder on their caps was a fungicide.

How to look

During a British Mycological Society foray some years ago, our party of mushroom hunters bumped into a party of bird watchers – we were all looking down and they were all looking up.

It is surprising how bad people are at spotting mushrooms when they first try – it takes a while to train your eyes to distinguish rocks or leaves from mushrooms. Incidentally, the best mushroom hunters are children as they are enthusiastic, generally have better eyesight than their adult companions and are much nearer the ground. Sometimes people confuse fungus foraging with hiking and march off as though the hounds of hell are after them, forgetting that they are already where they want to be! So, slow right down, scan the ground as you go and follow as erratic a path as the terrain will allow. Most people do well with a gentle wander around, but I usually resort to a certain amount of energetic thrashing about in the undergrowth for fear of missing something.

When you find some fungi, remember that you have found two things – fungi *and* a place where fungi like to grow. Stop and look carefully all around as there are likely to be other species very nearby.

I seldom cut mushrooms to pick them. I much prefer to gently ease the whole fruit body out of the ground with a knife and so preserve the entire specimen for identification. There are several important characteristics at the base of the stem of many mushrooms that are crucial in establishing their identity; a colour change on cutting, a small root, a volva (bag). If you cut above the ground, these are lost to you. Of course, if you are absolutely sure you know what you are picking, then cutting will do no harm and your supper won't get covered in dirt. There is no conservation reason for choosing one method over the other.

One last tip: don't walk backwards; you're bound to squash something.

How to tell one fungus from another

It would be wonderful if all the edible fungi came with a little green sticker and all the poisonous fungi with a red one. Unfortunately, nature is not so accommodating and there are no such short cuts, not one. However, I do often hear of sure-fire tests that have worked for people over many years. Those for whom they haven't worked I don't hear from quite so often.

Just for the record, here are a few tests that I've come across that, if applied rigorously, will eventually lead you to an early grave:

'It is OK if you can peel the cap.'
I often show people how easily the skin of the Death Cap can be peeled.

'If other animals can eat it, then so can you.'
Slugs have a totally different metabolism to humans and can munch on a Death Cap with impunity, as, in fact, can rabbits!

'If it doesn't turn a silver spoon black, it is fine.'
This is complete nonsense.

'No mushroom that grows on wood is poisonous.'
… except for the Funeral Bell (*Galerina marginata*), Sulphur Tuft (*Hypholoma fasciculare*) and half a dozen others.

*'It is fine if you only eat mushrooms with black gills …
or is it white gills?'*

My favourite piece of useless advice comes from the second-century physician and poet, Nicander:

*'The rank in smell, and those of livid show,
All that at roots of oak or olive grow,
Touch not! But those upon the fig-tree's rind
Securely pluck – a safe and savoury kind!'*

So how do you know whether a mushroom is edible or not? You need to find out its name. I concentrate here on mushrooms and toadstools, that is, anything with a cap and a stem. Other fungi, such as the Jelly Ear, Puffball, Truffle and Beefsteak Fungus, are so distinctive that they should not prove too difficult to identify and are not easily confused with poisonous species.

Mushrooms and toadstools are notoriously difficult to identify with any great certainty. With the flowering plants there are many clear characteristics that help you to distinguish one species from another – number and colour of petals, shape of leaf, hairiness and so on – but when it comes to mushrooms and toadstools they all have a stem and a cap and everything else is a matter of detail. This similarity of form exists because, of course, mushrooms are *organs*, not *organisms*. In fact, they are reproductive organs and their form is simply a matter of function, which is why they all look much the same. Imagine you were given the task of identifying a selection of mammals just by studying their reproductive organs and you will see the problem. (Don't imagine it for too long.)

This difficulty is compounded because a young fungus may look quite unlike a mature one and different environments produce strikingly different examples of the same species. If you find it a frustrating task telling one fungus from another, then I must tell you that so do I. Often I will spend an hour or two with piles of books and a microscope studying a single toadstool only to be forced to admit defeat, whereupon I tear the offending specimen to shreds, then stamp on it, then throw it into the bin, then set fire to the bin. I did say it was frustrating. On the other hand, the joy and satisfaction of achieving an accurate identification is complete and I hope that you will embrace the little bit of hard work as simply part of the fun. Let us then put potential frustration to one side and consider the following positive thoughts:

There are fewer than 100 species, both edible and poisonous, described in this book and, if your interest is purely of a culinary nature, these are all the fungi you will ever want to learn.

Although there are thousands of mushrooms and toadstools, they do, mercifully, fall into natural groups or genera that usually share certain characteristics. So, among others, there are the Amanitas (white gills, ring on the stem, bag at the base of the stem) and the Russulas (stocky, gills brittle). This helps enormously as the human brain is very good at categorising things and if you can work out which genus a fungus belongs to, you are three-quarters of the way there.

Learning what a mushroom or toadstool looks like is similar to learning what a particular person looks like. Superficially, one person looks much like another, but subtle differences enable us to easily recognise a friend in a crowd. So it is with fungi – once you have become familiar with a species, you will be able to name it at 30 paces.

But where on earth do you start? Well, the time-honoured way is to pick up a mushroom book and flick through the pictures until you spot something that looks a bit like the fungus you have in your hand. Don't do it. In fact, I suggest that you put your books back on the shelf for a moment and turn your mind to the most important thing of all – looking at the mushroom.

There is no single process for identifying a fungus. It all depends on which fungus you are talking about and how much you know about it already. Here, however, is the basic process:

1. Take notes in the field or wood
2. Obtain a spore print
3. Study the fungus
4. Follow a 'key' to find a possible name for the fungus or at least which genus or group it belongs to
5. Check the answer with pictures and descriptions.

1 Take notes in the field

Your study should really begin at the moment you find your fungus. Take a note of where it was growing, under what sort of tree, whether it was growing singly, in a ring or in tufts or on wood, and so on. Check the smell and any colour change when the flesh is cut as these can be terribly important considerations that freshly picked specimens usually exhibit best.

2 Obtain a spore print

You may think that spore colour is rather an esoteric characteristic to consider, but do believe me when I say that it is one of the most important. For reasons that will become evident, if you know the spore colour, you will know where to start looking in your book. I must add that if you already have a reasonably good idea about the identity of the mushroom in front of you, a spore print may not be strictly necessary – spore prints are most useful when you haven't got the faintest idea where to start.

Spores come in several colours – white is the most common, but they move through many shades of cream to yellow and warm and cool browns through to dark browns, then black. You will also find, quite commonly, pink spores and there is one toadstool, the highly poisonous False Parasol (*Chlorophyllum molybdites*), which has green spores.

It is often possible to guess the colour of the spores by looking at the gills on which they grow. Unfortunately, this short cut does not *always* work, as sometimes either the gills themselves are highly coloured or they are pale and the coloured spores have yet to form. A much better way is to take a spore print. Cut off the cap and lay it on a piece of white paper. Alternatively, make a hole in a piece of white paper, push the stem of the mushroom through the hole and sit it on a glass or cup. If you can cover the top, it will prevent the mushroom from drying out.

Depending on the freshness of your specimen, a reasonably useful spore print can be ready in a couple of hours though overnight is certainly better. Although we are talking about 'prints', the shape is immaterial – we are only interested in the colour of the spore mass.

So what use is this hard-won piece of information? Knowing the spore colour does not, directly, tell you what your specimen is, but it can tell you a lot about what it is not. If the spores are white, you have eliminated half of all the fungi it could have been. If the spores are pink, you have eliminated over 90 per cent. Several of the popular books have the fungi arranged according to spore colour, usually with white at the front and black at the back. Most important is the use of spore colour in multi-choice and dichotomous keys.

Taking a spore print

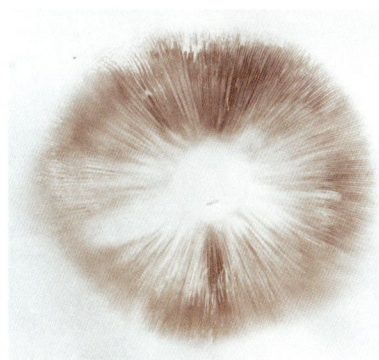

3 Study the fungus

The more you know about a fungus, the more certain you can be of its identity, so it is well worth examining your find carefully and even, dare I say it, make notes! The good news is that the subtle details of which I spoke earlier are, on closer consideration, not so subtle after all. Here is a list of some of the main characteristics used in identification:

CAP:	Size, shape, colour, surface texture, peelability of the skin.
STEM:	Size, shape, colour, surface texture. Is there a ring? Is there a bag at the base?
RING:	If there is a ring, is it like a collar or a skirt? Is it coloured? Does it have markings on it?
GILLS OR TUBES:	Colour. How are they attached to the stem? How thick are they? How close together? Are they brittle or soft or waxy? Do they fork?
FLESH:	Texture – fibrous, rubbery or crumbly? Smell, taste (be careful!).
SPORES:	Colour.
HABITAT:	Where is it growing? Are they in groups, tufted, single?
SEASON:	Spring? Autumn?

Take, for example, the fungus pictured here. A cursory description would be 'a medium-sized toadstool with a scaly brown cap'. Let us see if we can do better with what can be seen just from the picture:

CAP:	Russet brown, paler at the edge, smooth but with movable pink/grey scales. Skin peelable, flesh white.
STEM:	Fairly robust, distinctly swollen at base, slightly rooting. Pinkish to white, roughened and showing distinctly pink where it has been damaged. Has a faint ring of scales at the top of the swollen base.
RING:	Large and fragile, white with little grooves running down it.
GILLS:	Close together, white but bruising pink.

I hope that you did not find that list too daunting – it only took a couple of minutes to make. It contains over 20 observations and if I were to read it, I would know straight away that it was describing *Amanita rubescens*, the Blusher.

4 Follow a 'key'

This is where that hard work begins. A key is a series of questions. The answer you give to one question will take you to the next question. When you run out of questions to answer, you will discover either the actual name you are looking for or the group within which your specimen may be found. Some keys will only give an answer if the mushroom in question is described within the book.

A key may, for example, ask if the cap skin peels easily. If it does you go to, say, question four, if not you go to question seven, and so on. I shall be frank with you: keys are difficult things. They always seem to ask ambiguous questions or demand seemingly impossible judgements. This is not a plot by key writers to drive you mad; keys are just very difficult to write. Still, in general, they do work and often work well, especially after you have had some practice.

Most keys will give you some sort of answer, be it a name or just a genus; the key I have included on the following pages is one that only gives you an answer if your specimen is in the book. Of course, this is an answer of a sort. If you cannot identify your fungus using the key, it is not in the book and you must not eat it!

To use the following key, first determine whether your specimen has spines, gills or tubes (see boxes i, ii and iii opposite). If it has gills, you will need to know the colour of the spores. Go to the beginning of the appropriate section and answer question 1.

So if, for example, you have a gilled, white-spored fungus, you would find yourself answering question 1 on the page opposite. If it has some sort of ring on the stem, you would then go to question 2 and, if not, you would turn the page to question 6. If you go to question 6, you are asked if it has a bag at the base. If it has, it is likely to be a Tawny Grisette; if not, you are led to question 7, and so on.

And you thought it was going to be complicated.

5 Check the answer with pictures and descriptions

If the key gives an actual name of a particular fungus, carefully check it with the description in your book and any photographs or drawings, making sure that all the characteristics tally with your specimen. Photographs generally capture one or two stages in the life of a fungus, so details that vary a great deal over time, like the shape of the cap, may not match your expectations. However, with a little practice you will be able to allow for such variations. It is worth taking a look at closely related species just to make sure you have the one you think you have.

If a key just gives you a genus or some other grouping, you either have to find a key to that genus or check all the possibilities that you have been given. The key in this book sometimes gives a list of three or four possibilities, but these are all very similar species dealt with in the same section. Don't expect to get an answer every time and don't make wild guesses. Do practise and don't get despondent.

Key to species with a stem and a cap

Unlike most mushroom keys, this is just a partial key referring only to the species described in this book. In other words, it won't always give you a result. If you don't get a result, you still don't know what it is and must not eat it! If you do get a result, check it with the descriptions and any photographs on the relevant page. I know it looks complicated, but just work through the key as carefully as you can. It is not as daunting as many others – I have one that is nearly 500 pages long! The drawings that are referred to appear on pp.36–7.

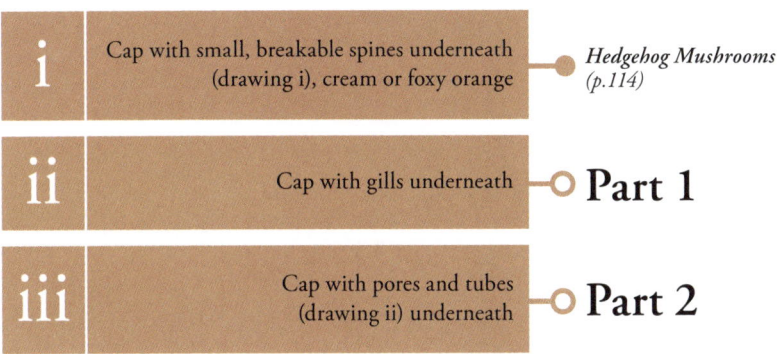

i	Cap with small, breakable spines underneath (drawing i), cream or foxy orange	*Hedgehog Mushrooms* (p.114)
ii	Cap with gills underneath	**Part 1**
iii	Cap with pores and tubes (drawing ii) underneath	**Part 2**

Part 1: Fungi with gills

SPORES WHITE OR CREAM TO PALE YELLOW

| 1 | i. Ring (drawings vi, viii, xiv) or sheath-like or shaggy ring zone (drawing iii) on stem or just a fleecy stem (drawing iv). | 2 |
| | ii. No ring or fleece on stem. | 6 |

| 2 cont. overleaf | i. Ring distinct, membranous (drawing xiv or vi) and not easily slid up and down stem. | 3 |
| | ii. Ring fragile or like a sheath or absent with just a shaggy ring zone or simply a fleecy stem. Caps usually less than 10cm diameter, with brown/orange scales (drawing vii). | *The Dapperlings* (p.146) |

2 cont.

iii. Ring complex, usually double, will slide up and down stem without damage (drawing viii). Cap large, usually over 10cm, with immovable brown scales (drawing v). — *Parasol, Shaggy Parasol (p.75)*

iv. Growing in tufts on wood. White, very slimy. — *Porcelain Fungus (p.58)*

3

i. Volva (bag) at base of stem (drawing x or xi). — 4

ii. No volva, stem base swollen and at least a little scaly (drawing xii or xiii). — 5

4

i. White with green cap or white all over. — *Death Cap (p.140) / Destroying Angel (p.143)*

ii. Brown cap with pure white movable scales. No grooves on top of ring (drawing xiv). — *Panther Cap (p.150)*

iii. Yellow cap, often with brown patches stuck to it. Smells of raw potatoes. Volva spherical (drawing xi). — *False Death Cap (p.143)*

5

i. Cap bright red or, rarely, orange, with white scales. Base fleecy (drawing xii). — *Fly Agaric (p.149)*

ii. All parts slowly bruising pinkish, especially where nibbled by slugs. Grey movable scales, striation on top of ring (drawing vi). — *The Blusher (p.64)*

6

i. Volva (bag) at base of stem (drawing x). Orange brown cap, distinct grooves at edge (drawing xxvii). — *Tawny Grisette (p.68)*

ii. No volva. — 7

7

i. Growing on wood. — 8

ii. Not growing on wood. — 9

8

i. Cap bright orange and sticky or slimy. Stem soon dark to black, velvety. — *Velvet Shank (p.81)*

ii. Stem lateral or missing. Cap shell-shaped (drawing xv). Spores sometimes have a very pale lilac tint! — *Oyster Mushroom (p.56)*

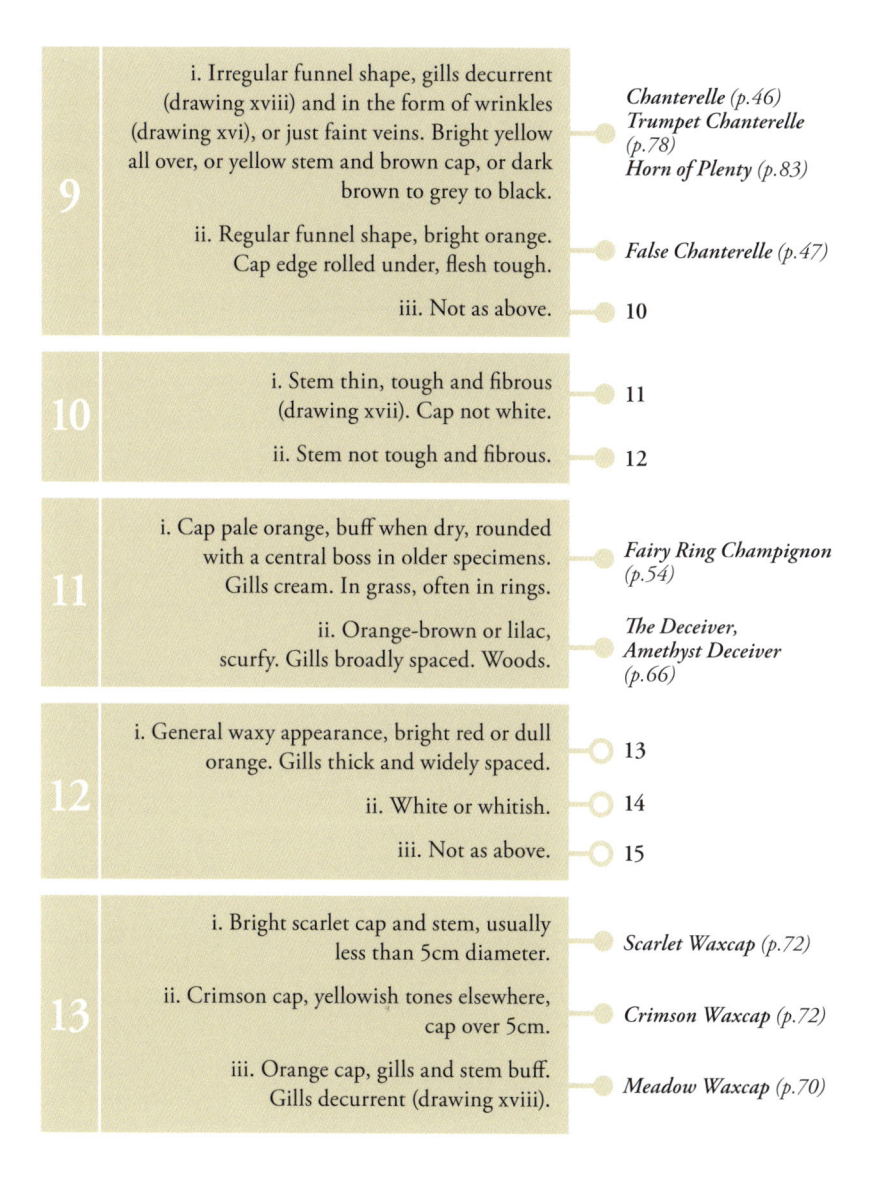

9	i. Irregular funnel shape, gills decurrent (drawing xviii) and in the form of wrinkles (drawing xvi), or just faint veins. Bright yellow all over, or yellow stem and brown cap, or dark brown to grey to black.	*Chanterelle* (p.46) *Trumpet Chanterelle* (p.78) *Horn of Plenty* (p.83)
	ii. Regular funnel shape, bright orange. Cap edge rolled under, flesh tough.	*False Chanterelle* (p.47)
	iii. Not as above.	10
10	i. Stem thin, tough and fibrous (drawing xvii). Cap not white.	11
	ii. Stem not tough and fibrous.	12
11	i. Cap pale orange, buff when dry, rounded with a central boss in older specimens. Gills cream. In grass, often in rings.	*Fairy Ring Champignon* (p.54)
	ii. Orange-brown or lilac, scurfy. Gills broadly spaced. Woods.	*The Deceiver, Amethyst Deceiver* (p.66)
12	i. General waxy appearance, bright red or dull orange. Gills thick and widely spaced.	13
	ii. White or whitish.	14
	iii. Not as above.	15
13	i. Bright scarlet cap and stem, usually less than 5cm diameter.	*Scarlet Waxcap* (p.72)
	ii. Crimson cap, yellowish tones elsewhere, cap over 5cm.	*Crimson Waxcap* (p.72)
	iii. Orange cap, gills and stem buff. Gills decurrent (drawing xviii).	*Meadow Waxcap* (p.70)

14
i. Large, white to off-white all over, growing in spring. Strong mealy smell. → *St George's Mushroom (p.62)*

ii. Small, white-frosted cap, mottled with brown/pink patches. Gills cream. → *Fool's Funnel (p.144)*

iii. Small, white all over, rather waxy in appearance, no frosting on cap. Gills very decurrent (drawing xviii). → *Snowy Waxcap (p.70)*

15
i. Gills produce a milky latex when broken, decurrent (drawing xviii). Funnel-shaped (drawing xxvi). → 16

ii. Not producing a latex. Fairly squat in stature. White gills and stems, caps coloured with yellows or greens or with bright red. Gills usually brittle except the Charcoal Burner). → 17

16
i. Milk bright orange, maybe pockmarks on stem (drawing ix). → *Saffron Milkcap (p.145)* / *False Saffron Milkcap (p.61)*

ii. Milk not orange. With birch or pine on acid soil. Smells of stock cubes when dried. → *Fenugreek Milkcap (p.145)*

iii. Milk not orange. Ring of pockmarks on cap. With oak. → *Oak Milkcap (p.82)*

17
i. Cap bright red. → *The Sickeners (p.152)*

ii. Cap yellow. → *Common Yellow Brittlegill, Yellow Swamp Brittlegill (p.51)*

iii. Cap with greens or blues. → *Powdery Brittlegill, Greencracked Brittlegill (p.48)*

iv. Cap with lilacs, greens and yellows, firm and slightly greasy. Gills not brittle. → *Charcoal Burner (p.48)*

SPORES PINK

1
i. Violet/blue stem, at least when young, fragrant. — *Field Blewit, Wood Blewit (p.86) Lepista sordida (p.89)*

ii. Grey/brown cap with rings of spots. In rings in grass. — *Lepista luscina (p.89)*

iii. Not as above. — 2

2
i. Cap grey/brown, quite large and robust. Gills not decurrent. — *Livid Pinkgill (p.154)*

ii. Cap about 5cm diameter, brown with innate silky fibres. Pasture. — *Silky Pinkgill (p.154)*

iii. Cap matt white, gills decurrent (drawing xviii). Strong mealy smell. Woods. — *The Miller (p.84)*

SPORES CLAY TO RUST-BROWN

1
i. On wood. Cap brown, but pale on drying. Stem white at the top, darker near base, ring on stem. — *Funeral Bell (p.160)*

ii. Not on wood. — 2

2
i. Decurrent gills (drawing xviii), funnel-shaped. Cap with broad grooves near edge, cap edge rolled under (drawing xix). — *Brown Roll Rim (p.164)*

ii. Gills not decurrent. — 3

3
i. White cap splitting radially (drawing xx), whole fruit body reddening with age. — *Deadly Fibrecap (p.156)*

ii. Small, cap splitting radially, white or lilac. — *White Fibrecap, Lilac Fibrecap (p.157)*

iii. Buff to brown cap often with darker centres. Whitish stem, some with water droplets on gills. Smells of radish. — *Poison Pies (p.162)*

iv. Orange and yellow colours, cap fibrous and finely scaly, young specimens may have fibres from the cap edge to the stem (drawing xxi). — *Deadly Webcap, Fool's Webcap (p.158)*

SPORES DARK BROWN, PURPLE-BROWN OR BLACK

1
- i. Tiny, tall and slender, cap yellow when dry, nipple-like projection on cap (drawing xxii). — *Magic Mushroom (p.167)*
- ii. Larger. — 2

2
- i. On wood, sulphur-yellow. — *Sulphur Tuft (p.168)*
- ii. Not on wood. — 3

3
- i. Cap tall and elongated when young (drawing xxiii). — *Shaggy Inkcap, Common Inkcap (p.97)*
- ii. Cap broader, permanent ring on the stem. — 4

4
- i. Cap edge, ring on stem and the outside and especially the inside of the base of the stem turn *intensely* chromium yellow on bruising. Slightly unpleasant smell. — *Yellow Stainer, The Inky Mushroom (p.172)*
- ii. Not yellowing at all or not so intensely. — 5

5
- i. Cap covered in scaly brown fibres (drawing xxiv). — 6
- ii. Cap white or whitish. — 7

6
- i. Flesh reddening when cut, quite small (5–10cm). Woodland. — *Blushing Wood Mushroom (p.99)*
- ii. Not reddening, large. — *The Prince (p.98)*

7
- i. Cap bruising slightly yellow, pendulous ring on stem with 'cogwheel' markings (drawing xxv). Woodland. — *Wood Mushroom (p.99)*
- ii. Large (10–30cm), in fields, often with 'cogwheel' marks on ring (drawing xxv). — *Horse Mushroom, Macro Mushroom (p.90)*
- iii. White, smaller, gills bright pink when young. In fields. — *Field Mushroom (p.93)*
- iv. Flat, compact, double ring. Growing in compacted soil, often in gardens and roadsides. — *Pavement Mushroom (p.95)*

Part 2: Fungi with tubes

1	i. With bright red on stem.	2
	ii. Without red.	3

2	i. Brown cap, yellow flesh that goes instantly and intensely blue. Stem covered in tiny red dots.	*Scarletina Bolete (p.110)*
	ii. Stem not swollen even when young, small.	*Red Cracked Bolete (p.106)*
	iii. Cap dingy white, flesh turns slowly pale blue. Stem covered in a red net. (Don't worry too much about this one; it is very rare.)	*Devil's Bolete (p.177)*

3	i. Stem long and rough with raised orange or black dots.	*Orange Oak Bolete, Orange Birch Bolete (p.108), Brown Birch Bolete (p.109)*
	ii. Cap sticky or slimy.	*Slippery Jack, Weeping Bolete (p.112)*
	iii. Not as above.	4

4	i. Stem relatively thin, brown, tubes pale yellow. Slightly bluing when bruised.	*Bay Bolete (p.106)*
	ii. Stem very swollen, at least when young.	5

5	i. Tubes and pores pink (except in very young specimens), brown net on stem.	*Bitter Bolete (p.175)*
	ii. Pores and tubes white, cream or yellow.	*Cep, Dark Cep (p.102) Oak Bolete (p.104)*

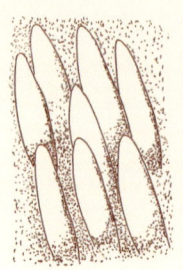

i
Hedgehog
Mushroom spines

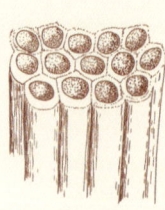

ii
Tubes and pores of
Boletus species

iii
Shaggy, zoned stem of
some Dapperlings

iv
Shaggy stem of some
Dapperlings

v
Immovable scales
on many Parasols

vi
Grooves on upper surface of ring

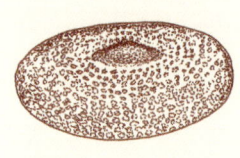

vii
Scaly cap of the Dapperlings

viii
Double ring of
the Parasols

ix
Pockmarked stem of the
Saffron Milkcap

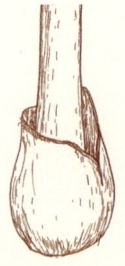

x
Volva at the base of
many Amanitas

xi
Volva at the base of
the False Death Cap

xii
Swollen, fleecy stem
base of the Fly Agaric

xiii
Swollen stem base

xiv
Pendulous ring

xv
Oyster Mushroom

xvi
Forked gills

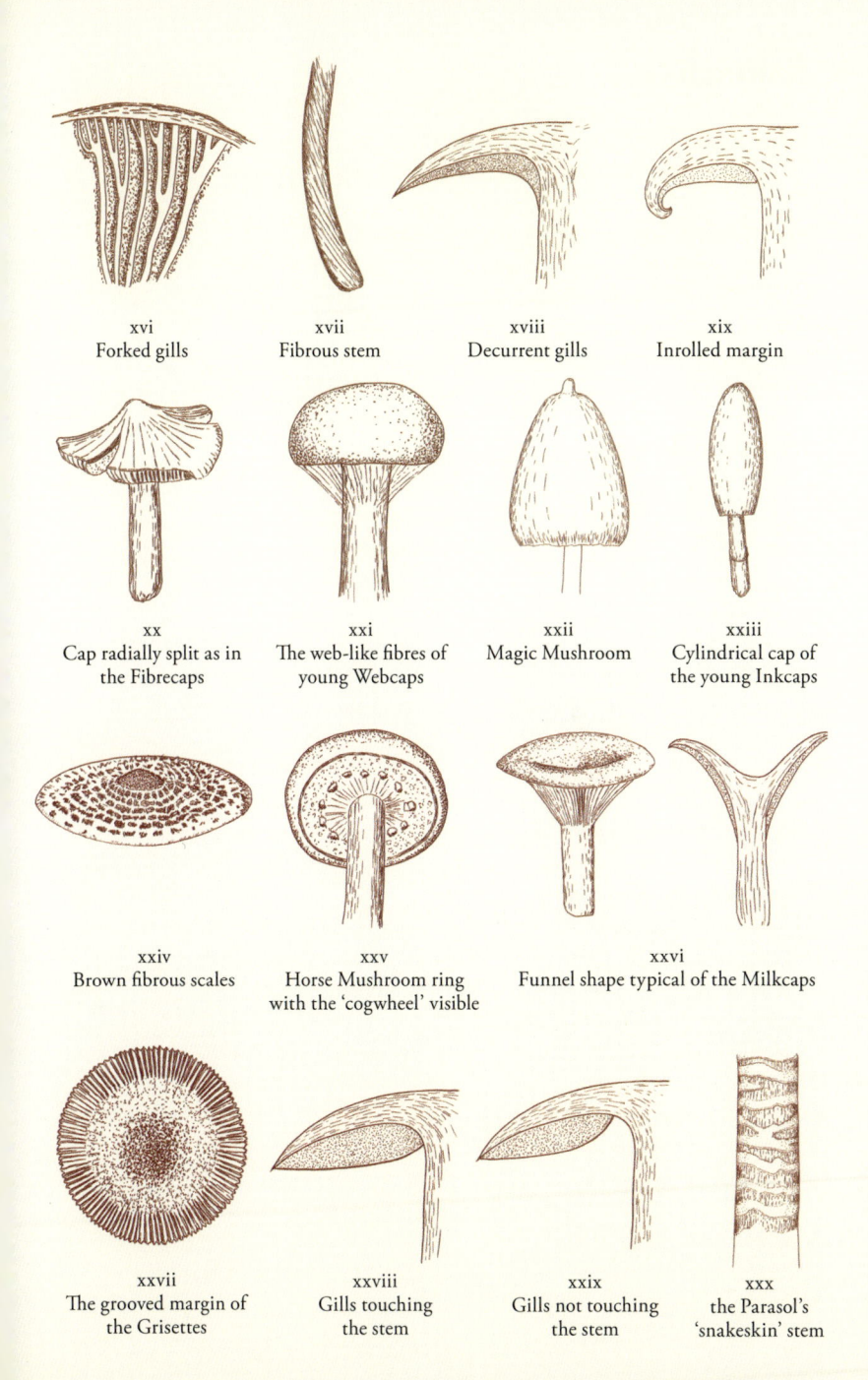

xvii
Fibrous stem

xviii
Decurrent gills

xix
Inrolled margin

xx
Cap radially split as in
the Fibrecaps

xxi
The web-like fibres of
young Webcaps

xxii
Magic Mushroom

xxiii
Cylindrical cap of
the young Inkcaps

xxiv
Brown fibrous scales

xxv
Horse Mushroom ring
with the 'cogwheel' visible

xxvi
Funnel shape typical of the Milkcaps

xxvii
The grooved margin of
the Grisettes

xxviii
Gills touching
the stem

xxix
Gills not touching
the stem

xxx
the Parasol's
'snakeskin' stem

Glossary

I have tried to avoid too much jargon in this book, but the following dozen or so words crept in because it was so difficult to do without them.

Ascomycete: A fungus that produces its spores, normally eight at a time, in little sausage-shaped cells then, usually, shoots them out of one end into the air, e.g. Morels, Truffles and yeast.

Basidiomycete: A fungus that produces its spores on little stalks, normally four at a time, at the end of cells called basidia, e.g. most mushrooms and toadstools.

Bracket fungus: A fungus with a fruit body that projects from a living or dead tree or branch and has the general appearance of a shelf.

Decurrent: Gills that run down the stem, e.g. Chanterelles (drawing xviii).

Genus: A closely related group of organisms, e.g. the genus *Russula* is all the so-called Brittlegills.

Hyphae: Long and very thin cells that make the bulk of a fungus.

Latex: A white, yellow or orange milky fluid that exudes from the broken gills and flesh of the Milkcaps.

Mycelium: A mass of hyphae.

Mycology: The study of fungi.

Mycophagy: The eating of fungi.

Mycophile: Someone who enjoys fungi.

Mycorrhizal: The relationship in which a fungus supplies water and minerals to a plant in exchange for sugars.

Saprotroph: An organism that lives off dead organic matter.

Species: A single type of organism. Usually defined as a group that can breed together.

Specific epithet: The last part of a scientific name, e.g. the '*cibarius*' part of '*Cantharellus cibarius*' (the Chanterelle).

Symbiotic: A relationship that is of mutual benefit between two organisms.

Taxonomy: The ordering of organisms into family hierarchies.

Umbo: A raised bump on the top of the cap.

Volva: The bag that is at the base of many mushrooms and toadstools (drawing x).

River Cottage Magic Seven Mushroom Challenge

With any subject it is always difficult to know quite where to start. If you have ever collected a dozen assorted species of fungi and tried to match them to any of the 2,000 pictures in a book, you will know just what I mean. They all look the same and your confidence just drains away. An easier way – certainly a safer way – is to concentrate on and actively look for just a small number of species that are relatively easy to recognise.

Below is a list of wild mushrooms that should not be too difficult to find and which will give you increasing confidence as you tick them off. I have arranged them in order of the amount of challenge they present and anyone who gets through this list can consider him or herself a proper mushroom hunter. Maybe we ought to have a badge.

Shaggy Inkcap (*Coprinus comatus*), p.97
Probably more familiar to most people than the Field Mushroom, this striking fungus frequently makes an appearance on grassy verges.

Jelly Ear (*Auricularia auricula-judae*), p.126
Very common on elder trees and can be found at most times of the year.

Fairy Ring Champignon (*Marasmius oreades*), p.54
Not only very common (urban even) but delicious.

Hedgehog Mushroom (*Hydnum repandum*), p.114
Quite unmistakeable, fairly common, excellent eating and unusual.

Cep (*Boletus edulis*), p.102
Common (though you might need to get out a bit!), extremely good to eat and not one that any self-respecting mushroom hunter could admit to not having found.

Morel (*Morchella elata*), p.133
This is likely to prove the most difficult to find – keep a look out in forest bark garden mulches in spring. Nevertheless, it is easy to identify and a gourmet treat.

The Blusher (*Amanita rubescens*), p.64
Extremely common in woods and very good to eat, this slightly more difficult to identify mushroom will provide a final (not too final, I trust) challenge.

Edible Species

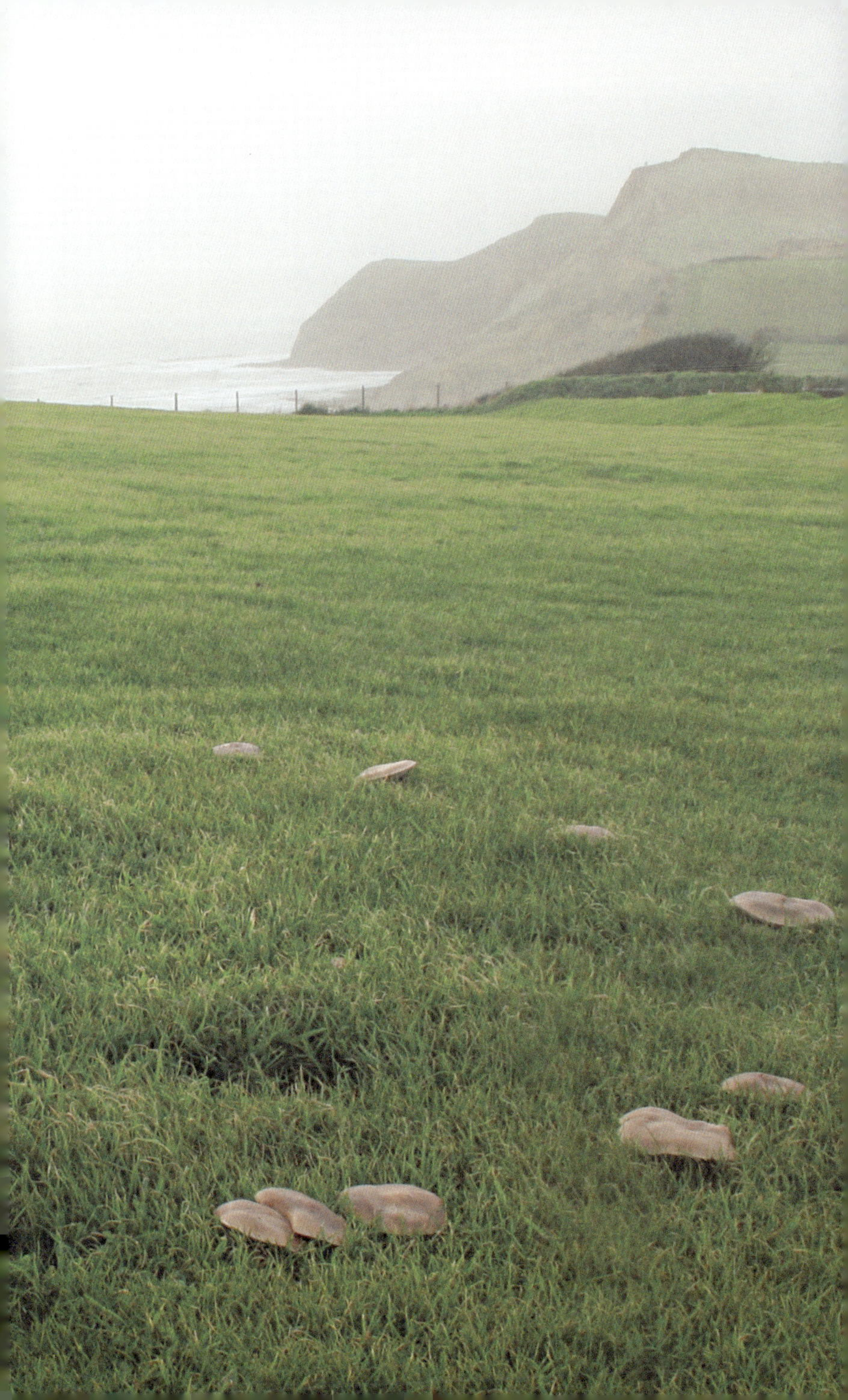

46
48
48
48
51
51
54
56
58
60
62
64
66
68
70
72
72
75
75
78
81
82
83
84
86
86
90
90
93
97
98
99
99
102
106

Edible Species *contents*

- 46 Chanterelle
- 48 Charcoal Burner
- 48 Powdery Brittlegill
- 48 Greencracked Brittlegill
- 51 Common Yellow Brittlegill
- 51 Yellow Swamp Brittlegill
- 54 Fairy Ring Champignon
- 56 Oyster Mushroom
- 58 Porcelain Fungus
- 60 Saffron Milkcap
- 62 St George's Mushroom
- 64 The Blusher
- 66 The Deceiver
- 68 Tawny Grisette
- 70 Meadow Waxcap
- 72 Scarlet Waxcap
- 72 Crimson Waxcap
- 75 Parasol
- 75 Shaggy Parasol
- 78 Trumpet Chanterelle
- 81 Velvet Shank
- 82 Oak Milkcap
- 83 Horn of Plenty
- 84 The Miller
- 86 Wood Blewit
- 86 Field Blewit
- 90 Horse Mushroom
- 90 Macro Mushroom
- 93 Field Mushroom
- 97 Shaggy Inkcap
- 98 The Prince
- 99 Wood Mushroom
- 99 Blushing Wood Mushroom
- 102 Cep
- 106 Bay Bolete
- 108 Orange Birch Bolete
- 108 Orange Oak Bolete
- 110 Scarletina Bolete
- 112 Slippery Jack
- 114 Hedgehog Mushroom
- 117 Common Puffball
- 117 Stump Puffball
- 117 Meadow Puffball
- 119 Giant Puffball
- 122 Cauliflower Fungus
- 124 Chicken of the Woods
- 126 Jelly Ear
- 128 Beefsteak Fungus
- 130 Summer Truffle
- 133 Morels

Of the approximately 4,000 species of larger fungi found in Britain, about a quarter are to some extent edible. The rest are too tough, too unpleasant or simply poisonous. Most of these edible species are either too small or tasteless to consider, too rare or too difficult to identify, and we are left with only 100 or so species that are commonly collected for food. Of these, I have chosen about 65 for this book. I have excluded a few of the popular species that are tricky to identify with any great confidence, so there are no *Tricholoma* species here and no red Russulas.

For many people, mushroom hunting is a matter of collecting Ceps, Chanterelles and one or two other 'high table' fungi. It is a pity that many other delicious fungi are disdainfully overlooked in the pursuit of their celebrated cousins, so I have made an effort to champion these underappreciated species. They are not always so straightforward to identify but their flavours can be just as good, and many of them are very common. Also it may be that a greater acceptance of these poor relations will take some of the pressure off the celebrities.

There is much more to mushroom hunting than the mere finding of a sustaining meal. Foraging for food is an instinctive activity and, as such, inherently pleasurable. One of the great joys of taking people on fungus forays is seeing the intense and primal delight in their eyes when they spot their quarry.

Nevertheless, wild fungi do have a nutritional value considerably greater than is often realised. Roughly speaking, fungi have a food value somewhere between that of meat and that of vegetables. Being low in fats and carbohydrates and high in proteins and vitamins, they are really very healthy foods indeed, though frying them in bacon fat can rather ruin their virtuous qualities. Most fungi contain good quality proteins, but do so rather unevenly with some like the Chanterelle containing almost none at all while certain of the *Agaricus* species contain over 40 per cent protein by dry weight. Most individual species lack certain of the essential amino acids and cannot be relied upon to provide all that is needed in a balanced diet, but since even the most enthusiastic mycophile is unlikely to rely entirely on mushrooms for sustenance, this is unlikely to be a problem. As their high levels of dietary fibre can be either a boon or a bane, depending on individual sensitivity, it is important to try a small portion the first time you eat any fungus.

I doubt if considerations of nutritional value or lack thereof are likely to be of major concern to the average mushroom hunter. He or she is concerned above all with taste, and in this wild fungi excel. The wealth of flavours that they provide remain unsuspected by those whose only experience of fungi comes from the ordinary cultivated mushroom, and there is much to look forward to.

A few words are in order about the names of the fungi. Very nearly every fungus in this book is provided with two names – one English, one scientific. Up until recently, there were hardly any English names for fungi, with fewer than one in twenty possessing one; an extraordinary state of affairs when one considers that nearly every last inconspicuous member of the flowering plants in Britain, down to the three-veined sandwort and the Portland spurge, sports at least one English name and often many more. In recent years, an effort has been made to provide an English name for most, if not quite all, of the larger fungi.

I cannot say that I have greeted this project with any enthusiasm; I like the scientific names because they are universal and precise and enable me to know what people are talking about when they use them. When, however, someone says that they saw some Scarlet Pixie Hoods or use some other ridiculous name for a perfectly respectable fungus, I seldom have the faintest idea what they are talking about. If only everyone would buckle down and learn the proper scientific names all would be well. Nevertheless, I understand that this is unlikely and I use the recommended list of English names with reasonable consistency throughout this book.

Finally a warning.

Although this book contains a certain amount of levity, the business of collecting wild fungi for food is a very serious matter. With good sense it is a perfectly safe way of enjoying the fruits of nature, but if, through carelessness, you get it wrong, you or your loved ones could die a horrible death. I have seldom set foot in a wood in the autumn without seeing at least one deadly fungus, so if you are at all careless, you will eventually succumb. It is encouraging, nevertheless, to consider that it is indeed carelessness that proves to be people's undoing. I doubt that anyone who has taken their collection home and studied it carefully has ever come to harm.

Here are some important things to remember:

- *Never* **eat a fungus if you do not know its name.**
- **Before you eat anything make sure that it agrees with the Key (pp.29–35) *and* the description *and* the photograph.**
- **Individuals within a species can vary greatly in size, shape and colour.**
- **Always consult more than one book. (I use dozens of them.)**
- **Many fungi can be eaten raw but some are seriously poisonous if they are not cooked. As a general rule it is safest to always cook what you pick.**
- **Some people react badly to even the most innocuous of mushrooms, so always try just a little the first time you try a new species.**

Chanterelle *Cantharellus cibarius*

CAP:	4–8cm but very variable in size. Irregular and wavy, funnel-shaped but often with a flattish top. The cap edge rolls down slightly. Bright yellow.
STEM:	3–8cm by 0.6–1.5cm. Tapers downwards, same colour as the cap, but may show white patches.
GILLS:	Not true gills but really 'wrinkles' on the underside of the cap. They **divide into pairs** (anastomosing) and run down the stem. Bright yellow.
FLESH:	Paler than the surface. Smell of apricots (very faint except where large numbers are kept together in a container).
SPORES:	White to yellowish.
HABITAT:	Woodland, chiefly oak, beech and pine. Often in moss.
FREQUENCY:	Very common.
SEASON:	Late summer to late autumn.

THERE ARE FOUR varieties of wild fungi that enjoy undisputed celebrity status – the Cep, the Truffle, the Morel and the Chanterelle. For me, the Chanterelle wins the Oscar outright for the delicate flavour that persists even after long cooking, its unsurpassed texture and, perhaps most of all, its beauty. No other mushroom is so versatile; no other mushroom retains its good looks so well in cooking.

Although the Chanterelle is content to grow with many different species of tree, a rule of thumb is to look for them under beech and oak in the south, and pine in the north. They are very at home on mossy banks or half hidden in leaf litter. Sometimes they grow in groups of a dozen or so, but occasionally an entire woodland glade can fill with hundreds of them. They fruit quite reliably and the same spot will produce Chanterelles year after year. They also grow quite slowly, so it may be worth waiting for small ones to turn into big ones and a single location will often remain productive for weeks or even months. Find your spot, remember it, don't tell anyone.

Beware of the poisonous (and slightly luminous!) Jack O'Lantern (*Omphalotus illudens*). It looks a little like the Chanterelle, but it is so very rare in Britain that I have not included it in this book. It is known only in a few locations in southern England, and mainly grows in tufts on oak stumps. Someone once mistook the Deadly Webcap (p.158) for a Chanterelle with disastrous consequences, but it is so unlike the Chanterelle that it is difficult to understand how such a mistake could have been made. There is one fungus,

however, that can fool just about anyone; it is called, unsurprisingly, the False Chanterelle (*Hygrophoropsis aurantiaca*). Fortunately, this mushroom isn't poisonous, but it does have flaccid, tasteless flesh far removed from that of its tasty twin. It is bright orange rather than yellow, is more symmetrical, has an in-rolled edge to the cap, is soft and fibrous in texture and has narrow, true gills rather than ridges. Sadly, in one of those little tricks that nature enjoys playing on us, it is even more common than the real Chanterelle.

Chanterelle

False Chanterelle

EDIBLE SPECIES 47

Charcoal Burner,
Powdery Brittlegill & Greencracked Brittlegill

Charcoal Burner *Russula cyanoxantha*

CAP:	7–12cm. Firm and rather rounded, colour very variable with violets, pinks, greens, yellows and white.
STEM:	5–8cm by 1.5–3cm. White and firm. (Get your chemistry set and rub the stem with iron sulphate; it won't go orange!)
GILLS:	*Flexible* and slightly greasy to the touch, white.
FLESH:	White.
SPORES:	White.
HABITAT:	Broadleaved woods, mostly beech and oak.
FREQUENCY:	Very common.
SEASON:	Summer to autumn.

Powdery Brittlegill *R. parazurea*

CAP:	5–10cm. Flat convex. Matt *grey/blue/green*.
STEM:	4–7cm by 1–1.5cm.
GILLS:	White to cream.
FLESH:	White.
SPORES:	Cream.
HABITAT:	Broadleaved woods, mostly beech and oak.
FREQUENCY:	Fairly common.
SEASON:	Summer to autumn.

Greencracked Brittlegill *R. virescens*

CAP:	7–12cm. Rounded then flattened out and wavy, dull ochre green with darker *scaly green patches* all over.
STEM:	5–9cm by 2–3cm. White, rusty spots later. (Goes orange with iron sulphate, so a lot of fun to be had here.)
GILLS:	Cream, fairly brittle.
FLESH:	White, firm.
SPORES:	White to pale cream.
HABITAT:	Broadleaved woods, chiefly beech.
FREQUENCY:	Occasional.
SEASON:	Summer to autumn.

Charcoal Burner

Powdery Brittlegill

EDIBLE SPECIES 49

Greencracked Brittlegill

THESE ARE a selection from a group of Brittlegills with mostly greenish or bluish caps. The most common of these is the Charcoal Burner. It is singular among the Brittlegills in not having brittle gills and thus is a fine example of biology refusing to have any regard for rules.

With any Brittlegill you are not sure of, a quick nibble of the cap edge will determine if it is acrid and inedible (spit it out!) or mild and edible. The very hot ones, such as the Sickener (*Russula emetica*), p.152, generally cause some sort of gastric upset and must be avoided.

All the mild Brittlegills have a nutty flavour and a pleasing texture that is suitable and safe for salads. As they are undervalued by the average mushroom hunter obsessed with 'A-list' mushrooms such as Ceps and Chanterelles, the Brittlegills are passed by as too difficult to identify and not tasty enough – which leaves all the more for us.

P.S. It is easy to tell a Brittlegill from anything else, but apart from 20 to 30 well-known species out of the 200 or so on the British list, it is all but impossible to tell one from another. Still, at least you can eat some of them. Far worse is the notoriously difficult genus *Cortinarius* – the Webcaps. Its 400 species are appallingly hard to identify and only one is edible. Most of them are extremely rare with a suspiciously large number having been recorded only once, so even the keenest *Cortinarius* twitcher is unlikely to spot more than a third of them in a lifetime. I often advise people new to mycology and overwhelmed by confusion to specialise in just one genus (an excellent piece of advice I have never taken myself). If you decide to take this path, don't choose *Cortinarius* – that way madness lies.

Common Yellow Brittlegill
& Yellow Swamp Brittlegill

Common Yellow Brittlegill
Russula ochroleuca

CAP:	6–10cm. Rounded when young, soon flattening out, yellow ochre.
STEM:	4–7cm by 1.5–2.5cm. White.
GILLS:	Brittle, white.
FLESH:	White. Tastes rather acrid.
SPORES:	White to cream.
HABITAT:	Woodland.
FREQUENCY:	Extremely common.
SEASON:	Summer to early winter.

Yellow Swamp Brittlegill
R. claroflava

CAP:	6–12cm. Rounded when young, often flattening out to form a completely flat disc, very bright shiny yellow.
STEM:	5–10cm by 1.5–3cm. White bruising grey to black.
GILLS:	Brittle, ivory at first, then ochre.
FLESH:	White.
SPORES:	***Ochre.***
HABITAT:	Damp birch woods.
FREQUENCY:	Common.
SEASON:	Late summer to autumn.

WALK INTO just about any wood in the autumn and you will immediately tread on a Common Yellow Brittlegill. The huge genus *Russula* contains over 200 species, but the Common Yellow Brittlegill is almost as common as all the rest put together. So it is rather a pity that, though perfectly edible, it earns a place in this book more for its super-abundance than its flavour. In fact, the flavour is not at all bad, just a bit peppery, which is fine if you like peppery, otherwise you can just add one or two to a mixed mushroom dish. The good news is that they are much less spicy when cooked than a nibble of a raw specimen will lead you to expect. Of course, as with all strong-tasting

Common Yellow Brittlegill

Young Yellow Swamp Brittlegill

Easily broken gills

mushrooms (and indeed all mushrooms), you should try a small amount first to make sure it agrees with you.

Perhaps better, though less common, is the under-appreciated and not at all peppery Yellow Swamp Brittlegill. I suspect that the 'Swamp' part of its name has protected it from the frying pan more than any inherent esculent failing. With its firm texture, nutty flavour and ability to retain its bright yellow coloration during cooking, it makes a tasty and decorative ingredient in most dishes. It is also one of the few that I am happy to recommend adding to a salad.

Beware of the Geranium Scented Brittlegill (*Russula felea*).

With their mostly bright caps, stocky outline and fragile gills, the Brittlegills are easily distinguished from other genera. Few Brittlegills are yellow, so the only one that need concern us here is the acrid Geranium Scented *Russula*. It has more of an orange tinge to its yellow colouring than the other two, and smells, you guessed it, of geraniums.

P.S. One would think that all mushrooms and toadstools, because they all look more or less the same, would be closely related to one another. They are not. The toadstool shape has been invented independently by no less than six different branches of the fungal family tree.

Brittlegills and the closely related Milkcaps are actually a long phylogenic way from other mushrooms and are closer to a lot of weird stuff that grows on twigs. In fact, strange as it must seem, Boletes, Puffballs and even the Beefsteak Fungus (p.128) are more closely related to, say, Field Mushrooms (p.93) than are the Brittlegills. This may appear extremely odd (it is rather like discovering that humans were more closely related to cows than chimps), until one remembers that mushrooms and toadstools are organs, not organisms. It should be no surprise that since they are designed for the same function they look the same. The technical term for this biological phenomenon is 'convergent evolution' and it can be seen throughout the natural world.

The Brittlegill's evolutionary distance from other mushrooms is hinted at in the character that gives them their name – brittle gills. In fact, the whole mushroom is brittle and this is because the Brittlegills are built from round cells quite unlike the long cells that make other mushrooms more fibrous and hence tougher.

Nature is endlessly and startlingly inventive and these evolutionary paths can lead on to some astonishing places. The Brittlegills and their friends the Milkcaps have Truffle-like descendents – the so-called Milk Truffles. Simply put, Milk Truffles are mushrooms that have made a massive change in shape and career and have taken themselves off to live underground. Some habits die hard though and at least one of them – *Zelleromyces stephensii* – will still produce a milky latex when you cut it.

Fairy Ring Champignon

Marasmius oreades

CAP:	2–5cm. Convex then flat with a ***central boss*** when mature, wavy margin. Tawny to ochre, paler when dry.
STEM:	4–7cm by 0.3–0.5cm. White to cream, ***tough and fibrous***.
GILLS:	Distinctly ***beige***, broad and ***spaced widely***.
FLESH:	Very thin, cream.
SPORES:	White.
HABITAT:	Short grass, lawns, parks, pasture. Often in rings.
FREQUENCY:	Very common.
SEASON:	Spring to autumn.
WARNING:	Must be cooked!

IF THE GARDENER'S No. 1 Most Hated Toadstool is the Honey Fungus, then No. 2 must be the Fairy Ring Champignon. The damage this fungus has inflicted on many a once spotless lawn has brought tears to the eyes of many a once proud gardener. It is all but impossible to eradicate and only the drastic measure of removing and then replacing half a metre of topsoil is guaranteed to work.

But there is good and surprising news – it is one of the very best of the wild mushrooms, in my opinion up there with the Ceps and Chanterelles. Better still it is very common, very prolific and so easy to identify that it would take heroic carelessness to mix it up with anything nasty. And who wants one of those dreary monoculture lawns anyway?

Fairy Ring Champignons are known to contain hydrogen cyanide, though they are perfectly safe to eat after being cooked. No, really. The quantities are tiny but the tell-tale smell of bitter almonds can still occasionally be detected. They suffer sometimes from maggots but seldom half-heartedly so; they are either all maggot-free or all infested. The stems are far too tough to eat, so just nip them off with a thumbnail as you pick them. The caps look and taste wonderful when pickled and preserved in oil (p.245) and, since they are viewed by many as toadstools, you get the irresistible chance to offer Pickled Toadstools to guests at tea time.

Beware of
the Fool's Funnel (*Clitocybe rivulosa*), p.144, which grows in similar habitats and is quite seriously poisonous. Don't worry too much as, with its 'frosted cake' bloom on the top of the cap, it is a very distinctive toadstool – just remember it is sometimes easy to lose concentration when picking lots of small mushrooms.

Fairy Ring Champignon

P.S. Few things in the fungal world stimulate more interest and puzzlement than fairy rings. These sometimes vast and ancient formations have received the attentions of productive imaginations for millennia. The largest one I know is around 70 metres in diameter and may be 200 years old, but they can live for a thousand years and grow up to half a mile across. Remember that we are talking about a half mile diameter single individual here – an individual organism that can dwarf any other on the planet! Well the mystery, if not the wonder, is now in the past.

Rings come about when the underground cotton wool-like mycelium of a fungus grows outwards from a central point and dies off in the middle. The mushrooms then grow from this underground ring. The ring zone of dead grass is caused by dehydration and by fungal toxins (cyanide again!), while the outer zone of lush grass is caused by the release of nitrogen from the feeding mycelium. The inner zone of lush grass is the result of nitrogen released from the dying mycelium. No fairies. Sorry.

Oyster Mushroom *Pleurotus ostreatus*

CAP: 5–12cm. Kidney-shaped, beige to grey, sometimes bluish.
STEM: Short, lateral.
GILLS: Whitish. Not branching.
FLESH: White, thick near stem.
SPORES: White to very pale lilac.
HABITAT: Usually on deciduous trees, most often beech. In tiers.
FREQUENCY: Very common.
SEASON: Spring to early winter.

OYSTER MUSHROOMS are almost unmistakable and their chief peril arises when less than agile mushroom hunters wielding sharp knives try to clamber over piles of slippery logs. They really are some of the best mushrooms, and can be found in enormous quantities. Before you fill your basket, just check to see if their maggot-to-mushroom ratio is too high for your personal taste – they are rather prone to this particular aggravation. Actually, all is not necessarily lost. A mycological friend of mine who (oddly) didn't much like eating mushrooms took a basket of them home, proudly informing me a couple of weeks later that he had succeeded in hatching 15 different species of mushroom fly from the maggots in his collection. Result!

Also look out for

the Pale Oyster (*Pleurotus pulmonarius*). If your Oyster Mushrooms seem to lack any stem, this is what they are more likely to be. Don't worry, they taste just as good. There is also the Branching Oyster (*Pleurotus cornucopiea*), which has gills down its stem and tastes of coconut. It became quite a common species a few years ago following an abundance of its favourite home, dead elm trees.

P.S. I am about to tell you more than you really want to know. Oyster Mushrooms grow on logs. Everyone is happy with this – Oyster Mushrooms are the good guys breaking down organic matter for future generations. But I am afraid they lead a terrible double life. Logs are made of cellulose and lignin, both of which are very low in nitrogen. Oyster Mushrooms need nitrogen and need to get it somehow. Until it fruits, the main part of an Oyster Mushroom exists as a cotton wool-like mass of fibres inside the log in which it is growing. On some of these fibres, tiny droplets of a powerful toxin form and proceed to stun passing nematode worms into immobility. Other fibres then grow to search out these hapless victims, enter their mouths and suck out their precious, nitrogen-rich fluids. Nasty. But nothing to worry about, unless, of course, you happen to be a nematode worm.

Oyster Mushroom

Oyster Mushroom

EDIBLE SPECIES

Porcelain Fungus *Oudemansiella mucida*

CAP:	2–10cm. Hemispherical, later convex. *Translucent* white/grey with an ochre flush in the centre of mature specimens. Very *slimy* indeed in wet weather, at least sticky in dry weather.
STEM:	3–8cm by 0.3–0.8cm. White, tough.
RING:	Distinct. Like a neat white collar.
GILLS:	White, distant.
SPORES:	White. This fungus is very productive of spores and a spore print can be formed inside an hour.
HABITAT:	In large tufts on beech trees, sometimes high up.
FREQUENCY:	Common.
SEASON:	Autumn to early winter.

DESPITE HAVING eaten around 120 species of fungi, I could never bring myself to try anything quite so slimy as the Porcelain Fungus. Then, quite recently, I met a couple with a basketful each of them. They dismissed my reasonably polite derision and assured me that they tasted a lot better than they looked. Thinking that they could hardly taste worse than they looked, I collected a few of them for supper. After the slime (and there is a lot of it) had been washed off and the stems removed, they sautéed well and had a surprisingly rich flavour. I am now a convert to the Porcelain Fungus.

Certainly it is a species well worth adding to your repertoire as during the season a mature beech wood can readily produce them by the hundredweight. Also there is not the slightest risk of mixing them up with anything else. I like to trim the stems as I pick and it is pretty essential to keep them away from other mushrooms in the basket because of the slime.

P.S. As you can see from the picture a Porcelain Fungus can completely take over a dead tree. It fights off rival fungi with its very own powerful fungicide. A study of this talent in the 1980s led to the creation of a new, very safe and very effective group of agricultural fungicides, the strobilurins, which have massively improved yields of crops such as wheat and fruits.

Porcelain Fungus

Porcelain Fungus – time for a ladder

EDIBLE SPECIES 59

Saffron Milkcap *Lactarius deliciosus*

CAP: 8–15cm. Convex, then flattened, then funnel-shaped. Dappled orange with darker concentric rings. Sometimes green in parts. Slightly sticky.
STEM: 4–7cm by 1.5–2cm. Pale and usually with *orange pits*.
GILLS: Slightly decurrent. Pale orange/cream, bruising green. Milk *bright orange*, then slowly green.
FLESH: Pale. Exuding orange milk fading to dull green.
SPORES: Cream.
HABITAT: Pines.
FREQUENCY: Fairly common.
SEASON: Autumn.

ANYONE ASKED to venture an opinion on the edibility of a fungus that is orange and exudes a bright orange milk that turns a lurid shade of green would probably give it the thumbs down. But of course, appearances count for nothing where edibility is concerned and the Saffron Milkcap is a good edible species, even if the 'deliciosus' epithet is something of an overstatement. Nevertheless, it is well worth collecting, especially if you like carrots, which it resembles in colour, texture and taste. Nineteenth-century authorities recommend baking halved Saffron Milkcaps with a little butter and salt in a covered dish for half an hour. And very good it is too.

The Saffron Milkcap is fairly common and restricted to pine woods. It does suffer from the attentions of insect larvae, so do check them before picking a basket full of maggots.

Also look out for

the rather censoriously named False Saffron Milkcap (*Lactarius deterrimus*). There are quite a few edible, orange Milkcaps,

Pockmarks often visible

Orange latex

but the False Saffron Milkcap is the most common (more common than the Saffron Milkcap). It is found only under spruce and is distinguished by the fact that the orange milk goes blood red and then green and by its tendency for the mushroom to turn green with age. The Traffic Light Mushroom would have been a better name. It is supposed to be less tasty than its companion, but the difference is slight. Most Milkcaps with bright orange milk are edible; make sure it is orange though, as there are a few very hot species with yellow milk.

P.S. Many trees are poor at extracting minerals and water from the soil; their fat rootlets present too small a surface area to absorb all they need. The huge mat of microscopic fibres (hyphae) that constitute the bulk of a fungus has no such problems. These fibres are able to absorb water and nutrients with great efficiency and will transfer them to a tree through a woolly sock of hyphae wrapped around its rootlets. The tree pays for its supper with sugar, and it is this sugar that forms the raw material from which many of our mushrooms are made. This equitable partnership is called mycorrhizal, and is of fundamental importance to the life of many fungi and trees.

Like our pine-loving Saffron Milkcap, many fungi are fussy when choosing a host tree and knowledge of which trees are around you will help you determine which mushrooms are at your feet. Some fungi, more catholic in their tastes, will grow with many types of tree, and if you have ever wondered why sycamore and ash woods are so useless for mushrooming, it is because they don't form such mycorrhiza at all.

Saffron Milkcap

St George's Mushroom
Calocybe gambosa

CAP:	6–12cm. Domed convex with the margin inrolled. White to beige with a brownish centre, often cracked, dry.
STEM:	3–6cm by 1–2cm. White.
GILLS:	White to pale cream, crowded.
FLESH:	White throughout. Very firm texture. ***Strong smell of fresh meal.***
SPORES:	White to cream.
HABITAT:	Short grass. Old pasture, lawns. Often in rings.
FREQUENCY:	Locally common.
SEASON:	*Spring.*

LIKE A LOT OF my mushroom hunting friends, I go into a decline in the winter and spring. I still wander the fields and woods and I do take a genuine interest in the flowering plants, especially the edible ones, but somehow it is not quite the same. And then, towards the end of April, my mood changes because I know that now is the time to look for that first big mycological treat of the year – the St George's Mushroom.

These appear with surprising reliability on and around 23 April – St George's Day, hence the name. They can be found a week or two before, but most finds take place in May with a few rare sightings in June. It must be said that my attempts to predict the date of their appearance based on what type of winter or spring we have had have been consistently useless; the St George's Mushroom, like all mushrooms, comes up just when it feels like it. It is, however, something of a joy to actually pick them for tea on St George's Day and it is seldom that I have had to forgo this pleasure. I once gave a basketful to a restaurateur friend of mine who put them on the menu as a St George's Day special. It is a sad reflection on the caution of the average diner that he did not sell a single order. Perhaps all his customers were Scottish that night.

The St George's Mushroom is typically a species of permanent grassland, so old pasture and downland give the best crops. But lawns, municipal parks and road verges are also permanent grassland as far as mushrooms are concerned, so you may well find them in an urban setting. It is not really a woodland species, but it will often make an appearance on grassy wood edges

St George's Mushroom

and paths. It does not seem to be at all fussy about whether the soil is acid or alkaline.

St George's Mushrooms often grow in rings although it is not always obvious as the grass is neither damaged nor stimulated by the mycelium. You can sometimes work your way around the circle picking the best ones. The older fruit bodies can look a little shabby, but don't let appearances deceive you; they are just as good to eat as their younger brothers. They grow very slowly so you will be able to revisit the same spot more than once in the season and their spring fruiting means that they are nearly always free of maggots.

The firm, dry flesh possesses a rather overpowering aroma of fresh meal, which has been known to deter faint-hearted foragers, but it is reduced to a pleasant level with cooking. I know it is a cliché, but butter, garlic and cream suit St George's Mushrooms perfectly.

Beware of the woodland species, the Deadly Fibrecap (p.156), which is really the only toadstool that might be mistaken for the St George's Mushroom. The similarity is superficial, so just the normal level of caution is required. The fact that the St George's Mushroom seldom, if ever, appears after the end of May and the Deadly Fibrecap is a toadstool of the summer months does help. But the real clincher is the unmistakably strong smell of the St George's Mushroom.

The Blusher *Amanita rubescens*

CAP:	8–15cm. Almost spherical when young, opening to a broad umbrella. Reddish brown with a covering of movable *grey/pink scales*. Damaged areas showing pink/red.
STEM:	8–15cm by 1.2–2.5cm. White, bruising pink/red with a swollen base covered in rings of scales.
RING:	Membranous and (this is important) has lots of *fine grooves* on its upper surface.
GILLS:	White, slowly bruising pink/red.
FLESH:	White, slowly turning pink/red.
SPORES:	White.
HABITAT:	Deciduous and coniferous woods. Most common with beech.
FREQUENCY:	Very common indeed.
SEASON:	Summer to late autumn.
WARNING:	Must be cooked!

I HESITATE to include the Blusher in this book. Not because it isn't delicious – it is – and not because it is an endangered species – it isn't – but because, like a Queen's Scout whose brothers are all in a young offenders' institute, it has some very unfortunate relatives. These relatives are, indeed, the very worst one could hope for, including as they do the Death Cap (p.140), Destroying Angel (p.143) and, most relevant in this case, the Panther Cap (p.150). Nevertheless, once you get a feel for its distinctive appearance you will be able to spot a Blusher at 30 paces. It is certainly one well worth learning as it is very tasty and very common, first appears in the summer when other mushrooms still have their heads down and, frankly, you aren't going to have a lot of competition from other mushroom hunters. Having just convinced you that maybe it is worth a try I am now going to ruin it by telling you that the Blusher actually contains a toxin. However this toxin, like the one in kidney beans, is destroyed by heat, so cook it and you will be fine. No salads.

It is an irritatingly variable species, differing in size and general shape enormously, but it has a most striking feature in that any damaged or bruised parts very slowly turn pinky red. This is usually most noticeable where slugs have had a nibble or at the base of the stem where it has been handled in picking.

Beware of the Panther Cap (*Amanita pantherina*), p.150, which has distinct separate white scales on the cap, has unchangingly white gills and stem and no grooves on the ring's upper surface. This is a seriously poisonous species, though seldom deadly.

The Blusher

Grooved ring and scaly base

Blushing where nibbled

P.S. Amanitas have quite a complex structure. The scales on the top and at the base of Blushers and the famous white spots on the Fly Agaric are the remains of the veil that once enclosed the young fruit body. In the Death Cap the veil remains intact as a sheath at the base of the stem. Amanitas also have a partial veil going from the middle of the stem to the edge of the cap, forming a ring on the stem that hangs down after detaching itself from the edge of the cap.

EDIBLE SPECIES

The Deceiver *Laccaria laccata*

CAP:	2–4cm but very variable, tawny, drying paler. A distinctly *scurfy* look to the surface and usually with a wavy, grooved margin.
STEM:	4–10cm by about 0.4cm. Similar colour to the cap, tough, fibrous and sometimes twisted.
GILLS:	*Flesh-coloured* and *very widely spaced*.
FLESH:	Thin, pale.
SPORES:	White.
HABITAT:	All types of woodlands.
FREQUENCY:	Very common.
SEASON:	Summer to early winter.

THE DECEIVER is so-called because it varies so confusingly in size and shape; so much so that after 30 years of familiarity with this species, I am still sometimes deceived. However, it does have some very straightforward characteristics that happily make identification certain.

With the tough stems discarded, this very common species, if not up there with the Chanterelles and Ceps, is a useful addition to a mixed mushroom dish. There – I said it. 'Useful in a mixed mushroom dish' is mushroom book code for 'tasteless, but you might not notice if you have anything decent to go with it'. Actually, it is not all that bad. Give it a try.

Beware of any of the anonymous 'Little Brown Toadstools' that often abound on the forest floor, which can look superficially like our Deceiver. The genus *Inocybe* (p.156) springs to mind, but these all have brown gills and spores. The Deceiver's scurfy cap, fibrous stem and widely spaced, flesh-coloured gills are distinctive characteristics.

Also look out for the Amethyst Deceiver (*Laccaria amethystina*), which is one of the most stunning mushrooms you will ever see. Its colour is quite amazing and the caps look splendid in a salad. (Remember to just try one or two the first time you eat them raw.) They fade with drying, so keep them covered in the fridge and perhaps soak them in water for a little while just prior to serving. The colour successfully survives cooking, however, and you can do no better aesthetically than serving them with saffron rice. It is, if anything, even more common than its cousin, and will often grow in large troops. The moderately poisonous Lilac Fibrecap (*Inocybe geophylla* var. *lilacina*), p.157, is similar in colour and size, but should not present a problem for the careful collector.

The Deceiver

Amethyst Deceiver

EDIBLE SPECIES 67

Tawny Grisette *Amanita fulva*

CAP:	5–8cm in diameter. Rounded then flattened. **Bright orange/brown** with a ***grooved margin***. Quite sticky, frequently with patches of the volva adhering.
STEM:	8–12cm by 1cm. Tapering from the bottom upwards. White to pale orange. Sheath-like volva at the base, which is white and spotted with rusty patches. There is *no ring or any sign that it ever had one*.
GILLS:	White, free of the stem.
FLESH:	White.
SPORES:	White.
HABITAT:	Beech and oak, but also sweet chestnut, birch and occasionally pine.
FREQUENCY:	Very common in small groups.
SEASON:	Autumn.
WARNING:	Must be cooked!

SINCE THE AMANITAS include several of the deadliest toadstools on the planet, many writers eschew the consumption of members of this genus altogether. This seems to me like plain cowardice. There are, in fact, a few Amanitas that with due caution you can quite safely eat. The Tawny Grisette is notably easy to distinguish from its lethal brethren because of the deep grooves on the cap edge, its bright colour and its lack of a ring. It can often be found in little groups of three or four and will sometimes dominate a woodland. It is one of the prettiest of the fungi with its lovely, slightly sticky orange-brown top pushing its way through the enveloping sheath, looking just like a fresh date. The flavour is mild and pleasant but you must remember to cook them. They are very fragile mushrooms, so do keep them separated from your weightier finds or they will get hopelessly squashed.

Distinctively grooved cap

Beware of the deadly Amanitas

and know what they look like (see pp.140, 149 and 150). Never pick one in the anonymous 'egg' stage.

Young Tawny Grisette   *Mature Tawny Grisette*

P.S. There is a mushroom, *Amanita vaginata*, that is simply called The Grisette. It is often collected for the table, but I have not recommended it here because its grey coloration makes it less easy to identify and because the Tawny Grisette is about ten times more common. You may also come across the beautiful but inedible Snakeskin Grisette (*Amanita ceciliae*). It was once gloriously known as *Amanita strangulata*, surely the best name for a toadstool ever.

If you are wondering how the Grisette got the last part of its Latin name, it just means a 'sheath', referring to the sheath-like volva at the base of the stem. There are several fungi with Latin names that would be unwelcome in polite company. Two that spring readily to mind are the Stinkhorn (*Phallus impudicus*) and the Earth Star (*Geastrum fornicatum*). As you will know if you have ever seen one, the Stinkhorn hardly needs to justify its scientific appellation but our otherwise retiring Earth Star does seem to have some explaining to do. This particular *Geastrum* raises itself from the ground in an arch. The Latin for 'arched' is '*fornicatus*' and it was underneath the arches that Roman ladies of the night could be found. I came slightly unstuck once at an adult education course I was running when I wrote the names of our finds on a table and forgot to wipe them off. During the week, an elderly art student found the foldaway table and complained bitterly about the 'filthy words' he had been exposed to.

Meadow Waxcap *Hygrocybe pratensis*

CAP:	4–8cm. Convex when young, eventually flattened except for a broad central bump. *Matt, pale orange.*
STEM:	3–6cm by 0.6–1.2cm. Cream.
GILLS:	*Thick*, broadly spaced, *waxy*, cream, *decurrent*.
FLESH:	Cream, thick at the centre.
SPORES:	White.
HABITAT:	Short grass on poor soils, nearly always with moss and often growing in rings.
FREQUENCY:	Locally abundant.
SEASON:	Late autumn, early winter.

I STILL REMEMBER my first sight of a field of Waxcaps. It looked as though some child had taken his box of toys and, in a shocking tantrum, had thrown them down the hillside. The incredibly bright colours of the Waxcaps are the most striking in the fungal world, ranging from white to yellow to orange to red to almost purple, with one beautiful pink species – the Pink Waxcap – and one extraordinary green one – the Parrot Waxcap. Several members of this dazzling genus are edible and the best of these is the Meadow Waxcap.

Its flavour is very pleasant but a little too mild to constitute a mushroom dish entirely unaided and I always try to mix it with stronger-tasting species such as the Horse Mushroom.

Also look out for the Snowy Waxcap (*H. virginea*).

It is really quite tasty although its diminutive size (only about 3cm in diameter) means that it will take a while to pick enough for a meal. It is very like the Meadow Waxcap in its general appearance, except that it is white, smaller and comparatively slender.

Beware of the seriously poisonous Fool's Funnel (*Clitocybe rivulosa*), p.144,

which could conceivably be confused with the Snowy Waxcap as it is white and also grows in grassland.

P.S. I have always taken a great delight in Latin names, but they do get me down sometimes. Many of the fungi, presumably in an effort to keep one step ahead of the police, are constantly changing them. I first knew the Meadow Waxcap as *Hygrophorous pratensis*, then it changed to *Camarophyllus pratensis*, then *Cuphophyllus pratensis*, and now *Hygrocybe pratensis* – and it may not stop there. It is hard enough learning them once without having to learn them four times. In the more cynical circles of mycology there is a general and not unfounded belief that if you wait long enough the name will always return to the one you learnt first.

Meadow Waxcap

Snowy Waxcap

EDIBLE SPECIES 71

Scarlet Waxcap
& Crimson Waxcap

Scarlet Waxcap *Hygrocybe coccinea*

CAP:	3–6cm. Convex. *Scarlet*, drying to yellowish in the centre. Scurfy and not slimy.
STEM:	3–5cm by 0.5–0.8cm. Dry. Yellow through orange to red. Paler at the base. Not blackening with age.
GILLS:	*Waxy*, creamy yellow, reddish when young.
FLESH:	Yellowish, thin.
SPORES:	White.
HABITAT:	Short mossy grass on poor soils. Often growing in rings.
FREQUENCY:	Common.
SEASON:	Late autumn, early winter.

Crimson Waxcap *H. punicea*

CAP:	8–12cm. ***Broadly conical. Crimson to slightly purple***.
STEM:	5–12cm by 1–2cm. Yellow, sometimes flushed orange.
GILLS:	*Waxy*, *thick* and broadly spaced. Yellow.
FLESH:	Whitish.
SPORES:	White.
HABITAT:	Short mossy grass on poor soils. Usually in small groups.
FREQUENCY:	Uncommon.
SEASON:	Late autumn, early winter.

THE SCARLET and Crimson Waxcaps must be among the most beautiful of all the mushrooms. The Scarlet Waxcap is really very common and it is a pity that its mild flavour does not entirely match its remarkable good looks. The larger Crimson Waxcap is less common and almost too pretty to pick, so I collect it just occasionally. As with all the Waxcaps, they like old, mossy grassland and are equally at home on blasted moors and slightly neglected suburban lawns. There are many other red Waxcaps, but they are generally smaller and often slimy. They are probably harmless, but it's best you avoid them.

The culinary strength of the bright Waxcaps lies chiefly in their striking colours. They look great in risottos or sliced thinly as an exotic garnish to an autumn salad. If the salad idea appeals, remember to try just a tiny amount the first couple of times you eat them to make sure they agree with you.

Scarlet Waxcap

Crimson Waxcap is much larger

EDIBLE SPECIES 73

The magnificent Parasol

Parasol & Shaggy Parasol

Parasol *Macrolepiota procera*

CAP:	15–35cm. Always with a little bump on the top. Fleecy and cream-coloured, covered in concentric, fixed, light brown scales. The scales form a central brown patch.
STEM:	Up to 25cm by 2cm. Bulbous base. Pale, covered in the typical '*snakeskin*' markings. With care it can be pulled out of its socket in the cap without damage.
RING:	Large and double, can be moved up and down the stem.
GILLS:	Cream/white.
FLESH:	White, unchanging when bruised. Smells of boiled milk.
SPORES:	White.
HABITAT:	Meadows, roadsides, parks.
FREQUENCY:	Common.
SEASON:	Summer to autumn.

Shaggy Parasol *M. rhacodes*

CAP:	8–15cm. Cream-coloured, covered in *shaggy* grey/brown scales.
STEM:	12–18cm by 1–2cm. Very *bulbous* base, smooth, dirty cream bruising orange/red. Top bruises orange when pulled out of socket in cap.
RING:	Double, can be moved up and down the stem.
GILLS:	Cream/white, *bruising red*.
FLESH:	White, bruising orange/red immediately on cutting.
SPORES:	White.
HABITAT:	Woodland, copses, roadsides, parks.
FREQUENCY:	Common.
SEASON:	Summer to autumn.
WARNING:	Must be cooked, disagrees with a few people!

NOTE: Both species come in a number of varieties, but the snakeskin markings and red bruising are, respectively, definitive characteristics.

THERE IS NO MORE astounding sight in an autumn field than a stand of Parasols. These stately, delicious and often enormous mushrooms can sometimes be spotted a quarter of a mile away and it can be difficult to stop oneself from running to pick them. The trouble is that, when you get there, they can look too good to pick and you may find your aesthetic and culinary sensibilities at war. I content myself with just a few of the more closed caps and leave the open ones to both produce their spores and grace the landscape. Honestly.

Fully open, they do look just like little parasols, and as long as the gills are soft and fresh, they are very good to eat. The smell is strikingly like that of warm milk, and the texture, when cooked, is fibrous and soft like the thigh meat of roast chicken. It is a pity to waste the tough stems, so I always find a place for them in the stockpot.

Now, whoever it was who said that life was too short to stuff a mushroom had clearly never come across the 'drumstick' Parasol. If anything ever cried out to be stuffed, it is these – they were clearly designed for this very purpose by a beneficent god. I will not burden you with a recipe here but merely point out that something involving bacon is not likely to disappoint.

Beware of the very similar and closely related genus *Lepiota* – the seriously poisonous Dapperlings (p.146) – which contains many species that look rather like their big cousins the Parasols. All of the Dapperlings are smaller than our two Parasols, so if your collection has any strangely diminutive individuals there is a chance that you have picked a Dapperling by mistake. Parasols grow to the drumstick stage and then open out; they do not start life as small fully open Parasols and just get bigger. My rule is to never pick a Parasol which is, or is likely to be when open, less than 12cm in diameter.

Note, too, that the Shaggy Parasol disagrees with some people, so always cook it before consuming and try only a small portion the first couple of times you eat it to check that it likes you as much as you like it.

P.S. The Parasol's smell of warm milk is so distinctive I could identify it from this alone. Smell is such an important clue to the identity of many fungi that anyone deficient in olfactory sensitivity suffers a severe handicap. The aniseed odour of the Horse Mushroom is well known, but there are more exotic experiences waiting out there. There is the Coconut Milkcap, the Curry Milkcap and the carrot-smelling Oak Milkcap. We have coal gas in the Sulphur Knight, rotting meat in the Stinkhorn and the foul smell of the Dog Stinkhorn. The more subtle fungal odours have taxed the ingenuity of writers over the years and they have sometimes resorted to an excessive floridity of language. The most notorious example is for *Hebeloma sacchariolens*, once described as 'reminiscent of harlots', a characterisation that has always put me at a serious disadvantage in determining this species.

Shaggy Parasol

Shaggy Parasols bruise red

Shaggy cap of the Shaggy Parasol

EDIBLE SPECIES 77

Trumpet Chanterelle

Cantharellus tubaeformis

CAP:	2–7cm. Dimpled, funnel-shaped, *scurfy grey/brown.*
STEM:	2–10cm by 0.5–1cm. Often flattened with broad grooves. Tough and fibrous. *Bright yellow.*
GILLS:	*Wrinkles* instead of gills. Yellow/grey then greyish brown.
SPORES:	White.
HABITAT:	Woodland. Usually in mossy leaf litter and on buried twigs.
FREQUENCY:	Common and often found in large numbers.
SEASON:	Late autumn. It will survive early frosts.

LIKE ITS RELATIVE, the Horn of Plenty (p.83), this mushroom seems to wear an invisibility cloak. After staring at an apparently barren patch of leaf litter for a minute or so you will suddenly notice a single mushroom and then another and another until you realise that you cannot really put your foot down without treading on one. This is one of those joyful moments that all mushroom hunters love. Its other close relative, the flamboyant Chanterelle (p.46), is much less reticent. The Trumpet Chanterelle has a thinner flesh but holds its shape well in cooking and looks great in soups and stews.

It is also one of the best mushrooms for drying as it will reconstitute completely after 15 minutes of soaking. Trumpet Chanterelles are seldom attacked by slugs and bugs and they have the happy trick of coming up in the same place year after year. I have one spot (one very well hidden spot before you ask) where I have picked them for more than 20 years.

Beware of getting carried away and absent-mindedly picking any of the small brown toadstools that habitually grow in similar habitats. If you check each mushroom for the bright yellow stem all will be well.

P.S. Learning how living organisms are related to one another is often a rather startling enterprise, as any child who has just found out that dolphins aren't fish could tell you. The fungi seem to be inordinately fond of such surprises. The Chanterelle group of mushrooms may look more or less like any other group of mushrooms, but it is, in fact, only distantly related. Its nearest cousins are *Clavulina cristata*, which resembles coral, and (if the DNA analysis can be relied on) a fungus found on wood called *Tulasnella violea*, which looks, quite simply, like a coat of pink emulsion.

Trumpet Chanterelle

Velvet Shank

Velvet Shank *Flammulina velutipes*

CAP:	3–7cm. Orange, paler at the edge. Very slimy in wet weather.
STEM:	1.5–7cm by 0.3–1cm. Usually curved, yellow at the top, brown to black below and distinctly *velvety* when mature. Tough and fibrous.
GILLS:	Pale yellowish.
FLESH:	Thin, pale orange/yellow.
SPORES:	*White*.
HABITAT:	On the dead stumps of deciduous trees, notably elm. In large, dense, tiered clusters.
FREQUENCY:	Common.
SEASON:	Late autumn to winter.

THE VELVET SHANK is one of my favourite mushrooms, reliably appearing even when that other aficionado of early winter, the Blewit, has called it a day. This pretty group was photographed (and eaten) on Boxing Day. There had been a severe frost just a day or two before, but frost is no problem to this mushroom as it can survive being frozen solid. Sometimes it can even be found covered in a layer of snow. The flavour is excellent and rather unusual – distinctly sweet and malty – and the texture is slightly and pleasantly chewy, but not at all fibrous. It sautés well and holds its shape and colour in cooking. The Velvet Shank is another of those mushrooms that lends itself to pickling and preserving in oil (p.245), though the sliminess survives the pickling process and is not to everyone's taste.

You might, in fact, have eaten Velvet Shanks without knowing it as the cultivated Enokitake mushroom that is sometimes found in delicatessens is the same species. Grown on sawdust and other organic material in plastic bottles, they attain their unnatural pallor and bizarre form by being kept in the dark.

Like certain other species, the Velvet Shank enjoyed something of a heyday in the 1980s when Dutch elm disease filled the countryside with an abundance of tree stumps.

Beware of the poisonous species

that grow on wood. Since the Velvet Shank grows in the depths of winter, there is seldom much else around with which it might be confused. Even so, it is important that you familiarise yourself with those species that might make an appearance in mild winters. The most dangerous is the Funeral Bell (p.160), but the Sulphur Tuft (p.168) is superficially similar to the Velvet Shank and will give you severe problems. If you are unsure, take a spore print (p.24) – unlike these two nasties, the Velvet Shank has white spores.

Oak Milkcap *Lactarius quietus*

CAP:	5–8cm. Convex then flattened and sometimes with a small depression in the centre. Cap surface shiny/felt-like, dull orange with concentric **pockmarks** near the edge.
STEM:	4–7cm by 1–1.5cm. Same colour as the cap.
GILLS:	Cream with an orange tinge. Milk abundant, white to pale cream, mild to slightly gingery in taste.
FLESH:	Cream. Smells a bit oily or carroty.
SPORES:	Cream.
HABITAT:	Always under oak.
FREQUENCY:	Extremely common.
SEASON:	Autumn.

THIS IS A SADLY overlooked species that has suffered from an often repeated accusation of 'smelling of bed bugs'. I have never knowingly smelled a bed bug so I cannot comment on this, but would rather compare their smell to that of carrots – a much more positive view. The slightly bitter taste of the fresh mushroom largely disappears with cooking and the final flavour is of carrot with a hint of ginger.

Beware of the Fenugreek Milkcap (*Lactarius helvus*), p.145. Most inedible Milkcaps can be detected by their peppery taste but the Fenugreek Milkcap is the exception as it is both mild in flavour *and* poisonous.

Horn of Plenty *Craterellus cornucopioides*

SHAPE: Like a very irregular black trumpet. Hollow right to the base. It is normally 6–10cm tall and up to around 4cm across. The inside is grey/brown to black and smoothly wrinkled. The outside is more grey.
HABITAT: Deciduous woods, chiefly beech and oak.
FREQUENCY: Uncommon, though locally abundant.
SEASON: Autumn.

ALONG WITH its close relative the Trumpet Chanterelle (p.78), the Horn of Plenty is a most retiring fungus that will often remain invisible, even when pointed out to you. Sometimes it stands out beautifully against bright green moss, but more commonly it will hide shyly in the leaf litter. If, however, you are lucky enough to spot one, stop just where you are and you will nearly always see many more, for it is in its abundance as much as in its shape that the Horn of Plenty earns its specific epithet.

It is well worth the effort of the hunt as, despite its outlandish appearance, the Horn of Plenty is a gourmet fungus sharing the top table with both the Cep and the Chanterelle. It is a happy companion of fish, particularly white fish, against which its colour provides a striking contrast. The delicate flavour is greatly intensified by drying.

The mushroom's funereal colours give rise to its alternative title: the Trumpet of Death – surely the most discouraging name for an edible fungus possible.

Horn of Plenty

The Miller *Clitopilus prunulus*

CAP:	3–8cm. Flat, wavy and often irregular in shape, white to cream with a texture like chamois leather. Rather soft and flaccid. Margin rolled under.
STEM:	2–4cm by 0.5–1cm. Same colour as cap.
GILLS:	White at first then *pink*, decurrent, often off-centre, thin and close together. *Can be peeled* away from the cap.
FLESH:	Smells very strongly of *raw pastry*.
SPORES:	Pale *pink*.
HABITAT:	Woodland, both broadleaved and coniferous.
FREQUENCY:	Very common.
SEASON:	Late summer to autumn.

I HOPE I HAVE convinced you that, with a little care, it is a fairly straightforward matter to tell most of the edible fungi from the poisonous ones. Most – but not the Miller. This looks so much like a seriously poisonous species, the Fool's Funnel (see below), that it was 20 years before I was able to summon up the courage to eat it. I collected it every year and I was 99.9 per cent certain I had got it right, but somehow that was never enough. The nineteenth-century mycologist Mrs Hussey bemoaned its reputation – 'neglected and despised in England, as one of that dreaded family, the Toadstools'.

While I cannot recommend the Miller as the ideal mushroom for the beginner, it is one that is well worth learning and I would be failing in my duty if I kept quiet about it. It is a delicious and very common mushroom. The powerful smell of raw pastry largely disappears when it is cooked, leaving a pleasant mushroomy taste.

The Miller grows in groups of half a dozen or so and for some reason (most probably parasitism) is fond of the company of Ceps. If you should find some, do take a moment to look around – there may be a particularly welcome bonus hiding nearby!

Beware of the Fool's Funnel (*Clitocybe rivulosa*), p.144. Fortunately, the Miller possesses several important characteristics that separate it from this villainous double and other dangerous *Clitocybe* species. It has pink spores, not white; gills that can easily be pulled away from the cap; a very strong smell of raw pastry; and a preference for woods, whereas the Fool's Funnel is a grassland species. With the Miller, be doubly sure to check that every expected characteristic is present. Also, remember that not all pink-spored species are edible, so do familiarise yourself with the Pinkgills (p.154).

The Miller on a wet day

EDIBLE SPECIES 85

Wood Blewit & Field Blewit

Wood Blewit *Lepista nuda*

CAP:	8–15cm. Convex, then flattened and wavy. Lilac, then brown but still with a hint of lilac, drying paler. Cold and damp looking.
STEM:	5–10cm by 1–3cm, often swollen at the base, lilac to brown and covered in paler lilac fibres, eventually brown.
GILLS:	Deep lilac, eventually fading as the spores mature.
FLESH:	Slightly rubbery, lilac. ***Smells strongly aromatic/perfumed***.
SPORES:	Pale pink.
HABITAT:	All types of woodland, in hedges and sometimes in grass.
FREQUENCY:	Common.
SEASON:	Late autumn to early winter.
WARNING:	Must be cooked!

Field Blewit *L. saeva*

CAP:	8–15cm. Rounded, then flattened with a 'sharp' edge. Cream to grey/brown, paler when dry, extreme edge whitish for a long time. Usually feels a bit damp.
STEM:	3–6cm by 1.5–2.5cm (very short). ***Intense lilac***, fibrous.
GILLS:	Similar colour to cap with a pink tinge on mature specimens.
FLESH:	Whitish to cream. ***Smells spicy/perfumed***.
SPORES:	Pale pink.
HABITAT:	In mature grassland, often in well-defined rings.
FREQUENCY:	Uncommon, but may be locally abundant.
SEASON:	Late autumn, early winter.
WARNING:	Must be cooked!

THE FIRST HARD frosts bring the mushroom season to a shivering halt and plunge the mushroom hunter into a mild depression. The Ceps and Chanterelles are gone; Giant Puffballs a distant memory. But there is one group of mushrooms that prefers the cold and the damp of early winter and can raise the spirits of bereft foragers right into the New Year – the Blewits. By no means poor substitutes for the mushrooms of warmer times, Blewits are among the best and not to be missed. Their oyster-like slipperiness is quite extraordinary and truly different to other fungi, as is their faint beetroot

Wood Blewit

Field Blewit

Lepista sordida

Lepista luscina

flavour. Lightly sautéed, their delicate flavour and texture is realised, and to those blessed dyads of 'strawberries and cream' and 'ham and eggs' I think we must add 'Blewits and garlic'. Garlic goes well with most, if not all, mushrooms, but none so well as the Blewit. Of course, a little cream may find its way into the saucepan as well.

The unprepossessing Blewits only reveal their stunning looks after they have been picked, when the beautiful lilacs and purples of stem and gills can be seen. The nineteenth-century writer Mrs Hussey refers to them as 'Fair faced the Bluette'. They can look too good to eat – almost.

Also look out for a few other Blewits that taste just as good as our familiar pair. Occasionally you may find what appear to be rather undernourished Wood Blewits; these are likely to be *Lepista sordida*. They sometimes grow in dense, inextricable clusters in grass. My favourite rare Blewit, however, is *Lepista luscina*. Though considered uncommon, I know of it from several locations where it grows in huge rings. Though it lacks the distinctive lilacs and blues of its cousins, it can be easily recognised by its spicy, flowery odour and the little brown dimples that form in rings on the cap. All Blewits are suspected of containing chemicals that can damage red blood cells. The chemical is unstable and is destroyed by cooking.

Beware of the Wood Blewit's slight similarity to some of the Webcaps. Two of the Webcaps may cause confusion: the common *Cortinarius purpurascens* and the beautiful and rare *Cortinarius violaceus*. Neither of these is poisonous and I have actually eaten *C. purpurascens*. However, several other Webcaps are deadly, and it may well be worth avoiding the entire genus. The tell-tale sign of any Webcap is the web of fibres connecting the stem to the cap edge. This is best seen on young specimens, though fibre traces can persist, clinging to the stem. If you are still uncertain, you can settle the matter with a spore print – Webcaps have rust-brown spores; Blewits, pale pink. The Field Blewit is much less problematic as the bright lilac stem and the pale cap and gills form a reassuringly distinct combination.

P.S. Most of the woodland fungi in this book are mycorrhizal. Blewits are quite different; they are saprotrophs living entirely on dead organic matter. This can be seen quite clearly if you pull a Wood Blewit out of the ground without trying to disengage it from its substratum – half the forest floor comes with it, all matted together by the mycelium of the fungus. The contribution of fungi to the wellbeing of the biosphere is little appreciated. Every year around one and a half trillion tons of cellulose, a material that only fungi can break down with any degree of efficiency, is produced. Without the fungi, the bulk of it would simply remain where it drops and life would soon become impossible for most organisms.

Horse Mushroom
& Macro Mushroom

Horse Mushroom *Agaricus arvensis*

CAP:	12–20cm. Almost spherical when young and unopened. Later, flattened convex. Creamy white and yellowing, especially when bruised. Smooth, sometimes a little scaly.
STEM:	8–12cm by 1.5–2.5cm. Cylindrical, sometimes club-shaped. Mostly smooth, but sometimes woolly just below the ring.
RING:	Large and pendulous with the typical *'cogwheel'* on the underside.
GILLS:	Pale cream, then pink, then brown.
FLESH:	White. Smells strongly of aniseed.
SPORES:	Dark brown.
HABITAT:	Pasture.
FREQUENCY:	Fairly common.
SEASON:	Late summer to autumn.

Macro Mushroom *A. urinascens*

Very similar to the Horse Mushroom except that the cap is scalier and sometimes grows to a massive 30cm diameter. The 'cogwheel' on the stem is less pronounced and the base of the stem is covered in woolly scales. Smells less aniseedy.

SINCE I SUSPECT that a good proportion of 'Horse Mushrooms' collected for breakfast are, in truth, almost identical to and just as edible as Macro Mushrooms, I have dealt with them both together.

As a single specimen will easily fill a plate, a Horse or Macro Mushroom can constitute a meal all on its own. And what a meal it is; black, pungent and dripping with an inky juice. Simply brush some melted butter onto both the top and bottom of the cap, sprinkle with salt and grill hot and quick. Younger, unopened specimens have an unsurpassed sweet aniseed flavour and lack the bitterness of their older sisters. The stems are perfectly edible but a little fibrous for some palates, and are perhaps best in soups and stocks.

It is a providential custom of Horse and Macro Mushrooms to grow in 'family pack' quantities of around a half dozen, often in a ring. This ring,

Horse Mushroom

Macro Mushroom with faint 'cogwheel'

EDIBLE SPECIES 91

'Cogwheel' typical of this group of Agaricus

which turns the grass brown on the outside and lush green on the inside, can be visible for a good part of the year, even when there are no mushrooms growing. This enables the observant mushroom hunter to spot a potential dinner months beforehand! They have one other accommodating habit – that of a long season, from as early as Easter to as late as the first carol singers.

Beware of the Yellow Stainer (p.172), which can look superficially just like our Horse and Macro Mushrooms. It is worth taking extra care in studying in detail any *Agaricus* species you collect, because the Yellow Stainer is the most common cause of mushroom poisoning in this country. The Horse and Macro Mushrooms both bruise yellow, like the Yellow Stainer, but less intensely and not at all in the stem base. Also, the yellow persists, whereas it fades to brown after a few minutes with the Yellow Stainer. Finally make sure that your collection smells of aniseed, not antiseptic.

P.S. *Agaricus urinascens* has sometimes been called *A. macrosporus*, hence Macro Mushroom. This refers to the large size of the spores and, indeed, examining these under a microscope is the best way of identifying *A. urinascens* for certain. Well, there is one other way. Young specimens and fresh fully grown ones smell pleasantly of aniseed, but if you take them home and leave them for a day or two the smell suggested by the last part of its Latin name can be detected. While you will be very pleased to hear that this smell disappears with cooking, eating them as fresh as possible is a sensible goal.

Field Mushroom *Agaricus campestris*

CAP:	6–10cm. White and silky, fibrous, often with browner fibres in the centre, rounded then flat, cap *skin overhanging*.
STEM:	5–8cm by 1–2.5cm. Spindle-shaped and not bulbous at the base.
RING:	*Simple* and *fragile*.
GILLS:	Pink from very young, then brown as the spores mature.
FLESH:	Turns slightly *pink* when damaged.
SPORES:	Dark brown.
HABITAT:	Grassland, usually in rings.
FREQUENCY:	Locally common.
SEASON:	Summer to autumn.

FEW SIMPLE PLEASURES compare with that of picking your way across a mushroom field in the mist of an autumn morning, except perhaps the breakfast that follows.

When Continental Europeans speak of wild mushrooms, they mean anything with a cap and a stem that they can eat; the British, with their centuries-old aversion to fungi, think only of Field Mushrooms. This was the mushroom that my grandmother got chased out of a farmer's field for picking; this is the mushroom that people fondly remember there being many more of when they were young.

Like all fungi of the field, the Field Mushroom has declined due to modern agricultural practices and is an excellent example of the conservation culprit being habitat loss and not the innocent mushroom picker. Ploughing and reseeding of long-established grassland, the application of fertiliser and the loss of grazing to cereals and oilseed rape have all taken a serious toll and it has become quite a rare fungus in some parts of the country. It will require the return of more gentle farming practices to restore this wonderful resource to its past abundance.

Nevertheless, it can be found in quantity wherever there is old pasture and it has a particular enthusiasm for fields with horses. Occasionally found in small groups, but more often in rings, Field Mushrooms can sometimes be picked by the tens of kilograms and I have seen them sold at the roadside by farmers with an unexpected cash crop on their hands. The most famous glut occurred in 1976 after the rains that followed the serious drought of that year – fields turned white with mushrooms.

Field Mushrooms are such delicate and attractive fungi that it is a pity to let them get dirty, so I always trim the base of the stem. Simplicity is the key to

Field Mushroom

Pavement Mushroom

cooking them and any urge to fry some in bacon fat and serve them on toast should not be resisted.

Also look out for
certain other *Agaricus* species. Around 220 species are accepted by various authorities, from *A. abruptibulbous* to *A. zylophilus*, easily half of which are good to eat. By far the best known of these is *A. bisporus* – our familiar cultivated mushroom. A few more are covered elsewhere in this book, but identifying the more obscure species (i.e. most of them) is a job for the specialist. Quite a few of them are virtually indistinguishable from Field Mushrooms and can be eaten without fear.

One particular *Agaricus* that does deserve a mention here is the Pavement Mushroom (*A. bitorquis*), so named because of its extraordinary ability to punch its way through tarmac. It is, unsurprisingly, a very solid mushroom, and is very good to eat if a bit chewy. The double ring on the stem together with the strongly inrolled cap edge in young specimens and very low stature make it easy to identify.

Fragile ring of the Field Mushroom

Beware of
the Yellow Stainer (p.172). Despite its firm place in our culture, the Field Mushroom is not really a species for complete beginners. Every year I speak to people who have been poisoned and it is almost invariably as a result of eating the Yellow Stainer in place of a Field or Horse Mushroom. Judging by the colourful and rather gruesome descriptions these people give of their symptoms, it would be well worth acquainting yourself with this treacherous impostor. Its key features are a long stem with a bulbous base, gills that are white when young, a large ring and a very strong yellowing on the cap edge and in the flesh of the stem base. It also has an unpleasant antiseptic smell, especially noticeable during cooking. In the Field Mushroom, the gills are always pink, the ring is thin and there is almost no yellow about it at all.

The Yellow Stainer will give you an unpleasant few hours, but that is all; far, far worse is the fate in store for someone mistaking a button Death Cap (p.140) or Destroying Angel (p.143) for a button Field Mushroom. Always be careful when picking immature specimens of any mushroom, as those all-important identifying characteristics may not have developed yet.

Shaggy Inkcap

Shaggy Inkcap *Coprinus comatus*

CAP:	Up to 12cm tall by 5cm. An elongated egg, curling up at the edges at maturity and turning to ink. Very shaggy, as you are entitled to expect. Pure white when young with a light brown patch on the top.
STEM:	10–20cm by 1–1.5cm. Cylindrical, hollow, white to pink, easily split into fibres.
RING:	Transient and fragile.
GILLS:	Extremely close together, cream at first then pink, then black.
FLESH:	Very thin.
SPORES:	Black.
HABITAT:	Grass, roadsides, often in disturbed ground.
FREQUENCY:	Extremely common.
SEASON:	Autumn.

THIS MUSHROOM demonstrates such a strange fondness for road verges and roundabouts that I sometimes wonder where it made a living before such things existed. It is a familiar and very distinctive mushroom and the only danger it presents comes from wandering around on busy dual carriageways when picking it. This was the very first wild mushroom I ever ate, but I cannot say that it is my favourite, tasting, as it does, of boiled polystyrene. However, many people say they like it, so maybe you will too.

Once Shaggy Inkcaps start to mature, the white flesh and gills redden and then go inky black, so pick only very young specimens that are white throughout. Not that they actually become poisonous with advancing age, but rather, like my Auntie Hilda, just more and more unpleasant.

Shaggy Inkcaps mature extremely quickly and because of this have the shortest sell-by date of any mushroom; it is therefore pointless trying to keep them for tomorrow's supper, even in the fridge. Eventually they reduce to the black ink from which they get their name by a process called 'auto-deliquescence' – a great word to use if you especially enjoy watching people's eyes glaze over.

Also look out for the Common Inkcap (*Coprinopsis atramentaria*), p.170, which is shorter, fatter and grey and, despite its unequivocal name, rarer than the Shaggy Inkcap. It is edible but – and let's face it, this is a big 'but' for many of us – if you drink alcohol within a few hours of eating it, you will be poisoned. Life can be very unfair sometimes.

The Prince *Agaricus augustus*

CAP:	12–20cm, occasionally larger. Cream-coloured with brown fibrous scales.
STEM:	12–20cm by 2–3.5cm. Club-shaped, white, covered with white, ***brown-tipped***, shaggy fibres when young.
RING:	Large and pendulous with ***brown scales*** on the underside.
GILLS:	Free of the stem, white then brown, eventually chocolate.
FLESH:	White, yellowing. Smells of ***aniseed or almonds***.
SPORES:	Purple/brown.
HABITAT:	Woodland, parkland, more often with conifers.
FREQUENCY:	Uncommon.
SEASON:	Summer to autumn.

'AUGUST' means 'inspiring reverence or admiration'. Considering that The Prince can grow to a magnificent 25cm in diameter and is one of the most beautiful and delicious mushrooms you will ever eat, I think that 'august' is just about right. It is rather a pity, therefore, that it so seldom makes an appearance.

The Prince is one of the many mushrooms that tastes and smells of almonds. The chemical involved in the process is benzaldehyde, the same as that found in sweet almond oil. This mushroom grows fairly indiscriminately in all types of woodland, but does seem to prefer conifers.

The Prince

Wood Mushroom
& Blushing Wood Mushroom

Wood Mushroom *Agaricus silvicola*

CAP:	7–12cm. Rounded, eventually flat. Smooth. Bright white, yellowing with age. Bruising yellow when handled.
STEM:	5–10cm by 1–1.5cm. ***Base very swollen.*** White, yellowing, especially when handled.
RING:	Pendulous with '*cogwheel*' markings underneath in younger specimens.
GILLS:	Grey/pink, then dark brown.
FLESH:	White, ***smells strongly of aniseed.***
SPORES:	Purple/brown.
HABITAT:	Oak and beech woods and also with coniferous trees.
FREQUENCY:	Fairly common.
SEASON:	Autumn.

Blushing Wood Mushroom *A. silvaticus*

CAP:	6–10cm, convex, then flattened, tawny-brown fibres forming larger scales on a paler background.
STEM:	6–10cm by 1–1.5cm, bulbous base, grey/white.
RING:	Pendulous when young, same colour as the stem and often with ***brown scales*** on the underside.
GILLS:	Pale, then pinkish, then dark ruddy brown.
FLESH:	Turns ***blood red*** when cut, then slowly dark brown. Thin in cap.
SPORES:	Dark brown.
HABITAT:	Coniferous woods, often in troops of a dozen or so.
FREQUENCY:	Common.
SEASON:	Autumn.

OF THE SEVERAL 'true' mushrooms (the genus *Agaricus*) that occur in woodland rather than pastures, these two are the most familiar. Despite the similarity of their names, they are not all that closely related and their taste is rather different. The white Wood Mushroom is a close cousin of the Horse Mushroom (p.90) with which it shares a sweet aniseed flavour and a disquieting tendency to bruise yellow (Yellow Stainer alert!). The Blushing

EDIBLE SPECIES

Wood Mushroom

Blushing Wood Mushroom

100 MUSHROOMS

Wood Mushroom, which acquired its name from its habit of turning blood red when handled or cut, is considerably less substantial and you will need a good collection to make a decent meal. It is an altogether more nutty fungus in both cap colour and flavour. It has, on occasions, been referred to by the worrying name of *A. haemorrhoidarius*, and you will be pleased to hear that this is a reference to that startling colour change and not a warning of what it might give you.

Blood-red stem of Blushing Wood Mushroom.

Beware of the Yellow Stainer group of toadstools (p.172). The fact that the Blushing Wood Mushroom goes blood-red when you cut it is a great encouragement as no Yellow Stainer does this. Just remember that the woodland version of the Yellow Stainer, the Inky Cap (p.172), also has dark fibrils on the cap, albeit distinctly grey ones. For collectors of the Wood Mushroom, however, great caution is needed to avoid confusion with the ordinary Yellow Stainer. It too is white and bruises yellow, but the smell (aniseed in the former and Elastoplasts in the latter) and colour change in the cut base of the stem (none and chromium yellow respectively) make identification certain.

It is well worth remembering that the Destroying Angel (p.143) is similar in shape to the Wood Mushroom, and is also white in cap and stem. It won't prove a problem to the careful forager because, unlike the Wood Mushroom, its gills are also pure white and it has a distinct volva at the base of the stem.

P.S. The way that fungi fall into natural groups or genera is an enormous help to the mushroom hunter desperately trying to make sense of the thousands of species that can be found. Well, further help is at hand. Many genera can be usefully split into smaller *sub*genera. The Brittlegills (or *Russula*), for example, can be divided up into lots of smaller groups depending on things like spore colour and cap colour, so if you know what the spore and cap colour are you will be very close to knowing what your specimen is called.

Agaricus is normally divided into the 'Flavescentes', which bruise more or less yellow, and the 'Rubescentes', which bruise more or less red. The Wood Mushroom and Horse Mushroom (p.90) are moderately yellowing fungi from the first group and the Blushing Wood Mushroom is an extremely reddening member of the second. Field Mushrooms redden mildly, Yellow Stainers yellow a great deal and so on. They can be divided up a lot more than this, but I am sure you get the idea.

Cep *Boletus edulis*

CAP:	12–25cm. Hemispherical to rounded, flattening at maturity. Various shades of ***brown, like the crust of a bread roll***, the extreme edge is often paler. ***Irregularly dimpled***, again just like a bread roll.
STEM:	6–15cm by 2–8cm. Usually very swollen, especially when young, grey/brown to white with a ***white network*** on the upper half.
TUBES:	Fine, white at first, then yellow, then green and spongy.
FLESH:	Firm and white throughout.
HABITAT:	Oak, beech, birch and coniferous trees. Prefers open situations.
FREQUENCY:	Common.
SEASON:	Summer to autumn.

IT IS A DANGEROUS business to judge a mushroom by its appearance, but the Cep, at least, is every last bit as good as it looks. The English name 'Penny Bun' neatly expresses its felicitous appearance. The Cep is the most prized of wild mushrooms and its collection is nothing short of an institution in several European countries. Long and unaccountably overlooked by the British, this mushroom is now highly prized here too, and every autumn the forests rustle to the sound of Cep hunters on the prowl.

The flavour is both subtle and rich, the texture both nutty and slippery. Being such a substantial mushroom, it does need more cooking than most; about ten minutes in the pan usually brings out the flavours and textures perfectly. The tubes on mature specimens are often peeled off by over-fastidious cooks who do not favour the frankly rather slimy texture of this component. I, for one, always leave them on. I work hard to find my Ceps and never waste any part of them – cap, tubes, stem, maggots – eat the lot, I say.

A young Cep looks so different from an old Cep that many people can hardly believe they are the same thing. While it is the firm, nutty young specimens that command the high prices, their middle-aged brothers have much more flavour. The elderly ones are best left

Tubes just maturing

The Cep

to release their spores, or, if you cannot resist them and they have not been too engaged in maintaining the mushroom fly population, used in soups.

A very rough guide is to look for Ceps with pines in Scotland, and with birch, beech and oak further south. As with many of the fungi, they seem to prefer open, park-like situations to the dark woodland depths, and a walk along a wooded path or roadside is most likely to meet with success. If you find a large number of Ceps, it takes a strength of personality beyond that given to most people to resist picking every last one. This is what I suggest: leave the babies and the elderly and pick two-thirds of the rest. It will be good for your karma.

Also look out for
several Boletes that are close to the Cep and every bit as good to eat as their famous cousin. Unfortunately, they are rather rare and I cannot recommend eating them unless you're able to find them in some abundance. The closest is the appropriately named Dark Cep (*Boletus aereus*), found mostly under oak. More distantly related and not quite so tasty is the Oak Bolete (*Boletus appendiculatus*), with its beautiful 'oranges and lemons' coloration. The cut flesh blues slightly and the pores are bright yellow.

Beware of
the very similar Bitter Bolete (*Tylopilus felleus*), p.175. While this aptly named toadstool is not at all poisonous, it would be most unwelcome at the dinner table. Its bitterness is quite extraordinary, and should one find its way into your *Ceps à la crème* you will have to throw the whole lot away. It is distinguished by the pinkish tinge taken on by the pores and the dark network on the stem.

P.S. The curse of the Cep hunter is not some dangerous look-alike species or even the unwelcome sight of another Cep hunter, but the humble maggot. Large specimens are seldom without these irritating competitors, and even young ones can become infested. Yet it is a great pity to despise these organisms, which have as much right to their dinner as we do. The most common maggots devoted to the annoyance of mushroom lovers are the fungus gnat larvae (*Mycetophilidae*) with their white bodies and dark heads. Most other fly larvae are whitish all over. If your maggots have legs, they are moth or beetle larvae. Larvae are generally found within the flesh of a fungus, but the 'fat-footed flies' (*Platypezidae*) feed between the gills. There are even some flies whose larvae feed on fungus larvae.

The ephemeral nature of most fruit bodies means that life cycles are necessarily short and many insect species manage to pack a whole lifetime into a very few days. Fruit flies (*Drosophilidae*) generally have the last bite of the cherry, living off the rotting gloop left by the disintegrated mushroom. My favourite maggot, however, is the gnat larva that harvests spores from bracket fungi by catching them in a slimy web, which it weaves underneath the tubes.

Dark Cep

Oak Bolete

EDIBLE SPECIES 105

Bay Bolete *Boletus badius*

CAP:	8–15cm. Hemispherical when young, viscid when wet but matt when dry, striking chestnut (bay!) in colour.
STEM:	5–10cm by 1–4cm. Very variable but narrow compared to Ceps, wrinkled and distinctly yellow/brown, paler at apex.
TUBES:	Pale yellow to greenish, bruising blue, pores small.
FLESH:	White to yellow, slowly bruising slightly blue/grey.
HABITAT:	Broadleaved and coniferous woods.
FREQUENCY:	Very common.
SEASON:	Autumn.

THE BAY BOLETE is a common, tasty and easily identified mushroom that is seldom prone to maggots. For the mushroom hunter it has it all. Its only downside is that, unlike mycologists, it does not improve with age. Pick only the reasonably young, firm specimens and avoid them in wet weather when they swell up like sponges and taste about the same.

Despite its benign character, the Bay Bolete was avoided by most nineteenth-century British mycophagists because it failed M.C. Cooke's 'golden' (and wrong) 'rule' for Boletes – 'don't eat them if they turn blue when cut'. The Bay Bolete lacks the meaty flavour of the Cep but is perfectly acceptable nonetheless. It also dries very well, a useful quality in a mushroom that can be gathered in such large quantities that reinforcements may be needed to carry your collection home.

Also look out for

a very common fungus called the Red Cracked Bolete (*Boletus chrysenteron*). It looks like a small Bay Bolete but is rather soft, the tubes are broader and greener, it has red on the stem and the cap surface usually has red cracks in it. A friend who was known for her fondness for road kill badger and garden snails, and whose frequent invitations to dinner always seemed to find me with a previous engagement, once collected a basketful of them. Her assessment, when I next saw her, that they tasted vile, I think we can take as definitive.

Red Cracked Bolete

Bay Bolete

Orange Birch Bolete
& Orange Oak Bolete

Orange Birch Bolete *Leccinum versipelle*

CAP:	8–15cm. Rounded, felt-like surface, dull orange. The *edge overhangs* the tubes.
STEM:	10–20cm by 2–5cm. Usually taller in relation to the cap than Ceps and slightly swollen at the base. Grey/white covered in woolly, *dark brown to black scales*.
TUBES:	Dull yellowish grey.
FLESH:	Whitish at first then faintly purplish grey and eventually black in parts.
HABITAT:	Under birch.
FREQUENCY:	Common.
SEASON:	Late summer to autumn.

Orange Oak Bolete *L. aurantiacum*

CAP:	10–20cm. Rounded, felt-like surface, bright orange-brown to brick red.
STEM:	10–20cm by 2.5–4cm. Pale at the top but the increasingly dense *russet* scales make it darker towards the bottom, sometimes blue-green at the base.
TUBES:	Cream to brown.
FLESH:	White at first, then faintly pink, green at the base and eventually turning grey to black.
HABITAT:	Under oak.
FREQUENCY:	Quite rare, so pick only when found in quantity.

THE *LECCINUM* species have tubes instead of gills and are close relatives of Boletes such as the Cep from which they are distinguished by their long scaly stems. The Orange Birch Bolete is by far the more common of the two and is distinguished by its grey stem. Both are solid mushrooms and take quite a bit of cooking, especially the stems, which need twice as long in the pan as the caps. Do not worry about the *Leccinum*'s tendency to go various shades of greens and pinks and blacks when cut – they are just trying to frighten you.

Also look out for one of the brown-capped *Leccinum* species, that constant companion of Birch trees, the

Brown Birch Bolete (*Leccinum scabrum*). This is pretty poor as edible mushrooms go, being rather tasteless and watery, but if you wish to try it, do pick the youngest and firmest specimens you can find. The Brown Birch Bolete has a brown cap and a long white/grey stem covered in dark brown scales, and the white flesh is unchanged when cut or slightly pink.

The Victorian mycologist Mrs Hussey certainly preferred the Orange Birch Bolete's 'trim grenadier' to the Brown Birch Bolete's 'dirty ruffian'. If we were left in any doubt of her opinion, she then goes on to call it a 'swarthy, shiny, scabrous, very vulgar individual'. I think it looks rather splendid, it is just a shame that its taste does not live up to its looks.

Scarletina Bolete *Boletus luridiformis*

CAP:	10–20cm. Dark brown with a velvet texture and hemispherical when young, later convex to flat, more leathery and a lighter brown.
STEM:	5–12cm by 2–4cm. Swollen at base. Bright orange/red made up of thousands of little raised ***orange dots*** against a yellow background.
TUBES:	Yellow/green, turning bright blue on cutting. Pores bright red.
FLESH:	Very firm when young. Yellow, ***immediately turning dark blue*** on cutting. The blue fades after a while.
HABITAT:	Woodland, mostly beech and oak, occasionally pine.
FREQUENCY:	Common.
SEASON:	Late summer to autumn.
WARNING:	Poisonous raw, but perfectly safe when cooked!

IF THERE IS ANY mushroom that seems to come with a health warning it must be this one. With its blood-red pores and stem, and bright yellow flesh that turns instantly an intense blue on cutting, it is surely shouting 'Don't eat me!' But this colourful relative of the Cep is harmless and very good to eat. Having such a fearsome appearance, it is one that tends to be left alone by the average mycophile, so if you are brave enough there is a feast waiting for you.

I am afraid there are a few caveats. It is one of those that *must* be cooked before eating; it is known to be indigestible to a few, so try just a little the first time; and there are one or two Boletes that are not at all edible with which it could conceivably be confused.

I seldom bother with the larger specimens, which are usually soft and full of maggots, choosing instead the young ones with their distinctive velvet cap. These have a firm texture, like the Cep, and a pleasant, nutty flavour. It is a great pity that the blue disappears with cooking – it would be great fun to be able to serve blue 'toadstools' to nervous friends.

Mature Scarletina Bolete

Young Scarletina Bolete

Beware of other Boletes with bright red colours on the stem and pores. The first check is to cut the flesh to see that it is lemon-yellow turning instantly and intensely blue (this is a good thing). The second check is to ensure that the stem is covered with orange-red dots and not a red net. The best-known, though very rare, poisonous Bolete is the scarily named Devil's Bolete (*Boletus satanas*), p.177, which is easily distinguished by its dingy white cap.

P.S. When considering something merely as an item of food, it is easy to lose sight of the fact that one is eating an organism of surpassing complexity and wonder. The Boletes, and many other fungi as well, produce their spores not on the surface of gills like, say, Field Mushrooms, but inside tubes. Now, these tubes may be 30mm long but less than half a millimetre internal diameter. The spores are formed on the inside surface of these tubes, in fours, on little stalks at the end of long cells called basidia. They are then propelled, by a mechanism that has taken a hundred years to understand, into the middle of the tube where they can float downwards and eventually out into the world. As you will appreciate this is a very delicate mechanism and the fungus goes to great lengths to keep its tubes absolutely vertical so that the spores don't stick to the sides.

The Boletes are no slackers when it comes to producing spores in this way, but the prize for outrageous fecundity must go to *Ganoderma applanatum*, a large bracket fungus, which can produce spores at the rate of 500,000 per minute, a rate it can keep up for several months at a time.

Slippery Jack *Suillus luteus*

CAP:	8–12cm. Broadly rounded to flattened. Date-brown, covered in slime, which dries to a sticky skin.
STEM:	5–10cm by 2–3cm. Pale whitish yellow.
RING:	Large, white and membranous, darker below, granular.
TUBES:	Pale yellow, very small.
FLESH:	Firm, white to yellow.
HABITAT:	Under two-needle pines such as Scots pine.
FREQUENCY:	Common.
SEASON:	Autumn.
WARNING:	Must be peeled and cooked!

THE PIRATICAL sounding Slippery Jack is the best of an otherwise poor bunch that is the genus *Suillus*. While its taste is too faint and its texture too uninteresting for it to form the centrepiece of any dish, in the hands of a good cook and mixed with superior mushrooms it can be perfectly acceptable. With its enormous ring it is certainly a striking mushroom and very common wherever there is Scots pine. If you find a rather orange one under larch, then it will be the Larch Bolete (*Suillus grevillei*), which is also edible.

Slippery Jack has a very, very slimy skin that is mildly poisonous (or to put it another way, an excellent laxative) and needs to be peeled off and discarded. The stem is not particularly worth eating either. It might be best not to discard the tubes as well, as there will be almost nothing left if you do. All *Suillus* species contain quite a lot of water, so it is very important to reduce this as much as possible during the cooking process.

One of the best things to do with any of the *Suillus* species is to dry them and then pulverise the dried slivers in a food processor. The resultant powder can be added to soups and stews. Choose the youngest and firmest and, as they are so watery, dry them as quickly as you can. However, there is one place where the Slippery Jack comes nicely into its own and that is on a pizza.

Despite my faint praise, do give Slippery Jacks a chance; you might well like them.

Also look out for the Weeping Bolete (*Suillus granulatus*). It too grows under pines, often in large groups, and gains its name from the watery drops that appear at the top of the stem in young specimens. The ringless, pale stem, bright yellow pores and rather sticky orange cap make it easy to identify. It is less common than our Slippery Jack, but its superior flavour makes it well worth searching out. Again, it is important to peel the skin.

Slippery Jack

Weeping Bolete

EDIBLE SPECIES 113

Hedgehog Mushroom
Hydnum repandum

CAP: 3–10cm. Irregular in shape, rounded when young, then flat with a central depression. The colour and texture of fine chamois leather.
STEM: 2–7cm by 1–3cm. Joins the cap to form a general funnel shape. Same colour as the cap or paler.
SPINES: Cream. Readily break off.
FLESH: Pale cream. Smell is faint, slightly bitter.
HABITAT: Woodland.
FREQUENCY: Very common.
SEASON: Late summer to early winter.

THE HEDGEHOG Mushroom is, for many reasons, the ultimate safe mushroom. It is common, very tasty and quite unmistakable. The kid-leather texture of the cap is clearly recognisable, even from some distance, and, once picked, its defining characteristic is revealed – the little spines projecting from beneath the cap.

It is a reasonably close relative of the Chanterelle (p.46), as its texture and irregular funnel shape suggest, but it is paler and bears its spores on hundreds of little spines instead of on gills. It is also very nearly as delicious as the Chanterelle, with the added advantages of sometimes being more common and much larger. On the Continent, it has long been held in high esteem and, judging by the names it has been given – Little Goat, Sheep's Foot and Little Rake – a certain amount of affection.

It has very catholic views on habitat and can appear in just about any woodland setting where mycorrhizal trees such as oak, beech, birch, hazel and pine occur. Although it often grows in small patches of three or four, occasionally you will be lucky enough to find a ring of them. My best find was a ring that contained 1.5kg of perfect

Hydnum rufescens

Hedgehog Mushroom

specimens. Sometimes you get a real Hedgehog Mushroom year and they can be found in huge numbers. If they have one drawback, it is this: those little spines break off and get everywhere.

The uncooked mushroom is quite bitter but this disappears with cooking. The flavour has been likened to that of oysters to which I can only say – maybe. Its texture is one of the best of all the mushrooms and it keeps its shape and size well during the fairly long cooking that its dry nature demands.

Also look out for the Terracotta Hedgehog (*Hydnum rufescens*). This is so much like the ordinary Hedgehog Mushroom that it has long been debated whether it is a separate species or not. It is distinguished by its red tones and smaller size. There are several other toothed fungi but most of them are rare and poor eating. I once tried, with high hopes, a single, endangered Scaly Tooth (*Sarcodon imbricatus*), which someone had picked for me and which is reputed to be edible. It is not.

P.S. A few years ago an experiment was carried out in China in which some mice were, over a period of six months, given powdered Hedgehog Mushroom to test its reputation as a fatigue suppressant. Various biochemical tests showed that chemicals associated with tiredness were at lower levels and excreted at a faster rate in mice that had eaten Hedgehog Mushrooms than in mice that had not. A gruesome clincher that does little to enhance the status of scientists in the public perception was that in a swimming test 'experimental mice drowned after a longer period of time than the control mice'. I cannot ascertain if these results were confirmed, but perhaps Hedgehog Mushrooms are the breakfast of the future.

EDIBLE SPECIES

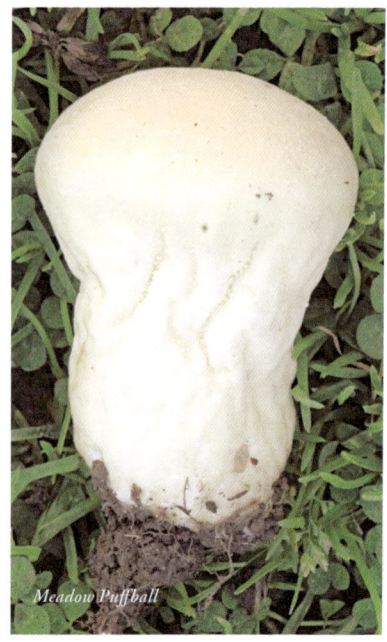

Common Puffball

Stump Puffball

Meadow Puffball

Common Puffball,
Stump Puffball & Meadow Puffball

Common Puffball *Lycoperdon perlatum*

SHAPE:	2–5cm in diameter. Rounded with a little bump in the centre and always with a definite stem. White when young, covered with easily broken brown/white spines that leave a mosaic pattern on the skin when broken off. Eventually brown and papery with a hole in the top for the spores to escape when mature. The flesh inside the thin skin is pure white when young, turning yellow then brown and dusty on maturity.
HABITAT:	Woodland.
FREQUENCY:	Extremely common.
SEASON:	Autumn.

Stump Puffball *L. pyriforme*

SHAPE:	Similar to the Common Puffball but is more pear-shaped, has much finer spines and is brown on top, even when very young.
HABITAT:	Grows in dense clusters on old tree stumps, unlike any other Puffball.
FREQUENCY:	Common.
SEASON:	Autumn.

Meadow Puffball *Vascellum pratense*

SHAPE:	Diameter up to about 4cm. The whole fruit body is usually ovoid when viewed from above. Even young specimens have a faint yellow tone. Minutely scurfy. The stem is less distinct and wrinkles at the base.
HABITAT:	Meadows.
FREQUENCY:	Common.
SEASON:	Autumn.

WHILE THE GIANT Puffball (p.119) is the undisputed star of the Puffball world, there are a number of much smaller Puffballs that taste just as good and are very common. For once, the 'Common' appellation is accurate – the Common Puffball is the one you are most likely to come across. Its easily detached spines make it fairly simple to distinguish from other Puffballs, but with the Puffballs it is really not necessary to know which Puffball you have collected as they are all edible and all taste much the same.

I confess that though I like the little Puffballs, I usually walk past them if there is anything else around that is worth eating. The reason for this uncharacteristic self-denial is that, while their soft marshmallow interior is a delight, they are the very devil to peel. I know that some people cook them whole, but all I can say is that they must have very strong teeth. Having gone to the trouble of peeling your Puffballs, lightly fry them in a little butter, perhaps having dipped them in beaten egg and breadcrumbs first.

With all Puffballs, it is important to only pick young specimens that are pure white throughout when cut in half. Any sign of yellow or green and they should be discarded. They are not poisonous; they just taste like wet cotton wool with a dash of vinegar!

Beware of Earth Balls, which are similarly round and can commonly be found in the woods. Earth Balls have been implicated in the odd poisoning incident, but they are not seriously toxic and are easy to distinguish from Puffballs. The chief reason for avoiding them is that they have much the same culinary virtues as tree bark – none at all. Unlike Puffballs, Earth Balls are never pure white inside; the youngest have yellow flesh, the mature purple black. If that isn't enough to reassure you, just check the skin, which is thin on Puffballs and thick and leathery on Earth Balls.

P.S. Latin names are handed out by taxonomists with little concern for the feelings of the organism involved. We have contrived to give ourselves the very respectable *'Homo sapiens'*, which means 'thinking man'. Our Meadow Puffball (*Vascellum pratense*) – 'Little vase that lives in a meadow' – doesn't do too badly either. However, the Stump Puffball (*Lycoperdon pyriforme*) was not so lucky. 'Pear-shaped thing that farts like a wolf' is not a name one would choose for oneself.

Puffballs are so-called because they 'puff' out their spores when squeezed. When mature, the spores sit in a cotton wool-like structure waiting for a drop of rain to land on the papery skin and puff the spores out through the little hole in the top. This, of course, is what the unfortunate Latin name refers to, though I have been unable to find out what wolves have to do with it. The Meadow Puffball is less sophisticated and the skin on its top simply breaks down to leave a little vase open to every drop of rain that might simply splash the spores into the air.

Giant Puffball *Calvatia gigantea*

SHAPE: Usually about 30cm in diameter, though occasionally much bigger. The largest one recorded was 84cm in diameter and weighed 22kg! When young, it has a pure white, kid-leather skin and the undifferentiated flesh is white and spongy throughout. There is no visible stem but the base wrinkles towards the fine mycelial strand that connects to the mycelium in the soil.

HABITAT: Pasture, nettle beds, sometimes rich soil in woods.

FREQUENCY: Occasional.

SEASON: Summer to autumn.

IF THERE IS ONE edible fungus that cannot possibly be mixed up with anything inedible, it just has to be the wonderful Giant Puffball. (Although I did once clamber into a field to try to pick a white duck.) Few things make the heart leap as much as spotting a ring of this enormous and supremely distinctive fungus in a meadow or on a distant hillside.

My best ever find was of 23 Giant Puffballs, all in one field and all in perfect condition. I picked half a dozen, which I then shared with friends, and virtuously left the rest to mature and produce their spores.

Giant Puffball

Giant Puffball

The texture of a Giant Puffball is rather similar to tofu, but I am pleased to report that the flavour is much, much better. ('Tofu' means 'rotten beans', which really says it all as far as I am concerned.) For a normal 30cm-diameter Puffball, it is worth cutting it in half and returning one half, in a plastic bag, to the fridge where it will keep for several days. The soft absorbent flesh is more suited to the frying pan than the stew pot, where it can become tasteless and soggy. I like them best in an omelette. Cut off the thin skin, slice the flesh about a centimetre thick, break up the slices into smallish pieces and fry both sides in butter with a little salt (it really needs the salt). When golden brown, pour in some beaten egg and you will soon be enjoying one of the world's greatest omelettes.

As Giant Puffballs start to mature, the flesh goes green and sweats profusely. Eventually, all the water is lost and the mature brown spores are suspended in a cotton wool-like mesh. Incidentally, this 'capillitium', as it is called, and the spores it holds have a clever knack of never getting wet, allowing the spores to be slowly released over a period of up to a year. We, of course, are only interested in the immature specimens, which are pure white throughout. If they feel dry and give a solid ring when tapped, they are likely to be okay. If you are unsure, just leave them in peace to produce their spores. Sometimes, if I find a maturing specimen in a vulnerable position (usually a field of cows), I rescue it and remove it to a hedgerow or adopt it and take it home to the safety of my garden. When the spores have matured, I wait for a windy day and give it a good kick; it's the least I can do.

They are most at home in rich soil in old grassland, but I have found them in nettle beds, ancient silage pits, hedges and even compost heaps. Giant Puffballs are so conspicuous that it is difficult to judge how common they really are. I give them the benefit of the doubt and pick just one or two.

P.S. The whole purpose of fruit bodies is to produce spores; this is something that Giant Puffballs do with Herculean single-mindedness. I haven't taken the time to check the assertion that a single average Puffball will produce no fewer than seven trillion spores, but it is in line with what is known about other large fungi. What I have done, and I realise I should get out more, is calculate what seven trillion spores would look like if they were each the size of a baked bean. Well, if you took four of the huge Millennium Stadia in Cardiff you could fill them to the roof. You would also have a particularly fine piece of installation art.

The immediate question, of course, is why are we not up to our necks in Puffballs? There are several answers: fewer than one spore in a thousand is viable; they are very fussy about where they grow; they have to face competition from other fungi; they are eaten by micro-organisms and invertebrates; and their mycelium may well be growing happily in that field down the road but just hasn't fruited yet.

Cauliflower Fungus *Sparassis crispa*

SHAPE: A more or less rounded mass of thin, branching, twisted lobes arising from a thick central stem. Almost white to creamy yellow, sometimes with a dark edge. Typically 30cm across, but occasionally much larger.
HABITAT: At the base of pine trees.
FREQUENCY: Fairly common, though scarce in some years.
SEASON: Late summer to autumn.

NOT EVEN THE most nonchalant of mushroom hunters can repress a whoop of delight at the sight of a Cauliflower Fungus resting at the base of a pine tree. For once, nature has supplied us with a fungus that both tastes very good indeed and comes in banquet-sized packages. It has a strong nutty/mushroomy flavour and can hold its own in a greater variety of dishes than just about any other mushroom. It is at home in frittatas, soups and stews and happy to be baked, braised and sautéed. Actually, there is a limit even to this highly adaptable species as I discovered when I tried to make a sweet milk pudding with it once – it was quite awful and the memory of it has haunted me ever since.

The Cauliflower Fungus can appear at the base of the same pine tree year after year. Still, I always feel guilty picking a whole one so unless I am throwing a dinner party for the entire village I usually just slice off what I need for tea.

The only fungus that looks remotely like it is the edible, if sometimes indigestible, Hen of the Woods (*Grifola frondosa*) – not to be confused with the Chicken of the Woods! It has a mass of small caps that are grey/brown on top and white below.

If there is one drawback with the Cauliflower Fungus, it is the amount of time needed to extricate pine needles, pine bark and earwigs. I minimise this effort by simply not worrying too much; there is just no point in being too precious about this sort of thing.

Wavy lobes

Cauliflower Fungus

Chicken of the Woods

Laetiporus sulphureus

SHAPE:	More or less semi-circular layered brackets, 10–40cm across. Upper surface velvety, zoned bands of **bright orange and yellow**, edge rounded and bright yellow. Lower surface bright yellow with very small pores. All these colours fade with age.
HABITAT:	On oak trees and some other trees.
FREQUENCY:	Common.
SEASON:	Spring to autumn.
WARNING:	Must be cooked, upsets some, avoid any growing on yew!

THERE IS NO FUNGUS that stirs people's imagination like Chicken of the Woods. Perhaps it is the intriguing name, or perhaps its amazing colour. It has a pleasant flavour, even if it is a little 'fungus-y' for some palates. The combination of mild flavour and soft fragility make it something of a fungal 'tofu', but the 'chicken' part of its name is no misnomer and it can replace chicken in many recipes.

Chicken of the Woods is extremely easy to identify and as such it is a safe bet. Unfortunately there is a problem – it doesn't agree with everyone. There are many credible reports of it causing dizziness, hallucinations and gastro-intestinal problems in a relatively small proportion of those who eat it. To minimise your chance of suffering any such misfortune, I suggest that you pick only specimens that are young and fresh, avoid any that do not grow on broad-leaved trees, make sure that the fungus really is thoroughly cooked and when you first eat it, try just the smallest of amounts.

Mostly they are found on living (though soon to be dead!) oak trees, but fruit bodies on willows, poplar, yew (do not collect any that grow on yew as they are known to be poisonous!) and some others are not uncommon. Rather than removing the whole thing from the tree, I just cut off some of the softer, milder flesh from the edge.

Beware of *Phaeolus schweinitzii*,

a large bracket fungus found at the base of conifers. It would take an inexcusable lack of concentration to confuse Chicken of the Woods with anything unpleasant, but *Phaeolus schweinitzii* does bear a passing resemblance. It is not poisonous, but you really wouldn't want to eat one. It is vaguely the same shape and it does have quite a bit of yellow about it. It is easily distinguished, however, because it also has a lot of brown and it is as hairy as a badger.

Chicken of the Woods

Jelly Ear *Auricularia auricula-judae*

SHAPE: Up to 7cm across. Cup-shaped when young, becoming irregularly lobed and uncannily ear-like on maturity. ***Very rubbery***. Red-brown. Inner surface smooth and shiny, outer surface scurfy.

HABITAT: Dead elder tree branches, and rarely on holly and other small trees.

CONSIDERING THAT Jelly Ears of one sort or another are cultivated at the rate of nearly half a million tons per year, it may seem surprising that few British mushroom hunters ever bother with them. The Jelly Ear, however, is something of an acquired taste. The undistinguished mild flavour and its unassailable crunchiness (I casseroled some for eight hours once and they stayed as crisp as when they were when picked) has assured them a place in Chinese cuisine, but has proved something of a challenge to western palates. A plate of boiled or fried Jelly Ears may be an unappetising prospect, but used with discretion in a spicy soup or stew where they can absorb the surrounding flavours, their unfamiliar qualities become clear assets.

The Cloud Ear (*Auricularia polytricha*) is the closely related cultivated species that can be bought in dried form from Oriental emporia. Our own native species, the Jelly Ear, is a very common fungus that is nearly always found on the dead branches of elder trees. The Jelly Ear, or Jew's Ear as it is often called (after the unlikely story that Judas Iscariot hanged himself on an elder tree – they are too springy for that grim purpose), is the most reliable of all the fungi; if I need some I just go to one of my local Jelly Ear trees and pick them. Only during the coldest and driest times of the year do they fail. If you acquire a particular liking for this fungus, it is worth drying some (p.243); 15 minutes of soaking in warm water will reconstitute them completely.

Jelly Ear collection

Beware of some of the Cup Fungi (from the *Peziza* family), as they can also look like ears, and often similar in colour. They are all inedible, but easily distinguished by their brittle rather than gelatinous flesh, and by always growing on soil. There are many other Jelly fungi but none of them look like ears and none of them are known to be poisonous.

Jelly Ear

EDIBLE SPECIES 127

Beefsteak Fungus *Fistulina hepatica*

CAP:	15–25cm across and 6cm thick. Dark liver-coloured, rubbery. Exudes a watery blood-like latex, especially when cut or squeezed.
TUBES:	Cream-coloured when young and easily separated from one another.
FLESH:	Red and marbled with white veins when young. Tastes acidic.
HABITAT:	On oak, rarely sweet chestnut.
FREQUENCY:	Common.
SEASON:	Autumn.

ONE REASON that fungi have for so long been treated with suspicion is their tendency to look like body parts – occasionally unmentionable body parts. Nowhere is this odd talent better demonstrated than in a young Beefsteak Fungus, which looks so very much like a tongue it is surprising that it was never adopted by proponents of the Doctrine of Signatures as a cure for stammering. As it ages, it starts to look more like a piece of liver (though if you saw it in a butcher's shop you would probably decide on lamb chops for tea that night), and it is from this appearance that it earns its name '*hepatica*'. At any stage, the cut flesh has a marbled, fibrous texture just like a rather fatty piece of braising steak and will exude copious amounts of a fluid easily mistaken for blood (you can clearly see a drop of this 'blood' on the leaf in the picture opposite). Altogether a thoroughly meaty fungus.

But does it live up to all this savoury promise? Well, not entirely. Its strongly acidic flavour, especially noticeable in young fruit bodies, is quite unlike the subtle, mild flavours we are used to with most mushrooms and will appeal only to those with more robust palates. If the acidity is too much for you, then soaking it in milk for 24 hours will certainly help. The rather rubbery texture survives the cooking process largely intact and is not to everyone's taste, so another possibility is to stew the sliced flesh with shallots and water for 20 minutes or so and to use only the ensuing gravy-like sauce, discarding the fungus itself. I am reminded of the good Dr Johnson's advice on the preparation of cucumber: 'A cucumber should be well sliced, and dressed with pepper and vinegar, and then thrown out, as good for nothing.' While I think that he would have said much the same about the Beefsteak Fungus, perhaps you ought to give it a chance. At least it is impossible to mix up with anything else and it provides an amusing way of frightening vegetarian friends at dinner parties.

Beefsteak Fungus

P.S. The Beefsteak Fungus is a cause of brown rot in oak and chestnut. As parasites go it is very well behaved, and will live quietly within the heartwood of the tree, gradually removing the structurally important cellulose to leave the brown lignin. Eventually it will make a career change from mild parasite to saprotroph, and proceed to hollow out the tree, releasing nutrients for the tree to recycle. If this process is, literally, cut short and the oak felled for timber, the planked boards will have a rich brown colour quite unlike the pale straw tones of uninfected oak and is referred to as 'brown oak'. Sometimes the infection has only taken partial hold and the result is the beautiful 'tiger-stripe oak'. You may have seen wooden bowls, usually of beech, at craft fairs and such like where the wood displays a pattern of black lines and irregular circles known as spalting. These are caused by fungal colonies spreading outwards in a roughly spherical manner and meeting another colony advancing in the other direction. The black lines mark the ensuing battle.

Summer Truffle *Tuber aestivum*

SHAPE: 2.5–9cm in diameter. Irregularly rounded, sometimes with hollowed-out areas. Surface consists of shiny black pyramidal warts. Flesh white at first then yellow-brown, marbled. When mature, smells strongly of Truffle!

HABITAT: In calcareous soil under a variety of trees, notably beech, hazel and oak.

FREQUENCY: Uncommon, though probably very under-recorded.

SEASON: Summer to early winter.

WITH EITHER great good fortune or a good deal of hard work it *is* possible to find Truffles in Britain. Although Truffle hunting has been an occasional occupation of the English countryside in the past, Truffles have never enjoyed anything like the adulation they receive in France and Italy. The noted French Truffle writer Jean-Marie Rocchia says that the Summer Truffle is found '… even in Southern England, where it is supremely disdained by the subjects of Her Gracious Majesty'.

As most people in this country will happily walk past a group of Ceps without a second glance, it is hardly surprising that few concern themselves with the rare and subterranean Summer Truffle. Pursuit of this elusive quarry has not been encouraged by the fact that the British Isles lack the Périgord Truffle and the White Truffle, both of which are orders of magnitude ahead of our Summer Truffle in both taste and price.

But how do you find them? My favoured method is to wait for someone who has discovered a handful of them, perhaps while digging over a rose bed near a beech hedge, to bring them along to ask for my expert opinion. I will say that I have no idea what they are but that if they leave them with me I will study them most diligently and let them know the results of my cogitations in due course.

Slightly more reliable is to simply find a suitable spot and scratch around in the hope of finding something. By far the best place to look is in open beech woods on chalky soil. There should be little in the way of ground cover, such as ivy and bramble, as Truffles dislike, and even suppress, surface vegetation, and their presence can sometimes be inferred from these exceptionally bare patches of ground. The little diggings of

Hollowed Truffle

Summer Truffle

squirrels searching for a snack can also provide a clue and I have even found partially nibbled Truffles just lying on the forest floor.

Start scraping away the soil close to the foot of a tree and work outwards for a metre or two. You will not need to dig deeply as Truffles seldom grow more than a few centimetres below the surface and will even push the soil up above them as though trying to burst through. Scratching away at the soil around a tree is very destructive of the mycelium of any of the fungi that may be there, including Truffles, so it is not a practice that I recommend you to use, except occasionally and then only on a small part of the area around each tree.

I once asked an Italian Truffle hunter if he used pigs to find Truffles. He said, with palpable derision, that only the French used pigs and then he spat on the ground. However, pigs can be used to find Truffles, though there are several drawbacks, not least of which is convincing the animal that you deserve the Truffle more than it does. Pigs are very large creatures and your powers of persuasion may not be up to the challenge. Much more sensible is to follow the Italians and use a dog. The main qualifications for being a Truffle hound are a good nose, a sweet temper and a manageable size. Something with a bit of spaniel in it is likely to fit the bill. Training a dog to find Truffles is actually not too difficult; contrary to popular belief, there is no need to have smeared Truffle paste onto its mother's teats when it was a pup, though you can if you want. Get hold of some dimethyl sulphide or (and I guess you are pleased to hear that there is an 'or') some Truffle oil and smear it on some small potatoes. Bury them for an hour or so, offer the smell to the dog and encourage it to locate the hidden potatoes (this is the hard part, but most dogs are very clever animals and should understand what is expected of them). When your dog finds the potato, reward him or her with fulsome praise and a treat. Alternatively, put some Truffle oil inside a cut-open tennis ball and play a game of 'catch', which should be allowed to develop into a game of 'hunt the tennis ball'.

If you are lucky or determined enough to find any Truffles, you could do no better than slice them onto scrambled egg.

Also look out for some of the other species of true Truffle in Britain, of which there are around 15. All of them are edible, though they are seldom large enough to be worthwhile. Pictured on p.130 are some small Hollowed Truffles (*Tuber excavatum*). This species is collected on the Continent and is used to make Truffle pâtés and oils. Hollowed Truffle is one of the Truffles that has a smooth surface.

P.S. Years ago, the British Mycological Society organised what can only be described as a pilgrimage to the various centres of the Italian Truffle industry. This memorable expedition has provided a lifetime's supply of anecdotes for its 20 or so participants, but apart from the searing embarrassment of once receiving a full, and unexpected, civic reception – mayor, town hall, brass band, the lot – while unshaven and wearing an anorak, the memory that stays with me most is that of the perfumed streets of Alba. In shop windows, on the plates of pavement diners and singly on little tables nervously attended by their owner, the White Truffles of Alba filled the air with their scent. The smell is intense, heady and overwhelming.

The White Truffle produces the most complex cocktail of aromatic chemicals, followed closely by the Périgord Truffle. Our own Summer Truffle lacks the more intriguing of these and so is less revered; but it does contain that most important of all the Truffle aromatics – the brain-numbingly smelly dimethyl sulphide.

Truffles produce their strong smells for a good reason. They belong to the ascomycetes – a group of fungi that disperse their spores by forcibly shooting them from the microscopic sausage-shaped structures in which they form. Living underground is in many ways a good lifestyle choice – it is safe, moist and relatively warm – but there is a serious drawback: there is nowhere to shoot your spores to. To circumvent this seemingly intractable problem, the mature Truffle produces a strong smell that attracts various animals, which proceed to devour it. In due course, the animals deposit the spores elsewhere and, with luck, a new Truffle mycelium is established.

Morels

Morchella esculenta

CAP: 6–10cm, irregularly rounded and deeply pitted like a honeycomb, hollow. Pale yellow to brown to grey.
STEM: White, hollow, grooved at base.
HABITAT: Copses, scrubby woodland, waste ground, gardens.
FREQUENCY: Uncommon.
SEASON: April and May.
WARNING: Poisonous raw, but perfectly safe when cooked!

M. elata

Generally similar to *M. esculenta* but with a pointed cap, which is grey/brown when mature. Most commonly found in forest bark mulch. It, too, must be cooked.

Morchella elata

SPRING FAMOUSLY brings many joys, but few match the sight of a group of Morels basking in the pale April sun. I spent a decade searching out this most thrilling of fungi. Every spring I would scour the New Forest, taking a special interest in the old forest fire sites, which Morels are said to favour, in the hope that this time my efforts would be rewarded. Years later I discovered that there is no record of Morels ever having been found in the New Forest and that I had been wasting my time. Hey ho.

What I did not know is that Morels are urbanites. They have, for the most part, given up their country ways and gone to live the high life in the big city. And so it is that every Morel I have ever found has been in someone's garden – in rose beds, in lawns, on compost heaps, on old Charlie's allotment and, most prolifically, in forest bark mulches. Even when Morels are found in natural locations, it is frequently on disturbed ground (that they like forest fire sites is quite true) and usually in unprepossessing locations.

The Morel you are most likely to find, *M. elata*, is the one that has taken to growing, sometimes in huge numbers, on forest bark mulches in municipal flowerbeds and domestic rose gardens. This species has a way of blending into the background and it can take a while to spot every one. It is not as tasty as *M. esculenta*, but it is still a great treat.

All the hollows and pits in a Morel provide excellent shelter for a variety of bugs, so you may have to spend some time serving eviction notices. On the other hand, their vernal habit means they are mercifully free of maggots.

As is witnessed by the imaginative prices they command in delicatessens, Morels have a very high epicurean standing. I am not too sure how well deserved this is as the flavour is really rather mild, but nevertheless they are strikingly beautiful fungi and it would be a pity not to treat them with some respect. I therefore favour recipes that preserve their good looks, like the one on p.196. However, should you be lucky enough to fill a couple of baskets with Morels, it would be worth drying and crushing a few (p.243). Powdered Morel is a fantastic thing to have in the kitchen as that mild flavour becomes highly intensified and can give a good mushroomy punch to any dish.

It is important to note that Morels are quite poisonous when raw, so, please, absolutely no salads and no lightly tossed stir-fries!

Beware of the False Morel (*Gyromitra esculenta*), p.178.

Although it is a related species, the resemblance to real Morels is only superficial – instead of having a honeycomb structure, the cap surface is convoluted. It is fairly uncommon in Britain, but still worth knowing about because it can be deadly.

P.S.

The domestic use of forest bark has turned the rather rare *M. elata* into a relatively common fungus, with 90 per cent of British finds occurring since 1985, when forest bark became popular. Why it should be so happy to grow on forest bark in people's gardens but not in forest bark in forests is something of a puzzler. It may be another example of 'stress fruiting', where fungi, running out of food, produce their reproductive organs (mushrooms) on the now-or-never principle. Experiments in Morel cultivation have found that if a single mycelium is grown in a medium half of which is rich in nutrients and half of which is not, then nutrients would be drawn from the rich part to feed Morels that start to grow in the poor part. (Do try to pay attention, there will be a test later.) This is exactly what we have when a nutrient-rich mulch is spread over a nutrient-poor soil. That my best ever find occurred where the mulch was on top of a weed-suppressing membrane of no nutrient value whatsoever seems to support my theory. As for where the spores come from, well, they're everywhere.

Morel

Poisonous Species

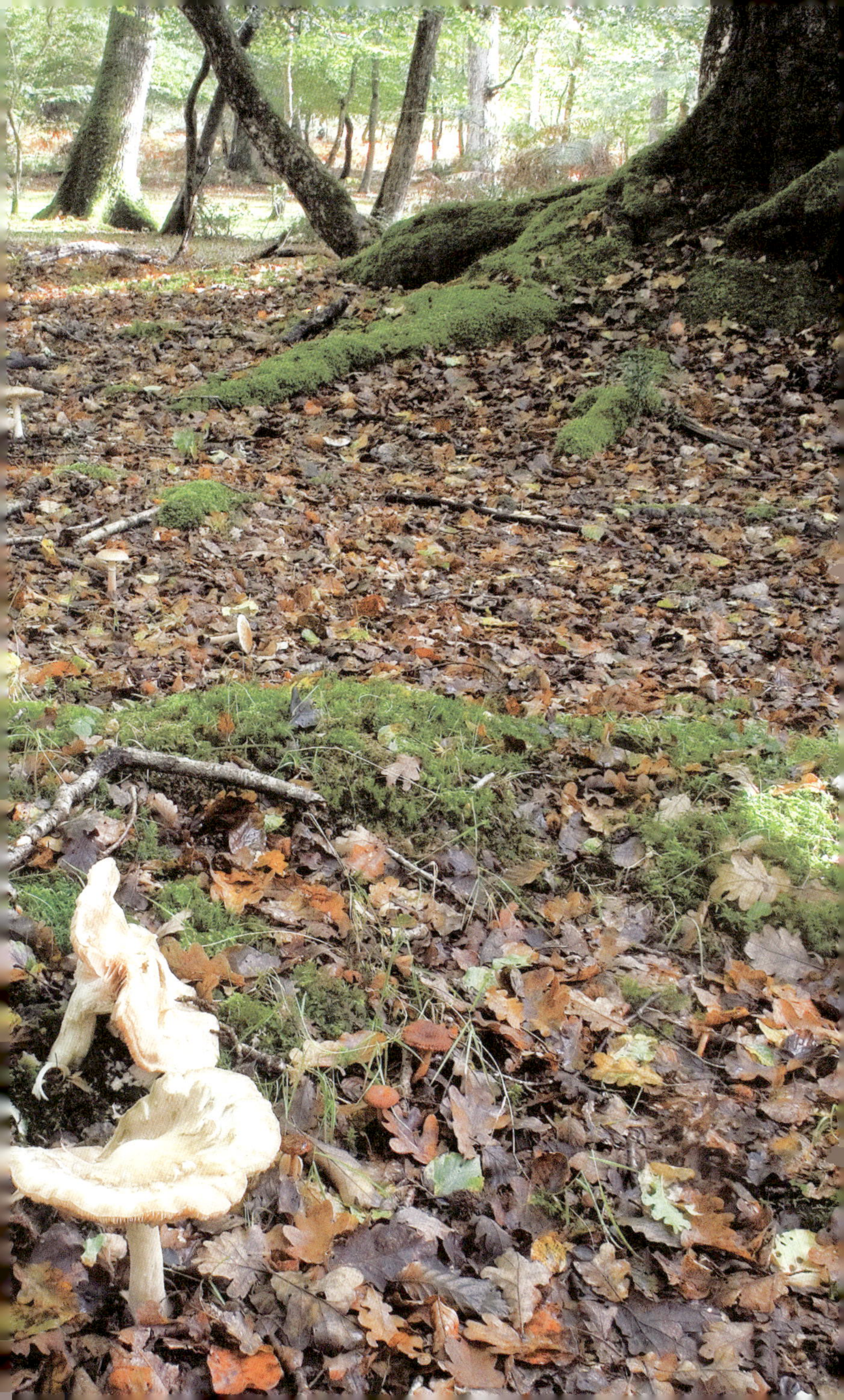

Poisonous Species *contents*

- 140 Death Cap
- 144 Fool's Funnel
- 145 Fenugreek Milkcap
- 146 The Dapperlings
- 149 Fly Agaric
- 150 Panther Cap
- 152 The Sickeners
- 154 Livid Pinkgill
- 154 Silky Pinkgill
- 156 Deadly Fibrecap
- 158 Webcaps
- 160 Funeral Bell
- 162 Poison Pies
- 164 Brown Roll Rim
- 167 Magic Mushroom
- 168 Sulphur Tuft
- 170 Common Inkcap
- 172 Yellow Stainer
- 172 Inky Mushroom
- 175 Bitter Bolete
- 177 Devil's Bolete
- 178 False Morel

As not all fungi have been tested for their toxicity, it is difficult to say how many of the 4,000 or so larger fungi that grow in this country are poisonous. My guess of around the 400 mark would give a random picker a one in ten chance of poisoning themselves. Don't do this. Fortunately, only around 20 are deadly poisonous and of these fewer than half are at all common. Less fortunately, the Death Cap (p.140), which causes a good 90 per cent of all fatalities due to fungal poisoning in Europe, is quite a common fungus. It is a toadstool I see three or four times a year and if you want to go mushrooming you really must learn what it looks like.

There are obviously nothing like 400 species considered here, but some groups (genera) of fungi contain many poisonous members and it is often sufficient to discuss just one of them accompanied by a warning to avoid some or all of its cousins. Nevertheless, if your specimen is not mentioned here this does not mean you can eat it! You must also have *positively* identified it as an edible species. The meanings of the ominous-looking 'X's are clear enough with an 'XXX' reserved for the deadly species.

Fungi can poison people in a whole range of fascinating ways and full and colourful details are provided with the appropriate species. The worst toxins are those that actually damage cells of the body. It is into this category that the Death Cap falls. The 'mildest' are those that simply cause gastrointestinal upset though it may not seem all that mild at the time. In addition, there are some that interfere with body chemistry. Muscarine, for example, stimulates the production of body fluids and coprine prevents the body from dealing effectively with alcohol. Finally, there are the toxins that produce primarily psychological effects, such as the one in the so-called Magic Mushroom (p.167).

In addition to the poisonous species, I have included one or two that, if not actually poisonous, would be unwelcome at the dinner table. The knowledge contained in the following pages is among the hardest earned in human history and we owe a huge debt to the many nameless martyrs who provided it.

Incidentally, I am occasionally asked what is the most deadly of all the fungi. The obvious answer is the Death Cap, but there is another species that has many, many more deaths on its conscience. It is called *Saccharomyces cerevisiae*, better known as brewer's yeast, and it produces a deadly toxin called ethyl alcohol.

Finally, do remember that even the most edible of fungi are poisonous if they have gone bad, so collect only the freshest of specimens and eat them as soon as you can.

Death Cap *Amanita phalloides* xxx

CAP:	5–12cm. Smooth and flatly convex at maturity. Sickly green, darker in the middle (the colour can be washed out in wet weather). Of particular importance for identification are the ***innate fibres*** radiating out from the centre of the cap.
STEM:	7–15cm by 1–2cm. Paler than the cap with an olive/grey mottled appearance. Swollen at the base and sitting in a distinct bag or ***volva***.
RING:	Large and pendulous with grooves on the top.
GILLS:	White, not touching the stem.
FLESH:	Pure white. Smells unpleasant, sickly, rancid.
SPORES:	White.
HABITAT:	It grows, usually in widely spaced groups of half a dozen or so, under oak and beech and in general mixed woods.
FREQUENCY:	Occasional.
SEASON:	Autumn.

I HAVE BEEN rather scathing in this book about using English names for fungi, but if any fungus needs one and deserves the one it gets, it is the Death Cap. A single specimen is quite enough to despatch you into the next world. Untreated, Death Cap poisoning has a 50 to 90 per cent mortality rate, and even with all that modern medicine can do it is fatal in 20 per cent of cases, tragically rising to around 50 per cent with children. It is responsible for 90 per cent of deaths by fungus so if you only ever learn to recognise one toadstool, then let it be this one.

The Death Cap is by no means uncommon; I usually find it three or four times a year, so it is no use just hoping that it won't cross your path. If you spend much of your time mushrooming, then one day you will find one. Death Cap fatalities in Europe and Russia run at a handful every year; in the UK it is around one per decade with just one or two non-fatal cases of poisoning every year. These are tiny percentages but of course if it is you, it is 100 per cent.

Dull green with innate fibres

Death Cap

It is customary in books on fungi to delight the reader with a gruesome description of the fate awaiting anyone unfortunate enough to consume a Death Cap, and I see no reason to depart from tradition. Here goes. The first symptoms have a relatively long incubation period of around 8 to 12 hours, a characteristic that is important in diagnosis. The symptoms suffered are gastrointestinal in nature, and they consist of abdominal pain, vomiting and cholera-like diarrhoea. The resulting fluid loss can cause lowered blood pressure, accelerated pulse, shock and leg cramps. This lasts for 12 to 24 hours, occasionally longer, and is followed by a period of recovery that also lasts 12 to 24 hours. But all this time the poison, amanitin, has been doing its terrible work and the signs of hepatic failure – pressure-sensitive liver, jaundice, intestinal bleeding and psychological disturbance – become evident, followed, in severe cases, by coma and death.

Loss of liver and kidney function ensures that a little of the poison goes a long way, so it helps to have only eaten a small amount in the first place, though it helps a great deal more not to have eaten any at all. There is no real cure, although high doses of penicillin and silybin (an extract of milk thistle!) have proved to be beneficial. Stomach washes and activated charcoal to remove the toxins from the stomach are employed, as are diuretics and blood treatments, such as haemodialysis. Apart from this, it is a matter of maintaining the body's electrolyte balance, general nursing care and hoping for the best.

I hope I have suitably frightened you about this fungus, but please do not become too paranoid about it; it is quite

Death Cap

False Death Cap

Destroying Angel

safe to handle one as long as you don't lick your fingers, and you must wash your hands before eating anything. Should you decide to collect one, and I am concerned as to why you would wish to do so, remember not to get it anywhere near other fungi – even the shed spores are deadly.

In its most typical form this is one of the easiest of all species to recognise, with several distinct characteristics. Dingy green caps, white rings on the stem and white bags at the base should all make the mushroom hunter pause for reflection. It is only when the fungus is damaged, very young or appears in its white form (a rare variety) that mistakes can understandably be made. The young 'button' Death Cap, when the whole fungus is covered with a white membrane, is particularly dangerous as it looks just like a button mushroom.

Also beware of other members of the *Amanita* genus, for, apart from *Amanita rubescens* and *A. fulva*, no Amanita should be eaten. Most of them are harmless, but many are rare and difficult to identify. At least one, the completely white Destroying Angel (*Amanita virosa*), is known to be every bit as deadly as the Death Cap. This beautiful whited sepulchre is quite rare in the south, but may be found with greater ease in Scotland.

Just as the edible species seem to have a poisonous or inedible double, the Death Cap has the False Death Cap. This is not poisonous, but the smell of raw potatoes does not inspire. It is distinguished from its evil twin by the smell, the yellow cap and by the 'gutter' around the top of the swollen base in place of the loose bag.

Fool's Funnel *Clitocybe rivulosa* xx

CAP:	3–5cm. Flattened to slightly depressed. Cap edge inrolled. Dirty white with a ***frosted*** look like the icing on a Belgian bun, usually with flesh coloured patches showing through.
STEM:	2–4cm by 0.5–0.8cm. Same colour as the cap, darker with handling.
GILLS:	Slightly decurrent, crowded, whitish to pale ochre.
FLESH:	Thin. Smells faintly mealy.
SPORES:	White.
HABITAT:	Pasture.
FREQUENCY:	Common.
SEASON:	Summer to late autumn.

THIS COMMON toadstool is seriously poisonous, even deadly. It contains high levels of the sweat-inducing toxin muscarine, and has sometimes been called the Sweating Mushroom.

The Fool's Funnel lives in small troops in grass and has the unhelpful habit of sometimes growing near the tasty, edible Fairy Ring Champignon (p.54). Fortunately, it does not look anything like it, although it is the same size. More worrying is its similarity to one of my favourite mushrooms: The Miller (*Clitopilus prunulus*), p.84.

There are several other poisonous little white *Clitocybe* species. They are all more or less funnel-shaped and have decurrent gills.

Fool's Funnel

Fenugreek Milkcap *Lactarius helvus* x

CAP:	6–12cm. Convex then flattened, often with a small central depression. Surface felt-like, later a little scaly, rather a dull greyish brick, later yellowish.
STEM:	5–12cm by 1–3cm. Similar colour to cap.
GILLS:	Pale ochre. ***Milk watery***, mild or slightly bitter.
FLESH:	Mild smelling when fresh, but smelling strongly of spicy stock cubes when dry.
SPORES:	Pale cream.
HABITAT:	In damp, mossy birch and pine woods.
FREQUENCY:	Uncommon.
SEASON:	Autumn.

LIKE THEIR cousins the Brittlegills, the Milkcaps can give warning of their poisonous nature by being very hot to the taste. The Woolly Milkcap and the Peppery Milkcap, for example, are unlikely to poison anyone because they are simply too hot to eat. Unfortunately, unlike the Brittlegills, the Milkcaps contain a rogue species that is poisonous even though it is mild in flavour. The poison is of the gastrointestinal variety and will give anyone who eats it an unpleasant few hours.

The Saffron Milkcap and its associates, all of which exude a bright orange milk, are very easily distinguished from the Fenugreek Milkcap, but the other Milkcap in this book – the Oak Milkcap (p.82) – requires more concentration. The most noticeable characteristic of the Fenugreek Milkcap is the strong smell of rather spicy stock cubes in dried or drying specimens. It is also fairly uncommon and found in damp pine and birch woods, not with oak.

The Dapperlings *Lepiota spp.* xxx

I will not describe any particular *Lepiota*, but sum up their main features.

CAPS:	Usually 6cm or less, the central patch is surrounded by concentric immovable scales. Umbrella-shaped, often with a central boss.
STEMS:	Often shaggy/fleecy.
RINGS:	Sometimes distinct, sometimes just a vague ring zone.
GILLS:	White and free of the stem.
SPORES:	White.
HABITAT:	Usually in ***woods***, occasionally in parks and pasture.
SEASON:	Summer to autumn.

AS AROUND one-quarter of the 40 or so Lepiotas contain the same poison, amanitin, as the Death Cap I have consigned the entire genus to outer darkness. The worst of a bad bunch is the Star Dapperling (*Lepiota helveola*), or possibly it is the Deadly Dapperling (*L. bruneoincarnata*), or maybe the Fatal Dapperling (*L. subincarnata*) which is pictured here. These and others have been implicated in a number of serious poisonings, including the occasional fatality. As the toxin is the same, the succession of symptoms is the same and I refer anyone who wants a good scare to the Death Cap entry (p.140) for the full gory details.

Lepiota species are quite distinctive, but they are still occasionally picked in error. The main concern for the mushroom hunter is their distinct similarity to *Macrolepiota* species, the eminently edible Parasols (p.75). The most straightforward way to avoid any Lepiota is to ensure that no open Parasol that you pick is less than 12cm in diameter. Most Lepiotas, including all the deadly ones, are less than 7cm in diameter and the only larger one, the rare *L. ignivolvata*, is not poisonous. Also make sure that your Parasols have good large rings that can be slid with reasonable ease up and down the stem. I met someone only recently who had picked and eaten some Dapperlings thinking they were young Parasols. It was a terrible mistake to make. She spent a week desperately ill in bed and was very lucky to survive.

One final consideration is that Dapperlings tend to have warm russet, orange or even pink colours, whereas Parasols are more chestnut in tone.

The other Dapperling pictured here is *L. magnispora*. As far as I know it is harmless, but I include it because it shows so well some of the characteristics of this dangerous genus.

Fatal Dapperling

Lepiota magnispora

POISONOUS SPECIES

Fly Agaric

Fly Agaric *Amanita muscaria* x

CAP:	10–20cm. Bright red and sometimes orange. Covered in pure white, movable spots (the remnants of the veil that covered the young fruit body).
STEM:	8–20cm by 1–2cm. White and faintly fleecy, base swollen and with fleecy bands.
RING:	Simple, pendulous.
GILLS:	White. Not touching the stem.
FLESH:	White.
SPORES:	White.
HABITAT:	Pine and birch.
FREQUENCY:	Very common.
SEASON:	Autumn.

THE FLY AGARIC is the consummate toadstool – beautiful, magical and deadly. Except that it is not deadly and, despite its fearsome reputation, it is not seriously poisonous at all. It does contain trace amounts of muscarine, but it would take about 70kg of Fly Agaric to cause any serious damage, a challenging meal for even the hungriest mushroom hunter. Its fairy tale beauty is in no doubt, however, and neither is its magical quality. The 'magic' comes from a substance called ibotenic acid, which turns into the powerful psychoactive drug muscimol. The symptoms start half an hour to three hours after ingestion and may include nausea and other physical symptoms. The psychological effects are not entirely unlike those caused by an excess of Chablis – including euphoria, difficulty speaking, confusion and sleep. As a bonus, one can look forward to feelings of floating, exaggerated movements, cramps, tremors and also muscle spasms.

These all sound rather too scary to me, but the Fly Agaric is commonly used as a recreational mushroom and there are some highly colourful reports of its use in north-eastern Asia from the eighteenth and nineteenth centuries. The famous ethnomycologist, Wasson, relates the practices of the robust Koryak people who exchanged reindeer skins for dried Fly Agarics from Russia. The Fly Agarics were scarce and highly prized but 'fortunately' (and I do use the word with considerable hesitation), muscimol is an eminently 'recyclable' compound and is excreted in the urine intact. The revellers would therefore carefully collect their urine and consume it in order to give themselves a 'second go', or maybe a friend (presumably a very close friend) their first. Cheers!

Panther Cap *Amanita pantherina* xx

CAP:	7–12cm. Chocolate brown with fine, **white fleecy scales**, fine striations on the edge.
STEM:	6–10cm by 1–2cm. White, swollen base with a distinctly **rimmed volva** like a little flower pot.
RING:	White. **Lacks grooves** on upper surface.
GILLS:	White, not touching the stem.
FLESH:	White.
SPORES:	White.
HABITAT:	Broadleaved woodland.
FREQUENCY:	Fairly uncommon, though locally abundant.
SEASON:	Autumn.

THIS IS THE neatest toadstool you will ever see. Dapper even. But one should never judge a fungus by how good it looks and this is a seriously poisonous species. It contains the same toxins, including the hallucinogenic ones, as its close cousin the Fly Agaric (p.149), but in concentrations that are high enough to cause dangerous physical symptoms in many and even death in someone weakened by heart disease.

The problem with the Panther Cap is two-fold: it is occasionally mistaken for the edible Amanitas and it is known to attract those collecting for purely 'recreational' purposes.

The Panther Cap is the bane of the careless Blusher collector (p.64). The similarity is superficial, but a lapse in concentration could see a Panther Cap finding its way into the mushroom basket. Its distinctly brown cap (which never shows any sign of pink), the white rather than pink/grey spots and the lack of grooves on the upper surface of the ring make differentiation certain, but a systematic check must always be made when picking Blushers.

The most problematic species, at least for those who like to indulge in extreme mushrooming, is the common and reputedly edible Grey Spotted Amanita (*Amanita spissa*). This looks almost *exactly* like the Panther Cap, but can be quickly distinguished by the fact that it *does* have little grooves on the top of the ring. Relying on one small detail is just not enough for me, but if you like the excitement of having your life hanging by a thread, then you could do worse than collect Grey Spotted Amanitas.

The Panther Cap is sometimes gathered for its mind-altering qualities, but as hallucinogenic mushrooms go this is a very poor choice. It is one of the few 'magic' mushrooms that is known to have caused fatalities and, as the active ingredients vary enormously depending on when and where they were picked, the effects are totally unpredictable.

Panther Cap

POISONOUS SPECIES 151

The Sickener *Russula emetica* x
& Beechwood Sickener *R. nobilis* x

CAP:	4–8cm. Bright red.
STEM:	5–8cm by 1–2cm. White.
GILLS:	White to pale cream, brittle.
FLESH:	White, pink below peeled cap. Very hot and acrid (spit it out!).
SPORES:	White.
HABITAT:	Sickener in coniferous woods, Beechwood Sickener in beech woods!
FREQUENCY:	Common.
SEASON:	Autumn.

THIS PRETTY PAIR is common in coniferous and beech woodlands respectively. No Brittlegill is particularly dangerous, but the intense acridity of many of them, including these two, is too much for most stomachs, which promptly complain in the colourful way they know best. Apparently, and I really don't intend to check this, parboiling can make many, if not all, of the acrid Brittlegills both palatable and safe.

While the safest way to avoid the two Sickeners is to avoid all red Brittlegills, some of them are, in fact, mild in taste and perfectly edible. The Brittlegills are notoriously difficult to identify but the simple test of nibbling a piece and spitting it out if it tastes hot is enough to settle the matter (this *only* works with Brittlegills!). The nineteenth-century Italian mycologist Vittadini is reported by Badham to have, unsportingly, fed them to his dogs and, observing no ill effects, fried up five good specimens and ate them. They were, he says, still acrid and unpleasant to the taste, but he suffered no more than 'praecordial uneasiness' and flatulence. Whatever the first of these is, I doubt if I would like it any more than I would the second.

P.S. The peppery taste of some of the Brittlegills and Milkcaps comes from a group of chemicals called the sesquiterpenes. If you have ever eaten a ginger biscuit, you will have eaten sesquiterpenes before. The flavour of ginger comes from a trio of these compounds – though, oddly, not its pungence.

There is reason to believe that the sesquiterpenes are synthesised chiefly after the fungus has been damaged, as is witnessed by the time it sometimes takes to taste them. It is very likely that they form a defence against attack by insect larvae; a defence that also works well against humans!

Beechwood Sickener

The Beechwood Sickener's pure white gills

Livid Pinkgill & Silky Pinkgill

Livid Pinkgill *Entoloma sinuatum* x x

CAP:	7–15cm. Convex then flattened/wavy. Cream to dirty grey/brown with age. Innate fibres radiating outwards.
STEM:	5–12cm by 1–2.5cm. Fairly cylindrical, sometimes with a swollen base. White, then off-white. Innate fibres run the length of the stem, slightly scaly.
GILLS:	*Pale yellow at first*, then pink as the spores mature.
FLESH:	White and firm, smells mealy.
SPORES:	Pink.
HABITAT:	Broadleaved trees.
FREQUENCY:	Uncommon.
SEASON:	Autumn.

Silky Pinkgill *E. sericeum* x

CAP:	5–7cm. Rounded then flattened, dark brown drying paler, *innate silky fibres*.
STEM:	2.5–6cm by 0.3–0.6cm. Brown, whitish below, fibrous.
GILLS:	Pink. Edge irregular.
FLESH:	Brown, smells mealy.
SPORES:	Pink.
HABITAT:	Pasture.
FREQUENCY:	Common.
SEASON:	Autumn.

THE LIVID PINKGILL is a splendid-looking toadstool that grows in large rings or groups in deciduous woods. Although believed to be responsible for 10 per cent of all poisonings, I cannot imagine which mushroom it is that people mistake it for, unless it is the barely edible Clouded Agaric; perhaps it just looks tasty. It is not clear what toxins it contains, but it does cause serious gastrointestinal symptoms, which include severe stomach cramps. It has also been associated with liver damage that might be fatal. Though again I do not know what one would mistake it for, the Silky Pinkgill is also worth knowing because it can cause vomiting and is a common denizen of fields and meadows.

There are several other Entolomas, but none are worth eating and most are known to be poisonous or are under suspicion. They all have flesh-pink spores that often colour the gills a fainter pink.

Livid Pinkgill

Silky Pinkgill

POISONOUS SPECIES 155

Deadly Fibrecap *Inocybe erubescens* xxx

CAP:	4–8cm. Conical with a central boss, cream with brown *radial fibres*, *reddening* with age, often *split* at the edge.
STEM:	4–8cm by 1–1.5cm. Slightly darker than cap, reddening, fibrous, slightly swollen at the base.
GILLS:	Buff at first with a white edge, then darker brown as the spores mature, reddening.
FLESH:	White.
SPORES:	Brown.
HABITAT:	Broadleaved trees, usually beech, can stray into neighbouring pastureland.
FREQUENCY:	Rare.
SEASON:	Summer.

I SUPPOSE the archetypal poisonous toadstool must be the Fly Agaric with its bright red cap and white spots (p.149). While it is indeed poisonous, its evil reputation is largely undeserved and comes more from its startling appearance than its actual toxicity. The little-known Deadly Fibrecap, on the other hand, contains no less than 100 times as much of the deadly muscarine as does the Fly Agaric. Furthermore, anyone who eats a Fly Agaric can hardly

Deadly Fibrecap

say they haven't been warned, whereas the Deadly Fibrecap is altogether more subtle in appearance and can fairly easily be mistaken for several of the collectable mushrooms.

Muscarine affects the peripheral nervous system and it produces an interesting range of symptoms of a 'productive' nature including sweating, lacrimation (tears), excessive urination, excessive salivation, vomiting and diarrhoea. It also, more dangerously, slows the heart and constricts the lungs. The effects wear off after an eventful 6 to 24 hours. The good news is that muscarine poisoning is seldom fatal and can be easily treated with atropine, which presents us with an intriguing possibility. Atropine is the deadly toxin found in Belladonna, so *in theory*, if you ate Deadly Fibrecap followed by Deadly Nightshade, you would be fine. Never, ever try this at home!

The chief concern with the Deadly Fibrecap is that when it is young, it is white to cream-coloured and so looks rather similar to a button mushroom. As a consequence, confusion with Field Mushrooms (p.93) and, given its early summer appearance, the St George's Mushroom (p.62), is conceivable. The Deadly Fibrecap does always grow with trees, but a field alongside a wood might well produce them, too. Do not become too alarmed, however. Its similarities with edible species are superficial and the differences profound; it is only the reckless that will succumb.

Lilac Fibrecap

Also beware of *all* the Fibrecaps, as every one is believed to be poisonous.

Apart from the Deadly Fibrecap and the two discussed below, they fall into the 'Little Brown Toadstool' category, and are unlikely to tempt the average mushroom hunter. However, they could be collected in error while gathering small mushrooms like the Trumpet Chanterelles (p.78) or The Deceivers (p.66).

The most common of the Fibrecaps are the White Fibrecap (*I. geophylla*) and the Lilac Fibrecap (*I. geophylla* var. *lilacina*). The latter is bright lilac and could be mistaken for the Amethyst Deceiver (p.66). All of the Fibrecaps have caps made up of fibres radiating out from the centre. Often the cap edges are split. The spore print is snuff brown.

Deadly Webcap & Fool's Webcap

Deadly Webcap *Cortinarius rubellus* xxx

CAP:	3–8cm. Conical or convex. Rusty/orange with fine scales.
STEM:	5–12cm by 0.5–1.5cm. Swollen at base. Paler than the cap, covered in a zigzag band of yellowish scales.
GILLS:	*Broadly spaced*, rusty yellow.
FLESH:	Pale yellow, staining rust in parts. Smells of radish.
SPORES:	Rust brown.
HABITAT:	Under pine and spruce.
FREQUENCY:	Rare. Most commonly found in Scotland.
SEASON:	Late summer to autumn.

NOTE: The Fool's Webcap (*C. orellanus*) and other dangerous members of this genus are similar, but the simple rule is to never eat any *Cortinarius* species.

IN 1952 THERE WAS a terrible mass poisoning in Poland. One hundred and two people were poisoned and eleven of them perished. The fungus that had wrought such havoc had undoubtedly caused untold suffering before, but it had evaded suspicion because of the very long delay – two to seventeen days – before its very serious effects became evident. This time it had, as it were, gone too far, and *Cortinarius orellanus*, the Fool's Webcap, was unmasked as a killer.

It is uncommon in Britain, as is the closely related Deadly Webcap, pictured opposite, which is just as dangerous. Some years ago the Deadly Webcap poisoned a trio of young people who were holidaying in Scotland. One of them recovered, but the other two, having suffered irreparable kidney damage, required transplants to restore them to reasonable health. There are one or two other species, such as *C. gentilis*, in this dangerous group, all of them members of the sub-genus *Leprocybe*.

The toxic syndrome is referred to as 'orellanus syndrome'. It is very similar to the Death Cap's 'phalloidin syndrome', which likewise assaults kidney function. The symptoms, expressed after the very long latent period (which evidently does not encompass any early gastrointestinal disturbance) are appetite loss, thirst, headache, vomiting, diarrhoea and shivering. Total kidney failure may follow and death soon afterwards.

The genus *Cortinarius* is very large and its members notoriously difficult to identify. It contains no fungus of even moderate culinary worth, but it does contain several deadly poisonous ones and a large number that live under a cloud of suspicion. I once managed to eat the Bruising Webcap (*C. purpurascens*), but it was not the most uplifting

Deadly Webcap

White cortina

experience – the faint but distinctive hydrogen cyanide flavour of bitter almonds is not one to be looked for in a mushroom; I shall not be repeating the experiment. It is worth having nothing to do with any of them.

As a genus, *Cortinarius* is quite easy to recognise as long as you are able to examine a young specimen. Instead of a ring from the stem to the cap edge, there is a web of fibres. This 'cortina', as you can see from the picture of the anonymous specimen pictured to the right, is clearly visible on immature fruit bodies, although spore-stained remnants of it can be seen stuck to the stem or cap edge on the more elderly. The youngsters sport either a white cortina or sometimes a blue cortina, a fact that I find endlessly amusing.

Funeral Bell *Galerina marginata* xxx

CAP:	2–7cm. Convex. Rusty brown, drying distinctly paler in the middle and/or at the edge. Margin slightly striate.
STEM:	3–9cm by 0.3–0.8cm. Similar colour to the cap or paler, darker below. Smooth.
RING:	Membranous ring.
GILLS:	Reddish brown.
FLESH:	Brown. Smells unpleasant.
SPORES:	Rust brown.
HABITAT:	In troops on dead wood, most often coniferous, but also broadleaved.
FREQUENCY:	Fairly common.
SEASON:	Autumn.

CONSIDERING the common occurrence and extremely poisonous nature of this toadstool, it is surprising that it is made so little of in the popular literature. Indeed, it has been described as being just unpalatable. In the 1960s, the presence of amatoxins in some *Galerina* species was detected and the treacherous character of this genus established. Amatoxins, the same deadly poisons found in the Death Cap, may come in lower concentrations in *G. marginata*, but meal-size portions of 100–150g of the fresh fungus are enough to cause death.

When I first began mushroom hunting I would often come across a species called *Kuehneromyces mutabilis*, which was recommended by the few books I possessed as an edible species. I am pleased that it never took my fancy as my books gave no warning that it is almost identical to the Funeral Bell, and the two can only be differentiated by the most careful examination.

Some grassland species of *Galerina* are also poisonous and the downfall of the careless 'recreational' collector. The rule that Little Brown Toadstools should be avoided is a good one.

P.S. If you spend much of your time reading books on mushrooms, you may have come across the names *G. autumnalis* and *G. unicolor*. Now, taxonomists (the people who name living organisms) come in two notoriously argumentative flavours: the 'lumpers' and the 'splitters'. At the moment, the lumpers are ahead of the game and these two toadstools are both now considered to be our *G. marginata*. But there are good reasons for believing that there are three separate species after all and the splitters may yet rule the day. For our simple purposes, however, the situation is straightforward enough – don't eat them. Any of them.

Funeral Bell

Funeral Bell in detail

POISONOUS SPECIES

Poison Pies *Hebeloma spp.* x

I will not describe any particular *Hebeloma*, but sum up their main features.

CAP:	Typically 2–7cm but one or two are larger. Convex. Russet to clay brown, sometimes sticky when moist.
STEM:	Often swollen at the base, white to cream-coloured, fibrous and often powdery. One or two have a ring.
GILLS:	Not touching the stem. Clay brown, white edged. Droplets often form **dark patches** on the gill edge.
FLESH:	Pale, sometimes smells of radish or bitter almonds.
SPORES:	Rusty brown.
HABITAT:	Mixed woodland.
FREQUENCY:	Very common.
SEASON:	Autumn.

POISON PIE is a nicely appropriate name for these gastrointestinal irritants. Their alternative name, Fairy Cake Mushrooms, is misleading to the point of irresponsibility. They may well be the smelliest of all fungi, with the various odours of radish, aniseed, flowers and chocolate reported.

Common in every type of woodland, often in large troops, their sometimes pale cap and brown gills could lead the unwary forager to mistake them for an ordinary mushroom. The genus *Hebeloma* contains over 70 species, none of which are welcome in the kitchen and most of which look pretty much like the one pictured on the right.

My favourite exception to this impenetrable uniformity is the Rooting Poison Pie, which has a ring on its taprooted stem and smells strongly of aniseed. Its already poor reputation as an edible fungus received a mortal blow when it was discovered where that taproot on the stem usually went: to the underground latrine of a mole.

Bitter Poison Pie

Typical Poison Pies complete with water drops

POISONOUS SPECIES 163

Brown Roll Rim *Paxillus involutus* xxx

CAP:	7–15cm. Generally funnel-shaped and usually with a central umbo at first. A variety of dingy-looking browns, viscid in wet weather. The cap edge is distinctively ***rolled under***, except on aged specimens. Cap margin with ***broad grooves***.
STEM:	3–7cm by 0.7–1.5cm. Cream-coloured and darker below.
GILLS:	Very decurrent, crowded, brown, bruising reddish. Easily separated from the cap.
FLESH:	Ochre.
SPORES:	Rusty brown.
HABITAT:	Woodland, most often with birch.
FREQUENCY:	Extremely common.
SEASON:	Late summer to autumn.

THE BROWN ROLL RIM is an oddity. While it can poison you in two quite separate ways, one of them occasionally deadly, it is still considered an edible species by some. Eaten raw it causes gastrointestinal disorders, but the guilty toxin can be removed by cooking and no ill effects will be felt. However, after the fungus has been eaten a number of times, another effect can come into play and haemolytic anaemia may occur. This may result in collapse, abdominal pain, vomiting and diarrhoea, along with renal symptoms, such as kidney pain and blood, or to be precise, haemoglobin, in the urine.

The Brown Roll Rim does not poison its victims but rather induces a severe allergy to itself in a process referred to as immunohaemolytic anaemia. Slowly, and largely without symptoms, it forms antigens in the blood serum until one meal too many is taken and catastrophic large-scale destruction of red blood cells occurs. Susceptibility varies from one person to another and the period of grace may stretch over years.

For a long time it was generally considered to be perfectly edible, provided it was prepared carefully – preferably parboiled before cooking, with the water thrown away. Then in 1940, the distinguished German

Deeply decurrent gills

Brown Roll Rim

mycologist Julius Schaeffer, famous for his work on the genus *Russula*, inadvertently contributed more to the body of mycological knowledge than he had ever hoped. After eating a series of dishes of Brown Roll Rim he promptly died and is, as far as I can discover, unique in being the only professional mycologist in history to have died by mushroom poisoning.

In my opinion, this drab and downright disreputable fungus – the ones pictured here are exceptionally neat examples of their kind – usually looks as though it should be helping the police with their enquiries and why anyone would wish to eat it is beyond me. Nevertheless, it is still regularly eaten in Eastern Europe, most notably in Poland, where it is the third most common cause of fungal poisoning.

Since the demise of the unfortunate Julius Schaeffer, a number of further deaths have been attributed to the Brown Roll Rim and, despite occasional and irresponsible attempts at rehabilitation, it is now properly considered to be a deadly species. Nevertheless, I know that people, presumably of East European origin, have taken to collecting it in the UK and it is only a matter of time before disaster strikes.

POISONOUS SPECIES

Magic Mushrooms

Magic Mushroom *Psilocybe semilanceata* x

CAP:	1–1.5cm. Acutely conical with a distinct 'nipple' on the top. Date-brown when young, maturing to a pale lemon, darkening at the cap edge. The cap is covered by a rubbery and peelable membrane.
STEM:	3–8cm by 0.1–0.2cm. Rather wavy.
GILLS:	Deep purple-brown.
SPORES:	Dark brown.
HABITAT:	Short grass in pasture or on heathland.
FREQUENCY:	Common.
SEASON:	Autumn.

THE MAGIC MUSHROOM is a singular fungus in many ways, not least in that it is the only one in this book that it is illegal to pick. If you don't know what it looks like, you *can* pick it legally though since you have seen the picture opposite I'm afraid that this excuse is now closed to you. The law changed in 2005; prior to then it was legal to collect it though not to prepare it. This meant that if you put your collection on a shelf and they dried out of their own accord that was fine, but if you put them on a shelf with the *intention* of drying them out, that became a preparation and wasn't. Now it is considered a class-A drug in any form and its possession or sale is a serious matter.

The 'magic' ingredients are psilocybin and psilocin, the former being the most important. Some 6–20mg, amounting to 12 to 24 specimens, is quite enough to cause intoxication. The effect is similar to that produced by LSD – elation, confusion, paranoia, formication (no not that, for*m*ication, which is the feeling of having things crawling under your skin), hallucinations and altered perception of space and time. These last for several hours, then wear off completely with no ill effects. Sometimes the experience is not at all a good one and people become locked, for a time, in a very frightening world. There is little evidence that Magic Mushrooms cause long-term damage, but excessive use over several years is unlikely to improve anyone's mental wellbeing.

For people who are determined to pick them, whatever the law says, the chief hazard is the possibility of picking something even worse and poisoning themselves as a result. While I do not wish to encourage dangerous experimentation, I must say that the Magic Mushroom is an extremely easy toadstool to identify. The key characteristics are the transparent rubbery membrane that covers the cap like a piece of cling film and the distinct nipple on the top.

Sulphur Tuft *Hypholoma fasciculare* xx

CAP:	4–7cm. Convex, sulphur yellow with an orange centre. Young specimens can have the remains of the partial veil attached to the edge.
STEM:	4–10cm by 0.5–1cm. Sulphur yellow turning foxy brown at the base.
RING:	Faint ring zone visible, usually dark with spores.
GILLS:	Sulphur-yellow, eventually black as the spores mature. Very crowded.
FLESH:	Yellow. Very bitter.
SPORES:	Purple-brown, almost black.
HABITAT:	Large and dense tufts on all sorts of dead wood.
FREQUENCY:	Extremely common.
SEASON:	Most abundant in the autumn to early winter, but often found earlier.

IT IS A POOR FUNGUS foray that does not encounter at least one group of Sulphur Tufts. This attractive toadstool appears in huge numbers on fallen logs and stumps and it is a great pity that it is not edible. The taste is extremely bitter and it causes quite serious gastrointestinal symptoms. It is highly distinctive and only by abandoning all caution could one pick this species by mistake. Unfortunately, this is just what an Italian restaurateur did quite recently, hospitalising all his customers with his mushroom special.

There have actually been a few fatalities attributed to this toadstool. It is, however, more likely that a mixed 'mushroom' dish containing some other nasty, such as the Funeral Bell (p.160), was responsible. If this is the case the unfortunate victims were worse mushroom hunters than even our Italian restaurateur, having managed to collect and consume not just one but two poisonous toadstools.

There is actually another *Hypholoma* species, the Brick Cap (*H. sublateritium*), which I know is quite a popular edible species but to my mind is too close to its poisonous cousin to be worth the risk. It has a brick-red cap and lacks sulphur-yellow gills.

Typical sulphur-yellow gills

A troop of Sulphur Tufts

Common Inkcap

Coprinopsis atramentaria x

CAP:	8cm high by 4cm wide. Ovoid then expanding to roughly conical. Grey or grey-brown. Striate.
STEM:	5–15cm by 0.8–1.5cm. White.
RING:	Ring-like zone near the base.
GILLS:	Extremely close together, white/grey, then brown to black. Disintegrating at maturity.
SPORES:	Black.
HABITAT:	Pasture, parks and gardens.
FREQUENCY:	Common.
SEASON:	Autumn.

THIS IS THE only fungus in the book that enjoys the dubious honour of a place in both the edible (with the Shaggy Inkcap, p.97) *and* the poisonous sections. This comes about because it is edible, but poisonous if you eat it with alcohol. For sensitive individuals there may even be a reaction from the tiny amount of alcohol absorbed through the use of aftershave or deodorant.

The Common Inkcap's duplicitous personality is due to a substance called coprine, which works its mischief by acting as an acetaldehyde-dehydrogenase inhibitor. This simply means that the liver becomes unable to break down alcohol completely and toxic levels of acetaldehyde build up in the body.

The symptoms are not life threatening. Unusually, for a poison of fungal origin there are no gastrointestinal problems. The chief effects are a feeling of hotness, reddening of the face and other parts of the upper body, tingling in the limbs and sometimes headache, sweating and shortness of breath. Sensitivity to alcohol can last for 72 hours, so you may be on the wagon for a while. As for what it tastes like, I am afraid that during the last 30 years or so my blood/alcohol ratio has not afforded me one single opportunity to find out.

Common Inkcap

POISONOUS SPECIES

Yellow Stainer & Inky Mushroom

Yellow Stainer *Agaricus xanthodermus* xx

CAP:	6–10cm, often flattened in the centre. White, sometimes grey, occasionally cracking, *strongly yellowing* when rubbed, notably so at the edge.
STEM:	5–12cm by 1–1.5cm, often *long* for the size of the cap. Base often swollen. White, *bruising an intense yellow*, especially in the *cut base*.
RING:	Large and complex, also yellowing when pinched.
GILLS:	White or pale in very young specimens (not pink as in the Field Mushroom). Mature specimens turn pink, then dark brown.
FLESH:	White but turns bright *chromium yellow* at the base of the stem and under the skin. The yellow *turns brown* after a few minutes. Smells unpleasant – carbolic.
SPORES:	Dark brown.
HABITAT:	Parkland, meadows, copses.
FREQUENCY:	Occasional.
SEASON:	Summer to autumn.

Inky Mushroom *A. moelleri* xx

CAP:	6–12cm, almost spherical when young, then flatly convex. A white background with grey/brown scales, darker in the centre. *Strongly yellowing* when rubbed, particularly at the edge.
STEM:	8–12cm by 1–1.5cm, usually *long* for the size of the cap. White, *bruising an intense yellow*, especially in the *cut base*.
RING:	Large and pendulous, yellowing when pinched.
GILLS:	White or pale in very young specimens, then pink, then dark brown.
FLESH:	The same as *A. xanthodermus*.
SPORES:	Dark brown.
HABITAT:	Parkland, woods, copses.
FREQUENCY:	Occasional.
SEASON:	Summer to autumn.

Yellow Stainer

Stained cap edge

Inky Mushroom

POISONOUS SPECIES 173

THE YELLOW STAINER is no killer, but its similarity to Horse, Field and Wood Mushrooms (pp.90, 93 and 99) makes it the single most common cause of mushroom poisoning in Britain. Many people assume that all 'mushrooms' (*Agaricus* species) are edible and pick them without discrimination. A mycological friend of mine was called upon to give his opinion on what turned out to be Yellow Stainers because, as his overly determined enquirer complained, 'they keep making me ill'.

The Yellow Stainer's woodland cousin, the Inky Mushroom (p.172), is quite frequent both in woods and at the roadside and, with its dark scaly cap, is sometimes mistaken for a Blushing Wood Mushroom (p.99).

Unfortunately, the Yellow Stainer is a very variable species that delights in appearing in many forms. It frequently foxes even the most experienced mushroom hunter who may have admired his or her fine collection of mushrooms for a minute or two before realising their mistake. Sometimes it is pure white, sometimes grey/brown. There are smooth ones and scaly ones, long-stemmed and short-stemmed. The violent colour change is your most reliable guide, though even then you must examine the effect on a fresh young specimen. It is worth noting that the chromium yellow seen in the Yellow Stainer fades to brown after a few minutes, whereas the yellow bruising seen in the edible *Agaricus* species is paler and persistent.

The other excellent identification point is the smell of Elastoplasts. If you miss it when you pick them, the smell gets even worse during cooking and provides you with a final warning!

Yellow Stainers contain a cocktail of unpleasant chemicals, but the main toxic constituent appears to be phenol. Phenol is rare in nature and is a very nasty poison indeed. In the Yellow Stainer, concentrations are quite low, so only 'mild' gastrointestinal symptoms occur and the unfortunate sufferer is at least spared the neurologic, cardiovascular and renal depredations that result from greater exposure. I doubt, however, that the average victim of this impostor would agree with the use of the word 'mild'. I have met people who have been very ill indeed for 24 hours – and that's 24 hours, apparently, of sitting in a small room clutching a bucket. Some people, however, suffer only mildly and others still say they can eat it with impunity. One authority suggests that the phenol is largely created during cooking, which would make it an exception to our rule that wild mushrooms should be cooked first. The possibility that they would be fine in salads is not something I have any intention of checking.

I was brought some rather elderly specimens once by someone who had managed to poison his entire family. They looked rather unusual and turned out to be the closely related but extremely rare *A. pilatianus*. When I informed him that he had poisoned everyone with one of Britain's rarest mushrooms he was thrilled.

Bitter Bolete *Tylopilus felleus*

CAP:	8–12cm. Beige to brown, ***suede-like*** at first.
STEM:	7–10cm by 4–6cm. Usually swollen at the base. Ochre, paler at the top, covered in a ***brown*** net.
TUBES:	White at first, then distinctly ***pale pink***.
FLESH:	Whitish, unchanging, ***intensely bitter***.
HABITAT:	Under broadleaved and coniferous trees.
FREQUENCY:	Occasional.
SEASON:	Late summer to autumn.

ALTHOUGH THIS toadstool is not poisonous, it is well worth getting to know because of the devastation it will inflict on any dish into which it finds its way. As bitter as gall, this charlatan looks very much like the Cep (p.102) and has ruined many a meal; just one, or even a quarter of one, will make an entire dish quite impossible to eat. It imitates the Cep in size, in shape and to some extent even colour. Yet it is on colour differences that we must rely to identify it.

The cap is a duller brown than the Cep; the tubes and pores are pale pink in mature specimens but, unfortunately, whitish in young ones, just like the Cep; the stem is ochre in colour, pale at the apex and covered in a ***brown*** net. Of course, if you are still not sure, you can always nibble a bit, then you will be left in no doubt at all.

POISONOUS SPECIES

Devil's Bolete

Devil's Bolete *Boletus satanas* xx

CAP:	15–25cm, convex, dingy white.
STEM:	7–10cm by 5–10cm. Very swollen at the base. Bright yellow at the top, ochre at the base, blood red in the middle and covered with a red net.
TUBES:	Dark yellow/green, pores small and blood red, more orange at the margin.
FLESH:	White, yellow in places, slowly turning *light blue*. Smells strongly of rotting flesh.
HABITAT:	Under beech and oak on chalky soils.
FREQUENCY:	Very rare.
SEASON:	Summer.

THE DEVIL'S BOLETE is rare enough to be on a Red Data List, so it is not likely to prove a frequent hazard to the mushroom hunter. Of course, should anyone actually manage to find and eat this endangered species, both dinner and diner would be that much the poorer.

It is very distinctive in appearance and mature specimens are reputed to smell sufficiently of rotting meat to take one's breath away if they have been kept in a box. Despite its portentous name, the Devil's Bolete is unlikely to cause anything more than severe gastrointestinal distress though, like many fungi, it is more poisonous raw.

While there are several other Boletes that look at least a bit like it, none of them are considered edible and confusion with these species is not an issue. The only Bolete I recommend that has any red on it – the Scarletina Bolete (p.110) – is distinctive in having a brown velvet cap and yellow flesh that goes violently blue on cutting. The Devil's Bolete is probably the toadstool that, in the nineteenth century, gave other bluing Boletes a mostly undeserved bad name. The blue reaction is 'simply' due to the enzymatic oxidation of yellow pigments.

For any organism, getting your name on a Red Data List is a sure-fire way of becoming relatively common – naturalists suddenly take an interest in your wellbeing and start finding you everywhere. Whereas the Devil's Bolete was once only known from two or three sites, it has now been recorded in over 30. Recently there was a find of around 250 fruit bodies in a single location; as with so many things they may be rare but if they find a spot they like, they can grow like weeds. The Devil's Bolete is still only really known from southern England, where it grows in open, sunny and south-facing locations, usually under beech, less often under oak.

False Morel *Gyromitra esculenta* xxx

CAP:	7–12cm. Irregularly rounded with brain-like convolutions. Yellow/brown to reddish brown.
STEM:	Up to 5cm long. Irregular, whitish to flesh-coloured.
HABITAT:	In sandy soil under pines.
FREQUENCY:	Uncommon.
SEASON:	March to April.

THIS IS THE PUFFER FISH of the fungal world. Raw or poorly prepared it is deadly, yet with proper treatment it is, by all accounts, delicious. I cannot corroborate this as I have not tried it, and eating a dish of False Morels is not on my to-do list. Here is why.

Although the poisonous agent is quite different to that in the Death Cap (p.140), the symptoms are similar and follow the same protracted path. There is a latent period of 6 to 12 hours, after which an unpleasant two- to six- day gastrointestinal phase begins, sometimes accompanied by psychological disturbances. After this there is likely to be a period of recovery, but by this time liver damage and sometimes haemolysis (destruction of the red blood cells) has occurred. In very serious cases, delirium, coma and death from circulatory or respiratory collapse follow within two or three days. Mortality is around 14 per cent.

There is considerable variation in people's susceptibility to the toxin, as is demonstrated by one well-documented incident in which four people out of a family of six suffered no symptoms while the other two were taken ill, one of whom died. This variable immunity is thought to be due to an inherited ability to metabolise the poison. The chemistry of the toxin involved in False Morel poisoning is horribly complicated but, simply put, the acid in people's stomachs reacts with gyromitrin to produce monomethyl-hydrazine, better known as rocket fuel.

Despite this, large quantities of False Morel are collected each year in Europe, though the sale of fresh specimens is banned in several countries.

The treatment I mentioned earlier is simply a matter of boiling it twice and discarding the water each time, although this is not without hazard as the kitchen can become filled with rocket fuel vapour. Drying them first (p.243) also renders them safe. If you really, really want to try the False Morel, you can buy it in tins in delicatessens.

Assuming you are not going to collect False Morels intentionally, they are still worth knowing about because of their similarity to, obviously enough, real Morels (p.133). Morels have a honeycomb structure whereas False Morels have convolutions, like a loosely screwed-up piece of brown paper.

False Morel

Recipes

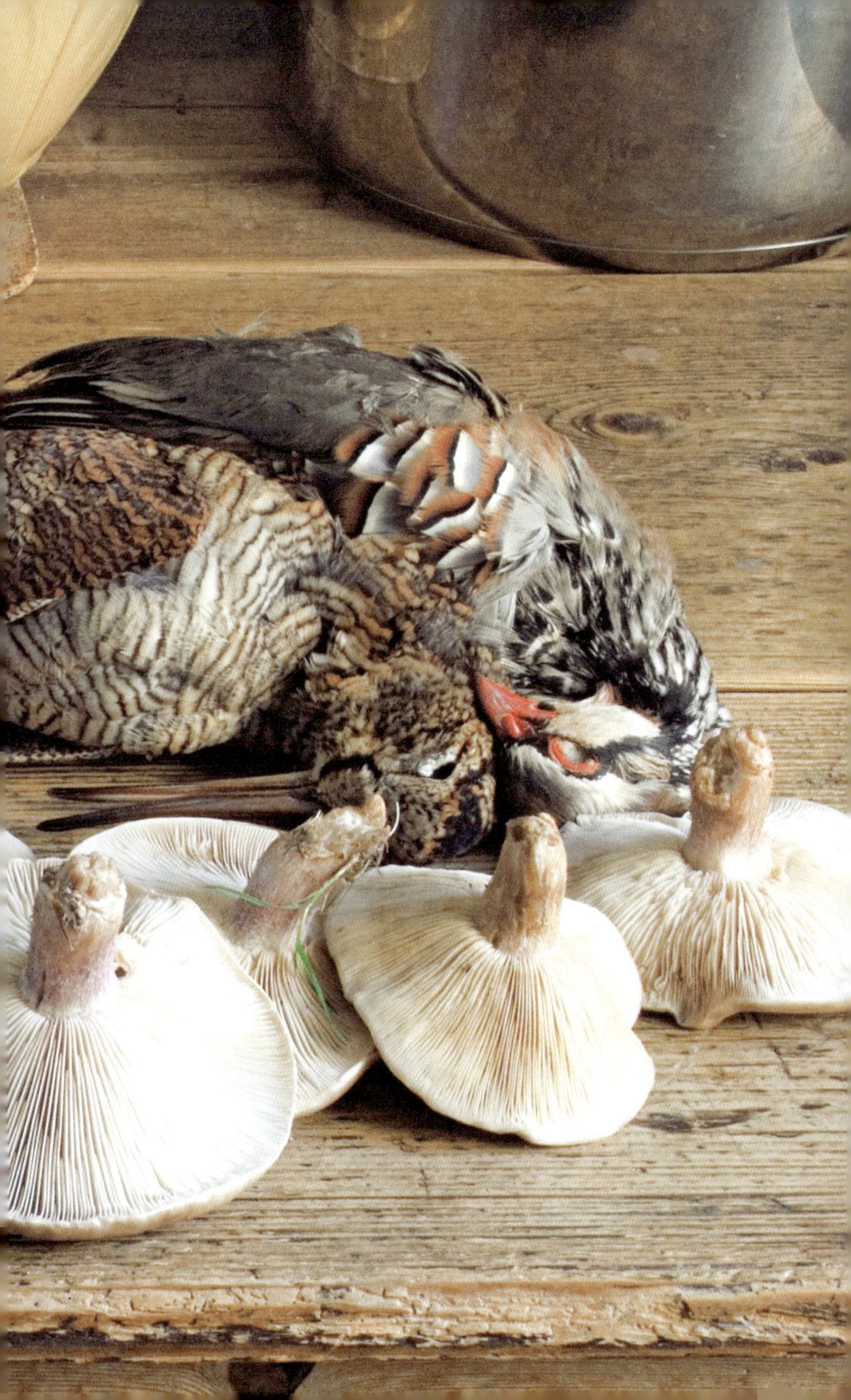

When it comes to wild mushrooms I must confess to being rather a lazy cook or, at least, not a terribly adventurous one. A gentle sautéing is all I usually bother with; at most I might add those old familiars – garlic and cream.

I do not think that there is anything wrong with this light approach. It is, after all, one of the most delicious ways to cook mushrooms, especially if you are trying a new, unfamiliar species and you want to experience its flavour as fully as possible, unchallenged by other ingredients.

Yet now I have learned that a good mushroom dish is not a matter of pointless elaboration but rather a way of enhancing and exploiting the qualities of a particular mushroom. It was Hugh and River Cottage that converted me. I had always had trouble with Parasols. Sautéed they can become soggy or tough. Then one day Hugh presented me with Deep-fried Parasols with garlic mayonnaise (p.236) and my moment of revelation had come.

Nevertheless, a great many of the recipes that follow still rely on a base of simply sautéed mushrooms – so it really pays to get that method just right. Fried mushrooms can be very disappointing if they're not done properly. Heart-breakingly disappointing.

While there are a few notable exceptions, mushrooms contain an awful lot of water. The moment they arrive in the frying pan this water is released and unless you like boiled mushrooms (and you really don't), it has to be removed – not by wastefully discarding it, but by evaporation. The juices soon reduce to a delicious glaze and the whole is then caramelised in the oil and butter. The basic mushroom-sautéing method is outlined in the first recipe of this section (p.184), but here is a fuller explanation of the principles behind it.

- Using a roughly half-and-half mixture of oil and butter for frying is a good idea. Butter gives an incomparable flavour but can burn easily. The oil will stop this and, if you use a decent olive oil, contribute some savoury flavour of its own. (Don't use a cold pressed oil though, as this also burns at a low temperature.)
- The bigger your pan, the more easily and quickly liquid will evaporate from it, so go for a large frying pan if you can. If you only have a small one or if you have a lot of mushrooms, cook them in batches. You don't want the uncooked mushrooms to form a layer more than one mushroom deep in your pan.
- Once you've added the mushrooms to a hot pan, throw in some salt and pepper too. Mushrooms need salt more than any other food and are quite forlorn without it.
- Use a medium heat to start with so that the water is released without burning the mushrooms, then increase it as the water starts to bubble.

- Keep cooking, stirring occasionally, until all the released moisture has evaporated, by which time the mushrooms are likely to have shrunk considerably. Continue until the mushrooms start to develop golden-brown patches. You now have a panful of mushrooms, ready to eat.

I should add that the amount of water contained by different types of mushroom – and even by the same types on different days – varies considerably, which means it is impossible to give precise cooking times. With very moist fungi, such as the Bay Bolete, it is sometimes worth removing the mushrooms from the pan for a few minutes and reducing the liquid on its own for a while to avoid overcooking. In contrast, with dry and firm fungi like Hedgehog Mushrooms and Chicken of the Woods, it can actually make sense to add a little water to extend the cooking time so the mushrooms don't brown or dry out on the outside before they are tender in the middle.

None of these details should obscure the fact that mushrooms are really very forgiving ingredients. Unlike fish and the finer cuts of meat, you do not need a thermometer and a stopwatch to get things just right, and while mushrooms should not be cooked to death it does little damage to leave them in the pan for a few minutes longer than originally intended. Some of the firmer mushrooms, like the Cep, need more cooking than their more delicate brethren – about ten minutes should do it – while others, such as the tiny Fairy Ring Champignon, can be ready in just two.

Another thing you can be pretty relaxed about is the actual choice of fungi for a given recipe. Nearly all the recipes here can be prepared with nearly any type of mushroom – which is fortunate if you're gathering your own as foraging strictly to order is a rare talent. There are exceptions, of course: Parasols and Puffballs would be poor ingredients for any type of stew, for instance, and the slippery Wood Blewit is unsuited to deep-frying. Notes at the beginning of each recipe indicate which mushrooms are likely to be most or least successful, but don't be afraid to experiment and improvise. The ideas that follow have certainly helped me expand my mushroom-cooking repertoire and plain old mushrooms on toast is now a thing of the past. Well, almost.

The recipes in this book have been a great joint effort by the River Cottage team. I cannot remember how each one came into being; a good number, of course, are Hugh's, some were created or donated by Gill and Dan, the resident River Cottage chefs, and some were suggested by Nikki and Helen on our editorial team. A few seemed to appear from nowhere at the last minute inspired by the fungi we had to hand. I had minimal involvement except in one important respect. When the recipes were tested and photographed I tasted all the finished dishes. Well somebody had to do it.

Fried mushrooms on toast

This is the simplest recipe in the book, but may well be the one you turn to most often. You're unlikely to meet a mushroom that doesn't respond well to this treatment so, if in doubt, get the frying pan out. The quantities here are for one, but, of course, you can easily scale the recipe up. If you're frying large quantities of mushrooms, it's best to do them in batches, or it will take ages for the liquid they release to evaporate.

Works with: just about anything.

Serves 1
150–200g wild mushrooms
 – either one variety or a mixture
1 tbsp olive oil
A knob of butter
1 small garlic clove, peeled and finely chopped

Salt and freshly ground pepper
Thick slice sourdough, granary or other good bread
1 tsp chopped flat leaf parsley
A squeeze of lemon juice (optional)

Clean and trim the mushrooms. Leave small ones whole, but cut any that are larger than a walnut into slices or chunks.

Heat the olive oil and butter in a frying pan over a medium heat, add the garlic and let it sweat for a minute or so, without colouring. Add the mushrooms and some seasoning. As they begin to release their juices, increase the heat under the pan so the liquid bubbles away. Keep cooking, stirring frequently, until the mushrooms are soft, all the liquid has evaporated and the mushrooms are starting to colour – how long this takes depends very much on the type of mushroom you're using.

While the mushrooms cook, toast and butter your bread. When the mushrooms are done to your liking, stir in the parsley and, if you like, a squeeze of lemon juice. Taste and adjust the seasoning, then pile onto your hot toast and eat straight away.

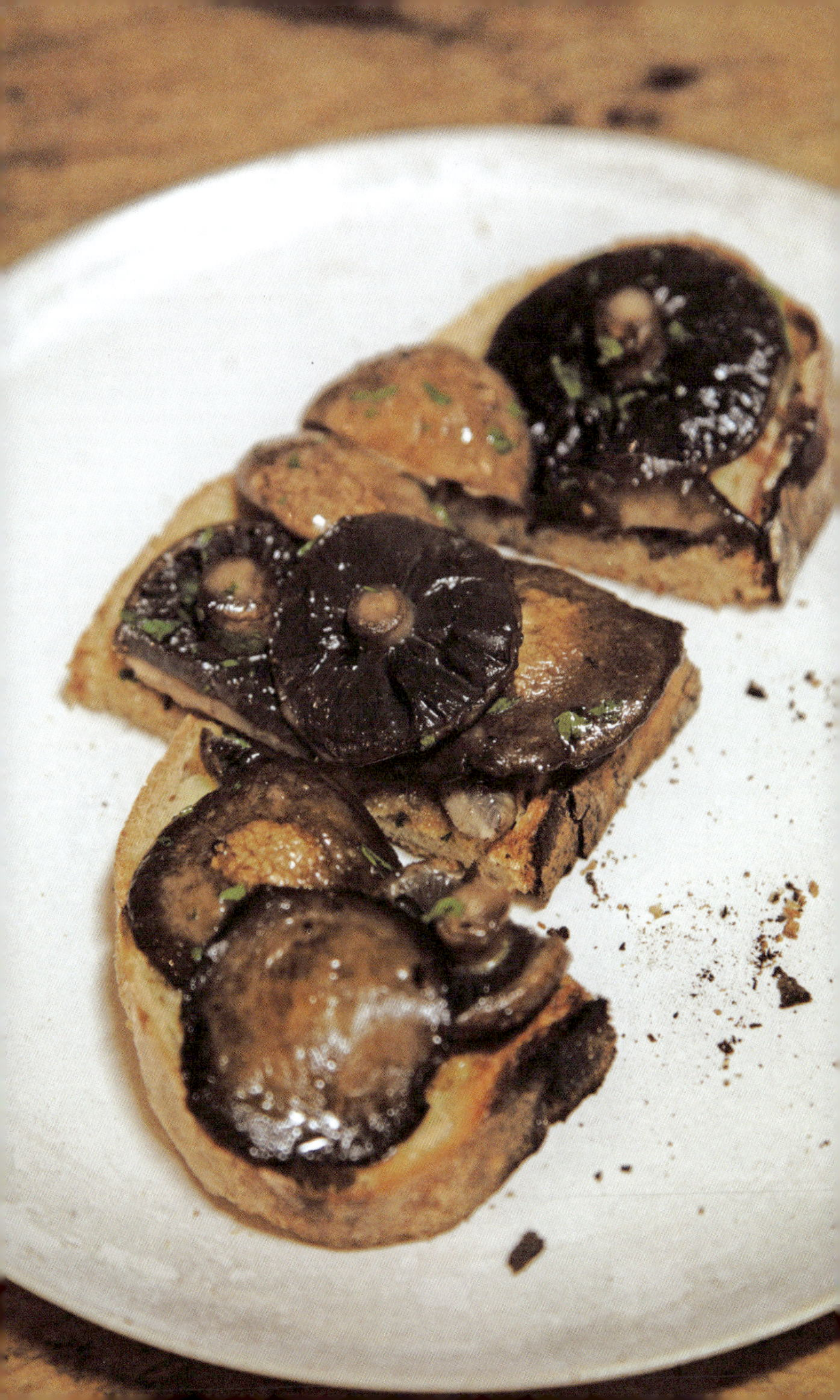

Scrambled eggs
with shaved Truffles

Should you find yourself in possession of a Summer Truffle, treat it with enormous respect. Use it with restraint, in only the simplest recipes, and with only the finest ingredients to partner it. To make your black jewel go as far as possible, begin by putting it in an airtight box with a few eggs and leaving it for a day or two so that its perfume subtly infuses them. You can then use a little of the Truffle for this recipe, and a little more, perhaps, for the Roast chicken with Truffles (p.241).

You probably don't need a recipe for scrambled eggs – everyone has their own favourite method – but here's a quick run-down anyway.

Serves 2
4 eggs
Salt and freshly ground black pepper
A large knob of butter
A few shavings of Truffle

Break the eggs into a bowl or jug. Season with salt and freshly ground black pepper and beat lightly with a fork. Heat a saucepan over a low heat and add a large knob of butter. When the butter is foaming, add the eggs. Stir gently, keeping the heat very low, as the egg cooks. The slower you cook the egg, the creamier and richer it will be. When the egg is nearly all set, with just the merest film of wetness still visible in places, remove from the heat. Give it another stir, then heap on to hot, buttered toast. Shave some of your Truffle very finely using a special Truffle shaver, or a mandoline, or cut it into slivers with a very sharp knife. Scatter over the eggs and serve immediately.

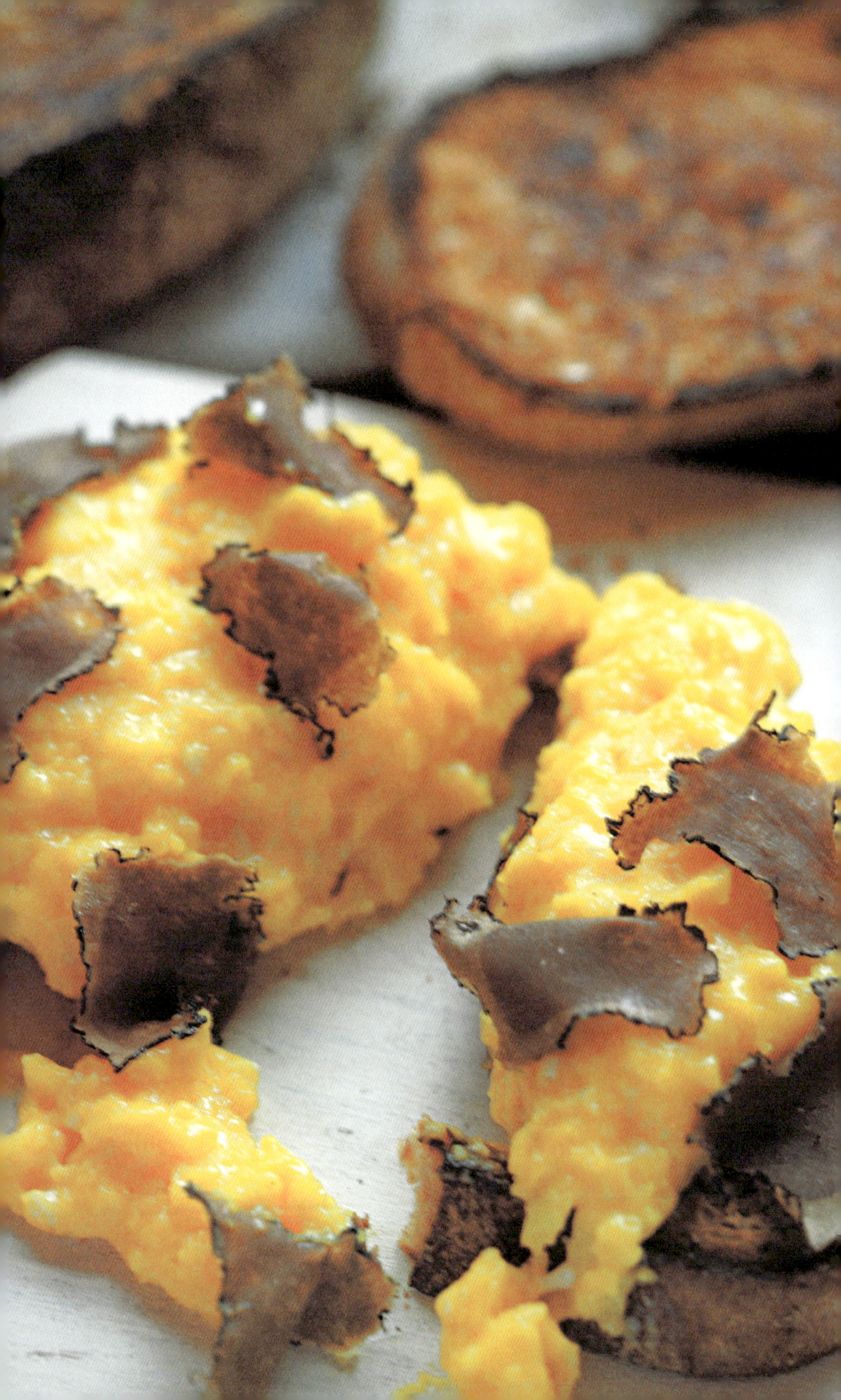

Salad of raw mushrooms

There are few fungi that are safe to eat raw, so this is a dish to make with the most flawless, freshly picked specimens of just a few species. Like all very simple dishes, it demands the very best ingredients so, as well as perfect mushrooms, you need a really good, peppery extra virgin olive oil, some dewy fresh herbs and perhaps a sliver or two of a fine aged Parmesan or Cheddar. An alternative to a top-notch olive oil would be a simple, slightly mustardy vinaigrette – and this would be a good option if you want to serve the mushrooms with a green salad.

Works with: Ceps, Field Mushrooms, Horse Mushrooms, Brittlegills.

Serves 2 as a starter

200g flawless, very fresh mushrooms
2 tsp very finely chopped herbs –
   flat leaf parsley, chives, chervil or
   wild sorrel would be good
Extra virgin olive oil
Flaky salt and freshly ground
   black pepper
A few shavings Parmesan or top
   notch Cheddar (optional)

For the vinaigrette (optional)
2 tbsp olive oil
2 tbsp sunflower oil
1 tbsp white wine
   or cider vinegar
½ tsp Dijon mustard
A pinch of sugar
Salt and freshly ground black pepper

If you want to use the vinaigrette, make it first by simply whisking together all the ingredients.

Clean and trim the mushrooms and slice them very thinly. Arrange them, overlapping the slices slightly, on two plates. Scatter on the herbs, trickle on the olive oil (or the vinaigrette, if you're using it), then sprinkle with a little flaky salt and black pepper. Add the Parmesan or Cheddar, if you like, then serve the mushrooms straight away.

Wild mushroom omelette

Any kind of mushroom can be used in an omelette and will taste delicious, but the more delicately textured varieties, such as Chanterelles, give particularly elegant results. This recipe enriches the eggs for the omelette with a good shot of melted butter, but this isn't essential.

Works with: pretty much any mushroom – large or meaty ones should be sliced first.

Serves 1 hungry forager, or 2 for lunch with bread and a salad
100g mushrooms
50g butter
Salt and freshly ground pepper
4 eggs
2 tsp chopped parsley

Clean and trim the mushrooms and cut into smallish pieces.

Set an omelette pan, or another good, non-stick pan, around 25cm in diameter, over a medium heat. Add about one-third of the butter. When it's foaming, add the mushrooms, with some seasoning. Sauté for 4–5 minutes or until all the liquid the mushrooms release has evaporated and they are starting to colour in the butter. Transfer them to a warm plate and set aside somewhere warm.

Beat together the eggs lightly, along with some seasoning. Melt the remaining butter in the mushroom pan over a medium heat, then pour most of it out of the pan and into the beaten eggs. Whisk it in lightly. (If you don't want to do this, just use a small knob of butter to grease the pan.)

Pour the eggs into the hot pan. As they cook, move the mixture around with a spatula or fork, pulling cooked egg up from the bottom of the pan and allowing runny egg to come into contact with the heat. Tip and tilt the pan a little at the same time. When the omelette is just set, but still slightly runny on top, pile the mushrooms on to one half of it. Scatter on the parsley. Remove the pan from the heat. Flip the un-mushroomed side of the omelette over onto the mushroomed side, and slip the whole thing out on to a warmed plate. Serve straight away, just as it is, or with a green salad to follow.

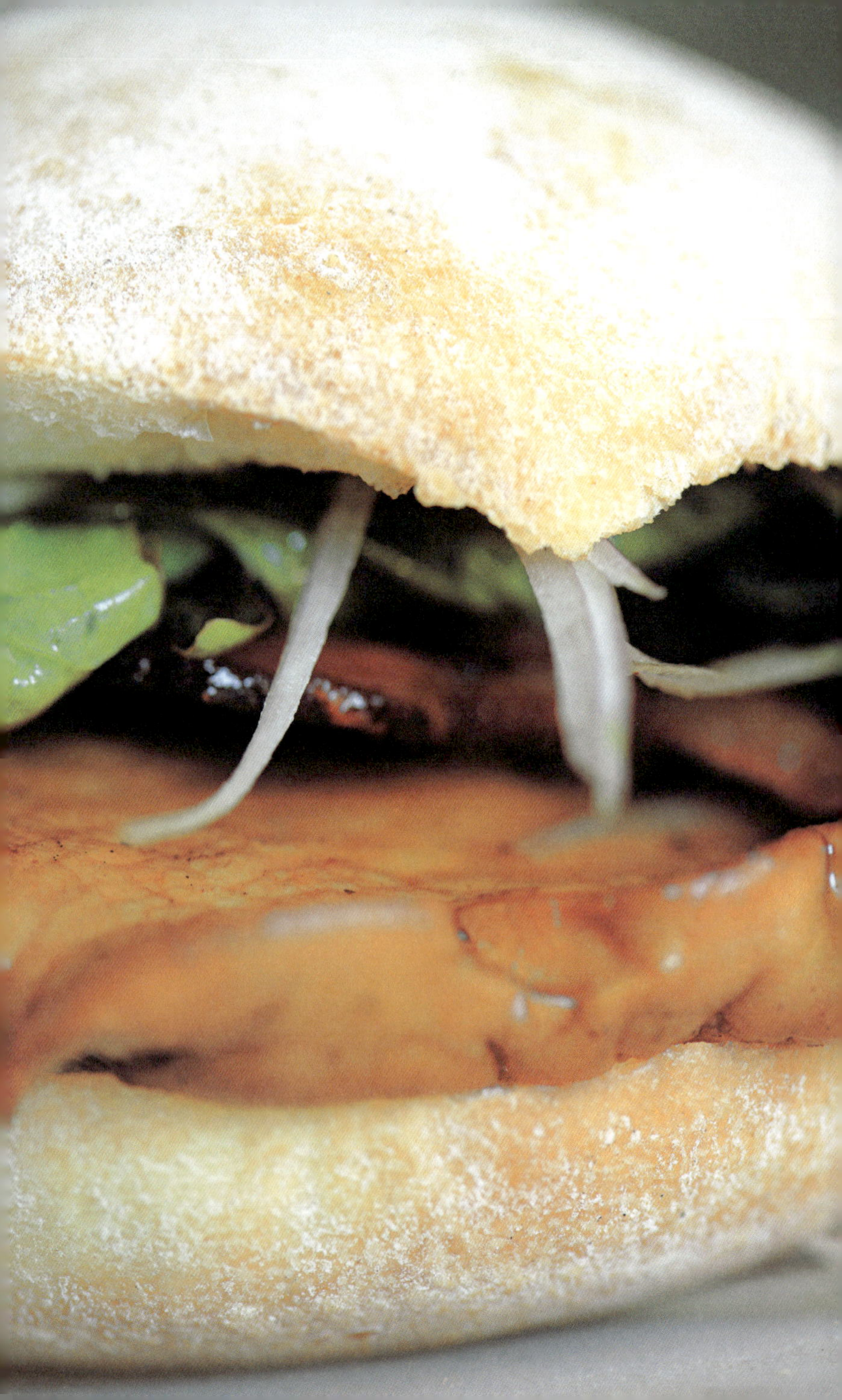

The Puffburger

This is an incredibly satisfying bit of fast food. You could make it with large, flat Field Mushrooms or something similar but, to be honest, it would be quite a different dish. The dense, savoury flesh of a Puffball, enhanced by being fried in bacon fat, is uniquely delicious.

Serves 2

1 tbsp oil or lard
4 rashers streaky bacon
4 slices Puffball, skin removed and cut into slices about 2cm thick, trimmed to roughly the same size as the baps
Salt and freshly ground black pepper
2 good soft baps
A few salad leaves – dressed, if you like, with a little vinaigrette (combine 3 tbsp olive oil with 1 tbsp wine, sherry or cider vinegar and season with salt, pepper and a pinch of sugar)

Put a frying pan over a medium heat, add the fat, then add the bacon and cook until it is as crisp as you like it. Remove the bacon and keep it warm. Add the slices of Puffball then turn them over immediately, to stop the first side absorbing all the fat, and fry for about 3 minutes, until golden. Flip them over again and fry the other side for the same amount of time. Season the Puffball. Cut open the baps, add two slices of bacon to each, then some of the dressed leaves, then a couple of slices of Puffball. (Some have been known to add ketchup at this stage.) Close the baps and serve straight away.

Asparagus
with St George's Mushrooms

The late spring discovery of a few creamy white St George's Mushrooms should be a cause for great celebration, as they are excellent, firm-textured fungi. As luck would have it, their appearance tends to coincide perfectly with the beginning of the British asparagus season. Combining these two delicious, highly seasonal ingredients in a very simple dish is an awfully good idea.

Also works with: the only other fungi you're likely to find during asparagus season are Morels and the occasional Horse Mushroom, both of which could be used in this dish.

Serves 2 as a light lunch
About 200g St George's Mushrooms
Salt and freshly ground black pepper
12 asparagus spears, trimmed
1 tbsp olive oil
50g butter

Clean, trim and halve the mushrooms (or quarter them if they're large).

Bring a saucepan of water to the boil, add a little salt, throw in the asparagus and cook for 3–4 minutes, until just tender, then drain them. Alternatively, you can steam the spears.

Heat the olive oil in a frying pan over a medium heat, add the mushrooms and sauté gently until they are tender and the liquid they release has evaporated. St George's Mushrooms need a fair bit of cooking and don't contain that much water, so keep the heat low to avoid drying them out before they're cooked through. Add the steamed asparagus spears to the mushroom pan, along with the butter. Season with salt and pepper, toss around once or twice, then transfer to warmed plates and serve at once, with bread and butter. A crusty white roll is rather good.

Steak, mushroom
& blue cheese sandwich

A good sandwich is no mere stopgap but something to marvel at before devouring in a cutlery-free frenzy. This is one for the real sarnie enthusiast because it does involve a little cooking, but it's worth the effort. Of course, it will be very special if you've gathered the mushrooms from the wild, but cultivated Portbells or other open-capped mushrooms will be fine. Don't stint on the steak. Some thin-cut sirloin, rib-eye or rump, with a decent bit of marbling, is essential to do the other ingredients justice. If blue cheese is not your thing, goat's cheese, Gruyère, Cheddar – or no cheese at all – work well.

Works with: any firm, meaty mushroom.

Serves 1 (amply)

A good handful of mushrooms
1 small baguette, or half a large one
1 tbsp olive oil
Salt and freshly ground black pepper
225g sirloin, rib or rump steak, about 1cm thick
Cold unsalted butter
1 tsp thyme leaves
100g mature blue cheese, such as Dorset Blue Vinney, Gorgonzola or dolcelatte, thickly sliced

Trim and clean the mushrooms, and slice them thickly if they are sizeable specimens.

Put the bread to warm in a low oven (or use a just-baked baguette that's still warm). Meanwhile, set a large frying pan over a high heat. When it's really hot, add the oil. Season the steak, put it in the pan and fry for about 20 seconds each side, if you like it rare, or more if you like it medium.

Remove the steak from the pan and leave it in a warm place to rest. Reduce the heat under the pan, add a little butter and then the mushrooms, some seasoning and the thyme. Sauté until all the liquid the mushrooms release has evaporated and they are starting to take a bit of colour.

Remove the bread from the oven. Open it up, butter thickly and then lay on the steak. Spoon over the mushrooms and any juices left in the pan, then finish with the blue cheese. Press the sandwich together firmly with the palms of your hands and dig in. This is particularly good with a pint of Guinness.

Oyster Mushrooms
with lemon & thyme

This is so simple, but incredibly tasty, the mushroom juices and butter making a lovely rich sauce. The mushrooms are delicious served on their own, just piled on hot toast, but also make a very good partner to some simply grilled fish or chicken. Alternatively, try them with a lemon zest mash. To make this, just boil some floury potatoes and mash them with a little warm milk and melted butter, a couple of tablespoons of extra virgin olive oil and the grated zest of a lemon.

Also works with: pretty much anything, except Puffballs.

Serves 2
150–200g Oyster Mushrooms
50g butter
Salt and freshly ground black pepper
2–3 tsp roughly chopped thyme
Juice of 1 lemon

Clean and trim the mushrooms. If they're large, tear them into pieces. Otherwise leave them whole.

Melt half the butter in a large saucepan over a medium–high heat. When foaming, add the mushrooms, season with salt and fry them briskly, being careful not to burn the butter. When the mushrooms are soft and golden, throw in the thyme, the lemon juice and plenty of black pepper. Add the rest of the butter and, as soon as it has melted, the mushrooms are ready to serve, piping hot.

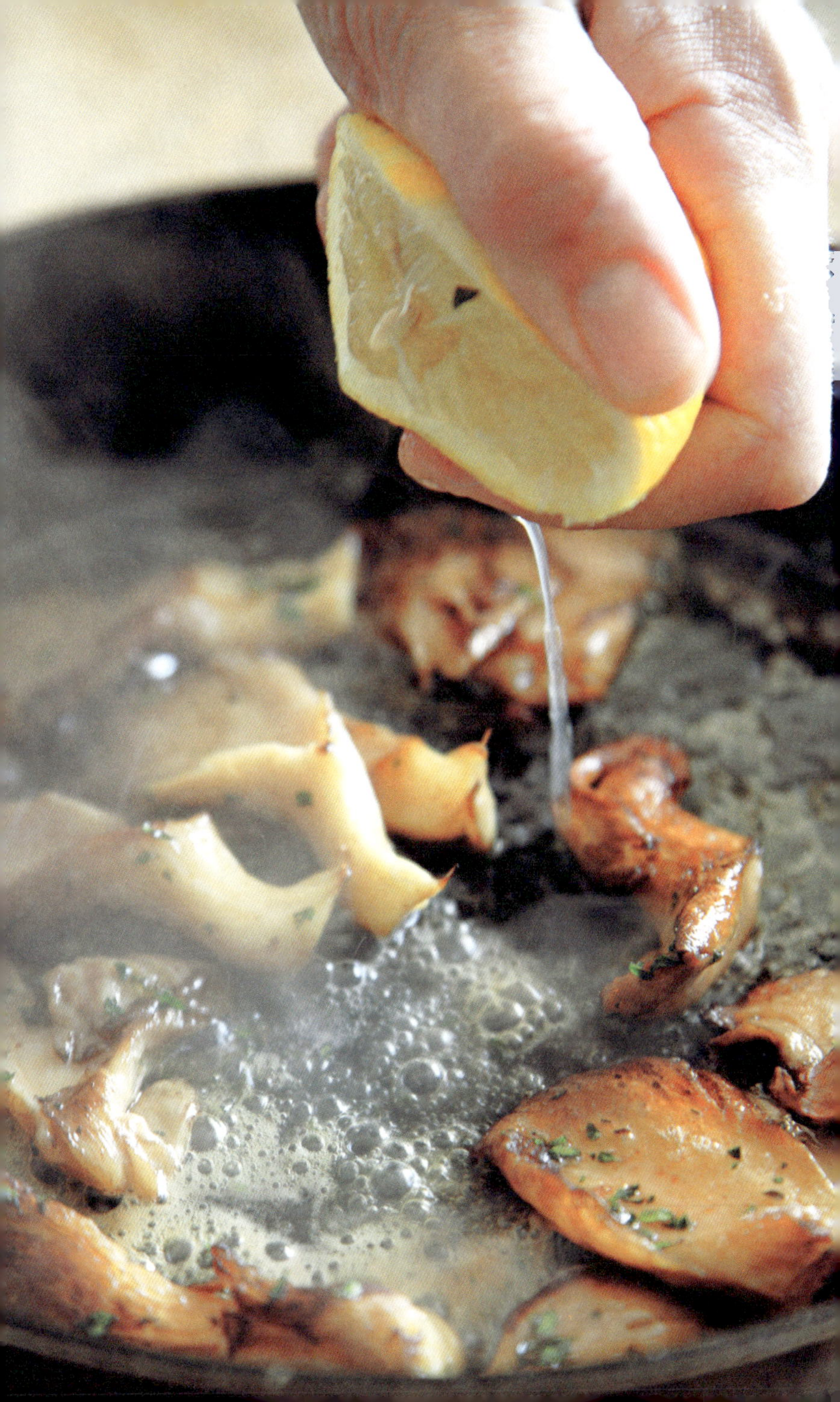

Chicken breast
with Morels, marsala & cream

The average *Morchella esculenta* (the finest of the Morels) is the size of a small fist, so you'd only need a few for this dish, and they would have to be cut into several pieces. If you're using bought, dried Morels, which are likely to be a different species and imported from the Continent, they'll be much smaller.

Serves 2
- 150–200g Morels
- 2 tbsp olive oil
- 2 boneless, skin-on chicken breasts
- Salt and freshly ground black pepper
- A knob of butter
- 1 small onion, peeled and finely chopped
- 2–3 tbsp marsala
- 200ml chicken stock
- 150ml double cream

For fresh Morels, clean and trim them, and cut into halves or quarters. For dried ones, put them to soak in the chicken stock (heated up). Give them 20 minutes or so, then strain, reserving the stock. Preheat the oven to 180°C/Gas Mark 4.

Add the olive oil to an ovenproof pan, large enough to take both chicken breasts comfortably. Place on a medium–high heat. Season the chicken all over with salt and pepper. When the pan is hot, add the chicken, skin down, and fry for a minute or so. Flip the breasts, cook for another minute, then flip skin-side down again and put in the oven for about 10 minutes, until about three-quarters cooked. Return the pan to the hob on a low heat, and transfer the chicken to a warmed plate.

Add the butter and onion to the pan. Fry gently for 5 minutes, until the onion starts to soften. Turn up the heat to medium and add the Morels. Fry for another few minutes, until the Morels are just about cooked, then add the marsala, then the stock, and boil until the liquid has reduced by half. Add the cream, then return the chicken to the pan, skin-side up, and simmer for a few minutes until the chicken is just firm when pressed and the sauce is reduced and thickened. If the sauce looks right and the chicken is not cooked, add a little more liquid and keep simmering. If the chicken is cooked and the sauce a little loose, remove the chicken and simmer the sauce until ready.

For an extra-special finish, turn the chicken a few times in the sauce and put it, skin-side up, under a hot grill to create a rich glaze. Serve with sautéed potatoes and wilted spinach or steamed broccoli.

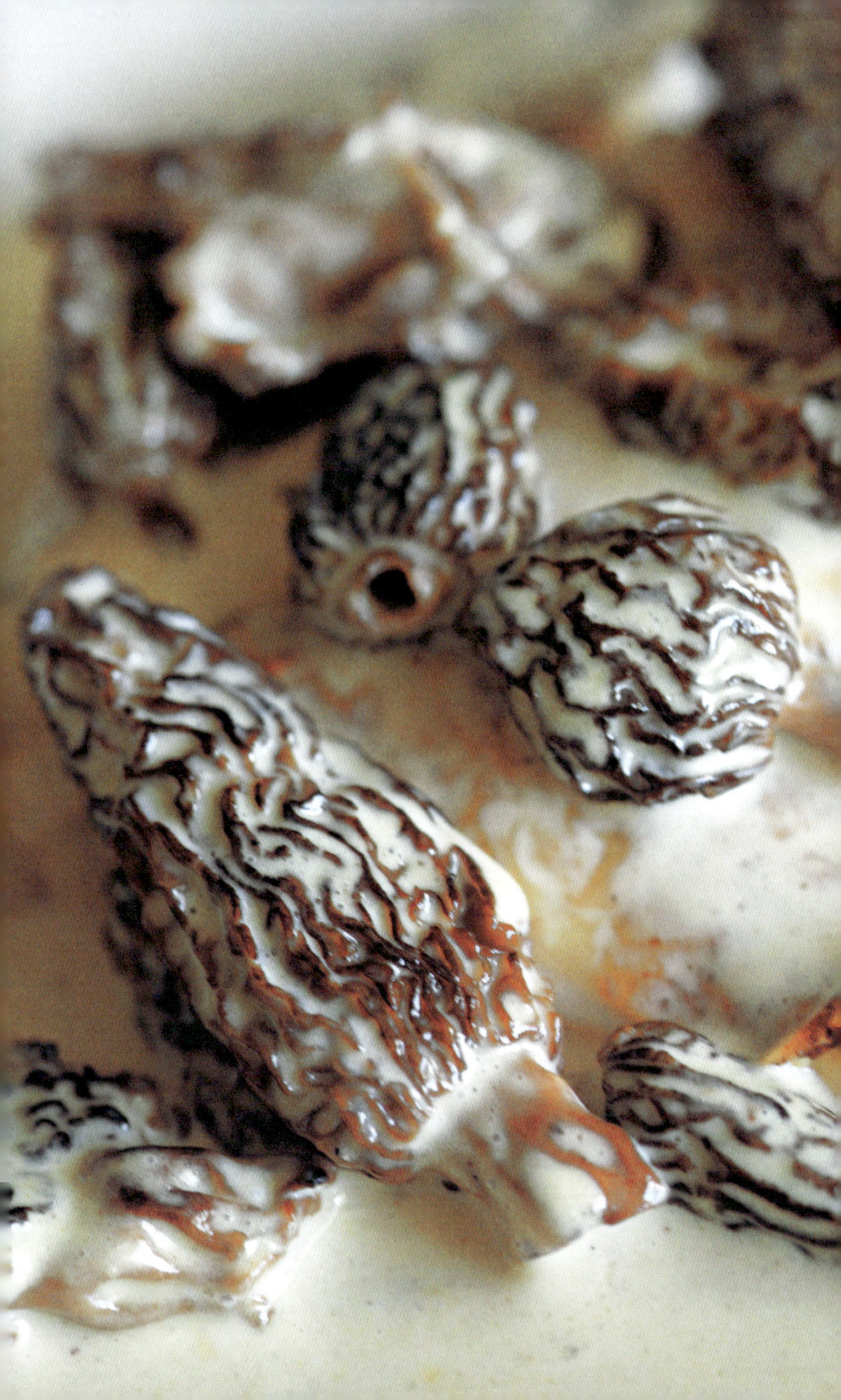

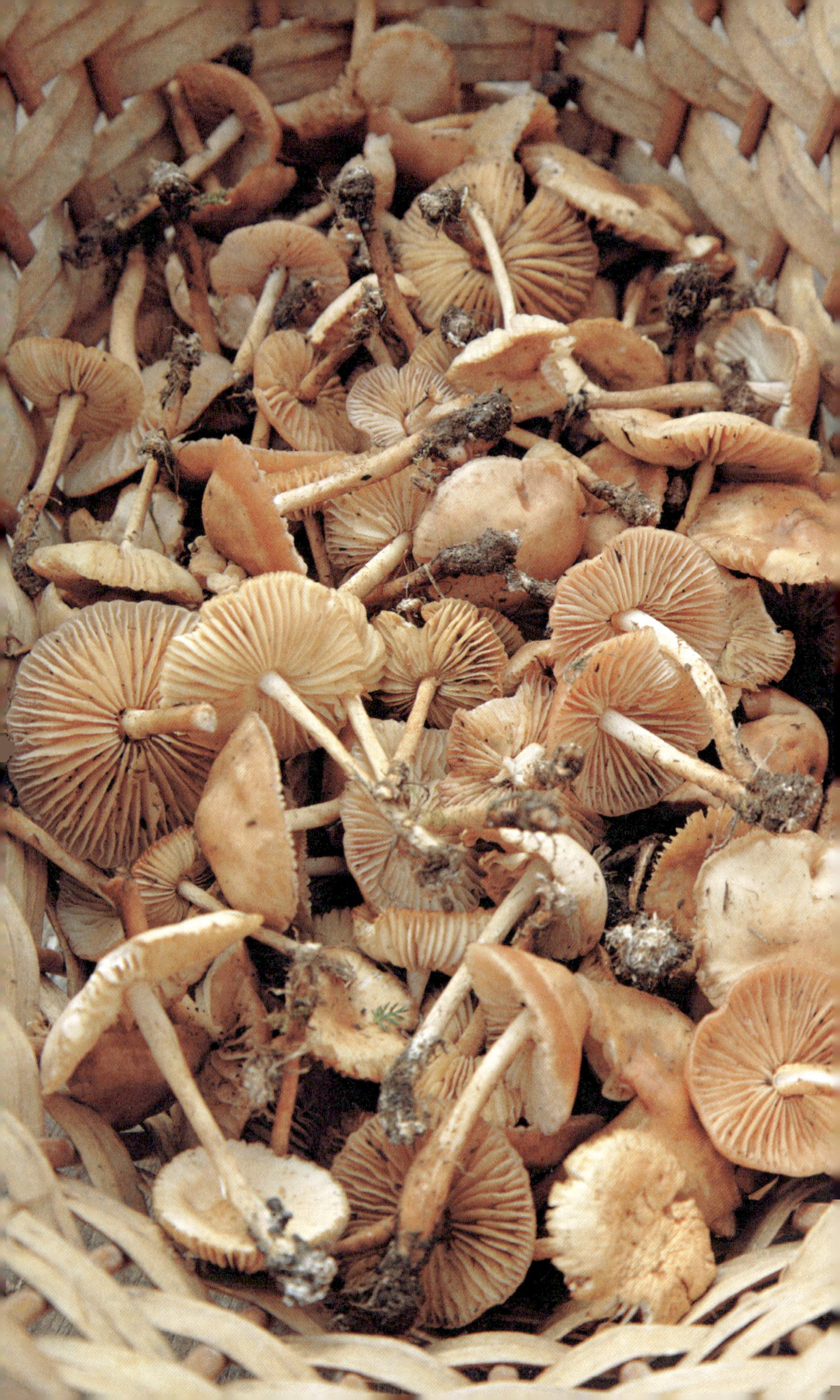

Venison
with Fairy Ring Champignons

The slightly nutty flavour of Fairy Ring Champignons works brilliantly in this dish. They certainly give Chanterelles (for which this recipe was originally devised) a run for their money.

Also works with: Chanterelles, Hedgehog Mushrooms, Deceivers and Winter Chanterelles (generally found in November, just in time for the venison season).

Serves 4

- A few handfuls of Fairy Ring Champignons
- 10 peppercorns
- 2 bay leaves
- 4 juniper berries
- 2 pinches flaky sea salt
- 500g piece of trimmed venison loin
- 1 tbsp olive oil
- 100g unsmoked bacon or pancetta, diced
- 1 tbsp white wine (optional)
- 25g butter
- Salt and freshly ground black pepper
- 1 tbsp chopped parsley

Preheat the oven to 200°C/Gas Mark 6.

Clean and trim the mushrooms. Put the peppercorns, bay leaves, juniper berries and sea salt in a coffee grinder or spice mill. Grind to a fine powder and scatter over the whole venison loin and rub it in lightly. Heat a medium-sized, ovenproof frying pan over a high heat, and add the olive oil. When it's hot, add the venison. Sear it, turning it so each surface gets a chance to meet the heat, until well browned on all sides. Transfer the pan to the oven and cook for 10 minutes.

Remove the meat from the pan and set aside on a plate to rest for 20 minutes. This is important, as it allows the juices in the meat to settle, making it more tender and juicy when you come to carve it. It also gives you time to cook the mushrooms.

Put the pan back over a medium heat. Throw in the bacon and cook until it just starts to crisp. Add the prepared mushrooms, toss them well with the bacon, and cook for 2–3 minutes, or until tender. Add a little wine if you like, but really only a splash – and let it bubble away to almost nothing. Add the butter to the pan and stir it in to the mushrooms as it melts. Season to taste and sprinkle over the parsley.

Spoon the mushrooms and bacon onto four warmed plates. Slice the venison and arrange alongside the mushrooms and serve with a mixed green salad.

Palourdes
with Chanterelles

Here's a recipe that you'll also find in *The River Cottage Fish Book*, on the basis that mycophiles deserve to know about it just as much as piscophiles.

Little palourde clams – or cockles, which would work just as well here – can be gathered at any time during the Chanterelle season (from August right up to late autumn, depending on where you are and what the weather's doing). This dish is a lovely, simple combination of those two delicious wild ingredients and incredibly quick to put together.

Serves 1–2
About 200g fresh Chanterelles
1 garlic clove, peeled and finely chopped
2 knobs of butter
2 tbsp white wine
24 palourde clams, purged by being left in a bucket of cold fresh water overnight
Freshly ground black pepper

Clean and trim the Chanterelles. If they are really big, cut them in half or quarters.

Put the garlic and a knob of butter in a lidded wide pan over a medium heat. When it's sizzled for a minute, add the wine. When the wine is bubbling, add the palourdes and cover the pan. Let them steam for 2–3 minutes, or until almost all the shells are open. Remove them from the pan and pick the meat from inside the shells, making sure you collect any juice from the shells as you go, returning it to the pan. Return to the heat and boil the liquid until it's reduced to about 1 tablespoon.

Heat a clean frying pan over a medium heat. Add another knob of butter and allow it to bubble, then throw in the Chanterelles. Sauté gently for 2–3 minutes, just until they soften, then add the palourde clams and toss them together with the mushrooms. Add the reduced palourde liquor and season with pepper – salt won't be necessary. Serve straight away, on a warmed plate, with bread and butter.

Warm salad of roast squash & fried mushrooms

A more elegant and satisfying autumn dish you could not wish for. There are few mushrooms that wouldn't work well here.

Works with: almost anything.

Serves 2 as a light lunch, or 4 as a starter

½–1 medium squash (about 1kg) – butternut or Crown Prince is ideal
12 sage leaves, roughly bruised
4 garlic cloves, peeled and thickly sliced
150ml olive oil, plus 1 tbsp
Salt and freshly ground black pepper
250g mushrooms
50g butter
A small bunch of wild rocket

200g softish blue cheese such as Cashel Blue or Oxford Blue, cut into chunks

For the vinaigrette
3 tbsp olive oil
1 tbsp wine, sherry or cider vinegar
Salt, freshly ground black pepper and a pinch of sugar

Preheat the oven to 200°C/Gas Mark 6.

Peel and deseed the squash and cut into 2.5cm chunks. Put these in a roasting tin with the bruised sage leaves, the garlic, 150ml olive oil and a generous seasoning of salt and pepper. Roast the squash for 35–45 minutes, stirring once or twice, or until soft and coloured at the edges. Leave until warm but not cold.

Meanwhile, clean, trim and slice the mushrooms. Whisk together the ingredients for the vinaigrette.

Put 1 tablespoon olive oil and the butter in a large frying pan over a medium heat. Add the mushrooms, season lightly with salt and pepper, and sauté for 4–5 minutes or until the liquid they release has evaporated and they're starting to turn golden. Leave to cool slightly but not completely.

The salad should be 'tiede' or warm room temperature, definitely not fridge cold, or even larder cold. In a large mixing bowl, gently combine the cooked squash, mushrooms, rocket and cheese. Lightly dress with the vinaigrette. Toss this all together and serve.

Mushroom pâté

If you think mushroom pâtés are always going to be a disappointment, then you've been eating the wrong ones. This very simple, deliciously garlicky version is based on a recipe from Julie Davies, of Crai Organics, who developed it using the organic Shiitakes she cultivates. It works just as well with other mushrooms, fresh, dried, wild or cultivated. If you have any of the pâté left over, try stirring it into a little hot béchamel sauce or some cream to make a delicious mushroom sauce.

Serves 10–12 as a canapé
250g mushrooms
30g butter
3–4 garlic cloves, peeled and
   finely chopped
250g cream cheese
Salt and freshly ground black pepper

Clean and trim the mushrooms and chop them finely.

Heat the butter in a large frying pan over a medium heat. Drop in the mushrooms and garlic and sauté, stirring frequently, for 10 minutes, or until all the moisture the mushrooms release has evaporated. Leave to cool for a few minutes.

Blitz the mushrooms in a food processor until smooth, then add the cream cheese and blitz again until well blended. Season to taste then leave to cool completely. Refrigerate for at least an hour for the garlic flavour to develop. Serve in generous dollops on crostini, or triangles of toast. This pâté keeps very well in the fridge for up to a week.

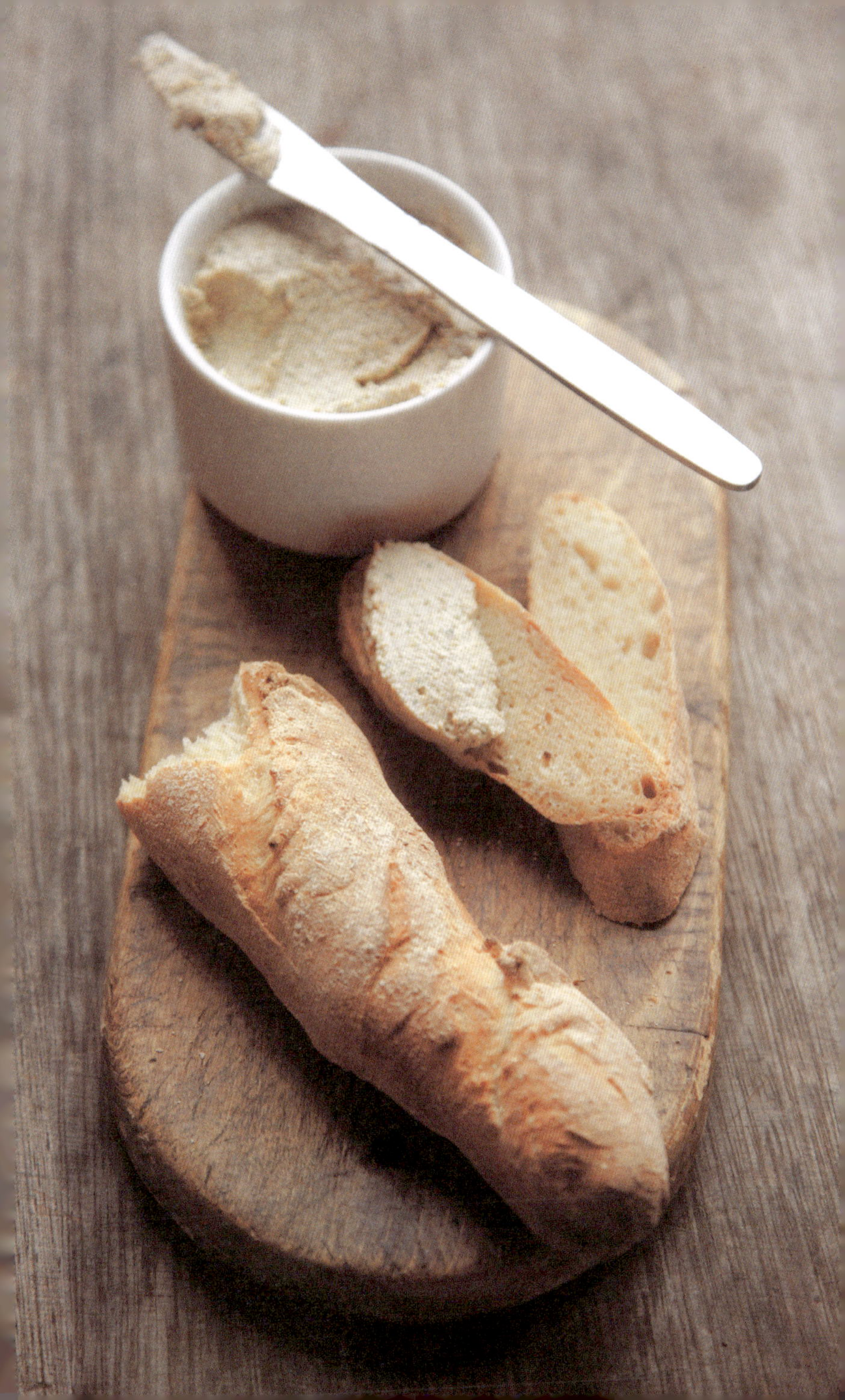

Mushroom soup

Mushroom soup should not be an also-ran, a repository for a haul of past-it, second-rate fungi that you wouldn't otherwise eat. However, it is actually a very good way of using mushrooms that don't look perfect, especially since these are often more mature specimens, which have lots of flavour. This particular soup is very smooth and creamy, but finished with a few whole, sautéed mushrooms. This gives a nice bit of texture as well as some individual mushroom flavours.

Works with: anything.

Serves 4–6
About 500g mushrooms – mixed or all of one type
35g butter
2 tbsp olive oil
1 leek, trimmed and sliced
1 small potato, peeled and diced
1 large onion, peeled and chopped
2 garlic cloves, peeled and chopped
1 tsp thyme leaves
Salt and freshly ground black pepper
1 litre mushroom stock, or vegetable or chicken stock, or a combination
100ml double cream
1 tbsp chopped parsley

Clean the mushrooms in the normal way, but don't be too fastidious about the trimming. As long as the stalks are clean and grit-free, they can go in to the mix. The same goes for slightly damaged or broken caps. Set aside 100g of the most aesthetically pleasing fungi to finish the soup with, and roughly chop the rest.

Put a large saucepan over a medium heat. Add about 25g of the butter to the pan with 1 tablespoon olive oil and, when foaming, add the leek, potato, onion and garlic. Cook for 10–15 minutes, or until soft but not coloured. Add the chopped mushrooms and the thyme and season with a little salt and pepper. Cook for a further 5 minutes. Pour over the stock, bring to a simmer and cook for 10 minutes.

Purée the soup in a blender until smooth and creamy. Return it to the pan, add the cream and bring back to a gentle simmer.

Meanwhile, in a separate small frying pan, heat the remaining butter and olive oil over a medium heat. Slice the reserved mushrooms (unless they're really small) and fry them until tender and starting to colour, making sure any liquid they release evaporates. Serve the soup in warmed bowls, topped with the sautéed mushrooms and some chopped parsley.

Mushroom loaves

These look really impressive and yet are very simple to cook. They make a great light lunch or supper, or a very generous starter.

Works with: pretty much anything.

Serves 4

- 4 large white crusty bread rolls – not too light and flaky, though
- 100g butter
- 350g mixed mushrooms
- 1 large leek, trimmed and finely sliced
- Salt and freshly ground black pepper
- 75ml white wine
- 150ml double cream
- 1 tbsp mixed chopped parsley and chives

Preheat the oven to 200°C/Gas Mark 6.

Slice a 'lid' off the top of each roll and scoop out most of the soft crumb from inside (use this to make breadcrumbs for another dish). Melt 75g of the butter and brush the hollowed-out rolls, inside and out, and the lids, with it. Place them on a baking sheet and bake for 5–10 minutes until golden and crisp. Turn off the oven, open the door and leave the rolls inside to keep warm.

Clean and trim the mushrooms and cut into fairly small slices.

Heat the remaining 25g butter in a large frying pan over a medium–low heat, add the leek and sauté gently until soft. Add the mushrooms and a pinch of seasoning and increase the heat a little. Cook, stirring frequently, until the mushrooms have released all their liquid, and it has evaporated. Add the wine and let it bubble away until the liquid has disappeared, then add the cream. Simmer gently for 5 minutes or so until thick – you don't want the mixture to be runny. Stir in the herbs and check the seasoning. Spoon the mushroom mixture into the hot, crisp rolls, put the lids on and serve straight away with some tender salad leaves.

Consommé
with dried mushrooms

Many fungi recipes are earthy, gutsy and rustic – and none the worse for that. This one, on the other hand, is the very soul of elegance. It's also quite unusual in that it works better with dried mushrooms than fresh. You could augment it with a few vegetables: finely diced carrot added with the mushrooms, for instance, or sliced spring onions thrown in at the end, but don't be tempted to add too many extra ingredients: you want the flavour of the mushrooms to shine through unchallenged. Dried Ceps are the perfect mushroom to use, but any well flavoured, sliced dried mushroom will do.

Works with: any dried, well flavoured mushroom.

Serves 4
50g dried, sliced mushrooms
800ml good clear beef or chicken stock
50ml white wine
1 tbsp olive oil
100g very small pasta, such as risoni or tiny pasta shapes
Salt and freshly ground black pepper
A little chopped parsley

Put the mushrooms in a bowl and pour over enough boiling water to cover them – around 200ml. Leave for about 20 minutes, then strain them, reserving the liquid. Pass this through a funnel or sieve lined with a coffee filter or some muslin, to remove any grit, then add it to the stock and white wine in a large saucepan. Bring to a simmer.

Meanwhile, heat the olive oil in a frying pan over a medium heat. Chop the soaked mushrooms fairly small, add them to the pan and sweat them gently for a few minutes before adding to the stock. Bring the stock to a simmer, then add the pasta and cook for 10 minutes or so, until the pasta is done. Taste and season accordingly, then ladle into soup bowls, scatter with just a little chopped parsley, and serve.

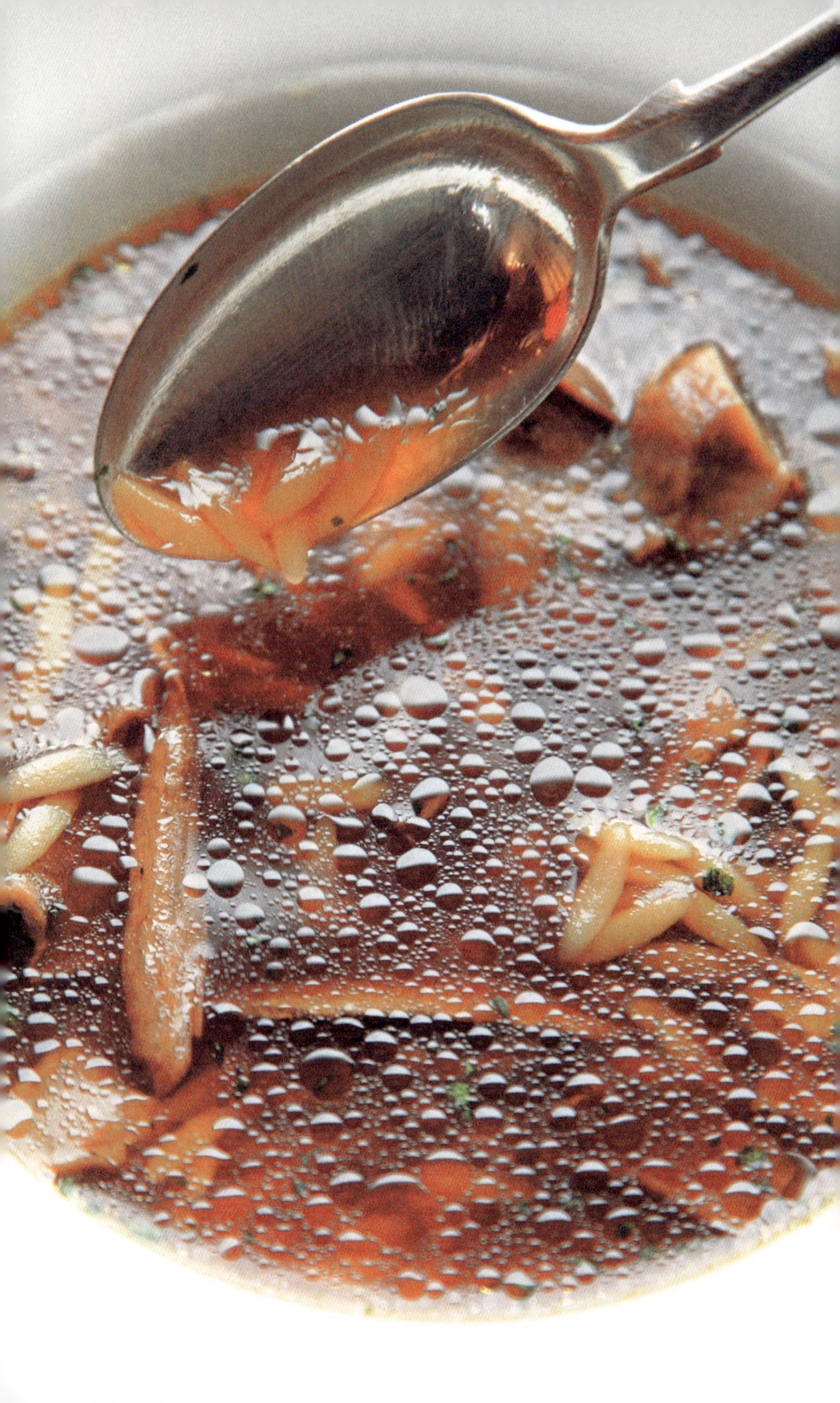

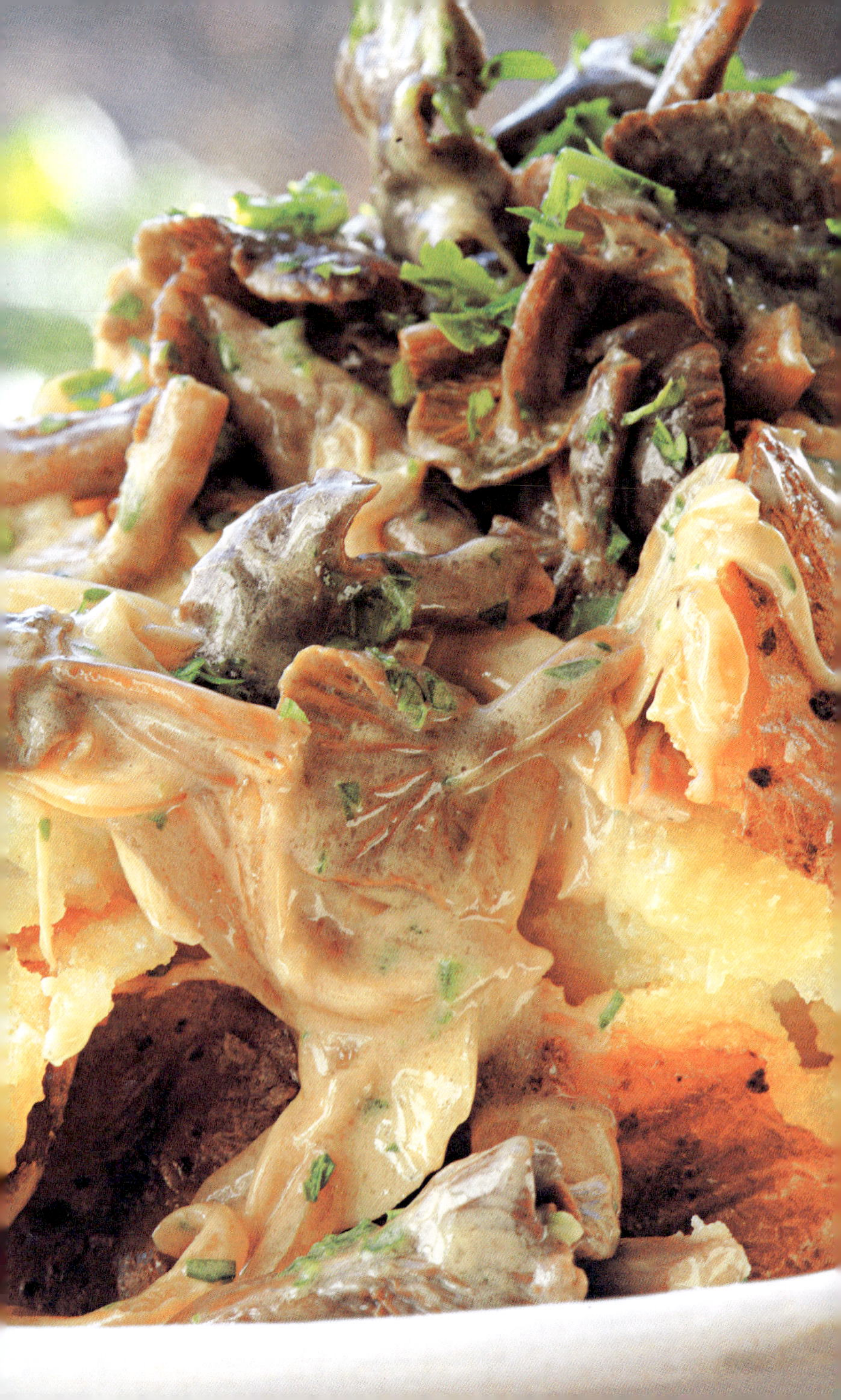

West Country stroganoff

This is so called because it was first cooked using Somerset cider, Devon cream and Dorset mushrooms. However, it would of course be best made with the local equivalents wherever you live. Winter Chanterelles are excellent in this dish, but by no means the only option, and also a mixture of types would work well.

Works with: Trumpet Chanterelles, Winter Chanterelles, Blewits, any Bolete, Blushers, Tawny Grisette, The Miller.

Serves 3–4

400–500g mushrooms	2 fat garlic cloves, peeled and finely chopped
1 tbsp groundnut or sunflower oil	150ml medium cider
2 onions, peeled and thinly sliced	150ml double cream
A large knob of butter	A squeeze of lemon juice
Salt and freshly ground black pepper	1 tbsp chopped parsley

Clean and trim the mushrooms and cut into walnut-sized chunks.

Heat the oil in a large frying pan over a medium heat. Add the onions and fry gently until starting to soften – about 10 minutes. Turn up the heat, add the mushrooms and knob of butter and fry, stirring, until the mushroom liquid has evaporated and everything starts turning golden. Season lightly, and toss in the garlic. Just as the garlic begins to colour, pour in the cider and stir well, then pour in the cream. Simmer for 5–10 minutes until the sauce is reduced and thickened. Add a squeeze of lemon juice. Taste and adjust the seasoning. Serve, with the chopped parsley scattered over, on a baked potato, or with rice.

Braised mushrooms
on pearl barley

Use large, dark-gilled Field Mushrooms or Horse Mushrooms for this – or organic cultivated mushrooms, such as Portobellos. Their substantial texture is delicious against the nutty grains of the barley and their inky juices contribute lots of flavour to the wine-infused sauce. If pearl barley is not to hand, you could serve them on a risotto (p.227) or on a mound of well seasoned, wet polenta.

Serves 4

For the barley
1 tbsp oil
A small knob of butter
1 onion, peeled and finely chopped
350g pearl barley
Up to 1.5 litres vegetable, mushroom or chicken stock (or use a mix of stock and water)

For the mushrooms
500g large Field or Horse Mushrooms
2 tbsp olive oil
A knob of butter
1 garlic clove, peeled and chopped
Salt and freshly ground black pepper
1 tsp chopped thyme
100ml red wine
200ml vegetable or chicken stock

Start with the barley. Heat the oil in a large-ish saucepan over a medium heat. Add the onion and cook for about 10 minutes, until soft and golden. Meanwhile, put the barley in another pan, cover with cold water, bring to the boil, then drain and rinse with cold water. Add the barley to the onions, stir it in, add about 1 litre of stock and bring to the boil. Turn down the heat to a simmer and cook, stirring often, for 45–75 minutes. After 40 minutes it should be tender but still chewy, whereas 75 minutes should render it pretty soft. As the barley cooks, add more stock or water – add it gradually because you don't want liquid left in the pan when the barley is cooked. Stir the knob of butter into the cooked barley and season well.

Meanwhile, clean and trim the mushrooms and slice them thickly. Heat the oil and butter in a deep frying pan over a medium heat. Throw in the garlic and cook for just a minute, without letting it colour, then add the mushrooms and seasoning. Cook, stirring from time to time, until they have shrunk to about half their original volume, and released their juices. Add the thyme, wine and stock. Bring to the boil, lower the heat and simmer for about 15 minutes, or until the mushrooms are very tender and the liquid has reduced by about half. Check the seasoning. Spoon the barley into warmed dishes, top with the mushrooms and their juices, and serve.

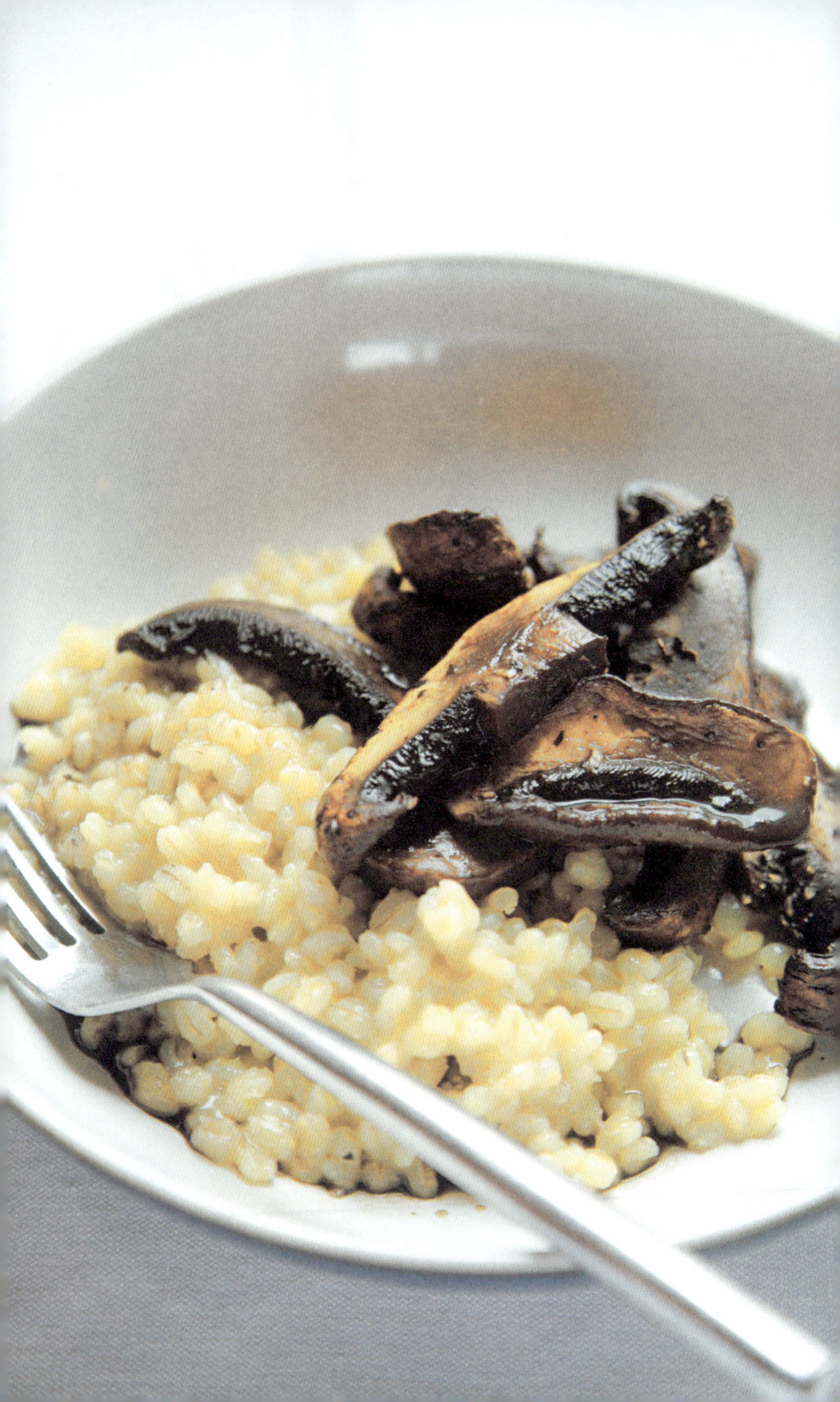

Cauliflower Fungus cheese

Cauliflower Fungus can look pretty daunting but, in fact, it's not difficult to prepare – treating it as you would an actual cauliflower is a pretty good approach. That is just how the idea for this dish came about and it turned out to be a delicious way to cook this spectacular-looking wild food.

Serves 4–6 as a side dish

About 1kg Cauliflower Fungus –
  either 1 whole small one,
  or part of a larger one (p.122)
1 small onion, peeled and grated
1 carrot, peeled and grated
500ml whole milk
1 bay leaf
Salt and freshly ground black pepper
50g butter
75g plain flour
100g mature Cheddar, grated
1 tsp English mustard

Preheat the oven to 180°C/Gas Mark 4.

Use a sharp knife to cut the Cauliflower Fungus into golf ball-sized florets. Work through the body, discarding any discoloured or damaged areas together with the tough core. You now need to get rid of all the unwelcome extras – pine needles, earwigs, etc. – that the fungus will inevitably contain. You might be able to do this with a thorough brushing, but you will probably need to wash the florets. Rinse them under the tap rather than soaking in water, and be as gentle as you can.

Put the grated onion and carrot in a small saucepan with the milk, the bay leaf and some black pepper. Bring almost to boiling, then set aside to infuse for 10 minutes before straining the milk into a warmed jug. Discard the bay leaf and vegetables.

Melt the butter in the milk pan (you don't need to wash it) over a medium heat and stir in the flour to get a loose roux. Cook this gently for a couple of minutes, then gradually add the warm, seasoned milk, stirring well after each addition to prevent lumps. When all the milk is added and the sauce is thick and smooth, bring it to a simmer and cook gently for just a minute. Add most of the cheese (reserving a little for the topping) and the mustard and stir well so the cheese melts into the sauce.

Place the prepared cauliflower fungus in a large mixing bowl, pour over the cheesy sauce and fold together with a large spoon (or use your hands). Spoon the mixture into a buttered, ovenproof dish. Sprinkle over the remaining cheese and bake for 15–20 minutes until bubbling and golden brown. This is particularly good served with steak or a piece of boiled bacon. It also makes a nice starter on its own.

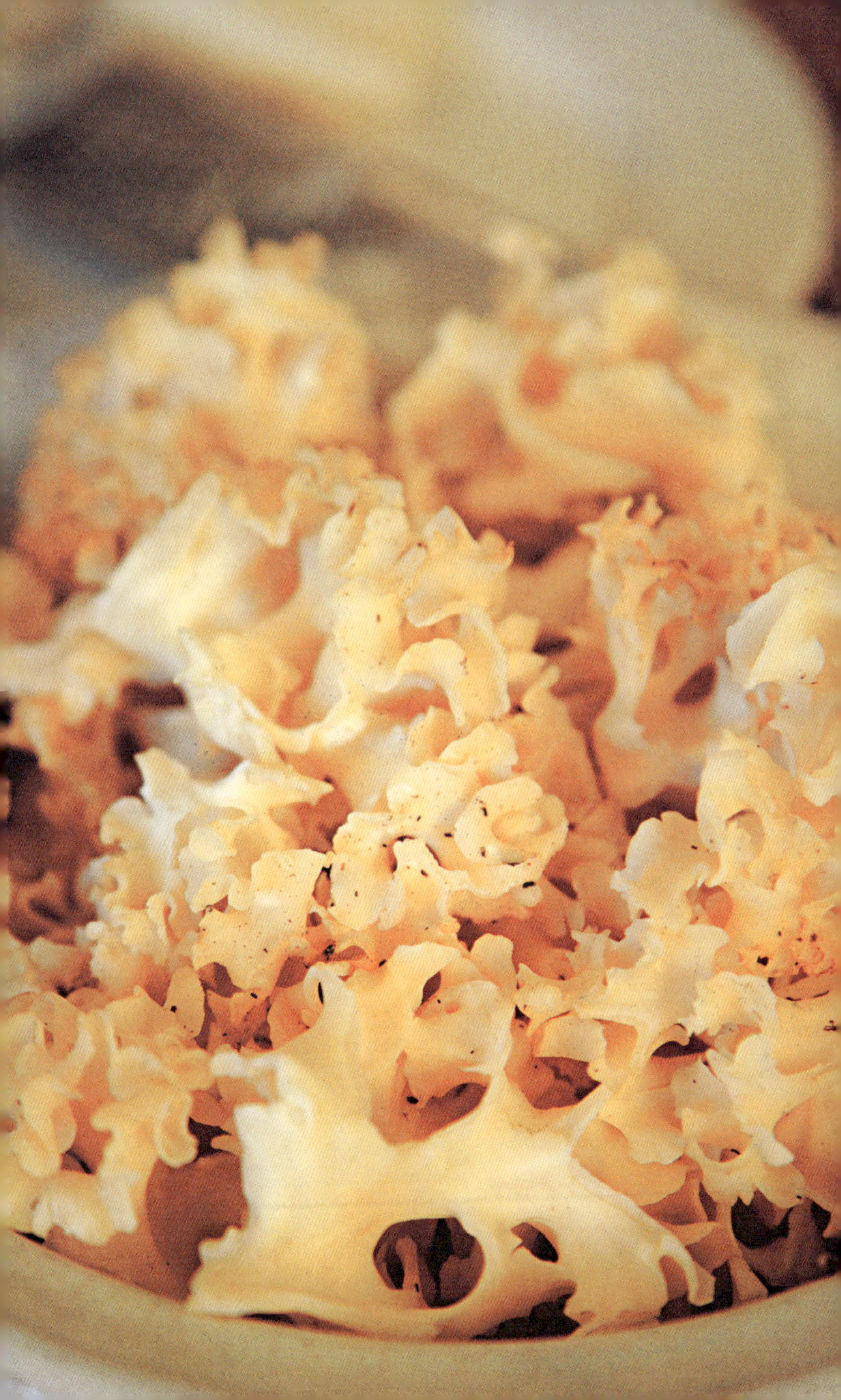

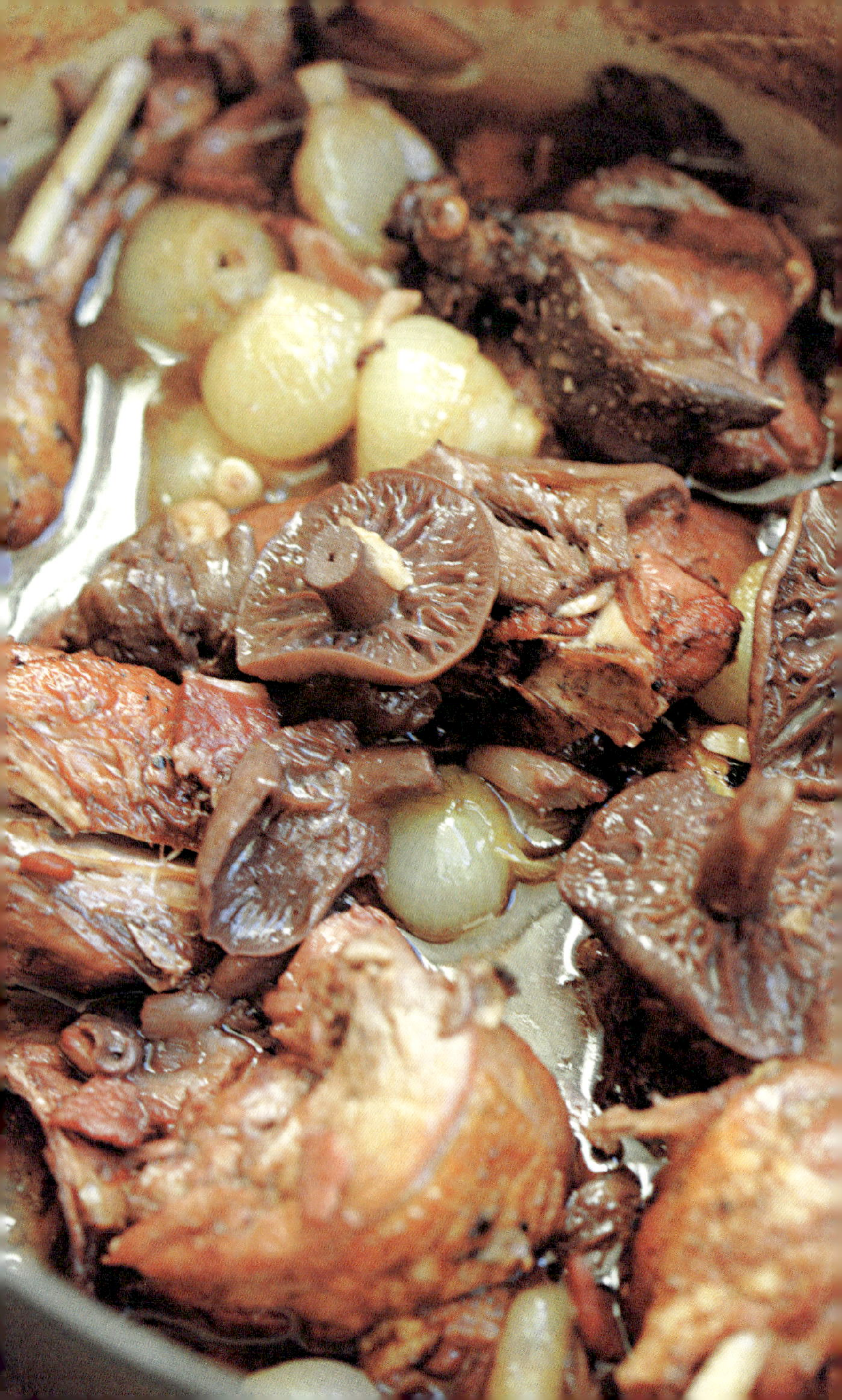

Braised pheasant
with wild mushrooms, shallots & bacon

Wild mushrooms always go well with game – and their seasons coincide neatly too – and you can use various different species of either here. If pheasant isn't available, try partridge or rabbit, for instance. Wood Blewits, as shown in the photo, are a good mushroom choice but this dish would also be excellent with Velvet Shanks, Deceivers, Winter Chanterelles or Saffron Milkcaps – all more unusual species that hold their shape during the long cooking.

Works with: almost anything, except Puffballs and Parasols.

Serves 2

- 150–200g mushrooms
- 2 tbsp sunflower or groundnut oil
- 1 pheasant, jointed into four pieces
- A little plain flour
- Salt and freshly ground black pepper
- 6 thick rashers streaky bacon, roughly chopped
- 12 baby shallots or pickling onions, peeled
- A knob of butter
- 2 fat garlic cloves, peeled and thinly sliced
- 2 glasses red wine
- About 250ml game, chicken or mushroom stock, or water
- 1 tbsp chopped parsley

Preheat the oven to 120°C/Gas Mark ½.

Clean and trim the mushrooms, and cut them into halves or quarters.

Heat the oil in a flameproof casserole dish over a high heat. Toss the pheasant pieces in the flour, shaking off any excess, then season them with salt and pepper. When the oil is hot, but not smoking, add the pheasant pieces, skin-side down. When they're a deep golden brown, turn them over, and add the bacon, shallots and mushrooms. Fry the whole lot, scraping and stirring as best you can, until everything has taken some colour. Toss in the butter and garlic, let it sizzle and foam, then pour in the wine and scrape up all the lovely caramelised bits from the bottom of the pan.

Add enough stock or water to nearly cover the pheasant, bring just to the boil, put the lid on and then transfer to the oven for about 1½ hours, until the meat is very tender and beginning to fall off the bone. Taste the juices, season if necessary, stir in the parsley and serve with mash or a baked potato.

Rabbit & mushroom puff pies

This is one of those forager-friendly recipes where almost any mushroom can be used. However, these pies are particularly good made with smaller fungi such as Deceivers, Winter Chanterelles and Fairy Ring Champignons. Hedgehog Mushrooms would be another good choice, not least because 'rabbit and Hedgehog pies' sound very intriguing. You could, though, use almost any game meat here. Pheasant works very well, for instance.

If you're in a hurry, you can skip the marinating and just flavour the meat by adding some garlic, bay and juniper to the pan as you brown it. Then again, if you have plenty of time you can make a sauce for the pies using the marinating liquid. Strain it, add another 150ml port and boil until reduced by half. Add 150ml stock, reduce by half again, then add a few tablespoons double cream and simmer until thick and rich.

Works with: anything except Parasols and Puffballs.

Serves 4

- 4 tbsp ruby port
- 2 bay leaves, torn
- 1 garlic clove, bashed
- 1 tsp crushed juniper berries
- About 800g boned-out rabbit (or hare, pheasant, pigeon or venison meat) from the saddle or leg, free of tendon or sinew
- 500g mixed mushrooms
- 50g butter
- 25g plain flour
- 250ml double cream
- Salt and freshly ground black pepper
- 2 tsp chopped parsley
- 300g puff pastry
- 1 tbsp olive oil
- 1 egg, beaten, to glaze

Combine the port, bay leaves, garlic and juniper, mix in the rabbit or other game and leave to marinate for an hour or two. Take the rabbit from the marinade, shake off the liquid, and cut the meat into thick slices.

Clean, trim and roughly slice the mushrooms.

Melt the butter in a large frying pan over a medium heat, add the mushrooms to the pan and cook gently for 4–5 minutes. Sift in the flour, and work it well in to the butter and mushrooms. Add the cream, turn down the heat and simmer gently for about 5 minutes, or until thick. Season with salt and pepper, add the parsley and leave to cool.

Roll out half of the pastry and cut into four thin discs, approximately 15cm in diameter, then roll out the rest and cut into four discs about 10cm in diameter. Put the larger discs in shallow saucers and spoon on the mushroom mix, leaving a wide rim at the edge.

Heat the olive oil in a large frying pan over a high heat. Add the sliced rabbit and fry it just until sealed and golden on the outside. Arrange the meat on top of the mushrooms on the pastry discs. Bring the edges of the pastry up over the filling, moisten the edges with water or a little milk, put the smaller discs on top and seal. Use a fork to crimp the edges together. Chill for half an hour.

Preheat the oven to 200°C/Gas Mark 6.

Transfer the pies to an oiled baking sheet, brush with the beaten egg and make slits in the top for steam to escape. Bake for 30 minutes, or until crisp and golden. Serve accompanied by some simply steamed seasonal veg – wilted spinach or shredded cabbage, perhaps – and some new or mashed potatoes.

Two mushroom tarts

A good mushroom tart is a very fine thing and there is no end to the possible variations on the theme. With a pastry case and a savoury egg custard being the two constants, you can create a filling with whatever you choose. Two excellent recipes follow, both combining specific mushrooms with aromatic and salty ingredients to delicious effect. Take these as templates and create your own tart filling with ingredients you have to hand. If the process of making and baking a pastry case seems a little too time consuming, consider the very easy, puff-pastry-based tart on p.222.

Cep, pancetta & thyme tart

This works really well with fresh Ceps but a combination of fresh and dried gives an even better flavour.

Also works with: for any tart, favour dryish mushrooms such as Hedgehog Mushrooms, Chanterelles, Winter Chanterelles or Charcoal Burners.

Serves 6

For the shortcrust pastry
250g plain flour
A pinch of salt
125g cold butter, cut into small cubes
1 egg, separated
About 50ml cold milk

For the filling
25–50g dried Ceps
Around 200g fresh Ceps
150g pancetta, cut into lardons
1 tbsp chopped flat leaf parsley
1 tbsp thyme leaves
A knob of butter
1 large onion, peeled, halved and sliced
2 whole eggs, plus 2 egg yolks
200ml full-fat milk
200ml double cream
Salt and freshly ground black pepper

To make the pastry, put the flour, salt and butter in a food processor and pulse until the mix reaches a breadcrumb consistency. With the machine running, add the egg yolk, followed by the milk, which should be added in a gradual stream. Watch carefully and stop adding the milk as soon as the pastry comes together. Turn out on to a lightly floured surface and knead into a smooth ball. Wrap in cling film and chill for half an hour.

Preheat the oven to 170°C/Gas Mark 3.

Roll out the pastry thinly and use to line a 25cm-diameter, loose-bottomed tart tin. Leave the excess pastry hanging over the edge. Prick the base all over with a fork, line with greaseproof paper and baking beans, put the tin on a baking sheet and bake for 15 minutes. Remove the beans and paper and return the pastry to the oven for 10 minutes. Then lightly beat the egg white and brush some of it over the hot pastry. Return it to the oven and bake for a final 5 minutes. This helps to seal the pastry and prevent any filling leaking out. Trim off the excess pastry using a small, sharp knife.

Turn up the oven to 180°C/Gas Mark 4.

Pour on enough hot water to just cover the dried Ceps and leave them to soak for 15 minutes. Swish them about in the bowl a few times to help loosen any grit (though if they are your own dried mushrooms, they really should not be gritty). Remove the Ceps with a fork, drain on a piece of kitchen paper, then chop them up roughly.

Pour the soaking liquid through a funnel lined with a coffee filter paper into a small saucepan. Set it over a high heat and boil until reduced to 100ml. Remove from the heat and reserve.

Clean, trim and slice the fresh Ceps.

Heat a large frying pan over a fairly high heat, add the pancetta lardons and fry until they are just starting to colour. Add the dried and fresh Ceps, along with the parsley and thyme. Cook until all the moisture the mushrooms release has evaporated, and they are starting to colour, then tip the mixture into a bowl.

Add the butter to the same pan, add the onion and fry over a medium heat until soft and just coloured. Combine with the pancetta and Ceps.

Beat the eggs and egg yolks with the milk, cream and the Cep liquor. Season with salt and pepper.

Fill the baked tart case with the Cep mixture (don't press it down too firmly), then pour over the custard. Make sure there aren't too many bits of Cep poking up out of the custard as these will dry out as the tart cooks.

Cook the tart in the oven for about 30 minutes or until golden on top and with only the hint of a wobble left in the middle. Leave to rest for at least 20 minutes before eating.

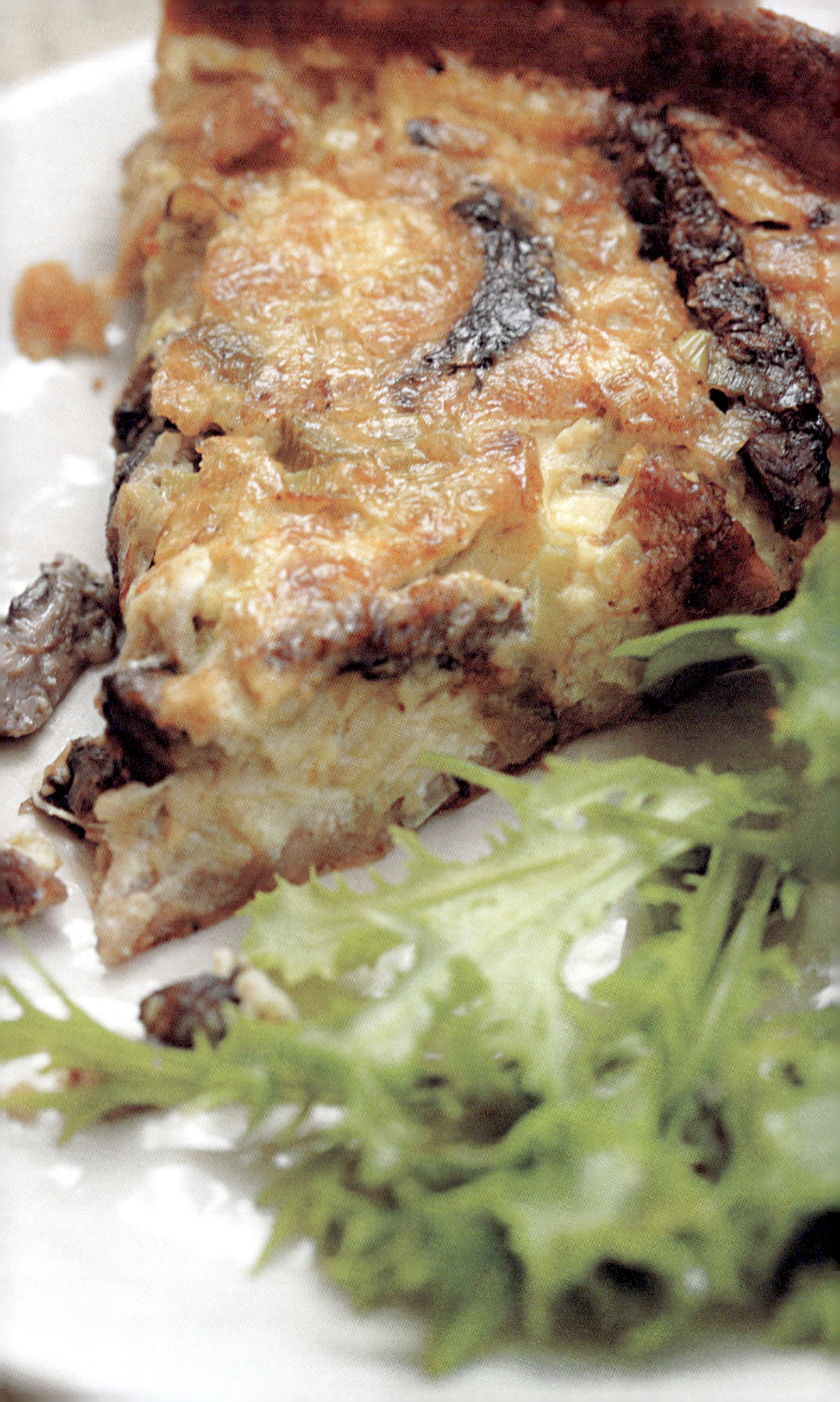

Parasol, leek & goat's cheese tart with walnut pastry

This follows the same basic method as the Cep tart, and is a lovely, earthy, autumnal dish. If you don't like walnuts, use the shortcrust pastry on p.218.

Serves 6

For the walnut pastry
60g walnuts
250g plain flour
A pinch of salt
125g cold butter, cut into small cubes
1 egg, separated
About 50ml cold milk

For the filling
200–300g closed or just-opened Parasols or Shaggy Parasols

50g butter
1 leek, trimmed, halved lengthways and finely sliced
2 whole eggs, plus 2 egg yolks
200ml full-fat milk
200ml double cream
Salt and freshly ground black pepper
100g hard goat's cheese, grated

First make the pastry. Preheat the oven to 170°C/Gas Mark 3. Put the walnuts in a food processor and chop them very finely. Then add the flour, salt and butter and proceed in exactly the same way as for the shortcrust pastry on pp.218–19. Roll out the pastry and use to line your 25cm-diameter, loose-bottomed tart tin, before baking as described on p.219. Turn the oven up to 180°C/Gas Mark 4.

Discard the Parasols' stalks, which can be fibrous, then clean and trim the caps and cut into slices about 5mm thick. Put half the butter in a large frying pan on a medium heat. Add the Parasols and a little seasoning and fry gently. They will shrink alarmingly, then, after their moisture has evaporated, they will turn golden and smell wonderfully nutty, even a little chickeny.

At the same time, melt the remaining butter in a lidded second pan, add the leek and cook gently. Stir every now and then, keeping the lid on between stirs, until soft but still bright green – about 10 minutes. Leave the mushrooms and leeks to cool.

Beat the eggs and egg yolks with the milk and cream, season with salt and pepper (allowing for the saltiness of the cheese) and stir in the mushrooms, leeks and cheese. Tip this mixture into the tart case and bake for about 30 minutes, until patched with gold on top and just a little wobbly in the middle. Leave to rest for at least 20 minutes before serving. This is also very good cold.

Easy wild mushroom tart

This is the simplest of tarts, and a good option if you don't have the time or inclination to make your own pastry. You can use any mushrooms you fancy and the whole thing takes little more than half an hour, start to finish.

Works with: just about anything.

Serves 2 as a starter or snack

About 200g mixed wild mushrooms
25g butter
Salt and freshly ground black pepper
1 garlic clove, peeled and finely chopped
Breadcrumbs made from 1 thick slice stale white bread, crusts removed
Finely grated zest of ½ lemon
1 heaped tbsp grated Parmesan
250g bought puff pastry or home-made rough puff pastry
1 tbsp finely chopped parsley
1 egg, beaten

Preheat the oven to 180°C/Gas Mark 4.

Clean, trim and slice the mushrooms.

Heat the butter in a small frying pan and add the mushrooms and a pinch of salt. As the mushrooms start to soften, throw in the garlic and fry gently for another 2–3 minutes or so. You want the mushrooms to be tender but not coloured and their liquid evaporated. Remove the pan from the heat and stir in the breadcrumbs, lemon zest, Parmesan, parsley and a few grinds of black pepper.

Roll out the pastry into a rough circle, no more than 5mm thick. Use this to line the base only of a 20cm-diameter tart tin or ovenproof frying pan and trim off the excess. Heap the mushroom mixture into the pastry, leaving a couple of centimetres uncovered around the edge – this will make a nice puffed-up, crisp, golden rim to the tart. Brush this edge with the beaten egg and bake for around 20 minutes, until the pastry is puffed up and golden. Serve hot or cold.

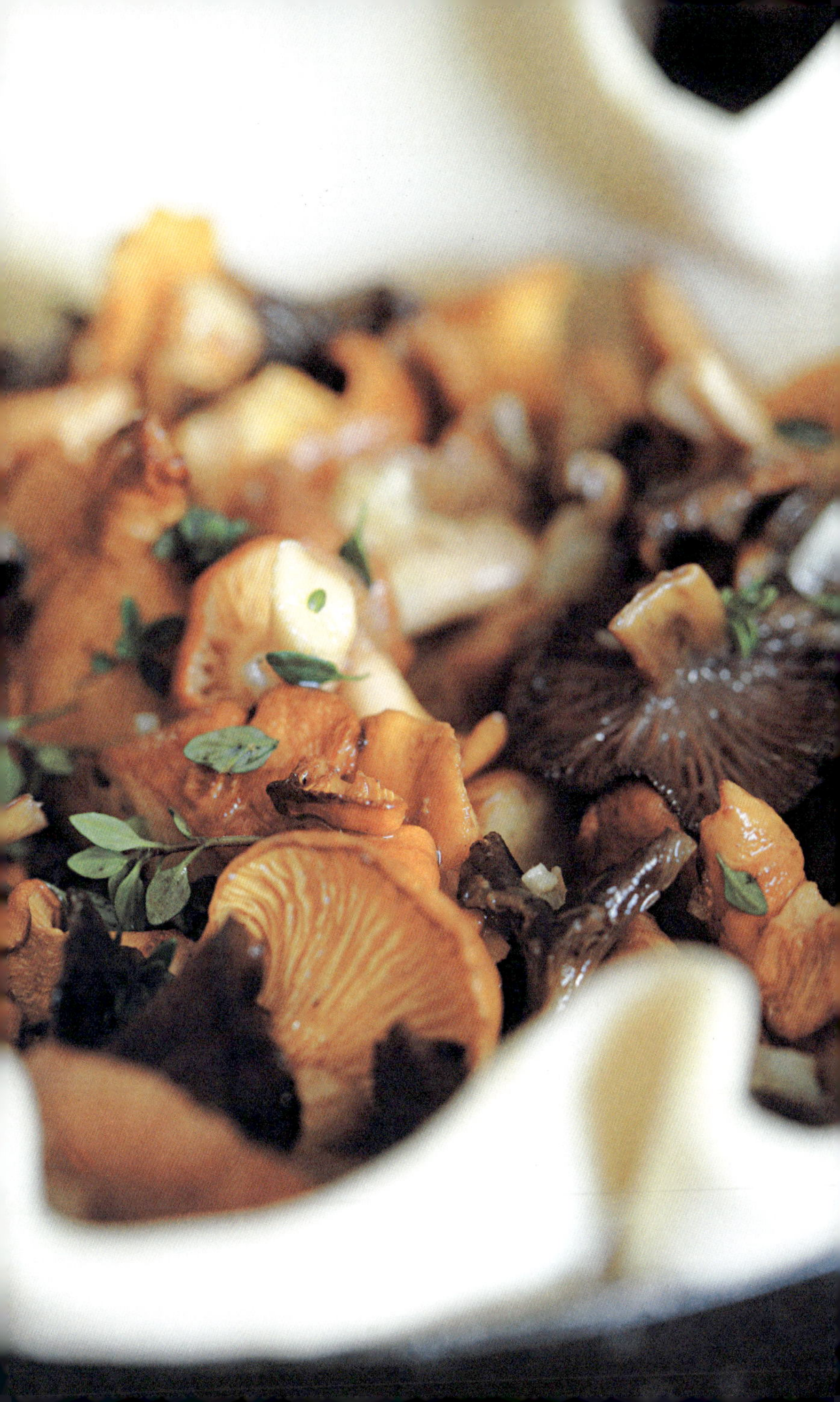

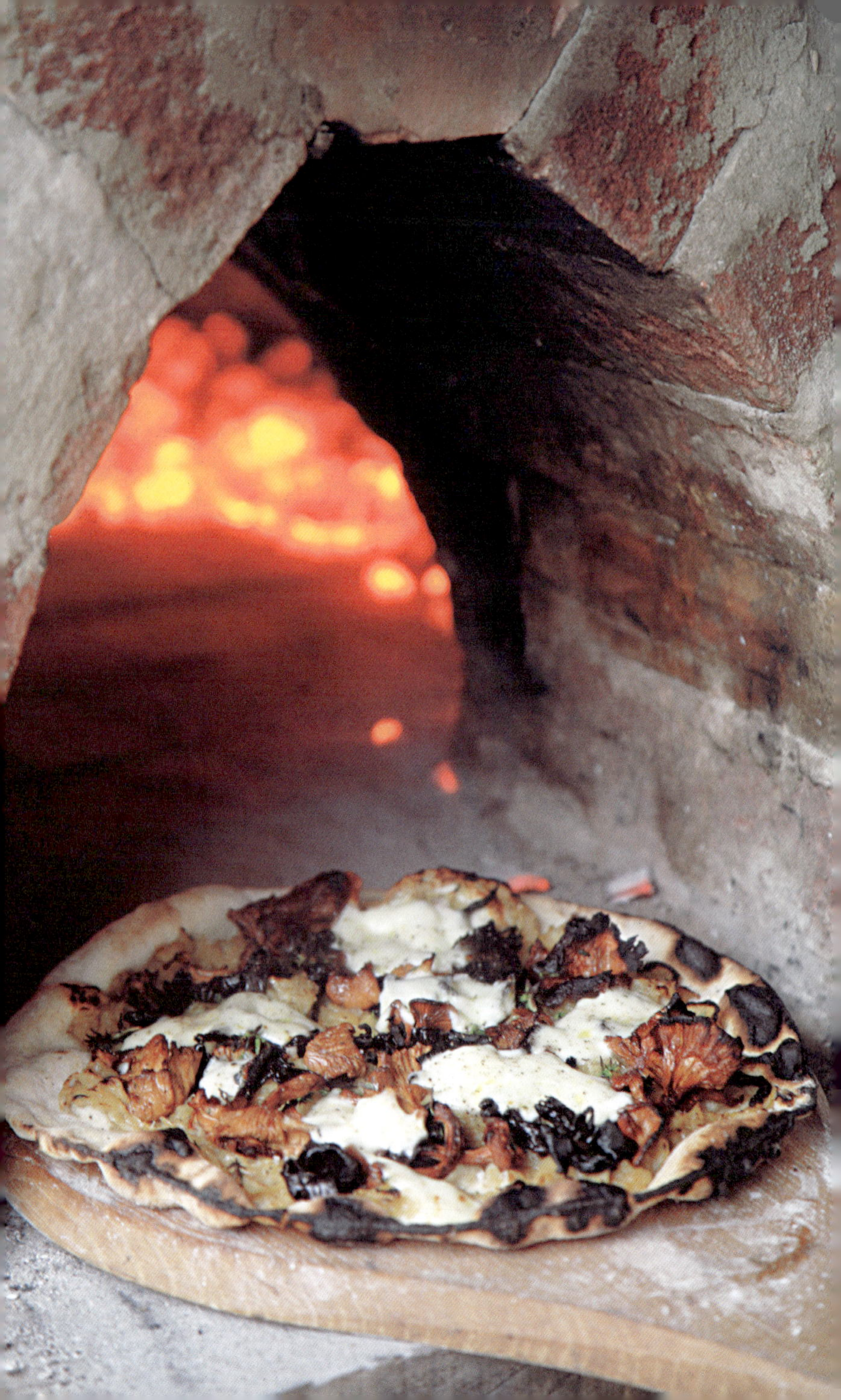

Pizza bianca
with mushrooms

Pizza bianca is a very simple pizza without tomato sauce. Given sweetness and softness with a topping of golden caramelised onions, it is a wonderful vehicle for a few, precious wild mushrooms as you don't need very many to create a big impact, visually and taste-wise.

Works with: just about anything, but perhaps the more colourful the better – try Chanterelles and Horns of Plenty (shown here), or Hedgehog Mushrooms and Blewits as well as Amethyst Deceivers or Waxcaps.

Serves 4

For the pizza dough
5g dried yeast
125g plain flour
125g strong white bread flour
5g salt
1 tbsp olive oil

For the topping
100–200g mushrooms
A large knob of butter
Flaky sea salt and freshly ground black pepper
3 tbsp olive oil
750g onions, peeled and very thinly sliced
2 heaped tsp fresh thyme leaves
A few tbsp crème fraîche or 1 ball buffalo mozzarella, sliced
Extra virgin olive oil

First make the dough: dissolve the yeast in 160ml warm water and leave for 10 minutes or so until it starts to froth. Meanwhile, combine the two flours and the salt in a large bowl. Add the yeast liquid and the oil, mix together into a rough dough, then turn out and knead on a floured surface for 5–10 minutes until silky and elastic. Leave it to rise in a warm place until doubled in size (at least 1 hour).

Meanwhile, prepare the mushrooms by cleaning and trimming them, then slicing thinly. Heat the butter in a large frying pan over a medium heat, add the mushrooms and a pinch of salt and fry gently until soft but not coloured. Remove them from the pan.

Add the olive oil to the pan. Add the onions, and a good pinch of salt, and cook gently on a low heat, stirring occasionally, for about half an hour until soft, golden and translucent.

Preheat the oven to 250°C/Gas Mark 9 and put in a baking sheet to heat.

Once the dough has doubled in size, knock it back and cut it in half. Use a rolling pin, or your hands, or both, to roll and stretch one half into a thin piece that will cover your baking sheet. Take the hot baking sheet from the oven, scatter it with a little flour or, even better, some cornmeal, fine polenta or semolina, and lay on the dough. Spread half the soft onions over the dough, scatter over half the mushrooms, then half the thyme, then add a few dollops of crème fraîche, or half the mozzarella. Scatter over some flaky salt and a few twists of black pepper, trickle on some extra virgin olive oil and bake for 10–12 minutes, until the base is crisp and golden brown at the edges. While it's cooking, roll out the second piece of dough, and prepare in the same way, so it's ready to go as soon as the first is cooked. Serve hot, in big slices.

Variation: Mushroom, ham & chard pizza

This alternative topping is slightly more substantial but just as delicious.

100–200g mushrooms
A large knob of butter
Flaky sea salt and freshly ground black pepper

8 chard leaves, stalks removed, torn and washed
8 slices air-dried ham
1 ball buffalo mozzarella, sliced
Olive oil

Make the dough as on p.225. Preheat the oven to 250°C/Gas Mark 9.

Clean, trim and slice the mushrooms. Heat the butter in a frying pan over a medium heat, add the mushrooms and a pinch of salt and fry gently until soft but not coloured. Remove the mushrooms from the pan, throw in the chard and cook for 30 seconds, just to wilt it a little.

Knock back the risen dough and use half of it to make your first pizza base with the method above.

Arrange half the mushrooms, ham, chard and mozzarella as artfully or artlessly as you like over the top, grind over some pepper and scatter on a little flaky sea salt, then trickle with a lick of olive oil. Bake for 10–12 minutes until the base is crisp and golden brown and the mozzarella sizzling. Repeat with the remaining dough and topping ingredients.

Wild mushroom risotto

The earthy flavour of mushrooms always works wonderfully in a risotto, and you can use almost any kind in this recipe. We like to use a real medley in ours: Ceps, Oak Milkcaps, Brittlegills, Bay Boletes, Hedgehog Mushrooms and Chanterelles. A mixture of fresh and dried mushrooms would work well too and the soaking liquid from rehydrated dried ones is a great addition to the stock.

We like to spoon the mushroom medley over the finished risotto, rather than stir it in: it makes for a nice clash of intense mushrooms with mildly fungal, creamy risotto. But if you like the idea of mixing everything up, go right ahead!

Works with: almost anything.

Serves 2

Around 300g fresh mushrooms, or a mixture of fresh and dried
75g butter
2 tbsp olive oil
4 shallots or 2 small onions, peeled and finely chopped
1 large garlic clove, peeled and finely chopped
Up to 750ml chicken, vegetable or mushroom stock
150g arborio or other risotto rice
Around 100ml white wine
Salt and freshly ground black pepper
2 tbsp chopped flat leaf parsley
2 tbsp double cream
50g grated Parmesan, plus extra to serve

If you're using any dried mushrooms, pour on just enough hot water to cover them and leave for 10–20 minutes. Strain them, reserving the liquid. If it looks gritty, pass it through a coffee filter, then add to the stock.

Clean and trim the mushrooms, and cut or slice them into fairly small pieces.

Melt about 15g of the butter with 1 tablespoon olive oil in a large, heavy-based saucepan over a medium heat. Add the onions and garlic and sauté gently for about 10 minutes, until soft – don't let them colour.

Meanwhile, bring the stock to a gentle simmer in a saucepan. Then turn down the heat very low – you need to keep the stock hot while you add it to the risotto.

Add the rice to the buttery onions and stir in well. Cook for a minute or two, then add the wine and let it simmer until absorbed.

Turn down the heat a little under the risotto pan. Add a ladleful of hot stock to the rice and let it cook, stirring from time to time, until nearly completely absorbed. Repeat with a second ladleful. Keep going, adding the stock gradually and stirring frequently, for about 20 minutes. By this time you should have used nearly all the stock, and the rice should be tender, with just the tiniest hint of bite left in it.

While the rice is cooking, heat a small knob of butter and 1 tablespoon olive oil in a large frying pan. Add the mushrooms and some seasoning and sauté for about 10 minutes until they are tender. Make sure that any liquid they release evaporates. Stir in the chopped parsley and keep the mushrooms warm while the rice finishes cooking.

When the rice is done to your liking, scatter the remaining butter, cut into little cubes, over the surface, along with the cream and the Parmesan. Turn off the heat and cover the pan for two minutes, then stir in the melted butter and cheese. Season well with salt and pepper. Check the consistency. If you like your risotto quite loose and wet, you can always add a little more hot stock now.

Spoon the rice into warmed dishes, spoon the mushrooms and any juices over the top, and serve with more grated Parmesan.

Pappardelle
with Ceps, sage & pancetta

Fresh homemade egg pasta, cut into thick ribbons, makes a wonderful vehicle for meaty slices of Cep. You can, of course, use a good shop-bought pappardelle instead, but find a fresh variety, made with egg, if you can – its tender texture will really make the dish.

Also works with: any Bolete and just about anything else, except perhaps Parasols, which would go soggy.

Serves 3–4

- 1 quantity pasta dough, as per the ravioli recipe on p.233
- Around 750g Ceps (more, if you've got them)
- 2 tbsp olive oil
- 150g pancetta or streaky bacon, cut into smallish dice
- 10 sage leaves, finely shredded
- 1 garlic clove, peeled and finely minced
- Salt and freshly ground black pepper
- A knob of butter
- Grated Parmesan, to serve (optional)

Make the pasta dough, following the recipe on pp.233–5. Trim the thin, freshly rolled sheets of pasta into lengths of about 20cm, then cut each into strips 2–3cm wide. Dust very lightly with flour and leave on a tea towel or hang up to dry – you can drape them over a coat hanger, or lay them on a flour-dusted tea towel hung over the back of a chair. Repeat with all the pasta. You can leave it for an hour or so, or use it straight away. Put a large pan of water on to boil.

Clean and trim the Ceps, cut them in half, then slice each half thinly.

Heat 1 tablespoon olive oil in a large frying pan, add the pancetta and cook until well coloured. Add the Ceps, sage and garlic, toss them with the pancetta and cook for a further 4–5 minutes or until the mushrooms' liquid has evaporated and they're starting to colour. Season with salt and pepper. Turn off the heat but keep warm.

Generously salt the pan of boiling water, drop the pappardelle into it and cook until al dente – probably no more than 2 minutes. Drain the pasta, tip it into the pan with the Ceps and pancetta, and add a good knob of butter and another tablespoon of olive oil. Toss well and serve on warmed plates. Parmesan is optional – the more Ceps you have, the less you need.

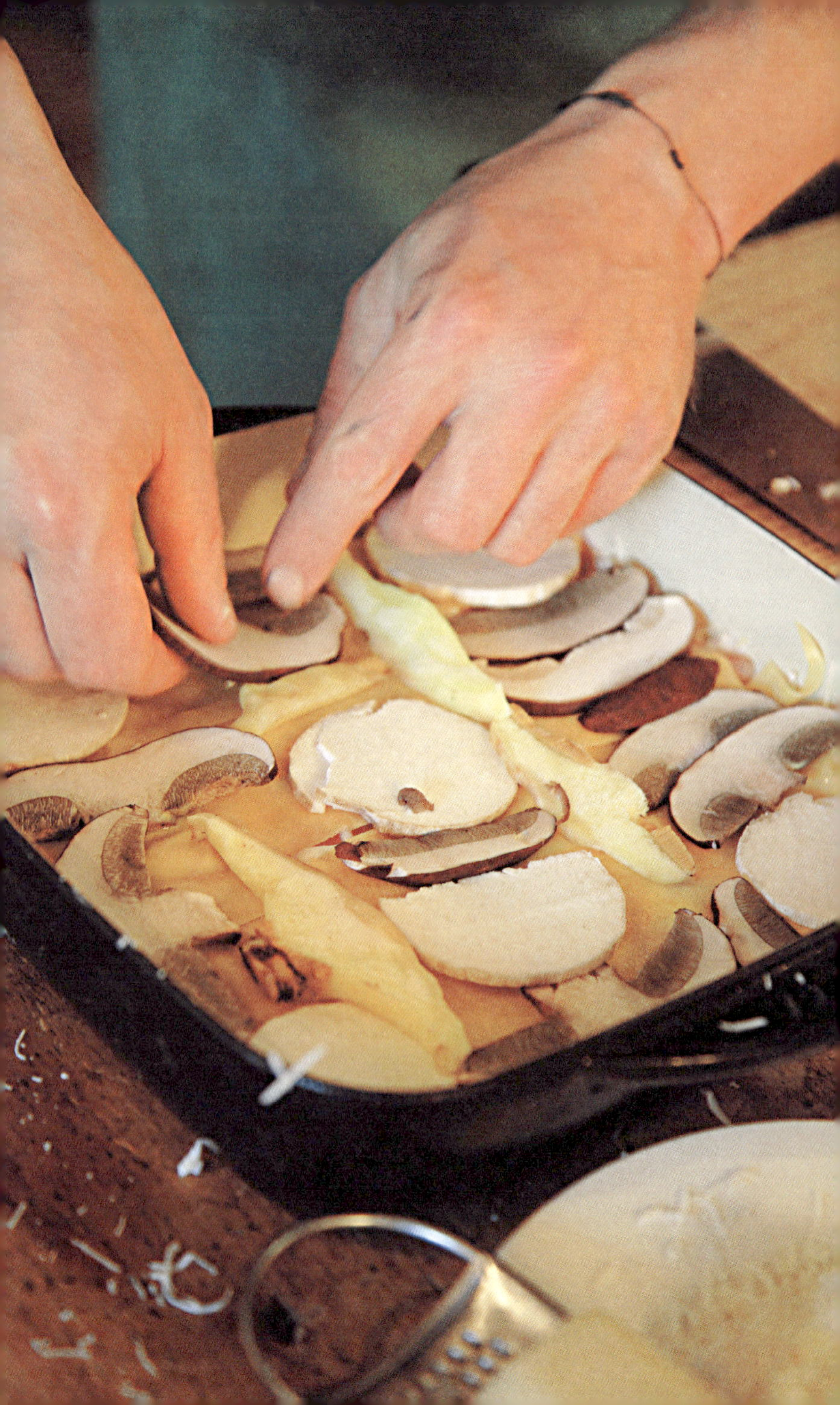

Boletus lasagne

This is a River Cottage classic, a variation on a porcini (Cep) lasagne cooked for Hugh many years ago by Mauro Bregoli of The Old Manor House restaurant in Romsey. It's a great way to make a really good meal from a relatively scant haul of mushrooms, as three or four good Ceps is enough for a lasagne to feed six. Any type of Bolete will work in this dish, or a combination of several different mushrooms. The lasagne you see here was made with Ceps, Bay Boletes and Slippery Jacks. You can use ready-made lasagne sheets but, if you have the time to make your own fresh pasta, it will contribute a lovely, tender quality and a superior flavour.

Works with: any Bolete, Wood Blewits, and large, firm Field Mushrooms.

Serves 6

For the béchamel sauce
500ml whole milk
½ onion, peeled
1 bay leaf
50g butter
50g plain flour
A pinch of grated nutmeg
Salt and freshly ground black pepper

For the lasagne
4–6 large firm Boletes – Ceps for preference
50g butter
4 tbsp olive oil
2 garlic cloves, peeled and finely chopped
Fresh pasta made with 200g flour, 2 eggs and 1 tbsp oil (p.233), cut into sheets the same length as your dish, or 250g fresh lasagne sheets
75g Parmesan, grated
75g hard goat's cheese, such as Woolsery, grated (or use all Parmesan)
4–6 very thin slices of air-dried ham (enough to make one good layer in the middle of your lasagne)

Begin with the béchamel sauce. Put the milk in a saucepan with the onion and bay leaf and bring to just below simmering. Set aside to infuse for 30 minutes. Melt the butter in a separate pan over a medium heat, stir in the flour to make a roux and cook for a few minutes. Now gradually add the hot milk, stirring after each addition to prevent lumps. When all is added, bring the sauce to a simmer and cook for 1 minute. Season with nutmeg, salt and pepper. The finished sauce should be a thick pouring consistency; add a little more hot milk if necessary.

Clean the Boletes and cut into fine slices. Since they aren't cooked before being added to the lasagne, they need to be thin enough to cook through easily, but not so thin that they disintegrate: about 3–4mm thickness is about right. If you have large Boletes, cut the stalk from the cap, slice the cap and then slice the stalk diagonally.

Melt the butter with the oil in a small saucepan. Stir in the garlic and then take off the heat. Preheat the oven to 190°C/Gas Mark 5. You are now ready to assemble your lasagne.

Brush the bottom of a large square or rectangular oven dish with some of the warm garlic and oil mixture. Put a layer of lasagne on the bottom then brush with more of the garlic oil. Pour a thin layer of béchamel, just a couple of tablespoons, over the pasta (you don't want to overwhelm the subtle mushroom flavours with too much sauce), then add a layer of sliced mushrooms. Brush with more of the oil mixture, then season with a twist of pepper and a sprinkling of the two cheeses. The cheese is simply a seasoning, it's not meant to form a thick layer, so keep it light.

Add another trickle of béchamel, then repeat the layering (lasagne, oil, béchamel, mushrooms, oil, pepper and cheese). Now add a layer of air-dried ham, top with béchamel, then repeat lasagne, oil, béchamel, mushrooms, oil, pepper and cheese, béchamel. Finish off with a final layer of pasta, a final, thick layer of béchamel and a final sprinkling of cheese.

Bake for about 25 minutes until nicely browned on top. Serve with a green salad.

Mushroom ravioli
with lemon & parsley butter

The filling for these elegant pasta parcels requires mushrooms with plenty of flavour. Horse Mushrooms and rehydrated dried Ceps is a particularly tasty combination.

Also works with: Chanterelles, Fairy Ring Champignons, Morels, Hedgehog Mushrooms, Horn of Plenty, Scarletina Boletes.

Serves 4

For the filling
350g mushrooms
1 onion, peeled and cut into quarters
1 garlic clove, peeled and halved
A large knob of butter
Salt and freshly ground black pepper
1 tsp chopped thyme
100ml white wine
75g soft, mild, rindless goat's cheese
   (or use ricotta or another
   soft white cheese)
25g grated Parmesan

For the pasta dough
300g '00' pasta flour
A pinch of salt
3 eggs
1 tbsp olive oil

For the butter
100g unsalted butter
Grated zest of ½ lemon
1 tbsp finely chopped flat leaf parsley

Clean and trim the mushrooms and break them into pieces.

Put the onion and garlic in a food processor and chop very finely. Heat the butter in a large frying pan and add the onion mixture, with a good pinch of salt and pepper. Fry, stirring frequently, until the onion is soft and most of the liquid has evaporated. Meanwhile, put all the mushrooms in the processor and chop them very finely. Add them to the pan with the onions, throw in the thyme, and cook for at least 15 minutes, stirring often, until you have got rid of all the mushrooms' moisture. Add the white wine, stir it in and cook until the liquid has evaporated. Then transfer the mixture to a dish and leave to cool. When it is cool, stir in the goat's cheese and Parmesan. Taste the mixture and add more seasoning if necessary.

To make the pasta, put the flour, salt, eggs and oil into a food processor and process until they just come together in a crumbly mass. Tip onto a lightly floured surface and knead for 5–10 minutes until smooth. The dough will seem dry and stiff but

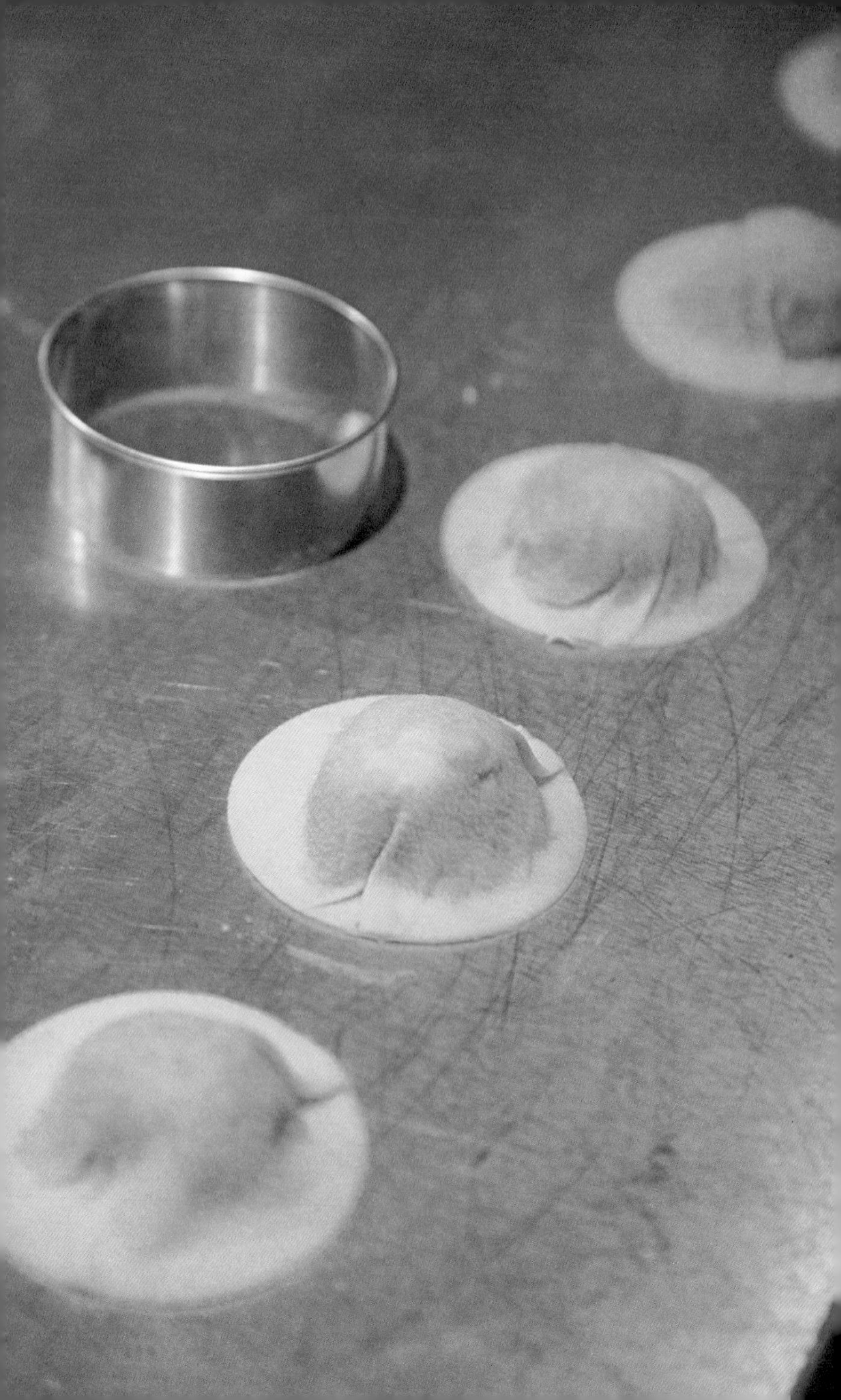

don't worry, it will soften a little as it chills. Wrap in cling film and chill for at least half an hour. Cut the pasta dough into four pieces and use a pasta machine to roll each one out. Dust one piece with a little flour and roll it through on the thickest setting. Fold in half and repeat, then repeat twice more. Then keep rolling the pasta through, gradually adjusting the machine so the pasta gets thinner and thinner. Dust with a little more flour if it starts to get sticky. You want the pasta thin enough that you can just about see the colour of your skin through it – probably at setting 5 or 6 (the second or third thinnest) on your machine.

To make the ravioli, use an 8cm cookie cutter to cut circles from the pasta sheets. You should get 24 ravioli from this recipe, so you'll need to cut 48 circles. Have a bowl of water and a pastry brush to hand, and a tray covered with a lightly floured tea towel. Put a blob of filling in the centre of one pasta disc. Dab a little water around the edge, top with a second pasta disc, and press the edges together to seal – work around the edge with your finger so no air is trapped inside. Place on the floured tea towel and repeat with the remaining pasta and filling. If you're not cooking the ravioli straight away, cover and refrigerate for up to 2 hours.

When you're ready to cook, put a very large pan of water on to boil. Prepare the lemon butter: melt the butter in a small saucepan over a very low heat, stir in the lemon zest and set aside to infuse.

When the pan of water is boiling, salt it generously. Depending on the size of your pan, you'll have to do this in two or three batches, maybe even four. So put 12, eight or six of the ravioli carefully into the boiling water. When the water returns to the boil, cook for 3 minutes, stirring once or twice so the ravioli don't stick together. Fish them out with a slotted spoon, letting the water drip off them, then transfer to warmed dishes. Repeat with the remaining ravioli. Stir the chopped parsley into the lemon zest-infused butter, spoon over the ravioli and serve straight away.

Variation: Mushroom piroshki, pasties or calzone

The intensely flavoured mushroom filling can also be folded inside pastry discs to make delicious little mushroom pasties, or piroshki as the Russians would call them. Either rough puff or shortcrust pastry will work. Alternatively, you can use small balls of pizza dough (p.225), rolled out very thinly, filled with the mix, and folded over, to make little wild mushroom calzone.

Deep-fried Parasols
with garlic mayonnaise

All the kinds of mushrooms could be given the deep-fried-in-breadcrumbs treatment but we honestly feel none will beat the Parasols. Their texture is excellent – almost chicken-like – and deep-frying is the perfect cooking method for them as it stops them turning into the wet rags you can end up with if you try to sauté them. Dipped in homemade garlicky mayonnaise, they really are wonderful. For best results, choose firm, heavy Parasols with their caps still closed, nearly closed or at least only recently opened.

Also works with: any *Agaricus* species, large thick-capped mushrooms only.

Serves 6 as a starter

For the garlic mayonnaise
1 very fresh egg yolk
1 anchovy fillet
1 garlic clove, peeled and
   finely chopped
½ tsp English mustard
1 small pinch each of salt, sugar
   and freshly ground black pepper
½ tbsp cider vinegar or lemon juice
100ml olive oil
150ml groundnut oil

For the Parasols
About 400g Parasols
Groundnut oil, for frying
2 tbsp plain flour
Salt and freshly ground black pepper
1 egg
100g fairly fine, fresh
   white breadcrumbs
Flaky salt and lemon wedges,
   to serve

Start by making the mayonnaise. Put the egg yolk, anchovy, garlic, mustard, salt, sugar, pepper and vinegar or lemon juice into a food processor and process until smooth. Combine the two oils in a jug. With the processor running, start pouring in the oil in a very thin trickle. When the oil starts to emulsify with the yolks, you can add the oil a little faster. By the time you've added all the oil, you'll have a thick, glossy mayonnaise. Adjust the seasoning and, if it seems too thick, thin it slightly with a little warm water. Cover and refrigerate until needed.

Remove the stalks from the Parasols and clean the caps well with a brush. Break the caps into segments – larger ones into eight, smaller ones into quarters.

Pour groundnut oil into a deep, heavy-based saucepan to a depth of at least 5cm. Heat it up to 180°C, or until a cube of white bread dropped in turns golden brown in about 50 seconds. Meanwhile, put the flour in a small bowl and season. Put the egg in a second bowl and beat lightly. Put the breadcrumbs on a plate.

Dust each piece of Parasol with flour, dip in the egg, then roll in the breadcrumbs, patting them on well. Drop a few carefully into the hot oil and fry for 2–3 minutes until golden brown. Scoop out and drain on kitchen paper. Continue until all the Parasols are cooked. Serve straight away with the garlic mayonnaise, some flaky salt and some lemon wedges.

Mushroom tempura

A lacy, crunchy tempura batter – much lighter than a traditional British batter – is a lovely coating for the more delicate members of the mushroom family. Don't try it with big, thick chunks of dense mushroom, as the water contained in them will make the batter soggy, but go for small pieces of thin, light fungi. You do need to be organised, getting your sauce and your mushrooms prepared before you even think about mixing the batter, and then frying the tempura quickly so you can get the whole lot to the table still piping hot. It's important also to leave the batter itself just barely mixed so it's thin, with plenty of lumps. This ensures a lovely, light, crunchy texture.

Works with: tender, delicate mushrooms such as Chanterelles, Oysters, Yellow Swamp Brittlegills or Oak Milkcaps.

Serves 4 as a starter

For the dipping sauce
2 tbsp soy sauce
2 tbsp mirin
½ garlic clove, peeled and finely chopped
½ hot red chilli, deseeded and finely chopped

For the mushrooms
About 300g mushrooms
Groundnut oil, for frying

For the batter
1 egg yolk
250ml ice-cold water
125g plain flour
Fine sea salt

Make the dipping sauce first. Put all the ingredients in a small pan, bring to the boil, then remove from the heat and leave to infuse. Prepare and trim the mushrooms. You want them in bite-sized pieces, so cut them up as necessary. Preheat the oven to 120°C/Gas Mark ½.

Heat about 8cm depth of oil in a deep frying pan, until it reaches 180°C (test with a cube of white bread – it should turn golden brown in about 50 seconds).

Meanwhile, prepare the batter: in a bowl, beat the egg yolk lightly, and add the cold water. Sift the flour into another bowl, then stir the cold egg mix into it very briefly – you want the ingredients barely combined, the batter should be lumpy. It also needs to be thin, to ensure a light, crisp coating, so add more water if necessary. When the oil is hot, dip a mushroom into the cold, lumpy batter and drop it into the hot oil. Repeat with just a few more mushrooms (too many and the temperature of the oil will drop) and cook for a couple of minutes until they are crisp (the batter should barely colour). Scoop out with a wire basket or 'spider' and transfer to a kitchen paper-lined plate. Scatter with fine salt straight away then transfer to the oven – or pass straight to your waiting guests. Cook the rest of the mushrooms in the same way, working as quickly as you can. Serve them piping hot, with the dipping sauce in one or two little bowls.

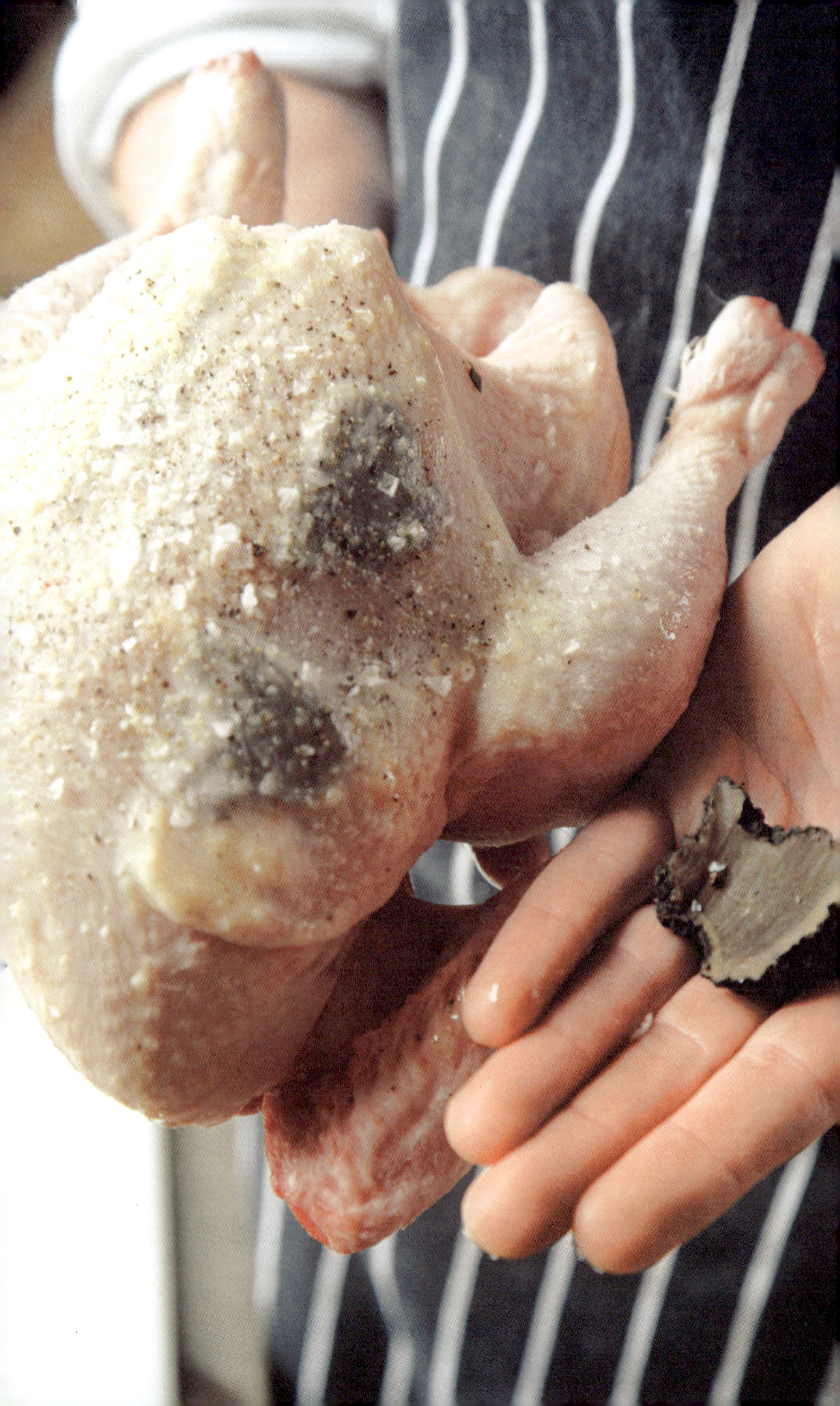

Roast chicken with Truffles

This is a lovely way to cook chicken, using just a little bit of Truffle to delicately perfume the breast.

Serves 4–5

100g soft butter
1 heaped tsp chopped thyme, plus an extra sprig
Salt and freshly ground black pepper
1 small but plump roasting chicken, weighing about 1.5–2kg
4–6 thin slices fresh English Truffle
8–10 small, whole shallots, unpeeled but rinsed clean
2 bay leaves
½ glass of white wine

Preheat the oven to 220°C/Gas Mark 7.

Beat the softened butter with the chopped thyme and season well.

Take off any string or elastic trussing from the chicken, place the bird in a roasting tin and spread out its legs from the body. Enlarge the opening of the cavity with your fingers, so hot air can circulate inside the bird.

Ease the skin of the breast away from the flesh by pushing your fingers gently down under the skin. Take great care not to tear it. You don't need to go all the way down, just create a large pocket of skin over the breast. Press half the thyme butter into this pocket, smearing it over the flesh of the breast, then carefully place the slivers of Truffle over the butter so they lie flat between skin and breast.

Smear the remaining butter all over the outside of the bird, and season it well. Put the whole shallots inside the bird (if they won't all fit, just put some in the tin), along with the bay leaves and sprig of thyme.

Roast for 20 minutes in the hot oven. Then baste the chicken, turn down the oven to 180°C/Gas Mark 4, pour the wine into the tin (not over the bird) and roast the bird for another 30–40 minutes, depending on its size. Open the oven door, turn off the oven and leave the bird for 15–20 minutes. This is usually enough time to roast a small chicken through without burning the skin. Check by pressing a skewer into the meat between the leg and the body: the juices should run clear.

Carve the bird in the tin, letting the pieces fall into the buttery pan juices, along with the cooked shallots, and letting the fresh juices from carving mingle with the rest. Then take the tin to the table and serve. A green salad is the only accompaniment you will need.

Mushroom stock

This makes a fantastic base for mushroom soups, stews, risottos and sauces, but can be used in all manner of other dishes where you need a good backbone of savoury flavour. There's little point being specific about quantities – use what you have, but it's not really worth making this stock with less than 500g mushrooms. You can use any fungi, wild, dried or cultivated, and this is an excellent and thrifty way to take care of excess mushrooms not needed for other dishes, clean stalks and other trimmings, and the more elderly or knocked-about fungi from your foraging trips. Don't, however, use anything that feels slimy or smells unpleasant.

Butter, lard or any other fat that's solid
   at room temperature
Mushrooms and mushroom trimmings
Onions, peeled and sliced – about
   one-sixth the weight of your mushrooms
1 leek, carrot and stick of celery
   (not essential, but desirable),
   all chopped fairly small
A bay leaf and/or a sprig of thyme

Heat a good knob of fat in a large frying pan, add a batch of mushrooms and fry until all their liquid has evaporated and they're golden brown. Repeat with all the mushrooms then put them in a stock pot with the onions, vegetables and herbs. Bring to the boil, reduce to a simmer and cook, with the lid on, for an hour or so.

Leave to cool until hand-hot but not scalding, then pass through a large sieve lined with muslin. Leave to cool completely, then refrigerate. When the stock is cold, remove the layer of solid fat that will have formed on top. Pour the stock slowly into a storage container, discarding any sludge at the bottom you don't like the look of. Store, covered, in the fridge, for up to three days, or freeze.

Preserving mushrooms

Whether you are fortunate enough to have a glut of mushrooms, or you simply don't want to use all the ones you've just gathered straight away, it's very handy to have a few preserving techniques up your sleeve. Almost without exception, a mushroom in good condition that's been properly preserved will perform just as well in a recipe as a fresh one. There are cases where preserved mushrooms are positively desirable, in fact. The Cep tart on pp.218–19 benefits from some dried mushrooms, which have a particularly concentrated flavour, while the oil, salt and vinegar used for pickling give mushrooms a unique, highly seasoned quality that makes them ideal for appetite-whetting canapés or antipasti.

Drying

This is perhaps the most popular way of preserving mushrooms, and the easiest. It works with just about any fungi, and enhances the flavour of most. Dried mushrooms can very quickly be rehydrated for cooking, but can also be powdered and added to dishes for a real boost of flavour.

You must start with good, unblemished, fresh mushrooms. Slice them thinly – but not too thinly. In most cases, that means 2–4mm thick. Then lay them on a rack – a cake cooling rack or grill rack is ideal – and put them in a warm place where air can circulate freely around them. A warm windowsill is perfect, or the top of an Aga, or a *very* low oven, with the door left slightly ajar. Commercial dryers are also available – though hardly necessary for most small-scale foragers.

Another technique, useful if you don't have a rack or you have lots of mushrooms to dry, is to thread the slices on to string, ideally with a piece of cardboard between each mushroom, and hang them over an Aga or radiator.

Speed is crucial – you must dry your mushrooms before they get any chance to spoil. However, it's also important not to toast them. The ideal drying temperature is 45–55°C, no higher, and you should expect the mushrooms to take five or six hours to dry properly. Good ventilation is essential or the mushrooms will spoil quickly and the unmistakable smell of elderly trainers will start to fill the air.

Once dried, store your mushrooms in clean, dry jars with sealable lids and keep for up to a year.

To rehydrate mushrooms, soak for 15 minutes in warm water. The soaking water, which becomes a sort of light mushroom stock, can be added to dishes too. If your mushrooms were gritty, rinse them once reconstituted, and pass the soaking liquid through a paper coffee filter to get rid of any debris, before using it in a dish.

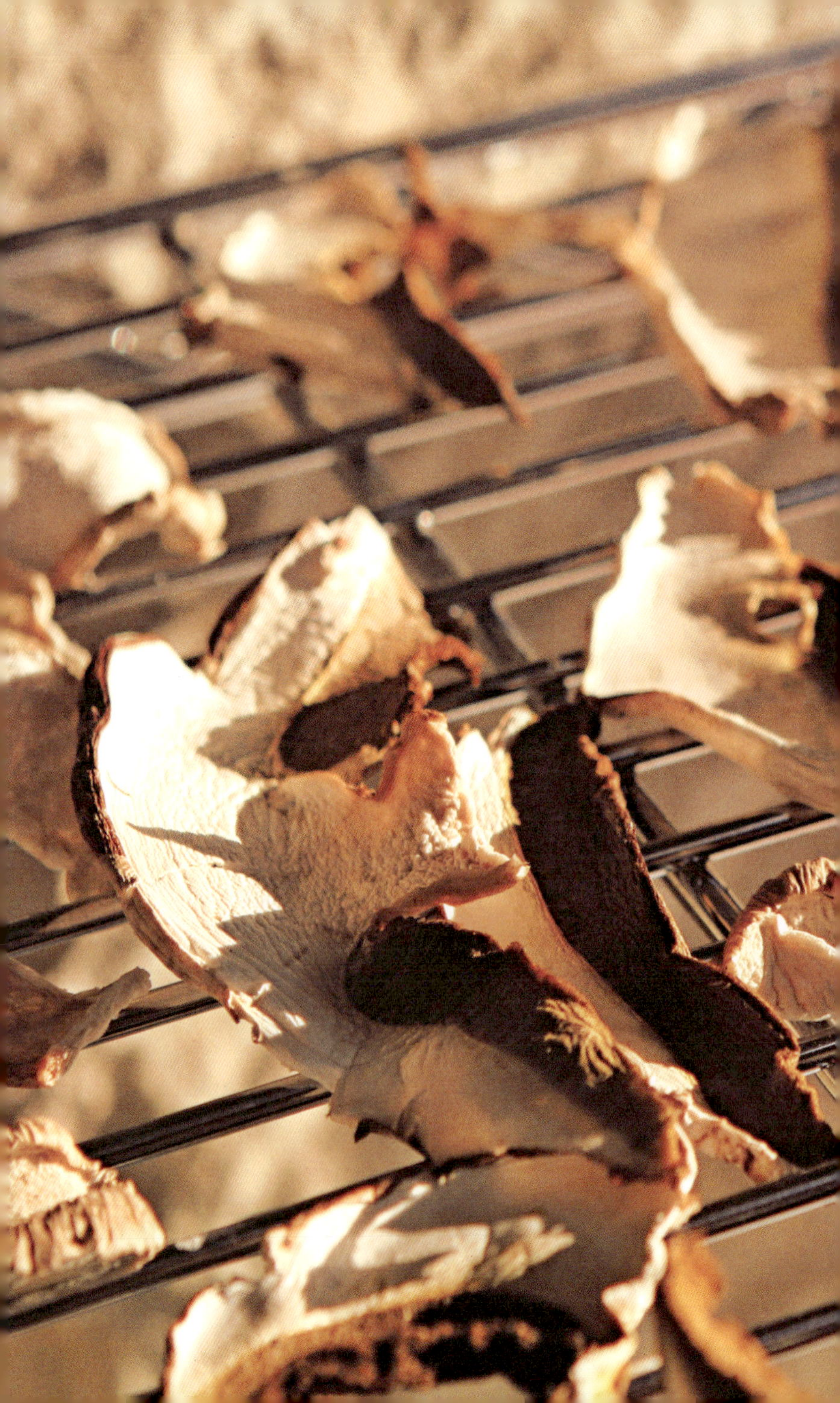

Freezing

You can freeze any mushroom. Very young ones freeze reasonably well raw, without any preparation, apart from basic cleaning. Once defrosted, you can use them just as you would fresh fungi. Slice and cook more mature specimens before freezing. Follow the basic sautéing technique used for mushrooms on toast (p.184) – without the garlic, as this can taste unpleasant after freezing – then let the mushrooms cool completely. Divide into portions and freeze in small bags or containers. After defrosting, revive them with a few minutes in a hot frying pan and then serve as they are, or incorporate in any recipe that uses sautéed mushrooms.

Mushrooms don't keep well for very long in the freezer, so use them within three months if you can, and certainly don't keep them for longer than six.

If you've had a good haul of mushrooms, but are unable to stow and stash them, make the wild mushroom soup on p.204, and freeze that instead.

Pickling

Pickling works best with whole small mushrooms such as Fairy Ring Champignons or very firm mushrooms such as button Field Mushrooms or firm young Ceps. This clever technique involves lightly pickling, or 'sterilising' the mushrooms, first with salt, then with vinegar, then preserving them in oil for safe keeping. Done well, they are delicious to eat straight from their jar of oil.

Clean your mushrooms and remove the stalks if they are tough. Cut them into fairly small pieces or, if they're small, leave them whole.

Put the mushrooms in a bowl and sprinkle liberally with fine-grained sea salt until all surfaces are covered. Leave for 1–2 hours, then pour off the accumulated liquid. Sprinkle on a fresh layer of salt and leave for a further 1–2 hours. Pour off the liquid again, then rinse the mushrooms under a cold, running tap to get rid of all the salt. Do it quickly so they don't have time to reabsorb any water.

Bring a pan of cider vinegar to a simmer (enough to cover the mushrooms). Drop them in and blanch for 2 minutes, then remove from the heat. Leave in the vinegar for at least 2 hours, and up to 24 for really big ones, such as whole Ceps. The longer they pickle, the longer you can keep them – but the more vinegary they taste.

Sterilise jam jars by washing them in hot, soapy water, rinsing and leaving to dry in a very low oven – or by putting them through a dishwasher cycle. Drain off the vinegar and transfer the mushrooms to the jars. Pour on enough oil to cover. Walnut oil is best in terms of flavour, but it only keeps a month or so. Sunflower or olive oil lasts longer. Give the jars a few firm knocks on the work surface to get rid of air bubbles and seal with lids. Label and keep in a cool, dry place, for up to six months.

The End

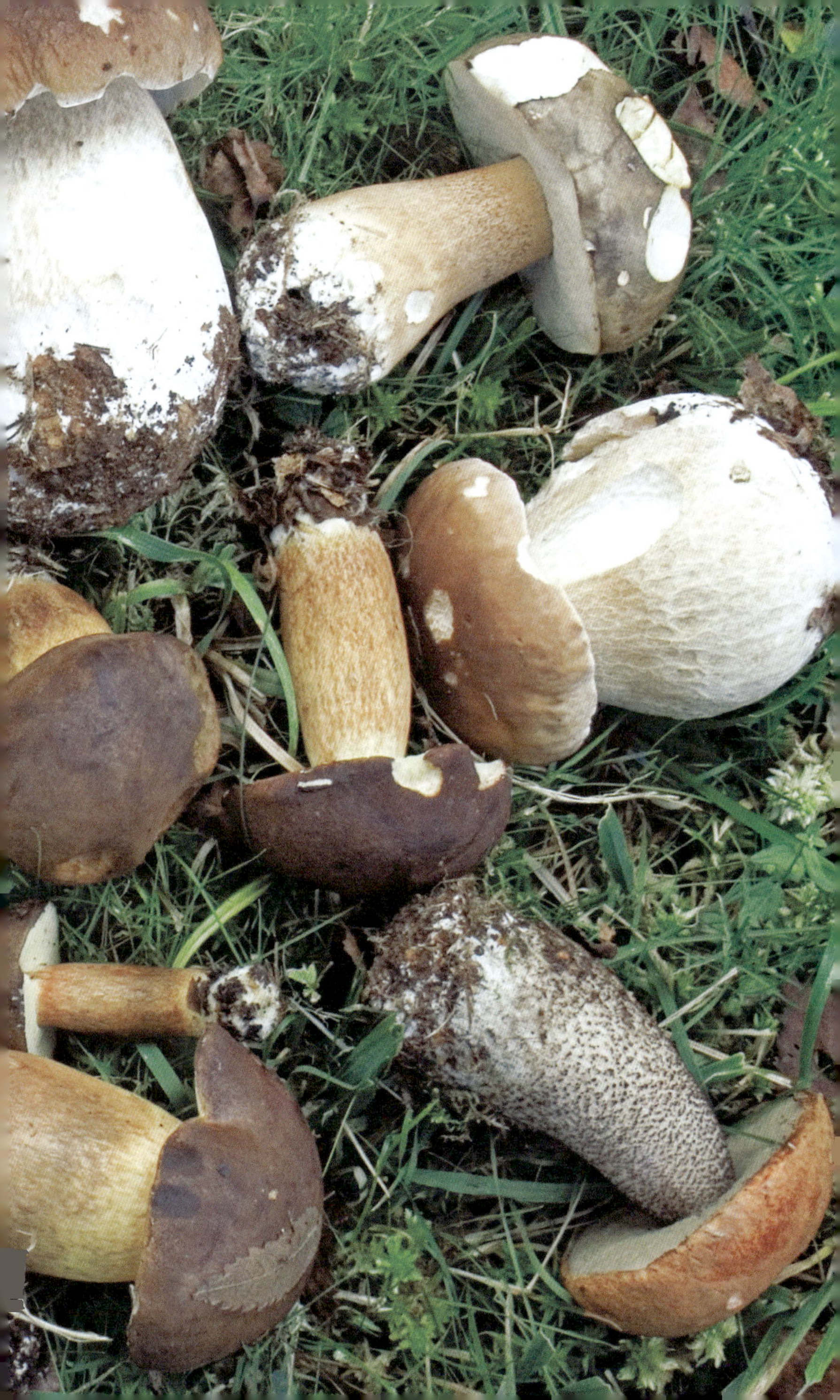

Useful addresses & further reading

It is quite impossible to have too many books on fungi but if you buy just one more you could do no better than *Mushrooms* by Roger Phillips (MacMillan, 2006). Also extremely helpful is Roger's website (www.rogersmushrooms.com), which is a stunning collection of photographs nicely laid out.

While there are many specialist and often impenetrable texts on individual genera, there are few books in print that make any attempt to cover the whole range of the larger fungi. If, however, you are prepared to take out a second mortgage it is really, really worthwhile getting hold of all six volumes (at around £80 each!) of *The Fungi of Switzerland*. Do not be put off by the mention of Switzerland, nearly all of the fungi in this vast work are found in the UK. The photographs are excellent and the descriptions technical but perfect. It is available from Richmond Publishing in Slough.

The venerable society devoted to the study of fungi, the British Mycological Society, is open to professional and amateur mycologists alike. It organises several forays each year, some of which are residential. It also publishes a number of journals ranging from the learned *Mycological Research* (which sports scientific papers with snappy titles such as 'Variability in Ribosomal DNA Genic and Spacer Regions in Phytophthora Infestans Isolates from Scottish Cocoa Plantations') through to the more digestible *Field Mycology* which has articles of actual use to the average mushroom hunter. Its address is British Mycological Society, The Wolfson Wing, Jodrell Laboratory, Royal Botanic Gardens, Kew, Surrey, TW9 3AB. The website address is www.britmycolsoc.org.uk.

Armchair mushroom hunters can obtain some of the species in this book from Smithy Mushrooms at www.smithymushrooms.co.uk. If you have ever thought of planting a Truffle tree do get in touch with Truffle UK at www.truffle-uk.co.uk.

There is nothing quite like going out with an expert to extend your knowledge of the fungi and many fungus forays are run each autumn by local societies and organisations, led by local experts. Fungus forays are among the many other day courses run at the River Cottage HQ on the Dorset/Devon border. If you would like to join me on one of these do contact us at www.rivercottage.net.

My own website is www.mushroomhunting.co.uk.

Acknowledgements

Writing is usually considered to be a very solitary enterprise, but I have found that in writing a book such as this one, it is not necessarily so. I have spent a great deal of time talking on the telephone to friends and reaping the benefit of their extensive knowledge. So it is a great pleasure to be able to thank them for their undue patience in helping me in my endeavour.

First I must thank Dr Peter Roberts and Gordon Dickson for their unstinting support. These are people of whom I can say, without the slightest hint of false modesty, know vastly more about the fungi than I will ever know, though I do believe that I am better looking than either of them. My good friend Dr John Cockrill has saved me considerable embarrassment by correcting some of my medical howlers in the section on poisonous fungi. It is gratifying to know that his years spent studying toxicology were not entirely wasted.

Alan Outen has kindly contributed photographs of fungi that proved too elusive for me and his general advice has been invaluable. The entries on the Boletus species would have been that much the poorer were it not for the support of King Bolete himself, Alan Hills.

I would also like to thank Dr Brian Spooner for his advice; Peter Chandler for his inspirational championing of maggots; Nigel Hadden-Paton for sharing his passion for Truffles. Also Tim Brodie-James from Natural England, Jim White and Bryan Edwards.

The team at River Cottage headquarters have put together a wonderful recipe section. The credit for this is due to Nikki Duffy, the River Cottage food editor, Gill and Dan and everyone else in the kitchen, and to Helen Stiles for organising the photoshoots. Also Colin Campbell for his superb food photography.

I have had enormous encouragement from the eternally patient editorial team at Bloomsbury, so much gratitude is due to Richard Atkinson, Erica Jarnes and Natalie Hunt, and to Emma Callery, the copy editor, for all her work. Also to Will Webb for his sterling work with the layout.

Many thanks are due to Gordon Wise for his invaluable guidance. I am immensely grateful for the enthusiastic support I have received from Rob Love and Antony Topping and hope that Rob now has the mushroom book he has always wanted.

Of course, this book would not have been possible without Hugh. So, quite simply, thank you Hugh.

Index

Agaricus 10–11, 17, 44, *92*, 92
    A. arvensis 10, 70, 76, 90–2, *91*
    A. augustus 98, 98
    A. bisporus 10, 95
    A. bitorquis 19, *94*, 95
    A. campestris 10, 93–5, *94*
    A. haemorrhoidarius 101
    A. macrosporus 92
    A. moelleri 172, *173*
    A. pilatianus 174
    A. silvaticus 99–101, *100*
    A. silvicola 10, 99–101, *100*
    A. urinascens 90–2, *91*
    A. xanthodermus 11, 172, *173*, 174
Alba, White Truffle of 132
Amanita 23, *36*
    A. ceciliae 69
    A. fulva 68–9, *69*, 143
    A. muscaria 148, 149
    A. pantherina 64, 150, *151*
    A. phalloides 140, 140–3, *141*, *142*
    A. rubescens 26, *27*, 39, 64–5, *65*, 143
    A. spissa 150
    A. strangulata 69
    A. vaginata 69
    A. virosa 143
Amethyst Deceiver 31, 66, *67*, 157
    pizza bianca with mushrooms *224*, 225–6
ascomycete 38
Ascomycota 12
ash trees 18
asparagus with St George's Mushrooms 192
atropine 157
Auricularia
    A. auricula 22, 39, *126*, 126, *127*
    A. polytricha 126

bacon, braised pheasant with wild mushrooms, shallots and *214*, 215
basidiomycete 38
Basidiomycota 12
baskets 16
Battarraea phalloides 15
Bay Bolete 35, 106, *107*
    boletus lasagne *230*, 231–2
    sautéed 183
    wild mushroom risotto 227–8
beech trees 18, 104
Beechwood Sickener 32, 152, *153*
beef, steak, mushroom and blue cheese sandwich 193
Beefsteak Fungus 12, 18, 22, 53, 128–9, *129*
Belladonna 157

birch trees 18, 104
Bitter Bolete 35, 104, *175*, 175
Bitter Poison Pie *162*
black spores 34
Blewit 17, 86–9
    Field 33, 86–9, *87*
    pizza bianca with mushrooms *224*, 225–6
    see also Wood Blewit
The Blusher 26, *27*, 30, 39, 64–5, *65*, 150
Blushing Wood Mushroom 34, 99–101, *100*
Boletus 17, 35, *36*, 53
    B. aereus 104, 105
    B. appendiculatus 104, *105*
    B. badius 106, *107*
    B. chrysenteron *106*, 106
    B. edulis 17, 18, 39, *102*, 102–5, *103*
    B. luridiformis 110, 110–11, *111*
    B. regius 15
    B. satanus 111, *176*, 177
    lasagne *230*, 231–2
    pappardelle with Ceps, sage and pancetta 229
bracket fungus 15, 38, 111, 124
braised mushrooms on pearl barley 210, *211*
braised pheasant with wild mushrooms, shallots and bacon *214*, 215
Branching Oyster Mushroom 56
bread
    fried mushrooms on toast 184, *185*
    mushroom loaves 205
brewer's yeast 139
British Mycological Society 19–20, 132
Brittlegill 48–53, 101, 152
    Charcoal Burner *48*, 48, 50, 218
    Common Yellow 32, 51–3, *52*
    Geranium Scented 53
    Greencracked 32, 48, *50*
    Powdery 32, 48, *49*
    salad of raw mushrooms 188
    wild mushroom risotto 227–8
    see also Yellow Swamp Brittlegill
Brown Birch Bolete 35, *109*, 109
Brown Roll Rim 33, *164*, 164–5, *165*
brown spores 33, 34
Bruising Webcap 158–9
Burglossoporus pulvinus 15

Calocybe gambosa 62–3, *63*
Camarophyllus pratensis 70
Cantharellus
    C. cibarius 17, 18, 38, 44, 46–7, *47*
    C. tubaeformis 78, *79*
caps
    colours 101
    identifying characteristics 26, *37*
'car park' effect 19
Cauliflower Fungus *122*, 122, *123*

cheese *213*, 212
Cep 17, 18, 35, 39, 44, 84, *102*, 102–5, *103*
    Cep, pancetta & thyme tart 218–19, 243
    consommé with dried mushrooms 206, *207*
    pappardelle with Ceps, sage and pancetta 229
    salad of raw mushrooms 188
    sautéed 183
    wild mushroom risotto 227–8
Chanterelle 17, 18, 31, 38, 44, 46–7, *47*
    cep, pancetta & thyme tart 218–19
    False 31, 47
    mushroom ravioli with lemon & parsley butter 233–5, *234*
    mushroom tempura 238–9, *239*
    palourdes with 200
    pizza bianca with mushrooms *224*, 225–6
    venison with *199*
    wild mushroom risotto 227–8
    see also Trumpet Chanterelle; Winter Chanterelle
Charcoal Burner 32, *48*, 48, 50
    Cep, pancetta & thyme tart 218–19
chard, mushroom, ham and chard pizza 226
cheese
    Cauliflower Fungus cheese *213*, 212
    mushroom pâté 202, *203*
    Parasol, leek and goat's cheese tart with walnut pastry *220*, 221
    steak, mushroom and blue cheese sandwich 193
chicken
    breast with Morels, marsala and cream 196, *197*
    roast chicken with Truffles *240*, 241
Chicken of the Woods *124*, 124
    sautéed 183
chitin 11
Chlorophyllum molybdites 24
clams, palourdes with Chanterelles 200
Clavulina cristata 78
Clitocybe rivulosa 54, 70, 84, *144*, 144
Clitopilus prunulus 84, 84, 144
Cloud Ear 126
Clouded Agaric 154
Coconut Milkcap 76
collecting fungi 13–20, 44
    and conservation 14–15
    cutting 16, 20
    how to look 19–20
    important points to remember 45
    law on 13–14
    picking 20
    toolkit 16
    when to look 17
    where to look 17–19
colours
    cap 101
    spores 24–5, 26, 29–34, 89, 101

Common Inkcap 34, 97, *170*, 170, *171*
Common Puffball *116*, 117, 118
Common Yellow Brittlegill 32, 51–3, *52*
conservation and mushroom hunting 14
consommé with dried mushrooms 206, *207*
coprine 170
Coprinus
    C. atramentaria 97, 170, *171*
    C. comatus 19, 39, *96*, 97
Cortinarius 50, 89
    C. orellanus 158
    cortina *159*, 159
    C. purpurascens 89, 158–9
    C. rubellus 158–9, *159*
    C. violaceus 89
Craterellus cornucopiodes 18, *83*, 83
Crimson Waxcap 31, 72, *73*
cultivated mushrooms 10
Cupophophyllus pratensis 70
Curry Milkcap 76
cutting mushrooms 16, 20

The Dapperlings 29, *36*, 76, 146, *147*
Dark Cep 35, *104*, 104
Davies, Julie 202
Deadly Dapperling 146
Deadly Fibrecap 33, 63, *156*, 156–7
Deadly Webcap 33, 46, 158–9, *159*
Death Cap 22, 30, 64, 65, 95, 139, *140*, 140–3, *141*, *142*, 146
    False 30, *36*, *142*, 143
Deceivers 31, 66, *67*, 157
    braised pheasant with wild mushrooms, shallots and bacon *214*, 215
    rabbit & mushroom puff pies 216–17
    venison with 199
    see also Amethyst Deceiver
decurrent gills *37*, 38
Destroying Angel 30, 64, 95, 101, *143*, 143
Devil's Bolete 35, 111, *176*, 177
digital cameras 16
Dog Stinkhorn 76
drying mushrooms 243

Earth Ball 118
Earth Star 69
easy wild mushroom tart 222, *223*
edible mushrooms 40–135
    and conservation 15
    identifying 22–3
eggs
    scrambled egg with shaved Truffles 186, *187*
    wild mushroom omelette 189
endangered species 15
English names of mushrooms 44–5
Enokitake mushroom 81

Entoloma
   E. sericeum 154, *155*
   E. sinuatum 154, *155*
esculenti 10

Fairy Cake Mushroom 162
Fairy Ring Champignon 31, 39, 54–5, *55*, 144, *198*
   mushroom ravioli with lemon & parsley butter 233–5, *234*
   pickling 245
   rabbit & mushroom puff pies 216–17
   sautéed 183
   venison with 199
fairy rings 18, 55
False Chanterelle 31, 47
False Death Cap 30, *36*, *142*, 143
False Morel 134, *178*, 178
False Parasol 24
False Saffron Milkcap 32, 60–1
family groups of fungi 12
Fatal Dappering 146, *147*
Fenugreek Milkcap 32, 82, *145*, 145
Fibrecap
   Deadly 33, 63, *156*, 156–7
   Lilac 33, 66, *157*, 157
   White 33, 157
fibrous scales *37*
Field Blewit 33, 86–9, *87*
field guides 16
Field Mushroom 10, 17, 18, 34, 53, 93–5, *94*, 157, 174
   boletus lasagne *230*, 231–2
   braised mushrooms on pearl barley 210, *211*
   salad of raw mushrooms 188
Fistulina hepatica 128–9, *129*
Flammulina velutipes 80, 81
flesh, identifying characteristics of 26
Fly Agaric 30, *36*, 65, *148*, 149, 150, 156
Fool's Funnel 32, 54, 70, 84, *144*, 144
Fool's Webcap 33, 158
forest bark 134
Forestry Commission 14
forked gills *37*
freezing mushrooms 245
fried mushrooms on toast 184, *185*
fruit flies 104
Funeral Bell 22, 33, 81, 160, *161*, 168
fungicides 58
Fungi (Spooner and Roberts) 12
fungus, origins of the word 11

Galerina
   G. autumnalis 160
   G. marginata 22, 160, *161*
   G. unicolor 160

Ganoderma applanatum 111
gardens 19
garlic mayonnaise, Parasols deep-fried with 182, 236–7, *237*
Geastrum fornicatum 69
genus 38
Geranium Scented Brittlegill 53
Giant Puffball 17, *119*, 119–21, *120*
gills
   decurrent *37*, 38
   forked *37*
   identifying characteristics 26, *37*
   key to fungi with 28, 39–34
   and spore colour 24
grassland mushrooms 17–18
grazing animals 18
Greencracked Brittlegill 32, 48, *50*
green spores 24
Grete Herball 10
Grey Spotted Amanita 150
Grifola frondosa 122
Grisette *37*, 69
   Tawny 28, 30, 68–9, *69*
Gyromitra esculenta 134, 178, *179*

habitat 26
   loss 15
haemolytic anaemia 164
hallucinogenic mushrooms 149, 150, 167
hand lens 16
hats 16
hay meadows 18
Hebeloma 162, 162, *163*
   H. radicosum 162
   H. sacchariolens 76
Hedgehog Mushroom *36*, 39, *114*, 114–15, 115
   Cep, pancetta & thyme tart 218–19
   mushroom ravioli with lemon & parsley butter 233–5, *234*
   pizza bianca with mushrooms *224*, 225–6
   rabbit & mushroom puff pies 216–17
   sautéed 183
   venison with 199
   wild mushroom risotto 227–8
Hen of the Woods 122
Hericium erinaceus 15
Hollowed Truffle 132
Honey Fungus 54
Horn of Plenty 18, 31, *83*, 83
   mushroom ravioli with lemon & parsley butter 233–5, *234*
   pizza bianca with mushrooms *224*, 225–6
Horse Mushrooms 10, 34, *37*, 70, 76, 90–2, *91*, 174
   asparagus with 192
   braised mushrooms on pearl barley 210, *211*
   salad of raw mushrooms 188

Hydnum
    H. repandum 39, 114–15, *115*
    H. rufescens 114, 115
Hygrocybe
    H. coccinea 72, *73*
    H. pratensis 70, *71*
    H. punicea 72, *73*
    H. virginea 70
Hygrophoropsis aurantiaca 47
Hygrophorus pratensis 70
hyphae 11, 38
Hypholoma
    H. fasciculare 22, 168, *169*
    H. sublateritium 168

ibotenic acid 149
identifying fungi 22–8
    edible and poisonous 22–3
    following a key 28, 29–37
        fungi with gills 29–34
        fungi with tubes 35–7
    note-taking in the field 24
    obtaining a spore print 24–5, *25*
    process of 24
    studying the fungus 26, *27*
Inkcap 19, *37*, 39, *96*, 97
    Common 34, 97, *170*, 170, *171*
    Shaggy 19, 34, 39, *96*, 97, 170
Inky Mushroom 34, 101, 172, *173*, 174
Inocybe 66
    I. erubescens 156, 156–7
    I. geophylla var. *lilacina* 66, *157*, 157
insect larva 15

Jack O' Lantern 46
Jelly (Jew's) Ear 22, 39, *126*, 126, *127*
Johnson, Dr Samuel 128

keys 28, 29–37
    fungi with gills 28, 29–34
    fungi with tubes 28, 29, 35–7
Kingdom Fungi 11
knives 16
Koryak people 149

Laccaria
    L. amethystina 66, *67*
    L. laccata 66, *67*
Lactarius
    L. deliciosus 60, 60–1, *61*
    L. deterrimus 60–1
    L. helvus 82
    L. quietus 82
Laetiporus sulphureus 124, 124
Larch Bolete 112
lasagne, boletus *230*, 231–2

latex 38
law on mushroom hunting 13–14
Leccinum 108–9
    L. aurantiacum 108, *109*
    L. scabrum 109, 109
    L. versipelle 108, *109*
leeks, Parasol, leek and goat's cheese tart with
        walnut pastry *220*, 221
lemon
    mushroom ravioli with lemon & parsley butter
        233–5, *234*
    Oyster mushrooms with lemon and thyme
        194, *195*
Lepiota 76, 146, *147*
    L. bruneoincarnata 146
    L. helveola 146
    L. ignivolvata 146
    L. magnispora 146, *147*
    L. subincarnata 146
Lepista
    L. luscina 33, *88*, 89
    L. nuda 86–9, *87*
    L. saeva 86–9, *87*
    L. sordida 33, *88*, 89
Lilac Fibrecap 33, 66, *157*, 157
Lion's Mane Fungus 15
Livid Pinkgill 33, 154, *155*
local authority land 14
Lycoperdon
    L. perlatum 116, 117
    L. pyriforme 116, 117, 118

Macrolepiota 146
    M. procera 74, 75, 76
    M. rhacodes 75, 76, *77*
Macro Mushroom 34, 90–2, *91*
maggots 104, 134
Magic Mushroom 34, *37*, *166*, 167
Marasmius oreades 39, 54–5, *55*
Meadow Puffball *116*, 117, 118
Meadow Waxcap 31, 70, *71*
metropolitan mushrooms 19
'middle aged mushrooms' 15
Milkcap *37*, 53, 152
    Coconut 76
    Curry 76
    Fenugreek 32, 82, *145*, 145
    Peppery 145
    Saffron 32, *36*, *60*, 60–1, *61*, 215
    Woolly 145
    see also Oak Milkcaps
Milk Truffle 53
The Miller 33, 84, *85*, 144
Morchella
    M. elata 39, *133*, 133, 134
    M. esculenta 133, 134

Morel 12, 17, 18, 19, 39, *133*, 133–4, *135*
    asparagus with 192
    chicken breast with Morels, marsala and cream 196, *197*
    cultivation 134
    False 134, *178*, 178
    mushroom ravioli with lemon & parsley butter 233–5, *234*
    powdered 134
    raw 134
muscarine poisoning 157
muscimol 149
mushroom, ham and chard pizza 226
mushroom hunting *see* collecting fungi
mushroom loaves 205
mushroom pâté 202, *203*
mushroom piroshki, pasties or calzone 235
mushrooms
    defining 10
    origins of the name 10
mushroom soup 204
mushroom stock 242
mushroom tempura 238–9, *239*
myccorrhizal 38
mycelium 11, 14, 17, 18–19, 38
mycography 38
mycology 38
mycophile 38

names of fungi 44–5
    specific epithet 38
Nicander 22
note-taking in the field 16, 24
nutritional value of fungi 44

Oak Bolete 35, 104, *105*
Oak Milkcap 32, 76, *82*, 82, 145
    mushroom tempura 238–9, *239*
    wild mushroom risotto 227–8
oak trees 18, 104
    brown rot 129
odours, fungal 76
omelette, wild mushroom 189
Omphalotus illudens 46
Orange Birch Bolete 35, 108, *109*
Orange Oak Bolete 35, 108, *109*
orellanus syndrome 158
Oudemansiella mucida 58–9, *59*
Oyster Mushroom 18, 30, *36*, 56, *57*
    with lemon and thyme 194, *195*
    mushroom tempura 238–9, *239*

Pale Oyster Mushroom 56
palourdes with chanterelles 200
pancetta
    Cep, pancetta & thyme tart 218–19, 243
    pappardelle with Ceps, sage and 229
Panther Cap 30, 64, 150, *151*
pappardelle with Ceps, sage and pancetta 229
Parasol 17, 30, *36*, *74*, 75–6, *77*, 146
    cooking 183
    deep-fried with garlic mayonnaise 182, 236–7, *237*
    False 24
    Parasol, leek and goat's cheese tart with walnut pastry *220*, 221
    Shaggy 30, 75, 76, *77*
    stem *37*
parks 19
Parrot Waxcap 70
parsley, mushroom ravioli with lemon & parsley butter 233–5, *234*
pasta
    boletus lasagne *230*, 231–2
    mushroom ravioli with lemon & parsley butter 233–5, *234*
    pappardelle with Ceps, sage and pancetta 229
Pavement Mushroom 19, 34, *94*, 95
Paxillus involutus 164, 164–5, *165*
pearl barley, braised mushrooms on 210, *211*
Peppery Milkcap 145
Périgord Truffle 130, 132
perniciosi 10
Pezizas 126
Phaeolus schweinitzii 124
Phallus impudicus 69
pheasant, braised pheasant with wild mushrooms, shallots and bacon *214*, 215
phenol 174
picking mushrooms 20
pickling mushrooms *244*, 245
pies
    mushroom piroshki/pasties 235
    rabbit & mushroom puff pies 216–17
pine trees 18, 104
pink spores 24, 25, 33
piroshki, mushroom 235
pizza
    bianca with mushrooms *224*, 225–6
    mushroom calzone 235
    mushroom, ham and chard 226
plastic containers 16
Pleurotus
    P. cornucopiea 56
    P. ostreatus 56, *57*
    P. pulmonarius 56
poisonous species 11, 44, 136–79
    frequency of 139
    identifying 22–3, 139
Poison Pies 33, *162*, 162, *163*
pollution 15, 19

Porcelain Fungus 30, 58–9, *59*
Portobello mushrooms 210
Powdery Brittlegill 32, 48, *49*
preserving mushrooms 243–5
The Prince 34, *98*, 98
Psilocybe semilanceata 166, *166*
Puffball 22, 53, 117–21
    Common *116*, 117, 118
    cooking 118, 183
    Giant 17, *119*, 119–21, *120*
    Meadow *116*, 117, 118
    Puffburgers *190*, 191
    spores 118, 121
    Stump *116*, 117, 118

rabbit & mushroom puff pies 216–17
ravioli, mushroom ravioli with lemon & parsley butter 233–5, *234*
Red Cracked Bolete 35, *106*, 106
rehydrating mushrooms 243
Rights of Way 13
'Right to Roam' land 13
rings, identifying characteristics of 26
risotto, wild mushroom 227–8
Roberts, Peter 12
Rocchia, Jean-Marie 130
Royal Bolete 15
Russula 23, 101, 165
    R. claroflava 51, *52*, 53
    R. cyanoxantha 48, *49*
    R. emetica 50, 152
    R. felea 53
    R. nobilis 152, *153*
    R. ochroleuca 51–3, *52*
    R. parazurea 48, *49*
    R. virescens 48, *50*

Saccharomyces cerevisiae 139
Saffron Milkcap 32, *36*, *60*, 60–1, *61*
    braised pheasant with wild mushrooms, shallots and bacon *214*, 215
    False 32, 60–1
St George's Mushroom 17, 32, 62–3, *63*, 157
    asparagus with 192
salads
    raw mushroom salad 188
    warm salad of roast squash and fried mushrooms 201
sandwiches, steak, mushroom and blue cheese sandwich 193
Sandy Sitball 15
saptrotroph 17, 38
Sarcodon imbricatus 115
sautéed mushrooms 182–3
Scaly Tooth 115
Scarletina Bolete 35, *110*, 110–11, *111*, 177

mushroom ravioli with lemon & parsley butter 233–5, *234*
Scarlet Waxcap 31, 72, *73*
Schaeffer, Julius 165
seasons for mushroom hunting 17, 26
seven mushroom challenge 39
Shaggy Inkcap 19, 34, 39, *96*, 97, 170
Shaggy Parasol 30, 75, 76, *77*
shallots, braised pheasant with wild mushrooms, shallots and bacon *214*, 215
The Sickeners 32, 50, *152*, 152
Silky Pinkgill 33, 154, *155*
sites of special scientific interest (SSSIs) 13
Slippery Jack 35, 112, *113*
    boletus lasagne *230*, 231–2
slugs 22
Snakeskin Grisette 69
Snowy Waxcap 32, 70, *71*
soups
    consommé with dried mushrooms 206, *207*
    mushroom soup 204
Sparassis crispa *122*, 122, *123*
species 38
Spooner, Brian 12
spore colour 24–5, 26, 29–34, 89, 101
    brown/black 34
    clay to rust brown 33
    green 24
    pink 24, 25, 33
    white/cream/pale yellow 25, 29–32
spore droppers 12
spore prints 24–5, *25*
spore shooters 12
spring season 17
squash, warm salad of roast squash and fried mushrooms 201
SSSIs (sites of special scientific interest) 13
Star Dapperling 146
steak, mushroom and blue cheese sandwich 193
stems, identifying characteristics of 26, 37
Stinkhorn 69, 76
stock, mushroom 242
studying the fungus 26, *27*
stuffed mushrooms 76
Stump Puffballs *116*, 117, 118
Suillus
    S. grevillei 112
    S. luteus 112, *113*
Sulphur Knight 76
Sulphur Tuft 22, 34, 81, 168, *169*
Summer Truffle *130*, 130–2, *131*
    scrambled egg with shaved 186, *187*
Sweating Mushroom 144
sycamore trees 18
symbiotic relationships 11, 18, 38, 61

tarts
- Cep, pancetta & thyme tart 218–19, 243
- easy wild mushroom tart 222, *223*
- Parasol, leek and goat's cheese tart with walnut pastry *220*, 221

Tawny Grisette 28, 30, 68–9, *69*
taxonomy 38
tempura, mushroom 238–9, *239*
Theft Act (1968) 13
thyme
- Cep, pancetta & thyme tart 218–19, 243
- Oyster mushrooms with lemon and 194, *195*

toadstools 24
- defining 10
- identifying 22, 23
- origins of the name 10
- *see also* poisonous species

toast, fried mushrooms on 184, *185*
toolkits 16
trees, symbiotic relationships with 11, 18, 61
trepass laws 13–14
Truffle 12, 18, 22, 38
- Hollowed 132
- Perigord 130, 132
- roast chicken with *240*, 241
- Truffle hunting 131–2
- White 130, 132
- *see also* Summer Truffle

Trumpet Chanterelle 78, *79*, 157
- West Country stroganoff *208*, 209

Trumpet of Death *see* Horn of Plenty
Tuber
- *T. aestivum 130*, 130–2, *131*
- *T. excavatum* 132

tubes
- identifying characteristics 26
- key to fungi with 35–7

Tulasnella violea 78
Tylopilus felleus 104, *175*, 175

umbo 38
urban environments 19

Vascellum pratense 116, 117, 118
Velvet Shank 30, *80*, 81
- braised pheasant with wild mushrooms, shallots and bacon *214*, 215

venison with Fairy Ring Champignons 199
volva (bag) 20, *36*, 38

walnut pastry *220*, 221
warm salad of roast squash and fried mushrooms 201
Waxcap 17
- Crimson 31, 72, *73*
- Meadow 31, 70, *71*
- Parrot 70
- pizza bianca with mushrooms *224*, 225–6
- Scarlet 31, 72, *73*
- Snowy 32, 70, *71*

Webcap *37*, 50, 89
- Bruising 158–9
- Deadly 33, 46, 158–9, *159*
- Fool's 33, 158

Weeping Bolete 35, 112
West Country stroganoff *208*, 209
White Fibrecap 33, 157
White Truffle 130, 132
Wildlife and Countryside Act (1981) 13, 15
wild mushroom omelette 189
wild mushroom risotto 227–8
Winter Chanterelle
- braised pheasant with wild mushrooms, shallots and bacon *214*, 215
- Cep, pancetta & thyme tart 218–19
- rabbit & mushroom puff pies 216–17
- venison with 199

Wood Blewit 33, 86–9, *87*
- boletus lasagne *230*, 231–2
- braised pheasant with wild mushrooms, shallots and bacon *214*, 215
- cooking 183

woodland mushrooms 17, 18–19
Wood Mushroom 10, 34, 99–101, *100*, 174
Woolly Milkcap 145

yeast 38
Yellow Stainer 11, 34, 92, 95, 101, 172, *173*, 174
Yellow Swamp Brittlegill 32, 51, *52*, 53
- mushroom tempura 238–9, *239*

yew trees 18

Zelleromyces stephensii 53

The River Cottage
Preserves Handbook

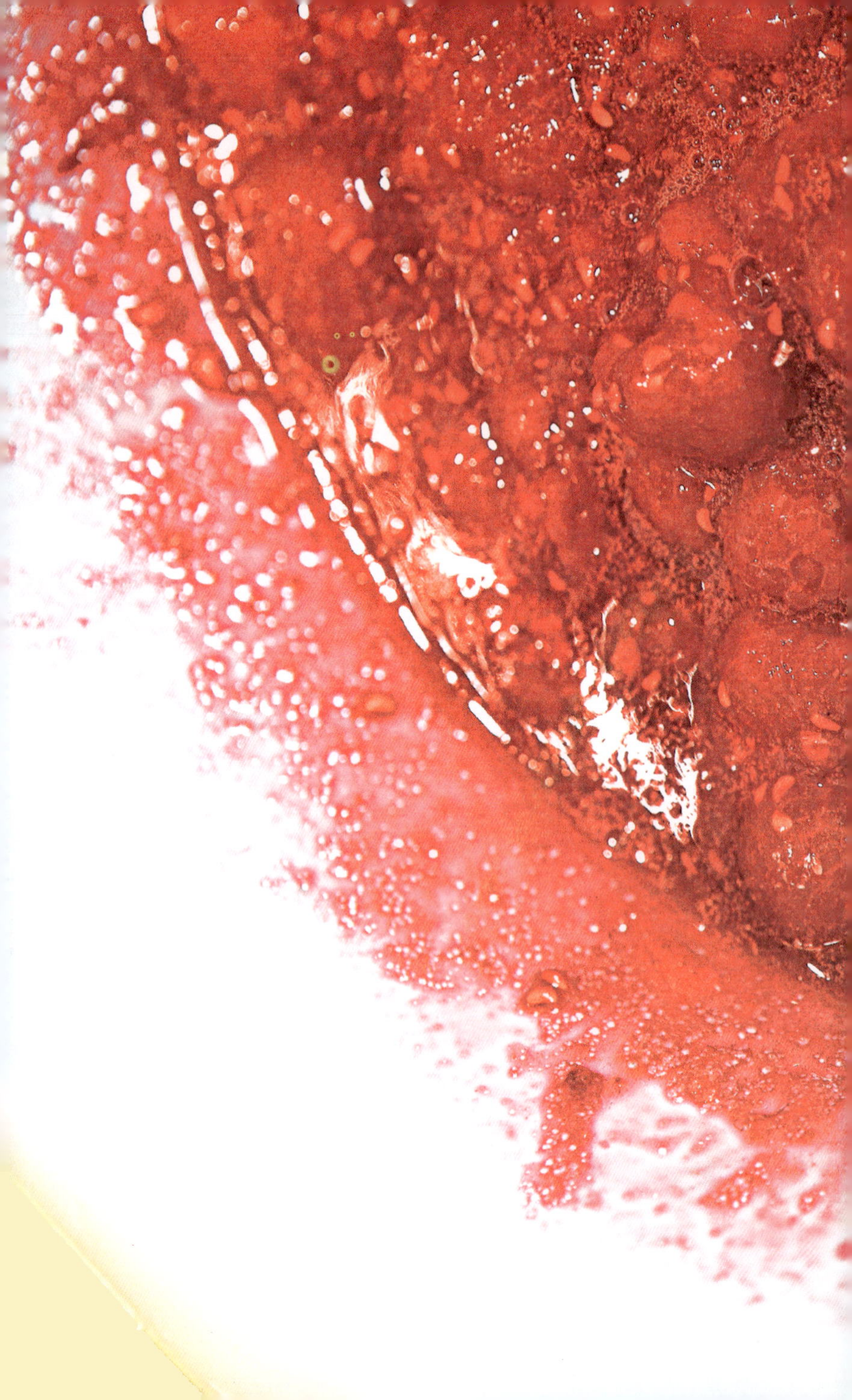

The River Cottage Preserves Handbook

by Pam Corbin

introduced by
Hugh Fearnley-Whittingstall

www.rivercottage.net

BLOOMSBURY
LONDON · NEW DELHI · NEW YORK · SYDNEY

*for my daughters
Pip and Maddy*

First published in Great Britain 2008
This paperback edition published 2012

Text © 2008 by Pam Corbin
Photography © 2008 by Gavin Kingcome
Additional photography © 2008 by Lois Wakeman

The beech noyau recipe on p.138 is reprinted by permission
of HarperCollins Publishers Ltd © Richard Mabey, 1972

The moral right of the author has been asserted.

Bloomsbury Publishing Plc, 50 Bedford Square, London WC1B 3DP
Bloomsbury Publishing, London, New Delhi, New York and Sydney

A CIP catalogue record for this book is available from the British Library.

ISBN 978 1 4088 3606 4
10 9 8 7 6 5 4 3 2 1

Project editor: Janet Illsley
Design: willwebb.co.uk
Printed in China by C&C Offset Printing Co., Ltd.

MIX
Paper from
responsible sources
FSC® C008047

www.bloomsbury.com/rivercottage

While every effort has been made to ensure the accuracy of the information contained in this book,
in no circumstances can the publisher or the author accept any legal responsibility or liability for
any loss or damage (including damage to property and/or personal injury) arising from any error in
or omission from the information contained in this book, or from the failure of the reader to properly
and accurately follow any instructions contained in the book.

Contents

Seasonality	8
The Rules	24
Jams & Jellies	42
Pickles, Chutneys & Relishes	92
Cordials, Fruit Liqueurs & Vinegars	128
Bottled Fruits	158
Sauces, Ketchups & Oil-based Preserves	186
Useful Things	208

I love jam and all its jarred and bottled relatives, the extended family we call by the rather austere name 'preserves'. Actually they're not austere at all. They are warm, forward and friendly, offering up both generous feisty flavours and intriguing spicy subtleties to all who embrace them.

Mostly, I love them for being so delicious. But I also cherish and admire them for something else. They epitomise the values at the heart of a well-run, contented kitchen. Firstly they embody and thrive on seasonal abundance. Secondly they are, or should be, intrinsically local, perfectly complementing the grow-your-own (or at least pick-your-own) philosophy. And thirdly, not to be sniffed at in these days of ecological anxiety, they are frugal, thrifty and parsimonious: they waste not, so we want not.

Jams, chutneys and pickles embrace the seasons, but they also, in an elegant and entirely positive manner, defy them. They do so by stretching the bounty of more abundant months into the sparser ones. We shouldn't underestimate this achievement. Over the centuries, wizards and alchemists have used all the power and magic they can muster to try and catch rainbows, spin straw into gold, and even bring the dead back to life. They've failed of course. Yet all the while, humble peasants and ordinary housewives have got on with the simple business of bottling sunshine, so that it may spread a little joy in the leaner seasons ... They call it jam.

More prosaically, I love the way that a couple of hours in the kitchen transforms a gardener's problem into a cook's delight. Come August and September, when it starts raining plums and you are wading through thigh-sized marrows, your conscience would be rightly pricked if you threw such bounty on the compost heap. But when you know how to bottle your own fruit and vegetables, a glut of apples or a pile of pears becomes an exciting opportunity rather than a headache.

Yet I know many keen cooks, even some gardener cooks, who never make preserves. They love eating them, they love receiving them as gifts, they love the *idea* of making them, but something is holding them back. What is it? A fear, perhaps, of the perceived paraphernalia of jam-making, a mild hysteria about the dangers of boiling sugar, a rumbling anxiety about the setting point. I know that such worries are unfounded, delusional even. So what can I do for these poor souls?

Well, I can introduce them to Pam Corbin. I first heard about 'Pam the Jam' when she was running Thursday Cottage Preserves, a small commercial jam company which operated in an almost domestic way, making old-fashioned preserves the old-fashioned way, with real ingredients. When we started planning our Preserving Days at River Cottage, I knew Pam was the person for the job. She shares her passion and wealth of knowledge with enviable clarity and enthusiasm. Many of her sentences end with, 'It's simple, really,' and with Pam to guide you, you really believe it is.

As this book has come together, my admiration for Pam has deepened. She is a great communicator who bestows infectious confidence on her charges. But more than that, she is a woman of decisive palate and impeccable good taste. Throughout the growing year that it took to produce this book, I was the lucky recipient of regular 'jamograms' – little parcels of tasting pots of recipes that she was developing for the book.

From her Early rhubarb jam to Roasted sweet beet relish, Bramley lemon curd to Roasted tomato ketchup, they were invariably exquisite. Your ambitions may be as modest as a few jars of perfect strawberry jam, but under Pam's guidance I'm quite confident that you will soon be dabbling with Blackberry and apple leather, Nasturtium 'capers', Figgy mostardo and Elixir of sage. Just writing their names makes me hungry.

Sadly there wasn't room for all of Pam's fabulous recipes in this book. But it is a tribute to her remarkable gifts that every time we decided to leave one out it felt like a minor tragedy. The upside is that every recipe that's in here is a tried and trusted gem. They met with universal approval from the River Cottage tasting panel – not a formal body, you understand, but a dangerous scrummage of whoever was around when Pam dropped by with a few more jars or bottles.

Pam's approach is not didactic, but encouraging and adventurous. Her message is that, once you've mastered a few basic techniques, there's really no stopping you. In this inspiring book she will show you the ropes and then give you the reins. I'm absolutely sure you will enjoy the ride.

Hugh Fearnley-Whittingstall, Dorset, May 2008

Seasonality

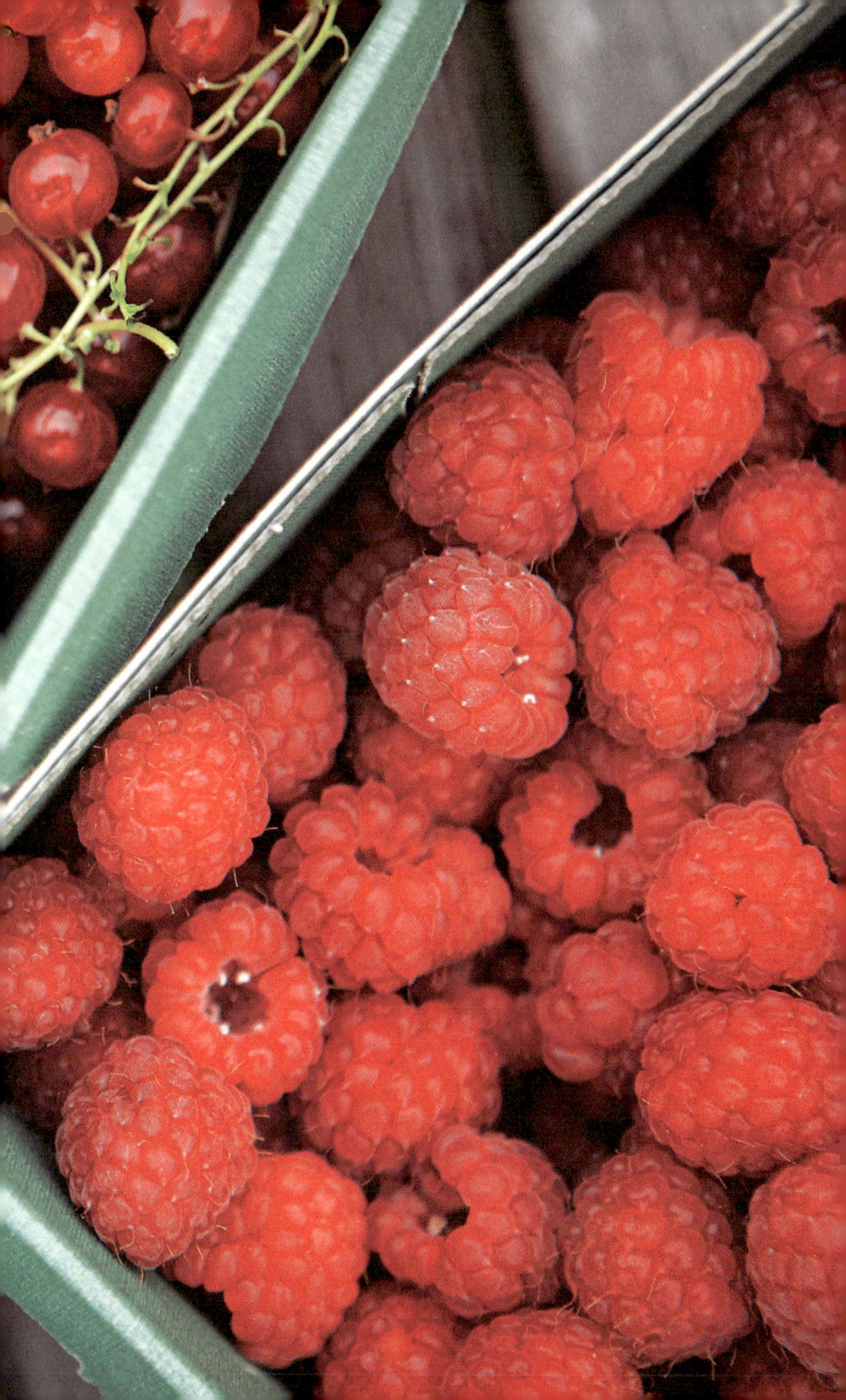

Preserving the bounties

of our fruitful summer and autumn was normal – a way of life – not so many years ago. It was essential to stock up the larder for leaner months, when fresh food was scarce or unavailable and the sealed bottles and jars full of 'summer' would help to allay the monotony of the winter diet. If soft summer currants and berries – and gluts of sweet-smelling tomatoes and trugs of veg – weren't *kept* in some form or another, then there would be no summer produce until the following year. There was no nipping down to the supermarket to buy, in the midst of January, a punnet of strawberries or even a bag of tomatoes.

You don't need to turn the clock back far, just a couple of generations to the 1950s, when to own a home refrigerator or a freezer was considered opulent, and of course fresh foods didn't arrive each day of the week, each week of the year by air and sea from all corners of the globe to flood shop shelves with produce that would otherwise be considered out of season.

The rationing of food during wartime Britain finally finished in July 1954, nine years after the war had ended. The war years had seen the government allocating sugar to the Women's Institute for jam-making so that surplus produce did not go to waste. The extent of food preservation by the WI did not stop at jam-making; these resolute ladies also canned fruit and vegetables for the national food supply. The end to those long years of rationing coincided with an increase in the variety of imported foods readily available throughout the year. Unquestionably, for many, this has meant the structure and meaningful importance of working and living the seasons, along with the necessity to preserve and not waste, have vanished from everyday life.

Following the seasons

Food is never more flavoursome nor as good as when it is fresh and in season, making the riches of a good harvest a just reward for anybody who is prepared to take notice of and be guided by the seasons. For me, there's not much to better a freshly dug new potato cooked up with a sprig of garden mint, and how these earthy roots can be thought of as humble is inexplicable as they are a staple food worldwide. If stored correctly (dark and between 5 and 10°C), their firm and starchy bodies will keep naturally for months without any further action to preserve them.

Or, what could surpass devouring a plateful of freshly picked raspberries? These soft juicy berries, however, will keep for barely a day or two before they begin to deteriorate, so action needs to be speedy to preserve them at their best. Raspberries are a wonderfully useful preserving ingredient, for they can be transformed into blissful jam, bottled, turned into berry cordial or used to make fruity vinegar, all to be put away and enjoyed later in the year.

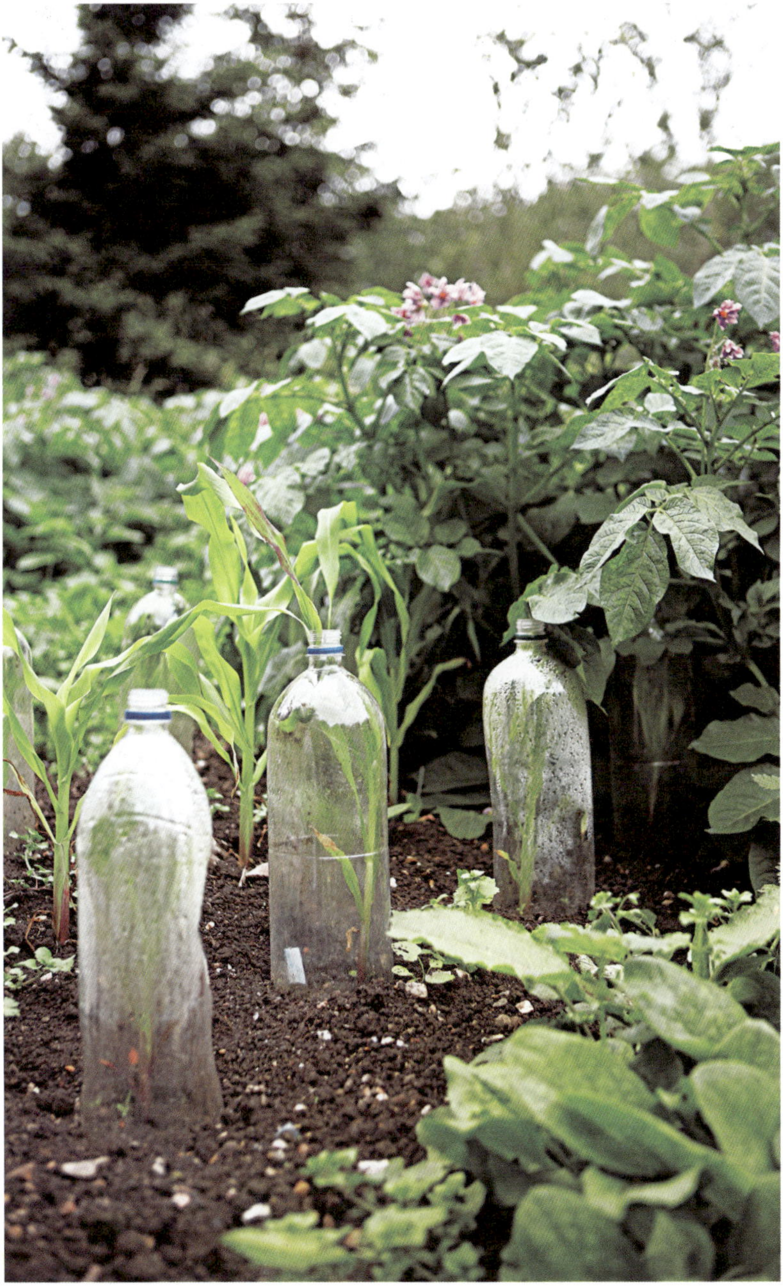

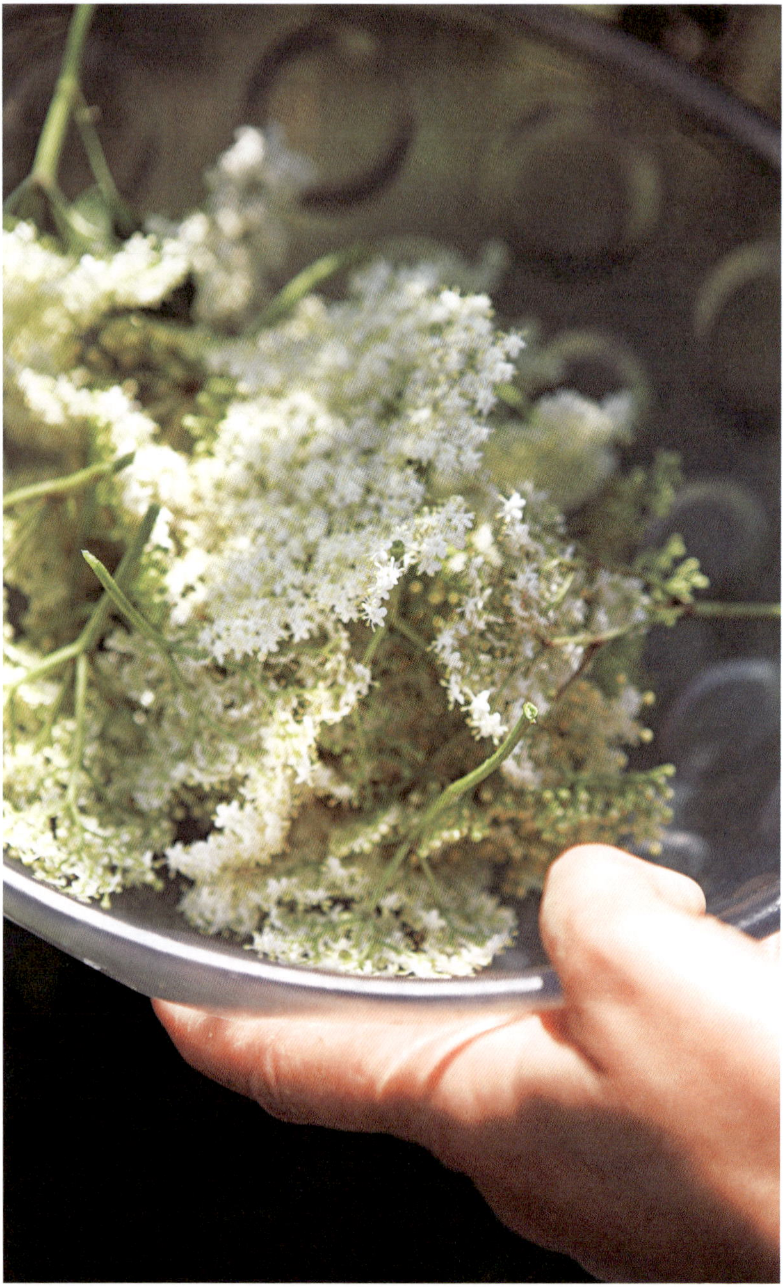

By the very nature of the variable climate linked with each of the four seasons, much of Britain's home-grown produce is available for limited periods, sometimes just a few swift weeks of the year, when crops of gluttish proportion are available to feast upon fresh, and any surplus will be at its best preserved in some way or another. Ideally, produce to be preserved should be as fresh and local as possible, so every tasty scrap of its character is unmistakably captured. However, there are a few exceptions to the *local* rule, and until we see citrus groves swathing the land, the long-standing tradition of making marmalade to preserve the bitter Seville orange will continue, in addition to the use of tart, acidic lemon in all number of preserving and culinary recipes.

The familiarity of the pattern of the seasons and what each offers is fundamental to understanding how the preserving year is entwined with the growing seasons. The *seasonal performance* is undoubtedly the greatest show on earth: a perennial show in four parts running for 365 days of the year with every month taking a worthy and significant role, where complementary ingredients 'brush shoulders' at their growing time. You'll find elderflowers add muscat perfume to gooseberries, pectin-rich redcurrants combine with low-pectin strawberries, and soft fleshy apples will partner seedy blackberries perfectly at autumn time.

The long slender stalks of rhubarb bridge the beginning and the end of each yearly cycle, starting around the time of the spring equinox, when the sun makes the first of its biannual crossings over the equator and the length of day and night are more or less equal. It is now that the first crinkled, sulphur-yellow rhubarb leaves begin to push their way up from the sleepy earth, unfurling to spread their towering umbrella leaves over silken red-green shoots. From here on, and until the quiescence of sleeping winter, there is usually something budding up and getting ready to yield some form of crop for us to harvest, so a sharp eye needs to be employed to avoid missing any of the seasonal gifts each month offers.

Spring

The spring months of April and May are the wake-up time, heralding the burst of new growth from latent pinky-tinged buds and shoots that rapidly change into blossom or velvety spring-green leaves. The feathery soft green foliage of the native beech begins to spill out from hedgerows in late April and early May, just ahead of the elderflowers who run riot in a showy-off way just about everywhere later in the month. Patches of nettles and wild garlic appear on sheltered banks, the tender young leaves just right to be turned into zesty pesto. Protected pockets of land will allow the first tiny green gooseberries of the season to be picked and, like the long red-green rhubarb stalks, these berries are sharp and tart too, almost as if it is nature's way of arousing our dulled taste buds, stimulating and preparing them for the rush of flavours to come. In preserving terms, these two months are still quite a lazy time, a teaser for the months ahead, but they are by no means idle. Use this time to check out your preserving gear (jars, bottles, lids and things) as well as making sure your stocks of sugar, spices and vinegar are plentiful for when the real season kicks off.

Summer

In June we encounter the summer solstice when the daylight hours are at their maximum and the increasing warmth gives rise to a frenzy of growing in all shapes and colours. We see the start of the soft fruit season with strings of shimmering redcurrants and the early varieties of strawberries and raspberries producing their first sweet berries. Aromatic herbs make themselves known and their heady, sweet-smelling leaves can be used to augment vinegars and oils, and to flavour pesto and relishes. The hedgerow shyly reveals diminutive silver-grey bramble buds, whilst the petals of *Rosa canina* (dog rose) can be gathered to add fragrance to jams, jellies, cordials and spirits. Down in the vegetable garden the first fattening roots of sweet beetroot and the swollen heads of Florence fennel will be beginning to show.

July is the month when the wooden spoon begins to get busy. The early soft fruit berries and currants of June extend to welcome maincrop varieties along with other currant and berry friends; blackcurrants, blueberries, tayberries and loganberries crop plentifully and gooseberries reach sweet maturity to end their productive reign. The silver-grey bramble buds of June break into pink-tinged white flowers, soon to metamorphose into the unmistakable drupelets of indigenous blackberries. Look closely at the elder bush and you'll see a mass of green under-ripe berries, which before long will glisten red-black as they ripen. Hips and haws are like hedgerow chameleons, disguised in their leafy green coats before they first tinge bronze and then blush red for their autumnal show. Cherries, the first of the stone fruits, will be ready, but be quick – they won't last long, and eagle-eyed birds will be waiting to gorge upon them. Greengages and plums are beginning to swell, but it won't be until late in the month or the beginning of August that the early varieties of these orchard fruits will be ready.

August is the true glut month when green beans, courgettes, tomatoes, cucumbers and summer veg invariably oversupply, resulting in a glorious month to preserve as much as possible. The summer-fruiting raspberries are soon replaced by the first flush of blackberries – always the sweetest and juiciest of the year. Watch out for hanging clusters of scarlet rowans, the berries of the mountain ash, for these, combined with a handful of crab apples, will make an outstanding jelly of carnelian colour.

Autumn

In September, you'll find your back step will become a home for refugee fruit, stuffed into bags and left by well-meaning friends who expect you to make all sorts of magnificent jams, jellies and other preserves. Trying to make sure all is safely gathered before the cooler and shorter days of autumn set in, this month might seem a race against time. But don't panic, you'll find marrows, onions, apples, pears and others have developed protective winter coats and, if carefully stored, will keep for a month or two, to use later in the year.

Orchard fruits will now be ripening. Plums, apples and pears yield freely, ahead of the fragrant quince ready at the tail end of the month – watch out though, for too much moisture will make these golden beauties split. For wild food foragers, hedgerows are ablaze with colour, intense with berries and fruits of all kinds; blackberries, rosehips, haws, elders, blue-bloomed sloes, scabby crabs (apples) and clusters of hazelnuts adorn native trees and bushes.

From here on, things really do begin to slow up. Much of the autumn harvest will be past its best. The woodland birds will have feasted well upon the hedgerow spread, although bitter sloes still clinging to thorny branches are for the taking, to imbue fruit liqueurs with their tartness. Apples and pears are still plentiful to turn into Christmas mincemeat or spicy chutney, and onions pickled now will be just right for the festive season. Sweet chestnuts, split from spiky armour, can be found in heaps of fallen leaves, while raspberries, of the autumn kind, stretch berry-picking to this time.

Winter

As the year spins towards the winter solstice, the shorter, darkening days and the lack of sunlight hours allow the earth to rest from growing. The dormancy of the winter begins and only hardy leeks, blue-green brassicas and a few rooty crops survive the cold. But still, within the cycle of the seasonal preserving year, there are two highlights yet to come. The bitter marmalade oranges from Seville arrive in early January, turning this month into a preserving stronghold of the year, when steamy citrus vapours fill our kitchens, and larder shelves are replenished with jars of golden, amber and tawny marmalade to last the year ahead.

Then finally, early rhubarb arrives to carry us through to the next perennial cycle. From late January to early March in darkened sheds and under tall forcing pots, the leaves force upwards to boast the beauty of their slender, translucent pink stalks, heralding the start of another seasonal year.

Seasonal availability

The chart overleaf gives an indication as to when seasonal produce is available. Inevitably though, it can vary by up to 4 weeks depending on how far south or north you live, or if you live in a frost pocket, exposed to cold winds, or a warm, sunny sheltered site. I've not included any indoor-grown crops (with the exception of forced early rhubarb) that rely on indoor heat for their growing cycle.

	JAN	FEB	MAR	APR	MAY
Apples (cooking)	•	•			
Apples (crab)					
Apples (eating)	•	•			
Asparagus					•
Beech leaves					•
Beetroot					
Blackberries					
Blackcurrants					
Blueberries					
Cherries					
Chestnuts					
Chilli peppers					
Cucumbers					
Damsons					
Elderberries					
Elderflowers					•
Fennel					
Figs					
Gooseberries					
Greengages					
Horseradish root					
Hedgerow berries					
Hazelnuts					
Lemons (imported)	•	•	•		
Nasturtium seeds					
Onions					
Pears					
Peppers					
Plums					
Quince					
Raspberries (summer)					
Raspberries (autumn)					
Redcurrants					
Rhubarb (forced)	•	•	•		
Rhubarb (field)				•	•
Rowan berries					
Seville oranges (imported)	•	•			
Runner beans					
Strawberries					•
Tomatoes (outdoor)					

JUNE	JULY	AUG	SEPT	OCT	NOV	DEC
			•	•	•	•
		•	•	•		
		•	•	•	•	•
•						
	•	•	•	•		
	•	•	•	•		
	•	•				
	•	•	•			
•	•	•				
				•	•	
		•	•	•		
	•	•	•			
		•	•			
		•	•	•		
•						
•	•					
		•				
•	•					
	•	•				
				•	•	
		•	•	•		
			•	•	•	
					•	•
	•	•	•			
	•	•	•	•		
			•	•	•	
			•	•		
	•	•	•			
			•	•	•	
	•	•	•			
			•	•	•	
	•	•				
•	•					
		•	•			
	•	•	•			
•	•	•	•			
	•	•	•			

SEASONALITY 17

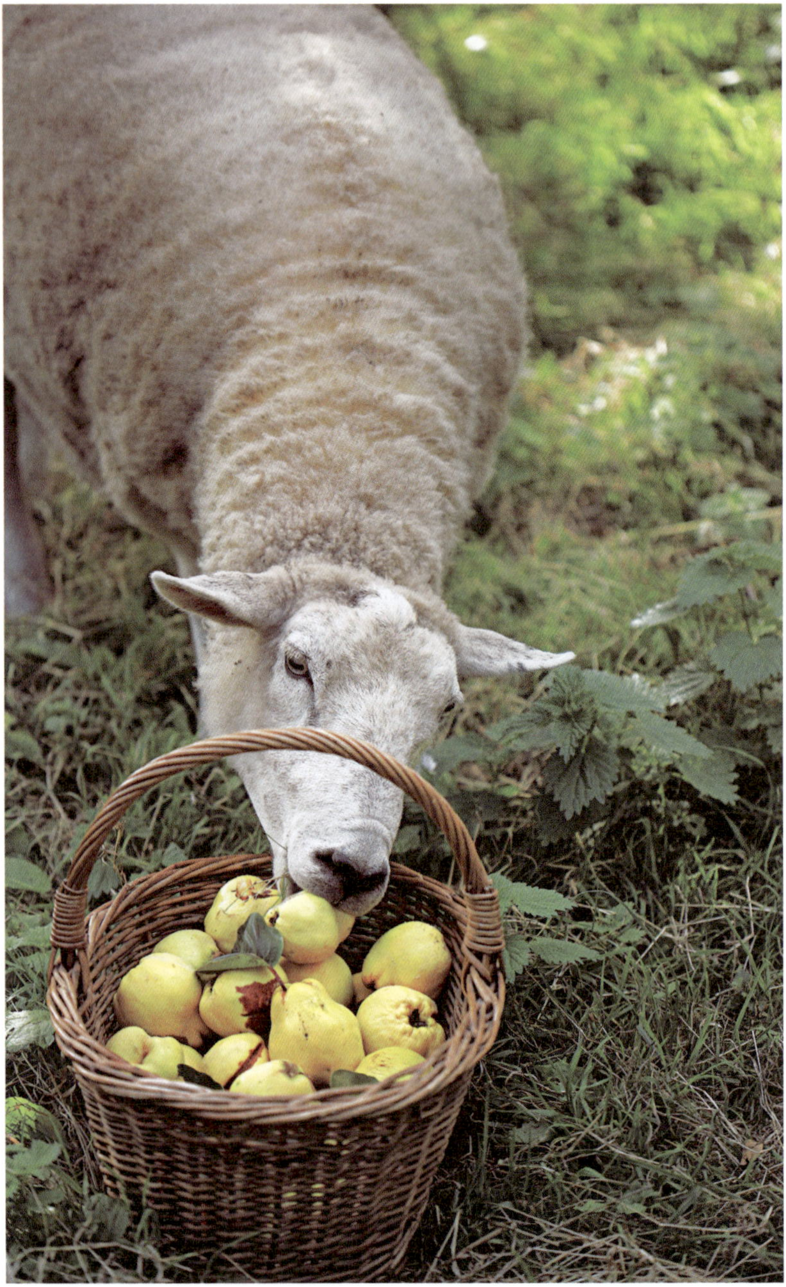

Fruit-growing regions in Britain

With an agreeable, temperate climate and a patchwork of differing soils, Britain bestows an abundance of fruit from all corners of the land. From the rich loamy lowland of the eastern counties to the verdant pastures of the West Country, the good earth not only gives crops the food and energy needed to sustain growth, but it also instils character in the fruit it bears. In turn, regions become strongly associated with their produce. Somerset is indelibly linked with cider apples, for example, while the fruit orchards of Kent give it the title 'garden of England'.

Some of these areas are mere pockets of land covering as little as a few hectares, like the rambling orchards along the river Fal in Cornwall, where the tart 'Kea' plum survives the salt-laden southwesterlies. Other larger regions embrace neighbouring counties, forming well-known commercial growing areas. The drier, colder eastern terrain, for example, is home to many British-grown strawberries, with names such as 'Early Cambridge', 'Cambridge Favourite' and 'Cambridge Vigour' sealing their origins. Grown too in this region is the unique and intensely flavoured darling 'Little Scarlet' strawberry, used for over a century by Essex jam-makers Wilkin & Sons. As many as seventy of these tiny sweet strawberries are packed into a jar of their highly acclaimed jam.

In western terrains you will find a network of ancient and established orchards crisscrossing and bordering pasture land. This large area splits down into smaller regions, which offer different varieties that assume native rights to the soil and climate they inhabit. Bittersweet, sharp and sweet, juicy apples for cider-making predominate the Devonshire and Somerset orchards, whereas the Vale of Evesham in southern Worcestershire is famed for the luscious plums, dessert apples and pears it bears. Here, in the wetter, warmer West, apples and pears put on their natural waxy waterproof coats to protect their fleshy fruit from the southwesterly precipitations.

Surprisingly, perhaps, despite the obvious contrast in climate, good commercial crops of soft berries and currants grow in both the North and South of the country. One noticeable difference is that 'high bush' members of the *Vaccinium* or blueberry family are cultivated in the safe and sheltered South, whereas 'low bush' relatives are those that are found growing wild on heath and moorland in the rather more vigorous climes of northern England and Scotland.

The rich fertile 'middling lands' sustain a fusion and miscellany of fruit-growing – from *ribes* to rhubarb and much in between. Good crops of blackcurrants flourish in the West Midlands, while the village of Timperley in Cheshire has long been famed for its field rhubarb 'Timperley Early' – a cultivar whose name and excellence dominates the rhubarb world. Gooseberries are another popular traditional crop in this part of the country.

The nineteenth century saw the start-up of gooseberry shows in the North and Midlands counties of Cheshire, Lancashire, Yorkshire, Derbyshire, Staffordshire and Nottinghamshire. Gooseberry enthusiasts grew (and still do in a handful of villages) outsize berries in the hope of winning the premier prize for the heaviest berry of the show. 'Ringer', 'London', 'Lancashire Lad', 'Lady Leicester' and 'Wonderful' are but a few of these weighty wonders. The berries were weighed by pennyweights (equivalent to 1.555g) and the heaviest 'London' ever recorded weighed in at just over 37dwt (58g) in 1852 – quite a monster to meet in a pie! Mind you, no show went without a tipple or two ...

Gooseberry growers' anthem

Come all you jovial gardeners and listen unto me
Whilst I relate the different sorts of winning Gooseberries
This famous Institution was founded long ago
That men might meet and drink and have a Gooseberry Show ...

Northwards, to the eastern edge of the Pennines, a district has become known as the 'Yorkshire Triangle'. Here, the heavy clay soil and the cold climate provide the right conditions for forcing rhubarb in darkened sheds during the short days of January and February; the frost is needed to kick-start the growth of the sweet, succulent soft shoots of this indoor-grown crop. The availability of coal from nearby mines was used to heat the forcing sheds until the mid 1980s but the miners' strike of 1984–5 obliged growers such as Oldroyd's to use kerosene and propane to heat the sheds, as they still do today.

To the west of the high Pennines in one of the wettest regions of Britain, the small Westmorland damson thrives in the hedgerows of the Lyth and Winster valleys. Related to the 'Shropshire' plum, it has grown here for three centuries or more. The flavour of this damson is unique and the skins provide a deep-purple dye for the northern woollen industry.

Over the border in Scotland, the cool conditions of the eastern and central counties of Perthshire, Angus and Fife provide excellent growing conditions for raspberries, strawberries and blackcurrants with such names as 'Ben Nevis', 'Ben Hope' 'Glen Moy' and 'Glen Ample' confirming their ancestral roots, whilst Tayside is the natural home to the red-black tayberry.

The chart overleaf gives an indication of principal growing areas in Britain, but by no means are these particular growing areas dedicated to growing *only* these fruits nor do the fruits listed *only* grow in them. Most regions, save for the highlands and moorlands, will grow a mixture of produce, and even here the odd elder or blackberry will flourish.

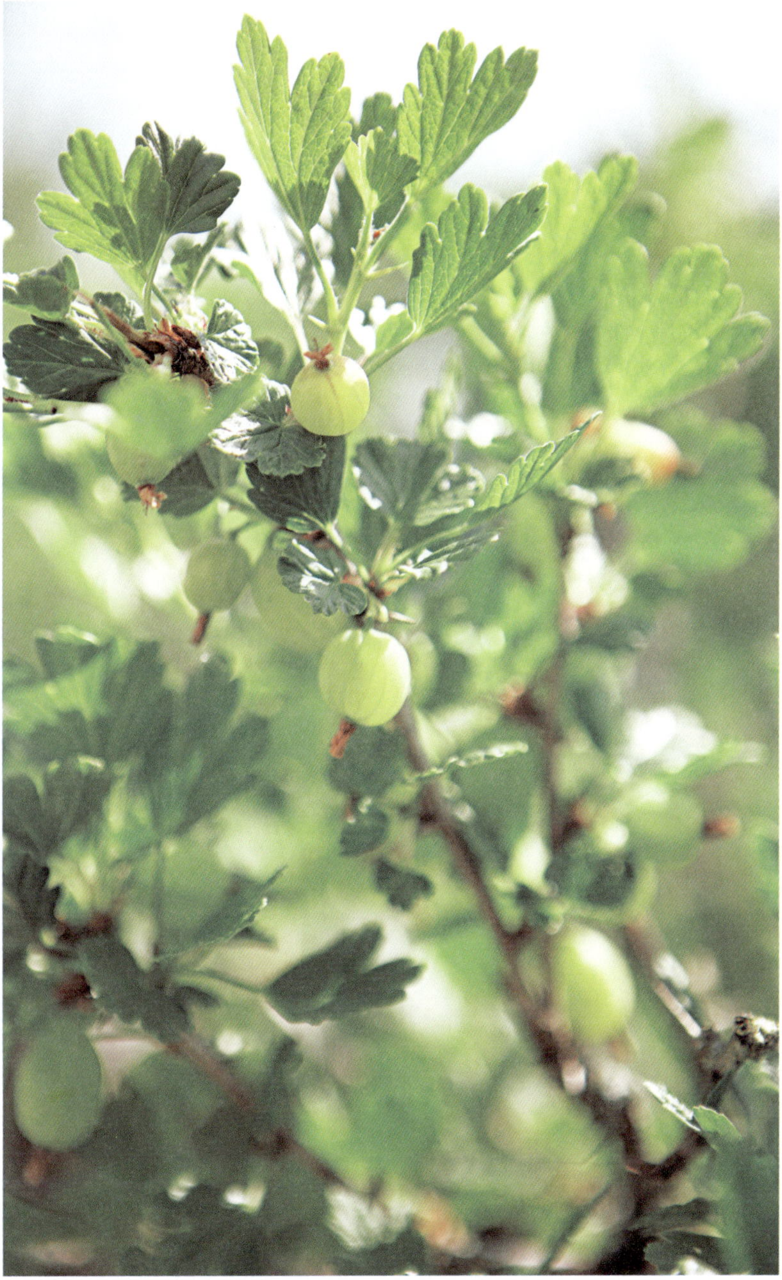

REGION	PRINCIPAL CROPS	SPECIALITIES
South-west – Cornwall, Devon, Dorset, Somerset	Cider apples Eating apples Blackcurrants Cherries Strawberries	'Dittisham Black' plum (Devon) 'Kea' plum (Cornwall)
Southern England	Cherries Blackcurrants Strawberries	Blueberries (south-east Dorset)
South-east England – Kent, Surrey, Sussex	Eating and cooking apples Blackcurrants Cherries Gooseberries Pears Plums Strawberries	Cobnuts (Kent)
Eastern counties – Essex, Cambridgeshire, Suffolk, Norfolk, Lincolnshire	Bramley apples Cherries Gooseberries Pears Strawberries	'Cambridge Gage' 'Worcester Pearmain' apple
West Midlands/ Welsh Border	Blackcurrants Damsons Eating apples Greengages Plums Pears	Perry pear 'Pershore' plum
North Midlands	Damsons Field rhubarb	
Northern England	Damsons Forced rhubarb	
Eastern and Central Scotland	Blackcurrants Strawberries Raspberries	Tayberries
National – rampant and everywhere	Blackberries Elderflowers/berries Hedgerow fruits and berries Apples	

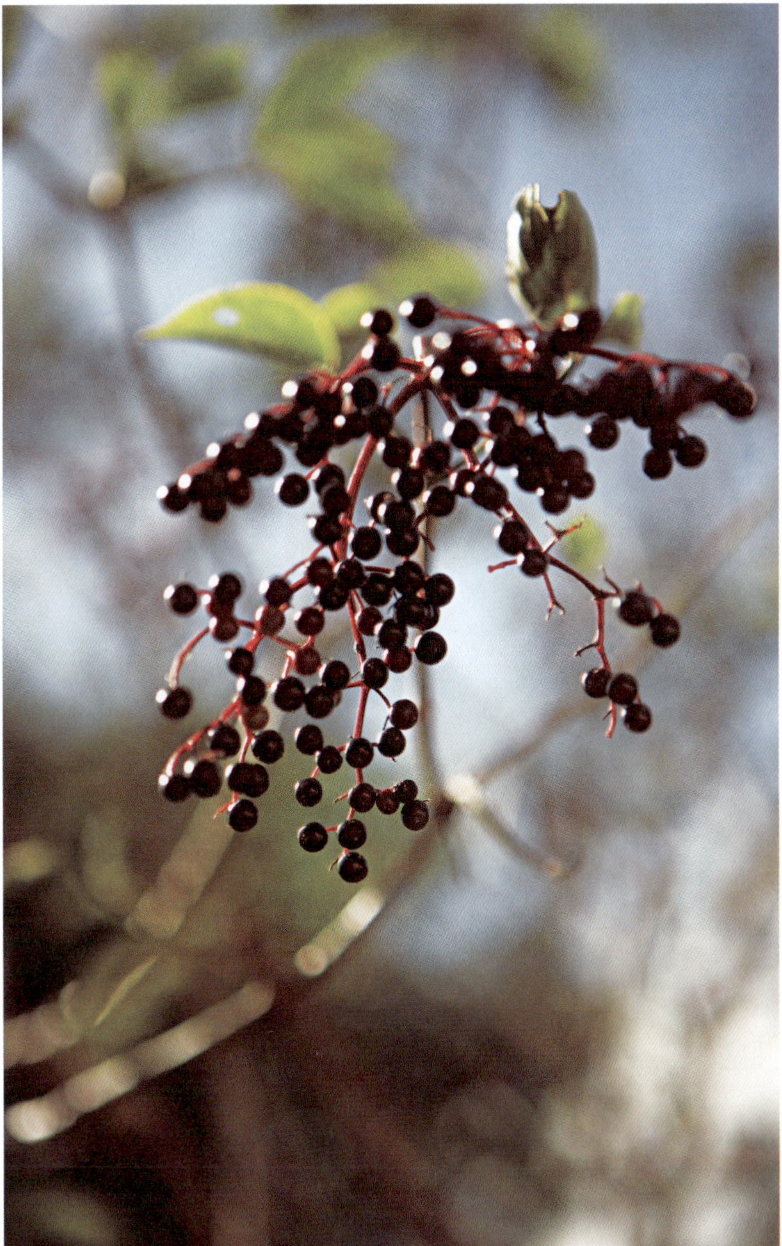

The Rules

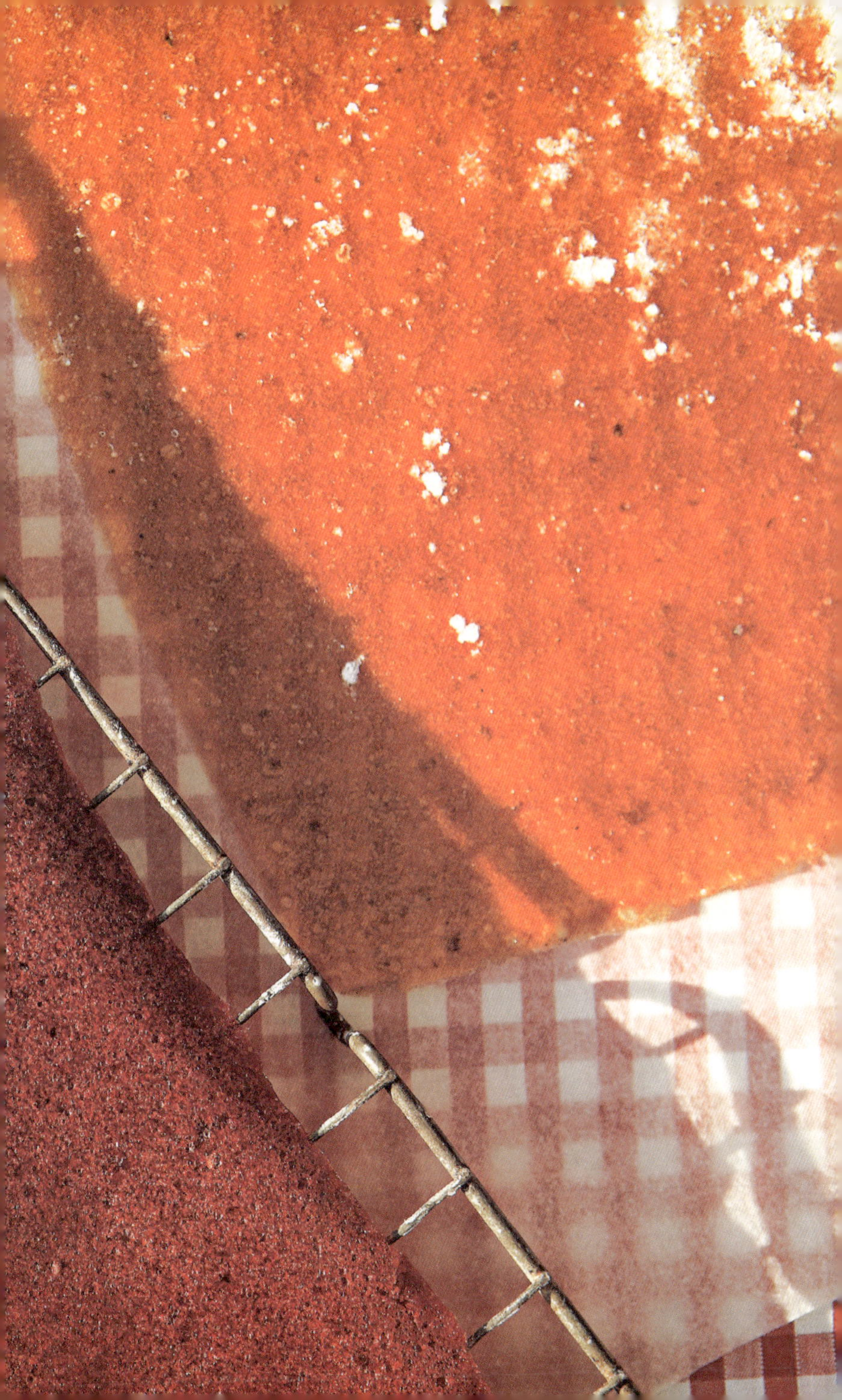

Preserving evokes deep-rooted, almost primeval feelings of self-sufficiency and survival, of gatherer and hunter, for this is how our ancestors stayed alive. These days this all sounds more than a little extreme, but unquestionably a home with a good store of home-made preserves will generate a feeling of warmth and confidence.

I admit that at times I can get quite carried away thinking of how I can fill shapely jam jars, of the glistening grains of sugar, the neroli-like perfume of Seville oranges ... But I've also found that it pays to be aware of a small amount of cold, hard science, and to be familiar with some basic but important practical techniques. Once you understand why food goes off, and how it can be prevented from doing so, your jam-, jelly- and chutney-making can reach new levels of success. Don't worry, you don't need a chemistry degree ...

The simple fact is that any fresh food, unless it is treated in some way, will inevitably decay and become unsuitable for consumption. There are four meddlesome elements that cause spoilage in foods – enzymes, bacteria, moulds/fungi and yeasts – but, if the cook intervenes to prevent or arrest their progress, most foods can be safely kept for extended periods of time.

The four spoilers

Micro-organisms are generally viewed as undesirable and if present in sufficient numbers they make food a health hazard. In certain conditions, all micro-organisms will flourish and increase. Some non-harmful micro-organisms are deliberately brought into play in food production, of course – mould in blue cheeses, and yeasts in beer- and bread-making, for example – but it is the harmful micro-organisms that concern us in preserve-making.

Good food hygiene is the first step in stopping the spoilers. It is essential that all food be handled with care, and all utensils, equipment and work surfaces be spotlessly clean, so as few micro-organisms as possible are present to start with.

The use of high temperatures is the second way to defeat the tricky foursome – hence cooking being an integral part of many preserving processes. They may thrive in warmth, but they cannot take real heat.

High concentrations of sugar, acid, alcohol or salt also kill these undesirables, or at the very least make it hard for them to flourish, and nearly all the preserving techniques in this book rely on large quantities of these ingredients to create conditions hostile to enzymes and micro-organisms.

The final line of attack involves excluding the air which these spoilers need to thrive. This is why well-sealed jars and bottles are essential, and why oil is another important preserving medium.

Enzymes

These are not actually organisms, but proteins found in all living things, animal or vegetable, and they perform a huge variety of roles. From a culinary point of view, it's important to know that enzymes remain active long after food has been harvested, and they function as catalysts for change, triggering and speeding up chemical processes. Enzymes trigger deterioration, for instance, by sparking off changes in tissue that in turn provide a fertile environment for the growth of micro-organisms. The discolouring of cut or damaged fruit or vegetables is also caused by enzyme action. However, if the exposed surface comes into contact with an acid or alkali, the discoloration will slow down. This is why prepared produce is often rubbed with lemon juice or plunged into lightly salted water.

Enzymes increase their activity at temperatures between 29 and 50°C and will begin to be destroyed at temperatures above 60°C. Their action is also halted at temperatures below freezing point but will increase again when warmth returns.

Bacteria

So small that they are only visible under a microscope, these are the most ancient and widespread form of life on earth. Bacteria increase rapidly at temperatures between 20 and 40°C. They become dormant in the freezer, and are destroyed at or near 100°C – the boiling point of water. Bacterial spoilage of food is sometimes difficult to detect, and although most bacteria are harmless – some even useful – some cause food to rot and become foul-smelling, and their toxins are harmful to health. It is therefore vital not to take any shortcuts with preserving procedures, and to follow all instructions carefully to avoid any form of bacterial contamination.

Moulds and fungi

The spores of these micro-organisms are present in the air around us and will take root in almost any food. Initially they produce fine threads, then the characteristic grey-green, cotton-wool-like bloom. Moulds and fungi are dormant at 0°C, thrive at temperatures between 10 and 38°C, and their spoiling activities decrease from 60 to 88°C, which is why cooking is an efficient way to get rid of them. A bit of mould on the top of an open jar of jam should not be scooped off and ignored; as they grow, some moulds produce mycotoxins that can be harmful if eaten.

Yeasts

The yeasts found in foods are generally not harmful to health but can cause spoilage. Most species are quickly destroyed at 60°C and above, and are inactivated by cold. Some grow in food containing as much as 60 per cent sugar and badly covered or half-used jars of jam stored in a warm kitchen are prime sites for yeasts to begin to ferment; also gases are produced, which may cause the preserve to 'blow' in the jar.

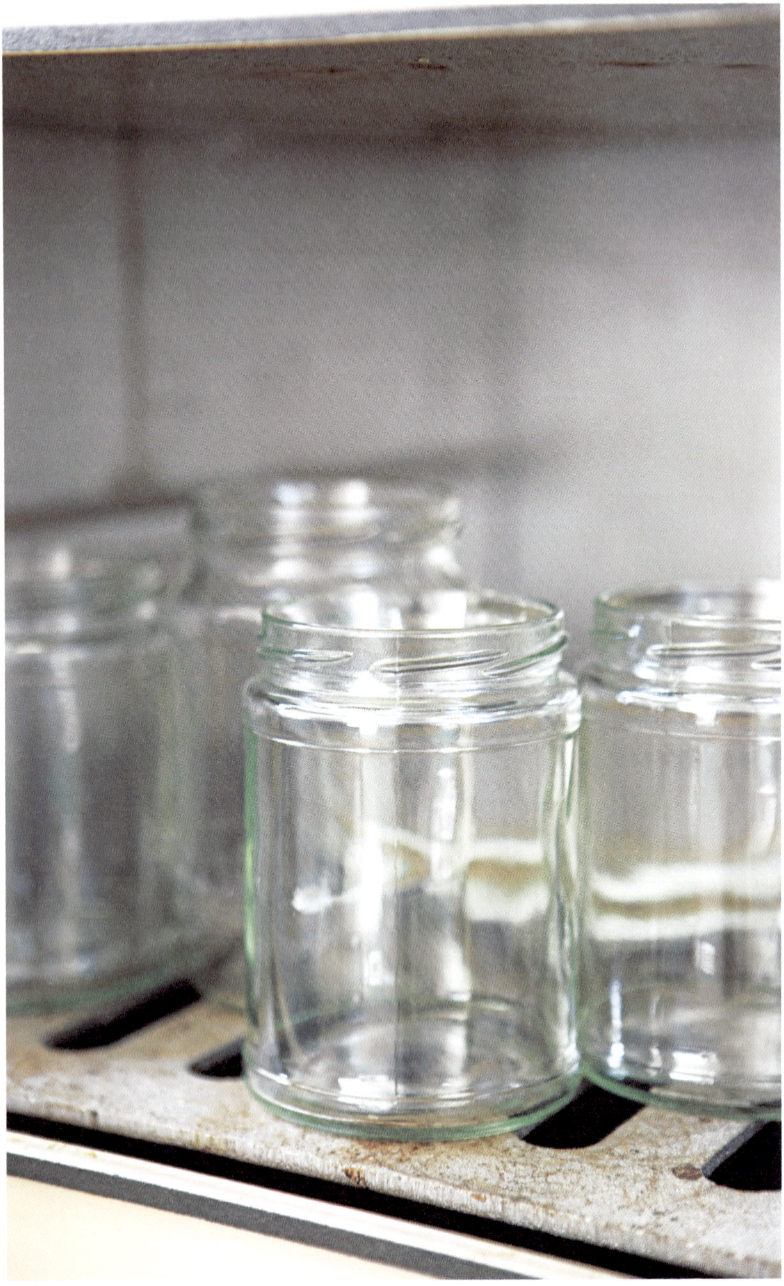

Potting, packing and sealing

Proper potting and sealing is one of the main pillars of good preserve-making. If done incorrectly, it can ruin a batch of otherwise perfect preserves. These days, some form of glass vessel with a secure seal is generally used. To reduce the risk of bacterial contamination, it is important to sterilise the container and fully fill or 'jam-pack' it with your preserve.

Sterilising jars

Any micro-organism lurking in the container you put your preserve into has the potential to grow and contaminate, which is why it is essential to use sterile jars. There are three simple ways to sterilise jars: you can immerse them in a pan of water and bring to the boil; or wash them in very hot, soapy water, rinse thoroughly, then dry them in a very low oven; alternatively, you can simply put them through a hot dishwasher cycle.

Whichever method you choose, only clean the jars shortly before they are to be used and make sure they are dry. This minimises time in which the jars might pick up new bacteria. Also, all hot preserves should be poured into warm jars (this helps to prevent the temperature dropping before the seal is applied), so you might as well use them before they have cooled down from the drying process.

Recycling jars and bottles

I like to reuse and recycle jars and bottles wherever possible. As well as keeping costs down, it gives me a wide variety of shapes and sizes to choose from. However, recycled jars should always be cleaned both inside and outside, then very carefully examined to make sure they are not damaged in any way. Cracks or chips are ideal breeding grounds for bacteria and can also shed tiny splinters of glass that could cause injury if swallowed.

Old labels on recycled jars should be fully removed. I find the best way of attacking this job is to fully immerse the jars in a pan of cold water, bring to simmering point and simmer for 10 minutes. I then let the jars cool and, when cool enough to handle, rub the label off with the blunt side of a knife. Tamper-seals and labels on lids can be removed in the same way.

If you do want to buy jars, they are available from specialist shops (see the directory, p.210) and are generally sold in certain sizes that comply with the requirements for commercially produced preserves. The sizes are always given as a volume rather than a weight, and the chart overleaf gives the equivalent approximate weight and volume capacities. However, if you are using an assortment of recycled jars, you might find it easier to measure their capacity in volume (just fill them with water then tip into a measuring jug).

Jar sizes

Before you start making a preserve, you should check the recipe to see how many jars you will need so you can have them ready.

METRIC WEIGHT	IMPERIAL WEIGHT	VOLUME
113g	4oz	100ml
225g	8oz	195ml
340g	12oz	290ml
454g	1lb	380ml
680g	1½lb	570ml
900g	2lb	760ml

Thankfully, almost all jars share just two or three lid sizes, so lids can often be mixed and matched between various jars and bottles.

Sealing jars

Having potted your preserve, the next vital thing is to seal it as quickly as possible to prevent entry of oxygen and airborne micro-organisms. For hot sweet preserves, chutneys and relishes there are two principal ways in which this can be done – with a cellophane cover or a twist-on lid. Pickles and vinegar preserves should always be sealed with vinegar-proof twist-on lids.

I like to seal fruit cheeses by pouring melted 'food grade' paraffin wax over the surface, giving a really traditional finish to the filled pots. The easiest way to melt the wax is to place it in a heatproof bowl (I keep one especially for this) and stand it in a pan of gently simmering water until the wax is liquid.

> **Cellophane covers** Place a waxed disc, wax side down, on the hot surface of the preserve, then cover the jar with a cellophane disc, securing it tightly with an elastic band. This is best done when the jar is still hot. Cellophane covers can also be applied when the jars are completely cold but should never be put on when the jar is tepid as this can cause mould growth.
>
> Before putting on the cellophane, make sure the rim of the jar is clean. With a drop of water, moisten one side of the cover to make it stretch, then position with the damp side uppermost. Secure with a rubber band. As the cellophane dries, it will contract to give a tight lid. Packs of waxed discs, cellophane covers, elastic bands and labels are available in supermarkets and kitchen shops, and from mail order suppliers (see the directory, p.210).

Twist-on lids The metal twist-on/off lids that come with most jars are very easy to use and create a good tight seal. Generally, these days, most lids have a plasticised lining that is 'food law approved' and suitable for use with both sugar- and vinegar-based preserves. Avoid the use of unlined metal lids with vinegar preserves because they will corrode and spoil the preserve. For the best possible results, I recommend always using new lids, even with recycled jars. Previously used lids are still an option but you must make sure they are not damaged in any way and they should be sterilised by boiling in a pan of water for 10 minutes before use.

Bottles

I stash away recycled bottles of various shapes and sizes to use when making cordials, fruit liqueurs, flavoured vinegars and oils. Vinegar bottles with screw-top lids are excellent for flavoured vinegars, cordials and squashes, while small, interesting-shaped spirit bottles are jolly useful for fruit liqueurs and make attractive gifts.

A good range of bottles can be purchased from specialist suppliers (see the directory, p.210), including old-fashioned preserving bottles with a swing-top lid fastening. I particularly like using these nice-looking bottles: made from toughened glass, they are easy to use, the lid is attached and they can be used time and time again. All bottles, lids and corks should be sterilised by boiling for 10 minutes in a pan of water before use.

Filling and sealing

Careful potting and sealing at the correct temperature for the particular preserve is important for the keeping quality.

TYPE OF PRESERVE	TEMPERATURE	NOTES
Jams, jellies, fruit butters and cheeses, marmalades	Hot-fill (preserve should be above 85–90°C) warm, dry jars, to within 3mm of the rim	Allow whole fruit jams and chunky marmalades to stand for 10–15 minutes after cooking, before putting into jars
Fruit curds	Fill warm jars as soon as the curd is cooked	For entry into local horticultural shows, fruit curds must be covered with wax disc and cellophane seal
Chutneys, relishes, sauces and ketchups	Hot-fill warm, dry jars	Remove air pockets by sharply tapping the jars. Use vinegar-proof lids. Some sauces may need to be sterilised in a water bath (see p.164)
Pickles and sweet pickles	Hot or cold-fill clean, dry jars to within 5mm of the rim	Use vinegar-proof lids. Remove air pockets by sharply tapping the jars
Fruit syrups	Hot-fill clean bottles and seal immediately	To extend shelf life, sterilise in a water bath or oven (see pp.164–6)
Bottled fruits	It is essential to follow individual recipes precisely	See Bottled Fruits (pp.158–85)
Oil and alcohol-based preserves	Cold-fill. Make sure ingredients are totally immersed before sealing	Remove air pockets by sharply tapping jars. Seal with a twist-on lid

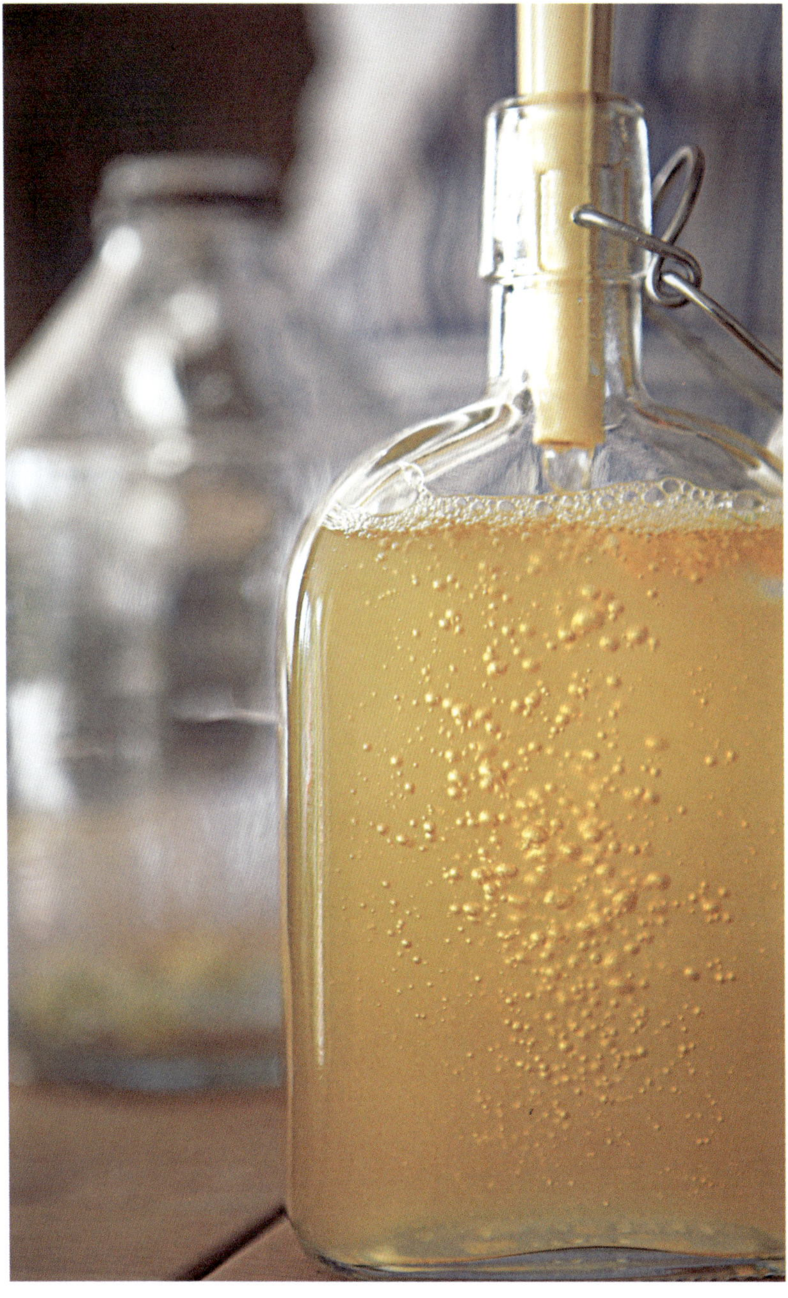

Labelling

Use self-adhesive labels with plenty of space to record what the preserve is and when it was made. Plain labels can be used but there are lots of attractive labels on the market designed especially for preserve-making. If you're a dab hand on the computer, you can even design your own. Don't try to stick a label to a hot jar – the glue will melt and it will fall off. Wait until jars are cold before labelling.

Safe keeping

A preserve with a good seal should last a long time, although the texture and colour may well deteriorate. None the less, I'd be the first to admit that a murky jar of some old concoction, discovered during a larder clear-out, will have little appeal – and there is always an underlying concern that it might have gone off. The following are guidelines for safe keeping and pleasant eating. (Chutneys, pickles and marmalades, by the way, improve with a maturing period so shouldn't be eaten straight away.)

Once opened, look after your preserves. Replace lids securely and keep the preserve in a cool place because, once the seal on a jar or bottle is broken, the contents are vulnerable and can be re-contaminated by micro-organisms.

PRESERVE	IDEAL SHELF LIFE
Fruit curds	Use within 4 weeks. Store in the fridge once opened
Vegetables in oil	Use within 4 months. Refrigerate one opened and use within 6 weeks
Pesto	Store in the fridge and use within 4 weeks
Fruit butters	Use within 9 months and refrigerate once opened
Jams and jellies	Use within 1 year
Fruit cheeses	Use within 1 year and refrigerate once opened
Mincemeat	Use within 1 year
Relishes	Use within 1 year. Store in the fridge once opened
Sauces	Use within 1 year
Chutneys and pickles	Store for 4–10 weeks before using. Use within 1–2 years
Marmalades	Use within 2 years
Alcohol preserves	Use within 3 years

In a cool, dry, dark place These conditions apply to the storage of all preserves. Few houses these days have good old-fashioned larders or cellars so you may find the best place to keep your preserves is in the garage or shed.

Key preserving ingredients

Most of the ingredients needed for preserving are in general use in a busy kitchen. It is, however, worth considering their different characteristics.

Sugar

A concentration of over 60 per cent sugar in a preserve creates an environment that is hostile to micro-organisms. Sugar can also be combined with vinegar in sweet-and-sour preserves such as chutneys and sauces. The sugar you use not only affects the cooking process but also influences the final flavour of your preserves:

Granulated sugar Available in pure white or golden, unrefined varieties, this is a good basic, inexpensive sugar that will work well in almost any of the recipes in this book. It has medium-coarse grains so takes a little longer to dissolve than fine-grained caster sugar but is less likely to stick to the bottom of the pan and burn. Granulated sugar is produced in Britain, from sugar beet (Silver Spoon is one brand), but an intensive refining process is involved. If you'd prefer an unrefined sugar, which will retain its natural golden colour and delicate caramel flavour, choose an imported one, derived from sugar cane. Billingtons produce an unrefined, organic, golden granulated, and also a fair trade variety. I use both unrefined and refined granulated sugar. Golden, unrefined sugar is ideal for marmalades, and with strong-flavoured fruits such as blackcurrants, but I prefer a refined white sugar for more delicate fruits and berries, for jellies and curds, and for flavoured liqueurs.

Large-grain preserving sugar This is more costly than granulated sugars. It's by no means essential for good preserves but the big, chunky crystals dissolve slowly, need less stirring and are less likely to stick to the bottom of the pan. They also produce less froth or scum. Preserving sugar does not generally contain added pectin.

Jam sugar This usually signifies a sugar with added pectin – and sometimes citric acid too. It's ideal for use with low-pectin fruits such as rhubarb and strawberries and will ensure a quick and easy set. However, don't use it with pectin-rich fruits like gooseberries, plums and Seville oranges – the set will be more like wallpaper paste.

Brown sugar Using unrefined demerara or muscovado sugar in a jam or chutney – either wholly, or in combination with a lighter sugar – changes the colour and taste. These dark sugars are not highly processed and are full

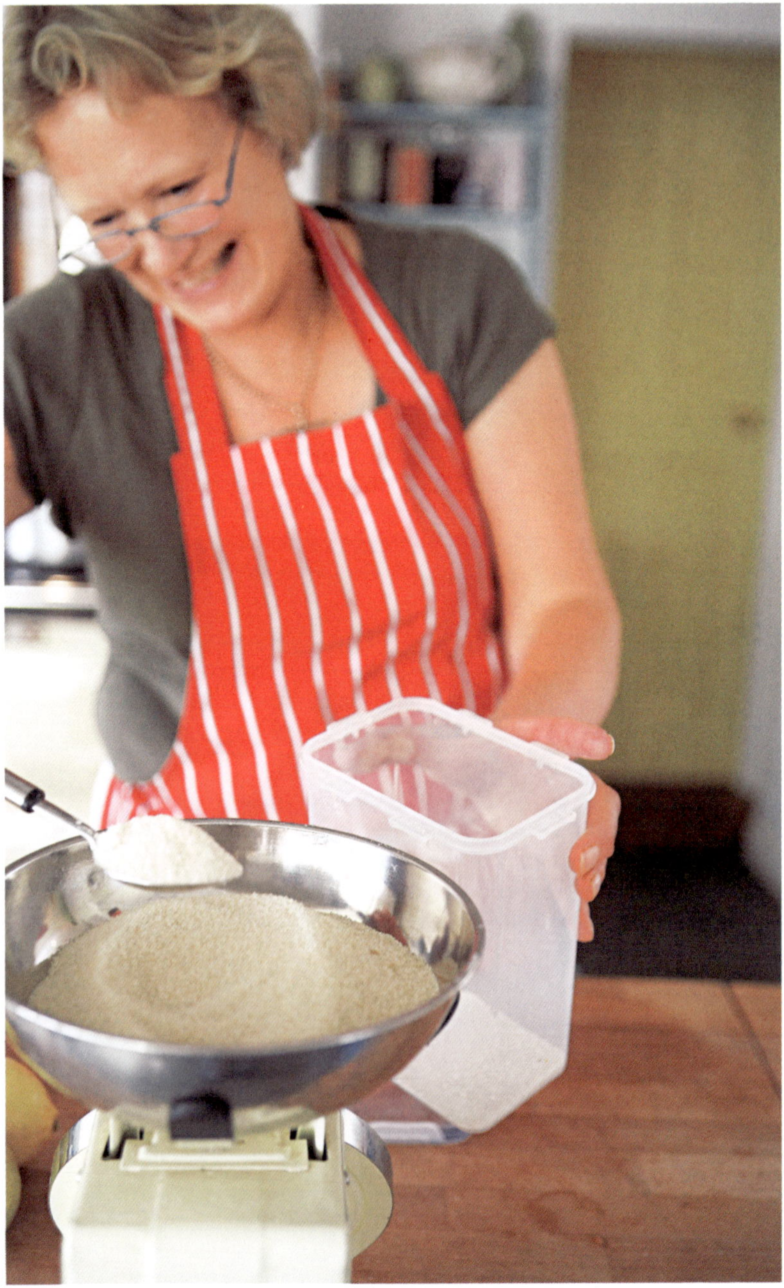

of natural molasses flavour. They can overpower delicate ingredients but are wonderful when used with citrus fruit in marmalades or with vinegar and spices in savoury chutneys and pickles.

Honey This can be used to add another layer of flavour to a preserve, although it cannot entirely replace the sugar as it burns very easily. Supplement 10–15 per cent of the total sugar in a recipe with honey and add it when the sugar has dissolved.

Vinegar

Vinegar has been used for centuries to preserve everything from onions to eggs, and foods preserved in this medium are generally referred to as being 'pickled'. The word 'vinegar' comes from the medieval French *vin-aigre,* meaning 'sour wine'. It is produced by a double fermentation of some form of fruit or grain. The first fermentation is brought about by yeasts turning sugar into alcohol, as in the production of wine, beer and cider. The second fermentation involves bacteria turning the alcohol to acetic acid, thereby creating vinegar.

In order to preserve successfully, the acetic acid content of vinegar must be at least 5 per cent – check the label. This level of acidity creates an environment where few micro-organisms can survive. The harsh flavour of vinegar can be mitigated by the addition of sugar and/or spices, while the choice of vinegar itself will also have a considerable effect on the final taste of your pickles:

Malt vinegar Produced from fermented barley, malt vinegar is inexpensive and has been the backbone of traditional pickling for many years. It has a very strong taste which some people love, but I often find it a bit too aggressive. Nevertheless, in a really hearty, well-spiced chutney or pickle, it can give precisely the right robust bass note of flavour and is a stalwart favourite for pickled onions. The colour in dark malt vinegars comes from the addition of caramel – pure, distilled malt vinegar is colourless.

Wine vinegars Derived from grapes, red and white wine vinegars are more expensive than malt but have a finer, more delicate flavour. I like to use them for pickling ingredients such as nasturtium pods, where I don't want the pods' fiery bite swamped by vinegar.

Cider vinegar This is sweeter and fruitier than wine vinegar and my choice for seasonal chutneys, pickles and relishes. Aspall's (see the directory, p.210) sells an excellent range of home-produced cider vinegars and, if you live in cider apple country, you may well find some excellent local varieties.

Salt

High concentrations of salt are of course inimical to yeast, bacteria and moulds, which is why this ingredient is so important in many preserving methods. Salt is also crucial for enhancing flavour. In addition, it is often used in the preparation of foods prior to pickling, where it draws out excess water, which would otherwise dilute and spoil the preserve (see Pickles, Chutneys & Relishes, p.92).

Sea salt This is produced by evaporating sea water. You can buy unrefined, natural flaky types, such as Maldon or Halen Môn, which are lovely sweet-tasting ingredients. They are also much more expensive than other salts so, while you might be happy to use them for seasoning, you may think it rather extravagant to use them in large quantities for dry-salting or pickling. A relatively inexpensive fine-grained sea salt, available from health food stores or supermarkets, is what I use most often in preserving. It's certainly the most suitable type for dry-salting vegetables for pickling, as it will coat them well. However, like many fine-grained, free-flowing salts, some fine sea salts contain an anti-caking agent, so do check labels before you buy.

Rock salt Generally the cheaper alternative to sea salt, this is mined from underground mineral deposits. It may also be sold as kitchen salt or table salt. Some is highly processed, purified and treated and tastes correspondingly harsh. I don't use salts like this in preserving as they can affect the final quality of the preserve. However, coarse, additive-free rock salts, such as Tidman's, are available, and make a good alternative to sea salt.

Alcohol

This is a very useful preserving medium but, to function effectively, it must be in the form of a spirit that is at least 40 per cent alcohol (80 per cent proof). Gin, vodka, rum, brandy and whisky are all suitable. Gin is a tried-and-tested favourite with fruits such as sloes and damsons, while stoned cherries will make a splendid liqueur when steeped in brandy. Colourless eau de vie (brandy or flavourless alcohol that has not been aged) is an ideal base for more delicate or subtle ingredients. Wines, fortified wines and cider can be used for preserving but need to be combined with other preservative ingredients such as sugar, or with sterilising methods such as bottling.

Oil

An effective means of sealing out oxygen, oil is a useful and potentially delicious part of many savoury preserves. The oil will be an integral part of the finished preserve and, as it will have taken on flavour from the preserved food, you might want to use it to enhance other dishes. So I'd advise always using the best you can afford.

Olive oil This is extracted by grinding olives to a paste and then pressing with large millstones. 'Extra virgin' refers to olive oil with very low acidity, which is completely unrefined and taken from the first pressing of the olives. It's considered to be the very best type. However, it is expensive, and often powerfully flavoured, and I rarely use it in preserves. 'Virgin' olive oil has a little more acidity, but is also unrefined and will have a good flavour. It is much more affordable, and my choice for most oil-based preserves. Anything labelled 'pure' olive oil, or just 'olive oil' will be a blend of refined and unrefined oils. Less exciting, they are still perfectly acceptable to use.

Sunflower oil Light in colour, almost flavourless, and much less expensive than olive oil, a good-quality sunflower oil is useful when you don't want the taste of the oil to intrude on the preserve. It can also be blended with other, more robustly flavoured oils (see below).

Rapeseed oil Golden in colour and nutty in flavour, this is extracted from the tiny, jet-black seeds of *Brassica napus*, a member of the mustard family, and is often home-produced. It contains less saturated fat than any other oil, is high in omega 3 and is a good source of vitamin E. I like to use it for flavoured oils.

Hemp oil Cold-pressed hemp oil is vivid green in colour and has a very strong nutty flavour. Again, it can be grown and processed in this country. Alone, it would be overpowering for many ingredients, but 10–15 per cent blended with sunflower oil creates a well-flavoured oil.

Equipment for preserving

Kitting yourself out for preserving will not entail a second mortgage. You probably already have most of the equipment you need in your kitchen. Here is a very quick run-through of essentials and useful items:

Preserving pan Sometimes called a maslin pan, this is almost an essential item – but a large, wide, heavy-bottomed stock pot could stand in. Preserving pans do have the advantages of sloping sides which maximise evaporation, a pouring lip and a strong carrying handle. Go for a robust stainless-steel one of approximately 9-litre capacity. This should be large enough for most jamming and chutney sessions. Your pan must be deep enough to contain the rapid rise in liquid that occurs when jam comes to a full rolling boil. It

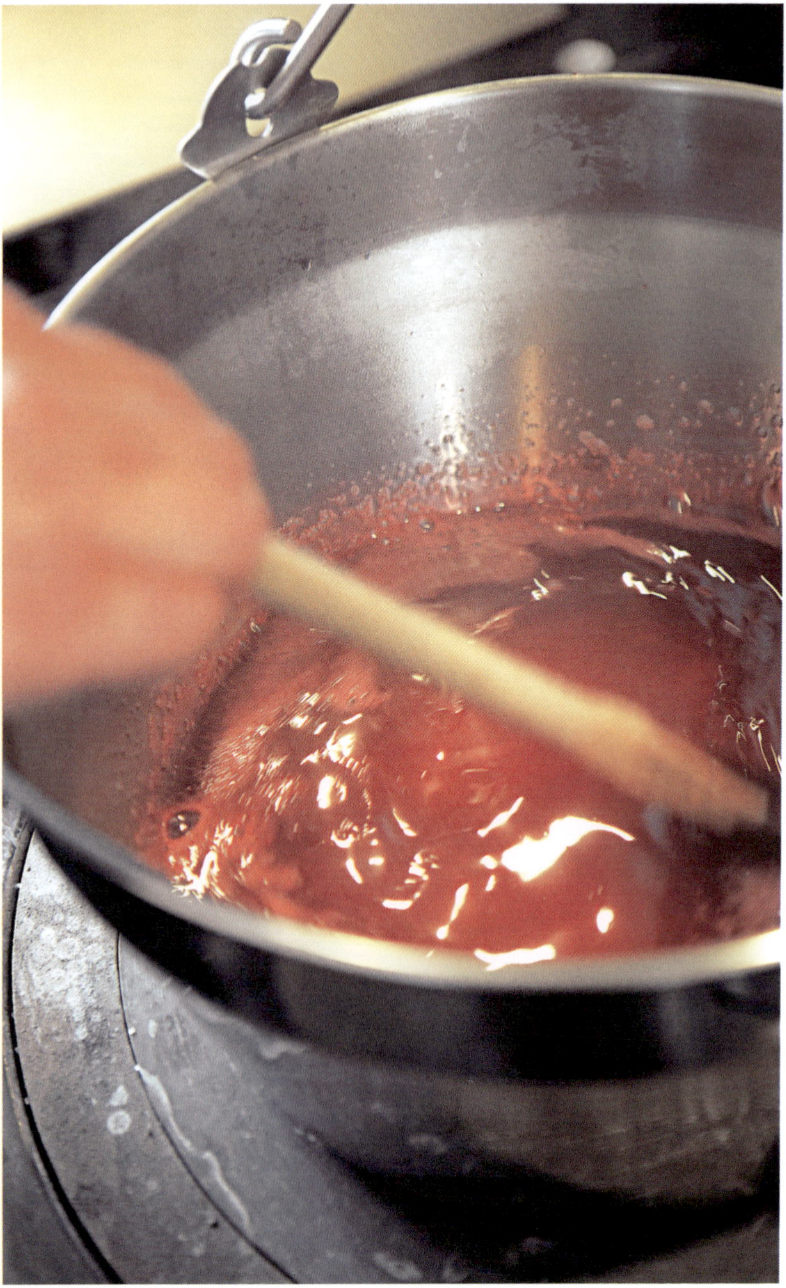

is useful to buy one with a calibrated volume measure on the inside of the pan which allows you to see by how much your ingredients have reduced.

Wooden spoons These need to be big and long-handled. If possible, keep one especially for jam and one for chutney-making (they will become impregnated with fruity and vinegary juices respectively).

Preserving or sugar thermometer This is not expensive and will help you to check that your preserves have reached the right temperature for setting point, as well as giving you an accurate guide to temperature when bottling.

Slotted spoon For skimming scum or fishing out fruit stones.

Sieves A couple of heatproof nylon sieves are useful for puréeing fruit – the acid from which can react with a metal sieve.

Paper coffee filters For straining small quantities of fruit vinegar or liqueur.

Mouli or food mill Great labour-saving tool for puréeing fruits and removing skins and pips simultaneously. Useful when making fruit butters and cheeses.

Jelly bag, or muslin, and stand These are essential for straining the juice from cooked fruit when making jellies. Purpose-made jelly bags and stands are available from specialist shops (see the directory, p.210). Or you can improvise, using an upturned stool with a double thickness of muslin tied to each leg to form a bag. Jelly bags and muslin can be re-used, even though they become stained by fruit dyes. Before use (even when new) they should be scalded by placing in a pan of water and bringing to the boil.

Spice infuser Not essential, but an alternative to tying spices in muslin for spicing vinegars and chutneys.

Measuring jugs and spoons One or two calibrated, heat-resistant measuring jugs are indispensable for measuring ingredients and pouring preserves into jars. A set of measuring spoons is also very useful for spices and seasonings.

Funnel A wide-necked pouring funnel can prevent spillages when filling jars but is not essential – a steady hand and a good pouring jug is often easier.

Accurate kitchen scales Very important for preserving success.

Jams & Jellies

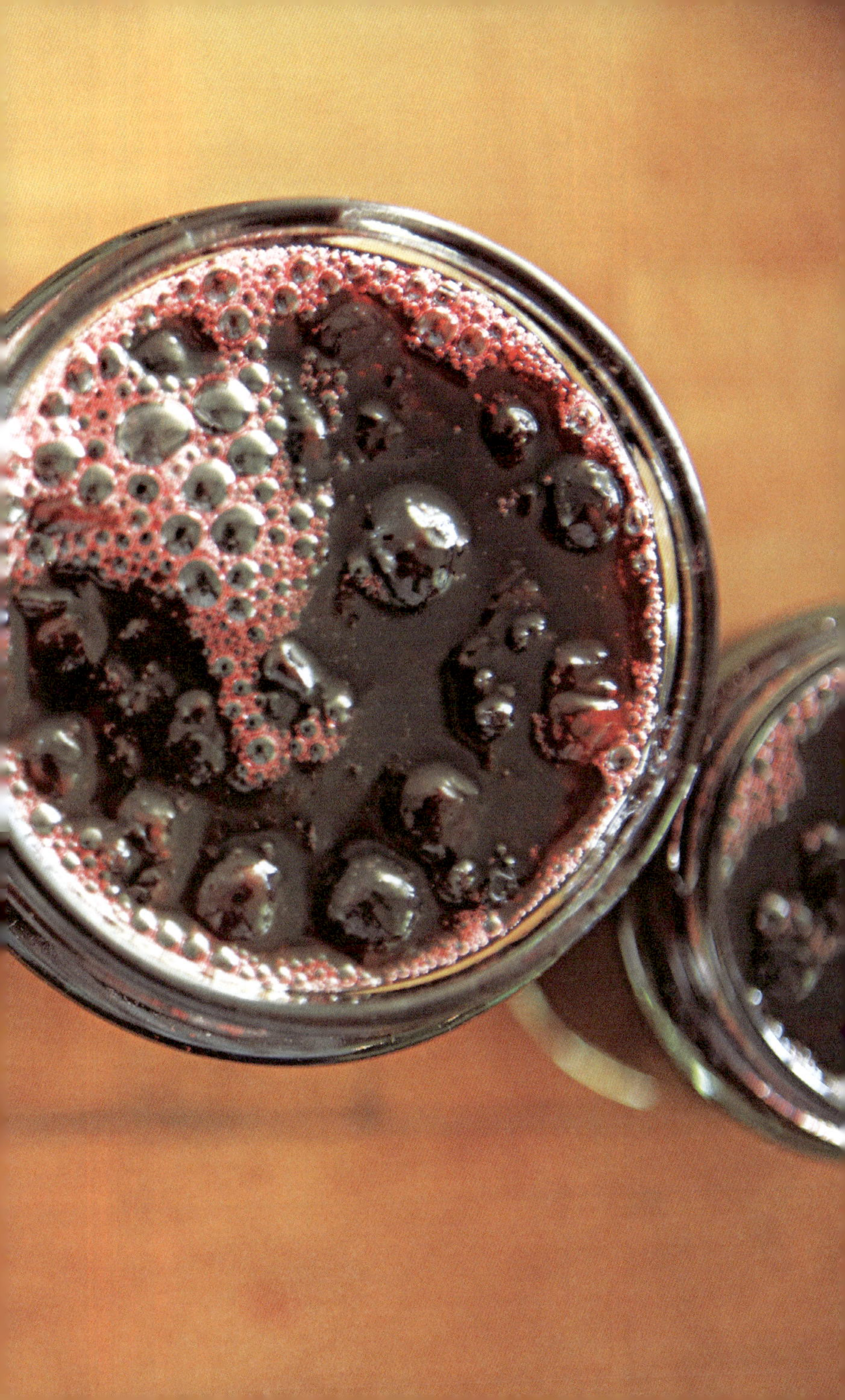

This is the sweetest chapter in the book, where you will meet what I call the 'sugar set'. In other words, recipes that rely purely on a high concentration of sugar to keep spoiling at bay. Sugar-based recipes form a broad and extensive branch of the preserving tree, and they are also the most familiar and perhaps widely used type of preserve. Here you will find out just how essential sugar is as a preserving ingredient and how, by means of various preserving techniques, it can be used to transform a host of fresh produce into goodies that can be safely stored away for the future.

The different types of sugar-based preserve that I make at home are as follows:

Jams Without doubt, jams are the most familiar of all the sweet preserves. They are simply mixtures of lightly softened fruit and sugar, boiled together until they gel into a mass.

Marmalades Although originally referring to a type of quince jam (*marmelo* being the Portuguese word for quince), the term 'marmalade' is now universally understood to mean a bittersweet preserve made from citrus fruit. Marmalades are made in a similar way to jams but the hard citrus peel needs long, slow cooking to soften it before sugar is added.

Conserves Made with whole fruit that has been steeped in sugar before cooking to draw out the juices, a conserve is similar to a jam but often has a slightly softer set. Commercially, the word conserve is often used to describe a posh jam with a high fruit content.

Fruit spreads and fridge jams These are relatively low in sugar and usually made with added pectin to help them set. In general, they still have a softer, looser set than traditional jams. Providing they are sealed when still over 90°C, they will keep for 9–12 months. However, once opened, they must be kept in the fridge as they do not contain sufficient sugar to prevent them spoiling at cool larder temperature.

Jellies Clear, translucent and smooth (no fruity bits), fruit jellies are the jewels of the store cupboard. They are made by boiling strained fruit juice with sugar. They are best made with fruits high in both pectin and acid, such as apples, crab apples, gooseberries and redcurrants – either on their own or in combination with other, lower-pectin fruits (see the pectin/acid content chart on p.48). The basic fruit juice and sugar mixture can also be used as a base for herb or flower jellies.

Fruit butters So called because they spread as 'soft as butter', these are made by boiling cooked, sieved fruit pulp with sugar. They are lower in sugar than traditional jams and will not keep as well. For this reason, they are best potted in smallish jars, which can be consumed in a relatively short time and stored in the fridge once opened.

Fruit cheeses These dense, solid preserves are similar to fruit butters in that they are made by boiling sieved fruit pulp with sugar. However, they are cooked for longer and taste richer and fruitier. You could make a cheese with almost any fruit but, because of the large quantity required, recipes usually favour prolific orchard, stone and hedgerow fruits such as apples, quince, damsons or crab apples. Fruit cheeses are normally packed in straight-sided jars or moulds so the preserve can be turned out whole and sliced.

Fruit curds These are not true preserves, being very low in sugar, but creamy mixtures of butter, eggs, sugar and an acidic fruit pulp or juice. To prevent the eggs curdling, they are cooked very gently in a double boiler or in a basin over a pan of boiling water. Curds are best eaten within 3–4 weeks, so they are usually made in fairly small quantities.

Mincemeats Again, these are not true sugar preserves, as alcohol plays its part in the process too. Mincemeats are mixtures of dried fruit, apples, spices, citrus zest, sugar, suet (sometimes) and alcohol. They are traditionally made in the autumn when the new season's apples are crisp and juicy, then kept for a couple of months to mellow and mature in time to make mince pies for Christmas.

Fruit leathers These rely on drying, as well as sugar, to preserve the fruit. A lightly sweetened purée is slowly dried in a low oven (or, in suitable climates, under the sun), producing a thin, pliable sheet. Fruit leathers store well for several months.

Candied fruits This is a generic term for fruits preserved by being steeped in sugar for a period of time. The sugar penetrates the fruit flesh, replacing some of the natural juices. Different types include glacé fruits, which are coated with a clear sugar syrup, and crystallised fruits, which are rolled in grains of sugar.

The essential foursome

In jam-, jelly- and marmalade-making, four ingredients are necessary to produce the magic result known as 'a set' – i.e. the right wobbling, spreadable consistency. These are fruit, pectin, acid and sugar. Getting to know them will help to ensure success.

Fruit

All fruit for preserve-making should be dry, as fresh as possible and slightly under-ripe. Over-ripe, wet fruit contains less pectin and acid and makes a poor-quality preserve. If you find yourself snowed under with produce during a particularly good cropping season, remember that most fruits, including Seville oranges, can be frozen and used later in the year quite successfully. Bear in mind that the pectin content reduces a little with freezing so sometimes extra pectin may need to be added.

With the exception of the citrus family, I have used only native British fruits in the recipes for this chapter. There are, of course, a whole host of imported exotics at our disposal these days, but buying these in the quantities required for jam-making can be expensive. In any case, with the abundance of home-grown fruits available to us, it's hardly necessary.

Pectin

This is a natural substance found in all fruit (and some vegetables) in varying quantities (see the fruit pectin/acid content chart overleaf). When combined with acid and sugar, it takes on a gum-like consistency – which is why it's essential in achieving a good set. Concentrated in cores, pith, skins and pips, it is released from the cell walls as the fruit is cooked. Pectin levels are at their highest in slightly under-ripe fruit and will decrease as the fruit ripens, or if it is frozen.

Fruit with lots of pectin will produce a jam or jelly that sets easily, while those containing lower amounts may well need a bit of help. This can come from other high-pectin fruits added to the mix (as with blackberry and apple jelly, for instance). Alternatively, extra pectin can be added in the form of a pectin stock (see right), or commercially produced liquid or powdered pectin (usually extracted from apples or citrus fruit). A third option is to use jam sugar with added pectin (see p.35). This is very handy for quick and easy jam-making and, provided the manufacturer's instructions are followed, will guarantee a set with low-pectin fruits such as sweet cherries, rhubarb and strawberries.

> **How to test for pectin** If you follow the chart overleaf, you shouldn't need to test for pectin. However, if you're using a fruit not covered here, there is a simple way to check the pectin levels. Add 1 tsp (5ml) of the cooked fruit juice to 1 tbsp (15ml) methylated spirits (or gin or whisky, as these work

too). Shake gently and leave for a minute or two. Juice from a pectin-rich fruit will form a firm clot. If the juice forms several small clots, this indicates a medium pectin content. Juice that remains fairly liquid signifies a low pectin level.

Home-made pectin stock A pectin-rich 'stock' is easily made from certain fruits. The procedure is much the same as the early stages of jelly-making:

Combine 1kg redcurrants, gooseberries or roughly chopped (but not peeled or cored) sour cooking apples with 600ml water. Bring to a simmer and cook gently for 45 minutes to 1 hour, or until the fruit is soft. Strain through a jelly bag (see p.41). The resulting pectin stock will keep for up to 4 weeks in the fridge. To keep it longer, either freeze it (but allow for a reduction in strength when using) or sterilise it.

To sterilise, bring the juice to the boil, pour into hot, sterilised preserving jars and seal immediately. Immerse the jars in a pan of hot water with a folded tea towel on the bottom. Heat the water until boiling, then boil for 5 minutes. Remove the jars carefully and store in a cool, dry place.

To use the stock, stir 150–300ml of it into every 1kg of low-pectin, softened fruit before sugar is added.

FRUIT	PECTIN	ACID
Apples (cooking)	HIGH	HIGH
Apples (crab)	HIGH	HIGH
Apples (dessert)	MEDIUM	LOW
Apricots	MEDIUM	LOW
Blackberries (early)	MEDIUM	LOW
Blackberries (late)	LOW	LOW
Blueberries	MEDIUM	HIGH
Citrus fruit	HIGH	HIGH
Cherries (sour)	MEDIUM	HIGH
Cherries (sweet)	LOW	LOW
Currants (red, black and white)	HIGH	HIGH
Damsons	HIGH	HIGH
Elderberries	LOW	LOW
Figs	LOW	LOW
Gooseberries	HIGH	HIGH
Greengages	MEDIUM	MEDIUM
Japonicas	HIGH	HIGH
Loganberries	MEDIUM	HIGH
Medlars	LOW	LOW
Mulberries	MEDIUM	HIGH
Peaches	LOW	LOW
Pears	LOW	LOW
Plums (sweet)	MEDIUM	MEDIUM
Plums (sour)	HIGH	HIGH
Quince	HIGH	LOW
Raspberries (ripe)	MEDIUM	MEDIUM
Raspberries (unripe)	MEDIUM	LOW
Rhubarb	LOW	LOW
Rowan berries	MEDIUM-LOW	HIGH
Sloes	MEDIUM	HIGH
Strawberries	LOW	LOW

Acid

This is naturally found in fruit and is essential for clear, bright, well-set preserves. It draws pectin out of the fruit, enabling setting point to be reached quickly without lengthy cooking, which would darken the jam. Acid also helps prevent crystallisation of the sugar. Levels of acid vary in different fruits (see chart, left) and are lower in over-ripe fruit. Lemon, gooseberry or redcurrant juice is sometimes added to low-acid fruit jams. It should be added before the fruit is cooked, so it can get to work on drawing out the pectin. If you're making jam with a low-acid fruit, such as strawberries or rhubarb, add 30ml lemon juice, or 150ml redcurrant, gooseberry or apple juice, per 1kg of fruit.

Sugar

The fourth vital ingredient for jam-making and the one that actually preserves the fruit and keeps it from spoiling. In order to do this, the proportion of sugar in a preserve needs to be 60 per cent or higher. Boiling the fruit and sugar mixture drives off water, which helps the sugar content reach this crucial level. Sugar also enhances the flavour of sharp, acidic fruits such as blackcurrants and gooseberries. See Key preserving ingredients, p.35, for in-depth information on different types of sugar.

Setting point

Providing the proportion of ingredients is correct, your jam or jelly should set once it has been sufficiently cooked. There are three simple methods you can use to check if setting point has been reached. Remove the jam from the heat while testing for setting point (it will lose more water as it cooks and may reach a point where it will set too firmly). If setting point has not been reached, return to the boil, cook for a further couple of minutes, then test again.

> **Crinkle or saucer test** Drop a little jam on to a cold saucer (I put one in the fridge when I start jam-making). Allow to cool for a minute then push gently with your fingertip. If the jam crinkles, setting point has been reached.
>
> **Flake test** Dip a clean wooden spoon into the jam, hold it up over the pan, twirl it around a couple of times, then let the jam drop from the side of it. If the drops run together to form a flake, setting point has been reached.
>
> **Temperature test** Place a preserving thermometer (see p.41) into the jam when it has reached a rolling boil. When it reads 104.5°C, setting point will have been reached. Pectin-rich fruits will set a degree or two lower.

Making perfect jams and marmalades

This checklist will help to ensure success every time:

1. Always use fresh, dry, slightly under-ripe fruit. Prepare and pick over according to type, i.e. hull strawberries, stone plums, top and tail gooseberries, shred citrus peel. Wash the fruit only if necessary and dry it well.

2. Simmer the fruit gently in a large, uncovered pan before adding the sugar. This softens the fruit and helps draw out the pectin. Soft fruits, such as raspberries and strawberries, will not need added water but tougher-skinned or semi-hard fruits, such as currants, gooseberries, plums, apples and citrus fruit, will.

3. Make sure that the fruit skins are well softened before sugar is added. Once the sugar is in, the skins will not soften further, no matter how long you cook them. Citrus peel for marmalade takes 1½–2 hours to soften.

4. A knob of butter (20g for every 1kg fruit) or a little cooking oil, added at the same time as the sugar, helps to prevent any scum forming on the jam.

5. After adding the sugar to the fruit or juice, stir it over a gentle heat to ensure it is completely dissolved before the mixture begins to boil. Adding the sugar before the jam is boiling helps to 'hold' the fruit in whole or chunky pieces. Warming the sugar in a low oven will speed up the dissolving process, but is not strictly necessary.

6. Once the sugar is dissolved, cook the jam, without stirring, at a full rolling boil, i.e. when the surface is covered by a mass of foamy bubbles that don't recede when stirred. Time your cooking from the point at which the rolling boil begins. Don't stir at this stage – it cools the jam so it would take longer to reach setting point.

7. Test for setting point, using one of the methods given on p.49, when the foamy bubbles have subsided and the boiling surface of the jam appears glossy and heavy.

8. When setting point is reached, remove the pan from the heat. To remove scum, stir the jam (always in the same direction so as not to introduce too much air) until it has dispersed. Alternatively, skim off scum with a slotted spoon. (Scum, by the way, is nothing to worry about – it's just air bubbles created by the intense cooking process.)

9. Allow jams with large pieces of fruit, and thick-cut marmalades, to cool for 10–12 minutes before potting. This allows the mixture to thicken slightly so that the fruit, when potted, should remain well distributed throughout the jar.

10. Pour into clean, sterilised jars (see p.29) while the preserve is still very hot (always above 85°C). Seal with suitable lids and, once cool, store in a cool, dry place.

Making perfect jellies

You will need to prepare the fruit in the same way as for jams (see left), but there are different watchpoints for jelly-making:

1. Soften the fruit by simmering it very gently for 45–60 minutes. With juicy fruits, like strawberries, raspberries, redcurrants and blackberries, allow 300–400ml water per 1kg fruit. For plums and damsons, allow 600ml per 1kg, and for blackcurrants 900ml per 1kg. Apples, quinces and hard fruits should be just covered with water.

2. Strain the cooked fruit pulp through a scalded jelly bag (this helps to make the jelly clear, see p.41) for at least 2 hours or overnight.

3. If you can't resist squeezing or poking the bag to extract more juice, be prepared for your jelly to be cloudy.

4. Allow 450g sugar for every 600ml juice. Bring the juice slowly to the boil and add the sugar only when boiling – this helps to keep your jelly clear and bright: the longer the sugar is cooked, the more the jelly will darken. Boiling time will be somewhere between 5 and 15 minutes, depending on the type of fruit used.

5. Test for a set in the same way as for jam.

6. Skim the jelly and pour into jars as quickly as possible.

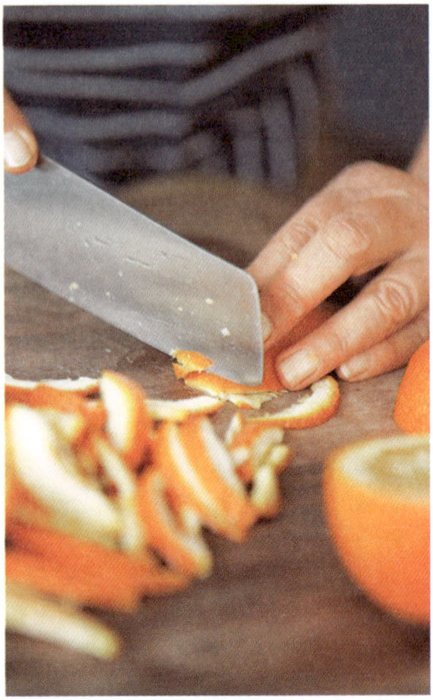
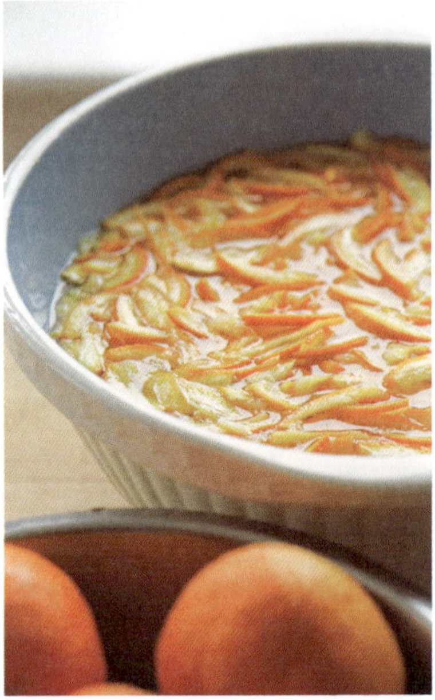
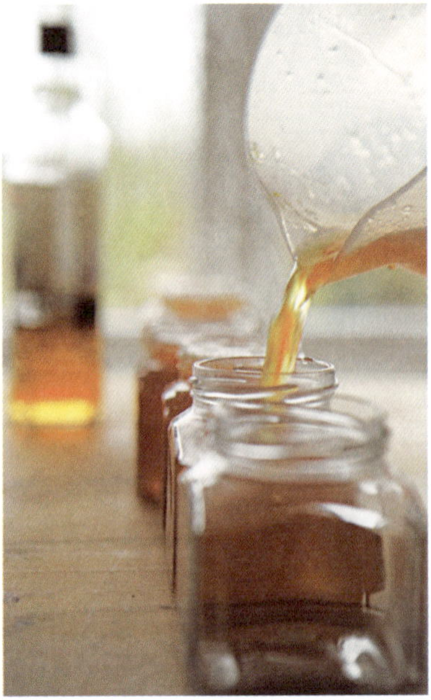
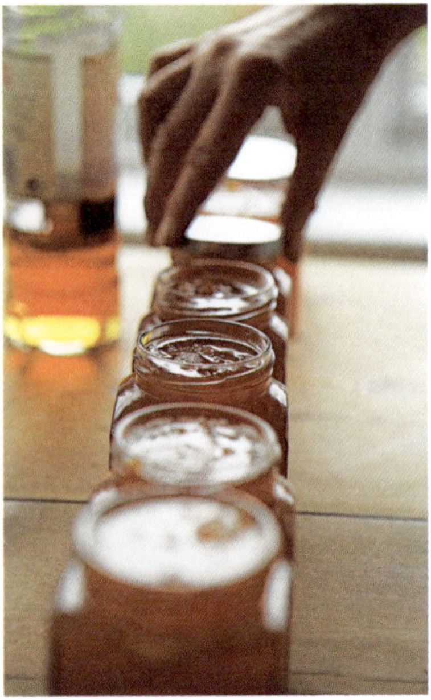

Seville orange marmalade

Season: January to February

The bitter Seville orange is the most traditional and arguably the finest marmalade fruit of all. Only available for a few short weeks from mid-January, this knobbly, often misshapen orange has a unique aromatic quality and is very rich in pectin. However, you can use almost any citrus fruit to make good marmalade – consider sweet oranges, ruby-red or blood oranges, grapefruit, limes, clementines, kumquats, or a combination of two or three (see my suggested variations overleaf).

There are two basic ways of making marmalade. My first choice is the sliced fruit method, which involves cutting the raw peel into shreds before cooking. I find this technique produces a brighter, clearer result. However, the whole fruit method, in which the fruit is boiled whole before being cut up, is easier and less time-consuming. It tends to create a darker, less delicate preserve – but that, of course, might be exactly what you want. I've given you both methods here…

Sliced fruit method

Makes 5–6 x 450g jars
1kg Seville oranges
75ml lemon juice
2kg demerara sugar

Scrub the oranges, remove the buttons at the top of the fruit, then cut in half. Squeeze out the juice and keep to one side. Using a sharp knife, slice the peel, pith and all, into thin, medium or chunky shreds, according to your preference. Put the sliced peel into a bowl with the orange juice and cover with 2.5 litres water. Leave to soak overnight or for up to 24 hours.

Transfer the whole mixture to a preserving pan, bring to the boil then simmer slowly, covered, until the peel is tender. This should take approximately 2 hours, by which time the contents of the pan will have reduced by about one-third.

Stir in the lemon juice and sugar. Bring the marmalade to the boil, stirring until the sugar has dissolved. Boil rapidly until setting point is reached (see p.49), about 20–25 minutes. Remove from the heat. Leave to cool for 8–10 minutes – a little longer if the peel is in very chunky pieces – then stir gently to disperse any scum, pour into warm, sterilised jars (see p.29) and seal immediately. Use within 2 years.

Whole fruit method

Makes 5 x 450g jars
1kg Seville oranges
75ml lemon juice
2kg granulated sugar

Scrub the fruit, remove the buttons at the top and put it, whole, into a preserving pan with 2.5 litres water. Bring to the boil then simmer, covered, for 2–2½ hours or until the orange skins are tender and can be pierced easily with a fork.

When cool enough to handle, take the oranges out. Measure and keep the cooking water – you should have about 1.7 litres. Make it up to this amount with more water if you have less, or bring to the boil and reduce if you have more.

Cut the oranges in half and remove the pips with a fork, flicking them into a bowl. Strain any juice from the pips back into the cooking water, then discard the pips.

Meanwhile, cut up the orange peel and flesh into thick, medium or thin shreds. Put the cut-up fruit into the strained cooking liquid. Add the lemon juice and sugar and bring to the boil, stirring until the sugar has completely dissolved. Bring to a rolling boil and boil rapidly until setting point is reached (see p.49), about 10–15 minutes.

Leave to cool for 10–12 minutes – a little longer if you've cut the peel into very chunky pieces – then stir gently to disperse any scum, pour into warm, sterilised jars (see p.29) and seal immediately. Use within 2 years.

Variations

You can use both methods for making many other delicious marmalades:

Lemon marmalade with honey Use 1kg lemons instead of oranges, and omit the extra lemon juice. Replace 250g of the sugar with honey, adding it at the same time.

Three-fruit marmalade Use a mixture of grapefruit, lemons and sweet oranges to make up a total of 1kg fruit.

Seville and ginger marmalade Replace 250g of the sugar with 250g chopped crystallised stem ginger, adding it along with the sugar.

Whisky marmalade Add 50ml whisky to the marmalade at the end of cooking.

'Ruby red' marmalade Both pink grapefruits and blood oranges make wonderful marmalades, though I prefer to use the sliced fruit method for these fruits. Add 100ml freshly squeezed lemon juice to every 1kg of fruit.

P.S. Don't limit marmalade to the breakfast table, for its traits and qualities can be well used in other culinary ways. I like to replace candied peel in fruit cakes with a tablespoonful or two of marmalade, and always add some to my Christmas mincemeat (see p.82). Marmalade makes a marvellous glaze for oven-baked ham, as well as sweet and sour chicken or pork dishes. Best of all, 3 or 4 tablespoonfuls will make a glorious golden topping for a good old-fashioned steamed pud.

P.P.S. For generations, marmalade-makers have cooked up the mass of pips found inside citrus fruits in the belief that they are full of pectin. However, most of the pectin is actually found in the citrus peel and I rely purely on this for the setting power in my marmalades.

Early rhubarb jam

Season: mid-January to late March

Early or 'forced' rhubarb has been produced in West Yorkshire since the 1870s, as growers discovered that the heavy clay soil and cold winter climate suited the plant (a native of Siberia). In the 'Rhubarb Triangle' between Bradford, Wakefield and Leeds, the tradition continues to this day. Sequestered in dark sheds, carefully cultivated rhubarb 'crowns' send forth slender, bright-pink stems, much more delicate in flavour than the thick green shafts of outdoor-grown rhubarb that appear later in the year.

This is one of my favourite ways to capture the earthy flavour of rhubarb. It's a plant that contains very little pectin so the jam definitely requires an extra dose. The shortish boil time helps to preserve the fabulous colour of the stems. I like to add a little Seville orange juice, but juice from sweet oranges works well too.

This light, soft jam is good mixed with yoghurt or spooned over ice cream, or you can warm it and use to glaze a bread and butter pudding after baking.

Makes 5 x 340g jars
1kg forced rhubarb (untrimmed weight)
900g jam sugar with added pectin
100ml freshly squeezed Seville or sweet orange juice

Wipe and trim the rhubarb and cut into 2–2.5cm chunks. Pour a layer of sugar into the bottom of a preserving pan, then add a layer of rhubarb. Repeat, continuing until all the sugar and rhubarb are used, finishing with a layer of sugar. Pour the orange juice over the top. Cover and leave for at least an hour or two – preferably overnight. This draws the juice from the rhubarb and the resulting syrup helps keep the rhubarb chunks whole when boiled.

Gently bring the mixture to the boil, stirring carefully without crushing the rhubarb pieces. Boil rapidly for 5–6 minutes, then test for setting point (see p.49).

Remove from the heat and rest for 5 minutes before pouring into warm, sterilised jars (see p.29). Seal immediately (see p.30). Use within 12 months.

Variations
Add 100g chopped crystallised stem ginger to the fruit, omitting the orange juice. Sharper-tasting maincrop rhubarb can also be used for this recipe – try adding a few young angelica leaves or a handful of fragrant rose petals.

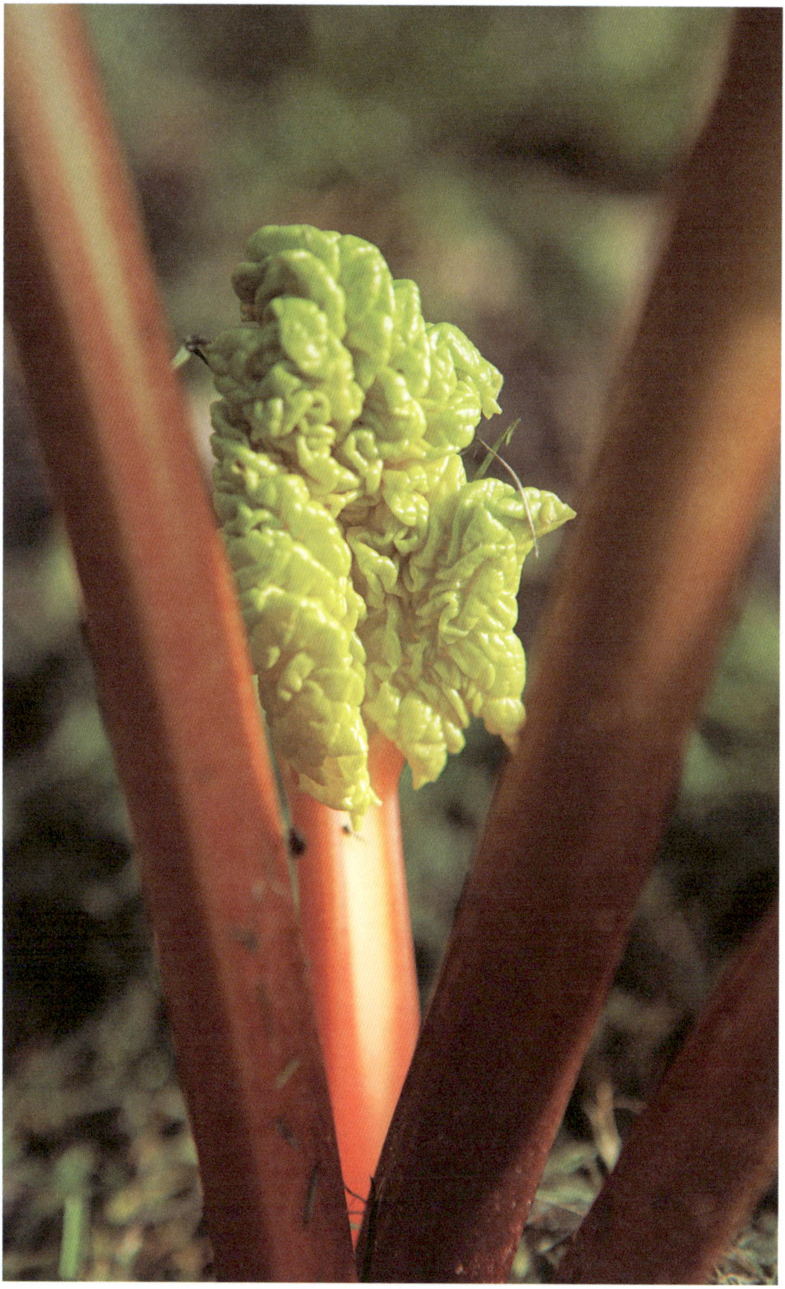

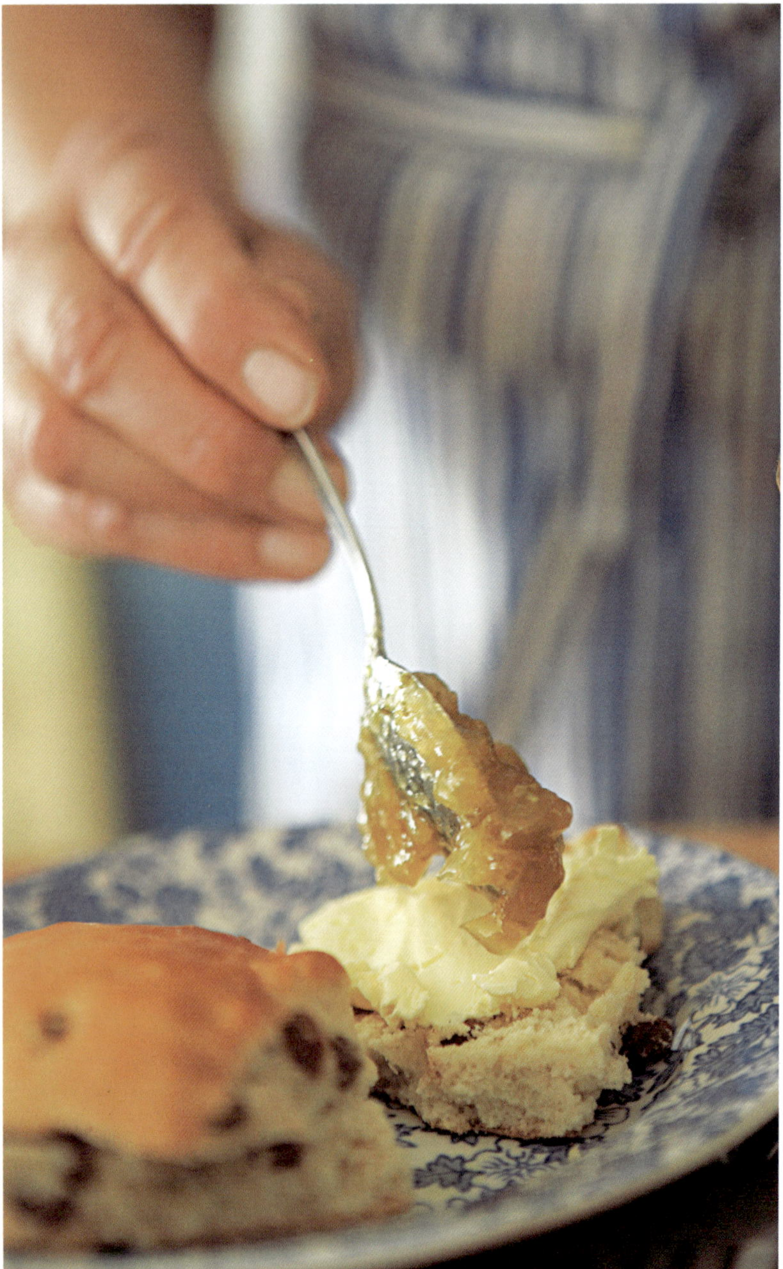

Green gooseberry jam
with elderflower

Season: late May to June

I welcome the first tiny gooseberries that appear in the month of May, just as the first boughs of elderflower are beginning to show. The berries are picked when no bigger than my little thumbnail, almost as a thinning process, allowing their brothers and sisters to fill out and mature on the bush. But these early green goddesses are full of pectin, sharp and tart, and make a divine jam. The fragrant elderflowers add a flavour which will remind you, when the days are short and dark, that summer will come again.

Makes 5–6 x 340g jars
1kg young gooseberries
Around 8 heads of elderflower
1kg granulated sugar

Top and tail the gooseberries (it's easiest to just do this with a pair of scissors) and put into a preserving pan with 500ml water. Check the elderflower heads for any insects, then place on top of the gooseberries. Cook gently until the berries are soft but still hold their shape. Remove the elderflowers.

Add the sugar. Stir carefully, so as not to break up the fruit, until the sugar has dissolved, then bring to a full rolling boil and boil for 9–10 minutes. Test for setting point (see p.49).

Remove from the heat, allow to rest for 10 minutes, then pot and seal (see p.30). Use within 12 months.

Variation
Use this recipe for later-season gooseberries, without the elderflowers. The fruit will be sweeter and the jam will have a soft pink colour.

P.S. To make a quick and easy piquant gooseberry sauce to go with mackerel, add a little cider or balsamic vinegar to warmed gooseberry jam (with or without elderflower). Let the flavours mix and mingle before spooning over the barbecued or grilled fish.

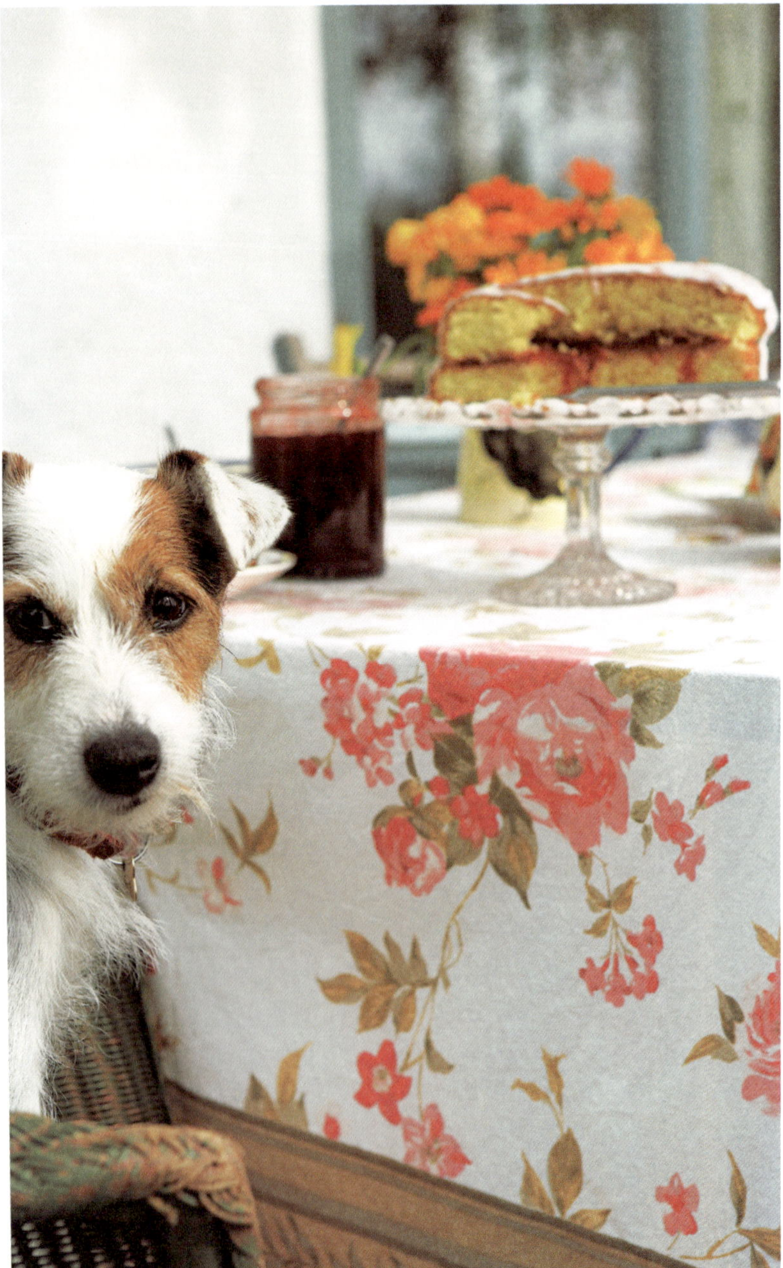

Strawberry jam

Season: May to August

After a dismal result with my strawberry jam at the 2007 Uplyme and Lyme Regis Horticultural Show, I decided to get my act together and work out a recipe that I could rely on to get me that much coveted first prize next time. My kitchen soon took on the appearance of a strawberry jam factory, with coded batches piled just about everywhere. I thought I'd nearly made the grade on batch three, but the tweaking for batch four caused mayhem in the jam pan. However, batch five seemed to come alive from the moment the lemon juice was added and I knew it was going to be just right – bright in colour with some soft whole fruit and, of course, that wonderful, intense strawberry taste.

Strawberries are low in pectin. Using sugar with added pectin helps to attain a lovely set and a flavour that isn't too sickly-sweet. Use freshly picked, dry fruit – not too big, or they'll blow to bits when the jam is bubbling away. However, if you're using very small fruit, make sure they're not too hard and seedy.

Makes 4–5 x 340g jars
1kg strawberries, hulled, large ones halved or quartered
500g granulated sugar
450g jam sugar with added pectin
150ml lemon juice

Put 200g of the strawberries into a preserving pan with 200g of the granulated sugar. Crush to a pulp with a potato masher. Place the pan on a gentle heat and, when the fruit mixture is warm, add the rest of the strawberries. Very gently bring to simmering point, agitating the bottom of the pan with a wooden spoon to prevent the fruit from sticking. Simmer for 5 minutes to allow the strawberries to soften just a little.

Add the remaining granulated sugar and the jam sugar. Stir gently to prevent the sugar sticking and burning on the bottom of the pan. When the sugar has dissolved, add the lemon juice. Increase the heat and, when the mixture reaches a full boil, boil rapidly for 8–9 minutes. Then test for setting point (see p.49).

Remove from the heat and, if the surface is scummy, stir gently until the scum has dispersed. Pot and seal (see p.30). Use within 12 months.

Redcurrant jelly

Season: June to mid-July

Redcurrants make a superb and very versatile jelly. In addition, their juice can be turned into a delicious alcoholic cordial (p.144). The redcurrant season is short, just a few weeks in midsummer, so make sure you don't miss it. If you haven't time to make your jelly straight away, you can pick the currants and freeze for later.

This is an endlessly useful jelly. A classic tracklement to accompany roast lamb or game, you can also use it to enhance the flavour of gravies, casseroles and piquant sauces. It makes an excellent glaze for fresh fruit tarts too.

Makes 4–5 x 225g jars
1kg redcurrants
Granulated sugar

You don't have to top and tail the currants, or even take them off their stalks. Simply wash them, put into a preserving pan with 400ml water, then simmer until they are very soft and have released all their juice. This will take about 45 minutes. Strain through a jelly bag (see p.41) for several hours, or overnight. Do not poke, squeeze or force the pulp through the bag or you'll get a cloudy jelly.

Measure the juice, put into the cleaned preserving pan and bring to the boil. For every 600ml juice add 450g sugar, adding it only when the juice is boiling. Stir until the sugar has dissolved, ensuring the sides of the pan are free of undissolved sugar crystals. Then boil rapidly for about 8 minutes or until setting point is reached (see p.49).

Remove from the heat and stir to disperse any scum, then pour into warm, sterilised jars and seal (see p.30). Tap the jars to disperse any air bubbles caught in the jelly. Use within 12 months.

Variation
Add a couple of tablespoonfuls of chopped fresh mint to the redcurrant jelly for the last 2–3 minutes of boiling.

P.S. Redcurrant jelly is the core ingredient of Cumberland sauce, a traditional partner to baked ham and game. Just add 50ml port, the grated zest of 1 orange and 1 lemon, 1 tsp cayenne pepper, a pinch or two of mustard powder and perhaps a pinch of ground ginger to 200g redcurrant jelly.

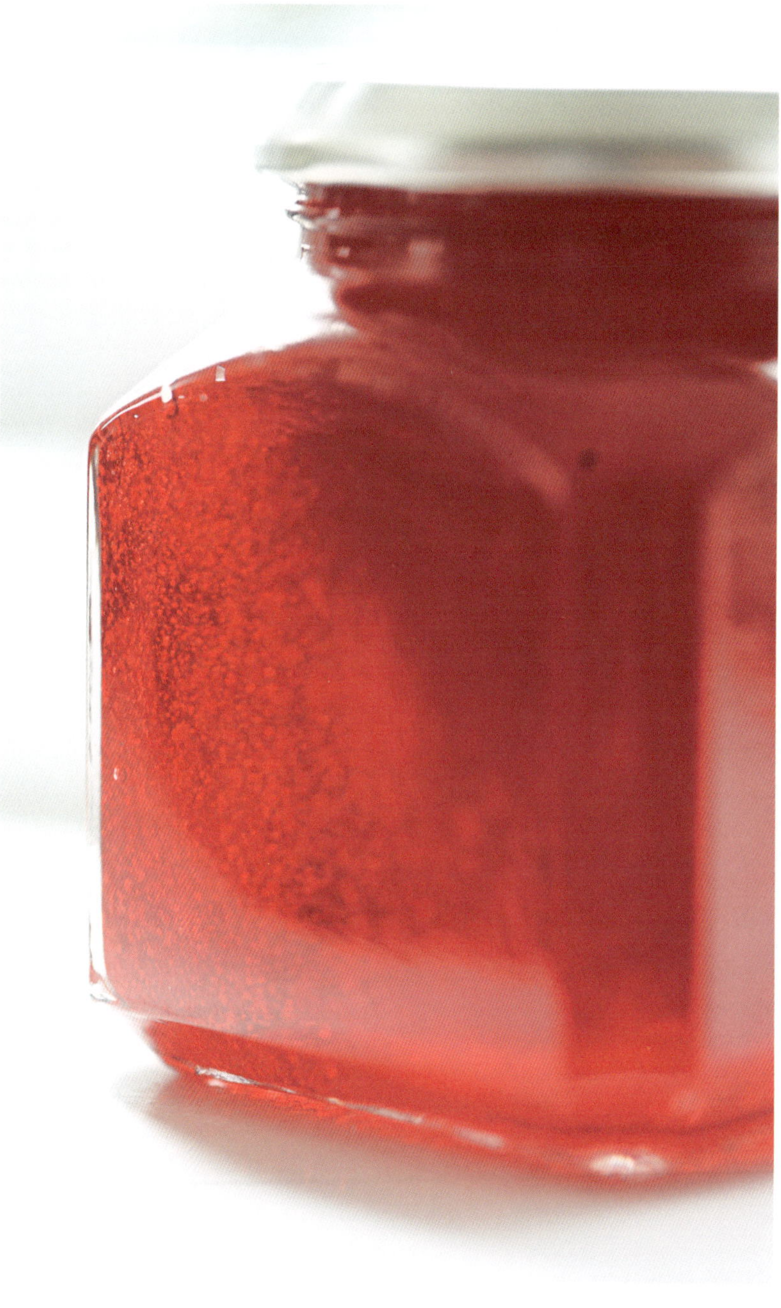

Mum's blackcurrant jam

Season: June to August

In my jam company days, when we would produce nearly 15,000 jars of preserves each week, my mum would still bring me jars of her home-made blackcurrant jam. Sometimes I wondered if I needed another jar in the house, but I always enjoyed it immensely – blackcurrant jam is an all-time favourite, with a flavour that is rarely rivalled. It's also very easy to make. The key is to ensure that the blackcurrants are softened sufficiently before the sugar is added, or the skins will toughen and be unpleasantly chewy.

Use this in all the usual jammy ways with bread, toast, pancakes, yoghurt, rice pudding, cakes, tarts and, of course, scones and clotted cream.

Makes 7–8 x 340g jars
1kg blackcurrants
1.5kg golden granulated sugar

Pick over the blackcurrants, removing any stalks, twiggy bits or damaged fruit (the dry shrivelled bit at one end is the remains of the flower and need not be removed).

Put the currants into a preserving pan with 600ml water. Place over a low heat and slowly bring to simmering point. Simmer for 15–20 minutes, or until the fruit is soft but not disintegrated into a pulp.

Add the sugar and stir until it has dissolved. Then bring quickly to a full rolling boil. Boil hard for 5 minutes. Remove from the heat and continue to stir gently for a couple of minutes to reduce the temperature. Test for setting point (see p.49).

Let the jam cool a little and make sure the currants aren't bobbing above the surface when you pour it into warm, sterilised jam jars (see p.29). If they are, then let the jam cool a little longer, and if they really won't submerge, then bring the pan back to the boil and boil for a couple more minutes.

P.S. The bittersweet leaves of the blackcurrant bush can be used as a substitute for tea. Simply infuse the leaves in boiling water, leave for 10 minutes then serve sweetened with a little honey.

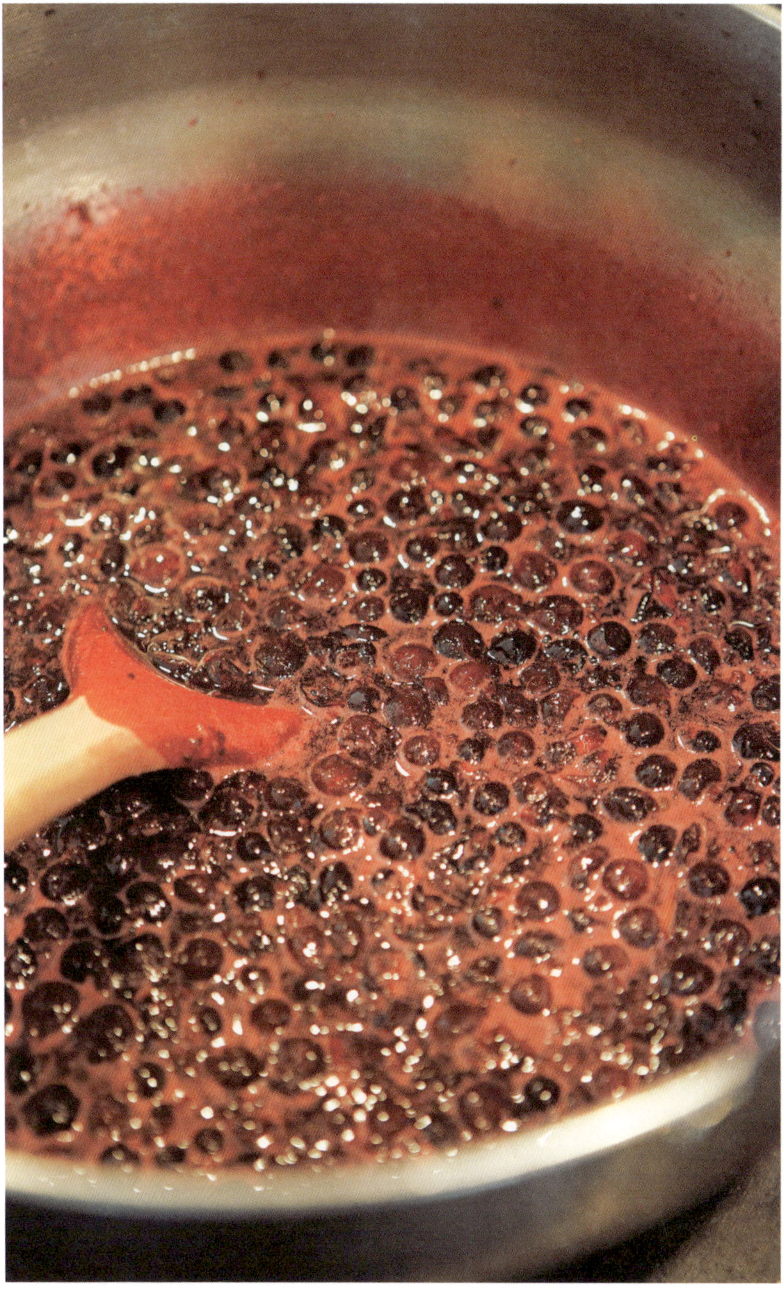

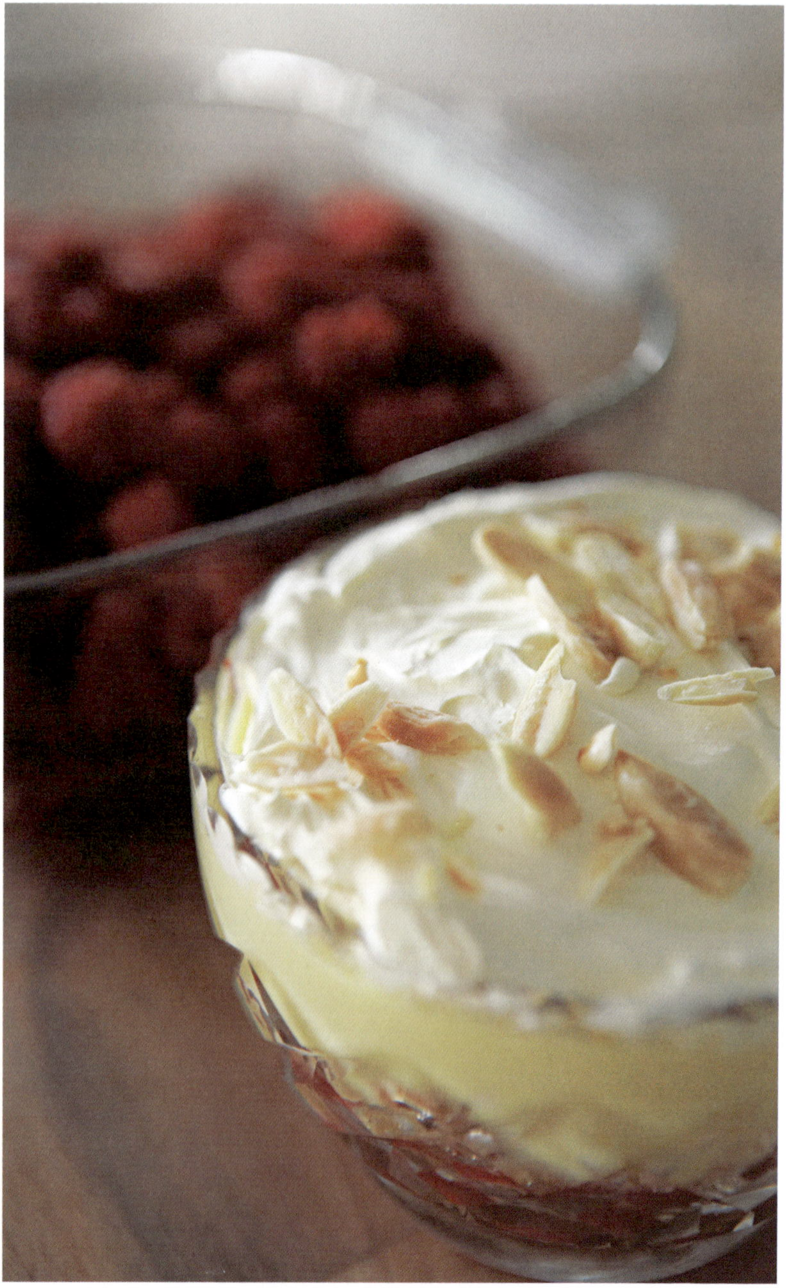

Hugh's prize-winning
raspberry fridge jam

Season: June to October

Hugh F-W, whose recipe this is, thinks the secret of success is to pick the raspberries on a hot, dry day, aiming for a good mixture of ripe and almost-ripe fruit, then to make the jam immediately – to capture the full flavour of the berries.

The light boiling and lower-than-normal quantity of sugar produce a loose, soft-set jam with a fresh, tangy flavour. Low-sugar jams of this type are often called fridge jams (see p.44). In fact, as long as it is capped when still above 90°C, this preserve will keep well in the store cupboard. However, once it is opened, you must keep it in the fridge. It won't last long after opening – maybe 2 or 3 weeks – but as it tastes so very, very good, this is unlikely to be a problem. It's one of those things you'll find yourself eating straight from the jar, maybe in the middle of the night!

This light, soft jam is fantastic in cakes or sherry trifles or stirred into creamy rice puddings. Best of all, layer it with toasted oatmeal, cream, Drambuie and honey for a take on the traditional Scottish pudding, cranachan.

Makes 6 x 340g jars
1.5kg raspberries
750g jam sugar with added pectin

Start by picking over the raspberries very carefully and discarding any leaves or stalks. Put half the fruit into a preserving pan and use a potato masher to roughly crush it. Add the remaining fruit and sugar (the mixture will look mouth-wateringly good).

Stir over a low heat to dissolve the sugar. Bring to a rolling boil then boil for exactly 5 minutes. (If you prefer a firmer jam, then continue boiling at this stage for a further 2–3 minutes). Remove from the heat, stirring to disperse any scum.

It is important to pour and cap this low-sugar jam quickly (see p.30), but you must allow it to cool just a little first (give it 5–6 minutes) to prevent all those little raspberry pips rushing to the top of the jar, leaving you with half a jar of raspberry jelly and half a jar of raspberry pips.

Variation
Flavourful ripe strawberries give very good results with this simple recipe too. Hull the strawberries, halve or quarter larger ones and continue as above.

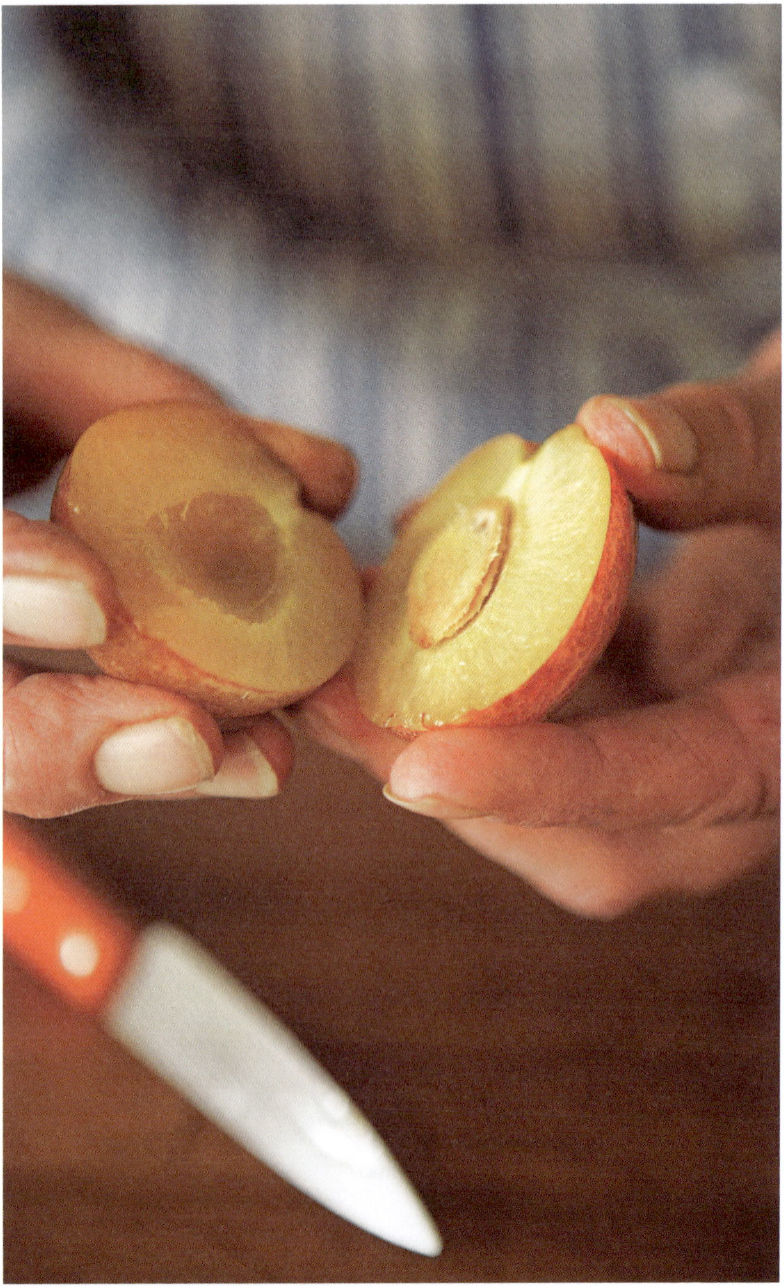

Plum jam

Season: August to September

Plums make a lovely jam and are rich in pectin and easy to prepare, so this is a great recipe for beginners. Just make sure the plums are tender and their skins well softened before adding the sugar. If not, the sugar hardens the skins and they'll be tough in the finished jam; they will also float to the top of the jar.

The widely available 'Victoria' is a first-rate jam plum but you can make a good preserve with others, including 'Early Rivers', 'Czar' and the yellow, egg-like 'Pershore', as well as greengages and smaller hedgerow plums such as bullaces and damsons.

Makes 8 x 340g jars
1.5kg plums
1.25kg granulated sugar

Halve and stone the plums. Crack a few of the stones open, using nutcrackers, and extract the kernels. Put these into a basin and cover with boiling water. Leave for a minute or so, then drain them and rub off the reddish-brown skin. The kernels will add a lovely almond-like flavour to the jam.

Put the plums, skinned kernels and 400ml water into a preserving pan. Bring to a simmer and cook gently until the fruit is tender and the skins soft – this should take about 20 minutes but depends on the variety and size of plum.

Add the sugar and stir until dissolved. Bring to boiling point and boil rapidly until setting point is reached (see p.49), usually 10–12 minutes. Remove from the heat. If the fruit is bobbing about at the surface, it's probably not cooked well enough (the sugar is heavier than the plums, and the jam must cook sufficiently for the fruit to absorb the sugar). If this happens, boil for a further 2–4 minutes.

Pot the jam and cover (see p.30). Use within 12 months.

Variations
Replace some of the water with freshly squeezed orange juice and/or add 2 cinnamon sticks. Another nice twist is to add 100g chopped walnuts to the jam towards the end of the boiling time.

Apple, herb and flower jellies

Season: late summer to autumn

The aromatic essences of fresh herbs and flowers can be captured beautifully in a jelly. These preserves are great to have in the kitchen as they add a sweet piquancy to all kinds of food, simple and rich. Cooking apples and crab apples are both ideal choices for the basic jelly. Excellent sources of pectin and acid, they nevertheless have gentle flavours that will not overwhelm the herbs.

Serve mint jelly with lamb, sage with fish, basil with poultry or game, parsley with ham or gammon, and rose-petal jelly (see below) with wafer-thin bread and butter. Any herb jelly will also be delicious with soft cheeses, pâtés and terrines.

Makes 5–6 x 225g jars
1.5kg cooking apples
1 medium bunch of sage, rosemary, mint, tarragon, thyme or basil

Granulated sugar
100ml cider vinegar

Roughly chop the apples, discarding any bad parts, but don't peel or core them. Place in a preserving pan with the herbs, reserving half a dozen small sprigs to put into the jars. Barely cover the apples with water. Bring to the boil then simmer gently, covered, for 45 minutes to 1 hour, until the fruit is very soft. Tip the contents of the pan into a jelly bag or piece of muslin suspended over a bowl (see p.41) and leave to drip for at least 2 hours, or overnight.

Measure the strained juice. For every 600ml, weigh out 450g sugar. Return the juice to the cleaned-out pan, with the vinegar. Heat to boiling point then add the sugar and stir until dissolved. Increase the heat and boil rapidly for 10–12 minutes or until setting point is reached (see p.49). Remove from the heat and skim with a slotted spoon to remove any scum.

Pour into small, warm, sterilised jars (see p.29), adding a herb sprig to each. Cover and seal (see p.30). Use within 12 months.

Variations

For stronger-flavoured jellies, you can add 3–4 tbsp freshly chopped herbs after removing the jelly from the heat. Allow to cool for 10 minutes before potting. For exquisite rose-petal or dandelion jelly, add 25g scented petals instead of herbs. The above method can also be used to make quince and medlar jellies, replacing the apples with your chosen fruit and leaving out the herbs.

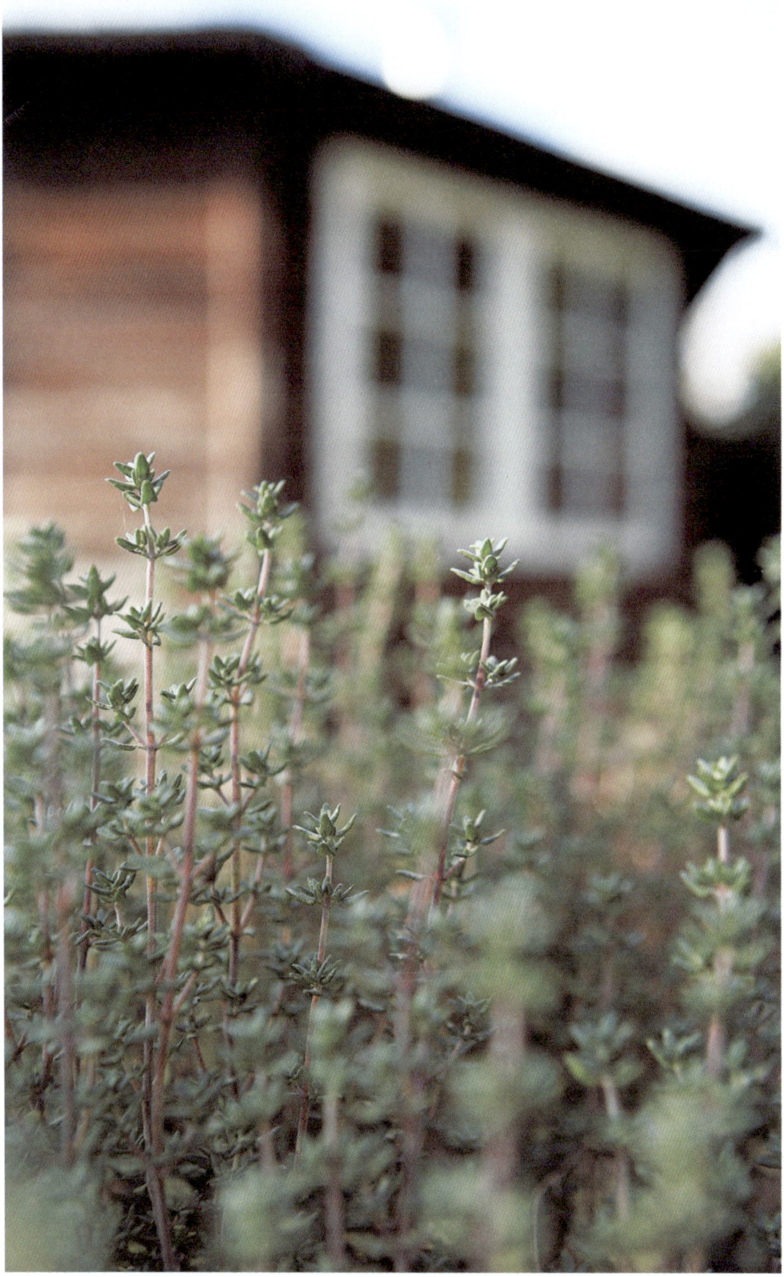

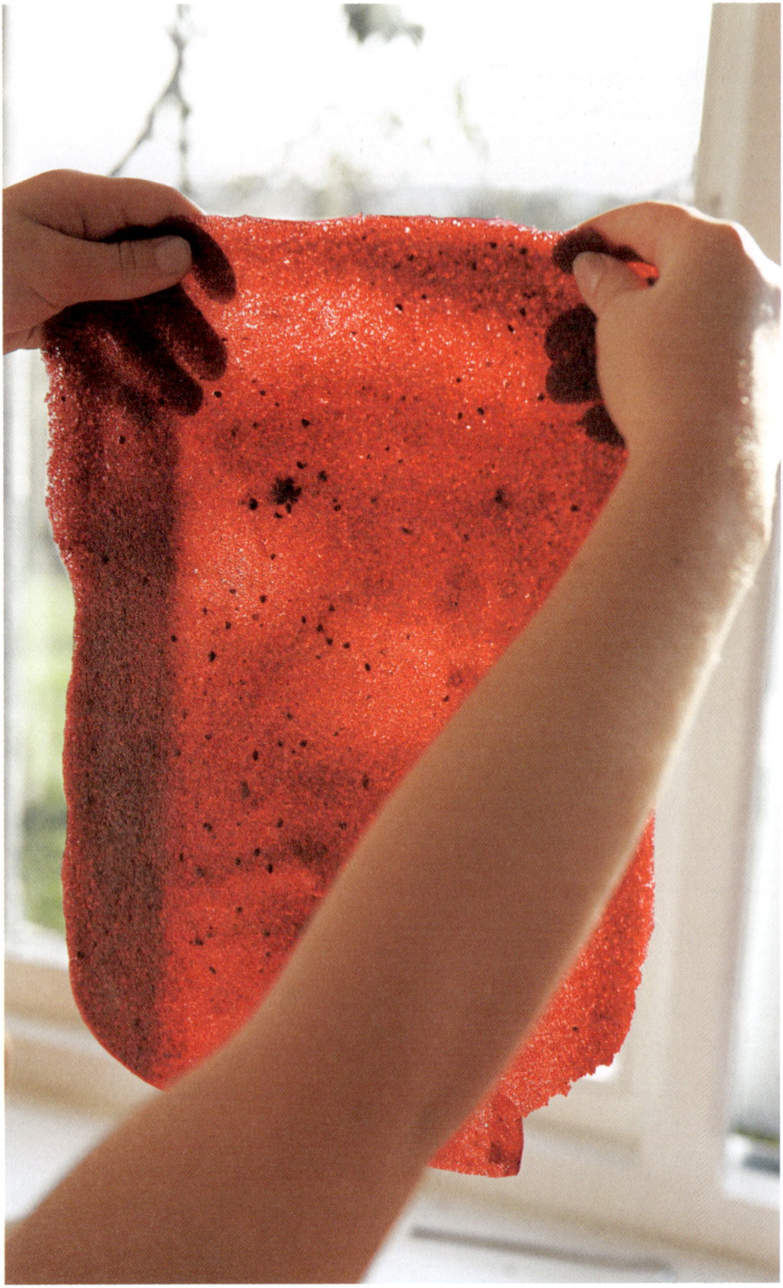

Blackberry and apple leather

Season: late August to September

Fruit leathers are thin, pliable sheets of dried, sweetened fruit purée with a flexible consistency exactly like leather. To be truthful, I had always avoided making them, thinking they sounded complicated. But, in a spirit of experimentation, I decided to try some out for this book. They were a revelation. I discovered how easy it is to create these strong, semi-transparent sheets, and how versatile they are. They are fun to use and eat – you can cut them, roll them, fold them and pack them away. Light and easy to carry, they're full of fruity energy, so great for lunch boxes or long walks. Snip off pieces to dissolve gently into fruit salads, or save them for the festive season when their translucent, jewel-like colours will look gorgeous on the Christmas tree.

Makes 2 sheets of 24 x 30cm
500g blackberries
500g peeled, cored and chopped cooking apples (2–3 large apples)
Juice of 1 lemon
150g honey

Preheat the oven to a very low setting – I use 60°C/Gas Mark ⅛ (approximately). Line two baking sheets, measuring about 24 x 30cm, with baking parchment.

Put the blackberries, apples and lemon juice into a pan. Cook gently until soft and pulpy, about 20 minutes. Rub the mixture through a sieve or mouli into a bowl; you should have about 700g smooth fruit purée. Add the honey and mix well.

Divide the purée between the two baking sheets. Spread it out lightly with the back of a spoon until the purée covers the sheets in a thin, even layer.

Put the baking sheets in the oven and leave for 12–18 hours, until the fruit purée is completely dry and peels off the parchment easily. Roll up the leather in greaseproof paper and store in an airtight tin. Use within 5 months.

Variations

There is no end to the possible variations here – you can turn any fruit into a leather. All you need do is create a smooth, thick purée with your chosen fruit before drying it out. Try plums, spicing the purée with a little cinnamon; or peaches, infusing them with a few honeysuckle blossoms as they cook. For a savoury leather use half and half apples and tomatoes seasoned with 2 tsp souper mix (see p.207) or celery salt.

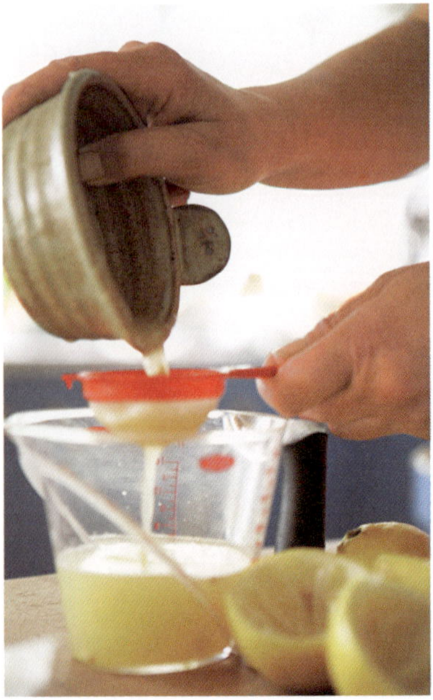

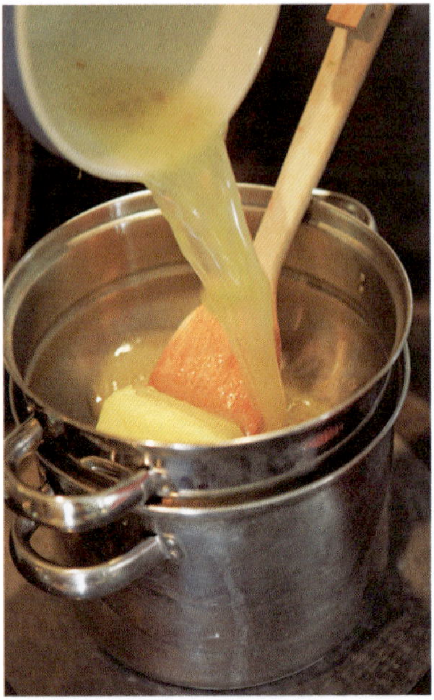

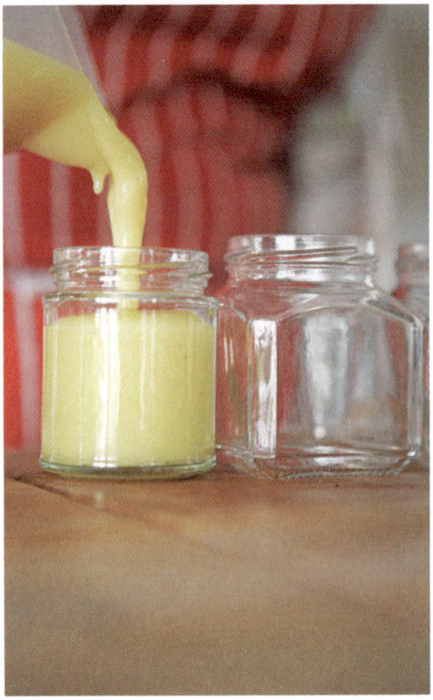

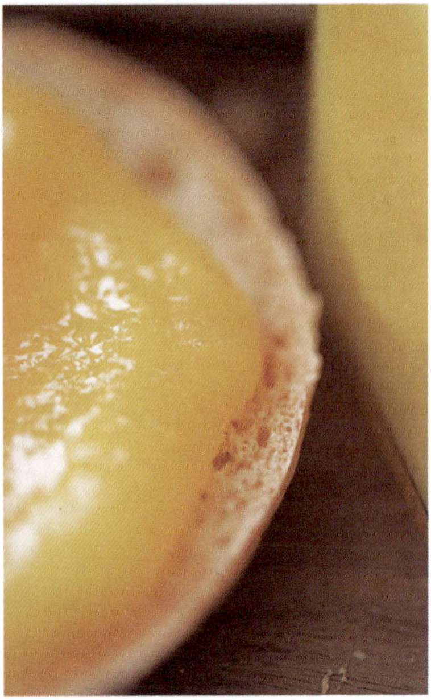

Bramley lemon curd

Season: late August to January

When I made preserves for a living, I tried all kinds of curds, from orange to passion fruit, but none of them was ever quite as popular as the good old-fashioned lemon variety. I didn't think I could improve on it until recently, when I came across an old recipe for an appley lemon curd. I tried it out and I now prefer it even to a classic straight lemon curd – it's like eating apples and custard: softly sweet, tangy and quite, quite delicious.

Makes 5 x 225g jars
450g Bramley apples, peeled, cored and chopped
Finely grated zest and juice of 2 unwaxed lemons (you need 100ml strained juice)
125g unsalted butter
450g granulated sugar
4–5 large eggs, well beaten (you need 200ml beaten egg)

Put the chopped apples into a pan with 100ml water and the lemon zest. Cook gently until soft and fluffy, then either beat to a purée with a wooden spoon or rub through a nylon sieve.

Put the butter, sugar, lemon juice and apple purée into a double boiler or heatproof bowl over a pan of simmering water. As soon as the butter has melted and the mixture is hot and glossy, pour in the eggs through a sieve, and whisk with a balloon whisk. If the fruit purée is too hot when the beaten egg is added, the egg will 'split'. One way to guard against this is to check the temperature of the purée with a sugar thermometer – it should be no higher than 55–60°C when the egg is added. If your curd does split, take the pan off the heat and whisk vigorously until smooth.

Stir the mixture over a gentle heat, scraping down the sides of the bowl every few minutes, until thick and creamy. This will take 9–10 minutes; the temperature should reach 82–84°C on a sugar thermometer. Immediately pour into warm, sterilised jars (see p.29) and seal (see p.30). Use within 4 weeks. Once opened, keep in the fridge.

Variations
To make gooseberry curd, replace the apples with gooseberries. If you'd like to go for a traditional, pure lemon curd, simply leave out the apples, increase the lemon juice to 200ml (4–5 lemons) and add the grated zest of 2–3 lemons.

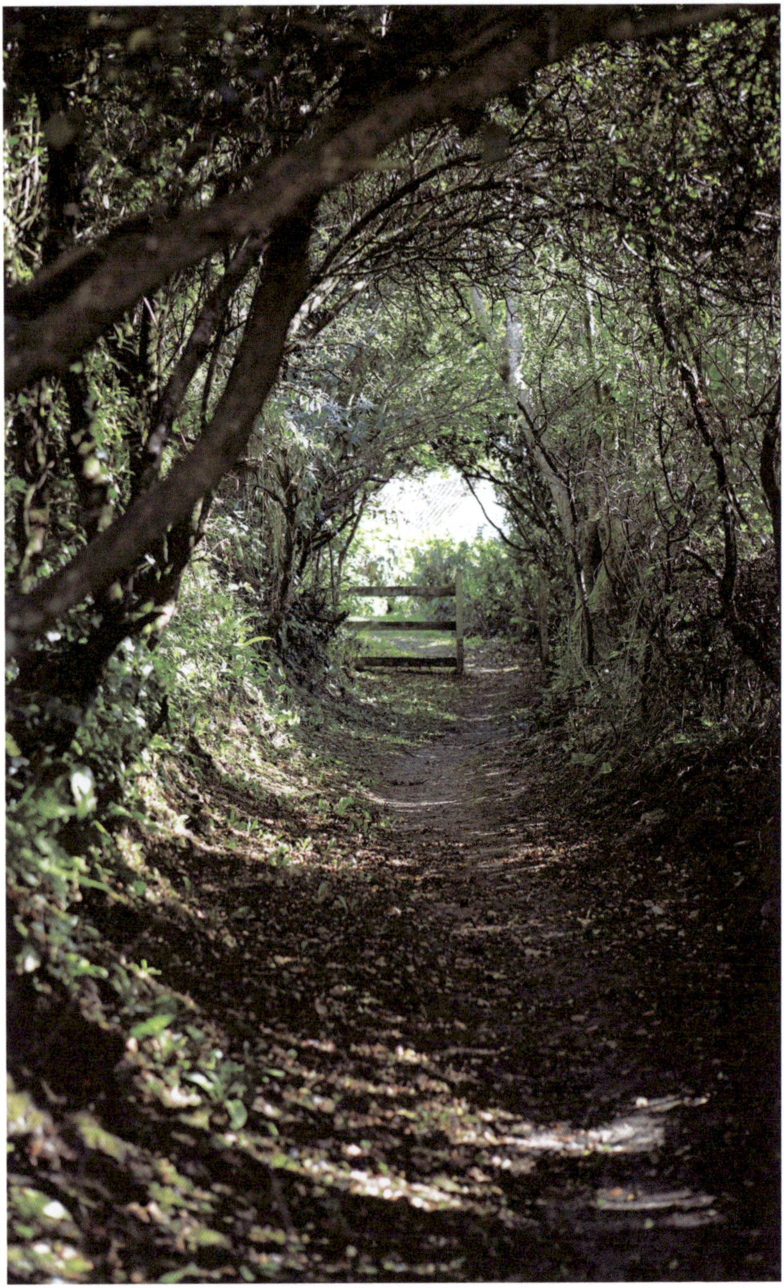

Hedgerow jelly

Season: September to October

The months of September and October allow us to reap the berried treasure of the hedgerows – a seasonal activity that is not without its dangers as many wild fruits are guarded by all sorts of thorns, prickles and entangling stems. However, with a little common sense and determination you should be able to overcome these country hurdles, and the basketful of fruit you bring home will be a just reward.

At the heart of all the best hedgerow jellies is the crab apple (*Malus sylvestris*). The pectin in this often scarred and scabby pomaceous fruit lends the setting power that many hedgerow berries lack. Crab apples produce a stunning pink jelly when used on their own, too.

For this recipe, you can use crab apples, sloes, bullaces, hips, haws, blackberries, elderberries or rowan berries. Usually, I go for about 50 per cent crab apples with a combination of two or three different berries. If I've gathered rosehips or rowan berries, however, I prefer to use them on their own, blended only with crab apple (see the variations overleaf).

Makes 7–8 x 225g jars
1kg crab apples (or cooking apples)
1kg mixed hedgerow berries (see above)
Around 900g granulated sugar

Pick over your fruit, removing stalks and leafy bits and rinsing the berries if necessary. Don't peel or core the apples (the peel and core are an excellent source of pectin), just chop them roughly. Place all the prepared fruit in a saucepan with 1.2 litres water. Bring gently to simmering point and simmer until all the fruit is soft and pulpy. Remove from the heat.

Have ready a scalded jelly bag or muslin cloth (see p.41) and turn the contents of the pan into it. Leave to drip overnight. The jelly will turn cloudy if you squeeze the juice through so just let it drip at its own pace.

The next day, measure the juice – you will probably have about 1.2 litres, though this will depend on the berries used. For every 600ml juice, allow 450g sugar. Put the juice into a large pan and bring slowly to the boil. Add the sugar as it just comes to the boil and keep stirring until the sugar has dissolved. Then boil rapidly, without stirring, for 9–10 minutes until setting point is reached (see p.49). Skim the jelly and pot and seal as quickly as possible (see p.30). Use within 12 months.

Variations

These are some of my favourite takes on the hedgerow jelly idea. In each case, follow the hedgerow jelly method and quantities (on the previous page); i.e. always use 450g sugar to each 600ml strained fruit juice.

Spicy crab apple jelly Use crab apples alone and add a few cloves and a couple of cinnamon sticks when the fruit is being cooked. This all-time classic hedgerow jelly is equally at home on thinly sliced hot buttered toast or as an accompaniment to succulent cold roast pork or turkey.

Rosehip and apple jelly Use 500g rosehips, first blitzed in a food processor, and 1.5kg crab or cooking apples. Excellent with roast pork.

Rowan jelly Use 1kg rowan berries and 1kg crab apples. Add the juice of 1 lemon before adding the sugar. For a really aromatic jelly, add a bunch of sage or thyme when the fruit is softening. Rowan jelly is lovely served with game.

Blackberry and apple jelly Use 1kg blackberries and 1kg apples. This is a nostalgic teatime treat for me, as I remember how good my grandmother's blackberry and apple jelly always tasted on wafer-thin slices of bread and butter.

P.S. Hedgerow jelly, or any other well-coloured jelly, can be used as a natural colouring for glacé icing. Just a teaspoonful or two will be sufficient to give your icing a wickedly deep hue that will be sure to liven up your cakes.

JAMS & JELLIES 79

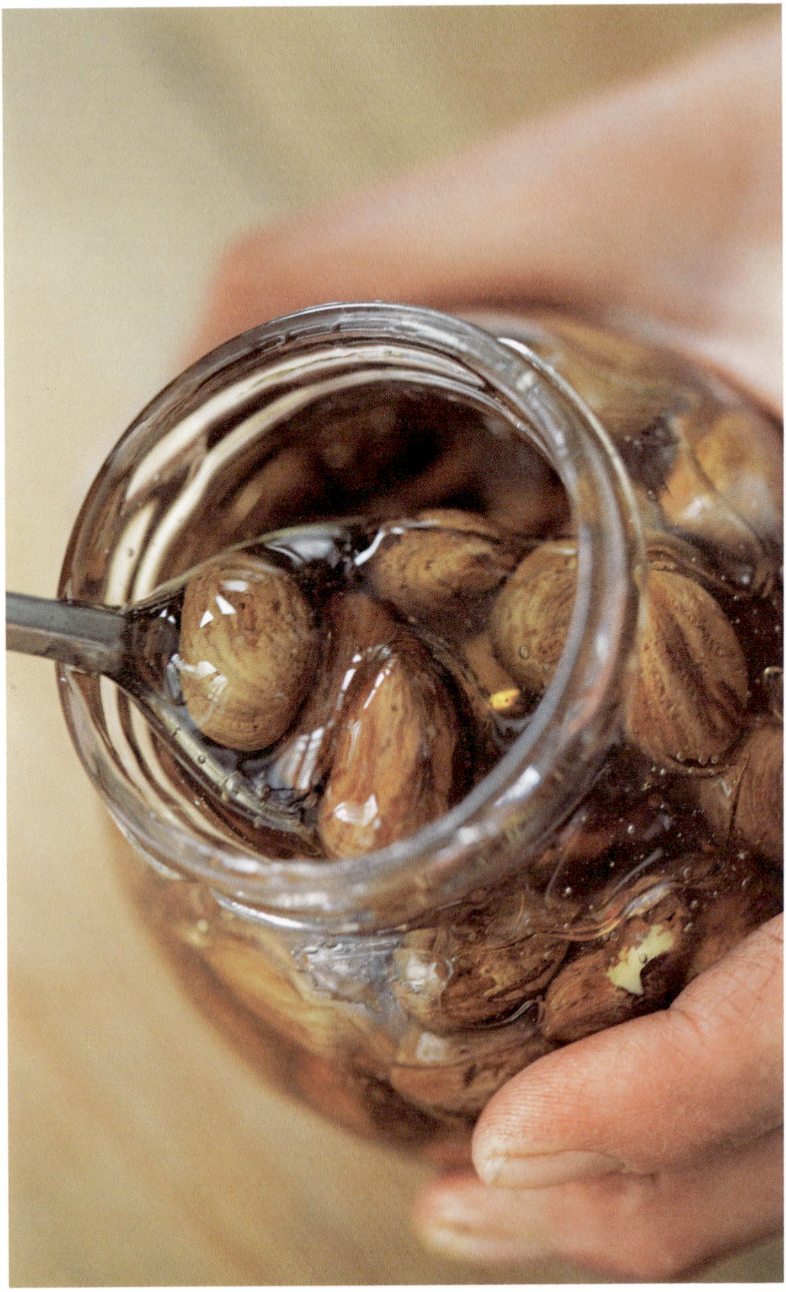

Honeyed hazels

Season: September

You've got to be quick to beat the squirrels to the hazelnuts each autumn. Once you've managed to find some, it's important to store them carefully. Even with their shells on, they have a tendency to dry out and shrivel up, but preserving them in honey will keep them fresh and fragrant for ages. Use wild hazels that you have gathered yourself, or British-grown cobnuts – which are simply a cultivated form of hazelnut.

Spoon your honeyed hazels over plain yoghurt, chocolate ice cream, porridge or muesli. They're also delicious as a topping for a steamed sponge pudding.

Makes 2 x 225g jars
500g hazelnuts or cobnuts
340g clear honey

Start by inviting your friends round for a nut-cracking evening (they'll come the first year, but maybe not the next). Crack all the nuts and remove the kernels.

Heat a frying pan over a low heat. Toast the shelled nuts in batches for 4–5 minutes, jiggling and shaking the pan to make sure they don't burn. Remove from the heat and allow to cool.

Pack the nuts into sterilised jars (see p.29), adding 1 tbsp honey at every third or fourth layer. Continue until the jars are chock-a-block full, making sure that the nuts are well covered in honey. Seal securely with a lid and store in a cool, dry, dark place. Use within 12 months.

P.S. 'Clear' honey is runny while 'set' honey is thick and opaque, but apart from this there is no real difference between the two types – it's just down to the feeding ground for the bees. Borage honey, a speciality of east Yorkshire, is one of the clearest honeys you will ever come across, whereas clover honey is favoured for its creamy thick texture and floral flavour. All honey, with the exception of heather honey, will eventually become cloudy as a result of the natural process of crystallisation. If you find this happens and you want your honey to be runny again, then just stand the jar in a bowl of hot water for a few minutes until it is liquid honey again.

Plum and russet mincemeat

Season: September to October

The term 'mincemeat' originated in the fifteenth century, when chopped meat was preserved with a combination of dried fruit, sugar and aromatic spices. During the seventeenth century, beef or lamb suet replaced the meat and has been used ever since – with vegetarian 'suet' a more recent option. This recipe is a departure on several fronts: it uses fresh fruit as well as dried, and contains no suet. In fact, it contains very little fat (only the oil in the walnuts). The result is light and fruity, but with all the rich, warm spiciness of a traditional mincemeat.

Makes 4 x 450g jars

1kg plums
Finely grated zest and juice of 2–3 oranges (you need 200ml juice)
500g russet apples, peeled, cored and chopped into 1cm cubes
200g currants
200g raisins
200g sultanas
100g orange marmalade
250g demerara sugar
½ tsp ground cloves
2 tsp ground ginger
½ nutmeg, grated
50ml ginger wine or cordial (optional)
100g chopped walnuts
50ml brandy or sloe gin

Wash the plums, halve and remove the stones, then put into a saucepan with the orange juice. Cook gently until tender, about 15 minutes. Blend to a purée in a liquidiser or push through a sieve. You should end up with about 700ml plum purée.

Put the purée into a large bowl and add all the other ingredients, except the brandy or gin. Mix thoroughly, then cover and leave to stand for 12 hours.

Preheat the oven to 130°C/Gas Mark ½. Put the mincemeat in a large baking dish and bake, uncovered, for 2–2½ hours. Stir in the brandy or gin, then spoon into warm, sterilised jars (see p.29), making sure there aren't any air pockets. Seal (see p.30) and store in a dry, dark, cool place until Christmas. Use within 12 months.

Variations

You can vary this recipe, but keep the fresh fruit purée to around 700ml and the total amount of dried fruit to 600g. For an apple, pear and ginger mincemeat, replace the plums with Bramley apples, the russet apples with firm pears, and 100g of the raisins or sultanas with 100g crystallised stem ginger. You could also exchange the walnuts for almonds and add a couple of teaspoonfuls of ground cinnamon.

JAMS & JELLIES

Quince cheese

Season: late September to October

A fruit cheese is simply a solid, sliceable preserve – and the princely quince, with its exquisite scent and delicately grainy texture, makes the most majestic one of all. It can be potted in small moulds to turn out, slice and eat with cheese. Alternatively, you can pour it into shallow trays to set, then cut it into cubes, coat with sugar and serve as a sweetmeat.

A little roughly chopped quince cheese adds a delicious fruity note to lamb stews or tagines – or try combining it with chopped apple for a pie or crumble.

Makes about 1kg
1kg quince
500–750g granulated sugar
Food-grade paraffin wax, for sealing
(see the directory, p.210)

Wash the quince. Roughly chop the fruit but don't peel or core them. Place in a large pan and barely cover with water. Bring to a simmer and cook until soft and pulpy, adding a little more water if necessary. Leave to stand for several hours.

Rub the contents of the pan through a sieve or pass through a mouli. Weigh the pulp and return it to the cleaned-out pan, adding an equal weight of sugar. Bring gently to the boil, stirring until the sugar has dissolved, then simmer gently, stirring frequently, for an hour and a bit until really thick and glossy. It may bubble and spit like a volcano, so do take care. The mixture is ready when it is so thick that you can scrape a spoon through it and see the base of the pan for a couple of seconds before the mixture oozes together again.

If you're using small dishes or straight-sided jars, brush them with a little glycerine (see the directory). This will make it easy to turn out the cheese. If you're using a shallow baking tray or similar, line it with greaseproof paper, allowing plenty of overhang to wrap the finished cheese.

When the cheese is cooked, pour it into the prepared moulds or jars. To seal open moulds, pour melted food-grade paraffin wax over the hot fruit cheese. Jars can be sealed with lids. Cheese set in a shallow tray should be covered with greaseproof paper and kept in the fridge.

For optimum flavour, allow the quince cheese to mature for 4–6 weeks before using. Eat within 12 months.

JAMS & JELLIES 85

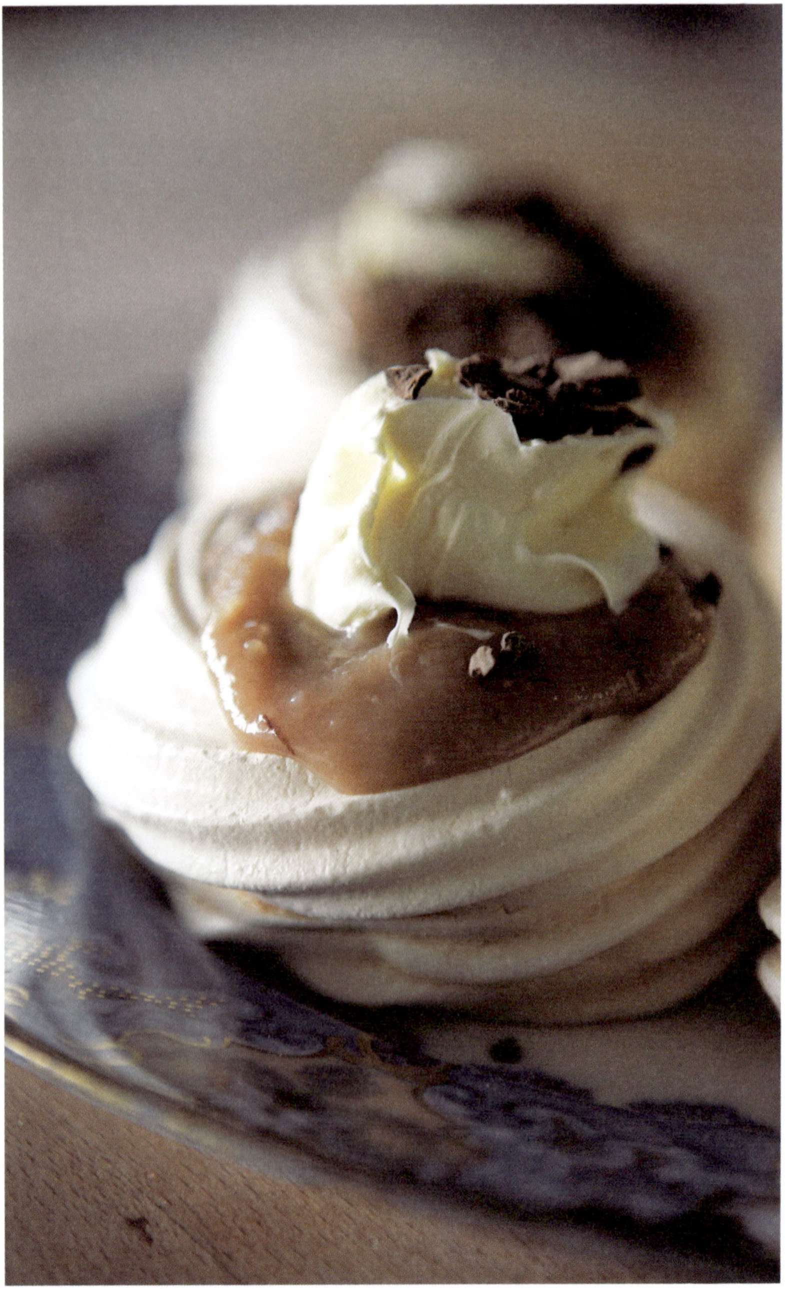

Melissa's chestnut jam

Season: October to December

I first made this deliciously sweet preserve while staying at a farm on Dartmoor. Melissa, who lived at the farm, came to help with the laborious job of peeling the chestnuts, and we whipped through them in no time. The addition of honey to the jam seemed entirely appropriate, since that's what 'Melissa' means in Greek.

I like to spoon chestnut jam into meringue nests and top with cream. Or stir a spoonful or two into chocolate mousse, or dollop on to vanilla ice cream before drizzling with hot chocolate sauce. This preserve also makes a lovely filling for chocolate cakes, and of course, it can be enjoyed simply spread on crusty bread.

Makes 5 x 225g jars
1kg sweet chestnuts
400g granulated sugar
1 tsp vanilla paste or extract
100g honey
50ml brandy

The first task is to remove the leathery shells and skin from the chestnuts. Use a sharp knife to make a knick in the top of each chestnut. Plunge them into a pan of boiling water for 2–3 minutes – sufficient time to soften the shell but not to let the nuts get piping hot and difficult to handle. Remove the pan from the heat. Fish out half a dozen or so chestnuts and peel off their coats. With luck, the thin brown skin under the shell will peel away too. Continue in this way until all are peeled.

Put the chestnuts into a clean pan and just cover with water. Bring to the boil and simmer for 25–30 minutes, or until tender. Strain, but keep the cooking liquid.

Purée the chestnuts with 100ml of the cooking liquid in a food processor or using a stick blender.

Pour a further 100ml of the cooking liquid into a pan and add the sugar. Heat gently until dissolved. Add the chestnut purée, vanilla paste and honey. Stir until well blended. Bring to the boil then cook gently for 5–10 minutes until well thickened. Take care, as it will pop and splutter and may spit. Remove from the heat and stir in the brandy. Pour into warm, sterilised jars (see p.29) and seal immediately (see p.30). Use within 6 months. Store in the fridge once opened.

88 PRESERVES

Candied orange sticks

Season: any time

I like to make several batches of these sweetmeats in November or early December. A dozen or so, wrapped in cellophane, are a charming gift. Needless to say, you don't need to stop at oranges: lemon and grapefruit peel work equally well and you can use milk, plain or white chocolate for dipping. The glucose syrup is optional, but does prevent the sticks becoming too hard. It is best to keep the candied sticks in an airtight container and only dip them in chocolate when you want them.

Makes about 100 sticks
4–5 large oranges
500g granulated sugar
1 tbsp glucose syrup (optional)
200g good plain chocolate

Scrub the oranges then remove the peel in quarters. To do this, cut through the peel with a sharp knife, going right round the orange, starting and finishing at the stalk, then repeat, at right angles to the first cut. Remove the peel, with the attached pith, from the fruit. Weigh out 250g peel and cut it into slices, about 6mm x 5cm.

Put the orange peel slices into a large pan and cover with 2 litres of cold water. Bring to the boil and simmer for 5 minutes. Drain and return to the pan with 1 litre of cold water. Bring to the boil and simmer, covered, for 45 minutes. Add the sugar and stir until dissolved (it won't take long). Simmer, covered, for 30 minutes. Remove from the heat and leave to stand for 24 hours.

Bring the pan to the boil again. Add the glucose syrup if using and boil gently, uncovered, for 30 minutes or until all the liquid has evaporated and the orange sticks are coated with bubbling orange syrup. Remove from the heat and allow to cool. Using a pair of tongs (or your fingers), carefully remove the orange sticks and place on a wire rack (with a tray underneath to catch the drips). Leave in a warm place, such as an airing cupboard, for 24 hours, or place in a very low oven at approximately 60°C/Gas Mark ⅛ for 2–3 hours to dry.

Break the chocolate into pieces, put into a heatproof bowl over a pan of simmering water and leave until melted. Remove from the heat. Dip one half of each orange stick in the melted chocolate and place on a sheet of greaseproof paper to dry.

Before dipping, the sticks will keep well for 3–4 months. Once they have their chocolate coating, they are best eaten within 3 weeks.

Cider apple butter

Season: September to November

Autumn is the season for apples. For centuries, the apple crop has been important and the apple tree cherished and celebrated for its fruit. Wassailing is a West Country tradition when, on Twelfth Night of old (17 January), country folk toast and drink the health of the largest and most prolific apple tree in the orchard for a healthy, fruitful crop the coming season.

The sharp and bittersweet qualities of cider gives this old-fashioned apple butter a special flavour. It's a sensational fruity spread to daub over hot buttered toast or crumpets.

Makes 5–6 x 225g jars
1.5kg cooking apples
600ml dry or medium cider
Granulated sugar
½ tsp ground cloves
½ tsp ground cinnamon

There is no need to peel or core the apples. However, if you are using windfalls (and this is a very good recipe in which to do so), cut away any damaged or bruised bits. Chop the apples into fairly big pieces (each into about 8). Place in a large pan with the cider and 600ml water. Cook gently until soft, then remove from the heat.

Push the apple mixture through a nylon sieve or use a mouli to reduce it to a purée. Weigh the fruit pulp and return it to the cleaned-out pan, adding 340g sugar for every 600ml fruit pulp. Add the cloves and cinnamon. Slowly bring to the boil, stirring until the sugar has dissolved, then boil rapidly for 10–15 minutes until the mixture begins to splutter and is thick and creamy.

Remove from the heat and pour immediately into warm, sterilised jars (see p.29) (it's best to use small jars as this low-sugar preserve has a relatively short shelf life, once opened). Seal immediately (see p.30). Use within 12 months. Store in the fridge once opened.

Variation

Blackberries make a beautiful fruit butter. Follow the above method using 1kg ripe blackberries, 500g cored and peeled cooking apples and 100ml lemon juice; allow 300g sugar for every 600ml fruit pulp.

Compost heap jelly

Season: any time

This is a wonderful, frugal recipe that complements some of the other fruity preserves in the book because it uses the apple scraps and citrus skins that would normally be destined for the compost heap or bin. These skins are full of flavour and rich in pectin, so it's a shame not to use them. For the cost of a bag of sugar (and a bit of your time) you can transform them into a really fruity, marmalade-flavoured jelly. It functions nicely as an emergency breakfast preserve when your last jar of marmalade has been eaten and the seasonal Sevilles haven't yet arrived in the shops.

Makes 3 x 225g jars
500g apple cores and peel
500g citrus fruit peel (unwaxed lemon, orange, grapefruit and/or lime), cut into roughly 1cm shreds

Granulated sugar
Juice of 1 orange, lemon or grapefruit (optional)

Put the apple cores and peel and the citrus peel into a saucepan. Add sufficient water to cover (you'll probably need about 1.5 litres). Bring to a simmer and cook slowly for 45–60 minutes – this softens the fruit and releases the valuable pectin. Turn the fruit into a scalded jelly bag or muslin (see p.41) and leave overnight to drip.

Measure the strained liquid and weigh 450g sugar for every 600ml juice. Return the juice to the pan and add the orange, lemon or grapefruit juice, if using. Bring to the boil, then add the sugar. Stir until dissolved then boil rapidly, without stirring, until setting point is reached (see p.49), about 10 minutes or so.

Remove from the heat and stir, always going in the same direction, until all the surface bubbles have disappeared. Pour into warm, sterilised jars (see p.29) and either swivel or tap the side of the jars to remove any remaining bubbles. Seal in the usual way (see p.30). Use within 12 months.

Pickles, Chutneys & Relishes

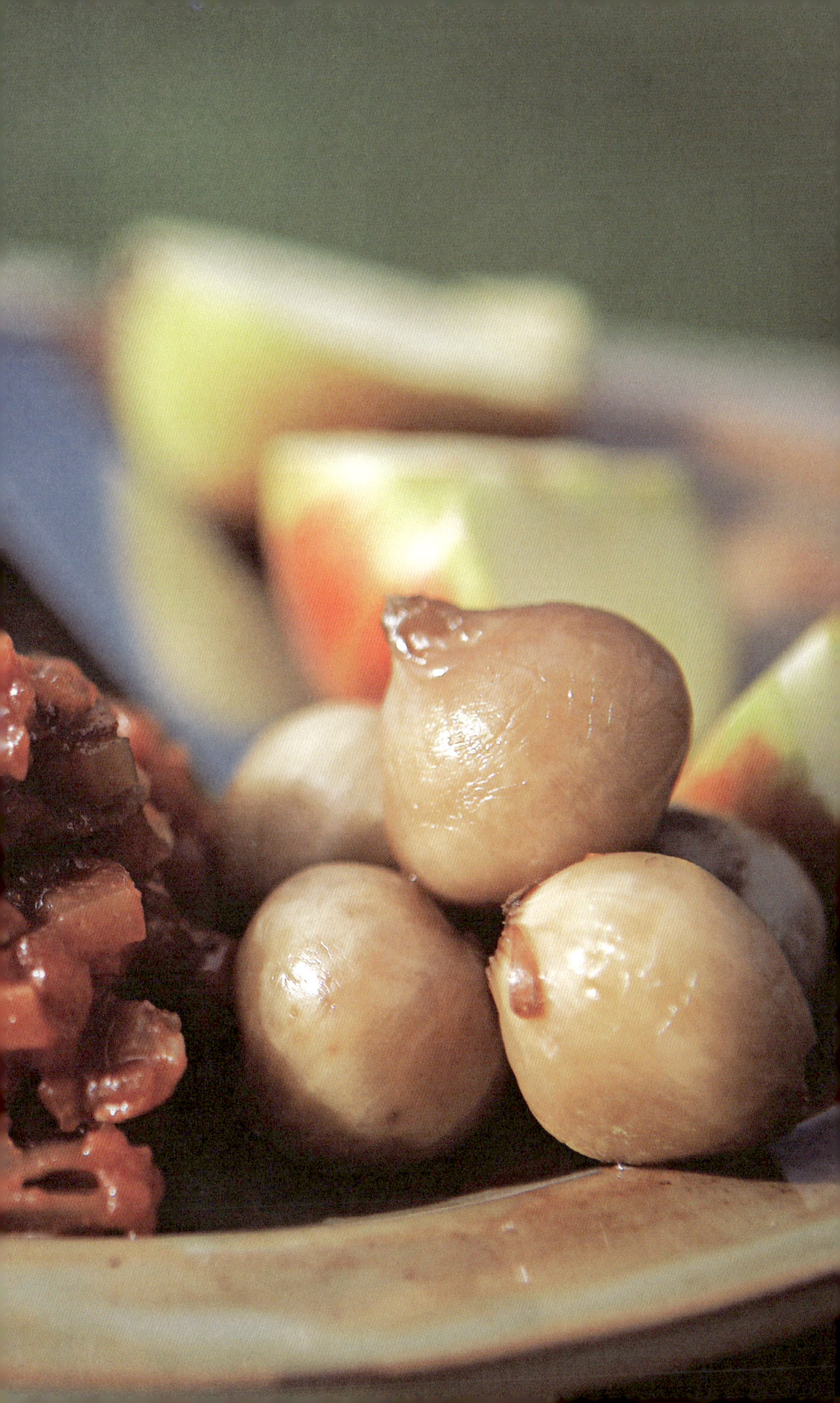

Time for vinegar vapours

to fill the air! This chapter is a little sharper than the last one – and full of recipes that feature piquancy, bite and spice. These sweet/sour preserves are generally inexpensive and easy to make. There are only a few guidelines to follow – you don't have to worry about pectin or acid, for instance, as in jam-making. Their uses extend far beyond cold meat and ploughman's lunches. They can be stirred into soups, added to meaty stews, curries or tagines, served with smoked or marinated fish and, of course, combined with other ingredients to make great sandwiches and picnic food. No home should be without them!

Often lumped together, pickles, chutneys and relishes are actually distinctly different and not prepared in the same way:

Clear pickles These are an age-old British way of preserving vegetables or fruit, which are usually left raw or only lightly cooked, and kept whole or in large pieces. Pickles rely predominately on vinegar and salt for keepability though sugar, honey, spices and herbs can all be added for extra flavour. After salting (see p.96), the ingredients are rinsed and drained before being packed into jars and fully covered with plain or spiced vinegar. Pickled onions are the classic example of this type of preserve.

Sweet pickles Made from fruits and vegetables, again in relatively large pieces, lightly cooked in sweetened vinegar, these are often flavoured with spices such as ginger, cloves and allspice. In some recipes – piccalilli, for instance – the vinegar syrup is thickened with cornflour to make a light sauce. The cooked produce is packed in warm jars and the vinegar syrup reduced and poured over the fruit to cover.

Chutneys We learnt about chutney-making from our Indian colonies in the nineteenth century, and authentic Indian chutneys are usually fresh preparations served with spicy foods. The British interpretation of a chutney is rather different: rich, highly spiced, sweet-sharp preserves, based on vegetables and fruit which are chopped small and cooked for a long time to create a spoonable consistency and mellow flavour. They often feature dried fruit too, which contributes natural sugar and textural contrast.

Relishes Somewhere between pickles and chutneys, these are made from diced or chunkily cut fruit and vegetables but they are cooked for a shorter time than a chutney. They can be spicy, sweet, sour (or all three), may be eaten soon after making and should be kept in the fridge once opened.

PICKLES, CHUTNEYS & RELISHES 95

Essential ingredients

Pickles and chutneys customarily rely on vinegar or a mix of vinegar, salt and/or sugar to preserve tender, young vegetables and fruit. Highly flavoured spices or herbs are added to augment the final flavour, but their often fiery potency will mellow as the preserve matures.

Salt

This plays a very important role in pickling and chutney-making and, indeed, can be used as the sole preservative, as in preserved lemons (p.126). However, it's more usually employed as a general flavour enhancer, and in the preparation of vegetables and fruit prior to pickling. It may be sprinkled straight on to the ingredients (this is known as dry-salting) or made into a brine (wet-salting) in which the ingredients are immersed and left for 12–24 hours. The salt firms up the vegetables and removes excess water which would otherwise dilute the vinegar and cause the pickle to turn mouldy. Dry-salting is ideal for watery vegetables such as cucumbers and marrows, and for very crisp pickles, whereas brine is less harsh and can be used for less juicy produce. A fine-grained salt is essential for dry-salting as it will adhere closely to the surface of the ingredient, but any good-quality salt can be used in a brine. See p.38 for more information on different types of salt.

> **To make brine** For a good all-purpose brine, allow 50g salt to 600ml water (a lighter brine is more appropriate for small ingredients such as nasturtium seeds). Simply dissolve the salt in the water and the brine is ready to use. The prepared ingredients should be covered with the brine and left overnight or for up to 24 hours, before being drained, dried, packed and pickled in jars. Many old recipes call for the brine to be 'strong enough to float an egg'; you will find this ratio will do just that.

> **To dry-salt** Layer your cut-up vegetables on a shallow dish, sprinkling fine salt between each layer. As in brining, the vegetables are left overnight or for up to 24 hours. After a few hours, you will see water being drawn from the vegetables. After salting, the ingredients need to be rinsed in very cold water (to keep them crisp), drained well and patted dry before being pickled.

Vinegar

Your pickles and chutneys will only be as good as the vinegar you use. If vinegar is the main preserving ingredient, as in most of the following recipes, it's important to use a good-quality variety with at least 5 per cent acetic acid content (you should find this information on the bottle). Beyond that, there are no hard and fast rules as to the type of vinegar you should go for – it's very much a matter of taste (see p.37 for more information on different types). However, in general, a translucent vinegar gives a better appearance in a clear pickle.

The vinegar used for pickling is almost always spiced. You can buy ready-spiced 'pickling vinegars', commonly based on malt vinegar. However, I prefer to make my own at home, so I can choose the type of vinegar and the precise spice mix.

Spices

These are essential to give fiery bite, flavour and aroma to pickles and chutneys. Whole spices are used for pickles – ground ones produce a cloudy result – but either whole or freshly ground spices can be used for chutneys. Whole spices should be tied in a muslin bag or enclosed in a tea or spice infuser (see the directory, p.210) so they can be easily removed after cooking.

To make a muslin spice bag, cut a piece of muslin, about 20cm square, put the spices in a heap in the middle and gather up the edges of the muslin to form a little sack. Tie the bag with string so that the spices are loosely but securely held in.

A traditional pickling spice blend can be bought ready-mixed but you'll get a much fresher flavour if you make up your own – I generally combine equal quantities of cinnamon stick, whole cloves, mace blades, whole allspice and a few peppercorns and allow 15–30g of this mix for every 1 litre of vinegar. I like to add a good tablespoonful of demerara sugar and a couple of fresh bay leaves when I brew up the spice. The mix can be kept in an airtight jar for at least a year and used as required. Other spices such as bruised root ginger, fresh or dried chillies, and fennel, dill or celery seeds can also be added to bring a different range of flavours to your pickles.

Always check the sell-by date on your spices and be ruthless about getting rid of any that are past their best. Once they reach a certain age, they'll lose the aroma and flavour you need. If you are using ground spice in a recipe, it is always worth taking the time to grind your own because, once ground, spices lose their pungency amazingly quickly. Give whole spices a light toasting in a dry frying pan then grind as finely as possible in a pestle and mortar, or a spice or coffee grinder. Prepare the spices in small quantities and don't keep the mix for more than a week or two.

Vegetables and fruit

These ingredients, which will make up the bulk and body of your preserve, should be young, firm and as fresh as possible. Almost any produce can be used, though soft berries are generally better in jams and jellies. I've made pickles and chutneys with just about everything else! Apples, gooseberries, pears, plums, marrows and tomatoes (ripe or green) form the base of most chutneys. For most recipes they should be peeled, washed and well drained, before being chopped, diced or left whole. Cut away any bruised or damaged flesh – this will not improve your pickles.

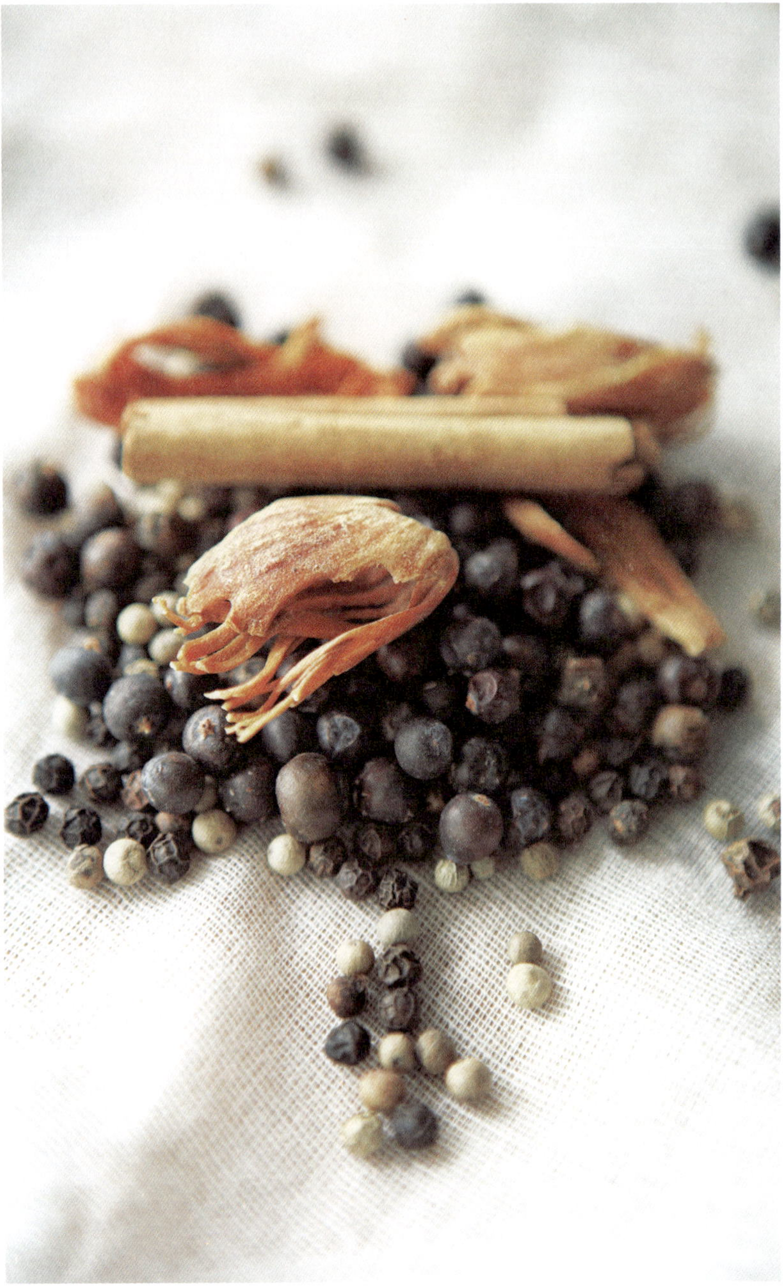

Making perfect pickles

Pickles are very easy to make and their success relies quite simply on good preparation of the raw ingredients, a well-spiced vinegar and an adequate maturing period.

1. After brining or salting your prepared fruit or vegetables, rinse and drain them well.

2. To prevent bruising, don't pack the produce too tightly into the jars.

3. Pack in an attractive way to within 2.5cm of the top of the jar, leaving enough room for the contents to be completely covered with vinegar.

4. Always use sterilised jars (see p.29) and vinegar-proof lids (see the directory, p.210).

5. Use cold vinegar for crisp pickles and hot vinegar if a softer texture is required.

6. Store your pickles in a cool, dark, dry place and leave them for at least 4 weeks before using.

Making perfect chutneys

Don't rush your chutney-making, for a good chutney will take several hours to make. The end result will be more than worthy of the time you've spent.

1. Use a stainless-steel pan and wooden spoon – other materials may react with the vinegar and cause discoloration.

2. Cut fruit and vegetables into small, even-sized pieces – this is time-consuming but really crucial in achieving a good final texture.

3. Long, slow cooking in an open pan is essential for the chutney to become rich, smooth and mellow.

4. Towards the end of cooking, stir frequently so the chutney doesn't catch on the bottom of the pan.

5. The chutney has reached the right consistency when you can draw a wooden spoon across the bottom of the pan and see a clear line for a few seconds before the chutney comes together again.

6. Fill jars to within 5mm of the top and cover with vinegar-proof lids. Badly covered chutney will dry out and shrink in the jar.

7. Store chutneys in a cool, dark, dry place and leave to mature for at least 8 weeks before using.

Spring rhubarb relish

Season: May to July

Made with the reddish-green stalks of maincrop or 'field' rhubarb, this is quick and easy, involving much less cooking than a chutney would require. It is light, very fruity, and not too sweet. Delicious with curries, oily fish, chicken, cheese and in sandwiches, you'll find it's a versatile addition to the larder.

Rhubarb, by the way, is very easy to prepare but do take care to always remove the leaves as they are poisonous.

Makes 4 x 340g jars
500g granulated sugar
100ml cider vinegar
1kg rhubarb (untrimmed weight)
125g raisins

For the spice bag
50g fresh root ginger, bruised
2 cinnamon sticks, snapped in half
6 cloves

First make your spice bag by tying up the bruised ginger, cinnamon sticks and cloves in a 20cm square of muslin.

Put the sugar, vinegar, 100ml water and the spice bag into a preserving pan. Heat gently to dissolve the sugar and allow the spices to release their flavours into the syrup. Remove from the heat and set aside to infuse for about 20 minutes.

Meanwhile, trim and wipe the rhubarb stalks and chop into 2–2.5cm chunks.

Add the rhubarb and raisins to the spiced syrup. Cook gently for 15–20 minutes until the mixture is thick, but the rhubarb is still discernible as soft chunks. Remove from the heat, pour into warm, sterilised jars (see p.29) and seal with vinegar-proof lids. Use within 12 months.

P.S. To bruise the root ginger for the spice bag, simply whack it gently with a rolling pin or similar blunt object.

Variation

Gooseberries will stand in quite readily for the rhubarb in this recipe. For the spice bag try using a mix of traditional Indian spices: 1 tsp mustard seeds and ½ tsp each of fennel, cumin, nigella and fenugreek seeds.

Chilli pepper jelly

Season: late summer to autumn

The beauty of this recipe is that it is so very simple. Moreover, you can turn up the heat or cool it down to suit your mood by the variety of the chilli pepper you use. Increasingly, these fiery fleshy fruits are being produced by specialist growers in this country (see the directory, p.210). Look out in the late summer and autumn for hot fruity Habanero, rich mild Poblano, tiny hot Thai chillies or flaming Jalapeños to use in this sizzling jelly relish. I like to use red bell peppers, as they are symbolic of the heat, but of course there's no reason why you can't use yellow, orange or green, or a mixture of all four.

Use this punchy jelly relish with cream cheese, smoked mackerel, rice dishes and crispy stir-fried veg.

Makes 4 x 340g jars
750g red bell peppers
100g Jalapeño or other chillies
50g fresh root ginger, peeled
350ml cider vinegar

1kg sugar with added pectin
50ml lime juice (1–2 limes)
1 level tsp salt

Start by slicing both peppers and chillies in half lengthwise and removing the fibrous tissue and countless seeds. Finely chop the peppers, chillies and root ginger or blitz them in a food processor. Place in a large pan, add the vinegar and slowly bring to simmering point. Add the sugar, lime juice and salt, stirring until the sugar has dissolved and the mixture begins to boil.

Boil for 4–6 minutes and then remove from the heat. Allow to cool for 5 minutes, then pour into clean, sterilised jars (see p.29) and seal with vinegar-proof lids. Use within 12 months.

P.S. If you find the pepper pieces rise to the top of the jar as you pot the jelly, leave until the jars are at room temperature, then give them a quick twist – the pepper pieces will redistribute and remain well suspended in the cooling jelly.

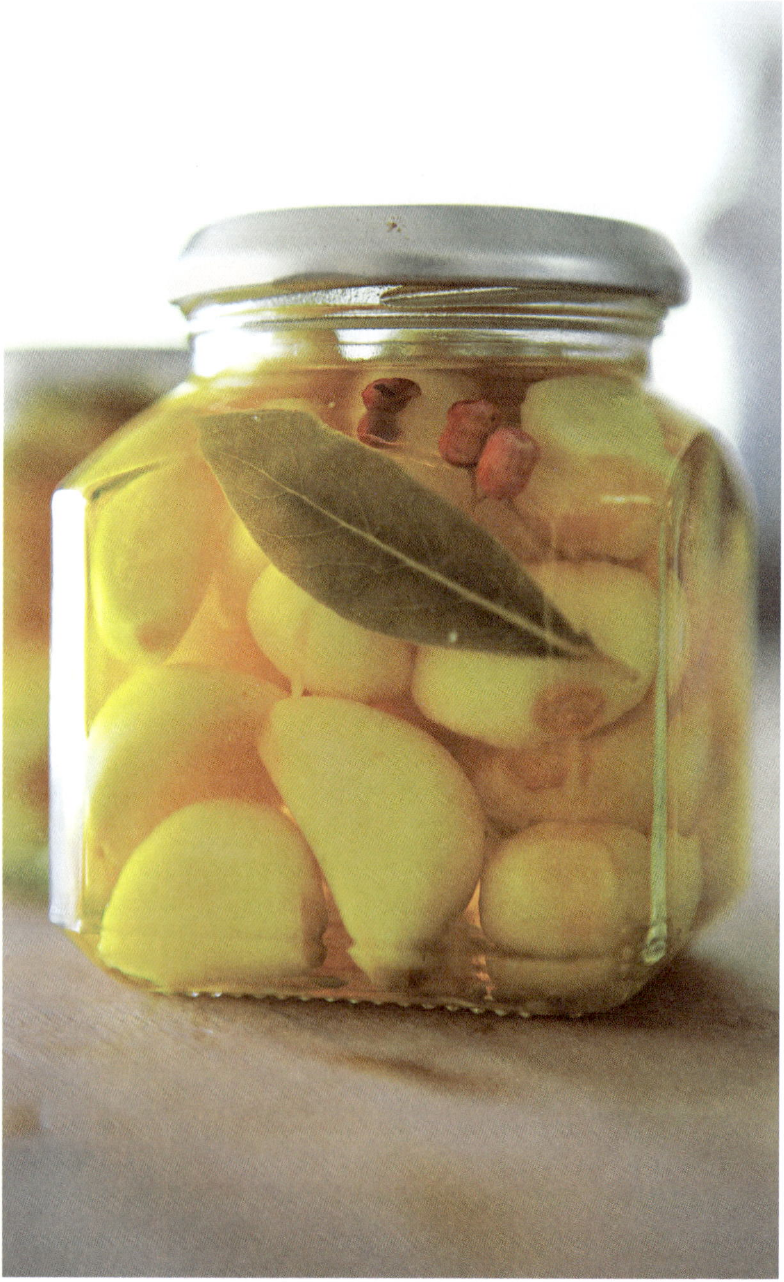

Pickled garlic

Season: May to August

Garlic is the strongest-tasting of the *Allium* family, and the moodiest too. It can change character considerably, depending on how it is treated. Left whole and cooked slowly, it is gentle and soft. Chopped up, it will release a little more of its pungent aroma, while crushed to a paste it attains the strong, sometimes bitter flavour that makes it notorious.

When pickled, it remains crisp to the bite, but the flavour becomes really quite mellow – you can eat the cloves straight from the jar. I like to slice the pickled garlic cloves finely and scatter them over salads, or serve them whole as antipasti, or nestle lots of them around a slowly roasting joint of lamb.

Garlic grows well throughout Britain – not just in the veg patch, but also in containers, tubs and even in flower borders, where it can help ward off invasive greenfly. New season's bulbs, with their soft white or purplish-pink skins, are mild and sweet – and much better for pickling than older, drier-skinned garlic, which can be bitter.

Makes 3 x 225g jars
500g new season's garlic bulbs
1 tsp fennel seeds
About 12 peppercorns (black, white or pink)
4–6 bay leaves
200ml cider vinegar
50g granulated sugar
Good pinch of saffron strands

Bring a large pan of water to the boil. Plunge in the garlic for a mere minute, to help loosen the outer skins. Remove from the water, drain and pat dry.

Have ready three warm, sterilised jars (see p.29). Break the garlic bulbs into individual cloves. Peel each clove and pack them into the jars, dropping in the fennel seeds, peppercorns and bay leaves as you go.

Put the vinegar, sugar and saffron into a pan. Bring to the boil and boil for a couple of minutes. Pour the hot vinegar over the garlic, then seal the jars with vinegar-proof lids. Use within a year.

P.S. There are two main types of garlic, hardneck and softneck. Hardnecks produce a flowering spike – or scape – which is usually snapped off to encourage the plant to put its energy into the bulb. These scapes have a delicate, fresh garlic flavour and can be used chopped up in salads, or to make a green and garlicky pesto.

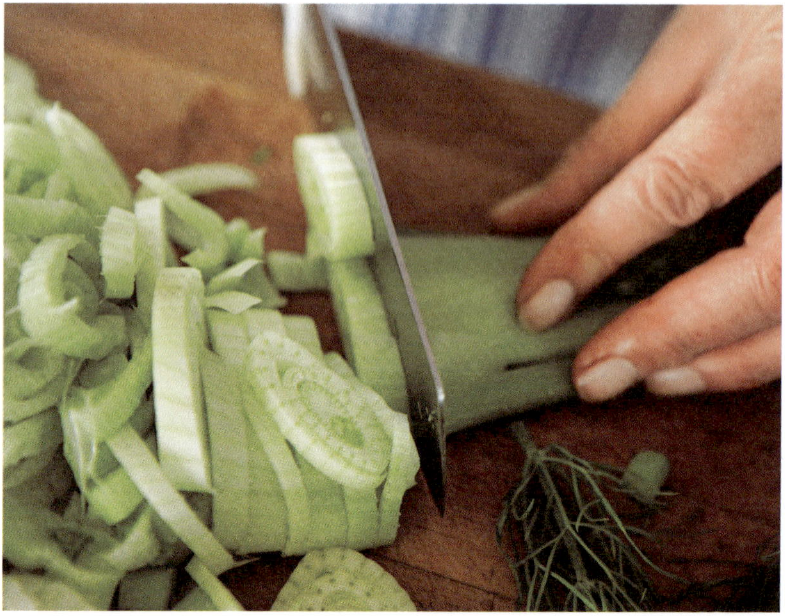

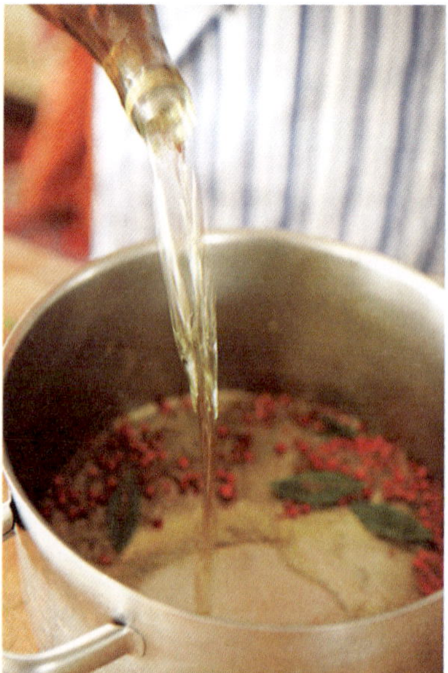

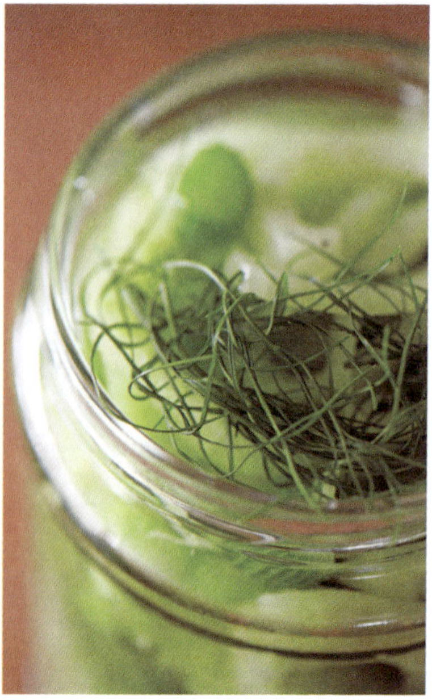

Pickled Florence fennel

Season: June to early July

Tall, willowy, feathered sweet Florence fennel, with its creamy-white, bulbous bottom, has to be one of the most alluring vegetables to grow in the garden. It's not easy to cultivate in every soil but, if it likes your particular situation, you should be able to grow plenty to use with gay abandon in the summertime, with some left over to preserve for later in the year.

It's only really worth making this pickle if you have a supply of freshly lifted bulbs when they are pale green and tender. All too often, the imported stuff is yellow and coarse. You have to discard much of the outer bulb and it certainly isn't worth the expense or trouble of pickling.

This lovely light pickle is delicious with smoked or oily fish and in winter salads. It nearly always makes an appearance at our Boxing Day lunch.

Makes 3 x 340g jars
Salt
1kg fennel bulbs, trimmed and thinly sliced, a few feathery fronds reserved
1 litre cider vinegar
15g peppercorns (black, white or pink)
75g granulated sugar
Grated zest of 1 unwaxed lemon
3 or 4 bay leaves
1 tsp celery or fennel seeds
3–4 tbsp olive, hemp or rapeseed oil

Pour 2–3 litres water into a large pan, salt it well and bring to the boil. Add the sliced fennel and blanch for no more than a minute. Drain in a colander, cool under cold water, then drain and pat dry.

Put the vinegar, peppercorns, sugar, lemon zest, bay leaves and celery or fennel seeds into a saucepan. Bring to the boil and continue to boil for about 10 minutes until the liquor reaches a syrupy consistency. The vinegar vapours will create quite a pungent atmosphere in the kitchen.

Pack the fennel into wide-necked, sterilised jars (see p.29), lacing a few fennel fronds between the slices. Remove the vinegar syrup from the heat and carefully pour over the fennel. You may well find all the spices remain at the bottom of the pan. If this happens, distribute them between the jars, poking the peppercorns and bay leaves down through the fennel slices. Pour sufficient oil into each jar to seal the surface. Seal the jars with vinegar-proof lids. Use within 12 months.

Roasted sweet beet relish

Season: June to August

I love the sweet, earthy flavour of beetroot and I hate to see it swamped in strong-tasting vinegar, as so often happens. This light preserve is quite a different proposition: roasting the young roots really concentrates their robust flavour, while the sharp pungency of horseradish adds a liveliness to the sweet beet. Serve this summery relish alongside smoked mackerel. It's also fantastic in sandwiches with cold meats.

Makes 5 x 225g jars

1kg young, small beetroot, trimmed
A little olive oil
250g granulated sugar
150ml red wine vinegar
2 tbsp balsamic vinegar
1 large red onion, peeled and finely chopped

50g freshly grated horseradish root (or pickled horseradish, see below)

For the roasted tomato purée
1kg tomatoes
2 level tsp sea salt
4 garlic cloves, peeled and sliced
50ml olive oil

Preheat the oven to 180°C/Gas Mark 4. For the tomato purée, halve the tomatoes and place them skin side down on a baking tray. Sprinkle with the salt, garlic and olive oil. Roast for an hour or so, on the bottom shelf of the oven, then remove. Rub through a sieve, or pass through a mouli or food mill, to remove the skins and pips – you'll end up with about 300ml of intensely flavoured purée.

Meanwhile, put the beetroot into a baking dish and trickle with a little oil. Roast, above the tomatoes, for 1–1½ hours (longer if necessary) until the skins are blistered, blackened and loosened. Leave to cool a little before peeling. You'll find the skins will slide off easily. Coarsely grate the beetroot (a food processor makes this job easy).

Put the sugar, vinegars, onion and horseradish into a large saucepan, bring to the boil and cook for 5 minutes. Stir in the tomato purée and cook for a couple more minutes. Finally, add the grated beetroot and cook for about 10 minutes, until thickened. Transfer to sterilised jars (see p.29) and seal with vinegar-proof lids. Use within a year. Refrigerate once opened.

P.S. It's easy to pickle horseradish root. Just grate enough freshly dug root to fill a jam jar, sprinkle over 1 tsp salt and 1 tsp sugar, top up with cider vinegar and seal with a lid. Use in sauces, dressings and soups – and, of course, serve with roast beef.

PICKLES, CHUTNEYS & RELISHES 107

Seasonal chutney

Season: any time from June to October

This is essentially Hugh F-W's classic Glutney, or River Cottage chutney, which first appeared in *The River Cottage Cookbook*. I have not been able to find a better basic chutney recipe. I love it because the flavour is so well balanced (neither too sweet nor too vinegary) and because it is so versatile – allowing you to use whatever gluttish fruit and veg you have to hand, as long as you stick with a similar ratio of fruit/veg to sugar and vinegar. I've included several seasonal variations here.

The fruit and veg chopping is reasonably time-consuming, but important. Whizzing everything up in a food processor would give a very different, sloppy-textured result. From start to finish, the chutney takes about 4 hours to make.

Makes 10–11 x 340g jars

1kg marrows or overgrown courgettes, peeled (if using marrows) and diced
1kg green tomatoes or tomatilloes, peeled and diced
500g cooking apples, peeled, cored and diced
500g onions, peeled and diced
500g sultanas
500g light soft brown sugar
600ml cider vinegar or white wine vinegar
2 tsp dried chilli flakes (optional)
Pinch of salt

For the spice bag
50g fresh root ginger, bruised
12 cloves
2 tsp black peppercorns
1 tsp coriander seeds

Make your spice bag by tying up the spices in a 20cm square of muslin. Put this into a preserving pan with all the other ingredients and bring slowly to the boil, stirring occasionally. This will take a while as there will be lots in the pan, but don't hurry it.

Let the mixture simmer, uncovered, for 2½–3 hours – maybe even a bit more. You do not have to hover, hawk-eyed, over the pan, but do keep an eye on it and stir regularly to ensure it doesn't burn. It's ready when it is glossy, thick, rich in colour and well reduced – but with the chunks of fruit and veg still clearly discernible. It is thick enough if, when you draw a wooden spoon through it, the chutney parts to reveal the base of the pan for a few seconds.

Pot the chutney while warm in sterilised jars (see p.29). Pack down with the back of a spoon to remove any air pockets. Seal with vinegar-proof lids. Store in a cool, dark place and leave for a couple of months to mature before using. Use within 2 years.

Variations

For each, use 500g light soft brown sugar, 600ml cider vinegar or white wine vinegar, a pinch of salt and 2 tsp dried chilli flakes (if liked); follow the basic method (left).

Gingered rhubarb and fig (spring)

1.5kg rhubarb, trimmed and chopped
1kg cooking apples, peeled, cored and diced
500g onions, peeled and diced
300g dried figs, chopped and soaked overnight in the juice of 3 large oranges with the grated zest of 2
100g crystallised ginger, chopped

For the spice bag

2 tsp mustard seeds
2 tsp black peppercorns
50g fresh root ginger, bruised

Plum and pear (late summer)

1kg plums, quartered and stoned
750g pears, peeled, cored and diced
750g cooking apples, peeled, cored and diced
500g shallots, peeled and diced
250g stoned prunes, roughly chopped

For the spice bag

50g fresh root ginger, bruised
2 tsp mustard seeds
2 tsp black peppercorns

Apricot and date (late summer)

500g unsulphured dried apricots, chopped, soaked overnight, drained
1kg marrow or courgettes, diced
500g cooking apples, peeled, cored and diced
500g onions, peeled and diced
250g stoned dates, chopped
250g raisins

For the spice bag

50g fresh root ginger, bruised
1 tsp cloves
1 tsp cumin seeds
1 tsp coriander seeds
2 tsp black peppercorns

Pumpkin and quince (early autumn)

1kg peeled, deseeded pumpkin, diced
1kg quince, peeled, cored and diced
500g cooking apples, peeled, cored and diced
500g red onions, peeled and diced
500g raisins
50g freshly grated horseradish root

For the spice bag

2 tsp peppercorns
12 cloves
2 cinnamon sticks

110 PRESERVES

Nasturtium 'capers'

Season: late July to September

After the vibrant trumpets of nasturtium flowers fade, you'll find underneath the foliage the knobbly green seed pods of the plant. They have a hot, peppery flavour and, when pickled, develop a taste very similar to that of true capers (the pickled flowerbuds of the Mediterranean *Capparis* plant). Collect the seed pods on a warm, dry day when all the flowers have wilted away. Gather only the green ones (sometimes they are red-blushed) and avoid any that are yellowing, as these will be dull and dry. The pods can also be used fresh to spice up salads, or as an ingredient in piccalilli (see p.114).

These feisty little pickled nasturtium seed pods are great in fish dishes and in herby, garlicky sauces. Try them in tartare sauce, or add to salads, especially with tomatoes. In fact, use them just as you would capers.

Makes 2 x 115g jars
15g salt
100g nasturtium seed pods
A few peppercorns (optional)
Herbs, such as dill or tarragon sprigs, or bay leaves (optional)
200ml white wine vinegar

Make a light brine by dissolving the salt in 300ml water. Put the nasturtium seed pods into a bowl and cover with the cold brine. Leave for 24 hours.

Drain the seed pods and dry well. Pack them into small, sterilised jars (see p.29) with, if you like, a few peppercorns and herbs of your choice. Leave room for 1cm of vinegar at the top. Cover the pods with vinegar and seal the jars with vinegar-proof lids. Store in a cool, dark place and leave for a few weeks before eating. Use within a year.

P.S. To make nasturtium tartare sauce, simply mix 100g mayonnaise with 2–3 finely chopped spring onions or 30g finely chopped white part of a leek, 1 tbsp coarsely chopped nasturtium capers, 1 heaped tbsp finely chopped parsley, a squeeze of lemon juice, and salt and pepper to taste. Serve the sauce with simple grilled or fried white fish, hot or cold salmon or trout, or a salad of freshly cooked baby beetroot, young broad beans and rocket or other leaves.

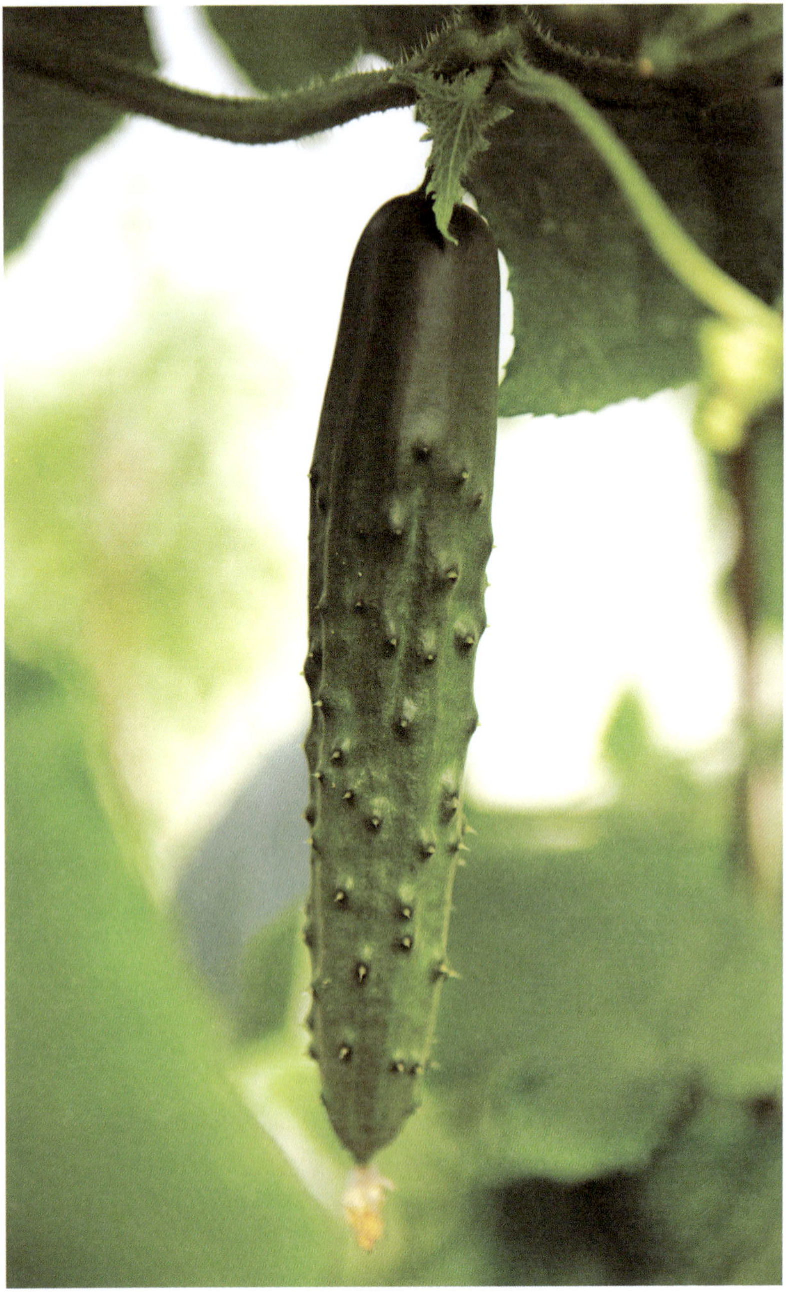

Sweet cucumber pickle

Season: July to September

This is a wonderful way to use up an abundance of cucumbers, be they long and uniform green, or the short, knobbly-skinned ridge type. It's also very quick and easy to make if you use a food processor. This is not a true preserve, as the cucumbers are not brined and the pickle is very light, but it will keep well in the fridge for a couple of weeks in a sealed container.

I love this sweet condiment with all manner of salads, and in sandwiches, but it's especially delectable with hot-smoked trout or salmon.

Makes 2 x 450g jars
1kg cucumbers
3 small onions, red or white
1 tbsp chopped dill (optional)
250g granulated sugar
1 level tbsp salt
200ml cider vinegar

Using the slicing blade of a food processor or a very sharp knife, very finely slice the cucumbers. Peel the onions and slice them very thinly too. Combine the cucumber, onion and dill, if using, in a large bowl.

Mix the sugar, salt and vinegar and pour over the cucumber and onion. Leave overnight for the sweet and sour flavours to mix and mingle or, if this isn't possible, leave for at least 3 hours before serving. Pack into a large airtight container or wide-necked jam jars. Store in the fridge and use within 2 weeks.

Variation

Creamy-white English winter celery makes a lovely sweet pickle, or you can use the more common green celery. Follow the recipe above, replacing the cucumber with 1kg celery. Run a potato peeler lightly down the stalks to remove any tough ribs, then cut into 6–7cm sticks (for crudités or dips) or chop into 1–2cm chunks. Use sweet, mild red onions and season the pickle with celery salt and 1 tsp caraway seeds. As celery does not contain as much water as cucumber, add 200ml water to the vinegar and sugar mixture.

Piccalilli

Season: August

This traditional sweet vegetable pickle, Indian in origin, is the ultimate August preserve for me. The time to make it is when garden produce is at its peak and there is ample to spare. You can use almost any vegetable in the mix but make sure you include plenty of things which are green and crisp. The secret of a really successful piccalilli is to use very fresh vegetables and to take the time to cut them into small, similar-sized pieces.

The recipe first treats the vegetables to a dry-brining, which helps to keep them really firm and crunchy, then bathes them in a smooth, hot mustard sauce.

Makes 3 x 340g jars

1kg washed, peeled vegetables –
   select 5 or 6 from the following:
   cauliflower or romanesco
   cauliflower; green beans;
   cucumbers; courgettes; green or
   yellow tomatoes; tomatilloes;
   carrots; small silver-skinned
   onions or shallots; peppers;
   nasturtium seed pods
50g fine salt

30g cornflour
10g ground turmeric
10g English mustard powder
15g yellow mustard seeds
1 tsp crushed cumin seeds
1 tsp crushed coriander seeds
600ml cider vinegar
150g granulated sugar
50g honey

Cut the vegetables into small, even bite-sized pieces. Place in a large bowl and sprinkle with the salt. Mix well, cover the bowl with a tea towel and leave in a cool place for 24 hours, then rinse the veg with ice-cold water and drain thoroughly.

Blend the cornflour, turmeric, mustard powder, mustard seeds, cumin and coriander to a smooth paste with a little of the vinegar. Put the rest of the vinegar into a saucepan with the sugar and honey and bring to the boil. Pour a little of the hot vinegar over the blended spice paste, stir well and return to the pan. Bring gently to the boil. Boil for 3–4 minutes to allow the spices to release their flavours into the thickening sauce.

Remove the pan from the heat and carefully fold the well-drained vegetables into the hot, spicy sauce. Pack the pickle into warm, sterilised jars (see p.29) and seal immediately with vinegar-proof lids. Leave (if you can) for 4–6 weeks before opening. Use within a year.

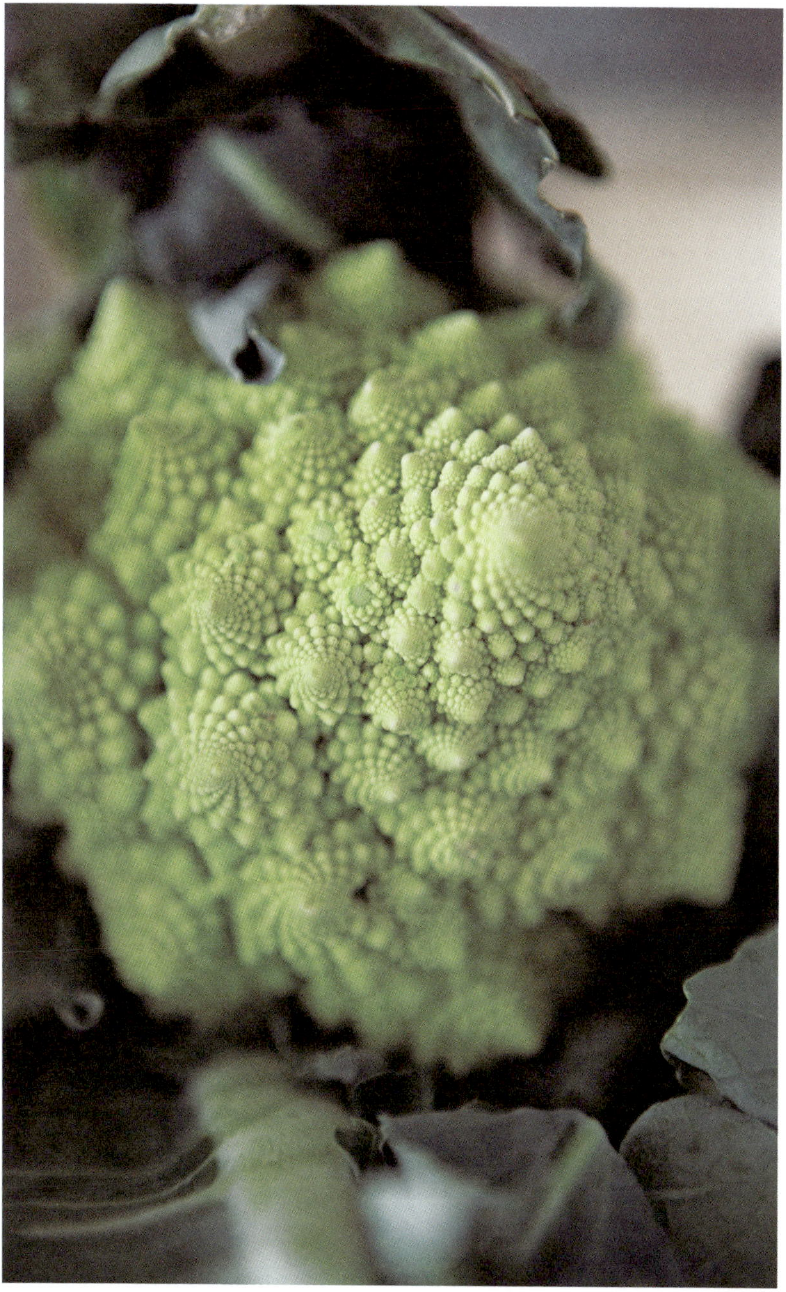

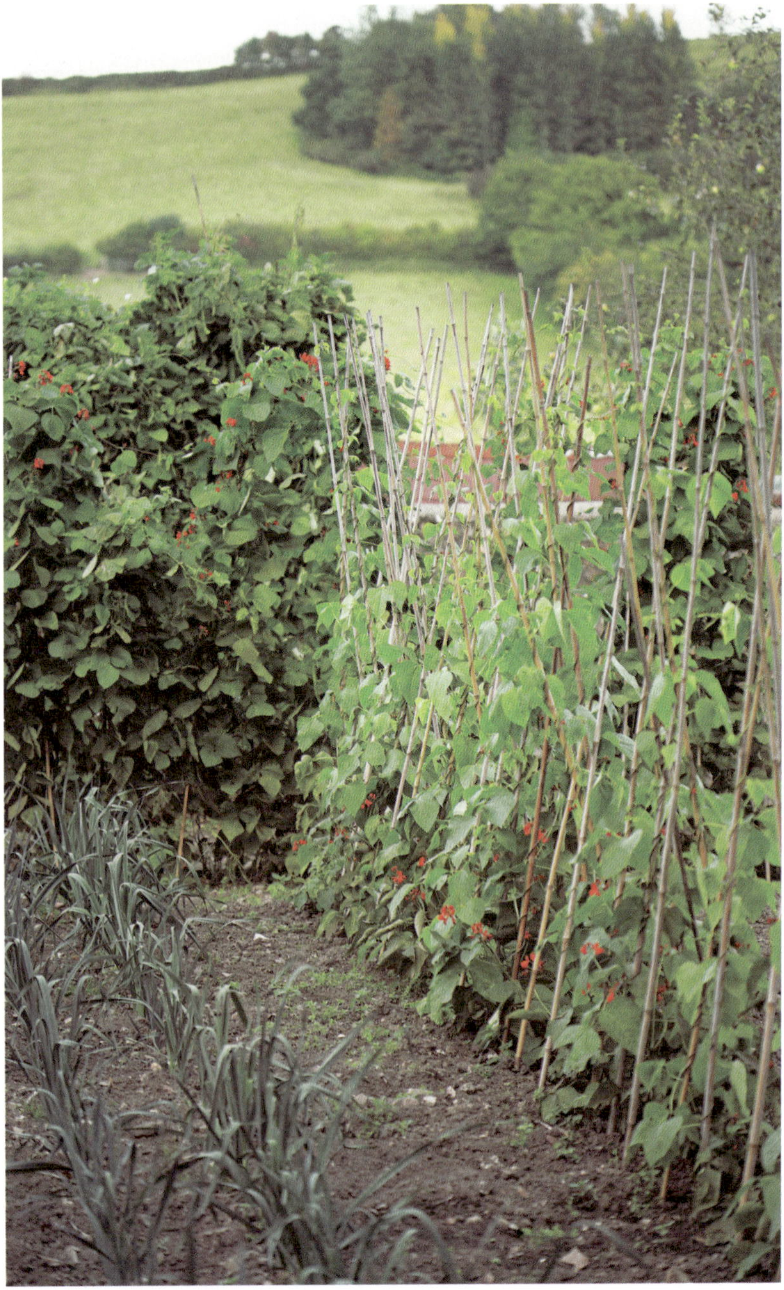

Runner bean pickle

Season: August to September

Runner beans are a bit of a love-or-hate vegetable and are often scorned in favour of other green beans. I do sympathise with those that don't eat them – we've all been served rubbery, greying old runners at some time or another and they're no fun at all. However, young tender green runner beans are altogether different and this recipe is just perfect for these guys. It has been eaten and enjoyed by just about everyone who has walked into my kitchen, so I hope that reproducing it here will convert a few more bean-haters.

I see the pickled beans as a preserved vegetable rather than a mere tracklement, and I think they're great alongside cold meats and salads.

Use a couple of jars that are at least 12cm high – taller, if possible – so that the beans can show off their length.

Makes 2 x 450g jars

1kg young runner beans	300g granulated sugar
Salt	1 tsp ground allspice
300ml cider vinegar or white wine vinegar	1 tsp coarsely ground black pepper
	6 juniper berries (optional)

Start by trimming the ends off the runner beans. If the beans are young and tender, there should be no need to string them. Cut the beans into lengths about 5mm less than the height of the jar you are using.

Bring a pan of lightly salted water to the boil. Add the beans and cook until tender; this should take 5–8 minutes.

Meanwhile, put the vinegar, sugar, 100ml water, allspice, ground pepper and juniper berries, if using, into a pan over a low heat, stirring until the sugar has dissolved. Bring to the boil and boil for a couple of minutes. Drain the runner beans, add them immediately to the spiced vinegar and simmer for 4–5 minutes. Strain the vinegar mixture into a small saucepan.

Pack the beans, upright, into warm, sterilised jars (see p.29); kitchen tongs and a knife are useful for doing this. Return the spiced vinegar to the boil then pour it over the tightly packed beans. Cap immediately with vinegar-proof lids.

Store in a cool, dark place and leave for several weeks to allow the pickle to mature. Use within 12 months.

Sweet pickled damsons

Season: late August to September

Dark-skinned, with a bluish bloom, small oval damsons are very tart and well flavoured, which makes them wonderful for preserving. This is a straightforward recipe that keeps the fruit whole and tender. I love warming cinnamon and allspice in the mix, but you can use any spices you fancy, or even a good tablespoonful of ready-made pickling spice (see p.97). These sweet spiced damsons are a lovely addition to any buffet table and splendid with cold poultry.

Makes 4 x 450g jars
600ml cider vinegar
5cm piece cinnamon stick
1 tsp allspice berries
Finely grated zest and juice of 1 orange
1kg firm, ripe damsons
750g granulated sugar

Put the vinegar, cinnamon, allspice berries, orange zest and juice into a pan and bring to the boil. Boil for 4–5 minutes then strain and allow to cool.

Prick each damson with a needle or skewer (this will prevent them splitting). Add the fruit to the cold spiced vinegar in a clean pan. Bring slowly to simmering point, then simmer very, very gently for 10–15 minutes until the damsons are just tender. Using a slotted spoon, lift out the damsons and pack them into warm, sterilised jars (see p.29).

Return the spiced vinegar to the heat, add the sugar and stir until dissolved. Boil for several minutes to reduce and thicken. Pour this hot spiced syrup over the damsons and seal immediately with vinegar-proof lids. Store in a cool, dark place. These pickled damsons are best kept for 6–8 weeks before eating.

Variations
You can use the same method to pickle firm green gooseberries or cherries. Rhubarb, cut into 5cm chunks, can also be dealt with in this way – but add the sugar with the rhubarb as it will help keep it whole.

Spiced pickled pears

Season: August to December

I love pickled fruits and always look forward to opening a jar to serve with cold poultry and ham. Small, hard pears such as 'Conference' are ideal for use in this recipe, and it's a very good way to deal with a barrel-load of them. If you stick with the basic quantities of sugar and vinegar, this recipe can easily be adapted for use with other fruits and different spices (see the variations below).

Makes 2 x 680g jars
300ml cider vinegar or white wine vinegar
400g granulated sugar
25g fresh root ginger, bruised
5cm piece cinnamon stick
1 tsp allspice berries
1kg small, firm pears
1 tsp cloves

Put the vinegar, sugar, ginger, cinnamon and allspice berries into a large pan over a low heat, stirring until the sugar has dissolved, then bring to the boil. Turn down the heat to a simmer.

Meanwhile, start peeling the pears, keeping them whole and with stalks attached. Stud each pear with 2 or 3 cloves and add to the hot vinegar. Simmer the pears very gently until they are tender but not too soft. Remove with a slotted spoon and pack them into warm, sterilised jars (see p.29).

Bring the spiced vinegar syrup to the boil and boil for 5 minutes, then strain it over the pears. Cover the jars with vinegar-proof lids. Keep for at least a month before using. Consume within a year.

Variations

Different spices can be used – try cardamom and coriander, with a flake or two of dried chilli.

Pickled peaches Plunge 1kg peaches into a pan of boiling water for 1 minute, then remove. Immerse them in cold water briefly, then peel. Proceed as for the pear recipe, but simmer the peaches for only 3–4 minutes.

Pickled crab apples Prick 1kg crab apples all over with a needle or skewer (this will prevent the skins bursting). Use well-coloured ornamental varieties such as 'Harry Baker', 'John Downie' or 'Pink Glow'.

Pickled onions

Season: September to November

A good pickled onion is perhaps the doyen of the preserves cupboard – but how do you like yours? Crisp or soft, sweet or sour, mildly spiced or chilli hot? The beauty of this recipe is that it can be used to make your onions (or shallots) just the way you like them. I like mine sweet, so use honey in this recipe, but you could dispense with honey or sugar altogether if you like a really sharp pickle. I also go for cider vinegar, rather than the more traditional malt, because the flavour is less aggressive. The blend of spices used here suits me nicely, but you could also use coriander, cumin or celery seeds – or any other spice you fancy. If you want crisp onions, use cold vinegar; if you like them soft, heat the vinegar first.

Makes 1 x 900g jar
1kg small pickling onions
50g fine salt
600ml vinegar (cider, malt or wine)
150g honey or sugar
15g fresh root ginger, lightly bruised
2 tsp allspice berries
2–3 mace blades
2 tsp mustard seeds
1 tsp black or white peppercorns
1 cinnamon stick
2 dried chillies (optional)
2 bay leaves

Using scissors, snip the top and the rooty bottom off the onions. Place in a large bowl and cover with boiling water. Count steadily to 20 (no more). Drain the onions and plunge into cold water. You will then find the skins will peel off easily.

Put the peeled onions into a shallow dish. Sprinkle with the salt, cover and leave overnight. Meanwhile, pour the vinegar into a pan and add the honey or sugar, ginger and spices (not the bay leaves). Cover and bring to boiling point. Remove from the heat and leave to infuse overnight.

Strain the spiced vinegar. Rinse the onions in very cold water, then drain and pack into a sterilised jar (see p.29), adding the bay leaves as you go. Pour over the vinegar (reheating it first, if you want softer onions) and seal with a vinegar-proof lid. Mature for 6–8 weeks before using. Use within 12 months.

Variation
Use shallots instead of onions and 300ml each red wine vinegar and white wine vinegar. Prepare as above, then pack the shallots into the jar along with 25g sliced fresh root ginger, 1 tsp coriander seeds and a couple of fresh mint sprigs.

PICKLES, CHUTNEYS & RELISHES 121

Hearty ale chutney

Season: October to January

Spices, onions and a traditional malty ale give this robust, pub-style chutney plenty of character, while the natural sugars in the root veg help sweeten it. It is delicious served with farmhouse Cheddar, crusty bread and a pint or two.

Makes 4–5 x 340g jars

400g onions, peeled and finely sliced
250g swede, peeled and chopped into 5mm pieces
200g carrots, peeled and chopped into 5mm pieces
250g apples, peeled, cored and chopped into 1cm pieces
150g cauliflower, broken into tiny florets
2 fat garlic cloves, peeled and crushed
100g stoned dates, finely chopped
150g tomato purée
300g demerara sugar
50g dark muscovado sugar
250ml malt or cider vinegar
2 heaped tbsp English mustard powder
2 heaped tsp ground ginger
1 heaped tsp ground mace
1 heaped tsp salt
½ tsp freshly ground black pepper
500ml traditional ale, bitter or stout (not lager)

Put all the ingredients, except the ale, into a large pan with 500ml water. Mix well, then place over a low heat and bring to a gentle simmer, stirring until the sugar has dissolved. Cook for about an hour – the vegetables will begin to soften and the juices will thicken and reduce.

Take the pan off the heat and add half the ale. Return to the heat and continue to cook for 30 minutes, by which time the mixture should be deep red-brown in colour. Add the remaining ale and cook for a further 30 minutes. By now the vegetables should be tender, but still retain their shape and a bit of crunch.

Remove from the heat and spoon into warm, sterilised jars (see p.29), making sure there are no air pockets. Seal with vinegar-proof lids. Store for 4–6 weeks before opening. Use within 2 years.

Figgy mostardo

Season: autumn to winter

The Italians use fiery-hot mustard oil to add a bit of passion to their classic fruit preserve *mostardo di cremona*. However, mustard oil is pretty well impossible to purchase in this country, so I have used mustard seeds and powder to pep up the dried figs in my own interpretation of the dish. Serve it with hot or cold meat, oily fish dishes, or with cheese in sandwiches.

Makes 4 x 225g jars
500g dried figs
Finely grated zest and juice of
    2 large grapefruit
1 good tbsp yellow mustard seeds
200g granulated sugar or honey
25g English mustard powder
100ml cider vinegar or white wine
    vinegar

Cut each fig into 4 or 6 pieces – it's easiest to do this using scissors. Place the figs in a bowl and add the grapefruit zest and mustard seeds. Measure the grapefruit juice and make it up to 500ml with water. Pour over the figs. Cover and leave overnight.

Put the figs and juice into a heavy-based saucepan. Heat gently until simmering then add the sugar or honey. Stir until dissolved.

Meanwhile, blend the mustard powder with the vinegar, add to the simmering figs and stir well. Simmer, uncovered, for 20 minutes, stirring occasionally, to reduce and thicken.

Remove the pan from the heat. Spoon the *mostardo* into warm, sterilised jars (see p.29) and seal with vinegar-proof lids. Store for 4 weeks before opening. Use within 12 months.

Variations

Dried apricots, apples or pears, or a good mix of them all, can be used in place of figs. For a stronger, hotter *mostardo*, use black mustard seeds instead of the milder yellow seeds. Orange, lemon or lime juice can replace the grapefruit juice. So you see, you can really make this recipe your very own ...

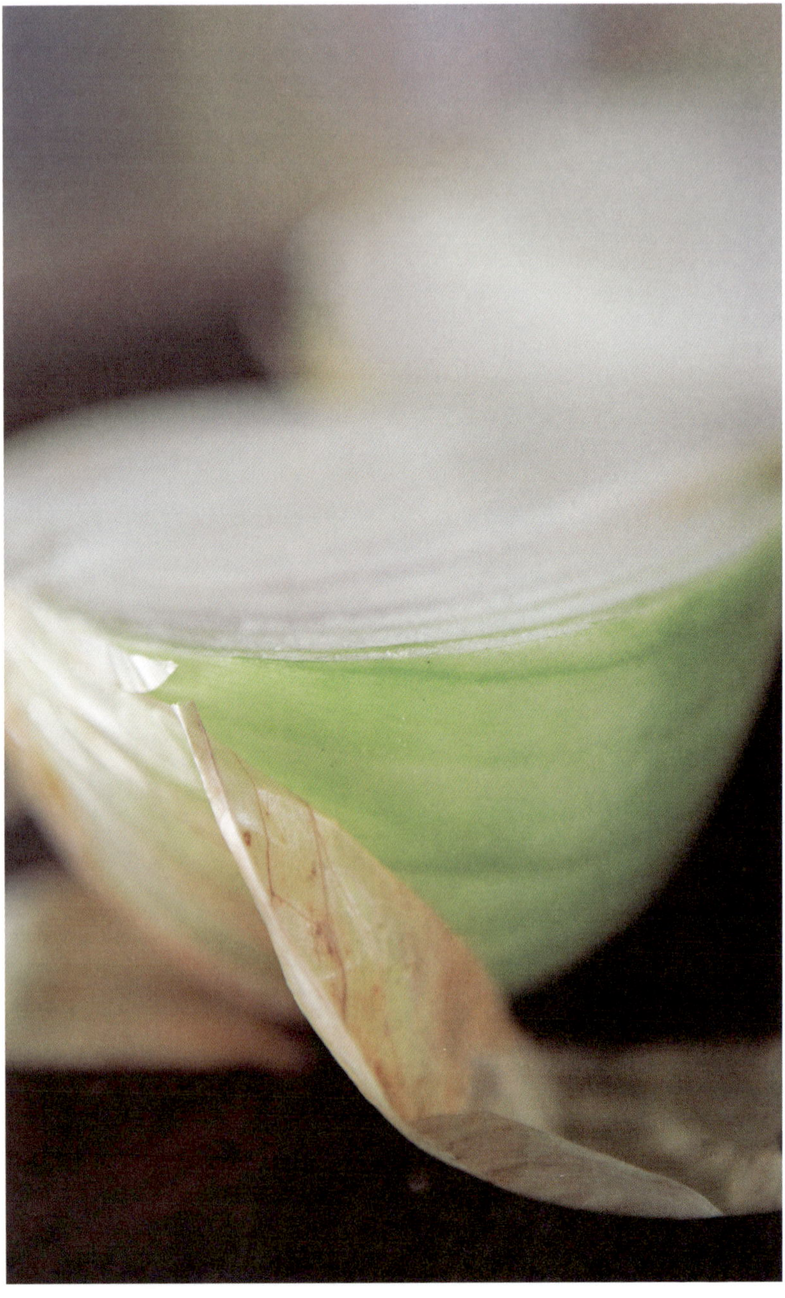

Onion marmalade

Season: winter

Onions are one of the most versatile ingredients in the culinary world, but not often given the chance to be the star of their own show. A recipe like this puts that right. Long, slow cooking turns a panful of red, white or yellow onions into a fantastic rich sauce-cum-jam that's brilliant served with bangers and mash and a heap of other dishes too. Try it with cheese on toast, with cold meat in sandwiches, or stir a spoonful into a creamy pumpkin soup.

Makes 5 x 225g jars
100ml olive oil
2kg onions, peeled and finely sliced
200g demerara sugar
150g redcurrant jelly
300ml cider vinegar
50ml balsamic vinegar
1 rounded tsp salt
½ tsp freshly ground black pepper

Heat the oil in a large pan over a medium heat and add the onions. Reduce the heat, cover the pan and cook over a low heat, stirring occasionally, for 30–40 minutes or until the onions are collapsed and beginning to colour.

Add the sugar and redcurrant jelly. Increase the heat and continue to cook, stirring more frequently, for about 30 minutes until the mixture turns a dark, nutty brown and most of the moisture has been driven off.

Take off the heat and allow to cool for a couple of minutes before adding the vinegars (if you add vinegar to a red-hot pan, it will evaporate in a fury of scorching steam). Return to the heat and cook rapidly for another 10 minutes or so, until the mixture becomes gooey and a spoon drawn across the bottom of the pan leaves a clear track across the base for a couple of seconds.

Remove from the heat and season with the salt and pepper. Spoon into warm, sterilised jars (see p.29) and seal with vinegar-proof lids. Use within 12 months.

P.S. Customarily made from citrus fruit, this marmalade is the exception to the rule. It takes its name and origins from the French, where historically the name 'marmalade' was used to describe fruit that was cooked for a very long time until it was reduced to a thick purée.

Preserved lemons

Season: November to March

Preserved lemons have a strong association with Middle Eastern and North African cuisines and their unique zesty, salty yet mellow flavour permeates many of the traditional meat and couscous dishes. Strips of preserved lemon can also be added to salads, soups and dressings, or mixed with olives and other appetisers. They are exceptionally easy to prepare and I like to make them around the turn of the year when the new season's lemons from Spain and Italy are in the shops.

Makes 2 x 450g jars
1kg small, ripe, unwaxed lemons
150g good-quality sea salt
1 tsp black or pink peppercorns
3–4 bay leaves
1 tsp coriander seeds (optional)

Wash the lemons in cold water and pat them dry. Set 3 or 4 of them aside – these will be squeezed and their juice poured over the salted lemons.

Using a sharp knife, partially quarter the remaining lemons lengthwise by making two deep cuts right through the fruit, keeping them intact at either end. Rub a good teaspoonful of salt into the cut surfaces of each lemon. Pack the fruit chock-a-block into sterilised, wide-necked jars (see p.29), sprinkling in the remaining salt, the peppercorns, bay leaves and coriander seeds as you go.

Squeeze the juice from the reserved lemons and pour over the salted lemons. They must be completely covered. You can top up the jars with a little water if necessary. Seal with a vinegar-proof lid. Leave for at least 4 weeks before opening to allow the lemon rinds to soften.

To use the lemons, remove one from the jar and rinse it well. Scoop out and discard the flesh (or purée it for use in dressings) and use the salted rind whole, chopped or sliced. Make sure the lemons in the jar remain covered with liquid and, once open, keep the jar in the fridge. Use within 12 months.

PICKLES, CHUTNEYS & RELISHES

Cordials, Fruit Liqueurs & Vinegars

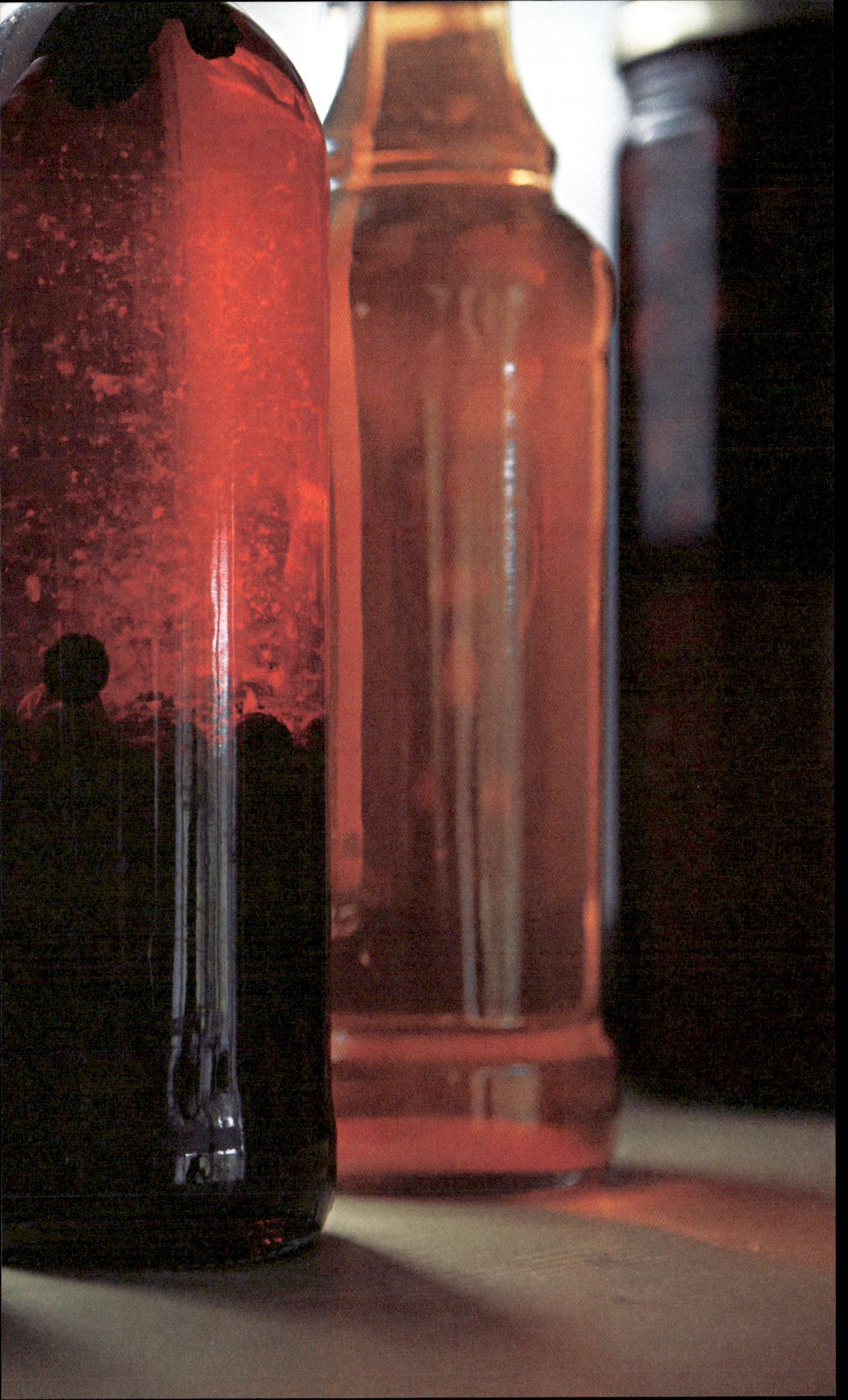

Preserving the essences

of fruits, flowers and herbs by steeping them in alcohol, vinegar or a sugar syrup is the core of these recipes. You might find yourself getting a bit bottled up in this chapter, but don't worry, you'll find it very refreshing and in parts quite intoxicating. Many of the techniques are age-old but are also enjoying a bit of a revival these days – fruit vinegars, in particular, are becoming increasingly popular.

Let me take you on a quick tour of the delicious liquors and infusions:

Cordials, syrups and squashes Essentially these are all concentrated fruity syrups. They are made from strained fruit juice, sweetened with sugar. Some herbs and flowers, such as elderflower, can also be used in a similar way. These smooth infusions can be diluted to taste (usually one part syrup to four or five parts water) to make delicious still or fizzy drinks, or added slowly (to prevent curdling) to ice-cold milk or yoghurt to create shakes and smoothies. Diluted half and half with water and frozen in suitable moulds, they make delicious ice pops. They can also be drizzled neat over ice cream for a quick and easy pudding.

Flavoured vinegars These are very simply made by steeping fruits, herbs or spices in vinegar. The vinegar is then strained (and the flavouring discarded) and usually sweetened. Flavoured vinegars can be used in dressings and mayonnaises, sauces, relishes, pickles and chutneys. They can be trickled neat over a salad, grilled cheese or avocado; diluted with ice-cold water to make a refreshing summer drink (these can be very good); or sipped in the winter to soothe sore, tickly throats. Fruit vinegars are usually made from soft fruits such as raspberries, strawberries or blackberries, which give up their juices easily.

Fruit liqueurs If immersed in alcohol and left in a warm place for several weeks, hedgerow berries, fruit, scented leaves and herbs will give up their flavours beautifully. Sugar is often added to the mix too, during or after steeping, to enhance the flavour. These tipples are not cheap to make but I really value them for their full, smooth flavours, and find a small sup can spirit away annoying thoughts.

Whole fruits in alcohol Raw or lightly cooked fruits can be preserved simply by being sprinkled with sugar and submerging in alcohol. Such fruits make a very special dessert, either on their own or served with a good vanilla ice cream. Be assured that any liquor left after the fruit has been eaten is unlikely to go to waste…

CORDIALS, FRUIT LIQUEURS & VINEGARS 131

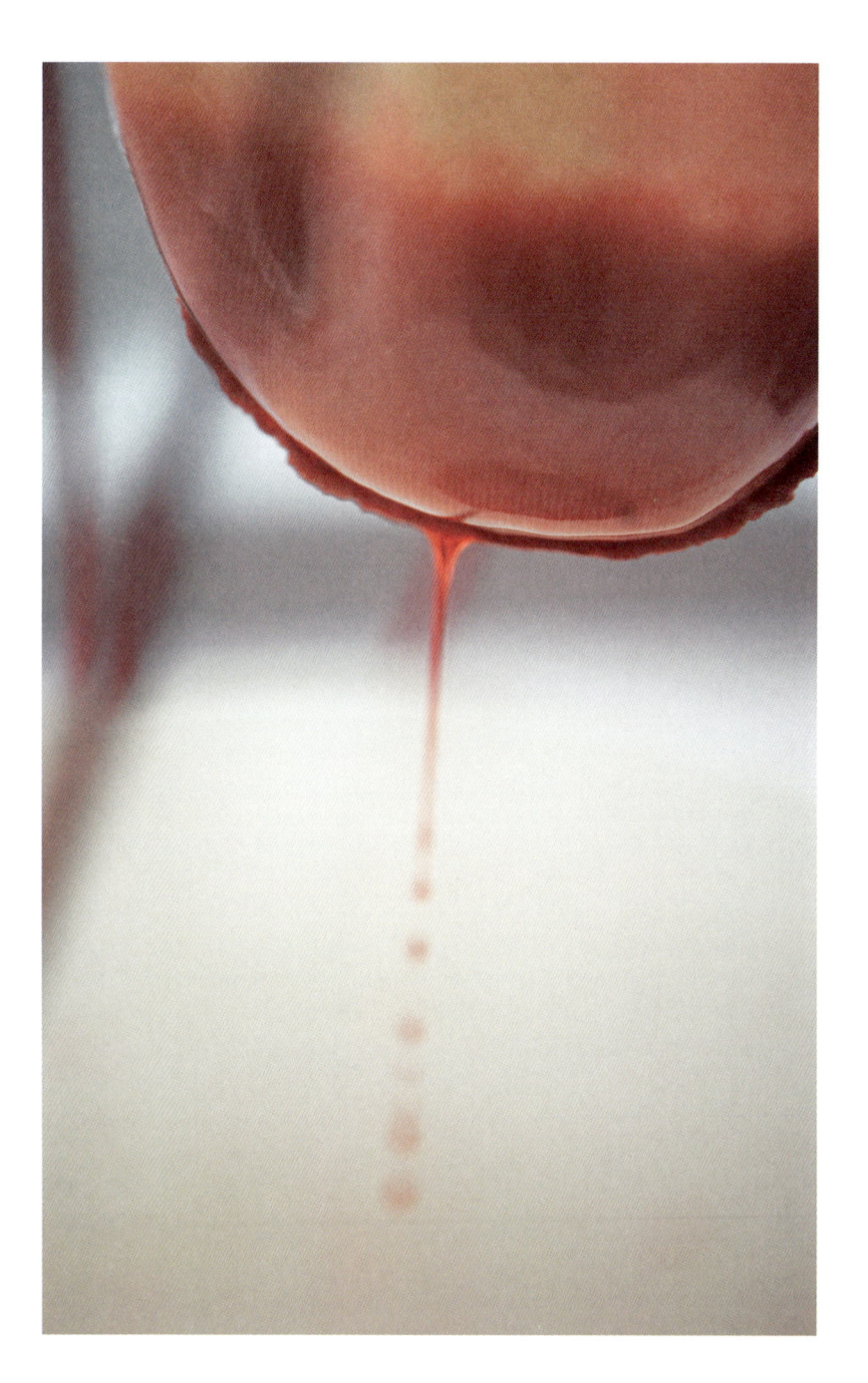

Key ingredients

You'll be amazed at how easily good fresh produce and simple store cupboard ingredients can be transformed into such wide-ranging and stimulating liquors.

Vinegar
Always use a good-quality vinegar with at least 5 per cent acetic acid. Light and fruity cider or wine vinegars are best for flavouring. Use the vinegar cold if it's to be steeped with soft, fresh leaves and flowers, but heat it for the best results with firm ingredients such as garlic, chillies and horseradish. For more on vinegars, see p.37.

Sugar
Refined white or light golden sugars are best in these recipes, to allow the flavours of the fruit, flowers or herbs to prevail. For more information on sugars, see p.35.

Alcohol
This is a very effective preserving medium, but needs to be in the form of spirit with at least 40 per cent alcohol (80 per cent proof). See p.38 for more information.

Fruit
This must be fresh, of the highest quality and definitely not under-ripe. In fact, fruit that is a little too ripe for jam, or for bottling, is ideal for fruit syrups. Perfectly ripe fruit should be used for preserved whole fruits and fruit liqueurs – prick it with a needle or skewer in several places to help the juices flow. Only wash the fruit if absolutely necessary. Otherwise prepare as follows:

> Strawberries and raspberries Remove the hull
> Cherries Stone or not, it's up to you
> Peaches and apricots Peel if you like, then slice or quarter
> Plums and damsons Halve or leave whole. If leaving whole, prick with a fork or skewer
> Pears Peel or not, then core, halve or quarter
> Grapes Remove the stems
> Early blackberries Pick over

Herbs, spices and flowers
It is important to gather herbs and flowers when they are fully dry and ideally when they have been gently warmed by the sun. This is when their characteristic oils and essences are at their best and most pungent. Likewise, spices and aromatics should be fresh and strong-smelling.

Shelf life and keepability

Fruit vinegars and liqueurs are best used within 2 years, although providing they are well sealed and kept in a cool, dry place, they will keep for considerably longer. Fruit syrups, cordials and squashes have a shorter shelf life – they can be kept in a cool, dry place, or the refrigerator, for a few weeks, or frozen. You can, however, extend their shelf life as follows:

Extending shelf life of fruit syrups, cordials and squashes to 4 months
Sterilise your bottles and their corks, swing-top lids or screw-tops by putting them all in a large pan of water and bringing to the boil. Leave them in the pan so they are still hot when you are ready to use them.

Bring the fruit syrup or squash to just above simmering point (check it reaches 88–90°C on a sugar thermometer). Using a funnel, fill the hot bottles to within 1cm of the brim if you're using screw-tops or swing-stoppers, or within 2.5cm of the brim if you're using corks. Fill each bottle and seal it before filling the next bottle. This method avoids using a deep-pan hot water bath (it is well-nigh impossible to find a pan deep enough to fully submerge bottles).

Extending shelf life of fruit syrups, cordials and squashes to 1 year To do this, you need to process the filled bottles in a hot water bath (see p.164). Fill the bottles with syrup to within 2.5cm of the tops for screw-tops or swing-stopper lids, and to within 3.5cm of the tops if you are using corks – this allows for expansion and prevents the tops blowing off. Screw-lids should be put on lightly and then tightened when the bottles are taken out of the water bath. Corks need to be held down and prevented from blowing off during the heating process by securing them with some strong insulation tape. Swing-tops should be fully sealed – the rubber ring will allow steam to escape.

Stand the filled, sealed bottles in a deep pan on a trivet or folded tea towel. Fill the pan with water, to within 2.5cm of the top of the bottles, and bring to simmering point (88°C). Keep at this temperature for 20 minutes. Remove from the pan and leave to cool.

Once cold, bottles that have been sealed with a cork can be made airtight by dipping the cork and the top 1cm of the bottle into melted paraffin wax or beeswax.

Storage after opening Whichever method you choose, once opened the bottles should be kept in the fridge.

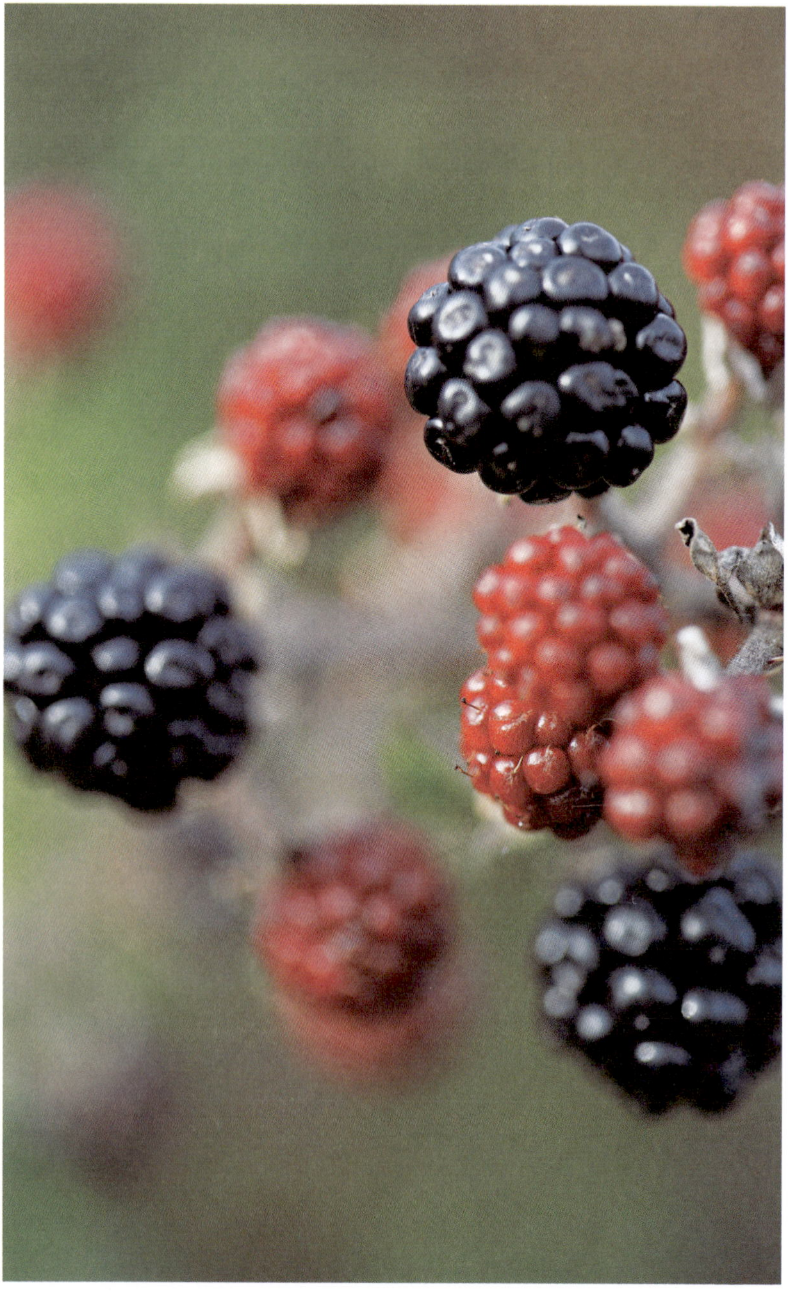

Family 'beena

Season: pretty much all year round

I'd like to introduce you to a group of cordials with a name inspired by a certain well-known fruit squash. These can be prepared throughout the year and are an excellent way of using fruit that's too ripe for jam-making. I've made rhubeena with rhubarb, berrybeena with summer berries, plumbeena with plums and dambeena with damsons – and currants, of course, work very well too. Use these fruits alone to make single variety 'beenas or, for a lighter and more economical cordial, use 50 per cent cooking apples.

Because the fruit pulp will be strained, you needn't be too fastidious with its preparation. Rhubarb should be cut into chunks. Strawberries should be hulled. Plums are best halved, but it's not necessary to remove the stones. Apples should be de-stalked and roughly chopped, but there's no need to peel or core them.

Makes about 1.5 litres
2kg fruit
Granulated sugar
Brandy (optional)

Place your chosen prepared fruit in a large saucepan. For each 1kg blackcurrants, apples or hard fruit, add 600ml water; for each 1kg plums or stone fruit, add 300ml water; for each 1kg soft berries or rhubarb, add 100ml water. Bring slowly to the boil, crushing the fruit with a wooden spoon or potato masher, and cook gently until the fruit is soft and the juices flowing. This will take anything up to 45 minutes depending on the type of fruit. Remove from the heat.

Scald a jelly bag or fine tea towel (see p.41) and suspend over a large bowl. Tip the fruit into it and leave to drip overnight.

Measure the resulting juice and pour into a clean pan. For every 1 litre juice, add 700g sugar (or to taste). Heat the mixture gently to dissolve the sugar, then remove from the heat. Pour immediately into warm, sterilised bottles (see p.133), leaving a 1cm gap at the top. At this point you may like to add a couple of teaspoonfuls of brandy to each bottle. Seal with a screw-top or cork.

'Beenas will keep for several months, provided they are sealed when hot and stored in a cool place. However, if you want to keep them for longer you will need to sterilise the bottles in a water bath immediately after bottling (see p.133).

Lemon squash

Season: November to March

A cool glass of this home-made squash knocks the commercially produced alternative into oblivion. Once tasted, this will become a favourite thirst-quencher. Serve diluted with cold water as a cool summertime refresher, or mix with tonic water and a splash of Angostura bitters for a non-alcoholic cocktail. You can also ring the changes and use oranges as well as lemons for a St Clement's squash.

Makes 2–3 x 500ml bottles
7–10 unwaxed lemons
650g granulated sugar

Scrub the lemons and pare the zest from four of them. Bring a pan of water to the boil, drop in the lemons and leave for 1 minute. Lemons are often quite hard and unyielding – this will soften them and they will give more juice when squeezed. Lift out the lemons and keep the lemon-infused water to one side. Squeeze the juice from the lemons and measure out 500ml of it.

Put the sugar, lemon zest and 500ml of the lemony water into a saucepan. Heat gently to dissolve the sugar, then bring to the boil. Add the 500ml lemon juice and bring just to boiling point. Remove from the heat and strain through a sieve into a jug. Pour immediately into hot, sterilised bottles (see p.133) and seal immediately with sterilised screw-caps, corks or swing-top lids.

Leave to cool, then store the squash in a cool, dry place or the fridge for up to 4 months. For longer keeping – up to a year – sterilise the bottles in a water bath (as directed on p.133).

To serve the squash, mix one part syrup to four parts water.

P.S. Another way to increase the yield of juice from citrus fruits is to roll the fruit back and forth over a work surface, pressing down firmly with the palm of your hand, for 2–3 minutes.

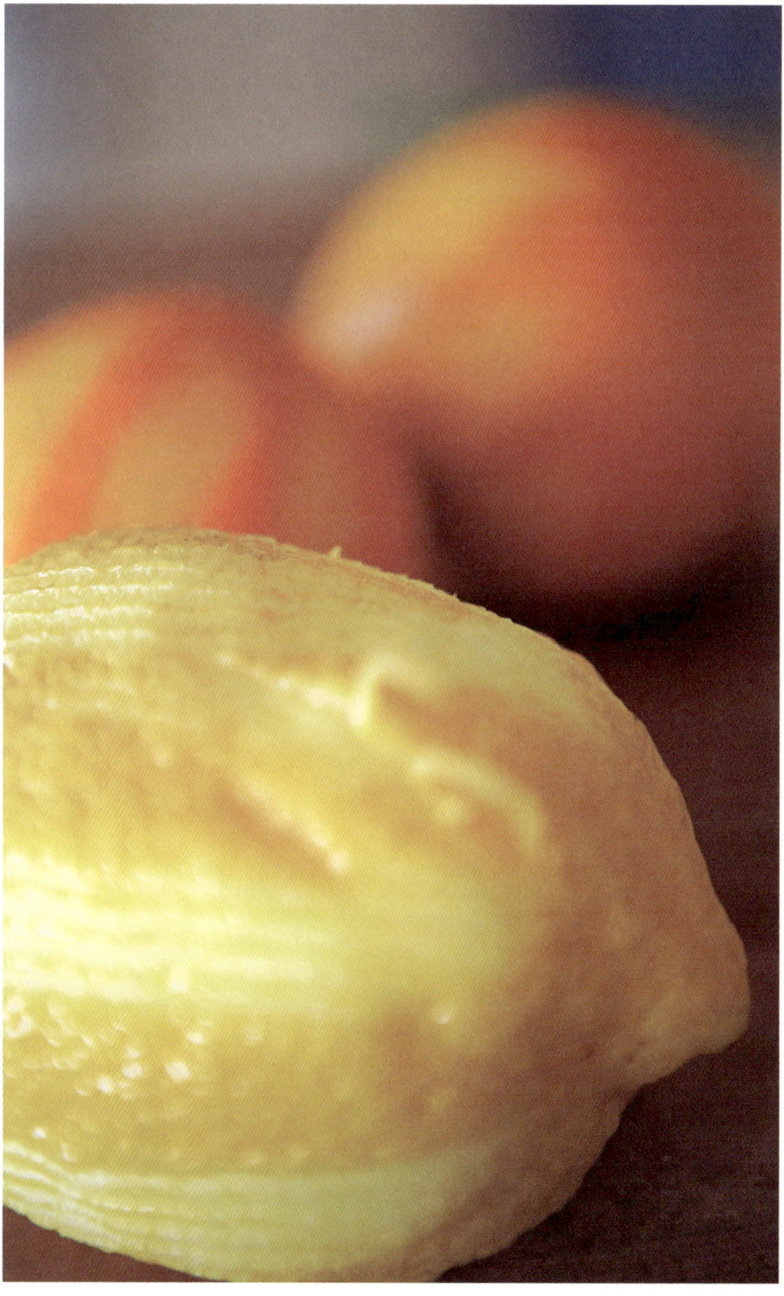

Beech leaf noyau

Season: late April to early May

The name for this unusual alcoholic cordial is actually the French word for 'fruit stone'. Traditionally, it was made from bitter almonds or peach stones mixed with gin, then left to steep in a warm place for several days before being cooked up with sugar then filtered through blotting paper. This recipe is from Richard Mabey's excellent *Food for Free*. It uses the young, silken leaves of our native beech tree (*Fagus sylvatica*), which first appear towards the end of April, to make an exquisite hedgerow version of the liqueur.

Makes 1 litre

1 loosely packed carrier bagful of soft young beech leaves
500ml gin
300g granulated sugar
Brandy

Pack the beech leaves into an earthenware or glass jar until it's about nine-tenths full. Pour the gin over the leaves, making sure they are well covered (they will oxidise and turn brown if left exposed). Leave to steep for 7–10 days so the leaves can release their striking green pigment. Strain the infused gin through muslin or a jelly bag (see p.41).

Put the sugar and 250ml water into a saucepan and heat gently to dissolve the sugar. Allow to cool completely before adding to the infused gin. Add a couple of capfuls of brandy too.

Put a couple of fresh beech leaves into a sterilised screw-top or stopper bottle (see p.133), then add the noyau and seal.

Wait for a cold winter night and a roaring fire, then partake of this potent liqueur. Use within 2 years (it may darken in colour over time).

P.S. If you miss the young beech leaves of early spring, you may get a second chance to make this noyau towards the end of June. Some beech hedges, when trimmed, will throw up new young shoots – not as prolific as the early crop, but still worth snatching.

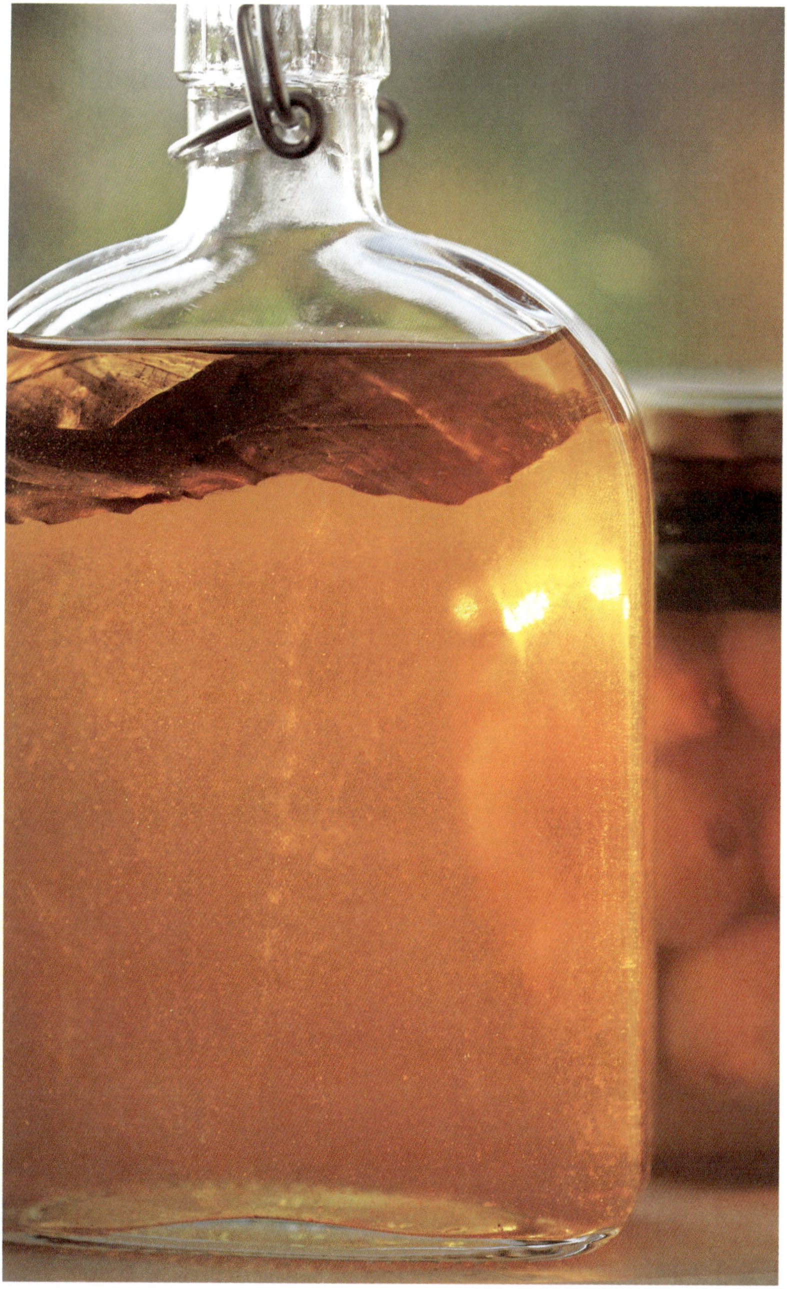

PRESERVES

Elderflower cordial

Season: late May to June

The sweetly scented, creamy-white flowers of the elder tree appear in abundance in hedgerows, scrub, woodlands and wasteland at the beginning of summer. The fresh flowers make a terrific aromatic cordial. They are best gathered just as the many tiny buds are beginning to open, and some are still closed. Gather on a warm, dry day (never when wet), checking the perfume is fresh and pleasing. Trees do differ and you will soon get to know the good ones. Remember to leave some flowers for elderberry picking later in the year.

This recipe is based on one from the River Cottage archives: it's sharp, lemony and makes a truly thirst-quenching drink. You can, however, adjust it to your liking by adding more or less sugar. The cordial will keep for several weeks as is. If you want to keep it for longer, either add some citric acid and sterilise the bottles after filling (see p.133), or pour into plastic bottles and store in the freezer.

Serve the cordial, diluted with ice-cold sparkling or still water, as a summer refresher – or mix with sparkling wine or Champagne for a classy do. Add a splash or two, undiluted, to fruit salads or anything with gooseberries – or dilute one part cordial to two parts water for fragrant ice lollies.

Makes about 2 litres
About 25 elderflower heads
Finely grated zest of 3 unwaxed lemons and 1 orange, plus their juice (about 150ml in total)
1kg sugar
1 heaped tsp citric acid (optional) (see the directory, p.210)

Inspect the elderflower heads carefully and remove any insects. Place the flower heads in a large bowl together with the orange and lemon zest. Bring 1.5 litres water to the boil and pour over the elderflowers and citrus zest. Cover and leave overnight to infuse.

Strain the liquid through a scalded jelly bag or piece of muslin (see p.41) and pour into a saucepan. Add the sugar, the lemon and orange juice and the citric acid (if using). Heat gently to dissolve the sugar, then bring to a simmer and cook for a couple of minutes.

Use a funnel to pour the hot syrup into sterilised bottles (see p.133). Seal the bottles with swing-top lids, sterilised screw-tops or corks.

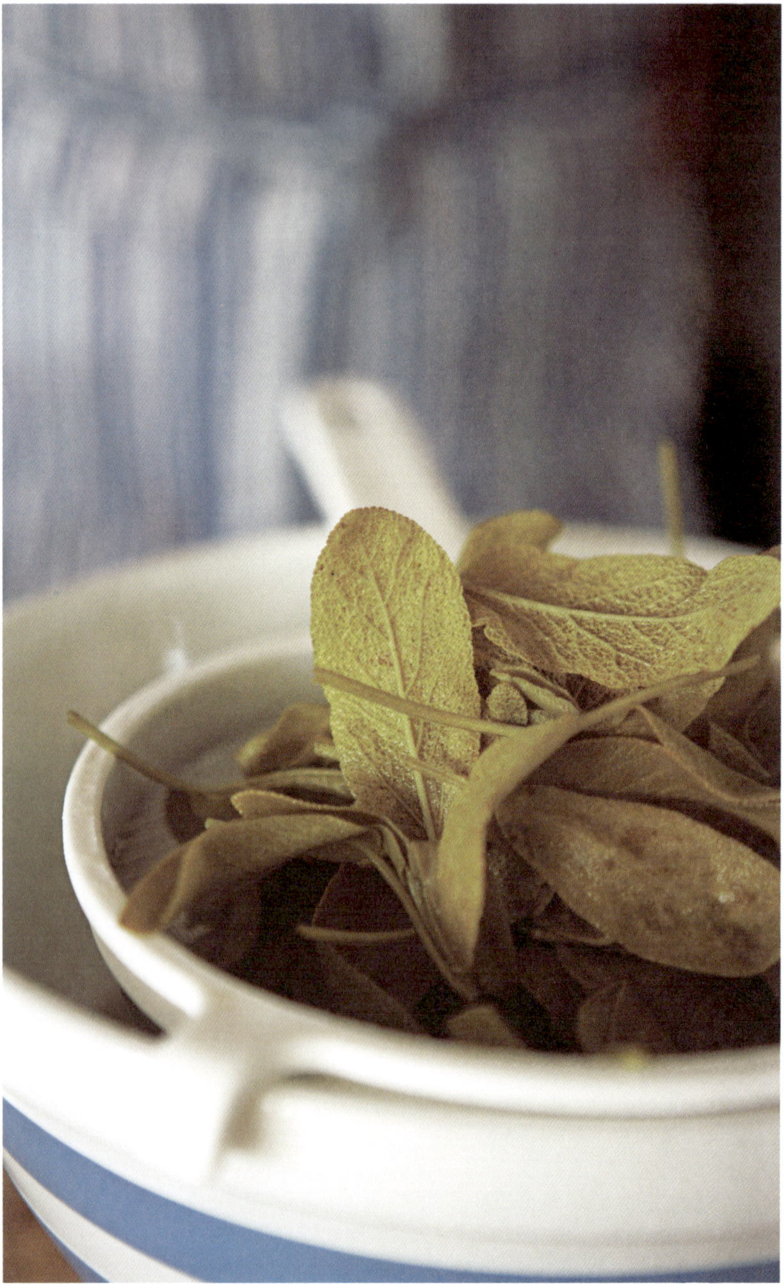

Elixir of sage

Season: spring and summer

The healing, warming properties of sage have long been recognised and one traditional way to imbibe them is by means of a liqueur, such as this one. The velvety, grey-green leaves are steeped in eau de vie and the resulting elixir should, I'm told, be drunk each day to ensure good health and a long life. I take just a capful (not a cupful) myself each morning and find it very restorative. Of course, this is not the only way to use this soothing herb liqueur – a glassful can be enjoyed as a comforting digestif or a capful diluted with tonic water for an aromatic pick-me-up.

Gather the sage on a warm, dry day. As an evergreen, this herb can be picked throughout the year but it's at its best during the spring and summer months.

Makes 1 litre
50–60g sage leaves (about ¼ of a carrier bagful)
500ml eau de vie
200g granulated sugar

Shake the sage leaves well to remove any wildlife (those that don't escape at this stage will become sublimely intoxicated). Pack the leaves into a large, wide-necked jar, of 600–700ml capacity. Fill the jar to the very top with eau de vie and seal with an airtight lid (if any leaves are uncovered they will oxidise and the colour of the liquor will become dull brown). Give it a good shake and then place on a sunny windowsill to steep for about 30 days, remembering to give it a shake every now and then.

When you're ready to complete the elixir, make a sugar syrup by gently heating the sugar with 200ml water until the sugar has dissolved. Allow this to cool.

Strain the sage liquor through a sieve into a bowl. Mix the strained liquor with the sugar syrup. Decant into clean sterilised bottles (see p.133), placing 2 or 3 of the soaked sage leaves in the bottle. Cork or cap with screw-caps. The elixir will be ready to use immediately. Consume within a year.

Currant shrub

Season: June to July

A shrub is an old-fashioned kind of drink: essentially a delightfully fruity, alcoholic cordial. Based on sweetened rum or brandy, it is traditionally flavoured with acidic fruit such as Seville oranges, lemons or redcurrants. Keep back some of the juice after straining redcurrants to make jelly (see recipe, p.62) and you will find this lovely tipple very simple to make.

Serve as an aperitif, either on its own or mixed half and half with dry martini and finished with a splash of fresh orange juice, which is my favourite way.

Makes about 1 litre
300ml strained redcurrant juice
600ml rum or brandy
Finely grated zest of 1 orange
1 tsp grated nutmeg
300g granulated sugar

Mix the redcurrant juice, rum or brandy, orange zest and nutmeg together in a large, wide-necked jar. You may find the mixture of acid and alcohol forms a gel – a perfect example of how adding fruit juice to spirit can determine pectin levels (see pp.46–7). Don't worry, the mixture will become liquid again when you add the sugar. Seal the jar tightly and leave for 7–10 days in a cool, dark place.

Transfer the currant and alcohol mixture to a pan, add the sugar and heat gently to about 60°C. When the sugar has dissolved, strain the liqueur through a jelly bag or muslin (see p.41). Decant the strained liquid into a sterilised bottle (see p.133) and seal with a cap.

Store for several months in a cool, dark place so the shrub can fully mature before you take the first tipple. Use within 2 years.

P.S. Redcurrants that grow on a standard (long-stemmed) bush, rather than at ground level, make picking very easy and also add interest to the garden. I pick 4–5kg redcurrants each season from my standard bush.

Variation
At marmalade-making time, buy an extra kilo of Seville oranges and use the strained juice in place of the redcurrant juice for an outstanding orange liqueur.

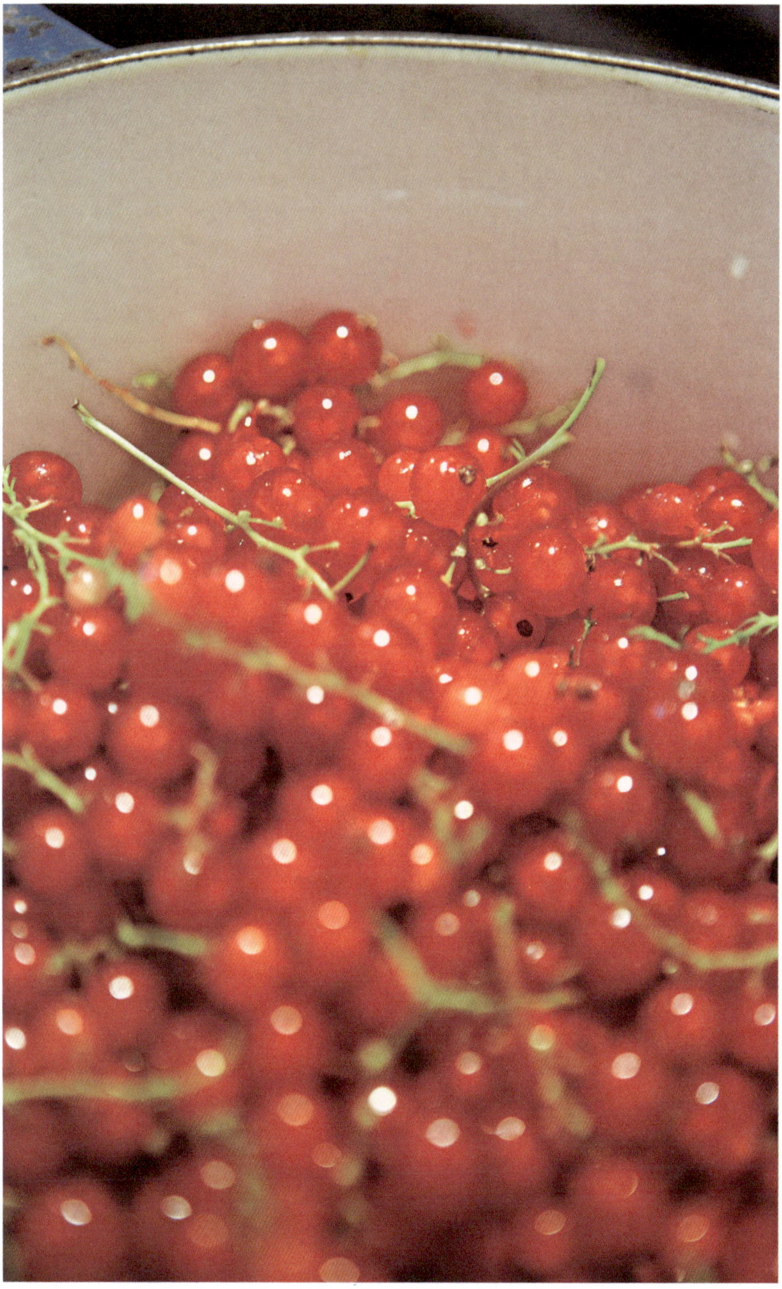

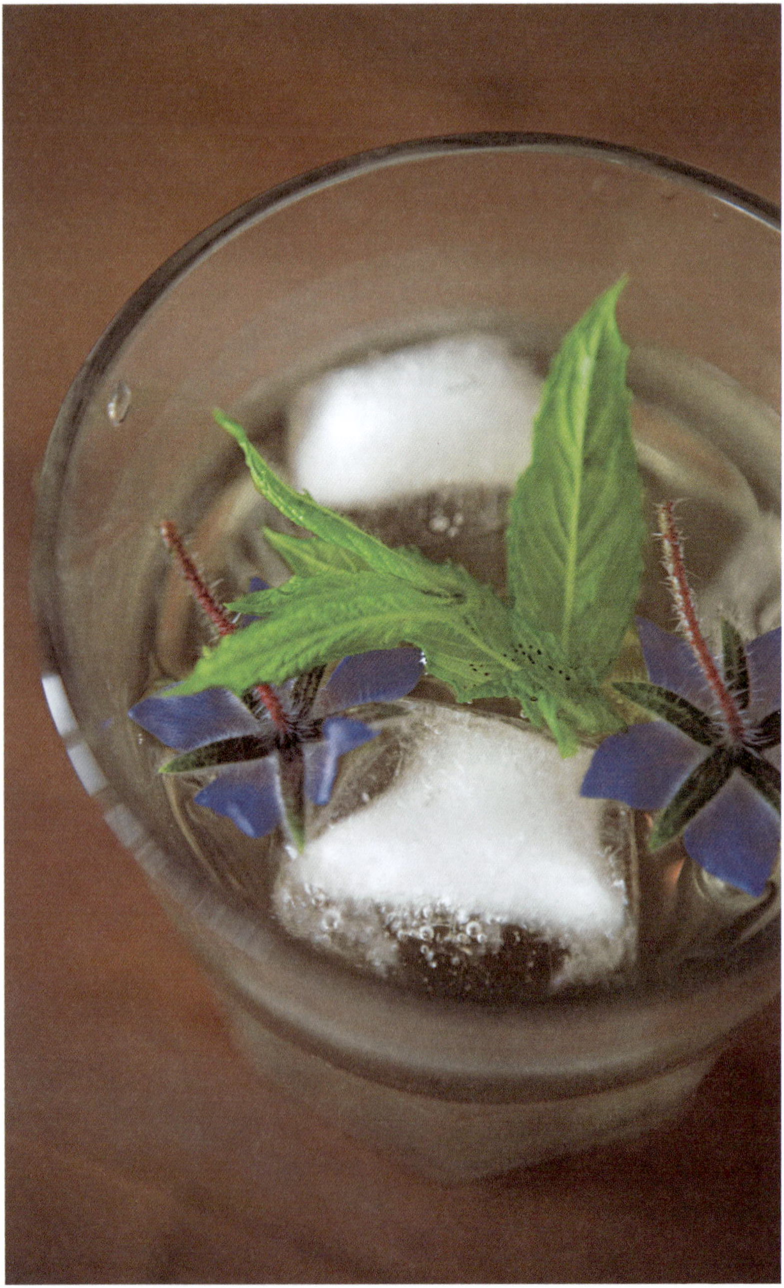

Mint syrup

Season: June to August

I can't help feeling that we should all make more use of garden mint (*Mentha spicata*). I'm sure that if it didn't run amok in the garden in a rather annoying way, we would prize it more highly not just as a nice thing to chuck in with the potatoes, but as the wonderful sweet-scented herb that it is.

This simple recipe is best made with young, bright green mint leaves, picked just before flowering, when the volatile oils are at their strongest. Gather them on a sunny day, when the plant is fully dry and the leaves are warm. Use the leaves immediately after picking to retain every bit of their amazing warming-and-cooling menthol character.

Mix 10ml mint syrup into a glass of ice-cold water, lemonade or tonic for a cooling summer drink. To make delicious hot, sweet mint tea, add 1 tbsp of the syrup to a pot (silver, of course, if you have one) of steaming green tea.

Makes 1 litre
50g freshly picked mint leaves
Juice of 1 lemon (50ml)

250g sugar
1 level tsp sea salt

Check the mint leaves for any insect life then tear the leaves into shreds. Put the lemon juice into a large bowl. Add the mint and pound with the end of a wooden rolling pin. Add the sugar and the salt and continue to crush the mint leaves to release their menthol essence. Leave to macerate for 8–10 hours or overnight.

Pour 600ml boiling water over the macerated mint mixture and leave to stand for a further 12 hours.

Strain the syrup through a very fine sieve or muslin into a saucepan. Gently bring to simmering point and simmer for a couple of minutes. Pour into warm, sterilised bottles (see p.133) and seal with screw-caps or corks.

This syrup will keep unopened for 4 months, but once opened, it should be stored in the fridge. If you want to keep it longer, it will need to be sterilised in a water bath straight after bottling (see p.133).

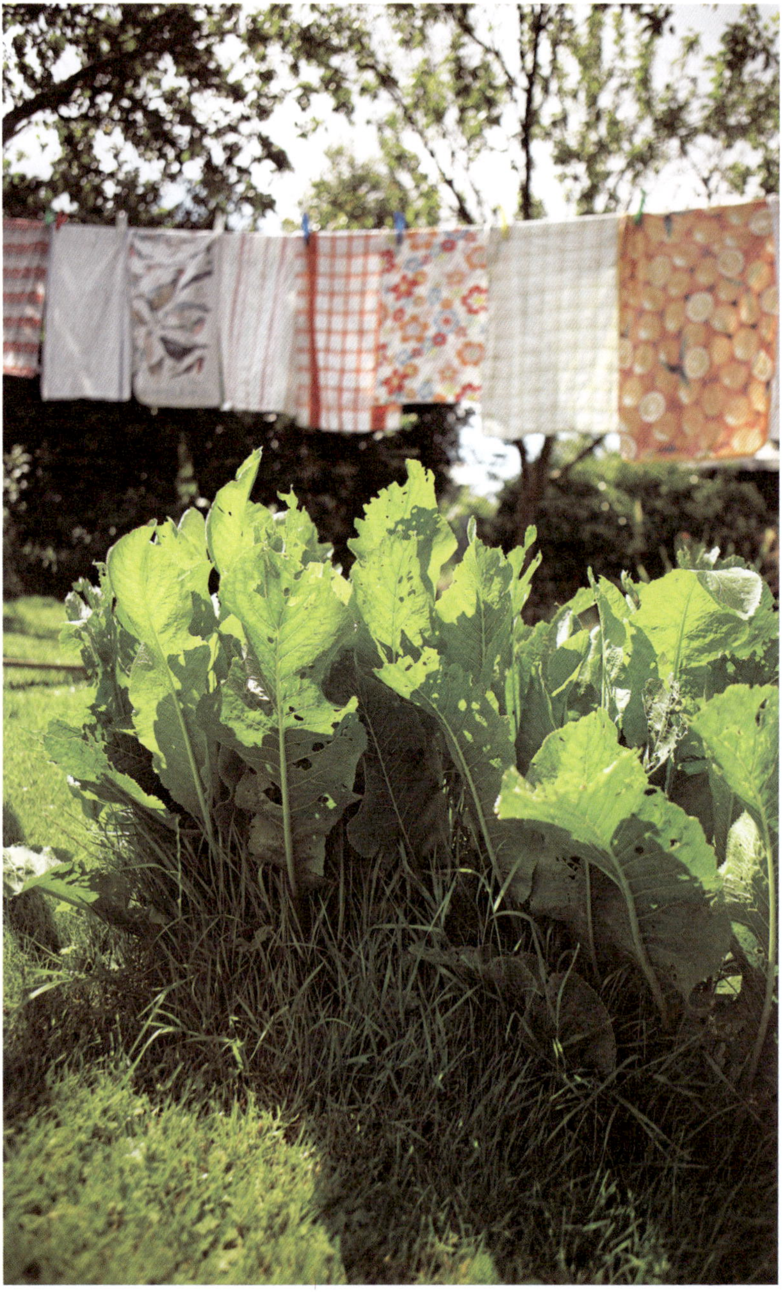

Flavoured vinegars

Season: June to November

These are very useful additions to the store cupboard as their distinctive flavours can revolutionise a simple salad dressing or sauce. The process is simple: aromatic herbs, flowers or strong-flavoured ingredients are steeped in vinegar for a period of time and are then strained out. The vinegar is then decanted into a sterilised bottle and sealed (see p.133).

Always pick leaves and flowers for steeping when they are dry and their perfume is at its best. Use cider vinegar or white wine vinegar, rather than the stronger malt – or perhaps try some delicate rice vinegar to give a hint of Asian flavour to the mix.

Horseradish vinegar

Peel and grate 50g freshly dug horseradish root and pack into a large sterilised jar with 2 finely chopped shallots, 1 tsp sugar and ½ tsp salt. Heat 600ml cider vinegar to just below boiling and pour over the mix. Seal and leave for a month or so before straining and bottling. I like to use this vinegar for pickling cucumber or beetroot.

Nasturtium vinegar

Fill a wide-necked jar of 570ml capacity with freshly gathered, brilliantly coloured nasturtium flowers, a few spicy nasturtium seed pods (see p.111), 2 chopped shallots, 8–10 peppercorns and ½ tsp salt. Pour over 500ml cold white wine vinegar. Leave for 30 days or so in a sunny spot, giving the jar a shake every now and then. Strain the vinegar and discard the flowers. Pack into a sterilised jar with a couple of fresh nasturtium flowers to identify the vinegar.

To make a splendid summer salad dressing, add 1 tbsp soy sauce to 100ml nasturtium vinegar and whisk in 200ml olive or rapeseed oil.

Mixed herb vinegar

Mix 4 heaped tbsp herbs – chives, parsley, tarragon, fennel, thyme, or whatever you have – with 500ml cold white wine vinegar or cider vinegar. Leave for 3–4 weeks in a cool, dark place. Strain, discard the herbs and bottle.

Spiced samphire vinegar

Pack 50g samphire, 6 allspice berries and 2 finely chopped shallots into a large jar. Pour over 500ml cold rice vinegar or cider vinegar. Leave for 2–3 months before straining and bottling. This is great for fish dishes, and in sweet and sour sauces.

Raspberry vinegar

Season: July to August

Sweetened vinegars are yet another way to preserve the flavour and character of summertime fruits such as raspberries. Historically, these concoctions were valued for their medicinal qualities, and were typically used to relieve coughs and treat fevers and colds. During the nineteenth century, raspberry vinegar in particular was recommended as a refreshing tonic to overcome weariness. But fruit vinegars have a multitude of culinary uses too and I certainly wouldn't want to be without a bottle or two in the kitchen.

Use raspberry vinegar on salads – either neat, or blended with olive oil. I also love it trickled over goat's cheese, pancakes and even ice cream. You'll also find that a spoonful adds a lovely piquancy to savoury sauces. For a revitalising summer drink, mix a couple of tablespoonfuls of raspberry vinegar with soda or tonic water and add ice.

The fruit for a vinegar needs to be gathered on a dry day. If the fruit is wet, it will dilute the vinegar and adversely affect its keeping quality.

Makes 1.5 litres
1kg raspberries
600ml cider vinegar or
  white wine vinegar
Granulated sugar

Put the raspberries in a bowl and crush them lightly with a wooden spoon. Add the vinegar. Cover the bowl and leave the fruit and vinegar to steep for 4–5 days, stirring occasionally.

Pour the fruit and vinegar into a scalded jelly bag or piece of muslin suspended over a bowl (see p.41) and leave to drain overnight. You can squeeze it a little if you like.

Measure the liquid then pour into a saucepan. For every 600ml fruit vinegar, add 450g sugar. Place over a low heat and bring gently to the boil, stirring until the sugar has dissolved. Boil for 8–10 minutes, removing any scum as it rises. Remove from the heat and leave to cool. Bottle and seal when cold. Use within 12 months.

Variations
Replace the raspberries with the same quantity of strawberries, blackcurrants or blackberries to create other fruit vinegars.

CORDIALS, FRUIT LIQUEURS & VINEGARS

Rosehip syrup

Season: late September to October

The shapely rosehip is the fleshy fruit of our native hedgerow rose. The orange-red berries that appear in the autumn contain a crowd of creamy white seeds, protected by tiny irritant hairs, which is why they should never be eaten raw.

Rosehips are rich in vitamins A and C and have long been used for making jams, jellies, wine, tea and, of course, syrup. This recipe is based on one issued by the Ministry of Defence during the Second World War when rosehips were gathered by volunteers. They were paid 3d (just over 1p) for each pound (450g) they collected and the syrup made from the fruit was fed to the nation's children.

Use this rosehip syrup, mixed with hot water, as a warming winter drink. I also love it drizzled neat over rice pudding or pancakes.

Or try this recipe of Hugh F-W's for a refreshing summer cocktail: pour 30ml rosehip syrup into a tall glass. Add 60ml white rum and mix well. Add a few ice cubes and pour over about 150ml tart apple juice. Garnish with a sprig of mint and serve with a straw.

Makes about 1.5 litres
500g rosehips
650g granulated sugar

Pick over the rosehips, removing the stalks, and rinse in cold water.

Put 800ml water in a pan and bring to the boil. Meanwhile, mince the rosehips or chop them in a food processor. Add them to the pan of boiling water, cover and bring back to the boil. Take off the heat and allow to stand for 15 minutes. Pour through a scalded jelly bag or muslin (see p.41) and leave to drip for an hour or so.

Set aside the strained juice. Bring another 800ml water to the boil, add the rosehip pulp, and repeat the boiling process. Tip the mixture back into the jelly bag or muslin and this time leave to drain overnight.

The next day, combine both lots of strained juice (you can discard the rosehip pulp). Measure the juice (you should have about 1 litre) and pour into a saucepan. Add the sugar and heat, stirring until dissolved. Boil for 2–3 minutes, then immediately pour into warm, sterilised bottles (see p.133) and secure with a screw-cap or cork.

Use within 4 months. If you want to keep the syrup for longer, you'll need to sterilise the bottles in a water bath (see p.133).

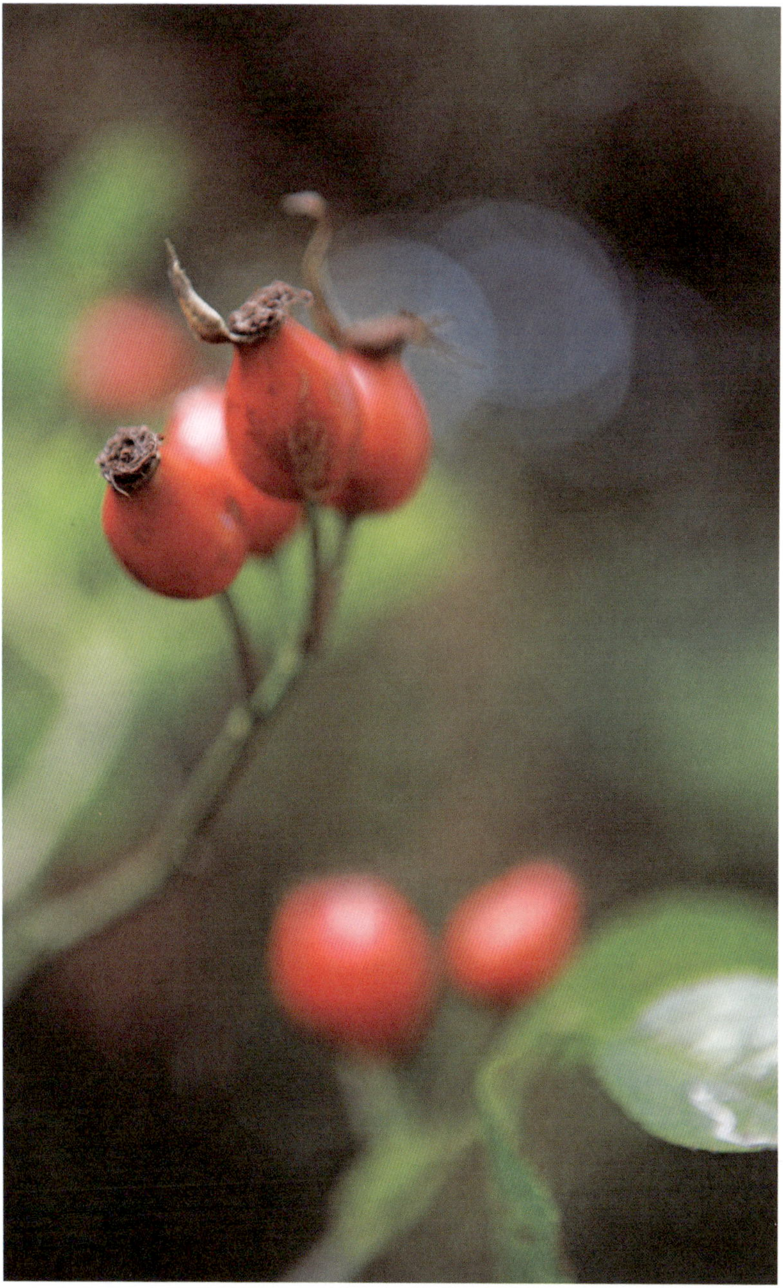

Sloe gin

Season: September to October

This is undoubtedly the best-known of the hedgerow liqueurs. It is best made with sloes that have been lightly frosted on the first cold nights of the year. (The frost helps to break down the internal structure of the fruit and get the juices flowing.) However, if the first frosts are late in arriving, you might miss the sloes because they'll have been eaten by birds. To avoid this, pick them late in September and pop in the freezer. Alternatively, prick the sloes all over with a skewer.

If you enjoy this hedgerow tipple, try some of my other favourites below. There is no reason why you cannot use vodka instead of gin.

Makes about 1 litre
450g sloes, frosted or pricked (see above)
450g sugar (or less for a more tart gin)
600ml gin

Put the sloes into a large clean jar or bottle. Pour over the sugar, followed by the gin. Secure the container with the lid and give it a good shake to mix up the contents. Shake daily for the next week to prevent the sugar from settling on the bottom and to help release the sloe juice. Thereafter shake and taste once a week for 8–10 weeks.

When the sloes have instilled their flavour, pass the mixture through a fine sieve. Pour the strained liqueur into bottles.

Ideally, you should leave sloe gin for 18 months before drinking, so it pays to have a year's batch in hand. Of course, that's not always possible – but do try and stash a bottle or two away to savour when it's mature and mellow.

And what to do with all those gin-soaked sloes? You can either eat them just as they are, or remove the stones and serve the fruit with ice cream, or fold into melted chocolate to make delectable petits fours.

Variations

In each case, follow the method for sloe gin, but with the following quantities:

Damson gin Use 450g damsons, pricked, 225g sugar and 600ml gin.

Blackberry and apple gin Use 225g blackberries, 225g cooking apples, peeled and chopped, 225g sugar and 600ml gin.

Cherry ratafia Use 500g cherries, pricked, 500ml eau de vie, 2 cinnamon sticks and 150g vanilla sugar.

Haw brandy Use 450g haws, 225g sugar and 600ml brandy.

Bachelor's jam

Season: June to October

This is also known as officer's jam but it's really not a jam at all. The German name, *Rumtopf*, seems far more appropriate for what is actually a cocktail of rum-soaked fruit. The idea is that the mixture of fruit, alcohol and sugar is added to gradually, as different fruits ripen throughout the growing season. This preserve is usually prepared with Christmas in mind, when the potent fruity alcohol is drunk and the highly spirited fruit can be served on its own or with ice cream and puddings. It's not essential to use rum, by the way – brandy, vodka or gin will work just as well.

You will need a large glazed stoneware or earthenware pot with a closely fitting lid, and a small plate, saucer or other flat object that will fit inside the pot and keep the fruit submerged.

Fruit in season (see p.132 for preparation)
1–2 litres rum, brandy, vodka or gin (40 per cent)
Granulated sugar (250g to every 500g fruit)

Choose just-ripe fruits as they appear through the summer and autumn. I normally kick off the pot with some of the first small, sweet strawberries of the season. Place these in the bottom of your pot or jar and, for every 500g fruit, sprinkle over 250g sugar. Leave this for an hour or so then pour over about 1 litre of your chosen alcohol. Place the saucer on top of the fruit to make sure the fruit remains immersed. Then cover the pot with cling film or plastic and, finally, a close-fitting lid.

Carry on like this throughout the summer and autumn, adding raspberries, cherries, peaches, plums, damsons, pears, grapes and blackberries as they come into season. (I avoid currants and gooseberries because their skins tend to toughen in the alcohol syrup, and I find rhubarb is too acid for the pot). Add the sugar each time too, and keep topping up the alcohol so that it always covers the fruit by about 2cm.

Do not stir the fruit at any point, just let it sit in its layers. When the pot is full to the brim, seal it tightly and leave for a couple of months before you start enjoying the contents. Just prior to using, dig deep and give the contents a good stir to combine all the scrumptious flavours. Use within 12 months.

P.S. If you're in a hurry, you can make bachelor's jam in one go in August, when lots of different fruits should be available. However, I do find it more fun to add the fruit over several months, whenever I have a surplus.

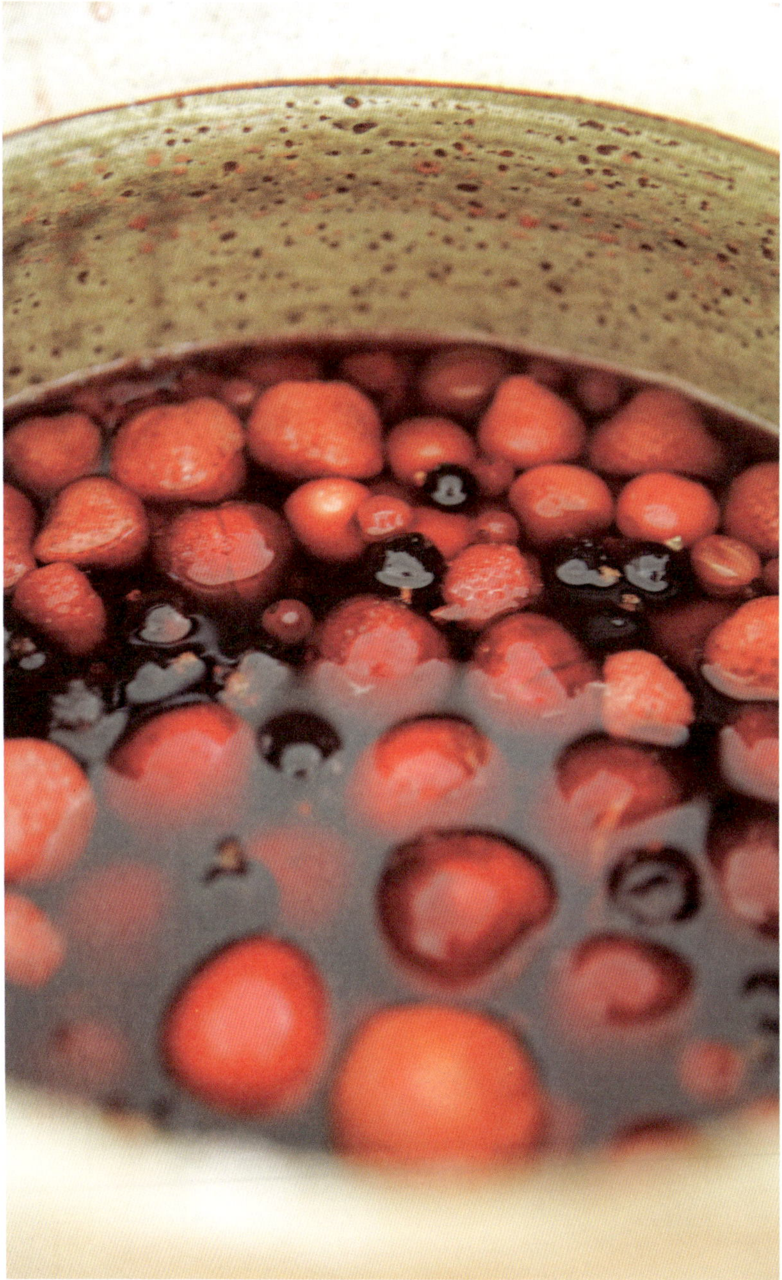

Bottled Fruits

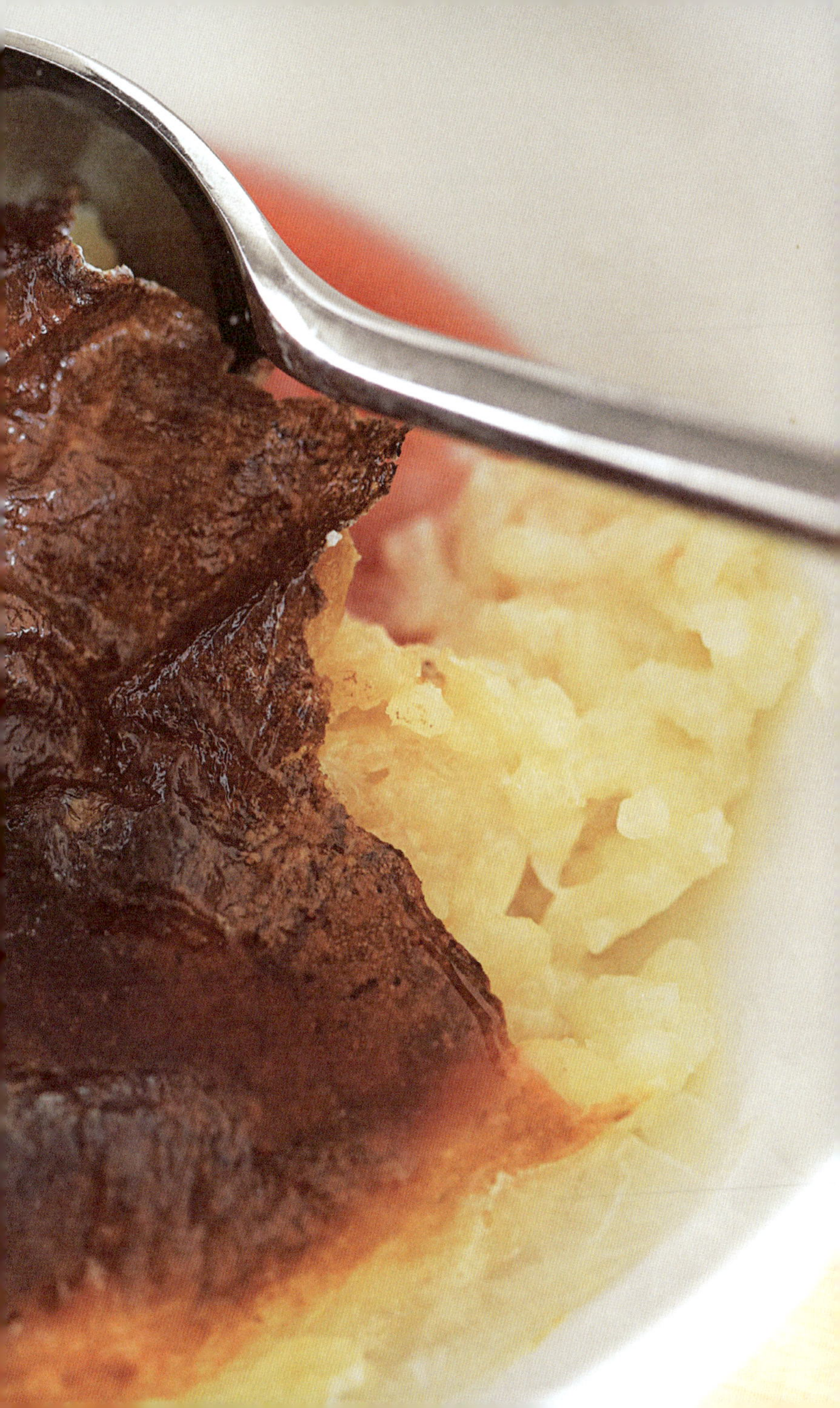

With the advent of the deep-freeze, bottling

has rather slipped from necessity and fashion. That's a shame as it is an excellent way of preserving fruits – far better than freezing for some – such as peaches, cherries, figs and apricots. These, when bottled, will remain closer in flavour and texture to their natural state. Another advantage of bottling is that the fruit is ready and waiting to be used at any moment – there's none of that ferreting about in the bottom of the freezer or waiting for a soggy mass of fruit to defrost.

Nevertheless, unravelling the bottling process can seem like cracking a secret code. There are so many methods to choose from – the slow water method, the quick water method, the very low oven, moderate oven or pressure cooker – as well as charts to navigate. To make it easier and to encourage you to have a go, I have whittled down bottling to two basic methods that can be used for most fruits – the water bath method and the oven method. To be successful, both rely on two simple points – the fruit must be sterilised by heating and the jars perfectly sealed.

Jars and bottles

The containers used for bottling are stronger than normal jam jars because they need to withstand a heating process. Two types are generally used (see below) and both are available in 250ml, 500ml, 750ml, 1 litre, 1.5 litre and 2 litre capacities (see the directory, p.210, for suppliers).

The jars, lids and rubber rings should be sterilised before the fruit is packed in. I find the easiest way to do this is to place them in a large pan of cold water and bring slowly to boiling point. I then remove the pan from the heat and leave the jars in the water until I need them. The safest way to remove the jars from the pan is with a pair of tongs. There is no need to dry the jars. Alternatively, before use, the jars can be washed in hot water, left inverted to drain, then put in a cool oven (140°C/Gas Mark 1) for 15 minutes.

> **Screw-band jars** Often referred to as Kilner jars, these have metal or glass lids and are fitted with rubber rings that separate the top of the jar and the lid. The screw-band is fully tightened only after the cooking process, to seal the jar and form a vacuum.
>
> **Clip jars** Often known as Le Parfait jars, these also have a rubber ring to separate the jar top from the lid but are fastened with a metal spring clip. These jars allow steam to escape, but no air can enter. They normally have a wider mouth than screw-band jars and are therefore more suitable for use with larger fruits such as pears or peaches.

BOTTLED FRUITS 161

In both cases, the rubber rings must be a perfect fit and in perfect condition – so check them before using. They will deteriorate with use and will need replacing from time to time. The rubber rings can either be sterilised with the jars and lids, or soaked in warm water for 15 minutes (this makes it much easier to stretch them on), then dipped in boiling water just before they go on the jar.

Preparing syrup

Fruit can be bottled in plain water but a syrup based on sugar or honey will improve the flavour. Alcohol, pure fruit juice, fruit cordials, scented leaves and spices can be added to give character and interest. The strength of the syrup depends on the type of fruit used and how you like your fruit to taste – the tarter the fruit, the heavier you'll want to make the syrup. Generally, you want a sweeter syrup for more tightly packed fruit too, because less is used. Syrups are always prepared by simply dissolving the required amount of sugar or honey in water and boiling for 1 minute.

Light syrup 100g sugar, 600ml water
Medium syrup 175g sugar, 600ml water
Heavy syrup 250g sugar, 600ml water

Fruit for bottling

This should ideally be perfectly ripe, but err on the side of under rather than over if you have to. Handle the fruit carefully as any bruising will spoil the preserve. Prepare it by removing stalks, stems, leaves and hulls, and rinsing in cold water if necessary.

Plums, damsons and cherries These can be bottled whole or stoned – stones will impart an agreeable almondy flavour. There's no need to prick the fruit.

Gooseberries These are best bottled when green and slightly under-ripe. The skins should be pricked or nicked to prevent shrivelling.

Pears and apples These should be peeled and cored before bottling. Pears can be cored and quartered or left whole. Once peeled, place in a bowl of salted water (25g salt to 1 litre water) to prevent discoloration until ready to pack.

Peaches, apricots and nectarines These should be peeled: immerse in boiling water for 1 minute then plunge into cold water, peel and pack immediately.

BOTTLED FRUITS 163

Rhubarb These stalks should be chopped into 2.5–5cm lengths and steeped overnight in a light to medium syrup prior to packing and processing.

Soft fruits Handle these as little as possible – just remove stalks or hulls.

Vegetables These require a very high-temperature process and are not suitable for home bottling by either of the methods covered in this book.

Packing tips

Fruit to be bottled should be handled as little as possible. Packing the fruit in neatly will mean you can get more in the jar.

1. Fruit will shrink during the heating process so should be packed into jars as tightly as possible, but without bruising.

2. Use a long-handled packing spoon, the end of a wooden spoon or a chopstick to position fruit and tease out any air bubbles.

3. Stand jars on a wooden surface or newspaper when filling with hot syrup.

4. Make sure the rim of the jar is free from pips or fruit fibres.

5. Give the jar a sharp knock or twizzle to remove any trapped air before sealing.

The water bath method

For bottling in this way, you need a pan deep enough to contain the jars completely submerged under water. The jars will crack if they sit directly on the base of the pan, so it needs a 'false bottom' such as a wire trivet or a folded tea towel. A thermometer is essential to check the temperature.

The fruit should be packed into jars and filled to the brim with hot syrup (about 60°C). If you're using screw-band jars, the band should be released by a quarter of a turn for steam to escape. Place the jars in the pan and cover completely with warm water (38°C). Heat to simmering point (88°C) over a period of 25–30 minutes, then simmer for the time given in the recipe or the chart (overleaf).

Remove the jars one at a time and place them on a wooden surface, newspaper or folded cloth – scooping out some of the water first will make it much easier to lift the jars from the pan. Tighten the bands on screw-band jars, then leave undisturbed for 24 hours until completely cool. Check the seal the following day (see overleaf).

BOTTLED FRUITS 165

The oven method

This takes longer than the water bath method but means you can process more jars at a time and you don't need to worry about finding a deep pan.

Preheat the oven to 150°C/Gas Mark 2. Stand the jars about 5cm apart (enough to allow the warm air to circulate) on a thick pad of newspaper, or stand them on newspaper or a folded tea towel in a baking tray filled with water to a depth of 3cm. Fill the packed jars with boiling syrup and cover with the rubber rings and jar tops, but do not fasten with clips or screw-bands at this stage.

Heat in the oven for the time given on the chart (see right). Remove the jars, one at a time, seal with the screw-band or clip immediately and place on a wooden surface, newspaper or folded cloth. Leave undisturbed until completely cool and check the seal the following day (see below).

Testing the seal

It's important to do this after bottling to check that the seal is absolutely airtight. When the jars are completely cool, undo the clips or remove the screw-bands. Put one hand underneath the jar and, with the other hand, carefully lift the jar by the lid. If it's well sealed, the lid will remain firmly on. You can then re-fasten the clip or screw-band and put the jar away for storage. If it comes away, either reprocess the fruit or eat it up immediately.

Storage

Store bottled fruits in a cool, dark and dry place. They will keep well for up to a year. After this, although there may be nothing wrong with them, the texture and colour will begin to deteriorate.

Opening jars

The round rubber seal on a Le Parfait jar has a small protuberance which when pulled should break the seal. However, it doesn't always work! So for awkward Le Parfait jars and Kilner jars, very carefully insert the point of a knife between the rubber ring and the rim and gently lever up. If the seal is still difficult to break, then stand the jar in hot water for a few minutes – this will help to release the seal.

Heating times for water bath and oven bottling methods

For safe bottling it is important to adhere to these timings. For the water bath method, check the water temperature with a thermometer; for the oven method, preheat the oven and check the temperature using an oven thermometer.

FRUIT	WATER BATH METHOD	OVEN METHOD
Apple slices **Blackberries** **Blueberries** **Currants** **Gooseberries** **Loganberries** **Mulberries** **Raspberries** **Strawberries** **Rhubarb**	Maintain at simmering point (88°C) for 2 minutes	30–40 minutes for jars up to 1 litre 45–50 minutes for 1–2 litre jars
Apricots **Cherries** **Damsons** **Greengages** **Plums, whole**	Maintain at simmering point (88°C) for 10 minutes	40–50 minutes for jars up to 1 litre 50–60 minutes for 1–2 litre jars
Nectarines **Peaches** **Plums, halved**	Maintain at simmering point (88°C) for 20 minutes	50–60 minutes for jars up to 1 litre 60–70 minutes for 1–2 litre jars
Figs **Pears** **Tomatoes, whole**	Maintain at simmering point (88°C) for 40 minutes	60–70 minutes for jars up to 1 litre 70–80 minutes for 1–2 litre jars
Fruit purées and pulps (these need to be poured at boiling point into hot jars)	Maintain at simmering point (88°C) for 5 minutes for fruit pulp, 10 minutes for tomato purée	Not applicable

Early rhubarb with honey

Season: January to February

The arrival of the early 'forced' rhubarb in January deserves a salutation of the greatest magnitude and I can never wait to savour its fresh, earthy energy. The blushing stalks, with their tart but delicate flavour, are strictly seasonal, so be sure you don't miss the chance to bottle a jar or two to enjoy later in the year.

Makes 2 x 500ml jars
150g honey
Juice of 1 large orange (you need 100ml)
1.5kg forced rhubarb

Put the honey and 500ml water into a pan and slowly bring to the boil to make a syrup. Remove from the heat and add the orange juice.

Meanwhile, wipe the rhubarb and trim the ends. Cut into even 2.5–5cm chunks. Place the rhubarb in a bowl and pour over the hot syrup. Leave to stand for 10–12 hours. This soaking makes the rhubarb much easier to pack in the jars.

Using a slotted spoon, take the rhubarb from the syrup and pack into warm, sterilised jars (see p.160). Bring the syrup to the boil again and pour over the rhubarb, filling the jars to the brim. Cover with lids, remembering to loosen screw-bands, if you're using them, by a quarter of a turn (see p.164). Stand in a pan with a folded tea towel on the base. Cover the jars with warm water (at 38°C). Bring to simmering point (88°C) over a period of 25 minutes. Simmer at this temperature for 2 minutes.

Carefully remove the jars from the pan and place on a wooden surface or a folded tea towel. Tighten screw-bands. Leave undisturbed to cool for 24 hours then check the seals before storing. Use within a year.

Variation
Instead of honey and orange, try using 50g very finely sliced fresh root ginger and liven up the syrup with ginger cordial or, better still, some ginger wine. Both natives of Asia, ginger and rhubarb are natural partners. So often ingredients that coincide, seasonally or locally, complement each other in the culinary world.

Blues and bay

Season: late July to September

This recipe, applying the oven method, can be used for bottling the many members of the *Vaccinium* family, which include the cultivated blueberry as well as the wild bilberry (also known as whortleberry, whinberry or blaeberry, depending on your region). These bushy plants can be found growing wild on heath and moorland in many parts of Britain. The cultivated blueberry also thrives in the acidic soil of coastal east Dorset, as well as other parts of the country, and it is now possible to buy excellent English-grown 'blues' (see the directory, p.210). The delicate, lemony nutmeg note of fresh bay complements their gentle flavour beautifully.

Serve these fragrant berries for a breakfast treat with thick vanilla yoghurt.

Makes 3 x 500ml jars
150g caster sugar
50ml lemon juice (about ½ lemon)
1kg blueberries or bilberries
6 fresh bay leaves

Preheat the oven to 150°C/Gas Mark 2.

Start by making a fruit syrup: mix the sugar with 600ml water in a pan and bring slowly to the boil to dissolve the sugar. Remove from the heat, add the lemon juice, cover and keep warm.

Pick over the berries, removing any twiggy bits or leaves. Pack them firmly, without crushing, into warm, sterilised jars (see p.160), sliding the bay leaves attractively around the side of the jars.

Bring the sugar syrup to the boil and pour over the blueberries, filling the jars to the brim. Cover with lids, but do not fasten the clips or put on the screw-bands. Put the jars, 5cm apart, in the oven for 30 minutes.

Carefully remove the jars, seal with screw-bands or clips immediately and place on a wooden surface, newspaper or folded cloth. Leave undisturbed until completely cool and check the seal the following day.

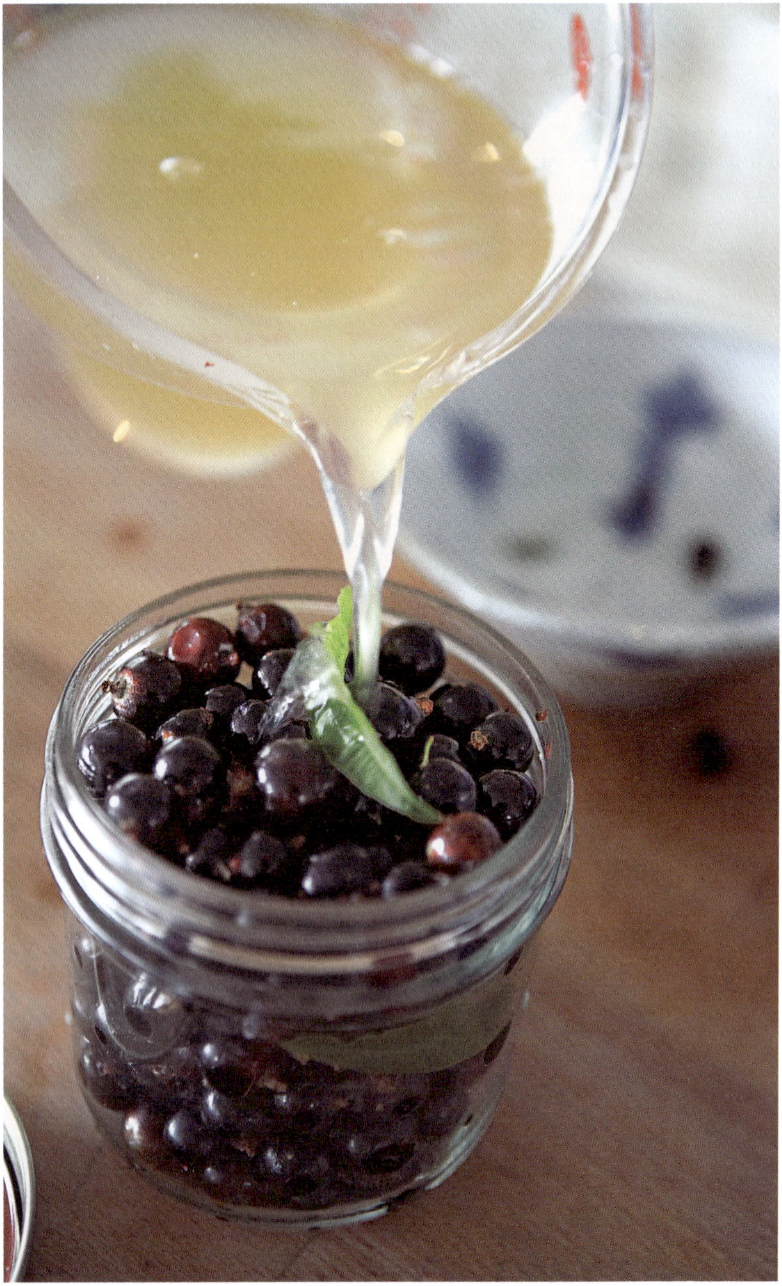

Bottled blackcurrants

Season: June to August

The rich, intense flavour of blackcurrants is well preserved by bottling and I find it very useful to have a few jars on the larder shelf. Bottled currants are delicious served with hot steaming custard, vanilla ice cream or good plain yoghurt. When friends drop by, I often open a jar for an instant pud.

Makes 2 x 500ml jars
200g granulated sugar
1kg large, firm, juicy blackcurrants
A few lemon verbena or scented geranium leaves (optional)

Put the sugar into a pan with 600ml water and heat gently to dissolve, then boil for 1 minute to make a syrup.

Prepare the blackcurrants by removing any twiggy stalks and rinsing the fruit if necessary. Pack the currants as tightly as possible, but without crushing, into warm, sterilised jars (see p.160). If using verbena or geranium leaves, layer 2 or 3 amongst the little purple-black fruits as you go.

Cover the packed fruit with the hot syrup (at 60°C), filling the jars to the brim. Fasten with screw-bands or clips. If using screw-bands, remember to tighten them and then release by a quarter of a turn (see p.164). Place a folded tea towel in the bottom of a large pan (which must be deeper than your jars are tall). Fill the pan with warm water (at 38°C) then submerge the jars completely.

Clip a sugar thermometer to the side of the pan. Bring the water slowly to simmering point (88°C) over 25 minutes, then maintain this temperature for just 2 minutes.

Lift the jars out and place on a wooden surface or a folded tea towel. Tighten screw-bands. Leave undisturbed for 24 hours. To check they are properly sealed, remove the clips or screw-bands and lift the jars by their lids. Store in a cool, dark place. Use within a year.

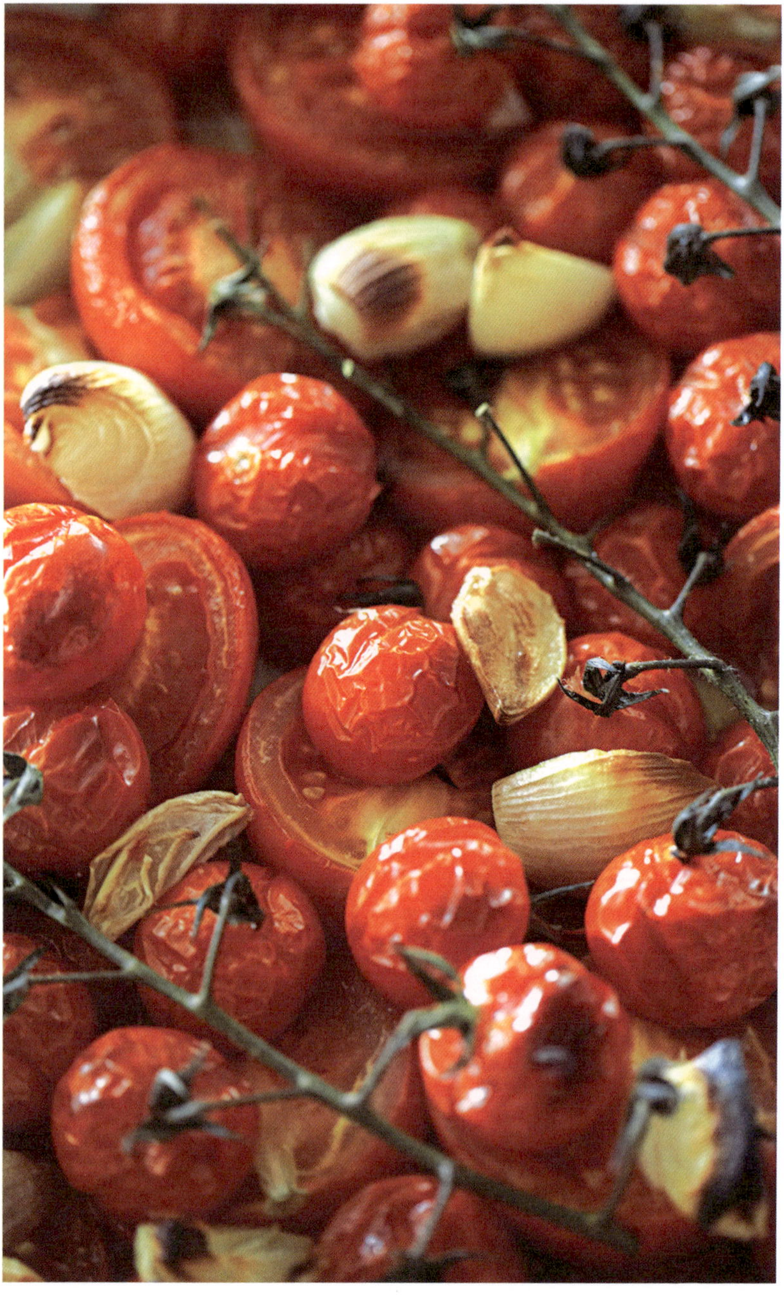

Roasted tomato passata

Season: August to September

For me, tomato passata is an essential store cupboard ingredient. I use it as a base for my roasted tomato ketchup (see p.195), as well as for pasta sauces and curries.

The best time to make this preserve is in August or September, when British tomatoes are at their cropping peak – smelling strong, sweet and aromatic when picked from the vine. This recipe uses 2kg fruit but, if you are using bought tomatoes as opposed to home-grown ones, I suggest you negotiate a good deal with your local grower and buy a boxful or two. You certainly won't regret it. You can't buy passata like this one!

Makes 2 x 500ml jars
2kg ripe tomatoes
200g shallots, peeled and thinly sliced
3–4 garlic cloves, peeled and thinly sliced
A few rosemary, thyme, basil or oregano sprigs
1 tsp salt
½ tsp ground black pepper
1 tsp sugar
50ml olive, sunflower or rapeseed oil

Preheat the oven to 180°C/Gas Mark 4.

Cut the tomatoes in half and place them, cut side up, in a single layer in a large roasting pan. Scatter the shallots, garlic, herbs, salt, pepper, sugar and oil over the top. Roast for about 1 hour, or until they are well softened. Remove from the oven and rub the tomatoes through a nylon sieve, or purée with a passata machine or mouli (see p.41).

Have your hot, sterilised jars ready (see p.160). Put the tomato purée into a saucepan and bring to boiling point. Pour it into the jars, filling them to the brim, and seal immediately with caps, clips or screw-bands. If you're using screw-bands, remember to release the lid by a quarter of a turn (see p.164).

Stand the jars in a large saucepan with a folded tea towel on the base. Cover with warm water and bring to simmering point (88°C) over a period of 25 minutes, then simmer for 10 minutes.

Remove the jars and stand them on a wooden surface or folded tea towel. Tighten the screw-bands, if using. Leave undisturbed until cold, then check the seal. Use within 12 months. Once opened, refrigerate and use within a few days.

Mulled pears

Season: late August to October

It always amazes me just how much fruit a gnarled old pear tree can bear in a good season. However, it's still a little tricky to catch pears at their point of perfect ripeness – somewhere between bullet hard and soft and woolly. Never mind, should you find yourself with a boxful of under-ripe specimens, this recipe turns them into a preserve 'pear excellence'.

These pears are particularly delicious served with thick vanilla custard, or used as a base for a winter fruit salad. Alternatively, try serving them with terrines and pâtés, or mix with chicory leaves drizzled with a honey mustard dressing and crumbly blue cheese.

Makes 2 x 1 litre jars
125g granulated sugar
500ml cider (dry, medium or sweet)
1.5kg small pears

Small handful of cloves
2 x 5cm pieces of cinnamon stick

Preheat the oven to 150°C/Gas Mark 2.

Start by making a cider syrup: mix the sugar with 500ml water in a pan and bring slowly to the boil to dissolve the sugar. Remove from the heat, add the cider, cover and keep warm.

Peel the pears, keeping the stalks attached. As you do so, place them in a bowl of lightly salted water to stop them browning. When all the pears are peeled, cut them in half and stud each half with a clove or two. Pack them into warm, sterilised jars (see p.160), adding a piece of cinnamon to each. Pears are very bottom-heavy of course, and I find the best way to pack them is head-to-toe.

Bring the cider syrup to the boil and pour over the pears. Cover the jars with lids, but do not fasten the clips or put on the screw-bands. Place the jars 5cm apart, in the oven, for 1 hour.

Remove the jars, seal with the screw-bands or clips immediately and place on a wooden surface, newspaper or folded cloth. Leave undisturbed until completely cool and check the seal the following day. Keep for up to 12 months.

Variation
Try replacing the cider with red wine and add a star anise to each jar if you like.

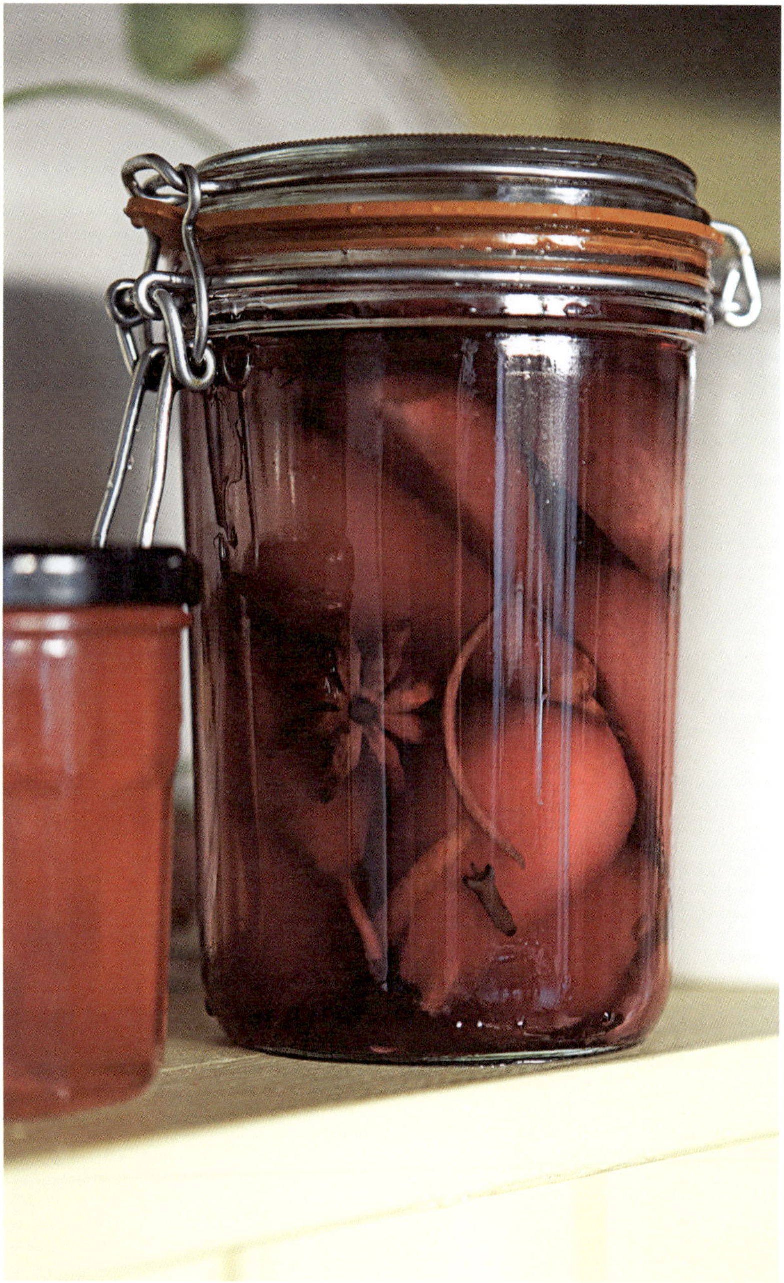

Spiced brandy plums

Season: August to early October

The Brogdale Trust in Kent is home to the National Fruit Collection – a bit like a Noah's Ark for the fruits of the earth. Among their many living specimens, they grow over 300 different cultivars of *Prunus domestica,* the European plum – also known as dessert plums. These fruits crop from high summer right through into October, giving us plenty to eat fresh, and loads to preserve for later in the year.

One of our great national fruits, plums are grown all over Britain and are often easy to find at farmer's markets and roadside stalls. So even if you miss the Early Rivers of late July, and you're away on holiday for the August Victorias, you should still be able to catch the Marjorie's Seedlings in September. Or you can bottle peaches, nectarines or apricot halves in the same way.

Makes 2 x 500ml jars

100g honey
Finely grated zest of 1 orange
100ml brandy
1kg plums, stalks removed
2 cinnamon sticks
2 star anise

Start by making a brandy syrup: put the honey and 400ml water into a pan, heat gently until the honey is dissolved, then add the orange zest and brandy. Set aside.

Halve the plums lengthwise with a sharp knife. Twist them apart and remove the stone with the point of the knife. Pack the plums into warmed, sterilised jars (see p.160) with the rounded sides of the fruit following the curve of the jar (you'll fit more in this way). Prod a cinnamon stick and a star anise down the side of each jar.

Pour the hot brandy syrup (at 60°C) over the fruit until the jars are full to the brim. Tap to remove any air bubbles. Seal with clips or screw-bands, remembering to release the screw-band by a quarter of a turn, if using this type of jar (see p.164).

Choose a large pan, deep enough for your jars to sit in and be totally immersed in water. Put a folded tea towel on the base and fill with warm water (at 38°C). Put the jars into the pan, making sure they are completely covered with the water. Bring to simmering point (88°C) over a period of 25 minutes, then maintain this temperature for 20 minutes.

Transfer the jars to a wooden surface or place on a folded tea towel. Tighten the screw-bands, if using. Leave undisturbed for 24 hours then check the seal is secure. Use within a year.

BOTTLED FRUITS 177

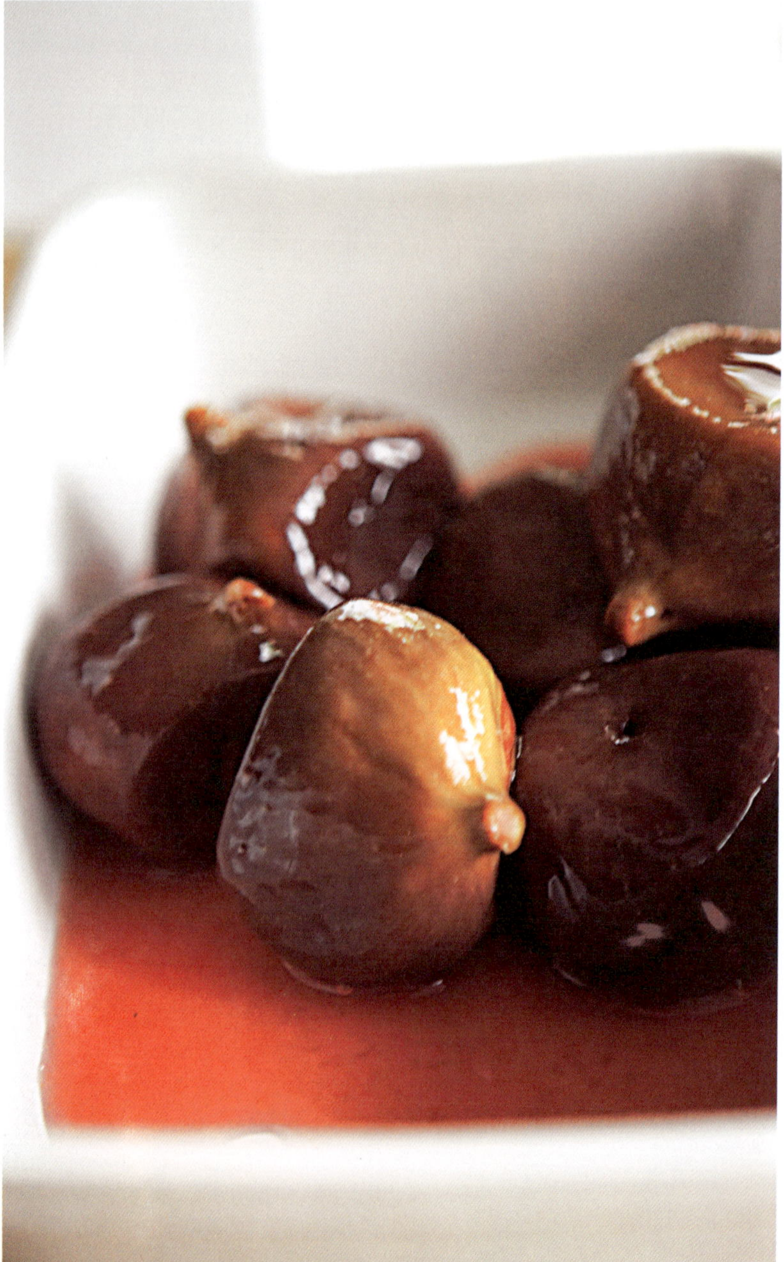

Figpote

Season: August to September

The fig is a member of the mulberry family and generally best suited to warmer climates than our own. However, a contented, well-positioned home-grown tree can still crop well, usually in August. In addition, September is peak season for imported figs, and they should be inexpensive and widely available. There are countless varieties, ranging in colour from purply-black to yellowy-green – any can be used for this recipe. Just make sure, when picking or buying, that your figs are ripe, as they do not ripen after picking.

This recipe uses a simplified version of the oven method. Everything is cooked and hot to start with, so it's not necessary to heat the jars for an extended time in the oven. A few jars of these honey-soaked fruits, stored away for the winter months, will be a blissful reminder that the hot days of summer were not just a fig-ment of your imagination…

Makes 2 x 250ml jars
12 figs (not too big) 450ml Earl Grey tea or green tea
150ml freshly squeezed orange juice 125g honey

Preheat the oven to 140°C/Gas Mark 1 and put your sterilised jars (see p.160) inside to heat.

Wash the figs and remove any hard, twiggy bits of stalk – but do not cut right back to the flesh, as this risks splitting the skin.

Put the orange juice, tea and honey into a pan and gently heat to simmering point to make a syrup. Add the figs and cook gently for 8–10 minutes, or until tender. Using a slotted spoon, take out the figs and carefully pack them into the hot jars (see p.164). It may be a bit of a squash, but figs quite like this. Return the filled jars to the oven to keep warm – it is important to keep the jars as hot as possible to create a successful seal.

Bring the fruit syrup to the boil and boil for 6–7 minutes to reduce it in volume. Stand the jars on a wooden surface or some newspaper and pour the hot syrup over the figs, filling the jars to the brim. Seal immediately with lids, clips or screw-bands. Leave undisturbed for 24 hours, then check the seal is secure. Use within a year.

Winter fruit compote

Season: winter

It may seem somewhat unnecessary to bottle dried fruit but I love having a few jars of this compote on the shelf. The once shrivelled fruits become plump and luscious and are quite delicious served alone for breakfast, or with yogurt or crème fraîche as a pudding.

I like to make this in early November, when newly dried prunes, figs and apricots are available. Keep a lookout for small, dried wild figs, which will plump up perfectly to their original shapely selves. The glistening black prunes from the Agen area in southern France are also key players – I prefer to use these unstoned because they infuse the compote with their almond-like essence. A handful of full-flavoured, unsulphured, sun-dried apricots complete the mix.

A simplified version of the oven method is used – everything is cooked and hot to start with, so the jars don't need to be heated for an extended time in the oven.

Makes 4 x 500ml jars
1 litre freshly made green tea, Earl Grey or breakfast tea
400g dried figs
200g unsulphured dried apricots
400g dried prunes, Agen prunes if possible, preferably with stones
200ml freshly squeezed orange juice
150g honey

Put the kettle on and make a large pot of tea (this is not for you, it's for the compote).

Combine the dried fruit in a large bowl. Pour the hot tea and orange juice over it and mix together, making sure all the fruit is totally immersed. Cover and leave to steep for 24 hours.

Preheat the oven to 140°C/Gas Mark 1 and place your sterilised jars (see p.160) inside. Carefully turn the fruit and liquid into a large pan. Bring slowly to simmering point and poach the fruit for 10 minutes.

Remove the pan of fruit from the heat. Using a slotted spoon, scoop out the fruit and pack into the hot jars. Return the jars to the oven to keep warm. Add the honey to the tea/orange steeping juice. Bring to the boil and boil for 5 minutes.

Carefully remove the jars from the oven and pour in the honeyed fruit juice so it comes to the very brim of the jars and completely covers the fruit. Seal immediately with lids, clips or screw-bands. Leave undisturbed for 24 hours, then check the seal is secure. Store in a cool, dry place and use within 12 months.

BOTTLED FRUITS 181

Liz's luscious raspberries

Season: July to late October

This recipe comes from Liz Neville, a virtuoso preserves maker with whom I run the River Cottage Preserved courses. You can make it with any raspberry, but we particularly like to use the big autumn berries which generously stretch the soft-fruit season well into October, even November. Bottle a few and you can extend your raspberry eating well into the dark winter months.

In an ideal world, the fruit for this preserve would be packed into the jars as you pick it from the canes. That may not be possible – but do make sure the fruit is in tip-top condition and handled as little as possible.

Makes 3 x 500ml jars
150g granulated sugar
1kg firm, just-ripe raspberries
100–150ml brandy, gin, vodka or raspberry liqueur

First make a syrup: put the sugar and 750ml water into a pan and heat slowly to dissolve the sugar then bring to the boil. Keep the syrup warm.

Pack the raspberries tightly into warm, sterilised jars (see p.160). Make sure you don't bruise the fruit – a chopstick or wooden spoon handle is useful for gently prodding it down. Pour the alcohol over the packed fruit. Fill the jars to the brim with the sugar syrup, tapping them to remove any air bubbles. Put the lids on the jars, loosening screw-bands by a quarter of a turn, if you're using them, to allow the steam to escape (see p.164).

Stand the jars in a deep pan and cover with warm water (at 38°C). Heat to simmering point (88°C), over 25 minutes. Maintain this temperature for 2 minutes.

Carefully remove the jars and stand them on a wooden surface or thick folded towel. Tighten the screw-bands then leave the jars undisturbed to cool. When cold, check the seal by removing the clips or screw-bands and lifting the jar by the lid. Use within 12 months.

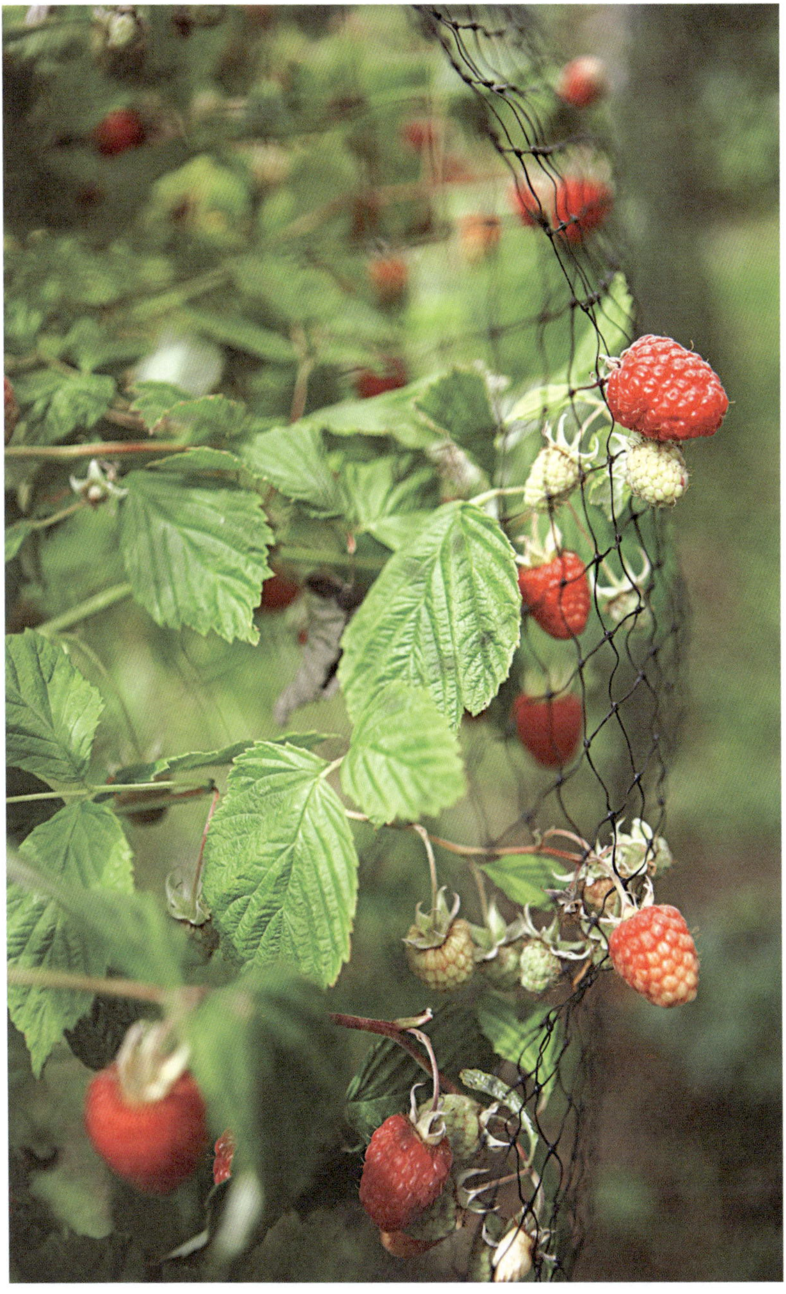

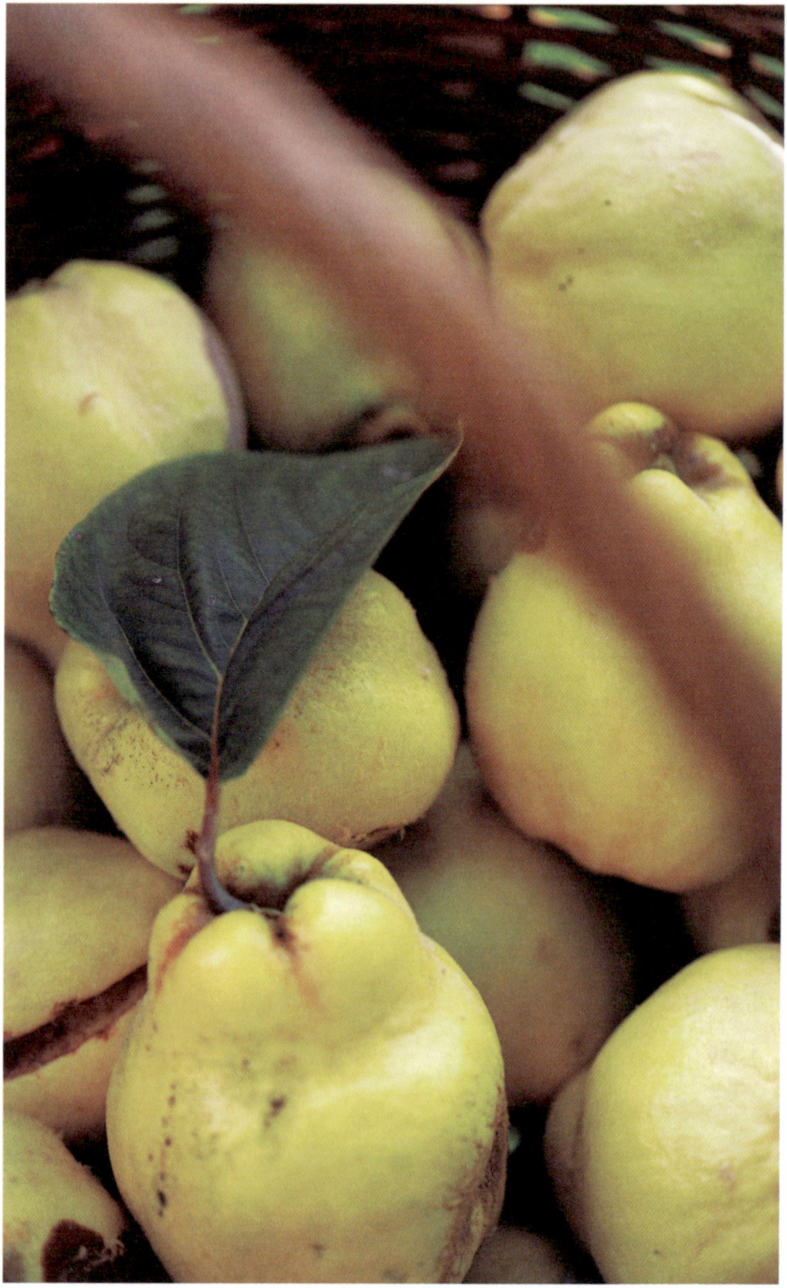

Quince and apple sauce

Season: September to October

The raw flesh of the lumpy yellow quince is dry and disagreeably sour. However, once cooked, it becomes pink and highly perfumed. Lightly sweetened and combined with good fluffy cooking apples, such as Bramleys, it makes a delightful accompaniment for roast pork or duck. I also love this aromatic fruity sauce on a home-baked rice pudding.

Makes 4 x 250ml jars

500g quince, peeled, cored and chopped	500g cooking apples, peeled, cored and chopped
Juice of ½ lemon	125g granulated sugar

Put the quince, lemon juice and 500ml water into a saucepan. Bring to the boil then simmer for 8–10 minutes (quince takes longer to soften than apple and needs a bit of a head start). Add the apples and sugar and cook for a further 10–15 minutes until all the fruit is well softened. Remove from the heat and either beat to a smooth pulp with a wooden spoon or rub through a sieve.

Meanwhile, preheat the oven to 140°C/Gas Mark 1 and place your sterilised jars (see p.160) inside.

Return the pulp to the pan and bring to the boil, stirring to make sure it doesn't catch and burn. Remove from the heat and pour immediately into the warm, sterilised jars. Seal with lids, clips or screw-bands, remembering to release the screw-band by a quarter of a turn if using this type of jar (see p.164). Place in a deep pan with a folded tea towel on the bottom. Cover with warm water, bring to simmering point (88°C), then simmer for 5 minutes.

Remove the jars from the hot water and place on a wooden surface or folded tea towel. Tighten the screw-bands, if using, and leave the jars undisturbed until cold. Check the seal. Store in a cool, dry place. Use within 12 months.

Sauces, Ketchups & Oil-based Preserves

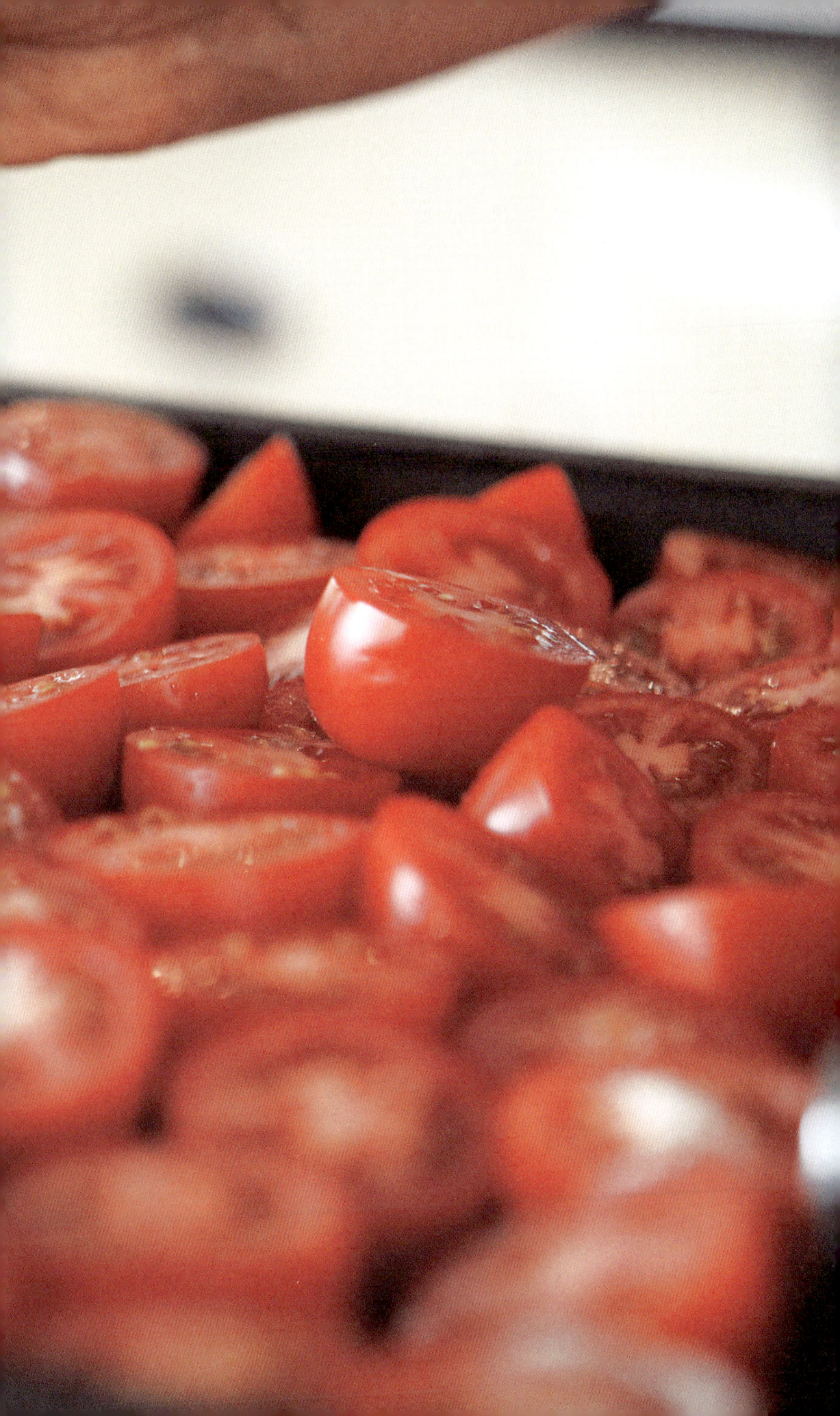

Sauces, pastes and condiments are among the tasty recipes in this chapter. Vinegar, sugar, salt and oil all come into play as preservatives; you will find more detailed information on these ingredients on pp.35–9. Oil has been used as an air-excluding ingredient since ancient times to keep foods from spoiling, but it is not a common preserving medium in this country. However, with the increasing availability of superb-quality oils, produced both here and abroad, this delicious and luxurious way of preserving is becoming much more accessible. It is certainly a branch of preserving that I find very exciting and rewarding.

This chapter will introduce you to the following range of preserves:

Sauces This is a generic term if ever there was one, but for the purposes of this book, I define a sauce as a smooth condiment generally made with similar ingredients to a chutney (see p.94). The cooked, spiced fruits and vegetables are either sieved or puréed to give a thick, pourable consistency.

Ketchups Sometimes referred to in old recipe books as 'catsups' or 'catchups', these are generally thinner than sauces and made from a single fruit or vegetable with vinegar and seasonings.

Vegetables in oil The technique of using oil to preserve lightly blanched or brined vegetables is strongly associated with Mediterranean countries, where olive oil is abundant. It is particularly suited to vegetables with strong flavours, such as globe artichokes, asparagus, dried tomatoes and mushrooms – not least because they will flavour the oil, which can also be used.

Pesto and pastes These intense condiments are made from aromatic or strongly spiced ingredients and do not contain high levels of salt, vinegar or other preservatives. For this reason, they need to be sealed off from the air with a layer of oil, refrigerated, and generally should not be kept for more than a month or two. After some has been taken from the jar, the oil covering should always be replaced, which may mean topping up with a little more.

Flavoured oils Easily made by steeping herbs, spices or other robustly flavoured ingredients in oil, these are among the simplest and most rewarding of preserves to make. They enliven everything from salad dressings and mayonnaise to marinades and stir-fries. Use warm oil for firm ingredients such as chillies and spices, and cold oil for green herbs.

Coulis Made from very lightly sweetened fruit that is simply sieved or puréed, coulis are usually based on juicy summer berries and currants.

SAUCES, KETCHUPS & OIL-BASED PRESERVES 189

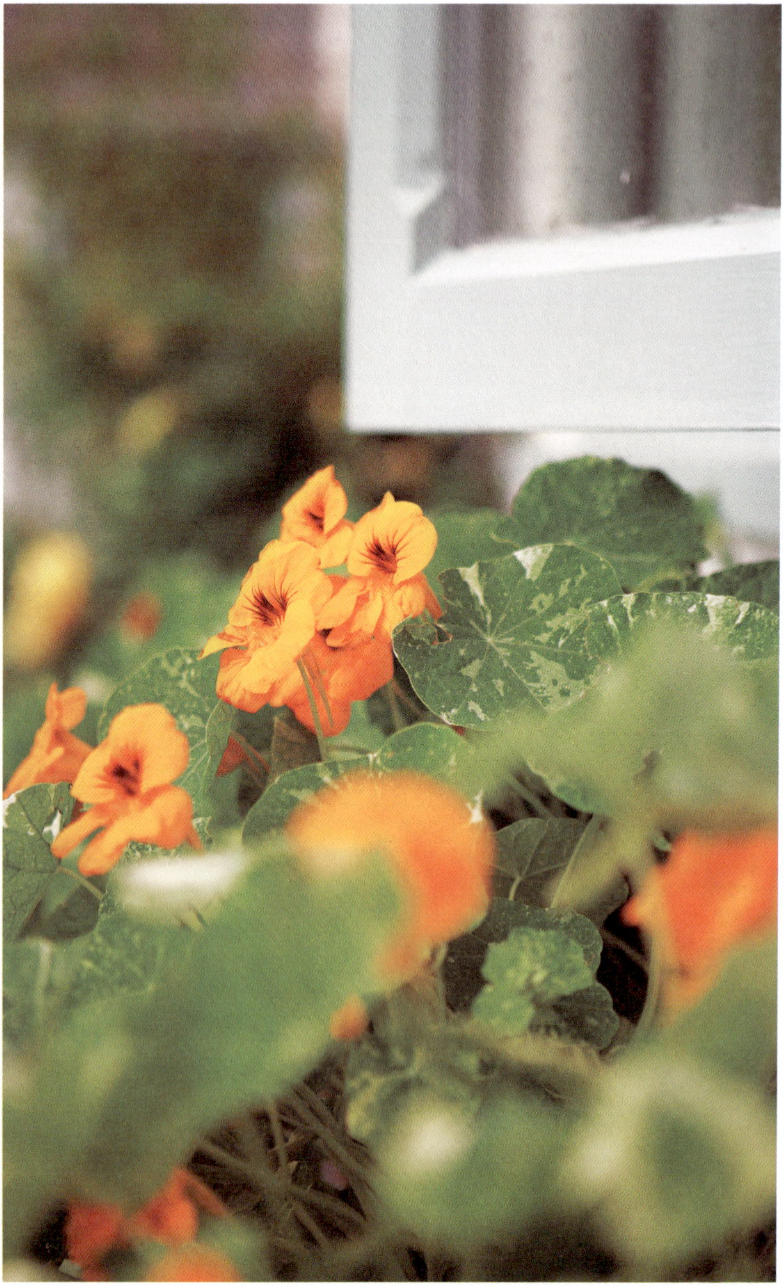

Garden pesto

Season: July to August

The big, plate-like leaves of the nasturtium plant (*Tropaeolum majus*) are abundant throughout the summer, and often well into the golden months of autumn. With their peppery flavour, they make the perfect base for a fiery pesto. Add a sprig or two of garden mint, a few golden marigold petals and some spicy nasturtium seeds and you have a wonderful sauce to stir into pasta, swirl on soups or just smear in a sandwich. Pick the leaves on a warm, dry day – ideally earlier in the summer, before the caterpillars have decided to feast on them.

Whenever I make pesto, I replace the traditional Parmesan with a local goat's cheese called Capriano. Made by Dorset-based Woolsery Cheese (see the directory, p.210), this is a hard goat's cheese, matured for a year. It makes an excellent alternative to Parmesan in all kinds of dishes. Using home-produced hemp oil instead of olive oil is another way to make your pesto more home-grown. If you find the pungent flavour of hemp oil a little too strong, you can combine it or replace it with rapeseed oil. See the directory for more details.

Makes 2 x 225g jars
50g nasturtium leaves
2–3 mint leaves (optional)
2 garlic cloves, peeled and crushed
6 or so nasturtium seed pods
 (see p.111)
50g pine nuts (optional)
75g mature, hard goat's cheese
 or Parmesan, finely grated

Juice of ½ lemon (50ml)
150ml hemp, rapeseed or olive oil,
 plus extra to seal
Petals from 2 marigold flowers
Salt to taste

Purists say that pesto should be made by pounding the ingredients together using a pestle and mortar. For this recipe, you can certainly do that, starting by crushing the mint leaves, garlic, nasturtium seeds and nuts, then adding the cheese, followed by the lemon juice and oil. Pound until well blended, folding in the marigold petals and salt at the very end.

Then again, you can do as I do and simply whiz everything (except the marigold petals and salt) in a food processor for a couple of minutes until you have a soft, well-blended mixture. Remove from the processor, and fold in the petals and salt.

(continued overleaf)

Either way, spoon the pesto into small, sterilised jars (see p.29) and pour a little oil over the surface to exclude any air. Cap with metal lids. Store in the fridge and use within 4 weeks. If you are making a lot of pesto, pack in small containers and freeze.

When you come to use the pesto, stir it well before spooning out. Make sure the surface of any pesto remaining in the jar is completely covered with oil before you return it to the fridge (this is very important if it is to keep well).

Variations

Traditionally, pesto is made with the leaves of the sweet basil plant (*Ocimum basilicum*). It's better suited to warmer climates than ours, where there are fewer slugs to devour the sweetly pungent leaves, but, if you manage to grow it in good quantities, do make use of it in this recipe. Alternatively, try some of our native herbs as the base for your pesto. Young, raw nettle tops and wild garlic leaves (both to be gathered in early spring) work beautifully together, as does parsley (flat leaf or curly). Hazels or walnuts can stand in for pine nuts, and a mature, robust Cheddar is a good alternative to Parmesan.

P.S. *Calendula officinalis*, or common garden marigold, is a really useful herb and should not to be ignored for culinary purposes. The golden pigment of the petals can be used, like saffron, to colour rice, cakes, desserts and butter. Alternatively, sprinkle the bittersweet, aromatic petals over mixed salad leaves, or toss a few into a fresh herb omelette.

Slow-dried tomatoes in oil

Season: July to September

I love the gutsy flavour of these tomatoes and like to serve them as part of a crisp smoked bacon and beetroot salad, or a hearty couscous salad with plenty of fresh coriander. There are times though, when I can't resist eating them from the jar!

Ideally the fruit would be sun-dried but we just don't have sufficient hours of sunshine in this country. Slowly drying them in a very low oven achieves similar and very pleasing results, although you do need a sizeable quantity of tomatoes.

Makes 2–3 x 225g jars

2kg tomatoes
2 tsp salt
2 tsp granulated sugar
100ml white wine vinegar
200–300ml olive, rapeseed or sunflower oil

Preheat the oven to 100°C/Gas Mark ¼. Cut the tomatoes in half around their middles and scoop out the pips with a teaspoon. Put the tomatoes, cut side up, on a wire rack with a baking sheet underneath to catch any drips. Sprinkle a few grains of salt and sugar on each cut tomato half. Leave for 10–15 minutes for the seasoning to begin to permeate the tomato flesh, then turn the tomatoes so their cut sides face down on the rack.

Set the rack of tomatoes over the baking sheet in the oven and leave them to dry for 6–10 hours; the drying time will depend on their size and juiciness. The tomatoes are ready when they are dry to the touch but still a little plump and fleshy. They'll have reduced by around 90 per cent and the total weight after drying will be about 200g. Don't let the tomatoes dry until they become brittle. Remove from the oven and allow to cool, then transfer to a shallow dish. Pour the vinegar over the tomatoes, cover and leave to stand for about 30 minutes.

Pack the tomatoes into sterilised jars (see p.29) to within 2cm of the top of the jar. Distribute the vinegar between the jars and then cover the tomatoes completely with oil, tapping the jar to expel any trapped air. Seal with lids. Store in a cool, dry place and use within 4 months. Once opened, store in the fridge, always make sure the tomatoes are fully covered with oil, and use within 6 weeks.

Variations

Use half balsamic and half white wine vinegar if you prefer. A tablespoonful or two of finely chopped preserved lemons is a flavourful addition.

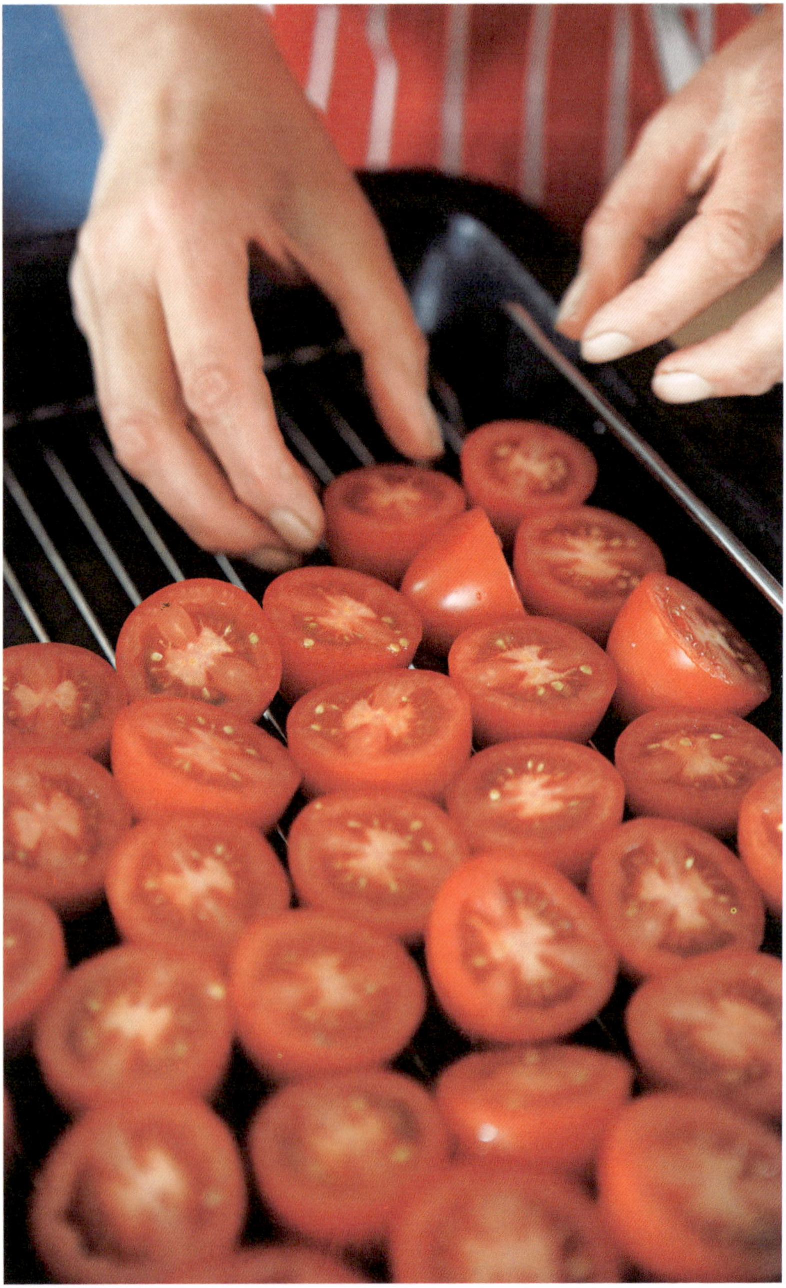

Roasted tomato ketchup

Season: July to September

Slow-roasted tomatoes provide a rich, intense base for this, my all-time favourite ketchup. The spices and seasonings I have used are good old-fashioned ones – those our grandmothers would have kept in their kitchens. However, if you like, you can fire it up by adding a couple of teaspoonfuls of chilli powder. Don't expect the ketchup to be the same colour as a commercial variety; it will be a warm orangey-red colour.

Makes 500–600ml

- 1 quantity (1 litre) roast tomato passata (see p.173)
- 100ml cider vinegar
- 50ml lemon juice
- 1 heaped tsp celery salt
- 1 heaped tsp mustard powder
- 1 heaped tsp ground ginger
- ½ tsp ground black pepper
- ¼ tsp ground cloves
- 100g demerara sugar

Put the passata into a heavy-based pan with the vinegar, lemon juice and spices. Bring to simmering point then add the sugar. Stir until dissolved then continue to simmer, stirring occasionally, for 25–30 minutes, until the sauce is reduced to a thick but pourable consistency.

Pour immediately into warm, sterilised bottles or jars (see p.160). Seal immediately with vinegar-proof lids. Store in a cool, dry place and use within 4 months. For longer keeping, sterilise the filled jars using the method on p.133. Once opened, keep in the fridge.

Variation

Rhubarb makes a delightful fruity ketchup and is a good way to use up the tougher, tarter stalks towards the end of the rhubarb season. Slow roast 2kg chopped rhubarb with 250g chopped red onions and 3–4 garlic cloves at 180°C/Gas Mark 4 for about an hour. Sieve the mixture and put into a heavy-based saucepan. Use the same quantities of sugar and vinegar as above, but leave out the lemon juice (as rhubarb is very acidic). Replace the mustard, black pepper and cloves with a good teaspoonful each of ground cumin and coriander. Continue to cook as for tomato ketchup.

Harissa paste

Season: July to September

Harissa is a North African ingredient, used to enhance many fish and meat dishes, as well as couscous and soups. I also like to use my version to make a fruity, fiery dipping sauce (see below) to serve with pork, fish or prawns.

The strength of the paste depends on the variety and quantity of chillies used. The chances are that this recipe, which I would describe as moderately hot, will merely tickle the palate of out-and-out chilli freaks. But all you need do, to make it fierier, is increase the amount of chillies, include more of their seeds (see below), or perhaps add one or two very hot little dried chillies.

Makes 2 x 112g jars

250g tomatoes
50g hot chillies
2 fat garlic cloves
50g shallots
1 tsp caraway seeds
1 tsp coriander seeds
½ tsp salt
50ml olive or hemp oil

Drop the tomatoes into a pan of boiling water for 30 seconds then scoop out and peel off the skins.

Remove the stalk and calyx from the chillies. The seeds contain most of the fruit's heat and, at this point, you can choose either to leave all the seeds in or, for a less intense paste, cut at least some of them out. Either way, make sure you wash your hands after handling chillies and avoid touching your eyes for a while, as the chilli oil will burn them.

Put the skinned tomatoes, chillies and all the other ingredients, except the oil, in a food processor and blitz until well blended. Tip into a small saucepan and heat until boiling then simmer for about 10 minutes until reduced and starting to thicken. Leave to cool. Pack into warm, sterilised jars (see p.29), leaving a 1cm gap at the top. Pour oil over the paste to completely cover it. Seal the jars.

Store in the fridge and use within 4 months. If you want to extend the shelf life, pack in small, sealable containers and freeze. Once opened, keep in the fridge, making sure the paste in the jar is completely covered by a layer of oil.

P.S. For a tasty chilli plum dipping sauce, simmer 50ml rice or cider vinegar, 100g plum jam (see p.69) and 1 tsp harissa paste until reduced and thickened.

SAUCES, KETCHUPS & OIL-BASED PRESERVES 197

Asparagus preserved in oil

Season: May to June

Spotting the first tips of asparagus pushing their way above ground in late spring is one of the greatest moments of the growing year. It means there will be asparagus to eat every day for the next few weeks; I also like to preserve a few jarfuls.

Use a good, but not really expensive olive oil (see p.39). When the asparagus has been eaten, the flavoured oil can be used to make a lovely salad dressing.

You will need one jam jar, about 20cm high, with a capacity of around 500ml, and a second jar of 250ml capacity.

Makes 2 jars (1 x 500ml, 1 x 250ml)

- 500g asparagus
- 300ml cider vinegar or white wine vinegar
- 2 fat garlic cloves or shallots, finely sliced
- 1 tsp peppercorns
- A few rosemary, thyme or basil sprigs
- 100ml lemon juice
- 400–500ml olive oil

Trim away the tough woody ends of the asparagus, then cut into lengths 1cm less than the height of your larger jar, keeping the tender trimmed-off bits to one side.

Put the vinegar and 200ml water in a saucepan and bring to the boil. Remove from the heat and cover to keep warm. Meanwhile, place a griddle pan over a high heat. Add the long asparagus spears and cook, turning once or twice, until lightly charred. Drop the spears into the hot vinegar bath and leave for 3–4 minutes. This sharpens the flavour of the asparagus, while the acidity assists in preventing bacterial growth.

Put about two-thirds of the garlic or shallot and peppercorns in the sterilised 500ml jar. Remove the asparagus from the vinegar bath and pack it, upright, into the jar. Add a few herbs. Pour over two-thirds of the lemon juice, then cover completely with oil. Seal with a lid. Repeat the entire process with the trimmed-off ends in the smaller jar, using up the remaining peppercorns, garlic, herbs, lemon juice and oil.

Keep in a cool, dark place for 6 weeks before using. Consume within 4 months. Once opened, keep in the fridge, making sure the asparagus in the jar remains covered with oil, and use within 6 weeks.

Variations
Substitute char-grilled peppers or lightly cooked artichoke hearts for the asparagus.

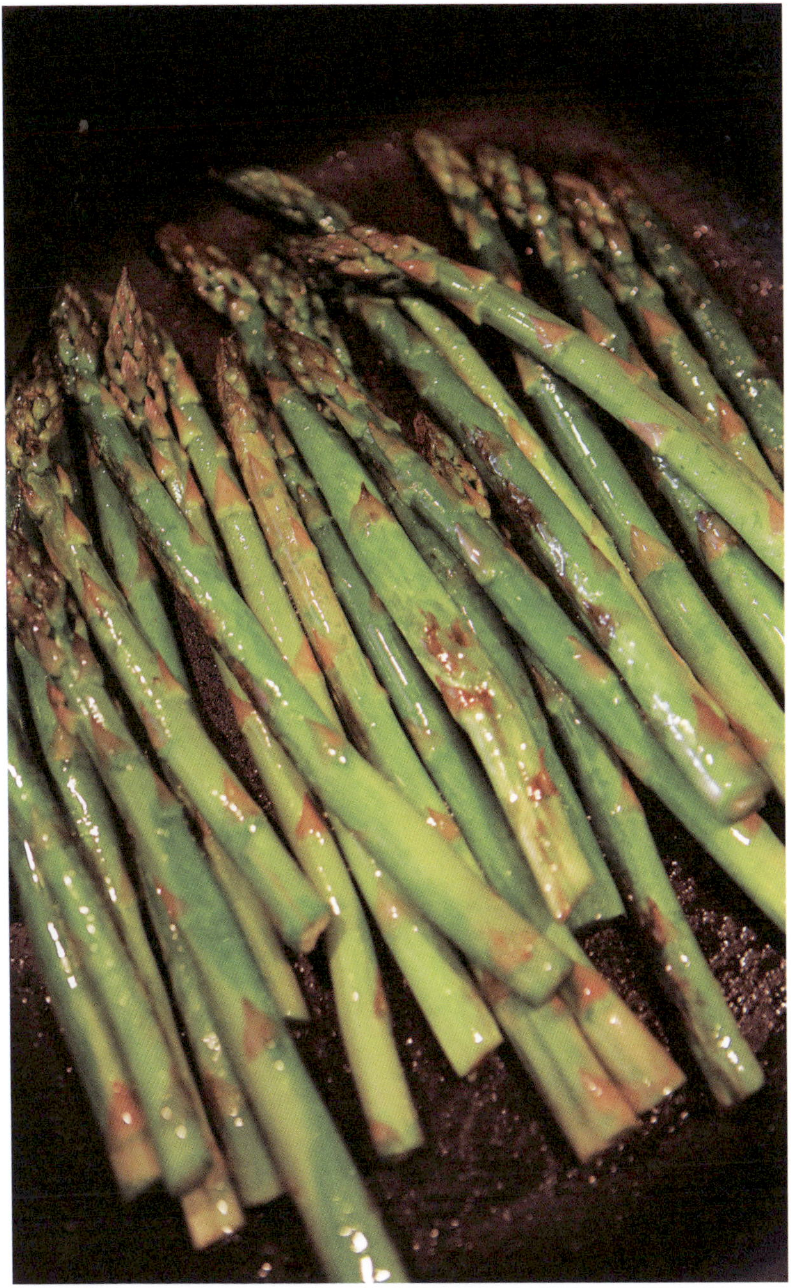

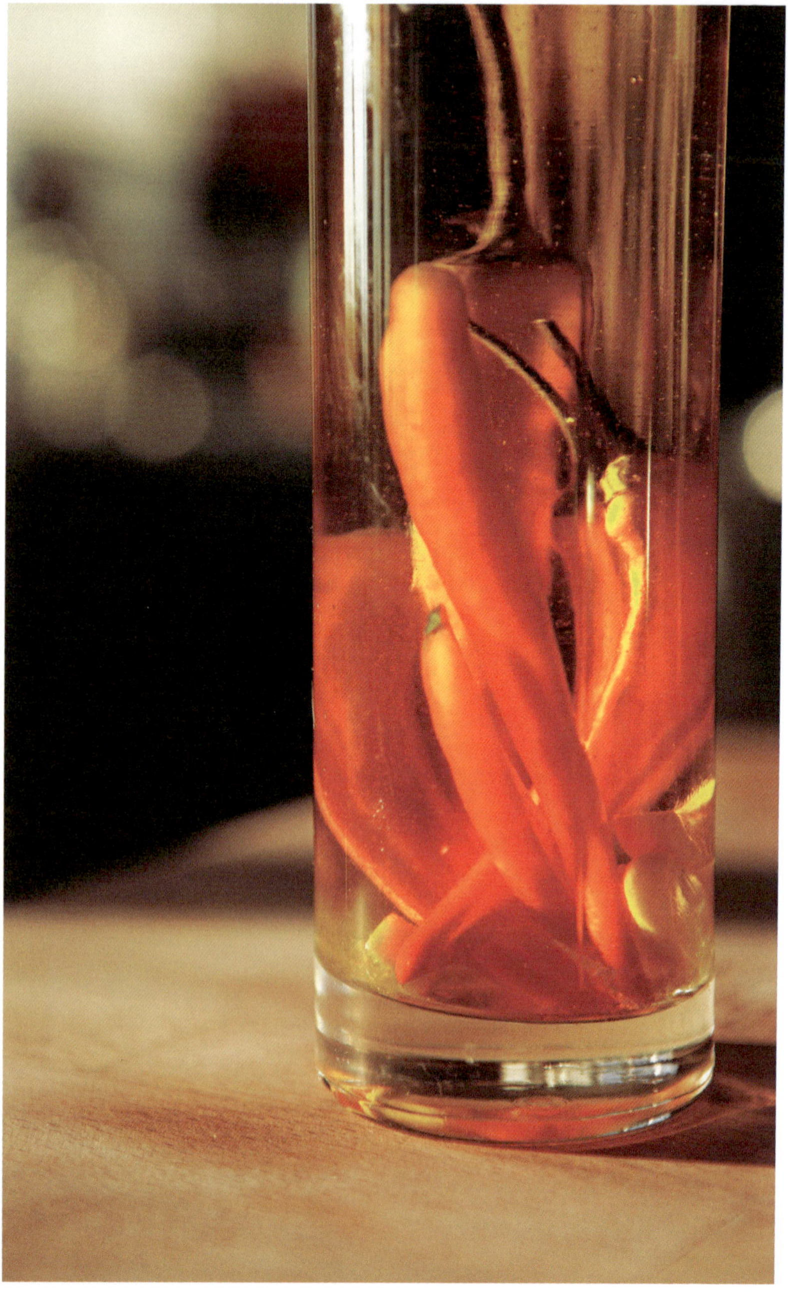

Flavoured oils

Season: more or less any time

These are dead easy to make and have endless applications in the kitchen. Use them to baste or brown ingredients and they will add pizzazz and excitement to stews and roasts. Likewise, they will jazz up a panful of onions or other veg for a soup or sauce, and impart character to fish dishes. Herb oils come into their own when drizzled over summer or winter salads; they are also excellent used in mayonnaises and dressings.

The basic principle is to choose robust flavourings and leave them for long enough to impart their mighty characters to the oil. Always use a good-quality oil as your base (see pp.38–9). In all cases, to prevent the oil becoming rancid, store in a cool place and use within 6 months.

Chilli oil

Split open 6–8 dried or fresh chillies. Pack into a dry, sterilised 500–600ml jar or bottle (see p.160), along with 1 tsp black peppercorns. Heat 500ml olive or rapeseed oil to about 40°C and pour over the chillies. Cover and leave to infuse for 14 days – a little more for a stronger oil. Strain and re-bottle.

Nice spice oil

In a dry frying pan, heat 1 tbsp each of coriander, cumin and fennel seeds together with a couple of dried chillies. Toast until they release their distinctive fragrances and just start to brown – shake the pan frequently to prevent them from burning. Crush the toasted seeds then transfer them to a dry, sterilised 500–600ml jar or bottle (see p.160). Pour over 500ml rapeseed oil. Leave for a couple of weeks before straining the oil and re-bottling.

Herb oil

Lightly pack a dry, sterilised 580ml jar (see p.160) with freshly gathered herbs such as basil, rosemary, thyme, sage or oregano. You can use individual herbs on their own or mix a few together. Pour over 500ml olive oil and leave in a cool place for a couple of weeks before straining and re-bottling the oil.

Pontack (elderberry) sauce

Season: August to September

This is kitchen alchemy at its most exciting and rewarding: a mysterious-looking brew of dark elderberries, vinegar and spices becomes a truly wonderful sauce, a secret weapon for the store cupboard that I don't like to be without. According to tradition, pontack sauce is best used after 7 years, but I'm hard pushed to keep it for 7 months. Pungent, fruity and spicy, it's an unrivalled partner for winter stews, casseroled liver, slow-roasted belly of pork, or anything wild and gamey. Besides serving this sauce alongside meat dishes, you can add a couple of tablespoonfuls to sauces and gravies.

The elderberry season is short and the berries are part of the hedgerow banquet for woodland birds, so don't delay – gather when you see them.

Makes 1 x 350ml bottle

500g elderberries
500ml cider vinegar
200g shallots, peeled and sliced
6 cloves
4 allspice berries
1 blade of mace
1 tbsp black peppercorns
15g fresh root ginger, bruised

Strip the berries from the stalks as soon as possible after picking – a table fork is useful for doing this. Place them in an ovenproof earthenware or glass dish with the vinegar and put in a very low oven (about 130°C/Gas Mark ½) for 4–6 hours, or overnight. Remove from the oven and strain through a sieve, crushing the berries with a potato masher as you do so, to obtain maximum juice.

Put the rich, red-black juice in the pan along with the sliced shallots, spices and ginger. Bring gently to the boil and cook for 20–25 minutes until slightly reduced (perhaps muttering some magic charm while you watch over the dark, bubbling potion). Remove from the heat and strain through a sieve.

Return the juice to the pan and bring to the boil, then boil steadily for 5 minutes. Pour the sauce into a warm, sterilised bottle (see p.160) and seal. Store in a cool, dark cupboard.

P.S. This sauce grows better with age, so try to lay some bottles down for a few months if you can.

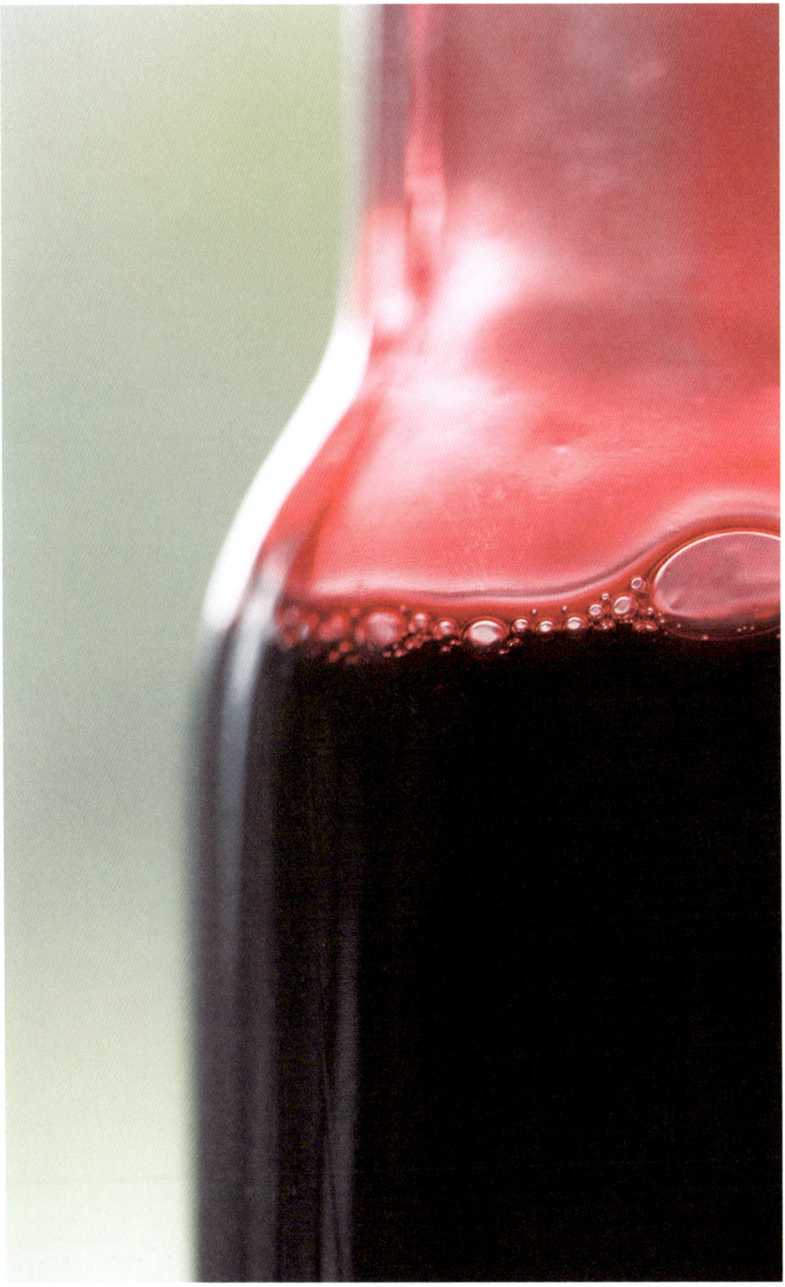

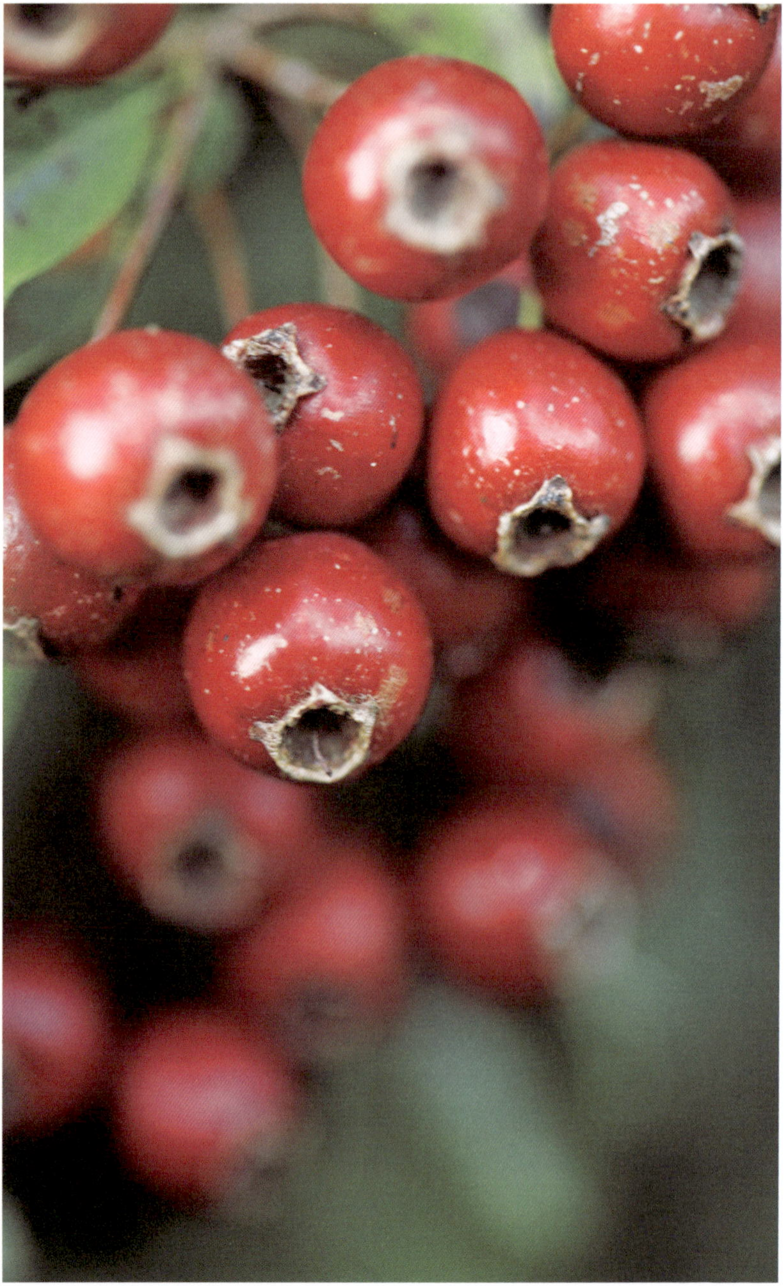

Saucy haw ketchup

Season: September to December

Hawthorn is widespread throughout Britain, and frequently used for hedging along farmland or roads. It's a lovely tree and provides vital natural accommodation for native birds, insects and invertebrates. Frothy white hawthorn blossom heralds the beginning of summer and the fading flowers later give way to developing clusters of blood-red berries, or haws. These swathe the hedgerows from early autumn well into winter – sometimes even through to the new year. The peppery, lemony little berries are too tart to eat raw, but I love them cooked into this sweet-sour hedgerow sauce.

Hawthorn tends to fruit prolifically, so you should have little trouble gathering enough haws. Do avoid picking from roadside bushes, however, as these may have absorbed fumes and pollution (although, for some reason, they often seem to be laden with the biggest and juiciest berries of all!).

Serve haw ketchup with rich meats such as venison or slow-roast belly of pork. It is also terrific drizzled over Welsh rarebit. My favourite way to enjoy this spicy sauce, however, is with a really good nut roast, served with a crisp green salad.

Makes 1 x 300ml bottle
500g haws
300ml white wine vinegar or cider vinegar
170g sugar
½ tsp salt
Ground black pepper to taste

Strip the haws from the stalks – the easiest way to do this is to snip them off with a pair of scissors or secateurs. Rinse in cold water.

Put the haws into a pan with the vinegar and 300ml water and simmer for about 30 minutes – the skins will split, revealing the firm, yellow flesh. Cook until the flesh is soft and the berries have become a muted red-brown. Remove from the heat. Rub the mixture through a sieve, or pass through a food mill, to remove the largish stones and the skins.

Return the fruity mixture to the cleaned-out pan. Add the sugar and heat gently, stirring, until it dissolves. Bring to the boil and cook for 5 minutes. Season with the salt and pepper. Pour into a sterilised bottle (see p.160) and seal with a vinegar-proof cap. Use within 12 months.

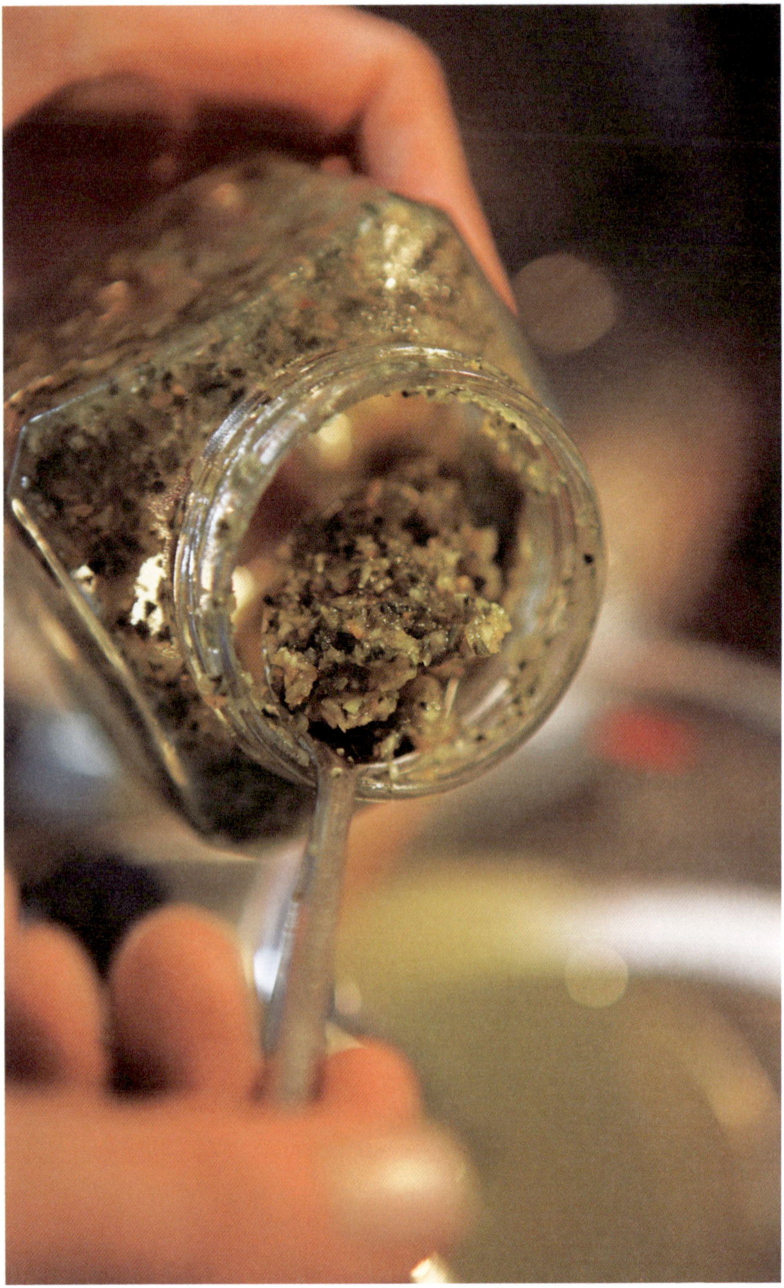

Souper mix

Season: more or less any time

A good vegetable bouillon or stock can be the making of many a soup, risotto or sauce. Preparing your own stock from scratch is easy enough – but it does take a little time, so an instant alternative is often welcome. The choice of vegetable bouillon powders and stock cubes on the market is pretty limited. There are one or two good products but, if you use them frequently, you might find an underlying uniformity creeping into your cooking. This is my solution. Whip up your very own souper mix – a concentrated paste of fresh vegetables simply preserved with salt. It's quick and easy to make and the stock it produces is delicious.

You can use just about any herb or vegetable you like – the important thing is that they are fresh and taste as *vegetabley* as possible. My preferred ingredients are indicated in this recipe, but you could also use young turnips, shallots, celery, swede, beetroot or peppers, as well as bay, thyme, lovage or mint – almost anything, really. Just bear in mind that the character of the stock will vary depending on the ingredients you choose.

The following are prepared weights, i.e. the ingredients should be washed, trimmed and peeled (where necessary).

Makes 3 x 340g jars
250g leek
200g fennel
200g carrot
250g celeriac
50g sun-dried tomatoes
2–3 garlic cloves
100g parsley
100g coriander
250g salt

The helping hand of a food processor is essential in this recipe. Simply put all the ingredients into the processor and blend together. The result will be a moist, granular paste. Spoon into sterilised jars (see p.29) and seal with vinegar-proof lids.

Keep one jar of the mix in the fridge – within easy reach for everyday cooking. The rest can be stored in a cool, dark and dry place. Use within 6 months.

To use souper mix, just stir about 10g (2 tsp) of it into 500ml hot water.

Useful Things

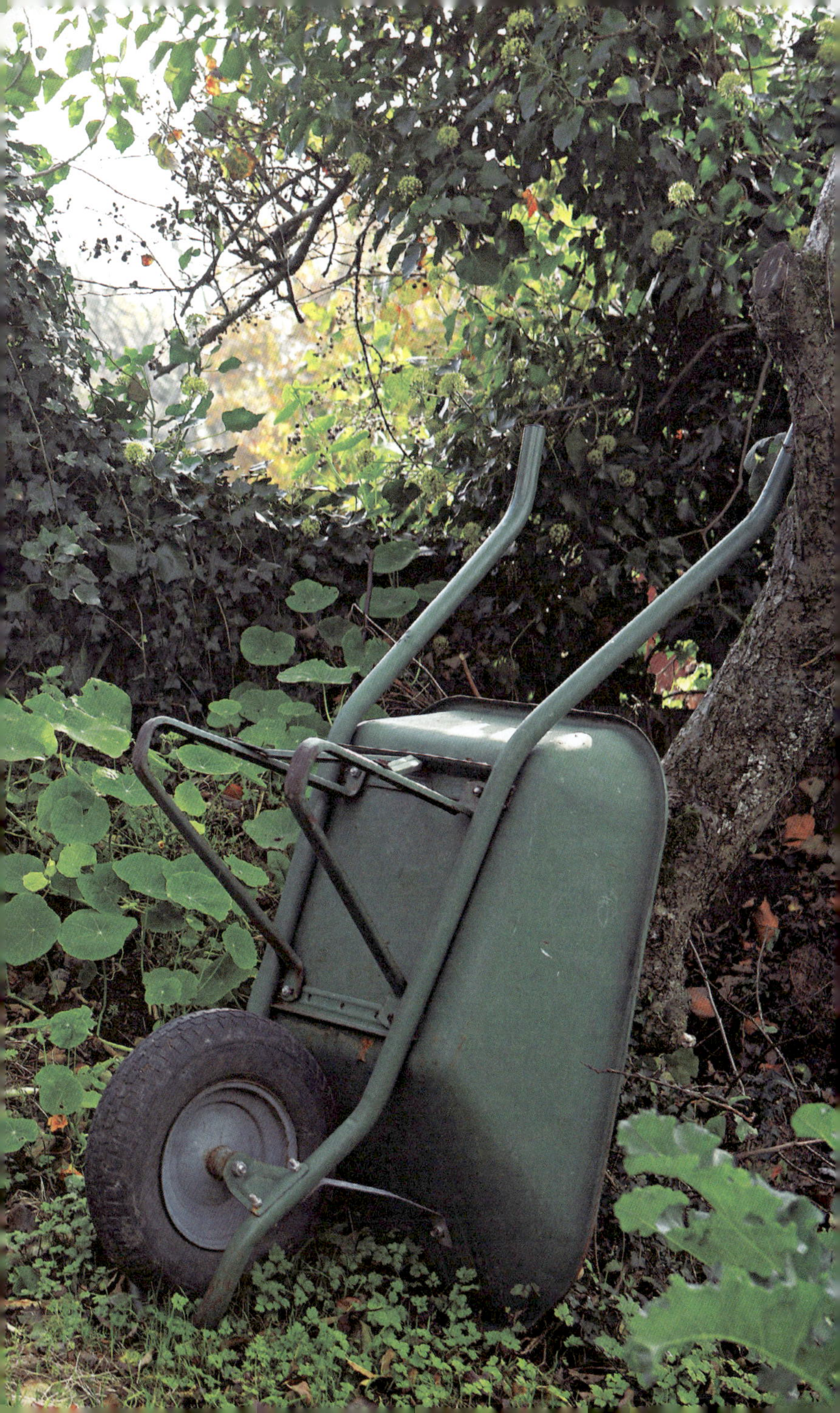

Directory

Preserving equipment and jam jar stockists

Kilner Jars (new jars and refurbishment of old rings)
www.kilnerjarsuk.co.uk
01372 372611

Rawlings & Son (Bristol) Ltd (jam jars)
www.rawlings-bristol.co.uk
01179 603989

Soap Kitchen (paraffin wax for sealing fruit)
www.soapkitchenonline.co.uk
01805 622221

Just Preserving
www.justpreserving.co.uk
01692 405984

Ascott, The 'Good Life' Store
www.ascott.biz
0845 130 6285

Lakeland Ltd
www.lakeland.co.uk
01539 488100

Wares of Knutsford
www.waresofknutsford.co.uk
0845 612 1273

Note that glycerine and glucose syrup are available from most chemists

Specialist ingredient suppliers

Oldroyd & Sons Ltd (forced rhubarb)
www.yorkshirerhubarb.co.uk
0113 2822245

Trehane Nursery (English blueberries)
www.trehanenursery.co.uk
01202 873490

Mr Trollope of Fingringhoe (quinces and medlars by mail order)
01206 735405

The Garlic Farm on the Isle of Wight
www.thegarlicfarm.co.uk
01983 865378

Peppers by Post
www.peppersbypost.biz
01308 897766

South Devon Chilli Farm
www.sdcf.co.uk
01548 550782

Steenbergs (organic and fair trade spices and spice infusers)
www.steenbergs.co.uk
01765 640088

The Anglesey Sea Salt Company Ltd (Halen Môn salt)
www.seasalt.co.uk
01248 430871

Cornish Sea Salt
www.cornishseasalt.co.uk
0845 337 5277

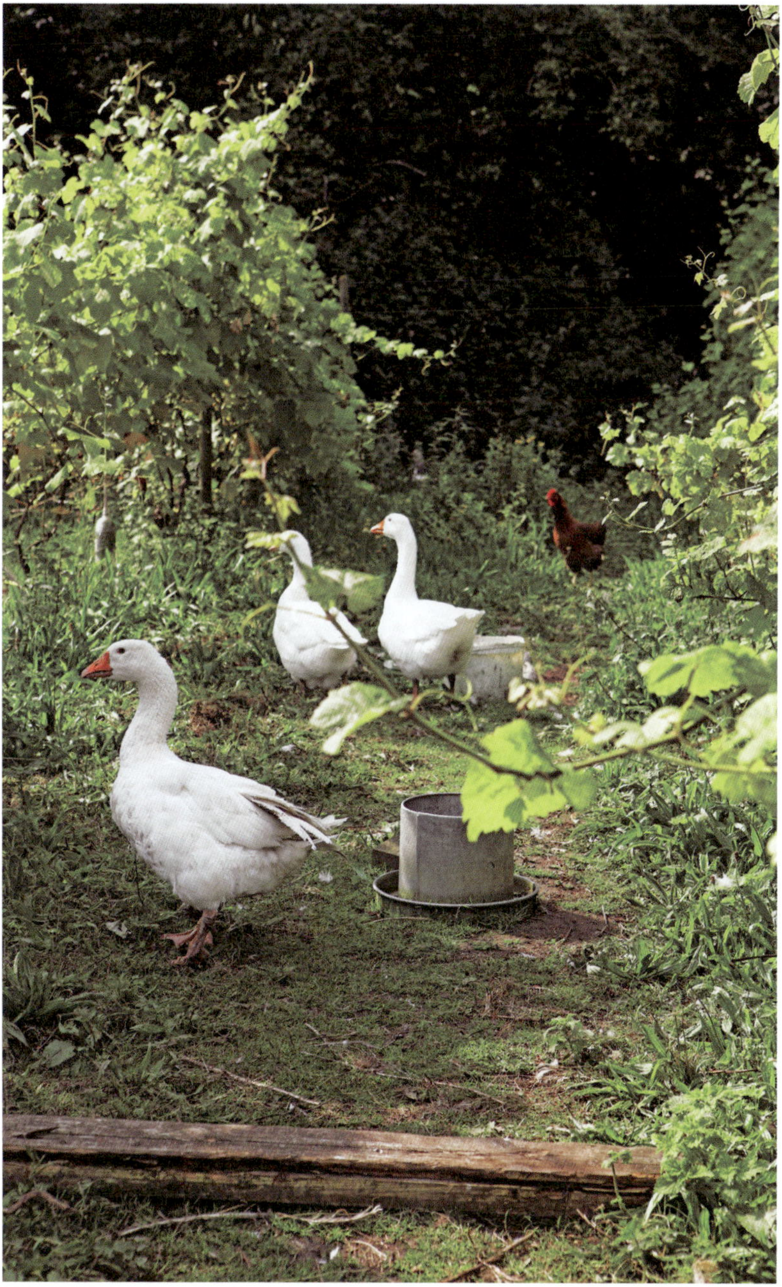

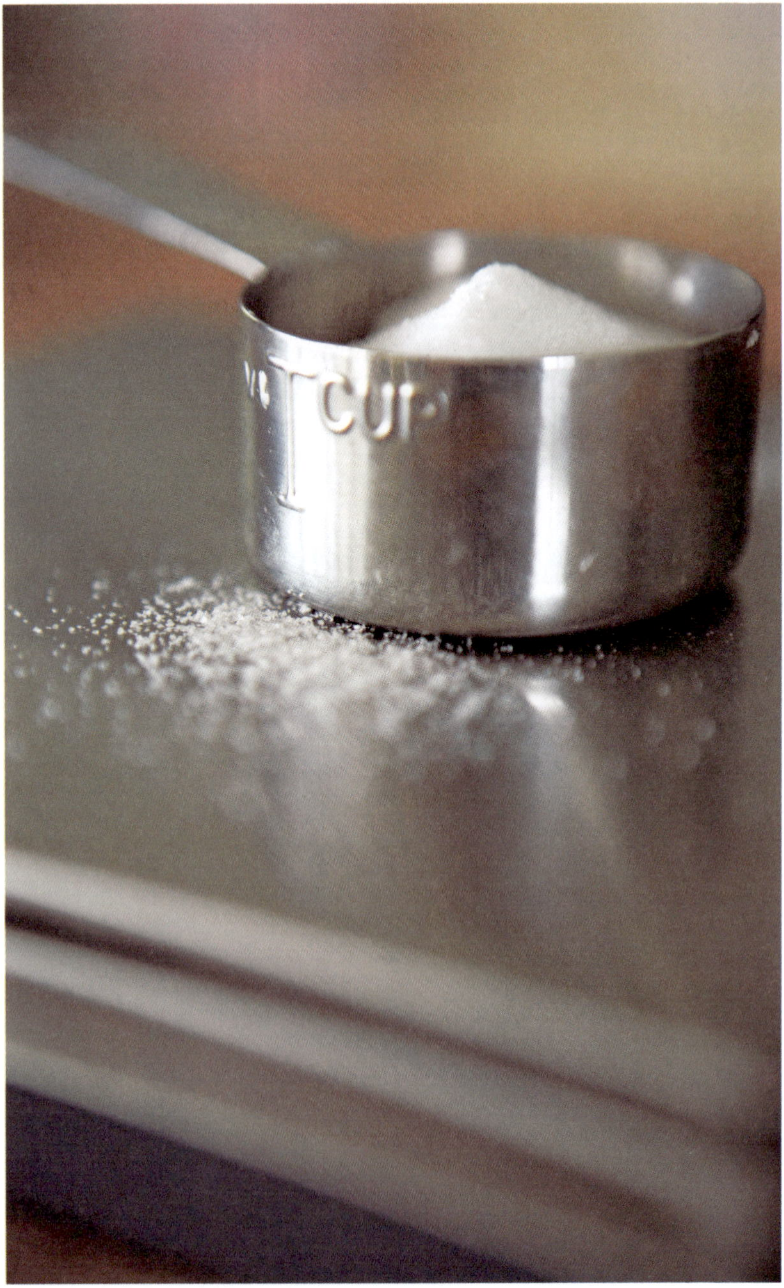
CUP

Maldon Salt (sea and rock salt)
www.maldonsalt.co.uk
01621 853315

Aspall (organic cider vinegar)
www.aspall.co.uk
01728 860510

The Somerset Distillery (cider vinegar,
eau de vie and cider brandy)
www.ciderbrandy.co.uk
01460 240782

Woolsery Cheese (Capriano cheese)
www.woolserycheese.co.uk
01300 341991

R Oil (rapeseed oil)
www.r-oil.co.uk
01451 870387

Yorkshire Hemp (hemp oil)
www.yorkshirehemp.com
01924 375475

Good Oil (hemp oil)
www.goodwebsite.co.uk

Billingtons Sugar Ltd (unrefined,
fair trade and organic sugar)
www.billingtons.co.uk
01733 422368

Silver Spoon (English beet sugar
and jam sugar with pectin)
www.silverspoon.co.uk
01733 422696

Food festivals

The last few years have seen a move to the organisation of many regional and local food festivals as well as a whopping increase in vibrant farmers' and country markets around Britain. These events provide a wonderful opportunity to buy from local growers and help keep rural communities alive. This list comprises a number of annual events, as well as organisations that link into seasonal events and food diversity.

Apples
National Apple Day is 21 October. Local events are held throughout the country on or around this date – see the charity Common Ground's website for venues.
www.commonground.org.uk

Citrus fruits (for marmalade)
The world's original marmalade event is held on the second weekend in February.
Marmalade Festival, Dalemain House, Penrith, Cumbria
www.marmaladefestival.com

Damsons
Damson Day is held in Cumbria in the middle of April, celebrating damson blossom with various walks.
www.lythdamsons.co.uk

Pears
Pear Day is a September pear harvest of the historic collection of pears at Cannon Hall, near Barnsley.
www.barnsley.gov.uk
01226 790270

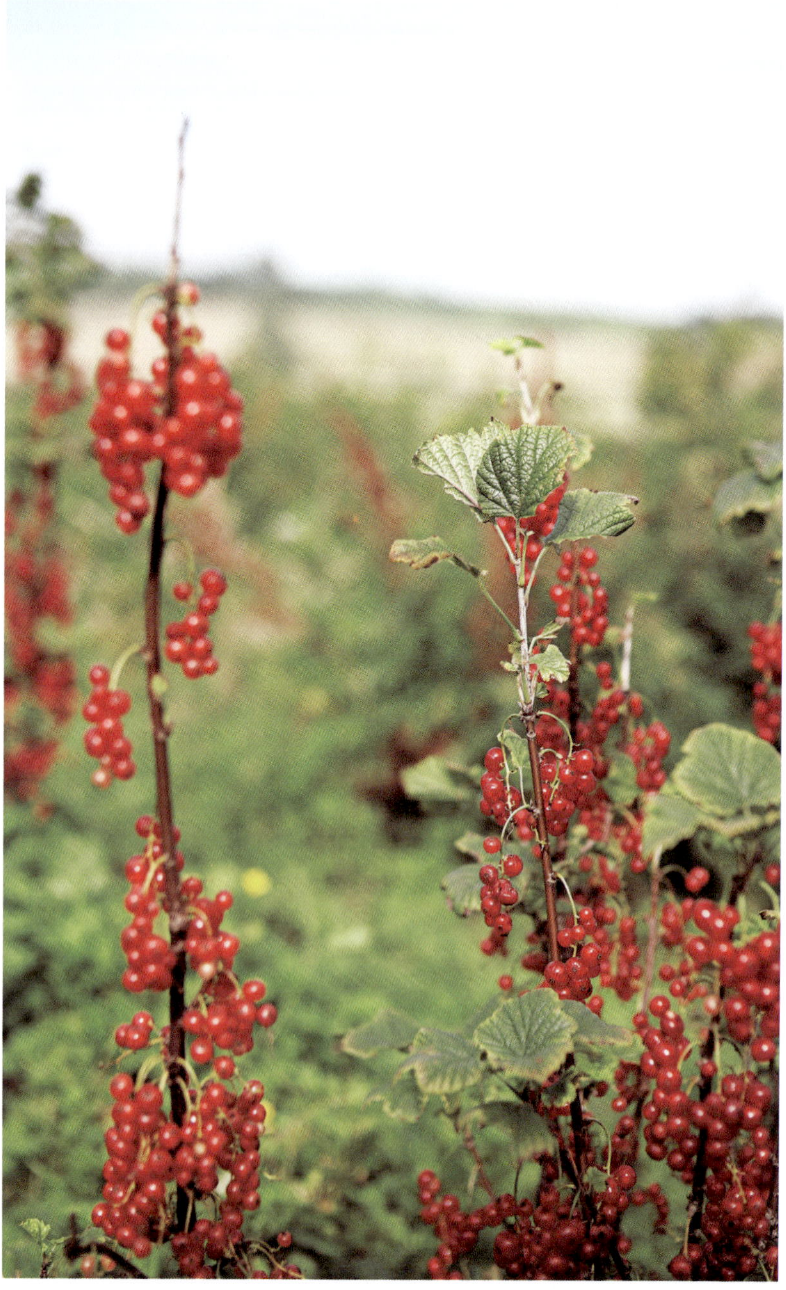

Plums
Pershore in Worcestershire hold a Plum Festival on August Bank Holiday.
www.pershoreplumfestival.org.uk

Rhubarb
A Spring Festival of Food, Drink and Rhubarb is held at the beginning of March.
www.wakefield.gov.uk

Asparagus
An opportunity for enthusiasts to taste and learn about this prize vegetable. Asparagus Festival, Pershore, Worcestershire
www.britishasparagusfestival.org

Chillies
Chichester holds a lively hot chilli festival in August.
www.westdean.org.uk

Garlic
The Isle of Wight Garlic Festival is an annual garlic harvest celebration held in the third week of August.
www.thegarlicfarm.co.uk

Associations and charities

British Beekeepers' Association (promoting bees and beekeeping)
www.britishbee.org.uk

Brogdale Horticultural Trust (home of the National Fruit Collection)
www.brogdale.org

Farm Retail Association (information on your local farm shop or pick-your-own farm)
www.farmshopping.com

National Association of Farmers' Markets (information on your nearest market)
www.farmersmarket.net

National Society of Allotment and Leisure Gardeners
www.nsalg.org.uk
01536 266576

The National Trust
www.nationaltrust.org.uk

Royal Horticultural Association (find your nearest horticultural group or club)
www.rhs.org.uk
0845 260 5000

Rural Revival
www.ruralrevival.org.uk

Soil Association (information on organic and local food)
www.soilassociation.org

Country Markets
www.country-markets.co.uk

Conversion charts

Metric quantities are given in the recipes. Use the following conversions if you prefer to work in imperial measures.

Weight

Metric	Imperial
25g	1oz
50g	2oz
100g–125g	4oz
170g	6oz
200g	7oz
225g	8oz
275g	10oz
340g	12oz
400g	14oz
450g	1lb
500g	1lb 2oz
900g	2lb
1kg	2lb 4oz

Liquid/volume

Metric	Imperial
150ml	5fl oz (¼ pint)
300ml	10fl oz (½ pint)
600ml	20fl oz (1 pint)
1 litre	35fl oz (1¾ pints)

1 tsp (1 teaspoon) = 5ml
1 tbsp (1 tablespoon) = 15ml

What is a gill? This old-fashioned term often crops up in old recipe books and one gill is equivalent to 150ml or ¼ pint.

Oven temperatures

	°C	°F	Gas Mark
Very cool	130	250	½
Very cool	140	275	1
Cool	150	300	2
Warm	160–170	325	3
Moderate	180	350	4
Fairly hot	190–200	375–400	5–6
Hot	210–220	425	7
Very hot	230–240	450–475	8–9

Acknowledgements

When asked if I would write this book, I hadn't realised just how many waking (and night-time) moments my thoughts would invariably be stuck in some form of jam jar or another. It's been a huge privilege, giving me the opportunity to adventure into new, exciting and often stirring territories, all contained in the amazing world of preserving. However, it would not have been possible for me to do so without the immeasurable help and support of family, friends and acquaintances, who have journeyed with me, solidly supporting me throughout.

First and foremost heartfelt thanks to Gavin Kingcome for his stunning photography, bringing ingredients and recipes alive, and for his steady patience on our photo-shoot days. Also to Nikki Duffy for her thoroughly attentive detail in checking recipes, thus reinforcing your success and victory in the jam pan.

Thank you to friends and neighbours in and around the Uplyme Valleys for their open generosity in allowing me to beg and sometimes steal produce from over the garden wall. I would particularly like to thank John and Henriette Wood for giving me a free rein to visit Rhode Hill Gardens – its rich bio-diversity quite the highlight of photo-shoot days.

On the technical front, thanks to Liz Neville for her invaluable fund of preserving knowledge, and to the outstanding technical team at Wilkin & Sons Ltd.

My thanks to the thoughtful and brilliant Bloomsbury team: Richard Atkinson, Natalie Hunt and Erica Jarnes; along with Will Webb for his outstanding work and ideas on the layout. Sincere thanks also to gifted editor Janet Illsley who meticulously and with great calm has perfectly potted, packed and sealed the book.

Thank you to Trisha Bye for keeping my kitchen and jam jars in apple pie order; and to her daughter Sophie for her jammy creativeness. Thanks also to Lois Wakeman for her 'on the spot' availability for eleventh hour photography.

At home, thank you to my husband Hugh for his support at all times, particularly for his lack of complaint when I dropped a full 2-litre bottle of his amazingly good sloe gin. To Pip and Maddy, who have never faltered with their help, advice and enthusiasm, and have seemingly always shared family life with a ton or two of jam.

A big thank you to Rob Love and the River Cottage team for their confidence that I could write the book. And last, but by no means least, immense thanks to Hugh F-W, warrior and leader of the *seasonal and local revolution* ... long may it last!

Index

acid 49
air, excluding from jars and bottles 26, 32
alcohol 26, 38, 132
   whole fruits in 130
alcohol-based preserves
   filling and sealing jars 32
   shelf life 34
apples 13, 15
   apple, herb and flower jellies 70
   apple, pear and ginger mincemeat 82, *83*
   blackberry and apple gin 154
   blackberry and apple leather *72*, 73
   bottled 162, 167
   Bramley lemon curd *74*, 75
   cider apple butter 90
   compost heap jelly 91
   family 'beena 135
   National Apple Day 213
   pectin and acid levels 48
   plum and russet mincemeat 82, *83*
   quince and apple sauce 185
   regional varieties 19, 22
   rosehip and apple jelly 78
   seasonal chutney 108, 109
   see also crab apples
apricots
   bottled 160, 162, 167
      winter fruit compote 180, *181*
   in fruit syrups and liqueurs 132
   pectin and acid levels 48
   seasonal chutney 109
artichoke hearts preserved in oil 198
asparagus
   Pershore Asparagus Festival 215
   preserved in oil 198, *199*

bachelor's jam 156, *157*
bacteria 27, 29
basil 192
beech leaf noyau 138, *139*
beer, hearty ale chutney 122
bees and beekeeping 215
beetroot 14
   roasted sweet beet relish 106, *107*
bilberries, bottled 169
blackberries 13, 14, 15
   blackberry and apple gin 154
   blackberry and apple jelly 78
   blackberry and apple leather *72*, 73
   bottled 167
   fruit butter 90
   in fruit syrups and liqueurs 132
   hedgerow jelly 77
   pectin and acid levels 48
   vinegar 150
blackcurrants 14
   blackcurrant leaf tea 64
   bottled *170*, 171
   Mum's blackcurrant jam 64, *65*
   pectin and acid levels 48
   regional varieties 19, 20, 22
   vinegar 150
blueberries 14, 19
   bottled 167, 169
   pectin and acid levels 48
blues and bay 169
borage honey 81
bottled fruits 158–85
   advantages of bottling 160
   heating times 167
   jars and bottles 160–2
      filling and sealing 32
      opening 166
   oven method 166, 167
   packing tips 164
   preparing syrup 162
   storing 166
   suitable fruits 160, 162–4
   testing the seal 166
   water bath method 164, *165*, 167
bottles 29, 31, *31*
   processing in a hot water bath 133
   recycling 29
   sterilising 31
brine 96
Brogdale Horticultural Trust, National Fruit Collection 176, 215
brown sugars 35–7
bullaces 77

candied fruits 45
candied orange sticks *88*, 89
Capriano cheese 191, 213
cellophane jar covers 30
cherries 14
   bottled 160, 162, 167
   cherry ratafia 155
   in fruit syrups and liqueurs 132
   pectin and acid levels 48
   sweet pickled cherries 118
chestnuts 15
   Melissa's chestnut jam *86*, 87
chillies
   Chichester Chilli Festival 215
   chilli oil 201
   chilli pepper jelly 101
   harissa paste 196
chocolate
   candied orange sticks *88*, 89

chutneys 94
    fruit in 97
    gooseberry 100
    hearty ale 122
    ideal shelf life 34
    making perfect 99
    salt in 96
    sealing jars 30
    seasonal 108–9
    spices in 97
    vegetables in 97
    vinegar in 96–7
    see also relishes
cider apple butter 90
cider vinegar 37
citrus fruit
    compost heap jelly 91
    pectin and acid levels 48
    see also marmalades
clear pickles 94
clip (Le Parfait) jars 160, *161*, 166
clover honey 81
cobnuts 22
    honeyed hazels 81
cocktail, rosehip syrup 152
coffee filters 41
compost heap jelly 91
conserves 44
conversion charts 216
cordials and liqueurs 130
    bachelor's jam 156, *157*
    beech leaf noyau 138, *139*
    currant shrub 144
    elixir of sage 143
    family 'beena 135
    ingredients 132
    rosehip syrup 152
    shelf life and keepability 133
    sloe gin 154–5, *155*
coulis 188
courgettes 14
crab apples 14, 15
    apple, herb and flower jellies 70
    hedgerow jelly 77
    pectin and acid levels 48
    pickled 119
    rosehip and apple jelly 78
    spicy crab apple jelly 78
cranachan 67
crystallised fruits 45
cucumbers 14
    sweet cucumber pickle *112*, 113
Cumberland sauce 62

damsons
    bottled 162, 167
    dambeena 135
    Damson Day 213
    damson gin 154
    in fruit syrups and liqueurs 132
    pectin and acid levels 48
    regional varieties 20, 22
    sweet pickled damsons 118
dates 109
demerara sugar 35–7
dog rose (*Rosa canina*) 14
dry-salting 96

Eastern counties, fruit-growing regions 19, 22
eau de vie 38
elderberries 14, 15, *23*
    hedgerow jelly 77
    pectin and acid levels 48
    pontack (elderberry) sauce 202, *203*
elderflowers *12*, 13
    elderflower cordial 130, *140*, 141
    green gooseberry jam with elderflower *58*, 59
enzymes 26, 27
equipment 39–41, 210

family 'beena 135
farmers' markets 215
figs
    bottled 160, 167
        figpote *178*, 179
    figgy mostardo 123
    pectin and acid levels 48
    seasonal chutney 109
filling jars 29, 32
flavoured oils 188, *200*, 201
flavoured vinegars 130, 132, 133, 149
Florence fennel 14
    pickled *104*, 105
flowers, in cordials, liqueurs and vinegars 132
food festivals 213–15
food mills 41
fridge jams 44, 67
fruit
    bottling fruit purées and pulps 167
    British fruit-growing regions 19–22
    in chutney and pickles 97
    in cordials, liqueurs and vinegars 132
    in jams and jellies 46
    see also bottled fruits
fruit butters 32, 34, 45
    blackberry butter 90
    cider apple butter 90
fruit cheeses 32, 34, 45
    quince cheese 84, *85*
    sealing jars 30
fruit curds 32, 34, 45
fruit leathers 45, *72*, 73

fruit liqueurs 130
fruit spreads 44
fruit syrups *see* syrups
fungi 27
funnels 41

garden pesto 191–2
garlic
    growing 103
    hardneck and softneck 103
    pickled garlic *102*, 103
    wild 13
gill 216
gin 38
ginger
    apple, pear and ginger mincemeat 82, *83*
    in early rhubarb jam 56
    Seville and ginger marmalade 54
glacé fruits 45
glacé icing 78
goat's cheese, Capriano 191, 213
gooseberries 14, *21*
    chutney 100
    curd 75
    green gooseberry jam with elderflower *58*, 59
    juice 49
    regional varieties 19–20, 22
gooseberries 13
    bottled 162
    green gooseberry jam with elderflower *58*, 59
    making pectin stock 47
    pectin and acid levels 48
    sweet pickled gooseberries 118
granulated sugar 35
grapefruit marmalades 54
grapes, in fruit syrups and liqueurs 132
green beans 14
green gooseberry jam with elderflower *58*, 59
greengages 14, 48
    bottled 167

harissa paste 196
haws 15, *204*
    haw brandy 155
    hedgerow jelly 77
    saucy haw ketchup 205
hazelnuts, honeyed hazels *80*, 81
hearty ale chutney 122
heather honey 81
hedgerow jelly 77–8
hemp oil 39, 191, 213
herbs
    apple, herb and flower jellies 70
    in cordials, liqueurs and vinegars 132
    herb oil 201
    mixed herb vinegar 149

honey 37
    'clear' and 'set' 81
    early rhubarb with honey 168
    honeyed hazels *80*, 81
    lemon marmalade with honey 54
horseradish
    horseradish vinegar 149
    pickled 106
Hugh's prize-winning raspberry fridge jam 67
hygiene 26

icing, glacé 78

jam sugar 35
jams 44
    acid in 49
    early rhubarb jam 56
    filling and sealing jars 32, 50
    fridge jams 44
    fruit for 46
    green gooseberry jam with elderflower *58*, 59
    Hugh's prize-winning raspberry fridge jam 67
    ideal shelf life 34
    making perfect 50
    Melissa's chestnut jam *86*, 87
    Mum's blackcurrant jam 64–5
    pectin 46–7
    plum jam 69
    setting point 49
    strawberry 61
    sugar in 49
japonicas 48
jars
    clip (Le Parfait) jars 160, *161*, 164
    filling 29, 32
    labelling 34
    lids 30, 31
    recycling 29, 31
    rubber rings on 160, 162, 164
    screw-band (Kilner) jars 160, *161*, 164
    sealing 30–1, 32
    sizes 30
    sterilising 29, 160
    stockists 210
jellies 44, 51, *51*
    apple, herb and flower jellies 70
    blackberry and apple jelly 78
    chilli pepper jelly 101
    compost heap jelly 91
    filling and sealing jars 32
    fruit for 46
    hedgerow jelly 77–8
    ideal shelf life 34
    ingredients 46–9
    jelly bags 41, 47
    making perfect 51

medlar 70
quince 70
redcurrant jelly 62, *63*
rosehip and apple jelly 78
rowan jelly 78
setting point 49
spicy crab apple jelly 78

ketchups 32, 188
rhubarb 195
roasted tomato ketchup 195
saucy haw ketchup 205
Kilner (screw-band) jars 160, *161*, 164
kitchen scales 41

labelling jars 34
large grain preserving sugar 35
leathers 45, *72*, 73
leeks 15
lemon(s) 13, *126*, *137*
Bramley lemon curd *74*, 75
marmalade with honey 54
preserved 126
squash 136
Le Parfait (clip) jars 160, *161*, 166
lids 30, 31
liqueurs *see* cordials and liqueurs
Liz's luscious raspberries 182
local produce 13
loganberries 14, 48
bottled 167

Mabey, Richard, *Food for Free* 138
malt vinegar 37
marigold (*Calendula officinalis*) 192
marmalades 13, 15, 44
culinary uses 55, *55*
filling and sealing jars 32
ideal shelf life 34
lemon marmalade with honey 54
making perfect 50
Marmalade Festival 213
onion marmalade 125
setting point 49
Seville and ginger marmalade 54
Seville orange marmalade *52*, 53–5
sliced fruit method 53
three-fruit marmalade 54
whisky marmalade 54
whole fruit method 54
marrows 15, 108
measuring jugs and spoons 41
medlars 48, 70, 210
Melissa's chestnut jam *86*, 87
meringue nests, chestnut jam in *86*, 87
micro-organisms 26, 29, 30

mincemeats 45
apple, pear and ginger mincemeat 82
ideal shelf life 34
plum and russet mincemeat 82, *83*
mint 62
syrup *146*, 147
moulds 27
moulis 41
mulberries
bottled 167
pectin and acid levels 48
mulled pears *174*, 174
Mum's blackcurrant jam 64, *65*
muscovado sugar 35–7
muslin 41
spice bags 97

nasturtiums
garden pesto 191–2
nasturtium 'capers' *110*, 111
nasturtium vinegar 149
nectarines, bottled 162
nettles 13
nice spice oil 201
Northern England, fruit-growing regions 19, 20, 22

officer's (bachelor's) jam 156, *157*
oil-based preserves
filling and sealing jars 32
harissa paste 196
pesto 34, 103, 188, 191–2, *192*
vegetables in oil 34, 188, *189*, 193, 198, *199*
oils 26, 38–9
flavoured oils 188, *200*, 201
olive oil 39
onions 15
onion marmalade 125
pickled onions 120, *121*
oranges
candied orange sticks *88*, 89
St Clement's squash 136
oven temperatures 217

paper coffee filters 41
peaches
bottled 160, 162
in fruit syrups and liqueurs 132
leather 73
pectin and acid levels 48
pickled peaches 119
pears 15
apple, pear and ginger mincemeat 82, *83*
bottled 160, 162, 167
in fruit syrups and liqueurs 132
mulled pears *174*, 174
Pear Day 213

pectin and acid levels 48
regional varieties 19, 22
seasonal chutney 109
spiced pickled pears 119
pectin 46–7, 55, 61
homemade pectin stock 47
peppers 210
chilli pepper jelly 101
preserved in oil 198
pesto 34, 103, 188, 191–2, *192*
piccalilli 94, 114
pickles
clear 94
figgy mostardo 123
fruit in 97
ideal shelf life 34
jars, filling and sealing 30, 32
making perfect 99
nasturtium 'capers' *110*, 111
pickled Florence fennel *104*, 105
pickled garlic *102*, 103
pickled horseradish 106
pickled onions 120, *121*
runner bean pickle 117
salt in 96
spiced pickled pears 119
spices in 97
sweet cucumber pickle *112*, 113
sweet pickled damsons 118
vegetables in 97
vinegar in 96–7
pickling spice 97
plums 14, 15, *68*
bottled 162, 167
spiced brandy plums 176, *177*
in fruit syrups and liqueurs 132
plum jam 69
leather 73
pectin and acid levels 48
Pershore Plum Festival 215
plumbeena 135
regional varieties 19, 20, 22
and russet mincemeat 82, *83*
seasonal chutney 109
pontack (elderberry) sauce 202, *203*
potatoes 10
preserved lemons 126
preserving pans 39–41
preserving thermometers 41
prunes 180
pumpkins 109

quinces 15, *184*, 210
pectin and acid levels 48
quince and apple sauce 185
quince cheese 84, *85*
quince jelly 70
seasonal chutney 109

rapeseed oil 39, 191, 213
raspberries 10, 14, 15, 20, *183*
bottled 167
Liz's luscious raspberries 182
Hugh's prize-winning raspberry fridge jam 67
raspberry vinegar 150, *151*
recycling jars and bottles 29, 31
redcurrants 13, 14, *47*, *144*
cordial 62
currant shrub 144
jelly 62, *63*
juice 49
making pectin stock 47
pectin and acid levels 48
relishes 94
chilli pepper jelly 101
filling and sealing jars 30, 32
ideal shelf life 34
roasted sweet beet relish 106, *107*
spring rhubarb relish 100
see also chutneys
rhubarb 13, 15
bottled 164, 167
early rhubarb with honey 168
early ('forced') 20, *57*, 210
early rhubarb jam 56
pectin and acid levels 48
regional varieties 19, 20
rhubarb ketchup 195
rhubeena 135
seasonal chutney 109
Spring Festival of Food, Drink and Rhubarb 215
spring rhubarb relish 100
sweet pickled rhubarb 118
rock salt 38
rosehips 15, *153*
rosehip and apple jelly 78
hedgerow jelly 77
rosehip syrup 152
rowan berries 14
hedgerow jelly 77
pectin and acid levels 48
rowan jelly 78
'ruby red' marmalade 54
rumtopf 156, *157*
runner bean pickle 117

safe keeping 34
sage, elixir of 143
St Clement's squash 136
salt 26, 38, 210, 213
dry-salting 96
making brine 96

in pickles and chutneys 96
samphire, spiced samphire vinegar 149
sauces 32, 34, 188
Scotland, fruit-growing in 19, 20, 22
screw-band (Kilner) jars 160, *161*, 164
sealing jars 30–1, 32
sea salt 38
seasonal produce 10–17
setting point 49
Seville orange(s) 13, 15, 46
    Seville and ginger marmalade 54
    Seville orange marmalade *52*, 53–5
sieves 41
sizes of jars 30
sloes 15
    hedgerow jelly 77
    pectin and acid levels 48
    sloe gin 154–5, *155*
slotted spoons 41
souper mix 73, *206*, 207
Southern/South-west England, fruit-growing regions 19, 22
spiced brandy plums 176, *177*
spiced pickled pears 119
spiced samphire vinegar 149
spices
    in chutney and pickles 97, *98*
    in cordials, liqueurs and vinegars 132
    grinding 97
    nice spice oil 201
    spice infusers 41
spoilage in food 26–7
spoons 41
spring rhubarb relish 100
squashes (fruit syrups) 130
    lemon 136
sterilising
    bottles 31
    jars 29, 160
    lids 31
    pectin stock 47
storage 34
strawberries 13, 14
    bottled 167
    in fruit syrups and liqueurs 132
    jam 61
        fridge jam 67
        pectin and acid levels 48
    regional varieties 19, 20, 22
    vinegar 150
sugar 26, 35–7, 132, 213
    in jams and jellies 49
sugar thermometers 41
sunflower oil 39
syrups 130
    for bottled fruit 162
    filling and sealing jars 32
    mint syrup *146*, 147
    rosehip syrup 152
    shelf life and keepability 133

tartare sauce, nasturtium 111
tayberries 14, 20, 22
thermometers 41
three-fruit marmalade 54
tomatoes 14
    bottled 167
        roasted tomato passata 173
        roasted tomato ketchup 195
        roasted tomato purée 106
    savoury leather 73
    seasonal chutney 108
    slow-dried tomatoes in oil 193
trifle *66*, 67
twist-on lids 31

Vale of Evesham 19
vegetables
    in chutney and pickles 97
    in oil 34, 188, *189*
        asparagus 198, *199*
        slow-dried tomatoes 193
    souper mix *206*, 207
vinegars 37
    flavoured 130, 132, 133, 149
        shelf life and keepability 133
    jars for vinegar preserves 30, 31
    mixed herb vinegar 149
    in pickles and chutneys 96–7, 99
    raspberry vinegar 150, *151*

walnuts
    plum jam 69
    plum and russet mincemeat 82, *83*
wassailing 90
Western England, fruit-growing regions 19, 22
whisky marmalade 54
white currants 48
wild garlic 13
wine vinegars 37
winter produce 15
Women's Institute (WI) 10, 215
wooden spoons 41

yeasts 27
Yorkshire Triangle 20

The River Cottage

Bread Handbook

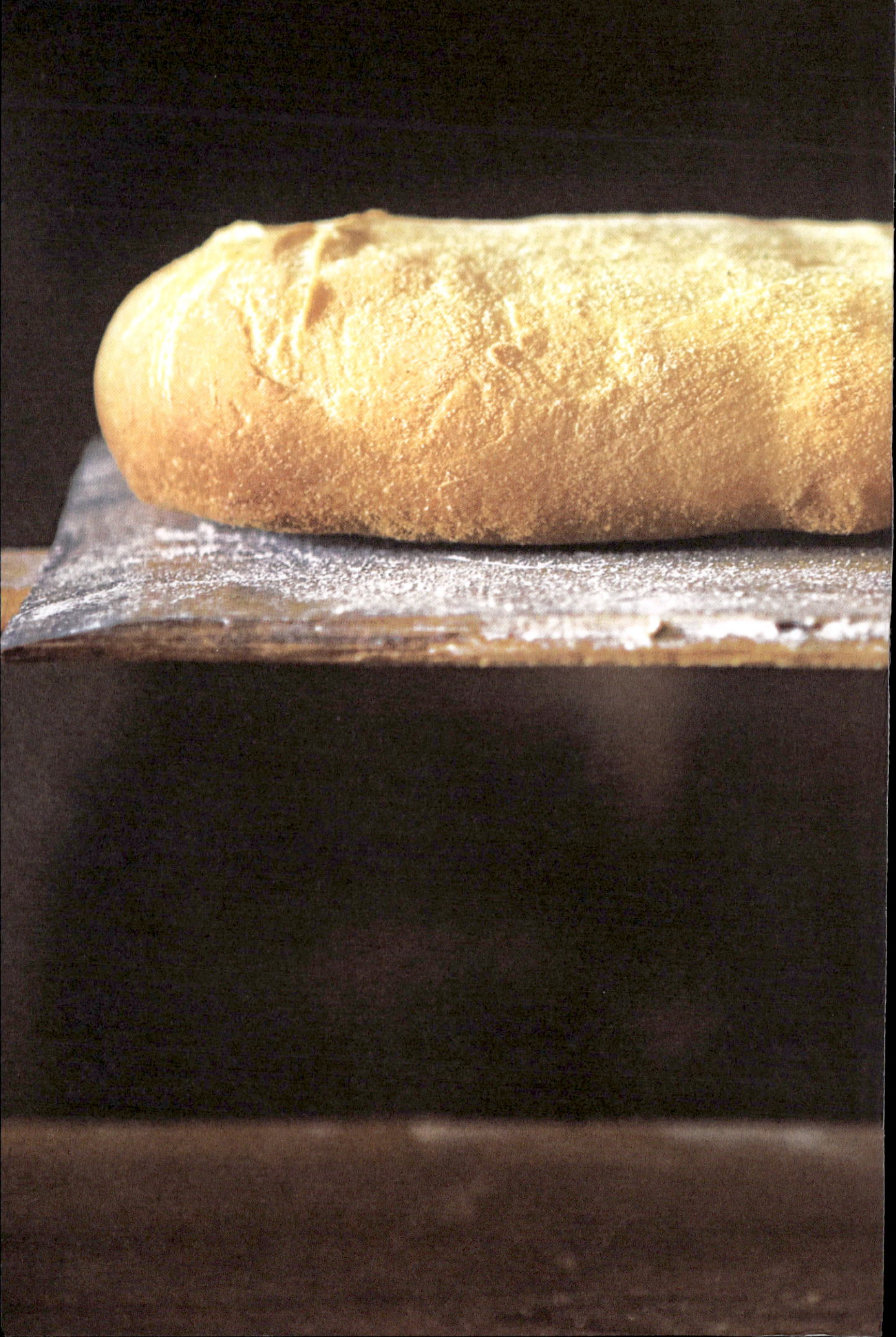

The River Cottage Bread Handbook

by Daniel Stevens

introduced by
Hugh Fearnley-Whittingstall

www.rivercottage.net

BLOOMSBURY
LONDON · NEW DELHI · NEW YORK · SYDNEY

First published in Great Britain 2009
This paperback edition published 2012

Text © 2009 by Daniel Stevens
Photography © 2009 by Gavin Kingcome

The quote on p.36 is from *The Tassajara Bread Book*, by Edward Espe Brown, ©1970 by the Chief Priest, Zen Center, San Francisco. Reprinted by arrangement with Shambhala Publications, Inc., Boston, www.shambhala.com

The moral right of the author has been asserted.

Bloomsbury Publishing Plc, 50 Bedford Square, London WC1B 3DP
Bloomsbury Publishing, London, New Delhi, New York and Sydney

A CIP catalogue record for this book is available from the British Library.

ISBN 978 1 4088 3607 1
10 9 8 7 6 5 4 3 2 1

Project editor: Janet Illsley
Design: willwebb.co.uk
Printed in China by C&C Offset Printing Co., Ltd.

MIX
Paper from responsible sources
FSC® C008047

www.bloomsbury.com/rivercottage

While every effort has been made to ensure the accuracy of the information contained in this book, in no circumstances can the publisher or the author accept any legal responsibility or liability for any loss or damage (including damage to property and/or personal injury) arising from any error in or omission from the information contained in this book, or from the failure of the reader to properly and accurately follow any instructions contained in the book.

Notes

Spoon measures are level unless otherwise stated:
1 tsp = 5ml spoon; 1 tbsp = 15ml spoon.

Use fresh herbs and freshly ground pepper unless otherwise suggested.

Use easy-blend (fast-action/quick) powdered yeast, rather than traditional dried yeast.

Oven timings in the recipes relate to fan-assisted ovens.
If using a conventional electric or gas oven (without a fan), increase the temperature by 15°C (1 Gas Mark). Use an oven thermometer to check the accuracy of your oven.

Contents

Why Bake Bread?	8
Getting Started	14
Bread Making Step by Step	34
The Basic Bread Recipe	72
Beyond the Basic Loaf	84
Bread Made with Wild Yeast	108
Bread Made without Yeast	126
Buns, Biscuits & Batter Breads	138
Using Leftover Bread	174
Building a Clay Oven	192
Useful Things	210

Bread is the staff of life, the saying goes. And in that sense

it is fundamental to our subsistence. But it is also fundamental to our pleasure – because good bread is the founding food of civilisation. So much greater than the sum of its humble parts, it defies all logic: it is the two-plus-two-equals-five of culinary evolution.

Bread is also like humanity itself. We come in many different shapes and sizes, colours and guises, yet underneath the skin/crust, we're all made of the same stuff. And the trick of achieving happiness and harmony is surely to celebrate and enjoy both our similarities and our differences, with equal vigour.

You only have to start reciting the names of the finest breads of the world to begin this process of celebration: cobber, baguette, chapati, sourdough, tortilla, ciabatta, brioche, bloomer… it's a litany of goodness. Wherever you are in the world, is there any better way of making yourself feel at home than breaking bread with the locals? Or, if you're feeling shy, at least going to visit the local baker.

But there's no doubt that for most of us good bread still seems much easier to enjoy than to make. And I must admit that for many years bread making was, for me, something of a culinary blind spot. I largely took the view that the making of bread, like the making of wine, was something best left to the experts. I felt I could enjoy it all the more for not knowing too much about its underlying mysteries. And then I met Dan!

When he first came to work with me in the River Cottage kitchen, Dan wasn't a particularly experienced baker – just a talented young chef long on the two qualities I look for in new recruits: curiosity and enthusiasm. But he soon decided to direct much of his energy and skill towards the blending of flour and yeast, in all its splendid forms. And as I watched him do so, I found myself revising my own rather hands-off approach to baking. His rapid and impressive progress was both engaging and infectious.

I saw that a form of cooking I had previously felt to be something of a dark art, was as ready to reveal itself to the energy of the open-minded, risk-taking enthusiast as any other. It had suited me to leave bread making on the side – I had enough other stuff on my plate. But I began to follow Dan's progress, picking up a few hints and tips even as they solidified in his own mind. And I found myself becoming a better baker, just by virtue of the occasional chat with Dan – and of course frequent sampling of his wares.

I'm not in Dan's league, of course. He has become a truly great baker. And a great teacher too, not least because, like all the best teachers, he is happy to acknowledge that he is still learning. What I love about this book is the irresistible way he passes on his knowledge. Like a nutty professor in his lab, he just can't wait to tell you how it all works. He hasn't lost the sense of wonder that his ingredients can really do the amazing things they do, or that the end results can be as delicious as they are.

This irrepressible enthusiasm now comes with a hefty dose of authority. Dan knows what he's talking about. He believes passionately in using the best ingredients, locally sourced where possible, and will guide you dependably to the right tools, edible and otherwise, for the job. And I can honestly say that I would now rather eat bread baked by Dan than anyone else (except perhaps my wife, who also bakes lovely bread, though sadly not nearly as often as Dan does).

And few, frankly, will be more delighted than I am to have in their hands, at last, the perfect book to help them bake better bread. This simple volume feeds my enthusiasm and knowledge, like a sourdough starter, so that I feel readier than ever to rise to the occasion. That's because Dan's creations, from the simplest flat bread to elaborate, multi-seeded concoctions, via the notoriously temperamental sourdoughs, are achievable and yet consistently delicious. And they are the real deal – about as far from the plastic-wrapped, machine-made monstrosities that shamelessly pass themselves off under the name of 'bread' as it's possible to get.

I'm thrilled that in this handbook, Dan will get to share with you, and with many, his passion and knowledge. Whether you want to know how to bash out a simple white loaf, delight your family with buttery croissants or fling together some Middle Eastern flatbreads to wrap up the meat on your barbecue, you can be sure you're in very safe, if rather floury, hands.

Hugh Fearnley-Whittingstall, East Devon, February 2009

Why Bake Bread?

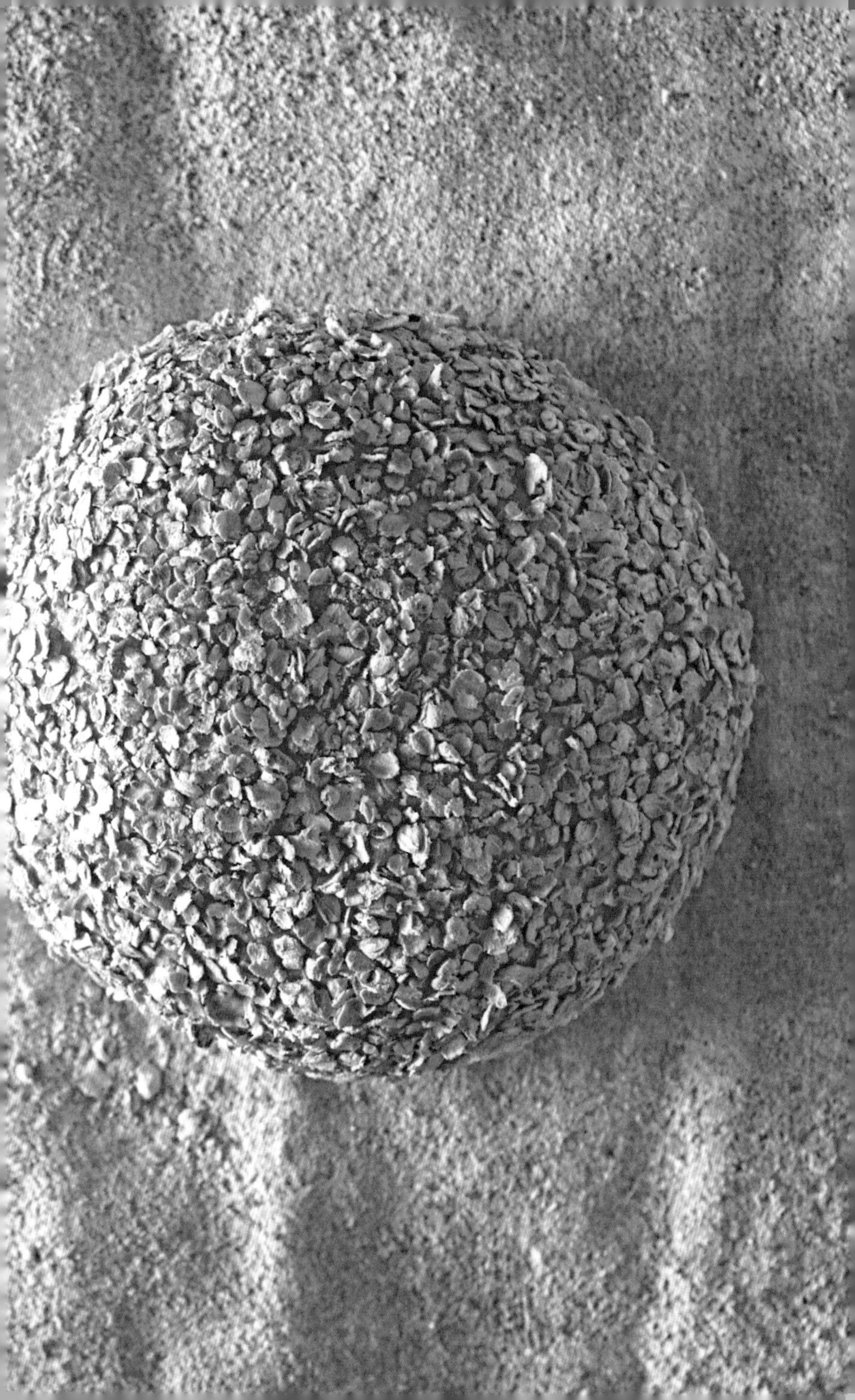

There is nothing in the world as satisfying to eat as home-baked, handmade bread. Of course, technically the artisan baker down the road is much better at it, but no amount of skill and craftsmanship can replace the utter joy of eating and sharing the stuff you make yourself. And it is practical to make bread – exceptional bread – with your own hands, in your own home, on a regular basis.

I know you are busy, so I have given you roti – a flatbread you can make, from cupboard to table, in less than 5 minutes. But I know that you also have free time, and I hope I can persuade you that free time spent in the kitchen – by yourself, with friends or with children, with music in your ears, wine in your glass, flour in your hair and magic in your hands – is time that could not be better spent.

If you are new to bread making, this sense of pleasure might not be immediate, but I am confident that you will reach it more quickly than I did. I remember my first loaf well – even the birds wouldn't eat it. I had followed the two-page recipe to the letter and the cookbook assured me that 'homemade bread is easy'. That was rather hard to swallow (as was my bread). Still, I soldiered on, day after day. After all, practice makes perfect.

There are two kinds of bread in the world: bread that hands have made, and bread that hands have not. In an ideal world, all bread would be hands-have-made – by your hands and my hands, and by the hands of those few professional bakers left in this country who are still doing it properly. I guess there will always be hands-have-not bread, and while it's not that bad, or at least it is surely edible, it seems a shame that bread has become so standard and commonplace, that we don't even consider what a small miracle a risen loaf is.

Mass-produced bread

Some would say that 1961 was a bad year for bread. It was the year the Chorleywood Bread Process came into being. Developed by the Flour Milling and Baking Research Association in Chorleywood, the process revolutionised the baking industry. This high-speed mechanical mixing process allowed the fermentation time to be drastically reduced, and meant that lower-protein British wheats could be used in place of the more expensive North American imports. Various chemical improvers and antifungal agents are necessary ingredients, as are certain hydrogenated or fractionated hard fats. This is high-output, low-labour production, designed to maximise efficiency and profit at the expense of the consumer.

Mass-produced bread is almost undoubtedly worse for you. Apart from the dubious additives and fats it contains, the short fermentation makes the wheat harder to digest. Indeed, some believe the Chorleywood processing method is partly to blame for a sharp increase in gluten intolerance and allergy. It is also probable that

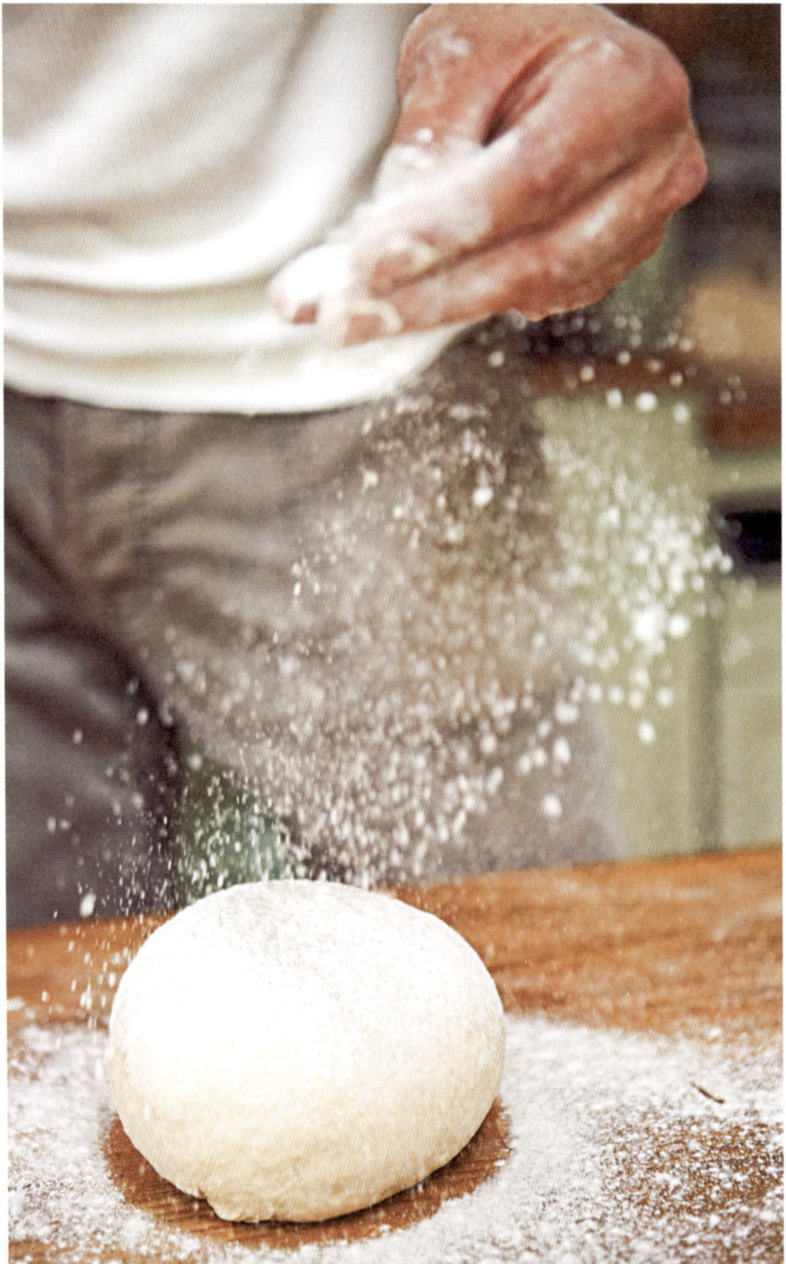

the prolific crossbreeding and modification of modern-day wheat, to produce stronger, tougher, harder-to-digest gluten, has contributed to wheat intolerance.

Somewhere in the region of 98 per cent of bread baked in this country is mass-produced, and most of it comes from around a dozen huge plant bakeries. Supermarkets love to crow about their in-store bakeries, but they are really nothing more than mini versions of these plants. 98 per cent is a lot. That means hands-have-not bread is not just the preserve of the supermarkets; it is the same bread you buy in most local 'bakeries'. I'm talking about the ones that sell white tin loaves with flat tops, apple turnovers and ham rolls with nasty pickle, where there is little hint of baking activity save for the oven-warming of sausage rolls, bacon-and-cheese slices and 'Cornish' pasties. The 'bakeries' whose bread looks the same as everyone else's... Well, nearly everyone else's.

Bread from real bakeries

Real bakeries are special places, where bread is made in small batches by real people's hands and baked on site. You can tell when bread is made by hand. For a start, it will look different from other bread in other shops, because every baker has his own, recognisable style. Shop at one regularly and you may spot changes in the bread from one morning to the next. You may even be able to tell if the baker was in a bad mood, so sensitive is real bread to the hands that make it. Some real bakeries sell their bread to local stores, which is excellent – the more places selling real bread, the better. Real bakeries are a rarity, though. If you are lucky enough to have one near you, then you would be mad not to use it. The bread will cost more... so it should.

Bread made at home

Home is the bakery where handmade bread does not cost more. At home, you can produce a large loaf, made with organic flour, for less than half the price of a similar-sized, mass-produced, non-organic loaf from a local shop. And your homemade bread can be great bread – even if it doesn't quite go to plan the first time.

I still have that first bread recipe I attempted – both pages of it. And now, years later, I realise why my first loaf was such a disaster. The basic method is fine, but to make good bread you need to understand the process. Some professional bakers and cookery writers skirt this all too briefly. As I discovered, being told 'what to do' is simply not enough. There is so much to know, and I really believe that the more you know, the better your bread will be. Two pages? Not even the best baker in the world could teach bread in two pages.

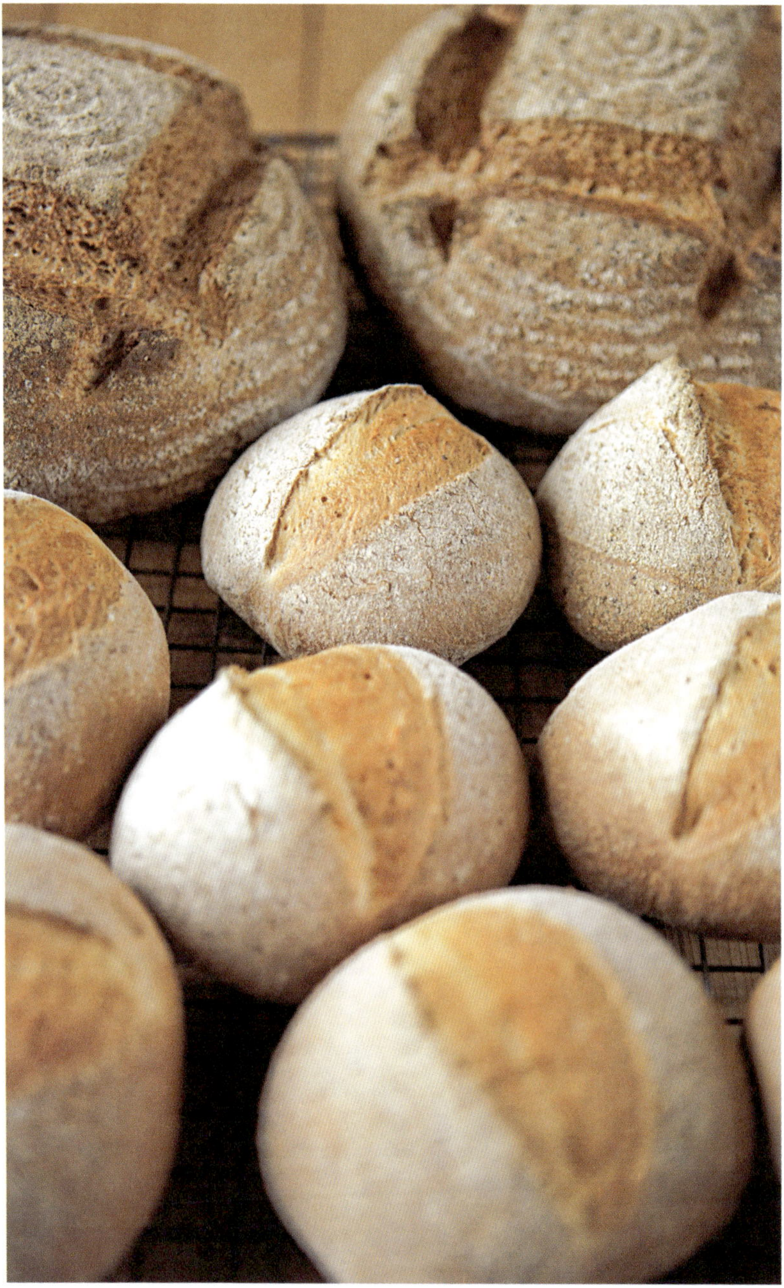

Getting Started

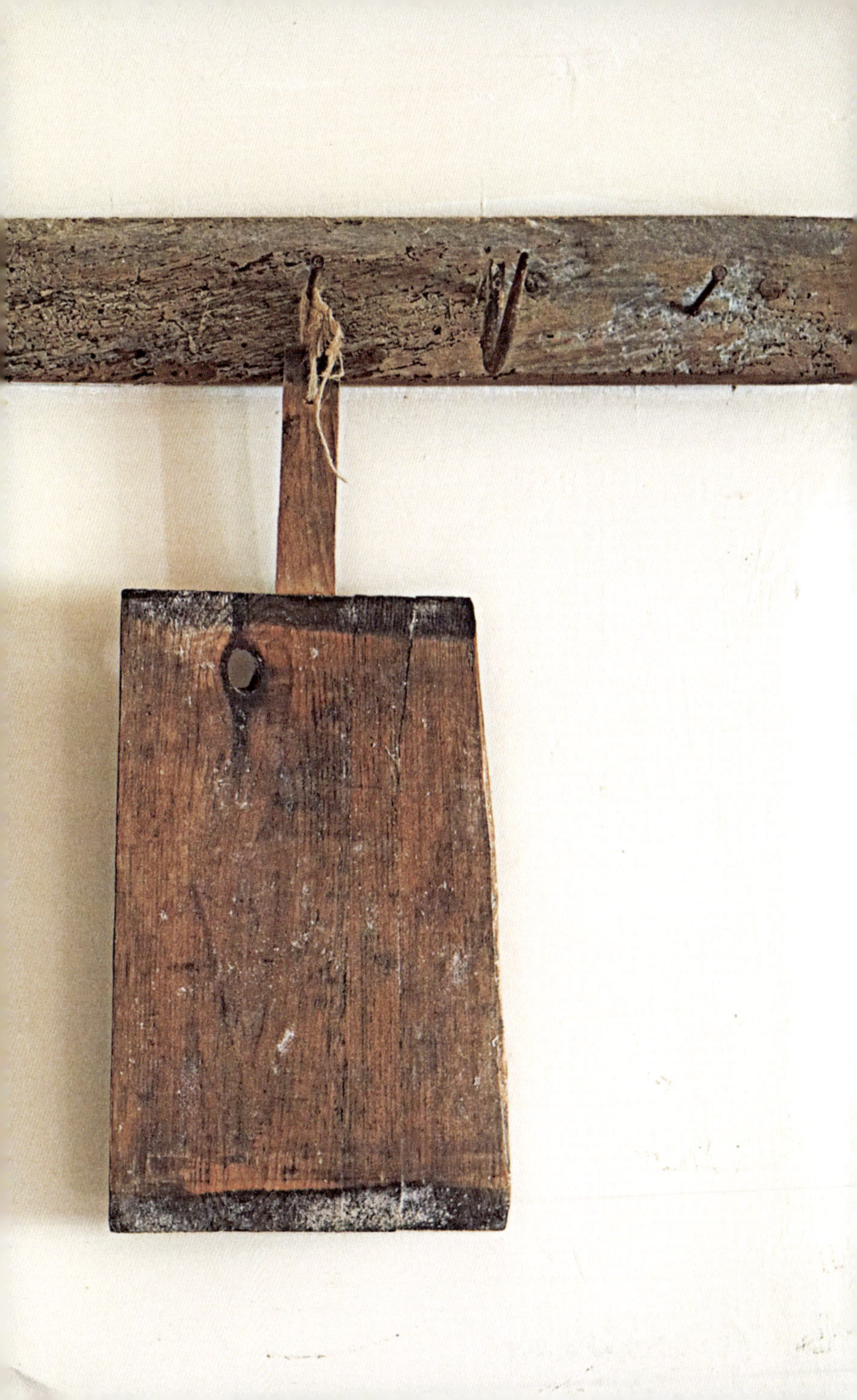

Baking kit

You don't need a vast inventory of special equipment to bake your own bread, but there are a few items that come in very handy, most of which are inexpensive. In addition to those described below, you'll find the following everyday kitchen tools useful: a measuring jug, a rolling pin, a set of pastry cutters, a pastry brush, a palette knife, a bread knife (which I also use as a dough slasher), several sturdy baking trays, a large wire cooling rack, and black dustbin liners (which I use over and over again for covering my doughs). I also have a lidded crock, where my sourdough starter (see p.110) lives.

Linen cloths

Linen draws a tiny amount of moisture from the surface of the dough, drying it just enough to prevent it from sticking. I have never found that dough sticks to a well-floured linen cloth, not even the wettest ciabatta. You can also fold and shape the cloth to make rucks and channels to keep your loaves in shape, and separate. Keep the cloths dry and you shouldn't need to wash them. At some stage of their life, you will want to replace them but I have had mine in regular use for well over a year. Fabric shops are the best place to buy linen; a metre will be more than enough and won't cost you very much. You can use clean tea towels instead, but they may stick; all-linen tea towels would be your best option.

Wooden boards

These are an alternative to cloths, to dust generously with flour and lay your bread on. We have two or three large (1.2 square metre) pieces of cheap, thin plywood at River Cottage, which are excellent for large batch baking. A couple of smaller ones would certainly be useful in your baking kit. They are less versatile than cloths in that you cannot ruck them up, but a little more practical as you can move them around with bread on. A board/cloth combination would be perfect.

Proving baskets

It is nice to own a couple of proving baskets. The best, and most expensive, are generally made of cane or reed, sometimes lined with linen, though you can buy cheaper wicker and plastic ones (see the directory, p.212). They come in different shapes and sizes and are excellent for holding the shape of your loaf as it is proving. Proving baskets are especially useful for wetter doughs, which cannot hold their own weight (large, airy sourdoughs, for example). Lower-gluten breads also benefit from the extra support. Dust the baskets heavily with flour and lay the bread in them, smooth side down.

Baking stone

The best way to bake bread is on a hot stone. Some kitchen shops sell them, but they are invariably too small, too thin and too expensive. Measure your oven, then go to your local hardware store and buy the paving stone that best fits. If you do not have a baking stone, you will need a baking tray – the larger and heavier the better.

Peel

A peel is a sheet of wood or metal with a handle, for sliding bread into the oven. You will need one if you are using a baking stone; either buy one (see the directory, p.212), make one, or use a rimless baking sheet instead. (My peel is simply a thin piece of wood, with a narrow piece nailed on as a handle – see pic on pp.14–15.)

Dough scraper

One of these is useful for handling and cutting the dough, and for scraping work surfaces and bowls clean. Small cheap plastic scrapers are adequate. You may already have something similar in your kitchen that will work; a plastic wallpaper scraper, for example.

Thermometer

A special-purpose thermometer is useful for checking the temperature of oil for deep-frying. A probe cooking thermometer will do the job.

Water spray bottle

I recommend one of these for spraying loaves before they go into the oven. You can buy them cheaply at garden centres and hardware stores.

Weighing scales

It is well worth investing in a set of digital scales. They should measure in increments of 5g or less, and have a capacity of at least 2kg. Alternatively, of course, you can use balance scales.

Large mixing bowl

Earthenware feels just right for making bread, but in truth, plastic and stainless steel bowls are both fine.

Food mixer

Although not essential for bread making, a food mixer fitted with a dough hook can be used for kneading and is particularly helpful for softer, wetter doughs that are difficult to work by hand.

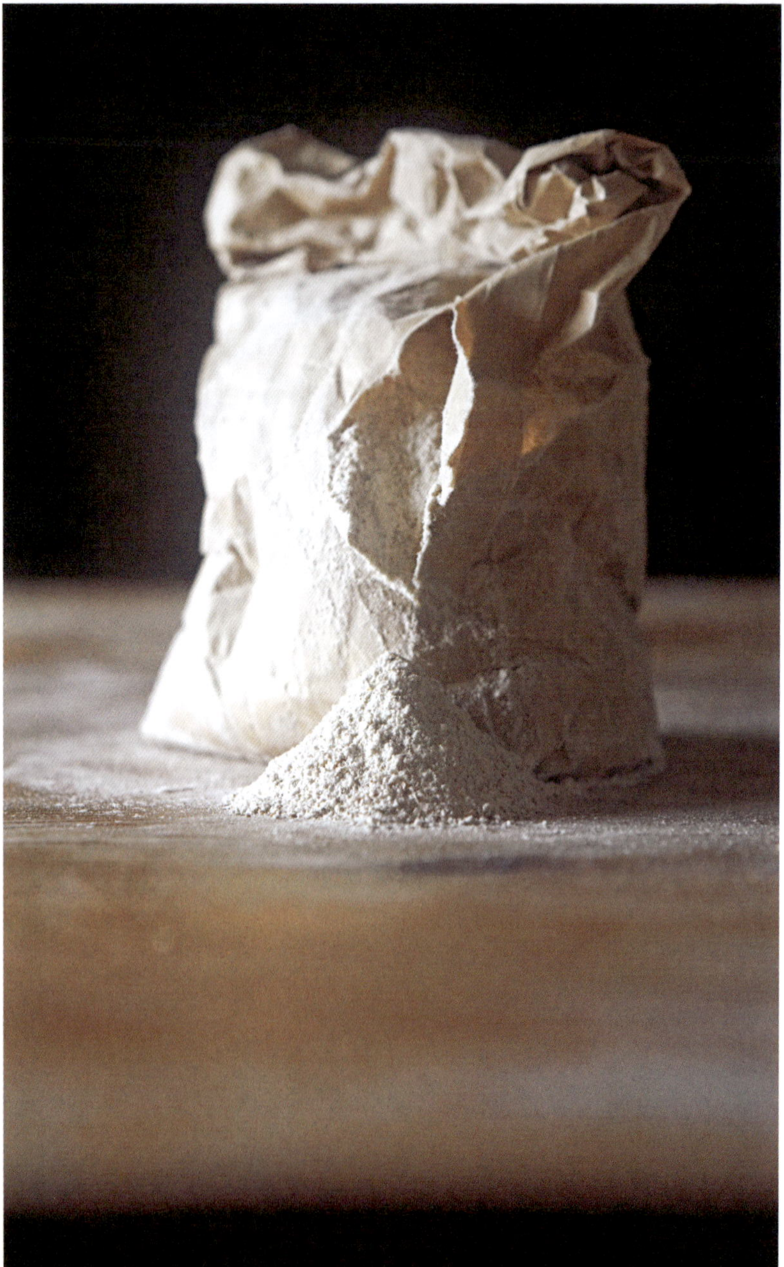

Ingredients

The best bread comprises four simple ingredients: flour, yeast, salt and water. It helps to know something about these – let's start with the most important: flour.

Flour

You must buy good flour – the best you can afford. The price of flour has increased dramatically, but making bread will always be cheaper than buying it, so you can afford the best. Wholefood stores are usually good places to buy flour, but I buy mine locally from my favourite bakeries, Leakers in Bridport and Town Mill in Lyme Regis, who sell the flour they use themselves. Many supermarkets sell good-quality flour too, alongside the cheaper stuff. I don't want pesticides, fungicides, or 'anycides at all' in my bread, and I'm sure you don't either, so I suggest buying organic flour.

Most of the flour on sale in this country is the product of roller milling. This is a large-scale, fully automated process in which the grains pass through a series of grooved rollers, sieves, aspirators and centrifuges, which cut, grind, sift and separate the grains to produce specified grades of flour. For white flour, the bran is removed early on, and only the pale endosperm is ground. Milling whole grains produces wholemeal flour, of course, which may then be sifted to produce a lighter brown flour. An unwelcome side effect of this super-efficient system is that the friction generated by the high-speed rollers can overheat the flour, destroying valuable nutrients. Fortunately, there is still another way.

Traditional stone milling, as you can imagine, is much rougher around the edges. Grain is poured into a hole in the middle of a huge stone disc, which rotates by whatever power is available (electricity/water/wind/donkey) on top of a second, stationary disc. The resulting meal falls away from the sides, and is sieved (or not) and bagged. A preliminary sifting of the wholemeal removes the coarser bits and gives brown flour. Subsequent siftings through finer meshes lighten and whiten the flour, but some bran will stay, so stoneground flour will never be as white as it would be from a roller mill. That is unless it is bleached, of course. Various substances have been used to whiten flour, both stone- and roller-milled, for the last 100 years or so, and the list reads a little scarily. Does anyone fancy a nitrogen peroxide/chlorine/chlorine dioxide/nitrosyl chloride/benzoyl peroxide/azodicarbonamide sandwich? No, I thought not. The function of bleach is purely aesthetic and I don't really approve of such chemical interference – it is vain and unnecessary.

I love using stoneground flour. It seems right that bread, such a basic and traditional staple, is made with basic and traditional methods. Stone milling still has the human touch, and if there is one foodstuff that should never have been sucked into the soulless, automated world of mass production, then surely it is bread. Bread that has been loved and cared for at every stage is better bread, no question.

Wheat flour

Of course, flours are produced from various grains, but in this country wheat flour is by far the most common. A grain of wheat is a seed and is made, basically, of three parts: the bran, which is the outside 'skin' and comprises about 13 per cent of the grain; the germ, which is the wheat plant in embryo (about 2 per cent); and the rest (about 85 per cent) is the endosperm, which supports and feeds the germ in its early stages of growth. The bran is full of flavour and protein; the germ full of vitamins; and the endosperm is packed with carbohydrates (in the form of starches and sugars), and contains proteins, minerals and oil.

All of these end up in your bread, of course, and they all have an effect. The starches and sugars feed the yeast, the proteins bond to form gluten, the minerals strengthen the gluten, and the oil rather gets in the way – wriggling in between newly bonding proteins and splitting them up. It's also the first to turn rancid (which is why it's important to stick to the use-by date on your flour). However, this oil is not all bad. By clinging to the starches, and also by retaining moisture, it helps soften the bread, and keep it soft for longer. Its benefits are such that extra oil (or butter, or lard) is often added to bread dough, though I don't add it straight away. I like to allow the proteins to bond, and become inseparable, first.

I would love to suggest that you only buy flour milled from grain grown in this country for bread making, but for reasons I will explain, I'm not going to. You see, there is wheat and there is wheat. Up to 30,000 different varieties, in fact. Wheats, or *Triticum*, are grasses, grown generally in temperate regions – mainly North America, Europe and the warmer south-western parts of Russia, India, China, Australia and Argentina. Different strains have different properties, the most notable of which is their protein content.

> Strong flour When you mix flour with water, certain proteins in the flour (gliadin and glutenin) bond together and form gluten. Gluten is an elastic, extensile substance that forms long chains when it is softened and stretched. The more it is worked, the longer and stretchier it gets (think of Blu-Tack). These elastic chains of gluten form a network, which acts like a membrane, trapping the carbon dioxide produced by fermenting yeast and making thousands of gas pockets inside the dough.
>
> The amount of gluten in the dough depends on the quality of the proteins in the grain. High-quality proteins will produce 'strong' flour with a high percentage of gluten (up to 15 per cent), which is what you want for leavened (yeasted) bread. Such flour is generally sold as 'strong flour' or 'bread flour' (or even 'strong bread flour'), and can be wholemeal, white or brown. Brown flour is sometimes sold as '81 per cent' flour, because a typical first sifting removes about 19 per cent of the total weight.

The problem for food-mile-conscious bread bakers in this country is that the strains of wheat with the best gluten-forming proteins simply will not grow successfully here. They flourish in nitrogen-rich soil and prefer cold winters and hot summers. Our climate is simply too placid, our soil too low in nitrogen. Canada, on the other hand, boasts the perfect conditions. Although it is possible to buy flour milled from 100 per cent Canadian wheat here, imported wheat is more heavily taxed, so the strong bread flours produced in this country are usually blends of British and Canadian wheat. Certainly the bread flour you buy in supermarkets is likely to be a blend of this kind.

However, several British millers are producing small quantities of purely local wheat flour (see the directory, p.212). I have found that bread made with these flours always tastes good, even if it is a little heavier. Indeed, the more I bake, the more I love heavy bread. It feels wholesome, satisfying and *real*. So if someone is growing and milling wheat near you, I would urge you to buy some. That said, when I buy local flour, I always buy wholemeal rather than white, as I find dense white bread much less appealing.

Plain flour 'Soft' flours have a gluten percentage of around 7–9 per cent and are usually sold as 'plain' flour. Their poorer-quality gluten is less extensile, and will struggle to form membranes and trap gas bubbles, so you end up with a weak structure and crumbly texture.

While this feature is not great for loaves of bread, it is perfect for biscuits, cakes and pastry. I sometimes use a combination of plain and strong flour when I am prepared to forgo some of the gluten strength in exchange for a yeast dough that is less resistant and easier to work – when I am making pizzas, for example.

Self-raising flour This is plain flour with raising agents added. It is most commonly used for cakes and sponge puddings, though it also forms the basis of some non-yeasted breads. I rarely have self-raising flour in my storecupboard, so I usually make my own version, by mixing 4g baking powder into every 100g plain flour (i.e. 4 per cent). With all baking, the fresher the flour the better, so I find it more convenient to have fewer open packets of different flours.

Malted grain flour Malting is a process by which whole grains are encouraged to germinate, producing sugars (amongst other things), which are then fixed by drying and browned by roasting. These now sweetly flavoured grains are then added to strong brown flour to produce different blends, which are variously named 'malted grain', 'malted seed', 'cobber', 'malthouse', and even, rather snazzily, 'maltstar'.

'Granary', by the way, is a trademark of Rank Hovis Ltd. It is the name given to a special blend of meal produced by Granary Foods Ltd. Bread can only properly be called Granary if it is made with Hovis Granary flour. You can buy this, and it is very good, but it is not the only malted flour available. Indeed, I am yet to find one that I don't like.

'00' flour This is an Italian grade of flour, usually milled from durum wheat. It is traditionally used for making pasta, but makes good bread too. Try using it to make ciabatta (see p.90) or focaccia (see p.89) in place of the strong white flour.

Other grain flours

While no other grain will make bread as light and well risen as wheat, other grains are used and each has its own character, flavour and history. It is well worth getting yourself acquainted with some of the alternatives, not least because wheat intolerance seems to be on the increase.

Spelt flour An ancestral cousin of modern wheat, spelt is an ancient grain, which has never been modified. The grain we use today is identical to that used by the Romans for their bread.

Spelt is becoming more widely available in this country, as flour/pasta/puffed sugary breakfast cereal, and is recognised as a genuine alternative to wheat. It contains gluten, but the gluten in spelt is more digestible than that in wheat. You can buy white spelt flour, but if the product doesn't claim to be white, assume it is wholemeal.

Traditional wholemeal spelt flour has an orangey tinge and tastes delicious – similar to wheat, and slightly nutty. It is excellent for making bread, but also good for biscuits, cakes and pastry. Spelt grows well in many places, including Britain.

Rye flour Rye thrives in cold climates and poor soil. It is widely cultivated and used across Scandinavia, Russia and Eastern Europe; it grows well in this country, too. Rye proteins form small amounts of weak gluten, producing dense, sometimes cakey, but very tasty bread. It is worth mixing rye with strong white wheat flour for a lighter loaf. I often use rye flour for dusting shaped loaves, and the baskets, boards and cloths on which I leave them to rise. Rye is sometimes sold as 'light' or 'dark', depending on the amount of whole grain left in it.

Kamut flour This yellowish flour is fairly low in gluten and makes decent, but not remarkable bread. It isn't a flour I use, but it is appearing more often in shops and has a tale behind it, which I thought you might find interesting. The story goes that a US airman, shot down over Egypt in the Second World War, discovered a few perfectly preserved grains in an ancient desert tomb. He managed to get himself and the grains to safety, and brought them home, where they were discovered to be an ancient North African wheat-related grain that was thought to be extinct. It was named 'kamut' (now a trademark), after the Egyptian for wheat. You can buy flour milled from the great-great-great-great grandchildren of the airman's grains, which are today grown exclusively in America.

Gluten-free bread flour This is usually made from a blend of rice, potato, tapioca and other flours, and typically contains xantham gum, as a sort of gluten replacement. Gluten-free flours generally come with a recipe on the bag, which you should follow; the method is usually rather different to traditional bread making. Bread made with such flour is, I would say, an acquired taste... one I'm yet to acquire.

GRAIN	FLOUR TYPE	GLUTEN	USES
Wheat	Strong white/wholemeal/brown	High	Bread
	Malted grain	High	Bread
	Plain white/wholemeal/brown	Low	Pastry, pancakes, biscuits. Also blended with strong flour for softer bread doughs (pizzas/flatbreads), soda bread, scones
	Self-raising white/wholemeal/brown	Low	Cakes, soda bread, scones
	'00' pasta flour	High	Pasta, bread
Spelt	Wholemeal/white	Medium high	Bread, biscuits, cakes, pasta
Rye	Dark/light	Low	Bread
Kamut		Medium	Bread
Gluten-free	White/brown	None	Bread

Water

Whether you use hard or soft water will make hardly any difference to your dough. Hard water is a little more alkaline than soft, and yeasts work a little more happily in a slightly acid environment, but it also has a higher mineral content, particularly of calcium and magnesium, which have a tightening and strengthening effect on the gluten. So, between hard and soft water, it's pretty much honours even.

I like the purity of baking with spring water. If you are lucky enough to live close to a natural spring, then you should use it; if you are happy to pay for mineral water, then do so. Otherwise, use tap water – it is perfectly good.

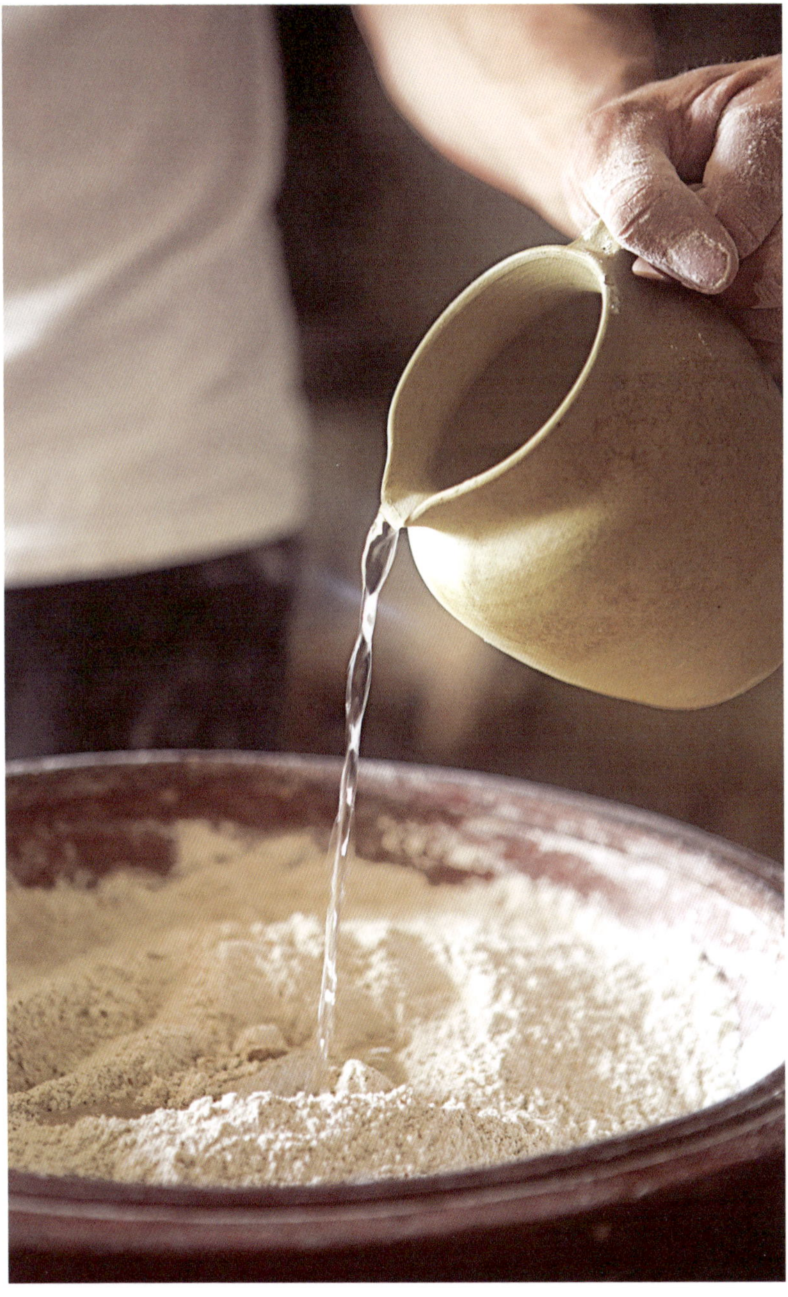

Yeast

The term 'yeasts' refers to a group of a hundred or so single-celled organisms, collectively known as *Saccharomyces,* which are a type of fungi. They depend on carbon but, because they do not contain chlorophyll, they cannot obtain carbon from carbon dioxide in the way plants do. Instead, fungi take carbon from carbohydrates. For yeasts, the carbohydrate of choice is sugar, hence their Latin name, literally 'sugar fungus'. One strain of yeast, known as brewer's sugar fungus, is cultivated commercially, though you can – and I hope you will – create and nurture your own culture of wild yeasts for raising sourdough, the most satisfying bread you will ever make (see pp.115–9).

Commercial yeast is cultivated in huge temperature-controlled, aerated vats filled with a solution of minerals and sugars, including molasses, or malted barley, or both, and known as 'wort'. Brewers, by the way, will find this virtually indistinguishable from the wort made in the first stages of beer making. Indeed, this method of yeast cultivation is no more than a controlled and refined version of the old practice of skimming off beer froth, then adding it to dough.

Yeast cells, known as 'seed' yeast, are grown in laboratory conditions from a single healthy cell. The seed yeasts are added to the wort and in this perfect feeding and reproducing environment – yeast heaven – a gluttonous orgy ensues. Yeast cells collect *en masse* on the surface, and are removed, washed, cooled and either pressed into cake form (fresh yeast) or dehydrated and crumbled (dried yeast).

One single yeast cell can be grown into hundreds of tons in a matter of weeks. As there are several billion cells to the gram, this is a reproduction rate of which rabbits could only dream.

Dried yeast This is readily available, consistent and reliable, and it has a long shelf life. It will become inactive eventually though, so pay attention to the use-by date. The kind of dried yeast you are most likely to buy these days is sold in powdered form, and may be labelled variously as 'fast-action', 'easy-blend', or 'quick'. This is the yeast used throughout this book, which I refer to simply as 'powdered dried yeast'. Traditional dried yeast, which comes in little pellets, requires activating and is used slightly differently. Some yeast packet labels bequeath special bread-making powers upon their contents, claiming they allow you to skip an entire period of rising. Don't be taken in by this. Yeast is yeast, and you can always skip a period of rising, but as you will learn, your bread will be less digestible for it.

Fresh yeast This is harder to come by than dried yeast. Try asking for fresh yeast at your local health food shop or bakery, where you may find it bagged for sale, in small pieces. And you should only ever buy it in small pieces, as

dried yeast

fresh yeast

GETTING STARTED 27

its active life is only around 2 weeks from manufacture. Fresh yeast in good condition will be a pale mushroom colour, and firm. If you break it, it will snap cleanly – and the smell should be pleasant. As it stales, it becomes darker, drier and smellier, until it breaks down into a disgusting, rancid putty (but you'll have thrown it away by then). As for freezing, it is generally purported that fresh yeast can be kept in the freezer, at least for short periods, but in my experience it dies more often than it lives, so I would never recommend it.

I enjoy using fresh yeast because I like the feel, and the snap, and the smell. But dried yeast's long shelf life makes it more practical, especially for occasional baking. As for the all-important performance – the ability to make good bread – frankly, I have no preference for fresh over dried. I just can't tell the difference. I nearly always use powdered dried yeast, which can be mixed straight into the dough. It is best to blend fresh, or dried pellet yeast with a little liquid first; if you do not, it is unlikely to fully blend.

For simplicity, all yeasted recipes in this book assume the use of powdered dried yeast. If, however, you prefer to use fresh yeast, simply double the quantity given in the recipe.

How yeast works When you mix yeast with flour and wet it, various things start to happen. In addition to the wheat's own enzymes, which begin to convert starch to sugar, the yeast cells produce several enzymes of their own, which convert the various sugars in the flour into forms the yeast can absorb. This is how yeast feeds. More enzymes inside the yeast cell convert these sugars into carbon dioxide and alcohol (amongst other things), which are excreted. The carbon dioxide forms into bubbles inside the dough, and causes it to rise. This is fermentation (from the Latin *fermo* meaning 'to boil', as the bubbles bear a resemblance to boiling). This enzyme activity helps to make the tough gluten in the flour more digestible. Not surprisingly, bread that ferments for longer is better for you.

After feeding heartily, and passing gas accordingly, the yeast cell's attention turns, inevitably, to reproduction. So it splits in two. Two become four, then eight, sixteen, and so on. Meanwhile, some of the excreted alcohol is converted into acetic acid, which slightly raises the acidity of the dough. Yeasts like that, and their activity increases because of it. All this rumpus noticeably raises the temperature of the dough. Other acids, including lactic and carbonic acid, are produced. And the heady combination of acid and alcohol creates esters, aromatic molecules that contribute to the flavour of the finished bread. The longer fermentation goes on, the more of these reactions take place, and the more reactions, the more flavour. Quite simply, bread that takes longer to rise tastes better.

Dough temperature is a key factor in the rate of yeast activity: between 25°C and 30°C it will be reasonably vigorous. Temperatures higher than this will increase this vigour, resulting in a dough that rises faster, but they will also cause the yeast to produce some undesirable sour flavours. Yeasts will start to feel a little uncomfortable above about 45°C; at around 60°C they will die – which is what happens in the oven, of course. Going the other way, activity will reduce to a steady rate, becoming fairly slow at around 20°C, and will practically stop at perhaps 2°C and below, where it will lie dormant until it either dies from not feeding (after maybe a couple of weeks), is warmed up (when it will pick up where it left off), or is frozen. Although I'm reluctant to advise freezing fresh yeast, I have never had problems freezing yeasted dough, at least for a short time (up to 6 months); it always reactivates on thawing.

While you can control the rate of fermentation by controlling dough temperature, you can also affect it by the amount of yeast you add. Obviously, the less yeast, the slower the rate. This can be literally as little as you like – remember what that single cell can do.

Salt

Although it isn't essential to add salt to bread, I would never consider leaving it out, as unsalted bread tastes so unlovely. Nevertheless, salt has a dark side (ask any slug). When it comes across yeast (and slugs), salt has a propensity to murder. So you must mediate, and you must keep them apart. That said, this only really applies to fresh yeast, or dried yeast that you have rehydrated; dry salt won't react with dry yeast.

Either way, as you mix and the salt is dispersed, so its capacity to harm becomes diluted. Yeast activity is nevertheless inhibited in salted dough, the result being that fermentation is slower than it would otherwise be. Also, salt has a tightening effect on the gluten network, making it stronger and more stable. Gas bubbles are trapped more effectively, and the bread rises higher and more evenly. Salt also helps bread to retain moisture, and salted bread therefore lasts longer.

So salt is a good addition, but which salt is best? There are several methods of harvesting salt from the earth. Rock salt is mined from salt beds, often deep underground. Water also percolates naturally (or is pumped) through to these beds, dissolving the salt and forming a brine, which can be pumped up to the surface and evaporated to form salt.

Sea salt comes from seawater, which is either allowed to evaporate naturally or boiled dry – the quicker method, which results in smaller, harder crystals. The more time-consuming natural drying results in beautiful large crystals, which are sold as flaky sea salt (Maldon is the best known), and are expensive.

Any salt you are likely to buy will contain impurities, although this is not necessarily a bad thing. Unrefined sea salt, for example, will contain traces of

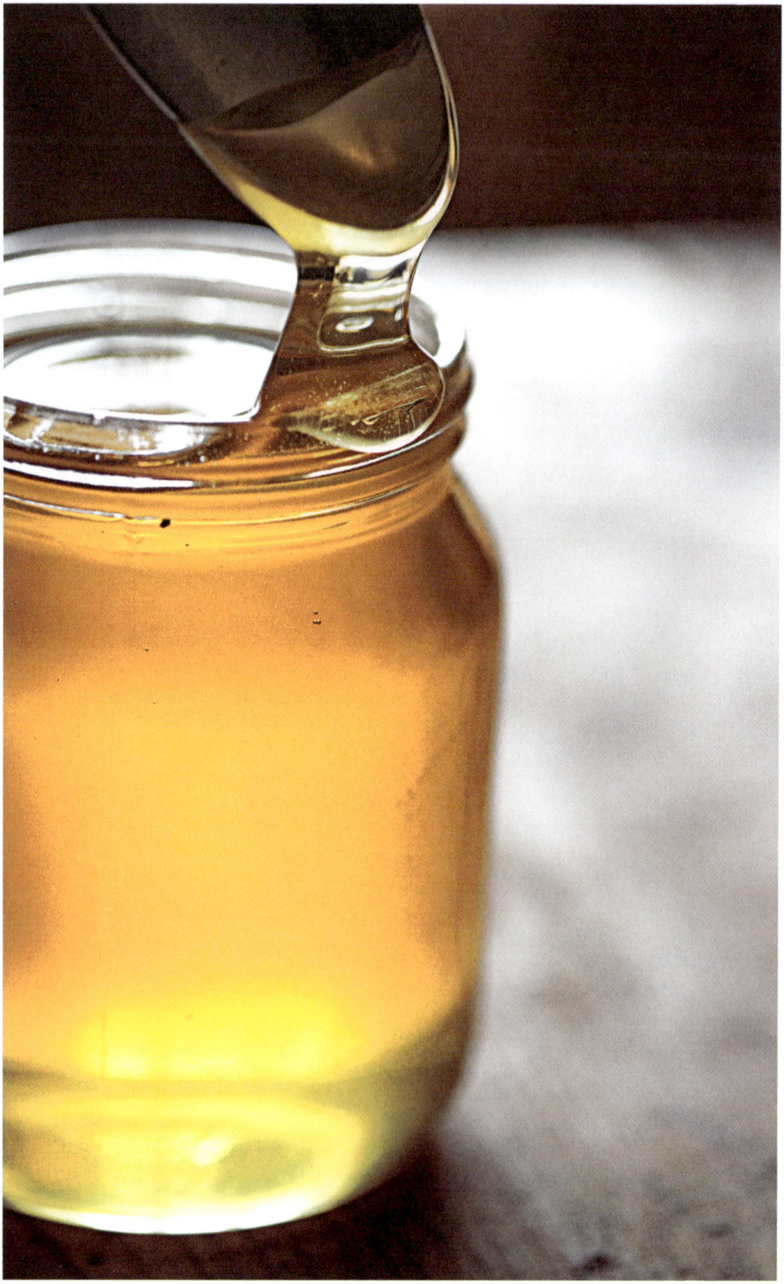

calcium, magnesium and other chlorides and sulphates. The content of salt (sodium chloride) and the concentrations of other minerals mixed with it vary according to where it comes from. This, along with the different methods of harvesting, accounts for the marked variety of natural salts available. French *sel gris* (grey salt), for example, is exactly that – grey, due to its high proportion of other minerals. By contrast, cheap, free-flowing table salt and cooking salt may be technically more 'pure' but will have additives, including anti-caking agents – E504 (magnesium carbonate) and E535 (sodium ferrocyanide).

Some of the impurities found in untreated salt will have an effect on your dough (calcium and magnesium will further tighten the gluten, for example), but I doubt you will notice the difference. My personal, perhaps romantic, preference is for unrefined sea salt, but in all honesty, for baking, I have found standard table salt to be absolutely fine.

Whatever salt you use, it must be ground finely, or it will not mix in properly. You can do this yourself, in a spice mill or a pestle and mortar.

Other ingredients

Now that you have the basics, you can take your bread in any number of directions, with the judicious addition of some choice ingredients. I have offered some suggestions here, though of course you can add what you please. Just don't add things for the sake of it. You could put olives in your bread, but they are better in a bowl. Cheese bread is good, but bread and cheese is better. I have seen bread made with fennel seeds and liquidised mussels. No, seriously. Give me some fennel seed bread, and a bowl of mussels, any day.

> Liquids You do not have to make bread with water. Milk, and even yoghurt, is excellent, and will make bread softer and (in the case of white bread) whiter. Cider and beer can be interesting, though I prefer to water them down a bit. Apple juice is lovely, as long as it is real apple juice.

> Fat As I have said, putting fat in your bread will make it a little softer, and will slightly improve its keeping qualities. Stronger-tasting fats will, of course, add their own hint of flavour, though these effects are not radical. Suffice to say that any animal fats, and any edible oils, can be used.

> Honey Natural and good for you, honey adds a beguiling sweetness to bread.

> Oats Essential in Scottish baking, oats are highly nutritious. I always have medium oatmeal, pinhead oatmeal and rolled oats in the cupboard and I eat them most days, in some form or other.

Cornmeal (or maize meal) In Italy, this is known as polenta and is often cooked as a porridge. It doesn't contain gluten and is therefore unsuitable for making risen loaves. However, cornmeal has a distinctive taste and cornbread (see p.167), which is usually cooked in a cast-iron skillet or frying pan, has a good flavour.

Millet This is a highly nutritional grain, tasting rather like oats. It can be cooked and eaten in a similar way to couscous. A couple of handfuls of millet, flaked or ground, can be added to bread dough for a bit of a health boost.

Barley Low in gluten, barley is unsuitable for making bread on its own, but I like to add barley flakes and barley meal to doughs. I also use them for dusting loaves.

Buckwheat In truth, this is not wheat; it is not even a grain. Surprisingly, perhaps, it is related to rhubarb. In Russia, buckwheat flour is used to make blinis (see p.168); a handful or two in your dough will add flavour and iron to your bread.

Semolina In Italian, this term means 'half-milled'. Semolina is a coarse grade of flour, usually made from durum wheat – the classic wheat for making pasta. I use it in ciabatta (see p.90), and for dusting the outside of English muffins (see p.99).

Seeds There is a simple rule here. If seeds taste pleasant, use them; if they taste strong, use less of them. Buy every seed packet on the shelf and have fun experimenting with them. I especially like sunflower, pumpkin, poppy and fennel; add sesame and linseed to these and you have my favourite six-seed blend.

Dried fruit As with seeds, use these with restraint. You cannot get away from the fact that adding fruit to bread turns it into fruit bread.

Nuts I use hazelnuts a lot, because I love them. To remove their skins, first shake the nuts in a dry frying pan over a medium heat until the skins turn dark and brittle like smouldered paper, then rub them in a clean tea towel and the nuts will shed their skins. Walnuts are worth a mention, too. Make wholemeal bread with walnuts and some honey, and a Stilton sandwich could hardly taste any better. As with seeds, if you like a nut, your bread will, too.

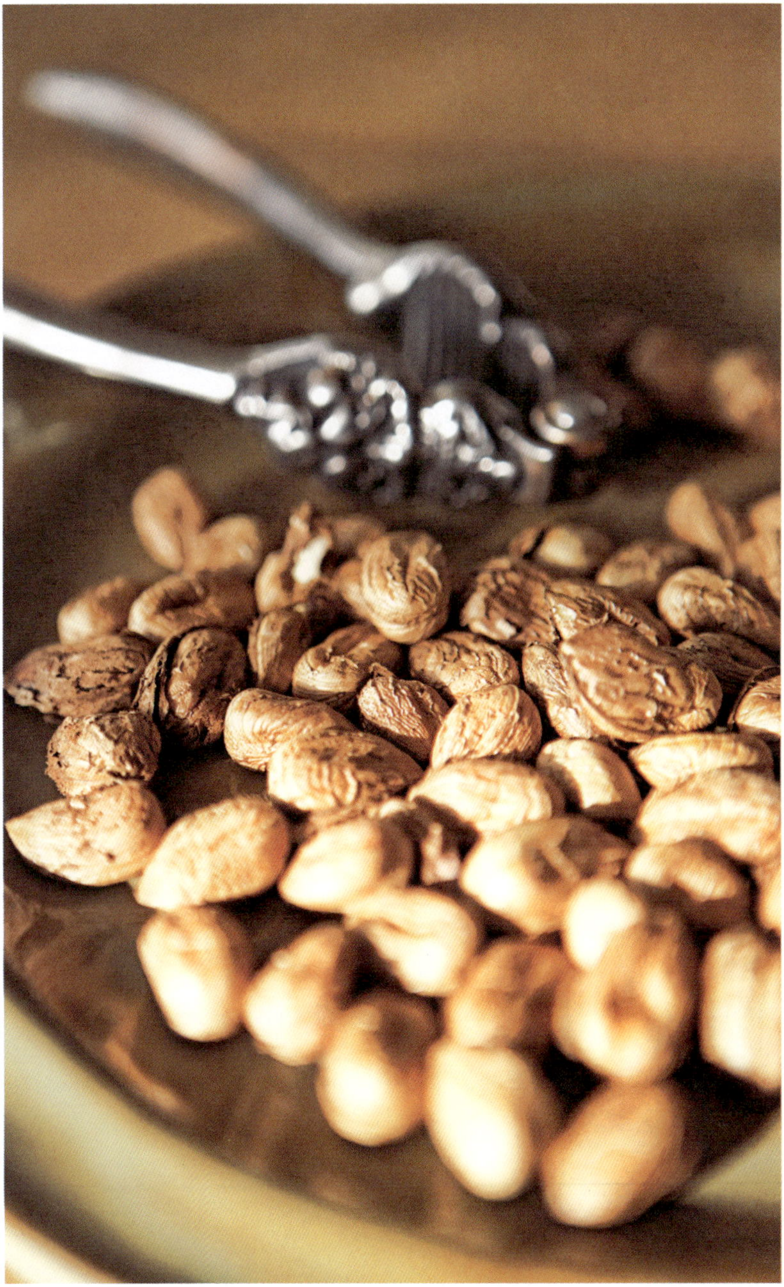

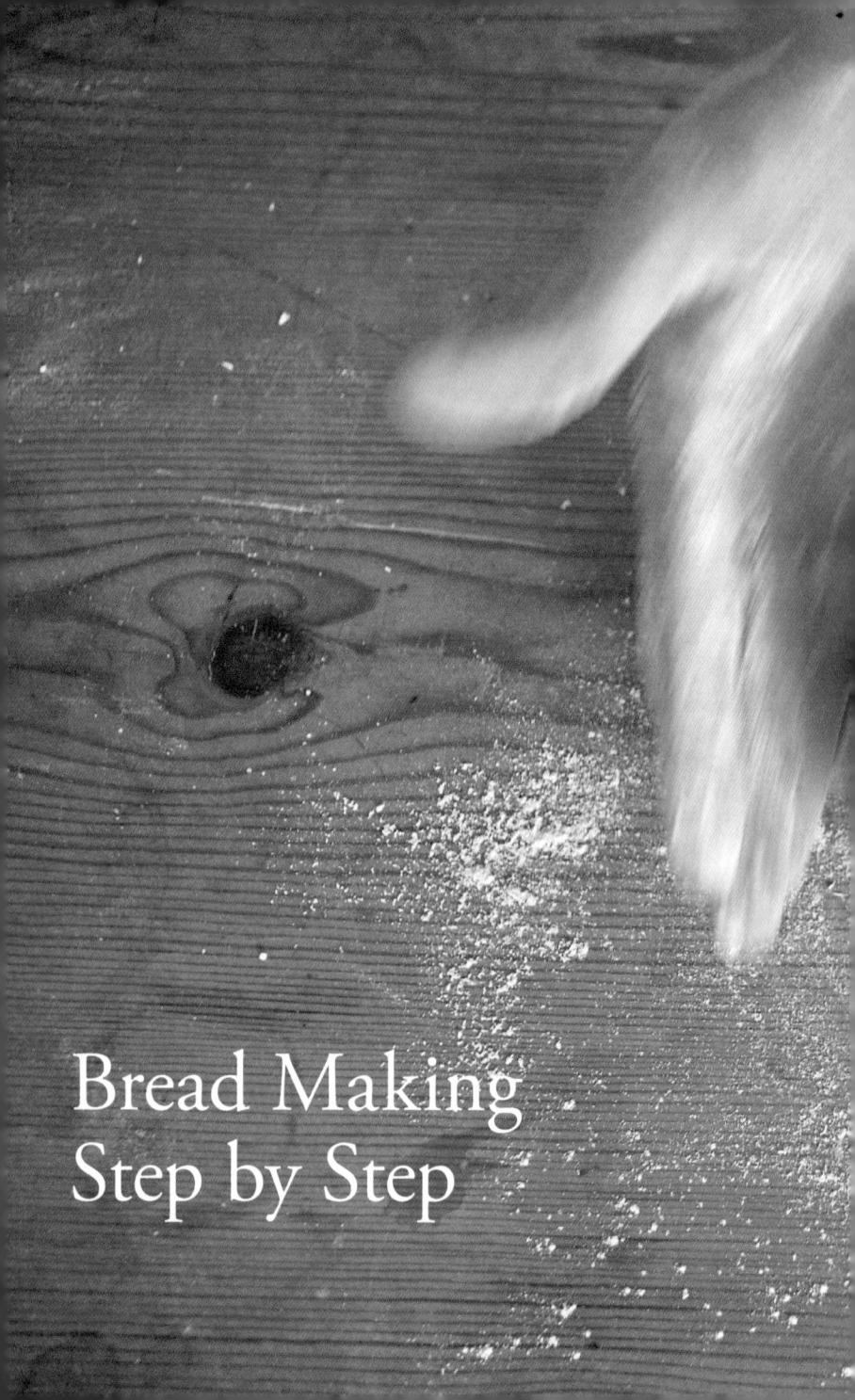

Bread Making
Step by Step

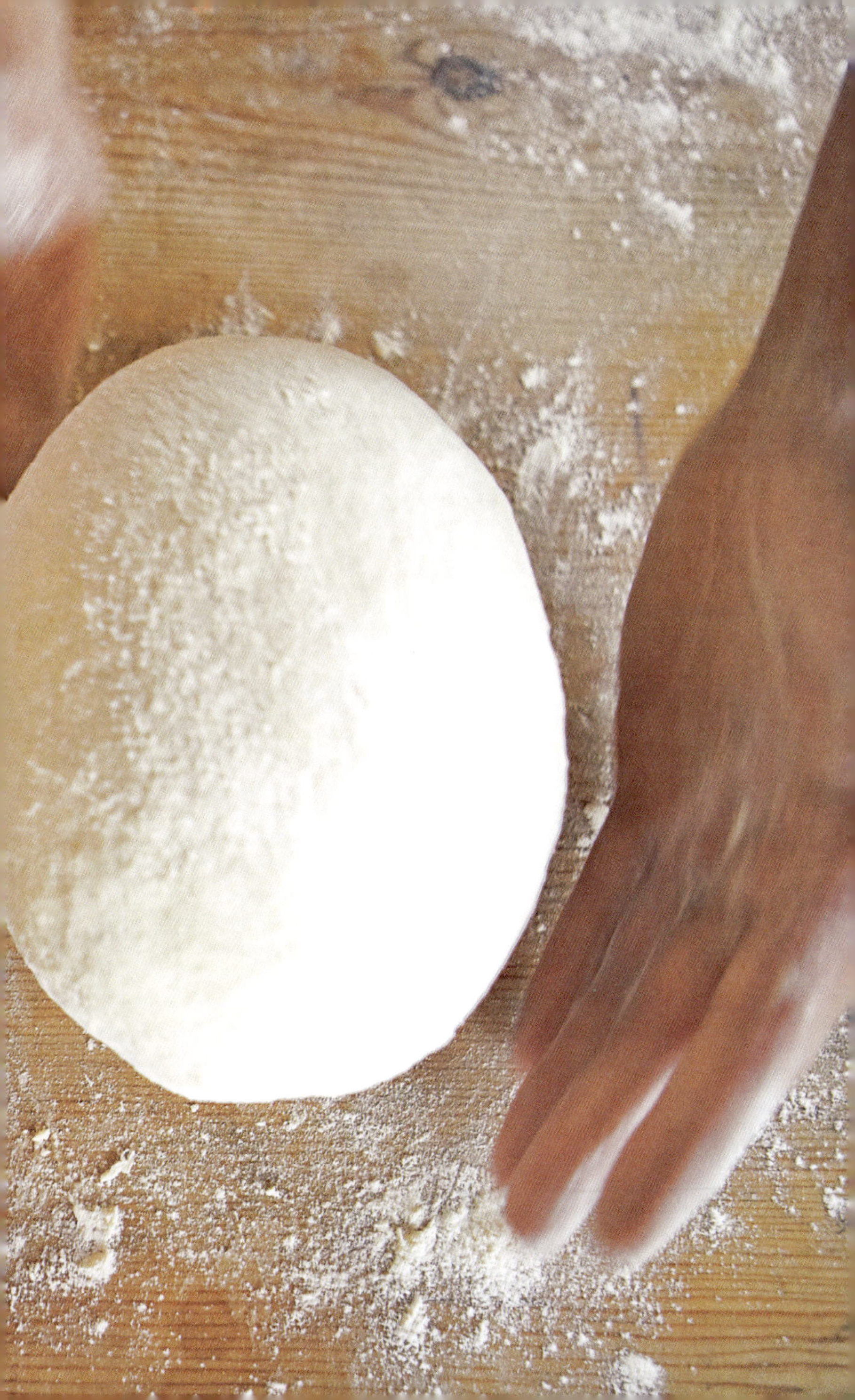

I'm not going to tell you that making really good bread at home is easy. To begin with, it may take you many attempts to make a loaf that you are truly proud of – and even then, the next one might let you down. But if bread making were a piece of cake, it wouldn't feel so amazing when you get it right. And no matter how many loaves you bake in your life, it *always* feels great when you get it right. Bread making is no mystery either, though it helps to know the science – to understand what happens when you make bread, and what affects it.

I have gone into a lot of detail in this section, and I make no apology for that. The more you understand, the better your bread will be. Take your time to absorb as much as you can about each of the bread-making stages before you begin baking. Once you are in the kitchen and the flour starts flying, you will find it easier to follow my own two-page bread recipe (see pp.76–7). It is actually a distillation of the basic method covered here; words highlighted in bold refer back to the headings in this section, for easy reference. I also show you how to adapt the recipe with infinite variations, including a few suggestions of my own, so that you may become master of your own bakery.

Anyone who bakes regularly will know that it is easy to get carried away in pursuit of the perfect loaf. I have often been unhappy with a totally decent batch of bread, for no other reason than that my last batch was better. Seek perfection, by all means, but please, don't be too hard on yourself. Always keep in mind the following wisdom, from the beautiful *Tassajara Bread Book* (see the directory, p.212):

> 'There are no mistakes. You might do it differently next time, but that's because you did it this way this time. Perfect, even if you say too much this, too little that. It's you and please be yourself.'

Bread making step by step

- Measure the ingredients (p.39)
- Mix the dough (p.42)
- Knead the dough (p.44)
- Shape the dough into a round (p.48)
- Leave to ferment (p.50)
- Deflate the dough (p.50)
- Leave to rise again (p.53)
- Prepare for baking (p.53)
- Divide the dough (p.54)
- Shape the loaves (p.55)
- Coat the outside (p.61)
- Leave to prove (p.63)
- Transfer the loaves for baking (p.63)
- Slash the tops (p.64)
- Bake the bread (p.66)
- Leave to cool (p.68)
- Look after your bread (p.68)

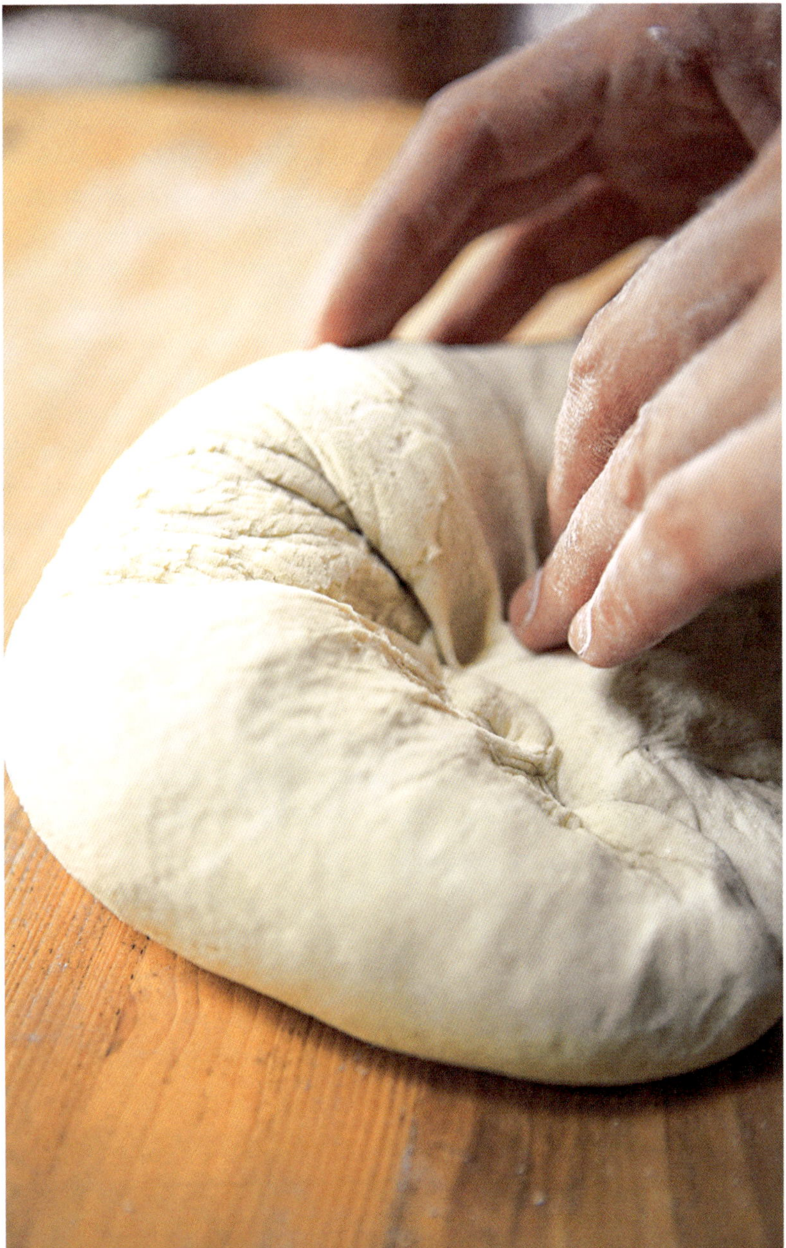

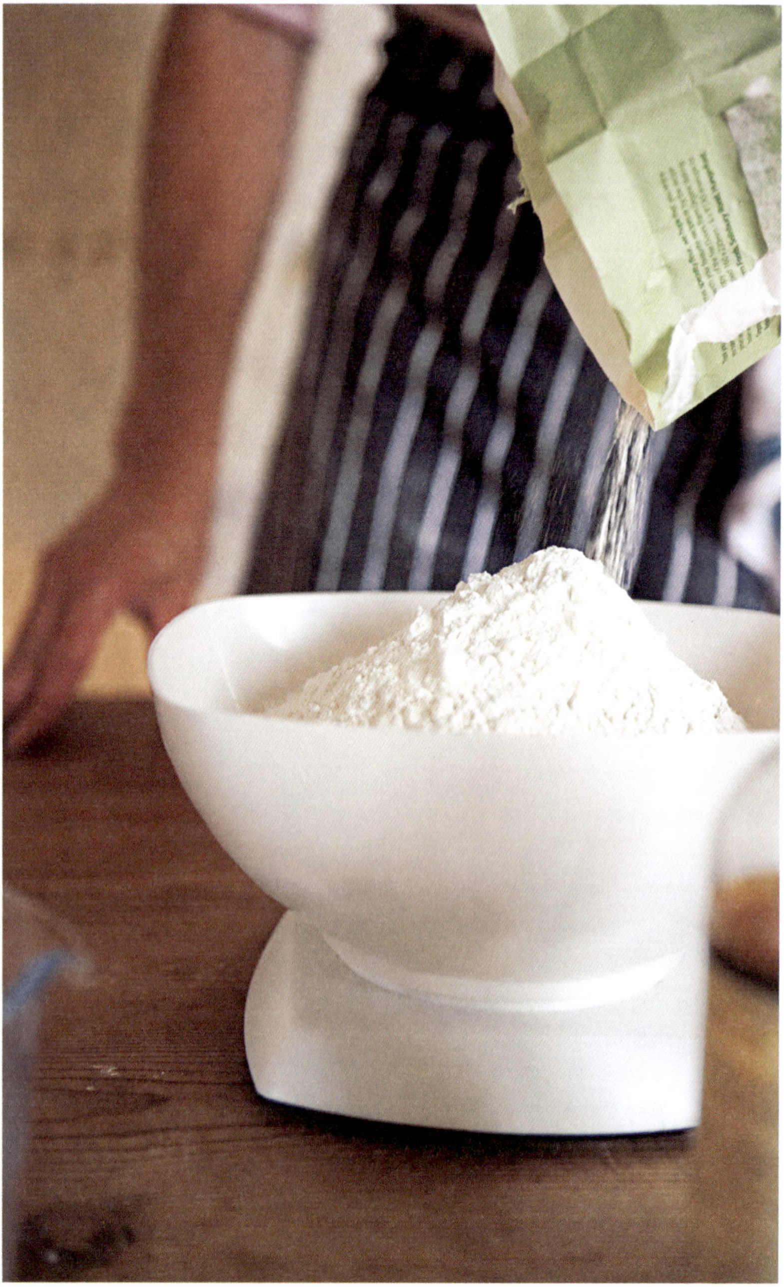

Measure the ingredients

There is a quick and easy formula for calculating the amount of each ingredient you need when making a batch of bread. Many professional bakers use this method, I use it, and you should learn it. It is known as the baker's percentage, and this is how it works.

First, decide how much flour you want to use. I suggest a kilo: the quantity of dough will be a comfortable size for kneading and will yield two large or three small loaves, or perhaps a dozen rolls – a good batch size for most ovens and most households (eat some, freeze some). Taking the weight of flour as 100 per cent, you measure every other ingredient as a percentage of this.

Water

The percentage of water to flour is sometimes referred to as 'hydration'. As I have indicated, different flours absorb different amounts of water, but a good starting point for a soft, kneadable dough using white flour is 60 parts water to 100 parts flour. This is 60 per cent hydration, or simply 60 per cent. So, for a kilo of dough (1000g) you would use 600g water. You can weigh it, but 1ml water weighs 1g, so 600g=600ml.

You may find that you need more water than this. For example, wholemeal flour, which often absorbs more water than white flour, may take 65 per cent hydration to produce a workable dough. Or you may want to make a wetter dough. For instance, if you are making ciabatta (see p.90), hydration is around 80 per cent. However, you will never want to make a drier dough, so use 60 per cent as your starting point.

Yeast

As a general rule, use 1 per cent for dried yeast, and 2 per cent for fresh. You can use less than this, which makes for a longer, slower fermentation, but you shouldn't really use more otherwise your bread may taste 'yeasty'.

Salt

The standard amount of salt is 2 per cent. There is a little flexibility here, but only a little. I generally use 2½ per cent for sourdough, for example. A loaf containing 3 per cent salt will taste a bit salty for most people. With 1 per cent salt, your bread will be a little bland.

Fat

Though I would not call this a basic ingredient, I usually add fat to bread dough in some form (usually sunflower or olive oil, occasionally melted butter or lard). You could certainly leave it out. But fat will give you bread with a slightly softer crumb, which keeps slightly better. I generally go for a good slug per kilo. I've just measured a good slug – it was a little over a tablespoon, about 20g. That's about 2 per cent, the same as the salt.

So our kilo batch looks like this:

Flour	1000g (100 per cent)
Water	600ml (60 per cent)
Dried yeast	10g (1 per cent), or 20g (2 per cent) if using fresh yeast
Salt	20g (2 per cent)
Fat (optional)	A slug, about 20g (2 per cent)

Before long, you will become so accustomed to these percentages that they become second nature, allowing you to confidently make bread, any time, anywhere. It is best to own a set of electronic scales, which will enable you to accurately measure your ingredients to within a few grams. If you do not, you will have to rough it a little; in which case it will help you to know that 20g fine salt is about 2 level tsp; as is 10g powdered yeast.

In addition to the above, all manner of ingredients can be added in small quantities to dough – to enhance the flavour and/or add interest to the texture.

Extras
Small dry ingredients, such as seeds or grains, are generally added in with the flour, yeast and salt. Nuts and dried fruit are better kneaded in later.

Adding a little old dough or a starter
A common practice in artisan bakery is to keep back a little dough from each batch to incorporate into the next day's baking. Old dough has had time to mature and develop flavour from the yeast activity, so adding a lump (as much as you like) of this a day or two, even a week after you made it, adds depth and character to a new batch. You can do this with any of the mixing methods; add it to your dough just before, or just after, you add the fat. Of course, you will not have any old dough the first time you bake.

If you keep a sourdough starter (see p.110), you can add a ladleful to your yeasted dough with similar results; this is what I do.

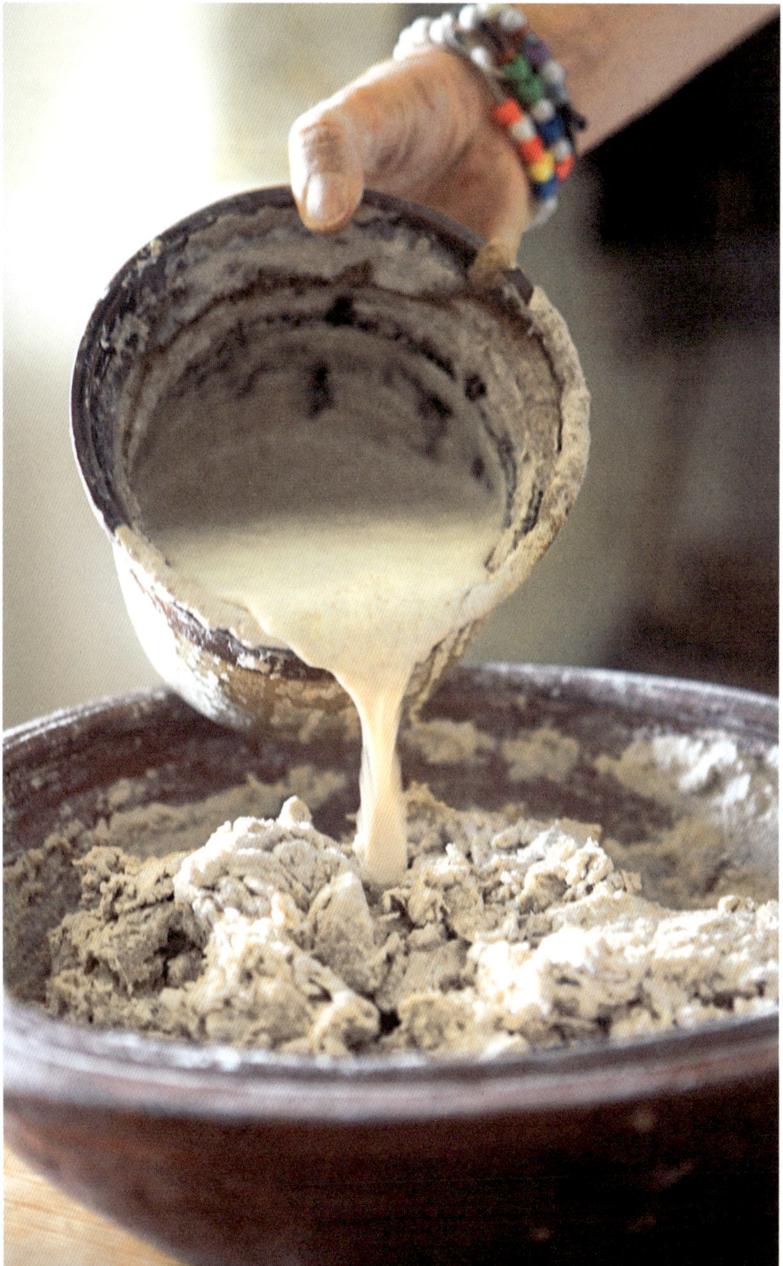

Mix the dough

There are three methods that I use to make a dough. Any of these will work for pretty much any bread; try them all and see which you are most comfortable with.

The one-stage mixing method
This is the simplest method. All the basic ingredients are mixed to a dough and kneaded straight away. At home, I nearly always make bread this way.

Add the flour, water, yeast and salt to your mixing bowl. Using two fingers of one hand, mix until you have formed a very rough, soft dough, adding more water if the dough is dry. Add the fat, if using, and squidge it all together.

The two-stage mixing method
Here, a flour and water dough is made and left to rest, before the yeast and salt are added. This allows the gluten to develop by itself. The effect is remarkable – the dough is easier to work, and it takes less time to knead. It is particularly good for a large amount of dough, which can be hard on your arms; I often use this method at River Cottage, where we generally make 4-kilo batches. The downside is that the yeast and salt don't blend as easily. They will eventually, but the dough will be slower to start fermenting.

Mix the water with the flour in the mixing bowl to form a rough dough, adding more water if you need to. Cover and let it rest for about half an hour, then add the salt, yeast and fat, if using, and squidge it all together.

The sponge method
This method is particularly good for sourdough (see pp.115–125), but will benefit any bread. You start with a yeasted, unsalted batter (the 'sponge'), which is left to ferment and mature for several hours. This wet, salt-free environment allows the yeast to ferment vigorously, and the extra-long fermentation will produce bread with more flavour. I would like to use this method more often, but you need to start it off the night before, which I'm inclined to forget to do. Hopefully, you will be more organised and remember to do so.

Before bedtime, mix half of the measured quantity of flour with all of the water and all of the yeast. Beat the mixture to a thick batter, using a stiff whisk if you wish, though stiff fingers work better. The following morning, add the rest of the flour and the salt. Mix to a rough dough, adding a little more water if it is too dry, then add the fat, if you are using it.

BREAD MAKING STEP BY STEP 43

Knead the dough

First, a note on your work surface: it needs to be flat and smooth. A craggy surface will trap bits of dough; even worse, the dough will pick up whatever is already trapped there. It should also be solid; a flimsy table won't stand up to your vigorous kneading. If you have a wooden work surface, so much the better – wood is generally warmer than formica, granite or stainless steel. What is more important is that you have plenty of room – a good metre width, and maybe an arm's length in depth – for effective kneading. It also makes sense to clear the area a bit. Put the washing up away and move the toaster, as flour and dough tend to get everywhere. And wear an apron.

Tip and scrape your dough out of the bowl on to your work surface. Clean and dry your hands – rub them together with a little flour to get the worst of the dough off, then wash them. By now, your dough is probably well glued to the work surface. Good... you want it to stick. Kneading is all about stretching the gluten; if the dough sticks to the surface, it's doing most of the work of one hand. It is going to stick to your hands as well. This is ok, but the faster you work, the less it will stick. You will get better at this, I promise.

Flour your hands a little. Now, with your left hand if you're right-handed, right hand if you're left-handed, press down on the dough with your fingertips, about a third of the way up (pic 1). With the heel of your other hand, in one smooth, quick motion, press into the dough just above your first hand and push down and away, a full arm's length if you have room (pic 2). Now cup the fingers of this hand and scrape/roll the torn, ripped-up dough back on top of itself (pic 3). Turn the whole dough around roughly 90° (pic 4). Repeat. Repeat. Repeat. Have a look at the dough as you stretch it. You will see long, thin strands developing – this is gluten.

At first, dough will stick all over you. From time to time, stop and clean your hands with more flour. With time, and practice, the whole thing will become one smooth operation. In fact, the 90° rotation will merge seamlessly into the next stretch. With each stretch, the dough will become a little less sticky. After a good 5 minutes, it probably won't be sticking much to anything. The dough will have tightened considerably; it will no longer be breaking into pieces and you will find it more resistant to your stretching. Adapt your kneading action as the dough changes. Start to use shorter and shorter strokes, until you are only stretching it to around double its length. From time to time, spend half a minute or so shaping your dough into a nice tight round, following the method on p.48. Get used to shaping dough into a round; it keeps you in control. If ever your dough is sticky, or slack, or unruly, and getting the better of you, shape it into a round, and you will tame it instantly.

You can knead bread in a machine, of course. Domestic food mixers often have a dough hook attachment, and can just about take a kilo batch of dough. Be warned, though, they get pretty hot with the effort, and mine has a tendency to 'walk'

1

2

3

4

1

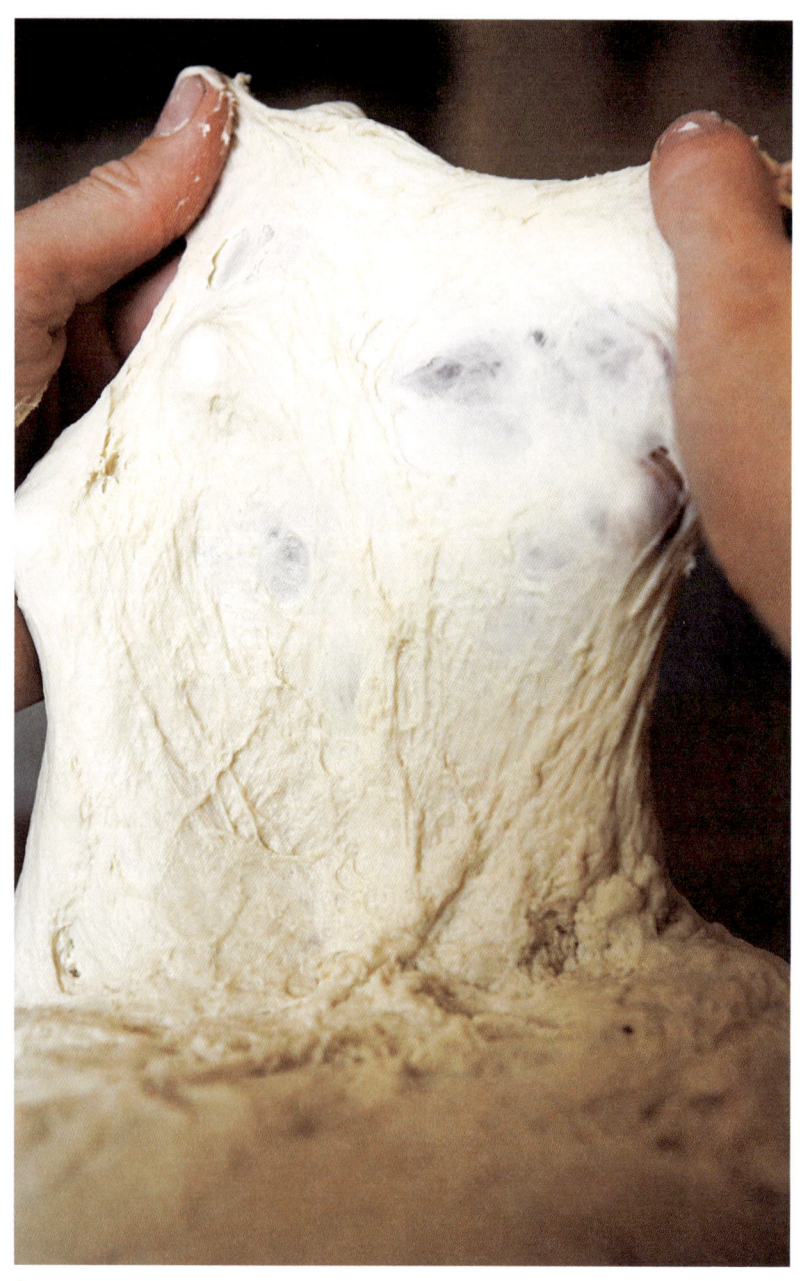

alarmingly across (and once, when I wasn't looking, off) the worktop. I now only use my mixer for softer, wetter, less strenuous doughs, and it is happier for it.

Kneading can take anywhere between 5 and 15 minutes, depending on the flour, your chosen mixing method, your kneading speed, and the size of the dough. Every now and then, try and form a membrane by stretching the dough thinly. Do this every couple of minutes. Each time, you should be able to stretch it thinner than the last. How thinly you can eventually stretch it will depend on the flour you are using. A white dough can usually be stretched quite thinly (pic 1), more so than a wholemeal dough (pic 2). Dough made from a low-gluten flour, such as rye, will snap readily (pic 3), despite your best efforts. When you feel your dough cannot be stretched any thinner, it is ready. As a guide, a dough made from strong wheat flour should stretch thinly enough to let daylight through, at least. Get it as thin as a pair of tights, and either your dough is amazing or your tights are too thick.

A small word of caution: it is possible for dough to be over-kneaded. At some point, the gluten structure will collapse, and the dough will revert to being soft and sticky, a calamitous position from which it will not recover. This is rare when kneading by hand. It is a peril more associated with kneading by machine, in which case vigilance and a slow mixing speed are your best safeguards.

If you are using larger extras, like nuts and fruit, you will need to incorporate them at the end of kneading. Stretch the dough out on the work surface, scatter over the ingredients, then fold, roll and knead briefly, to disperse them.

2   3

Shape the dough into a round

When you are satisfied with your dough, you should shape it into a round. It will then rise evenly, and you can more easily gauge its progress. This also encourages the yeast to work for you during rising. As it ferments, the gas bubbles gently stretch the strands of gluten and this stretching is most effective if the strands are taut to begin with, which they will be, if you do this.

Lay your dough, smoothest side facing down, on the work surface and prod a little with all your fingers to flatten it (pic 1). Now, with one or two fingers and a thumb, lift an edge, fold it into the middle and press down (pic 2). Make about an eighth turn of the dough, pick up the edge at the side of the fold you just made and press into the middle. Repeat, until you get back to where you started (pic 3). Now flip it over (pic 4). You should have a nice, smooth, round dough. Put your hands flat on the work surface, palms up, either side of the dough, one forward, one back (pic 5). Now, in a fluid motion, bring your hands together under the dough, at the same time sliding the forward hand back and the back hand forward (pic 6). This both spins the dough and stretches the upper surface down and under. Repeat this 'spinning' action two or three times. With practice, you can start to cup your hands around the dough; the point of the flat hands is to discipline yourself to use the inside edges of your palms and little fingers to do the stretching work.

BREAD MAKING STEP BY STEP 49

Leave to ferment

First you need to find a container in which your dough can comfortably double in size without billowing over the top. This may well be the mixing bowl you started off with, but give it a quick wipe first and dry with a tea towel.

Now, you can either flour the dough all over, or oil it. If you added oil to the dough, it makes sense to use the same type of oil, but any oil will be fine. Oiling is slightly better than flouring, as it makes an airtight coating, which prevents the dough from drying out. It also enables you to oil the container, which makes it easier to turn the dough out later. (Don't oil the container if you have floured the dough, though; you will just make oily flour lumps.)

Either way, put the dough into the container and cover it. I find the simplest way is to put the container in a bin liner and tuck the opening underneath. This makes a lovely environment for your dough – a little humidity from the fermentation process, and a little extra warmth from the bag (black absorbs and radiates heat). Covering the bowl with cling film would be nearly as good, though a little more wasteful, as you can't reuse it.

Now you need to leave your dough to rise in a warmish place. A pleasantly heated kitchen is ideal, but a slightly cold room is still fine – the dough will just take longer to rise. An airing cupboard, with the boiler going, is likely to be too warm. On top of the Aga is too warm. For a really slow overnight rise, you could put the covered dough in the fridge, but you will rarely want to (unless you are making brioche, see p.95).

During this period of rising, we want the gluten to be stretched by the activity of the yeast to the limit of its elasticity, at which point the dough will have roughly doubled in size. Beyond this, the dough noticeably loses its structure and elasticity; it will start to look flaccid and a bit holey. This is not a disaster, but the dough will be a little weaker for it.

Deflate the dough

Once the dough has risen sufficiently, uncover and tip it out on to your lightly floured work surface (pic 1). Gently press into the dough with your fingertips and squash it all over (pic 2), until it is roughly the size you started with. A common term for this is 'knocking back', which suggests punching and battering – a level of domestic violence not conducive to a happy relationship with your bread. You have spent a long time loving it... Don't ruin it all now.

1

2

BREAD MAKING STEP BY STEP 51

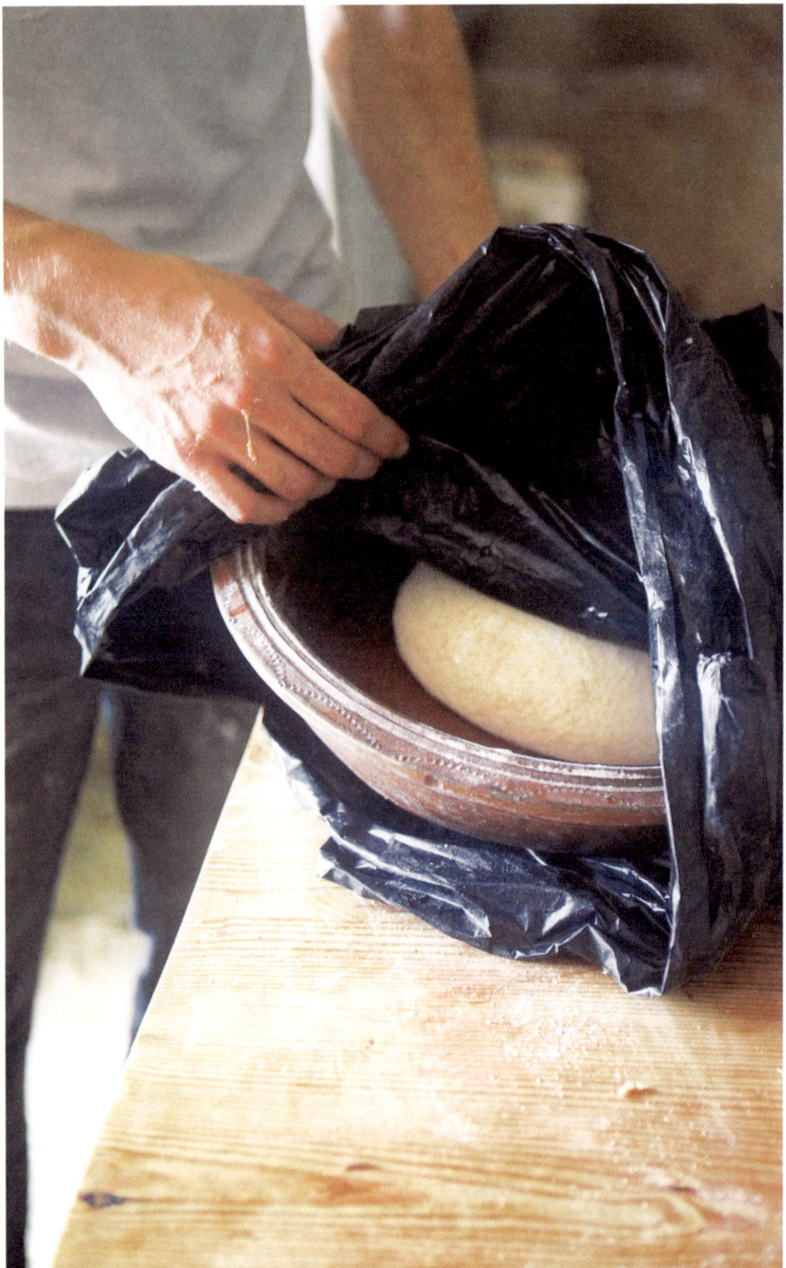

Leave to rise again (optional)

You can now leave your dough to rise a second time, following the same spinning and shaping process as before, in order to further mature and improve it. You can even repeat the rising and deflating process three, four, maybe five times. Each time you'll notice the dough becoming more satiny and pillowy. You cannot do this indefinitely, though. Eventually there will be no sugars left for the yeast to feed on, and you need it to have enough oomph for the final prove (see p.63) before baking.

Prepare for baking

Before you shape your loaves, which you are about to do, it is worth getting ready to bake them. Timing becomes fairly critical later and you don't want to get caught out, with a cold oven, for example. So, turn the oven on now – to maximum.

With the odd exception, for the first 5–10 minutes of baking you want two things in your oven (besides the bread). The first is as much heat as you can get. With enough heat, your bread will rise dramatically in the oven. Known as 'oven spring', this rising is caused by the heat-induced expansion of the gas bubbles in the dough; this expansion will continue until the crust hardens enough to suppress it. I think 260°C is the upper limit, but most domestic ovens don't get that high, so my advice is simply to turn up the dial as far as it will go.

If you have a baking stone (see p.17), it should be in the oven from the start, on the middle shelf or thereabouts (remember your bread needs plenty of headroom). If not, find your largest, heaviest baking tray and use it in the same way. You will be baking your bread directly on this, somewhat replicating the old, traditional brick-floored bakers' ovens. (You can replicate these even better by building one of your own, see Building a clay oven, pp.192–209.) If using a baking tray, you can remove it from the oven to load the bread, but this is not practical with a heavy stone. You will need to leave it in the oven and use a 'peel' (see p.17) to slip the bread on to it.

The second thing you want is steam. If the air in your oven is humid, the crust will take longer to dry so it stays soft for longer, and the bread can rise higher and more evenly. To mimic a professional baker's steam-injected oven, I heat a heavy roasting tin in the bottom of the oven, then pour in boiling water from the kettle as I put the bread in. This gives a nice whack of steam straight away, as well as some slow-release steam for a few minutes afterwards. I also use a spray bottle, the kind you get in a garden centre, to wet the bread just before it goes in. This goes some way towards making up for the lack of sophisticated technology in a domestic oven.

With your oven set up, you should clear space around it. You'll need to work fast so move anything you might crash into. You will also need a sharp serrated knife, for slashing the loaves, if you so wish, and an oven glove if you are using a baking tray. Have these within grabbing distance of the oven, along with your spray bottle if you have one. Put some water in the kettle, ready to boil. With everything in place, and your oven gently warming your kitchen, you are ready to shape your bread.

Divide the dough

First, divide your dough as precisely as you can. Make your loaves or rolls the same size and shape, and they'll cook in the same time. If you started with a kilo batch of flour, the weight of dough will be a little over 1.6kg (1kg flour and 600g water, plus a little salt, yeast, etc). Halve this and you'll make two 800g loaves. I never make loaves much larger than this. My preference is for loaves of 500–600g, so I usually divide my batch into three. If you want rolls, weigh them at 120g and you'll get a baker's dozen. Keep some dough back for your next baking session, if you wish.

Thus divided, your loaves-to-be must be shaped into rounds (see p.48), lightly floured and left to rest, on the worktop, covered with plastic. This intermediate shaping stage is key to getting an even, uniform finish to your loaf. About 10–15 minutes' rest is ideal, just to relax the gluten, in preparation for the final shaping.

Shape the loaves

You can make any shape of loaf you like, but I tend to stick to just four shapes: a round, a tapered baton, a baguette-type stick and a sort of stubby cylinder, which is my favourite. I rarely bake bread in a loaf tin, because I much prefer the appearance of a naturally formed loaf; also I don't much like the texture of the pale lower crust of a tin loaf. But for those of you who would like to use a loaf tin, I will show you how to shape the dough for it.

However you want to shape your bread, I will make the assumption that your dough is already formed into loose rounds and lightly floured.

A baguette-type stick

I usually make four of these long, thin loaves from a kilo batch, so they weigh about 400g each. With the dough smooth side down on your work surface, prod it flat, then roll it up towards you fairly tightly. Now working with both hands flat, roll and stretch the dough like a Plasticine snake, as thin and long as you like, remembering, of course, that it still has to fit in your oven. You can leave the ends rounded, but I like to taper them into a tight point, in which case do as for a tapered baton (see p.56), but press a little harder.

A tapered baton

With your dough smooth side down, prod all over with your fingertips to flatten it (pic 1). Fold the top edge down to the middle (pic 2) and press along the seam. Fold the two top corners in towards the middle, at a 45° angle (pic 3) and press down along the edges. Roll it up tightly, starting from the top (pic 4), and press all along the seam to seal (pic 5). Now, with your hands cupped over the dough, roll it back and forth, using increasing pressure on the outsides of your hands to taper the ends (pic 6).

A stubby cylinder

There is rather more to shaping this loaf than may be apparent from its appearance. Of the various loaves described, this shaping is the most complicated procedure and it takes a little more practice to perfect. The result is a really tightly moulded loaf that holds its shape brilliantly and rises dramatically in the oven. It is the loaf I bake more often than not, partly because it delivers just the right proportion of lovely, crisp crust and soft, chewy interior.

To shape a stubby cylinder, lay the dough smooth side down and prod it flat with your fingertips. Roll it up tightly towards you, using the fleshy part of your thumbs to really tuck it in (pic 1). With the seam upwards, press all along the seam with your fingertips (pic 2). Now flatten and stretch the dough sideways to about twice its width (pic 3). Fold one end in by a third and fold the other over it (pic 4). Flatten with your fingertips to a rough square (pic 5), then roll up tightly (pic 6). Seal the seam by pressing with your fingertips, then roll gently to get an even shape (pic 7).

A tin loaf

With your dough smooth side down, prod it fairly flat with your fingertips until it is as wide as your tin is long. Now roll up the dough towards you as tightly as you can, then press along the seam with your fingers and lay seam side down. Smooth and stretch the ends down and tuck them underneath. Lift up the dough and drop it into the loaf tin.

Rolls

Weigh or slice off pieces of dough between 100g and 150g, according to how large you want your rolls to be, but do try to keep them roughly the same size. Choose any shape you like – I favour a round or a tapered baton. To shape rounds, simply follow the technique for shaping a batch of dough (see pp.48–9); for tapered batons, shape as for a large loaf (see p.56).

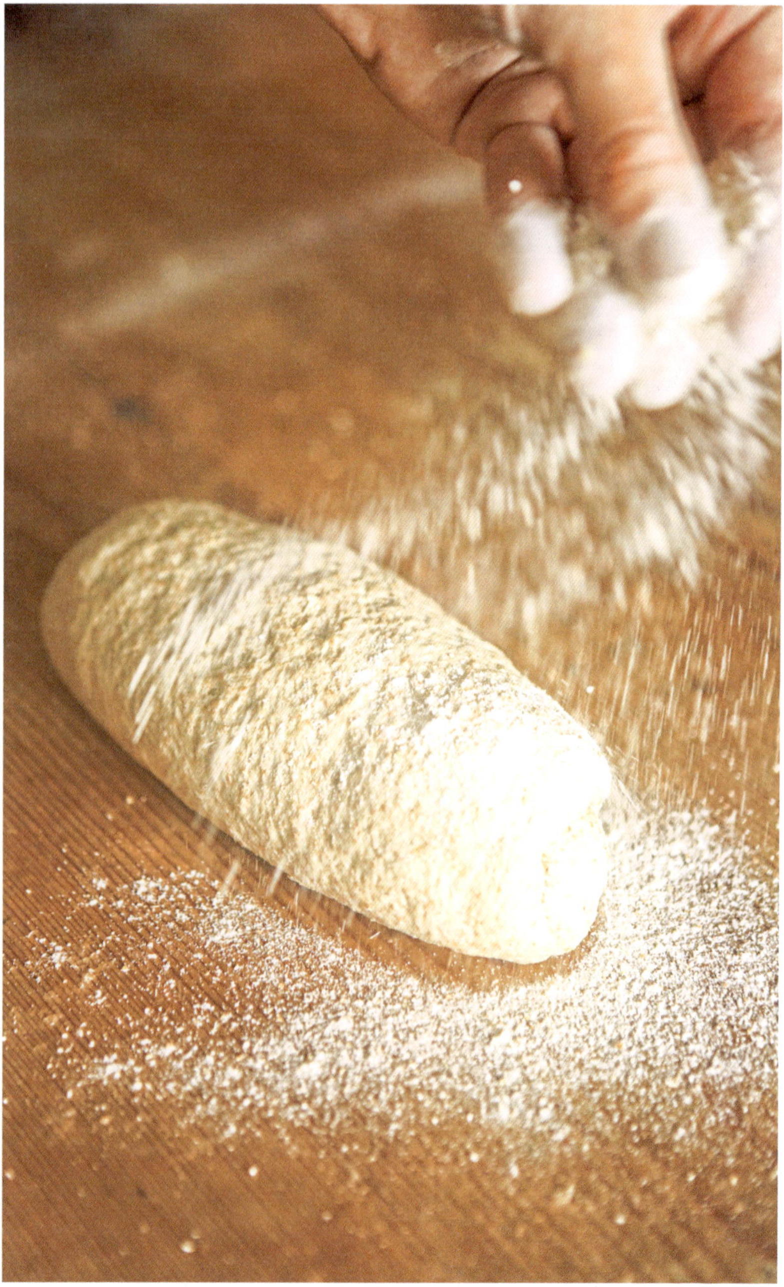

Coat the outside

You can leave your loaves naked, but they will be much more grateful – and feel much more beautiful – if you give them a lovely coat to wear. Select a flour, or choose grains and seeds.

Flour
You can use the same flour that you made your bread with, but I usually use rye flour. It gives a pleasing greyish, matt surface to the finished loaf that contrasts beautifully with the golden brown of the opened-out slashes. Coarse-milled flours – wholegrain rather than white – give a better finish, in my view. Drop a fistful of flour on top of the shaped loaf and roll it about to coat it all over and under.

Grains and seeds
Roll your bread thoroughly in a bowl of milk or water, then in a bowl of one or more of the following: rolled oats, oatmeal, barley, rye or millet flakes, bran, cracked wheat, linseed or other mild-tasting seeds, such as poppy, sesame, pumpkin or sunflower seeds. You could also include a small amount of stronger-flavoured seeds like cumin, caraway, coriander and fennel in your mix. Coat the loaves generously – they should be totally covered. Pat all over to help everything stick.

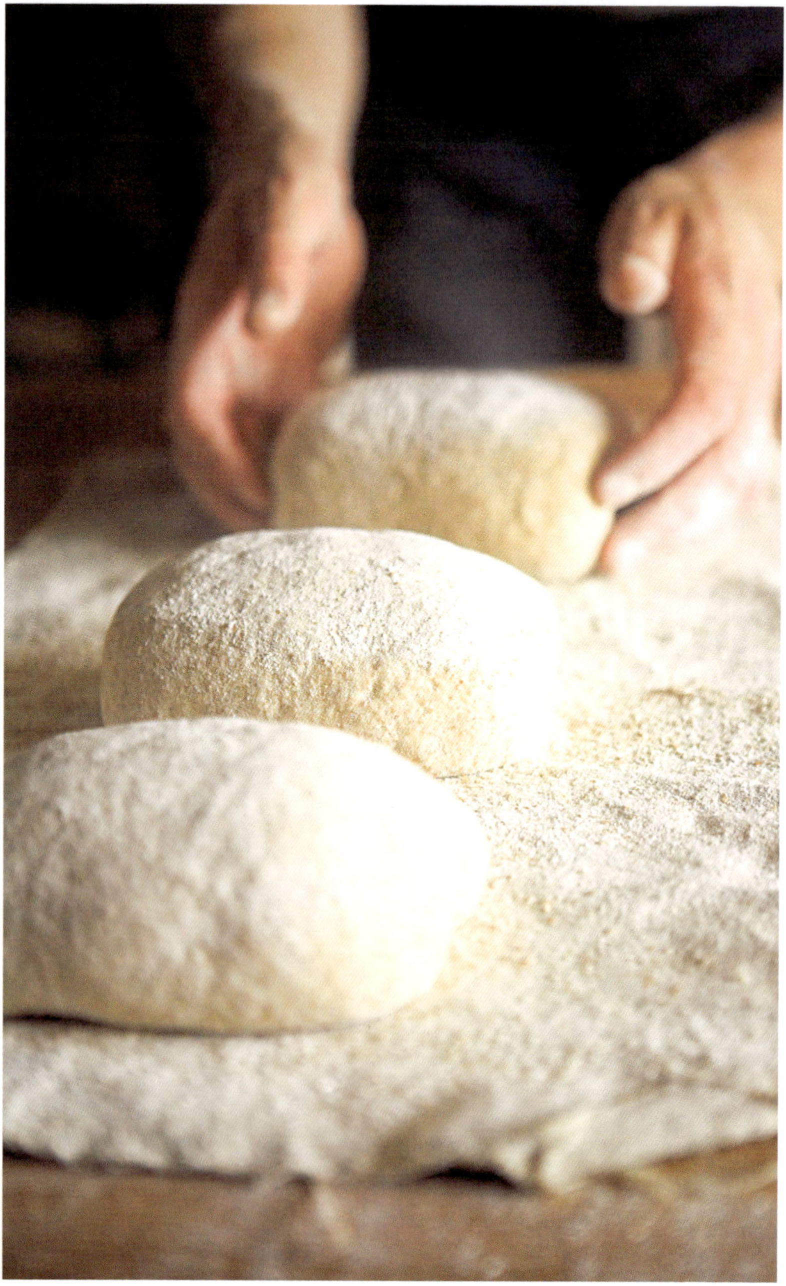

Leave to prove

Proving is the final rising of your shaped loaf before baking (the fact that your dough rises a final time 'proves' that it is still active). If you are not baking in a loaf tin, you will need to sit it in a basket, or on a cloth or board (see p.16). Whichever you use, dust it generously with flour – I usually use rye, for reasons given earlier, but any will do. Loaves in proving baskets should always be smooth side down. With linen cloths or wooden boards, I suggest proving loaves the right way up, as they will keep their shape better this way. If you are using cloths, you can ruck them up a little to give some support to the sides of the loaves. This is particularly effective with baguettes. Always cover your dough with plastic bags.

Giving precise times for proving is not helpful but, again, you want the dough to roughly double in size; this could take as little as 20 minutes, or as long as 2 hours, depending on the vigour with which the dough is fermenting.

Keep an eye on the dough as it proves. When it's looking significantly bigger, give it a gentle squeeze at the sides. Do this every so often and you will feel it getting lighter and airier. If, after such a gentle squeeze, the dough springs airily back to its original shape, and if it has almost (but not quite) doubled in size, it is about right. It is hard to describe the perfect moment in words. The best I can say is that a really well-shaped, tightly moulded, perfectly risen loaf has a certain look and feel about it, as if it is just bursting to be baked.

If the bread is over-proved, the gluten will lose its structure, the dough will start to look a little saggy, and the finished crumb will end up coarse, and too 'holey'. Under-proved bread will be a little dense and heavy – and also prone to the dreaded 'flying crust' syndrome, whereby the top crust deceitfully balloons away from the rest of the dough in the oven.

You should err on the side of under- rather than over-proving, though; it will rise some more in the oven.

Transfer the loaves for baking

If you are using a baking tray, get it out of the oven, shut the door quickly and set the hot tray close to your bread. If you are using a baking stone, lay the peel on the work surface.

If you've proved your bread in baskets, use one hand to gently support the bread as you tip it out on to the tray or peel; it will now be the right way up. If you have used cloths or boards, the loaves are already the right way up. To pick one up, roll it towards you so you can get your hands on the underside, then roll it back on to your hands, and lift it.

If you are using a baking tray, leave as much space as you can between the loaves. If you are using a peel, then you will need to work one loaf (or a few rolls) at a time. Flour the peel if your bread is in any way sticky, then lay one loaf (or a few rolls) along the leading edge.

Slash the tops

Making cuts in a loaf helps it to expand in the oven. Proved bread already has a slightly dry crust from contact with the air, which inhibits rising, and slashing through this crust exposes the soft, stretchy dough inside. I nearly always slash my bread, but there are a couple of exceptions. I usually leave round rolls just as they are – they stay rounder that way. And low-gluten breads, such as rye, rise very little in the oven, so the slashes are, in effect, redundant – they would open only a little, which looks ugly. Low-gluten breads have a beauty all their own. During proving, because of the low surface tension, the dough crackles all over as it expands, like a shattered windscreen.

Many bakers use an old-fashioned razor blade for slashing. I prefer a sharp, long-bladed, serrated knife – a bread knife, in fact. Don't just pile in. Imagine a line on the dough then cut along it, using your spare hand just to hold the loaf in place. Use long strokes and be controlled, but confident. It is crucial that you don't press down when you cut – you will squash the dough, and press out precious gas. Work swiftly, but don't rush – you will end up snagging and stretching the dough. Slash up to 1cm (half an inch) deep, using two or three strokes on each cut if you need to. Make your slashes evenly deep, and evenly spaced.

Your slashes should be simple. Beautiful though they can be, they are not made purely for decoration – they have a job to do, which is to help the bread expand. And they will do their job that much better if you let the gluten help, too. Let me explain how.

When you shaped the loaves tightly, you put tension on the gluten; now you can use this tension to pull the slashes open. Round loaves have equal tension all around, pulling outwards and downwards, so a cut in any direction will open well. All the longer-shaped loaves (see pp.55–8) have lateral tension. They have been rolled up, like a carpet, or a coiled spring. The more you cut across (perpendicular to) this tense gluten, the more the cuts will open. So a lengthways cut opens most, crossways cuts open least. Experiment with the different options and decide which you like the look of best. Scoring the loaf on the diagonal is a good compromise.

Slashing is a very good test of the quality of your dough. If it is well kneaded and perfectly risen, the cuts will open out, even as you make them.

BREAD MAKING STEP BY STEP 65

Bake the bread

Once you've slashed your loaf (or not), spray it all over with water, if you want to (see p.53). Now either put the baking tray in the oven or slip the dough from the peel on to the baking stone. To do this, lay the front edge of the peel in position, resting on the stone, then pull it away, like a tablecloth party trick.

As soon as all the loaves are in, pour a good slosh of boiling water from the kettle into the roasting tray (keep your face back), and shut the door. Do all this as fast as you possibly can, to keep the precious heat in.

Now, for a few minutes at least, you must leave the door shut, to keep the heat in; this is the time for 'oven spring', the final rise before the crust hardens. After 10 minutes, have a look. Shuffle the bread about if it is colouring unevenly and lower the temperature to:

200°C/Gas Mark 6	if the crust is still very pale
180°C/Gas Mark 4	if the crust is noticeably browning
170°C/Gas Mark 3	if the crust seems to be browning quickly

These temperatures apply to fan-assisted ovens. If you are using a conventional non-fan-assisted gas or electric oven, you will need to have your oven approximately 15°C/1 Gas Mark hotter. Continue baking, adjusting the temperature as you see fit. The total baking time will depend on your particular oven and the size of your loaves. If during baking the crust appears to be fully browned, cover it loosely with foil to prevent over-browning.

Use the following timings as a guide, but rely on your own judgement. These represent total baking time in the oven:

12 rolls	10–20 minutes
3 small loaves	30–40 minutes
2 large loaves	40–50 minutes

When your bread is fully baked, it will feel lighter than when it went in. This is because it will have lost about 20 per cent of its weight through evaporation. The crust should feel firm (though less so on rolls), and it should sound hollow when tapped on the base. This is no definitive test, though – a loaf will also sound hollow when it could really do with another 10 minutes' baking. So, if in doubt, bake for a bit longer. If your bread is a little over-baked, all it will have is a slightly over-thick crust… and there is nothing wrong with that.

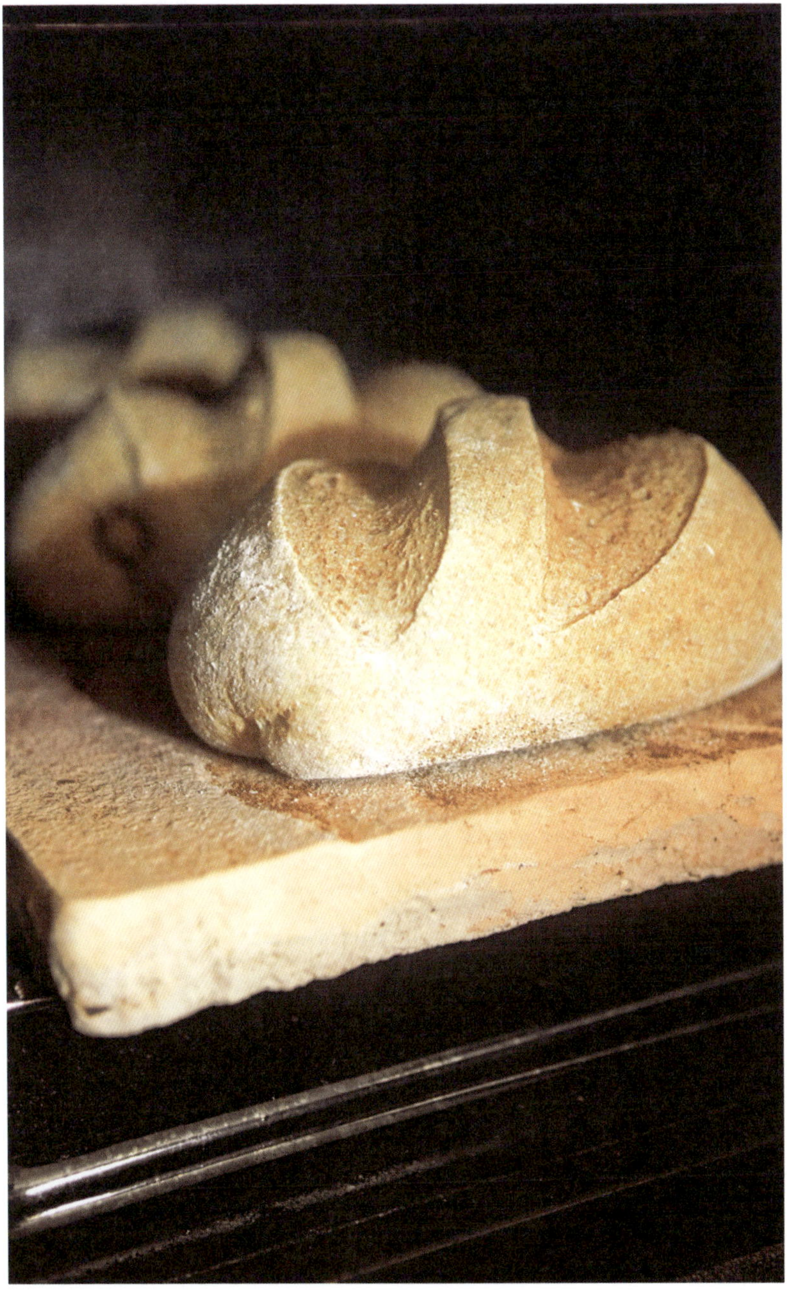

Leave to cool

If you have a cooling rack, put your bread on it. If not, a propped-up oven shelf would do fine. Now leave it alone to cool. Your bread is full of steam, and is in fact still cooking. You must let it finish, in its own time. If you cut hot bread, it will be steamy, heavy and doughy. Hot rolls are about the only exception to the leave-it-alone rule, but only if you pull them apart. Don't squash or cut them.

Look after your bread

Having lovingly produced your handmade bread, it makes sense to treat it properly, whether you are serving it straight away or storing it.

Slicing
Telling you the best way to slice bread may seem totally unnecessary, but I've seen too many people squashing, ripping and hacking at once-beautiful loaves. You should use a sharp serrated knife and avoid pressing down as you cut. Use a rhythmic sawing action and the weight of the blade will be enough. Brace the sides of the loaf with your other hand, close to where you are cutting, so it holds its shape.

Storing
The advice is anywhere but the fridge. According to Harold McGee, the food science guru, bread stored in the refrigerator stales as much in one day as bread held at 30°C does in 6 days. So, store your bread at room temperature, wrapped in paper, or in a bread bin, or both. Plastic and foil keep too much moisture in and make the crust soft. Uncovered loaves let too much moisture out. Bread freezes successfully, but it must be well wrapped – in plastic, this time. After defrosting, your bread will probably benefit from refreshing.

Refreshing
Day-old bread can be returned (almost) to its former glory with a short stint in the oven. Staling is the re-hardening of starch granules that had been softened in the oven. By reheating the bread – to 60°C or above – the starch softens again. You can do this again and again, but each time the crust will dry out a little more and become thicker and harder. You will not be able to refresh bread after more than a couple of days' staling, though. It will have lost too much moisture. But all is not lost – you just need some ideas for Using leftover bread (see pp.174–191).

To refresh bread, I suggest a moderate oven, preheated to about 170°C/Gas Mark 3: allow 5–10 minutes for rolls; 15–20 minutes for loaves.

BREAD MAKING STEP BY STEP   69

Troubleshooting

Problem	Possible reasons
Heavy bread, with a dense, 'cakey' texture	Low-gluten flour Under-kneaded
Heavy bread with a solid, rubbery texture	Under-proved
Solid, rubbery bread with large air holes at the top ('flying crust')	Under-proved
Flat, 'tired' shape	Low-gluten flour Under-kneaded Initial oven temperature too low Loaf not shaped tightly enough Dough not supported enough during proving
Well risen, but uneven shape	Over-proved Loaf not shaped tightly enough Dough not supported enough during proving
Slashes don't open out fully	Low-gluten flour Under-kneaded Initial oven temperature too low Loaf not shaped tightly enough Dough not supported during proving Slashes too deep Slashes cut too 'crossways' instead of 'lengthways' (except round loaves)
Soft crust	Under-baked Oven too cool
Hard, thick crust	Over-baked
Doughy texture	Under-baked Sliced while still hot
Coarse, dry, 'holey' texture	Over-proved

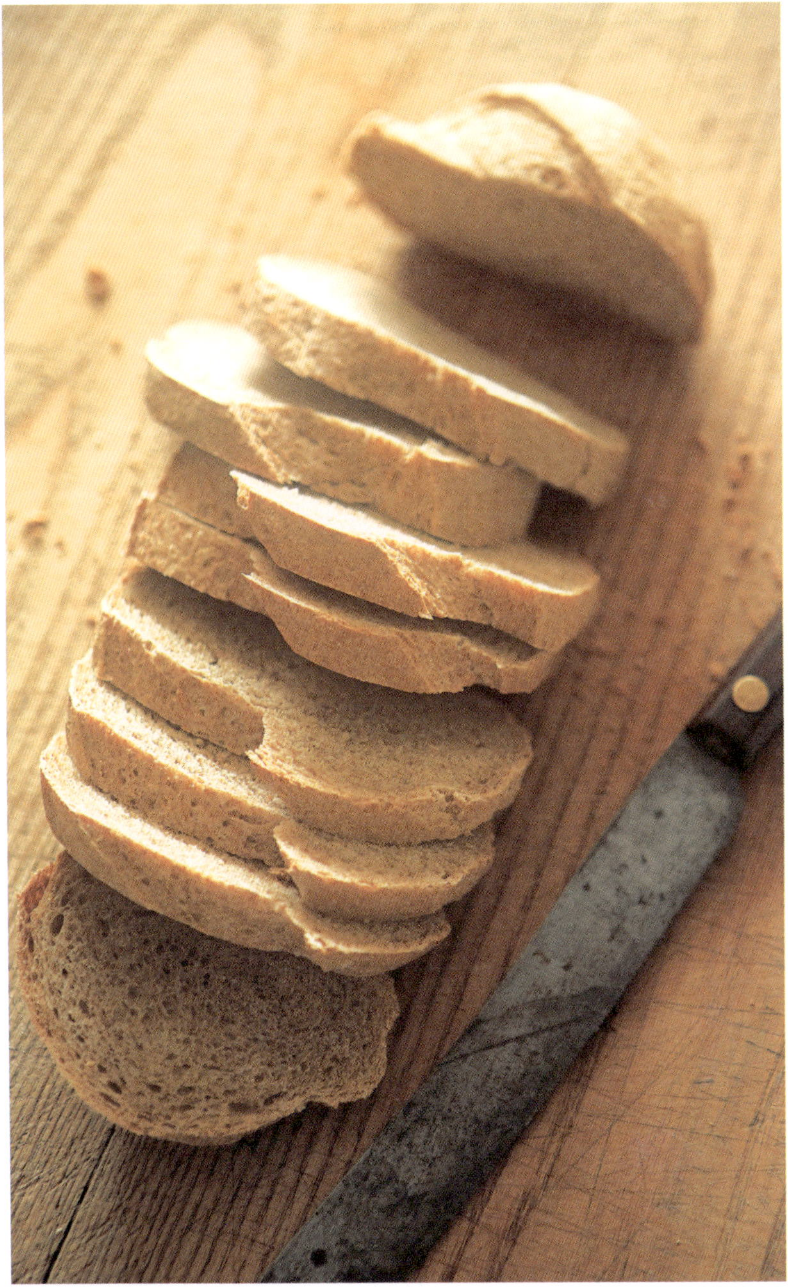

The Basic Bread Recipe

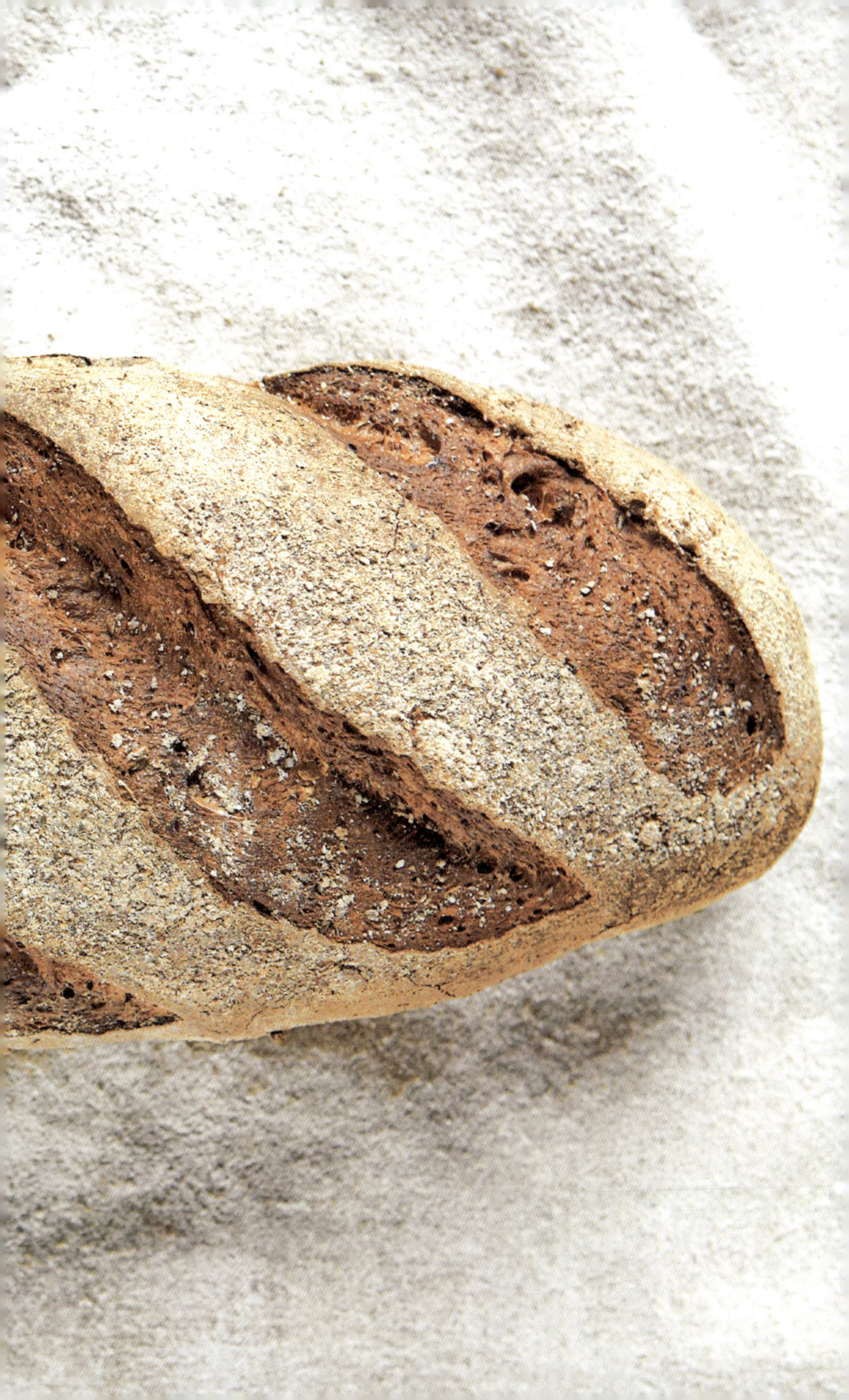

This basic bread recipe

is the most important recipe in the book. As you will gather, it is a condensed version of the previous section: Bread making step by step (pp.34–71). It is the recipe that I hope you will use the most to begin with, as it is your route to making good, everyday bread. The more you make it, the more you will get used to the feel of the dough in your hands, and the changes it goes through during the various stages of bread making. You will start to recognise how one day's baking differs from another. And hopefully, with the help of the previous section, you will start to understand why. Get good at this recipe and you will be much better at all of the others in the book.

In time, I hope it will become the recipe you will use the least. I expect that you will soon memorise the 'baker's percentage' – the ratio of one ingredient to another – so that you no longer need to look it up. I hope the method will become so familiar that you can fit it into your daily life without even thinking about it. And I'd like to think that, before long, you will never need to look at these pages again.

Once you are comfortable with the basic principles of flour-water-yeast-salt, and the effects of different liquids, and once you understand the boundless fun you can have with the addition of a few grains, seeds and spices, I hope you will discover your own favourites. By all means go wild with your experiments (after all, you don't know until you try), but please remember one thing: bread is beautiful all by itself. As Robert Browning wrote:

> *'If thou tastest a crust of bread, thou tastest all the stars and all the heavens.'*

So there you go... now you know what stars taste like.

Ingredients for bread making

My basic bread recipe is infinitely adaptable. Simply choose one or more options from the ingredients listed below (or add your own), and slot them into the ingredients list (overleaf), in place of the *italics*.

Essential	Choices
Flour	Strong white, strong brown, strong wholemeal, '00', malted grain, wholemeal spelt, white spelt, rye, kamut
Yeast	Powdered dried yeast
Salt	Fine sea salt
Liquid (warm)	Water, milk, yoghurt, apple juice, cider, beer; 1 tbsp honey can be added to any of these
Optional	
Fat	Oils, such as sunflower, vegetable, corn, rapeseed, hempseed, olive, groundnut or any other nut oils; or melted hard fats, such as butter or lard
Old dough/starter	A piece of old dough (see p.40), or a ladleful of sourdough starter (see p.110)
Extras	Flakes, meal or flour of oats, barley, rye, millet, buckwheat, maize, chickpea or rice, or semolina; seeds, such as pumpkin, sunflower, linseed, poppy, sesame, fennel, caraway, cumin, coriander or alfalfa; bashed nuts, such as hazelnuts, walnuts or any other nuts; dried fruit, such as raisins, dried apricots or chopped dates
Coating	Rye or any other flour; anything on the extras list except nuts and dried fruit; plus about 200ml milk or water, if coating with anything other than flour (to help it stick)

The basic bread recipe

This is my simplified bread recipe, which can be adapted to create a host of different breads (see chart on p.75). You will find more detail on the essential stages (highlighted in bold below) in the previous chapter. To begin, you need to measure the ingredients.

Makes 2 large or 3 small loaves, or 12 rolls

Essential
1kg *flour*
10g powdered dried yeast
20g fine salt
600ml *liquid* (warm)

Optional
2 handfuls of *extras*
A piece of old dough, or a ladleful of sourdough starter
About 1 tbsp (a good slug) of *fat*
2 handfuls of *coating*
About 200ml milk or water (if coating with anything other than flour)

First, mix the dough. This is the one-stage method; you can adapt it for other methods. Combine the *flour*, yeast and salt in a large mixing bowl. Add smaller *extras* if you are using them (save nuts and dried fruit for after kneading). Add the *liquid*, and with one hand, mix to a rough dough. Add a piece of old dough or the starter if you are using one. Add the *fat* if you are including and mix it all together. Adjust the consistency if you need to, with a little more flour or water (or your chosen liquid), to make a soft, easily kneadable, sticky dough. Turn the dough out on to a work surface and clean your hands.

Knead the dough until it is as smooth and satiny as you can make it – as a rough guide, this will take about 10 minutes. If you are using larger *extras*, like nuts and fruit, stretch the dough out on the work surface, scatter over the ingredients, then fold, roll and knead briefly, to disperse them.

Shape the dough into a round once you have finished kneading. Then oil or flour the surface and put the dough into the wiped-out mixing bowl. Put the bowl in a bin liner and leave to ferment and rise until doubled in size. This could be anywhere between 45 minutes and 1½ hours – or longer still, if the dough is cold.

Deflate the dough by tipping it on to the work surface and pressing all over with your fingertips. Then form it into a round. If you like, leave to rise again up to four times. This will improve the texture and flavour.

Now, prepare for baking. Switch the oven to 250°C/Gas Mark 10 or its highest setting, put your baking stone or baking tray in position and remove any unwanted shelves. Put the roasting tin in the bottom if you are using it for steam (in which case, put the kettle on). Get your water spray bottle ready if you have one, your serrated knife if using, an oven cloth, and your 'peel' if you are using a baking stone. Clear the area around the oven.

Divide the dough into as many pieces as you wish (I suggest two large or three small loaves, or a dozen rolls). Shape these into rounds and leave them to rest, covered, for 10–15 minutes.

Shape the loaves as you wish, and coat the outside with your chosen *coating*. Transfer the loaves to well-floured wooden boards, linen cloths, tea towels or proving baskets and lay a plastic bag over the whole batch, to stop it drying out. Leave to prove, checking often by giving gentle squeezes, until the loaves have almost doubled in size.

Transfer the loaves for baking to the hot tray (removed from the oven), or one at a time to the 'peel'. Slash the tops, if you wish, with the serrated knife, and before you bake the bread, spray it all over with water if you can. Bring the boiling kettle to the oven, if you are using it. Put the tray in the oven, or slide each loaf on to the stone, pour some boiling water into the roasting tin, if using, and close the door as quickly as you can.

Turn the heat down after about 10 minutes to: 200°C/Gas Mark 6 if the crust still looks very pale; 180°C/Gas Mark 4 if the crust is noticeably browning; 170°C/Gas Mark 3 if the crust seems to be browning quickly. Bake until the loaves are well browned and crusty, and feel hollow when you tap them: in total, 10–20 minutes for rolls; 30–40 minutes for small loaves; 40–50 minutes for large loaves. If in doubt, bake for a few minutes longer.

Leave to cool on a wire rack, or anything similar that allows air underneath. Bread for tearing can be served warm, but bread for slicing must be cooled completely.

Look after your bread and enjoy it. After all, you have put a lot of work into it... and don't waste a crumb.

P.S. Remember that timing in the recipe relates to fan-assisted ovens. If using a conventional electric or gas oven (without a fan), increase the temperature by 15°C (1 Gas Mark). Use an oven thermometer to check the accuracy of your oven.

Variations
on the basic bread recipe

There is no end to the possibilities, of course, but to get you going, here are a few combinations of my own. You might make one, or all, or none of them… though I'd like to insist that you make my favourite malted and seeded loaf (see p.80).

Malted grain bread

There is something special about malted flour. I don't know what it is, but like candlelight or a soft-focus lens, it is flattering – the Don Juan of home baking. As Elizabeth David wrote in her excellent *English Bread and Yeast Cookery*, 'Homemade granary bread is very good-tempered, exceptionally easy to mix and bake. It has so much to recommend it, especially to beginners in bread-making.' I couldn't agree more.

Makes 2 large or 3 small loaves, or 12 rolls
1kg malted grain flour
10g powdered dried yeast
20g fine salt
600ml warm water
About 1 tbsp melted butter
A piece of old dough, or a ladleful of sourdough starter (optional)
No extras
2 handfuls of rye flour, for coating

Follow the basic bread recipe method (see pp.76–7).

White bread

With full-flavoured brown and wholemeal breads, you can get away with a loaf that is firm or dense – in fact, it can be a bonus. However, if white bread isn't soft, light and crusty, it is pretty disappointing. It is far harder to make good white bread than any other kind of bread, so don't feel downhearted if it takes you a while to get it right. Adding milk, or better still yoghurt, makes a softer, richer crumb.

Makes 2 large or 3 small loaves, or 12 rolls
1kg strong white flour
10g powdered dried yeast
20g fine salt
600ml warm water (or half water, half milk or yoghurt)
About 1 tbsp sunflower oil
A piece of old dough, or a ladleful of sourdough starter (optional)
No extras
2 handfuls of strong white flour, for coating

Follow the basic bread recipe method (see pp.76–7).

Spelt bread

Due to its comparatively low gluten content, spelt bread is often considered to be rather dense and heavy. That's because it often is, but it shouldn't be. Spelt dough just needs to be treated properly. I reckon there are two secrets: a little more kneading than normal – an extra 5 minutes or so; and proving in baskets to hold the loaves up (or make small loaves if you do not have any baskets). It is very satisfying to make bread from the same grain the Romans baked with.

Makes 2 large or 3 small loaves, or 12 rolls
1kg wholemeal spelt flour
10g powdered dried yeast
20g fine salt
600ml warm water
About 1 tbsp sunflower oil
A piece of old dough, or a ladleful of sourdough starter (optional)
No extras
2 handfuls of spelt flour, for coating

Follow the basic bread recipe method (see pp.76–7).

Oaty wholemeal

This bread is coated in three grades of oatmeal for a really interesting texture and a beautiful look. I have been making it a lot recently, with a variety of wheat called 'Einstein' which I buy from a local grower. The pale oats contrast strikingly with the wonderful chestnut-coloured crust. It is a perfect example of how bread should taste.

Makes 2 large or 3 small loaves, or 12 rolls
1kg strong wholemeal flour
10g powdered dried yeast
20g fine salt
600ml warm water
About 1 tbsp sunflower oil
A piece of old dough, or a ladleful of sourdough starter (optional)
No extras
2 handfuls of mixed pinhead oatmeal, medium oatmeal and oat flakes, plus about 200ml milk, for coating

Follow the basic bread recipe method (see pp.76–7).

Malted and seeded loaf

I can't stop making this at the moment. Everyone at River Cottage is going mad for it. The recipe is inspired by a five-seeded malted grain flour made by Bacheldre Watermill (see the directory, p.212). I have added a sixth seed – poppy, because I love it. Go a little easier on the fennel, as they are the most strongly flavoured of the seeds.

Makes 2 large or 3 small loaves, or 12 rolls
1kg malted grain flour
10g powdered dried yeast
20g fine salt
600ml warm water
About 1 tbsp sunflower oil
A piece of old dough, or a ladleful of sourdough starter (optional)
2 handfuls of extras: a mix of sunflower, pumpkin, linseed, sesame, poppy and a few fennel seeds
2 extra handfuls of the above seed mix, plus about 200ml milk or water, for coating

Follow the basic bread recipe method (see pp.76–7).

Breakfast rolls

You could get up before the birds to make rolls in time for everyone else's breakfast, or you could bake them ahead and freeze them in batches. Simply grab a batch out of the freezer, give them about 15 minutes in a moderate oven, rub a bit of flour in your hair and pretend you've been up half the night. Much better… and it should get you out of the washing up.

Makes 12 rolls
1kg strong brown flour
10g powdered dried yeast
20g fine salt
600ml warm milk
About 1 tbsp melted butter
A piece of old dough, or a ladleful of sourdough starter (optional)
No extras
2 handfuls of white (or brown) flour, for coating

Follow the basic bread recipe method (see pp.76–7).

Festival bread

As a celebration of the inaugural River Cottage Festival, we thought we'd have a bit of fun. So, from a choice of five or six different flours and a couple of dozen other ingredients, around sixty guests, my co-host Steven and I came up with this unlikely recipe – through nominating, voting and a little cajoling. The alfalfa seeds got in on novelty rather than merit. Steven was the only voice in favour of poppy seeds, so we put one in... to keep him happy.

Makes 2 large or 3 small loaves, or 12 rolls
1kg wholemeal spelt flour
10g powdered dried yeast
20g fine salt
300ml warm water
300ml warm cider
1 tbsp honey
1 tbsp rapeseed oil
A piece of old dough, or a ladleful of sourdough starter (optional)
2 handfuls of extras: a mix of barley flakes, oat flakes, golden raisins, chopped dried apricots, bashed hazelnuts, alfalfa seeds and a poppy seed
2 handfuls of spelt flour, for coating

Follow the basic bread recipe method (see pp.76–7).

Monastery bread

If you prefer bread that is soft, airy and light as a feather, skip this one. If, however, you are of wholesome and earthy ilk, make it. But be warned: this one hurts. The dough is solid and uncooperative when it comes to kneading. You will notice the ample quantity of extras in the form of rolled oats; this bread is all about oats. I like it sliced thinly, with butter or cheese, or honey... and a flagon of mead. Sitting in the refectory, after vespers, might be just the place to enjoy it.

Makes 2 large or 3 small loaves, or 12 rolls
1kg strong brown flour
10g powdered dried yeast
20g fine salt
600ml warm water
1 tbsp honey
About 1 tbsp melted butter
A piece of old dough, or a ladleful of sourdough starter (optional)
6 handfuls of extras: rolled oats
2 handfuls of rye flour, for coating

Follow the basic bread recipe method (see pp.76–7).

Hazel maizel bread

This bread is sweet and delicious. The maize meal gives a pleasing, slightly cakey texture, along with an alluring undertone of sunshine. The honey, nuts and apple juice make it a natural accompaniment to cheese. As you are shaping the bread, you will find bits escape everywhere. This is the nature of nuts in bread – and this is why you should only add them after kneading.

Makes 2 large or 3 small loaves, or 12 rolls
800g strong wholemeal flour
200g maize meal
10g powdered dried yeast
20g fine salt
300ml warm water
300ml warm apple juice
1 tbsp honey
About 1 tbsp melted butter
A piece of old dough, or a ladleful of sourdough starter (optional)
2 handfuls of extras: bashed hazelnuts
2 handfuls of wholemeal flour, for coating

Follow the basic bread recipe method (see pp.76–7).

Empty-the-shelf bread

Peasants of old would often bulk out their bread with whatever they could lay their hands on: oats, millet, bone meal, even sawdust. I felt a little peasanty recently as I was clearing out my kitchen cupboards and found myself with various near-empty packets of flour, meal and seeds that needed using up. Feel free to adapt this recipe to use whatever you have around... within reason, of course. Empty-the-cereal-box bread would be interesting; empty-the-Hoover-bag bread... perhaps rather less so.

Makes 2 large or 3 small loaves, or 12 rolls
1kg strong wholemeal flour, or a mixture of bag-ends
10g powdered dried yeast
20g fine salt
600ml warm water
About 1 tbsp fat (whatever needs using up)
A piece of old dough, or a ladleful of sourdough starter (optional)
2 handfuls of extras: a mix of any or all of wheatgerm, bran, oats or oatmeal, millet flakes, barley flakes, seeds (sunflower/poppy/pumpkin/linseed/sesame)
2 extra handfuls of these extras, plus about 200ml water, for coating

Follow the basic bread recipe method (see pp.76–7).

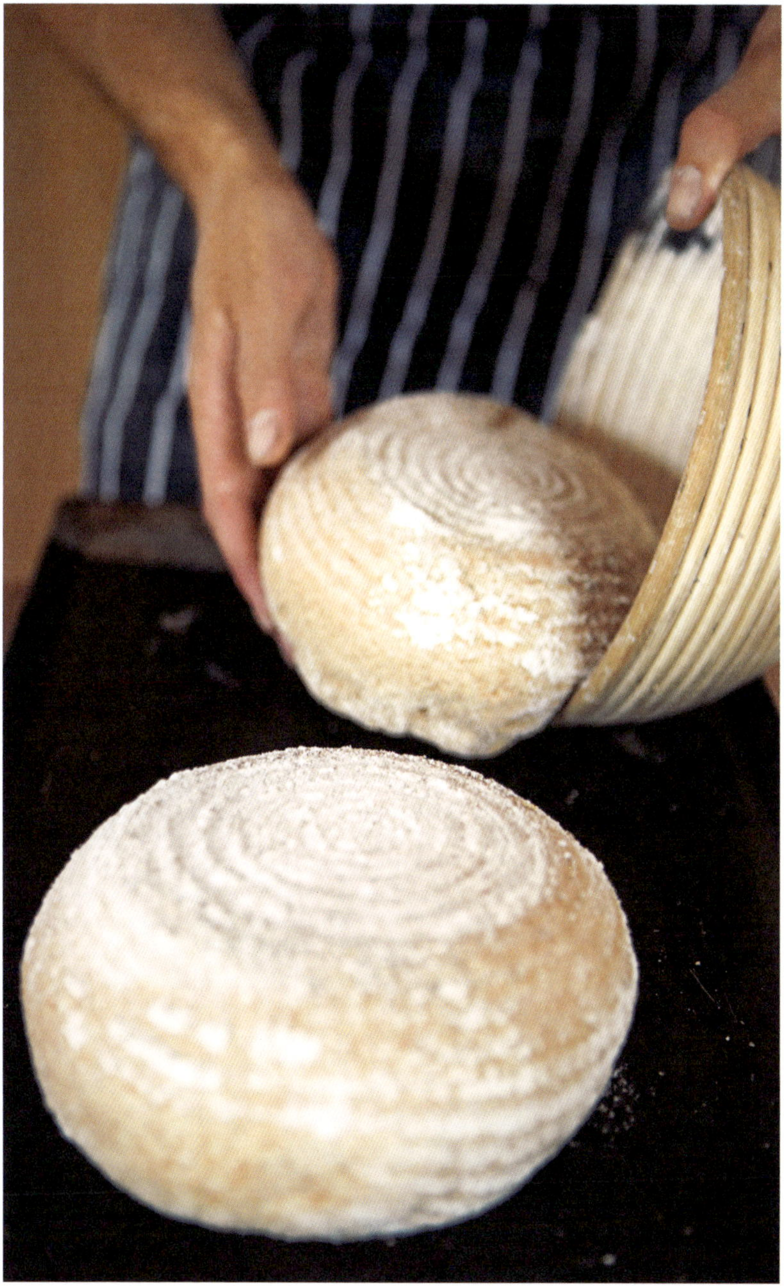

Beyond the Basic Loaf

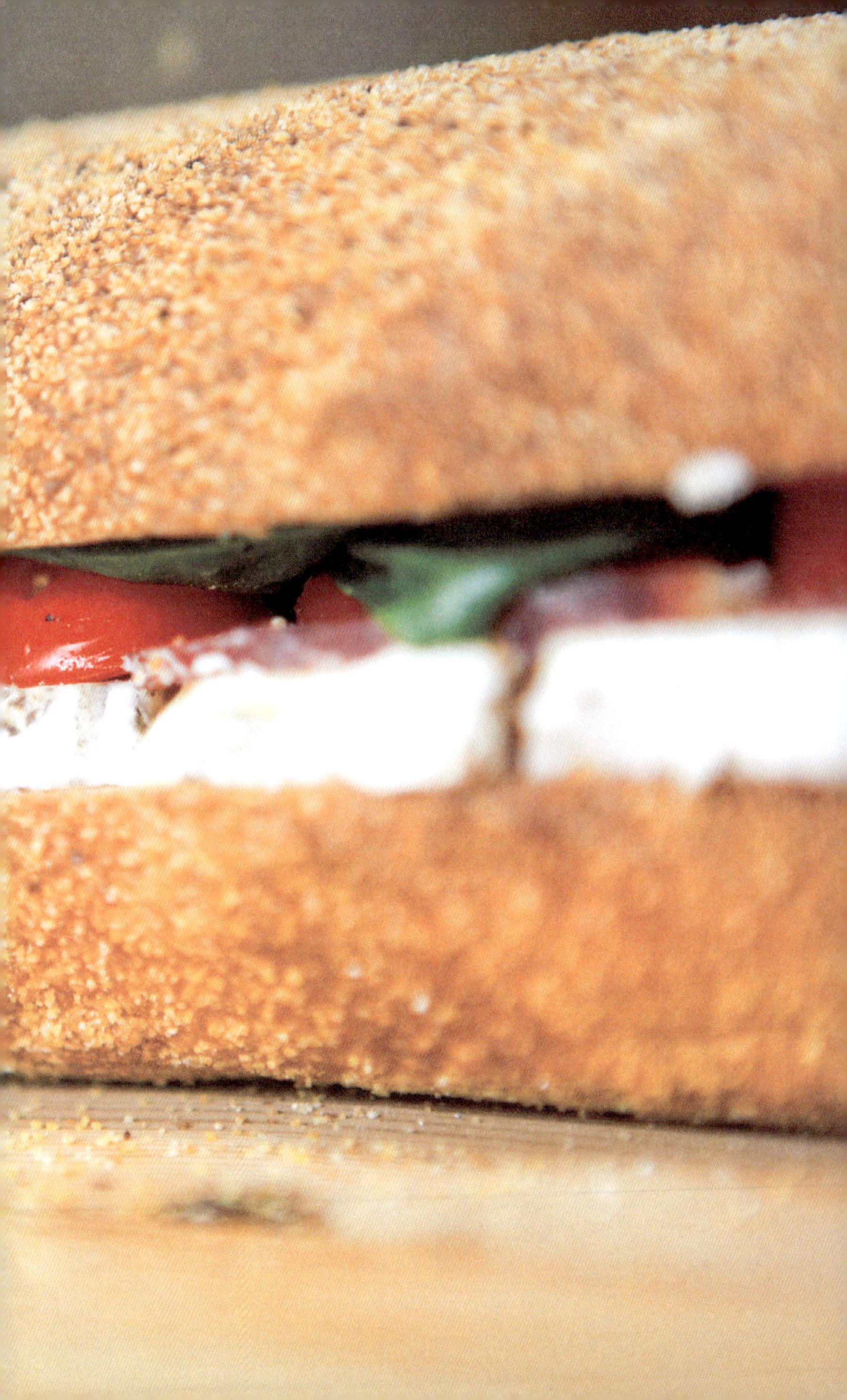

If you skipped

Bread making step by step (pp.34–71), you really need to go back and un-skip it. You will be much better at all of the breads in this section if you do. Some are more difficult than others.

Ciabatta, for example, is tricky, to say the least. I suggest you don't attempt it until you are a reasonably proficient baker, or it will make you feel disheartened. The dough you make it with is wet... impossibly wet. It has to be this way, to create the big air holes and the classic irregular, slightly saggy shape, supposedly mimicking the carpet-slipper that gives it its name.

Focaccia, on the other hand, is quite forgiving – perfect for less experienced bakers. Because it is shallow, and supported by a rimmed tray, the strength and structure of the dough is not so critical; it can be under-kneaded or over-proved, and you will still end up with bread you can be proud of.

I also want to introduce you to the delights of traditional English muffins, real bagels and proper pizza… this chapter is all about expanding your repertoire of bread doughs. Dive in and have fun. Choose from the following:

Beyond the basic loaf

- Focaccia (p.89)
- Ciabatta (p.90)
- Breadsticks (p.92)
- Brioche (p.95)
- Bagels (p.96)
- English muffins (p.99)
- Vetkoek (p.100)
- Flatbread (p.103)
- Pizza (p.104)
- Barbecue breads (p.107)

Reminder: Oven timings in the recipes relate to fan-assisted ovens.
If using a conventional electric or gas oven (without a fan), increase
the temperature by 15°C (1 Gas Mark). Use an oven thermometer to check
the accuracy of your oven.

BEYOND THE BASIC LOAF 87

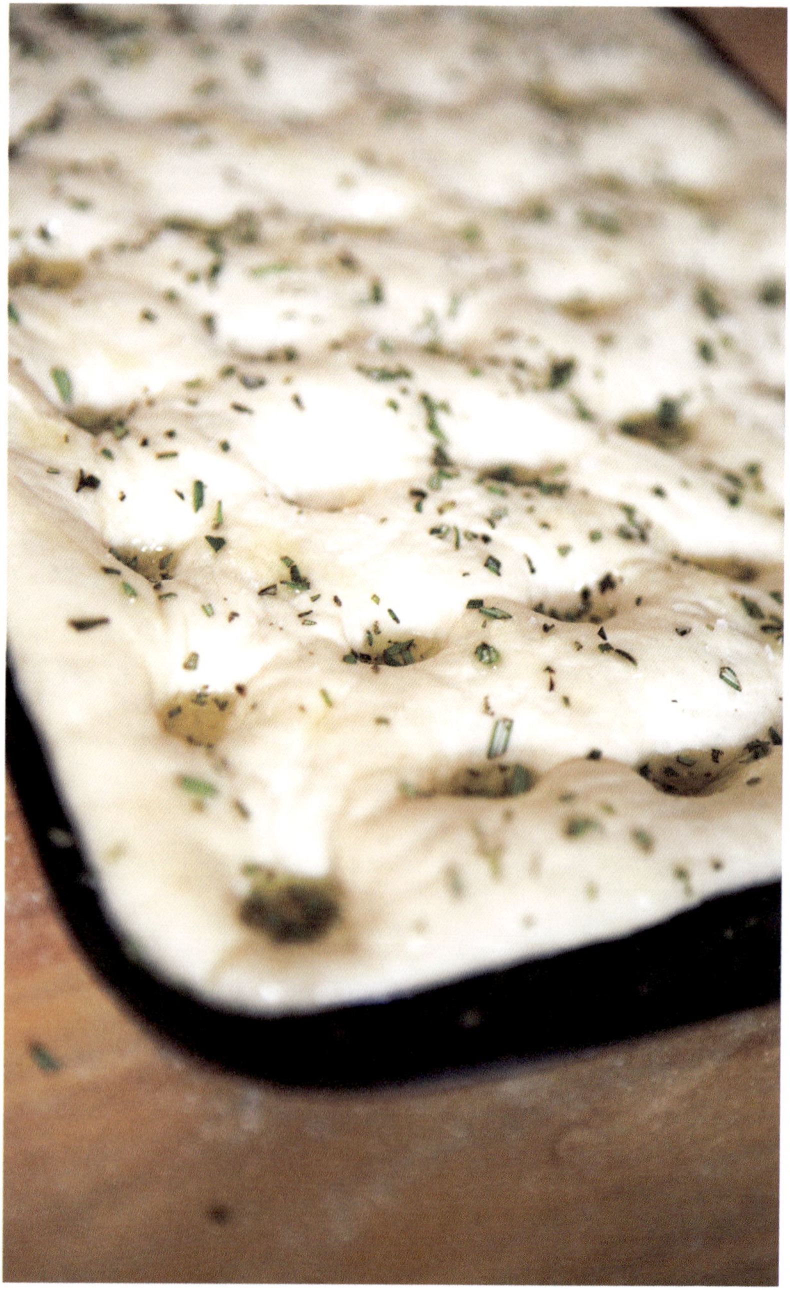

Focaccia

Focaccia is excellent sharing bread for serving with supper, and is really easy to make. You can certainly miss out the rosemary, and you don't have to sprinkle the top with salt, though it is authentic. You could expand this recipe and experiment as I have often done, mixing various herbs and other flavourings into the actual dough, though I think you'd have to ask an Italian if you can still call it focaccia. You could use a food mixer to knead this soft dough.

Makes 1 focaccia
500g strong white bread flour
5g powdered dried yeast
10g fine salt
325ml warm water
About 1 tbsp olive oil, plus extra for coating

To finish
A generous drizzle of olive oil
A sprinkle of flaky sea salt
A couple of rosemary sprigs, leaves stripped and finely chopped

To knead by hand: mix the flour, yeast, salt and water in a bowl to form a sticky dough. Add the oil, mix it in, then turn the dough out on to a clean work surface. Knead until smooth and silky, about 10 minutes.

Or, to use a food mixer: fit the dough hook and add the flour, yeast, salt and water to the mixer bowl. Mix on low speed until evenly combined, then add the oil and leave to knead for about 10 minutes, until smooth and silky.

Shape the dough into a round (see p.48) and coat with a little extra oil. Leave to rise in a clean bowl, covered with a plastic bag. When it has doubled in size, tip it on to the work surface and press into a rough rectangle. Place in a lightly oiled shallow baking tray, measuring about 26 x 36cm. Press the dough in with your fingers, right into the corners. Now leave to rise, covered, for about half an hour.

Preheat your oven to 250°C/Gas Mark 10, or as high as it will go. When the bread looks puffed up and airy, use your fingertips to poke deep holes across the whole surface, almost to the bottom. Drizzle the top generously (but not swimmingly) with olive oil and sprinkle with salt and rosemary. Bake for about 10 minutes, then turn the oven down to about 200°C/Gas Mark 6 and bake for a further 10 minutes.

Focaccia is best eaten warm, but not hot; leave to cool on a wire rack for about 10 minutes before serving, or leave to cool completely.

Ciabatta

This bread is pretty special. I love the flavour from the olive oil, the really big air holes and the roughness of the semolina-coated crust. I highly recommend a baking stone in your oven for this bread. It cannot hold its own weight and the instant fierce heat from beneath gives an essential lift. If you use a baking stone, you will of course need a peel, or a rimless baking sheet, for sliding the bread on to it. You will notice the salt content is slightly higher than usual; this takes into account the large amount of extra semolina flour you will need to use later, for shaping and coating. A food mixer would be useful for kneading this very wet dough.

Makes 6 small loaves

750g '00' flour or strong white bread flour
250g fine semolina, plus up to 500g for dusting
10g powdered dried yeast
25g fine salt
800ml warm water
A generous tbsp extra virgin olive oil, plus extra for drizzling

To knead by hand: mix the flour, semolina, yeast, salt and water together in a very large bowl, then add the oil. You won't be kneading this in the conventional manner. Instead, form your strongest hand into an 'eagle-claw' and beat the mix for about 5 minutes, until smooth.

Or, to use a food mixer: fit the dough hook and add the flour, semolina, yeast, salt and water to the mixer bowl. Mix on low speed until evenly combined, then add the oil and mix for about 5 minutes.

Put the bowl in a bin liner and leave to ferment. Every half an hour for the next 3 hours, do the following: uncover the bowl, slug in some olive oil, smooth it all over, and underneath, then make an attempt to fold the whole thing in two in one direction, then in three in the other (a bit like folding a blanket). The first time this will not really work, but this repeated action over the next 3 hours gives real structure to the gluten, and the dough will become more cohesive and elastic.

Now, prepare yourself. Have ready some linen cloth and dust this, the work surface, the dough and your hands generously with semolina. Make a big pile of semolina to one side, so it's easy to grab. Now tip the dough out on to the work surface. Dust with more semolina. Divide the dough into six, using a dough cutter, a fish slice, or a knife. Use quick chopping motions, dusting as you go. Everything is sticking to everything, I know. Add more semolina.

Now, one piece at a time, fold the edges in to make a rough rectangle. Flatten the rectangle, roll up lengthways, press along the seam to seal, coat in semolina and lay on the cloth. Stretch it out as you do this, so it is roughly four times as long as it is wide.

Cover your bread with plastic and leave to rise until doubled in size. Meanwhile, preheat your oven, with your baking stone (or tray) inside, to 250°C/Gas Mark 10, or as high as it will go.

You will probably see big, satisfying blisters all over the loaves – these are your big air pockets. When you are ready to bake, flip the loaves, one at a time, on to your dusted peel (or straight on to the hot tray), give them a little stretch lengthways, and slide into the oven. Do all this as fast as you can, to minimise heat loss. Bake at maximum heat for 10 minutes, then at 200°C/Gas Mark 6 for about another 15 minutes. Remove from the oven, drizzle with olive oil, then leave to cool on a wire rack, where everyone can see them.

P.S. To make a real Italian-style panino from one of your freshly baked ciabatta, split it lengthways and layer with a few slices of good air-dried salami, pieces of soft, ripe goat's cheese, 1 sliced fat tomato and lots of basil leaves. A little sea salt on the tomatoes would be good, but check the saltiness of the cheese. Add a grinding of black pepper. Close the sandwich and squash down with both hands. Rub the top and bottom with olive oil. Heat a ridged griddle pan and toast your panino, pressing it down often. When nicely charred on the bottom, turn it over and press down again, using a fish slice now, as the top will be hot. After 10 minutes or so, the cheese will have melted and your panino should be nicely stuck together and ready to eat.

Breadsticks

Breadsticks are brilliant. You can make lots in no time at all. They come out long and rough and misshapen, not remotely resembling anything you can buy. Make these if you have friends coming round for drinks. You may not want to bake all of the dough – freeze any you don't need now, in batches, and use within 6 months. This is another soft dough, so a food mixer would be useful for kneading.

Makes about 30

250g strong white flour, plus extra for dusting
250g plain white flour
5g powdered dried yeast
10g fine salt
325ml warm water
A drizzle of sunflower or olive oil, plus extra for coating

To finish
Olive (or other) oil, for brushing
A sprinkling of any of the following:
　　Flaky sea salt
　　Black pepper
　　Poppy seeds
　　Smoked paprika
　　Chopped rosemary leaves
　　Finely grated Parmesan

To knead by hand: mix the flours, yeast, salt and water in a bowl to form a sticky dough. Add the oil, mix it in, then turn the dough out on to a clean work surface. Knead until smooth and silky.

Or, to use a food mixer: fit the dough hook and add the flours, yeast, salt and water to the mixer bowl. Mix on low speed until combined, then add the oil and leave to knead for about 10 minutes, until smooth and silky.

Shape the dough into a round (see p.48), coat with a little extra oil and place in a clean bowl. Leave to rise, covered with a plastic bag, until doubled in size.

Turn the dough out on to the work surface, and using plenty of flour, roll out to between 5mm and 1cm thick. (You may have to do this in batches – it depends how much room you have.) Dust the top evenly with more flour, then flip the whole thing over and dust the other side.

Now cut into strips, about 1cm wide and as long as you like (pic 1). If you want to flavour the breadsticks, brush the tops with oil and sprinkle lightly with your chosen flavouring(s) (pic 2). Now oil your baking trays and lay the bread strips out on them, curling some if you like (pic 3). Leave to prove for about half an hour, then bake at 200°C/Gas Mark 6 for about 20 minutes until golden and just dried out through to the middle. Cool on a wire rack. Stand in a jug or pot (pic 4) to serve.

1

2

3

4

BEYOND THE BASIC LOAF 93

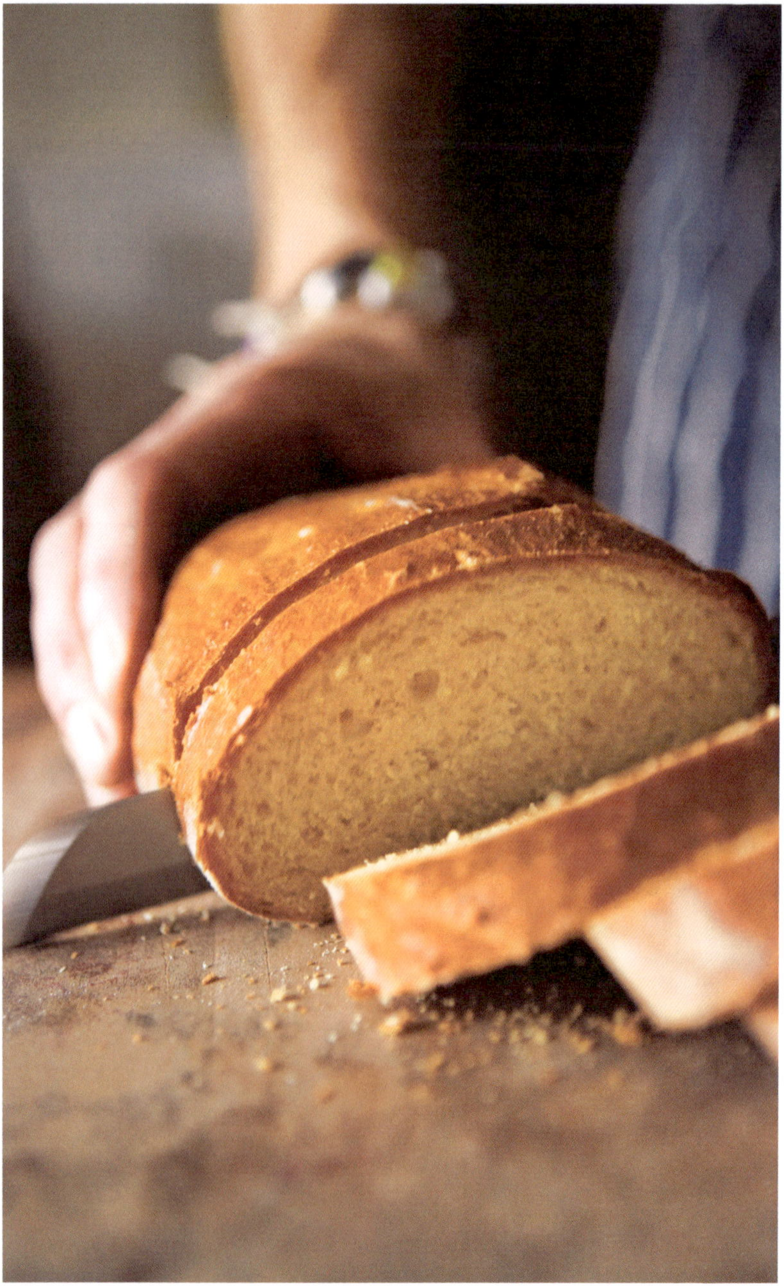

Brioche

This classic French bread is rich and slightly sweet, with a soft, golden crust and a yellow, buttery, cakey crumb. It is widely eaten in France – with coffee for breakfast, as a roll with dinner, or as a base for any number of desserts. At River Cottage, we like to toast brioche and serve it with a smooth chicken liver pâté, and a little fruit jelly.

Contrary to popular belief, as bread goes, brioche is pretty straightforward. The dough is very soft to handle though, so kneading in a food mixer is easier. You can make and bake brioche all in one day, but it benefits from sitting overnight in the fridge – the very soft dough stiffens as it chills, making it easier to shape.

Makes 2 small loaves

400g strong white bread flour, plus extra for dusting
5g powdered dried yeast
10g fine salt
90ml warm milk
2 tbsp caster sugar
100g butter, softened
4 medium free-range eggs, beaten

To glaze
1 medium free-range egg
2 tbsp milk

To knead by hand: mix all the ingredients in a large bowl, and bring it all together to form a dough. Knead for about 10 minutes, until smooth and shiny.

Or, to use a food mixer: fit the dough hook and add all the dough ingredients to the mixer bowl. Mix on low speed until combined, and leave to knead for about 10 minutes, until smooth and shiny.

Shape the dough into a round (see p.48), place in a bowl and cover tightly. Leave in the fridge overnight.

The next day, divide the dough in two and form into the shape of your choice (see pp.55–59). Lightly flour the loaves, lay them on a wooden board or linen cloth and cover with a plastic bag. Leave them somewhere nice and warm to prove until almost doubled in size; this could take 3 or 4 hours, as the dough is cold.

Preheat the oven to 200°C/Gas Mark 6. For the glaze, beat the egg and milk together. Transfer the risen loaves to a baking tray and brush all over with the glaze. Bake for about 10 minutes, then lower the oven setting to 180°C/Gas Mark 4 and bake for a further 30 minutes or until golden brown. Cool on a wire rack.

Bagels

Until recently, most of the bagels I had eaten seemed bland, somewhat dry and rather boring. That was until I came across a bagel recipe in an old Jewish cookbook and was enlightened. Good bagels, like the ones you are about to make, are slightly sweet and curiously chewy, with a soft, shiny, tasty crust. You poach them for a couple of minutes in water before you bake them – the oddest thing you are ever likely to do to a piece of dough.

Makes 12

500g strong white bread flour
5g powdered dried yeast
10g fine salt
250ml warm water
20g caster sugar
50ml vegetable oil, plus extra
   for coating

To finish
1 medium free-range egg, beaten
Poppy or sesame seeds (optional)

In a large bowl, mix together all the ingredients to make a dough. Knead on a clean surface until smooth and elastic. Shape into a round (see p.48), coat with a little extra oil and place in a clean bowl. Leave to rise, covered with a plastic bag.

When the dough has doubled in size, deflate it and divide into 12 pieces. One at a time, roll into a sausage shape, about 15cm long. Wet the ends and press them together to make a ring. Leave to prove, covered, on a lightly oiled plastic board or metal baking sheet (not floured cloths or boards).

Preheat the oven to 200°C/Gas Mark 6. Lightly oil a couple of baking sheets and in a wide pan bring around a 10cm depth of water to the boil.

When the bagels have roughly doubled in size, they are ready for poaching. You will need to do this in batches. Turn the pan of water down to a simmer, then slip as many bagels as will fit comfortably into the water (allow room for them to puff up). Cook for a minute on each side, then remove and drain on a clean tea towel (not kitchen paper as it will stick).

When they are all poached, lay the bagels on the baking sheets, gently sticking any that uncurled in the water back together again. Brush all over with beaten egg, then sprinkle with seeds if you like. Bake for 15 minutes, until the bagels are a uniform, glossy golden brown. Cool on a wire rack.

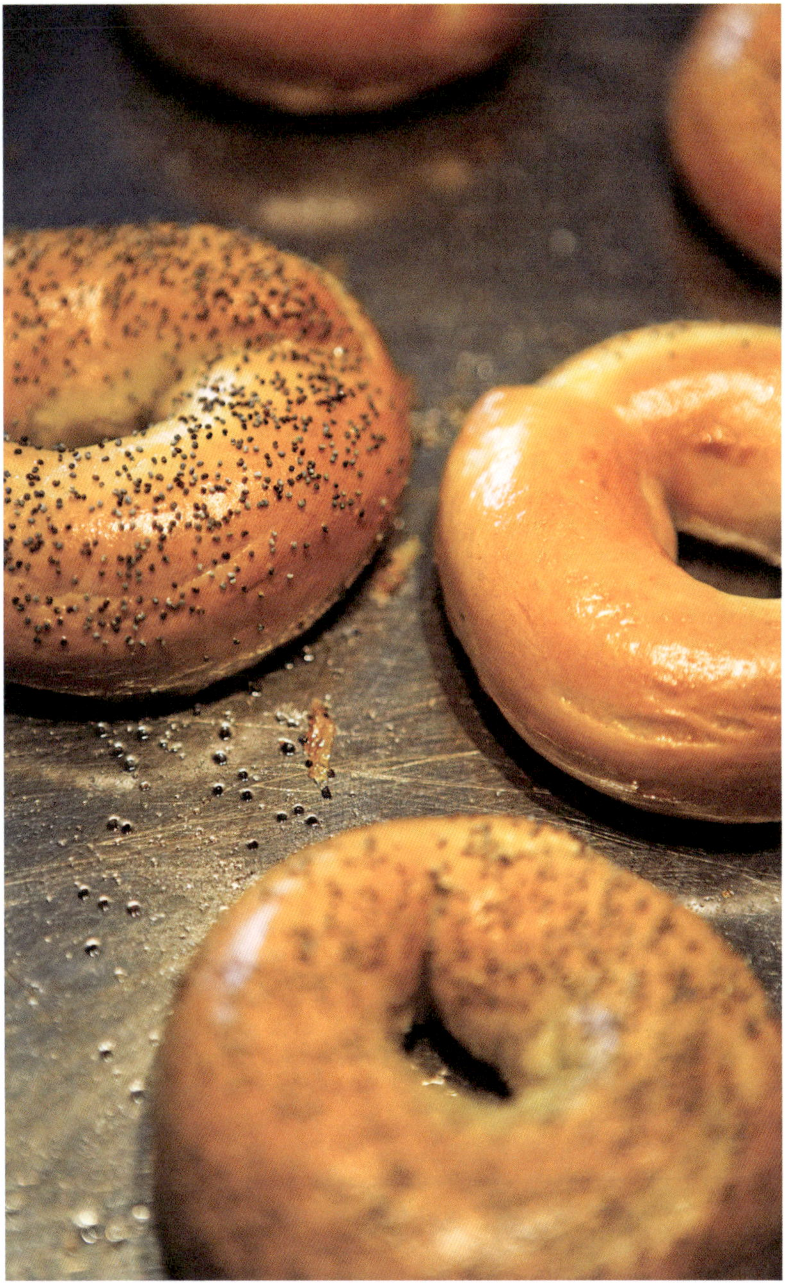

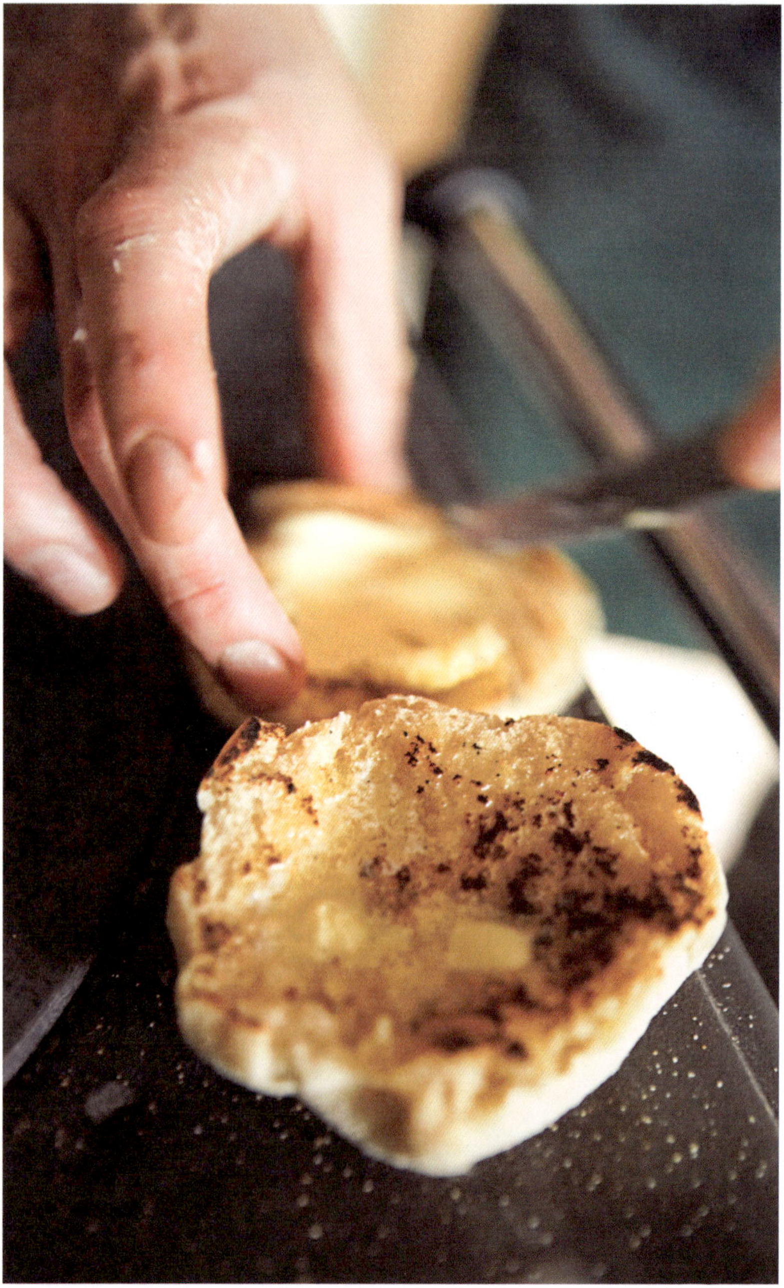

English muffins

A muffin – split, toasted and buttered – is my very favourite bread to have with eggs for breakfast. If you own an Aga, then lucky you – muffins were made for cooking straight on the top. If not, you will need a couple of heavy-based frying pans (each large enough to hold 4 or 5 muffins). This dough is soft, so you might prefer to use a food mixer to knead it.

Makes 9

500g strong white bread flour, plus extra for dusting
5g powdered dried yeast
10g fine salt
325ml warm water

A drizzle of sunflower oil, plus extra for coating
A handful of semolina flour, for coating

To knead by hand: mix the flour, yeast, salt and water in a bowl to form a sticky dough. Add the oil, mix it in, then turn the dough out on to a clean work surface. Knead until smooth and silky.

Or, to use a food mixer: fit the dough hook and add the flour, yeast, salt and water to the mixer bowl. Mix on low speed until combined, then add the oil and leave to knead for about 10 minutes, until smooth and silky.

Shape the dough into a round (see p.48), coat with a little extra oil and place in a clean bowl. Leave to rise, covered with a plastic bag, until doubled in size.

Tip the dough out on to the work surface and press all over to deflate. Divide into 9 pieces, shape each into a round and flatten to about 1–2cm. Dust them all over with semolina flour; this gives a lovely texture to the crust. Leave to prove on a linen cloth or wooden board, covered with a plastic bag, until doubled in size.

Heat a couple of large heavy-based frying pans over a medium heat. Lay the muffins in the pans and cook for a minute or so, then turn them over gently. Cook slowly for a further 10 minutes, turning every now and then. You may need to adjust the heat if they seem to be colouring too fast, or not fast enough. Alternatively, if you are using an Aga, cook the muffins directly on the warm plate for up to 15 minutes, giving them a quick blast on the hot side at the end, if you think they need it. Leave to cool on a wire rack.

Vetkoek

Vetkoek, pronounced 'fet cook', is an Afrikaans word, meaning 'fat cake'. I once knew a guy called Andre, a South African taxidermist, who lived in a tiny caravan. He made me four things: a badger tooth necklace, boiled rabbit, coffee so strong you could chew it... and *vetkoek*. The *vetkoek* were excellent.

Makes 12

500g strong white bread flour, plus extra for dusting
5g powdered dried yeast
10g fine salt
300ml warm water
At least 1 litre sunflower or vegetable oil, for deep-frying

In a bowl, mix together the flour, yeast, salt and water. Turn out on to a clean work surface and knead until smooth and silky. Shape into a round (see p.48), coat with a little extra flour and place in a clean bowl. Leave to rise, covered with a plastic bag, until doubled in size.

Divide the risen dough into 12 pieces, shape into rough rounds and dust lightly with flour. Cover these and leave them for about 10 minutes, to rise a little.

Heat a 5–8cm depth of oil in a deep, heavy-based pan to 170°C. If you do not have a frying thermometer, check the oil temperature by dropping in a cube of bread; it should turn golden in less than a minute. Deep-fry the *vetkoek*, a few at a time, for 3–4 minutes each side. Let them cool a little before eating.

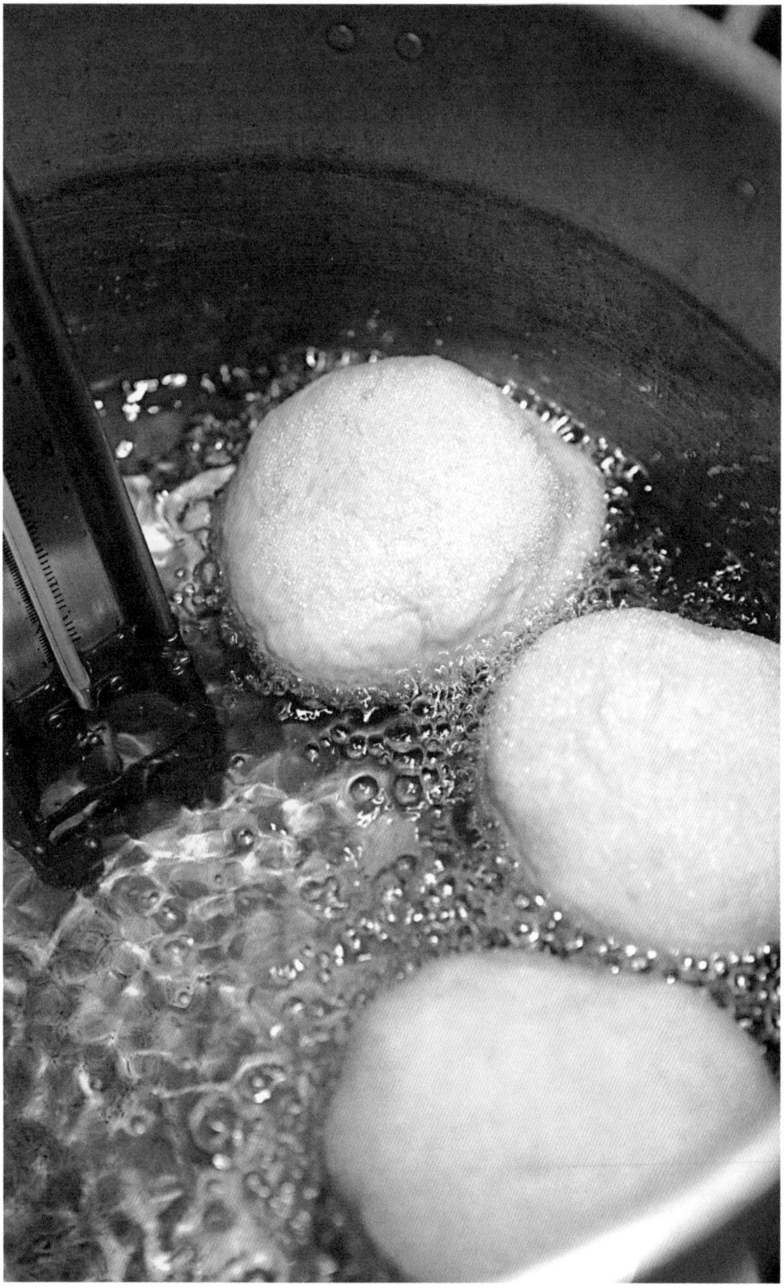

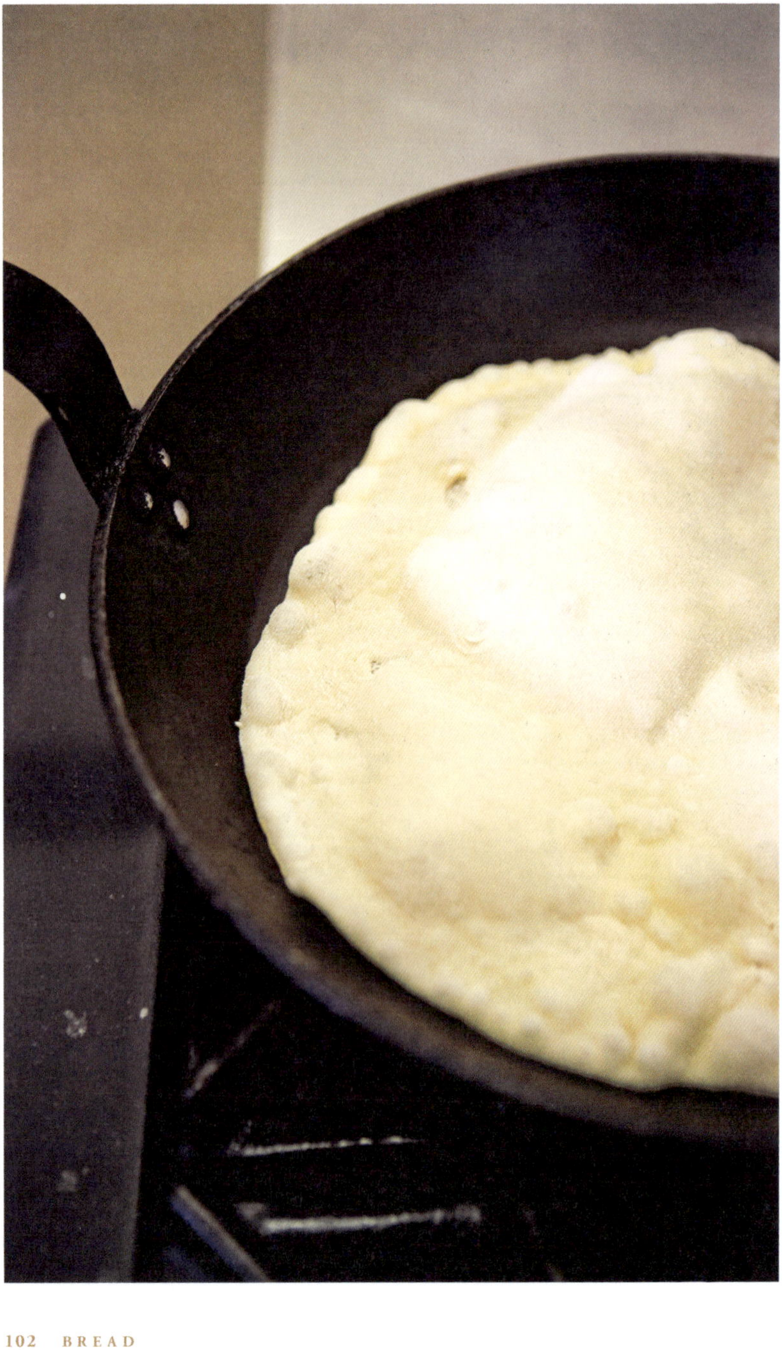

Flatbread

In restaurants in southwest Turkey, fantastic bread is served – steaming hot and cooked to order. It's a bit like pitta, but lighter, softer, and as long as your table. You can make similar bread at home, though you may struggle to make it the size of your table. The dough is soft, so use a food mixer to knead it, if you can.

Makes about 12

500g plain white flour, plus extra for dusting
500g strong white bread flour
10g powdered dried yeast
20g fine salt
325ml warm water
325ml natural yoghurt, warmed
2 tbsp good olive oil, plus extra for coating

To knead by hand: mix the flours, yeast, salt, water and yoghurt in a bowl to form a sticky dough. Add the oil, mix it in, then turn the dough out on to a clean work surface. Knead until smooth and silky.

Or, to use a food mixer: fit the dough hook and add the flours, yeast, salt, water and yoghurt to the mixer bowl. Mix on low speed until combined, then add the oil and leave to knead for about 10 minutes, until smooth and silky.

Shape the dough into a round (see p.48), then place in a clean bowl. Leave to rise, covered with a plastic bag, until doubled in size. Deflate the dough, then if you have time, leave to rise a second, third, even a fourth time (this improves the dough but is by no means essential).

Tear off pieces the size of small lemons (or smaller, or larger, if you like). One at a time, shape into a round, then using plenty of flour, roll out to a 3–4mm thickness and leave to rest for 5 minutes or so; this improves the finished bread dramatically.

Meanwhile, heat a large, heavy-based frying pan over the highest heat and set the grill to maximum. When the pan is super-hot, lay the first bread in it. After a minute, or possibly less, the bread should be puffy and starting to char on the bottom. Slide the pan under the hot grill, a good 15cm from the heat, and watch your creation balloon magnificently.

Remove the bread when it starts to char on the top, slip a lick of olive oil over, and feed your awestruck friends. They will need something to dip the bread into, such as taramasalata (see p.179), and/or beetroot houmous (see p.178). Repeat and repeat, to use all the dough.

Pizza

The best way to bake pizza is in a fiercely hot (400°C+) brick-floored, wood-fired oven. Cooked this way, your pizza will be charred, blistered and ready in as little as 1½ minutes. It will also taste sensational. If you do not have a wood-fired oven or home-built clay oven (see pp.192–209), the next best way is on a baking stone in a domestic oven. The base won't char as much and it will take longer, but it will still be amazing. You'll need a peel, or rimless baking sheet, to slide the pizza on to the stone. If you do not own a baking stone, you can lay pizzas on baking trays. They will cook more slowly and won't blister, but they'll still taste good. Make either the roast tomato sauce or garlicky olive oil, and choose as many toppings as you wish.

Makes at least 8 small pizzas
250g strong white bread flour
250g plain white flour
5g powdered dried yeast
10g salt
325ml warm water
About 1 tbsp olive oil
A handful of coarse flour (rye, semolina or polenta), for dusting

For the roast tomato sauce (optional)
500g tomatoes
2 large garlic cloves, peeled and sliced
2 tbsp olive oil
Salt and black pepper

For the garlicky olive oil (optional)
6 large garlic cloves, peeled and grated
6 tbsp extra virgin olive oil

Toppings to add before baking
- A small bowl of: grated Parmesan; grated Cheddar; sliced buffalo mozzarella
- A ramekin of: good salami; chopped dry-cured bacon; air-dried ham; anchovy fillets; thinly sliced cooked artichoke hearts; wild mushrooms fried gently in olive oil with garlic and thyme.
- A sprinkling of: capers; finely chopped rosemary leaves; black pepper; thinly sliced mild red chilli

Toppings to add after baking
A scattering of: basil leaves; rocket leaves; chopped parsley; wild garlic flowers

To make the dough by hand: mix the flours, yeast, salt and water in a bowl to form a sticky dough. Add the oil, mix it in, then turn the dough out on to a clean work surface. Knead until smooth and silky.

Or, to use a food mixer: fit the dough hook and add the flours, yeast, salt and water to the mixer bowl. Mix on low speed, then add the oil and leave to knead for about 10 minutes, until smooth and silky.

(continued overleaf)

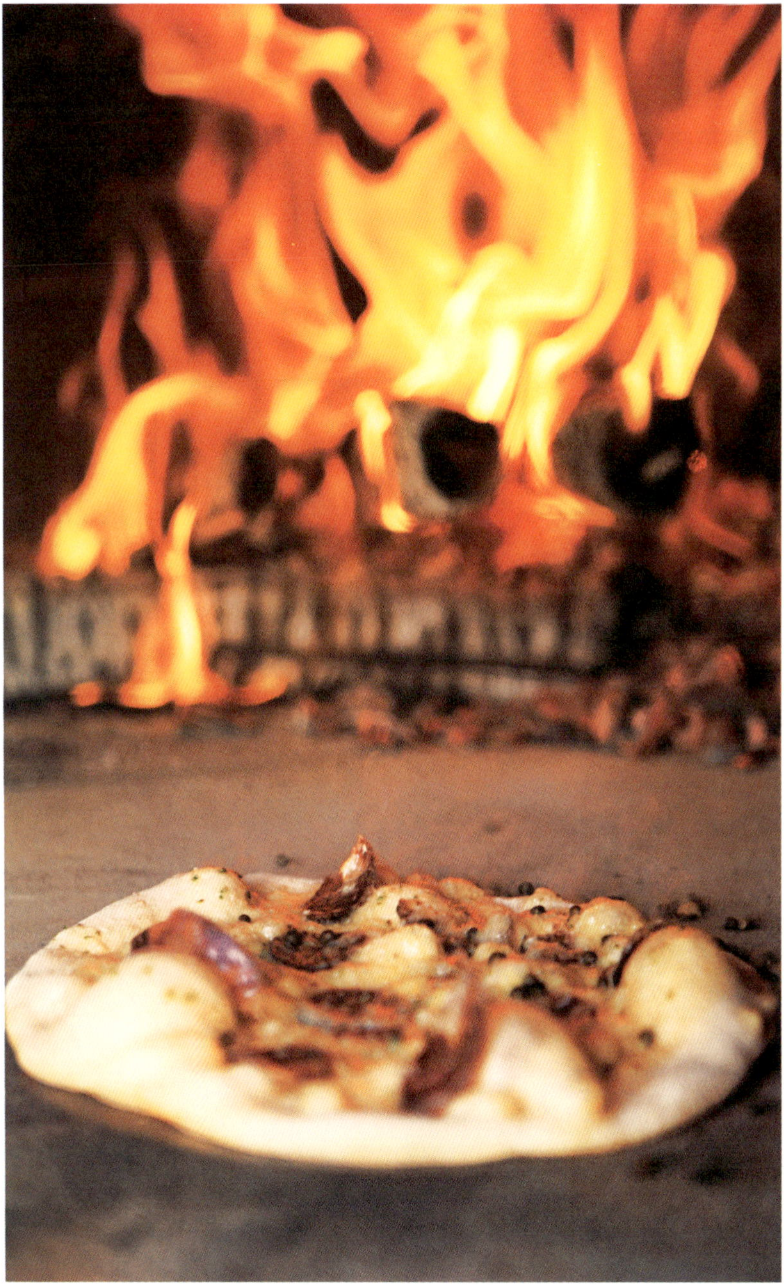

Shape the dough into a round (see p.48), then leave to rise in a clean bowl, covered with a plastic bag, until doubled in size.

To prepare the roast tomato sauce, if using, preheat the oven to 180°C/Gas Mark 4. Halve the tomatoes and lay them, cut side up, in a roasting tin. Mix the garlic with the oil, pour over the tomatoes and shake the tin a little, to distribute the oil. Season with salt and pepper. Roast for 30–45 minutes, until the tomatoes are soft and slightly charred. Rub through a sieve into a bowl.

Or, for the garlicky olive oil, simply mix the garlic with the oil.

Have your toppings laid out in little bowls, or in piles, so everyone can make their own selection.

If using a domestic oven, preheat your oven, with your baking stone (or tray) inside, to 250°C/Gas Mark 10, or as high as it will go. (Alternatively, have your clay oven raging hot and rake the embers out.)

To shape and bake the pizzas

If using a wood-fired oven or a baking stone in a domestic oven, take a lime-sized piece of your risen dough and roll it out until about 5mm thick, keeping it as round as you can. Dust the peel or rimless baking sheet with coarse flour, and lay the dough on it. If you are using a baking tray: either roll out a lime-sized piece as above, or you could take a larger piece, and press it into the tray, to fit.

Think thin and delicate with your toppings, including the cheese, as befits thin, delicate bases. Overloaded pizzas will be hard to handle and will quite probably tear; they will also come out soggy. Try to use only three or four toppings on each pizza. The following combinations work well:
- Garlicky oil, artichokes, Parmesan and basil
- Garlicky oil, anchovy, capers and Parmesan
- Roast tomato sauce, mozzarella, black pepper and basil (Margherita)
- Garlicky oil, chilli, mozzarella and rocket
- Garlicky oil and rosemary
- Roast tomato sauce, salami, Parmesan and parsley
- Fried wild mushrooms with their oil, Parmesan and parsley (my favourite)

Apply the toppings to be added before baking, then either slip the pizza briskly but carefully on to the baking stone (or brick floor), or transfer the baking tray to the top shelf of the oven. Bake until the cheese is melted and bubbling: this should take about 1½ minutes in a wood-fired oven; more like 7–9 minutes in a domestic oven. Remove from the oven and scatter over any leaves or other raw toppings you may be using. Cut your pizza up and dig in… while somebody else bakes the next one.

Barbecue breads

Like the *vetkoek (*on p.100), this is not so much a recipe as a different way of cooking bread dough. If you want to make your dough outdoors, and have no suitable surface for kneading, you could employ my (no longer) secret 'soggy tea towel' technique (described below).

Makes at least 8

500g strong white bread flour (or other bread flour of your choice), plus extra for dusting
5g powdered dried yeast
10g fine salt
300ml warm water
A drizzle of sunflower or other oil

In a bowl, mix together the flour, yeast, salt and water. Drizzle in a little oil and squidge the dough together. Turn out on to a clean work surface and knead until smooth and silky. Alternatively, to use the 'soggy tea towel' technique: wring the dough between your hands, as if you were wringing a tea towel. Fold it in half every few wrings as it gets too thin, and keep wringing until the dough becomes smooth and springy.

Shape the dough into a round (see p.48), coat with a little extra flour and place in a clean bowl. Leave to rise, covered with a plastic bag, until doubled in size.

You can be very flexible about proving. Make the dough in the morning if you like, then keep deflating it through the day until it's time to eat. At this point, tear off pieces of dough and pull and squash them into roughish rounds, as thin as you can get them by hand.

Leave to rise for about 10 minutes, or until you have space on the barbecue, then slap them on. How long they will take to cook depends on how thick they are, and how hot the barbecue is, but around 7–10 minutes should be about right – tear one open and check it is cooked in the middle. Let cool slightly before eating.

Bread Made with Wild Yeast

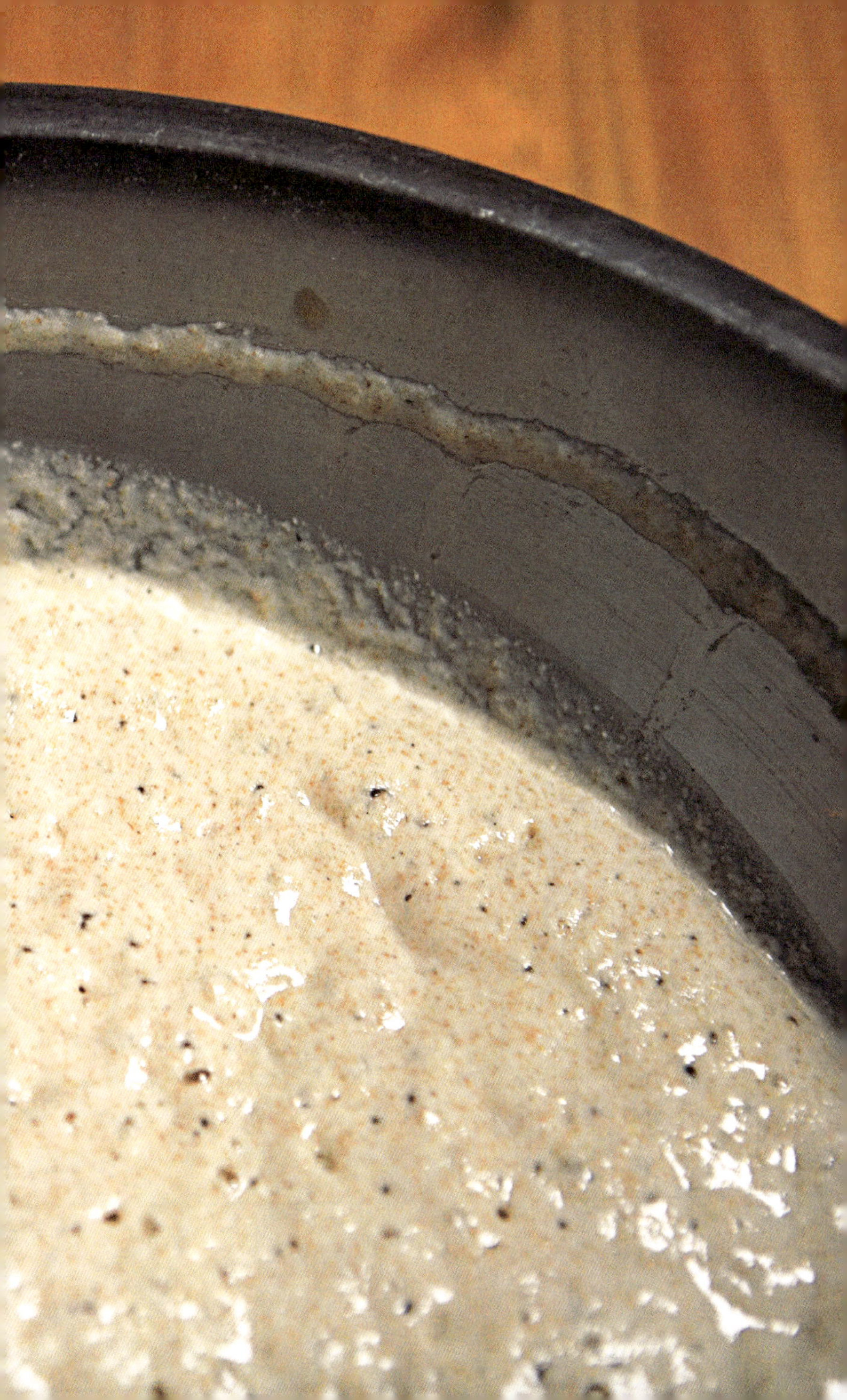

You don't have to buy yeast from the shop to make your bread.

You can get your own, from the wild. What's more, you don't need any special equipment, local knowledge or expert tuition. There are dormant yeast spores all around you – in the air, in your fruit bowl, and in that lovely bag of organic flour in your cupboard. As wild foraging goes, it's a bit of a doddle – you don't even need to leave the house, unless, of course, you need to buy that bag of flour. You just need to create an environment in which the yeast spores will become active.

Sourdough starter

A starter (also known as a *poolish*, or *levain*) is a fermenting dough or batter, all or part of which is used to raise a batch of bread. The term sourdough broadly applies to bread raised with wild yeasts. Defining characteristics of such breads are a slower fermentation and a distinctly sour (but by no means unpleasant) flavour. Both are the result of high acidity caused by the presence of certain bacteria, among them lactic acid bacteria (the same bacteria used to make yoghurt), which colonise the starter along with the yeasts. Making a starter is easy. We know that yeasts need sugar, warmth and moisture to reproduce. All you need to do is provide these. Here's the recipe, if you can call it that.

For the first stage
A cupful of flour (about 150g)
A cupful of warm water (about 250ml)

For the first 'feeding'
A cupful of flour (about 150g)
About 100ml warm water (about 250ml)

For each subsequent feeding
A cupful of flour (about 150g)
A cupful of cold water (about 250ml)

The first stage
You really need a plastic or earthenware container with a lid to make your starter in. It should be big enough to allow plenty of room for frothing – at least four times the volume of your initial batter (because you will add more later). You can use any type of flour you like; I have made excellent starters from rye, spelt and wheat. I recommend that you use wholemeal rather than white flour though; it will ferment sooner – and more vigorously.

1: the first signs of fermentation

2: vigorous fermentation

There is no need to be precise about the quantities of flour and water. For the first stage, just use roughly equal volumes of each to make a thick batter and whisk it well – this incorporates more air, and therefore more yeast spores. If you have a food mixer, then 10 minutes at high speed would be ideal. Put the batter into the container, put the lid on and leave it somewhere fairly warm – a warm kitchen is fine; an airing cupboard would do, but don't put it too close to the boiler.

The first feeding

At some point, your starter will begin to ferment. This depends on many factors, such as the flour used, how much you whisked it, which yeasts and bacteria happen to be around, and how warm it is. To give you some idea, a white wheat starter I made at home took two full days to puff a couple of little air bubbles to the surface; a wholemeal spelt starter I made at work was frothing rapidly after only a few hours. So, check every 12 hours or so, and when you see the first signs of fermentation (p.111, pic 1), give your starter its first 'feeding' by whisking in another 150g or so of flour and another 250ml warm water. Replace the lid and leave it again.

Check your starter again after another day (though in reality you will be so fascinated by now that you won't be able to keep away from it). Don't worry if all this takes longer than you expected – it will get there in the end. And when it does, I should warn you about the smell. You will either love it, or hate it. It might be sickly sweet or sickly sour, smelling of vinegar, or rotten apples, or brandy, or gone-off milk, perhaps. Breathe in deeply; I want you to remember this smell.

Subsequent feedings

Now tip out half of the starter (into a plastic bag or an old milk carton) and discard it. Replace this with another 150g flour, and 250ml cold water this time, and leave it another day, at a fairly cool room temperature now. In fact, find it a permanent home – it may be with you for life, after all. Hereafter, you are into a feeding programme, and you need to find one that suits you.

I suggest for the first week at least, while your sourdough starter is getting established, you feed it daily, discarding half and replacing it. Keep smelling it and you'll become aware of the aroma changing, becoming less harsh and more complex as it matures. You will also notice different smells at different stages of fermentation. Without sounding too cosy, you should develop a living relationship with your starter. It is very much like keeping a pet. You will get to know when it needs feeding, when it is most active, when it is tired and sluggish, and (sorry about this) when it could do with a good beating (I whip mine in the food mixer every couple of weeks – the oxygen does the yeast a lot of good). About a week into your routine of daily feeding, when fermentation is vigorous (p.111, pic 2) and regular, and the smells have become recognisable and established, you are ready to use your starter.

If you are likely to bake regularly, as we do at River Cottage, keep your starter as it is – as a thick batter, at room temperature, feeding it daily. But if you will only be using it every couple of weeks or less, you may as well slow the fermentation; then you'll need to feed it less. To do so, you can either make it colder or drier, or both:

- Keep your starter in the fridge and it can go a week without being fed.
- Alternatively, add enough flour to make a stiff dough and you could happily feed it every three or four days. To feed a dough, discard half (or better still, bake with it), make a new flour and water dough the same volume as the discarded part, and knead it into the remaining starter. A dough that is fed like this will still be pretty active. Many bakers keep starters permanently in the form of a dough (when it is more usually known as a *levain*), and bake with them daily.
- Or do both: keep it as a dough in the fridge and you only need to feed it every couple of weeks.

What is important, though, is that your starter is really active when it comes to baking, so at least a couple of days ahead, remove it from the fridge and/or bring it back to a thick batter by adding water, then feed it daily until you bake.

Nurtured this way, your starter will live for ever. However, you may get to a stage where you have no room in your life to look after it but you don't want to throw your starter away. It is worth freezing it for the future – well sealed and labelled clearly.

Currently at River Cottage, we have two starters: a wheat one, an offshoot of my own 3-year-old starter; and an older rye starter, given to us by Clive Mellum from Shipton Mill. Clive's batter has been continuously fermenting for 12 years. But at 12, it is still young. Aidan Chapman, an outstanding baker at the Town Mill bakery, tells me his rye starter was first made 30 years ago in Russia. It is the tradition in many communities to hand down starters from one generation to the next. How satisfying it must be to bake with them – a little piece of ancestry in every loaf.

Making bread with your starter
Sourdough baking is different from conventional bread baking only in that the process takes longer. You should familiarise yourself with the detailed section: Bread making step by step (pp.34–71), as the following recipes refer back to it.

Bread made with wild yeast

- Sourdough (p.115)
- My sourdough (p.117)
- Sour rye bread (p.120)
- Spelt sourdough (p.122)
- Pumpernickel (p.124)

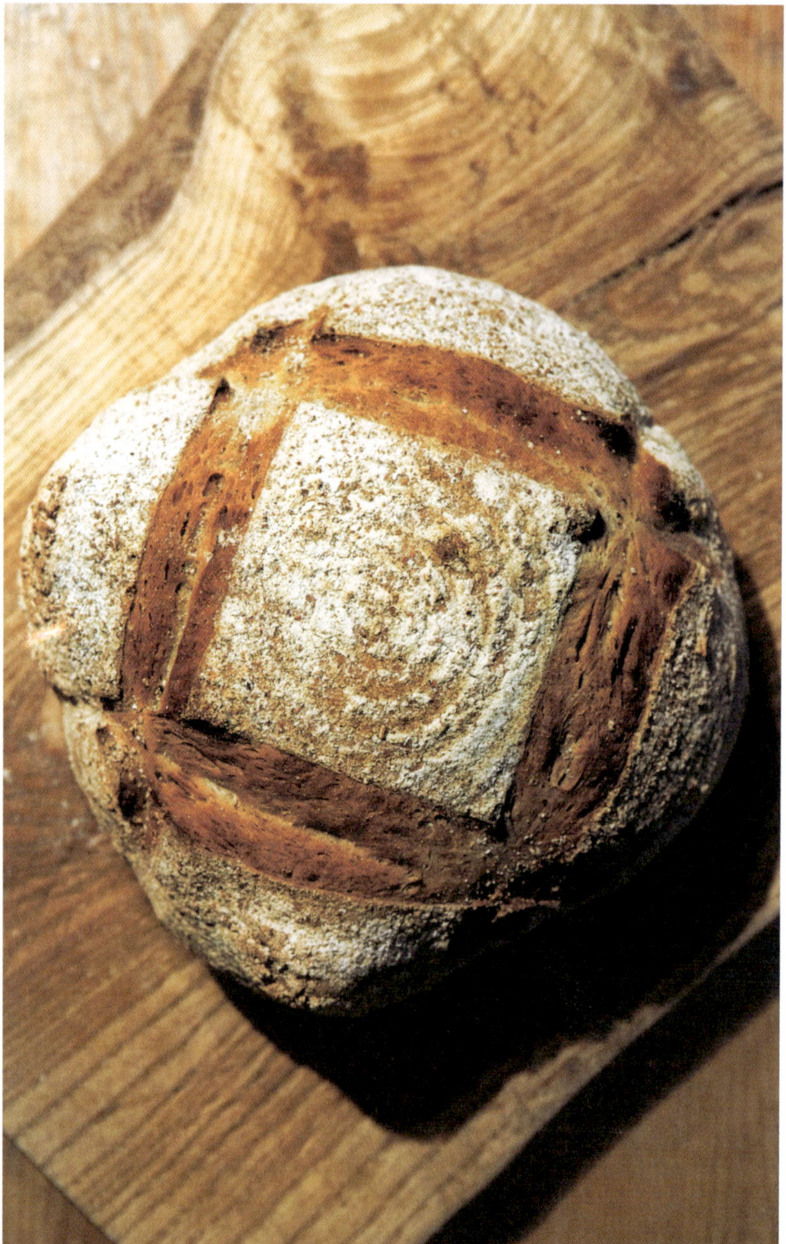

Sourdough

This is a simple wholemeal sourdough, which you can adapt infinitely, in the same way as the basic bread recipe (see pp.72–7). I have also given you the River Cottage variation (see p.116).

Makes 2–3 loaves

For the sponge
500g strong wholemeal wheat flour
600ml warm water
A ladleful of very active sourdough starter (see p.110)

For the dough
600g strong wholemeal wheat flour, plus extra for dusting
25g salt

Before you go to bed, make the sponge: mix all the ingredients together by hand in a large bowl or plastic container. Beat for a while, squeezing the lumps of flour out as you come across them. Put the container in a plastic bag and leave it somewhere fairly warm until the morning.

The next day, mix in the flour and salt, and squash it all together, adding more flour or water as necessary, to make a soft, easily kneadable, sticky dough. Turn it out on to a clean work surface and knead for about 10 minutes, until smooth and springy.

Form the dough into a tight round (see p.48), flour it all over and place in a clean bowl. Cover with a plastic bag and leave to rise. After an hour, tip it out on to your work surface (it may not have risen much at this point). Form it into a tight round again, return to the bowl, cover and leave to rise for another hour. Repeat this process once, or even twice more – you will notice the dough becoming increasingly airy.

After the final rising period, tip the dough out on to the work surface and deflate it by pressing all over with your hands. Divide into two or three, and shape into loaves (see pp.55–9). Coat with flour, then transfer the loaves to well-floured wooden boards, linen cloths, tea towels or proving baskets. Lay a plastic bag over the whole batch, to stop it drying out, and leave to prove until almost doubled in size; this could be anywhere from 1–4 hours, depending on the temperature of the dough and the vigour of your sourdough starter.

When the loaves are almost ready, switch the oven to 250°C/Gas Mark 10 or its highest setting, put a baking stone or a heavy baking tray inside, and place a roasting tin on the bottom shelf. Put the kettle on. Have a water spray bottle, a serrated knife and an oven cloth ready, as well as a peel or rimless baking sheet, if you are using a baking stone. Clear the area around the oven.

(continued overleaf)

When the loaves are ready, either transfer them to the hot tray (removed from the oven), or one at a time to the peel. Slash the tops with the serrated knife and spray the bread all over with water. Put the tray into the oven, or slide each loaf on to the baking stone, pour some boiling water into the roasting tin and close the door as quickly as you can.

Turn the heat down after about 10 minutes to 200°C/Gas Mark 6 if the crust is still very pale; 180°C/Gas Mark 4 if the crust is noticeably browning; or 170°C/Gas Mark 3 if the crust seems to be browning quickly. Bake until the loaves are well browned and crusty, and feel hollow when you tap them: in total allow 30–40 minutes for small loaves; 40–50 minutes for large loaves. If in doubt, bake for a few minutes longer. Leave to cool on a wire rack.

Variation

To make River Cottage sourdough, use strong white rather than wholemeal flour. For the sponge, use a 50:50 mix of wheat and rye flour (250g each). Add a good slug of sunflower oil after you have formed the dough.

My sourdough

Deliciously chewy and tangy, with enormous air holes and a fine savoury crust, this is one of my favourite breads. The large holes are due to a wetter than usual dough, so you will find it a little trickier than usual to handle. The shaped loaves will be rather saggy and would certainly benefit from the support of a rucked-up linen cloth or, better still, proving baskets. In any case, this sourdough will rise dramatically in the oven and will always end up looking glorious, if occasionally perhaps a little misshapen.

Makes 2–3 loaves

For the sponge
650ml warm water
500g strong white bread flour
A ladleful of sourdough starter
    (see p.110)

For the dough
600g strong white bread flour,
    plus extra for dusting
25g salt

To finish
A handful of rye flour

Before you go to bed, make the sponge. Mix the water, flour and starter together in a bowl. Cover and leave in a fairly warm place overnight.

The next morning, to knead the dough by hand: mix the flour and salt into the sponge. Bring it together and squidge in the oil if using. The dough should be soft and sticky – just kneadable, but rather wetter than a normal dough. You will need some extra flour – for your hands, the dough and the worktop. It will be quite messy to begin with. Every now and then, clean your hands and scrape the worktop. Use more flour when you need to, but be sparing with it – you don't want to make the dough stiff, or you won't get the big air holes.

Or, to use a food mixer: fit the dough hook and add the sponge, flour and salt. Mix on low speed until combined, then add the oil and knead for about 10 minutes.

When your dough is smooth and satiny, shape it into a nice tight round (see p.48) and place in a bowl. Cover and leave somewhere warm for about an hour.

Now lightly flour the dough, tip it out on to the work surface and press it out flat with your fingertips. Shape into a round again, put it back in its bowl, cover and leave in a warm place for another hour. Do this twice more. You will see and feel the dough becoming smoother, shinier and more airy.

(continued overleaf)

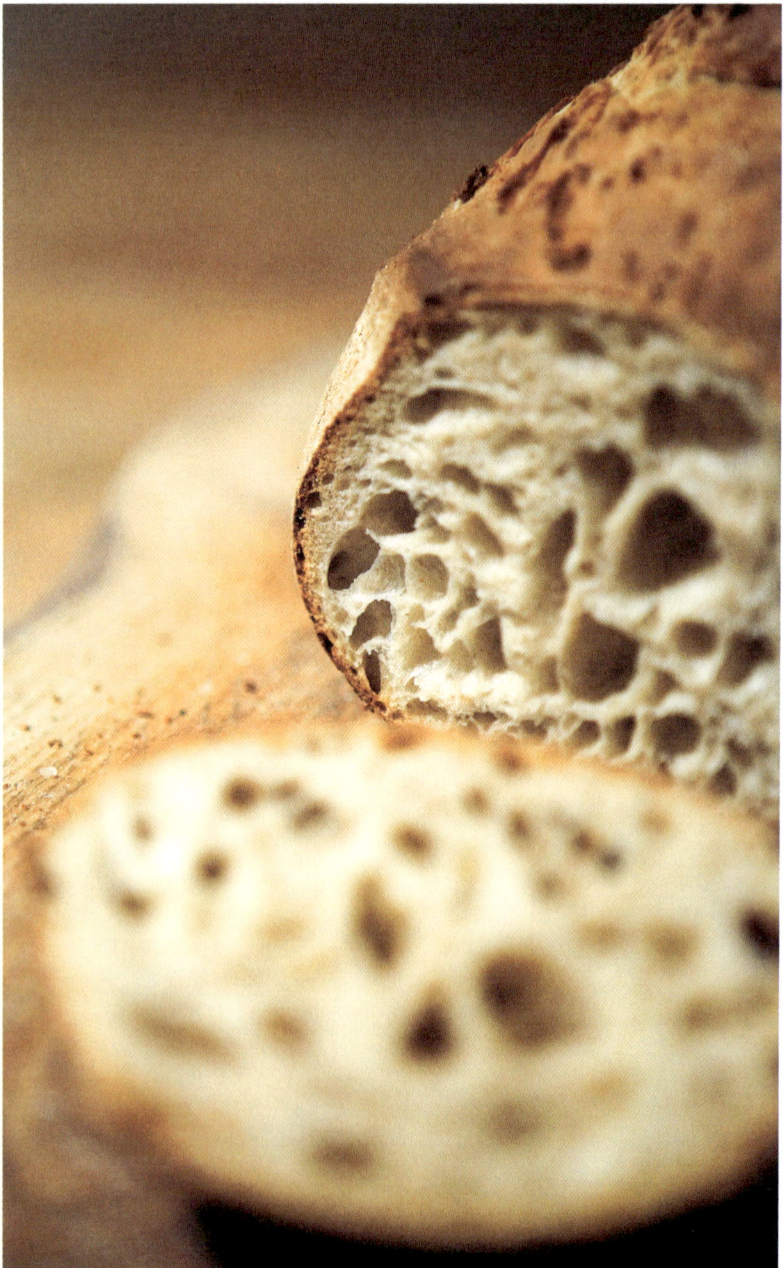

After these 4 hours of rising and deflating, the dough will feel soft and puffy, like an angel's pillow. Sink your hands in and deflate it once more. Divide into two or three and shape into loaves (see pp.55–9). Coat with the rye flour and transfer to well-floured wooden boards, linen cloths, tea towels or proving baskets.

Lay a plastic bag over the whole batch, to stop it drying out, and leave to prove for 2–3 hours or until doubled in size; you will probably notice big air holes developing near the surface. Unlike with other breads, you should err on the side of over-proving; the loaves may end up a little misshapen, but the air holes will be bigger.

When the loaves are almost ready, switch the oven to 250°C/Gas Mark 10 or its highest setting, put a baking stone or a heavy baking tray inside, and place a roasting tin on the bottom shelf. Put the kettle on. Have a water spray bottle, a serrated knife and an oven cloth ready, as well as a peel or rimless baking sheet, if you are using a baking stone. Clear the area around the oven.

When the loaves are ready, either transfer them to the hot tray (removed from the oven), or one at a time to the peel. Slash the tops with the serrated knife. Spray the bread all over with water. Put the tray into the oven, or slide each loaf on to the baking stone, pour some boiling water into the roasting tin and close the door as quickly as you can.

Turn the heat down after about 10 minutes to 200°C/Gas Mark 6 if the crust is still very pale; 180°C/Gas Mark 4 if the crust is noticeably browning; or 170°C/Gas Mark 3 if the crust seems to be browning quickly. Bake until the loaves are well browned and crusty, and feel hollow when you tap them: in total allow 30–40 minutes for small loaves; 40–50 minutes for large loaves. If in doubt, bake for a few minutes longer. Leave to cool on a wire rack.

Sour rye bread

Rye makes dense, heavy bread, as it has very few gluten-forming proteins. It is very tasty, though, and well worth making. You could replace some of the flour (perhaps 250g) with strong white bread flour to lighten it if you like, but I love the full flavour of pure rye and as long as it is sliced thinly, its texture is a pleasure, not a chore. Kneading it is somewhat less satisfying than with high-gluten doughs, in that it doesn't become stretchy, or resilient, or silky. In fact, it doesn't seem to change much at all. This means less work for you, though; 5 minutes should be quite enough. I also suggest shaping the loaves straight away, giving them a single, long rise. Rye bread doesn't seem to benefit from the usual longer process of rising and deflating, which mainly serves to develop the structure of high-gluten breads.

Makes 2–3 loaves

1.1kg dark rye flour, plus extra for dusting
25g salt
600ml warm water
A ladleful of sourdough starter (see p.110)
A good slug of sunflower oil (optional)

Combine the rye flour, salt, water and starter in a large bowl and mix to a dough, adding more flour or water if needed, to make a soft, easily kneadable dough. Mix in the oil, if using. Turn the dough out on to a clean worktop and knead for about 5 minutes; you'll probably need extra flour as it will be quite sticky. Divide the dough into two or three, shape into loaves (see pp.55–9) and dust well with flour.

Leave to rise somewhere fairly warm, covered, ideally in well-floured proving baskets. You can use linen cloths or wooden boards, but as it is so low in gluten, unsupported rye bread tends to spread outwards rather than upwards, giving you flat loaves. Loaf tins would give higher, though less attractive loaves. Your dough needs to double in size, which can take anywhere from 1–4 hours, depending on the temperature of the dough and vigour of your starter. When almost ready, place your baking stone or tray in the oven and preheat the oven to 250°C/Gas Mark 10, or as hot as it will go.

When ready to bake, turn your loaves, one at a time, on to a peel and slide them on to the baking stone in the oven or remove the tray, turn the loaves on to it and return to the oven. There is no need to slash rye bread. It will hardly rise, so slashes would barely open up anyway, and it is likely to crack attractively in the oven, especially if it has been well floured. Bake at the high temperature for about 10 minutes, then lower the heat to 180°C/Gas Mark 4 and bake for a further 20–30 minutes. Cool on a wire rack.

BREAD MADE WITH WILD YEAST

Spelt sourdough

Enriched with hemp seeds, this sourdough is deeply flavoured, savoury and nutty. As with any bread made with spelt, a little extra kneading and some proving baskets to hold the shape of the loaves work wonders. I love to eat this bread with hearty winter soups.

Makes 2–3 loaves

For the sponge
500g spelt flour
600ml warm water
A ladleful of sourdough starter
  (see p.110)

For the dough
50g hemp seeds
600g spelt flour, plus extra for dusting
25g salt
A good slug of hemp oil

Before you go to bed, beat all the sponge ingredients together in a large bowl, cover and leave somewhere fairly warm overnight.

In the morning, toast the hemp seeds in a dry frying pan over a medium heat, tossing them often, for about 2 minutes until they smell strong and nutty. Grind them, using a pestle and mortar if you have one; otherwise use a spice grinder or small blender. I like to leave them quite coarse, for a bit of texture. Add the seeds to the sponge with the flour and salt, mix to a dough, then incorporate the oil. Use more water or flour as necessary to give a kneadable dough.

Turn the dough out on to a clean work surface and knead for about 10 minutes, until smooth and springy. Form the dough into a tight round (see p.48), flour it all over and place in a clean bowl. Cover with a plastic bag and leave to rise. After an hour, tip it out on to your work surface (it may not have risen much at this point). Form it into a tight round again, return to the bowl, cover and leave to rise for another hour. Repeat this process once, or even twice more – you will notice the dough becoming increasingly airy.

After the final rising period, tip the dough out and deflate it by pressing all over with your hands. Divide into two or three, and shape into loaves (see pp.55–9). Coat with flour, then transfer to well-floured wooden boards, linen cloths, tea towels or proving baskets. Lay a plastic bag over the whole batch, to stop it drying out, and leave to prove until almost doubled in size; this could be anywhere from 1–4 hours, depending on the temperature of the dough and the vigour of your starter.

When the loaves are almost ready, switch the oven to 250°C/Gas Mark 10 or its highest setting, put a baking stone or a heavy baking tray inside, and place a roasting tin on the bottom shelf. Put the kettle on. Have a water spray bottle, a serrated knife and an oven cloth ready, as well as a peel or rimless baking sheet, if you are using a baking stone. Clear the area around the oven.

When the loaves are ready, either transfer them to the hot tray (removed from the oven), or one at a time to the peel. Slash the tops with the serrated knife. Spray the bread all over with water. Put the tray into the oven, or slide each loaf on to the baking stone, pour some boiling water into the roasting tin and close the door as quickly as you can.

Turn the heat down after about 10 minutes to 200°C/Gas Mark 6 if the crust is still very pale; 180°C/Gas Mark 4 if the crust is noticeably browning; or 170°C/Gas Mark 3 if the crust seems to be browning quickly. Bake until the loaves are well browned and crusty, and feel hollow when you tap them: in total allow 30–40 minutes for small loaves; 40–50 minutes for large loaves. If in doubt, bake for a few minutes longer. Leave to cool on a wire rack.

Pumpernickel

Pumpernickel originated in the Westphalia region of Germany, invented by bakers as a way of making the most of the residual heat of their wood-fired ovens once the usual bread had been baked. The recipe includes rye or wheat berries, which you can buy in many health food shops. Please make this once, at least, just for the experience. It is a drawn-out affair, to say the least (two and a half days from start to finish), but each stage is very simple.

Use a medium cast-iron (Le Creuset-type) casserole dish with lid, or something similar, for baking this bread. Alternatively, you could use a couple of loaf tins.

Makes 1 loaf

For the soaker
200g rye bread, or other brown bread, sliced (stale is fine)
200g rye berries (or wheat berries)
Enough water to cover

For the sponge
300g rye flour
300ml warm water
About 1 tbsp sourdough starter (see p.110)

For the dough
300ml warm water (use the water from the soaker)
250g rye flour
250g rye flakes
20g salt
50g blackstrap molasses
A little oil

The evening before baking, make the soaker: preheat the oven to 200°C/Gas Mark 6 and lay the slices of bread on a baking tray. Bake until they are brown all the way through to the middle – snap one in half to check. Go as dark as you dare without burning. When you are happy, place the bread in a bowl with the rye berries and cover with cold water. Press the bread down every now and then to get it nice and soggy. In a separate bowl, make the sponge: beat together the flour, water and starter until smooth. Cover and leave both, at room temperature, until the morning.

The next morning, strain the soaker in a sieve set over a bowl, squeezing the bread out and reserving the liquid. Measure 300ml of this liquid (or make it up to 300ml with water if you don't have enough). Heat in a pan until tepid, then pour into a large mixing bowl and add the bread and rye berries, the sponge, rye flour, rye flakes, salt and molasses. Mix, stickily, until it all comes together. Oil your baking container(s), then scoop the mixture in, filling no more than half-full. Cover with a plastic bag (or lid) and leave to double in size – this could take up to 4 hours.

When you are nearly ready to bake, cover tightly with a double layer of foil (if your container doesn't have a lid). Preheat the oven to 200°C/Gas Mark 6. Place the tins on the middle shelf and bake for an hour. Turn the oven down to 190°C/Gas Mark 5 and bake for another 30 minutes, then at 180°C/Gas Mark 4 and 170°C/Gas Mark 3 for 30 minutes each. Finally, bake at 150°C/Gas Mark 2 for 3 hours, then switch the oven off and leave the pumpernickel inside until morning.

If you are baking your pumpernickel in a clay oven, put the tins in when it is nice and hot, seal the door and chimney up, and leave to bake until morning.

The morning after, remove the almost-black breads from the tins (they may be quite well stuck – running a knife around the sides will help), wrap them in greaseproof paper and leave to mature at room temperature for a day before eating. Delicious with cheese, cold meats and smoked fish.

Bread Made without Yeast

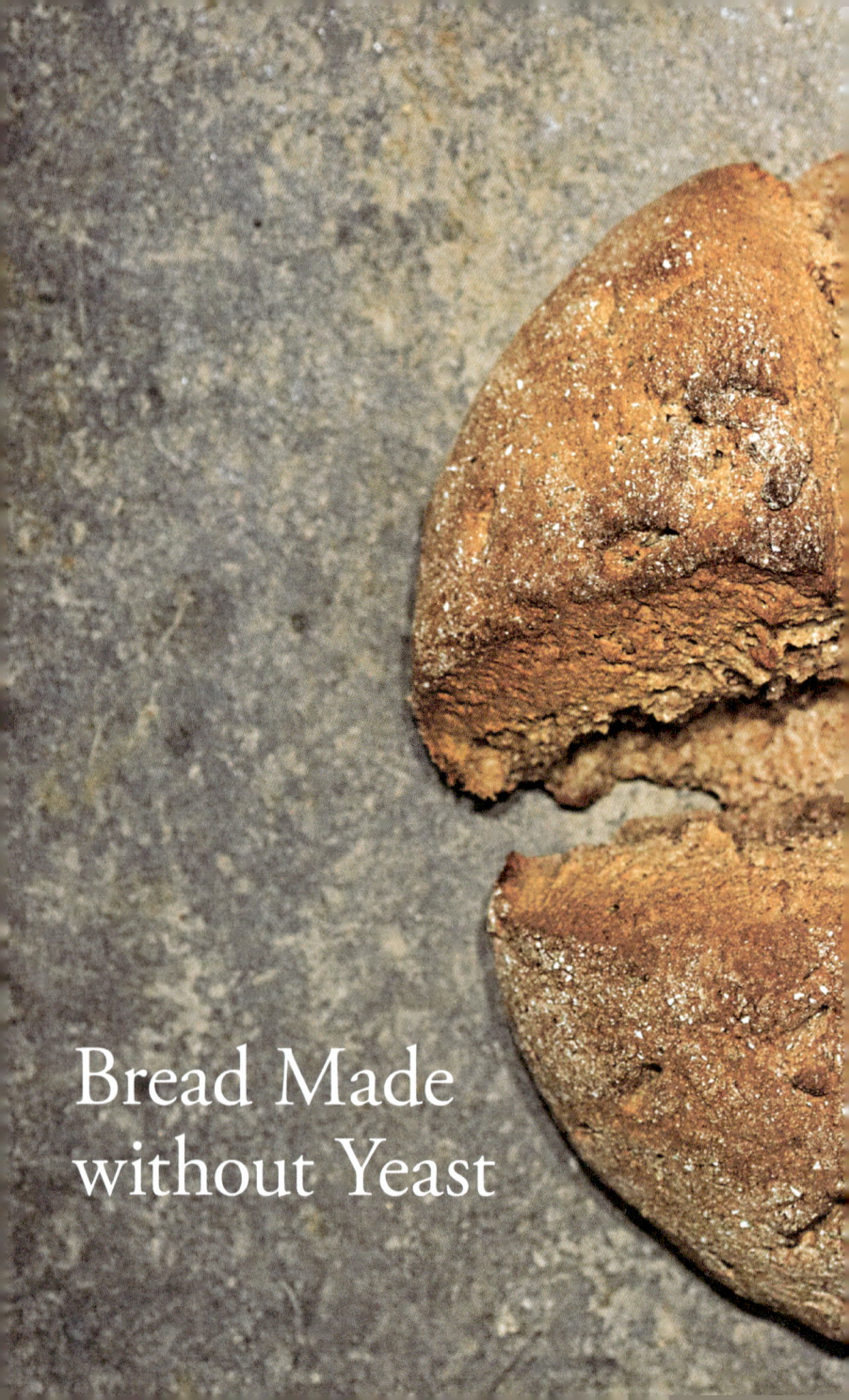

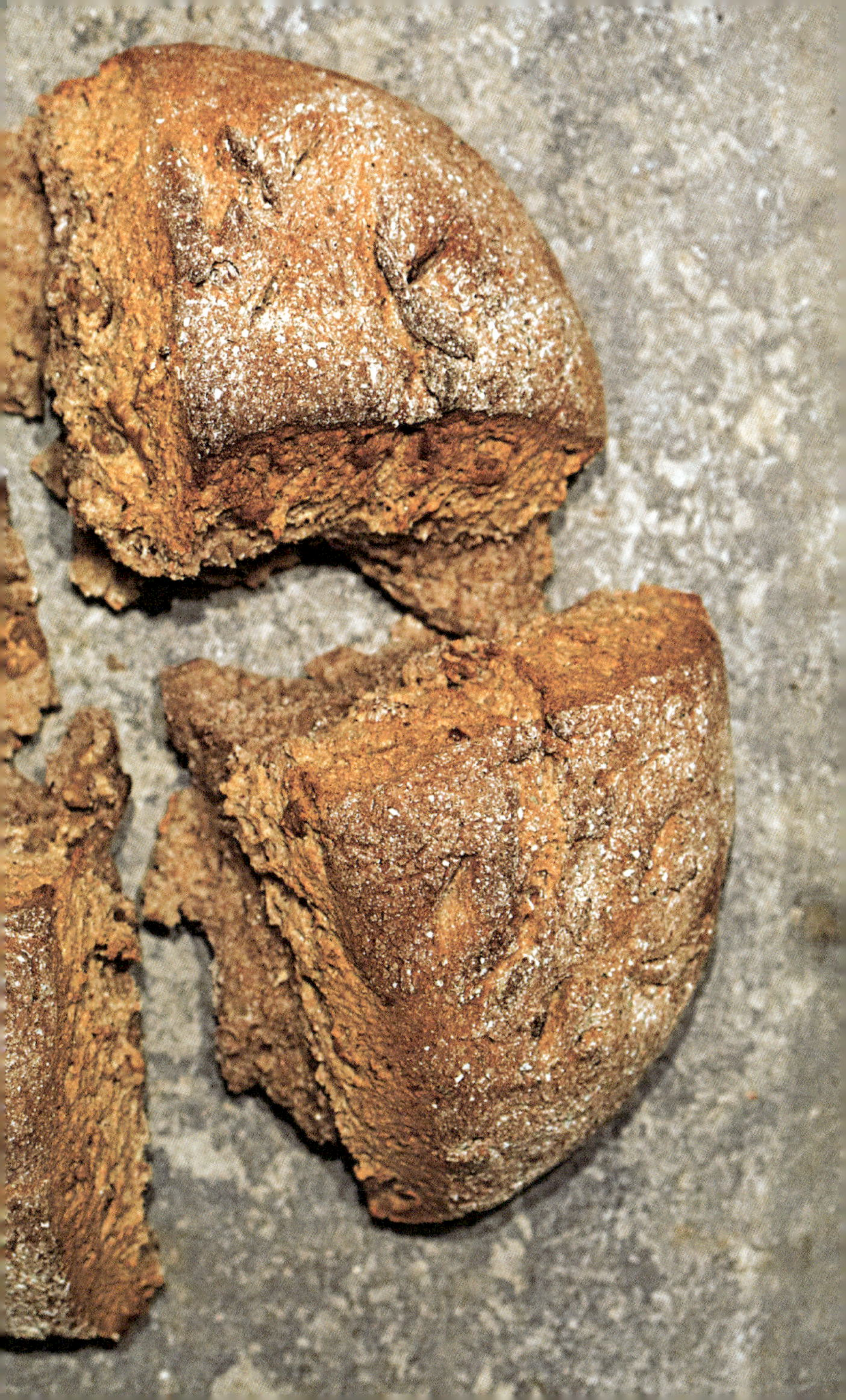

If time is tight, or it's lunchtime and you've forgotten to go shopping, then this is the chapter for you. Yeast-free breads are much easier and far less demanding of your time than the yeasted kind. For most of these recipes, you simply mix everything together and cook it.

There are also a few flat breads in here. These are unleavened, meaning they contain no raising agent at all. However, roti, the staple bread of southern Asia, still manage to puff up impressively all by themselves.

As you become confident with these recipes, you can adapt them to suit yourself – adding a few herbs, spices or some dried fruit perhaps. If there was ever a good place to spread your floury wings, it is here. These are such simple, basic breads that before long, making them – and your own variations – will become second nature.

Bread made without yeast

- Soda bread (p.130)
- Walnut and honey bread (p.131)
- Roti (p.133)
- Tortillas (p.134)
- Bannocks (p.137)

Reminder: Oven timings in the recipes relate to fan-assisted ovens. If using a conventional electric or gas oven (without a fan), increase the temperature by 15°C (1 Gas Mark). Use an oven thermometer to check the accuracy of your oven.

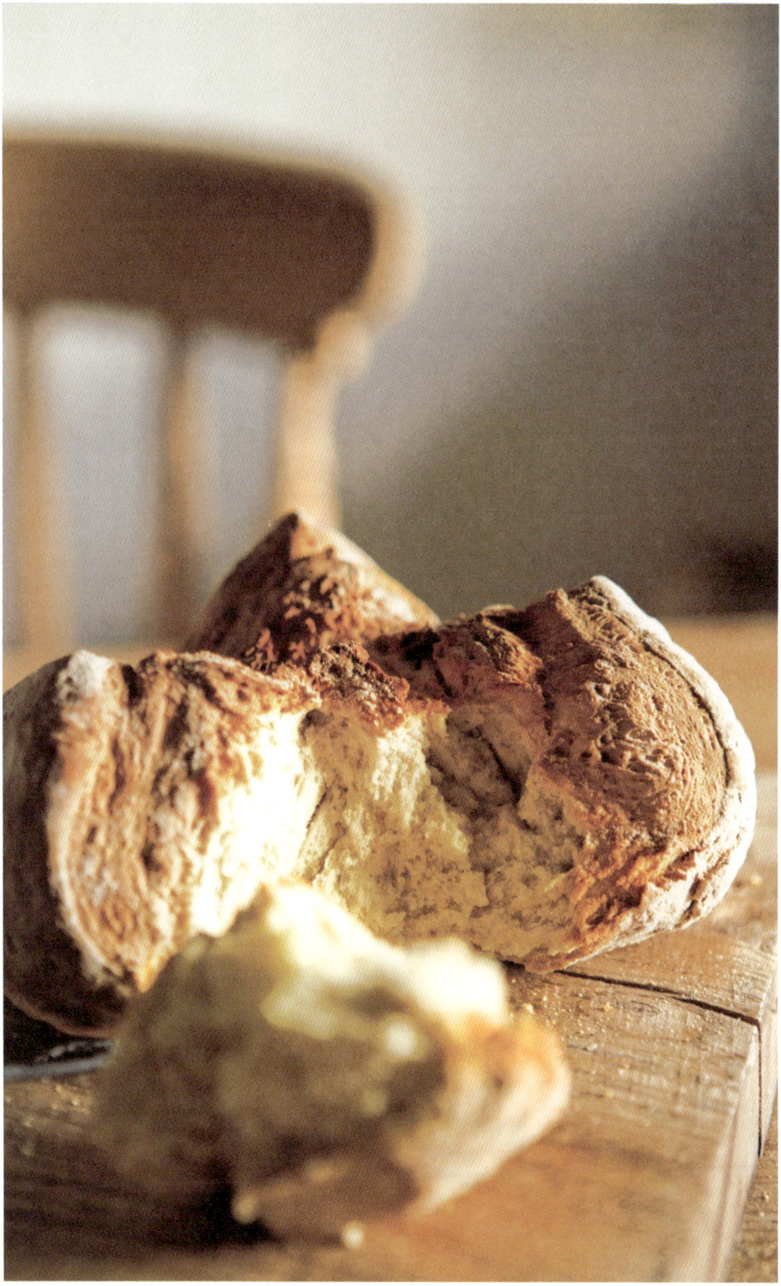

Soda bread

Soda bread is so easy to make. No kneading, no proving – just mix the ingredients together, shape into rough rounds and throw in the oven. Buttermilk is relatively easy to buy, but you can also make this bread with thin yoghurt, milk or water, or any combination of these.

Makes 2 loaves
500g plain white flour, plus extra
   for dusting
10g salt
4 tsp baking powder
300ml buttermilk, thin yoghurt,
   milk or water

For coating
A little flour (rye would be good)

Preheat the oven to 200°C/Gas Mark 6. Combine the dry ingredients in a bowl and mix in the buttermilk or other liquid to make a dough.

Knead briefly, divide into two, then shape into rough rounds. Pat to flatten until about 5cm high, flour the loaves all over and place on a baking tray. Now cut a cross in the top of each loaf, almost through to the bottom, then stab lightly all over.

Bake for 20–25 minutes or until the bread sounds hollow when tapped on the base, then allow to cool for a few minutes on a wire rack. Best eaten warm, with butter.

P.S. If you have time, try making your own buttermilk, which will also give you fresh butter to spread on your bread. Cream will eventually turn to butter when beaten, but it takes a while. Using a food mixer, beat 1 litre double cream until it thickens, then stiffens, then eventually (and very suddenly) separates. When it does, pour it through a fine sieve into a bowl. The liquid in the bowl is buttermilk. The residue in the sieve is butter. Squeeze and squidge the butter together, then hold it under cold running water and squeeze it a bit more to rinse off any buttermilk.

Variation
To make brown soda bread, replace the white flour with wholemeal and add a good tablespoonful of black treacle. This makes a sweeter, slightly heavier bread – excellent with a pint of Guinness and an Irish stew.

Walnut and honey bread

This is a lovely flavoured soda bread to serve with cheese. To vary the flavour, you could replace the honey with the same quantity of dried fruit (dates are excellent), and replace half the water with apple juice.

Makes 2 loaves

200g honey
200g walnuts
500g plain wholemeal flour,
  plus extra for dusting
10g salt
4 tsp baking powder
300ml water

Preheat the oven to 200°C/Gas Mark 6. Soften the honey in a pan over a gentle heat. Using a pestle and mortar, crush half of the walnuts very finely, almost to a powder. Crush the other half very coarsely. This gives the ideal combination – lots of flavour from the crushed nuts, and texture from the large pieces.

Combine the flour, salt, baking powder and walnuts in a bowl. Add the honey and water, and mix together until evenly combined. Knead briefly to a firm dough.

Divide the dough in two and shape into rough rounds. Flatten to about 5cm high and cut a deep cross in each, almost through to the base. Bake for 20–25 minutes or until the bread sounds hollow when tapped on the base.

Allow the bread to cool a little on a wire rack. If you're wondering what to have it with, a lump of Stilton and a ripe juicy pear would be perfect.

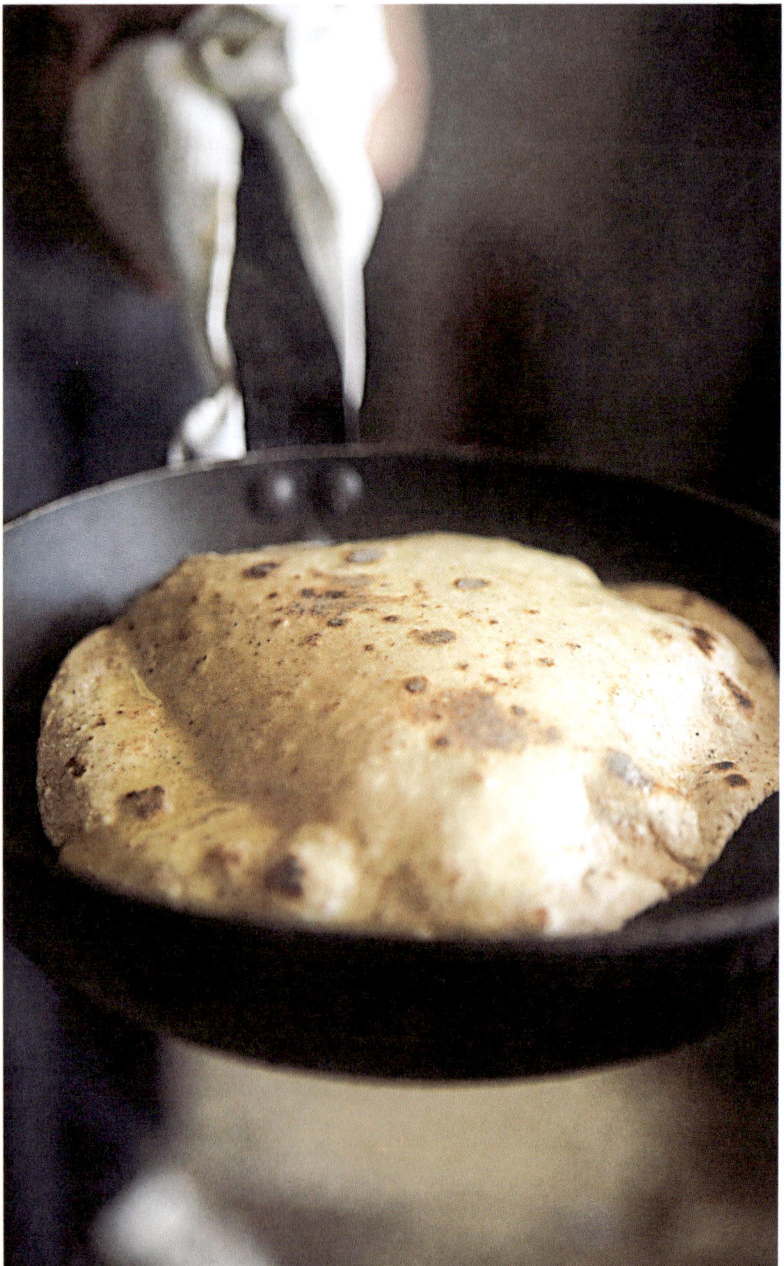

Roti

This is daily bread in India and Nepal, perfect for scooping up stews and curries, and lentils. Once you've grasped the method you will make roti all the time – it is so easy, and the way the bread balloons in the pan will delight and amaze you. If you use wholemeal flour, as I often do, sieve it to remove the coarser bits; your roti will puff up better.

Makes 6
100g strong brown or wholemeal flour, plus extra for dusting
A small pinch of salt
60ml water
A large knob of butter, melted

Mix the flour, salt and water together in a bowl and knead between your hands for a couple of minutes until smooth. Divide the dough into six and roll into balls, as round as you can. Place a heavy-based frying pan over a medium heat. Using plenty of flour, roll each ball out to a thin circle, about 15cm across.

When the pan is hot, lay the first roti in. After about half a minute, you should see a few bubbles. Flip the roti over – it should be slightly browned, with the odd dark spot. Cook the other side for another 30 seconds; the bubbles should get bigger. Flip again, and the whole thing should puff up. I say should – about one in three of mine don't quite make it. Turn a couple more times, if you want a bit more colour, then remove and brush with melted butter.

Keep the roti warm, wrapped in a tea towel, while you cook the rest. Serve as soon as they are all ready.

Tortillas

Perfect for wrapping around any food you like for a portable lunch, tortillas are quick and easy to make. This Mexican flatbread was so called by the Spanish conquistadors because it reminded them of the classic omelettes from their homeland. If your tortilla reminds you of an omelette, throw it away and start again… it has gone badly wrong.

Makes 8
250g plain white flour, plus extra for dusting
5g salt
150ml water

Mix the ingredients together in a bowl to form a rough dough. Knead for a few minutes, until the dough is smooth and no longer sticky. Cover and leave to rest for about half an hour; this relaxes the gluten and makes the dough easier to roll out.

Divide the dough into eight and shape each piece into a round. Lightly flour the work surface and roll the rounds out thinly – to a 2–3mm thickness. Place a large frying pan over a medium heat, and have ready a clean tea towel.

When the pan is hot, lay a tortilla in it and cook for half a minute or so, until the underside is patched with dark brown. Flip over and cook for another 30 seconds, then wrap it in the tea towel while you cook the next one. Keep adding the tortillas to the tea towel as you cook them – this holds the steam in as they cool, and keeps them soft.

If you are not planning on eating the tortillas straight away, wrap them in foil to stop them drying out. When ready to serve, reheat in a low oven at 140°C/Gas Mark 1, still wrapped in foil, until just warm.

Variation

Corn tortillas are made in the same way – just substitute cornmeal (maize meal) for wheat flour. To turn corn tortillas into nachos, cut them into wedges. Heat some oil for deep-frying in a suitable pan to 175°C (the temperature at which a cube of bread will turn golden brown in a minute). Deep-fry the nachos for up to a minute, until crispy. Drain on kitchen paper and serve with a dip or two, such as beetroot houmous (see p.178) or taramasalata (see p.179).

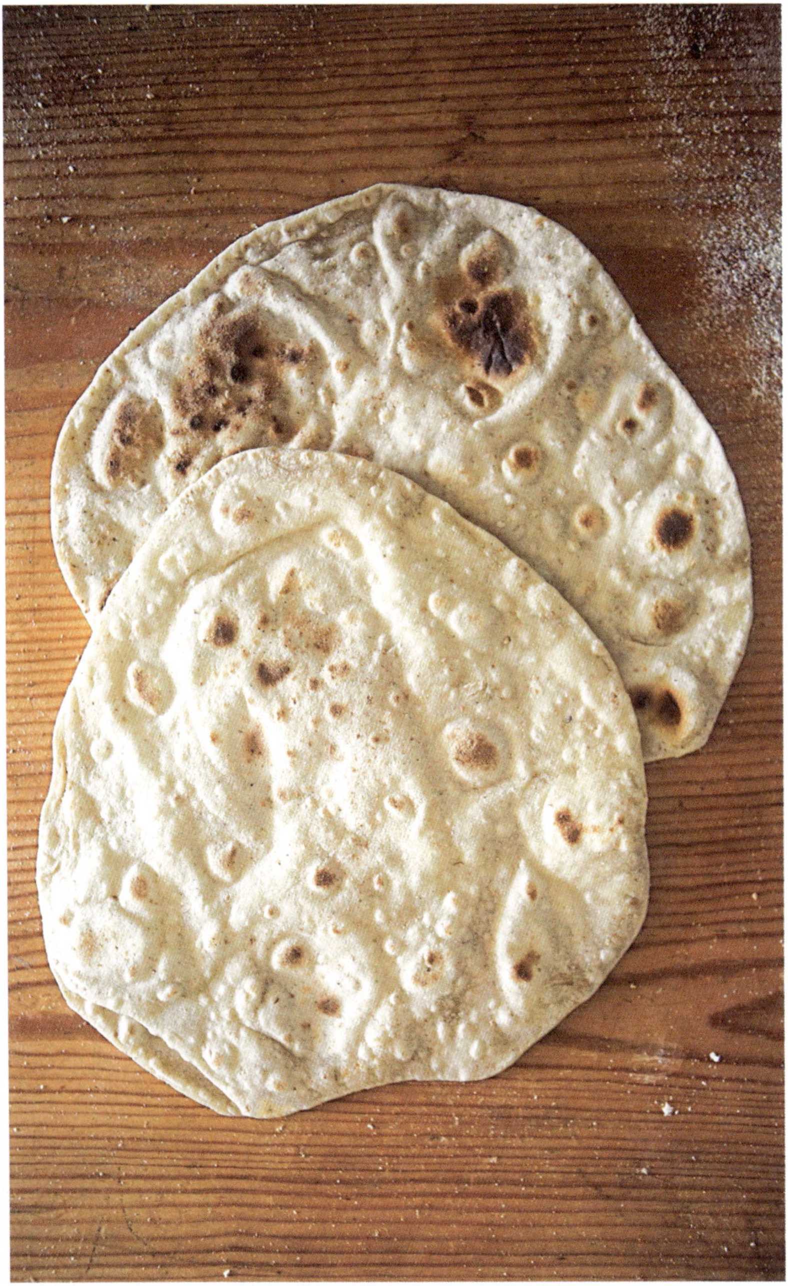

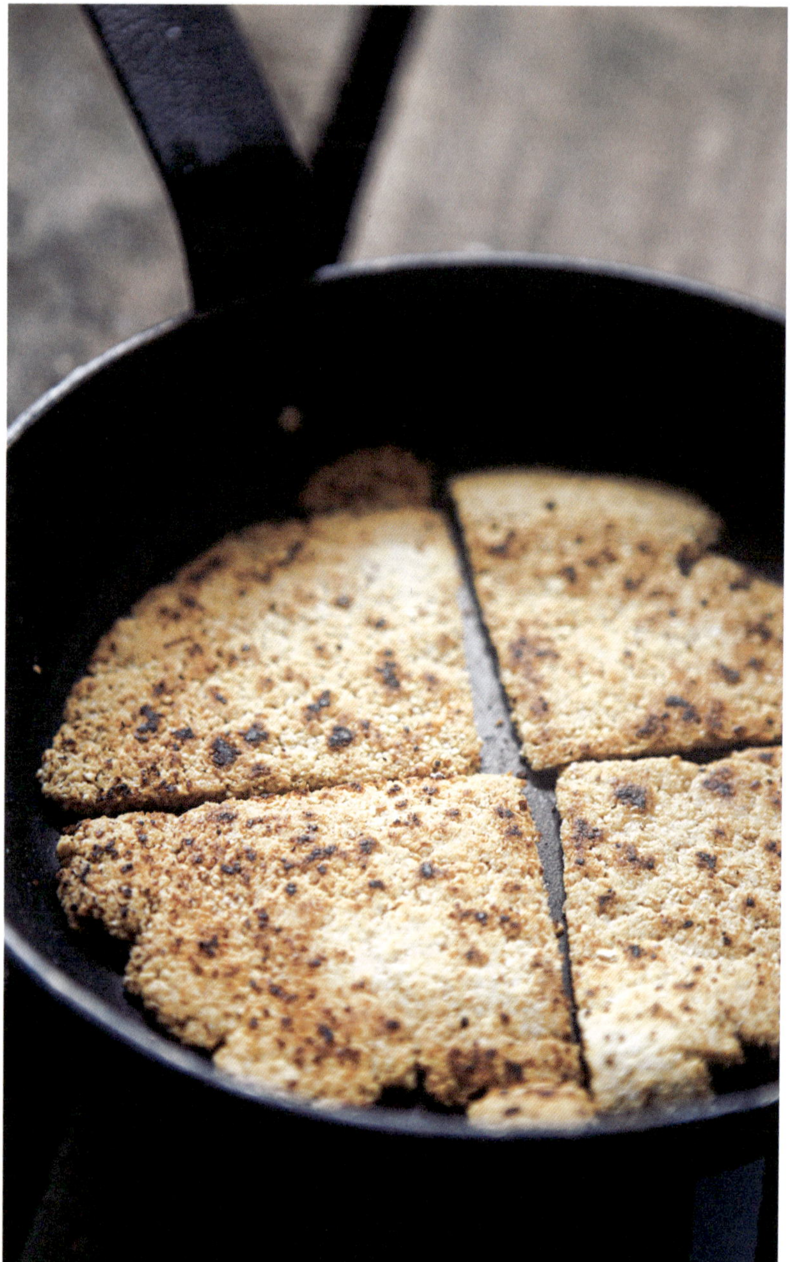

Bannocks

This Scottish, oaty, frying-pan bread should be made fast and eaten warm. You can store bannocks and reheat them later, but they are better served straight away. I love to eat them in winter, with butter and thick soup. Have the rest of your lunch ready and make the bannocks at the last minute.

Makes 2

125g medium oatmeal, plus extra
   for dusting
A small pinch of salt
A slightly bigger pinch of
   baking powder
About 2 tsp melted bacon fat (or lard,
   butter or oil), plus a little extra for
   greasing the pan
3–4 tbsp hot water

Mix the oatmeal, salt and baking powder together in a bowl and pour in the melted fat, along with enough water to mix to a stiff paste. Place a heavy-based frying pan over a medium heat.

Dust your work surface with oatmeal and scrape the mixture on to it. Sprinkle with more oatmeal and divide the dough in two. Roll each out to a round, a little less than ½cm thick. You'll need to work fast because the dough stiffens as it cools. Cut each round into quarters.

Add a little fat to the hot pan, and cook the bannocks, one at a time (that is four quarters together), for a couple of minutes on each side. Eat warm, with butter.

Buns, Biscuits & Batter Breads

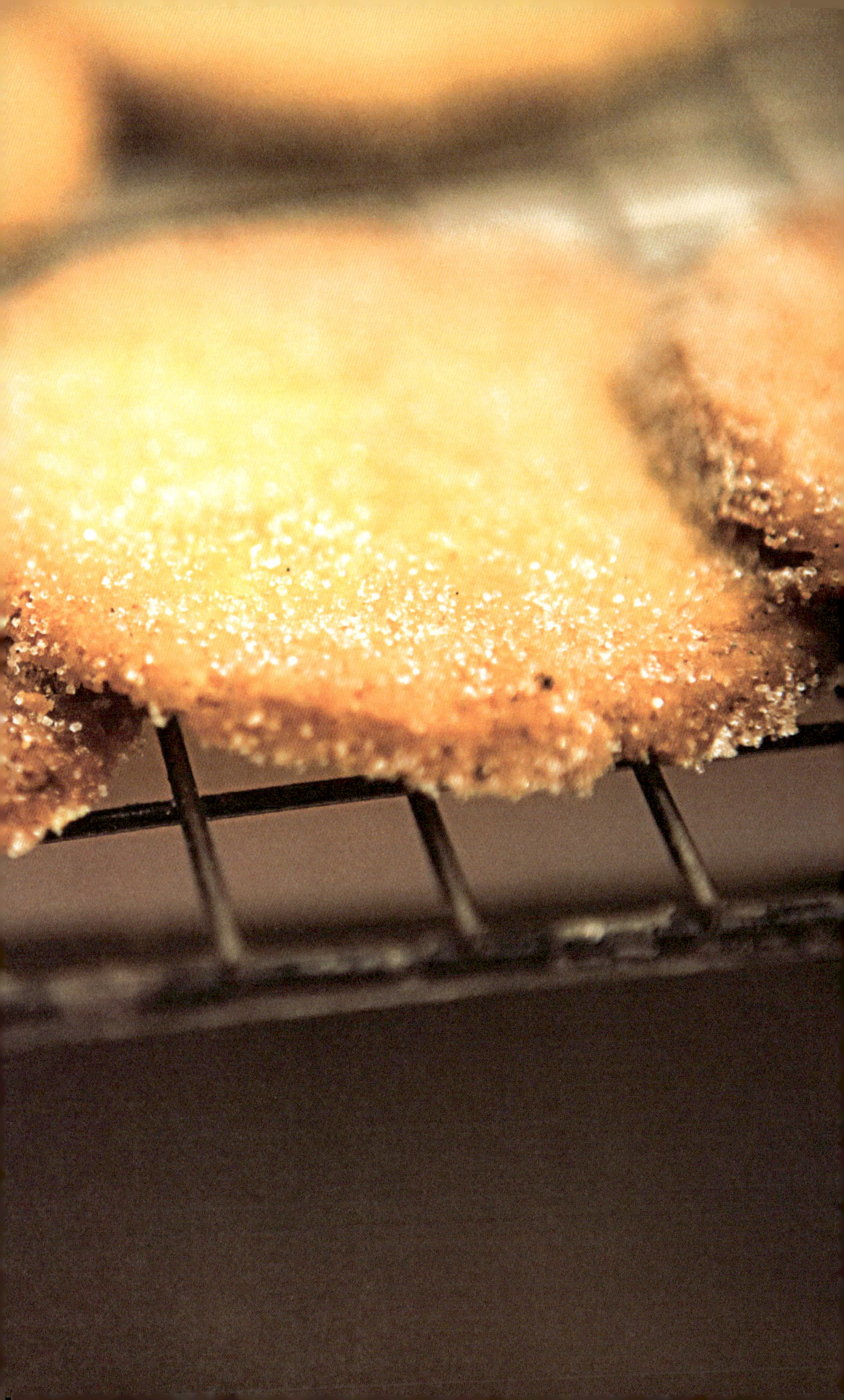

This collection of recipes goes beyond a basic flour-and-water dough, to include enriched doughs and batter breads. I've also been liberal with the definition of 'bread' here by including a few biscuits, which is entirely for your benefit, of course. Guests will be awestruck when you offer handmade oatcakes and spelt digestives with the port and Stilton, rather than 'assorted biscuits for cheese'… with the best ones gone.

Now is the time to try your hand at English teatime classics, such as lardy cake, hot cross buns and Chelsea buns. Enriched with eggs and butter (or lard) and enlivened with fruit and spice, these are truly delicious. And everyone should know the pleasure of a homemade doughnut – still hot and buried in sugar. Doughnuts are made in much the same way as bread rolls, up to the point where you deep-fry them, of course.

Croissants are rather more time-consuming and a little tricky, but perhaps not as difficult as you might think. Get it right, and it may well be the proudest moment of your culinary life. But take my advice – do not make croissants if you are in a really hot kitchen, in a hurry, or in a bad mood. They will not work.

The batter breads, which include crumpets and blinis, are all cooked in a frying pan or on a griddle and are relatively easy to make. There is no kneading, or concern about perfect rising. In truth, you can wow your friends with little skill or precision on your part. Not that I'm suggesting you lack skill or precision, of course… I'm just suggesting you save it for the croissants.

Buns, biscuits & batter breads

- Doughnuts (p.142)
- Churros (p.144)
- Croissants (p.147)
- Lardy cake (p.151)
- Hot cross buns (p.152)
- Chelsea buns (p.154)
- Scones (p.156)
- River Cottage shortbread (p.158)
- Spelt digestives (p.161)
- Poppy and caraway crackers (p.163)
- Scottish oatcakes (p.164)
- Crumpets (p.165)
- Cornbread (p.167)
- Blinis (p.168)
- Staffordshire oatcakes (p.171)
- Socca (p.172)

Reminder: Oven timings in the recipes relate to fan-assisted ovens.
If using a conventional electric or gas oven (without a fan), increase
the temperature by 15°C (1 Gas Mark). Use an oven thermometer to check
the accuracy of your oven.

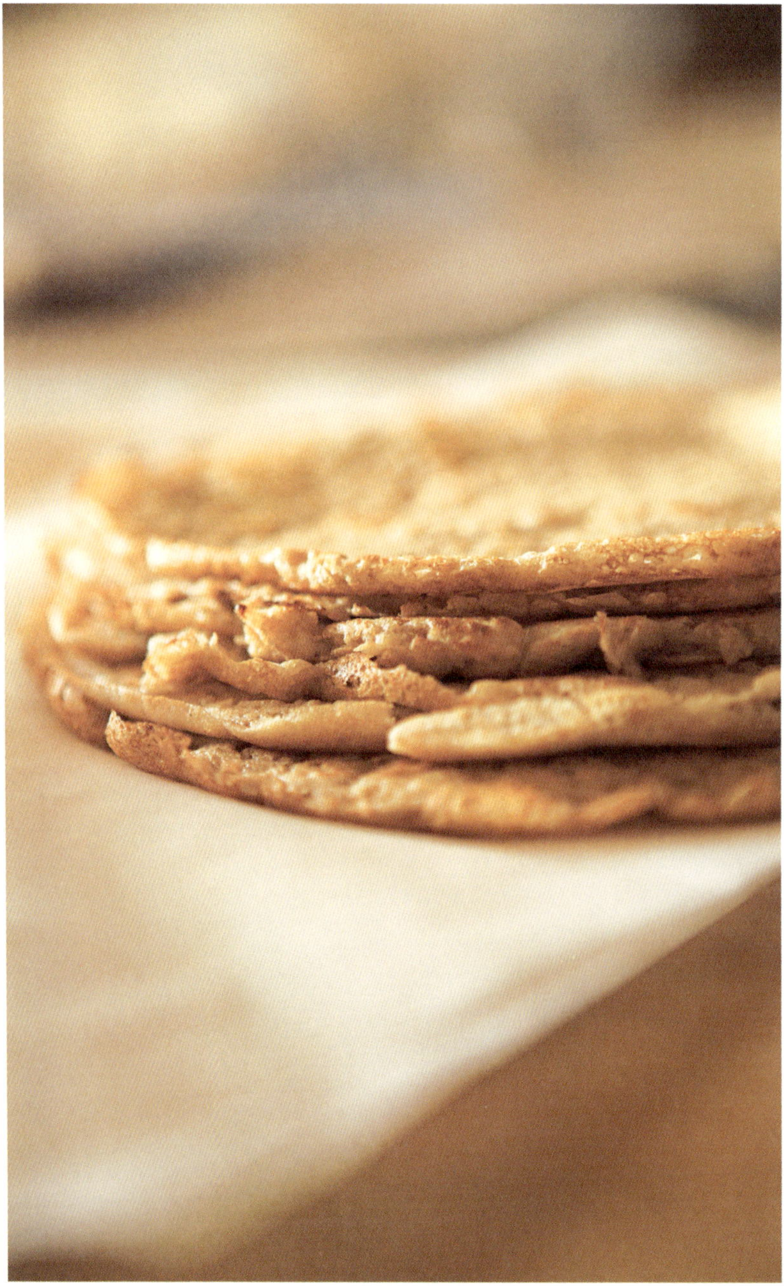

Doughnuts

This method will give you tangerine-sized doughnuts, but you can make them any size you like – simply adjust the frying time accordingly. Little golf-ball-sized doughnuts make a brilliant pudding with something to dip them into – try sieved raspberries and cold custard.

Makes 20

250g strong white bread flour
250g plain white flour
200ml warm milk
100g unsalted butter, softened
100g caster sugar, plus extra for dredging
2 medium free-range eggs
5g powdered dried yeast
10g salt
At least 1 litre sunflower or vegetable oil, for deep-frying

You really need to use a food mixer fitted with a dough hook for this recipe. Mix by hand if you like, but it will be a rather sticky affair. Put the flours, milk, butter, sugar, eggs, yeast and salt into the bowl of the mixer and knead with the dough hook for approximately 10 minutes. Dust the dough with a little flour, turn it out on to a floured surface and shape into a round (see p.48).

Clean and dry the mixing bowl, put the dough back in it and cover with cling film or a plastic bag. Leave to rise until it has doubled in size.

Turn the risen dough out on to the work surface, press out all the air and divide into 20 equal pieces. I find it easiest to weigh them – each piece should be around 50g. Roll them into balls and place on a floured cloth or board. Cover with cling film or a plastic bag and leave to prove until doubled in size.

Heat a 5–8cm depth of oil in a deep, heavy-based saucepan to 175°C; the oil must not fill the pan by more than a third. If you do not have a frying thermometer, check the oil temperature by dropping in a cube of bread; it should turn golden brown in a minute. Deep-fry the dough balls in batches for about 5 minutes, turning them over every now and then so they brown evenly.

Remove the doughnuts from the oil with a slotted spoon and drain well on kitchen paper for half a minute or so. While they are still warm, toss in caster sugar to coat generously. Keep warm while you deep-fry the rest, then enjoy your doughnuts – as soon as possible.

Variations

Add any of the following to the mixer along with the other ingredients:
- Finely grated zest of 1 lemon or orange
- 1 tsp natural vanilla extract (or use vanilla sugar rather than caster sugar)
- 2 tsp ground cinnamon (ideally freshly ground in a spice mill)

You could also flavour the sugar the doughnuts are tossed in with ground cinnamon, ground star anise, or ground mixed spice. Or fill your doughnuts with some runny jam, using a syringe or small piping bag fitted with a thin nozzle.

Churros

Traditionally eaten for breakfast in Spain, churros are deep-fried and tossed in sugar like doughnuts, but they are made with a thick, non-yeast batter rather than a risen dough. Eat them with coffee or dipped in hot chocolate, as the Spanish do.

Serves 4

- 300g plain white flour
- 1 tsp baking powder
- A good pinch of salt
- 375ml boiling water
- At least 1 litre sunflower or vegetable oil, for deep-frying
- Caster sugar, for dredging

Mix the flour, baking powder and salt together in a mixing bowl. Add the boiling water and beat with a wooden spoon until smooth. Transfer to a saucepan and cook gently for a couple of minutes, stirring, until the mixture comes away from the side of the pan. Cover and leave to rest for half an hour.

Heat the oil in a suitable deep, heavy-based saucepan to 175°C; it must be at least 3cm deep, but not fill the pan by more than a third. If you do not have a frying thermometer, check the oil temperature by dropping in a cube of bread; it should turn golden brown in a minute.

Traditionally, the mixture is piped straight into the oil and you can do this if you wish, using a piping bag fitted with a 3cm nozzle. You'll need to deep-fry the churros a few at a time. Carefully pipe lengths (as long as you like), straight into the hot oil. Alternatively, drop tablespoonfuls of the mixture into the oil. Fry, turning every now and then, for 3–4 minutes until golden all over.

Remove the churros with a slotted spoon and drain on kitchen paper, then toss in a bowl of caster sugar. Serve as soon as possible, while still warm.

BUNS, BISCUITS & BATTER BREADS 145

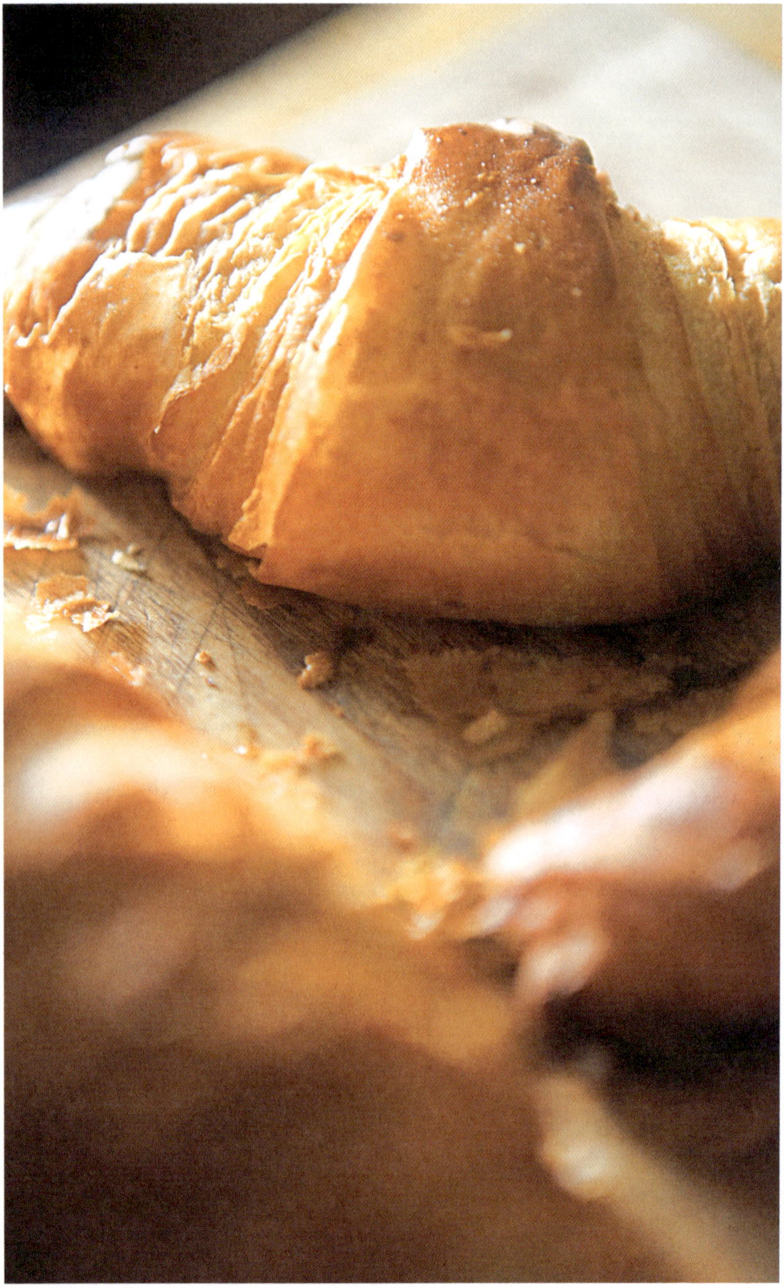

Croissants

I love croissants and everything about them. They take their name, which translates as 'crescent', from their shape of course. It also means growing or rising, which fits nicely because they billow beautifully in the oven.

The technique for making croissants is somewhat similar to puff pastry in that a sheet of butter is sandwiched in the dough, which is repeatedly rolled and folded to produce hundreds of wafer-thin layers. It is best to start the night before, as you need the dough to be cold when you roll it. If too warm and soft, it ruptures easily squeezing out butter everywhere.

Makes about 24–28
**1kg strong white bread flour,
   plus extra for dusting
20g salt
330ml warm water
330ml warm milk
10g powdered dried yeast
140g caster sugar
500g unsalted butter**

**For the glaze
2 medium free-range egg yolks
50ml milk**

It is best to use a food mixer for the first stage as the dough will be soft, sticky and difficult to knead by hand. So, put all the ingredients, except the butter, into the mixer bowl and fit the dough hook. Knead on low to medium speed until the dough is soft, stretchy and satiny – about 10 minutes. Put the dough in a decent-sized polythene bag (it needs room to rise), suck out the air, tie a knot in the bag and put it in the fridge to rest overnight.

First thing in the morning, get the butter out of the fridge. You need it to warm up a bit so it is workable, but not soft. The idea is that the dough and butter have a similar degree of firmness.

As soon as it seems ready, lightly flour the butter, lay it between two sheets of cling film and bat it out with a rolling pin to a fairly neat square about 1cm thick. Take your time to get the thickness and shape as even as possible, then put to one side.

Take your dough out of the fridge, flour it and roll out to a rectangle, a little more than twice the size of the butter (allow a couple of centimetres extra all round). Now lay the butter on one half leaving a border, fold the other half over and press down all the way round to seal the butter in.

(continued overleaf)

1

2

3

4

Next, roll the dough away from you until it is twice its original length, then fold the top and bottom edges in by one-sixth. Fold them in again by another sixth, so the folds meet in the middle, then fold one on top of the other.

Give the dough a quarter-turn and roll it out again to about the same size as before. Fold the top and bottom edges in to meet at the middle, then fold one on top of the other. Roll this out slightly and seal the edges with the rolling pin.

Put the dough back in the plastic bag and return it to the fridge to rest for an hour or so. (You've given the gluten a good workout and it must relax now, otherwise it will be resistant and uncooperative later.)

In the meantime, you need to cut a template from a piece of cardboard (the back of a cereal box or something similar). You want an isosceles triangle, measuring 20cm across the base and 25cm tall. (The easiest way is to draw an upside down capital T and join the points, like a cartoon sail.)

When your dough has rested, unwrap and roll it out to a neat rectangle, a little larger than 140 x 50cm (pic 1). Now trim the rectangle to these measurements, leaving perfectly straight edges. Cut the rectangle in two lengthwise, to give two 25cm wide strips. Now using your template as a guide, cut 12–14 triangles from each strip (pic 2).

Lay each triangle pointing away from you and roll up from the base (pic 3). Wet the pointed end and seal it. Curl the tips around to form a crescent and pinch them together to hold them in place (pic 4); or you can leave them straight if you prefer. (At this point you could freeze some if you like. Space them out on a tray and freeze, then pack into bags. Allow an extra hour for rising when you come to use them.)

Lay your croissants, with the sealed point underneath, on baking trays lined with greased baking parchment or (better still) silicone mats. Cover with cling film or a bin liner and leave to rise until doubled in size. As the dough is cold, this could take a couple of hours, or longer.

When ready to bake, preheat the oven to 200°C/Gas Mark 6. Beat the egg yolk and milk together, then gently brush all over the croissants. Bake for about 10 minutes, then lower the setting to 170°C/Gas Mark 3 and bake for a further 5–10 minutes until they look beautifully golden. Transfer to a wire rack and let cool slightly, while you make coffee.

P.S. If your work surface isn't large enough to roll the dough out to a 140 x 50cm rectangle, cut it in half. Roll out one portion at a time to a rectangle a little bigger than 70 x 50cm, then cut into strips as above and cut 6 or 7 triangles from each strip, using your template as a guide.

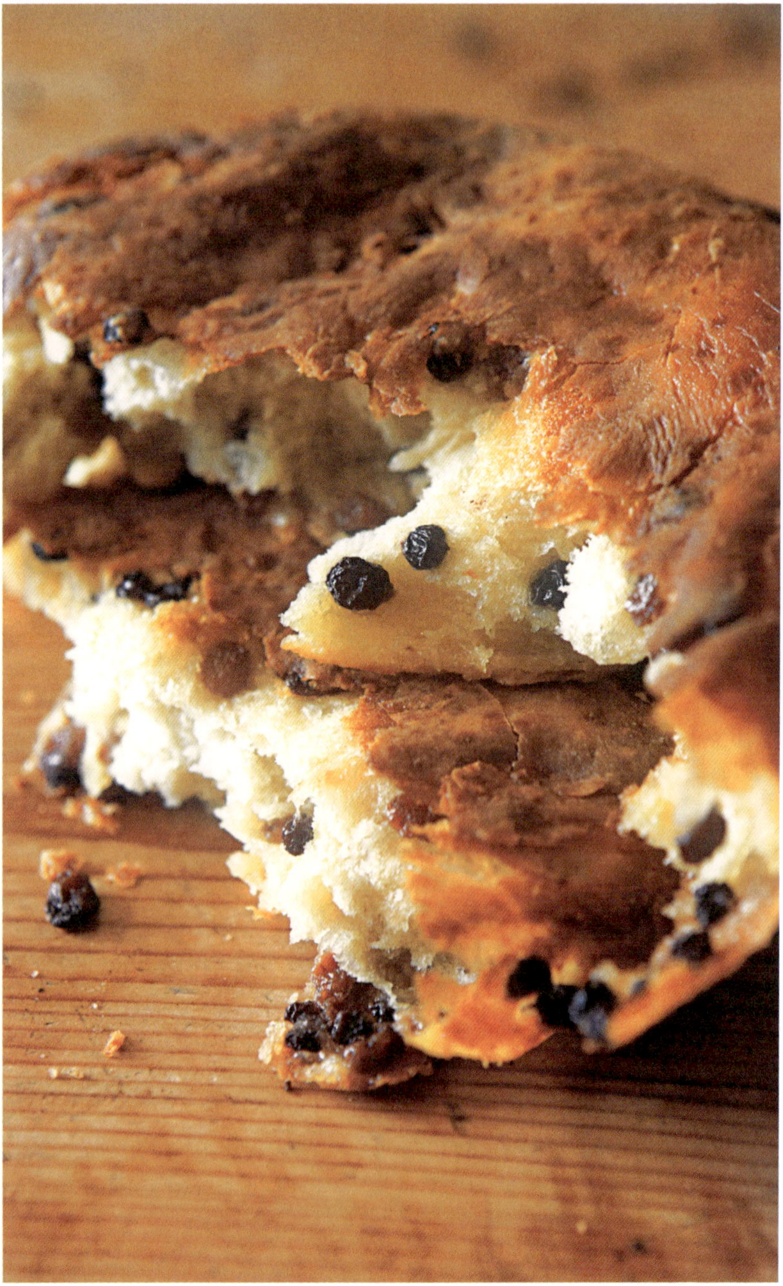

Lardy cake

Apparently, Northumberland lardy cakes are made with milk and currants, while Hampshire lardy cakes have no fruit at all. I have seen Wiltshire lardy cake made with various combinations of dried fruit and spices. Call it what you will, you can be sure of two things: plenty of lard, but no cake – lardy cake is bread. A footnote in Elizabeth David's *English Bread and Yeast Cookery* makes me smile: 'If you can't lay your hands on pure pork lard, don't attempt lardy cakes.' Say no more.

Serves 8

250g strong white bread flour, plus extra for dusting
150ml warm water
5g powdered dried yeast
5g salt
160g lard
50g sultanas
50g currants
50g chopped candied peel
50g caster sugar
1 tsp ground cinnamon (ideally freshly ground in a spice mill)

Put the flour, water, yeast and salt into a bowl and mix to a soft dough. Melt 10g of the lard and incorporate it into the dough, then turn out on to a floured surface and knead until smooth and elastic. Put into a clean bowl, cover and leave to rise until doubled in size.

In a separate bowl, toss the dried fruit and candied peel together with the sugar and cinnamon. Cut the rest of the lard into small dice.

Tip the dough out on to a clean work surface and press all over with your fingertips to deflate. Roll out to a rectangle, about 1cm thick. Scatter over half of the dried fruit mixture and lard pieces, then roll up from a short side to enclose the filling.

Give the dough a quarter-turn and roll it out again to a rectangle, as before. Scatter over the remaining fruit and lard and roll up again. Now roll out the dough to a 20cm square and place in a greased deep 20cm square baking tin. Leave to rise for another 30 minutes.

Preheat the oven to 200°C/Gas Mark 6. Bake the lardy cake for 30–40 minutes until well risen and golden brown. Leave to cool slightly in the tin for 10–15 minutes, then invert on to a wire rack to finish cooling. Placing the lardy cake upside down will allow the melted lard to be reabsorbed into the dough as it cools. Serve warm or cold, cut into slices.

Hot cross buns

Freshly baked or toasted, I love these buns and bake a batch whenever it takes my fancy, leaving off the crosses if it isn't Easter. I also like to vary the dried fruit – a mix of chopped dates, cranberries, apricots and cherries is particularly good.

Makes 8

250g strong white bread flour, plus extra for dusting
250g plain white flour
125ml warm water
125ml warm milk
5g powdered dried yeast
10g salt
50g caster sugar
1 medium free-range egg
50g butter
100g raisins, currants or sultanas (or a mixture)
Finely grated zest of ½ orange
1 tsp ground mixed spice

For the crosses
50g plain white flour
100ml water

To finish
1 tbsp apricot (or other) jam, sieved
1 tbsp water

If you have a food mixer, combine the flours, water, milk, yeast, salt and sugar in the bowl and fit the dough hook. Add the egg and butter and mix to a sticky dough. Now add the dried fruit, orange zest and spice and knead on low speed until silky and smooth. (You can do this by hand, but it will be sticky to handle.) Cover the dough and leave to rise in a warm place for about 1 hour until doubled in size.

Knock back the risen dough and divide into 8 equal pieces. Shape into rounds (see p.48) and dust with flour. Place on a floured board, cover with plastic or linen and leave to prove for about half an hour until roughly doubled in size.

Preheat the oven to 200°C/Gas Mark 6. To make the crosses, whisk together the flour and water until smooth, then transfer to a greaseproof paper piping bag and snip off the end to make a fine hole (or use a plastic food bag with a corner snipped off, as I do). Transfer the risen buns to a baking tray and pipe a cross on top of each one, then bake in the oven for 15–20 minutes.

Meanwhile, melt the jam with the water in a pan. Brush over the buns to glaze as you take them from the oven. Transfer to a wire rack to cool. Serve warm, cold or toasted.

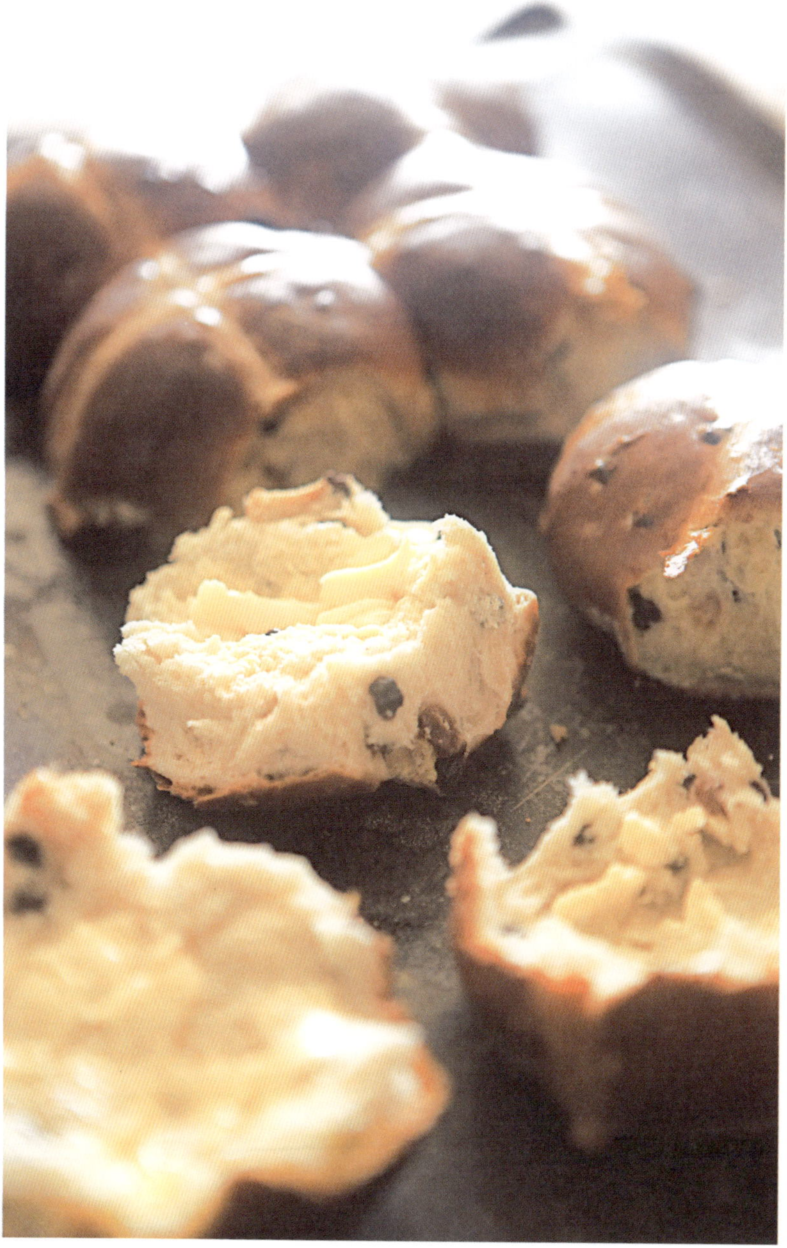

Chelsea buns

According to Mrs Beeton, Chelsea buns are sweet rolls made with dried fruit... similar to hot cross buns but without the cross. However, these are Chelsea buns as we know them – sticky, curranty, swirly and square.

Makes 9

550g strong white bread flour,
  plus extra for dusting
50g caster sugar, or vanilla sugar
5g powdered dried yeast
10g salt
150ml warm milk
225g butter, melted
1 medium free-range egg

For the filling
25g butter, melted
100g caster sugar
200g currants

For the glaze
50ml milk
50g caster sugar

In a bowl, combine the flour, sugar, yeast and salt, then add the milk, butter and egg and mix to a sticky dough. Turn out on to a floured surface and knead until smooth and silky. Return to the cleaned bowl, cover and leave to rise for about an hour until doubled in size.

Brush the base and sides of a deep 30cm square baking tin with a little of the melted butter and coat with a little of the sugar (for the filling), shaking out the excess.

Tip the dough out on to a floured surface, dust with flour and roll out to a rectangle, about 60 x 40cm. Brush the melted butter all over the dough to the edges, leaving a 2cm margin free across the top (long) edge. Sprinkle with the sugar and scatter the currants evenly on top, right to the edges, but leaving the top margin clear.

Press the currants into the dough, then starting from the edge closest to you, roll up the dough to enclose the filling and form a long sausage. Moisten the margin at the top with water and press to seal. Cut the roll into 9 equal pieces. Turn each piece on its end and press with your hand to flatten slightly, until no more than 3cm high. Arrange in rows of three in the baking tin – they should just touch each other.

Preheat the oven to 200°C/Gas Mark 6. Leave the buns to prove for about half an hour until doubled in size again. Sprinkle a little of the sugar for the glaze over them and bake for about 20 minutes until golden brown.

Warm the milk and remaining sugar together in a pan until dissolved, then brush over the buns to glaze when you take them out of the oven. Best served warm.

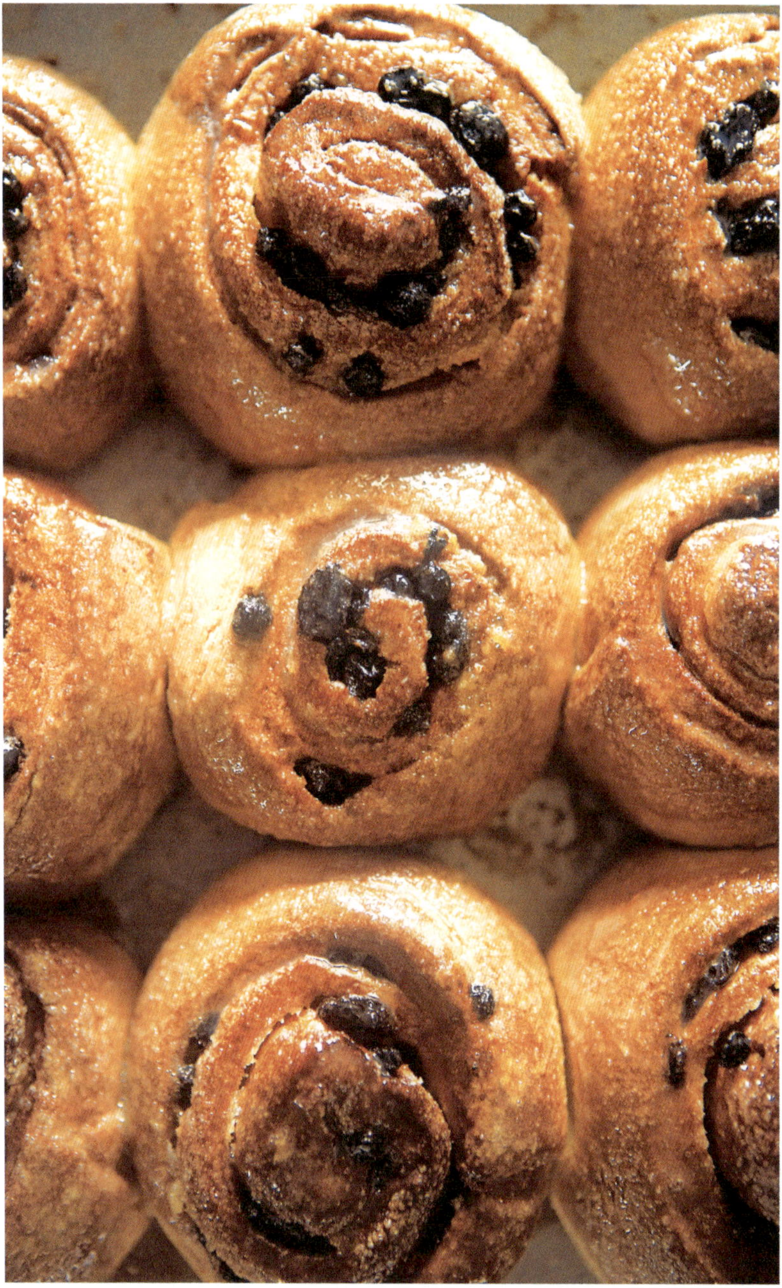

Scones

Of course you can put what you like on your scones, but I'll usually opt for a cream tea. Cream tea etiquette is fiercely disputed in the West Country. The Cornish put strawberry jam on their scones first, then the cream; in Devon and Dorset it is customary to do it the other way round. Personally, I prefer raspberry jam and I always put jam on first… even though I live on the Devon/Dorset border.

Makes about 8

300g plain white flour, plus extra for dusting
2 tsp baking powder
A good pinch of salt
75g unsalted butter, at cool room temperature (neither fridge-cold nor soft), cut into cubes
50g caster sugar
1 medium free-range egg
1 tsp natural vanilla extract
120ml double cream
A little milk, for brushing

Preheat the oven to 200°C/Gas Mark 6. Using a food processor if you have one, whiz together the flour, baking powder, salt, butter and sugar until the mixture resembles fine breadcrumbs. (Otherwise, sift the flour, salt and baking powder into a mixing bowl, rub in the butter with your fingers, then stir in the sugar.)

In a separate bowl, beat the egg, vanilla and cream together, then add to the rubbed-in mixture and bring together with your hands to form a soft dough.

Turn the dough out on to a floured surface and knead very briefly, for 10 seconds or so, to make it a little smoother. Now, using a little more flour, pat or gently roll out to a thickness of about 4cm.

Using a 6 or 7cm pastry cutter (or a larger one, if you like), cut out about 8 scones – pressing the cutter straight down, rather than twisting it, as this gives the scones a better chance of rising straight up.

Lay the discs on a lightly greased baking sheet, brush the tops with milk and bake for about 15 minutes, or a little longer if the scones are large. To check that they are cooked, insert a wooden cocktail stick into the middle; it should come out clean. Transfer to a wire rack to cool for a few minutes, then serve warm.

BUNS, BISCUITS & BATTER BREADS 157

River Cottage shortbread

This is quite different from a traditional thick Scottish shortbread. Rather than rubbing butter into flour then adding sugar in the usual way, we cream the butter with the sugar first as you would for a sponge cake, which makes the mixture really light. We also add egg yolks, and roll the dough out thinly – to make rich, delicate biscuits.

Makes about 24
175g butter, softened
90g caster sugar, plus extra
    for sprinkling
A generous pinch of salt
2 medium free-range egg yolks
200g plain white flour, plus extra
    for dusting

Flavourings (optional)
One (or more) of the following:
    1 tsp natural vanilla extract
    Grated zest of 1 lemon or orange
    1 tsp ground cinnamon (ideally
        freshly ground)

In a food mixer fitted with the paddle beater, or using a hand-held electric beater, cream the butter and sugar together on medium-high speed until very pale (almost white) and fluffy, scraping the sides down regularly with a spatula.

Lower the speed to medium, and add the salt, egg yolks and any extra flavourings at this stage. Beat for another half a minute, then switch the machine off. Fold the flour into the mixture, using a spatula. You will have a very soft sticky dough.

With floured hands, scrape the dough out of the bowl on to a floured surface. Pat it into a wide, flat disc, using more flour if you need to, then wrap in cling film and refrigerate for about 1 hour, as the dough needs to firm up before you can roll it out.

Preheat the oven to 180°C/Gas Mark 4. Unwrap the dough and roll it out on a floured surface to a thickness of about 3mm. Using a 6cm pastry cutter, cut out about 24 rounds. With a palette knife, carefully transfer them to a non-stick baking sheet, or one lined with baking parchment.

Bake for 7–10 minutes, until just golden around the edges, but pale on top, checking every minute after 7 minutes. The shortbread biscuits will still be soft; they firm up on cooling. As you remove them from the oven, sprinkle generously all over with caster sugar. Leave on the baking sheet for a minute or two, then carefully transfer to a wire rack to cool.

P.S. These delicate biscuits will keep for a couple of days in an airtight container.

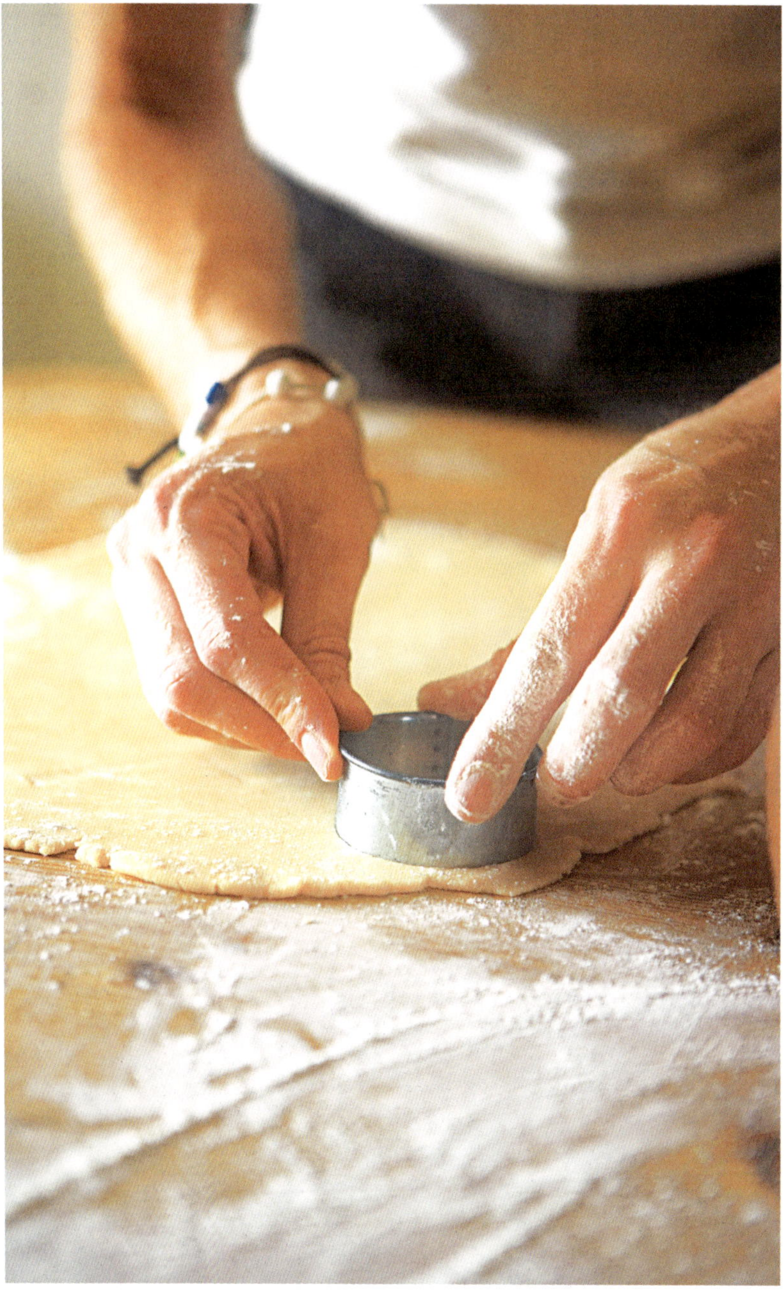

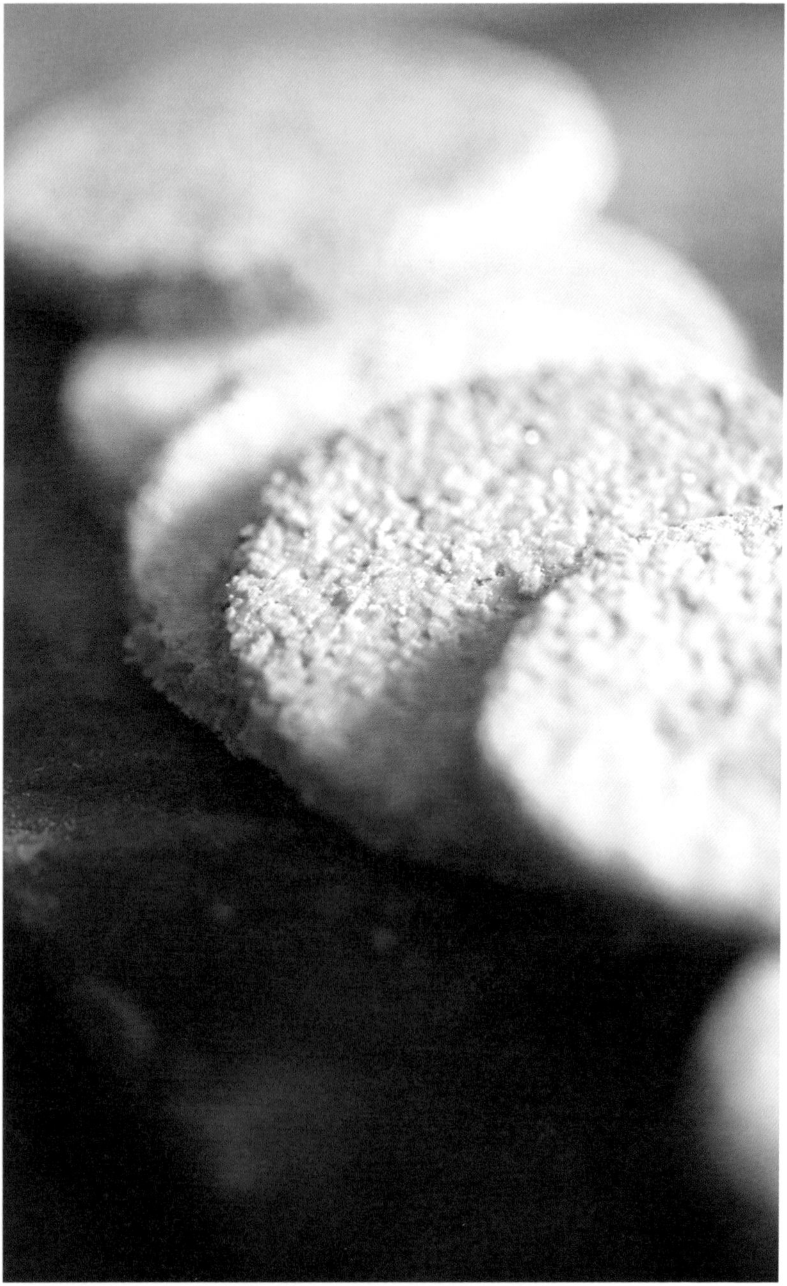

Spelt digestives

We often make these at River Cottage, usually to serve with cheese, but they are also delicious with cold meats, particularly pâtés and terrines. We prefer a less sweet biscuit with meats, so we reduce the sugar content slightly. I have given both options here.

Makes about 40
250g unsalted butter, softened
250g spelt flour, plus extra for dusting
250g medium oatmeal
125g soft brown sugar (or 100g for a less sweet biscuit)
10g salt
2 tsp baking powder
A little milk, to mix

Rub the butter into the flour until it resembles fine breadcrumbs; the easiest way to do this is in a food processor, if you have one. Add the oatmeal, sugar, salt and baking powder, and mix together until evenly combined. Add enough milk, a few drops at a time, to bind the mixture and form a slightly sticky dough.

Turn the dough out on to a lightly floured surface and dust with more flour, then press into a round, flat disc. Wrap in cling film and refrigerate for at least half an hour, to rest and firm up a bit. (This dough will keep well in the fridge for a few days, but it will become rock-hard, so if prepared ahead you'll need to let it soften out of the fridge before you roll it out.)

When ready to cook, preheat the oven to 180°C/Gas Mark 4. Flour the dough well and lay it between two sheets of greaseproof paper or cling film. (As the dough is sticky and brittle, this makes it much easier to handle.) Roll it out carefully to a thickness of 3–4mm, dusting regularly with flour to stop it sticking.

Using a 7cm pastry cutter, cut out about 40 rounds and lay them on non-stick baking sheets, or ones lined with baking parchment. Bake for 7–10 minutes, checking regularly after 7 minutes; the biscuits should be brown around the edges and lightly coloured on top. Leave on the baking sheet for a minute or two, then carefully transfer to a wire rack to cool.

P.S. These biscuits will keep for several days in an airtight container.

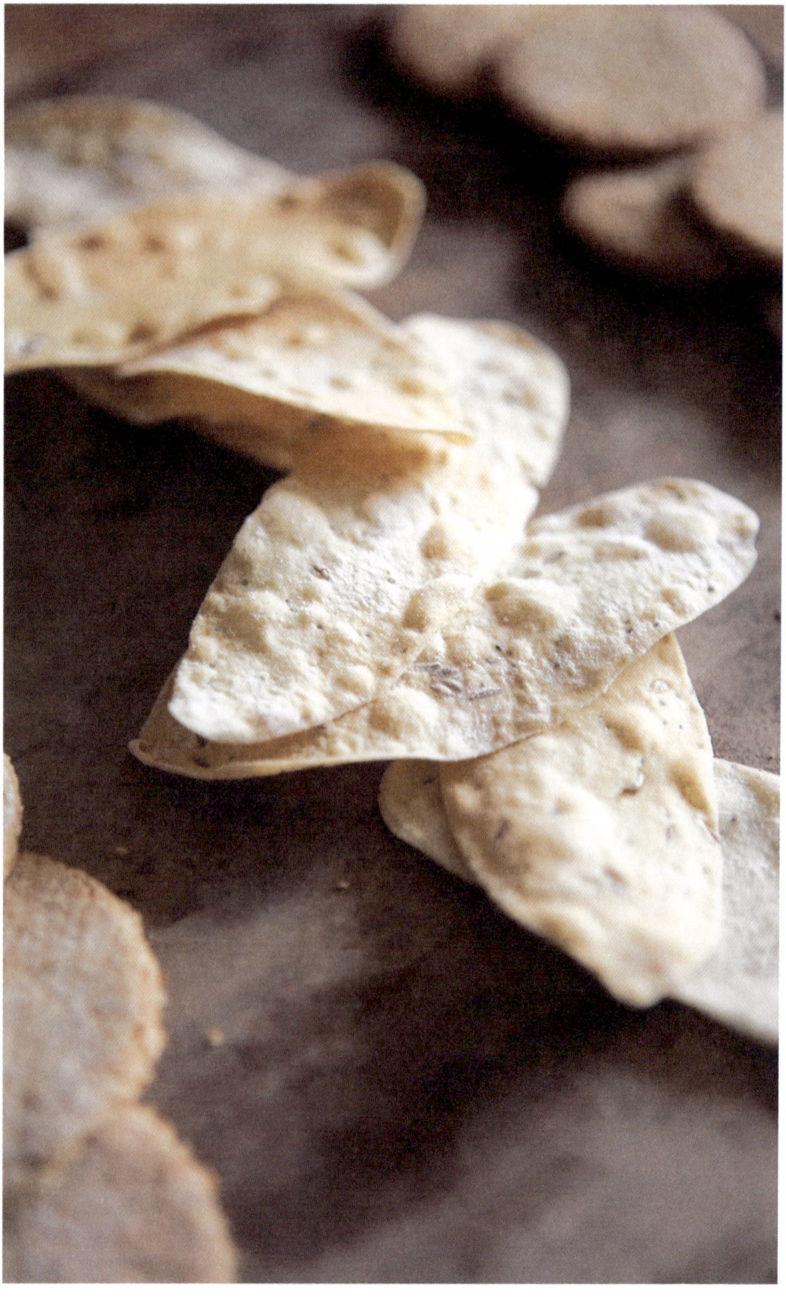

Poppy and caraway crackers

These are tasty, crispy and light as a feather. So light, in fact, that you should switch the oven fan off if you have one – they have a tendency to take off.

Makes about 25

250g plain white flour, plus extra for dusting
½ tsp baking powder
½ tsp poppy seeds
½ tsp caraway seeds
½ tsp salt
40ml olive or sunflower oil
100ml water

In a bowl, mix all the dry ingredients together, then make a well in the middle and add the oil and water. Gradually mix together until evenly combined and bring together to form a rough dough. Knead briefly, using more flour if you need to; the dough should be soft, but not sticky. Wrap in cling film and leave to rest in the fridge for half an hour or so.

Preheat the oven to 180°C/Gas Mark 4. Lightly flour your work surface, then roll the dough out until about 5mm thick. Using a 5cm cutter, cut out about 25 rounds, then roll out each round again, in one direction, as thinly as you can. Lay them on baking sheets and bake for up to 10 minutes, but be watchful – it is easy to overcook these crackers. They are ready when they are just showing the first signs of browning, but still predominantly pale.

P.S. These crackers don't keep very well once cooked, so if you don't think you need this quantity, it is best to freeze half of the dough.

Scottish oatcakes

This is one version – and there are many – of the classic Scottish biscuit. I have made oatcakes simply with oatmeal and cold water, as I suppose was once customary. I quite liked them, but they were terribly fragile. Using hot water softens the oats, and the oil helps to bind them.

Makes about 20

140g medium oatmeal, plus extra for dusting
140g porridge oats
A little pinch of salt
75ml sunflower oil
About 2 tbsp just-boiled water

Preheat the oven to 180°C/Gas Mark 4. Mix all the dry ingredients together in a bowl. Add the oil and enough hot water to mix to a firm dough. Pat into a flat disc, cover and leave for 10 minutes or so – this makes the dough a little easier to roll.

Dust your work surface and the dough with oatmeal and roll out until it is about 5mm thick. Using a 6cm cutter, cut out about 20 discs. Place on baking sheets and bake for about 20 minutes until just browned at the edges. Leave on the trays for about 5 minutes to firm up, then transfer to a wire rack to cool. Either eat straight away, with cheese if you like, or keep for up to a few days in an airtight container.

Crumpets

Crumpets are an English teatime classic, not for a refined cucumber-sandwich-and-best-china tea, but eaten fireside with a big pot of tea – and very likely butter down your shirt. To make real crumpets, you need metal crumpet rings to hold the batter in while they are cooking. If you don't have any suitable metal rings, try the variation for pikelets below.

Makes about 12
450g plain white flour (approximately)
350ml warm milk
350ml warm water (approximately)
5g powdered dried yeast
10g salt
1 tsp baking powder
A little sunflower or vegetable oil

In a bowl, whisk together the flour, milk, water and yeast. You will end up with a rather runny batter (the consistency of single cream). Cover with cling film or a plastic bag and leave to one side for at least an hour, until it is really bubbly. You can leave it for 3 or 4 hours if it suits you.

When you are ready for tea, heat a large, heavy-based frying pan or flat griddle over a medium-high heat. Whisk the salt and baking powder into the batter. Grease your crumpet rings and pan, using a scrunched-up piece of kitchen paper dipped in oil.

Now I suggest you do a test run. Put one crumpet ring in the pan, fill to just below the top and see what happens. If the batter is the correct consistency, it should stay contained within the ring and lots of holes should appear on the surface after a minute or two. (If it dribbles out underneath, the batter is too thin so whisk in a little more flour. If lots of holes don't appear, the batter is probably too thick, so whisk in a little water.) Do another test run if necessary.

After 5 minutes or so, when the surface is just set, flip the crumpet over, ring and all. (If the base is too dark, turn the heat down.) Cook for 2–3 minutes until golden on the other side. Once you have a successful test run, cook your crumpets in batches. Either butter and eat straight away, or cool on a wire rack for toasting later.

Variation

To make pikelets, whisk another 50g flour into the batter to stiffen it, so you won't need to use crumpet rings to prevent it spreading out like a pancake. Dollop spoonfuls of this batter into your greased pan and cook for a couple of minutes only on each side. Pikelets will be less than half the thickness of crumpets.

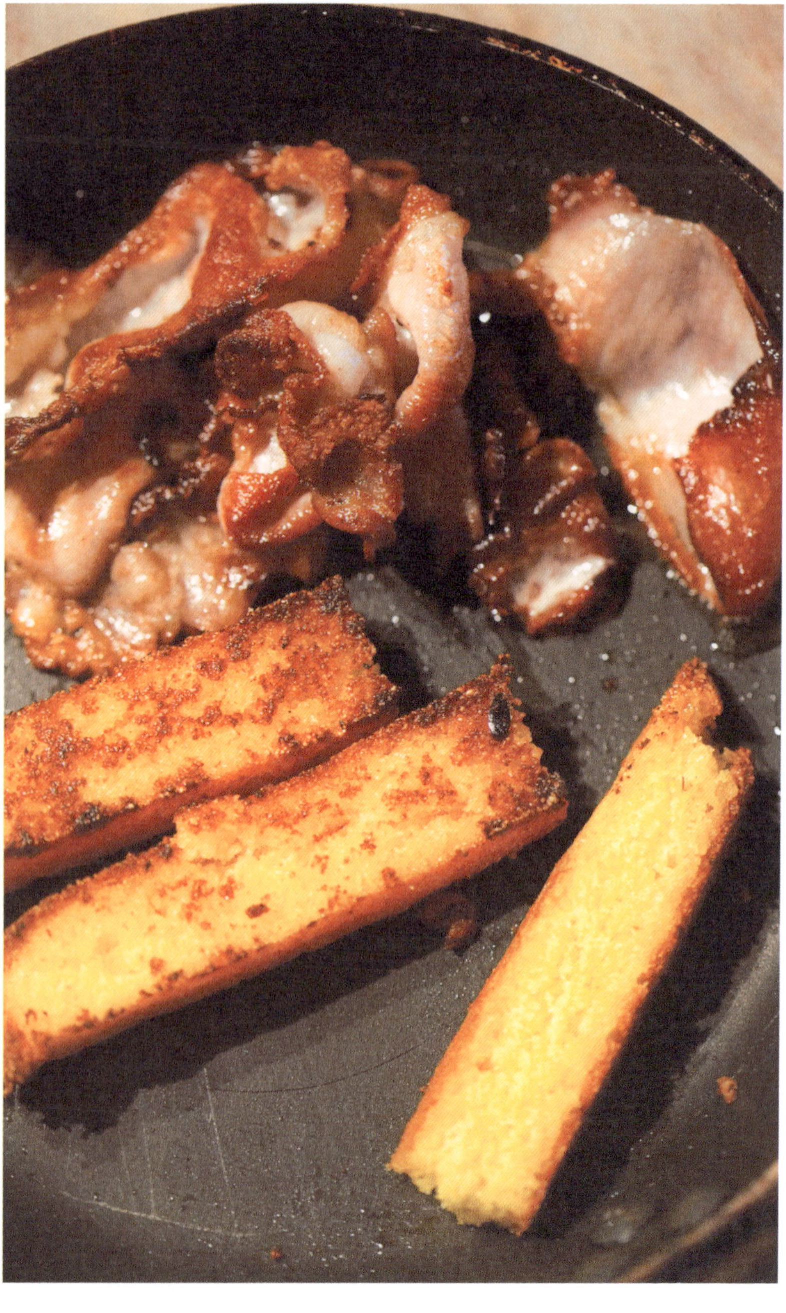

Cornbread

Cornbread is delicious, one of the defining tastes of the Deep South of America. It is traditionally made with bacon fat, but butter and lard are both excellent substitutes. Eat it warm with butter, or fry slices in butter or bacon fat. Cornbread would be at home at a barbecue – alongside a sticky rack of ribs and a big salad. Or try it my favourite way (see below).

Makes 1
250g cornmeal (maize meal)
10g baking powder
5g salt
1 tbsp bacon fat, butter or lard,
    plus an extra 1 tbsp for cooking
125ml milk
125ml yoghurt

Preheat the oven to 180°C/Gas Mark 4. Place a good heavy-based medium ovenproof frying pan over a medium heat to warm up.

Meanwhile, mix the cornmeal, baking powder and salt together in a large bowl. Melt the bacon fat or other fat in a small saucepan, then add the milk and yoghurt. Warm through, then add to the dry ingredients and stir it all together.

Melt the 1 tbsp fat for cooking in the frying pan, then immediately pour in the cornbread mixture. Let it cook for a minute, then transfer to the oven and bake for about 20 minutes, until firm and golden. You can eat it straight away or leave it to cool for a while if you prefer.

P.S. To make my perfect breakfast (for one or two, depending on appetite): wipe out the pan you made the cornbread in and cook 5–6 rashers of smoked dry-cured bacon until crispy; remove and keep warm. Add ½ finely diced small onion to the pan with a knob of butter and fry over a medium heat until soft and golden. Meanwhile, strip the kernels from a corn cob and cook in boiling water for 2 minutes. Drain and toss with the onions. Season with salt and a good grinding of pepper, and serve with the bacon, cornbread and maple syrup. To turn breakfast into supper, serve after sundown with a large sip of bourbon.

Blinis

These traditional Russian pancakes are properly made with buckwheat flour. At River Cottage, we love to make blinis but rarely have buckwheat, so we use a mix of rye and wheat flours. They are totally delicious.

Makes about 12 (or 50 mini-blinis)

- 225ml milk
- 200ml natural yoghurt or crème fraîche
- 2 large free-range eggs, separated
- 100g rye flour
- 100g strong white bread flour
- 1 tsp salt
- 5g powdered dried yeast
- A little melted butter or sunflower oil, for greasing

Warm the milk and yoghurt or crème fraîche together in a pan until just tepid, then remove from the heat and whisk in the egg yolks.

In a mixing bowl, whisk together the flours, salt, milk mix and yeast until smooth. Cover with cling film and leave for at least an hour to ferment. You can leave it for 3 or 4 hours, if you like.

When ready to cook, heat a large, heavy-based frying pan or flat griddle over a medium-high heat. Whisk the egg whites in a separate bowl until stiff, then stir a spoonful into your bubbling batter to loosen it. Now gently fold in the rest of the egg whites.

Grease the pan with a scrunched-up piece of kitchen paper dipped in melted butter or oil. Dollop tablespoonfuls of the batter into the pan – as many as you can fit, but not too close together as they will spread slightly. Cook for a minute or so, then flip over and cook for another minute. Remove and keep warm, wrapped in a cloth, while you cook the rest. Serve hot, with butter or savoury toppings.

Variation

'Mini-blinis' – teaspoonful-sized dollops that cook in half the time – make excellent party food. Top them with smoked salmon and crème fraîche, or caviar perhaps, or the River Cottage way – with slices of home-cured mackerel and a little dill yoghurt.

BUNS, BISCUITS & BATTER BREADS

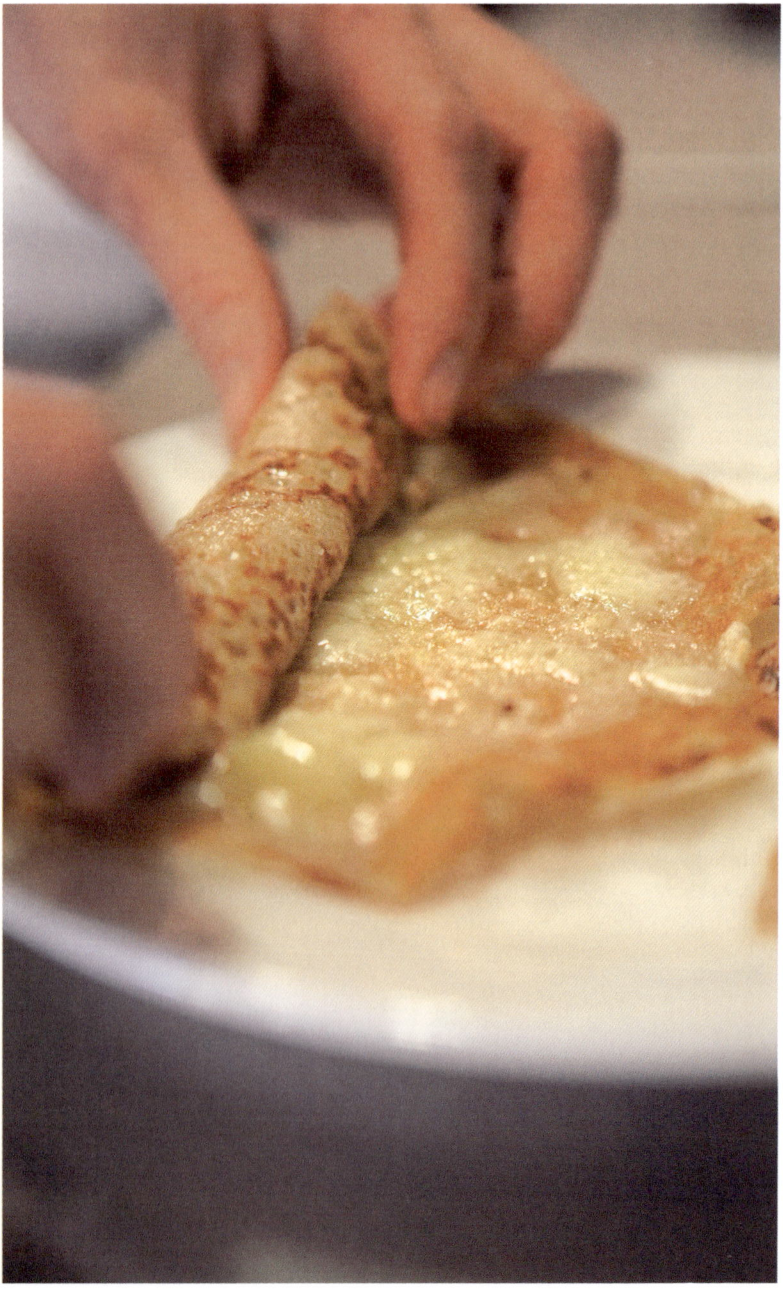

Staffordshire oatcakes

My best friend at university came from a village near Stoke-on-Trent. He loved Staffordshire oatcakes, which we ate for breakfast on Sundays – three each, stacked up with the 'full English', plus loads of ketchup. They also make a great lunch (two is more than enough) rolled around cheesy béchamel sauce and bacon lardons, with some salad on the side. Make a whole batch and cook as many as you need – the batter keeps well in the fridge or freezer. I've also found that cooked oatcakes can be warmed in the oven or in a pan successfully.

Makes 10–12

225g wholemeal flour
225g fine oatmeal
500ml warm water
500ml warm milk
5g powdered dried yeast
10g salt
A little sunflower (or other) oil

Whisk everything together, except the oil, in a large bowl until smooth. At this stage the batter will seem too thin, but it will thicken as the oatmeal swells. Cover and leave for at least an hour, until the batter is really bubbly and frothy.

Heat a large, heavy-based frying pan over a medium-high heat, then grease it with a scrunched-up piece of kitchen paper dipped in oil. Give the batter a good whisk then pour a ladleful into the pan, tipping and swirling the pan so the batter thickly coats the base.

Cook for a couple of minutes, during which time the surface will become pocked with holes. Flip over and cook for a further minute, then remove from the pan. Wrap in a clean tea towel to keep warm. Cook enough oatcakes for breakfast (or lunch); keep the rest of the batter in the fridge or freeze for later.

Socca

Made with chickpea flour, this thick pancake from the South of France is summer tearing and sharing food. Serve it outdoors, with some good tomatoes, cheese, salad leaves, salami and olives, perhaps, or a ragu of beans. You could try adding flavours to the pancake batter too: finely chopped rosemary and black pepper would be excellent. You'll notice the recipe uses equal volumes of flour and water, and the flour is measured by volume, not weight for convenience. Use a measuring cup, or a jug, or any other container, to measure first the flour, then the water. The quantities are easily adjusted to make the number of pancakes required.

Makes 1
About 100ml chickpea flour
About 100ml water
Small pinch of salt
Extra virgin olive oil, for frying

Tip the flour and water into a mixing bowl. Add a pinch of salt, then whisk until most of the lumps have gone.

Heat a slug of olive oil in a small frying pan. When it is hot but not smoking, pour in enough batter to give a 5mm thickness. Cook until it has set, but keep checking the underside.

When it is dark in patches, even very slightly charred, flip the pancake over, trickle a little more oil round the side of the pan and give it a shake. Cook for another couple of minutes, until the other side is similarly coloured. Tear a bit off the side to check it is cooked through.

Serve the pancakes straight away, or keep warm while you cook some more.

P.S. You can buy chickpea flour from health food shops, or Asian food stores where it may go by the name of *besan* or gram flour.

BUNS, BISCUITS & BATTER BREADS 173

Using Leftover Bread

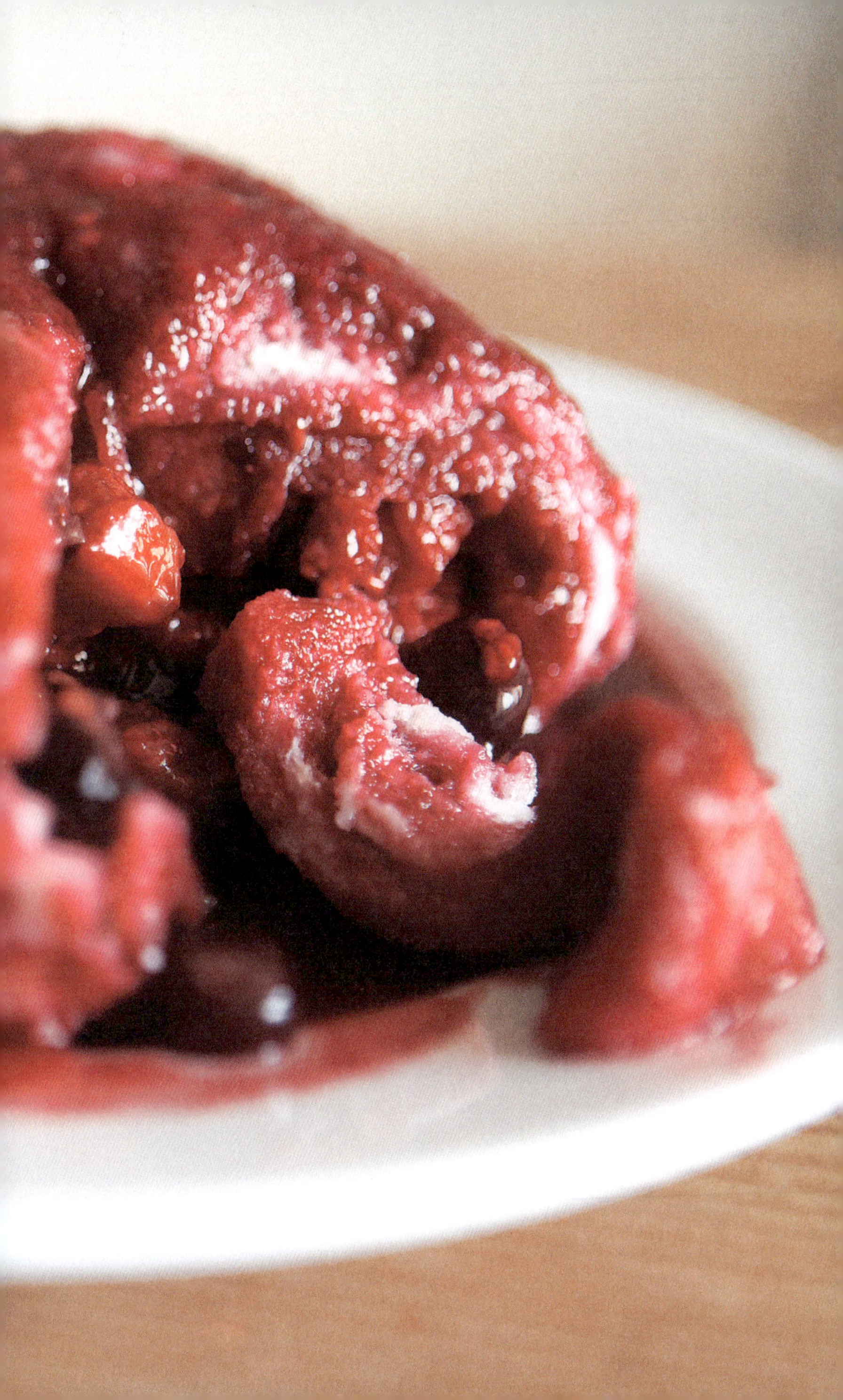

I never throw bread in the bin and neither should you

– unless, of course, it is mouldy, which it shouldn't be if you've stored it properly. Consider these possibilities for your ageing loaf:

Cut the whole bottom crust off your loaf and use as a plate for a stew. Afterwards, eat the plate. It may sound silly, but this was an old English staple, known as a 'trencher'. A good, thick slice of stale bread in the bottom of a bowl of stew is still an excellent idea.

Rip bread up into big chunks keeping the crusts on. Toss them in olive oil and bake until golden for wonderful croûtons to drop into soup. You could add some grated cheese as you toss – for a tastier, more stuck-together affair.

Make a bread sauce to serve with roasted poultry or game. Remove the crusts, tear the bread into chunks and soak in just-boiled milk infused with a small onion, a bay leaf and a few cloves for half an hour. Reheat and season generously with sea salt and freshly ground pepper to serve.

Rip bread into smaller chunks to make Spanish *migas*. Fry the bread in lard or bacon fat until crispy, throwing in some bacon lardons and sliced onion for extra flavour if you like. Season with salt and pepper, and finish with chopped parsley. Serve topped with a fried egg for the perfect breakfast.

Make breadcrumbs by blitzing chunks of bread, a handful at a time, in a food processor to make coarse crumbs. Freeze any breadcrumbs you won't use straight away. They freeze brilliantly and you'll find endless uses for them:
- Use to thicken soups, or sprinkle over dishes to be flashed under the grill for a crisp topping.
- Or to coat fish: season fillets of fish, dip into flour, then into beaten egg, then into breadcrumbs and shallow-fry. (For a thicker, crunchier coat double-dip them in the egg and breadcrumbs.)
- Or to make 'poor man's Parmesan': shallow-fry breadcrumbs in olive oil with a little salt until crisp, drain on kitchen paper and scatter over pasta.

Dry breadcrumbs completely spread out on a tray, in a very low oven or somewhere else warm, then blitz again until super-fine.
- Use to make Scotch eggs: seal just-softer-than-hard-boiled eggs inside good-quality sausage meat (100g per egg), dip first in flour, then into beaten egg, then into fine, dry breadcrumbs to coat. Deep-fry in hot oil at 170°C for about 5 minutes, until the sausage meat is cooked through.

- Or, if you make your own sausages, use these dry breadcrumbs as rusk – they will soak up fat and moisture, keeping the sausages juicy.
- Or use to coat your own homemade fish fingers.

And don't forget toast – one- or two-day-old bread makes better toast than fresh bread. Or do as Benjamin Franklin once said, 'Give me yesterday's Bread, this Day's Flesh, and last Year's Cyder.' Sounds good to me... Or, try the recipes on the following pages.

Beetroot houmous

For this shocking-purple variation of the classic chickpea dip, bread is used as a thickener because beetroot makes a thinner purée than chickpeas. I've given exact quantities here, but the way to make houmous is to add the ingredients a little at a time, tasting and tweaking as you go, until you think it is perfect. You could make a larger batch – it will sit quite happily for several days in the fridge, ready to dip raw vegetables into when you fancy a snack. Illustrated on p.87.

Serves 4

1 tbsp cumin seeds
25g crustless, stale bread
200g cooked beetroot
1 large garlic clove, peeled and crushed
About 1 tbsp tahini
(sesame seed paste)
Juice of 1 lemon
Salt and black pepper

Toast the cumin seeds in a dry frying pan over a medium heat, shaking the pan almost constantly, until they start to darken and smell amazing (less than a minute). While still hot, crush the seeds using a pestle and mortar, or a spice grinder.

Break the bread into chunks and whiz in a food processor to crumbs. Add the beetroot, most of the garlic, 1 tbsp tahini, a good pinch of the cumin, half the lemon juice, a sprinkling of salt and a good grinding of pepper. Blend to a thick paste.

Taste the houmous; you should be able to detect every flavour. If not, add a little more of whatever is lacking and blend again. Keep tasting and adjusting until you are happy. Serve with flatbread (see p.103) and/or vegetables for dipping.

Taramasalata

If pollack are obliging enough to come into the River Cottage kitchen laden with roe, we salt, poach and hang the roe in our cold smoker quicker than you can say taramasalata backwards. This is our recipe.

Serves 8
250g smoked pollack or other fish roe
About 100g stale white bread, crusts removed
150ml whole milk
1 garlic clove, peeled and crushed
100ml extra virgin olive oil
200ml sunflower oil
Juice of 1 lemon
Salt and black pepper

To serve
Smoked paprika, for sprinkling
About 1 tbsp finely chopped parsley
A little preserved lemon rind, cut into very thin strips (optional)

Cut the smoked roe open and scrape them out with a spoon, discarding the skins. Tear the bread into chunks and soak in the milk for a few minutes, then squeeze out excess moisture and put into a food processor, along with the fish roe and garlic.

With the machine on low speed, trickle in both oils through the funnel in a steady stream. Add the lemon juice a little at a time, tasting as you go, until you are happy. Season with salt if needed (this depends on the saltiness of the roe), and a generous grinding of pepper.

Transfer the taramasalata to a serving bowl, sprinkle with a little smoked paprika and scatter over the chopped parsley and preserved lemon if you have any. Serve with loads of flatbread (see p.103) or toast.

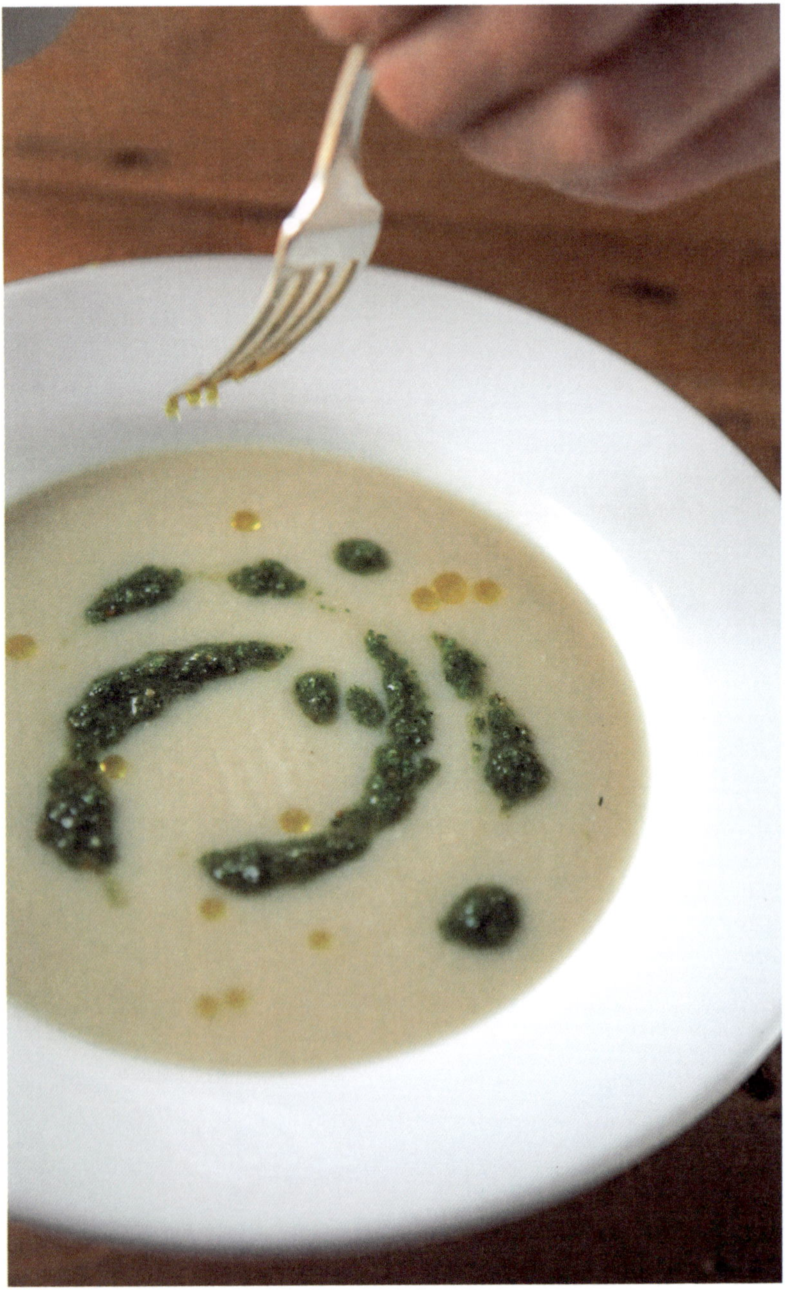

Nettle pesto

This is a rural Devon, River Cottage version of the classic Italian sauce. We substitute nettles, rapeseed oil, Cheddar and breadcrumbs for basil, olive oil, Parmesan and pine nuts. Use it wherever you would use pesto – it is excellent swirled on top of creamy soups, or tossed through pasta.

Makes about 450g
20g breadcrumbs
100g young nettles (or the top few leaves of older ones)
20g strong Cheddar, grated
½ garlic clove, crushed to a paste with a little salt
150–200ml rapeseed oil
Salt and black pepper

Preheat the oven to 180°C/Gas Mark 4. Scatter the breadcrumbs on a baking tray and bake for about 10 minutes until dry and golden, checking them frequently towards the end as they burn quite quickly. Tip on to a plate and allow to cool.

Wearing gloves, pick over the nettles, discarding all but the thinnest stalks, then wash well. Fill a bowl with iced water. Find a pan large enough to take the nettles and half-fill it with water. Bring to the boil and cram in the nettles, pushing them down with a wooden spoon to immerse them. Cook for just 1 minute, then drain through a sieve over a bowl to save the cooking water. Immediately plunge the nettles into the iced water. As soon as they are cold, remove and squeeze them as dry as you can – they will not sting you once they are cooked.

Put the nettles into a food processor along with the breadcrumbs, cheese and garlic. With the machine on low speed, trickle in enough rapeseed oil to make a loose paste. (Alternatively, you can grind the nettles, breadcrumbs, garlic and cheese to a paste using a pestle and mortar, then slowly incorporate the oil.)

Season your pesto with salt and pepper to taste. It is now ready to use. As for the nettle cooking water you saved, drink it – it's too good to waste.

Panzanella

This Tuscan bread salad is excellent eaten on its own for lunch, but also just right with barbecued food, or anything else you want to eat outdoors with a bottle of wine on a hot summer's day. As with all peasant food, there are limitless variations, so feel free to adjust this recipe. That said, I would never attempt to make it if I didn't have some really good ripe tomatoes and decent extra virgin olive oil.

Serves 4

About 500g stale white bread
   (ideally ciabatta or sourdough)
150ml extra virgin olive oil
1 large red onion, finely chopped
½ cucumber, chopped quite small
4 good-sized ripe tomatoes,
   chopped quite small
A handful of small capers
25ml good-quality white wine vinegar,
   or cider vinegar
A pinch of caster sugar
Flaky sea salt and black pepper
A big bunch of basil, leaves only

Preheat the oven to 180°C/Gas Mark 4. In a roasting tray, toss the bread with half the olive oil then bake it, shaking the pan occasionally, until golden and crispy. You can miss out this step – many Italians would – but it adds texture and flavour, which I like. Leave to cool, then toss with the onion, cucumber, tomatoes (including all their juices) and capers in a large serving bowl.

In another bowl, whisk the rest of the olive oil together with the wine vinegar and sugar. Pour this dressing over the salad and season generously with salt and pepper. Tear the basil over and toss it all together. Taste for seasoning.

You can either serve the salad straight away, or leave it to stand at room temperature for an hour or so, to let the flavours blend.

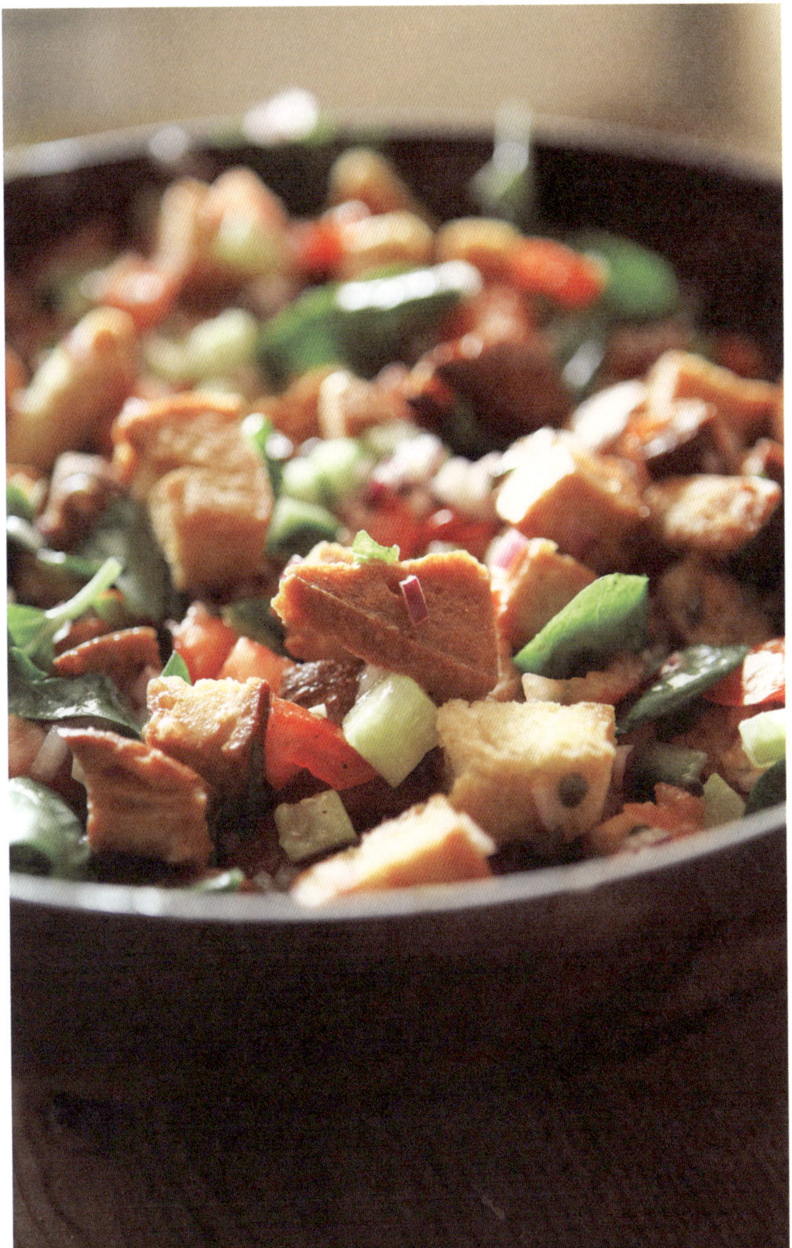

Pain perdu

This is a classic French dessert, which translates as 'lost' or 'forgotten' bread. Basically, it is sugary, eggy bread, which is truly delicious topped with seasonal fruit. Try it with poached rhubarb, or with summer berries – some of them puréed. Serve for dessert, or brunch if you prefer.

Serves 6

3 thick slices stale white bread, crusts removed
4 large free-range eggs
100g caster sugar
200ml whole milk
A few drops of natural vanilla extract
About 100g unsalted butter

To serve
Poached fruit or summer berries

Cut the bread slices in half diagonally. In a mixing bowl, whisk the eggs and sugar together for a couple of minutes to help dissolve the sugar, then add the milk and vanilla extract, and whisk again. Tip this mixture into a shallow dish (large enough to take all the bread in a single layer). Lay the bread slices in the dish, leave to soak for a minute, then turn them over and leave for another minute.

In the meantime, set a frying pan over a medium-low heat. Once the bread has soaked, add a generous knob of butter to the pan – enough to just cover the bottom of the pan once melted. As soon as the butter is frothing (don't let it brown), lay as many bread slices in the pan as will comfortably fit, and fry for 2–3 minutes on each side until golden brown.

Remove the *pain perdu* from the pan and keep warm while you fry the rest of the bread slices, adding more butter to the pan as necessary. Serve straight away, with poached fruit or berries.

Variation

You can flambé the bread, too, if you like. Add a splash of Cognac, Grand Marnier or whatever you fancy, right at the end. Set alight with a match and leave until the flame has subsided.

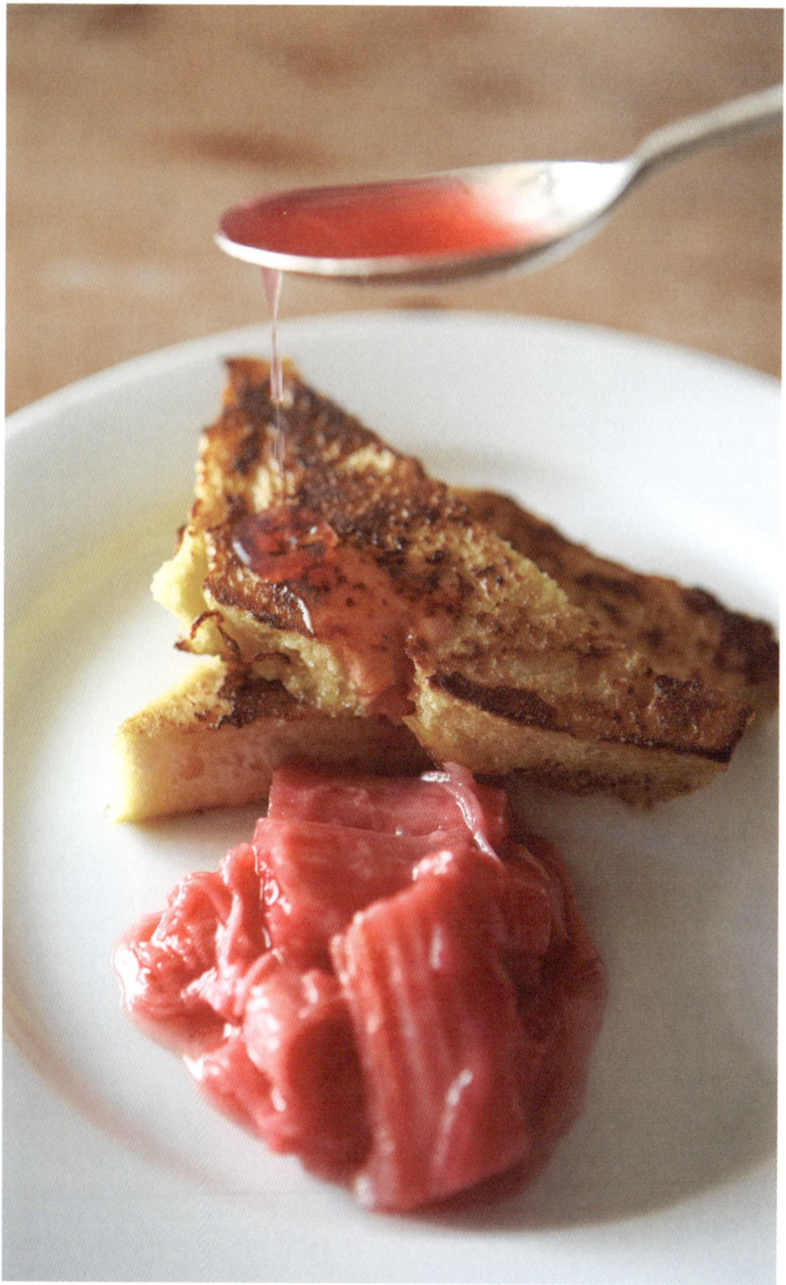

Bread and butter pudding

If you don't like bread and butter pudding, the chances are that you've never had one that's been made properly. This recipe should change your mind.

Serves 6
About 600g one- or two-day-old white bread
About 50g unsalted butter, softened
300ml double cream
300ml whole milk
1 vanilla pod
6 medium free-range egg yolks
200g caster sugar
A good handful of raisins

Butter a shallow oval baking dish, about 30 x 20cm. Cut the bread into medium-thick slices, butter them, then cut the crusts off and halve the slices on the diagonal to form triangles.

Pour the cream and milk into a saucepan. Split the vanilla pod lengthways, scrape out the seeds with a teaspoon and add them to the pan with the empty pod. Bring just to the boil over a medium heat, then take off the heat and leave to infuse for 10 minutes. In a large bowl, briefly whisk together the egg yolks and 150g of the sugar to combine. Pour in the hot milk and cream mix, including the vanilla, whisking all the time. This is your custard.

Arrange the triangles of bread in the baking dish – in rows, propped up and leaning on each other so they come just proud of the dish, sprinkling the raisins in between. Continue in this way until you've filled the dish and used all the bread, cutting the triangles up and tucking the pieces in as you need to. Don't try to be neat – the point of layering like this is that the propped-up ends, which stand clear of the custard, turn golden and crispy in the oven. Try not to leave too many raisins exposed, as they are liable to scorch during baking.

Now, pour over the custard, making sure you moisten all the pieces of bread. Let the pudding stand for 20 minutes or so, to allow the custard to soak in. Heat the oven to 180°C/Gas Mark 4 and boil the kettle.

When you are ready to bake, sprinkle over the rest of the sugar. Sit the dish in a roasting tin and pour in enough boiling water to come halfway up the side of the dish (this bain-marie will help to keep the pudding soft.) Bake for 20–30 minutes, until the custard is just set in the middle – prod the top with your finger to check. Serve hot or warm, with cream or ice cream.

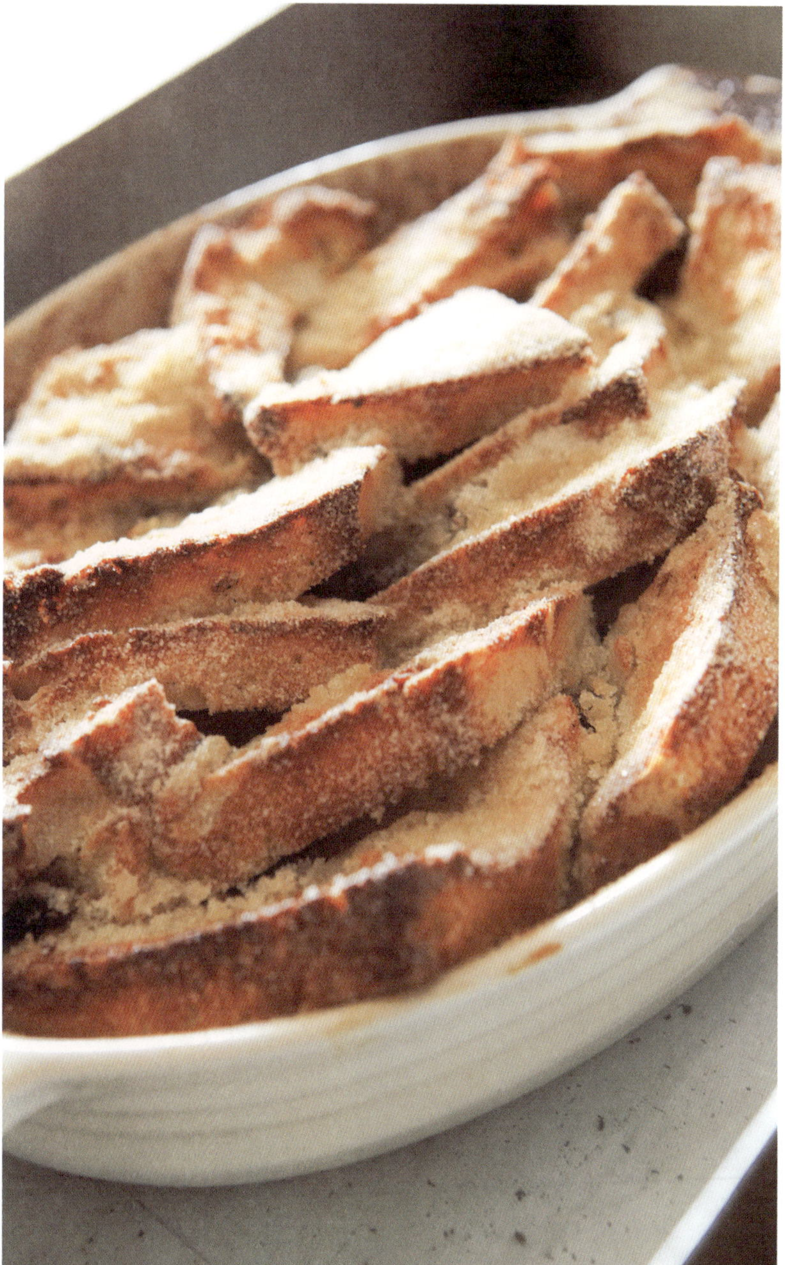

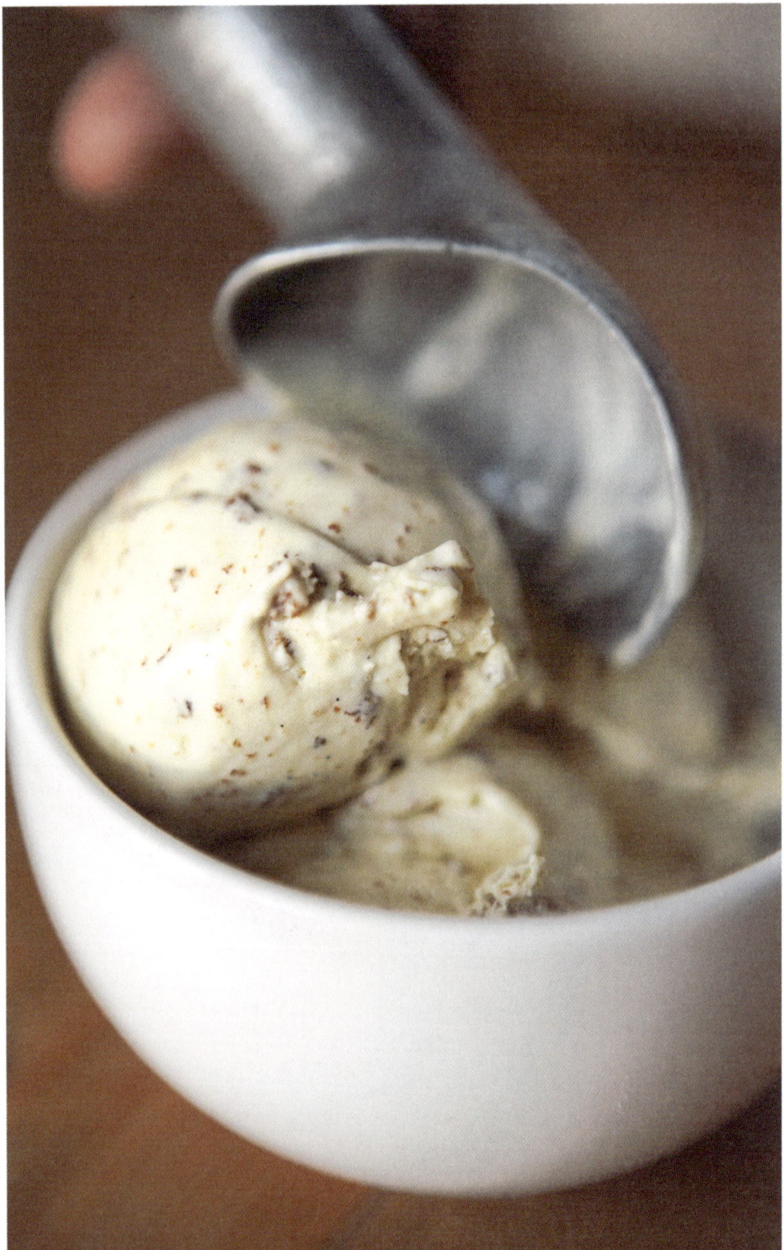

Brown bread ice cream

This is vanilla ice cream, dappled with little golden, sweet, nutty-tasting, chewy treats, so it tastes that much better. Ideally you would make this in an ice-cream maker, but if you don't own one, there is another way (see below).

Makes about 600ml

100g fresh or one- or two-day-old wholemeal bread
100g soft light brown sugar, or demerara
250ml whole milk
1 vanilla pod
6 medium free-range egg yolks
125g caster sugar
250ml double cream

Preheat the oven to 180°C/Gas Mark 4. Tear the bread into smallish pieces, toss with the brown sugar and scatter on a baking tray. Bake in the oven for 10 minutes or so, until quite dark and caramelised. Leave to cool on the tray.

Meanwhile, pour the milk into a heavy-based pan. Split the vanilla pod lengthways, scrape out the seeds with a teaspoon and add them to the milk together with the empty pod. Slowly bring just to the boil.

Meanwhile, in a large mixing bowl, briefly whisk together the egg yolks and caster sugar, then slowly pour in the hot milk, whisking constantly. Tip in the vanilla pod too. Pour the mixture back into the saucepan and set over a low heat. Stir constantly with a wooden spoon or silicone spatula for about 5 minutes until the custard is thick enough to coat the back of the spoon; do not let it overheat or it may curdle.

As soon as it is ready, pour the custard into a cold bowl, cover with cling film to prevent a skin forming, and leave to infuse for at least 10 minutes.

Remove the vanilla pod, stir in the double cream and churn the mixture in an ice-cream maker according to the manufacturer's instructions. When the ice cream is thickened and almost ready but still a little soft, crumble in the toasted bread and churn until frozen.

P.S. If you do not have an ice-cream maker, freeze the mixture in a suitable bowl in the freezer, taking it out and whisking or beating it every half-hour over the next few hours until it becomes too firm to beat, then allow to freeze completely. Ice cream made this way will be harder when fully frozen, so you will need to allow extra time for it to soften slightly before serving. It will be delicious nonetheless.

Summer pudding

This is a celebration of the English summer, so make it with homegrown fruit if you possibly can. The mix of fruits should be governed by what is in season. Try for a balance of sweet and tart fruits – say, strawberries, raspberries, redcurrants, blackcurrants and blueberries. You will need a 900ml pudding basin and a plate small enough to fit inside the rim. The whole pudding is illustrated on pp.174–5.

Serves 4

600g mixed ripe soft fruits (see above)
100g caster sugar
6–8 medium thick slices of one- or two-day-old white bread, crusts removed

Put the fruits and sugar into a heavy-based pan over a medium heat, stir together and bring just to the boil, stirring regularly. Simmer for 1 minute only, then remove from the heat. The fruits will release a fair amount of juice.

Line the base and sides of a 900ml pudding basin with slices of bread, overlapping them slightly and cutting them to fit as necessary. Reserve a slice or two for the lid.

Now fill the basin with all of the fruit and most of the juice, saving a few tablespoonfuls (or more) for serving. You may find you have more juice than you need; this depends on the fruit and its ripeness.

Cut the reserved bread to fit the top, sit a plate on top that just fits inside the rim and weight it with a couple of tins from the cupboard. Refrigerate for about 8 hours.

To serve, invert the pudding on to a large plate and pour over the reserved juice. Serve with cream.

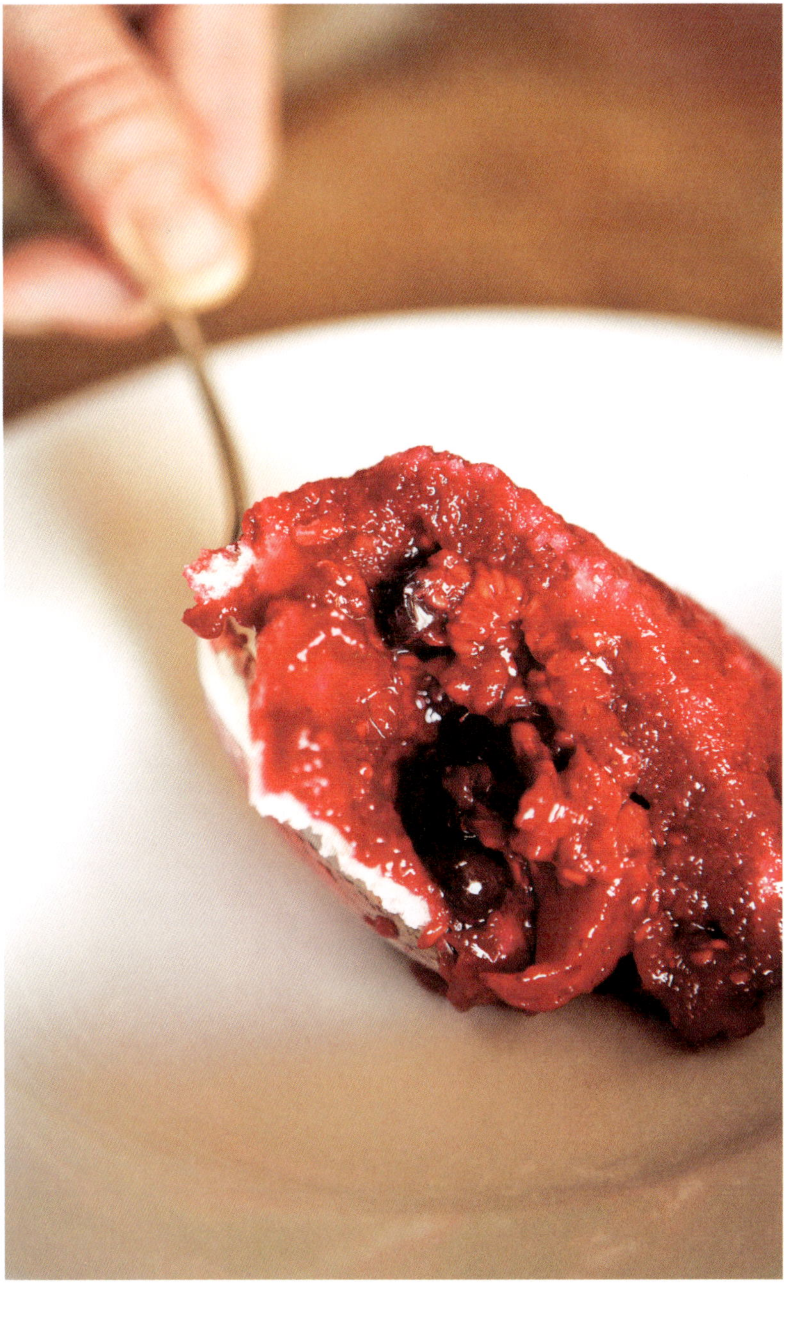

Building a Clay Oven

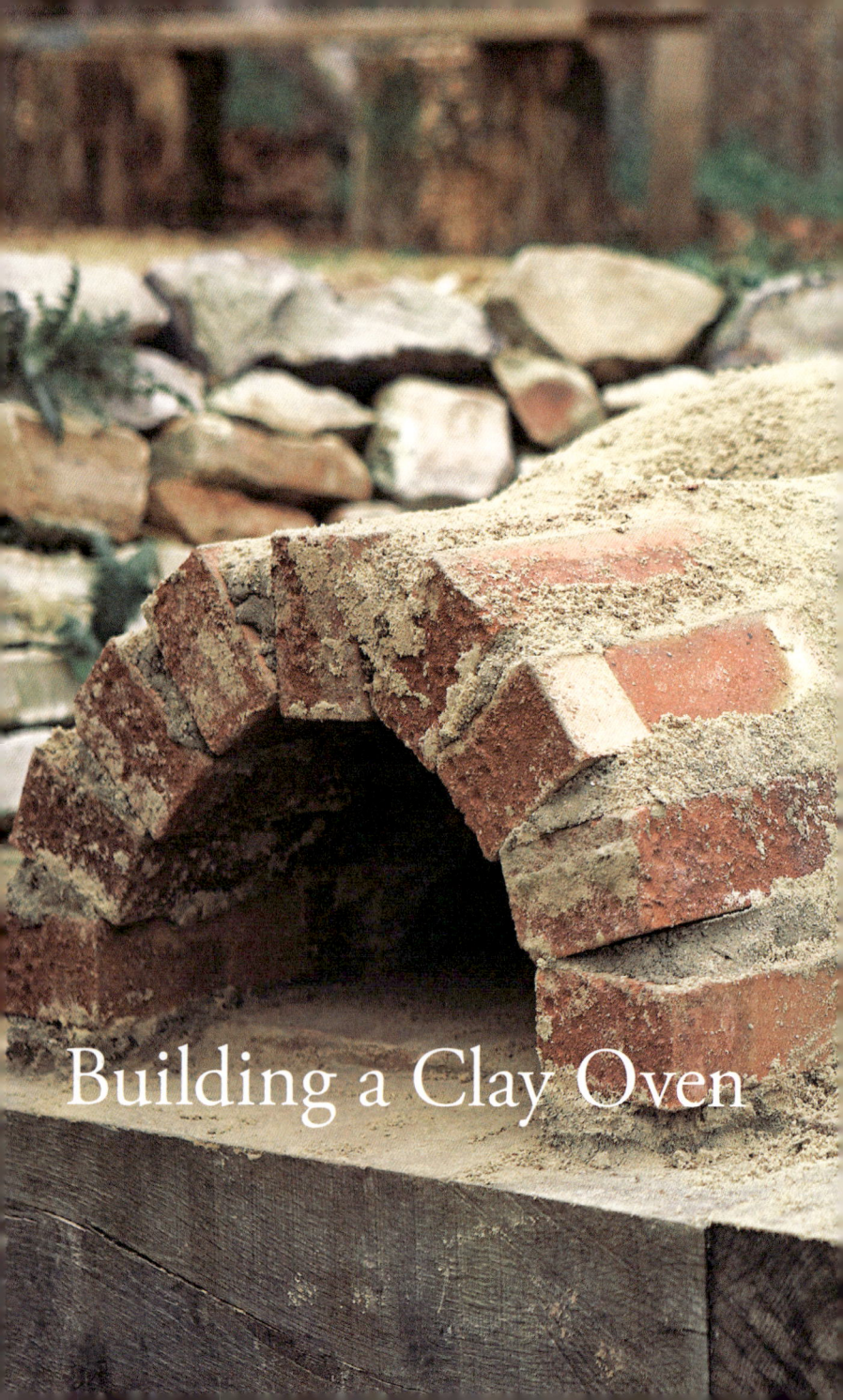

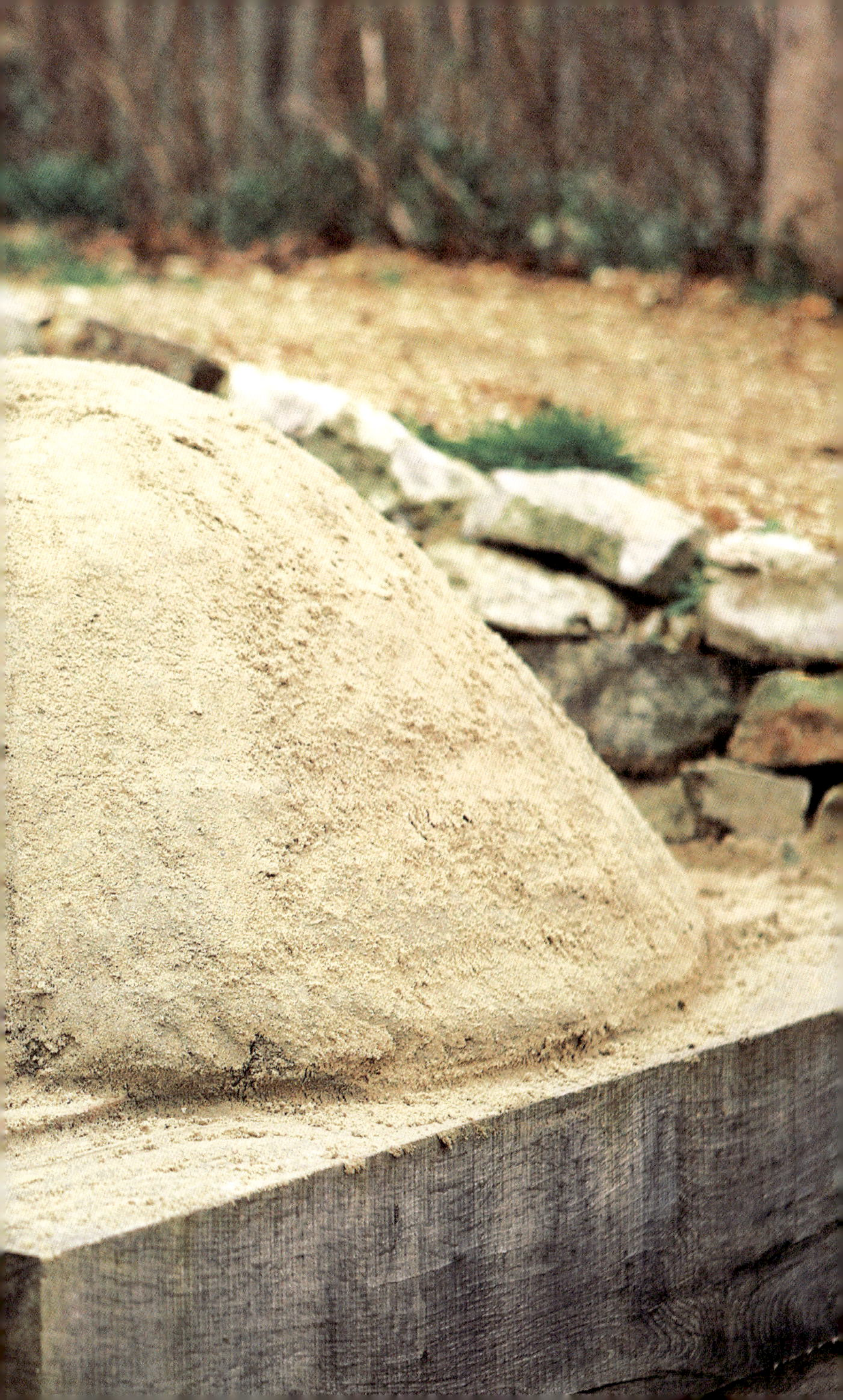

If I was a lump of dough, proving my final minutes away and contemplating the manner of my passing, I'd choose the old-fashioned way to go – to be slipped, bare-bottomed, straight on to the ash-covered floor of a hell-hot wood-fired oven. However, these days I'd be hard pushed to find such an oven. A few small artisan bakers still use one, so do some authentic pizzerias; you might even find one in an old house – nestled in the side of an inglenook fireplace. Your best bet, however, is to build your own.

This is not as ridiculous as it may sound. With a little effort and not too much money, you can build yourself an oven from clay, sand and bricks in your back garden – an oven that is capable of reaching temperatures of 400°C and above, in which you could bake bread or pizzas, or even your Sunday roast.

Almost anything you can cook in your domestic oven, you'll be able to cook in a clay oven, and in most cases the food will be better for it. I would probably draw the line at a sponge cake, or a soufflé, which are fragile affairs that need a temperature dial and an airtight door. On the other hand, I would certainly give scones and Yorkshire puddings a go.

So, if you can find around two square metres in your garden, and three spare days in your life, you could build yourself something truly special. Your humble backyard could be transformed into a Mecca of gastronomy.

How a clay oven works

The principle is simple: you light a fire inside the oven and keep it stoked long enough for the heat to fully penetrate the walls and floor. You then remove some or all of the embers and bake using the residual heat. A well-built oven with a close-fitting door will retain heat for many hours, even with all the embers removed.

Building your oven

You will be building a simple igloo-shaped clay-and-sand oven, set on some sort of raised plinth. You can tailor the size of your oven to suit your needs, so consider what they will be. Will you be baking two or three loaves at a time, or a dozen? Do you want to be able to fit a whole shoulder of pork in it, or will you never cook anything larger than a leg of lamb?

There is more chance of scorching food in a small, cramped oven because the oven is hottest around the edges (as the heat radiates from the walls and floor). On the other hand, a large oven will take more fuel to heat, so I wouldn't make it any larger than you think you will need.

To make things simpler, I will give measurements for an oven that is a good size to bake a few loaves, or three or four pizzas at the same time, or take a large roasting tin. It will have an internal oven space about 80cm in diameter and 40cm high, and the oven will need to sit on a square plinth 150 x 150cm. In practice, it is quite straightforward for you to scale this up or down. The entire oven size is dictated by a single measurement: the diameter of a hemisphere of sand, which you will build, and around which your oven will be moulded.

The plinth

Technically, you could build an oven at ground level, but in practice you'd be bending down too far to see into it. The nearer to eye level you get, the easier it will be on your back, but an eye-level oven would mean an awful lot of plinth, which you may find rather obtrusive. You should also take into account the fact that you will be scraping hot embers out of the oven. These need to drop into something, and the further they have to fall, the more chance they will miss your container and land on your foot. Ideally, you want to raise the floor of the oven to somewhere between 1 and 1.5 metres.

There are any number of possible ways to build your plinth and I am sure you will want to think aesthetically as well as structurally. As it will be purpose-built, it may as well look good and be designed to fit in with your garden. As I'm not familiar with your garden, I can't tell you whether your finish should be timber, sandstone or jewel-encrusted mirrors, but I can tell you that the structure must be solid and stable – as indeed must be the ground you build it on.

You should allow yourself a good 1.5 metres of clear space in front of the place where your oven door will be sited: this area becomes your 'kitchen' and you will need room to move about in it. The top of the plinth should be made of brick, stone or concrete. Remember that this will become the floor of the oven, and as such, needs to be made as flat as possible.

Our plinth at River Cottage is 120cm square and 70cm high. The walls are railway sleepers, set on solid, level ground and fixed with right-angled brackets on the internal corners. The plinth is in-filled with rubble, the top of which is levelled with sand, to about 5cm below the top of the sleepers. Plain London bricks are set on this, upside down (flat side up), in a herringbone pattern, to form a level top. The gaps between the bricks are filled with more sand.

This construction works a treat, but there are other options. I once had an ugly square concrete-walled coal bunker in my garden, which would have made an ideal plinth. A stack of breezeblocks would do the job too.

Weather proofing

You may wish to construct a simple roof to protect your oven, though this is not essential; you could just keep it covered with tarpaulin when you are not using it. A roof can be anything you want it to be – it just needs to keep the worst of the rain off. A little water isn't going to hurt, but a soaking wet oven will not get hot enough, and badly weather-beaten clay will start to erode.

Bear in mind, too, that a lot of smoke will be coming out of the oven and your roof is bound to affect the airflow around it. I suggest it should clear the top of your oven by at least a metre. You may wish to make provision for a chimney if you feel the space is too enclosed – say, if you are building up against a wall. The roof over our clay oven at River Cottage is made of corrugated iron.

The three stages of building your oven

There will be three layers to your clay oven and you will need a separate day to build each one, as each layer needs to dry fully before you start the next one. Drying time depends largely on the weather, but you can – and should – accelerate the process by lighting a fire inside.

The oven consists of an inner skin, made of a mixture of sand, clay and water; an insulating layer, made of clay, wood shavings and water; and an outer wall, made again of sand, clay and water, with a brick-arch doorway, if you wish.

This is an uncomplicated project, but it does require some work, and I strongly recommend that you rope in a few able bodies to help with the grafting. A merry band of three or four helpers will make light of a job that you might find a little daunting alone. Plan roughly when you will tackle each of the stages and let them know, but ask them to be flexible, as the weather will determine how much time you'll need between the three building days.

Sourcing your materials

Before you begin, you will need to obtain 8 buckets of clay and 18 buckets of sand. By 'bucket', I mean a large metal pail, rather than a household mop bucket. You will also need two carrier bags full of wood shavings, a large heavy-duty tarpaulin, a newspaper, and a thin stick. This will become your measuring stick and you'll need to mark it 7cm from one end – with a pen or tape, or by cutting a notch. If you want to build a door and a chimney lid, you will need about half a square metre of wood (hardwood is best), 2–3cm thick, and a decent saw.

> **Clay** The easiest way to get hold of some clay is to go digging. It is very easy to find, though away from a source of water clay is likely to be pretty dry. At River Cottage we have a man-made pond in the lower field and we dig our clay from its banks. If you have access to such a pond, or a stream or small river, you will be able to do the same – with permission from the landowner, of course.
>
> Your clay should be squidgy, and reasonably free of other soils and stones; take a small piece and work it with your hands until it is supple, then roll into a snake and wrap it around your finger. It should not snap.
>
> You may prefer to buy your clay, of course. I am yet to find a nearby builder's merchant that sells it, but a friendly local potter or perhaps an art school should be able to point you in the right direction.
>
> **Sand** This is a natural material too, of course, and if you can get it for free so much the better. Otherwise, builder's merchants sell it pretty cheaply. Any grade will be fine.
>
> **Bricks** A builder's merchant again is probably your best option, or a reclamation yard if you happen to have one locally. Buy whatever bricks take your fancy.
>
> **Wood shavings** Any timber merchant or sawmill will probably be happy to sell you wood shavings. These should not be too coarse, or too fine – the texture of muesli would be good.

The first day

To do list:
- Mix the clay and sand
- Build the sand former
- Build the inner skin
- Remove the sand former
- Begin drying

Mix the clay and sand

Lay the tarpaulin out on the ground and tip 6 buckets of sand and 3 buckets of clay on to it (pic 1). This will give you enough for today's work, but if you want to get ahead of yourself, you could double the amount, which will give you enough for the outer wall too.

Now, stick a pair of wellies or stout boots on as many friends as you can muster and start stomping (pic 2). Throw out any stones as you come across them. Every so often, get hold of both corners of one end of the tarpaulin and pull it over to meet the other end (pic 3); this will turn the sand and clay over on itself, helping to mix it thoroughly.

You may feel the mix is just too firm, dry and difficult to work, in which case you need to add some water – this is likely if the clay was very dry to begin with. If you dug clay from a riverbank or pond, it will probably be wet enough already. The final consistency of the mix should be soft enough to mould and shape easily, and strong enough to hold its own weight.

When your mix is looking pretty well blended, test the consistency. Take a small piece of dough (the size of a lime) and spend a minute or so compacting it. Now hold it at shoulder height and drop it on to the ground. On impact it should crack, but roughly hold its shape (pic 4). If it crumbles, the mix is too sandy and you need to add more clay. If it 'splats', it is too wet and you should add more sand. When you are happy with the consistency, your building material – or 'mud' as I prefer to call it – is ready to use.

Build the sand former

The first stage of building is to make a dome of sand, which will be the 'former' around which you build the inner skin of the oven. First, trace a circle 80cm diameter, centrally on the plinth. Next, heap sand into the circle and start forming a dome – or almost a dome (p.200, pic 1). The mound should rise vertically to start with, to about a hand's depth, before it starts to curve inwards; this gives much more headroom for anything cooking next to the wall. The finished dome should be about 40cm high.

Mix the clay and sand

1

2

3

4

Build the sand former

1

2

3

4

From time to time, stand on the plinth, centre your eyes over the dome and get a bird's-eye view of your work (pic 2) – it is much easier to spot imperfections from up there. When you are happy, the next step is to cover the dome with a layer of wet newspaper. You will be digging the sand out later; this newspaper layer tells you when to stop digging. Soak whole sheets and lay them over the dome (pic 3); you don't need to be neat, by any means – just make sure you completely cover the sand (pic 4). This is slightly harder in practice than it sounds, but only slightly; the paper won't stick to the sand as well as you might hope, but it will stick to itself.

Build the inner skin

You are now ready to start building your oven. The technique is simple. Pick up a good handful of your clay and sand 'mud' and pat and mould it into a rough brick shape. Sit this adjacent to the dome and, using the edge of one hand as a mallet and the other hand as a buffer, pack the brick down to a width of around 7cm (pic 1), using your measuring stick as a guide. Make a second brick and sit it alongside, packing down in the same way. The 'bricks' should merge into one (pic 2). Compacting is essential. Apart from giving the structure more solidity, it removes air pockets, which can expand with the heat of the oven and cause cracks.

Build the inner skin

1

2

Continue like this until you get all the way round, then start your second layer, and so on. You don't need to measure every time, but poke your stick in every now and then to make sure you maintain the thickness. And don't forget your bird's-eye view – this is still your best guide. Once you reach the top and close the gap, take some more time to depth-check and smooth your dome; the more even the structure, the stronger it will be.

When you are happy with the shape, have a cleanup. Your work is almost done. Save any leftover mud – splash a little water over it, shovel into plastic sacks or bin liners, tie the tops to stop it drying out and keep it for later. Now would be a good time to have lunch. You should leave your oven to settle on itself and firm up a bit for at least a couple of hours; you could even leave it overnight if it suits you better. You want it to get used to being there.

Remove the sand former

Now comes the fun bit: you are going to take away your oven's support. With a decent knife (a bread knife, funnily enough, is perfect), cut an arch where you want your door to be (pic 1). This will not be the finished doorway so don't worry about making it perfect. Decide how wide you want it. Do you have a particular roasting tray that needs to fit through? A reasonable size would be 30cm wide, and perhaps 20cm high.

Pull the mud out from the arch that you have cut (pic 2), then with one hand, start hollowing out the sand (pic 3). Keep digging, inwards, sideways and upwards. You won't be able to see what you're doing – your arm will be in the way – but at some point you will reach your layer of newspaper (pic 4). As you expose it, peel it away; this is too satisfying for words.

Keep digging and peeling, ignoring the little voice in your head that is telling you the whole thing will collapse at any minute. It won't. As you get deeper, be aware of your arm – it is easy to bash the side of the archway if you don't concentrate. When you finally scrape out the last bit of sand, take a step back and marvel at your oven. It really is still standing.

Begin drying

Over the next few days, you want your oven to dry out completely. Light a fire inside as often as you can. This can be tricky, as there is a lot of moisture inside and not much oxygen, but I suggest you resist using cheaty methods such as firelighters/barbecue fuel/petrol (unless you want your bread to taste of these). It is best to light a small fire near the doorway, where there is more air, then push it to the back once it is going strong. Your oven is fully dry when it has stopped steaming during firing; the colour will be considerably paler too.

Remove the sand former

1

2

3

4

BUILDING A CLAY OVEN

1

The second day

To do list:
- Build the door arch and chimney
- Make a clay slip
- Build the insulating layer
- Continue drying

Build the door arch and chimney

You can form the door arch from your clay and sand mud, but I recommend that you make it from bricks. It will look more attractive and bricks are stronger, withstanding little knocks far better.

Build a sand former the same size as your doorway, extending forward a brick's length from the base of the oven. Now build an archway around the front section of the former, using some of your reserved clay and sand mix as mortar between the bricks (pic 1). Use more clay and sand to extend the doorway back to meet the receding wall of the oven (pic 2). Cut a hole in the top of this, roughly 20cm diameter, and form a chimney around the hole, around 20 cm high (pic 3). Remove the sand former after a few hours.

Make a clay slip

1    2

Make a clay slip
Get your wellies on again. Drag your tarpaulin out and empty one bucket of clay on to it. Tip about half a bucket of warm water on to the clay and start stomping. As the water gets blended in, keep adding more until you have a sludgy gloop, the consistency of thick yoghurt – this is called 'slip'. You can make the slip in a dustbin, mixing it with your hands (pic 1) if you prefer. Next, start to mix in the wood shavings with a shovel. Keep going until the whole thing looks like a stone giant's cornflake crunchie: the slip should bind the shavings together, just as the chocolate binds the cornflakes (pic 2).

Build the insulating layer
Using the same method as you used on the first day to build the inner skin (see pp.201–2), pack your wood and clay mixture over the dome, again to a thickness of about 7cm, using your measuring stick as a guide. Skirt around the doorway – you don't need to insulate the arch.

Continue drying
Dry this insulating layer out completely, building the odd fire as before (see p.202), over the next few days to hasten the process.

Build the insulating layer

The third day

To do list:
- Build the outer wall
- Make a door and chimney lid (optional)

Build the outer wall
You need to apply exactly the same method as you used to build the inner skin (see pp.201–2), though you'll find this stage much more satisfying. Keep fussing over your outer wall until it looks the way you want it to. You could decorate it, if you like – using some natural paints perhaps, or stud it with stones. The important thing is that the oven can breathe, or it will retain moisture – so don't smother it in tiles, or anything else that is not porous. Dry it out, building fires (see p.202), as before.

Make a door and chimney lid
Measure and cut a piece of wood to fit snugly inside the door arch. Cut a short baton for a handle and glue or nail it to the outside of the door. Cut a circle from another piece of wood to sit on the chimney. These will not be fireproof, of course; they are for retaining heat after the fire has been removed. Soaking them in water before every use will help stop them warping. Your oven is now ready to use.

Build the outer wall

Using your oven

The oven will need 3–4 hours' firing to get up to temperature. Start a small fire just inside the doorway, using paper and small kindling, then build it up with larger pieces of wood until it is burning well. When it is established, use sticks to slide the burning wood carefully right to the back, then keep feeding it with more wood as you need to, in order to maintain a good, rolling flame. The heat will become ferocious. I cannot give precise timings – you will get used to your own oven – but if the outer wall feels fairly warm you can be pretty sure the inside is scorching. For the last 10 minutes, spread the embers out to get extra heat into the whole floor.

When you are ready to cook, scrape or shovel all the embers out into a metal dustbin, or better still, something with a flat side that can sit flush to the wall of the plinth. At River Cottage we use a pig-feeding trough, which is ideal.

For most cooking, you will need to wait for the oven to cool a bit. The internal air temperature can be as high as 450°C, even with the fire removed completely. The surface temperature of the floor will be even hotter. This is perfect for cooking pizza, which will be ready in little over a minute, but nothing could withstand this heat for any longer. A loaf of bread would be black in no time. An oven thermometer would be helpful, but I have not found one that can measure above 300°C. In time, you will become a reliable temperature gauge. As you get to know your oven, you will get used to the searing heat – the feel of it on your skin as you reach in. I reckon if I can hold my hand just inside the doorway for a couple of seconds, I can probably bake a batch of bread without too much scorching. If I can't, I wait.

When I'm making bread, I shape a couple of small balls of dough (the size of a lemon) for testing. I put one into the oven and check it after a couple of minutes. If it shows signs of scorched patches, particularly on the bottom, I wait 5 minutes or so, then test the other ball. If this one is only turning golden after 2 minutes, I go for it. If it scorches again, I give it another 10 minutes or so before putting the loaves in.

To bake bread, follow your chosen recipe, then slip your loaves into the clay oven one at a time. Keep an eye on them; you will almost certainly want to shuffle them around so they colour more evenly. To bake pizza, follow the recipe (pp.104–6).

Once the bread is baked, I always feel it is a shame to waste the residual heat, so I almost always have something ready to follow it with – the temperature would now be perfect for a joint of meat, for example. Also, don't forget that your oven will make an effective, if rather immobile, patio heater.

As your oven settles into life, you may find cracks appearing. Don't worry unduly about this. If they become large, fill them in with clay, otherwise the efficiency of your oven may be affected. Some day, depending on how well it is sheltered and how often it is used, it will be time to knock your oven down and build a new one. Don't feel too downhearted about this. After all, everything returns to earth… in the end.

Useful Things

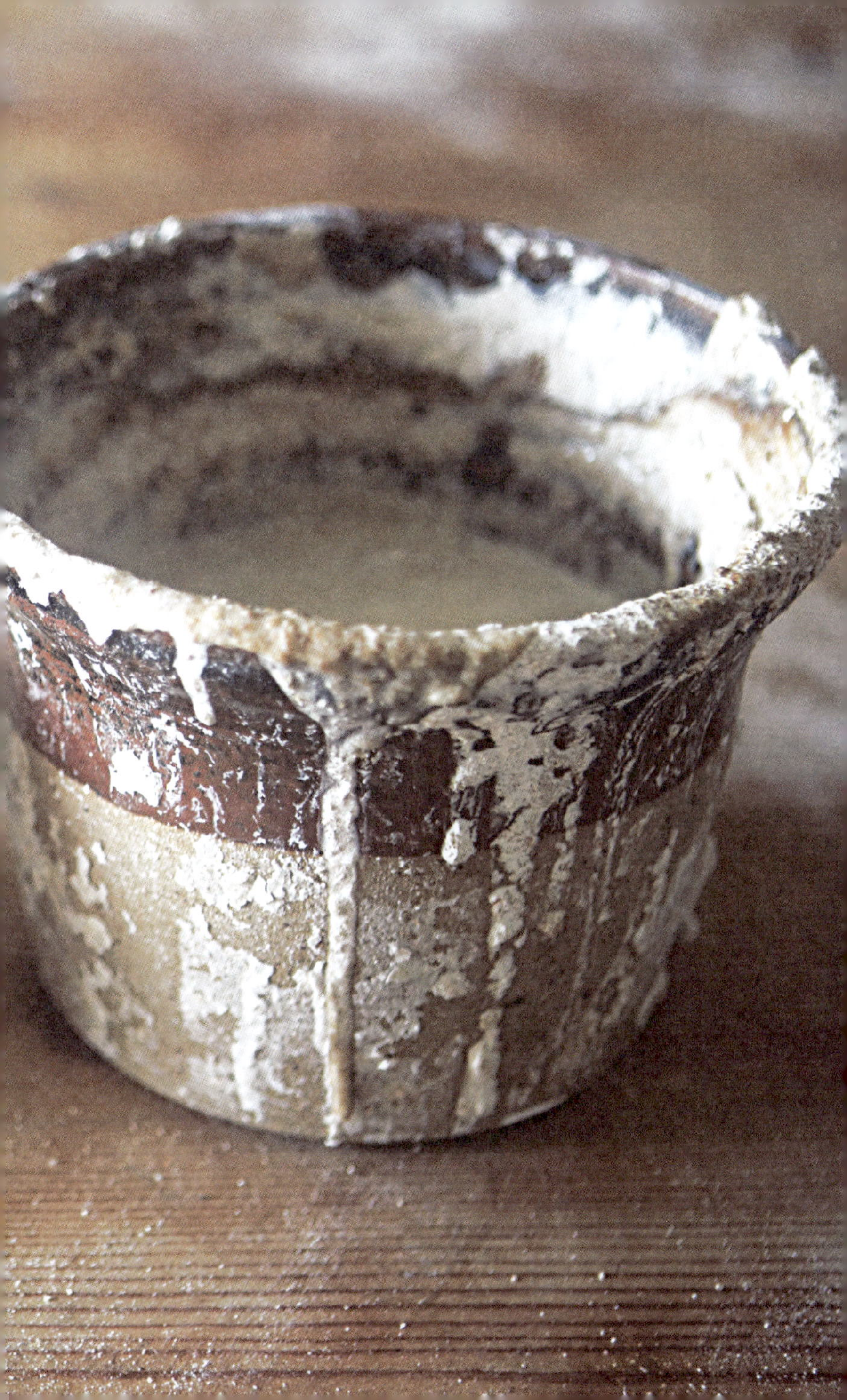

Directory

Flour suppliers

Doves Farm
Hungerford, Berkshire
www.dovesfarm.co.uk
01488 684880
Wide range of organic flours,
including speciality and gluten-free

N R Stoate & Sons
Cann Mills, Shaftesbury, Dorset
www.stoatesflour.co.uk
01747 852475
Mainly organic flours,
stoneground by Michael Stoate,
a fifth-generation miller

Bacheldre Watermill
Churchstoke, Montgomery, Powys
www.bacheldremill.co.uk
01588 620489
Lovely range of stoneground
flours, mostly organic

Shipton Mill
Tetbury, Gloucestershire
www.shipton-mill.com
01666 505050
Many organic and speciality flours

Sharpham Park
Glastonbury, Somerset
www.sharphampark.com
01458 844080
Spelt flour, grown and milled
on an organic farm

Equipment suppliers

Creeds Ltd
Aylesbury, Buckinghamshire
www.creeds.uk.com
01296 658849
Suppliers of general baking equipment
(including proving baskets and peels)

Nisbets
Avonmouth, Bristol
www.nisbets.co.uk
0845 140 5555
Full range of catering-standard
kitchen equipment

Further reading

English Bread and Yeast Cookery
Elizabeth David
(Penguin Books, 1977)

The Tassajara Bread Book
Edward Espe Brown
(Shambhala Publications, 1970)

Baking with Passion (Baker & Spice)
Dan Lepard and Richard Whittington
(Quadrille, 2003)

McGee on Food and Cooking
Harold McGee
(Hodder & Stoughton, 2004)

SHIPTON
MILL
organic semolina
1kg
CERTIFIED UK 5
SHIPTON MILL, TETBURY, GLOUCESTERSHIRE, GL8 8RP

Conversion charts

Metric quantities are given in the recipes. Use the following conversions if you prefer to work in imperial measures.

Weight

Metric	Imperial
25g	1oz
50g	2oz
100g–125g	4oz
170g	6oz
200g	7oz
225g	8oz
275g	10oz
340g	12oz
400g	14oz
450g	1lb
500g	1lb 2oz
900g	2lb
1kg	2lb 4oz

Liquid/volume

Metric	Imperial
150ml	5fl oz (¼ pint)
300ml	10fl oz (½ pint)
600ml	20fl oz (1 pint)
1 litre	35fl oz (1¾ pints)

1 tsp (1 teaspoon) = 5ml
1 tbsp (1 tablespoon) = 15ml

Oven temperatures

	°C	°F	Gas Mark
Very cool	130	250	½
Very cool	140	275	1
Cool	150	300	2
Moderate	160–170	325	3
Moderate	180	350	4
Moderately hot	190	375	5
Moderately hot	200	400	6
Hot	220	425	7
Hot	230	450	8
Very Hot	240–250	450–475	9–10

Acknowledgements

I could not have done this without...

Everyone at Bloomsbury:

Richard Atkinson, you have always had something good to say about me, your encouragement makes such a difference.

Janet Illsley, you have put so much work into this, thank you. I am so impressed by how you have brought it all together and made sense of my ramblings.

Will Webb, you have made such a good-looking book. Thank you for everything you've done. Oh, and I'm still waiting to try your bread...

Penny Edwards, thank you for your hard work and attention to the production of this book.

Erica Jarnes, thank you so much for your help, and for always looking pleased to see me.

And Natalie Hunt, you have guided me through this brilliantly. I have felt properly looked after... I will miss my trips to the big city. Thank you so, so much. I hope we have made a book you are proud of.

And everyone at River Cottage:

Thank you to Rob Love and Hugh Fearnley-Whittingstall, for giving me this opportunity, for believing in me, and for sticking by me.

And to Gill Meller, you have given me great help and massive support. I've run out of excuses now... I'd better get back in the kitchen. Cheers blood.

Thank you to Nikki Duffy for starting me off so well, for your time and energy and endless, endless patience.

Debora Robertson, you have been amazing. You have worked so hard for me, and given me so much encouragement, and so much belief in myself. Thank you also for 'conquistadors' – the best word in the book!

Not forgetting:

Aidan Chapman at the Town Mill Bakery: You have always been very generous with your knowledge. Thank you, I am a much better baker because of you.

Niamh, my lovely little bun. I hope you like the book I've made.

And Michelle Rose, Mia and Olivia... thank you for letting us cover your kitchen in flour. I had a wonderful day making wonderful bread with you.

Hazel Maxwell... thank you for everything. I wish I was more like you. I love you.

And last of all:

Thank you to Gavin Kingcome. Working with you was a complete pleasure. Your photographs are amazing... your camera makes the world so much more beautiful. This started out a word book with pictures; it ended up a picture book with words. It is our book.

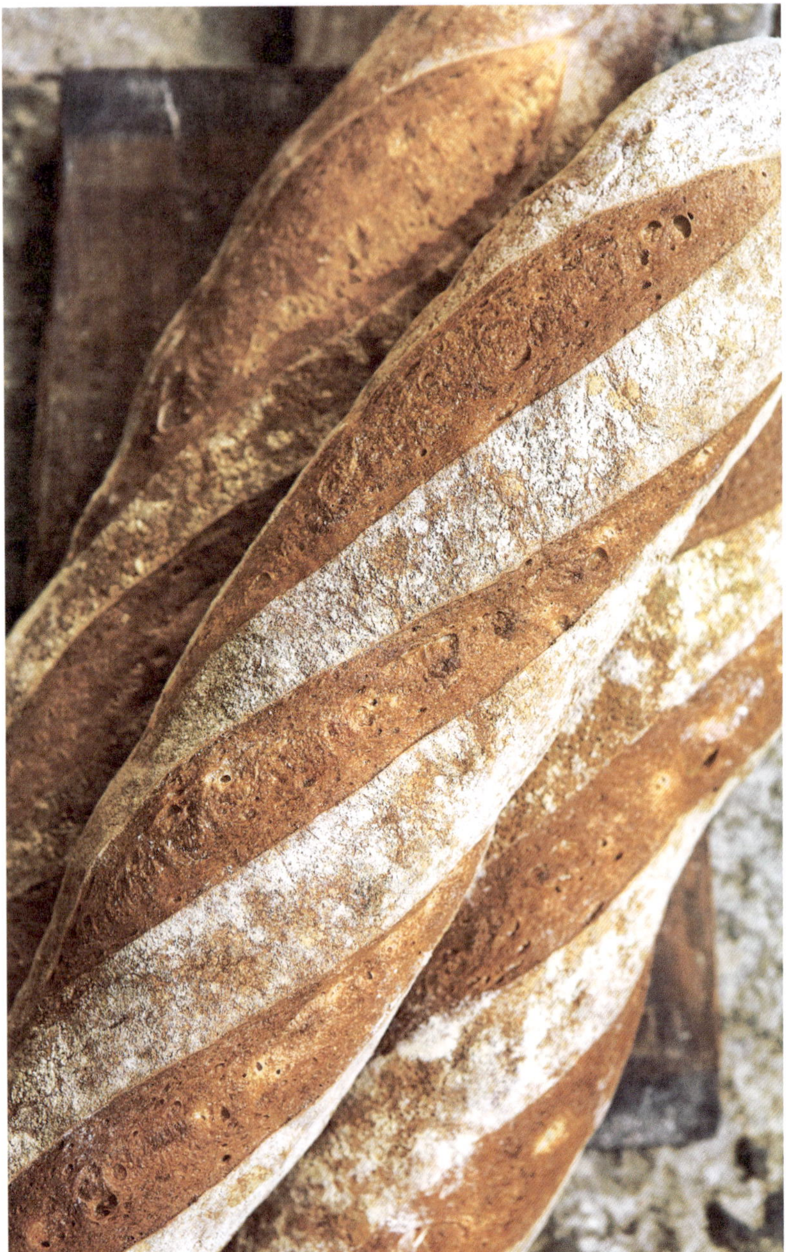

Index

acetic acid 28
additives
    in mass-produced bread 10
    in salt 31
alfalfa seeds
    festival bread 81
apple juice 31
    hazel maizel bread 82

bacon
    cornbread 167
    migas 176
bagels 96
baguettes, shaping 55
bakeries 12
baking bread 66
    in clay oven 209
    timings 66
    see also bread making
baking powder, self-raising flour 22
baking stones 17, 53
    baking bread 66
    pizza 104
    transferring loaves for baking 63–4
baking trays 17, 53
    transferring loaves for baking 63–4
bannocks 137
barbecue breads 107
barley flakes 32
    festival bread 81
basic bread recipe 72–7
    variations 78–83
basil
    panino 91
baskets, proving 16, 63
batons, shaping 56
beer 31
beetroot houmous 178
bin liners 50
biscuits
    poppy and caraway crackers 163
    River Cottage shortbread 158
    Scottish oatcakes 164
    spelt digestives 161
bleaching flour 19
blinis 168
boards 16
bowls 17
bran 19, 20
bread and butter pudding 186
bread flour 20
bread making 34–70
    baking bread 66
    coating the outside 61
    cooling bread 68
    deflating dough 50
    dividing dough 54
    kneading dough 44–7
    leaving dough to ferment 50
    leaving dough to prove 63
    measuring ingredients 39–40
    mixing dough 42
    preparing dough for baking 53–4
    shaping dough into a round 48–9
    shaping loaves 55–9
    slashing the tops 64
    transferring loaves for baking 63–4
    troubleshooting 70
bread sauce 176
breadcrumbs 176–7
breadsticks 92
breakfast 167
breakfast rolls 80
bricks, building a clay oven 197, 205
brioche 95
brown bread ice cream 189
brown flour 19, 20
brown soda bread 130
buckwheat 32
buns
    Chelsea buns 154
    hot cross buns 152
buttermilk
    soda bread 130

calcium 24, 31
Canadian wheat 21
candied peel
    lardy cake 151
caraway seeds
    poppy and caraway crackers 163
carbon dioxide 28
    see also gas bubbles
carbonic acid 28
cheese
    nettle pesto 181
    panino 91
    pizza 104
Chelsea buns 154
chickpea flour
    socca 172
chimney, clay oven 196, 205, 208
Chorleywood Bread process 10–12
churros 144
ciabatta 86, 90–1
cider 31
    festival bread 81
clay
    for clay oven 197, 198
    clay slip 206

clay ovens
    building 192–208
    using 209
cling film 50
cloths 16
containers, oiling 50
conversion charts 214
cooling bread 68
corn tortillas 134
cornbread 167
cornmeal 32
crackers, poppy and caraway 163
cream
    bread and butter pudding 186
croissants 147–9
croûtons 176
crumpets 165
crust
    coating 61
    'flying crust' syndrome 63, 70
    slashing tops 64
    steam and 53
    troubleshooting 70
    using as a plate 176
cucumber
    panzanella 182
currants
    Chelsea buns 154
    hot cross buns 152
    lardy cake 151

deflating dough 50
digestives, spelt 161
digital scales 17, 40
dips
    beetroot houmous 178
    taramasalata 179
dividing dough 54
doors, clay ovens 208
dough
    coating the outside 61
    deflating 50
    dividing 54
    intermediate shaping 54
    kneading 44–7
    mixing 42
    'oven spring' 53, 66
    preparing for baking 53–4
    proving 63
    rising 28–9, 48, 50, 53
    shaping into a round 48–9
    shaping loaves 55–9
    slashing tops 64
    starter 40
dough scrapers 17
doughnuts 142–3

dried fruit 32
    adding to dough 40
    festival bread 81
    hot cross buns 152
    lardy cake 151
dried yeast 26, 28
durum wheat 22

eggs
    bread and butter pudding 186
    migas 176
    pain perdu 184
    scotch eggs 176
empty-the-shelf bread 82
endosperm 20
English muffins 99
equipment 16–17
esters 28

fan-assisted ovens 66
fat 31
    quantities 39–40
fermentation 28–9
    rising dough 48, 50
    sourdough starter 112
festival bread 81
fire, in clay oven 209
fish, coating with breadcrumbs 176
fish fingers 177
flambéed pain perdu 184
flatbread 103
    roti 133
    tortillas 134
flour 19–24
    coating loaves 61
    gluten-free bread flour 23
    hydration 39
    kamut flour 23
    leaving dough to ferment 50
    milling 24
    quantities 39, 40
    rye flour 23
    spelt flour 23
    wheat flour 20–2
Flour Milling and Baking Research Association 10
'flying crust' syndrome 63, 70
focaccia 86, 89
food mixers 17
    kneading dough 47
former, for clay oven 198–201
freezing
    bread 68
    breadcrumbs 176
    dough 29
    yeast 28
fresh yeast 26–8

fridges, storing bread in 68
fruit
    summer pudding 190
    see also dried fruit

garlicky olive oil 104
gas bubbles
    'oven spring' 53, 66
    rising dough 28–9, 48
germ 20
gluten 24
    effect of salt on 29
    gluten intolerance 10
    kneading dough 44
    proving dough 63
    relaxing 54
    rising dough 48, 50
    slashing tops 64
    in spelt flour 23
    in wheat flour 20–2
gluten-free bread flour 23, 24
goat's cheese
    panino 91
grains
    adding to dough 40
    coating loaves 61
Granary flour 22

hazelnuts 32
    festival bread 81
    hazel maizel bread 82
hemp seeds
    spelt sourdough 122–3
honey 31
    walnut and honey bread 131
hot cross buns 152
houmous, beetroot 178
hydration 39

ice cream, brown bread 189
ingredients 19–32
    basic bread recipe 75
    measuring 39–40
insulation, clay ovens 206
intermediate shaping 54

kamut flour 23, 24
kneading dough 44–7
knives
    bread knife 16
    slashing tops 64
    slicing bread 68
'knocking back' 50

lactic acid 28
lardy cake 151

leftover bread 174–91
    beetroot houmous 178
    bread and butter pudding 186
    breadcrumbs 176–7
    brown bread ice cream 189
    nettle pesto 181
    pain perdu 184
    panzanella 182
    summer pudding 190
    taramasalata 179
levain 110
linen cloths 16
liquids 31
loaf tins 55
loaves
    coating the outside 61
    shaping 55–9
    size 54
    slashing the tops 64
    transferring for baking 63–4
low-gluten breads 64

magnesium 24, 31
maize meal 32
    corn tortillas 134
    cornbread 167
    hazel maizel bread 82
malted and seeded loaf 80
malted grain bread 78
malted grain flour 22
mass-produced bread 10–12
measuring ingredients 39–40
migas 176
milk 31
millet 32
mineral water 24
'mini-blinis' 168
mixing bowls 17
molasses
    pumpernickel 124–5
monastery bread 81
muffins, English 99
my sourdough 117–19

nachos 134
nettle pesto 181
nuts 32
    adding to dough 40
    festival bread 81
    hazel maizel bread 82
    walnut and honey bread 131

oats and oatmeal 31
    bannocks 137
    coating loaves 61
    festival bread 81

monastery bread 81
oaty wholemeal 79
Scottish oatcakes 164
spelt digestives 161
Staffordshire oatcakes 171
oil 31
    leaving dough to ferment 50
    in wheat flour 20
olive oil
    ciabatta 90–1
    focaccia 89
    garlicky olive oil 104
one-stage mixing method 42
onions
    migas 176
    panzanella 182
organic flour 19
'oven spring' 53, 66
ovens 53
    clay ovens 192–209
    for pizza 104
    preparing for baking 53–4
    refreshing bread 68
    steam 53
    temperatures 53, 66, 215

pain perdu 184
pancakes
    blinis 168
    socca 172
panino 91
panzanella 182
Parmesan, 'poor man's' 176
peels 17, 53, 66
    transferring loaves for baking 64
pesto, nettle 181
pikelets 165
pizza 104–6
plain flour 22
plinth, clay oven 195–6
poolish 110
'poor man's Parmesan' 176
poppy and caraway crackers 163
proteins 20–1
proving baskets 16, 63
proving dough 63
pumpernickel 124–5

racks, cooling 68
raising agents, self-raising flour 22
raisins
    bread and butter pudding 186
    festival bread 81
    hot cross buns 152
refreshing bread 68
refrigerators, storing bread in 68

rising dough 28–9, 48, 50, 53
    'oven spring' 53, 66
    proving dough 63
    slashing tops 64
River Cottage shortbread 158
River Cottage sourdough 116
rock salt 29
roe
    taramasalata 179
roller milling, flour 19
rolls
    breakfast rolls 80
    refreshing 68
    shaping 59
    size 54
roof, clay oven 196
rosemary
    focaccia 89
roti 133
rye berries
    pumpernickel 124–5
rye flour 23, 24
    blinis 168
    coating loaves 61
    pumpernickel 124–5
    sour rye bread 120

salads
    panzanella 182
salami
    panino 91
salt 29–31
    focaccia 89
    quantities 39, 40
sand
    for clay oven 197, 198
    former 198–201
sandwiches
    panino 91
sauces
    bread sauce 176
    nettle pesto 181
    roast tomato sauce 104
sausage meat
    scotch eggs 176
scales 17, 40
scones 156
scotch eggs 176
Scottish oatcakes 164
sea salt 29–31
seeds 32
    adding to dough 40
    coating loaves 61
    malted and seeded loaf 80
sel gris 31
self-raising flour 22

semolina 32
    ciabatta 90–1
shaping, intermediate 54
shaping loaves 55–9
shortbread, River Cottage 158
slashing tops 64
slicing bread 68
slip, clay 206
smoked pollack roe
    taramasalata 179
socca 172
soda bread 130
    walnut and honey bread 131
'soggy tea towel' technique 107
sour rye bread 120
sourdough 115–16
    my sourdough 117–19
    pumpernickel 124–5
    River Cottage sourdough 116
    sour rye bread 120
    spelt sourdough 122–3
    sponge method 42
    starter 40, 110–13
spelt flour 23, 24
    festival bread 81
    spelt bread 79
    spelt digestives 161
    spelt sourdough 122–3
sponge method, mixing dough 42
spray bottles 17, 53
spring water 24
Staffordshire oatcakes 171
staling 68
starter 40
    sourdough 110–13
steam
    cooling bread 68
    in oven 53
stoneground flour 19
stones *see* baking stones
storing bread 68
strong flour 20–1
stubby cylinders, shaping 56–7
sultanas
    hot cross buns 152
    lardy cake 151
summer pudding 190

tapered batons, shaping 56
taramasalata 179
temperature
    in clay oven 209
    dough 28, 29
    oven 53, 66, 215
texture, troubleshooting 70
thermometers 17, 209

tin loaves, shaping 58
tins 55
toast 177
tomatoes
    panino 91
    panzanella 182
    roast tomato sauce 104
toppings, pizza 104, 106
tops, slashing 64
tortillas 134
trays, baking 17, 53
troubleshooting 70
two-stage mixing method 42

vetkoek 100

walnuts 32
    walnut and honey bread 131
water 24
    quantities 39, 40
water spray bottles 17, 53
weighing scales 17, 40
wheat 20–1
    flour 20–2, 24
    wheat intolerance 12, 22
wheat berries
    pumpernickel 124–5
white bread 78
white flour 19
wholemeal flour 19
    hydration 39
    oaty wholemeal 79
wild yeasts 26, 108–25
wood-fired ovens, pizza 104
wood shavings, for clay oven 197
wooden boards 16
work surfaces, kneading dough 44
wort 26

yeast 26–9
    how yeast works 28–9
    quantities 39, 40
    rising dough 50, 53
    sourdough starter 110–13
    wild yeasts 26, 108–25
yeast-free breads 126–37
yoghurt 31
    blinis 168
    cornbread 167
    flatbread 103
    my sourdough 117–19

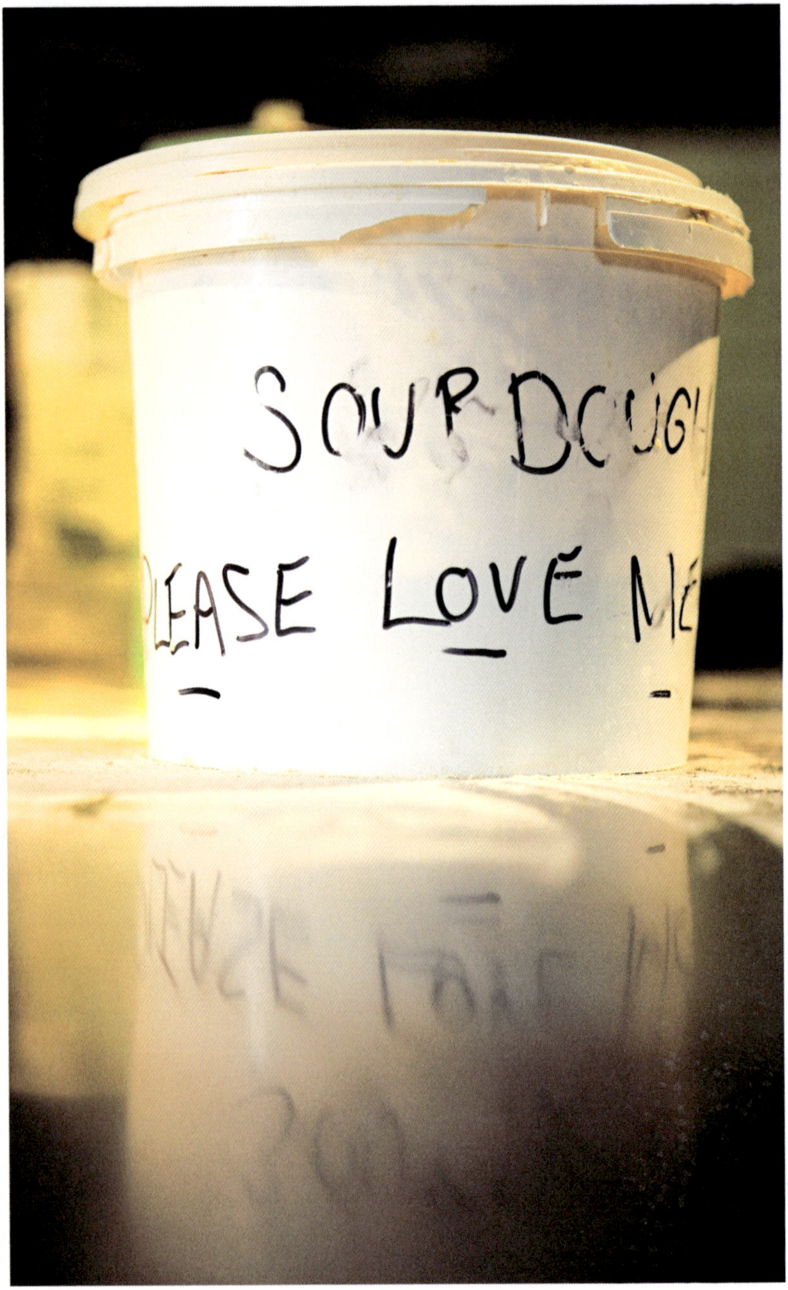
SOURDOUGH
PLEASE LOVE ME

The River Cottage

Veg Patch Handbook

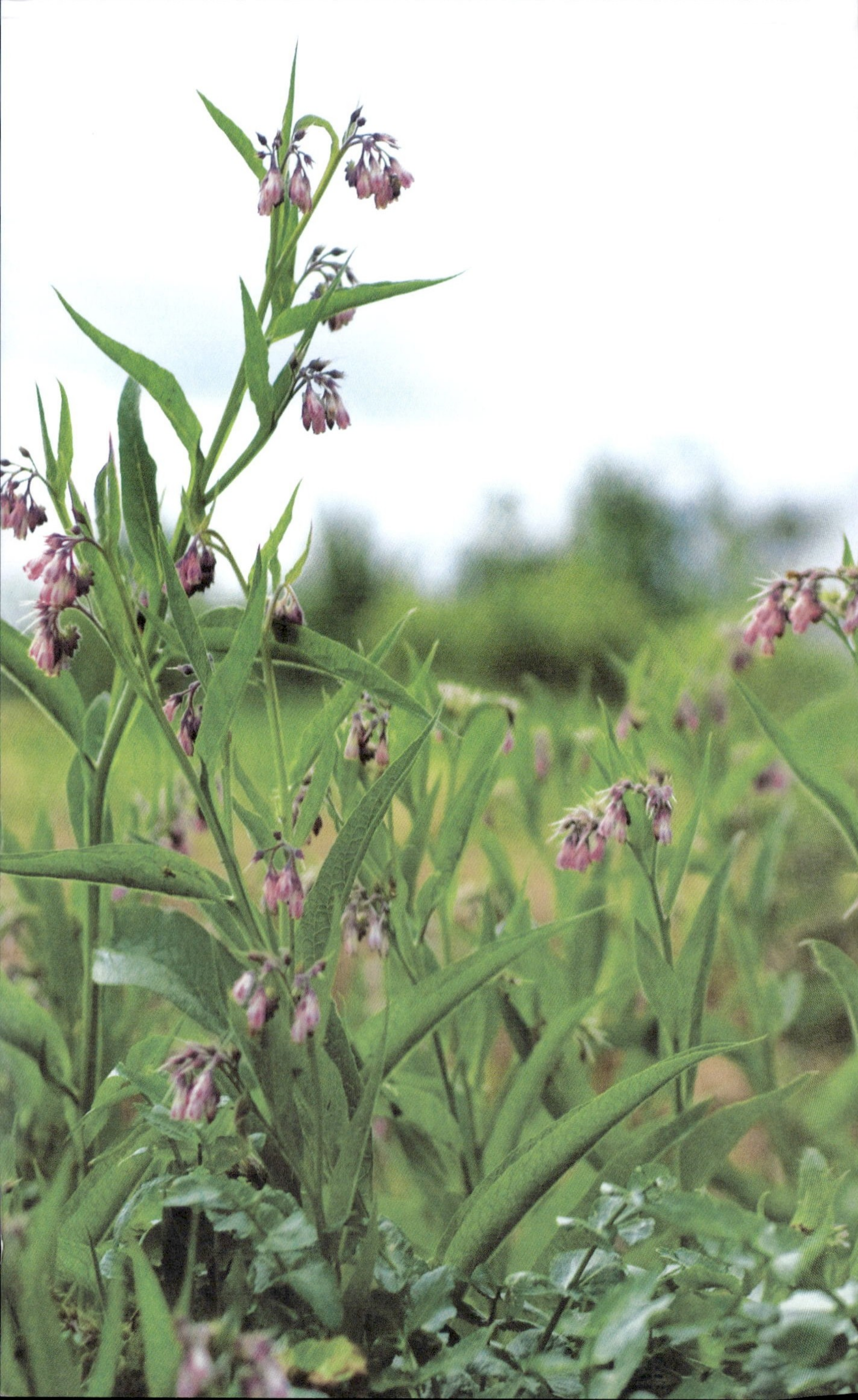

The River Cottage Veg Patch Handbook

by Mark Diacono

introduced by
Hugh Fearnley-Whittingstall

www.rivercottage.net

BLOOMSBURY
LONDON · NEW DELHI · NEW YORK · SYDNEY

for Candida

First published in Great Britain 2009
This paperback edition published 2012

Text © 2009 by Mark Diacono
Photography © 2009 by Mark Diacono
Additional photography on pp.51, 197 (left), 205, 224, 231, 232,
235, 236, 241, 245, 249, 252 © 2009 by Gavin Kingcome

The moral right of the author has been asserted.

Bloomsbury Publishing Plc, 50 Bedford Square, London WC1B 3DP
Bloomsbury Publishing, London, New Delhi, New York and Sydney

MIX
Paper from responsible sources
FSC® C008047

A CIP catalogue record for this book is available from the British Library

ISBN 978 1 4088 3608 8
10 9 8 7 6 5 4 3 2 1

Project editor: Janet Illsley
Design: willwebb.co.uk
Printed in China by C&C Offset Printing Co., Ltd.
www.bloomsbury.com/river cottage

While every effort has been made to ensure the accuracy of the information contained in this book, in no circumstances can the publisher or the author accept any legal responsibility or liability for any loss or damage (including damage to property and/or personal injury) arising from any error in or omission from the information contained in this book, or from the failure of the reader to properly and accurately follow any instructions contained in the book.

Contents

Growing your own Food · 8

Vegetable A–Z · 20

Plant Groups · 154

Planning your Veg Patch · 170

Creating your Veg Patch · 184

Maintaining your Veg Patch · 200

Recipes · 220

Directory · 265

Index · 268

I wish I'd had this book in my hands when I first set out on my River Cottage adventure more than ten years ago. I can say with some certainty that it would have saved me from many mistakes, but its author would no doubt find that unduly negative. And this is the joy of Mark's thoroughly upbeat approach to growing your own food. His philosophy is that 'There are no mistakes, just experiences you probably shouldn't repeat.' I can safely say that, if I'd had this book ten years ago, I would not only have had fewer experiences that I don't wish to repeat, I would also have had many more experiences that it would be an unqualified pleasure to repeat again and again, season after season.

I have watched Mark's progress from enthusiastic amateur to passionate teacher with admiration and great pleasure. I'm thrilled that he's now our head gardener at River Cottage. Both on our courses and in the pages of this book, I can think of no better person to share our philosophy with a wider audience. There are few people better placed than Mark to tell you how to deploy home-grown veg to improve the quality of your life, because that's precisely what he's been doing for the best part of the last decade. His great strength lies in choosing and growing vegetables and fruits that are 100 per cent relevant and therefore 100 per cent rewarding. In other words, he grows food that he knows he will use, and will bring him and his family great enjoyment. He recognises of course that these guiding principles will result in a different harvest for everyone. But one of the joys of this book is the way it helps you decide what that harvest should be for you.

One of Mark's personal passions is to explore the fringes of what it's possible to grow in our unpredictable but undeniably shifting climate. With characteristic verve, he seized the opportunity to look at gardening in a fresh way and started planting pecans, olives and apricots at Otter Farm, his own smallholding in Devon. The inevitably mixed results have included some fantastic successes – among them the most delicious apricots I have tasted anywhere in the world!

Mercifully, Mark's a better grower than a fisherman. When we first met, we went fishing together out of Weymouth, in pursuit of bass. Sadly, Mark spent most of the time with his head over the side of the boat, generously redistributing his breakfast to the local marine life. He didn't say much that morning. Yet when we got talking back on dry land, I quickly realised this was someone who had something interesting to say about food. Then he began running a few courses for us at River Cottage and I saw what a great teacher he is. It's down to him that we now have Szechuan pepper, allspice, almonds and olives nestling on the slopes around River Cottage. But also that we have sent many hundreds of visitors home with the inspired notion that they will, from that moment on, make home-grown food a vital part of their family life.

In addition to his experimental high-risk crops, Mark's 'let's not take anything for granted' approach has led him – and us – to push at the margins of our seasonality and try out innovative growing methods with some of our best-loved veg crops. Consequently you'll find this book is far more than just a digestion of received veg garden wisdom. It is a passionate polemic for growing your own that is full of fresh insights and surprising practical suggestions, such as growing your spuds in stacks of car tyres.

I don't think it's overstating it to say that growing your own food will change your life. It may start with a few pots of herbs, a row of radishes, a tub of lettuce, but it rarely ends there. Change is incremental, but inevitable. The pure, sweet pleasure of podding your own peas seconds after picking them will lead to new adventures, new crops. If you grow it, you're more likely to eat it, to share it with friends, and even find yourself making new friends (that happens a lot when people come to River Cottage HQ).

Once you have made the connection between plot and plate, you'll expect more, and demand more, from your food. Anaemic, shrink-wrapped cabbage from the supermarket can never taste as good as one you tended from a seed, saved from slugs and caterpillars, nurtured through too little rain or too much. You'll cherish it for the miracle it is and, because of that, you're less likely to waste it.

Food miles, packaging and food waste are three of the biggest challenges that face us as a society, but when you grow your own, you are no longer contributing to the problem. And, without doubt, when you're connected to the land you have more of a stake in its welfare.

Mark and I believe that this adventure is out there for everyone. You just have to choose it. Whether you live in the middle of the city or are nestled in your own green acres, whether you have a terrace with tubs, a regimental allotment or a sprawling vegetable garden, you can have a go. Growing vegetables is a forgiving activity. Try new things, experiment, and as long as you hang on to your optimism and sense of wonder, your veg patch – however tidy or raggedy, big or small – will be a kingdom of earthy delights. As Mark says, 'Plants want to grow, all we have to do is let them, rather than make them'.

I'm very excited about this book. Whether you want to grow a few beans or tend a huge spread, Mark's your man. His wisdom will stand you in great stead as you embark on the adventure of growing your own. And at a time when it's easy to fall prey to all of the gloom that surrounds the food we eat, Mark's sense of what is possible is the perfect antidote.

Hugh Fearnley-Whittingstall, East Devon, March 2009

Growing your own Food

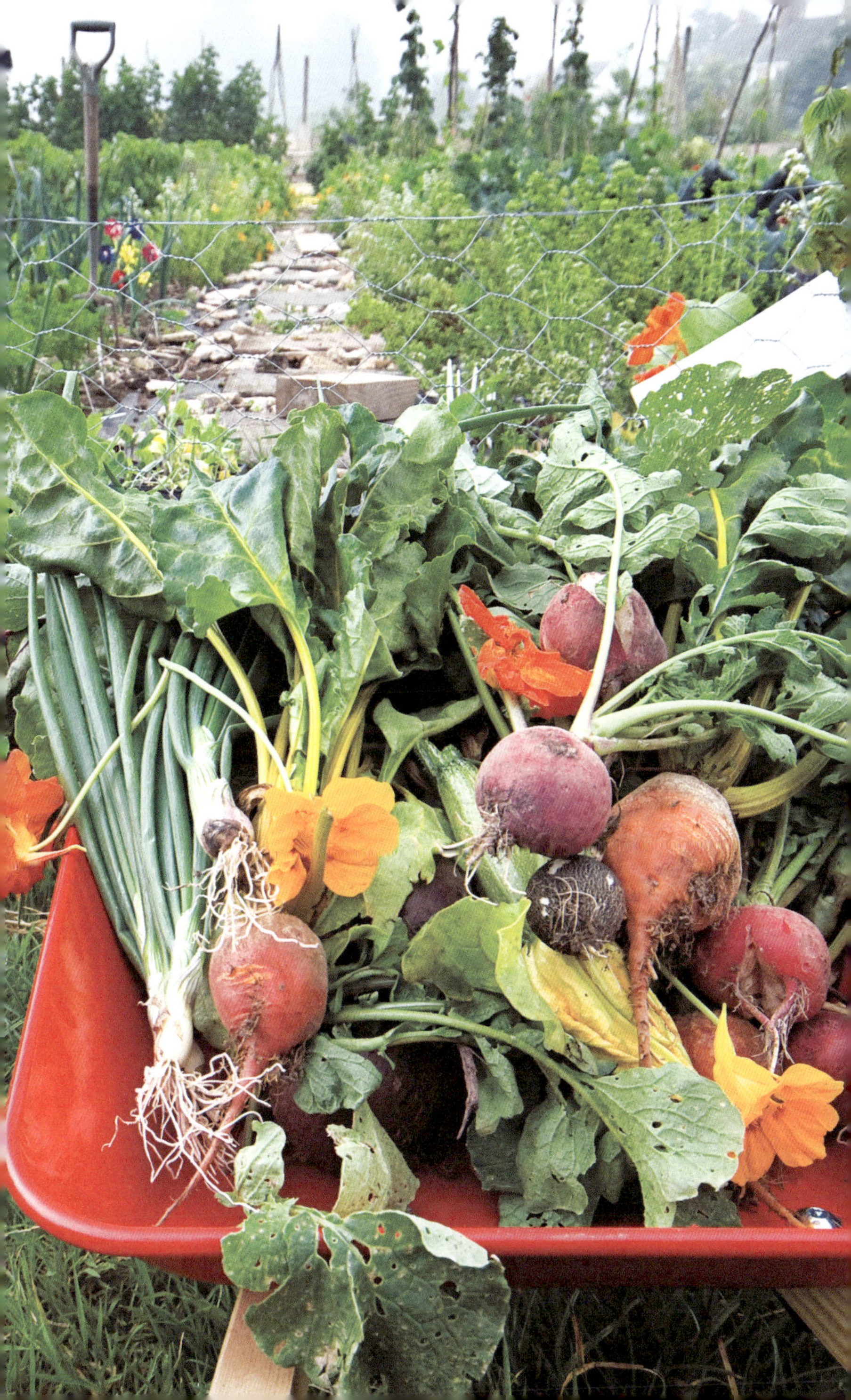

There are few pleasures that beat sitting in your veg patch in May with people you love, your just-cut asparagus cooking on a camping stove and almost ready to eat with a little butter, salt, pepper and Parmesan. Pour a glass of something dry made from grapes or apples and you'll be enjoying the best that the good life has to offer.

Such moments – and there are many of them – are unique to the home-grower. As the asparagus ends, so come the peas, the beans, the baby carrots – each one incomparable to its shop-bought cousin. And so it goes through each of the seasons. If you're looking for a reason to start a veg patch, these moments alone make a compelling case.

You may also find (as I did) that you become a better cook. When you have played a part in its growth, you understand why this tomato tastes so special or why that one's only okay, and why waiting to pick your parsnips until after the frosts makes them taste so sweet. But you'll get much more than amazing food from your plot.

One of the essential beauties of having a veg patch is that the simple act of growing and eating your own food decorates life in often unexpected ways. Whether you need more time alone or more time with loved ones, space to think or more time doing, your plot can provide. If you have children, take some time to involve them; if they see sweetcorn pop up in a pot, having sown it a few days earlier, they're almost certain to follow it along its journey until they are eating their own popcorn. And once you start, it sows the seeds for more.

You may well find that your veg patch turns food into something you do rather than just what you eat. It takes you into the outside world and brings it into your home; it roots you in your landscape, and acts as the seasonal clock around which family, friends – and the soil that supports them – come together. Simply, I know of no one with a veg patch whose life hasn't been greatly enhanced as a result.

Aside from the personal, there has never been a more important time to grow your own food. Our dependence on oil-based chemicals to beef up the plant and beat up its competition means that it typically takes ten times more energy to grow it than it delivers as food. Add to that the packaging, the food miles and the energy budgets of supermarkets (using more per square metre than most factories), and it's hardly surprising that our shopping basket accounts for as much as a quarter of our carbon footprint.

With our climate changing and oil peaking, we have little choice but to move towards a low-carbon diet and there's simply no better way of doing that than by growing our own organic food. As writer Michael Pollan put it: 'Growing even a little of your own food is one of those solutions (to climate change) that, instead of begetting a new set of problems – the way "solutions" such as ethanol or nuclear power inevitably do – actually beget other solutions, and not only of the kind that save carbon.' It creates new habits that give us low-carbon food at its best and that dilute our reliance on big business and reconnect with our ability (and need) to provide for ourselves. It strikes a blow for independence.

If it sounds laughably idealistic to contend that a veg patch can really make a difference, remember that our dependencies on oil and supermarkets for our food are only as they are thanks to so many similarly small, repeated actions: we vote them in every time we shop, and we vote them out every time we sow.

A veg patch is also the perfect place to remind ourselves of one of the fundamentals of life itself: we depend on plants. For all our evolutionary advances, they can do something we can't: create food for themselves from little more than sunlight and air. Happily, many of them do it in such a way that's not only edible for us, it's delicious. And we get much more than flavour from eating seasonal food that is harvested at the top of its game and full of vitality. Vitamins, minerals and antioxidants are all at their peak when first picked, so every mouthful brings with it more of what your body needs. It also gives them to us as we need them – in frequent, small, combined doses. So it's not just that we need to eat plants, we were built to eat them.

This book is about everything to do with that fundamental relationship. It's still a food book, it just happens to be about the whole journey – from plot to plate. Most of us are a little more familiar with the eating than the growing, but start your own veg patch and I hope you'll quickly find the plants a fascinating means to a delicious end.

You needn't feel intimidated if you are new to growing. It isn't the great mystery that so many would have it. On the contrary, it's compellingly, wonderfully simple. It is even (dare I say it) fairly hard to mess up; you just may not know how to do some of it yet. Think of it like directions to a new place – follow them and getting there is simple, and you'll soon be doing it without thinking. Growing is mostly a matter of helping everything along – caring for the soil, bringing things together at the right time and removing any obvious obstacles. Plants want to grow, all we have to do is *let* them rather than make them.

Nor do you need an acre, an allotment or even a garden: a veg patch is simply a space, however small, where you can grow even a little of what you eat. Everyone can do it and this book offers you a series of invitations to do just that.

So if it's time, space, money or inspiration you're short of, don't worry: all are common obstacles but none of them are insurmountable, as I hope this book will reassure you. Clear a patch or fill a few pots with compost and you'll be glad you did. Your food will not only be the finest you've ever tasted, it will come with no packaging, no branding, no food miles, no hydrogenated this or saturated that. Food simply doesn't get any better, but more than that, you'll find everything about it is positive – for you, your family and even for the wider world.

Making a wish list

When I began growing food I spent so much time pondering which plants fitted in where that I almost forgot the point – getting mouthwatering food to the table. A lazy bath reading *Jane Grigson's Vegetable Book* jolted my mind back on track in a second. I got out all the food books and put away the growing ones and started scribbling an unfettered list of food I liked. Everything went in regardless of whether it would grow in the UK, avocado included, and I'd recommend you do the same. Think firstly of flavour and you won't go far wrong.

The Vegetable A–Z (pp.20–153) is a great place to start with your wish list. I hope it will remind you of some of your favourite flavours as well as challenge you to step out of the familiar – to try new tastes, new varieties and run the risk that you might find a few prejudices threatened.

From that initial wish list you can start whittling or embellishing, depending on the limitations and opportunities of your life and your veg patch. There is no ready-made plan for the ideal patch – all the best gardens (edible or otherwise) express the grower's personality, fit their life, their tastes, and reflect their inquisitiveness, so try to make sure yours does too. What you grow really is up to you, but deciding can be daunting. Here are a few pointers that may help:

Grow what you most like to eat

Although it can (and should) be much more, a successful vegetable patch has to be functional, providing you with at least some of the food you most enjoy. If your plot is delivering in spades it will justify the time spent out there with your hands in the soil. It may seem obvious, but you'd be surprised how many people grow what they think they should be growing rather than the food they most like to eat.

Challenge your taste buds

Always, always, always grow something you've never eaten before. No matter how long you've been growing your own, no matter how gargantuan your appetite, there will always be something you've yet to munch on. Supermarkets tend to offer the same food week in week out – it simplifies the supply chain and maximises profits. Over time this establishes and reinforces a peculiar mistrust of the unfamiliar: just how good can borlotti beans be if I have never seen them before? The answer: wonderfully, reassuringly appetising. If you're new to them, try Jerusalem artichokes, salsify, kai lan and mizuna, and you'll see what I mean.

You might also consider planting at least one vegetable that you actively dislike, or think you dislike. The likelihood is you'll offer at least a begrudging acceptance that your hated veg is in fact not bad at all. This is partly because the bond between grower and growee confers upon you the pride of the parent, but largely because you'll have the harvest as it should be – at its perfect peak, which is often alarmingly dissimilar to its shop-bought brother. Broadcaster John Peel once said of The Fall that if they were to bring out an album that he didn't like he'd feel it was somehow a failing in him. I'd urge you to think that way a little about food, and assume that you just haven't found the way that it's delicious yet. If, even in its just-picked prime, you find you still can't abide it then you can at least consign it to Room 101 safe in the knowledge you gave it (and yourself) a fair go.

Go for variety

A little of lots rather than lots of a little is what you're after from your veg patch. Sow a broad range of veg and you'll open up all sorts of kitchen possibilities. You'll also find that there can be a huge difference between varieties of the same food – 'Edzell Blue' and 'Pink Fir Apple' potatoes, for instance, not only look, cook and taste completely different, they are harvested months apart. More importantly, by growing a few varieties you'll be taking out a little edible insurance – some varieties resist diseases more readily than others, and having a range greatly reduces your chances of being cleaned out.

Grow through the seasons

Many of the harvests in the colder months will be up there with anything the summer can throw at you – the purple sprouting broccoli, salsify and giant red mustard leaves in winter are a match for the best any season can offer, so I would encourage you to plan and plant for the whole year.

Some gardeners treat their patch a little like their tent – happy to enjoy it in the sunnier months and even happier to pack it away as the nights draw in. There is absolutely nothing wrong with taking this approach if it suits you best, but do it consciously. Many's the allotmenter who tidies away the last bedraggled courgette and squash plants wondering what's coming next, to find themselves with nothing to follow. Rest assured you can have year-round home-grown feasts, but you have to plan for them in the same way you do for the stars of the main summer show.

Prioritise plot-to-plate veg

Some harvests keep hold of their best characteristics for weeks or even months – parsnips, for example – and we should love them for it. Others, such as asparagus, sweetcorn and peas, are altogether more delicate, happy to lose texture, vigour or (most distressingly) their sugars from the second they are detached from the plant. Without exception, they're delicious, so do grow some and get them from plot to pot as soon as you can – hours are crucial, even minutes for some – and you'll have the best that any veg patch can offer.

Top 8 plot-to-plate veg

Asparagus	see p.28
Peas (and pea shoots)	see p.110
Broad beans	see p.39
New potatoes	see p.117
Sprouting broccoli	see p.137
Summer carrots	see p.50
Sweetcorn	see p.145
Tomatoes	see p.149

Prioritise the transformers

Garlic, chillies and herbs may be delicious in their own right, but their great gift is in offering other crops any number of costumes to dress up in, transforming great harvests into outstanding meals.

Summer carrots, brushed clean and munched straight out of the soil, may be as sweet as it gets, but your winter harvest will shift a couple of notches up the culinary ladder with the addition of rosemary or coriander. What makes a tomato seem even more tomatoey? Basil. And where do you start with the wonderful contribution garlic makes to any number of dishes? And think visually too – edible flowers, with their colour as much as their flavour, add a punctuating spike to any number of salads.

For the most part, the transformers are expensive to buy, yet easy to grow, taking up very little of your precious space, so make room for as many as you can – they'll multiply your kitchen possibilities endlessly.

Top 5 transformers

Garlic	see p.81
Herbs	see p.87
Chilli peppers	see p.65
Edible flowers	see p.72
Shallots and spring onions	see p.128 and p.135

Prioritise the most 'expensive' foods

Growing your own is as much about old chestnuts as it is about new shoots, and one standard line that you can fairly well rely on is that by the time you've factored in your time, growing your own may well not be the most rewarding economic activity. But that doesn't mean it can't knock a fair-sized hole in your weekly shop or save you the expense of that gym membership. Check through the veg you buy across all four seasons and identify the most expensive – many are surprisingly easy to grow, and are often expensive only because they are limited to a short period of production, or are tricky to harvest on a commercial scale. Asparagus is a classic, commanding a high price, yet requiring little more than planting once and keeping reasonably free of weeds.

Top 5 money savers

Asparagus	see p.28
Globe artichokes	see p.85
Sprouting broccoli	see p.137
Most herbs	see p.87
New potatoes	see p.117

Cut down on food miles

Growing everything we eat may not be a realistic option for all of us, but putting a sizeable dent in your food-related carbon emissions may be easier than you think. Growing your food organically is the biggest step you can make in reducing your food's footprint, but there is a little extra targeting that can make all the difference in greening up your larder. If you enjoy fruit normally sourced overseas (like peaches and apricots) climate change is making it easier to grow them here in the UK, but bizarrely many of the veg we import the most can also be grown here with ease. Green beans and peas top the list, so if you like them, grow them for yourself.

Top 5 imported veg

French beans	see p.79
Peas	see p.110
Sweetcorn	see p.145
Asparagus	see p.28
Onions	see p.102

Grow something beautiful

A beautiful plot is a more enticing place to spend your time. Make room for some flowers, some are edible (see p.72), many suit cutting for the house, and most will bring beneficial insects to your patch and encourage the biodiversity that should underpin any piece of the planet, however small.

A good-looking plot doesn't necessarily equate to neatness, and everyone's idea of what is pleasing to the eye is unique, but nurture your own sense of the beautiful and your patch will become the place you most want to be for your morning coffee, to read your Sunday paper, or to sip that early-evening cider. And every time you're there – even if you're not gardening – you'll notice something, attend to something small, pick up on progress, and get to nibble at the emerging harvests.

Top 5 ornamental veg

Globe artichokes	see p.85
Jerusalem artichokes	see p.92
Runner beans	see p.124
Borlotti beans	see p.36
Florence fennel	see p.76

Get some seed catalogues

Catalogues aren't just the source of your seeds – they're the inspiration for trying new foods, different varieties, and for stirring up anticipation through the colder months. Get on the internet, check the directory (p.265) for catalogue suppliers and nose around – they're not all the same. Many specialise, and (as with anything) prices and quality will vary, so it pays to invest a little time reading a few through the winter.

Essential tools

If you've ever tried putting up a shelf you'll be familiar with the spirit-sapping tedium that comes with poor-quality tools. Think of them as an investment – spend your money well and they'll pay you back for years, take short cuts and you'll regret it every time you pick them up. Take time to try some, ask around, borrow a few and buy them for how they feel in your hands and how they perform in the soil, not for how they look.

There are a few tools that you simply shouldn't be without:

A fork This is the workhorse of your veg patch, used to loosen or break up ground as well as for lifting your root crops. Get your hands on a good one before you buy any other tools.

A spade For digging, cutting straight edges, and turning compost.

A hoe For weeding between plants or larger areas. Some work by pushing, others by pulling – try some out before you buy as you'll have your hoe in your hands a fair bit. At the same time, get a sharpening stone – it will save you endless energy.

A rake For levelling and working the surface of your patch. Go for a sturdy rake rather than one of those spindly things designed for collecting leaves.

A trowel and a hand fork These let you get in close to dig small areas for planting into and spot-weeding. They'll be in your hand more than any other tools – so make sure they feel comfortable – and if you can stretch to it, get a couple of spares for those times you have extra help.

A wheelbarrow, watering can and two buckets are also indispensable. The rest of the items you might need can be homemade – a line of string between sticks makes as straight a guideline for planting as anything, and you can use a sturdy stick to make holes for dropping your leeks into rather than use a dibber.

The cost can mount up, so do investigate second-hand shops, car boot sales, the local recycling centre, and the possibility of sharing tools. And there are always the on-line auction sites. Some good starting places in your search are included in the directory (pp.265–6).

Essential terms

Growing, like most things, has its fair share of jargon – much of which can obscure rather than illuminate. Most terms are explained as you come across them in the book, but it's worth being familiar with the following as they crop up regularly.

Annual An annual plant is a plant that germinates, flowers and dies (or is harvested before it dies) in one year.

Biennial A biennial plant takes two years to complete its life-cycle.

Blanching As far as the veg patch is concerned, blanching refers to the exclusion of light (usually intentionally) from parts of a plant, with the aim of producing a more succulent, sweeter crop.

In the kitchen, blanching describes the brief boiling of vegetables (for a minute or so) before plunging into cold water, in order to arrest the conversion of sugars to starch and/or retain maximum texture. Vegetables are usually blanched before freezing.

Cut-and-come-again Some vegetables, such as lettuces, do not have to be grown to full maturity. Instead, you can harvest their leaves by cutting or picking, after which the plant will keep growing to give you further harvests. The main advantages are that harvesting in this way avoids gluts, makes harvesting mixed leaves in usable quantities easier, and you can get a longer, steadier harvest from a small space.

Cut-and-come-again

F1 varieties/F1 hybrids These are the result of a cross between two distinct varieties. Many F1s offer vigorous, predictable, disease-resistant and high-yielding plants. The disadvantages include the higher cost of seeds, the fact that the seed is not worth saving as new plants will be weak at best, and that all your F1 seeds of the same variety tend to mature simultaneously – the home-grower usually aims for a more gradual harvest.

Forcing The process of accelerating growth, usually by increasing the temperature and/or light manipulation. The aim is usually either to get an earlier crop and/or a sweeter, less bitter one.

Hardening off If you've started off any plants under cover, most seedlings will adjust much more quickly to life in your veg patch if you give them the chance to acclimatise first. To do this, move your seedlings outside in the morning, taking them back under cover for night. This is usually done for 4 or 5 days for vegetables, and is the process known as hardening off.

Perennial A perennial plant is a plant that lives for more than two years.

Pollination Before a plant can bear fruit and create seed, its flowers need pollinating. This involves the transfer of pollen from the anther (a structure at the tip of the stamen where pollen is produced) to the stigma. Self-fertile plants can do this themselves using their own pollen. Others require pollination from another variety of the same plant.

Potting on The process of moving your seedlings to a larger pot, to ensure they have sufficient space for the roots to develop unhindered.

Running to seed/bolting This is when a plant begins to try to form seeds; usually accompanied by rapid formation of flowers. It is generally triggered by a cold spell, or by changes in day length, or by an extended dry period.

Sowing direct To sow seeds straight into the soil rather than start them off in modules etc.

Sowing under cover To sow seeds in a polytunnel, greenhouse, or even on a windowsill, in order to protect from pests and/or provide more warmth.

Tilth Refers to the condition and texture of the soil surface – usually a 'good tilth' implies an even, fine texture into which you can sow seed.

Vegetable A–Z

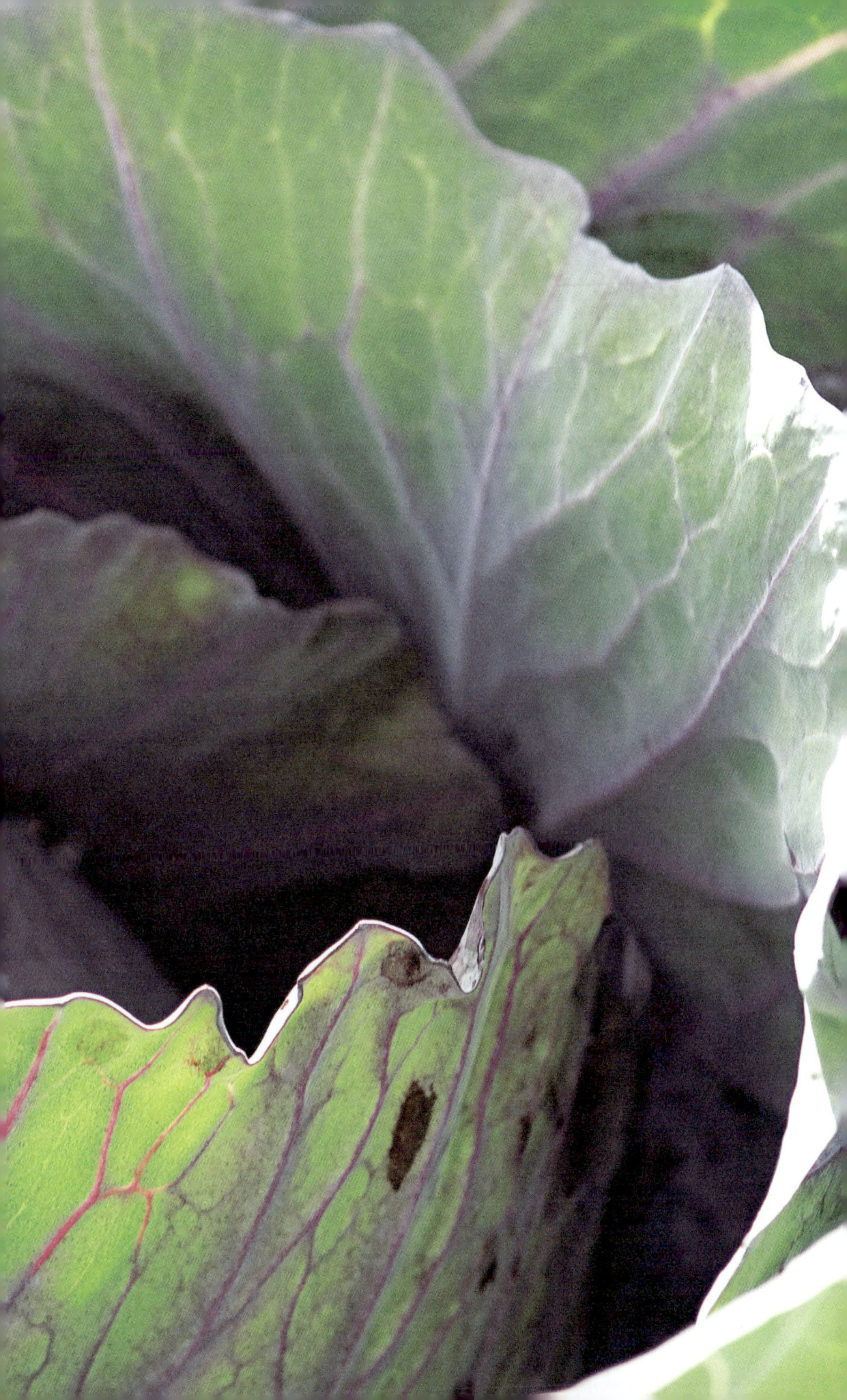

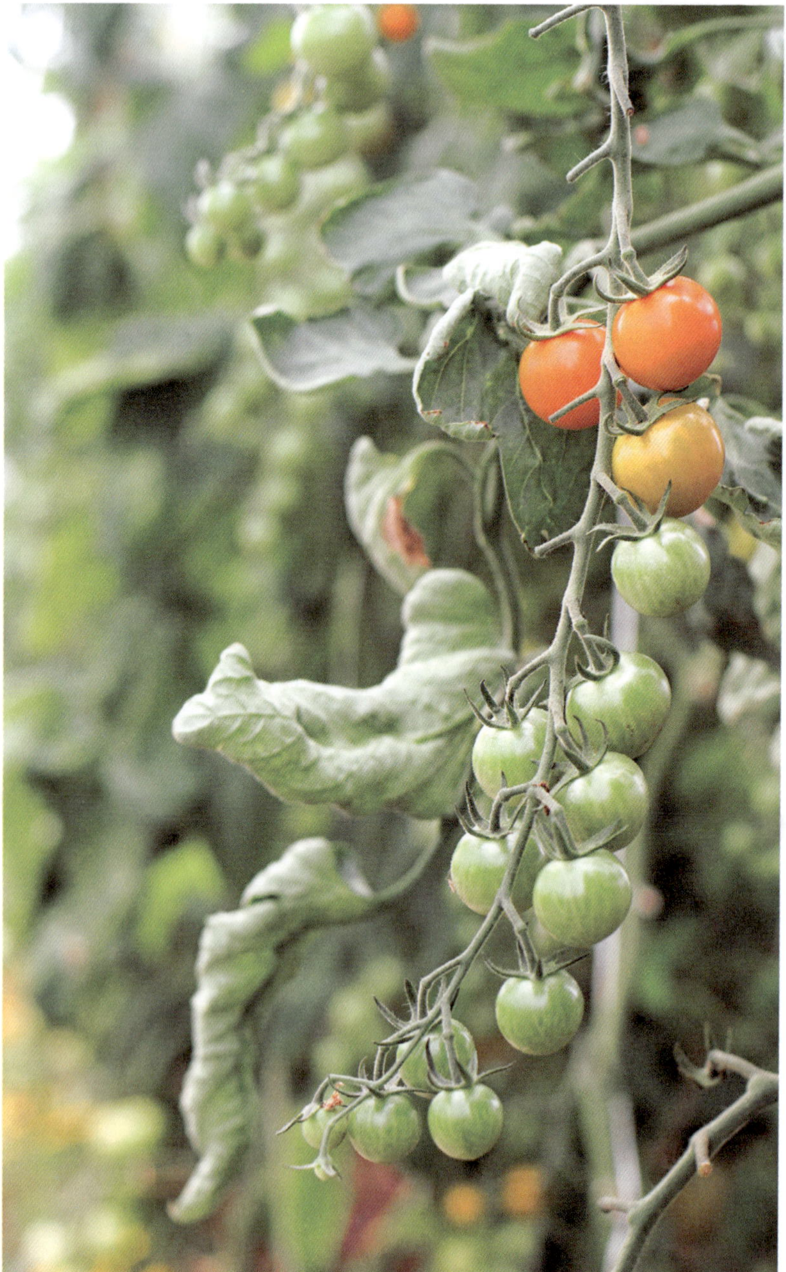

I've included all the vegetables, herbs and edible flowers that I love, and a few even that I just quite like. Inevitably there are some that didn't make the cut for one reason or another – okra is too unreliable for most people here in the UK, oka (a South American tuber) is lovely, but hard to source. Don't let this stand in your way of adding more to your wish list. Seed catalogues, on-line forums, blogs and cookbooks are great sources of inspiration – you're bound to find another food you want to try and any number of varieties worth giving a go.

Sowing times are included as a guide – they can vary considerably depending on whether you live in the Highlands or High Wycombe, and of course from year to year. The seasons are delightfully fluid – I am no more able to name the date that I expect the first frost here than I can tell you when it will come where you are. But it's not worth getting too hung up on. If it says to sow in early March but it's unseasonably cold, leave it a week or two. The essential thing is not to worry about getting it right all the time, but to do it. You'll learn as much from what doesn't work out as what does, and you'll develop a feel for it surprisingly quickly.

If you want to push the odds slightly more in your favour, then you can start many plants off under cover – in a polytunnel, under a cloche or even on a windowsill. Where this is possible, I've included times for sowing under cover – along with an idea of when these seedlings should be moved outside for planting.

You can grow many plants all the way through to harvest under cover if you are fortunate enough to have a polytunnel or greenhouse. Both take the edge off the outside temperatures and allow you not only a head start in getting things under way, but also a few precious weeks at the end of the summer to ripen things fully. It's a pretty reliable rule that you can sow direct in a polytunnel a month or so earlier than you can outside, and harvest a month or so longer than you can outside. In some cases, you'll even be able to coax a year-round supply in this protected space where it would be impossible to do so outside. Bear this in mind when reading the sowing times.

I have also included an idea of how to get to grips with each of the foods when they reach your kitchen, and suggested particular ways to prepare and cook them that I think show them off at their best. If you are unfamiliar with any of the foods then this should give you a good approach to trying them out. But that's just the start – be adventurous, play around with different vegetables and get the most from your harvests.

You'll come across plenty of sources of inspiration. Talking of which, I'd really recommend you invest in Pam Corbin's *River Cottage Preserves Handbook*. In many ways, the art of preserving is the final step on that perfect journey that begins in the soil and ends at your table. Get yourself familiar with the many ways of arresting the process of decay and you'll not only stretch your harvest further, you'll have even more reminders of why it was all worth it.

Vegetable sowing, planting and harvesting times

	JAN	FEB	MARCH	APRIL	MAY	JUNE	JULY	AUG	SEPT	OCT	NOV	DEC
ASPARAGUS												
Start under cover		•										
Plant out			•	•								
Harvest					•	•						
AUBERGINES												
Start under cover		•	•									
Plant out					•	•						
Harvest								•	•	•		
BEETROOT												
Start under cover			•	•	•							
Plant out					•	•	•					
Sow direct				•	•	•	•					
Harvest							•	•	•	•		
BORLOTTI BEANS												
Start under cover			•	•	•	•	•					
Plant out					•	•	•					
Sow direct				•	•	•	•					
Harvest								•	•	•		
BROAD BEANS												
Start under cover		•	•	•	•							
Plant out				•	•	•	•					
Sow direct				•							•	
Harvest				•	•	•	•	•				
BRUSSELS SPROUTS												
Start under cover		•	•	•								
Plant out					•	•						
Harvest	•	•	•	•						•	•	•
CABBAGES (summer/autumn harvest)												
Start under cover			•	•								
Plant out					•	•						
Harvest						•	•	•	•	•		
CABBAGES (winter harvest)												
Start under cover				•	•							
Plant out						•	•					
Harvest	•	•	•								•	•
CABBAGES (spring harvest)												
Start under cover							•	•				
Plant out									•	•		
Harvest			•	•	•	•						
CALABRESE												
Start under cover			•	•	•							
Plant out				•	•	•						
Sow direct				•	•							
Harvest						•	•	•	•			

	JAN	FEB	MARCH	APRIL	MAY	JUNE	JULY	AUG	SEPT	OCT	NOV	DEC
CARDOONS												
Start under cover			•	•								
Plant out					•	•						
Harvest										•	•	
CARROTS												
Sow direct				•	•	•	•					
Harvest						•	•	•	•	•	•	
CAULIFLOWERS (summer harvest)												
Start under cover	•	•	•									
Plant out			•	•	•							
Harvest						•	•	•	•	•		
CAULIFLOWERS (winter harvest)												
Start under cover				•	•	•	•					
Plant out							•	•	•	•		
Harvest	•	•	•	•	•	•					•	•
CELERIAC												
Start under cover		•	•									
Plant out					•	•						
Harvest	•	•	•						•	•	•	•
CELERY												
Start under cover		•	•									
Plant out					•	•						
Harvest								•	•	•		
CHARD & PERPETUAL SPINACH												
Start under cover			•	•	•	•	•	•	•			
Plant out				•	•	•	•	•	•	•		
Sow direct				•	•	•	•	•				
Harvest	•	•		•	•	•	•	•	•	•	•	•
CHICORY												
Sow direct					•	•	•					
Harvest	•									•	•	•
CHILLI PEPPERS												
Start under cover		•	•	•								
Plant out						•						
Harvest								•	•	•		
COURGETTES												
Start under cover				•	•	•						
Plant out					•	•	•					
Harvest							•	•	•	•		
CUCUMBERS & GHERKINS												
Start under cover			•	•	•							
Plant out					•	•						
Harvest							•	•	•	•		
ENDIVE												
Sow direct					•	•	•	•				
Harvest	•	•	•					•	•	•	•	•
FLORENCE FENNEL												
Sow direct				•	•	•	•					
Harvest						•	•	•	•	•	•	

	JAN	FEB	MARCH	APRIL	MAY	JUNE	JULY	AUG	SEPT	OCT	NOV	DEC
FRENCH BEANS												
Start under cover				•	•	•	•	•				
Plant out						•	•	•	•			
Sow direct				•	•	•	•					
Harvest						•	•	•	•	•	•	
GARLIC												
Sow direct		•	•							•	•	
Harvest						•	•	•	•	•		
GLOBE ARTICHOKES												
Start under cover		•	•									
Plant out						•	•					
Harvest						•	•	•	•	•		
JERUSALEM ARTICHOKES												
Sow direct	•	•	•									
Harvest	•	•	•							•	•	•
KALE												
Start under cover				•	•	•	•	•	•			
Plant out					•	•	•	•	•	•		
Harvest	•	•				•	•	•	•	•	•	•
LEEKS												
Start under cover		•	•	•								
Plant out						•	•					
Harvest	•	•	•	•	•					•	•	•
LETTUCES												
Start under cover	•	•	•	•	•	•	•	•	•			
Plant out				•	•	•	•	•	•	•		
Sow direct			•	•	•	•	•	•	•			
Harvest	•	•	•	•	•	•	•	•	•	•	•	•
ONIONS												
Sow direct				•	•					•	•	
Harvest						•	•	•	•	•	•	
PARSNIPS												
Sow direct				•	•	•						
Harvest	•	•	•						•	•	•	•
PEAS												
Start under cover		•	•	•	•							
Plant out					•	•						
Sow direct			•	•	•	•				•	•	
Harvest						•	•	•	•	•	•	
PEPPERS												
Start under cover		•	•									
Plant out						•	•					
Harvest									•	•	•	•
POTATOES												
Sow direct		•	•	•								
Harvest						•	•	•	•	•		
RADISHES												
Sow direct				•	•	•	•	•	•	•		
Harvest					•	•	•	•	•	•	•	

	JAN	FEB	MARCH	APRIL	MAY	JUNE	JULY	AUG	SEPT	OCT	NOV	DEC
ROCKET												
Sow direct			•	•	•	•	•	•	•			
Harvest				•	•	•	•	•	•	•	•	
RUNNER BEANS												
Start under cover				•	•	•						
Plant out					•	•	•					
Sow direct				•	•							
Harvest						•	•	•	•	•		
SALSIFY & SCORZONERA												
Sow direct				•	•							
Harvest										•	•	
SHALLOTS												
Sow direct		•	•									
Harvest							•	•	•			
SORREL												
Sow direct			•	•								
Harvest						•	•	•	•	•	•	
SPINACH												
Sow direct			•	•	•	•	•	•	•	•		
Harvest	•	•	•	•	•	•	•	•	•	•	•	•
SPRING ONIONS												
Sow direct		•	•	•	•	•	•	•		•	•	
Harvest	•	•	•	•	•	•	•	•	•	•	•	
SPROUTING BROCCOLI												
Start under cover			•	•								
Plant out						•	•					
Sow direct				•	•							
Harvest	•	•	•	•								
SQUASH, PUMPKINS & GOURDS												
Start under cover				•	•	•						
Plant out						•	•					
Harvest										•	•	
SWEDE												
Sow direct				•	•	•						
Harvest	•	•							•	•	•	•
SWEETCORN												
Start under cover				•								
Plant out						•	•					
Sow direct					•							
Harvest								•	•	•		
TOMATOES												
Start under cover		•	•									
Plant out				•	•	•						
Harvest							•	•	•	•		
TURNIPS												
Sow direct			•	•	•	•	•					
Harvest						•	•	•	•	•		

Asparagus *Asparagus officinalis*

PLANT GROUP	Perennials (see p.169)
START UNDER COVER	February
PLANT OUT	Seedlings: June; Crowns: March–April
HARVEST	May–June

The arrival of spring and the warming soil promise so much, yet I can't help feeling impatient at this time of the year as it's still the best part of a month until the first asparagus appears. I suffer from what food writer Simon Hopkinson calls 'asparagus fever'. Obsessively, I check for their emerging green noses every morning and most afternoons from April Fools' Day. When those tips eventually do break the surface, it feels like the new season's harvest is really getting under way and about to offer one of the finest flavours a veg patch can provide. How fitting that it comes first in the A–Z... if it hadn't I'd have considered misspelling it 'aasparagus'.

Be prepared to develop the addiction once you've tasted asparagus fresh from the ground. Fortunately, in Britain we have the ideal conditions for producing the finest there is, so do grow some and chill some good dry white wine in anticipation.

Varieties

'Connover's Colossal' and 'Mary Washington' are older varieties that produce good yields of particularly delicious spears. Plants can be male or female, with the former tending to give greater overall yield, the latter usually producing larger spears.

The newer F1 varieties, such as 'Jersey Knight', produce all-male plants so the harvest is likely to be larger and more uniform. However, I prefer using non-F1s and the variety in size that comes with them.

How to grow

Asparagus can be raised from seed (sown in modules in February for transplanting in June), but most people go for young dormant plants known as crowns. Being a year older, they cost more, but the reward of an earlier crop justifies the price.

Growing asparagus is easy. Choose a well-drained site, or raise the bed if you've slightly heavier soil, and dig up any perennial weeds. In late March or early April, dig a trench to a spade's depth, incorporating a little compost or well-rotted manure into the bottom. Shovel in around 10cm of soil and mound this up into a ridge at the bottom of the trench. Space the crowns at least 50cm apart along the ridge and spread the roots out evenly on either side. Cover the crowns with 10cm or so of soil and water well. Allow about 80cm between rows. If you cover the rows with a mulch of grass cuttings or manure you'll help to retain moisture and suppress weeds.

Asparagus 'Mary Washington'

There's usually one stage where a vegetable needs a little extra attention. With asparagus this comes early and involves keeping the bed weed-free, as asparagus hates competition. This is best done by hand as hoeing damages the shallow roots. In autumn, when the foliage yellows, cut the stems back to 5cm above the soil. A tip I learnt from Ray Smith (the River Cottage butcher) is to support plant rows with a ring of string. Simply place canes along either side of the lines of asparagus and link them with a loop of string – this prevents a hole forming at the base of the plant as it sways in the wind, where water can get in and rot the roots.

That's it – that's all that stands between you and just about the finest lunch you could wish for. After that, barring a little self-restraint in the first years, it's slippery chins every May and June.

How to harvest

Sit on your hands, go on holiday in May, do whatever you have to, but don't take spears in the first 2 years, or 3 years if growing from seed. The plant needs the top growth to direct energies towards getting a root system established.

After that, clear a space in your diary for when the asparagus spears break the surface as May approaches. When they reach 15cm or so, use a bread knife (or a specialist asparagus knife) to cut them a couple of centimetres below the surface. Stop harvesting by the longest day.

Carefully tended, asparagus plants should crop for 20 years or more, with each crown yielding around 10 spears each season.

Problems and pests

Asparagus beetle can be a nuisance, but is easy to spot with its black and white back and distinctive red rim. If the beetle (or its larvae) shows itself, simply pick off and squash them, or feed them to the chickens.

How to eat

Enjoying asparagus is not so much about recipes as it is about time. Seconds seem to matter, minutes definitely do. It's no exaggeration to say that if you have the water boiling before you cut the spears you'll notice the difference. Just boil or steam your spears within seconds of picking and enjoy with butter, salt, black pepper and Parmesan, or with hollandaise sauce (see p.258). Hugh's soft-boiled egg accompaniment is delicious, and there is something very satisfying about the scruff-meets-toff of asparagus soldiers with soft-boiled eggs.

Most other recipes are based on the assumption that you will tire of eating asparagus simply (as above), which I think is nonsense, but if you've a genuine glut they will take happily to a gratin (see p.127), and make a delicately flavoured houmous (see p.229). For more recipes, see pp.244, 248, 250.

Aubergines *Solanum melongena*

PLANT GROUP	Solanaceae (see p.168)
START UNDER COVER	February–March
PLANT OUT	May–June
HARVEST	August–October

Along with courgettes and sweetcorn, aubergines make up the holy trinity of barbecue veg. Maybe it's those oily griddle lines that cart your mind off to the Med, but they are a must when the charcoal comes out.

Shop-bought aubergines rarely offer much in the way of flavour, yet home-grown, they have a real creaminess with a finer flavour. It does, however, take a little effort to ensure a late-summer harvest. Aubergines like sun and are comparatively easily knocked off their steady course to maturity, so grow them under cover and take out a little edible insurance. I start some in the polytunnel, some on windowsills, and I still sow a second batch a couple of weeks later as a backup.

Varieties

Most varieties are indistinguishable in taste, apart from 'Moneymaker' (F1), which is particularly delicious, and the beautiful 'Rosa Bianca', which is creamier than most. 'Black Beauty' is a very dependable cropper. 'Slim Jim' is a slender, smaller-fruiting variety that needs less ripening, so should give you more chance of a crop if you live in the North or are growing them in containers.

How to grow

I start aubergines off under cover in Jiffy 7s (see p.197) or modules in March, potting on regularly as they grow. Get them into the soil under cover (in a polytunnel or cloche) in May, or if you're an optimist outside in June. Attention to detail is vital in swinging the odds of a good harvest your way. Add some good compost before planting, and remember that growing them in a polytunnel, greenhouse or on a windowsill is likely to offer your best chance of success.

Support the plant as it grows by tying it to a sturdy cane. Take care when weeding or picking as the stems are easily damaged. Fortnightly comfrey or seaweed feeds (see p.215) from immediately after flowering will help to bring the fruit to its peak.

How to harvest

Expect to harvest from August through until mid-October. Don't wait until the aubergines reach supermarket proportions – snip them off any time after they get to 8cm in length (and up to 18cm or so) to get them at their best.

Aubergine flower

Aubergine 'Black Beauty'

Problems and pests

Apart from a less than belting summer, aphids and red spider mites are likely to be the main obstacles between you and tasty late-summer aubergines. Try companion planting with basil (see p.212), rubbing off any aphids that appear. If you still find your plants under attack then parasitic controls are the best solution, see the directory (pp.265–6) for suppliers.

How to eat

Aubergines are perfect sliced, brushed with olive oil and griddled on the barbecue. Cut them into slightly larger pieces and they also take well to roasting.

Aubergine caviar makes a delicious dip or topping for toast. Top and tail a few aubergines and boil them until tender. Drain in a colander and let them dry out and cool a little before peeling. Mash the flesh with a little lemon juice, olive oil and salt and pepper to taste, then serve warm.

Although not essential, before cooking, you can salt your aubergine slices for half an hour, then rinse and pat them dry with a clean tea towel or kitchen paper. This removes any hint of bitterness, which is absent in most newer varieties, but also reduces the amount of oil they take up, allowing their delicate flavour to shine through. For more recipes, see pp.248, 256.

Beetroot *Beta vulgaris*

PLANT GROUP	Roots (see p.162)
START UNDER COVER	March–June
PLANT OUT	May–July
SOW DIRECT	April–July
HARVEST	July–October

I'm still mystified as to why carrots are so much more popular than beetroot. Both plants give up deliciously sweet, versatile, easy-to-grow roots, yet beetroot also has outstanding leaves, heavy with vitamin A to go with the vitamin C-rich beets. And this isn't one of those veg where the root is the prize and the leaves merely edible. Swiss chard is the same plant – bred to swell at the stem rather than the root, so rest assured of a quality double harvest.

Sow beetroot early in the spring and you'll have tender, sweet salad leaves before the summer arrives, followed by purple marbles to crunch raw through the hottest months, and snooker-ball-sized globes to boil or roast as the heat starts to dip off in the autumn. Sow them successionally and you can even have the three-stage harvest at once.

Naturally, we associate beetroot with the familiar ruby-red swollen roots, but there are also golden, white and candy-striped varieties, which can be cooked and eaten in much the same way.

As with carrots or fennel, beetroot offers so much more than just a side-veg supporting role – happily transforming any course from the canapés through to puddings. If you're growing beetroot for the first time, try some of the recipe ideas (see p.35) and prepare for them to take over your kitchen.

Varieties

'Barabietola di Chioggia' is a traditional, hard-to-beat beet with wonderful concentric pink and white circles within. This Italian favourite is good grated raw, but really comes into its own once cooked, when it turns particularly sweet. If you are after the longest season, 'Egyptian Turnip Rooted' and 'Pronto' are early varieties which don't easily run to seed. Both have outstanding leaves for salad, and roots that take very happily to the roasting tin, as well as being outstanding raw.

I've also grown 'Moneta' this year for the first time and it's been excellent for both beets and leaves. For added aesthetics as well as top-drawer flavour, try sowing a row of 'Burpees Golden', adding the sweetly delicious golden beets to any recipe to contrast with their purple cousins.

Beetroot 'Barabietola di Chioggia'

How to grow

I sow early beetroot under cover in modules in March for planting out around 6 weeks later, but the majority I sow direct from April through to July. Sowing every few weeks will ensure a successional crop.

Space and size are yours to play with. Give them more room and you'll get larger beets; give them less and you'll have more, but smaller, beets from your veg patch. I prefer not to sit around tending to swollen prize-winning veg – we are growing them for the table rather than the local show after all. So, I pull them when they are golf-ball- to snooker-ball-sized. I still tend to sow reasonably close though, thinning them gradually to 8cm apart and taking the young plants to use in the kitchen. The rows should be around 20cm apart.

How to harvest

The smallest plants make delicious raw, leafy throw-ins to salads, with anything that has more than a marble of beetroot worth a few minutes of steaming. Expect the main harvest around 3 months after sowing.

If, as many people do, you find you've sown too many and your harvest is too large, leave some to grow on over winter. They'll look fantastic and give you a fine hungry-gap harvest of new leaves.

Problems and pests

If birds nipping at leaves or seeds are a pain, do whatever works best for you – CDs swinging in the wind, netting, scarecrows, falconry, blunderbuss...

How to eat

Beetroot is incredibly versatile. The young leaves are perfect in salads, and when they're a little larger and coarser, you can steam them like spinach. The roots make a wonderful houmous (see p.229). When roasted or boiled, they transform into sweet tender globes. They also make a delicious substitute for potatoes in a gratin dauphinoise, and a perfect alternative for their orange cousins in carrot cake. Sweet and earthy, beetroot has a particular affinity with soft cheese (especially goat's cheese), garlic and thyme.

Roast or boil them in their skins with a few centimetres of the leaves and all of the roots on – this prevents the sweet purpley juices leaching out. The result is sweeter, more tender and somehow more 'beetroot' – its very essence magnified. Leave until cool enough to handle before peeling.

For more recipes, see pp.223, 233, 240, 242, 260.

Borlotti beans *Phaseolus vulgaris*

PLANT GROUP	Legumes (see p.157)
START UNDER COVER	March–July
PLANT OUT	May–July
SOW DIRECT	April–July
HARVEST	August–October

Borlottis are worth growing for the beauty of their stunning speckled pods alone, but the beans also happen to be luscious and versatile. Although superficially similar to kidney beans, their red and cream speckle, finer texture and sweeter flavour set them apart. You can use them fresh in salads or on toast, dried in earthy winter stews and soups, or save them for next season's sowing. They are rarely available to anyone but the home-grower, so give them some space – and yourself a treat.

Varieties
'Lingua di Fuoco' is reliable, delicious and the most widely available variety.

How to grow
Start borlotti seeds under cover from March until early July for an autumn harvest; root trainers (see p.197) allow their roots to develop well. Let them get to at least 5cm tall before planting out, from mid-May. You can also sow seeds direct from late April until early July. Most varieties are climbers and will require a tepee or other structure to support them as they grow. They love the sun, so give them a good light site, with around 20cm between plants. And keep them well watered from flowering onwards, using comfrey tea (see p.215) every other week to promote a longer harvest.

How to harvest
The main harvest is August and September, but if you are after a long season, early and successional sowings can stretch this from June to November. Pick borlottis when the pods begin to turn cream – you can always pop one if you're unsure.

For dried beans or seed saving for next year, leave the beans in place until the weather is about to turn wet, then cut the plant and hang it upside down somewhere light and airy until the pods really desiccate. Next, shell the beans and allow them to dry for a few more days on paper, before storing in a paper bag or airproof jar.

Problems and pests
Marigolds (*Tagetes* sp.) are a good companion plant, deterring aphids and attracting the ladybirds and hoverflies that will finish off any aphids that do appear. Starting

borlottis (or any legume) under cover is the best way to minimise the impact of slugs and snails, but be prepared for slug-picking duty every other evening.

How to eat

Borlotti beans are lovely dried, but get them fresh and they are softer, slightly more flavoursome and cook more quickly. They have that rare quality of taking on other flavours yet being distinctive enough to shine on their own or alongside saltier sheep's and goat's cheeses. Robust in texture, they are ideal in stews and soups, but also suit a softer approach – try borlotti houmous (see p.229). Once dried, they are usually soaked overnight before cooking. Be aware that cooking tends to fade the speckles. For more recipes, see pp.223, 230, 248.

Borlotti beans 'Lingua di Fuoca'

Broad bean 'Aquadulce Claudia'

Broad beans *Vicia faba*

PLANT GROUP	Legumes (see p.157)
START UNDER COVER	February–May
PLANT OUT	April–July
SOW DIRECT	November or April
HARVEST	April–September

Take a mid-spring trip to Worth Matravers in Dorset and follow the footpath that loops east from the pub before turning south to meet the cliffs. Head west, following the coastline for a mile or two, turning inland at the signpost before you reach Chapman's Pool. Here, if you're lucky, you'll find a full field of broad beans in flower. Hold your breath and walk quickly to the centre, then close your eyes and breathe in the loveliest, most intoxicating perfume there is.

While their perfume is indisputably superb, broad beans themselves seem to divide people into believers and detractors, with few sitting on the fence. I'm firmly with the believers. This is one of those prime harvests that really must be home-grown to be enjoyed at its peak. If you are one of those unfortunates that doesn't like broad beans, I'm convinced it is just that you don't like them yet. Indeed, you are one of the fortunates. How wonderful to have the revelation of just-picked, just-cooked broad beans as a discovery to come. I'm genuinely envious.

Varieties
Offering delectable, reliable harvests, 'Bunyards Exhibition' and 'Green Windsor' are hard to beat for springtime sowing. With their long pods filled with so many small, tender beans, 'Aquadulce Claudia' is the best for autumn sowings. 'The Sutton' is a good hardy dwarf variety, which grows half a metre high and does well in a fairly exposed site. It will even give a decent crop when grown in large pots.

How to grow
I start most of mine off under cover, in toilet roll inners or root trainers (see p.197), every 3 weeks from late February through to the end of May, to plant out a month later. This successional sowing gives a nice steady harvest from late May onwards.

If you want a slightly earlier harvest, you can sow broad beans direct in November (ready to harvest in April), but be prepared for birds, mice and the wet to deplete any direct-sown seed.

Sow or plant the seedlings 20cm apart, 5cm deep, and in rows 60cm apart. You'll need to pinch out the top few centimetres of growth on the main stem when the flowers have just wilted and the first pods are starting to appear. This directs energy to the developing pods and (as this is their favourite part) reduces the likelihood of aphid infestations. Taller varieties may need supporting with a hoop of string around canes placed along each side of your rows and at row ends. Water the beans through any dry periods.

How to harvest

If you sow in November you may get your first beans in late April, otherwise expect to be picking around 3 months after you've sown your seeds in spring and summer. Before cooking you'll need to remove the beans from the pods. Allow for the beans to be around a third of the weight of the unopened pods.

Problems and pests

Keep a watch for ants on your plants. They won't be causing any harm, but they are there for a reason – looking for aphids. Aphids secrete honeydew, which the ants can detect in minute amounts, so if you see them it may be that your broad beans are about to come under attack from the aphid militia. Get your spray hose ready. Better still, if you have a few nettles growing nearby, leave them. You may find, as I do, that they work as a perfect sacrificial plant, drawing almost all of the aphids to them and away from your precious pods.

Pea and bean weevil may leave its characteristic notches in the foliage, but damage is cosmetic. As is chocolate spot, looking as the name implies. Good air circulation and keeping your plants watered through dry patches helps minimise the likelihood of this fungal disease.

How to eat

Broad beans are as versatile as it gets – happy with most fresh herbs, lemon juice and many of the saltier cheeses like feta, sheep's or goat's cheese. The perfect spring beans on toast, they also lend themselves to endless salads, and make a wonderful alternative in the houmous recipe (see p.229).

Generally, you'll be looking to give them a couple of minutes in simmering water to bring out maximum sweetness. But it's not only freshness that makes the home-grown haul so superior to the shop-bought; they are simply that much more delicious eaten young and smaller than a thumbnail. Get them early enough and they are even wonderful raw. Do try steaming whole pods when small (no more than a few centimetres) for a few minutes. Later-season beans can run with stronger flavours, such as garlic and ginger. And if broad beans are particularly large, slip them out of their skins, as these are likely to be a bit tough.

Don't discard the leafy pinched-out tops. One of the top treats for the greedy gardener, they are fantastic in risotto, as a steamed side dish or wilted in butter.

For more recipes, see pp.226, 230, 244, 248, 251.

Brussels sprouts
Brassica oleracea var. *gemmifera*

PLANT GROUP	Brassicas (see p.159)
START UNDER COVER	February–April
PLANT OUT	May–June
HARVEST	October–April

We think of Brussels sprouts as Christmas veg on a stick, yet by growing a few different varieties, you can enjoy these wonderfully nutty nuggets for around 3 months either side of the festive season. I can't get enough of them, but for some reason, sprouts seem to split the nation: you either love them or loathe them. Perhaps as a child you were, quite rightly, repelled by them being overcooked. The characteristic house-filling sulphurous smell that results is enough to put anyone off. Put aside any preconceptions that you might have and try boiling or steaming sprouts lightly instead. Discover their friendship with cream, nuts and bacon, and you'll surely start to enjoy them.

Varieties
'Noisette' and 'Groninger' are outstanding pre-Christmas sprouts, with 'Seven Hills' taking you through the festive season. 'Wellington' and 'Red Rubine' (with its wonderful deep-red sprouts) will give you a fine late winter harvest.

How to grow
Growing Brussels sprouts requires a touch of patience, but very little in the way of effort. Start them off under cover in pots or Jiffy 7s (see p.197) as winter turns to spring, then plant them out about 60cm apart as spring becomes summer when they are around 10–15cm tall. The plants are shallow-rooting yet tall, so firm them in really well, and tread the bed over.

To make the most of the space, you can always squeeze in a few fast-maturing salad leaves, radishes or leafy herbs around the base of the plants, to give you a quick harvest before the Brussels sprouts grow to any size.

Planting early and later varieties of sprouts, which mature at different rates, will ensure a harvest from October through to Easter. Check the catalogue or seed packet for planting and harvesting times.

Brussels sprouts require little in the way of care while they are getting up to size. Just keep an eye out for pests that show interest, and water the plants during an extended dry period.

Brussels sprouts 'Wellington'

How to harvest

With its tight nobbles dotted along its chunky stem and an umbrella of rubbery leaves, you could be forgiven for wondering which part of the plant is destined for the kitchen. It's those mini-cabbages along the stalk that are your primary prize, but don't neglect the leaves. These make fine cut-and-come-again greens, often tasting milder than the sprouts themselves. Take just a few at a time and leave the rest for the plant.

If you're after all the sprouts on a plant at once, chop the top of the plant off in October and, for some mysterious reason, they'll all mature together for Christmas (fingers crossed). Otherwise, leave the top on and nip the sprouts off as they mature. And if you have chickens, hang the leftover stalks upside down, as they make fine edible pecking posts.

Problems and pests

Cabbage white caterpillars and slugs will almost certainly try to beat you to your harvest. Picking them off is the most effective remedy (see pp.216–17 for other methods). Pigeons will either bother your veg patch intensely or not at all. Be prepared to net against them, string CDs up to swing in the wind and flash reflected light, or look up a good pigeon pie recipe.

How to eat

Steaming sprouts should only take around 6 minutes or so, unless they are large in which case they'll need longer. As with any green leafy vegetable, add them to a pan containing plenty of well-salted boiling water and cook until just tender, then drain and serve at once. Or, once cooked, immediately plunge them into cold water to retain that lively green colour, then drain; reheat in a pan with a little butter when ready to serve.

Sprouts tossed in a little melted butter or olive oil are a truly delicious side veg. And any that don't get eaten will be perfect sliced and combined with other veg to make bubble and squeak.

You can dress sprouts up with any number of partners. Once steamed, push them around a pan with melted butter, seasoned with salt, pepper and nutmeg, before serving with grated Parmesan. They will take to various other flavourings: lemon, almonds, garlic, chives, peppercorns are all worth playing around with. However, my favourite way to eat Brussels sprouts is creamed with chestnuts and bacon (see p. 255).

Cabbages *Brassica oleracea* var. *capitata*

PLANT GROUP	Brassicas (see p.159)
START UNDER COVER	Summer/autumn cabbages: March–April Winter cabbages: April–May Spring cabbages: July–August
PLANT OUT	Around 6 weeks after sowing, when 7 or 8cm tall
HARVEST	Year round, depending on variety:– Summer/autumn cabbages: June–October Winter cabbages: November–March Spring cabbages: March–June

You could be forgiven for thinking that cabbages are a pretty ordinary bunch, with the limited range on offer in supermarkets. But grow your own and you'll soon appreciate how diverse and delicious they are, and how choice of variety is critical to enjoying them at their finest. For visual as well as culinary impact, varieties such as 'Red Drumhead' and 'January King' are up there with any ornamental plant.

You'll find cabbage varieties for harvesting throughout the year. However, much as I love them, I grow few cabbages through the summer because I don't want them to crowd out too much of my valuable plot through the busier, sunnier months.

Varieties

For summer and autumn harvesting: 'Red Drumhead', which is tasty and stunning to look at, is a must. 'Marner Early Red' is another beautiful red cabbage, excellent raw. 'Greyhound' is a reliable, flavoursome green summer cabbage.

For winter harvesting: 'Cuor di Bue', 'January King' and 'Best of All' (the finest Savoy) cannot be equalled for flavour or looks. Grow all three.

For spring harvesting: 'Hispi' – a delicious and quick to mature green cabbage.

How to grow

Start cabbages off under cover in modules or guttering: in March/April for summer- and autumn-hearting varieties; April/May for winter-hearting ones; and in July and August for spring-maturing types. Plant them out around 6 weeks after sowing, when 7 or 8cm tall, at the distance recommended on the seed packet (usually 25cm for smaller varieties, and twice that for larger ones). Water them in well, and tread around them to firm the ground.

Don't let them dry out, as you're after good steady growth. You'll find little else to do in the way of maintenance, apart from picking off the odd caterpillar.

Savoy cabbage 'Best of All'

How to harvest
Timing will depend on your choice of varieties, but you will easily recognise the moment when the centre forms a relatively solid heart – use secateurs or a fairly solid knife to cut the head free. I don't let all of my cabbages mature. Instead I take a cut-and-come-again approach to them, diving in early to harvest odd leaves from at least half of the plants, and leaving the rest to form hearts for harvesting later.

Problems and pests
Caterpillars can decimate your cabbages, so either net plants through the growing season, or pick the pests off regularly and squash any eggs you come across. They seem less attracted to red varieties, so there's another reason to grow some. Slugs can be a problem even to established plants, so keep checking for them.

How to eat
Some cabbages, including Savoy, are wonderful raw, or sliced thinly and sautéed in olive oil, with tomatoes and herbs. Cabbage (and other brassicas) makes a tasty pasta sauce. Steam leaves until tender, then chop finely and throw into a pan for a few minutes with a little oil and garlic. Toss with the pasta and a touch of cream. Add chilli, herbs, Parmesan, etc, as you prefer. For more recipes, see pp.223, 255.

Calabrese *Brassica oleracea* var. *italica*

PLANT GROUP	Brassicas (see p.159)
START UNDER COVER	March–May
PLANT OUT	April–June
SOW DIRECT	March–May
HARVEST	June–September

This is the ever-popular vegetable most of us call broccoli. I must confess that although I like calabrese my heart really lies with sprouting broccoli, so I don't give these plants the space others might do. More recently, they've started to creep over a bit more of the plot, as my 3-year-old daughter loves eating their florets snapped straight from the plant. And if you're trying to grow your own and have young children, you'll know that anything which can keep them happily occupied for a few precious moments (while you do something they construe as 'dull') is gold.

Varieties
'Crown and Sceptre' and 'Chevalier' (F1) are top varieties for taste and reliability.

How to grow
Start them off under cover in modules or Jiffy 7s (see p.197) in early March, or sow the seed straight into your plot a couple of weeks later. Final spacing should be at least 30cm between plants. Spread your sowings by a fortnight to give a steady supply over a couple of months. If you are especially keen on calabrese, you can grow the plants in the ground in a polytunnel or greenhouse, sowing as late as early October for an early spring crop.

Calabrese is fairly low maintenance once established, but do keep your plants from drying out. It is steady, unchecked growth that you are looking for, after all.

How to harvest
You should get a harvest around 3–4 months after sowing, depending on the variety you are growing and the weather. Cut the heads from the plant with a good bit of stalk, and you should get side florets following on.

Problems and pests
Calabrese can provide hostelling facilities to any number of caterpillars, so look out for them and pick them off the plants as you spot them. And do soak the heads well in salty water before cooking to procure any that have kept hidden. Good job my daughter can't read that last bit.

How to eat

Calabrese takes very well to the pasta sauce treatment suggested for cabbages (see p.45). It also makes an excellent addition to your veg tempura (see p.233). If you are serving calabrese as a side veg, first steam it and then give it a good dressing. This can be as simple as good olive oil, black pepper and sea salt, or a classic vinaigrette. Or try this favourite dressing: mix a little finely chopped parsley with ½ tsp wholegrain mustard, a chopped garlic glove, ½ finely chopped red chilli, a pinch of sea salt and 100ml natural yoghurt. Pour over the hot calabrese and serve.

For more recipes, see pp.244, 250, 251.

Calabrese 'Chevalier'

Cardoons *Cynara cardunculus*

PLANT GROUP	Perennials (see p.169)
START UNDER COVER	March–April
PLANT OUT	May–June
HARVEST	October–November

Belonging to the thistle family, the cardoon looks a little as you might imagine a thistly celery on steroids. It is easily mistaken for the globe artichoke, whose flavour it somewhat resembles, but don't be tempted to investigate the flowerheads. It is the deliciously succulent inner stems and heart that you are after.

Many believe that to enjoy cardoons at their best you need to exclude the light, by binding the leaves tightly to the plant (a process known as 'blanching'). But even if you don't make time for blanching, the young stems are a truly delicious autumnal treat. If all you grow them for is their beauty and insect-attracting flowers, they are well worth the little effort required.

Varieties
Cardoons are often sold as an unnamed variety, but if you can source it, try 'Gigante di Romagna' as it is large and deliciously reliable.

How to grow
I sow them under cover in Jiffy 7s (see p.197) or pots in early spring, getting them out in the plot as soon as they are several centimetres tall. Planting at least 80cm apart should give them plenty of room to develop. Add compost or manure to the soil to get them growing quickly.

If you have planted cardoons in a windy site, stake them well as they grow. In autumn, when the flowers and long stems dry out, chop them back hard to encourage fresh growth.

How to harvest
Cardoons will quickly make a good height to add structure to your veg plot, and by late summer you can always tie up the stems and leaves to blanch the tender hearts for eating – a process that takes around 6 weeks. The stalks quickly flop when cut, so be sure to harvest them when you're ready to cook.

Problems and pests
You'll need to avoid slugs during the first weeks after planting out, but thereafter pests shouldn't be a problem.

Cardoon flowerheads

How to eat

Whether or not your cardoons are blanched, you will need to snip out the leafy part from the midrib. For the simplest cooking treatment, braise or steam the stalks for around half an hour until tender. They will be gorgeous with any of the sauces that suit globe artichokes, or you could try serving them with a mustardy/garlicky/anchovy mayonnaise.

Cardoon stalks are also worth the trouble of breadcrumbing and frying. Use a peeler to strip off the tough outer strings from half a kilo of stalks and chop them into 5cm lengths, popping them into a bowl of water acidulated with some lemon juice or white wine vinegar as you go. Boil for half an hour, then drain, dry and let them cool. Beat 2 egg yolks and 1 whole egg together. In another bowl, mix a handful of breadcrumbs with as much Parmesan and salt and pepper as you like. Heat a shallow layer of vegetable oil in a large frying pan until fairly hot. Dip the chopped stalks in the egg mix, then into the crumbs to coat, then add them to the pan. Fry until crisp and golden, drain on a wire rack and sprinkle with salt. Serve hot, with lemon wedges and mayonnaise.

Carrots *Daucus carota*

PLANT GROUP	Roots (see p.162)
SOW DIRECT	March–June
HARVEST	May–November

Recently I've come to see carrots in a new light. I now think of them as two very distinct vegetables: summer carrots and winter carrots, and use them accordingly. Think 'S' for summer carrots – small, sweet, salad, stir-fry, six-minutes' steaming. Winter carrots can be equally, if differently, delicious – roast them slowly with robust flavours, such as garlic and rosemary. Carrots also have an affinity with the seeds from most of their Umbelliferae cousins, including cumin, parsley, dill and fennel, although the judicious cook may want to steer clear of hemlock recipes.

The first time I grew carrots I set up an elaborate fence around them: rabbits eat carrots, everybody knows. The rabbits came and munched the brassicas to pieces. The fence blew over, but it made no difference – the rabbits tore through the cabbages. I've still never seen a rabbit eat a carrot... apart from Bugs Bunny. I've since discovered that his casual carrot-crunching wasn't anything to do with our toothy friends favouring them out in the field. Rather it came about from Clark Gable eating carrots while nonchalantly leaning against a fence talking to Claudette Colbert in the movie *It Happened One Night*. So now I know who to blame...

Varieties

Spring-sown 'Nantes' and 'Chantenay' give speedy returns in summer; summer-sown 'Autumn King' is good for harvesting from late autumn onwards. If your soil is on the heavier side, try the spring-sown 'Parabell', a small, almost-spherical carrot, best eaten at squash-ball size.

Carrots were originally purple, and can also be grown in red, white or yellow varieties. Resist the temptation to grow these novelties – almost without exception, they are as tasty as a trowel.

Choice of variety is particularly important, but to get the maximum taste out of your harvest it's worth going to the trouble of planting a few complimentary herbs, such as coriander and rosemary.

How to grow

Carrots are best sown direct. The lighter the soil the better, but carrots will do fine in whatever your soil type if you take time to prepare a good deep tilth. Pick a site with few stones, and don't be tempted to add manure to the ground, unless (like me) you find eternal amusement in forked carrots.

Early summer carrots lifted in May

Rake and water the bed well, and sow your seeds direct from March through to June. Sow seed every 30cm for larger winter roots, or as I prefer, mix the seed with a little sand and sow thinly, to give bunches of smaller carrots in the warm months. Cover the seed with a thin layer of compost. Sow summer carrots successionally (small sowings, every few weeks) for a steady supply rather than a glut. Whatever size you're after, try to sow as close to the final spacing as you need, as thinning releases volatile chemicals that attract carrot flies.

Little ongoing care is required, other than ensuring that your carrots don't dry out and that they are well weeded.

How to harvest

Pull summer carrots as soon as they are ready (from May onwards), leaving any smaller ones in the ground to develop a little. Winter carrots are usually fine left in the ground until you're ready to eat them. However, if you know you're approaching a really rainy period, pull to prevent them sending out extra fine roots. If you're lifting them well before eating, store them unwashed in a wine crate (or similar) full of slightly damp sand, or in paper sacks that exclude the light.

Problems and pests

Carrot fly is the pest you will need to guard against. Comfrey or seaweed solution (see p.215) helps to discourage the fly as well as encourage the plant. Companion planting from the strong-smelling onion family (try chives or spring onions) works pretty well as the fly navigates by smell. That said, a protection of horticultural fleece is an accessory often worn in the second year as a lesson learned from the first.

How to eat

Eat carrots straight from the ground especially during the summer, brushing off the soil with your hands. Or steam them for a few minutes until tender but retaining a bite and serve with a light dressing or good butter. Juice winter carrots with apples for a beautifully tasty vitamin boost, or roast them with honey (see p.253). Carrots also make a wonderful soup, especially with the addition of coriander and/or parsley, and no stock is complete without them (see p.259). For more recipes, see pp.223, 225, 233, 250, 260.

Cauliflowers *Brassica oleracea* var. *botrytis*

PLANT GROUP	Brassicas (see p.159)
START UNDER COVER	Summer cauliflowers: January–March; Winter cauliflowers: April–July
PLANT OUT	Summer cauliflowers: March–May; Winter cauliflowers: July–October
HARVEST	All year, depending on sowing time:– Summer cauliflowers: June–October Winter cauliflowers: November–May

This is one of those vegetables that few dislike but fewer really love. I suspect it's because few of us have enjoyed them at their best. They may never be the most flavourful feast from your plot, but grow your own and you'll be bowled over by their stunning smell alone.

I certainly didn't like cauliflower when I was young. I'd seen a brain on TV when I was tucking into cauliflower cheese as a child and a switch was clicked. Fortunately, a few years ago, my favourite Indian takeaway reaquainted me with the delights of this vegetable and I now find cauliflowers creeping across the plot in ever-increasing numbers.

You can grow cauliflowers all year round, but I'd urge you to grow them through the winter when they are easy and productive, serving up tasty heads during the leaner months into early spring. Cauliflowers grown through the summer are high maintenance, needing endless watering and feeding if you're to get perfect white globes to harvest. It's not to say that they are impossible, but you'll need to be a real devotee and prepared to commit the time, the care, and a little love to get what you're after. I prefer it slightly easier – I'm busy enough in the summer with all the others in the veg patch to be over-attending a 'special' one.

Varieties

With a spread of varieties you can have delicious cauliflowers all year round. Unsurprisingly, 'All Year Round' does what it says, producing good-sized white cauliflowers whenever you want them, although most people sow from early spring until June for a late summer through autumn crop. I prefer to go for some of the winter varieties such as 'Purple Cape' that are ready in March to May when there's not a whole lot about.

The conical 'Romanesco' variety, with its incredible fractal, self-replicating pattern is as impressive on the plate as it is in your plot. It is also sold by some as a variety of calabrese.

Cauliflower 'Romanesco'

How to grow

This is the ultimate seed packet veg: check the sowing times and stick to them. If you sow them any earlier, your cauliflowers will probably bolt on you. I sow all mine under cover, in modules, planting them out when they are around 7–10cm tall. Steady growth is what you're after, so give them a sheltered site in full sun, prepare the bed well in autumn with compost, plant them out 65cm apart and tread the soil down well to anchor the shallow-rooting plants.

If you want to produce really beautiful cauliflowers, then it's worth the trouble of bending a few of the outer leaves over the developing curd to protect it – part snapping the central rib of the leaves helps keep them in place.

How to harvest

Cut off the globe when it has formed a dense hemisphere, before it gets a chance to bolt. You will need to keep a keen eye on them as this can happen almost overnight if the weather's hot.

Problems and pests

Cauliflower seedlings can be troubled by slugs and caterpillars, so pick off any you find. Once you've got your plants past the seedling stage, your troubles should be behind you.

Bolting – where the cauliflower bursts its globe skywards in little florets – is your main headache if you're growing cauliflower in summer. In warm sun, they grow rapidly, forming heads very easily and are liable to run to seed. Although bolting tends to be caused by the extra light and heat that comes with long summer days, watering seems to arrest this urge, so get ready with the watering can if you've not had much rain.

How to eat

The complex, subtle taste of cauliflower is wonderful either raw or cooked laden with spices – somehow it survives even a fairly robust heat treatment. If you break or cut your cauliflower into florets, steaming takes only 10 minutes or so. If you're in any doubt, err slightly on the underdone side – the last thing you want to do is overcook it. Rarely has a home-grown vegetable shown the importance of fine texture better than the cauliflower.

Another lovely way of serving cauliflower is to cook and serve it whole, smothered in a dressing made from ½ finely chopped garlic clove, 6 chopped anchovies, 50ml lemon juice and a pinch of cayenne pepper, whisked together with 100ml olive oil.

For more recipes, see pp.223, 233.

Celeriac *Apium graveolens* var. *rapaceum*

PLANT GROUP	Roots (see p.162)
START UNDER COVER	February–March
PLANT OUT	May–June
HARVEST	September–March

Not someone addicted to celery, but a root of the same family with a comparable, yet sweeter, slightly peppery, nutty flavour. Shop-bought, you'll get a knobbly fighter's fist of a root, but home-grown celeriac has the added bonus of a crown of celery-like stalks – great chopped finely into soup bases. Celeriac has the ability to absorb flavours without losing itself and it works well with many partners, not least cream. Distinctive and versatile, it features in many culinary classics.

Varieties
'Prinz' is the most widely available variety and rarely disappoints.

How to grow
You can sow celeriac direct, but you'll risk slugs and snails attacking the emerging seedlings. I sow mine under cover in February–March in modules. Hardening off for a week or so works really well with celeriac, resulting in fewer failures and reducing the number that go to seed. Plant them out in May, 40cm apart. Celeriac will tolerate light shade, but the soil should be kept moist in dry weather.

How to harvest
Although celeriac can take over 4 months to reach maturity, it will keep in the ground until March. After harvesting, store with the leaves removed for longevity.

Problems and pests
Other than slugs attacking emerging seedlings, you're unlikely to suffer any other nuisances. Celery fly maggots might (if you're very unlucky) damage plants in early spring. To avoid this, you can plant seedlings out a little later, from May onwards.

How to eat
Peel celeriac and drop into water acidulated with lemon juice to prevent discolouring. Blanching celeriac in boiling water for 1 minute then refreshing in cold water takes the edge off any bitterness – worth doing if you're using it raw in salad. Try layering slices alternately with potato for a lovely variation of dauphinoise (see p.254); or in a half-and-half mix for mash. For more recipes, see pp.225, 227, 228, 250.

Celeriac 'Prinz'

Celery *Apium graveolens* var. *dulce*

PLANT GROUP	Roots (see p.162)
START UNDER COVER	February–March
PLANT OUT	May–June
HARVEST	August–October

As their names suggest, celery and celeriac are closely related. Even if you're not one of those who love the unusual tang of raw celery, grow it for its marvellous ability to bring out the best in others, notably in stocks, stews and soups.

Varieties
Older varieties are grown in trenches, gradually earthed up as they grow. Happily, new self-blanching varieties avoid this palaver. 'Golden Self Blanching', 'Daybreak' and 'Green Utah' are all excellent varieties that need no blanching (see p.18).

How to grow
Sow seed under cover in early spring in modules or Jiffy 7s (see p.197), shifting them into pots, 7.5cm across. Harden off for a few days when the first proper leaves have formed in May or June, before planting out 25cm apart. Celery likes a moisture-retentive, well-drained soil in a sunny spot – add compost and/or well-rotted manure a few months before if you can. Keep celery from drying out, and keep it well weeded until the plants are large enough to shade out any competing weeds.

How to harvest
Harvest self-blanching varieties before the frosts, when the sticks are recognisable in their usual form, from around August to October.

Problems and pests
Starting celery off under cover minimises slug and snail damage. Planting out from May onwards avoids celery fly maggots (which tend to trouble celery in April).

How to eat
In my view, celery works best in combination with garlic, onions and carrots, as the underpinning base of any number of stocks and stews. If you're looking for it to take centre stage, then try serving it as a gratin: boil in salted water for 10 minutes, drain and lay in a buttered ovenproof dish, then just cover with béchamel sauce, dot with a few knobs of butter and grate over lots of Parmesan. Bake at 190°C/Gas Mark 5 for 15 minutes or until golden. For more recipes, see pp.228, 256, 259.

Celery 'Green Utah'

Chard *Beta vulgaris* var. *flavescens* and Perpetual Spinach *Beta vulgaris* var. *cicla*

PLANT GROUP	Others (see p.169)
START UNDER COVER	March–August
PLANT OUT	April–October
SOW DIRECT	April–August
HARVEST	All year

As their Latin name attests, chard and perpetual spinach are almost one and the same, each giving you delicious year-round leaves for the minimum of trouble. I have a few chard plants that are still throwing out tasty leaves 17 months after sowing, somehow avoiding the attention of the slugs, snails and caterpillars. Many growers undervalue those plants that almost seem to cut themselves and hop into your basket, but don't take offence at their lack of reliance on you – love them all the more for their quiet self-sufficiency.

Beyond being as easy as it gets to grow, they'll do much to liven up the look of your patch. Green-and-white Swiss chard was made for the frosts to dust with ice crystals, and the richly coloured varieties add a vibrant flourish to any plot.

Varieties

Swiss chard and perpetual spinach are often sold as unnamed generic seed, but it's worth searching out 'White Silver' for its delicious green-and-white leaves. Colourful rhubarb and rainbow chard make tasty additions to the plot – 'Bright Lights' is the variety I grow every year. Most varieties picked small will give you tender salad leaves, but 'Canary Yellow' chard (with its yellow ribs) is perhaps the best. 'Popeye' is, appropriately, the best named variety of perpetual spinach.

How to grow

Success with either chard or perpetual spinach is pretty well assured. Germination rates are high, and so good is their ability to regrow, you'll only need two sowings to get cut-and-come-again leaves all year. Your first sowing should be in March. Sow under cover in Jiffy 7s (see p.197) or modules and plant out 6 weeks later at least 50cm apart, or sow direct in April. Your second sowing, for winter and early spring eating, should be in August, direct or under cover. Don't get anxious if your sowings take a little while to appear – a few weeks for any sign of growth is normal.

Apart from giving them a little water in a drought, chard and perpetual spinach need no routine care other than weeding.

How to harvest
You'll be harvesting your first cut of leaves around 10 weeks after sowing – either cut leaves or tear them off from the outside of the plant or chop the whole lot a few centimetres above ground level, and new leaves will grow in their place.

Problems and pests
Slugs and snails may trouble young seedlings. Starting them off under cover helps get the plant to a size that limits the extent of the damage, but keep an eye out.

How to eat
Strip the stems from the leaves and steam them for 3–4 minutes before adding the torn-off leaves for another 2 minutes. As a side vegetable, olive oil and salt is all that is needed, although a little chopped chilli won't go amiss. Both chard and perpetual spinach are lovely chopped and cooked with Puy lentils, and work well as the leaves in half the garden soup (see p.223). For more recipes, see pp.244, 248.

Chard 'Bright Lights'

Chicory *Cichorium intybus*

PLANT GROUP	Salad leaves (see p.166)
SOW DIRECT	May–July
HARVEST	October–January

I grew chicory for the first time only a couple of years ago and it won me over immediately, although the bitterness can be an acquired taste for some. You can grow chicory either for salad leaves or for hearts, which are usually cooked. Think of chicory and endive (see p.74) as the 'olives' of the salad bowl. The first taste of each may leave you uncertain, but once it's clicked with you – and it will – you'll not want to be without them.

Bear in mind that chicory hearts tend to be sweeter than the individual leaves, so it's worth growing some for leaves and others for hearts, giving you two very different leafy flavours from just one sowing. Added to that, chicory looks good, grows well in the darker months and delivers in the leaner weeks.

Varieties

The hardy 'Rossa di Treviso' (also known as 'Treviso Rosso'), one of the radicchio types of chicory, has been the taste and visual success of all the chicories I've tried – both for its hearts and its reddy-purple/acid-green leaves. 'Palla Rossa' is similarly beautiful, easy to grow, very hardy, and forms delicious dense heads. 'Sugar Loaf', with its crisp green hearts and leaves, is wonderfully tasty, and has a good resistance to bolting even when grown in a polytunnel. 'Variegata di Castelfranco' is an excellent traditional variety that I have found to be happily reliable for either cut-and-come-again leaves or for allowing to heart up.

How to grow

Sow direct in late spring and early summer, thinning the plants to 5cm apart for small leaves, 25cm for larger leaves or hearts, in rows around 25cm apart.

How to harvest

Chicory is one of those delightfully useful harvests that not only endures the cold, it positively thrives in it. With good care, regular picking, and a little bit of luck, you can expect leaves and hearts right through the coldest months of the year, with cut-and-come-agains staying slowly productive for up to 4 months. Once you've had some success with chicories and taken them to heart, investigate a few more varieties. There's an amazing range of textures and tastes out there – check the catalogues and seed packets.

You can force chicory, but lovely as it may be, it has always seemed one step too far for me, involving digging up and so forth, so I've never bothered.

Problems and pests

Rather in the way we don't tend to do 'bitter' flavours very much in this country, few pests do either, which is fortunate.

How to eat

A few leaves work well in a salad, where chicory's slight bitterness will offset a range of milder wintery leaves beautifully. Chicory is also delicious braised, and works well in risottos.

If you're looking for it to take centre stage, quarter 3 chicory heads and blanch them in water acidulated with lemon juice for a couple of minutes. Drain thoroughly and allow them to cool. Crumble 100g blue cheese into a small pan, add 80ml double cream and warm through until the cheese just starts to melt. Take off the heat and season with freshly ground black pepper (the cheese will add the saltiness). Heat 20g butter in a frying pan and add the chicory, cooking it until it starts to colour. Serve the chicory warm, dressed with the blue cheese dressing and scattered with a few crushed toasted walnuts. For more recipes, see pp. 248, 250.

Chicory 'Rossa di Treviso'

Picking chillies 'Cayenne Long Slim'

Chilli peppers *Capsicum annuum*

PLANT GROUP	Solanaceae (see p.168)
START UNDER COVER	February–April
PLANT OUT	June
HARVEST	August–October

Chilli peppers are one of the most potent of 'transformers', lending a gastronomic hand to so many of your other harvests. All that flavour from such a little pod makes them a real must, whether you've a rural smallholding or an urban window ledge. Everything from potatoes to salads is lifted by the spicy punch of chilli, and with careful selection of variety to suit your preference for heat, you'll find them a hugely rewarding harvest.

If you do not have a polytunnel or greenhouse, pop your chilli plants on your sunniest windowsill. Many varieties love the restricted root run they get in a pot, and in your home they'll benefit from you being able to keep a close eye on them as they develop. Once under way, chilli plants grow quickly from tiny seedlings into beautiful (almost Christmassy) bushes. Even on a windowsill, don't be surprised to get a couple of dozen chillies or more from each one.

Varieties

'Hungarian Hot Wax' is a favourite, producing its long and pointed fruit over a relatively short season. This gives them a racing chance of maturing even in a disappointing summer. Not only that, their heat alters with its colour – pick them green and mild, through yellow to fiery red. 'Jalapeño' is similarly excellent.

If you are looking for the best variety for indoor pot growing, go for 'Apache', which is a smaller variety and pretty much in the centre of the heat spectrum. 'Poblano' is hard to beat for times when you're after something on the milder side of hot and is ideal for stuffings or salsas. If you can handle it, try any of the ridiculously hot Habanero varieties – keep some yoghurt handy as it alleviates the burning sensation (from your mouth at least).

How to grow

I sow mine under cover in March in Jiffy 7s (see p.197) or small pots and keep them either at bench height or on a windowsill in the house for the extra warmth – chillies hate the cold and the wet. Don't start them off after April – they are sun lovers and need a long season to make it to their best. Peppers are slow to germinate, taking up to a month, so try popping them in the airing cupboard to speed things up – by as much as two-thirds. Make sure, however, that you take them out as soon as they poke out of the compost. Pot them into 9cm pots and on to larger ones as soon as the roots start to poke out. Get them into the ground (ideally under cover) or into their final pot in June.

Chillies are less trouble to the grower than tomatoes, but less reliable in coming to full ripeness. Comfrey waterings (see p.215) or sprays given from flowering onwards will nudge you ever nearer to a top crop, but don't overwater them, and do tie the plants to a stake for support. It is also a good idea to limit the height (essential if you're growing them in pots), so pinch out the growing tips to encourage them to bush out.

How to harvest

Pick and use them fresh at their peak – usually September or so, depending on how sunny the summer has been. Then, as the sunlight hours fall in mid-autumn, pick any that remain and dry them in an oven on its lowest setting overnight for use over the following months.

Problems and pests

You'll rarely find your chilli plants troubled. If you do, it will probably be aphids (see pp.217–18 for remedies).

How to eat

Chilli adds heat and colour to a host of dishes. Use it where you like, but be adventurous as it works surprisingly well with many less obvious partners. The confit chilli (see p.230) will go with just about anything.

For a deliciously different take on scrambled eggs: add ½ finely chopped onion and ½ finely chopped garlic clove to a drop of olive oil in a hot pan. Cook for a few minutes, then add a couple of peeled, chopped tomatoes, a few chopped oregano leaves (go easy on these) and ½ finely chopped medium-hot chilli. In a bowl, beat 6 eggs lightly and add them to the pan, mixing everything together well with a wooden spoon. Push the eggs around the pan with the spoon and, just as they begin to scramble, throw in a few pitted olives. Serve with toast.

For more recipes, see pp.242, 256, 259.

Courgettes *Cucurbita pepa*

PLANT GROUP	Cucurbits (see p.165)
START UNDER COVER	April–June
PLANT OUT	May–July
HARVEST	July–October

An ideal plant for the beginner or the nervous grower – once planted out, you can almost ignore courgettes. They really do grow quickly, easily and abundantly to the point where they are almost reviled for their productivity. This is one harvest you needn't worry about maximising. The secret of enjoying it to the full is to grow only a few plants, harvest them as tasty cigars, and have a few belting recipes up your sleeve for the excess that's coming your way.

Growing courgettes also lets you in on one of those unique home-grown harvests – their flowers. These store and travel poorly, so growing your own is the only way to lay your hands on them at their peak. They are truly delicious, with a distinctive sweet, mildly peppery flavour that almost feels like you are tasting the pollen.

Varieties
Try 'Arbarello di Sarzarno' or 'Soleil' (F1) for delicious, long cigars; 'Rondo di Nizza' for wonderful green globes, ideal for stuffing; and 'Trombomcino' as a tasty climber ideal for tepeeing in pots.

How to grow
Start courgettes off under cover in small pots in April, hardening them off for a couple of days before planting them out about 60cm apart when you're confident you've seen the last frost. Two sowings – one in early spring, one in early summer – should keep you in fruit right into autumn.

Make sure they have plenty of water during the first weeks after planting out. Also water the plants through dry periods, though you'll probably find that their leaves help to retain soil moisture, and handily suppress weeds. A fortnightly comfrey feed (see p.215) from flowering onwards will give them a boost if you're after maximum yield, though you should find them perfectly productive without.

How to harvest
In truth, it's pretty hard to go wrong with courgettes – all you have to do is avoid leaving them to get too large. If you do, flavourless exhibition fruit will result and the plant will stop producing those sweet cigars that should be your aim. The only rule is 'keep picking'.

Problems and pests

Starting courgettes off under cover ensures that they get to a good size before arriving in your veg patch, by which stage slug and snail damage will usually be minimal. There are a range of viruses and mildews that may affect your courgette plants. For the most part you will still get a crop, but you'll need to remove any badly affected plants and burn them.

How to eat

Delicious though ratatouille can be, maximising the versatility of courgettes will help you make the best of what will be plentiful. Try them grated raw in salads, or dress thin slices with oil and lemon, salt and pepper and any of the annual herbs. Chilli and pine nuts will happily sit by their side, and they make a perfect partner for Parmesan. Courgettes are also the ideal barbecue veg, taking to the griddle almost as well as a steak.

Torn into salads, the flowers make a vibrant addition, but are perhaps best as a wonderful cup for stuffing and deep-frying (see p.234). Go for the male flowers, as they have no young courgette developing behind them.

For more recipes, see pp.223, 237, 248, 256.

Courgettes 'Arbarello di Sarzarno'

Cucumbers and Gherkins
Cucumis sativus

PLANT GROUP	Cucurbits (see p.165)
START UNDER COVER	March–May
PLANT OUT	May–June
HARVEST	July–October

If you want to see the importance of texture to culinary pleasure and just what a difference it can make to the very best ingredients, grow your own cucumbers and gherkins. They may not be at the top of the in-your-face flavour bombs that the gardener can grow, but try 'Crystal Lemon' cucumbers and 'Vert Petit de Paris' gherkins and I'm sure you'll find them a revelation of cool crunch. I'd no sooner be without my own than I would salad leaves.

Added to that, the plants look beautiful and could be grown by the most inexperienced gardener, so find room for even just a couple of plants. Sea salt, freshly ground pepper, olive oil – and a hot day on which to appreciate their coolness – are all the accompaniments they need.

Varieties

'Crystal Lemon' is outstanding, giving you cool, yellow globes of summer freshness. 'Marketmore' is a great all-rounder, suitable for indoors and out. Some cucumber seed is sold as an outdoor variety (check the catalogue or seed packet). If you're growing these then leave all flowers on, but don't grow more than one variety as they may cross-pollinate, leading to bitterness in the fruit.

'Eureka' (F1) and 'Vert Petit de Paris' are wonderfully delicious and reliable gherkin varieties that grow really well outside, either over a structure or allowed to scramble over the ground.

How to grow

Jiffy 7s (see p.197) and small pots are best for starting off cucumbers and gherkins. I get them going under cover in March or April, potting them on as needed until planting out in May (after hardening off for a couple of days). Choose a sunny, sheltered site, and leave a good half-metre between plants. Some varieties will do well outside in a good summer but all will be more reliable under cover, cropping earlier and for longer. Cucumbers and gherkins like to climb and scramble, and although you won't need to support the fruits themselves, canes give the plant a good structure to wind around.

The plants will need watering most days if grown under cover, and through any dry periods if they are outside. Increase watering as they grow. As with other cucurbits, comfrey feeds (see p.215) every fortnight after flowering starts will really give the plants – and hence your crops – a boost. Pinching out the shoot and growing tips helps focus the plant's energies on fruit production, but once in a while I haven't got round to it and I've still had excellent yields.

If you are growing cucumbers under cover, do check whether your chosen varieties are all female (many modern F1 cultivar are) or look for emerging male flowers. These have no small cucumber behind them in the way that female flowers do. You'll need to remove male flowers as they appear, because if female flowers are pollinated their fruit (and its eater) will turn bitter.

How to harvest

If you sow in April you can expect a good harvest from August onwards, although you can always try a March and May sowing too if you are particularly keen to maximise your chances of a long and heavy haul. Most varieties, especially 'Crystal Lemon', will be at their best if you pick them before they get too large and firm, before the skin thickens too much. Judging the best size is largely a matter of experimentation. Peel them if you leave it late and they'll still be delicious.

Problems and pests

Starting your plants off under cover minimises the chances of slug damage while the seedlings are small and vulnerable. After that, they should remain relatively untroubled. Cucumbers can be susceptible to mildew. Comfrey or seaweed solutions (see p.215) sprayed on the plants help to lessen the risk, but 'Burpless Tasty Green' (F1) is resistant to mildew, so growing a few of this variety ensures you'll have a cucumber crop even if the others succumb.

How to eat

Cucumber is a refreshing, cool addition to many summer salads, none finer than the classic Greek salad: put a thinly sliced cucumber into a large salad bowl with 4 large, juicy tomatoes, cored and cut into wedges. Crumble in 250g feta cheese (or similar crumbly, salty cheese) and add a couple of handfuls of pitted black olives. Drizzle over 90ml good olive oil and 30ml lemon juice, and season with freshly ground black pepper to taste. Mix very gently and sprinkle with a few torn basil or oregano leaves to serve.

For a sweet-sour treatment, marinate 2 peeled and thinly sliced cucumbers in a mixture of 50ml olive oil, 25ml white wine vinegar, 2 tbsp caster sugar, a small handful of finely chopped dill and plenty of salt and pepper to taste for an hour.

For more recipes, see pp.250, 251.

Cucumber 'Marketmore'

Edible flowers

| PLANT GROUP | Others (see p.169) |

I'm sure the idea of eating flowers won't appeal to some macho allotmenters, but the chances are they are eating some already... blissfully unaware. Cauliflower, broccoli, calabrese and artichokes are just a few of the flowers that most of us put away quite happily in their semi-mature state, but somehow it seems altogether weirder to give 'proper' flowers like nasturtiums a whirl.

I have to take my hat off to Sarah Raven who inspired me to try edible flowers. If you sit, as I did, grim-faced at the prospect, then I'd like to suggest courgette flowers as the best bridge for crossing the divide. It looks like a flower, it is a flower, but you can take comfort that at least it comes from a vegetable. Try them deep-fried (see p.234) and marvel at their pepperiness.

Most edible flowers won't give you any trouble, nor call on your time. Sow direct or in pots, at spacings advised on the packet. Don't let them dry out, and if you're growing them in pots most will welcome the odd comfrey feed (see p.215). Snip off unblemished flowers at their peak for eating, and tatty ones for the compost heap. This ensures the plant will keep producing new flowers over the following weeks.

Top flowers for the kitchen

In addition to my favourite courgette flowers (see p.67), try growing the following:

Borage This is the beautiful bee-attracting flower that adds colour to a jug of Pimms, along with leaves that bring a wonderful cucumber coolness to salads. Buy one packet and sow in spring. Borage's ability to self-seed ensures that you'll then have it for life. Freeze the flowers in ice cubes to drag your harvest into the winter.

Nasturtiums Happy in poor soil, nasturtium flowers taste almost as good as they look, bringing their sweet pepperiness to any summer salad. They are also perfect in tempura (see p.233). Sow them in spring, either in lines (5–10cm apart) or just broadcast in a patch and thin if you think they're getting too cramped. Some, like 'Black Velvet', will climb if you give them structure, or creep over the ground if you don't. 'Tip Top Mahogany' is probably the pick of the bunch – its peppery leaves are the strongest of the ones I've grown. Even the seed pods are edible – and, if you eat a couple of dozen at the first inkling, reputedly ward off colds.

Viola Start them off in spring under cover and the pansy-like flowers will bring a colourful, sweet and fragrant twist to mid-summer, autumn and winter salads without having the peppery hit of many of the other edible flowers.

Calendula (pot marigold) Sprinkled over salads, the petals add a bright-orange dash, and if you're after something different try using them with rice, where they bring a colour and taste close to saffron but for a fraction of the price. Not to be confused with marigold (*Tagetes* sp.), which is a fine companion plant (see p.212).

Herb flowers The flowers of most herbs are also edible; some – like chive flowers – are particularly delicious. As a rule of thumb, you'll find they taste very much like the more-used parts (if perhaps slightly stronger or milder). Fennel, dill, thyme and oregano flowers are all worth trying, allowing you to add their familiar flavour to your food in a beautifully different way.

Borage

Endive *Cichorium endivia*

PLANT GROUP	Salad leaves (see p.166)
SOW DIRECT	May–August
HARVEST	August–March

With its tasty bitterness, endive – like chicory – adds to your cooking options over the colder half of the year. As with chicory, you have the choice of growing it for leaves or hearts, although endive plants are altogether more floppy and informal. I love endive, though not in large quantities, so I grow only a few plants and I suggest you do the same if you're new to them.

If you are not convinced by the bitterness of this salad veg, you can always take the edge off it with a little simple blanching. When your endive resemble upturned mop heads, place a large pot over a couple of them (with the holes blocked to exclude all light). Uncover them after 3 weeks or so and they should be paler, sweeter, and delicious. Leave the unblanched endive to grow on slowly until you are ready to blanch a few more.

Varieties

'Fine de Louvier' is excellent for leaves, 'Blond Full Heart' for hearts, while 'Cuor d'Oro' is hard to beat for productivity and doesn't need blanching – it turns itself white. Consider 'Cornet de Bordeaux' if you want to grow endive through winter.

How to grow

Endive seeds are best thinly sown straight into your plot, thinning the plants as they grow to allow 25cm between plants. Sow from late spring until mid-summer, – exactly when will depend on the variety, so check the catalogue or seed packet. If you are growing endive for hearts, sow them successionally in smaller batches to avoid them all maturing at the same time.

Endive plants are pretty low maintenance, although you may need to water them a little in a hot, dry patch to prevent bolting.

How to harvest

You can crop endive for a good 6 months or more from August onwards, which makes them a wonderfully enduring addition to your autumn and winter options. Endive is excellent for cut-and-come-again leaf harvesting, or if you have a hearting variety such as 'Blond Full Heart', you can let them develop until the hearts are saucer-sized and try the quick blanching technique. If you're harvesting the whole blanched head, slice it off at soil level using a long knife.

Problems and pests

Problems are rare. Slugs and snails are usually put off by endive's bitterness, but do check the plants occasionally, especially if you are blanching them under pots.

How to eat

If you are unsure about bitter leaves, try a few 'Fine de Louvier' endive as your way in. The cut leaves make a bright, edgy contrast scattered sparingly into a mixed leaf salad, or as a leafy salad on their own with a honey mustard dressing.

Surprisingly perhaps, endive is also delicious fried: blanch in boiling water for a couple of minutes, drain and dry well. Season generously, then fold the outer leaves around the paler centre to keep it crisp and succulent. Heat a little olive oil in a frying pan and fry the endive on one side until it starts to brown, then flip over to fry the other side. It's lovely eaten on its own, but particularly good with fish.

Or try sliced endive hearts fried in tempura batter (see p.233) – they're fantastic. For more recipes, see pp.226, 250.

Endive 'Cuor d'Oro'

Florence fennel
Foeniculum vulgare var. *azoricum*

PLANT GROUP	Others (see p.169)
SOW DIRECT	April–July
HARVEST	June–November

Closely related to the feathery fennel herb, grown predominantly for its leaves and seeds, Florence fennel varieties bulk up at the base into the classic aromatic bulbs. Their distinctive flavour comes from a compound also found in star anise, and I love the cool taste as much cooked as I do raw. Aniseed may not be everyone's glass of Pernod, but even if you are unsure it's really worth giving fennel's mild, sweet bulbs a try. As with celery, even if the naked veg isn't to your taste, it has the ability to make others shine a little brighter. Try the various different ways of serving it and let fennel work its magic throughout a meal.

Easy to grow and one of the most beautiful vegetables there is, fennel is worth its place in your patch for its striking presence alone.

Varieties
Reliable, delicious and tender, 'Romanesco' is a must. If you have trouble with fennel bolting, try 'Finale', which is slower to run to seed than other varieties.

How to grow
Sow direct from late April–May onwards for best results, thinning out the emerging seedlings to 25cm each way. If you're desperate for an early start, then you can sow varieties that resist bolting, such as 'Finale', as early as the end of February since they'll happily grow through the heat of high summer. You can leave some to produce into the colder months, cutting them back often to encourage more succulent growth. Fennel isn't fussy when it comes to soil. It will do well anywhere, but do give it some sun and regular (but not too much) water.

Problems and pests
Fennel is very rarely troubled by anything.

How to harvest
The bulbs will be ready from late July through to November (or from late June if you have sown early varieties). If you've sown a good number, you can start harvesting earlier when they're smaller.

While the bulbs are developing, pinch off some of the tendrilly top growth too – use it to add a clean aniseedy hit to salads and dressings. If you cut the bulbs about 3cm above ground, the remaining stump may well sprout again through the following months. Do leave some to grow on unharvested – they add decorative structure to the veg patch... and the insects will love you for it.

How to eat

Fennel has proven to be a real four-course favourite of mine, turning out refreshing cool soups, livening up salads, finding a heaven-made match with fish and cheese, and, as the Italians do, you can take it one course further and serve it with fruit.

It delivers not just in flavour, but equally importantly in its texture. Wonderfully crisp raw, firm to squidgy when roasted or boiled, fennel is a classic whatever-the-weather vegetable that is resilient enough to work just as well as leftovers the following day. It makes a perfect addition to the crudités list, a wonderful griddled partner to fish and chicken, and if the bulbs flower try the umbrella in tempura batter (see p.233). For more recipes, see pp.242, 244, 259.

Florence fennel 'Romanesco'

French beans 'Blauhilde'

French beans *Phaseolus vulgaris*

PLANT GROUP	Legumes (see p.157)
START UNDER COVER	March–July
PLANT OUT	May–August
SOW DIRECT	April–July
HARVEST	May–October

Smaller and rounder than runner beans, French beans come in climbing and dwarf varieties. Give both sorts a go, as there are some delicious varieties of each. They not only deliver in the kitchen, they'll add colour, variety and height to your plot too. Indeed many varieties were originally grown as ornamentals.

French beans are also just about as easy, productive and versatile as veg go. Not only do you get a great return from each plant, you have any number of opportunities to use the beans. Picked small they are delicious raw; left a little larger they are wonderful briefly steamed; once fully grown the beans can be podded and eaten in soups and stews, or saved for sowing the following year. A must for any plot.

Varieties

'Purple Teepee' (purple, dwarf), 'Blauhilde' (purple, climbing), 'Rocquencourt' (yellow, dwarf) and 'Blue Lake Climbing' (green, climbing) are all excellent.

How to grow

Bean seeds are pleasingly large for handling. It's worth soaking them for half an hour to soften their skin and encourage germination before you sow them. You can sow direct from mid-spring onwards, under cover from March for a June crop, and as late as July for an autumn haul. If you're starting them off indoors, try toilet roll inners or root trainers (see p.197) to allow their roots to develop a good run.

Don't be tempted to sow too many. Some varieties, including those above, are heavy croppers and you'll end up with a rather full chutney cupboard. Instead, sow three small batches 6 weeks apart for a steady supply. They'll germinate quickly in a bright, cool (but not cold) place. Let them get to a few centimetres tall before planting out, to increase their chances of dodging slugs.

The climbing varieties will need something to grow up or over. This can be anything from a few canes tied into rows or a tepee, to more elaborate arches and screens. If you're going for the tepee, ensure the pattern of canes in the ground is in a 'C' shape rather than a full circle so that you can get to the beans that grow towards the centre. If left unpicked, these will continue to develop far beyond the picking stage and take valuable resources from the plant, slowing production of the succulent beans you are after. If you are growing French beans in a line, give them a good 20cm between plants. Most beans love the sun, but watch the taller varieties for the wind. These energetic climbers can easily reach 2 metres, so pick a fairly sheltered spot... or don't, and watch them fall over as I did last year.

Beans love water from the stage when they are flowering, and watering with comfrey tea (see p.215) will promote healthy and extended production.

How to harvest

The main harvest is August and September, but if you're a fan you can stretch this from June through to November by sowing them successionally as recommended. Regular picking is essential, partly because the beans are at their best small, but also as it stimulates the plant to grow more and for longer. Try a few beans when they're small and smooth – they should snap easily in the middle when you bend them. It's worth using scissors or secateurs to harvest them as pulling often tears the plant itself. Once you can see the beans bulging in their pod they've got too large to be ideal, but still pick them to encourage more to grow, or if it is towards the end of the season let some fatten and the pods turn golden. Leave in place until the weather is about to turn wet, then cut the plant and hang it upside down somewhere light and airy until the pods really desiccate. Then shell the beans and allow them to dry for a few more days on paper. *Voilà*: haricot beans. Or next year's seed.

At the end of the season don't pull up the plants unless you've a crop going straight in. If you cut the plants clear, leaving the roots to breakdown into the soil, you'll be leaving a nutritious present for the next crop to enjoy (see p.157).

Problems and pests

Green and black aphids love beans almost as much as we do, so it's well worth planting a few flowers as companion plants in with the beans. Marigolds (*Tagetes* sp.) are particularly good at attracting the aphid-eating ladybirds and hoverflies. If you still get bothered, the best remedy is to rub or spray the aphids off with the hose. Slugs and snails can quickly decimate your crop – get in early and get in hard with as many remedies as you can manage (see p.216).

How to eat

Add beans to boiling salted water and cook until tender, but retaining a bite, then plunge briefly into ice-cold water to preserve colour, flavour and vigour. Most of those that are not already green, will be once cooked, but if you're after preserving a little of that garden colour try adding 1 tsp sugar to the cooking water.

French beans are fantastic with most of the dressings and sauces that work with asparagus, globe artichokes, sprouting broccoli and peas, but are perhaps best with a Japanese-style dressing (see p.251). For more recipes, see pp.223, 244, 256.

Garlic *Allium sativum*

PLANT GROUP	Onions (see p.164)
SOW DIRECT	October–November or February–March
HARVEST	May–September

I don't think there's another smell to match garlic for getting the gastronomic juices going. Chopped and thrown raw into salsa verde, or fried gently with onions, or roasted alongside tomatoes, the effect is the same – that aroma makes you hungry. And it's all thanks to the plant's defence system. As with all members of the onion family, garlic releases sulphurous compounds, predominantly allicin, when it is nibbled by an inquisitive animal, ensuring that only an initial munch is taken rather than a more comprehensive feasting. We take advantage of this release of allicin as the welcome taste and aroma we know as 'garlic' in our kitchens, but it is also responsible for many of the benefits that garlic is famous for – being antibacterial, blood-thinning, spirit-lifting, cholesterol-lowering, and detoxifying.

Legend has it that garlic also bestows upon those that eat it a lucky charm, protection and good fortune; it discourages the devil, and even returns lost souls. It's pretty good to cook with too.

Varieties

There are many reasons not to bother with growing your own garlic. It is easily sourced, cheap to buy and keeps well, but growing your own can give you access to more varieties, to fresh (or 'green') garlic, and you get the added bonus of its beneficial properties as a companion plant. 'Printanor' and 'Thermidrome' are good reliable varieties that should do as well as any in this country.

Although botanically closer to a leek than true garlic, 'Elephant' is definitely worth trying. Eaten green, it's a real treat, or you can roast it to bring out its full mild sweetness. It lives up to its name too, growing up to a hefty 10cm across.

A word of warning: don't bother trying to grow from cloves you've bought in the shops as most are grown in warm climes overseas and are prone to viruses that properly sourced garlic isn't.

How to grow

Garlic loves the sun and a free-draining patch, and it can be planted as a companion to ward off a range of nuisances, including carrot fly. You will buy either individual cloves or a whole head of garlic. If the latter, then separate the cloves, discarding the tiny ones at the centre. Plant them direct in October/November ideally, or in February/March, and they'll all be ready for harvesting in the summer. The

Garlic 'Printanor'

autumn-sown garlic, however, will be larger and slightly earlier to your kitchen than the ones sown later. Pop them in around 7cm deep (a little deeper for 'Elephant') with the flat base downwards, allowing around 15cm between them, with rows at least 20cm apart.

Garlic loves to flower, so if you are after a good-sized bulb, cut off the stem as it heads skywards in order to concentrate the plant's energies towards developing good bulbs.

How to harvest

Harvest time really depends on you. Pull the plants from June as green garlic for immediate use, or wait a while until any leaves yellow to investigate whether it's time to dig your garlic up. Once pulled, dry them in the sun for a day or two, then store indoors somewhere cool. Most varieties will last for around 4 months or so.

Problems and pests

As with other members of the onion family, rust (see p.98) can be a problem; crop rotation is your best prevention.

How to eat

Using garlic raw (crushed or chopped) makes the most of its beneficial qualities, as cooking diminishes them to a degree. Remember: the finer you chop, the stronger the flavour.

Roasted garlic is a delicious addition to many other dishes. Place a whole bulb in a small roasting tin, drizzle with olive oil and roast in the oven at 170°C/Gas Mark 3 for about 40 minutes. Squeeze out the soft, sweet pulp from the papery skins and stir into soups, dressings or sauces, or simply spread on toasted sourdough and top with soft cheese and roasted tomatoes.

Green garlic is altogether sweeter and gentler than its pungent relative, remaining in the background, yet enhancing its cooking pot companions to delicious effect. The late-spring/early-summer harvests – broad beans, lamb, artichokes, new potatoes and peas, in particular – take really well to green garlic. It's difficult to overuse, so don't be shy with it.

For more recipes, see pp.225, 227, 228, 229, 230, 234, 240, 242, 254, 257, 259.

Globe artichoke 'Romanesco'

Globe artichokes *Cynara scolymus*

PLANT GROUP	Perennials (see p.169)
START UNDER COVER	February–March
PLANT OUT	May–June
HARVEST	May–September

You'll end up with more on your plate after you've eaten a globe artichoke than was there to start with. Somehow piles of green material appear seemingly endlessly from this tight spiky ball. This deconstruction is inspired by the search for every scrap of the delicate nutty flesh that hides at the base of each petal, and at the heart of the flower itself. And it's well worth the effort – this is gourmet food for the lazy gardener – sow artichokes once, and they'll keep on giving harvest after harvest.

Globe artichokes tick all the right boxes – they are low maintenance, reliable croppers, easy to start off, have unbelievable flavour, and they are expensive in the shops. *And* this Mediterranean perennial is a looker. It can grow over 2 metres tall, bringing some wonderful structure to the plot, and throwing out delicious buds. If left to flower, these attract a whole range of beneficial insects, particularly bees, into the garden. The globe artichoke even makes a wonderful cut flower.

Varieties

Don't bother with the new varieties, which are geared very much towards commercial production. In my experience, they don't have the flavour of the older established varieties. 'Gros de Laon' and the purply 'Violetta di Chioggia' are a brilliant combination, or try 'Romanesco'. If you live in the North, then you may appreciate the extra hardiness of the 'Green Globe' variety.

How to grow

Sow under cover in Jiffy 7s (see p.197) or in modules in early spring – germination is usually quick. Pot on seedlings as soon as they are large enough to handle. Plant them out a pace or so apart in a sunny, well-drained spot in May or thereabouts.

During the first year, don't be tempted to let your taste buds get the better of you. Let the plant establish, and cut off any buds as soon as you see them. This will concentrate the plant's energies on developing its root system.

As for maintenance, it really couldn't be simpler. Add compost in winter as a mulch that will work its way into the ground and enrich the soil for the spring. And although some gardeners cut back the old stems to ground level in autumn, frankly I've never bothered. The plants will tire after 4 or 5 years, so you'll need new ones to take their place. Small plants, known as offsets, form at the base of the plant.

Select ones that are at least 30cm tall, with a couple of shoots and reasonable roots, and carefully detach them. Some people prefer to pot these offsets on for a year before planting out, but to my mind, that's an unnecessary step. I plant mine straight out, chop the leaves down by about half and water them well. I find they soon establish, ready to crop the year after.

How to harvest

The yield can be variable, but if you bank on getting eight or so globes from each plant every July–August you shouldn't be disappointed. Mediterranean they may be, but you can get a very long season if you're lucky. We've even picked them on Christmas Day, and some favour these winter treats. During the colder months the artichokes may be darker than usual or 'winter-kissed' – blistered white by the frost – but they should still be delicious and tender if they are green on the inside of the petals. Dodge any that are mouldy, drying out or wilting.

Problems and pests

None.

How to eat

Artichokes, if you're new to them, look as though they could do some damage in the wrong hands, and it's certainly not obvious how one cooks and eats them, so here's a crash course: firstly boil the globes whole until tender, which can take anything from 15–45 minutes depending on their size. To test, pull a leaf away from the base of the stem – it should come away easily. Once that's done, it's time to choose how you want to eat them.

The classic way to serve artichokes is whole, just boiled as they are, ready for guests to tear off the petals, dip in vinaigrette or melted, salted butter and strip the succulent flesh off from the base of each petal with their teeth.

Alternatively, once cooked you can strip all the petals off and chop out the hairy choke (the immature flower) to get to the fleshy heart that lies underneath. This succulent prized part is delicious with any number of dressings, or it can be preserved in oil, but my favourite way to eat it is made into houmous (see p.229) and served on crostini.

Catch artichokes young and small and try them raw, dipping each tender petal into your favourite dressing, without the fiddle of cooking or dealing with the choke. You can even braise these small artichokes to eat whole.

For more recipes, see pp.242, 244, 250.

Herbs

| PLANT GROUP | Others (see p.169) |

Herbs deserve a River Cottage Handbook of their own, so rather than attempt to be exhaustive I'm focusing on a few favourites. These are the herbs, well known and less so, that do their main job better than all the others, adding value to good produce, turning healthy harvests into great meals. Many also work well as companion plants (see p.212) and/or bring beneficial insects to your veg patch. Do try to grow at least a few, as you really can't afford to do without them – either out in the garden or in your kitchen.

There is much variety when it comes to spacing and timing of sowing. Check the seed packet and catalogue and follow the advice.

Herbs fall into two groups: the annuals, generally leafy, that you sow, grow and use within a year; and the perennials, generally woody, that will keep on giving over a longer period. I tend to grow the annual herbs scattered around the veg plot (although many gardeners prefer a dedicated bed for them). You can keep tender annuals going for at least some of the winter by bringing them indoors if they're in pots. I use the low-growing perennial herbs oregano and thyme to edge paths. A combination of cold and damp will kill off many herbs, so avoid such locations.

Perennials

Most of the woodier perennial herbs are from southern Europe, so give them what they're used to – sunny, drier, sheltered sites in well-drained soil. Add sand, grit and/or organic matter if your soil isn't up to scratch, but don't be tempted to compensate for the poor soil with feeds for the perennial herbs – they like it tough, and they'll only produce lush and more weakly flavoured growth. Perennials like to be divided in early spring. Prune them in March and don't be afraid to be fairly brutal, they'll bounce back with healthy new growth.

Bay *Laurus nobilis* An essential in any stock, stew or soup, bay brings a wonderfully aromatic edge that's surprisingly good in rice pudding too. Although expensive to buy as plants, it's the best way to start. You'll be repaid by endless leaves and the plant itself gets hardier as it ages, growing ever more vigorously to tree size if allowed. Any fish, whether baked, grilled, fried or barbecued, will benefit from a few leaves.

Chives *Allium schoenoprasum* These grow easily from seed, or you can divide existing plants. The best leaves come from young plants, so give yourself fresh plants at least every other year. Chives are an exception to most perennial herbs, favouring a good, rich, moist soil. They also do really well in pots and are fine grown indoors

Bay

Chives in flower

Moroccan mint

Oregano

for winter use. Their long thin leaves add a mild oniony bite to salads, fish dishes and soups, but do try the flowers as they're also delicious in salads. After flowering, cut chives back hard and you may well get a decent second flush of growth. Garlic chives, tasting as you'd imagine, are a variation well worth trying too.

Lemon verbena *Aloysia triphylla* The truly mouthwatering, cleansing smell of lemon that comes off these leaves is magnified by steeping them in boiled water. Lemon verbena can be a touch sensitive to the cold, so mulch around the roots with straw or similar, and to protect them through the winter – the plant will regrow when things warm up again. Water regularly and prune back hard in preparation for winter. The plant also does very well grown in pots. Fresh lemon verbena leaves are incredible; if dried, the leaves last and last. Use them to make a lovely refreshing tea, as the base for lemonade, and scattered over fruit salads.

Lovage *Levisticum officinale* A lesser-known and much-underrated herb, tasting a little like celery, lovage is an excellent addition to vegetable stock and many other recipes. It grows well from root propagation and seed, as long as you keep it moist and give it some room to grow. If you're growing it in a pot, make sure it's a good-sized one. Try it (sparingly at first) as a partner to peas, lettuce or potatoes in soup. For an amazing sauce that goes with just about any meat but is particularly special with pork: melt 2 tbsp butter in a pan, add 12 finely chopped lovage leaves, and cook for 3–4 minutes – don't worry if they turn dark green. Add a good splash of white wine and let it all simmer for a minute or two. Stir in 1 tsp wholegrain mustard and season well.

Mint *Menthe* sp. Another essential for your patch, although keep it in pots or otherwise restricted as it's very invasive. Try growing a few varieties as they all have their strengths – Moroccan makes the finest tea, peppermint's a great all-rounder, and spearmint is slightly milder than the rest. Mint favours a moist soil and does best in sun, but it will do okay in shade too.

Oregano *Origanum vulgare* An absolute must in a Bolognese sauce and many Mediterranean dishes. You can grow either tender or hardy varieties. Both are delicious, but the tender ones are usually fuller flavoured, while the hardy ones live longer. As with thyme, oregano is no problem to grow and look after, bringing bees and butterflies on to your patch. Give them a sunny site.

Rosemary *Rosmarinus officinalis* Rosemary is slow-growing, so it's understandably tempting to buy in plants to enable you to begin harvesting immediately. These can be expensive, however, so it may be a good idea to sow at least some of the plants you'll want. Once established, you'll get year-round aromatic leaves to go with your lamb, pasta sauces, roasted root veg, and anything else that will take this robust herb. Rosemary grows perfectly happily in a pot, so even if your space is limited, do try to grow at least one plant. As well as the flavoursome spiky leaves, the strikingly beautiful blue flowers bring the bees to your garden.

Sage *Salvia officinalis* Sage grows well from seed or from cuttings, lasting perhaps 5 years (though less in pots) before you need to replace them. Prune them back hard in spring to promote good strong growth, and don't be tempted to feed or water this sun lover. Little trouble to grow, you should get an all-year harvest to go perfectly with your pork, or to make tea that apparently refreshes the memory.

Tarragon *Artemisia dracunculus* A classic aniseedy herb, not to my mind at its best straight up, but wonderful in combination with receptive partners – classically with chicken, mayonnaise and fish. Grow sweet, punchy French tarragon, rather than the more bitter, tougher Russian variety. Divide or sow new plants every 3 years, and don't attempt tarragon in pots – it hates them.

This herb is worth growing if only to make your own tarragon vinegar: wash and chop 6 good handfuls of tarragon leaves and throw them into a large bowl. Pour in 1 litre white wine vinegar and decant into a large sterilised jar. Leave the jar on a sunny windowsill for a month or so, shaking it occasionally. Then pour the vinegar through muslin and decant into sterilised bottles or jars. Add a small fresh sprig of tarragon to each and seal.

Thyme *Thymus* sp. An aromatic low-growing herb that couldn't be easier to grow. There are endless varieties to try, but start with common thyme (*T. vulgaris*). It germinates and develops well from seed, and doesn't need watering other than during a drought. Plants will eventually tire though, and should be replaced every 5 years or so. Thyme doesn't really like growing indoors, so if you want some to hand, try a pot on an outside window ledge or by the back door. Beyond the beautiful aromatic flavour it lends to many dishes, thyme has another advantage: bees love the flowers and will pollinate lots of other plants for you while they're about.

Annuals

The annuals tend to prefer things more moist, the soil richer, a little shade, and with plenty of room to develop and to ensure air circulation. Generally they grow easily from seed, and as a result are inexpensive. If you prepare a good bed, adding organic matter, you'll get them off to a good start and have every chance of unchecked progress. Quick growth is what you are after for succulent leaves, so unless otherwise suggested for your variety, don't let them dry out, and give them the odd comfrey feed (see p.215) to top up nutrients if you're growing them in containers. Unlike most perennial herbs, the majority of annuals deteriorate rapidly after picking, so pick them as you need them, and if there's any wait at all, pop their stems in a jar of water.

Basil *Ocimum basilicum* You'll find numerous varieties of this aromatic classic, but start with 'Sweet Genovese' as your main crop around which to experiment. Basil is the smell of summer to many, making an excellent companion for tomatoes in the kitchen and in the garden. Sow seed thinly from spring, planting out after frosts if you've started them in modules, and ensure you don't let your basil dry out. In your veg patch basil can be a little hit and miss, even in the summer, but it's easy to grow under cover, doing well in pots. If you want to extend your harvest, cut back your plants before flowering to encourage fresh growth. Pesto (see p.258) is the obvious avenue for any surplus, although you can freeze leaves whole in oil – in ice cube trays – to pull the scent of summer into the autumn and winter.

Chervil *Anthriscus cerefolium* If you're new to chervil, its taste is something like parsley with a slight hint of aniseed. As you can imagine, that makes it excellent in salads, with fish and in many sauces. Happiest in shade, doing well in pots, chervil should not be allowed to dry out. Sow direct from early spring until autumn and you should get a harvest in most months.

Coriander *Coriandrum sativum* With its amazing leaves, followed later by wonderful seeds, coriander will give you two essential harvests. Sow seeds in April and May, give them a rich soil and water them only in a drought. The leaves add a pungent freshness to salads, salsas, curries and other dishes, while the seeds lend a light aromatic spiciness to meat and fish dishes, as well as a punchy spike to bread.

Dill *Anethum graveolens* A delicious, though much underused herb, dill is essential for gravadlax, and outstanding with poached fish, cucumber, gherkins and potatoes. Sow direct or in pots in spring, don't water unless there's a really dry patch, and don't cut it back as it sulks. Dill is one of those herbs that the more you eat it, the more you want to eat it, so pinch the odd bit as you're walking around your veg patch and you'll find you come up with endless possibilities for it. It's fantastic in dressings and sauces for most seafood, chicken and cool crunchy lettuces.

Parsley *Petroselinum crispum* You can choose between curly and flat-leaved parsley; the latter has slightly more flavour. Although usually treated as an annual, parsley will often survive all year round, though I've found to get the best leaves you should replace the plants after 6 or 7 months. Sow direct, only just covering the seeds with soil, and keep them from drying out. And sow a lot... you'll use it.

Jerusalem artichokes
Helianthus tuberosus

PLANT GROUP	Perennials (see p.169)
SOW DIRECT	January–March
HARVEST	October–March

Some plants should be in every veg patch and this is one. Where else would you get a beautiful late-summer cut flower, a seasonal windbreak, kilos of compostable material, and – as if that wasn't enough – a delicious, yet underrated food year after year? And all for doing little other than planting them once.

Contrarily, they are neither artichoke nor from Jerusalem, but a sunflower originally named girasole after the Italian for sunflower. Girasole gradually morphed into Jerusalem, but their apparent similarity in taste to the globe artichoke that spawned the rest of their name is one that passes me by. To my palate, this veg has a wonderfully savoury flavour that shouts out its origins in the earth.

With a leafy, flowering stem that can reach 3 metres, Jerusalem artichokes are a tasty root, high in potassium, iron, fibre and endless other vitamins and minerals, so why are they comparatively uncommon? Perhaps it is their reputation for digestive disturbance. In *Gerard's Herbal* of 1621, John Goodyer observed that they 'cause a filthy loathsome stinking wind within the body, thereby causing the belly to be pained and tormented, and are a meat more fit for swine than men'. An exaggeration perhaps, but there's no denying their gas-giving qualities do affect some. Fortunately the more frequently eaten, the more effectively the body deals with the starch. That's not only cause for celebration among sufferers (and their companions), but also an invitation to eat more of this unappreciated vegetable.

Varieties
There are a few varieties about but 'Fuseau' is the one to go for. Less knobbly than most others and therefore less grief in preparing, it has an outstanding flavour.

How to grow
In early spring, plant the tubers direct, 15cm down and 60cm apart, in a permanent bed, or plant them as a windbreak… and wait. By mid-summer they'll throw up stems, slowly forming sunflower-like heads that burst open towards the end of September. Let the frosts hit them to kill off the flowers that you haven't cut for decorating the house and (as with parsnips) the chill will improve the flavour of the tubers. You may have heard of the potential for Jerusalem artichokes to become

invasive. As with raspberries, the notion of a self-expanding harvest sounds like a bonus to me, but if you prefer things neat and tidy, beware of their lateral creep.

How to harvest

The artichokes will be ready to harvest from October through to May, depending on when you sow. They store unreliably, so dig them when you're about to use them, leaving a few tubers for next year's growth. In practice it's pretty hard not to leave some behind. Each of your planted tubers should return around 2kg of delicious artichokes for eating.

Problems and pests

None.

How to eat

Smooth-skinned tubers, such as 'Fuseau', can be simply washed thoroughly before use, whereas knobblier varieties are best par-boiled, refreshed with cold water and rubbed to remove their skins. They make an amazing soup (see p.227), the perfect vegetable crisps, and take to the roasting tin especially well. Yet my favourite way to eat them is finely sliced, softened in a pan with butter, then blitzed with cream and stirred at the last minute into risotto. For more recipes, see pp.238, 253.

Jerusalem artichokes 'Fuseau'

Kale *Brassica oleracea* var. *acephala*

PLANT GROUP	Brassicas (see p.159)
START UNDER COVER	March–August
PLANT OUT	April–September
HARVEST	June–February

It would be hard to find a lower-maintenance, yet more highly nutritious and flavourful leaf that offers such variety. From the robust, dark 'Cavalo Nero' to the more delicate 'Red Russian', picked for baby salad, you're spoilt for choice. If you're pushed for space and have to prioritise, make sure kale makes the cut.

Varieties
'Cavalo Nero', 'Red Russian', 'Redbor' (F1), and 'Walking Stick' kale are all worth growing. They're very different in appearance and taste, yet equally delicious.

How to grow
Sow in March for summer picking, or as late as August for autumn and winter harvesting. Start them off under cover in Jiffy 7s (see p.197) or modules if you're after full-sized plants, or sow in guttering if you want cut-and-come-again leaves. Plant out as little as 10cm apart for the latter, to around 50cm for plants to reach full size. They are slowish to mature, long at their peak and keep producing if you pick leaves, so two or three sowings over the year should give you constant kale.

How to harvest
Expect to harvest kale leaves 3–4 months after sowing. If it's variety you're after, adopt a cut-and-come-again approach. 'Red Russian' is perfect for planting closely and picking the leaves when only a few centimetres long – toss raw into salads.

Problems and pests
Cabbage white butterflies can be a pain in spring and summer. I find companion planting (see p.212) and picking off the caterpillars prevents any real harm, but you could try 'Pentland Brig' and 'Redbor' as these seem less attractive to them.

How to eat
Use kale in any recipes that are suited to cabbage or Brussels sprouts. For a great pasta sauce: steam the leaves until tender; drain, chop finely and throw into a pan with some olive oil and garlic for a few minutes. Add a touch of cream – and chilli, herbs, capers, Parmesan etc, as you prefer. For more recipes, see pp.223, 242, 255.

Kale 'Pentland Brig'

Leeks 'Hannibal'

Leeks *Allium ampeloprasum* var. *porrum*

PLANT GROUP	Onions (see p.164)
START UNDER COVER	February–April
PLANT OUT	June–July
HARVEST	September–May (earlier for baby leeks)

Grow leeks once and you'll become attached very quickly. They are delicious, versatile veg that make the plot look special even through the cold months when the frosts are around. There's something about that almost algal green-blue that just suits the cold.

With a good selection of early and late varieties, you can harvest from September through winter and into early spring, adding to your arsenal of 'hungry gap' fillers. You can even add a month or two on at the early part of your harvest by growing some of your leek seedlings just a little longer instead of transplanting them. Pick these when they are just the size of spring onions for a late-summer treat.

Do leave a few plants to flower through late spring and into the summer. Extraordinarily beautiful, they add the third dimension to the plot, keeping a satisfying connection with what has been, and providing you with all the seed you need for the coming year.

Varieties

'Monstruoso de Carentan' (early), 'D'Hiver de Saint-Victor' (late), 'Saint Victor' (late) and 'Musselburgh' (late) are delicious, reliable yearly fixtures in my veg garden, and having tried 'Hannibal' as an early variety for the first time I've a feeling it will be making a return. 'King Richard', a very early variety, is particularly excellent for baby leeks.

How to grow

Start early- or late-harvesting leek varieties in guttering under cover in March–April, sowing 3cm apart. Plant out in June or July, in the roots/onions patch or to follow your early spuds if you have lifted them.

Planting out is quite a particular process: tease the leek, which should be 20cm or so tall, out of the guttering; trim its roots to 5cm; make a hole 15cm deep with a pencil and lower the leek gently into it. Keep the plants at a distance of around 15cm from their neighbours, in rows 30cm apart. Fill the holes with water, but don't infill with soil.

Baby leeks are well worth adding to your summer menu. Sow them thinly and successionally – a few weeks apart – in a bed with a very fine tilth. Thin the emerging seedlings, allowing 3cm between them. It is important to water baby leeks frequently.

If you are after a larger ratio of white to green, you can always earth your leeks up a little, or even set the seedlings into slightly deeper holes.

Problems and pests

Rust, evident as orange or brown blotches on the leaves, can affect your harvest but usually only decoratively. The odd seaweed or comfrey feed (see p.215) helps prevent it, but rotating your crops strictly (see p.172) is the main way of minimising any problem with rust. If you do have a more serious infection, dig up all affected plants and burn them.

How to harvest

Harvest leeks as you need them from September onwards, or in the case of baby leeks, when they are pencil-thick and look very much like spring onions.

If you're leaving some to flower (which you really must) you can always save the seed for the following harvest. Be aware that they won't replicate the original variety unless that is the only variety you are growing.

How to eat

Leeks lend a wonderful base flavour to any number of soups, most famously the classic vichyssoise (creamed leek and potato), which is traditionally served cold, but equally delicious hot. They are also excellent in stews, pies, pasta sauces, risottos and stir-fries.

Most recipes call mainly for the milder white part of the veg, but don't discard the green part. Instead use it to flavour stocks and marinades, or to add flavour to a roast chicken pop a piece of green leek into the cavity with a wedge of lemon and some parsley stalks.

Where a recipe calls for whole leeks, these can be a bit tricky to clean. The easiest way is to slit them along the length of the green part at intervals, then immerse in cold water to tease out the soil.

Try steaming small or medium leeks until just tender, then hit them with olive oil, a little lemon juice and some chopped parsley for a lovely side dish or light lunch. Baby leeks are even better friends with cream and sage. Steam or griddle them to bring a wonderfully intense leekiness into your summer. For more recipes, see pp.227, 228, 248.

Lettuces *Lactuca sativa*

PLANT GROUP	Salad leaves (see p.166)
START UNDER COVER	January–September
PLANT OUT	April–October
SOW DIRECT	March–September
HARVEST	All year

Generally high-yielding and easy to grow, lettuces offer a fantastic variety of colour, texture and taste. They also reward a little careful investigation. Most of us think of lettuces as either tight cones (hearting lettuce) or slack-headed roses (loose-leaf lettuce), which of course they can be, but there is another way of getting the most from them. As well as letting some lettuces develop fully, we can also tuck in a little earlier by treating the lettuce bed as a salad orchard. Pluck a few young leaves here and there and in a few short weeks they'll regrow for another harvest – a cycle of cut-and-come-again cropping that can last for months.

By nipping off a few leaves from different varieties of lettuce you'll also be opening up all sorts of mixed salad possibilities for the table. Add in edible flowers (see p.72), oriental leaves (see p.105), herbs (see p.87) and other leaves such as rocket, and this really is one area of your harvest where you can let your imagination run riot.

Varieties

Lettuces love the sun but they like it cool too, so if you're happy to put in a little effort, and you go for the right varieties, you can grow lettuce all year round, enjoying a different leafy salad every day of the year.

For summer and autumn harvesting: 'Little Gem' is a classic. This fast-growing cos lettuce is a must for every patch and perfect for container growing, followed closely by 'Pinokkio', which makes an excellent (some say superior) alternative.

For winter and spring harvesting: 'Marvel of Four Seasons' lives up to its name deliciously, while 'Winter Density', 'Rouge d'Hiver' and the soft-headed 'Valdor' are all good varieties. And from 'Green Oak Leaf', you can pluck perfect cut-and-come-again leaves right through winter.

How to grow

Getting a steady harvest rather than a glut is the key with lettuces and there are some simple ways of ensuring a good succession: sow every few weeks; every time you sow, start some off direct and others under cover in modules as they'll mature at different times; and if you grow some for leaf supply and let others develop hearts from the same sowing you'll have an automatic successional harvest. Plant out

Lettuce 'Winter Density'

those sown in modules when 5–10 cm tall. Spacing is very flexible. Sow close for cut-and-come-again leaves (maximising your yield per area and minimising bare soil) or further apart (check the packet) if you're growing them to full maturity.

For spring and summer lettuces, sow under cover from New Year and outside in your patch from March. Lettuces like sunny yet cooler conditions for germination, so beware the hottest weeks (mid-June to mid-August) as they'll tend to bolt. Sow in the evening and water the ground first at this time of year. Give summer lettuces a shady spot, don't let them dry out, and treat them as cut-and-come-agains – to avoid them going to seed in the heat.

For leaves through winter into spring, sow in late summer and autumn (check the catalogue or seed packet for times). They'll do better under cover but with luck you may be successful outside, especially if you give them a little fleece protection.

Keep an eye on your lettuces as they start to heart – usually around 3 months after sowing. Given half a chance, too much sun and/or too little water they'll happily bolt, which makes most varieties taste bitter. Water regularly during this delicate time. But don't overwater winter lettuces – indeed, you may not need to water them at all.

Keep plants well weeded – lettuces hate competition.

How to harvest

One of those essential foods that you can harvest every day. Taking a cut-and-come-again approach to at least some of your lettuces will enable you to get the most from your plot. Either pick up to half of the young leaves, or cut them all 3cm or so above ground, and in a few short weeks they'll grow back.

Problems and pests

You'll not be the only one after these succulent, tender leaves – slugs and snails will need to be deterred (see p.216). Bolting in the summer months is also a risk, lessened by taking a cut-and-come-again approach and watering well in dry periods.

How to eat

For the most part, lettuce isn't a flavourfest. Most varieties are neutral, but that's not to say they are flavourless. The differences are often subtle but they are present, awaiting a simple dressing of good oil and salt, or (for a crispy cos) griddling. Good on their own, they also make the perfect mixed salad base, a platform on which smaller amounts of the more exhibitionist leaves can play.

And if the idea of salad in December doesn't appeal, firstly give it a whirl – you may be surprised; and secondly try lettuce cooked. It makes a marvellous risotto (chopped and wilted into the rice for the last few minutes of cooking) and a clean, refreshing soup (see p.226). For more recipes, see pp.238, 248, 250.

Onions *Allium cepa*

PLANT GROUP	Onions (see p.164)
SOW DIRECT	Seed or sets March–April, or September–October for sets of overwintering varieties
HARVEST	May–October

Most of us use onions every day so they are a prime candidate for inclusion in your veg patch, but don't sacrifice your valuable space without some judicious selection. I grow only a few white maincrop onions in the summer, because they are cheap to buy, locally available, store for a long period and take up a fair amount of the veg patch at the busiest time of the growing year.

Instead I give priority to the sweetness of shallots and red onions, and the punch of spring onions (see p.135). Red varieties and shallots are no more trouble to grow than their white cousins, and are inexplicably expensive to buy. So if you're in any way short of space, knock a hole in your food budget by growing these onions and shop for the white ones. You also have the option of growing your white varieties over winter, taking up room when there's likely to be less in your veg patch and giving you a springtime harvest.

Varieties

Delicious and reliable, 'Red Baron' is the outstanding red onion. 'Stoccarde' is a tasty, reliable white main cropper, and 'Radar' is worth a go if you're after a reliable overwintering white onion.

How to grow

Most onions can be grown from either seed or mini-onions known as sets. Sets are easier to deal with, but seed is considerably cheaper if you're going for a big harvest.

Plant maincrop sets during the first half of spring, and overwintering varieties in September or October. For both, the tips should be just slightly below the level of the soil. The rule of closeness and harvest size applies: plant 4–10cm apart for small onions; or 15–25cm apart for larger ones.

With seed, sow direct in early spring – thinly in lines, 1cm deep and 15cm apart. You are likely to have to thin the seedlings, spacing them according to the size of onion you are after.

Although reasonably low maintenance, onions do like a sunny, well-drained spot... they'll happily run to seed if they get the opposite. Also, make sure your onions are clear of weeds. This enables your crop to get the nutrients it needs, and ensures good airflow around the bulbs, minimising the risk of disease.

Onions drying before storing
'Red Baron' and 'Sturon Globe'

How to harvest

As onions mature, the leaves will start to yellow and at this stage you can bend the tops over to aid ripening. Lift your onions when you like the size they are. You should be pulling larger maincrop onions from mid-summer. Leave them to dry for a day or two in the sun, then store them somewhere light for up to around 6 months. An ideal airy way to store them until you're ready to use them is in pairs of tights, knotted between the bulbs. Start using them from the toe end, snipping below each knot as you go. Overwintering onions don't store for long so pull them as needed, don't bother with drying, and use them immediately.

Problems and pests

Onion downy mildew and white rot are possible problems, though not overly common. You can't do much about it if you encounter either of these, but rotating your crops (see p.172) is vital to minimising the likelihood.

Neck rot, should it occur, is more likely to be visible in stored onions. Sort through your harvest well before storing, discarding any that are soft, and use any that seem borderline straight away.

How to eat

Preparing onions may not be the most popular kitchen task, but the chemical that causes eye-stinging is released (mainly from the leafier end) to protect the plant from being munched by pests as it grows. If you hold the leafier end, chop off the bottom of your onion and slice from that end, you'll reduce those tears.

As well as all the everyday uses, onions are really worthy of a starring role. French onion soup and onion tart are deserving classics, but if you've a glut – of red onions especially – try making them into a tasty preserve.

Red onion marmalade is my favourite companion to sausages, goes brilliantly with cheese, and couldn't be easier to make: peel and slice 1kg red onions and slowly fry them in a little sunflower oil, stirring once in a while, until they are quite soft. Turn the heat up to quickly drive off any moisture and pour in 80ml red wine vinegar and 100g soft brown sugar. Continue to cook, stirring more frequently, until the mixture thickens and becomes a touch sticky. For extra bite, stir through 1–2 tsp wholegrain mustard, if you like. Spoon into sterilised, airtight jars, refrigerate and use within a month or two.

For more recipes, see pp.223, 225, 227, 228, 247, 248, 256, 259.

Oriental leaves

| PLANT GROUP | Others (see p.169) |

There are so many outstanding oriental leaves, and so much flexibility about when to grow and harvest, and how to use them, that the best I can offer is an introduction to the indispensable favourites – the rest is up to your sense of inquisitiveness. They can do much to liven up your kitchen, particularly during the leaner weeks.

How to grow

Many oriental leaves are happily sown and grown in full sun. Follow your catalogue/seed packet advice, as even varieties of the same plant can be grown differently. These leaves will give you tasty harvests from the end of summer through to early December outside, and right through winter if grown under cover. Most develop quickly, giving you a fast return, but they will ask for water to maintain unchecked growth. Pests love them too, so try growing most of your oriental leaves later in the year – to follow on from peas, beans and lettuce. Through the winter you may not get excessive growth but you can still pinch off a small harvest, and as soon as there's a hint of warmth you'll find new leaves to perk up the lean weeks.

I tend to start some off under cover in modules, and sow some direct under cover and outside. This provides a succession in harvest and some insurance should pests make hay in the outdoor leaves or if some run to seed. Spacings vary considerably, so follow what it says on the packet. Nearly all the oriental leaves do well from a cut-and-come-again approach – it ensures you get a harvest early and tender, and stimulates more growth. When harvesting, pick the leaves when you want to eat them, as many deteriorate rapidly once picked, and it's usually better to cut with small, sharp scissors as many are shallow-rooting and are easily dislodged. All of this wonderful group will do well in containers or on your windowsill.

Varieties

Confusingly, lots of oriental leaves are sold under more than one name, and/or have different spellings. Also, many are sold as generic rather than named varieties, so be guided by catalogue/packet descriptions, and source seed from a good supplier.

Amaranth This nutritious leaf is used all over the world; it is particularly popular eaten as calaloo in the Caribbean and horta in Greece. Also known as Chinese spinach, the taste is somewhere between spinach and artichoke and you can use it in the same ways as spinach – particularly when small and young for salads, or wilted with lemon juice and olive oil. It has the advantage of being slow to bolt, even when grown in the hottest months when many others want to run to seed.

Chop suey greens Often sold under this generic name, but also as the superior 'Shungiku' variety, these are very easy to grow. When the plant reaches 15cm or so, only 6 or 7 weeks after sowing, you get beautiful aromatic leaves to add variety and punch to salads, or to sauté with bacon and serve as a side veg through all but the coldest months. And you can leave some to grow on as a bee-friendly flower, cutting some for the house.

Giant red mustard These vibrant crimson and green leaves make a stunning addition to your patch and your kitchen, providing a harvest into and right through the colder months. The larger you let the leaves grow, the hotter they get, adding a horseradishy hit to a beef sandwich in February. One of my favourite winter leaves.

Kai lan This is the first year I've grown this oriental leaf and I've found something special. It looks very much like a slightly less rufty-tufty sprouting broccoli, throwing up sweet succulent shoots through the warmer months. It needs next-to-no steaming, loves all the sauces and dressings you'd hope it would, and no matter how much you eat you never get tired of it. I'm genuinely wondering if this hasn't the potential to be the veg that makes up the fourth leg of the culinary relay, that starts with sprouting broccoli, asparagus and peas. It's that good.

Mibuna Untidy and with slightly rounder leaves and a milder flavour than mizuna (see below), mibuna will offer itself for salads, wilting and stir-fries all year. To get it at its best, avoid sowing this one in the hottest months as it may well bolt.

Mizuna Looking a little like wild rocket that's filled out, mizuna's delightfully scruffy leaves give you a not-too-intense mustardy addition, either raw in salads or cooked in any number of ways. Apart from the flavour, the best thing about mizuna is its year-round harvesting time.

Pak choi Mild, juicy and crisp, yet succulent when small, pak choi is a real must. It will also give you a quick return – mid-summer leaves within a month of planting. Add to mixed salads, eat raw on its own, toss into stir-fries or have as an alternative side veg to any leafy brassica. It is often sold as a generic variety, but 'Green Revolution' (F1) and 'China Choi' are particularly tasty, and reliably fast-growing.

Wong bok This is one of those Chinese cabbages that looks like a 'Little Gem' lettuce that's been to the gym. Maybe I'm just lazy, but there's something very appealing about a vegetable that keeps its prize tucked away from mud and doesn't need washing or fiddling with. Peel off its gloriously sweet crisp leaves to use in salads, or slice thinly and stir-fry.

Giant red mustard

Pak choi

Mibuna

Amaranth (foreground)

VEGETABLE A–Z

Parsnips *Pastinaca sativa*

PLANT GROUP	Roots (see p.162)
SOW DIRECT	March–May
HARVEST	August–March

Easy to grow, the parsnip is a fine source of fibre and rich in vitamins and minerals. It also loves a frost, turning its stored starches into more sugars, just waiting to come out with a slow roasting in your kitchen. It's shape may lend itself to showmanship, but don't be tempted to try and impress with the size of your parsnips, as woody, bland tapering roots will be your reward. Buy a sports car instead, and keep your parsnips small.

Varieties
'Tender and True' has a fantastic flavour, getting to a decent size (about 7cm across the shoulders) before edging anywhere near fibrous territory. This year I also grew 'Gladiator' (F1) and they were outstanding, giving me a heavy, deliciously sweet crop of unwoody parsnips.

How to grow
Parsnips prefer a sandy, loamy, well-worked soil. These are not veg for the impatient: slow to germinate and slow to grow, they can be in the ground for 10 months. Sow them direct in early spring in rows 30cm apart, thinning to 15cm between plants.

Parsnip seed deteriorates rapidly, so buy fresh each year. And don't add organic matter to the ground before sowing parsnips as they will probably fork.

How to harvest
Traditionally you start to harvest after the first frost and continue through winter, but you can keep the spacing smaller and harvest delicious baby roots in summer.

Problems and pests
Parsnips are usually trouble-free, though wireworm can be a problem. Keep your plants well weeded and dig over an affected area (see p.219).

How to eat
Parsnip's sweet, aromatic flesh adds comfort to many dishes. Roasted with honey (see p.253) or flavoured with warm spices, such as cumin and coriander, they are a treat. Try alternating them with spuds in dauphinoise potatoes (see p.254), or use them to replace carrots in a cake (see p.260). For more recipes, see pp.223, 225.

Parsnip 'Halblange White'

Peas *Pisum sativum*

PLANT GROUP	Legumes (see p.157)
START UNDER COVER	February–May
PLANT OUT	May–June
SOW DIRECT	October–November for overwintering varieties, and/or March–June
HARVEST	May–October

When he'd done with being President of the USA, Thomas Jefferson went back to tending his patch, and with such vigour and success that to many his greater achievement lies in his gardens at Monticello. He trialled endless varieties of any veg he could lay his hands on, but he wasn't such an anorak that he didn't know how to welcome in a harvest. Every year he held a competition to find the grower of the first peas of the season. The winner then invited all contestants to supper with the peas taking centre stage. There's far too little of this seasonal celebration going on now, so we've decided to reinstate the tradition here at River Cottage and encourage you to do likewise. I'm expecting inventive methods, underhand dealings and outright cheating.

Peas will take up a little of your time. Most will need support while they grow, and if you have a family gathering, you'll certainly find podding is best done by a few people. But time spent on peas is rarely better spent. I guarantee one taste of your home-grown own and they'll become a permanent fixture on your plot. As with asparagus, the speed of the conversion of their sugars to starches means that minutes count. If you can't eat them straight away, then get them cold or frozen as this arrests the loss of sweetness.

Personally I don't think it's worth buying fresh peas. At best they'll have been picked several days before, and frozen peas taken straight from the field to the freezer within a few hours generally have a much better taste. However, to fully appreciate the taste of fresh peas at their absolute peak, there really is no other way than growing your own. Once you've tasted them, most of your peas won't even make it to the pan as they are among the finest grazing treats you can award yourself as you go about some task or other. Treat them as sweets.

And it's not only the peas that you're after from your plants. The side shoots and growth tips, known as pea tips (or 'green gold' to the Japanese) will add a succulent, sweet crunch to any salad; they are also delightful eaten just as they are. You will end up with fewer pods if you pick them, but if you have a lot of plants or you've had more successful germinations than expected, grow the reserves on just for

Peas 'Purple Podded Pea'

these tips. You can even get an indoor crop of tips all year round by sowing some in autumn – to bring a touch of springtime zing to the darkest months.

As well as the pea we all know and love, you may want to try growing mangetout peas, which are eaten whole, as their name suggests. Or sugar snaps, which are eaten in the same way and have a lovely crunchy texture and delectable sweetness.

Varieties

Pea seed is sometimes sold as either wrinkle-seeded or round-seeded varieties. Both are good for spring sowing, but round varieties can also be sown in October–November to give an early harvest in May.

There are many excellent varieties but I've found 'Alderman', 'Douce Provence' (my favourite round-seeded variety) and 'Hurst Green Shaft' to be especially tasty, reliable and heavy-cropping. 'Purple Podded Pea' makes a stunning addition to the veg patch and tastes as good as it looks. If you can't wait to sample your fresh peas, try 'Kelvedon Wonder' – not only delicious, but very quick to crop (about 75 days from a spring sowing). 'Markana' is a good dwarf variety choice if your patch is exposed or you have limited space; it grows to only around 75cm and is reasonably self-supporting. Expect most pea varieties to mature in around 100 days.

And don't overlook sugar snaps (usually sold as generic 'sugar snap' rather than as named varieties), or mangetout – 'Norli' and 'Weggisser' are particularly tasty varieties. Try half a row of each as a taster and you'll soon be sowing more.

How to grow

Peas will do okay on most soils, but if you're after a fantastic crop, incorporate plenty of organic matter and dig the bed well, but don't be tempted to add manure. If you do, you'll get plenty of encouraging growth but a disappointing crop of peas.

It's best to start peas off under cover in root trainers or toilet roll inners (see p.197) to help them develop a healthy root run that should get them off to a fine start when planted out. Sow too many, to ensure you'll have enough backups should the birds or slugs invade, using any spares for pea tips. Plant them out when they are around 10–15cm tall.

If you want to sow straight into your plot, avoid doing so in wet, cold conditions as the seeds are likely to rot. Spacing varies with variety (check the packet) but allow around 10cm between plants and keep rows around 75cm apart.

To give you a long, steady season and avoid a huge glut, sow them successionally a fortnight apart, and pick them regularly – to encourage more pods to form.

The taller pea varieties will need some support. Twiggy hazel prunings, thrust fat end into the soil, are traditional and work best. These hold the plants upright and offer something for the growing tendrils to latch on to. The dwarf varieties tend to provide each other with mutual support to a degree, but you may have to supply a helping stick or two if they need it. As with climbing beans, the taller peas can easily make 2 metres tall, so avoid exposed areas of your plot, and be aware of any shadowing likely to result. Radishes and salad leaves are a top choice to fill any affected area, as they'll enjoy the shade.

Do keep your plants from drying out. The occasional comfrey feed (see p.215) from flowering will boost pea production a little, but it's not essential.

How to harvest

Many varieties reach harvest within 2 months and should be picked at their peak.

Problems and pests

Mice and birds love the seed, so start most, if not all, of your peas off under cover. This also helps get them past their most vulnerable stage, when slugs and snails are particularly damaging.

You're quite likely to see small stamp-edge notches appearing on the young spring leaves, caused by pea and bean weevils. This is rarely a problem as the damage is usually insignificant and your harvest will be unaffected. More frustratingly, the caterpillar of the pea moth goes about its business unseen, burrowing into the pod and your precious peas, yet visible only when you pop the pod to taste them. The best way to deal with this nuisance is to avoid it. The caterpillar hatches to enjoy its main feeding in July and early August, so time your sowings to mature before and after this period. Mangetout are unaffected as they are picked before the peas develop – use them as a mid-summer harvest between your early and late peas.

How to eat

Cook peas briefly (if at all) to enjoy them at their best, and do try Jane Grigson's suggestion for young and tender peas: boil them in their pods so the peas steam, plunge briefly in cold water and pick them up by the stalk, dip in butter (or any sauce you fancy), and suck out the peas, crunching the pods at the end.

If you miss peas when they are small and sweet, don't discard them. Pick the larger pods to encourage more to form and use their peas for purées, fritters, burgers and minty mushy peas.

Once you've shelled your peas, don't throw the pods away. Make 'compost soup': wash the pods, add them to a pan of boiling stock or water and simmer for 6–7 minutes, then throw in 8–12 washed outer lettuce leaves and continue to cook until the pods are soft. Purée in a blender or using a hand-held stick blender until smooth. Season with a pinch of sugar, salt and freshly ground black pepper. Serve with a spoon of yoghurt half stirred in. Apart from being delicious, there's the added satisfaction that much of it was otherwise destined for the compost heap.

For more recipes, see pp.223, 226, 229, 233, 237, 239, 244, 248, 258.

Peppers *Capsicum annuum*

PLANT GROUP	Solanaceae (see p.168)
START UNDER COVER	February–March
PLANT OUT	May–June
HARVEST	August–November

Last year I harvested two peppers, hardly enough to keep body and soul nourished, but they were spot on – sweet, edgy and bright. It was just enough of a carrot to get me trying once more. I've rarely had the success with sweet peppers that I have with their fiery cousins... perhaps I'm sending out signals that I prefer to eat chillies. But I do quite like peppers, enough to grow them for sure, not least because they have plenty of uses in the kitchen.

Even growing peppers in the Southwest, I have found them to be just short of the heat and light they crave to crop and ripen reliably to their peak. They are worth a try though, as they're wildly different from those you buy in supermarkets. And they are undoubtedly more successful grown in a greenhouse or polytunnel (or even on a windowsill) than out in the veg patch.

Varieties

I may have had limited success over the years, but I can tell you there's a world of difference between the best varieties and the rest. 'Californian Wonder', 'Marconi Rossa' and 'Sweet Nardello' are so good that even a miserable harvest will get you growing them in hope next year.

How to grow

Sow pepper seeds under cover in early March in Jiffy 7s (see p.197) or small pots. Keep them either on a bench or on a windowsill in the house as they'll love the extra warmth. Peppers need a long sunny season to mature, so don't start them off after April, otherwise they won't have time to get there.

Peppers can take a month to germinate. You can pop them in the airing cupboard to speed it up, but do get them out as soon as they start to emerge. Pot them into 9cm pots and on to larger ones when the roots start to poke out. Get them into the ground or into their final pot in June – and if you are after optimum results, grow them under cover.

As with chillies, peppers are less trouble to the grower than tomatoes, but less reliable in coming to full ripeness. Comfrey waterings (see p.215) or sprays given from flowering onwards are invaluable, but don't overwater them. Also, do tie the plants to a stake for support. It's also a good idea to limit the height (essential if

Pepper 'Marconi Rossa' early ripening

you're growing them in pots), so pinch out the growing tips to encourage them to bush out. Hand-pollinating the first flowers with a soft paint brush seems to improve the chances of getting more fruit.

How to harvest

Peppers vary in colour but many move through the classic green to red ripening process. You can pick them at any point along this timeline, even when small and green. Try one at each stage (snipping them off the brittle plant) and see how you prefer them. There is the added advantage that picking a few early in mid-summer will stimulate others to follow, ready through to early autumn.

Problems and pests

Pepper plants are rarely subject to any problems. If they are troubled by anything, it will most probably be aphids (see pp.217–18 for remedies).

How to eat

If you've had a half-decent pepper harvest, you deserve to celebrate it. Now you've grown them, you can see for yourself just what a revelation of sweet tender heaven they can be.

Roasting peppers is the best way to go with them: place in a roasting tin, drizzle with a little olive oil and roast in the oven at 190°C/Gas Mark 5 for half an hour or so until softened and a little charred. When they're ready, pop them hot into a polythene bag or seal them in a plastic container (anything that is airtight), for 5 minutes or so. This steams them slightly and makes it easy to slip the skins off. Once skinned, slit open the peppers and remove the core and seeds. Now they're ready to transform into rich, sweet soup – with the same weight of roasted tomatoes, good veg stock and a little chilli for punch. Alternatively, cut into strips and scatter over pizzas (see p.242) or into salads to add sweetness and colour.

Fortunately peppers are robust enough to keep their shape and substance when roasted crammed full of all manner of stuffings: capers, olives, anchovies, garlic, aubergines, tomatoes – really anything with a Mediterranean touch works well.

For more recipes, see pp.230, 233, 244, 256.

Potatoes *Solanum tuberosum*

PLANT GROUP	Solanaceae (see p.168)
SOW DIRECT	February–April
HARVEST	May–October

Dedicate your space to the truly delicious, less common potato varieties and you'll find them one of the crops that really passes the home-grown taste test. Most of the varieties named below are waxy, flavoursome and less widely available in the shops, and I'd urge you to concentrate on growing these.

Unless you do not have a local supplier you can buy from, or you have more space than you need, or you are aiming for self-sufficiency – and you can live with the frequent disappointment of blight – then I'd urge you not to bother with many (if any) maincrop bakers or mashers. New potatoes and some late-season waxy varieties are not only amazing to eat, they're expensive to buy in the shops. Prioritise these and your pocket will notice the difference, as well as your taste buds.

The exception to the maincrop rule is the knobbly 'Pink Fir Apple', the finest potato of them all, yet famously susceptible to blight. This is the one variety that's worth the trouble. Boiled and dressed as a salad potato it is only surpassed by the leftovers sliced and pushed around a pan with a little garlic and bacon the day after.

Varieties

Potatoes are usually classified by when they are ready to harvest, and by their main use – new or salad potatoes, multipurpose, bakers and mashers.

For earlies: I'd recommend 'Belle de Fontenay' and 'International Kidney' (also known as 'Jersey Royal') for outstanding salad potatoes. 'Pink Duke of York' is a tasty all-rounder that you can dig up early for new potatoes, or grow on larger.

For second earlies: 'Yukon Gold' is excellent for chips, baking and roasting. 'Charlotte' is a reliable and tasty all-rounder and, along with 'Duke of York', well worth considering if you have room for only one or two varieties.

For early maincrop: 'Ratte' is excellent in late summer and early autumn.

For maincrop: 'Pink Fir Apple' is as good as a potato gets.

How to grow

Dig the bed before planting, but don't add lime. Potatoes love soil that's mildly acidic, and scab will be more of a problem in alkaline soils (see pp.189–90 for more information on soil pH).

'Chitting' is simple but essential. Left in the light in the early spring, the seed potatoes develop nodules (or chits). These are the start of new growth, which while

Harvesting potatoes 'Belle de Fontenay'

desirable, need limiting to focus the growth as you want it. The 'essential' number of nodules is a matter of debate, but two or three chits should see you right. Planting is simple: dig a hole 20cm down (10cm for earlies), place your potato in, chits up, and infill, forming a small mound to help you to spot new shoots coming through. Repeat at 30cm intervals. A handful of wet newspaper or straw plus one of manure in the bottom of each hole is said by some to encourage the potatoes along.

As the leafy tops emerge, tradition holds that you 'earth up' – simply raking up the surrounding soil to create a ridge along the line of potatoes. The idea is to prevent light reaching the top few potatoes, in so doing stopping them from turning green and unpalatable. Earthing up also pretty much takes care of any weeding at the same time. Removing the flowers as they appear is an easy way to increase yield.

How to harvest

Lift early and second earlies as you need them – they'll keep for a week or so only. Allow your maincrop potatoes to dry for a day or two in the sun before storing them somewhere dark in hessian or paper sacks. Whatever happens, ensure you dig up every last scrap of your potatoes each year, to avoid 'volunteer potatoes' the following year, which can harbour blight.

Problems and pests

Your two main problems are likely to be scab and blight (see p.219). The former is a largely cosmetic blotching of the skin – just peel your potatoes. The latter is a fungal disease that can decimate your crop. The best way to deal with blight is to concentrate on early varieties, which are harvested before blight usually attacks.

Blight strikes when it has the heat and moisture it loves, usually in late summer if there is a period of high rainfall. The disease can cause the potatoes to rot (accompanied by one of the worst smells you can imagine), but if you act quickly when you see the telltale dark blotches on the leaves, you can save your harvest. At the first sign, cut all foliage down from any of the infected varieties. With luck you will have caught the disease before it spreads down the stem into the tubers. Leave your potatoes in the ground for 2 or 3 weeks to allow the skins to mature and keep your fingers crossed that when you lift them you'll have your harvest intact.

'Pink Fir Apple' is the one later-maturing variety on which I think it is worth taking the gamble with blight.

How to eat

There's not much you can't do with a potato, as they take happily to just about every cooking method there is. For recipes, see pp.225, 227, 228, 246, 254.

Radishes *Raphanus sativus*

PLANT GROUP	Brassicas (see p.159)
SOW DIRECT	March–September
HARVEST	April–November

Radishes seem to be ubiquitous: if a person has a veg patch, there will most likely be some radishes growing in it. I've always grown radishes, but had the feeling that I was missing a treat when it came to eating them, and then I discovered the reason: imagination. It's not that I don't like the flavour of their peppery roots or their tight crunch – I do, I love it – but there just didn't seem to be much you can do with them, other than bend down and crunch on one when you're wandering past.

Inspired to investigate, I dug out *Jane Grigson's Vegetable Book*. She enthuses passionately about them and mentions a Claudia Roden recipe: thinly slice a few handfuls of radishes, mix with orange slices, dress with orange and lemon juice, add a splash of orange blossom or rose water, plus plenty of chopped coriander. It's amazing. She also tells me that there is a radish festival where they are eaten with brown bread and butter – oh rejoice, I sneer, but on trying it I see why the fuss – it's simple, but delicious. And that's the beauty of the radish. It's worthy of adventurous time spent in the kitchen, yet stands up equally well to a good munch taken fresh from the ground.

Varieties

Radishes come in summer varieties, such as 'French Breakfast' and 'Scarlet Globe', which crop in around a month, as well as the larger-growing autumn/winter varieties sown from late July to early September. If you are growing radishes for the first time, go for a few varieties, sowing them successionally (small amounts, every week or two) to ensure a steady supply, and do your own taste test. For winter use: I'd recommend the strongly flavoured 'Rosa'. For summer use: I suggest 'French Breakfast' (long and of medium intensity); 'Pink Beauty' (sweet, round and mild, even when large); and 'Cherry Belle' (crisp, sweet and mild).

How to grow

Sow straight out from March through to September, dotted about in groups or thinly in rows 15cm apart. Botanically in with the roots, in practice you can sow them wherever you like as they're in the ground for such a short time, but avoid areas recently enriched with organic matter as this tends to make radishes split.

Avoid letting your radishes dry out. Steady growth is what they need to avoid splitting or bolting.

How to harvest

There is no quicker-to-harvest food. It only takes a month or so for summer varieties to mature, so a little, sown often, is best. Pick them young and eat straight away.

Problems and pests

Flea beetles may well be drawn to your radishes. Fortunately they usually just pepper the leaves with small holes, leaving the tasty root unaffected.

How to eat

Encouraged by a rather hefty harvest this year, I've found a few more treatments for the supposed humble radish. For Hugh's punchy take on the classic raita: finely slice 200g washed and topped radishes. Mix 300ml natural yoghurt with 100g soft goat's cheese until smooth, then gently fold in the radish and a few chopped mint leaves. This makes a wonderful dip for crudités, and a cool side for spicier food.

For a thrifty, yet tasty soup (also Hugh's), blanch 20 radishes and their leaves with 12 mint leaves in boiling water for a minute, then drain and plunge into cold water. Purée in a blender together with 1 small peeled, cored and diced apple, 250ml vegetable stock (see p.259), 2 tbsp crème fraîche and a pinch each of salt and cayenne pepper, until smooth and creamy. It's delicious warm, but amazing chilled and garnished with a little mint and a few raw radish slices.

For more recipes, see pp.250, 256.

Harvesting radishes 'Scarlet Globe'

Rocket 'Rucola'

Rocket *Rucola coltivata*
and Wild rocket *Diplotaxis tenuifolia*

PLANT GROUP	Salad leaves (see p.166)
SOW DIRECT	March–September
HARVEST	April–November

Rocket – both salad and wild varieties – has livened up the salad bowl no end with its peppery, hazelnutty taste. Both varieties are easy to grow, which is good news considering the price of this salad leaf in the shops. With a little care, rocket will give you a harvest all year round, so make sure you've always got some on the go.

Varieties
Wild rocket and salad rocket are usually sold as generic rather than named varieties. Wild rocket plants tend to be at their best for a little longer than salad rocket, and have leaves that are more incised and slightly milder in flavour.

How to grow
Both types of rocket are happy growing under cover or outside, but will crop slightly more easily under cover in the winter than outside. Sow the seed thinly, direct to your plot any time from early spring to autumn, and harvest either as a cut-and-come-again leaf or pull up the whole plant if you want to use the space. Planting distance is flexible, but 10cm between plants and at least twice that between rows is usual.

Rocket likes to run quickly to seed, so be sure to keep it watered.

How to harvest
Grow rocket for year-round harvesting if you've indoor space for the coldest months. Pick leaves frequently, and at the first signs of toughness, sow replacement plants.

Problems and pests
Flea beetle can be a problem, but damage is usually limited to small holes on the leaves that don't affect the taste.

How to eat
Rocket's peppery hit makes a wonderful addition to mixed salads, yet stands up as a salad on its own – dress with olive oil, a few drops of balsamic vinegar and salt.

Also try it thrown late into a risotto to wilt; as a spiky alternative to basil in pesto; or in place of radish in a soup (see p.121). For more recipes, see pp.238, 242, 248.

Runner beans *Phaseolus coccineus*

PLANT GROUP	Legumes (see p.157)
START UNDER COVER	April–June
PLANT OUT	May–July
SOW DIRECT	April–May
HARVEST	June–October

I doubt there's an allotment in the country without at least one scrambling pyramid of runner beans. They have everything going for them: they're easy to grow, prolific, go on for months, and many varieties put the infamous stringy ones to shame.

If you're already growing your own, you'll need no persuasion to sow them every year. And if you're just starting, then put aside any preconceptions. Just go for a couple of plants though – you'll be amazed at how many beans you get from them.

Varieties
'Polestar' is fantastic – stringless, tasty, and with gorgeous bright-red flowers. 'Kelvedon Marvel' and 'Scarlet Emperor' run closely behind.

How to grow
Sow direct, 5cm deep, when you're confident the last frost has passed, or start them off under cover in root trainers or toilet roll inners (see p.197) in early April, planting them out at a spacing of 25cm a month later. One sowing of a few plants is likely to be plenty as runner beans are prolific – the more you pick the more they produce, pumping out beans for around 3 months. If you don't want to be without them, a July sowing will give you a new supply into the autumn.

Most varieties will easily make 2 metres tall, so they'll need canes or support, either as a tepee or in rows. Applying a mulch will help to retain moisture.

Unlike French beans, which pollinate themselves, runners need to be pollinated by bees, so a few sweet peas or other flowering plants nearby will help to bring them in. Give your plants a warm, sheltered position too, as bees hate the cold and wind.

As with most beans, give them regular watering and comfrey tea (see p.215) from flowering onwards, especially if they're in pots. You can pinch out the tops to get them to bush out below when they reach the height that suits you best.

How to harvest
From June onwards, pick the beans young, small (from 10cm) and often. And pick any larger pods you've missed first time round and try them – continual picking

will ensure your bean factory keeps delivering new pods for longer, and some varieties will still make good eating. When you've had your fill, leave a few pods to grow on – the beans inside swell and are a great butter bean alternative. The flowers are delicious too, but you'll have fewer beans to harvest if you decide to eat them.

Problems and pests

Halo blight (spots with a paler ring around them on the leaves) is usually carried by the seed, so ensure you buy from a good source. Slugs love everything about runner beans, so give this part of your patch particular attention (see p.216).

Blackfly can be an issue. I plant marigolds next to the beans to draw in lots of ladybirds and other insects that feast on these aphids, so I rarely have a significant number. Also, birds may peck off flowers, preferring the red-flowering varieties.

How to eat

I tend to eat almost all of the runner beans I grow either in salads or as a side veg, where they take well to any of the dressings and sauces that work well with brassicas. They're also amazing with a Japanese-style dressing (see p.251).

As the beans get larger, it may be worth peeling off the potentially stringy edges, but there should be no need to do so if they're under 12cm or so.

For more recipes, see pp.223, 256.

Flowering runner beans 'Polestar'

Runner beans 'Scarlet Emperor'

Salsify *Tragapogon porrifolius*
and Scorzonera *Scorzonera hispanica*

PLANT GROUP	Roots (see p.162)
SOW DIRECT	April–May
HARVEST	October–November

Hugely popular in France and Italy, salsify and scorzonera are unquestionably among my desert island veg and I'm shamelessly evangelical about them. They both look a little like a size-zero parsnip, and their flavour, according to fable, is reminiscent of oysters, though I would describe it simply as slightly nutty and sweet. They are also indistinguishable from each other in taste, though not in looks, with salsify paler than its narrower, dark cousin the scorzonera.

If you are hesitant about trying something new, I would urge you to sow half a row of each – partly because both veg are so delicious, and partly to encourage your sense of culinary inquisitiveness. When I first started growing vegetables, I was instinctively averse towards those I hadn't tried before... even more so to ones that I hadn't heard of at all. After all, my logic ran, if they were so good, why were they so little known? Well, this has proved so wrongheaded an approach to food (and maybe even to life) that I have entirely reversed it, taking it as a challenge to find the ways in which any vegetable can be exquisite. Step forward salsify and scorzonera, the first of my vegetable adventures a few years ago, and a fixture in my veg patch ever since.

Varieties
Salsify: 'Mammoth' and 'Giant' are reliable and delicious varieties.
Scorzonera: 'Russian Giant' (also known as 'Black Giant of Russia') is the most widely available variety and the most reliable I've grown.

How to grow
Both veg are pleasingly easy to grow. Sow direct in April or May, 15cm apart, 1cm deep – into soil with few stones that hasn't been manured recently.

You'll need to water the plants during dry periods, but otherwise they will take care of themselves.

How to harvest
They are usually ready to lift in early autumn but can be left in the ground until needed (unless a big freeze is imminent). This is particularly useful if the veg appear

Salsify 'Mammoth' and Scorzonera 'Russian Giant'

small, as their hardiness allows you to grow them on for another year. Simply cut them to ground and earth up in autumn for a chicory-like leaf in spring. These leaves are particularly good to eat, as the local rabbits will attest. Lift the veg very carefully – their roots can be very long and are easily snapped. The flowers are also edible, although not remarkable in my view.

Problems and pests
None.

How to eat
Salsify and scorzonera are delicious braised, baked, boiled or sautéed. It is best to parboil them with the skins on, peeling them after refreshing in cold water.

For an easy side dish to accompany red meat: put the peeled roots into a roasting tin, drizzle with olive oil and scatter with thyme sprigs, then roast in the oven at 200°C/Gas Mark 6 for 20 minutes or so.

My favourite way with either salsify or scorzonera is to enjoy them in a creamy gratin: boil until tender, plunge into cold water, then peel and chop into pieces. Sauté gently in butter, without browning. Tip into a gratin dish and stir in enough double cream to make a sauce without drowning them, plenty of black pepper and a little lemon juice. Sprinkle with parsley and Parmesan and grill until bubbling and lightly browned. Two mouthfuls in you'll resolve to grow them every year.

For more recipes, see pp.225, 233.

Shallots *Allium cepa*

PLANT GROUP	Onions (see p.164)
SOW DIRECT	February–March
HARVEST	July–September

If you're even vaguely short of space but want to grow some onions, then grow shallots (and spring onions) in preference to 'ordinary' white onions. Shallots take up less room on your plot and they're expensive to buy, while you can get maincrop onions cheaply anywhere. If you think that maincrop onions are somehow a larger, better-value harvest due to their size, or you're anticipating fiddly peeling and chopping with their smaller cousins, let me reassure you that shallots are not just small onions. Get ready for a milder yet finer flavour, superior in every way to all the maincrop white onions.

Varieties
'Red Sun' takes some beating as an unusual red shallot, and 'Matador' is a top-notch sweet, yet edgy, shallot.

How to grow
Most shallots can be grown from either seed or mini-onions known as sets. Sets are easier to deal with, but seed is considerably cheaper if you're going for a big harvest.

With seed, sow direct in early spring, thinly in lines 1cm deep and 30cm apart. You're likely to have to thin the seedlings to around 20cm apart.

Plant sets during the first half of the spring with the tips just slightly below the level of the soil. Space sets around 20cm apart, in rows 30cm apart.

Keep your shallots clear of weeds and your crop will enjoy the nutrients it needs. This also ensures good airflow around the bulbs, minimising the risk of disease.

How to harvest
July to September is the time to lift shallots, as their leaves begin to yellow. Let them dry in the sun for a day or two before using immediately, or storing them in net bags for later use.

Problems and pests
Rotating your crops (see p.172) helps to minimise the likelihood of getting onion downy mildew and white rot, though both are comparatively rare. Neck rot can occur during storage. Sort through your harvest well, discarding any that are soft, and use any that are borderline immediately.

How to eat

Shallots can be used in much the same way as maincrop onions in recipes and this is how many people choose to use them. However, I like to save mine for roasting long and slow in their skins to draw out maximum sweetness; for throwing quartered on to pizzas; and for slicing thinly and marinating in red wine vinegar with a pinch of sugar, to add to salads.

If anyone needs convincing that shallots are a bit special, try this way of cooking them: heat a little butter in a large frying pan, add 250g peeled shallots and a couple of rosemary sprigs. As the shallots start to colour, add 2 tsp sugar, followed by a large glass of red wine and 1 tsp balsamic vinegar. Cover and simmer for about 20 minutes. To finish, remove the lid, turn up the heat and let bubble to reduce the liquid until it just forms a colourful glaze on the shallots.

For more recipes, see pp.242, 244, 256.

Shallots 'Matador'

Sorrel *Rumex acetosa*

PLANT GROUP	Salad leaves (see p.166)
SOW DIRECT	March–April
HARVEST	June–November

If you're new to sorrel, it's a perennial that we tend to grow as an annual to keep the leaves from getting tough. Lemony and sharp, sorrel has an acidity reminiscent of rhubarb and gooseberries, yet the leaves are tender, like spinach. They are excellent with oily fish, potatoes, and in soups. And when young and small, you can toss them sparingly into salads. Sow a line and you'll find any number of uses for it.

Varieties
You can gather wild sorrel if you have it nearby, as long as it's not near polluting traffic, but 'Buckler-leaved' and 'Broad-leaved' sorrel are best for your patch.

How to grow
Sow direct in March or April for a steady supply through summer and autumn. Distance between plants is up to you, depending on the size of plant and leaf you are after, but 30cm should do between rows. Water the plants in dry periods to avoid bolting.

How to harvest
Pluck or snip off sorrel leaves regularly for a cut-and-come-again harvest from June until November, or by cutting a few centimetres above the ground to encourage fresh growth.

Problems and pests
None.

How to eat
Don't be put off by the colour change on cooking – from vibrant green to khaki. To prepare, strip out the main veins of larger leaves, then wash the leaves well.

My favourite way to eat sorrel is with new potatoes: cut the prepared sorrel into 1cm strips, toss with the just-cooked potatoes, a little olive oil and butter, then rest for a minute or so until wilted. Season and serve as a side dish or snack on its own.

Sorrel also makes a lovely, punchy soup, combined with a little potato and cream (like a leek and potato soup). And try a few small, young leaves in a salad to pep it up. For more recipes, see pp.223, 246, 248.

Harvested sorrel 'Broad-leaved'

Perpetual spinach seedlings

Spinach *Spinacia oleracea*

PLANT GROUP	Salad leaves (see p.166)
SOW DIRECT	March–October
HARVEST	All year round

Welcome to the incredible shrinking harvest. You'll be sat watching the leaves wilt in the pan and you'll swear you put two dustbinfuls on to cook. Luckily for us, everything that is 'spinach' – the green, the beautifully sharp edge to the flavour – remains after the cooking.

You don't have to cook spinach. It works equally well as a salad leaf when picked small and young, before the leaves begin to thicken. Pick them larger and you'll find they will happily combine with anything from pulses and potatoes to meats. And if you go for the right varieties, you can pick spinach all year round, giving you another versatile leaf to add to your armoury in bridging the so-called 'hungry gap'.

Spinach is also particularly good for you. It's high in both iron and vitamin C, and it just so happens that the vitamin C boosts your body's ability to absorb the precious iron, so you get the maximum benefit.

Varieties

'Dominant' and 'Bordeaux' (F1) are hard to better for autumn and winter leaves, making wonderful salad leaves when picked small. 'Matador' is an excellent variety to try in the summer, as it's slow to bolt – and delicious.

New Zealand spinach (*Tetragonia expansa*) is a must. Although it's not a true spinach, it delivers a similar flavour and importantly grows merrily through the hottest times (even indoors) when many true spinaches tend to bolt. Sow it April–June and watch it sprawl across your patch. You shouldn't need to water it in anything other than drought times, and you can pick the tender leaves frequently when they are just a few centimetres, from mid-summer into the autumn.

Perpetual spinach (*Beta vulgaris* var. *cicla*) (see p.60) is unrelated but gives you similar(ish) leaves seemingly endlessly. It's well worth sowing a few to ensure a year-round factory of versatile leaves.

How to grow

Sow direct once a month from March through to early autumn (depending on your varieties) for a year-round crop. Any variety can be sown early in spring and early autumn, but try Matador for June–August sowings. Go for rows about 30cm apart, and try to sprinkle thinly – 3cm or so apart. Thin to 20cm if you are after large leaves. If you are picking small leaves as a cut-and-come-again crop, you should get a harvest in little over a month in optimum conditions, perhaps twice as long when it's cooler. Watering is vital to steady growth of the plants and it minimises the likelihood of bolting – little and often is ideal.

How to harvest

Keep cutting leaves, when they are around 3cm or so above ground level, to encourage more growth.

Problems and pests

Apart from the stage when spinach is at its most vulnerable to slugs as it emerges, it is rarely troubled by any pests or diseases.

How to eat

Pick spinach small and it's a fantastic addition to most leafy salads, but as soon as the leaves are medium-sized, they will have lost their succulence and are better cooked. Spinach makes a lovely partnership wilted with chick peas or potatoes, taking perfectly happily to the milder end of the curry spices.

Hugh's creamed spinach is particularly good: strip the stalks from 500g spinach and wash the leaves well. Cook with only the water clinging to the leaves from washing in a covered large saucepan until just wilted. Refresh briefly with cold water, drain well and squeeze with your hands to extract as much water as you can, then chop roughly. Put 250ml milk in a pan with a sliced onion and 2 bay leaves. Bring almost to the boil, take off the heat and leave to infuse for 10 minutes, then strain into a jug, discarding the onion and bay. Melt 50g unsalted butter in the pan and stir in 25g plain flour to make a loose roux. Cook gently for a couple of minutes, then stir in half the warm, infused milk. Cook, stirring, until the sauce is thick and smooth, then incorporate the rest of the milk. Bring to the boil and simmer gently for a minute. Season well with salt, pepper and a generous grating of nutmeg. Next, stir in the chopped spinach. Heat through, but don't let it bubble for more than a minute. Taste and adjust the seasoning with salt, pepper, and a touch more nutmeg perhaps. Serve at once, ladled into large warm bowls. Simple, yet delicious, and if you're in the mood, a little Gruyère or Parmesan grated over the top works a treat.

Or for a tasty snack, wilt 500g spinach, refresh, dry and chop as for creamed spinach (above). Beat 2 eggs with a little Parmesan, a good grating of nutmeg and a good pinch each of salt and pepper. Add the spinach and just enough breadcrumbs to hold the mix together fairly stiffly, then shape into squash-ball-sized nuggets. Heat a good glug of olive oil in a frying pan until just smoking, and fry the nuggets for 5 minutes or so until golden all over. Let them cool a little, then serve warm rather than blisteringly hot, with a punchy (garlicky or mustardy) mayonnaise.

For more recipes, see pp.223, 244, 248.

Spring onions *Allium cepa*

PLANT GROUP	Onions (see p.164)
SOW DIRECT	October–November for overwintering varieties; or February–August
HARVEST	February–November

As soon as I munched through a 'White Lisbon' I was hooked, and everything from salads to tarts to mashed potato to cold meats gets the mild punch of spring onions now. On top of that incredible flavour, they're easy to grow, and take up next to no room to generate all that flavour. Treat them as a salad, but also get used to them as one of those multi-purpose transformers that add to – and make more of – so many of your other harvests.

They work wonders for some of your plants in the garden as well as the kitchen, acting as an ideal companion plant (see p.212) for carrots, with their oniony smell disguising the carrot scent that would otherwise attract the damaging carrot fly.

Varieties

'North Holland Blood Red' looks and tastes the best of the spring onions, although 'White Lisbon' isn't far behind. 'White Lisbon Winter Hardy' is the best for overwintering to get an early crop.

How to grow

Sow them thinly direct into your patch in lines around 10cm apart, thinning (and eating) them as they grow. Give them a sunny, well-drained spot. Sowing them in small amounts every few weeks from the end of February until the start of August will give you a steady supply into autumn. Winter-hardy varieties sown in October and November will give you an early harvest, starting around Valentine's Day.

As for routine care, a little careful weeding (avoiding the shallow roots) is all they'll ask of you.

How to harvest

With a range of varieties successively sown, you can have spring onions from February right through to November. Pull them up as you need them, using the thinnings as you go.

Problems and pests

Onion downy mildew and white rot are rare and incurable, but if you avoid growing onions in the same place 2 years in a row, you're unlikely to get either.

How to eat

Sliced thinly, spring onions bring punch and crunch to any salad, and they take well to the griddle or barbecue. I particularly love them sliced as thinly as possible in salad dressings. If you've any mashed potatoes left from a meal, then throw in chopped spring onions along with any leftover chopped greens, and shape the mix into cakes for shallow frying as the classic bubble and squeak.

For more recipes, see pp.226, 239, 244.

Spring onions 'White Lisbon'

Sprouting broccoli

Brassica oleracea var. *italica*

PLANT GROUP	Brassicas (see p.159)
START UNDER COVER	March–April
PLANT OUT	June–July
SOW DIRECT	April–May
HARVEST	January–April

The 'hungry gap' at the back end of winter and early spring can feel like the garden's annual holiday. It's certainly a lean time compared to summer, but what is around can be truly special. Step forward sprouting broccoli. Admittedly, when there's little to harvest, there can be a temptation to overhype the average, but these flavoursome spears make it a true veg patch essential. It comes in either white or purple varieties, which not only help fill the hungry gap, but almost make you glad there's little else about so you can concentrate on getting your teeth stuck into them.

I'm not sure how sprouting broccoli has managed to remain a relative secret, given that it is one of the very, very finest foods your garden can produce. I suspect it may be a triumph of the supermarkets. Sprouting broccoli has a delicate, complex flavour and is more tender than calabrese. It's also comparatively short-lived and tricky to pick in large quantities – all of which points the supermarkets towards calabrese. They've managed to divert our attention with ease, with calabrese not only winning the race to our shelves over sprouting broccoli, but even managing to pinch its name on the way.

Varieties

Sprouting broccoli is available in a range of varieties that produce at slightly different times, allowing you to stretch this delicious harvest over a longer period. For earlies, try 'Rudolph' and 'White Eye'; for mid-season, I'd recommend 'Red Arrow'; for lates, 'Claret', 'Late Purple Sprouting' and 'White Star' are all good choices. You could even try one of the new summer-cropping varieties, such as 'Bordeaux', but there's something about sprouting broccoli in the heat of full summer that doesn't seem quite right to me – I prefer to enjoy it in its season.

How to grow

Start them off under cover in Jiffy 7s (see p.197) or small pots in March/April, planting out when they are around 10cm tall in June or early July. Give them 50cm between plants. Alternatively, sow direct in April/May.

Sprouting broccoli 'Purple Sprouting'

Make sure you water your sprouting broccoli plants if there's a dry period in the first few of months after you've planted them, but don't water them through winter – they'll do fine on their own.

Problems and pests

Slugs and snails are the main threat. Patrol regularly and deal with them in whichever way you prefer (see p.216).

How to harvest

Sprouting broccoli is a cut-and-come-again veg, and if you choose the right varieties, you can help yourself from New Year through to April. As with most cut-and-come-agains, regular harvesting pays dividends, prompting the plant to keep on throwing out tasty arms, so make sure you get out there with the basket every few evenings. Slice off entire shoots when they're young and tender – and certainly before they risk going to seed as this halts production.

How to eat

In the finest of edible baton-passing, the sprouting broccoli starts to dip off just as the asparagus kicks in, and you can treat them exactly the same: steam the spears quickly before dipping in hollandaise or dressing with good olive oil, lemon juice and freshly grated Parmesan.

If you find yourself with too much on your hands (an impossibility surely), then blanch in boiling water for a couple of minutes only, drain, cool quickly in cold water and freeze in batches.

For more recipes, see pp.233, 244, 258.

Squash, pumpkins and gourds
Cucurbita maxima, C. pepo and *C. moschata*

PLANT GROUP	Cucurbits (see p.165)
START UNDER COVER	March–May
PLANT OUT	June–July
HARVEST	October–November

This threesome comes in almost any shape and colour imaginable and there's little to touch them for spectacular productivity. If you're a first-timer, try a few as they'll reward you on every front – they're very hard to mess up, they look incredible, they swamp out the weeds locally, and not only do they pump out a sizeable harvest, they also keep well, allowing you to enjoy them long afterwards.

The distinction between pumpkins, squash and gourds is bizarrely vague, and even their botanical names provide little guidance. If it helps, I tend to think that pumpkins are generally orange, gourds are mostly inedible, squash are almost always delicious. So, concentrate on squash for the kitchen, a pumpkin or two for Hallowe'en, and decorative gourds to weird up your plot.

Varieties
There is such a variety of delicious and peculiarly shaped squash available that you can try a new cultivar every year if you like, but there are three you should start off with: the creamy and versatile 'Early Butternut' is a real must, as is 'Crown Prince' (F1), which looks, tastes and stores as good as any, and the onion-shaped 'Red Kuri' (aka 'Uchi Kuri') with its deliciously sweet, nutty flesh. Other possibilities are 'Jaspée de Vendée', a heavy cropper with a delicate flavour, and the flatter 'Tancheese' with its slightly sweeter salmon-coloured flesh. If you're after an outstanding edible pumpkin, look no further than 'Rouge Vif d'Etampes'. For Hallowe'en, 'Atlantic Giant' is perfect as it lives up to its name impressively.

How to grow
Start them off under cover in spring in small pots or Jiffy 7s (see p.197), sowing each seed on its edge to prevent rotting. When they have reached a good size with four leaves or so and you're sure the frosts have passed, plant them out at least a metre apart – the leaves will fill up the sea between them, keeping weeds out and soil moisture in. Dig a good-sized scoop and fill the hole with compost, planting your seedling in and watering well. Squash and pumpkins will repay any investment in richness and moisture at this stage.

Squash 'Red Kuri'

How to harvest

Don't be too impatient when it comes to picking pumpkins and squash – leave them to ripen as long as you can. If the weather turns wet for more than a few days, slip a roof tile or something similar under them to prevent them from sitting in the damp. Ready or not, when the frosts approach it's time to cut them. Pick them with a short stalk, as this seems to ensure against (most) rotting in storage. Place them somewhere light but not too warm – they'll continue to ripen a little for a week or two longer. Most will store well into the winter.

It isn't advisable to save seed from squash or pumpkins. Any cross-pollination that may have occurred will come through in the next generation, leading to unpredictable taste.

Problems and pests

Slugs and snails are a threat for a few weeks after planting out, so you'll need to keep these in check (see p.216).

How to eat

Squash and pumpkins roast so well you'll probably find that's the first port of call for much of your harvest. Don't bother with peeling them first, just slice them up chunkily, scrape the pips and fibres out and toss then in a roasting tin with a splash of olive oil, a good sprinkling of sea salt and black pepper, and a few garlic cloves. Roast in a preheated oven at 200°C/Gas Mark 6 for half an hour or so until tender, turning them at least once.

To make a tasty soup, roast a reasonable-sized pumpkin or squash as above, then cut away the skin and peel the garlic. Using a blender, purée the roasted squash or pumpkin flesh with the garlic and 1 litre vegetable stock (see p.259), in batches if necessary. Return to the pan and warm through gently. Thin with a little extra stock (or milk) to the desired consistency, check the seasoning and serve scattered with thin strips of crispy bacon.

Don't discard the seeds from your pumpkin or squash, as they're both delicious and highly nutritious. Wash and dry them, then spread out on a roasting tray, scatter with flaky sea salt and roast in a hot oven at 200°C/Gas Mark 6 for a few minutes to bring out the flavour.

Both squash and pumpkin also work well finely diced and gently cooked in olive oil with a little garlic. Use as a risotto base (outstanding with a little rosemary), or – with the addition of a little vegetable stock and/or cream – as a pasta sauce.

For more recipes, see pp.248, 254, 262.

Swede *Brassica napus* var. *napobrassica*

PLANT GROUP	Brassicas (see p.159)
SOW DIRECT	April–June
HARVEST	September–February

This is very possibly the least glamorous vegetable of them all. It has rivals (notably the turnip) but swede has the edge, I think. With its rough, matt skin and tendency to become fibrous when allowed to grow too large, swede offers little in the way of initial culinary promise, yet it is a really valuable addition to your veg patch. The secret is to focus on its qualities and keep it simple. Although we think of it as a root veg, swede is a member of the brassica family, and therefore botanically in with the cabbages and broccoli. So as well as harvesting the deliciously sweet root, have confidence that the leaves are not just there for photosynthesising – these are top-notch greens for the table.

Famously popular in Scotland, swede is an essential element of Burn's Night celebrations, when it is traditionally served with haggis. South of the border swede was, until recently, the pre-pumpkin vegetable hollowed out and carved with faces to make Hallowe'en lanterns. Ugly maybe, delicious double-croppers certainly, good for you definitely, and you can carve a novelty face out of them: what more could you want from a vegetable?

Varieties
'Willemsburger' has a green top rather than the usual purple one, producing good-sized roots with pale orange flesh of excellent quality. It's also resistant to club root (the main disease you might encounter), and keeps well, so even if you try other varieties, give this one a go too.

How to grow
Sow swede direct from April–June, thinning the emerging seedlings to at least 20cm apart.

Keep the plants well weeded to minimise competition. Water them through dry periods, but note that a steady amount for a few days is better than a lot in one go, as they'll happily split if there are serious fluctuations in water supply.

Problems and pests
Slugs may damage the leaves and tops of swedes as they emerge, which can lead to rotting from the top. Make sure you include your swedes as part of your regular slug patrol (see p.216).

How to harvest

Lift swedes throughout the autumn and winter, twisting off their leafy tops. If you find you have a surplus, store them in a wooden box of moist sand.

How to eat

Treat the tops as cut-and-come-again leaves, picking half and leaving the rest for the plant. The cabbage pasta sauce treatment (see p.45) works wonderfully well with swede tops – a little chilli in the mix is particularly fine.

The skin is quite thick and uneven, so when preparing, first quarter the swede and then peel with a knife rather than a vegetable peeler. Roasted or mashed, swede is a wondrous, sweet accompaniment to roast meat, game and poultry. Just bear in mind that roasting or steaming concentrates the flavour, whereas boiling dilutes it. Drain swede thoroughly before mashing and don't be shy with butter, cream and freshly ground black pepper.

For more recipes, see pp.225, 253.

Swede 'Willemsburger'

Sweetcorn *Zea mays*

PLANT GROUP	Others (see p.169)
START UNDER COVER	April
PLANT OUT	May–June
SOW DIRECT	May
HARVEST	July–September

Sweetcorn is the ideal crop for beginners and even more so for children as it grows quickly, vertically and obviously, communicating the wonder of growth and life as well as any vegetable there is. And on top of that, of course, you get to look forward to popcorn.

If you intend to eat the cobs fresh rather than as popcorn, remember that they're right up with asparagus and peas when it comes to minimising plot-to-pot time. As their name implies, it's the sweetness you're after. In this respect, every hour counts, as the sugars quickly convert to starches after the corn leaves the plant – eat them on the day you pick them if you can.

When it comes to cooking, it's worth knowing that sweetcorn is one of those rare crops that, if overcooked, is in fact better for you. Although their vitamin C quickly reduces, the levels of ferulic acid shoot right up with long cooking at high temperature. Why is this a big deal? Ferulic acid is an antioxidant – one of those great caretakers of our internal system running about sweeping up potentially damaging free radicals that can contribute to physical changes we perceive as ageing, as well as heart disease and cancer. Most ferulic acid is held in the cell walls and fibres within the sweetcorn and cooking breaks these down, liberating the bioactive bodyguards to go about their rather wonderful business. So, for once, you can boil the backside out of this veg with impunity.

Varieties

A lot of the newer varieties are known as 'supersweet', having higher levels of sugars – 'Sweet Nugget' (F1) and 'Sweetie' are the best I've tried.

It is well worth giving some of the older varieties a whirl too. Many prefer what they feel is a better balance of sweetness with the sweetcorn's other flavours – 'Golden Bantam' is reliable and tasty. Be sure to check whether the seeds you are buying are supersweet or normal, as you'll need to allow significantly more room if you grow some of each (see page 147).

If you (or your children) are after popcorn, 'Strawberry Sweetcorn' is hard to beat and a beautiful ornamental addition to the veg patch.

Sweetcorn 'Golden Bantam'

How to grow

April is the best time to get sweetcorn started under cover in pots or Jiffy 7s (see p.197), planting them out when around 7cm tall and the frosts are definitely past (around May or June).

Leave it until May if you're sowing sweetcorn direct. Plant the seeds knuckle deep, with spacing 30cm each way.

Sweetcorn are wind pollinated (unlike most other vegetables which are pollinated by insects). It's therefore better to plant them in groups rather than rows if you can, to maximise pollination. You should allow at least 8 metres between supersweet and normal varieties, as cross-pollination may reduce their sweetness. The plants grow well if there is a reasonable blend of rain and sun, giving you a harvest from mid-summer into autumn.

Water them well after flowering if there's an extended dry period.

How to harvest

By early summer (depending on variety) the flowers will have appeared at the top of the plant, puffing out clouds of pollen that can turn you, the soil and hopefully the tassels on the plant yellow. Each of these untidy tassels is actually a thin tube connecting the outside world with a grain, patiently waiting to be fertilised. If you're lucky, the pollen hits its target, and in a few short weeks you'll be munching the results. The cobs are ready when the tassels turn dark brown. Stick a thumbnail into one of the niblets, and if the liquid released is milky, your sweetcorn is ready for the pan; if it's clear, then leave it a while.

After picking, if you can't eat your sweetcorn immediately, keep the leaves on as this helps retain freshness, and get them in the fridge quickly to slow the conversion of sugar to starch.

Problems and pests

None.

How to eat

You can mess around with sweetcorn to your heart's content, adding it to any number of salads, but little beats boiling and eating them simply with butter, salt and pepper. (Don't salt the cooking water though or it will harden the kernels.)

Or you might like to try barbecuing them, leaves on – the slight burnt flavour combines well with their sweetness, and gives you another opportunity to use any leftover confit chilli (see p.230).

For more recipes, see pp.242, 248.

Tomatoes 'Costuluto Fiorentino'

Tomatoes *Lycopersicon esculentum*

PLANT GROUP	Solanaceae (see p.168)
START UNDER COVER	February–March
PLANT OUT	April–June
HARVEST	July–October

A tomato at its best, wrapped in a basil leaf, is summer in a succulent globe. Warm from the sun, your first home-grown 'Gardener's Delight' is likely to be up there with any harvest you grow, but if you want to ripen it to its perfect peak, it pays to know a little about the deceptively complex tomato. There's a fine line between reaching this peak and overdoing the physical compromise that comes with it. As the flavour develops, the tomato becomes softer, more prone to damage – and judging that is half the fun of growing them. Erring on the cautious side, supermarkets focus on getting them intact from soil to shelf, so their tomatoes are picked early and firm, never attaining the flavour of vine-ripe tomatoes and often bland.

Yet a home-grown crop can sometimes be little better, or utterly delicious, or anywhere in between. Why such uncertainty when other foods that ripen, bananas, say, are pretty much the same every time? With around 400 sugars, acids and volatiles contributing to the mix, tomatoes are just that much more complex. With so many variables, it's not hard to see how we can get anything from a tinny trebly tune to a bassy bottom-heavy boom.

And that's not all. Not only are there endless permutations when it comes to these compounds, but they are far from stable within the tomato itself. The colour change from green to red isn't just a change of wallpaper, it indicates a deeper chemical transition within. The acid balance moves from appley malic acid towards the sharper citric acid, with the sugars shifting from glucose to the far sweeter fructose. Added to this, the volatiles are jumping about too. And then there's our easily fooled senses – the sharper citric acid makes the sweeter fructose seem even sweeter to us, as does the change to a softer texture. So ripening, it seems, is far from a linear process: every last tweak of chemical ripening can multiply itself in terms of our experience of it.

But the tomato is no soup of sugars, acids and volatiles washing about willy-nilly – it holds many of these compounds separately in its structure, and the act of slicing, chewing or heating breaks down the constraining boundaries, causing enzymes to hit compounds, sweetness to touch acid, flesh to merge with juice, giving us a tomatoey jumble of jostling flavours. Ripening involves essentially the same breakdown and intermingling, increasing towards the peak, which contributes much to our enjoyment of that elusive hit of whole, perfect tomatoeyness.

It's good to understand why the tomato can be anything from delightful to disappointing, but more importantly it hints at why it can be so tricky to get to the tomato we are after. So, safe in the knowledge that it's not your fault if your tomatoes turn out so-so, relax, and enjoy giving them a go. What you must do is prepare well, choose a range of good varieties, and keep the plants fed and watered (as outlined below). You'll still need an element of luck, though, to get all those sugars, acids and volatiles to line up just so. But as with the old adage, the more you practise the luckier you'll get – there's simply no short cut to getting to know which tomatoes do best on your patch. Talk to your dad, your neighbour, the oldest allotmenter you can find and ask what works for them, as they may have some great ideas. And trust yourself too – developing a little touch and a knack is all about trying things out and watching and encouraging a little luck to come your way.

Varieties

Tomatoes are particularly sensitive to place, so try at least four varieties to start off with and stick with the ones that thrive, trying a few more each year.

Unless you've a compelling reason to do otherwise, it's well worth trying each of the different types: 'Gardener's Delight' is rightfully the ubiquitous cherry, although 'Orange Bourgain' makes an excellent alternative; 'San Marzano' is a flavoursome plum; of the extra-large tomatoes, 'Costuluto Fiorentino' and 'Brandywine' are outstanding and reliable, with 'Burpees Delicious' living up to its billing.

Of the yellow tomatoes, look no further than 'Sungold' – it's deliciously sweet. 'Tumbling Tom' is the one to try for growing in hanging baskets. 'Black Krim' is another variety worth growing, not only for its remarkable red-black skin, but for its firm yet juicy texture and incredible flavour – perfect for tomato salads and salsas.

If you're going for some outdoor tomatoes, plump for varieties that ripen early – they may just give you the edge you need to get a mature crop, as they'll need less sun. Most cherry tomatoes should give you a good chance.

How to grow

Start tomatoes off under cover in February or March in Jiffy 7s (see p.197) or modules. When they get their first true leaves (following the initial pair of 'seed' leaves), move each plant into a 10cm pot, planting them 5mm below the height of the seed leaves.

Plant them out when they reach around 20cm tall, with flowers starting to open on the lowest truss. A sheltered, sunny spot is vital, as is a good, fertile medium in which to grow, so incorporate well-rotted manure and/or compost a couple of months ahead of planting them if possible.

Your plants will need a little support – canes for tying the taller cordon varieties (single-stemmed plants, occasionally sold as 'indeterminate' varieties) to, or netting and/or a few shorter sticks for bush varieties (also known as 'determinate' varieties).

The key to success is simple – tomatoes want sun, water and feeding, so make sure they get them. Tomatoes have one set of roots at the surface for feeding and other deeper roots for drinking, so bear this in mind when caring for them. You can bury a piece of pipe or an upturned plastic bottle with its base cut off next to the plant and use it to get the water down to where it counts. This isn't essential, but there are those who swear that surface watering dilutes flavour. After flowering, the fruit will start to set and a good drenching once a week with comfrey tea (see p.215) or seaweed feed will make all the difference. Remember that 'little and often' is the mantra – split fruit is all you'll get for drought followed by overwatering.

Shoots that develop between the stems and the main leaves must be removed as they use up valuable nutrients and water that your fruit needs, increase shading and reduce air circulation. Simply pinch them off. Cutting off the top of outdoor plants when six trusses have set fruit is usually advised to focus energies on the fruit, and most people do this on indoor plants too. Another thing I tend to do is pull off some leaves as the fruit ripens to promote air and light access, and so reduce the chance of disease. It's a balancing act between leaving plenty of leaves for the plant to photosynthesise but still getting the sun and air around your fruit.

How to harvest

The indoor harvesting stretches from July to early autumn, but outside you may be waiting into September for it to kick off. For that reason alone I prefer to grow most indoors. Any unripe outdoor fruit can be picked in the second half of September and ripened on a sunny sill – the ethylene given off by a nearby banana can shunt the process along, though they won't quite match up to those turned by sun alone.

Problems and pests

Companion planting works wonders with tomatoes. Garlic and nasturtiums repel aphids with their smell, whereas basil draws the aphids to it and away from your prize crop for you to deal with as you like (see p.212).

Tomatoes can suffer from the same blight as potatoes (see p.219), so avoid planting any outside if yours show any signs of the disease. Growing them under cover (as I do) will much reduce your chances of getting blight, but do make sure you don't grow them in the same spot year after year in your polytunnel or greenhouse to avoid the risk of disease building up in the soil.

How to eat

Tomatoes have an affinity with many ingredients – basil of course, but also cheeses, olives and anchovies – offering delectable salads and endless other culinary treats. Cold dramatically affects their flavour, causing an irreversible decline in the aromatics especially, so don't refrigerate! For more recipes, see pp.230, 256, 259.

Turnips *Brassica rapa*

PLANT GROUP	Brassicas (see p.159)
SOW DIRECT	March–July
HARVEST	June–October

I grow turnips every year for the pigs to nose through in autumn, but this year I allowed them (the turnips that is) to cross the line between field and garden, and I'm glad I did. With their sweet, peppery roots and outstanding leafy tops (spicy, like mustard greens) they have been one of this year's garden surprises. A couple of varieties disappointed, but this is to be expected, as turnips are famously unreliable in taste. Any variety can be delicious on one patch, bland on another, so try a few, and persevere with the winners.

It may be that as a nation we have been alone in missing out on a classic double harvest. As I write on the first weekend in November, I discover that I am but one tantilising Saturday shy of the annual turnip festival held on the banks of Lake Zurich in Switzerland. Apparently this is Europe's largest turnip festival, the rather scary implication being that there are other rival turnip festivals out there desirous of our attendance. Web-searching confirms how widespread these root raves are, and how almost unique we are in consigning the turnip to livestock fodder.

Varieties

As turnips vary in performance depending on location, recommending particular varieties is tricky. Try three or four and see which do best in your conditions. For me, 'Atlantic', 'Snowball' and 'Purple Top Milan' have come out tops.

How to grow

Sow direct in a shady spot every 3 weeks from late March to July, although be aware that early sowings can tend to bolt. Thin gradually until the plants are at least 15cm apart, using the discarded thinnings as greens.

You can also keep sowing (with no need for thinning) through August and September for delicious cut-and-come-again green tops to harvest in early spring.

Keep the plants watered through dry periods, but keep the watering consistent as fluctuations may cause them to split.

How to harvest

Pick your turnips when the roots are no bigger than a snooker ball, ideally smaller, through summer and autumn if you've sown successionally. Late-summer sowings (or early autumn under cover) will give you delicious leafy greens in March.

Problems and pests

Don't be fooled by your eyes, turnips are brassicas not roots, and they can suffer from the same ailments as most of the others. Club root is best avoided by rotating where you grow your plant groups each year (see p.159). Flea beetle may well leave its trademark peppering of tiny holes in the leaves, but they shouldn't be more than a passing nuisance.

How to eat

I do think we can learn a trick from the French and Swiss who braise or sauté turnips. They are also delicious roasted in a little honey, or try them – as the Italians favour – in risotto. They also make a deliciously different 'risotto' of their own, taking the place of the rice itself (see p.247). And turnips are surprisingly good when sharing the main duties with potatoes in the dauphinoise recipe (see p.254).

Turnip tops are one of the finest greens you'll eat – they'll take well to anything from a simple steaming to a spicier treatment. Try them with the pasta sauce that works so well for cabbages (see p.45).

For more recipes, see pp.225, 253.

Turnips 'Purple Top Milan'

Plant Groups

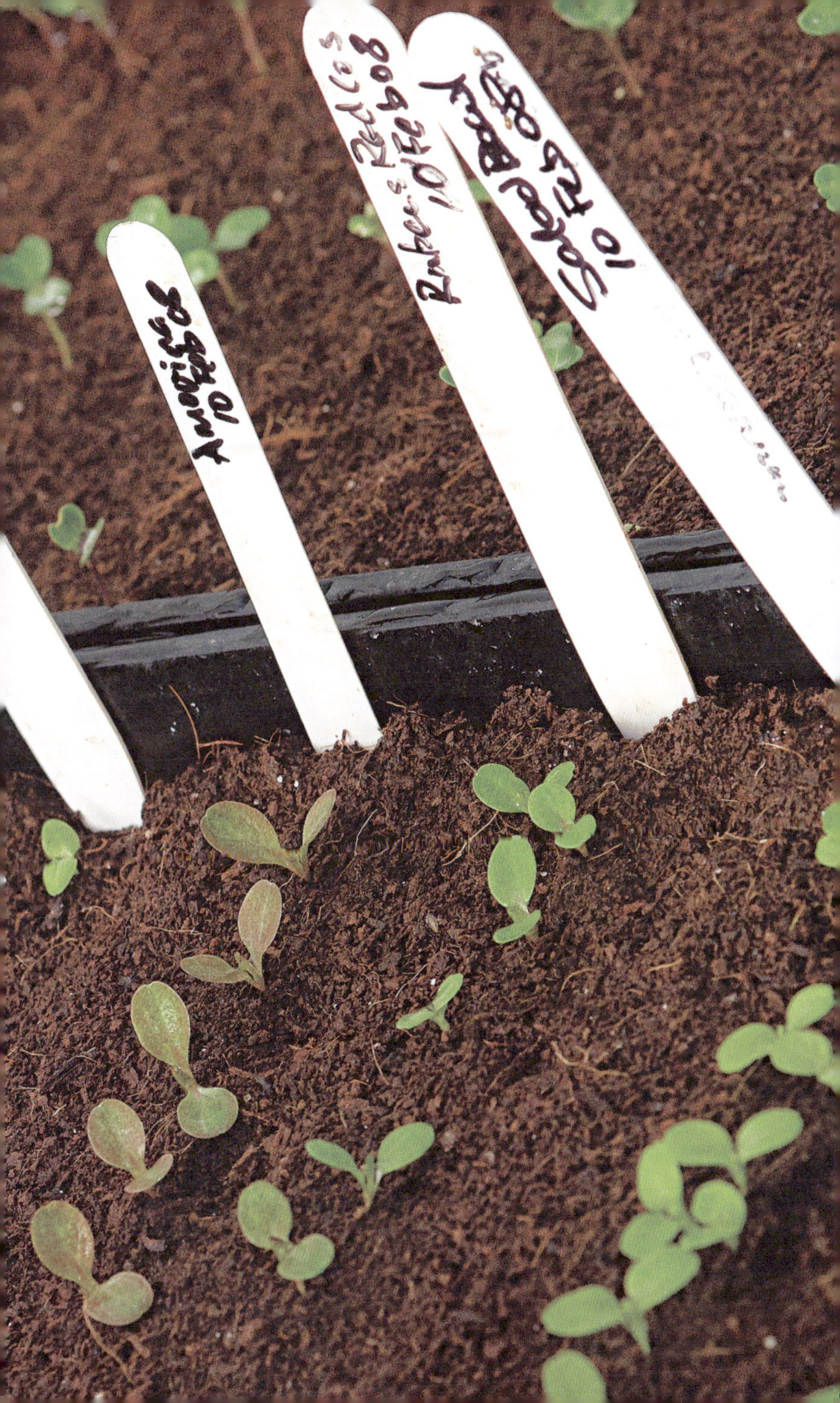

Almost all the food

on your wish list falls readily into one of the main plant groups – legumes, brassicas, roots, onions, cucurbits, salad leaves, Solanaceae and perennials. The rest I've thrown into a catch-all group I've called 'Others'. It's worth looking through the next few pages and familiarising yourself with what each of these groups gives and takes from your veg patch, as they will be key to guiding you on how you organise your plot. Check out the tips for growing each group successfully too. Remember, time invested now pays dividends all through the rest of the year.

Legumes

Borlotti beans	see p.36
Broad beans	see p.39
French beans	see p.79
Peas	see p.110
Runner beans	see p.124

If you've got better things to do at 8 o'clock on a mid-June evening than pop freshly shelled peas into your mouth as you amble around your vibrant plot with a glass of what you fancy, then life must be pretty special.

Peas and beans are packed with protein, they're cheap and easy to grow, and many arrive early in the growing year to encapsulate the taste of spring and welcome in the warmer days. They also come with the almost unbelievable bonus that they nourish the garden as well as the gardener. Nodules in the roots convert nitrogen from the air into compounds that feed the plant as it grows. When the plant dies or the top is cut off, the nitrogen is released into the soil as the roots break down, naturally fertilising your patch for subsequent plants. So plant legumes in spring and miraculously that bed will be more fertile in autumn.

With many of the legumes, every minute between plot and pot counts towards retaining their sweetness, so growing your own is really the only way to get to enjoy them at their sweet succulent prime. Having said that, the more I grow, the fewer seem to make it to the kitchen. Caught young and small, so many of them make delicious fast food as you wander about your patch.

Peas and beans are best started off under cover, planting out when they've reached several centimetres tall. Mice and birds love to tuck into seeds, so if you sow direct be prepared to lose a few, especially from autumn and early spring sowings.

Grow legumes in a well-drained plot to get them at their best, and remember to give them their rightful place in your crop rotation (see p.172), as this minimises the likelihood of disease. Pea and bean weevil can be a pain, producing the stamp-edge notches you'll see in leaves, but they rarely get beyond nuisance status. It's the slugs and snails that are your main enemy. Hit them early and hit them hard – go out every other night at dusk, disposing of any you find.

As well as the edible legumes, you're likely to come across a few others that are grown with the purpose of benefiting the soil. Known as green manures, most do as their edible cousins do and leave the soil enriched with nitrogen, so it pays to get familiar with how they can help bump up your harvests (see p.208).

In growing legumes you're not only feeding yourself and your soil, you may also be doing something for the planet. I can think of few things that better illustrate the wrongheadedness of our food supply than green beans and peas topping the list of the most air-imported fruit and veg – above exotics such as grapes and pineapples.

Growing legumes in small spaces

All of the legumes will grow happily in containers, although (like those grown outdoors) most will be grateful for any support you can give them. Canes and twigs can be tied into supporting tepees (see p.211), and with the help of a little netting or wire mesh, the climbing legumes will happily crawl up walls, taking up very little of your ground space.

Don't let containers dry out, and do give them a weekly watering of comfrey tea (see p.215) from flowering time onwards.

Tips for success with legumes

- Sow successionally
- Start them off under cover in root trainers or toilet roll inners (see p.197)
- Plant them where you grew potatoes last year
- Give them a sunny site
- Many climb, so do give them a sheltered spot
- Remember to give them support or grow dwarf varieties
- Pinch out the tops to encourage lower, bushier growth
- Water with comfrey tea once a week after flowering to encourage maximum pod production

Brassicas

Brussels sprouts	see p.41
Cabbages	see p.44
Calabrese	see p.46
Cauliflowers	see p.53
Kale	see p.94
Radishes	see p.120
Sprouting broccoli	see p.137
Swede	see p.143
Turnips	see p.152

All stemming from a wild original species, the brassicas provide an exhibition of natural and professional selection at its most varied. Coloured purple, white, black, green, red, yellow, blue – and everything in between – they offer the cook an array of edible roots, stems, flowers and leaves, yet we usually lump them together as 'greens'. They are generally regarded as narrow variations on a theme, though the reverse is true. How many of us even clock that we are eating flowers when we tuck into our calabrese, sprouting broccoli or cauliflower?

Not only do they offer diversity for the kitchen, many are stunning. Choose the right varieties and grow them at their happiest time of the year and the brassicas can deliver something delicious for the table every week of the year – beautiful and productive, the perfect combination.

You'll need to spend a little time getting to know the brassicas as varieties are particularly idiosyncratic – happy on one plot, poor on the next. Try a few of each and persevere with your favourites, dropping the others for new trials. It's worth the effort. With most brassicas, you won't notice a difference if they hit the plate a minute rather than an hour after picking, but grow the right varieties well and you'll appreciate their home-grown flavour is far superior to any in the supermarkets.

As with any plant group, a few rules will guide you to success. Although brassicas germinate well if sown direct, slugs, snails and birds will be rubbing their imaginary hands with glee as the leaves poke up. So start them off under cover in pots, modules or Jiffy 7s (see p.197), planting out when there's at least four leaves on the plant.

If you need convincing about rotation (see p.172), let the prospect of club root clarify your mind. The disease infects the roots, creating cysts which impair the flow of nutrients to the upper parts of the plant. Your crop will be poor at best, but worst still, the disease persists. Once you have it, you are stuck with it. There is no cure.

Cabbage 'January King'

The best way to tackle it is prevention – and rotation helps ensure that there is less risk of build-up. Sowing your own brassicas (rather than buying in seedlings) also helps to ensure they are free from the disease.

Cabbage root fly can be a nuisance, attacking brassicas when they're vulnerable after planting out. If you want to be preventative, put a flat cardboard collar around the stem to block the flies getting to the join with the soil to lay eggs. Interplanting with pungent herbs also helps to confuse those pests that navigate by smell. Hand-pick caterpillars (mostly cabbage whites) that show up in the sunnier months. I prefer this to netting, which usually works but detracts visually and impedes access.

Flea beetle can be a pain to most brassicas, but they particularly target radishes – nibbling small holes in their leaves that cumulatively impair the plant's ability to photosynthesise. Tolerance is usually the only alternative to chemical remedy, or you could try the ever-inventive Bob Flowerdew's remedy (see p.218).

Growing brassicas in small spaces

Brassicas are the plant group that takes least well to growing in containers. Their typically long growing time from sowing to harvest not only takes up space to the exclusion of quicker harvests, it often exhausts the nutrients found available in a confined space. Most won't die but your chances of getting a top-quality harvest are limited by your dedication in feeding them.

Given how strikingly beautiful many brassicas are, you may be better to use them in any garden space you have, to add extra appeal to your flower beds.

Tips for success with brassicas

- Club root loves acid conditions, so neutralise your soil pH with lime if you need to (see p.190)
- Never grow them in the same place within 3 years
- Grow them where legumes grew last year to benefit from the residual nitrogen in the soil
- Incorporate organic manure well ahead of planting
- Start them off under cover
- Try a number of varieties of each and persist with the ones that work best on your veg patch
- Plant in firm ground (and/or tread in well after planting) to ensure anchorage
- Give each plant some room, brassicas like air circulation
- If possible, give them a shady site rather than full sun
- Go out on regular slug, snail and caterpillar patrol – it will really up your harvest

Roots

Beetroot	see p.33
Carrots	see p.50
Celeriac	see p.56
Celery	see p.58
Parsnips	see p.108
Salsify	see p.126
Scorzonera	see p.126

With the early-summer sweetness of baby carrots, the autumnal earthiness of parsnips and the wintery possibilities of celeriac, I doubt there's another food group to touch root veg for year-round variety. Yet they have a rich history of under-appreciation and are subject to inconsistent prejudices. Roots may have seen many through wartime scarcity, but several European countries seem to have had their fill and their particular staple has lost its appeal: the French love a turnip, but not a parsnip. Then there's mistrust of the unknown: in England few savour salsify, while in Italy it is worshipped. Every root is revered and reviled with seemingly equal enthusiasm.

Roots may not be helped by their looks, but don't judge this book by its less-than-glamorous cover – their typically rough, thickish skin is precisely what we should be grateful for. It protects the body of the root and retains water, allowing us to store them until we need them. The root itself is the energy store full of sugars (providing immediate energy for the plant) and starches (its long-term reserves) and it is this wonderful combination we prize for its sweetness and fine texture. We also owe a debt to the defence system of some roots. It prompts the starches to quickly convert to more sugars should the plant feel under threat – hence parsnips taste sweeter after a frost. Some even produce sulphurous compounds to ward off attack, which we taste as the mustardy hit behind radishes and horseradish.

The key to giving roots the prominence they deserve in your patch is to focus on variety. Most of us eat our fair share of potatoes, onions and carrots, but we can readily source them locally. Cutting back on maincrops of each will free up some of the precious plot to try lesser-known, yet tasty roots like salsify and scorzonera.

You'll need patience and a little trust to grow roots. There's not the usual visual encouragement, nor a moment's stolen grazing: it's all going on, but mostly unseen. As a rule, roots are unfussy and most of your work comes before planting – in ensuring a good deep tilth for uninhibited growth. Avoid adding compost to the soil, as this encourages most roots to fork. You're after steady, deep-rooting growth, which allows the plant to draw up and accumulate minerals as a tasty prize.

For culinary perfection, size is often critical. The world of sport offers the best guide to prime harvests – golf and snooker balls for the best beetroot, baseballs for celeriac. But in truth, optimum size (and therefore spacing) is pretty flexible, and should reflect how you like to eat them. Close spacing gives a larger harvest of smaller veg, and vice versa. For what it's worth, I prefer small to medium root veg in the warmer months, slightly larger ones as the weather gets colder.

Growing roots in small spaces

Many of the roots will do well in containers of at least 25cm diameter and depth. If you want larger specimens of any roots, a stack of three tyres filled with compost is perfect, but you'll need to keep them well watered. Even if you're not short of room, this is an excellent way of getting an early crop of summer carrots under cover.

Tips for success with roots

- Prepare a good deep, fine bed
- Only add compost as a top dressing
- Think of roots as year-round harvests rather than just winter warmers
- Space closely for smaller crops (mainly in the warmer months), and further apart for larger veg
- Don't let them dry out, especially those closely planted, as they will have a greater tendency to bolt, becoming woody to eat. Remove any that do immediately, as they are thought to release chemicals that induce their neighbours to follow suit.

Onions

Garlic	see p.81
Leeks	see p.97
Onions	see p.102
Shallots	see p.128
Spring onions	see p.135

The onion family is right up there in that group of culinary transformers, taking many of your other harvests to a higher place in the kitchen. Stew without onions, vichyssoise without leeks – both unthinkable. From sharpness and crunch, through to soft, sweet and mellow tastes, family members have different qualities to offer. They also stand up on their own with the right treatment – typically long slow roasting to refocus the flavours and bring their natural sweetness to the fore.

Happily most members of the onion family are pretty easy to grow, and if you rotate your veg beds you should have little trouble from diseases. That said, this is one area of your patch that you can look to rationalise if you're stuck for space. Most maincrop onions are cheaply available and of pretty high quality in the shops. In most cases these maincroppers are not the home-grown flavour revelation that, say, peas are. So unless you have a real desire to grow all your onions, and have plenty of space to do it in, consider dropping at least some maincroppers for shallots, red onions, spring onions and a few garlic varieties – the real gastronomic treats.

Growing onions in small spaces
Spring onions are perfect for containers, trays, and even small spaces between other plants in the ground. Similarly, if you've only a small patch of ground I'd recommend growing even a few heads of garlic, as they make a beautiful addition to any garden.

Tips for success with the onion family
- Grow them together with roots as part of your 4-year rotation (see p.173)
- Use some of the smaller members of the onion family as companions with carrots to deter carrot fly
- Concentrate on growing shallots and other more unusual and expensive members of the onion family
- Sow into warm soil to reduce the tendency to bolt
- Give them a sunny open site for best results – they need good air circulation to discourage diseases
- Keep them well weeded – they hate competition

Cucurbits

Courgettes	see p.67
Cucumbers and gherkins	see p.69
Squash, pumpkins and gourds	see p.140

If you're either a novice, or lazy or have little time, cucurbits should come right near the top of your wish list as a delicious, varied easy-to-grow lot. All you need to make the cucurbits happy is a moist rich soil to grow them in, a sunny spot and a willingness to water at the first sign of dryness. If your soil needs enriching, add well-rotted manure and/or compost before planting.

Such is their apparent desire to reach your table, your main difficulty may well be in avoiding an over abundant crop. Known (at least in my house) as cucurbiquity, the result is squash, cucumbers and courgettes (especially) seemingly everywhere. The best advice to avoid your harvest becoming more of a hassle than a joy is: not to plant too many; to have a handful of fantastic recipes ready for the inevitable surplus; and to pick your courgettes, cucumbers and gherkins small and frequently. This will give you maximum flavour to minimum volume, and avoid that 'not again' feeling when they do rather better than you had envisaged.

If you are after the ideal place to grow them (or are short of room) any of the cucurbits will grow very happily in your compost heap, drawing on the rich nutrients therein, and getting a gentle nudge from the heat of the decomposition process.

Growing cucurbits in small spaces

Cucurbits are rambling space takers, but with the right varieties you can train that growth vertically over canes, netting, arches, or indeed anything you might like to hide in your garden. Check the catalogue description for squash, cucumber, courgettes and gherkins that are happy to scramble.

Most of the cucurbits will do well in containers, though you will need to make sure these are large enough. You'll also have to water them well and give them the occasional feed once they start to develop fruit.

Tips for success with cucurbits
- Start them off under cover
- Give them room to grow
- Water them regularly
- Harvest courgettes, cucumbers and gherkins small and frequently
- Mulch them early on to help retain water (see p.210) – the leaves should do this for you as they grow

Salad leaves

Chicory	see p.62
Endive	see p.74
Lettuces	see p.99
Rocket	see p.123
Sorrel	see p.130
Spinach	see p.133

For years, I couldn't see the point of eating something that didn't even provide me with enough calories to finish eating it, but now that I've come to concentrate on the range of salad leaves I can grow, rather than just hearting lettuces, my attitude has changed. As I write, I have lettuce leaves of 'Marvel of Four Seasons' and 'Green Oak Leaf', the bitterness of chicory and endive leaves, peppery wild rocket, the lemony sharpness of sorrel, along with pea tips, endless herbs and edible flowers, as well as a few oriental leaves to choose from. I'm after a salad with a variety of flavours, textures and colours, and my plot now reflects this.

Focusing on leaves has been the single largest revolution in my veg patch. Gone is the waste that usually comes with too many lettuces hearting all at once, and I get deliciously different salads every time.

Most salad leaves are packed full of antioxidants – those mysterious beneficials that appear to help the body to deal with all manner of ills. But there's little point in getting your daily dose from bags of ready-washed supermarket leaves. Apart from all that packaging, the likelihood is they've been 'washed' in a chlorine solution. The positive side of supermarket salad bags is that they've given many of us a taste for eating mixed leaves, and the seed suppliers have been quick to catch on.

The variety of leaves available to grow is vast compared to even a few years ago. There's the crunchy, the floppy and the multi-coloured, the peppery, the lobed, the mustardy, the crinkly, the bitter. And salad leaves are just as much of a taste sensation in the winter as the summer. With a little forethought, you can have their crunch, punch and goodness right through the winter, as well as through the warmer months. Happily, they are easy to grow, pretty forgiving of site, need little more than the odd watering, and many will grow again if you take a harvest of leaves. Added to that, salad bags are expensive to buy, so you've every reason to grow them.

The very notion of salad is also becoming increasingly and deliciously blurred. Many of the leaves traditionally grown for cooking are finding their way (usually picked small and tender) into salads. Spinach, chard, some kales, oriental leaves, edible flowers, pea tips and herbs all add to your salad-making choices. You can even turn salads into delicious main courses with the addition of meat, fish, seeds, nuts and cheese. The possibilities are further multiplied if you experiment with interesting dressings. So, if like me you've been a bit indifferent when it comes to salad, it's time to elevate them above the 'good for you' part of the plate. Give them their own stage, afford them at the very least some good oil and some sea salt. You'll be amazed.

Growing salad leaves in small spaces
This is the easiest of all the plant groups to grow in small spaces. Most are quick to mature, take up little room and will give you leaves from any container. To save time and space, sow leaves for cutting rather than hearting. Try leaves for repeated cutting in guttering, seed trays or in pots on your windowsill.

Tips for success with salad leaves
- Most can be sown direct, but all do better started in modules or in guttering
- Unless noted for a particular variety, don't let the soil dry out or the plant will feel stressed and run to seed
- Weed little and often
- Regular slug and snail patrols will greatly increase your harvest
- Cut or pick leaves a couple of centimetres above the soil and your plant will resprout a number of times before they tire

Solanaceae

Aubergines	see p.31
Chilli peppers	see p.65
Peppers	see p.114
Potatoes	see p.117
Tomatoes	see p.149

The potato shares its family with a rather unlikely crew of Mediterranean favourites – the aubergines, peppers, chillies and tomatoes. In theory, this means that they should share the same bed. In practice, all but the potatoes tend to be grown in a polytunnel, greenhouse, in a growbag or in a pot.

If you're feeling optimistic and are trying any of the sun lovers outside, then it's sensible to start them off under cover and plant them out where you've just lifted your earliest potatoes. If any of your potatoes have blight, then grow your tomatoes indoors or in a container as they are susceptible to the disease too.

Growing Solanaceae in small spaces

A stack of three tyres filled with compost is the perfect growing medium for a crop of early indoor new potatoes whether you've a shortage of space or not. Tomatoes, aubergines, chillies and sweet peppers are just about ideal for small spaces.

You might construe having no room outside, or only concrete next to the house, as possible limitations, but it needn't be the case with these sun lovers. It simply means that you'll end up growing them either on a sunny windowsill, or on a balcony, or in pots or a growbag against a wall – all of which will give them the light, heat and shelter they'll love.

Keep the plants well fed with comfrey tea (see p.215) from flowering onwards to ensure they have the nutrients required for fruiting.

Perennials

Asparagus	see p.28
Cardoons	see p.48
Globe artichokes	see p.85
Jerusalem artichokes	see p.92

Most of the inhabitants of your veg patch are annuals – germinating, maturing and being eaten within a year – but there are also a few absolutely prize long-livers that every patch should have. This group is the edible equivalent of the self-refilling pint. plant them once and almost unbelievably you'll be in for harvest after harvest, year after year. Each is easy to establish, fairly low maintenance, top of the flavour charts and expensive in the shops – the perfect qualifications for growing your own.

You can plant the perennials anywhere you like, but life is likely to be simpler if you give them a bed (or beds) of their own.

Others

Chard and perpetual spinach	see p.60
Edible flowers	see p.72
Florence fennel	see p.76
Herbs	see p.87
Oriental leaves	see p.105
Sweetcorn	see p.145

The rest fall into a catch-all group I've called 'others'. This disparate bunch is either outside the main plant groups or in the case of oriental leaves (many of which are brassicas) do not need to be grown with the rest of their family. Plant them where you like around your veg patch.

Planning your Veg Patch

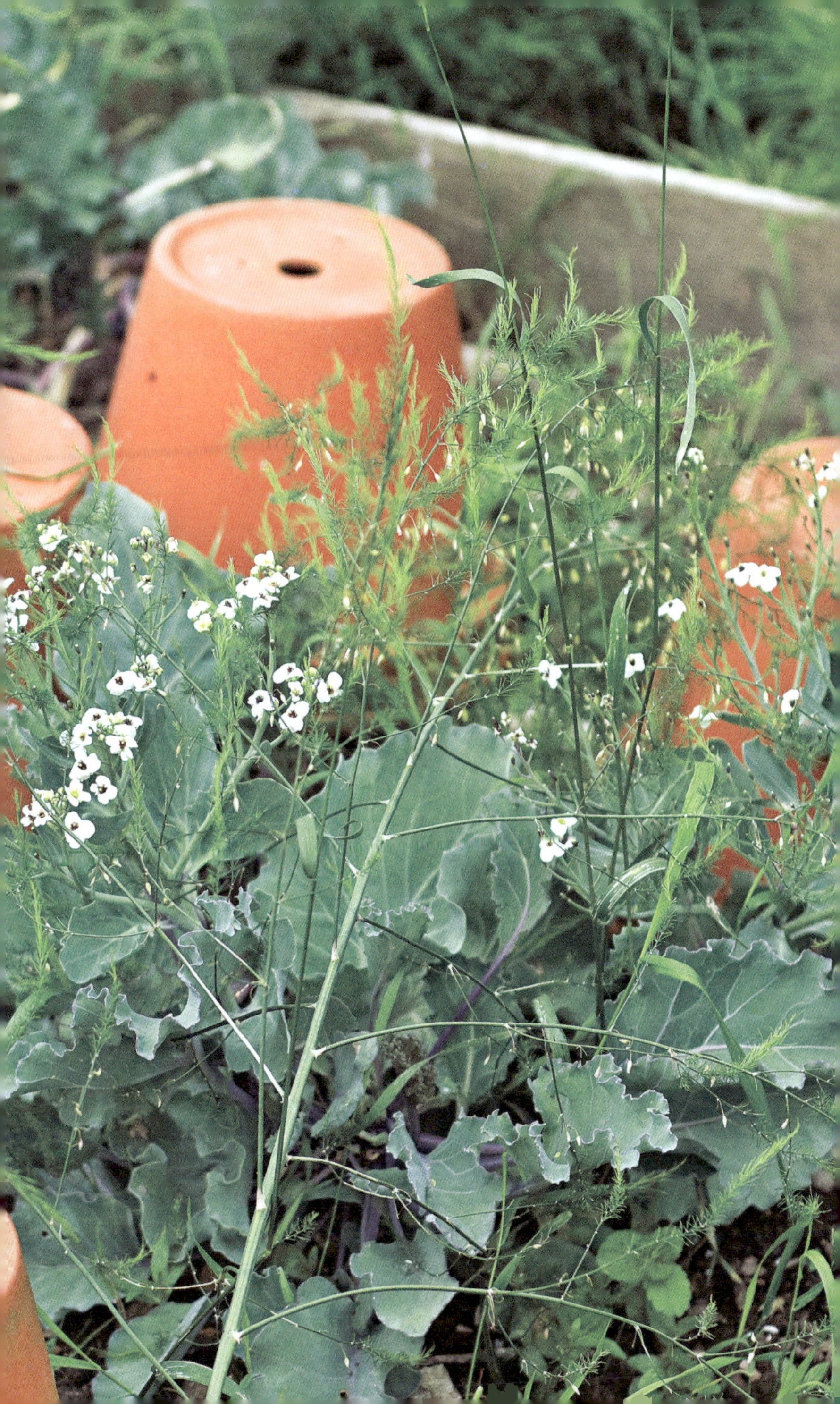

Every mid-November when the fire's working hard and I feel the need for the beer to be kept out of the fridge rather than in it, I know it's time to look through seed catalogues. Part of me knows it's a bit ridiculous to love this time so much, but what I read now is what I'll be eating in a few short months and I can't help but get hungry at the prospect. It's a menu of sorts, it's just that the service takes a little longer.

You may not be drenched in mid-summer sweat or digging up the plot in early winter, but as you stretch out in front of the flames with a glass in one hand and a catalogue in the other, the work you are doing is every bit as important as the graft at any other time of the year.

As well as choosing and ordering varieties, this is the time to organise your plot a little, and to do that you'll need to know a little about plant rotation.

Planning your rotation

If you're looking for an easy life as well as the Good Life, you'll need to start thinking early about how you want to organise your patch. To do that you'll need to understand the principle of plant rotation – the fundamental process that will minimise pests and diseases and maximise your harvests.

The idea of plant rotation couldn't be simpler: most of your plants will do better if you grow them together in their plant groups and if you don't grow them in the same place each year. There are a number of reasons for this.

Plants from the same group:
- Tend to enjoy the same conditions – growing them together makes it easier to provide them with this
- Often grow and mature at similar times – grouping them makes it easier to clear larger areas and prepare for the next crop
- Are often planted/sown at similar times, making most effective use of prepared ground and ensuring that bare earth is minimised
- Are usually susceptible to the same diseases – grouping them together and moving them each year helps minimise the risk of diseases building up
- Often have specific nutrient requirements – growing them together helps provide this, while rotating helps ensure that the soil doesn't become depleted

There are endless ways of planning your rotation but at River Cottage we use the simplest: the 4-year cycle – it's easy to split your patch into four, and to my mind the plant groups fall most naturally into this rotation plan. Start with this and you'll not go far wrong.

The beds for a 4-year rotation

THE LEGUMES BED
Where we put all the legumes – broad beans, beans, peas, etc. Notable for the ability of the roots of these plants to take nitrogen from the air and make it available in the soil for other plants.

THE BRASSICA BED
For all the brassicas, such as broccoli, cabbages and kale. This bed also includes a couple of those oddities that we think of as roots, but that are botanically brassicas, notably turnips and swede.

THE ROOTS AND ONIONS BED
Although separate families in their own right, these two are often grouped together for the purposes of the veg patch. The root family includes many of our underground tasties – carrots, celeriac, parsnips, etc. As well as onions themselves, the onion family includes garlic, leeks and shallots.

THE POTATO BED
Potatoes, although gastronomically treated as root vegetables, are in fact tubers and usually given a bed of their own. They belong to the Solanaceae family, which also takes in aubergines, peppers and tomatoes – all of which, if you grow them outside, can go in this bed.

Each of these four beds influences its part of the plot in specific ways, with its own associated diseases and nutrient needs. To ensure that this pattern of giving and receiving is balanced and that diseases are not given the opportunity to build up, the beds are moved around the garden in rotation.

Following our system, rotation involves splitting the heart of your patch into four sections and keeping a very particular order to the rotation. Where you grow legumes this year you should grow brassicas next, roots and onions the year after, potatoes in year 4, and then back to legumes.

The order is important for many reasons, most notably to ensure that the plants which produce nitrogen in the soil (the legumes) are followed by plants that benefit most from more nitrogen in the soil (the brassicas).

	Year 1	Year 2	Year 3	Year 4
Plot 1	LEGUMES	BRASSICAS	ROOTS & ONIONS	POTATOES
Plot 2	BRASSICAS	ROOTS & ONIONS	POTATOES	LEGUMES
Plot 3	ROOTS & ONIONS	POTATOES	LEGUMES	BRASSICAS
Plot 4	POTATOES	LEGUMES	BRASSICAS	ROOTS & ONIONS

As mentioned earlier, perennials – asparagus, artichokes, the perennial herbs, etc – are best given a permanent home out of the main rotation. Cucurbits, annual herbs, salad leaves and the 'others' can be happily slotted into your plot anywhere you like.

Making a paper plan

The more you do indoors, the less you'll run into trouble later outside. Get some graph paper (or print some from a web source) to help plan out your plot. But before you think about plants, consider your infrastructure: where's the water coming from, where do you want your main paths and where will you put the compost bin?

Water

Alongside the health of the soil and the amount of sunlight, the availability of water is the major influence on the success of your crops, but you'd be amazed how many aspiring growers convince themselves that they can happily haul a couple of watering cans back and forth from a distant tap: don't make that mistake.

If you've any way of harvesting rain water then take it, and leave yourself outside the grasp of any hosepipe ban. Shed and greenhouse roofs have a surprisingly large surface area and guttering secured to them can direct much of the water you'll need to a storage tank. Water butts are invaluable (check with your local council, many have offers for them), as are at least two watering cans. If you have water on tap, invest in a long and durable hose, and a reel for it.

Paths and access

In your eagerness to get as much out of your patch as possible, don't overlook the need to get to your plants regularly as they're growing – a plateful of tomatoes loses something of its reward when you've tripped over the squash, become tangled in the borlottis and flattened the basil in the process. Give yourself room to get about.

For your paths, work out the breadth you think you need to get yourself and a wheelbarrow around, then widen them by another 30cm. Believe me, a few well-placed narrow paths amongst your beds won't be enough.

Compost bin

This is the ultimate recycling centre – you'll turn to this stack of nutrients regularly to enrich your soil, and in turn care for your plants. There are a number of options to choose from, including making your own compost bin (see p.203), but whichever you take, don't be tempted to put it too near your veg. Snails and slugs love breeding in compost and will happily make short journeys at night to eat anything close by.

The beds

Once you've taken care of water supply, main access paths and where the compost is going, you'll need to define your beds and what you plan to grow in them. If you're looking to grow your veg in four main beds plus one or two for perennial plants, then I'd recommend you consider the perennial bed first. Decide how much you want to grow and determine its size from that. Then split what remains of your plot into quarters, allowing for more paths to give you access to them.

The key measurement when mapping out your beds is your reach. Don't have beds that you can't comfortably reach the middle of, otherwise sooner or later, you'll tread on your precious soil, compacting it in the process: 1.5 metres is an ideal width for beds, if you have access from all sides. If for any reason you want a wider bed than you can reach to the middle of, source a few wooden planks to walk on, as this spreads your weight and compacts the soil much less. Old scaffold boards are ideal.

Keep referring back to the patch itself, and ask yourself if your paper plan feels right looking at it on the ground. Amend it as you go. Take every opportunity to look at other plots, and take advice from neighbouring allotmenters. All can help you get to the design that best suits you and what you're growing.

Tips for your paper plan
- Measure your patch and use graph paper to help you draft out a plan
- Give yourself plenty of room for paths and easy access
- Visit open gardens and allotments, and stare over hedges for inspiration
- As your plants may need extra water, plan for where your supply will come from
- Site your compost bin away from your main beds
- Remember, your reach is most important – don't plan to grow more than you are confident of coping with, and make sure that you can reach all of it from your paths (or planks)
- If your space is more than you need, you can always grow into it – use green manures (see p.208) or cover unused areas with durable mulch mat (see p.210)

Growing seasonally and successionally

Now that you've organised your plot spatially, your concern is what happens over the course of the year. To get the most from your plot, you'll need to plan not only what goes in to start with, but also what follows. You'll need to think successionally. This is more straightforward than it might at first appear. All the information you need to help you plan when to sow and when you're likely to harvest each food is to be found in the A–Z. Successional thinking is about paying as much attention to the harvest time as to the initial sowing, and getting seedlings ready to take the place of crops as they finish. So when you're drawing up a plan for where you'll be growing your veg, write down next to each when it is harvested, and it will become second nature to ask yourself questions such as 'When the potatoes come up, what goes in?'

You'll also want to ensure that you don't have great gluts of one food all at once. When it comes to your plot 'little and often' is usually best, and this goes as much for your harvests as any other part of growing your own. Apart from the food that keeps for months (such as parsnips and squash), you should aim for a slow supply to match your consumption. This becomes increasingly important the shorter the shelf life of each harvest. Salad leaves, radishes and summer carrots are quick to go past their best, so a glut inevitably means wastage.

To combat this, you have two main strategies, Firstly, sow at intervals to ensure your harvest comes gradually. Secondly, sow your seeds under different conditions (some indoors, some under glass, some outside) and they'll reach maturity at different times. A good tip: as you go to plant out any seedlings you've started under cover, sow a fresh batch. That way you'll always have seedlings following on behind.

With year-round availability in supermarkets, seasonal produce has rather taken a back seat. There can be some strange comfort in buying pretty much the same food every week, but having any food any time you want it comes at a price. The eating calendar necessarily uncouples from the growing year, losing its subtlety. You may be able to buy asparagus on bonfire night, but it'll be a pale imitation of the real thing, and have been flown halfway around the world. It also robs asparagus of that dimension that comes with it and many other foods: anticipation.

If you're taking the step to grow your own food then try not to supplement your harvest with too much imported veg. Give yourself a chance to appreciate the wonder of each season and what it brings to your plate. If you celebrate your harvests as they come, your home-grown menu will never tire – there'll always be a new crop around the corner. Little can match the heavenly baton-passing of purple sprouting broccoli to asparagus and on to peas, except perhaps the anticipation of it. To be out of step with the rhythm of the seasons is to assume that tomatoes are somehow 'better' than parsnips, or that summer is superior to winter – and when you're in step every flavour is something to relish in its place in the seasonal swing.

Common garden considerations

A veg patch works best when gardener and garden are in harmony, so it pays to spend a little time being sensitive to the limitations and opportunities provided by both. The balance between ambition and practicality is a tough one to strike, and if you have to make a choice I'd urge you to come down on the side of practicality – better to make a success of something smaller than be overwhelmed.

Be realistic about the shortcomings as well as the opportunities of your plot. If you stare cold-eyed at what you have, the chances are you'll make the best of it and turn as many of the seemingly negative aspects to your advantage as is possible. Make a list of what's good and bad, and ask your partner or a friend to check it over – we aspiring gardeners can be beautifully blinkered in our enthusiasm! You may have one or two of the following common garden 'shortcomings', but don't worry, they are far from insuperable.

Limited space

The classic. What you have never seems enough – if you have a balcony you want a courtyard, if you've a courtyard you want a garden, if you've a garden then gimme a field. Everyone has limited space as far as they are concerned. In truth, no matter what size of patch, we can all grow more on it than we think we can, and whether you've a tiny garden, an urban courtyard, or a high-rise windowsill you can still claim your share of the harvest.

The secret lies in making the most of what you have, taking innovation and integration to the max, and searching out new and space-saving ways of growing your food.

One of the best ways of squeezing a harvest out of a small area is to grow your plants in containers. Pots, small raised beds, hanging baskets and planters all allow you to tailor your growing area to suit where you are. You'll need to keep a more vigilant eye on watering, replace the compost in pots every year, and perhaps offer the occasional comfrey feed (see p.215) to keep the nutrients topped up. Be inventive and look for recycling and reusing opportunities, such as colanders, large food cans and ceramic sinks – anything with drainage. This year I grew potatoes in tyres, and carrots in leaky wellies that would otherwise have been thrown out. They were both prolific and delicious.

Even a square metre patch on the ground extends skywards for as high as you like: use it. Supported by canes, tepees, netting or wires, many tall growers will give you a substantial harvest while taking up only a minimal footprint on the ground. And don't forget 'vertical' doesn't just mean upwards – balconies and hanging baskets provide the perfect base from which to grow dangling crops like tomatoes ('Tumbling Tom' is a great cascading variety) and strawberries.

Growing veg in small spaces

		SMALL BED	POTS	TYRE STACK	WINDOWSILL
LEGUMES	Broad beans	●	●		
	Borlotti beans	●	●		
	French beans	●	●		
	Peas	●	●		
	Runner beans	●	●		
BRASSICAS	Brussels sprouts	○	○		
	Cabbages	○	○		
	Calabrese	○	○		
	Cauliflower	○	○		
	Kale	○	○		
	Radishes	●	●		●
	Sprouting broccoli	○	○		
	Swede	○	○		
	Turnips	○	○		
ROOTS	Beetroot	●	●	●	
	Carrots	●	●	●	
	Celeriac	○	○		
	Celery	○	○		
	Parsnips	●	●	●	
	Salsify	○	○	○	
	Scorzonera	○	○	○	
ONIONS	Garlic	○	○		
	Leeks	○	○		
	Leeks (baby)	●	●		●
	Onions	○	○		
	Shallots	○	○		
	Spring onions	●	●		●

		SMALL BED	POTS	TYRE STACK	WINDOWSILL
CUCURBITS	Courgettes	○	●	○	
	Cucumbers and gherkins	○	●	○	
	Squash and pumpkins	○	●	○	
SALAD LEAVES	Chicory	●	●		●
	Endive	●	●		●
	Lettuces	●	●		●
	Rocket and wild rocket	●	●		●
	Sorrel	●	●		●
	Spinach	●	●		●
SOLANACEAE	Aubergines	●	●		●
	Chilli peppers	●	●		●
	Peppers	●	●		●
	Potatoes	○	●	●	
	Tomatoes	●	●		●
PERENNIAL	Asparagus	●	○		
	Cardoons	●	○		
	Globe artichokes	●	●		
	Jerusalem artichokes	●	●	●	
OTHERS	Chard and perpetual spinach	●	●		
	Edible flowers	●	●		
	Florence fennel	●	●		
	Herbs	●	●		●
	Oriental leaves	●	●		●
	Sweetcorn	●	●		

● = recommended
○ = feasible

Look for inventive ways of growing plants together. A traditional way of growing in a small space, known as the Three Sisters, allows you to grow a climbing legume, sweetcorn and a cucurbit together in mutually supporting harmony. The climber will feed the other two with its nitrogen-fixing roots while taking advantage of the sweetcorn for scaffolding, while the cucurbit (such as squash or courgette) crowds weeds out, keeps water in and cools the roots of all three. You may also find you have chances to snatch a quick crop from alongside your main harvest. If you sow salad leaves, radishes and other fast-maturing crops alongside a chilli plant in a pot for example, they will reach picking time before the chilli needs all the space in the pot.

If you have a small garden, you might wonder whether you can free up any space for vegetables. Even if you are attached to the loveliness of the flowers, you may find that the ornamentals you grow can give you something for the table too. Globe and Jerusalem artichokes, purple cabbages, fennel, giant red mustard, nasturtiums and chives are all attractive inhabitants of a border that will give you a delicious harvest.

It also pays to match up your conditions with your plants. If you've a small garden with a warm wall, get the sun lovers next to it to benefit from its extra heat, and consider painting it white to bounce those rays around even more. If you've a cool, shady or north-facing wall, get the plants which like it out of direct sun there, and consider training a morello cherry against it. You can even introduce a mini greenhouse into your small space by investing in a cloche (shown below), building a cold frame (a short, glass-lidded box), or using plastic water bottles with the bottom cut off to bring the benefits of extra heat and frost protection to your patch.

Lettuce under a cloche

You should also consider bringing the outside inside. Windowsills and porches can make your house the engine room for your plot. Great places to start seedlings off, they are also ideal for taking many plants through to harvest. As well as pots and other containers, you can keep guttering or seed trays on windowsills filled with cut-and-come-again salad leaves, giving you a continual harvest from a small space.

The secret to growing your own in a limited space is to be positive and creative. If you look hard enough, there'll be a way to grow at least some of your own food.

Extreme soil conditions

Soil pH can range anywhere from strongly acidic to strongly alkaline, and texture varies from sand to clay, with the ideal for growing most plants being somewhere in the middle of both. If you find yourself out at either end, don't worry, there is much you can do to nudge yourself towards the centre of the spectrum (see p.189).

An exposed site

While a little breeze is desirable to help air circulate, strong winds can severely limit the success of your crops. If you find yourself at their mercy more than occasionally, then I'd urge you to put up a fence at the outset. Fences, hazel or willow hurdles, or the usual array of hedging shrubs will all do the job, but if you're after a return from your boundary, consider making it edible. Many of our hedgerows offer up a seasonal harvest – of crab apples, cherries, elderberries, sloes, plums, hawthorns and more. Perhaps include something different, such as cherry plum or bay. Italian alder grows quickly with the added bonus of feeding your plot with its nitrogen-rich leaves as they fall, or get the best of both worlds with the autumn olive (*Elaeagnus umbellata*), which not only grows rapidly, it also fixes nitrogen (see p.212) and gives you lovely fruit for jam. Plant what suits your patch and your taste buds. Anything but leylandii.

A sloping site

If your patch is on a steep incline, you may think the pinnacle of your troubles is in getting your wheelbarrow from the bottom to the top, but the likelihood is that a slower, less visible process is your main enemy. As it rains, your precious soil will begin to wash away, running off with the downpour and taking with it not only your most valuable resource, but denying it the full benefit of the water soaking in.

The solution is terracing. The idea is simple – divide your slope into as few level patches as you can and as many as you need to make the steps between them practicable. It can be a tough task, and if you ask me, this is where a driver with a digger is a good investment – they'll have it done in no time. Short hedges across the slope also work wonders to arrest the downhill slip of soil, but your prime concern is to always keep the soil covered – if not with edible crops, then with green manures (see p.208) as this greatly reduces erosion.

Common gardener considerations

Never mind the soil, the climate or the aspect – your key consideration is what *you* can and can't do when it comes to dedicating time with your hands in the earth. Time, money and access are the big three limitations as far as the gardener is concerned, but these need not be obstacles, merely realities to accommodate. The soundest advice, as before, is not to bite off more than you can chew.

Starting up is all about anticipation and planning, carrying on is all about confidence and momentum. The most essential ingredient is to make sure your time in the veg patch is something you enjoy. Don't let it become a bind or chore.

Limited time

Chances are you'll not be short of competing calls for the time you'd like to spend on the plot. You'll want to get there twice as often, you'll want to stay there twice as long when you do. But do try to dedicate a little time as often as possible, rather than make lengthy but infrequent visits – and be realistic about your time commitment from the start. Match that to your plan and your reach will meet your grasp.

Creativity is your saviour when it comes to limited time. There's *always* a way of doing something smarter. Try integrating some of the high-maintenance harvests with your life rather than relying on you going to them. Keep the needy crops where you spend more of your time, whether it's outside the back door, on a windowsill, or in the office. Keep much-munched herbs in pots near the kitchen, and go for cut-and-come-again leaves on your balcony and windowsills. Let your plot come to you.

The less time you'll have to tend your plot, the more important your initial preparation is. The quality of your infrastructure becomes even more crucial, as you don't want to spend all your precious evening hauling water from a distant pipe to seedlings, nor re-edging your paths as they seek to recolonise your once-pristine beds. If time is tight then take a day's holiday in the winter before you even think about planting, to create paths that don't grow: you'll never have to spend time stopping a concrete slab encroaching on your lettuces. Keep everything simple.

Limited money

Having a veg patch will involve more than a few beans changing hands, especially in the start-up year. There are many ways of keeping costs to a minimum, and which works best depends on what you can offer.

Money is not the only exchangeable resource – time, surplus harvest, skills and machinery are the classic smallholder's currency, equally acceptable to many gardeners. Swap, sell, exchange in any way you can think of – part of the harvest in exchange for the seeds to sow it, a morning's weeding for some seed potatoes, a few hours' loan of a rotovator for help laying a path.

Seeds are often inexpensive, but if you're short on cash, planning a larger plot or are after some of the more expensive varieties the price can add up considerably. Bear in mind that your first year is likely to be the most expensive. In subsequent years you can save seed, use the remainder of the first year's and exchange some of what you have left for new varieties. To get off to an affordable start in year one, talk to friends, neighbours and fellow allotmenters. Many will have some seeds left from the previous year and be happy to barter them for a slice of the harvest.

Organised seed swaps are also becoming much more common again. If you haven't already, get used to the idea of shoeboxes and drawers full of half-empty seed packets that to everyone else are half full. That is just about the best definition of the conditions that create a market as you can get. All you have to do is link the owners of all those shoeboxes, and the best way to do that is to join a group, either physical or virtual. Sign up to local horticultural societies or try allotment groups, pin a notice up at work, tell everyone you know.

And don't forget to sign up to the River Cottage Community (see p.266). Run independently, it relies on the combined experience of thousands of members, and that's an awful lot of virtual garden fences to peak over. There's an organised seed swap every year, along with a lively Farmers' Market section for selling or requesting anything at all to do with bringing your own food to the family table.

If you're looking to turn a profit, you may be up against it, but those who are time-rich and well schooled in the art of preserving and household thrift might, just might, make growing food a sensible economic exercise. Factoring in the costs of alternative ways of getting the benefits you glean from your plot (such as going to the gym) certainly helps balance the books, but in all probability your reward will be more to do with health, happiness, and the genuinely life-enhancing pleasures that come with eating rather than feeding.

Limited access

Many aspiring growers find their nearest allotment is at the other side of town, which can limit ease of access. The issues thrown up often equate to limited time, and many of the ways of alleviating them also apply. Going for low-maintenance plants, investing in preparation and avoiding grass patches that need mowing and edging are all sensible routes to take. It's also vital to keep your seedlings where you spend more of your time – this is the stage of their lives when they need most frequent attention, so use those windowsills, balconies and porches.

On-site storage can make all the difference too, and although these may be at greater risk due to infrequent time spent at your plot, having your tools on site can make a real difference if your main mode of transport is anything other than a car. Get yourself a shed or a lock-up container (a galvanised feed bin does fine) to keep your most used tools in.

Creating your
Veg Patch

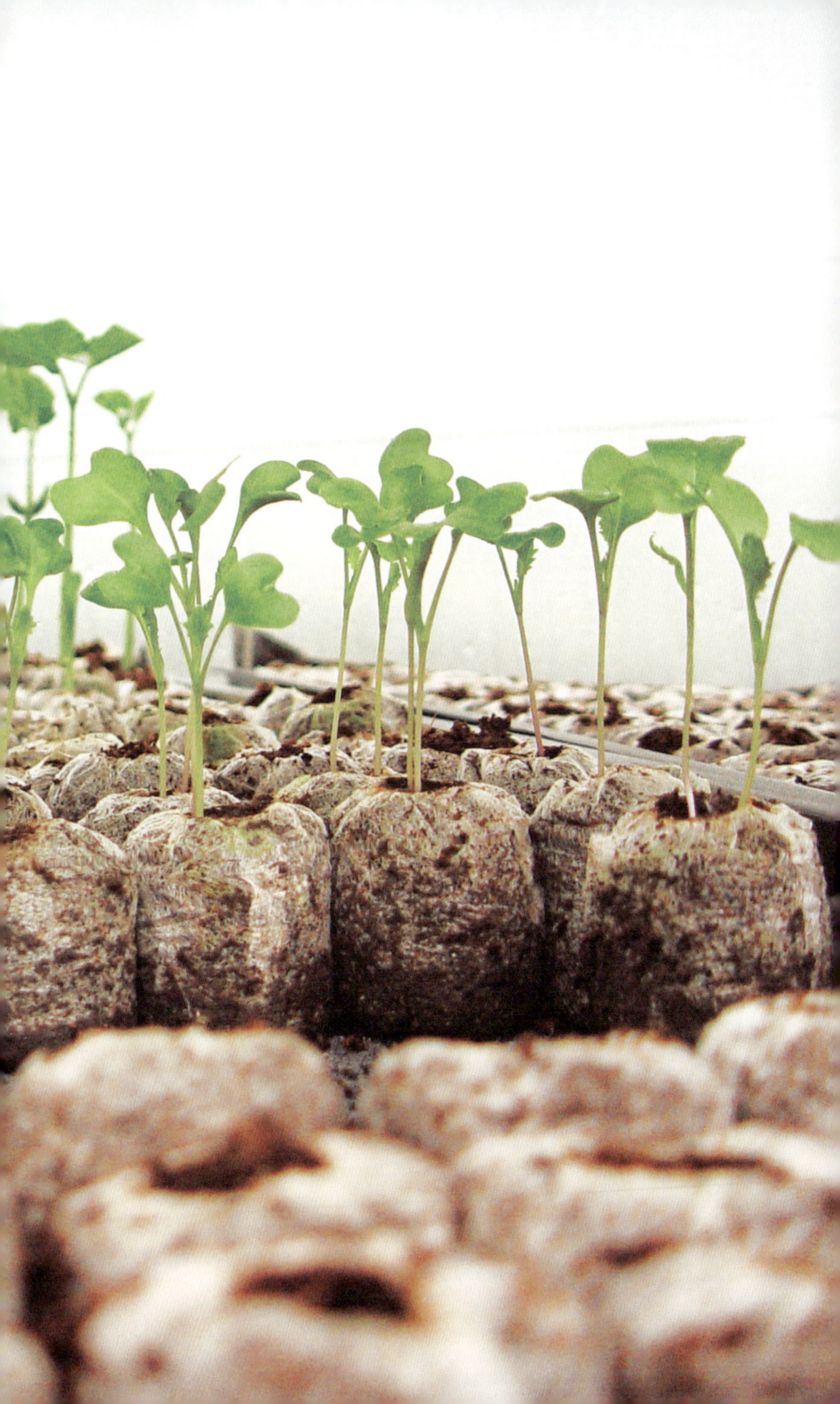

Gardeners tend to fall into two groups: those who put the majority of their energies into looking after the plants, and those who concentrate on the ground they grow in. Belong to the second group. Your primary job is to care for the soil, and it will (for the most part) look after the plants. Remember, however much of a slight it may be to your ego, it's not you that grows the plants, it's the soil – so treat it as a close friend.

I make no apologies for repeating the importance of planning: the growing year magnifies what you do well and what you do less well. Get it right and life on the plot will feel incrementally rewarding, take short cuts and you'll find you're paying for it exponentially as the ramifications compound. Every second spent bending your back in January on preparation saves a minute on your knees in April when you're busy sowing, and rewards you with an extra hour on your backside enjoying your harvest at its height. So it pays to be a little patient early on. Hold back the urge to get planting and spend a little time investing.

Clearing

The closer you can get to starting with a weed-free patch, the better. If your plot is a jungle of perennial weeds (such as ground elder, bindweed and creeping thistle), the ideal approach is to dig up any large brambles and cover the ground with a light-excluding mulch for at least a year to kill them off. Digging and ongoing weeding will only engage you in an endless wrestling match, rotovating will only multiply the enemy. The likelihood is that your plot is a step or two back from this jungle, and if so, there's little else for it but to acquaint your palms with the handle of a fork.

If you can, dig over your plot in late autumn or early winter, as this will allow a long period for the weather to break down the clods into something approaching the tilth you're aiming for. Some growers will tell you to double-dig your veg patch, which involves digging down to twice the depth of your spade's blade. I favour a minimum-dig approach, disturbing the soil structure only when essential. So, I'd recommend you dig only to the depth you have to, in order to clear the plot.

Dig up any perennial weeds like docks, roots and all, and either burn them or tie them up in a bin bag to decompose fully before incorporating them into your compost. Any annual weeds can be composted, although if you're in any doubt about what's annual and what's perennial, throw it in with the perennials to be safe. If you think you have many annual seeds in there (if it's an allotment that's been used for a while, chances are there will be), cover the plot with clear plastic for a fortnight to encourage them to germinate quickly, then hoe them off.

There are alternatives to the traditional dig-it-all-clear method, notably the no-dig approach whereby beds are created above the existing soil surface (see p.193).

Getting to know your soil

It's a good idea to learn to love your soil right from the off. You and your plants will be relying on it for sustenance and if you understand a little about its character you'll form a much stronger partnership with it. The two qualities you'll need to familiarise yourself with are soil texture and soil pH, both of which will play a large part in influencing the health of your plants... and therefore the quality of your suppers.

You can tell a lot from your soil by how it feels (see soil texture, below) but if you really want to get inside it, a professional soil analysis is undoubtedly the most thorough way to go. It's simple: send off a few trowelfuls to a soil analyst and they'll tell you about its texture and its pH (see p.189). See the directory (p.266), for those offering this service. With a professional analysis, you will also learn a little about the nutrient balance within your soil. Don't be too daunted by this: it can be interesting to uncover more about the wonderful stuff that nurtures your plants. In truth, however, if you keep adding organic matter – ideally in the form of your own compost – you'll right any significant imbalances naturally.

If you prefer the DIY approach you can also get good basic information from a few simple tests that you can carry out for yourself (see below and p.190).

Soil texture

The main mineral components of soil are clay, silt and sand. Sand particles are the largest, followed by silt, with clay particles the finest. Soils with a lot of sand are free-draining, whereas those comprised of predominantly clay particles are water-retentive and lie at the other end of the soil spectrum. It's no surprise that a reasonably equal mix of each – namely, a loamy soil – is what you're after.

The perfect loam blesses few of us. Thankfully there is much we can do to nudge things towards the happy medium, but to get there we need to know where our soil is starting from. Almost all soils will fall into one of the groups described overleaf. There are soil types outside these groups, but they are rare. In such cases, the area is unlikely to be used for cultivation (thin moorland soils, for instance) or will be famously productive (some fen soils, for example). If this applies to you, you're best to seek professional advice specific to your location.

You can do a rough-and-ready texture test yourself. Take a little of your soil, the size of a golf ball, and squeeze it gently together in your hands. If you need to, add water, a little at a time – you want just enough – until you get a putty-like consistency. Keep kneading and squeezing until you have broken any clumps down. Try to make it into a ball: if it won't hold together you have a sandy soil. If it has formed a ball, try to roll it to form a worm: if it won't you have a sandy loam (i.e. between a loam and sandy soil); if it forms a worm up to 3cm long you have a loam; a 3–6cm worm indicates a clay loam, and a longer one suggests a clay soil.

Testing soil texture

Loamy soils Loams are the gloriously desirable average, a middle ground derived from reasonably equal amounts of sand, silt and clay. These soils enjoy something of the good-draining qualities of the sand, balanced with some moisture-retaining capabilities from the clay and have good levels of nutrient availability. If you are lucky enough to have one of these soils, rejoice.

Sandy soils These freely draining soils are easy to work for most of the year and have much going for them, notably that they warm up very quickly in spring. However, their easy drainage can be a problem: the large particle size of sand creates air spaces, which allow water to move through the soil, flushing nutrients away from the roots. The soil may become more acidic and dry out as a result, which in turn can limit the availability of the remaining nutrients. This can create a 'hungry' soil, dependent on feeds. The secret is to regularly add organic matter in the form of compost, well-rotted manure and/or green manures (see p.208). Get it right and a well-balanced, yet tweaked sandy soil can be highly productive.

Clay soils When it comes to drainage, clay soils are at the other end of the spectrum to sandy soils. Clay's small particle size limits air spaces, so these soils hold on to moisture, making it harder to work, easy to compact and slower to warm up in the spring. On the upside, these soils usually have excellent reserves of nutrients – your main task is to free them up by getting air and fibre into the mix. And as with sandy soils, incorporating organic matter helps even out the imbalance and move your soil's character towards the loamy ideal. One thing you should avoid at all costs is damaging the soil structure through compaction. Never be tempted to walk, work or use machinery on a clay soil while it is wet.

Soils developed over limestone and rock These are usually alkaline, stony and fairly shallow. These characteristics combine to seriously limit the range of vegetables you can grow, so it's best to create raised beds (see p.193), infilling with bought-in topsoil, and any other organic matter you can lay your hands on.

Soil pH

This gives an indication of the relative acidity or alkalinity of the soil, which governs much of what happens in your veg patch in two ways. Firstly, plants and soil organisms tend to perform at their best within fairly narrow pH limits. As far as your veg patch is concerned, most are happiest somewhere in the middle of the scale (i.e. reasonably neutral conditions), so the nearer you get to this, the broader the range of veg you can grow. Secondly, pH affects the availability of soil nutrients. Most pertinently for the veg patch, acidic soils often have high nutrient levels but for various reasons your plants are unable to get at them.

If you've gone for a professional soil test, the results will tell you all about the pH and may offer advice about any action you may want to take. There is a good DIY alternative though, with most garden centres selling inexpensive pH testing kits. The process is a simple one: put some soil in the tube supplied, add a few drops of test solution, shake it up and leave it to settle. Comparing the colour of the resulting solution with the colour chart supplied indicates the pH of your soil. Chances are you'll have a result somewhere towards neutral, neither strongly acidic nor alkaline, but if not you may wish to take some action.

With acidic soils the usual course of action is to neutralise the acid by applying an alkali, usually lime in one form or another. Agricultural lime (naturally occurring calcium carbonate) is probably the cheapest form of lime for the grower and it can be applied at any time of the year, although best in late winter. You simply cast it over your patch at the rate suggested on the packet. This method may be slow-acting but this makes its effect on soil pH and fertility (as well as plant growth) both steady and long-lasting. Lime is available from most garden centres, countryside suppliers and specialist businesses, but make sure it comes from a sustainable source.

Very alkaline soils are extremely rare, and while it is possible to rectify them with sulphates of one sort or another, you're highly unlikely to find yourself in this position – even if your soil's starting point is alkaline to a degree. The answer to extreme alkalinity is effectively dilution, by incorporating as much organic matter in the form of compost, topsoil and well-rotted manure as you can lay your hands on.

Few of us have the time, money or inclination to aim for the holy grail of the perfect neutralish loam. Nor should we. It is worth remembering that some plants prefer conditions slightly off-centre anyway – potatoes and strawberries like it slightly acid, brassicas slightly alkaline. In practice, as long as you address extremes at the start (or you're planting to suit those conditions) you're likely to find most of what you plant will grow perfectly well. My garden is a little too acidic to be ideal, but although I haven't bothered liming, I do make sure I keep adding organic matter every year. The real point is that with just a slight increase in knowledge about your soil you'll not only understand what's going on in your patch, you'll know what to do about it should you need to. Once you've eliminated any extremes and you're somewhere in the ballpark, my advice is to relax about any limitations, plant appropriately, forget 'perfection', and enjoy the successes and the odd failure.

Creating paths and access

Life will be much easier if you make a very clear distinction between where you grow and where you walk: don't walk on your beds and don't grow your paths. To avoid walking on your beds, make sure they aren't too wide to start with (see p.175), and lay your hands on a couple of wooden planks – old scaffolding boards are ideal, being long and comparatively light. These will allow you to access the middle of your beds but spread the weight of your steps out along its length, minimising compaction. I suggest you chop one of the boards into three sections. You can then use one section if you only want to go a little into the bed, and it means that those less able to manhandle a whole plank can lay out small ones as stepping stones.

The idea of grass paths might sound lovely and green, but unless you have all the time in the world to mow and edge them, forget it. I prefer to dedicate my time to the food. Light-excluding mulch mat makes an immediately effective path; see the directory (pp.265–6) for suppliers. I used mine like that for a couple of months before covering it with a few centimetres of sand and a row of salvaged slabs.

Preparing your beds

Now that your paths are in place, you can set about preparing your beds. Imagine you're a seedling with delicate, fibrous roots branching out in search of anchorage, water and nutrients. The last place you're looking to settle in is a bed full of boulders. You want something soft and fine to nestle into, and if you get it you'll be off to as good a start as you can get.

Once you've cleared your patch of weeds (see p.186), you'll have a choice about how you take your beds to the next stage. You're after a soil of crumble-mix consistency, and there are a few ways of getting there. Hiring a rotovator can be a great timesaver. Churning up the soil as they go, rotovators are the easy way of breaking your soil down to a finer consistency, although they're not without effort on the part of the operator. If you've not used one before, imagine a loud, heavy wheelbarrow with a rather more destructive wheel. Whatever you do though, don't get the rotovator out when the soil is wet, as you'll only smear it and destroy any of the soil structure that you've worked so hard to achieve.

If there's no rotovator option, then I'm afraid there's nothing for it but to bend your back. Any time after the Christmas lights start to go up, dig your patch over to a depth of at least one and a half spits (the height of your spade's blade) and you'll have a few months of rain and frost to weather the lumps down. Around Valentine's Day, when the ground is dry, rake your whole patch over, using the back of the rake or a fork to smash up any remaining clods. Do it well, but not fanatically – it's better to do your whole patch reasonably thoroughly than concentrate madly on a quarter, then lose heart. Rake towards you, taking larger lumps to the side to bash them up some more (or out to the compost bin), then repeat at right angles.

If you have a supply of compost, now's the time to spread it about – this will give it time to start to be taken into the soil by rain and earthworms.

Tagetes and tomatoes in a raised bed

If the idea of so much digging with the upset it causes to the existing soil structure doesn't appeal, or the thought of a little exercise leaves you cold, then you can always opt for the no-dig approach. The method is championed by many who believe that the benefits of digging don't outweigh breaking apart the structure, releasing carbon from the soil and upsetting what may be a healthy ecosystem operating perfectly happily.

One of the most popular no-dig approaches is to lay decomposable material (such as thick cardboard) on the ground and cover it with a layer of compost or topsoil, at least 15cm deep. As well as allowing you to sow or plant directly into the compost layer, the cardboard kills off any weeds and grass before subsequently breaking down. It's a fantastic 'fast-forward' method, and especially effective in colonising areas of lawn. This method, with its mass of added compost or topsoil, creates a raised bed of sorts, but if you're considering the no dig approach I'd recommend that you create proper raised beds, with sides, as maintenance will be much easier.

Creating raised beds

I love raised beds. An edge around 8–10cm high looks good, makes the cultivated area distinct, and allows you to build up the soil height over time with added compost and organic matter. If it seems like a palaver, let me assure you it's another of those instances where a molehill of work upfront saves a mountain of messing about later on. Not only are edges crisp, it is easy to keep them that way. Strimming and mowing are straightforward, and the edging boards present a pretty decent barrier to weed and grass encroachment.

Raised beds also give you instant good drainage, which is what most plants prefer, and they warm up quickly in the spring allowing you to get on with growing a little earlier. So, if you're on heavy ground or shallow soil or in a cool area, I'd really recommend going for them. That little extra height also helps if you have trouble with (or an inherent resistance to) bending.

Your boards should be at least 13cm wide, 2.5cm thick and the length required. You'll also need some stakes to secure them with: 5 x 5cm and 20cm long should be fine. Allow one stake to screw the boards into in each corner and every metre or so along the sides. As with your walking boards, there are endless sources to choose from (including recycled scaffolding boards), but your nearest sawmill may well prove the best bet for locally sourced wood. Douglas fir is a great one to go for, as it is relatively cheap, looks great and ages beautifully. Also it's one of the harder softwoods, so you can use it without the chemical pressure treatments that are both unsustainable and far from ideal next to where you grow your food.

You can buy your own kits for raised beds, see the directory (p.266) for suppliers. With these, you are up and off almost immediately and you can raise them higher, change bed shapes, pick them up and move them to another site. Not surprisingly, their flexibility makes them popular with many.

Starting off your plants

With your veg patch prepared, you can start the real business of growing some food. You'll be growing most of your vegetables and herbs from seed, every one of which is a little grain of potential. It has all the ingredients within it to become the plant, its flowers and its fruit. Your job is simple: put the seed in contact with a medium that will allow it to reach this potential, when the climate is at its best to suit its needs. Mostly that's a case of sowing it on to some well-prepared ground at a particular time of year, covering it with a thin layer of compost or soil, and watering it.

Occasionally it makes sense to either start plants off indoors or to grow them in protected conditions throughout. In the Vegetable A–Z (pp.20–153), I've outlined what suits each plant best, and where there are options. Of course, you should feel free to try whatever else suits you too.

Getting started outdoors

Sowing the seed straight into your veg patch (direct sowing) is the most time-efficient way of starting off your plants. It misses out the indoor step, any potting on, the increased watering required in the warmer indoors, and saves you time and money.

Direct sowing suits the hardier plants – the salads, spinach, beans and peas, and most of the roots. As long as there is some warmth around, from mid-spring you'll be able to sow these straight into your garden with every chance of success.

Tips for starting your plants outdoors

- Prepare the ground well to give your seeds the best start in life. A fine tilth ensures easy root development
- The smaller the seed, the finer the tilth required. Larger seeds have more reserves and can live with a little hardship on the way if they really have to
- Develop a feeling for where you are. The timings in this book and on the seed packets are a great guide, but there can be a month between the earliest sowings on well-drained soils in the Southwest, and the latest in exposed or heavier soils in the North
- Water the ground lightly before you sow. It stops seed being displaced so easily and speeds germination
- Sow thinly. You can sow large seeds like peas straight from your hand, but smaller seed needs sowing from a pinch – and do it quickly to ensure thinner coverage
- Sow in drills (shallow lines). Even if you are aiming for crops to be in blocks, sow them as a series of rows. It helps ensure good spacing, plus when they start growing, you'll know if it's not in the line it's probably a weed
- Generally the larger the seed, the deeper it is sown. Broad beans to your first knuckle; carrots only with a dusting of covering soil or compost

- The seeds will generally need watering twice a week until they germinate. If the rain doesn't do it for you, fill in the gaps with the watering can
- Thin mercilessly. I have to fight sentimentality every time and remember to think of the ones that are left – they will be healthier, with access to more reserves and space
- Thin the seedlings out to their final spacing when they are a few centimetres tall, and if they are herbs and salad leaves you'll find yourself with a mini-snack to keep you going
- Weed. Weed some more, then weed again. Other plants will compete with your crops for resources, and you don't want them to. So get the hoe out – little and often is best for your sanity. It really is only a chore if you avoid it for a good while. Early in the morning on a sunny day is ideal as the severed weeds will dry up quickly. Give yourself 10 minutes' hoeing every time you go to your patch. You'll be amazed at the immediate transformation, and it will become a pleasant part of your time there
- Every month, make a habit of sharpening your hoe. It will make your weeding so much more pleasurable and efficient

Broad beans emerging

Getting started indoors

It is better to start some plants indoors, or 'under cover' – partly for convenience and in some cases for necessity. Many (such as French beans, tomatoes, courgettes) are not resistant to the cold, so you are unable to sow them outside until the temperature reaches a certain level. Starting them off indoors (in a polytunnel, greenhouse, cloche, or on your windowsill) ensures they have this temperature earlier in the season, and allows you to get them to a reasonable size before you plant them out – when the outdoor temperature is warm enough. And if your plants are ahead, then your harvest will be too.

Also, you may want an earlier crop than from those you sow direct. Peas, beans and salads all get started off in my polytunnel to go outside around the same time as I sow more direct, giving me an earlier crop to go alongside my outdoor-sown one.

Growing under cover gives you much more control over the environment, so you can be more certain that your plants have a gentler start. Strong winds won't be damaging them, and pests aren't given free rein. Germination and survival are usually more successful, so for the extra work before they hit your patch you get extra rewards, and you save the thinning time. They'll also be less vulnerable to the nibblers that like to munch on them. And don't forget, sowing indoors doesn't just provide a protected environment for the plants, it means you are okay to get on with growing when the soil's cold, the weather's wet and the wind's howling.

The chance of your seeds turning into plants and then into delicious food rests very much with their start in life, and the growing medium you choose is a big consideration. Don't mess about, get yourself some good stuff. It needs to be of a fine texture, and of the right nutrient balance, see the directory (pp.265–6) for suppliers. And don't be tempted to go for those growing mediums containing environmentally unsustainable peat. Its extraction releases greenhouses gases and reduces an already endangered and valuable habitat.

Using your compost couldn't be easier. Fill whatever you're sowing into around three-quarters full of compost; this will allow for it to swell when watered. Sow your seed to the depth advised on the packet (see also p.194). It's that simple.

There are a few ways of starting your plants off indoors, each with its own advantages, as follows:

Module trays A great way of starting off your seedlings, these trays are separated into cells, one for each seed. It's simple: the initial spacing is done for you, the plant gets to a good size before it requires moving, and you don't damage any plants when you're taking them out. It's also a great way of starting off all those that hate root disturbance, including most of the brassicas and the Mediterranean favourites like tomatoes. You can always sow two seeds to a cell if you want to be sure of at least one coming up per cell.

Jiffy 7s

Seedlings in a module tray

Jiffy 7s These small cylinders contain a growing medium of coir (recycled coconut fibre) with just about enough nutrients to get your seeds off to a good start. Coming as dehydrated flat counters, a few minutes in water swells them into shape ready to use. Sow one or two seeds into each and keep them watered, preferably in a tray lined with capillary matting to retain moisture. Plant them straight out when the seedlings are 3cm or so high, tearing the tissuey covering a little to let the roots through. Avoid the Jiffy 7s made with peat.

Root trainers Essentially long modules, root trainers are especially suited to plants that enjoy a long root run early in life – the peas and beans in particular. They are worth the investment, or you can take the homemade approach: toilet roll inners filled with compost are cheap and effective, and just as good – with the cardboard decomposing when you plant them out.

Seed trays I am not a great fan of seed trays. With all those plants squashed in together, you damage half of them getting the other half out, and then there's all that separating and potting on. If you really want to use them, remember that when your seedlings have reached 3cm or so tall and have their second pair of leaves, they'll need separating and transferring into a bigger pot, before planting out into your patch when they get to the right size. This is the process known as 'pricking out'. As you try to tease the seedling out of the soil in the seed trays, hold the leaves rather than the stem, as the plants can regrow leaves more easily if they get damaged. You do get more seedlings for less space than in modules so if space is short, seed trays may be for you.

Guttering Sarah Raven introduced me to the idea of using guttering to raise seedlings indoors and I can't recommend it highly enough. It may seem a touch ridiculous at first, but this method really does pay off. All you do is saw the guttering to the length that you want, fill it with compost and sow in the usual way. Try it. Its semi-circular profile saves compost, fits on a windowsill, and is cheap to get hold of. On top of that, guttering *feels* right. It sits in your hands perfectly, making carrying your seedlings about simpler. I also think that the extra surface area of black plastic treats your emerging plants to a little extra heat too. Everything about it makes sense: the compost is concentrated where the plant needs it, watering is reduced as a result, and you can either gently ease the whole length of seedling-filled compost into a prepared ditch in your plot, or tear them off one at a time for planting out.

Pots These use a lot of compost compared to the other methods, so I tend to use them only for the big-seeded cucurbits which appreciate the extra room from the off. For starting your plants off, you have a choice between biodegradable and plastic pots. Coir pots are made from an otherwise unused by-product of the coconut industry and on the face of it are excellent green alternatives to plastic (i.e. oil-based)

Growing seedlings in guttering

containers. However, their green credentials are partly compromised by the distance they travel to reach you and the fact that they are designed to biodegrade. Although this sounds like an advantage, it actually means that all the energy that goes into their creation is used only once. Being 'green' is rarely black and white. Sturdy plastic pots can, of course, be used again and again. I can't make up my mind which is greener, so I tend to use some of each. It's worth remembering that some garden centres will take (and make available) pots for recycling.

Tips for getting off to a good start indoors

- Get your timing right. Refer to the Vegetable A–Z (pp.20–153) for sowing times for each plant. Although the seasons are famously unpredictable, a useful guide is to work back 5 or 6 weeks from when you'd normally expect the last frost and sow then. This gives just the right length of time for the plants to establish themselves before going out into the big wide world with confidence
- As with outside, sow thinly – that way you'll avoid having to thin too much
- Water very, very lightly until your seeds germinate. Try one of those misters usually used for cacti. You want moist but not wet soil, as seeds can easily rot
- For smaller seeds, put your pot (or whatever you're sowing in) on a tray and pour water into the tray – the water soaks up into the pot, which avoids disturbing the delicate seeds
- If you can see roots at the bottom of your chosen container it's time to plant them out. If the weather's not right, then you'll have to pot them on

Planting out

When your seedlings reach the right size, indicated in the Vegetable A–Z (pp.20–153), they are ready to be planted out, and this is the point at which they are at their most vulnerable. As with children heading off to their first day at school, anything you can do to smooth the transition the better it will be for them, and in turn for you.

Any plants started off under cover will benefit from hardening off. For 4 or 5 days take them outside in the day, and get them back under cover for the night. They'll get accustomed to the shift in conditions and be less shocked when planted out.

Water your seedlings well an hour or so prior to planting out, and, if possible, plant them out in the early morning. This will give them all day to get used to their new home, enjoy the sun and get ready for the dark, cooler evening.

Dig the hole or trench *before* you ease the seedling out of its first home, to avoid it drying out – even a little. And do take great care when extracting your seedlings from whatever they've begun life in. If you've sown into modules, gently squeeze around each cell from beneath and (if you have to lend a persuasive tug) grab hold of a leaf (it can grow another) rather than the stem.

Once in place, firm the soil around your seedling, and water in well.

Maintaining your Veg Patch

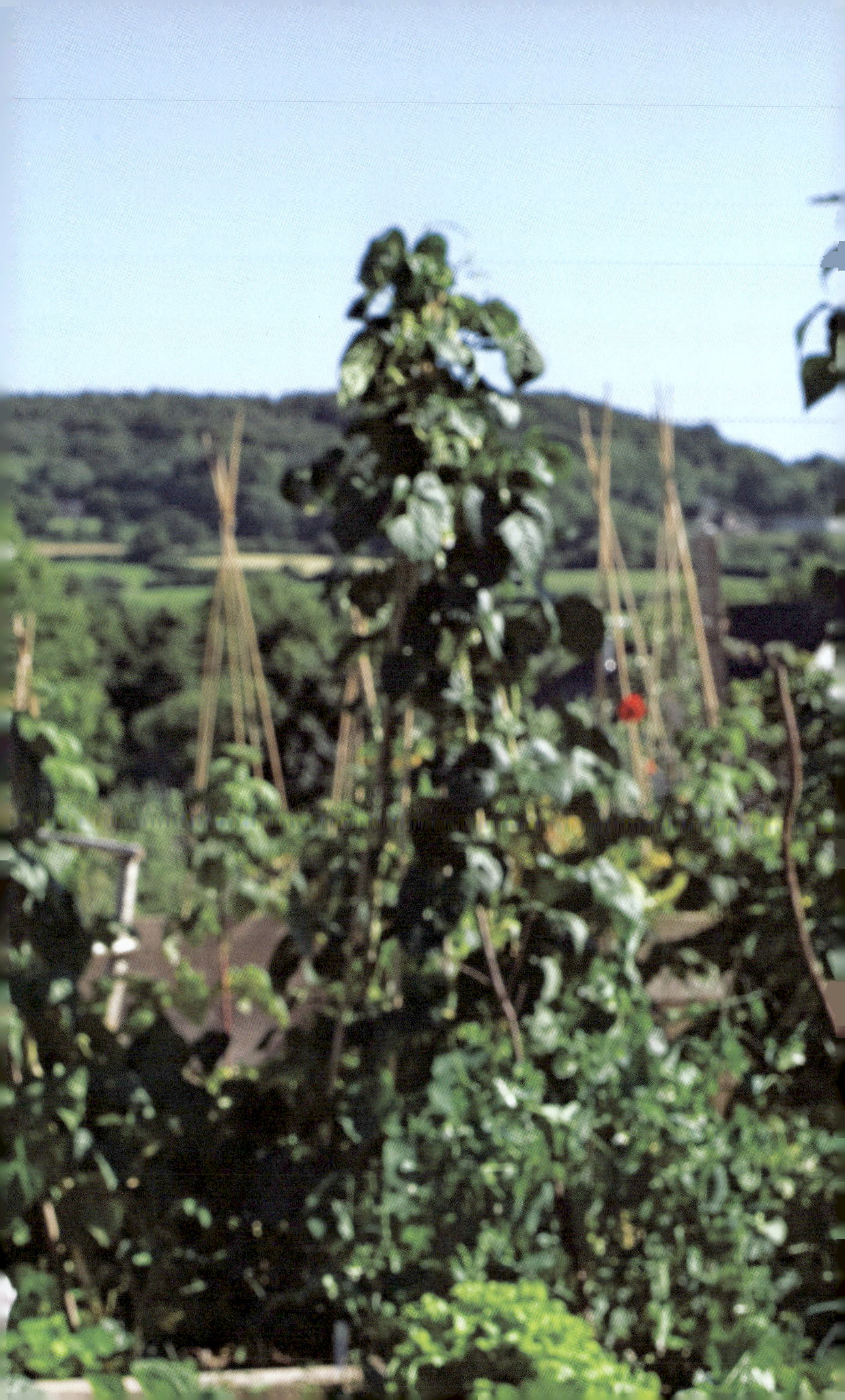

Ensuring your veg patch

is at its fittest is largely a matter of developing some good habits. You'll need to look after the soil, take care of the plants and keep a regular eye out for pests. Keep this hierarchy in mind and you'll give yourself every chance of a healthy and productive plot.

Your focus should be very much on the soil, as it is the cornerstone of maintaining your veg patch. Organic matter in general and compost in particular are vital to its health. Take the time to learn how to make compost and use other forms of organic matter (see pp.207–10) and you'll encourage a balanced environment for growth. As a consequence, your plants will be healthier, and less troubled by pests. You'll also ensure that, as the years roll by, your soil increases in vitality and health, rather than diminishes.

Once in a while the plants themselves will require your attention – some will need supporting, or an extra feed to help them keep pumping out their harvest. Mostly it's a matter of detail, but it can make all the difference to maximising your harvests, so take time to become familiar with ways of lending your plants a helping hand (see pp.211–15).

Once in a while, despite your best efforts, the pests will come and you will need to know how to deal with them, though you are unlikely to encounter a biblical plague. Pests are more inclined to be quietly tedious – so it's best to be quietly tedious back. Get out there every few evenings and you'll spot them early and be able to deal with them quickly. I've included a guide to recognising and dealing with the main nuisances (see pp.216–19).

If you find yourself looking for the section on pesticides, weedkillers and man-made fertilisers, I'm afraid I'll have to disappoint you. Given that these cause long-term harm for short-term gain, there's no reason to carry on growing that way. In any event it's easy not to, it's healthier not to, and – as endless studies show – yields from organic growing are typically higher over time.

Looking after your soil

The act of growing, for the most part, takes from your soil. As well as using sunlight and water for growth and development, your plants draw in nutrients from the soil (such as nitrogen and potassium) in order to produce the roots, leaves, stems and flowers that you eat. Rotation helps to keep this reduction in soil reserves to a minimum, but the nutrient cycle will spiral downwards unless you step in and play an active part in replenishing it, and that means putting a few sustainable practices in place from the start.

The best ways to do this are to make your own compost and to grow nourishing crops, known as green manures, between your main harvests.

Compost

Nosing through Jane Perrone's excellent *Allotment Keeper's Handbook*, I was slapped across the face by a Bette Midler quote:

'My whole life had been spent waiting for an epiphany, a manifestation of God's presence, the kind of transcendent, magical experience that lets you see your place in the big picture. And that is what I had with my first compost heap.'

I'd been wondering how to convey the enormity of what composting is all about, to try and tie what is on the face of it a faintly ridiculous, grubby little pastime with our place in the world, and our world's place in the whatever, and I have to confess I was struggling. The last thing I was prepared for was Bette Midler doing it in a few dozen well-chosen words.

Compost is about the best all-round treatment you can give your soil. It boosts nutrient status, helps retain moisture, improves soil structure and if laid straight on top of your soil makes a wonderful mulch. Most of what your household throws out can go in it, and that's the beauty of making compost. You're turning the waste from today's meal into something that nurtures your supper tomorrow. Added to that, you're cutting down the contribution to landfill.

Making a compost bin

Strictly speaking you don't need a bin to make your own compost, but in reality it is easier to contain and manage your compost if you do. Plastic bins look neat and are an instant solution – your local council may offer them at a reasonable price. Alternatively, you can also make your own.

The simple, classic design is for a square enclosure with a front that can be opened to make adding material easy. The cheapest construction uses wooden pallets or corrugated iron securely fixed in place to form three of the sides, with a front of wooden slats or another pallet (loosely tied in place) for access. It functions satisfactorily, especially to get you started in producing your own compost. If, however, you're looking for something a little more aesthetically pleasing and with a longer lifespan, then you can create sturdy wooden compost bins without huge expense or any tools other than a saw and a hammer.

Having one compost bin in your garden will work perfectly well, but you need to keep turning the compost in order to aid decomposition. In an ideal world, it is best to have three adjacent bins, as this makes turning easy and ensures that compost that's almost ready to use isn't being added to. The process is simple: use the first bin to add to, then when it's full, turn it into the second bin and begin filling the first with new material. Keep turning the compost in bin 2 from time to time, watering as you do so – this will accelerate the decomposition dramatically. When it's almost ready (or bin 1 becomes full), turn bin 2 into bin 3, and use when it's ready.

Siting your bin on a level, well-drained sunny spot on top of soil allows excess water to get out, worms to get in, and the sun to warm it and speed up the process of decomposition. If concrete is your only option, start the bin off with a layer of soil or (if you have it) your own compost – this will bring in the worms and ensure a population of beneficial organisms gets to work.

Making compost isn't tricky. It's something that will happen anyway – try stopping a potato peeling from decomposing. All you need do is foster the conditions for it to happen quickly and efficiently, and you'll have brown gold aplenty.

Suitable material for your compost bin

Your compost bin will happily convert much of what you'd otherwise throw out into compost, but a little organisation will make it happen quickly and efficiently. Think of your ingredients as belonging to one of two groups: the Greens and the Browns.

The Greens are rich in nitrogen and many are activators that stir the slower-rotting Browns into quicker action. These prime greens include:
- Diluted urine (half a pint of urine to a gallon of water)
- Grass cuttings
- Nettles
- Comfrey leaves

Other Greens you should happily add include:
- Raw vegetable peelings
- Tea bags and coffee grounds
- Young annual weeds, but avoid weeds with seeds at all costs
- Unwoody prunings
- Animal manure from herbivores such as cows and horses (organic is ideal)
- Poultry manure and bedding

The Browns are carbon-rich, and slower to rot than the Greens, but the incorporation of the Green activators breaks them down at a fair pace. The Browns include:
- Waste paper – shredded or torn up is best
- Cardboard
- Bedding from vegetarian pets such as rabbits
- Tough hedge clippings
- Woody prunings – shredded or chopped is best
- Old bedding plants
- Sawdust and wood shavings
- Bracken
- Fallen leaves

'Reuse' comes above 'recycle' in the environmental hierarchy, so where possible it's greener to pass the magazines to your local doctor or dentist for others to read rather than putting them in your compost.

There are a few very definite no-gos when it comes to your compost bin. Meat, fish, dairy and cooked food (including bread) are all likely to attract pests, especially rats. Cat litter and dog faeces can bring any number of parasites and unwanted organisms into your food chain. Avoid putting these in your bin at all costs. Although some plant diseases will be killed off in your compost heap, I tend to lean towards safety and tie any infected plants in a bin bag along with nutrient-rich perennial weeds such as docks, leaving them to break down for a few months (until the larger weeds are unrecognisable) before adding it to the compost heap. Quarantining them in this way means you kill them off no matter how long it takes, rather than leaving a hostage to fortune in your compost.

Any wood shavings, especially if from shredded conifers, not only take a while to decompose in the heap but (if they haven't completely broken down in the compost) can also lock up valuable soil nitrogen, depriving your precious plants for at least a season. It's best to add shavings only in small quantities along with Green activators, or if you have the space, leave them in a pile for a couple of years to break down. Avoid using them at all if the wood has been treated with preservatives. The golden rule in adding to your compost heap is 'if in any doubt, leave it out'.

Wooden compost bins

With compost (as with most things) the more you put in the more you get out. Generally your compost will be ready in 9 months to a year, but if you're after a quick turnaround it can be made in as little as 2 months. The secret is in the turning. The more you mix your compost, or turn it into a neighbouring compost bin, the more air gets incorporated, and air is exactly what decomposing organisms love. Air and water that is. As you turn your compost, give it a good watering, even better if you can make that from your own (ahem) personal tap.

The amalgamated ingredients will begin to break down, reducing in volume, and gradually turning dark brown when the process is complete. It may not be as crumbly and lump-free as you're used to seeing in compost bags from the garden centre, but as long as it is sweet-smelling and earthy it will be perfectly usable. If you can sieve it or pull out any big bits (such as twigs) then do, and return them to your bin to break down some more.

Tips for the best compost

Given time, even the most clumsily constructed pile will decompose, but if you're after the finest compost there is, here are a few steps to help you along the way:

- Use more or less equal volumes of Greens and Browns, but your own mix will need to take into account your site, the weather and the time you're able to put into it – learn from your experiences, and remember...
- Greens and Browns regulate each other: if your compost is too wet, add more Browns; if it's too dry, add some Greens
- Ensure that you don't use too thick a layer of either at once – the best compost is formed most efficiently when Greens and Browns are as integrated as possible
- Use green activators like grass cuttings to activate otherwise slow-rotting Browns
- Don't shy away from using some of the tougher Browns. They may break down more slowly on their own, but in combination with the Greens they provide essential bulk and structure to your finished product. If you maximise their surface area by chopping or shredding, you'll find the accelerating Greens will nudge them along
- If you can, have three bins side by side and keep turning and watering them.

Speeding up your compost

If you're feeling particularly enthused and want to make fantastic compost in record time, you can always have a bash at adding a bit of heat to your heap. The principles are the same as for any compost, but the smaller you shred your material before adding it to the heap the better, as this creates a greater surface area for decomposition to take place. Shears are good for chopping up small amounts, but for woodier material, if your mower is sturdy enough, make a low pile and mow over it to take it down a grade or two. If you've a lot to get through, consider hiring a chipper.

The key to heat is thorough and frequent mixing, and ensuring everything is damp as you do it, as the two big agents of decomposition are water and air. After a week or so you'll notice the heap is getting warm. This is a good sign, as it indicates biological action is under way. It may even get positively hot – a neighbour even baked a potato in his (it took only a couple of hours to cook through).

A week or two later the compost may start to cool. As soon as you notice this turn it again, trying to get the centre of the heap to the outside and vice versa. Add more water (or urine) if you need to, or more material if it is more than damp. The heap should warm up well again as the aerobic organisms get back to full steam. You can repeat this a few times if you want, but at some stage the heating effect will diminish. When you reach this stage, you can leave the heap to finish off by itself.

You can add compost at any time of the year, but a month or two before spring kicks in will ensure your beds get a much-needed boost for the hard work ahead.

Other sources of organic matter

The ideal is to create a closed system of nutrients for your veg patch, whereby your life adds all the nutrients to rebalance those taken out by the plants you eat, but sometimes practical considerations make it unattainable. Luckily, there are endless off-site sources for organic matter that will enrich your soil.

Farmyard manure Full of beneficial nutrients, source it from an organic holding if you can. You'll need to let it compost well (for at least 6 months) before you add it to your patch, to allow it to settle chemically and biologically. This also allows time for any worming treatments to degrade – they don't just kill the animals' worms, they'll do for earthworms too!

Chicken manure Very high in nutrients, this is best added to your compost to dilute it, rather than added direct to your soil, as it can be very concentrated.

Mushroom compost Having been used for growing mushrooms, this spent compost is low in nutrients but an excellent source of fibre for the soil, helping its structure and in so doing raising the availability of the nutrients in it. It may be mildly alkaline, so not the one to go for if you're on chalky ground (see p.189).

Seaweed Pick a carrier bag full of this potassium-rich plant yourself if you live near the coast, washing it clean of salt, before adding it to the surface as an excellent feeding mulch. Or you can mix into your compost bin.

Straw, hay, grass and old animal bedding From chickens and pigs, these are good sources of organic matter, but best added to your compost to decompose first.

Green manures

This magical group of plants acts as a living manure, soil improver and/or fertiliser. They tend to be short-term crops that grow a mass of foliage rapidly, covering the soil and suppressing weeds, thereby minimising erosion, nutrient leaching and compaction. On top of that, some green manures root deeply, aerating the soil, drawing minerals to the surface and helping to break up the ground, which is particularly useful if you have clay soil. Some (such as clover) belong to the legume family, taking nitrogen from the air and making it available in the soil to feed the vegetables that follow. When you need the space again, your green manures can then be composted or dug in to improve soil structure.

There are many green manures to choose from to suit your purpose, although they are particularly good to grow over winter, acting like a duvet for the soil as well as improving its structure and fertility through what for many are the least productive months. The table opposite covers the best green manures, an idea of when to use them and the benefits they offer.

Crimson clover

Green manure	Sow	Cut/Dig in	Nitrogen fixer?	Characteristics
Agricultural lupins	March–June	Sept–Nov	Yes	Does well in an acid soil. Treat as a legume in the rotation.
Agricultural mustard	March–Sept	Sept–Nov	Yes	Very fast-growing, giving good quick coverage. Treat as a brassica in the rotation.
Alfalfa	May–July	3 months later or overwinter	Yes	Rich in elements needed for good growth. Treat as a legume in the rotation.
Buckwheat	April–Aug	3 months later or longer	No	Very quick growing. Flowers attract beneficial insects. Does well on poor ground (which it improves).
Crimson clover	March–Aug	3 months later or overwinter	Yes	Flowers attract beneficial insects (especially bees). Treat as a legume in the rotation.
Field beans	Sept–Nov	After winter	Yes	Excellent coverage.
Hungarian grazing rye	Aug–Sept	March–May	No	Good, quick coverage.
Phacelia	March–Sept	3 months later or overwinter in the South	No	Beautiful flowers that attract beneficial insects, especially bees. Quick, tall growth.
Red clover	April–Aug	2 months to 2 years later	Yes	Flowers attract beneficial insects. Ideal for growing long term. Treat as a legume in the rotation.
Tares	March–Sept	March–May	Yes	Excellent fertility builder. Treat as a legume in the rotation.
White clover	April–Aug	3 months later or longer	Yes	Low-growing. Flowers attract beneficial insects. Ideal for growing long term. Treat as a legume in the rotation.

Mulches

A mulch is simply any layer of material placed on the surface of the soil. Its primary role is to suppress weeds, but most mulches help to retain water in summer, reduce run off in winter, deter pests, and limit temperature fluctuations simply by acting as an insulating blanket. There are endless possibilities to choose from. Flattened cardboard boxes do the basic job perfectly well, but compost is the best all-rounder – bringing all of those benefits while adding nutrients and improving soil structure as it gradually works its way into the soil (or rather rain and worms work it in for you). Hay, straw, seaweed and spent mushroom compost are also excellent choices, working well as suppressors, barriers and insulators but they usually need clearing away, composting and replacing after a while.

Loose mulches are easy to use. Water the ground well first to ensure the soil has a good initial reserve, then spread a reasonable layer (at least 5cm) of your mulch around your plants to reap the benefits. If you have large uncultivated areas or are leaving a bed (or even your whole plot) without crops for a while, then you're best going for a living mulch in the form of a green manure (see p.208). Anywhere that requires long-term mulching, such as paths, will need a more durable covering. Permeable, breathable, hardwearing mulch mat is ideal, and comes in rolls of anything from 1–5-metre widths, see the directory (pp.265–6) for suppliers.

Squash growing through biodegradable cornstarch mulch

Looking after your plants

The best thing you can do to promote healthy plants is to look after the soil. The rest is largely detail, but in the detail lies the few per cent that can make all the difference. Some plants require physical support while they attempt to scramble skywards for the space, light and ventilation they need to deliver a really bountiful crop.

It also helps to understand companion planting (see p.212), whereby plants work in sweet partnership, often to mutual advantage. Learning to foster these happy alliances will do much to maximise your harvest and minimise the pests.

There are also a few highly productive food factories, like courgettes and beans, which really benefit from a nutritious boost to keep them at maximum productivity. You don't need to rush out and buy these, all you need is a few nettles (easy to source) or a corner dedicated to the marvel that is the comfrey plant.

Supporting plants

Although most of your plants will happily throw out edible bits for you to feast on, the odd one will need a little help on its way to harvest time. Most peas, some beans, and a few varieties of sweetcorn will all be grateful of either canes, netting or twine to help them keep to the vertical. Where possible, take advantage of what's already there. Grow climbers along a wire fence, tack a little netting to a wall or try the Three Sisters method (see p.180).

If you're growing rows of climbers, push canes or stakes of at least 2-metre length into the ground a few centimetres away from your seedling or the place you intend to plant it, tying them together at the top with their opposite cane. What you'll end up with is a triangular tunnel with your plants growing up the sides.

Another way that looks beautiful and is equally suitable for pot growing is training your climbers up a tepee. Spacing will vary a little depending on your crop, but 30cm between stakes is usual, with two plants growing up each cane. Push the stakes in well, and tie them together at the top – preferably leaving one 'side' open to form a C shape, so that you can get to the inside to harvest any crops before they over-mature. If you have it to hand, hazel lengths work really well, otherwise bamboo canes are probably your cheapest option. A tip I picked up from Simon Hansford, head gardener before me at River Cottage, is to grow beans on an 'X' frame so that the beans hang on the outside of the canes, making harvesting easier. Whatever you're growing, using whatever supporting system, plant on the inside of the canes as you're less likely to damage the plants with the hoe or your size 10s.

Dwarf varieties supposedly do perfectly well without support, but many (especially peas) will benefit from some of the twiggier hazel growth pushed fat end into the soil, lending the tendrils something to latch on to and preventing any pods trailing along the ground.

Companion planting

This technique of growing plants in close proximity with the aim of benefiting at least one of them is enchanting. Careful partnering can achieve so many ends. Sow in the right combinations and you'll attract beneficial insects to your patch for pollinating flowers and hoovering up aphids; you'll be able to disguise the scent of crops vulnerable to pests that navigate by smell, accumulate otherwise unavailable minerals and/or nitrogen for neighbouring or subsequent crops, or simply provide physical help such as shelter and support. Some (such as nasturtiums) even lay down their leaves, to attract pests away from the crop destined for your kitchen.

For the organic vegetable grower, companion planting ranks alongside rotation and soil health as one of your foremost weapons against pests and diseases, so it pays to know a little about it. I've noted some of the more commonly used companions earlier, but the table opposite should help influence your planting plans. It won't leave you pest-free, but it will form a harmonious, eco-friendly first line of defence. And once you start exploring the possibilities of companion planting, you'll be hooked.

If you only have time to experiment with a few companions in your first year then try the following:
- Plant spring onions or chives in with your carrots – carrot fly can smell carrots from up to a mile away, but the onion family mask their carroty smell
- Plant basil near your tomatoes as it attracts aphids to it, and away from your precious tomatoes
- Sow nasturtiums near your beans and lettuces – they are a great sacrificial plant, attracting cabbage white butterflies away from your more precious harvests.

Pot marigold attracting pollinators to the veg patch

Companion	Companion for	Benefit
Onion family	Many vegetables	Disguises the scents of other vulnerable harvests, notably protecting carrots from carrot fly
Basil	Tomatoes, aubergines	Attracts aphids away from more vulnerable harvests
Borage	Tomatoes, squash	Attracts pollinating insects and repels tomato worm
Coriander	Most vegetables	Repels aphids and carrot fly, and attracts bees when allowed to flower
Hyssop	Brassicas	Repels cabbage white butterflies and attracts pollinating insects if allowed to flower
Marigolds (*Tagetes* sp.)	Most vegetables	Produces chemicals in its roots, which deter nematodes, slugs and wireworms
Mint	Cabbage, tomatoes, radish	Deters cabbage white butterflies, aphids and flea beetles
Nasturtiums	Brassicas	Attract cabbage white butterflies away from brassicas and lettuces
Nettles	Legumes and brassicas	Attract aphids and cabbage white butterflies away from legumes and brassicas
Oregano	Brassicas	Repels cabbage white butterflies, and attracts beneficial insects when flowering
Pot marigold (*Calendula officinalis*)	Tomatoes, asparagus	Repels tomato worm, whitefly and asparagus beetle
Rosemary	Legumes, brassicas, carrots	Repels cabbage white butterflies, bean beetle and carrot fly, and attracts beneficial insects when flowering
Sage	Brassicas, carrots, radish	Repels cabbage moth, carrot fly, and flea beetle
Thyme	Brassicas	Attracts beneficial insects when flowering, and may repel whitefly, cabbage worms

Comfrey

Comfrey feeds

Looking a little like untidy borage, comfrey grows rapidly with roots that drive deep down into the soil, dragging otherwise inaccessible minerals up to accumulate above ground. It is these reserves that make comfrey such a star in your garden. Nitrogen, potassium and phosphorus form the holy trinity of nutrients that most plant growth depends on, and comfrey has them in abundance.

Forget the artificial chemicals. Growing comfrey is a natural, cut-and-come-again way of adding a few nutrients while you water. Its quick-growing nature makes for a natural fertiliser factory, which you can utilise in a number of ways. Cut leaves, laid as a mulch, will gradually liberate their minerals as they break down, or act as a wonderful accelerator if incorporated into your compost heap, but I use comfrey most as a liquid feed.

Making your own comfrey feed is simple: fill an old onion net or similar with torn-up comfrey leaves and suspend it in your water butt. Over the next few weeks it will decompose in the water to create comfrey tea. I'll warn you, it smells like a tram driver's glove, but you'll soon learn to love it when you see the lift it gives to any of your fruiting plants – tomatoes, courgettes and beans in particular will thank you for a drink of it. Give them a good watering, or spray the leaves, any time from flowering onwards and they will repay you with a heftier harvest.

If you do not have a water butt, chop the bottom off a large upturned water bottle and fill it with comfrey leaves, placing half a brick or something similar on top to keep the leaves under pressure. Over the next week or two, they will begin to breakdown and leach their dark liquid into the neck. Then you simply undo the lid, decant, and dilute the goo with water in the ratio of 15:1 for use. You can also make tea in the same way using nettles, though their chemical balance is more towards nitrogen (good for growth) than potassium (best for fruiting), so use it when it's growth that you want to encourage. Bought seaweed feeds do a similar job but they are comparatively costly.

There are a number of varieties of comfrey, but lay your hands on the Bocking 14 comfrey if you can, see the directory (pp.265–6) for suppliers. It's a sterile variety and therefore doesn't set seed, which allows you to control its footprint (comfrey can be very invasive). If you want to expand your supply of this marvellous resource, dig up a root in winter and slice it into counters the thickness of a pound coin. Sow each counter 3cm deep in a pot filled with compost. Roots will soon form, ready for planting out any time from late spring.

It's hard not to be a little evangelical about comfrey once you start using it and see the results. It has the big-hitting macronutrients that are essential for plant growth, it looks amazing and its flowers bring endless beneficial insects to your plot. And it's pretty much free.

Pests and diseases

Pests and diseases could fill a whole (admittedly rather dull) book of their own. That said, the main threats to the frequency and enormity of your haul are largely predictable, easy to identify and few in number. If you rotate your crops and look after the soil, and pair up your crops with their helpful companions you will be giving yourself every chance of minimising troubles, but some pest and disease tedium comes with the territory.

I've tried to cover the most probable causes, along with prevention and any remedies, for each of the foods in the Vegetable A–Z (pp.20–153), and gone into further detail below about the most likely troublemakers. But there will come a time when something cleans you out of a tasty crop – the one you were most looking forward to, no doubt. It's rare, but it happens. Learn what you can from it, but get used to it: pests and diseases are part of life's rich travesty in the veg patch.

If you're unfortunate enough to turn up some weird malady that doesn't seem to fit these descriptions, don't be shy of getting on the internet if you have access. Any number of sources will be able to help you, see the directory (see pp.265–6) for a few starting points. Otherwise this is where having signed up to a club or society, or growing on a shared space, really comes into its own. Bending the ear of fellow allotmenters or gardeners is all part of the sociable fun of it.

Slugs and snails These will almost certainly be your number one enemy, clearing vast tracks of seedlings and stripping larger leaves to their bones. In my experience there is no universal panacea when it comes to dealing with them – so hit them with a range of methods for limiting their number. Copper tape gives them an electric shock (it cheers my heart just to read those words), but is usually impractical for defending your whole patch. Still, if you've any particularly precious plants in smaller beds or pots this is well worth investing in. Slug pubs are another favourite: sink a yoghurt carton or similar down to soil level and fill it with beer, which seems to attract the slimemakers for one last drink in the saloon before they fall in and drown. It's what 3 per cent lager was made for.

There are biological controls available to you as well, see the directory (p.266) for suppliers. Most are tiny nematodes, worms that are harmless to us and delightfully harmful to slugs in particular. They can be expensive if you're relying on them to police a large area, but excellent for particularly intensive or smaller areas. Slugs and snails are not overly keen on sandy, gritty surfaces, although I usually find that the simple act of gardening soon covers the grit I've put down. If you ask me there's little to beat dusk patrol, harvesting them in a bucket for the chickens or snipping them in half. You need to get used to them too, they'll always be there – but if you hit them hard and keep knocking them back (and accept a little loss here and there) the balance of things will remain on your side.

Common striped snail

Cabbage white caterpillar

Caterpillars Butterflies, especially the cabbage white, come to your plot looking for somewhere to lay their eggs; more specifically they're looking for a food supply for the caterpillars that will eventually emerge. Luckily for you, it's pretty much just one corner of your patch that flashes 'Caterpillar food' to them in huge neon lights – the brassicas. If you've too much time on your hands then here's an excuse to buy one of those pocket-sized identification books, otherwise you'll be happy to know that caterpillar ID is irrelevant to the remedy – here we have the perfect daytime use for your dusk patrol slug bucket. Birds will help you out to some degree, but there's no substitute for regular checks. And don't wait for the caterpillars, go looking for the eggs as soon as you see the butterflies about and rub them off. Fine netting can work in excluding butterflies, but I hate that barrier between me and the plants so I don't bother with it.

Aphids Most aphids will come to your plot in the form of tiny green- and blackfly. You'll find they mainly target soft young growth in spring, the underside of new leaves and growth tips in particular. For the most part they are a relatively harmless nuisance, but if they establish in larger numbers they can seriously weaken a plant, as well as passing on diseases as they move from plant to plant. You're much less likely to encounter them in numbers if you encourage their natural predators to set up house on your plot. It's the lacewings, ladybirds, hoverflies and the like that you're after, so get the flowers and the companion plants in that attract them. You may also want to consider investing in horticultural fleece to cover the most vulnerable plants and exclude the aphids in the process.

If aphids still show up – and sometimes they will – just rub or hose them off, or if they are really persistent, use horticultural soft soap made from naturally occurring fatty acids.

Asparagus beetle and flea beetle

Both may nibble at your crops, but rarely do serious damage. That said, nothing should mess with asparagus. Pick off and destroy any asparagus beetles, and burn end-of-season foliage to prevent them overwintering. Try Bob Flowerdew's inspired method for dealing with flea beetle: smear a square of cardboard with treacle and wave it just above the leaves. This causes the disturbed beetle to leap up and stick to the card, for you to take off and feed to the chickens or throw on the fire – brilliant.

Asparagus beetle

Soil worms Wireworms and cutworms can be a nuisance, although luckily they rarely reach more troublesome status. Wireworms are the larvae of a group of click beetles that like to channel into roots, potatoes in particular. This can lead to rotting, or at least act as a guide hole for slugs to excavate. Cutworms are the larvae of specific moths and they do as you'd expect from their name, slicing off the roots of vulnerable seedlings. Both are easy to detect from their damage, and tend to be more of a problem in plots that were previously grass.

A little damage is almost inevitable although early lifting of crops, such as potatoes, helps limit wireworm damage. But, if you feel that the balance has swung a touch too much away from you, then try digging your patch over when it's convenient to expose the pests to hungry birds. If wireworms really get out of hand (this is reassuringly rare) there's always the nematode (*Heterorhabditis megadis*) route for you to try. August or September is the best time to use it as the wireworms are hatching, and bear in mind that you may have to repeat its use the following year.

If you detect cutworm damage, then carefully dig around the affected plant. You'll usually discover cutworms near the soil surface – destroy them as you find them. They feed (and do their damage) at night, so keep on the lookout for them above ground at dusk.

Blight If your potatoes, tomatoes or any of the other Solanaceae family develop brown blotches on their leaves, get ready to act – your plants have been infected by the fungal disease *Phytophthora infestans*, or blight. If not caught early, the disease will move on to the rest of the plant, attacking the edible parts you prize most.

Blight needs warmth and moist conditions to spread and is most common in late summer. Spores are spread by wind and rain so indoor crops are rarely affected, but if you're growing Solanaceae outside, then consider sourcing more resistant varieties, such as 'Verity', 'Lady Balfour', 'Cara' and 'Remarka' maincrop potatoes; 'Legend' and 'Ferline' (F1) tomatoes, and/or early-maturing varieties, which are likely to be harvested before blight is a threat.

If blight strikes, chop back and burn the foliage in the hope that it hasn't spread to the roots. Allow 3 weeks for the spores on the surface to die (and the skins of your tubers to thicken a little more) before digging them up.

Hygiene is vital. Ensure good air circulation indoors, get your seed from a reputable supplier and, to be on the safe side, don't save any seed for the following year. With potatoes, it is important to remove every single scrap of plant and root you can find, even when harvesting an unaffected crop as the merest morsels can potentially harbour blight. They may regrow into rogue potato plants, known as 'volunteers', that can infect your subsequent crop. If you spot any volunteers that have sprung up from remnants of last year's harvest, dig them up and burn them. It pays to be meticulous.

Recipes

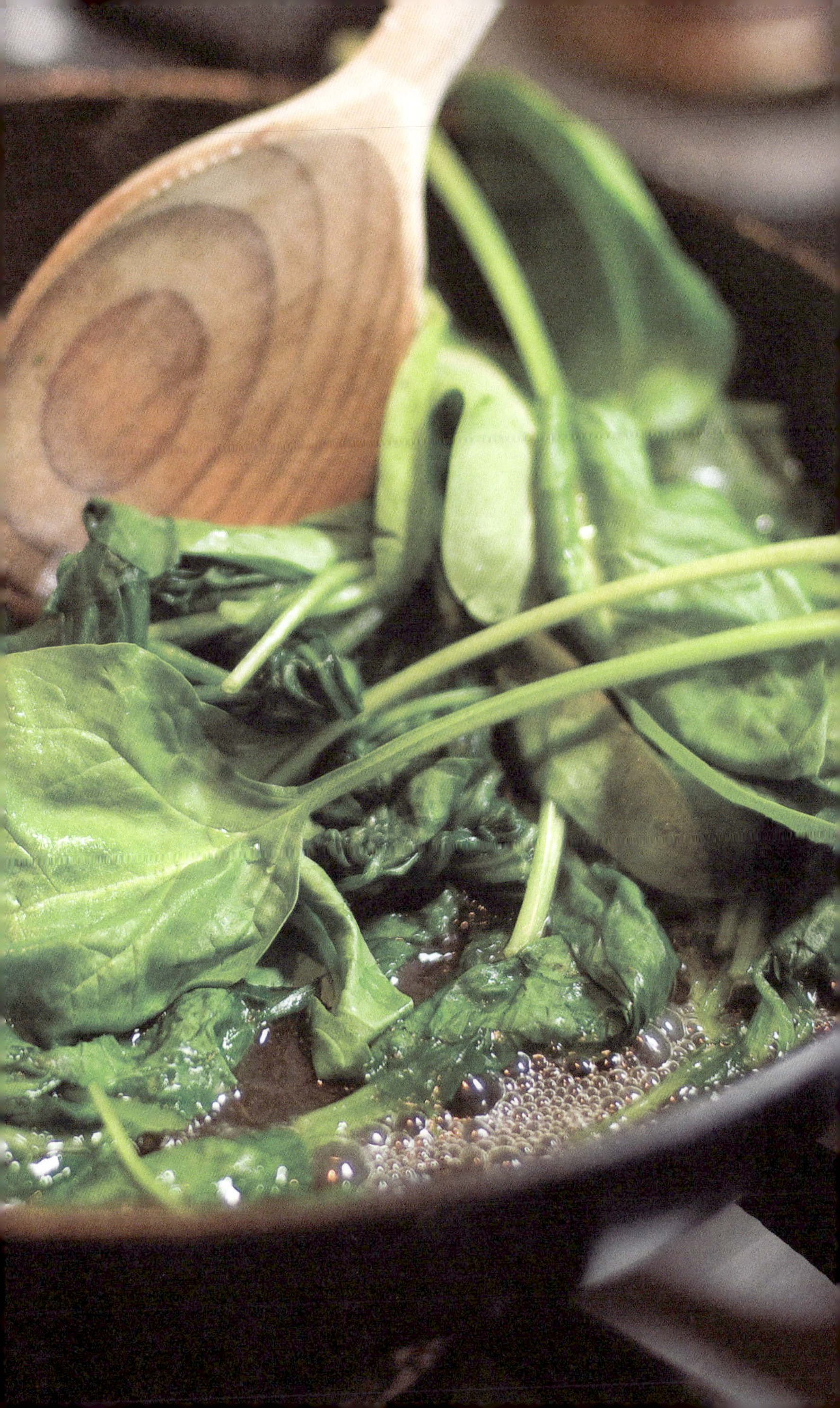

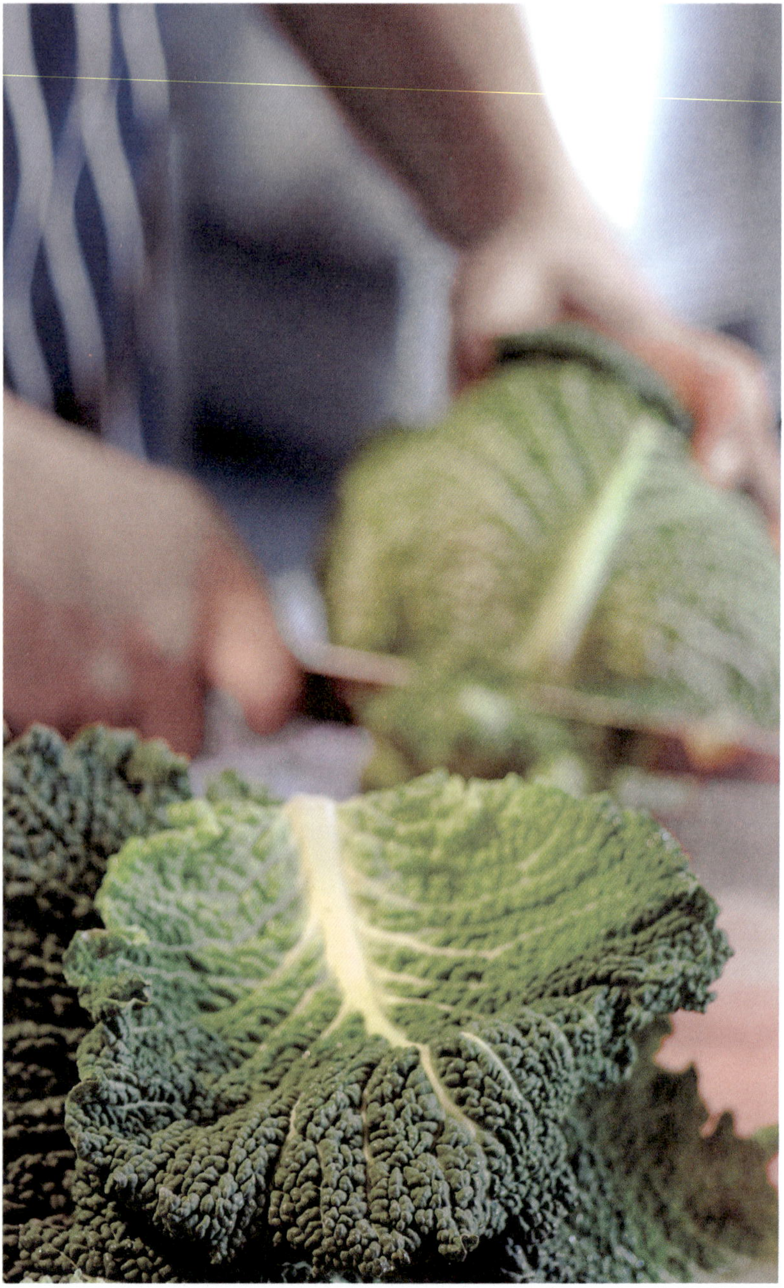

Half the garden soup

What better way to start off the recipes than this wonderfully adaptable celebration of high harvest on your veg patch? You won't need to use any stock as the vegetables add so much flavour of their own. Apart from the tomatoes and onions, all the headliners can be substituted for whatever you have plenty of. From late August onwards, you can add whatever fresh beans are about. Apart from the lovely borlotti, try a few beans plucked from overgrown French or runner bean pods – just give any beans a few minutes' cooking time before you add the other vegetables.

Serves 4–6
A little olive oil or butter
500g onions, peeled and sliced
½–1kg ripe tomatoes
Sea salt and freshly ground
    black pepper

Some or all of the following
3–4 medium carrots, peeled and diced
3–4 medium beetroot, peeled and
    diced
3–4 medium courgettes, diced
A few handfuls of peas
A fistful of French or runner beans,
    roughly chopped
A fistful of chard or spinach leaves,
    finely shredded
A fistful of kale or cabbage leaves,
    finely shredded

To serve
Extra virgin olive oil, to drizzle

Heat a little olive oil or butter in a large pan and sweat the onions until softened. Meanwhile put the tomatoes into a bowl, pour on boiling water to cover and leave for a minute, then drain and peel off the skins. Chop roughly and add to the onions. Cook gently for about 15 minutes until thick and pulpy, then add about 500ml cold water (or light stock) and a good pinch of salt.

Now add the vegetables of your choice, except the leafy veg. Bring to the boil, lower the heat and simmer for 10 minutes. Now add the shredded leafy veg and top up with a little more boiling water if necessary. Simmer for another 5 minutes, stirring regularly, until all the vegetables are tender, but only just.

Taste and adjust the seasoning, then serve immediately, in warm bowls. Drizzle a little olive oil over each serving.

Variations
Pretty much any harvest you have available can be swapped for a similar weight of one of the same family: 3–4 medium parsnips instead of 3–4 carrots, for example.

224 VEG PATCH

Curried root soup

It may be a bit strange to start by telling you to ignore the recipe, but that's what I'm going to do here. Well, not ignore it exactly, but do adjust the veg to suit yourself and what you have to hand. Just make sure that you end up with about 700g roots and potato, chopped into 2cm (or so) cubes. No parsnips? Substitute 200g turnips, or up the other vegetables slightly, and so on. This is just a great basic recipe for creating a tasty, satisfying soup and I do hope you'll make it your own.

Serves 4

1 tbsp olive oil
1 large onion, peeled and finely chopped
4 garlic cloves, peeled and sliced
1 thumb-sized piece of fresh root ginger, peeled and chopped
1 tsp cumin seeds, ground
1 tsp caraway seeds, ground
1 tsp coriander seeds, ground
3 tsp medium curry powder
200g carrots, peeled and chopped
200g celeriac, peeled and chopped
200g parsnip, peeled and cut into small dice
100g potato, peeled and chopped
1.5 litres light vegetable stock (see p.259) or chicken stock
Sea salt and freshly ground pepper

To serve

1 tbsp chopped coriander leaves
Natural yoghurt, flavoured with a little chopped mint
Flat breads or naan

Heat the olive oil in a large saucepan over a medium heat. Add the onion, garlic, ginger, ground spices and curry powder. Fry gently, stirring frequently, for 5–10 minutes until the onions are soft, then add the chopped roots and potato. Cook gently for another 10 minutes.

Add the stock and bring to a simmer, then cover the pan and simmer gently until all the vegetables are tender, about 15 minutes.

Purée the soup in a blender, in batches if necessary, until smooth, then return to the pan and heat through. Taste and adjust the seasoning.

Ladle the soup into warmed bowls, scatter over the chopped coriander and add a little minted natural yoghurt. Serve with some warm flat breads or naan.

Variations

Vary the roots according to what you have available. Just keep the total weight approximately the same, and don't substitute the potatoes.

Lettuce soup with spring onions, broad beans and chorizo

Sweet broad beans and salty, spicy chorizo are made for each other. Easy to prepare, this soup is lovely as a solo treat, yet alluring enough to grace the smartest of dinners. It is delicious served hot or cold.

Serves 4
20g unsalted butter
1 large bunch of spring onions, finely sliced
400ml light vegetable stock (see p.259)
3 lettuces (Cos, Romaine or similar), shredded
250g freshly picked, shelled broad beans
Sea salt and freshly ground black pepper
1 tbsp olive oil
About 60g chorizo sausage, cut into small chunks

To serve
Handful of mint leaves (optional)

Melt the butter in a medium heavy-based saucepan over a low heat. Add the spring onions and cook until soft, about 5 minutes. Pour in the stock and bring to a gentle simmer. Throw in the shredded lettuces and half the broad beans. Allow the lettuce to wilt, giving an occasional stir, then cook for a further 5 minutes.

Purée the soup in a blender, in batches if necessary, until smooth. If it seems a little thick, thin with a dash more stock. Season well with salt and pepper.

Blanch the remaining broad beans in a small pan of boiling water for 2 minutes. If using baby beans, you don't need to skin them; if they're larger, cool slightly, then squeeze them between your finger and thumb until they pop out of their skins.

Heat a frying pan, add the olive oil, then throw in the chorizo and fry until it crisps up. Add the blanched beans and toss to coat in the sausage-seasoned oil.

To serve the soup hot, heat it through and ladle into warm bowls, then top with the fried chorizo and broad beans. Alternatively, cool then chill, adjusting the seasoning before serving, scattered with the broad beans, chorizo and torn mint leaves.

Variations
Although not quite as perfectly as broad beans, peas work very well in this recipe – just throw them in a minute or two before the end.

Jerusalem artichoke soup

Peeling Jerusalem artichokes is a labour of love, owing to their knobbly surfaces, but the intensely earthy and luscious flavour of this soup makes it all worthwhile, I promise. Once peeled, drop them into a bowl of water with a squeeze of lemon juice added, so they don't discolour while you prepare everything else.

Serves 4–6
50g unsalted butter
1kg Jerusalem artichokes, peeled and larger ones halved
350g leeks, washed and finely sliced
100g potato, peeled and diced
1 medium onion, peeled and diced
2 garlic cloves, peeled and chopped
750ml good chicken stock or vegetable stock (see p.259)

100ml double cream
Sea salt and freshly ground black pepper

To serve
Snippets of crisp-fried bacon, or 4–6 spoonfuls of pesto (see p.258)

Melt the butter in a large, heavy-based saucepan and sweat all the vegetables and the garlic until soft, about 10 minutes. Pour in the stock, bring to the boil, then turn down the heat and simmer for 20–30 minutes until the vegetables are very soft.

Purée the soup in a blender, in batches if necessary, until smooth. Return the soup to the pan and bring to a simmer, then turn down the heat. Stir in the cream and season well with salt and pepper. Warm through, being careful not to let it boil.

Ladle the soup into warm bowls. Scatter over some snippets of crispy bacon or stir a spoonful of pesto into each serving.

Variations
For this creamy soup, you can easily substitute similar veg for the leeks, artichokes and potato, but I'd recommend halving the overall weight of veg if you're not using Jerusalem artichokes. A particularly delicious combination is 500g diced celeriac and 100g each of potato and leeks. If any variation seems slightly too thick once puréed, simply thin with a little milk.

Leek and celeriac soup

I find it incredibly satisfying that a vegetable as unglamorous as celeriac can create a soup which is so elegant and rich. Of course, the addition of oysters makes it particularly sophisticated, but it's also good simply splashed with a little cream and sprinkled with some finely chopped chives.

Serves 6–8
50g unsalted butter
1 tbsp olive oil
About 500g peeled celeriac, roughly chopped (peeled weight)
2 tender inner sticks of celery, chopped
2 leeks, washed and sliced
1 potato (about 150g), peeled and roughly chopped
1 medium onion, peeled and chopped
2 garlic cloves, peeled and chopped

About 1.25 litres light chicken or fish stock, or vegetable stock (see p.259)
½ glass white wine
16 fresh oysters in their shells scrubbed clean (optional)
100ml double cream, plus a little extra
Sea salt and freshly ground black pepper

To serve
Finely chopped chives (optional)

Place a large saucepan over a medium-low heat and add the butter and olive oil. When the butter is foaming, stir in all the chopped vegetables and garlic. Cook gently for about 10 minutes until everything is softened but not coloured. Pour in the stock and wine and bring to a gentle simmer. Cover and cook for 20–25 minutes, stirring once or twice, until all the vegetables are tender.

Purée the soup in a blender, in batches if necessary, until smooth. If it seems a little thick, thin with a bit more stock or water. Return to the pan.

If using oysters, place a large saucepan containing half a glass of water over a high heat and bring to the boil. Place half the oysters in the pan, cover with a tight-fitting lid and allow them to steam for 2 minutes; this will lightly poach the oysters and open the shells just a crack. Remove from the pan and finish the job – carefully opening up the shells and taking the meat out, without spilling the juice in the shell – tip this into a small bowl. Repeat with the remaining oysters.

To finish the soup, stir in the cream and the reserved oyster juice, if including. Warm the soup through gently and season with salt and pepper to taste. Ladle into warm bowls and pop the poached oysters on top or add a splash of cream and a sprinkling of chives to serve.

Minted artichoke houmous

Try to time the making of this dip to coincide with listening to something on the radio, or a new CD. Removing the flesh from the artichokes takes a while, but it's a soothing way of passing the time, and the results are definitely worth it. It might be an unorthodox houmous, but the earthy taste of the artichokes contrasts beautifully with their surprisingly silky, creamy and rich texture. It makes a great dip for veggies and is really delicious spread on bruschetta (see overleaf).

Serves 4–8 as a starter
7–8 globe artichokes
Sea salt and freshly ground black pepper
1 garlic clove, peeled and finely chopped
Handful of mint leaves, roughly chopped
2–3 tbsp olive oil

Add the artichokes to a pan of boiling salted water and cook for 25–40 minutes, depending on size; they are ready when you can pull one of the leaves off easily, and when a knife inserted into the base meets with little resistance.

Leave the artichokes until cool enough to handle, then pick off the leaves. If these have any substantial flesh on them, use a small paring knife or teaspoon to scrape it off and reserve it for the houmous. Once you reach the artichoke's heart, pull off the choke (the hairy immature flower which sits beneath the leaves) and remove any tough or fibrous parts of the stems.

Put the artichoke hearts into a food processor or blender, along with any flesh you have taken from the leaves. Add the garlic and mint. Now pulse, adding enough olive oil through the funnel as you go to give you a thickish consistency – just like that of a traditional chickpea houmous. Season with salt and pepper to taste and serve immediately.

Variations
This is also wonderful with asparagus, broad beans, peas or beetroot replacing the artichoke hearts.

Tomato bruschetta
with blue cheese and confit chilli

Sweet, salty, sharp and punchy – this recipe has it all. You'll need very ripe tomatoes, preferably on the large size: 'Brandywine', 'Black Krim' and 'San Marzano' are ideal. For the cheese, Stilton is good, although Dorset Blue Vinny is worth seeking out.

The intensely flavoured confit chilli oil is particularly special and you'll be glad that the quantities here make more than you need for this recipe. Keep the rest in a sealed bottle in the fridge and use to add zing to salad dressings and marinades.

Serves 4 as a starter or snack

4 slices of good, rustic white bread
1 garlic clove, peeled
4 ripe tomatoes, sliced
200g blue cheese
Freshly ground black pepper

For the confit chilli oil
6 mildish chillies, such as 'Poblano'
250ml olive oil
1 tsp thyme leaves
1 garlic clove (unpeeled)

To make the confit chilli oil, slice the chillies open from tip to tail, then remove the seeds with a spoon and discard. Slice the chilli into strips and place them in a small saucepan with the olive oil, a few thyme leaves and the unpeeled garlic clove. Heat slowly until the oil is simmering very gently and cook the chillies until soft, about 25 minutes. Remove from the heat and allow the oil to cool.

For the bruschetta, preheat the grill to high. Drizzle or brush a little of the confit chilli oil over the bread slices. Toast on both sides until golden, then rub them all over with the garlic clove.

Place the tomato slices on to the bruschetta, crumble over plenty of blue cheese and flash them under the grill until bubbling. Place on warm plates and season with pepper (the cheese will probably provide enough saltiness). Spoon over a little more of the confit chilli oil and serve immediately.

Variations
All manner of vegetables lend themselves to tasty bruschetta, including roasted peppers, broad bean or borlotti bean purée, and globe artichokes in the form of minted artichoke houmous (see p.229).

RECIPES

VEG PATCH

Vegetable tempura

The key to creating perfect, crispy tempura is to ensure that the water is very cold and the fat is very hot. Mix the batter just before you want to use it and don't over-mix – a few lumps are fine. In fact, a few lumps are very good as they create extra crunch. Get everything ready to go and whisk up the batter as the oil is heating up.

Serves 4 as a starter or snack

About 1 litre groundnut or vegetable oil for deep-frying

For the tempura batter
125g plain flour
Good pinch of sea salt, plus extra for sprinkling
1 egg yolk
175ml ice-cold sparkling water

For the vegetables
A selection (or one) of the following:
Sugar snap peas
Baby carrots
Baby beetroot
Cauliflower florets
Broccoli florets
Or anything else you can batter...

Heat a 10cm depth of oil in a suitable deep, heavy-based saucepan until it registers 180°C on a frying thermometer, or until a cube of white bread dropped into the oil turns golden brown in just under a minute.

For the batter, sift the flour and salt together into a large mixing bowl, then whisk in the egg yolk and sparkling water.

Cook the tempura a few pieces at a time: dip the vegetables into the batter to coat and then carefully drop them into the hot oil. Fry for a minute or so until golden brown, using a fork or spoon to drizzle a little more batter over the vegetables as they are frying. Don't overcrowd the pan.

Drain the tempura on kitchen paper, sprinkle with sea salt and serve immediately, while piping hot.

Variations
Try any veg you have to hand. Baby carrots and other tender small roots, and non-leafy harvests are suitable.

Deep-fried courgette flowers

These are surprisingly easy to make once you've mastered the technique, and they look incredibly pretty on the plate. You might also like to try stuffing the courgette flowers with some soft goat's cheese flavoured with a little chopped thyme before coating them in batter and deep-frying, as below.

Serves 3–4 as a starter or snack
12 courgettes, with flowers
A little olive oil
3 garlic cloves, peeled and crushed
Flaky sea salt
About 1 litre sunflower or groundnut oil for deep-frying

For the batter
125g plain flour
Good pinch of sea salt
1 egg yolk
175ml ice-cold sparkling water

To serve
Lemon wedges

Firstly, separate the flowers from each courgette and check your flowers for insects (especially if you have vegetarians coming for supper). Set the flowers aside.

Slice the courgettes as thinly as you can. In a large frying pan, warm a slug of olive oil over a medium-low heat, then add the courgette slices with the garlic. Season with a sprinkling of salt to help draw out moisture and cook slowly for about 10 minutes until they are concentrated and oily, but not at all watery, stirring from time to time; don't let them brown more than a shade. Let cool slightly.

Carefully spoon the cooked courgette mixture into the courgette flowers. You should get 2–4 heaped teaspoonfuls into each one, depending on the size of the flowers.

Heat a 10cm depth of oil in a suitable deep, heavy-based saucepan until it registers 180°C on a frying thermometer, or until a cube of white bread dropped into the oil turns golden brown in just under a minute.

In the meantime, make the batter: sift the flour and salt together into a large mixing bowl, then whisk in the egg yolk and sparkling water.

Cook 2–4 courgette flowers at a time, depending on their size and the diameter of your pan: dip the stuffed flowers into the batter to coat, then carefully lower them into the hot oil. Deep-fry for 1–2 minutes, until puffed up, crisp and golden brown. Drain on kitchen paper. Sprinkle with flaky salt and serve at once, with lemon wedges for squeezing.

RECIPES 235

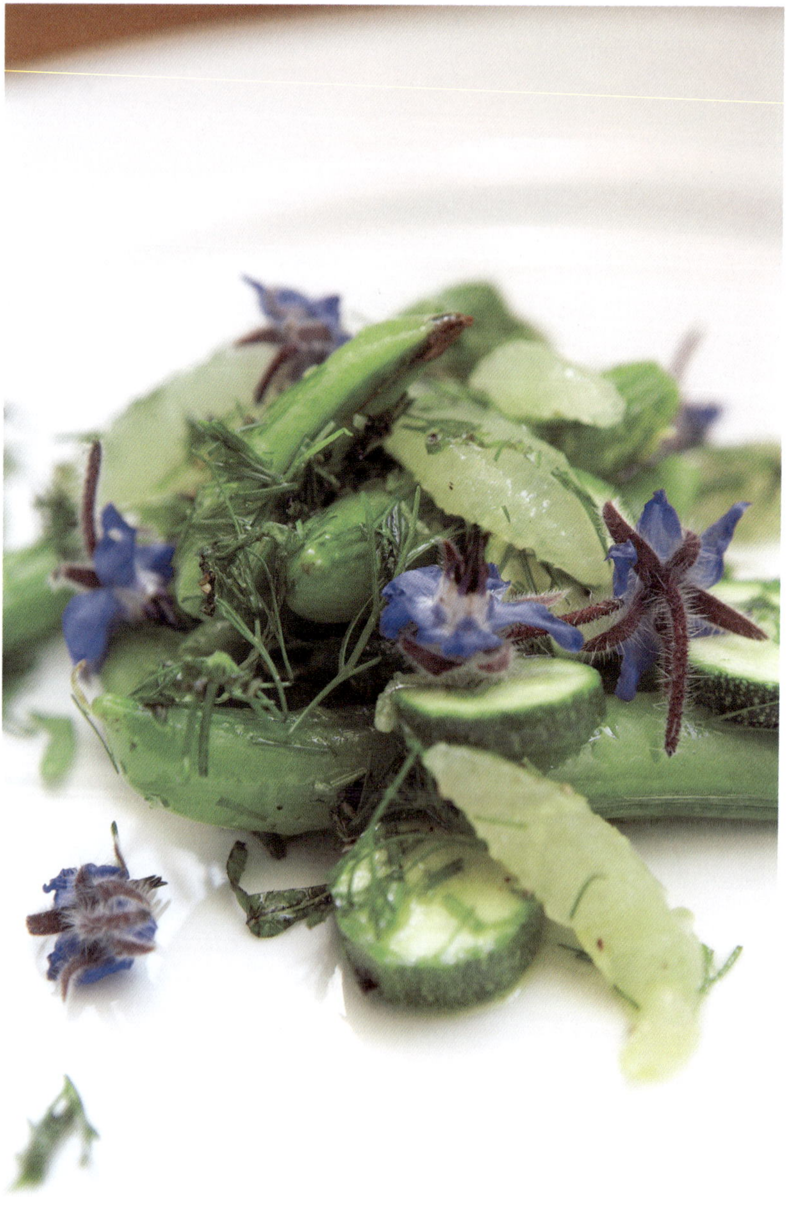

Baby courgette salad
with lemon and sugar snap peas

This is as refreshing as it gets. It just cuts through, like the first mouthful of the perfect gin and tonic. Don't be tempted to hold back on the lemons – you'll be pleasantly surprised. It makes a great, zingy starter for a summer lunch, or a lovely side dish alongside some grilled or barbecued lamb chops.

Serves 4 as a starter, 6 as a side dish

- 4–6 baby courgettes
- 130g young, tender sugar snap peas
- 2 organic (unwaxed) lemons
- Small bunch of mint, tough stems removed, finely chopped
- Small bunch of dill, large stems removed, finely chopped
- 2 tbsp olive oil
- Sea salt and freshly ground black pepper
- Borage flowers, to garnish (optional)

Slice the courgettes into rounds, 3mm thick. Throw them into a bowl with the sugar snap peas. Peel one of the lemons, removing all the white pith, then cut out the segments, free from their membranes. Add to the courgettes.

Grate over the zest of the other lemon, being careful to avoid any of the bitter white pith. Halve the lemon and squeeze over the juice. Add the chopped herbs, along with the olive oil, salt and pepper, and toss well.

Leave the salad to stand for 5–10 minutes before serving, to allow the flavours to mingle. Toss again lightly before serving and check the seasoning. Scatter some borage flowers over the salad to garnish if available.

Jerusalem artichoke salad
with goat's cheese and hazelnuts

This is a lovely way to enjoy Jerusalem artichokes. Don't expect them to roast like potatoes – you should get crisp and golden skins, but the insides will be fluffy and may break up a bit. If they do, it just means they will absorb more of the flavours of the hazelnut oil and lemon juice, which is exactly what you want.

Serves 4–6 as a starter or light lunch

80g shelled hazelnuts
650g Jerusalem artichokes
4 tbsp extra-virgin olive oil
Maldon sea salt
1–2 bay leaves
1 tsp hazelnut oil
½ lemon
Freshly ground black pepper
80g firm goat's cheese, cut into small chunks
2 handfuls or so of winter salad leaves, such as mizuna, rocket and green salad bowl lettuce (many of the oriental leaves also work well)

First, toast the hazelnuts. Preheat the oven to 180°C/Gas Mark 4. Spread the nuts out in a single layer on a baking sheet and roast for 8–10 minutes, until lightly coloured and the skins are blistered and cracked. Tip them on to a clean tea towel and wrap them up. Leave for a minute, then rub vigorously in the tea towel until the skins fall off. Set aside to cool, then chop the nuts roughly (or leave them whole, if you prefer).

Turn up the oven to 190°C/Gas Mark 5 and put a large roasting tin inside to heat up. Scrub the artichokes thoroughly and halve or quarter them lengthways, depending on their size (you want chunks about 1.5cm thick). Put the artichokes into a bowl and add 3 tbsp of the olive oil, along with 1 tsp salt and the bay leaf. Toss to mix, then tip into the hot roasting tin and roast until lightly golden, about 35 minutes, giving the tray a good shake after 15 minutes to turn the artichokes over in the oil. Set aside to cool slightly.

Meanwhile, whisk together the remaining 1 tbsp olive oil and the hazelnut oil. Drizzle over the warm artichokes, squeeze on a good spritz of lemon juice and season with salt and a few grinds of black pepper. Turn it all over gently with your hands until well combined, then add the hazelnuts, goat's cheese and salad leaves. Toss lightly, divide between plates and serve.

Baby pea and ricotta salad
with spring onions

This salad is a great summer favourite at River Cottage HQ. The sweetness of the peas combined with the creaminess of the ricotta and sharpness of the spring onions is a real winner.

Serves 4 as a starter or light lunch

500g very fresh baby peas
3 tbsp olive oil
10–12 spring onions, trimmed and halved lengthways
1 tbsp lemon juice
Sea salt and freshly ground black pepper
200g ricotta (or other soft, fresh curdy cheese)
1 tsp thyme leaves, roughly chopped

Bring a saucepan of water to the boil, drop in the peas and cook for a maximum of 2 minutes, then drain well.

Heat 1 tbsp olive oil in a frying pan, add the spring onions and sweat gently for 4–5 minutes, until softened.

For the dressing, in a large bowl, combine the rest of the olive oil with the lemon juice and plenty of salt and pepper.

Toss the warm peas and spring onions in the dressing, then divide between individual serving bowls. Crumble the ricotta and scatter over the salad, along with the thyme. Serve warm or at room temperature.

Feta and beetroot salad
with parsley

This makes a gorgeous salad – I promise it tastes just as good as it looks.

Serves 4 as a starter or lunch
500g whole baby beetroot
1 garlic clove, peeled and roughly chopped
Sea salt and freshly ground black pepper
2 tbsp olive oil
200g feta, or semi-hard goat's cheese, such as Woolsery, crumbled into small chunks
20g flat-leaf parsley leaves

For the vinaigrette
3 tbsp olive oil
1 tbsp wine, sherry or cider vinegar
Pinch of sugar

To serve
Slices of brown bread

Preheat the oven to 200°C/Gas Mark 6. Scrub the beetroot well and place them on a large piece of foil. Scatter with the garlic, salt and pepper, and trickle over the olive oil. Scrunch up the foil to make a loose parcel and place on a baking tray. Roast until tender – about an hour, although they make take longer. Test with a knife: the beetroot are ready when the blade slips in easily.

Leave the beetroot to cool, then top and tail them and remove their skins. Cut into chunks (quarters or eighths) and place in a large bowl. Add the cheese and parsley leaves and toss the lot together with your hands.

In a small bowl, whisk together the ingredients for the vinaigrette, seasoning with salt and pepper to taste. Drizzle over the salad and toss lightly. Serve straight away, with some brown bread on the side.

RECIPES 241

Roasted beetroot pizza
with kale and anchovies

Beetroot is so underrated. Its rich, earthy flavour, silky smooth texture and wonderful sweetness make it able to star in both sweet and savoury courses. The combination of beetroot, kale and anchovies makes for a stunning warm salad with some sliced boiled eggs or a bit of sirloin steak, but it also makes a rather spectacular winter pizza topping, with the fragrant oil drizzled over the top.

Roast the beetroot with the skin on, and the roots and leaves intact, to keep in all the flavour. Garlic and thyme are a must – the combination infuses both beetroot and olive oil with the most delicious savour.

Serves 4

For the pizza bases
250g strong plain white bread flour
250g plain flour
2 tsp salt
5g fast-acting dried yeast
350ml warm water
Slug of olive oil

For the topping
5–6 smallish beetroot, with leaves and roots intact
4 tbsp olive oil
5 garlic cloves, unpeeled and bashed a bit
5–6 thyme sprigs, plus about ½ tsp thyme leaves for sprinkling on the pizzas
2–3 rosemary sprigs
Sea salt and freshly ground black pepper
100g young kale, stalks removed
2 dried chillies, deseeded and chopped
About 300g good mozzarella, torn
24 anchovies or salted pilchards

First make the pizza dough. Sift the flours and salt into a large mixing bowl, stir in the yeast, then make a well in the centre and add most of the water. Using two fingers of one hand, mix until you have a very rough, soft dough, adding more water if the dough is dry. Add the olive oil and squidge it all together.

Turn the dough out on to a well-floured surface and knead until smooth and silky (or you could use an electric mixer with a dough hook attachment). Place the dough in a bowl, cover with a damp tea towel and leave to rise in a warm place until doubled in size, which should take about an hour or so.

Meanwhile, roast the beetroot. Preheat the oven to 200°C/Gas Mark 6. Put your beetroot into a roasting tin with 2–3 tbsp of the olive oil, 3 garlic cloves and the thyme and rosemary sprigs. Roll the beetroot around a bit so that they are nicely coated and season well with salt and pepper. Roast for about 40 minutes, shaking the tin from time to time, until the beetroot are very soft when pierced with a knife. Leave until cool enough to handle, then rub off the skins, chop off the roots and leaves, and slice the beets into wedges. Reserve any of the tasty oil for later.

Turn your oven up as high as it will go and place a couple of sturdy large baking sheets inside to heat up.

Chop the kale roughly. Peel and slice the remaining 2 garlic cloves. Warm 1–2 tbsp olive oil in a frying pan over a high heat and toss in the kale, along with the garlic and chillies. Keep moving the kale around the pan until it's wilted, very soft and any liquid has evaporated. Season with salt and pepper to taste.

When the pizza dough has doubled in size, turn it out on to a lightly floured surface and divide into four. Shape one of the quarters into a circle and then roll it out with a rolling pin until you have a pleasingly thin base. Repeat with the rest of the dough.

Carefully place the pizza bases on the hot baking sheets, then quickly divide the roasted beetroot among them, along with some torn mozzarella and anchovies. Season with salt and pepper, and sprinkle lightly with thyme leaves, then spoon over any leftover beetroot roasting juices.

Bake the pizzas for about 8–10 minutes until the cheese has melted and the base is crisp and browned.

Variations

The pizza dough can be used as the base for so many mouthwatering toppings – you'll probably already have your own favourites. Almost any veg will work if you find its best partners.

Spring into summer tart

If you ever wondered what 'green' would taste like – try this tart. It's bursting with all kinds of fresh and delightful flavours and is exactly what I'd like to eat on a warm summer's day, with a simply dressed salad of baby leaves on the side. More green, I know, but you can't have too much of a good thing.

Serves 6

For the pastry
125g plain flour
Good pinch of salt
75g unsalted butter, chilled and cut into small cubes
1 egg, separated
3–4 tbsp cold milk

For the filling
100g fresh garden peas
100g baby broad beans
Knob of butter
1 large bunch of spring onions, finely sliced
100g broad bean and pea tops
Small handful of chard leaves, washed
Sea salt and freshly ground black pepper
A few feathery fennel tops, chopped
Small bunch of young, flat-leaf parsley, stalks removed, leaves roughly chopped
Small bunch of mint, stalks removed, leaves roughly chopped
Small bunch of chives, finely chopped
75g hard goat's or sheep's cheese, coarsely grated
100ml whole milk
200ml double cream
2 whole eggs, plus 2 egg yolks

To make the pastry, put the flour, salt and butter into a food processor and pulse until the mixture is the consistency of coarse breadcrumbs. Add the egg yolk, then with the motor running, pour in the milk, in a thin stream through the funnel. Watch carefully and stop adding the milk as soon as the dough comes together. Tip the pastry on to a lightly floured surface, gently shape into a smooth ball and then flatten slightly to a circle. Wrap in cling film and chill in the fridge for 30 minutes.

Preheat the oven to 170°C/Gas Mark 3. In the meantime, for the filling, blanch the peas and broad beans in a pan of boiling water for 1 minute then refresh in ice water. Drain and set aside. Heat the butter in a frying pan over a medium heat and gently fry the spring onions for 2–3 minutes until soft. Add the broad bean and pea tops, and the chard, and cook for just a couple of minutes until wilted. Season well.

Lightly grease a loose-bottomed 25cm tart tin. Roll out the pastry thinly and line the tin with it, leaving the excess pastry hanging over the edge. Prick the base all over with a fork, line the case with baking paper and baking beans and put the tin on a baking sheet. Bake 'blind' for about 15 minutes. Remove the paper and beans and bake for another 10 minutes.

Lightly beat the egg white, brush some of it over the hot pastry and return the pastry case to the oven for a further 5 minutes; this helps to seal the pastry and prevent any filling leaking out. Trim off the excess pastry using a small, sharp knife or by rolling a rolling pin over the top of the tin so that all of the overhanging pastry falls away.

Turn up the oven to 180°C/Gas Mark 4. Arrange the chard, spring onion and pea top mixture over the bottom of the pastry case. Scatter over the blanched peas and broad beans and then the chopped herbs. Sprinkle on the grated cheese. In a jug, whisk together the milk, cream, eggs and egg yolks, season well with salt and pepper, and pour into the tart case. Bake for about 40 minutes or until lightly set and golden brown. Serve warm or cold.

Variations

Any green spring or summer veg – including asparagus – will work, and the leafy herbs can be altered to suit your taste.

Mackerel with sorrel sauce

This takes only a couple of minutes to throw together and makes a great quick supper. The sharp, lemony tang of sorrel is the perfect foil for the rich, oily flesh of the mackerel.

Serves 2
200g sorrel
4 very fresh mackerel fillets
Sea salt and freshly ground black pepper
1 tsp olive oil
50g unsalted butter

1 egg yolk
1 tbsp double cream

To serve
New potatoes

Wash the sorrel thoroughly, remove and discard the stalks and chop the leaves coarsely. Set aside.

Season the mackerel fillets with a little salt and pepper. Put a heavy-based frying pan over a medium heat and add a thin film of olive oil. When the oil is fairly hot, lay the mackerel fillets skin side down in the pan and cook until the flesh is almost completely white. Flip the fillets over for just a minute to finish cooking – the whole process should take no more than 5 minutes. Transfer to a warm plate and keep warm while you make the sauce.

Add the butter to the pan in which you cooked the fish and melt over a medium heat. When it is foaming, throw in the sorrel, which will quickly wilt and turn a dull greeny-brown. Give it a swift stir, remove the pan from the heat and let it cool for 30 seconds, then beat in the egg yolk to thicken the sauce. Season with salt and pepper to taste, and stir in the cream to enrich the sauce.

Serve the mackerel with the warm sorrel sauce and some waxy new potatoes.

Turnip 'risotto'

Turnips are often seen as rather modest fare, which is a great shame as I really love their peppery flavour. If you need convincing – or are just after a top supper – try this recipe by Italian-American chef Mario Batali from his book *Simple Italian Food*. It turns the humble turnip into the star, giving it the full-on glamour treatment. It's lovely as it is, but sometimes I add a little fried pancetta or bacon just for a change.

Serves 4 as a main course, 6 as a starter

500ml hot chicken stock
90ml extra-virgin olive oil
1 medium red onion, peeled and finely diced
700g turnips, peeled and cut into 4–5mm dice
Sea salt and freshly ground black pepper
30g unsalted butter
20g Parmesan, freshly grated
Small handful of parsley, tough stalks removed, leaves finely chopped

Heat the chicken stock in a pan to a simmer and keep hot. Warm the olive oil in a large, heavy-based frying pan over a medium-low heat. Toss in the onion and cook until softened, about 10 minutes. Add the turnips and cook for 2 minutes.

Ladle in some of the hot chicken stock and cook until absorbed, stirring from time to time. Continue until all of the stock has been added, about 10–15 minutes.

Season with salt and pepper to taste. Stir in the butter and Parmesan, then remove from the heat, scatter over the chopped parsley, and serve in warm bowls.

Squash risotto
with crispy sage

If the taste of tomato encapsulates summer, then squash is surely the same for autumn. It shares a perfect partnership with sage's meaty, aromatic warmth – used here as an undercurrent of flavour and a crispy topping. As the evenings cool and darken, you'll be hard-pressed to find a more comforting supper.

Serves 4 as a main course

900ml vegetable stock (see p.259) or chicken stock
1 medium onion, chopped
3 tbsp olive oil
12 sage leaves, finely chopped, about 2 tbsp
1–2 garlic cloves, chopped
250g arborio rice
Small glass of white wine

375g squash or pumpkin (peeled weight), diced small

To finish
3 tbsp sunflower oil
About 16 sage leaves
75g butter
Piece of Parmesan or Pecorino
Sea salt and freshly ground pepper

Heat the stock in a pan until almost boiling, and then keep hot over a very low heat. In a heavy-based saucepan, sweat the onion in the olive oil until soft but not browned, about 10–15 minutes. Add the chopped sage and garlic and cook for a couple of minutes. Now add the rice and stir to coat the grains with the oil, then add the wine and stir until most of the liquid has been absorbed.

Pour in about a third of the hot stock and bring to a gentle simmer. Cook until almost all the stock has been absorbed, stirring regularly but not all the time. Add the squash and a little more stock, and continue to simmer gently, stirring occasionally, until the stock has been absorbed. Continue to add more stock a little at a time until the pumpkin is soft and the rice is nicely al dente. You may not need all of the stock. The texture of the finished risotto should be loose and creamy.

When it is almost ready, heat the sunflower oil in a small pan and fry the whole sage leaves for a few seconds until crisp. Drain on kitchen paper.

Now it's time for the final stage that adds so much of the creaminess to the dish. Stir the butter and a little grated cheese into the risotto and season well. Divide between warm serving bowls and throw a few crispy sage leaves over each portion. Bring the rest of the cheese and a grater to the table for guests to help themselves.

Variations

Courgettes, asparagus, broad beans, peas, lettuce, spinach and many others will happily take the place of the squash in this recipe. And rosemary (used lightly) works well in place of the sage.

Celeriac rémoulade

Rémoulade is, strictly speaking, a mustardy French dressing that could be used with whatever you fancy, but such is its happy friendship with celeriac, I've never known it served in any other way. This is the dish to give anyone who might need convincing about the wonder of celeriac.

Serves 6–8 as a side dish
2 tsp hot English mustard
2 tsp cider vinegar
1 scant tsp sugar
Pinch of sea salt

75ml olive oil
75ml groundnut or sunflower oil
1 celeriac, about 750g

Combine the mustard, cider vinegar, sugar and salt in a bowl. Pour the oils into a jug, then very slowly whisk them into the mustard mixture until you get a creamy, emulsified dressing. Taste and adjust the seasoning with salt if necessary.

Peel the celeriac and cut it into fine matchsticks, then toss them in the dressing to coat evenly.

You can serve this salad with almost anything, but it is especially good with cold pork or ham and sourdough bread.

Variations
Although perfect with celeriac, this dressing works really well with almost anything hot or cold. Try it with some of the brassicas, salad leaves, asparagus, globe artichokes or summer carrots.

French beans
with Japanese-style dressing

I love the contrast between the intensely green beans and dramatic black dressing in this recipe. It's great alongside simply grilled or barbecued fish. Alternatively, you can add some shredded leftover roast chicken or pork to transform it into a main course in its own right. The dressing is good with other vegetables, too, especially carrots and courgettes.

Serves 4 as a side dish

300g French beans
50g black sesame seeds
1 tsp hemp seeds
1 tsp sunflower seeds

2 tbsp caster sugar
1 tbsp soy sauce
½ tbsp mirin
1 tsp toasted sesame oil

Top the beans (tail them, too, if you want, though I rather like the curling tails, so tend to leave them on). Plunge them into a pan of boiling water and cook for a couple of minutes until they're just beginning to soften but haven't lost their bite. Drain, refresh in a bowl of iced water, then drain again and pat dry.

Warm a small frying pan over a medium heat and toss in the sesame seeds, hemp seeds and sunflower seeds. Shake the pan until the seeds are just toasted and releasing their fragrance – this will take only a couple of minutes. Lightly crush the toasted seeds using a pestle and mortar, then add the sugar, soy sauce, mirin and sesame oil, and mix to a paste. It should have the texture of coarse, damp sand.

Use your hands to toss the blanched French beans with the dressing, making sure that they are all well coated, then serve.

Variations

This fantastic dressing works well on anything from broad beans to salad leaves. Try it with whatever you like to dress.

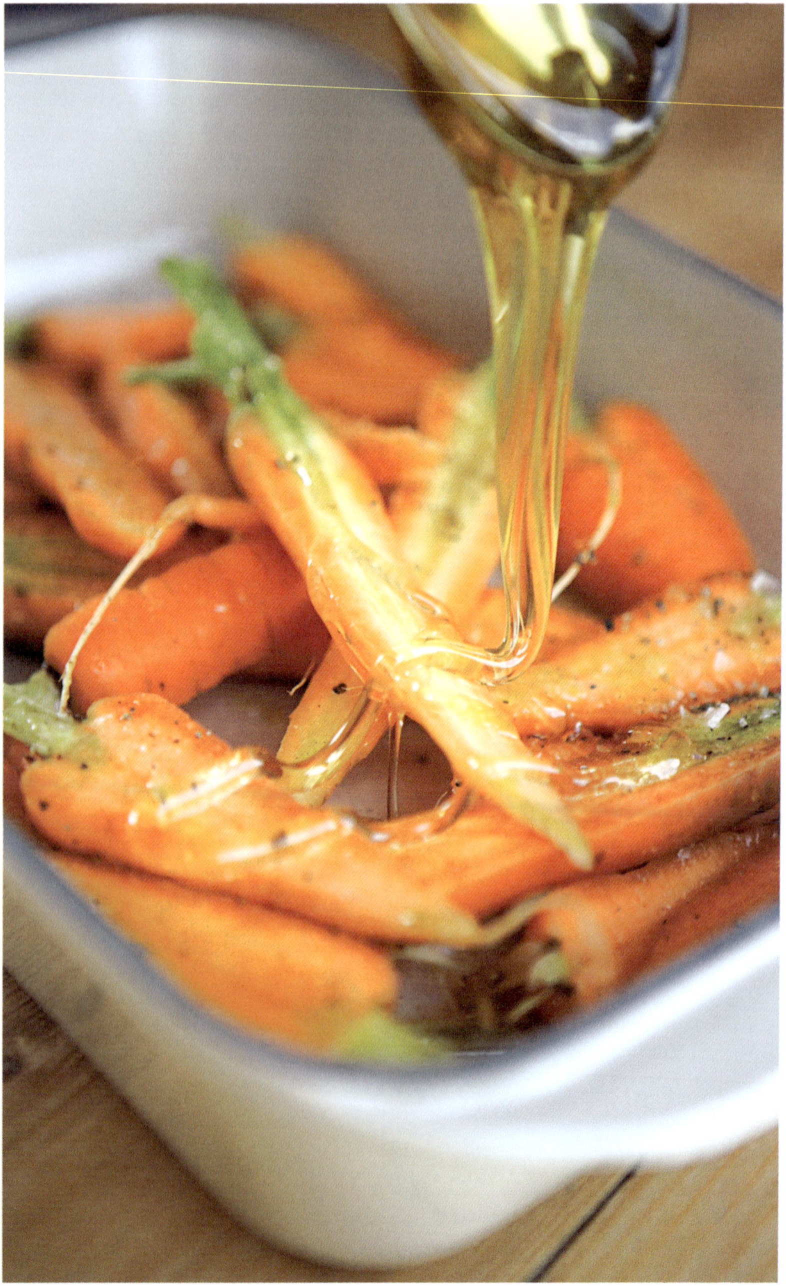

Honey roast carrots

These are a great favourite over the winter months at River Cottage HQ – we make them all the time. They are so easy and quick to throw together, but be warned – their luscious, caramelised sweetness is quite addictive.

Serves 6 as a side dish

2–3 tbsp olive oil or goose fat
1kg good-quality carrots (either from your garden or organic), peeled
1–2 tbsp good runny honey (preferably local)
Sea salt and freshly ground black pepper
40g unsalted butter
Small bunch of flat-leaf parsley, tough stalks removed, leaves roughly chopped

Preheat your oven to 200°C/Gas Mark 6. Put the olive oil or goose fat into a roasting tin and put the tin into the oven to heat up.

Slice the carrots and tip them into the hot roasting tin. Spoon over the honey and season with salt and pepper, then shake the tin a little until the carrots are well coated. Roast for 35–40 minutes, giving the tin a good shake halfway through the cooking time. The carrots are done when they are tender, crisp and darkened around the edges. Stir in the butter and chopped parsley and serve immediately.

Variations

Parsnips and the other root vegetables take to this treatment really well. Jerusalem artichokes work too, but I'd recommend halving the amount of honey.

Dauphinoise potatoes

This meltingly delicious dauphinoise has more of a garlicky kick than the traditional recipe, where the gratin dish is simply rubbed with a single clove, which is then discarded. By all means substitute any other root veg for the potato, or better still, use half potato and half a different root veg.

Serves 6 as a side dish

25g unsalted butter, softened
600g waxy potatoes, such as 'Belle de Fontenay' or 'Duke of York'
300ml double cream
2 large garlic cloves, peeled and crushed or grated
Sea salt and freshly ground black pepper

Preheat the oven to 170°C/Gas Mark 3. Rub a gratin dish liberally with the butter.

Peel the potatoes and slice them thinly, either with a sharp knife or a mandoline. In a large bowl, whisk together the cream and garlic and season well with salt and pepper. Toss the potatoes in the mixture and layer them in the gratin dish, then pour over any remaining cream.

Bake for 1¼–1½ hours, pressing down all over with a fish slice or spatula every 15 minutes or so, to compress the potatoes and stop them from drying out. Alternatively, cover tightly with foil for the first hour of cooking, then remove the foil and turn up the heat to 200°C/Gas Mark 6 for the last 15 minutes. The potato bake is ready when the top is bubbling and golden, and the potatoes are soft and yielding when pierced with a knife. Leave to stand for a few minutes before serving.

Variations

Turnips, celeriac, parsnips and squash all work particularly well in this dauphinoise – but are best as a half-and-half split with the potatoes rather than used exclusively, as their sweetness can be a little too much on its own.

Creamy Brussels sprouts
with chestnuts and bacon

If you know anyone who's yet to be convinced by Brussels sprouts, put them out of their misery and cook this dish for them. It's so undeniably magnificent that it will convert them in a second.

Serves 6 as a side dish, 2 for supper

250g fresh chestnuts (or use vacuum-packed chestnuts)
500g Brussels sprouts
Sea salt
Knob of butter
2 tbsp double cream
4–6 thick streaky bacon rashers

Roast the chestnuts well ahead: make a little cut in each one (to prevent explosions) and dry-fry them in a heavy-based frying pan over a medium-high heat for about 10–15 minutes (or, better still, toast them on a shovel in an open fire). Turn them frequently until they are cooked through and probably a little charred. Let the chestnuts cool, then peel away both the shell and the thin brown inner skin. Chop or crumble them up and they're ready to go.

Just before serving, add the Brussels sprouts to a saucepan of well-salted water and simmer for around 6–8 minutes, depending on their size, until just tender. Drain well, then purée with the butter and double cream in a food processor, or using a hand-held stick blender. You're after creaminess, but the texture doesn't have to be totally smooth.

Cut each bacon rasher into bite-sized pieces and fry them in a dry pan until crispy.

Add the chestnuts to the creamed sprouts and heat through gently but thoroughly. Spoon the mixture into a warmed serving dish and sprinkle over the crispy bacon bits. Serve immediately.

Variations
All of the leafy brassicas will happily partner the chestnuts, cream and bacon.

Glutney

This is one of those marvellous recipes that you'll turn to again and again. Try it once and you'll see how easy it is to play around with the ingredients – stick to the approximate overall amount and you'll find it's very forgiving. This year I made it with squash instead of courgettes, and plums in place of tomatoes, and (if you'll forgive the immodesty) it was outstanding.

Makes about 10 x 340g jars

1kg courgettes, unpeeled if small, peeled if huge, cut into 1cm dice
500g onions, peeled and diced
1kg red or green tomatoes, scalded, skinned and roughly chopped
1kg cooking or eating apples, peeled and diced
500g sultanas or raisins
500g light brown sugar
750ml white wine (or cider) vinegar
1–3 tsp dried chilli flakes
1 tsp salt

For the spice bag
1 thumb-sized nugget of fresh or dried ginger, roughly chopped
12 cloves
12 black peppercorns
1 (generous) tsp coriander seeds
A few blades of mace

Put the vegetables and fresh fruit into a large, heavy-based pan with the sultanas and sugar. Make the wine vinegar up to 1 litre with water and add to the pan with the chilli flakes and salt.

Make up the spice bag by tying all the spices together in a square of muslin. Add the spice bag to the pan, pushing it into the middle.

Heat the mixture gently, stirring occasionally until the sugar has dissolved, then slowly bring to the boil. Simmer, uncovered, for 2–3 hours, stirring regularly to ensure it does not burn on the bottom of the pan. The chutney is ready when it is rich, thick and reduced. To test, drag a wooden spoon through the mixture: it should part to form a channel and reveal the base of the pan. If it starts to dry out before this stage is reached, add a little boiling water. Allow to cool slightly.

Pot the chutney while still warm in sterilised jars. Seal with plastic-coated screw-top lids (essential to stop the vinegar interacting with the metal). Leave to mature for at least 2 weeks – ideally 2 months – before using.

Variations
Vary the summer veg and fruit with whatever takes your fancy.

Salsa verde

The sauce as far as I'm concerned. I've yet to find any meat, fish or poultry it doesn't go with – and the more you make it the better it gets, as you develop a feel for how you like it. The herbs, and their individual quantities, are yours to choose. I favour tarragon and chervil, but tend to avoid rosemary and sage, as they are inclined to dominate the others. Try the recipe below and take it off in your own direction.

Serves 4

1 garlic clove, peeled
Small bunch of flat-leaf parsley, leaves stripped from stalks
Small bunch of basil
Slightly smaller bunch of mint, leaves stripped from stalks
2 anchovies
2 tsp capers
1 tsp mustard
A few drops of lemon juice
½ tsp sugar
Pinch of sea salt
Freshly ground black pepper
2 tbsp olive oil

Roughly chop the garlic, then add the herbs and chop together until combined. Add the anchovies and capers and continue until everything is finely chopped.

In a bowl, combine the mustard, lemon juice, sugar, salt and pepper, then stir in the herby mix. Stir in the olive oil a little at a time, to obtain a thick, glossy consistency. Now's the time to taste it – and add a little of this or that until it's as you want it.

Pesto

Of course you'll be tempted to use a food processor to make this classic dressing, but try to make it with a pestle and mortar, at least once. The texture is better and it's a satisfying thing to do. Pesto is something you should taste and tweak as you go along, so adjust the quantities until you get the flavour that is right for you.

Serves 4

½ garlic clove, peeled and chopped
Sea salt and freshly ground black pepper
3 good handfuls of basil, leaves picked from the stalks and roughly chopped
Handful of pine nuts, very lightly toasted
Good handful of freshly grated Parmesan
Extra-virgin olive oil
Squeeze of lemon juice (optional)

Pound the garlic with a little pinch of salt and the basil leaves in a pestle and mortar, or pulse in a food processor but be careful not to over-process. Add the pine nuts and pound again. Turn into a bowl and add half the Parmesan. Stir gently and add just enough olive oil to bind the sauce and get to an oozy consistency. Season to taste, then add most of the remaining cheese. Pour in some more oil and taste again. Keep adding a bit more cheese or oil until you're happy with the taste and consistency. You may like to add a squeeze of lemon juice at the end to give it a little tang, but it's not essential. Try it with and without and see which you prefer.

Hollandaise sauce

Hugh's cheaty hollandaise is *the* match for all the headline veg that one by one herald in the warmer months – purple sprouting broccoli, asparagus, peas, etc.

Serves 4

150g unsalted butter
1 egg yolk
Good squeeze of lemon juice
Sea salt and freshly ground pepper

Melt the butter gently, cool slightly, then whisk it, a little at a time, into the egg yolk, aiming for a loose mayonnaise consistency. Whisk in the lemon juice and season with salt and pepper. Serve soon after making, as this sauce has a tendency to split after a while. Even if it does start to split, fortunately it's still quite palatable.

Roasted tomato sauce

As simple and delicious as it gets, this is perfect as a quick midweek sauce for pasta, a pizza topping, the base of any number of soups and much, much more. Any flavoursome tomato variety will work well, but in truth, this sauce even brings out redeeming qualities in a fairly ordinary harvest. And you can always throw oregano, thyme and/or a little chilli into the mix before roasting if you fancy.

Serves 4–6, or more
1kg ripe tomatoes ('San Marzano' are perfect)
3 garlic cloves, peeled and chopped
3 tbsp olive oil
Sea salt and freshly ground black pepper

Preheat the oven to 180°C/Gas Mark 4. Halve the tomatoes and lay them cut side up in an ovenproof dish. Mix the garlic with the olive oil and spoon it over the tomatoes. Season with salt and pepper. Roast for 40 minutes or so, until the tomatoes soften and begin to char slightly. Push the garlicky, tomatoey mix through a sieve to remove the skins and seeds. Taste the sauce and adjust the seasoning if you need to. That, believe it or not, is it.

Vegetable stock

This recipe from the River Cottage kitchen makes a lovely, fresh, well-flavoured stock that you can use as the base for any number of soups, risottos, stews and more. The quantities listed show you the proportions – simply multiply up if you're in the mood to make plenty to freeze.

Makes about 1.5 litres
3 large onions
6 carrots
1 head of celery
Handful of parsley sprigs
Handful of thyme sprigs
4 bay leaves

Optionals
Fennel
Parsley stalks

Finely shred everything you're using, place in a large pan and just cover with water. Bring to the boil, simmer for 2 minutes, then take off the heat. Leave to infuse for 30 minutes, then strain. Freeze any stock you're not using in half-litre batches.

Carrot and walnut cake

Fragrant with spices and deliciously moist, this cake is about as far away from the dry and dreary 1970s health-food shop incarnations as you can get. The unusual addition of apple sauce keeps it really juicy. You can either make your own apple sauce by cooking one large Bramley apple in a couple of tablespoons of water until fluffy, or use good-quality ready-made.

Makes 12 squares

- 80g sultanas
- Knob of butter, for greasing
- 220g wholemeal self-raising flour
- 1 tsp baking powder
- 1 tsp ground cinnamon
- 1 tsp ground ginger
- ½ tsp salt
- Good pinch of ground cloves
- 220g light muscovado sugar, plus an extra 3 tbsp for the syrup
- 120ml sunflower oil
- Finely grated zest and juice of 1 orange
- 2 eggs, lightly beaten
- 225g apple sauce (see above)
- 270g carrots, peeled and coarsely grated
- 80g walnuts, roughly chopped
- 1 tbsp lemon juice

Preheat the oven to 170°C/Gas Mark 3. Put the sultanas into a small bowl, pour on hot water to cover and leave to soak for 20 minutes.

Lightly grease a loose-bottomed 20–22cm square cake tin, about 8cm deep, line the base with greaseproof paper and butter the paper. Sift together the flour, baking powder, cinnamon, ginger, salt and ground cloves.

In a large bowl, whisk together the 220g muscovado sugar, oil and orange zest until well combined, then whisk in the eggs until the mixture is creamy. Fold in the apple sauce, followed by the flour mixture until just combined. Next fold in the grated carrots and walnuts. Finally, drain the sultanas and fold these in.

Spoon the mixture into the prepared tin and smooth the surface with a spatula. Bake for about 1¼ hours, until a fine skewer inserted into the centre comes out without crumbs clinging to it. If the cake appears to be overbrowning before it is done, cover the top loosely with foil.

While the cake is in the oven, make the syrup. Put the orange juice into a small saucepan with the 3 tbsp light muscovado sugar and 1 tbsp lemon juice. Warm over a low heat, stirring until the sugar dissolves, then increase the heat and simmer until slightly syrupy, about 4–5 minutes.

As you remove the cake from the oven, run a knife around the edge and pierce the top a few times with a fine skewer. Now pour over the syrup, trying to make sure that you cover the surface fairly evenly. Stand the cake tin on a wire rack and leave to cool for a while before cutting into squares. You can serve this cake warm as a pudding with a dollop of crème fraîche, or cold as a treat at any time.

Variations

For a different sweet alternative to the carrot, try using parsnip or beetroot.

Pumpkin meringue pie

This ginger-spiked pastry case with its silky, spicy pumpkin filling and wispy topping of crisp-on-the-outside, soft-on-the-inside meringue makes a pretty spectacular autumn dessert. You'll hardly believe anything quite so glamorous started life in the veg patch.

Serves 10

For the filling
1.4kg pumpkin(s)
30g unsalted butter
50g light muscovado sugar, plus an extra 20g for sprinkling
1 tbsp syrup from the stem ginger jar
1 tsp ground ginger
1 tsp ground cinnamon
Good pinch of ground nutmeg
Good pinch of cloves
Pinch of salt
3 egg yolks
100ml double cream

For the pastry
450g plain flour
140g unrefined icing sugar
Pinch of salt
½ tsp ground ginger
30g preserved stem ginger in syrup, drained and finely chopped
225g unsalted butter, well chilled and cubed
2 egg yolks
3–4 tbsp iced water

For the meringue
3 egg whites
175g golden caster sugar

To serve (optional)
Whipped cream, a little extra chopped stem ginger and a drizzle of syrup from the jar

Preheat the oven to 180°C/Gas Mark 4. Halve the pumpkin(s) and scoop out the seeds. Put a small knob of butter and sprinkle 1 tsp light muscovado sugar into each cavity. Place in a roasting tin, cavities facing up. Put a splash of water into the bottom of the tin, cover tightly with foil and bake until the pumpkin is completely tender, about 1 hour.

Meanwhile, make the pastry. Sift together the flour, icing sugar, salt and ground ginger. Tip into a food processor and add the stem ginger and cubes of butter. Pulse until the mixture resembles coarse sand, then add the egg yolks and pulse quickly until it comes together in a ball, adding a little iced water if you need to, 1 tbsp at a time. Wrap the dough in cling film and chill in the fridge for about 30 minutes.

Let the pumpkin cool slightly, then scoop out the flesh and buttery juices into a food processor (you should have about 500g). Add the muscovado sugar, ginger syrup, spices and salt, and purée until very smooth. In a separate bowl, whisk the egg yolks and cream together, then fold in the pumpkin mixture until well combined.

Lightly grease a loose-bottomed 30cm flan tin, 3cm deep. Unwrap the pastry and roll out between two sheets of lightly floured baking parchment (this makes it slightly easier to handle) to a large round. Gently lower the pastry into the flan tin, easing it into the edges and being careful not to stretch it. Allow the excess pastry to hang over the side of the tin and stand the tin on a baking sheet.

Line the pastry case with baking paper and baking beans and bake 'blind' for 20 minutes. Remove the paper and beans, prick the tart base with a fork and return to the oven for 10 minutes. Leave to cool completely. Use a sharp knife to remove the excess pastry from the edge, or roll a rolling pin over the top and let the excess fall away. Heat the oven to 150°C/Gas Mark 2.

For the meringue, whisk the egg whites in a large clean bowl until they form stiff peaks. Whisk in the sugar, 1 tbsp at a time, until the mixture is thick and glossy.

Spoon the pumpkin filling into the pastry case, smooth with a spatula, then spread the meringue over the top with a palette knife, making sure it seals the edges completely. Swirl decoratively with your knife. Bake for 45 minutes.

Serve the pumpkin meringue pie warm or cold, with whipped cream, a scattering of chopped stem ginger and a drizzle of ginger syrup if you like.

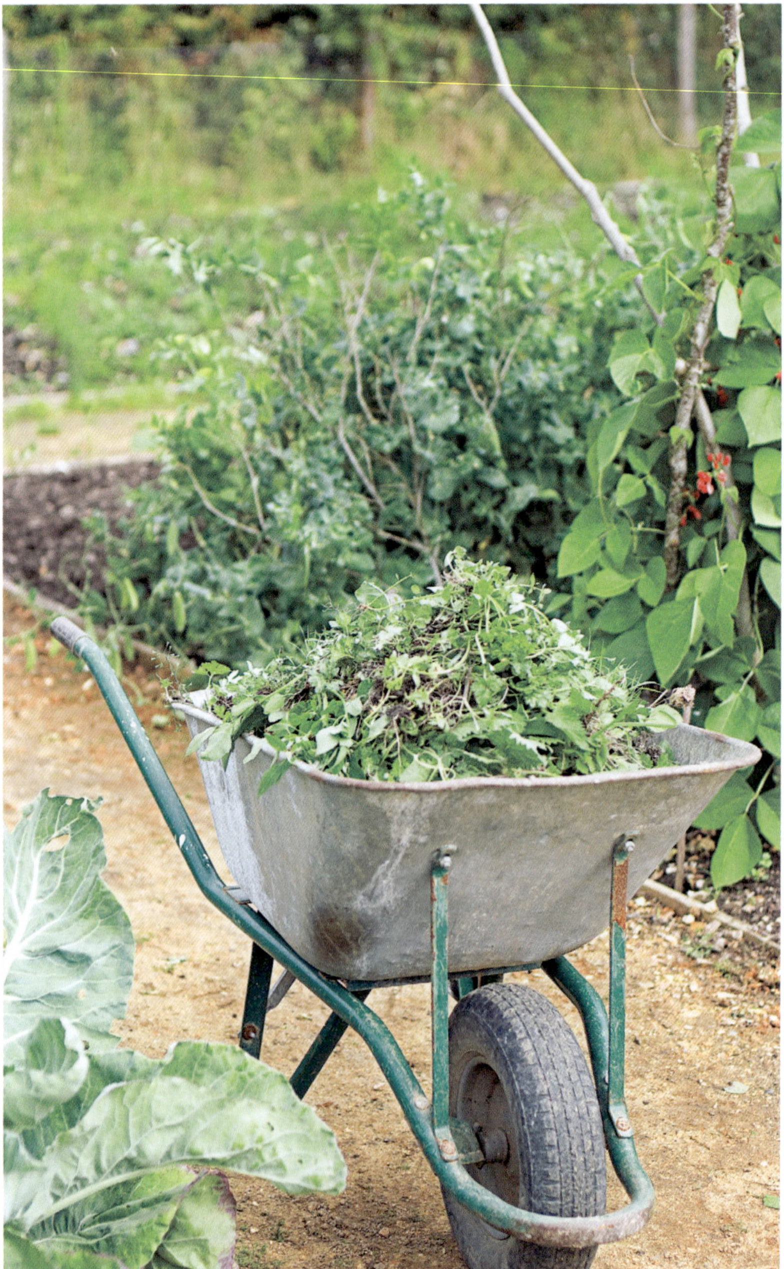

Directory

Seeds and seedlings

The Heritage Seed Library
www.gardenorganic.org.uk/hsl
024 7630 8210
Members receive free heirloom varieties, which helps to conserve our edible heritage

The Real Seed Catalogue
www.realseeds.co.uk
01239 821107
Excellent small supplier – no F1 or GM seeds

Kings Seeds
www.kingsseeds.com
01376 570000

Edwin Tuckers
www.tuckers-seeds.co.uk
01364 652233

Thomas Etty
www.thomasetty.co.uk
01460 57934

Jekka's Herb Farm
www.jekkasherbfarm.com
0845 290 3255

Nickys Nursery
www.nickys-nursery.co.uk
01843 600972

Sarah Raven's Kitchen and Garden
www.sarahraven.com
0845 092 0283

Rocket Gardens
www.rocketgardens.co.uk
01209 831468
Suppliers of organic vegetable and herb seedlings to create instant gardens

Delfland Nurseries
www.organicplants.co.uk
01354 740553
A nursery specialising in organic vegetable seedlings

The Chilli Pepper Company
www.chileseeds.co.uk
01539 558110

South Devon Chilli Farm
www.southdevonchillifarm.co.uk
01548 550782

Other supplies

Fertile fibre
www.fertilefibre.com
01432 853111
Organically certified peat-free compost and more

West Riding Organics
www.wrorganics.co.uk
01484 609171
Organically certified compost

The Natural Gardener
www.thenaturalgardener.co.uk
01568 611729
Coir and biodegradable pots, compost and sustainable pest control

LBS Garden Warehouse
www.lbsgardenwarehouse.co.uk
01282 873370
General garden supplies, including mulch mat/ground cover

The Little Veg Patch
www.earthwormlandscapes.co.uk
01202 882993
Instant raised veg patch

Link-a-bord
www.linkabord.co.uk
01773 590566
Instant raised beds made from recycled plastic

Wiggly wigglers
www.wigglywigglers.co.uk
01981 500391
Worms, wormeries and general veg patch supplies

Implementations
www.implementations.co.uk
0845 330 3148
Bronze/copper tools – hardwearing and beautiful

The Green Gardener
www.greengardener.co.uk
01603 715096
Range of biological pest control, plus general veg patch supplies

Defenders
www.defenders.co.uk
01233 813121
Biological pest control for the garden

Useful organisations

The River Cottage Community
http://community.rivercottage.net
A community of thousands to call on for advice and to share experiences

Garden Organic
www.gardenorganic.org.uk
024 7630 3517
A charity (formerly the HDRA) dedicated to organic growing. Well worth joining to give you access to a wealth of advice. Also an excellent source for seeds and everything to do with growing

Royal Horticultural Society
www.rhs.org.uk
0845 062 1111
A great source of advice, with numerous excellent gardens to visit, and also offers a soil analysis service

Slow Food
www.slowfooduk.info
01584 879599
Promoting the locality, diversity and enjoyment of food

National Society of Allotment Holders and Leisure Gardeners
www.nsalg.org.uk
01536 266576
Protecting, preserving and promoting allotment gardening

My own website is:
www.otterfarm.co.uk

Acknowledgements

Before I had the fun of writing one of my own, I'd never have suspected what a team effort turning the words into a book really is. So this is the part where I come clean about not having done absolutely everything on my own.

If you've tried any of the recipes in this book, you may be convinced that I'm a better cook than I am. Hopefully some of you won't get to read this as it's tucked away at the back and will carry on in blissful ignorance. In truth, without the River Cottage kitchen team as a whole, and Gill Mellor and Debora Robertson in particular, this book's final step on the journey from plot to plate would have been a far less tasty one. Thank you. And to Hugh for letting me pinch the odd classic of his.

Huge thanks also to Gavin Kingcome for his fine photography. And to Cristian Barnett for photographic inspiration, encouragement and advice in equal measure.

I owe much gratitude to Richard Atkinson, Janet Illsley, and Natalie Hunt in particular, at Bloomsbury, for their patience, vision and tireless enthusiasm. And to Will Webb, an inspired designer with a fantastic eye. Together they have done much to make this book what it is.

Thanks also to my agent, the rather wonderful Caroline Michel at PFD, whose enthusiasm and faith in me I hope to repay with endless sales and the second bottle of my own sparkling wine.

To my family, the first bottle. Candida and my lovely daughter Nell, thank you for being entirely unselfish in giving me the time and freedom to write this. As I tend to take half an hour over five minutes, I have much to repay.

Lastly, to those at River Cottage. To Emma Stapleforth, Victoria Moorey and Will Livingstone – they do most of the work and I get too much of the credit – thank you. To Simon Hansford (the previous Head Gardener) and Nikki Duffy: thanks for your contributions early on. To Steven Lamb, who I work so closely with: it's a total pleasure. To Rob Love: I hope this will help you stop fishing (for veg) so much. And Hugh: without whom there would be no book... thanks for thinking I could do it. And to everyone else at RCHQ: going to work couldn't feel less like going to work.

Further reading

I recommend: *Bob Flowerdew's Complete Book of Companion Gardening*; *Salad Leaves for All Seasons: Organic Growing from Pot to Plot* by Charles Dowding; *Oriental Vegetables* by Joy Larkcom; *Jekka's Complete Herb Book* by Jekka McVicar; and *The Allotment Keeper's Handbook: A Down-to-Earth Guide to Growing Your Own Food* by Jane Perrone. And if you're looking for more ideas for what to do with your harvest, these three classics are indispensable – *Jane Grigson's Vegetable Book*, *Sarah Raven's Garden Cookbook* and *The River Cottage Year*.

Index

access 183, 190–1
acidic soils 181, 189–90
alder, Italian 181
alfalfa 209
alkaline soils 181, 189–90
allotments 183
amaranth 105
animal manure 207
annuals 18
    herbs 90–1
antioxidants 166
aphids 212, 217–18
apples: glutney 256
artichokes *see* globe artichokes; Jerusalem artichokes
asparagus 24, 28–30, 169
    companion planting 213
    in small spaces 179
asparagus beetle 218
aubergines 31–2, 168
    companion planting 213
    seasonal guide 24
    in small spaces 179
autumn olive 181

bacon, creamy Brussels sprouts with chestnuts and 255
basil 91, 213
    pesto 258
bay leaves 87
beans 157–8
    supports 211
    see also individual types of bean
beds: planning 175
    preparing 191–3
    raised beds 189, 193
    seed beds 194–5
    width 175
beetles 218
beetroot 24, 33–5, 162–3, 178
    feta and beetroot salad with parsley 240
    roasted beetroot pizza with kale and anchovies 242–3
biennials 18
biological pest controls 216
birds 157
blackfly 217–18
blanching 18
blight 168, 219
boards 175, 191, 193
bolting 19
borage 72, 213
borlotti beans 24, 36–7, 157, 178
brassicas 159–61
    companion planting 213
    crop rotation 173–4
    in small spaces 178
    see also individual types of brassica
broad beans 24, 38–40, 157, 178
    lettuce soup with spring onions, chorizo and 226
    spring into summer tart 244–5
broccoli, sprouting 27, 137–9, 159, 178
bruschetta, tomato with blue cheese and confit chilli 230
Brussels sprouts 24, 41–3, 159, 178
    creamy Brussels sprouts with chestnuts and bacon 255
buckets 17
buckwheat 209

cabbage root fly 161
cabbage white butterflies 161, 212, 217
cabbages 44–5, 159
    companion planting 213
    seasonal guide 24
    in small spaces 178, 180
cake, carrot and walnut 260–1
calabrese 24, 46–7, 159, 178
calendula 73
carbon emissions 15–16
cardboard: mulches 210
    no-dig approach 193
cardoons 25, 48–9, 169, 179
carrot fly 212
carrots 50–2, 162–3
    carrot and walnut cake 260–1
    companion planting 213
    honey roast carrots 253
    seasonal guide 25
    in small spaces 178
catalogues, seed 16, 172
caterpillars 161, 217
cauliflower 25, 53–5, 159, 178
celeriac 25, 56–7, 162–3, 178
    celeriac rémoulade 250
    leek and celeriac soup 228
celery 25, 58–9, 162, 178
chard 25, 60–1, 169, 179
cheese: baby pea and ricotta salad with spring onions 239
    feta and beetroot salad with parsley 240
    Jerusalem artichoke salad with goat's cheese and hazelnuts 238
    pesto 258
    spring into summer tart 244–5
    tomato bruschetta with blue cheese and confit chilli 230
cherry, morello 180
chervil 91
chestnuts, Brussels sprouts with bacon and 255
chicken manure 207

chicory 25, 62–3, 166, 179
chilli peppers 64–6, 168
    seasonal guide 25
    in small spaces 179, 180
    tomato bruschetta with blue cheese and confit chilli 230
chives 87–9, 180
chop suey greens 106
chutney: glutney 256
clay soils 187, 189
clearing ground 186
climate change 16
climbing plants, supports 211
cloches 23, 180, 196
clover 208, 209
club root 159–61
coir 197, 198–9
cold frames 180
comfrey feeds 215
companion planting 212–13
compost 202–7
    compost bins 175, 203–5
    mulches 210
    no-dig approach 193
    preparing beds 191
compost, potting 196
containers 177
    cucurbits in 165
    legumes in 158
    onions in 164
    root vegetables in 163
    salad leaves in 167
    Solanaceae in 168
    sowing seeds in 196–9
coriander 91, 213
corn on the cob 145–7
courgette flowers, deep-fried 234
courgettes 67–8, 165
    baby courgette salad with lemon and sugar snap peas 237
    glutney 256
    seasonal guide 25
    in small spaces 179, 180
crop rotation 172–4, 202
    brassicas 159–61, 173
    legumes 157, 173
    onions 164, 173
cucumbers 25, 69–71, 165, 179
cucurbits 165, 179, 180
curried root soup 225
cut-and-come-again crops 18
cutworms 219

dauphinoise potatoes 254
digging 186, 191–3
dill 91

direct sowing 19, 194
diseases 172, 205, 216–19
    see also individual vegetables
drainage: raised beds 193
    soil texture 187, 189
drills, sowing in 194

edible flowers 72–3, 166, 169, 179
Elaeagnus umbellata 181
endive 25, 74–5, 166, 179
equipment 17
erosion 181
exposed sites 181

F1 hybrids 19
farmyard manure 207
fences 181
fennel, Florence 76–7, 169
    seasonal guide 25
    in small spaces 179, 180
fertilisers 202
    comfrey feeds 215
feta and beetroot salad with parsley 240
field beans 209
flea beetle 218
fleece, horticultural 218
Florence fennel *see* fennel
flowers, edible 72–3, 166, 169, 179
food miles 15–16
forcing 19
forks 17
French beans 78–80, 157
    French beans with Japanese-style dressing 251
    seasonal guide 26
    in small spaces 178

garlic 26, 81–3, 164, 178
germination 195, 196
gherkins 25, 69–70, 165, 179
giant red mustard 106, 180
globe artichokes 84–6, 169
    minted artichoke houmous 229
    seasonal guide 26
    in small spaces 179, 180
glutney 256
gluts 176
gourds 27, 140–2, 165
grass: in compost 207
    paths 191
green fly 217–18
green manures 157, 208–9, 210
greenhouses 23, 196
guttering, sowing seeds in 198

half the garden soup 223
hand forks 17

hardening off 19, 199
harvesting 24–7, 176
　　see also individual vegetables
hay 207, 210
hedges 181
herbs 87–91, 169
　　edible flowers 73
　　in small spaces 179
hoeing, seed beds 195
hoes 17
hollandaise 258
honey roast carrots 253
horticultural fleece 218
horticultural societies 183
houmous, minted artichoke 229
hyssop 213

imported vegetables 15–16, 176
insects: beneficial 217–18
　　companion planting 212

Japanese-style dressing, French beans with 251
Jerusalem artichokes 92–3, 169
　　Jerusalem artichoke salad with goat's cheese and hazelnuts 238
　　Jerusalem artichoke soup 227
　　seasonal guide 26
　　in small spaces 179, 180
Jiffy 7's 197

kai lan 106
kale 26, 94–5, 159, 178
　　roasted beetroot pizza with kale and anchovies 242–3

leeks 26, 96–8, 164, 178
　　Jerusalem artichoke soup 227
　　leek and celeriac soup 228
legumes 157–8
　　companion planting 213
　　crop rotation 173–4
　　green manures 208
　　in small spaces 178, 180
lemon verbena 89
lettuces 26, 99–101, 166, 179
　　lettuce soup with spring onions, broad beans and chorizo 226
lime, neutralising soil 190
limestone, soils over 189
limitations: access 183
　　money 182–3
　　space 177–81
　　time 182
loamy soils 187, 189, 190
lovage 89
lupins, agricultural 209

mackerel with sorrel sauce 246
mangetout peas 112
manure 207
marigolds 73, 213
meringue pie, pumpkin 262–3
mibuna 106
mice 157
mint 89, 213
　　minted artichoke houmous 229
mizuna 106
module trays 196
money-saving ideas 15, 182–3
morello cherry 180
mulch mat 191, 210
mulches 186, 210
mushroom compost 207, 210
mustard: agricultural 209
　　giant red 106, 180

nasturtiums 72, 180, 212, 213
nematodes 217, 219
nettles 213
nitrogen 202
　　comfrey feeds 215
　　in compost 204
　　crop rotation 173
　　green manures 208
　　legumes 157
　　wood shavings and 205
no-dig approach 193
nutrients 202

oka 23
okra 23
onions 102–4, 164
　　companion planting 213
　　crop rotation 173–4
　　half the garden soup 223
　　seasonal guide 26
　　in small spaces 178
oregano 89, 213
organic matter 190, 202
　　compost 203–7
　　green manures 208–9
　　mulches 210
　　sources of 207
oriental leaves 105–7, 166, 169, 179
ornamental vegetables 16

pak choi 106
paper plans 174–5
parsley 91
　　salsa verde 257
parsnips 26, 108–9, 162, 178
paths 174–5, 190–1
pea and bean weevil 157

peas 110–13, 157
    baby pea and ricotta salad with spring onions 239
    pea tips 110, 166
    seasonal guide 26
    in small spaces 178
    spring into summer tart 244–5
    supports 211
peat 196, 197
peppers 26, 114–16, 179
perennials 19
    herbs 87–90
    vegetables 169, 175, 179
perpetual spinach 25, 60–1, 169
pesticides 202
pesto 258
pests 202, 216–18
    companion planting 212–13
    see also individual vegetables
pH values, soil 181, 189–90
phacelia 209
phosphorus 215
pizza, roasted beetroot with kale and anchovies 242–3
planks 175, 191, 193
planning veg patch 170–83
plant groups 154–69
planting out 199
planting times 24–7
    see also individual vegetables
plastic pots 199
plot-to-plate vegetables 14
pollination 19
polytunnels 23, 196
porches 181
pot marigolds 73, 213
potassium 202, 207, 215
potatoes 117–19, 168
    blight 219
    crop rotation 173–4
    dauphinoise potatoes 254
    seasonal guide 26
    in small spaces 179
pots *see* containers
potting on 19
pricking out 197–8
pumpkins 27, 140–2, 165, 179
    pumpkin meringue pie 262–3

radishes 120–1, 159, 161
    companion planting 213
    seasonal guide 26
    in small spaces 178, 180
rain water harvesting 174
raised beds 189, 193
rakes 17

raking soil 191
rats 205
red onions 164
rice: squash risotto with crispy sage 248–9
River Cottage Community 183, 266
rock, soils over 189
rocket 27, 122–3, 166, 179
root trainers 197
root vegetables 162–3
    crop rotation 173–4
    curried root soup 225
    in small spaces 178
    see also individual types of root vegetable
rosemary 89–90, 213
rotation of crops *see* crop rotation
rotovators 191
runner beans 27, 124–5, 157, 178
running to seed 19
rye, Hungarian grazing 209

sage 90, 213
    squash risotto with crispy sage 248–9
salad leaves 166–7, 179, 180
salads: baby courgette salad with lemon and sugar snap peas 237
    baby pea and ricotta salad with spring onions 239
    feta and beetroot salad with parsley 240
    Jerusalem artichoke salad with goat's cheese and hazelnuts 238
salsa verde 257
salsify 27, 126–7, 162, 178
sandy soils 187, 189
sauces: hollandaise 258
    pesto 258
    roasted tomato 259
    salsa verde 257
scorzonera 27, 126–7, 162, 178
seasonal vegetables 13–14, 176
seaweed 207, 210
seed catalogues 16, 172
seed trays 197–8
seedlings: hardening off 199
    planting out 199
    pricking out 197–8
    thinning 195
seeds: saving money 182–3
    seed swaps 183
    sowing 194–5
shallots 27, 128–9, 164, 178
sheds 183
silty soils 187
sloping sites 181
slugs 157, 175, 216
small gardens 177–81
snails 157, 175, 216

soil 187–90
    clearing ground 186
    crop rotation 173
    digging 186, 191–3
    erosion 181
    extreme soil conditions 181
    green manures 157
    improving 202–10
    mulches 210
    no-dig approach 193
    pH values 189–90
    preparing beds 191–3
    raised beds 193
    sowing under cover 196
    texture 187–9
    tilth 19
soil worms 219
Solanaceae 168, 179
sorrel 27, 130–1, 166, 179
    mackerel with sorrel sauce 246
soups: curried root soup 225
    half the garden soup 223
    Jerusalem artichoke soup 227
    leek and celeriac soup 228
    lettuce soup with spring onions, broad beans and chorizo 226
sowing: sowing direct 19, 194
    sowing times 23, 24–7
    successional sowing 176
    under cover 19, 23, 196–9
    see also individual vegetables
spades 17
spinach 27, 132–4, 166, 179
spinach, perpetual 25, 60–1, 169, 179
spring into summer tart 244–5
spring onions 27, 135–6, 164, 178
sprouting broccoli 27, 137–9, 159
squash 140–2, 165
    companion planting 213
    seasonal guide 27
    in small spaces 179, 180
    squash risotto with crispy sage 248–9
stock, vegetable 259
straw 207, 210
successional sowing 176
sugar snap peas 112
    baby courgette salad with lemon and sugar snap peas 237
supports 211
    cucurbits 165
    peas and beans 158
swede 27, 143–4, 159, 178
sweetcorn 27, 145–7, 169, 179, 180

tares 209
tarragon 90

tart, spring into summer 244–5
tempura, vegetable 233
tepees, supporting plants 211
terminology 18–19
terracing, sloping sites 181
testing soil pH values 190
texture, soil 187–9
thinning seedlings 195
Three Sisters method, supports 180, 211
thyme 90, 213
tilth 19
time, limited 182
tomatoes 148–51, 168
    blight 219
    companion planting 213
    glutney 256
    half the garden soup 223
    roasted tomato sauce 259
    seasonal guide 27
    in small spaces 179
    tomato bruschetta with blue cheese and confit chilli 230
tools 17, 183
transformers 14–15
trays, sowing seeds 196, 197–8
trowels 17
turnips 27, 152–3, 159, 178
    turnip 'risotto' 247

vegetable stock 259
vegetable tempura 233
vegetables: planning veg patch 170–83
    what to grow 12–16
violas 72

walls 180
walnuts: carrot and walnut cake 260–1
watering 174
    seed beds 199
    seeds 195
    water butts 174
    watering cans 17
weeds: clearing ground 186
    in compost bins 205
    green manures 208
    mulches 210
    no-dig approach 193
    weeding seed beds 195
    weedkillers 202
wheelbarrows 17
wild rocket 122–3, 179
windowsills 181, 196
windy sites 181
wireworms 219
wong bok 106
worms 204, 207, 218

The River Cottage

Edible Seashore Handbook

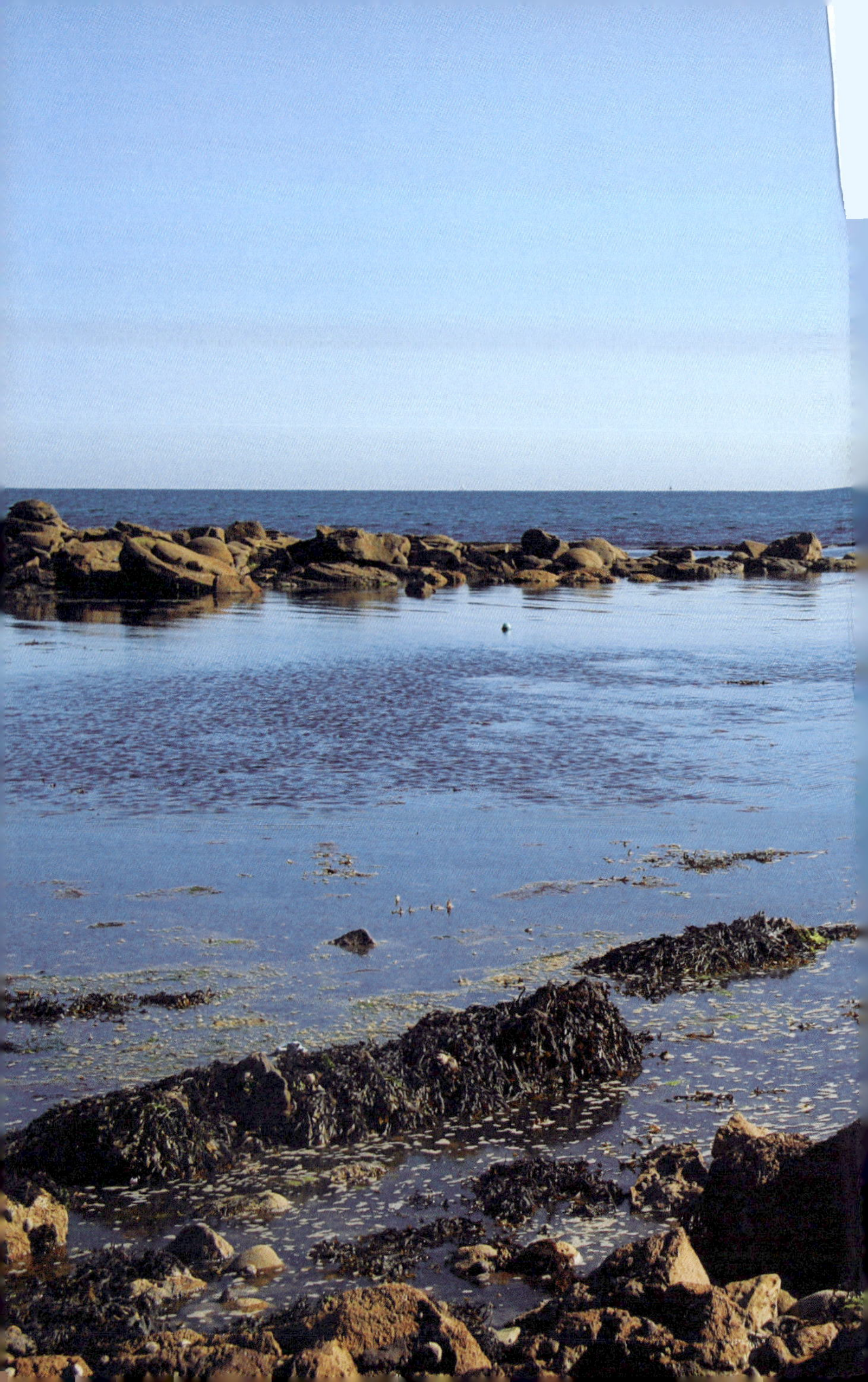

The River Cottage Edible Seashore Handbook

by John Wright

introduced by
Hugh Fearnley-Whittingstall

www.rivercottage.net

BLOOMSBURY
LONDON · NEW DELHI · NEW YORK · SYDNEY

For Trish

First published in Great Britain 2009
This paperback edition published 2012

Text © 2009 by John Wright
Photography © 2009 by John Wright
Recipe photographs © 2009 by Colin Campbell, except
pp.166–7, 169, 179, 192, 195, 213 © 2009 by John Wright

The moral right of the author has been asserted

Bloomsbury Publishing Plc, 50 Bedford Square, London WC1B 3DP
Bloomsbury Publishing, London, New Delhi, New York and Sydney

A CIP catalogue record for this book is available from the British Library

ISBN 978 1 4088 3609 5
10 9 8 7 6 5 4 3 2 1

Project editor: Janet Illsley
Designer: willwebb.co.uk

Printed in China by C&C Offset Printing Co., Ltd.

MIX
Paper from responsible sources
FSC® C008047

www.bloomsbury.com/rivercottage

While every effort has been made to ensure the accuracy of the information contained in this book, in no circumstances can the publisher or the author accept any legal responsibility or liability for any loss or damage (including damage to property and/or personal injury) arising from any error in or omission from the information contained in this book, or from the failure of the reader to properly and accurately follow any instructions contained in the book.

Contents

Starting Out	8
Foraging Safely	24
The Rule Book	32
The Flowering Plants	44
The Seaweeds	86
The Molluscs	106
The Crustaceans	140
Recipes	166
Useful Things	230

Who can resist the great primal, elemental pull of the sea? Even if you're no sailor, it's a near certainty that you have been drawn to the sea's edge at some point in your youth, to stand on the brink of the vast ocean, and dabble on the margins of our known universe: our shores.

Childhood memories of building sandcastles, rummaging in rock pools and splashing in the surf stay with us like little else. Whether netting plump prawns in a weedy rock pool, or plucking weed itself, silky and wet, from the fringes of a reef, or hauling in a crab pot with hope in my heart, these salt-scented, windswept, sand-encrusted endeavours have imprinted themselves on my mind with particular clarity. For me, those precious moments have been equally nourishing in adulthood. And just as they are always a pleasure to recall, they are also a pleasure to repeat, as often as time allows.

This is a phenomenon that John Wright, the author of this brilliant little book, understands well. The Edible Seashore foraging days that he leads at River Cottage are among the most popular of all our events and he puts this down to the fact that they allow people to escape into that wonderful, truly wild, yet accessible world where the sea meets the land. It's the ultimate antidote to the daily grind.

Take a group of adults out of their work environment, give them some buckets and nets and let them go paddling among the rock pools, and they invariably have a whale of a time. Foraging allows you to leave behind your humdrum concerns and routines and inhabit a world full of fresh air, foaming spray and genuinely exciting discoveries. The fact that so many of them are edible – delicious even – is the great and under-appreciated bonus.

There is no better companion on such a jaunt than John. This is not his first River Cottage book. If you own a copy of his volume on mushrooms, you will know that he is not only a great expert on mycology, but one of the most engaging and amusing writers on the subject. Within this new book you will discover – what you may already have suspected – that the breadth of John's knowledge and the width of his wit and wisdom go way beyond our fungal heritage. He is just as much at home with estuarine mud, golden sand, or salty water between his toes as he is with the bosky forest floor beneath his boots.

The fact is that John's knowledge of wild foods across the board is greater than that of anyone else I know. But, as with mushrooms, the delight of this book is not only the erudite precision with which he selects from his vast store of knowledge, but also in the sheer joy, the sense of wonder and fun, with which he puts it across. You know that few people will get quite as much pleasure from stumbling on, say, a good thick cliff-top run of Alexanders as John. But when he describes its taste, its surprising role in our history, and a nifty way for you to prepare and taste it at home, then all that fun and excitement is yours for the taking.

The result is that even the armchair forager can take much pleasure from this book. I'm convinced, though, that it will inevitably lure most of you, sooner rather than later, down to the coast. If you are even remotely interested in our culinary heritage, then you must. As he reveals in the pages that follow, there is a wealth of delicious food to be found on the strands, reefs, mud flats, cliff tops and marshes of Britain's glorious and varied coastline. Shellfish and crustaceans, leafy greens, herbs, flowers and seaweeds are waiting to be discovered.

Gathering wild foods is one of the most satisfying and energising projects a person can undertake and doing so by the seaside – rain-whipped, salt-scoured, sun-baked or otherwise – is foraging at its most carefree and joyous. Nevertheless, it would be disingenuous to suggest that foraging is always straightforward and easy. You need to have more than an inkling of where to go, what to look for, what to avoid, and what to do with the wild foods you find. And with all that in mind, John has risen admirably to the task of producing a truly practical guide.

This handbook is meant to find its way into pockets and rucksacks. Taking this book with you is about as close as you can get to actually having John walking alongside as you comb your chosen beach. These pages are packed with indispensable advice and information, from clear photographs of the hole a razor clam forms in the sand, to instructions on how to create your own first-rate shrimp net. John even makes a good fist of unravelling the unremittingly complex laws and lore that relate to walking along, and taking things from, our seashores.

River Cottage HQ is situated on the Devon-Dorset border and down here we have access to some of the most beautiful, clean and richly populated shores in the country. We are particularly lucky, I'll grant you, but I can't emphasise enough that seaside foraging is a pleasure that's open to all of us. We are blessed throughout the UK with a stunning and varied coastline, which is largely well looked after and usually accessible to walkers, bathers and foragers. Even if you don't live very close to the sea, nowhere in the land is more than about 70 miles distant from it. If you're feeling a little jaded or in need of some fresh inspiration, perhaps it's time for a trip to the beach? You could be amazed at what you find and, as everyone knows, there's nothing like the sea air to give you an appetite...

Hugh Fearnley-Whittingstall, East Devon, May 2009

Starting Out

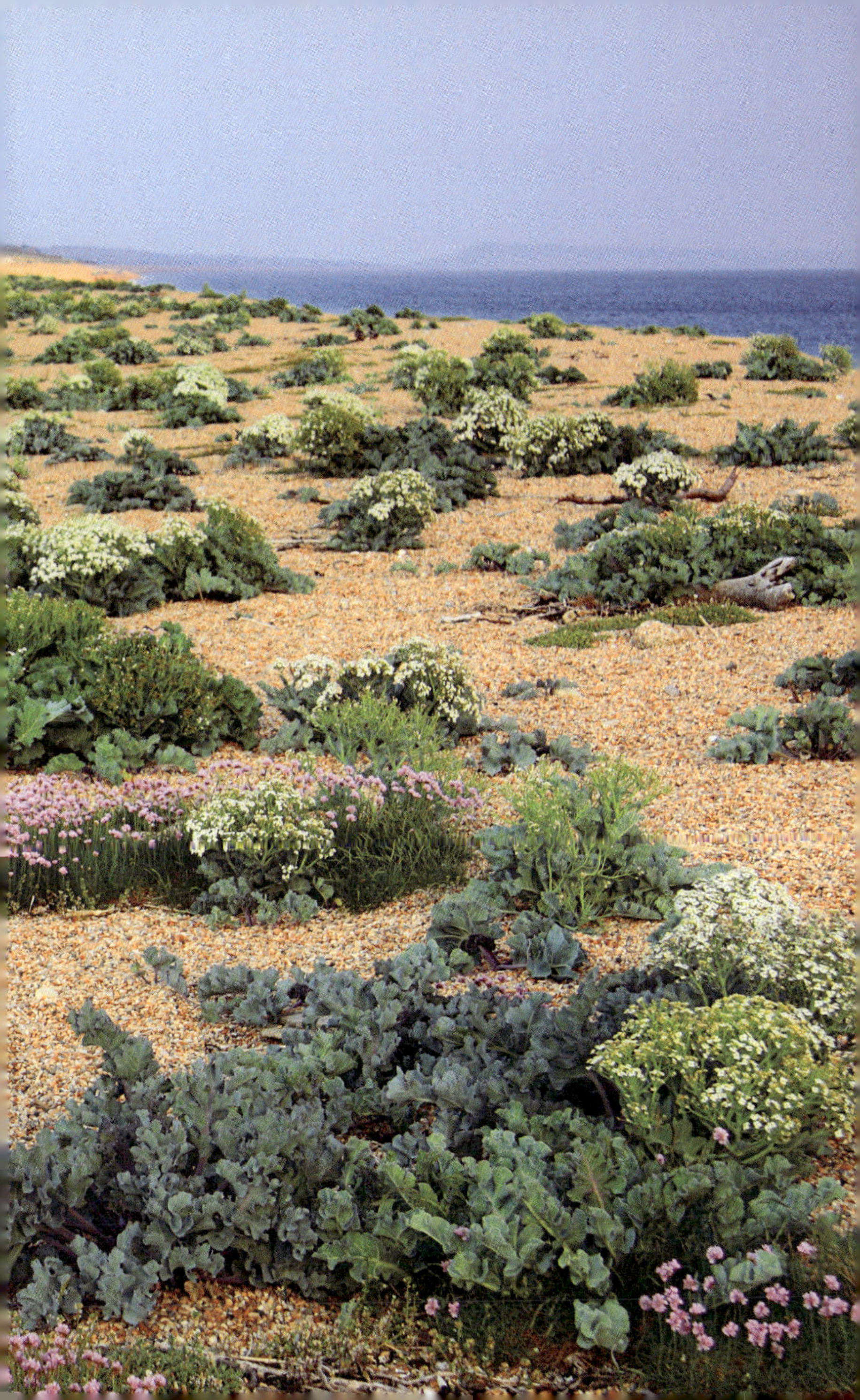

We are blessed in these islands with a vast and fruitful coastline yet few of us collect for ourselves any of the abundant edible plants and animals that can be found there. It is a very anthropocentric view to consider that the food plants and animals that are left uncollected around our shores are wasted, but it is certainly true that countless tons of vegetables, seaweeds and animals that could be gathered and eaten without any noticeable effect on the populations concerned are left to 'rot on the vine'. The aim of this book is to encourage the careful collection of some of this bounty.

Collecting shellfish near my childhood home in Portsmouth was a regular family pastime led by my father; he was a keen fisherman and, as the son of a Lowestoft trawler skipper, one who had fishing in his blood. I learned most of my seaside plants and seaweeds many years later in the springtime when mushrooms (my second foraging love) were scarce. I would roam the coastal paths of the West Country with my *Food for Free* and my *Wild Flowers of Britain and Northern Europe* in my hand. Now, if I ever need to find wild food reliably and in abundance the seaside is my first destination. There is just so much to be found there.

I have imposed some limits on what to include in this book. Generally speaking everything described here can be gathered from somewhere between the top of a seaside cliff to out to sea as far as waist deep on a low spring tide. You might need to get wet to collect some of what is described here but not *too* wet and you won't need a boat. The plants in this book include strictly maritime species but also a few that are particularly common by the sea. Many plants which are found just as commonly inland have been excluded – one of my favourite seaside foraging spots provides blackberries, elderflowers and horseradish, but these species are not covered here.

The last time I caught a proper fish (apart from inadvertently in a crab pot) was in 1960 – a small whiting if you are interested. With this level of expertise established I have decided to avoid mentioning fish entirely. All the animals in this book are generically called 'shellfish', a term which covers the molluscs (Cockles, Mussels, Oysters, etc.) and crustaceans (Crabs, Lobsters, Prawns, etc.). Some creatures that one might expect to be here, such as ormers, scallops, sea urchins and crayfish, have been omitted either for conservation reasons or because they are too hard to catch in shallow water. A few likely plants are also missing – the sea pea, for example, is edible in small quantities but sufficiently rare to put it out of bounds and sea campion, although you can eat it, just doesn't taste very nice.

All the techniques in this book for catching or finding shellfish I learned over the years for myself or from fishermen friends. One thing I have found is that there are as many methods and variations of methods as there are fishermen, and every time I talk to someone new I learn something new. I have not been able to include everything I have discovered and I certainly have not discovered everything there is to know. Do not be disappointed if your favourite trick for catching your prey is missing.

The instincts for foraging and hunting are deep within us all and we have lost much in failing to fulfil these needs. I would ask you to enjoy your days wandering and paddling by the sea, looking for your supper, but I know I do not have to; such pleasure is written in your genes.

Conservation

We are so far from our food these days. We seldom have to think of where it comes from or how it got to our kitchen (though things are improving). A bag of Prawns from the supermarket freezer is just a commodity, a fuel to be mixed with other fuels to produce a passable dish for the table. But spend a couple of hours with a shrimp net and the resultant meal is an occasion. In foraging, the natural order is restored; a relationship, albeit an asymmetric one, between gatherer and gathered is established. We come at last to truly value food and to understand how hard it can be to come by.

To the forager and the hunter the seasons are a matter of great importance; the weather and, at least where the subjects of this book are concerned, the tides, an intimate part of everyday life. Most importantly the collector quickly gains an understanding of living organisms and will learn of the problems and pressures they face. It is my belief that anyone who enjoys this close a relationship to the natural world will seek to protect it. As Richard Mabey suggests in his seminal *Food for Free*, if they see a threat to a wood, a meadow, a beach, they will take it *personally*.

I am often asked if it is entirely appropriate for anyone in this overpopulated world to plunder the wild for food. Which is, when one considers it, an extremely odd question. A moment's reflection will reveal that foraging, together with hunting, is the *only natural* way that a human being can obtain sustenance. All other methods of acquiring food, from supermarket ready-meals via farmers' markets all the way to the virtuous allotment garden, are a matter of human artifice. To live the truly natural life one has to forage.

Implicit in the question is an assumption that cultivation is somehow less morally suspect – when, clearly, cultivation has its own massive environmental impact. If one grows a field of soya beans one must first kill everything that was growing there before, and then continue to deny that area of land to any competing organism. As knock-down arguments go this is not a bad one, though nothing, of course, is ever that simple. Nevertheless, I think it is a good starting point and the presumption that we have a moral right to collect food from the wild, a birthright even, can be maintained.

When it comes to asserting that right the careful forager will judge every species and every situation individually and make a judgement. This judgement must be based on a knowledge of an organism's biology, ecology and conservation status.

There is the argument that this is all very well, but what if everybody went foraging? This has no *moral* weight. It is not immoral, though it may be unwise, to visit Swindon on Tuesdays – but if everybody did it there would be a major crisis. It would be a minor ecological disaster if everyone picked as much Sea Beet as they could find – but, like the Swindon Catastrophe, it is simply not going to happen. Ultimately, that best distributed commodity, common sense, must be employed.

If, for example, a plant is moderately rare, one could only feel justified in removing, carefully, a leaf or two from each specimen, and then only occasionally, while checking to make sure that there was no evidence of someone else having done the same. Some species are so rare that one must avoid disturbing them at all and eating them would be out of the question. Most (though not all) of the species in this book are common and it would require much dedicated foraging by large bands of foragers for any problem to arise. Those problems that do occur when wild food is gathered are almost invariably the result of commercial, and often mechanised, harvesting. The individual, collecting for personal use, will pick things individually and not resort to damaging practises such as dredging. For once the individual is in control of the source of their food and able to make informed decisions.

There is one moral trap that someone concerned with species conservation may fall into, and that is the sin of what might be termed 'environmental colonialism'. This takes the form of refusing to gather something locally, yet happily buying the same plant or animal collected in questionable circumstances in another country. Importing food while exporting environmental damage.

These are general suggestions for those who wish to be written among the righteous:

- Only pick a few leaves from each plant.
- Keep on the move when collecting shellfish – pick a few from each spot then look elsewhere.
- Avoid collateral damage to other organisms – walking about carelessly on vegetated pebble beaches, for example, can easily wreck the delicate plants that grow there.
- Return rocks to their rightful place in rock pools.
- Do not leave piles of mud when digging for shellfish – the mud will smother organisms beneath it.

Finally, there is a great deal of legislation designed to protect native species and habitats; details of these, sometimes blunt, instruments can be found in The Rule Book (pp.32–43).

The nationally scarce Wild Cabbage

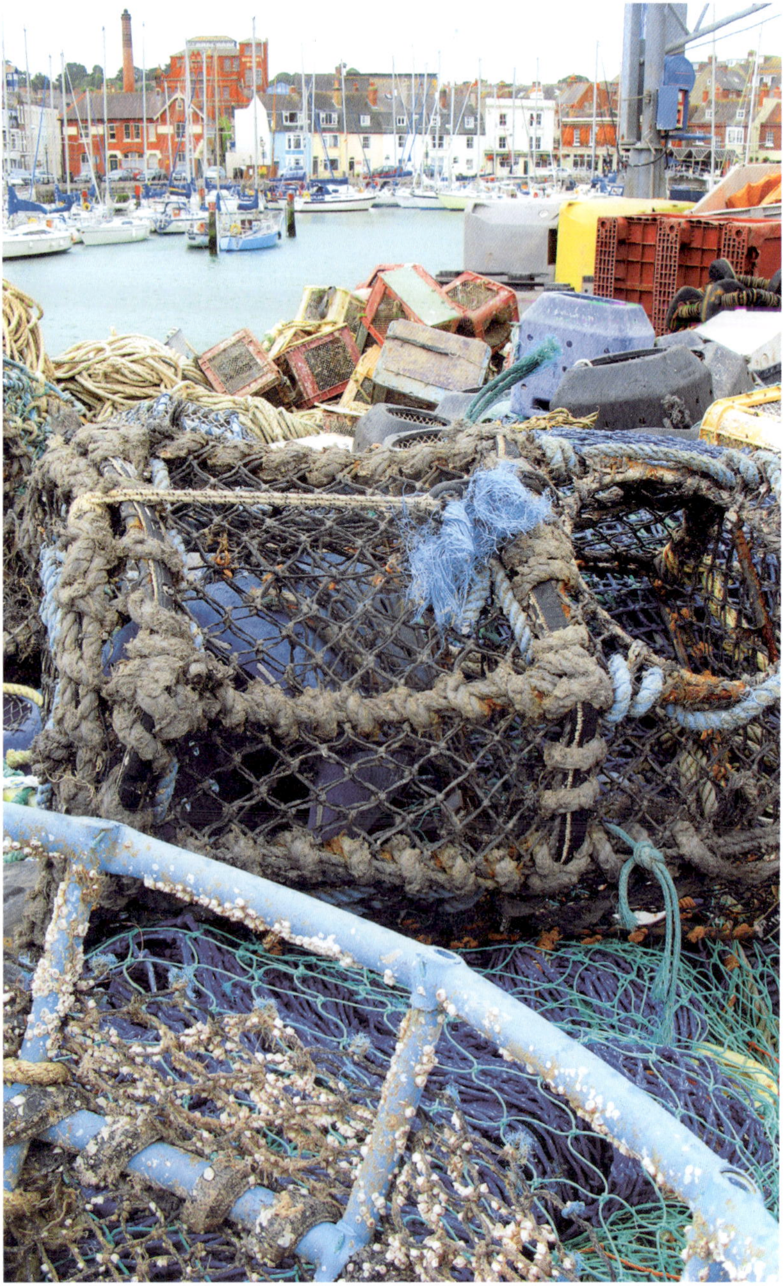

Equipment

Much of what is needed by the seaside forager will be common pieces of household and garden equipment, but to be the complete seaside forager you will need some much more serious pieces of kit. These are the pots and nets needed to catch crustaceans. You can spend a lot of money on such things and you might decide it would be preferable to make some of these. You may also need safety equipment, so do read pp.29–30.

Knives and scissors

To avoid uprooting entire plants (generally an illegal operation) you will need to cut off the bits you want with a knife or a pair of scissors. A penknife is sufficient for most occasions and it is legal to carry one around at all times. If you feel you need a bigger blade (over 75mm) it is perfectly legal to bring one with you while foraging as you will have a good reason so to do. Be careful though. On my way to a foraging location in Wales, I stopped off in Swansea to buy some new boots. I wanted to wear them straight away and proceeded to cut off the various tags with my 5-inch blade. The shop assistant screamed, 'He's got a knife!' and took a little persuading that I wasn't an axe murderer after all.

Kitchen scissors are the most useful of foraging implements and essential for any seaweeding expedition.

Spade

Walking around with a spade under your arm can similarly gain you unwelcome attention, though, provided you do not have a rolled-up carpet with you as well, not the sort that invites the arrival of the police. A spade will be necessary for the extraction of some of the deeper Clams such as the Sand Gaper. It will need to be very sturdy and as narrow as possible.

Rake

An ordinary garden rake will suffice for cockling. In Hampshire and Dorset there is a minimum gap between the tines of 22.5mm.

Containers

A bucket is the most suitable container for collecting crustaceans and molluscs – cover your catch with some seaweed to keep it in good condition. Canvas bags are best for plants unless you are collecting small quantities when a plastic container will suffice. Seaweeds are best kept in string bags as this allows them to drain – the best are the ones used by divers. Using a different bag for each species will spare you the hour or so it takes to sort out a mixed bag of seaweed.

Heart-shaped prawn net

Triangular prawn net

Prawn net

The simple child's prawn net is not suitable for any but the most casual prawning expedition. To take the matter seriously you need something like the two pictured above – and you may have to make your own. The triangular one is used for the 'up and under' manoeuvre; the heart-shaped net for the 'sideways sweep'. The frames are made from 8mm steel rod, bent and bound tightly by twine to a broom handle which has had two shallow grooves carved into one end for the prongs of the frame to sit in. Heavy-meshed net is best as it hangs better and is not so easily tangled in weed. I am afraid that you are on your own when it comes to sewing the seam in the net and the net to the frame – my net-making talents are on par with my knitting skills. My only advice is to use a blanket stitch wherever possible – it usually works. It will help to use copper wire as well as twine to attach the net to the frame as this will protect the twine and the net from the rough surface of rocks.

Shrimp net

As a good shrimp net (or pandle or push net, as it is often known) is hard to find I have given instructions for making one. The commonest size is about 120cm wide, though larger ones have been used. Its size and unweildy nature mean that it must be collapsible, making it slightly more of a challenge to construct. The trickiest part is attaching the net evenly – mine hangs with a distinct list to starboard, which at least adds character.

The drawings on p.18 will, I hope, give you a good idea of how a shrimp net is made. The whole thing can be disassembled (for storage and transport) simply by untying the triangular length of cord. If, when assembled, all the cords are kept in tension it is a surprisingly sturdy affair.

A hardwood such as beech is the best material to use, but a decent bit of softwood will do. All three major members should be made from timber about 3cm by 5cm in section. The bevelled piece at the front of the push bar and the triangular piece halfway up the shaft must be screwed in place. The push bar and its attached bevelled piece both have a triangular section cut out of them into which the end of the shaft will fit – make sure you cut these bits out before you screw the pieces together as it is twenty times easier than doing it afterwards.

Critically important is the chamfer at the base of the push bar – without it you will quickly grind to an embarrassing halt!

Once again you are, I am afraid, largely on your own when it comes to attaching the net. It can either be threaded on to the cord as you attach this to the frame with twine and the leather straps, or you can sew it on afterwards. The net in the drawing has two vertical seams at the back to give it some shape. If the whole construction is held horizontally, the net should hang down by about 60cm.

Shrimp net

Making a shrimp net

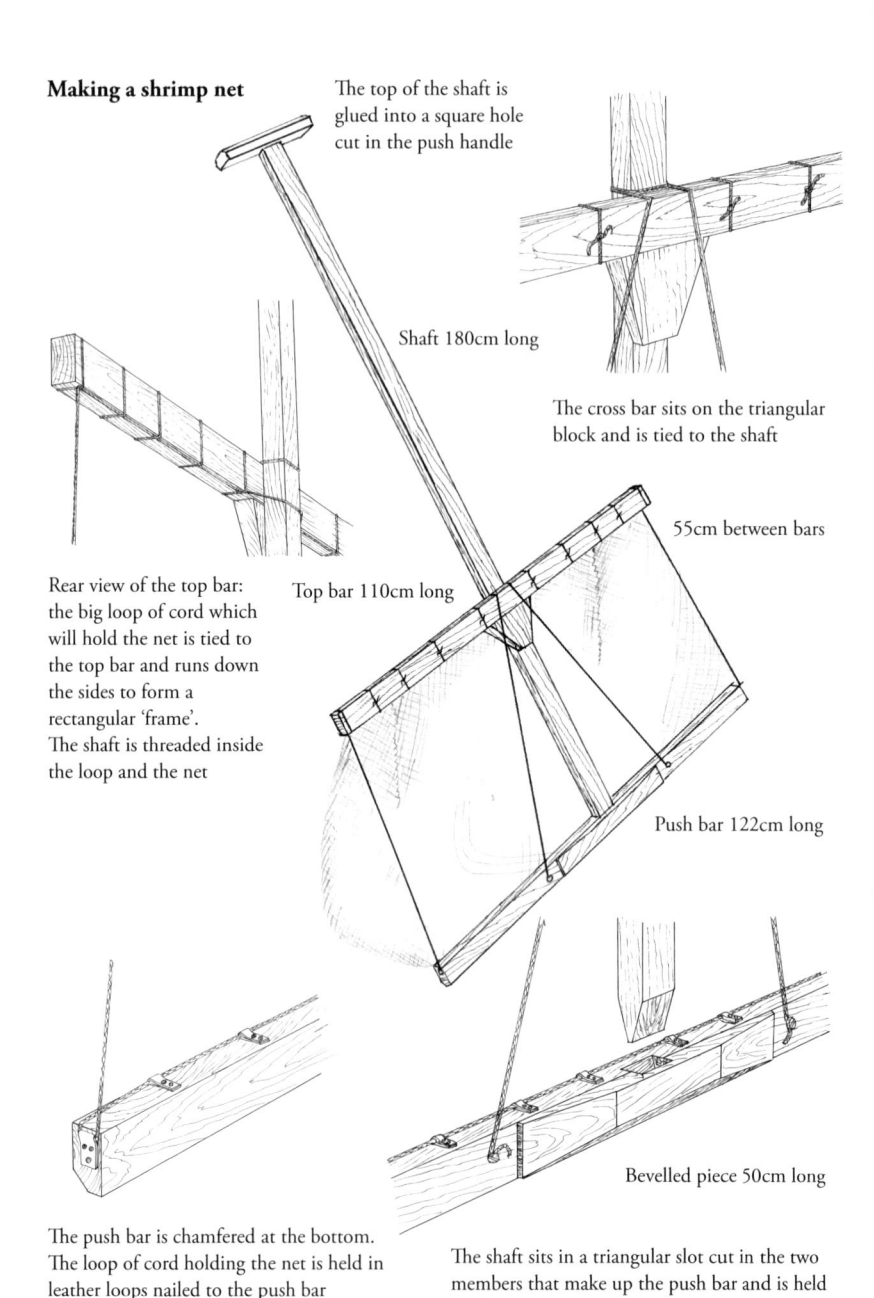

The top of the shaft is glued into a square hole cut in the push handle

Shaft 180cm long

The cross bar sits on the triangular block and is tied to the shaft

55cm between bars

Rear view of the top bar: the big loop of cord which will hold the net is tied to the top bar and runs down the sides to form a rectangular 'frame'.
The shaft is threaded inside the loop and the net

Top bar 110cm long

Push bar 122cm long

Bevelled piece 50cm long

The push bar is chamfered at the bottom. The loop of cord holding the net is held in leather loops nailed to the push bar

The shaft sits in a triangular slot cut in the two members that make up the push bar and is held rigidly in place with a length of cord looped around the top bar

Drop net

Crab hook

Drop or hoop net

The cheap drop nets that you can buy from seafront shops are actually rather good, just a little small. However, there is a simple and time-honoured way of making your own – remove all the spokes from a bicycle wheel and string a net to it, then attach three short ropes to hold it level, plus a hauling rope. These ropes should be held out of the net with small buoys so that your prey doesn't have its suspicions raised when you start to haul your net in. Finally you need two pieces of twine running together across the frame with two pieces of thick leather threaded on them, to hold the bait.

While it is possible to wade out with your drop nets, it is better, and much warmer, to lower them into rock pools or into deeper water from rocky promontories, jetties or quaysides. Drop nets are fairly indiscriminate in what they catch and herein lies the excitement of using them – at a new spot there is no knowing what might be found. Sometimes one finds Prawns, sometimes Shore Crabs, sometimes Velvet Swimming Crabs, occasionally a large fish. The key to using them is to pull them up quickly so that the catch does not escape. How long you leave them in the water is a compromise between good sense and patience. I think that 20 minutes is about right, but having never managed more than five I am only guessing.

Crab hook

It is not difficult to make one of these – a broom handle, a bent piece of 8mm steel, a couple of Jubilee clips and it is done.

Pots

This is where your bank account will be emptied as your garage fills up. Pots are beautiful things and it is easy to become a pot collector rather than a pot user. However you can sidestep these problems by buying a few of the cheap collapsible 'pots' that are readily available. These are good for catching Prawns, Velvet Swimming Crabs and even Lobsters if you buy a big one. As well as being fairly cheap, they have the great advantage of portability. Their disadvantages are that they quickly develop holes and will seldom last more than one season, and they must be tethered or weighted down to stop them being washed away.

Also fairly light, though not collapsible, is the prawn pot. It comes in a bewildering variety of shapes and sizes but the 'cylinder' type seen here is the most popular. These pots are designed to catch *only* Prawns; the small diameter entrance hole (about 30mm) will exclude unwanted by-catch such as Velvet Swimming Crabs, which would normally spend their time in captivity cheerfully eating your Prawns. There will be an easily accessed central compartment for the bait.

For Velvet Swimming Crabs a side-entry creel is best. They *can* be caught in the larger crab pots but are usually small enough to escape through the mesh once they get bored. Side-entry creels may be simple affairs with two side entrances and one chamber, or the more complicated 'parlour pot' type with a second chamber. The bait can be attached to a doubled length of twine strung somewhere in the middle of the pot. These pots are also good at catching Lobsters.

If Brown Crabs, Spider Crabs or Lobsters are your intended quarry then something altogether larger and heavier is required. This will usually mean a top-entry 'parlour pot'. These are fiendishly clever devices which trap their prey *when they try to escape* from the pot. The bait is attached to the outside surface of the plastic flowerpot-shaped entrance. The Crab or Lobster enters the 'chamber' of the pot to get at the bait but cannot get a good hold of the smooth-sided entrance when it tries to escape. It will then make a bid for freedom through the entrance into the adjoining 'parlour', usually via a net 'valve', and become trapped beyond all hope of escape. In practice you will normally find Crabs or Lobsters in both compartments. The problem for the seashore forager with these pots is their weight. Carrying a pot weighing 27 kilos 400 metres over rocks covered in seaweed is jolly good exercise but no fun at all.

A third type of pot (not pictured) is also available; the 'inkwell' pot. These pots owe their attractive shape to their basket-weaving origins though the modern variety uses a netted frame and often a 'flowerpot' entrance hole. They trap their prey by having an entrance which is simply out of reach to all but the most athletic of Crabs and Lobsters. A fan of the inkwell pot explained to me once that they are better than parlour pots for catching Lobsters because the animals will not suffer damage due to fighting – they just chase each other round and round in circles.

Collapsible pot

Prawn pot

STARTING OUT 21

Side-entry creel

Top-entry parlour pot

I have been told a great number of fishermen's stories over the years and this one is fishier than most.

Having placed my pots at low tide I nearly always go back to empty them on the next low tide but one – this will be around 25 hours later. There is no reason why you could not leave them for another day if you have the patience for it.

Once actually inside a pot, many Crabs and Lobsters show a strong disinclination to leave. Removing one that has attached itself by a claw is a straightforward exercise if you know how – and impossible if you don't. Either put the pot back in the water and wait until the animal releases its grip or give the claw a sharp tap with any convenient implement.

Putting out pots from the beach is an interesting and unusual pastime. I am always worried that my pots are going to be stolen so I usually carry them down to the beach in bags then wait, or try to wait, until there is no one around before proceeding. Unfortunately, as soon as the pots are unveiled people appear from nowhere and settle down to watch what they consider to be a spectator sport. Fortunately my audiences so far have all proved to be upstanding citizens without felonious intent. In some parts of the country there is a legal requirement to mark the position of all pots with a buoy. In my area there is no such necessity so I never use one and rely on landmarks to find them again. I even use special weighted ropes that sink out of sight of inquisitive eyes. I have never lost a pot. Paranoia pays.

Pots laid this near to the shore can be subject to much more violent conditions than those laid in deeper water. Tidal flow and wave action are more intense close to shore. For this reason it is important to choose calm weather for any pot-laying expedition both for safety's sake and to ensure that pots do not get washed away. Lost pots do not just disappear, they become 'ghost pots'. These will lie on the seabed somewhere and an animal will enter to eat the bait but be unable to get out. It eventually dies and becomes bait itself and something else enters the pot. Pots have been dredged up after being lost for a couple of years, packed tightly with the shells and decomposing carcasses of trapped Crabs and Lobsters.

There is always much discussion on what type of bait to use for which prey and how rancid or fresh it should be. I really do not think that it matters too much for the casual pot-thrower and a few fish heads stored in the freezer will keep you well supplied. Do not use Limpets as bait – they perform a useful service in preventing certain seaweeds taking over rocky shores. The invasive Slipper Limpet, however, is fair game and an extremely good bait for Prawns (sorry, no fisherman can resist recommending his favourite bait).

Foraging Safely

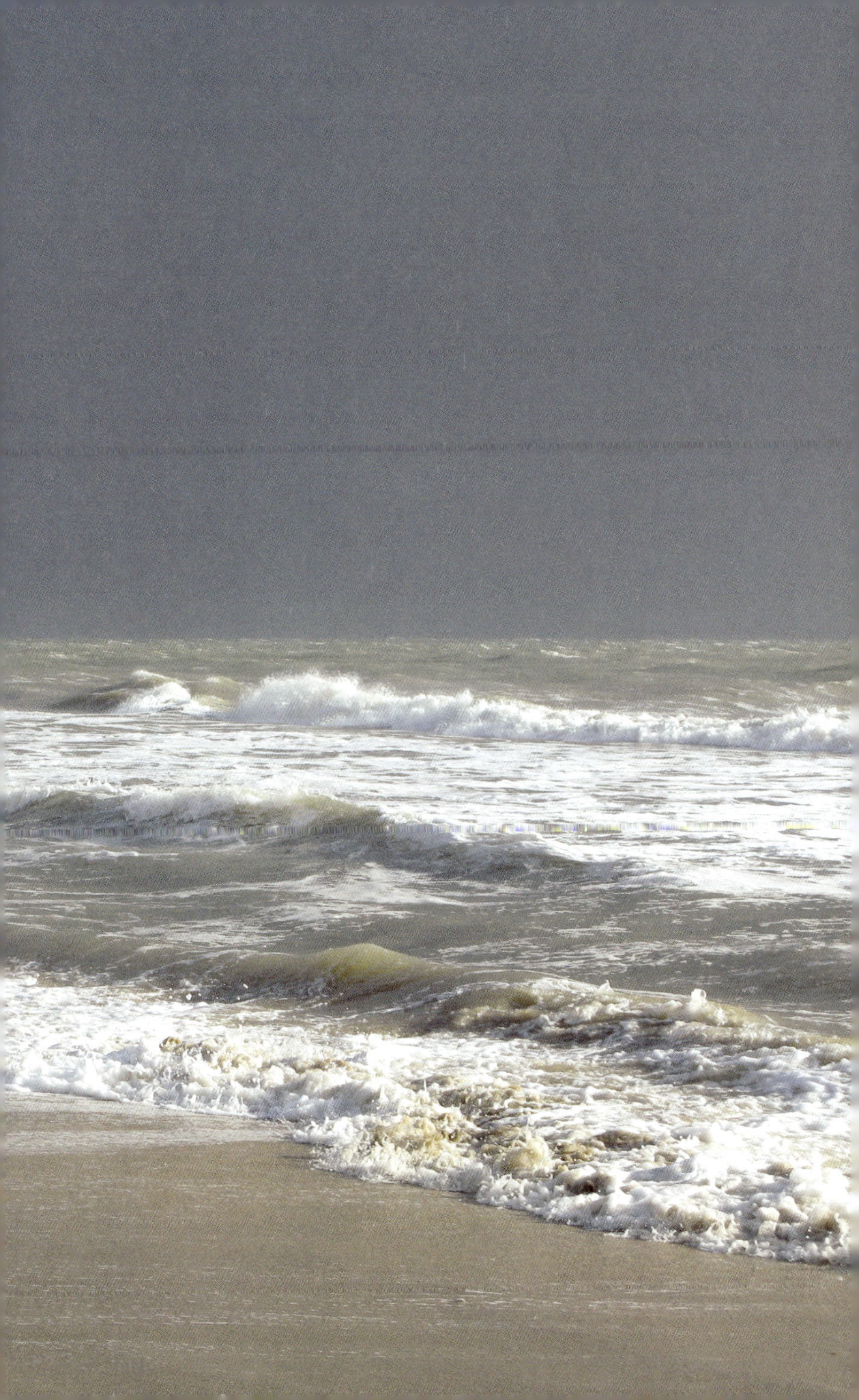

There are more, and more interesting, ways of killing yourself along the coast than anywhere else. You can drown, fall off a cliff, get hit by something else falling off a cliff, poison yourself with hemlock water-dropwort, become cut off by the tide and die of exposure, or get run over by a jetskier. In addition to these fatal encounters there are innumerable opportunities for injury and illness. A broken leg incurred by slipping off a seaweed-covered rock; a partially severed finger courtesy of an ill-disposed Lobster; sunstroke; food poisoning... the list is endless.

Few people suffer these indignities and calamities through sheer misfortune; it is nearly always a matter of being either under-prepared or over-reckless. I do not lecture you from a position of superiority – it is by simple good fortune that I am here to pass on this bitterly acquired knowledge. Three times while taking pictures for this book I became hopelessly stuck in mud. On each occasion I had gone just that little bit too far (with mud, too far can be about a metre) and, instead of retracing my steps, I carried on. Drowning while up to your thighs in mud is not a pleasant end – and anyway, you feel such a fool. I speak lightly of such matters but the dangers are all too real and tragedies a frequent occurrence.

As any boy scout will tell you, the key to survival is to be prepared. Here are a few things that must be considered if you want to return from your endeavours alive and in good working order. Most are fairly obvious, but ignoring the obvious has been the downfall of many, so I mention them anyway.

Weather

Always check the forecast, and always take into account the possibility that it may be wrong. Remember that the coast can have its own ideas about the weather, and sea mists and onshore and offshore breezes can confound the general forecast. The Met Office supplies an inshore forecast for the entire coast, and you should check this as well.

Tides

One of the joys of foraging is that one becomes attuned to the natural world and its many cycles. For beach foragers, the second most important of these cycles (the most important being the seasons) is the tide. Much collecting requires a low tide and you will obviously need to know when this is, but even if you are just picking plants from the upper shore a knowledge of the tide may be essential to ensure that you do not become stranded.

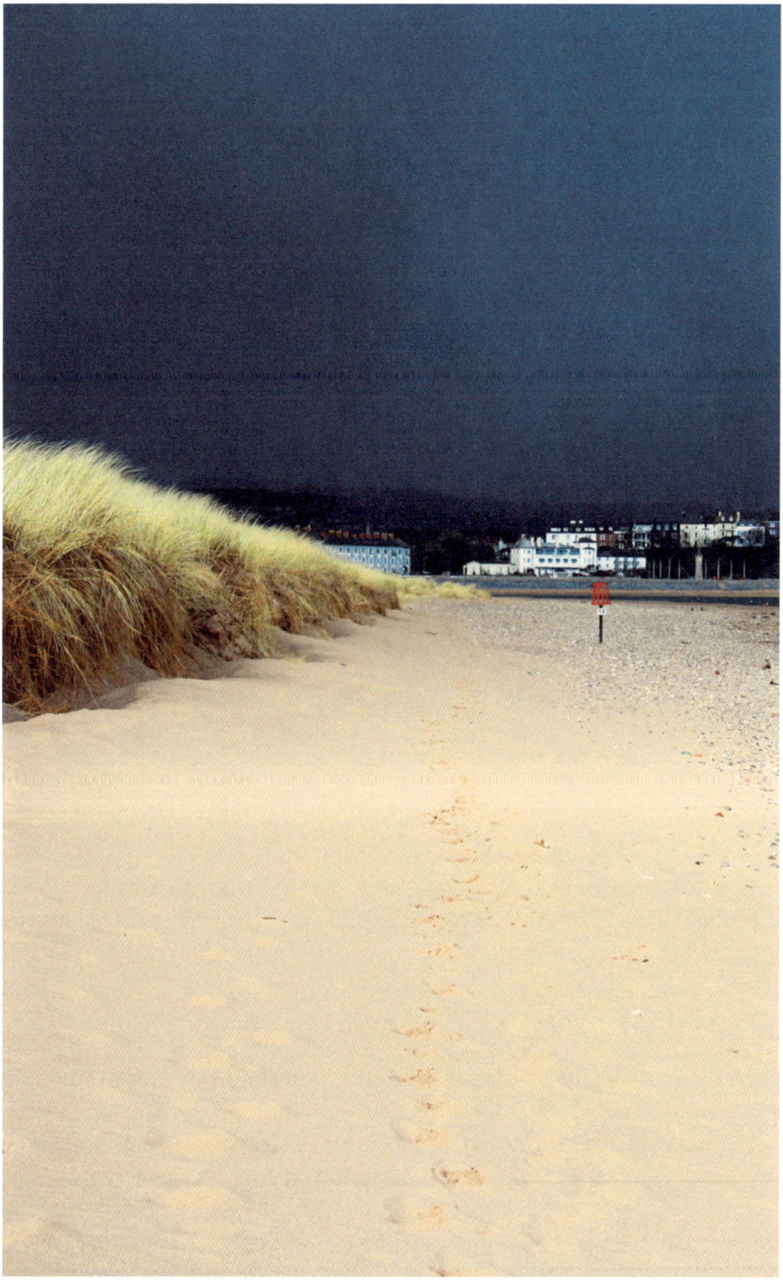

The most important thing to know is that tides and the tidal streams that accompany them are *local*. Some places have tidal ranges of barely 2 metres while at others it may be a massive 16 metres. The returning waters may creep back slowly and imperceptibly or they may race up the shore at a terrifying pace. Where I live we have a double low, but 50 miles to the east there is a double high (due to an interference pattern caused by the shallow waters of the Solent, I am told). You may be intimately acquainted with tidal conditions on one part of the coast, but this knowledge is all but useless elsewhere.

An essential purchase for every seashore forager is one of those little tide almanacs that are available in all our coastal towns. More detailed information, in the form of graphs, is available online for the week ahead at least. These are enormously helpful if your local tide is complex in any way.

Remember that while tides are governed by those most regular of bodies – the Moon and the Sun – they are not easy to predict. Weather conditions can have a dramatic effect on the tide with low and high pressures raising and lowering tidal heights respectively (1cm per millibar), and on- and offshore winds having the same effect. I have frequently gone to my favourite Razor Clam beach only to find the tide 'held in' by an onshore breeze. Remember when you are checking tide times to take account of daylight saving time. This can put your calculations out by an hour if you get it wrong, or even 2 hours if you are prepared to take the time to make a real hash of it.

The theory that describes our tides is horribly complicated (it involves cosines, which is never encouraging) but, simply put, tides depend on the position of the Moon and the Sun. The Moon and the Earth swing around each other with their mutual centre of gravity just below the Earth's surface. This causes the sea nearest to the Moon to bulge in that direction due to the Moon's gravity *and* the sea on the other side, away from the Moon, to 'fly outwards' due to what is commonly termed 'centrifugal' force. The seas on the 'sides' of the Earth are correspondingly lower. As the Earth rotates, most places where tides occur (they don't happen everywhere) enjoy two high tides (the bulges) and two low tides (the dips) a day. In fact there are slightly fewer than this as, of course, the Moon will have moved each day as it revolves around the Earth. The time between tides is, in fact, 12 hours and 25 minutes.

Every 14 days the Sun shows its gravitational effect when it becomes roughly aligned with the Moon and the Earth, at the new and the full Moon, and the tidal range becomes amplified. These are the 'spring' tides, named for the fact that they 'spring up' and not for the season. When the Moon is at 90° to the Sun/Earth line, again twice every lunar month, the tidal range becomes smaller; the 'neap' tides. In fact spring and neap tides lag behind these positions of the Moon by a day or two. Finally the spring tides in the spring and autumn are larger than at other times and these are the best tides for finding the more elusive of the seaside fauna.

Tidal streams

You are only likely to need to know about tidal streams (currents) if you are snorkelling or wading out further than knee deep. As with the tides it is local knowledge that is needed or, failing that, a great deal of caution and careful observation. One place where I often snorkel is as still as a mill pond, but stray just a metre or two into the channel and you can be whisked out to sea in moments.

Tidal streams do not just happen, they are all dependent on the tide. At low and high water there is *usually* very little current, these times being termed 'slack water'. However, in some places low tide is when the tidal streams are at their fastest.

Clothing

Anyone intent on making frequent and serious seaside foraging trips is likely to see a considerable expansion of their wardrobe. A genuinely waterproof coat, trousers and boots and an interesting hat or two are basic necessities, with wetsuits, drysuits and waders being the more specialist items of sartorial equipment that might find their way into the closet at some point. It is often said (usually by superbly equipped people in trying circumstances) that there is no such thing as bad weather, just the wrong clothing. At the seaside your life may depend on appropriate attire, so always consider carefully what you need to wear.

Wellington boots are an item of clothing about which I have mixed feelings. Generally they are useful, though they can be treacherous on seaweed-covered rocks, and in the one place where they appear to be essential – mud – they can be an outright liability. I have frequently performed the amusing dance where one stands on one leg while trying to extricate an errant boot from the mire, all the time sinking deeper and deeper. Wellington boots will desert you without a second thought and I have been unable to rectify the situation with 'Wellington boot suspenders', which seem not to be available, even from 'specialist' suppliers.

Equipment

There are several things that can be of great use in an emergency and that may be worth taking, depending on how adventurous you are planning to be.

A mobile phone, kept in a waterproof case (the sad voice of experience talking here), can be very useful – though they are not always reliable companions in far-flung places. A waterproof torch – you can buy waterproof versions of those stylish affairs that you strap to your forehead. A whistle to keep in touch with companions, or just to blow like mad to let the rescuers know where you are in the fog. (My fungus-foraging friend Reg used to have a 'wife whistle' which he would blow to inform Lil that he was lost in the woods again.) There is a lot to be said for collecting shellfish in buckets rather than bags – they can provide a wonderful third 'foot', should you find yourself in softer and stickier mud than you expected.

Other people

Always tell someone where you are going and when you are likely to return, and, though this is not necessary in all circumstances, bring a companion with you. Other people are not, however, always an asset. If you are snorkelling in an area infested with jetskiers, kitesurfers and fast boats it is wise to increase your visibility dramatically by towing a large bright buoy behind you. This will ensure that no one will have to explain to you, or your next-of-kin, that they just didn't see you.

Animals

Having been frightened by the film *Jaws* at a highly impressionable age (27), I am not one to blithely swim across seaweed-infested waters wearing nothing but a small swimsuit and an innocent smile. Nothing will convince me that the sea is anything other than an alien environment full of hideous creatures intent on doing me harm. I have never swum in water more than 5 feet deep and any excursion into the sea always finds me with full wetsuit, boots, gloves and hood to protect me from venomous fauna and killer seaweed. While it may be that my imagination is a little overdeveloped (I will admit to killer seaweed being one of its figments), there are several creatures that the forager may encounter that can cause injury.

To get the big one out of the way first, sharks do exist in British waters though attacks are almost unheard of. It is true that most of the larger ones are harmless basking sharks but the porbeagle desires larger prey than plankton and has frightened one or two of my diving friends. However, as I do not take my 'Observer's Book of Sharks' with me into the sea and the merest suggestion of a sharky outline will see me out of the water in under a second, such fine differentiations are of academic interest only.

A considerably more realistic peril is posed by the claws of Lobsters and Crabs. I have never been caught out by a Lobster or Brown Crab but I did suffer a close and bruising encounter with a Velvet Swimming Crab. Only my thick rubber gloves prevented blood (mine) from being spilt and its grip was so strong I thought I might have to wear it on my finger as a bizarre piece of jewellery until it got bored. I can only imagine what a Brown Crab could do. The best place to hold the shell on these animals is just above and slightly behind the place where the claws join the body.

Few fish will take a bite out of you but there are several which produce venom. One of the worst is the weever fish. This ugly little demon hides in sand with its venomous spikes sticking upwards. It is the bane of the shrimp-netter and the reason why no shrimping expedition should be attempted without robust footwear. If you are unfortunate enough to be stung, your foot may go green, purple and then black, and it will hurt.

Gathering seaweed or Winkles from a rock pool seems safe enough but do be wary of the snakeslock anemone. A sting from this flamboyant little green beast is only moderately painful but will leave a memorial to itself in the form of a cluster of brown scars from the iron oxide which the venom releases from the blood. These scars can, amazingly, last for 2 years.

Poisoning

As the whole point of foraging is, obviously, to find things to eat, an entire new area of danger is opened up to you. Many people worry about collecting shellfish from the wild and there are, indeed, potential perils to face there. Always follow the rules I give for the safe gathering and preparation of these creatures. There are several seriously poisonous plants and fungi that can be mistaken for edible species, so never eat anything unless you know precisely what it is called and that it is edible. Full details will be provided on the relevant pages.

Hemlock water-dropwort – poisonous

Bittersweet – poisonous

FORAGING SAFELY

The Rule Book

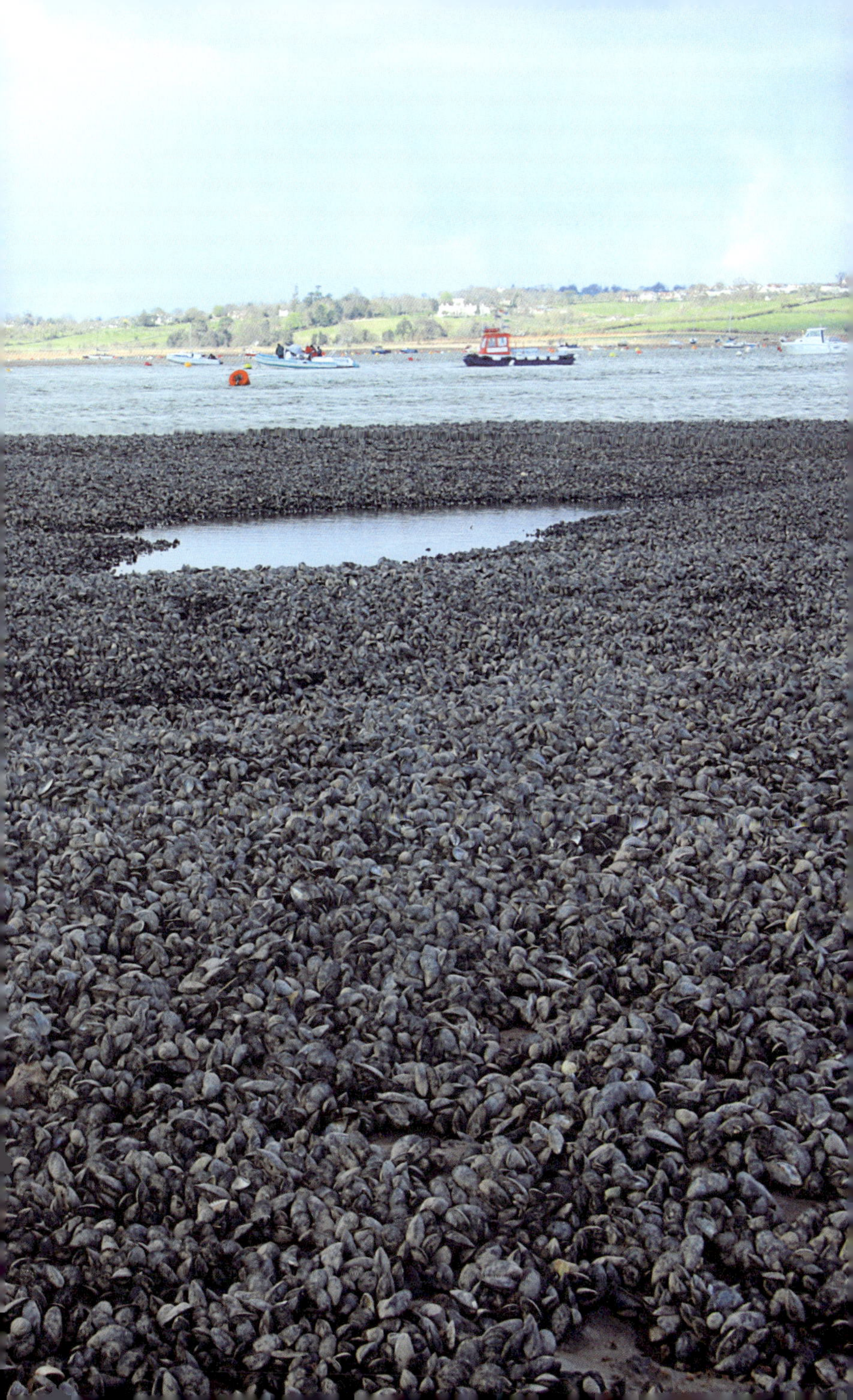

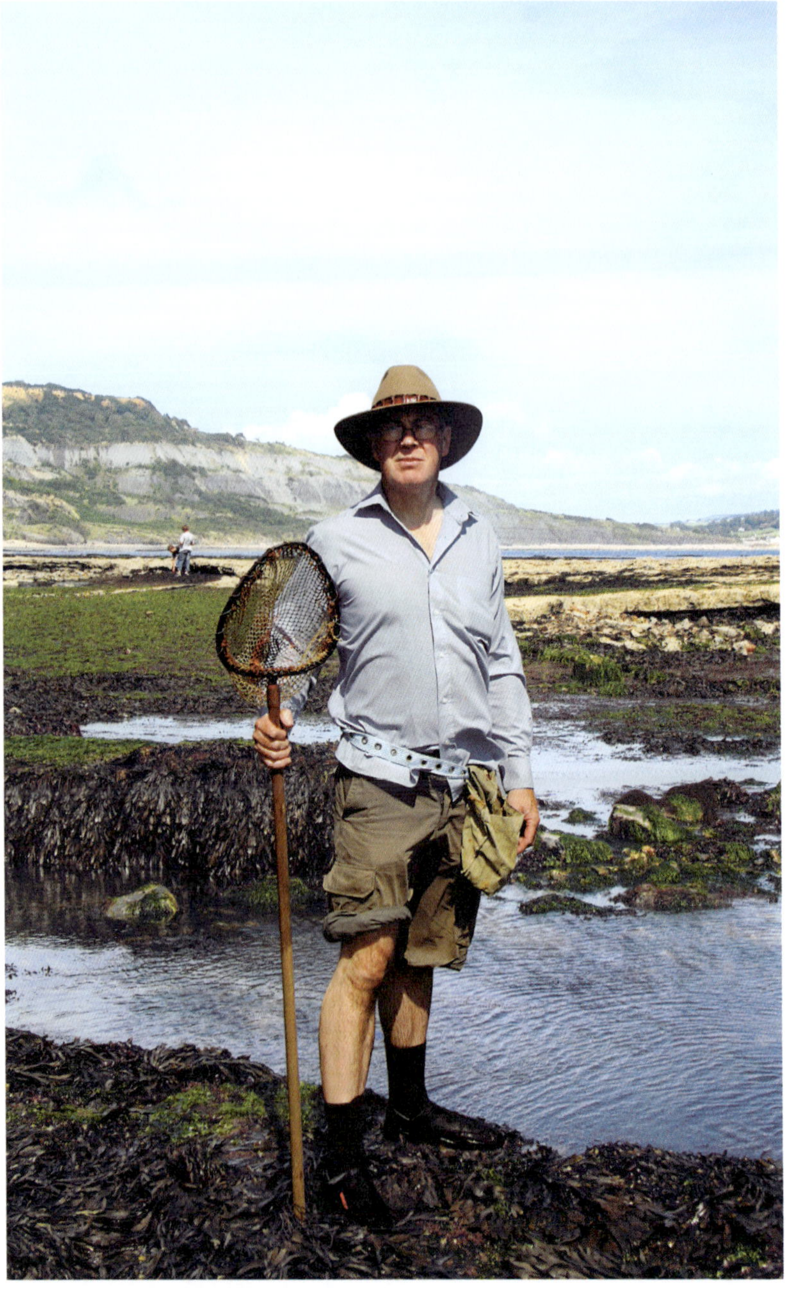

I will warn you straight away: this is a nightmare. I defy anyone not having a firm and comprehensive grip on the law to collect half a dozen different things from the beach for his or her tea without committing an offence. There are so many exciting crimes and misdemeanours to choose from – trespassing, theft,[1] digging up weeds,[2] collecting Mussels in Hampshire east of a line running north/south through the Needles Lighthouse after 4 p.m. during the Oyster season,[3] or Winkles in Sussex during late May,[4] or six Prawns in Northumberland[5] (though five is legal). I could go on. A lot.

So, all I can do is give you a rough overview of the many laws and regulations that affect the average forager; to do the subject justice would require the whole book and more. What follows is the law as I understand it, so please don't quote me should you find yourself up in front of the beak. Two complications make a confusing situation worse: laws and regulations are constantly changing, and they are often different in the four countries that make up the UK, not to mention the Channel Islands and the Isle of Man. Nevertheless, I will do my best to cast light where there is shadow and spread hope where there is despair. As you can see I am giving references throughout this chapter. This is to facilitate further study, and to allow you to check that I am not making things up.

We are interested in just two issues – where we can go and what we can do when we get there.

Where can we go?

Before we start I will need to clarify my use of four words. 'Beach' is the strip of land above the high-tide mark, 'foreshore' is the land exposed periodically between the low- and high-tide mark and 'shore' is the two combined. The 'sub-tidal zone' is the seabed below the low-tide mark. All this is important. Honestly.

A tender belief lodged firmly in the bosom of most people in these islands is that they have a legal right to walk along any shore that does not actually sport a 'private, keep out' or 'MOD Property – unexploded shells on beach' sign.[6] Sadly, they are wrong. There is no general right of access to the coast and the shore is not some briny species of common land. The only part of the UK where there is such a right is in Scotland where access to nearly all the land, including the shore, is an historic right enshrined in the recent Land Reform Act.[7] However, the good news is that things may soon change for England and Wales with legislation tabled to provide a coastal corridor, albeit an intermittent one, complete with 'spreading room' so that anyone can wander off the path and get on to the shore.[8]

The British coast is about 7,000 miles long (depending on how carefully you do the measuring – it's a bit like working out the surface area of a hedgehog) and, at the time of writing, the public has unquestionable legal access to very little of it. Around half of the British coast is served by public footpath, but the existence of one does not necessarily mean that there is any access to the shore itself. There is no public right of access over the beach or across the foreshore, both of which will belong to someone, and probably to two different someones. Precisely who owns a beach is often obscure, but ownership will be in accordance with general land law principles – it is seldom common land. Some beaches will be owned by the person who owns the land adjoining, some by the local authority, and some exist in a state of limbo complicated by their sometimes moveable nature. So while you might get near the seaside along one path or another, you should not, strictly speaking, venture on to the shore. The access we enjoy at present is usually a formal or informal permissive arrangement or is simply *de facto*, meaning that we go there even though no right of access exists.

It does get slightly more complicated when we come to the foreshore. Just over half of the foreshore is owned by the Crown Estate with the rest in the possession of local authorities, the National Trust, various duchies and private individuals and organisations.[9] There is a general right of navigation over the sea, including the foreshore; however, when the tide goes out the right of traversing the foreshore no longer exists. The only exception to this, and one which is relevant to our interests, is the common-law right to collect shellfish as part of a general right to fish in tidal waters.[10] This right implies a right of access.[11] So, you can legally be on the foreshore if collecting Cockles but not if you are collecting seaweed or walking your dog.

The Crown has a *prima facie* right to the sub-tidal zone[12] and this ownership will be administered by the Crown Estate.

Despite these concerns, the forager is unlikely to be challenged in most of the places he or she is likely to go. The National Trust, for example, permits access to over 800 kilometres of coast.[13] There are, nevertheless, places and occasions where difficulties could occur, a private beach being an obvious example. If you are challenged for trespassing by the owner or the owner's agent (invariably embarrassing social encounters, or so I have been told) you must leave immediately by the shortest route practicable. You cannot be prosecuted, whatever the signs say, though you could, in principle, be sued; trespassing is a 'civil wrong', not a crime. Problems can occur where the status of the beach or land is uncertain. If you are unsure of where you can legally go, enquire locally and do so as diplomatically as possible.

Remember that trespassing is a matter of permission not position. If the owner *says* that you can go on to his land you will not be trespassing.

It is my hope that the proposed changes to the law will remove all these tiresome uncertainties. Jerome K. Jerome, in *Three Men in a Boat*, was inspired to greatness on these matters, relating a tale of the three protagonists lunching under some willows by Kempton Park. They were asked by a scruffy-looking character, whose authority they doubted, if they knew that they were trespassing. They replied that they 'hadn't given the matter sufficient consideration as yet to enable them to arrive at a definite conclusion on that point, but that, if he assured them on his word as a gentleman that they *were* trespassing, they would, without further hesitation, believe it'. They then offered him some bread and jam and continued with their picnic.

What can we do when we get there?

This is where the fun really begins. I will sum up the various rights, responsibilities and limitations, then explore them in more detail.

1. There is a general right under common law and statute to collect wild 'fruit, fungi, flowers and foliage' on any land, for private use.[14] This does not apply to seaweeds.
2. Organisms cannot be collected or damaged if they are protected by law.[15]
3. Many places have byelaws which may control or ban the collecting of wild plants or animals.
4. No plant may be uprooted on private land without the landowner's permission.[2]
5. There is a general right to fish, including shellfish, in tidal waters.[10]
6. Many bivalve molluscs (Mussels, Oysters, Clams) are in private fisheries of various sorts or fished (commercially) under licence.
7. EU and national laws, and also byelaws, cover what, whether, when, where, how and how many shellfish you can catch.

1. The right to collect plants and fungi

In England and Wales it is part of common law that a person may collect the 'four f's' – fungi, fruit, foliage and flowers. They must be growing wild (so apples from an orchard or planted crops cannot be taken), and they must be collected for personal use only – if gathered for reward or commercial gain the act becomes one of theft. This common-law right is specifically incorporated in the Theft Act 1968, which states that such a person 'does not steal what he picks'. It is generally presumed that this applies only on land to which the picker has legal access, but the act uses the phrase 'any land' twice, and may actually mean what it says. If so, you are entitled to collect anywhere. Of course if you are trespassing you shouldn't be, but it seems that the landowner is unable to insist that you give him what you have collected, as the contents of your basket, having had no owner before, are now owned by you. Such encounters may not of course present the most opportune occasion to discuss legal niceties. Landowners under these circumstances are invariably accompanied by

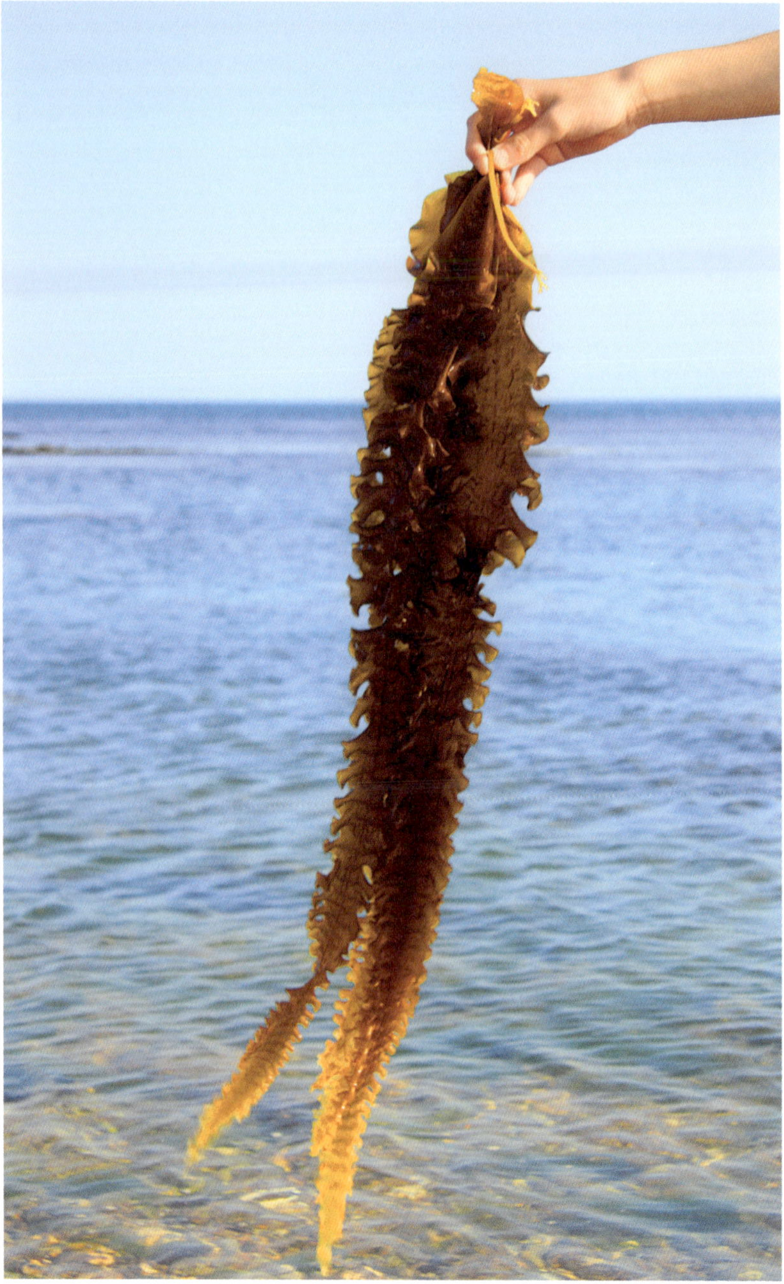

a dog and a large brother-in-law and are generally disinclined to engage in amiable banter. As, in principle, it is possible to be sued for trespass, it is likely that the only recourse for a landowner is to sue for the value of what was removed. It would be helpful to test the principle in court, so if there are any volunteers, do let me know how you get on. Scotland has a law similar to the 'four f's' which upholds an established right to collect from the wild. Again it is applicable only for private individuals picking their own supper.

Sadly there is no 's' among the 'f's. A general right to collect seaweed does not exist, unless it has become detached from the seabed in which case it is considered fair game. A right to collect attached seaweed can be granted by whoever owns the foreshore or the sub-tidal zone (in the latter case it will usually be the Crown Estate) and will be acquired by anyone who has collected the stuff, unopposed, in one place for 30 years. Despite these obstacles it is unlikely that you will face the wrath of either the law or a landowner for collecting a couple of kilograms of seaweed.

The new 'right to roam' legislation has confused a confusing situation further as it states that a person is not entitled to be on land designated as open access under the act if he 'intentionally removes, damages or destroys any plant'.[16] This goes against the spirit, though not the letter, of the Theft Act, removing the common-law right of foraging, albeit on only a part of the land open to the public. The CROW Act, as it is called, grants access to 'mountain, moor, heath, down and registered common land', very little of which applies to the coast. But a concern is that the entire coast could come under the auspices of the Act in the future and that foraging for coastal plants will become illegal. The same schedule also effectively bans any sort of hunting or fishing; a perfectly reasonable position inland, but disastrous were it ever applied to a beach. Fortunately, sea fishing is unlikely to be affected in any new legislation due to the riots that would surely ensue. By the way, should you fall foul of these parts of the CROW Act, you will not have committed theft but merely become a trespasser; you must remove yourself immediately and not return for 72 hours. Incidentally, you cannot take your cat with you on to such land, though your dog is acceptable and you must not 'annoy' people. I said it was fun.

2. Conservation legislation

There are many plants and animals specifically protected under the Wildlife and Countryside Act,[15] none of which are recommended here as suitable for dinner. Nevertheless one must always be aware that such species exist and that they may be inadvertently damaged by careless foraging.

Of more concern to us is the status of plants and sometimes animals that can be found on Sites of Special Scientific Interest (SSSI). If they are cited in the original declaration of the site then it is an offence to damage them.[18] Many quite common plants, some of them in this book, may be cited in these declarations, Sea Kale being a good example. It is my opinion that the odd leaf may be taken from the occasional plant without damage (the act does use the word 'recklessly'), but a nature warden or, heaven forbid, a magistrate may take a different view. This problem is a frequent possibility as about half the coast of England and Wales is an SSSI.

SSSIs also come with a list of activities which Natural England thinks might damage the site and for which permission is required. These usually include such things as changing the level of the water table and extraction of minerals but the more relevant activity of removing plants and animals is also likely to be on the list. Natural England, however, takes a pragmatic view and accepts that the careful collection of small quantities of common species will not do any damage.

Of slightly more concern are things called 'Special Areas of Conservation'. These are 'super' SSSIs coming under the auspices of the EU: there are over 600 in the UK and many are maritime. They enjoy even more protection than SSSIs, which simply means that you can get into more trouble, quicker.

3. Byelaws on collecting

Some places where access is permitted will have byelaws controlling the activities of the forager, perhaps banning the removal of all or part of any plant. The National Trust, for example, has such byelaws (though few in Scotland) as do some local authorities. Byelaws are sometimes challenged; there was an important case in Strangford Lough in Northern Ireland where a winkle picker successfully objected in court to a National Trust byelaw banning the collection of shellfish.[11]

4. The prohibition of uprooting a plant

The most difficult part of the law for the forager is the clause in the 1981 Wildlife and Countryside Act which states that if anyone 'not being an authorised person, intentionally uproots any wild plant... he shall be guilty of an offence'. This effectively removes the (fairly tasteless) Sea Beet root and the (delicious) Alexanders root from the forager's menu.

The only way around this blunt piece of legislation is to become an 'authorised person' and get permission. Since finding out who the owner is *and* getting their blessing is unlikely (Alexanders, for example, grow most readily along the roadside and the county council will not be keen to have it dug up) most (law-abiding) foragers will have to forgo these interesting vegetables.

5. The general right to collect shellfish

The right to collect shellfish (marine molluscs and crustacea) in tidal waters is a common-law right.[10] They can be gathered when the tide is out, and when it is in, and there is a concomitant right of access. However, this right is qualified and beset by a bewildering array of restrictions and regulations.

6. Private fisheries etc.

Bivalve molluscs (Mussels, Razor Clams, Oysters, etc.) are big business, and the places they are found, or can be grown, are valuable real estate. It is no surprise, then, that many of them have come under private control of one sort or other. There are three ways in which this is, or has been, done.

The oldest arrangement is a 'private fishery'. This is granted by the Crown and is simply what it says. Whether the owner has ownership of all the fish in the area specified or just certain species is not always clear, as the knowledge may have been lost over the years. Private fisheries, you see, are ancient affairs dating (mostly) from before Magna Carta when the Crown's right to grant them ended. If you haven't got one already you have really left it too late. There are thousands of them scattered around the coast, nearly all in estuaries, some in deep water, some right up to the beach, some large, some tiny. By their nature they are usually in the most promising areas and if, for example, on an exceptionally low tide, you come across a decent number of native Oysters you are very likely to be in a private fishery. Despite, or maybe because of, their archaic nature, they are often jealously guarded by their owners or, at least, their supposed owners. Anyone collecting shellfish from certain parts of the Thames Estuary, for example, where there are several hundred small private fisheries, has a fair chance of becoming engaged in vigorous conversation with distressed, and invariably large, gentlemen waving photocopies of ancient decrees. The rule is to check with your local Sea Fisheries Committee if you are at all unsure.

The second type, a 'several order', is so called because the public right to fish has been 'severed'.[18] These are obtained through statutory instrument by application to the Secretary of State and are designed to encourage individuals and organisations to establish or improve a fishery by giving them exclusive rights in specific areas. They are granted for certain species only, so you could collect Mussels where an order has been granted for Oysters, though you must not disturb the Oysters in so doing. Several orders can apply to molluscs or crustaceans. They are granted for up to 99 years but 20 to 30 years is much more common, and 7 years is more typical of recent orders. The locations of such fisheries are usually well signposted with buoys and notices. Local Sea Fisheries Committees occasionally possess such orders which they 'sub-let' to others, but apart from this have no authority to administer them. However, they are likely to be well informed as to their existence and location if you need to find out where they are.

Lastly we have 'regulating orders'.[19] These are granted to the local Sea Fisheries Committee, local authority (parish council even) or other body, which then has the power to restrict the collection of certain species in certain well-defined areas by the granting of licences to individuals or organisations, the setting of quotas and the operation of closed seasons. Again, this is to encourage the establishment and maintenance of shellfisheries. Crucially for us, the public's right to fish for the species for which an order is given is removed, but there is often an accommodation whereby the individual can collect relatively small amounts, perhaps in certain restricted locations. To be sure of your rights you will need to check with the administering authority. Few regulating orders exist in Scotland.

Oh, and there are also 'hybrid orders', where a regulating order can apply to a several order. While this is no doubt important, I cannot work out what it could possibly mean and am long past caring.

7. Regulations governing what you can catch, when and how

Finally we come to the rules and regulations set out in EU regulations,[20] Statutory Instrument[21] and local byelaws which tell people what they can catch, when and how they can catch it, and how big it should be before they can take it away with them. These are baroque pieces of legislation which apply mostly to the practices of the much-put-upon commercial fisherman. However, it is essential that you know about such things as permits, closed seasons and minimum landing sizes before you try to catch or collect shellfish of any sort. I have given much of this information in the appropriate chapters.

EU and national law give overarching restrictions but you will also need to know the local byelaws. These are set, in England and Wales, by twelve local Sea Fisheries Committees, the bodies set up to regulate inshore fishing out to the six-mile limit. These very helpful people will give you all the information you need with no fuss. They all have their own set of byelaws which differ enormously; this is partly to reflect local conditions and partly (it seems to me) just for the fun of it. Only one has any regulation on Shrimps; in the Northeast you will need a permit to collect Lobsters whereas in Sussex you can collect two a day and in the other ten areas you can collect as many as you like; the southern and Sussex regions have closed seasons for Winkles, while none of the others do; some require pots to be marked with buoys and telephone numbers, and others don't mention buoys at all. You will just have to ask. At present there is less local control in Northern Ireland and Scotland and the best body to ask if you are unsure is the local council.

Finally, please remember that the law changes all the time and the various organisations which administer it will come and go. At the time of writing a new Marine Bill, which could change almost any of the above-mentioned laws and regulations, is making its way through Parliament and the two Welsh Sea Fisheries Committees may be subsumed into central government. The English SFCs are due for a new name – the 'Inshore Fisheries and Conservation Authorities' and the powers that they have will be extended.

I have provided contact information for many of the organisations that will be able to help you keep on the straight and narrow in the Directory (see pp.232–3).

Good luck. If you ever find yourself in trouble, pretend you are Norwegian.

Reference notes

[1] Theft Act 1968

[2] Wildlife and Countryside Act 1981 Part 1. Section 13(1)(b)

[3] Southern Sea Fisheries District Committee, Byelaw 7

[4] Sussex Sea Fisheries District Committee, 'Winkle closed season byelaw'

[5] Northumberland Sea Fisheries District Committee, Byelaw 13

[6] Ramblers' Association 'Sea Change for the coast'

[7] Land Reform (Scotland) Act 2003

[8] Access to the English Coast, DEFRA website

[9] Natural England NCAF 22/2 Options for improving access to the English Coast

[10] Essay on the Rights of the Crown and the Privileges of the Subject in the Sea Shores of the Realm, Hall 1830

[11] Adair v National Trust (1998) NI 33

[12] A-G v Emerson (1891) Appeal Cases p.649

[13] Consultation on proposals to improve access to the English coast, National Trust 2007

[14] Theft Act 1968 Definition of 'theft' section 4(3)

[15] Wildlife and Countryside Act 1981 Schedule 8

[16] Countryside and Rights of Way Act 2000 Schedule 2: Restrictions to be observed by persons exercising right of access 1(l)

[17] Wildlife and Countryside Act 1981 28 P(6)

[18] Essay on the Rights of the Crown and the Privileges of the Subject in the Sea Shores of the Realm, Hall 1830 p.47

[19] Seafisheries (Shellfish) Act 1967

[20] EU Regulation 850/98 is the main one

[21] For example 'The Undersized Velvet Crabs Order 1989'

The Flowering Plants

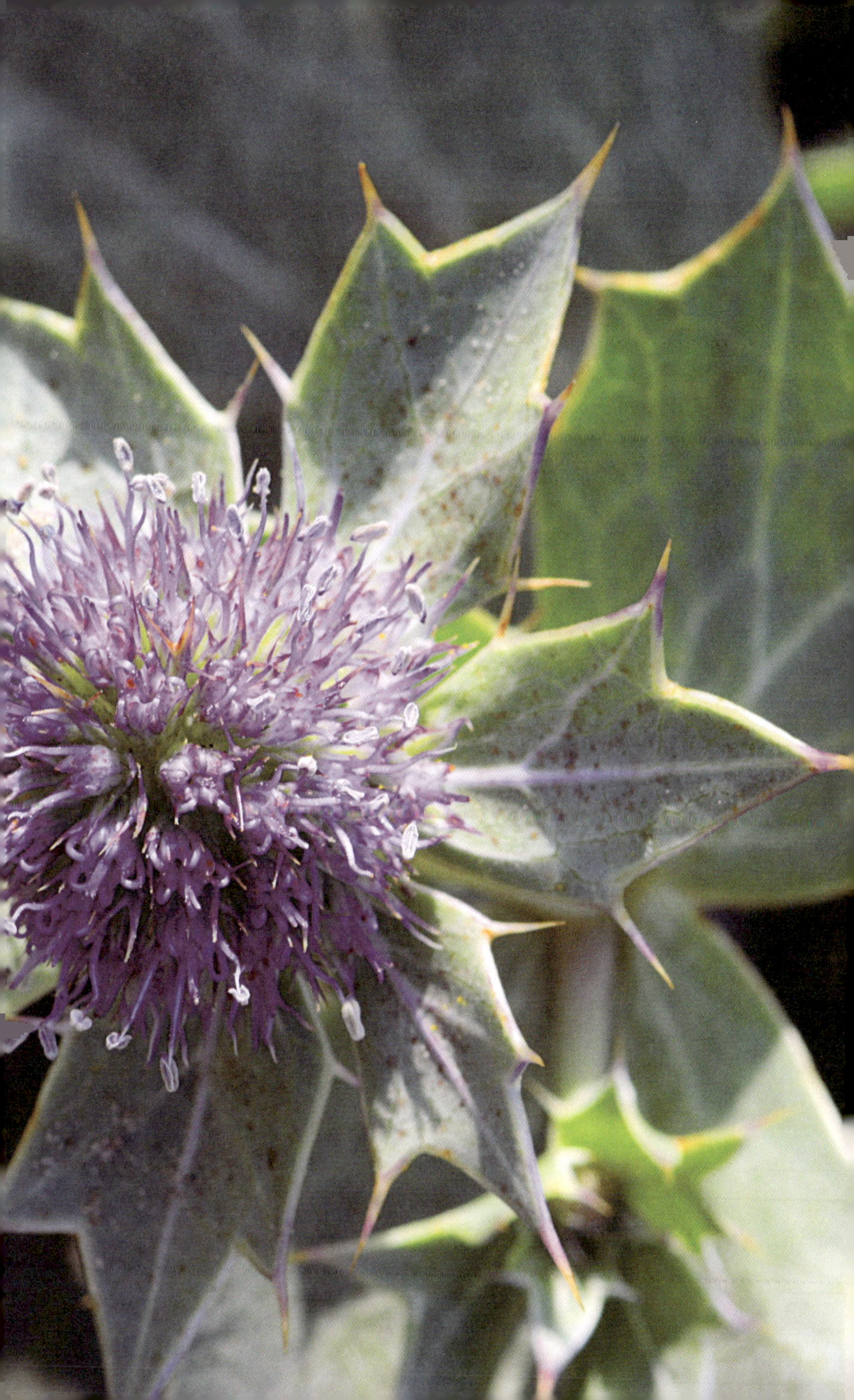

Alexanders *Smyrnium olusatrum*

Foraging for wild plants

is generally seen as a rural pursuit, carried out in woods, fields and hedgerows. The sea's edge, by contrast, with its abundance of shellfish and other creatures, is considered to be the domain of the hunter. Yet if I am looking for large quantities of interesting edible plants it is to the seashore that I am invariably drawn.

Quite why the seaside is so extraordinarily productive of edible plants seems a mystery at first but it is likely to be due to the defence strategy they employ to survive in their exposed and salty habitats – their succulence. This property is lacking in most of our inland species, but Sea Beet, Wild Cabbage, Sea Kale, Sea Purslane, Marsh Samphire and the Oraches all have the thick, succulent leaves that we enjoy.

It is easy to be confused by wild plants; there are at least 1,500 species in Britain and one can despair of making a correct identification. Some of the genera described here are challenging – the Oraches are difficult to tell apart and the Samphires impossible. However, confusing your Babington's Orache with your Spear-leaved Orache, or your *Salicornia ramosissima* with your *S. europea*, will not result in a ruined dinner or a ride in an ambulance. These genera apart, most of the species in this book are distinctive enough and should not confound the forager. The four members of the carrot family recommended here, though, should be approached with a degree of caution as, although they are easily identified, they do have some superficially similar and deadly relatives. The photographs and brief descriptions I have supplied should be sufficient to ensure accurate determinations of the various species, but I do recommend using a field guide if you are in any doubt.

One great aid to identification is to bear in mind that plants, like animals and fungi, come in family groups. So here we have the 'cabbage' family – Sea Kale, Wild Cabbage and the Rockets; the 'carrot' family – Alexanders, Rock Samphire, Fennel and Sea Holly; and the 'goosefoot' family – Sea Beet, the Oraches, Sea Purslane and Marsh Samphire. Plant families, like all families, will share certain characteristics, so the cabbages sport smallish flowers in the shape of a simple cross; members of the carrot family usually have their flowers in little umbrella-like 'sprays'; and goosefoots generally have long spikes of inconspicuous flowers. However, biology is famous for having no real principles and no generalisations are ever possible. Sea Holly, for example, though in the carrot family, has flowers and leaves which look just like those of a thistle. And the flowers of the Marsh Samphire – one of the goosefoot clan – are tiny, inconspicuous and not on separate spikes at all.

Mushrooms are something of an anomaly in this section as they are not plants at all – they just didn't fit anywhere else.

As well as a few familiar flavours and textures, there are some unusual ones to be found among the coastal plants. The exquisite young shoots of the Sea Kale, the powerfully aromatic Alexanders stems and the intensely acidic Sea Buckthorn are almost unavailable to anyone but the seaside forager.

48   EDIBLE SEASHORE

Sea Kale *Crambe maritima*

HABITAT	Pebble beaches
DISTRIBUTION	Periodically all around the coast, but mostly south from Norfolk round to Cornwall, then again on the coast of the Irish Sea
SEASON	Mid March–end April for the shoots; May–June for the 'broccoli' heads. Summer for the flowers and seed pods
CONSERVATION STATUS	Uncommon but not specifically protected. Can appear in vast numbers at certain good sites

Sea Kale must be the most magnificent of all British plants. I still remember the first time I found one – a monstrous and solitary cabbage ensconced on a shingle beach, looking like a forgotten prop from a sci-fi B movie. The leaves were 30cm across and the whole thing close to 2 metres in diameter. The size is all the more impressive for the fact that the plant disappears each winter, with no sign of its imposing presence save a few dried leaves and wisps of flower stalks. It overwinters as a mass of thick, brittle roots which contain all the food for next year's early shoots. It is a long-lived plant; some are still in existence that were old when I first met them 25 years ago.

Sea Kale is one of the select plants that can make a living on pebble beaches. The seventeenth-century herbalist John Gerard says with inadvertent poeticism:

> '*Groweth naturally upon the bayche and brimmes of the sea where there is no earth to be seene, but sand, and rolling pebble stones.*'

It can occasionally be found on cliffs and in gravel. The Channel coast and up the east coast as far as Great Yarmouth is its main stronghold, with another population range on the coast of the Irish Sea.

Sadly Sea Kale is a fairly rare plant, or rather, its habitat is rare. Vegetated pebble beaches are globally uncommon and northwest Europe has a large proportion of them. The threats to these wonderful habitats come, at least in Europe, from human interference. The main problem is us trampling all over them. This is easily observed on long beaches where all vegetation is lacking within 300 metres of the car park, gradually increasing in density as people, or their dogs, decide they have walked far enough. It is best to keep away from the vegetated areas and stay nearer the sea edge. If you want to walk among the plants you will need to adopt a comic mincing gait to avoid the delicate sea pea, sprouting Sea Kale and carpets of sea sandwort.

But what about collecting for the pot; does this seriously damage the plant's viability? Certainly it would if everyone did it, but I do not think it likely that many people will (though they have in the past). I restrict myself to one or two meals a year, removing no more than two young leaves from each plant and only building one blanching mound. Sea Kale is not a protected plant though it frequently grows at protected sites (SSSIs). Although damaging plants that are 'cited' in the establishment of an SSSI is illegal, picking a leaf or two is not likely to get you into trouble as it does not constitute real damage (your honour).

Sea Kale has long been domesticated and Victorian horticulturalists expended much time and paper on long and intricate instructions for its cultivation. Seeds are available from specialist suppliers (do not confuse them with seakale beet) and, while a good Sea Kale bed takes some time and effort to establish, it is not actually a difficult process and may be the best route to take if you acquire the taste.

How to eat

While it is possible to eat a mature cooked Sea Kale leaf, it may require a day or two to accomplish the task. It has the flavour and texture of a damp, thick face flannel. As the Victorian horticulturalist, Charles McIntosh, lamented, 'This Kale cannot be too much boiled.' Indeed not.

So how can the plant be eaten? There are actually several ways. Picked while they are no longer than 12cm from the base of the stalk to the tip of the leaf, the young, purple leaves are perfectly edible and full flavoured, if a little bitter.

Secondly, one can eat the young flower spikes. These are very similar to broccoli and quite delicious. However, I feel rather uneasy about removing the reproductive parts of an uncommon plant and, having tried them just the once, have now taken the pledge.

The third and best way is to blanch and force the young leaves. This is how you do it: find a good-sized plant in January or early February (you can spot them from the remains of last year's foliage) and build up a mound of pebbles above where the leaves will grow. Remember where it is (the part of the proceedings where I always fall down) then go back some time around the middle of March until the end of April and gently scrape the pebbles away. If all is well you will find some tender and gloriously tasty shoots like those shown in the picture; these can be lightly steamed and served with butter or even eaten raw. A useful variation on this technique is to wander about until you find *someone else's* mound, thus saving yourself, though obviously not them, a lot of effort.

Once the plant is fully developed there are two more treats in store for the forager. Sea Kale flowers are surprisingly sweet and can be added to a salad and, later still, the young, pea-shaped seed pods can also be eaten. These are strange things indeed; they look like a pea and taste like a cabbage!

P.S. Though the Latin names of plants and animals deter many people, the esoteric rules that govern their creation combined with some commendable human ingenuity has produced some entertaining results.

Though related, Sea Kale is not the wild ancestor of the kales with which we are more familiar; these belong, with all our other cabbage-like plants, to the genus *Brassica*. The Latin name, *Crambe maritima*, is unexceptional as *Crambe* means 'cabbage' and *maritima* means 'associated with the sea'. More bizarre is *Crambe crambe* meaning 'cabbage cabbage' which, oddly, turns out to be an animal – actually a species of sponge. It does, in fact, look a little like a cabbage, albeit a brilliant orange one.

Zoology, unlike botany or mycology, is plagued by taxonomic rules which allow such tautologies. One of my favourites is the greenfinch, a bird which is known to eat the seeds of the Sea Kale. Its Latin name is the splendid *Chloris chloris chloris*. Unsurpassable, however, is the magnificent *Gorilla gorilla gorilla*!

Forced Sea Kale shoots

THE FLOWERING PLANTS

Wild Cabbage *Brassica oleracea*

HABITAT	Cliffs
DISTRIBUTION	Scattered location around Britain but rare in Scotland
SEASON	Spring and early summer
CONSERVATION STATUS	'Nationally scarce', so collect just a few leaves very occasionally

There is little doubt that the much-burdened Romans, never able to leave anything out of their suitcases, brought cultivated varieties of cabbage to the British Isles. However, it is likely that a wild form of the plant was already in existence here and eaten by the native Celts. How much of today's Wild Cabbage is original and how much is hybridised with cultivars is not really known but the beautiful plants that grace cliffs south from Dundee round to Morecambe have an incongruous domestic appearance born of our familiarity with garden varieties.

Its status of 'nationally scarce' means that it is not a wild food that should be collected with abandon, but if you do come across some in the spring or early summer it is well worth trying a few smaller leaves just to say that you have. Despite food writer Jane Grigson's assessment of Wild Cabbage being 'very nasty indeed', I find it to be similar in texture and flavour to 'spring greens'. Should you catch it at just the right moment you can also enjoy a rather thin, but still tasty, 'sprouting broccoli'. (As an aside, one can only weep for historians whose sources allow entire civilisations to pass unmentioned and unmourned while meticulously recording that someone as obscure as Drusus Caesar, son of Augustus, did not like broccoli.)

Wild Cabbage is very particular about where it grows – it is found at the tops of cliffs, the bottom of cliffs, the space in between and seldom anywhere else. As you might imagine, collecting some for the pot can be perilous. It is a very distinctive plant which can be mistaken for only one other denizen of the coast – the pebble-beach-loving Sea Kale. Wild Cabbage usually nestles in the cliff face on a straggling stem, but occasionally one comes across a specimen – like the splendid example pictured here – which is determined to become a palm tree.

Wild Cabbage is the ancestor of all of our cabbages from Savoy to cauliflower, from broccoli to Brussels sprouts. The virtues and vices of the wild native are much the same as these cultivars, though the old herbalists considered the former to be the more virtuous. All cabbages are packed with vitamin C and folic acid and all are believed to offer some protection against malignant disease. What your mother told you about greens is quite true and you would have done well to heed her entreaties.

The vices, however, are familiar to all and as much sociological as physiological. The health-giving properties of cabbage come, it seems, at a price.

How to eat
A plant as uncommon as Wild Cabbage is unlikely to make a frequent appearance on any menu, so it is worth enjoying it at its best when the opportunity to try it arises. Use only the youngest of leaves and steam for 5 minutes. Serve tossed in oil and toasted sesame seeds.

P.S. My all-time favourite medicinal use for cabbage is provided by Culpeper who suggests mixing the ashes of the stalk with hog's grease and rubbing it on any place afflicted with melancholy or windy humours. Sounds like fun – if, that is, you can get hold of the hog's grease.

Sea Rocket *Cakile maritima*

HABITAT	Sand dunes
DISTRIBUTION	All around the coast
SEASON	Spring and early summer
CONSERVATION STATUS	Common

Perennial Wall Rocket
Diplotaxis tenuifolia

HABITAT	Waste ground
DISTRIBUTION	Patchily around the English coast especially the Southeast. Less common in Wales
SEASON	Spring and early summer
CONSERVATION STATUS	Common

It was with high hopes that I took my first taste of Sea Rocket. All the other wild Rockets are delicious and I thought that Sea Rocket's succulence would make it the best of them all. The fact that it was not mentioned in any of my reference books as being edible I took to be an oversight by writers who should have known better. Well, they certainly knew better than me. The taste was so intense I was sure I had poisoned myself. Sea Rocket is not actually toxic – but it is certainly the last word in acquired tastes.

Seldom more than 15cm high, it is a pretty plant of the otherwise unattractive strand-line on sandy beaches. The delicate pink flowers appear in spring, to be succeeded by spicy seed pods in the summer. It can be found, intermittently, around the entire coast of Britain wherever sandy shores occur. All Rockets are members of the cabbage family, hence the mustard-like flavours (from a group of chemicals with antioxidant properties called the glucosinolates). Sea Rocket is an annual plant relying on its corky floating seeds to produce next year's growth. It is fairly common and, as it is unlikely to be over-troubled by gourmets, will probably remain so.

A more substantial Rocket (80cm tall) frequently found by the seaside, usually in unprepossessing situations like car parks, is Perennial Wall Rocket. It is not strictly a maritime plant but seems to have a vague preference for the more equable climate of the coast. It is also known simply as Wild Rocket and is one of two or three species found in small, and expensive, packets in supermarkets under that name. How it is that an obviously cultivated plant can be sold as 'wild' is a mystery without solution. The 'wild' Wild Rocket is a perennial plant, as is indicated by its other name, and the new shoots arise from amongst the dried twigs of last year's growth.

How to eat

Despite my earlier condemnation, Sea Rocket's pungent quality and crisp texture is not entirely out of place in a salad provided you use only a small amount and find yourself in good physical shape. Steamed for 5 minutes, much of the bitterness disappears, making it just about palatable. The seed pods are spicy and have been used to make a sauce similar to horseradish (a plant also in the cabbage family) and the dried roots ground to form a type of flour, but this is really a famine food.

Perennial Wall Rocket is a wonderful salad plant. The initial flavour of the truly wild variety is just as nutty as one would hope, followed by a considerably more powerful peppery punch. The pungency varies from plant to plant so it may be worth choosing and picking; it is also stronger after flowering. While most people would be more content to mix it with other, milder salad vegetables, Perennial Wall Rocket on its own, dressed with a good oil and a fruity vinegar, is a spicy delight.

P.S. I always wondered how the Rockets acquired their odd name. It turns out that it comes from the Latin *eruca*, a type of cabbage. This became *ruca* in Old Italian, with the diminutive form *rochette*. The *Cakile* part is from the Arabic for Sea Rocket. All disappointingly dull in the end.

Sea Rocket

Perennial Wall Rocket

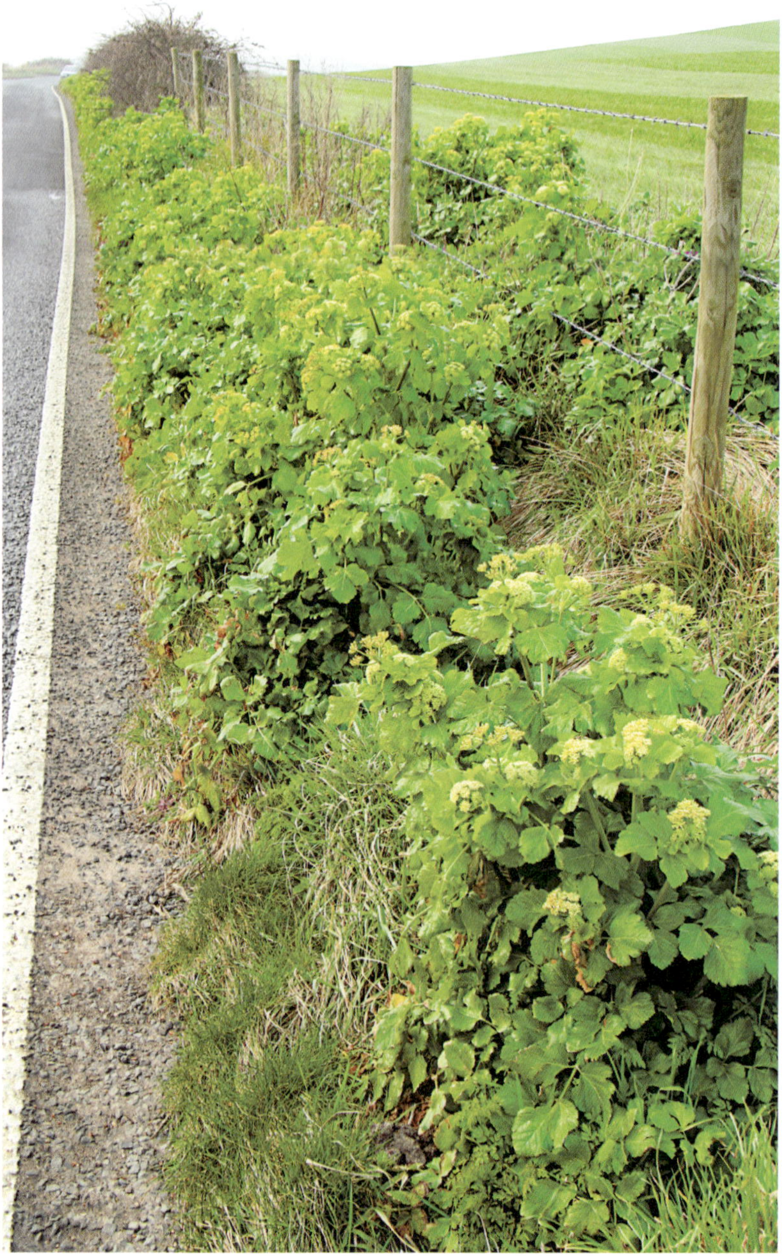

Alexanders *Smyrnium olusatrum*

HABITAT	Roadsides and waste ground within a mile or two of the sea
DISTRIBUTION	All around the Welsh and English coast, less common in the North; rare in Scotland
SEASON	November–April/May; seed heads in autumn
CONSERVATION STATUS	Very common

It is odd that a vegetable with so venerable a history as that enjoyed by Alexanders should have been so completely lost from the kitchen garden. But, just as ground elder was replaced by parsley, so Alexanders was replaced by celery. While ground elder has refused all invitations to leave its garden fastness, Alexanders has, for the most part, retreated to the coastal fringes of Britain where it lingers as though awaiting a ship to return it to its Mediterranean home. The simple reason for its usurpation is that Alexanders is something of an acquired taste – one of those robust flavours that can easily offend the bland modern palate. However, as there is much to be said in its favour, perhaps it is time for this neglected plant to enjoy a revival.

Alexanders' winter appearance and known appeal to horses may explain why it arrived with the Romans – it provides excellent fodder when little else is available. The name is generally understood to come from Alexander the Great who was born in Macedonia where the plant was abundant, or possibly after Alexandria. An alternative is that it is a phonetic corruption of its Latin name *olusatrum* (meaning black herb – the seeds and root are black); more unlikely derivations have proved to be true, so it may be so. From the first until the eighteenth century it took its happy place in the kitchen. It was also, since classical times, prized for its medicinal uses. Culpeper, in his famous Herbal, says that it was good 'to move women's courses' (whatever they might be), effective against 'the biting of serpents' and useful in relieving 'the stranguary', so it was obviously a handy thing to have around. Celery, itself a wild plant found near the sea, had long been viewed with some suspicion and little used, but by the seventeenth century, new, more succulent varieties had been developed and Alexanders' days were drawing to a close.

The startling bright green of Alexanders is a joy to see amongst the otherwise dead vegetation of winter. Indeed it has often flowered before many other plants have put up a single shoot. While Alexanders is sometimes found on the upper beach it is more common as a roadside plant within half a mile or so of the sea, and with a particular fondness for lay-bys. Quite why it needs to be near the sea but not necessarily near enough to see it or smell it is something of a mystery. The most likely explanation is that, as a plant of warmer climes, it is not tolerant of inland frosts; indeed where it still persists inland it is usually in sheltered situations such as against a garden wall. It is less frequent north of a line drawn from Liverpool to Newcastle, again indicating a preference for a milder climate. Alexanders is a biennial and you will see the new plants growing around those that are mature and in flower. It is the latter which provide the hollow stems, flower buds and leaves that one can eat. The young growth will form a remarkably substantial black root by the end of the year and this too can be eaten.

How to eat

The flavour, as I have suggested, is a powerful one; the *Smyrnium* part of its name means 'myrrh'. If you know what angelica tastes like you will know the aromatic component, but it is also rather bitter. Some people will find these flavours mightily refreshing in a salad but I do not share their enthusiasm and I suspect that few would. Fortunately Alexanders is very accommodating when cooked and one can enjoy as much or as little of its potency as one desires.

The parts most commonly eaten are the stems. Collect them when they are fat, succulent and young – the very young and slender stems can be surprisingly tough and the really old ones like bamboo. Use the straight lengths between the branches. Peel away the fibrous outer layer with its baler-twine texture. Since the strong aromatics are destroyed with heat there is a trade-off which depends on the cooking time: 5 minutes for crisp and highly aromatic; 10–12 minutes will give you soft and (relatively) mild. Add butter and serve with fish or just on its own. The very young, early shoots and the unopened flower buds can be treated in the same way.

Alexanders grows in large swathes and can be used with abandon, leaves included, as a stock vegetable in soups and stews. The wonderfully sweet and aromatic root could also be used for this simple purpose and is excellent sautéed or roasted. Unfortunately it is illegal to dig up wild plants without the landowner's permission and permission to dig up roadsides is seldom obtainable. The good news here is that Alexanders is easy to cultivate and can be grown just like its cousin the parsnip. By August the black seeds have set and can be collected, dried and used in pickles, as a fragrant 'black pepper', or to restore the flavour of Alexanders lost in cooking.

Alexanders has a strong affinity for sugar and can be used to make a startlingly green and powerfully flavoured liqueur (p.183). It can also be candied in just the same way as its relative angelica, see candy Alexanders (p.172). It was with some reservation that I first attempted this process but the result was a vast improvement on the foul green candied angelica my mother used to frighten me with when I was a young child. Dangerously encouraged by my success, I then invented Alexanders and rhubarb jam (p.180). It should have been a disaster but in fact is really rather delicious. It is my gift to the world.

Alexanders' distinctively broad, pink-tinged leaf base

P.S. Important!

Alexanders is a member of the carrot family, the umbellifers. This family contains a huge number of notoriously hard to identify plants, many of them important as food and a few among the deadliest plants known to science. Alexanders is relatively easy to identify, but one must always be very careful. Here are a few key characteristics that make identification certain: *yellow* flowers; a *broad*, veined, *pink*-tinged sheath at the base of the stems and flower buds; *shiny* leaves which are relatively shallowly lobed and have a *sharply* serrated edge; a strong sweet aromatic smell like that of angelica: if broken, the young stems *do not* exude a sticky fluid.

The most likely plant to be disastrously mistaken for Alexanders is hemlock water-dropwort (illustrated on p.31). A decent helping of this plant will finish you off in 3 hours.

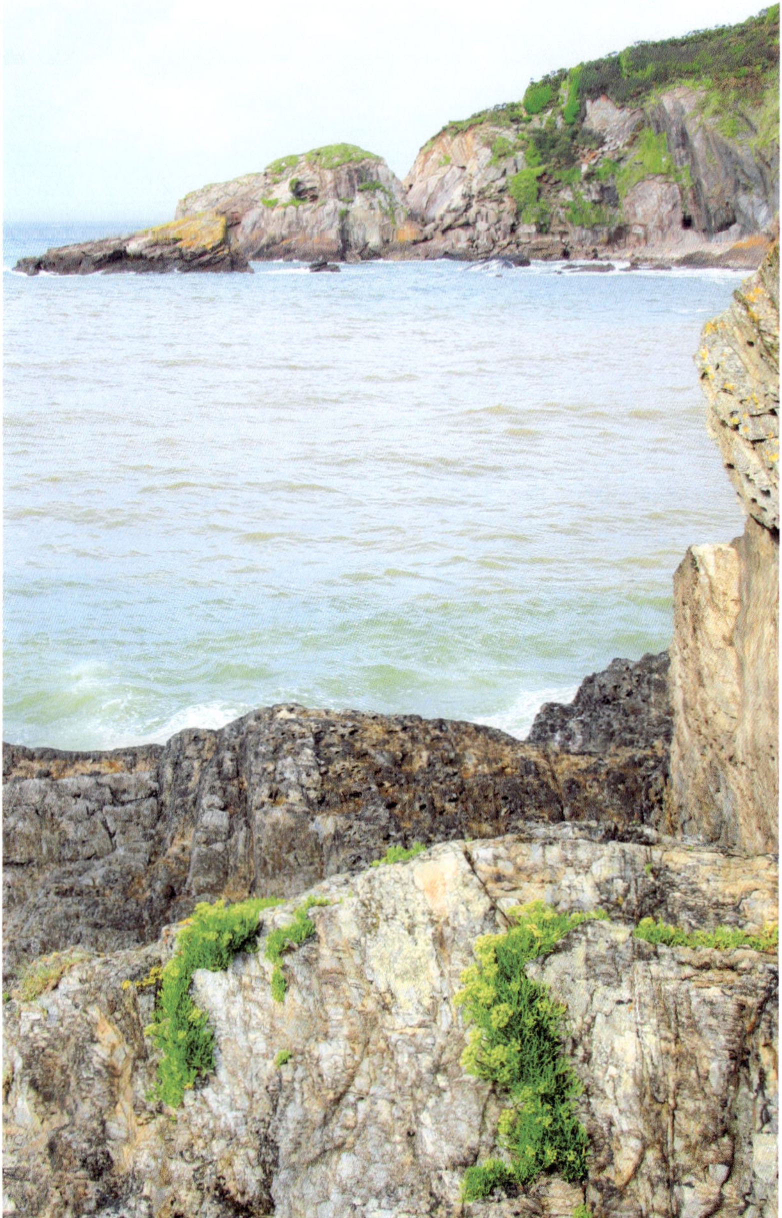

Rock Samphire *Crithmum maritimum*

HABITAT	Cliffs and sea walls; pebble beaches
DISTRIBUTION	South from Great Yarmouth and round as far north as southern Scotland
SEASON	All year, but best in spring
CONSERVATION STATUS	Common

I have tried very hard to like Rock Samphire but I must, sadly, report that all my efforts have come to nothing. It is, I think, a plant that will appeal only to the connoisseur of unusual flavours – raw, boiled, steamed, braised or pickled, the 'carrots and kerosene' flavour remains overpowering and undiminished. The taste comes from a cocktail of aromatic chemicals, one of which is pinene. This is a major constituent of turpentine, a substance not known for its culinary merit.

Rock Samphire was once, however, much esteemed and considered far superior to its namesake, the unrelated Marsh Samphire; indeed there were complaints of its pickled form being adulterated with this plant. Its popularity in the nineteenth century gave rise to a minor cottage industry in Dorset, as Bridport captains would ship entire plants extracted from the cliffs of Portland (complete with no less than one ton of cliff!) to discerning gardeners in London. Incidentally, the name 'Samphire' comes from a phonetic corruption of the French *Herbe St Pierre* after St Peter, doubly appropriate for being the patron saint of fisherman and also Jesus' 'rock' – *Petros*.

If there is anything that Rock Samphire is famous for it is its habit of growing on cliff faces. There is a well-known quote from King Lear about the 'dreadful trade' of Samphire gathering, where the collectors dangle precariously on ropes to gather their prize. This method is still open to anyone with an exaggerated sense of adventure but, with its reduction in popularity, plants are now just as likely to be found growing out of the cracks in the sea wall or on the upper beach as anywhere so dangerously inaccessible.

Despite having unaccountably acquired a reputation for being rare, or even 'almost extinct', Rock Samphire is actually a fairly common plant and if you enjoy its flavour you will not need to restrain your collecting hand too much. It can be found around the coast running south from Great Yarmouth all the way to the southeast of Scotland. As with most plants collected for their leaves, the spring is the best time to pick it. A perennial member of the carrot family, it is a distinctive and rather beautiful plant with succulent grey-green leaves and delicate white flower heads. Only the most careless could confuse it with something inedible. It was,

The succulent leaves of Rock Samphire

however, carelessness that once had me chewing a sea aster leaf by mistake; not a pleasant experience – it was like sucking on a mothball.

How to eat

Of course you must not be swayed by my poor assessment of Rock Samphire's value in the kitchen – do try some steamed or boiled and served with a little butter – you might like it; after all there are some people who like seed cake. Or pickled Rock Samphire (p.178) might be more to your taste.

P.S. The fact that Rock Samphire never grows where it might get its feet wet once saved the lives of four sailors. Shipwrecked off Beachy Head in a storm in 1821, they found themselves clinging to rocks in total darkness with the tide coming in fast. About to take the desperate step of trying to swim to shore before the rising tide overwhelmed them, a flash of lightning revealed a patch of Rock Samphire. They now knew that the sea would never cover the rock completely and that they would be safe until daybreak when they were rescued. A story worth remembering should you find yourself in the same situation.

Fennel *Foeniculum vulgare*

HABITAT	Roadsides and waste land
DISTRIBUTION	England and Wales. Less common in the North
SEASON	Spring and summer. Seeds appear in the autumn and may persist until Christmas
CONSERVATION STATUS	Common

Like Alexanders, Fennel is a Mediterranean plant which has taken the same journey of escaping the kitchen garden to enjoy the warmer climes of the coastal fringes. Also like Alexanders, it prefers the southern half of Britain. Not that it is exclusively a maritime plant – a spectacular specimen grows, magically, out of the pavement near my house every year, a whole 12 miles from the sea. As with many introduced plants Fennel seems a little uncertain of the welcome it might receive in its preferred habitat and spends a lot of time hanging around seaside car parks and other less than pristine locations.

There is an old adage which tells us that 'He who sows Fennel, sows trouble.' With this warning in mind I make certain that all my Fennel comes from the wild (I'm sure it is just nonsense but I don't like to take any chances). The delicate hair-like leaves with their potent aniseed flavour are unmistakable and available from late spring through to the autumn, though the fresh early ones are the best; sometimes they get a second wind and new leaves will appear in December. Fennel grows in such abundance that it is worth collecting entire plants in the summer to hang up to dry for winter, though you will have to like the smell a lot if you do. The appearance of the dried herb gives us both the common name and the Latin name – *Foeniculum*, meaning 'little hay'.

How to eat

The seaside situation of this feral plant is fortuitous because of the strong association it has with fish, allowing the shoreline mackerel fisherman to grab a handful on his way home. The freshness of Fennel moderates the oiliness of some fish and mackerel grilled on a bed of Fennel is a perfect combination. Fennel sauce has been a mainstay of the kitchen for centuries: steam the leaves for a few minutes, then chop finely and mix with soft butter. Traditionally, parsley and mint were used in addition to Fennel. For more recipes, see pp.202, 210.

Do not forget that there is a second harvest to be had from Fennel – in the autumn the seed heads form to give you an enormously useful spice which can be ground up to flavour fish dishes, curries and bread. I have even made an alcoholic drink similar to Pernod, by crushing the seeds and steeping them in vodka for half an hour, then re-bottling, using a coffee filter to remove the bits. The result is remarkably good – sweeter and lighter than its commercial cousins. The seed, and indeed the drink, is considered to be a great aid to digestion. As this translation of a medieval Italian guide to health, *Regimen Sanitatus Salernitatum* has it:

'In Fennel-seed, this vertue you shall finde,
Foorth of your lower parts to drive the winde.'

I am not sure if this a vertue or a vyce.

Sea Holly *Eryngium maritimum*

HABITAT	Sand dunes
DISTRIBUTION	Southern Scotland; England and Wales
SEASON	All year
CONSERVATION STATUS	Uncommon and rarely collected as it needs to be unearthed to get at the edible roots

Although not specifically protected by law or on any red data list, Sea Holly is a fairly uncommon plant, which, since it is mostly the roots that are eaten, has to be unearthed in order to be consumed. Its normal habitat nearly always has SSSI status, so the chances of getting the required permission to uproot one approaches zero. I thought I would never get the chance to try some of this once-popular delicacy. Then one day I found a spot where they grow in their thousands, and, lying on the beach where the edge of a dune had been eroded away, a solitary Sea Holly that had been exhumed by nature herself. I wrestled fiercely with my conscience for half a second, then broke off a handful of roots and replanted what I could of the rest.

Sea Holly is a beautiful plant, so much so that it is occasionally cultivated. Although it looks very much like a thistle or a strangely diminutive variety of holly, it is actually a member of the carrot family. In late summer the flowers blossom a bright blue. It is almost invariably found on or near sand dunes where, its sharp spines poised, it preys on barefooted holidaymakers. The numerous roots, though less than a centimetre thick, are very long at a metre or more and, with so much root to a single plant, one can understand why they were once collected for food.

How to eat

The white-fleshed roots have a carroty texture, a slightly bitter, carroty taste and a smell that is a powerful and pleasant mixture of carrots and Brazil nuts. Wanting to enjoy my small harvest at its best, I wondered if this unexceptional flavour could be improved by using the roots in one of the few ancient recipes using 'eryngo' (as it was once called) that survive. I passed quickly over marrowbone pie and then considered 'substitute ass's milk', an extraordinary concoction given to consumptives who could get neither real ass's milk nor the even more beneficial 'woman's milk'. People whom, one would think, had suffered enough already. The recipe calls, in addition to the roots, for pearl barley, shaved hartshorn, 18 mashed snails and syrup of Tolu. It was the last ingredient that had me stumped.

I settled eventually on Sea Holly's best-known recipe, 'candied eryngoes'. Well, they taste nice enough – like candied carrots. But 'candied eryngoes' are not just eaten

THE FLOWERING PLANTS 67

for their flavour. Certainly not. Sea Holly has long been considered an aphrodisiac. Gerard speaks of it being good for people 'that have no delight or appetite to venery'. More direct is the reliable Culpeper, who speaks of it being a 'venereal' plant, 'hot and moist', which 'strengthens the spirit procreative'. Until the middle of the nineteenth century, Colchester (worryingly also known for its Oysters) was proud to have in its midst a purveyor of candied eryngoes. A box of these was famously presented to Queen Charlotte on her arrival in England, just prior to her marriage to George III. History fails to record whether or not they were efficacious but her subsequent delivery of fifteen children shows, at least, that they did no harm.

I have my precious jar locked in the safe waiting for the day, not far in the future, when I might need it.

The edible roots of Sea Holly

Sea Beet *Beta vulgaris maritima*

HABITAT	Upper beach, paths, cliff tops
DISTRIBUTION	Southern Scotland; England and Wales
SEASON	Best in spring, but individual plants can be productive at any time of the year
CONSERVATION STATUS	Very common

It is a pleasure, for once, to be able to recommend a wild plant for the table without dark warnings of its imminent extinction or damnation from faint praise of its flavour. Sea Beet is common, abundant and delicious. These felicitous qualities were recognised by our ancestors and traces of its use – in the form of barbecued Sea Beet root – have been discovered in Mesolithic Denmark dating from around 7,000 years ago. After a mention in a Babylonian text of it being one of the (more unlikely) plants grown in the Hanging Gardens of Babylon, Sea Beet enjoys a long, detailed and largely dull history as it was gradually developed into the variety of cultivated plants we know today.

Sea Beet's adventurous genetic makeup has enabled it to take on a multitude of domesticated forms. The nearest to the wild original is that substantial standby of many a kitchen garden, perpetual spinach (ordinary spinach is a different, though related, species). There is also chard, grown for its leaf stems as much as its leaves. A more surprising result of all this experimentation is sugar beet, the source of about half of our sugar. When we consider that an important fodder crop – the exquisitely named mangelwurzel – is also one of Sea Beet's children, it becomes clear that we owe a considerable debt to this unassuming plant.

While few would dispute the benefits accrued from these four crops, not all is well. If ever there was an example of the dangers of genetic meddling it surely comes in the form of that vile purple abomination, beetroot. I do know that some people consider it to be edible, but the cloying aromatic sweetness and invasive colour surely argue otherwise. If you spend much time looking for Sea Beet you will come across plants that exhibit a purple tinge to their stems. It is probably varieties like these that were doomed to become the modern beetroot. Incidentally, while the reds and yellows of most of our cultivated plants, from capsicum to carrots, are carotenes, the colours in beetroot are the botanically uncommon betalains – a group of pigments that also give us the brilliant red of the fly agaric toadstool.

Sea Beet is a denizen of the upper shore and is seldom found elsewhere. Apart from this preference it seems unconcerned about its substratum, happily growing in sand, pebbles, soil or even the cracks in the sea-wall concrete. Its bright-green and

A Sea Beet plant showing its swollen root

thickly succulent leaves make it impossible to confuse with anything else though it can vary enormously in leaf size, stem colour and general shape. The best time to pick it is in April and early May when the sweeter new growth appears, but in sheltered areas it is quite possible to collect enough for a meal at any time of the year. I once picked some from a cliff top on Christmas Eve ready for a side dish of Sea Beet, smoked salmon and cream cheese terrine on Christmas Day. It is extremely common all around the coast, though, as with many seashore plants, it is less so in Scotland.

How to eat

The tastiest part of Sea Beet is the very young flower shoot – complete with its attendant pale leaves – just before it launches itself in a great spike of tiny blossoms. But even the thickest and darkest leaves are good eating as long as the tougher leaf stems and ribs are removed. While it is quite unpalatable raw, steaming for 5 or 6 minutes will bring out its sweet flavour and remove the excess bitterness. It can be used in any recipe that requires spinach, and in my opinion, is far superior. As well as an excellent flavour, it has the virtue of retaining its texture rather better than its cousin.

The roots of Sea Beet are also edible (and often quite large, as you can see) but you will need permission from the landowner to dig them up. While the concentric rings of the cut root are like those of beetroot and the taste the same, if very mild, we are, at least, spared the colour. If you ever get the chance to try this throwback to the world of those Mesolithic Danes do not demur. It will take you back to your roots.

For more recipes, see pp.177, 190.

The young flower shoot

Sea Purslane *Atriplex portulacoides*

HABITAT	Salt marshes
DISTRIBUTION	England and Wales; almost completely absent from Scotland
SEASON	Best in spring and summer
CONSERVATION STATUS	Common

This is a tough little plant. With its feet stuck in stony, salty mud and its head exposed to the worst that the elements can offer, it endures conditions that would kill most plants within hours. Yet it dominates many of our estuaries and mud flats, forming vast sinuous tracts of vegetation. It can be found in salt marshes all around the coast, though it is uncommon in Scotland and Northern Ireland.

The thick oval leaves, seldom more than 2cm long, are protected from the drying effect of the wind by a covering of tiny papery scales, giving the plant its pretty silvery appearance. Such survival mechanisms define the flavour and texture of the leaves – salty, thick and furry. Sprinkle some salt on one of those little stick-on felt pads used to protect French-polished sideboards from heavy pieces of Staffordshire and you will have it perfectly.

How to eat

While the young leaves of May are the best, Sea Purslane is a perennial plant that can be collected at any time of the year. The leaves provide a salty and crunchy addition to salads, though you would not want too many of them. Cooking has little effect on their palatability, though boiling for 5–10 minutes will reduce the saltiness to an acceptable level. The flavour is not unpleasant – simply unremarkable. No amount of cooking will reduce the leaves to a purée, so they are sometimes used in fishy risottos, or with couscous.

The best use for Sea Purslane leaves, however, is to employ their saline nature as a natural condiment and sprinkle a handful over roast potatoes or other roasted vegetables during the final 10 minutes of cooking.

P.S. Like just about every plant known to man, Sea Purslane has been credited with numerous medicinal virtues. Culpeper excels himself on this occasion with much to say in favour of its cooling properties. Among them is an ability to cool '... the outrageous Lust of the Body, Venerious Dreams, and the like'. I've been eating the stuff for some years now and I think it's just starting to work.

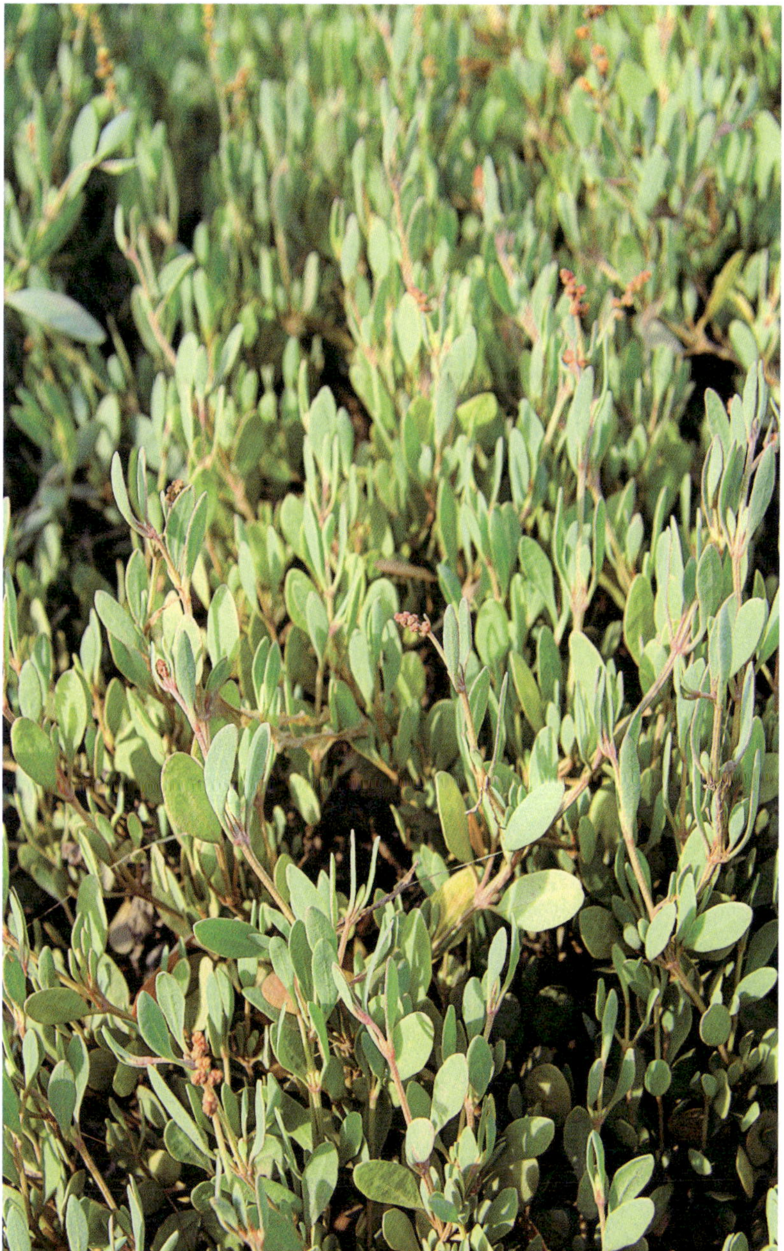

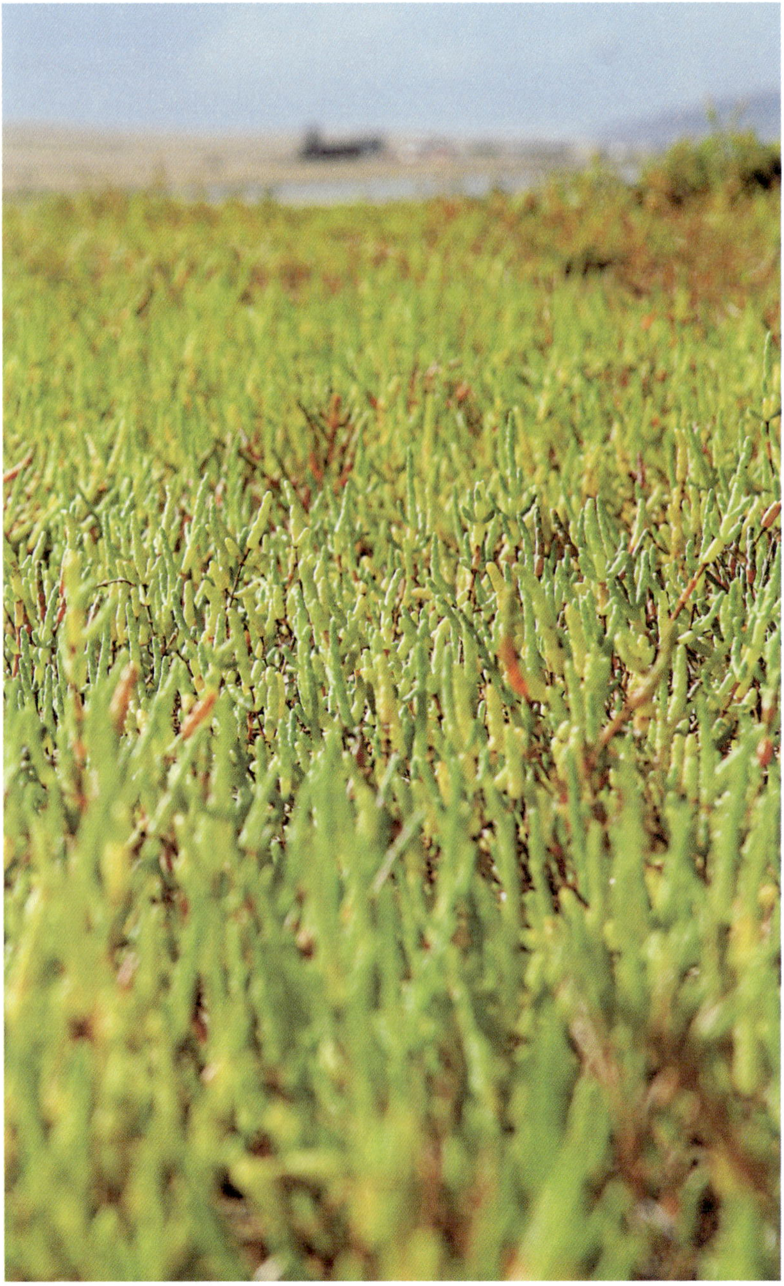

Marsh Samphire *Salicornia* spp.

HABITAT	Salt marshes and mud flats
DISTRIBUTION	All around the coast, but with large gaps due to lack of habitat
SEASON	June–September; early crops more succulent
CONSERVATION STATUS	Common, though one or two species less so. Unfortunately it is not easy to tell them apart

Neither cactus nor seaweed, this fleshy genus is like Sea Beet, the Oraches and Sea Purslane – a member of the goosefoot family. Marsh Samphire does not look remotely like any of these plants, but taxonomies are all about relationships, not appearances. Although the practical consequences are slight, we have here a group of species, not just one. The bright-green *Salicornia europaea* is the most familiar, but if your collection has a purple tinge it may be *S. ramosissima*. There may be half a dozen species to be found in Britain but, as even experts find them confusing, there is little point in worrying about such things.

Unlike many of our edible wild plants – once familiar, now neglected – Marsh Samphire has taken the opposite road; from total obscurity to moderate fame. William Turner in his sixteenth-century herbal had to make up a name for it as he 'could never meet a man that knew it'. He chose 'Glaswede' from its use in glassmaking and the later 'Glasswort' is still used now. In the nineteenth century it earned its modern name 'Marsh Samphire' (pronounced, for some reason, sam*fur*) from its culinary association with the unrelated Rock Samphire (sam*fire*). It was used as a 'poor' substitute for this plant in pickles; 'a saltish mawkish flavour' as Anne Pratt, a naturalist of the time, had it. Now it is highly esteemed and commands a good price at the fish stall.

Most of what is eaten in Britain is imported from France, Israel and even Saudi Arabia, but there is still a tradition of benign commercial collecting in eastern England. There are good, if scattered, populations all around the British Isles so it is not a hard plant to find. If you come across a good spot it can look like a meadow, or perhaps a green shag-pile carpet with all the 'shags' standing on end.

Marsh Samphire is a tidal plant of the mud flat and expeditions to pick it are messy affairs, best prepared for with appropriate clothing and an attitude of resignation. It is a low plant, seldom more that 20cm high, and you will need to get down in the mud to pick it. Scissors are a necessity as, of course, it is illegal to uproot it without permission. I once got into terrible trouble with a nature warden when, scissorless, I inadvertently uprooted a couple of plants while trying to break pieces

Marsh Samphire plants often grow singly

off. With tall specimens at least, it is best to snip off the more succulent top half of the plant, though whether or not this mitigates the damage to what is an annual plant is debatable. It rarely reaches collectable size until late June, with Midsummer Day being the traditional start of the season. By mid-September it usually looks pretty tired and it disappears with the frosts of autumn. When you get home with your collection you will need to wash it, and yourself, thoroughly to remove all the mud.

How to eat

Marsh Samphire is very good indeed raw in a mixed salad, the saltiness being a boon in small doses and a bane if overdone. Only use the tips of young plants for salads, as these will lack the stringy central fibre. Steaming is the best way to cook it, with 6 minutes in the pot being perfect. The result is a pleasant, succulent vegetable that is none the worse for a little butter, or, best of all, dipped in any fishy sauce that you find on your plate. Again, the younger tips can be eaten whole, but if the plants are more mature, or you have most of the plant, you will have to strip the flesh off the tough woody middle with your teeth. The young stems of late June and early July can be pickled – just follow the recipe on p.178. See also the recipe on p.175.

P.S. There is one more 'Marsh Samphire' which you might encounter – Perennial Glasswort, *Sarcocornia perennis*. Although in a separate genus it is very similar to its annual cousins, excepting that it grows from prostrate wiry stems. It is also good to eat, though you will always have to contend with that central fibre.

The Oraches *Atriplex* spp.

HABITAT	Upper beach, waste land
DISTRIBUTION	All around the coast
SEASON	Spring and summer
CONSERVATION STATUS	Common

There are a bewildering number of Oraches that seem happy to be beside the seaside, and telling one from the other is not particularly easy. The two most common are the Spear-leaved Orache (*Atriplex prostrata*), with distinctly arrow-shaped leaves, and Babington's Orache (*A. glabriuscula*), which has more rounded and distinctly mealy leaves. If you are not sure exactly which Orache you have, no harm will be done as long as you know it is an Orache. If you are uncertain even of this, it is best to wait until the spiked clusters of tiny flowers appear. These will enable you to safely distinguish an Orache from any of the poisonous inhabitants of the shore which have very different flowers.

The Spear-leaved Orache is common all around the coast and also inland except in Scotland; Babington's Orache is only happy by the sea. Both are common and may be picked with a clear conscience. However they spread themselves rather thinly and collecting a kilo of leaves would likely clear 20 metres of beach, so pick just a little from any one spot. Both varieties can be found in straggling mats on the strand-line all mixed up with seaweed and less attractive flotsam. Sometimes the Spear-leaved Orache will grow on the upper shore, forming more erect plants.

One more seaside Orache is worth a mention: Frosted Orache. This is a decidedly maritime species and distinctive too – looking as though it has been dusted with icing sugar.

How to eat

The Oraches taste like spinach and can be cooked in the same way. They have a pleasant texture, though they can be quite bitter if eaten raw in a salad, so cooking is the only option. For recipes, see pp.177, 190.

P.S. I feel I should clarify the relationships between these plants. The above species are all Oraches, which means they belong to the genus *Atriplex*, in turn a member of the goosefoot family (the *Chenopodiaceae*, meaning 'goose foot'). In addition to the Oraches and several other genera, there are also goosefoots in the goosefoot family; these belong to the genus *Chenopodium*, which means 'goose foot'. Sea Purslane (*A. portulacoides*) is a slight anomaly in that despite being an *Atriplex* it is not called an Orache and despite being called a 'Purslane' it does not belong to the Purslane family (*Portulacaceae*). If you want to tell a goosefoot from an Orache, the female flowers of the latter are enclosed in a pair of roughly triangular bracteoles. Simple.

Spear-leaved Orache

Frosted Orache

Sea Buckthorn *Hippophae rhamnoides*

HABITAT	Sand dunes, shrubby areas and waste ground
DISTRIBUTION	All around the coast
SEASON	Berries can be found from July until the winter; early berries are the best
CONSERVATION STATUS	Common

As God cast the errant Adam and Eve from their forager's paradise he cursed the ground that had previously been so fruitful: 'Thorns also and thistles shall it bring forth to thee.' Then, to prove he meant business, he created the Sea Buckthorn.

This attractive plant is covered in great clusters of bright orange berries and the novice might assume that collecting a couple of kilos would be the work of minutes. Not so. The berries burst as soon as you touch them and the branches are defended by the wicked spines that give the plant its local Norfolk name – the splendid 'Wywivvle', a reference to the 'adder'. Like tiny, fragile balloons of orange juice glued to a barbed wire fence, there is simply no easy way to pick them. Rolling your finger around the branch to push them off is the only way I find effective, but it is still very inefficient. As it is only the juice that is needed, an alternative method is to squidge the berries while holding a bucket underneath. If you ever want to try, you should bring along a supply of Elastoplasts and, to protect yourself from the juice which will squirt everywhere, wear either a mackintosh or a Hawaiian shirt with a lot of orange in it.

With a few substantial gaps in Wales and Scotland, this is a common plant all around the coast on sandy upper shores and sand dunes. Sea Buckthorn has been introduced away from its native east and southeast coast, as a plant useful for stabilising dunes. Unfortunately, it has taken its job a little too seriously and made a thorough nuisance of itself. So invasive a plant is fair game, and you may take as many berries as you like, or, perhaps I should say, can. The berries typically ripen in September, though they can be found as early as late July, and may last into the winter. Those that have endured a frost will have lost some of that glorious tartness, so pick early. By the way, if you ever find a Sea Buckthorn bush that refuses to produce berries then you are expecting too much of it – it's a boy.

How to eat

So are the berries worth all the pain of picking? Indeed they are. The juice has an acidic intensity that makes the prosaic lemon seem quite bland. Some years ago there existed a 'sour cherry' boiled sweet which could remove the skin from the

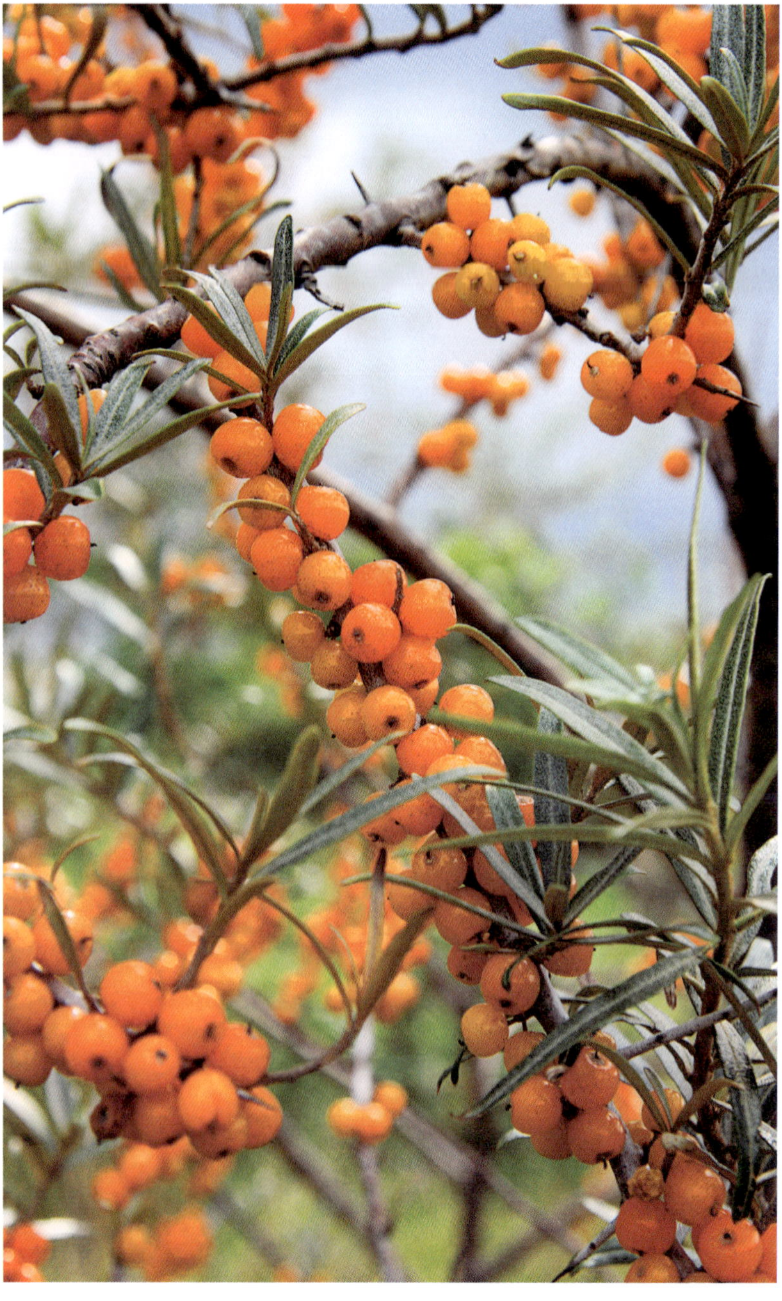

mouths of small children. (It is still available, albeit as a pale imitation of its former toxic self. Perhaps there had been some hospitalisations.) This is the only other food I know that comes close to the acidity of Sea Buckthorn.

The smell of the berries is a surprise too – distinctly of cider. This becomes overpoweringly strong after picking and decidedly rancid during cooking (see below). Don't worry, the smell disappears later. Malic acid, as found in apples, is the cause of Sea Buckthorn's sharpness. The fresh juice will not keep for very long, quickly turning vinegary, but if you can get your timing right, or simply keep some in the freezer, it is a superbly maritime alternative to lemon on fish.

Where Sea Buckthorn excels is in puddings and preserves. It is always best to strain out the skin and substantial pips. This can be done either before or after cooking. The best jam I have ever made, and I make a lot of jam, is Sea Buckthorn and crab apple (p.179). There is no great subtlety to the flavour, but the breathtaking tartness is one of life's more straightforward pleasures. It goes well with fish, of course, but my favourite way to eat it is by the spoonful – straight out of the jar. Sea Buckthorn juice can be added to fruit pies, made into a sorbet or used to make a cordial.

Much has been made of the health benefits of Sea Buckthorn. In Eastern medicine it is something of a cure-all, although Western medicine has not been entirely supportive of this oriental enthusiasm. It certainly contains high levels of vitamins C and E, antioxidants and endless other chemicals apparently conducive to human wellbeing, and these have elevated Sea Buckthorn to the fashionable status of a 'functional food'. I do not know how beneficial Sea Buckthorn really is, but Genghis Khan apparently swore by the stuff. Here is a man who, judging by the fact that he has 16 million living descendants, faced a gruelling daily schedule and needed to keep his strength up. If it was good enough for Genghis, then it's good enough for me.

P.S. My thirteen-year-old daughter showed me one of her diary entries, it reads: 'Came downstairs. Dad's been cooking berries again and the whole place smells of sick. Iona came round. She said, "Why does your house smell of sick?" We went to Iona's.'

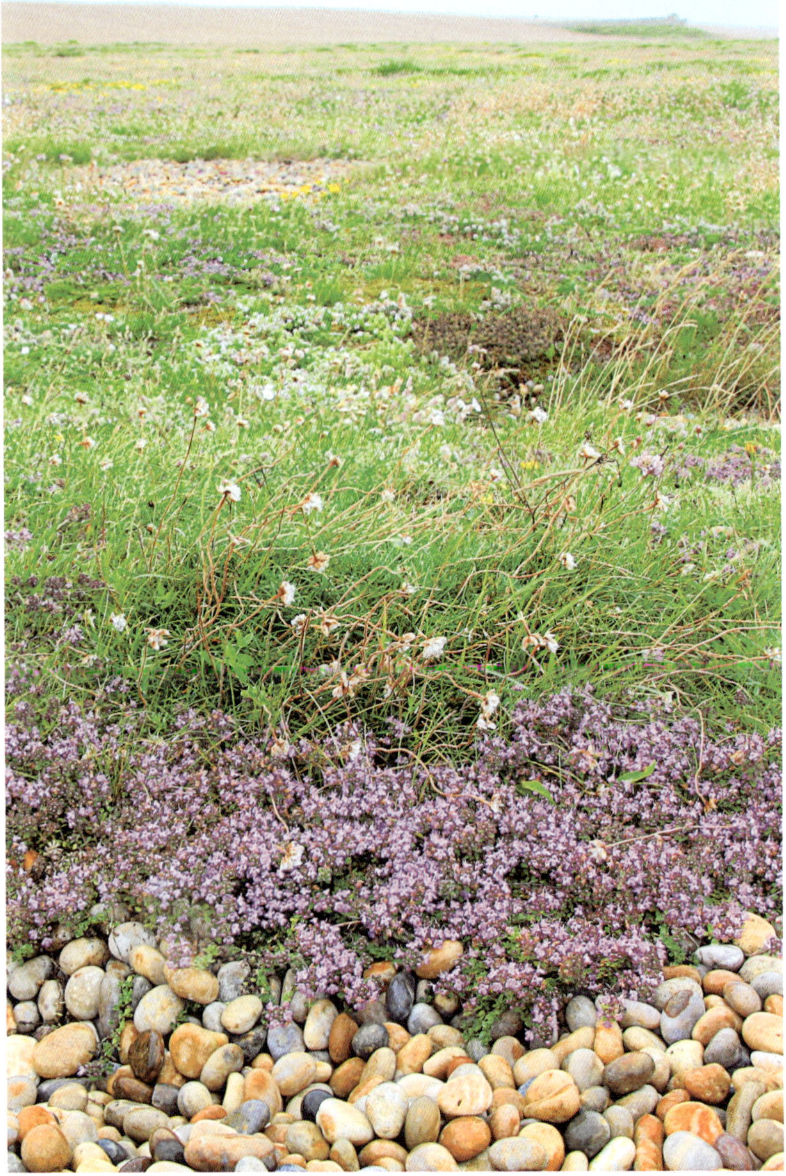

Wild Thyme *Thymus polytrichus*

HABITAT	Short turf
DISTRIBUTION	All around the coast, though largely missing from the east and southeast coasts of England
SEASON	Late spring and summer
CONSERVATION STATUS	Common

Garden herbs seem to come in two varieties – those that drop dead if you look at them too severely, and those that have to be destroyed with Agent Orange and flamethrowers before they take over the garden completely. No amount of love, attention, pH adjustment or prayers to St Jude seem to make any difference to the thyme I plant in my garden. It just dies. So I am pleased to be able to sidestep all this trauma and simply collect a handful of sprigs whilst searching out my larger seaside quarry.

Few people think of Wild Thyme as a maritime plant and, of course, it is found inland too on heath and down, in close-cropped pasture and on limestone pavement. However, maritime heaths, mature sand dunes and cliff tops are also prime locations for this pretty and useful little plant. I find most of mine in amongst the thrift of a grassy upper beach. It can be quite hard to locate and I usually have to wait until the bright tufts of two-toned pink flowers appear before I can find my spot. It is worth waiting for the flowers anyway as they, too, have some flavour. Either strip the leaves and flowers from the woody stems or just snip off entire stems with scissors. It is not a difficult plant to identify; the small oval leaves sit opposite one another on those long straggling stems, the plant forming a mat.

The cultivated plant is a different species (*Thymus vulgaris*), which has been much selected for its aroma; the wild variety is nowhere near as pungent but the very idea of 'Wild' Thyme is romantic enough to assure it a place in the kitchen. If you do find some strong-smelling thyme, it is most likely to be 'large thyme' (*T. pulegioides*), a plant only found in the southeastern half of England.

How to eat

The mild flavour of Wild Thyme means that you will have to use it quite generously. Its culinary uses are endless – in casseroles, in (slightly chewy) sandwiches, or in an omelette – but my favourite use is to add it to a yoghurt-based white sauce to go with mushrooms.

For more recipes, see pp.198, 201, 202.

Mushrooms

HABITAT	Short, unploughed grass
DISTRIBUTION	All around the coast
SEASON	All but the coldest and driest times of the year, but autumn is best
CONSERVATION STATUS	All mentioned below are common except for *Agaricus bernardii*

The seaside is not a place where many people would expect to find mushrooms, but there are few better venues for a fungus foray than cliff tops and grassy coastal paths. There are two reasons why. As much of our coastal fringe comes with a permanent grassy path, and cliff edges and tractors do not form a happy combination, there is little disturbance of the soil and the mycelium from which the fungi grow can flourish. Secondly, few fungi tolerate frosts and the coast is remarkably free of them for much of the year. This means that while autumn is still the best time for mushrooms the coast can enjoy an extended season with treasures such as the Horse Mushroom growing from April to December. I have found Fairy Ring Champignons clinging to a cliff edge in March and Field Blewits and St George's Mushrooms in February.

There are a handful of fungi that insist on a maritime location – mostly sand dunes – though only one of these, the excellent *Agaricus bernardii*, is a good edible species. However, those that will interest the forager most are familiar species from inland that just happen to like to be beside the sea.

The short turf found commonly next to the beach or on cliff tops is perfect for all of the grassland fungi. *Agaricus* species such as the Field Mushroom (*A. campestris*) and the Horse Mushroom (*A. arvensis*) are common, as is the delicious Fairy Ring Champignon (*Marasmius oreades*) – a species that loves to grow in caravan sites. Small Puffballs abound and you may be lucky enough to find a Giant Puffball (*Calvatia gigantea*). Later in the year huge rings of Field Blewits (*Lepista saeva*) will appear and, scattered colourfully everywhere, the glorious Waxcaps (*Hygrocybe* spp.).

I must make the usual plea for caution when it comes to collecting fungi for the pot. The golden rule is to eat something only if you can positively identify it as an edible species. You will certainly need a good book or two. I will put modesty to one side for a moment and recommend *The River Cottage Mushroom Handbook*, but there are other good titles available. Really nasty species like the Death Cap (*Amanita phalloides*) are normally found in the woods. The dangerous Mushroom you are most likely to encounter is the 'mildly' poisonous Yellow Stainer (*Agaricus xanthodermus*) which, just to be trying, looks very similar to a Field Mushroom.

A splendid ring of Fairy Ring Champignons

The Seaweeds

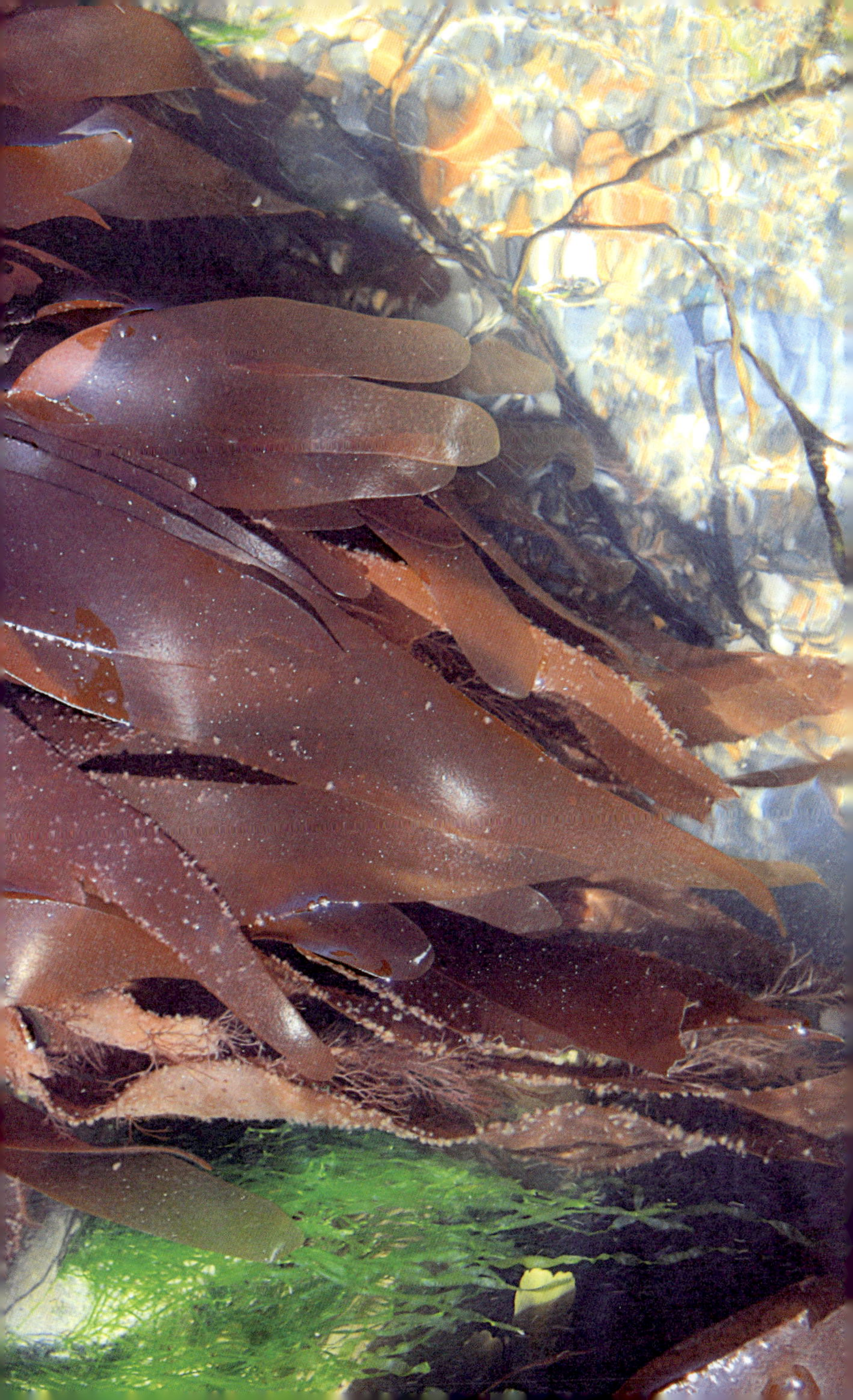

While it would take little to convince most people that eating, say, Velvet Swimming Crabs or Razor Clams is likely to be a rewarding experience, I fear that selling seaweed is going to tax my persuasive talents to their limit. There is a valiant history of such attempts and the several charming books I own on the edible seaweeds all display an evangelical zeal better suited to the pulpit. Well, you will get none of that nonsense here. I am an enthusiastic collector and eater of seaweeds but I appreciate that not one of them actually looks, or indeed smells, remotely edible.

There is little tradition of eating seaweeds in the British Isles and among the English almost no history of eating them at all. The Orient, however, has long embraced seaweeds, and it is mostly in Japanese restaurants and sushi bars that the Western palate encounters them. One notable, yet rarely noted exception to the Western neglect of seaweed is Carragheen. This is eaten by most people at some point during the course of a week as an additive to ice cream, milkshake and many processed foods, though few know what they are eating.

If few eat seaweed, fewer still collect it themselves; indeed I have only met one other person that does so. This is a great pity because they are so common, so useful in the kitchen, so nutritious and, best of all, free.

No seaweed is poisonous, with the exception of the *Desmarestia* species, which unhelpfully contain fairly large amounts of sulphuric acid within their cells. Fortunately these seaweeds grow in deep water well away from our grasp. Of the hundreds of species that grow around these islands only a tiny fraction are ever eaten, maybe just half a dozen; most of the rest are too rare, too tough, too slimy or just don't taste very nice. Some of the edible species are available commercially, usually dried, but there is absolutely no fun in buying something you can pick in quantity for nothing.

The absolute key to eating seaweeds is to cook them appropriately. You cannot boil up a saucepan of Carragheen, or sauté half a kilo of Kelp, and expect to get anything you would want to eat. Of the seaweeds dealt with in this book, Dulse alone is suitable as a simple cooked vegetable; the green seaweeds are just used in salads or dried to form an unusual condiment; the Kelps are mostly employed as flavour enhancers, being removed from the soup or stew before serving; and Carragheen itself is never eaten, but used for the thickening/setting agent it contains.

The spring is generally the best time to embark on a seaweed-collecting expedition, but most of them can be found, perhaps in reduced quantity or quality, throughout the year. Most of the seaweeds in this book can be gathered without getting one's feet wet, but the Kelps at least may require some serious paddling. It is always best to gather plants which are attached to their substrate, but detached individuals are perfectly safe to eat providing they look healthy enough. Always leave at least one third of the plant behind so that it might re-grow.

One of their more unfortunate accomplishments is an ability to concentrate heavy metals and other pollutants. This is seldom a problem now, after so much clean water legislation, but seaweed on rocks near an old tin mine or other industrial venture is probably best left to glow gently and peacefully in the dark. I never worry about the bacterial pollution that is such a concern with the bivalve molluscs as seaweeds will not absorb bacteria and, in any case, are cooked or at least washed well before being eaten.

Seaweeds are extraordinarily nutritious. Most people know that they contain a lot of minerals (most famously iodine), but they also provide many vitamins and high proportions of good-quality proteins. Dulse, for example, can be an impressive 35 per cent protein by dry weight. I understand that it is possible to live on an exclusive diet of seaweed and almonds but I intend to leave the fieldwork on this one to someone else.

As with everything in this book, collect carefully (use scissors), picking a little here and a little there. A string bag (preferably the type used by divers) is ideal for collecting seaweed as you will not have to carry a lot of sea water around with you as well. Make sure you use a different bag for each species – sorting out hopelessly mixed-up collections of seaweed is an irritating waste of time.

The taxonomic place of seaweeds is still a matter of debate. They are classed as algae but this is just a convenient box in which to place what is believed to be a disparate group. For the sake of convenience I refer to them in this book as plants. It may be that some of them *are* plants but it is also highly probable that some are not. In other words, not only is their relationship to other organisms unclear, so is their relationship to each other. There are three groups of seaweeds – green, red and brown – and I will discuss species from all three. Green seaweeds are members of the division *Chlorophyta*, with species such as Sea Lettuce and Gutweed; red seaweeds of the division *Rhodophyta*, such as Dulse and Carragheen; and the brown seaweeds are the *Phaeophyta*, a class that includes the Kelps.

Lastly I would encourage you to enjoy the little-appreciated beauty of our seaweeds. The colours can be quite breathtaking, especially the reds and greens of the typical rock pool. With their flamboyant good looks they can put our domestic gardens to shame.

Gutweed *Ulva intestinalis*

HABITAT	Sheltered areas. Rock pools and mud flats. Entire intertidal zone, especially upper shore
DISTRIBUTION	All around the coast
SEASON	All year; best in spring and summer
CONSERVATION STATUS	Very common

I cannot think of any other item of food with such a discouraging name, though why it is called what it is will be immediately obvious from the picture. As with so many things, we are talking here about a group of species, but the one in the picture opposite is true *Ulva intestinalis*. This beautiful seaweed is at home on the upper shore, often living cheerfully in the hostile environment of warm and fast-drying rock pools of wildly varying salinity.

On a sunny day the little tubes will fill with the oxygen expired during photosynthesis, allowing them to float as a layer on the tops of the pools to soak in yet more sunlight. Gutweed always starts life attached to a rock or a shell, but the floating layers have been known to float freely on the surface, forming great rafts of green. The other species commonly found is *Ulva linza*; it is very similar but distinctly flattened.

How to eat

Extremely common all around the coast, Gutweed (and its associates) is an annual species which may be collected with abandon by anyone who acquires a liking for it. The question is – does anyone like it enough to bother? Frankly, for those who try a mouthful while on the beach, the answer is certainly no. There is nothing wrong with it – it just doesn't taste of anything but salt. Yet there are three ways of preparing it that will bring out the best of what it has to offer.

In each case it will need a thorough rinsing first. The simplest way is to use it in a salad, dressed with copious amounts of cider vinegar and walnut oil (my favourite oil and vinegar combination). The next possibility is to dry it to make 'green nori' flakes: thoroughly dry your Gutweed either on non-stick trays in the oven at 50°C, or spread out thinly on a clean sheet in the garden if the sun is shining; then crush and blitz in a blender for a few seconds. This actually has quite a lot of flavour and can be used as a condiment sprinkled on to pizza, pasta, noodles or even incorporated in bread or a fishy sauce. Finally, dried Gutweed can be deep-fried for a few seconds in a light oil to produce delicious crispy seaweed (see p.186). See also recipe on p.210. Gutweed is one of the seaweeds cultivated in Japan where it is called 'aonori'.

Another edible, and beautiful, member of the *Chlorophyta* or 'green seaweeds' is Sea Lettuce (*Ulva lactuca*). It too can be used in a salad, though it does take a bit of chewing, or dried and fried. It has also been employed as a (poor) alternative to Laver. One more thing: it is bursting with proteins, vitamins and minerals and is jolly good for you.

Ulva intestinalis

Ulva linza

This picked rosette of Dulse is about half a metre long

Dulse *Palmaria palmata*

HABITAT	Rocky shore. Just above and just below the low-tide mark
DISTRIBUTION	All around the coast, but largely absent from north Kent coast and north to Scarborough
SEASON	All year, but best in the spring
CONSERVATION STATUS	Common

I suspect that H. G. Wells in *The War of the Worlds* had Dulse in mind when he wrote of the tumultuous 'red weed' that the Martians brought with them on their ill-advised excursion to Surrey. The thick carpet of venous foliage that sometimes covers the lower shore at low tide has a very alien appearance. In the water it is one of the most beautiful of all the seaweeds, forming huge red rosettes set strikingly against a background of bright-green Sea Lettuce. The large size, blood-red colour and finger-like terminations of the fronds (well illustrated on pp.86–7) make Dulse an easy species to identify – there is just nothing else like it.

Dulse can be collected throughout the year, though spring, when the new growth appears and protein content is at its highest, is the best time. St Patrick's Day marks the start of the season in Ireland, and you could do worse than follow this tradition. It is a long-lived plant in a turbulent environment, and the leaves can look tattered once collected, but it is sufficiently profuse to allow for picking and choosing.

Dulse has a long history of use in the UK but, as with all the seaweeds, it is a use restricted largely to the Celtic west and north. Its name is also of Celtic origin, being a variation of its alternative name 'Dillisk', which means 'leaf of the water'. In Ireland it is sufficiently popular for cultivation to be an economic possibility and is grown on ropes hanging in the water in the same way as Mussels. This is an impressively benign form of aquaculture which actually improves the quality of the sea water by acting as a buffer for excess nitrogen caused by run-off from over-fertilised agricultural land.

How to eat

In Ireland and Canada, Dulse is most commonly consumed in a dried state as an 'on the move' snack just like the humble crisp. Its flavour is salty, iodic and fishy, and it takes a great deal of chewing; not a food which is easy to like unless learnt at your mother's knee. Some eat Dulse completely raw – I once met an Irishman in a pub who recalled it being in the cheese sandwiches of his youth – but the texture is completely unassailable (shirt collar) and, strangely, the flavour too mild to warrant the effort of chewing.

Cooked, it is a superb and unusual vegetable. The flavour can be lost in boiling so I normally steam it. It takes from 10 minutes to half an hour to soften depending, it seems, on the will of the gods – just keep a close eye on the saucepan to avoid overcooking. Served unadorned, it can be too strong for the modern palate – cabbage with a hint of the medicine cabinet to follow – but as an addition to a smoked fish tart it is perfect (see p.190).

A traveller in Ireland once observed a woman boiling potatoes and Dulse together to form a sticky, starchy paste. It sounds awful but it formed the inspiration for Dulse potato cakes (see p.189). Another possibility is to deep-fry dried Dulse for a few seconds to give you some ready-salted seaweed crisps (see p.184). These can be eaten plain or crumbled on to other dishes as a condiment. See also recipe on p.204.

P.S. There is another 'Dulse' though it is not related, called 'Pepper Dulse', *Osmundea pinnatifida*. Pepper Dulse is a very common seaweed and can be found anywhere in the intertidal zone, growing in layers attached to rocks. The specimens near the high-water mark tend to be a light brown, with those further down the shore progressively darker and usually bigger.

The small fern-like fronds, picked fresh from the rocks, have the flavour of raw fish – very peppery raw fish – and this is where their strength lies. Pepper Dulse works well in fishy salads, especially when raw fish is part of the meal; the texture is a rather unusual variety of crunchy and (be warned) the fishy flavour is one that will stay with you for about 3 hours. The pepperiness (and the fishiness) can be concentrated and preserved by drying the fronds and either leaving them as flakes or ground into a powder to make an extraordinary pepper for use with fish. But only fish.

Pepper Dulse

Pepper Dulse frond, 20mm long

Carragheen

Chondrus crispus (and also *Mastocarpus stellatus*)

HABITAT	Rocky shores. Below and just above low-tide mark
DISTRIBUTION	All around the coast, but absent from parts of East Anglia and Lincolnshire
SEASON	All year, but best in spring and summer
CONSERVATION STATUS	Common

While even the most enthusiastic phycophagist (seaweed eater) will admit to seaweed being something of an acquired taste, this cannot be said of Carragheen. Its singular feature is that it has almost no flavour at all and, if anything, must be considered an acquired *texture*.

Carragheen is a purely practical food. A gelatinous substance, a trio of polysaccharides collectively called carragheenan, is extracted from it by boiling and used to set sweet or savoury jellies and mousses, and to thicken soups. This may all seem rather dull, but it is so useful in the kitchen that it is surprising how infrequently it is employed. Carragheenan is an excellent gelatine substitute for use by vegetarians or for those who look in vain on a packet of gelatine for a reassuring provenance. I always think it extraordinary that something that smells so much like a bucket of Oysters can be used in sweet puddings – the seaside smell disappears completely (well, almost completely) with cooking. Anyway, the chance of offering dinner guests Seaweed and elderflower panna cotta (p.194) for dessert is not to be missed.

Carragheen is one of the red seaweeds and is extremely variable in appearance. Its branches can be broad or narrow, flat or twisted, brown, red, yellow or even white. Its lack of grooves, warts or bladders is the best way to distinguish it from its lookalikes. It is often confused with a very warty seaweed called *Mastocarpus stellatus*, also pictured overleaf, but – and for once nature has taken our side – this has all the beneficent properties of true Carragheen and one will do just as well as the other. It, too, is rather variable in shape but often has pointed tips to its branches and is always covered in little papillae (warts).

A common seaweed of rock pools, Carragheen can usually be collected without the need to get one's feet wet. However, it is seldom out of the water except during spring lows, so a certain amount of paddling may be required. The main season, from May to September, nicely places Carragheen collecting as an ideal seaside holiday diversion, though I have collected it all year round. In common with most

Carragheen

Mastocarpus stellatus, life size

other edible seaweeds, Carragheen is identifiable by touch alone. It has a wiry, bushy consistency, unlike that of any other species. Carragheen sometimes appears to be covered in iridescent blue patches. These are just little bubbles of oxygen sticking to the surface, and the whole plant will 'fizz' as the bubbles are shaken loose. As with all the seaweeds, it is best to cut them, with scissors, at least one third of the way up from their holdfasts.

How to eat

Having collected your Carragheen you must wash it thoroughly to remove all the salt and the invariably present Winkles. If you are not going to use it immediately, it can readily be preserved for later use by drying. It *can* be dried in a low oven (50°C), but you will either need to live alone or with some very forgiving people who are extremely fond of you. The entire house will become filled with the heady aroma of low tide and the smell may persist for 24 hours.

Much better is to spread your seaweed on an old (but clean!) sheet pinned down with bricks or spikes on the lawn to dry. (In fact, I use my daughters' trampoline which is perfect for the purpose, though I do receive complaints.) Leave it for a few days, turning it over occasionally (the odd shower of rain is of no consequence), and when it is crispy, collect it into plastic boxes or cloth bags. Apart from humanitarian considerations, drying your seaweed outdoors will tend to remove the last olfactory reminders of the seaside and also to bleach it, thus removing the green coloration that may be unwelcome in a sweet mousse.

When needed, dried Carragheen should be reconstituted for a few minutes in cold water, then drained and put in a pan covered by a centimetre or two of fresh water. Heat it through very gently and stir frequently. The mix will become stickier and stickier and will be ready after 20 minutes to half an hour. While still hot, it must be strained through a muslin bag (you will need clean rubber gloves to protect your hands from the heat) or a fine sieve. You will now have the setting agent which can be mixed immediately with other hot ingredients to make your mousse or fruit jelly. Many recipes call for the Carragheen to be boiled in milk, but I find this always causes the milk to separate out. Extraction in water first is the best option.

To thicken a soup or stew, just soak the seaweed for a few minutes, place it in a small muslin bag and hang it in the pot.

See also the recipe for Brown Crab mousse with Carragheen on p.219.

P.S. You may think that you have never eaten seaweed in your life, but if you like ice cream or milkshakes or have eaten any number of other processed foods, then you certainly will have eaten Carragheen. Carragheenan is extracted from various seaweeds in vast quantities and, in the EU, goes by the snappy name of E407.

Kelp *Laminaria digitata*

Kelp and Sugar Kelp

Laminaria digitata and *Saccharina latissima*

HABITAT	Rocky shores below the low-tide mark
DISTRIBUTION	All around the coast, but largely absent from north Kent coast and north to Scarborough
SEASON	All year
CONSERVATION STATUS	Common

These large seaweeds are almost completely ignored as food in Britain, yet in the Far East they are so highly regarded that commercial cultivation has long been necessary. I am sure I must be missing something here, but for once I think the British might be right.

There are several species of Kelp found in British waters but *Laminaria digitata*, with its hand-shaped fronds and round stem, is the commonest of them. It forms massive and ecologically important Kelp beds all around the coast, the tops of which can often be seen protruding from the sea at low tide. And, as it seldom grows further up the beach, low tide is the only time you will be able to collect it. While it is often possible to grab some Kelp from the safety of a rock, on many shores you will just have to get wet. It is common enough to permit the removal of entire individuals if you wish, though the gentlest way of collecting is to just cut off the finger-like fronds with scissors. Sugar Kelp grows less densely and is similarly inaccessible to the fully clothed forager.

How to eat

All Kelps dry well, though their presence on the washing line tends to invite comment. Don't worry about the white deposit that appears on the surface. It is not mould, but the sugar alcohol 'mannitol', and should be left. Dried Kelp reconstitutes in a few minutes.

Kelp (several species) is referred to as 'Kombu' in Japan and employed on a grand scale in a vast array of dishes. Its most familiar use is in the stock, dashi, an ingredient considered essential in Japanese cuisine. Dashi is made by boiling Kombu with fermented, smoked, dried and flaked tuna, with the solid contents thrown away after cooking (and the strong temptation to ditch the lot stoically resisted). This, in turn, is used to make one of Japan's most famous dishes – miso soup.

One of the main uses for the Kelps in Asia is as a flavour enhancer – they contain considerable quantities of glutamic acid. I have frequently added a frond to soups and stews in the belief that it works, but a controlled experiment with a leek and potato soup revealed the unpalatable truth of the matter – it just makes everything taste faintly of iodine.

Another alleged virtue of Kelp is its ability to speed up the cooking of beans – it doesn't, I've tried – and also to reduce the collateral damage for which beans are justly famous. (Unfortunately I have been unable to determine the veracity of this second putative virtue as experimentation in that area has been banned in the Wright household.) Our native Kelp is a different species from those used in the Orient but that is unlikely to be the reason for my failures – they are undoubtedly all of my own making.

One recipe that does work is to use Kelp in its dried state to produce seaweed crisps. These are really delicious (see recipe on p.184), although Sugar Kelp works best. Just make absolutely sure that you do not overcook them – burnt seaweed has a flavour that sears itself into the memory.

Sugar Kelp *Saccharina latissima*

Laver *Porphyra* spp.

HABITAT	Rocky shores. All levels of the shore depending on species
DISTRIBUTION	All around the coast with the occasional gap due to lack of rocks
SEASON	One species or another will be available all year
CONSERVATION STATUS	Common, though under pressure in some areas due to commercial collecting

The seaweeds generally known as Laver are extraordinary plants. They consist of a single membrane which looks sufficiently like a piece of purple/brown polythene to cause a moment's consternation in those concerned about litter. Seen in this raw state for the first time, they are an unappetising prospect, yet cooked properly Laver is one of the best and most nutritious of all seashore foods. It is worth noting here that Laver is the seaweed, laverbread is a coarse purée of cooked Laver. The name Laver comes directly from the Latin word for 'water plant'.

The Laver that is collected in the British Isles consists of four or five species of varying habit, season and quality, the most familiar of these being *Porphyra umbilicalis*. As a genus *Porphyra* is extremely distinctive, but it is all but impossible for anyone other than an expert to distinguish one individual species from another. My advice is to search for something that looks like the Lavers pictured overleaf and just see what you think of it.

From November to April a species called *Porphyra linearis* can cover rocks on the upper shore with what looks like a coat of cheap varnish. It is the easiest of the *Porphyra* species to identify, consisting as it does of very slender fronds only a few millimetres wide. Unusually for seaweeds it does not require complete immersion in water in order to grow, often being content to live in the 'splash zone' at the top of the beach.

The winter habit of *P. linearis* can make collecting it a chilly exercise and I recall once being completely drenched by an exceptionally large wave which broke on the rock I was picking from. It is best picked on a receding tide before it dries to a papery membrane so that you don't find yourself scraping grit from the rock to eat with your breakfast. Even wet it is a frustrating seaweed to pick and 'combing' the strands out with a fork, twirling them like spaghetti and then pulling seems to work best. It produces a tasty (some would say the tastiest) dark laverbread when cooked and is the 'fast food' of the Laver world, taking a mere 5 hours to cook.

The species that are typically found hanging from rocks (or piers, or groynes) like rows of sleeping bats, are most likely to be either *Porphyra umbilicalis* or *P.dioica*. Both can be found all year round, though the most abundant growth occurs in the late summer when rocks can be thickly draped with their flowing fronds. Cut the fronds one third of the way from their holdfast with scissors.

The one I pick most often is *Porphyra leucosticta*. I find it in abundance in the shallow water at low spring tides, growing attached to *Fucus serratus* (serrated wrack). Floating like a silk handkerchief, it is seldom out of the water and can be identified as a species of Laver by touch alone. It is easy to gently tear the waving fronds from the wrack and it comes away completely clean. It grows from April to September, making it a fair-weather seaweed. It does seem to take more cooking than the others and will remain resolutely green no matter how long it spends in the pot.

All of the species grow very rapidly, with rates up to 5mm per day being typical, and some can disappear even more suddenly as their season ends or a storm sweeps them away. Their fast growth means that an area picked nearly clean may be completely repopulated within a month provided that the collecting has been done with care. With two of our species to be found all year and the other two taking more or less six-monthly turns, Laver is always in season. None of them are threatened at a national level though there has been local pressure in a few places due to commercial gathering.

How to eat

Given the unappetising appearance of raw Laver and the even less photogenic nature of laverbread (it looks like a cow pat), it is strange that *Porphyra* species (mostly *P. yezoensis*), in the processed form of nori, is frequently used in that most visually aesthetic of cuisines – sushi. Here the cultivated seaweed is shredded and dried on frames to form the familiar paper-like sheets that one finds wrapped around little pieces of fish or rice. Nori production is now a highly mechanised process of considerable economic importance to the Japanese economy.

The traditional British way of preparing Laver is an unsophisticated affair which consists, metaphorically speaking, of beating it into submission. The cooking process is one of the longest in the culinary canon with only whole, roasted wildebeest and my Auntie Hilda's Brussels sprouts taking longer. Around 6 hours of boiling is just about enough, but the Laver sold in Swansea market is cooked for a majestic 8–10 hours. The result is a forbidding, almost black and slightly sticky purée and it is this that is called laverbread. It has a strong savoury flavour with the faint maritime tang one would expect.

Different Laver species, and the same species collected at various times of the year, often require different cooking times so a certain amount of experimentation will be required.

Porphyra leucosticta attached to its normal host – serrated wrack

Porphyra linearis – the tastiest of the Lavers

THE SEAWEEDS

Porphyra umbilicalis

Served plainly, Laver is, frankly, a food best learnt before the age of five, but in any of those dishes for which it is slightly famous it is really rather good. Mixed with oatmeal and shaped into little cakes then fried in bacon fat and served with Cockles, it provides a bracing alternative to bacon and eggs for breakfast; see also the recipe for Laverbread with Clams and bacon on toast (p.193). It also makes an unusual canapé spread on small rounds of toast and sprinkled with lemon juice.

Among the several important amino acids packed into Laver's unlikely form is glutamic acid. This is the acid of the undeservedly maligned organic salt 'monosodium glutamate' (science has long dismissed its reputation as the cause of 'Chinese restaurant syndrome'). It explains the strong savoury flavour of laverbread and its occasional use as a flavour-enhancing sauce, traditionally on lamb.

P.S. It is perfectly possible, if mildly eccentric, to make your own nori. Coarsely liquidise the raw Laver in plenty of water, using an electric blender, then empty the slurry as evenly as you can on to one or two of those table mats made from thin strips of bamboo. Place another mat on top and squeeze out the water with the help of tea-towels. Use pegs to hold everything together while it all dries out in the garden or conservatory.

The nori sheets shrink to about half the size you expect and, though my own creations have all been lumpy, holey and crude, I have been proud of every one. Perhaps you will make a neater job of it than me.

Laver large enough for instant nori

The Molluscs

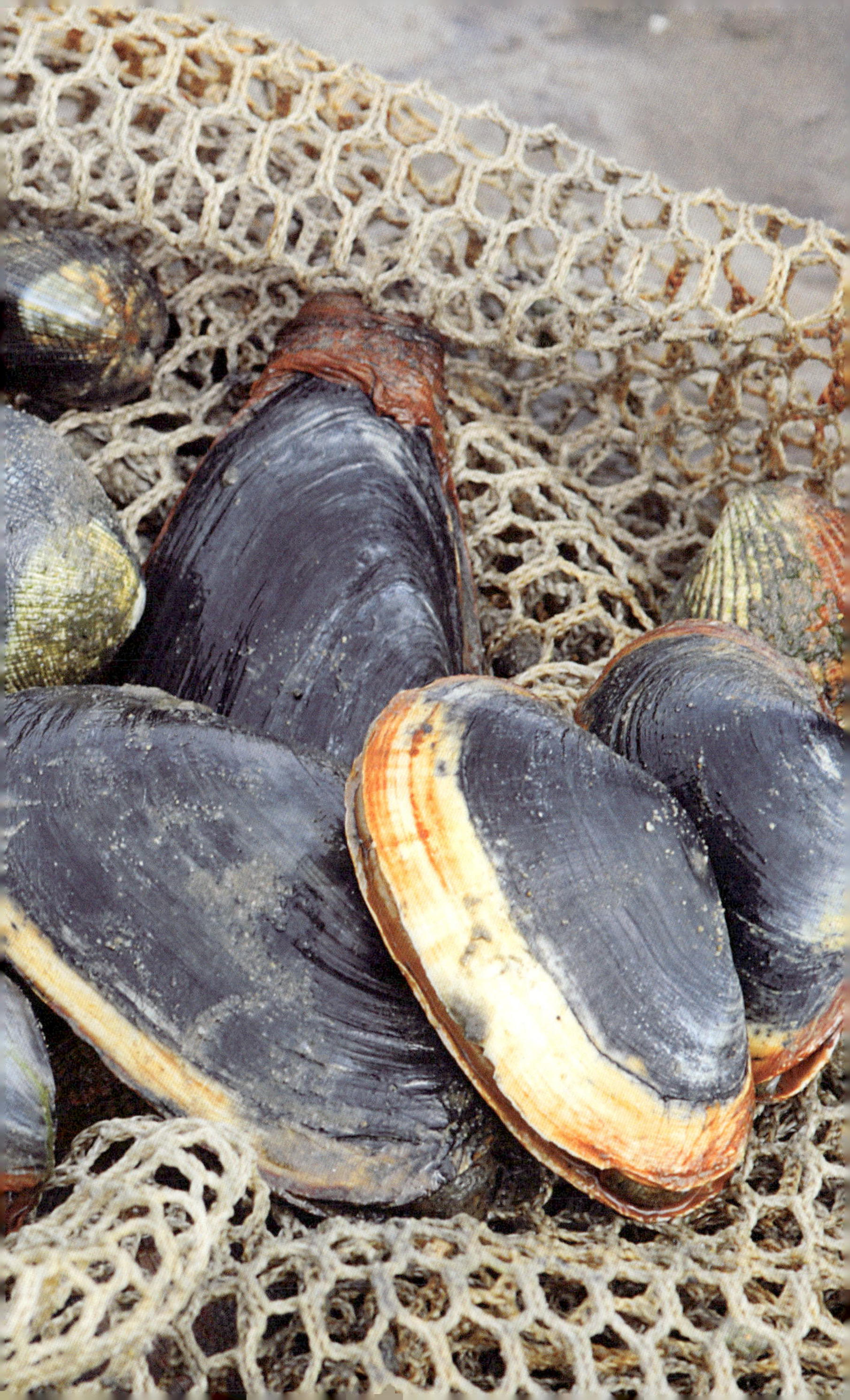

There are three types of marine mollusc – the bivalves, the gastropods and the cephalopods, though it is only the first two categories that will interest us here; we will not be trying to catch squid. The bivalves – Cockles, Mussels, Oysters and Clams – are the gourmet stars of the show, with the lowly Winkle, Dog Whelk and Limpets very much in the chorus line.

Before setting out remember that many shellfish are protected by closed seasons, minimum landing sizes (MLS) and other restrictions, so do check with your local authority first.

The thing everyone worries about when it comes to collecting wild shellfish is the risk of food poisoning. My plan is first to frighten you all to death by relating the terrible things that could happen to you, then explain how to avoid them.

Only the bivalves pose a serious potential health problem. They are filter feeders, passing litres of sea water through their bodies every hour, extracting the tiny particles of food suspended therein. Unfortunately, if the food contains anything unpleasant, the bivalve will consume that too. This unpleasantness comes in four general forms: bacteria, viruses, algae and chemicals of a regrettable nature.

Bacteria

Bacterial contaminants such as *E. coli* come from sewage or agricultural run-off. Although you are already host to billions of these tiny organisms living harmlessly in your lower intestine, certain strains can cause gastro-intestinal upset. This is generally all over quite quickly (in a good way) but the effects can be much more serious in those with a weak constitution. Shellfish from over 300 areas around the UK, a large proportion of them in estuaries where they are gathered or farmed commercially, are regularly tested for *E. coli*. The observed level of *E. coli* is used as an indicator of the general level of all bacteria and the waters accorded a category status (A, B, C and unclassified). Shellfish from category 'A' waters have less than 230 *E. coli* per 100g flesh and are fit for immediate human consumption. Category 'B' shellfish have less than 4,600 *E. coli* per 100g of flesh and must be depurated (purified), or heat-treated, or re-laid in category 'A' waters before sale. Category 'C' shellfish (less than 46,000 *E. coli* per 100g of flesh) must be re-laid in cleaner waters and given time to rethink their lives. The 'unclassified' will contain even more *E. coli* and are beyond all redemption. The fishery will be closed.

With the exception of category 'A' shellfish, commercially farmed or gathered bivalves will at some time be made safe by a process called depuration. The shellfish are stacked in crates inside a tank full of sea water which is continually pumped through an ultra-violet irradiated chamber, destroying all bacterial contaminants. The process usually takes 42 hours and the purified shellfish are safe enough to be eaten raw.

Viruses

Viruses, such as the Norovirus, can be a more intractable problem, both in their detection and elimination. These are the main cause of gastro-enteritis from shellfish and cause problems somewhere in Britain every year. They *can* be removed by depuration but it may take longer than the normal 42 hours. Commercially, it comes down to monitoring viral levels, re-laying in cleaner waters, heat treatment, optimistic depuration and a certain amount of hoping for the best.

Algae

Algal blooms are caused by such organisms as diatoms and the dino-flagellates and generally, though not always, occur in the warmer months. They can cause serious illnesses, but most victims suffer no more than an uncomfortable couple of hours. The commonest of them, DSP, or diarrhoetic shellfish poisoning, results, as its name makes clear, in gastro-intestinal problems.

The most serious, PSP or paralytic shellfish poisoning, is mercifully rare. You do not have to wait long before the symptoms arrive – usually within 30 minutes of consuming your *moules marinières*. They include tingling in the mouth, shortness of breath, muscular weakness, gastro-intestinal problems and, very rarely, death.

There are two more syndromes. NSP, neurotoxic shellfish poisoning, is relatively mild, causing a burning sensation in various, and sometimes unfortunate, parts of the body. The last of this unhappy crew, ASP, or amnesic shellfish poisoning, is very rare indeed and, although it is known to exist in UK waters, no cases have been reported here. Its effects may be serious but I cannot remember what they are.

Chemicals

Finally there is always the possibility of contamination from heavy metals such as mercury and zinc, or scary-sounding chemicals such as the organohalogens. Any problem of this nature is likely to be known to the local Sea Fisheries Committee or other authority and the beds will be closed.

If you have ploughed your way through the above, you may well have decided never to eat another Oyster except under medical supervision. Please do not despair. Things are much improved with new water treatment technologies being introduced and various EU directives (shellfish waters and shellfish hygiene) implemented. Furthermore there is much that you can do personally to eliminate the risk.

Here are my six top tips for safe wild bivalve consumption:

1. Talk to local fishermen and the local authorities about water quality.
Of the first importance is local knowledge. There are several people worth consulting, such as local fishermen and bait diggers. The ultimate source of wisdom in this matter, however, is your local Port Health Authority. This may have been subsumed into the local Environmental Health Authority or the town or county council, in which case you may need to dig deep to get to the right person. Wherever shellfish are caught or farmed commercially there is a strict testing regime to ensure public safety. This means that the water quality in an area may be known with some precision. This information is in the public domain; ask and it shall be given you. Not all areas are good for shellfish and it is unlikely that these waters will have been tested. The Food Standards Agency also takes a keen interest in shellfish safety and publishes the test results on the internet.

2. Collect only from obviously clean areas. Do not collect from narrow estuaries, from harbours or marinas.
A certain amount of common sense is useful when deciding whether to pick or not to pick. Murky estuaries and marinas, litter-strewn beaches, nearby disused tin mines and worrisome outflow pipes should not reassure the casual shellfish gatherer.

Wild rocky shores are the safest for Mussel collecting

3. Use the very sensible old adage of avoiding months that lack an 'r'.
While it does not fit every situation, the idea that it is safer to eat shellfish if there is an 'r' in the month is a sound one. The late spring and summer are the times when bivalves are at their most active, filtering through vast quantities of sea water. It is also when bacterial and, more importantly, algal contamination is at its peak. Algal blooms do occur at other times of the year but they are quite rare. Remember that there may be legal restrictions on when shellfish may be collected and that beds can be closed if a health issue is identified.

4. Give the shellfish time to clean themselves for a few hours in well-aerated salted water.
I am afraid that purging shellfish in saline (35g salt per litre of fresh cold water) has minimal effect on their safety and is no substitute for professional depuration. Nevertheless, it is something I always do to remove as much of their intestinal contents as possible. (Sorry – I can't think of a more delicate way to put it.) Cockles certainly need this chance to clean themselves to remove the sand. Bivalves open up their shells in water and will quickly drown once they have used up the dissolved oxygen. I use big, shallow trays for the purpose so that oxygen can be easily absorbed from the air, and I lay the shellfish no more than one deep. I keep the water cool and splash it about a lot for the same reason, changing it at least once. The absolute maximum time that should be allowed for the process is 10 hours and the shellfish should be cooked immediately after.

5. Unless you are sure they are from category 'A' waters, always thoroughly cook any shellfish you gather.
Some people, for reasons best known to themselves, consider raw shellfish to be tasty. Unfortunately they will have to forgo this odd preference when it comes to wild-caught animals. Unless you are absolutely sure that your shellfish come from category 'A' waters they *must* be cooked. Cooking kills all bacteria and viruses, so, unless there has been an unseasonal algal bloom that has escaped the attention of your local authority (algal toxins are *not* destroyed by heat), or a mysterious, unreported heavy metal pollution incident, such shellfish will be safe.

6. Check for signs of life before you cook them.
Finally, do tap your bivalves on the side of the pot so that they might prove their vitality by snapping shut. After cooking make doubly sure by only eating those which have opened.

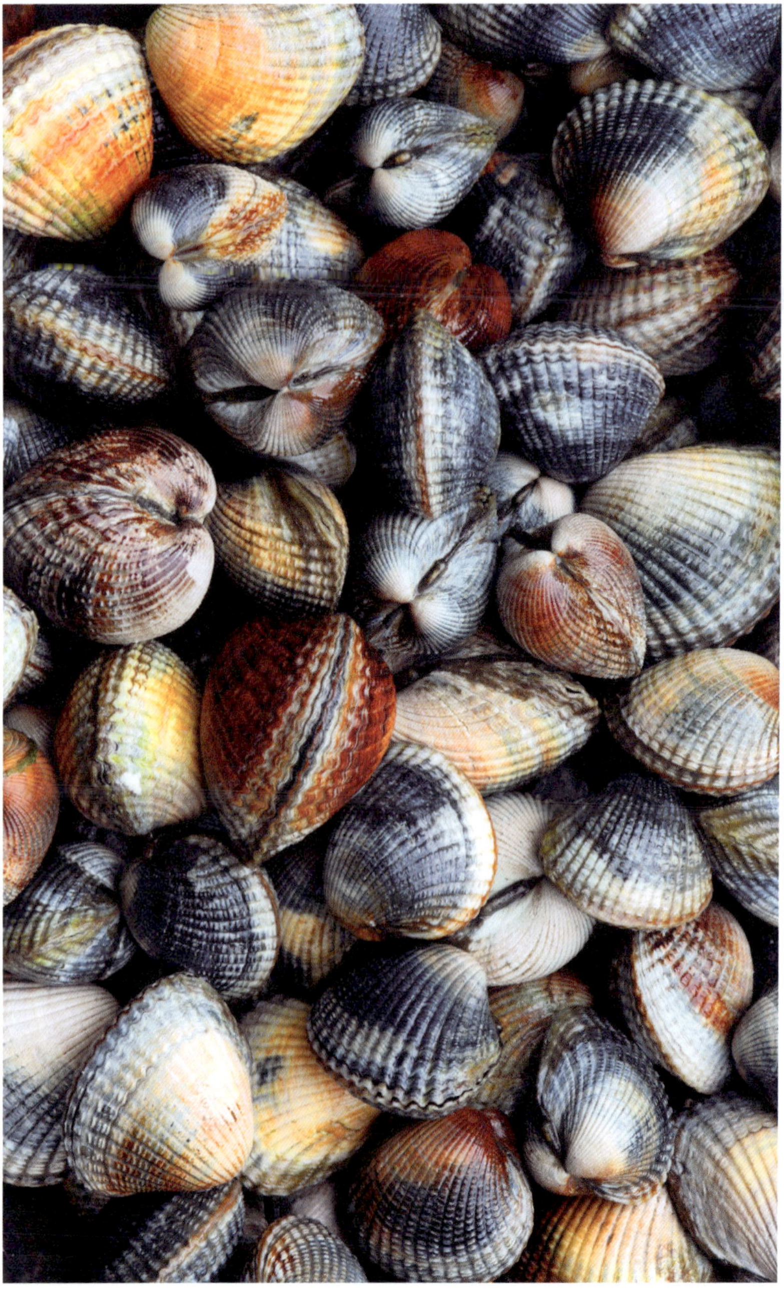

Cockle *Cerastoderma edule*

HABITAT	Intertidally and just below low-tide mark in sheltered sandy/gravelly/muddy bays and estuaries
DISTRIBUTION	All around the coast, but patchily due to lack of habitat
SEASON	All year, but summer months generally avoided
LANDING RESTRICTIONS	Varies from none to 19mm–23.8mm MLS
CONSERVATION STATUS	Very common, but permits and quotas exist in many locations to prevent over-picking

One of my most powerful childhood memories is of the many cockling expeditions I made with my family to Langstone Harbour near our home in Southsea. We used to travel there in my father's 1928 Morris, a splendid vehicle known to us as 'The Bus' which was kept mothballed from November to March as it refused to run if the temperature was not to its liking. We never used rakes to find our Cockles – the feel of the black mud through our fingers and the little triumph every time the hard round shell of a Cockle was encountered was too enjoyable to permit any mechanical intermediary. I recall watching the briny buckets of Cockles sat in the kitchen overnight, bubbling quietly with mysterious life, but what I cannot remember is actually eating them – the hunt itself, I suppose, was always the main reward.

After Mussels, Cockles are our most abundant bivalve, with around 20,000 tons being gathered every year. Unlike Mussels, which are extensively cultivated, they are harvested mostly from wild populations. Cockles seem to like an occasional breath of fresh air as they grow almost entirely in the intertidal zone. They can be found in any type of sand, from gravelly to muddy.

The major Cockle beds are at Morecambe Bay, the Thames Estuary, Burry Inlet in South Wales, the Solway Firth and the Dee Estuary. Most coastal counties have populations of Cockles but there are a few places where they are rare, such as the south coast of Kent and the Bristol Channel.

Most Cockles are collected commercially using highly efficient methods such as hydraulic dredging; these are victims of their own success and are carefully regulated to prevent over-exploitation and limit damage to other organisms. The relatively gentle practice of hand gathering, still used by the professionals in South Wales, is more benign, but even this needs to be closely controlled in certain areas as a hundred people collecting 100kg each in a day can quickly clean out an area of

Cockles completely. However, the individual forager, collecting half a bucket, need never worry about his or her effect on Cockle populations.

Cockles can be enormously prolific and densities of 10,000 per square metre have been recorded (a mental calculation tells me they would need to be small Cockles, shoulder to shoulder and four deep to fit). It may be that these high numbers are due to a process called 'rouching'. This occurs where the Cockles in a dense bed outgrow the area and start to pile up, one on top of the other. Strong currents and spring tides accelerate the process and the animals may collect in gullies and form 'rouches' a foot thick. The collector will need to replace his rake with a shovel and has about a day to claim the prize before the unfortunate animals perish from dehydration. Such abundance is rare, with much lower densities to be expected, but in a reasonable spot it doesn't take long to collect enough for a substantial tea. Licensed cocklers are sometimes limited to 100kg in a day, a figure which suggests that regular higher catches are possible.

As an occasional cockler I revert to my childhood method of plunging my hand into the muddy sand and hoping for the best. However, it is much more efficient to bring a rake with you. Cockles are always found in the top centimetre or two, so you will not have to work too hard. It is important to return the sand or mud to where you found it as 'spoil heaps' will kill any Cockles or other organisms they cover.

There are two, even gentler, ways of finding Cockles. Many are so near the surface that the edges of their shells, where their siphons appear, are clearly visible to the careful searcher. Some may also betray their position by firing a little jet of water into the air as the tide ebbs, but they always do so in one's peripheral vision and can seldom be accurately located. Lazier still is to collect the larger ones that simply sit

Cockle typically partially concealed in the mud

on the surface. These are often elderly Cockles which appear to be too decrepit to bury themselves. It is possible that they are able to rely on their large size and thick shells to protect themselves from predators. Unfortunately, like an old broiler hen, these are not likely to provide the most tender of meats.

Although Cockles are often collected all year round, the summer months should be avoided as that is when they spawn. The best time is September to October when they have put on weight over the summer but not yet expended it during winter.

Wherever you go, do check on the local regulations and status of the beds. There may be a closed season and normally open beds can be closed at any time for various reasons. There might be a minimum size (MLS) of 19mm, 20mm, 22.5mm, an extraordinarily precise 23.8mm or no minimum at all; it just depends where you are. Some areas have personal quotas and some require a permit. With all these things you will just have to ask your local Sea Fisheries Committee. The 2004 tragedy in Morecambe Bay reminds us of the dangers of cockling. This bivalve's preferred habitat of muddy sand is also where fast tides can overwhelm the unprepared.

How to eat

As Cockles are not happy out of their environment and will, for unknown reasons, drop dead at the first opportunity, it is essential to eat them as soon as you can. But unless you do not mind eating little purses full of sand, it is necessary to give your Cockles time to purify themselves. Overnight in a shallow tray of salt water (35g salt per litre of water) and kept cool and as well aerated as possible is all that is needed. Do check them for signs of life before cooking. Dead ones gape slightly, will not close when disturbed and should be discarded; live ones will snap shut. A double check, after cooking, is to only eat those that open. Live – closed tight; cooked – opened wide. I need not describe the flavour – few of you will not have tried them, but I will make a plea for more imagination to be used in their cooking. For the cook Cockles are largely indistinguishable from most Clams and can be used in the same recipes. I hope that the recipe on p.196 will inspire you to great things.

For more recipes, see pp.202, 204, 209, 216.

P.S. Cockles live life on the edge. Although they may live for 4 or 5 years, such aged individuals are quite rare and 2 years is more common. Predation, parasitism, pollution and bad weather all conspire to make life difficult for them. But sometimes they appear too eager for the next world and will perish in their millions. These mysterious die-backs, as they are known, occur quite frequently in the spring – and will usually consist of last year's recruitment, which will be a year old and just about big enough to collect. These events can be catastrophic for those whose livelihoods are linked to the Cockle's wellbeing, but quite why they occur is, at the time of writing, unknown.

Mussel *Mytilus edulis*

HABITAT	Rocky shores, occasionally attached to seaweed on sand. All shore levels
DISTRIBUTION	All around the coast with gaps due to lack of habitat
SEASON	Avoid the summer months; autumn is the best time
LANDING RESTRICTIONS	From none to 45mm–51mm MLS
CONSERVATION STATUS	Very common

One has to admire the common Mussel. Exposed to pounding waves, scorching sun and freezing temperatures, consumed by Dog Whelks, Crabs, starfish and human beings, it still manages to maintain its foothold all the way around our coast, sometimes in astronomical numbers. I once walked across a mussel bed in Wales that must have contained a billion; it took half an hour to get from one end to the other. Yet even in such vast numbers it is never a pest, providing food and shelter for countless other organisms such as the Netted Dog Whelk, the beautiful leaf green worm, and, most of all, barnacles.

Why, one must wonder, is this huge supply of a gourmet food left uncollected? Apart from us having generally lost the habit of foraging, the reason for this is straightforward: fear. Dark (and often true) stories of terrible poisonings lurk at the back of everyone's mind and the cautious Mussel lover will inevitably play it safe and choose the cultivated version.

Farmed Mussels are merely wild Mussels that have been gathered when young and collected in one place, often hanging on ropes from pontoons in estuaries. This is, incidentally, an impressively benign form of aquaculture, with almost no environmental drawbacks. Except when they are grown in the purest of waters (certified grade 'A'), the only reason these cultivated Mussels are safe to eat is that they have been placed, for a minimum of 42 hours, in tanks of sea water, which is sterilised by being constantly pumped through an ultra-violet light chamber.

Yet, even without the cultivated Mussels' process of depuration, as it is called, the wild Mussel is perfectly safe, so long as it is collected and treated with care. The precautions to be followed are described in detail in the introduction to this section.

Wild Mussel beds can be found almost anywhere in the intertidal zone; muddy sand, sandy mud (technically speaking there is a difference!), gravel, jetties, bedrock and boulders. The only requirement is that the substrate does not move about too much (which is why pebble beaches are not suitable). Exposed rocky shores with fast

THE MOLLUSCS 117

tides are my preferred hunting grounds as they are more likely to be free from pollution. While there is generally no closed season for Mussels, May to August should be avoided as they will be underweight and susceptible to the dangerous algal blooms of the warmer months, and also higher levels of bacterial pollution. By the autumn they will be much safer to eat and at their plumpest, having put on weight to see them through the winter.

There is no EU minimum landing size but local byelaws often set one – anything from 45mm to 51mm. Mussels can grow to a massive 15cm and live up to 20 years, but such aged monsters are rare, with most beds consisting of just three year classes (one-, two- and three-year-olds) and 70mm being about the largest you will find. If you encounter a bed where the Mussels are clean, neat and all about the same age, it is very likely to be a commercially laid bed and will be, alas, out of bounds.

There is an unfortunate complication that clouds Mussel collecting in Scotland. In that fine country all the Mussels (and Oysters) are owned by the Crown and, technically at least, it is illegal to gather them without the express permission of the Crown Estate. Fortunately the collecting of Mussels (though not Oysters) for personal use is tolerated and it is most unlikely that the Scottish forager would face the prospect of explaining his or her activities to the local magistrate.

Collecting Mussels is a straightforward matter – just gently twist them free, taking care not to dislodge too many of their diminutive neighbours. Never worry about encrusting barnacles; they will just make your dinner seem all the more authentically wild.

Sometimes you will find that the Mussel contains one or two tiny pea crabs, *Pinnotheres pissum*. These are rather startling creatures when first encountered as they live, permanently, *within* the Mussel and not just in the shell. However, there is no reason why they cannot be eaten along with their host – they taste of crunchy Mussel. The relationship between host and guest has been the subject of much fanciful speculation over the years, the wildest notion being that the Crab acts as 'lookout' against marauding cuttlefish. In fact the relationship is one of mild parasitism, with host Mussels tending to be underweight.

How to eat

Just before cooking, give your Mussels a good scrub under cold running water to remove anything you don't like the look of, and debeard them by pulling away the byssal threads, which will otherwise remain attached to the Mussel flesh (I use pliers to do this, they can be very tough on the wild animal).

There is nothing complicated about cooking Mussels. The simplest and arguably the best way is to simply steam them with a splash of white wine, a knob of butter and a chopped garlic clove for 3–4 minutes in a tightly covered frying pan.

For more recipes, see pp.198, 199, 216.

P.S. The byssal threads that anchor Mussels to rocks are remarkable pieces of biochemical engineering. These tough little protein tethers are much more complex than they look, consisting of a rigid part, a shock-absorbing spring section, an adhesive 'foot' and a protective 'varnish' layer. The 'foot' is the most interesting part as it contains one of the best glues on the planet. It can stick to rock (obviously), glass, plastic, metal, skin and even Teflon. It also works (again obviously) underwater. Much effort has been expended by industrial chemists in synthesising this glue. It *can* be extracted from Mussels but you need approaching 10 million Mussels to produce 1kg of adhesive. So far it's been used primarily in medical situations, but I can't wait for the day when I'll be able to buy a tube of 'mussel glue' from my hardware store.

P.P.S. *Mytilus edulis*, meaning 'edible Mussel', is an unfortunate name and not one the Mussel would have chosen for itself. We did not, after all, call ourselves *Homo edulis* (edible man), though most large predators would think the specific epithet more apt than *sapiens* and there are certainly enough of us to go round. No, the name *Mytilus edulis*, like that of *Ostrea edulis*, the native Oyster, the Mushroom, *Lactarius deliciosus*, or the second-century theologian, Justin Martyr, is one that rushes to meet trouble halfway.

A typical colony of Mussels with different age classes

The native Oyster, a rare find

Oyster *Ostrea edulis*

HABITAT	Muddy sediment below the low-tide mark
DISTRIBUTION	Scattered locations, chiefly south coast England, Thames Estuary and west Scotland
SEASON	November to February
LANDING RESTRICTIONS	70mm diameter MLS
CONSERVATION STATUS	Nationally scarce

Pacific Oyster *Crassostrea gigas*

HABITAT	Muddy sediment and on rocks and harbour walls. Lower shore and below the low-tide mark
DISTRIBUTION	Isolated populations all around the coast
SEASON	All year, though the summer should be avoided
LANDING RESTRICTIONS	None
CONSERVATION STATUS	Invasive species and fair game

Oysters are very special; the truffles, perhaps, of the shellfish world, and if there is any fish that tastes better I will be pleased to hear of it. The question for us is, 'can they be collected from the wild in the UK?' The answer, I am delighted to say, is 'yes', but it is a qualified 'yes'.

The native Oyster was common enough to be a food of the Victorian poor – though not, it is worth pointing out, the very poor. While a penny could buy three Oysters it could also buy a more rewarding '… ha'porth of bread and a ha'porth of cheese, or a half-pint of beer, with a farthing out' (*London Labour and the London Poor*, Henry Mayhew, 1851). The same authority tells us that 124 million Oysters were sold in London alone every year. Those days are long past and the native Oyster much declined.

The human oyster-catcher nowadays faces no less than three problems. The Oyster is now a fairly rare species with scattered populations, mostly in the South – the Solent and the Thames Estuary being strongholds – and also on the west coast of Scotland and in Northern Ireland. These reduced circumstances are partly a result of the excesses of the past and partly a matter of disease, pollution and predation.

The Oyster's conservation status is now one of 'priority species' and it is subject to various biodiversity action plans. Second, many of the Oyster beds that do exist will be part of an ancient and jealously guarded private fishery or otherwise in private ownership and thus out of bounds. For those in Scotland the news is all bad. Scottish native Oysters are the property of the Crown and it is illegal to collect them without a permit. Since the Crown takes Oyster conservation very seriously, a permit will not be forthcoming. Third, the Oyster is not at its happiest on the foreshore; it is considered to be a sublittoral (below the low tide) species and is rarely found out of the water.

Putting this all together: the native Oyster is too rare to pick, too hard to find and probably belongs to someone else anyway. If that is not enough, it enjoys a closed season for half of the year in most of its strongholds, with 1 March to 31 October being closed in the Solent area, and there is a minimum landing diameter of 70mm.

Having said all this, one does very occasionally come across native Oysters, usually in ones and twos but sometimes more, and if they are in a public fishery and in season it is possible to collect some for tea. Their preferred habitat is estuaries, and similar sheltered situations, on muddy, pebbly sand.

Now for some good news. In 1926 the Pacific Oyster (*Crassostrea gigas*) was introduced into the UK for the first time. Since then this large, fast-growing species has been extensively cultivated and if you order a dozen Oysters in a restaurant it is generally these that the waiter will bring to your table. Until recently there was little concern that this foreign import would cause any ecological problems. It spawns only

These feral Pacific Oysters are about 13cm long

when summer sea temperatures reach around 18°C – a temperature, it was thought, unlikely to be attained in the bracing waters around Britain (in cultivation they are spawned in special nursery tanks). However, a slight general warming of British waters and the odd exceptionally hot summer have provided, intermittently, conditions suitable for the Pacific Oyster's thwarted reproductive aspirations to be realised. This alien species is now established in the wild in scores, perhaps hundreds, of locations and has given cause for worry over its environmental effects.

As ecological disasters go, the Pacific Oyster is one of the best. Some would talk of a 'plague of Oysters' but this is as oxymoronic as a 'plague of chocolate'. The large Oysters pictured here were collected from a location in the south of England (if you think I am going to be any more precise, think again). They were fat, juicy and, fried for a minute or two in butter, among the best things I have ever tasted.

Pacific Oysters like to cement themselves to jetties, harbour walls – and even to each other, forming solid crusts of Oysters on the beach. In such situations they cannot be picked, they must be quarried; a crowbar is the most suitable implement to take with you (a handy-sized rock sufficing for the unprepared). Industrial gloves are also useful; Oysters don't bite, but their shells can be very sharp.

The south coast of England, round to the Thames Estuary, has been the chief 'beneficiary' of the warming sea and it is here that most feral Pacific Oysters will be found. The intermittent opportunities for breeding have resulted in populations that often consist of one age class only; there were a thousand or more Pacific Oysters where I picked the ones shown, but they were all of the same generation. Unless you too are worried about them perpetrating environmental mischief it is best, therefore, to leave a good proportion of what you find to await the next warm summer. Whether or not we will enjoy this bounty indefinitely depends on future water temperatures, a completely unpredictable parameter.

How to eat

The Oysters' fondness for warm and murky estuarine conditions means that more consideration than usual must be given to the possibility of contamination (see pp.108–9). Oysters can drown quickly so only give them about 4 hours to purify themselves. Immediately after this they must be cooked. Yes, I did say cooked. There really is no choice unless you know for certain that they come from class 'A' waters. I see no problem with this; cooked Oysters are superb. (There is nothing wrong with raw ones either – for anyone who enjoys sticking their head in a bucket of sea water and taking a deep breath they are a delight.) My favourite way is to remove them live from their shells (you will need a proper oyster knife and a cloth or glove to protect your hand from serious injury) and sauté them for a couple of minutes. Their mild flavour and soft texture is perfect in a chowder – just add the Oyster flesh a minute or two before removing from the heat. For more recipes, see pp.210, 212.

Cross Cut Carpet Shell or Palourde	**Manila Clam**
Warty Venus	**Hard Shell Clam**
Surf Clam	**Sand Gaper**

Clams

HABITAT	Sandy, muddy and pebbly sediment in sheltered bays and estuaries. Lower shore
DISTRIBUTION	All around the coast, though many species are highly localised
SEASON	Avoid months without an 'r'
LANDING RESTRICTIONS	Few Clams have an MLS
CONSERVATION STATUS	Most Clams worth eating are common and you probably won't find the rare ones!

Clams are little regarded in this country, with much of what is collected exported to countries whose inhabitants sensibly appreciate these superbly sweet delicacies. Being by their nature hidden from view, they are not the easiest of prey to find, but a 'clam dig' can be a satisfying and social affair with a prize at the end well worth the labour.

The word 'Clam' is a loose term referring to any number of bivalve marine molluscs (having two halves to their shell) that make a living hiding in the sea bottom, filtering particles of food from the water. Two Clams – the Razor Clam and the Cockle – are dealt with elsewhere in this chapter; this section describes some of the other main species. It would require a whole volume to do the Clams thorough justice so I will just describe some of the most important ones that might be found by the seaside forager.

Unless you have a particular spot in mind, most of the Clams you find will be a by-catch of cockle raking. Apart from this, locating them is all a matter of observation, local knowledge, exploration and luck. When you discover a likely spot it is often possible to find your prey precisely.

Clams are siphon feeders and will frequently betray their presence with little holes in the sand or mud. Most holes are indistinguishable from those produced by marine worms, but some, like the 'keyhole' of the Razor Clam or the double holes of the Carpet Shell Clams are distinctive. The large Sand Gaper has an appropriately big siphon hole which can be differentiated from a worm hole by the bubbly squirt of water that may be produced when the nearby mud is disturbed.

Clam-rich areas, just as the tide recedes, can be exciting places (well, they excite me) with tiny intermittent fountains appearing everywhere, the whole ground seething with hidden life. Locating a Clam by its fountain, however, is seldom easy as the little squirt of water always seems to appear in one's peripheral vision. When I decide I have found one I usually just scrabble around in the mud, but sometimes they dig in deep and a spade is needed. Clams are, unfortunately, extremely hard to tell apart, with colouration being particularly variable. The good news is that it matters little – they are all good to eat.

The real aristocrats of the edible bivalve world are the Venus Clams, the *Veneridae*. The Pullet Carpet Shell, *Venerupis senegalensis*, is the easiest Venus Clam to find, occurring patchily around much of our coast in sheltered locations, with particular strongholds on the south coast of England and the west coast of Scotland. It is not pictured here but looks just like the Cross Cut Carpet Shell but without such deep grooves. It lives in sand, muddy sand and gravel substrates from around the low-water mark down. The Warty Venus, *Venus verrucosa*, restricted to shelly gravels of the south coast of England and the west coast of Scotland, is a splendid-looking and highly regarded species but not one that is easy to find.

Two ex-pat American Venus Clams can be found in scattered populations on the south coast of England. The muddy creeks at the top end of Hampshire and Sussex harbours and in some of the Essex estuaries are home to the slightly chewy Hard Shell Clam, *Mercenaria mercenaria*. Supposedly imported to this country from America when they were jettisoned from a transatlantic liner in Southampton Water, they formed the basis of a fairly lucrative fishery back in the 1970s. They can grow to a substantial 12cm across (most Venus Clams are little more than 5cm) and, as a non-native, are fair game in public fisheries. The second species is the very tasty Manila Clam, *Venerupis phillipinarum*. At present it is found only in Poole Harbour, though it is likely that it will spread further.

The greatest prize of all is the Cross Cut Carpet Shell or Palourde, *Tapes decussatus*. This beautiful Clam, the sweetest-tasting of them all, can be 5cm or more across. Its clinching identification characteristic is the shell ornamentation, which consists of deep grooves running both ways across the shell.

One of the commonest groups of Clams is the Trough Shells, their presence in the locality often evident from the thousands of white shells on the upper beach. Pictured (on p.124) is one of the most frequent of these, the Surf Clam, *Spisula solida*. Trough Shells typically live in sand just below the low-tide line. They are all rather mild in flavour, with the advantage of being less chewy than Cockles.

One extraordinary-looking Clam which I often find (oddly enough) in muddy creeks is the Sand Gaper, *Mya arenaria*. Known more appetisingly in North America as the Soft-shelled Clam, this is an essential ingredient in a Clam bake. These large Clams, which betray their location with a large siphon hole that squirts water when disturbed, dig themselves in deep – and the older and bigger they are, the deeper they go. A reasonably mature specimen would be about 10cm long and 30cm down.

Digging a Sand Gaper out is a skilled and energetic operation. You will need a narrow but very strong spade and will have to ease up a large clod of estuary to ensure that you have found a Clam and not a worm. The Sand Gaper has an enormously long siphon (it is, necessarily, at least as long as the Clam is deep), which can often be seen withdrawing rapidly into the shell. The trick is to get the creature out without breaking its very fragile shell with the spade. I am not entirely convinced they are worth all the effort and inevitable ecological disturbance. The flesh is watery and the only part really worth eating is the siphon – an organ of worrisome appearance. You will need to remove the sheath-like skin which surrounds it to reveal the muscular tube beneath. It can be eaten raw as long as you wash it thoroughly and don't look at it.

How to eat

Clams, like Mussels, are usually steamed open in a little water or white wine plus, of course, butter and garlic, in a covered frying pan. I like to remove the cooked Clams from the pan, discarding the top half-shell, and serve them with a sauce made from the reduced liquor. The most famous recipe for Clams, however, is Clam chowder. The essential ingredients of this superb class of soups are stock, bacon or salt pork, potatoes, cream and Clams. It is difficult to see how anyone could go wrong with such a combination.

For more recipes, see pp.193, 201, 202, 204, 216.

P.S. A common group of bivalves, not mentioned above as its members are too small to eat, is the genus *Abra*. Here in Britain we have *Abra alba* and *A. nitida* but sadly lack the most interesting of them all. Taxonomists are only human and cannot always be trusted to approach their work with due seriousness. Thus it was that *Abra cadabra* came into being. Unfortunately not all taxonomists have a sense of humour; *Abra cadabra* has now been renamed *Theora cadabra*, which is no fun at all.

Carpet Shell Clam double siphon holes

The large Sand Gaper siphon hole

Razor Clams *Ensis* spp. and *Solen marginatus*

HABITAT	Sheltered sandy or gravelly bays and estuaries. Low-tide mark and below
DISTRIBUTION	All around the coast, but rare on the east coast of England and the north coast of Devon and Cornwall
SEASON	Avoid months without an 'r'
LANDING RESTRICTIONS	10cm MLS
CONSERVATION STATUS	Not threatened, but sometimes overfished by dredging

Because of the extraordinary way that it is done, there is an excitement and drama to catching Razor Clams that is like no other, and for many it is the ultimate foraging enterprise. Yet it is not at all difficult to extricate them from their sandy hiding place once you find them – it is the finding that is the challenge.

There are four, fairly common, native species of Razor Clam: *Ensis ensis*, *E. siliqua*, *E. arcuatus* and *Solen marginatus*. For the forager the differences between them are slight and they all taste the same – very good indeed. The first two prefer fine, sometimes muddy, sand and the last two a grittier environment. *E. siliqua* is the largest at a massive 20cm, *E. arcuatus* 15cm, *E. ensis* and *S. marginatus* the babies of the bunch at around 12cm. Razor Clams are long-lived shellfish with *E. siliqua* sometimes making it to its twentieth birthday. They can be found all around the coast though are less common on the east coast of England and the north coast of Cornwall and Devon.

Razor Clams live in vertical burrows with their siphons more or less flush with the seabed. These siphons, although seldom visible themselves, are the key, or should I say 'keyhole', to finding these elusive creatures. Go to a sheltered sandy beach (the presence of empty shells is encouraging, though no more than that) at the lowest tide you can manage, when the wind is slight and the sea is calm. Such a happy conjunction of conditions is rare so a certain amount of patience may be necessary. Such exploration may reward the effort but a better strategy may be to rely on local knowledge. Many people will already know if and where there are Razor Clams in the area and if you ask around you should soon find out all you need.

Having found your spot and a perfect day to go there, paddle out slowly and with a gentle tread. There is no point wading out much past knee depth unless you don't mind getting soaked when it comes to catching them. Polarising sunglasses will help you see past the sea's reflective surface, with the added advantage of making

Razor Clam, *Solen marginatus*, with foot extended

you look cool. Razor Clams betray their presence with little keyhole-shaped holes in the sand, 10–20mm long, caused by the activity of those siphons. These holes are sometimes small slits, sometimes flattened 'figure eights', such as the one pictured on the right. If you are extremely lucky this is what you will find and you will have struck gold. Stand still; look around to see if there are any more.

You will have brought with you one of those plastic tubs of table salt which has a small opening at one end (best to bring two pots – you will run out quickly). *Gently* squirt some salt *on to* the hole and wait. If all goes well, 10–20 seconds later you will see a flurry of activity, followed by the amazing sight of a Razor Clam rising, like magic, from the sand. Quickly grip the shells by their *edges*, hold on, then pull very gently. The 'foot' will still be anchored firmly in the sand, pulsing to regain a foothold and if you tug too hard it is easy to pull the animal in two. Speed is essential as the Clam will quickly withdraw into its burrow if you don't grab it straight away. If all has gone to plan you will soon be holding up a splendid, gloopy (the 'foot' usually hangs forlornly out of the bottom of the shell) Razor Clam.

Occasionally, if the tide is very low the 'keyholes' can be found out of water and are all the easier to spot. A more professional approach is to snorkel for them. This is possible in poorer weather as you no longer need to see through the surface of the sea to spot the keyholes. The other advantage is that it allows you to go a little deeper and access the denser beds further offshore. If there are lots of keyholes, it is possible to 'broadcast' the salt over several at once and grab them all as they come up. This is how they are commercially hand-fished, though normally using full diving gear.

There is one more species which you might find if you live near The Wash or the Essex and Kent coast. It is *Ensis americanus*. As the name suggests it is a foreign import which arrived in Europe as larvae in ballast water in the late 1980s. This animal is now gradually working its way west along the English Channel. Like most invading species it is not at all welcome for reasons of conservation and may – indeed, must – be collected with abandon. Of course in order to do this you will need to be able to recognise it when you see one. It has a much broader shell than the natives (6:1 as opposed to 8:1), but if this doesn't clinch it you will be looking out for things such as 'Pallial sinus reversed S-shape pointing to posterior adductor scar', as it says in one of my reference books. Means nothing to me either.

The shoreline forager will find mature, full-size specimens fairly elusive as those near the shore are predated more readily (not least by *Homo sapiens*) and it may be that juveniles settle in the shallow water at the edge and move downhill to join the grown-ups as they mature. One might sensibly ask how a bivalve buried in sand could possibly do this and the answer is simply that they can swim.

The minimum commercial landing size for all species is 10cm so it is best to leave any smaller specimens where they are – the size of the keyhole is a very good indicator. Apart from hand-collecting, Razor Clams are commercially harvested by

Razor Clam just out of its burrow

A keyhole in the seabed

hydraulic dredging, a ruthlessly efficient way of extracting the animal from its sandy home. The Razor Clam's slow growth means that populations can easily be fished out by such industrial methods, and there can also be some collateral damage. Hand-collecting by divers, though more benign, can also be fairly destructive if carried on for too long. By contrast, the individual forager, collecting a few specimens from around the low-tide mark away from the offshore population centre, is a virtuous being and richly deserves his or her supper.

How to eat

Like all shellfish, the Razor Clam contains a lot of 'anatomy' inside its shell and it is best not to enquire too closely as to what all the bits are for. The only part you should leave in the shell (though I have eaten it and lived) is the distinctive black stomach. The tastiest part, and fortunately the largest, is the 'foot'. This consists of a long tube, swollen at the end. It is very slightly tougher than a good scallop but quite a bit sweeter.

Razor Clams are cooked when the meat loses its watery, translucent appearance. Simple is best with this wild delicacy and barbecued Razor Clams, plus a little lemon juice perhaps, takes some beating.

For more recipes, see pp.196, 201, 202, 204, 207.

P.S. *Solen marginatus* (the species pictured on p.129) performs a clever trick when, having been disturbed, it rises from the sand. The top part of the siphon will come off and drift away before the remainder of the Clam withdraws to its burrow with a sigh of relief. The piece of flesh appears to be a sacrificial offering to whatever predator the Clam 'thinks' might be attacking it. This behaviour is familiar to us in the disposable tail of certain lizards and is known technically as 'autotomy'.

THE MOLLUSCS

Winkle or Periwinkle *Littorina littorea*

HABITAT	Rocky shores and seaweed-rich estuaries
DISTRIBUTION	All around the coast
SEASON	Avoid the summer months – some areas have a closed season from mid-May to mid-September
LANDING RESTRICTIONS	Usually none, but South Wales has an MLS of 13mm
CONSERVATION STATUS	Very common

There is surely no item of food that is taken less seriously than the Winkle and I am not really sure why this should be so. Maybe a long association with the poor is to blame, possibly its familiarity as a playground euphemism or just the fact that it is impossible to eat one with any degree of decorum. In Britain it has seldom found its way on to the menus of the type of restaurant that is comfortable with the word 'drizzle' and is an infrequent choice for a dinner party hors d'oeuvre. Yet many people, myself included, have fond childhood memories of this most time-consuming of foods. Incidentally the name 'Periwinkle' comes from the old English for 'winding Mussel'. I will use the more familiar 'Winkle' throughout.

Many seashore species can be a foraging challenge, taking skill to locate or cunning to catch. Not so the Winkle. Visit any rocky shore or any weedy mud flat and you will find some. Millions of them. As gastropods in the same sub-class as garden snails, they live a similar life and you can often see them nibbling on a Sea Lettuce. They are very important browsers of the algae which grow on rocks, helping to prevent dominance by any one species and allowing the slower-growing seaweeds such as Carragheen to establish themselves. For this reason it is wise to leave behind a fair proportion of what you find to continue this essential work.

There is little mistaking the Winkle's relatively large dark-brown or green shell and if you do collect some Top Shells in error no harm will be done as these are just as tasty though usually smaller and even more fiddly. The superficially similar Dog Whelk (p.135) is normally white and has a little groove at the base of the shell opening rather than being completely round. When removed from a rock, the Winkle will make a distinctive and satisfying sucking sound and squirt out a little jet of water.

The collecting of Winkles is sometimes regulated with a closed season from mid-May to mid-September and it is probably best to avoid them in the summer anyway so that they can breed in peace. There is often a minimum size; in South Wales the

Winkle should not pass through a 13mm square mesh, in Devon and Cumbria this is 16mm. If in any doubt, ask your local Sea Fisheries Committee.

How to eat

The flesh of the Winkle is remarkably sweet and rich in flavour and, as long as you do not cook them beyond 5–10 minutes, nicely tender. It helps to have put them into a well-aerated bowl of salted water for a couple of hours to give them a chance to purify themselves. Whether or not you eat the unappetising-looking bit at the end is up to you. It is very tasty, if a little gritty, but not for sensitive souls who wonder, anxiously, exactly what it is they are eating. The traditional method of consumption is to extricate them with a pin and eat them, one at a time, dipped in vinegar. I have a pointed pair of tweezers which speeds up the whole process considerably. My Auntie Margaret, in 1950s London, used to patiently remove a couple of dozen from their shells and eat them with vinegar in a sandwich. Sounds awful to me. She and her friends would also take the little (and inedible) trapdoors, or opercula, and stick them on their faces as instant Margaret Lockwood beauty spots. They had to make their own entertainment in those days.

There are a thousand recipes for Mussels and very few for Winkles. It's just not that sort of mollusc. However, the plain Winkle can be improved by steaming it in a covered shallow pan of white wine and herbs and reducing the resultant sauce to form a dip. One proper recipe involves gently frying quartered small button mushrooms with shallots and a little cumin. Once the shallots have softened, throw in some cooked, shelled Winkles and turn up the heat for a minute or so until everything is lightly browned. Serve with bread.

See also the recipe on p.209.

P.S. That Winkles were popular in Victorian times is known, almost instinctively, by everyone. They seem, somehow, to embody the rather suspect cuisine of those interesting times. One of the best social histories ever written is Henry Mayhew's magnificent 1851 *London Labour and the London Poor*. In volume one of this masterly piece of observation he writes of the poor, but evidently loquacious, 'wink' men of the city. One of them explains that 'winks' are 'reckoned a nice present from a young man to his sweetheart'. (Don't try this at home.) Another seller, we are told, made no 'speeches' but all day sang:

Winketty-winketty, wink-wink-wink,
Wink, wink,
Wicketty-wicketty-wink,
Fine fresh winketty-winks, wink-wink!

He must have driven people mad. A third 'wink' man explains that the 'unfortunate' women who live near Waterloo are among the best of his customers, especially, for reasons he does not explain, on Sundays. Mr Mayhew tells us that 3,600,000 pints of Winkles are sold each year on the streets of London – this works out to a colossal 1,620 tons and 300 million individual Winkles.

P.P.S. Unlike many other invertebrates that may recklessly change sex in middle age or even manage to be both sexes at the same time, the Winkle leads a pretty straightforward sort of a life, though not one entirely without drawbacks. The girls fare well enough but the boys face a terrible ordeal after the mating season: their, er, winkle drops off. It does, mercifully, grow back in time for next year, but it must be a terribly traumatic experience the first time it happens.

Dog Whelk *Nucella lapillus*

HABITAT	Rocky shores, mid-shore to below the low-tide mark
DISTRIBUTION	All around the coast
SEASON	Avoid the summer months and April and May
LANDING RESTRICTIONS	None
CONSERVATION STATUS	Very common

The large and familiar Common Whelk is a fairly infrequent visitor to the lower shore, much preferring deeper water; one does, however, occasionally come across them at low tide, in ones and twos and looking rather lost. Commercially they are caught in special barrel-shaped whelk pots and there is no reason why you shouldn't put one out at a spring low tide to see how you get on. I did come across a more interesting method of catching them in Jeffreys' 1862 *British Conchology*. He relates that Cheshire fishermen would place a dead dog under a pile of stones at the low spring water mark. The Whelks were evidently attracted to the smell but unable to get at its source. At the next low tide they were simply picked off the stones in large numbers. I haven't tried it but it may be that road-kill badger has at last found a purpose.

The Dog Whelk, though considerably smaller, is much more accessible and a common inhabitant of the intertidal zone. It is usually viewed suspiciously by the casual collector of shellfish as something that looks like a Winkle but probably isn't, or as just a small Common Whelk. It is neither of these. While not closely related to the Whelk, being in a different family, it *is* edible, having a similar taste and texture. The Dog Whelk appears in a variety of forms and colours and has a close relative in the more colourful and elaborately incised Netted Dog Whelk. All Dog Whelks have a little groove at the base of the opening (where their 'radula' emerges to drill into their prey) which distinguishes them from Winkles.

As these little creatures are less common than Winkles and have been a cause for conservation concern, mostly in the past due to pollution by anti-fouling paints, it is best to collect no more than a handful, and then just occasionally. The 'r' in the month rule should be obeyed with this species, avoiding April as well, when they start to form their breeding groups.

How to eat

Recipes for Dog Whelks are even less common than those for Winkles, though I did once come across one which involves cooking them in a tomato sauce with kidney

Dog Whelks feeding on Mussels

beans. Apart from eating them like Winkles, I think that the best recipe is a 'doggy' version of Hugh's Whelk fritters, made from chopped and fried bacon and onion mixed with the minced Whelks, egg and a little curry powder. Complete details are supplied in *The River Cottage Fish Book*, but you can probably work it out for yourself from the ingredients. Dog Whelks are carnivores so, rightly or wrongly, I never fancy the dark 'gooey bit' that some people swear by in the Winkle.

See also the recipe on p. 209.

P.S. The Dog Whelk feeds mostly on Mussels and barnacles, inserting a long feeding tube into its unfortunate prey through a shell opening or through a little hole it drills itself. To make the hole it employs a rasp on the end of its proboscis, and chemical secretions from a specialised piece of kit in the sole of its 'foot' called, unimaginatively, an 'accessory boring organ'. The prey is immobilised with narcotic saliva, dissolved by enzymes and sucked up the feeding tube. I hope I haven't put you off. Apart from predation by Crabs and by birds, which will swallow them whole, they can also suffer retribution from their victims. The byssal threads that Mussels use to anchor themselves are sometimes employed as lassoes, holding Dog Whelks immobile until they starve to death. Not that they are great travellers as long as their food supply holds out. Marked specimens were found to have strayed no more than 30cm from where they were placed a year previously.

Limpet *Patella vulgata*

HABITAT	Rocky shores, intertidal zone
DISTRIBUTION	All around the coast
SEASON	Avoid months without an 'r'
LANDING RESTRICTIONS	None
CONSERVATION STATUS	Very common but easily over-collected

Slipper Limpet *Crepidula fornicata*

HABITAT	Generally below the low-tide mark but often thrown higher up the shore
DISTRIBUTION	South of a line drawn across from Grimsby to mid-Wales
SEASON	Avoid months without an 'r'
LANDING RESTRICTIONS	None
CONSERVATION STATUS	Invasive species – eat all you can

Anyone who enjoys eating pencil rubbers dipped in fish paste will find the common Limpet a treat. I have been assured by a friend who runs a fish restaurant that it is possible to cook Limpets in a way that renders them fairly tender but I think he is simply lying. However, there is one way that does, just about, work (see below).

Although extremely common, Limpets play an important role in the ecology of the seashore. Their grazing activities ensure that a variety of organisms can obtain a foothold on our rocky shores and that no one species (typically the green algae) will come to dominate. In view of this, I think it is wise to collect Limpets just very occasionally and even then only one or two from each rock. Important for the conservation of this creature is the fact that they change sex halfway through life, giving up the struggle and responsibility of the male to enjoy the easy life of the female. If you only pick the large ones you will cause an imbalance in the population's sex ratio, an effect that has caused problems in some parts of the world.

If you wish to avoid damaging our native species, then I have an excellent alternative for you: Slipper Limpets. This invader from North America has caused much damage to marine ecosystems in the southern half of the British Isles by virtue of their huge numbers; in particular, many traditional Oyster beds have had to be abandoned because of their smothering influence. As such, Slipper Limpets are the

The architecturally inclined Limpet, *Patella vulgata*

fairest of game and if you could eat your way through every last one you would be doing a great service to the nation and deserve a knighthood.

They can be found from the low-water mark down, but quite often a neat little stack of them will be washed up, still alive, further up the beach. Their vitality is easily determined: if they are stuck firmly to the one below then they are alive.

If it is worrying you at all, the second part of their name comes from the Latin for 'arched', a reference to their shape. It is not a slur on their moral fortitude.

How to eat

Cook the Limpets whole for 20 minutes, then purée everything inside the shells in a blender. The black innards are very tasty and the rubbery 'foot' is turned into a more assailable collection of little pencil rubbers. Mix in some oil and lemon juice and serve on small pieces of toast with a garnish of raw Marsh Samphire. Not bad at all.

To prepare Slipper Limpets, I normally scrub the entire stack, having discarded the usually long-deceased bottom one, with a stiff brush and throw it into boiling water for 15 minutes. Inside each shell is a little 'foot' the size, shape and consistency of a tap washer and, cunningly tucked up on a little mezzanine shelf, a small collection of vital organs. The most extraordinary thing from the cook's point of view is the marvellously rich savoury smell that fills the kitchen when Slipper Limpets are cooked. Liquidised, with or without the rubbery 'foot', and added to a fish stew or stock they impart a superb and entirely guilt-free flavour.

Two stacks of Slipper Limpets

The Crustaceans

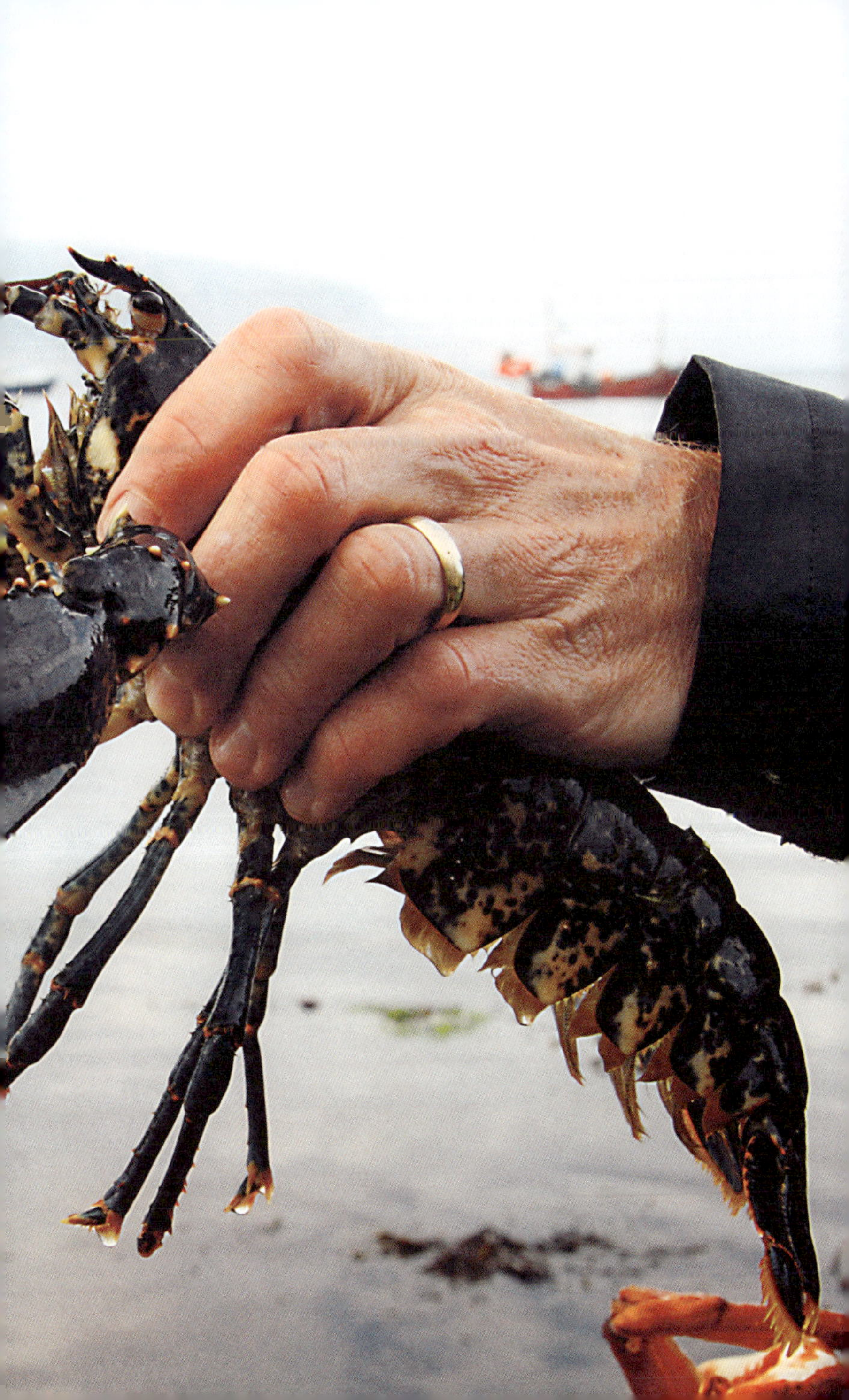

This is where the gentle forager turns into a ferocious hunter and the pleasures become primal and intense. I used to consider digging potatoes an exciting activity (we live very quietly here in Dorset), but it is absolutely *nothing* compared to the drama of lifting a crab pot to discover what lies within. And the joy of catching Shrimps in a push net is not to be missed.

The prizes and flavours in this chapter are mostly familiar from the fishmonger's slab, but we have an opportunity here to enjoy them at their very freshest and, like everything else in this book, we can be completely assured of their provenance. To enjoy your catch safely it is important to transport and store crustaceans properly. At room temperatures ammonia is created rapidly in the bodies of crabs and lobsters and, out of water, they are unable to use their gills to remove it. They will normally die within 24 hours. At 5°C they can be kept for 2 or 3 days. The rule is to keep them cool and moist on the way home and dispatch them as soon as possible.

There are many regulations that cover the catching of crustaceans. The more general ones, such as 'minimum landing size' (MLS), are mentioned where appropriate but you should always check with your local Sea Fisheries Committee to see if you need a permit to put out a pot, or are limited to how much of any one thing you can catch, and so on. These regulations exist to protect the species involved from over-exploitation, an aim both practical and ethical. With crustaceans, however, there is another ethical issue that no thoughtful forager can ignore – the problem of pain.

As yet another televised gazelle was torn apart by yet another televised lion, my mother, with awe-inspiring predictability, would always say, 'Isn't nature cruel?' As carnivores, and even to some extent as voluntary herbivores, we are complicit in nature's mindless iniquity. Many of us worry about such things and with crustaceans such as Crabs and Lobsters we must wonder if they suffer when they are boiled alive. Small creatures like Prawns and Shore Crabs perish so quickly when dropped in boiling water that, arguably, ethical problems do not arise. Brown Crabs, Spider Crabs and Lobsters, however, take an appreciable time to die and a real concern may exist here.

Several methods are employed to kill Lobsters and Crabs 'painlessly'. Placing them in a saturated salt solution for half an hour, or in fresh water, or cooking them from cold so that they 'pass out' before the water becomes unbearably hot, or even zapping them in a microwave oven have all been recommended. I have grave doubts about these practices, which may be worse than straight boiling.

If the nervous system of a crustacean is cooled it becomes very sluggish and any consciousness that it possesses will be lost. It is then possible to perform a *coup de grâce* to finish the animal completely before boiling it. Place the animal in a freezer for about 2 hours. Do not allow it to freeze solid as this will ruin the texture of the meat.

With Crabs you must then destroy two of their ganglia (nerve clusters) with a bradawl or small cross-headed screwdriver. Drive it first of all into the small indentation underneath the tail flap and then into the head between the eyes and through the mouth; in both cases wiggle the implement about to inflict the necessary amount of damage.

With Lobsters you must destroy the main ganglion in the head, which must be cleaved in two with a knife by inserting the point into the 'cross' at the top then quickly slicing down.

Not everyone is convinced by these methods: they do require a certain amount of skill and it is possible that crystals form in the joints of the animals during freezing which may cause the animal pain. However, it is the only method likely to be effective in the domestic kitchen and is the one recommended by the RSPCA.

By far the best method of humanely dispatching crustaceans is electrocution using a machine called the 'Crustastun'. This destroys the creature's nervous system completely and reliably. It is a costly piece of commercial kit at present, but it is hoped that one day a domestic version will be produced.

But are we worrying unnecessarily? Almost anyone who has watched a Lobster thrashing around in a pot of boiling water before it finally succumbs can be in very little doubt that we are not, but this is biology and there is no pressing reason to believe that this frantic activity is accompanied by any conscious experience. What conciousness actually is, what causes it, how to know whether it is present or not, or even what it is for, are all largely unknown. In order to address worrying questions such as 'can invertebrates feel pain?' we must at present rely entirely on inference.

It can reasonably be assumed that most vertebrates having brains not too dissimilar from ours (though not fish) also possess consciousness at some level and may experience pain. Vertebrates have a great lump of neural tissue (a brain) where conscious experience is generated. Lobsters and other invertebrates have a distributed neural structure with a few small and scattered clusters called ganglia. They also have relatively little nervous tissue (humans have a thousand times more than a Lobster). Given these enormous differences in neural structure it is difficult to believe that crustaceans can experience pain in anything like the form or to the degree we do, or even that they feel it at all. On the other hand it may be that pain has so much survival value in encouraging an animal to 'get the hell out of there' that a fair proportion of what little nervous system it possesses is devoted to feeling it.

Research, or at least the interpretation of the research, into invertebrate pain, often cited by those who believe that such a phenomenon exists, is plagued by anthropomorphism. Science will settle the matter eventually but for now we just do not know.

If Crabs and Lobsters feel no pain, there is no problem; if they do, then every time we boil one alive we are perpetrating an unspeakable horror. The only moral response to this possibility is either to not eat them at all or to take steps to ensure a quick and 'painless' end.

144   EDIBLE SEASHORE

Brown Shrimp *Crangon crangon*

HABITAT	Sandy and muddy estuaries and coasts
DISTRIBUTION	All around the coast
SEASON	Spring mostly, but also in the autumn
LANDING RESTRICTIONS	None
CONSERVATION STATUS	Common

'He's down at Bognor for the shrimping.' Thus Bertie Wooster defiantly explains the absence of his valet to a concerned Aunt Dahlia. Ever since I read, many years ago, of the inimitable Jeeves' enthusiasm for Brown Shrimps I have had a bright watercolour vision of this gentle pastime; of wading knee deep in a mirror-calm sea, my push net before me, the horizon lost in the warm haze of a June morning. When, eventually, I tried it for myself, the pleasure was all I had hoped for. The excitement of the hunt, the gentle paddling, mild exercise and fresh air are a conspiracy of joy.

Brown Shrimps are found, intermittently, all around our coast in fine sand and muddy sand and are particularly fond of estuaries and estuary-like conditions. As usual it is local knowledge that counts, so I am unable to tell you exactly where you might find them. There are, nevertheless, many well-known shrimping hot spots, which can be located simply by asking local fishermen. You might also look up natural history records for your area or talk to naturalists (diplomatically; information on local species will not be readily given if your declared intention is to eat them).

Trial and error may well be worth the effort as the habit of shrimping has been lost in many places and there may be numerous sandy shores that go unshrimped. Precisely where on the tide and whether it should be springs or neaps depends to some extent on where you are, but an hour either side of slack water on spring low tides is generally best. (It may be that Shrimps move down shore as the tide recedes and become squeezed into an ever-narrowing band.) In some places there will be too much weed or too many rocks at low water (rocks and push nets do not co-exist happily) and a neap low tide may be better. There is, at least, some agreement as to the best time of year to go shrimping. April is considered the prime month, with any time from March to the end of June providing a good chance of success. There is a second season from September to the end of November though the Shrimps, many of which only hatched in the spring, can be a little smaller.

Unlike their larger relatives, the Prawns, which hide in crevices and amongst seaweed, Shrimps hide in sand. All that can be seen of them during the day is their antennae and their eyes, two tiny periscopes, protruding nervously from the sandy bottom. To remove them from their hiding place we cruelly use their defence strategy against them. Brown Shrimps, if disturbed, will flick themselves out of the sand to make their escape. Clever creatures that they are, they will even shoot off in random directions to prevent any predator learning to take advantage of regular behaviour.

To catch Shrimps you will need to go equipped. Shrimp nets are not easy to come by and you may have to make your own, see pp.16–18. The bottom bar is designed to disturb them into their escape response by squeezing their sandy burrows as it is pushed across the sand. The Shrimps then jump high enough to be caught in the net, their random direction of escape being of no help at all.

Push your net across the sand, usually parallel to the beach, in about 0.5–1 metre of water. The 'handlebar' should be just above waist height; a slight paunch (or 'alpha-male secondary sexual characteristic' as I call mine) will help cushion the odd buffeting you will receive every time you hit a rock. You will see the disturbed sand swirl from the front bar of your push net and, occasionally, a Shrimp as it jumps. Sometimes a particularly athletic Shrimp will leap right over the net and you will have to hope to catch it on your next pass. Stop every 30 metres or so to clear your net of weed and unwanted creatures and to empty any Shrimps into your collecting box or bag. The by-catch is likely to include the odd Prawn and, every now and then, something larger, such as a Velvet Swimming Crab (p.161), a few sand eels, or even a flounder.

There is one much less welcome by-catch that reminds us of the importance of good footwear when shrimping. The dorsal spines of an evil-looking little demon called the weever fish stick upwards from the sand in which the fish hides. These spines are quite venomous and if you get one in your foot it will hurt, a lot. Be careful too when removing any that get into your net. An old pair of trainers are sufficient protection and with a pair of shorts, if you don't mind getting a bit cold, or a wetsuit if you do, you will be suitably attired for your expedition. Some people like to wear a pair of open-topped waders, though they are not an item of clothing for the self-conscious. Vanity apart, I always worry about what happens if you fall over wearing a pair or are swamped by a large wave. There is just no standing up when you share your waders with 20 gallons of water.

How to eat

The taste of Shrimps is incomparable; sweeter and richer than that of Prawns. They are best boiled in sea water from live (or *very* recently deceased) for just a couple of minutes. This can be done in a saucepan on the beach if you like, or you can take some sea water home with you. The only way to avoid the fiddly business of peeling them is to eat them whole, or to just remove the head. Personally I would rather take the time. A large plate of Shrimps, complete with a suitable snifter, can be peeled and consumed in the time it takes to read a chapter of Jeeves' favourite light reading, Spinoza's *Ethics*. He would be proud. For more recipes, see pp.215, 217, 219, 220.

Prawn *Palaemon serratus*

HABITAT	Rocky shores, rock pools
DISTRIBUTION	West coast of Wales and Scotland, Orkney, southwest England; scattered elsewhere
SEASON	Summer through to November. Some areas have a closed season from January to end July
LANDING RESTRICTIONS	Permit requirement or maximum catch may apply in some places
CONSERVATION STATUS	Common

For some reason, catching Prawns seems to be an activity reserved either for gentlemen of a certain age or for young children. The cheap prawn nets beloved of younger foragers will certainly catch the odd Prawn, but for serious work something altogether more substantial is required. Prawn nets come in two main shapes: heart-shaped and triangular (see p.16). Personally I prefer the latter type which allows for an 'up and under' scooping manoeuvre on a sandy bottom. The former, on the other hand, can get into some of the more awkward corners and gullies.

Prawns are migratory in that they only come close to shore during the summer and autumn; they overwinter in deeper water. Early-summer Prawns are usually too small, so late July is the earliest one would attempt a prawning expedition, with September to early November being the high season. They can be found around most of our coast, though the West, and particularly the Southwest, is the most productive, the Northeast being largely barren. Some areas have restrictions on the amount caught, or even have a closed season (1 January to 31 July), so you should check with the relevant local authority before you venture forth. There are no size restrictions but small Prawns are not really worth catching and will have had no time to reproduce. Slightly later in the year it is possible to find the very similar but smaller Prawn *Palaemon elegans*. It is called Billy Winters in Dorset, reflecting its season and I have seen them on sale in Dorchester just before Christmas.

Here's how you catch Prawns. They are largely nocturnal, hiding under ledges and in seaweed during the day. An hour or two before a spring low tide, go to a beach which has lots of large rocks on it or where the shore is made of rock ledges; that is, any beach where the rocks form overhangs under which Prawns will hide. They disperse a little in the cloudy water of the returning tide, so stick to a receding tide and the slack water at low. Wade out about knee deep and push a triangular net along the sea floor under the overhang, then when it has gone as far as it will, lift it upwards and draw it back out, scooping any Prawns into the net. Alternatively, use a heart-shaped net in a long sideways motion. This net is also good for dragging through the seaweed around the inside edges of rock pools. Empty your catch into a bucket of sea water.

A more leisurely alternative to the prawn net is the drop net. Cheap ones, normally sold to children intent on crabbing, are readily available, but a larger net (like the one pictured on p.19) is better. Use the smelliest bait you can find and lower the net into a rock pool or from a suitable rock or promontory for 5 minutes, then quickly pull it clear of the water. Unfortunately, the nocturnal habit of the Prawn will limit the number you are likely to catch, although I have found that those murky waters of an incoming tide will provide enough cover for some of them to risk venturing forth.

A drop-netting expedition on a dark October evening, when the Prawns will be at their most active, is likely to prove fruitful though it will certainly be safer to do so from a pier or jetty. The chief problem with the drop net is the amount of by-catch in the form of Shore Crabs and undersized Velvet Swimming Crabs you are likely to encounter.

My preferred method of catching Prawns is to use a pot. Very cheap lightweight pots (as shown on p.21, top picture), which can be easily collapsed and carried, are easy to obtain. The convenience they afford compared to more substantial pots must be weighed against their short life span – they quickly rust and their thin netting will soon develop holes. Such light pots will also have to be weighted down or tethered in some way to stop them wandering off. Also, most of these have entry holes large enough to allow a by-catch of Crabs, which will proceed to eat your Prawns before you can.

The best solution, if you don't mind the inconvenience of carrying them around, is the professional prawn pot (shown on p.21, bottom picture). These have thumb-sized holes which will allow the entry of a Prawn but nothing larger.

As with other crustaceans, take the pot out to a clear area between the weed and rocks at low tide and come back at the next, or the next but one, low tide, to see what you have caught. On a really good beach it may not be necessary to leave your pots for so long. At my favourite spot I can usually collect enough for tea in the hour it takes for the tide to turn.

How to eat

Prawns can survive for some hours if kept in a bucket of fresh sea water, and for about an hour in a bucket of fresh air. Cook them alive in salt water as soon as you get home, though there is no need to worry if some have expired during the journey – they will still be very fresh. Remember that these are the same Prawns as the ones you will buy from the fishmonger and are cooked in just the same way. They are ready to eat as soon as they have turned, magically, bright pink, after which they will become progressively tougher.

For more recipes, see pp.216, 217, 219, 220.

P.S. A dark cloud of environmental guilt hangs over the commercially fished Prawn, making the humble Prawn and mayonnaise sandwich a shameful indulgence. Some seafloor damage is inevitable in any trawling operation, but there is also the vexed question of by-catch where unwanted and sometimes endangered species are discarded. The good news, however, is that trawling in the North Atlantic is reasonably benign with a small by-catch which is being reduced all the time.

Warm-water trawling, by comparison, is notoriously damaging with a by-catch of up to 95 per cent of what is caught being thrown away. This includes iconic threatened species such as the turtle. The tropical farming of certain species of Prawn, with the exception of some of the more carefully regulated operations, is seriously suspect, managing to commit nearly every environmental and social sin in the book. If you want to eat your sandwich with a completely clear conscience, search out Prawns commercially caught in a pot where the by-catch is minimal and seafloor damage non-existent. Unfortunately, discovering the exact provenance of Prawns is not always easy. Best of all, of course, is to catch them yourself. Virtue is a dressing sweeter even than mayonnaise.

Squat Lobster *Galathea squamifera*

HABITAT	Under flat rocks on sandy/rocky shores
DISTRIBUTION	Orkney, west coasts of Scotland and Wales, southeast Scotland, southwest and south England
SEASON	Late summer, autumn
LANDING RESTRICTIONS	None
CONSERVATION STATUS	Common

Despite the impressive aspect of the Squat Lobster shown here, this is actually a tiny creature, smaller than a decent-sized Prawn. There are several species of Squat Lobster living around the British Isles, of which *Galathea squamifera* is the easiest to find. A much larger species, the Rugose Squat Lobster, *Munida rugosa*, is fished commercially with creels in Scotland (its main haunt) and it can sometimes be found on the supermarket shelf; however, this animal prefers deep water and will be out of range of most shoreline pot layers.

A really good low tide and a shore covered in moveable flat rocks and a bit of sand is the best territory for our little Squat Lobster. Gently lift up any rock which has at least some water beneath it and watch carefully to spot the flurry of activity that betrays the presence of your quarry. They swim backwards at great speed and you will need to be quick to catch one before it hides under something you cannot move. I sometimes find one clinging sneakily to the bottom of the rock I am lifting, trying to evade my all-seeing hunter's eye.

Squat Lobsters are common all around the coast but most especially in the West and South, with inevitable gaps due to geography. With this abundance and no legal restrictions on its collection, it is fair game for the forager, who may gather with a clear conscience. However, for me at least, it is a most charming little creature which, like the closely related hermit crab, strays a little too far for comfort into the mental category of 'pet'.

How to eat

If you can find it in your conscience to eat them, cook from live in a little salted water for just a minute or two. Apart from a minute amount in the claws, the only meat you will find is in the small tail which curls under the carapace, but what meat it is! Sweeter than any other I have tasted.

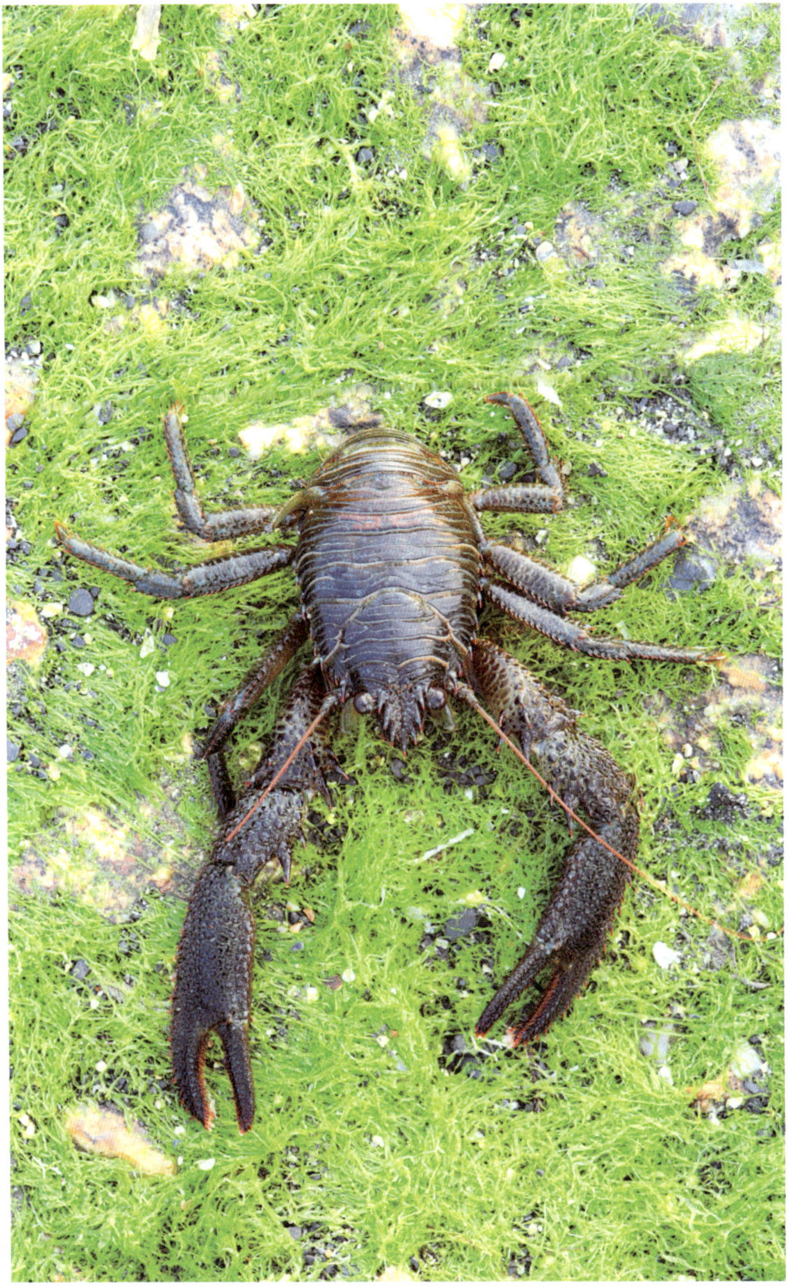

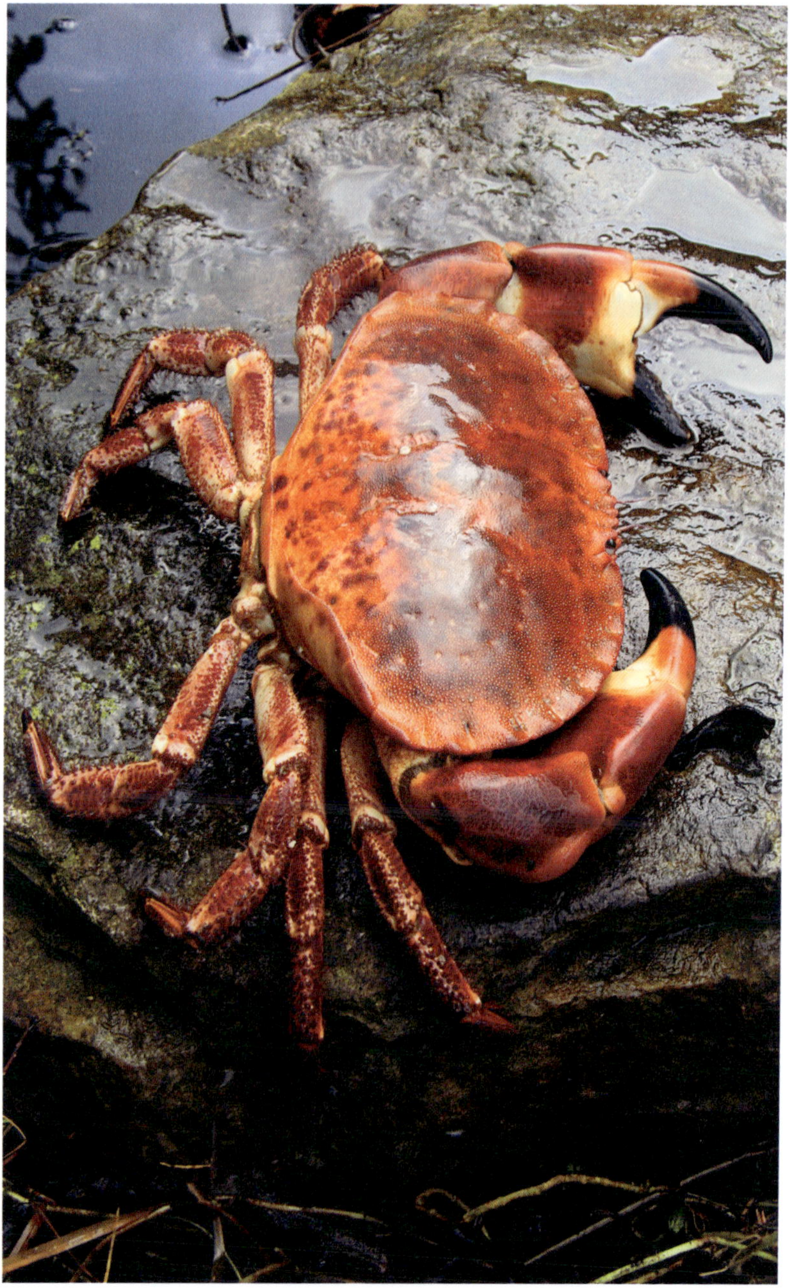

Brown Crab *Cancer pagurus*

HABITAT	All types of marine habitat, but in shallow water best found on rocky shores
DISTRIBUTION	All around the coast
SEASON	All year, but nearer the shore in summer
LANDING RESTRICTIONS	MLS of 140–160mm across the carapace. Berried females may be off-limits
CONSERVATION STATUS	Very common

Of all the creatures and plants contained in this book the Common or Brown Crab is the most difficult to bag. Not, as the unequivocal name indicates, that it is uncommon; one can find, quite literally, thousands of them in the summer and autumn hiding under intertidal rocks. But, sadly, these will all be juveniles and too small to collect. Mature individuals *can* be found around low tide but these too will be smaller adults; the really big ones are found in much deeper water.

Thus it is that I have had limited luck using a pot from the shore, with only a very small proportion of those I have caught being above the legal minimum size of 14cm (15 or 16cm in some places) across the carapace. To stand any chance of success it is necessary to get your pot out as far as possible. If you can (safely) lower them from rocks this will help, as will having an exceptional spring low tide and a good tidal range. The main problem with a big tidal range, however, is the strong currents that accompany them. These can quickly dash a pot to pieces or just sweep it away. As with Lobster, rocky, seaweedy shores are the best as they provide good cover and food for the hunting Crab. A flat seabed is also helpful for keeping the pot level. I always use a top-entry parlour pot (see pp.20, 22) to catch Crabs but these are heavy pieces of equipment to carry around.

There is another, more sporting, way of catching them. Again you will need a rocky shore, a good low tide, a really big tidal range and also a hook on a stick (see p.19). Quite large Crabs will hide out in mini, crab-sized caves, during low tide, patiently waiting for the water to return and always ready to confront an interloper. Find a likely-looking hole in the rock and gently probe with your stick, slowly moving it from side to side. If you are lucky a large Crab will grab hold of it. Slowly pull the attached Crab towards you, then, when it is within reach, slide your free hand over the top of its shell and grab hold. (I have found this to be an operation more suited to the slender female arm.) The key to this technique is stealth; roughly poking the stick around will ensure that the Crab will retreat to the deepest recess and you are likely to damage the animal. I have seen it done badly, with nothing but

Hooking a Brown Crab | *Brown Crab caught!*

broken bits of Crab to show for the effort. You are likely to find the odd 'soft-shelled' individual. These are Crabs that have recently moulted and which will be waiting, anxiously, for their new shell to harden. It always makes me shiver to touch their jelly-like shell and I am happy to leave the poor things to fight another day.

Apart from the size restriction there are also a variety of regulations depending on where you live. For example, it may be illegal to land berried (egg-carrying) females or unattached claws, or to use soft-shelled Crabs for bait.

How to eat

How to humanely kill a Crab is covered in the introduction to the crustaceans. Cooking Brown Crabs is simple: place them in boiling salted water then, after the water comes to the boil again, boil for 12 minutes for the first 1kg, plus another 4 minutes for every subsequent 500g. Leave the Crab to cool, but do not try to speed the process by putting it into cold water as some of this will be absorbed, making the meat very soggy. Extensive details of how to prepare a Crab are given in *The River Cottage Fish Book*, but you can eat everything soft except the yellow/white papery sac of a stomach situated just behind the mouth, the conspicuous 'dead man's fingers' and any papery membranes you don't like the look of.

For more recipes, see pp.219, 220, 224.

Shore Crab *Carcinus maenas*

HABITAT	Everywhere!
DISTRIBUTION	All around the coast
SEASON	All year
LANDING RESTRICTIONS	None
CONSERVATION STATUS	Very common

Some Shore Crabs must spend their whole summer being dragged out of the sea, kept in a brightly coloured bucket for a few minutes, then thrown back in again. The holiday pastime of catching Crabs is often the only chance children ever get to express their instinctive desire to hunt and the joy to be seen on their faces is primal. However, it never seems to cross their minds to consider eating what they catch – perhaps the lure of ice cream is too distracting.

Shore Crabs are clearly not hard to catch – a crab line from a jetty or pier, using any bait, can yield dozens in half an hour. More efficient still is the drop net. Left in for 10 minutes it can be swarming with Crabs, both in the net and hanging on from below. As soon as they are landed the origin of their Latin epithet *maenas* or 'frenzied' becomes clear, as they frantically scuttle for cover or escape back into the sea – you will have to be quick to bag your catch. Shore Crabs like sheltered conditions, which is why harbour walls and jetties are the best hunting grounds. In the winter they tend to be rather inactive and are less easy to catch.

The Shore Crab is easy to identify as it has pointed rear legs, whereas the Velvet Swimming Crab has rear legs in the form of paddles. The colour is very variable with the common 'green all over' variety being interspersed with those sporting pink undercarriages. If you are still unsure, they have three blunt projections between the eyes and five sharp ones either side.

How to eat

Shore Crabs are perfectly edible, although there is not a great deal of meat on one – tiny, and very tasty, pieces in each leg segment and a little more in the claws; that is all. Unless you are prepared to take the time to extract these morsels the best way of using them is in a soup, or more specifically, a bisque. Such a soup will be made from cooked and crushed Crabs and with the shells sieved out at a late stage of the preparation. My favourite recipe for bisque made with Shore Crabs is on p.220.

Spider Crab *Maja squinado*

HABITAT	Rocky, weedy shores
DISTRIBUTION	Wales, south and southwest England
SEASON	Spring
LANDING RESTRICTIONS	MLS of 120mm for females and 130mm for males. Some areas limit catch to five a day
CONSERVATION STATUS	Common

The first time I ever encountered a Spider Crab was over 25 years ago when a party of fishermen returning from a day in Weymouth crashed their car just outside the remote farmhouse where we lived. They repaid our offerings of tea and sympathy with two large buckets of the things. I have, I think, received more unwelcome gifts, but at least they didn't wander about the kitchen. I would be a great deal more appreciative these days.

There is one major advantage in catching your own Spider Crab. It is the only way you are likely to get hold of one. For some reason, perhaps the memory of John Hurt having something very similar stuck to his face in the movie *Alien*, they are not popular in the UK and are almost never available from fishmongers. Nearly all of the catch from the British Isles is shipped to France and Spain and we, yet again, miss out on one of our great natural assets.

The *Maja* of their Latin name, meaning 'May', is a clue to the best time to find them; *squinado* ultimately derives from a word meaning 'angles', describing them rather well. There are two ways of catching them. The simpler is very simple indeed, relying only on luck and a little courage. In April and May Spider Crabs return from their warm winter quarters in deep water and can be found wandering around sandy, seaweedy bays, sometimes in their thousands. Under such conditions it is possible to wade out thigh deep during a spring low tide and reach down to pick them up. They have long been gathered this way in Jersey and the historian Nicolle (*Channel Islands*, E. Nicolle, 1893) tells of women and children feeling for them with their feet (which is where that courage comes in handy).

The more reliable alternative is to put out a pot or two. Wade out waist deep at low water and place your pots in 'thoroughfares' between seaweedy rocks. Return at the next, or the next but one, low tide to see what you have collected. They are large animals and an appropriately substantial pot will be needed. I normally use a top-entry parlour pot (see pp.20, 22). The first time I tried it I caught over twenty Spider Crabs in two pots – most were too small, but several were of sufficient size to make it to my kitchen.

158 EDIBLE SEASHORE

Spider Crabs have spread slowly north and east, but at present they can be found south of a line drawn from Holyhead to Dover, with a few populations on the west coast of Scotland. In some regions of England and Wales a permit may be required, or there may be a daily quota.

There is a landing restriction of 12cm for females and 13cm for males (males have a narrow abdominal flap while in the female it is the full width of the abdomen). The size is measured from the back end of the shell to the front, just behind the two projecting spines. These minimum size restrictions must be adhered to, but they are blunt instruments. In order to grow, all Crabs create new shells and discard the older, smaller one in a process called moulting. Spider Crabs, unlike many other Crabs, reach their adult size and then perform a final moult and stop growing completely. So, adults can be found at just 8.5cm while immature specimens can be well over 13cm. It may be that such restrictions impose an 'unnatural' selection and that Spider Crab sizes will gradually decrease.

Spider Crab moulting habits are important to us for another reason – their effect on meat quality. Growing a new shell is an enormous drain on an animal's resources and around moulting time the flesh becomes very 'watery' and reduced in quantity. The best Spider Crabs to catch are the adults from previous years as they arrive in the spring – these will have had time during their winter foraging to fatten themselves up nicely and will not have moulted for many months. They can be identified by the disreputable state of their carapace, which is likely to have a generally knocked-about appearance and will sport an interesting array of seaweed and other wildlife that will have had time to grow. By the autumn, when they are ready to go to deep water to do whatever a Spider Crab does, most will have a shiny new shell and not be worth eating.

How to eat

Spider Crabs are quite fiddly to prepare but well worth it and, though there is not as much meat on them as their size might lead you to believe, the leg and claw meat is marvellously sweet – some say better than Lobster. They should be cooked for about 20 minutes for the first kilo, plus 15 minutes per kilo after that. Allow to cool, then drain. Twist off the legs and claws and crack them to get at the meat with a crab pick or the plain flat handle of a teaspoon. Everything in the opened shell is edible except the black stomach and the feathery 'dead man's fingers'; scoop out the brown meat and dig out as much of the white meat above where the legs were as possible.

For more recipes, see pp.219, 220, 224.

160 EDIBLE SEASHORE

Velvet Swimming Crab *Necora puber*

HABITAT	Slight preference for rocky shores
DISTRIBUTION	West coast of Scotland and Wales, south and southwest England, northwest England
SEASON	All year
LANDING RESTRICTIONS	MLS of 65mm across carapace
CONSERVATION STATUS	Common

Although most people, used to the much larger Brown Crab, would think the Velvet Swimming Crab too small a morsel to consider, it is fortunate that God in his great wisdom did not make them any larger than he did. Had he done so, the peaceful rock pool would have become a place of terror. This little Crab has a great deal of personality – and it is mostly a sociopathic one. While it can run or swim away, it will just as often stand and fight, waving fierce little claws in an unmistakable 'come and get some' manner.

Picking one up is a most hazardous endeavour. If held carelessly, it will quickly rotate its body until your fingers are within claw range and then grip on tenaciously and bloodily. (For some reason seeing someone else jumping up and down screaming with a Crab attached to a finger is one of the most amusing spectacles known to man.) They are a little less aggressive when discovered in a romantic embrace; a protracted affair in which the male protects the female by carrying her around while she moults prior to mating. If disturbed while in this intimate state they will seldom attack but merely look affronted.

The Velvet Swimming Crab is quite unmistakable. It has a brown velvet coat, rear podomeres (fancy name for a segment of leg) flattened into stylish swimming paddles and a pair of the most terrifying red eyes you will ever see. It is a common inhabitant of rocky shores from the intertidal zone down to 60 metres deep and you should have little trouble getting hold of enough for a meal.

Lifting up rocks in rock pools at low tide (and putting them carefully back, of course) should meet with some success, as should dragging a prawn net (not to be confused with the much wider shrimp net) through the Kelp and wrack on which they often feed when not terrorising the local Prawns. I have even caught them by hand from amongst seaweed on sandy beaches miles from the nearest rock. Drop nets cast from a pier, jetty or convenient large rock can be very productive too.

The best way, however, is to use a pot. Normal-size crab pots are not really suitable as they are unnecessarily heavy for the task at hand and the relatively tiny Velvet Swimmer can escape from them quite easily. I have had considerable success with collapsible pots, though the disadvantage here is that the Crabs will chop the bait purse into shreds. The ideal pot, however, is a lightweight creel with an opening between 65 and 85mm – the parlour variety (see pp.20, 22) being the best as it will hold more Crabs and will prevent your catch from escaping. The minimum commercial landing size is 65mm across the carapace and it is only cricket to leave soft-shelled animals, amorous pairs and 'berried' (egg-carrying) females to continue unmolested.

Until the mid 1980s the Velvet Swimming Crab was considered by British lobster and crab fishermen an annoying, bait-stealing by-catch. Then the Spanish, who had long considered this species a delicacy, and had consumed nearly every last Velvet in their own waters, were forced to cast their eyes elsewhere. In Scotland and many other parts of the UK, catching Velvet Swimming Crabs is now a small but important part of the fishing industry with a few thousand tons caught each year. They are sent, alive in tanks, on long and expensive journeys to foreign parts with only the occasional, probably re-imported, 'eight pack' of frozen Crabs appearing in British supermarkets. It is a great pity that, with most of Europe's Velvet Swimming Crabs caught in British waters, so very few are eaten by the British. As with our historic aversion to wild mushrooms, we are missing out.

How to eat

Although small, these Crabs contain a surprising amount of meat and it is every bit as delicious as that of the Brown Crab – and often sweeter. The 'dead man's fingers', the stomach and papery bits must be removed, but after that you can eat everything that isn't actually crunchy. The meat in the legs is often particularly easy to get at as the bony exterior can be wafer thin. Pull one from the shell and you will be able to squeeze out the meat like toothpaste from a tube. Do not forget the meat hidden in the carapace above the legs – fiddly to get at but well worth it. Eaten simply (see p.223), or traditionally in a thick fishy stew, it is the sort of food that requires a lack of self-consciousness, good company and a glass of something relaxing.

P.S. Anyone who has only eaten ready-prepared Crab will view the contents of any unprepared crab shell, including that of the Velvet Swimming Crab, with a degree of trepidation. They will wonder what it is they can eat or indeed want to eat. In fact you can eat everything except the dead man's fingers, the stomach, anything crunchy and any tough papery bits. Dead man's fingers are not as deadly as their name suggests. They are the gills of the Crab and simply unpalatable and indigestible. The tasty brown meat, which can often fill the shell, is the 'hepatopancreas', an organ which performs several functions, one of which is to store fat. Just beneath the shell you will often come across a pale layer of 'meat'. This is the new shell being formed and it too is edible, as is the bright red roe sometimes found in hen Crabs.

Lobster *Homarus gammarus*

HABITAT	Rocky, weedy shores
DISTRIBUTION	All around the coast
SEASON	All year
LANDING RESTRICTIONS	MLS of 90mm carapace length, some areas have permit requirements. 'V-notched' animals and berried females must be returned
CONSERVATION STATUS	Still common but overfished

Extraordinary as it may seem, Lobsters are amongst the easiest of all creatures to catch by the shore. The reason for this good fortune (ours, not theirs) is that, in rock-strewn, seaweedy bays at least, they can be found right up to the low-water mark.

To catch a Lobster you will need a pot. A full-size parlour pot (see pp.20, 22) is ideal, though rather heavy to carry around on treacherous, seaweed-strewn beaches. Lobsters are able to squeeze through the tiniest of holes, so it is only prawn pots with their small openings which will be entirely unsuitable. However, I would recommend a side-entry parlour pot with an entrance aperture of 85mm. Even collapsible, lightweight pots can catch Lobsters, though you will need a large one.

Unless you lower your pot by rope from a suitable rock, you will have to get wet and wade out up to chest deep to find a good spot. Choose the best spring low tide you can and, of course, plan your expedition with a close eye on the weather forecast. The best place to leave your pot is on a sandy floor between weed-covered rocks. This will be prime hunting ground for the Lobster, with thoroughfares between the rocks and plenty of cover. Spring and early summer are the best times to catch Lobsters near the shore, a seasonality that ties in well with the 'getting wet' part. Go back the next day, or the next but one, and see what you have caught. I cannot describe the excitement of finding a Lobster in a pot – you will just have to experience it for yourself. One thing which might rather spoil your day, however, is a severed finger. Handle Lobsters with great care, holding them so that your fingers are just above where the pincers join the body.

There are two general restrictions on catching Lobsters (though you must also check local byelaws). The first is a landing size restriction: the carapace, measured from just behind the eyes to its back edge (where the tail starts), must be not less than 87mm (or 90mm in some parts of the coast). This ensures that no individual is captured before maturity. The second restriction is that 'V-notched' Lobsters must be released. These are females (or 'hens' as they are quaintly called), which have had a little 'V'-shaped cut made in their tail. This is a conservation measure to increase

164 EDIBLE SEASHORE

the number of females and hence the number of eggs produced. Beyond these two there is, in some areas, a ban on landing 'berried' (egg-carrying) females. Even if no formal restriction exists, it is only sensible to return such animals to the sea.

How to eat

The vexed question of how best to dispatch a Lobster is discussed in the introduction to this section, but cooking them is simple enough. A very large pan of salted boiling water is all that you need: drop the Lobster into the water, wait until the water boils again, then cook for 15 minutes for the first 750g, plus 5 minutes for every 500g thereafter. Full preparation details are given in *The River Cottage Fish Book* but, briefly, cut the Lobster in half starting with the head, the knife facing forward, then the rest of the body with the knife facing backwards. Discard the black line (the gut) that runs the length of the body, the stomach which sits just behind the mouth and the gills. Every other soft part is edible, although the bright pink 'tomalley' is an acquired taste.

For more recipes, see pp.220, 227.

P.S. Deciding whom to mate with, and obtaining an enthusiastic response from the object of one's affections, is a task faced by nearly every animal on the planet. Generally speaking it is a matter of impressing and being impressed. For birds a large and colourful tail might do the trick, or perhaps a particularly beautiful song; for other animals it may be a magnificent mane, a slim ankle or a gift of roses. Lobsters have their own special currency of worth – urine. A female Lobster will track a prospective partner to his lair by the smell of his urine. She will then hang around outside and urinate in his direction and if, from the smell, the male thinks she might be the girl for him he will urinate back. If love has found a way the female will move in for a couple of weeks and that is that. I shall stick to saying it with flowers.

Recipes

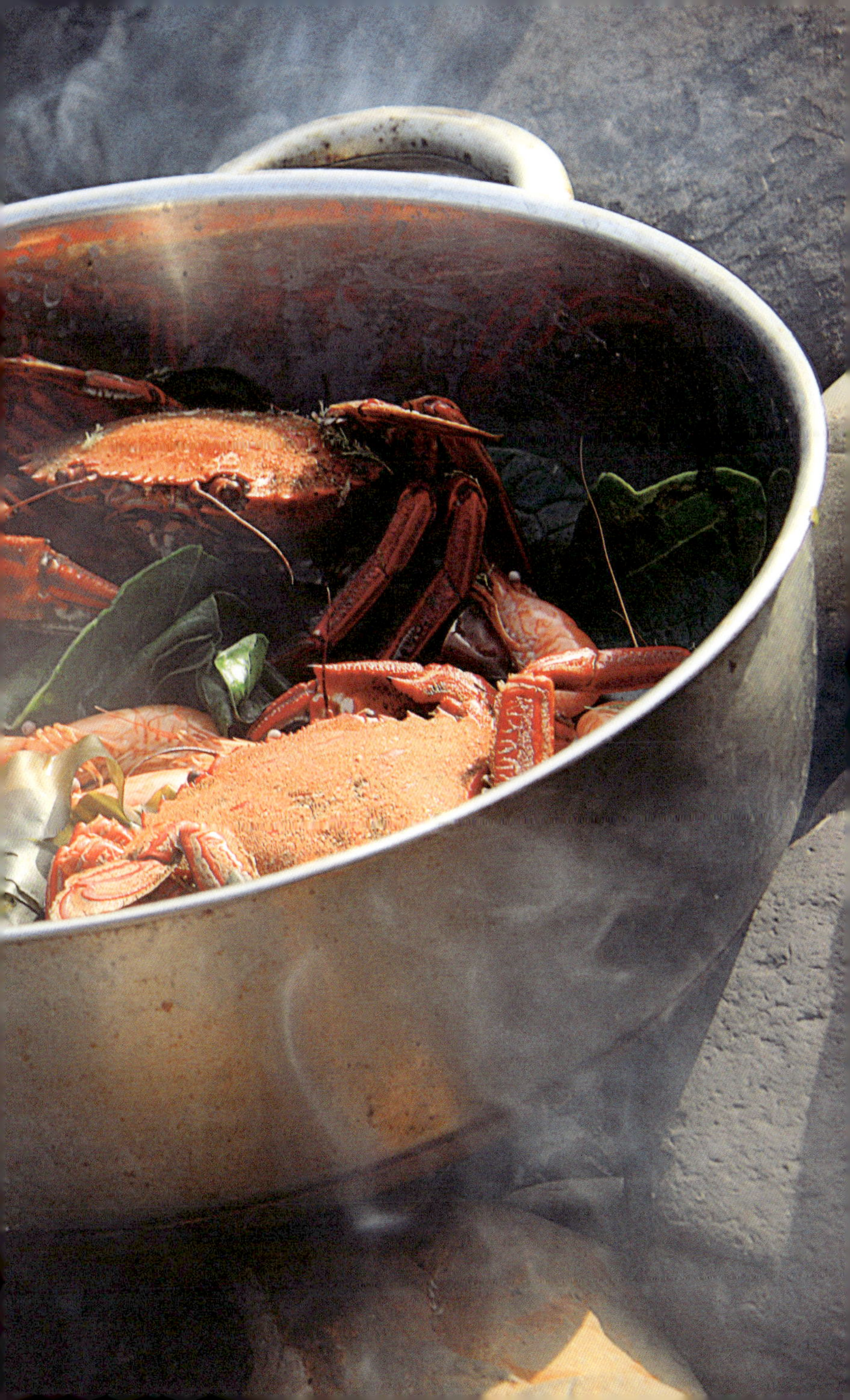

The reputation generally enjoyed by 'wild food' is not one of great sophistication – boiled nettles, grubby roots and bitter herbs are worthy and wholesome but not items destined for the high table. Yet the wild foods described in this book are the antithesis of such prosaic fare. Crab, Lobster, Marsh Samphire, Rocket and exotic seaweeds are all gourmet foods of the highest standing. Forage by the sea and you can eat like a king.

I look back at the days spent with my friends at River Cottage HQ testing the recipes and getting the photographs with a misty-eyed gladness. Apart from finding the ingredients I was given the important jobs of making useful suggestions, getting in the way and tasting the finished dishes. Onerous tasks indeed.

I think that the recipes here do justice to the quality of your hard-won ingredients and will provide a perfect end to a perfect foraging day.

Recipes

- Steamed Alexanders (p.171)
- Candy Alexanders (p.172)
- Marsh Samphire with poached eggs (p.175)
- Smoked pollack with Sea Beet (p.177)
- Pickled Rock Samphire (p.178)
- Sea Buckthorn and crab apple jam (p.179)
- Alexanders and rhubarb jam (p.180)
- Alexanders liqueur (p.183)
- Kelp crisps (p.184)
- Crispy seaweed and toasted sesame seeds (p.186)
- Dulse potato cakes (p.189)
- Dulse and smoked fish tart (p.190)
- Laverbread with Clams and bacon on toast (p.193)
- Seaweed and elderflower panna cotta (p.194)
- Cockles with chorizo (p.196)
- West Country cider Mussels (p.198)
- Mussels with chilli and tomato (p.199)
- Stuffed Hard Shell Clams (p.201)
- Steamed Clams with sausage (p.202)
- Clam arancini with arrabbiata sauce (p.204)
- Razor Clams with almost wild gremolata (p.207)
- Winkles with garlic butter (p.209)
- Oyster risotto with deep-fried Gutweed (p.210)
- Hangtown fry (p.212)
- Potted Shrimp (p.215)
- Spicy Prawn soup (p.216)
- Prawn and courgette salad with a chilli dressing (p.217)
- Brown Crab mousse with Carragheen (p.219)
- Crab bisque made with Shore Crabs (p.220)
- Velvet Swimming Crab with garlic mayonnaise (p.223)
- Devilled Crab cakes with herby mayonnaise (p.224)
- Lobster with charmoula butter (p.227)
- Fish stock (p.228)
- Shellfish stock (p.229)

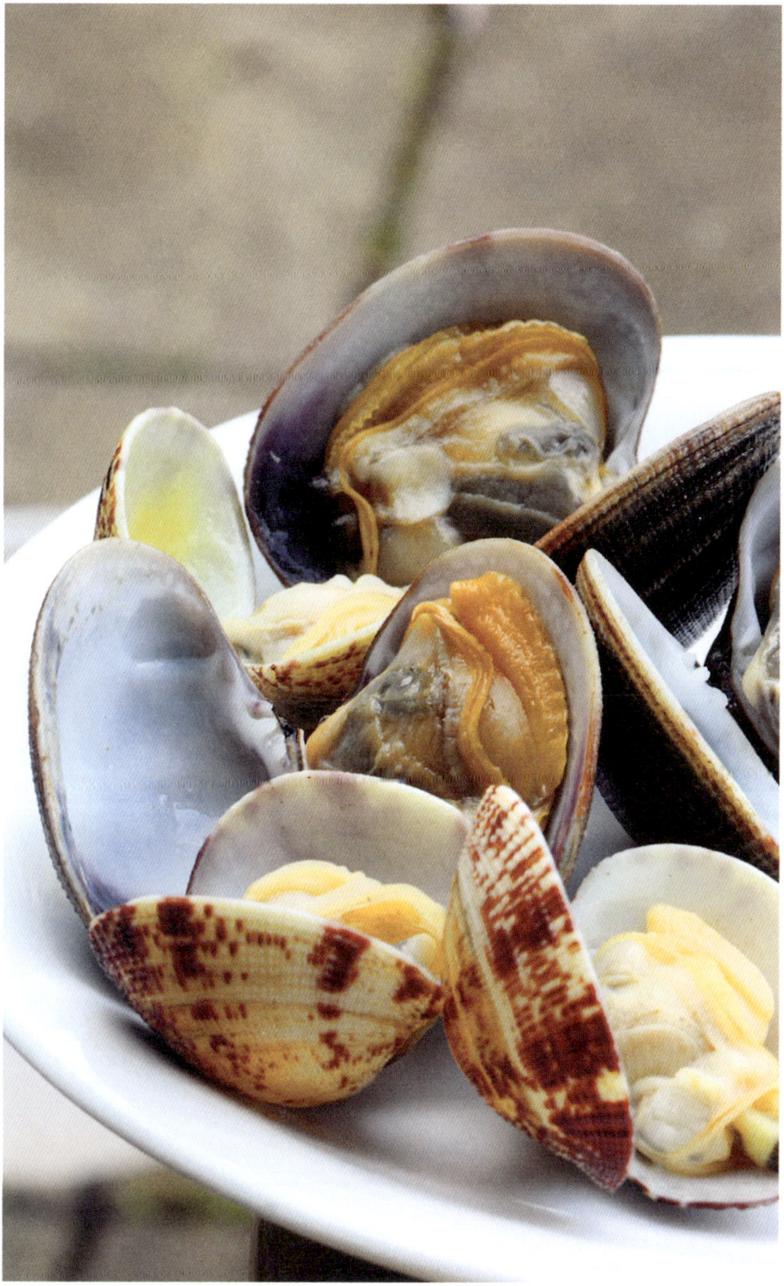

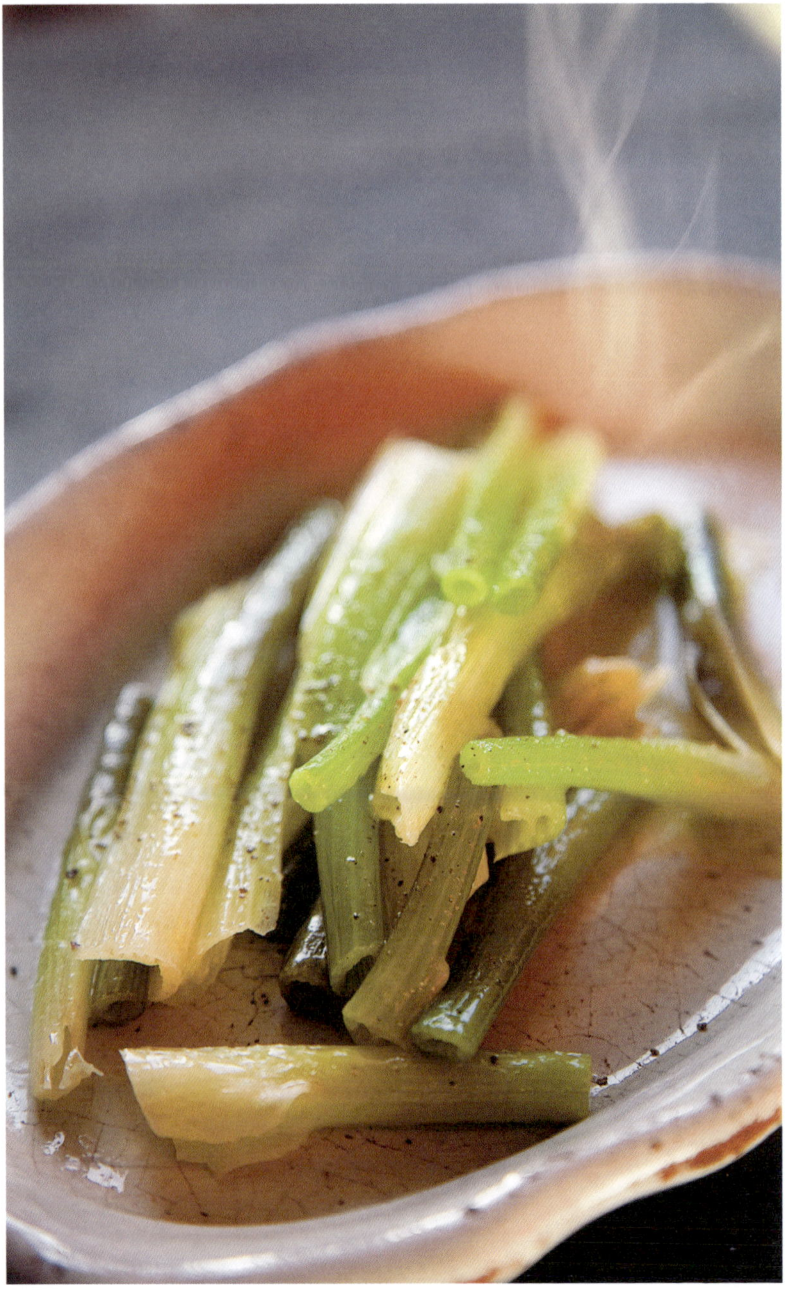

Steamed Alexanders

Alexanders have a strong and distinctive flavour that completely defies description. Enjoy them simply steamed, on their own, as a special first course, with a few slices of sourdough bread.

Serves 2 as a starter
250g Alexanders stems or shoots
30g unsalted butter
A few grinds of black pepper

Remove any fibrous outer skin from the Alexanders, trim the rough ends, then cut into 10cm lengths. Place them in a steamer, or if you don't have one, in a sieve or colander over a pan of boiling water and put a lid over the top. Steam for 5–10 minutes, depending on how strong you like the flavour, but at least until they are tender enough to be easily pierced with a knife.

Toss the Alexanders in the butter and a few grinds of pepper until well coated. Serve immediately on warm plates.

Candy Alexanders

Success in making this unusual delicacy (which is named after a nightclub singer of my close acquaintance) depends on using only the fattest and juiciest of stems and taking things slowly. I have always been a fan of the candying process; it is one with a forgiving nature, well suited to the more absent-minded cook. Replacing most of the water contained within fruits or stems with sugar is a slow matter and if you suddenly rediscover a dish of half-glacéd cherries or half-candied Alexanders after a week or two's neglect the process can be continued without detriment. Should some Sea Holly roots legitimately come into your possession, you can use this recipe to make the candied eryngoes mentioned on p.66.

The flavour of Alexanders is quite fugitive, which is why I suggest reinvigoration with some of the pungent seeds if you have them. The Alexanders turn a beautiful shade of palest, translucent amber and make a delicious addition to cakes and pastries... or you can eat them just as a sweetmeat. Candy would have loved them.

Makes about 20 sticks
500g fat Alexanders stems
About 500g caster sugar
1 tbsp Alexanders seeds
   (if available)

Trim the Alexanders stems to about 10cm in length and put them into a saucepan with enough water to cover by 2cm. Simmer until tender, about 10 minutes. Remove from the pan, reserving the water, and peel away any tough fibres.

Weigh the stems, then add the same weight of sugar to the pan of cooking water. If you have them, add the Alexanders seeds (preferably tied up in a little muslin bag) and bring the syrup to the boil. Lay the Alexanders stems in a flat-bottomed dish and pour over the syrup. Cover and leave for a day.

Pour the syrup and any seeds (or use fresh seeds) into a saucepan and bring to the boil. Simmer for a few minutes to reduce slightly. Pour back over the Alexanders and leave another day.

Repeat this process for another 2 days, then drain off the remaining syrup and lay the Alexanders stems on wire racks. Either dry them in a low oven at 40–50°C for 4 hours or on a sunny windowsill over several days. Do make sure they are completely dry before you store them, to prevent them going mouldy.

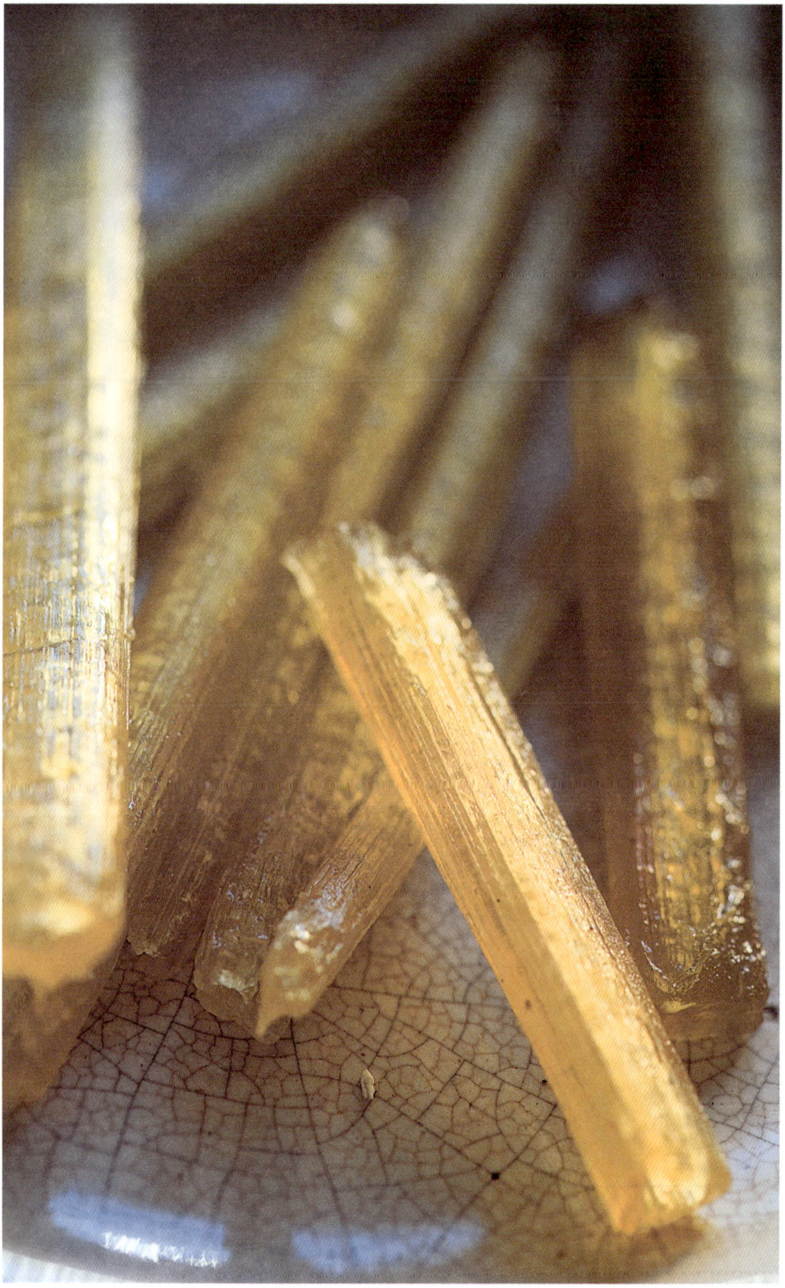

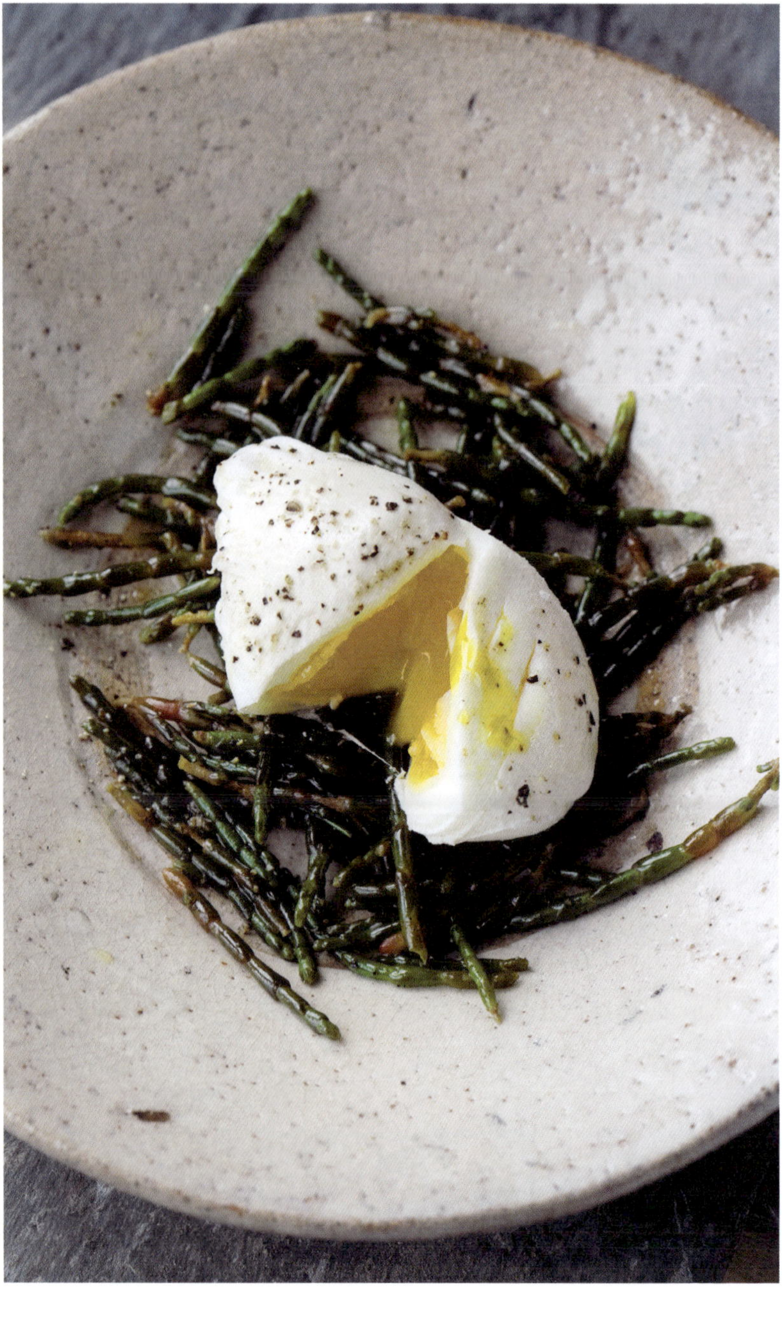

Marsh Samphire
with poached eggs

This briny take on eggs florentine makes an unusual starter or light lunch. You will need the very youngest of Marsh Samphire tips which lack the central tough fibre for this dish. If you like your Marsh Samphire salty, then instead of boiling it, place it in a covered frying pan with a dessertspoonful of water and the butter over a medium heat. Uncover after a minute, then quickly reduce the water to nothing and sauté for a few seconds.

Serves 2
350g young Marsh Samphire tips
A knob of butter
Freshly ground black pepper
2 eggs
2 tbsp cider vinegar

Bring two pans of water to the boil. Toss the Samphire into one of the pans – do not add salt as the Samphire is already very salty – and boil for a couple of minutes. Drain well and toss with a knob of butter and some freshly ground pepper and return to the pan to keep warm.

Crack the eggs into a saucer. Make sure the second pan of water is boiling steadily, add the vinegar and stir the water with a wooden spoon to create a whirlpool. Tip the eggs into the whirlpool. Turn the heat down and poach for about 3 minutes until the whites are set.

Remove the poached eggs with a slotted spoon and drain on kitchen paper. Divide the Samphire between two warmed plates, place a poached egg on top of each serving and grind on some black pepper. Serve immediately.

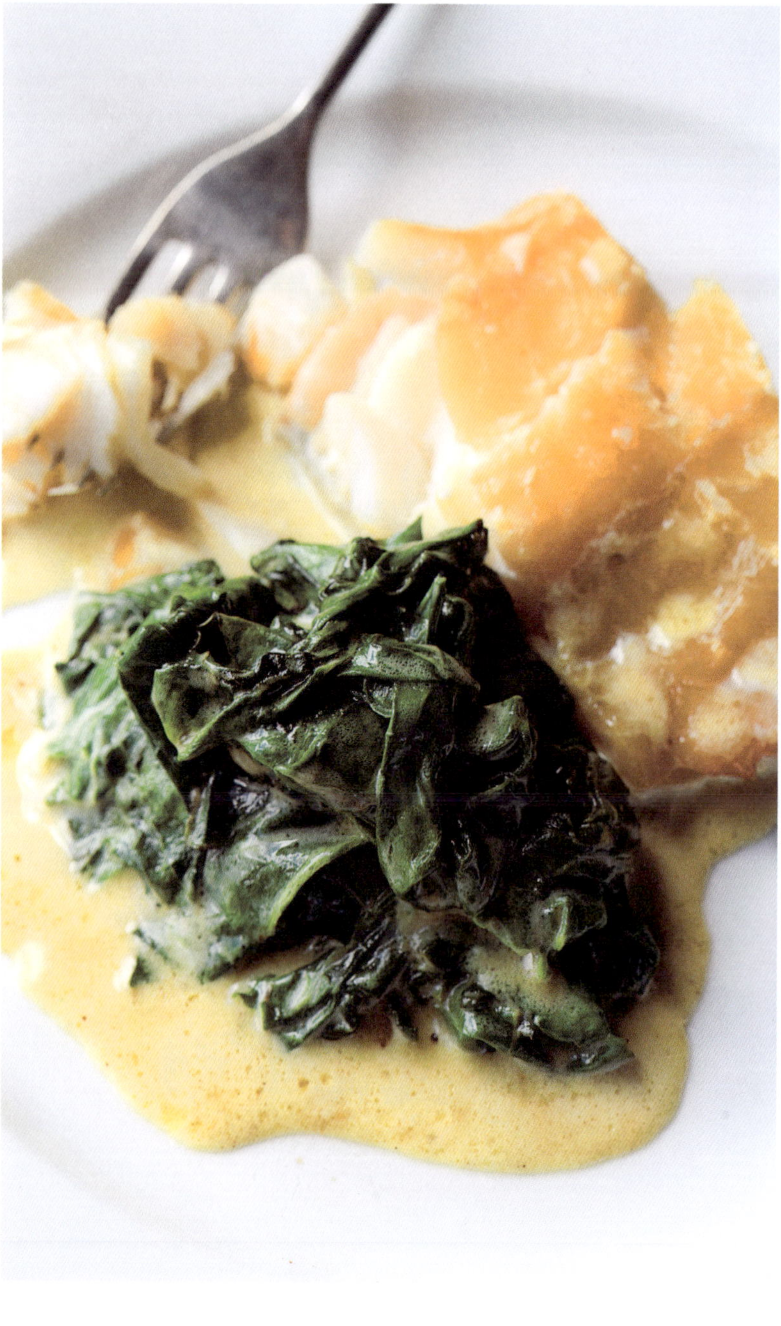

Smoked pollack
with Sea Beet

Sea Beet is one of the seaside's greatest culinary treasures. It is available for most of the year, can be found in large quantities and, best of all, is quite delicious. There are endless possibilities for this versatile plant, but this fishy, creamy recipe takes a lot of beating.

Serves 2

2 fillets of smoked pollack, or other smoked white fish
150ml whole milk
150ml double cream
A knob of butter

2 big handfuls of Sea Beet (or you can use any of the Oraches), washed and shredded into 3–4cm pieces
A squeeze of lemon juice
Freshly ground black pepper

Put the smoked pollack fillets into a medium saucepan and pour over the milk and cream. Cover the pan and bring to a gentle simmer, then turn off the heat and leave the fish to cook in the hot liquid – this may only take another minute. Lift out the pollack fillets and keep warm. Turn up the heat and let the liquid bubble until reduced by half.

Warm the butter in a frying pan and sauté the Sea Beet until just wilted and still bright green. Add the reduced milk and cream mixture to the frying pan and cook until the liquid thickens and the Sea Beet is well coated. Add a squeeze of lemon juice and some black pepper (it probably won't need salt as the fish is quite salty).

Divide the Sea Beet between two warm plates and top with the smoked pollack fillets. Serve immediately with lemon wedges and slices of brown bread and butter.

Pickled Rock Samphire

Despite all the horrid things I have said about Rock Samphire, this recipe is really rather good. The 'kerosene' flavour remains slightly in evidence, but is much moderated by the sweetness – and by the pickling process. Use the young shoots of May. Eat with cheese and bread or with a mackerel salad.

Makes 1 jar
300ml cider vinegar
1 tsp white peppercorns
25g sugar
Finely grated zest of ½ lemon
1 bay leaf
70g Rock Samphire leaves (use the topmost sprigs), washed
1 tbsp olive, hemp or rapeseed oil

Put the vinegar, peppercorns, sugar, lemon zest and bay leaf into a saucepan. Bring to a simmer and let it bubble for 10 minutes to reduce a little. Blanch the Rock Samphire in salted water for a few seconds, then, without rinsing, pack into a sterilised jar, leaving a 2cm space at the top. Pour on the hot pickling liquid, cover with a thin layer of oil and seal the jar with a vinegar-proof lid. Keep in a cupboard for 2 years, then throw it away (just kidding).

Sea Buckthorn
and crab apple jam

This is one of the best jams there is – and one that is not easily come by unless you make it yourself. The tartness will take your breath away.

Makes 3 or 4 x 340g jars
500g crab apples
500g Sea Buckthorn or Sea Buckthorn juice
400g granulated sugar

Chop up the crab apples, but don't remove the pips or the peel, both of which contain pectin. Place in a heavy-based saucepan with the Sea Buckthorn and add 600ml water. Bring to a simmer and cook until the fruit turns to a pulp.

Strain the pulp through a fine sieve into a preserving pan and add the sugar. Heat gently, stirring frequently, until the mixture boils, then boil for another 10 minutes or so, until setting point is reached, i.e. 104.5°C. (To test for a set, see p.180.) Skim off any scum. Pour the jam into warm sterilised jars. Cover and seal.

Alexanders and rhubarb jam

This is simply rhubarb jam with half the rhubarb replaced with Alexanders. If you want the stems to keep their shape during cooking it is necessary to place them in sugar for a few hours first. If you omit this stage the result is likely to be Alexanders stems suspended in a clear pink jelly – rather pleasing I think. The flavour of Alexanders, so powerful in the raw plant, soon dissipates with cooking. To replace it I often add a muslin bag of Alexanders seeds (or, at a pinch, leaves) for the last 2 minutes of cooking.

Makes about 4 x 340g jars
**500g Alexanders – young and thick
   stems are best
500g rhubarb, tough stems trimmed
900g jam sugar with added pectin
1 tbsp Alexanders seeds or
   a handful of leaves (optional)**

If your Alexanders are anything other than the most tender of plump, young stems, peel off any stringy outsides, rather as you would with celery. Cut the stems into chunks of about 2cm. Cut the rhubarb into similar-sized pieces too.

Put the Alexanders stems into a steamer over boiling water. Cover and steam for 10 minutes.

Scatter a layer of sugar over the bottom of your preserving pan and add a layer of rhubarb and Alexanders. Repeat, continuing until all of the sugar, rhubarb and Alexanders are used up. Pour 100ml water over the surface, then cover and leave for an hour or two at least, or overnight.

If you do not have a preserving thermometer, put a saucer into the freezer to chill (ready to test for setting). Gently bring the pan of rhubarb and Alexanders to the boil, stirring carefully to ensure you don't break up the stems. Boil rapidly for 5–6 minutes then, if you wish to boost the flavour, add a muslin bag of Alexanders seeds or leaves. Cook for another 2 minutes until setting point is reached, i.e. 104.5°C. To test for a set if you do not have a thermometer, drop a little of the mixture on to your chilled saucer and push with your finger; if the jam wrinkles it is ready.

Remove from the heat and allow to rest for 5 minutes – this ensures all of the fruit won't rise to the top of the jars. Pour the jam into warm, sterilised jars, then cover and seal in the usual way.

RECIPES 181

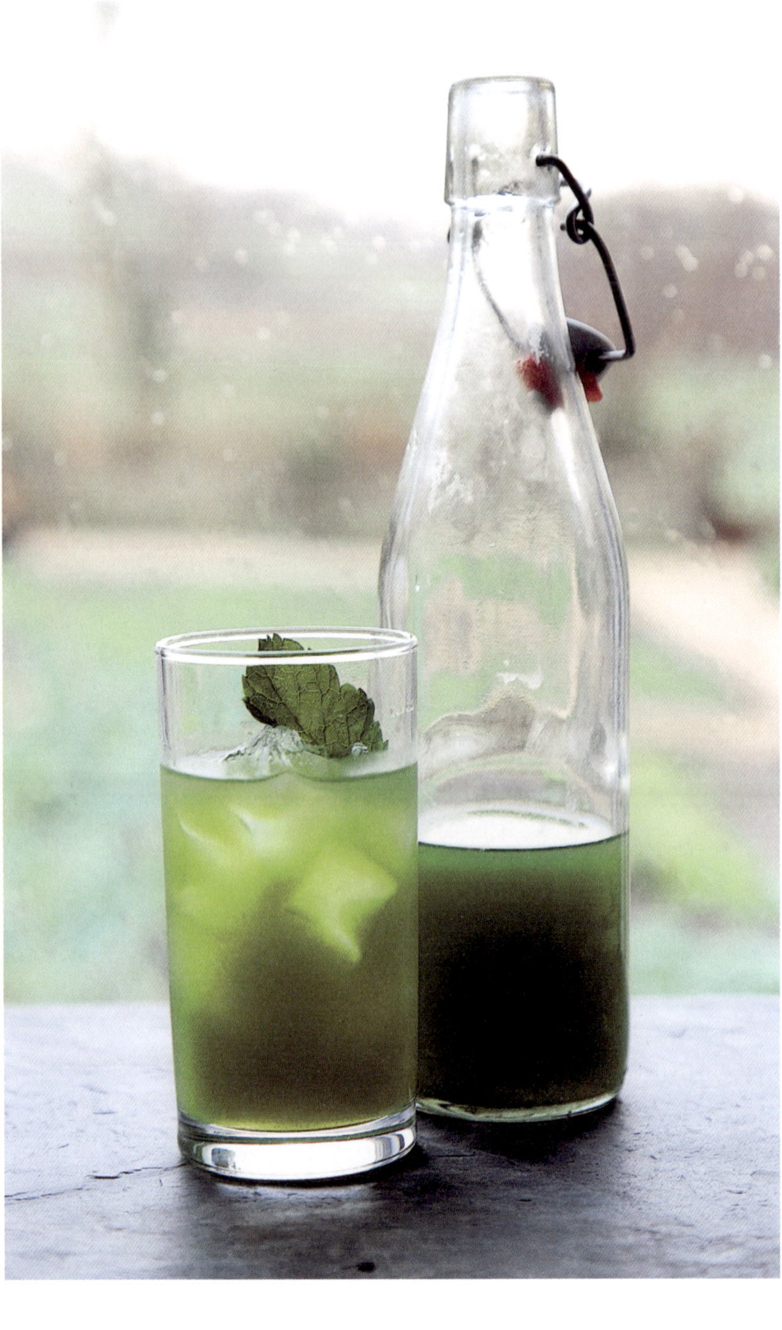

Alexanders liqueur

I am rather excited about this. Completely on its own, it is a little too powerful – both in flavour and alcohol content – but over ice, in a martini or even in a forager's mojito, it is something special. In summer, it would make a very interesting addition to a refreshing granita too.

Makes 1 bottle
500g Alexanders, including a few leaves for colour, well washed and chopped into 2cm chunks
caster sugar
vodka

In a blender, blitz the Alexanders stems and leaves until you have a fine, bright green purée. Set a coffee filter over a jug. Tip the purée into a clean tea-towel and squeeze out the juices into the filter – you'll have to squeeze quite hard to extract as much liquid as possible.

Measure the liquid, then measure half of its volume in caster sugar and combine the two. Stir to dissolve the sugar. Measure the volume and add about triple the volume of vodka, so the proportion is approximately 25 per cent Alexanders sugar syrup to 75 per cent vodka. Pour into a sterilised bottle and seal.

Serve the liqueur over ice, with an Alexanders leaf to garnish if you like. Don't worry about the floaty, cloudy green bits – it wouldn't be the same without them.

Kelp crisps

These make a great ready-salted snack. Be careful not to overcook, as the flavour of burnt seaweed is one that will stay with you for some days. Sugar Kelp is the best and you can also use Dulse.

Makes 1 bowl
A length of dried Kelp (dried straight from the sea, without rinsing)
Sunflower or groundnut oil for deep-frying

Use scissors to cut the Kelp into 3–4cm squares.

Heat a 10–12cm depth of oil in a deep, heavy-bottomed saucepan until it registers 180°C on a frying thermometer, or until a cube of stale white bread dropped into the oil turns golden within a minute.

Deep-fry the Kelp in small batches: carefully drop about 4 pieces at a time into the hot oil and fry for about 5 seconds – they will be ready when the surface bubbles up. Remove with a slotted spoon and drain on kitchen paper while you cook the rest. Eat them straight away.

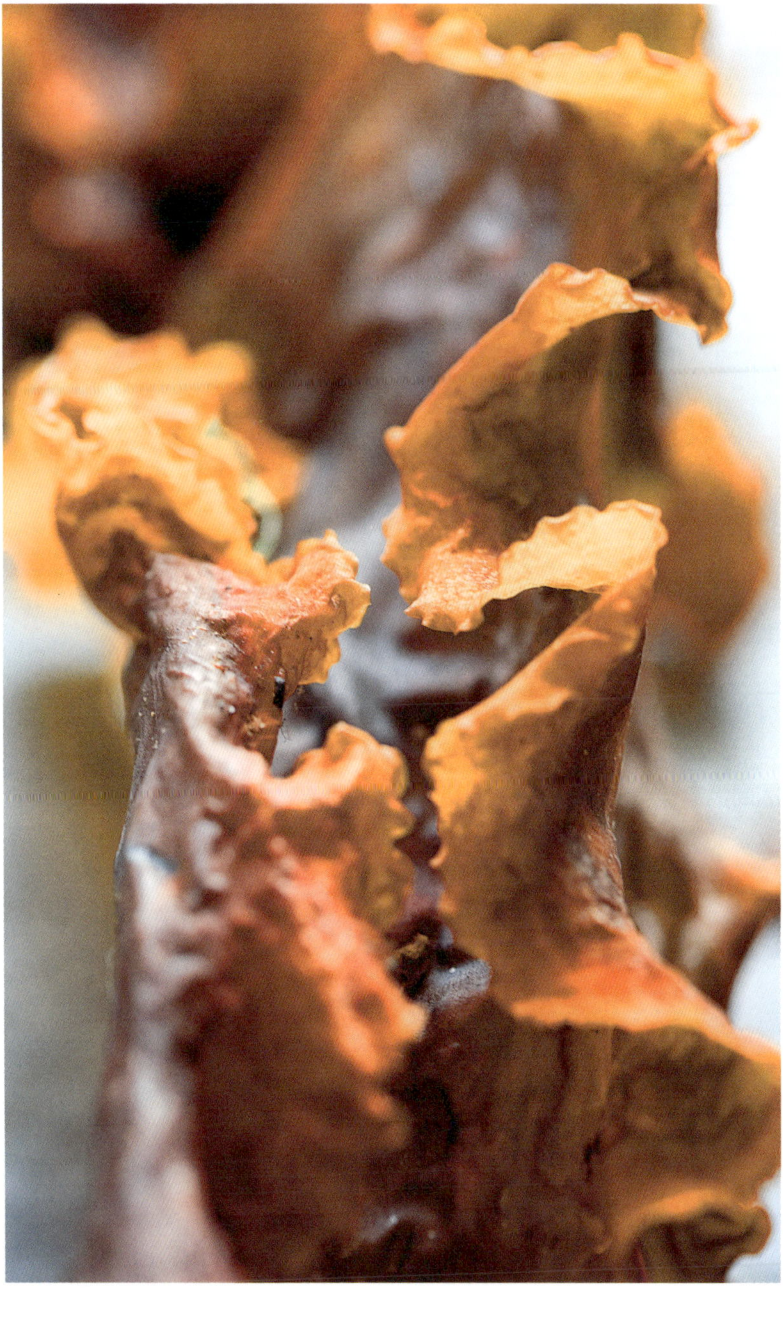

Crispy seaweed
and toasted sesame seeds

This Japanesey mixture makes a great condiment to sprinkle on fried fish. You can also dip cooked Crab, Lobster or Prawns into it if you like.

Makes 1 bowl
Sunflower or groundnut oil for deep-frying
A handful of Gutweed, rinsed and patted dry (see p.210 for warning about spitting!)
3 tbsp sesame seeds
1 tbsp golden caster sugar

Heat about an 8cm depth of oil in a deep, heavy-bottomed saucepan until it registers 180°C on a frying thermometer, or until a cube of stale white bread dropped into the oil turns golden within a minute.

Deep-fry the Gutweed in batches: carefully lower into the pan using tongs and fry for 4–6 seconds only, then remove with a slotted spoon and place on kitchen paper to drain while you deep-fry the rest.

Warm a dry, small frying pan over a medium-high heat and add the sesame seeds. Toast gently, shaking the pan occasionally, for about 40 seconds until golden and fragrant. Tip the Gutweed into a warm bowl, add the toasted sesame seeds and sugar and toss gently to mix. Eat straight away.

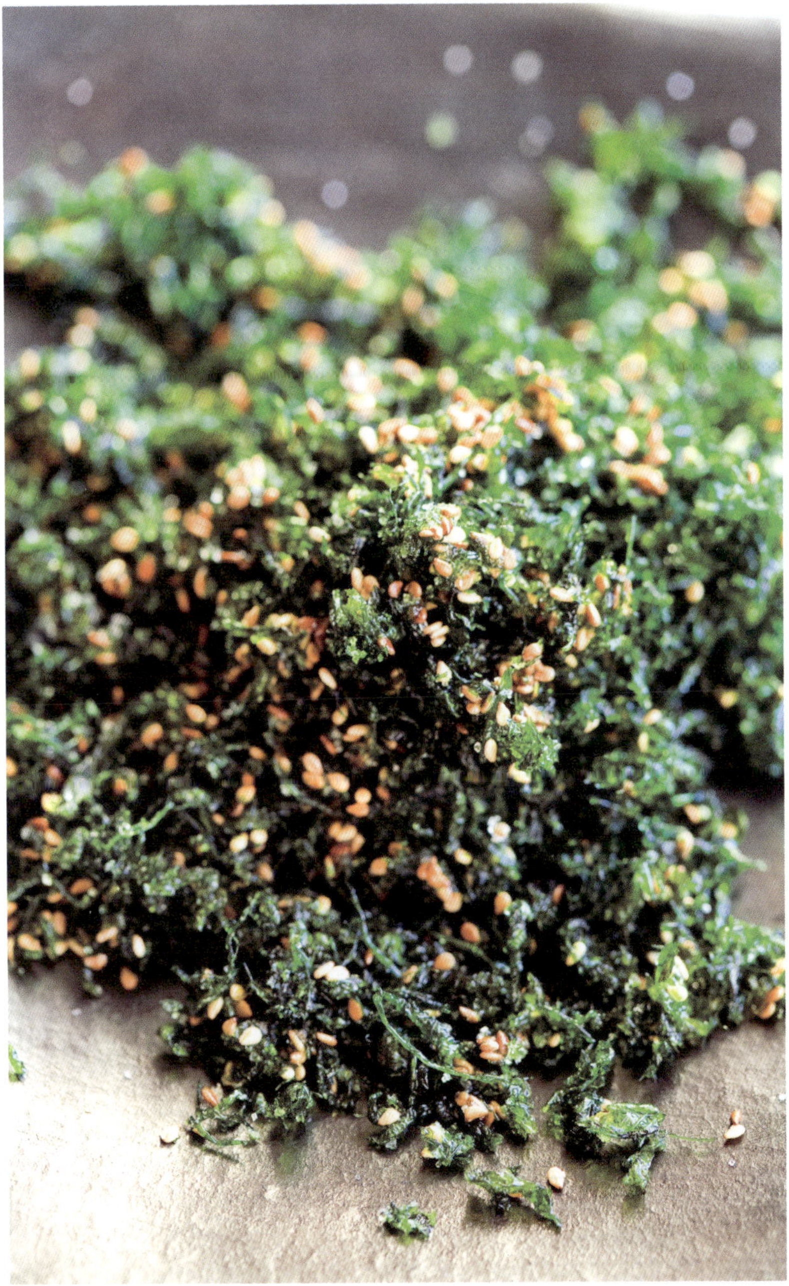

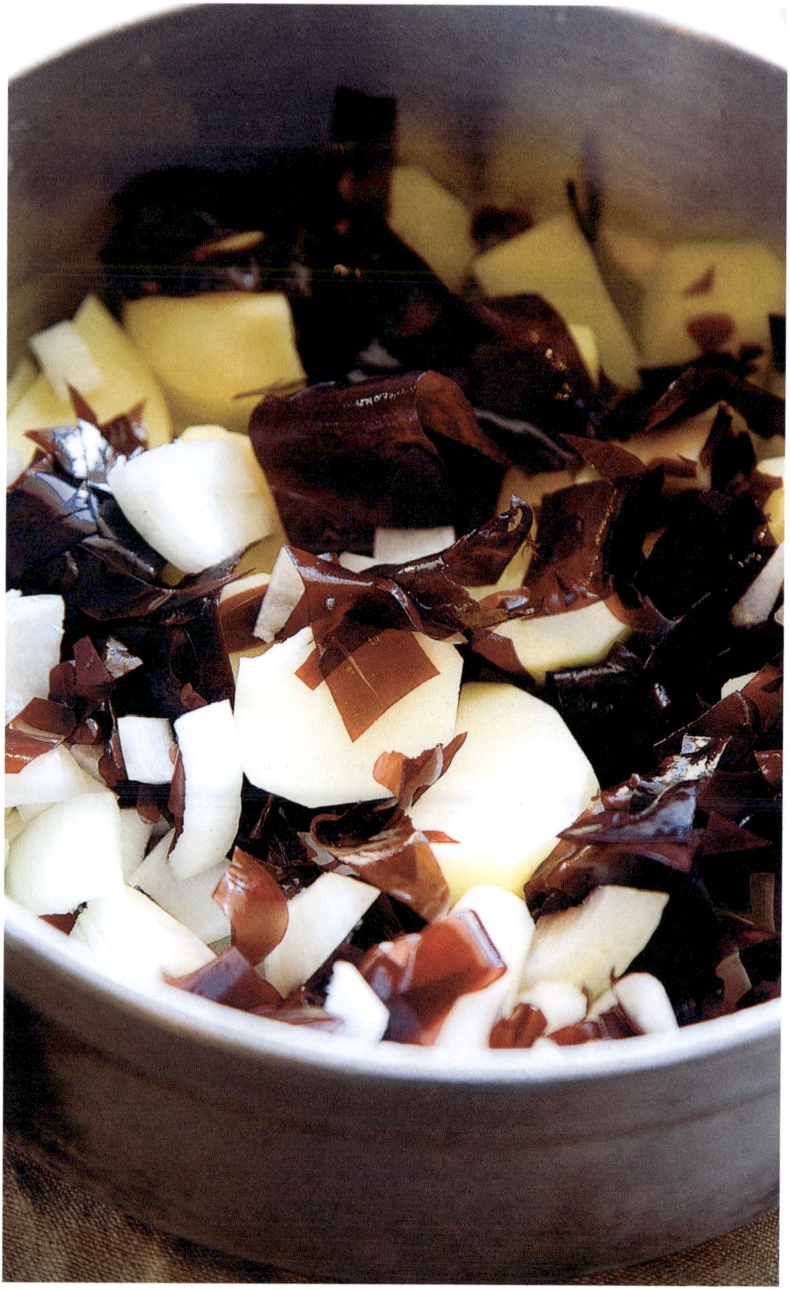

Dulse potato cakes

These are a great addition to a cooked breakfast and, if fried in sunflower oil rather than pork fat, they make delicious vegetarian 'fish cakes'.

Makes 10–12
500g potatoes, peeled
500g Dulse, well rinsed and chopped
2 medium onions, peeled and
 finely chopped
2–3 tbsp sunflower oil or
 bacon fat

Cut the potatoes into 4–5cm chunks and put into a saucepan with the Dulse, onions and enough water to cover by about 4cm. Bring to the boil, lower the heat and simmer until the potatoes are tender and most of the liquid has evaporated – keep an eye on the pan so that the contents don't stick or burn.

Mash the mixture very coarsely or beat into a rough 'mash' with a wooden spoon and shape into 6–7cm diameter patties.

Heat the oil or bacon fat in a large frying pan over a medium-high heat. Fry the Dulse cakes, in batches if necessary, for about 4–5 minutes on each side or until cooked through and slightly crispy on the outside. Drain on kitchen paper and serve.

Dulse and smoked fish tart

A deliciously savoury tart – like licking the sea wall, but in a good way. I sometimes use Sea Beet or one of the Oraches in addition to the Dulse to make it even more of a maritime treat.

Serves 6–8

For the pastry
200g plain flour
A pinch of salt
100g cold, unsalted butter, cut into small cubes
1 egg, separated
About 50ml cold milk

For the filling
350g smoked mackerel or pollack fillet
200ml whole milk
About 140g Dulse, well rinsed and finely shredded
A knob of unsalted butter
2 onions, peeled and finely sliced
200ml double cream
2 eggs
2 egg yolks
Freshly ground black pepper

To make the pastry, put the flour, salt and butter into a food processor and pulse until the mixture has the consistency of breadcrumbs. Add the egg yolk and then, with the motor running, trickle in the milk through the funnel, stopping as soon as the dough comes together; don't overprocess. Tip the dough on to a lightly floured surface and knead gently to make a smooth ball. Wrap in cling film and chill for half an hour.

Preheat the oven to 170°C/Gas Mark 3. Roll out the pastry on a lightly floured surface and use to line a 28cm loose-bottomed tart tin, allowing the excess pastry to overhang the rim of the tin. Prick the base in several places with a fork, line with a sheet of greaseproof paper and fill with baking beans or rice. Bake for 15 minutes, then remove the paper and beans and return to the oven for 10 minutes until the base looks dry and cooked through. Lightly beat the egg white and brush all over the pastry to seal, then bake for a further 5 minutes until golden. Trim off the excess pastry from the edge with a small, sharp knife.

For the filling, flake the fish from its skin, removing any bones. Tip the flaked fish into a bowl and set aside. Put the skin into a pan with the milk and bring to a bare simmer. Take off the heat and leave to infuse while you get on with everything else.

Put the Dulse into a pan and cover with about 3cm cold water. Bring to the boil and simmer for about 7 minutes until tender. Drain well.

Heat the butter in a frying pan over a medium-low heat, add the onions and fry very gently until soft and just beginning to turn golden, about 15 minutes. Gently stir in the Dulse and flaked fish, then tip the mixture into the tart case.

Strain the infused milk into a bowl and add the cream, eggs and egg yolks. Whisk together, then season with pepper and pour over the filling. Bake at 170°C/Gas Mark 3 for 40 minutes until lightly set and browned. Serve warm or cold.

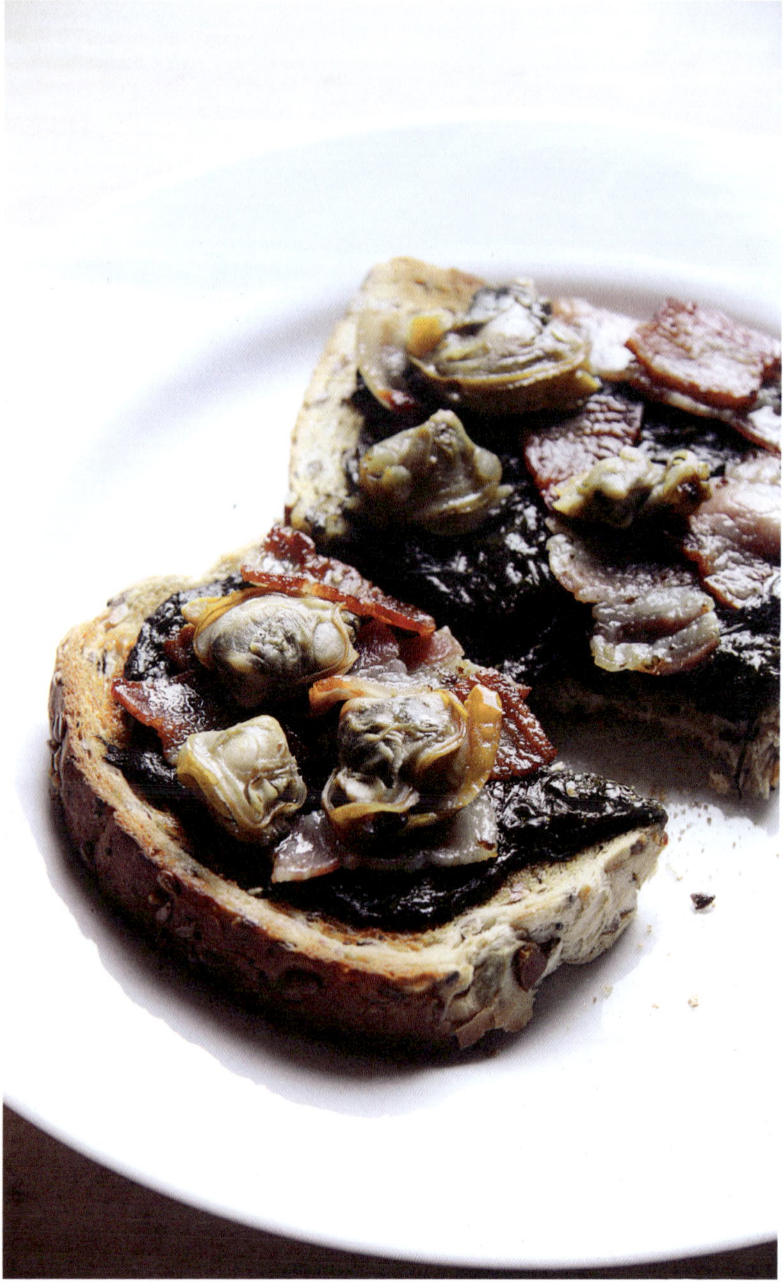

Laverbread with Clams
and bacon on toast

The unusual and unfamiliar taste and texture of Laver is something that should be enjoyed at its very best the first time you try it. This, I think, is it.

First you need to make your laverbread. It takes an extraordinarily long time to cook, anywhere between 5 and 10 hours depending on species and time of year, but the process can be speeded up enormously if you use a pressure cooker. Place your well-washed Laver in a heatproof bowl, cover it with an upturned heatproof plate and sit in 4–5cm water inside a pressure cooker. Cook for about an hour. This is a long time in a pressure cooker and is best done in two stages to prevent the water boiling dry and the aromatic calamity that would follow. When the Laver is cooked, transfer it to a clean saucepan, then heat and stir until the excess liquid is reduced and a coarse, sticky purée is formed.

If you are determined to follow tradition and cook for the whole 5 to 10 hours the best pot to use is a thick-bottomed preserving pan with a lid. Stir occasionally and then reduce the cooking liquor until a sticky consistency is reached. Whichever way you use, there is a considerable investment in time and energy so it is worth cooking a large quantity and freezing whatever is not needed immediately.

Serves 4
100g laverbread
6 rashers of best streaky bacon
20 or so Venus Clams or 40 Cockles
A squeeze of lemon juice
4 large slices of warm toast

Once you've made your laverbread, chop the bacon into bite-sized pieces, then gently fry in a dry frying pan until just crispy. Remove with a slotted spoon to a warm plate and keep warm.

Carefully add a little water to the pan, then add the shellfish. Cover with a tight-fitting lid and cook until the shells steam open, about 3 minutes. Remove from the heat and take the shellfish out, emptying any juice back into the pan. Shell the Clams and keep them warm.

Throw the laverbread into the clam juice and bacon fat, stir and gently fry, reducing to that sticky consistency again. Towards the end add a little lemon juice. Spread the laverbread on toast and top with the bacon and Clams.

Seaweed and elderflower
panna cotta

This is the very last word in wild-food desserts and something of a revelation for those who cannot believe that seaweed could actually be useful in the kitchen. If elderflowers are out of season you can use elderflower cordial, or infuse the milk with a split vanilla pod or two and make a vanilla panna cotta instead. The quantities given here make enough to fill six small coffee cups or darioles.

Serves 6
25g dried or 80g fresh Carragheen
200ml milk
50g caster sugar

12 elderflower heads, flowers stripped with a fork
200ml double cream

If you are using dried Carragheen, soak it in cold water for 20 minutes.

Pour 600ml water into a saucepan, add the Carragheen and bring to the boil. Lower the heat and simmer gently for 20–25 minutes, stirring occasionally.

Pour the milk into another pan and add the sugar, along with the elderflowers held in a muslin bag. Heat slowly until the liquid is about to boil, then remove from the heat and take out the flowers.

Spoon the hot, sticky (and strangely aromatic) mess from the Carragheen pan on to a large double layer of muslin. Don some clean rubber gloves – you will need them badly. Gather up the muslin and hold it over the infused milk. Squeeze tightly to extract the setting agent from the Carragheen through the muslin into the milk, whisking at frequent intervals.

Lightly whisk the cream into the mixture, then quickly pour into darioles or cups. Refrigerate until set (you won't have to wait long).

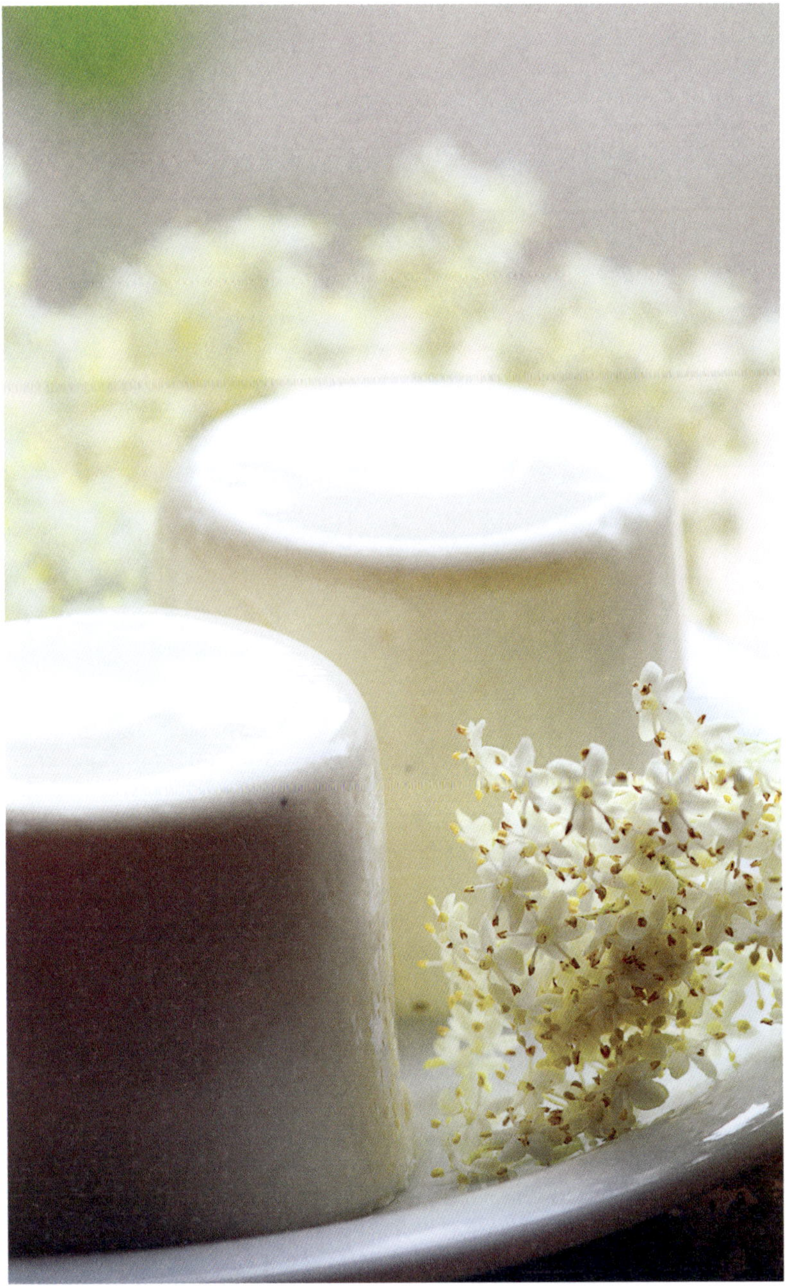

Cockles with chorizo

The day to day cuisine of the 1950s and '60s was a plain affair, untroubled by innovation or an excessive variety of ingredients. It was then, circa 1961, with horror that I greeted the arrival at the dinner table of gammon served with a slice of inexplicable pineapple. In garnishing the main course with what was clearly the dessert we presumed that our dear mother had strayed from the path of reason and was wandering the foothills of insanity. I now blame Fanny.

Years later I was similarly surprised to be served – this time by a restaurateur friend – lemon sole with crispy bacon. Unlike the gammon and pineapple transgression, this marriage works extraordinarily well and the idea of fish with meat is now widely accepted. Not that any meat will do. Chicken works in certain fish dishes such as paella, but it is pork in the form of sausage or bacon that really does the trick. Nor is every fish suitable – the mild flavours of white fish and bivalve molluscs being a requirement. The following simple exploitation of this happy relationship, served with bread, makes a quick and delicious lunch. It also works with Oysters and other Clams – you can see in the picture some Clams that crept unbidden into the pan.

Serves 2
400g Cockles, cleaned (see p.115)
1 tbsp olive oil
150g cooking chorizo, sliced into
    rough chunks

Juice of 1 lemon
A small handful of flat-leaf parsley,
    finely chopped

Have the Cockles cleaned and ready to cook. Heat the olive oil in a frying pan over a medium heat and sauté the chorizo until its lovely red fat runs, about 4 minutes. Now throw in the Cockles, cover the pan tightly and cook until the shells open.

Squeeze over the lemon juice, stir in the chopped parsley and serve immediately, in warmed bowls.

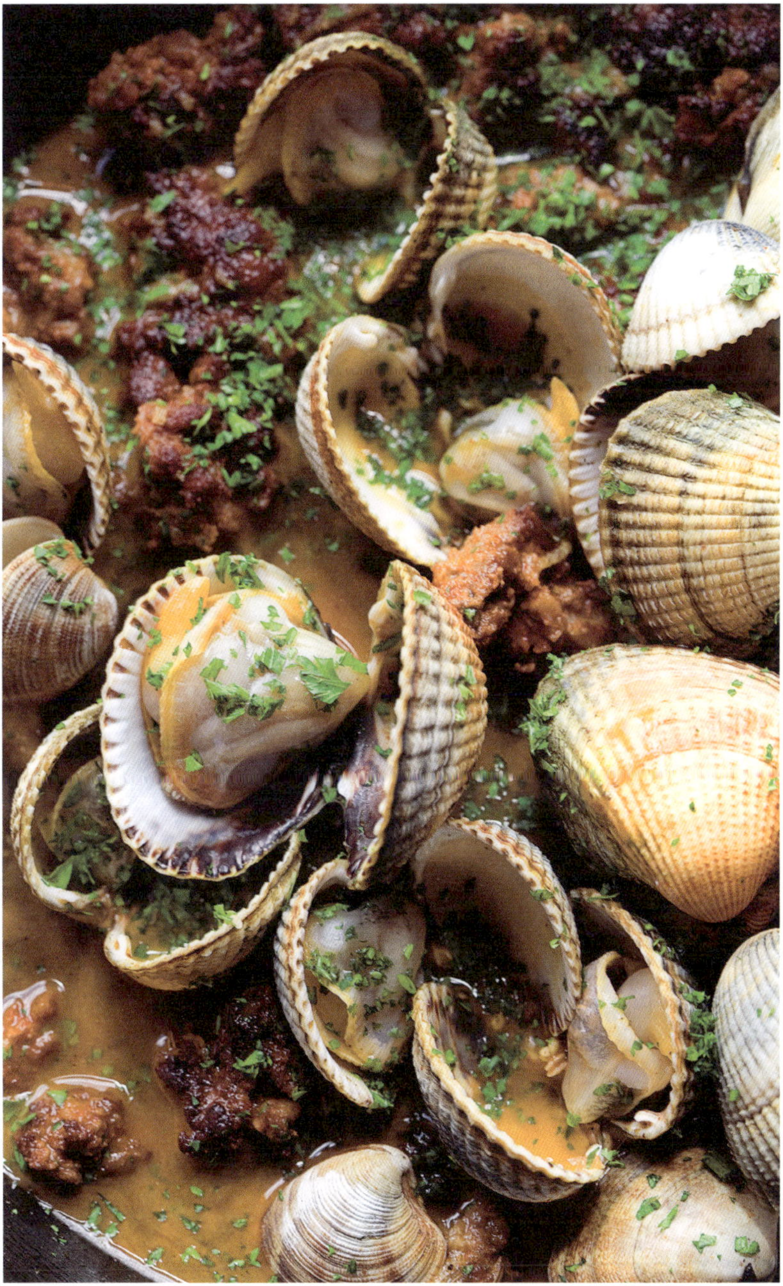

West Country cider Mussels

When you have gone to the trouble of collecting your own Mussels, you really want a recipe that brings out the best in them. This Anglicised take on *moules marinières*, which I pinched straight from *The River Cottage Fish Book* (they won't mind), is one of my favourites.

Serves 2 as a main course

- 50g unsalted butter
- 1 onion, peeled and finely sliced
- 2 garlic cloves, peeled and finely sliced
- 1 tsp thyme leaves, or 2 tsp Wild Thyme (if you can find any!)
- 1½ tsp cider vinegar (optional)
- ½ glass of medium cider
- 1kg Mussels, purged (see p.111), scrubbed and debearded (see p.118)
- Sea salt and freshly ground black pepper
- 2 tbsp double cream (optional)

Heat the butter in a deep, wide pan over a medium heat. Add the onion and garlic, then cover and sweat for 5 minutes or so, stirring occasionally, until softened but not coloured.

Increase the heat and add the thyme. When it releases its scent, add the cider vinegar, if using, and cider, then the Mussels and some salt and pepper. Give them a quick stir and a shake, then cover with a tight-fitting lid. Cook for 3–4 minutes, shaking the pan a couple of times, until the Mussels are open (discard any that remain closed). Add the cream, if you like, to the juices in the pan.

Spoon the Mussels into warmed bowls, pour the juices over and around them, and serve with good bread and a glass of cider.

Mussels with chilli
and tomato

A warming dish to serve in early autumn, when Mussels have finished spawning and home-grown tomatoes are still good.

Serves 2 as a main course, 4 as a starter

- 1 tbsp olive oil
- 1 small onion, peeled and finely chopped
- 1 garlic clove, peeled and finely chopped
- 1 red chilli, deseeded and finely chopped
- 100ml dry white wine
- 1kg Mussels, purged (see p.111), scrubbed and debearded (see p.118)
- 500g large tomatoes, skinned, deseeded and roughly chopped
- Sea salt and freshly ground black pepper
- Chopped parsley, to serve

Heat the olive oil in a large, wide pan over a medium heat. Add the onion, garlic and chilli and fry gently for 5 minutes until soft. Add the wine and Mussels, cover the pan tightly and cook for 3–4 minutes until the Mussels are open. Discard any that remain closed.

Scoop the Mussels out with a slotted spoon and divide them among warmed bowls. Add the tomatoes to the juices in the pan and cook for a few minutes, crushing them slightly, until you have a rough-textured sauce. Season with salt and pepper.

Spoon the sauce over the Mussels, scatter with chopped parsley and serve, with plenty of bread to mop up the juices.

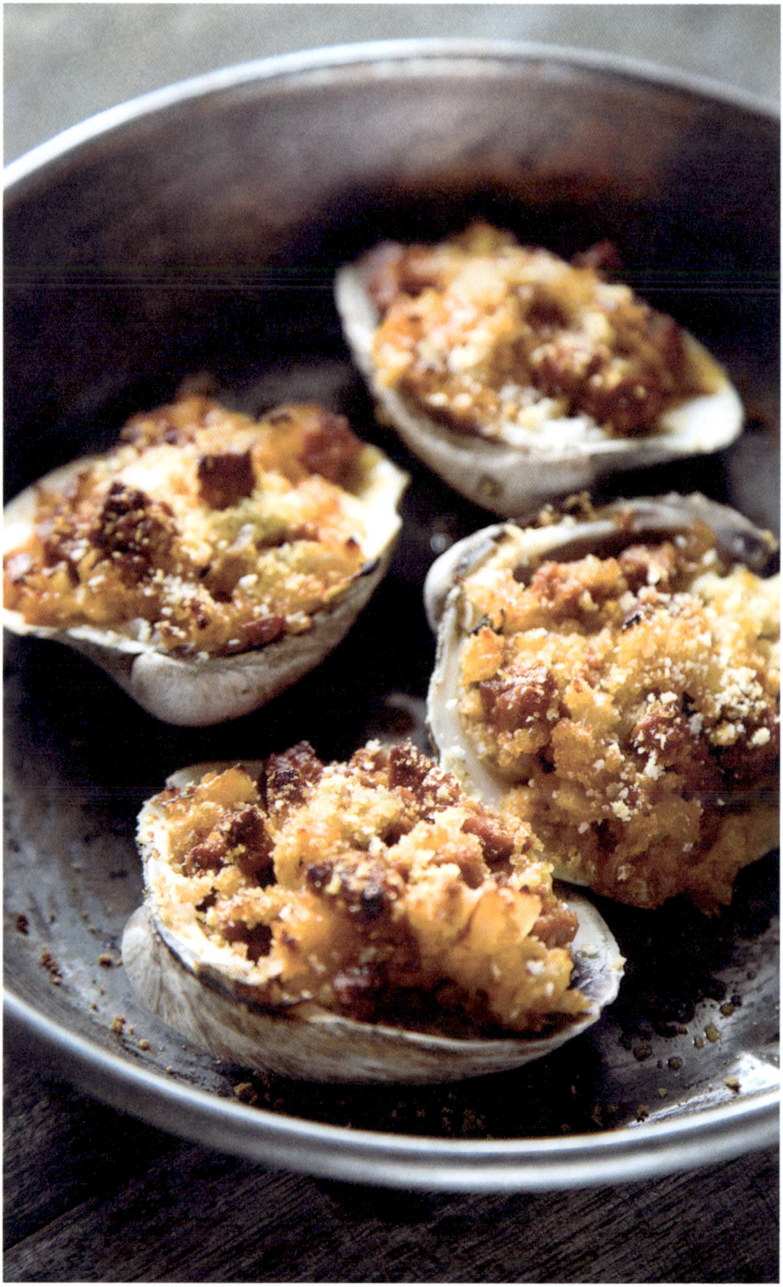

Stuffed Hard Shell Clams

These are a great favourite on the east coast of America, where Hard Shell Clams enjoy the rather marvellous name of quahogs. They've become something of a favourite of mine too, though these large Clams are not that easy to come by. However, the recipe can be made with the smaller Clams, or even Mussels – they will just be more fiddly to handle.

Serves 6 as a starter

6 Hard Shell Clams, well scrubbed
1 tbsp olive oil
250g cooking chorizo, cut into small chunks
1 onion, peeled and finely chopped
1½ tsp thyme leaves, or 2 tsp Wild Thyme leaves (if available), chopped

A small handful of fresh white breadcrumbs
Freshly ground black pepper
About 30g unsalted butter, for greasing and drizzling

Preheat the oven to 200°C/Gas mark 6.

Bring a pan containing 2–3cm of water to the boil. Add the Clams, then cover and boil for 1 minute only, until they just start to open. Remove them from the pan with a slotted spoon and open as you would an Oyster (see p.123), tipping the juices from the shell into a small bowl. Remove the Clams from their shells and chop the flesh roughly.

Heat the olive oil in a frying pan over a medium-high heat and sauté the chorizo for 3–4 minutes until the fat runs, then transfer to a bowl using a slotted spoon. Lower the heat, add the onion and thyme to the pan and sauté until the onion is soft, about 5 minutes. Toss into the bowl with the chorizo, then stir in the breadcrumbs and chopped Clams, along with their juices and a few grinds of black pepper.

Lightly grease 6 half-clam shells with butter and spoon in the Clam and chorizo filling. Melt the rest of the butter and trickle over the filling. Bake for 10 minutes until golden on top.

Steamed Clams with sausage

This unlikely-sounding dish is one of the best things I have ever tasted and I kneel at the feet of Debora who cooked it for me at River Cottage. It is very easy to make. A variation is to use Cockles in place of Clams. You will never waste a Cockle by dipping it in vinegar again.

Serves 4 as a main course, 6 as a starter

25g butter
1 medium onion, peeled and finely chopped
1 leek, white part only, trimmed and finely sliced
1 tbsp Wild Thyme leaves (ok – it doesn't *have* to be wild!)
1 tsp fennel seeds, roughly crushed
200g herby pork sausages, skinned and roughly broken into 2cm pieces
1 tbsp fresh oregano, chopped
400g tin chopped tomatoes
120ml dry white wine
1kg Clams, well scrubbed
2 tbsp flat-leaf parsley or Wild Fennel fronds (or a mixture), chopped

Melt the butter in a large, heavy-bottomed frying pan over a medium-low heat. Add the onion, leek, thyme and fennel seeds, and sauté gently until the vegetables begin to soften, about 10 minutes.

Add the sausage pieces and cook, stirring frequently, for about 5 minutes until evenly browned. Stir in the oregano, chopped tomatoes and wine. Turn up the heat and bring to a simmer.

Add the Clams, cover the pan tightly and cook just until they open, which should take no longer than 4 minutes. Discard any that remain closed. Sprinkle over the parsley and/or fennel fronds. Divide between warmed bowls and eat immediately.

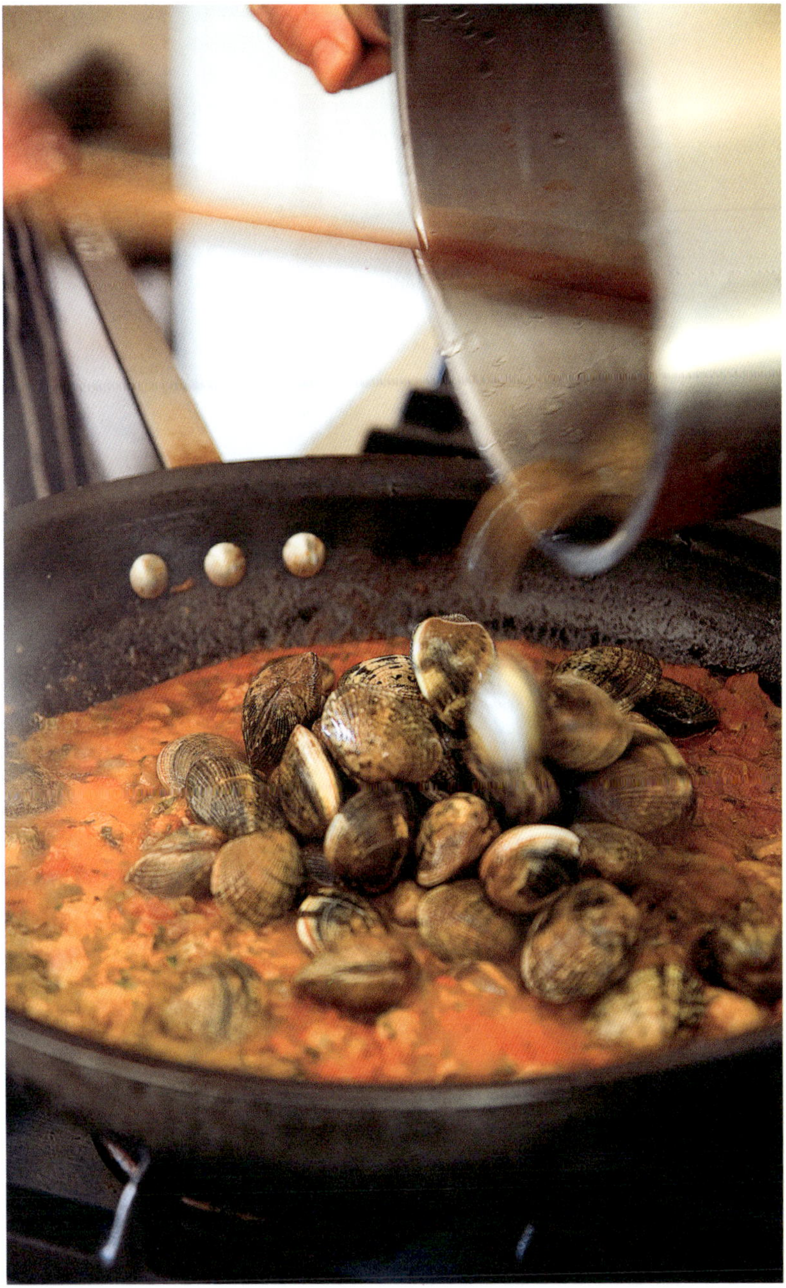

Clam arancini
with arrabbiata sauce

This is a superb dish but not one you should embark upon if 'time's wingèd chariot hurries near'. My first attempt took the best part of a day, though tea breaks, a trip to the pub and a well-deserved afternoon nap may have accounted for most of it – an hour and a half would probably be enough for a more efficient cook.

It helps if you can visualise what you are making – basically it is deep-fried, breadcrumb-coated balls of sticky risotto, which contain a Clam or two, served with a spicy tomato sauce (*arrabbiata* means 'angry' in Italian). Of course 'Clams' can be replaced by Cockles or Oysters or even Mussels.

Serves 4 as a main dish

For the risotto
1 tbsp olive oil
40g butter
1 onion, peeled and finely chopped
2 garlic cloves, peeled
300g arborio or other risotto rice
1 litre hot fish stock (see p.228), or vegetable stock
Sea salt and freshly ground black pepper
About 50g Dulse, well washed
2 eggs, separated
A handful of Clams (one or two for each rice ball) depending on size, well scrubbed
80g fine white breadcrumbs
About 1 litre sunflower or groundnut oil for deep-frying

For the arrabbiata sauce
3 tbsp olive oil
1 garlic clove, peeled and finely chopped
1–2 medium-hot red chillies, deseeded and membrane removed, then finely sliced
200g ripe tomatoes, skinned (if preferred), cored, deseeded and roughly chopped
A good pinch of sugar

To make the risotto, heat the olive oil with half of the butter in a large, heavy-bottomed frying pan over a medium-low heat. Add the chopped onion and sauté gently until soft and translucent, about 10 minutes. Meanwhile, finely slice one of the garlic cloves. Add this to the pan and sauté with the onion for another couple of minutes. Tip the rice into the pan and stir until all of the grains are well coated in the buttery oil.

Add the hot stock a ladleful at a time, stirring until almost all of it is absorbed before adding more. The final result should be smooth and slightly drier than a normal risotto, with the rice still a little *al dente*. You may not need to use all of the stock. Season well with pepper and leave to cool.

While the rice is cooling, make the arrabbiata sauce. Heat the olive oil in a small frying pan over a medium-low heat. Add the garlic and chilli and sauté for a couple of minutes until soft and fragrant. Add the tomatoes and cook, stirring from time to time, for 5 minutes. Season with a pinch of sugar, a little salt and a few grinds of black pepper. Keep the sauce warm.

Next, steam the Dulse for about 10 minutes or until tender. Drain and chop very finely. Mix it into the cooled rice, along with one of the egg yolks.

Bring a pan containing a splash of water to the boil. Add the Clams, then cover tightly and steam until they just open, about 3–4 minutes. Discard any that remain closed. Remove the Clams from their shells and set aside.

On a chopping board, mash the remaining garlic clove to a paste with a scant pinch of fine sea salt and then mix into the remaining butter until evenly blended.

Once the rice is cooled, wet your hands and take a heaped tablespoonful in the palm of one hand. Make a small hole in the middle of it and place a small scrap of the garlic butter and a Clam in the cavity. Press the rest of the rice around it, ensuring the filling is completely enclosed by the rice, to make a fairly firm little ball.

Whisk together the remaining egg white and whole egg. Dip each rice ball into the beaten egg and then roll in the breadcrumbs until well coated.

Heat the oil in a deep, heavy-bottomed saucepan until it registers 180°C on a frying thermometer, or until a cube of stale white bread dropped into the oil turns golden within a minute. Deep-fry the rice balls 3 or 4 at a time: lower them into the hot oil with a slotted spoon and fry for a few minutes until golden. Drain on kitchen paper and keep hot while you cook the rest; allow the oil to come back up to temperature between batches.

Serve the arancini at once, with the warm arrabbiata sauce for dipping.

P.S. As an alternative to Dulse, you could use uncooked, puréed Laver – or cheat completely and substitute 3 sheets of 'nori', pre-soaked for 10 minutes.

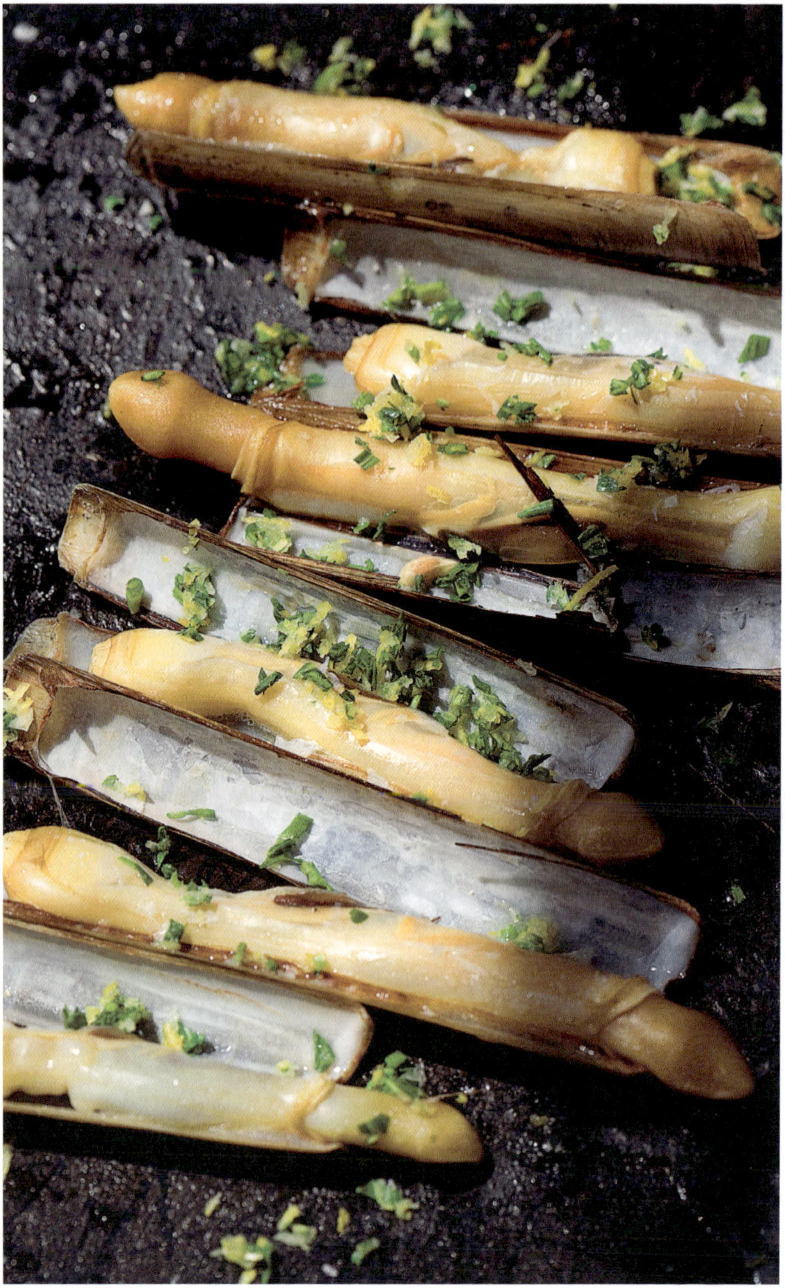

Razor Clams
with almost wild gremolata

When I came across some crow garlic (by the sea as it happens) and some Wild Rocket, they seemed like great ingredients to transform into gremolata to go with these Razor Clams. Unfortunately, I am yet to find wild lemons growing in the Southwest, hence the 'almost' – maybe some sorrel would fit the bill. You can also barbecue the Razor Clams until just open before sprinkling with the gremolata. This recipe will work with any other Clams you can lay your hands on.

Serves 4 as a starter
12 Razor Clams

For the gremolata
Grated zest of 1 large lemon
1–2 crow garlic (or ordinary garlic) cloves, peeled and grated
A small handful of Wild Rocket, very finely chopped

Preheat the grill until it is as hot as it will get.

Lay the Clams on a sturdy baking sheet and place under the grill until they open. Remove from the grill and allow to cool for a minute while you make the gremolata.

In a small bowl, mix together the lemon zest, garlic and chopped Rocket.

Carefully prise open the clam shells until they are flat and remove the black stomach. Sprinkle on the gremolata. You can serve the Clams like this or pop them under the grill for a further minute if you like.

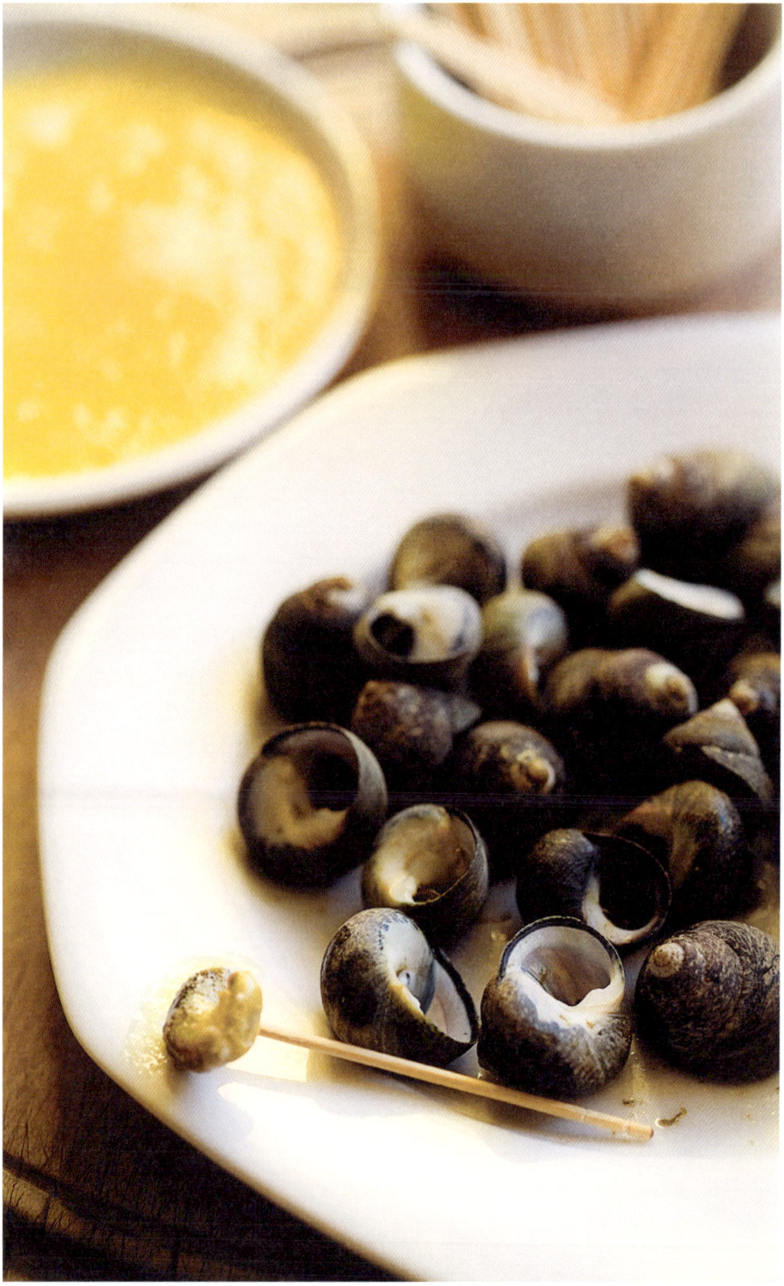

Winkles with garlic butter

This maritime version of the terrestrial classic will also work with Dog Whelks if you can get enough, or even Cockles.

Serves 2 as a snack
A pint of Winkles, well scrubbed

For the court bouillon
2 carrots, peeled and finely sliced
4 celery sticks, finely sliced
1 leek, white part only, trimmed and finely sliced
2 onions, peeled and finely sliced
3 garlic cloves, smashed
2 bay leaves
A large sprig each of thyme, tarragon and parsley
2 tsp cracked black peppercorns
2 tsp salt
A small glass of dry white wine

For the garlic butter
2 garlic cloves, peeled
Flaky sea salt
100g butter
1 tbsp very finely chopped parsley

Start by making the court bouillon. Put all of the ingredients into a large pan and add 1.5 litres of water or sea water. Bring to the boil and simmer for 20 minutes.

Meanwhile, make the garlic butter. Cut the garlic cloves in half lengthways and remove the green germ running through the middle if there is one. Mash the garlic to a paste with a good pinch of salt. Melt the butter in a small pan over a medium-low heat, add the garlic paste and cook very gently for a minute. Remove from the heat and add the chopped parsley.

Add the Winkles to the court bouillon, bring back to the boil and simmer gently for 5 minutes. Drain, discarding the court bouillon and bits of vegetables and herbs.

You will need to use a pin to remove the fingernail-like 'door' that seals the shell before skewering the meat inside and pulling it out. Dip into the garlic butter and eat immediately.

Oyster risotto
with deep-fried Gutweed

This truly spectacular and luxurious starter is the clincher in any argument about whether raw Oysters are better than cooked Oysters – they aren't. When preparing the Gutweed, make sure you dry it very well and use a heavy-bottomed, deep pan to fry it in. It spits ferociously (to be honest, it explodes), so do take care!

Serves 6 as a starter

For the risotto
2 tbsp olive oil
20g unsalted butter
2 leeks, white part only, trimmed and finely chopped
1 small onion, peeled and finely chopped
1 garlic clove, peeled and finely chopped
150g arborio or other risotto rice
A small glass of white wine
500ml hot fish stock (see p.228)
1–2 tbsp Wild Fennel fronds, finely chopped (optional)
A dash of Pernod (optional)
Sea salt and freshly ground black pepper

For the Gutweed
Sunflower or groundnut oil for deep-frying
A small handful of Gutweed, well rinsed and patted dry (see above)

For the Oysters
20g unsalted butter
6 large Oysters, shelled (see p.123), juices reserved

To make the risotto, heat the olive oil and butter in a large, heavy-bottomed frying pan over a medium-low heat. Add the leeks and onion and sweat gently for about 10 minutes until softened. Add the garlic and cook for another couple of minutes. Add the rice and stir until the grains are coated with buttery oil, then add the wine and bring to a gentle simmer. Cook, stirring, until most of the liquid is absorbed.

Now start adding the hot fish stock, a ladleful at a time, waiting for each ladleful to be almost completely absorbed before adding the next one. Add the reserved oyster juices to the rice. If you run out of stock before the rice is cooked, add some boiling water instead. The final result should be smooth and creamy, with the rice still a little *al dente*. Stir the Fennel into the risotto, along with the Pernod, if using.

When the rice is almost done, prepare the Gutweed and Oysters. Heat about an 8cm depth of oil in a deep saucepan until it registers 180°C on a frying thermometer, or until a cube of stale white bread dropped into the oil turns golden within a minute. Deep-fry the Gutweed in batches: carefully lower into the pan using tongs and fry for 4–6 seconds only, then remove with a slotted spoon and place on kitchen paper to drain while you deep-fry the rest.

Melt some butter in a heavy, non-stick frying pan and sauté the Oysters until nicely browned. Check the seasoning of the risotto and divide between warmed plates. Arrange an Oyster on each one and sprinkle on the fried Gutweed. Eat at once.

Hangtown fry

This is the omelette to end all omelettes. The story goes that it was a great hit with gold prospectors who had struck it rich in the California frontier town – they were the only ones who could afford the luxurious combination of Oysters, bacon and eggs! Another story, probably apocryphal, would have us believe that it was the 'last breakfast' of a condemned man, about to be hanged, who was trying to combine all of his favourite foods in one dish.

Serves 1

3 rashers of streaky bacon, halved
2–3 eggs, beaten
Sea salt and freshly ground black pepper
½–1 tbsp finely chopped flat-leaf parsley
6 Oysters, shelled (see p.123)
A handful of seasoned fresh white breadcrumbs
20g butter

In a dry frying pan, cook the bacon over a medium heat until just crisp. Drain on kitchen paper and keep warm.

Season the beaten eggs with plenty of salt and pepper and add the chopped parsley. Dip the Oysters in the beaten egg and then into the breadcrumbs to coat. Melt the butter in an ovenproof frying pan over a medium heat and fry the Oysters for a couple of minutes until golden. At this stage, heat up the grill.

Pour the rest of the egg mixture over the Oysters in the frying pan and let it set slightly. Pull the set egg away from the sides with a spatula, tilting the pan and allowing the uncooked egg to run towards the edges.

Just before the egg has all set, lay the bacon rashers over the top of the omelette and finish off under the grill for a minute or so, but only until it has set. Serve immediately, sprinkled with gold dust... not really.

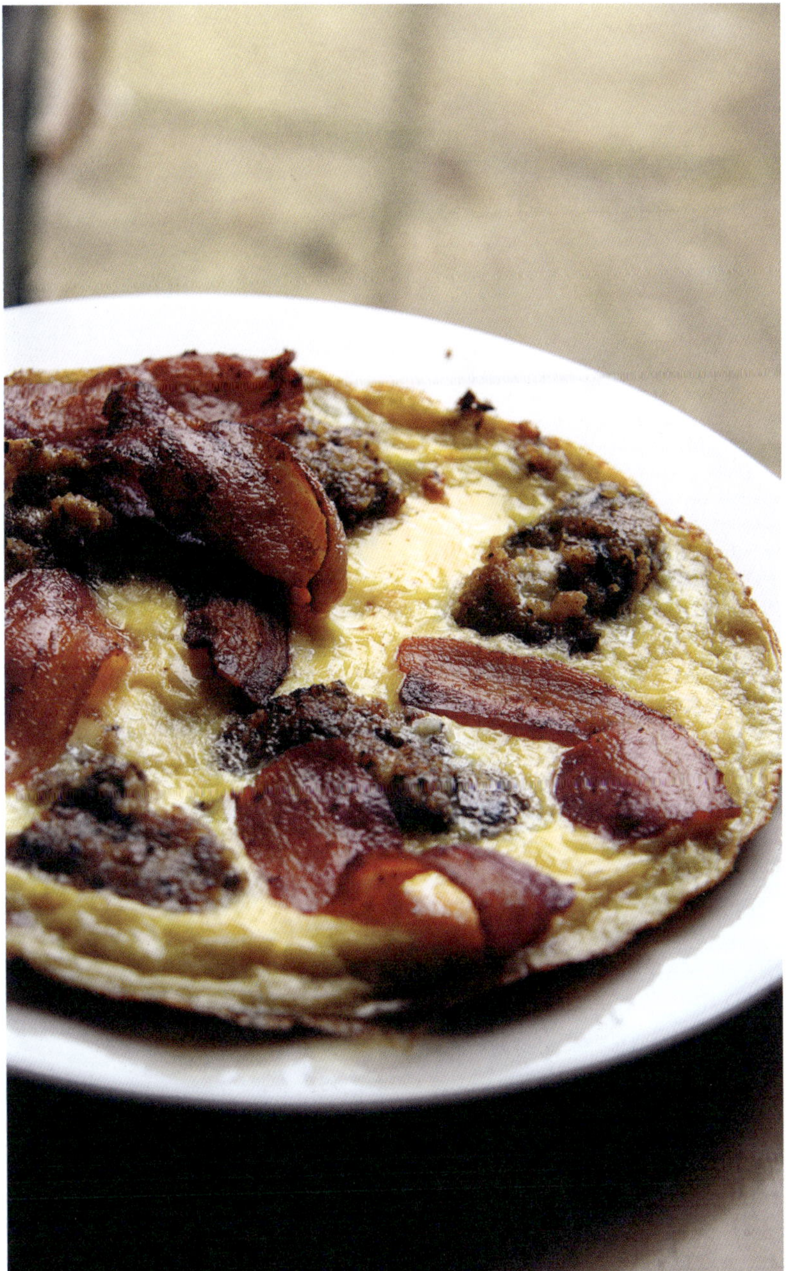

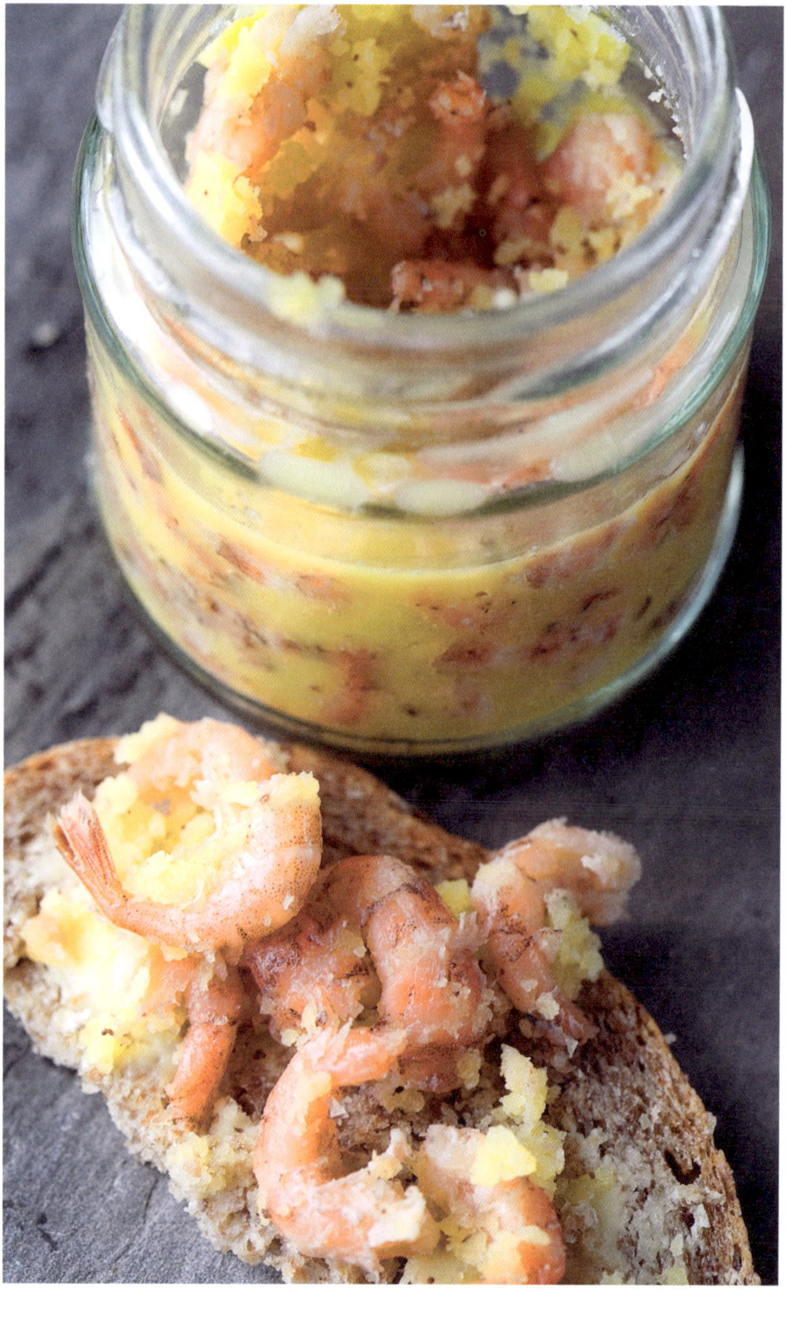

Potted Shrimp

Peeling Brown Shrimps is truly a labour of love, but the results are worth it. The Shrimps will need the barest of flirtations with a pan of boiling salted water – a minute is more than enough – before peeling.

Serves 2
120g unsalted butter
A pinch of ground mace
A pinch of cayenne pepper
1 bay leaf
200g peeled, cooked Brown Shrimps, Shrimps or rock pool Prawns

A squeeze of lemon juice
Fine sea salt and freshly ground white pepper

To serve
Hot brown toast

Gently melt the butter in a small saucepan. Carefully pour the clear butter into another saucepan, leaving behind the milky solids. Pour 2–3 tbsp of the clarified butter into a warmed, small jug and set aside.

To the rest of the clarified butter in the pan, add the mace, cayenne and bay leaf. Simmer very gently for 2 minutes. Discard the bay leaf, then add the cooked, peeled Shrimps and a squeeze of lemon juice. Stir for a couple of minutes, season with a little salt and white pepper, and remove from the heat.

Spoon the Shrimps and butter into two ramekins or small jars, pour on the reserved clarified butter to cover in a thin layer and put into the fridge to set.

Remove the potted Shrimp from the fridge 20 minutes or so before you want to serve them. Spread on to hot brown toast.

Spicy Prawn soup

A rich, spicy soup with lots of Asian flavours. You can alter the fish/shellfish content according to what you have managed to gather or buy.

Serves 4

- 1 tbsp sunflower oil
- 1 onion, peeled and finely chopped
- 1 thumb of fresh root ginger, peeled and grated
- 3 fat garlic cloves, peeled and finely chopped
- 1 small, hot red chilli, deseeded and finely chopped
- 2 lemongrass stalks, tough outer layers removed, finely sliced
- 400ml fish stock (see p.228)
- 400ml tin coconut milk
- 150g dried egg noodles, broken up a bit
- 500g cooked, shelled Prawns – or a combination of Prawns and just-cooked Mussels, Clams, Cockles, or other seafood
- Soy sauce, to taste
- Juice of 1–2 limes, to taste, plus lime wedges to serve
- 1 heaped tbsp chopped coriander

Heat the oil in a large saucepan over a medium heat, then add the onion, ginger, garlic, chilli and lemongrass. Sweat gently, stirring from time to time, for 5 minutes or so, until the onion is soft and golden.

Add the stock, bring to a simmer and cook gently for 10 minutes. Add the coconut milk, stir well and bring back to a simmer. Drop in the egg noodles and simmer until they're done – about 3 minutes.

Add the Prawns and any other cooked shellfish and simmer for just 1 minute to heat through. Taste the soup and season with the soy and lime juice.

Ladle the soup into warmed bowls and serve straight away, scattered with the coriander and accompanied by lime wedges.

Prawn and courgette salad
with a chilli dressing

A very simple dish, with just a hint of chilli and garlic in the dressing to enhance the sweetness of the Prawns. If you are using courgettes, make sure they are really small. Fully grown raw courgettes are inedible, as a friend of mine once discovered when he found one impersonating a cucumber in his cheese sandwich.

Serves 2

1 or 2 small courgettes or
  ½ cucumber
2 large handfuls of mixed salad
  leaves
150g cooked, shelled Prawns
1 tbsp roughly chopped mint leaves

For the dressing
½ red chilli, deseeded and
  finely chopped
½ clove garlic, peeled and crushed
A squeeze of lemon juice
3 tbsp olive oil
A pinch of sugar
Sea salt and freshly ground black
  pepper

First make the dressing: put all the ingredients into a small jar. Put on the lid and shake well to emulsify. Taste and adjust the seasoning, adding a little more lemon juice if you like.

Using a swivel potato peeler, slice the young courgette(s) or cucumber into fine discs or long ribbons.

Divide the salad leaves between two individual bowls and toss with a little of the dressing. Scatter over the courgette, then arrange the Prawns on top. Trickle a bit more dressing over the salad (you may not need all of it) and finish with a sprinkling of mint.

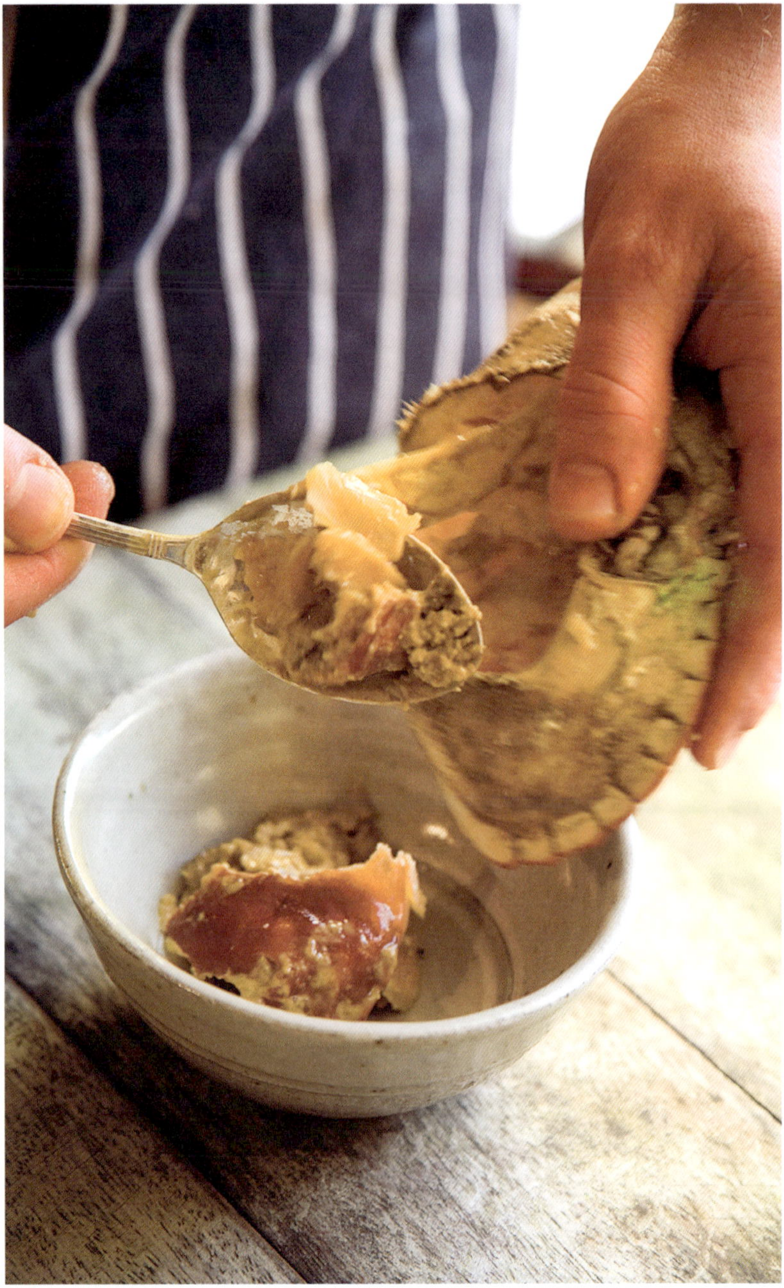

Brown Crab mousse
with Carragheen

It is most satisfying to bring together two of our best forage ingredients in one dish, especially two that are likely to be found on the same day. My best spot for Crabs and Lobsters is also covered in Carragheen, making the excursion doubly worthwhile. The recipe calls for Crab meat, which could be Brown Crab, Spider Crab or Velvet Swimming Crab. Of course there is no reason why Lobster, Prawns or Shrimps could not be used instead.

Serves 6

150g Crab meat
Grated zest and juice of ½ lemon
1 tbsp finely chopped parsley, or a mixture of parsley and dill
Sea salt and freshly ground black pepper
25g dried or 80g fresh Carragheen, well rinsed
150ml double cream
150ml semi-skimmed milk
A few drops of Tabasco
A small pinch of chilli flakes

In a small bowl, mix together the Crab meat, lemon zest, lemon juice and parsley. Season with salt and pepper, being fairly generous with the salt. If you are using dried Carragheen, soak it in cold water for 20 minutes.

Pour 500ml water into a saucepan and add the Carragheen. Bring to the boil, lower the heat and simmer gently for 25 minutes, stirring occasionally. In a separate pan, warm the cream and milk with the Tabasco and chilli flakes.

Strain the hot Carragheen mixture through a double layer of muslin directly into the pan of warm creamy milk, whisking all the time. To do this effectively, don a pair of rubber gloves, gather the muslin and squeeze it to extract as much setting agent as possible.

Quickly stir in the Crab meat mixture, then spoon into ramekins or similar moulds. Cover and refrigerate until set.

Turn out the mousses on to individual plates and serve with a green salad and buttered sourdough toast.

Crab bisque
made with Shore Crabs

It is astonishing that something as humble as half a bucketful of Shore Crabs can transform itself into something quite so sophisticated as this sublime soup.

Serves 8

- 1kg Shore Crabs or other shellfish
- A knob of butter
- 1 tbsp olive oil
- 1 large onion, peeled and finely chopped
- 1 large fennel bulb, finely chopped
- 3 celery sticks, finely chopped
- 2 garlic cloves, peeled and crushed
- 1 bay leaf
- 1 tsp paprika
- A pinch of cayenne pepper
- ½ glass of white wine
- 250g skinned, deseeded and chopped ripe tomatoes (prepared weight), or tinned chopped tomatoes
- A small glass of cider brandy
- 1.75 litres fish stock (see p.228)
- A large sprig of tarragon
- 50ml double cream
- 1 tbsp lemon juice
- Sea salt and freshly ground black pepper

Place the Crabs in a plastic bag in the freezer for an hour. Bring a large pan of well-salted water to the boil (allow 10g salt per litre of water). Drop the Crabs into the boiling water, bring back to the boil and cook for 2 minutes. Remove the Crabs and let them cool a little, then chop them roughly with a large, heavy knife.

Melt the butter with the olive oil in a large heavy-based pan over a medium-low heat. Add the onion, fennel, celery, garlic and bay leaf. Sauté gently, without browning, for about 5 minutes until the vegetables are softened. Add the paprika and cayenne and cook for another minute.

Add the wine, tomatoes and Crab, and give the mixture a good stir. Cook for a further 5 minutes, then pour in the brandy and bring to a simmer. Take off the heat and ignite the brandy. When the flame dies down, add the stock and tarragon. Return to the heat, bring to a low simmer and cook gently for 25–30 minutes.

In small batches, strain the soup through a conical strainer into a bowl, pushing as much liquid and vegetables through as you can. Then, pass the soup through a fine strainer into a clean pan and return to the heat. Bring to a simmer and stir in the cream and lemon juice. Season with salt and pepper to taste. Serve in warmed bowls, with some good bread.

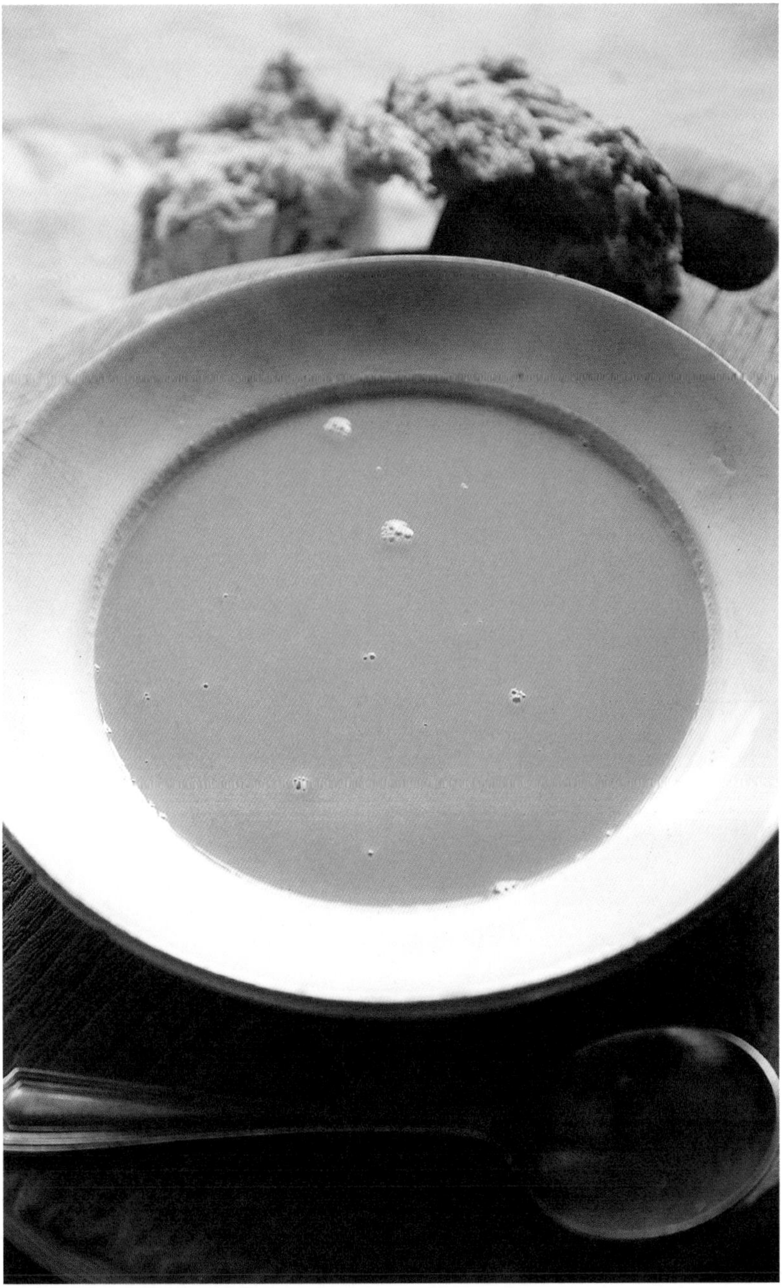

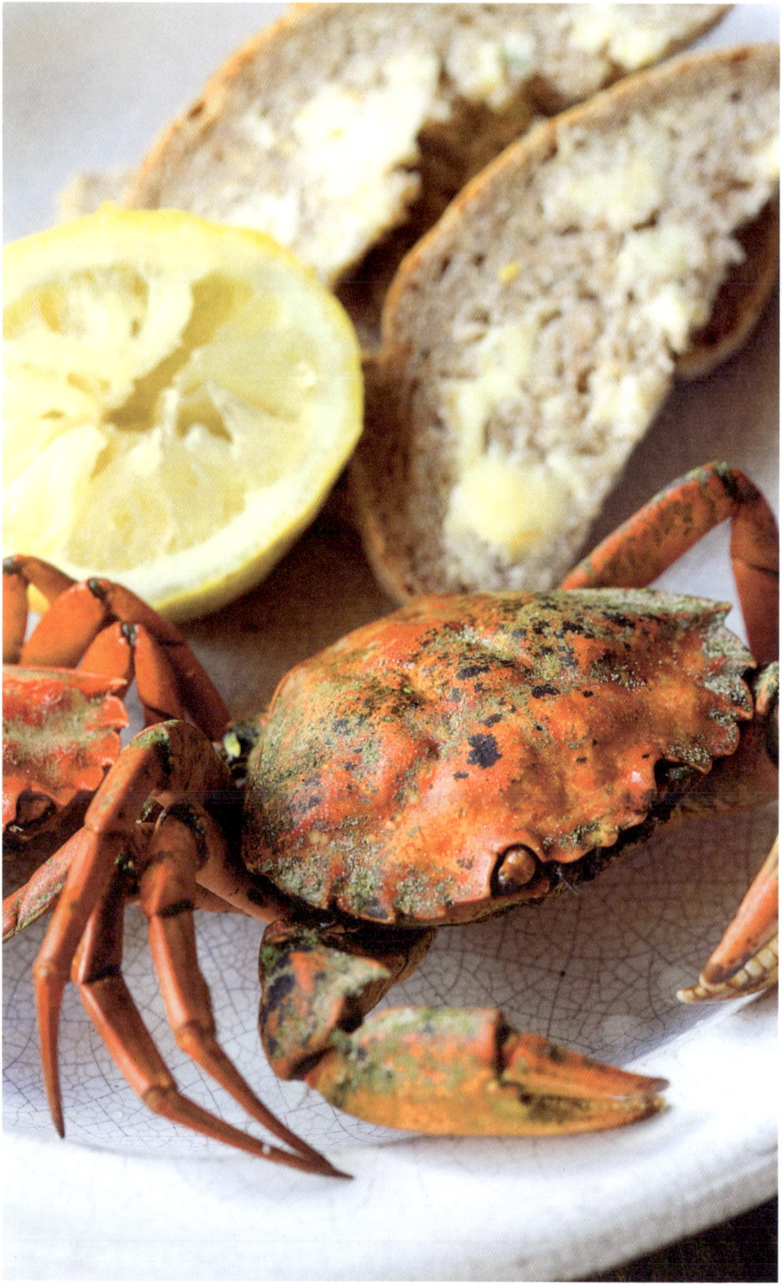

Velvet Swimming Crab
with garlic mayonnaise

This is a rather messy and time-consuming start to a dinner party but one which is sure to break the ice. Don't forget to pick the meat out of the shell from above the legs. The lovely, garlicky mayonnaise is the perfect partner.

Serves 4

A dozen or so Velvet Swimming Crabs (allow 1 or 2 per person, depending on their size)
Salt

For the garlic mayonnaise

2 garlic cloves, peeled and crushed to a paste with a little salt
2 small anchovy fillets (optional)
2 very fresh egg yolks
1 heaped tsp English mustard
1 tbsp cider vinegar or lemon juice
A small pinch of sugar
Sea salt and freshly ground black pepper
100ml olive oil
200ml groundnut oil

To serve

Brown bread
Unsalted butter
Lemon wedges

Put the Crabs into the freezer for half an hour – small crustaceans like these perish quickly in boiling water so this is long enough to make them insensible.

Meanwhile, make the garlic mayonnaise: in a bowl, mash the garlic with the anchovies, if using, then mix in the egg yolks, mustard, vinegar, sugar and seasoning. Start adding the oils, a few drops at a time, whisking constantly, until the mayonnaise starts to emulsify. Then add the rest in a thin stream, beating well all the time. (Or, put everything except the oils into a food processor and process until smooth, then with the motor running, add the oils slowly through the funnel until you have a thick, glossy mayonnaise.) Adjust the seasoning and, if the mayonnaise seems too thick, thin it slightly with a little warm water. Cover and chill until needed.

Bring a large pan of well-salted water to the boil (allow 10g salt per litre of water). Drop the Crabs into the boiling water and cook them for 5 minutes. Remove the Crabs and allow to cool.

Serve the Crabs with thinly sliced brown bread and butter, lemon wedges and garlicky mayonnaise.

Devilled Crab cakes
with herby mayonnaise

These make a great starter, or you could shape smaller ones to serve as canapés. If you find some wild sorrel, you can chop a few leaves very finely and use it instead of the lemon zest; it would be good in the herby mayo too.

Serves 4 as a starter; makes 10–12 canapés

For the Crab cakes
20g unsalted butter
2 shallots, peeled and finely chopped
2 tbsp very finely chopped celery
1 egg yolk
1 tbsp soured cream
½ tsp English mustard powder
½ tsp Worcestershire sauce
½ tsp cayenne pepper
1 tbsp finely chopped chives
Finely grated zest of 1 small lemon (or some finely chopped sorrel)
Freshly ground black pepper
¾ tsp salt
About 120g fresh white breadcrumbs
250–300g Crab meat, picked over
clarified or unsalted butter, for shallow-frying
Lemon wedges, to serve

For the herby mayonnaise
4 tbsp good mayonnaise
2 tbsp soured cream
A squeeze of lemon juice
Freshly ground black pepper
1 tbsp finely chopped chives (or finely chopped sorrel)

First make the herby mayonnaise: whisk all of the ingredients together, spoon into a bowl, cover and refrigerate until needed.

For the Crab cakes, melt the 20g butter in a small frying pan over a low heat, add the shallots and celery, and sauté gently until softened, about 8 minutes. Leave to cool.

Put the egg yolk, soured cream, mustard powder, Worcestershire sauce, cayenne, chives, lemon zest, a few grinds of black pepper and the salt into a large bowl and whisk together until evenly combined. Stir in the shallots and celery, together with 2 tbsp of the breadcrumbs.

Gently stir in the Crab meat, then form the mixture into 4 cakes, about 5cm in diameter. Spread the rest of the breadcrumbs out on a plate and coat each Crab cake generously. Place on a tray, cover loosely and refrigerate for an hour, or up to a day.

Melt the butter in a frying pan and fry the Crab cakes for 3–4 minutes on each side. Drain on kitchen paper and serve hot, with the mayonnaise and lemon wedges.

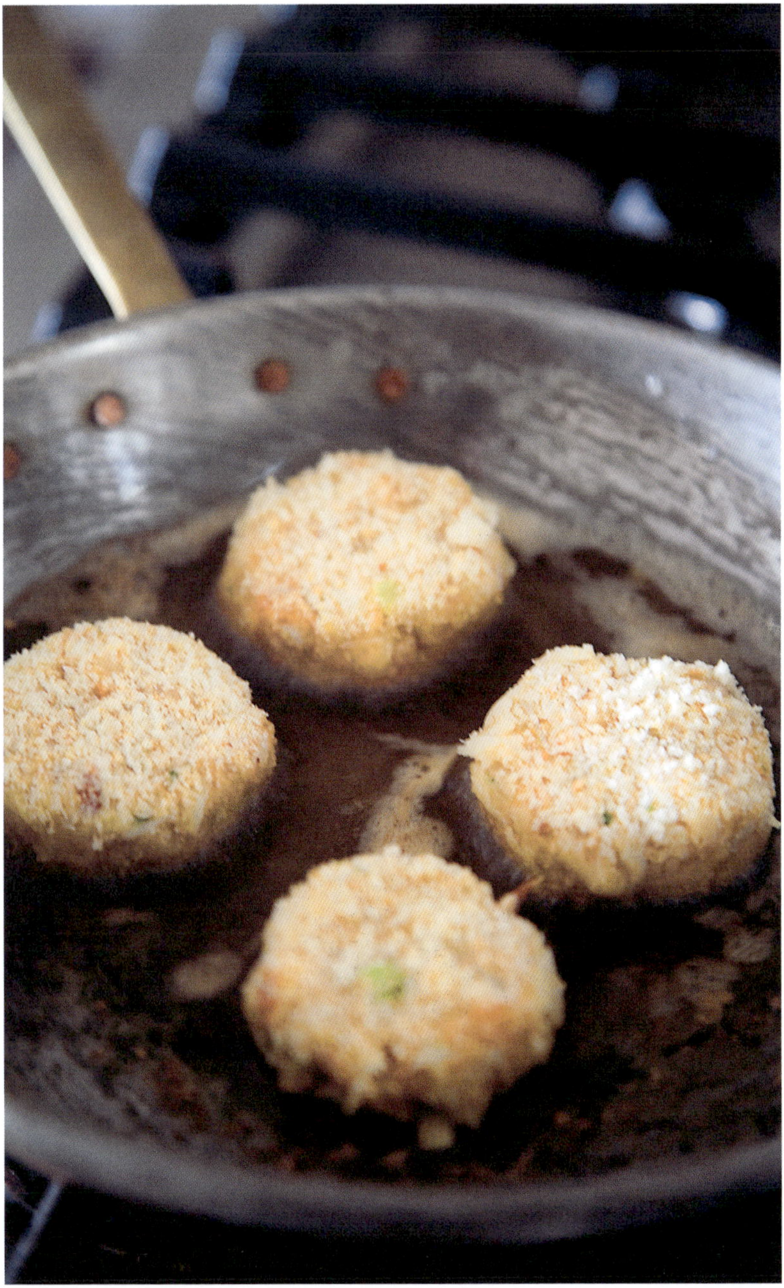

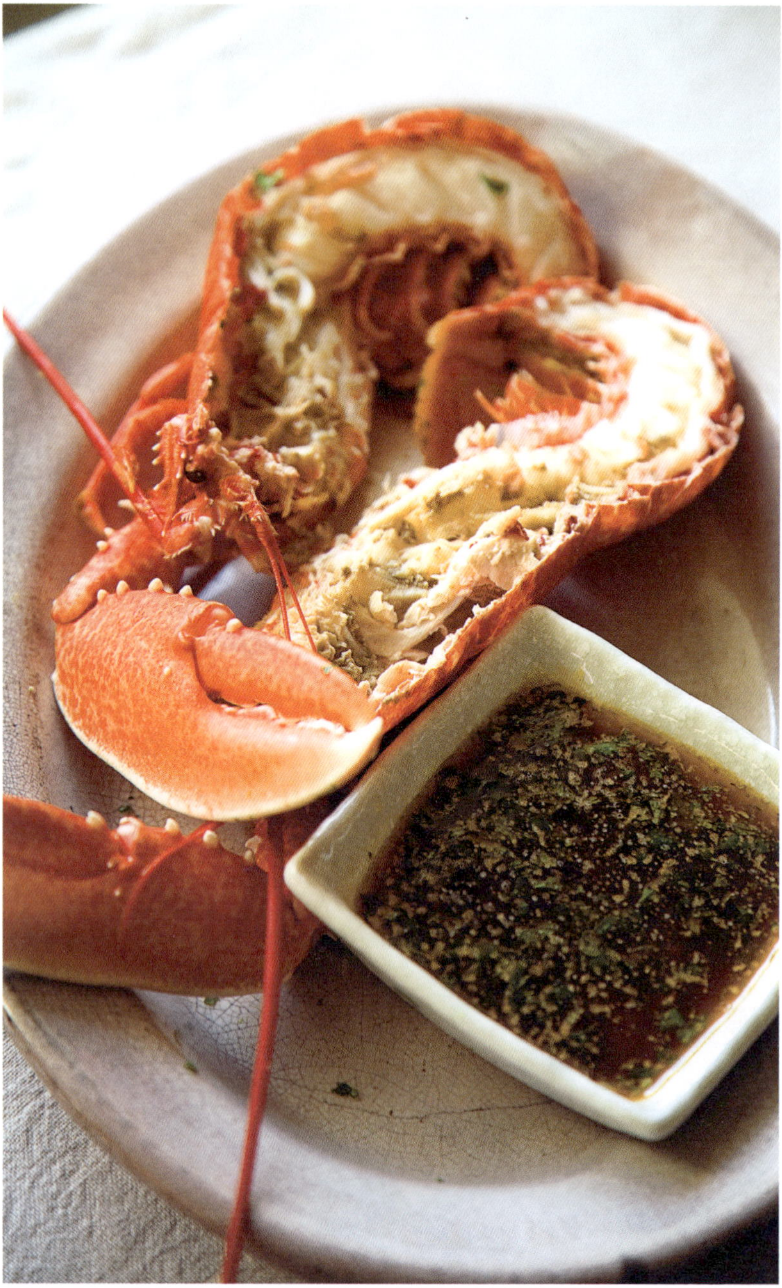

Lobster with charmoula butter

If you have reached the 'ninth dan' of foraging and caught your own Lobster, you will want to enjoy it at its very best. I do not think that the smoky, herby flavours of this North African sauce will disappoint.

Serves 4 as a starter, 2 as a main course

2 live Lobsters
salt

For the charmoula
90g unsalted butter
2 garlic cloves, peeled and finely chopped
2½ tbsp finely chopped coriander leaves
1½ tbsp finely chopped parsley
2 tsp lemon juice
A few gratings of lemon zest
A pinch of chilli flakes
½ tsp ground cumin
¼ tsp hot smoked Spanish paprika
Sea salt

Do follow the advice given on pp.142–3 for the gentle dispatch of Lobsters.

Bring a large pan of sea water or well-salted fresh water to the boil (allow 10g salt per litre of water) and drop the Lobsters into it. Cover, return to the boil and then remove the lid. From the moment the water returns to the boil, boil steadily and time the cooking as follows: allow 10 minutes for a 500g Lobster, 15 minutes for one weighing 750g, and an extra 5 minutes for every 500g after that. Remove the Lobsters from the pan and allow them to cool a little until comfortable to handle.

While the Lobsters are cooling, make the charmoula. Melt the butter in a small pan over a medium heat. Add the garlic and let it bubble very softly for a minute. Stir in the rest of the ingredients, season with a little salt and divide between individual serving bowls.

To divide the Lobsters in two, you will need a chopping board and a large, heavy knife. Lay one belly-side down on a board, its legs splayed out. Steadying the Lobster with one hand, place your knife in the centre of its head, with the blade facing the Lobster's nose and press down hard until the knife meets the board and the Lobster's top half is split down the middle. Swivel the knife around and repeat the process in the opposite direction, splitting the Lobster from middle to tail.

Arrange the lobster halves on plates and serve with the charmoula.

Fish stock

Several of the recipes in this book call for a fish stock, so I thought it worth including instructions for making this indispensable ingredient. I must confess to being a bit of a stock bore. I will wag a reproachful finger at anyone who unwisely confesses to throwing out a chicken carcass without making a stock from it first, and then encourage them to live a better life by relating interesting anecdotes about my past stock-making triumphs. Making something superb out of what would otherwise be discarded is so satisfying I cannot imagine why anyone would forgo the pleasure. My obsession has now reached the point where I buy fish for its stock-making potential alone – the flesh is just a bonus.

Creating a stock is easy, and with fish stock it is also quick. Very fishy fish, such as herrings, do not work well. White fish make the best and unfishiest stocks, followed by salmon and trout which are a bit fishier. Flatfish (like dabs) are my favourite – the first-class stock they produce being a suitable compensation for the sometimes pitiful amount of flesh they contain. The strong flavours of salmon and trout are a challenge, but these can be removed by frying all the bits in a hard-setting vegetable fat before adding to the stockpot. The only problem with this is that it can make the stock a little cloudier than normal.

It is important that the fish bits you use are really fresh as any existing off-flavours will tend to be accentuated. You can use the head, tail, bones and skin of the fish, but the gills impart a bitter flavour to the stock so they will need to be removed (use wire-cutters – they are the only things that work!). The line of blood underneath the spine must be stripped out and any remaining blood washed away in cold water.

About half an hour is long enough to produce a good fish stock – much longer and the bones will begin to impart a 'chalky' flavour and the fish will start to break down chemically to produce some unwelcome fishy odours.

Makes about 1.5–2 litres
2kg fish heads, tails, bones and skin, all rinsed
2 medium onions, peeled and finely chopped
2 carrots, peeled and finely chopped
4 celery sticks, finely chopped
4 bay leaves

Put all the ingredients into a large pan, press down and add enough water to cover by about 2cm water. Bring to a low simmer and cook for about 30 minutes. Do not stir as this will cloud the stock, though you can press down the ingredients with a potato masher if you like.

Strain the stock into a bowl through a large sieve lined with a double layer of muslin. The stock can be used immediately, though it may be worth allowing the oil to rise to the surface so that it can be skimmed off. Alternatively, cool and then place in the fridge. The cooled stock will set to a jelly consistency and any fat can be scraped off the surface easily.

The fish stock will keep for about 2 days in the fridge, or it can be frozen.

Shellfish stock

A major variation on this stock, and one which is more in the spirit of this book, is to use the shells, legs and other tough bits of Crabs, Lobsters, Prawns and Shrimps instead of, or as well as, ordinary fish bones and heads. This stock is quite superb in almost any stewy or saucy fish dish and is the basis of all bisques. You will need at least a kilo of trimmings but you can always stockpile them in the freezer until you have enough. Don't use the bigger bits such as claws and Brown Crab shells as they impart little flavour and can make everything taste rather chalky. All the rest should be crushed, in a plastic bag, with a rolling pin.

The flavour can be enhanced enormously by first frying the crushed trimmings in butter for 2–3 minutes. Alternatively, spread them in a large roasting tray and roast at 200°C/Gas Mark 6 for no more than 10 minutes. (I baked some for 45 minutes once and the flavour of burnt Spider Crab remains with me to this day.)

Finally a plea. We are all used to removing the cooking water of boiled carrots and potatoes by straining them in a sieve. Do not, as I once did, make the novice stock-maker's mistake of straining the stock into the sink and keeping the cooked bones – it will result in a wail of despair and some unfortunate language.

Useful Things

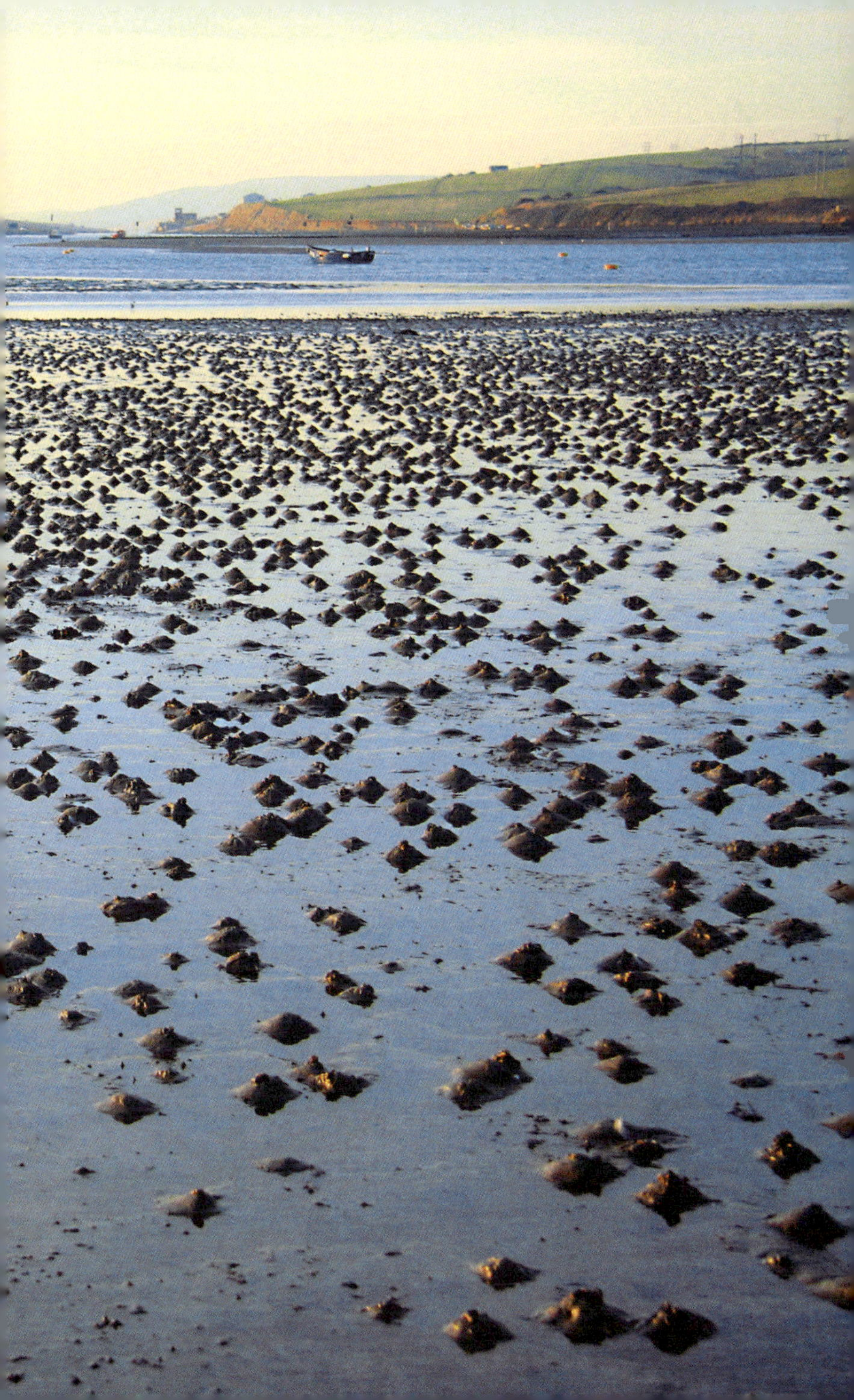

Directory

Conservation

The main government conservation bodies of the UK are:

Natural England
0114 241 8920
www.naturalengland.org.uk

Scottish Natural Heritage
01463 725000
www.snh.org.uk

Council for Nature Conservation and the Countryside
028 9054 3076
www.cnccni.gov.uk

Countryside Council for Wales
0845 130 6229
www.ccw.gov.uk

These organisations come under one unifying body:

Joint Nature Conservation Committee (JNCC)
01733 562626
www.jncc.gov.uk

Access to the countryside

Access and several other matters of interest to the forager come under:

Department for Environment, Food and Rural Affairs (DEFRA)
Defra
0845 933 55 77
www.defra.gov.uk

The Ramblers' Association has been tirelessly defending and extending access to the countryside for well over 100 years.

The Ramblers' Association
020 7339 8500
www.ramblers.org.uk

Major coastal landowners

Crown Estate
020 7851 5000
www.thecrownestate.co.uk

National Trust
0844 800 1895
www.nationaltrust.org.uk/main

National Trust for Scotland
0844 493 2100
www.nts.org.uk/home

In England and Wales byelaws and other matters governing the collection of shellfish out to the six-mile limit (far enough for us) are governed by twelve Sea Fisheries Committees. Their contact details can all be found at:

The Association of Sea Fisheries Committees
www.asfc.org.uk

Safety issues

Food Standards Agency
Offices in England, Scotland and Wales
020 7276 8829
www.food.gov.uk

Met Office
www.metoffice.gov.uk/weather/marine/inshore_forecast

As well as general and inshore weather forecasts, the BBC has a first-class online tide-forecasting service. Hundreds of locations are covered giving detailed tidal prediction with graphs for 7 days.

BBC
www.bbc.co.uk

Organisations that take an interest in the conservation, study and production of shellfish:

Centre for Environment, Fisheries and Aquaculture Science
www.cefas.co.uk

Shellfish Association of Great Britain
020 7283 8305
www.shellfish.org.uk

Marine Stewardship Council
www.msc.org

Fishonline
www.fishonline.org

Marine Conservation Society
www.mcsuk.org

Pots and nets

Coastal Nets Limited
01308 427885
www.coastalnets.co.uk

Medley Pots
01405 764465
www.medleypots.com

Useful Reference Books

Philip's Guide to Seashores and Shallow Seas of Britain and Europe
by Andrew C. Campbell
(Philip's Reference, 2005)

The Wild Flowers of Britain and Ireland: A New Guide to Our Wild Flowers
by Marjorie Blamey, Richard Fitter and Alastair Fitter
(Tandem, 2003)

The Wild Flower Key: How to identify wild plants, trees and shrubs in Britain and Ireland (Revised Edition)
by Francis Rose and Clare O'Reilly
(Frederick Warne Publishers, 2006)

The River Cottage Mushroom Handbook
by John Wright
(Bloomsbury, 2007)

The River Cottage Fish Book
by Hugh Fearnley-Whittingstall and Nick Fisher
(Bloomsbury, 2007)

North Atlantic Seafood
by Alan Davidson
(Macmillan, 1979)

Acknowledgments

I have had to get to the bottom of quite a few mysteries in writing this book: Why does the Laver I collect seem to move around the shore? (It is two different species.) Should I stop gathering food plants from right-to-roam land? (Yes, it is trespass.) Do I really need a licence to put out my lobster pot? (No, but I might elsewhere.)

These questions and a thousand others were answered largely by a small army of experts and enthusiasts who have been kind enough to receive my many enquiries with patience. Not least among these were a number of fishermen.

Fishermen come in two varieties: those that won't talk and those that won't stop. It is in the last, blessed, category that the following fine fellows belong:

Richard Lunt, without whom the chapters on crabs and lobsters would hardly have been possible. I have spent many hours with Richard by the sea and he has been endlessly generous with his incomparable knowledge. Peter Talbot-Elsden and Andy Horton shared their passion for the humble, and very tasty, Brown Shrimp. David Wiscombe took time out from his bees to show me the finer points of prawn netting. Rod and James Barr, of whose net-making abilities and anecdote-telling I stand in awe. Dave and Sue from Fowey Sea Farms, who not only revealed the mystery of mussels, but also let me into an amazing secret. Dave from the Gower, whose courage with an angry crab I will forever be unable to match. Kelvin Moore, who has taught me much over the years about Clams in general and that most elusive of prey, the Razor Clam, in particular. Also Troy Matthews, Michael 'Luggs' Baber, George Hurst, Graham Jolliff and many others.

Many professionals have also helped me:

The chapters on bivalve molluscs would have been much the poorer but for the massive and unstinting support of Dave Palmer from Cefas. Dr. Tom Pickerell from the Shellfish Association of Great Britain has cheerfully answered all my questions and offered invaluable advice throughout. I have spoken to people at nearly all twelve Sea Fisheries Committees and received from them an enormous amount of graciously given assistance. Tim Robbins from Devon has suffered my questioning more than most, so particular thanks go to him. Anita Carter from JNCC helped me determine the conservation status of the species mentioned here.

Many members of staff from Defra have been enormously helpful regarding the laws of foraging, as have those from the Ramblers' Association and Natural England. David Harris from Crown Estate helped me get to grips with property law as it relates to the coast. Liz Thompson solved many legal puzzles for me.

Dr Carl Meyer from the Hawaii Institute of Marine Biology (no less) clarified the strange life choices made by Spider Crabs. Professor Juliette Brodie of the Natural History Museum was particularly helpful in sorting out those pesky Laver species. Nigel Emery from Weymouth's Port Health Authority introduced me to the complexities of shellfish safety, and I also received much assistance on this matter from the Food Standards Agency. The UK Hydrographic Office kept me within my depth regarding tides and currents.

I am only sorry that I have had to refer to many of the above by their organisation and not by name. There were many more people who helped me with this book and I regret not being able to mention them individually. My profound thanks to all.

The River Cottage food editors Debora Robertson and Nikki Duffy created most of the recipes in this book. Thank you both for your sparkling professionalism.

Thanks to Colin Campbell for annoying me, yet again, with his consummate photographic skills. I am also grateful to Bryan Johnson for so splendidly cooking most of the recipes.

The team at Bloomsbury has been ever encouraging, ever helpful. I am indebted to Richard Atkinson for diligently and diplomatically trimming the rough edges from my manuscript while letting me keep most of my jokes; to Will Webb for taking my raw materials and fashioning them into something we can be proud of and also for teaching me how Anglo-Saxon my aesthetics are; to Janet Illsley for her light touch in ironing out the many wrinkles that would have otherwise left this book looking unloved; but most of all to Natalie Hunt who, with her customary charm and professionalism, has kept the whole project (and me) together and on time.

Thanks are also due to Gordon Wise for leading this stranger in a strange land, to Rob Love for being the eternal enthusiast and to Antony Topping for driving this project forward.

My thanks go, as always, to Hugh – for writing such a lovely introduction, for trusting me yet again with a large project and for his tireless work in keeping us all firmly rooted in our own back yards.

Finally, a special thanks to my daughters Florence and Lily and my wife Diane for accompanying me on so very many seaside jaunts, not always in good weather, and for putting up with the interesting smells that came from the kitchen.

Index

Page numbers in *italic* refer to the illustrations

Abra alba 127
  A. cadabra 127
  A. nitida 127
access, right of 35–6
Agaricus arvensis 84
  A. bernardii 84
  A. campestris 84
  A. xanthodermus 84
Alexanders 40, *46*, 47, *56*, 57–9, *59*
  Alexanders and rhubarb jam 180, *181*
  Alexanders liqueur *182*, 183
  candy Alexanders 172, *173*
  steamed Alexanders *170*, 171
algal blooms 109, 111
almanacs, tide 28
Amanita phalloides 84
anemone, snakeslock 31
angelica 58
arrabbiata sauce 204–5
ASP (amnesic shellfish poisoning) 109
Atriplex 77–8, *77*–8
  A. glabriuscula 77–8, *77*
  A. portulacoides 72, *73*, 78
  A. prostrata 77–8, *78*

Babington's Orache 77–8, *77*
bacon: Hangtown fry 212, *213*
  laverbread with Clams and bacon on toast *192*, 193
bacteria: on seaweeds 89
  in shellfish 108, 111
bait, pots 23
basking shark 30
beaches: definition 35
  ownership 36
berries, Sea Buckthorn 79–81, *80*
Beta vulgaris maritima 69–71, *70*–*1*
bisque, Crab 220, *221*
bittersweet *31*
bivalves 108
blanching Sea Kale 50, *51*
Blewit, Field 84
boots 29
Brassica oleracea 52–3, *53*
Brown Crab *152*, 153–4, *154*
  Brown Crab mousse with Carragheen 219
  catching 20, 153–4, *154*
  safety 30–1
Brown Shrimp 42, *144*, 145–6
  Potted Shrimp *214*, 215

buckets 15, 30
Buckthorn *see* Sea Buckthorn
buoys, marking pots 23
butter: garlic butter *208*, 209
  Lobster with charmoula butter *226*, 227
by-catch, prawn fishing 149
byelaws 37, 40, 42
byssal threads, Mussels *117*, 118, 119, 136

Cabbage, Wild *13*, 47, 52–3, *53*
cabbage family 47
Cakile maritima 54–5, *55*
Calvatia gigantea 84
Cancer pagurus 152, 153–4, *154*
candy Alexanders 172, *173*
Carcinus maenas 155–6, *155*-*6*
Carpet Shell Clam 125
Carragheen 88, 89, 95–7, *96*, 132
  Brown Crab mousse with Carragheen 219
  Seaweed and elderflower panna cotta 194, *195*
carrot family 47
celery 57
Cerastoderma edule 112, 113–15, *114*
charmoula butter, Lobster with *226*, 227
chemical pollution, shellfish 109
chillies: Mussels with chilli and tomato 199
  Prawn and courgette salad with a chilli dressing 217
  spicy Prawn soup 216
Chlorophyta 89, 91
Chondrus crispus 95–7
chorizo: Cockles with chorizo 196, *197*
  stuffed Hard Shell Clams *200*, 201
cider Mussels, West Country 198
Clams 108, *124*, 125–7
  Clam arancini with arrabbiata sauce 204–5
  laverbread with Clams and bacon on toast *192*, 193
  steamed Clams with sausage 202, *203*
  stuffed Hard Shell Clams *200*, 201
  see also individual species
cleaning shellfish 111
clothing 29
Cockle 108, 111, *112*, 113–15, *114*
  Cockles with chorizo 196, *197*
  laverbread with Clams and bacon on toast *192*, 193
collapsible pots *21*
'colonialism, environmental' 12
conservation 11–13, 39–40
containers 15
courgettes: Prawn and courgette salad with a chilli dressing 217
crab apples: Sea Buckthorn and crab apple jam 179, *179*
crab hooks 19, *19*

236 EDIBLE SEASHORE

Crabs: catching 20–3, 153–4, *154*, 155–6, 157–9
    Devilled Crab cakes with herb mayonnaise 224, *225*
    holding 31
    killing 142–3
    safety 30
    see also individual species
Crambe crambe 51
    C. maritima 48, 49–51, *51*
Crangon crangon 144, 145–6
Crassostrea gigas 121, 122–3, *122*
crayfish 11
creels, side entry 20, *22*
Crepidula fornicata 137–9, *139*
crisps, Kelp 184, *185*
crispy seaweed and toasted sesame seeds 186, *187*
Crithmum maritimum 60, 61–3, *62–3*
Cross Cut Carpet Shell *124*, 126
CROW Act 39
Crown Estate 36, 39, 118, 122
crustaceans 140–65
    killing 142–3
    regulations 142
    several orders 41–2
    storing 142
    see also individual species
Culpeper, Nicholas 53, 57, 68, 72
currents, in sea 29

'dead man's fingers' 159, 162
Death Cap 84
Desmarestia 88
Devilled Crab cakes with herb mayonnaise 224, *225*
Diplotaxis tenuifolia 54–5, *55*
Dog Whelk 108, 132, 135–6, *136*
drop nets 19, *19*, 148
DSP (diarrhoetic shellfish poisoning) 109
Dulse 88, 89, *92*, 93–4
    Clam arancini with arrabbiata sauce 204–5
    Dulse and smoked fish tart 190–1, *191*
    Dulse potato cakes 189

E. coli 108
eggs: Hangtown fry 212, *213*
    Marsh Samphire with poached eggs *174*, 175
elderflowers: Seaweed and elderflower panna cotta 194, *195*
Ensis americanus 130
    E. arcuatus 128
    E. ensis 128
    E. siliqua 128
'environmental colonialism' 12
Environmental Health Authorities 110
equipment: catching shellfish 15–23
    safety 29–30
EU regulations 42

Fairy Ring Champignons 84, *85*
Fennel 47, 64–5, *65*
    Crab bisque made with Shore Crabs 220, *221*
    Oyster risotto with deep-fried Gutweed 210–11, *211*
Field Blewit 84
fish, safety 30, 31
fish stock 228–9
fishing: by-catch 149
    fisheries 41–2
    legislation 39
flowering plants 44–85
Foeniculum vulgare 64–5, *65*
food poisoning, shellfish and 108–11
Food Standards Agency 110
footpaths 36
foreshore: definition 35
    ownership 36
    right of access 36
freezers, killing crustaceans 142–3
Frosted Orache 78, *78*
Fucus serratus 102
fungi 84, *85*
    right to collect 37–9

Galathea squamifera 150, *151*
garlic: Velvet Swimming Crab with garlic mayonnaise *222*, 223
    Winkles with garlic butter *208*, 209
gastro-enteritis 108–9
Gerard, John 49, 68
ghost pots 23
Giant Puffball 84
Glasswort *see* Marsh Samphire
glutamic acid 99, 105
Goosefoot family 47, 75, 78
gremolata, Razor Clams with 206, *206*
Grigson, Jane 52
Gutweed 89, 90–1, *91*
    crispy seaweed and toasted sesame seeds 186, *187*
    Oyster risotto with deep-fried Gutweed 210–11, *211*

Hangtown fry 212, *213*
Hard Shell Clam *124*, 126
    stuffed Hard Shell Clams *200*, 201
heavy metal pollution, shellfish 109
hemlock water-dropwort 26, *31*, 59
herby mayonnaise 224
Hippophae rhamnoides 79–81, *80*
Homarus gammarus 163–5, *164*
hoop nets 19, *19*
Horse Mushroom 84
hybrid orders, fisheries 41
Hygrocybe 84

inkwell pots 20
Inshore Fisheries and Conservation Authorities 42

jam: Alexanders and rhubarb jam 180, *181*
    Sea Buckthorn and crab apple jam 179, *179*
Jeffreys, John Gwyn 135
Jerome, Jerome K. 36–7

Kelp 88, 89, *98*, 99–100
    Kelp crisps 184, *185*
killing crustaceans 142–3
knives 15

Lactarius deliciosus 119
Laminaria digitata 98, 99–100
land ownership 36
Laver 89, 101–5, *103–5*
    laverbread 101, 102
    laverbread with Clams and bacon on toast *192*, 193
legislation 32–43
Lepista saeva 84
Limpets 23, 108, 137–9, *138*
liqueur, Alexanders *182*, 183
Littorina littorea 132–4, *133*
Lobsters 163–5, *164*
    catching 20–3, 163–5
    killing 142, 143
    Lobster with charmoula butter *226*, 227
    regulations 42
    safety 30
    see also Squat Lobster
local authorities, fisheries 41

Mabey, Richard 11
McIntosh, Charles 50
mackerel: Dulse and smoked fish tart 190–1, *191*
Maja squinado 157–9, *158*
Manila Clam *124*, 126
Marasmius oreades 84
Marine Bill (2008) 42
Marsh Samphire 47, 61, *74*, 75–6, *76*
    Marsh Samphire with poached eggs *174*, 175
Mastocarpus stellatus 95–7, *96*
Mayhew, Henry 121, 134
mayonnaise: garlic 223
    herb 224
Mercenaria mercenaria 126
mercury, in shellfish 109
minerals, in seaweeds 89
molluscs 41, 106–39
    see also individual species
Moon, and tides 28
mousse, Brown Crab with Carragheen 219
Munida rugosa 150
mushrooms 47, 84, 119

Mussels 35, 41, 108, 116–19, *117*, *119*
    Mussels with chilli and tomato 199
    West Country cider Mussels 198
Mya arenaria 126–7
Mytilus edulis 116–19, *117*, *119*

National Trust 36, 40
Natural England 40
neap tides 28
Necora puber 160, 161–2
nets: drop nets 19, *19*, 148
    prawn nets 16, *16*, 147–8
    shrimp nets 16–17, *17–18*, 146
Netted Whelk 135
Nicolle, E. 157
noodles: spicy Prawn soup 216
nori 102, 105
Norovirus 109
Northern Ireland, byelaws 40, 42
NSP (neurotoxic shellfish poisoning) 109
Nucella lapillus 135–6, *136*

omelettes: Hangtown fry 212, *213*
Oraches 47, 77–8, *77–8*
ormers 11
Osmundea pinnatifida 94, *94*
Ostrea edulis 119, *120*, 121–3
Oysters 41, 108, 119, *120*, 121–3
    Hangtown fry 212, *213*
    Oyster risotto with deep-fried Gutweed 210–11, *211*

Pacific Oyster 121, 122–3, *122*
pain, killing crustaceans 142–3
Palaemon elegans 147
    P. serratus 147–9, *148*
Palmaria palmata 92, 93–4
Palourde *124*, 126
panna cotta, Seaweed and elderflower 194, *195*
parlour pots 20, *22*, 153, 163
Patella vulgata 137–9, *138*
pea crab 118
Pepper Dulse 94, *94*
Perennial Wall Rocket 54–5, *55*
Periwinkle *see* Winkle
permits 42
Phaeophyta 89
pickled Rock Samphire 178
Pinnotheres pissum 118
plants: conservation legislation 39–40
    flowering plants 44–85
    poisonous plants 31
    right to collect 37–9
    see also individual species
poisons 31
    mushrooms 84

seaweeds 88
pollack: Dulse and smoked fish tart 190–1, *191*
    smoked pollack with Sea Beet *176*, 177
pollution 89, 109
porbeagle shark 30
Porphyra 101–5
    P. dioica 102
    P. leucosticta 102, *103*
    P. linearis 101, *103*
    P. umbilicalis 101, 102, *104*
    P. yezoensis 102
Port Health Authorities 110
potato cakes, Dulse 189
pots 20–3, *21*, *22*
    catching crabs 153, 161–2
    parlour pots 153, 163
    prawn pots 148–9
Potted Shrimp *214*, 215
Pratt, Anne 75
prawn nets 16, *16*, 147–8
prawn pots 20, *21*
Prawn 147–9, *148*
    catching 20, 147–9
    killing 142
    laws 35
    Potted Shrimp *214*, 215
    Prawn and courgette salad with a chilli dressing 217
    spicy Prawn soup 216
private beaches 36
private fisheries 41–2
protein, in seaweeds 89
PSP (paralytic shellfish poisoning) 109
Puffball, Giant 84
Pullet Carpet Shell 126

rakes 15
raw shellfish 111
Razor Clams 41, 125, 128–31, *129*, *131*
    Razor Clams with almost wild gremolata 206, *206*
regulating orders, fisheries 41–2
regulations 32–43
Rhodophyta 89
rhubarb: Alexanders and rhubarb jam 180, *181*
rice: Clam arancini with arrabbiata sauce 204–5
    Oyster risotto with deep-fried Gutweed 210–11, *211*
rights: of access 35–6
    to forage 37–9
    'right to roam' legislation 39
risotto: Clam arancini with arrabbiata sauce 204–5
    Oyster risotto with deep-fried Gutweed 210–11, *211*
Rock Samphire 47, *60*, 61–3, *62–3*
    pickled Rock Samphire 178

Rocket, Wild 47, 54–5, *55*
    Razor Clams with almost wild gremolata 206, *206*
roe, Crab 162
Royal Society for the Prevention of Cruelty to Animals (RSPCA) 143
Rugose Squat Lobster 150

Saccharina latissima 99–100, *100*
safety: eating shellfish 108–11
    foraging 24–31
St George's Mushroom 84
salad, Prawn and courgette 217
Salicornia 74, 75–6, *76*
    S. europaea 75
    S. ramosissima 75
Samphire *see* Marsh Samphire; Rock Samphire
Sand Gaper 15, *124*, 125, 126–7, *127*
Sarcocornia perennis 76
sausage, steamed Clams with 202, *203*
scissors 15
Scotland: collecting Mussels 118
    legislation and regulations 35, 39, 42
    Oysters 122
sea aster 63
Sea Beet 12, 40, 47, 69–71, *70–1*
    smoked pollack with Sea Beet *176*, 177
Sea Buckthorn 47, 79–81, *80*
    Sea Buckthorn and crab apple jam 179, *179*
sea campion 11
Sea Fisheries Committees 41, 42, 142
Sea Holly 47, 66–8, *67*, *68*
Sea Kale 39–40, 47, *48*, 49–51, *51*
Sea Lettuce 89, 91, 93
sea pea 11, 49
Sea Purslane 47, 72, *73*, 78
Sea Rocket 54–5, *55*
sea sandwort 49
sea urchins 11
seaweeds 86–105
    containers 15
    crispy seaweed and toasted sesame seeds 186, *187*
    right to collect 39
    Seaweed and elderflower panna cotta 194, *195*
    see also individual species
serrated wrack 102, *103*
sesame seeds, crispy seaweed and 186, *187*
several orders, fisheries 41
sharks 30
shellfish: cleaning 111
    right to collect 40
    safety 108–11
    shellfish stock 229
    when to eat 111
shore, definition 35

Shore Crab 148, 155–6, *155–6*
    Crab bisque made with Shore Crabs 220, *221*
    killing 142
Shrimp *see* Brown Shrimp
shrimp nets 16–17, *17–18*, 146
side entry creels 20, *22*
Sites of Special Scientific Interest (SSSI) 39–40
slack water 29
Slipper Limpet 23, 137–9, *139*
smoked mackerel: Dulse and smoked fish tart 190–1, *191*
smoked pollack with Sea Beet *176*, 177
Smyrnium olusatrum 56, 57–9, *59*
snakeslock anemone 31
Soft-shelled Clam 126
Solen marginatus 128–31, *129*, *131*
soups: Crab bisque made with Shore Crabs 220, *221*
    spicy Prawn soup 216
spades 15
Spear-leaved Orache 77–8, *78*
Special Areas of Conservation 40
Spider Crab 20, 142, 157–9, *158*
Spisula solida 126
spring tides 28
Squat Lobster 150, *151*
Statutory Instruments 42
stock: fish 228–9
    shellfish 229
sub-tidal zone 35, 36
Sugar Kelp 99–100, *100*
Sun, and tides 28
Surf Clam *124*, 126

Tapes decussatus 126
tart, Dulse and smoked fish 190–1, *191*
Theft Act (1968) 37, 39
Theora cadabra 127
Thyme, Wild *82*, 83
Thymus polytrichus *82*, 83
    T. pulegioides 83
    T. vulgaris 83
tidal ranges 28
tidal streams 29
tides, safety 26–8
toast, laverbread with Clams and bacon *192*, 193
tomatoes: Clam arancini with arrabbiata sauce 204–5
    Crab bisque made with Shore Crabs 220, *221*
    Mussels with chilli and tomato 199
    steamed Clams with sausage 202, *203*
Top Shells 132
torches 29
trawling, by-catch 149
trespassing 36–9
Trough Shells 126
Turner, William 75

Ulva intestinalis 90, *91*
    U. lactuca 91
    U. linza 90, *91*
Umbellifers 59

Velvet Swimming Crab 148, *160*, 161–2
    catching 20
    identifying 156
    safety 30
    Velvet Swimming Crab with garlic mayonnaise *222*, 223
Venerupis phillipinarum 126
    V. senegalensis 126
Venus Clams 126, *127*
    laverbread with Clams and bacon on toast 192, 193
Venus verrucosa 126
viruses, in shellfish 109
vitamins, in seaweeds 89
vodka: Alexanders liqueur 182, *183*

Warty Venus 124, 126
water quality 110
Waxcap 84
weather 26, 28
weever fish 31, 146
Wellington boots 29
Welsh Sea Fisheries Committees 42
West Country cider Mussels 198
Whelks *see* Dog Whelk
whistles 29–30
Wildlife and Countryside Act (1981) 39, 40
Winkle 108, 132–4, *133*
    laws and regulations 35, 40, 42
    Winkles with garlic butter 208, *209*
wrack, serrated 102, *103*

Yellow Stainer mushroom 84

zinc, in shellfish 109

The River Cottage

Sea Fishing Handbook

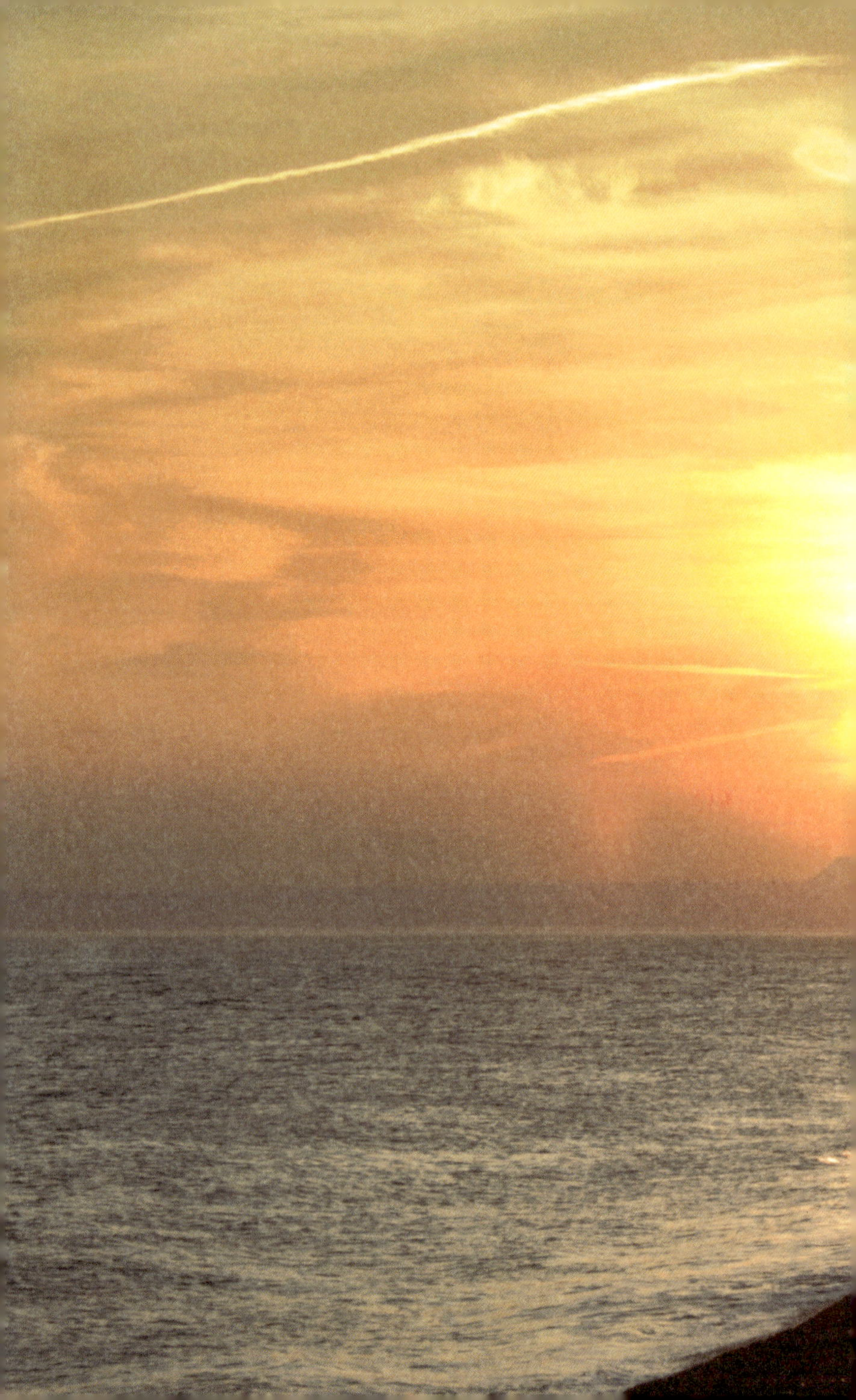

the RIVER COTTAGE

The River Cottage Sea Fishing Handbook

by Nick Fisher

introduced by
Hugh Fearnley-Whittingstall

www.rivercottage.net

BLOOMSBURY
LONDON · NEW DELHI · NEW YORK · SYDNEY

To my own Fisher-family crew, Helen, Rory, Rex, Patrick, Kitty and our dog Spike, without whom there would be no point to my fishing or cooking

First published in Great Britain 2010
This paperback edition published 2012

Text © 2010 by Nick Fisher
Photography © 2010 by Paul Quagliana
Recipe photography © 2010 by Gavin Kingcome
except the following: p.35, p.91, p.105 (bottom), p.108 (top and middle) © Mike Thrussell;
p.92 © Chris Caines; p.98 © Dr Richard Roberts; p.106 (bottom) © Richard 'Tiny' Daw;
p.118 © Matthew Toms; p.147 © John Wright. Cover image © Ed Pavelin/Alamy
Illustrations © 2010 by Toby Atkins

The moral right of the author has been asserted

Bloomsbury Publishing Plc, 50 Bedford Square, London WC1B 3DP
Bloomsbury Publishing, London, New Delhi, New York and Sydney

A CIP catalogue record for this book is available from the British Library

ISBN 978 1 4088 3610 1
10 9 8 7 6 5 4 3 2 1

Project editor: Janet Illsley
Designer: willwebb.co.uk

Printed in China by C&C Offset Printing Co., Ltd.

MIX
Paper from responsible sources
FSC® C008047

www.bloomsbury.com/rivercottage

While every effort has been made to ensure the accuracy of the information contained in this book, in no circumstances can the publisher or the author accept any legal responsibility or liability for any loss or damage (including damage to property and/or personal injury) arising from any error in or omission from the information contained in this book, or from the failure of the reader to properly and accurately follow any instructions contained in the book.

Contents

My Fishing Mission	8
When to Go Fishing	14
Where to Go Fishing	24
Fish You Might Catch	42
Tackle and Kit	110
Bait	148
Fishing Skills	160
Fish Preparation Skills	180
Cooking Fish	200
Directory	249
Index	252

I've been bewitched by the sea for as long as I can remember. Some of my earliest memories are of paddling around in rock pools, bottom in the air and eyes fixed firmly on the salty puddle in front of my nose, marvelling at blood-red sea anemones and pulling up tiny crabs or shrimp in my neon-yellow nylon net. Forty years on, and I'm at it again, ostensibly tutoring my own brood in the fine art of rock-pool fishing, but in reality just as thrilled and beguiled as I was then, and they are now.

Catching my first fish is a moment firmly etched on my memory too, though my pride is tinged with mild embarrassment. I was five. My dad, taking pity on my lack of success, covertly placed a very dead mackerel on the end of my hook. I was fifteen before the scam was revealed. I should have realised long before then that Richmond Park is not one of the world's great sea-fishing destinations. My first 'real' catch was a 2½lb perch I landed on Lough Corrib in Ireland. Mum cooked it. I ate it. It was delicious. From that point on I was as firmly hooked as that perch.

Since then, what was a passion has become a near obsession. I seize every chance to go out fishing on my little boat, *Louisa*. Even when that's not possible, fishing is never far from my mind. I sort my tackle on winter evenings in front of the fire, browse fishing catalogues and even, when I can get away with it, watch fishing programmes on the telly. That's how I first found out about the author of this book. Stuck on dry land, I discovered Channel 4's *Screaming Reels*, presented by one Nick Fisher. Fishy name, fishy guy. And, I was delighted to find, presenter of the best fishing programme ever made.

Nick's approach was about as far away from a damp day on a river bank as you can get. He was wild, irreverent, slightly dangerous, funny. I decided to stalk him, to reel him in with a view to collaborating on some fishy telly. We met. We fished together. He caught a small roach and I caught, er, nothing. The telly didn't quite happen. I'd like to say we enjoyed our fishing too much to let work get in the way, but since meeting more than ten years ago, we have at least managed to write *The River Cottage Fish Book* together. It's a sizeable tome, which did require us to spend rather too much time at our desks. But it also allowed us a fair bit of time on the water – earnestly researching our subject, of course.

Nick's first fishing memory is, characteristically, rather more swashbuckling than mine. There he was, at the end of a rock pier in Millport on the Ayrshire coast, dipping his toy rod into the sea, surrounded by fishermen with years of experience, buckets of succulent bait, bags of expensive equipment. A tug on the line. A wrasse on the end of it. As the tiny kid struggled to land it, the adults swarmed around him, offering to help. But Nick was having none of it. He insisted on landing it himself.

We've come a long way from bent-pin hooks and plastic rods these days. As our wives are only too quick to point out, we both have far too much tackle cluttering up the house. And we're never short of an excuse to acquire more. Yet in our heart of hearts we know it's unnecessary. That what really marks us down as fishermen is not the extent of our kit, but the fact that we still get that same sense of anticipation when we get our tackle together, and the same surge of excitement when we feel a fish tugging on the end of the line, as we did with our first-ever fish.

Now that you've picked up this book, we'll soon be counting you as one of us. Even if you've never fished before, don't be anxious about your beginner status or your lack of experience. We often fish with beginners who catch more than us on their very first time out. As Nick emphasises from the outset, you really don't have to spend much on tackle to get great pleasure, and great results, from your sea fishing. One well-chosen rod-and-reel combo will see you through a multitude of shoreline scenarios. And an hour or two with this book will put you in with a shout of a memorable catch on your first-ever outing.

Whether you're a beginner or an old-timer, there's no one better than Nick to take you fishing – even if it is a virtual fishing trip taken from the comfort of your favourite armchair. Nick is the one to communicate the vital philosophy that every fishing day is a good day, whatever the outcome. His enthusiasm, knowledge and passion shine from these pages. And the message, above all, is that fishing is not an exclusive pastime, far from it. It's the most convivial way to spend time with old friends, or indeed make new ones. When pursued solo, it's inspiring and contemplative, the perfect antidote to the mayhem of modern life. It is also one of the most fun family days out you can imagine.

And to cap it all, you will, if you're lucky, get the most fantastic prize at the end of it. A delicious supper. I once said to Nick, as we bobbed about somewhere off the Dorset coast, 'So much better than golf, isn't it?' 'Yeah,' he said, 'you can't eat a hole in one.' How very true, I thought…

To eat a fish that you've pulled from the sea yourself is a culinary pleasure, surpassed only by that of sharing it with the friends or family you've just been fishing with. And to make a just-caught fish taste delicious is hardly a chore. A flash of heat, a slug of oil, a bit of butter, a few herbs, some garlic, perhaps a splash of wine, is often all that's needed. But in the spirit of far-flung seafaring adventure, we both enjoy exploring other ideas too – thyme and parsley might be replaced by chilli and soy, a classic crisp chip-shop batter one day, pure, clean escabeche the next.

But whatever the recipe, one thing holds true. Fresh sustainably caught fish from British waters is some of the finest in the world. And, in a country where you're never more than 70 miles from the sea, it is accessible to all of us. I hope you'll pack your rod and reel (and perhaps a bucket barbecue and a travelling selection of seasonings) and treat yourself to a day's fishing soon. In fact, just writing this has got me longing to check the tides, and rummage in my tackle box…

Hugh Fearnley-Whittingstall, East Devon, March 2010

My Fishing Mission

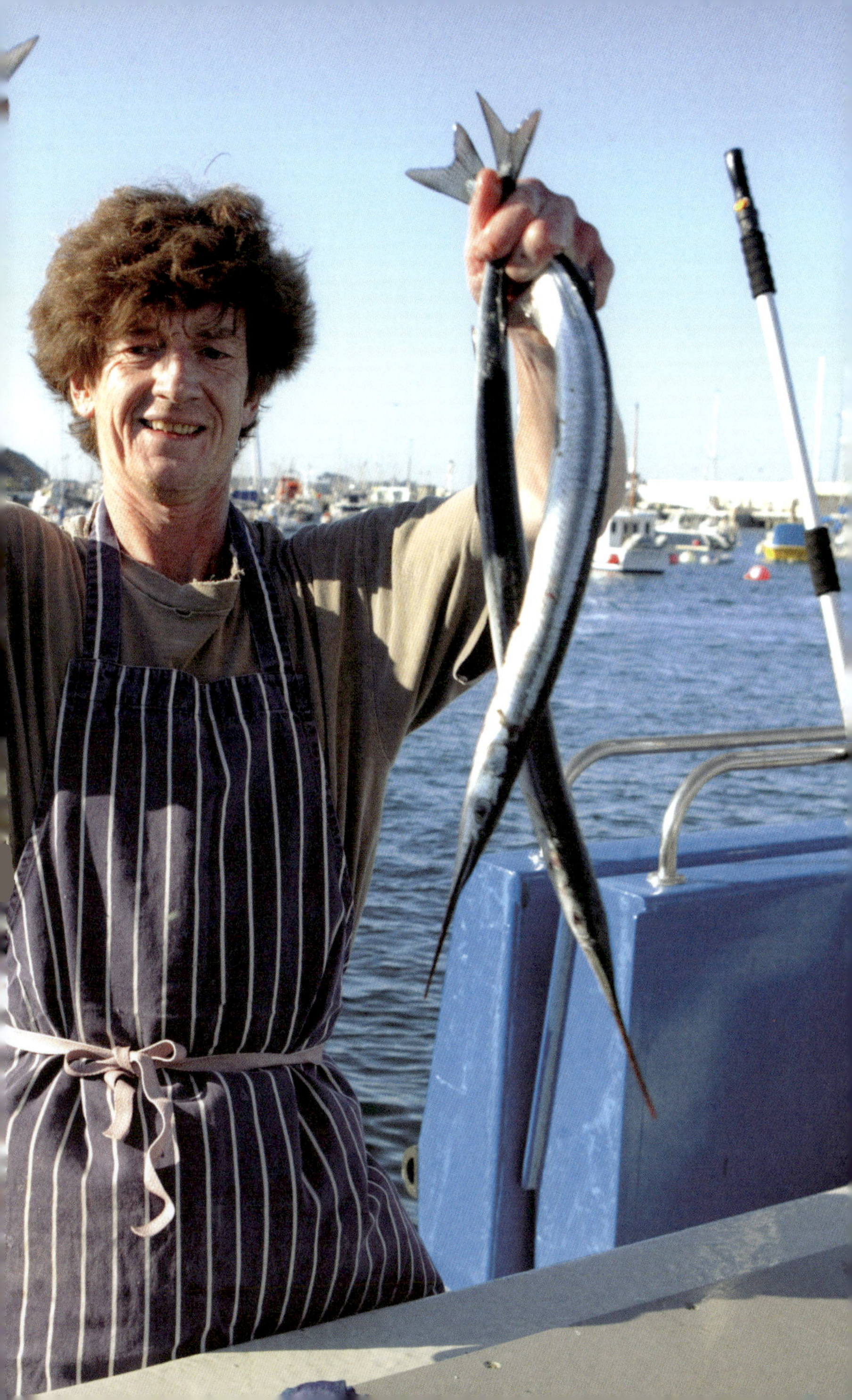

Fishing is a beautiful thing.

It is a rich, satisfying minestrone of emotions and experiences that engage your brain, heart, soul and stomach. By its very nature, a fishing trip involves the Great Outdoors in a gloriously active and interactive way. Unlike other outdoor pursuits, fishing is not simply about observing or photographing, or ticking off lists. Nor is it just about cutting a swathe through the Outdoors, fast or slow, under sail, or hanging from a paraglider, or standing on a surfboard.

Fishing is about getting down to the sea and investigating it. Challenging it. Using your brain – maybe parts of it you don't get to use in everyday life – coupled with some well-chosen equipment, to extract something alive from the water. Not wishing to be too dramatic, fishing is about life and death. It's one of the very few interests you can pursue in modern society that still involves going out to hunt and kill your dinner; where you can still feed your family or friends from the fruits of your hunting adventure.

A fishing trip, at its best, has many parts. First there's the preamble – time spent in anticipation and day-dreaming – a period which can take up anything from a snatched moment during a busy day at work, to a lengthy reverie staring out the window of a packed bus. Part of the preamble includes planning the trip: choosing where to go and when to go; deciding whether to plump for a quick mackerel-bashing boat trip or a two-tide, all-day session on some fabulous Victorian pier. It's a time of maps and charts and tide tables, of mates and books, of internet chat rooms and tea-stained lists. Or maybe, for some more confident anglers, this is also a time for thumbing through recipes and amassing ingredients.

All this planning blossoms into the day of 'actually being there'. A day when, if things go well, you might catch a bucket of mackerel, a jaw-dropping sea bass or a thick-scaled, spiny-finned black bream – great fish on which to practise with your descaler and filleting knife.

If the fish capture and the following fish preparation have been successful, they should neatly segue into the fish cooking part of your expedition. A marvellous time of creativity – hot pans, sharp knives, fresh herbs and great smells – which in turn spills over into the very best of all times: the eating experience.

The joy of fishing is that it delivers on all manner of levels from the spiritual to the nutritional. Fishing has a purpose. A point. An end game. And I have to confess, it's the end game – the cooking and eating of fishing – that interests me just as much as the hooking, playing and netting part. I fish mostly because I love to cook and eat what I catch.

In Britain we are fortunate, because there are still an awful lot of fish in the seas around our coast. A multitude of edible species lurk in our inshore waters, from salmon and sardines to cod and pollack. There are beaches, piers, rocks, breakwaters, estuaries and harbours, peppered all around our islands, which provide easy access to fishing, fish and ultimately great seafood. Even at a time when global fish stocks are in a fairly catastrophic state, in our inshore British waters we are still in reasonably good shape.

In order to catch some of our inshore fish, you could, if you choose, fill a couple of sheds with assorted fishing tackle. You could buy yourself an array of fishing rods and reels and rigs and lures to cover every eventuality. Or, like me, you could be pragmatic, limiting your scope and curbing your budget by focusing on fishing for the species that you are most likely to catch, and the ones that you are most likely to want to eat.

With that in mind I've tried to keep rigs, baits and tackle-faffing to a minimum in this book. You may soon outgrow my basic approach, but if I only manage to help you get out and catch a few of your first fish, I will have achieved my goal. Even better if I can help you to prepare and to cook the fish you catch – either on the beach or at home.

My cooking is like my fishing: it's not always clever or fancy or neat. What makes me happiest is when I use every single scrap of every single fish I've killed, in order to feed the ones I love. For me, wasted food – or wasted fish – can spoil the whole experience. Taking fish from the wild to feed ourselves is a privilege, not a necessity. So apart from doing it with a little style, a lot of passion and gratitude, it's also important that we do it with a clear conscience.

Like Hugh, I've been inordinately fortunate in my fishing 'career', and have fished all around the world. I have hunted some very exotic species in some wildly exotic places. All of which is very nice, but ultimately, it does feel a little irrelevant in the big scheme of things. The irony of all that travelling is that I've come to realise now that the greatest pleasure I derive from fishing today is fishing for British fish, catching them as best as I can, doing as little damage as possible along the way, and cooking them into a simple homespun, homemade feast.

Nick Fisher

Glossary

Fishing, like any hobby or passion, is made all the more intriguing and satisfying by having its own special language. At first, this may seem off-putting and exclusive, but once you get the hang of it, this language will become the much-loved lexicon that separates you, the angler, from the non-angler.

Here are a few much-used terms, which are well worth having in your vocabulary. I've included the definitions, too, so that when you use them you have some idea what they mean:

Artificial lure A lure is an example of any 'terminal tackle' that will 'lure' a fish to bite it. It can be anything from a rubber fish mounted on a hook (made to imitate small bait fish), to a mackerel feather (made to imitate tiny fry fish), to a hook-mounted jelly worm (made to look like a marine worm). Rubber baits are also known sometimes simply as 'artificials'. And 'lures' can also refer to metal, wooden or mechanical baits, such as spinners, plugs or spoons, which are 'retrieved' through the water in such a way that they, too, imitate small fish that are slow or wounded and are therefore easy prey for predator fish.

Bleeding Releasing blood from the circulatory system by cutting the gills of your fish, after you've banged it on the head. Bleeding makes the flesh appear 'cleaner' and slows down the rate at which it will spoil, thus prolonging its shelf life.

Bottom-fishing Also known as 'ledgering', this is a method of fishing when your bait is held firmly on the seabed.

Casting The act of propelling your bait or lure some distance out into the water, using a rod.

Demersal fish Fish that live mostly in the demersal region of the sea, which is right down on the bottom, just above the seabed.

Feathering The act of fishing with a string of feathers.

Float fishing Fishing with your bait suspended under a float.

Ground bait Extra bait that you add to the water around your hook bait, to create a focus and act as an attractant to fish in the vicinity. Also known as 'chum'.

Handlining Fishing with a handline rather than a rod and line. A handline is a thick line that is wound on to a wooden frame.

Hook bait Whatever you put on your hook – something a fish wants to eat, that will bait it to bite.

Ledgering See bottom-fishing.

Ledger rig General term used to describe any static rig that is weighted on the bottom, with the bait presented on or near the seabed.

Marks A 'rock mark' is a specific location, on the rocks of a cliff or beach, where you would expect to catch fish. A 'good beach mark' is a place on a beach known to be productive. Even on a boat, the skipper might lower the anchor or else drift over a certain 'mark' because he knows it has given up fish in the past.

Pelagic fish Species, like mackerel, herring and tuna, which are able to feed up and down the water column from the seabed to the surface. Pelagic means 'wandering' or 'nomadic' and these fish also wander from area to area in search of the best food.

Priest A purpose-made instrument of death. The tool you use to bash a fish over the head with; so called, because it administers the last rites.

Retrieving The action of winding in; the opposite to casting.

Rig The construction of the 'terminal tackle'. The type of rig or construction you use might be referred to by the method of angling you're using, such as a 'float rig', or it might be named after the species of fish you're targeting, such as a 'plaice rig'. It can also relate to the location in which you're fishing, such as a 'pier rig'.

Snood Another name for a short hook length. The piece of line on a rig (especially a paternoster rig) which actually connects to the hook. A snood may be stronger than the reel line if a fish has teeth. Or weaker, if the fish (mullet, for example) are easily spooked by thick line.

Spinning A method of angling using a spinner (or spoon or wedge) as bait.

Striking The action of reacting to a 'bite' – the feeling of something nibbling at your bait – by quickly raising the rod tip to the 11 o'clock position, with the intent of driving your hook into the fish's mouth and effect a 'hook up'.

Tackle Anything you take fishing with you, from a rod and reel to rigs and weights, spinners and feathers. All of these constitute part (or all) of your 'tackle'.

Terminal tackle The business end of your line. 'Terminal' refers to the end of your line that interfaces with the water and, hopefully, the finned things. A hook and a weight is all part of your 'terminal tackle'; a reel isn't.

Trolling The practice of fishing from a slow-moving boat, by dragging a bait, feathers or lure along 30 yards or more behind the boat.

When to Go Fishing

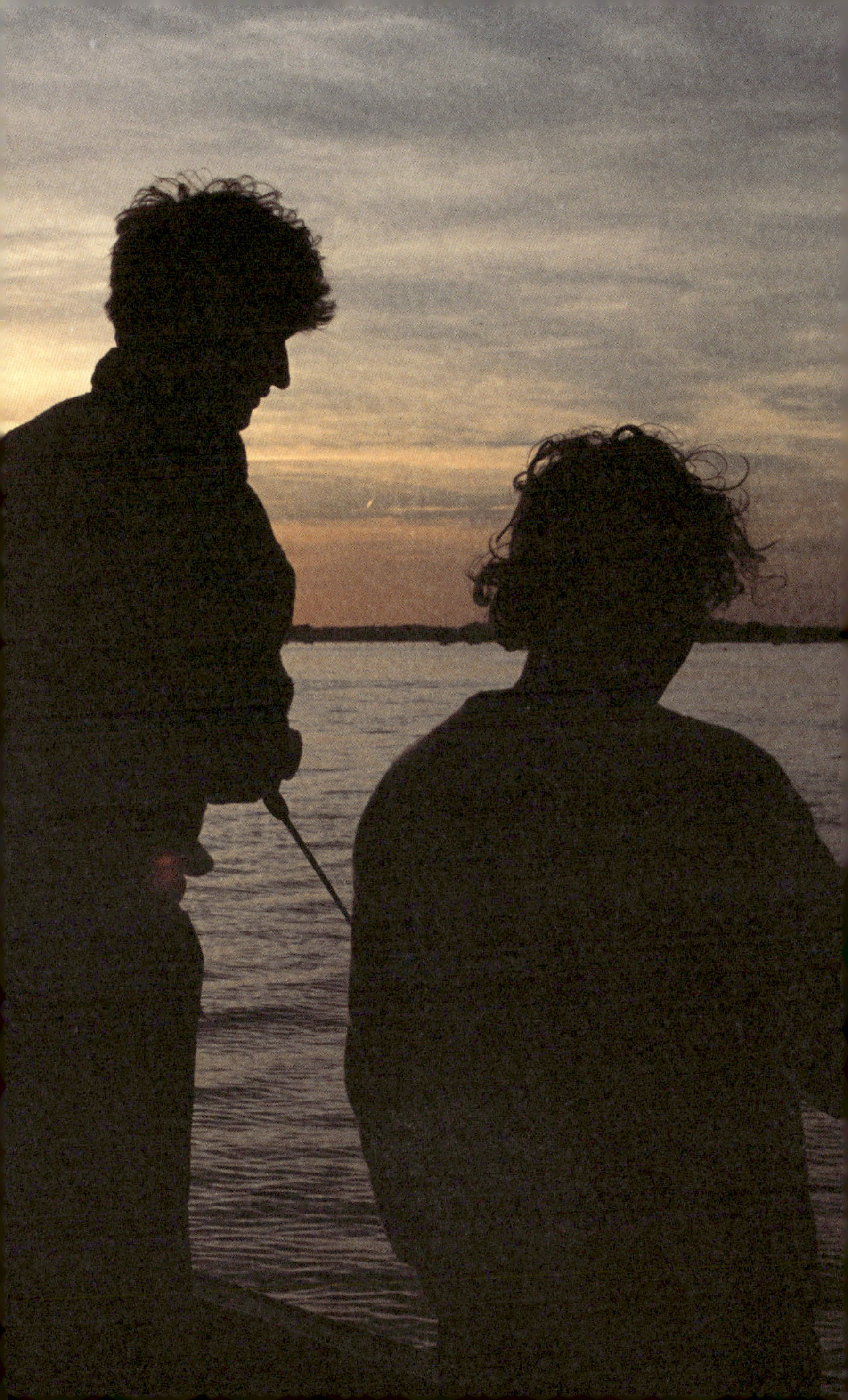

When it comes to outdoor pursuits, we can all so easily get obsessed with tackle, kit and clothing. It's human nature to assume that success or failure in any sort of outdoor quest boils down to what you choose to take with you. But I know, from bitter fishing experience, that it's not *what* you take that matters most. It's *where* you choose to go and *when* you choose to go there.

Tides, past weather and future weather all have an effect on how fish behave and how they feed. You can never guarantee to catch fish, but you can narrow the margin for failure by learning a few basic rules about seasons, weather, tides and time of day.

Time of year

In fishing 'season' has two meanings. There's the natural season when certain migratory fish that live part of the year in deep offshore waters are present in our inshore waters and accessible to the angler. And there's the imposed legal season, which denotes when you're permitted to try and catch certain species. This restriction is a way of protecting vulnerable fish, namely salmon and sea trout, when they're in the process of migrating out of the sea into rivers in order to spawn. The law is designed to give them a better chance of successful spawning and to stop fishermen targeting these fish when they're preoccupied with sex rather than survival.

Although the legal season applies only to salmon and sea trout, it is worth considering in relation to other species. Any fish in the act of spawning, or that have recently finished spawning, are not good to catch. If you catch fish before they spawn, you're depriving them of the ability to reproduce and potentially destroying millions of fish eggs before they've had a chance to be fertilised. What's more, a fish that has recently spawned is not particularly good to eat, because its energy and nutrition have been devoted to creating healthy eggs to the detriment of the rest of its body, particularly its muscle flesh – the part that you most want to eat.

There are no laws to stop you catching sea fish that are just pre- or post-spawning. And at certain times of year it's impossible to know if you're going to catch one in either condition before you do. But if you catch a fish, either swollen with eggs, or with a telltale slack belly and flabby muscle tone, then try to release it safely back into the sea (see p.176). If you then catch another in the same condition, it makes sense to move to another location or change bait or technique, and try for a different species.

Most sea fish are in their prime in the late summer months and through the autumn, mainly because they have spent the last few months of the year gorging on abundant high-protein food and are therefore fat, fit and full of omega-rich oils and life-enhancing minerals like selenium, taurine and zinc.

The adjacent chart breaks down the year into seasons and indicates the best possible time to take each of the most catchable species from the sea.

Seasonal fishing for sea fish

	SPRING	SUMMER	AUTUMN	WINTER
MACKEREL	2	3	3	1
DOGFISH	2	3	3	2
POUTING	3	3	3	2
POLLACK	2	3	3	2
COD		3	2	3
WHITING			3	3
GARFISH	1	3	2	
RED GURNARD	1	2	3	1
BLACK BREAM	1	3	2	
PLAICE	3	2	2	1
SEA BASS	1	3	3	
DAB & FLOUNDER	1		1	3
HORSE MACKEREL	2	3	3	1
HERRING	1	2	2	
SQUID			3	2
SLOB TROUT	2	3	2	
GREY MULLET	1	3	1	

🐟🐟🐟 = most likely to catch
🐟🐟 = likely to catch
🐟 = a slim chance

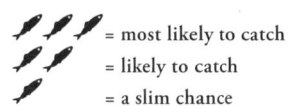

Weather

The perfect weather conditions for sea fishing are a day with light cloud cover and a steady light onshore wind coming from one direction, which gives some movement to the surf and should ideally colour the water just a little by churning up small clouds of sand in the shallows.

Always check the weather 24 hours in advance of your intended trip (see Directory, p.249, for weather forecast websites) and be prepared to cancel if the weather is forecast to turn ugly. Don't get me wrong, fishing in bad weather can sometimes be a lot of fun when you already have some sound angling experience. But if you're still near the start of your learning curve it's only going to make the basics, such as tying knots and casting, that much more difficult.

Rain

Even if you've got top-notch waterproof clothing, persistent rain will still mess up a day's fishing. It makes everything so much more difficult to do, and will create a stack of wet kit to deal with when you get home. In saying that, rain splashing on the water can actually help to cover a multitude of angling sins, like bad casting and noisy wading, and rain hitting the water can sometimes put the fish at their ease.

Sunshine

A day of bright sunlight can be surprisingly unproductive weather for going fishing. Fish generally don't like too much sun as most of them don't have eyelids, so they skulk goth-like in darkened depths. This is a tactical move because bright sunlight illuminates the water and airborne predators, like cormorants and gannets, can spot fish much more easily. In addition, most of our native fish don't like water that is too warm as it makes them sluggish and puts them off their food.

The middle of a very hot summer's day might *seem* like the perfect time to sit next-the-sea, rod-in-hand, but bright sunlight really isn't ideal for fishermen either. Believe me, some of the most excruciating sunburn I've ever experienced (and I'm a freckled ginger Scot!) came courtesy of hot summer fishing. I know it sounds very Nanny State, but if you do choose to go and fish in the middle of a summer's day, take lots of fresh water, a hat and lashings of sun cream. And if you're wearing sandals, don't forget to cream your toes!

During hot weather, it's always best to go fishing at dawn and dusk, because the fish come out to feed when the light levels are low and the water is cool. For the angler with a throbbing vein of romance in his soul, it's also the most special time of the day to be by the water, when most non-angling civilians haven't yet ventured out, or have already gone home. Being able to sit and savour dawn and dusk next to the sea is one of the many unexpected privileges of being an angler.

Wind

High winds (20mph plus) are rarely an advantage in fishing. Some locations are more affected by wind than others, as are some fishing techniques. The direction of the wind is also an issue. Here's a rough rule of thumb summary, to help you understand the impact of wind on your fishing:

In an inshore boat It's the responsibility of the skipper to make a judgement on whether the wind is too strong to allow his anglers to fish comfortably and safely. Generally, anything above a Force 5 is deemed to be too 'lumpy' for fishing.

On the beach The main issue is direction. Wind can be offshore (coming from the land heading out to sea), onshore (coming from sea to land), or it can be blowing across the beach in either direction parallel to the sea. An offshore wind is the most comfortable for fishing, because it's at your back and will help your casting by giving it extra wind propulsion. The exact opposite is true of a strong onshore wind. Having a hard wind in your face all day is uncomfortable and tiring, and it'll make casting more difficult and even potentially dangerous. Light to moderate cross winds aren't so much of an issue, except an easterly wind which is colder and rarely the best for a day's fishing, hence the uncannily true adage: 'When the wind's in the east, the fish bite least'. But strong cross winds are a pain to fish and many anglers will find real trouble keeping their weight and bait where they want it on the seabed, due to the sideways drag of the wind and water pulling on the line, moving it off to one side.

Rock fishing A strong wind in any direction is going to make a potentially dangerous place to fish even more dangerous. Erratic winds cause erratic seas and being stuck on an exposed rock above deep water in a strong wind is too much of a risk. I haven't been washed off a rock, but I've been drenched by big waves I didn't see coming. Dragging soaking gear back to the car, knees knocking with fright, is really no fun.

Tides

Tides give me goosebumps – especially when I try and get my head around the micro and macro mechanics of what happens in the period between high tide and low tide. Tides influence the creation and flow of plankton, as well as the movement and feeding patterns of all fish, molluscs and crustaceans. But before focusing on life under the water, first we need to stand back, look up and try to get some kind of handle on how the life of everything in the sea – from a tiny shrimp to a huge bucket-mouthed conger eel – is connected to, and controlled by, the movement of our moon and the sun in outer space.

Along most parts of our coastline, in any given 24-hour period, the tide will be high twice and low twice. When you check the local newspaper's tide table for the times of high water and low water, you'll often find a symbol that depicts the corresponding phase of the moon. Most of us understand that the moon is somehow responsible for tides – and that its influence has got something to do with the moon's magnetic or gravitational pull. And that's all you really need to know (plus the fact that the times of high water and low water will shift forward by about 40 minutes every day. So, if high water is at noon today, it'll be at around 12.40pm tomorrow.)

But for me, grasping a little more about the cause and effect, about *why* the sea behaves the way it does, helps to increase my pleasure and interaction with it.

The moon

The moon revolves around the earth, and the earth and moon together revolve around the sun. The sun is much bigger than our moon, but the moon is much closer. And so the moon has the greater gravitational effect on the earth.

As the moon passes over and around the face of the earth, it acts like a magnet trying to pull the earth towards it. The earth, in its own orbit of the sun, won't shift under the pull of this massive magnet, but the seas – covering over 70 per cent of the planet – will. The sea on the side of the earth nearest to the magnetic moon will bulge upwards towards the moon, drawn by its gravitational pull. This bulge of water on one side of the earth creates a high tide.

The sun

Although it is not so pronounced, the sun also has a gravitational pull that affects the sea on the surface of the earth. And because the moon rotates around the earth and together they rotate around the sun, there are phases when the moon is in between the earth and the sun. Also, there are phases when the earth is in between the sun and the moon, like piggy in the middle. There are phases, too, when the moon and the sun are at right angles to the centre of the earth. If you imagine the earth as being the centre of a clock, this is when the sun is at 12 and the moon is at 3.

Each of these combinations of moon, earth and sun has a distinct effect upon the magnetic pull exerted on the seas, creating a different-sized bulge that affects the height of tides.

Spring tides and neap tides

Spring tides have nothing to do with the season of spring. 'Spring' relates to the notion of the tide 'springing' up; in other words, being at its most mobile and most fierce.

Neap tides are the opposite. These are the weakest or smallest tides, when the difference in height from low water to high water (the tidal range) is much smaller than the difference during spring tides.

WHEN TO GO FISHING 21

Neap and spring tides alternate every two weeks; halfway through each complete phase of a new moon, or lunar month (28 days).

The spring tides occur when the moon's gravitational pull is at its strongest; when it's furthest away from the sun and the earth is piggy in the middle, then both planets are pulling at the sea in opposite directions, which creates a bulge in the seas on both sides of the earth. Springs also occur when the moon is on the same side as the sun and together, with their combined magnetic force, they're pulling the surface of the seas dramatically in one direction.

Neap tides occur when the sun and moon are at right angles to the earth, in the first and third quarters of the new moon. This is when the sun's magnetic power is directly cancelling out some of the moon's magnetic strength.

But all you absolutely need to remember from this celestial dance of moon, earth and sun is that spring tides are strong and big, and neap tides are weak and small.

How tides affect fisherman Knowing the times of high and low water is essential to fishermen. If you're fishing on a shallow, sandy surf beach in Norfolk or Cornwall, the sea could be an awfully long walk away at low tide. And if you set up an elaborate fish camp way down the beach as the tide is coming in, you'll find yourself having to re-site your camp before you've even had a chance to get your first brew on.

So do check the time of tides as a matter of course. The daily shift forward by 40 minutes each day is caused by the incremental movement of the moon on its 28-day orbit of the earth. This means that if the fish came on the feed at a certain time yesterday, chances are they'll do the same towards an hour later today.

How tides affect fish Developing a mental image of how tides work is hard enough, and even if we do get our heads around the physics, most of us will imagine tides as something constant and gradual.

Unsurprisingly, the sea isn't that straightforward or predictable. Most importantly, tide movement – from low to high – *doesn't* happen at an even and constant speed. When the tide comes in, it starts off slow, gets fast, *very* fast, slows down, stops and slowly starts running again, in the opposite direction. The specific pace that a tide is running during the flood (incoming) tide or ebb (outgoing) tide is something that wreck-fishing charter skippers and yacht skippers need to know intimately. Arguably though, if all we intend to do is chuck a float-fished mackerel strip off the end of the pier in our quest to catch garfish for tea, then all we really need to know is when the tide is going to be low and when it's high.

And yet, just knowing that the state of the tide and formation of local geography – in terms of where there are headlands and bays – make a difference to the direction and pace of the sea will ultimately help us to think a little more like a fish. To keep itself alive, well fed and safe, a fish depends on its knowledge of the tides.

Every aquatic life form in our inshore waters is influenced by tide. Some fish and shellfish can use the tide and even *second-guess* tidal movements, to ambush prey or avoid being ambushed. Other life forms, like plankton, are totally at the mercy of tidal currents, which will carry it hither and yon, sometimes straight into the mouths of plankton predators.

Moving up the chain from plankton are the fish that feed on it. These small fish, also known as 'bait' fish, have some ability to swim against the tides, but only up to a certain point. When the tidal run is too strong they get pushed around, while larger predator fish, who are able to swim against the tide whenever they need to, are able to use the corralling power of the tide to their advantage. Bait fish that are bunched and bullied by tidal currents become easy prey for fish like pollack, bass and cod, who make good use of the all-you-can-eat buffet that a fierce tide creates.

Understanding how the tides influence the food chain in turn helps us second-guess what certain fish might be doing at certain times.

As a general rule of thumb, tidal movement is a good thing for encouraging life to exist in the sea. A run of tide is a physical movement of the water and when it flows around rocks, gullies and structures, it will create bubbles of air in the water, pumping it full of life-enhancing fresh oxygen. At the same time, it transports food such as plankton, worms and crustaceans into the mouths of predators.

And yet, when a tide is too fierce, which it does become in some locations around the coast at certain times of the year, even the big fish will have to stop feeding. This is because holding themselves head-on into the full force of the tide starts to demand too much effort and valuable energy. So instead, they'll find somewhere sheltered in the lee of a structure to hunker down and let the bite of the tide pass.

Tides, crabs, worms and clams High and low tides cover and expose areas of mud, sand and gravel on beaches, estuaries and harbours. This twice-daily movement of sea water back and forth across these areas is vital to the creatures that live there.

At low tide, when the water recedes and exposes swathes of the seabed to the open air, crabs and worms bury themselves under the damp sand for safety. Then later, the fresh run of tide will bring them up out of their hiding holes to feed. Clams are filter feeders; they mostly want to filter the first run of a new tide because they know it will be carrying the maximum amount of sediment and plankton and algae as it sweeps them up across the exposed flats. Fish in turn know what the crabs and clams and worms want to do. Fish like dabs, flounders, plaice and mullet will use the new tide to carry them on to the flats to hunt the worms and crabs as they pop out to savour the new wet.

Conversely, when the tide is out and the mud and sand banks are exposed, it's time for anglers to become fork-wielding predators and to dig in the soft mud for fresh live baits with which to tempt those foraging fish species on the next flush of the tide.

Where to Go Fishing

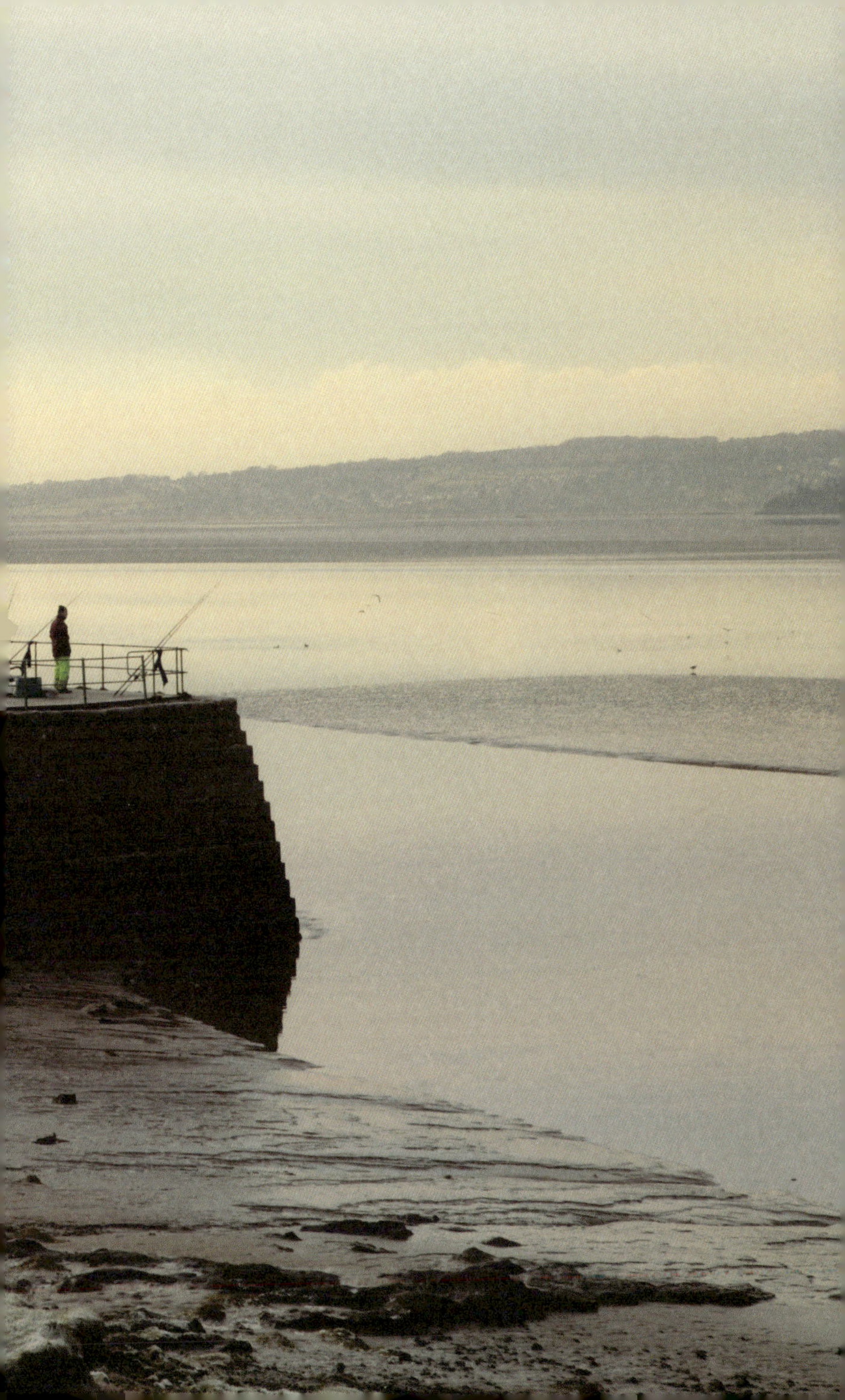

Very tasty and exciting sea fish can be caught from either the shore or from a boat. Undoubtedly, more fish are caught from boats, simply because they can cover a larger area and deeper water much more quickly and efficiently. However, boat fishing is always going to be more expensive and more complicated to arrange. Shore fishing, on the other hand, is instantly accessible to anyone able to wander on to a beach. Pier fishing and rock fishing have the added advantage of allowing you to drop directly down into deeper water than you would normally be able to reach from the beach.

Boat fishing

Boat fishing is, without a shadow of a doubt, one of the easiest ways to get yourself on the other end of a fishing line from an edible sea fish. However, understandably not everyone wants to be spoon-fed their first fish, or wants to invest in an outing they're not sure they'll enjoy. So, although heading out to sea might logically be the quickest way to get a bend in your rod, staying on dry land might be what you feel you'd rather do. And if that's the case, there's plenty of information in this book designed to help you hook up (see pp.30–41).

If you do decide to go boat fishing first as a way of learning the ropes, then unless you happen to be lucky enough to own a boat or have a friend with a boat, the chances are you'll be reliant on booking yourself on to a charter fishing boat.

Charter boats come in all shapes and sizes, from custom-made high-speed craft that only take half a dozen anglers, through large open-decked day boats that specialise in seaside-resort mackerel trips, to serious deep-water charter boats, which normally carry ten anglers and two crew. And then there's always the odd trawler which might take out 'trippers' on days that it's not going out to sea to drag a net.

For anyone new to sea fishing, I would advise against booking yourself on any boat trip that lasts more than 2 hours, simply as a precaution. Because, if you don't like it, or if you don't feel well, at least you know it's going to be over soon. Serious sea-angling charters are normally a minimum of 4 hours, and some are 8 hours or more. Avoid these until you've got your feet wet with a few shorter trips first.

The most effective way to get your hands on something worth cooking is to sign yourself up for a one-hour mackerel trip. There are lots of these mackerel-trip boats in harbours all around the country that run during the summer and sometimes into the autumn months, when the weather allows.

Often these boats provide tackle and some instruction, too. On some boats you will be equipped with a simple handline, or a basic rod and line, attached to a string of mackerel feathers. On others, the handline is standard supplied kit but a rod and line can be provided for an extra charge. Make sure you ask what the arrangement

Locations for catching sea fish

	MACKEREL BOAT	INSHORE FISHING BOAT	SANDY BEACH	SHINGLE BEACH	ROCKY LEDGE	PIER	ESTUARY	HARBOUR
MACKEREL	best	best	best	best	best	best	lucky	best
DOGFISH		best	lucky	lucky	lucky	best	lucky	lucky
POUTING		best	best	lucky	lucky	best	lucky	lucky
POLLACK		best	lucky	lucky	best	lucky	lucky	lucky
COD		best	lucky	best	lucky			
WHITING		best	best	best	best	best		best
GARFISH	best	best	lucky	lucky	best	best		best
RED GURNARD		best	best	best	best	best		best
BLACK BREAM	best	best	lucky	lucky	best	best		best
PLAICE		best	best	best	best	best	lucky	lucky
SEA BASS		lucky	best	best	best	lucky	lucky	lucky
DAB & FLOUNDER		lucky	best	lucky	lucky	best	best	best
HORSE MACKEREL	best	best	lucky	lucky	lucky	best		best
HERRING	best	best			lucky	lucky		lucky
SQUID	lucky	lucky				best		best
SLOB TROUT							best	lucky
GREY MULLET					lucky	best	best	best

🐟 = best   🐟 = might get lucky

is before you sign up. Some mackerel boats will encourage you to bring your own rod, others advise against it. The simple reason is that it's harder for a skipper to avoid anglers getting into tangles if they're all using different tackle with different line thicknesses and different weights. If everyone is using the same basic tackle, the lines will all behave in the same way and it's then easier for the skipper to control the dangle of the terminal tackle as he manoeuvres the boat.

There is, however, likely to come a point once you've been on a mackerel-trip boat a few times when it dawns on you that, fun though it is, you're not really controlling the whole process. You're on someone else's boat, using someone else's tackle. The skipper has decided where, and when, and how you will fish. And, suddenly, being shoulder to shoulder with a load of people doing exactly the same thing makes you feel less a master of your own mackerel destiny.

This might well be all you really want from a sea-fishing experience – a chance to bag up with mackerel in the simplest and most efficient tackle-lite manner. But, in my experience, the more you can take control of where and how you fish, the fewer fish you might catch, but the more pleasure you'll derive from catching them. In which case, assuming you don't have your own boat, you'll have to think about beach, pier or shore fishing to get your mackerel.

Often people will start off on mackerel boat trips, then get a bit bored and frustrated, so move on to beach and pier fishing, to get the hang of using tackle, tying knots and learning about techniques and baits. Many then progress *back* to boats again in the form of short charter reef trips (also called 'reef-fishing trips' or 'inshore trips') to enable them to go in search of other species of fish which are easier to catch from a boat. These fishing trips are slightly more technical, last about 2–3 hours, and might involve bringing your own tackle.

Boat fishing equipment

ROD	Boat rod, carp rod or spinning rod (see pp.113–17)
REEL	Multiplier or fixed-spool reel (see pp.119–20)
LINE	15–20lb line (see p.121)
HOOKS	1–4/0 hooks (see pp.122–3)
TERMINAL TACKLE	Weights, swivels, booms, beads, feathers, other lures (see Tackle and Kit, pp.125–9 and pp.132–44)
RIG ASSEMBLY	Paternoster, running ledger, float, spinner, pennel (see pp.163–7)
BAIT	Mackerel, squid, lugworms, ragworms (see Bait, pp.153–5 and p.158)

A note on seasickness

Seasickness seems so unfair. Some people will feel seasick just standing on a boat tied up alongside a harbour, while others can be bounced around like a pea on a kettle-drum and never feel even the slightest bit queasy.

In fact, seasickness doesn't have anything to do with the sea; it's simply motion sickness – the same as you might get travelling on a plane, train, car or bus. The brain just gets confused. The inner ear is your balance centre, and your eyes provide your visual information reference. When the two don't agree, vomiting may soon follow. Inside a cabin or a wheelhouse, it's even more confusing. Your eyes tell your brain you're in a stable environment, but your inner ear knows you're pitching around.

According to experts, fatty foods are best avoided for at least 12 hours before a sea trip. And it's always better to travel on deck, rather than inside the wheelhouse or cabin. The best position to plant yourself on a boat is right at the back where it's low down and most stable. And the best place to look is at the horizon, but don't fixate on it. Keep your head as level and still as possible, to avoid further confusion. The sickness is caused by your sensory perceptions being out of synch, so don't use binoculars or try to read – focusing your eyes on close subjects or artificially magnified ones will only exacerbate the symptoms.

Seasickness sufferers – skippers, too – often say that if you feel sick, it's best to be sick: let it happen, rather than try to hold on to your breakfast. Out is better than in, ideally from the back of the boat into the sea or a bucket with the wind behind you.

Shore fishing

As an island, we are surrounded by a stunning range of shore-fishing venues, including sandy beaches, pebble beaches, rocky cliffs, piers, estuaries and harbours.

Choosing where to go on your first few exploratory shore-fishing trips should really be dictated by what's easily accessible to you. Whether you're on holiday and there's water in the vicinity, or you're heading out from home and planning a trip to some nearby stretch of sea, the three most useful tools you can use are a map, a telephone directory and an angling website.

A detailed OS map of your planned destination will show where the water meets the land, the nearest parking spots and passable footpaths to the shore. If it is an estuary, a map will help you identify where and how the river flows into the sea. And if you're intent on trying your luck at a beach, you can study what's on either side of the spot you fancy. Features like rocky headlands, open bays and tight coves all affect the tidal flow and even the weather, especially the wind. If you know the forecast wind direction you can make an informed choice as to which side of a headland or a bay to fish, making sure the wind is on your back, rather than hard in your face.

A phone directory will list fishing tackle shops in the area. And a good tackle shop is a fount of useful knowledge. A quick conversation with a local tackle dealer can save you a lot of time. You might not feel qualified to conduct an in-depth conversation, but never be afraid to admit you're a novice and need all the help you can get. You'll be amazed how helpful anglers and tackle dealers can be if you give them the opportunity. Fishermen love their fishing and love to be able to show how knowledgeable they are. Obviously, it's much easier to have this sort of conversation face to face. And any canny tackle purveyor will realise that you're much more likely to part with cash if you're actually standing in front of his till.

Angling websites are just as important when you're exploring new locations. Anglers are a proactive bunch, who love to expound their wisdom. I've listed the best websites in the Directory (see pp.249–50), but there are many more local ones, and personal blogs that you can track down with a little cybersleuthing. There's so much angling information available that a trawl of the internet is very worthwhile before heading out in the hope of getting your own net wet.

Sandy beaches

Most people love to spend a day hanging out on a warm sandy beach. To be able to swim and paddle, to play with your children, dog or inflatable swim-toys one minute and catch a fish from the self-same sun-kissed sea the next would be a perfect scenario. In reality, it's unlikely to happen. Swimmers and anglers don't make for naturally sympathetic and symbiotic bedfellows. Apart from the obvious hook-in-flesh danger aspect, there's also the problem that humans splashing around in the water are likely to scare away any fish. The best time to try fishing in this type of location is just after dawn and just before dusk, when the light levels are low and there is no glare from the sun on the water. This is when the fish will feel safe to venture into shallow water. And conversely, the best time for beach fun is when the sun is high.

Best tides The most effective stage of the tide for sandy beach fishing is when it's going out or coming in. Not when it's at its lowest or its highest. Tide movement is significant on sandy and pebbly beaches because the motion of the sea on to sand or through pebbles might dislodge any resident fish or aquatic life.

Sand fleas, shrimps, tiny crabs, sand eels and other small sea creatures live in wet sand and among tiny gravel-like pebbles. These creatures also like to be covered by a layer of sea water, as this allows them to move around easily and seek out food and mating partners. All these life forms are acutely aware when the tide is going out or coming in, either because of the change in its direction or the change in pressure as it ebbs and flows. So they know when their covering of sea water is about to disappear. And when this is imminent, they have two choices: either dig into the wet sand and hunker down for the duration, until the water layer returns with the next incoming tide; or else move with the outgoing tide, slipping further and further down the sloping beach, until the tide stops ebbing and starts to come back in again.

Fish such as dogfish, plaice, bass, gurnard and, to some extent, mackerel feed on these beach-dwelling aquatic critters and they know that as the outgoing tide slides down a beach, it is going to be washing a selection of these critters in their path.

Fish also know that when the tide is flowing in over the sun-warmed sand or pebbles, all manner of edible critters who have hunkered down for the duration will pop out of their hiding holes to take advantage of new oxygen and better mobility.

Sandy beach fishing equipment

ROD	Spinning rod (see pp.113–14) or carp rod (see p.116–17)
REEL	Fixed-spool reel (see p.119)
LINE	10–15lb line and shock leader (see pp.121 and 131)
HOOKS	1–4/0 hooks (see pp.122–3)
TERMINAL TACKLE	Floats, weights, swivels, beads, feathers, other lures (see Tackle and Kit, pp.123–9 and pp.132–44)
RIG ASSEMBLY	Running ledger (see p.164)
BAIT	Mackerel, squid, lugworms, ragworms, peeler crab (see Bait, pp.153–5 and pp.158–9)

Shingle beaches

Steep shingle beaches like Chesil in Dorset are also known as 'storm' beaches, because their 45° slope of shingle or gravel leading down to a plateau of sand is the result of fierce wave action. The joy of fishing this sort of beach is that you never need to cast out very far. Most fish feeding takes place along the line where the shingle meets the sand. The onshore waves will erode the sand under the shingle slope, displacing food and attracting various fish, from bass to plaice, to gurnard and small pollack.

Chesil Beach stretches for 17 miles, from Portland to West Bay, so it can be very hard to decide exactly where to stop and cast your bait. One way is to examine the high water line along the upper part of the beach, looking for concentrations of flotsam and seaweed. These indicate that there's an unseen feature, or a convergence of currents just off the beach or further out to sea, propelling floating and submerged matter up the beach at a particular point. This is a good place to start, because the sea in this spot is obviously carrying a lot of matter: sea rubbish and weed that will contain all sorts of small aquatic life, which in turn will attract feeding fish.

Any protruding bumps of shingle breaking the even sweep of the shoreline suggest there is something happening in the deeper water that keeps the build-up of shingle at this position. Any hint of a feature or a tidal anomaly is worth investigating. And it always helps the angler to see what a beach looks like at low water. Any hollows, rocks or ridges represent features. Fish love features. Mark the position of any you spot by taking a visual bearing in relation to the cliffs or background. This way you can aim your bait in that direction once the tide has started to flood.

The tackle is the same as you'd use on a sandy beach. The steep-angled shingle will give you deep water close in on high tide, so mackerel feathers and spinners are easier to use for more of the tide than on a shallow sandy beach. A short lob cast on a shingle beach at high tide will easily put you in water deep enough to hold fish.

Shingle beach fishing equipment

ROD	Spinning or carp rod (see pp.113–14 and pp.116–17)
REEL	Fixed-spool reel (see p.119)
LINE	10–15lb line and shock leader (see pp.121 and 131)
HOOKS	1–4/0 hooks (see pp.122–3)
TERMINAL TACKLE	Floats, weights, swivels, beads, feathers, other lures (see Tackle and Kit, pp.123–9 and pp.132–44)
RIG ASSEMBLY	Running ledger (see p.164), float rig (see p.165)
BAIT	Mackerel, squid, lugworms, ragworms, peeler crab (see Bait, pp.153–5 and pp.158–9)

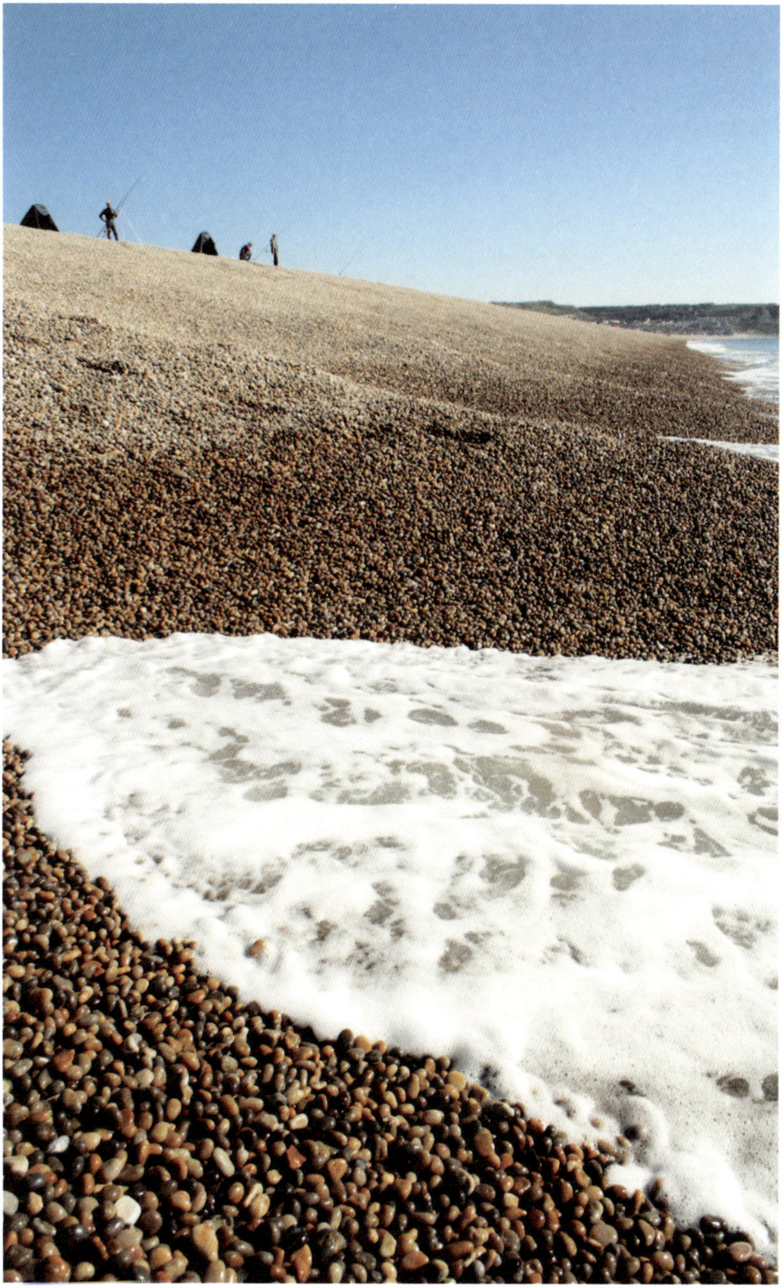

Rough ground or rocky beaches

Some beaches are just not suitable for enjoyable fishing, especially for the beginner. Beaches that contain a large amount of big boulders and craggy rock are dangerous and tackle-hungry. Fishing on very rocky, rough ground requires specialist tackle and a solid knowledge of local tides and weather. What's more, the species these beaches attract, like conger eel, bull huss and smoothhound, are complicated to hook and land, and not species that I would encourage you to eat.

There is nothing more soul-destroying than getting all excited about going on a fishing trip, only to end up somewhere scary, where you snag against rock at every cast, leaving you confused, bruised and tackle-less.

Pier fishing

Most fish like structure in their lives. Literally. Much of the seabed is a desert – miles of flat nothingness that is constantly scoured by a continually shifting, incessant Sirocco-like 'wind' in the form of tidal currents. Water is pushed and pulled four times a day across this landscape, which, if there's no structure growing out of it, makes it a very inhospitable environment for fish and shellfish, except those that can burrow into the sand to seek sanctuary.

A pier is a sanctuary – a glorious multi-layered, multi-faceted sanctuary – which provides all manner of seductive nooks and crannies for things to lodge and grow, or else hide and dine. Classic Victorian piers have iron legs and stone feet. They stick out at 90° to the coastline, causing all sorts of confusion to the natural flow of the tide, which normally travels parallel to the shore.

So a pier acts as a spit, jutting across the tide, creating eddies and swirls, lees and races – all the things that fish, shellfish and worms favour, rather than the constant exposed stream of tides that exist on a barren, featureless seabed.

The legs and feet of a pier obstruct the sideways movement of the tide, acting as barriers to the flow. This creates a shadow or lee in one direction of the tide, while the side of the pier foot facing the advancing tide will be eroded, creating a series of pockets which, in time, join up to form a trench. The base of a pier becomes a moonscape of craters and hollows, pockets and trenches, all of which impede the flow of worms, crabs and other fish-edible species that drop into the hollows as the tide pushes them in one direction or another.

The pier structure provides footing for seaweeds, algae, mussels, limpets and winkles, while the pier 'floor' is carpeted with compartments to hold various washed-along foodstuffs. All of this food attracts fish. Congers, codling, coalfish, dogfish and pouting get their snouts down in the troughs, while mackerel and mullet and garfish will sit higher in the water, using the vortexes of tide to deliver food. A pier is like a massive seafood buffet that caters for every species of bait fish and predator at some stage of the tide.

End of the pier syndrome Most anglers' natural instinct is to cast to the far side – of anything. If I turn up on one bank of a river, I inevitably try to cast my bait to the opposite bank. If I fish a lake, I try to cast my bait at least into the middle. And the same is also true when I go pier fishing. My natural instinct is to walk to the furthest end of the pier, jostle for position with other anglers and cast as far as I can. In all of us there lurks some competitive desire to cast our bait the furthest, in the erroneous belief that by so doing we'll catch more fish. But, given that the troughs and hollows on the underside of the pier are an advantage for fishing, obviously the best place to fish is actually around the middle of the pier.

Gear and the pier When you arrive at a pier, check which way the tide is running. If it's flowing from right to left, you might feel it's better to fish on the left side, as your tackle and bait will be dragged away from the structure, down the tide, so you'll be able to see your line and more easily recognise any bites. Otherwise, if you drop your bait on the right-hand side, your tackle is going to be dragged *under* the structure by the tide, right into the tackle-snagging, barnacle-encrusted legs of the pier.

The fish, however, are most likely to be tight *under* the pier, feeding in the gullies and holes. And they'll probably be pointing head-on into the tide, watching for food being pushed their way. So, any angler dropping their bait on the down-tide side is actually dropping their bait *behind* the feeding fish, with the scent being washed even further away down tide.

If you drop the bait on the up-tide side of the pier, the scent will be wafted towards the underside, where the fish will notice it quickly and hopefully move to grab it. Fishing the up-tide business-side of the pier is much more snaggy, but you can learn to tune your rigs to make it possible, by fishing with heavier weights and a 'rotten-bottom' or sacrificial link. This is simply a length of weaker line that you attach to your weight when you're fishing over rocky and snaggy ground. The idea is that this weak length with a lower breaking strain will break before the main line does. This way you sacrifice only the lead when it gets stuck, because the weak link will snap, and you won't lose your entire rig. Another way of creating a weak link is to tie a paper clip to the bottom of your line and hook the weight on to it. When the lead gets stuck, the paper clip will bend straight under strain as you pull hard, letting your weight fall off but freeing the snag and saving your rig.

Pier fishing equipment

ROD	Spinning rod (see pp.113–14) or carp rod (see p.116–17)
REEL	Fixed-spool reel (see p.119)
LINE	10–15lb line and shock leader (see pp.121 and 131)
HOOKS	1–4/0 hooks (see pp.122–3)
TERMINAL TACKLE	Floats, weights, swivels, beads, feathers, other lures (see Tackle and Kit, pp.123–9 and pp.132–44)
RIG ASSEMBLY	Paternoster or running ledger rig (see pp.163–4)
BAIT	Mackerel, squid, lugworms, ragworms, peeler crab (see Bait, pp.153–5 and pp.158–9)

Estuary fishing

Not all harbours have a river running through them, but all estuaries do. The estuary is where the river widens out from a clear channel cut through the land to an open plain, where it meets the sea. The estuary is the point where fresh water meets sea water and it mixes together to make 'brackish' water.

For some fish, such as sea trout and salmon, this brackish water zone acts as a kind of no man's land, where they stop to make the difficult transition from sea fish to river fish for the purposes of breeding.

For other fish, like slob trout (see pp.97–9), the brackish water and intertidal zone is like a bizarre purgatory – a place where they stay because they can't make up their minds whether to remain in the river and be brown trout, or else bite the bullet and take to the ocean, to become pukka sea trout.

For yet others, like immature juvenile bass, the estuary is a safer option than the outside sea. Less likely to contain 'A list' predators, the estuary acts as a nursery area, providing somewhere for the young fish to feed and grow in relative safety.

Mullet cruise around estuaries for much of their lives as they like warm shallow water and the weed, maggots and algae it offers. Flounders and dabs love estuaries, too, because the soft silty mud provides camouflage and is normally home to their favourite food: shrimps, crabs and worms. Flounder fishing is an ideal way to fish an estuary. While targeting flounder with ragworm, you might also accidentally catch sea trout, slob trout, bass, pollack, dab or plaice, so it's a practical catch-all approach.

The best way to start is at low tide and follow the incoming tide upwards from the estuary mouth towards the source of the river. Travel light, with just one rod, a couple of spare rigs and a pair of wellies or waders to navigate the muddy spots. In fact, be very careful of muddy spots, don't venture away from the rocky shoreline by too far. If the mud is exposed then wait for the tide to cover it. Don't try to cross it.

As you move up, look for gullies and hollows which are exposed but soon to be filled by the incoming tide. These are good spots to fish, and are places where dabs or flounders will hole up, waiting and feeding while the incoming tide covers the ground ahead, forging the way. Dabs like to hunt in small packs too. So, if you do hook a fish, send your next cast back to the very same spot; there may well be a bunch of his hunting buddies waiting to chomp your bait.

There's nothing to stop you float-fishing up an estuary too, with a worm suspended just a couple of feet below an easy-to-cast but not-too-bulky float.

Estuary fishing is best when you're mobile and covering a lot of water. You're unlikely to catch a monster, but you'll be surrounded by wading birds, wild mussels, cockles, winkles and maybe even the occasional wild oyster, seal or otter. All of which go to make the estuary experience in the world of brackish water really quite special.

Estuary fishing equipment

ROD	Spinning rod (see p.113–14)
REEL	Fixed-spool reel (see p.119)
LINE	10–15lb line and shock leader (see pp.121 and 131)
HOOKS	1–2/0 hooks (see pp.122–3)
TERMINAL TACKLE	Floats, weights, swivels, beads, feathers, other lures (see Tackle and Kit, pp.123–9 and pp.132–44)
RIG ASSEMBLY	Float rig (see p.165)
BAIT	Mackerel, squid, lugworms, ragworms, peeler crab (see Bait, pp.153–5 and pp.158–9)

Rocky cliffs and ledges

Fishing off rocks works well because, unlike gently sloping beaches, the water around rocky outcrops is often instantly deep. Rocks also attract algae, which attract larger life forms, which in turn attract fish. Rocks provide cracks and crevices for seaweed to root and this provides food and shelter for all manner of aquatic life, including fish and larger crustaceans such as crabs, shrimps, prawns and lobsters. A rock face that is always partially submerged by sea water is like a mini reef, providing a permanent habitat which can support a whole food chain of sea life.

Fishing off rocks that always have sea around them is easier in some ways than a beach, because there's always water, whatever the state of the tide. And a simple drop of a bait from the rocks gives you instant access to this reef-like habitat.

However, the disadvantages of rock fishing are numerous. It's a naturally snaggy environment, which will rob you of tackle. And it adds an extra dimension of difficulty when landing a fish. Trying to drag a fish up a snaggy rock face so often turns a moment of triumph to one of tears and regret. To overcome this, use a drop net (see pp.146–7) or a long-handled landing net.

The most worrying aspect of rock fishing is that it's potentially very dangerous. I've known experienced anglers who have broken ankles climbing to rock marks. One of the most common accidents befalling rock fishermen is tripping on a rabbit hole, while lugging fishing tackle across cliffs. And these accidents are ones which happen *before* they've even got to the really dangerous spot. The bit where the rocks meet the sea.

Every year a number of anglers are swept off rocks by crashing waves. And even more have to be rescued by lifeboat crews, because they get stranded by rising tides and frighten themselves rigid by climbing down to places which they then discover they can't climb back out of. Make no mistake, rock fishing is fraught with danger. If you're determined to try it, then:

- Make sure you go somewhere that is recommended by an experienced angler or tackle shop.
- Before you go, listen to a relevant local weather forecast and check the tide table so you know what the tide is doing and when (see Directory, p.249). Don't go in bad weather.
- Take a mobile phone and put the coastguard number on speed dial. In some rock-fishing locations, mobile phone signals are poor or non-existent, so as an added precaution, let someone at home know exactly where you're going and what time you intend to return. That way, if you don't pitch up, they can contact the coastguard and let him know exactly where you went.
- Pack a torch – just in case of emergency.
- Wear good boots with ankle support and a decent grip.
- Travel light.
- Don't take young children with you.

Rocky cliff fishing equipment

ROD	Spinning rod (see pp.113–14) or carp rod (see p.116–17)
REEL	Fixed-spool reel (see p.119)
LINE	10–15lb line and shock leader (see pp.121 and 131)
HOOKS	1–4/0 hooks (see pp.122–3)
TERMINAL TACKLE	Floats, weights, swivels, beads, feathers, other lures, drop net or landing net (see Tackle and Kit, pp.123–9, pp.132–44 and pp.146–7)
RIG ASSEMBLY	Float rig (see p.165)
BAIT	Mackerel, squid, lugworms, ragworms, peeler crab (see Bait, pp.153–5 and pp.158–9)

Harbours

Harbours are built to provide a safe haven for boats, giving them somewhere to moor protected from the direct force of the prevailing wind and weather. And what works for boats works for fish too. A harbour is like an office foyer with fish passing in and out through the doors, some just to drop off or pick up, others to hang around and wait, and a few more going straight through to the elevators and on up to higher levels.

In the event of storms, some fish will take refuge inside harbours, especially small fish like sprats, which don't have the strength to fight against stormy seas and strong currents. Where there are sprats or other bait fish, then sure enough bigger fish will follow. Bass and big mackerel are opportunistic feeders and will cruise into any harbour that's providing a temporary home to some nervy sprats. And so, just before and just after stormy weather, the temporary population of harbours might explode with refugees and refugee predators.

In the late summer and autumn, when the sea temperature is at its warmest, prawns are attracted to the weed and algae that grow on the submerged harbour pilings. And, where there are prawns, there are always cruising fish, trying their hardest to eat them.

Cold weather can have an effect on the aquatic population of a harbour too, by offering a shivery siren call to certain species. The first frosts of winter attract squid as they migrate in from deeper water. Like any of the finned predators, these violent cephalopods are on the hunt. They target small fry – fish born earlier in the year – who are taking cover in the shadow of the harbour walls. Squid also have huge eyes, which gives them a night-hunting advantage.

Winter fish like whiting will gravitate towards harbour mouths, especially at night when, like squid, they feel less conspicuous.

As most harbours also have a river running into them from their landward side, there's a continual flow of fresh water which flushes food along the river bed and into the harbour itself. Sea fish will hang out where the fresh water spills into the harbour in order to intercept this conveyor-belt of food. The more rain that's falling inland and the more swollen by flood the river is, the more potential food it will carry. (That said, there is a limit to how much fresh water the average sea fish will stand.)

Certain fish 'smell' fresh water and get excited by it, for reasons other than food. Salmon, sea trout and eels all require fresh river water for their breeding cycle. Mature salmon and sea trout return from feeding at sea and seek to enter specific rivers, in order to run upstream to search out tiny gravel-bedded tributaries where they can lay their precious eggs in cool, well-oxygenated fresh water.

One fish which is synonymous with harbour cruising is the grey mullet. These fish are the 'homies' of the harbour neighbourhood, who cruise around the calm water, simply seeing and being seen. Grey mullet are understandably often mistaken for bass by novice harbour groupies who see a big silver fish (often in excess of 5lb) cruising in the sunlight as if he owns the place. Many assume it must be a high-ranking predator like a bass, rather than a vegetarian algae-sucking pacifist mullet.

The truth is that bass are much more wary and inconspicuous than mullet, who are conspicuous in their disregard for prying eyes. You'd be forgiven for thinking that a fish that makes himself so easy to spot would also be easy to catch. Nothing could be further from the truth (see grey mullet, pp.100–103).

Harbour fishing and the law Many harbours will have local restrictions about where you're allowed to fish. A quick chat, or a phone call to the harbourmaster, or even a look at the website, will clarify what you're allowed to do, when and where.

As a rule, boat owners are unhappy about people fishing around their craft. I've seen mooring ropes snagged, tackle left snapped and hanging from fenders, and gel-coat yacht surfaces chipped and scratched by carelessly cast terminal tackle. As a boat owner myself, I've experienced all manner of madness in the harbour mouth during summer, and believe me, getting someone's terminal tackle wrapped around your propeller is extremely annoying, potentially dangerous and expensive.

It's these accidents and discourtesies that create bad feeling between anglers and boaters in harbours and, because it's boaters who pay the mooring fees (and, thus, the harbourmaster's wages), boaters will always have the greatest leverage. Antagonising boaters will only ever restrict your fishing.

Harbour fishing equipment

ROD	Spinning rod (see p.113–4)
REEL	Fixed-spool reel (see p.119)
LINE	10–15lb line and shock leader (see pp.121 and 131)
HOOKS	1–4/0 hooks (see pp.122–3)
TERMINAL TACKLE	Floats (waggler and bubble), weights, beads, swivels, feathers, other lures, drop net or landing net (see Tackle and Kit, pp.123–9, pp.132–44 and pp.146–7)
RIG ASSEMBLY	Running ledger (see p.164), float rig (see p.165)
BAIT	Squid, mackerel, ragworm, bread (see Bait, pp.153, 155, 158 and 159)

Fish You Might Catch

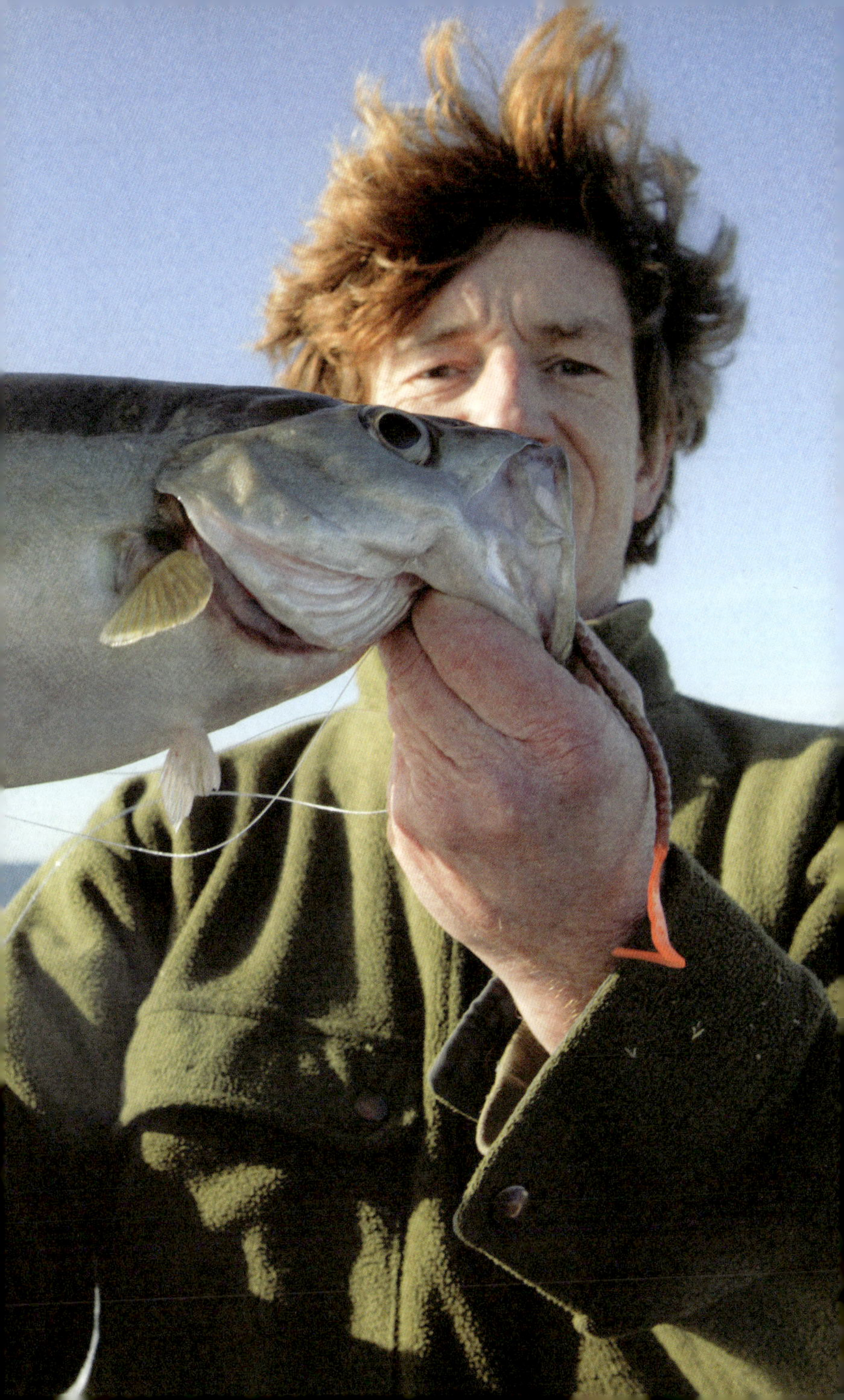

'If you caught something every time, it would be called "catching" not "fishing", wouldn't it?' This is the sort of philosophy that gets bandied about amongst sea anglers to make you feel better about going home with an empty cool box. These words alone might be enough to heal your disappointment, but I doubt it. However, you should be aware that even anglers like me and Hugh, who have spent decades in the pursuit of fish, often come home fishless – even on the most promising of days in the most ripe and fertile fish locations.

Most of the fish that you can catch around our shores are not only edible but delicious, and the species in this chapter are arranged roughly in order of the ones most likely to put a bend in your rod, to those least likely to put in an appearance.

Some species don't taste as good, or take too much effort to prepare, or are too small to bother with; I've identified these (on pp.104–6). And there are some fish that taste good, but are in serious danger of being overfished and should be released, as they're much better for the marine environment alive than dead (see pp.107–9).

Unlike wild mushrooms or berries, there aren't any fish that will poison you if you eat them, although there is one British fish – the weaver fish (see p.106) – that *will* poison you if you accidentally stand on it with bare feet, or prick yourself with its three stiletto-sharp fin spines. But if you pan-fry it and eat it on toast with butter and horseradish sauce it will do you no harm.

One myth that I feel should be exploded at this point is that learning to sea-fish is a means to access cheap fish. It isn't. If cheap fish is what you want from sea fishing, then stop now. Don't fool yourself that learning to fish will save you money, it won't. The ratio of spend – in terms of money, time and effort – to fish on plate doesn't make any personal economic sense whatsoever. And yet, what fishing does give you, if you catch the bug and really take to it, is ultimately priceless. The joy and satisfaction of learning new skills and being able to convert a day out at the seaside into a smashing feast of bitingly fresh fish is a gift for life.

The location (see pp.27) and season (see pp.17) affect what you might catch. Where fish dwell in the water column is also a factor (see adjacent diagram).

Key:
1. Garfish (top, middle)
2. Grey Mullet (top, middle)
3. Herring (top, middle)
4. Horse Mackerel (top, middle, bottom)
5. Mackerel (top, middle, bottom)
6. Black Bream (middle, bottom)
7. Sea Bass (top, middle, bottom)
8. Squid (middle, bottom)
9. Pollack (middle, bottom)
10. Cod (bottom)
11. Red Gurnard (middle, bottom)
12. Dogfish (bottom)
13. Whiting (bottom)
14. Pouting (bottom)
15. Dab (bottom)
16. Flounder (bottom)
17. Plaice (bottom)

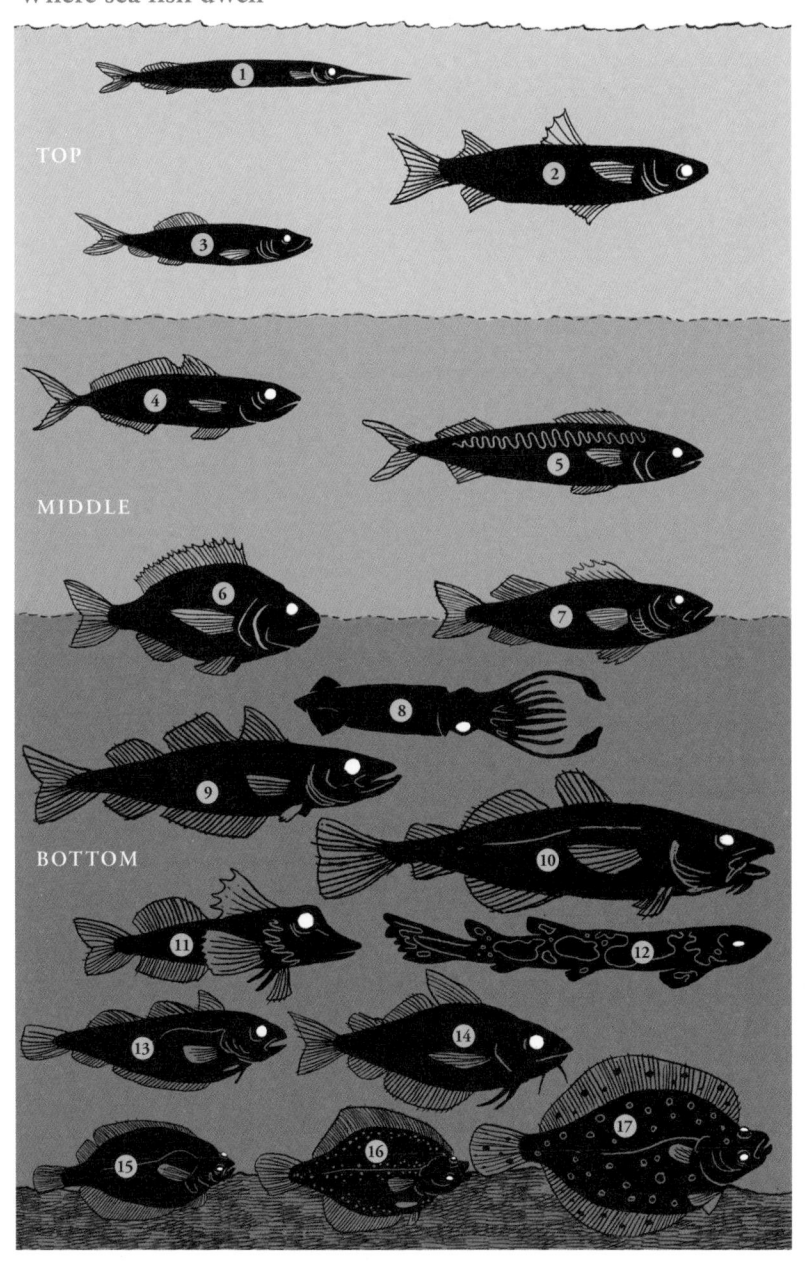

Where sea fish dwell

TOP

MIDDLE

BOTTOM

FISH YOU MIGHT CATCH

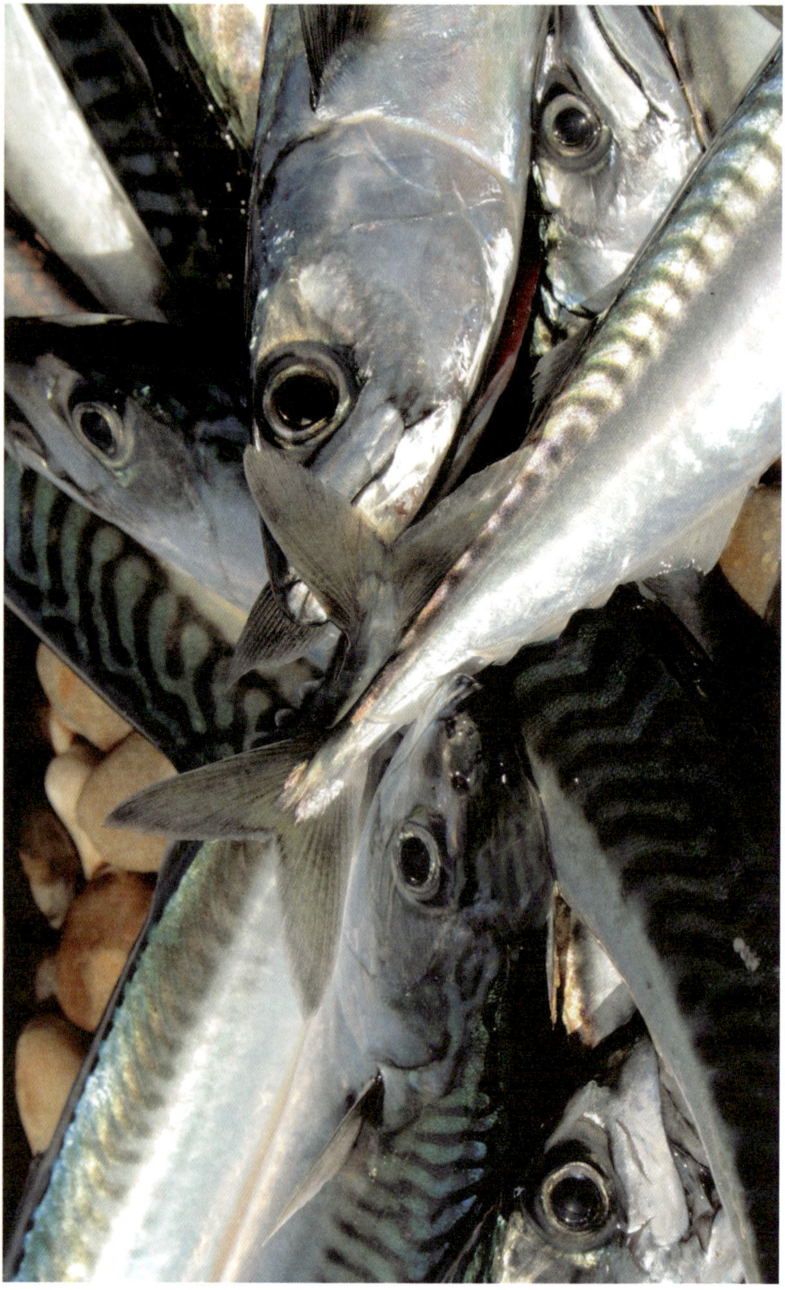

Mackerel *Scomber scombrus*

SEASON	All year in the Southwest. Generally April–October in the rest of the UK
LOCATION	Beach, pier, rocks, boat
METHOD	Spinning, feathering, float-fishing with small strips of bait (mackerel or squid)
CONSERVATION STATUS	Healthy

So many love affairs with sea fishing have started with a mackerel bite. Without a shadow of a doubt, these are our finest sea fish. Not only are they plentiful, they are co-operative, they taste good and they're chock full of life-enhancing omega-rich oils and other nutrients.

Always excitable and hungry, mackerel are like perennial puppies. The reason why they are so ravenous and therefore happy to attack practically any sort of bait – from a bare shiny hook to a fancy thrumming spinner – is because they are 'pelagic' or wandering fish. These are fish that are continually on the move, both in terms of migration, as well as moving up and down the water column, hunting food at various depths, from the surface to the seabed. Mackerel are in effect the British equivalent of tuna or marlin, which criss-cross entire oceans in the pursuit of top-class feed.

Mackerel behave in the same way as these big-scale pelagic fish, only they do it over a smaller range. They might not cross oceans, but mackerel will migrate up and down the English Channel, or along hundreds of miles of our coastline, in their quest for top nourishment. And their pelagic nature, this continual searching and swimming, necessitates that their flesh be oily. Mackerel require a continual ready source of energy on tap, as 'fuel' for their hard-working muscles. Conversely, white fish, such as cod and pollack, have a much less active lifestyle and so can carry their oil energy supplies in the reservoir of their liver.

Finding them

Mackerel are eternally obliging fish, which can be caught from a range of locations (see chart, p.27), using various methods, from small baits float-fished, to cast spinners, feathers or plugs.

During the spring, mackerel migrate to inshore shallow waters as the sea first begins to warm. In winter, the deeper water offshore maintains a higher temperature than the shallower inshore water, so mackerel move offshore to follow the food and more consistent water temperatures. When spring returns, they move back inshore as the food supplies migrate and the sea temperature rises.

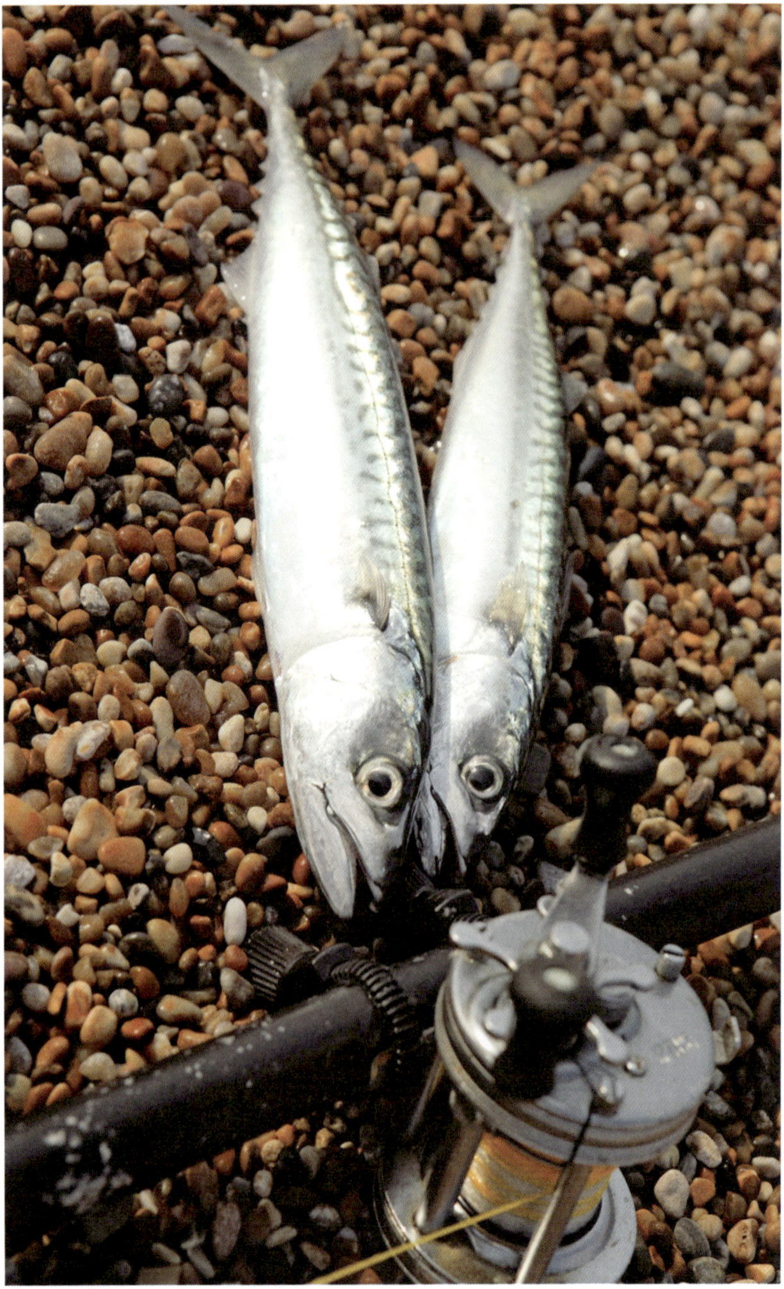

Most of the time you won't actually catch sight of mackerel, even though they may be feeding near the surface. Occasionally during the late summer and autumn you may detect evidence of their presence in two ways: showers of tiny fry fish hopping out of the sea and seagulls diving into it. The fry leap out of the water in an attempt to escape mackerel, which are hunting the shoal from below. And the sea birds dive in to take advantage of the mackerel's endeavours, picking off bait fish that have been wounded or disoriented by the mass mackerel attack.

Catching them

If you're fishing from a boat, the easiest way to catch mackerel is with a string of mackerel feathers (see pp.134–5). You just have to lower them over the side and jig them up and down at various depths, or let them hang out the back, 20 or 30 yards behind, as the boat putters slowly along. This latter method is known as 'trolling' (see p.13).

Using mackerel feathers is trickier if you're casting from a shallow sandy beach, where they'll sink and possibly get caught up on the seabed. But it's still likely to be the most productive method. I often cut a string of six feathers down to three, which still gives three chances to attract a mackerel but reduces the weight of your string and the possibility of accidentally hooking the seabed. Choosing the right weight – just enough for a decent cast but not too much to take it down to the seabed too quickly – is another way of fine-tuning your beach feathering approach.

Because of their high oil content, mackerel spoil much more quickly than white fish like whiting, cod or pollack. So, they need to be killed, bled and chilled soon after they're caught (see pp.177–9); there's a particular method for killing mackerel which bleeds them at the same time (see p.178). And to enjoy them at their best, you really need to eat mackerel as soon as possible – ideally on the day you catch them, or at least within the next couple of days.

Eating them

Mackerel are laughably easy to cook; their natural oils make them conveniently self-basting and hard to spoil, either on the grill or in the oven. I love mackerel made into sashimi (see pp.206–8), pickled (see pp.210–11) and in escabeche (see p.213 and pp.216–17).

It is also delicious barbecued with bay leaves (see p.230), baked with potato chunks and lemon wedges (see p.233) or fry-poached and then generously drizzled with lemon juice or crab apple juice (see pp.242–3). And a great way of cooking mackerel on the beach is to poach it in a bucket of sea water (see p.228).

Dogfish *Scyliorhinus canicula*

SEASON	All year
LOCATION	Beach, pier, boat
METHOD	Fish a bait (worms, squid or mackerel) on a bottom-fishing rig
CONSERVATION STATUS	Healthy

Most fish are hard to catch and easy to eat. Dogfish are the opposite: sometimes catching them is too easy. Their rabid hunger and terrible table manners makes them suckers for swallowing hook bait. If you happen to alight upon a whole pack of doggies, then you might find *all* you catch is one dogfish after another. A rowdy pack can scare every other self-respecting species away and then squabble amongst themselves over the pickings left on the feeding ground.

Dogfish are tricky to eat, but it's not because they don't taste good, far from it; a bite-sized nugget of deep-fried beer-battered dogfish is about as delicious a fish-eating experience as any sane angler could wish. No, it's the *packaging* that dogfish goujons come in that is the problem.

The Lesser Spotted Dogfish (aka the LSD), our most common dogfish, and our most prolific member of the shark brotherhood, is covered in a thick, gritty sandpaper-like skin, which is so tightly fitted that it requires a real knack to get it off without shedding your own blood, or tears, in the process. So tricky is the art of dogfish skin removal that I've devoted a whole section to the techniques (see pp.194–7).

But please don't be put off. Think of a dogfish as the marine equivalent of a pomegranate – there's some serious fiddling to be done to get to the good stuff. However, when you succeed, the hidden fruit is sweet and succulent, easy to cook, and well worth the effort.

Finding them

Dogfish don't go anywhere. Even in the depths of winter, when most other species have sought out warmer and deeper climes, the dogfish, bless him, can still be found snouting around all his usual haunts searching for food. Sometimes the cold weather or a change in feeding patterns causes them to hunt in packs, which means there may be a thinner spread of dogfish over a large area, but a large concentration at specific marks.

Most of the year, dogfish like to feed over sandy, gravelly or muddy ground, but they'll occasionally hunt over rocky ground too. They can be found in deep as well as very shallow water.

Catching them

Catching dogfish isn't too difficult. They'll eat more or less anything, so baits don't have to be fancy, or fresh – sometimes stinkier is better. Dogfish are used to hunting out baits in dark murky depths, so they've developed a highly tuned sense of smell, and use their snout more than their dark, beady satanic eyes to find food. Baits don't need to be carefully presented on the hook either: a doggie will bite chunks out of a whole dead dolphin if it needs to. So a lump of old mackerel, rancid from defrosting and refreezing, ragworms, fish guts, tails, heads, limpets, whelks or hermit crabs will all work. Dogfish are very partial to a cocktail, so don't be scared to be inventive and mix squid and worm or fish and crab on the hook. But remember, like all true scavengers, dogfish are members of the bottom-feeding fraternity, so whatever bait you do use, it needs to be well weighted, so it's in contact with the seabed.

I generally prefer to use fine wire hooks when I'm fishing for any of the species I've covered in this book. However, dogfish do have thick cartilage in their jaws, covered by that incredibly tough sandpaper skin, which can make hook removal quite tricky. Thin wire hooks are inclined to bend very easily in a dogfish's jaw as you try to remove them, and then they become useless. (It always helps to have a pair of long-nosed pliers in your box to help remove hooks.) If you're in the middle of a dog pack, and are catching more dogfish than you intend to keep, it makes sense to swap to using thick wire hooks (a 2/0 or 3/0), which bend less easily, and then also use the

How to hold a dogfish

pliers to squeeze the barb down flat. That way you'll be able to unhook the dogfish easily and return the ones you don't want to eat totally unharmed.

Unhooking a dogfish can be a painful business for the angler, because a dog's flapping and curling tail can easily wind itself around your wrist as you fumble at the hook, inflicting a very nasty graze with its highly abrasive skin – one which will take a long time to heal.

To get around this, some anglers take a rag with them to wrap around the fish while they perform hook removal surgery. Another technique I often use is simply to fold the fish sideways so that the tip of its tail is level with its chest, and hold the tail fin firmly against its body with the thumb and fingers of one hand (as shown above), while you deal with the hook with your other hand. The friction of its skin against skin makes it easy to hold it still.

Because they're such primeval thick-skinned sharks, dogfish don't die easily. To despatch one properly, it's necessary to club it hard, two or three times across the centre of the head, with a well-weighted 'priest' (see p.146). And remember there are special techniques for skinning dogfish (see pp.194–7).

Eating them

Dogfish is easy to cook. It doesn't flake or fall apart like white fish or oily fish, so it makes fantastic stew (see p.224). And because it's a cartilaginous fish, which doesn't have skeletal bones, it is a popular choice with even the fussiest fish eaters. Simple dogfish goujons, deep-fried in breadcrumbs (see pp.238–9) and dipped in homemade tartare sauce (see p.205), are about as eminently edible as any fish can be.

Pouting *Trisopterus luscus*

SEASON	All year
LOCATION	Boat fishing is best. Also try the beach, rocky cliffs and harbours for small pouting
METHOD	Bottom-fishing with mackerel strip for bait, or ragworm, lugworm or squid strip bait
CONSERVATION STATUS	Healthy

Pouting are members of the cod family, so they're related to whiting and pollack, yet they don't get treated with anything like the respect that their cod cousins receive. For as long as I've been sea fishing, I've known pouting to be sneered at by serious sea anglers, mostly because they're regarded as an unwanted accidental catch landed during the more serious business of targeting fish like cod, bass or black bream. Pouting are not even considered worth keeping for crab-pot bait or for hook bait, and because they rarely survive being released back into the water, they are often left to drift away at the torturous mercy of eye-plucking seagulls.

The reason why pouting don't survive when they're released is because they're very sensitive to pressure change. Being brought up from a depth of even as little

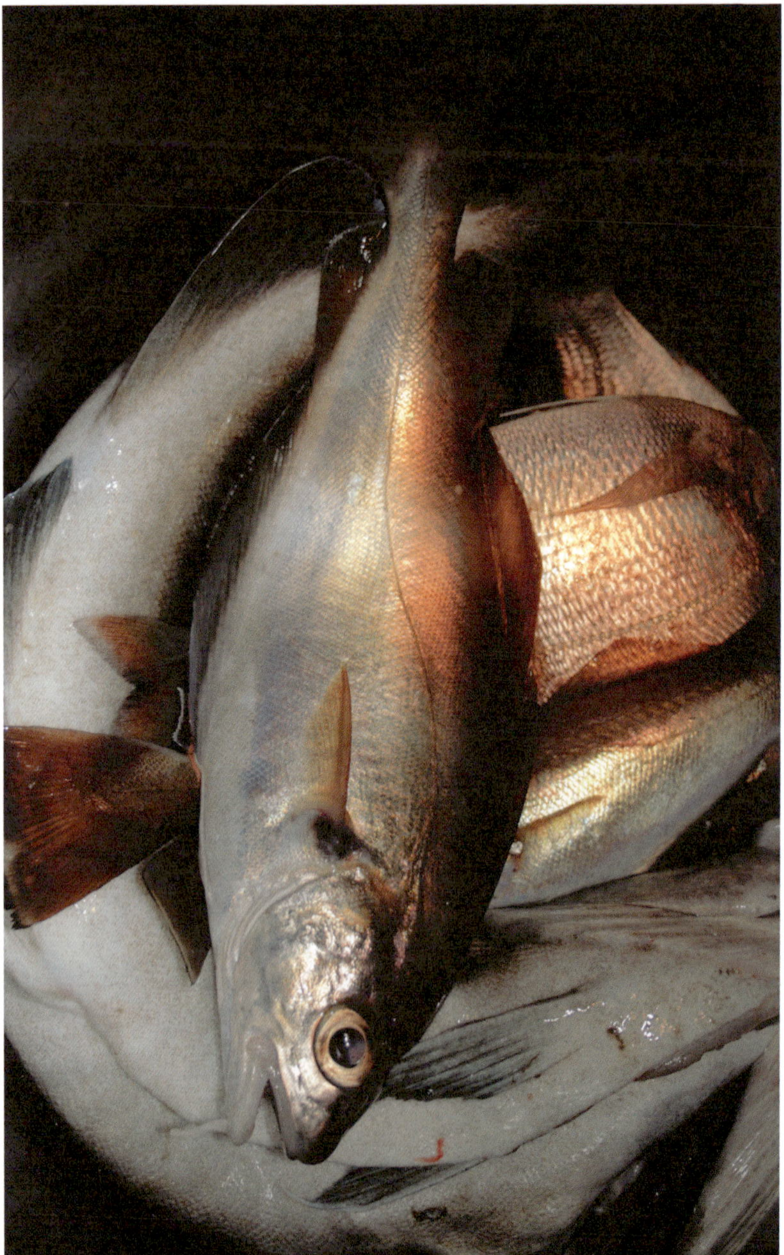

as 30 feet can cause their swim bladder to 'blow' and the membrane over their eyes to inflate (as a consequence, they've been given the uncharitable moniker 'bug eyes'). In this inflated state, they're unable to swim back to the seabed, and so float helplessly on the surface.

If you catch a pout, especially from a boat, then the chances are it's going to die. This may be a tragedy for the pout and his family, but it is good reason for the fish-loving angler to celebrate because pouting, despite their ill-deserved reputation, are very good to eat.

Finding them

Pouting can be caught nearly all year round, the spring, summer and autumn months being the most pout productive. The bigger ones tend to stay in water over 40 feet deep, so the best method for catching them is from a boat, but occasionally big ones will be caught from beach marks too, especially in the evening and at night. Rocky cliffs and harbours usually hold a resident population of small pout.

Catching them

As pouting are bottom-feeding fish, you need to use a bottom-fishing rig baited with a mackerel strip/chunk, worm or squid. They also respond well to mackerel feathers with a chunk of bait attached to the bottom couple of hooks. Pouting have big mouths and greedy bellies, so hook size and even bait size is unimportant. They'll wrap their gums around anything vaguely edible.

If you catch a pouting, bleed it, gut it and chill it as soon as you can. Removing guts swiftly is the key to pouting success. Many pouting detractors claim they smell bad, and it's true their guts do have a distinct smell, which is more 'composty' than other fish. This is simply because they eat more weed in their diet and have a different digestive system. But if you gut them and chill them within an hour or two of catching, they smell and taste as fine as any white fish in our seas.

Eating them

The proof of the pouting is in the eating. In countries where they worship freshly caught fish of all species, like Spain, Portugal and France, you'll see pouting or *faneca* fillets in every local fish market. And in my house, they're a firm favourite too. Usually I serve them as fried breadcrumbed fillets (see pp.238–9) or battered fillets (see p.240), sometimes popped into a crusty roll with a dab of homemade tartare sauce (see p.205), garlic mayonnaise (see p.204) or tomato ketchup.

Pollack *Pollachius pollachius*

SEASON	Inshore during summer and autumn
LOCATION	Over rocky ground, weed beds and near inshore reefs and structures
METHOD	Ragworm bait, spinner, rubber worms, rubber fish. Caught on paternoster rigs, trolled lures and float-fished ragworm
CONSERVATION STATUS	Healthy, but more vulnerable now they're commercially fished as a replacement for cod

In the last few years, pollack has gone from zero to hero. A fish once considered fit only for cat food now regularly sells for the same, if not more than, cod. Chefs rave about pollack now, when not so long ago cod and haddock were the only white fish deemed worthy of note. And anything you might do with cod, you can do with pollack, in the knowledge that it's a faster-growing, more plentiful fish, which doesn't carry anything like the same conservation issues that cod does.

Unlike herring and mackerel, which are pelagic oily-skinned fish, pollack and cod are white demersal fish. They inhabit the demersal zone of the sea, close to the seabed, where currents are less strong and life is less frenetic. Unlike pelagic fish, they don't swim around all day long, and instead hide around features out of the force of the current where they can ambush their prey.

As pollack don't need a constant ready supply of fuel oil, they store it in their liver, where it can be slowly tapped when needed. Pollack liver oil shares the precious health-giving properties that have made cod liver oil so famous. (In Iceland, I've stayed in hotels where at the end of the breakfast buffet line stands a decanter full of chilled cod liver oil and a stack of shot glasses, for diners to dose themselves for the day ahead.) It's mad not to do something with the livers of any pollack you catch; personally I would highly recommend keeping the liver for popping into the pot whilst making fish stock, to add extra flavour and nutritious oils.

Finding them

Really big pollack of 15lb plus are a deep-water fish, so they are rarely caught from the shore or from inshore boats. However, when the water is warm during the summer and autumn months, small pollack (around 2lb) are often found in shallow water around rocky outcrops or kelp seaweed beds. Pollack love a feature, such as a small reef or ledge, a sunken wreck, or ancient concrete pilings – somewhere to lie in ambush for small fish and crabs that are washed along by the tide.

FISH YOU MIGHT CATCH 57

Catching them

Being voracious predators and sometimes opportunistic bottom-feeders, pollack can be caught on all sorts of baits and rigs, from feathers and baited feathers to ragworm and peeler crab. From a boat they can be caught trolling, drifting or even while sitting at anchor. My favourite way to catch pollack from a small boat is to drift while fishing a lightly weighted paternoster rig on a spinning rod, or light boat rod, with 15lb line and a fat trailing ragworm as bait. Of course you can use rubber worms and artificial baits instead, which are a lot cheaper and will work well in most conditions. But there's just something very satisfying and exciting about fishing with what you know in your heart is a pollack's favourite meal. The bites are rapacious. A pollack will chase a big ragworm with all the enthusiasm of a hungry lurcher.

An important thing to note, though, is that even fishing into no more than 20 feet of water, pollack, like pouting, don't fare well after being brought out of the sea. Catch and release doesn't really work with pollack, so if you do happen upon a good pollack spot, stop as soon as you've caught your feed. Don't be tempted to go on fishing for 'sport' afterwards; it will only cause more pollack demise.

I recommend gutting your catch at sea or on the shore, because it's less messy than doing it in the kitchen, and more importantly, it gives you a chance to put ice directly into the belly cavity.

Eating them

Small pollack make very good eating. Because of their delicate white flesh, they're not really suitable for barbecue cooking, unless you cook them in a protective foil parcel. But they're a very good fish to practise your filleting skills on.

I always save the heads and skeletons of my pollack (along with the liver), because they make such excellent fish stock (see pp.218–20). Like a cod's head, a pollack's head is full of cartilage. When boiled and then allowed to cool, this creates the most magnificent fishy jelly, which is wonderful as a base for fishy risottos and soups. If you make stock from pollack, you don't have to use it straight away. More often than not, I pour the cooled stock into a double layer of freezer bags and pop it in the freezer for another day.

To cook pollack fillets, I lightly salt them first, distributing 1 tbsp salt over both sides of each fillet and leaving them to stand for around 15 minutes, before giving them a good rinse in cold water and a pat dry with a tea towel.

I then coat the fillets in a tempura-style batter or breadcrumbs and deep-fry (see pp.238–9), draining them well on kitchen paper before serving. Or I shallow-fry the fillets in olive oil, with some capers and lemon juice.

Otherwise fillets of pollack can be steamed and served with a soy, chilli and garlic sauce (see pp.236–7) or baked with green beans and stock, and topped with a pesto crust (see p.234).

Cod *Gadus morhua*

SEASON	Winter (October–February). In recent years, early-summer runs appear in the Channel
LOCATION	Shore fishing over rough, rocky ground or shingle beaches. Early-summer inshore boat fishermen concentrate their efforts over beds of brittle starfish
METHOD	From shore, use big baits (peeler crab, lugworm, mussel and black lug) ledgered on pennel rigs. Over starfish beds, boat anglers use rubber fish, wedges and baited feathers
CONSERVATION STATUS	Not too healthy; use discretion

Cod is not a smart fish. In fact, I'd go as far as to say that it's really quite a stupid fish. When cod are present in any number, they're easy to catch. They're greedy, lazy big-mouthed slobs, who'll eat just about any bait you put in front of them, and swallow it whole – from a single ragworm on a size 1 hook, to a pennel rig-mounted cocktail of baits the size of your foot.

A few years ago, I was evangelical in my cod preservation stance and put more than a few noses out of joint when I insisted every cod caught while drift fishing from our boat off the Portland Race, outside Weymouth, was returned. They often get caught in amongst the bass and bream shoals feeding in the fast current. Since then, I've become more easy-going and have even kept one or two cod myself as I've seen their numbers inshore increase. But that's one or two fish over the same number of years. Even if we know there's good cod fishing to be had, we have to be abstemious and careful. Make no mistake, if the cod species is abused, it will disappear.

In saying all that, anyone who has the opportunity to catch a couple of cod, now and again, would be mad not to make the effort and, if successful, to take the odd fish home. Yet, here is where we need to have a healthy fish conscience. In my opinion, one fish from a trip is acceptable, two is an absolute maximum, and if you keep catching cod, for whatever reason – because the planets are aligned and you find yourself 'in the zone' – then you need to have the discipline to stop.

Finding them

The trick of cod fishing is almost entirely down to location: being in the right place at the right time, either on a rocky beach mark when a bunch of feeding fish are passing during the winter months; or in early summer on a boat drifting over a bed

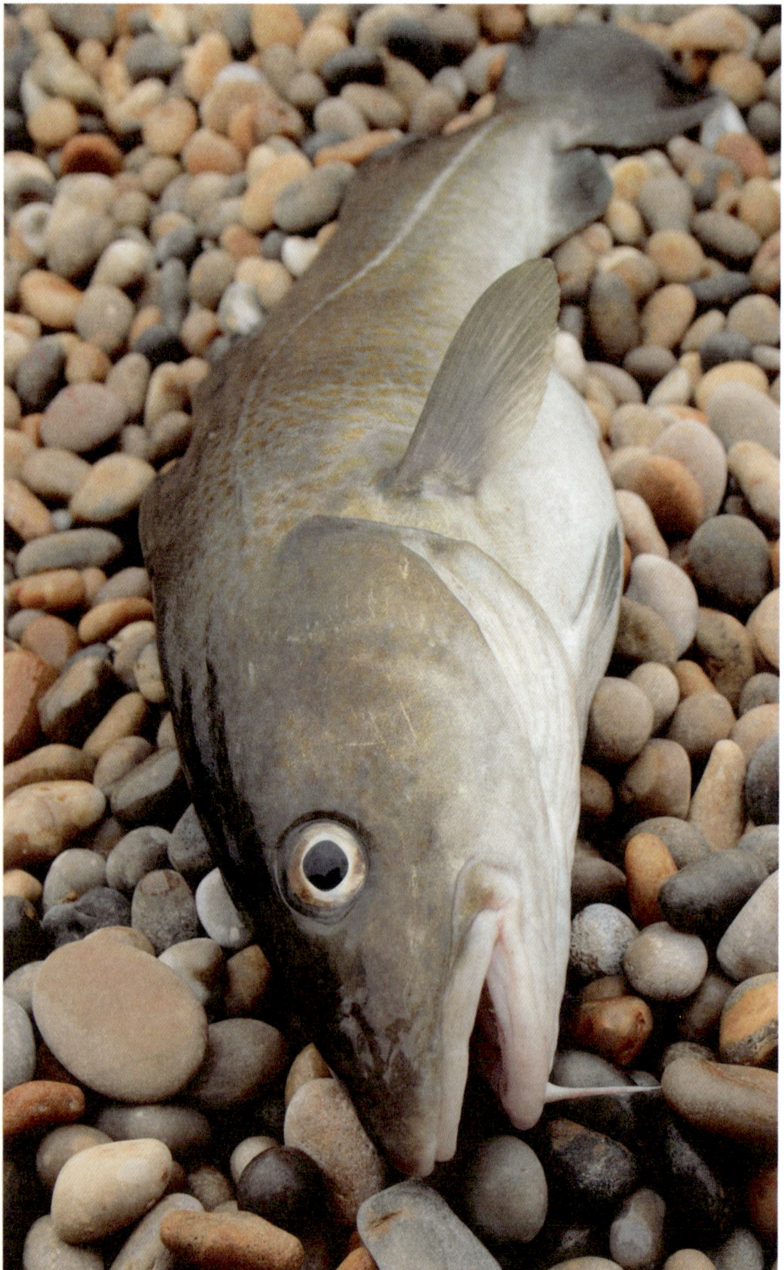

of brittle starfish, which have caught the attention of a feeding shoal. Sometimes beach fishing at night works best as the cod will come closer to the shore under the cover of darkness. When I was living in Norfolk, in my very early teens, night fishing was considered the only way to catch cod from the beach. Along with my dad, I would crunch over miles of pebbles carrying a ghostly glowing Tilley lamp and just occasionally we'd get lucky and tease a couple of codling from the wind-chilled North Sea.

Catching them

I take my hat off to anyone who catches a cod from the beach. It takes dedication and perseverance to track down cod; it might even require cold, blustery night sessions, many blank trips and much investment in bait. So, if you're someone who likes a challenge and is prepared to put in the hours and the effort, then you definitely deserve your cod. Use big baits – peeler crab, lugworm, mussel and black lug – on a pennel rig (see p.167).

Boat fishing for cod is slightly less noble and deserving, in terms of the ratio of effort to reward. Unless you're skippering your own boat, chances are you're going to be taken out by a skipper who knows where the cod are, and can put you above a co-operative feeding shoal (of which, let's face it, there aren't statistically that many). There you'll be able to pretty much fill your boots fairly easily. Usually a few drifts over a feeding shoal with rubber fish Storm lures (see pp.143–4) or baited feathers (see pp.134–6) will result in multiple hook-ups. In this situation, it's not unusual with feathers to even hook two or three cod at a time.

This is when recreational cod fishing is dubious, in my opinion. Any cod caught and killed should be justly earned. Cod is not a fish we can afford to get greedy or complacent about, nor is it one that we recreational anglers can over-target or abuse from boats, while commercial fishermen are governed by strict quota restrictions.

If you do catch a cod – well done. And if you do kill it, just make sure you treat it with total respect from the killing, chilling, preparing cooking and eating perspectives, so that you leave not a single morsel unloved.

Eating them

Cod bones, skin, head and fins all make fabulous fish stock (see pp.218–20). The cod head alone, if it's big enough, can be roasted (stick a couple of rashers of thick streaky smoked bacon on top and a bunch of rosemary inside) with fennel root to make a finger-licking, bone-picking, eye socket-sucking feast.

Fillets of cod can be steamed (see p.235) or baked with green beans and stock, and topped with a pesto crust (see p.234). And there is no finer fish to wrap in an eggy batter and deep-fry (see pp.238–41), then drain and serve with tartare sauce (see p.205) or a sweet chilli or soy and garlic dipping sauce (see p.205).

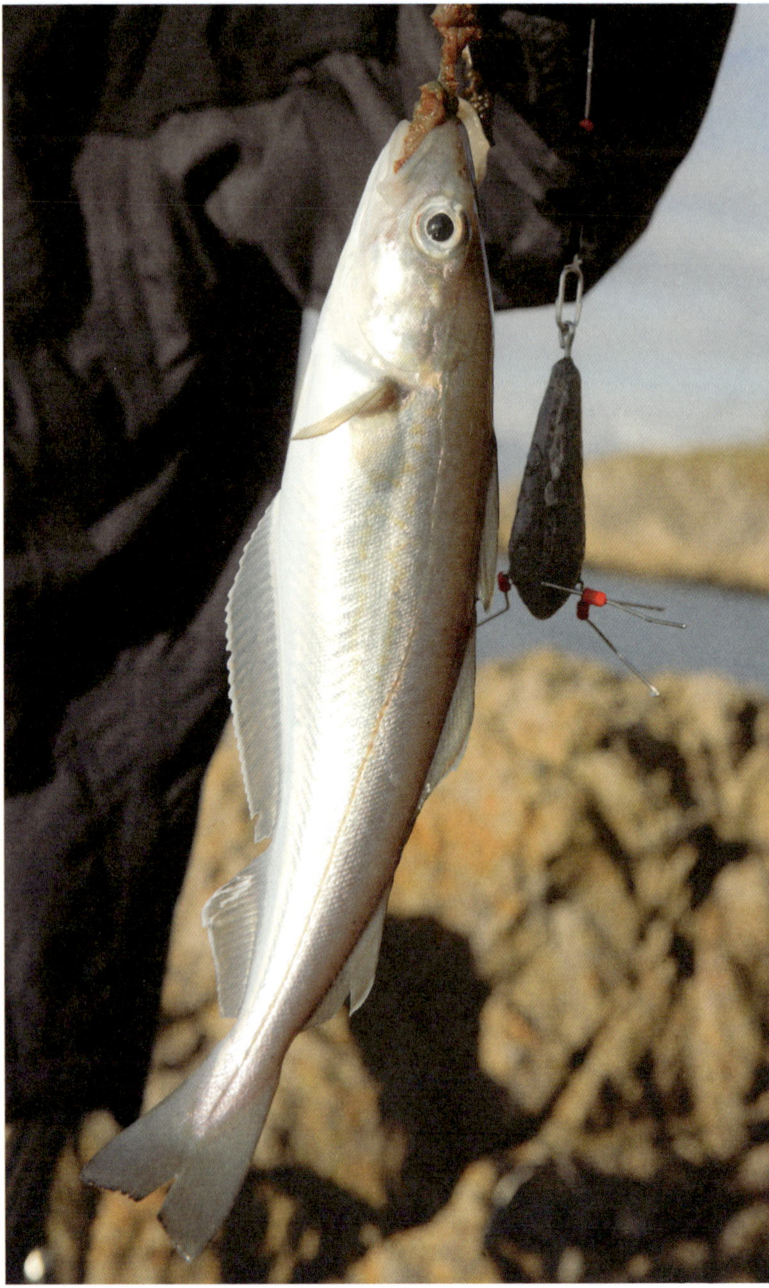

Whiting *Merlangius merlangus*

SEASON	Autumn and winter
LOCATION	Inshore boats over sandy, muddy or shingle ground. Occasionally from the shore too, especially at night, when fishing on to a sandy seabed
METHOD	From a boat, mackerel feathers baited with chunks of fish work, as will any paternoster rig baited with worm and fish baits. From the shore, use a bottom-fishing paternoster rig with small fish baits such as mackerel, sprat, herring and even strips of fresh whiting
CONSERVATION STATUS	Healthy

My most clearly etched memory of whiting lingers from my childhood in Scotland, where these fish were used in a perverse form of culinary torture executed upon sick people. Whiting poached in milk is the Protestant equivalent of Jewish chicken soup: a cure-all for the bilious and nauseous. In my granny's kitchen, the pressure cooker was the most prized instrument of torture. Sadly, poaching whiting until it's the consistency of zoo plankton really does its flaky muscular flesh a terrible disservice.

Since moving to Dorset, I've learned to let go of my lowland Scots Presbyterian roots and recognise fresh whiting for the fabulous Arctic white-fleshed fish that it really is. Not only delicious to eat, but satisfying and challenging to catch at times too. I now love cooking and eating whiting. And I can say, with unabashed pride, that I've managed to turn the whiting legacy around, and now my whiting fish fingers or tempura fillets in a sweet chilli dipping sauce are firm crunchy favourites with my own four children.

In so many ways, it is hard to find a more boring fish than whiting. They are the masters of beige. Beige in flavour, beige by nature, and beige in their behaviour, preferring to inhabit the most middle-of-the-road patches of seabed – not too deep, not too shallow, not too rocky. They like a nice sandy patch where they can ferret around *en masse* for crabs and worms.

Whiting don't appear to have any very interesting friends either. Winter shoals are often mono species. It's as though no self-respecting species wants to be associated with whiting. This is probably a result of their timing though, arriving inshore when most of the other more interesting fish have departed offshore to deeper, warmer, more constant and less storm-affected seas.

Finding them

Like a winter version of the mackerel, whiting arrive in our inshore waters around September, usually travelling in large shoals. The peak period for catching them around Britain is probably between late October and late November, but certainly on the south coast, they can often hang around right through until February and even into March. After Christmas is when the big ones (up to 2lb in weight) are normally caught. These tend to be more the lone wolves with big teeth and big appetites, unlike the smaller shoal fish that busy themselves along as members of a pack in the autumn.

The trick with catching whiting is location. They love clean sandy ground, but also have a penchant for a bit of flat muddy ground too if there's plenty of food to be found. Along shingle and surf beaches they'll cruise any gutters or troughs that have been scoured out behind the breaking surf. At night they'll venture into very shallow water, less than a couple of feet in depth, if they're finding good food.

The big spring tides of the late autumn are the ones that bring whiting right in to the beach. Then, in sporadic shoals, they hug the coastline in the same way that mackerel do in summer. Whiting will move along the shore against the flow of the tide. They're hunting for crabs and small fish being pushed along by the current and by heading into the flow they're able to use their keen hunter's sense of smell to its best advantage.

Catching them

Once you've found a shoal, the hard work is over; whiting are normally very easy to catch. Oddly, for such a cautious fish, they are actually not too fussy about what they'll pop in their mouths. Place just about any bait in their face and they'll hang themselves on your hook like floppy wet lemmings, limply pursuing mass suicide.

Unlike mackerel, whiting are demersal or bottom-feeding fish, closely related to cod. So they'll always be caught on, or very near, the bottom, usually using ledgered baits of mackerel or squid, or ragworm or lugworm. They are suckers for baited feathers too. Mackerel feathers, baited with chunks of mackerel flesh or squid, fished in the usual jigging manner, but down deep, bouncing off the seabed, is one very productive method to haul a few in, once you've found your shoal.

And for all their beigeness of character, whiting are, rather surprisingly, not averse to a bit of bling. Many committed and serious whiting anglers (which may seem like a cruel contradiction in terms) will fix silver flashing and rattling beads (known as Booby beads) to their feathers or paternoster rigs in order to attract the fishes' attention.

For all their lack of pizzazz, a whiting's mouth does conceal an impressive array of small pointy teeth. These teeth can eventually rasp right through fishing line, especially if you're banging out a bucket in a session. So use a 20–25lb hook length.

Normally, however, whiting weigh less than 1lb, although there are shoals of larger ones, known as Channel whiting, which can regularly be found weighing 2–4lb. These are the real bad boys of the otherwise bland whiting world. Not surprisingly they put up much more of a fight than the beige 1lb clones and, if you're lucky, might well put an unexpected curve in your carbon.

As with their close but sadly misunderstood cousins, the pouting (also known as the pout whiting), they should be cracked on the head, bled and chilled quickly. Warm whiting will deteriorate fast because their muscle flakes are very small and tightly packed, and the flesh will turn soft if it's not kept well chilled.

Eating them

A bunch of whiting, big or small, will always give terrific fillets – as well as some cod-like heads and frames that provide the basis of a truly classic fish stock (see pp.218–20). Most of the whiting I catch I'll fillet and fry in breadcrumbs or tempura batter (see pp.238–9), or possibly grill with bacon lardons or chorizo (see p.245).

I also like to fry-poach whiting fillets with olive oil, garlic and lemon and serve them over a bowl of brown rice (see pp.242–3).

Sometimes I'll just coat them lightly in a mix of cornflour, salt and black pepper and fry them quickly in very hot corn oil (see p.239).

Alternatively, neatly trimmed slices are perfect candidates for a quick ceviche marinade (see pp.214–15), especially with thinly sliced peppery-hot red chilli.

Garfish *Belone belone*

SEASON	Spring, summer and early autumn
LOCATION	Around piers, rocky headlands and from inshore boats
METHOD	Mini mackerel feathers, baited feathers and float-fishing with small mackerel, sand eel or even garfish strips for bait
CONSERVATION STATUS	Healthy

Garfish are extraordinary-looking creatures – rather like a cross between a swimming dinosaur, a baddie from *Thunderbirds* and an early blueprint for the Trident missile. They have a long pointed beak and a sleek, hydrodynamic body, with a sharply forked tail to provide them with forward thrust. But these are not their only distinguishing features. Garfish have luminescent green scales and a remarkable turquoise skeleton. You can always recognise anglers who have had a successful garfish catching experience, because their hands, bag and clothing possess an unmistakable green glow from all the dislodged scales.

I've often heard even experienced anglers say that garfish can't possibly be eaten because the green colouring is poisonous. This is totally untrue. The green of their scales and the deep green pigment of their bones is caused by a harmless mineral called vivianite, which is commonly found in rock formations around the English Channel. If you can get over the radioactive sheen of their scales and bones, you'll find that garfish are truly delicious to eat. Their lovely white flesh has the consistency of very firm mackerel and, because they are an oily pelagic fish, they're packed with beneficial nutrients.

Finding them

Summer is the best time to catch garfish. They're known in some areas as 'the mackerel guide' because they'll appear just in front of the spring shoals of migrating mackerel. And generally they'll hang around the same places as mackerel for the rest of the summer. This means that piers, seaward harbour walls and rocky headlands are classic garfish haunts.

Being oily pelagic fish, garfish tend to favour warmer water, and they'll happily swim in the very top layer of the sea during the summer. In fact, they're one of the few British sea fish that you might actually witness leaping out of the water. Their slender acrobatic design makes it possible for them to leap over rocks and navigate into very shallow water close to cliffs and rocks, in their predatory hunt for small fish, and to avoid less agile predators.

FISH YOU MIGHT CATCH 67

Catching them

Because they hunt small bait fish, garfish are occasionally caught on micro feathers or small baited feathers. Some adventurous anglers even pursue them with a fly rod, using small white or silver lures, although, in my experience, these flies work much better if they're tipped with a tiny strip of fish flesh or fish skin.

However, the most enjoyable and successful way to catch garfish is from a rock jetty or pier, using a light spinning rod and a sea float or bubble float rig, with a small hook size 1 suspended a few feet beneath it, weighed under by a drilled bullet lead. The hook should then be baited with a tiny sliver of mackerel flesh, sand eel fillet, or whole small sand eel. If you get lucky, try using a sliver of garfish flesh instead. (Like so many other sea predators, they are enthusiastically cannibalistic.)

Garfish are immense fun to catch. They'll put a serious bend in your rod and will often leap out of the sea during the ensuing fight, like a mini marlin or super-streamlined rainbow trout. The rows of sharp teeth inside their bony beak of a mouth does make them a little tricky to unhook. It helps to keep a wet tea towel and pair of pliers handy. Hold the garfish in the wet towel, use the pliers to turn the hook bend back on itself, and pull it from its mouth. If you've already caught enough for a meal, or feel a bit unsure about eating the fish and so intend to let them go, the wet towel minimises abrasion of scales, which might otherwise damage a garfish's chances of survival. Indeed, if you're not intending to keep many or any, you can squeeze the barb flat on your hook before you start fishing and the garfish will probably release themselves during the battle unharmed.

To kill a garfish, I would normally grab it in a rag or towel and give it a sharp crack over the back of the head; you don't need to wield the priest (see p.146) with a heavy hand. There's very good flesh in the neck and 'shoulders' so keep your killer blow accurate. You can hold them by the beak too, if you find this an easier way to keep the head perfectly still while you aim.

Eating them

My first garfish eating experience was in Guernsey, the Mecca of garfish fishing and eating. I had two cooked for me by a delightful septuagenarian who ran a local B&B. She grilled them briskly and served them with mushy peas, horseradish sauce and toast. It was a meal I'll never forget and I've cooked garfish in various ways since. My favourite is probably baking them in an open dish with wedges of par-boiled potatoes and lemon (see p.233). Horseradish sauce (see p.205) is a fine accompaniment.

Escabeche (see p.213 and pp.216–17) is another great option for garfish fillets. The oiliness of the flesh lends itself perfectly to being flour-dusted, quick fried and then doused with a tangy, vinegary marinade. Or you can simply grill chunky batons of garfish with a handful of chorizo slices and let the paprika-coloured oil baste the green-tinged garfish for a quick dish that is as colourful as it is delicious.

Red gurnard *Aspitrigla cuculus*

SEASON	Summer and autumn
LOCATION	Most easily caught from an inshore boat. They favour sandy, muddy or gravelly ground. Gurnard can be caught from beaches and piers too, though usually smaller fish
METHOD	Bottom-fishing with running ledger or paternoster rigs, using bait of worm, squid or mackerel, works well. Occasionally caught on mackerel feathers or baited mackerel feathers
CONSERVATION STATUS	Healthy

Catching a red gurnard always feels like winning the lottery. They are a gift of a fish; a ruby-red jewel that comes rising out of a grey sea in an explosion of colour, so bright you practically have to shade your eyes from the glare. My heart always skips a beat when I catch a gurnard, not least because I can practically taste the fish feast that lies ahead.

To look at, a gurnard has the face and forehead of a Glaswegian pub-brawler, and skin the colour of a Moroccan sunset. The Dutch call gurnard the 'Englese soldaat', in reference to the scarlet red coats of the traditional English battledress.

In centuries past, soused gurnard was considered a delicacy, which in truth it is. But then the tide of gourmet taste changed and they were relegated to the bottom rung of the dinner ladder. Until recently, red gurnard were rarely ever eaten or sold by fishmongers in Britain, and they were most commonly used as crab-pot bait.

Gurnard were favoured by potters because they had tough skins and lots of firm flesh, which meant they lasted for a couple of days or more in a crab pot. They do, it's true, make for great pot bait because of their handy size and because their delicious flesh is held together very tightly in a thick wrapping of skin. This means that crabs and lobster are forced to pick away at them for ages, trying to get all the flesh off and attracting even more crabs and lobster into the pot in the process. Using them as pot bait is such a terrible waste of great food though.

Thankfully gurnard is now being appreciated for the fabulous fish it is and has cruised on to menus around the country. The best gurnard I've ever eaten was served up in a small hotel restaurant in Penzance. The fish was coated in a spicy flour and fried whole, head and all, in very hot oil. Done this way, all the fins and skin became golden and crispy. Served with a green salad, new potatoes and huge chunks of fresh lemon, it was a finger-licking, flesh-picking, fin-crunching joy.

Finding them

Spring through to autumn is when most gurnard are caught. The best time, as for so many of our inshore species, is towards the end of summer and beginning of autumn when the sea is at its warmest and the fish are all well fed.

With their low-slung mouths and large fin feet, gurnard are ostensibly bottom-feeders. They feel their way across sandy and muddy flats, as well as rock-strewn portions of seabed, using their hook-like fin 'toes' to grip on to the seabed, and their feeler feet to poke around in the sand and unearth small crabs and tasty molluscs. They aren't glued to the seabed though; gurnard will move up in the water column to chase prey fish if there's nothing available on the floor. Most gurnard are caught from boats although smaller fish can be caught from sandy and pebble beaches too.

Catching them

If the weather is right and the tides are not too strong, it's not actually that difficult to catch gurnard, because they're not a fussy fish. Most are caught by accident, either when feathering from a boat for mackerel (they especially favour baited feathers), or when bumping a bait across sandy ground in search of flat fish like plaice or sole. When trying to catch bream on paternoster rigs bottom-fished with squid and ragworm baits, it's very common to pick up gurnard too. They're not faddy feeders – if they see bait, they'll usually eat it.

Although they look a bit prehistoric and slow, don't be fooled. Gurnard will often snatch a bait (such as squid, mackerel or worm) immediately after it's been cast into the surf. Their extra big eyes give them great quality of vision, even in murky conditions. And they're lightning quick to move in on anything that flashes silver or kicks up dirt. If you feel a bite on your line before your bait's even properly touched the bottom, it's likely to be a gurnard.

If you catch a gurnard that's under 8 inches, it should be released if it appears well enough to swim away. If you're catching a lot of small fish, then squeeze down the barb on your hook to make it easier to unhook and release them.

And when you handle your gurnard, don't be surprised if it starts making bizarre croaking noises. The Scottish colloquial name for gurnard is 'crooner', a name which refers to their habit of singing or snoring when caught.

This fish has a monstrously hard head and a square-topped bar-fighting forehead. So when you want to kill a gurnard for the pot, it'll need to be walloped extra hard. And I always snip through the gills with my fishing scissors in order to bleed them.

Eating them

Gurnard are without doubt one of the best eating fish in British waters, like a cross between sea bass and monkfish. There's a lot of bony head on a gurnard too, which makes fabulous fish stock (see pp.218–20). I like to dust the fish in spicy flour and fry them in very hot vegetable oil to crisp up their skins (see p.239), then finish them for a few minutes in the oven.

Gurnard also makes very impressive sashimi (see pp.206–8), sushi (see p.209), and is a shoe-in for a great fish soup (see pp.222–3). It is also one of the all-time best fish stew ingredients, because of its robust nature and its righteous refusal to flake up and break up in a pan (see pp.224–5).

Black bream *Spondyliosoma cantharus*

SEASON	Late spring, summer and autumn
LOCATION	Boats over inshore reefs and rocky ground. Occasionally beaches and cliffs
METHOD	Bottom-fishing with running ledger or paternoster rigs, using small mackerel and squid strip baits
CONSERVATION STATUS	Commercial targeting is on the increase but is still relatively light

I have to confess I couldn't help myself from jumping around like an over-excited schoolgirl the first time I hooked one of these off my own boat in Dorset. I've always had a soft spot for black bream. They fight hard and they taste better than practically any other fish from our local waters. In fact, I'd swap a bass for a black bream any day of the week.

Bream fishing is such an exciting, pleasing affair. Bream bites are so positive and their fight so tenacious, teasing and rod-rattling. Then the sight of a black bream as it appears at the surface, nearing the landing net, is inspiring. And unforgettable, as bream flare their great long spiny dorsal fin and the male fish also gleams with steel-blue and black mating colours. Then, tragic as it is to kill them, this is offset by the promise of great eating. Raw, marinated, grilled or fried, few other fish can equal them. If ever there was a prince among fish, the black bream is he.

Finding them

Black bream fishing on the south coast is a summer and autumn affair. They're migratory fish that come to our shores in the warmer months from warmer seas. Some early fish may be caught close to the foot of cliffs or around deep inshore rocky marks in springtime, when the fish are spawning. But the main bream-catching season is during the summer, when they're hanging around reefs and wrecks, hunting for protein to recondition themselves after the rigours of reproduction.

Whilst a few black bream get caught from beaches and cliffs or rocks, most are caught from inshore boats. So check with local charter boats that do half-day inshore reef trips and ask about the potential for black bream. Huge numbers of bream are caught along the south coast every season, within just 2 or 3 miles of land.

When you hit upon a good black bream mark, they can be a surprisingly co-operative fish. They are not overly fussed about tide and will happily feed through the slack periods, unlike bass and many of the other Channel fish.

FISH YOU MIGHT CATCH 73

Catching them

The way most good skippers catch black bream from a boat is to anchor over a reef, ledge or wreck in a position where the baits will sit just up tide of the structure. The scent of the baits is then dragged into the wreckage by the movement of the water, which in theory teases fish out of the protective structure to investigate.

Bream tackle couldn't be simpler. You need a spinning rod or carp rod or light boat rod. Use a simple one- or two-hook paternoster rig with size 1 or 2 Aberdeen hooks. Black bream average around 1–3lb in weight, with the occasional big one coming in around 4–5lb. But even at this size they still have very small mouths, so hooks need to be small and strong. Their limpet-crunching teeth can easily bend or break hooks that are too wiry and weedy.

The baits you use should be small, too. Strips of squid, about the width of a pencil and half as long, work best. Just hook them once through the tip of the widest end and they'll flutter enticingly in the current. Black bream also respond well to tiny chunks of fresh mackerel (about half the size of a first-class stamp), single small lugworms, ragworms or scallop frills. And a bream will even take frozen worms or frozen prawns. Don't fill a hook with loads of bait hoping to make your offering seem too irresistible to ignore, as the bream will just nibble away at it, leaving you with no bait and no dinner. (Or else, you'll simply attract the bigger-mouthed pouting to your bait.)

A black bream will never just grab a bait and gobble it down; they're more inclined to worry a bait, pecking away like a demented bantam cock. Sometimes after a series of half-hearted bites, if you reel in, you'll see teeth marks all along the length of the bait, where black bream have nibbled but never fully committed to necking your offering.

You do need to strike a bream bite. 'Striking' is simply the action of sharply lifting the rod tip upwards in response to the pecking, hoping to drive the small hook home into the cartilage around the bream's toothy mouth. The timing of a bream bite strike is worthy of a thesis all of its own. Strike too early and you pull the un-mouthed bait away from the fish, probably spooking it off in the process. Strike too late and the bream will have fleeced your hook, leaving you bare-hooked and unlikely to catch anything.

What happens so often is that you'll strike a bite and miss, and then you're left wondering if there's any bait still on your hook or not. Then an internal debate starts: *should I reel in and check?* Which, of course, would be the sensible thing to do. But, if you do still have bait on your hook, you'll be wasting precious fishing time. The world of bream fishing can be fraught with frustration and insecurity.

Hooking a black bream on light tackle in a steady tide makes for a really decent bit of rod-bending action. As the fish come up in the water they'll turn and get their heads down, taking line in fast jerky pulls. Their fighting technique is very distinctive

– they use fast movements and jaggy head-shaking lunges. You'll know you've got a black bream on immediately it's hooked.

Once you've reeled in your catch, be very careful of the skin-puncturing spines along their fins and around their gills. They also have thick scales, which make them great for cooking on a barbecue, as the scales help to protect the flesh from the heat.

If you're taking the fish home, then consider descaling them on the beach or harbour first, as it can be a messy business at home. If, however, you do descale them in the kitchen, hold the fish underwater, either in a bucket or in the sink, to stop the scales flying around.

Eating them

Black bream are ideal for baking (see pp.231–3) or grilling (see p.245). Their laterally flat shape makes them perfect for scoring across the flank – squeeze butter mashed with garlic and rock salt into the slashes and it will ooze delectably into the flesh as the fish cook, giving a crispy garlicky coating to the skin. Baby new potatoes and carrots from the garden are all you'll need for a fantastic meal.

I particularly like to fry-poach black bream fillets with garlic, lemon and fresh herbs (see p.244). They also make great sashimi (see pp.206–8), sushi (see p.209) and a classic ceviche (see pp.212–13 and 214–15).

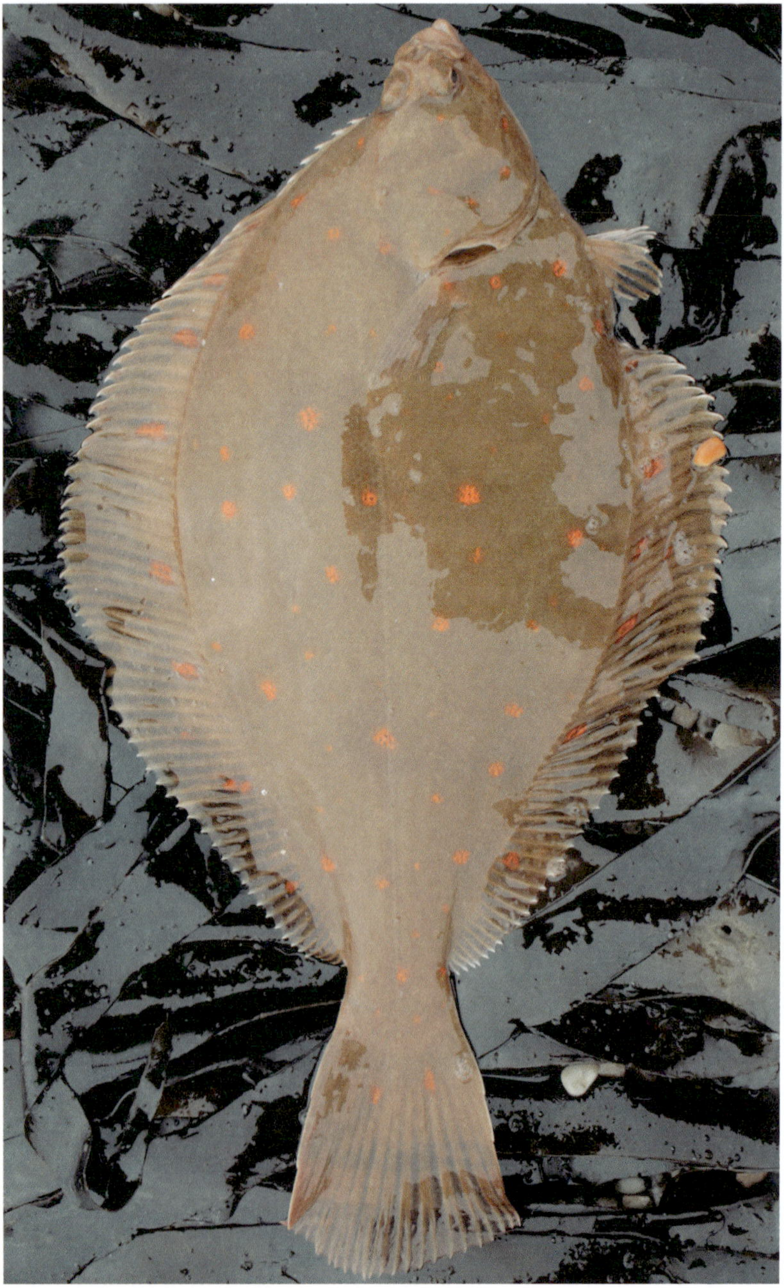

Plaice *Pleuronectes platessa*

SEASON	Spring, summer and autumn
LOCATION	Shore fishing from sandy beaches and shingle beaches, or an inshore boat fishing over a sandy seabed or mussel beds
METHOD	Use long baits made up of lugworm and squid, fished on the bottom, either ledgered from the beach or slowly dragged along the bottom from a drifting boat with a plaice rig or a plaice spoon
CONSERVATION STATUS	Healthy

The Florida-orange splodges on a plaice's top side make it an instantly recognisable fish. And it's one of the few common inshore fish that has always been regarded as a 'proper' fish. Like cod and haddock, which have – rather unfortunately for their own sustainable safety – become the staple fodder of the great British fish and chip eater, plaice is one of those fish that commands respect. Trotting home with a couple of pouting and a dab might not make you a hero, but walk through the door carrying a plaice and respect is guaranteed. Because of its heroic nature, plaice is one of those fish that serious anglers can get rather obsessed and compulsive about.

Finding them

Plaice are usually caught fishing from the shore over sandy ground, or drift fishing or anchor fishing from a boat over a sandy bottom or mussel beds. Fishing around the south coast can be at its best in the late spring and early summer, when adult fish are ending their mating and spawning period and starting to feed voraciously in order to put some real girth back on their shrinking love handles.

Catching them

All tackle shops sell 'plaice rigs' if you don't fancy tying your own. And there are even special devices you can buy or make, known as plaice 'spoons'. These were originally made by serious plaice specimen hunters from teaspoons. The handle is sawn off to leave just the bowl of the spoon, into which a hole is drilled in one end, and a ring looped through for attaching to a swivel.

The plaice spoon is attached a few inches above the bait and it is designed to attract a big flattie's attention by kicking up puffs of sand, as the bait is dragged along the sandy ground from a slowly drifting boat. These mini sand clouds suggest that something crustacean-like is feeding on the bottom, and the plaice, in theory, will then venture over to investigate and happen upon a tasty-looking bait.

According to purists, a perfect plaice bait is made of lugworm and squid, woven together in a tantalising cocktail, and big – up to 6 inches long. Trouble is, a bait that good will also attract practically every other fish feeding on or near the bottom, from a dab to a dogfish, so it's hard to be too selective.

Even if you're fishing in the spring/summer post-spawning period, when plaice are in desperate need of a post-coital blow-out, they can still be very hard to catch. This is because they become totally focused on one particular food source and won't even look at a mouthful of anything else. They particularly love eating mussels at this time of year and get their love-weary heads down to gorge themselves silly on the small cherry-sized seed mussels that lie in beds often close to rocky shorelines.

When plaice are grazing on bite-sized mussels, which an angler cannot duplicate for bait, experienced plaice hunters may resort to cheap sensationalism – flashing glittering baubles and beads to solicit intrigue. Plaice rigs at this time of year may include rattling Booby beads, spinning vanes and sequins; anything flashy enough to distract a plaice who has his nose hard-pressed to the mussel trough. But often the feeding plaice are unmoved and remain uncatchable to rod and line anglers.

Plaice baits might be huge, but plaice bites aren't. Even very large plaice will often only have a pathetic nibble bite like a two-day-old sparrow chick. And because they use their wing-like fins to stir up the sand as they feed, they often simply disturb a bait with their fins rather than truly mouth it. This can be a crucial moment, because if you strike a nervy bite too early, you'll scare any serious-sized plaice away. They don't grow big and fat from being stupid. So patience definitely pays dividends when pursuing the picky plaice.

Sometimes big flat fish, which already have what looks like a very squashed head, appear hard to kill with a priest or bosher (see p.146). Being flat to begin with means there's not much skull to fracture. A couple of proper hard cracks to the head will usually suffice, but with some fish you might also want to puncture the brain cavity with a screwdriver or blunt knife.

Eating them

If handled well, plaice make for epic eating, although I personally wouldn't choose to cook mine on the beach. They need, and deserve, a little more special treatment and controlled heat, either on the hob in a large non-stick pan, or under the grill (see pp.246–7), or else baked whole in the oven, head and flesh still on the bone (see pp.232–3). I've recently taken to slashing the top side of my baked plaice as they go into the oven and adding a few small strips of smoked streaky bacon across the slashes. Then, when I take it out of the heat after a short fierce baking, I'll squeeze lemon juice or even half an orange into the gaping gashes.

Sea bass *Dicentrarchus labrax*

SEASON	Summer and autumn
LOCATION	Rocky outcrops and storm beaches, inshore boats over rocky ground and reefs
METHOD	Use ragworm or sand eels for bait. Use spinners, plugs or rubber fish as lures
CONSERVATION STATUS	Healthy. MLS of 40cm

Sea bass are the Holy Grail of sea anglers. Both shore and boat anglers talk of sea bass in hushed tones, because they're considered so special. The reasons for this are manifold. With their gleaming silver flanks and hydrodynamic torpedo shape, bass look magnificent. They also have a reputation for being hard-fighting, rod-bending apex predators, and to top it all, their culinary repute is second to none.

Then of course there's the monetary value. Just a portion of pan-fried sea bass in a modest seaside restaurant could cost you north of twenty quid. And a whole 5–6lb sea bass, bought over the counter in a fishmonger's shop, would cost you a fortune.

In short, bass look great, fight well and are among the top three most sought-after and expensive of British fish – so, why *wouldn't* any angler want to catch one?

It's worth noting, before we start plotting how to get a portion of rod-caught heaven on your plate, that sea bass are one of the few British sea fish to have a minimum legal landing size limit. Measured from tip of the nose to fork of the tail, this is currently set at 40cm or 16 inches (though some regions have variations; these should be posted in the harbourmaster's office.) This regulation applies to *everyone*, from the recreational angler to the commercial fisherman. Even if you're only idly flicking a spinner from the beach – and not trolling or netting from a commercially registered fishing vessel – it doesn't exempt you from this important byelaw.

The MLS for bass exists primarily because they are slow-maturing fish, which only become sexually mature when they're at least 5 years old. So in order to protect our inshore breeding populations, the size restriction is instigated to allow all sea bass around our coastline a chance to spawn and reproduce. Mostly bass spawn in estuaries and shallow protected bays, which is why you'll find many estuaries have restrictions on bass fishing, to prevent juvenile fish from being disturbed or killed.

Finding them

Bass can be found in pockets around most of our shoreline. In the South and Southwest they're predominantly a summer and autumn fish. They'll sometimes hold in small areas right through into the depths of winter too, depending on what

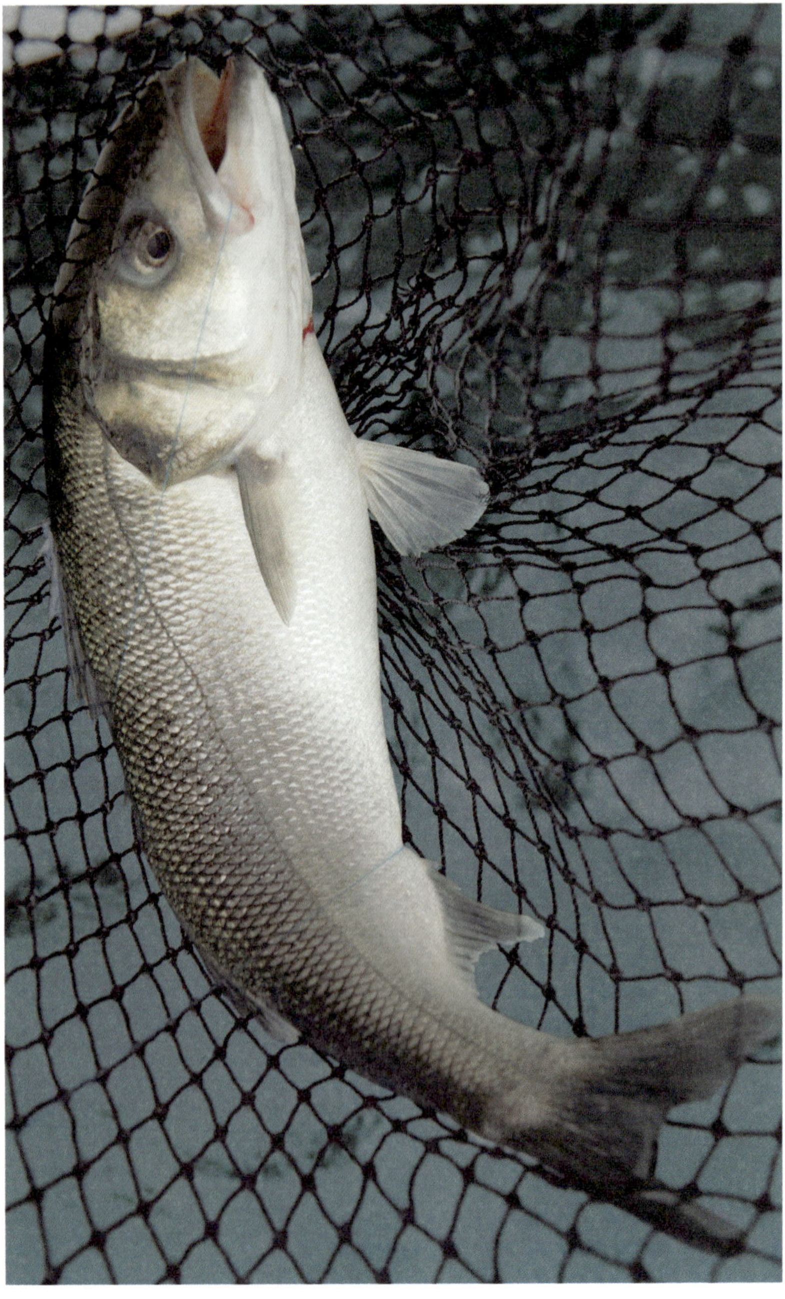

food is available to them. Bass like to hunt small fish and crabs, so wherever these are in abundance – over reefs, in rocky patches of seabed, around pier pilings or close up to rocky cliffs – you might just get lucky and catch one.

Catching them

For all their kudos, small bass are not hard to catch. They're young, stupid, hungry and fearless. And they'll wrap their gums around anything that looks even potentially edible. Catching bigger bass does get more difficult, not least because the biggest fish have lived the longest, seen the most, and developed the greatest sense of suspicion and self-preservation.

The two most likely ways that you'll actually catch a bass yourself from the shore are spinning with a plug, spoon or wedge, or else fishing a big whole squid bait, ledgered just behind the surf line.

Spinning for bass

Spinning for bass is really no different from spinning for mackerel or pollack from the beach. The same spinner or lure that will catch a pollack will catch a bass. However, some big bass will more happily take a bigger-sized spinner, spoon or plug than a similar-sized mackerel or pollack. This is simply because bass have huge mouths and are more aggressive and predatory than mackerel or pollack, so they will attack much bigger prey.

There are two schools of thought concerning summer spinning for bass. One is the careful and exacting approach, the other is the chuck-it-and-suck-it approach. The careful, thoughtful bass angler will go to the beach at break of dawn, when all is calm, the shore is as yet undisturbed by humankind, and the sun hasn't started to shine its glaring spotlight on the haunts of the wary bass. But I've also heard tales, told in tackle shops up and down the coast, of 'grockle' anglers who buy their first-ever rod, reel and Toby spoon, walk down to a known mark and catch a 3lb bass on their first cast. Nothing about angling is predictable.

So it's definitely worth having a bash for bass. Stick on a big plug or spoon and go for a wander along the beach or fish off some rocks. Fish with an open mind and a hungry belly – who knows what might tug your string. And the joy is, if your plug or spoon isn't too large, you might be compensated for your effort and lack of bass with a big pollack or jumbo-sized mackerel instead. Both of which are every bit as good as bass to eat.

Surf ledgering for bass

Ledgering with one whole or even two whole squid on a pennel rig (see p.167) is a tactic that only really works after a storm. The water needs to be rough from the earlier storm winds, but beginning to calm down, and the sea needs to be cloudy.

The theory behind this technique is that the bigger bass will come close inshore (as close as 10–15 yards) to feed on crabs and other shellfish that have been dislodged by the crashing waves and scouring action of the storm surf. The cloudy, stirred-up, sediment-filled water affords them a feeling of security, where they would otherwise be nervous and flighty if the sea was sun-illuminated and clear.

Bass feel safe surrounded by murk, and with their armour-plated heads and steel-like gill rakers, they're properly equipped to feed nose down into the whirlpool of sand and gravel. They also have a highly tuned sense of smell, so in this murk they can still home in on a free meal.

The noise of the surf and constant churning up of the sand and gravel helps the angler too. The sea noise will mask the vibrations of your movements on the beach, which in calm circumstances would easily spook a bass. You need to use big fresh succulent squid baits and to refresh them regularly, so they emanate maximum scent. The more attractive a bait smells, the easier it is for a big bass to find it.

If you try this method, by all means do use a tripod rod rest, but make sure you stand close to it at all times; a big bass will easily pull a rod off a rest and out to sea. It's happened to a surprising number of experienced anglers. You'll also need to use a minimum of 15lb reel line and a 40lb shock leader too if you're fishing near snags or sharp rocks. It's not easy to hook one of these surf-hunting bad boys, but if you do, it's usually even harder landing him. Don't even attempt to do it on light line. Tears and regret will be the only possible outcome.

Bass are every sea angler's dream fish. If you should be so lucky as to catch one above the MLS of 40cm, by all means kill it, bleed it and chill it. Then descale it, cook it, and make stock with every morsel you don't eat. But should you catch two, then I'd urge you to think hard about letting the second one go. A 3lb bass is the thing of anglers' dreams, but it's also a very important marine resource, capable of one day spawning and producing many more sea bass. One bass is more than enough to keep on any day's fishing. Two is starting to take them for granted.

Eating them

One of the most impressive things about bass is how easy it is to cook. You can't really go wrong, unless you desperately overcook it. And even then, a good bass can be quite forgiving. From sashimi (see pp.206–8) and ceviche (see pp.212–13 and pp.214–15) to fry-poached fillets (see pp.242–4), to baked whole in the oven (see pp.231–3), even to barbecued, scales on (see pp.226–8), bass will taste fantastic. Lemon juice, olive oil, salt and black pepper are all the flavourings you'll ever need to add to this great natural-tasting fish. If you get lucky and have a lot of bass to eat, try it cold (or rather at room temperature, not chilled) maybe with a tiny smidgen of horseradish sauce (see p.205) just to eke the flavours out, or mixed with warm lentils and a splash of sweet vinegar like balsamic or rice vinegar.

Dab *Limanda limanda*
Flounder *Platichthys flesus*

SEASON	Late summer, autumn and winter
LOCATION	Estuaries, creeks and off sandy beaches
METHOD	Bottom-fishing with worm or shellfish baits
CONSERVATION STATUS	Healthy. Rarely sold commercially

Most anglers and fishmongers tend to group dab and flounder together. They certainly look very similar and both are poor cousins of the mighty plaice. In fact, the flounder is often mistaken for a plaice, because it can sometimes have a smattering of orange spots across its back – though flounder spots rarely have the same eye-watering Florida-orange intensity of the plaice's big abstract blotches.

The best way to tell the difference between a plaice and a flounder is by examining its bumps. A plaice has a smooth even skin, sloping all the way over its back, gently continuing right down to the tips of its dorsal and anal fins. A flounder, on the other hand, has a row of weird sharp bumps called tubercules which lie in a line separating its body from the base of both of its major fins. It also has a line of the same tubercules running along and behind its head.

You can easily distinguish between a dab and a flounder by touch. The skin of the dab is much rougher, spinier and more abrasive than the smooth skin of the flounder. (The Latin name for dab, *Limanda limanda*, is derived from *lima*, meaning a file or rasp.) Another obvious difference between the two fish is that flounders can grow a bit larger than dabs (12 inches on average as opposed to 10 inches), but otherwise they're fairly similar in terms of their diet, seasons, and indeed the methods you might adopt to try and catch them.

Finding them

To catch these fish in tip-top condition it is better to fish in the autumn, when they're well past spawning and have fed hard through the summer. Neither dab nor flounder worry too much about tides; they'll feed on both the biggest 'springs' and the smallest 'neaps' (see pp.20 and 22). And what they like best of all is feeding close to the shore just after a storm, while the sea is settling down. They come close in to hoover up crabs or shellfish that have been dislodged by the storm's wave action. Although both dabs and flounders can be caught during the day, even in bright sunlight, the most productive time to fish for them is after the sun has gone down. They feed voraciously at dusk and during the night too.

Flounder

Both flounders and dabs like to feed over sandy or muddy ground, either off a beach or particularly in, or adjacent to, a river estuary. Although both are committed sea fish, they also have a love affair with fresh water. The flounder is the most passionate about river water and will migrate so far up rivers that it will pass beyond the furthest reach of the sea, where it no longer experiences any aquatic salinity. Because of this love of fresh water, flounders are often found in lochs, and in the Netherlands they have even been farmed entirely in freshwater ponds.

Dabs don't do fresh water with quite such abandon. They will venture up estuaries, feeding in small packs through the hollows and depressions in mud and sand, but they'll always return to the sea proper with the outgoing tide.

Neither dabs nor flounders are freaked by shallow water or too much sunlight. Their camouflage abilities, which involve burrowing into or covering themselves over with sand and silt, make them abnormally brave in the shallows.

Catching them

The flounder's habit of moving into shallow muddy creeks has given rise to one bizarre method of fishing for them, known as tramping. Every year in Palnackie in Scotland, there is the World Flounder Tramping Championships, which involves contestants stepping through thigh-high water in bare feet, in the hope of treading on a flounder hidden under the mud. The fish is then pinned down by the tramper's foot, and either stuck with a barbed spear, or else grabbed by the head and slipped into a wet sack tied around the waist of the tramper.

Dabs are not subject to tramping, but they were once fished in the shallow creeks around Blakeney on the North Norfolk coast by spearing with long bamboo poles.

The more conventional way to fish for dab and flounder is by bottom-fishing with baits such as ragworm or lugworm or any form of shellfish that you can get to stay on a hook, from mussels to razor clams; flounder in particular won't turn their pug-like nose up at a strip of fresh fish or squid. Use small size 1 and 2 Aberdeen hooks, casting on to sandy or muddy ground from beaches, piers and harbours.

Dab and flounder bites often take the form of three or four swift 'knocks', which happen with such machine-gun-like rapidity it's hard to react to them. So don't. Just wait. And if another series of taps occurs, simply pick up the rod and start to reel in. You don't need to 'strike' (see p.174) on a dab or flounder bite, they'll normally hook themselves, simply from pulling against the weight of the lead.

Eating them

Both flounder and dab are delicious grilled with a well-massaged smear of butter (see pp.246–7), pan-fried (see pp.242–3), or baked with a splash of cider or wine (see pp.231–3). And they're great eaten in a crusty bap with garlic mayonnaise (see p.204) or tartare sauce (see p.205) and a smattering of salad leaves or chopped chives.

Horse mackerel *Trachurus trachurus*

SEASON	Spring, summer and autumn
LOCATION	Inshore boats and mackerel-trip boats, or from piers, rocks and outer harbour walls
METHOD	Feathering, or float-fishing with mackerel or squid strips
CONSERVATION STATUS	Healthy

Horse mackerel is also known as 'scad' or 'scad mackerel' or even occasionally 'Jack mackerel'. Although it shares a name with our Atlantic mackerel, it isn't actually related to it in any way. Scad are part of the global Jack family (along with fish like blue runner, Jack Crevalle and amberjack), a very tasty and much-loved variety of fish that appears all the way down the eastern American seaboard and across the Atlantic to South Africa. The name 'horse' mackerel is said to have been given to these silver-sided, fork-tailed fish because legend has it that other species would ride upon their backs to cross the wide Atlantic.

Like so many of our 'forgotten' species, scad has got something of an undeservedly bad reputation. Just the other day, I was told by an experienced charter boat skipper that horse mackerel are impossible to eat because they're full of bones. This sort of prejudice against certain fish is rife amongst British anglers and skippers, and cooks too. People say things about eating – or rather not eating – fish like scad, pout and garfish as though they're giving you established facts, yet often they're simply repeating what they've heard, without ever trying them. I've eaten scad mackerel hundreds of times and I can honestly say that it's firm fleshed and delicious. So please don't pay any attention to anti-scad propaganda.

Scad mackerel is not only delicious, its flesh is full of omega-rich oils and has high levels of taurine, an organic acid often added to energy drinks. Taurine is thought to be essential for skeletal muscle development, useful in reducing high blood pressure, helpful in avoiding congestive heart failure, and even thought to promote better neurotransmission in the brain. In other words, the scad mackerel is not just edible, it's a super fish super-food.

And if you really want to hear how totally brilliant scad are, listen to the Japanese, who religiously hunt a very close relative of the scad called aji. This is a fish so revered by Japanese sushi and sashimi chefs it's even honoured with its own special celebration day know as Aji Himono Day. If you're ever lucky enough to get your hook into one, be grateful, be gracious and treat it with respect, because this is a crowned prince amongst fishes.

FISH YOU MIGHT CATCH 87

Finding them

Just like mackerel, scad mackerel are most prevalent in summer and autumn. And like mackerel, they will follow and hunt any shoals of small fry or sprats around the coastline, so they're often found feeding very close in to shore, especially as it starts to get dark. It's difficult to set your sights on catching scad alone, because they rarely seem to occur in mono-species shoals, but are instead mixed into mackerel shoals.

Generally speaking, scad are normally found nearer the seabed than mackerel, except in the darkness of twilight or night where, in calm water, they may head up to feed nearer the surface.

Catching them

Strings of feathers, especially the smaller-sized or even micro feathers, are, in my experience, probably the most reliable scad seducers. Next in line I would plump for using small strips of squid on a paternoster rig (see p.163) just as you might for targeting black bream. Float-fishing 1-inch to 3-inch squid strips is another reliable method. It helps to give the float rig a tweak from time to time to make the float splash and the squid strip move up then flutter down in the water. Scad are used to hunting for sprats, so any small splashes at or near the surface are likely to attract their attention.

If you do catch yourself a scad or two, kill them swiftly, bleed them and keep them cool. They're an oily fish, not quite as oily as mackerel or herring, but they'll go off quickly if they get warm.

Eating them

When you prepare scad for cooking, you need a slightly different approach from mackerel. Scad have scales that need to be removed (see p.183) and the distinctive bony ridge along either side of its mini tuna-like tail needs to be sliced off with a sharp knife, or trimmed off with your sharpest kitchen scissors.

Contrary to the myth, scad meat is less bony and easier to fillet than mackerel because the fish has more of an oval profile, like a black bream. The flesh is firmer than mackerel flesh and perfect for light pickling (see pp.210–11) or escabeche (see p.213 and pp.216–17), or plain grilling or frying. The Japanese use scad for sushi (see p.209) and sashimi (see pp.206–8).

Another favourite Japanese way is to coat scad fillets in wheat flour, then lightly fry them, let them cool and then marinate in vinegar and soy sauce with slices of sweet red pepper.

Being an oily fish makes scad perfect for grilling (see p.245) or barbecuing (see pp.226–8), as they self-baste and don't spoil too quickly under the heat of the grill or over hot charcoal.

Herring *Clupea harengus*

SEASON	In the Southwest herring turn up in summer swimming with mackerel shoals. North of the Bristol Channel and the Thames Estuary they tend to be around more during late autumn and spring
LOCATION	Mackerel boat, or from the beach, piers and harbour breakwaters
METHOD	Mostly caught using mackerel feathers or micro mackerel feathers
CONSERVATION STATUS	Healthy

Victorian naturalists referred to herring as a 'gregarious' fish. This always makes me think of herring as a happy-go-lucky party animal, forever in search of the right crowd to hang out with. In truth, I think it simply refers to their habit of travelling around in large shoals.

In Dorset, we very rarely come across any large shoals of herring; instead, the few we do catch are normally mixed in among mackerel shoals. I don't really know if this is because these herring get lost and just hook up with any old shoal that appears to know where it's going, or because they're suffering from some deep-seated identity crisis. Whatever the cause, all the recent ones I've caught have been on mackerel feathers and plucked from the centre of a mackerel shoal.

Along the east and northeast coast, herring shoals are more plentiful, but they are nothing compared to the biblical shoals that existed before the 1950s trawler-fishing boom. At that time, herring shoals typically measured several miles wide and tens of yards deep, containing trillions of fish. These once provided massive seasonal employment all the way down Britain's east coast – from Wick to Great Yarmouth.

Sadly, the diesel-powered trawler revolution and the use of massive purse seine nets was devastating for our national herring stocks. The overfishing had such a damaging effect that a ban was imposed on commercial herring fishing in the 1970s. There has been some recovery in certain areas since then, and there's now even a certified sustainable herring fishery in the Thames Estuary. Herring do crop up, here and there, all around the coast, caught from angling boats, often when least expected, and normally sandwiched in amongst shoals of other species.

Although herring stocks have been decimated by industrial-scale commercial fishing fleets, the recreational angler doesn't have to fear inflicting damage by catching a few for tea. In my experience, fishing on the south coast in particular, there might be a run of herring for a week or so, in tightly packed shoals, easily as big as mackerel shoals and often mixed among them, but they won't stay like the mackerel do; they move on, only to leave us all wanting more.

Finding them

Herring are a pelagic fish, like mackerel, so they wander around the coast, but also up and down the water column. They are plankton feeders, so they move up to the surface at dusk, as the clouds of zooplankton rise upwards with the cooling water. (Zooplankton is the collection of minute animals that in turn feed on phytoplankton, the near-microscopic plant plankton.)

Most herring are caught from mackerel-fishing boats, but like other fish species they are occasionally caught from the shore, especially from piers and deep-water rock marks. There may be some reliable herring spots along the east coast where herring shoals are most prolific (see Directory, p.249, for websites to investigate further), but down on the south coast it's hit and miss.

Catching them

The best way to catch herring is on mini or micro feathers. These are arranged just like normal mackerel feathers but on much smaller hooks, sometimes with glow-in-the-dark luminescent colours.

The smaller your feathers, the more chance there is that a herring or two will mistake them for the tiny sea creatures they voraciously hunt. Should you ever be lucky enough to hook into a couple of strings of herrings, then you are destined for a tremendous feast. Pound for pound, herring are the most nutritious fish in our waters. They contain even more omega-rich oils, essential minerals and life-giving fatty acids than mackerel, which takes some doing.

Just like mackerel, their high oil content means herring spoil very quickly once they're dead, as the oils in their flesh will oxidise and attract bacteria – a process that you can slow down by getting them on ice as quickly as possible.

Eating them

In medieval times, a suitable portion of herrings was defined in law, by the monks of Westminster Abbey. The religious fervour of the day imposed a staggering 215 fasting days each year, during which the eating of meat was forbidden. Fish was the preferred food on fast days and, according to the monks, a suitable portion for a devout brother was firmly set at four or five herrings, depending on size (of the herring that is, not the monk). Personally, I would wholly concur that about four or five herrings apiece is a very good portion. Any less is sacrilege.

Because herring were so plentiful, but also very perishable, many different methods of preserving them were devised during their heyday, ranging from salting to pickling, to curing in wine and mustard, to smoking – either hot or cold – as red herrings, kippers, bloaters or buckling. Pickled and smoked herrings are certainly delicious, but fresh herrings offer great potential, too.

If you do manage to catch a few and the weather's amenable, you'll find that fresh herrings barbecue beautifully, with a taste and texture somewhere in between a mackerel and a sardine (see pp.226–8). And because herring come ready infused with their own self-basting oil, they're also perfect for grilling (see p.245).

I love herring cooked escabeche-style (see p.213 and pp.216–17) too, because the fillets crisp up well on the outside, remaining soft inside, and their oiliness contrasts perfectly with a vinegar marinade and slightly crunchy shallots.

But I have to say that my mum's traditional Scottish recipe of coating filleted, splayed herring in coarse oatmeal and frying them in butter or beef dripping, then serving them with a dollop of stewed rhubarb or gooseberries, takes a lot of beating.

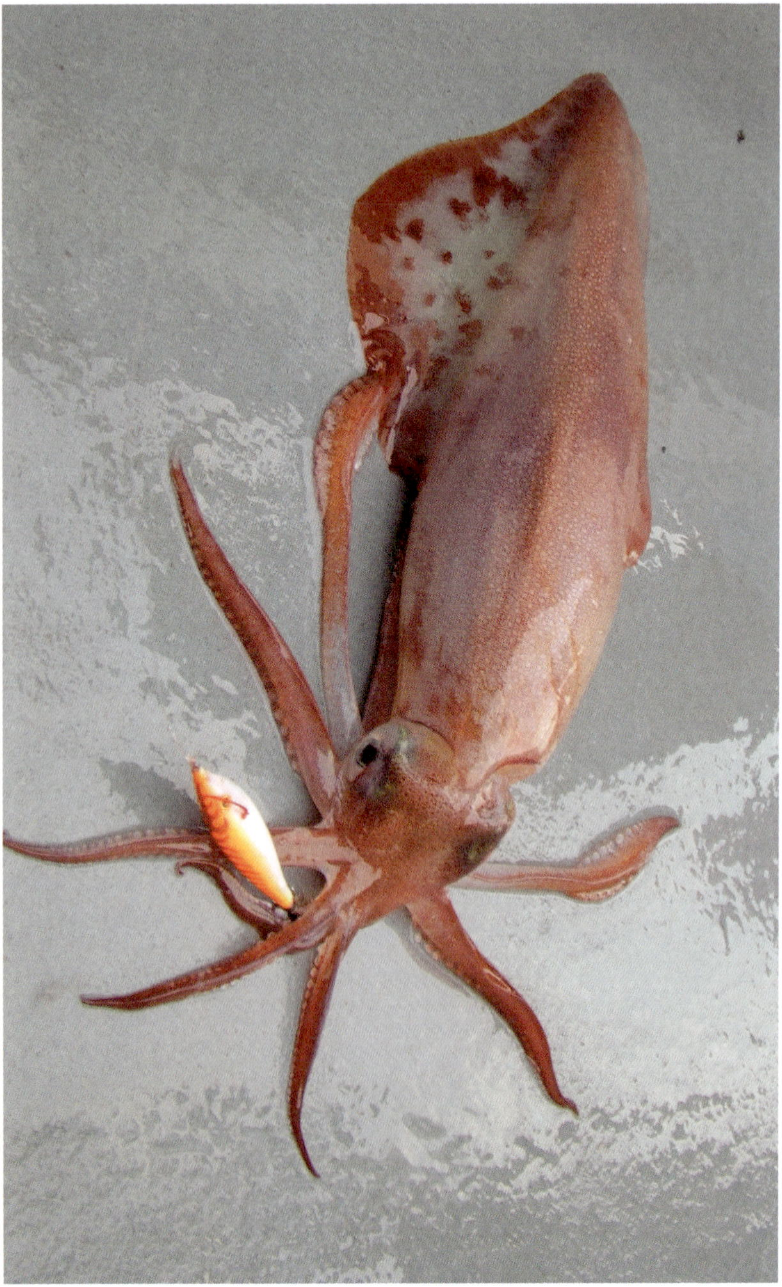

Squid *Loligo forbesi*

SEASON	Winter
LOCATION	Harbours, piers and breakwaters
METHOD	Using squid jigs or slow-retrieving a small dead fish bait, mounted on a treble hook
CONSERVATION STATUS	Healthy

Most people know squid as 'calamari', which they generally encounter only on menus, in pickled seafood salads, or occasionally on the fishmonger's slab. I often find people are shocked to learn squid not only inhabit our inshore waters, but that they can actually be caught relatively easily. The biggest bother about catching squid, in fact, is that it's only really possible in the cold winter months, from November onwards, and that the best time to fish for squid is when night is falling.

A cold winter's evening is, understandably, not everyone's favourite time to sit for hours on a pier, breakwater, harbour wall or inshore boat. But, if you do brave the elements and the gloom, you could be in for one of the most extraordinary experiences you'll ever have with a rod in your hand and a bucket at your feet.

Finding them

Squid migrate to shallow inshore water from their normal haunts of deep offshore waters in the winter months to breed and to hunt. Although they appear to be passive almost jellyfish-like creatures, squid are in fact active and aggressive predators, who will bite big chunks out of any small fish, alive or dead, with their sharp, horny parrot-like beak, situated in the centre of their web-like cluster of tentacles.

The fish squid like to hunt best are small juvenile whiting and poor cod. These vulnerable fish know there are a lot of hungry predators in the big sea eager to swallow them whole, and so they make an effort to protect themselves by moving into shallow safe havens in the evening – places where big fish are loath to tread. Small whiting and poor cod seek sanctuary alongside harbour walls, deep breakwaters and piers at dusk, where they'll also find some bonus sustenance in the form of shrimps and snails, who too are hiding amongst the weed and algae growing from the shadowy underwater structures.

Squid are blessed with enormous eyes, which give them enhanced night vision. This means they're very well equipped to slope into the shadows, in search of the nervy small fry, and are able to pick them off with sniper accuracy using their sucker-encrusted tentacles. The place to find squid, then, is close against these structures, at nightfall.

Catching them

The best way to catch squid is to use either a small dead fish as bait, or a factory-manufactured squid jig.

Using squid jigs

There are two types of squid jig available in tackle shops. One is made of glow-in-the-dark luminescent material. It has a skirt of upward-pointing hooks encircling its base and a body which glows green in the dark. The other type looks like a prawn, wearing a tight velour tiger-striped jacket (which comes in a variety of colours), with a spiked dorsal fin and a couple of layers of hook-bristling skirts around its tail.

Both of these lures are supposed to attract the squid's attention: the dumpy one because it glows with mesmeric luminosity and the fat prawn one because, well, it looks like a fat prawn. On sight of a jig, the squid should shoot out its sucking tentacles, wrap them around the lure and attempt to drag it towards its beak.

Meanwhile, the angler, in theory, made aware of some action occurring underwater through the vibrations at his rod tip, will start to reel in – pulling the jig in the opposite direction to the squid. This should entangle the tentacles in those needle-sharp hooks, which means with a constant reeling pace the squid should stay attached, until he's lifted from the sea, destined to become lightly battered tempura squid rings. Oh, if only it were that simple!

In my experience, the glow-in-the-dark dumpy lures don't work so well around our stretch of coastline. I don't know why. In Weymouth harbour, I've found it's the prawn variety that works best.

Using a small fish as bait

Using a small dead fish as bait to attract the tentacle attentions of a squid is often more successful than a jig. I suppose that when the water is slightly cloudy, squid can detect the dead fish bait through smell, as well as using their amazing sight. If the water is clear, jigs can attract them from a long distance but jigs rely totally on the fish being able to see. The scent of the dead fish provides a whole other sensory attraction. A poor cod is, after all, a real example of what they're hunting, rather than an optical imitation.

Normally, I'd suspend a 4-inch freshly killed poor cod a couple of feet above a lead weight of 3 or 4oz. The best rig to use is a two-hook rig, with one hook to hold the poor cod on the end of the line and the other hook, preferably a small treble, just nicked into the skin of its flank, with two of the three treble hooks facing out, ready to snag into the squid's inquisitive tentacle. The two hooks of the treble facing out will never work as well as the multi-hook skirts on the prawn-shaped jigs do. And so, the technique of fishing the small dead fish rig is slightly different from the jig. Because it doesn't have the same grappling skirt of hooks, it won't snare the squid so

Prawn-style squid jig

Glow-in-the-dark-style squid jig

easily, so you need to reel in much more slowly and evenly. While the squid is busy nibbling at the bait, you're trying to coax him up to the surface, without him becoming aware of what's occurring.

Using this technique, once you get your squid to the surface, you'll need to get a net under him quickly. Often the squid isn't actually hooked at all, he's simply holding on, munching at your bait, quite unaware that you're slowly reeling him in. So unless he's actually entangled and snagged by one of the small treble hooks, he can just let go at any time and disappear back down to the deeps. It's a tense and tricky moment.

Once you've got him in the net, the best thing you can do is to leave him inside it, holding the net out over the water to see what he does next. Often, but not always, squid will squirt their load of ink at this moment, when they feel themselves trapped by the netting. This ink is better unloaded into the sea than all over the deck of your boat, or all over your clothes. Getting fresh squid ink out of clothing is not an easy task. Whether he does or doesn't squirt at this point, it's still best to put him into a bucket of water next, because if there is more ink to come, containing it in the bucket makes for less washing. Do not underestimate the indelible blackness of a fresh squid squirt. It's so unbelievably black and sticky I have a couple of squidding shirts that have been boil-washed umpteen times and yet still bear the black residue of a November night's fun.

To kill a squid, you can either just leave it in a bucket of water, which is a slow way to go, or you can put it on ice, which will kill it quicker. Or you can clamp it hard, on either side of the head, with a pair of long-nosed pliers. If I have ice I'll use it, but as we normally fish for squid in the depths of winter I rely on the bucket of sea water technique. Keeping them alive for a while in the bucket also allows them to purge more of their ink.

Eating them

Preparing squid (see pp.198–9) is almost as satisfying as catching them. Seeing such an alien-like creature turned into pure snow-white slabs of sweet calamari flesh is indescribably gratifying. And squid rings or squid strips dipped in spicy flour and fried in hot oil (see pp.238–9), then served with lemon wedges and a homemade sweet chilli dipping sauce (see p.205), are just about the most wonderful hot tangy squid experience you can have.

It's also possible to fry squid pieces in a very hot pan with just a smidgen of oil and then squeeze over lemon and lime juice (see fry-poaching, pp.242–3). They take only a couple of minutes and once cooked you can toss them in a dressing of oil and rice vinegar spiked with a little chilli.

Squid rings and pieces are perfect for adding to a risotto (see p.221), or to a light tangy fish soup (see pp.222–3) too.

Slob trout *Salmo trutta*

SEASON	Spring, summer and autumn
LOCATION	River estuaries
METHOD	Earthworms trundled along the river mouth with a light weight
CONSERVATION STATUS	Healthy

The trout family, aka the salmonids, are an awe-inspiring tribe. Brown trout inhabit water from the clear mountain streams of the Himalayas to the shopping-trolley-strewn creeks of central London. And one shocking, otherworldly thing that brown trout do – or at least *some* brown trout do – is suddenly decide, during their infancy, to stop being a freshwater fish and, instead, convert to become a sea fish. And so, over a period of a couple of years, a spotty, fragile river-dwelling trout, no longer than your middle finger, will transform to become a huge silver-sided gleaming beast of a trout, weighing up to 6lb. Big enough and tough enough to eat at least five finger-sized brownies for breakfast.

The point of this bizarre transformation is to venture out to sea, to become big and strong and exceedingly fertile, and then to return to the river, packed full with millions of eggs, in order to multiply and thus enhance the evolution of the species. The fuel that powers this survivalist evolution is high-protein seafood, such as shrimps and crabs, which are much more nutritious to trout than any food to be found back home in the babbling brook of their birth. The place for a brown trout to put on serious weight, then, is in the all-you-can-eat seafood buffet that lurks beyond the mouth of the river estuary.

Making the passage from lean-pickings fresh water to fat-boy sea buffet sounds easy. Geographically it's only a couple of miles, or less, but physiologically the leap is enormous. The difference between living as a fish surrounded by fresh water, and living as a fish surrounded by sea water, is akin to you or me deciding we're going to live on the moon. Then, over the space of a couple of months, actually growing the physical equipment to help us survive in an alien environment.

The brown trout who undergo this unbelievably fundamental and dynamic metamorphosis and go to live and feed in the sea, then come back to rivers to spawn, are called sea trout. Sea trout, in other words, are simply brown trout who have chosen to go and live some of their lives at sea.

There's a huge amount we don't know about sea trout, including how far a sea trout will migrate out to sea in order to find good food. We know salmon swim all the way to Greenland, but sea trout are generally believed to stay within a 5-mile radius of the shoreline. They might migrate along the coast a greater distance, but they don't feel the need to go far out.

Slob trout, on the other hand, are lacking in motivation. A slob trout is a brown trout that *thinks* it wants to become a sea trout, but lacks the bottle to go the whole hog. Instead of leaving the river, traversing the estuary, and forging ahead to pastures new and menus large, a slob trout starts the journey – then wimps out. It gets as far as the estuary and goes no further, deciding instead to live an in-between life, moving up and down the estuary from the edge of the scary sea to the mouth of the safe river, with every ebb and flow of the tide. Probably saying to itself, 'That's it. I'm going. I am. I'm off. Er… No I'm not. I'm staying. No. I'm going. I'm *definitely* going. Nope. I'm staying…' and so on, for tide after tide, year after year.

I've always liked to believe that slob trout are so called because they live a slob-like existence, committing to neither one thing nor another. I may be wrong, there may well be another totally different explanation. But if there is, I don't want to know it. To me, they will always be estuarine couch potatoes, who like to pretend they've left home, but keep coming back every weekend, bringing their washing with them.

Finding them

Slob trout move up and down the muddy and gravelly terrain where the flow of the river cuts across the wide open estuary. They will lie head towards the flow, usually on either side of the fast-moving water rather than in the middle of it, watching for any food washed along towards them. At this point they're becoming opportunistic feeders and may take from the bottom or the top of the water, especially if it's shallow. Slob trout are always easiest to catch in the summer and autumn months. In theory they're still stuck in their intertidal purgatory during the winter but they may seek places to lie low and sulk rather than feed when the water's too cold.

Catching them

The best bait I've come across to catch slob trout is worms. In the west coast of Ireland where I've caught plenty of slobs, the preferred bait is actually garden lobworm. It seems to work very well. The tackle and rig I always use for estuary slobs is a spinning rod with 10lb line, a drilled bullet weight, with a 6lb hook length to a thin-wire size 1 or 2 Aberdeen-style hook, which has a perfect long shank to thread on a worm halfway with plenty of tail left hanging off.

I normally wear waders and walk to a point where I can cast near the centre of the river flow as it cuts across the estuary, although the near edge of the flow is perfectly good enough, especially if the flow is strong.

The start of the ebb tide is my favourite, as the flow of the river begins to beat back the push of the tide. All you need to do is cast out, let your weight hit the bottom and then keep a gently taut line and a well raised-up rod tip, so you're able to feel the weight bump along the bottom. When fishing using this method you always want to keep your lead weight gently on the move, which is why it helps to use the marble-sized drilled bullet leads. If your weight is too heavy it will sit firm and not trundle. And if it does get caught up on something, just raise the rod tip to lift it out of its snag, and then bump on.

It takes a bit of practice, but it's a fabulous way to fish. It keeps you in touch with your bait, and you can keep walking or wading upstream with the tide or downstream with the flow, depending on which is stronger, so you're always covering new ground. What you should picture in your underwater mind is the slob trout facing into the oncoming current, nose down, looking for food being washed out by the flow.

You'll often pick up dabs, flounders, the odd small pollack, a miracle mullet or possibly a bass with this technique. If you find a suitable estuary site to fish it's really worth a try. I think it's a wonderful engaging and exciting method to fish.

Once you've made your catch, a sharp crack with a priest (see p.146) and a scissor cut across the gills to bleed slob trout is all that's required. Then you only have to gut them and they can be cooked whole.

Eating them

Grilled trout (see p.245) is my favourite, with a knob of butter, salt, pepper and chives. But cold trout is also a treat with lemon mayonnaise and chopped herbs. Another great way to cook trout is whole in the oven (see pp.231–3), or on the barbecue, or in wet newspaper parcels over an open fire (see pp.226–8).

Grey mullet *Chelon labrosus*

SEASON	Spring, summer and autumn
LOCATION	Harbours, estuaries and sometimes several miles up river
METHOD	Float-fished bread flake on tiny hooks, float-fished maggot, ledgered bread flake on a single running ledger rig, or Mepps spinner tipped with ragworm
CONSERVATION STATUS	Healthy

Of all our native sea fish, grey mullet are without a shadow of a doubt the greatest rod tease. They are by far the most conspicuous sea fish, so often seen cruising around harbours or nudging their way up shallow estuaries, unafraid of the sunlight, basking in the glare of a hundred frustrated anglers' eyes, yet there is no easy way to catch them on rod and line.

Grey mullet are more or less vegan in their approach to life. They live by a Buddhist philosophy of doing no evil to other swimming finned things and exist on a diet of algae, weed and the very occasional worm or maggot. They are also the world's pickiest nibblers, and show no passion or real appetite for food. Like harbour-dwelling supermodels, they seem to exist on nothing but sunlight and sips of chilled water. When it comes to bait, they have only one weakness, and you'll need an awful lot of skill and patience to catch one out…

Finding them

Summer is the mullet's favourite season. Unlike most fish, they like to see and be seen, unless cormorants are flying overhead. Mostly you'll see them close to shore. They're found most easily in harbours where they cruise round at any stage of the tide, and sometimes they appear in shoals edging their way around rocky headlands.

Rarely have I ever been aware of them out at sea, mainly because they're not attracted to normal boat-fishing methods. However, netsmen who set gill nets across the direction of the tide runs will often pick them up miles out to sea. So they are there, they just don't make themselves obvious to anglers.

Catching them

There are many ways you can try and catch mullet by rod and line, but the four most successful methods are float-fished bread flake, ledgered bread flake, spinner and worm or float-fished maggot. None of them are easy. But the heady satisfaction of hooking and landing a big mullet, because it is so difficult to do, is unsurpassed.

Float-fished bread flake method

A grey mullet's only Achilles heel, in his vegan-esque diet, is bread. The cheapest, whitest, nastiest, cotton-woolliest white bread, broken into minuscule granules, is just about the only thing that can tempt a grey mullet to part its luscious Angelina Jolie-esque lips.

To employ the float-fishing technique, use a bread 'flake': a torn first-class stamp-sized portion of the fleshiest, most crust-free section of the slice. This is then dipped in sea water and pinched between thumb and forefinger to expel excess moisture. And finally it's mounted on a tiny size 14, or smaller, freshwater coarse-fishing hook. The wetting and squeezing is done to help the flake to stay on the hook longer, because bread is a very fragile, easily unseated bait. For this reason, cast it with care.

If this sounds fiddly and faffy to you, believe me, it is. Seriously so. And it gets worse. Really dedicated mullet anglers don't use sea-fishing gear at all, they only use coarse-fishing tackle, designed for catching small things like a ½lb roach. Mullet maestros use 12- or 13-foot coarse float rods, a small fixed-spool reel, fitted with 6lb main line, tapering to 2lb tip section. This rig is then fished under a skinny, delicate waggler float. Their approach is all about achieving perfect presentation of a tiny bread bait, with zero visible evidence of the angler. Basically, if your teeny-tiny hook isn't completely and neatly covered by your minuscule morsel of hand-wrung bread flake, and a glint of steel should shine through, then you might as well be fishing with a crane hoist and a sack of spuds, because no self-respecting mullet is ever going to give it the time of day.

To increase your chances, you can try hanging an onion sack of dried, stale mushed-up bread just upstream of where you intend to fish. I've seen this done on the river Medway estuary in Kent, the home of the Mullet Club, with pretty impressive results. Done on an outgoing tide, tiny fragments of bread are taken downstream with the flow, siren-calling mullet to follow the stream of morsels towards the source. The waggler rig is then fished close to the bread chumming sack, so that a feeding mullet might suck in the hook bait instead of a free chum offering.

If you're faffily inclined, it's worth a try. The fight of a grey mullet on a float rod with light line is as sensational a battle as you'll ever experience from any British fish.

Ledgered bread flake method

In Guernsey, I once fished with a mullet fanatic who used a totally different technique, fishing on the harbour basin floor. He would wade out across the exposed mud at very low tide and lay a bed of broken-up white bread in a sofa-sized patch. Then he'd wait on the harbour wall and watch as the tide came in and covered his bread. He would cast a pinch of bread flake on a tiny hook, weighed down with a ½oz lead, and so the bait was 'ledgered' on the bottom close to the bread patch. He'd then wait as the tide filled the harbour and the mullet nudged their way along the bottom, entering with the fresh flood of tide. They'd happen upon his tempting patch of bread and eventually suck up his sneakily positioned hook bait.

Spinner and worm method

This is probably my favourite mullet technique, because it's active and immediate and doesn't involve too much fiddling.

Basically this is a way of spinning for mullet using a conventional spinning rod with a small size 5 Mepps spinner, which is slightly modified to increase your chances. The modification is simple: remove the treble hook from the spinner and replace it with a 1½-inch length of 6lb monofilament line with a size 14 carp hook tied on the end. Now, take an inch of fresh ragworm and very lightly snag it on to your hook.

In my experience this method works best in cloudy tidal water. I've fished this way off the back of my boat when it's been tied up to a harbour buoy and caught several passing mullet. If you see signs or splashes of cruising fish, just cast near them and retrieve the spinner at a quickish pace. Slow down and speed up until you find the pace that the fish best respond to. For a peace-loving species, it's hard to explain what it is about half a ragworm and a French-designed spinner that suddenly gets them all excited (which it does *some* of the time). There are times, of course, when this method has zero effect. And then there are other times when the spinner will keep being bumped and plucked by mullet without any proper hook-ups.

The last method involves maggots…

Float-fished maggot method
This will work in two locations, either from the beach fished over rotting seaweed in the summer, or over a sewage outflow pipe where the mullet are used to seeing maggots as an opportunistic source of food.

Fishing near sewage pipes Mullet like nothing better than hanging around sewage outflow pipes and snacking on assorted effluent solids. I know, for a fish that acts like a committed vegan Buddhist most of the time, this behaviour seems outrageous. The truth is, most fish and shellfish love an outflow pipe pumping effluent. Thankfully these pipes are much rarer around our coastline than they used to be.

One of the consequences of outflow pipes is the preponderance of maggots. Grey mullet, in the right mood, love a maggot. I've fished a heavy-bodied waggler float straight into the brown river of an outflow (ironically on one of the prettiest stretches of the country's coastline) with a double maggot on a size 16 hook, and had stunning rod-bending success. But telling you to 'First find a sewage pipe' really doesn't feel like a healthy way to set you on course for a tempting mullet supper.

Fishing amongst rotting seaweed The other maggot technique is a lot less nausea-inducing, but it does require an awful lot of complicated cosmological things to happen, in just the right order. First you need a storm. A storm that washes a large amount of kelp and seaweed far up a beach. Then you need a period of hot weather, to make the now rotting seaweed warm enough to encourage flies to lay their eggs in the stinking bacteria-ridden weed mounds. Then, as the eggs hatch into maggots, you need a super-big spring tide to wash up to and through the line of rotting weed and flush out the adult maggots.

In a calm but high sea, these maggots will get carried out into the water, acting like a dinner gong to any grey mullet in the vicinity. Sea fly-anglers like to fish a maggot-imitating fly pattern at these incoming mullet. You could also fish a tiny clear waggler float with a small hook and single maggot on the outgoing current.

If you've been successful with your mullet-fishing quest, firstly, you have my sincerest respect, and secondly, remember that mullet need to be killed, bled, chilled and gutted swiftly after landing. A solid crack across the back of the head with a priest (see p.146) will suffice.

Eating them

Big mullet can be cut into cutlets and cooked in foil parcels or baked (see pp.231–3). Smaller mullet are great baked whole, stuffed with herbs and lemon slices. Recently I ate one stuffed with feta cheese and chutney, which tasted delicious. Nothing wrong with filleted and grilled either. Mullet does benefit from a tasty sauce (see pp.224–5), as it has a good meaty, flaky texture but not a huge amount of flavour of its own.

Fish you might catch… but can't eat

One of the most exciting things about sea fishing is that you really don't know what you might catch. Even within just a few miles of my local harbour, I've seen sun fish, normally found in the Caribbean, and caught trigger fish, which hail from the eastern seaboard of America. There are resident colonies of reef-dwelling sea horses, and local anglers who have caught such oddities, and exciting hook-ups with mako sharks and thresher sharks are reported practically every summer. The sea is full of rather astonishing surprises. But that also means that you're fairly likely to hook into a few inedible species, which I'd really recommend you release (see pp.176–7 for details on how to release fish).

The reasons for not attempting to add these particular species to your menu are twofold: either it's simply a waste of time and a waste of fish trying to eat them, because no matter what you do to them, they're never going to taste good; or else, it's because they're too small to warrant your culinary attentions and would be much better returned to remain part of the indigenous food chain.

The fish you're most likely to catch but can't eat include three types of wrasse – ballan, cuckoo and corkwing. Then there are the rocklings (they sound like a delightful boy band, don't they?), which include the three-bearded rockling and the five-bearded rockling. There's the blenny brothers (a Country and Western duo), which include the tompot blenny and the common blenny or 'shanny'. Finally there's the weaver fish. The weaver is occasionally caught on rod and line, but it's mostly encountered by shrimpers, pushing their hand-held shrimp nets through shallow sandy-bottomed tidal lagoons. Weaver fish are very easy to recognise and are worth being aware of, because they have three sharp spines protruding from their backs which can give you a ferociously painful sting. The weaver is about the only fish in British waters (apart from jellyfish) that is likely to cause you any sort of harm.

Ballan wrasse
Labrus bergylta

Usually caught over rocky ground, either from beach, boat or cliff marks. They will eat practically any bait and can be used to make fish stock, if they've been badly hooked or have 'blown' (see p.176). Otherwise, always release them, gently.

Cuckoo wrasse
Labrus mixtus

Mostly caught from boats when fishing over rocky ground or kelp beds. They are impossible to confuse with any other British fish. Always release them when you can. If you have to kill them, because they've 'blown' (see p.176), use them for stock or give to crab potters to use as bait.

Corkwing wrasse
Crenilabrus melops

Usually caught over rocky ground and kelp beds. They are a little more colourful than a ballan, but not nearly as exotic as the cuckoo (above).

Poor cod
Trisopterus minutus

Poor cod can be caught from the shore or a boat, usually over rocky ground or reefs. They can be used as an effective bait for bass or squid, but otherwise always release them. If you do catch one that accidentally dies, you can eat it; they're just very small and much better for the marine environment left alive.

Tompot blenny
Parablennius gattorugine
Shanny/Common blenny
Lipophrys polis

Both types of blenny are caught in shallow water from the beach, or around man-made structures such as piers and breakwaters. They're extraordinary-looking fish, which have no food value and are just too pretty and too unusual to use for bait.

Weaver fish
Echiichthys vipera

Weaver fish tend to be caught from sandy beaches. Be careful how you release a weaver – you need to avoid getting stuck by the obvious spines. If you're fishing at night or twilight check any small fish on your line with a torch first before you grab hold of it, just in case it's a weaver.

Fish you might catch... but shouldn't eat

If you're going to be an angler and start taking home your catch to cook, then I think it's important to understand, right from the start, that there are some species in our UK waters which we have all to agree not to kill.

These species, which take in all of the rays and also the shark relatives, including the smoothhound, starry smoothhound, bull huss and tope, should be off-limits to all anglers because the stocks of these species are in danger of being overfished to a potentially disastrous level.

The reason why this cluster of shark relatives is so at risk is because they don't breed in the same way as other species. Unlike pollack, cod or pouting, which can produce several million eggs a year, rays and huss and hounds produce a small number of eggs, which are fertilised inside the mother's body, greatly reducing their overall number of young. Rays and hounds will lay large purse-like eggs, which already have partially developed young inside them. This means the ratio of eggs laid to young produced is high, but the number of overall eggs is only a fraction of the number laid by fish who fertilise their eggs externally.

As a consequence, when stocks get low, it can take a great many successful years of breeding to slowly boost them back up again to sustainable proportions. Hounds and rays do not repopulate their numbers anywhere near as efficiently as other egg-laying fish, but they do survive well after being caught and released.

Cartilaginous fish (sharks and rays) don't have swim bladders like demersal fish, which are very sensitive to pressure change caused by being reeled to the surface from a depth. In contrast, dogfish, hounds, huss, sharks and rays are all seemingly unaffected by being reeled in and can return to the depths again quickly. For this reason, it's safe and ecologically sensible to let them go (see pp.176–7 for details on how to release fish). A ray or a huss will return to the depths and get on with its life, unharmed, if you release it carefully. So there is every reason to release them and no reason, other than greed, to keep them.

Tope
Galeorhinus galeus

Tope are mostly caught from boats, but can sometimes be caught from the shore too, especially during the summer. Tope is our largest inshore shark (record weight of 82lb). It is often caught while bream fishing over rocky ground with small squid baits. This is now a protected species and must be released.

Bull huss
Scyliorhinus stellaris

Mostly caught from boats, though sometimes from the shore. Bull huss tend to be caught over rocky ground, and are fond of crab bait. They often turn up in crab pots, having been attracted by the bait. Also known as the greater spotted dogfish, the bull huss is much bigger than the dogfish and has larger spots.

Smoothhound and Starry smoothhound
Mustelus mustelus and *Mustelus asterias*

These are shallow-dwelling sharks, often found in the mouths of estuaries because they like a muddy bottom to hunt for crabs, worms and small fish. A female will only have 10 pups maximum every 2 years, so they are very sensitive to overfishing.

Undulate ray

Skates and rays
Rajidae family

Most rays are caught from boats but they can be caught from the shore too. They like clean open sandy ground or muddy flats where they can pounce on crabs, small fish and sand eels. The thornback ray (*Raja clavata*) is our most common ray species. (A useful skate and ray identification chart is available from www.sharktrust.org.)

Conger eel
Conger conger

Mostly caught over very rocky broken ground or near wrecks or reefs. Also may be caught at night-time from the shore, as they're nocturnal feeders and like to feed in shallow water. There are many conger recipes, but I've yet to find one I like. Exciting to catch, this is one fish that truly deserves to be released.

Tackle and Kit

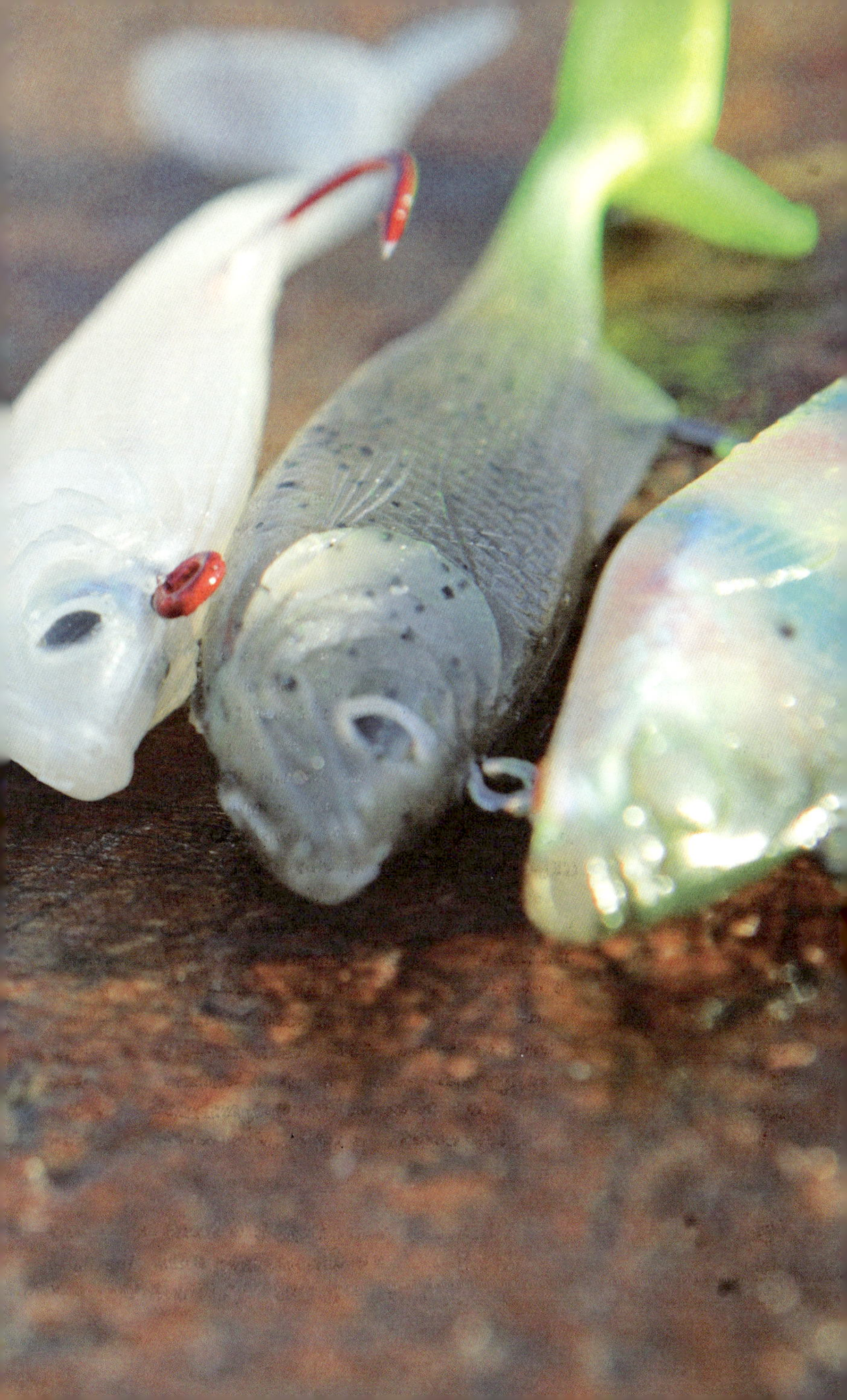

One of the most exciting aspects of taking up any new hobby is buying kit. It's a form of identifying and engaging with your sport. *I have a fishing rod – therefore I am an angler.*

In my 40-odd years of fishing, I have coveted all sorts of tackle, from all over the world. Through an over-exposure to tackle fanaticism I've now achieved an almost Zen-like state where I've satisfied all my wants. I've accumulated so much kit over the years that recently I've turned into a kind of tackle-vegan, and now enjoy going fishing virtually kit-less.

Where I might enjoy the sensation of being almost naked (in a tackle sense) while heading out fishing, a lot of anglers will experience a lack of tackle as a rabid insecurity. Many anglers' greatest fear is that they'll go fishing somewhere and discover once they get there that they haven't brought along the right gear. As a result, most anglers hideously overcompensate when they pack their kit and take far too much tackle.

Having gone through my own tackle addiction and come out the other side – one day at a time – I do feel uniquely qualified to reduce the weight of your tackle box, by detailing only the essentials.

Main tackle: rods, reel and line

The rod, reel and line can be thought of as the 'hardware' of your fishing tackle, and are the first essentials when you're getting your kit together. It's worth spending money on a good-quality reel and line because these are the constants of your fishing trips. The reel and line in particular have a lot demanded of them every time you cast and retrieve, they receive the most wear and tear, so they're the pieces to invest in. Without a working reel and reliable line, your fishing trip will soon end in tears.

Rods

To catch the fish you most want to eat, you'll probably need a rod too. You can catch fish with a handline (see p.118) but I think it's safe to assume that most anglers will need at least one rod. The rod has two main functions. It acts as a springy whip-like device with which to cast out your bait from the shore, and it's used as a lever to help you lift your weight and hopefully your fish out of the sea.

Rods get named after functions, such as spinning rods, or after locations, such as beach rods and boat rods, or after species, such as carp rods or bass rods.

Spinning rod A spinning rod has been given its name because it is designed for use with a spinning reel (otherwise known as a 'fixed-spool reel') and for casting an artificial lure called a 'spinner' (see pp.138–40). So it's designed for 'spinning' as a technique, which you might use to catch mackerel, pike, salmon, pollack, bass or grey mullet. But most rods are capable of performing a lot more functions than their name implies.

For instance, you might think a carp rod is only good for catching carp, but in fact it's great for a whole range of species. Really these are only manufacturers' names, given to certain designs of rod to afford the purchaser confidence that one particular rod will perfectly suit the species he's setting his sights on. In reality, it's a bit of a ruse to make anglers buy a different rod for every species. This is by no means necessary.

An 8–9-foot spinning rod is capable of catching and landing all of the fish mentioned in this book. It is the most versatile rod you will ever buy.

Spinning rods normally come in two sections: butt section and tip section. You can also buy four-piece or six-piece 'travel' spinning rods, or 'telescopic' spinning rods, which concertina down into their own handle section. These rods will fit in a suitcase, so they are great if you're travelling on a plane and want to avoid having to check-in your rods separately to the oversized baggage section.

If you're tempted to buy a travel or telescopic spinning rod, be warned, you get what you pay for. Because they require complex engineering to fit all the pieces together, very cheap telescopic and multi-piece rods do tend to break more easily. Unless they've been carefully engineered (which costs money), the sections often don't slot together very well and fishing with the resulting rod feels like using a giant stick of wholewheat spaghetti that's been chopped into sections and then 'Araldited' back together again.

The most reliable and most effective spinning rod is a two-piece rod, rated to cast a weight of up to 20–50g (about ¾–2oz); this rating is normally printed on the shaft, just above the handle.

You can buy rods with either cork or rubber handles. My personal preference is cork. I like the way it looks and feels. However weather-resistant rubber handles are practical, last longer and require zero maintenance.

The most important part of any rod is the 'blank' it's made from. The blank is the body or spine of the rod; the carbon-fibre stick on to which the rings, handle and reel fixtures are all attached. The definition of a good blank is one that is light but strong, and which bends in the right place for the job you want it to do. Tackle dealers and manufacturers talk in terms of 'fast tapered blanks', and 'powerful upper sections flowing into a stiff butt', etc. Getting your head around rod technology and design when you're new to angling is unnecessary, unless it's something that grabs your curiosity. You certainly don't need to know how rods are designed and made; so long as you're buying from a reputable dealer, buying a reputable brand, and it's a rod that feels comfy to hold, then you can't go far wrong.

Just as with men's fashion or designer sports cars, there is an elite top-end of manufacture, which is crazily expensive. There are spinning rods that will cost you upwards of £600 which, frankly, is just silly. When you're starting out, don't pay more than £50 for a spinning rod. Buy a reputable make. By all means buy online – there are usually stacks of customer reviews on websites where you can compare makes – but I confess I'm a sucker for buying a rod in a tackle shop, because I like to buy a rod from a man or woman who knows what they're talking about. And you just can't beat *feeling* a rod – giving it a good waggle and just seeing if you like it. Even if you don't really know what you like, you'll get a much better idea if you're holding it in your hands rather than reading about it on a website or in a catalogue.

There are other considerations to rods, like rings, reel-seat fixtures and 'action' (the way a rod bends when it's under strain from a fish), but my advice is to assume all that stuff is okay. If you like the colour, the grip, the price and the way it waggles, go ahead and buy it.

Boat rods I'm not going to cover deep-sea, wreck and reef fishing in this book. It's not really appropriate to anyone who is starting out, because the commitment required, in terms of both tackle and time (the average deep-sea trip is 6–8 hours), is too much. If you've never been sea fishing before, then a deep-sea trip is not the place to start. I want to stick to inshore, shallow-water fishing, where there are lots of great fish to be caught without having to use complicated or heavy gear.

Boat rod-bending action

So, the long and the short of it is; you don't really *need* a boat rod. Even if you go out on a summer mackerel trip, the chances are you'll use tackle provided by the skipper, which might be rod and line or else handlines (see p.118). (If you're booking a trip, don't forget to ask about tackle.) Or, with the skipper's permission, you could even use your own spinning rod, set up with a 3 or 4oz weight and a line of mackerel feathers (see pp.134–7). But it can get tricky for mackerel-trip skippers if anglers are using a mixture of rods and handlines. They all sink at different rates and have differing degrees of water resistance and drag, which can soon turn a mackerel trip into a tackle-knitting session. So be sure to check with the skipper before booking that he's happy for you to have your own rod on board.

At 9 feet, a spinning rod takes up a lot of room on a boat. Most boat rods are around 7 feet, which makes them easier to use on a confined deck space. Apart from being shorter, boat rods are stronger than spinning rods. They need to be able to lift ½lb of lead off the seabed, occasionally attached to a fish of 10–15lb, which also has tidal current to help it fight.

In saying this, the mistake most people make when buying a boat rod is to buy one that is too thick and too strong. It's hard to resist, I know. We're only human, and by nature we assume that the beefier the rod we buy, the beefier the fish we'll catch. This is absolutely not the case. Some of the biggest fish I've caught – fish well over 100lb – have been landed on spinning rods or carp rods. I've seen enormous conger eels brought to the boat on light bream rods and a 15lb line. It's not the breaking strain that matters so much as the technique you use to land it.

If you do want to buy your own boat rod for mackerel trips and inshore reef-fishing trips, all you need is a one-piece or two-piece rod. Boat rods don't have casting weight printed above the handle like spinning rods, they are sold by line class. So they'll say something like 20–30lb, or 50–60lb. I personally haven't used a boat rod in this country in excess of 20lb class in years. There's no need. Don't spend more than £50–100. And be aware that you'll need a boat reel, otherwise known as a 'multiplier' reel (see pp.119–20) to go with it too. Boat rods are not designed to be used with ordinary spinning reels.

Carp rods Even if you never intend to fish for carp, a carp rod is a good weapon to have in your carbon-fibre armoury. Carp rods aren't that different from spinning rods, they're just stronger, less bendy at the tip and capable of casting a heavier weight. They are very versatile and are becoming increasingly affordable.

A new carp rod shouldn't cost you more than £50–100, and there are loads of great secondhand bargains to be had, because the truly committed carp angler is a tackle fiend who will change and upgrade his rods about as often as normal people change their socks. And a carpist's castoff casting stick is certainly good enough for sea fishing. So check out local classified ads and auction sites.

Look for a carp rod with a 'test curve' of 1½–2lb. I often use carp rods to fish from the beach and one with a 2lb test curve will cast a 4oz weight and a bait with ease. Of course, a carp rod isn't going to chuck a lead 200 yards out to sea, like a proper beachcaster rod (see below) would. But at most of the beach marks suitable for a relative novice, a carp rod will cast far enough to catch fish and they're so much easier to use and to store than beachcasters.

Fly rod You'll only need a fly rod if you want to go fly fishing. Fly fishing requires a very different set of tackle, skill and knowledge from the other styles of fishing I cover in this book, and revolves around a different command of mechanics.

All other forms of fishing involve casting something weighted, whether it's a bait, a float, a spinner or a set of feathers with a lead weight attached. And so the rod acts as a simple flexible lever, with a weight at one end. Get the weight moving through the air, using the whip action of the rod, and the moving weight will pull the line off the reel as it goes.

Throwing an imitation fly, weighing a fraction of a gram, more than a couple of feet is impossible because it has no weight or inertia, and it will be held back by even the slightest breeze. You can't add a weight to the fly, because then it'll just sink in the water, and flies are meant to float on the surface. So the only way to propel a weightless fly with a rod is if the line that carries it is heavy, yet buoyant. This can be achieved, but it requires a completely different style of casting and another set of specialised tackle. So if you want to learn how to fly-cast, I'd recommend taking one or two casting lessons from a qualified instructor (see Directory, p.250).

If you want to buy a fly rod that will work for catching trout, sea trout, mackerel, garfish, grey mullet, sea bass and even pike, buy a two-piece 8 weight (this refers to the weight of the fly line), in either a 9-foot or 9-foot-6-inch rod. Again, don't spend more than £100. And don't buy a fancy fly reel, the cheapest one will do perfectly well to begin with. But do spend money on getting a medium-to-good quality weight-forward floating or slow-sinking fly line. 'Weight forward' describes the design of the fly line itself. This means the line is designed and profiled so that the inherent weight of the line is distributed towards the forward end. This is done specifically to make it easier to cast.

Beachcaster rod This is a huge and powerful rod designed to cast large weights over long distances from the shore. Beachcasters can range from 12–14 feet long and cast huge lumps of lead up to 6–8oz.

In my opinion they are not easy things to use and not much fun – either to cast or to land fish. If you progress at beach fishing you may want to buy a beachcaster and try for long-distance casts. But I'd prefer to leave the mechanics and techniques of beachcasting to more technically advanced books than I intend this to be.

Handlines These are simply thick lines used without a fishing rod or reel. They're normally stored on a wooden frame and can be unwound, weighted, hooked and baited, and then dropped over the side of a boat or from a pier. They can be fished with baits or with mackerel feathers.

Handlines are great pieces of kit, especially when used from a boat. They're hard to find in tackle shops, except for the ubiquitous orange nylon stranded crab line, which does the job for mackerel and small pollack, but is a pretty horrible thing to use. My preference is for a very thick monofilament line (see p.121) or thick braided nylon line (illustrated below), with something in the region of 150–200lb breaking strain. Old-fashioned handlines wound on wooden frames are particularly good – look out for secondhand ones in car boot sales and household auctions.

Handlines are the opposite to rod and reel lines: rod anglers strive to fish with a light rod and a thin line to increase sensation through the rod; however, with handlines, thicker is better. The beefier the handline, the more movement and information will be transmitted from the hook to the hand. With thin handlines there is less 'communication' travelling down the line, and if you do hook a fish thin lines bite into your flesh more.

The true joy of handlining is about having direct contact with the fish. Being able to feel every nibble and bite with your fingers on the line, as well as every lunge of the ensuing fight, is so much more exciting than having the sensations filtered through line, reel, rod and padded handle before they reach your fingertips.

Reels

A good reel is more important than a good rod, because it's working much harder and there are many more parts that can go wrong. Unless you want to go fly fishing, the only two types of reel you'll need to cope with are spinning reels (also known as 'fixed-spool reels') and multiplier reels (also known as 'boat reels'). Most usually, spinning reels are used from the shore and multipliers from a boat. Both types of reel are illustrated on the following page.

Spinning or fixed-spool reel A spinning or fixed-spool reel is a vital and versatile piece of kit. Technically speaking, the very same reel can be used in sea water and fresh water, but some fixed spools are made specifically for sea use. These tend to be bigger, because they're used for casting more weight and thicker line. They also have more protection against the corrosive effect of salt water.

Even fixed-spool reels that are designed for sea fishing will grind to a halt after a few outings if they're not maintained. The simplest and most basic precaution to prolong their life requires that you rinse your fixed-spool reel in fresh water after use at sea, then roughly dry it with a rag and spray with WD40.

In a perfect world, you would have two spinning reels: one for sea, one for fresh water. Apart from anything else, you can get away with a smaller-sized reel in fresh water. The most versatile-sized reel you can buy is a 5000 or 050.

In terms of its internal engineering, a spinning reel works hard. If you're casting and retrieving all day long, chucking out a couple of ounces of lead with each cast, then the stresses and strains on such a compact mechanism are considerable.

For this reason alone, very cheap reels don't last. The gear wheels in cheap reels are made of plastic or soft metal and really won't survive much abuse. And, be warned, if your reel does die in the middle of a day out fishing, there's not much you can do to improvise. It's an essential and fundamental part of the fishing process. Sadly, a broken reel equals an early bath.

So, for a reel you intend to use in sea water, be prepared to invest around £40 plus. Most reels come with a free spare spool, which can prove very useful. Buy or beg a third spool too, because then you can fill each spool with different thicknesses (or types) of line to cover a range of eventualities. Having an extra spool of line is like having an extra reel without having to carry the extra weight.

Multiplier or boat reel The difference between a spinning/fixed-spool reel and a multiplier/boat reel is like the difference between a two-wheel-drive car and a 4x4. The multiplier is mechanically a much more efficient piece of machinery. It is mounted on the rod just like a proper winch, at 90° to the line. It has a handle at one end, which cranks a bobbin, creating a simple and direct drive, rather than the complicated system a fixed-spool reel uses.

Spinning (fixed-spool) reel

Multiplier reel

A multiplier can handle more weight and it can reel a line in quicker, which means it's most suited to fishing from a boat, particularly in deep water where you might be using a heavy lead and reeling in is hard work. The multiplication of revolutions of the spool, created by the clever engineering of the reel's internal gears, means the reel gears take some of the strain out of reeling up from a depth. The downside of the multiplier reel is that it's a very tricky thing to cast. However, when you're simply using a multiplier from a boat, you don't need to be able to cast. You just lower your gear over the side, by taking the reel out of gear and letting it drop.

For shallow-water boat fishing, multiplier reels don't need to be expensive. If you're never fishing in more than 100 feet of water then a reel is not being asked to do too much grunt work. But they still need to be resilient to the gear-clogging salt water. Very cheap multipliers do tend to rot and jam quickly, sometimes within half a dozen outings. The lower end of mid-range reels will do the job. You shouldn't have to spend more than £30–50.

Multipliers don't come with spare spools. Unlike spinning reels, spools are not easy to remove and change. So, when you choose the line for your multiplier, make sure it's the line you want, because changing it again later is a very finicky job.

Fly reel You'll only need a fly reel if you're using a fly rod. Fly reels are the most simple and basic design of any reel. Normally fly anglers don't even use the reel for retrieving a fish, it's only used as a line holder and the fish is played by holding the line in the hand, feeding it through the fingers. For this reason alone, fly reels aren't worthy of much consideration. Any old thing will do.

Line

There are two types of fishing line that you're likely to encounter: monofilament and braid. Monofilament is the most common. It's what most people think of as fishing line: clear or translucent single-core nylon polymer line, which is extruded by machine and ranges in strength from ½lb breaking strain to 1000lb. The most useful range for you to have is between 10 and 15lb. It is also helpful to have a spool of 30–40lb to use to make up rigs and to tie to the reel line as a shock leader if you're casting hard from the beach.

If you've got a spare spool or two for your spinning reel, you might want to consider loading them with braid of about 20–25lb breaking strain. Braid is a fairly recent invention. It is composed of interwoven strands of Kevlar-like man-made fibres which create a very strong, very thin line.

The key characteristic that makes braid interesting to anglers is that, unlike monofilament line, it doesn't stretch. Monofilament line is inherently elastic: the more line you have out in the water, the greater the amount of stretch and recoil it will have. The downside of this elasticity or stretch is that it 'muffles' sensation over distance.

At 50 yards, you'll feel a bite on the braid line much more clearly than you will on monofilament line. Braid also cuts through the water more efficiently than monofilament, because pound for pound it has a much slimmer profile and so it creates less resistance to the water current.

The disadvantages of braid are that it can be very tangly and it's trickier to tie efficient knots with. Braid's inelasticity can sometimes prove problematic too. A little amount of stretch is useful at the hook end of the line. Without it, braid can be too unforgiving and will rip a hook right out of a fish's mouth, or else straighten out the bend in your hook, making it useless.

Using braid is a subjective issue and you probably won't have a view on it until you've had a few years' experience of different types of sea angling. In very deep seas (which probably you won't be fishing, at least for some time) it's more common as it causes less water drag and gives better 'communication' at depth. In shallow-water fishing you don't need to use braid, but you might at some point like to experiment.

If you do use braid, you'll need to join it to a short length (8 feet) of monofilament line in order to tie on your hook. Braid should never be used all the way through to the hook; it isn't translucent like monofilament, so it can spook fish and prevent them taking your bait.

Terminal tackle

This is the 'software' that you add to the 'hardware' of your rod, line and reel to transform them into something that can catch fish. The term 'terminal tackle' describes everything that interfaces with the sea (and hopefully with the fish), including hooks, floats, weights, swivels and lures. These pieces of terminal tackle can be assembled into various types of 'rig'. Different types of rig, such as running ledger (see p.164) or paternoster (see p.163), are used either for specific locations, to catch specific types of fish, or to present baits on or just above the seabed.

Hooks

Hook technology is mind-boggling. There are so many sizes, shapes and metallic compositions of hook to choose from, I could easily fill this whole book with amazing hook facts and still barely scratch the surface. There is a hook designed for every fish, every bait and every technique of angling known to man. My personal approach though, is Forrest Gump-like in its simplicity.

In the early days of your fishing adventures, a lot of terminal tackle that you might use (such as spinners, plugs, feathers, Storm lures and pre-made terminal rigs, such as 'pier rigs') will already come with hooks fitted. Experienced and purist anglers may well baulk at the quality of some of these hooks, but when you're learning the ropes, I think it makes perfect sense to be thankful that one part of the puzzle is already in place. If it comes with a hook already tied on it, then use it. You may lose

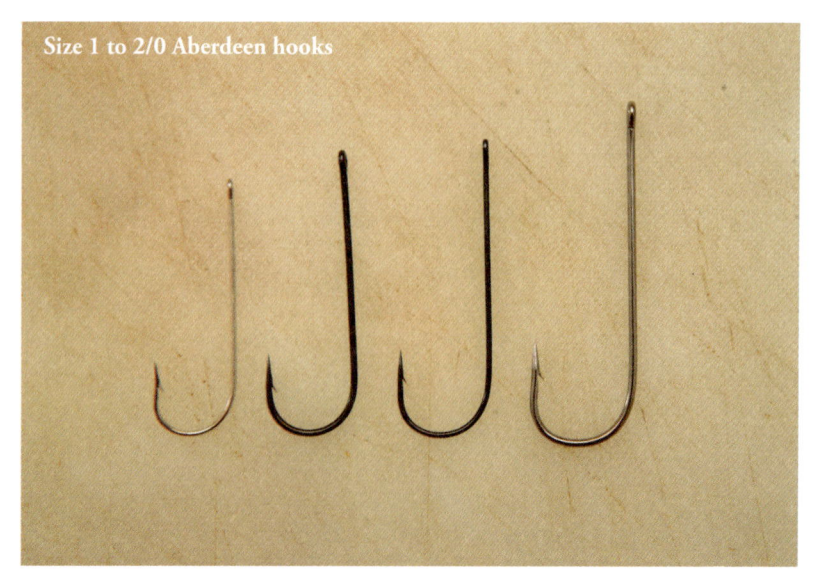

Size 1 to 2/0 Aberdeen hooks

a fish or snap a hook because they're not up to spec, but I think it's better to get to the point of losing a fish rather than never even getting your tackle wet because you haven't quite mastered the knots.

This is my must-have hook shopping list, from the smallest to the biggest. With this selection in your tackle box, you'll be covered for all the species you're likely to catch or want to catch. (One thing to remember is that small hooks catch big fish but big hooks rarely catch small fish.)

- Size 14 freshwater hooks are a specialist size used for catching finicky mullet, when bites are hard to come by. Otherwise most mullet anglers would normally use a size 10 freshwater hook.
- Size 1 and 2 Aberdeen are perfect all-round hooks for catching any of the species mentioned in this book, particularly black bream, pouting, whiting, mackerel, dogfish and garfish. The 'Aberdeen' part of this name refers to the shape of the hook and the length of the shank (the straight bit of the hook before the bend). You might find, if you're catching a lot of dogfish, that the 1 and 2 hooks bend rather too easily when you're trying to remove them from a dogfish's tough mouth. In which case, move to a bigger size (below) and squeeze the barb flat with a pair of pliers to make it easier to remove.
- Size 3/0 is a better hook to use for catching pollack, bass and gurnard. The smaller ones will also work, they just might straighten during the fight if the fish are a decent size.
- Size 4 treble hooks are ideal for squid rigs and for replacing broken spinner hooks.

Floats

A float is simply a flotation device, fixed to a specific point on your line, from which your chosen bait is suspended (see diagram on p.165). A float keeps your bait at a fixed depth in the water. Depending on the location and the species you're trying to catch, you might suspend your bait just under the surface (for example, using bread flake for mullet in a harbour), or in mid water (targeting mackerel with squid strip). Or you might want to suspend the bait (sand eel or ragworm for bass) deep down, just above the seabed, especially if it's weedy or snaggy with sharp rocks, which you want to avoid.

Floats are very sexy. They're shiny, colourful, and come in a range of figures from the anorexic supermodel profile to the chubby big-bottomed bung. The shape of the float and its overall size relates to the type of sea that you are going to use it in.

If the sea is dead calm you can get away with a small float, which is a good thing because a big float might, if the bait is suspended close to it, spook any nervy fish. A big float makes a big splash and casts a big shadow on the water. The smaller the float the sneakier you can be. And small slim waggler floats are best for finicky fish like mullet, because they're easy to pull under. So if a fussy mullet pulls on a suspended

Useful selection of floats

Split shot

bait, he'll feel minimal resistance and might commit to bite. But a fat float will create too much pull against the bait and the wise old mullet will smell a rat.

Over the years, I have owned thousands of floats. Having said that, out of all those that have seduced me into buying them, pitifully few ever venture out of the tackle box on to my line. By all means, indulge any natural predilections, but being pragmatic, these are the floats you'll actually use:

Thin bodied, self-cocking waggler This is used for grey mullet, perch in rivers and grayling. The important feature of this float is that the body has a built-in weight, which makes it easy to cast and forces it to stand upright in the water, without having to hang extra weight beneath it.

Sea float A simple polystyrene wide-bodied float, which comes in a range of sizes. Perfect for mackerel, garfish, bass and pollack, it also works in fresh water for pike.

Bubble float These come in bright orange for long-distance sea fishing, and clear plastic for more sneaky stuff in fresh water, harbours and estuaries. Bubble floats are an old but brilliant invention. Some even have two plugs which allow you to add water to the float to give it weight, but won't make it sink. The bubble float is fabulous for casting, but its spherical profile means it is not a very sensitive instrument. It's heavy and suspicious to fish. It can, however, be used successfully for mackerel, garfish, pollack, grey mullet or perch.

Bullets and bombs

Weights

A weight exists to make things sink. Baits and lures and feathers are shackled to a lead weight in order to get them down deep enough in the water to where the target fish are feeding. In poorer countries around the world I've fished with fishermen who use pebbles, rusty bolts or old spark plugs attached to the line to provide sinkability. Needless to say, in this country you can buy weights in a dizzying selection of shapes, sizes and materials. Carp anglers have a penchant for lead weights that are carefully manufactured and disguised to look like stones!

Of all the tackle you buy, weights are the thing you're most likely to lose. Every time you get snagged, it's the weight that gets lost first. So don't bother to buy anything but the cheapest. Some anglers even make their own. It's also worth noting that they are by nature heavy, so the fewer you decide to take, the less of a burden your tackle box will be.

This is all you really need to keep in your weight munitions:

- A small selection of bombs, from 1–5oz, used when ledgering or feathering (see pp.135–7).
- A small selection of drilled bullets, from ⅛–2oz, used under big floats and for worming or touch-ledgering (see pp. 102 and 165).
- A box of various lead-free split shot, which are nipped on the line beneath smaller floats to make lightweight baits sink. Never use more weight than you need. The more weight you attach, the bigger the splash and the bigger the lump of lead falling through the water, both of which will spook fish.

Swivels

Swivels are useful for creating joins between two lengths of line of different strength. For example, if you have 20lb line on your reel, but only want to present 10lb line to the fish on your hook line, then a swivel makes the joint easy to tie and it will also minimise the potential for tangles.

Swivels are great for joining rigs to the main line. Because of their mechanical construction, swivels can rotate in the water, with either end of the swivel turning in either direction, which means they stop the line from getting kinked or twisted up. In water with a strong tide, the swivel allows a rig to twist and twirl in the current without winding itself into a hideous tangle.

A swivel also makes a perfect stop for a running ledger rig (see p.164). It stops the weight from sliding all the way down to the hook, as well as providing a tangle-resistant buffer between reel line and hook line.

Clip swivels These are most useful when you tie them to the end of your line as the junction between your line and a weight, or between your line and a type of terminal tackle like a spinner, wedge or plug (see pp.138–42), all of which need to be able to rotate as they pass through the water. Without a clip swivel, they would be constantly twisting and kinking the reel line. The clip swivel allows them to rotate freely – and allows you to change them as often as you want without having to tie any knots.

Swivels, clip swivels and three-way swivels

Clip swivels are used to connect to the weight because they can be easily undone, so you can change the size of your weight quickly to match the tide, current or fishing technique. A larger or smaller weight can be attached without the bother of cutting line and tying new knots. They also provide some protection for your line. If you tie your line directly to the loop in your bomb weight, it'll get damaged and nicked every time the weight hits a rock, eventually fraying and breaking, so you'll lose your lead. Because the clip is metal, it won't be affected.

Clip swivels are perfect for using with spinners because you can chop and change as often as you like without having to tie new knots. In fact, if you're new to fishing, knots might still be a bit of a challenge, in which case you can use clip swivels at *both ends* of your mackerel feather string, from the reel line as well as to the weight. That way, you can swap from feathers (see pp.134–7) to spinner (see pp.138–40) to paternoster rig (see p.163) without having to tie knots.

The most useful-sized swivels to have are:
- rolling swivels size 1 or 2
- clip swivels in size 2/0
- three-way clip swivels

Three-way clip swivels are used to make quick paternoster rigs, with the reel line from the top eye, weight link line from the bottom eye, and hook link (snood) from the middle.

None of the fish in this book are big enough to break any medium-sized swivels. Size isn't too much of an issue, but avoid having a huge swivel or clip swivel that's almost as big as the spinner it's clipped to, and similarly avoid anything that's made of such fine wire that it's hard to fit your line through the swivel eye! Tackle shops stock perfectly serviceable swivels. I've fished for decades and still don't fully understand how swivels are sized. Use common sense. If you can't break a swivel or a clip with your bare hands, chances are a 2lb fish can't break it either.

Booms

The function of a boom, on a one- or two-hook paternoster rig (see p.163), is to provide a stiff right-angled 'branch' to the main vertical 'spine' of your rig. The end of the boom, furthest from the spine, is where you hang your hook, suspended on a 'hook link': a piece of monofilament line no more than 8 inches long.

The function of a boom in these basic rigs is to put some distance between the hook and the main line of the rig, in order to stop them becoming tangled together when you cast out or drop your bait down from a pier or boat. If your hook and bait get tangled around the main line of the rig, it'll make your bait presentation ineffective and obscure the bait from a fish's hungry eyes. A boom holds your bait out on a cantilever, keeping it separate and suspended away from the main line, where it can flutter and float attractively in the water, begging to be eaten.

Small booms for paternoster rigs

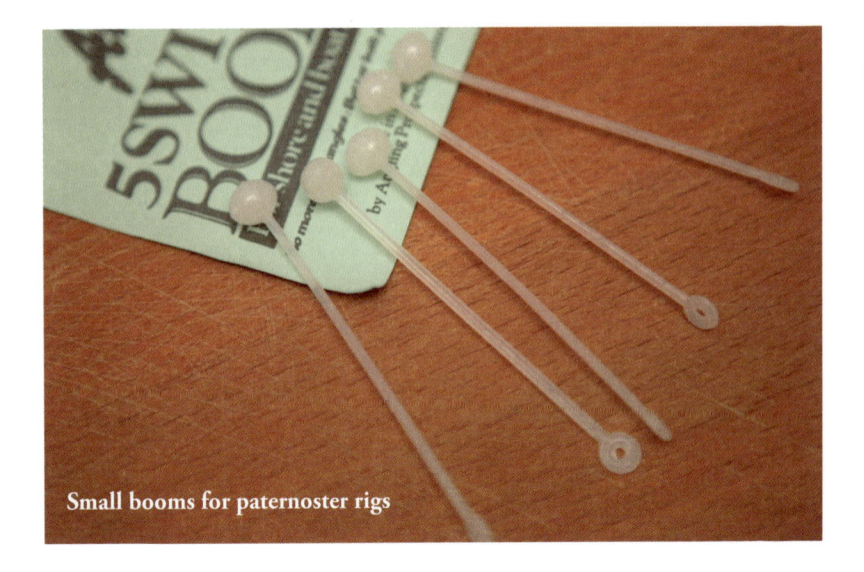

Most booms can be moved up and down the line, so that you can position them at the preferred distance from the weight. And when you're fishing vertically, either from a boat or from a pier, or off a rocky cliff into deep water, you can determine the depth you want your bait to be presented at by setting the boom height above the weight. By setting the boom 3 feet above the weight you know your bait will be stationed 3 feet off the seabed. This can be useful if you're trying to keep your hook and bait above a bed of seaweed or a bunch of snaggy rocks; the boom holds it in open water, just above the structure where fish will find it easily and where it avoids getting caught up in tackle-thieving snags.

There are various booms on sale. Some are hollow tubes that can be used like zip sliders for making running ledger rigs (see p.164), some are wire. The booms you want for simple paternoster rigs or single-hook rigs are solid plastic, 3–5 inches long, with a hole at one end through which to tie a short hook link. At the other end is a means of attaching the boom to the 'main spine' line of your rig. The method of attaching can vary according to the type of rig; some require knots, most don't.

I'd advise you to buy a basic, cheap boom (because you're bound to lose plenty, we all do), which is easy to attach under adverse conditions. Check out a few shop-bought rigs that include booms. Consult websites like worldseafishing.com and see what patterns they have on offer. And do ask in a local tackle shop which pattern they would advise. Even ask them to show you exactly how to tie one on. There's nothing worse than getting a boom out of your box on the high seas or on a crowded pier and not having the faintest idea how to fit it. All the more reason to keep your tackle purchases simple.

Beads

Beads

Beads are used as a shock absorber between the swivel and the weight's wire loop on a running ledger rig (see p.164). In theory, they prevent the monofilament line from being crunched between the metal of the loop and the metal of the swivel, which will eventually cause it to snap.

I don't always use beads. In fact, if my hands are cold or sticky from bait or fish, I won't even bother to try. They're so annoying to use in bad weather conditions that I think I've lost more beads than I've ever used. However, they are important if the loop on your weight is bigger than the size of your swivel. If the swivel can pass through the loop, then it won't work as a stop. Sticking a big bead between them will prevent the swivel slipping through the weight loop.

Another way of using beads is when you're tying simple rigs for plaice or flounder fishing. Threading eight or ten beads along the line just above the hook will provide something eye-catching and alluring that flat fish respond to and which will, in theory, draw their attention to your bait. Whether you believe this or not, it can't do any harm, and you never know, the extra resistance of the beads in the current may make the bait flap a little more enticingly.

Zip sliders

The zip slider is normally a rigid tube of plastic with a clip attached to one side. The reel line is threaded down the centre of the tube and the weight is attached to the clip. This allows the line to pass freely through the tube, without moving the weight. So, when a fish pulls on a bait, the line slides through the slider without disturbing

Zip sliders

the bait. This way the fish isn't spooked by feeling any resistance of the weight, and yet, the pulling of the line will still register on the flexible rod tip as a bite. This type of set-up is known as a running ledger rig (see p.164). A zip slider is so called because it acts like the handle on a play-area zip slide, where you can slide down a taut wire, holding on to a handle.

Hook link

The line which is attached to your hook is known as the 'hook link' or 'snood' or even, just to complicate things further, the 'leader' – not to be confused with the shock leader (see opposite). It makes sense for this hook link to be no thicker than absolutely necessary, because some fish are particularly aware and wary of thick line near the bait and will refuse to bite if the mouthful looks strange or acts suspiciously.

Most anglers carry a spare spool of line, which they'll use only for hook links – in other words, the final section of line in your rig that leads to the hook. Some serious anglers will buy a very good-quality line for this short but important section, often a fluorocarbon line, which is specifically designed to appear less visible in water. It's thin and transparent, but strong.

Personally I don't think fancy and expensive fluorocarbon line is necessary, unless you're targeting a really finicky species, like grey mullet. A spare spool of ordinary monofilament is always useful to have, though, as it means you can tie a new hook length without having to cannibalise your reel line.

Shock leader

A shock leader, for general beachcasting, is a length of 40–60lb mono line, which should be about twice the length of your rod. It is designed to absorb the initial shock of heavy lead weights (2oz or more) when you're casting hard from the shore.

The strength of main reel line you'll want to use while casting with a spinning rod or a carp rod (or even a beachcasting rod) is no more than 15lb. Heavy line increases aerodynamic resistance. Anything upward of 15lb is too heavy to be practicable casting over any distance. But just using 15lb line with a 3 or 4oz weight will end in potentially painful disaster, because the force of the cast with that weight is greater than the strength of your reel line. It will snap like straw, unless you use a shock leader to cushion the force of the cast.

A shock leader is a beefed-up extension of your reel line which takes all the initial strain of casting. It is tied to the business end of your reel line and runs to the top of your terminal tackle rig. The important thing is that the shock leader is long enough to wind a few times around your reel spool, up the rod and down to the start of your rig when you're in the casting position. A shock leader should be between 20 and 30 feet long. This will absorb all the shock of the cast, thus protecting the more fragile reel line. Shock leaders also combat abrasion when fishing over rough seabeds.

There's a formula for judging the necessary breaking strain of shock leaders, which equates to 10lb of shock leader for every single ounce of weight cast. Given that you will have a minimum of 10lb line on your reel to begin with, no shock leader is needed for a 1oz weight. If you've got 15lb line on your rod, you will probably get away with casting 2oz, if you're careful. Above 2oz you'll definitely need to add a shock leader, and remember that each extra ounce requires an extra 10lb breaking strain:

- 3oz weight: 30lb shock leader
- 4oz weight: 40lb shock leader… and so on.

If, like me, you prefer to use a spinning rod or carp rod for beach fishing, you'll never cast more than 4oz, so a 40lb shock leader will more than suffice.

I always keep a spool of 30lb or 40lb in my tackle box and tie on a 20-foot length if I'm fishing hard with a string of mackerel feathers and a 3 or 4oz weight. There is a special knot for tying shock leaders on to your reel (see p.170).

Bait elastic

If you want to use peeler crab, mussels, hermit crabs or razor clams as bait, buy a spool of bait elastic from a tackle shop. It is gossamer-fine elastic, which you can just wind and wind around a squidgy bait. Even herring baits, which can quickly turn mushy, benefit from being lashed to a hook with bait elastic. It's very easy to use because it has a sticky, self-gripping surface and doesn't need to be knotted, just wound around itself a dozen times or more.

Artificial lures

An artificial lure is quite simply any piece of terminal tackle that is designed to attract or even annoy a fish, to the extent that the fish then attacks and tries to eat the lure. So, a lure might be designed to look like a tiny fish, or a worm. Or it might simply be made with a reflective surface or from brightly coloured material that creates a flash in the water, interesting enough to make the fish strike.

Artificial lures are used instead of a bait (see pp.150–9). A bait is just a piece of recognisable food hung on a hook to try and attract the hungry attentions of a fish. Lures are used either because a bait isn't available, or because the thing a lure does a good job of imitating, such as a small sprat or a sand eel, is impractical to find and keep alive for use. Baits can be messy and smelly; artificial lures are clean and re-usable. Artificial lures may cost a bit to buy, but they can last for years. Fresh live baits are very hard to buy because not many tackle shops stock them and if they do, they're far from cheap.

Spinners, plugs, jelly worms, rubber fish, mackerel feathers, spoons and wedges are all examples of artificial lures.

The adjacent chart gives you some idea of the best luring or baiting approaches for different types of fish. Thank God there will always be mind-boggling exceptions to every rule and fish, bless them, will always surprise you in their determination to break any rules we devise. But as a rough 'how to get started' guide, this marries up the most likely species with the most likely techniques.

Surface popper plug for bass fishing

Bait and lure techniques for sea fish

	MACKEREL FEATHERS	MINI FEATHER	BAITED FEATHERS	SPINNER OR PLUG	JIG/ STORM LURE	FLOAT-SUSPENDED BAIT	BOTTOM-LEDGERED BAIT
MACKEREL	Best	Best	Best	Best	Best	Best	Lucky
DOGFISH			Lucky				Best
POUTING	Lucky		Best				Best
POLLACK	Lucky		Lucky	Best	Best	Lucky	Lucky
COD	Lucky		Best		Best		Best
WHITING	Lucky	Lucky	Best				Best
GARFISH	Lucky	Best	Lucky	Lucky		Best	
RED GURNARD	Lucky	Lucky	Best	Lucky	Lucky		Best
BLACK BREAM			Lucky		Lucky	Lucky	Best
PLAICE							Best
SEA BASS	Lucky	Lucky	Lucky	Best	Best	Lucky	Lucky
DAB & FLOUNDER							Best
HORSE MACKEREL	Best	Best	Best	Best		Best	Lucky
HERRING	Best	Best	Lucky	Lucky	Lucky	Lucky	
SQUID					Best	Lucky	Lucky
SLOB TROUT				Lucky		Lucky	Best
GREY MULLET				Best		Best	Lucky

KEY: Best = BEST   Lucky = MIGHT GET LUCKY

Feathers

Feathers probably account for more sea fish catches around the coast of Britain than any other form of terminal tackle. Mackerel feathers are an absolute must for any sea angler who wants to catch fish to eat.

A string of mackerel feathers, at its most basic, is a combination of three, four or six hooks, each tied about 18 inches apart, along a length of clear monofilament fishing line. The individual hooks each have a small pluck of chicken feathers lashed to them.

Shop-bought mackerel feathers come in a variety of colours; mostly these sets are all white, or all orange, or multi-coloured with each of the hooks sporting a different hue of plumage including red, blue, white, orange and black.

I refuse to get too colour conscious about mackerel feathers. It really doesn't hurt to have a colour selection of feathers in your tackle box, to ring the changes when the fish aren't biting. But to get hung up on one mackerel feather colour or another is a sure sign of madness.

I do believe in having more than one *size* of feather though. The size of the feather relates to the size of the hook it's mounted upon. There are several types of small feathers available from tackle shops. The smaller feather sets (which may also be called micro feathers, mini feathers, Sabikis or Hokkais) are really worth having in your collection simply because they might work when bigger ones won't, or they

Mackerel feathers

might work on different species. They may lure mackerel who are being a bit shy, and they may also work on some of the smaller species like herring, sprats, horse mackerel, garfish and even large sand eels.

The size of the feather (or mini lure, as it really is) and its efficiency at attracting fish will relate to the size of the prey prevalent in the water at that time. If all the mackerel are busy feeding on ¼–½-inch-long fish fry, then a great big 3-inch-long feather isn't going to successfully imitate what the mackerel are feeding on. It might even scare them off.

The smaller-sized 'feathers' often don't involve any feather plumage at all. They are simply mini fish lures, tied with flashy and sparkly man-made materials. I would recommend having a couple of sets of smaller feathers in your box.

The little micro feather sets sometimes contain even more than six hooks to each string. I've come across sets of eight or ten mini lures on a string, which are set closer together than the big feathers, but they can be very tangly and tricky to use. However, without too much faffing, you can simply cut a long string of micro feathers in half and make two shorter, more manageable ones.

Why feathers work A string of feathers will attract fish, especially mackerel, because of the way they move and glint. Some feathers have silver flashy material tied into the feather, but also the hooks themselves, if kept clean, will gleam and reflect sunlight as they're jigged through the water. Movement is key. A stationary feather hanging limply in the water will rarely attract a bite, as it won't resemble anything a mackerel might regard as food. Movement makes it interesting. It makes capture seem more urgent.

A hungry mackerel, hunting in a competitive group, sees a movement and a flash of reflected light, and instantly nails what it assumes is a small fish, before any of his mates get a look in.

The mackerel-seducing movement that you can induce in your feathers will differ depending on whether you're afloat on a boat, perched high above the water on a pier, or else down at sea level on the beach.

Feathering from a boat This is the easiest and most effective way to use feathers, because you can simply drop them down to the seabed, weighted by a bomb-shaped lead, and then wind them back up again. Fish will take either on the way down or up; they're not fussy about direction, just movement.

Instead of simply letting the feathers fall through the water, it's more effective to lower them 10 or 15 feet at a time and stop, then jig them up and down, two or three times, at each new level. The 'jigging' should be done in rhythmic sweeps, moving your rod from waist height to head height and down again. This way you can cover the water column efficiently, jigging the feathers through every stage from the boat to the seabed. Mackerel can feed at any depth; sometimes they're only 5 feet under the boat, other times they're way down deep, practically on the seabed. When you're reeling the feathers back up, do the same jigging sequence in reverse. Keep stopping every half a dozen reel turns, to jig up and down at least two or three times.

If you do feel a 'rattling' on your line, it means a mackerel is hooked up. Mackerel will hook themselves, you don't have to 'strike' (see p.174) to drive the hooks home. Mackerel feather hooks always have a pronounced barb on them, so fish rarely escape if they're properly hooked in the mouth. Instead of winding up furiously when you first feel the telltale rattle, to bring your precious quarry up to the boat, try 'hanging' your line for 10 seconds. Hanging means suspending it without jigging or retrieving it.

More mackerel will often hook themselves on your spare feathers while the string hangs in the water with the first mackerel already hooked up. The simple explanation for this is that if one mackerel sees another mackerel obviously engaged in some hunting and eating activity, it's very likely to pile in and try to get some action for itself. So by hanging, you can make competitive feeding and unchecked mackerel greed really work in your favour.

Feathering from the beach For the very reasons that feathering from a boat is so easy (you're surrounded by water deep enough to contain fish), feathering from the beach is much more difficult. In order to get to water deep enough to contain fish, say upwards of 10 feet, you'll normally need to be able to cast your feathers at least 20 or 30 yards. Apart from anything else, this can be a hazardous business. Casting a string of stainless-steel brutally barbed hooks from a standing position out to sea is fraught with potential danger.

At the same time, feathering from the beach is one of the most satisfying ways of catching a feed of mackerel. So, I feel it's my duty to help you to catch some mackerel from the beach without maiming anyone. In order to do this, there are some things we need to rule out. The first of these is the use of a beachcaster rod.

If you walk along Chesil Beach in Dorset in the summer, you'll see lots of anglers chucking out strings of feathers with enormous rods. These are beachcaster rods (see p.117) and they're normally around 13 feet long or more.

As I mentioned earlier, I don't enjoy using these big rods at all. This is for two reasons: firstly, they're not easy to cast and definitely not by anyone new to fishing; secondly, they're uncomfortable to hold and not very pleasant to play a fish on. Beachcasters are unwieldy, uncomfortable sticks, capable of chucking a weight and bait up to 300 yards. But you will only achieve distances of 100 yards or more if you practise and have a well-tuned, expensive and tricky-to-use multiplier reel attached to it. I'm not saying you won't one day progress to using a beachcaster and casting further than I could even dream of, but for the sake of getting started, let's forget beachcasters altogether.

The next option is to use a beach rod. This is usually 11–12 feet long and is built like a very beefy spinning rod. It's designed to take a big, beefy spinning reel with heavy-duty 20lb line. It's much easier to use than a beachcaster, not much more difficult than a spinning rod or carp rod, but it is a hefty, ungainly thing that has no use other than to chuck out big baits and feathers off the beach or rocks.

A simple spinning rod (or carp rod or bass rod – all basically the same thing) has myriad uses in the sea and fresh water, but more importantly it can be used by practically any size of person – man, woman or child – with ease and comfort. To fish from the beach with a spinning rod or a carp rod with feathers, you will need at least 15lb line on your spinning reel, a shock leader (see p.131) and no more than a 3oz lead. The trick is to keep the tackle light and well balanced in terms of weight to rod ratio. I never use anything heavier than a carp rod and I can cast far enough to catch fish in comfort. I also never use more than three feathers – to reduce the chance of snags.

When you're fishing with feathers from the beach, you have to keep the feathers moving through the water, not just to attract fish, but also to avoid them sinking to the bottom and getting snagged as you wind them shorewards. Remember, even with only three feathered hooks there are still at least three opportunities to get your tackle hung up on rocks. And because of the low angle at which you have to retrieve them, it's often impossible to pull them free without breaking your line once they've snagged. This means leaving a string of dangerous tackle wrapped around a rock, uncomfortably close to the shore where people are likely to go swimming.

Your retrieve should be fast. You can intersperse each few winds of the reel with a long steady jig upwards, which, if you hold the rod high, will make the feathers 'swim up' in the water.

Tangles and knots need to be avoided, so keep your line simple and in good working condition. An unwanted knot in your reel line, which forces you to stop winding in order to untangle it, will cause your feathers to sink and might then lead you to hook up with the seabed.

Spinners and wedges

Simple spinners have been around for hundreds of years. They are clever pieces of mechanical engineering, which work on the principle that as they're retrieved through the water, the force of the water passing through the spinner blades will make them rotate like a propeller. The rotation of this blade (or blades) causes vibrations in the water (imitating a wounded fish) as well as creating flashes and glints of light from the shiny metal surfaces as they revolve. The flashing and the vibrations will both attract fish, either out of curiosity or an intention to attack.

The 'Mepps' spinner is an ancient French design, which has been copied and 'improved' upon many times by many manufacturers. But I have to confess I have a real soft spot for the original Mepps, which are very efficient at spinning and creating a vast amount of vibration and flashing, because of their simple but effective design. Original Mepps tend to be more expensive than the myriad imitations, and yet I don't mind paying the extra.

Mostly sea fishermen these days only use the smaller Mepps for mullet spinning, and the rest of the sizes often get left for freshwater pike anglers to use. Mepps is a design classic and you really should have one in your box – there's not a predator species in the world that hasn't been caught by a Mepps.

A wedge (aka Dexter) is like a heavy version of a spinner. It's usually got a much heavier body and an aerodynamic shape, which makes it easy to cast, even into a head-on wind. It can also be used from a boat, either cast out and allowed to sink and then retrieved, or just dropped down over the side, allowed to flutter down to the seabed and then retrieved up 20 turns of the reel handle and dropped back down again. So with this method you're working your wedge up and down in the bottom 20–30 feet of the sea beneath the boat. A wedge doesn't rotate like a spinner and it doesn't have mechanical blades to whirl as it's retrieved. Instead it is carefully designed to wobble and kink as it's retrieved, moving in the way a wounded fish might swim.

The wedge is aerodynamically designed to cast efficiently. The bigger the wedge, the further you should be able to cast. But the bigger the wedge the fewer fish you're likely to attract, simply because a small wedge of ¾–1oz looks like potential prey to a small mackerel, horse mackerel or pollack, but a big wedge of 1½oz could scare them away because they might think it's about to prey on them. Certainly, a big bass might attack a big wedge, but remember there are far fewer big bass around than there are small mackerel. And big bass are a lot smarter too. So if you're just looking for a fun couple of hours with the prospect of a decent nosebag at the end of it, stick to smaller wedges.

Using a spinner or wedge from the shore Casting a spinner or a wedge from the beach is a much easier alternative to casting a string of feathers. A spinner or wedge has only one hook (even though it'll probably be a treble hook with three barbs),

Spinners, including the Mepps spinner (middle left)

Dexter wedge

TACKLE AND KIT 139

so it's less likely to get snagged on the seabed as you retrieve, and less likely to tangle up during repeated casting. Both a spinner and a wedge are normally used without additional weight. All of their weight is intrinsic to their body shape, and so they sink more slowly than a string of feathers, which has a weight attached to the terminal end of the string. A string of feathers with a weight at one end can be cast out further than most plugs or spinners or spoons, because it is normally heavier. However, because spoons and plugs are lighter, they sink more slowly and are less likely to snag on the bottom, which makes them more relaxing to fish with.

Feathering from the beach will also normally require tying on a shock leader (a plug or spoon won't) and fishing at a frantic rate, retrieving fast, to avoid snagging on the seabed. With spinners, spoons and wedges, the pace of retrieve can be slowed down to a much less frenetic pace. Personally, I can only stand half an hour of frantic feathering before I want to swap to a more sedate method.

With spinners and wedges and spoons (see below), which imitate one single bait fish, rather than a small string of them, as feathers do, there is also the strong possibility of attracting the attention of bigger, more selective predators in the area like sea bass or pollack. It's unlikely (though by no means impossible) that you'll hook a big bass on mackerel feathers, but there's every chance you'll hook one on a lure like a spoon or plug.

Using a spinner or wedge from a boat You can cast a spinner or a wedge from a boat and let it sink, then slowly retrieve it. This can work well when the fish (especially bass and pollack) are hunting near the surface, or else if you let your lure drop into the tide and be taken away from the boat with the current for a few minutes, before you start a long slow retrieve. I should add, though, that most mackerel boats or charter boats don't allow or don't encourage clients to cast lures from the boat, mostly for safety reasons. When a group of paying clients are dropping their feathers or baits over the side, it's possible to limit any accidents. When a bunch of punters are casting plugs with up to three huge treble hooks mounted on them every couple of minutes, wheeling back behind them to cast, lurching with every wave, the health and safety issue becomes a nightmare.

So, if you've got your own boat, or have a friend with one, or else have chartered a boat all to yourself, then you'll be able to cast plugs, spoons and anything you like, but when you're cheek by jowl with your fellow anglers in the care of an experienced skipper, you're unlikely to be allowed to cast your spinner from their boat.

Toby spoons

Tobys are more like wedges than spinners. They wobble and they rotate too, but not with the ferocity and frequency of a spinner. They also imitate a wounded fish's behaviour. Tobys can be really effective when cast and retrieved, or else trolled slowly

Toby spoon

behind a moving boat. Being generally lighter, they don't usually cast as far as a wedge, but nor do they sink so fast. So a Toby can be retrieved more slowly than a wedge, which can be handy in shallow water to avoid hooking up with the seabed.

However, like wedges, bigger Toby spoons look great and cast further. They do offer the opportunity of catching a big fish, but a ½lb mackerel (which would be delicious to eat) is going to swim in fear of his life from a big Toby spoon, rather than try to swallow it.

Plugs

There are two distinct types of plug: floating and diving. Both might be used from the shore or possibly from a boat. The depth you desire your plug to dive under the surface depends on where you think the fish may be feeding. Bass, for example, will feed on wounded fry right on the surface, practically grabbing them out of seagulls' mouths, while pollack like to hunt a few feet down from the surface at least.

A floating plug stays on the surface all the time, even when it's being reeled in, because it's very buoyant and simply wiggles its way across the surface of the water. A diving plug, on the other hand, may well float on the water when it's still, but as soon as you start to wind it towards you, the diving vane at its head forces it under the surface of the water.

Some diving plugs are deep divers, some are shallow, depending on the size and angle of the diving vane. And some are integrally weighted too, so they sink down in the water as soon as they're cast out.

Plugs

Plugs are beautiful. Irresistible, perfectly proportioned pieces of tackle that sing to anglers and wannabe anglers with a siren song that will have you parting with your cash faster than you can say John Dory. I once had a guest on my angling radio show, *Dirty Tackle*, who had a collection of plugs worth over £10,000. These weren't antique or vintage collectors' plugs. They were brand-new ones; and none of them were ever used in anger. He just hoarded them in huge multi-drawered tackle boxes and pored over them with gloating obsession. He was a man totally smitten by the lure of the lure. But be warned, there are plugs designed specifically to catch the cash-rich angler first, and fish second.

Apart from simply casting and retrieving a plug or a spinner, both can be used as a 'trolled' bait, let out behind a slow-moving boat. Trolling is a method of fishing originally developed for bluewater game fish, such as marlin and sailfish. All it means is that you tow a lure (plug, spinner, wedge or large fly) 30–100 yards behind the boat, which must be moving very slowly. The lure is positioned either on the surface, near the surface, or deep down, depending on the type of lure and the species of fish you're after.

Plugs are not essential kit. Yes, they are sexy, alluring, and fun to use. They just don't as a rule catch an awful lot of fish. If you really *must* have a plug, then buy a floating plug and a shallow-diving plug of around 3½–4 inches. Try casting them off rocks or a steep, sloping beach, so they're working in at least 10 feet of water. You might get lucky and pick up a pollack. Work hard at dawn and dusk, and you might even attract the homicidal attentions of a bass. But don't hold your breath.

Rubber fish, 'Shads' or 'Storm lures'

Just as all vacuum cleaners get called 'Hoovers' and plastic food wrap is always 'cling film', so any rubber fish lure usually ends up being called a 'Shad' or a 'Storm lure' after the most famous of the rubber fish manufacturers.

Rubber fish come in a variety of colours, sizes, shapes and designs. They are sold both with and without hooks, and some also come with an integral weight fitted inside the body. A plain rubber fish, to which you add your own hook and then attach a weight, is obviously much cheaper than the sophisticated, pre-weighted option. However, for simplicity's sake, I'd recommend buying a couple of packets of the luxury version just to get you started. You can always experiment with rigging your own when you've got a feel for what you like.

Using a rubber fish lure from the shore Pre-weighted rubber fish are enormously versatile lures, which can be used – like spinners – for casting out from the beach or rocks, as well as for drift fishing from a boat. One cunning aspect of the pre-weighted rubber fish is the fact that the bend of the hook is upturned so the point appears upwards out of the back of the rubber fish.

The design of the integral weight means the fish always stays the right way up when it's being retrieved with the hook sticking proud out of its back. This greatly reduces the possibility of the hook catching on the seabed as it's retrieved, without reducing its effectiveness for hooking into a predator's mouth.

On a beach terrain that's not too rocky, you can even 'bounce' your rubber fish along the bottom as you wind it in, by occasionally slowing or stopping the retrieve to let the lure sink and skip on the seabed. The skip kicks up sand, causing vibrations, which might just grab the attention of a hunting bass, pollack or mackerel.

Using a rubber fish lure from a boat Rubber fish are most effective fished from a drifting boat. They can work from an anchored boat too, but not as well, simply because the lure is covering less ground.

Around Portland Bill, where we are lucky to have probably the best sea bass fishery in the British Isles, the technique of using Storm lures fished under a drifting boat is the most effective bass-catching technique. (Using live sand eels as bait is a possible exception, but much more complicated to obtain and keep alive for long enough to use from a drifting boat.)

To understand how drifting with these lures works, imagine a boat drifting along with the tide over a rocky seabed. Around Portland, we're usually fishing in less than 100 feet of water. Now, imagine connecting a line between your rod and a rounded lead weight, which then bounces across the rocks, directly beneath, or slightly behind the drifting boat. With the line held tight from your rod tip, you'd be able to feel every bump of the lead on the rocks as it is dragged over them by the moving boat.

Rubber fish and a jelly worm (right)

Now, imagine attaching your sexy rubber fish, which wiggles so enticingly in moving water, suspended a couple of feet above the weight, as it bounces over those rocks, just far enough up the line to avoid getting snagged in rocks or seaweed. And just far enough above the rocks to be silhouetted against the light above, perfectly positioned in the line of sight of any hungry predatory fish holding position in the lee of a rock, where it's ducked down out of the tiring tidal current, head pointing into the flow. This is how these big predators hunt when the tide is running fast; they hunker down behind rocks and look up, waiting for potential dinner to drift overhead.

Rubber fish lures also catch fish as they're being reeled upwards, from the seabed towards the boat. Some fish – pollack, cod, coalfish, bass and mackerel – are more than happy to chase a bait fish upwards. And because rubber fish look so much like the fish these predators hunt, a Storm lure has every chance of being attacked, simply by being in the right place at the right time. When a lure looks and behaves like a bait fish, then it's perfectly likely to get eaten.

Rubber worms or 'jelly worms'

These work on the same principle as rubber fish, although you can't normally buy them with a weight and hook already fitted. Jelly worms are slightly more limited in the fish they attract too. By all means chuck a packet in your tackle box and experiment with them one day when you're on a boat and have already filled your boots. To begin with though, stick to the pre-weighted rubber fish.

Other pieces of useful kit

Here are a few extra items of kit, which might not mean the difference between success and failure (except in the case of the drop net), but are all things you should get into the habit of taking with you.

Insulation winder

It's a special sort of person who's prepared to unclip their mackerel feather set at the end of a fishing session, dry them carefully and then wind them up neatly, returning them to the packet whence they came. Sadly, I am not made of such patient and meticulous stuff. However, after years of having a rusty, tangled, dangerous mess of used mackerel feathers lurking at the bottom of my tackle box, I have discovered the joys of insulation foam pipe lagging. A mere 12 inches of this stuff will marshal rigs and feathers, keeping them in one place, virtually tangle-free, until they're required again.

Scissors

Heavy-duty kitchen scissors with plastic handles are one of the most versatile tools you can take along with you on a fishing trip. Everything from trimming knots to chopping up bait and unwanted fishing line can be achieved with these. Buy a pair with brightly coloured handles and you're less likely to leave them behind.

Knife

There are three obvious reasons for having a knife with you when you're sea fishing: to chop bait; to gut fish; and to fillet your fish. The first two jobs don't really require a very sharp knife and, in any case, cutting bait on a bait board will blunt a sharp edge in seconds. However, filleting fish can only be done effectively with a very sharp knife. In order to do all these knife jobs capably, you either have to take along an efficient knife sharpener, or else have two knives: one for bait and one for fish preparation. The choice is yours. If you do choose to invest in a sharpener, I would recommend taking one that's easy to use, like a Chantry-style pull-through type. Using a steel or a whetstone on a boat can very quickly and easily result in a messy blood-and-sticking-plaster situation.

Pliers

If you're putting together a fishing kit for the first time, it is worth buying yourself a new pair of pliers. Don't splash out – cheap ones will do – but do make sure they have a decent cutting edge. Thin-nosed pliers are probably the most useful because they're more versatile, but don't get hung up on searching too hard for the perfect pair because, if you're anything like me, they'll be lost or rusted solid within their first few months. And don't make the mistake of taking your favourite pair from your toolbox, because they'll never be the same again.

A stout pair of pliers is brilliant for pulling buried hooks out of cartilaginous jaws, or for snipping the shaft of a hook that has got buried in a rope, your thumb, jumper or boot. Pliers can be used for mending outboard motors, squeezing flat barbs on hooks, and stripping skin off dogfish. In short, you never really know what you might need a pair of pliers for, so just make sure you have some with you.

Priest or bosher

A hammer handle, a length of copper pipe filled with sand, a truncheon, a long-shafted screwdriver, a shop-bought 'priest', a short hardwood shillelagh club, a toffee hammer, an adjustable spanner, 18 inches of blue nylon water pipe… I've seen fish despatched with all of these objects. It doesn't really matter what your chosen assassination device is, so long as it's effective and handy. Don't wait to improvise on the spot and grab for a rock or a boat skipper's best torch; either of these will cause unnecessary mess. Pack something suitable for killing fish. For cracking them with a fatal blow across the head. Pack it and know where it is when you need it.

Drop net

A drop net is a circular (or occasionally square) frame which has a 'basket' of netting hanging down from its underside. The hoop of the net is suspended from a rope in such a way that it can be lowered, off a pier or harbour wall, while the mouth of the net will remain open and parallel to the water surface below. A drop net has two main uses: for lifting a fish that's hooked to your rod line up a steep harbour wall; and for catching crabs and prawns from a pier, harbour or breakwater.

If you're fishing from a pier or rock face, high above the water's surface, the job of hauling a fish and a lead weight perpendicularly upwards may well be enough to snap your rod. By lowering the net, swinging the fish and weight into it, and hauling the net up by its attached rope, you'll minimise the risk of losing the fish or busting your fishing rod. Except, it has to be said, that getting the fish to swing into your drop net is in itself no mean feat.

The other purpose of the drop net is curious exploration. If you stick a stone in the centre of your net and lower it to the seabed, it will sit there like an inviting carpet. If you also tie a lump of alluring bait, like a mackerel head and guts, to the centre of the net, who knows what might stray on to your rug trap for a nibble.

The mesh size of the net will limit what you can catch. But, even if your drop net has a wide mesh, too big for prawns or shrimps, you can always carry a smaller-meshed lining to tie inside it. That's if your fishing trip starts to evolve more into a shore crab and prawn exploration event. There is a point to crabbing like this. Shore crabs can make good bait (see p.159), wild prawns are the pink-shelled food of the

Drop net

gods, and an amazing array of other things will occasionally crop up in your drop net too. Potentially anything from lobsters to eels and from dabs to dogfish.

Apart from anything else, a drop net is a great diversion on a slow day's fishing. And any haul from the harbour floor is a fascinating snapshot of sea life. I spent a whole day with my boys fishing off Cromer pier with just a drop net. We had a plastic bucket full of sea water in which to empty and admire each haul of shore crabs, before releasing them all back to the wild. It may sound pointless, but actually it was a thoroughly enjoyable expedition.

Cool box

An insulated cool box or a cool bag with a handful of cool blocks is an essential piece of kit for anyone who is serious about keeping their fish in its finest condition. Even in the winter, fish can spoil very quickly if left exposed to light and air. Any fish you catch need to be killed, bled and preferably gutted and chilled within an hour of being caught. I am evangelical about keeping fish cool and I always take a cool box with blocks or ice. I like the solid cool boxes and I've got one that is big enough to fit my tackle box into. So I only have to carry the one box on the way out. Insulated cool bags can be folded up and carried inside your tackle bag or box, or they can be used to carry your bait and lunch. Either way, a cool box or bag guarantees your best fish comes home in the best condition.

Bait

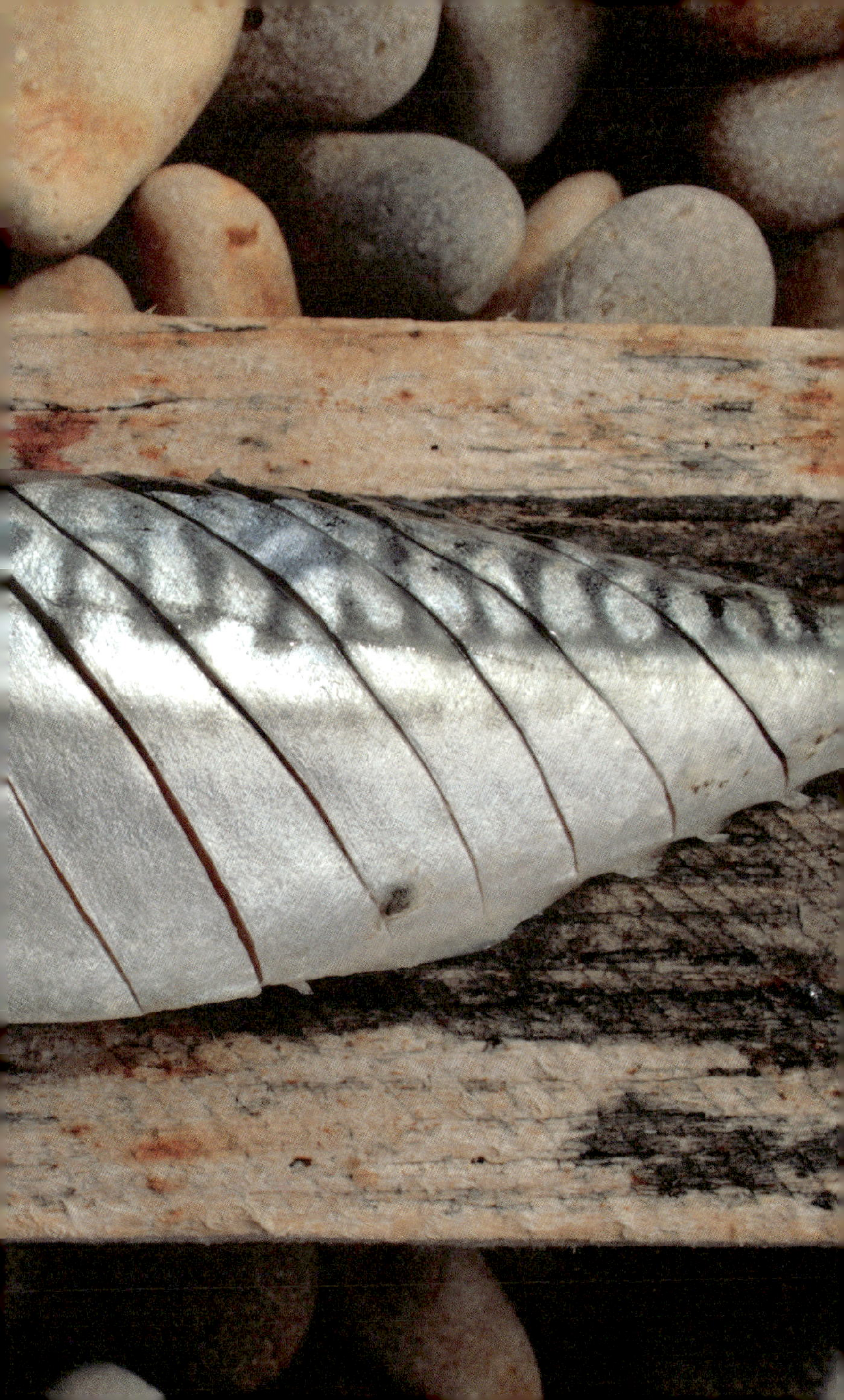

The best bait to choose to put on your hook is the bait that the fish you most want to catch will most want to eat. Some fish are omnivorous and will eat a whole range of baits. The dogfish is a prime example of such a survivor fish. It will adapt to any circumstances and have a go at digesting practically any sort of food, from a mouthful of decomposing shark to a single cockle. Mullet are the opposite. They're obsessive in their finickiness and won't even consider a mouthful unless it meets their anorexic criteria exactly.

In turn, some anglers are obsessive about their bait too. Really serious beach anglers who fish in competitions will spend hours on bait acquiring and bait storing. You can, if you want, dig your own lugworms and ragworms and collect your own peeler crabs. But most anglers, myself included, are handicapped by time and sloth and would rather buy bait when we need it. However, there is a limit to the range of good baits you can buy. Most ordinary seaside tackle shops will sell frozen squid, frozen mackerel (usually whole, sometimes whole but headless, and occasionally in fillets), live lugworms and live ragworms. Some may also stock frozen sand eels and possibly frozen peeler crabs.

If I'm off on a boat fishing trip, I'll normally grab a small block of frozen squid and a couple of quids' worth of ragworms. The squid is a great all-round bait and the ragworm will always work on pouting, plaice, whiting and black bream. In the summer, I wouldn't bother about buying any mackerel because I'd assume we would be able to catch some on feathers fairly easily and we could use the fresh mackerel, filleted and cut into slices, as bait. In the winter, I might buy a couple of frozen mackerel too (or better still, take a couple from my freezer – if I've been wise enough to lay some down for the lean times).

If I'm going shore fishing I would take some squid and some ragworms, possibly a frozen mackerel, but I'd also have a forage around, looking for fresh mussels and limpets when I arrived at my chosen destination, if there were suitable rocks and crevices to be searched.

Time and time again fish will gleefully prove anglers wrong by sticking up two stubby fingers (or fins) every time we think we've made a new angling rule. So, don't expect what a fish eats to be what you think it should eat; they'll trip you up as often as they can. But, as a rough rule of thumb, the adjacent chart indicates the baits that consistently work best for the species you're most likely to encounter.

Bait for sea fishing

	SQUID STRIP	WHOLE SQUID	MACKEREL STRIP	WHOLE MACKEREL	SAND EEL	LIMPET/MUSSEL	PEELER CRAB	LUGWORM/RAGWORM	BREAD
MACKEREL	Best		Best		Best	Lucky	Best	Lucky	
DOGFISH	Best	Best	Best		Best	Lucky	Best	Best	
POUTING	Best	Lucky	Best		Best	Lucky	Best	Best	
POLLACK	Best	Best	Best	Best	Best			Best	
COD	Best	Best	Best	Best	Best	Lucky	Best	Best	
WHITING	Best		Best		Lucky	Lucky	Best	Best	
GARFISH	Best		Best		Best				
RED GURNARD	Best		Best		Best	Lucky	Lucky	Best	
BLACK BREAM	Best		Best		Lucky	Lucky	Lucky	Best	
PLAICE	Best		Lucky		Best	Best	Best	Best	
SEA BASS	Lucky	Best	Lucky	Best	Best		Best	Best	
DAB & FLOUNDER	Lucky		Lucky		Lucky	Lucky	Best	Best	
HORSE MACKEREL	Best		Best		Best	Lucky	Lucky	Best	
HERRING	Best		Best		Lucky				
SQUID				Best	Best				
SLOB TROUT								Best	Lucky
GREY MULLET								Best	Best

Key: Best = Best   Lucky = Might get lucky

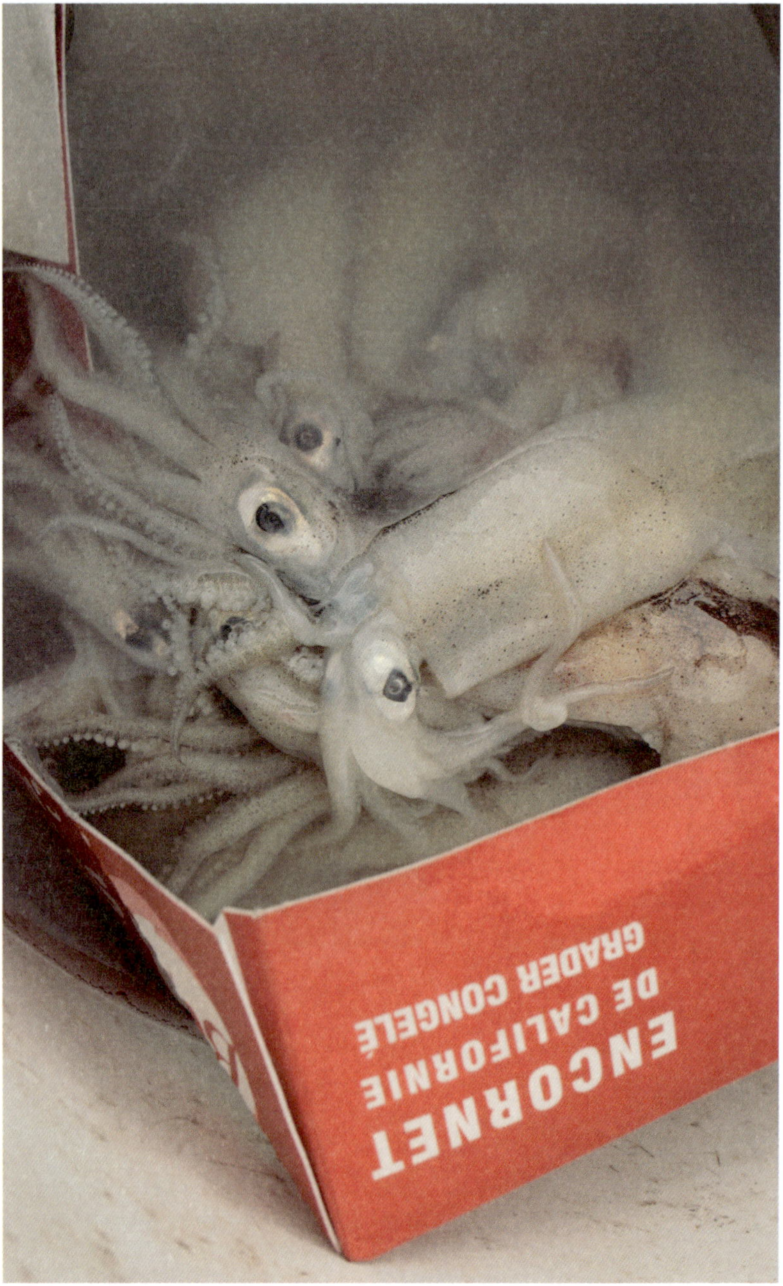
ENCORNET
DE CALIFORNIE
GRADER CONGELÉ

Squid

Squid is one of the most versatile baits you can use. Nearly all of the fish mentioned in this book will wrap their gums around a mouthful of squid if given half a chance.

Squid is very convenient to use because it freezes and keeps well. You can even refreeze it (once or twice at the most) if you don't use it all on a fishing session. You can buy squid from tackle shops in frozen 5lb lumps, or in smaller bagged portions, which contain just a handful of individual squid.

Bait squid are usually about 4–8 inches long, but sometimes you can buy much smaller squid, often known as Japonica, which are only an inch or two long at the most and can be used whole.

The larger squid can be used whole too, if you're targeting large-mouthed fish, like bass. In fact, a whole squid, or even two, threaded on a large 4/0 hook or on a 4/0 pennel rig (see p.167), is a very popular bait for bass, fished off a beach, close in, just behind the surf breaking line. This approach works especially well just after stormy weather, when bass will come in close under the cover of murky water looking for food that's been scoured out by the storm waves.

A squid head and tentacles are terrific bait too; good for bream, pouting and gurnard. The head and tentacle cluster have a thick, almost cartilaginous texture, which will stay on the hook well, through several casts.

The classic way to fish squid is with the mantle (the white bell-shaped body) cut into cigarette-sized strips. These work best when they're very lightly hooked, just through one end, so they can flutter and flap in the current in an enticing and irresistible way. The fact that squid is so white means that it shows up well in the water too. Cuttlefish strips, and even whole small cuttlefish, can be used in exactly the same way as squid.

Lugworms

Lugworms are dug by bait diggers from sandy and muddy beaches when the tide is at its lowest point. You can dig your own lug if you like, but it's a back-breaking and often fruitless, frustrating business. Having said that, the few times I have successfully dug my own marine worm bait, each worm in the bait box has felt like a major achievement. And subsequently it is hook-mounted and used with great care and expectation. But for simplicity's sake, to begin with, just buy your lugworms from a tackle shop.

Normally, lug are sold either by number or by weight. A dozen lug is plenty to get you started. Lug are traditionally sold in a folded newspaper package and if you don't use them all in one session, they'll keep for a few days, wrapped in damp newspaper, stored in the fridge. They work best for cod, bass, flounder, dabs and whiting when fished on a fine-wire Aberdeen hook.

There's a knack to threading lug on to a hook. Start by inserting the hook point in the centre of the bulbous head end, then try to slide the worm all the way up the hook shank and push an inch of the worm over the knot. Don't squeeze the lug too hard with your thumb and forefinger as you thread it, or else you'll get showered with lug juice and your bait will end up looking shrivelled and anorexic.

Ragworms

Treat ragworms the same as lugworms; keep them in the fridge wrapped in wet newspaper. There are king rags (very big ones), ordinary rag, white rag (very rare and sought by serious competition anglers) and even farmed rag (some purists baulk at ragworm farmed in the hot-water outflow of power stations, but in truth, any rag is worth a try if you can get hold of it without having to re-mortgage your house).

Like lug, you should thread them on a thin wire hook, though rag have the added frisson of possessing a pair of clamp-like pincers in their mouth parts. Getting a nip from these hairy, wiggly critters as you're trying to slide a hook down their throat can really make you jump and even squeal like a schoolgirl at a Jonas Brothers gig. Which all adds to the fun of a day out fishing.

An inch or two of ragworm used on the tip of a Mepps No. 5 spinner (see pp.138–40) sometimes works a treat for harbour mullet too.

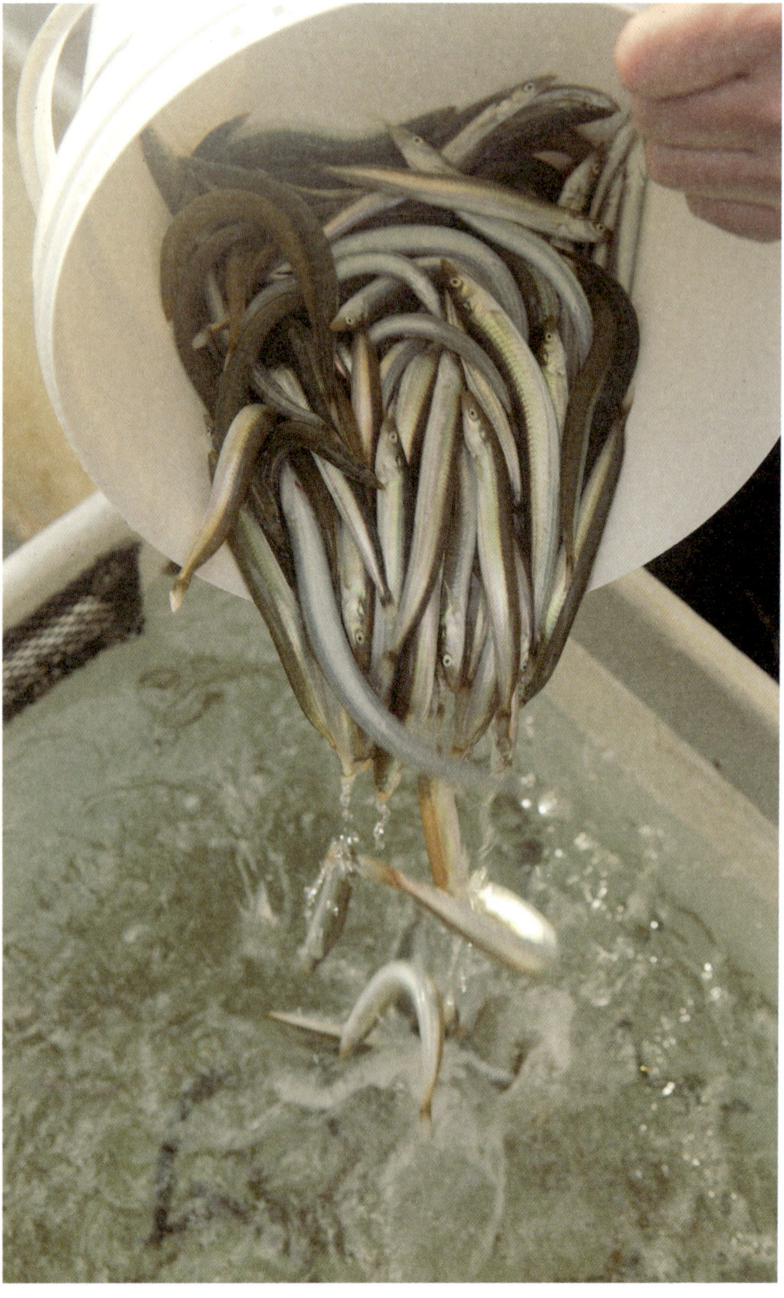

Sand eels

Live sand eels are a bass's favourite food, but they're often very difficult to find for sale in tackle shops, and are even harder to keep alive. They require a large bucket of sea water with a bubbling battery-operated aerator device to provide a constant stream of oxygen to keep them alive. And even then, with oxygen bubbles and fresh sea water, they'll still die with alarming and disturbing regularity.

Packs of frozen sand eels are the alternative. They never seem to work quite as well as live eels, but if the fish are hungry and you're in the right place at the right time, they're the next best thing.

There is more than one way to hook a live sand eel. Different anglers will swear by different methods and the bigger-sized eels (sand eels can vary from 3–10 inches in length) might require a different technique from the smaller ones. What you're trying to achieve is a position for your hook that is unobtrusive enough to allow the (live) sand eel to swim as freely and as unhindered as possible. You also want to avoid sticking your hook through a part of your sand eel which will kill it. If you've gone to all the trouble of finding and storing live sand eels then you want them to stay alive on your hook as long as possible.

The two simplest methods to hook a live sand eel are either through the tip of its beak-like mouth, from under its chin and up through the top of its nose, or alternatively sideways, from one side of the head through to the other, just in front of the sand eel's eyes.

You can hook a dead sand eel in exactly the same way, but most anglers prefer to stick the hook right through the eyes on a dead sand eel so the curve of the hook is threaded through both bony eye sockets.

With a very big sand eel, whether it's alive or dead, it's better to thread the hook down through its mouth and out through one side of its gills, then nick the point of the hook in and out through the flesh an inch below its head and pull the line taut so the hook shank lies flat and straight, up through its gill and mouth. This method holds a big eel more securely, which reduces the chance of it being accidentally pulled off. It also sets the point of the hook further down the sand eel's body, which means there's a better chance of a big attacking fish being hooked.

Limpets

If you're fishing off rocks or a rocky beach, then limpets are always likely to be close at hand. Take a blunt knife or screwdriver along with you and use it to lever them off a rock, then scoop the foot and flesh out of the shell. The foot is very rubbery, like thick squid, and it will stay on the hook for ages. It always feels good to me to be using fresh bait from the location in which I'm fishing, but sadly limpet is not every species' favourite lunch.

Mussels

Fresh mussels, teased off rocks or harbour pilings, are soft, juicy and laced with pungent attractants. Many more species will make an effort to eat fresh mussel than they would fresh limpet. The only trouble with de-shelled fresh mussel is that it's so soft and succulent, it's very difficult to keep on a hook unless it's been lashed on with a foot or two of bait elastic. It's well worth a try though, as some fish, such as plaice, will sell their souls for a mouthful of fresh mussel. It will also get nibbled off a hook by small-mouthed scavengers like crabs faster than you can blink.

Mackerel

Fresh or frozen mackerel is one of the best baits to use. For most of the fish featured in this book it works most effectively in small strips cut from a medium-sized fish fillet. A whole fillet, fished 'flapper' style (with the central spine removed so the two fillets flap in the current), works well for large flat fish and for rays, conger eel and tope. A mackerel head, cut off at an angle with some of its guts still attached, is cracking bait for a large bass.

Although mackerel is a bait much loved by many fish, it's also the bait that is all too often badly presented. Mackerel works well because it's oily, and gives off lots of exciting smells, as well as having a flash of iridescent skin to attract sight feeders. However, if you simply stick a fat, misshapen lump on your hook, it won't attract anything except a brain-dead, half-starved dogfish, or crabs.

The best bait is one that hangs delicately and enticingly from the hook and can flutter in a natural fashion in the current. Size isn't nearly as important as presentation. Ideally, your mackerel strip bait should look like the one shown below.

Mackerel strip bait

Peeler crab

This is the name given to a common shore crab when it's about to moult its shell, which it does once a year between early May and late June. The crabs are filled with yellow body fluid and have soft, squidgy internal organs at this point, which makes them irresistible to cod, bass, smoothhounds and dogfish, to name but a few.

You can collect your own live peeler crabs, especially at the higher reaches of the tide around muddy estuaries, though they are tricky to catch. Peelers that are just about to shed their shells are the best. To identify a peeler, look for cracking between the top shell and the leg sockets. To check, remove the tiny pointed end of one leg; if a perfectly formed leg is revealed, rather than just white sinew, you have a peeler.

Peelers will stay alive in the fridge for several days and peeler aficionados often hold them there until they're at their peak. Collecting your own bait is undoubtedly satisfying, but peeler 'farming' in your fridge might feel like a step too far.

If you do get hold of a peeler or two, remove the soft shell before you either lash it to a hook with bait elastic (see p.131) or cut it in half, remove the legs and carefully 'weave' your hook through the leg sockets.

Bread

Bread is only really used for catching grey mullet. It can either be fished under a sensitive float (see p.165), pinched on to the hook, or else squeezed on to a hook and ledgered in one lump on the harbour bed. This is usually presented amongst a 'carpet' of ripped-up tiny pieces of bread, laid out to act as ground bait, to attract a cruising mullet's attention. The worst cotton-woolly white sliced bread works best.

Fishing Skills

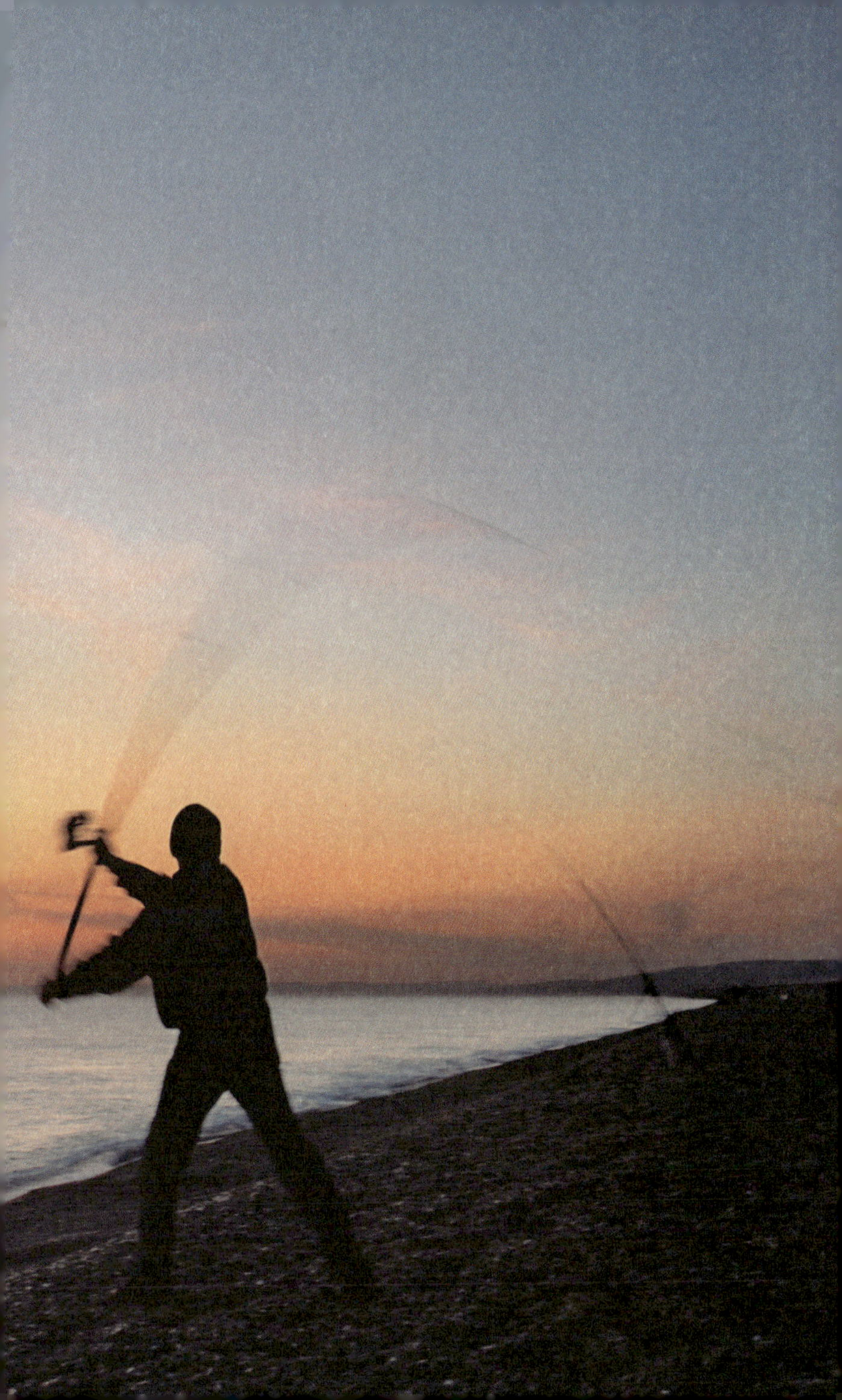

There are a few things you can do beforehand to prepare for the day you first go down to the sea, armed and dangerous, such as practising tying essential knots, and unpacking a rig and working out how to attach it to your line.

You can't practise killing a fish, or releasing a fish, but you can take yourself down to the local park or football field with your rod and reel to practise casting – carefully. Instead of flinging a lump of lead around your local park, try attaching a small rubber super-ball to your line, either by drilling a hole through it or taping your line to it with duck tape. Or else use a rubber fish lure with the hook snipped off, or a Toby spoon lure with the treble hook removed for safety.

Obviously you'll need to watch out for runners, dog walkers, cyclists and any other park users. When I started out, I spent hours practising like this, casting with a fly rod or even practising with a beachcaster rod and a tricky multiplier reel. At times, I may have looked like a bit of a twonk, but it made all the difference to my fishing when I eventually got to the water's edge.

Assembling a rig

A rig can be location-specific; a pier rig is a tackle set-up which works well when fished from a pier, for example. A rig can also be technique-specific; a float rig is a set-up of line, hooks, weight and float that allows you to float-fish. A rig could also be species-specific. A bream rig might vary slightly from a whiting rig in its construction or choice of hook size, even though they're both used in roughly the same location, fishing the same technique.

There are hundreds of different rigs. Proficient, experienced anglers take great pride in inventing new ones and customising existing ones. But there are only a handful that you really need to know about.

Shop-bought rigs

Before going into the individual rigs, a quick word about shop-bought ones. Serious, experienced anglers will shake their heads and make tut-tutting noises at the mention of shop-bought rigs. In their opinion, such things are expensive, badly made, and an unnecessary luxury, only indulged in by those with more money than sense. Taking this kind of stance is fine if you know how to tie knots and are confident about what you're hoping to achieve.

Personally, I believe you should never be embarrassed about buying a rig from a shop. Tackle dealers will love you, and you'll be able to get your bait wet quickly instead of fumbling around, all fingers and thumbs, for half an hour before your terminal tackle ever makes a splash. Even purist home-rig-building, experienced sea anglers would agree that you can't catch fish if your bait isn't in the water.

Paternoster rig

The paternoster rig, also known as the 'pier rig', 'bream rig' and 'boat rig', includes one, two or three hooks suspended above the weight. In other words, when the weight is on the seabed and the line above it is held tight, your baited hooks, spaced 12–18 inches apart, hang off the side of the main line on their own individual branches, known as 'snoods'. These snoods should flutter around in the current, presenting your hook baits in a visible position just above the seabed where bottom-feeding fish will easily notice them.

The paternoster rig can be fished from the shore too, as long as the ground you're fishing over isn't too snaggy with rocks. A two- or three-hook paternoster fished from the shore is good for flat fish as the shallow angle of the line will position the baits on or near the seabed.

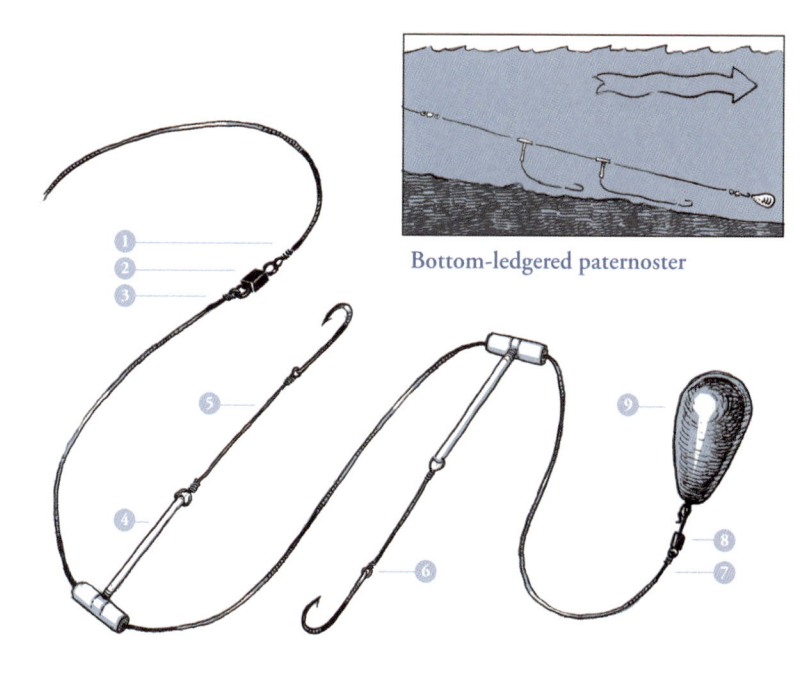

Bottom-ledgered paternoster

① Half-blood knot
② Swivel
③ Half-blood knot
④ Boom
⑤ Hook link
⑥ Half-blood knot
⑦ Half-blood knot
⑧ Clip swivel
⑨ Bomb weight

FISHING SKILLS

Running ledger rig

In angling speak, a ledgered bait is a bait that is located on the seabed by the use of a lead weight. And, just to make life more confusing, a 'running ledger' is often used from a drifting boat, where the bait is not resting on the seabed, but is bouncing along the seabed, or is even held, suspended a couple of feet above the seabed. So in fact it's not really a 'ledgered' rig but a moving one.

The 'running' part refers to the fact that the reel line, if pulled from the hook end, will 'run' through the weight. So, if a fish grabs the hook, it can run with it for a few feet before it feels the strain of the rod bending. The weight isn't fixed to the line, so when a fish pulls the hook it doesn't initially feel any resistance of the weight which might make it suspicious and cause it to drop the bait. Of all rigs, this is the easiest to make.

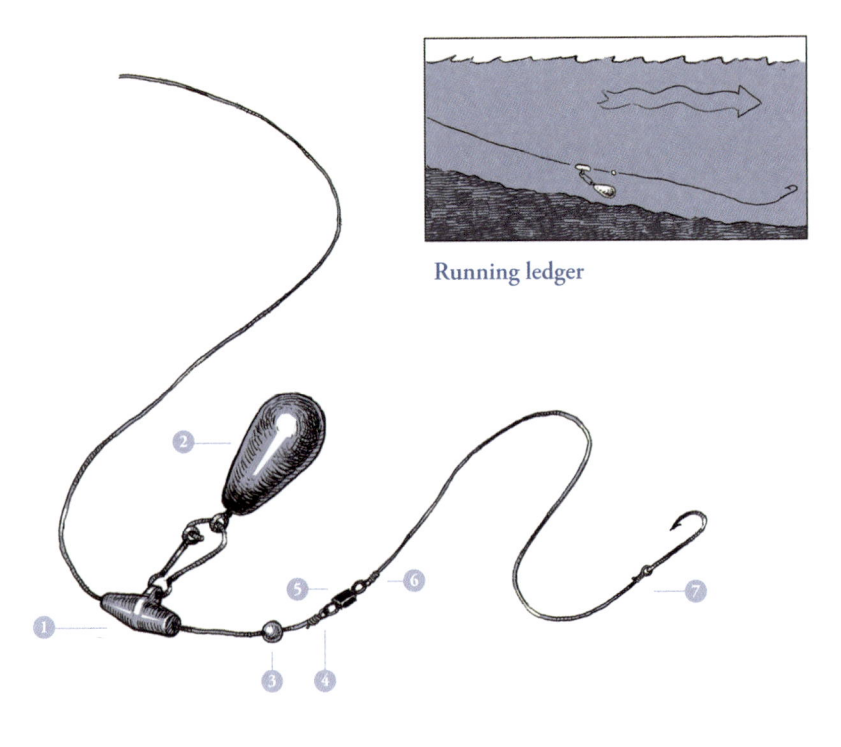

Running ledger

1. Zip slider
2. Bomb weight
3. Bead
4. Half-blood knot
5. Swivel
6. Half-blood knot
7. Half-blood knot

Float rig

Use a float rig when you want to keep your bait clear of a snaggy or weedy seabed, or if you want to present your bait near the surface of the water rather than near the seabed, because that's where the fish you're targeting are feeding. A float rig allows you to present a small bait high in the water, where certain species like garfish, mackerel and mullet prefer to feed.

If you're fishing from rocks over snaggy ground, a float rig suspends your bait out of reach of the snags, allowing it to travel naturally with the current, presenting the bait in clear water just above the rocks or weed where fish should be lurking and waiting to ambush their food.

The key to keeping your bait at exactly the right depth under the water is the stop knot (see pp.169–70), which stops your float from sliding up the line.

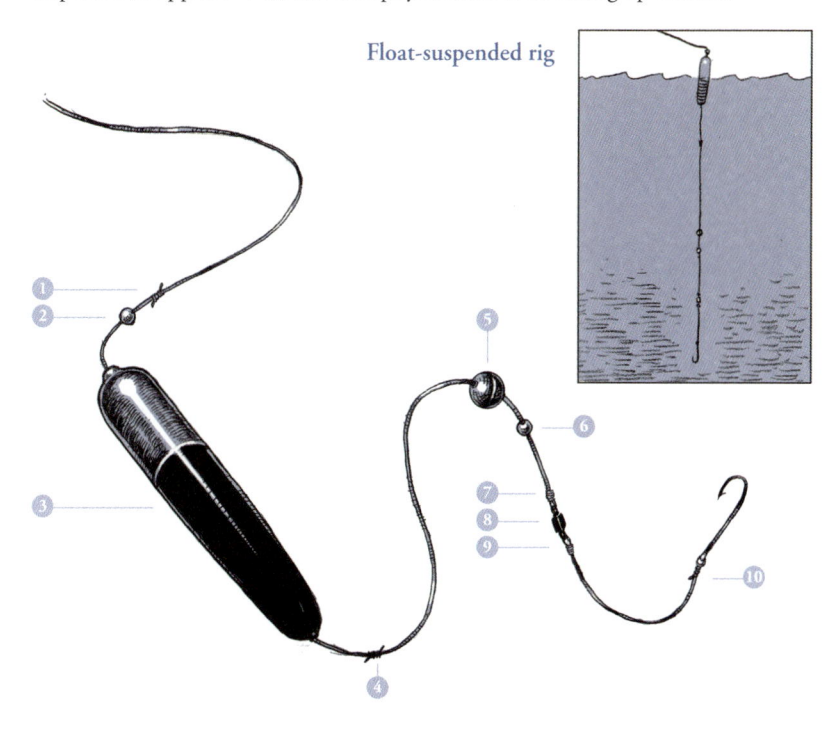

Float-suspended rig

1. Stop knot
2. Bead
3. Float
4. Stop knot
5. Drilled bullet weight
6. Bead
7. Half-blood knot
8. Swivel
9. Half-blood knot
10. Half-blood knot

FISHING SKILLS

Spinner/wedge/spoon rig

You can just tie a clip swivel to the end of your line and clip on a spinner, wedge or spoon (see pp.138–41). This will work adequately most of the time. You can add an extra swivel 2 or 3 feet above the clip swivel, to give the line greater protection from becoming twisted by the spinner's revolving action. This is most valuable if you're fishing in very strong currents, or across the mouth of an estuary with a strong outgoing or incoming tide. It also provides a little extra weight, which might help with casting, especially if you're using a very lightweight spinner, or else you're fighting against a facing wind. In extreme windy cases, or where you want your spinner to work deeper in the water, you can add a 'drilled bullet' lead weight, which you thread on to the line above the swivel (towards the reel). This provides extra overall weight which makes casting easier.

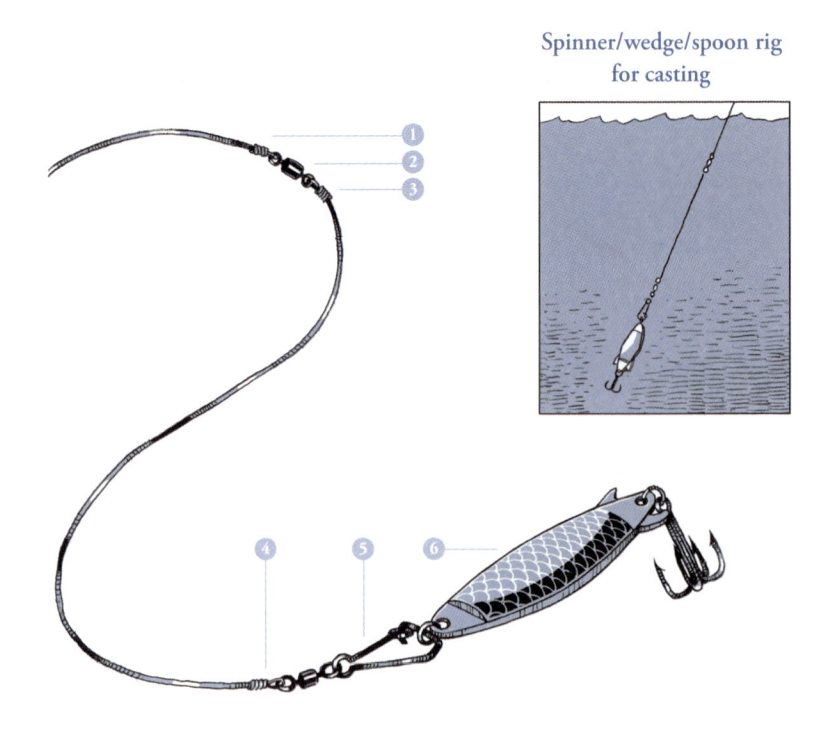

Spinner/wedge/spoon rig for casting

1. Half-blood knot
2. Swivel
3. Half-blood knot
4. Half-blood knot
5. Clip swivel
6. Toby spoon

Pennel rig

The pennel rig performs two functions. Firstly, by putting two hooks on one line, it allows you to mount a much bigger bait than you could safely secure on a single hook. Secondly, it increases your chances of hooking into a fish, because it gives you two potential hook points on the same bait.

If you fish with a big bait that only has one hook threaded through it, at the head end, then you can easily miss a fish if it bites at the tail end. The fish gets a mouthful of your bait for free, and you, most likely, get *half* a bait back, but no fish. With a pennel rig your hooks are spread across a big bait, making both ends deadly.

To tie a pennel rig, thread the line through the eye of the upper hook, wind the line five times or more around the shank, and tie it to the eye of the second hook, so the first hook can be easily moved up or down the line. This increases or shrinks the distance between the two hooks, in order to match the size of the bait you're using.

Not only is the pennel rig useful for beach or boat fishing, presenting big baits on your line, and holding them in place whilst casting, but the rig also has its uses when squid fishing. If you use a pennel rig – either with two single hooks as shown, or even with a small treble hook at the terminal end – you're simply increasing the number of sharp, barbed hook points that stick out of your bait.

When fishing for squid, the more potentially snaggy points you have protruding from your bait fish, the better. If you're squidding with pennel-mounted small dead pouting, or poor-cod baits, the squid will explore them with his tentacles as he tries to drag the dead fish to his beaky mouth. The more hooks there are, the more chance you have of snagging him on the barbed points as you reel him up to the surface.

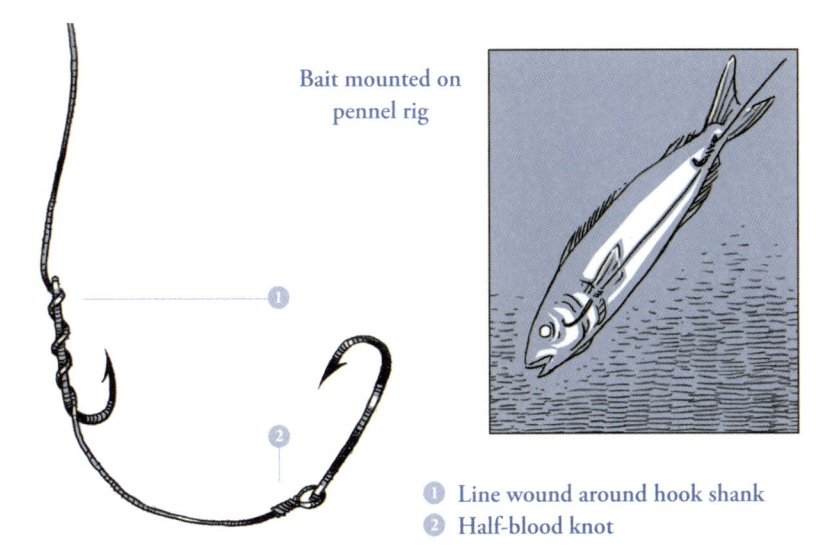

Bait mounted on pennel rig

① Line wound around hook shank
② Half-blood knot

Tying basic knots

Knots are things of deep joy. We can so easily freewheel through life never needing to know more than a simple granny knot, but once you learn a couple of new ones, suddenly you'll find all manner of uses for them. Being able to tie knots is unexpected food for the soul. Whilst you don't need to know many knots for fishing, the half-blood knot is the essential one for attaching your hook to your line.

Whenever I'm learning a new knot, I take a spool of line, a big blunted hook and I practise while I'm watching telly. Tying and re-tying the same knot when you're only half paying attention to what you're doing is the best way to learn, because your hands get used to the movements and you learn them by heart and by touch. This way you can avoid the sad and soggy business of referring to a book when you're on a boat or the beach.

Half-blood knot

This is the most used knot in angling. It works well with monofilament but not with braid.

- Put your line through the eye of the hook, pull 3 inches through and hold it parallel to the reel line (step 1).
- Twist the short end around the reel line five or six times while holding the hook or swivel eye still (steps 2–4). After the last turn, bend the end down and poke it through the hole created in the line just above the eye (step 5).
- Pull it through slowly, while easing the knot down towards the eye. Lick the knot as you're doing this. Saliva helps lubricate the line, which stops it kinking or causing too much friction on the line as you pull the knot into place.
- Pinch the knot down with your fingernails as you give the last tug to the reel line to make it sit hard on top of the eye.
- With a pair of kitchen scissors, trim off the tag end close to the knot (step 6).

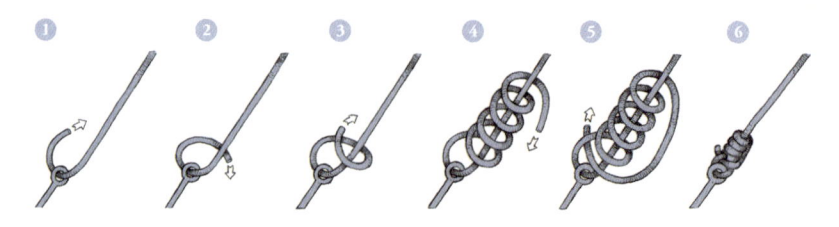

Tucked half-blood knot

This is the cautious belt-and-braces version of the half-blood knot. In an ordinary half-blood, when you pull the tag end of the line tight, you then simply trim it off. But in the tucked half-blood you make the knot even more safe by tucking the tag end through the topmost loop (steps 4–5). The extra tuck through the loop created at the top of the twists, furthest away from the eye, secures the knot better than the simple half-blood.

I'm ashamed to admit that I never tuck my half-bloods. I know I should, but I'm too impatient to do that extra bit of work and I don't like the look or feel of a tucked one, especially on monofilament line of 15lb or more. It's a bit like choosing whether to tuck your shirt into your trousers and cinch it with your belt, or let it hang loose and risk having a draught up your tummy. I'm not proud of it, but I have to confess, I don't give a tuck.

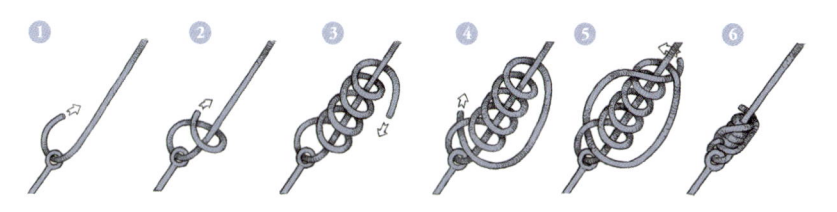

Stop knot

A stop knot is a handy knot to know because you can use it whenever you want to create a 'stop', either for a sliding boom or, most commonly, when you're float-fishing and want to create a stop to mark the furthest point the float will slide up the line, which sets the predetermined depth that your bait will be suspended beneath the float.

There are two types of stop knot that I normally use: one is a cheaty, quick one, which can be tied as a simple overhand knot with a thinnish rubber band. The elasticity helps it grip the line, just enough to hold the bead and float in position, but, at the same time, not so much that it can't be easily repositioned if you want to alter the depth.

The other stop knot can be tied with ordinary monofilament line (usually it's better to use slightly thicker line than the reel line, but it's not essential). Or there's some lovely rubbery string stuff sold in tackle shops for rig-building called Powergum, which makes a quick and efficient stop knot that can be repositioned up and down the line easily to alter the depth of your float-suspended bait. (See diagram and tying instructions overleaf.)

FISHING SKILLS

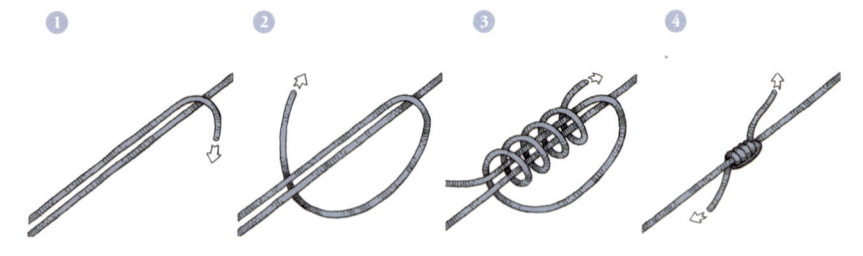

Monofilament line or Powergum stop knot
- Decide where you want the knot to sit on the main line.
- Cut a length of about 4 or 5 inches of monofilament or Powergum, just enough to comfortably tie an overhand knot with. Lay it alongside your main line and then curve your stop knot line into a loop (steps 1–2).
- Hold the loop against the main line and pass one end of your line through the loop four or five times (step 3).
- Now moisten the loops with spit and pull both ends of your line apart so that the loops begin to close into each other (step 4). The harder you pull the tighter the coils of the loop will grip around the main line.
- Trim off the excess monofilament or Powergum from the ends, leaving the tight knot with ½ inch at either end.
- Whenever you want to slide this knot up or down your main line, use a lick of spit to lubricate the knot and the line.

Elastic band method
- Snip through an elastic band (I love those red ones postmen leave) so that it becomes an elastic length rather than a circular band.
- Determine the position you want it to sit on your main line above the float and simply tie it around your line in an overhand granny knot.
- Pull it tight and trim off the excess rubber. It should still move up and down the line if you want to shift it. But so long as you pulled it tight enough in the first place, because of the friction of the grippy nature of the rubber, it will hold itself on the line.

Casting shock leader knot

This is a very important knot. It is used to join your reel line of 10–15lb to your shock leader of 30–40lb. Because of the job that it does – providing a small, neat join between two vastly different diameter lines undergoing the enormous strain and shock of casting several ounces of lead with great force from a standing start – it needs to be tied efficiently. This is definitely a knot to practise at home until you've really got the hang of it.

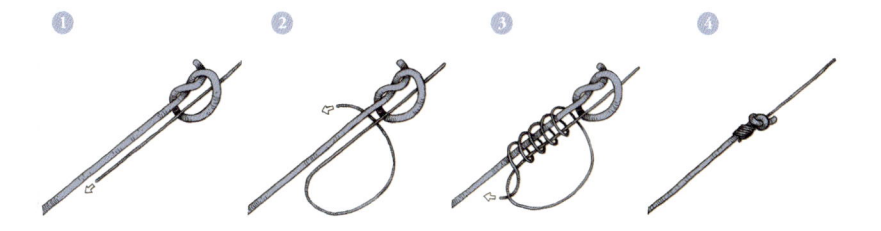

- First, tie a simple overhand knot at the end of the shock leader. Then thread the reel line through the centre of the leader knot, pull 4 or 5 inches through and lie it alongside the leader (step 1).
- Now twist the reel line loosely five or six turns around the leader (steps 2–3).
- On the last turn, fold it back towards the overhand knot and tuck it under the first twist, between the reel line and the leader.
- Pull the tag end of the reel line gently as you work the tightening twists down towards the overhand leader knot. The trick is to lubricate these turns with spit and help them to sit evenly butting up against the leader knot.
- Pull the leader knot tight with your teeth and make sure the turns are neat together and snug against the leader knot (step 4).
- Test it by pulling hard on both ends of line leader and reel.

Braid knot

There are some very complicated braid knots. Generally, it's much more difficult to tie knots in braid than monofilament because braid is very thin and shiny (see p.121). A lot of conventional monofilament knots just won't work on braid. They slip open. The easiest braid knot to tie, and to remember, is also called the Uni-Knot.

- Pass the end of the line through the eye and pull it back up the line for a few inches and then bend it back to form a loop (step 1).
- Wrap the end around the two parallel lines, passing it through the loop.
- Do this five times or more (step 2) and then pull the tag end away from the hook until the knot tightens (steps 3–4).
- Then lubricate the knot with spit and push it down the line to the eye.
- Pull the reel line firmly to seat it neatly above the eye.

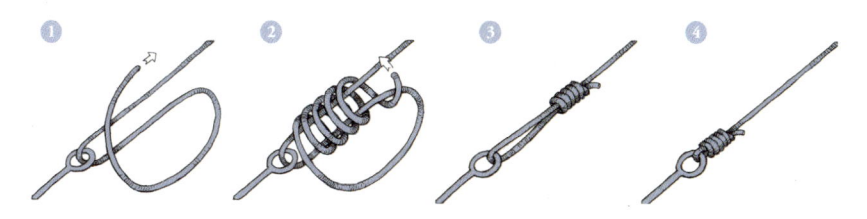

Casting

The most casting you are ever going to do is when you're spinning or mackerel feathering from the beach. That's because both these techniques involve fishing a moving lure through shallow water, and in order to stop your lure or feathers from sinking and snagging on the bottom, you have to keep reeling in, which of course means you then have to keep casting out again, over and over. This may seem like I'm stating the obvious, but it's a valid point, especially if you're new to casting, or you're fishing with a child, or someone else who's new to casting. Don't attempt a technique that revolves around being able to cast passably well when you're not sure if you can.

Easier venues for first-timers or children, or those unsure of their casting ability, are piers, harbours and rock marks, where you can float-fish for mackerel, for instance. Float fishing from a pier involves occasional casting. After one cast, you could leave your bait suspended beneath your float, dangling seductively in the current, for half an hour or more before you have to reel in and cast again. On the other hand, while feathering off the beach, you'll probably have to cast every 2 minutes.

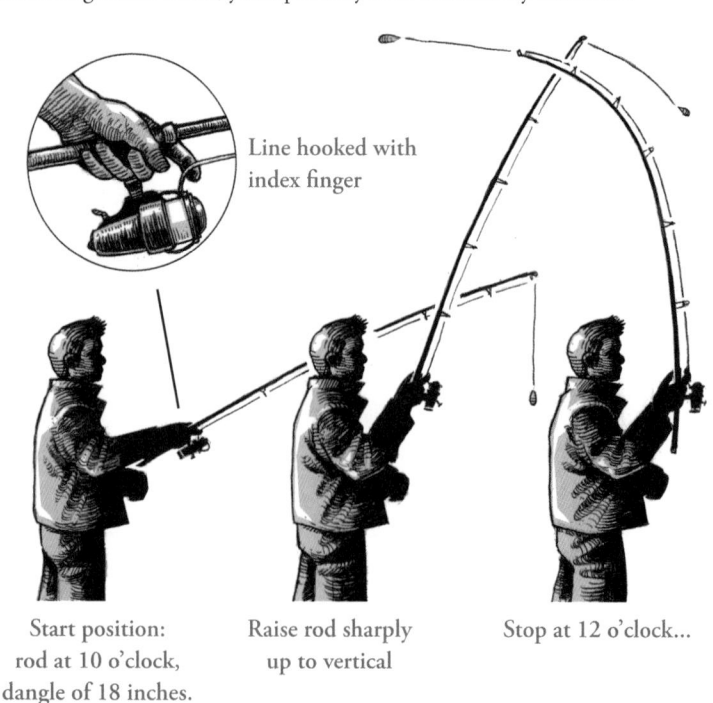

Line hooked with index finger

Start position: rod at 10 o'clock, dangle of 18 inches. Cock back bale arm

Raise rod sharply up to vertical

Stop at 12 o'clock...

How to cast a spinning rod

Hold the rod in your dominant hand, fingers either side of the reel seat stem. Your forefinger and middle finger should be on the up side, your two other fingers on the down side.

- Point the rod upwards at 10 or 11 o'clock.
- Next, reel in your casting weight until it hangs between 18 inches and 2 feet below your rod tip (this is the optimum casting 'drop').
- Wind the reel, so that the roller on the bale arm of the reel is in the nearest position to your index finger.
- Now, you should be able to extend your index finger and hook it around the line.
- Take the weight of the line in the crease of your finger beneath your fingertip, and hold it, while you cock the bale arm back using your other hand. You don't need to trap the line between your finger and the rod shaft. You just need to hold it far enough back towards the reel handle so that line doesn't fall from the spool. You're simply putting enough tension on the line to keep it on the spool.
- Now, with the rod still pointing at 10 or 11 o'clock, make like you're a crane, swivelling your waist, so the rod goes from being just in front of you to being

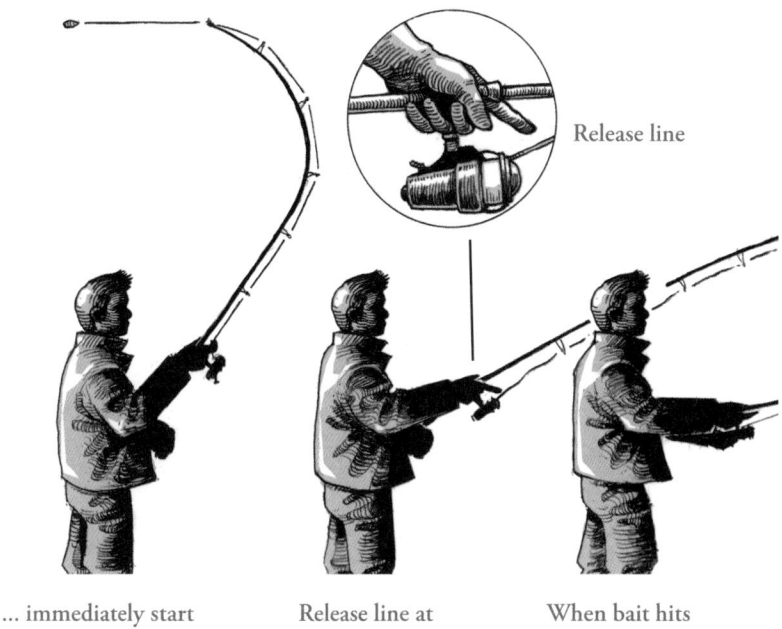

Release line

... immediately start forward cast

Release line at 10 o'clock position

When bait hits water, wind reel to release bale arm

FISHING SKILLS 173

just behind you. So you're turning your body, not your feet, half a turn. During this action, your other hand should be on the lowest point of the rod butt.
- Now, the rod is still at 10 o'clock position, only it is pointing behind you. So if you imagine you're the centre of a clock face, it's now at 2 o'clock.
- At this stage, you need to turn your wrist over, so you rotate the rod through 180°. Basically, instead of the reel and rings pointing towards the ground, you need to turn your wrist so they point to the sky.
- Now, you are locked and loaded and ready to cast.
- Keep your rod behind you, but turn your head to face forward – towards where you want to cast. Imagine the rod as a big flexible pole, which you're going to whip forward by pulling your bottom hand towards you as your reel hand punches out, thus whipping the tip of the rod forward.
- As you bring the rod over, snapping it forward, stop as you reach the 10 o'clock position. At the same moment, straighten your index finger to release the line. The rod tip shouldn't come lower down than 9 o'clock in the forward cast.

Describing it makes it sound more complicated than it really is. I'd urge you to practise. Spend time casting away from the waterside and try to 'feel' when it goes right. Casting is like hitting a tennis ball on the 'sweet spot' of a racquet, or a rounders ball with the meat of the bat. You soon *know* when you've done it right.

Striking and playing a fish

'Striking' is what you do when you feel a bite on your bait. But 'striking' is a misleading word really, because it suggests a lot of action – a big violent, powerful movement, which it actually shouldn't be. More people lose fish by striking too hard, or else by reeling in too fast and too furiously, than at any other time. (Losing a fish whilst you're reeling is known as 'bumping' a fish.)

A strike should be when you raise the rod tip quickly and firmly, but not with a heavy hand, from your normal fishing position of rod at 9 o'clock, up to 11 o'clock.

Most of the time, you don't really need to 'strike' so much as simply raise the rod tip up to the 11 o'clock position and start reeling, steadily. When the rod is starting to bend in the 11 o'clock position it's already exerting pressure on the line, pulling it taut and pulling the hook point upwards.

The only time you need to strike with any real determination is when you're bottom-fishing for black bream or possibly float-fishing for garfish. But even then, with the black bream's nibbly bites and the garfish's sometimes tentative takes, you may well find that it doesn't work, even though you strike fast and positively. In these circumstances, you'll often find that reverting to not striking, instead simply raising the rod tip and reeling steadily, solves, or at least reduces, the problem of missed fish.

FISHING SKILLS 175

Releasing your catch

Some fish, like wrasse, rockling and poor cod, are simply not worth eating. Wrasse are too bony, with flesh like soggy cotton wool, and rockling and poor cod are just too small and fiddly to process. So if you catch any of these, they need to be handled and released carefully in order to survive. Similarly, bass less than 40cm from the tip of their nose to the fork of their tail are classed as undersized, and you are required by law to release them. Also, you'll most probably catch various individual fish, which, although they belong to an edible species, are just too small for the pot, and so deserve a second chance to return to the sea to do some more growing.

Releasing fish is something you need to do carefully and quickly. The more you handle a fish, either to admire it, or possibly photograph it, the more chance there is that you'll damage it. With smooth small-scaled fish like mackerel, even the merest contact with dry hands will remove and abrade enough scales to cause it potentially terminal damage. So, if you can, always dampen your hands before you handle a fish that you intend to release. If it's too slippery to hold, you can use a damp cloth to help, but the cloth must be properly wet. A dry cloth will rasp off scales even quicker than dry hands.

If you're on a boat, or fishing from rocks or a harbour wall where you have water directly beneath you, it is possible to release small fish without even touching them, simply by taking the shaft of the hook in your thumb and forefinger, turning it upside down, so the point is aiming downwards, and then giving a firm flick with your wrist. The fish should just fall off and land back in the sea.

Some fish, the wrasse family in particular, are very sensitive to the change in pressure when they're being reeled up from any depth over 20 feet. They're normally bottom-dwelling fish, and the pressure change that occurs when they are reeled to the surface causes them to 'blow'. This means their insides, including their swim bladder, may start to protrude out from their anal vent. Their eyes will also expand and pop out (see pouting, pp.53–5), as the air pockets in them rapidly expand as they ascend.

In this 'blown' state, they're unable to swim back down to the seabed and are best killed and saved for the stock pot. But, with a little experience, you'll soon get to recognise when you've hooked a wrasse. Wrasse bites and subsequent fights are very distinctive: a sharp rattle at your rod tip, followed by a short-lived, but very aggressive head-shaking fight. So, if you think you've hooked a wrasse from a boat, or a pier, or any depth of 20 feet or more, simply reel it in very slowly. I know it's hard if you're excited and just want to see what it is that's fallen for your bait, but, if they're raised from the seabed super-slow, they often won't 'blow'. Without bug eyes and protruding swim bladders they can be released successfully, to continue their important, rudely interrupted wrasse work.

If you reel in a fish on the beach, and you instantly know that you want to release it, then don't bump it up the pebbles to your tackle box. Leave it in the shallows while you locate your pliers.

Try to keep any fish at least semi-submerged at all times. And never just 'throw' a fish back. Hold it in a few inches of water for half a minute, if you can, to give it enough time to re-orientate itself and get water flowing through its gills. This movement of water through its gills will give it a boost of oxygen, which should be enough to make it flick its tail and depart.

Killing fish

The best way to kill any of the fish you're likely to catch is with a swift, sharp crack to the head with a blunt instrument. Take something suitable with you – don't rely on finding something deadly at the scene of your catch. Scrabbling around trying to find the 'right' stone on the beach, or a heavy enough screwdriver on a boat, or a lump of driftwood at your rock perch, causes delay.

Delaying a fish's death while you hunt for a murder weapon is cruel; it prolongs the suffering of the fish out of water, and it is also detrimental to the quality of the flesh that you want to eat. A fish, lying alive on the deck of a boat or on sand, shingle, rock or the timbers of a pier, is going to flap and struggle, and beat its tail madly, trying to escape the only way it knows how: by attempting to swim. In so doing, it will thrash itself against a hard surface which will bruise its flesh, causing its naturally firm, muscular texture to deteriorate, and creating tissue damage that will potentially attract bacteria and make it go off quicker.

Allowing a fish to flap longer than necessary also depletes the energy reserves within the muscle tissue. These energy reserves would otherwise be kept within the dead muscle and would be used to maintain the cellular metabolism, which slows the onset of rigor mortis and subsequent spoiling.

In other words, if you do not have a rolling pin, priest, hammer handle, long-handled screwdriver or a shop-bought bosher at the ready, you will unduly extend the fish's death throes and deliver yourself a substandard portion of prime fish flesh for supper.

To kill a fish, the method is quite simple. You need to hold the fish down on a stable, flat surface. Keep a clean rag or tea towel handy to hold it firmly while you hit it hard on the head, at least twice. This should kill the fish instantly. Don't mush the head in some crazed axe-murderer-like frenzy – you want to be able to use the head later for fish stock. But don't be too soft either. You need to hit it hard enough and accurately enough – across the back of its head – to bring its life and its flapping to a swift and decisive end.

Killing mackerel

Instead of banging mackerel across the head, I prefer to snap their necks. Killing them by this method does two jobs at once. It kills the fish and it bleeds them in one swift movement.

The easiest and most effective way to simultaneously kill and bleed a mackerel is to put a thumb or forefinger in its mouth, and bend its head back acutely, at 90° to the body. This snaps the neck and at the same time rips the gills out from where they're attached under the throat. This kills the fish instantly and the rip in the gills starts the bleeding process all in one move.

This method is used with mackerel and not with other fish because, quite often, you'll catch a few mackerel in quick succession if you luck into a shoal. In order to continue fishing and maximise on the brief bright window of non-stop rod-bending action, you need to employ a method that kills and bleeds quickly, leaving your hands free to fish on. Mackerel are also suitable for killing this way because they tend to be small fish, and their necks are easily broken. They don't have sharp spines or razor-sharp gill covers, like bass or bream do, and they don't have thick, fat unbreakable necks like cod or pollack.

Snapping mackerel necks and tearing their gills upwards will not be everyone's cup of tea. And it may well just be too brutal for the gently acclimatising novice fisher. If so, then don't do it. Stick to a simple bosh with a blunt instrument. Just kill your fish quickly and efficiently in the manner that suits you best and feels right.

Bleeding fish

I don't promote 'bleeding out' as an alternative to boshing it on the head. Death by bleeding out, which involves cutting an artery and allowing the fish to die through loss of blood and lack of oxygen, is too cruel for me. And the fish will still flap and thrash in the process of its death throes, causing bruising to the flesh.

I do like to bleed my fish, but I advocate cracking them on the head first. A fish's heart will continue to beat for 2–3 minutes after it's been killed by a blow to the head. So a crack over the head will stop the flapping, and because the heart continues pumping, the majority of blood can still be flushed from the flesh.

The reason I advocate bleeding any fish is because when a fish is killed and it isn't bled, its blood remains within its circulatory system throughout its flesh. This blood will coagulate, creating weblike patterns and streaks through any fillets you might later cut from the bones. This blood doesn't really do any damage or affect the flavour of the fish too much, but without it, the flesh is cleaner-looking and potentially it will keep much longer because it's the blood in the flesh that will normally first attract bacteria.

Bleeding a fish

In order to bleed a fish, I crack it over the head and then, as soon as I can, I snip through one set of bright-red gills with a pair of tough kitchen scissors. A major artery runs through the fish's gills. So by snipping all the way through a gill arc, just after the fish has been dealt a firm blow, this will open up the artery to allow the thick crimson arterial blood to be evacuated from the body by the still-beating heart.

Chilling fish

The single biggest threat to your life-enhancing fish supper is heat. Most people like going fishing in good weather, yet excessive warmth will spoil your fish stunningly quickly. One of the worst things you can do with your lovely fresh-caught fish – and I've seen it often – is to stick it in a black dustbin liner bag and leave it in the sun.

It helps to take the fish's guts out before you chill it (see gutting, pp.183–6). It's not essential and it might not be possible, depending how and where you're fishing, but a fish's gut, incorporating decomposing food, will attract bacteria quickly. So, the sooner you can safely remove the fish's insides, the better. But even if you can't gut the fish soon after catching, you should still chill it whole and gut it later.

To keep your fish in peak condition, put it in an insulated cool box with some ice or a few freezer blocks. I usually carry my lunch in the same box and hopefully swap lunch for the raw materials of my fish supper during the day. It doesn't have to be a big cool box. I'll often take a 2-litre cool box with one ice block, and sometimes I'll even fillet fish as I catch them, in order to keep them compact and well chilled.

Fish Preparation Skills

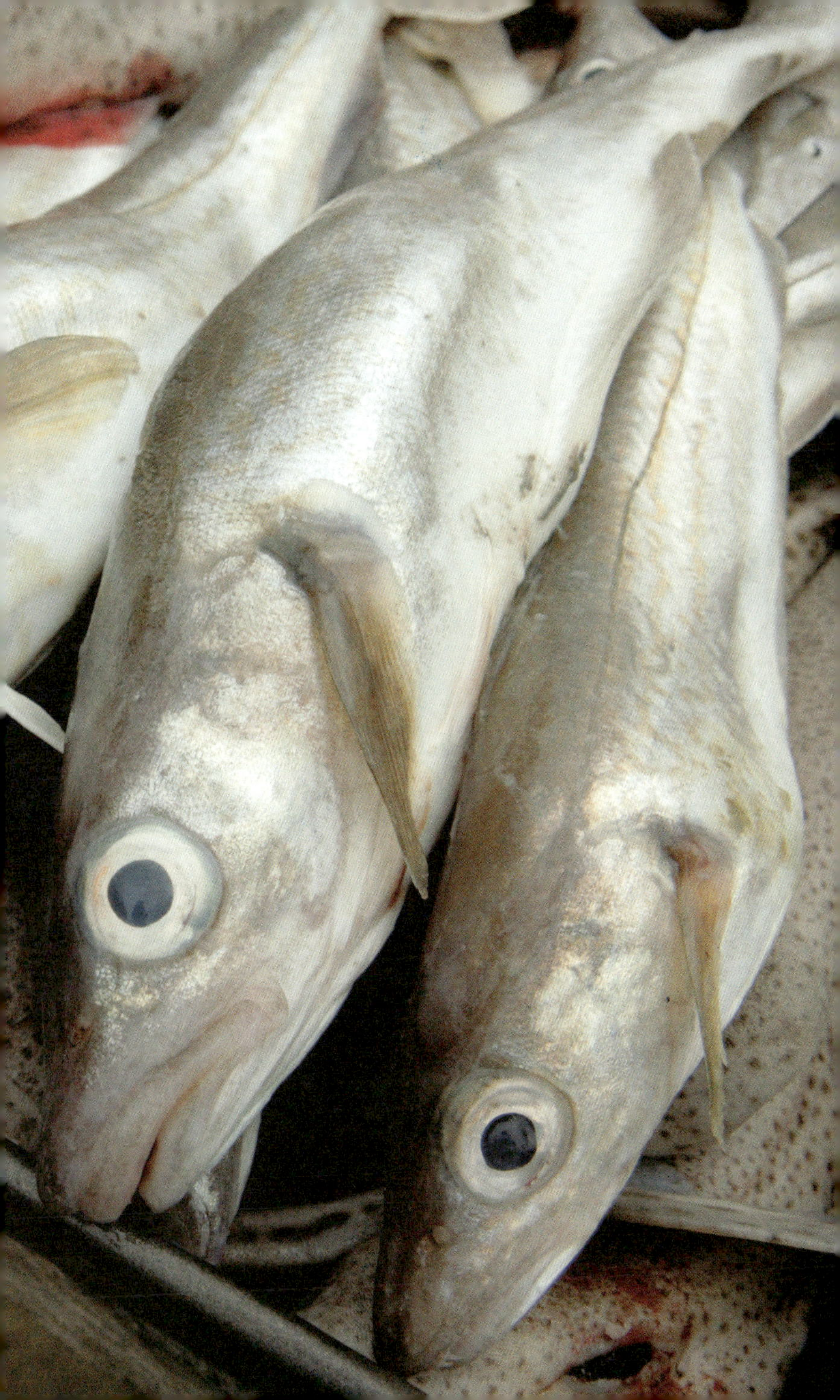

I've always really enjoyed the job of preparing fish. It's

a hard thing to explain. You either want to take fish apart, or you don't. From the very first mackerel I ever caught, aged five, I had an urge to take its insides out. Now, transforming a fish – fresh from the sea – into a perfect glistening portion of flesh, begging to be cooked, gives me great satisfaction. Fish cookbooks often suggest you 'ask your fishmonger' to do every task from filleting to cutlet cutting, but thankfully, as a fisherman, you don't have that luxury. Instead you have a duty to learn how to get the fresh, flapping thing you've caught into the best possible shape for cooking.

How you treat the fish you've landed and how you then transport them to where you intend to cook them is an issue of respect. Nothing depresses me more than seeing anglers leaving a charter fishing boat with a black dustbin liner bag, bulging with once beautiful wild fish, which I know will already be halfway to becoming slime-covered mush, fit only for cat food or fertiliser.

To enjoy the great fish you catch – and get the best out of them in terms of flavour and texture – you need to understand the basics of good fish prep.

Once a fish is dead, your first two concerns should be scales and guts. Only certain fish will need descaling (such as bass, black bream, pollack and grey mullet, which have very heavy scales), and it's easiest to descale them before they've been gutted, when the belly cavity is still intact. (However, don't fret if you haven't time to descale the fish before you gut them; it's still feasible, just not quite so easy.)

It is most crucial to gut your fish as soon as possible after catching it, because the longer you leave the guts inside, the more potential 'harm' they'll do, as they start to attract bacteria, which break down and spoil the fish flesh from the inside. Ideally the fish should be gutted within an hour or two of being caught, and the belly cavity filled with ice.

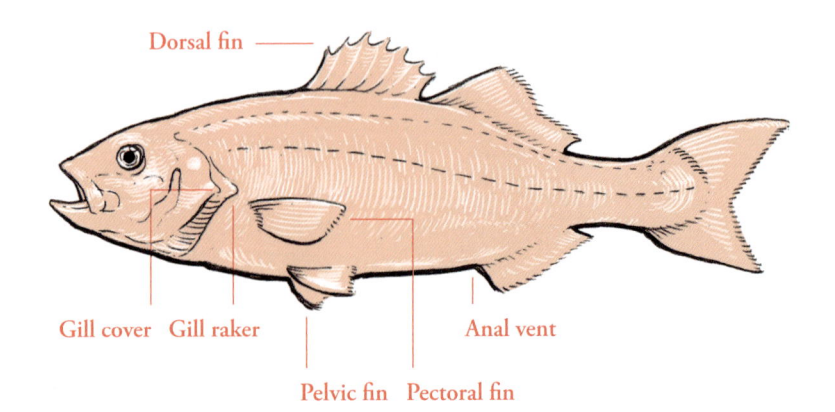

Scaling

Obviously, you remove scales from a fish because you don't want to eat them. But, if you are going to skin a fish, it's easier to do so with the scales intact, as the skin can become very thin and papery once the scales are removed.

I also leave the scales on my fish if I'm intending to barbecue it, as they help to protect the flesh from the intense heat of the coals, keeping the flesh more moist.

Removing scales from fish is easy. You just rub them up the wrong way, from tail to head – opposite to the way they overlap and lie. You can use the back of the blade of a short, strong knife. Some proper fishing knives sold in tackle shops come with a special crinkle-cut pattern along the back of the blade designed for descaling fish. Alternatively you can use a shop-bought descaler. These come in a variety of forms and shapes; my favourite are the plastic-handled descalers with a semi-circle loop of crinkle-edged steel mounted off the top of the handle. You can even make your own descaler by nailing upturned bottle caps on a handle-sized lump of wood.

It's best to descale a fish in running water or in a bucket of water, to stop the scales flying around. Work from tail to head and rinse the fish when you've finished.

The fish you really need to descale are black bream, bass and grey mullet, unless you're going to barbecue them.

The fish that could do with a quick rub over with a descaler but aren't heavily scaled are pollack, pouting, garfish, whiting and herring.

Flat fish, dogfish, squid and mackerel don't require any descaling.

Gutting

Gutting is the messiest prep stage, so even if you intend to take your fish home with you (rather than cook them on the beach), it's a job which is better done at sea or at the water's edge. Fish guts and scales are best returned to the sea, because they provide food for crabs and gulls and other carrion-feeding fish. Fish heads and frames are best taken home, for making stock. However, do be sensible and sensitive about where you deposit any fish guts. Don't just dump them into a harbour at slack tide or leave them on the beach in the belief that the next high tide will take them away, causing a sight and stench for other beach users to endure in the meantime.

The two main types – or rather shapes – of fish that you're most likely to catch are 'round' fish, or, if you're very lucky, 'flat' fish. These are fishmongering terms, which describe the shape of the fish's cross section. A mackerel sliced in half would be round. A plaice would be flat. Arguably, there are a few oval-shaped fish too, such as black bream, John Dory and trigger fish, but these can be treated in the same way as round fish.

Gutting a round fish

To gut a round fish, such as a mackerel, pouting, pollack or even a dogfish, the best place to start is by inserting the tip of your knife into its anal vent. This is the downstream end of the digestive tract, so if you cut upwards from here, slicing the belly wide open, you'll expose all of the fish's stomach and internal organs.

The safest way to do this is with the fish lying on its side, tail towards you. Place the flat of your hand on its upper side to hold it steady and insert your knife at about a 5 o'clock angle, with the tip pointing headwards and the cutting edge facing outwards (pic 1), in order to slice the belly from the inside out, as you work the knife upwards (pic 2).

Then stick your thumb inside the belly to hold the belly flaps open while you scoop out the contents (pic 3). Drag as much as you can out, either with your free hand or with the blade of the knife (pic 4). Some of the insides will naturally still be attached to the gullet or throat end, and if they won't come away with a pull, snip them off with kitchen scissors or carefully cut with the knife (pic 5) as close to the head as you can manage.

If you're intending to cut the fillets off your round fish, then you need to do no more; if, however, you're going to cook it 'on the bone' you might want to finish cleaning out all the internal residue. What's left in the belly cavity can be scraped out with the blade of your knife (pic 6). You'll find a line of dark goo, held beneath a thin membrane along the underside of the spine where the two ribcages meet. This looks like thick coagulated blood, and functions as the fish's kidney. It's preferable to remove this, because when cooked it can give the flesh that presses against it a slightly bitter, coppery flavour. And, for the more visually sensitive diner, it can appear somewhat off-putting.

The best way to remove the kidney blood is to puncture the membrane with the tip of your blade, slice it from one end to the other, and scrape the dark goo out with the blade, or with the back of your thumbnail, while holding it under a trickling tap or rinsing it in a bucket of water. It's not the end of the world if you don't remove this blood line. And often, if I'm cleaning and cooking a whole bunch of mackerel on a barbie, I'll leave it in and simply pack the belly cavity with a few extra bay leaves to cover the blood line and counteract any possible bitterness.

First and foremost, the importance of gutting round fish is to rid the tasty muscle flesh of possible contamination by the digestive juices, or decomposing food that is inside the fish's belly. Organs such as heart, liver, sex organs, roe or milt (sperm) can be left in and cause no detriment to the fish flavour whatsoever.

Personally, I love most fish roe and I'm quite happy to pick around any amount of liver and heart. Again, the fastidiousness of your gutting, beyond taking out the digestive essentials, is really down to personal taste.

FISH PREPARATION SKILLS 185

Gutting a flat fish

Unlike a round fish, the innards on a flattie are found quite close to the mouth. To locate the internal cavity, feel around the flat fish's collar. To one side of the head you'll feel firm neck muscle, on the other a soft, squidgy spot. Sometimes, especially on good-sized plaice, you'll sense what feels like a collection of stones just under the skin. These are seed mussel shells, sometimes crunched up, often whole, which the plaice has sucked up, cramming his belly pouch-style, for consumption later.

To eviscerate a flat fish, stab the point of a sharp knife into the flesh on his upper side, just below the single pectoral fin (pic 1). Once you've cut through the skin and the knife point is in the belly cavity, cut sideways for 2 inches, following the curve of the skeleton (pic 2), creating an incision just big enough to poke a finger and thumb inside (pic 3) and extract the digestive tract and contents of the stomach (pic 4). The liver and roe can be left in, and the heart too, if you like, or you can pull everything out, finishing off with a good rinse to remove any digestive goo.

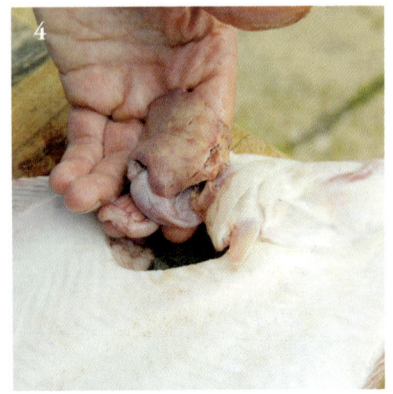

Removing gills

The only time I bother to remove the gills from a fish is if I'm going to cook it whole with its head on. Gills extract oxygen from the water and transfer it to the lungs. They also work as a filtration system, trapping potentially harmful bacteria, which can accelerate the decay of a fish once it's dead. They are one of those indicators that you should look at when you're assessing how fresh a fish is, for example if it's lying on a fishmonger's slab and you're considering buying it for your tea.

Bright red gills, on which the gill strands stand apart and proud – like the teeth on a comb – is the sign of a truly fresh fish. Grey, gummy, gooey, sticky gills suggest that a fish is past its best.

It's easy to remove gills. Lift the gill plate (pic 1) and snip through either end of the gill arch with kitchen scissors (pic 2). Cut around the base of the gills where they attach to the body (pic 3) and pull them away with your fingers (pic 4).

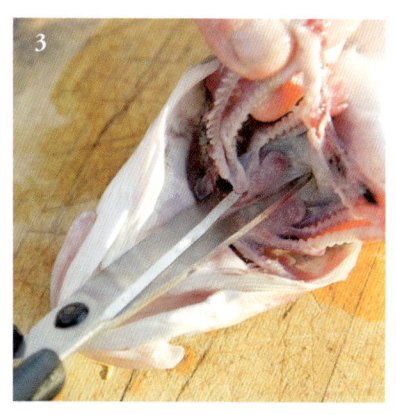

Filleting

Filleting is a wonderful skill to learn. It's not nearly as easy as it looks when someone professional is doing it. Nor is it as difficult as it first seems. It's a case of learning the basic principles and then letting yourself loose on some fish. Don't rely on the fish you catch. Buy some unfilleted fish from the fishmonger, such as mackerel, dabs or whiting. Once mastered, it's an impressive and useful skill for life.

Filleting a round fish

There are many ways to fillet a round fish and this is my preferred method. The approach is simple, repetitive and designed to remove maximum flesh. If you feel you've left more flesh on the bone than you wanted to, don't be scared to take your knife and carve any little clinging morsels off. So what if they're not attached to the rest of the fillet? They'll still taste the same. And don't forget the stock pot (see pp.218–20) is the absolver of all filleting sins and oversights.

First cut off your fish's head with an angled cut that goes from behind its head, at the top of its neck, across and under its pectoral fin, on the lower side of the fin, in a line that cuts through the top of its belly. Use a strong-bladed knife for this. If it's a big fish with a thick spine, a flexible filleting knife won't be man enough and will quickly blunt or get chipped if regularly used to chomp through the bone. Once the head is off you should have a fish body with a 45° angled slice where its head once was (pic 1). The apex of this angle is where your first fillet-cutting slice starts.

Keep your fish flat on the board at all times. Angle your knife across the sharp corner of the sliced neck and start with the heel of your blade, where the blade joins the handle (pic 2). Position the blade just above the central line of the spine, aiming to cut the uppermost side of the dorsal fin. The first cut should ideally penetrate about ½–¾ inch into the flesh, about two-thirds of the way down towards the tail.

Stop two-thirds of the way down and then, keeping the blade level and parallel to the board, work the point across the fish, over the top side of the central spine until it pokes out of the belly side of the fish. Now your knife should look like its stabbed right through the fish (pic 3). From here, work it down in one, two, or three (fewer is better) cuts towards the tail, with the cutting edge of the blade angled very slightly downwards so that it effectively 'shaves' the flesh off the central bone.

Once you've cut right down to the tail, move back up to the start of the first cut at the sharp pointed neck angle. Using the thumb on the hand that isn't holding the knife, fold open the cut to expose the spine. Your next cut wants to deepen the first cut, keeping the knife at a gentle angle, but striving to cut to where the ribcage starts to bulge upwards (pic 4).

Then, work this cut down to the point where the free-flapping tail section starts (pic 5). If your knife is sharp, these cuts shouldn't require much pressure. Don't force

FISH PREPARATION SKILLS 189

your way through the flesh. Use smooth, gliding, angled cuts and try to use all of your blade, not just the tip.

Your next cut should be your last. It should take you up over the curve of the ribcage and down across the belly cavity (pic 6, p.189).

To remove the other fillet, flip your fish over. This time start with the head towards you and commence your first cut at the tail end, working up to the head end. Then stab through to release the tail fillet. And finally, use two or three more cuts to remove the whole fillet, working across the ribcage and down across the belly as you did on the first side. Trim each fillet of excess skin.

Now you need to remove the line of small bones from the centre of each fillet. To do this, cut lengthwise down each side of the line of bones (pic 7, p.189). Angle these cuts into a V-shaped trough. Then, using the tip of the knife, carefully lift out the central line of flesh containing the bones (pic 8, p.189).

Filleting a flat fish

Filleting a flat fish is more straightforward than filleting a round fish, mainly because the anatomy and skeleton are easier to navigate. The body is squashed flat, so it's a two-dimensional puzzle, rather than a three-dimensional one. Because of this, there's no central ribcage and belly cavity to have to cut around.

Having said that, it's only really worth filleting flat fish that are at least 1½–2lb. Smaller flat fish are best cooked whole in the oven as the flesh depth is very shallow and filleting is simply too wasteful. Eating flat fish 'off the bone' is so easy anyway; a grilled or baked flat fish sits flat on your plate, you peel back the skin and eat the flesh off one side of the bone, and then flip it over and eat the other side.

But should you find yourself happily in possession of a nice plump plaice or an enormous flounder that you want to fillet, what you need to do first (after removing its guts) is lay it white side down, on your board.

Your first cuts should be a V shape of two cuts, which run down either side of the head. From the bottom of this V, the next cut, turning your V shape into a Y shape (pic 1), should run right down the centre of the fish from neck to tail, dividing the upper side into two sections. Each of these sections are known as quarter fillets, because there's two on each side, and four in total. Your downward cuts will always cut down to the wide flat skeleton – so you can't cut too deep. The bone is your end point, so just cut to the bone and stop.

The central cut will fall to one side or the other side of a small central ridge of bone, which is where the spines of the skeleton meet in the middle. For the next cut, angle the tip of the blade under one side or the other (pic 2) – I usually go for the right-hand side (because I'm right-handed) – and just ease the tip ½ inch under the flesh. Then with the tip scraping flat against the skeleton, cut all the way down the length of the fish.

FISH PREPARATION SKILLS   191

The next cut is exploratory, allowing you to slide the blade of your flexible filleting knife deeper under the flesh, with the blade always scraping against the fan of the skeleton bones. Effectively you're working from the centre of the fish outwards, scraping the fan of the bones, until you reach the outer edge and are able to cut out through the skin that meets the outer ribbon of fins (pic 3, p.191). Then remove the quarter fillet (pic 4, p.191).

Do this on both sides, left and right (pics 5, 6, 7 and 8 p.191), then flip your fish over. Now you need to repeat the process on the white side. This will give you four almost identical fillets, with the two upper ones being slightly thicker with brown skin, and the underside ones thinner but with white succulent skin. Trim the fillets with your knife or scissors to remove any fin spines or tag ends of skin.

Skinning

Skinning a fillet always looks an impressive feat, but it is much easier to achieve than you might think. One thing worth bearing in mind though, as I mentioned in the scaling section, is that it is more difficult to skin the fillet from a fish that has been rigorously descaled than one which still has its scales intact, or one that has only had a quick swipe or two to clean the worst of the moulting scales. This is because rigorous descaling can leave the skin paper thin and therefore more likely to tear under the knife.

The mechanics of skinning a fillet are easy. Lay the fillet flesh side up, skin side down on a clean flat board. Start from the tail end. If the tail's very slippy to hold with your fingertips, a pinch of salt will give you a little more grip.

Hold the tip of the tail firmly down on the board and cut down through the flesh with your blade angled slightly towards the head end. Stop when you reach the flesh side of the skin.

Now, turn your blade so that it's steeply angled towards the head, just as though you were trying to shave the flesh side of the skin. Hold the tail down and move the blade ½ inch, to start the cut. Then stop. Don't move the blade any more. Instead, wriggle the tail with your other hand and pull it towards you, away from the blade. This is where that sprinkle of salt helps with the gripping.

The trick is to move the tail, not the blade. The blade is held rigid while you wriggle and pull the tail towards you. You'll soon see how easy it comes. Keep the downward pressure on the blade constant, but not too hard. Make sure the fillet always remains flat to the board as you tug and wriggle the tail.

FISH PREPARATION SKILLS 193

How to skin a dogfish

Skinning a dogfish is a skill really worth learning. Dogfish are as easy to catch as mackerel, but nowhere near as easy to cook and eat, because their delicious flesh comes wrapped in a thick, sandpaper-like skin, which appears to have been fitted with super-glue. There is, however, a surprising amount of satisfaction to be had from mastering the technique of peeling off this skin, as well as the more obvious culinary reward. Of the various techniques I've come across, I use the following two methods (both illustrated), as I've found them to be the most reliable.

Skinning with pliers

This involves removing the two fins on the fish's back, with deep horizontal slices, to cut the fin off right down to its root (pic 2), then doing the same on the underside with the tail fin.

Now slice beneath the anal fins, cutting across the fish, deep into the belly cavity, and then turn and slide the knife upwards towards the head, slicing away the whole belly and stomach walls (pic 3). This can be done in one long deep cut, which removes everything abdominal, right up to the underside muscular column of the main body.

Remove all guts and stomach flaps right up to the throat, before turning the knife from the horizontal to the vertical and cutting downwards under the throat, right through to the back of the neck, removing the head. This leaves a headless, finless, gutless dogfish, with a tail (pic 4).

Then, using just the point of the knife, while holding the fish by the tail, head end pointing away, cut a skin-deep line between the holes where the fins once were. This cut ideally penetrates just below the skin, and continues in a line from tail right up to decapitated neck, all along the back (pic 5).

Then flip it over and make the same longitudinal cut along the underside of the tail, joining up the oval-shaped hole (where the fin was) to the gaping hole that was the belly. So the skin is now divided longitudinally in two halves. The thinking is that to strip the skin from two halves, one down each side, is easier than trying to take it off in one sock-like piece.

In order to start peeling the skin, you need to cut a ring around the tail, just to the depth of the skin, and then lift up a tab-end of skin, big enough to clamp with the jaw of the pliers. Each half of the skin is then stripped off, using pliers, from tail to head (pic 6).

With practice it's possible to peel the skin off in two long pulls, one on each side (pic 7). And when that happens, believe me, it is a supremely satisfying feeling. Not only is the sensation of one long peeling action very pleasing, but to see the perfect skinned eminently edible-looking flesh appear from under what previously looked

FISH PREPARATION SKILLS 195

like something you'd use to sand your kitchen floorboards is like discovering the Holy Grail over and over again. But do be prepared for it to go wrong. Often the pliers keep slipping and failing to hold on to the slimy tag and you'll find the skin coming off in tiny pieces, which makes the process slow and irritating.

A few tips:
- Dogfish skin is phenomenally tough stuff and will dull the edge of a sharp knife in seconds, so avoid using one of your best knives. My favourite dogfish knife is a cheap nylon-handled meat boning knife, which will stand a lot of abuse, yet can still be re-sharpened easily.
- Use square-nosed rather than thin-nosed pliers.
- Use a tea towel or rag to hold the pliers and even a thick rubber glove to hold the tail. The skin is very abrasive and unless you've got hands like a pot hauler, you'll easily rasp some skin off. It's very painful and takes ages to heal!
- When you manage to get a good grip, pull like you mean it. Try to get a whole side off in one rip – restarting on a half-stripped side is never easy.
- When I was first shown this technique I was told that it could be done without pliers, using just your teeth instead. Which of course I had to try. And yes, it can be done, but I grazed the tip of my nose and my top lip in the process, and really wouldn't recommend it, unless you're desert-island desperate.

Skinning by hand

This method doesn't require pliers, but a glove or a rag, to protect your skin and give you some grip, won't go amiss.

As for the previous technique, cut off the back fins right down to the root, so that it leaves two oval-shaped holes in the back, exposing white flesh.

Flip the fish over, slice off the fins under the tail and the anal fins too, but don't slice off the belly. Instead, cut the belly open all the way up from the anal vent to the throat, like you would to gut any round fish (pic 1). But continue the cut right up through the chin, effectively splitting the underside of the head wide open in two. Then remove all the guts (pic 2).

With the fish on its back and the flaps of the belly opened out, make two cuts at 45° between the head and the pectoral fins at either side of the head (pic 3), almost through to the spine. This creates two flaps, incorporating the fins, which can now be used as 'handles' (pic 4).

With one foot planted firmly on the dogfish's head, and what's left of its chin facing downwards, it's now possible to peel each flap around towards the spinal column, ripping the skin at the neck. Then, holding the head and body down with your foot while pulling the two flaps together (pic 5), it's possible to remove the entire skin in one long pull (pic 6). Finally, cut off the head (pic 7).

FISH PREPARATION SKILLS 197

How to prepare squid

Freshly caught squid are very satisfying to prepare. They're just so weirdly beautiful, and when you've successfully deconstructed one, they're so simple to cook. All the flesh is more or less the same thickness; there are no bones or cartilage or skin to bother fussy fish diners and the bulk of the flesh is easy to cut into any shape or size you desire, from butterflied curls, to rings, chunks or cubes. And then there's those delicious tentacles, which in my house we all fight over.

Squid is best cleaned under a slowly running tap. First rinse it to remove any ink, which might have leaked out of the ink sac (pic 1).

Then pull the head (hopefully still attached to the guts) out of the mantle (body). To do this, hold the mantle in one hand, take the head and tentacles in the other and pull. Be careful though, if the head feels like it might part company with the guts, leaving them inside, then you need to slide your fingers into the head end of the mantle and tease the guts out (pic 2), by detaching them from their fixings on the inside. This might take a couple of attempts. Just keep gently tugging at the head until you can feel the insides come free. Then draw the whole lot out.

Lay the head and tentacles and guts on your board and cut through the head just on the tentacle side of the eyes (pic 3). This should leave you with a bunch of tentacles just joined together at their base, which you keep, and a set of eyes attached to a set of guts, which you throw away.

Now rinse out the mantle; put your fingers in and give it a slosh around. Then turn it tail end up and grab both fins in one hand (pic 4). Depending on how big your squid is and how thick its covering membrane of stretchy translucent skin is, this will either simply peel off in your fingers, or else need to be poked and prised off by puncturing the membrane skin with your fingernail (pic 5). Having watched Korean and Chinese women clean squid, I realise a tough fingernail is a most useful tool for removing the membrane from fins, mantle and tentacles. Sadly, I bite mine.

Once you've teased as much membrane off as you can, or can be bothered to, you're good to go – and start cooking. However, if you're going to cook squid rings, one last thing you can do is invert the mantle. Turn it inside out by pushing the tail up through the neck, just like you're turning a sock inside out. Use a wooden spoon handle to push the thin end in and up.

The reason for doing this is twofold: first it allows you to clean out all the residue of the guts which might cling to the interior of the mantle, without having to cut it open. And secondly, because it reverses the stresses of the cylindrical wall of the mantle, it means you'll always cook perfectly round squid rings, rather than floppy figure-of-eight ones, which you get if you don't flip the mantle inside out. It's not compulsory, but it's a neat little trick that never fails to impress! The mantle and fins are now ready to cut as required and cook with the tentacles (pic 6).

FISH PREPARATION SKILLS 199

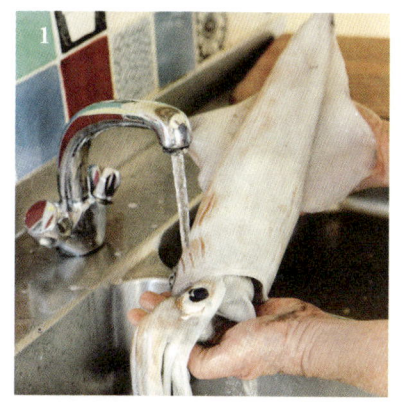

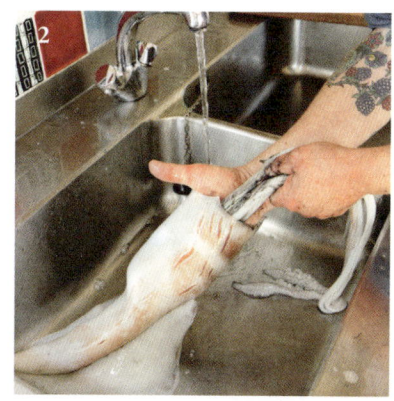

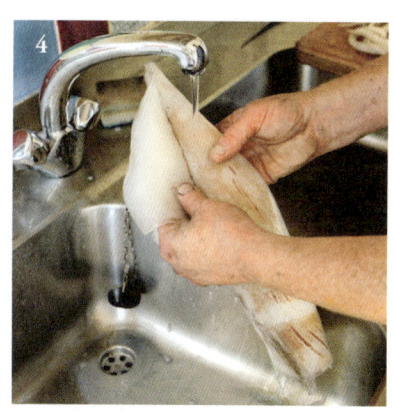

Cooking Fish

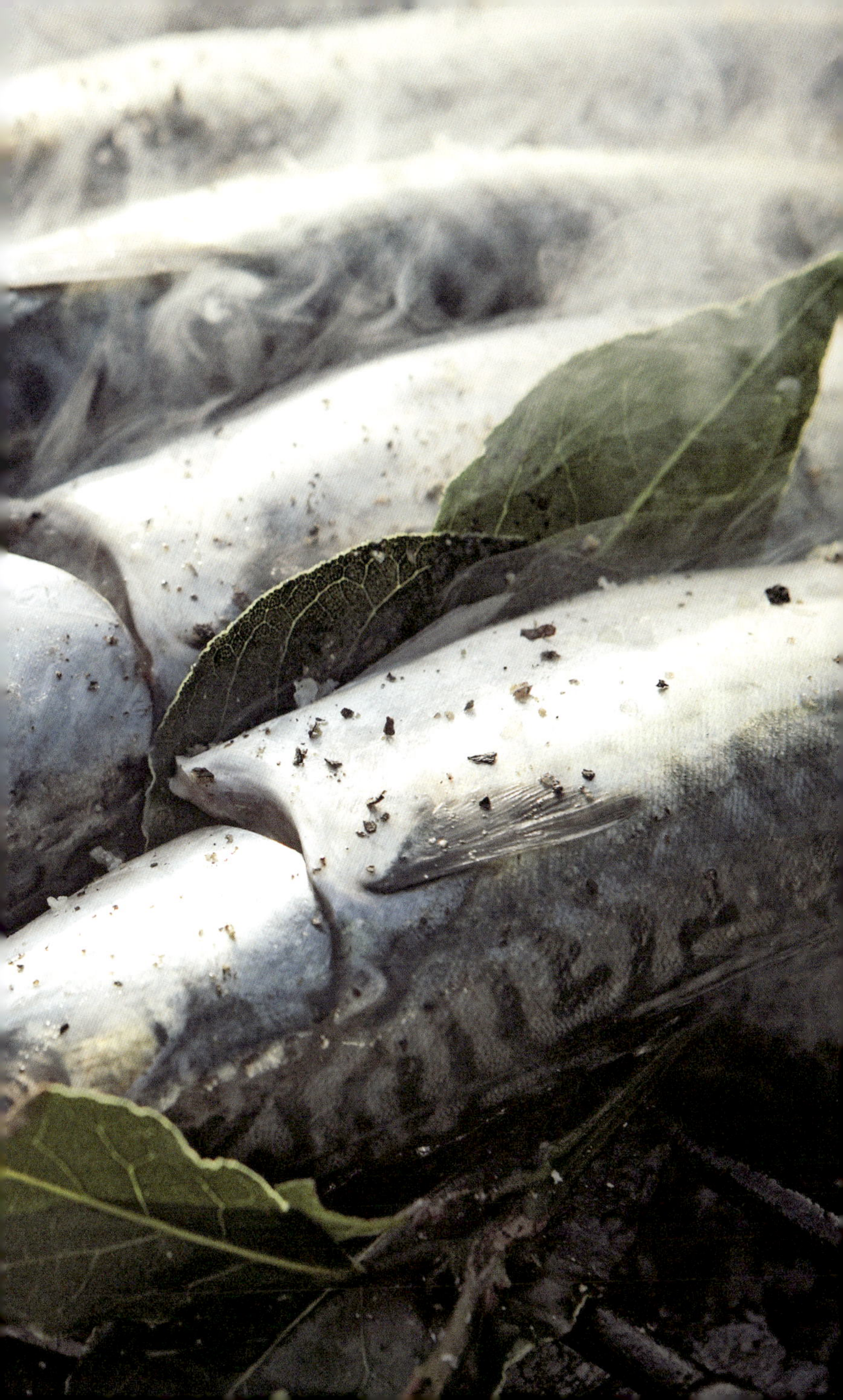

I rarely do anything fancy or faffy with the fish I catch,

mainly because I usually cook it and eat it while it's still blisteringly fresh. Good fresh fish requires very little cooking and very little in the way of extra flavouring. If it's straight from the sea, then it has the freshness and sea flavour that I most want to taste. I rarely use specific recipes – and I never use complicated ones. Instead, I just choose the cooking method that I think will best suit the particular bit of fish I've caught, and the people I'll be serving it to. Added ingredients, seasonings, accompaniments and quantities are all very flexible.

So, in this section, I am simply giving you my general fish cooking techniques. You will find some recipes here, but they're intended as guides, rather than prescriptions. I'm hoping that you'll customise them to your heart's content. The way to become a happy fish cook is to feel your way along, turning the basic principles of good fish cookery into your own recipes. If you still feel like getting stuck into some slightly more structured fish cookery, Hugh and I have included a whole range of tried and trusted recipes in *The River Cottage Fish Book*.

There are really no absolute 'wrongs' in my approach to fish cookery, other than overcooking, which is the most common mistake. But this is easily avoided. Just remember that fish flesh is very different from animal flesh. This is largely to do with the creatures' different lifestyles.

Fundamentally, fish don't have to deal with gravity. They don't have to bear their own weight all day long whilst trying to keep themselves propped up on two or four legs. Instead they have the luxury of water to take their body weight and so their muscles don't need to be encased in membranes and lashed into place by sinews and ligaments. Fish muscle is much softer, held together in precisely stacked flakes and bound only by layers of collagen, a substance which dissipates at very low cooking temperatures. In short, fish flesh is much more delicate than meat or fowl, and it's a lot quicker to cook.

The adjacent table matches different species with different cooking techniques, simply as a quick reference guide. As always, these are suggestions, not rules. Just because flounder sashimi hasn't lit my fire, it doesn't mean it won't work for you.

Sea fish cooking techniques

	SASHIMI	SUSHI	CEVICHE	STOCK	BARBECUE	PAN-FRY	DEEP-FRY	WHOLE FRY	GRILL	BAKE	FOIL PARCEL	STEAM
MACKEREL	✓	✓			✓	✓			✓	✓		
DOGFISH				✓		✓	✓		✓	✓	✓	
POUTING	✓	✓	✓	✓		✓	✓		✓	✓		
POLLACK	✓	✓	✓	✓		✓	✓		✓	✓		
COD				✓		✓	✓		✓	✓		
WHITING	✓	✓		✓		✓	✓			✓	✓	✓
GARFISH						✓	✓	✓	✓			
RED GURNARD	✓	✓	✓	✓	✓	✓	✓	✓	✓	✓	✓	✓
BLACK BREAM	✓	✓	✓	✓	✓	✓	✓		✓	✓	✓	✓
PLAICE					✓	✓	✓		✓	✓	✓	
SEA BASS	✓	✓	✓	✓	✓	✓	✓		✓	✓	✓	✓
DAB & FLOUNDER					✓		✓	✓	✓	✓		
HORSE MACKEREL	✓	✓			✓	✓			✓	✓		
HERRING					✓	✓	✓		✓	✓		
SQUID					✓	✓	✓	✓	✓			
SLOB TROUT	✓	✓	✓	✓	✓	✓			✓	✓	✓	✓
GREY MULLET					✓		✓	✓	✓	✓	✓	✓

✓ = recommended cooking technique

Herbs, seasonings and accompaniments

I tend to ignore the kind of rules about seasoning and saucing fish that have been handed down over the years from various messiahs of fish cookery. The selection of herbs and seasonings that I would deem essential to fish cooking is pretty small, mostly interchangeable, and can be used with all the species I cover, although some flavourings do work better with certain styles of cooking.

One notion I am inclined to agree with is that oily fish are best served with a piquant, citric accompaniment such as salsa verde, while white fish works better with a creamy sauce, like tartare. Citrus flavours cut the richness of oily fish flesh perfectly, of course, but then a fried mackerel fillet smeared with a dollop of creamy horseradish sauce is equally gorgeous, which totally contradicts the theory. So, rather than offer you rules about cooking and serving fish, I'm simply going to list my most-used herbs and seasonings and favourite fishy accompaniments:

My essential seasonings are:
- Sea salt
- Black pepper
- Garlic
- Chilli
- Wasabi
- Horseradish
- Chives
- Thyme
- Bay leaves
- Parsley
- Lemons
- Limes
- Capers
- Crabapple juice (verjuice)
- Vinegar

My top accompaniments for fish are:

Homemade mayonnaise

Put 2 egg yolks in a bowl with a scrap of crushed garlic, some salt and pepper, a pinch of caster sugar, 1 tsp Dijon mustard and 1 tbsp cider vinegar or lemon juice. Whisk lightly together. In a jug, combine 150ml rapeseed or light olive oil with 150ml sunflower oil. Whisk the oils very gradually into the yolk mixture: start with just a few drops, then slowly increase to a thin stream. Keep whisking all the time so the oil is emulsified into the yolks. (You can also do this in a blender.) When you've added all the oil, adjust the seasoning with more salt, pepper, sugar and lemon juice if necessary. Cover and chill until needed. Keep in the fridge for up to 3 days.

Garlic mayonnaise

Follow the mayonnaise method above, but start off with more garlic – 2 fat cloves, crushed to a paste with a little salt, should be about right.

Tartare sauce

Combine 2 heaped tbsp good mayonnaise with a roughly chopped hard-boiled egg, 1 tbsp chopped parsley, 1–2 tsp chopped dill or chives (optional), 2 tsp chopped capers and 2–3 chopped gherkins or cornichons. Add a squeeze of lemon juice to taste and season with pepper, and salt if necessary.

Salsa verde

Roughly chop the leaves from a large bunch of flat-leaf parsley, along with a few basil and/or mint leaves if you have any. Add 1 finely chopped garlic clove, a few capers and a couple of anchovy fillets if you like. Chop it all together until quite fine. Scrape into a bowl and mix in 1 tsp hot mustard, a good squeeze of lemon juice and enough olive oil to make a thick paste. Season with salt, pepper and more lemon juice if needed. Use within a day or two.

Dill hollandaise

Put 1 egg yolk in a bowl. Melt 150g unsalted butter (or salted if that's all you have), cool until tepid, then trickle it gently on to the egg yolk, whisking all the time, until it's all incorporated. Add 2 tbsp finely chopped dill, a squeeze of lemon juice, and some salt and pepper. Serve straight away.

Sweet chilli dipping sauce

In a small saucepan, combine 3 tbsp redcurrant (or other fruit) jelly or jam with 1 tbsp cider or white wine vinegar, a dash of soy sauce, 1 finely chopped hot chilli and 1 finely chopped garlic clove. Heat gently, stirring, until the jelly melts, then simmer gently for a couple of minutes. Season with pepper. Leave to cool. Before serving, whisk in a little warm water and/or more soy sauce to give a runny dipping consistency. Once cooled, this will keep in the fridge for at least a week.

Soy and garlic dipping sauce

Combine 3 tbsp soy sauce with a good dash of Worcestershire sauce, 3 tbsp mirin or rice wine (or cider or apple juice), 3 tbsp water, 1 finely chopped red chilli, 1 finely chopped garlic clove, 1–2 tsp grated fresh root ginger and a good pinch of sugar. Bring to a simmer and cook gently for 2–3 minutes. Let cool slightly. Serve warm as a dipping sauce for deep-fried battered fish or tempura, or dribble over mackerel fillets or any sort of hot fish. Once cooled, it'll keep in the fridge for a week or so.

Horseradish sauce

Combine about 100g grated fresh horseradish root with 2 tsp cider or white wine vinegar, 1 tsp hot mustard and a pinch of sugar. Leave for 10 minutes, then stir in 125g crème fraîche or soured cream. Season with salt and pepper. Use within 24 hours.

Raw fish: sashimi and sushi

Sashimi

Sashimi is simply bite-sized pieces of raw fish fillet served with a splash of soy sauce and a smidgen of wasabi (or strong English mustard). In some respects, it's the most basic way to prepare fish because it doesn't involve any cooking. But that doesn't mean it's the easiest. Sashimi involves a certain knowledge of fish anatomy and skill with a filleting knife. It's arguably a lot easier to throw a whole head-on guts-out mackerel on a barbecue than to render it into elegant, boneless, uncooked bite-sized pieces.

I'd seriously encourage you to try sashimi-making. There's something undeniably exciting about eating fresh raw fish – especially fish you've caught yourself. There's no more natural way to enjoy freshly caught fish. A little goes a long way though – you don't necessarily need a whole plateful of it. Every summer, when the black bream fishing starts, I like to ceremonially carve a few slices of a just-caught new-season bream on my boat. It's a joyous nature-taster of things to come.

'On board' sashimi should be a quite rough and ready affair, where you simply slice off some nice boneless strips of just-caught fish flesh and dunk them in soy and wasabi. But an accidental mouthful of bone or gristle can be off-putting, so it's worth developing a bit of a technique of your own, a little sashimi routine that'll help you to deliver a clean, boneless, scale-free result. In my experience that means at least keeping a spare cutting board just for sashimi, and pack some kitchen roll or a clean tea towel too.

You could argue that cramming the finer points of sashimi preparation into a few paragraphs is impossible. Sushi and sashimi chefs train for up to 10 years to perfect the deep and complex art of raw fish preparation and presentation. So, this is a cheat's guide, but it's all you'll need – as long as you're working with top-notch super-fresh fish, and you don't mind fairly free-form presentation…

There are a few bits of essential equipment:
- A sharp filleting knife (and a sharpener)
- A clean tea towel and/or some kitchen roll
- Two chopping boards. Whether you're making sashimi on board a boat, on the shore, or in your kitchen, your gutting and filleting board must be different from your sashimi cutting board. Cross-contamination from one to the other can ruin the end result. Doesn't hurt to have a separate knife too.
- A bowl of clean tap water or sea water: this helps to freshen a piece of fish while you prepare it, and is essential for dipping your knife into between cuts. The dipping of the blade stops the steel 'dragging' in the flesh. If you use a sticky knife, it can create furry, broken edges in even the firmest fish flesh, rather than clean, crisp-cut lines.

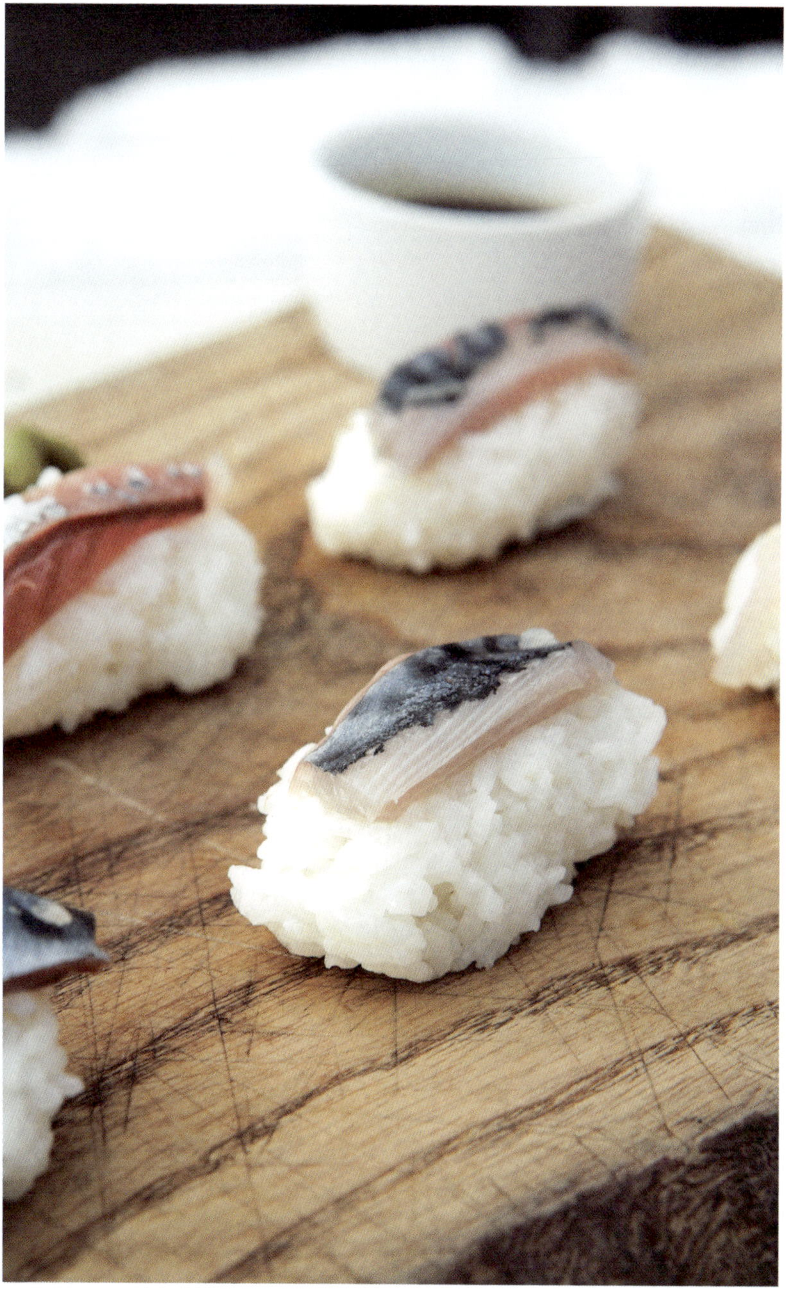

Things to remember:
- Keep cutting surfaces clean.
- Keep your cutting knife very sharp and very clean. Dip it frequently in clean water as you work.
- Accept that there will be some waste when you fillet. Sashimi-cutting requires you to jettison anything that might have bones or membranes (use these bits for stock). And don't use anything that has got too warm or looks unappetising.
- Try and handle the fish as little as possible. Warm hands will make the flesh soft and slimy.

My all-time favourite sashimi fish are:
- Sea bass
- Red gurnard
- Pollack
- Pouting
- Mackerel

My basic technique:
Don't descale your fish. You'll need to remove the skin and it's easier to do this with the scales on. (Descaling makes the skin thin and more likely to tear.) However, be careful not to let any scales transfer from the skin side of the fish to the flesh side.
- Working on your filleting board, gut your fish (see pp.183–5). Rinse it really well to get rid of any traces of blood, innards or scales.
- Fillet the fish as carefully as you can (see pp.188–90), then remove the skin from each fillet (see p.192).
- Pat the fillets dry with a clean cloth or kitchen paper and transfer to the clean cutting board. Trim and tidy each fillet, discarding any remaining bones and any membranes or unappetising bits. You should now have a couple of very neat and clean-looking naked fillets.
- Cut the fillets into bite-sized pieces, remembering to keep dipping your knife into clean water. It's best to work at a 45° angle to the grain of the flesh, cutting it first into thick strips, then slicing these into smaller 'bites' if necessary.
- Arrange your sashimi on a clean plate. Top each piece with a mere smear of wasabi or hot mustard, sprinkle on a few drops of good light Japanese soy sauce (such as Kikkoman), and serve immediately.

Sushi

If you can cut sashimi, the next step is to have a go at sushi. At its most basic, sushi is nothing more than a mouth-sized oval of perfect rice with a smear of wasabi and a sliver of thinly sliced good fresh fish (i.e. sashimi) draped on top (shown on p.207). Cooking, seasoning and storing the rice correctly is 95 per cent of the art of good home sushi-making. It's not difficult, nor does it require a lot of special equipment. Once cooked, the rice can be shaped by simply pressing it into balls, then flattening slightly. But, if you fancy a cheap, clever gadget, buy yourself a sushi portion press.

My favourite sushi fish are:
- Sea bass
- Red gurnard
- Pollack
- Pouting
- Black bream
- Pickled mackerel (see p.210)

Sushi rice

A failsafe recipe for cooking rice to make nigiri sushi – simple finger-shaped sushi.

Serves 6

200g sushi rice
100ml rice wine vinegar
1 tbsp caster sugar
¼ tsp fine sea salt

Rinse the rice in a sieve under cold running water until the water runs clear, then rinse it again. Drain and tip into a large saucepan. Cover with plenty of cold water. Leave to stand for half an hour, then drain, return to the pan and add fresh water to cover by an inch or two. Bring to a fast boil. Cook for 5 minutes, then turn the heat down and simmer gently for a further 15–20 minutes, until nearly all the water has been absorbed. Take off the heat, cover the pan and leave to stand for 10 minutes.

Meanwhile, put the wine vinegar, sugar and salt in a small pan and heat gently until the sugar has completely dissolved. Leave to cool. Add the mixture to the warm cooked rice, combining it well. Tip the seasoned rice on to a large tray and spread it out to help it cool. Perfectionists will also fan it at this stage. Don't refrigerate it.

To make nigiri sushi, have a small bowl of clean water to hand. Dip your fingers into it frequently as you work, to stop the rice sticking to them. Take a roughly bite-sized portion of rice (it can be still slightly warm, or completely cooled – warm is best). Roll it between your palms to form a ball. Squash it slightly and smooth and mould it with your fingers to form an even oval shape. Repeat with the rest of the rice.

Once the rice ovals are all formed and cooled, top each with a smear of wasabi or hot mustard, then a piece of sashimi (see p.207). Serve with soy sauce for dipping.

Lightly pickled mackerel

Mackerel makes great sashimi, eaten with no more than a smudge of green wasabi and a dribble of soy sauce. However, when mackerel is used to make sushi portions, it's traditionally lightly pickled first: quickly salted, then marinated in vinegar. This is because, being an oily fish, it deteriorates very quickly, and in its raw state it can be prone to parasitic worms. Hugh and I eat yards of raw mackerel every year without any problems, but then our mackerel is always fresh and straight from the sea. If yours is more than 24 hours old, or you're not quite sure how super-fresh it is, or if you just fancy a new flavour, try this quick mackerel-pickling recipe.

Makes enough for 40 sushi pieces
100g fine sea salt
4 large mackerel fillets

For the marinade
500ml rice vinegar
50ml mirin, apple juice or sweet cider (or water with 1 tsp sugar added)
10g sea salt

Sprinkle about one-third of the fine salt over a non-metallic dish. Lay the mackerel fillets skin side down on top, without overlapping them, then sprinkle over the rest of the salt in an even layer. Leave for just 5 minutes, then turn each fillet in the salt and transfer to a bamboo basket or a plastic colander. Leave for another 10 minutes, so the salt continues to draw out the juices. Then quickly but *thoroughly* rinse each fillet in cold water and pat dry with a cloth or kitchen paper.

Mix all the marinade ingredients together and put into a non-metallic container, such as a ceramic dish, or a plastic box. Add the mackerel fillets and leave in the fridge for 1–1½ hours by which time the flesh will have turned creamy white.

Remove the fillets, shaking off the marinade, and pat them dry. Discard the marinade. Carefully peel off the papery, thin outer skin of the mackerel, from the head to the tail, leaving the iridescent pattern underneath on the fillets (but don't worry if a little of it comes away with the skin).

Lay the fillets skin side down again. Use tweezers to remove the pin bones from the lateral line along the middle of the fillet. Or you can cut each side of the line of bones and lift them out with a filleting knife (see p.190; pic 8, p189).

Your pickled mackerel is now ready to cut for sushi. Slice across each fillet at ½ inch intervals at a 45° angle, to get roughly diamond-shaped pieces. Place each one on a shaped oval of sushi rice (see pp.207 and 209) on to which you've first smeared wasabi or mustard.

COOKING FISH 211

Marinated fish

Marinating is an incredibly simple way to add flavour to fish. You can do it with raw fish, using a cold marinade – a technique that generally works best with white fish. Alternatively, you can bathe cooked fish in a hot marinade to get a quite different result – usually best with oily fish. There are a couple of classic dishes, both South American in origin, which make the most of these techniques and I frequently turn out a version of one or both of them at home. They share two particularly attractive characteristics: first, they can be excellent make-ahead dishes, which don't rely on split-second timing. Secondly, they're just begging to be tweaked and tinkered with, depending on the ingredients you have to hand.

Cold marinating: ceviche

Cold marinating can be as simple as tossing chopped or sliced super-fresh raw fish with a few aromatic flavourings and herbs – maybe olive oil, Tabasco, parsley, chopped red onion – and serving it up as a kind of fish 'tartare'. However, I nearly always include some citrus juice in a cold marinade and, as soon as I do that, I am entering the exciting realms of 'ceviche'.

Ceviche is a way of 'cooking' fish, but without heat. It relies, instead, on the chemical properties of citric acids. When fish is cooked in the conventional way the protein fibres, which resemble coiled springs running through the flesh, begin to unwind and straighten out. This starts to occur at about 55°C and, within a short time, the fibres will have straightened out and begun to merge and coagulate. At this point, fish is deemed to be cooked. The exact same reaction can be created by immersing fish flesh in citric acid, which in the case of ceviche means a delicious marinade of lemon, lime and orange juices. When you immerse fish flesh in these juices, there's an almost immediate visible chemical reaction. As the acid is absorbed, the translucent flesh becomes opaque and milky (just as it does when you heat it).

Ceviche celebrates the natural textures and flavours of good fresh fish, without being quite as hardcore an experience as eating sashimi or sushi. If you find totally raw Japanese-style fish preparation just too alien, but like the idea of eating fish in its natural state, ceviche is definitely worth a try. Firm white-fleshed fish, such as black bream, bass, pouting, whiting and pollack, work best. I'd certainly consider using salmon or trout too. But really oily fish like mackerel, while they can make an interesting addition, don't tend to work as a main ingredient. Ceviche is often made with a mixture of fish species but it's equally good with just one type.

You can vary the amount of time you allow the fish to marinate before you eat it. When I first started making ceviche, I would leave it for an hour at least. Over the years, my marinade time has got shorter and shorter, and quite often now I'll just prepare it and eat it straight away – especially if I've made it with some eye-wateringly fresh bass or black bream, because I can't keep my hands off it. It's actually perfectly safe to keep your marinated fish in the fridge and eat it the next day, when you'll find the texture much softer and less 'raw'. But my own preference is for a just-marinated fresh, zingy, crunchy experience.

Hot marinating: escabeche

When I find myself looking for something a little different to do with oily fish, such as mackerel, herring or garfish, and I have a little bit of time on my hands, I'll plump for the hot marinade option. While this involves cooking the fish, the final dish itself is served at room temperature. It's a great recipe for using up a glut of oily fish, and it's perfect for a large group of fish diners. Or as a tapas-style dish, served alongside other delicious fish treats.

All I do is fillet the fish then fry the fillets quickly over a fairly high heat to give them some colour on the flesh side and just a little crispy edge. I might dip the fillets in flour first too so they'll have an extra crispy coating – this crispness works well with the marinade as it soaks up the flavours a little more than the flesh alone might do. Over these cooked fillets I'll then pour a hot and fragrant marinade: a mix of, say, vinegar and apple juice, spiked with garlic, shallots, grated ginger, lemon zest and chilli. The fish will then be left to cool in its aromatic bath, and I'll serve it later with some good crusty bread to soak up the juices. A dish like this is great to make in advance because it actually improves with being chilled for a day, although I always serve it at room temperature, never cold.

What I'm describing in my ad hoc way is actually a Latin American classic called escabeche. Like ceviche, it exists in many forms, so you should feel totally at liberty to create your own version. For my money, it's a great way to use up an excess of oily fish. I'll often use it on a few skinny, sad mackerel that I've got left after a barbecue, or with the results of filleting accidents. I'll even do it with bony fish like sprats or small herring or garfish, where the bones are too tiny to remove without a full surgical team as back-up. In this case, I'll fry the fish hard, cranking the oil up a few degrees and crisping them good and proper. This way, the bones, fins and skin become crunchy, and the marinade soaks into them deliciously. The result is both soft and crisp, spicy and sour, turning something that could have been wasted fish into a sweet, tangy, crunchy delight.

My ceviche

A ceviche marinade must contain strong citric juices – lime, lemon and orange are all essential, in my view – but everything else is optional and variable. What you're after is a marinade that is bitter and acidic, but which also has sweet tones. I always add a little sugar and salt to take the edge off the acid taste. The rest is up to you. Try soft brown sugar instead of caster, try Tabasco instead of fresh chilli, add smoked paprika or a few glugs of peppery olive oil. I also love to mix in some raw salad vegetables to bulk out the mixture and give it some crunch – thinly sliced celery and onion are my favourites, but use whatever you like. I've made very good ceviche with sliced carrots. Even tomatoes can work, though I'm not a huge fan unless they're partly green and very tart and firm.

Serves 5–6

500g fish fillets (black bream, sea bass, red gurnard, pouting and pollack are ideal)
Juice of 3 limes
Juice of 2 lemons
Juice of 1 orange
1 red chilli, deseeded and chopped
1 clove garlic, peeled and crushed
1 tsp caster sugar
1 red onion, peeled and sliced
2 inner stems of celery, sliced
Salt and freshly ground black pepper

Trim your fish fillets carefully, as for sashimi (p.208). You need completely 'clean' fillets, without bones, skin, scales or membranes. Slice the fillets into pieces, about 2 inches long and at least ½ inch thick. If the pieces are too thin, they'll 'overcook' and turn mushy. Pour the lime juice over the fish and toss lightly. Limes have more acid than other citrus fruits, so adding this first kick-starts the 'cooking' process. Refrigerate or keep in a cool box while you prepare the rest of the marinade.

In a bowl, mix the lemon and orange juices with the chilli, garlic, sugar, a good pinch of salt and lots of pepper. Taste the marinade and tweak the flavours to your liking: it should be citrus-sharp, but also fragrant and with a hint of sweetness. Once you're happy, pour the marinade over the fish chunks. Add the onion and celery and mix it all together. Leave in the fridge for a minimum of 15 minutes to 'cook'. I personally wouldn't leave it longer than an hour, but you can leave it overnight if you choose.

Serve in little bowls, making sure that each has a generous portion of the marinade along with the fish and vegetables. Toasted crusty bread is a great accompaniment. When you've eaten all the fish and crunchy salad, the leftover marinade is a joy to drink. It's sour and fruity-fishy – in a good way – and truly wakes up your tongue. In Ecuador, they call these few gulps of marinade *leche de tigre* or 'tiger milk'. Mixed with a generous shot of vodka, it's a customary hangover remedy!

COOKING FISH 215

My escabeche

Try adding your own blend of flavourings to the marinade. Spices such as cumin, coriander or allspice, and aromatic herbs like thyme or marjoram all work well. Orange zest could replace the lemon. Thinly sliced onion, carrot, celery or pepper can be added too: sauté them until soft in the fish frying pan before you add the marinade liquid. It's sometimes nice to finish the dish, just before serving, with a sprinkling of a fresh herb, such as parsley or even mint. I'll also add some thinly sliced raw onion and hot chilli – and maybe even very thinly cut carrot – right at the very end. The crunch and bite of the onion and chilli set against the sweet, crunchy-coated softness of the fish fillets is enough to make you start writing sonnets.

Serves 6

Olive or rapeseed oil, for frying
12 fillets of mackerel or scad mackerel, garfish or herring

For the marinade
100ml cider or balsamic vinegar
200ml apple juice
1 hot red chilli, finely chopped
2 shallots or garlic cloves, peeled and chopped
A couple of bay leaves
Grated zest of 1 lemon
Salt and freshly ground black pepper

Heat a thin layer of oil in a non-stick frying pan over a medium-high heat. Fry the fish fillets, in batches, for a couple of minutes each side, until lightly coloured and just cooked. Transfer to a large dish in which they will fit snugly in one layer.

Combine the vinegar and apple juice and add to the frying pan with the chilli, shallots, bay leaves and lemon zest. Heat until simmering, then cook for a couple of minutes, scraping up any crispy bits from the pan as you do so. Season well with salt and pepper. Pour this hot marinade over the warm fish fillets in their dish, to cover them completely.

Leave to cool, then chill for a few hours – or up to 24 hours – before bringing back to room temperature. Serve with lots of bread for mopping up the marinade.

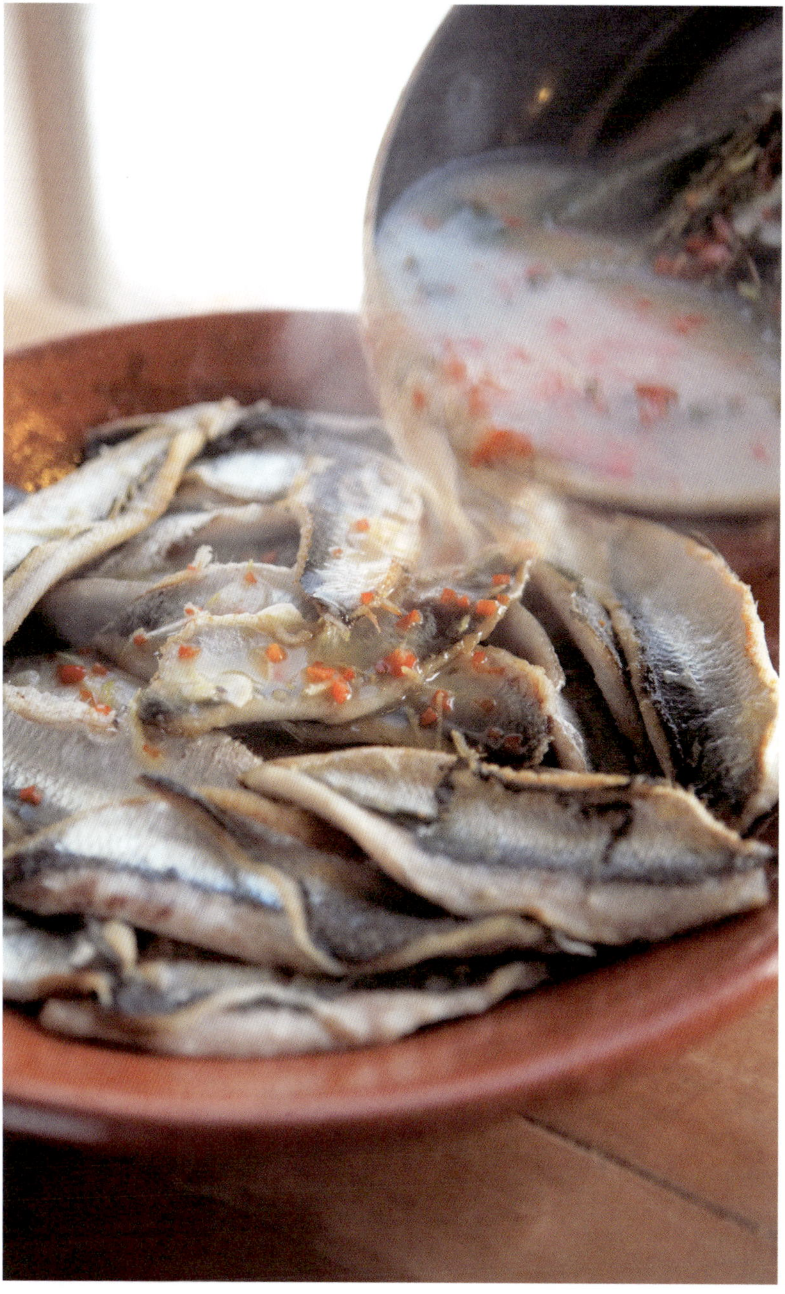

Fish stock

Stock is a precious thing, a commodity that opens the door to all manner of fast and flavoursome meals. It freezes well, but I'll often keep a bowl of jellied stock in the fridge for a week, where frankly it seems to improve with age. It's incredibly useful for quick fish dishes. If, for instance, I'm frying a couple of fillets, I often add half a ladleful of stock to the pan after the first few minutes of cooking. The liquid semi-poaches the fish and reduces to form a rich and tasty little 'gravy' in the pan.

I make my own fish stock because it's easy – and far better and far cheaper than any stock I could buy. I have some on the go most days, primarily so I know there'll always be plenty of tasty base for soups and risottos. Stock-making also enables me to render raw offcuts of fish edible to my dog, chickens and pigs. However, the stockpot has another purpose: it is a salve for a guilty conscience. If I've made a hash of filleting a fish, or have only used the very best bits – for sushi or sashimi – leaving lots of odd morsels of flesh clinging to the bone, then I feel absolved of guilt knowing that nothing is going to waste: all these odds and ends will contribute to a perfect stock. I view the stockpot as a filleter's confessional, into which all the sins of the flesh (left sticking to the bone) can be washed away and made good.

The only special equipment you need for stock is a good large pot. I have two actually: one has a 9-litre (about 2-gallon) capacity; the other's about 13 litres (nearer 3 gallons). Both are heavy-based so they conduct heat evenly, and have well-fitting lids to stop excess evaporation. Big, easy-to-grab lug-like handles help too.

What do I put in? Skin, heads, bones, fins, livers and roe (eggs or milt) all go into my stockpot. In fact, with the exception of the guts, I'll put in any part of any white or semi-white fish (pollack, cod, pouting, whiting, bream, bass, gurnard or dogfish). Flat fish are great for stock too – the frames, heads and skins of plaice, dabs and flounders make some superlative stock.

I don't normally use oily fish, like mackerel or herring. I find they make the stock too greasy and too fishy in flavour. On occasion, I'll chuck in the odd mackerel frame, but rarely the heads. (Incidentally, even these still get used – generally on my next fishing trip. I'll freeze mackerel heads and use them singly as bait, or put several together in a tangerine sack and use for baiting crab pots. I might also mince up the heads to make chum – rubby dubby – for a special black bream trip.)

It's impossible to be precise about quantities when you're using up trimmings, bones and oddments. But, as a rough guide, I don't think it's worthwhile making stock with less than 500g of fish trimmings – 1.5kg would be better. If you don't eat as much fish as I do, try saving up a stash of fish trimmings in the freezer, adding to it whenever you can. (See recipe overleaf.)

My three favourite recipes using fish stock are fish risotto (see p.221), fish soup (see pp.222–3) and fish stew.

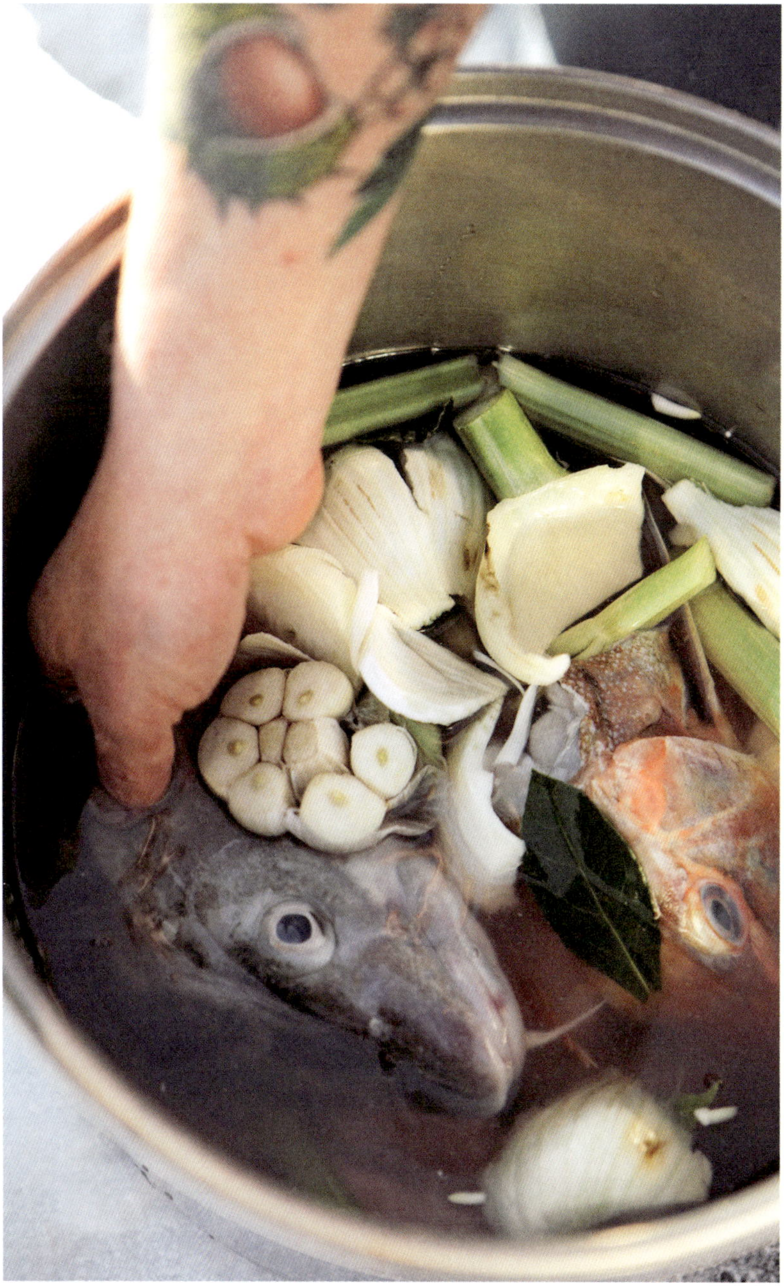

Simple fish stock

I never really use the same combination of flavouring veg and seasonings twice, though I regard celery, carrots, onions and bay leaves as essential. The rest largely depends on what I find in the bottom of the fridge or in the garden.

Makes 2–3 litres

500g–1.5kg fish trimmings (see p.218)
2–3 stems celery, roughly chopped or whole
2–3 carrots, chopped or whole
2–3 onions, peeled and halved
6 bay leaves
Salt

Plus any of the following:
A few green peppercorns
A couple of dried chillies
A head of garlic, sliced in half
A couple of slices of fennel bulb, plus a handful of feathery tops and a few seeds if available
Leek tops
Parsley stalks
Thyme sprigs

Simply chuck all your fish heads, bones, skins and filleting sins into a large pot, then add the all-important seasonings and vegetables. Now cover the lot with water and add some salt – I use 2 tsp to every 5 litres water. But don't go overboard, the saltiness will increase as the stock reduces; you can always add more salt later.

Bring to the boil, reduce the heat, cover and let it simmer gently for a minimum of 20 minutes; ideally no more than 30 minutes. And it'll probably be fine if you forget about it and leave it on for a bit longer, as long as it's not boiling hard.

Taste the stock to make sure you're happy with it. I normally make mine quite watery. (You can always reduce it later by boiling it hard once the bones and veg have been strained out.)

While the stock is still hot, or at least warm, attack the contents with a potato masher, pulping up the veg, knocking all the flesh off the bones, and mushing up any heads. Then pour through a colander into a bowl. I use a wide-holed colander rather than a sieve because I like bits in my stock. You can strain it through a fine sieve, or even through muslin, if you're anally retentive and prefer a clear, translucent result.

When the fishy contents are in the colander, give them another bashing with the spud masher or the end of a rolling pin to extract every last drop of juice. Then leave the stock to cool, before putting it in the fridge, or possibly bagging and freezing it. My fish and bone mush goes to the chickens or the pigs, after I've hived off a few of the better-looking bits for my dog Spike.

A simple fish risotto

The fresh fish you add to your risotto at the end of cooking can be almost anything: oily fish, white fish, shellfish, squid or cuttlefish. Just make sure it's all carefully skinned, deboned and cut into large bite-sized pieces (except prawns or shrimp, which can be put in whole). To be honest, though, if I've got a really stonking fish stock, I sometimes don't add any fresh fish at all – a plain, soupy fish stock risotto is simply one of the most flavoursome and soothing dishes.

Serves 4

**A large knob of butter
2 tbsp olive or rapeseed oil
1 onion, peeled and chopped
1 garlic clove, peeled and chopped
About 700ml fish stock
350g risotto rice (arborio or carnaroli)
1 glass dry white wine or cider
(optional)
About 300g fresh fish and/or shellfish
(chunks of white or oily fish fillet, whole scallops, squid rings, whole shell-on prawns or shrimp)
½ lemon
A little chopped parsley or chives
(optional)
Salt and freshly ground black pepper**

Heat half the butter with 1 tbsp oil in a large saucepan. Add the onion and garlic and sauté gently for 5–10 minutes. Meanwhile, bring the stock to a low simmer in another saucepan.

Add the rice to the onion, stir and cook for a couple of minutes. If you're adding wine, do so now, and let it simmer until all the liquid has evaporated. Now start adding the stock, one ladleful at a time. Stir well after each addition and add the next ladleful as the previous one is absorbed. Keep the risotto simmering gently, and stir frequently. It should take about 18 minutes to add all the stock, and for the rice to be just cooked. When it's done, season with salt and pepper.

When the rice is nearly done, cook the fish and/or shellfish. You can steam it, but I usually fry it. Heat the remaining butter and 1 tbsp oil in a large frying pan over a medium heat. Add the fish and shellfish and fry gently for about 2 minutes until just cooked, or even a little undercooked. Finish with a generous squeeze of lemon juice.

Add the fish and shellfish to the rice for just the last minute or so of cooking, folding them in very gently so they don't get broken up. Remove the risotto from the heat and serve right away, sprinkled, if you like, with some parsley or chives.

Variation
If you've got a good rich stock, simply bring to the boil and pour it over couscous. Add a knob of butter, cover and leave to stand until it has soaked up all the stock.

My fish soup

I've never made this exactly the same way twice, but it's always very quick, simple and deeply satisfying. All I do is create a tangy, salty thin soup base – really just a poaching medium for the fish – add a few noodles and thinly sliced vegetables then, at the last minute, some chunks of fresh fish.

Everything about this soup should be fresh and very lightly cooked. I can make it in 4 minutes once I've got the stock up to temperature. It's very easy and adaptable, so do play with it – try it without noodles, add some broccoli sprigs or kombu seaweed, or make it really spicy, or squeeze in a lime at the end to make it sour. The soup should change through the seasons, reflecting the vegetables and fish that are at their best. You can even make it with just stock and white fish and nothing else.

If I've got a good batch of stock ready, I'll use that alone for the soup base. But, if I only have a small amount, or it's a bit watery, I'll augment it with miso (Japanese fermented soya bean paste) or dashi-no-moto (a Japanese soup base made from dried bonito fish flakes). There are lots of different kinds of miso; it doesn't matter much which you use, but a paste is preferable to granules.

The most important issue with this soup is timing. You must avoid overcooking the vegetables and fish. If in doubt, err on the side of undercooking and you'll probably hit it right. If I've made you feel nervous about timing, you can always cook the fish separately by steaming or frying it, then add it to the hot soup just before serving. Small quarter-fillets of dab and flounder work well fried first and then placed on top of a bowl of soup, or risotto for that matter.

Serves 4
500ml–1 litre fish stock
1–2 tbsp miso paste or ½–1 sachet of dashi-no-moto
About 150g medium dried egg noodles
1 large leek, trimmed and sliced
1 fennel bulb, trimmed and sliced
1 garlic clove, peeled and sliced
1 red chilli, sliced
300–400g mixed white fish and shellfish, such as 4–5cm pieces of skinless, boneless pollack, pouting or gurnard, squid rings, whole or halved scallops, shell-on prawns
Toasted sesame oil or chopped parsley or coriander, to serve
Salt and freshly ground black pepper

Put the fish stock into a large saucepan; you need roughly a mugful for each person. If you're using miso paste or dashi, first mix this with some boiling water to a sloppy paste. Once in the pan, bring up to a simmer, stirring to make sure the miso or dashi is all dissolved.

Now add your noodles: break flat bundles in half first; let nests open out in the water, helping them along with a big-pronged fork. Simmer for 3 minutes, stirring occasionally, until the noodles are pliable but not fully cooked.

Now add the leek and fennel (or other veg) and start your mental clock. Once the veg is in, you're about 3 minutes from pouring this into bowls. You want the veg to be still crisp when it's served, so don't dither. Taste the broth and add salt and pepper if you think it needs it. Turn the heat right down, then add the garlic and chilli and, finally, the fish. Thicker, denser items like scallops or squid should go in first: they'll need a couple of minutes to cook through. White fish pieces will only take a minute, so add these right at the end (they'll go on cooking even once you've served up).

When the fish is just cooked, take off the heat and ladle the soup immediately into warm bowls. Finish with a trickle of sesame oil, or chopped parsley or coriander.

Gurnard with tomato and fennel

This is a gloriously rich, warming braise. You can make it using only tinned tomatoes as the liquid element, but I think it's immeasurably enhanced by the addition of some lovely homemade fish stock. If you can't get hold of gurnard, try thick cutlets of grey mullet or dogfish goujons or cutlets (both of these need only 10–15 minutes in the oven). To make this more substantial I've included a can of chickpeas, but you can leave these out if you prefer it more soupy.

Serves 4

- 2 tbsp olive or rapeseed oil
- 100g chorizo or smoked streaky bacon, cut into small chunks or lardons (optional)
- 2 onions, peeled and chopped
- 4 celery sticks, sliced
- 2 fennel bulbs, trimmed and roughly chopped
- 4 garlic cloves, peeled and chopped
- 1 fat red chilli, deseeded for less heat if preferred, and sliced
- 400g tin chopped tomatoes
- 2 tbsp tomato purée
- About 400ml fish stock (or use another 400g tin of tomatoes)
- 400g can chickpeas, butterbeans or other pulses, drained and rinsed (optional)
- 2 tsp smoked paprika
- 2 bay leaves
- A pinch of sugar
- 4 red gurnard or mullet cutlets (about 400g each), descaled and gutted
- Salt and freshly ground black pepper

Heat the oil in a large casserole or saucepan over a medium heat. Add the chorizo or bacon if using and fry for a couple of minutes, until the fat starts to run. Add the onions, celery, fennel, garlic and chilli. As soon as they all start to sizzle, reduce the heat, cover the pan and let the vegetables sweat and soften, stirring them from time to time, for about 15 minutes.

Add the tomatoes, tomato purée, stock, chickpeas if using, paprika and bay leaves. Bring to a simmer and then cook, uncovered, for about 40 minutes, until you have a thick, rich sauce. Season to taste with sugar, salt and pepper. Meanwhile, preheat the oven to 180°C/Gas mark 4.

If you're using a large casserole dish, you may be able to fit the gurnard in it – nestle them snugly into the hot sauce. Otherwise, transfer the sauce to an ovenproof dish and add the fish, pushing the portions down gently into the sauce. Bake in the oven, uncovered, for 15–20 minutes, or until the fish is cooked through.

Serve each portion of fish with plenty of the chunky tomatoey sauce, and mashed potato or crusty bread to mop it all up.

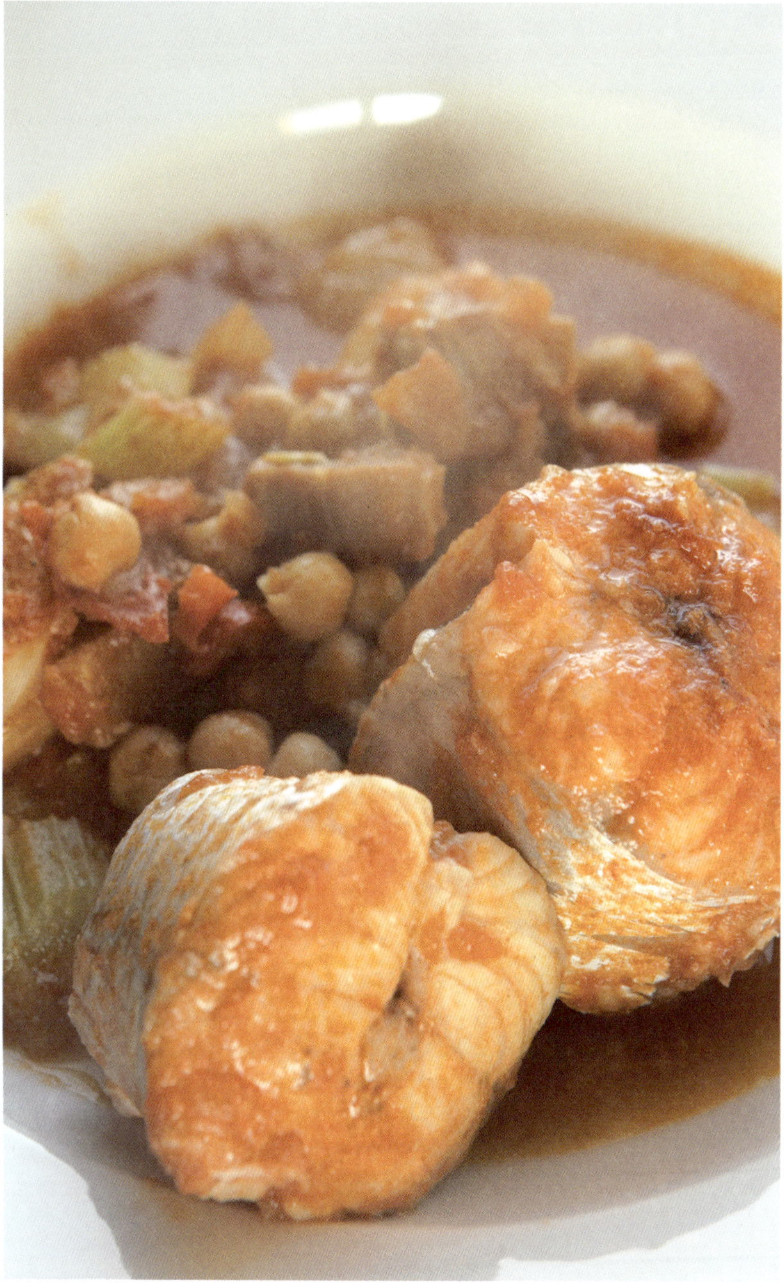

Barbecued fish

When I think of barbecues, I think of the beach – that's where I tend to do a lot of open-air cooking. Lit by the setting sun, accompanied by friends, family and a cool box brimming with freshly caught fish, there is just nothing better. But of course you can enjoy the wonder of a fresh fish barbecue, with all its smoky, fire-cooked, lip-smacking, finger-licking flavours, in your garden, on a roof terrace, or wherever.

One thing I really would encourage you to do is barbecue in the autumn and winter. I love an outdoor fire when the weather is cold and cooking is a cosy joy, rather than a sweating chore. In my opinion, the best time for beach barbecues is late October. This time of year can produce some stunning clear but mild days. What's more, the mackerel are plentiful and at their best, absolutely chock-full of omega oils – they've spent all summer feeding on high-grade protein and slowly converting it to oil to keep them fuelled through the winter months.

Whenever you choose to do it, there are just a few simple things to be aware of in order to make your barbie the thing of joy it should be. And, believe me, I've done my research over the years: my advice on how to run a successful barbie is inspired by my multiple failures as well as my modest successes.

The right kit

When it comes to equipment, I suggest you buy a bucket barbecue. I think they are the safest and easiest to use, particularly on the beach. Here in Dorset, where beaches are mostly made up of pea shingle, a bucket barbie works best because it keeps the main concentration of heat well up off the shingle, which has a habit of splitting when it gets too hot and pinging around like ricocheting bullets. Bucket barbies are also great for beach cooking because they're easy to carry (they come with a handle) and you can stash your charcoal and firelighters or kindling inside the bucket.

I abhor disposable barbies. The coals inside them are made of reconstituted coke-mush and they come ready-impregnated with evil ignition chemicals that make your fish taste like diesel fuel. Most of all, I hate them because too many people think 'disposable' means 'just leave on the beach when you're finished'.

For fuel, I always use local hardwood charcoal made from coppiced wood – it's increasingly easy to buy these days. I never ever use charcoal briquettes – the fuel of Satan – ungodly things that shouldn't be used to cook good fish. I don't like the chemicals put into them and I find they always get too hot, too late – they don't give the good hour of steady heat that a well-laid hardwood charcoal fire will provide.

Personally, I can't see any point in cooking on the beach if you've got to lug tons of gear along with you. So, when we barbecue as a family, we don't take knives and forks. We eat our mackerel like a fleshy corn-on-the-cob, using fingers and teeth to tease off the flakes of flesh. All the kit I ever take is one big sharp knife – and a pair of tongs when I remember. If we bother to take plates, which doesn't happen often, we'll pack plastic ones that can be washed in the sea or recycled paper ones that can be burned. However, most of the time I just serve grilled fish on flat beach stones. Hunting for their own stone plate is a great game for the children too.

One other bit of kit I often take with me when I'm barbecuing on the beach is a pair of thick leather gardening gloves. They are a godsend when things are suddenly getting too hot and you need to move searing hot metal around in a hurry.

Lighting your fire

Despite my dim view of disposables and briquettes, I'm not a fanatical purist: I do often use firelighters to get a barbecue going (my justification is that these are all burnt away and obliterated by the time any food gets near the fire). Thin, dry twigs or scraps of cardboard make good kindling too. If you're using these, they should go into the bed of the barbecue first.

Lay your charcoal out in a thick layer in the barbecue – one golden rule is to always use more charcoal than you think is needed. If using firelighters, distribute a few bits of them between the coals. Now light your kindling, cardboard or firelighters, pile more charcoal on top, stand back and let things start to catch. As soon as the charcoal starts to burn in places, start piling up the coals over these hotspots, fuelling the flames. Don't be afraid to redistribute and rearrange the coals several times during this firing-up period, so that all the coals get a chance to start burning. Tending the fire is as much of a creative role as cooking the food. Once all the coals are burning well, knock them down again into an even layer. Now you've got to wait, wait, wait before you put your fish anywhere near the fire. Do not cook anything until all flame and smoke has died away and the coals are glowing and covered in grey ash.

Cooking your fish

The best fish to barbecue are oily ones because they're self-basting and won't dry out over the intense heat, as white fish can. My absolute favourite for the barbie is mackerel (see p.230), but I've also had wonderful feasts of barbecued garfish, herring and scad mackerel. I don't particularly like to barbecue white fish like pouting or pollack because the intense heat of charcoal doesn't do white fish flesh any favours; it just scorches it and makes it too dry.

If I've got pouting or pollack to cook on the beach, I'll take an old heavy-bottomed frying pan along and shallow-fry fillets or small, whole gutted fish. Alternatively, I'll parcel them up in foil or wet newspaper so they can steam-cook on the barbecue grill. Little dabs and flounders, with their relatively thick skin can work surprisingly well on a barbie, especially one that's cooling down, and where the fierce heat has gone from the coals. A slow-cooked whole dab or flounder, turned regularly and then picked apart with a sharp knife and eaten straight from the blade, feels like fresh fish at its freshest. And one of my favourite ways to cook fish on a barbecue is in a pot or bucket of fresh sea water (see below).

A barbecue can descend into disaster when great fish get ruined by being burned or stuck to the grill. It's nothing short of a tragedy when you've carefully landed, killed and chilled a fabulous fish to see it cremated on the spars of your barbie, inedible to man or beast. So, a crucial investment in my view is a good-quality 'sandwich'-style grill basket – one you can fit a few fat mackerel in and still be able to close properly. It needs to have an inch or two of depth on each side, and the bars need to be made of good-quality steel (preferably stainless) and be strong. The puny wire ones will rust, buckle, break and slice through your dearly beloved fish.

The best grill baskets I've found came from Susmans, a South African import company I found online. South Africans seem to know a lot about eating outdoors and make seriously heavy-duty kit. I'd spend more on a decent grill basket (that will last for years) than I would on the barbecue itself, which really is just a receptacle for hot coals.

You don't have to buy a grill basket: you can just cook on the flat grill that fits on top of your barbecue, of course. However, I find I can never get a fire-threatened fish off quickly enough, without major risk to life, limb and mackerel. If you're going to cook whole fish directly on the barbecue grill, leave the heads on. And, when you gut the fish, try not to make the slice in the belly too long. A head-on fish with a mostly complete belly will hold together better on the flat grill, while the head gives you something to grab hold of when you turn them over.

Barbecuing using a bucket of sea water

One of the most delicious and natural ways to cook mackerel on the beach is to poach them in a bucket of sea water. Of course, you don't have to use a bucket; a pan or a stockpot will do perfectly well. And it doesn't hurt to use a vessel with a lid – it'll help the water heat up faster. If you don't have a lid, lay a chopping board or a sheet of tin over the top of the bucket as you bring it up to boiling point.

The way I normally cook mackerel by this method is to heat a gallon of sea water in a pot on top of my barbecue, making sure there's enough water in the pot to completely cover the fish. When it's about to start boiling, I take the pot off the heat, submerge the head-on, guts-out mackerel in the water and cover the pot to keep the heat in. You can throw bay leaves or fennel tops into the water before you submerge your fish, but I'm happy to just enjoy the simple, natural seasoning of the sea.

It will take only 10 minutes to poach a one-portion-sized mackerel, weighing ½ –¾lb, in the residual heat.

The texture of mackerel poached in sea water is firm and deliciously moist. I like to peel the skin off and then gnaw at the flesh, eating it flake by flake, chunk by chunk, straight off the bone.

Barbecued mackerel with bay

Barbecued mackerel with bay or fennel

The smoky flavour of a freshly grilled mackerel, cut with the aromatic punch of bay or fennel, is unbeatable. I would definitely advise using a grill basket, so that as soon as you think the fire is too hot, or the dripping juices are making it too smoky and everything is about to go pear-shaped, all you need do is lift the basket off entirely and set the fish aside while the fire dies down.

Serves 6
A little olive or rapeseed oil
6 whole mackerel, gutted but heads left on
Lots of bay leaves or fennel tops and/or lightly crushed fennel stalks
Salt and freshly ground black pepper
A couple of lemons (optional)

Prepare your barbecue (see pp.226–7).

Massage the fish all over with a little oil, then season them generously with salt and pepper inside and out. Scatter a layer of bay leaves or fennel in the base of your grill basket. Lay the mackerel on top. Tuck some more bay or fennel inside the fish cavities. Put some more bay or fennel over the top of them. Close the grill basket.

When the fire has died down and the coals are glowing and covered with a good layer of white-grey ash, put the basket of fish on the barbecue, low down and very close to the hot coals. This technique is very dramatic: you'll often get clouds of thick scented smoke and even crackling flames roaring up if the oil in the bay leaves ignites. But the fish doesn't come to any harm – in fact, quite the opposite. The herbs actually protect the fish from the intense heat of the grill and they create a scented steam – fresh fennel tops in particular – which penetrates and cooks the fish while keeping it moist. When you come to eat, you'll probably find bits of charred bay leaf or fennel stalk clinging to your mackerel flesh like lumps of shrapnel, but these only enhance the flavour and crunchy skin texture of the cooked fish.

Cook the mackerel for 4–5 minutes each side. Open the grill basket and check one fish to see if it is done, then serve straight away, with a squeeze of lemon juice if you happen to have some, and some good bread. A salad of some sort – maybe peppery green leaves, or sliced ripe tomatoes – is a great accompaniment.

If you don't have a grill basket, make sure the barbecue grill itself is good and hot, then lay the bay or fennel directly on to it when the coals are ready. Stuff more bay or fennel inside the fish, and lay them directly on top of the smoking herbs on the grill. Turn the fish after about 5 minutes and cook the other side. Remove the mackerel as soon as it's cooked to the bone and serve.

Baked fish

The foil parcel method

Nothing could be easier than cooking fish in a foil package. It's a wonderfully simple and very forgiving technique, yet the result is really quite elegant. All you're doing is sealing your fish – which could be a whole gutted specimen, or a couple of fillets, or even thick cutlets, cut from the fish at right angles to the spine – inside a little chamber with a bunch of aromatic flavourings. These create a fragrant steam in which the fish will cook. The parcel goes into the oven or on the fire, and in just 15–20 minutes you'll have beautifully cooked moist fish in a little pool of aromatic juices.

When cooking fish in this way, my favourite additions are lemon juice and lemon zest (loads of it), fresh garlic, bay leaves, fennel tops, sliced ginger, chives, black pepper, butter, lime juice and, most important of all, salt. I can never resist a hit of hot too, so I'll add some sliced fresh chilli, seeds and all, which never fails to deliver a little extra frisson.

The liquid might be a splash of cider, beer, wine, verjuice or apple juice. The more you add, the more of a poaching technique you'll achieve. Conversely, if you don't use any liquid – only add butter or oil – the cooking that takes place will be like a combination of frying and poaching, which is also very good. Don't be shy about experimenting with flavourings when you're doing your own foil-baked fish.

If you're cooking your parcels in the oven, one sheet of foil should be enough. Put it, shiny side down, on a sturdy baking sheet, give it a lick of butter, add the fish, then draw up the foil to fashion a 'pot' around it. Pasty-shaped packages work well. Into your foil-fashioned pot, put your herbs or spices, oils and liquids, then scrunch the foil closed at the top. The parcel should be well sealed but baggy: there should be room inside for hot air and steam to circulate. Put it in an oven preheated to 190°C/Gas mark 5. Keep an eye on it, checking it every 5 minutes or so. A small fillet will be cooked in about 10 minutes, whereas a whole 1.5kg fish could take 35 minutes. Just keep opening the parcel and prodding until you see the flesh flake invitingly and peel away easily from the bone (if there is any).

If you want to cook a foil parcel of fish over, or in, a wood fire or a pile of glowing coals, you'll need a couple of layers of foil at least, but the technique and the timings are similar to oven-cooking.

Sometimes, if I'm doing parcels with small fillets, I'll stick some veg in too. Calabrese and purple-sprouting broccoli, celery and green beans all cook at the same rate as a white fish fillet and chucking them all in the same parcel saves on pans.

When it's time to serve, bring the foil parcel – or parcels – to the table and open them up so everyone can enjoy the cloud of delicious scent that's released. Share out the fish and don't forget to pour some of the sauce from the bottom of the foil parcel over each portion.

Baking without foil

This is what I think of as 'naked baking', without a foil parcel to protect the flesh and hold in juices. The fish I most like to bake naked are large whole plaice, whole headless mackerel, whole bass, whole pollack and slob trout.

I choose this technique for these fish because I want their flesh to be cooked in a harsher way – a way that forces out moisture more quickly from the flesh, crisps the skin and turns the ends of the fins crunchy and even singed. It's a more violent and dynamic way of attacking your fish with heat, which produces different textures and flavours from steaming, poaching or parcel-style 'wet' methods.

You can cook whole fish more or less naked, with perhaps just a splash of oil or butter, or maybe a rasher or two of streaky bacon to provide a little extra oil to lubricate the skin. However, baking also works well with cutlets or fat fillets, which can be smeared with oil and herbs to create a 'crust' as the exterior dries out in the intense heat.

To prepare a whole fish for baking, I'll leave the skin on but take the scales off – either when I'm still at sea or in the sink as soon as I arrive home with my catch. I dry the fish with a tea towel and then, using my hands, massage oil or butter all over its skin, fins and head. Fish heads and fins love to stick to baking trays. They will do their level best to stick, whether you oil them or not, but the more time you devote to putting oil on them, the easier it will be to part them from the pan when you finally take them from the oven. I then fill the bellies of my fish with bay leaves and a generous knob of butter.

The skin of the fish acts almost like a porous, natural foil parcel to hold the heat and the moisture inside. However, the skin can also be slashed open two or three times, which makes the skin retreat from the cut and the flesh start to gape underneath. This can look very dramatic and it provides a great opportunity to add a little extra seasoning of salt, pepper or lemon juice directly on to the grain of the flesh – which can then penetrate deep into the fish.

Slashing works especially well on flat fish like large plaice, but be a little careful when you put slashes in the sides of a round fish – don't cut too deep or do too many slashes. I've gone overboard in the past with Jack-the-Ripper-style slashes only to watch my beautiful whole fish fall apart in the oven as the skin retreats and shrivels, leaving the flesh to tumble out.

The prepared fish go on to a baking tray and into the oven, which I've preheated to around 200°C/Gas mark 6. The time taken depends a great deal on the size of the fish, and the position in the oven (see right), but, as a rough guide, a few fish cutlets can take as little as 12 minutes, while a big plaice might need to be in there for upwards of half an hour.

Positioning your fish in the oven

How aggressively a fish is baked is partly a result of where in the oven you choose to place it. Baking at the top of the oven, in the hottest zone, isn't really that much different from grilling. In my oven, if I bake a mackerel or a slob trout on a flat baking tray, with nothing more than a smear of butter and a sprinkle of salt and pepper, I'm able to cook it all the way through in 15 minutes, and just begin to crisp up the top layer of skin. It won't be quite as crisp as it would be if it was cooked under a grill, but it's enough to give the skin a roasted look and a sharp tangy flavour.

The middle and bottom rungs of the oven are where I'll put fish that's fairly thick and needs a longer, slower cooking time in order for the heat to penetrate the flesh right to the bone.

Sometimes when I'm baking a big fish, I'll move it around the oven – up or down, depending on whether I want to put more heat on to the surface of the fish or into the centre. With a big plaice, for example, I'll start it low in the oven for 10 minutes before moving it up to the top rung for a further intense skin-crinkling, flesh-roasting 10 minutes to finish it off.

I also do a bit of moving around with one of my favourite mackerel dishes, where the fish is baked on a bed of par-boiled chunky potatoes with onions, olive oil, whole garlic cloves and huge chunks of peel-on lemons. This I'll start in the bottom of the oven and progress upwards every 10 minutes, before giving it a final skin-crisping blast at the top. I often cook garfish in the same way.

If I think a fish is cooked in the middle but I want it to be crisper on the top then I'll migrate it upwards to where the heat is greatest. And the opposite is true if the topmost skin of the fish looks ready, but, from a quick prod with a fork, I can feel the flesh in the centre, near the spine, is still firm and clinging to the bone. If it's underdone in the centre it needs to be left for a few minutes in the bottom of the oven where the lower heat can penetrate deeply without overcooking the surface.

Baked cod or pollack with green beans and pesto

This simple little dish is a real winner. It's very easy to just knock it up for one person, and no more work to make it for two or more. Instead of beans, you could use tender stems of purple-sprouting broccoli or, in early summer, some slender spears of asparagus.

Serves 2

About 200g trimmed French beans
About 150ml hot fish stock
2 thick fillets of cod or pollack (about 250g each), skinned and boned
3 heaped tbsp pesto (homemade or good-quality bought)
Salt and freshly ground black pepper

Preheat the oven to 200°C/Gas mark 6. Scatter the green beans in an ovenproof casserole dish and pour the stock over them. Lay the fish fillets on top, then sprinkle on a little seasoning (remember that the pesto will be quite salty). Spread the pesto in a thick layer over the fish. Bake in the oven for 10–15 minutes, until the fish and beans are cooked, and the pesto has formed a delicious crust. Serve straight away, with new potatoes.

Steaming

Any kind of fish – white, oily, flat or cartilaginous (dogfish) – can be steamed quickly and easily. Any cut or portion will work too, from whole fish to cutlets to individual fillets. The joy of steaming is that it's gentle. Lightly steamed fish will retain its shape and size; it doesn't wrinkle, crisp, buckle, shrink or harden. It stays moist, flaky and, once steamed, it is extremely easy to deconstruct. Bones will just fall out of steamed fish and skin will peel off with minimum effort. Steaming is also very fast – it can take just a few minutes – and so easy to control. All you need to do, to check how your fish is doing, is lift the lid and give the fish a gentle prod with a fork – if the flesh is cooked it will easily break into flakes.

Steaming seems to me a very pure and honest way to cook fish, but also if I'm honest, a bit boring. Mostly I steam fish when I'm planning to do something else with it *after* it's been steamed – to make fish cakes perhaps, or add to a risotto just before serving. Or I might let it cool and serve it with salad, or possibly mix it with mayonnaise and make sandwiches.

I might occasionally steam a whole fish or a large fillet if I want to eat it cold. Slob trout is fabulous steamed then flaked off the bone, allowed to cool and served with lemon or garlic mayonnaise and steamed vegetables, or with salad and rice.

So steaming is a useful tool in the fish cook's armoury. Granted, simply steamed fish can be a bit bland, but I do love the texture, and a plain piece of steamed fish is a great backdrop to other ingredients. Sometimes I serve up plain steamed fish and vegetables drizzled with something punchy – a splash of warmed sesame oil, warmed olive oil, or a spicy chilli and rice vinegar sauce – to put a little edge to the flavour.

The two best fish-steaming tools are a fish kettle and a collapsible stainless-steel steaming basket (also called a 'petal' basket) which fits inside one of your saucepans or your wok. Put a little water into the base of the kettle or the pan and bring to the boil. Then put your fish on the fish kettle tray or into the steaming basket, add to the pan and cover tightly. Single fillets can be cooked in a matter of minutes. A large whole fish in a fish kettle might take 20 minutes.

Always make sure that the water you add to create your steam isn't deeper than the tray at the bottom of the fish kettle, or deeper than the feet on your petal steamer. You don't want the boiling water to actually touch the fish, only the steam that it delivers. It takes a remarkably small amount of water, in a pan with a good tight-fitting lid, to sufficiently steam even the firmest of fresh fish.

I rarely bother to flavour the water that I use to create the steam. Sometimes I might add a handful of fennel tops or a couple of bay leaves to make the steam aromatic, but I'll never do more than that because the fish is in the steam for such a short time so it's not worth going to too much trouble. Any additional seasoning is going to happen after the fish is taken out of the steam.

Steamed white fish and broccoli with soy, chilli and garlic

This is a very puritanical recipe that makes me feel very righteous. It's the type of meal I like to make best of all at lunchtime, just for my wife Helen, and myself, when all the children are at school. Personally I'm an addict of hot chilli and will always liven up what is quite an Amish-type meal with a Mexican-style kick.

Serves 2

- 2 fat fillets of white fish, such as pollack or pouting (about 250g each)
- A good handful of purple-sprouting broccoli, tough ends trimmed
- 3 tbsp soy sauce
- 3 tbsp mirin or rice wine
- 1 clove garlic, peeled and chopped
- 1 red chilli, chopped
- 1 tsp grated fresh root ginger
- A good pinch of sugar
- Toasted sesame oil, to finish

You'll need a collapsible steel steaming basket, or 'petal' basket, for this. Put a little water in the base of a large saucepan, deep frying pan or wok, into which the basket will fit snugly. Bring the water to the boil.

Put the fish fillets, skin side down, in the basket, trimming them to fit if necessary. Tuck the broccoli stems around the fish. Transfer the basket to the pan (making sure the water doesn't touch the fish). Cover tightly and steam for 5–7 minutes, until the fish is done.

Meanwhile, combine the soy sauce, mirin, garlic, chilli, ginger and sugar in a small pan with 3 tbsp water. Bring to a simmer and cook gently for 1 minute, then remove from the heat.

Serve the fish and broccoli on warmed plates and trickle some of the warm soy mixture over them. (You probably won't need it all, but it will keep well in the fridge for at least a week.) Finish with a splash of toasted sesame oil and serve with rice.

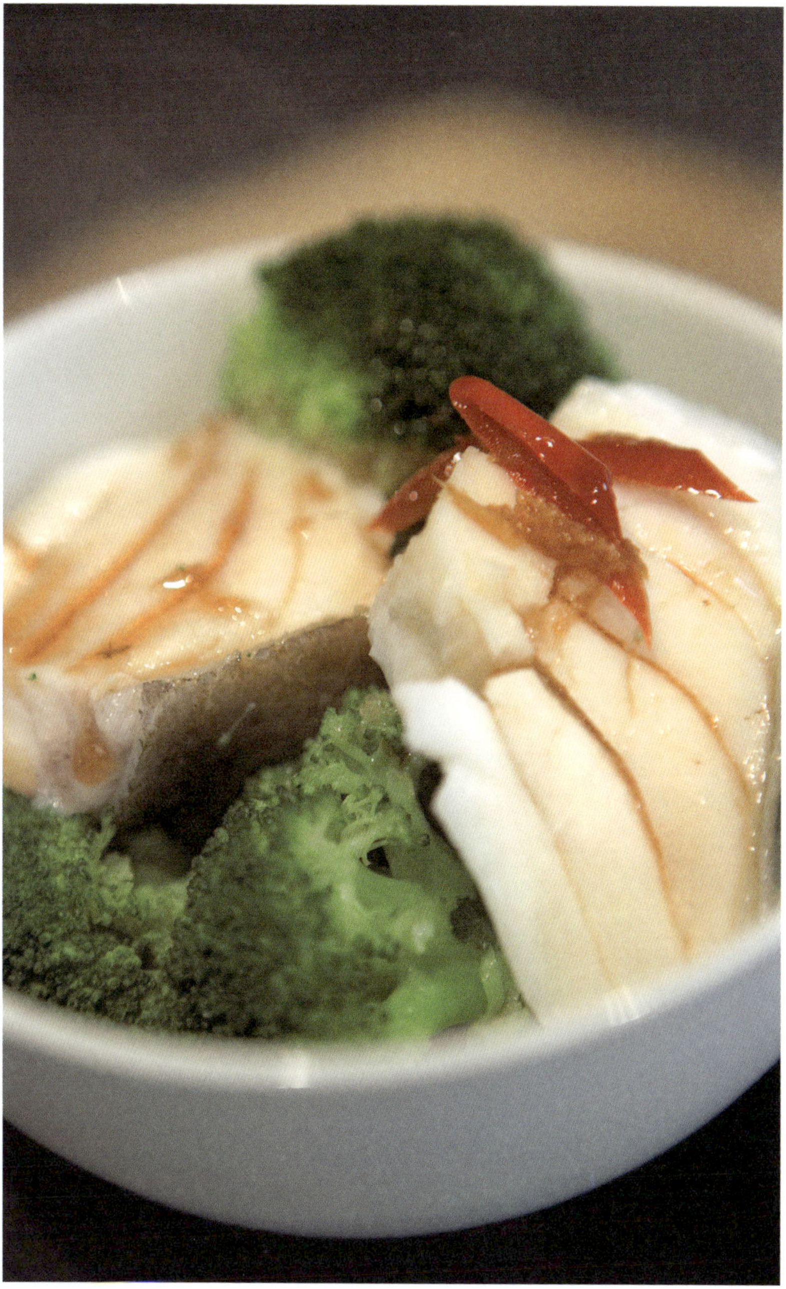

Deep-fried fish

I passionately enjoy deep-fried fish. I love to cook it. I love to eat it. And I love to see all my children's hungry, greasy-chinned mouths devouring my deep-fried fish.

The things I deep-fry most are:
- Fish fillets in 'chip shop' batter or tempura batter
- Fish fillets in homemade breadcrumbs
- Fish fillets in Japanese panko breadcrumbs
- Squid rings dusted in spicy flour
- Fish fillets dusted in spicy flour
- Whole small fish (head on, guts out) dusted in powdered spices

Some people are put off deep-frying because they think it requires special equipment and gallons of oil. But, to me, it's not a specialist technique: it's just a way of blitzing fish in a couple of inches of really hot oil – either sunflower or groundnut. I don't use more than 2 inches of oil – if the piece of fish isn't submerged, I can always turn it over halfway through cooking. And, because I don't use a great depth of oil, I can deep-fry in a flat-bottomed wok, or even a 12-inch thick-bottomed frying pan.

The key to success is heat. I always use my biggest, hottest gas ring and I never start cooking until my oil is searing hot. To be honest, I deep-fry at temperatures higher than are generally advised. Most sources will tell you that around 180°C – or when a cube of bread browns in 50–60 seconds – is ideal. I'm not going to argue with that as I'm well aware that overheated oil can spontaneously ignite. And if I'm cooking a large item, such as a chunky fillet encased in thick batter, I'll stick to around 180°C or a little lower. If the oil is too hot, the fish will burn on the outside before the heat has had a chance to penetrate to the centre. But if I'm fast-frying tiny little whole fish, or scraps of squid, or thin fillets, I cannot resist taking the oil over 180°C to ensure that irresistible, super-crispy effect. But please be safe: if your oil registers over 200°C on a cook's thermometer, or if it is smoking, turn off the heat.

Choosing a coating

My choice of coating is fairly random and to some extent based on what's in the cupboard), but there is a size factor. My homemade 'chip shop' batter is a substantial eggy affair, which works best on large fillets. Incidentally, the hot oil should crisp and seal the batter crust very quickly, so the fish inside isn't in contact with hot oil and never becomes greasy.

Tempura batter is much less substantial and I use it with any sized fillet of fish. All I do is mix half-and-half plain flour and cornflour with enough ice-cold sparkling water to make a thin, lumpy batter (the lumps are important – don't overmix it).

Breadcrumbs can go two ways. If you dip your fish in flour, then egg, then breadcrumbs, you can end up with a really hefty, but delicious coating to your fish. Or you can leave out the egg-dipping part of the process, as I do with Japanese panko-style breadcrumbs. Pressing the breadcrumbs straight on to the fish flesh gives a light, crispy, crunchy sheen of breadcrumbs, rather than a thick coating.

And then there's the simple light-dusting-of-well-seasoned-flour approach, which I often use with squid and small fish fillets. Sometimes I'll use cornflour to coat small fillets, or small whole fish like sprats or little whiting, really just to stop them sticking together in the pan. But this also gives them an irresistible crunchy golden sheen. Small fillets of dab or flounder will cook in the blink of an eye in a hot oil with no more than a dusting of seasoned flour to keep them decent. And then they can be slipped between the crusty embrace of a nice white bap with some salad leaves and eaten straight away.

I will occasionally deep-fry a whole head-on, guts-out fish such as a gurnard, whiting or small pollack – anything up to about 250g. I'll dust it first in spiced flour or even just in a blend of ground spices. Normally I'll opt for cumin, curry powder, chilli powder and fenugreek, but I have used only paprika (which looks wonderful) or cayenne pepper. A spicy deep-fried whole fish is tremendous fun to cook and also to eat. The idea is to get the outside as crisp as possible – even the fins and tail should be crisp and spicy and edible – while the flesh inside remains moist and tender. This requires a couple of inches of oil so hot that it practically crisps flesh on contact.

Timings

If your oil is hot and the fish is small, it will cook in next to no time. Little fishfinger-sized morsels will only need 1–2 minutes. A battered fat fillet will need 3–4 minutes, while a whole fish normally takes about 5 minutes to cook through.

My golden rules for successful deep-frying are:
- Let the oil get really hot before you start.
- Use tongs to put your fish pieces or fillets in the oil, and do it very carefully.
- Cook in small batches. Don't overload the pan or the fish bits will start to stick together and the temperature of the oil will drop.
- If you're using batter, always let the excess drip off a fillet before slipping it into the hot oil. Excess batter will break off and dirty your oil more quickly.
- Don't prod fish or turn it over too early. Leave until it's at least honey-coloured, preferably tea-coloured, then turn it. The second side will cook in half the time.
- When you remove fish from the hot oil, put each piece straight on to a couple of layers of kitchen paper. Don't stack the pieces of fish on top of one another, as this will make your batter soggy, which is a sin.
- Never use your frying oil more than twice. Just once is better.

Battered pollack

When I say 'pollack' here, I mean any decent-sized white fish fillet, so that could include gurnard, coley, mullet, cod, whiting and pouting. They'll all work. In fact, *any* fillet of fish will be delicious if you fry it in this batter. Arguably, you could dip your welly socks in this batter, deep-fry them and serve them with homemade tartare sauce and no one would complain!

Serves 4
200g plain flour
1 egg yolk
About 250ml whole milk
Sunflower or groundnut oil, for frying
4 fillets of pollack, skinned
Salt and freshly ground black pepper

To serve
Lemon wedges
Tartare sauce (see p.205)

Sift the flour into a deep bowl and season it well with salt and pepper. Whisk the egg yolk with about 100ml milk. Make a well in the centre of the flour and start adding in the egg and milk mixture, whisking well and gradually incorporating the dry flour from the sides. Once all the eggy liquid is in, start adding more milk – you'll probably need around an additional 150ml. Keep going, whisking all the time, until you have a smooth batter with a consistency a little thicker than double cream. Leave this to rest for 10 minutes.

Heat a couple of inches of oil in a deep-sided, heavy-bottomed saucepan (or use a deep-fat fryer) until it reaches 175–180°C (when a cube of bread dropped into the oil turns brown in less than a minute.

Pat the fish fillets with a tea towel or kitchen paper so they're nice and dry. Give the batter another quick whisk. Dip one fillet into the batter, hold it up and let it drip for a minute, then dip it a second time and let it drip again. Transfer to the hot oil. If your pan is big enough, repeat with a second fillet.

Cook for about 3 minutes, then turn the pieces of fish over in the hot oil, using tongs. Cook for another 1–2 minutes, or until the batter is a rich golden brown all over. Lift out and drain on kitchen paper. Repeat with the remaining fillets, then serve at once, with lemon wedges and tartare sauce.

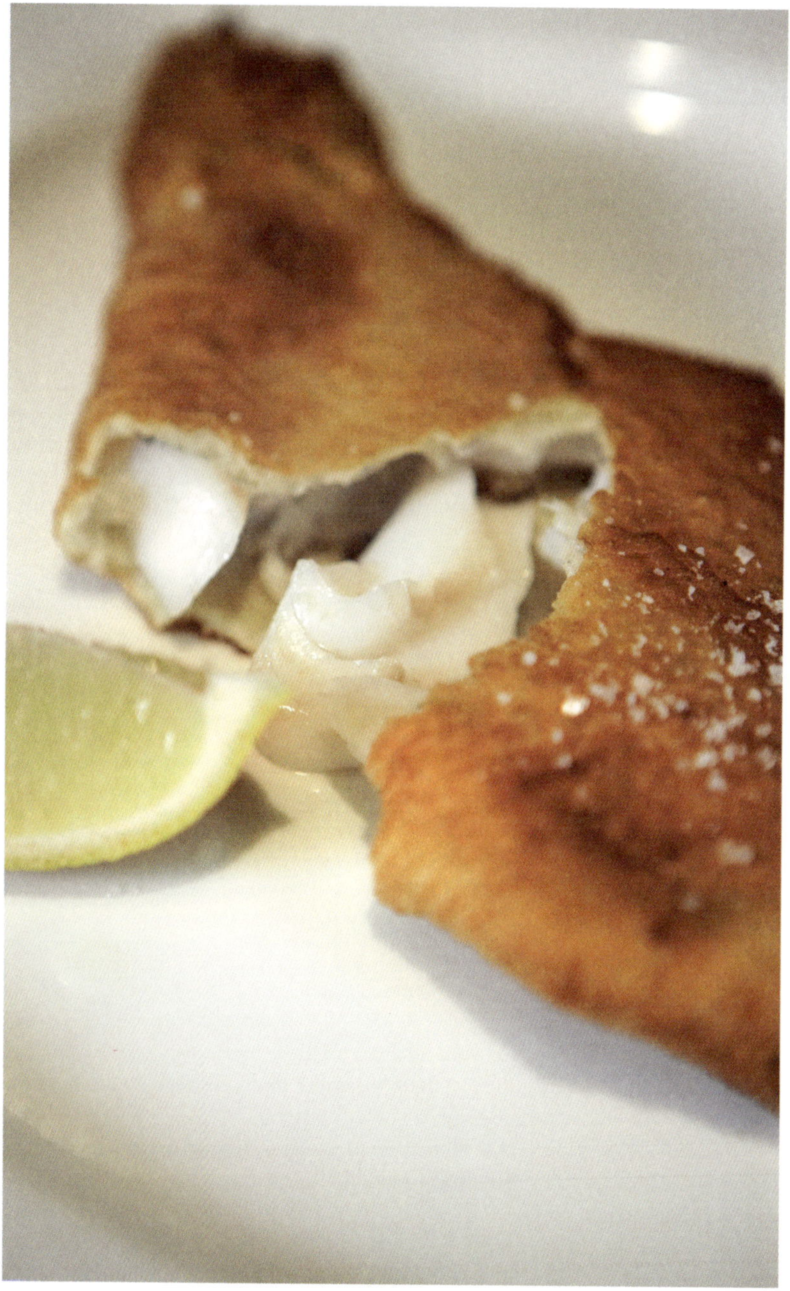

Pan-fried fish

I know 'pan-frying' is one of those terribly cheffy phrases that gets some people's backs up. 'What *else* would you fry it in – if not a pan?' retorts Gill at River Cottage. Fair enough, but I find the term useful. For me, it neatly describes the simple frying I like to do, day in day out, with all kinds of fish.

I could call it 'shallow-frying' but that would be a bit of a misnomer as it suggests the use of a fair amount of oil. What I'm talking about here is cooking fish in a frying pan with a mere lick of grease – a smear of lubrication between pan and fish to stop the flesh or skin sticking. A tablespoon of oil or butter will do it, or a bit of melted bacon fat, or the lovely salty fat from a couple of slices of chorizo sausage.

Fry-poaching

Pan-frying, at its most basic, is a very quick and simple way to produce a beautifully browned and slightly crisped fillet. But over the years I've modified the technique a little. For starters, I don't whack the heat up too high. I do not like to 'sear' fish, because in my opinion all fish flesh is too delicate to be seared. Searing, to me, means intense heat or, in the context of fish, 'spoiling by overcooking'. The only time I'll really crank up the heat when I'm pan-frying is when the fish is not at its best. Searing and crispy-crispy pan-frying is a good way to disguise fish that has slightly outstayed its welcome.

If the fish I'm frying is really fresh and in tip-top condition, then I'll treat it as gently as possible. In fact I'm more than happy to start my fish cooking in a warm rather than a hot pan, letting the temperature increase as I go. And just to cosset my fish even more, what I usually do is to fry my fish a little bit, then finish the cooking by poaching it. A whiting fillet, gently 'fry-poached' in a touch of good olive oil with fresh garlic and an obscenely generous squash of lemon, is far preferable to anything that's been 'seared' against super-hot metal.

This is how fry-poaching works: I'll start the cooking process with just a little oil in the pan to sizzle the surface of the fish, but as soon as it's sealed and partially cooked, I'll flip the fillets over and spoon a little liquid into the pan. That could be fish stock, lemon juice, verjuice or even cider or apple juice. The liquid simmers and steams, semi-poaching the fish and, at the same time, reducing down to a soupy gravy. The result is less crisp than straight frying, but more tender – and the intense little 'jus' that forms in the pan is a real bonus.

This fry-poaching technique works best with fillets – for me, usually fillets of mackerel, whiting, bream, small bass or small pollack. And, unless you cover the pan with a tight-fitting lid while you're doing the poaching bit, it only really works on fillets less than 1½ inches thick. Fry-poaching doesn't have the penetrating power needed to cook really thick fillets or whole unfilleted fish.

You can fry-poach fillets with their skin on or off. If I'm cooking fillets at the larger end of the scale, I'll usually skin them – it helps the steam from the poaching liquid to penetrate. I'll cook small fillets, like those from small mackerel, skin on. Mackerel skin is thin and fiddly to remove, plus it can also be delicious when cooked. I normally fry fillets flesh side down first, because I find that frying the skin first makes the flesh side bulge and curl as the skin shrinks. This can make the fillets slightly more delicate to turn. I'll cook them until they just begin to brown, then flip them over on to their skin sides and add my poaching liquid a few moments later. In another couple of minutes, they should be done.

If I've put the fish in skin side down by mistake (which I often do), I wait until the skin is browning nicely, then douse the flesh with lemon juice or stock before very gently rolling the fillets over and letting them bubble for a minute or two.

With this fry-poaching technique, I'm never in a hurry to take the cooked fish out of the pan. I use a heavy-bottomed frying pan and I like to let the contents settle and finish cooking very slowly in the residual heat. To be honest, if I'm just cooking a quick fish fillet lunch for myself, what I like to do most of all is to actually eat it straight out of the pan. That little pool of fish gravy never tastes better than when it's wiped out of the bottom of the pan with a chunk of good crusty bread!

Fry-poached fillets of bream, with garlic, lemon and herbs

This is one of the ways of cooking bream that I'll never tire of. I love the filleting, the cooking – with all the lemony herb smell – and the eating. All moist and sour and sweet and hot, with a little olive oily thing going on, this is my kind of heaven. In fact I'd die happy if fry-poached bream fillets were my last supper.

Serves 2

- 3 tbsp olive oil
- Small knob of butter
- 1 large black bream, descaled, filleted and pin-boned
- 1 garlic clove, peeled and chopped
- Juice of 1 small or ½ large lemon
- 1 tbsp mixed chopped 'soft' herbs, such as parsley, chervil, chives, basil and/or mint
- Salt and freshly ground black pepper

Heat 1 tbsp oil and the butter in a pan over a medium heat. When the butter is sizzling gently, season the bream fillets well and add them to the pan, flesh side down. Cook for about 2 minutes until starting to brown underneath. Scatter the garlic over and around the fish, then carefully flip the fillets over. Add the lemon juice and the remaining 2 tbsp oil. Increase the heat a little and cook for about 2 minutes more, until the fish is cooked through and the juices have reduced a little. Remove from the heat. Transfer the fillets to warmed plates. Scatter the chopped herbs in the pan and stir them into the juices, then spoon the herby juices over the fish and serve.

Grilled fish

Grilling is like upside-down barbecuing. You can achieve a similar crisp-skinned result, but in the comfort of your own kitchen and with the sort of temperature control that barbecuers can only dream of. You simply have to raise your grill pan a notch or two nearer the flame to increase the burn, or move it down to give your fish more gentle heat. And the easy-access nature of an overhead grill makes it easy to tweak your fish as it cooks – brush on a little extra olive oil, baste with a bubbling sauce, add an anchovy or two, or drench it with lemon juice.

For some fish, grilling is the best cooking method. Sprats, sardines and fish cutlets (cuts taken across the body of the fish at right angles) are particularly delicious grilled. It's also probably the best way to cook small flat fish like dabs and flounder, which need little more than a smear of butter or a lick of olive oil and a generous shake of salt and pepper to make them sing.

You can, of course, simply cook your fish directly on the wire grill rack, bare flesh against bare metal, if you're happy for moisture and oil to drip out of your fish. If you grill a cutlet or a whole sardine on a rack, flipping it over when the top side has browned, then cooking the underside the same way, you'll end up with a crispy, dry-cooked fish with a relatively dense flesh texture. If it's a very oily fish, like a sardine, sprat, herring or mackerel, the hot oil bubbles and burns on the surface as it escapes, making the skin crisp, sweet and chewy.

Alternatively, you could put the same piece of fish in an open parcel of foil, either on the rack or in your grill pan, or simply lay it directly in the grill pan without any foil. Cooked in this way, cupped or sealed from below, it'll be much more moist and more 'steamed' in texture.

For another kind of dish, try grilling some fillets of white fish directly in the pan, or in a foil 'bucket', with a creamy mustard or dill sauce spooned over them. The sauce will ploop-ploop around the fish, steaming and poaching the underside of the fillet. Meanwhile, any sauce on top of the fish will begin to brown and crisp, providing a contrasting crunchy top layer.

I like to add flavouring ingredients to fish when I'm grilling, like streaky bacon or chorizo. Whenever I can, I'll grill something like a fillet of whiting or pollack sprinkled with little lardons of chopped streaky bacon (smoked if possible). The bacon exudes its delicious salty fat, which bastes the white fish flesh and stops it from getting too dry. Its saltiness helps season the fish too, and the crispy bacon crunch is a fabulous complement to the moist fish flakes underneath.

If you have an overhead grill, do make the most of it, because grilling fish – from small whole pollack and trout to segments of garfish mixed with chorizo – is a great way to cook it. And don't miss out on flame-roasting fat sardines, herrings or sprats until their silver paper-like skin bubbles, crisps and browns – a real treat.

Grilled flounder (or dab or plaice) with lemon

Never underestimate the pleasure of eating a freshly grilled, freshly caught flattie. Normally I butter the fish thoroughly and whack it straight on to the tray for the fish-to-metal contact. This gives an almost caramelised crispy finish to the white-skinned underside. But, you can, if you fancy, put some thick wedges of lemon under the fish; this helps stop it sticking and adds a tang of lemon steam to assist the cooking. It also gives you hot wedges to squeeze over the fish as you eat it.

Sometimes, I'll remove the head and stomach cavity with one 45° angled cut across the neck before I start cooking. This reveals a perfect cross-section of the flattie, making it easy to tell when it's perfectly cooked through to the bone.

Serves 1
1 dab, flounder or smallish plaice
A big knob of salted butter, slightly softened
1 lemon, cut into wedges
Salt and freshly ground black pepper

Preheat the grill as high as it will go. Meanwhile, massage your whole fish with the butter, using your hands. Really work the butter into every inch of skin, like you were putting sun screen on a toddler. Work that butter right up to the tips of the fins – you don't want them sticking to your grill pan. Season the fish generously with salt and pepper.

Now lay your fish, dark side up, white side down, on the floor of the grill pan or a flat grill tray and grill for no more than 5 minutes, without turning. The thinner underside will 'fry' sufficiently from its contact with the grill tray. Let that salt-and-peppery top skin boil and bubble, erupting into little geyser puffs of steam. The crispy, chewy skin is a perfect contrast to the soft moist flesh within, which when it's all doused in a squirt of searing lemon juice will take your tastebuds to a sacred heavenly place.

Serve each whole fish still spitting and sizzling from the grill. Pour over any butter and fish juices from the grill pan and accompany the fish with grilled or fresh lemon wedges, new potatoes, rice or couscous and steamed lemony greens.

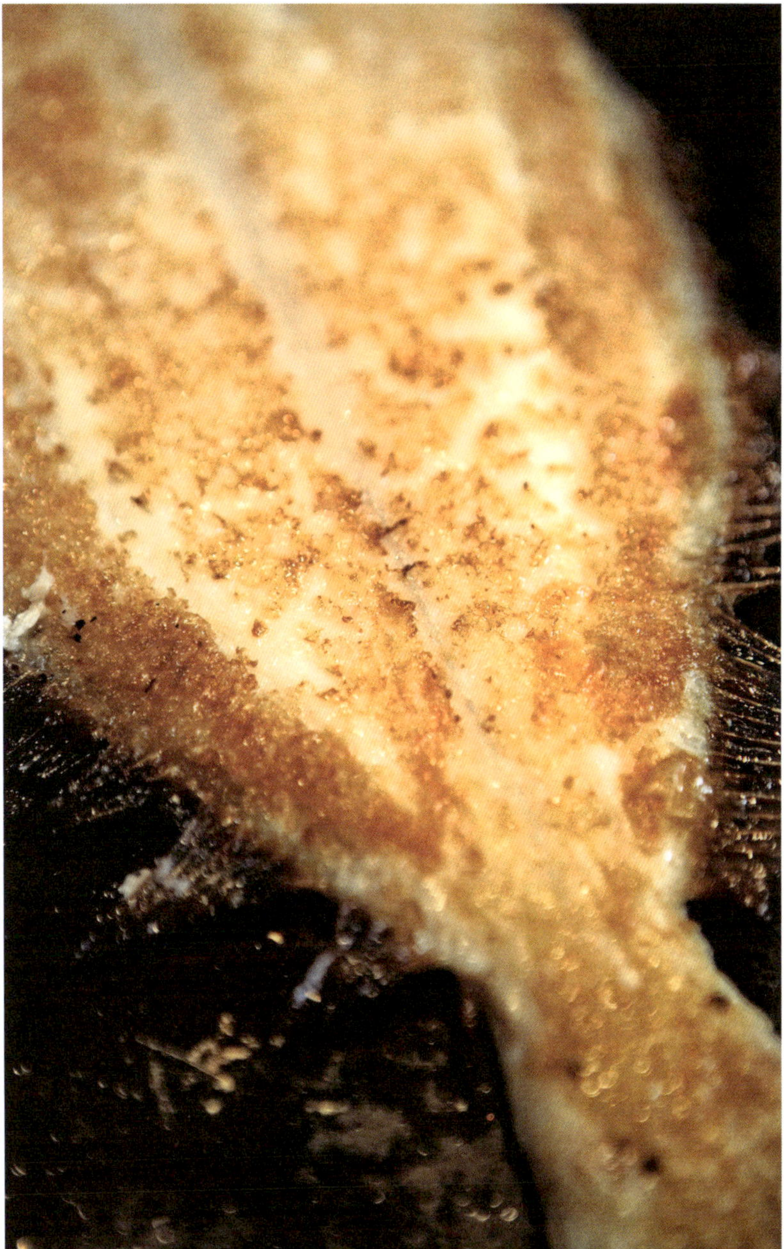

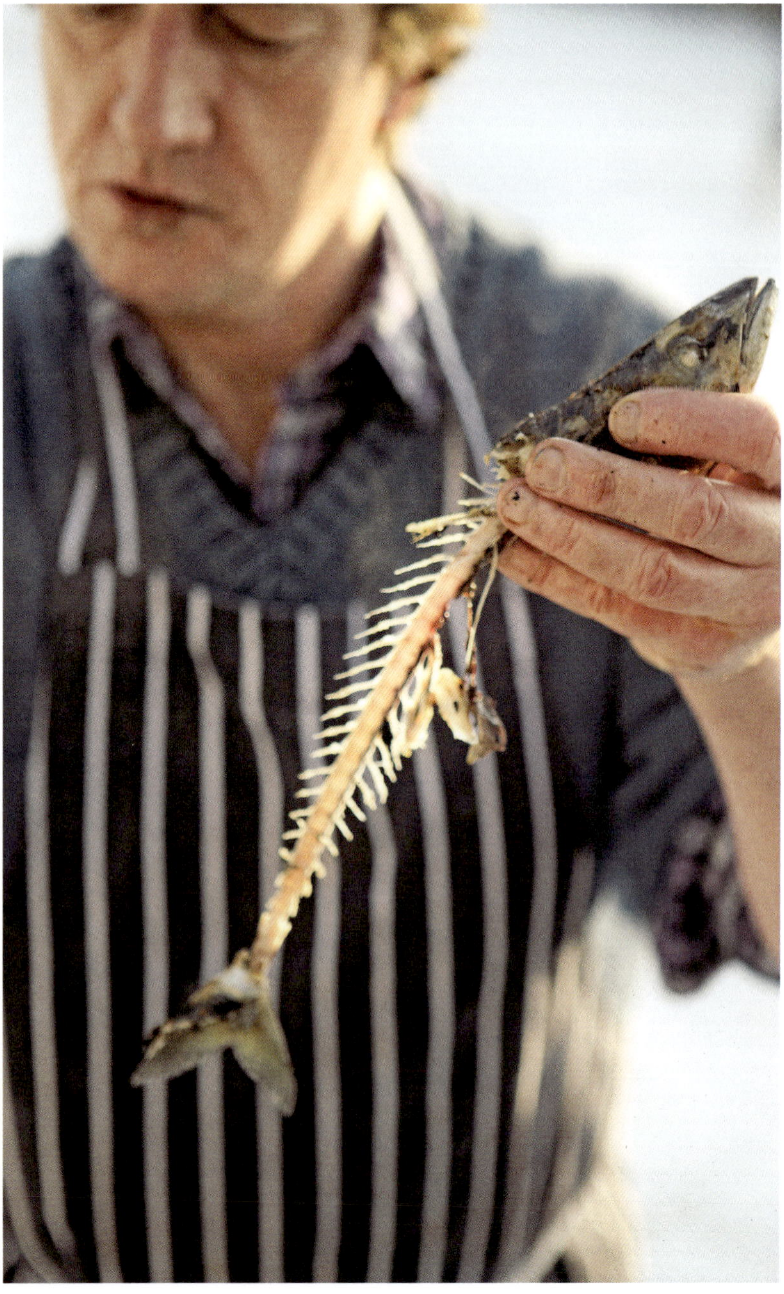

Directory

World Sea Fishing
www.worldseafishing.com
An amazing one-stop site run by good friend and consummate sea angler Mike Thrussell. Everything from a beginners' guide to area-by-area, up-to-the-minute catch reports, angling features, online tackle shop, tips, knots, rigs, boat recommendations and more.

Get Hooked
www.gethooked.co.uk
West Country-biased guide to fishing spots and accommodation.

General weather forecasts:
Inshore Met Office
www.metoffice.gov.uk/weather/marine/inshore_forecast.html

BBC Weather
www.news.bbc.co.uk/weather/forecast

XC Weather
www.xcweather.co.uk

Met Office Shipping Forecast
www.metoffice.gov.uk/weather/marine/shipping_forecast.html

Wind forecasts:
Windfinder.com
www.windfinder.com/forecasts/wind_british_isles_akt.htm

Windguru
www.windguru.cz/int/best.php
Designed for windsurfers, excellent.

Tidal forecasts:
Admiralty Easy Tide
easytide.ukho.gov.uk/EasyTide/EasyTide/SelectPort.aspx

BBC
www.bbc.co.uk/weather/coast/tides

Proudman Oceanographic Laboratory
www.pol.ac.uk/ntslf/tidalp.html

Angling bodies:
Angling Trust
www.anglingtrust.net
Represents all game, coarse and sea anglers and angling in England. Campaigns on environmental and angling issues, including pollution and commercial overfishing at sea.

Angling boats:
The Deep Sea Directory
www.deepsea.co.uk
UK directory for angling and diving boats, run by top skipper and friend Chris Caines. Forums, catch updates, accommodation and recommended charter boats all around the country.

West Bay Fishing Trips
www.westbayfishingtrips.co.uk
Local site for me. My favourite local skipper is Matt Toms 07967 944781.

Guides:
Guided Fishing
www.guidedfishing.co.uk
A directory of fishing guides; details of affordable fishing guides for both sea and freshwater angling around the UK.

Fly-casting instruction:
AAPGAI
www.aapgai.co.uk
Association of Advanced Professional Game Angling Instructors.

Knots:
Animated Knots by Grog
www.animatedknots.com
Great guide to tying knots. Watch different knots being tied and stop and start at will. Practically knot porn!

Fisheries conservation bodies:
Marine Stewardship Council
www.msc.org
An independent charity promoting the certification of sustainable species around the world. Its blue fish tick labels appear on fish products from areas the MSC has certified as well managed and sustainably fished.

Fishonline
www.fishonline.org
Clear up-to-date information about the sustainability of fish and shellfish, run by the Marine Conservation Society.

Marine Conservation Society
www.mcsuk.org
A UK charity dedicated to the conservation of our seas and seashores.

The Association of Sea Fisheries Committees
www.asfc.org.uk
Covers all sea fisheries committees by area and also quotes local minimum fish landing sizes, etc.

Useful Reference Books

The River Cottage Fish Book
by Hugh Fearnley-Whittingstall and Nick Fisher
(Bloomsbury 2007)

The River Cottage Edible Seashore Handbook
by John Wright
(Bloomsbury 2009)

The New Encyclopedia of Fishing
by John Bailey
(Dorling Kindersley 2002)

North Atlantic Seafood
by Alan Davidson
(Macmillan 1979)

The End of the Line
by Charles Clover
(Ebury Press 2004)

The Guinness Guide to Saltwater Angling
by Brian Harris
(Guinness World Records Ltd 1977)

The Sea Angler Afloat and Ashore
by Desmond Brennan
(A&C Black Publishers Ltd 1985)

The Field Guide to the Marine Fishes of Wales and Adjacent Waters
by Paul Kay and Dr Frances Dipper
(Marine Wildlife 2009)

Fish
by Michael Pritchard
(Collins Gem 2004)

Acknowledgements

The construction of a book about fish catching and fish cooking requires an unholy combination of skills and kindness from a bizarre collection of people.

On the fishing front: Mike Thrussell and his son Mike Thrussell Jnr. have been endlessly generous with their time, extensive knowledge, patience, contacts and photographs. Without Mike senior's help, I would have torn my hair out in clumps. Chris Caines, Matt Toms, Richard English and Pat Carlin are all excellent Dorset charter skippers who have helped me time and time again, over the years, with their superlative fishing skills. They've also let me raid their tackle boxes and photo albums mercilessly for this book too.

On the photography stuff: Good friend and talented angler Paul Quagliana has accompanied me on countless fishing trips. He takes great action angling pictures and yet still manages to catch more fish than me, or anyone else. Gavin Kingcome's cookery photographs make me feel hungry, and I'm in debt to anglers such as Dr Richard Roberts who have kindly let me use their own hard-won fish portraits. Thanks to Toby Atkins for his top-drawer illustrations too. Also to Xa Shaw-Stewart who did great sleuth tracking down photos of odd fish.

On the cookery end of things: I can't thank Gill Meller and his crew (Emma and Richard) at River Cottage HQ enough, for letting me run amok in their kitchen. And respect is due to Jess Upton who arranged for fish, photographer and me to all be in the same place at the same time. While Nikki Duffy deserves a big shout for turning my cooking style into something resembling a recipe.

On the book production business: Natalie Hunt should be canonised for her saintly patience and unerring professionalism in collating and editing the many complicated elements of this book. Meanwhile her boss, Richard Atkinson, kept a firm hand on the tiller, while Janet Illsley got down and dirty with the editing. Will Webb then skilfully made it all look pretty once it was hung out to dry. Old friend and work colleague Helen Stiles inspired me to get on with writing the book, while my wife, Helen, provided, as always, unflinching enthusiasm, much needed encouragement, multi-fingered typing skills and endless delicious food to bolster the process. Thanks, also, to my book agent Antony Topping.

And eternal gratitude to my children Rory, Rex, Patrick and Kitty for eating all my fish meals and putting up with my various fish obsessions. And lastly, I must thank Hugh for making the whole thing possible and still being the most enthusiastic and generous angler I know.

Index

Page numbers in *italic* refer to the illustrations

Aberdeen hooks *122*, 123
accompaniments 204–5
artificial lures 12, 132–44
assembling rigs 162–7
autumn, seasonal fishing 17

bait 148–59
  bait elastic 131
  booms 127–8
  bread 151, 159
  floats 123
  ground bait 12
  hook bait 12
  ledgered bait 164
  limpets 150, 151, 157
  lugworms 150, 151, 154, *154*
  mackerel 158, *158*
  mussels 150, 151, 158
  peeler crabs *150*, 151, 159, *159*
  ragworms 150, 151, 155, *155*
  sand eels 150, 151, *156*, 157
  squid *152*, 153
'bait' fish, tides and 23
baked fish 203, 231–4
ballan wrasse 105, *105*
barbecued fish 203, 226–30
bass *see* sea bass
batter, tempura 238
battered pollack 240, *241*
beach fishing
  bait 150
  casting 172
  feathering 136–7
  winds 19
beach mark 13
beachcaster rods 117, 136
beaches
  rocky beaches 34
  sandy beaches 27, 28–9
  shingle beaches 32, *33*
beads 129, *129*
black bream *see* bream, black
blanks, rods 114
bleeding fish 12, 178–9, *179*
blenny 106, *106*
boat fishing
  bait 150
  feathering 135–6
  rubber fish lures 143–4
  seasickness 29
  spinners and wedges 140
  tackle 28
  trolling 142
  where to go 26–8
  winds 19
boat reels 116, 119
boat rig 163
boat rods 114–16, *115*
bombs 125, *125*
booms 127–8, *128*
boshers 146
bottom-fishing 12
bottom ledgered paternoster rig 163
braid knot 171, *171*
braid line 121
bread 151, 159
bread flake method, catching grey mullet 101–2
breadcrumb coatings, fried fish 239
bream, black 72–5, *73*, *75*
  bait and lure techniques 133, 151
  cooking techniques 203
  fry-poached fillets of bream 244, *244*
  locations 27, 44, *45*
  season 17
bream rig 162, 163
broccoli, steamed white fish and 236, *237*
bubble floats 124
bull huss 107, 108, *108*
bullets 125, *125*
'bumping' a fish 174

carp rods 116–17, 137
cartilaginous fish 107
casting 12, 172–4, *172–3*
casting shock leader knot 170–1, *171*
catch
  playing a fish 174
  releasing 176–7
  striking 174
ceviche 203, 212–13, 214, *215*
charter boats 26–8
chickpeas
  gurnard with tomato and fennel 224, *225*
chilli dipping sauce 205
chilling fish 179
citrus juice
  ceviche 212–13, 214, *215*
clip swivels 126–7, *126*
coatings, fried fish 239
cod 59–61, *60*
  bait and lure techniques 133, 151
  baked cod with green beans and pesto 234, *234*
  cooking techniques 203
  locations 27, 44, *45*
  season 17
conger eel 109, *109*
cooking fish 200–47

cool boxes 147, 179
cork handles, rods 114
corkwing wrasse 105, *105*
crab lines 118
crabs
    peeler crabs 150, 151, 159, *159*
    tides and 23
cuckoo wrasse 105, *105*

dab 83–5
    bait and lure techniques 133, 151
    cooking techniques 203
    grilled dab with lemon 246, *247*
    locations 27, 44, *45*
    season 17
deep-fried fish 203, 238–40
deep sea fishing 114
demersal fish 12
Dexter wedge 138, *139*
dill hollandaise 205
diving plugs 141
dogfish 50–2, *51*, *52*
    bait and lure techniques 133, 150, 151
    cooking techniques 203
    locations 27, 44, *45*
    season 17
    skinning 194–6, *195*, *197*
drop nets 146–7, *147*

eels
    conger eels 109, *109*
    sand eels 150, 151, *156*, 157
eggs (fish) 16, 107
elastic, bait 131
elastic band method, stop knot 170
equipment
    cooking 206–8, 226–7
    see also tackle
escabeche 213, 216, *217*
estuaries 27, 36–7

feathers 12, 134–7, *134*
fennel, gurnard with tomato and 224, *225*
filleting fish 188–92, *189*, *191*
fires, lighting 227
fish soup 222–3, *222*
fish stock 203, 218–20, *219*
fishing
    bait 148–59
    fishing skills 160–79
    inedible fish 104–6
    off-limits fish 107–9
    tackle and kit 110–47
    when to go 14–23
    where fish dwell 44, *45*
    where to go 24–41

fixed-spool reels 119
flat fish
    filleting 190–2, *191*
    gutting 186, *186*
float rig 165, *165*
float-fishing 12
    bread flake method 101–2
    floats 123–4, *124*
    maggot method 103
floating plugs 141
flounder 83–5, *84*
    bait and lure techniques 133, 151
    cooking techniques 203
    grilled flounder with lemon 246, *247*
    locations 27, 44, *45*
    season 17
fluorocarbon line 130
fly reels 120
fly rods 117
foil parcels, baking in 203, 231
freshwater hooks 123
fried fish 203, 238–44
fry-poaching 242–3

garfish 66–8, *67*
    bait and lure techniques 133, 151
    cooking techniques 203
    locations 27, 44, *45*
    season 17
garlic mayonnaise 204
gills, removing 187, *187*
gravity, tides 20–2
green beans, baked cod or pollack with pesto and 234, *234*
grey mullet *see* mullet, grey
grilled fish 203, 227–8, 245–6
ground bait 12
gurnard, red 69–71, *70*
    bait and lure techniques 133, 151
    cooking techniques 203
    gurnard with tomato and fennel 224, *225*
    locations 27, 44, *45*
    season 17
gutting fish 179, 183–6, *185*, *186*

half-blood knot 168, *168*
handles, rods 114
handlines 12, 118, *118*
handling fish 176
harbours 27, 40–1
herbs 204
herring 89–91, *91*
    bait and lure techniques 133, 151
    cooking techniques 203
    locations 27, 44, *45*
    season 17

hollandaise, dill 205
hook bait 12
hook links 130
hooks 122–3, *122*
horse mackerel 86–8, *87*
  bait and lure techniques 133, 151
  cooking techniques 203
  locations 27, 44, *45*
  season 17
horseradish sauce 205
hounds 107
huss 107, *108*

ice, cool boxes 147, 179
inedible fish 104–6
insulation winders 145

jelly worms 144, *144*
jigs, squid 94, *95*

killing fish 177–8
kit *see* tackle
knives 145, 183
knots 168–71
  braid knot 171, *171*
  casting shock leader knot 170–1, *171*
  half-blood knot 168, *168*
  stop knot 169–70, *170*
  tucked half-blood knot 169, *169*

laws
  fishing seasons 16
  harbour fishing 41
lead weights *124–5*, 125
ledgering 12
  bait 81–2, 102, 164
  rigs 13, 129, 130
legal seasons 16
limpets, as bait 150, 151, 157
lines 121
  casting 172–4, *172–3*
  handlines 12, 118, *118*
  hook links 130
  knots 168–71
  shock leaders 131
  swivels 126–7, *126*
  zip sliders 129–30, *130*
lugworms 150, 151, 154, *154*
lures, artificial 12, 132–44
  feathers 134–7, *134*
  plugs 141–2, *142*
  rubber fish 143–4, *144*
  rubber worms 144, *144*
  spinners and wedges 138–40, *139*
  Toby spoons 140–1, *141*
  trolling 142

mackerel *46*, 47–9, *48*
  as bait 150, 151, 158, *158*
  bait and lure techniques 133, 151
  barbecued mackerel with bay or fennel *229*, 230
  cooking techniques 203
  killing 178
  lightly pickled mackerel 210, *211*
  locations 27, 44, *45*
  mackerel trip boats 26–8, 116
  season 17
  see also horse mackerel
mackerel feathers 134–6, *134*, 172
maggots, catching grey mullet 103
marinated fish 212–16
marks 13
mayonnaise 204
'Mepps' spinner 138, *139*
minerals 16
monofilament line 121
  stop knot 170, *170*
moon, tides 20–2
mullet, grey 100–3, *101*
  bait and lure techniques 133, 150, 151
  cooking techniques 203
  locations 27, 44, *45*
  season 17
multiplier reels 116, 119–20, *120*
mussels, as bait 150, 151, 158

neap tides 20–2
nets, drop 146–7, *147*

oil, deep-fried fish 238, *239*
overfishing 107

pan-fried fish 203, 242–4
paternoster rig 127, 128, 163, *163*
peeler crabs 150, 151, 159, *159*
pelagic fish 13
pennel rig 167, *167*
pesto, baked cod or pollack with green beans and 234, *234*
pier rig 162, 163
piers 27, 34–6, *35*
plaice *76*, 77–8
  bait and lure techniques 133, 151
  cooking techniques 203
  grilled plaice with lemon 246, *247*
  locations 27, 44, *45*
  season 17
plankton 23
playing a fish 174
pliers 145–6
  skinning dogfish 194–6, *195*
plugs *132*, 141–2, *142*

poaching fish 228
  fry-poaching 242–3
pollack 56–8, *57*
  bait and lure techniques 133, 151
  baked pollack with green beans and pesto 234, *234*
  battered pollack 240, *241*
  cooking techniques 203
  locations 27, 44, *45*
  season 17
poor cod 106, *106*, 176
popper plugs *132*
pouting 53–5, *53*, *54*
  bait and lure techniques 133, 151
  cooking techniques 203
  locations 27, 44, *45*
  season 17
Powergum stop knot 170, *170*
preparing fish 180–99
priest, killing fish 13, 146, 177

ragworms 150, 151, 155, *155*
rain 18
raw fish 206–10
rays 107, 109, *109*
red gurnard *see* gurnard, red
reef fishing 28, 114, 116
reels 119–20
  boat reels 116
  fly reels 120
  maintenance 119
  multiplier reels 116, 119–20, *120*
  spinning reels 119, *120*
releasing catch 176–7
retrieving 13
rice
  simple fish risotto 221
  sushi *207*, 209–10
rigs 13, 162–7
  assembling 162–7
  booms 127
  float rig 165, *165*
  paternoster rig 163, *163*
  pennel rig 167, *167*
  running ledger rig 164
  shop-bought rigs 162
  spinner/wedge/spoon rig 166, *166*
risotto 221
rock fishing 19, 27, 38–9
rock mark 13
rockling 176
rocky beaches 34
rods 113–17
  beach rods 137
  beachcaster rods 117, 136
  boat rods 114–16, *115*
  carp rods 116–17

fly rods 117
spinning rods 113–14, 116, 137
round fish
  filleting 188–90, *189*
  gutting 184, *185*
rubber fish lures 143–4, *144*
rubber handles, rods 114
rubber worms 144, *144*
running ledger rig 164, *164*
  beads 129
  zip sliders 130

salmon, legal season 16
salsa verde 205
sand eels 150, 151, *156*, 157
sandy beaches 27, 28–9
sashimi 203, 206–8, 210
sauces 205
scad *see* horse mackerel
scaling a fish 183
scissors 145
sea bass 79–82, *80*
  bait and lure techniques 133, 151
  cooking techniques 203
  locations 27, 44, *45*
  season 17
seasickness 29
sea trout 97–8
  legal season 16
sea water, poaching fish in 228
seasonal fishing 16–17
seasonings 204
seaweed, catching grey mullet 103
self-cocking waggler floats 124
shanny 106, *106*
sharks 107–8
shingle beaches 32, *33*
shock leader knot 170–1, *171*
shock leaders 131
shore fishing
  bait 150
  beachcaster rods 117
  rubber fish lures 143
  spinners and wedges 138–40
  where to go 30–41
shot, split *124*, 125
skates 109, *109*
skinning fish 192–6, *193*, *195*, *197*
slob trout 97–9, *98*
  bait and lure techniques 133, 151
  cooking techniques 203
  locations 27
  season 17
smoothhound 107, 108, *108*
snoods 13, 163
soup, fish 222–3, *222*

INDEX   255

soy and garlic dipping sauce 205
spawning 16, 107
spinning 13
   for grey mullet 102
   reels 119, *120*
   rig 166, *166*
   for sea bass 81
   spinners 138–40, *139*
spinning rods 113–14, 116
   casting 172, 173–4
   feathering 137
split shot *124*, 125
spoon rig 166, *166*
spoons 140–1, *141*
spring, seasonal fishing 17
spring tides 20–2
squid *92*, 93–6
   as bait 150, 151, *152*, 153
   bait and lure techniques 133, 151
   cooking techniques 203
   locations 27, 44, *45*
   preparation 198, *199*
   season 17
squid jigs 94, *95*
starry smoothhound 107, 108, *108*
steamed fish 203, 235–6
stock 203, 218–20, *219*
stop knot 169–70, *170*
striking 13, 174
summer, seasonal fishing 17
sun
   and tides 20, 22
   when to go fishing 18
surf ledgering, for sea bass 81–2
surface popper plugs *132*
sushi 203, *207*, 209–10
swivels 126–7, *126*

tackle 13, 110–47
   artificial lures 132–44
   bait elastic 131
   beads 129, *129*
   boat fishing 28
   booms 127–8, *128*
   estuary fishing 36
   feathers 134–7, *134*
   floats 123–4, *124*
   handlines 118, *118*
   harbour fishing 41
   hook links 130
   hooks 122–3, *122*
   lines 121
   pier fishing 34
   plugs 141–2, *142*
   reels 119–20
   rock fishing 39
   rods 113–17
   rubber fish lures 143–4, *144*
   rubber worms 144, *144*
   sandy beach fishing 31
   shingle beach fishing 32, *33*
   shock leaders 131
   spinners 138–40, *139*
   swivels 126–7, *126*
   terminal tackle 13, 122–44
   Toby spoons 140–1, *141*
   useful kit 145–7
   wedges 138–40, *139*
   weights *124–5*, 125
   zip sliders 129–30, *130*
tackle shops 30
tartare sauce 205
tempura batter 238
terminal tackle 13, 122–44
thornback ray 109
tides 19–23
   pier fishing 34–6
   sandy beaches 31
Toby spoons 140–1, *141*
tomato, gurnard with fennel and 224, *225*
tompot blenny 106, *106*
tope 107, 108, *108*
trolling 13, 142
trout *see* sea trout; slob trout
tucked half-blood knot 169, *169*

undersize fish 176

waggler floats 123, 124
weather 18–19
weaver fish 44, 106, *106*
websites 30
wedge rig 166, *166*
wedges 138–40, *139*
weights *124–5*, 125
whiting *62*, 63–5, *64*
   bait and lure techniques 133, 151
   cooking techniques 203
   locations 27, 44, *45*
   season 17
winders, insulation 145
winds 19
winter, seasonal fishing 17
worms
   jelly worms 144, *144*
   lugworms 150, 151, 154, *154*
   ragworms 150, 151, 155, *155*
   tides and 23
wrasse 105, *105*, 176
wreck fishing 114

zip sliders 129–30, *130*

The River Cottage
Hedgerow Handbook

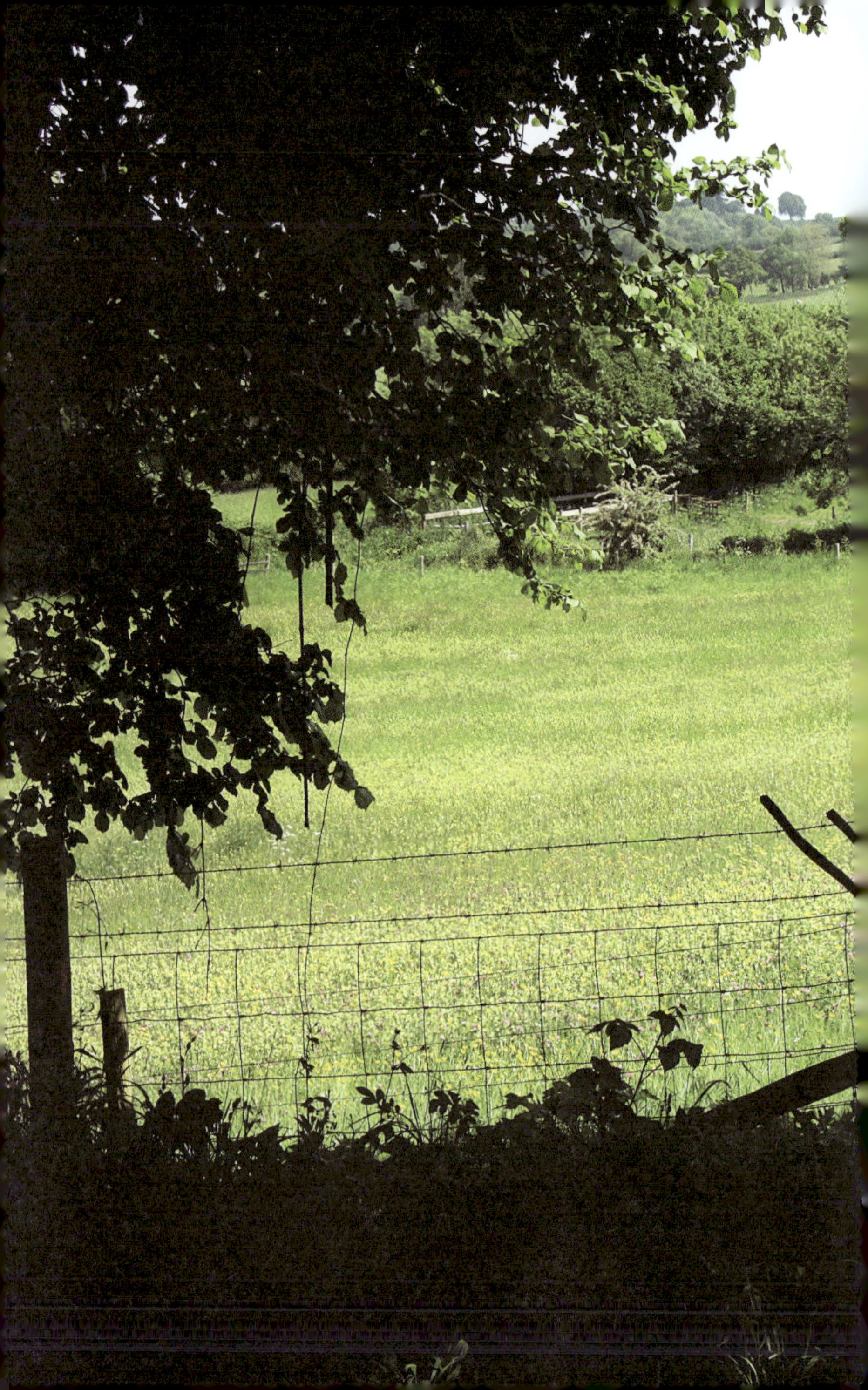

The River Cottage Hedgerow Handbook

by John Wright

introduced by
Hugh Fearnley-Whittingstall

www.rivercottage.net

BLOOMSBURY
LONDON · NEW DELHI · NEW YORK · SYDNEY

For my girls – Diane, Flossie and Lily

First published in Great Britain 2010
This paperback edition published 2012

Text and photography copyright © 2010 by John Wright

The moral right of the author has been asserted

Bloomsbury Publishing Plc, 50 Bedford Square, London WC1B 3DP
Bloomsbury Publishing, London, New Delhi, New York and Sydney

A CIP catalogue record for this book is available from the British Library

ISBN 978 1 4088 3611 8

10 9 8 7 6 5 4 3 2 1

Project editor: Janet Illsley
Designer: willwebb.co.uk

Printed in China by C&C Offset Printing Co., Ltd.

MIX
Paper from responsible sources
FSC® C008047

While every effort has been made to ensure the accuracy of the information contained in this book, in no circumstances can the publisher or the author accept any legal responsibility or liability for any loss or damage (including damage to property and/or personal injury) arising from any error in or omission from the information contained in this book, or from the failure of the reader to properly and accurately follow any instructions contained in the book.

www.bloomsbury.com/rivercottage

Contents

Starting Out	8
Conservation and the Law	20
Edible Species	30
Poisonous Species	166
Recipes	198
Useful Things	244
Index	251

This is not the first time I've taken up my pen to introduce a book written by John Wright. I did so back in 2007, when John produced the very first River Cottage Handbook, *Mushrooms*, and I did it again a couple of years later when he wrote another, *Edible Seashore*. So to find myself musing on his work is not a novel experience, although it is one filled with pleasure and admiration. It's clear to me that there really is no limit to this man's enthusiasm and excitement about the great outdoors – the edible bits of it in particular. And this compact manual is just like its forerunners: erudite, authoritative, confidence-building, witty. It will tell you all you need to know to turn any little walk or ramble into a foraging expedition, and it will inspire and entertain you at the same time.

Foraging is, and has long been, a great timeless, life-enhancing pursuit. It is deeply satisfying, deeply grounding. It gets us out into the fresh air and brings us closer to the natural environment from which we can so easily become estranged. It's a lovely thing to do on your own and often even more fun if you get your family or a group of friends to join in. There are, of course, a few serious foraging dangers in the form of poisonous plants, but most perils are fairly minor… the odd nettle sting and the occasional muddy trousers, perhaps.

However, for me there is a certain risk attached to foraging when it is performed *à deux* – especially when I am one part of the *deux* and John is the other. Because, while foraging really shouldn't be a competitive sport, with John around, it becomes so at times. The pair of us don't seem to be able to resist seeing who can gather the greatest number of nuts, the hardest-to-reach damsons, or the rarest bit of edible greenery. For me, I suppose it's a chance to prove myself, to enhance my foraging street-cred. For John… well, I think it's just showing off.

But don't let our rivalries deter you from engaging in your own foraging adventure. Antler-locking is absolutely not an essential part of wild food gathering. It should be neither a race nor a contest, but simply a highly enjoyable, very productive pastime. What's more, foraging is something that can be done by almost anyone, almost anywhere. You don't need a four-wheel-drive vehicle, waders, orienteering skills or a plethora of specially shaped sticks to be able to gather some of your own wild food. As John has said on many previous occasions, 'You're never more than five minutes from a patch of nettles,' a phrase I think he poached from *A Cook on the Wild Side*. The strength of this book is that it brings home this accessibility.

What John also celebrates so marvellously is the sheer joy of the hunt. 'Finding one's own food is such a fundamental drive,' he says, 'it is unsurprising that it is so much fun – nature has a delightful tendency to reward us for doing things that are essential for life, but which are hard work, complex or even absurd.' I couldn't have put it better myself (though that won't stop me from trying).

John's approach is egalitarian and inclusive and he makes the point that we are all hunter-gatherers at heart. It may be the case that most of us don't do much hunting or gathering any more, but that doesn't mean we can't. His view – and mine too – is that 'instincts do not disappear just because we do not use them'. What's more, freed from any urgent necessity to find food for ourselves in the wild, we can now enjoy the search all the more. The hedgerow is perhaps the most accessible and least daunting type of wild food environment. Few of us are very far from some kind of woodland, field edge, heathland, allotment or, indeed, garden, and these habitats are all included in John's 'hedgerow' bracket. And, just to encourage you a little more, plant identification in these areas is generally more straightforward and less nerve-racking than in the world of, say, fungi.

One of the many things I love about John is the sheer relish he displays for consuming his wild harvest. He never loses sight of the fact that, at the end of the day, once you've filled your lungs with fresh air and put roses in your cheeks, foraging is about getting something good to eat. What you do with your booty once you get it home is very important and John is no less an expert on this than he is on finding it in the first place. He shares my view that simple dishes are, almost without exception, the best ones for wild food. From a simple Nettle Soup to a stunningly refreshing Watermint Sorbet and excellent Chestnut Florentines (a personal favourite of mine), the recipes alone will have you itching to don your wellies and start hunting.

However, should the weather, minor illness or some other misfortune curtail your foraging efforts at any point, you needn't be too disappointed. For this book, like all John's work, is so beautifully and entertainingly written that there's as much enjoyment to be had from reading it curled up on the sofa as under a tree or beside a stream. It's a book that I know will stay on my shelf well beyond the day when I have to hang up my boots and confine myself to armchair foraging permanently. I take every opportunity to rib John about the fact that this point of retirement is considerably further off for me than it is for him. But I sometimes wonder about that. As this piece of work testifies, wild food finding is in John's very blood and I imagine he'll be tramping his way along the hedgerows, basket at the ready and stick in hand, for many, many years to come. I certainly hope so.

Hugh Fearnley-Whittingstall, East Devon, June 2010

Starting Out

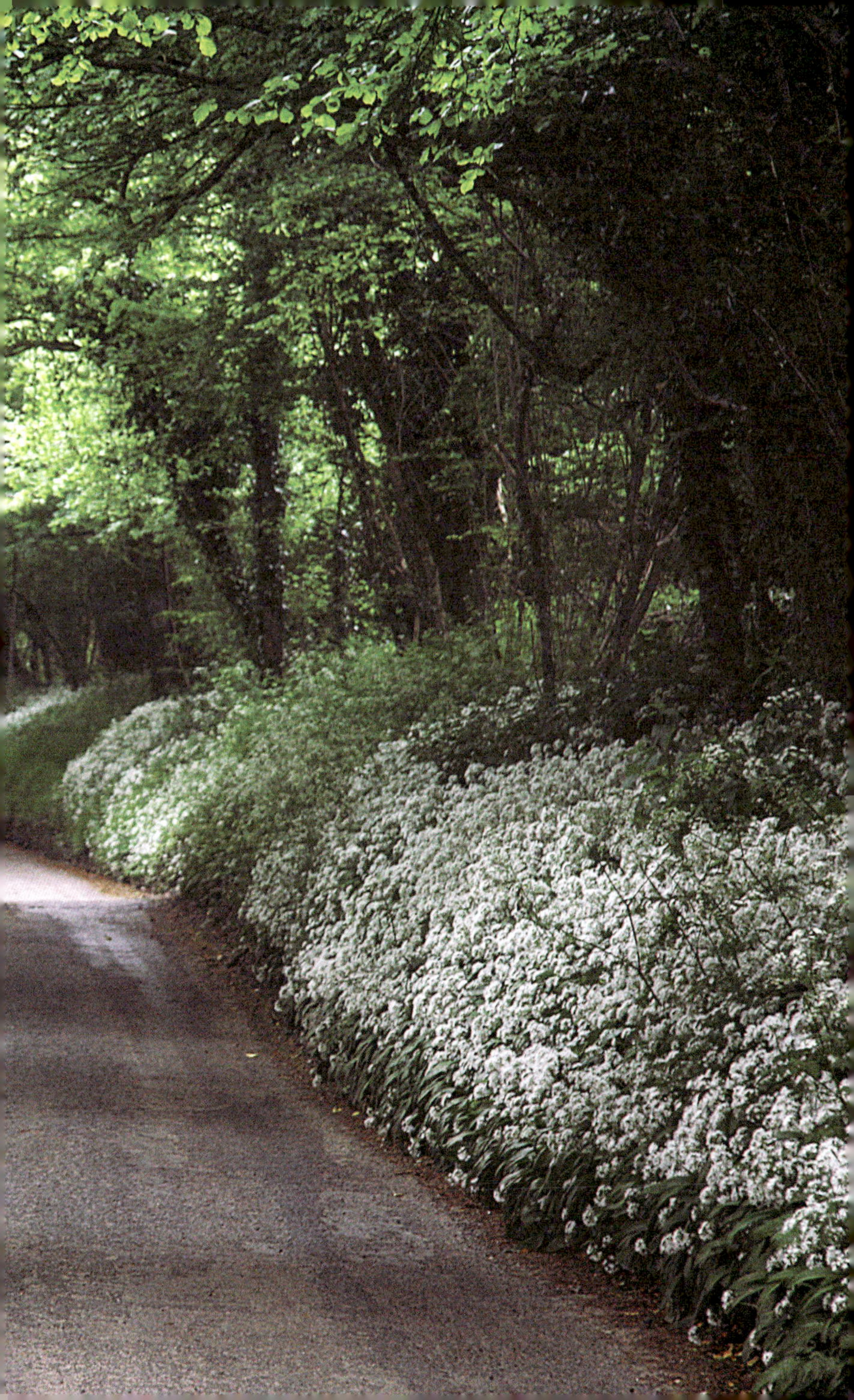

I am frequently told that going on a walk with me can be rather disconcerting. Except for the occasions when I offer my companion the odd leaf to chew upon, I appear to be strangely distracted and barely listening to what is being said to me. Well, I am – usually – listening; it is just that I am doing something else as well – looking.

Once one learns the foraging way of life, it is difficult to stop. Every walk, every car or train journey is an opportunity to find a new patch of Watermint, a likely spot for Pignuts or a promising-looking wood. If my walking is absent-minded, my driving is lethal. Foraging at 50mph, with eyes darting left and right and the occasional abrupt punctuations of the forager's emergency stop, has made me a danger to all road-users.

I hope that you come to love foraging and learning about foraging as much as I do. I know for certain that you will enjoy the food you find on your travels – eating wild Raspberries on a summer evening, for example, is difficult to beat. While many of the foods here are wild versions of familiar plants, there are several which may be new to you. Pignuts, Brooklime, Bulrush shoots and Silverweed roots are not readily found at even the best of greengrocers and are delicacies available only to the forager. Of course, there was a time when life was quite different, a time when there were no shops, no farms to supply them and not even a garden.

Ten or eleven thousand years ago in the Near East, not far from the mythical Garden of Eden, human beings made their greatest ever innovation: agriculture. For all the aeons before this, there was only one way our ancestors could obtain food – from the wild. Agriculture has been the backbone of our civilisation, relieving us of the time-consuming and unreliable daily hunt for food, but it has also deprived us of one of life's great pleasures.

While gathering wild food is still a matter of everyday life in many rural parts of the developed world (though much less so in Britain), nowadays the culture of hunting and foraging persists for most people largely as a pale remnant. Hunting has become a formalised and often ritualised sport; the true purpose, acquiring food, frequently forgotten. And few people now will forage for much more than a basket of Blackberries or a bag of Elderflowers. But, of course, instincts do not disappear just because we do not need them as we once did. Most of us now sublimate our foraging urges in supermarket aisles, which have been cunningly designed by Machiavellian retail psychologists to mimic the ancient experience.

Given that finding one's own food is such a fundamental drive, it is unsurprising that it is so much fun – nature has a delightful tendency to reward us for doing things that are essential for life but which are hard work, complex or even absurd. I take people out every year on various forays and it is wonderful to see their primal delight; all other concerns and thoughts flee and the single-minded nature of the enterprise becomes almost meditative.

With the need to find food in the wild no longer pressing, and most people living in an urban environment, the knowledge of what can be eaten, and where and when to find it, is no longer learned at a mother's side. Books can tell you the 'what' and to a large extent the 'when', but the 'where' cannot be described beyond generalities. The precise location of particular plants was knowledge passed down through the generations; Pignuts are always found *here* and there is a plum tree *here*, *here* and *here*, with the second one producing the best fruit. Such things now have to be learned anew. I have a mental map of exactly where hundreds of different wild foods can be found and a sense of my chances on any particular day, but this is hard-earned knowledge acquired from years of searching – if my mother knew where to find Pignuts she has kept the information to herself.

This book won't tell you exactly where to find Pignuts either, but I hope it will fill in some of the gaps and point you more or less in the right direction. As your life no longer depends on knowing where to find wild food, you have the leisure to enjoy the search, with every new discovery an exciting one. Coming across an unsuspected woodland clearing full of ripe Raspberries or a Chestnut tree producing good-sized nuts is a wonderful experience.

There is so much to enjoy here and I hope you will become the hunter/gatherer you were designed to be.

Where to look

The title of this book is 'Hedgerow' but it actually covers plants found in many more places than this. Wood, mountainside, moor, bog, heath, stream, meadow, field edge, seashore, urban wasteland, garden and allotment can all produce an abundance of wild foods. Most people can make a good start by looking in their own flower-beds – Hairy Bittercress, Dandelion, Ground Elder, Silverweed and Corn Salad can all be found in the average flower garden and it is rather satisfying to be able to eat your weeds. The vegetable garden can supply even finer delicacies, such as Fat Hen and Spear-leaved Orache.

One of my favourite spots for foraging is other people's veg patches and I am something of a familiar figure at the local allotments. There was some suspicion at first from the gardeners, but when my requests to pick some of their weeds proved *not* to be a cover for theft or sabotage, I was welcomed as a harmless idiot. In fact, few places are more packed with wild edible greens than the disturbed ground of an allotment garden – with Fat Hen, Spear-leaved Orache, Red Goosefoot and Chickweed available by the sackful. You may not be quite so lucky as I am – some allotments have fallen under the firm hand of an officious parish clerk or allotment association and will be scrupulously weed free. Also, the organic revolution has not touched the hearts and souls of all who practise horticulture, so the patch of Fat Hen you have been eyeing up for the last week may have recently been sprayed with 2,4-Dichlorophenoxyacetic acid or something equally unappetising. Always check with your friendly gardener first.

Even without the wildlife refuge of many gardens, the urban forager need not feel left out. Around twenty species mentioned in this book are commonly found in odd corners of our cities and suburbs. Fennel, Perennial Wall Rocket, Rowan, Blackberry, Stinging Nettle, Wild Strawberry and others are all as much, or even more, at home in town as out. Not that urban foraging is without its perils. Herbicidal sprays, pollution and, most of all, dogs, can make a forage around town a dicey business. There is good news though: pollution from motor vehicles is not what it was when lead was an ingredient in petrol. All that lead has now been washed away and is, mercifully, not being replenished. Other fuel and exhaust residues such as oil and carbon particles do not travel far from the road and will be no problem unless you pick your plants very close to the traffic. It is usually perfectly obvious whether a plant is growing in acceptably clean conditions so just use your common sense.

The countryside too has its pitfalls. Roadside pollution can still be a menace, though usually less so than in town. Problems from agricultural sprays are a rare concern but you should still be careful when picking from the edge of crop fields. Cars on the move can be a nuisance and I often find myself squeezing into a prickly hedge when two cars perversely choose that particular spot to pass one another. Probably the worst problem, though not dangerous unless you happen to be in the hedge at the time, is hedge-trimming. This operation is essential – left untrimmed, hedges would cease to be hedges and attempt to join the other side of the road to make a long wood. Despite efforts by councils and farmers to cut at the right time of year (usually to accommodate nesting birds), they often seem to do so at the wrong time for the forager. Promising Redcurrant bushes, Gooseberry bushes and Hazel trees are devastated in seconds by the voracious blades of these vertical lawn mowers. In any new world order, I will have the whole process placed under my personal control. Nevertheless, we can often be lucky and find a crop that has managed to escape. My favourite hedgerow harvest – the relatively tall Elderflower – normally evades the hedge-trimmers.

Woodland edges are seldom trimmed and will often contain many edible species. The modern version of the planted hedgerow is the swathes of trees and shrubs planted by imaginative council and highway authorities along dual carriageways and even on roundabouts. My best spot for Wild Cherries is on a bypass (I won't tell you which) and the largest patch of Sea Buckthorn I have ever come across is alongside the A1 just south of Newcastle. Sometimes these places are accessible, but often they are a forage too far.

The heart of a wood is surprisingly poor foraging territory; it is generally too dark and fails to provide the 'edge habitat' required by so many plants. Wood Sorrel and Sweet Chestnut are the most likely woodland finds. Heath and bog bring Bilberry and Cranberry respectively, while streams will supply two of my favourite edible plants – Watercress and Watermint. Fields and meadows are also excellent hunting grounds with Pignut, Sorrel, Wintercress and Dandelion.

I have included a few of the plants that can be found at the seaside though you'll find them explored more thoroughly in my *Edible Seashore* handbook. I repeat them here either because they are particularly tasty or because they also occur inland.

How to look

Foraging for plants requires very little in the way of equipment, but a certain amount of preparation will make it a great deal easier – and safer. I have waded out into a chalk stream to pick Watercress in bare feet on several occasions, having forgotten my wellies. You *can* do it, but it is not fun – the water temperature feels about zero even in July. Feet are not the only parts endangered – with so many berry trees armed with spines and thorns, thick gloves and robust clothing are often an absolute necessity. I also highly recommend a hat as this will shade your eyes, protect your head, keep you dry, and double as an emergency foraging basket.

A collection of real baskets, buckets, small pots with lids and canvas bags will bring your finds home intact and, if you take enough, not hopelessly mixed together. A knife is an important part of the forager's kit, but there is now a serious obstacle to this innocent necessity. Carrying a knife in a public place with a blade longer than 75mm, or any knife with a fixed blade or a blade that can be locked in position (many penknives are like this), is a criminal offence with up to four years available to catch up on your reading. It is, however, fine if you have 'lawful excuse' – a carpenter on his way to a site job or a fisherman off to the seaside would have a good reason to carry a fixed blade, but the wild food hunter may have a harder time convincing a suspicious member of the constabulary of his innocent intentions. Of course, if you popped into the bank while on your way to your favourite Wild Garlic spot with a bowie knife tucked down your trousers you would be asking for trouble. Scissors are indispensable and I never go anywhere without a pair, even to the bank, but even these could conceivably be misconstrued as a fixed blade. A spade will be necessary for unearthing Horseradish and other roots, though how you are going to explain one of those I do not know.

Berry-pickers are the love-child of a comb and a dustpan. They can speed up the picking of Bilberries, though, by the time you have removed all the twigs and leaves in your collection, not as much as you might hope. You can either spend a day and

Forager's kit: boxwood berry-picker, knife, scissors, drainpipe picker and stick with crooked end

a half handcrafting one in finest boxwood like I did, or buy a perfectly serviceable plastic and wire one from a specialist supplier for under a tenner. Much more useful, though this time you *will* have to make it yourself, is a plum/apple/hazelnut/cherry picker fashioned from a 40mm plastic waste pipe. The fruit rolls magically down the tube into your hand or even into a bag secured at the bottom. The prongs are made by cutting and shaping the pipe into a fork, then carefully bending them by warming the plastic over a gas flame. The last bit is fraught with danger but if you keep the pipe at least 15cm above the flame you shouldn't burn yourself too badly.

A sturdy stick with a crooked end for pulling fruit- and nut-bearing branches within your grasp – and for waving at rival foragers in a threatening manner – is de rigueur.

There is one potential hazard in using these implements, or at least carrying them around in a public place – the innocent forager may be open to the accusation of 'going equipped'. Such a situation might arise, for example, if you walked past a cherry orchard on your way to pick some hedgerow plums while carrying your trusty drainpipe picker over your shoulder. This sounds, and is, ridiculous, but the penalty is up to three years inside and the police and courts do not always pursue the path of good sense.

Finally, a little-used hedgerow foraging technique that is my gift to you is the 'standing on the roof of your car' method. This is seriously effective – I once picked many kilos of plums from a tree whose lower branches had been stripped bare by less adventurous collectors. A proud moment.

When to look

Wild food can be found at any time of the year – even January – but the warmer months are always best. Spring will bring succulent new growth and Hawthorn blossoms, and summer has its Strawberries and Redcurrants, but if I were to choose the best time of all, it would be early September. Many summer fruits are still around and the autumn ones just beginning, roots are plump and green vegetables such as Watercress and Fat Hen still in leaf.

For each species I have indicated when they are most likely to appear. This is summarised in the Forager's Calendar (pp.16–19). The dates given are inevitably approximate as they can vary by a few weeks with the weather, which in turn will be influenced by geographical location. 'May' blossom from the Hawthorn, for example, is so called because of the time of its appearance, but it can often be found in June.

Forager's calendar

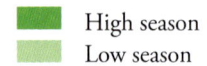

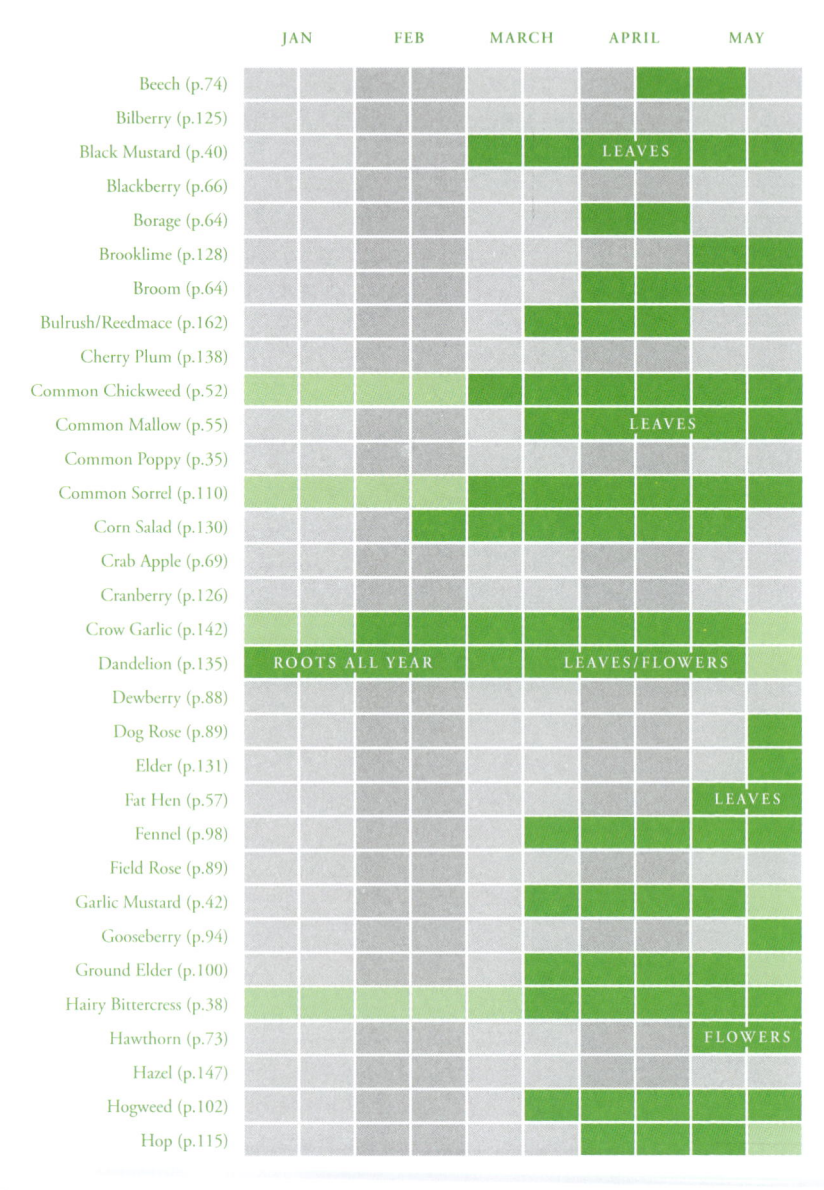

■ High season
■ Low season

	JAN	FEB	MARCH	APRIL	MAY
Beech (p.74)				■	
Bilberry (p.125)					
Black Mustard (p.40)			■	LEAVES	
Blackberry (p.66)					
Borage (p.64)				■	
Brooklime (p.128)					■
Broom (p.64)				■	
Bulrush/Reedmace (p.162)			■		
Cherry Plum (p.138)					
Common Chickweed (p.52)	▨	▨	■		
Common Mallow (p.55)			■	LEAVES	
Common Poppy (p.35)					
Common Sorrel (p.110)	▨	▨	■		
Corn Salad (p.130)		■	■		
Crab Apple (p.69)					
Cranberry (p.126)					
Crow Garlic (p.142)	■	■	■	▨	
Dandelion (p.135)	ROOTS ALL YEAR			LEAVES/FLOWERS	
Dewberry (p.88)					
Dog Rose (p.89)					■
Elder (p.131)					
Fat Hen (p.57)					LEAVES
Fennel (p.98)			■	■	
Field Rose (p.89)					
Garlic Mustard (p.42)			■	■	▨
Gooseberry (p.94)					■
Ground Elder (p.100)			■	■	
Hairy Bittercress (p.38)	▨	▨			
Hawthorn (p.73)					FLOWERS
Hazel (p.147)					
Hogweed (p.102)			■	■	
Hop (p.115)			■	■	

Seasons vary greatly from year to year so this is a rough and ready guide to the best times to look. Some plants have more than one crop and this is noted on the chart. The low season (shaded pale green) is when a plant may sometimes be found but is not necessarily at its best or so easy to find.

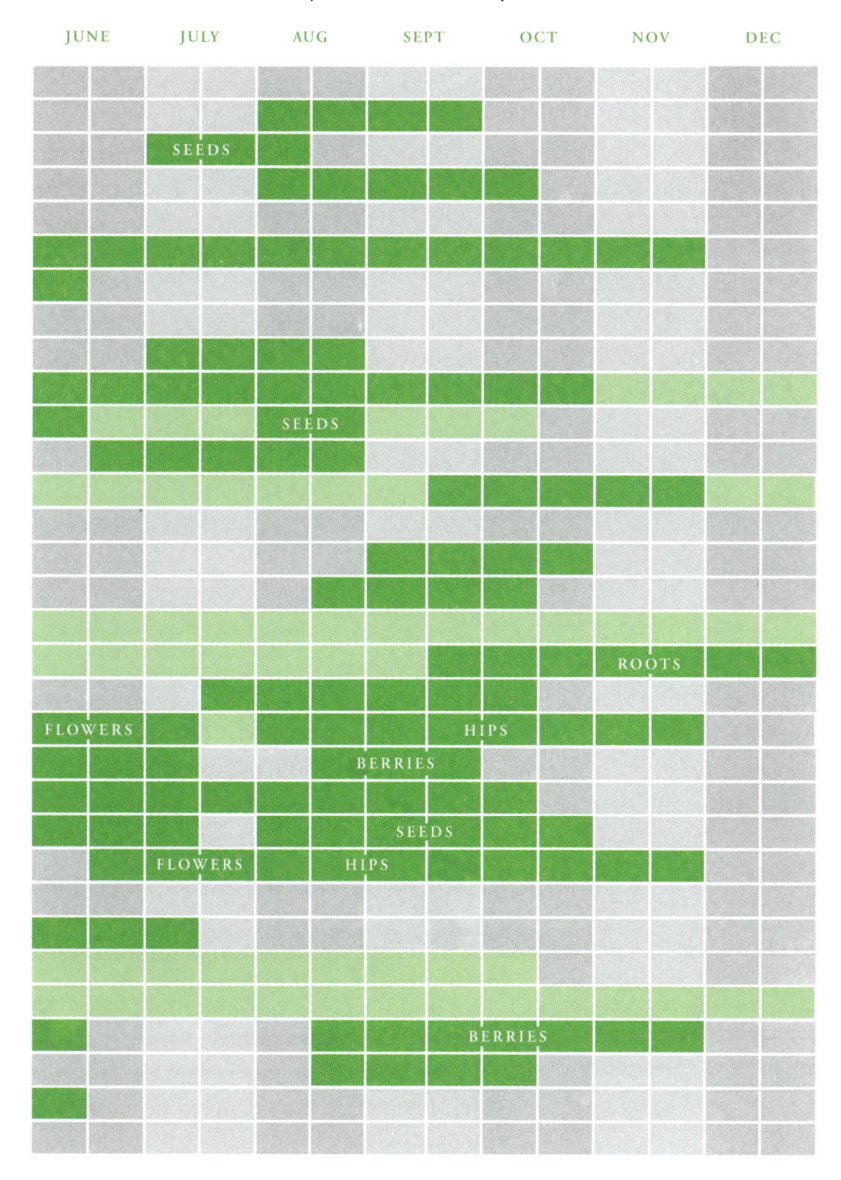

JUNE	JULY	AUG	SEPT	OCT	NOV	DEC

SEEDS

SEEDS

ROOTS

FLOWERS · HIPS

BERRIES

SEEDS

FLOWERS · HIPS

BERRIES

STARTING OUT 17

	JAN	FEB	MARCH	APRIL	MAY
Horseradish (p.44)				▨▨	▨▨
Japanese Rose (p.91)					
Juniper (p.153)					
Lime (p.74)					■■
Perennial Wall Rocket (p.50)			■■	■■	■■
Pignut (p.104)			■■	■■	■■
Raspberry (p.87)					
Redcurrant (p.97)				FLOWERS	
Red Goosefoot (p.59)					▨■
Round-leaved Mint (p.120)					■
Rowan (p.75)					
Sea Buckthorn (p.156)					
Sheep's Sorrel (p.111)			■■	■■	
Silver Birch (p.159)			■	▨▨	
Silverweed (p.78)				▨▨	▨
Sloe/Blackthorn (p.81)					
Spearmint (p.120)				■■	■■
Spear-leaved Orache (p.60)					■■
Stinging Nettle (p.112)			■■	■■	■■
Sweet Chestnut (p.151)					
Sweet Cicely (p.107)			■	LEAVES	■
Watercress (p.47)			■■	■■	■■
Watermint (p.117)				■■	■■
Wild Carrot (p.108)					
Wild Cherry (p.83)					
Wild Garlic (p.144)			■■	■■	
Wild Marjoram (p.123)				■■	■■
Wild Parsnip (p.108)					
Wild Plum (p.138)					
Wild Strawberry (p.92)					
Wintercress (p.36)	■■	■■	■■	■▨	▨▨
Wood Sorrel (p.62)	▨▨	▨▨	■■	■■	■■
Yarrow (p.141)					■■

| JUNE | JULY | AUG | SEPT | OCT | NOV | DEC |

FLOWERS THEN HIPS, BUT OFTEN TOGETHER

BERRIES

FRESH LEAVES FROM PLANTS CUT BACK EARLIER

SEED PODS   ROOTS

Conservation and the Law

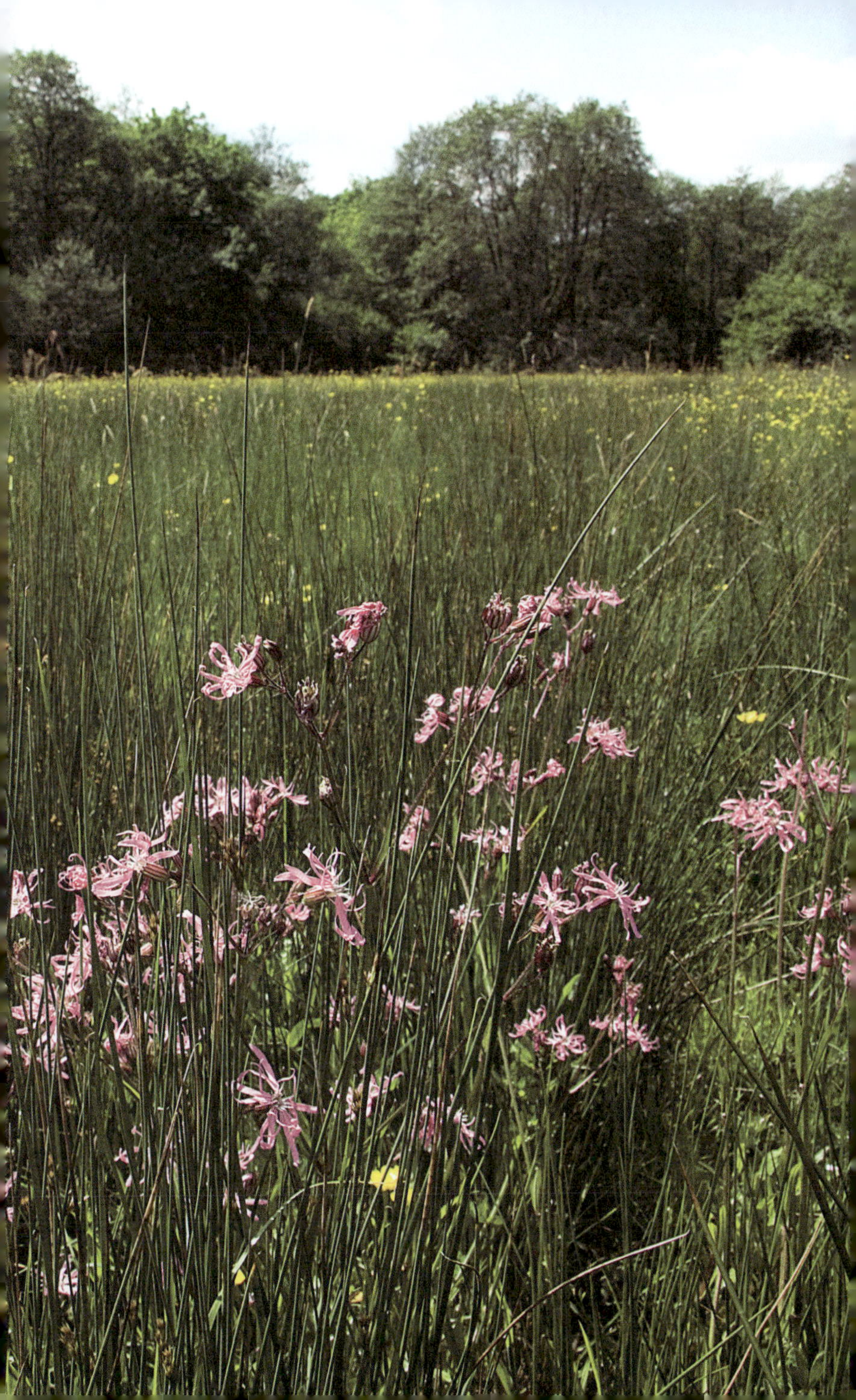

People can become very disquieted over the matter of conservation and foraging. Surely, they argue, we should not be taking things from the wild for our own purposes; surely nature has been injured by us enough without this further imposition. This is not an argument with which I have a great deal of sympathy. It is, of course, perfectly possible to forage in a manner that is damaging to the natural world, but it is not actually all that easy.

Many of our native species *are* under threat but it is not from the forager. Invasive species take a toll of habitats by usurping ecological niches; Japanese knotweed and Himalayan balsam being among the worst hedgerow offenders here. But most damage is done by human-induced loss of habitat. The ploughing of meadow and downland, uprooting of hedges, felling of mature woodlands, urbanisation, golf courses, industrial development or even something as simple as walking on a pebble beach (one of the problems faced by sea kale) all have a major effect on biodiversity. Habitat is everything – if the correct habitat exists, so will the species that thrive in it, foraged or not.

The commercial collection of plants has the potential to cause problems because of its likely scale, but there are few records of this actually happening. The reason for this is not hard to see. Some shellfish and some fungi are well worth the effort of gathering for reward, but it is much harder to make a living from wild plants – a kilogram of Wood Sorrel may command a high price but it will take several hours to collect.

But what if *everybody* picked wild plants? There are two ripostes to this. First of all, not everybody will. I recall watching a popular television programme where one of my favourite edible plants – Sea Beet – was enthusiastically recommended to the viewers. I worried that families would set off with baskets, boxes and large appetites on weekend trips to collect every last plant. The following season, in the half-dozen highly accessible places where I pick it myself, I could find not the slightest evidence that anyone had picked a single leaf. If anything, I rather hope that my powers of persuasion are greater than those of that television presenter. Secondly, for most of the plants in this book, it would make very little difference if everybody *did* pick them. Dandelions, Sorrel, Blackberries, Elderflowers, Sloes, Nettles, Crab Apples, Fat Hen, Hawthorn, Sweet Cicely, Sweet Chestnut, Wild Garlic, Wood Sorrel and more are so hugely abundant that it would effectively be beyond our abilities to damage them by collecting.

Remember also that when one is picking fruits the plants themselves are completely unaffected. Fruit are created, of course, in order that the plant may reproduce and not so that we might feed ourselves; it could, therefore, be argued that picking fruit might damage the long-term reproductive success of a species. This is clear nonsense because of the vast numbers of fruit (or seed) that a plant produces in its lifetime, out of which only one or two need to develop into new

Southern Marsh Orchid, *Dactylorhiza praetermissa*

mature plants. For example, how many Crab Apples would you have to gather before populations of Crab Apple trees started to decline? Well, nearly all of them, and for several decades.

There is also the plea that we should always leave some wild fruit to feed the birds. Now I like birds as much as the next man (woodcock and teal are particular favourites) and I think that if they can get to the berries before I do then jolly good luck to them.

I suspect that at least some of the concerns expressed by individuals and organisations over foraging and wildlife are not about conservation but protecting their patch – good old-fashioned territoriality. Certainly one or two of the nature wardens with whom I have 'had words' over the years, even when I was carrying no more than a camera and tripod, seemed more interested in 'seeing me off' than in seriously protecting the species on their site. Fortunately, organisations such as Plantlife and the National Trust are now, with publications and courses, actively encouraging the idea of careful foraging as a way of helping people feel that the natural world actually has something to do with them.

One sin occasionally committed by the conservation-minded is that of 'environmental colonialism' – refusing to buy or gather local wild food while cheerfully buying the imported article. A typical example of this is when a restaurant is banned, or at least discouraged, from using locally collected ceps and chanterelles on conservation grounds with no concern expressed about their being imported from who knows where. I once observed the same mindset at play in a national nature reserve where all the gates were made from tropical hardwoods.

When one considers the ethics of a particular position, they must be weighed against those of its alternative – one cannot assume that cultivated food has no negative environmental impact. Whatever food you eat, it must have come from *somewhere* and eating from the wild is, in principle at least, *more* virtuous than eating cultivated food. There are a handful of food crops which may be considered positive or at least neutral in their environmental effects – hill-grazed sheep, oysters and seaweeds being the only three I can easily bring to mind – but most are inevitably negative. Any crop – rice, wheat, potatoes, vines, olives, apples – requires that whatever wild organisms were there originally must be destroyed and then kept at bay, and we must remember that most husbanded animals are fed on crops of some sort or another.

A truly committed environmentalist who also eschewed foraging (and hunting) would probably starve to death. Foraging, by contrast, is a thoroughly virtuous exercise. If one forages from the wild, it is *still wild* afterwards and, far from being a dangerous aberration, foraging (and hunting) are the *only* natural means by which we can obtain sustenance – all others being a matter of artifice. My concern is not that we forage too much, but too little. It is admittedly a human-centred view, but there are vast quantities of wild food in our hedgerows, woods and fields and most of it goes to waste. More food taken from the wild would, in theory at least, mean that some land could be released from agriculture and reserved for wildlife.

I hope that my arguments have convinced you that foraging is not only harmless but positively beneficial. But, of course, with a bit of effort, it is still perfectly possible to turn yourself into a walking ecological disaster. For example, picking Blackberries is clearly a benign activity, but trampling over lady slipper orchids to do it is not. Always tread carefully where there might be delicate organisms that could be damaged. This applies particularly to things like Marsh Samphire, Watercress and Watermint, which are found in sensitive habitats.

Here is a brief, and rather obvious, guide on how to get it right:

1. Take care not to damage habitats by trampling all over them.
2. Most of the plants in this book are very common but one or two are not and should be picked with extreme care and only occasionally. I have indicated the conservation status of most of the species I describe.
3. Obey the laws that cover conservation.
4. Although it hardly applies to such things as Blackberries and Haws, in general it is wise to pick a little here and a little there of whatever you are collecting. A woodland floor stripped of its Wood Sorrel, for example, is a forlorn sight.

You may now enjoy your foraging in the certain knowledge of your virtue.

The law

The law of foraging has never been an entirely settled matter and many pitfalls exist to catch out the unwary forager. There are three legal areas to consider – access, ownership and conservation. If you cannot bear to plough through this section, and who can blame you, there's a more digestible summary at the end.

First things first. If you venture on to private land for whatever purpose, without explicit or implicit permission from the owner, then you are trespassing. (Note that there is no law of trespass in Scotland, where there is an admirable and long-established right to roam almost everywhere.) If you do stray on to private land without permission then you will not be committing a crime. It will be, rather, a civil wrong so you cannot be prosecuted, no matter what the signs say. You could, however, be sued, even if you do not damage anything or make a thorough nuisance of yourself – the landowner could sue for the hypothetical advantage you receive from being on his or her land. If asked to leave, you must do so by the nearest exit. There are many places where implicit permission may be given – land owned by the Forestry Commission, National Trust and local authority land, Wildlife Trust nature reserves and so on.

The fundamental law governing foraging is the common law right to collect the 'four 'f's – fruit, flowers, fungi and foliage'. This applies with two provisos – first that the material picked is for personal use, not commercial gain, and second that it is growing wild. You could, for example, pick five kilos of Crab Apples from a farmer's hedge but could not sell the jelly you made from it at the local bring-and-buy sale. You could *not* pick five kilos of apples from an orchard – that would be stealing. Similarly if the Crab Apples had been purposely planted as a crop then again that would count as theft.

This principle is helpfully enshrined in the 1968 Theft Act which states that *'A person who picks mushrooms growing wild on any land, or who picks flowers, fruit or foliage from a plant growing wild on any land, does not (although not in possession of the land) steal what he picks, unless he does it for reward or for sale or other commercial purpose. (For purposes of this subsection 'mushroom' includes any fungus, and 'plant' includes any shrub or tree.)'*

Note that the act refers twice to *'any land'*, and uses the phrase *'although not in possession of the land'*, meaning that even if someone is trespassing they will not be stealing. The picking would merely constitute a further act of trespass and this is not a matter for the criminal law. One interesting practical consideration here is that if a landowner caught you with a basket of those Crab Apples picked from a wild tree growing on his land he could not demand them from you, though explaining this to him would likely tax your debating skills. His only redress would be to sue for the value of the apples.

The main message from this, however, is that gathering wild food in a place to which you are permitted access is legal and can be done without having to look over your shoulder. There are, inevitably, exceptions. On some land this right has been withdrawn with a byelaw forbidding the collection of any plant, fungus or animal. There should be a sign to this effect somewhere near the entrance. It is possible to challenge these byelaws if you feel really strongly about them (and you have money lying around the house in drifts) and this has been done successfully in the past, such as at Strangford Lough, N.I., where a winkle picker successfully contested a National Trust byelaw banning the collection of shellfish.

A second, and even more irritating, exception is on land made newly accessible under the Countryside and Rights of Way Act 2000 (CROW). This generally welcome act has made large tracts of land legally accessible to walkers, but confers no right to collect wild food (or anything else) that exists there. The act states that a person is not entitled to be on the land if he '... *intentionally removes, damages or destroys any plant, shrub, tree or root, or any part of a plant, shrub, tree or root.*' Fortunately this does not remove existing rights of foraging in places such as where

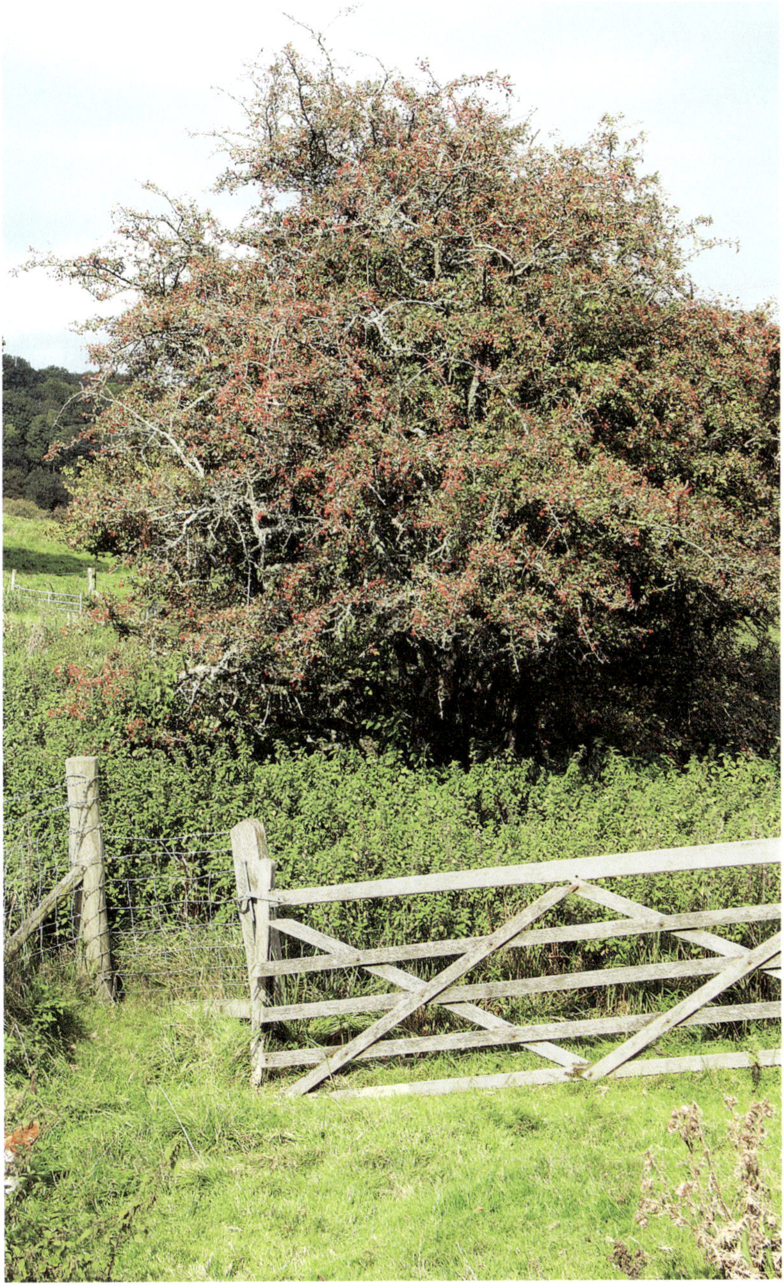

a footpath passes over land now within the act or any common land which the act may encompass. The wording of the act makes the picking of, say, Blackberries on land where access was not previously allowed an act of trespass (not, it must be stressed, theft) and the law requires that a person doing such a thing remove themselves immediately for a period of 72 hours, presumably to give them a chance to reconsider their lives.

There is, in fact, almost nothing you can do on CROW land other than walk across it. It is, for example, technically against the provisions of the act to go on to such land if you have head lice as the only animal you are allowed to take with you is a dog; you are also not allowed to annoy people or engage in a Scrabble tournament (no organised games). While you are sat there, peacefully not scratching your head or playing Scrabble, you can at least enjoy a picnic which *is* allowed. I have read quite a few acts of Parliament over the years while studying the law as it pertains to foraging and have concluded that they are largely drawn up by lunatics.

Conservation law is an added burden. The popular works of Beatrice Potter seem to be the main authority for much of this legislation, not scientific studies or common sense. It is the bluntness of the laws that cause the problems, not their good intentions. The 1981 Wildlife and Countryside Act states that: '... *if any person... not being an authorised person, intentionally uproots any wild plant... he shall be guilty of an offence.*'

This seems like a perfectly reasonable law until one tries to imagine the problem it was intended to solve. It does not, of itself, prevent a farmer from ploughing up a field containing plants, rare or otherwise, as the farmer would be an authorised person. Foragers, on the other hand, have never been a threat to wildlife when collecting Dandelion or burdock roots. Apart from the casual or commercial (and remember, commercial collecting is already an offence) uprooting of bluebell and snowdrop bulbs and maybe the odd collector of rare plants digging up a lizard orchid, there never was a problem to solve. Now the roots of common plants are out of bounds and the absurd situation exists where an annual plant can be cut off at just above ground level, effectively killing it, but pulling it up by the roots is a criminal offence – Hairy Bittercress and Marsh Samphire are two plants to which this applies. The answer, such as it is, is to become an authorised person and obtain permission from the land owner.

Certain plants mentioned in the 1981 act are on the famous 'schedule 8' list and it is illegal to damage them in any way. None of these rare plants are recommended in this book.

Some of the best foraging sites are, inevitably, on Sites of Special Scientific Interest (SSSIs). There are approaching 10,000 of these in Britain. Many are on private land with no public access, but some are open to the public. There are a couple of problems for the forager under the terms of the 1981 act which establishes these sites. When a site is registered as an SSSI, a list is drawn up of species which made it interesting in the first place and it is illegal to damage any of these organisms. This is unlikely to affect most foraging excursions, but a few plants in this book are sufficiently special to warrant a mention in the declaration of an SSSI – Cranberry and Juniper are two which come to mind.

More serious is something else that is published with the declaration of a site – an ominous list of 'operations likely to damage' the SSSI. These activities are not necessarily banned, but consultation with, and permission from Natural England, the government agency that administers the act, would be required before they could take place. A list will often include such obvious things as quarrying and tree-felling, but there is also a catch-all along the lines of 'removal of or damage to any plant, fungus or animal'. Natural England and the other conservation authorities are, however, generally sensible bodies, which understand that picking Blackberries, Sloes or Sorrel is not going to do any harm at all and are unlikely to seek prosecution for the restrained collection of such common plants.

If you manage to negotiate these arcane rules and miss out on your fun day in court there is one further (and potentially more serious) pitfall awaiting the unwary forager – the law which deals with the carrying of knives and other foraging equipment. See Starting Out (pp.13–15) for the hair-raising details.

Good luck. I hope you don't need it.

Here is that summary:

1. You need permission to go on to land you do not own, otherwise you will be trespassing. This does not apply in Scotland.
2. There is a common law right, enshrined in law, that you may collect 'fruit, flowers, fungi and foliage', providing it is for personal use only and is growing wild.
3. Byelaws exist in some places which have removed these rights.
4. This right does not exist on CROW land unless it existed before the land was registered under the act.
5. It is illegal to uproot any plant without permission from the owner of the land on which it grows.
6. Some (rare) plants are protected by law.
7. Plants cited in the declaration of an SSSI are protected.
8. Picking any plants on an SSSI may, strictly, be illegal but it is unlikely that picking common plants such as Blackberries and Sorrel will result in prosecution.

Edible Species

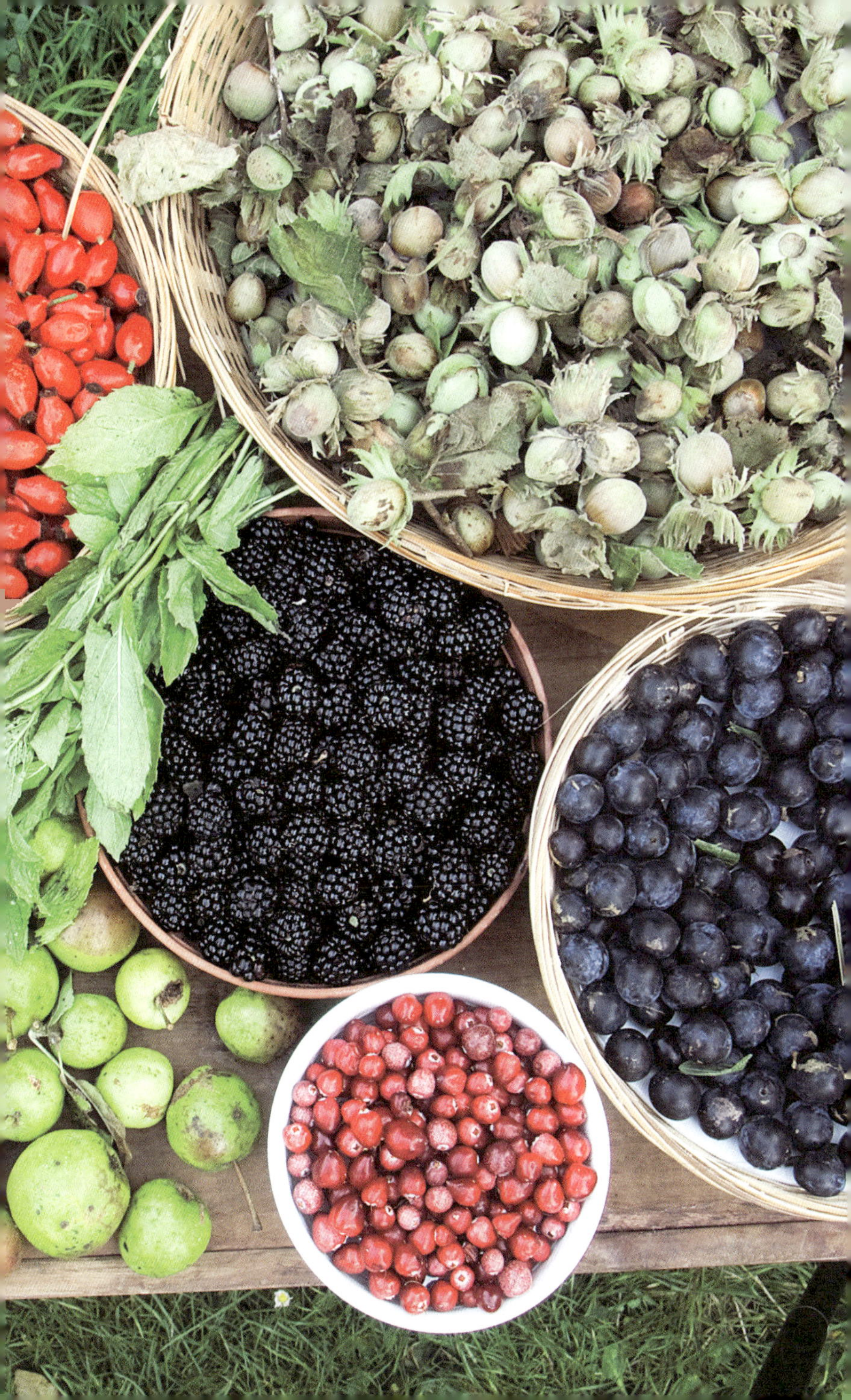

The seventy or so species described here are the best wild food plants that the British Isles have to offer. It is not a comprehensive list – there are many more edible plants than this, but most are uncommon or just don't taste all that great. I have chosen those you are most likely to find and most likely to enjoy. There are a few omissions which may seem odd to the seasoned forager. For example, I have left out bistort and tansy because I don't think they taste very nice, and Comfrey because it is seriously poisonous if eaten in large quantities. There are also a few oddities which I've included because they are interesting for some reason or other – Yarrow and Brooklime being two such. For a more complete list I highly recommend Richard Mabey's justly famous *Food for Free*.

If you are new to foraging I suspect the one thing that will surprise you is not necessarily the number of species that can be found, but just how much of many of them can be easily (and sustainably) collected. A small, expensive packet of supermarket salad looks quite pitiful next to a basketful of Wild Rocket that has been gathered for nothing in a few minutes. And a punnet containing half a dozen under-ripe cultivated plums looks rather dismal compared to a car boot full of glorious, and free, wild Cherry Plums.

I know that many people are concerned that a walk on the wild side will quickly see them in hospital. But although there are plants that will kill you before you can get to the nearest A&E, the sensible forager need not worry. Most edible plants are distinctive enough (everyone knows what a Stinging Nettle, Hazelnut and Raspberry look like) and if you are not sure whether you can tell a Red Goosefoot from a Black Nightshade then you should just not bother with it. I have eaten around one hundred species of wild plant and one hundred and thirty species of wild fungi and have never – well, not yet – had as much as a mild stomach ache. It is just a matter of being extremely careful and, above all, not jumping to conclusions. Remember, accidentally killing yourself by eating a poisonous plant for your tea may be a painful tragedy for you and your nearest, but, worse still, it is so *embarrassing*.

The good news is that identification is much, much easier in the plant world than it is in the fungal world, where there is little obvious difference between an edible Blusher and a poisonous Panther Cap – like most mushrooms and toadstools they both have a cap and a stem and accurate identification is all down to the fine details. With plants, however, there are enormous differences in general size, leaf shape, flower structure, growth habit and so on. Still, you will need to proceed carefully with some species, observing each characteristic in turn.

Most plants in this book present no problem – few people will confuse a Blackberry, Raspberry, Crab Apple or even Fennel with anything else. Nevertheless, identification is not always straightforward. Since we are often interested in just the young leaves, we may not always have the most useful identifying feature, the flower, to help us.

While there are endless ways of getting things wrong, there are three areas of particular concern: berries, the potato family and the carrot family. Many berries are good to eat but some equally tasty-looking ones can be seriously poisonous. Fortunately, most are quite distinctive and you will have the added assistance of leaves and growth habit to make you certain of your identification. Plants are put into families for the simple reason that they are related to one another. This also means that, like all families, they share certain characteristics.

There are two seriously treacherous families in this book, the carrot family and the potato family. Both contain plants that are very good to eat, but also plants that will have you in A&E – if you are lucky enough to get there in time. No wild member of the potato family in this country is edible, but some species do have leaves which can look superficially like those of some edible plants, particularly the goosefoots. The carrot family does include native edible species; the issue here is distinguishing between these and the poisonous carrots, most notably Hemlock Water-dropwort. I have tried to warn of these possible confusions so that when, say, you pick Fat Hen, you will be quite sure that you have not picked Black Nightshade by mistake.

I have avoided technical terms as much as possible – too much, my botanist friends might say – as most people will throw their hands up in despair when presented with phrases such as '*lvs oblong, sinuate-dentate to pinnatifid, lower narrowed into the stalk, the upper sessile or amplexicaul*', and I decided that general clarity was preferable to academic precision.

A mistake I see again and again is people making up their mind about something and ignoring clear features that indicate that it cannot possibly be what they think it is. A typical example would be, 'I am sure it is Fat Hen though the leaves are a bit hairy.' Fat Hen *never* has hairy leaves so it *must* be something else. Another mistake is to flick through a book to find something that 'looks a bit like it'. There is nothing wrong with flicking through books, we all do it, but it is essential to double check that all the characters you are expecting are actually there.

This handbook alone should suffice when it comes to identifying the various wild foods, but there is nothing wrong with double checking in a wild-flower field guide. Not that I recommend you join me in Anorak World with fifteen books to plough through. The internet is also a good place to find pictures of plants, but it can be unreliable. To use our example above, an image search for Fat Hen may well present you with a picture of Black Nightshade instead because it just happens to be on the same web page as Fat Hen as a comparison – so do be careful.

Eventually you will be able to spot a member of the goosefoot family from ten paces and provide its Latin name at five – it is all a matter of practice.

For more information on identifying plants – and a few extra species that you might want to look out for – go to www.rivercottage.net/foraging.

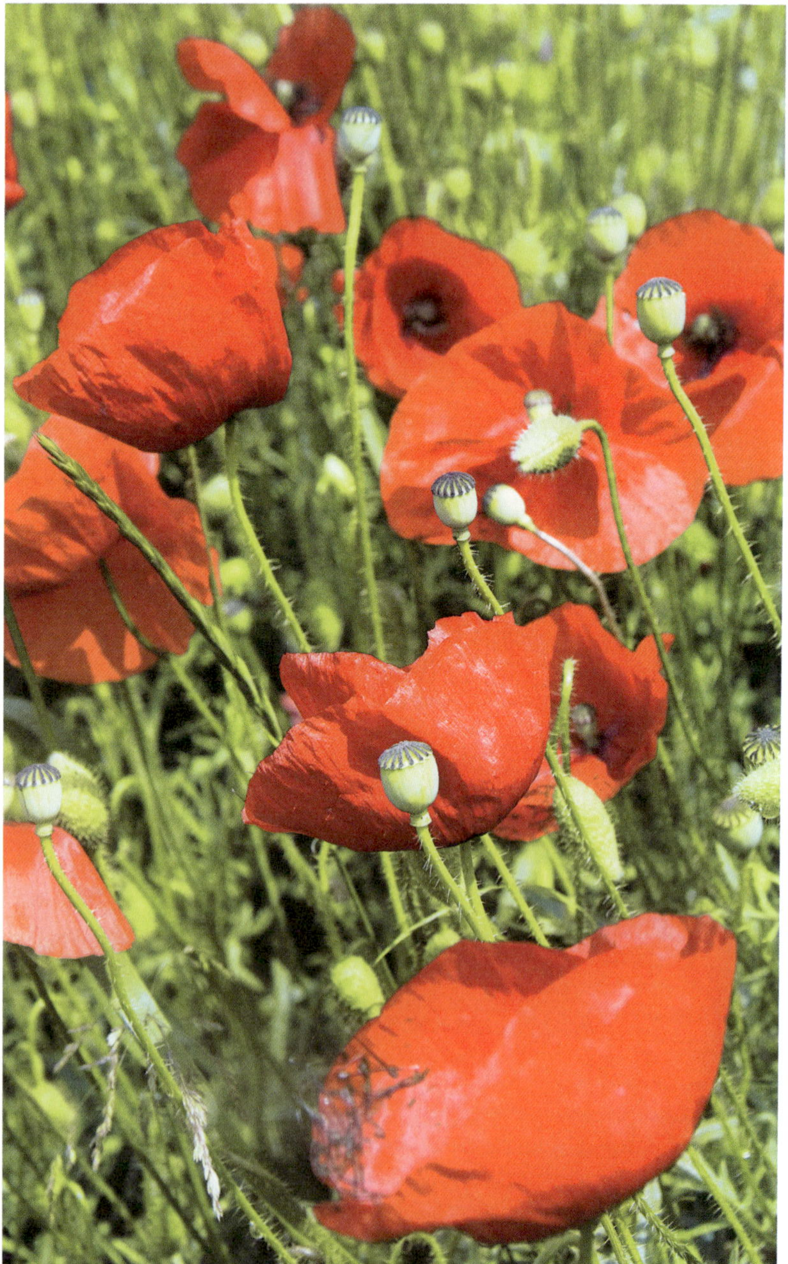

Common Poppy *Papaver rhoeas*

DESCRIPTION	Medium annual, to 90cm. Leaves deeply divided, with pointed irregular lobes, hairy. Stem hairy. Flowers scarlet, often a small dark patch at base of petals, many successive flowers on one plant. Seeds in lidded cups
HABITAT	Cornfields, disturbed ground
DISTRIBUTION	Very common in England, except the Northwest. Scarce in central Wales, Northern Ireland and in Scotland, except the Southeast
SEASON	Seed heads mature from late June until August

Nothing is more evocative of high summer than an inadvertent field of Poppies. These are less frequent today, but sometimes a corner or a strip of field escapes the herbicidal sprays and the dormant Common Poppy takes its chance to turn it scarlet. The ephemeral flower is the colour of fresh blood and a reminder of the Western Front where so many lost their lives; the plant germinates in disturbed soil and none were so disturbed as those of Belgium and France during the First World War.

Apart from fields, the Common Poppy is common everywhere from gardens to grassy banks. All parts are poisonous except the seeds and it is these that we eat. Timing is everything as the seed heads should be picked just as they ripen and open – before this the seeds are not ready; after and the seed heads will likely be empty. Pull the seed heads off and place them in a bag or plastic box – a basket is obviously not suitable as the seeds will fall through.

If necessary leave them a few days to ripen and when the heads rattle with their seeds turn them upside down and shake, or, to speed things up, prise the lids off first. The nutty flavour of the seeds is very familiar baked on bread and there really is no better way of using them, although they are also used to flavour cakes.

Also look out for the Opium Poppy (*P. somniferum*). The seeds of the Common Poppy and all our other native poppies are tiny and you will need to find a large number of seed heads for a worthwhile collection. Much more rewarding are the seed heads of the Opium Poppy, which are comparatively huge and full of large seeds. These seeds can be used, as above, in bread- and cake-making. The Opium Poppy has almost the same distribution as the Common Poppy but with a preference for the seaside in the North. Roadsides and gardens are typical habitats for this flamboyant and distinctive plant. With its broad blue/green leaves and large pink flowers it is unmistakable.

Wintercresses *Barbarea* spp.

DESCRIPTION	Medium/tall perennial, 40–80cm. Upright from basal rosette of leaves. Leaves with deep leaflet-like lobes, in several pairs. Hairless. Flowers four-petalled, yellow
HABITAT	Hedges, stream banks, damp ploughed fields
DISTRIBUTION	Common Wintercress: very common in England, rare in the west of Scotland and central-west Wales. Fairly common in Northern Ireland. American Wintercress: occasional in southern and western England, coastal in Wales, scarce elsewhere
SEASON	All year, but best in winter and early spring

It is a pleasure to see the rosettes of dark, shiny green leaves of Wintercress amidst the barren landscape of January. Common Wintercress (*B. vulgaris*) is the most common of the four species of *Barbarea* in the British Isles, followed by the very similar but alien American Wintercress (*B. verna*), which actually originated in southwest Europe – it is just popular in America. Both these provide a winter salad from their basal leaves when almost nothing else is growing. Not that everyone will be pleased to see it on their plate – the leaves are peppery and quite bitter and perhaps unsuitable for the effete modern palate. In 1847 a gardening manual dismissed both plants, saying they were '*subordinate to the Watercress in every character, and our pages may be occupied with more useful subjects*'.

The only thing to do, of course, is find some and try it. The place where the photograph (opposite) was taken is a typical habitat – a damp field edge. Sadly this was the only plant intact – the others had been nibbled by roe deer, judging by nearby signs (you know you have lived in the country too long when you can identify animals by their poo). In fact any damp but not boggy area is likely to be a good hunting ground.

The two species are difficult to tell apart when young (not that it matters very much, except that American Wintercress is a little milder). If you want to know the difference, the Common Wintercress has only two or three pairs of lobes to the American Wintercress's half-dozen. In the mature plant the former has unlobed side leaves and shorter seed pods.

The leaves can be cooked, though this seems to enhance rather than diminish the bitterness. The best thing is to use them in a salad with some other milder-flavoured leaf. A first-class oil and some cider vinegar will help.

American Wintercress

Hairy Bittercress *Cardamine hirsuta*

DESCRIPTION	Small annual. Leaves form a small rosette about 10cm across. Leaves sparsely hairy, opposite, with one terminal leaflet. Flowers tiny, white, four-petalled. Seed pods slender, upright and explosive!
HABITAT	Waste ground, gardens, walls, field edges, path edges
DISTRIBUTION	Extremely common throughout the British Isles, though rare in the Scottish Highlands
SEASON	All year

Most of the weeds sent to build the characters of gardeners are tenacious perennials such as bindweed and Ground Elder, but one annual – Hairy Bittercress – is a match for them all. This uncommonly short-lived little plant will appear suddenly in any neglected corner of the garden and has a particular liking for flower tubs. A single plant can, from germination to explosive dissemination, produce five hundred seeds in a couple of months and an unweeded flower bed can be quickly overrun. Hoed, sprayed or uprooted, it is almost invariably discarded as the pernicious weed it certainly is, but this is a sad waste. Neither particularly hairy nor bitter the 'cress' part of its name, at least, is appropriate, for the flavour is indistinguishable from that of the familiar sandwich ingredient. This prosaic weed is fresh and nutty in flavour and, in my opinion, the very best of the wild salad vegetables.

Hairy Bittercress is a member of the cabbage family and has several close relatives which are all edible. If you find Bittercress in woodland it is more likely to be Wood Bittercress (*C. flexuosa*) and if it is unusually large then it is probably Large Bittercress (*C. amara*). The Reverend Johns in his *Botanical Rambles* describes Hairy Bittercress as having 'few pretensions to beauty', but there is a member of the *Cardamine* genus which needs no pretence; it is that denizen of wet meadows, the lovely Lady's Smock (*C. pratensis*). Although edible, this plant is both bitter and too pretty to pick.

Hairy Bittercress is best collected by snipping off the leaves with scissors although I often uproot entire plants (legal niceties being more than usually absurd in this instance), then trim away the root to avoid getting dirt everywhere. Some of the best plants are found growing at the edges of pavements but these tend to suffer much in the way of pollution, particularly that of a canine nature.

There is really nothing dangerous with which the various Bittercresses might be confused, but the related Scurvygrasses look superficially similar. They have a rosette of single, heart-shaped leaves. These are edible, though only in the loosest sense of the word, being extremely bitter.

EDIBLE SPECIES 39

Black Mustard *Brassica nigra*

DESCRIPTION	Large annual up to 2 metres high. Large, deeply lobed, stalked leaves, very rough surface. Flowers yellow, four-petalled. Seeds black, in small erect pods. All parts taste very strongly of mustard
HABITAT	Seaside cliff edges, waste ground, river banks
DISTRIBUTION	Fairly common, local. Chiefly in England south of the Wash. Almost entirely coastal in Wales
SEASON	Leaves are at their best in spring, but can be found for much of the year in sheltered places. Seeds in July and August

This native annual has long been cultivated and is the original mustard. It is found most readily on cliff edges, explaining perhaps its neglect by the average forager. Although commonly used as a spice and salad ingredient, historically its main use has always been as a medicine. Anything with so potent a flavour as mustard is bound to attract the attention of herbalists who, sometimes rightly, assume that such a plant must have considerable power over the body. Of potential interest to the forager is its reputed ability to resist '*the malignity of mushrooms*'; however, Culpeper is not only the most entertaining herbalist, he is also the most unreliable. He also tells us that it is good for the '*falling down sickness*', the '*drowsy and forgetful evil*' and that it '*helps toothache*'. The latter has some truth in it. A mouthful of mustard tends to take your mind off your molars.

Three crops can be obtained from Black Mustard – the leaves, the young flower heads and the seeds. Seen in a greengrocer's, the leaves would most likely be passed over by most customers. They are fairly tough and have the surface texture of a scouring pad. None of this really matters; the flavour is worth it. I well remember my first taste, many years ago. There was a certain amount of running around and a lot of gasping. It was the surprise as much as the heat.

Black Mustard is great in a beef sandwich as a pleasant cross between horseradish and a green salad. The hot mustard taste of the raw leaves only appears after a bit of chewing. For this reason a pesto is the best way of using it – the mastication has effectively been done for you.

The bright yellow/green young flower heads are succulent and spicy, if a little bitter. Steam them for just a few minutes and serve with butter, or you could use them in the pesto. Don't pick every one you can find, however, as you will then miss out on Black Mustard's third crop – the seeds.

These are the hottest of all the mustards; English mustard is a blend of Black and the milder White Mustard, together with some flour and turmeric. As Black Mustard seeds are tiny and form in short pods, they are very difficult to collect. Timing is difficult too – I arrived a week late at one of my Black Mustard spots and could find barely a half-teaspoonful – the rest had been scattered. The surest way is to cut the flower spikes while the pods are slightly under-ripe, then thresh out the seeds on to a sheet when ready.

Garlic Mustard *Alliaria petiolata*

DESCRIPTION	Erect biennial, usually single-stemmed, 1 metre tall. Leaves bright, light green, hairless; heart-shaped, more pointedly so with upper leaves, more rounded with the lower leaves; bluntly toothed edge. Flowers four-petalled, white. Smells of garlic when crushed
HABITAT	Shady hedgerows, woodland edges
DISTRIBUTION	Very common throughout the British Isles, except in north and west Scotland and in Northern Ireland
SEASON	March–May, although new leaves can appear in the autumn

This cheerful-looking spring cabbage seems to harbour an odd desire to become a garlic plant. Untouched, the leaves are odourless, but when crushed or chewed the garlic aroma becomes immediately apparent. In addition to the name given here it is also commonly known as Hedge Garlic, Jack-in-the-hedge and, in the past, Sauce-alone – the latter being a reference either to its comprehensive talents as a flavouring or an unlikely corruption of *Sauce-ail* where *ail* is the French for 'garlic'.

As few shady hedgerows will fail to support a colony or two of this stately herb and it is a very easy plant to identify, Garlic Mustard is a reliable hedgerow favourite. Although it is familiar as a tall and erect plant, the rounded kidney-shaped basal leaves can be found from early in the year. The best time to pick it, however, is just as the flowers start to appear – much later and the flavour becomes rather rank. The small, bright leaves towards the top of the plant are the best. The roots, too, taste powerfully of garlic but they are rather thin.

Not everyone appreciates Garlic Mustard's virtues. In North America its introduction as a herb has been a small ecological disaster as, having no natural enemies there, it has displaced many native plants. The nineteenth-century writer Anne Manning described it thus: '*as ugly a Jack as one need wish to see, breathing odiously of garlic*'. For most people the flavour will be a pleasant mixture of mild garlic and mild mustard. It is most often employed as a salad vegetable or in a sauce to go with lamb. However, there is no reason why it should not be cooked; it is, after all, a type of cabbage. Serving it as a boiled vegetable is not a rewarding activity, but crispy Garlic Mustard, where the leaves are rolled up, shredded and deep-fried gives an interesting wild equivalent of the crispy 'seaweed' sold in Chinese restaurants. Perhaps most sensible is to employ it as a filling in Hen Chicken (p.215), instead of Fat Hen. Of course you will ruin the pun if you do.

P.S. Despite the unsurprising fact that Garlic Mustard tastes of garlic and mustard there are no garlic or mustard flavours in the plant – technically it is almost tasteless. When the leaves are bruised or chewed, however, chemical precursors are transformed, through a series of complex reactions, into these flavours. The mustard component is allyl isothiocyanate and the garlic flavour diallyl disulphide (the same as in true garlic). Mustard and garlic are not, generally speaking, welcome flavours for most animals and it is for this reason that the plant creates them. It is, however, a strategy that seriously backfired when it encountered the catholic palate of *Homo sapiens*.

Horseradish *Armoracia rusticana*

DESCRIPTION	Medium, leafy perennial, to 70cm, or 1.2 metres when flowering. Leaves in upright clusters, highly distinctive, large, broad, crinkling, 'fish-bone'-like pattern of veins, bright, fresh green. Flowers four-petalled, white – but flowers irregularly in the British Isles
HABITAT	Waste ground, roadsides, field edges
DISTRIBUTION	Very common in England though less so in the North, and coastal in the far Southwest. Coastal in Wales. Rare in Scotland and Northern Ireland
SEASON	All year, but best in the autumn (after this the leaves are gone and you can't find them!)

I distinctly remember trying some of my father's Horseradish Sauce when I was just nine years old. I decided immediately that it was, like girls, something I would only come to appreciate later in life. Well, it took much longer to learn to love the former than the latter, and only in the last few years have I taken to having it with my beef.

Horseradish is a fairly recent addition to our landscape, having been introduced from eastern Europe in the Middle Ages. Like so many invaders it has never found a truly wild home here, being content with disturbed and peripheral land, such as roadsides. In some parts of England, Norfolk for example, it has become a dominant roadside plant, its startlingly bright-green summer foliage extending for miles.

The leaves that will lead you to the edible root are very distinctive, but confusion with superficially similar large dock leaves is not impossible. Not that such a mistake is dangerous – you just won't find any Horseradish roots. A differentiation is simple: dock leaves usually have a little bit of red about them; they are not so bright a green; they do not have the distinct 'fish-bone' vein markings; and the base of the stem does not exude a white fluid which tastes of Horseradish.

It is possible to eat Horseradish leaves, though they are pretty tasteless – like a poor and slightly bitter cabbage. But it is, of course, the roots that are eaten, and these are not at all without taste. Being roots, they will obviously have to be dug up and Horseradish collecting suffers more than any other foraging pursuit from the prohibition against uprooting plants without permission. Considering the vast swathes of the plant that go uncollected, this is a great pity, but if you want to keep within the law, permission is what you must get. The end of October and beginning of November is the best time – the roots are full and fat and, a most practical consideration, if you leave it any longer the leaves will wither and disappear and you

EDIBLE SPECIES 45

won't be able to find the roots at all (I know, I have tried). Seeing the leaves will also ensure that the roots you are digging up *are* Horseradish and not some other, perhaps deadly, root such as Hemlock Water-dropwort.

It is fair to say that Horseradish roots are not easy to unearth. They are branched and twisted and tend to grow in soil with more than its fair share of large stones. Once you have your prize, take it home and wash off all the soil. The roots will keep for a long time if they are stored in sand to keep out the light and stop them drying. One other possible way exists for preserving Horseradish – scrub, slice thinly across the root, dry the slices very slowly on a warm windowsill or in a low oven, then powder the dried slices in a blender.

But Horseradish ideally should be used raw and freshly grated. I have tried cooking it as a vegetable, but the spiciness turns to bitterness and the texture is that of wet kindling wood. To prepare Horseradish, peel off the thin skin with a potato peeler, then grate the root across the grain. I have never been caught in a tear-gas attack but I can't imagine it is as bad as grating Horseradish. Do it outside on a windy day. One cooked dish which does work very well is Horseradish and Chestnut Dumplings (p.216). The very light cooking the grated root receives ensures that the aromatic flavour does not turn bitter.

There are many recipes for Horseradish Sauce, each seeming to outdo the next in potency. Ignoring those that call for chilli powder, cloves or anchovies, the simplest recipe is to mix 100g grated Horseradish root with 2 tsp cider vinegar, 1 tsp ground mustard seed, 125ml double cream and a little salt and black pepper. The sauce should be kept in the fridge and used within 24 hours.

Watercress *Rorippa nasturtium-aquaticum*

DESCRIPTION	Large trailing aquatic perennial. Leaflets more or less opposite plus terminal leaflet, *very shallowly lobed* edges, dark green, often with a bronze tinge. Young leaves form a rosette around emerging flower heads. Taste *peppery*. Flowers small, white, four-petalled
HABITAT	Shallow streams, often chalk streams, ditches
DISTRIBUTION	Common, less so in the North
SEASON	Late March until November

Few wild plants come in such abundance as Watercress. It is usually possible to pick a sackful of leaves in a few minutes with little noticeable effect on the local plant population. The high price it commands in the shops makes this all the more welcome. Watercress is exactly the same delicious plant cultivated or wild – there has been no effort, or need, to improve it.

There *are* a couple of problems, however. The first comes in the form of a look-alike – Fool's Watercress (*Apium nodiflorum*). This is not nearly as bad as it sounds, for it too is edible, though much inferior, with a mild taste of carrots. It grows in precisely the same locations, often found unhelpfully intertwined with true Watercress and still gives me pause even after years of familiarity with both species. The distinguishing features of Fool's Watercress are finely and bluntly toothed edges to the leaflets, shiny yellow/green opposite leaflets and a taste of carrots.

The second problem is less easy to overcome. There is a little creature, a fluke, called *Fasciola hepatica*, which spends part of its time stuck to aquatic plants waiting to enter the digestive tract of a sheep or other herbivore. It has a baroquely complex life-cycle with about ten stages, three of which it enjoys inside a small snail. The last of these stages, the cercarium, leaves the snail and swims around until it finds a plant to attach itself to, turns into a cyst called a metacercarium and waits. The process generally requires a habitat which includes grazing animals, slow-flowing or stagnant water, muddy river banks to harbour the snails, and suitable vegetation.

F. hepatica is not a natural parasite of humans, but the tiny metacercarium will gradually develop and eat its way through you until it is at the 3cm, flat, slug-like adult stage, whereupon it finds its way into your liver. There it will be a further nuisance – blocking bile ducts, causing infections and hepatitis and eating more bits of you. As an infected person will often have many flukes sitting in their bile ducts it is sometimes, unsurprisingly, fatal. Although around two and a half million people are infected worldwide by various routes, it is difficult to quantify the problem in this

Watercress

Fool's Watercress

country where little wild Watercress is eaten. However, *F. hepatica* is very common here (millions of sheep suffer its depredations every year), so the risk is a real one.

I presume you will not be wanting a family of slug look-alikes taking up residence in your liver so my advice must be not to bother with raw wild Watercress. There is of course one simple way of removing the parasite – cooking. This would mean that salads are off the menu but there are still many excellent recipes which use cooked Watercress. But if you still want to eat it raw and wild I offer the following suggestions. Collect in fast-moving water upstream of any grazing animals. Avoid streams with muddy banks – these can harbour the snail, which acts as an unwilling accomplice to the fluke. Pick from plants that are growing in the middle of streams – you never see snails doing the breast stroke so these plants are less likely to be infected by snails climbing the stems. Choose leaves that are never submerged in water and thus out of reach of the swimming cercaria – this is easier with the large mature plants of summer. When you get home soak the collection in 10 per cent white vinegar solution for 10 minutes, then rinse very thoroughly. Alternatively, and more reliably, chlorine-based proprietary sterilisers (such as the ones used to sterilise baby's bottles) will both kill and remove the metacercaria. The latter rather detracts from the wild, natural quality of your salad but is no worse than the chlorine sterilisation of domestic water supplies.

In the eighteenth century, the writer George Saville Carey penned a slightly invigorating poem about a watercress girl, Phoebe, he met on the way to London.

When hoary frost hung on each thorn,
Ere night had well withdrawn her gloom,
Poor Phoebe went one wintry morn,
From Colnbrook, down to Langley-broom,
When from the brake or from the rill,
Half clad and with neglected tresses,
Her rushy basket try'd to fill,
With fresh and green SPRING WATER CRESSES.

There is more but I think we have had enough. I always go fully clothed and brush my hair, but the basket is a good idea. Wellies and a large pair of scissors complete the essential Watercress foraging kit. Every part of the plant is edible, but I usually collect the rosette around the developing flower head.

Assuming you successfully navigate the dreaded fluke peril, Watercress has genuine health-giving properties, as it is packed with copious quantities of vitamins, minerals and phytochemicals. The peppery taste is immediately recognisable and is common to many other members of the cabbage family. Its potency is diminished with cooking so quickly sweating it for a sauce or adding it at the very last minute to a soup is the best way to retain the flavour.

Perennial Wall Rocket
Diplotaxis tenuifolia

DESCRIPTION	Medium bush-like perennial, to 1 metre. Leaves long and irregularly lobed, tasting nutty at first then hot and peppery. Last year's stems usually visible amongst the leaves. Flowers yellow, four-petalled. Long, thin seed pods
HABITAT	Mostly coastal or urban
DISTRIBUTION	Largest population in the far southeast of England including London, but also Bristol, Liverpool and several other cities. Rare in Scotland and absent from Ireland. Scattered elsewhere, mostly coastal
SEASON	March–July

One naturally assumes that the country mouse will have the edge over the city mouse when it comes to foraging, but it is not always so. I have never seen Perennial Wall Rocket in a truly wild location, the nearest to this being a seaside car park near Weymouth, which is skirted with a couple of dozen substantial bushes. My best find of this plant ever was in the old industrial centre of Bristol where Perennial Wall Rocket grows from every crack in the concrete. It was a fairly dog-free place so I happily filled a couple of bags.

The leaves grow in little bunches all the way up the stem and you can simply cut these off. There is really nothing nasty that can be confused with Perennial Wall Rocket and the nutty, peppery flavour alone will be sufficient to reassure you. Just watch out for those dogs.

Perennial Wall Rocket is an alien invader, though a well-behaved and welcome one, and the same plant as the wild rocket one often sees in supermarkets and greengrocers. I have made polite enquiries to a couple of retail outlets, asking how they justify the 'wild' part of the name (the staff do not collect the stuff from the hedgerow on their way to work) and received charming, evasive replies in return. I guess we will never know.

The flavour of the truly wild plant is the same as that of the cultivated 'wild' plant, except that it is considerably nuttier and very considerably more peppery. If you are man enough, or indeed woman enough, there is no reason why you could not eat it alone in a salad, but I generally mix it with other milder salad leaves. Either way, I love it.

EDIBLE SPECIES 51

Common Chickweed *Stellaria media*

DESCRIPTION	Low, sprawling annual. Tangled habit, individual strands up to 50cm long. Leaves 1–2.5cm, oval, mostly hairless, slightly frosted. Stems straggling, *single line of hairs* down one side. Flowers five-petalled, though petals are very deeply divided and look more like ten
HABITAT	Gardens, dung heaps, field margins. Prefers damp areas
DISTRIBUTION	Very common throughout the British Isles
SEASON	Can be found all year, but only in sheltered locations during the winter. Summer growth can be stringy

Common Chickweed is not a popular plant, as anyone who has spent an hour uprooting it from their vegetable garden, only to have it defiantly reappear a couple of weeks later, will tell you. Yet as one who has forsaken the embattled life of the gardener for the lazy pursuits of the forager, it is something I am always pleased to see. Common Chickweed is one of the tastiest of the wild greens and the enlightened gardener should view it not as a threat, but as a welcome bonus crop.

The name comes from the practice of feeding it to poultry who love the stuff. Generations of budgerigars have also enjoyed this plant, and it has been used as an occasional fodder crop for cattle. Apart from its edible uses, Chickweed has found employment in a variety of dubious medical remedies. An eye lotion is one such, and its habit of closing its leaves at night has inspired its use as an inducer of sleep.

Chickweed is clearly not a hard plant to find, and its almost continual appearance throughout the year will ensure you a fairly constant supply. Avoid, however, the thin and stringy growth of summer. Both leaves and stems are good to eat when young and fresh. Scissors are a must when collecting this plant, otherwise you will uproot the entire plant, tough stems, roots, mud and all. Watch out for any entwining speedwell plants which are superficially similar but nearly always show their distinctive tiny blue flowers.

Chickweed is easily distinguished from potential impostors, such as the larger and slightly edible Greater Stitchwort (*Stellaria holostea*), by the single line of fine hairs running the length of the stem.

The flavour is mild and pleasant, not unlike lettuce but with a bit of freshly mown cricket pitch thrown in. It is fine in a salad as long as only the youngest stems are used. It works well in a soup and makes for an excellent stir-fry, but my favourite recipe is for Chickweed Pakoras (p.211).

Single line of fine hairs on stem

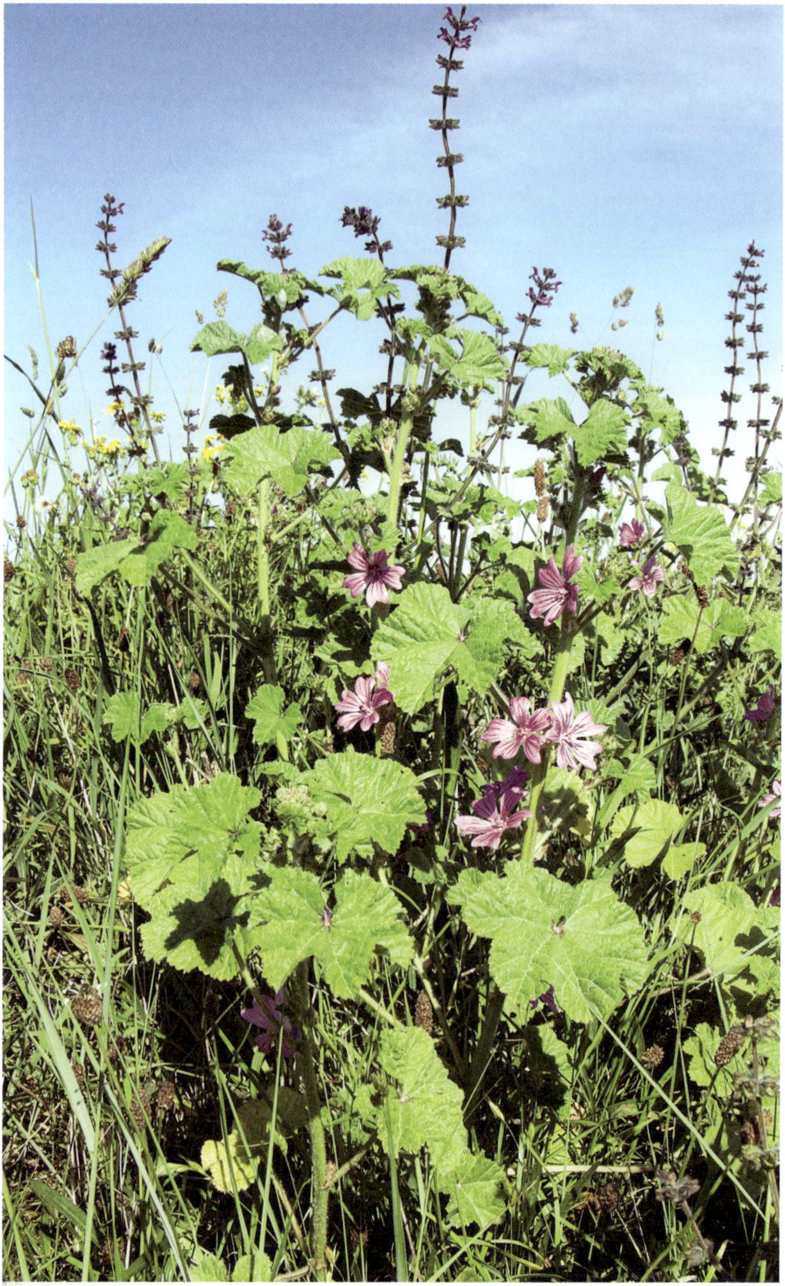

Common Mallow *Malva sylvestris*

DESCRIPTION	Medium annual/perennial, 0.8–1.5 metres, usually upright. Leaves rounded palmate (palm-shaped), lower leaves more rounded, often with a central dark spot, downy/hairy, on long stem. Flowers five-petalled, pink/mauve. Seeds in a ring like a ring doughnut
HABITAT	Roadside, waste ground, field edge. Frequently coastal
DISTRIBUTION	Very common throughout much of the British Isles but scarcer in northern England, Scotland and Wales. Very scarce in Northern Ireland
SEASON	Spring for the leaves, though they can be found through much of the year. Late summer for the seeds

The marshmallows we buy today were once, of course, made from the mucilaginous roots of real marsh-mallows. But this is quite a rare plant these days, found only in the upper reaches of some marshes and in brackish ditches from the Wash southwards. Common Mallow, however, is what it says it is – common. I do not think you will be making any sweetmeats from this plant as the roots are too small, but the leaves and the little seeds are edible.

The mucilage found in its leaves has given this plant its reputation as a soothing plant rather like aloe vera. Culpeper prescribes it for scaldings, burnings, swellings, dandruff and, most worrying of all, excoriations of the bowels. And also for '*the stinging of bees, wasps and the like*'. One of its old names is Round Dock, and it may be Common Mallow that we should rub on Stinging Nettle rashes not Common Dock.

The mildly nutty seeds were once commonly eaten by children, but they are fiddly to collect and it is primarily the leaves that are used. Common Mallow can be found easily everywhere, particularly near the sea. The young leaves of spring are certainly the best, but even these will pick up a considerable amount of dust on their slightly furry surface. Just wash them well before cooking. Mallow leaves start to wilt the moment they are picked, so seal them in a plastic box to take them home.

The flavour is mild and pleasant, and the texture slightly slimy. As a plain vegetable it is a non-starter, though I did make a slightly slippery bubble and squeak with it once. There is really only one 'proper' thing that can be made from the Common Mallow – the Middle Eastern dish, Molukhia or Jew's Mallow soup. It is not a complicated dish, consisting mostly of chicken meat, chicken stock, garlic and lots of finely chopped Common Mallow leaves. It looks a little like 'grass-cutting' soup to me but tastes good.

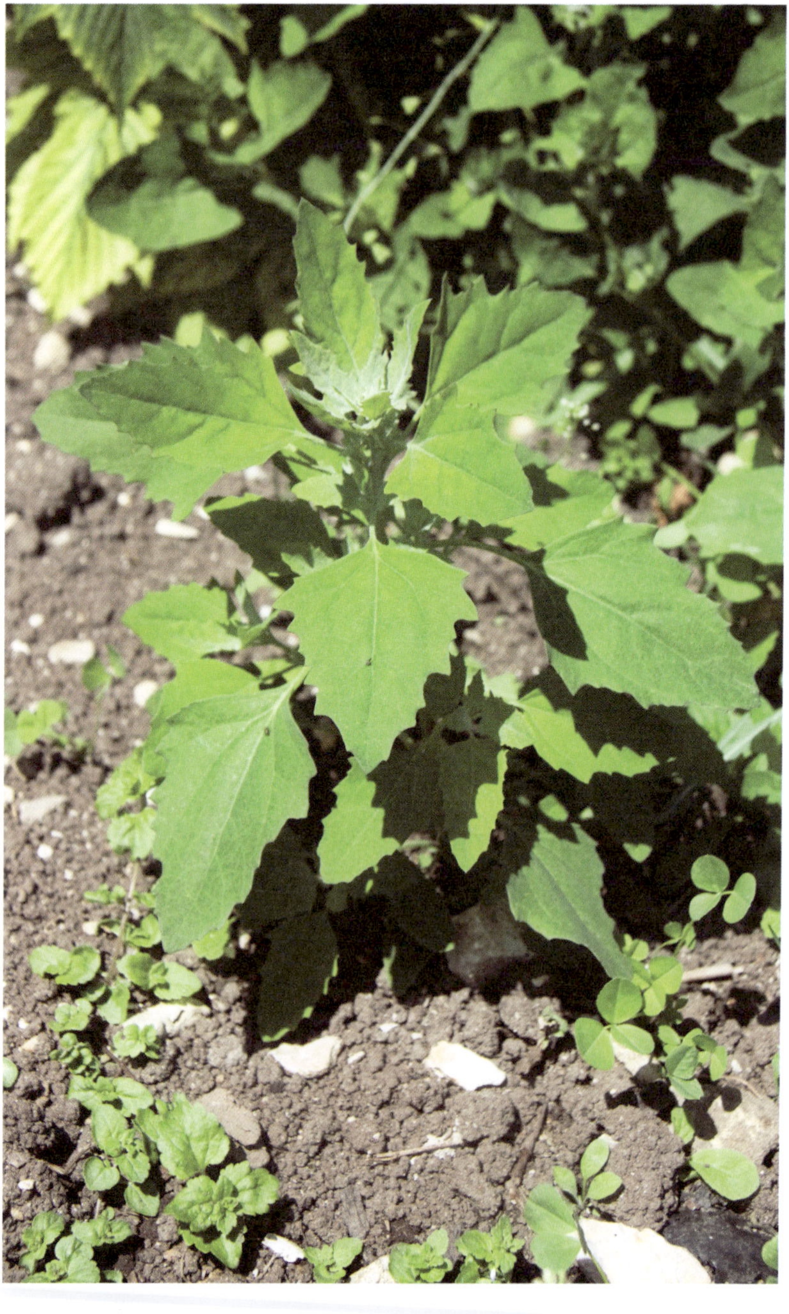

Fat Hen *Chenopodium album*

DESCRIPTION	Upright, medium annual, to 1 metre. Leaves very variable but roughly rounded triangular, narrower at top of mature stem, covered in white meal – especially when young, feel slightly greasy. Flowers grow from leaf joints on spikes
HABITAT	Disturbed, cultivated ground. Compost heaps. Not on high ground
DISTRIBUTION	Extremely common throughout the British Isles, but rare in the east of Scotland
SEASON	May–October

Having some years ago been evicted from my allotment for taking an over-relaxed view of cultivation, it is still nice to visit the old place from time to time to see how my more diligent successors are getting on. Of course it is not just nostalgia that draws me there – it is the weeds. Chief among these is Fat Hen. Any piece of nitrogen-rich cultivated ground, left for a couple of weeks in the summer, can start to sprout a perfect crop of this tasty vegetable. Being a generous sort and not wanting to keep it all for myself I tell the gardeners that it is edible and tasty, but they always proceed to dig it in and, with much labour, plant the inferior spinach instead.

Fat Hen has been around for millennia but was probably introduced and, like so many other once-popular plants, has overstayed its welcome. It was used as a favourite green vegetable until a few centuries ago when it was replaced by the related spinach. The seeds can last in the soil for decades; there appear to be four different varieties, all with different germination requirements and longevity, and seed densities can reach tens of thousands per square metre. It is a persistent and troublesome weed not just in allotment gardens but also on agricultural land, where much effort is expended in suppressing it. The forager, of course, cares not for the woes of others and this information just tells him or her where to look.

Fat Hen is easy to identify once you have the hang of it. It is, unfortunately, rather variable in its appearance (*morphological plasticity*, don't you know) and it hybridises with other members of the goosefoot family, which already look like it anyway. Furthermore, the young plants and leaves look unlike the mature plants and leaves. None of this would matter too much if there was nothing nasty to confuse it with but, inevitably, there is. These are members of the treacherous Solanaceae (potato family) such as Black Nightshade and Datura. The safest way to be sure you have Fat Hen is to pick the young plants at 15cm or so, with their more

Red Goosefoot

highly distinctive mealy surface, or the fully grown ones, with their unmistakable flower spikes. Two or three crops of young plants a year are easily available from the same piece of land if it is dug over after picking (this counts as gardening if you do it yourself and foraging if someone else does it). You should never be short of Fat Hen between May and October.

The flavour is similar to spinach but a little less bitter, and can be used in similar situations. The delicate leaves do not steam well and are best sweated with a little butter for 5 minutes. Hen Chicken (p.215) is a good way of using a substantial amount of Fat Hen in a tasty dish. I suggest serving it with a salad of Chickweed.

Also look out for quite a large number of other goosefoots. These are members of the goosefoot genus (*Chenopodium*), not necessarily the overarching goosefoot family (*Chenopodiaceae*), which also includes the edible Sea Beet and Marsh Samphire. Principal among these is Red Goosefoot (*C. rubrum*). The leaves of this plant are unhappily like those of some nightshades, so do be careful and wait until the flower spikes start to appear if you are unsure (the nightshades have five-petalled and often rather flamboyant flowers). The leaves are unusually shiny for a goosefoot. The stem normally exhibits a red coloration in amongst the green, as do the flowers. By far the best place to find this neat plant is on a compost heap.

The best-known goosefoot, other than Fat Hen, is Good King Henry (*C. bonus-henricus*); sadly it is now a fairly uncommon plant though it was once extensively cultivated. The strange name, repeated in the Latin epithet, is from the German *Guter Heinrich*. Heinrich was probably an elf and the 'Good' part was to differentiate the plant from the unrelated and poisonous 'Bad Henry' – Dog's Mercury. Quite where the 'King' bit comes from no one knows.

Further than this, there are over thirty other goosefoots in the British Isles. Fig-leaved Goosefoot, Many-seeded Goosefoot and Nettle-leaved Goosefoot are all fairly common and all with a roughly southern and eastern distribution; most of the rest are extremely rare. It is likely that nearly all are more or less edible, though Foetid Goosefoot and Stinking Goosefoot do not sound too promising.

Spear-leaved Orache *Atriplex prostrata*

DESCRIPTION	Medium annual, to 1 metre. Often upright, but seaside plants especially can be straggling. Lower leaves fairly large, triangular with straight base approximately at right angles to the leaf stem, broadly toothed, slightly mealy. Upper leaves narrow on maturity. Flowers grow on spikes from leaf joints
HABITAT	Waste ground, cultivated ground, compost heaps, upper beaches
DISTRIBUTION	Very common in England, though rare in the Northwest. Coastal elsewhere
SEASON	May–October

I find Spear-leaved Orache more often than its relative Fat Hen. It too can be found in cultivated soil and waste ground, but Spear-leaved Orache also has a holiday home by the sea. Sometimes you will find a substantial crop in an unusual place; my best find of this plant was underneath the steps at Dorchester South Railway Station – there was also a nice patch of Wild Strawberries just outside the main entrance and I nearly missed my train.

As with other members of the goosefoot family, this plant does have certain similarities to the Solanaceae family, the nightshades. Black Nightshade, for example, has similar-shaped leaves but lacks, among other things, the distinctly straight base to its triangular leaves. One plant you will almost certainly confuse it with, given the chance, is Good King Henry. This is much less common, shorter, its leaves are less lobed and it has a different flower structure – apart from that there is little between them so it is just as well that it too is edible.

All the oraches mentioned here are good spinach substitutes though too bitter to be used raw in a salad.

Also look out for several other oraches, Common Orache (*A. patula*) being the most obvious. Again it is a weed of cultivation with a liking for the seaside. Babington's Orache (*A. glabriuscula*) and Frosted Orache (*A. laciniata*) are exclusively seaside plants, often forming long mats of vegetation above the strand-line. The first has small triangular/oval leaves; the second does what it says it does and looks as though it is covered in frost.

If you are confused by the oraches and the goosefoots then I welcome you to a not very exclusive club. Even my most enthusiastic botanical friends despair at giving a positive identification for many of them. Serious floras, such as the excellent *New Flora of the British Isles* by Clive Stace, has for one of the goosefoots '… *lower leaves trullate to triangular-ovate, acute to rounded, and mucronate at apex, cunate to truncate at base…*' and so on. For the forager the main thing to know is that they *are* oraches or goosefoots – most are good to eat and none will do you any harm. All those mentioned here have some degree of mealiness on the leaves and tiny flowers which grow in long spikes originating from where the leaf joins the stem.

Wood Sorrel *Oxalis acetosella*

DESCRIPTION	Low creeping perennial. Leaves trefoil, leaflets heart-shaped with central fold, finely hairy, yellowish green. Stems red/brown. Leaf and flower stems *unbranched* and arising from a single base. Flowers five-petalled, white to pale pink with mauve veins, yellow centres. Carpeting woodland floor. All parts taste acidic
HABITAT	All types of woods including coniferous; shady places
DISTRIBUTION	Very common throughout the British Isles, except the Fens
SEASON	All year, though best in the spring and early summer

Wood Sorrel is a refined and delicate plant, quite unlike its rough grassland namesake, Sorrel. The flavour, however, is the same – powerfully acidic. Found all over the country, it can carpet the woodland floor with pretty leaves which fold up at night like automatic origami. *Oxalis* comes from the Greek *oxys* meaning 'sharp' (oxygen has the same derivation though unjustified, due to the mistaken belief that it is essential for making acids; a job done, in fact, by hydrogen). The name Sorrel is also a reference to the taste, being derived from *sur*, the French for 'sour'.

The trefoil nature of the leaves has made it one of the candidates for the shamrock, with which St Patrick demonstrated the nature of the Holy Trinity (in fact the Trinity is a mystery and resists metaphor). Another familiar religious association is due to its flowering at Easter time, giving it the occasional name of Alleluia.

The flowers are unusual in that while they are nearly always infertile, the plant always sets seed. In fact the seeds are produced by tiny, unopening and self-fertile flowers near the roots in a process called cleistogamy ('closed marriage' – 'open marriage', if you're wondering, is called chasmogamy). The visible flowers are, it seems, just for show.

Many people confuse Wood Sorrel with clover. This is a terrible novice mistake to make and will cause you much embarrassment on any natural history society ramble. Clover leaflets are oval, never heart-shaped. An easier, and more dangerous, error is confusion with the related Procumbent Yellow Sorrel (*Oxalis corniculata*). This contains potentially dangerous levels of oxalic acid and has caused deaths in grazing animals if not in humans. Its stems are branched, the flowers are yellow and it seldom grows in woods, so you should have no trouble with it.

It is pleasantly refreshing on a hot spring day to nibble a few leaves of Wood Sorrel, but if you want more, then scissors will be needed to avoid bringing the woodland floor home with you too. The plant is tiny and it does take a while to collect a reasonable amount. A newspaper report complaining about commercial collecting and the fairly substantial price obtainable for a kilo of Wood Sorrel showed not the slightest inkling of how long such a quantity would take to collect – about a day in my opinion.

The stems and flowers are edible as well as the leaves, with the same lemony grape-skin flavour. Although it is available almost all year, the fresh growth of the spring is better flavoured and textured.

As it is attractive, Wood Sorrel is sometimes used as a decorative and fruity garnish. I once used it (rather daringly, I thought) on a lemon torte. It is a perfect alternative to lemon with fish, either alone or in a mixed wild salad. (It is worth mentioning here that not all wild salads work – I once tried Wood Sorrel, Ramsons and Hairy Bittercress all together – it was unspeakably vile.)

Wood Sorrel can also be made into an excellent sauce by chopping the leaves finely, then sweating them in some double cream for a couple of minutes – just perfect with salmon or trout.

The taste of Wood Sorrel comes from oxalic acid and calcium oxalate, which are poisonous but present in Wood Sorrel in sufficiently small quantities to be harmless unless you eat a great deal. See entry for Sorrel (p.110).

Broom *Cytisus scoparius*

DESCRIPTION	Wiry shrub up to 2 metres. Lower leaves small trefoil. Stems spineless, angular in section, green. Flowers brilliant yellow, like tiny sweetpeas when open
HABITAT	Heath, roadsides, open woods. Often on sand
DISTRIBUTION	Common throughout the British Isles, except the Fens and northwestern extremity of Scotland
SEASON	Buds from April until early June

Geoffrey Count of Anjou, father of Henry II, wore a sprig of Broom as an emblem. The medieval Latin name of the Broom is *Planta genista* and is the origin of Plantagenet. This is the sort of story that will make you the centre of attention at parties and is worth remembering.

There are several flowers that can be eaten on their own and Broom buds are the most accessible of them all. The shrub is visible for some miles on a sunny day because of the dazzling intensity of its yellow flowers. The related and unpalatable gorse has furry buds and spiny leaves. Broom buds (the bright-yellow but unopened flower) are available in the spring and are best when small and tight.

Broom is in the pea family so it is little surprise that the flavour is that of pea, or perhaps another relative, the runner bean. They provide a tasty decoration on a spring salad and can be added to a stir-fry at the last moment. You can also pickle them, if you must.

My recommendation of Broom is wholehearted, but comes with two small warnings. All parts of the Broom, including the flower buds, contain trace amounts of toxins – sparteine and isosparteine being chief among them. These can depress heart function, cause paralysis and restrict peripheral blood vessels. You may need to eat around two kilograms of the buds before noticing the effects, so a dozen on a wild green salad are unlikely to do you any harm. Rarely, you might encounter the Spanish Broom (*Spartium junceum*), distinguished by its pine-like leaves. The buds of this Broom contain significantly higher levels of toxin and must not be eaten.

P.S. There are a few other wild flowers that can be used for their decorative qualities – Bramble, Rose and Borage on a salad, or Primroses set on top of a Champagne jelly. Primroses can even be candied by brushing on a strong sugar solution and letting them dry. Sweet Violets, if you can find them, may also be preserved in this way. (A piece of advice to any male readers who tread this floral path is not to tell your mates about it in the pub.)

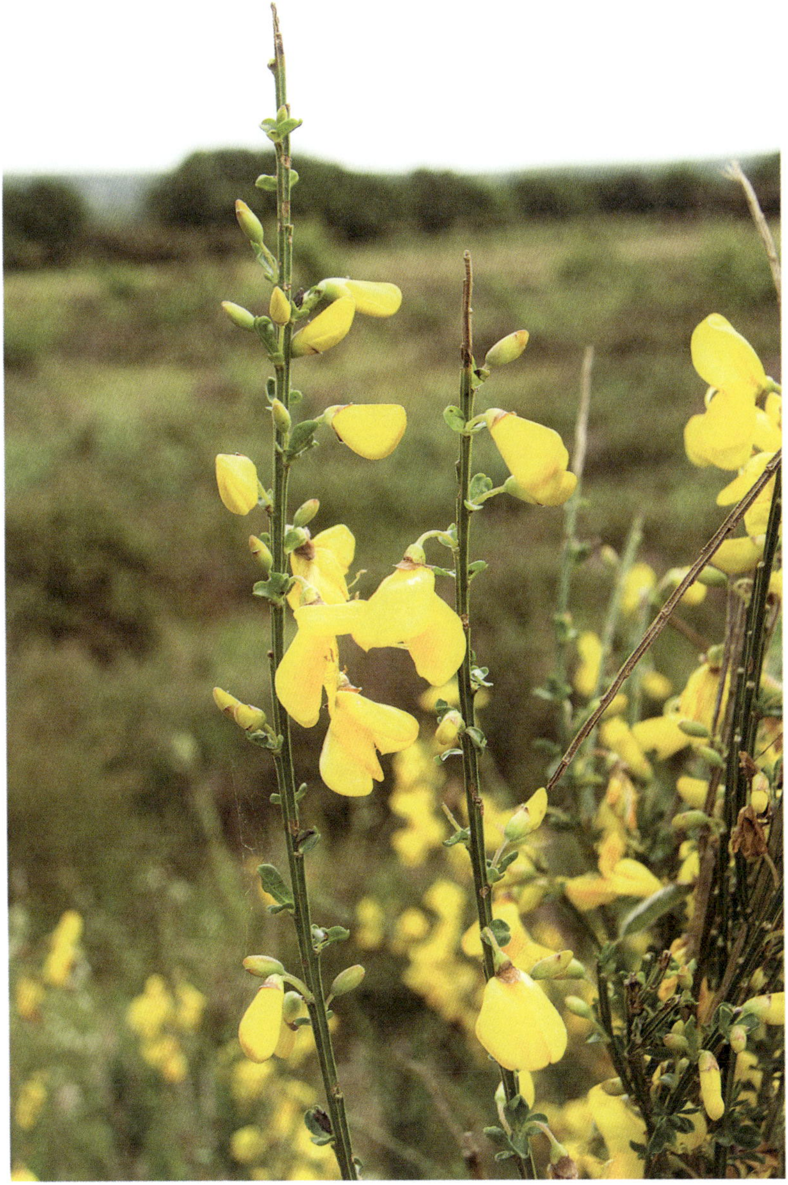

Blackberry *Rubus fruticosus* agg.

DESCRIPTION	Scrambling, arching shrub, to 3 metres. Leaves with three to five leaflets – oval/pointed, serrated edge, hairy white underside. Stem with backward-pointing strong, sharp thorns. Flowers five-petalled, white to pale pink. Fruit consisting of many dark purple/black segments
HABITAT	Woods, hedgerows, waste ground, gardens. All soil types, but does not like very wet conditions
DISTRIBUTION	Extremely common throughout the British Isles, except the Scottish Highlands
SEASON	Berries from August until mid-October

Plants often possess a distinct personality but few have one quite as large as that of the common Blackberry. This untidy, sprawling, invasive shrub is self-confident to the point of boorishness, yet more generous than any other plant in this book. Foraging for fruit can be hard work – the Redcurrant and the Raspberry, the Wild Strawberry and the Bilberry are all difficult to find in any quantity – but the Blackberry may be regularly picked by the bucketful.

My record for one season's Blackberry picking is 65 kilograms (it was a good year for field mushrooms, too, with 50 kilograms from the field just above the Blackberry patch). Such quantities are not unusual and the imagination and operational schedule of the cook can be taxed to the limit. Of course there is always the freezer – but they can languish there neglected and forgotten for years (I once inherited several ancient bags of Blackberries from a friend who was emigrating).

No one has any trouble identifying a Blackberry – it is something we seem almost born to recognise; the only berry that will cause confusion is the very similar and equally edible Dewberry. Finding them will also not be hard. As Gerard says, '*The bramble groweth for the most part in every hedge and bush*' and it is indeed common in hedgerows everywhere, odd corners of farms, scrub, woodland, unruly gardens and waste ground. It is the one plant that the town-dwelling forager will always be able to find – usually in otherwise unattractive corners of the urban environment.

Few people will have missed out on the singular pleasures of Blackberry picking – it is something nearly every child has, or should have, done at some time. I did once go Blackberry picking with a young lady for whom these fruit were things that came in ready-made pies. She wore medical latex gloves to protect her hands from contamination with the real world. They lasted 4 seconds but she still survived to tell of her ordeal.

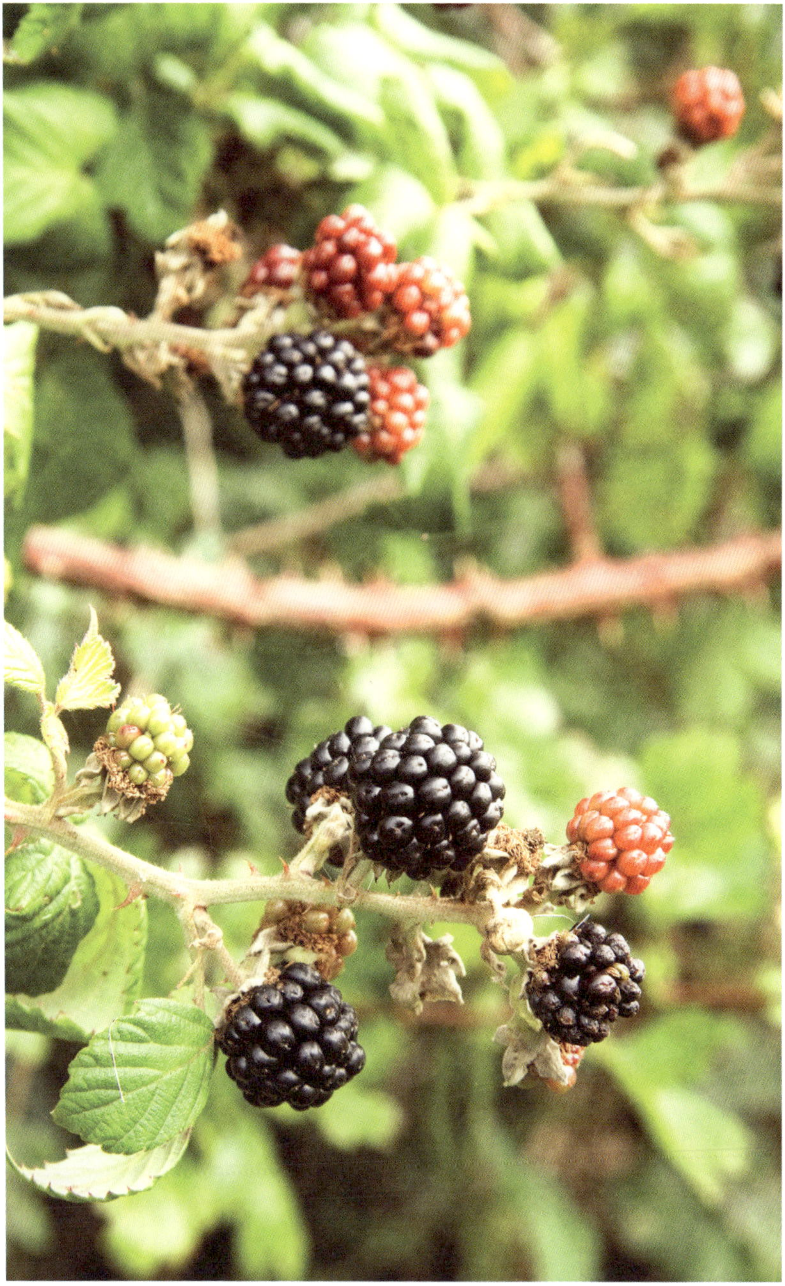

I recall the Blackberry-picking trips of my childhood. These were military operations involving unseasonably thick clothing, leather gloves, baskets and buckets, and a search of the house for the walking stick with a crook on the end. I recommend this sort of preparation if you want to pick in quantity. There is much to be said for using one leather-gloved hand to hold the stalk, and the other ungloved hand to pick the berries. A walking stick to hook out-of-reach bunches and beat down the undergrowth is essential. Long sleeves and Wellington boots will protect you from most of the vicious thorns, though you will be very lucky to get away completely unscathed. The late August and early September days that form the peak of the Blackberry season are also a good time for the flies that infest both them and you. Blackberrying, as I am sure you know, is a very uncomfortable enterprise but worth every single scratch.

There is a well-known superstition that Blackberries should not be picked after Michaelmas because the Devil has spat on them, fallen on them (having been cast out of heaven on that day), thrown his cloak over them or stamped on them. Michaelmas is 29 September or, if you use the old calendar, 10 October. The best Blackberries tend to be early in the season when the sun is strong, before the flies have pierced them and the grey mould *Botrytis cinerea* has taken hold. But there is no genuine reason for not picking them late in the year, so long as you can find good ones.

The biggest and sweetest berry is usually the one at the end of the stalk. This ripens long before all the others and is the one to eat raw; the rest are best for cooking. Quite what a Blackberry will taste like is a bit of an unknown until you actually eat it. Ripeness and weather seem to have a large bearing, but the Blackberry comes in many microspecies, which may vary greatly in taste.

Blackberries do not keep. Not even for a day. The mould spores are sat on the surface of the berries waiting to do their worst, so whatever it is that you hope to make with your precious cache you should start straight away. If there is no time to make your jam or crumble, at least cook the berries through by simmering them on a low heat for a few minutes.

The sheer quantity of Blackberries that you can collect opens up possibilities that would be wasteful or impractical with other berries. The best country wine I've made was Blackberry, and the best jelly I ever made – well, that was Blackberry too. Blackberry jelly, vinegar, sorbet or ice cream, Blackberry and apple pie or crumble, summer pudding and fruit leather – I could list a hundred ways of cooking this adaptable fruit, but many will already be familiar to you. Three ideas from three giants of the hedgerow harvest are, however, of particular note. Hugh adapts a Sloe Gin recipe to make a Blackberry whisky, which gets better and better with keeping if you have the self-restraint to allow it to. Richard Mabey tells us of Blackberry 'junket', made by keeping the juice of ripe berries in a warm room overnight until it sets, and Pam Corbin has the perfect recipe for Bramble Mousse (p.221).

Crab Apple *Malus sylvestris*

DESCRIPTION	Small tree. Leaves broadly oval/pointed, toothed edge, alternate. Twigs and branches intricately entangled, true Crab Apple trees quite often have occasional thorns
HABITAT	Woods, hedgerows
DISTRIBUTION	Common in England south of Cumbria and in lowland Wales and Scotland, uncommon elsewhere
SEASON	September–October

A fully burdened Crab Apple tree is a wonderful sight in autumn, but chiefly from a distance. The apples themselves are, as one Edward Long put it in the eighteenth century, '*never admired for loveliness of aspect*'. Small, misshapen, spotty and scabby, and full of pips, they do not inspire the cook. Nor are they remotely edible raw – they must be cooked. Yet when prepared properly they are a treasure.

Old woodland and farm hedges away from habitation are the most likely places to find the true Crab Apple. Roadside trees are much more likely to have arisen from discarded pips – 'wildings' as they are called. The Crab Apple has a malleable genetic makeup, which has allowed it to be developed into the two thousand or so domesticated apple varieties that exist today. A tree grown from the pip of a cultivated apple can produce a totally unpredictable fruit. It may be similar to its parent apple; often it will be just like a Crab Apple, or sometimes it will be completely different from either. The forager must always take a pragmatic view of what is on offer. Apples growing on any wild tree – whether true Crab Apple or wilding – must be judged solely on their merits, not on their racial purity.

The true Crab Apple is a fine fruit with some useful qualities. Chief among these is the sharpness which makes it inedible raw. This is principally down to the tongue-dissolving malic acid, beloved of 'extreme candy' eaters. Verjuice is a venerable substitute for lemon juice or vinegar, which exploits this quality well. (The name, incidentally, comes from the French *verde* or 'green', most verjuice being made from under-ripe grapes.) It can also be produced from apples that have been left in a pile for a month to mature; those that have matured too far are discarded and the remaining apples mashed and pressed. The juice is kept for a few weeks to mature a little more, then bottled. The intensely sharp flavour makes it a particularly good accompaniment to fish.

I use Crab Apples in an (almost) entirely wild version of Pam Corbin's 'leathers'. Hawthorn and Crab Apple Leather is a first-class way of dealing with two fruits that

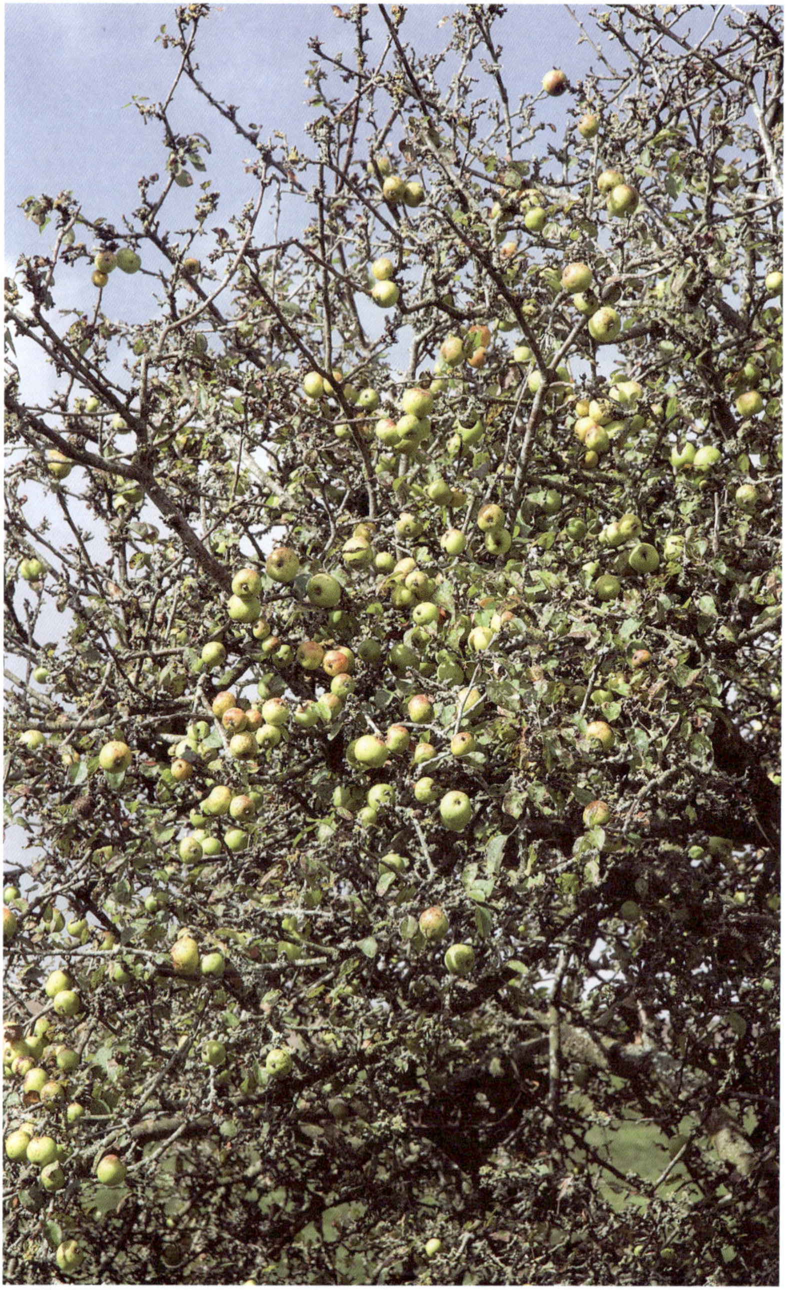

are mostly pips and skin. To prepare, chop 500g Crab Apples and stew with 500g Haws and 100ml water for 20 minutes. Push the cooked mixture through a fine sieve into a saucepan, add 150g sugar and heat the pulp, stirring until the sugar dissolves. Now spread the purée on baking trays lined with baking parchment and place in a low oven (at 50–60°C/Gas mark ⅛) for 12–18 hours until dry and leathery.

Of course, the recipe for which this tart apple is best known is Crab Apple jelly. The very high pectin content means that it will always set well, and other fruits can be added to make a variety of jellies. Cooked, strained and with sugar added, Crab Apples also make a sharp apple sauce – just use extra sugar if it takes the roof of your mouth off. Although Crab Apples are not very lovely whole, they can still be used sliced as decoration, as in Cranberry and Apple Tart (p.222).

P.S. I cannot resist passing on this medicinal recipe from the early 1800s; it is for a concoction called Black Drop:

> *Take half a pound of opium sliced, three parts of good verjuice, one and a half ounces of nutmeg, and half an ounce of saffron. Boil them to a proper thickness; then add a quarter of a pound of sugar, and two spoonfuls of yeast. Set the whole in a warm place near the fire for six or eight weeks, then place it in the open air, until it become a syrup; lastly, decant, filter, bottle it up, adding a little sugar to each bottle.*

I am not sure what it was supposed to cure; everything perhaps.

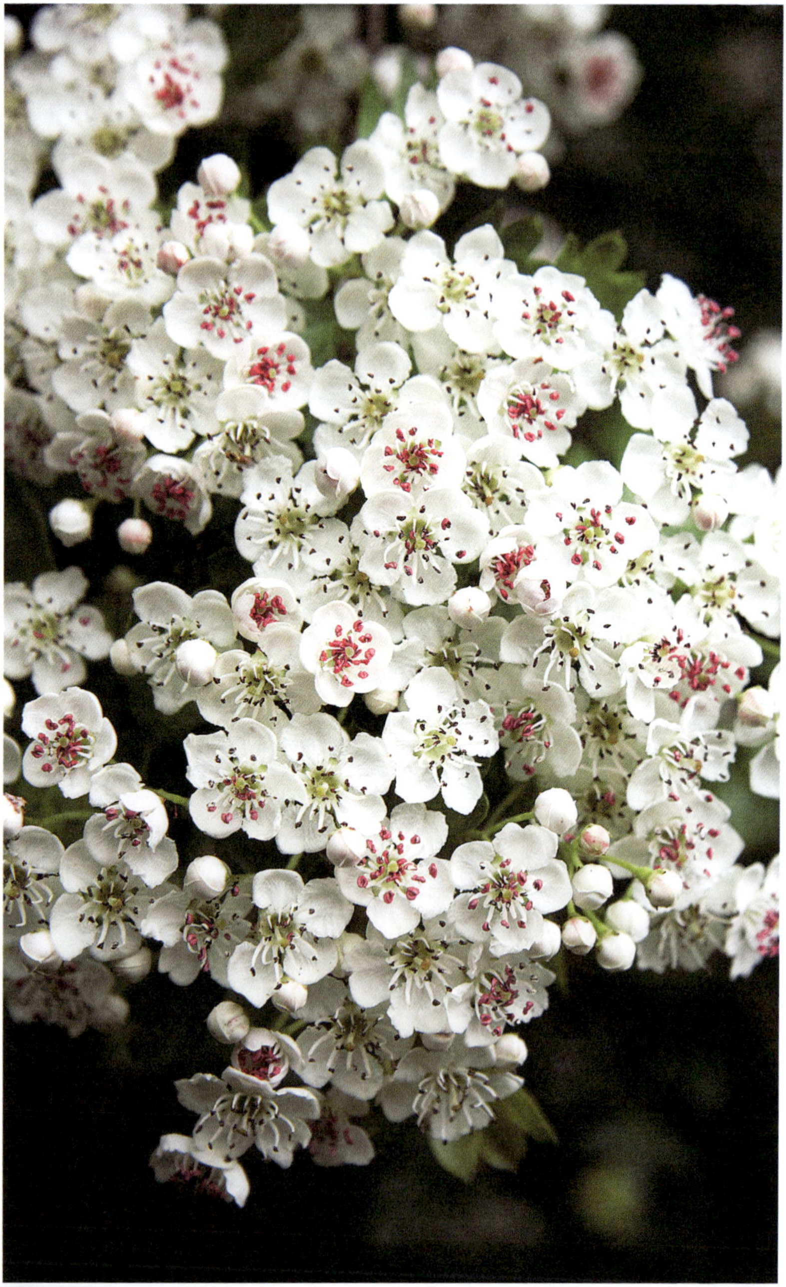

Hawthorn *Crataegus monogyna*

DESCRIPTION	Shrub or small tree. Leaves with deeply divided lobes, stalked, pair of stipules (tiny leaves) at the base. Spiny branches. Flowers in sprays, five white petals, stamens pink. Berries red, like miniature apples, single large seed
HABITAT	Hedgerow, or occasionally singly as well-shaped trees
DISTRIBUTION	Very common everywhere, except the north of Scotland
SEASON	Flowers May–June, berries August–November or even December

The Hawthorn is Britain's most abundant hedgerow tree. Millions were planted as dividing hedges to fulfil the eighteenth- and nineteenth-century Inclosure Acts. A bright legacy of a tragic past. From the middle of May until June, Hawthorn's heady and dazzling 'May' blossom enlivens the countryside and from August to November its rich red berries are the very stuff of autumn.

This humble tree has more folklore and tradition associated with it than any other plant, save perhaps the Elder, and I recommend Richard Mabey's *Flora Britannica* and Geoffrey Grigson's *Englishman's Flora* for full expositions. Chief among its associations are those constant preoccupations – love (or to be frank, sex) and death. The love bit owes something to the tree's flamboyant springtime fecundity though mostly it is the smell – heady and fragrant, but also with a strangely moving undertone, trimethylamine. This chemical is one of the first products of putrefaction (most familiarly of fish), leading the pessimistically inclined to connect the blossom with death, while the optimistic mind turns to a more cheering association.

You will certainly have no trouble finding May blossoms or Haws (the usual troublesome name for the berries), with only the rounder-leaved Midland Hawthorn likely to cause any confusion. This is less common but can be used in the kitchen in the same way, although the blossom is very potent indeed. Hawthorn is in the apple sub-family, as a cursory look at either flower or berry will tell you. Another member – the much-cultivated and sometimes naturalised cotoneaster – may confuse the extremely unobservant, but it has quite different leaves. Nevertheless, do familiarise yourself with the poisonous red berries described later in this book if you are at all unsure. As with most of the plants that provide both flower and berry, pick the flower early and the berry late. Flowers about to drop will have lost their perfume and early berries will be low in sugar and flavour.

Another crop available from the tree is the young leaves. These are the 'bread' of 'bread and cheese' collected by country children, though very much in the past. The 'cheese' is the unopened flower buds. Many people say they like them and they are entitled to do so; however, in common with all other leaves of trees, what little flavour they possess is pretty awful.

If you can come to amicable terms with the superstition that bringing May blossom into the house is bad luck you will be able to make Wild Flower Syrup (p.237). This is very similar to maple syrup and considerably cheaper. If you are concerned about the slightly indecent smell, it does disappear, well almost.

The berries are a bit of a challenge to the forager. There are so many of them – it must amount to millions of tons a year – yet they are time-consuming (and prickly) to pick and not easy to use. The flavour of the flesh is mildly fruity and slightly starchy – like an over-ripe apple. They are not particularly pleasant eaten raw and consist largely of pip. Cooking, therefore, is the only course of action. They will make a passable jelly when mixed with apples, a good wine and an excellent sauce (see Pam Corbin's *River Cottage Preserves Handbook*). However, the best way of doing justice to their sheer numbers is to make a fruit leather (p.69).

P.S. Hawthorn leaves, eaten on the hoof or in a mixed salad, are not that bad, though I have given them to adults who are always disappointed with the taste which is not at all what they remember from their childhood. A few tree leaves are edible – Beech, Hawthorn and Lime being the best known. I have managed to eat Oak leaves when extremely young (them, not me) and sometimes they are nice enough, at other times mouth-numbingly bitter. Lime is the best of them, having good-flavoured young leaves with a decidedly mucilaginous texture. Beech leaves? Don't bother.

Rowan *Sorbus aucuparia*

DESCRIPTION	Small tree. Leaves pinnate (lots of leaflets, like an ash tree), with many opposite leaflets and one terminal leaflet. Blossom in umbrella sprays, white, with an unpleasant smell. Berries bright red
HABITAT	Often solitary in hilly or mountainous areas to nearly 1000 metres. Planted in urban areas. Uncommon with lime
DISTRIBUTION	Common in suitable habitats throughout the British Isles
SEASON	Berries August–November

This little tree is one of our hardiest plants, happy to cling to precipitous mountainsides and at a higher altitude than any tree other than the Juniper. Not that you will have to put on your climbing boots to find one – it can easily be found in lowland heath and wood, and is a frequently planted suburban tree.

Most of our native trees have some magical associations, but it is usually the smaller ones that are considered the most powerful. The Elder and the Hawthorn are two such trees and the Rowan is a third; perhaps it is due to their more human size. It is likely that the name Rowan is a reference to the dazzling colour of the early-autumn tree when both berry and leaf turn red; Rowan may simply mean

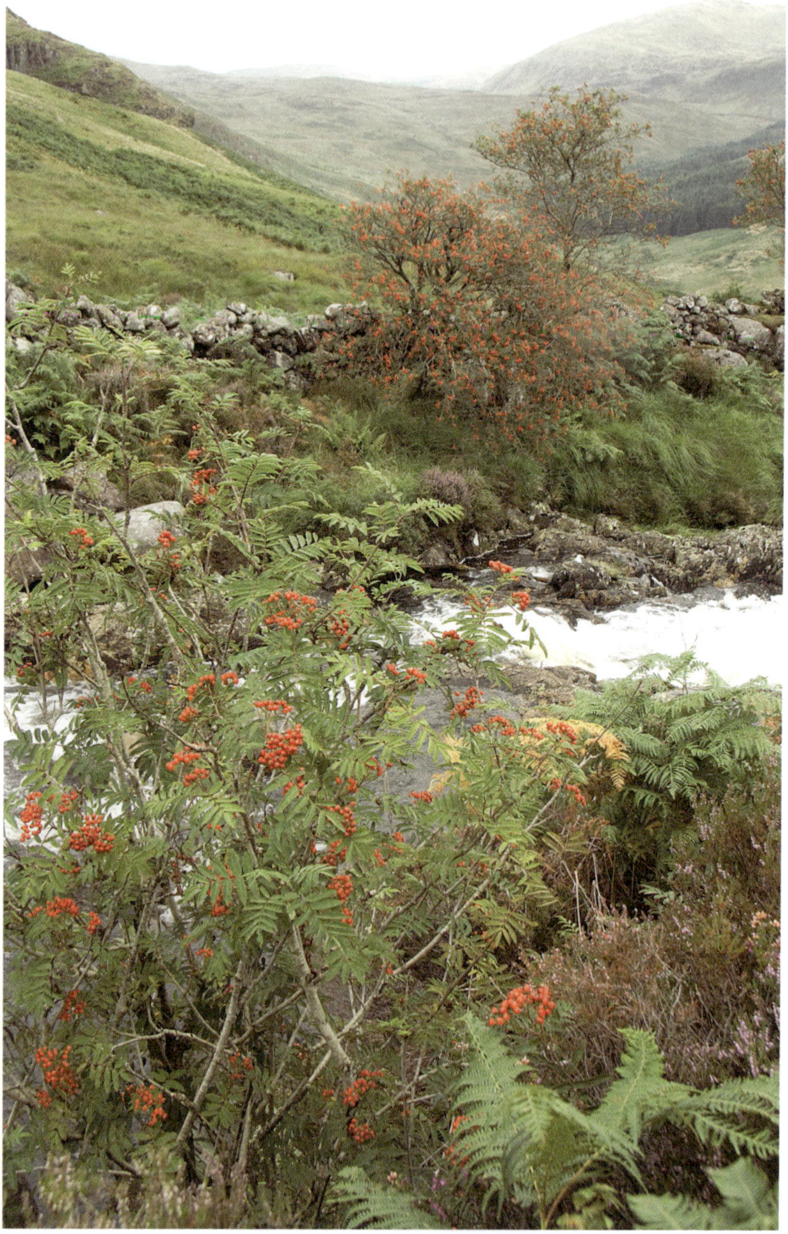

'red-one'. Red is the colour of protection and it is for this property that Rowan is planted outside dwellings. In *The Laidly Worm of Spindleston Heugh* (a tale of a Northumberland dragon) we learn:

> *Their spells were vain. The hags return'd*
> *To the Queen in sorrowful mood,*
> *Crying that witches have no power,*
> *Where there is Rown-Tree wood.*

Even in Northumberland, neither witches nor dragons are the problem they once were, but it is still an attractive tree to have in the garden. If it has a failing, it is the smell of the blossom – it smells of rotting flesh.

Identification of the Rowan is simple while the ash-like leaves are still in place. Unfortunately the berries are commonly picked quite late in the year and the leaves may have long gone. The answer is to select your trees before the leaves fall. Whitebeam produces very similar berries on a very similar tree but has totally different-shaped leaves. Fortunately the berries are not poisonous.

It is a pity that so common and productive a tree has not seen fit to grow berries of a better flavour, but the fact is they are both tart and bitter, and full of pips. They are also poisonous raw. Cooking does little to reduce the bitter quality, so even something like a Rowan and apple tart is likely to be less than delicious. As a soft fruit it is therefore something of a failure but, of course, it has one use which rescues it from foraging oblivion – Rowan jelly. Again I will refer you to Pam Corbin's *River Cottage Preserves Handbook*, where a full recipe for a doubly wild jelly (it also contains Crab Apples) is given.

P.S. In 2006, in an episode that defies irony, a gentleman in his sixties from Gloucestershire reportedly climbed over a fence on to private land while on a walk in Cheshire and picked some Rowan berries. There were, it seems, words spoken between the picker and a security guard from a nearby building who had spotted the misdemeanour and had remonstrated. Three months later, back in Gloucestershire, the local police, having been notified of the putative felon's address by the Cheshire constabulary (who themselves discovered it from CCTV footage of the gentleman's car), called on the berry-picker and took him to the police station. He admitted an offence under the 1968 Theft Act and accepted a caution.

It is unclear whether or not this was a miscarriage of justice. If the Rowan berries were cultivated – and it has been said that they were 'cultivated' as food for birds – then it was theft. If they were growing wild, then under the 1968 Theft Act it was most definitely not. The berry-picker's wife made half a dozen jars of Rowan jelly from the berries, making the principle of law '*de minimis non curat lex*' – 'The law does not concern itself with trifles'– doubly appropriate.

Silverweed *Potentilla anserina*

DESCRIPTION	Short, creeping perennial with runners. Leaflets with saw-toothed edge, silvery due to fine hairs, at least on the underside. Flowers yellow, five-petalled
HABITAT	With grass, waste ground, garden borders
DISTRIBUTION	Very common throughout the UK
SEASON	Roots best dug in late summer and autumn. Leaves visible from spring until mid-October

The old name for Silverweed was Wild Tansy. The 'other' tansy has similarly shaped leaves but is unrelated and a member of the daisy family. Culpeper notes this, saying:

> Now Dame Venus hath fitted women with two herbs of the same name, the one to help conception, and the other to maintain beauty, and what more can be expected of her?

What indeed? Silverweed performs the first function, being the '… *best companion, their husbands excepted*' that a woman desiring a child might have.

Silverweed is related to the various cinquefoils and to the familiar tormentil, and is in the rose family. Its Latin name *Potentilla* means 'little powerful one' and it certainly seems to survive just about anywhere. There is never any problem finding such a tough little plant and you will probably have some in your garden as a persistent weed of your flower borders. The edible roots can be dug up at any time of the year but it is best to do so after they have put on weight during the summer and certainly before the leaves have died completely and you can't find them. This is any time from September to mid-October. The leaves are very distinctive with their saw-toothed edges and silvery coating of hairs. Digging them up will reveal a mass of roots, not all of which will be Silverweed, so do be careful. A good Silverweed root will have nodules along its length and may be the thickness of a French bean.

It is fair to say that unless you have absolutely nothing else to do, digging up Silverweed roots is not necessarily the best use of your time. They have long been considered a famine food, but as famine foods go, they are really rather good. The flavour is of chestnuts or perhaps Jerusalem artichokes; they are just very fiddly to collect and prepare. Times can change of course and in post-apocalyptic Britain you may yet save your tribe with the arcane knowledge imparted here.

Use a nylon scouring pad or knife to remove the skin and then boil, steam or sauté them. In the past, a flour has been ground from the dried roots, and pancakes made from this, though that really would be wasting your time.

Silverweed roots and leaves

EDIBLE SPECIES 79

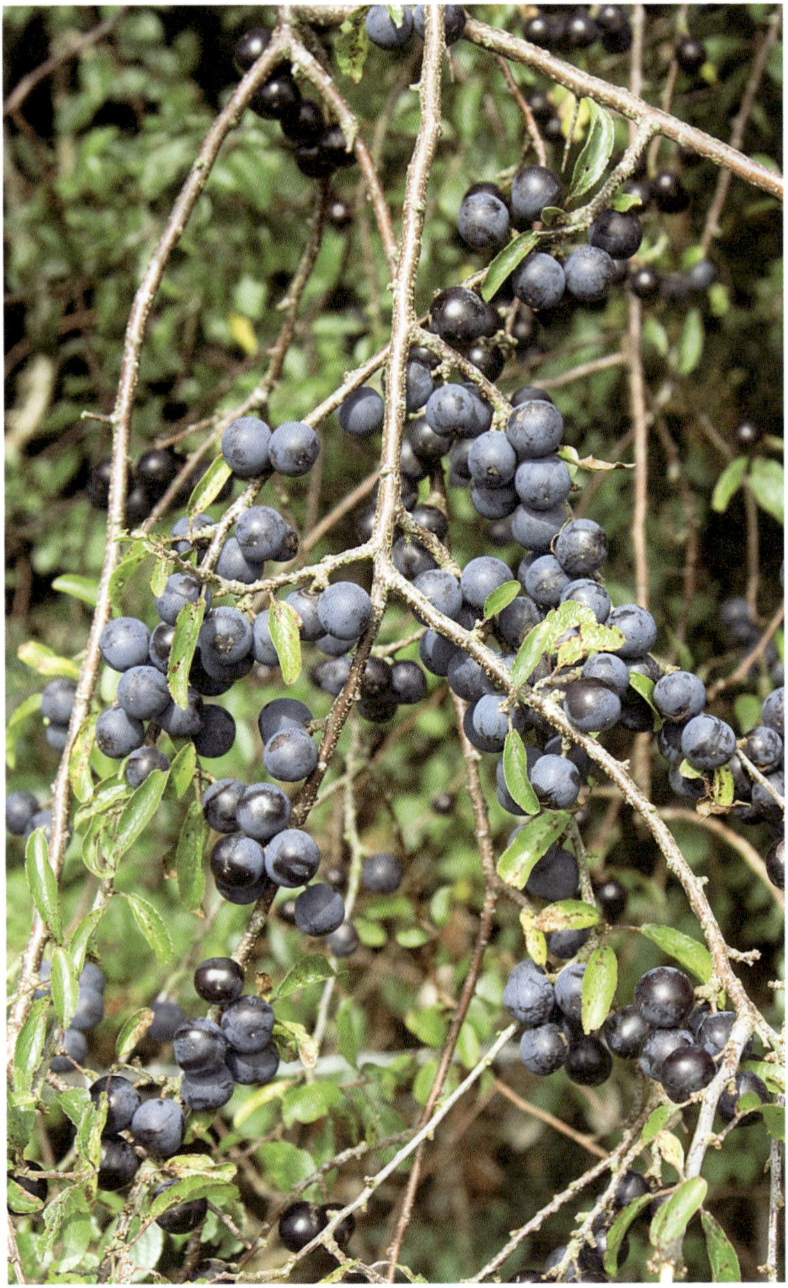

Sloe/Blackthorn *Prunus spinosa*

DESCRIPTION	Shrub or small tree. Leaves oval, toothed. Trunk and branches dark brown to almost black, long, tough, sharp thorns. Flowers white with red stamens, five-petalled, appearing in March before the leaves. Fruit 1–1.5cm, dark blue/purple/black, with a bloom
HABITAT	Wood edges, scrub, hedgerow
DISTRIBUTION	Very common throughout the British Isles, though increasingly scarce in the north of Scotland
SEASON	September–November, sometimes in December

Most foragers have a secret Sloe patch of which they speak proudly and guard jealously. As one who lives in an area in which the Blackthorn seems to be the dominant shrub and who can pick 50 kilograms before breakfast, I shake my head disdainfully at such talk. Not that I am without pity for those less fortunate.

With its almost black bark of winter, white blossom of spring and grape-like fruit of autumn, the Blackthorn is a lovely tree. It can fill a hedgerow or form dense, impenetrable thickets, providing a safe nesting site for many bird species. The blossom is the earliest in the year (except for that of the closely related Cherry Plum), appearing and usually falling before the leaves are unfurled. A very excitable nineteenth-century traveller, one William Anderson, described the berries in prose more purple than they themselves are: '*distilled in tears… ethereal globules; now blue… now black, with the play of the raven's wing…*'

Along with the Plums, the Blackthorn is a member of the genus *Prunus*, in turn a member of the rose family, the Rosaceae. The second half of its Latin name is clear enough in meaning if you have ever had a close encounter with a Blackthorn. The spines are vicious in the extreme, seemingly designed to kill rather than deter. Indeed they were once considered to be poisonous, since the wounds they inflict often refuse to heal.

Following the blossom and an inconspicuous few months, August sees the new berries forming. These green acid drops are quite inedible, though at one time the juice was squeezed from them and slowly boiled dry to form *Acacia Germanica*. It was said (without risk of exaggeration – it must have tasted like battery acid) to be a powerful astringent and was '*given in fluxes, etc. from a scruple to a dram*'. The acidity of Sloes is down to our old friend malic acid, but there is also tartaric acid and tannic acid, the latter chemical being the one responsible for sticking your tongue to the roof of your mouth.

The mouth-numbing properties of even the ripest berry is familiar to most, and the longer you can leave the berries on the tree the better. A mild and wet November can, however, ripen them to a plump softness and raw edibility, at least for the stout-hearted. October is probably the time when most people pick them, though I have on occasion found them persisting until Christmas. The berries form in huge numbers around the branches and would be fairly easy to pick were it not for those terrible thorns. At least one gardening glove should be used when gathering Sloes, and a hat would be a wise addition to protect your head.

Although there are several delicious things that can be made with Sloes the word that twins with it most often is gin. There seem to be as many methods for making this simple liqueur as there are people who make it and I did some selfless research one Christmas, going around my village tasting as many recipes and vintages as I could talk people into giving me. Unfortunately I did not take notes and have unaccountably forgotten the details beyond the fact that they were all 'jolly nice'. However, one thing about Sloe Gin, which I knew already, was amply confirmed – the older the vintage, the better it is. The best one I tried was fourteen years old – it was like a fine Madeira.

The basic recipe could not be simpler: Prick 500g Sloes with a fork and place them in a large jar. Add 500g sugar and 600ml gin. Shake to mix everything up and give the jar a further shake every now and then over the next week, at least. It will be just about drinkable after a couple of months but if you can keep it for the next year it will be much improved. If you decide to keep it, then remove the Sloes after 3 months.

The only other familiar recipe for this fruit is Sloe and Crab Apple jelly. A jam is also possible if you sieve out the pits from the well-cooked Sloes; unless you use a pectinised sugar you will need to add the same weight of cooked Crab Apples (or cooking apples) to provide the pectin it needs to set. Finally, there is the excellent standby for any fruit that needs straining to remove pips or pits – a fruit leather.

P.S. Sloes form an important ingredient in a heroic recipe from the *Family Save-all* of 1861. It also contains Elderberry juice, so it would make an appropriate forager's nip (or bath):

> *Take twelve gallons of soft river water, forty-eight pounds of raisins, fourteen pounds of Lisbon sugar, twelve quarts of elder juice, three quarts of juice of sloes, and half an ounce of isinglass; mix all together; when this has stood two months, or till it is fine, draw it off into a clear cask, and add six pounds of loaf sugar and three quarts of brandy. Bottle it in the April following, and keep it two years before drawing the corks.*

Wild Cherry *Prunus avium*

DESCRIPTION	Small to medium tree. Leaves long, pointed oval, saw-toothed edge. Blossom white and abundant. Fruit generally smaller than cultivated varieties, hanging down on *separate* stalks
HABITAT	Woodland edges and occasionally in hedgerows. Often planted in streets and along dual carriageways, etc.
DISTRIBUTION	Frequent throughout the British Isles, though less common in the North and parts of the west of Scotland
SEASON	Late June and July

'*Beautiful berries! Beautiful tree! Hurrah! for the wild, wild cherry tree*' go the enthusiastic if slightly awkward lines of a nineteenth-century song. The sentiments at least are ones with which we can concur.

There are several varieties of Cherry that grow wild in the British Isles, but the native Wild Cherry is the one most likely to produce useful fruit. The modern cultivated varieties are largely its descendants, crossed and selected over the years to produce heavier and sweeter fruit. The 'wild' Wild Cherry is usually found as a forest tree but it does like the light and normally clings to the wood edge.

Cherry pits travel around a great deal and some of the more productive roadside trees will be the result of felicitous littering. The best Wild Cherry trees I know were actually planted by the Highways Agency on the steeply sloping banks of a local bypass, though they make for rather dangerous foraging. I take an entirely pragmatic view of collecting this lovely fruit; if the tree is growing more or less wild and produces decent Cherries, I will pick them – provenance does not concern me. Cherries do grow on trees of course, so you may need to engage in a little climbing, adding to the experience rather than detracting from it, and the 'standing on the roof of the car' technique (p.15) can be very useful.

'*Oh where is a wild cherry tree?*' If you do not know of any Wild Cherry trees in your area keep your eyes open for the flamboyant April blossom that has overexcited poets for centuries: '*… what are those living hills of snow, or of some substance purer in its brightness even than any snow that falls…?*' The fruit will start to appear at the end of June and you will have to be quick to beat the birds. Normally it is necessary to pick slightly under-ripe fruit and ripen them at home; though, as the picture overleaf shows, sometimes you can be lucky. Like other *Prunus* species, such as Plums, the fruit is variable in quality – '*grateful to the Stomach, and whet the Appetite*', as one writer has it, or '*harsh and crude to the taste*', according to another – you will just have to pick and taste.

Wild Cherries are relatively small, but can be used in all the recipes devised for their cultivated cousins. The strong acidity of some of the wild fruit lends itself to glacé cherries (the home-made ones put the commercial variety to shame). Sweet Cherry Pickle is quick and easy: simply pit the Cherries, pack them in a clean jar and cover with a mix of hot, lightly spiced cider vinegar and sugar to taste. You can also make a jam, though take care – Cherry jam is one I regularly manage to burn before it sets. Best of all, and most likely to do justice to your hard-won cherries, is Wild Cherry brandy – just replace all the appropriate ingredients in the recipe for Sloe Gin (p.82).

P.S. When I am not out foraging, I work as a cabinet maker. I cannot therefore talk about Cherry without mentioning its wood. Cherry is one of the finest cabinet-making woods in existence, rivalling mahogany in its depth of colour and grain, but without the accompanying concerns about rainforest destruction. Sadly most Cherry trees are too scattered for commercial harvesting, ending their lives as logs (though very good logs), their potential for becoming a chair or table lost for ever. The wood is fairly easy to work, though the grain often changes direction several times over the length of a plank and planing is necessarily done against the grain with a finely set and extremely sharp blade. The most noticeable thing about cherry wood is that when it becomes overheated during machining it smells of Cherries.

P.P.S. Cherry-pit is an old game involving throwing stones or cherry pits into a small hole. There is also cherry-pit spitting, something most of us have indulged in at one time or other (well, I have). If you think you are good at it, the world record stands at 29.12 metres.

The traditional game is celebrated by the likeable seventeenth-century poet Robert Herrick of *Gather ye Rosebuds* and *Cherry Ripe* (he liked cherries) fame:

Julia and I did lately sit
Playing for sport at cherry-pit:
She threw; I cast; and, having thrown,
I got the pit, and she the stone.

This rhyme seems innocent enough, if a little impenetrable, but Herrick was a wistful bachelor with other things on his mind; Julia was his muse, and 'pit' and 'stone' coy allusions.

EDIBLE SPECIES 85

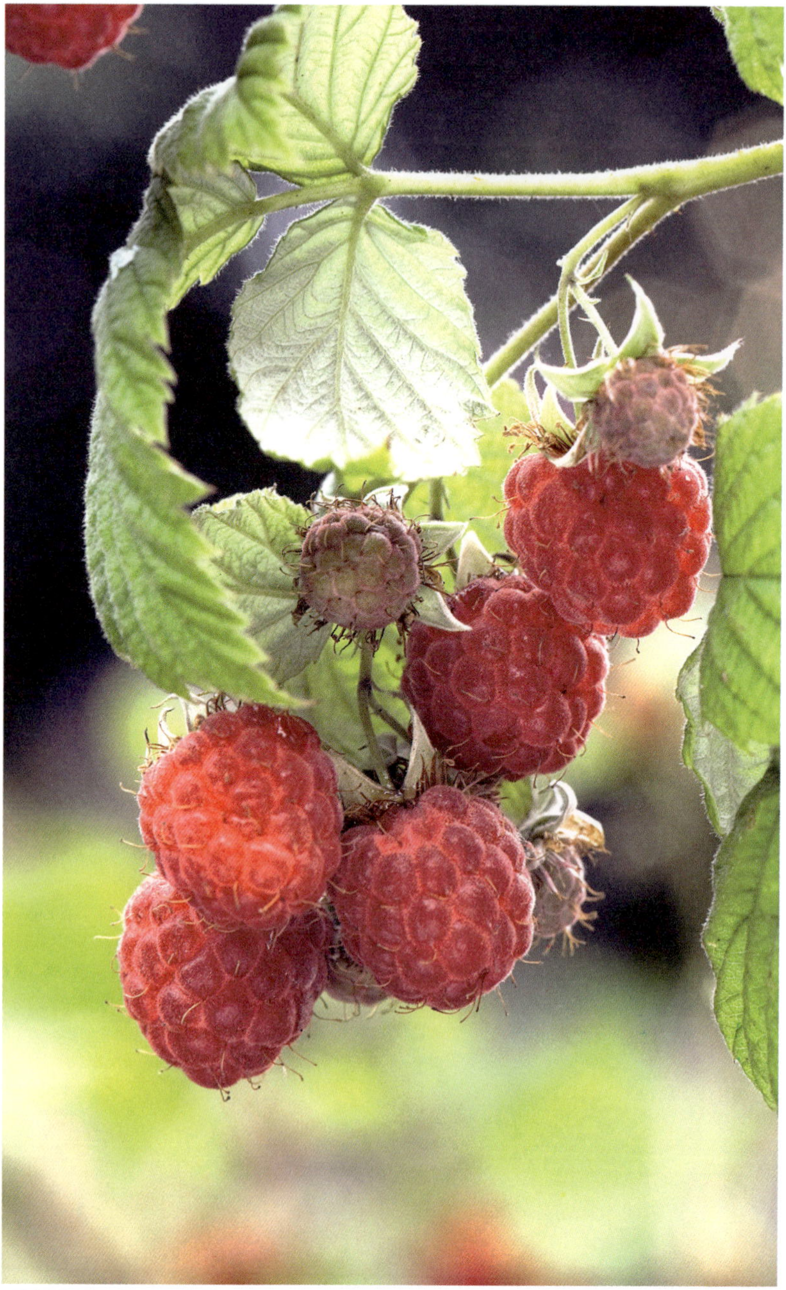

Raspberry *Rubus idaeus*

DESCRIPTION	Cane-like perennial 1–1.5 metres. Leaves pointed oval, serrated edge, finely hairy and light green above, densely hairy and white below. Stems with soft thorns and minute hairs. Flowers like small Blackberry flowers. Fruit smaller than cultivated varieties and often paler
HABITAT	Hedgerows, woods – usually in a clearing
DISTRIBUTION	Throughout the British Isles, except the Fens
SEASON	Late June–late August

There aren't many wild foods I am as pleased to see as the wild Raspberry. I know half a dozen locations where it grows and I am always on the lookout for more. Fortunately, I seldom need to worry about competition from other foragers – until the berries redden most people pass them by as slightly odd-looking brambles.

The Raspberry is a native of the British Isles, although there has been some naturalisation of cultivated strains. Their old name was Raspis or Raspis-berry, from a French sweet rose-coloured wine called *Raspise*. A common alternative name was Hindberry and, less common, Mount Ida Bramble – from Pliny's description of it on the mountain in Crete and reflected in its Latin name.

The fruit is exactly the same as the garden variety, save being a little smaller, so needs neither introduction nor warning of deadly look-alikes. The Raspberry is a perennial, with the berries growing on last year's canes. Even before the berries arrive it is easily distinguished from Blackberry by the very soft thorns and pale leaves. Broadleaf woodland clearings are by far the best place to find them, sometimes in abundance. I know of one clearing that contains half an acre of Raspberries, though exactly where is the sort of information I impart only to my direct descendants. Sadly wild Raspberry canes are not as burdened with fruit as the Blackberry and you will have to work hard to collect a good amount. They are not that easy to pick either. Less than perfectly ripe, they cling on until you squash them with pulling and the moment you touch the ripe ones they drop off to disappear frustratingly into the undergrowth. Do not take children with you to pick them – they will eat them all.

Raspberries do not keep well so deal with them as soon as you get home. There are many recipes for Raspberries but only one which does justice to the wild variety – eat them raw with a little caster sugar. If you find more than you can eat you should just try harder to eat them; failing that you could make Raspberry vinegar or retain their beauty by using them on a cheesecake.

Dewberry

Also look out for the Dewberry (*Rubus caesius*). The humble Dewberry has a tendency to look like a failed Blackberry. The individual druplets are larger, fewer, dusty-looking and irregular in size. It does, however, taste very good, being consistently sharper in flavour than a Blackberry. The plant is low and rather rambling, and grows in damp woods, along grassy paths and scrubland. Like the Raspberry, its thorns are relatively soft. The main problem with the Dewberry is picking the berries. These are soft, succulent and burst with great ease. Either take the time to be very careful or use a fork to pull the berries away. Alternatively you could take Richard Mabey's advice by snipping them off at the stem with scissors and eating them like cocktail cherries.

P.S. The Raspberry is not a plant that has enjoyed a great medicinal reputation. Even Culpeper, a herbalist who found miracle cures everywhere, says, '*I find no great virtue in the leaves.*' There does persist, however, the belief that a tea (or, heaven help us, a pessary) made from the leaves stimulates the uterus during (and after) childbirth. A grim account from the nineteenth century details a meddling intervention in delivering an afterbirth which would no doubt have made an appearance when it was good and ready. The story in St Mark's Gospel of the woman who '*had suffered many things of many doctors, and had spent all she had, and was nothing bettered, but rather grew worse*' is peculiarly relevant here. Modern science has not found an unequivocal medicinal effect for Raspberry leaves so there probably isn't one.

Dog Rose *Rosa canina*

DESCRIPTION	Long arching shrub to 2.5 metres. Leaves oval/pointed, serrated edge. Stems woody, green when young, with strong, sharp red thorns. Flowers usually pink, sometimes white. Hips red, pointed oval
HABITAT	Hedgerow and scrub
DISTRIBUTION	Very common throughout the British Isles
SEASON	Petals May–July, hips from August

Field Rose *Rosa arvensis*

DESCRIPTION	Trailing plant to 1.5 metres. Leaves oval/pointed, serrated edge. Stems woody, green when young, with curved thorns and wiry hairs. Flowers always white, styles forming a *central column*. Hips red, smaller and rounder than those of the Dog Rose
HABITAT	Hedgerow, wood and scrub
DISTRIBUTION	Very common south of the Humber, rare elsewhere
SEASON	Petals June–August, hips from August

These roses are delicate and modest affairs of white and pink – a far cry from the brash cultivars that fill our gardens. Yet there is much joy to be had from our native roses. If we include the many hybrids, there are around a hundred roses to be found wild or naturalised in the British Isles. Of these, fourteen are native and only the two mentioned above are really common.

Anyone who has walked along a country lane in June will not have failed to notice the lovely blossoms of the Dog Rose – it is a constant and familiar part of a British summer. The petals are edible in jams and jellies, but their slight fragrance is easily lost in cooking and the best way to use them is scattered on a summer salad. The white petals of the straggling Field Rose are even less fragrant and lack the pretty pink of its cousin. A tea can be made from the leaves, if you like that sort of thing.

With both these species, however, the real value comes from the hips. These can be gathered from August until November, though I have often found them hanging on past Christmas. The flavour varies a great deal with ripeness and whether or not

Dog Rose

Field Rose

Japanese Rose

Rosehips

they have endured a frost, but I will collect them as long as they look reasonably healthy. The uncompromising thorns make picking them hazardous work and you will need to take things slowly, with gloves and scissors a must.

The taste of Rosehip Syrup is imprinted pleasantly on my mind from the bottles of the stuff my mother gave me as a child. (The memory is not entirely unsullied by dark thoughts, however, because the spoonful of syrup was always preceded by a spoonful of cod-liver oil.) The syrup is fruity and not quite like anything else.

The hips are an extension of the stem and not actually the fruit – the real fruits are inside, covered in hairs. These hairs can be quite a serious irritant so if you wish to make a syrup, or anything else, they must be removed. This can be done by the messy and time-devouring process of splitting the hips open and taking them out. This way the flesh is preserved more or less intact, not reduced to a juice or purée, and can be used in such historical delicacies as Rosehip tart.

More sensible, however, is to cook the hips whole in water, occasionally and gently mashing them with a potato masher after they have softened and continuing to simmer for a total of 15 minutes. The juice is squeezed through a double layer of muslin, the muslin is then cleaned and the juice passed through again.

If you want to make Rosehip Syrup, use 250ml water for every 150g of hips. Put the finished juice in a pan with 150g granulated sugar and stir over a low heat until dissolved, then bring to the boil and take off the heat. This is fairly low in sugar so should be used quite quickly and kept in the fridge, but it will keep for longer if poured hot into hot sterilised jars and sealed with a lid – as you would a jam.

Rosehip Syrup is the basis for nearly everything that can be made from hips – ice cream, sorbet, ice lollies – it is even used to flavour cakes and biscuits. I use it with a vanilla panna cotta, on pancakes and for Rosehip Babas with Blackberries (p.224). You can, of course, just eat it by the spoonful – it contains a lot of vitamin C and is terribly good for you – with or without the cod-liver oil.

Also look out for the Japanese Rose (*R. rugosa*). This plant is an enthusiastic immigrant, common in gardens, but also in hedgerows, roadsides and on sand dunes by the sea, often becoming the dominant plant wherever it finds a home. The flowers are a deep pink, of medium size and intensely perfumed. In addition it has, like my Auntie Hilda from Lowestoft, enormous hips. Unlike most other roses, the hips and flowers are often on the bush at the same time. Being so large, the hips are a shortcut to making Rosehip Syrup, but not one as good as that made from our own roses. It is scattered throughout the British Isles, with a distinct coastal preference.

Our native roses can have a lovely perfume, but it is faint and fleeting. The Japanese Rose, however, is breathtakingly fragrant and the one to use in Turkish Delight (p.232) and in the glorious Rose Jelly (p.242). Nor need you stint on your main ingredient since, being an invader, the Japanese Rose can be picked freely.

Wild Strawberry *Fragaria vesca*

DESCRIPTION	Low, straggling perennial. Leaves trefoil, leaflets pointed/oval, sharply toothed edge, grooved, shiny, green/yellow. Long runners. Flowers five-petalled, 12–18mm diameter, white. Fruit about 1cm diameter
HABITAT	Dry grassy places, woodland clearings, hedgerow, old gardens, waste ground, old railway lines
DISTRIBUTION	Common throughout the British Isles, though rare in the extreme north of Scotland
SEASON	June–August, but may continue to autumn

'*Doubtless God could have made a better berry, but doubtless God never did.*' So the writer Dr William Butler inarguably asserted in the seventeenth century.

The tiny Wild Strawberry that we find in the hedges and woods is not an escapee from our gardens, reverted to its wild form, but a genuine native plant. In fact the cultivated strawberry that we know today did not originate with our own Wild Strawberry. It is a cross between two species from the Americas – the large but tasteless Chilean strawberry, *F. chiloensis,* and the small but flavoursome Virginian strawberry, *F. virginiana*. This garden strawberry was first bred in the mid-eighteenth century, but both prior to this and for some time after, the wild native was brought into gardens and tended with appropriate care. The Alpine strawberries one sees at garden centres and in seed catalogues are mostly cultivars of the native species, thus continuing this practice.

Although a common species, the Wild Strawberry does not appear in abundance everywhere and you really need to find your patch in order to gather them in any quantity. A good spot, such as a recently felled woodland clearing, can provide a red carpet of berries. My best place is a disused railway embankment where the poor, thin, dry soil and the open light provide the perfect habitat. Even where they grow in huge numbers, Wild Strawberries are not the easiest of fruits to pick. They are, of course, very small – their Latin name, *Fragaria vesca*, means 'the small fragrant one' – and they crush easily. Use a shallow basket or box, preferably with a tea-towel in the bottom to protect your prize. This, of course, assumes that you will be taking them home; just remember that such an action may result in sharing them with people who will be grateful but never quite grateful enough.

Wild Strawberries have a long fruiting season – in exceptional years you can start picking in early June and continue until October. The food writer Jane Grigson talks of brushing away some snow one winter to find a good quantity of Wild

Strawberries lying beneath, though it is possible that these were yet another species, the occasionally cultivated, hardy and delicious Hautbois strawberry, *F. moschata*.

Wild Strawberries are time-consuming delicacies to pick and seldom come by the bucketful. It is therefore wise to use your precious find carefully – jams, pies and wines, sadly, are off the menu. I favour keeping the berries whole and visible, preserving their flavour, beauty and texture – a decoration on a cheesecake or fruit flan, preserved in brandy and sugar (p.239), or eaten simply with cream.

P.S. Talking of Strawberries and cream, Robert Herrick, who wrote so naughtily about Cherries (see p.84), writes about them again but, being a bit of a soft-fruit fan, this time includes Strawberries in his verse. For the sake of decency, I have omitted the second half of the poem and the title – you'll just have to look it up.

Have ye beheld, with much delight,
A red-Rose peeping through a white?
Or else a Cherrie, double grac't,
Within a Lillie? Center plac't?
Or ever mark't the pretty beam,
A Strawberry shows halfe drown'd in Creame?

Gooseberry *Ribes uva-crispa*

DESCRIPTION	Shrub 1–2 metres tall. Leaves broad, lobed, dark green, finely hairy. Branches spiny. Fruit green with pale striations taking on a reddish hue with maturity, dried petals persisting at the end
HABITAT	Hedgerow, wood margins, river gorges, areas of previous habitation
DISTRIBUTION	Fairly common throughout the British Isles, except for mountainous and high hill country, and the Fens
SEASON	Late May until July

Having managed to lose a Gooseberry up my nose at the age of four (a story of which my mother has not tired in over half a century), I have always had an intimate relationship with this most comforting denizen of the school dinner hall. There is something very British about the understated Gooseberry. It is indeed a native plant, preferring our damp and mild climate – and its finer points seem more appreciated here than anywhere else.

Wild Gooseberry bushes are found only occasionally, so do keep a lookout for them on your country walks and make a mental note of any you encounter, especially in the spring when the bush will advertise its existence by showing green before most of its neighbours. Even should you find one, disappointment may still be yours as they do not always fruit and that bane of the hedgerow harvester – the farm hedge-trimmer – may devastate in seconds any crop that does appear.

If you have negotiated these problems then you have a great prize. The wild form is inevitably smaller than its many cultivated cousins, though the welcome garden escapees that are often found in the hedgerow may be larger. As with the cultivated Gooseberry, the later the fruit is picked the sweeter it becomes, except that the later you pick it the more likely it is that some other forager (may he or she rot in hell) has helped themselves.

Cooking with Gooseberries is a straightforward matter. The really sweet ones can be eaten raw, though these are rare in the wild variety. Sauce and chutney, jam and jelly, sorbet and fool, pudding and pie, cake and crumble – all wonderful and simple foods, though they can be improved. There is another hedgerow favourite which complements the Gooseberry perfectly – the Elderflower. If you ever try Gooseberry and Elderflower fool then you will never go back to plain Gooseberry.

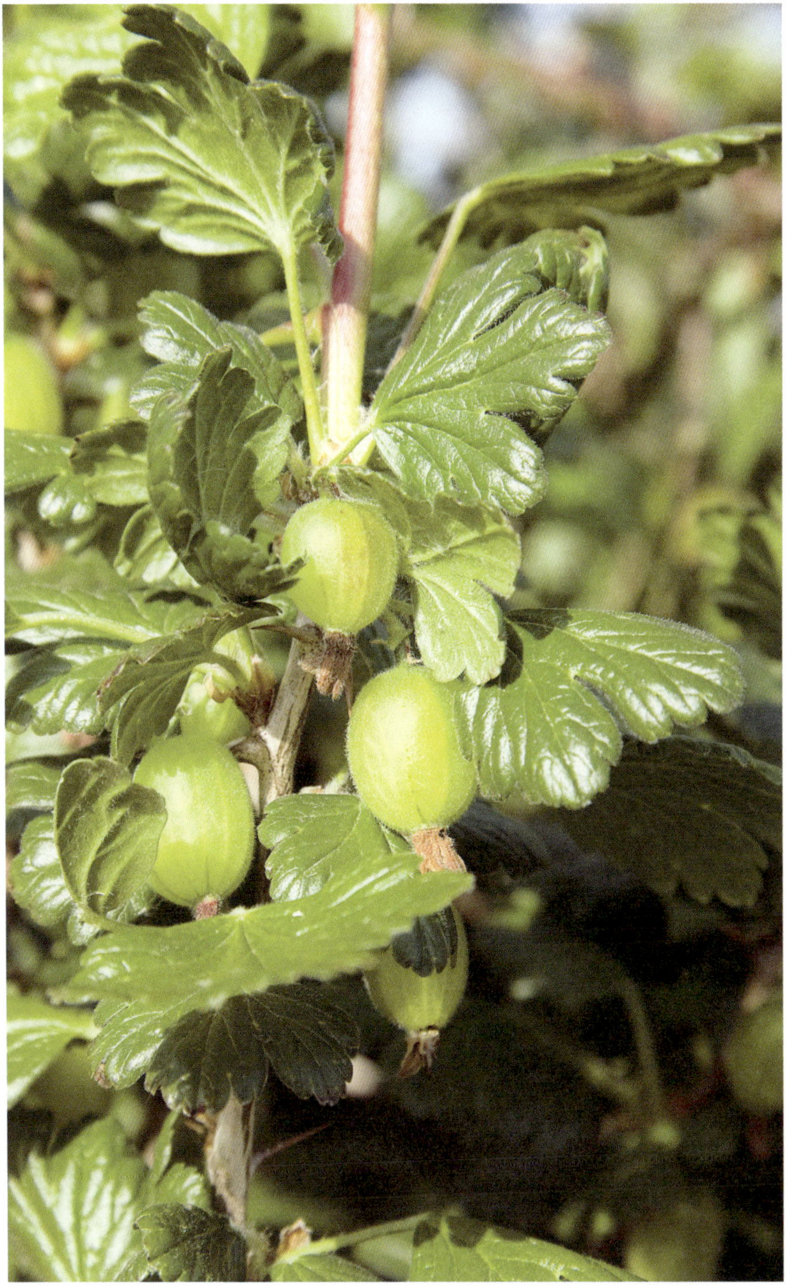

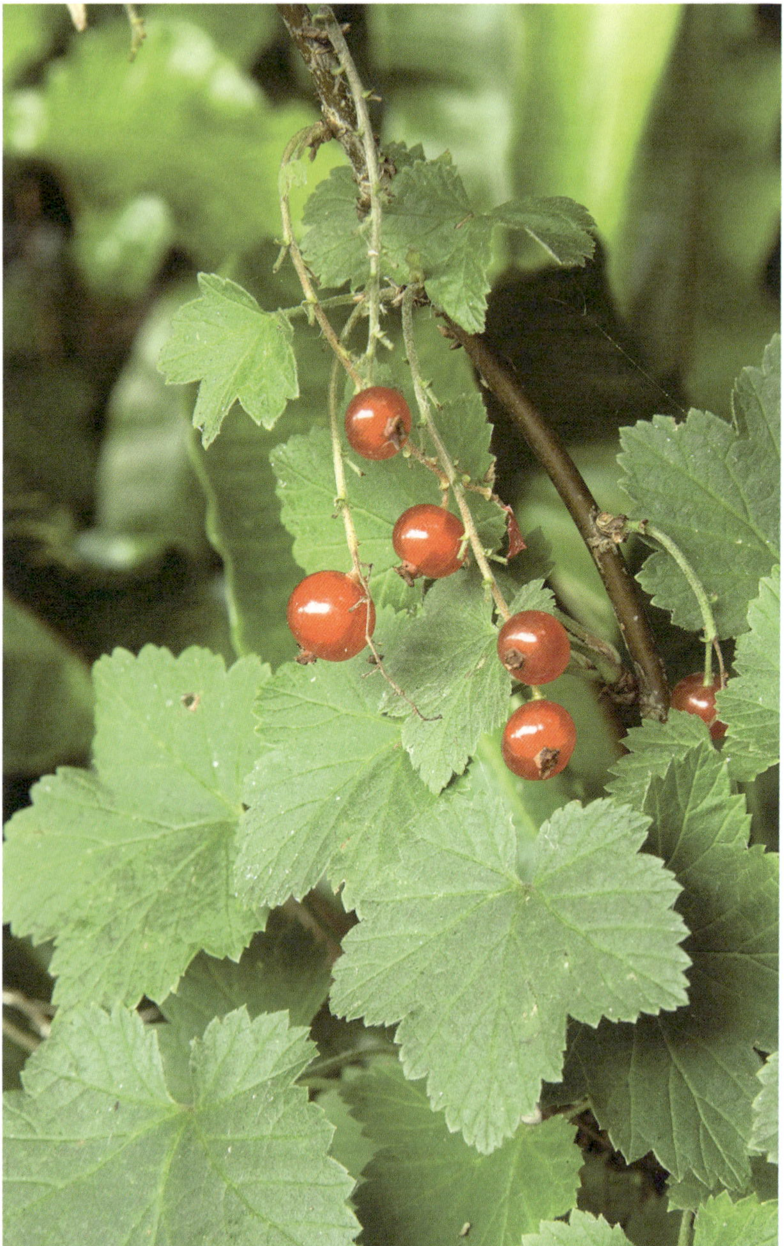

Redcurrant *Ribes rubrum*

DESCRIPTION	Shrub 1–1.5 metres tall. Stems erect. Leaves maple-like, mostly hairless. Flowers tiny, five-petalled, pink. Bright-red berries, hanging down
HABITAT	Hedgerows, shady woods, overhanging river banks
DISTRIBUTION	Common in England, more so in the South; central Northern Ireland, central and northeast Scotland
SEASON	Flowers April–May. Berries June–July

I have a fondness for the humble Redcurrant which can only be regarded as a triumph of optimistic anticipation over experience. In spring its frothy pink flowers can fill the hedgerows and woodland clearings and every year a bumper harvest is promised. Then attrition sets in. Most of the hedgerow blossoms disappear with the attention of the summer hedge-trimmers and most of those that survive refuse to set. The green berries remain stubbornly green for weeks and many either commit suicide and drop off or fall victim to colour-blind chaffinches. A pitiful few red berries develop for the once-hopeful forager and picking a useful amount will involve several hours' work and much travelling.

Nevertheless, it is a common plant so you should have little trouble in finding some. A few plants are clear garden escapees and likely to be better fruited than wild natives. Look out for Redcurrant's distinctive leaves in spring and go back in the summer. My best patch is mixed in with the overhanging trees on a stream edge, but this does mean that harvesting requires wading up and down in wellies.

It would be nice to say that wild Redcurrants are worth the wait and the work, but frankly they are not. They are sharp in flavour but not unpleasant and, while they would look good decorating a cheesecake, most sensible recipes involve straining out the large number of unwelcome pips. Redcurrant jelly is the favourite of course, but the best way to do justice to the few berries you are likely to find is by making a table jelly dessert with another summer fruit such as Strawberry, Raspberry or Cherry set inside, whole. Simply cook the Redcurrants with a little water, strain, add sugar to taste and some soaked leaf gelatine (about 5g for every 250ml of liquid). Heat through until the gelatine has dissolved, then cool for 10 minutes. Scatter the fresh wild fruit in a glass bowl, pour the liquid redcurrant jelly over and refrigerate to set.

If the berries prove too much work there is Redcurrant leaf tea. It is one of the best of the hedgerow drinks, but tea made from the flowers is even better. I will confess to being a bit of a builder where herbal tea is concerned, but that made from Redcurrant blossom is superb – it tastes like tea.

Fennel *Foeniculum vulgare*

DESCRIPTION	Tall, upright, branched perennial, 1–2.5 metres. Leaves exceedingly fine and feathery, grey/green. Flowers in a yellow umbrella spray. Seeds with black edge. All parts smell strongly of aniseed
HABITAT	Near habitation, waste ground, coastal
DISTRIBUTION	Fairly common in southern England, scarce in the North and Scotland, coastal in Wales. Absent from Ireland
SEASON	Spring until summer for the leaves, late summer and autumn for the seeds

Fennel is not a native of these islands and it still seems a little unsure of itself even after two thousand years, preferring odd corners of the urban environment and seaside car parks to any pristine wilderness. It probably just likes the milder climate such places afford. Fennel is in fact a Mediterranean plant and probably one of the things the Romans did for us. The ancient Greek name for it is *Maratha*, after the city-state of Marathon, where it grew in profusion before it all got trampled to death by runners.

There will never be any problem in identifying this plant because of the unusually fine, feathery leaves and the distinctive aniseed smell. The leaves can appear as early as December in sheltered spots, though March is more typical, and will continue until the summer. The plants can be enormous and usually come in little colonies, so there will be plenty to gather – you often see Fennel in expensive and tiny packets in supermarkets and it is more than usually rewarding to pick it for nothing. It is one of the safest urban plants to collect because its height puts it out of reach of all but the tallest and most talented of dogs.

In late summer and autumn a second crop appears – the seeds. These are tiny compared to the commercially grown ones, but just as good to eat. They will need to be collected just before, or just as they ripen.

Finally, one more crop can be obtained – a diminished and slightly tough form of Florence Fennel from the swollen stem bases. This is best collected in spring as the young shoots appear. The problem with this, of course, is that you will destroy the whole plant and have nothing for next year.

The main use for Fennel is as an accompaniment to fish. This felicitous association goes back to antiquity. For some reason, maybe for pious fear of the sin of gluttony, relatively few recipes survive from earlier times; nearly all references to what we consider to be foodstuffs are to their medical application, not their culinary ones. Nevertheless, some were written down and survive to this day. Here is a surprisingly modern-sounding one from *The Cook's and Confectioner's Dictionary* of 1723:

> *Gut and wash your Mackerel, then either slit or gash them down the Back, that they may take the Seasoning, then lay them a while in Oil, Salt, Pepper and Fennel; then wrap them up in the Fennel, lay them upon a Gridiron, and broil them. Make a Sauce for them, of clarified Butter, sweet Herbs shred small, Salt, Nutmeg, Gooseberries, Fennel, a little Vinegar and Capers.*

Quite why Fennel works so well with fish I do not know. Culpeper, determined to find the explanation for all things in the heavens, suggests that it is '*because it is a herb of Mercury, and under Virgo, and therefore bears antipathy to Pisces*'.

Pork also benefits from the addition of Fennel leaves or seeds, and of course the leaves can simply be added to any salad. My most unusual success was a home-grown anise made by adding a dessertspoonful of the seeds to a bottle of white rum, which takes on the sweet anise flavour almost immediately.

EDIBLE SPECIES

Ground Elder *Aegopodium podagraria*

DESCRIPTION	Creeping, medium perennial, to 30–60cm. Leaves compound, up to nine leaflets with pointed/oval or irregular serrated edge. Young leaflets bright, shiny, yellowish. Flowers white, umbrella-shaped spray
HABITAT	Gardens, woods, hedgerow. Most often near habitation
DISTRIBUTION	Very common throughout the British Isles, except the north of Scotland
SEASON	March and through until October if you keep cutting it back

I think it is fair to say that Ground Elder is not a popular plant. It was introduced to these islands at some point lost to history by a person who would sap our strength and will. Quite why certain plants have the ability to survive everything nature and human ingenuity can throw at them, while others give up the ghost even when lavished with love, is a mystery.

We have 'tomato blight' and 'pea root rot' but never 'Ground Elder wilt' or 'bindweed botrytis', or if we do they are not doing their jobs properly. The only gardening I am prepared to engage in is the careful removal of Ground Elder from a much-loved lily of the valley patch. It takes an hour of back-breaking work and has to be repeated three times a year. The weed even grows in my lawn and not even grass likes growing there.

Yet this pernicious plant has one saving grace – it is edible. This usefulness in the kitchen is why, of course, Ground Elder was introduced to the British Isles, not malign intent. No doubt the first person to plant it here was delighted to see how well it liked its new home, but as it grew out of favour it continued to grow in the garden regardless.

In the Middle Ages Ground Elder was used extensively as a (totally ineffective) remedy for gout – even carrying some around was believed to be efficacious. This is testified by one of the plant's names – Goutweed – and also by the second part of its Latin name, *podagra* meaning 'gout'. It was also known by the similar Goatweed, though this may be a reference to the shape of the leaves, and indeed the first part of the Latin name means 'goat's foot'. The common name arises because the leaves and flowers are similar to those of the unrelated Elder tree.

Ground Elder is clearly a plant you will have no trouble finding; if you are lucky enough *not* to have any in your garden you will be a welcome visitor at the house of anyone who *does* have it in theirs. Failing this, it can be found easily in woods and hedgerows, especially near habitation. Although Ground Elder is a member of the dangerous carrot family, along with the deadly Hemlocks, it is an easy plant to identify. The leaves are unusually broad and lacking in deeply incised edges. The new shoots, with their folded, shiny yellow-green leaves, appear as early as March and these are by far the best ones to collect. The leaves are, however, edible up until the stage when the plant flowers, at which point their chemistry changes somewhat and they become tough, odd in flavour and slightly laxative. Continual picking and cutting back will ensure renewed growth until the autumn, so there will be a constant supply.

The flavour of the very young leaves is indistinguishable from a good parsley, but more succulent, so it is as a garnish, like parsley, that I normally use it. The leaves can also be cooked as a vegetable like a (slightly stringy) parsley-flavoured spinach and served with butter. I have made Ground Elder soup and Ground Elder quiche, all the tastier for being made from the bodies of an enemy. If you keep guinea pigs it is well worth feeding them with as much Ground Elder as you can – it gives a lovely fresh flavour to the meat.

Hogweed *Heracleum sphondylium*

DESCRIPTION	Tall, robust biennial/perennial to 2 metres. Leaves broad, deeply divided, bristly. Stem bristly, green or dull red. Flowers in umbrella sprays, greyish white
HABITAT	Roadsides, field edges, waste ground
DISTRIBUTION	Very common throughout the UK, except the north of Scotland
SEASON	March–June, though often available later

This rather furry-looking plant does not appear particularly appetising, yet its young shoots are one of the best hedgerow treasures. Once the leaves have opened they lose much of their charm, though. As the various names – Hogweed, Pig's Parsnip and Pigweed – suggest, they have long been fed to pigs. Hogweed has also been called Cow Parsnip and it was no doubt a general fodder plant.

You will have no trouble finding Hogweed – barely a roadside or field edge in the country is bereft of it. While it is an easy plant to recognise, it does belong to the notorious carrot family and you will need to take care. The famous Giant Hogweed is also superficially similar, but produces a sap which causes dermatitis on exposure to sunlight. Most botanicals tell us that the two plants are easy to tell apart as one is seldom more than 1.5 metres tall, while the other reaches 4 metres or more, but as it is the young shoots that are eaten, this distinction is of little help. Normally, however, last year's dry flower stems will persist from both plants and if any are 4 metres tall you will have an excellent clue. In addition, the leaflets of Giant Hogweed are more pointed and are softly hairy on the underside, while its stems are a blotchy red.

Normally you will cut the individual young Hogweed shoots from a plant that is less than half a metre high, slicing with a knife as low down as you can. The younger they are and the less formed the leaf, the better they will taste. The root has plenty of food in store and will continue to send up young shoots for a couple of months or more, making Hogweed a genuine 'cut-and-come-again' plant. Some of the shoots are particularly fat. These are the sheathed flower shoots and, when very young, are even tastier than those of the leaves.

The flavour of cooked Hogweed shoots is frequently likened to asparagus. Well, they are certainly succulent, retaining little of the fibrous texture of the raw shoot, but the taste is nearer parsley than asparagus. The longer they are cooked, the less of the parsley flavour remains and the sweeter (and unfortunately, soggier) they become. They can be steamed and eaten with butter and black pepper, but the best way to serve them is dipped as Hogweed Tempura (p.202).

EDIBLE SPECIES 103

Pignut *Conopodium majus*

DESCRIPTION	Small upright perennial. Height around 30cm. Basal leaves fine and fern-like, later leaves forming delicate fronds from the stem joints. Flower heads white and umbrella-shaped. Tuberous root, irregular, rounded, up to 25mm diameter at the end of a long, fine root thread
HABITAT	Hedgerow banks, woods, old pasture. Prefers dry soil
DISTRIBUTION	Common all over the UK, except for the Fens
SEASON	All year, but tubers can only be found easily from February to July when the plant is visible

The hunt for the Pignut is like no other – something between a search, a puzzle and a test of dexterity. The 'nut' (really it is a tuber, like its relative, the carrot) cannot just be dug up, it must be searched out by following the infuriatingly delicate root fibre down, and north a bit then maybe southeast until the prize is located. Break the fibre and all is lost. The feeling of triumph at locating the tiny reward is a great foraging moment. On one of the wild-food forays I lead, hard-hearted stockbrokers were on their hands and knees begging for time to find just one more Pignut.

To find the nut you must first learn the plant. The feather-like fronds of the young plant are fairly distinctive, though Fool's Parsley is not too dissimilar and may cause confusion. Fool's Parsley tends to grow as a weed of cultivation – vegetable gardens being its preferred habitat. It has more substantial leaves, the flower heads have conspicuous long, thin spikes projecting from underneath them and – even if you are still fooled – there is no nut to find. Pignuts nearly always grow in fairly large groups so you may find yourself in one place for a long time. I know a field in Devon that seems to grow little else. As you need to dig up the nuts, permission will be required if it is not on your own land. Since their frequent habitat is old wildlife-rich pasture you should be careful not to disturb the turf too much – dig up a few here and a few there and do it as carefully as you can. Although the nuts are available all year they are only findable when the plant is visible – from February to July. It seems likely that Pignuts are the heroes of the otherwise inexplicable rhyme 'Here we go gathering nuts in May'.

Pursuit of this earthy treasure has long been a children's pastime, but I know of none that enjoy it now, even in my rural village. It's a pity that such a simple pleasure has been lost. Pignuts have not found much of a place in the primitive medicine cabinet though Culpeper tells us that being a plant under Venus '… *they provoke lust exceedingly, and stir up those sports she is mistress of…*'. You have been warned.

Are they worth all that effort to find? If you were planning a wild dinner party, Pignuts would not form more than a tiny part of the meal. Collecting enough for any more would be the work of several days. As an occasional treat, though, they are highly recommended. Uncooked the flavour is faintly sweet and similar to a Hazelnut. Cooked it is more like Sweet Chestnut. They take a bit of cleaning, though there is no pressing reason to peel off the thin brown skin. They can be added raw to salads or cooked in stews. Sliced and toasted in a little oil, they are excellent added to a stir-fry or a Wild Garlic Pesto (p.205). Of course you can just sit in the grass for an hour, digging, scrubbing, nibbling and meditating.

P.S. The existence of Pignuts in a location is a good sign of its biodiversity. Unfortunately, this is something of a two-edged sword. Pignuts were not given their name for nothing as pigs, which can smell them from some distance, will go to great lengths to dig them up. Wild boar have long been extinct in these islands but have made an inadvertent comeback as farm escapees – either accidentally or as part of an ill-advised blow for animal rights – and are now breeding in southwest England and elsewhere. The snout of the wild boar is a formidable instrument, able to overturn large areas of turf in search of this favourite food. I have seen hundreds of acres of downland – previously rich in flowers, fungi and invertebrates – ploughed up by these animals looking for a tasty morsel. This assault obviously damages all that grows there, but it also releases nitrogen which encourages coarse grasses to grow and inhibits recovery. Maybe we ought to eat all the Pignuts we can after all.

Young Pignut with early spring leaves

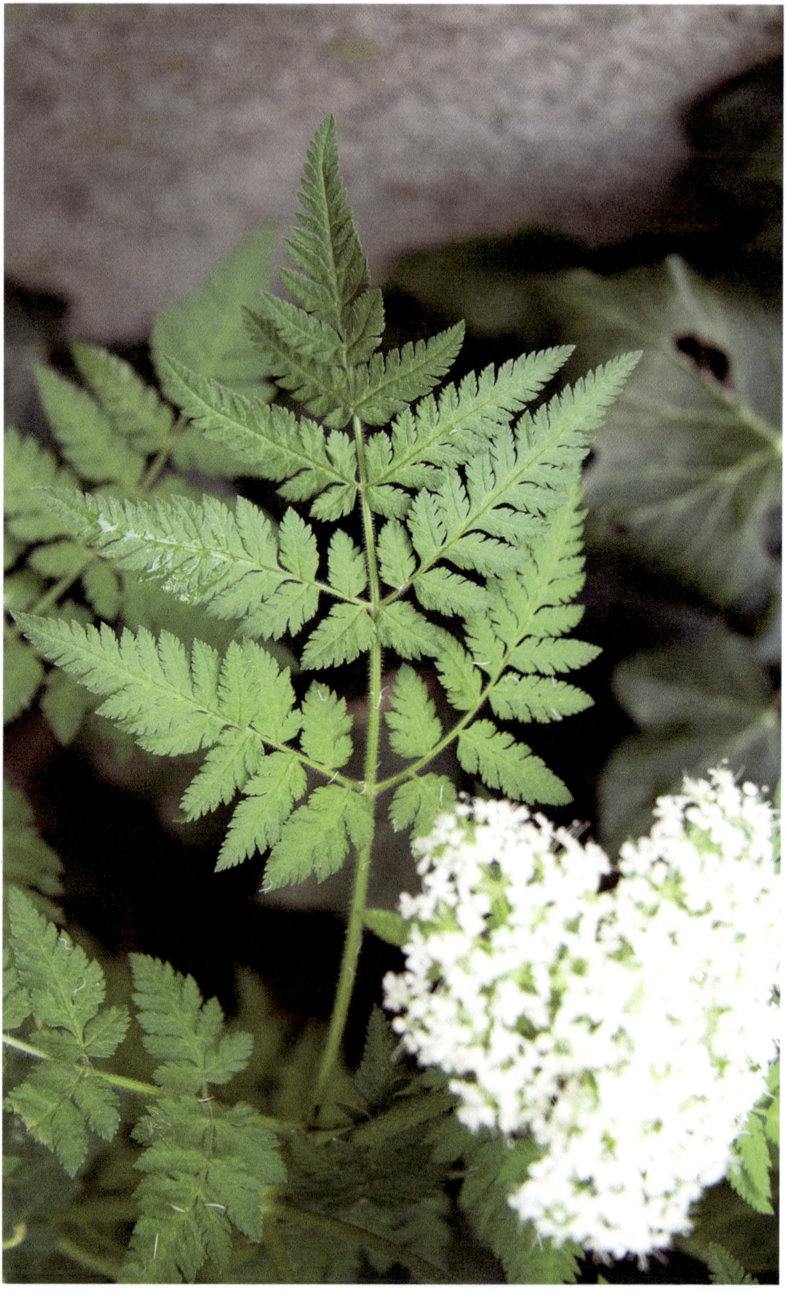

Sweet Cicely *Myrrhis odorata*

DESCRIPTION	Medium tall perennial, to 1.5 metres. Leaves fern-like. Stems hollow, hairy. Large tap root. Seed pods vertical, ribbed and long. Flowers in white umbrella. All parts smell of aniseed
HABITAT	Hedgerows, wood margins, often near water
DISTRIBUTION	Common, but with a northern distribution. England north of a line from Birmingham to Scarborough, Scottish lowlands and east-central Northern Ireland. Sparse in Wales
SEASON	Leaves from March until October, best early. Seed pods in June and July. Roots in October

As a confirmed southerner this is a plant I seldom get to see, yet in the North it can fill the roadside much as Cow Parsley does in the South. Superficially the two hedgerow scenes look the same, but they certainly don't taste the same and I envy my northern friends their good fortune. Sweet Cicely's distribution is rather odd, but its frequent appearance near habitation suggests it was introduced, then became naturalised in the cooler North where the climate was more like its mountainous central European home.

It is not a hard plant to identify but it *is* a member of the notorious carrot family and care must be exercised, especially if you intend to eat the root. The easy test is to rub the leaves and sniff. If you smell aniseed you are probably on the right track, with only the equally edible Fennel smelling the same. The 'sweet' part of the name is well deserved – the chemical which provides the aniseed flavour is a sweetener too. It has also been called Sweet Chervil and even the rather nice Candy Carrot.

The uses of Sweet Cicely are endless and some employ the sweetness to advantage – the leaves can be sprinkled on trifles or strawberries, or used as an additional sweetener for rhubarb. They can be included in a salad, of course, but also in place of Fennel in any number of dishes, fishy ones being the most obvious. The young and strongly aromatic pods are eaten too, sometimes as an on-the-go snack, and the roots may be sliced in a salad, roasted or boiled or even, as suggested by the herbalists, candied to protect against the plague.

Finally, the last two wicked lines of an eighteenth-century poem:

Sing, sweet Cicely, sing no more,
Till Love be deaf, as well as blind.

Wild Parsnip *Pastinaca sativa*

DESCRIPTION	Medium/tall biennial, to 1.5 metres. Pinnate leaflets opposite, irregularly lobed, toothed, hairy. Stem ribbed, hairy. Flowers in yellow umbrella sprays
HABITAT	Bare places, roadsides, sand dunes
DISTRIBUTION	Complex distribution. Southeast of a line from the Humber to the Severn, though rare in north Devon and Cornwall. Frequent in South Wales, locally common in coastal northern England. Scarce elsewhere
SEASON	Roots in the autumn

Wild Parsnips are the same species as garden parsnips and their complex distribution suggests that much of the wild population has returned to the wild after a domestic sojourn. Although the fully grown plants look vigorous enough, the only bit we eat – the roots – are pathetic affairs compared to the giants we are used to. Nevertheless, they taste splendidly of parsnip.

The roots are best dug in the autumn, but by then most of the plant will be skeletal and will have lost many identifying features. The best thing is to get to know your plants and observe the older members of the population develop their distinctive yellow flowers before they die back. This will help you avoid confusion with several poisonous members of the carrot family, such as the Hemlocks. Parsnips are, of course, biennials and the plants you will be digging up are those that have completed one season's growth. Parsnip is rather like its relative the Giant Hogweed in that contact with it can sensitise the skin to sunlight and cause dermatitis. It is by no means as dangerous in this respect, but it may be worth using gloves to be safe.

There is really only one way of cooking Wild Parsnips which will do justice to the small amount you are likely to find – parsnip crisps. Just slice them thinly and deep-fry in a good cooking oil until they are, well, crisp.

Also look out for the Wild Carrot (*Daucus carota*). This is the ancestor of the cultivated carrot, which now possesses subspecies status as *Daucus carota sativus*. As with the Wild Parsnip, you are not going to be able to replace your home-grown or bought-in crop with the wild ancestor, but it is common enough to try out occasionally. It has a similar southeastern distribution to the Wild Parsnip, but with a distinctly maritime preference, though this is quite likely to be another subspecies – *gummifer*. At no more than 70cm, it is a fairly low plant, with typical feathery leaves and dense white/grey flower heads with conspicuous bracts growing out from the edge. The root is, again, rather a disappointment, but it does look like a carrot (except for its colour, which is pale) and taste like a carrot.

Both these plants are included for their interest more than their genuine usefulness in the kitchen. The fact that they must be dug up argues against their extensive collection because of the collateral damage that is caused and permissions that must be obtained. Frankly I do not expect many will try them more than once or twice – conservation and legal worries aside, they are too much like hard work.

Wild Parsnip

Common Sorrel *Rumex acetosa*

DESCRIPTION	Upright, medium perennial. 30–100cm tall. Basal leaves forming a rosette, arrow-shaped with sharply pointed lobes. Higher leaves clasping stem. Mature leaves reddening. Single stem, seldom branched, reddening. Flower spike tall, flowers and seeds rusty pink. All parts taste acidic
HABITAT	Rough pasture, hedgerow, woods. Prefers neutral to acid soils
DISTRIBUTION	Very common everywhere
SEASON	It is often possible to find some all year but the spring and the second growth in the autumn are best

Sorrel is a very close relative of the dozen or so docks that live in these islands. They are all members of the Polygonaceae, a family which includes other familiar plants such as bistort, redshank, buckwheat and Japanese knotweed. Most familiar of all is rhubarb with which Sorrel shares its fruity flavour. Sorrel has long been used as a food and also as a medicine, most usually for its cooling properties.

You will have no trouble finding Sorrel – almost any field and hedgerow will sport some, although it is less common on chalk. The mature plants are highly conspicuous in summer with their rusty pink flower spikes, which slowly turn red brown as the seeds mature. These tall plants of late spring and summer provide little in the way of fresh leaves, but from February the bright new rosettes appear from the perennial root and a second growth follows in late summer through to early winter.

Identification is not difficult though the docks may distract you for a moment. The most worrying look-alike is the poisonous Lords and Ladies (*Arum maculatum*, p.191). This is a vastly different plant but the leaves are superficially similar and sometimes almost identical (as the picture on p.193 shows). On a recent walk a friend accidentally picked Lords and Ladies leaves and put them in my basket thinking they were giving me a present of Sorrel. This, at least, is my charitable assessment of the incident. There are two ways to be sure – Lords and Ladies leaves are relatively thin compared to the rather succulent leaves of Sorrel and its backward-pointing lobes are always *rounded* whereas those of Sorrel are sharply *pointed*. Do not use the taste test here unless you want your tongue and lips to go numb and swell up.

Sorrel is often added to a salad of milder leaves as it is a little too strong on its own. More often it is used to make a sauce, for example with yogurt, the shredded leaves being sweated for a couple of minutes, then for a minute or two longer in the yogurt. Alternatively, you can just mix the shredded leaves in raw. Fish dishes are the most obvious targets for Sorrel sauce, but meats such as veal, chicken and pork benefit too. Sorrel's capabilities do not stop there. It makes a terrific omelette – either straight into the mix or as a creamy sauce inside – and it can even be used to provide acidity to puddings.

The taste of Sorrel comes from oxalic acid and calcium oxalate. These are quite seriously poisonous and in a sufficiently reckless dose will cause vomiting, muscular twitching, convulsions, renal failure, cardiac arrest and even milk-fever (though I think you need to be a cow for the last one). Oxalic acid removes calcium from the bloodstream, turning it into calcium oxalate (from which you can make your very own kidney stones) and resulting in hypocalcaemia. There is at least one recorded occasion in which a fatality occurred due to eating Sorrel; it was in Spain. One serving of the guilty soup contained a substantial (though not *that* substantial) half kilogram of the plant and the unfortunate victim was not at all in the best of health even before his final meal. As long as you are reasonably fit a small amount of Sorrel will do you no harm, just don't eat it by the bucketful.

Also look out for Sheep's Sorrel (*Rumex acetosella*), a smaller but very similar plant. The key difference is the lobes on the leaves which are more like wings, or halberd-shaped as they are often described. It is strictly a lover of acid soils.

Stinging Nettle *Urtica dioica*

DESCRIPTION	Upright perennial, to 1.5 metres. Leaves heart-shaped, opposite on stem, serrated edge, covered in stinging hairs. Stems tough and fibrous, also with stinging hairs
HABITAT	Woods, waste ground, hedgerow, near habitation
DISTRIBUTION	Throughout the UK
SEASON	Spring – before the flowers form, though the younger the better. New growth will appear in summer and autumn from cut-back plants

Revered and reviled but ignored only at a cost, the Stinging Nettle is among the best known of our plants. Indeed it is often the first one we learn, as the splendidly named Reverend Tipping Silvester wrote in 1733:

There grows the Product of a scatter'd Seed,
The Nettle, Plant ignoble, baleful Weed.

Despite its familiarity and long history of use in the kitchen and sickroom, it is shamefully under-exploited these days. Everyone has heard of Nettle Soup but few have ever made it.

Any plant with such overt potency as the Stinging Nettle was likely to accumulate a large number of putative cures to its name. Culpeper lists nearly thirty diseases for which it is the answer and, bringing us up to date, Piers Warren, in his book *101 Uses for Stinging Nettles*, has forty-seven. (Incidentally, don't try the 'X-rated' number '101', it isn't nice… or safe). A few of these remedies make some sense. Stinging Nettles contain vitamin C, so will prevent scurvy, and the substantial levels of iron will alleviate some types of anaemia. In the roots there are antihistamines, making them a likely palliative in hay fever and other allergies. The one disease for which they show most promise went unnoticed by the old herbalists – enlargement of the prostate. One more complaint which Stinging Nettles, used as a poultice, are reputed to cure is haemorrhoids. Just remember to boil them before applying.

I will not need to tell you where to find a supply of Stinging Nettles – few plants are more ubiquitous – and while there are look-alikes in the dead nettles and yellow archangel these are equally edible. Picking Stinging Nettles is always going to be a trial – even with decent gloves. The long stems whip around and invariably get you somewhere. The brave, or foolhardy, can pick them without gloves by moving their fingers upwards and grasping the stem just below the young half-dozen or so leaves at the top. This manoeuvre, which can take a fair amount of painful practice, breaks

EDIBLE SPECIES 113

the hollow silica hairs from the side so that they do not penetrate the skin. The stinging toxin was long thought to be formic acid – the poison produced by ants – but modern analysis has revealed a cocktail of histamines, acetylcholine, tartaric acid and oxalic acid. Whichever of these is the main culprit, it hurts, and the pain can last a couple of days. The idea of rubbing dock leaves on to the affected area seemingly goes back at least to Chaucer who uses the phrase '*Nettle in Docke out*' in his *Troilus and Criseyde*. Despite its antiquity, it is doubtful if it works and there is also the possibility that it is Common Mallow – formerly known as Round Dock – that the old writers were referring to.

Only young, fresh leaves should be collected. In March the whole plant can be picked, but as they mature, just pick the developing leaves from the top. At the first sign of flowers developing you must stop picking. The plant will now start producing cystoliths – microscopic rods of calcium carbonate – which can be absorbed by the body where they will mechanically interfere with kidney function. By this time the texture and flavour has deteriorated anyway and the plants are not worth picking. Cut-down plants will produce a second fresh growth and it is sometimes possible to pick Stinging Nettles up until November.

Picking them without gloves is one thing but eating them without cooking is quite another. There are some notorious nettle-eating contests held around the country, the best known being at the Bottle Inn in West Dorset. I have never entered this competition but I have eaten raw nettles. The trick is to fold two or three into a large pill first then apply a crushing bite with the molars. It's like eating sandpaper. Beer helps.

A more gentle introduction to nettle consumption is tea. To make one cup, just pour boiling water over half a dozen leaves, steep for 5–10 minutes, then scoop the leaves out. If you like the water left over from boiling Brussels sprouts you'll love it. Of greater interest is Nettle beer. This is more of a sparkling wine than a beer (when I make it anyway) and downing a pint has much the same effect as downing a pint of Champagne.

The flavour of cooked Stinging Nettles is halfway between spinach and a mild cabbage and there is no reason why it cannot be served straight as a vegetable. Thin leaves do not always take well to steaming, so just gently sweat them for 10 minutes in a covered pan with the little bit of water that adheres to the leaves from washing. Serve with some butter and black pepper stirred in. You will be relieved to hear that cooking completely destroys the nettle's ability to sting.

The cooked and coarsely puréed leaves can be dolloped on to a pizza or used to stuff cannelloni. Continuing this distinctly Italian theme, the cooked and finely chopped leaves, squeezed almost dry, are added to flour to make Nettle Ravioli (p.206). Nettles can be used in several of the recipes in this book calling for green leaves but the best of them is the simplest – Nettle Soup (p.201).

Hop *Humulus lupulus*

DESCRIPTION	Long climbing perennial, 2–6 metres. Mature leaves *palmate* (like a hand), edges serrated like a Stinging Nettle. Stems coarsely hairy. Flowers green, male branched sprays, female cone-like, on separate plants
HABITAT	Hedgerow
DISTRIBUTION	Fairly common in England, except for the North and far Southwest. Uncommon in Wales and Scotland, rare in Northern Ireland
SEASON	April and May for the shoots, September for the flowers

The Hop is the only native member of the Cannabaceae family, though I am given to understand that its well-known relative is occasionally and mysteriously seen in remote woodland clearings. While Hops have long been considered a soporific – the Kentish hop-pickers are reputed to have added the Hop resin from their knives to their roll-ups – it is their other recreational use as a flavouring of ale to make beer for which they are famous. In Britain the medicinal and culinary uses of Hops predate their employment in ale. The seventeenth-century writer John Evelyn in his *Discourse of Sallets* considered Hops to be more medicinal than fit for a *sallet* and Culpeper suggests it as a cure for French diseases, whatever they are. Putting the sickroom and bar-room aside, it is the young shoots that are eaten.

The plant disappears to its roots in the winter and cannot be found. In April and May the young shoots trail themselves all over hedges and – provided they do not fall foul of the hedge-trimmer – you should be assured of a good harvest. The leaves are very distinctive with their hand-like shape and serrated edges so you will not risk confusing them with the other trailing hedgerow plants, such as bindweed, or the poisonous Black and White Bryonies (p.195).

While I fancy some of the beeriness comes through in the shoots, the flavour is an unusual one and not easily described – you will just have to try some. They can be enjoyed in a soup, a stir-fry or in pakoras (p.211).

P.S. Hop shoots are the delicacy of but a few and the Hop is best known for its use in beer-making. Hops add not only bitterness and flavour but also stability to a beer. The herbalist Gerard has reassurance for those of us particularly fond of this drink:

> *The manifold virtues in hops do manifestly argue the holsomnesse of beere above ale; for the hops rather make it phisicall drinke to keepe the body in health, than an ordinarie drinke for the quenching of our thirst.*

Young Hop shoots

Before the beneficial properties of Hops were fully appreciated, various other hedgerow plants were used to add bitterness and flavour to ale. The very common and aromatic Mugwort and that denizen of acid peat bogs, Sweet Gale, were two of the most common; Yarrow (p.141), Ground Ivy and the wonderfully named Horehound also found their way into the barrel. Another plant which was employed occasionally is Wormwood (*Artemisia absinthium*). This fairly uncommon plant, famous for its inclusion in another alcoholic drink – absinthe – is one of my favourites due to the heady perfume of its leaves. If you ever find any, just break off a leaf, roll it in your fingers and sniff – it smells like a Turkish tobacconist's.

Watermint *Mentha aquatica*

DESCRIPTION	Medium upright perennial to 80cm, more often 20–30cm. Leaves dark green, pointed/oval, sometimes with a purplish tinge, finely hairy, toothed edge, opposite. Stem square in section, hairy, reddish brown. Flowers lilac, some axial flowers but also a rounded flower head at the top. All parts smell strongly minty
HABITAT	Stream sides, boggy places, damp meadows
DISTRIBUTION	Common throughout the British Isles, except the northern Highlands of Scotland
SEASON	April–November

Even someone as dedicated as I am to not gardening has mint growing by the back door – it is one of those plants that is needed in small quantities just occasionally and has the commendable property of growing vigorously without the slightest effort. Although the particular flavour that the garden varieties supply is hard to find in the wild, there are many native mints to be enjoyed. The most common and most useful of them all is Watermint.

The upright nature, the furry and slightly bronzed leaves and the damp habitat make Watermint an easy plant to spot. Identification is easier than normal as the peppermint-like smell is unmistakable. It is, perhaps, possible to mix it up with another mint, but that is the worst that can happen. Nevertheless remember that this is the preferred home of the deadly Hemlocks so you must be careful.

Watermint is really not hard to find – nestling among the Watercress and Brooklime along a stream edge, or hiding in the reeds and meadowsweet of a wet meadow – but you may need to search a little before you find your spot. When found it is usually in some quantity so you will not have to stint on your recipes. Picking is often an exercise requiring Wellington boots – even if there is a nice patch within reach of the unbooted there is always a nicer one just a little too far away. Scissors are essential tools for collecting this perennial plant – the stems are quite tough and it is all too easy to uproot the whole thing, leaving nothing to grow for next year.

The smell is almost peppermint but not quite. True peppermint is a hybrid of Watermint and Spearmint. Hybrids abound in the mint world, making life difficult for the botanist and interesting for the cook. The smell of Watermint varies from plant to plant and from season to season. The first growth in the spring is the sweetest, with a slight turpentine tone appearing by the autumn. Even the time of

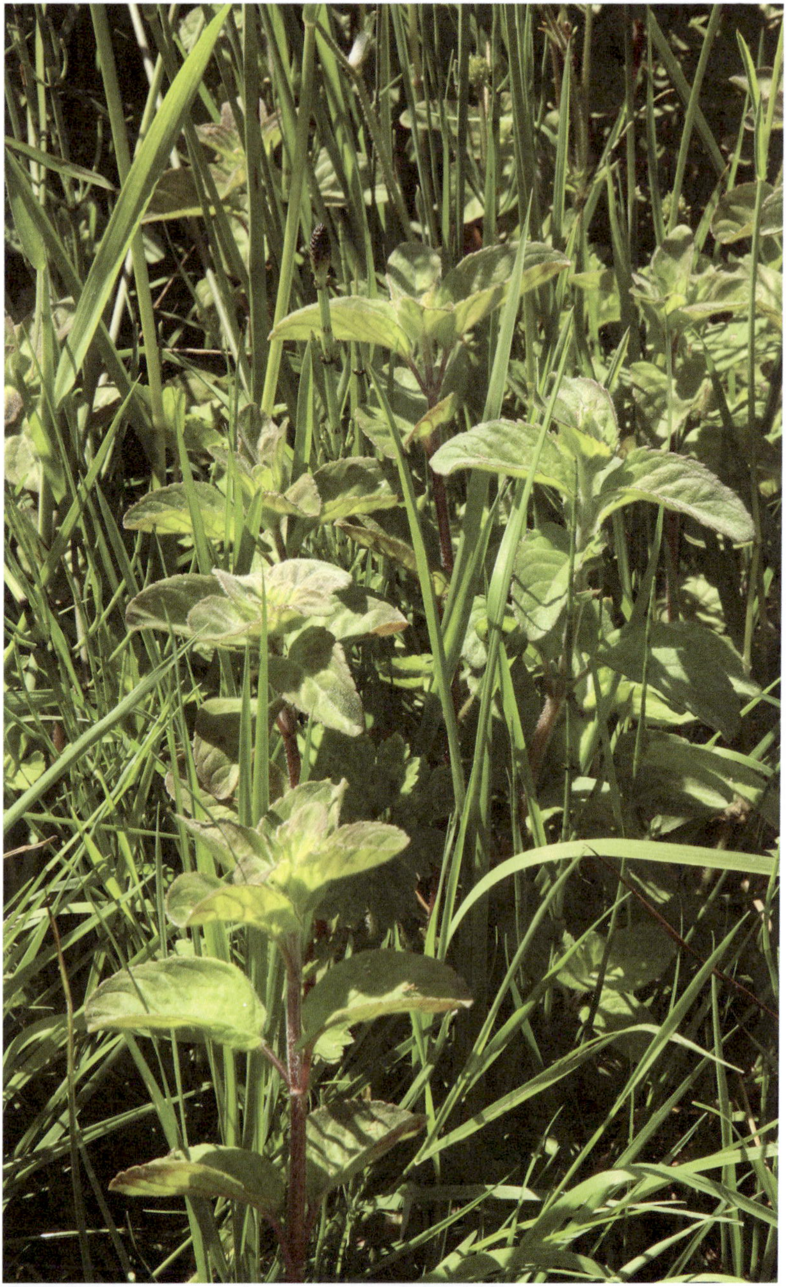

day has some effect – Mary Randolph, writing in 1838 as *The Virginia Housewife*, implores the forager to '*Pick the mint early in the morning while the dew is on it.*'

Many recipes involving the mints require steeping the leaves in a liquid for a period of time. The simplest of these is mint tea. I have always considered a fondness for herbal teas an inexplicable affectation but I tried this and find it less vile than some others. A high recommendation indeed. Back to Mary Randolph, who was picking her mint for a higher purpose, mint cordial, evidently in industrial quantities to see her through the winter.

> *Put two handsful into a pitcher, with a quart of French brandy, cover it, and let it stand till next day; take the mint carefully out, and put in as much more, which must be taken out next day – do this the third time; then put three quarts of water to the brandy, and one pound of loaf sugar powdered; mix it well together – and when perfectly clear, bottle it.*

I highly recommend the recipe for Watermint Sorbet (p.219). It is one of the few desserts that is both delicious and invigorating. Watermint has long been used as a carminative, which is why we still eat mints at the end of the meal (rather ruined when they come in large boxes and are covered in chocolate). As the herbalist Gerard says, '*Mint is marvellous wholesome for the stomacke.*' Watermint *can* be used wherever garden mint is used, but the peppermint flavour may not suit everyone.

P.S. Culpeper has to be quarantined as a p.s. for his comments on mint. Among the many recommendations he has for it is a '*remedy for those that have venereal dreams and pollutions in the night, being outwardly applied*'. How you 'outwardly apply' it he doesn't say. I have given the matter considerable thought and suggest stuffing the leaves in your Y-fronts.

Spearmint *Mentha spicata*

DESCRIPTION	Medium, upright perennial, to 70cm. Leaves distinctly pointed/oval, with neat saw-toothed edge, bright green, almost unstalked, mostly hairless. Stems square in section. Flowers lilac, central spike and some on stalks from the leaf joints. Smells intensely of spearmint!
HABITAT	Roadsides, waste ground. Often a garden escapee
DISTRIBUTION	Frequent throughout the British Isles, but less common in Scotland, Wales and Lincolnshire. Rare in Ireland
SEASON	May–October

Apart from the ubiquitous and delightful Watermint, the most common of all *Mentha* species is Corn Mint (*M. arvensis*). Unfortunately this is not a great asset in any kitchen so I have passed it by; the naturalist and writer Geoffrey Grigson famously describes it as smelling of 'mouldy Gorgonzola'. There are, however, several other, more useful mints which the habitual country rambler is likely to encounter. Perhaps the best of these, certainly the smelliest, is the ancestor of many of our garden varieties, Spearmint.

The flavour of Spearmint needs no introduction but the wild plant will not be familiar to many people. It is, however, one of the easiest of the mints to identify with its ragged-edged, bright-green leaves and, most of all, its toothpaste smell. I know it from several locations, though nowhere near as many as Watermint, and in one of these (a country lay-by) it grows in vast profusion. Spearmint is an introduced species which has become naturalised. For this reason it is often found near habitation.

As with Watermint, Spearmint is best employed in sweet dishes and in drinks, though it has been used in the past – as its garden descendant is today – with lamb.

Also look out for any number of other mints. There are at least a dozen of these if the hybrids are included. The one pictured here is Round-leaved or Apple-scented Mint (*M. suaveolens*), a native species found scattered all over the British Isles but more frequent in the Southwest. It is one of the commonly cultivated species and you are quite likely to find it near habitation.

Spearmint

Round-leaved Mint

EDIBLE SPECIES 121

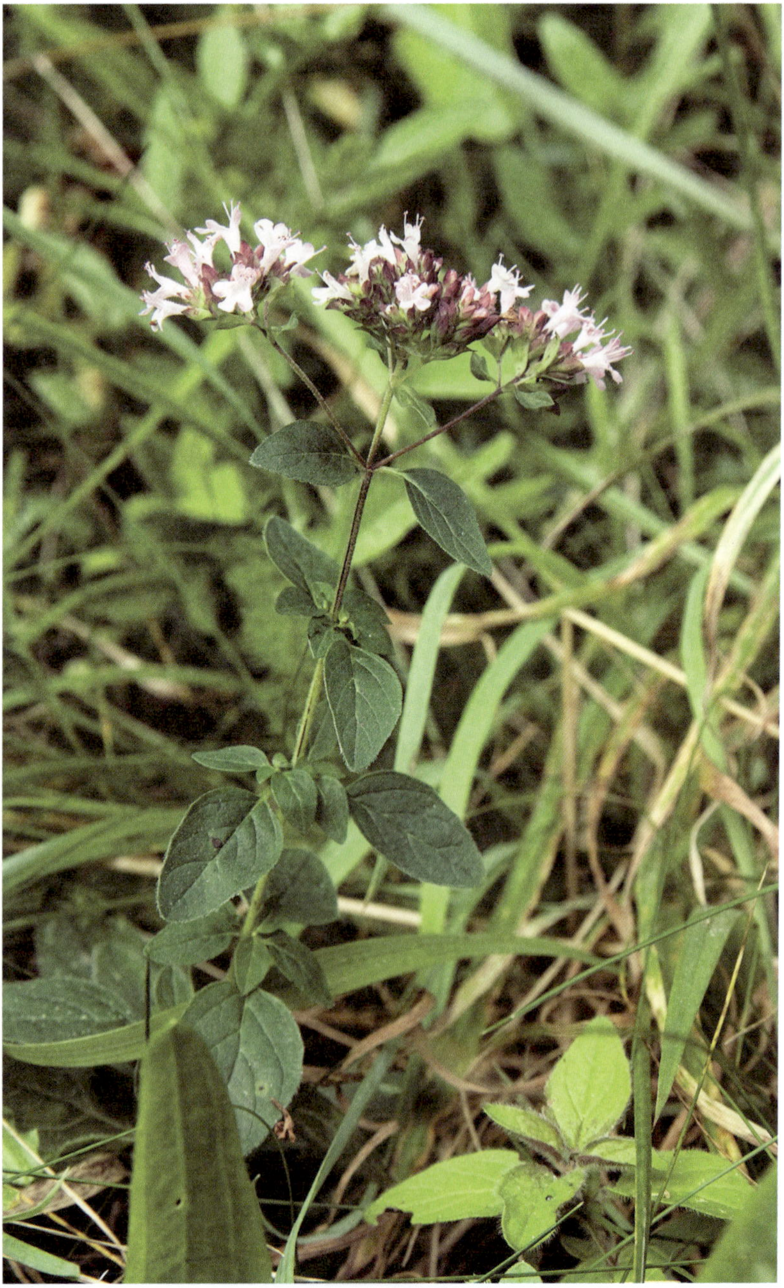

Wild Marjoram *Origanum vulgare*

DESCRIPTION	Medium perennial, to 50cm. Leaves pointed/oval, finely and sparsely downy especially the edge, short dark green stalks. Stem thin, reddish brown, square in section. Flowers pink, arising on long stems from the leaf joints. Smell strongly aromatic
HABITAT	Dry grassland, roadsides, scrub. On lime
DISTRIBUTION	Occasional. Scattered throughout the British Isles with a southern bias. Rare in northern Scotland and Northern Ireland
SEASON	May–October

This is the oregano that we find in our pasta sauces and on pizzas; thus we associate it with Italy, yet it is a native species, long appreciated in these islands for its medicinal and culinary properties. The marjoram we typically grow in the garden is one of several related species, such as sweet marjoram (*O. majorana*) and pot marjoram (*O. onites*).

Wild Marjoram is most common in the south of England and it likes chalky soils. As it is a perennial you only have to find it once to have an annual supply. I have a spot – a roadside verge – half a mile from my house where it appears in abundance every year. The six months of the year when it is not producing useful leaves are easily filled as it keeps very well indeed when dried.

The taste is the familiar one – perhaps a little fainter than from plants grown in warmer climates – and it is hardly necessary to describe how it might be deployed. The eighteenth-century food writer Louis Lémery writes: '*Marjoram is an Herb us'd in Sauces, to give your Meat the more Relish*', and it is hard to disagree.

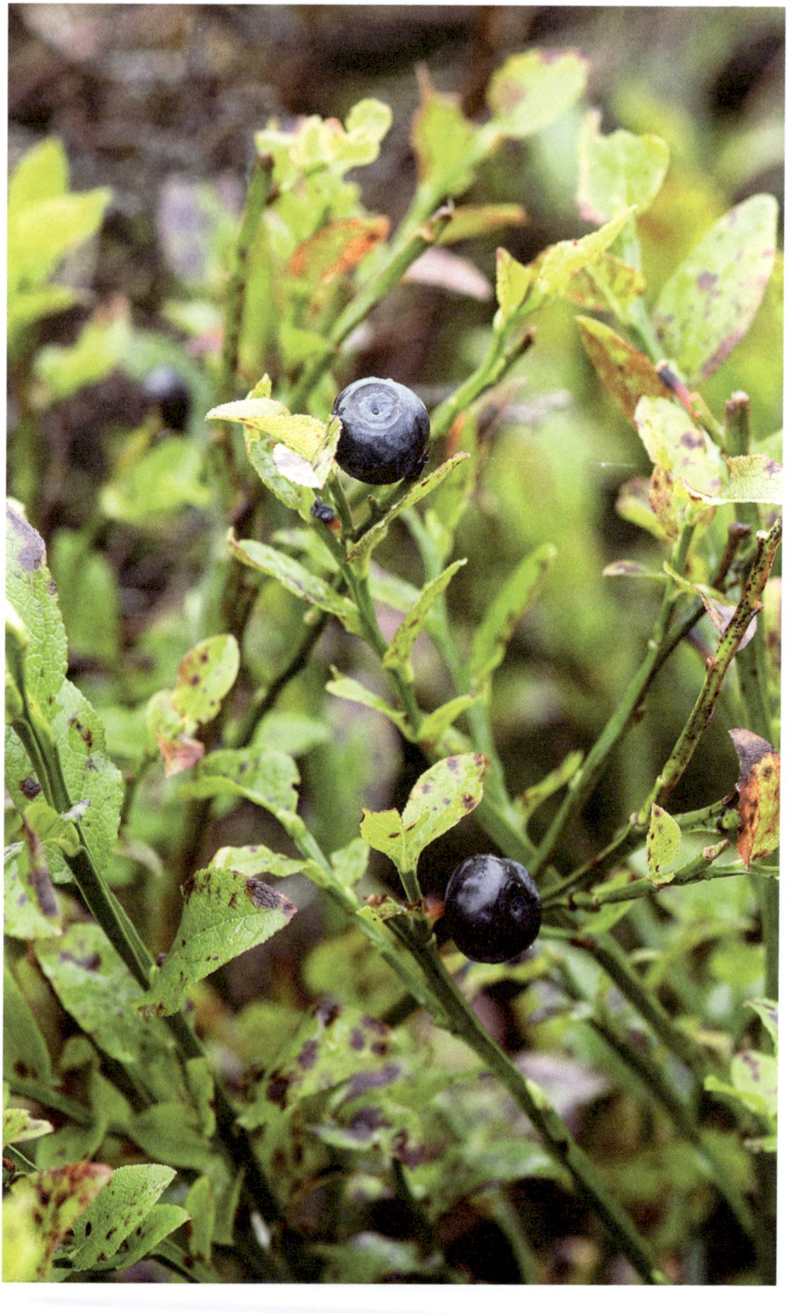

Bilberry *Vaccinium myrtillus*

DESCRIPTION	Short shrub, to 50cm. Leaves oval, 1–3cm, reddening with age, deciduous. Stems green, angled in cross-section. Berries dark blue, almost black, a bloom like a plum, end flattened slightly
HABITAT	Heaths, moors, open woodland – acid soils, never chalk
DISTRIBUTION	Common west of a line drawn from Scarborough to Exeter and scattered on the heaths of south and southeast England
SEASON	August and September

The native Bilberry (or Whortleberry, Blaeberry, Huckleberry or half a dozen other names) is much superior to its North American cousin, the blueberry. But the imported species has one major advantage – you don't have to pick it.

I have spent many, many hours knelt among the huge tracts of Bilberry bushes on Exmoor and Dartmoor with very little to show for my efforts. Although the bushes are common, the berries hang upon them sparsely, and at a back-breaking height. A reasonable rate for handpicking is considered to be 250g per hour. If you are determined to make a better job of collecting your Bilberries then it might be time to invest in a berry-picker (p.13); this is the very best type of berry to use it on but there are the usual disadvantages of damaged berries and unwanted leaves. Peasant children have, in the past, been employed to collect large quantities of Bilberries for market but the less disciplined modern child will most likely come back with nothing more than a smiling purple face and an empty basket.

Largely missing from the rich soils of central and eastern England, this is a berry of wild heath and moor – the picture opposite was taken on a wet and blowy Scottish mountainside. It also grows in open woodland but I have seldom seen berries on these plants, no doubt due to my being out-foraged by deer and ponies.

As you might guess I am one with the child forager when it comes to Bilberries. Not a single Bilberry has ever made it back to my kitchen. But if you are luckier, harder-working or more self-controlled than me, there are wonderful things to be done with half a kilo of Bilberries. The flavour is sharper than the blueberry and richer, but the berries are similarly blessed with a lack of hard pips. Better still, they look wonderful.

I favour recipes that show off the beauty of these berries and speak of the selfless toil that went into their collection. The excellent tart on p.222 does just this but uses the much rarer Cranberry. It would look every bit as good with Bilberries.

Cranberry *Vaccinium oxycoccos*

DESCRIPTION	Slender, low, creeping perennial. Leaves small, sparse, alternate, oval, shiny dark green. Stems thin and straggling. Berries rounded/pear-shaped, red, often mottled
HABITAT	Acid bogs and heaths, open boggy woods. Usually nestled in sphagnum moss
DISTRIBUTION	Uncommon, restricted to wild areas of central and southern Scotland, northwest England, west Wales, central Northern Ireland. Occasional elsewhere. Gather seldom and with care
SEASON	August–October

Fen Berry, Moss Berry, Moor Berry – these names leave us in no doubt where this splendid little plant is to be found. Sadly the Cranberry is much less common and widespread nowadays due to the draining of land for agriculture. It was once found in many parts of southern England but is now almost extinct in this region.

Most of its current strongholds are sensitive and often protected habitats, and even there it is seldom found in abundance. The berries pictured here and on the Cranberry and Apple Tart (p.222) were found on a magnificently grim bog (or 'moss' as it is called) in Galloway after a three-day search during their wettest August week on record. Not exactly easy foraging.

In the eighteenth century, at Longtown on the northern border of Cumberland, 20–30 pounds of Cranberries were sold every day during the five- or six-week season. They were used to make Cranberry tarts. This sort of bounty is not possible today; our commercial Cranberries are all American Cranberries (*Vaccinium macrocarpon*).

Along with Bilberries, Cranberries are a member of the Ericaceae family and are often found nestling in the sphagnum under tufts of heather, itself an ericaceous plant. Finding them is quite a task as the berries are hard to see and the thin plants almost invisible. Once you find a plant there are likely to be more nearby. Do collect with care and restraint, and be careful of the delicate habitat around you.

Cranberries have received a certain amount of attention recently as being half food, half medicine – a 'functional food' as such are called. Its list of nutrients is no more than one would expect from an average fruit, but it does seem to have some ability to ameliorate certain infections, such as those of the urinary tract, by preventing the bacteria from sticking to cells and also a possible benefit in treating cardiovascular disease.

The berries are very beautiful and, while you can make them into sauces and drinks, are best used in a way that shows them in all their rare glory. They are rather sharp and some consider them inedible raw. However, they are certainly not poisonous and if sufficient sugar is used in the recipe the berries will simply add a tart note to the dish – popping in the mouth with a pleasant sharpness if used raw. Like Bilberries, and unlike most other wild berries which can be rather pippy, they contain very small seeds which are hardly noticeable when eaten.

For some reason Cranberries have the longest use-by date of any fruit. I have kept them in an unrefrigerated pot for 3 months with no sign of decay and an eighteenth-century botanical states that '*They may be kept for several years by wiping them clean and closely corking them up in dry bottles.*' Of course, you could just eat them.

Brooklime *Veronica beccabunga*

DESCRIPTION	Low, straggling aquatic perennial, to 60cm. Leaves rounded oval, bright green – paler below, opposite pairs at 90° to each other. Stem hollow, roots issuing from leaf joints part of the way up. Sky-blue, four-petalled flowers
HABITAT	Streams and pond sides, wet paths
DISTRIBUTION	Common throughout the British Isles, except the northwest of Scotland
SEASON	May–November

I am going to be straight with you: Brooklime doesn't taste all that great. This is not a personal opinion – although it is undoubtedly edible, no one I know has a good word to say about it. So why is it here? Four reasons. It *is* edible, it's good for you, it's very common and the Latin name is fun.

Brooklime is a plant found in slow-moving streams and sometimes along wet footpaths. The bright-green leaves are very neat and do look rather tasty. It is just that they aren't. Mixed with other salad ingredients such as Watercress (with which it often grows) and dressed with oil and vinegar, Brooklime is really not bad – this is how it is eaten in mainland northern Europe. Do not even think of cooking it.

Brooklime is one of the speedwells, with the same pretty blue flowers. The leaves are rather rounded, however, and you will not easily confuse it with the other water-loving speedwells. Brooklime suffers the same problems as Watercress regarding liver fluke, so you must read about it (p.47–9) before you embark on a Brooklime salad.

P.S. *Veronica beccabunga* is one of the most remarkable Latin names in existence, which is saying something when you consider it is up against glories such as *Upupa epops* and *Apolysis zzyzxensis*. The name always makes me think of Carmen Miranda. The origin of Veronica is undecided and why it was given to the speedwells obscure. Where *beccabunga* comes from is also uncertain. Most probably it is the German *Bachbunge* meaning 'brook bunch' – the plant does fill up streams with large bunches of itself. Or it could be 'brook bung' – the Norse 'bung' being a reference to it blocking streams, or maybe from the Flemish *beckpunge* meaning 'mouthsmart', a reference to its bitter flavour.

The origin of the common name is also unclear. 'Brook' is straightforward enough, but 'lime' could refer to stream or mud or plant, or the Old English name for speedwell. Nice to get these things sorted out.

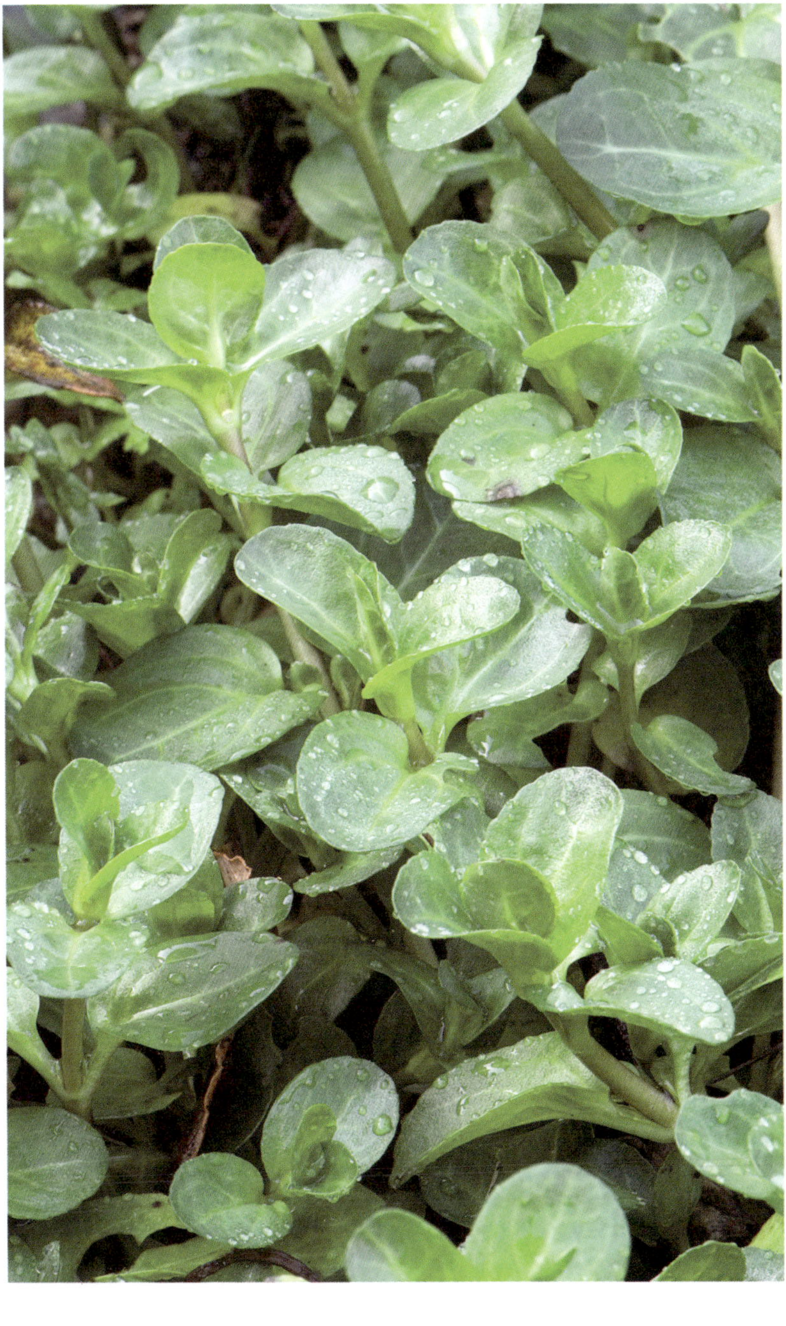

Corn Salad *Valerianella locusta*

DESCRIPTION	Low, short, branching annual, to 15cm. Lower leaves spoon-shaped, almost hairless, slightly succulent, opposite. Flowers with five petal-like lobes, tiny, in clusters, pale lilac
HABITAT	Waste ground, agricultural land, gardens
DISTRIBUTION	Frequent in England, increasingly rare in the North. Generally coastal in Wales
SEASON	Late winter and spring

Corn Salad, or Lamb's Lettuce as it is often called, is a mild-flavoured salad plant historically more popular in France than here. The cultivated version, which can be bought from the greengrocer's or grown at home, is larger but even milder. The clusters of tiny pale-lilac flowers make it an easy plant to spot and impossible to mix up with anything nasty. I find it mostly as neat little plants growing in flower beds or on waste ground, but it is also a common weed of agriculture.

It can quickly go to seed so the young growth of winter and spring is the best. I doubt if a salad made entirely from Corn Salad would satisfy many people so it is best used mixed with other, stronger-flavoured leaves and dressed well. The flowers, too, are edible and they add a pleasantly powerful fragrance to a salad.

Elder *Sambucus nigra*

DESCRIPTION	Shrub or small tree. Leaves formed from two or three pairs of opposite leaflets plus one terminal leaflet. Leaflets oval and pointed with serrated edge. Flowers in stalked umbrella sprays, five-petalled, cream with yellow stamens. Berries purple/black with three small pips
HABITAT	Hedgerow, disturbed ground near habitation, nitrogen-rich area such as around rabbit warrens
DISTRIBUTION	Very common everywhere, except central and northern Scotland
SEASON	Flowers late May–early July, berries August and September

This untidy weed of a plant has been the source of both comfort and fear for millennia; a tree to both court and counter disaster. Despite its unkempt appearance it is, above all, a plant of power. The superstitions associated with the Elder are legion. To fell the tree is unlucky as it is home to the unforgiving Elder Mother; burning the timber in the house will release the devil within; and to make a cradle from its timber is sheer folly. Yet it has been attributed with innumerable virtues.

Every part, flowers, berries, leaves, bark – and even the soil it grows in and any spring that passes its roots – has been used as a cure for some ailment or other. Warts and sorrows can be transferred to an Elder stick and buried, and an Elder planted near a house (there is one by my back door) will protect the occupants from evil. It will even provide refuge during a thunderstorm as it is, we are told, never struck by lightning. Once you learn of these charming absurdities it is difficult to get them out of your head. I often accidentally break thin branches when collecting flowers or berries and always, without thought or hesitation, say sorry.

How and when the Elder earned its fearful reputation is lost in time but it appears to be pre-Christian. Christianity, however, as it has done so skilfully so often, picked up the pagan tradition and turned it to its own use. The tree from which the remorseful Judas hanged himself was deemed to have been an Elder, and the Cross of Christ was said to have been made from its timber. This association with the Easter story accords perfectly with the ambivalent Elder, for the death of Jesus was, of nature and necessity, both disaster and triumph.

In common with a handful of others species included in this book, the Elder provides two crops, flowers and berries, though there is a third in the Jelly Ear

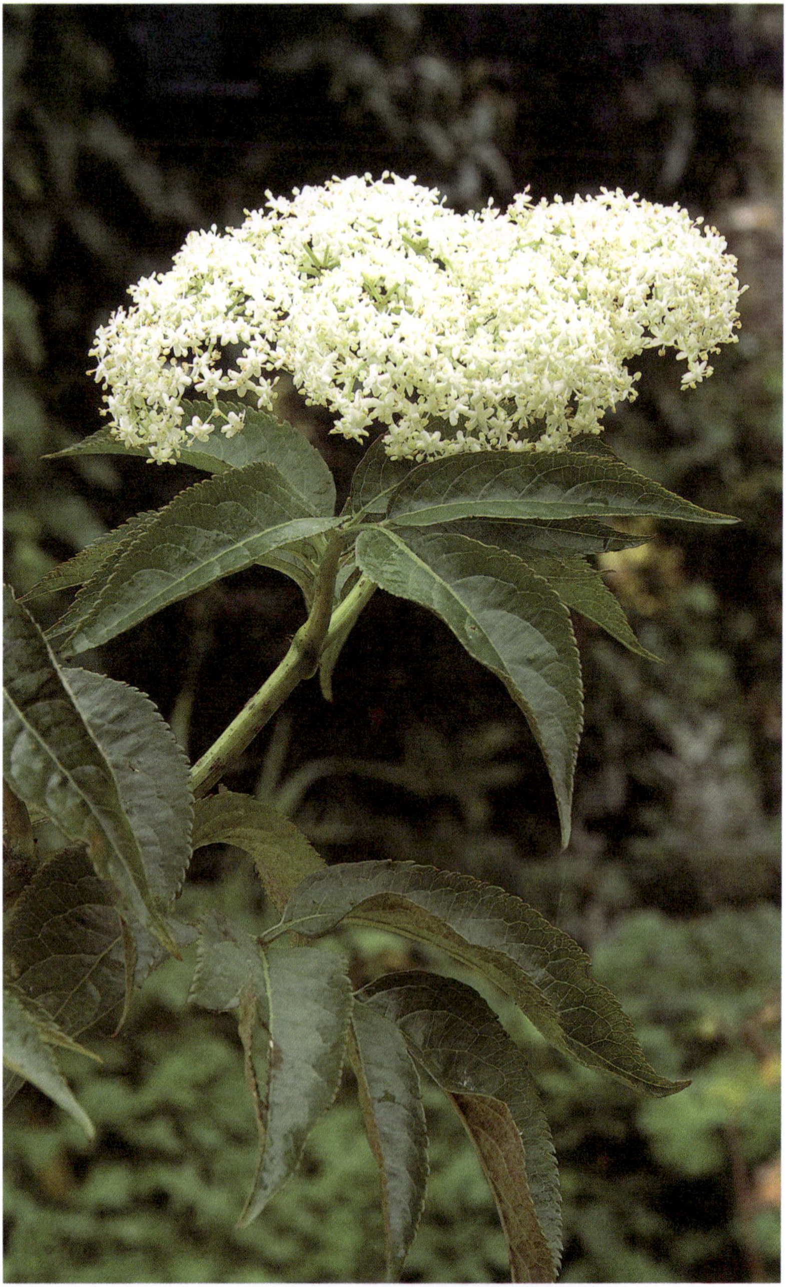

fungus which grows on the dead branches. There is one novice mistake that I must warn you about. Do not pick all the flowers from a tree, then go back expecting to find some berries. You won't. Find any, that is. Fortunately the Elder is sufficiently common to provide both in great abundance. Its popularity, however, has made some of the more urban and suburban trees the subject of friendly and sometimes not-so-friendly rivalry among springtime cordial and 'Champagne' makers.

The tree is easy to recognise, though a few species such as the related, broader-leaved and earlier-flowering Wayfaring Tree can provide a false dawn for the Elderflower hunter. Later in the year it is even possible to be distracted by the tall umbel of the Hogweed. If you are still uncertain, the smell of the flowers will reassure. The aroma is that of muscat – glorious, sweet, rich and heady. Indeed it is too heady for some. Many detect a certain sickliness; perhaps even a whiff of cat's wee. There is something in these accusations, so if you are a sensitive soul, pick the blossoms before the heat of the day has brought on their full potency. If you can *only* smell cat's wee you probably have a Rowan tree on your hands. Only pick the fully open flowers, which retain the rich yellow stamens in the centre. Over-the-hill blossoms are always a little grey and drop their petals easily.

The flower heads can be cut with scissors or simply snapped off at the first joint. Once you have enough, go home straight away and start work – fresh Elder blossoms do not keep well. I usually remove the fresh flowers from their green umbels with a fork – not worrying too much about the occasional green bit of stalk. If I am making a Champagne I will chuck the whole flower head into the pot. The berries too can be removed with a fork.

If you are unable to deal with your collection immediately, it is possible to dry it. Indeed it is wise to dry as many flowers as you can as they retain their aroma quite well and provide a supply into the next season. Place the umbels upside down on a flat surface and leave in a warm dry place out of the sunlight. The dried flowers come away easily from the stems – just shake. Since Elderflowers are always used as an infusion, dried petals can be employed in just the same way as fresh ones.

There is no hedgerow glory finer than the Elderflower. As a Champagne, cordial or sorbet it is a treat beyond compare. Yet I think it is still under-used – supermarket shelves are not overburdened with Elderflower yogurt or Elderflower ice lollies. At home, of course, the limits are set only by our imaginations, a particularly successful exercise of which resulted in my proudest creation – Elderflower Delight (p.232). A few more suggestions are: a jelly (with added lemon juice, or even Sorrel, to lend some bite), a syrup to go on pancakes or ice cream (p.237), a mousse or even some blossoms tied in a cloth and added to your bath (a bit girly this one, forget I said it). The best Elderflower recipes bring in another hedgerow treasure – the Gooseberry. Gooseberry jam infused in the final boiling stage with a muslin bag of Elderflowers is just wonderful, and Gooseberry and Elderflower fool is a dessert made in heaven.

Apart from their familiar use in Elderberry wine, the berries are a little more of a challenge. They are mildly poisonous raw so they should always be cooked. There was a tradition that Elderberries were as good as grapes until their unfortunate encounter with Judas Iscariot; now they are rather tart and pippy. Despite this they have a good fruity flavour and will make a passable jelly, especially when mixed with Blackberries. Elderberries always seem halfway to vinegar when you pick them and this quality can be exploited in a superb Elderberry vinegar. My favourite way of using them, however, is simply as a juice. Cook a kilo of berries, strain through a sieve and add sugar (quite a bit) to taste. It is one of the best hedgerow drinks and puts all that imported cranberry juice to shame.

Dandelion *Taraxacum* agg.

DESCRIPTION	Small perennial. Rosette up to 30cm across. Leaves sharply indented with saw-toothed edges, hairless. Flowers rise on hollow stems from the centre. Flowers bright orange-yellow, composite. Stems and leaves produce a bitter white latex
HABITAT	Recently disturbed grassland, wasteland, roadsides
DISTRIBUTION	Extremely common everywhere
SEASON	Leaves best in spring before the main flower crop, which is between late March and early May. The occasional flower can be found through much of the year. Roots in autumn and winter

I think that most people have a deep affection for the Dandelion; along with the daisy, it is a wild flower that even the most urban of urbanites will recognise. There has certainly been a great deal of appreciative, but truly terrible poetry written in its honour:

Said young Dandelion,
With a sweet air,
I have my eye on
Miss Daisy fair.

and purple prose:

When the children of the plant arrive at maturity, each one of them with parental care is furnished with a handsome balloon filled with provisions; a gust of wind separates the family…

A field of Dandelions is indeed a wonderful sight, so we must forgive such excess. For the forager the Dandelion is a treasure. It provides three crops – leaves, roots and flowers. The leaves can be collected at any time, but they are less bitter and more crunchy just before the flowers appear. The roots are best disinterred in the autumn or winter when they will be at their plumpest. It is possible to find the odd Dandelion flower at all but the coldest times of the year, but the main flush happens in early spring. Gather them in the morning, in full sun if possible, then rush home and deal with them straight away before they close up for the night. There are numerous similar-looking plants, such as the catsears and hawkbits, but the flowers of these tend to be smaller and are not toxic should you make a mistake.

The Dandelion has long been collected for its medicinal benefits. It is, above all things, a diuretic; a talent confirmed by modern science and probably down to its high potassium content. Its unfortunate common name of 'piss-a-bed' testifies to this reputation. The huge number of ailments it is reputed to cure is largely a matter of wishful thinking, but it *is* an exceptionally healthy food, containing vitamins A, C and K, along with potassium and calcium and a reasonable amount of protein.

The leaves should be collected before the flowers appear, but they are always rather bitter. Mixed with milder salad plants, however, they provide an acceptable bite to a sandwich. The intensity of the bitterness can be reduced by covering the young leaves with a pot for a few days to force them – though this is perilously close to gardening and not entirely in the spirit of the book.

The flowers have a limited use in the kitchen – they make an interesting (i.e. horrible) tea, or they can be dipped in batter and fried to make fritters (even more horrible). One recipe that works very well is Dandelion Jelly Marmalade (p.240) as the petals impart a pleasant bitterness and colour; the petals also make an excellent floral syrup (p.237). Where they really come into their own, however, is in Dandelion wine – one of the best of all the country wines.

The roots are very bitter raw and just about edible cooked. They are best known for their use in Dandelion and burdock beer. One other odd use is well known though seldom tried – Dandelion coffee. The roots are scrubbed, dried thoroughly in a low oven, then roasted at 200°C/Gas mark 6 for 30 minutes and then ground up like coffee. This is the sort of report that no sensible person will ever believe but for once it is true – it genuinely works. The result is almost indistinguishable from real coffee in smell, appearance and taste, lacking perhaps just some of the more subtle aromas. It contains no caffeine of course so you will be able to get to sleep very easily. How long for, though, is another matter – just remember that vulgar common name.

P.S. The agg. part of the Dandelion's Latin name given above is an abbreviation of 'aggregate'. This means that we are talking about several microspecies – in this case (the British Isles) no less than 235 – from *T. aberrans* to *T. xiphoideum*. You may well have noticed that not all Dandelions are the same – some larger, some smaller, some with sharply serrated leaves, some more rounded and so on. Among the general mass of botanists there is a small band who live on a higher plane than their colleagues and study nothing but Dandelions. They are called Taraxacologists. Two of these grand masters, Dudman and Richards, in their great work *Dandelions of Great Britain and Ireland*, say that they suspect other botanists consider them mad. How right they are. But to study a subject of interest to no one but a tiny coterie and which is, as far as we can tell, totally inconsequential, is strangely commendable. *Salute*, taraxacologists!

Several other common plants are apomictic (as this microspeciation is called), most famously the Blackberry, which has a subspecies for every day of the year. Apomictic species have all but given up sex as a messy waste of time and effort and their offspring are nearly always clones. This is a slightly dangerous strategy for, although the overheads involved in sexual reproduction no longer have to be borne, the advantages of genetic interchange and the removal of harmful mutations are lost. However, they dabble in sex occasionally, which prevents them entering an evolutionary dead end. Parthenogenesis (meaning virgin birth) in certain animals, such as stick insects and some lizards, is a related process.

With the Dandelions it seems that a huge number of these microspecies were created thousands of years ago and their genetic makeup became fixed seemingly for ever. The weakest became extinct, leaving us with the few hundred we have now.

Wild Plum *Prunus domestica*

DESCRIPTION	Small tree or shrub. Leaves pointed/oval, coarse blunt-toothed edges, slightly hairy both sides, alternate. Thornless. Fruit with bloom, purple, sometimes green or yellow, groove on one side
HABITAT	Hedgerows, wood edges, often naturalised around deserted buildings
DISTRIBUTION	Fairly common everywhere, except central northern England and the Scottish Highlands
SEASON	September–October

Cherry Plum *P. cerasifera*

DESCRIPTION	Small tree or shrub. Leaves pointed/oval, blunt but *finely* toothed edges, slightly hairy on underside of midrib, alternate. Mostly thornless. Fruit the size and shape of a very large cherry, but with a typical plum groove down one side. Red or yellow
HABITAT	Hedgerows – frequently planted, often near habitation
DISTRIBUTION	Common throughout the British Isles, though much more so in the Midlands and the Southeast
SEASON	July

There are variations within *Prunus domestica* that have attained subspecies status but they are unclear and inconsistent and hybrids between them confuse the picture further. Plums can therefore be confusing, but for all practical purposes (we just want to eat them) Plums, Bullaces and Damsons are the same thing. Cherry Plums, however, are not, and I will talk about them separately.

Wild Plum trees are hot property and if you find one it is best not to mention it to your 'friends'. Pick the Plums as ripe as you can, remembering that someone else may be watching the tree. There will be particularly enticing fruit out of reach at the top, and ladders, fruit-pickers and even standing on the roof of your car may be required. If the tree is safe from other foragers you can place a large sheet on the ground to catch fallen fruit, but not for long – they will not be safe from animals.

Wild Plum

Cherry Plum

The Cherry Plum is a sadly overlooked fruit – passed by as an inedible unknown, fallen and squashed on the roadside. It has very early blossoms – the beginning of March being typical and long before nearly any other tree. Herein lies the problem with Cherry Plums. The blossoms are often affected by cold weather and fail to set. If it is mild at the right time, however, you can look forward to an extraordinarily large crop. In July the fruit will hang like grapes from the tree, the branches brought to breaking point with their colourful burden, and it can be difficult to carry home all you have picked. Time, perhaps, for reinforcements.

Both Plums are enormously variable in texture and taste, as was noted in typically outrageous fashion by Culpeper:

> *All plums are under Venus, and are, like women, some better, some worse.*

This is due as much to growing conditions and time of picking as species and variety, but it is true that Plums can, indeed, delight or disappoint in equal measure. There is never any way of guessing what a Plum will taste like – you will just have to eat it. I have, however, consistently found the yellow Cherry Plums to possess a superior flavour to the red.

All Plums will suit recipes for their cultivated sisters. Jams and jellies, Plum wine and Plum gin, crumble and cake, pudding and pie, bottled or dried – there is really no need to detail the many ways you can cook with Plums – it is just that the flavour is so much better for being freely acquired.

P.S. Geneticists must have larger brains than the rest of us in order to carry around the endless amount of detail encountered in their discipline. Nothing in genetics is ever easy; every rule has an exception and the only firm rule is that there isn't one. *Prunus domestica* is the name of the cultivated plum and the wild form is the same species escaped from the garden. Most organisms (including us) have two sets of chromosomes but some, including a large number of plants, are not content and will have more. This is called polyploidy and is important. *Prunus domestica* has no less than six and is thus referred to as being hexaploid. These six sets come from three ancestors. It is possible that four of them came from two Blackthorns and two from a Cherry Plum but more likely that all six are former Cherry Plum chromosomes. If the latter is the case then Wild Plums are *super* Cherry Plums.

Chromosomes contain most of an organism's DNA and control most of what goes on inside the cell. One would think that having more than your fair share of chromosomes would be like having three cooks in the kitchen – miserable confusion. But it is generally not so and polyploid organisms are often, like our plum, large and vigorous. We have much to thank this quirk of nature for: potatoes, wheat, oats, sugar cane, bananas, and many more food species have been developed using artificially induced polyploidy.

Yarrow *Achillea millefolium*

DESCRIPTION	Medium/short, upright perennial, to 50cm when flowering. Leaves very feather-like. Flowers in an umbrella of florets, which have five white petals and a yellow centre
HABITAT	Grassy banks, garden borders, hedges and grassland
DISTRIBUTION	Very common throughout the British Isles
SEASON	May–November

The strikingly feather-like leaves can be found growing in amongst grass almost everywhere and you are very likely to have some in your garden.

The Latin name derives from the Greek hero Achilles, who was supposed to have learned from his centaur mentor Chiron about its beneficial properties as a herb for healing battle wounds. Not a particularly effective one, evidently, considering Achilles' fate. The second part of the Latin name is a plain description of the leaves – 'thousand-leaved'.

Yarrow normally finds only one use in the kitchen. I have been particularly scathing of herbal teas and generally speaking I think they deserve it. Yarrow tea, however, is really quite good, I will put it no stronger than that, and I feel it is one I can recommend.

Crow Garlic *Allium vineale*

DESCRIPTION	Medium perennial, 30–60cm. Leaves stiff, grass-like, semi-cylindrical, hollow and grooved. Flowers mixed with the bulbils (tiny bulbs) or just bulbils, these emerging from a papery sheath. Underground bulb, onion-like, 1–2cm diameter
HABITAT	Grassy banks, field edges, cultivated land
DISTRIBUTION	Common in southern England, except the moors in the Southwest. Rare in Northern Ireland. Largely coastal elsewhere and increasingly scarce in the North
SEASON	Leaves during winter and spring, bulbs late spring and early summer

Some plants are revered, some reviled. Crow Garlic is definitely in the latter camp. The word garlic comes, it is believed, from the Anglo-Saxon *gār lēac* meaning 'spear leek' – a reference to the leaf shape of cultivated garlic. Crow Garlic comes from *crāwan lēac* meaning 'crows' leek' – a leek fit only for crows.

In fact it was not the flavour of Crow Garlic that gave it such a poor reputation; it is what it did to milk. Crow Garlic has always been a common weed of pasture, and cows will eat it with the grass. Even a small amount makes the milk from these animals undrinkable, so a great deal of effort was expended in eradicating it from the land. It was not only milk that was spoiled. Wheat could also become contaminated; it seems that garlic bread was sometimes on the menu long before it became fashionable or desirable. A gossip paper from 1796 has some '*Ironical Advice to Bakers*', suggesting that as well as ground bones the baker should also use '*cheap wheats that are plentifully mixed with crow-garlick*' because of its '*excellent perfume*' and '*leeky flavour*' which will be much requested by his Welsh customers. In 1739 there was even a complaint that the truffles found in Richmond Park were tainted with the odour of nearby Crow Garlic. In fact truffles naturally have a slight garlicky flavour due to some related organic sulphur compounds.

None of this need worry the forager, who will be welcome in places where it is unwanted. In southern England it is common in hedgerows and grassy places, especially near the sea. One problem with foraging for this plant is seeing it, even if it is in front of you. The leaves are just like those of a coarse grass – a near perfect, if accidental camouflage. As with most foraged items you will soon learn their subtle differences of growth habit and shape. Early spring is a good time to collect Crow Garlic as the leaves stand in clearly visible clumps above the still sleeping grass.

The leaves have a good, chive-like flavour but they are a bit stringy unless very young. The best crop from Crow Garlic, however, is the bulb. This can be difficult to dig up from amongst the dense grass in which it often grows, but if the flower stem is visible you can use it as a handle to uproot the whole plant. The bulb looks like a silverskin onion but tastes halfway between garlic and onion. It can be used – raw or cooked – with discretion, in place of either. The flavour is not as strong as garlic so you can use more in your recipe.

Wild Garlic *Allium ursinum*

DESCRIPTION	Short/medium perennial, to 50cm. Leaves broadly elliptical and pointed, soft and often damp to the touch. Flowers white, star-like, five-petalled in round sprays. All parts smell strongly of garlic
HABITAT	Shaded hedgerow, woodland
DISTRIBUTION	Very common throughout the British Isles, except for the north of Scotland. Also less common in central eastern England
SEASON	Leaves February–June. Flowers and seed heads April–June. Root bulb all year, if you can find them

Wild Garlic, or Ramsons as it is also known, is a wild food that nearly everyone has heard of, even if they have never seen it. This is an extremely common plant and a gift of nature to the wild gourmet. From March until June shady roadsides and open woodlands are filled with the elegant lanceolate leaves and in May and June the pretty star-shaped flowers. They are also filled with the smell of garlic. This is pleasant enough in small amounts and at the beginning of the season, but as the leaves start to disintegrate, it becomes rancid and overpowering. While the culinary possibilities of this plant were not unknown it was more often used in the past for its medical virtues:

Eate leekes in Lide, and ramsins in May,
And all the yeare after physitians may play.

In this old West Country rhyme 'Lide' is a name for March. The health-giving properties of garlic in its several forms are well known – antioxidant, antiseptic and more – but its true potential in the kitchen has only relatively recently been appreciated in this country.

Wild Garlic abounds in the countryside but it is not particularly happy in an urban environment, preferring shaded hedgerows and open woods. The younger the leaves the better they will be – certainly try to pick them before they flower – after this the flavour becomes fainter and coarser. When you find your patch you will have an over-abundance of riches, as there will be many more than you can possibly eat. Scissors are a must for picking the leaves and a largish flat basket will help keep them safe. If you have travelled to your picking spot by car you may encounter a small problem – unless the smell of garlic is to you a joy beyond compare do not put your collection on the back seat – a warm car can bring out the overwhelming best

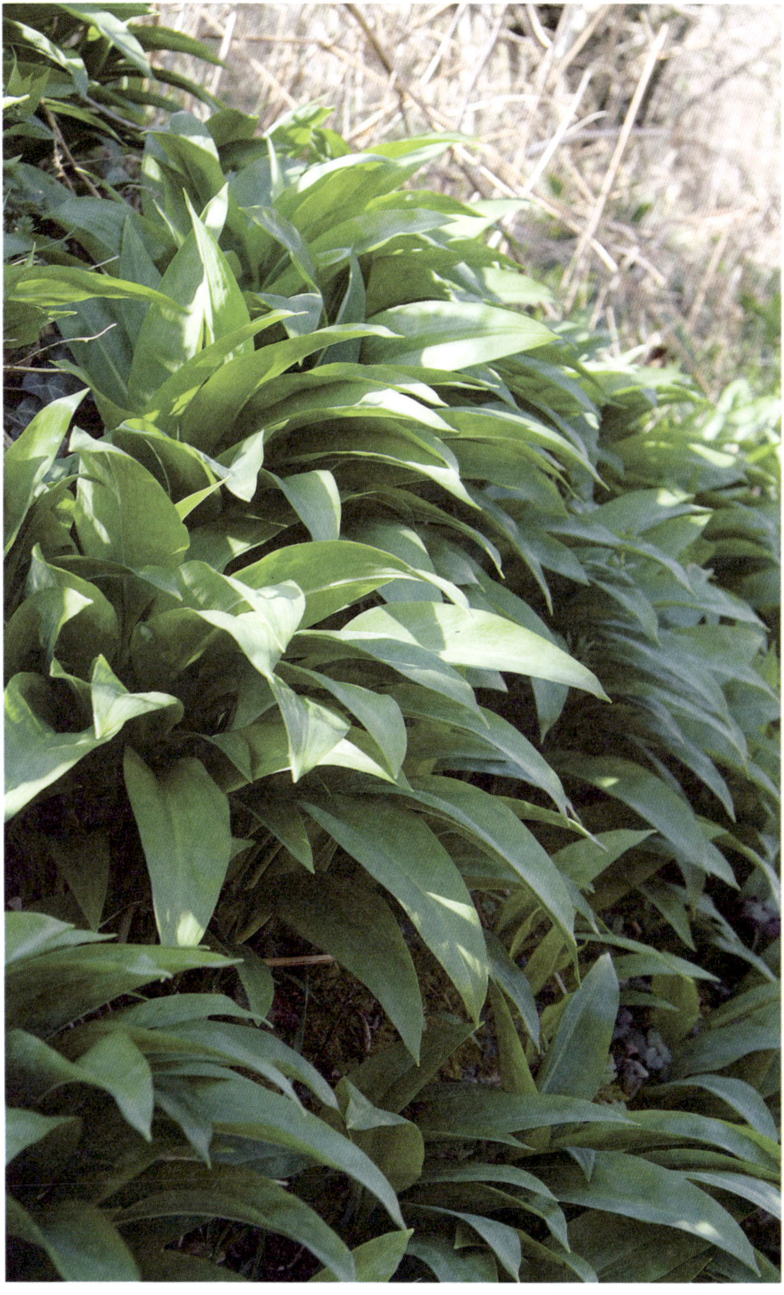

(or worst) that Wild Garlic has to offer. The leaves wilt very quickly so either use them as soon as you get home or keep them covered in the fridge.

It is the leaves which are almost invariably eaten, but the decorative flowers and the young seed heads are also edible, both tasting strongly of garlic. Whether or not the leaves are around, it is still possible to gather the underground bulb – even in December. This tubular structure is a modified leaf stem and similar in flavour to a familiar garlic bulb, if a little milder. Do take all the necessary legal and safety precautions for collecting wild roots.

There are, unfortunately, several poisonous plants which lie in wait for the careless Wild Garlic collector. Lily of the valley bears a striking similarity to Wild Garlic and is a common garden plant occasionally found escaped to the wild. Do be careful, therefore, if picking near habitation as it is quite seriously poisonous. The Autumn Crocus (or Meadow Saffron) also has long pointed leaves and has caused at least one death in the UK quite recently after being mistaken for Wild Garlic. Much more common is Lords and Ladies (p.191). The fully grown leaves are quite unlike those of Wild Garlic but the immature ones could confuse, especially as they too appear from the barren ground of early spring. This may all sound rather worrying, but there is no need for concern – Wild Garlic smells strongly of garlic when crushed and none of these impostors do.

Wild Garlic is considerably milder in flavour than its cultivated cousin, but it can be used in all the familiar situations. As it is used mostly in the form of a leaf, however, it does provide some extra culinary avenues to explore. Two simple uses come straight away to mind – chopped in a salad or whole in a cheese sandwich. Finely chopped it looks great mixed into cream cheese or in an omelette. Perhaps one of the best recipes is Wild Garlic Pesto (p.205) – a real wild delight. A wild British version of the Greek dolma, Wild Garlic Parcels (p.204), can be made from the larger leaves.

P.S. It is a strange but fortuitous fact that the tasty members of the lily family (onions, garlic, chives, Wild Garlic and many others) are edible to humans. We are almost unique in the animal kingdom in finding them both palatable and non-toxic. Most animals will not happily touch them (sheep are apparently an exception) and when forced through circumstance to eat them may be poisoned. Most dog and cat owners know not to give their animals onions in any form – a compound *n-propyl disulphide* causes serious anaemia and deaths have occurred.

Grazing animals will commonly eat a little Wild Garlic and, more commonly still, small amounts of Crow Garlic. This seldom causes ill health in the animal, but its milk will be undrinkable and, if some is consumed just prior to slaughter, the meat will be spoiled.

Hazel *Corylus avellana*

DESCRIPTION	Small tree or shrub. Sometimes single stem, more often multiple stems. Leaves large and roundish, but with a pointed end. Stems straight, grey-brown, horizontal markings. The flowers in catkins. Nuts enclosed in overlapping bracts, in clusters of two, three or four
HABITAT	Understorey in broad-leaved woods, hedgerow, scrub
DISTRIBUTION	Very common throughout the British Isles, save the odd mountain top
SEASON	Nuts late August until mid-October

We all have our favourite places. Mine is a Hazel coppice about a mile from where I live in Dorset. It is a peaceful place with overarching ash trees, snuffling, scratching badger cubs in April, a dazzling carpet of bluebells in May and some rare, if inedible, fungi in October. The wood was established centuries ago to supply fencing and hurdles for the local sheep farms, but hurdles are mostly, though not entirely, a thing of the past. Nowadays the Hazels, some more than 2 metres across, wait in vain for the coppicer's lopper. In the dark centre of the coppice few nuts ripen, but the trees at its bright edge sometimes produce more than I can pick.

The wild Hazelnut is the ancestor of the large, carefully cultivated cobnut, which appears in the shops in August and September. There are around seventy varieties but they are still all *Corylus avellana*. This gentle form of agriculture once thrived in Kent, but is now much reduced from its heyday, so do supplement your wild harvest by buying them when you see them in the shops. There are also filberts (named after St Philibert whose feast day, 20 August, coincides with the start of the nutting season). These large nuts are a different species (*C. maxima*), which seldom grows wild in the British Isles.

Wild native Hazelnuts have been picked since antiquity, but few people bother with them now and it can indeed be a frustrating exercise. The hedgerow-grown Hazel sometimes produces nuts but most will have been lost to the voracious council hedge-trimmer. Of course hedges have two sides and you may be luckier if you venture on to the field side if there is one. Untrimmed woodland edges like my own patch are the best hunting grounds. It will probably not be news to you that squirrels eat nuts and they do take a fair toll of the crop; but if there are enough nuts about, the squirrels simply cannot get round to eating them all – even squirrelling them away. You could solve the problem by eating the squirrels (only grey ones!) – they are rather good and squirrel offal kebabs are among the best things I have tasted. If

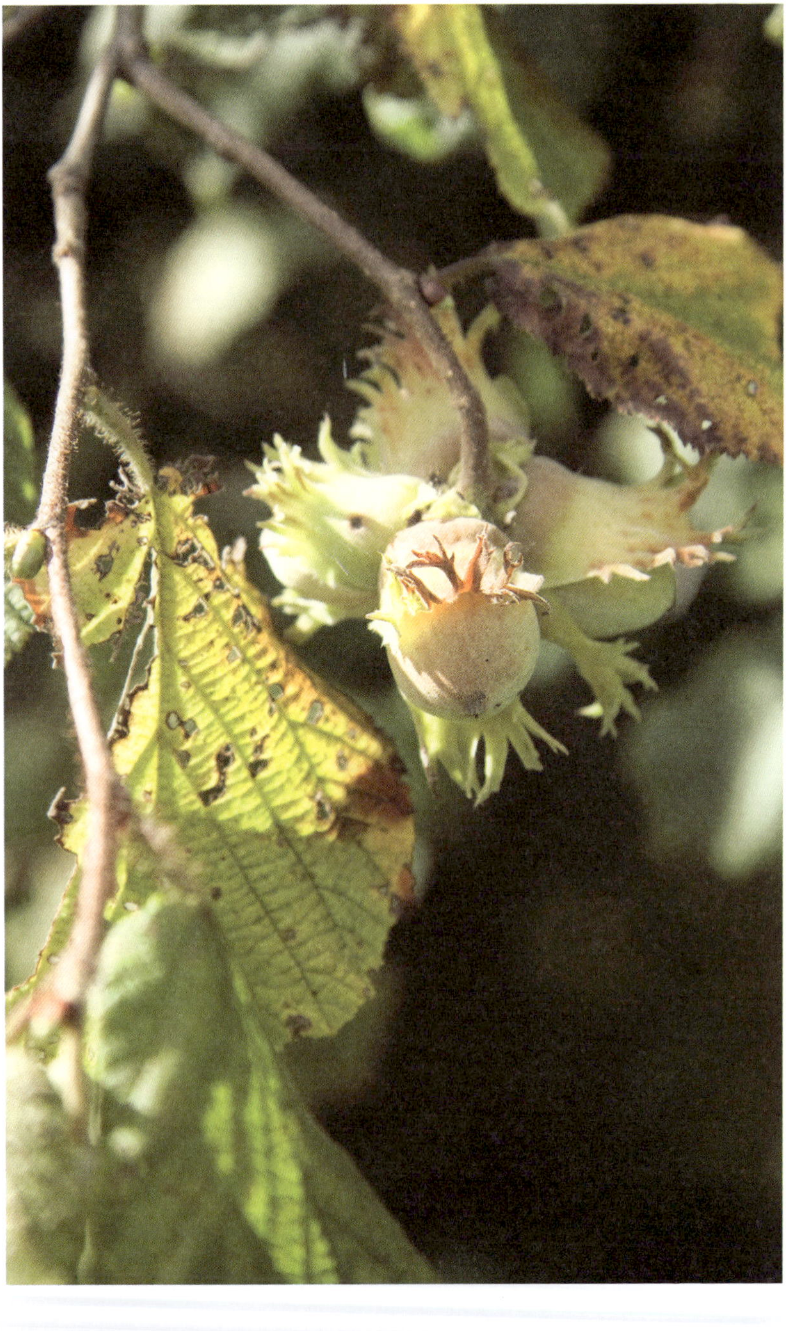

you manage to find a tree covered in nuts you may still face disappointment. Many of the nuts are empty, or 'blank' or 'hedge' nuts as the Kentish growers call them, though unfortunately it is not possible to tell this until you crack them open. Some years are excellent, however, producing a bumper crop with most of the shells full.

The nuts are edible as soon as they reach a good size in August and early September. The early green nuts are milky and slightly fruity in taste but lack the oily richness of the mature nut. They do not keep or ripen further once picked, so eat them straight away. One advantage with the green nuts is that the squirrels seldom bother with them. The fully ripe nut is brown and tends to fall off the branch as soon as you look at it with any degree of anticipation. I often bring a blanket with me to catch these strays. You can also shake the tree to dislodge the ripest nuts but it is hard work for a poor result. It will be well worth checking a few nuts as you go to make sure you do not go home with a basket full of empty shells.

Ripe Hazelnuts will keep for several months, but my wild crop is very precious and gets eaten as soon as I can find the time (or someone else) to shell them. However, this does mean that you are released from the yoke of seasonality and can use them long after their growing season. As with most wild food you will want to do something special with them.

Several recipes in this book use Hazelnuts to their very best effect – ground to make the pastry case for Cranberry and Apple Tart (p.222) and sprinkled artistically on to Chestnut Macaroons (p.231). You can also use them instead of Pignuts in Wild Garlic Pesto (p.205). One odd use which works best with the fresh nuts is Hazelnut milk. The basic method is to soak a handful in water overnight, rinse, then blitz them in a blender with about 400ml water or skimmed milk. Strain through a muslin bag and drink.

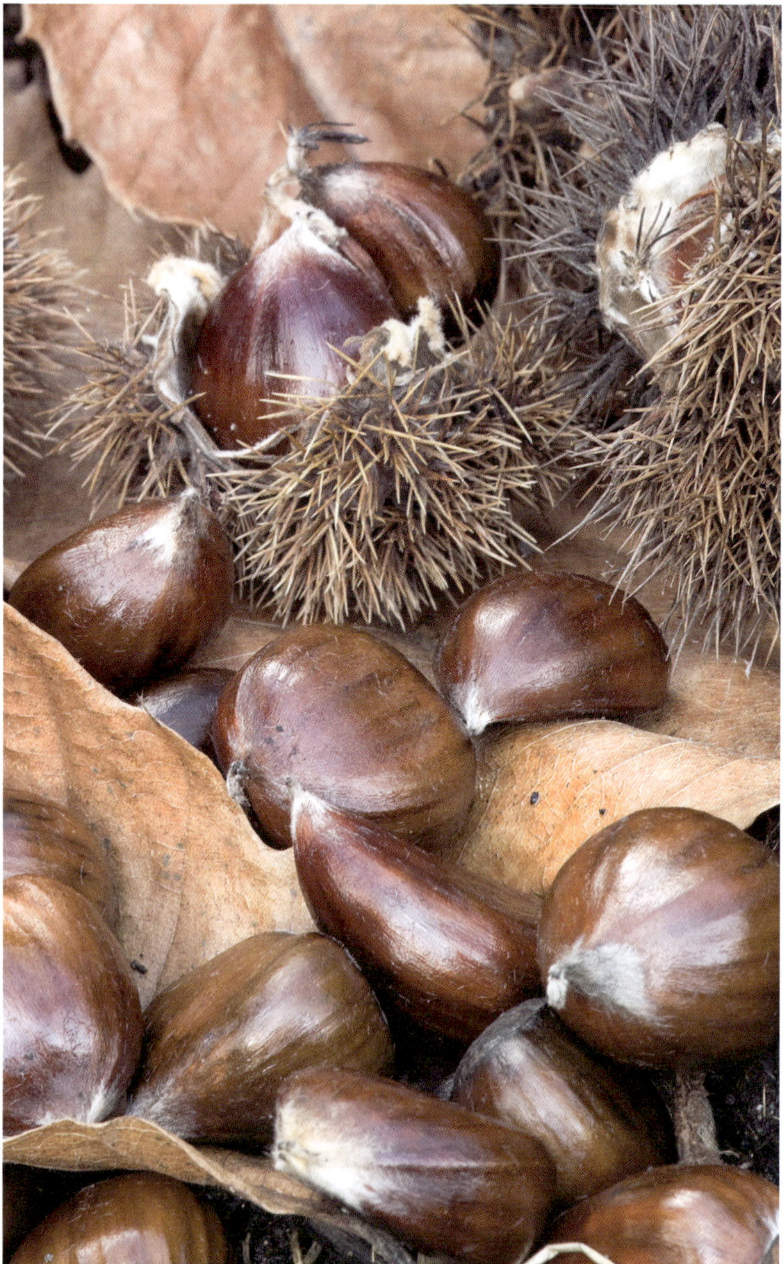

Sweet Chestnut *Castanea sativa*

DESCRIPTION	Large tree. Leaves large, long, pointed/oval, saw-toothed edge. Husk covered with very sharp spines. Nuts two or more to a husk, slightly hairy!
HABITAT	Park or woodland. Not on lime
DISTRIBUTION	Common, scattered around England but with a southern preference. Less common in Scotland, Northern Ireland and central Wales
SEASON	October

Like so many plants that are not native to the British Isles the Sweet Chestnut is less than perfectly at home here, even after two thousand years. The nut is often unformed and even when it does reach an edible size is rarely more than a third of the size of its southern European sister, the single nutted marron. Also, it seldom grows from self-set seed in this cooler clime, normally having to be planted. Not that the tree itself appears to struggle – Sweet Chestnuts are among our most impressive trees, some many centuries old and vast in size.

Sweet Chestnuts of an edible size are not necessarily found every year, but sometimes the weather suits them and we get a bumper crop. The ones pictured here are genuine Dorset Chestnuts, a very good size – and very sweet. A search around the forest floor in September and early October will often find hundreds of husks containing pathetically small or unformed Chestnuts. These are usually just nuts that the tree has discarded, saving its energies for the remaining fruits, which will contain useable nuts. These should be ripe and ready in the second half of October. Sometimes only one or two trees in a forest will set good fruit, so do not be too despondent if the first few trees you find produce only empty husks.

There is nothing to confuse the would-be Chestnut gatherer beyond the obvious and unrelated Horse Chestnut or conker tree. I think it a pity that the substantial nut of the latter is not edible and have tried to find out if there is a way of removing the toxin; there isn't. If you're in any doubt, the husk of the Sweet Chestnut is covered in a large number of long, fine bristles and contains more than one nut, whereas the Horse Chestnut has a few rather stumpy spines and only ever contains a single nut. Sweet Chestnut spines are extremely sharp, '*As troublesome to handle as a hedgehog*', as an eighteenth-century writer has it, and the husk cannot be held even gently without a finger being pricked. Rubber or leather gloves are the best defence against this peril. The traditional method of removing the nuts is to make a small pile in the woods, stamp on it and search through the debris for the bright shiny treasure.

The Chestnut is a sadly neglected food, seldom used in Britain other than around Christmas. The seventeenth-century writer and gardener Evelyn laments: *'But we give that fruit to our swine in England, which is amongst the delicacies of princes in other countries.'* I have tried to compensate for this continuing oversight by providing no less than four recipes that use Chestnuts (see below).

Finding carbohydrates is always a problem for the forager – fruits and leaves contain little, and roots are often more trouble than they are worth. Chestnuts, however, contain large amounts – and provide it in a delicious and accessible form. A typical value is around 40 per cent of the fresh peeled weight. The chestnut contains much less fat (3 per cent) than the other wild nut in this book, the Hazelnut (60 per cent); it is fairly light on protein but unusual in containing vitamin C and also some of the B vitamins. Altogether a healthy and useful food. I have a theory that one could survive on my favourite chestnut recipe alone – Chestnuts and Brussels sprouts. 'Alone' is appropriate here.

The Chestnut's sweet, starchy nature allows it to be used with great success in both sweet and savoury dishes. Whether used whole or puréed, chestnuts must be at least part-cooked to make removal of the skin possible. Boil them for 10 minutes in small batches then, using rubber gloves, remove one at a time from the hot water, cut open and peel. Both outer and inner skin will come away easily.

The traditional way of eating Chestnuts of course is by roasting them in the fire. The nuts must have a slit cut in them to release the steam which would otherwise build up to explosive pressures. Richard Mabey's playful suggestion that one Chestnut should be left unslit to indicate when the others are ready should be ignored unless you want lots of holes burnt in your carpet. There is something very special about sitting there, perspiring vigorously, carefully arranging your batches of chestnuts so that they cook just right, then burning your fingers when you try to peel them.

The high starch content is obvious from the crumbly consistency of the cooked nut. This starch enables Sweet Chestnut to be turned into a wonderful flour, making it one of the most versatile wild foods. If you find yourself in possession of a large quantity of the nuts – and time – it is well worth making. Peel slightly undercooked Chestnuts, then flake using a Mouli grater. Dry the flakes in a low oven at 40°C and then pulverise in a blender. This flour can be used for gnocchi, pancakes, biscuits, pasta, polenta, pastry, cakes and even bread, though as it is lacking in gluten it does not rise well and should be used half and half with a strong bread flour. An extremely rich roux can be made using Chestnut flour, and one of the best meals to serve on a cold December evening is a game pie packed with as many woodland creatures as you can get your hands on, the juices thickened with a Chestnut roux.

Finally there is the most famous of all Chestnut treats – marron glacé. See also the recipes for Horseradish and Chestnut Dumplings (p.216), Chestnut Pancakes (p.226), Chestnut Macaroons (p.231) and Chestnut Florentines (p.229).

Juniper *Juniperus communis*

DESCRIPTION	Small tree. Sometimes upright, but more usually sprawling, evergreen. Berries 6mm–1cm diameter, green for a long time, blue/black when ripe. Usually grows in colonies
HABITAT	Dry limestone in the South, acid areas in the North
DISTRIBUTION	Main population in northern Scotland. Also in the north of England, north of Northern Ireland and northern Wales, and in central southern England
SEASON	August–November

The Juniper is one of only three conifers native to the British Isles (Yew and Scots Pine being the others), but despite this it is not really common. It also has an odd distribution pattern. I have never seen one in Dorset outside a garden centre, but in nearby Wiltshire at Britain's very own Area 51 – Porton Down – there are thousands of them, constituting 20 per cent of the southern England population. These are not exactly accessible to the forager. All the trees here are either around one hundred years old or fifty years old, coinciding with periods when rabbit numbers were very low, so it may be that it is rabbits eating the seedling plants that restricts Juniper populations. In Scotland, at least in the northern half, they are much more common and where I found those pictured overleaf.

To be precise the berries are not berries, they are cones; if you look carefully you will see the overlapping layers on the surface. The relatively soft and rather sticky outer layer is sweet and aromatic, while the central part is highly aromatic and crunchy. Eating a plain berry is a little like drinking a straight gin downwind of a pine forest. The gin connection is obvious, of course, because Juniper gives this drink its flavour and indeed its name – from the French for Juniper – *genévrier*. The reputation of gin is a long-standing one, summed up rather well in the *Compleat Confectioner* of 1742:

> *It is indeed true, that the Liquor call'd Geneva, or, more vulgarly, Gin, becoming of late Years but too common, has been the Occasion of much Mischief and many Disorders; but the best Things may be abus'd.*

It is probably just as well that the domestic manufacture of gin is illegal and that we must turn our minds to more temperate uses for this unusual food.

Those Juniper trees that can be found are often in ecologically sensitive areas and the tree itself is the subject of various biodiversity action plans. A certain amount of

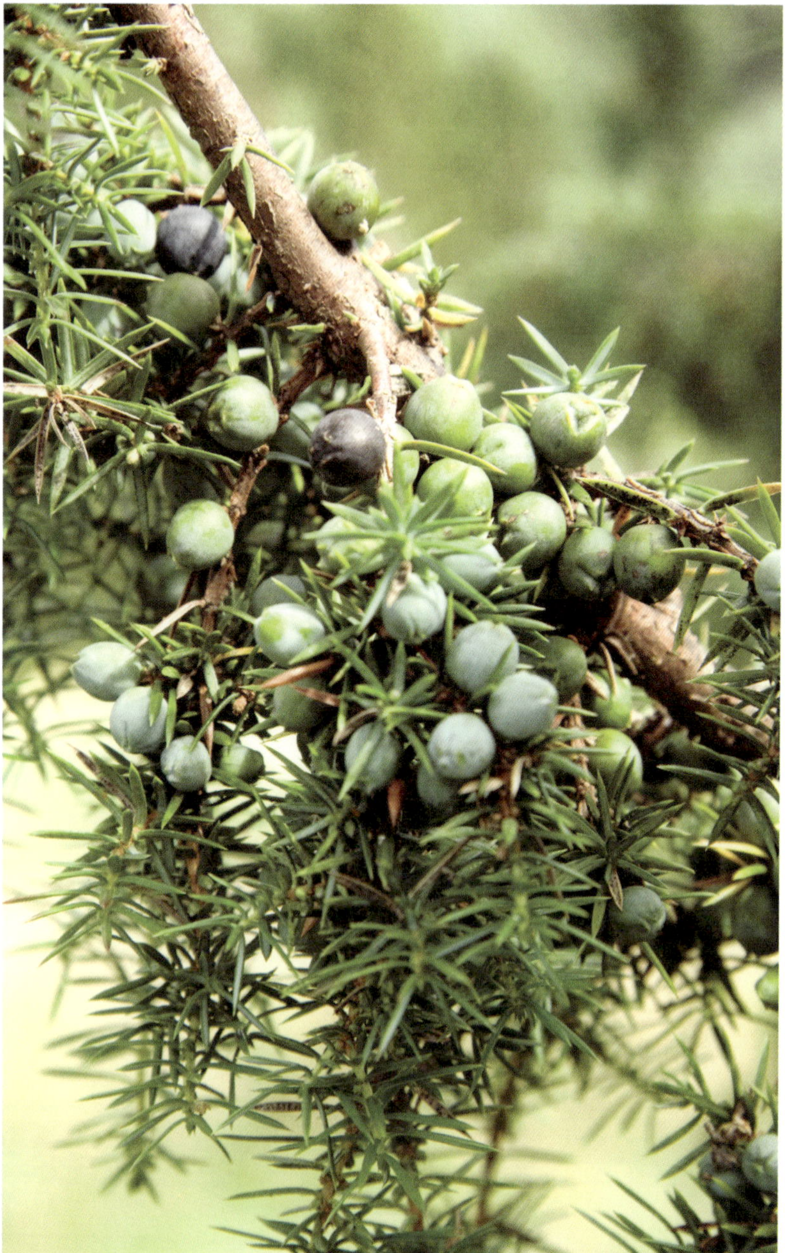

care and restraint should therefore be exercised when collecting (though how much good this will do if there are rabbits around I cannot say). You will certainly need to take care, as the needles are the sharpest of any plant I know. An alternative to picking by hand is to lay a sheet underneath the tree and shake or beat it, but it is better just to use gloves.

Since Juniper berries are not true berries they cannot be expected to follow a typical berry lifestyle, and indeed they do not. The green berries will remain on the plant for a year or two, only ripening blue/black in the second or third year. Also, different-aged berries can be found on the same branch with maybe just a few ripe ones among the green. As a fairly substantial proportion of trees (mostly the males) do not produce berries, it can sometimes seem a miracle to find a bush that actually has some. Fortunately a few berries go a long way and, providing you can locate some trees in the first place, you should not face an entirely unrewarding quest.

The strong clean flavour of the berry is used to moderate rich, gamey or fatty meats, such as pork, venison and duck. Juniper Pot (p.213), a delicious Danish recipe, uses loin of pork. Marinades, sauces and pickles can all usefully employ the berries and if you want your Sloe Gin (p.82) to taste more of gin than of Sloes then add Juniper berries. Considering the rather medicinal taste, it is unsurprising that Juniper berries have long found a place in the medicine cabinet. They have been employed against the biting of snakes, against dropsy, colic and a dozen or so other ailments. One of the more likely remedies, which I found in an eighteenth-century travelogue, is for a chesty cough. It is this which inspired what is perhaps the most unusual recipe in this book – Juniper Toffee (p.234). Not that I make any claims for its efficacy – it just tastes great.

One small word of warning – Juniper really does contain pharmacologically active compounds, the principal of which is an abortifacient. It has long been employed domestically for this doubtful purpose – copious quantities of gin and a very hot bath being the normal modus operandi. As well as expectant mothers, those suffering kidney problems should also avoid Juniper berries.

Sea Buckthorn *Hippophae rhamnoides*

DESCRIPTION	Shrub or small tree, to 2.5 metres. Leaves long and thin, grey/green with grey dots. Stems thorny. Bright-orange berries in very dense clusters, extremely sharp-tasting
HABITAT	Seashore, sand dunes. Frequently planted elsewhere as a roadside shrub
DISTRIBUTION	Fairly common around the entire coast of Britain, though only native on the east coast. Occasionally inland, mostly through being planted
SEASON	Berries ripe from late July and persist into the winter. Early berries, before the frosts, are by far the best

This striking plant with its intensely bright-orange berries and pretty grey/green leaves is becoming more familiar now that it is being planted as a roadside shrub. It is actually a seaside plant native to the east coast, and if it is seen elsewhere on the coast it has, again, been planted. Sea Buckthorn is useful for firming up sand dunes and providing coastal protection, but a little too good at its job, sometimes turning the ecologically sensitive dunes into dense, impenetrable thickets.

While it may be thoroughly despised by the naturalist, for the forager it is a great delicacy. If it has a drawback it is the near impossibility of picking the berries. The branches are covered in ferocious spines and the berries burst as soon as you touch them. As it is only the juice that is wanted, I usually just squidge it straight into a little plastic tub held underneath the branch and sieve out all the unwanted debris later. Another possibility, which can only be justified where the plants are clearly unwelcome for environmental reasons, is to cut off whole branches with secateurs or even a saw, put them in the freezer and then shake off the frozen berries.

The flavour of Sea Buckthorn berries has to be experienced to be believed. If you have ever eaten what is sometimes called 'extreme candy' you will have a vague idea, though you will have to imagine it without the sugar. The berries contain large quantities of malic acid, a natural acid an order of magnitude sharper than the more familiar citric acid. The juice can be used, diluted and with sugar, to make a spine-stiffening drink, or as a fierce wild substitute for lemon with fish. I make Sea Buckthorn and Crab Apple jam, and, though I say so myself, it is a marvellous work among all nations.

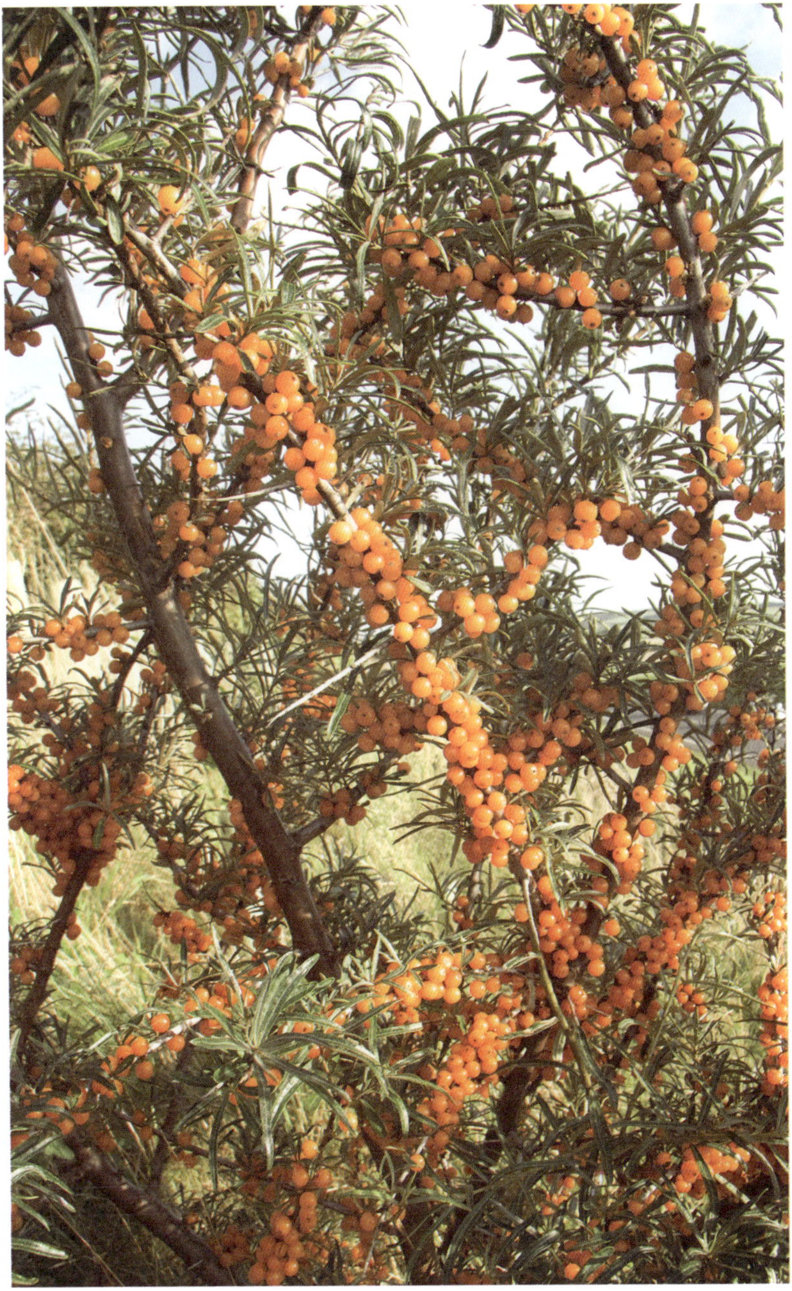

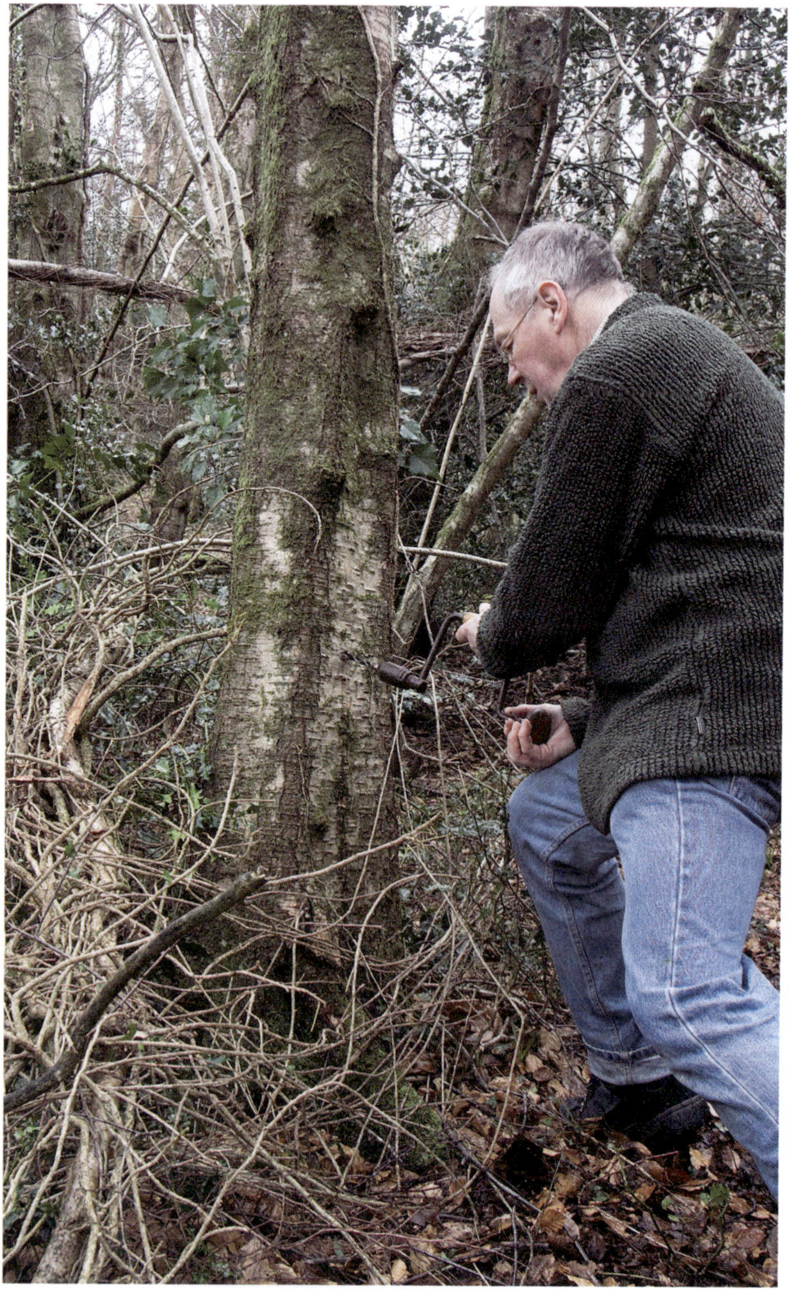

Silver Birch *Betula pendula*

DESCRIPTION	Medium-sized tree. Leaves triangular, base straight with rounded corners, other two sides doubly serrated. Branches drooping. Bark silver/white with dark raised horizontal markings, diamond-shaped on mature trees
HABITAT	Prefers light sandy soil
DISTRIBUTION	Very common, except in the far north of Scotland
SEASON	March and early April

Although most of what a forager looks for can, generally speaking, be gathered legally and with a clear conscience, tapping birch trees may involve a small excursion to the dark side.

Unless the trees are your own or you have permission from the owner, tapping a birch tree always feels like a commando raid and on those (rare) occasions when I put righteousness to one side I will take a daughter with me to act as lookout. The enterprise is made all the more exciting by the necessity of returning to the crime scene the next day to collect the prize. But what is this prize, what can you do with it and is it worth so much damage to your karma?

Birch sap, for it is this that is drawn from the Silver Birch, is easy to collect provided you are well equipped and visit your tree at precisely the right time of year. Birch tapping consists simply of drilling a hole into the side of a tree and guiding the flow of sap into a suitable container. I have tried many ways of doing this but the semi-professional method used by the occasional North American maple tapper is by far the best.

The most critical piece of kit is the spile or spout. You won't find these devices in your local ironmonger's in the UK, so you will have to search online for a supplier. A spile is a tapered tube with a hole at one end and a spout at the other. In the middle there is a hook from which a bucket may be hung. The bucket should ideally be galvanised and with a little hole to attach it to the spile, and a cover to keep the rain out. You will also need a wood bit or auger bit, which should be the diameter of the narrow end of the spile – this ensures a tight fit. A brace, or for the modern forager, a battery-operated drill, a mallet, a container to keep the sap in, and some tapered dry wooden pegs – the pores sealed at the narrow end with candle wax – completes the inventory for the well-equipped birch tapper.

Drilling a hole in a tree and bleeding it for 24 hours requires a healthy specimen with a minimum trunk diameter of 25cm. It should also have had at least a couple of years' rest from the last time it was tapped. The hole should be about a metre from the ground, drilled at a slightly upward angle and about 3cm deep. If the tree is ready the sap will pour out as soon as the drill is halfway in. If no sap appears then stop drilling, drive a prepared plug into the wound and try another tree. If, however, all is well, hammer home your spile, attach the bucket and retire for 24 hours. When you have collected your sap remember to firmly fill the hole with your wooden plug as otherwise the sap will continue to run for several days and the tree may not survive this added imposition.

A single tree may produce up to 5 litres in a day, though half as much is more likely. I usually tap about half-a-dozen trees at the same time as birch sap sours quicker than milk and you cannot stockpile it. You will have to gather all you want while you can as the season is very short. Precisely when a birch tree starts to produce sap will depend a great deal on the weather, but around the second week of March is fairly typical. Overall the season is about a month long and ends a little before the buds start to show green. By this time the character of the sap has changed, and not for the better – it can have an overpowering popcorn flavour; soon after this it stops altogether. For the best flavour, gather sap as early in the season as you can.

Silver Birch is very easy to identify so you should encounter no problems, even though the leaves will not be on the tree to help you. A closely related species, Downy Birch, (*B. pubescens*), is also widespread if not quite so common. It produces a rather bitter sap but is easily distinguished by its red-brown bark. Several other trees produce a sap, though I have had little success in finding the right time to tap them. Sycamore and Field Maple are both maples and thus related to the North American Sugar Maple. They can produce a more sugary sap than Silver Birch but I have never been able to get any out of them. Walnut can also provide sap but as it is a tree which struggles in the UK anyway it is best to leave it in peace.

If Silver Birch trees were able to express an opinion they would no doubt object to having some of their lifeblood drained away, but it seems to have little effect on their viability as long as it is performed only occasionally and with care.

So what can you do with the stuff now you have 20 litres sat in your kitchen? If you have taken a swig of sap while in the woods you may well be wondering what it is good for – its taste is almost indistinguishable from water. But it is very good water indeed. In Scandinavia, where birch trees grow in astronomical numbers, the sap is bottled and sold as a tonic. It does have a slight flavour, with a hint of sweetness, but both are very faint.

Apart from drinking it straight, there are two other uses for the sap – Birch sap wine and Birch Sap Syrup. A lot of people swear by the wine, but apart from a mild woodiness I suspect it contributes little more than water. No doubt I am betraying an insensitive palate here so I suggest you try it for yourself. Much more interesting is the syrup. This is similar to maple syrup but with its own distinctive flavour – molasses maybe, or caramel with slightly acidic or bitter undertones. It is terrific on pancakes, especially Chestnut Pancakes (p.226), but really comes into its own when used for that 1970s dinner party standby – crème caramel.

The low sugar content of Birch sap (less than 1 per cent) means that an awful lot of water needs to be evaporated off: 10 litres will produce a frankly pitiful 100ml of Birch Sap Syrup if fully concentrated. Sugar Maple by comparison produces two and a half times as much. I start the process in a preserving pan then, when 90 per cent of the water has gone, transfer the thin syrup to a bain-marie, or a heatproof bowl over a saucepan of simmering water. The point of this is to prevent the fructose-rich syrup burning. (Make sure the bowl is a big one – you will need to get your head inside to lick it out later.) If you continue reducing you will obtain a sticky brown substance. This is strong-flavoured and bitter, so, if you are unconcerned about authenticity, it is better to stop the process earlier and add some white sugar – the Birch sap effectively being used as a flavouring. As long as it is sticky enough it will keep well in a sealed bottle – certainly the full ten months until next Pancake Day.

Bulrush/Reedmace *Typha latifolia*

DESCRIPTION	Tall upright perennial grass, 1–2.5m. Leaves in two rows, topmost extend above the flower head. Stem enclosed in the leaves, up to 4cm in diameter, completely round in cross-section. Male flower spike directly above the thicker female flower spike
HABITAT	Swampy areas, ditches, garden ponds
DISTRIBUTION	Frequent in England, except the Northwest. Occasional in Scottish and Welsh lowlands and Northern Ireland
SEASON	Early spring for the young shoots

I become unaccountably excited whenever I see a stand of Bulrushes. All other large grasses seem like poor impostors, but for some reason the Bulrush seems like the real thing. Beyond its beauty there is another reason to love this plant – you can eat it. Although by no means as common as it once was – due to the drainage of wetland for agriculture – Bulrushes are still a familiar sight in the countryside, especially the English countryside.

It is, however, not a plant I would recommend collecting whenever you find it – its habitat is often a delicate one and may even be protected. Also, since you will have to remove nearly all of the plant you may need permission from the landowner in order to comply with the law on uprooting plants. Nevertheless, it can sometimes be found in large quantities and the collecting of half a dozen for the kitchen once or twice a year is unlikely to do any harm. Because they look so attractive Bulrushes have frequently been planted in domestic ponds – a habitat they love not wisely but too well, and the hapless pond-owner may be delighted to see you take away as many of the damn things as you wish.

For some reason almost no one collects this plant for food, yet much of it is edible. The strange rope-like roots contain a great deal of starch, which can be eaten raw or baked to make a flour; the immature flower spike can be eaten raw or cooked and tastes like sweetcorn; one can make flour out of the mature seeds; even the pollen can be collected. In my opinion, however, the best way to eat Bulrushes is to cook the young spring shoots.

A Bulrush patch will be easy to spot, even in early spring, as last year's highly distinctive maces will still be around. From late February to April or even May the young shoots will grow from the starch-rich underground roots. Shoots 50–80cm tall are about the right size. They can be cut off at any distance from the roots, but

EDIBLE SPECIES 163

Distinctive cross-section pattern of the Bulrush shoot

I get my knife right into the mud and cut at the bottom of the stem. The shoots look almost exactly like leeks and are prepared for cooking in the same way.

With last year's seed heads as a clue, it is difficult to confuse Bulrushes with anything else. However, the young yellow flag iris is superficially similar and can cause severe gastrointestinal upsets if eaten. The plant resembles the young Bulrush but the stem is flattened in cross-section instead of perfectly round.

If you have ever sat, bored to distraction, at the edge of a cricket pitch watching a dull game, you may have tried to alleviate the tedium by nibbling on the succulent base of a piece of grass. The flavour is exactly what you get from Bulrush shoots, but of course the size is much greater. A decent-sized shoot will be 3–4cm across, and not much less when the tough outer layers have been peeled back. If you would rather reduce the grassy flavour to a more moderate level, the peeled shoots can be chopped and stir-fried – not unlike bamboo shoots. One of the best stir-fries I ever ate was Bulrush shoots, seaweed, Crow Garlic and Jelly Ear mushrooms (p.203) – an extraordinary combination of wild, and *only* wild, ingredients.

Also look out for several other reeds and rushes. Common Sedge (*Carex nigra*) is the easiest to spot, with its black flowers and three-sided stem. It is much smaller than a Bulrush but there will still be a reasonable amount of succulent stem left after peeling and it is sufficiently common to permit picking a dozen or so.

P.S. Many of you will have noticed that I am following popular usage in calling this plant a Bulrush despite the insistence of many that this name should be restricted to a different grass-like species, *Schoenoplectus lacustris*. What I am calling a Bulrush should, it is said, be called a Great Reedmace. In making my stand I am following Richard Mabey, who calls this a '*rare victory for common English over botanical protocol*'. The Botanical Society of the British Isles hedges its bets by accepting enough names to satisfy and annoy everyone – Bulrush, Great Reedmace and even False Bulrush.

The confusion has long been blamed on the famous late-nineteenth-century painter of 'Victorians in togas', Sir Lawrence Alma-Tadema. The accusation, frequently repeated, is that his painting *Moses in the Bulrushes* depicts the baby Moses nestling in a clump of Great Reedmace and that this image has so imprinted itself on the common mind that the misconception has continued to this day.

The main problem with this nice story is that Alma-Tadema never produced a painting called *Moses in the Bulrushes*. He did, however, paint one called *The Finding of Moses*. Unfortunately this contains neither 'true' Bulrush nor Reedmace. Furthermore, the confusion, if confusion it be, predates not only the painting but also the painter. In 1819, seventeen years before Alma-Tadema's birth, a writer complains of '*reed mace*' being '*vulgarly called bulrush.*'

It is probable that artists when painting the biblical scene have merely continued this 'vulgar' tradition. For example, in 1828 Delaroche paints unmistakable Reedmaces (and a Pharaoh's daughter who seems to be having a little trouble with her clothing) in his depiction of the story.

Still, I am of the opinion that if something has been popularly called by a name for getting on for two hundred years we might as well stick with it.

As it happens neither Reedmace nor the true Bulrush (*S. lacustris*) would have been found in ancient Egypt – a fact apparently known to Alma-Tadema. The infant Moses would have been discovered amongst papyrus (*Cyperus papyrus*). One final, unhelpful twist in this tale is the fact that the word Bulrush comes from the Middle English *bulrish* meaning papyrus.

Poisonous Species

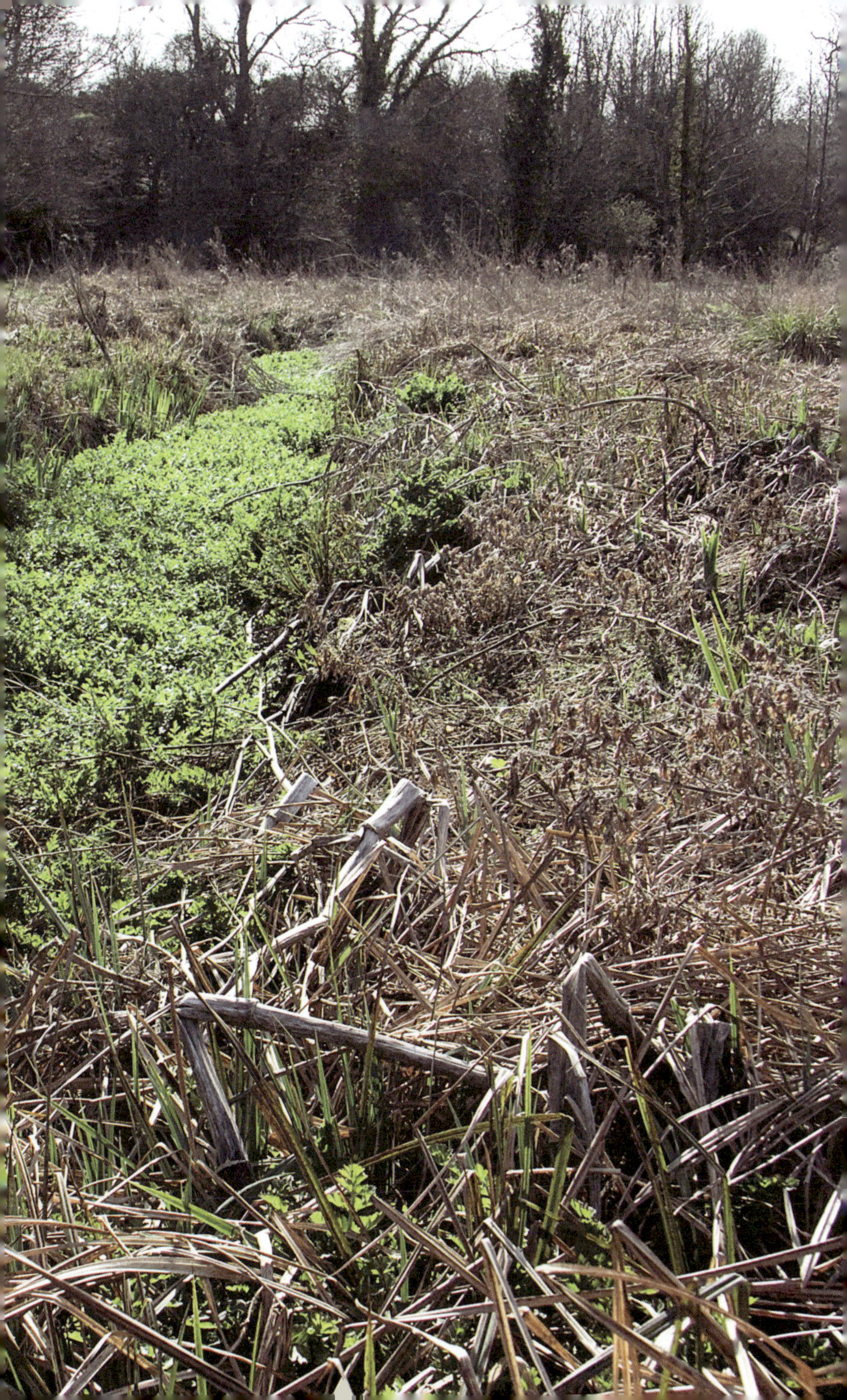

Foxglove, *Digitalis purpurea*

Alongside 'don't play with matches', 'remember to clean your teeth' and 'mind the cat', something that most children learn at their mother's knee is 'never eat wild berries or plants'. Childhood lessons are difficult to unlearn. I was in my twenties when I found out that it wasn't a criminal offence for men to thread a needle – my mother having told me as a five-year-old that it was. But if you want to enjoy what nature has put before us you will have to put aside parental pleas and your own fears. Of course, mothers are right on most things and there is a very real danger in eating wild plants – if you get it wrong, even once, you can die.

A positive identification of an edible plant is essential if you want to eat it, but it is very encouraging if you can also assure yourself that it is not some deadly look-alike. There are more than two hundred poisonous plants in the UK, so I have selected just those that could conceivably present a problem to the forager; they may look like an edible species or they happen to be very common. I have tried to indicate how poisonous each plant is with a star rating. 'X' plants make you quite ill, 'XX' make you very ill and 'XXX' make you dead.

Two families dominate this section – the carrot family and the potato family, more properly called the Umbelliferaceae and the Solanaceae respectively. These are highly ambivalent families – in addition to their many seriously poisonous members, both contain several important edible species as their names carrot and potato suggest. Some of the edible Umbelliferaceae grow wild in Britain, but, apart from the odd self-sown urban tomato, there are no wild edible Solanaceae here – they are all poisonous or unpalatable and usually both. The most serious Solanaceae, Deadly Nightshade, is quite rare and resembles nothing edible. The worst of the Umbelliferaceae is the most deadly of all British plants, very common, *and* looks a bit like several edible species. It is Hemlock Water-dropwort and if you want to collect leaves or roots it is one you really must learn – if you make a mistake with this plant you could be dead within 3 hours.

As with the poisonous fungi, plants do not come with a little label to tell you whether or not you can eat them. You just have to work out what they are from characteristics such as leaf shape, whether or not it is hairy, number of petals and so on. Refer to the specific advice on how to identify plants under individual entries, bearing in mind the most important thing is never to jump to conclusions. And for more information on identifying plants – and a few extra species – go to www.rivercottage.net/foraging.

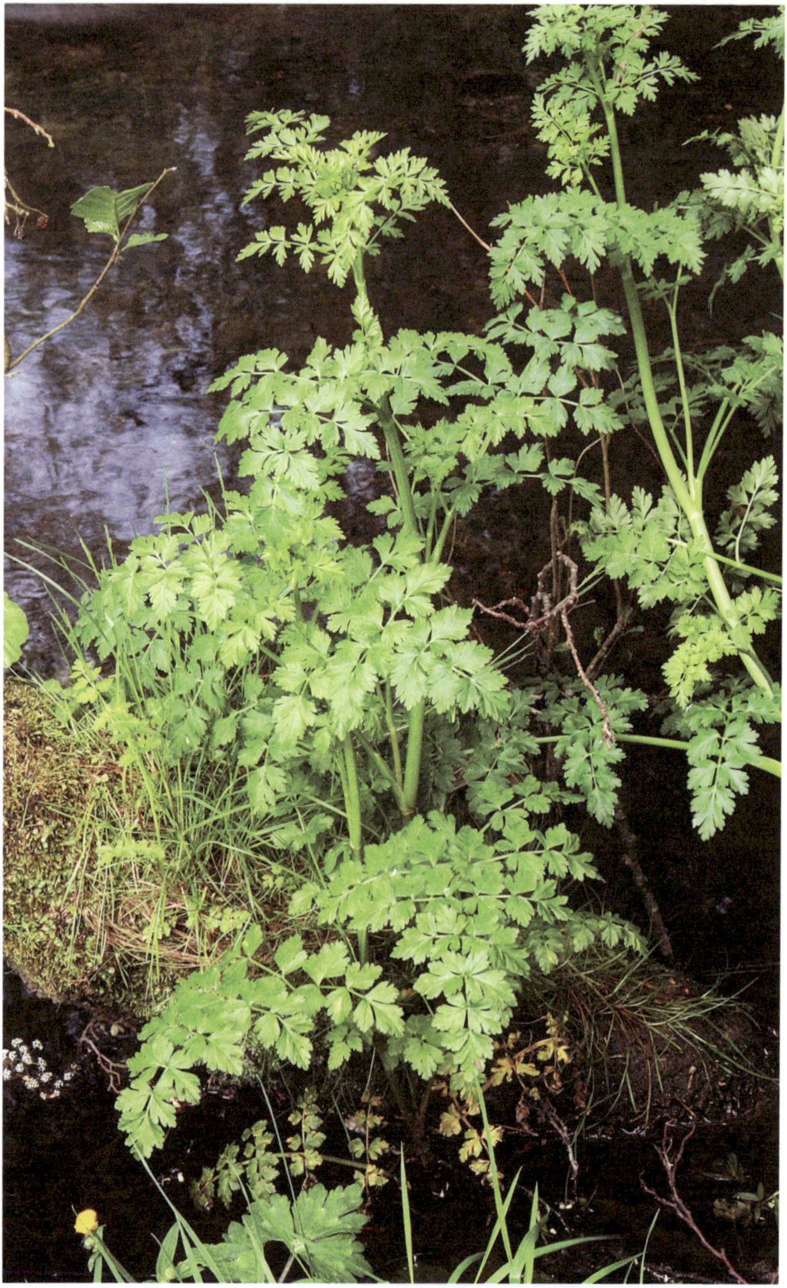

Hemlock Water-dropwort

Oenanthe crocata **XXX**

DESCRIPTION	Medium perennial, 50–150cm tall. Leaflets approximately opposite and with a terminal leaflet, deeply lobed. The narrow young leaf stems sheath the stem, sometimes pink tinged. Stems grooved, hollow, young ones especially exude a strong-smelling, sticky fluid which turns slowly yellow. Flowers form in umbels of separate white half-globes. Clusters of swollen white roots
HABITAT	Wet areas, particularly streams, ditches, marshes, damp path edges
DISTRIBUTION	Common and often abundant south of Oxford and on the whole western side of Britain. Generally coastal in northeast England and east Scotland. Largely absent elsewhere
SEASON	Roots exist all year. Young shoots seen from February, flowers in June and July

This is the most poisonous of all British plants and one of the most poisonous in the world, yet it is sufficiently common to fill large tracts of wetland with its bright-green growth in early spring. Its dread power has long been known as is attested by the numerous and often colourful reports of fatal poisonings over the centuries. Occasionally several fatalities will occur when a group partake in a deadly meal. In 1834 four convicts from Woolwich Prison died and ten others survived after supplementing their meagre rations with the roots of this plant; in 1857 two labourers died horribly, again from eating the roots. Much more recently, in 2002, a group of eight young people on holiday in Argyll narrowly escaped death when they made a more than usually toxic vegetable curry. Fortunately, as the poison is diminished with heat and they ate only a little of the sliced root, they suffered only a very uncomfortable couple of days and made a full recovery.

This is such a common plant in many parts of the country that every forager must learn to recognise it. Deadly Nightshade is famously poisonous but quite a rarity, not easily confused with anything edible – not so Hemlock Water-dropwort. Hogweed, Alexanders, Carrot, Parsnip, Ground Elder and several other plants in this book are all excellent edible species, but they belong to the same treacherous

The swollen, deadly roots of Hemlock Water-dropwort

family as Hemlock Water-dropwort – the carrot family (Umbelliferaceae). These are notoriously tricky to tell one from the other and include some of the deadliest species known. The leaves of Hemlock Water-dropwort are fresh-looking and similar to flat-leaved parsley. The roots, too, look temptingly tasty and substantial, as you can see from the picture, and are (I am told) not too unpleasant in flavour. Apart from acts of straightforward foolhardiness, it is generally the edible root of the water-parsnip for which Hemlock Water-dropwort is mistaken. A single bite of the raw root has been known to cause death. The rule, as always, is only to eat something if you are absolutely sure of its name.

The toxin in Hemlock Water-dropwort, oenanthotoxin, assaults the central nervous system, causing vomiting, fast heart rate, abdominal cramps and seizures in all who partake of it. All parts of the plant are toxic, but the fleshy roots have the highest concentration of poison, higher still in winter and spring.

Finally it is worth mentioning that there are several other Water-dropworts – mercifully none as deadly as Hemlock Water-dropwort. Most are fairly rare though the Corky Water-dropwort (*O. pimpinelloides*) is quite common in grassland in the southwest of England. There is little point in learning these relative rarities as there is nothing edible in this book with which they can be confused.

Hemlock *Conium maculatum* xxx

DESCRIPTION	Upright biennial up to 2 metres. Leaves fern-like, dark green. Mature stems *red spotted*, hollow and cylindrical. Unpleasant mouse-like smell. Flowers white in an umbel. White tap root
HABITAT	Generally damp places, often coastal. Waste ground, ditches, stream sides, roadsides – especially where salted
DISTRIBUTION	Common throughout the British Isles, but largely absent from higher ground and much of Northern Ireland and Scotland, except for the east coast and eastern lowlands
SEASON	First visible in March, flowers in June and July

This stately plant is famously deadly with at least one famous victim to its name – Socrates. His death, however, was no foraging accident but a judicial execution by poisoning. Capital punishment in the ancient world was generally not a cheerful process and Hemlock poisoning may well have been the best of a bad bunch. Francis Bacon states that '*Hemlock is noted for procuring the least painful Death*', although paralysis followed by respiratory failure while the subject is fully conscious is not without its drawbacks.

Hemlock's distinctive red-spotted stem (*maculatum* means 'spotted' – hence 'immaculate' meaning 'unblemished') and imposing size make it an easy plant to recognise and avoid, and its unpleasant mousey smell has not encouraged careless foraging. Nevertheless, a superficial similarity to parsley and a fleshy root not unlike that of Wild Parsnip have led some to make terrible mistakes. All parts of the plant are poisonous, but the seeds particularly so. The principal toxin in Hemlock is coniine, an alkaloid rather similar to nicotine. It affects the central nervous system, causing respiratory failure.

Modern cases of Hemlock poisoning do occur, but even now are not always accidental – in 2006, for example, a biochemist from Devon committed suicide with a lethal cocktail of Hemlock and alcohol. More common is accidental ingestion – often, and tragically, by children. In 1994 a three-year-old Australian boy died when he ate some he had found in his back garden, and in 2002 a thirteen-year-old girl perished in North America. There is no antidote to the several alkaloid poisons contained within Hemlock, survival depending on the original dose, the victim's constitution and energetic nursing care.

Hemlock stems

Hemlock leaves

One rather absurd way of poisoning yourself would be to follow the advice of a seventeenth-century writer on '*How to make... small birds drunk, that you may take them with your hands*' – you mix grain with Hemlock juice. In fact birds are seldom affected by the poison, but their flesh becomes highly toxic, as some who tried it have discovered. Accidental poisoning from eating wild birds inadvertently tainted with Hemlock became a problem in Italy a few years ago with seventeen cases, four of which were fatal, reported between 1972 and 1990.

Inevitably, so powerful a plant found its way into the ancient medicine chest and is still occasionally used in some (highly doubtful) homeopathic preparations. In the mid-eighteenth century, at the instigation of one Dr Storck of Vienna, it became a fashionable remedy for a variety of tumours before the cure was discovered to be worse than the disease. Hemlock's 'cooling' properties (it causes paralysis) are no doubt the reason Culpeper tells us that '... *applied to the privities, it stops its lustful thoughts*'. Best of all is Boyle (of Boyle's Law fame – the one about pressure and volume in a gas being inversely proportional – though I am sure you remember), who suggests rubbing crushed Hemlock on to the chest '*To reduce flaggy Breasts to a good shape and consistence*'. It worked for me.

Fool's Parsley *Aethusa cynapium* xx

DESCRIPTION	Low to medium annual, to 50cm. Leaves fine and deeply incised, fern-like, hairless. Stems ribbed. Flowers white umbrella spray, with conspicuous *long bracts* hanging down below the flower head. All parts smell unpleasant, especially when crushed
HABITAT	Weed of cultivation, waste ground
DISTRIBUTION	Common in England south of Cumbria, scarcer elsewhere
SEASON	Leaves from June to October

The name Fool's Parsley tells you most of what you need to know about this plant. It is another treacherous member of the carrot family, mimicking some of its edible cousins very well. It does look remarkably like cultivated parsley, though not curly-leaved parsley. If you see it in flower all doubts flee as it has highly distinctive long bracts hanging below the flower heads like a beard.

As Fool's Parsley grows happily, indeed chiefly, in the garden, often alongside its cultivated and harmless relative, it is a blessing that the smell and taste are very unpleasant. If you still manage to make a mistake your final warning comes in the form of a burning sensation in the mouth – the plant's Latin name, *Aethusa*, means 'burning one'. The leaves of Fool's Parsley could conceivably be confused with those of Pignut, but Pignut's edible root is rounded while that of Fool's Parsley is like a tiny parsnip.

It is not quite as poisonous as some other members of the carrot family, though it does contain the toxin found in Hemlock – coniine and causes similar symptoms. A nineteenth-century writer refers to the case of two ladies who '*ate a little of it in a sallad instead of parsley, and who were soon seized with nausea, vomiting, headache, giddiness, somnolency, pungent heat in the mouth, throat, and stomach, difficulty in swallowing, and numbness of the limbs*'. It appears that they survived the experience. In 1845 three children ate the roots of Fool's Parsley, thinking them to be parsnips. Two survived, but Ellen Williams, aged just five, died within a few hours. The doctor, one Evan Thomas, House Surgeon to King's College, who reported this incident became fascinated by the plant and its effects and went on to perform some particularly gruesome and fatal experiments on cats and dogs. Modern cases of poisoning are rare and we must hope they stay that way.

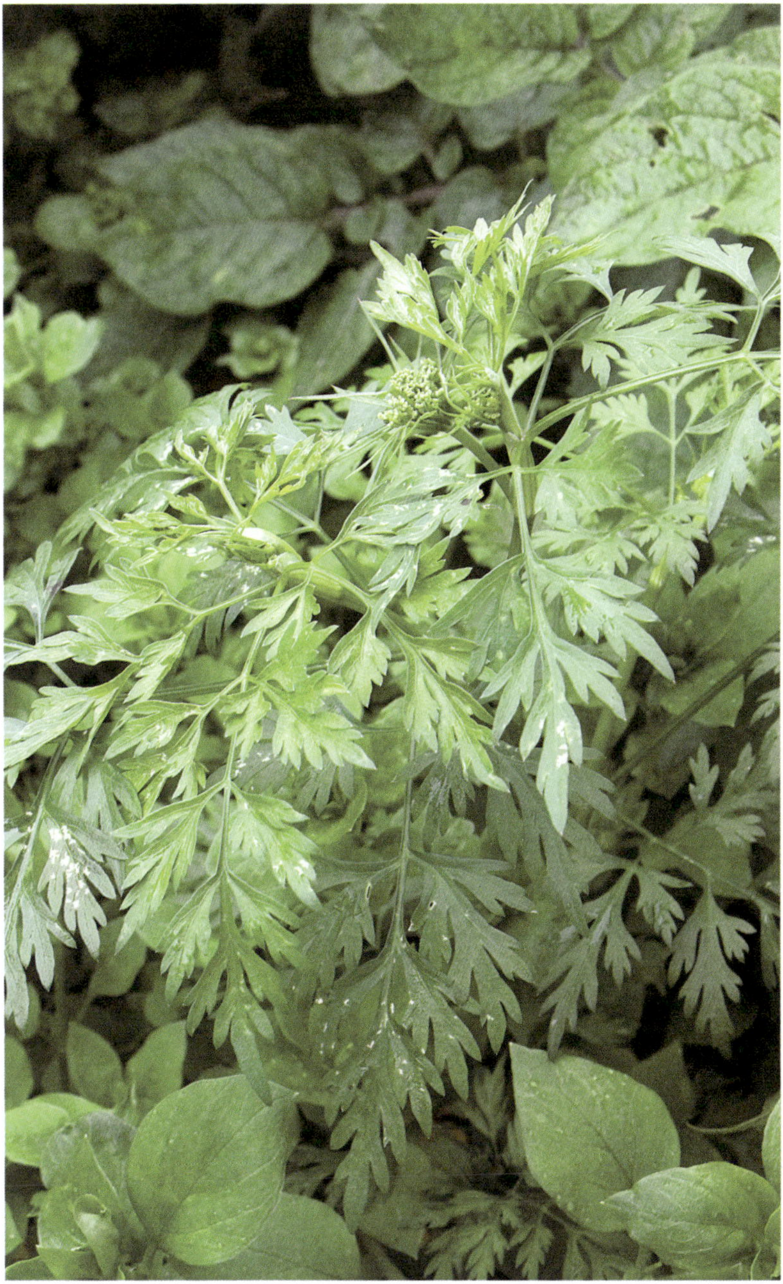

Dog's Mercury

Annual Mercury

Dog's Mercury *Mercurialis perennis* xx

DESCRIPTION	Short to medium upright perennial, to 35cm, growing from underground rhizomes. Leaves pointed/oval, opposite, bluntly serrated edge, slightly downy. Flowers on stalks, no petals, whitish
HABITAT	Shady woods and hedges. Forms large patches of vegetation
DISTRIBUTION	Very common throughout the British Isles, save the Fens and northern Scotland
SEASON	From February, but can be found in sheltered locations all year

Annual Mercury *M. annua* x

DESCRIPTION	Short to medium, upright annual, to 50cm. Sometimes branched. Leaves pointed/oval, more coarsely serrated than Dog's Mercury, paler green. Flowers on stalks, white
HABITAT	Weed of cultivation
DISTRIBUTION	Common in England south of the Wash, except Devon and Cornwall. Rare or absent elsewhere
SEASON	May–November. Sometimes overwinters

These closely related species have an uncertain culinary reputation. Dog's Mercury is certainly poisonous, but Annual Mercury was once eaten as a green vegetable and my inclusion of it here in the poisonous section may be a slur on its good character. However, it does have a medical reputation as a 'useful laxative' and this alone may give one pause.

Dog's Mercury is a fairly distinctive plant growing in a distinctive manner in a distinctive habitat so there really should be no reason why anyone would mistake it for anything edible. But, of course, they have. The most reported story of poisoning by this plant is from 1693 when an entire family from Shropshire was laid low with a dinner of Dog's Mercury and bacon; everyone recovered fully save one daughter who sadly perished. There are scattered reports of poisonings over the centuries, including – in 1831 – three women in Boston who mistook the plant for Good King Henry (p.59), a common edible plant of their native Ireland (or *'sweet isle of their nativity'* as the *Boston Medical Journal* prettily puts it). They all survived. Much more recently – in the 1980s – a couple in North Wales mistook Dog's Mercury for Brooklime (p.128). Quite how they managed this I cannot guess, but they suffered severe gastrointestinal problems, inflammation of the kidneys, flushing of the cheeks and jaw, and destruction of some of their red blood cells (haemolysis). Although they consumed a large quantity they were fortunate in that they cooked it first, thus destroying some of the toxins. They made a complete recovery.

Dog's Mercury is very different from Brooklime but it has a resemblance to some of the goosefoots, such as Good King Henry and Many-seeded Goosefoot. Both have tiny flowers on spikes and similar-looking mature leaves arranged around a central stem. The names of these two unrelated groups of plants have intertwined in the past, so that Good King Henry was once known as English Mercury, Annual Mercury as French Mercury and Dog's Mercury (in Germany) as Bad Henry. If that is not enough confusion for you, both Dog's and Annual Mercury were once called *Cynocrambe*, meaning Dog Cabbage.

There should be no problem for the careful forager. The goosefoots tend to have a mealy surface texture on the young leaves at least, while Mercury leaves are very slightly hairy. Dog's Mercury also has underground rhizomes, whereas the goosefoots just have a mass of thin roots. Habitat will also be a reassurance as Dog's Mercury is a plant of shady woods whereas the goosefoots like light and open ground.

Assuming that Annual Mercury *is* poisonous, it presents slightly more of a problem. It often grows in association with other weeds of cultivation – in fact there is a Fat Hen plant clearly visible in the picture on p.178. The long and neatly serrated bright-green leaves are mostly hairless but they also never have that granulated, mealy surface to their young leaves. Remember, it is quite rare outside its stronghold of southern England, so you may not have to worry about it at all.

Henbane *Hyoscyamus niger* xxx

DESCRIPTION	Upright, annual/biennial to 80cm. Single-stemmed. Leaves alternate, deeply toothed edge, hairy, sticky. Stem hairy, sticky. Flowers distinctive, yellow with purple centre. Whole plant smells unpleasant
HABITAT	Disturbed ground, rough agricultural land, coastal dunes
DISTRIBUTION	Uncommon. Southeast England, largely coastal elsewhere
SEASON	May to September

Apart from the common nightshades, such as Black Nightshade and Woody Nightshade, there are several other unpleasant but relatively rare members of the Solanaceae. Their rarity and distinctiveness suggest that they are unlikely to cause you any problems, but it is still important to be aware of them – and they are very pretty too.

Henbane is fairly typical of the nightshades with large berries, flamboyant five-petalled flowers and a generally sinister appearance. Being implicated in the death of Mrs. Crippen, it is also something of a celebrity in the plant world. This association with dastardly deeds long predates Dr Crippen's malfeasance, as we may judge from the eighteenth-century poet William Coombes:

While whisp'ring Murder tells them that she knows,
Where the sharp Dagger's forg'd, and Henbane grows.

Despite its murderous reputation, Henbane seldom causes death. But it causes more than its fair share of hair-raising symptoms including thirst, dilated pupils, photophobia, fever, vomiting, accelerated heart rate, hypertension, convulsions, coma and about a dozen more. Hallucinations and euphoria are also among Henbane's extensive arsenal of effects and it is for these that the plant is sometimes, and dangerously, used today.

Pliny the Elder gives us a tip on how Henbane might be so employed: '… *an oil is extracted, which is injected into the ears, and deranges the intellect*'. One wonders how he found this out.

When in flower Henbane is unlikely to confuse anyone as its flowers are so distinctive (pictured overleaf), but the leaves are superficially similar to those of some of the goosefoots, notably Red Goosefoot. Just remember that the latter is hairless, whereas Henbane is covered in long hairs.

Henbane in flower

The closely related and seriously poisonous Thorn Apple (*Datura stramonium*) also has leaves similar to some goosefoots, but they are larger with more pointed, almost holly-like lobes. Also, the flowers are bell-shaped – not spikes of clustered flowers growing from where the leaf joins the stem. Thorn Apple makes the occasional appearance on waste ground and sometimes, unhelpfully, grows in vegetable gardens. It is also known as Jimson Weed after an unfortunate incident in Jamestown involving intoxicated British soldiers during the American War of Independence, and, more tellingly, Loco Weed. Herein lies the main reason why people are poisoned by this plant – its occasional use for 'recreational' purposes. As a fun thing to do at weekends eating Thorn Apple must be near the bottom of the list; the effects are weird, unpredictable and unpleasant, and the chance of killing yourself high. I am going to stick to my Saturday night Ovaltine.

Perhaps the most famous poisonous plant is Deadly Nightshade (*Atropa belladonna*). Nothing about this rare native plant resembles any of the edible species mentioned in this book. Nearly all poisonings from this plant are from children eating the shiny black berries.

P.S. One utterly bizarre use for Henbane from 1657 is in the catching of panthers – animals which, we are told, find Henbane irresistible. Simply hang the plant out of the panther's reach and it '*never leaves off leaping and frisking up and down*' until, exhausted, it '*so dyeth on the place*'.

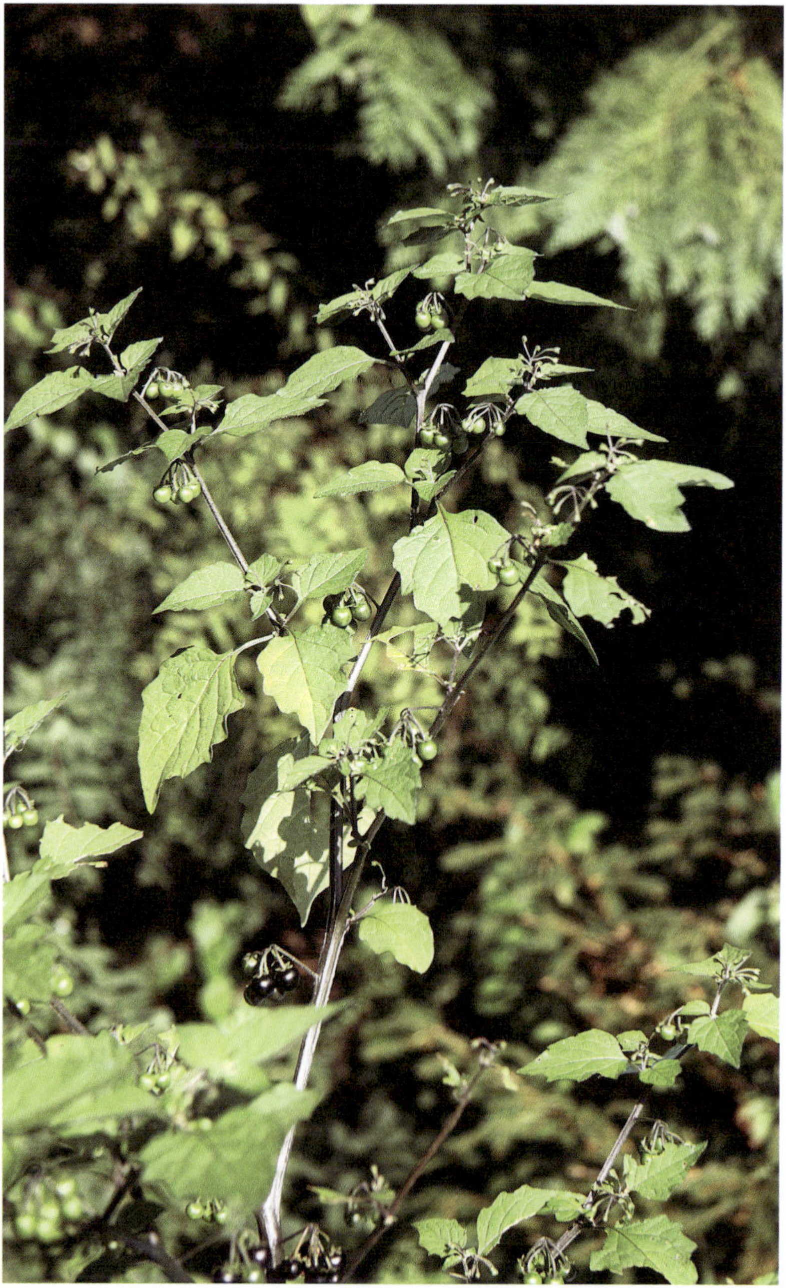

Black Nightshade *Solanum nigrum* x

DESCRIPTION	Low to medium upright annual, to 60cm. Leaves pointed with rounded base and shallow lobes, hairless or sometimes downy. Flowers white. Berries black
HABITAT	Cultivated ground, waste ground
DISTRIBUTION	Common in England south of Hull, rare in Scotland and Northern Ireland, coastal in Wales
SEASON	Berries July–October

Another very common nightshade, though neither as familiar nor as attractive as Woody Nightshade. Black Nightshade is frequently found in vegetable patches and is often mistaken for a potato plant. Fortunately it does not produce tubers so no harm is done. The young leaves and thoroughly mature berries are not, or at least, not *very*, poisonous and have occasionally been eaten in the past. With so much else to eat I really do not think it is worth the risk.

The immature berries are certainly poisonous, causing headache, diarrhoea and even, very rarely, death due to cardiac and respiratory failure. The toxin is solanine, a glycoalkaloid, which is also known from the skin of poorly stored green potatoes, where it occasionally causes mischief. The mature leaves also contain this toxin and are rather similar to the leaves of some goosefoots, most notably Red Goosefoot. The latter has a mealy coating (little granules) on the young leaves, is hairless and shows a certain amount of red on the mature stems. It also tends to be more of an upright, single-stemmed plant with the leaves forming a rosette and, of course, the flowers are reddish spikes (not five white petals) and the fruit or seeds are inconspicuous – not inside black berries as they are with Black Nightshade.

Woody Nightshade
Solanum dulcamara **xx**

DESCRIPTION	Clambering perennial, up to 2 metres, sometimes forming low sprawling bushes. Leaves pointed with a round base or sometimes a wing, downy. Stems straggling, reddish brown. Flowers have five purple petals folded back with bright-yellow anthers in a column. Berries green, then orange, then red, pointed/oval, hanging down in bunches, usually showing ripe and unripe berries in the same bunch
HABITAT	Hedgerows, on shingle beaches, waste ground
DISTRIBUTION	Very common in England, though less so in the North. Common in central Scotland and the southern half of Northern Ireland
SEASON	Berries May–September

This very familiar plant is also known as Bittersweet owing to the taste of the berries, which is bitter at first then sweet (don't try it). Woody Nightshade is frequently thought to be Deadly Nightshade (*Atropa belladonna*), but they are two distinct, if related, plants. Deadly Nightshade is a fairly rare plant and quite different in appearance, producing single large cherry-like black berries as opposed to Woody Nightshade's clusters of small red berries.

Woody Nightshade is a very beautiful plant with colourful flowers and berries showing all the colours of a traffic light on a single branch. There is little it can be confused with, but is sufficiently common to be worth knowing. There have been poisonings by this plant, usually children attracted by the bright-red berries; flushing of the skin, thirst and abdominal pain are among the symptoms. Normally recovery is complete, but there is one recorded case of a nine-year-old girl who died from internal haemorrhaging after eating them. The level of toxin drops dramatically when the berry is *fully* ripe, presumably to allow birds to distribute the seeds without falling out of the sky. Technically, at this point, one could eat them but this, of course, is a prime example of 'don't try this at home'.

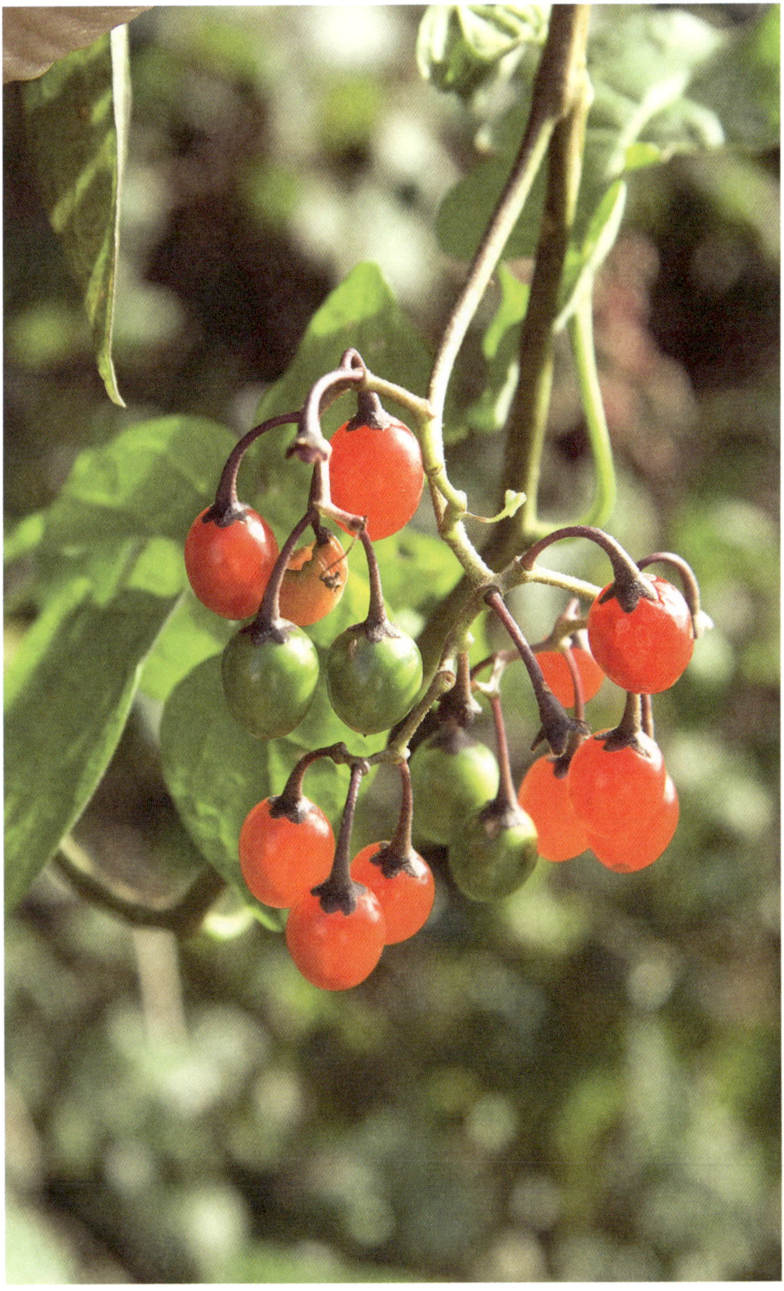

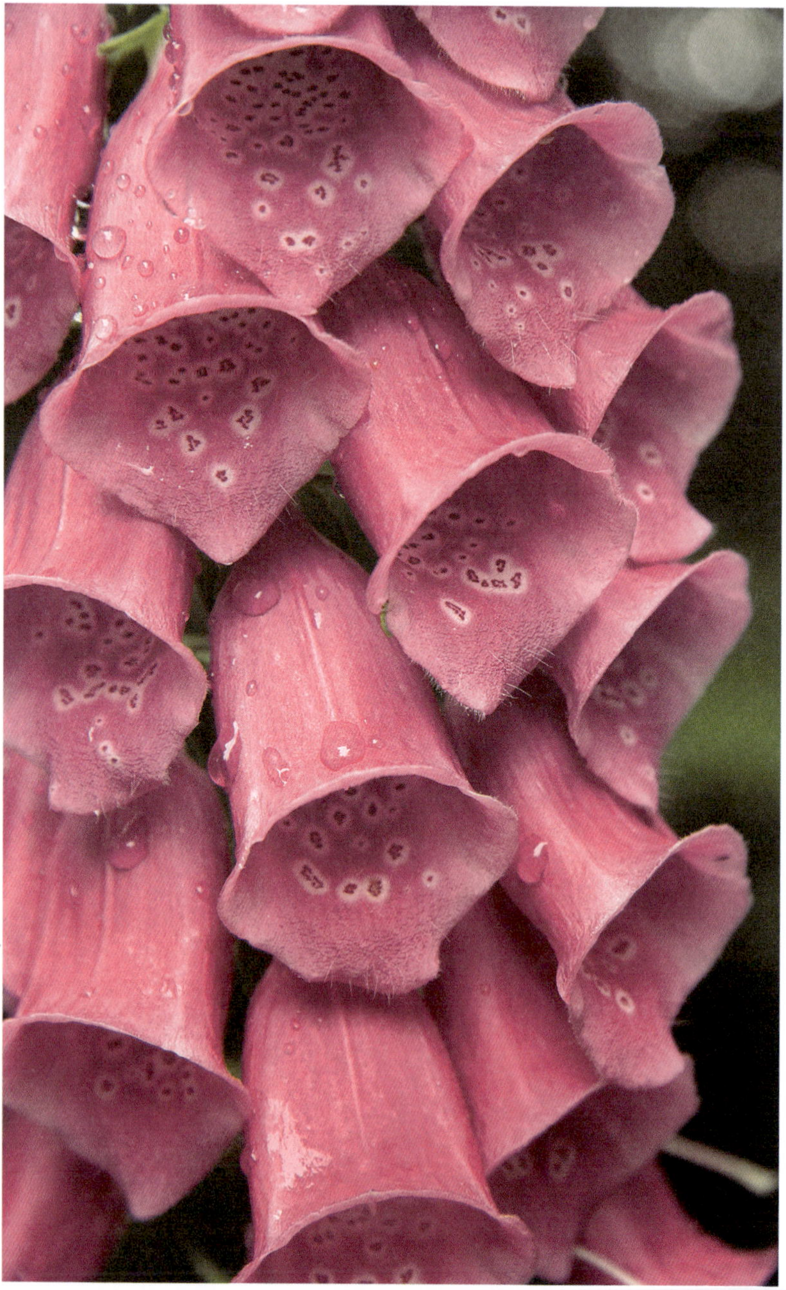

Foxglove *Digitalis purpurea* xxx

DESCRIPTION	Tall, upright perennial, to 1.5 metres. Thick, soft, furry leaves arranged around a central stem. Flowers a distinctive purple/pink bell shape, in a tall spike
HABITAT	Woods, scrub, hedgerows and heath
DISTRIBUTION	Very common throughout the UK, save the Fens
SEASON	Flowers June–September. Leaves much of the year

No visitor to the countryside in high summer will have failed to notice this handsome plant; it graces many of our roadsides and fills many woodland clearings, buzzing with its attendant bees. In full bloom no one could mistake this plant for anything else, but the leaves are rather similar to those of Comfrey, a plant which is sometimes eaten (see below). Should, as has happened, any such mistake be made it is going to be a big one as this plant is utterly deadly.

The poison is a group of chemicals generically called digitalin, which affects the heart and is deadly in even tiny doses – 10mg (one fiftieth of the weight of a single paracetamol tablet) is invariably fatal. This quantity is easily contained in one or two leaves and it was two leaves that, sadly, an amateur botanist used recently to end his life, carefully avoiding a larger dose which would have caused vomiting.

P.S. The father of modern pharmacology is the admirable doctor, botanist and chemist, William Withering. In 1775 he learned from an old woman (some say, romantically, that she was a gypsy) a remedy for the oedema caused by heart failure, better known then as dropsy. The mixture consisted of twenty herbs, but Withering managed to settle on Foxglove as being the active ingredient. To his great credit he then proceeded to carefully measure its effect in differing doses (starting with a very low dose) on 163 patients. He recorded his results, publishing them *whether or not* they supported his tentative contention that the herb was of use in curing dropsy. This thoughtful and systematic procedure was a major break with the superstitious guesswork of the past and marks the birth of true medical research.

Before Wittering, Foxgloves had been considered to have little application in herbal medicine. Gerard talks of them being '*of no use, neither have they any place amongst medicines*', and Culpeper unenthusiastically lists a dozen ailments that Foxgloves might alleviate, none of which is dropsy. Digoxin and digitoxin are now extremely important drugs, strengthening and slowing the heart beat, but dosage is extremely critical and one may forgive the old herbalists for wanting little to do with the plant that contains them. In medicine there is something called the therapeutic index, which, crudely put, is the ratio between the dose that will cure you and the dose that will kill you (or at least do considerable harm). A comfortable index is about 100 – with digitalin it is around 2 or 3.

Withering himself died young at the age of 58, probably from consumption. As he lay dying a friend wrote, in a remarkable congruence of wit, admiration and tactlessness, 'The flower of English botany is Withering.'

P.P.S. Comfrey, the plant that Foxglove is sometimes confused with, has long been considered an edible plant, albeit not a particularly popular one. It has also been used for centuries in herbal remedies – internally for a variety of ailments and, more usefully, externally as a poultice of the leaves or roots to aid the healing of sprains, burns and broken bones. This latter use is reflected in the Latin name *Symphytum* which means 'to make whole'.

Unfortunately a dark suspicion has fallen on Comfrey and it is now considered to be quite seriously poisonous, causing dangerous liver conditions and even liver cancer. In 2001, the US Food and Drugs Administration banned its use in herbal preparations, expressing serious concern over the plant's safety and citing a number of incidents of disease and at least one death. Cirrhosis and veno-occlusion (blockage) of the liver are the main problems. Only after a considerable amount has been consumed over a period of months do the cumulative effects of the highly poisonous pyrrolizidine alkaloids manifest themselves. The roots, which have occasionally been consumed as a vegetable, contain large quantities of the toxins and young leaves relatively small amounts. The mature leaves contain less still.

It could be argued that the occasional Comfrey fritter made from older leaves would do little harm, but the Velcro texture never completely disappears and I don't think that the forager will lose a great deal by banishing Comfrey from the menu.

Lords and Ladies *Arum maculatum* x

DESCRIPTION	Short perennial, to 40cm. Leaves large, arrow-shaped, stemmed, often spotted. Flowers a single brown club enclosed in a large open sheath. Berries clustered on a spike, red
HABITAT	Woods, hedgerows, copses. Shade-loving
DISTRIBUTION	Very common throughout the British Isles, except central Wales and the Scottish Highlands
SEASON	Leaves January–May, Flowers April–June, berries May–September

The leaves of Lords and Ladies often dominate the woodland and hedgerow of late winter and early spring, and will persist for several months before the plant transforms itself into the second of its three manifestations. It is this stage, the flowering stage, that gives the plant a fair proportion of its one hundred or so common names.

Lords and Ladies is a coy reference to the impressively vertical central spadix resting in its sheath-like spathe. Another familiar name is Cuckoo Pint. The Cuckoo part is either derived from 'cuckold' or a reference to the energetic behaviour of the male cuckoo. Pint is clear enough, being shortened from 'pintle'; the Wiltshire name

A spike of Lords and Ladies berries

Dog Cock puts it more straightforwardly. Incidentally 'Pint' should be pronounced to rhyme with 'mint'. My favourite piece of rural circumlocution is Wake Robin – 'Robin' is an affectionate name similar to Dick or John Thomas and 'Wake' just tells you what mood he is in. Like all good things, this flowering stage eventually passes to be replaced by the berries on a spike.

The leaves of Lords and Ladies are not terribly poisonous, acting mostly as an irritant. However, they do have the potentially serious effect of swelling up the tongue and throat. As an inveterate nibbler of wild plants (worth doing only if you are *very* careful and are familiar with the dangerous plants), I once tried the tiniest piece of Lords and Ladies, spitting out as much as I could after a few seconds. The tip of my tongue went numb and my lips swelled as though I had been using lip-plumping lipstick (not that I would know). After a few minutes my whole throat and oesophagus started to feel on fire. It is for this reason that the plant seldom causes problems – few can eat enough to poison themselves.

The main potential for confusion is with Sorrel. The two plants are completely unrelated, but the leaves sometimes look worryingly similar. There are many differences but the easy one, if you are in doubt, is that the backward-pointing lobes of Sorrel are always sharply pointed, whereas those of Lords and Ladies are slightly rounded. A few of the goosefoots have arrow-shaped leaves, but they always grow from a central stem and will often have a granular surface, especially when young.

The berries are the most poisonous part of Lords and Ladies, but their growth habit as solitary spikes is unlike that of any edible plant – only children or the foolhardy are ever poisoned.

Sorrel above, Lords and Ladies below

Black Bryony

White Bryony

Black Bryony *Tamus communis* xx

DESCRIPTION	Perennial climber, up to 4 metres long. Leaves distinctly heart-shaped, light green. Flowers small, pale yellow/green, six-petalled. Bright-red berries appear, along with the immature yellow and green ones, in long strings
HABITAT	Woods, hedgerows, scrub
DISTRIBUTION	Very common in England, except the North. Rare in central Wales, absent elsewhere
SEASON	Berries September–November

The bright-red, yellow and green strings of Black Bryony berries festoon the autumn hedgerow like early Christmas decorations. They are larger in size than most hedgerow berries and do look quite tasty, but their colourful 'pearl necklace' growth habit makes them very easily distinguishable from the edible berries. Black Bryony is quite poisonous, the commonest effect being an irritation of the skin and mouth caused by tiny needles of calcium oxalate penetrating the skin. The berries also contain irritant histamines and bitter saponins.

Black Bryony is unusual in being the only member in the British Isles of the otherwise exotic yam family. Another bryony, much less common than Black Bryony and totally unrelated to it, is White Bryony (*Bryonia dioica*). This, too, is the only wild British representative of its family, the cucumbers. It is also seriously poisonous and grows as a climber. Its leaves are maple-like and it clings to the hedgerow with spiralling tendrils. It produces clusters of poisonous red berries.

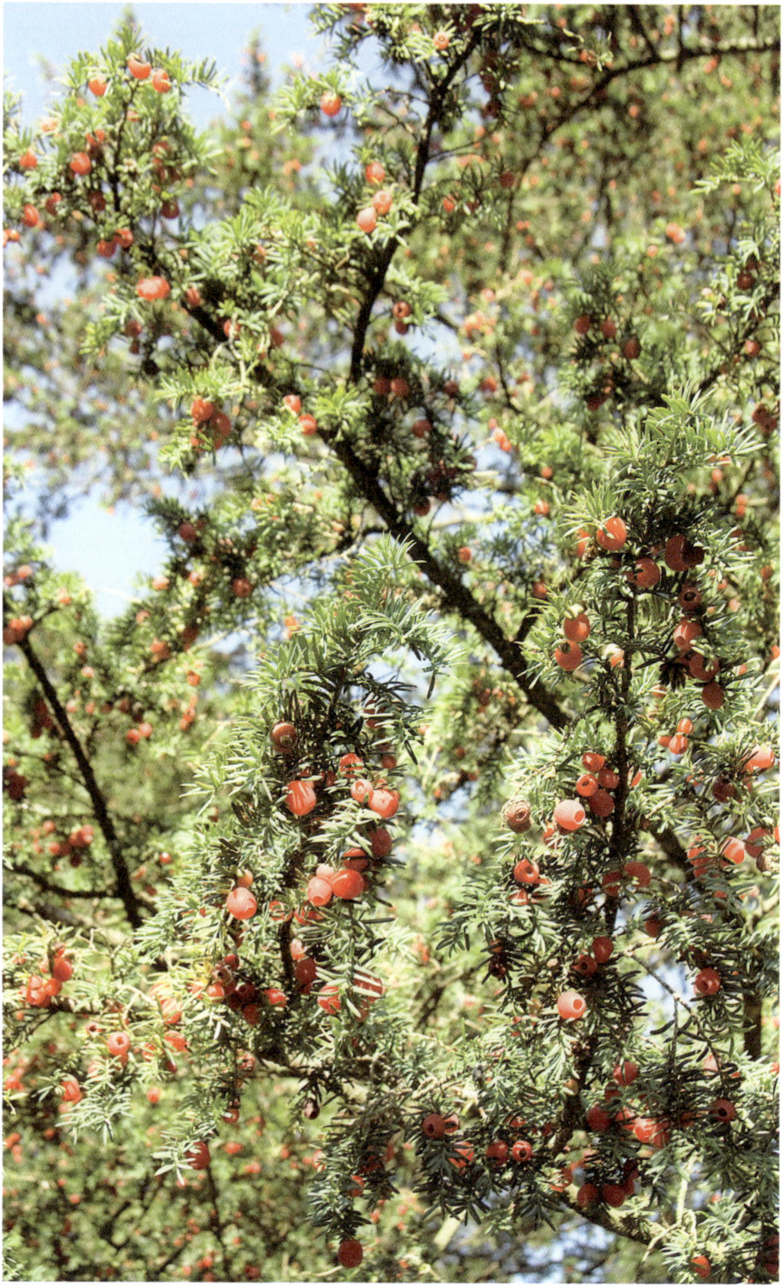

Yew *Taxus baccata* xxx

DESCRIPTION	Large tree. Needles in opposing rows. Berries bright scarlet
HABITAT	Frequently planted, often on lime. Churchyards, old gardens
DISTRIBUTION	Very common; uncommon or missing in northern Scotland and Northern Ireland
SEASON	Berries September and October

I cannot really imagine anyone eating any part of the splendid Yew by mistake, but it certainly has happened. The most usual victims are children, attracted by the bright berries – they do look rather tasty and a woman in Germany in 1975 unaccountably ate four or five handfuls of leaves and duly died. In fact nearly all parts of the Yew are seriously poisonous and often deadly, containing as they do the chemical *taxin,* which interferes with heart action. The one exception is the soft part of the fruit. This means that you can eat the berries as long as you spit out the pips without chewing them. Obviously I have tried them and find them to be slightly mucilaginous and pleasantly sweet, though not very fruity. I suppose a jelly could be made out of it, or perhaps a sorbet for an extreme dinner party. Maybe not.

P.S. The Yew is one of only three native British conifers, the others being Juniper and Scots Pine. Since they are all conifers one is entitled to expect them all to bear cones. The cones of Scots Pine are quite obvious but the other two appear to have berries instead. However, if you look closely at a Juniper berry you can see that it is a tiny, soft pine cone. But what of the Yew? In fact the red fleshy part of the berry – the aril – is a highly modified cone scale. If you look at the immature berry it actually looks like a tiny acorn.

Recipes

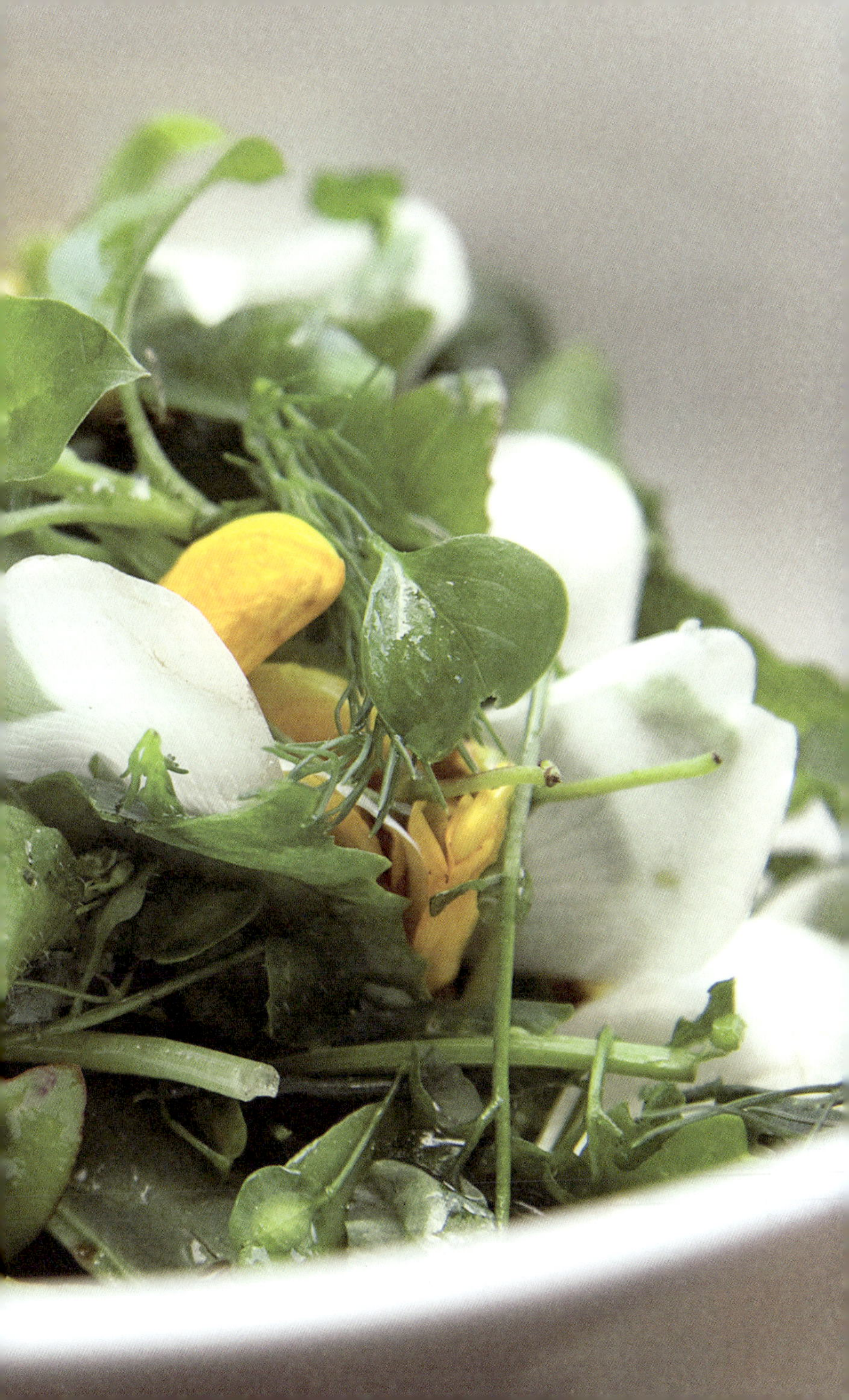

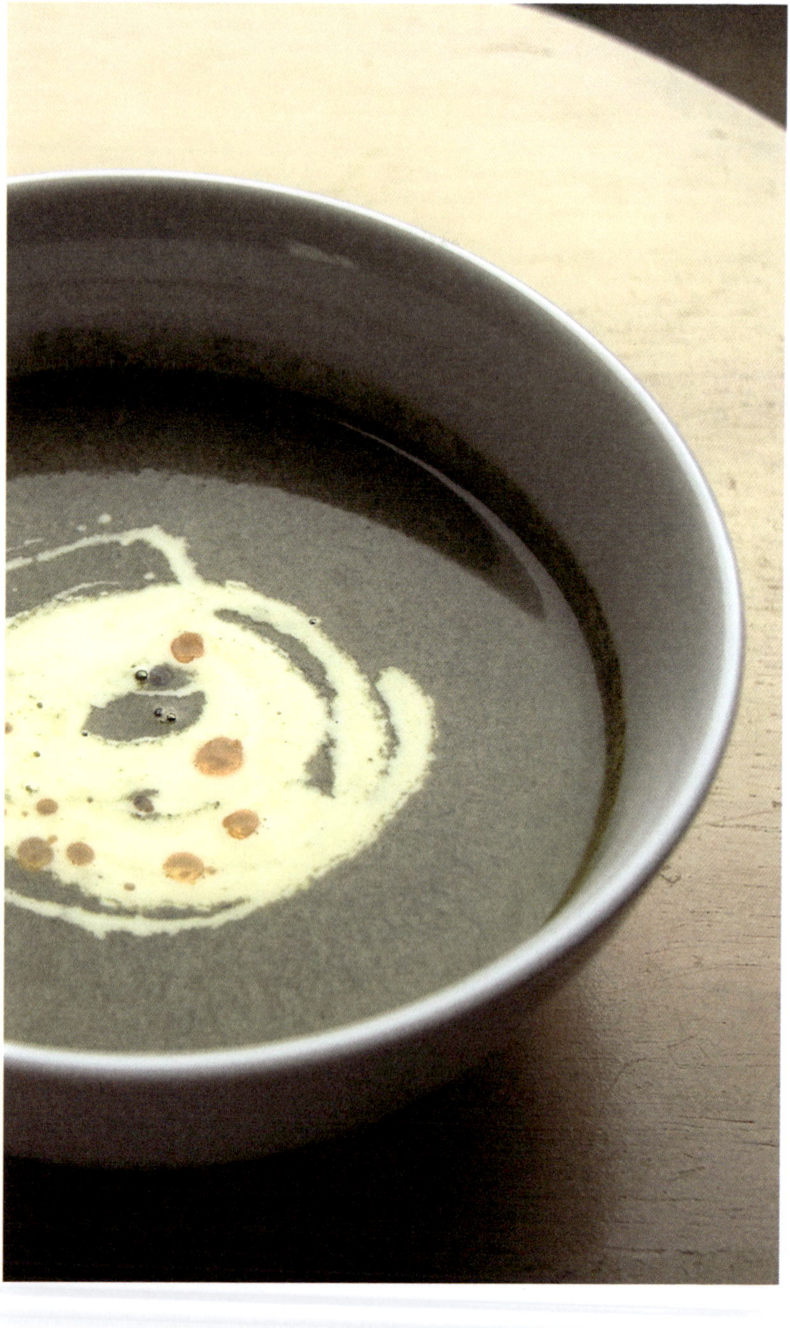

Nettle soup

Nettle Soup is probably what most people first think of when they consider cooking on the wild side, so I could hardly leave it out. The keys to an excellent Nettle Soup are potato – to give it body – and really good stock – to give it spirit. Without these the wild food cynic's worst suspicions of boiled weeds will be confirmed. Note that a carrier bag is the standard measure for Nettles.

Serves 4

- Half a carrier bagful of Stinging Nettle tops, or fresh-looking larger leaves
- 50g butter
- 1 large onion (or a dozen Crow Garlic bulbs if you want to be truly wild), peeled and finely chopped
- 1 litre vegetable or chicken stock, or even light fish stock
- 1 large potato, peeled and cut into cubes
- 1 large carrot, peeled and chopped
- Sea salt and freshly ground black pepper
- 2 tbsp crème fraîche
- A few drops of extra-virgin olive oil
- A few drops of Tabasco

Wearing rubber gloves, sort through the Nettles, discarding anything you don't like the look of and any thick stalks. Wash the Nettles and drain in a colander.

Melt the butter in a large saucepan, add the onion and cook gently for 5–7 minutes until softened. Add the stock, Nettles, potato and carrot. Bring to a simmer and cook gently until the potato is soft, about 15 minutes. Remove from the heat.

Using an electric hand-held stick blender, purée the soup and then season with salt and pepper to taste.

Ladle into warmed bowls and float a teaspoonful of crème fraîche on top. As this melts, swirl in a few drops of extra-virgin olive oil and Tabasco.

Hogweed tempura

There is something incongruous about this name, a bit like 'Winkles Beurre Meunière'. 'Hogweed in Batter' would be a little more straightforward but just doesn't sound the same and, of course, it isn't the same. Japanese tempura is on a higher plane than humble batter and once you have mastered the necessary oriental incantations is very easy to make.

Before you embark on those incantations do make sure to read the chapter on picking Hogweed shoots – it has some very dangerous look-alikes.

Serves 4
200ml lager or light beer
12–16 young Hogweed shoots
Sunflower oil, for deep-frying
50g plain flour
50g cornflour
½ tsp salt

For the dipping sauce
2 tbsp soy sauce
2 tbsp mirin (rice wine)
1 level tsp sesame seeds

Put the lager in the fridge (or in the freezer as long as you can trust yourself not to leave it there for longer than 30 minutes). Rinse the Hogweed shoots, drain and pat dry. Mix together the ingredients for the dipping sauce in a serving bowl.

Heat the oil in a suitable deep, heavy pan until it registers 180°C on a frying thermometer. Meanwhile, mix the flour, cornflour and salt together in a bowl and make a well in the middle. Just before the oil reaches the required temperature, pour the lager into the flour and mix to a batter *very quickly and leaving in lots of lumps*.

Immediately dip a batch of the Hogweed shoots into the batter, shaking off the excess and quickly lower them, one at a time, into the hot oil. The cooking time is very brief at only a minute, or possibly two for any thicker pieces.

Drain the cooked Hogweed pieces on kitchen paper to absorb the excess oil; keep hot. Use a slotted spoon to remove any stray bits of batter in the oil before cooking the next batch. Eat while hot, with the dipping sauce.

Wild stir-fry

This is a spring recipe for the purist – everything in it is wild. Well, everything except the oil. The only thing in this book that contains any quantity of oil is Hazelnut, but unless you have a three-ton oil press to hand, there is no sensible way of getting to it. I have come to terms with this small failing.

Rather than restricting the stir-fry to plants, I have introduced wild foods from my other River Cottage Handbooks: *Edible Seashore* and *Mushrooms*.

Serves 2
2 or 3 Bulrush shoots, washed
Handful of dulse, washed
Handful of Jelly Ears (if you can find some), cleaned
1 tbsp pepper dulse, washed
About 10 Crow Garlic bulbs, peeled
Handful of Sea Beet leaves or shoots
1 tbsp good-quality oil
2 tsp seawater

Remove the tougher outer leaves of the Bulrush shoots, then cut into 1cm lengths. Slice the dulse and the Jelly Ears into strips. Finely chop the pepper dulse and the Crow Garlic. The Sea Beet leaves or shoots should be left whole, unless they are particularly large.

Warm the oil with the seawater in a wok or large frying pan. Add the dulse, Crow Garlic and Jelly Ears, cover and simmer gently for 5 minutes. Remove the lid, add the remaining ingredients and turn up the heat. Stir-fry for 3 minutes, then serve in warmed bowls.

Wild Garlic parcels

Wild Garlic Parcels are a decidedly temperate-zone take on the Greek dolma – the stuffed vine leaves of many a sunshine holiday. This is a meaty version, but the sausage could easily be replaced with vegetables.

Serves 4

32 large young Wild Garlic leaves
100g arborio rice, cooked
250g sausagemeat (or black pudding, or a mixture of both)
200ml good chicken or vegetable stock
Sea salt and freshly ground black pepper

Preheat the oven to 190°C/Gas mark 5. Clean the Wild Garlic leaves, separate the stalks and chop these finely. In a bowl, mix the chopped garlic stalks with the rice, sausagemeat and some salt and pepper. Lay the Wild Garlic leaves shiny side down on a board, in pairs to form a cross. Place a teaspoonful of the rice mixture on the centre of the cross then, starting with the bottommost leaf, wrap them around to form little parcels. Turn the parcels over and place in a baking dish. Pour the stock over them, then cover with a lid or foil and bake for 45 minutes.

Wild Garlic pesto

Wild Garlic lends itself perfectly to a pesto and Pignuts make an excellent wild replacement for the familiar pine nuts.

Makes 1 small jar

50g Wild Garlic leaves, washed
30g Pignuts, sliced and briefly toasted in a little oil in a frying pan, then chopped
30g Parmesan cheese, freshly grated
80ml olive oil, plus extra to cover
Sea salt and freshly ground black pepper

The simplest method is to put everything except the oil in a food processor, blitz for a few seconds, then continue to whiz while slowly adding the olive oil through the funnel. I prefer to leave things a little coarser and take the traditional path of finely chopping the Wild Garlic leaves, then grinding them with the Pignuts, Parmesan and seasoning, using a large pestle and mortar, and adding the olive oil towards the end. Whichever you decide upon, transfer to a jar, pour sufficient olive oil on top to keep the pesto covered, close the lid and store it in the fridge. Under its layer of oil, the pesto will keep for several weeks.

Nettle ravioli

These look magnificent and will convince everyone of your wild foody credentials. Years ago, I watched my friend Rosanna, a Neapolitan mamma of classic proportions and character, rolling out pasta sheets and cutting tagliatelle with the expertise that came from a lifetime's experience. For mortals, a cheap pasta-making machine is a safer route to take. Making your own pasta with one of these is fun and not at all difficult, unless your machine has more personality than is good for it. The commonest type has little scrapers underneath the rollers designed to remove errant pieces of pasta that get stuck. Unfortunately these bend easily and the machine becomes bunged up with pasta. We are only allotted a certain amount of patience and mine ran out about twenty years ago, so I removed these useless pieces of metal with a pair of pliers. I haven't looked back. Apart from this necessary piece of engineering, the real key to keeping everything moving is to scatter flour about the place as though you are not the one who will have to clear it up later.

Serves 4

For the pasta
100g Stinging Nettle leaves
500g Italian '00' pasta flour
4 large eggs
½ tsp sea salt

For the filling
50g Stinging Nettle leaves
25g Pignuts, plus a little oil (or Hazelnuts or pine kernels)
25g Wild Garlic leaves (or an ordinary garlic clove)
1 egg
Sea salt and freshly ground black pepper

To serve
Melted butter, freshly grated Parmesan or Wild Garlic Pesto (p. 205)

Wash the Nettles (for the pasta and filling), simmer in a little water for 10 minutes, then drain thoroughly. For the pasta, take two-thirds of the Nettles and squeeze out as much water as you can, then chop them very, very finely, almost to a powder.

Heap the flour into a mound on a clean surface, make a well in the middle and add the eggs and salt. Start to mix to a dough, then add the Nettles and continue kneading until it is an even green colour. The dough should be quite firm; if it gets too sticky, sprinkle on a little flour; if too dry, knead in a little water. Wrap in cling film and refrigerate for 20 minutes.

Meanwhile, make the filling. Slice the Pignuts and briefly sauté in a little oil (or just chop other nuts). Chop the remaining (cooked) Nettles and the Wild Garlic (just crush ordinary garlic). In a bowl, mix the Nettles, Pignuts, Wild Garlic and egg together and season with salt and pepper to taste.

Roll out the pasta into thin sheets, using a pasta machine; keep the sheets covered with a very slightly damp tea-towel as you work, to prevent them drying out.

One sheet at a time, cut out rounds, using a 6cm pastry cutter. Spoon a little of the filling into the centre of half of the pasta discs and place another disc on top of each. Press firmly with a ravioli press (if you have one) or just press the edges together firmly and crimp with the handle of a knife. Keep covered while making the rest.

Bring a large pan of salted water to a rolling boil. Add the ravioli and cook at a fast boil until *al dente* (tender but firm to the bite), about 3–4 minutes. Drain thoroughly and serve on warmed plates, topped with melted butter or grated Parmesan or, best of all, with Wild Garlic Pesto.

Watercress omelette with cream cheese and smoked salmon

Despite looking uncannily like a certain variety of foam-rubber carpet underlay, this is a rather delicious soufflé omelette. The whisking and folding of the egg whites is a labour of love but it does make a lighter omelette. Just about everything could be changed if you want – the Watercress could easily be Chickweed, Fat Hen or several of the other wild greens in this book and the filling could be just about anything you fancy.

Makes 2 (each serves 1 generously or 2)
85g Watercress, washed
4 eggs, separated
2 tbsp crème fraîche
Sea salt and freshly ground black pepper
A little oil for cooking

For the filling
75g cream cheese
100g smoked salmon slices
Handful of Sorrel leaves, washed and shredded (optional)

Blitz the Watercress, egg yolks, crème fraîche and some salt and pepper together in a blender for a few seconds.

Beat the egg whites in a scrupulously clean bowl with a balloon whisk until they form soft peaks, then carefully fold into the Watercress mixture.

Heat a little oil in a medium frying pan and pour in half of the omelette mixture. Cook for a couple of minutes until set and golden brown underneath, then carefully transfer to a warmed plate. Repeat to cook the second omelette.

Top with the cream cheese and smoked salmon and sprinkle with shredded Sorrel if you have some to hand. Fold to enclose the filling and eat straight away.

RECIPES 209

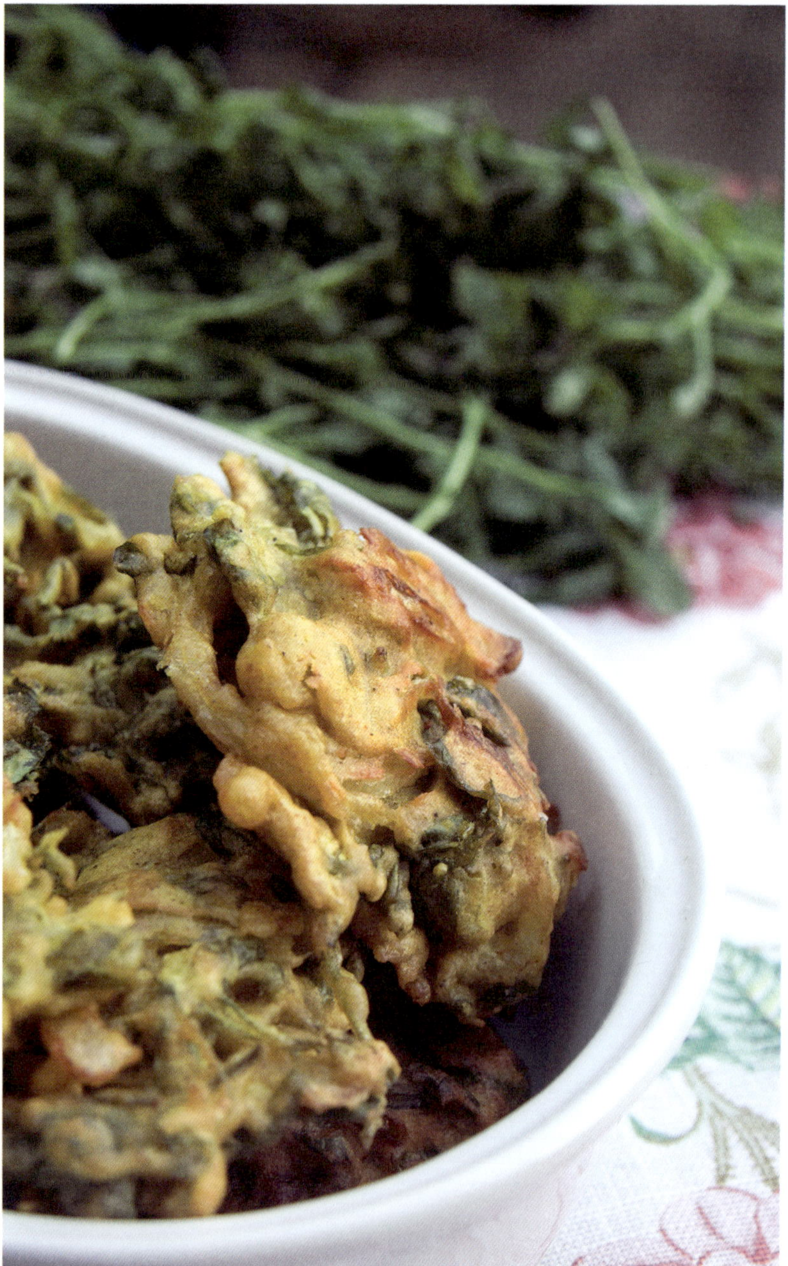

Chickweed pakoras

The slightly stringy nature of Chickweed can make it something of a trial in the kitchen and Pakoras are by far the best way to use it. This is a difficult recipe to get wrong – almost any quantities of the various ingredients will work – just make sure you use plenty of salt. The tablespoonful of medium-hot curry powder I suggest gives a mild flavour with a little warmth; if you like it hot then up the quantity or use a hotter powder. There may be purists who baulk at the idea of ready-made curry powder; if you are one, then feel free to use coriander, cumin, turmeric, chilli and so on – in whatever proportions you like.

Fat Hen, Sea Beet and several other green leaves in this book will work just as well in this incredibly quick, cheap and delicious recipe.

Makes 8

100g gram (chickpea) flour
1 tbsp medium curry powder, or to taste
½ tsp baking powder
½ tsp sea salt (or more)
About 120ml water

50g Chickweed, washed, dried and roughly chopped
10 Crow Garlic bulbs, or 1 small onion and 1 ordinary garlic clove, peeled and finely chopped
Vegetable oil for shallow-frying

Mix the flour, curry powder, baking powder and salt together in a bowl, then slowly stir in enough water to form a paste the consistency of mustard. Mix in the Chickweed and Crow Garlic and stir until they are well coated in the paste.

Heat a thin layer of oil in a heavy-based frying pan. When hot, spoon in heaped dessertspoonfuls of the pakora mixture to form little cakes, spacing them well apart. Cover with a lid and cook over a medium heat for about 5 minutes until crisp and golden brown on one side. Turn the cakes over to brown the other side. Drain on kitchen paper and serve at once.

Sorrel and Fat Hen tart

This is a substantial and delicious tart recipe, which allows for an endless variety of fillings. It would be particularly good with Sorrel and Hop tops.

Serves 6–8

For the pastry
200g plain flour
A pinch of salt
100g cold, unsalted butter, cut into small cubes
1 egg, separated
About 50ml cold milk

For the filling
A knob of unsalted butter
1 onion, peeled and finely sliced
30g Sorrel, washed
70g Fat Hen, Watercress or Stinging Nettles, washed
200g goat's cheese
3 eggs, plus 2 egg yolks
200ml double cream
Sea salt and freshly ground black pepper

To make the pastry, put the flour, salt and butter into a food processor and pulse until the mixture resembles breadcrumbs. Add the egg yolks and then, with the motor running, trickle in the milk through the funnel, stopping the moment the dough comes together. Tip on to a lightly floured surface and knead gently to make a smooth ball. Wrap in cling film and rest in the fridge for 30 minutes.

Preheat the oven to 170°C/Gas mark 3. Roll out the pastry on a lightly floured surface and use to line a 28cm loose-bottomed tart tin, allowing the excess pastry to overhang the rim of the tin. Rest in the fridge for 20 minutes.

Prick the pastry base with a fork. Line with a sheet of greaseproof paper and fill with baking beans or rice. Bake for 15 minutes, then remove the paper and beans and return to the oven for 10 minutes until the base looks dry and cooked. Lightly beat the egg white and brush all over the pastry to seal, then bake for a further 5 minutes until golden. Trim off the excess pastry from the edge with a small, sharp knife.

For the filling, heat the butter in a frying pan over a low heat, add the onion and fry very gently until soft and pale golden, about 15 minutes. Remove from the heat. Roughly chop the Sorrel and Fat Hen and wilt in a steamer for 2–3 minutes. Scatter the wilted greens and onions evenly in the pastry case, then crumble over the goat's cheese. Whisk together the whole eggs, egg yolks and cream with some salt and pepper and carefully pour over the filling.

Bake for 40 minutes until the filling is lightly set and browned. Serve warm or cold.

Juniper pot

The extremely rich nature of this unusual dish is cut back nicely by the Juniper berries and by the lactic acid in the crème fraîche. I am grateful to my friend Helle for passing on this Danish triumph. This is one of the few savoury dishes I know that contains neither onions nor garlic.

Serves 2
500g pork loin
8 Juniper berries (or more if you really love the flavour)
Leaves from 1 rosemary twig
20g butter
125ml single cream (or more if you like lots of sauce for your mash)
125ml crème fraîche
Sea salt and freshly ground black pepper

Trim any excess fat from the pork, then cut into small steaks. Crush the Juniper berries and rosemary using a pestle and mortar.

Heat the butter in a wide heavy-based saucepan. Add the meat and brown lightly on both sides. Stir in the cream, crème fraîche and some salt and pepper. Place the lid on the pan and cook on a very low heat (at a bare simmer) for 1 hour, stirring occasionally. If it appears too dry, then stir in a little more cream.

Serve with mashed potato or rice and a green vegetable.

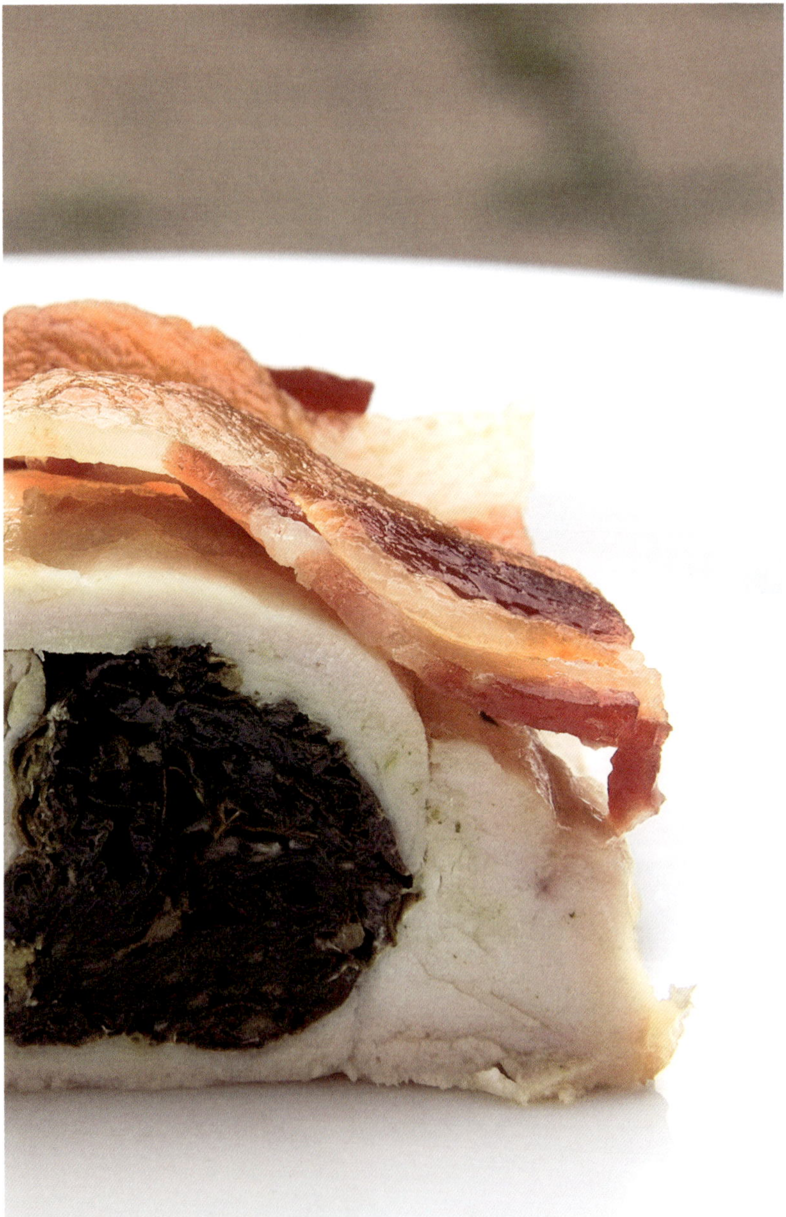

Hen chicken

Basing a recipe on word play is not necessarily a good idea but works quite nicely on this occasion. It is a pretty straightforward recipe with a reassuringly short list of ingredients – only the stuffing of the chicken breasts presents anything in the way of a challenge.

Serves 4

200g Fat Hen (or any other wild green vegetable that tastes good when cooked), washed
30g Wild Garlic leaves, washed
20g butter
4 large free-range chicken breasts, boned and skinned
100g streaky bacon rashers
300ml good-quality chicken stock
Sea salt and freshly ground black pepper

Preheat the oven to 190°C/Gas mark 5. Coarsely chop the Fat Hen and Wild Garlic. Sweat them together with the butter in a covered frying pan for 5 minutes, adding a splash of water to prevent sticking. Season with salt and pepper to taste. Allow to cool, then squeeze out excess water.

Here is the technical bit. A chicken breast is made up of two muscles – one large, one small. Carefully cut them apart. Take the larger piece, hold it flat on a board with the palm of your hand and, using a really sharp knife held horizontally, cut a pocket in the meat. Stuff the pocket with a quarter of the cooked greens, then place the smaller fillet over the gap. Wrap with a single layer of streaky bacon. Repeat for the other three breasts.

Lay the stuffed chicken breasts in a baking dish (with lid), season with salt and pepper and pour over the stock. Put the lid on and place in the oven. Cook for 20 minutes, basting at least twice, then remove the lid and continue to cook for a further 20–30 minutes depending on size, until the chicken is cooked right through and the bacon is slightly crisp.

Transfer the chicken breasts to warm plates and pour over the cooking juices. (If the stock is a little too thin, bubble vigorously to reduce before pouring over the chicken.) Serve with rice or new potatoes and a green vegetable.

Beef casserole with Horseradish and Chestnut dumplings

Horseradish is almost invariably used to make a sauce and is seldom cooked. The hot taste so appreciated with roast beef normally disappears during cooking, but the gentle and fairly brief cooking it receives here ensures a certain amount of bite is retained – but not too much. The Chestnuts add richness and sweetness, helping to make these the best dumplings I have ever tasted. The basic beef casserole is slightly stolen from Hugh's *River Cottage Meat Book*. I am sure he won't mind.

Serves 4
25g butter
250g onions, peeled and chopped
125g salt pork, pancetta or bacon off-cuts, cut into smaller chunks
750g boneless shin of beef or other stewing beef, cut into chunks
25g plain flour, sifted
500ml stout or beef stock (or any combination of the two)
2 bay leaves
1 tsp thyme leaves

For the dumplings
75g self-raising flour
25g Chestnut flour
A pinch of baking powder
50g freshly grated Horseradish
50g shredded suet
About 75ml water
Sea salt and freshly ground black pepper

Preheat the oven to 120°C/Gas mark ½. Heat the butter in a large frying pan. Add the onions with the pork or bacon and brown lightly, then transfer to a casserole dish with a slotted spoon, leaving the fat in the pan. Now brown the beef, in batches, in the pan. Once it is all browned, return the beef to the pan, sprinkle on the flour and stir to mix with and thicken the juices. Transfer the beef to the casserole dish.

Pour the stock/stout into the frying pan, stirring to mix with the sediment, then pour into the casserole dish. Add the herbs and some salt and pepper. Cover and cook in the oven for 2¾ hours if using shin, otherwise 2¼ hours, stirring occasionally. If necessary, add a little water halfway through cooking to keep the meat moist.

Meanwhile, make the dumplings. Mix the flours, baking powder, Horseradish and suet together in a bowl, then incorporate enough water to make a soft dough. Knead lightly and shape into balls, about 3cm in diameter.

Take out the casserole and sit the dumplings on top of the stew. Put the lid back on and return to the oven for a further 25 minutes or until the dumplings are cooked.

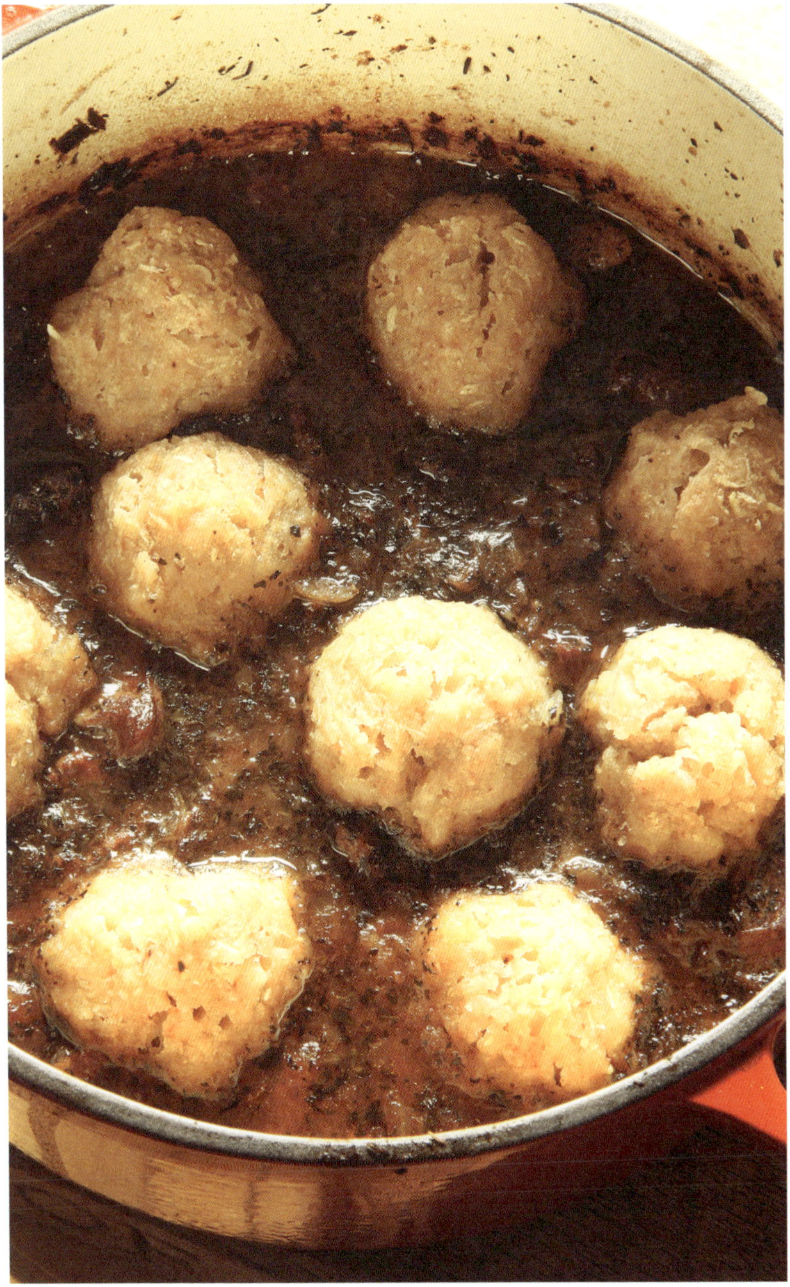

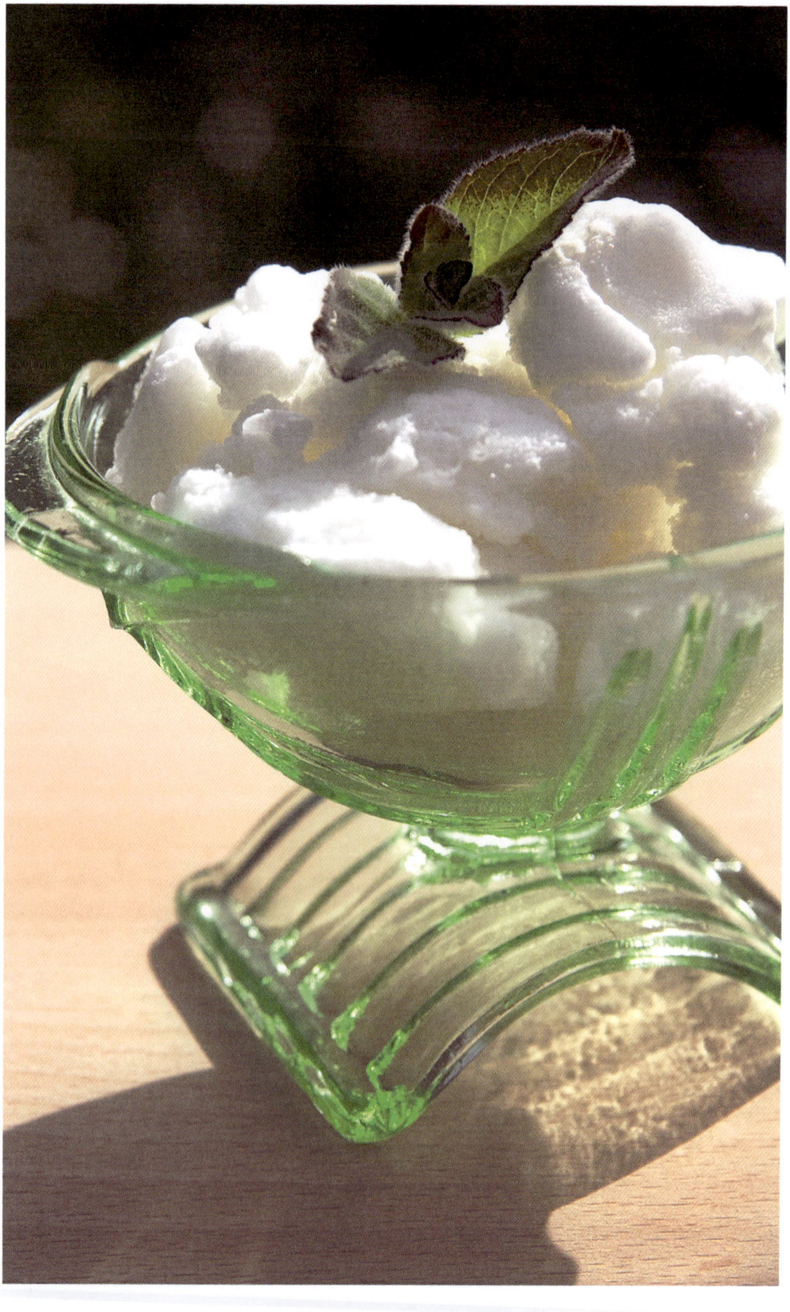

Watermint sorbet

This is one of the lightest and most refreshing desserts there is. Lemon sorbet is sometimes used to restore the palate between courses and this is even better. Interestingly – well, I think it's interesting – sometimes it comes out pale pink and sometimes pale green – it all seems to depend on the infusion temperature and when you add the lemon juice. Unfortunately I have never quite worked out the details and the colour always comes as a surprise.

The best alternative to Watermint is Elderflower, but it also works nicely with Japanese Rose or Spearmint.

Serves 6
650g caster sugar
800ml water
Juice of 4 lemons
Small handful (about 20g) Watermint, plus a few nice sprigs to finish

Put the sugar and water into a large saucepan and heat gently, stirring to dissolve the sugar, then add the lemon juice and Watermint. Set aside to cool, then pass the infused sugar syrup through a fine sieve to strain out the Watermint.

Churn the sugar syrup in an ice-cream machine until very thick, then transfer to the freezer to set firm (unless serving straight away). If you do not have an ice-cream maker, then put the mixture into a shallow container and place in the freezer until it is nearly frozen but still with some liquid. Take it out, crush into manageable chunks with the end of a rolling pin and whiz in a blender to break down the ice crystals, then return to the container and freeze. Do this a couple more times until a consistent, smooth sorbet is formed.

This dessert is certainly best served soon after making, but if you store it in the freezer for a while, take it out 10–15 minutes before serving to allow it to soften. Serve in glass dishes, topped with Watermint sprigs.

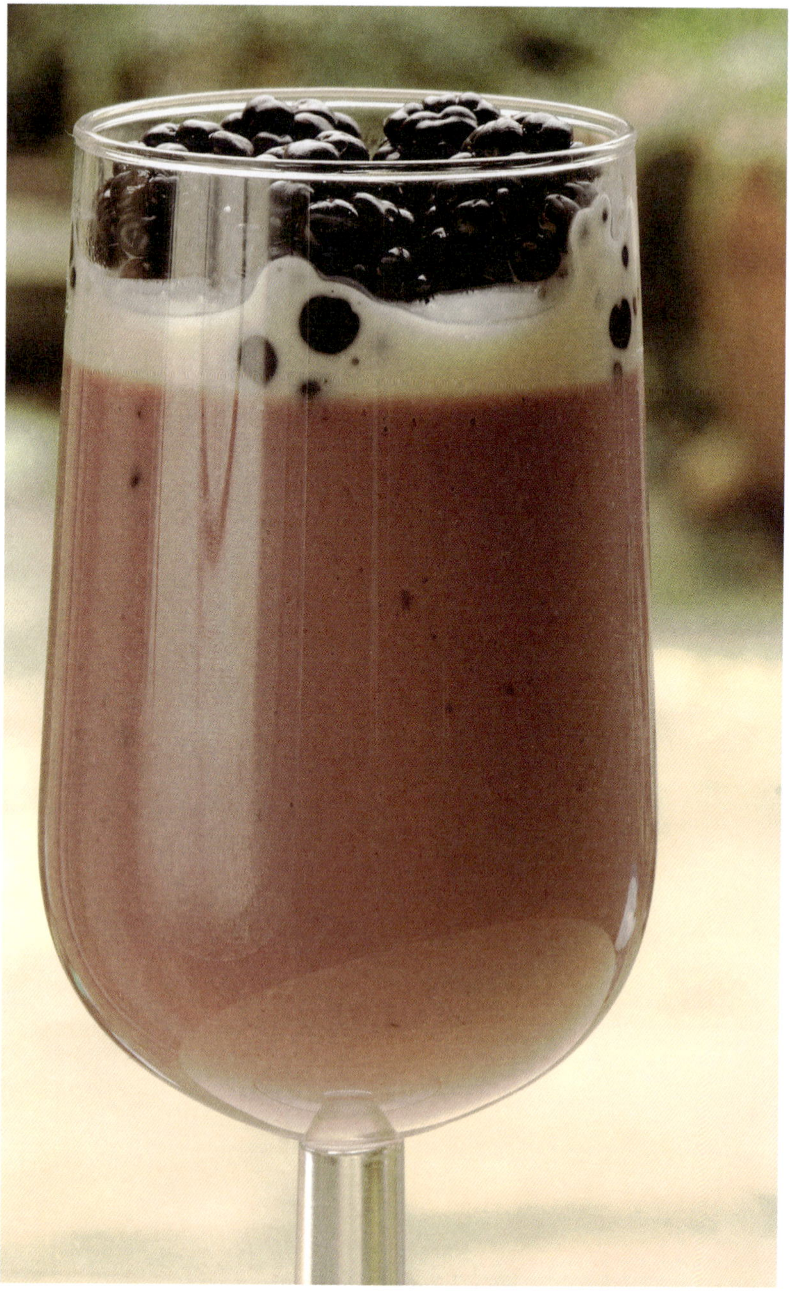

Bramble mousse

I am most grateful to my friend Pam Corbin for this substantial recipe. Blackberry picking is gruelling, exacting and dangerous work, so you deserve the best reward for your labours. Here it is.

Serves 4
500g Blackberries, washed
7g leaf gelatine
Juice of ½ lemon (omit if your Blackberries are strongly acidic)

3 large eggs
100g caster sugar
200ml double cream

Set aside 50g of the best Blackberries for serving. Put the rest into a saucepan, cover and cook gently for 5 minutes until softened. Meanwhile, soak the gelatine leaves in a shallow dish of cold water to soften.

Crush the cooked Blackberries in the saucepan using a potato masher, then pass through a sieve into a bowl, pressing with the back of a wooden spoon to extract as much juice as possible. If you want to get every last drop of juice out (and you should), squeeze the pulp left in the sieve in a muslin bag. Rinse out the saucepan.

Pour the Blackberry juice into the pan, add the lemon juice and heat gently until almost simmering, then take off the heat. Squeeze the gelatine leaves to remove excess water, then add them to the hot blackberry juice and stir until dissolved. Set aside to cool until tepid.

In a large bowl, whisk the eggs with the caster sugar until thick, pale and mousse-like. Continuing to whisk, slowly pour in the Blackberry juice, followed by 150ml of the cream.

Pour the mixture into glasses and place in the fridge for a couple of hours until set. Before serving, pour a little cream on top and decorate with the remaining berries.

Cranberry and apple tart

The Cranberries on this tart were hard won on a trip to a remote Scottish bog and I wanted to make the most of them. Thankfully Pam Corbin came up with a recipe that would show the berries in all their glory. If you cannot afford the time to wander hopefully around northern bogs then almost any autumn fruit will do. Bilberry is an obvious alternative, but Blackberries would look great too.

Serves 6

For the Hazelnut pastry
30g shelled Hazelnuts
175g plain flour
100g butter, cut into small cubes
50g caster sugar
1 egg, beaten

For the filling
500g cooking apples
25g butter
50ml water
50g sugar
50–75g Cranberries
8–10 Crab Apples
Juice of ½ lemon
Caster sugar for sprinkling

Preheat the oven to 200°C/Gas mark 6. Scatter the Hazelnuts on a baking tray and toast in the oven for about 5 minutes. Chop the nuts very finely or blitz in a food processor. Put the flour into a large bowl, add the butter and rub in until the mixture resembles fine breadcrumbs. Stir in the sugar and Hazelnuts. Finally, mix in the egg to form a smooth dough. Wrap in cling film and rest in the fridge for 30 minutes.

Peel, core and roughly chop the cooking apples and place them in a saucepan with the butter and water. Cover and cook gently until the apples are soft and fluffy. Stir in the sugar and half of the Cranberries (less if you do not have many).

Roll out the pastry on a lightly floured surface and use to line an 18–20cm flan tin. Prick the base lightly. Line the pastry case with greaseproof paper and baking beans or rice and bake for 15 minutes. Remove the paper and beans or rice and return the flan to the oven for 5 minutes to dry and cook the base. Let cool slightly.

Spread the apple and Cranberry filling in the pastry case. Finely slice the Crab Apples crossways, pushing the pips out to reveal a star-shaped pattern. Toss the slices in the lemon juice to stop them browning. Arrange the Crab Apple slices around the edge of the tart and sprinkle them with a little caster sugar. Return the tart to the oven for 15–20 minutes until the Crab Apple discs are cooked. Place the tin on a wire rack and allow to cool. Pile the remaining Cranberries in the centre of the tart to serve.

RECIPES 223

Rosehip babas with Blackberries

In the early 1970s I spent a few unsettling months living in the Tahiti Hotel in Aldershot. It was not a nice place to live. The kitchen facilities mercifully did not exist so I ate out every day in any one of Aldershot's many fine cafes. My diet consisted almost entirely of egg, sausage, chips and babas. Rum babas were popular at the time but have now fallen out of favour; perhaps it is the fabulous number of calories they provide. I would like to see them back, just for old times' sake.

Ideally, you need to get hold of the special baba tins, although mini flan dishes may just fit the bill.

Makes 6
7g sachet dried yeast
75ml warm milk
1 tbsp caster sugar
125g plain flour
2 large eggs
75g unsalted butter, softened

For the syrup
150ml home-made Rosehip Syrup (p.91)
100ml rum or brandy

To serve
200g Blackberries
150ml single cream

Mix the yeast, warm milk and sugar together in a large bowl and leave in a warm place for 15 minutes until it starts to froth. Butter six individual baba tins.

Add the flour and eggs to the yeast mixture and beat thoroughly with a spoon. Add the softened butter and continue to stir until you have a smooth mixture.

Half fill your baba tins with the mixture and leave the tins in a warm place until the mixture has risen to the top of the tins. Preheat the oven to 180°C/Gas mark 4.

Bake the babas for 20–25 minutes until golden. They are rather unforgiving when it comes to cooking times; the difference between undercooked and slightly burnt is about 2 minutes! Leave to cool a little on a wire rack, then carefully remove from their tins – not the easiest of manoeuvres, but using a thin plastic knife will help.

While the babas are still slightly warm, mix the Rosehip Syrup and rum or brandy together and pour over the babas. Fill with Blackberries and serve with cream.

RECIPES 225

Chestnut pancakes with Birch Sap Syrup

It is always good to have more than one wild foraged ingredient in a recipe and to put two distinctly woodland foods together is particularly satisfying. Of course you can substitute home-made Chestnut flour with a commercial one, or Birch Sap Syrup with imported maple syrup if you need to. This is one of the simplest recipes in the book, with the plain wheat flour of an ordinary pancake being replaced with Chestnut flour. The flavour is fairly intense and complex, and also quite sweet, so that only a small amount of syrup will be needed.

Before we start, here is an easy way to make Chestnut flour: Place the Chestnuts in a pan of cold water and bring to the boil. Cook gently for 10 minutes, or 15 minutes if they are large. Turn off the heat, but leave the Chestnuts in the hot water. Don a pair of rubber gloves. One at a time, remove the Chestnuts, cut into the pointed end on the flat side and start to peel the skin. Usually, both layers come away together.

Cool the peeled Chestnuts in the fridge, then grate them in a Mouli grater. Spread thinly on a non-stick baking tray and place in a very low oven (40°C), with the door slightly ajar, for an hour or until perfectly dry. Blitz the dried Chestnut flakes in a blender to a powder. The result will not be as fine as wheat flour but this does not matter, not a bit.

Serves 2
2 eggs
100g Chestnut flour
250ml milk

Sunflower or corn oil, for frying
Birch Sap Syrup (p.161) or Wild Flower Syrup (p.237)

Crack the eggs into a bowl, add the flour and mix to a paste. Slowly add the milk, stirring all the time to prevent it going lumpy. Alternatively (and much easier), put all three ingredients into the bowl at the same time and mix with an electric hand-held stick blender. Leave the batter to stand for an hour.

Heat a little oil in a small non-stick frying pan. Stir the pancake batter, then pour or spoon in enough to thinly cover the base of the pan or, if you want interesting shapes (like those in the picture), a little less.

When the top surface takes on a translucent appearance, turn the pancake over and cook the other side for a minute or two. Repeat with the rest of the batter. Serve immediately, with a small quantity of syrup trickled over.

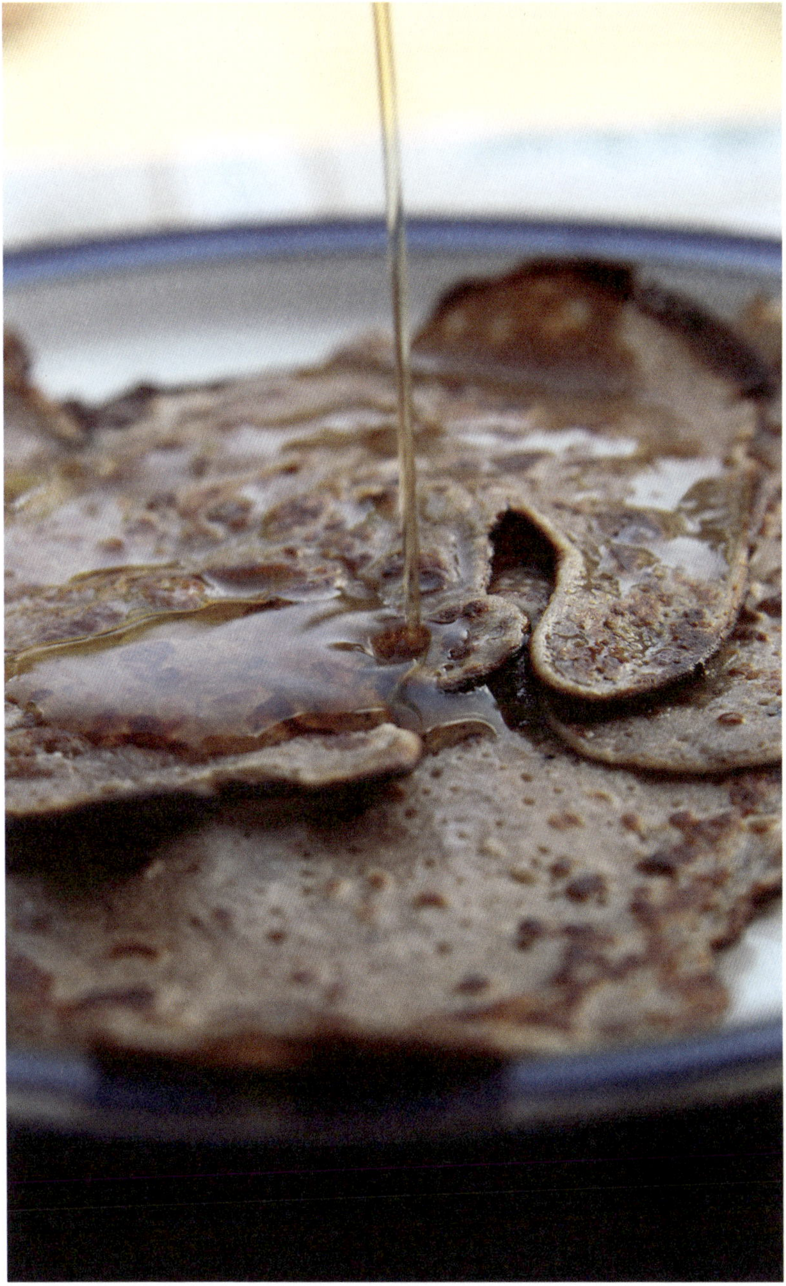

228 HEDGEROW

Chestnut Florentines

As you may have noticed I have become a bit of a Chestnut flour bore, insisting that everyone puts it into every conceivable recipe. Certainly if you want your sauces, cakes, dumplings or biscuits to be sweeter and richer there is no better way. Commercially bought Chestnut flour is very expensive, but the forager laughs at such things – his or her Chestnut flour costs nothing. To make it, see the recipe for Chestnut Pancakes (p.226).

Makes about 10

50g butter
50g caster sugar
50g honey
25g Chestnut flour
40g shelled Hazelnuts, coarsely crushed

2 tsp double cream
About 20 Rosehips, carefully seeded and coarsely chopped

To finish (optional)
About 40g dark chocolate

Preheat the oven to 170°C/Gas mark 3. Line a large baking tray with baking parchment.

Put the butter, sugar and honey in a small saucepan and heat gently until everything has melted. Turn off the heat and stir in the Chestnut flour, crushed Hazelnuts, cream and chopped Rosehips until evenly combined.

Using a dessertspoon, drop small mounds of the mixture on to the prepared baking tray, leaving plenty of space in between to allow for spreading. Bake in the oven for 8–10 minutes until golden. Leave the Florentines to firm up on the baking tray until almost cold, then carefully lift off on to a wire rack.

I think these are lovely just as they are, but if you like you can melt the chocolate in a bain-marie (or heatproof bowl over a pan of simmering water) and use to carefully coat the bottom of each Florentine; place them upside down on a wire rack to set. This can be a messy business, but there are worse things.

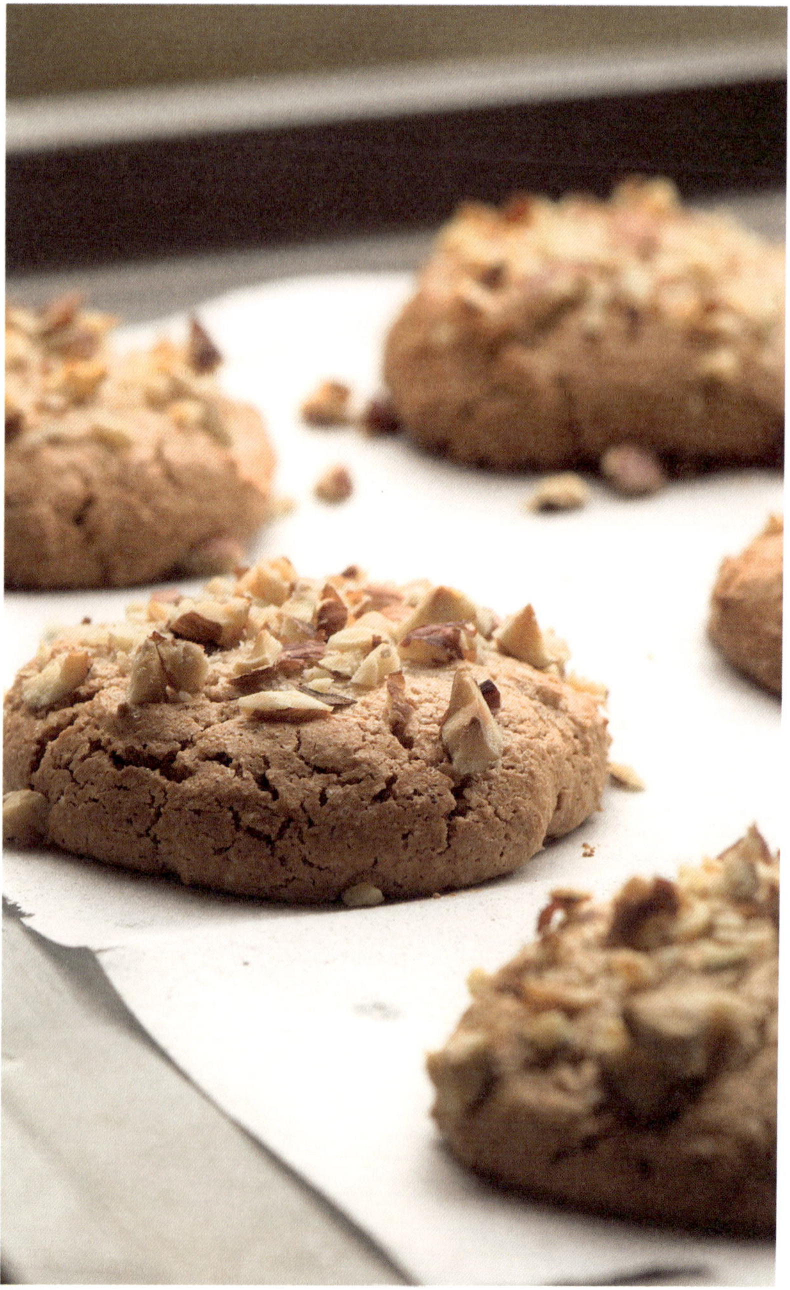

Chestnut macaroons

Chestnut flour can be a difficult ingredient in bread and cakes, refusing to allow them to rise in quite the way the cook would like. In this recipe, however, it behaves better than the ground almond it replaces, making perfectly formed macaroons every time.

Makes about 8

100g Chestnut flour (p.226)
20g rice flour
200g caster sugar

2 large egg whites
25g shelled Hazelnuts, coarsely chopped

Preheat the oven to 170°C/Gas mark 3. Line a large baking tray with rice paper (which is usually made from potatoes, by the way).

Mix the Chestnut flour, rice flour and sugar together in a bowl. Beat the egg white lightly (don't worry if it is not perfectly frothy) and stir into the mixture.

Drop heaped dessertspoonfuls of the mixture on to the prepared baking tray, spacing them well apart. Sprinkle the chopped Hazelnuts on top. Bake in the oven for 20–25 minutes until golden brown.

Leave the Chestnut Macaroons on the baking tray for a few minutes to firm up, then transfer to a wire rack to cool.

Elderflower delight

I seriously considered leaving this recipe out of the book, not because there is anything wrong with it, but because I didn't really want you to have it. My generous good nature has won through, however, so here it is. While I would maintain that this is the best hedgerow delight imaginable, the Elderflowers could easily be replaced with Japanese Rose petals. A further possibility would be to use Rosehip Syrup (p.91) to make Turkish delight, adjusting the sugar and water amounts accordingly.

Makes about 60 cubes
20g leaf gelatine
20 Elderflower sprays
700g granulated sugar
Juice of 2 lemons

400ml water
130g cornflour
30g icing sugar

Soak the gelatine in a shallow dish of cold water to soften. Strip the Elderflower blossom from the stems with a fork and tie them in a piece of muslin to form a bag, leaving a length of string. Put the granulated sugar, lemon juice and 300ml water in a heavy-based saucepan, heat gently until the sugar is dissolved, then leave to cool.

In a bowl, mix 100g of the cornflour with the remaining 100ml water until smooth, then stir into the lemon sugar syrup. Return the saucepan to a low heat. Squeeze the gelatine to remove excess water, then add to the mixture and stir with a balloon whisk until the gelatine has dissolved.

Bring the mixture very slowly to the boil and simmer for 10 minutes, stirring almost continuously to prevent the mixture sticking and any volcanic build-up of steam. Suspend the muslin bag of Elderflowers in the mixture and simmer, still stirring, for a further 15 minutes, giving the muslin bag an occasional squeeze with the back of the spoon to release the Elderflower fragrance. The mixture will gradually clarify and become extremely gloopy. When ready, leave to cool for 10 minutes.

Mix the remaining 30g cornflour with the icing sugar. Line a shallow baking tin, about 20cm square, with baking parchment and dust with a heaped tablespoonful of the icing sugar and cornflour mixture. Remove the muslin bag from the gloopy mixture, then pour it into the baking tin and place in a cool place (but not the fridge) to set. Now refrigerate for a few hours until it becomes rubbery.

Cut the Elderflower Delight into cubes with a knife or scissors and dust with the remaining icing sugar and cornflour.

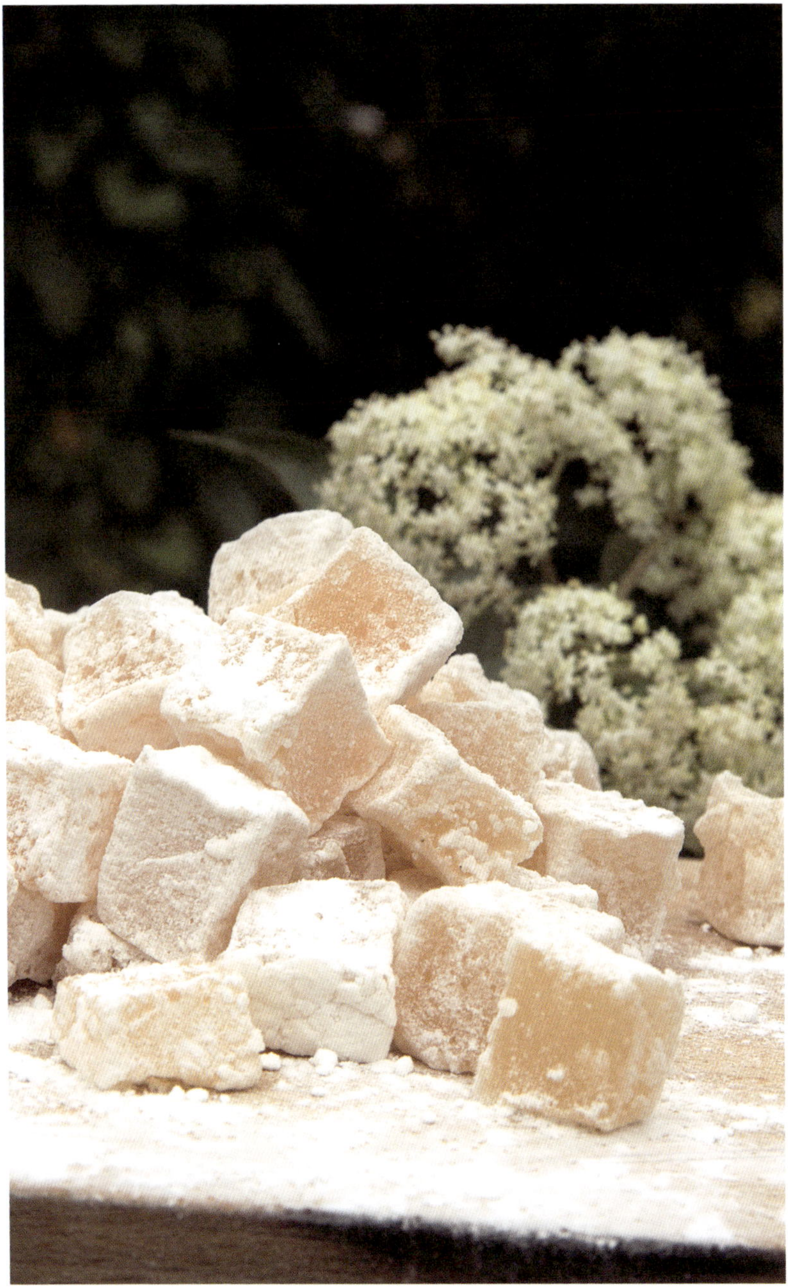

Juniper toffee

During a visit to the Falkland Islands in 1762 a traveller, one Antoine-Joseph Pernety, spent a pleasant afternoon conversing in Latin with an unnamed friar at the local monastery. The friar helpfully passed on a large number of extraordinary remedies of the 'Take thirty-one live crayfish, caught when the moon is in Cancer' variety. Among them is a cure for 'malignant fevers', which entailed binding a live tench to each of the patient's feet for 12 hours; one for colic where the sufferer held the root of a sunflower under the armpit; and, most entertaining of all, sticking the short and curly hair of someone of the opposite sex up your nose to stop it bleeding. There are far, far worse, but I will spare you.

The one recipe which might just work – and the inspiration for my Juniper Toffee – is for '*A moift Afthma, Colds, and Diforders of the Breaft*'. A pound of crushed Juniper berries is simmered in a pound of unsalted butter for half an hour, then the berries are strained out and discarded. An equal weight of best honey is added to the remaining infused butter and the mixture put on '*an exceeding low fire till it has gained the consistency of syrup*'. My version of the recipe uses less overpowering quantities of honey and berry and makes a set toffee, not a syrup. And the flavour? Well, I absolutely love it – halfway between an English toffee and a pine wardrobe. You will need a good cooking thermometer.

Makes 1 tray

8g (about 80) Juniper berries
100g unsalted butter
350g granulated sugar
100g honey
½ tsp cream of tartar
A pinch of salt
150ml water

Lightly butter a shallow baking tin, about 30cm square. Crush the Juniper berries and tie them in a piece of muslin to form a bag, leaving a length of string. Set aside.

Combine all the other ingredients in a heavy-based saucepan. Place over a low heat and stir frequently until the mixture comes to the boil. Turn the heat right down and hang the muslin bag over the side of the pan so it is suspended in the mixture. Continue to simmer, stirring gently and giving the bag of berries a squeeze with the spoon every minute or two. The toffee is ready when the temperature registers 137°C on a cooking thermometer, about 25 minutes after the start of cooking.

Remove the pan from the heat and put the lid on for a couple of minutes so that a little steam builds up inside (to dissolve the sugar crystals that have formed on the sides). Take off the lid and stir the toffee very gently for a few minutes as it cools a little, then pour into the prepared baking tray. Leave until set but still slightly warm. Remove from the tray (not always that easy), lay on a flat surface and score with a knife or pizza cutter into squares. Cover loosely with greaseproof paper and leave until set. When the toffee is quite cold, break it into pieces.

P.S. Toffee-making is something of a black art and there are several things that can go wrong. One of the worst problems is the butter separating out, but the pinch of salt and stirring after removal from the heat help a lot. If sugar crystals from the side of the pan make it into the finished toffee they can crystallise the whole batch (like Kurt Vonnegut's fictional *Ice Nine* does to water).

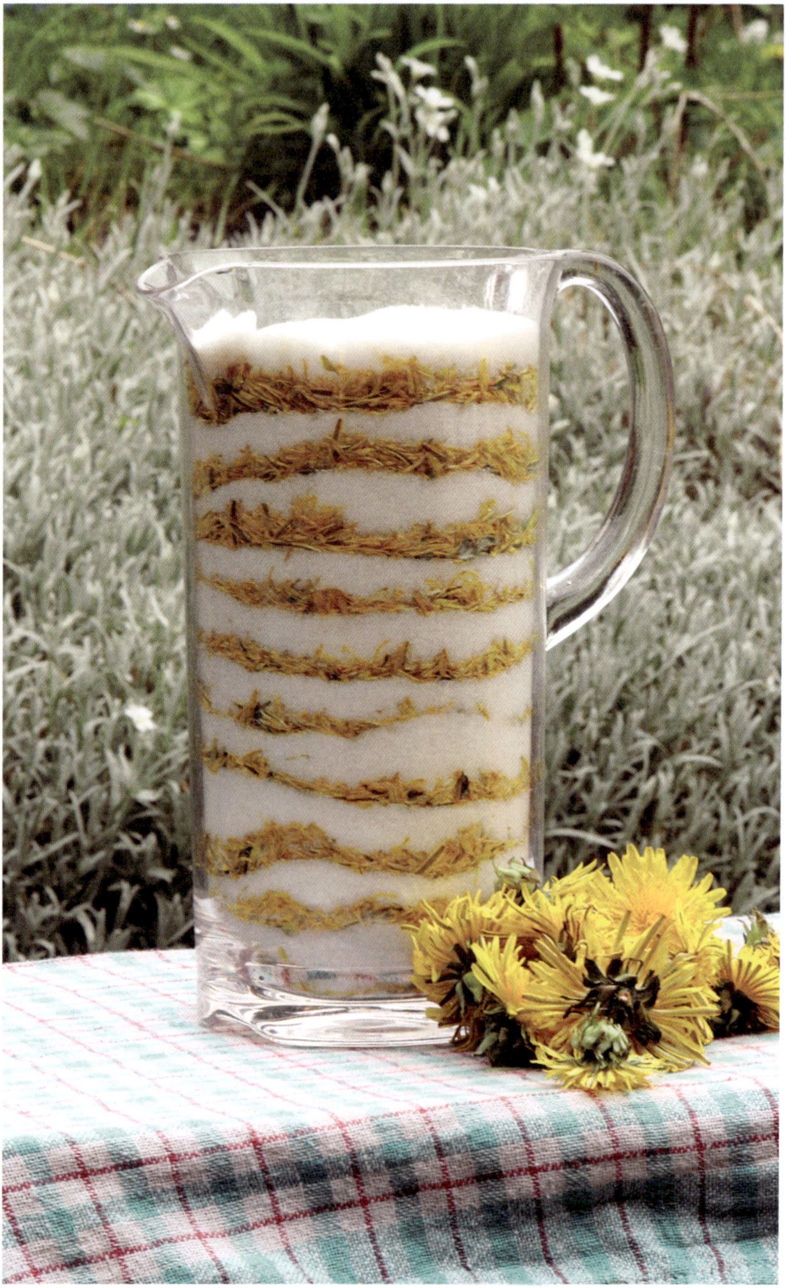

Wild flower syrup

The heady smells of May blossom – Japanese Rose, Elderflower, Hawthorn and even Dandelion – pack quite a punch, but capturing them is not that easy. Dried petals retain but a faint echo of their former glory, but syrups leave much of the perfume intact. Syrups can be used in several ways – on pancakes and ice creams, in drink mixes, or as a replacement for sugar in cakes and desserts. To make a syrup that will keep, you need to maintain a sugar concentration above 65 per cent. Boiling up blossoms in a strong sugar solution would quickly destroy the delicate aromas, but this way is gentle, if sticky.

Makes about 1 litre
Lots of freshly picked blossoms (about a litre)
About 1kg granulated sugar
About 550ml boiling water

Put a 2cm layer of blossoms in the bottom of a large jug, minimum 2 litres capacity. Pack the blossoms down, then sprinkle on a 1cm layer of sugar – don't worry if things all get mixed up. Continue these alternate layers of sugar and blossoms until the jug is full, keeping a note of the amount of sugar used. Cover the jug and leave to stand for 24 hours.

Empty the mixture into a saucepan and pour on 55ml of boiling water for every 100g sugar used. Heat the mixture gently, stirring, until the sugar has dissolved, then strain into a clean jug.

Pour any syrup that you are not using straight away into sterilised bottles and seal. Stored in a cool, dark cupboard, it will keep for up to a year.

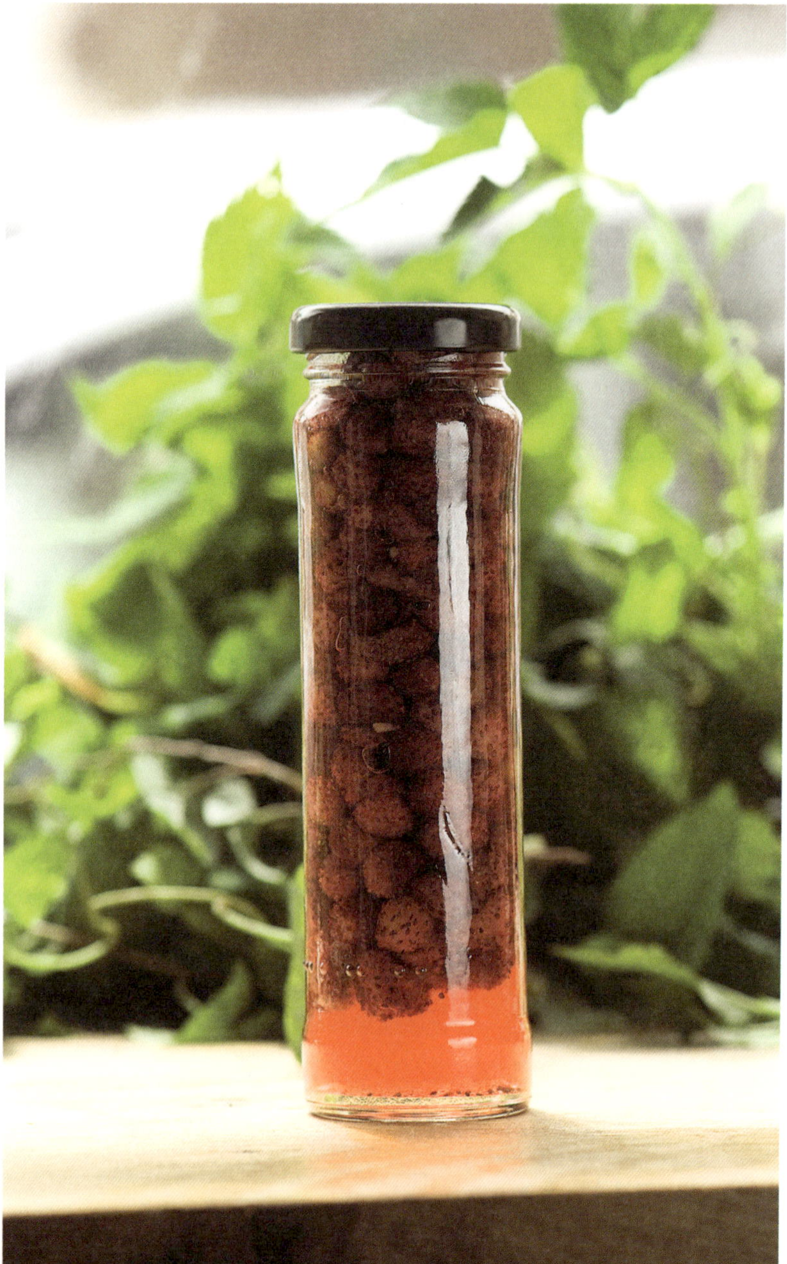

Wild Strawberries
in brandy syrup

In the unlikely event that you find more Wild Strawberries than you can possibly eat fresh, it is nice to use some to make what is effectively a rumtopf. This is a powerful thing to eat on its own but goes wonderfully well with ice cream or better still, panna cotta, such as the one in my *Edible Seashore* Handbook.

Makes 1 jar
Wild Strawberries (as many as you can spare)
An equal weight of granulated sugar
Brandy

Place alternate layers of Strawberries and sugar in a sterilised jar until you reach the top. Now pour in brandy, so that the jar is brimming. You will need to have a more or less equal weight of Strawberries and sugar in the jar (though quite how you ensure this I will have to leave to you as an exercise).

Screw the lid on, shake so that any bubbles float to the top, then unscrew the lid and top up again with brandy. Gently shake occasionally and eat within a couple of months. This recipe works with any other soft wild fruit.

Dandelion jelly marmalade

This refreshing springtime marmalade is very easy to make, provided you use a good quality, sharp and unfiltered (cloudy) apple juice and jam sugar (sugar with added pectin). The colour is a lovely golden and the apple juice takes on a pleasant bitterness from the Dandelion petals.

Makes about 5 jars

1 litre good-quality sharp, fresh apple juice (do not use juice from concentrates)
80g Dandelion petals, (snip them off with scissors)
100ml freshly squeezed lemon juice (2–3 lemons)
750g jam sugar (i.e. sugar with added pectin)

Pour the apple juice into a saucepan and stir in 60g of the Dandelion petals. Bring to simmering point and remove from the heat. Cover and leave to infuse overnight.

The following day, strain the juice through a sieve to remove the petals (they will have discoloured slightly). Return the juice to the pan, add the lemon juice and heat slowly to boiling point. Add the sugar and stir until dissolved, then add the remaining dandelion petals. Increase the heat and boil rapidly for 6–7 minutes or until setting point is reached (see below).

Remove from the heat and skim the surface with a slotted spoon to remove any scum. Pour into warm sterilised jam jars, cover and seal. If you find the Dandelion petals are floating to the surface, leave until the jelly is at room temperature and then give the jar a sharp shake. You will find the petals distribute evenly throughout the setting jelly.

P.S. To test for setting, put a teaspoonful of the marmalade on to a chilled saucer. Leave for about a minute, then push the surface with your finger – if it wrinkles and the marmalade appears to be setting it is ready.

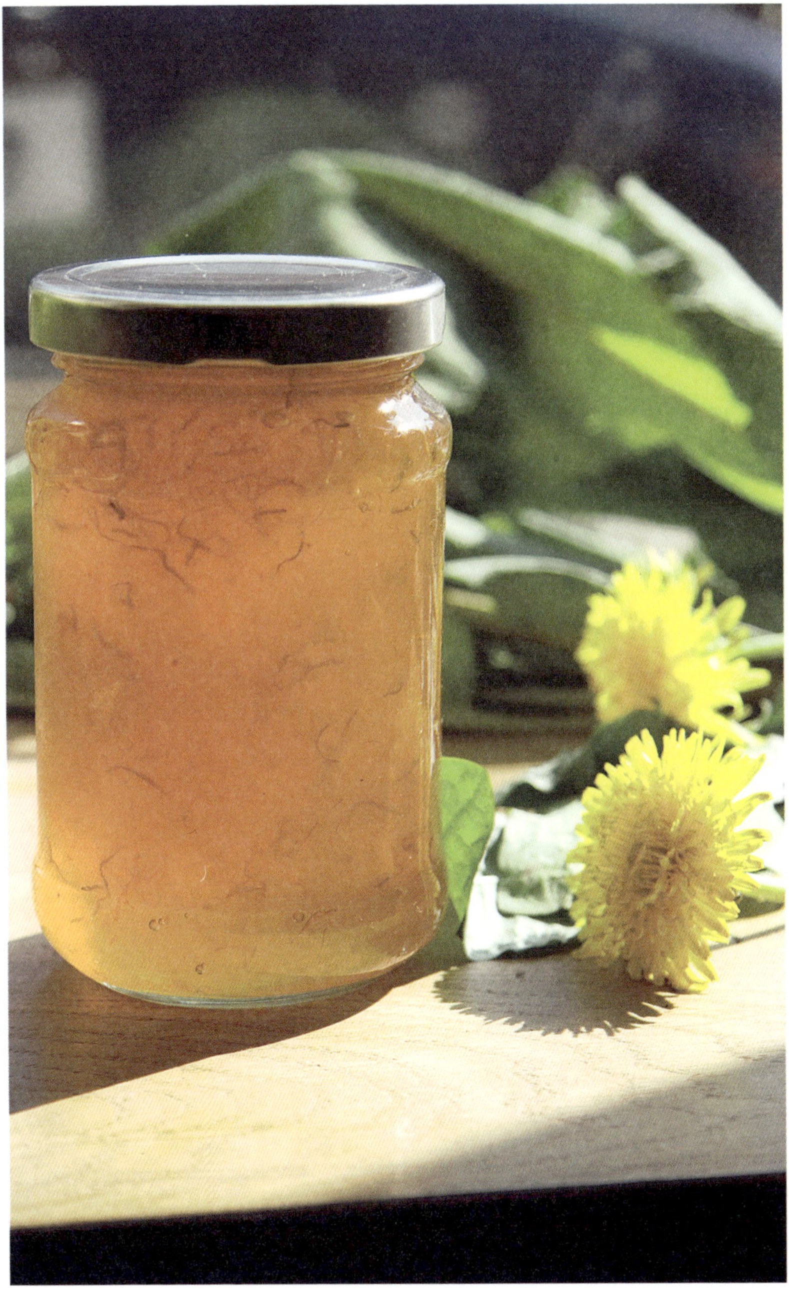

Rose jelly

The gentle native species are too light of fragrance to make this jelly so I always use the potent and heady Japanese Rose. There are many ways to do it, but this is the simplest and quickest I know. As with Dandelion Marmalade I'm using the answer to a maiden jam-maker's prayer – pectinised jam sugar – so you will not have any trouble with the set. I like Rose Jelly with a lot of flavour, so I use a lot of petals and you can up the flavour even more if you like, by hanging a muslin bag of fresh petals over the side of the pan during the last minute of cooking. Bit sticky though. And don't set fire to the muslin.

You could use Elderflowers in the same way and make Elderflower Jelly.

Makes 2 small jars
250ml water
250ml Japanese Rose petals
  (gently pressed down)
350g jam sugar (i.e. sugar with
  added pectin)
Juice of ½ lemon

Pour the water into a medium saucepan and bring to the boil. Take off the heat and stir in the petals. Pour into a bowl, cover and leave for an hour at least, or overnight if you have the time.

Strain the liquid through a fine sieve back into your pan and place over a low heat. Add the sugar and stir to dissolve, then add the lemon juice and bring to a scary, fast boil. Keep this rolling boil going for 4 minutes, then take the pan off the heat.

Allow the mixture a couple of minutes to calm down, then pour into hot sterilised jam jars, filling them to the brim before screwing on the lid.

Elderflower cordial

I have a bad habit of putting off my annual Elderflower Cordial production until mid-July and have to roam around for hours, picking a spray here and a spray there. Had I started in early June I could have picked the lot from any two trees and in a fraction of the time.

This is the best of the hedgerow soft drinks, its heady perfume an essential accompaniment to summer picnics. You should easily be able to make enough to last you the whole year, but this will be in vain if your cordial starts to go mouldy by August. There are two ways to stop this small catastrophe:

The first is to put your cordial into swing-top bottles, place the full bottles, upright, stoppers in place, into a large pan of water, carefully cover the bottle with a tea-towel to keep the hot water vapour in, and heat to about 80°C for 30 minutes. It is worth putting an old tea-towel in the saucepan first to prevent the base of the bottles overheating.

The second, much easier method is to add a Campden tablet for every 4 or 5 litres of cordial you make. The tablet should be ground up and mixed with a little water before stirring into the cordial. Campden tablets contain the preservative sulphur dioxide, which some people cannot tolerate. However, the concentration after the cordial has been diluted is tiny and considerably less than that found in many wines.

The following recipe uses a fairly high proportion of sugar, so it should last several months without either of the above treatments.

Makes about 1.8 litres
3 unwaxed lemons
Blossoms from 30 Elderflower heads, removed from the stems with a fork
1.3 litres water
2kg granulated sugar
75g citric acid – or tartaric acid, which is a little less sharp

Cut the zest from the lemons and squeeze the juice. Put both into a large bowl and add the Elderflowers. Bring the water to the boil in a saucepan, turn off the heat and add the sugar, stirring until dissolved. Allow to cool for 10 minutes.

Pour the warm syrup over the lemon and Elderflowers and stir in the citric or tartaric acid. If you wish to use Camden tablets add half a tablet now. Cover and leave for 24 hours. Stir, then strain through a sieve lined with a sterilised muslin cloth into sterilised bottles.

Useful Things

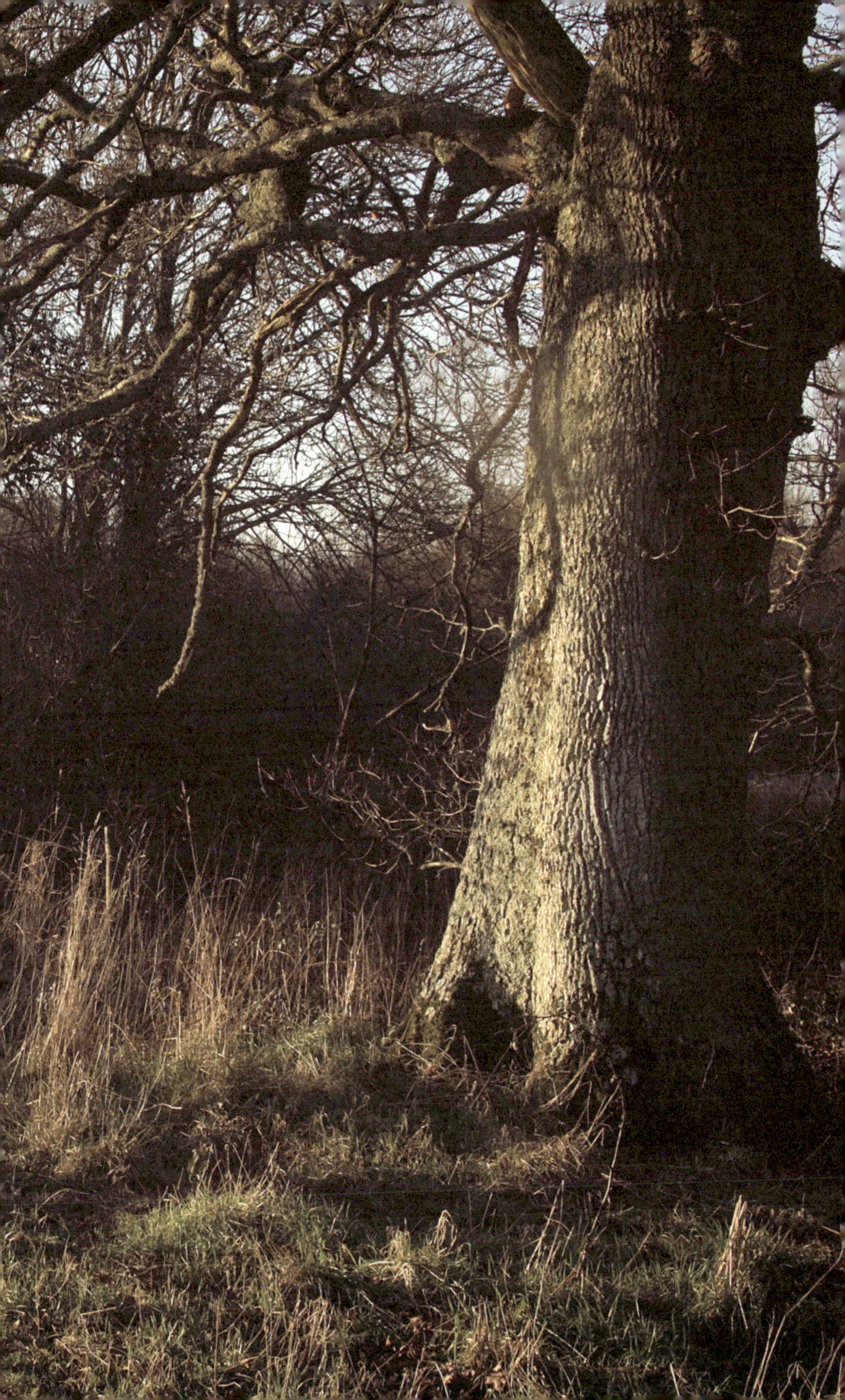

Glossary

Alternate: Leaflets on opposite sides of a central leaf stem but in staggered positions. Compare the term 'opposite' (below).

Annual: A plant which lives for less than a year.

Axial: Arranged around a stem.

Basal: At the base of a plant – normally referring to leaves.

Biennial: A plant which grows for a year and produce flowers and fruit in the second year. Sometimes it may take three years to fruit.

Bract: A modified leaf around a flower or fruit.

Composite: A flower made up of many tiny flowers, like a daisy or dandelion.

Compound: A leaf made up of leaflets.

Leaflet: The divisions of a compound leaf.

Lobed: Divided into rounded sections.

Terminal: At the end or apex – normally of a compound leaf or a flower.

Opposite: Leaflets on opposite sides of a central leaf stem in matched pairs. Compare the term 'alternate' (above).

Perennial: A plant that lives for an indefinite length of time, but longer than one year. May flower and fruit many times.

Pinnate: A compound leaf with leaflets immediately opposite one another.

Trefoil: A leaf in three parts.

Terminal leaf

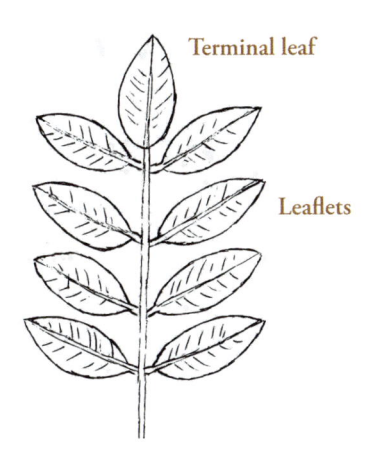

Leaflets

A compound leaf with opposite leaflets

A compound leaf with alternate leaflets

Bract

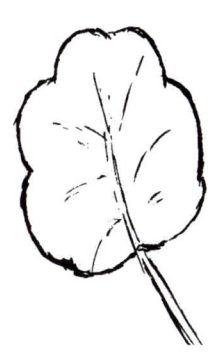

Shallowly lobed leaf

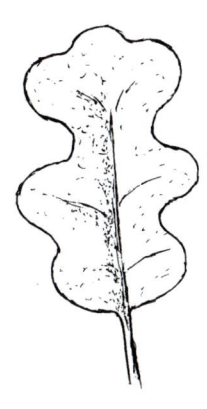

Lobed leaf

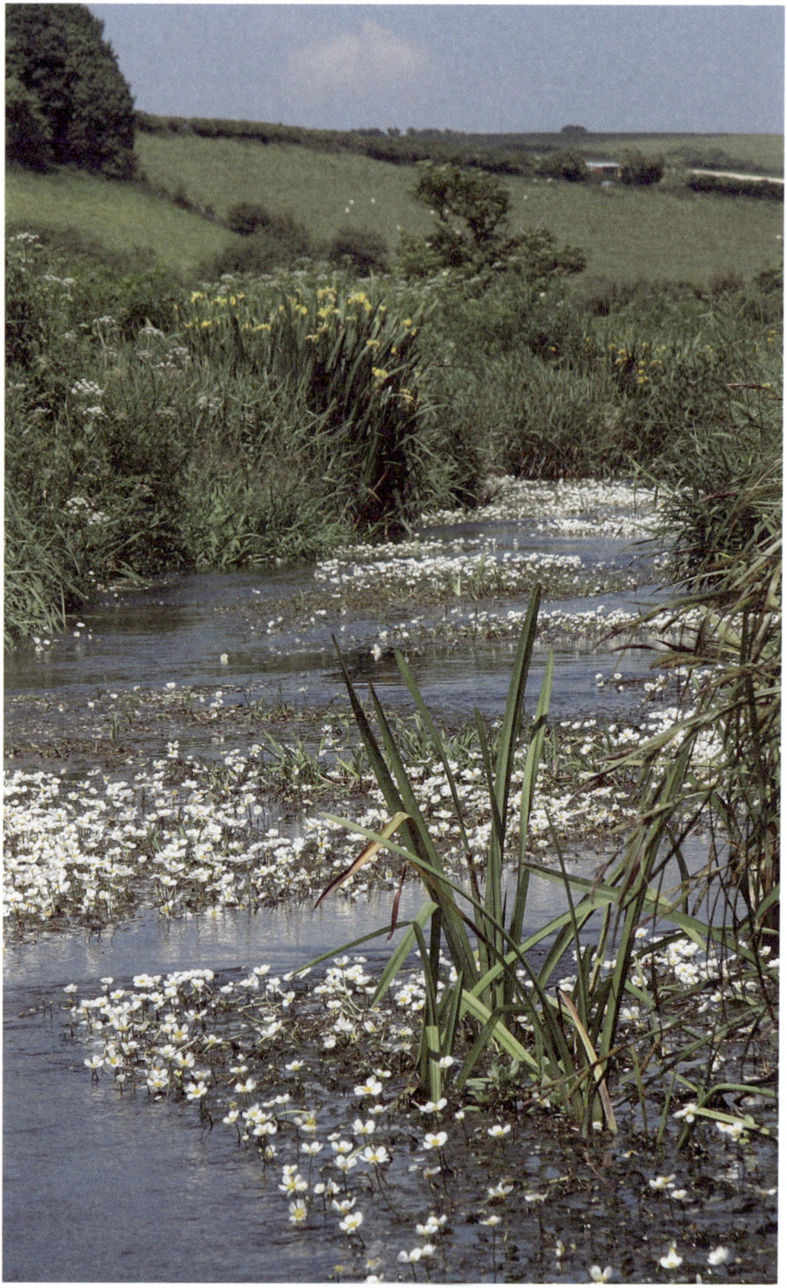

Directory

Conservation:

The four main government conservation bodies of the UK are:

Natural England
0845 600 3078
www.naturalengland.org.uk

Scottish Natural Heritage
01463 725000
www.snh.org.uk

Council for Nature Conservation and the Countryside (Northern Ireland)
02890 254835
www.cnccni.gov.uk

Countryside Council for Wales
0845 1306229
www.ccw.gov.uk

These organisations come under one unifying body:

Joint Nature Conservation Committee (JNCC)
01733 562626
www.jncc.gov.uk

Access to the countryside:

Access and several other matters of interest to the forager come under:

Department for Environment, Food and Rural Affairs (DEFRA)
0845 933 55 77
www.defra.gov.uk

The Ramblers
Defends and extends countryside access.
020 7339 8500
www.ramblers.org.uk

Societies:

Botanical Society of the British Isles
www.bsbi.org.uk

Useful reference books:

The Wild Flower Key: How to identify wild plants, trees and shrubs in Britain and Ireland (Revised Edition)
by Francis Rose and Clare O'Reilly
(Frederick Warne Publishers, 2006)

Food for Free
by Richard Mabey
(Collins new edition, 2007)

The River Cottage Preserves Handbook
by Pam Corbin (Bloomsbury, 2008)

The River Cottage Edible Seashore Handbook
by John Wright (Bloomsbury, 2009)

The River Cottage Mushroom Handbook
by John Wright (Bloomsbury, 2006)

My own website, which deals with many foraging matters is:
www.wild-food.net

For more information on identifying plants and a few extra species and recipes:
www.rivercottage.net/foraging

Acknowledgements

This is a thank you to the charming, accommodating and supremely knowledgeable people who have helped me with this book.

There are two people in particular without whom I would have thrown in the towel before I started. Bryan Edwards is the most accomplished naturalist I have ever met. I have enjoyed our many plant-hunting walks and thank him for his unflagging patience in answering my constant question: 'So what's this one called, Bryan?' The recipe section, and much else besides, owes a very great deal to my good friend Pam Corbin. Her culinary talents are legendary and I am ever thankful for the advice that she has selflessly given me.

My thanks go to Steve Alton for checking my assertions on natural history (and for finding some real howlers), to John Cockrill for his help with matters medical, to Mike Gardner for imparting his knowledge of genetics, and to Luke Hindmarsh for helping us all stay out of the magistrates' court. My thanks also to the allotment holders of Maiden Newton, for not calling the police.

My many friends at Bloomsbury have been ever helpful, ever tolerant. Many thanks to Richard Atkinson for wielding the red pen so accurately and, I am afraid, so needfully. Also to Will Webb for his sterling work on the layouts and to Janet Illsley for accomplishing her difficult task of fixing my many errors and ensuring it all looks good and makes some kind of sense. I am particularly grateful to Natalie Hunt for her steady editorial hand and for being so kind to me.

Thank you to Gordon Wise for his continuing support. Also to Rob Love and Antony Topping for having faith in my abilities and, of course, to Hugh for his terrific introduction and for inspiring me – and a whole generation.

Index

Page numbers in *italic* refer to the illustrations

access 25–8
Achillea millefolium 141, *141*
Aegopodium podagraria 100–1, *101*
Aethusa cynapium 176, *177*
Alexanders 171–2
Alliaria petiolata 42–3, *43*
Allium
   A. ursinum 144–6, *145*
   A. vineale 142–3, *143*
allotments 11–12
Alma-Tadema, Sir Lawrence 165
alternate leaflets 246, *247*
Anderson, William 81
Annual Mercury *178*, 179–80
annuals 246
Apium nodiflorum 47
apple juice
   Dandelion jelly marmalade 240, *241*
apples *see* Crab Apple
Armoracia rusticana 44–6, *45*, *46*
Artemisia absinthium 116
Arum maculatum 110, 191–3, *191–3*
Atriplex
   A. glabriuscular 60
   A. laciniata 60
   A. patula 60
   A. prostrata 60–1, *61*
Atropa belladonna 183, 186
Autumn Crocus 146
axial 246

bacon
   Hen chicken *214*, 215
Bacon, Francis 173
balsam, Himalayan 22
Barbarea 36
basal 246
Beech 16–17, 74
beef casserole with Horseradish and Chestnut dumplings 216, *217*
beer
   Hogweed tempura 202
berries
   berry-pickers 13–15, *14*
   poisonous 33
   see also individual types of berry
Betula
   B. pendula 158, 159–61, *160*
   B. pubescens 161
biennials 246
Bilberry 13, 16–17, 66, *124*, 125
biodiversity 22
Birch
   Downy 161
   Silver 18–19, *158*, 159–61, *160*
   Birch Sap syrup 161
      Chestnut pancakes with Birch sap syrup 226, *227*
birds 24
biscuits
   Chestnut Florentines *228*, 229
   Chestnut macaroons *230*, 231
bistort 32
Bittercress
   Hairy 16–17, 28, 38, *39*, 63
   Large 38
   Wood 38
'Black Drop' 71
Blackberry 12, 16–17, 22, 25, 28, 29, 66–8, *67*, 137
   Bramble mousse *220*, 221
   Rosehip babas with Blackberries 224, *225*
Blackthorn 18–19, *80*, 81–2
bogs 13
Borage 16–17, 64
Boyle, Robert 17
bracts 246, *247*
Bramble 64
   Bramble mousse *220*, 221
brandy
   Wild Cherry brandy 84
   Wild Strawberries in brandy syrup *238*, 239
Brassica nigra 40–1, *41*
'bread and cheese' 73–4
Brooklime 16–17, 32, 128, *129*
Broom 16–17, 64, *65*
   Spanish 64
Bryonia dioica 194, 195
Bryony
   Black 115, *194*, 195
   White 115, *194*, 195
Bullace 138
Bulrush 16–17, 162–5, *163*, *164*
   wild stir-fry 203
burdock 28
Butler, Dr William 92
byelaws 26

calendar, forager's 16–19
candied Primroses 64
Cardamine
   C. amara 38
   C. flexuosa 38
   C. hirsuta 38, *39*
   C. pratensis 38
Carex nigra 164
Carey, George Saville 49
Carrot, Wild 18–19, 108–9, 171–2

carrot family 33, 101, 102, 107, 108, 169, 172, 176
cars, standing on roof of 15
Castanea sativa 150, 151–2
Chaucer, Geoffrey 114
cheese
    Sorrel and Fat Hen tart 212
    Watercress omelette with cream cheese and smoked salmon 208, *209*
    Wild Garlic pesto 205, *205*
Chenopodium
    album 56, 57–9
    C. bonus-henricus 59
    C. rubrum 59
Cherry, Wild 12, 18–19, 83–4, *85*
    Cherry-pit 84
    Sweet Cherry Pickle 84
    Wild Cherry brandy 84
Cherry Plum 16–17, 32, 81, 138–40, *139*
Chestnut
    Horse 151
    Sweet 13, 18–19, 22, *150*, 151–2
        beef casserole with Horseradish and Chestnut dumplings 216, *217*
        Chestnut Florentines *228*, 229
        Chestnut macaroons *230*, 231
        Chestnut pancakes with Birch sap syrup 226, *227*
chicken, Hen *214*, 215
Chickweed, Common 11, 16–17, 52, *53*
    Chickweed pakoras *210*, 211
clothing 13
clover 62
cobnuts 147
coffee, Dandelion 137
'colonialism, environmental' 24
Comfrey 32, 189, 190
composite flowers 246
compound leaves 246, *247*
confectionery
    Elderflower delight 232, *233*
    Juniper toffee 234–5, *235*
Conium maculatum 173–5, *174–5*
Conopodium majus 104–5, *105*
conservation 22–5, 28–9
containers 13
Coombes, William 181
Corbin, Pam 66, 69, 74, 91
cordial, Elderflower 243
Corky Water-dropwort 172
Corn Salad 16–17, 130, *130*
Corylus
    C. avellana 147–9, *148*
    C. maxima 147
Countryside and Rights of Way Act (2000, CROW) 26–8
Crab Apple 16–17, 22, 24, 26, 64, 69–71, *70–1*

Cranberry and apple tart 222, *223*
    Hawthorn and Crab Apple Leather 69–71
Cranberry 13, 16–17, 29, 126–7, *127*
    Cranberry and apple tart 222, *223*
Crataegus monogyna 72, 73–4, *74*
cream
    Bramble mousse *220*, 221
cream cheese
    Watercress omelette with cream cheese and smoked salmon 208, *209*
Crippen, Dr 181
Crow Garlic *see* Garlic, Crow
Cuckoo Pint 191–3
Culpeper, Nicholas 40, 55, 78, 88, 99, 104, 112, 115, 119, 140, 175, 189
Cytisus scoparius 64, *65*

Damson 138
Dandelion 13, 16–17, 22, 28, 135–7, *136*
    Dandelion jelly marmalade 240, *241*
Datura 57
    Datura stramonium 183
Daucus carota 108–9
Delaroche, Paul 165
Dewberry 16–17, 66, 88, *88*
Digitalis purpurea 188, 189–90
Diplotaxis tenuifolia 50, *51*
Dock, Common 44, 55
Dog's Mercury 59, *178*, 179–80
dulse
    wild stir-fry 203
dumplings, Horseradish and Chestnut 216, *217*

eggs
    Watercress omelette with cream cheese and smoked salmon 208, *209*
Elder 12, 16–17, 22, 75, 131–3, *132*
    Elderflower cordial 243
    Elderflower delight 232, *233*
'environmental colonialism' 24
equipment 13–15, *14*
Evelyn, John 115, 152

Fasciola hepatica 47–9
Fat Hen 11, 15, 16–17, 22, 33, *56*, 57–9
    Hen chicken *214*, 215
    Sorrel and Fat Hen tart 212
Fennel 12, 16–17, 98–9, *99*
fields 13
filberts 147
Florentines, Chestnut *228*, 229
flour, Chestnut 152
flowers
    as decoration 64
    wild flower syrup *236*, 237

flukes, on Watercress 47–9
Foeniculum vulgare 98–9, *99*
Fool's Parsley 176, *177*
Fool's Watercress 47
foraging
  conservation and the law 22–9
  equipment 13–15, *14*
  when to look 15–19
Forestry Commission 26
Foxglove *188*, 189–90
Fragaria
  F. chiloensis 92
  F. moschata 93
  F. vesca 92–3, *93*
  F. virginiana 92
fruit 22–4
fungi 32

Garlic
  Crow 16–17, 142–3, *143*
    Chickweed pakoras *210*, 211
    wild stir-fry 203
  Wild (Ramsons) 18–19, 22, 63, 144–6, *145*
    Hen chicken *214*, 215
    Wild Garlic parcels 204, *204*
    Wild Garlic pesto 205, *205*
Garlic Mustard 16–17, 42–3, *43*
Gerard, John 66, 115, 119, 189
gin, Sloe 82
gloves 13
goat's cheese
  Sorrel and Fat Hen tart 212
Good King Henry 59, 60, 180
Gooseberry 12, 16–17, 94, *95*
Goosefoot 33, 57, 59, 60–1, 193
  Fig-leaved 59
  Foetid 59
  Many-seeded 59, 180
  Nettle-leaved 59
  Red 11, 18–19, 32, *58*, 59, 181, 185
  Stinking 59
Grigson, Geoffrey 73, 120
Grigson, Jane 92–3
Ground Elder 16–17, 100–1, *101*, 171–2
Ground Ivy 116

habitat loss 22
hats 13
Hawthorn 15, 16–17, 22, *72*, 73–4, *74*, 75
  Hawthorn and Crab Apple Leather 69–71
  Midland Hawthorn 73
Hazel 12, 16–17, 32, 147–9, *148*
  Chestnut Florentines *228*, 229
  Chestnut macaroons *230*, 231
  Hazelnut pastry 222

heath 13
Hemlock 108, 117, 173–5, *174–5*
Hemlock Water-dropwort 33, 46, 169, *170*, 171–2
Hen chicken *214*, 215
Henbane 181–3, *182*
Heracleum sphondylium 102, *103*
Herrick, Robert 84, 93
Himalayan balsam 22
Hippophae rhamnoides 156, *157*
Hogweed 16–17, 102, *103*, 171–2
  Hogweed tempura 202
Hop 16–17, 115–16, *116*
Horehound 116
Horse Chestnut 151
Horseradish 16–17, 44–6, *45*, *46*
  beef casserole with Horseradish and Chestnut dumplings 216, *217*
Humulus lupulus 115–16, *116*
Hyoscyamus niger 181–3, *182*

identifying plants 32–3

jelly
  Dandelion jelly marmalade 240, *241*
  Elderflower jelly 242
  Redcurrant jelly 97
  Rose jelly 242
Jelly Ears
  wild stir-fry 203
Jimson Weed 183
Johns, Reverend 38
Juniper 18–19, 29, 153–5, *154*, 197
  Juniper pot 213
  Juniper toffee 234–5, *235*
Juniperus communis 153–5, *154*

knives 13, 29
knotweed, Japanese 22

Lady's Smock 38
Lamb's Lettuce 130
laws 13, 15, 25–9
leaflets 246, *247*
leaves
  edible tree leaves 74
  shapes *247*
legislation 13, 15, 25–9
Lémery, Louis 123
lemon
  Watermint sorbet *218*, 219
lily of the valley 146
Lime 18–19, 74
lobed leaves 246, *247*
Loco Weed 183
Lords and Ladies 110, 146, 191–3, *191–3*

INDEX 253

Mabey, Richard 32, 66, 73, 88, 152, 165
macaroons, Chestnut 230, 231
Mallow, Common 16–17, 54, 55, 114
Malus sylvestris 69–71, *70–1*
Malva sylvestris 54, 55
Manning, Anne 42
Maple, Field 161
Marjoram, Wild 18–19, *122*, 123
marmalade, Dandelion jelly 240, *241*
May blossom *72*, 73
meadows 13
Mentha
   M. aquatica 117–19, *118*
   M. arvensis 120
   M. spicata 120, *121*
   M. suaveolens 120, *121*
Mercurialis
   M. annua *178*, 179–80
   M. perennis *178*, 179–80
Mercury
   Annual *178*, 179–80
   Dog's 59, *178*, 179–80
Mint
   Corn 120
   Round-leaved 18–19, 120, *121*
   Spearmint 18–19, 120, *121*
   Watermint 13, 18–19, 25, 117–19, *118*
      Watermint sorbet *218*, 219
mousse, Bramble *220*, 221
Mugwort 116
mushrooms 32
Mustard, Black 16–17, 40–1, *41*
Myrrhis odorata *106*, 107

National Trust 24, 26
Natural England 29
Nettle, Stinging 12, 18–19, 22, 32, 55, 112–14, *113*
   Nettle ravioli 206–7, *207*
   Nettle soup *200*, 201
Nightshade
   Black 32, 33, 57, 60, *184*, 185
   Deadly 169, 171, 183, 186
   Woody 186, *187*
nightshade family 59, 60, 181

Oak 74
Oenanthe
   O. crocata *170*, 171–2
   O. pimpinelloides 172
omelette
   Watercress omelette with cream cheese and smoked salmon 208, *209*
opposite leaflets 246, *247*
Orache
   Babington's 60
   Common 60
   Frosted 60
   Spear-leaved 11, 18–19, 60–1, *61*
Origanum
   O. majorana 123
   O. onites 123
   O. vulgare *122*, 123
Oxalis
   O. acetosella 62–3, *63*
   O. corniculata 62

pakoras, Chickweed *210*, 211
pancakes
   Chestnut pancakes with Birch sap syrup 226, *227*
Papaver
   P. rhoeas 34, 35
   P. somniferum 35
parasites, flukes 47–9
Parsnip, Wild 18–19, 108, *109*, 171–2
pasta
   Nettle ravioli 206–7, *207*
Pastinaca sativa 108, *109*
pastry, Hazelnut 222
pepper dulse
   wild stir-fry 203
perennials 246
Perennial Wall Rocket 12, 18–19, 32, 50, *51*
pesto, Wild Garlic 205, *205*
pickers *14*, 15
Pignut 13, 18–19, 104–5, *105*
   Nettle ravioli 206–7, *207*
   Wild Garlic pesto 205, *205*
Pine, Scots 197
pinnate leaves 246
Plantlife 24
Pliny the Elder 87, 181
Plum
   Cherry 16–17, 32, 81, 138–40, *139*
   Wild 18–19, 138–40, *139*
poisonous plants 32–3, 166–97
pollution 12
Polygonaceae 110
Poppy
   Common 16–17, *34*, 35
   Opium 35
pork
   Juniper pot 213
potato family 33, 169
Potentilla anserina 78, *79*
Primrose 64
private land 25–6
Prunus
   P. avium 83–4, *85*
   P. cerasifera 138–40, *139*
   P. domestica 138–40, *139*
   P. spinosa 80, 81–2

Ramsons *see* Garlic, Wild
Randolph, Mary 119
rare plants 28
Raspberry 18–19, 32, 66, 86, 87–8
ravioli, Nettle 206–7, *207*
Redcurrant 12, 15, 18–19, 66, *96*, 97
Reedmace 16–17, 162–5, *163*, *164*
   wild stir-fry 203
Ribes
   R. rubrum 96, 97
   R. uva-crispa 94, *95*
rice
   Wild Garlic parcels 204, *204*
Rocket, Perennial Wall 12, 18–19, 32, 50, *51*
Rorippa nasturtium-aquaticum 47–9, *48*
Rosa
   R. arvensis 89–91, *90*
   R. canina 89–91, *90*
   R. rugosa 90, 91
Rosaceae 81
Rose 64
   Dog 18–19, 89–91, *90*
   Field 16–17
   Japanese 16–17, *90*, 91
      Rose jelly 242
rose family 81
Rosehips 90–1, *90*
   Chestnut Florentines *228*, 229
   Rosehip babas with Blackberries 224, *225*
   Rosehip syrup 91
Rowan 12, 18–19, 75–7, *75*, *76*, 133
Rubus
   R. caesius 88, *88*
   R. fruticosus 66–8, *67*
   R. idaeus 86, 87–8
rum
   Rosehip babas with Blackberries 224, *225*
Rumex
   R. acetosa 110–11, *111*
   R. acetosella 111

safety 13, 32
Sambucus nigra 131–4, *132*, *134*
Samphire, Marsh 25, 28
sausage meat
   Wild Garlic parcels 204, *204*
'schedule 8' list 28
scissors 13
Scotland, right to roam 25
Scurvygrasses 38
Sea Beet 22
   wild stir-fry 203
Sea Buckthorn 12, 18–19, 156, *157*
seaside 13
Sedge, Common 164
Sheep's Sorrel 18–19

Silverweed 18–19, 78, *79*
Silvester, Rev. Tipping 112
Sites of Special Scientific Interest (SSSIs) 28–9
Sloe 18–19, 22, 29, *80*, 81–2
   Sloe Gin 82
smoked salmon
   Watercress omelette with cream cheese and smoked salmon 208, *209*
Solanaceae 57, 60, 169, 181
Solanum
   S. dulcamara 186, *187*
   S. nigrum 184, 185
sorbet, Watermint *218*, 219
Sorbus aucuparia 75–7, *75*, *76*
Sorrel
   Common Sorrel 13, 16–17, 22, 29, 110–11, *111*, 193
      Sorrel and Fat Hen tart 212
   Procumbent Yellow Sorrel 62
   Sheep's Sorrel 18–19, 111
   Wood Sorrel 13, 22, 62–3, *63*
soup, Nettle *200*, 201
Spartium junceum 64
Spearmint 18–19, 120, *121*
Stace, Clive 61
Stellaria
   S. holostea 52, *53*
   S. media 52, *53*
Stinging Nettle *see* Nettle, Stinging
Stitchwort, Greater 52, *53*
Storck, Dr 17
Strangford Lough 26
Strawberry
   Alpine 92
   Chilean 92
   Hautbois 93
   Virginian 92
   Wild 12, 15, 18–19, 66, 92–3, *93*
      Wild Strawberries in brandy syrup *238*, 239
streams 13
Sweet Cicely 18–19, 22, *106*, 107
Sweet Gale 116
Sycamore 161
Symphytum 190
syrup
   Birch sap syrup 161
   Rosehip syrup 91
   wild flower syrup *236*, 237

Tamus communis 194, 195
tansy 32, 78
Taraxacum 135–7, *136*
tarts
   Blackberry or Bilberry tart 222
   Cranberry and apple tart 222, *223*
   Sorrel and Fat Hen tart 212

Taxus baccata 196, 197
tempura, Hogweed 202
terminal 246
Theft Act (1968) 26, 77
Thorn Apple 183
toffee, Juniper 234–5, *235*
trespassing 25–8
Typha latifolia 162–5, *163*, *164*

Umbelliferaceae 169, 172
urban foraging 12
Urtica dioica 112–14, *113*

Vaccinium
  V. macrocarpon 126
  V. myrtillus 124, 125
  V. oxycoccos 126–7, *127*
Valerianella locusta 130, *130*
verjuice 69
Veronica beccabunga 128, *129*
Violet, Sweet 64

Wall Rocket, Perennial 12, 18–19, 32, 50, *51*
Walnut 161

Warren, Piers 112
Water-dropwort
  Corky 172
  Hemlock 33, 46, 169, *170*, 171–2
Watercress 13, 15, 18–19, 25, 47–9, *48*
  Watercress omelette with cream cheese and smoked salmon 208, *209*
Watermint 13, 18–19, 25, 117–19, *118*
  Watermint sorbet *218*, 219
Whitebeam 77
wild boar 105
wild flower syrup *236*, 237
wild stir-fry 203
Wildlife and Countryside Act (1981) 28
Wildlife Trust 26
Wintercress 13, 18–19
  American 36, *37*
  Common 36
Withering, William 189, 190
wood, cherry 84
woodlands 12, 13
Wormwood 116

Yarrow 18–19, 32, 116, 141, *141*
Yew *196*, 197

The River Cottage

Cakes Handbook

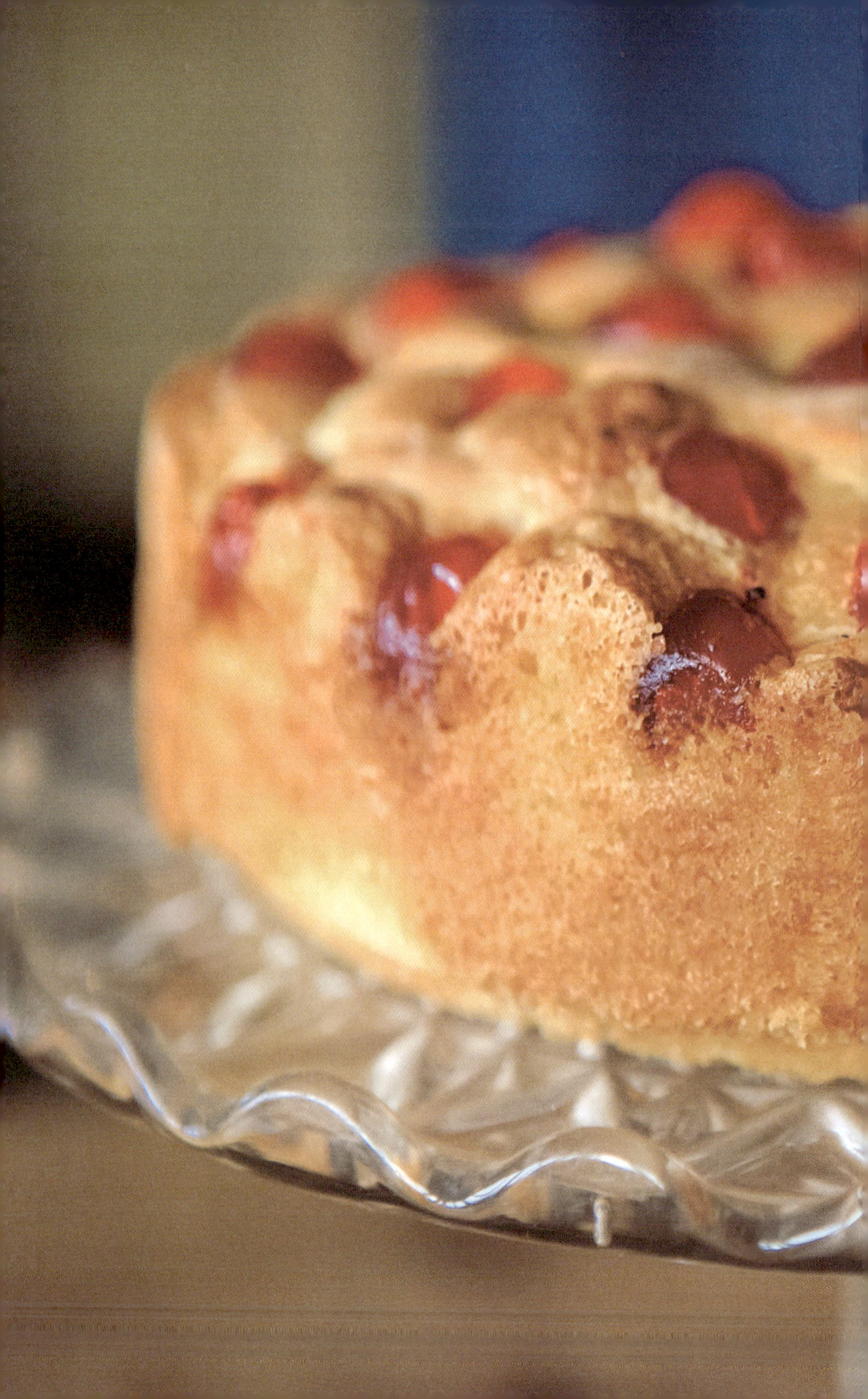

The River Cottage Cakes Handbook

by Pam Corbin

introduced by
Hugh Fearnley-Whittingstall

www.rivercottage.net

BLOOMSBURY
LONDON · NEW DELHI · NEW YORK · SYDNEY

In memory of lovely Philippa

First published in Great Britain 2011
This paperback edition published 2012

Text copyright © 2011 by Pam Corbin
Photography © 2011 by Gavin Kingcome

The moral right of the author has been asserted

Bloomsbury Publishing Plc, 50 Bedford Square, London WC1B 3DP
Bloomsbury Publishing, London, New Delhi, New York and Sydney

A CIP catalogue record for this book is available from the British Library

ISBN 978 1 4088 3612 5

10 9 8 7 6 5 4 3 2 1

Project editor: Janet Illsley
Designer: Will Webb
Photographer: Gavin Kingcome

Printed in China by C&C Offset Printing Co., Ltd.

While every effort has been made to ensure the accuracy of the information contained in this book, in no circumstances can the publisher or the author accept any legal responsibility or liability for any loss or damage (including damage to property and/or personal injury) arising from any error in or omission from the information contained in this book, or from the failure of the reader to properly and accurately follow any instructions contained in the book.

www.bloomsbury.com/rivercottage

Contents

Getting Started	8
Fillers & Toppers	46
Small Cakes & Bakes	68
Big Cakes	120
Fruity Cakes & Gingerbread	184
Party Cakes	216
Useful Things	242

You may already know of Pam Corbin through her wonderful *River Cottage Preserves Handbook*, or perhaps you have attended one of her preserving courses down here at Park Farm. Her expertise relating to jams, jellies, chutneys, cordials and liqueurs is unsurpassed, and her down-to-earth way of sharing that knowledge has made her one of the most popular members of our team. That's why, when Pam agreed to channel her considerable talents into a book dedicated to cake, I was filled with pleasure and, indeed, greedy anticipation. You won't be surprised to hear that I stepped up to my professional responsibilities and made myself available for sampling as the book progressed. It was a tough job… Now, having read the book, cooked a number of the recipes for my family at home, and eaten many others hot from Pam's tins (or picked up from my special cake sample drop box at River Cottage HQ), I would venture to say that this may be the only cake-baking book you'll ever really need.

What I love about Pam is that she's a champion of the art of the possible. Having proved that there is nothing mysterious or arcane about the art of preserving, and that fabulous preserves are within the reach of any cook, Pam has performed a similar magic on the subject of baking. While many of us enjoy whipping up a batch of muffins or a chocolate sponge – and many more need very little encouragement to sample the results – a lot of cooks are under the misapprehension that they're not great cake-makers, or somehow lack the special touch needed to produce great results. If that strikes a chord with you, then this book should set you right. Not only is it an invitation to rediscover an enormous range of delectable cakes and biscuits, it's also a confidence-inspiring demonstration that we can all create them if we want to.

There are literally thousands of different cakes, bakes, scones, biscuits and cookies that Pam might have chosen to showcase here, but I think there's something rather brilliant about the range she has selected. She's combined a raft of wonderfully nostalgic regional recipes, such as Cornish fairings, Grasmere gingerbread and Dundee cake, with some intriguing and often rather sophisticated options, such as Italian certosino or her delicate little marzipan-filled Simnel cakelets. There are a few surprises – I absolutely love Pam's 'Veg patch' gnome cakes and her homemade Jammy dodgers. But all the recipes are based on the principles we try to stick to at River Cottage: many focus on seasonal ingredients, several use up leftovers and, of course, Pam encourages us to make use of local produce, including herbs and fruit we might have growing in our own gardens.

You won't find elaborately decorated cakes here, or swathes of fondant icing and sugarpaste – and thank goodness, I would say. Pam never goes down the route of novelty for novelty's sake, which is very liberating for the cook. Who wants to worry about piping and moulding when there's cake to be eaten? And it doesn't mean these cakes and bakes aren't beautiful to look at. As Pam says, she simply believes in allowing a cake's natural charms to speak for themselves. The result is that while Pam's cakes always look stunning to me, there's nothing here that doesn't taste at least as good as it looks...

It's got to be said – and I think this is very sad – that cake has rather fallen out of favour in some quarters. It can be seen as an over-indulgent foodstuff without nutritional value. But, with the best homemade cakes, that's just not fair. While I'm not suggesting we should all be cramming ourselves with macaroons and Battenberg every day, I think sweet baked treats have an important part to play in a well-balanced, life-enhancing diet. There are cakes for special occasions, of course – the birthday cakes and Christmas tree biscuits, or Pam's elegant pudding cakes such as the Seville orange polenta cake – but plenty of others which fulfil a more everyday need. A slab of fruity 'Elevenses' lumberjack cake, a slice of Banana bread or a chunk of Pam's lovely 'Bird table' bread cake are all fantastic ways to fill a hungry gap between breakfast and lunch, or to fuel yourself on a long walk. And Pam packs so many of her cakes with fruit, seeds and vegetables, as well as the obvious eggs, milk and flour, that she demonstrates time and again that cake can be a sustaining, wholesome option, not just 'empty calories'.

Pam also has an eye on the clock. She understands that, while it's lovely to spend an entire afternoon ensconced in the kitchen, turning out Swiss rolls, tray bakes and buns, it's not always possible. Consequently, there are plenty of cakes here, including the divine Banana and chocolate cake as well as the classic Victoria sandwich, which you could have on the table, warm and irresistible, within the hour. And I also love the fact that many of these cakes are great 'keepers': invest a little time in mixing and baking them, and they'll sit happily in a cake tin for days, even weeks – in a few cases, months – improving all the while.

This book, then, is much more than a collection of scrumptious treats to be enjoyed once in a while. It's a comprehensive call for the revival of cake, in all its many glorious guises. It's a celebration of home-baking with good, well-sourced ingredients, an argument for the revival of elevenses and four o'clock tea, an acknowledgement of the simple pleasure of offering a cuppa and a slice of something nice to someone you care about. You may be a seasoned baker with a string of village-show rosettes to your name – in which case, you will find plenty here to expand your repertoire, and probably garner a few more gongs! But even if you are a novice who has only dabbled on the shores of flapjacks and fairy cakes, I urge you to feast your eyes on Pam's work. These carefully crafted, inspiring and utterly delicious recipes will bring out the baker in you, I promise.

Hugh Fearnley-Whittingstall, East Devon, January 2011

Getting Started

Mention the word cake and it seems to touch the heart and find the soul – communicated in a mistiness of the eyes and an affirming whisper of *'I love cake'*. These days, in this world of cup-cake cornucopia, the weekly baking day has been almost swept away amidst the candy-coloured, swirly-topped cakes that are so freely available from countless retail outfits. Now, I don't want you to think I'm a spoilsport, and I'll be the first to admit the chance of a coffee, slice of cake and a chat is always high on my list of priorities. But what could be more pleasurable, or time better spent, than an hour or two of baking in the kitchen, radio on, with cake fumes airily wafting into every corner of the house? What better gift can we hand down to our children than the skill to take natural ingredients and turn them into something to nourish and sustain; and more often than not in the case of the cake, make something special to mark and celebrate an important occasion?

My mum made cakes and so did her mum. Baking day generally fell on Friday, ensuring that there was always cake in the tin for the weekend, especially for tea on Sunday. These treasured bakes were offered only when the bread and butter – or come to that, anything else vaguely filling – had been eaten up. This was the moment that the cake was cut. After that, the supplies in the cake tin were rationed to last the rest of the week, although sometimes, thankfully, there was a midweek boost of freshly made flapjacks. As a consequence, the cake tin itself prompted rushes of pleasure or disappointment with a *'thank goodness'* when reassuringly heavy, or *'oh bother'* when light and empty.

I can't remember a time when I didn't make cakes and I have certainly never considered baking in the slightest way a chore. You don't have to be extraordinarily talented or have heaps of time to make cakes. A simple baking session requires a few store-cupboard ingredients, plus a little of your time. From mixing to devouring, a panful of muffins can be ready within 30 minutes and the quintessential and much-loved Victoria sandwich doesn't take much longer. Of course, it makes economic sense, too. Not only will the cost of these home-baked goodies be a fraction of their commercial counterparts, your sense of fulfilment will be priceless. And those lucky enough to be nurtured by cake will keep the memories of your baking long into old age; a good cake lingers in the memory long after the last crumb has been eaten.

The history of cake goes back a long way, its evolution spanning thousands of years. It would appear our Neolithic ancestors made cakes in some form or another, but these early attempts were a far cry from our notion of a cake. Their cakes were flat and hard, made from little more than a mix of moistened crushed grain and baked on a hot stone – an early prototype of our oatcakes today. Since then, cakes as we know them have evolved bit by bit. The ancient Egyptians added honey, while the Romans included raisins, nuts and fruit.

Sweet spices, eggs and sugar were incorporated into recipes during the sixteenth century and records show that yeast was used to leaven these lavishly enriched cakes. By the beginning of the eighteenth century, cakes were beginning to be made without yeast. Instead, eggs were whisked for up to an hour until they were light and voluminous. As a consequence, dutiful cooks, who were keen to ensure their cakes rose, ended up with 'wrestler's wrists'. Mercifully, during the 1840s, Alfred Bird (who, incidentally, also devised custard powder) created a mix of bicarbonate of soda (alkaline) and cream of tartar (acid) and formed what has become known as modern-day baking powder. After that, and with the help of more easily regulated ovens, cake-making became more or less… a piece of cake.

Even the shortage of food, along with its strict rationing, during the war did not stop cake-making. While land girls dug for victory by growing vegetables, determined housewives improvised and made frugal cakes without eggs – using carrots or potatoes and whatever sort of fat was available.

Bearing in mind the enforced parsimony of those adverse times, baking with the wealth of fabulous ingredients we can tap into these days has never been quite so easy or universally accessible. From simple-to-make daily treats to those gorgeous goodies we dream about, take pleasure in your baking – it's a lifetime skill, which will only get better.

Baking gear

Cake-making isn't a dressy affair – just swap your kid gloves for oven gloves and wear an apron and comfy clothes (heels are optional). However, if you are going to get serious about cake-making (and I hope you do), investing in a few pieces of useful equipment will certainly make it easier and more satisfying. When a cake pops out of its tin perfect, whole and undamaged, it's a real moment of joy.

You'll be able to find all the items I mention here in a well-stocked kitchen shop (which will also be a pleasure to browse around), or from various internet sources. It's always advisable to buy the best quality you can afford: top-notch items, chosen with care, will become reliable kitchen aids that last a lifetime. But there is no need to go into debt to keep the family in cakes. The chances are, you'll already have most of the things you need – and too much stuff will clutter up the kitchen drawers.

Electric mixer

Buying a simple hand-held electric whisk is a shrewd move: it will save you time and elbow grease. Many recipes require butter and sugar to be beaten together until 'very light and creamy'. By hand, with a wooden spoon, it can take 10–15 minutes to get to this stage. With a hand-held whisk, it can be reached in about 5 minutes. A free-standing electric mixer is a real boon for creaming, whisking and rubbing-in methods. A food-processing attachment or a separate machine is useful for processing nuts, etc. But these large bits of equipment are expensive and, in general, all cake-mixing processes can be undertaken by hand or with a hand-held electric whisk.

Mixing bowls

A selection of different-sized mixing bowls is helpful. The roomy proportions of good old-fashioned earthenware basins are excellent for most cake-making methods and the bowls are sufficiently heavy to sit firmly on the work surface without moving whilst ingredients are being mixed together. A 30–32cm bowl will be adequate for most average cake mixes. Do keep a lookout in charity shops and market stalls for vintage mixing bowls, a lovely addition to your kitchen.

Scales

A good set of scales is essential. Good results rely on accurate measuring. Flat-bed digital scales are handy to weigh ingredients straight into the mixing bowl.

Wooden spoons

These are useful for beating, mixing and stirring, as they do not scratch non-stick surfaces or conduct heat. The unsealed wood can hold strong flavours, such as garlic and spices, so it is worth dedicating one or two spoons to cake-making alone.

GETTING STARTED 13

Metal spoons
Large metal spoons are best for folding a lighter or drier mixture into a heavy one.

Measuring spoons
A set of graded measuring spoons, from ¼ tsp/1.25ml to 1 tbsp/15ml, will give you the exact spoon quantities necessary for successful baking.

Measuring jug
An angled jug that can be read from above is useful for measuring liquid ingredients, particularly for recipes such as muffins that use several liquids.

Spatula
A spatula or 'scraper' with a flexible head is helpful for folding in, as well as scraping out the mixing bowl so that all the cake mix gets into the baking tin.

Sieve
A fine-meshed sieve is essential for aerating compacted flour and icing sugar. It is worthwhile having a couple of sieves, one for dry ingredients and one for wet. A good sharp tap over the kitchen sink will remove any residual floury grains from the mesh of your 'dry' sieve and will save you having to wash it.

Citrus zester or fine grater
This will enable you to easily remove the highly flavoured and aromatic zest from citrus fruit without the bitter pith underneath.

Wire cooling racks
These footed metal grid racks allow air to circulate around cakes so they can cool more quickly. You'll need at least two to enable you to turn a cake out of its baking tin, then straight away re-invert it onto a second rack. This double action helps to prevent criss-cross grid markings on the top of the cake. Cooling racks are usually either rectangular or round. Look out for tiered racks that fold away, which are a tremendous aid for a big baking session or a kitchen short of space.

Oven thermometer
An inexpensive but good oven thermometer is well worth investing in, so you can check how accurate your oven temperature is. If you discover the temperature of your oven is not what it says on the dial (a not uncommon occurrence), the thermometer will help you achieve the correct temperature for each recipe.

Baking tins
For good results, it is essential to use the right-size tin for a recipe. However, this doesn't mean you have to use a round (or square) tin if that's what the recipe says. A 20cm round tin is roughly the same as an 18cm square one. Keep in mind the volume of a square tin is about the same as a round tin that is 2cm bigger.

Loose-bottomed tins are ideal for easily turning out cakes that won't come to any harm if inverted, such as the two halves of a Victoria sponge. But cakes with delicate or streusel-type toppings are best baked in a clip-sided springform cake tin. The following assortment should be sufficient for most baking requirements:

- 2 x 20cm sandwich tins
- 1 x 23cm springform tin (with spring-release clip on the side for easy release)
- 1 x 23cm garland or ring mould (circular, with a hollowed-out centre)
- 1 x 1 litre loaf tin (about 20 x 10cm)
- 1 x 2 litre loaf tin (about 25 x 13cm)
- 1 x 30cm x 20cm Swiss roll tin
- 1 x 18cm square tin
- 1 x 12-hole muffin tray
- 1 x 12-hole fairy cake tin
- 1 or 2 large baking sheets (for biscuits)

Good baking tins can be pricey but they are a sound investment and should last a lifetime. My favourite tins are made by Alan Silverwood Ltd (see directory, p.244).

Manufactured in the UK, the light anodised alloy conducts heat evenly and speedily and you may well find baking times can be reduced a little. The tins also release their cakes easily. The range includes a good choice of shapes and sizes, including an ingenious multi-size tin and a special Battenberg tin. Although the tins are not dishwasher safe, the smooth surfaces are very easy to clean with hot soapy water.

Otherwise, go for good heavy-duty, non-stick bakeware, such as the Masterclass range from Kitchen Craft (see directory, p.244), available from most good cookshops, or the Cook and Bake range from Lakeland (see directory, p.244). Much as I've tried, I seem to have little success with silicone baking moulds, usually ending up with a crumby-looking cake plus the laborious job of cleaning out the mould. But perhaps it's me, and somewhere along the line I've got it wrong.

Lining and baking papers

Used to line tins, these prevent cakes sticking. The various options are as follows:

Greaseproof paper This needs to be lightly greased before using to line baking tins. It's also ideal for wrapping cakes and biscuits to be stored in an airtight container.

Baking parchment A silicone-coated non-stick paper, this is easy to use and effective; there's no need to grease it. Look out for unbleached baking parchment. You can keep the baking parchment used for rolling out biscuits, etc. Just wipe over, roll up and keep till next time.

Bake-O-Glide The satin of the baking world. A Teflon-coated non-stick fabric, it can be reused hundreds of times. Although it may seem a bit costly, a moderate-sized roll will kit out your favourite baking tins in silky smooth underwear that will have your cakes slipping out of their corset-like armoury quite effortlessly. The downside is that it's not biodegradable – but of course this is offset by the fact that you are not using hundreds of pieces of baking parchment.

Baking parchment cake-tin liners Shaped to fit neatly into specific sizes of baking tins, these quick-release liners withstand oven temperatures up to 230°C/Gas mark 8. They are particularly time-saving if you are batch-baking.

Muffin, cup cake or fairy cake papers These are ideal for making small yet perfectly formed cakes. Use them singly to line the cups of muffin or cup cake trays, or tripled if you want them to stand free on a baking tray.

Edible wafer paper Made from potato or rice starch, this is used to line baking trays and helps light, sugary bakes like macaroons hold together and release easily.

GETTING STARTED 17

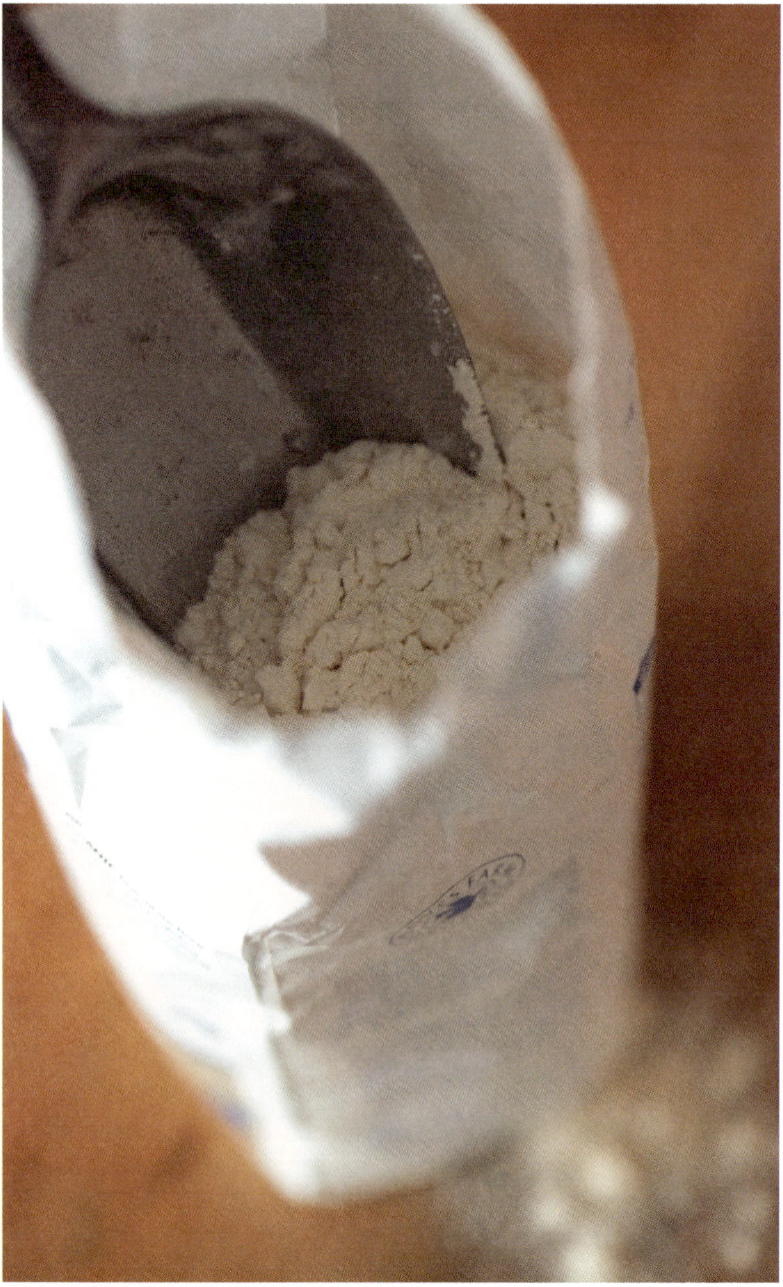

Cake ingredients

From quick-to-make homely griddle cakes to fabulous, light and billowy egg-blown sponges, the vast majority of cakes are made from four store-cupboard ingredients: flour, eggs, sugar and fat (usually butter). It's quite incredible how varied cakes can be, considering the basic elements most of them have in common – but of course, ever since humankind has been baking, we've been using a few extra choice ingredients to work small but crucial changes. Dried fruit, spices, nuts, coconut, fresh fruit, vegetables, honey, treacle and coffee all spring to mind, as well as the temptress Ixcacao, the goddess of chocolate. These added ingredients can transform a plain cake into anything from a hearty family filler to a gâteau to die for.

One of the greatest advantages of home-baking is that it gives us choice. Home cooks have control over their own ingredients and we can choose local, sustainable, organic or fairly traded options if we want to. A cake won't go horribly wrong if you don't use free-range eggs or fair-trade bananas, but I always keep in mind the saying, 'What you put in, is what you take out'. I think that's true on many levels, not just in terms of simple flavour. Remember, too, that your time is precious: you owe it to yourself to use good ingredients because they add untold value to your baking.

Before you get going, it's well worth taking a little time to learn how ingredients work together, so that every cake you bake will be a triumph. I'll start with the key players, the ones that combine to form the foundation of most cakes.

Flour

Flour is the backbone of a cake. Cakes can be made without eggs, sugar and fat, but rarely are they made without some sort of flour. Cake flours are generally sold as either 'plain' flour, without raising agents, or 'self-raising', which has the correct ratio of raising agent added. Plain flour is ideal for biscuits, fruit cakes, gingerbread and fine-textured cakes that rely on tiny air bubbles trapped in beaten egg to give lift. Self-raising flour is very handy for quick-mix batter cakes where the recipe does not rely on creaming or whisking to incorporate air into the mix. All flour needs to be sifted, sometimes twice, to aerate it and free up any compacted particles. If you sift wholemeal flour, don't throw away the husky bits left in the sieve. Re-combine them with the sifted flour – it's the goodness of the whole grain you are after.

Wheat flour This baking staple introduces protein, in the form of gluten, to a cake, and it's this gluten that gives a cake its structure, allowing the crumb to stretch and expand as the cake bakes, then 'holding' the risen shape. Wheat is graded into three different strengths, depending on the quantity and type of gluten it contains: finely textured 'soft' flour is best for cakes; 'hard' or 'strong' flour is best for bread-making; very hard durum wheat flour is used for pasta.

Wheat flour is available as white or wholemeal. Wholemeal is milled from the entire wheat grain, whereas white flour is milled from grains with the nutrient-rich bran and wheatgerm removed. Although white flour is used more often than not for cake-making, wholemeal flour can replace it partially, or completely, in most recipes. The coarser texture of wholemeal flour may give a slightly more dense texture to a cake – but sometimes that's just what we want!

If you like to use a mix of white and wholemeal flour, it's useful to keep a dedicated container of half-and-half mix for easy weighing out. Always check the best-before date as the higher concentration of oils in wholemeal flour can cause it to go rancid relatively quickly. Store all flours in sealed containers and keep in a cool, dark and dry place.

There are many different brands of wheat flour to choose from. I favour those which are neither bleached nor over-processed. My favourite flours come from Doves Farm and Marriage's (see directory, p.244); both can be sourced from most health food shops and some supermarkets.

Non-wheat flour

Non-wheat flours, such as rice, corn, polenta, potato and chestnut, can be used in conjunction with wheat flour to add specific flavours and textures to a cake. With the exception of spelt, they contain no gluten, so you can use them on their own if you need to exclude wheat from your diet. However, the results will be different – a little denser or heavier, but still delicious.

Spelt A distant cousin of wheat, spelt produces a deep nutty well-flavoured flour. Although it contains gluten, the structure is rather more delicate and brittle than the gluten in wheat flour and it is more easily absorbed by the body. Sharpham Park (see directory, p.244) produces excellent spelt flour from UK-grown spelt.

Cornflour Milled from the heart of the maize kernel, cornflour is very fine and powdery. It does not contain any gluten and is rarely used in cake-making. However, when combined with wheat flour, it makes extraordinarily good shortbread.

Rice flour Produced from either white or brown rice, this is often used in gluten-free recipes, in combination with other ingredients such as ground almonds, coconut or grated vegetables.

Polenta This is produced from ground maize kernels and is therefore gluten-free. It is rich yellow in colour and is either fine- or coarse-ground. Fine-ground polenta is generally used for baking and is sometimes combined with ground almonds to produce a slightly grainy, yet moist cake.

Potato starch flour This is made by grinding potatoes to a pulp, removing the starch and then drying it until it can be ground into a powder. Potato starch is gluten-free and often used as one of the ingredients in pre-mixed gluten-free cake flours.

Oats Rich in protein and fibre, and with a lovely nutty flavour, oats are the main ingredient in flapjacks and muesli-type bars. More often than not, rolled (porridge) oats are used, but some recipes, such as parkin, call for oatmeal or oat flour.

Chestnut flour High in carbohydrate and starch, chestnuts contain no gluten or cholesterol and can be ground to a glorious, nutty-sweet flour to be used in special cakes and biscuits.

Gluten-free and wheat-free flours Excellent gluten-free cake flours, blended from a mix of non-wheat cereals with added raising agents, such as cream of tartar and bicarbonate of soda, are available from Doves Farm and Bia Nua (see directory, p.244). These flours also usually contain xanthan gum – a natural substance derived from corn syrup, which is often employed as a substitute for gluten because it improves crumb structure. You can buy it in most health food shops. Made with Bia Nua's gluten-free cake flour, my Victoria sandwich works a treat.

Raising agents

Some cakes rely wholly on the actual method used to make them rise, i.e. the whisked method, whereas others make use of raising agents. Baking powder is a mix of alkaline and acidic substances (bicarbonate of soda and cream of tartar respectively). When combined in the presence of moisture, they release gas which forms thousands of tiny bubbles and inflates the cake batter. This instant reaction is why, traditionally, it has always been important to get a cake mix into the tin and into the oven as soon as possible after adding liquid. However, these days, most modern baking powders are described as 'double action' and require heat as well as moisture for the real rise in the cake, giving the cook a bit more time. Bicarbonate of soda can be used on its own as a raising agent, but only works if there is acidity present from other ingredients. Yoghurt, buttermilk, apples, citrus fruit, cocoa, honey and treacle are all acidic and will give the necessary reaction when combined with bicarb.

Always measure raising agents precisely, so for 1 level tsp, level the measure off with the back of a knife or your little finger. Sift raising agents with the flour and make sure they are well mixed before adding to other ingredients. The easiest way to do this is to give it a quick whiz with a whisk – electric or a basic balloon whisk.

If you want to turn plain flour into self-raising, add 1 level tsp baking powder for every 125g plain flour. Make sure raising agents are fresh – within their best-before date – or they may fail to produce the desired effect.

Sugar and other sweeteners

Sugar, with its alluring sweetness, enriches the flavour and texture of cakes. Until the mid-1970s, most sugar used for home-baking was refined white, with a small amount of demerara or other brown sugar. But today, there is a glorious array of sugars to choose from. Billington's (see directory, p.244) produce some fabulous unrefined sugars, from light, buttery, fine-grained golden caster sugar to rich, toffee-flavoured dark muscovado. I love these unrefined sugars and I know their warm aromas add depth of flavour and sincerity to my baking.

It is, however, caster sugar that picks up the accolade of most used sugar in home-baking. Its free-flowing small grains are perfect for creaming with butter to make the lightest of sponges. The larger crystals of everyday granulated sugar would take ages to beat to the light and fluffy state required in the creamed cake method. Caster sugar is available in refined (white) or unrefined (golden) varieties, the latter having a mellow, faintly caramelly flavour.

With soft brown and muscovado sugars, you will find they sometimes harden and clump together on storing. If this happens, put the sugar in a basin, cover with a damp tea-towel and leave overnight. Hey presto, in the morning you'll find your sugar will be lump-free and easy-going.

The soft browns With their soft, fine grains, these sugars range in colour from light caramel – ideal for light fruit cakes and chocolate cakes – to rich dark brown, which is perfect for sticky gingerbreads.

The muscovados With approximately 6% molasses, muscovado sugars are richer in natural minerals than the soft browns. Intense and nutty in flavour, light brown muscovado is ideal for light or medium fruit cakes, whereas its dark, toffee-flavoured brother adds colour and depth to rich festive-type fruit cakes.

Demerara Caramel-flavoured golden crystals are this sugar's defining characteristic. It is delicious in tray bakes and biscuits and those recipes where butter and sugar are melted together. Less expensive than the soft browns, demerara is a simple way to introduce the robust distinctive flavour of unrefined sugar.

Molasses and treacle These dark, sweet syrups are by-products of the sugar-making process and to all intents and purposes are the same thing. Extracted from the raw cane during refining, they contain all its nutrients and a great deal of concentrated flavour. Their trademark stickiness is crucial to gingerbreads, but their oily brown-black colour and intense taste bring richness and goodness to other cakes too.

Golden syrup With its unique much-loved flavour, golden syrup is often used in crunchy biscuits and gingerbreads. A little in fruit cakes lends a homely flavour, and helps to keep the cake fresher for longer. Bear in mind that golden syrup is about 40% sweeter than standard sugar, so a spoonful or two is probably all you will need to bring that deep, toffee-ish taste.

Honey This can be used in place of some of the sugar in baking recipes and its moisture-absorbing qualities will help cakes stay fresh for longer. If using, substitute roughly 25% honey for sugar. Reduce the oven temperature slightly to prevent over-browning, as honey burns more easily than sugar.

Flavoured sugars These add subtle fragrance and flavour to your baking. Use them to enrich classic sponge cakes and biscuits – by adding to the mixture, or sprinkling them on after baking. While they can be ridiculously expensive to buy, flavoured sugars are simple to make at home (see overleaf). Caster sugar is the best carrier for delicate aromas such as lavender or rose-scented geranium, whereas soft brown sugar is ideal for more robust flavours such as cinnamon. Unquestionably, the most widely used is vanilla sugar. A close second (well for me at least) is orange sugar, which I like to use in fruit cakes and gingery things. Keep jars of flavoured sugar on the go by perpetually topping them up with more sugar and flavouring.

To make a flavoured sugar, simply place the measured sugar and flavouring in a sealed container and combine thoroughly. A large jam jar will do for lavender and cinnamon sugars (the types you might use only in fairly small amounts), whereas it makes sense to use a much larger container for vanilla and orange sugars or any others that you like to use in quantity.

FLAVOUR	SUGAR	ACTION
Vanilla	Caster, preferably unrefined	Add 2 split vanilla pods to 1kg caster sugar. Leave for at least 2 weeks before use. For a more intense flavour, cut the vanilla pods into small pieces and place in a food processor with a quarter of the sugar. Blend until the pods are ground to a coarse powder. Mix with the remaining sugar.
Orange or lemon	Caster, preferably unrefined	Finely pare some citrus zest and cut into 1mm shreds. Place in a very cool oven or a warm airing cupboard until completely dry. Combine with the sugar, using the peel of 1 entire orange or lemon for every 1kg sugar. Leave for at least 2 weeks before using.
Cinnamon	Light soft brown	Add 1 tsp ground cinnamon for each 100g sugar. You can use this straight away.
Lavender	Caster	Add 1 tsp dried lavender flowers, or half a dozen fresh lavender heads, for every 100g sugar. Leave for a month before using. You can sift it to remove the flower heads before using, if you like.
Rose-scented geranium	Caster	Dry a good handful of rose-scented geranium leaves in a warm place for a couple of days. Layer them in a jar with 1kg sugar. Leave for a couple of weeks before using. This is a lovely sugar to use in simple sponges or in other recipes instead of rose water.

Icing sugar The finest-textured of the sugars, icing sugar is of course perfect for icings – whether water, butter or cream cheese based. In addition, a snowy dusting will finish many cakes, as well as covering up any cracks on the surface. Use white refined if you want a pure white finish. Or, for a delicious, light brown, natural caramel icing, use unrefined icing sugar. A few biscuit recipes call for icing sugar in the mix itself as it gives very light, crisp results (see Jammy dodgers, p.84).

Eggs

This key ingredient contributes moisture, volume, lightness, flavour, colour and nutrition. What's more, eggs come in their own recyclable packaging. Rich in protein, fat and essential vitamins, they really are little wonders. Brown, white, blue or speckled, it really doesn't matter what the shells look like. The most important thing is that the eggs are fresh and have come from healthy free-range hens that have fed and foraged on natural and/or organic food. For cake-making, to get the best out of eggs, they should be used at room temperature. If the weather is particularly cold, warm the eggs by placing them in a bowl of hot but not boiling water for a minute. If these fundamental principles are in place, the rich flavour and deep golden colour of the yolks will be reflected in the finished cake.

All eggs are pretty much the same shape, but their sizes can vary considerably. Commercial egg producers use the following grading:

Very large	73g plus
Large	63–73g
Medium	53–63g
Small	53g and under

And then of course, there are duck and goose eggs, much bigger than hen's, prized for their deep, golden yolks and renowned for the cakes they make.

So how do you know which egg to use? I generally use good medium-sized or smallish large hen's eggs when baking i.e. ones that weigh around 63g.

If you have a supply of small bantam eggs or big goose eggs instead, weigh them with their shells on. Then, bearing in mind the 63g factor, you can work out how many you will need. A medium-sized goose egg is usually equivalent to three 63g hen's eggs, while one monstrous, emerald-green emu egg will replace ten hen's eggs. Admittedly, I've not yet had the opportunity of making a cake with one of these, though three emus live a stone's throw from my house.

P.S. Egg whites freeze well. Place in a small container and label with the number of whites. Or freeze single egg whites in ice-cube trays, then put into a bag, seal and store for up to 6 months. Once thawed they are perfect for making meringues.

Fats

Fat brings flavour and texture to a cake and home-bakers have a choice far removed from the bland, omnipresent palm oils that saturate commercial baked products.

Butter Most often of all, I reach for butter, because the flavour is just incomparable. Unsalted butter, sometimes called sweet butter, is best for baking. Its pure, nutty flavour and soft texture are perfect for baking. However, you can use salted butter if you prefer – but make sure it's only lightly salted, or the flavour of the finished cake may be adversely affected. (In fact, these days, most butter is only lightly salted.)

For most baking purposes, especially if it needs to be creamed, butter should be soft (though not oily) and at room temperature. Provided it is, you'll find creaming a satisfying task, rather than an exhausting one.

Other fats and butter substitutes You may, for health or dietary reasons, opt to use one of the processed margarine-type fats instead of butter. Indeed, many cake-makers prefer to use these soft, whipped-up emulsions that can be beaten quickly and easily, straight from the fridge, to make quick-mix and unquestionably light sponge cakes. If you do go for margarine, then use one that is non-hydrogenated and therefore free from trans-fatty acids. Look for margarines that state they only use palm oil from a sustainable source.

I rarely use soft margarines myself but I do like to use rapeseed or sunflower oil in some of my baking. These pure vegetable oils are quick and easy to incorporate in muffins, tea breads, some fruit cakes and other recipes that contain a relatively small amount of fat and do not rely on creaming butter to incorporate 'lift' into the mixture. In the spirit of experimentation, I made a Victoria sandwich with sunflower oil, and although it rose and looked the part, the texture was quite dense and the flavour rather unpleasant.

Although little used these days, dripping, the rich sweet fat left after roasting a joint of beef, can be used to replace butter in farmhouse fruit cakes.

Optional extras

With the above basic ingredients in place, do take the time, before you get baking, to consider how other ingredients are brought into play and how they can influence the simplest of cakes.

Citrus fruits The peel or zest of citrus fruit is bursting with fragrant oil that helps to protect and preserve the fruity flesh inside – remove this thin outer layer of waxy skin and within a day or two the fruit shrivels and the flesh inside spoils. Citrus zest will bring acidity and a zesty vibrancy to your baking. Finely grated citrus zest is a valuable ingredient and is frequently added to cakes, biscuits and icings – quite literally for its absolutely fabulous zestiness.

To get the maximum flavour out of citrus zest, add it with the butter: its flavour will be fully released when the butter is pounded to a cream. Use a citrus zester or a fine grater to remove the aromatic zest from the fruit, without including the bitter white pith underneath.

The squeezed juice of citrus fruit has a less pungent and pervasive flavour, but it is very useful for soaking dried fruit and flavouring icings and drizzle toppings.

Candied peel The bitter-sweet citrussy tang of this ingredient contributes to the complex mix of flavours in many fruit cakes and gingery recipes. Made by softening and preserving thick slices of citrus peel in sugar, it can be bought ready diced in small bits (though I find these rather hard with little flavour), or in larger pieces, which can then be cut using a sharp knife to the size you require. To prevent candied peel becoming hard and gristly, store it wrapped in polythene in an airtight container. You can also make your own, which is straightforward and very satisfying.

Homemade candied peel

3 medium unwaxed oranges
3 unwaxed lemons
400g granulated sugar

Scrub the oranges and lemon, then, using a sharp knife, cut the peel from the fruit, removing it in quarters.

Put the citrus peels into a large pan and cover with 2 litres cold water. Bring to the boil and simmer for 5 minutes. Drain, return to the pan and add 1 litre fresh cold water. Bring to the boil and simmer, covered, for a good hour until the peels have softened. Add the sugar and stir until dissolved. Simmer, covered for about 20 minutes. Remove from the heat and leave to stand for 24 hours.

Bring the pan to the boil again. Simmer, uncovered, for about 30 minutes or until the peels have become translucent and most of the liquid has evaporated. Remove from the heat and allow to cool. Using a pair of tongs, remove the peels and place on a wire rack, filling the centres with any remaining syrup.

Pack, when cool, in a sterilised jam jar or airtight container. Cut and use as required. This candied peel will keep unopened for 3–4 months.

P.S. The 'juiced out' shells of citrus fruit can be turned into fragrant fire-lighters. Place on a wire tray in a warm airing cupboard, cool oven or the bottom of an Aga and leave for 2–3 days until the peel has dried out. Keep in a dry place. When laying a fire, pop a few pieces in with the paper and kindling wood. As you light your fire, the volatile, aromatic citrus oils will fill the room with their gorgeous aroma.

Other fresh fruit and vegetables These can add volume, moisture, fibre and nutrients to a cake. Both carrots and apples have long been used in sweet baking, but parsnips, courgettes, rhubarb, pears and other orchard fruits can all be employed to create airily light, mouthwatering cakes. Prepare vegetables and fruit just before adding them to a mixture by grating with a very fine grater or the grating disc on a food processor. Fold into the batter as quickly as possible to prevent discolouration.

GETTING STARTED 29

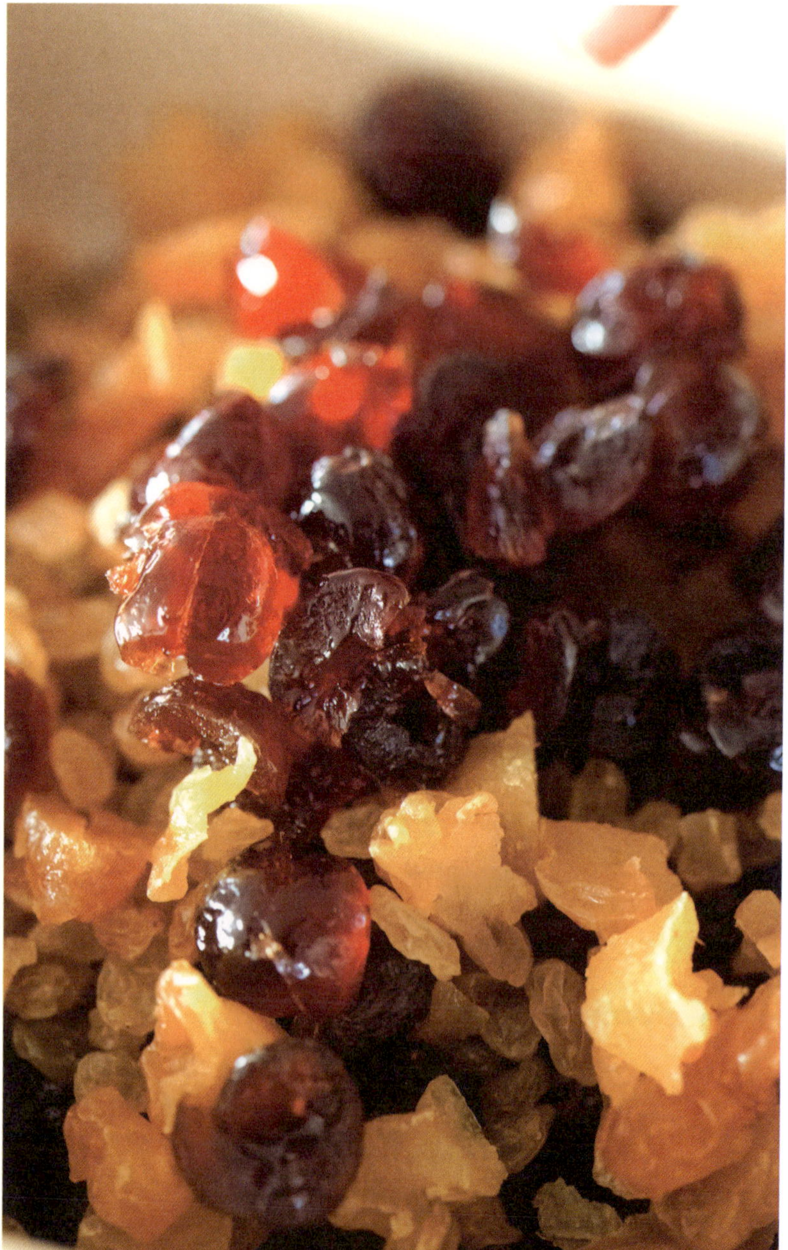

Glacé cherries Quite the queen of the preserved fruits in cake-making, these little gems bring a hint of sweet almond flavour along with a succulent yet crunchy texture. Avoid very brightly coloured red cherries for they will almost certainly contain E127 colouring. Natural glacé cherries, although much darker in colour, have a delicate taste.

To prevent cherries sinking to the bottom of a cake, rinse them in a little warm water to remove the sugar syrup (the sugar is the heavy bit). Dry them well, halve and toss in a little flour before using.

Dried fruits With their sweet intense flavours, dried fruits lend character and texture to a cake. They are, of course, simply fresh fruits that have been preserved by drying – either naturally in the sun or in a commercial drying unit.

Conventional dried fruit may contain sulphur dioxide; this is added to keep the colour and halt natural oxidisation. Organic dried fruit is produced without chemical intervention, which usually results in the fruit being much darker and, I think, better flavoured.

When you are buying dried fruit, bear in mind that the plumpest fruits are not necessarily the best. Often the most shrivelled-looking fruits retain the most flavour and, as they are so dehydrated, you get better value for your money. I buy most of my dried fruits from my local health food shop. Crazy Jack (see directory, p.244) produce an excellent organic range, which is available from many health food stores and supermarkets.

When it comes to cake-making, you are most likely to use dried vine fruits and, although technically they are all raisins, they split into three categories:

Currants are small, seedless and intensely sweet. Sometimes called 'raisins of the sun', they are dried black Zante grapes and come mainly from Greece.

Sultanas are pale golden, seedless and succulent. Most of our sultanas come from Turkey.

Raisins are dried white grapes usually of the muscatel variety and are mainly from the USA, Turkey, Greece and Australia.

Aside from this holy trinity, other dried fruits to use in your baking include apricots, dates, figs, prunes, cherries and cranberries.

Coconut The sweet white flesh from the mature fruit of the coconut palm is readily available as grated desiccated coconut and shredded dried coconut, in both sweetened and unsweetened forms. Sweetened desiccated coconut is the product most often used in baking. It brings natural moisture and that unmistakable coconut flavour to a cake. It is imported from many developing countries, but I do like to make sure the coconut I use is from a fair-trade source. Both desiccated and shredded dried coconut can also be lightly toasted and used as a decoration.

Nuts Used whole, chopped or ground, these bring texture, moisture, immense flavour and exceptional nutritional value to a cake. For flavour and freshness, it's best to buy nuts in relatively small quantities. They soon become stale and turn rancid on storing. Buy almonds and hazels with their skins on – they'll have a much better flavour and are less expensive. Once you have cracked the technique of removing their skins (see below), you'll find it a quick and easy job to do.

Chopping nuts is much easier if you warm them slightly first, by tossing them for a minute or so in a frying pan over a medium-low heat, or placing them on a baking tray in a low oven. This simple action will prevent them from shooting all over the place as you chop them. Also, the end result will be much nicer if you chop nuts by hand, rather than use a food processor.

The sweet almond, in the culinary world, is considered the doyenne of nuts. It can be used whole, split, flaked and/or blanched (skin removed), but perhaps its greatest contribution to baking is when it is ground. Ground almonds can be used to replace a proportion of flour and give a cake an appealing moistness without making it too heavy. Bought ready-ground almonds are very fine and delicate, though they need to be used quite quickly as they have a tendency to go stale and rancid. Alternatively, you can grind your own almonds in a food processor; the texture will be a little coarser and the flavour a little fresher (see below). The dark-tan skin of almonds can taste quite bitter and is best removed before using.

To blanch (or skin) almonds: place the nuts in a small bowl, cover with boiling water and leave for 1 minute. Drain, pour on fresh boiling water and leave for another 2–3 minutes. Drain again and set aside until cool enough to handle. Pinch the nuts between your finger and thumb and you will find they will shoot out of their loose, baggy skins at great speed. Dry with a tea-towel or kitchen paper.

Sometimes slivered almonds are called for in a recipe. Indeed using slivered, rather than roughly chopped, nuts will give your baking more style. You can buy slivered almonds or, better still, slice blanched almonds lengthways two or three times into shapely splinters.

Hazelnuts are delicious in cakes, or on top of them, whether whole, chopped or ground. The trees or shrubs are common in the UK and hazelnuts can be foraged from hedgerows and woods. (Note that when cultivated they are called either cobnuts or filberts.) The summer needs to be long and hot to produce good-sized nuts. Not only that, our native squirrels are mindful of nut-collecting time. For this reason, I often find myself relying on imported nuts. Hazels have a thin dark red-brown skin which is best removed before using.

To skin hazelnuts: toast them in a non-stick frying pan over a medium heat, shaking the pan to prevent them from burning, for 3–4 minutes until their skins begin to crack and flake off. Remove from the heat and leave until cool enough to handle. Now this is where the fun starts. Place 8–10 nuts between the palms of your hands. Rub vigorously until the skins flake off and you are left with creamy-yellow naked nuts. Alternatively, you can rub them in a tea-towel.

Walnuts, with their soft, yet crunchy texture, are invaluable either in cakes or used as a decoration on the top. Unlike hazels and almonds, it is unnecessary to skin them. To restore slightly stale walnuts, toss them in a warm small frying pan for a couple of minutes to release their flavoursome oil.

To prepare your own ground nuts: whiz the skinned nuts in a food processor until they are very finely ground. To retain freshness, store the ground nuts in an airtight container and use within 2–3 weeks.

Praline is a sweet nutty confection – lovely sprinkled onto cakes or blended with melted chocolate as a filling or topping. It takes just 10 minutes or so to make. Have ready a lightly oiled baking sheet. Put 125g granulated sugar in a heavy-based saucepan and place over a low heat until the sugar has dissolved to a clear syrup. Add 125g almonds or hazelnuts (skins on). Swirl the pan around until the nuts are evenly coated with the sugar syrup. Continue to cook until the syrup turns nutty brown (watch carefully as it can quickly go too far and start to burn). Tip the mixture onto the oiled baking sheet and leave until cool. Place the cooled praline in a food processor and whiz to a coarse powder. Store in an airtight jar for up to 3 months.

P.S. To remove fragments of shell from a batch of freshly shelled nuts, place the nuts in a large bowl of cold water and the shells will float to the surface.

Spices Rich with the exotic and beguiling essences of their native lands, spices are wonderful additions to many cakes. To get the best flavour from spices, buy them in small quantities and use them up relatively quickly to ensure they are fresh; out-of-date ground spices can be severely lacking in flavour. Many independent health food shops sell spices loose, so you can buy them little and often. Steenbergs (see directory, p.244) have a first-rate range of organic and fair-trade spices and other baking ingredients. Store spices in airtight containers, such as little jam jars.

Cinnamon, with its warming, fragrant tones, is often used in cakes made with orchard fruits. It complements apples particularly well, but also pears and plums.

Nutmeg, with its mellow, sweetly aromatic qualities, is a key ingredient in mixed spice, but it is also lovely to use independently in rich fruit cakes and everyday apple cakes. Nutmeg can be bought ready ground, but I prefer to use it freshly grated from a whole nutmeg kernel.

Mixed spice is a harmonious medley of ground sweet spices. Typically it includes cinnamon, nutmeg, coriander, ginger, allspice and cloves – a perfect mix to add to fruit cakes and spicy biscuits.

Poppy seeds, with their sweet, slightly nutty flavour and distinctive slate-blue colour, give aroma and texture to otherwise plain cakes.

Caraway seeds have been used for centuries in spice cakes, biscuits and breads for their pungent aniseed-like flavour.

Vanilla is used very often in cake-making – its unique mellow, fragrant sweetness being highly prized in no end of recipes. It is available as whole pods, a ground powder or a liquid extract. None of the options are cheap, but investment in pure vanilla is a must in my book. If using extract, make sure it is pure vanilla extract, not a synthetic vanilla 'essence'.

Ginger adds fiery warmth and true spiciness to cakes and biscuits. Ground ginger is commonly used; this is root ginger, dried and ground to a powder. Sticky glacé stem ginger and preserved stem ginger in syrup can also be chopped and added to cakes to give bite, texture and flavour.

Salt Although not strictly necessary, a little salt will fine-tune and enhance the final flavour. It may appear somewhat contradictory to use unsalted butter and then add salt, but I can assure you, the pinch of salt usually specified in recipes is far less than the amount contained in salted butter. Use a fine-grained sea salt.

Chocolate Lending a divine smooth richness and untold seductiveness, chocolate is quintessential in baking. Don't we all love a chocolate cake? In cake-making, it is used in both powder form (cocoa) and as a solid (chocolate). Cocoa powder is rich in flavour and colour, but rather bitter; it is ground from the dried solids of the fermented cocoa bean after the cocoa butter has been removed.

Chocolate itself contains cocoa solids and cocoa butter, and often sugar as well. It is the proportion of cocoa solids that determines the grade of chocolate. Plain (dark) chocolate ranges between 35% cocoa solids (the legal minimum) and 100% (for a very dark, bitter bar). White chocolate doesn't contain any cocoa solids but is a blend of cocoa butter, milk and sugar, resulting in a very low melting point.

I like to use a good plain, semi-sweet or bitter-sweet chocolate with a cocoa solid content around 60–70%, which yields a delicious smoothness with a relatively low melting point. Green & Black's (see directory, p.244) produce excellent well-priced organic cocoa powder and chocolate. If you are using really intense 100% dark chocolate, such as Willie's (www.williescacao.com), use roughly 30% less than the recipe states.

Flowers and herbs Look no further than the summer garden or hedgerow to find flowers and herbs to add heady or aromatic fragrance to your baking. The early-summer hedgerows, more often than not, are alive with the creamy white blossom of elderflowers. A little later, the summer garden will provide breathtaking scents from roses, lavender and jasmine, while the leaves from aromatic herbs such as rose-scented geraniums, lemon verbena and peppermint can be used to impart their unique sweet, fresh savour to your baking.

Simply steep the flowers or foliage in a little water to add to simple sponges and icings, or lightly sweeten to make a fragrant sugar syrup to drizzle over freshly baked cakes (see Scent from heaven cake, p.160).

Likewise, more concentrated, yet still delicately perfumed, orange flower and rose waters add blissful tones to fruit or almondy cakes and marzipan. These can be bought from specialist baking suppliers such as Steenbergs (see directory, p.244).

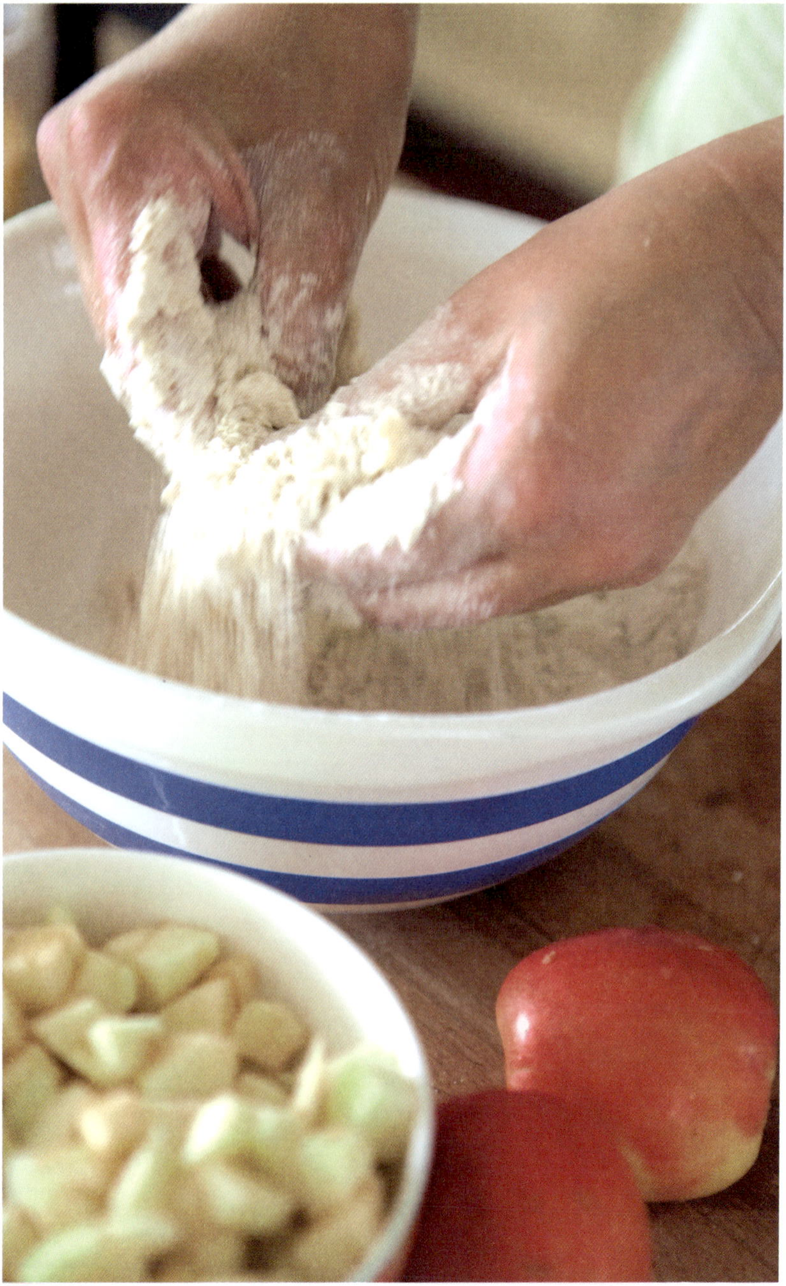

Baking methods

There are five basic ways to combine ingredients for a cake. These methods all have similar aims: to thoroughly blend dry, lighter ingredients with moist, heavier ones and to incorporate air into the batter in order to give lift and lightness.

Rubbing-in method

This is often used for biscuit-making and for cakes that contain little fat. Butter or other fat is cut into small pieces, then added to sifted flour and lightly rubbed in with the fingertips until the mixture resembles breadcrumbs. You will get much better results if your hands are cool, and if you work the mixture lightly, lifting the crumbs high to keep the blend soft, airy and free-flowing.

Creaming method

This is probably the most widely used cake-making technique and it is best employed for large egg- and butter-rich cakes, such as Victoria sandwiches and some fruit cakes. Softened butter or margarine is first thoroughly beaten, or 'creamed', until light and fluffy, then fine-grained caster sugar is added. The key to success (so please don't skimp) is then to cream the butter and sugar together energetically to create a mass of tiny air bubbles. Once surrounded with an egg-based batter and baked, these bubbles 'set' and provide the light, airy structure of the cake. It is important to make sure all the gritty bits of sugar are completely blended into the creamy mix, so always scrape down the sides of the bowl a couple of times while creaming.

Creaming properly by hand will take 10–15 minutes. If you are using a hand-held electric whisk, you should allow 5–6 minutes; with a free-standing electric mixer, it will take about 4 minutes. If using an electric whisk, start off on the lowest speed, increasing to moderate once the butter and sugar are thoroughly combined.

Whisking method

This technique involves vigorously beating eggs and sugar to incorporate air until a thick, creamy mousse is formed, then folding in sifted flour, and sometimes a little melted butter. It is particularly used for light sponges and fatless cakes, such as Swiss rolls. The egg-and-sugar mousse is very delicate and care must be taken to minimise the loss of volume when folding in the flour. Before you begin, do make sure that your bowl and whisk are spotlessly clean, as any grease in the bowl will prevent the eggs from whisking up properly.

If you are using a balloon whisk or an old-fashioned hand whisk, the eggs and sugar need to be placed in a heatproof bowl sat over a pan of just-off-the-boil water (don't allow the bowl to touch the water). The heat from the steam helps the sugar to dissolve and thickens the egg very slightly. If, however, you are using a hand-held

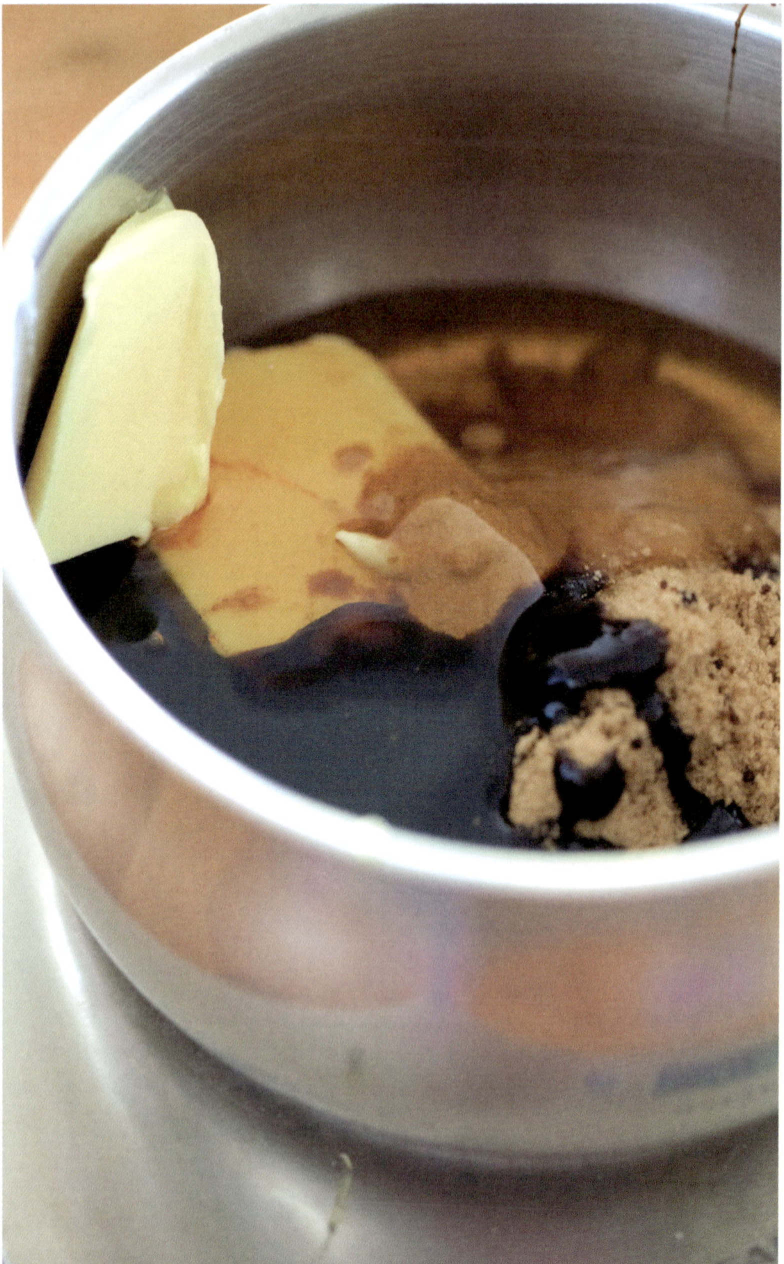

electric whisk or free-standing electric mixer, it is not necessary to do this. Having said that, you will certainly find that placing the bowl over hot water when using a hand-held electric whisk speeds up the operation.

Melting or warming method

This is frequently used when making damp cakes, such as gingerbreads and tray bakes, as well as crunchy biscuits. It is a lovely, straightforward technique that involves melting butter, syrups, sugar and liquids together before adding them, often with a beaten egg or two, to the dry ingredients.

Blitz or 'all-in-one' method

The simplest and fastest way of making a cake, whereby all the ingredients are beaten together with an electric mixer for no more than 1½–2 minutes. This method is ideal if you want to whip up a sponge cake very quickly, but success relies on all the ingredients being at room temperature when you begin. (This is one instance when soft margarine wins hands down over butter, because it can be used straight from the fridge.) Though quick and easy to make, I always feel that a blitzed cake lacks the dignified demeanour of a traditionally creamed one.

Lining tins

Greasing and/or lining baking tins will help any reluctant or shy cakes to be released after baking. I find butter the best greasing medium. I prefer it to processed margarines, while I've found oils do not always give a completely non-stick surface. You can use either a bit of butter wrapper with a knob of soft butter on it, or dab a pastry brush in a little melted butter and paint over the base and sides of the tin.

For most cakes, I simply grease the sides of the tin with softened butter, then smear a little on the base to just hold a piece of baking parchment in place. Gluten-free cakes are more likely to stick, so make sure you grease the tins for these very well. Richer, deeper fruit cakes demand a bit more comfort so run a piece of baking parchment around the sides of the tin too. For cakes with crumbly toppings such as Somerset cider cake (p.168) or Hugh's fresh cherry cake (p.174), do make sure you use a springform tin or one with a loose bottom so you can remove it easily.

Dusting the tin with flour after greasing it gives fatless sponges a crisper and more defined outline and will also help them to cling and 'climb' up the side of the tin in the oven. Use flour on its own, or mixed with an equal quantity of caster sugar. Dust the flour round the inside of the greased tin until it is evenly coated, removing any excess by shaking the tin upside down over the sink. For chocolate cakes, dust the tin with a mix of cocoa powder and sugar.

Lining a round tin
For the base, either use a pre-cut baking parchment circle (available from independent hardware stores and supermarkets) or make your own by placing the tin on a sheet of baking parchment, drawing around the base and cutting out with scissors.

For the sides, cut a strip of baking parchment approximately 2.5cm longer than the circumference of the tin and about 3cm wider than the height of the tin. Fold down a 1.5cm strip along one long edge, then unfold and use scissors to snip to the fold line, roughly at 2.5cm intervals. Press the strip around the inside of the greased tin, allowing the frilled edge to fit snugly around the base. Place the baking parchment base disc on top. Look out for narrow rolls of baking parchment (10cm wide), which are just the job for lining sides; these are available from Lakeland (see directory, p.244).

P.S. For garland or ring moulds, there is no need to line. Simply grease the tin well with butter. Turn the cake out 5–10 minutes after removing from the oven.

Lining a square tin or Swiss roll tin
Measure the base of the tin, adding on the depth of the sides plus an extra 1cm. Cut a piece of baking parchment this size. Place the tin in the middle of the paper and mark each of the corners. Then cut from the outer-edge corners of the baking parchment to the marked corners in the centre. Dab a little butter on the base and the sides of the tin (this is just to hold the paper in place). Ease the paper into the tin, folding the diagonally cut flappy ends neatly around each corner. For deep-sided tins you may need to smear a tiny bit of butter to keep these pieces in place.

To line a loaf tin
Use the method above or, more simply, just cut a piece of baking parchment long enough to cover the base and the long sides, then liberally grease the unlined ends. If the cake is reluctant to release, then run a small knife around the edge of the unlined ends.

P.S. To give a hint of perfume to light summer sponges, place 3–4 sweet scented geranium or lemon verbena leaves on the lined base of the tin. Remove them from the baked cake when it is turned out.

GETTING STARTED 41

Baking expressions

As time goes by, and with increasing experience, you'll begin to have baking conversations with yourself: *'Needs a little longer'* or *'Mmmm, that looks good'*. These unconscious thoughts will appear to be fitting for whatever stage the cake is at. However, there are a few customary terms which repeatedly crop up in baking methods and it's well worth understanding their meanings:

Curdling

Curdling describes when a beaten mixture breaks down into tiny grainy curds. It can occur when eggs are added to creamed butter and sugar, for one of three reasons. Firstly, it could be that the butter and sugar have not been creamed thoroughly and the sugar is still gritty when the egg is added (see the creaming method, p.37). Secondly, it may be that the eggs are too cold. If you are using eggs straight from the fridge, warm them up by placing them in a bowl of hot but not boiling water for a minute. Finally, curdling can occur when the eggs are added too quickly to the creamed butter and sugar.

It is to prevent curdling that you are often told to add 1 tbsp flour with each egg, and to ensure an egg is thoroughly beaten in before adding the next. Another trick to help avoid curdling is to add 1 tbsp flour before the first egg. A curdled mixture cannot hold air well and will result in a heavy cake. If, despite all precautions, your mixture does curdle, add 1 tbsp sifted flour to prevent it breaking down any more.

Folding in

This is a gentle cutting and folding action used to incorporate light ingredients into a heavier mixture. This term most frequently applies when adding flour to creamed or whisked mixtures. It is also the technique used to incorporate whisked egg whites into a cake mixture. Folding should be done using either a large metal spoon or a rubber spatula.

To fold in, you need to cut vertically through the mix with a deft, clean stroke, while at the same time rotating the bowl a quarter-turn with your other hand, bringing the spoon out and 'folding' the mixture over on itself. This gentle repeated action will turn the ingredients over on top of each other, combining them without losing too much of that precious trapped air.

Dropping consistency

This describes the texture of a cake mixture when a spoonful of it will fall from the spoon when it is tapped on the side of the bowl or lightly shaken. A soft dropping consistency is the stage at which a mixture will drop from the spoon by itself when the spoon is tipped.

Ribbon consistency

This is the term used to define when a whisked mixture is very thick, light in colour and falls away in a ribbon-like fashion when the beaters are lifted up out of the mix. It is most often applied to whisking eggs and sugar together, for example when making a Genoese or whisked sponge.

Turning out

This simply means removing a freshly baked cake from its tin. Turning out onto a footed wire rack allows heat to escape quickly and makes for a lighter cake. Light sponge cakes need to be left in their tins for 5–10 minutes after coming out of the oven, to settle and firm up, whereas more robust fruit and drizzle cakes are often left in their tins until cold.

To turn out a cake, place a wire rack over the top of the tin and invert both the cake and the rack then, with care, lift the tin off. (To prevent a criss-cross grid marking the top of the cake, place a clean folded tea-towel on the rack first.) Remove any lining paper and then turn the cake back the right way up with the help of a second rack. With experience, you will find you'll be able to use your hand for this stage, so you won't require a second rack.

Cake-makers' tips

This handful of baking tips should help your cake-making session to run smoothly. Enjoy your baking – your pleasure will be reflected in the finished cake.

Get organised before you start to bake Weigh out all the ingredients for the recipe and put them on a tray. For recipes with lots of ingredients, tick them off as you go. There are two advantages to doing this. The first is that you won't leave anything out (I speak from experience: my Christmas cake has, on more than one occasion, been missing the odd ingredient). The second plus is that your cupboard door handles won't get sticky.

Before you begin, sift the flour with any salt, raising agent or spices This will aerate and separate the fine flour particles and evenly distribute the other dry ingredients.

Place a damp, folded tea-towel underneath the bowl This will prevent it from slipping or skidding on the worktop.

Get to know your oven Resolve any idiosyncrasies it might have. Is it hot or cool or decidedly moody on a Monday morning? Adjust baking times and temperatures accordingly. More often than not, the most favourable cake-baking temperature is 180°C/Gas mark 4 and this is well worth remembering.

Once the cake is in the oven *Do not* open the door until at least three-quarters of the way through the recommended baking time. Open it too soon and both you and the cake will get a sinking feeling as that magical rise disappears, never to return. Remember too, if baking your cake in a larger than recommended tin, the cooking time will be less. Conversely, in a smaller tin, the cake will be deeper and take longer. Indeed, you may well need to reduce the heat a little towards the end of baking, or cover the top with a double thickness of baking parchment to prevent it browning too much while the centre finishes cooking.

Avoid any aerobic exercise near the oven This includes children playing hop-scotch on the kitchen tiles. Cakes thrive in a secure atmosphere. Bumps and thumps, in a baking environment, will frighten the cake and there is a good chance it will sink.

Cakes, when done, will shrink away slightly from the tin or the lining paper For creamed and whisked mixtures, the cake should spring back into shape when lightly pressed with your fingertip. For fruit cakes and heavier cakes, a fine skewer or small, sharp knife inserted into the centre of the cake should come out clean.

Recipe essentials

For the recipes in this book, unless otherwise stated:
- Spoon measurements are level.
- Eggs, with shell on, weigh approximately 63g.
- Bake your cake in the centre of the oven.
- Cooking times are a guide, not written in stone. Check your cake three-quarters of the way through the suggested cooking time.
- For fan-assisted ovens, reduce the given temperature by 10–20°C depending on your oven.

Storage

Homemade cakes have best-before dates, just like shop-bought ones. I have recommended a conservative keeping time for each recipe in this book. In general though, cakes tend to fall into four types:

Muffins and fatless sponges These are best eaten freshly baked; I don't mean scoffing the lot as soon as they are out of the oven, but certainly eat within a couple of days.

Vegetable/fresh fruit-baked cakes The high moisture content of these cakes means they should be stored in a cool place and eaten within 3–4 days.

Creamed cakes (For example, a Victoria sponge.) Best eaten within 5–6 days.

Dried fruit-based cakes These are the long-term keepers and, more often than not, actually improve with time. Wrap these cakes lightly in greaseproof paper and store in an airtight container or cake tin.

Most cakes freeze well and slicing and freezing them is one way to avoid uncontrolled cake consumption and have ready a wedge or two for a lunch box.

Cakes are best kept in airtight containers or cake storage tins. When used over a period of years cake tins will become much loved and well respected 'friends' in your kitchen. Sometimes it can be a bit of a tight squeeze to transfer a finished (especially a decorated cake) into a tin. A nifty and easy way to do this is to cut a strip of greaseproof paper about 15cm x 50cm. Place the cake in the centre of the strip and use the ends to carefully lift and then lower the cake into the tin. Leave the paper strip in place, either folding the ends over the cake or the outside edge of the tin. You can then use the ends to lift the cake out of the tin when required.

Fillers & Toppers

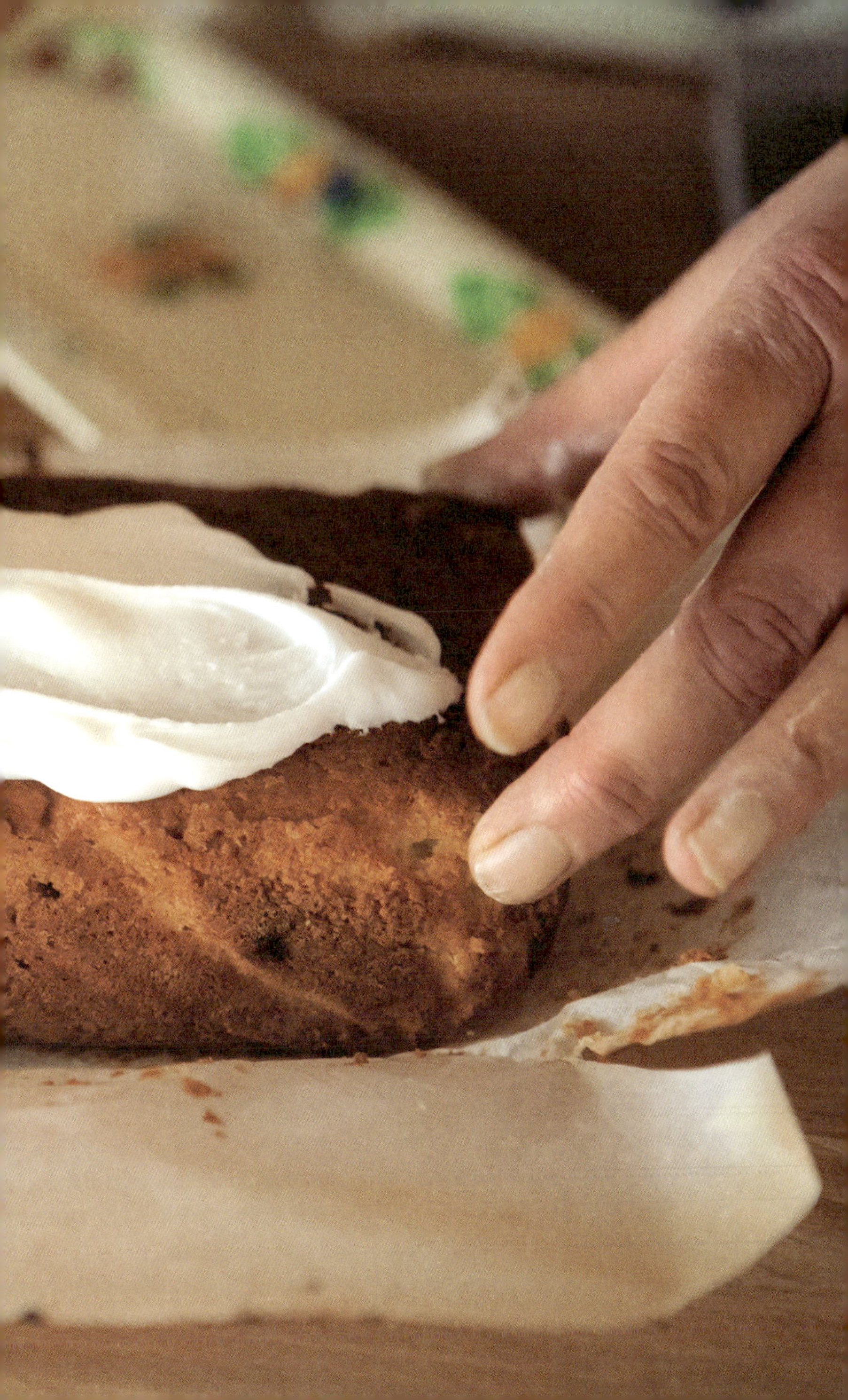

I'm not an expert cake decorator, but I do love to prettify some of my cakes. Unquestionably, there are some cakes which can be transformed into little seductresses with a touch or two of glitz or glamour. However, I generally steer clear of too much tarting up. I much prefer to keep my cakes naturally beautiful with just a few simple decorative touches – some arty feather icing, perhaps, or a few well-chosen dainty flowers to enhance their inherent charm.

Simple icings are the obvious choice. A coating of soft, sweet buttercream, gently smoothed across the top of a cake, is often enough, but a drizzle, which is poured over a cake, is even easier and its essence permeates right through to the core.

Nature offers up a number of amazing decorative gifts too. Fresh, fragrant edible flowers, such as primroses, marigolds, borage and roses, will beautify a simple iced sponge cake, while the juice of fresh summer berries – used in place of water in icings – gives outstanding flavour and colour. Likewise, the heavenly scents of aromatic flowers and herbs can be captured by infusing them in liquids, their vivacity bringing unexpected pleasure to the simplest of toppings. And the intricate patterns and beautiful shapes of leaves can be transferred to chocolate to make feather-light edible foliage.

Keeping decorations simple makes your life easier and means the cake itself remains the focus of attention.

Fillers

There is a fine line between what constitutes a cake filler and a topper. Many of these delectable fillers will feel equally at home on top of the cake as they do sandwiched in between the layers. Conversely, you will find some of the soft toppers will adapt very comfortably to the role of a filler. The moral of this is that it gives you the chance to do a little mix and matching, as well as using the ingredients you happen to have to hand.

Vanilla buttercream

This classic all-rounder doubles as a velvety smooth topper and filler in many cakes. It can work solo or partner up on the adhering job with a few spoonfuls of hold-fast jam. The rich, sweet taste of buttercream works particularly well with plain cakes and is perfect for topping cup or fairy cakes.

To fill a 20cm sandwich cake or top 12 fairy cakes
60g unsalted butter, softened and cut into small pieces
125g icing sugar, sifted
½ tsp vanilla extract

Place the butter in a mixing bowl and, either using a wooden spoon or a hand-held electric whisk, beat until creamy. Incorporate the icing sugar in three lots, beating well before adding the next. When it is all added the mixture should be a light cream. Finally mix in the vanilla extract.

Variations

Chocolate Replace 25g of the icing sugar with cocoa powder.

Coffee Add 1 tbsp coffee essence or 1 tbsp instant coffee dissolved in 1 tbsp hot water and cooled.

Nut Add 75g finely chopped nuts or 2–3 tbsp praline (see p.33).

Honey Replace half the icing sugar with 2 tbsp runny honey.

Jammy fillers

Whole-fruit jam or fruity jammy jellies are a blissful and easy way to glue a sandwich cake together, as well as a resourceful use of homemade preserves. Although red jams are customarily used, there is no prescriptive flavour to use, so choose your favourite. Gooseberry, for example, works particularly well in a cake topped with elderflower-infused glacé icing.

Lemon curd

Freshly made lemon curd makes a delectable filling for sponge cakes and Swiss rolls. You can make it while the cake is baking – it really doesn't take long. Add a crushed meringue (see p.112) to the finished curd for a crunchy lemon-meringue filling.

To fill a 20cm cake or Swiss roll (with some to spare)
Finely grated zest and juice of 1 large unwaxed lemon
75g caster sugar
50g unsalted butter
2 eggs, well beaten

Have ready a pan of barely simmering water. Put all the ingredients, except the eggs, into a heatproof bowl that will sit snugly on the pan without touching the water. Place the bowl over the water and, stirring once or twice, leave until the butter has just melted. Briskly whisk in the eggs using a balloon whisk, until thoroughly combined into the buttery lemon mixture. Scrape the sides down and whisk occasionally until the mixture is glossy and thickened. Either cool in the bowl and use immediately to fill a cooled cake, or pour into a couple of small clean jam jars, seal with a metal lid and store in the fridge; use within 2 weeks.

Meringutan

This is my quirky name for a delightful filling that can be whipped up in an instant. Simply blend a crushed meringue (see p.112) into 150ml lightly whipped double cream to give you enough to layer two 20cm sponges. Double the quantities for a three-layer cake.

Caramel cream

A glorious confection to squeeze between layers or ooze over cakes. It can be made simply (and I hope you don't think this a cheat's way) from a tin of condensed milk. Place a tin of condensed milk on a folded tea-towel (this will stop it rattling around) in a deep stainless-steel saucepan. Cover completely with warm water. Bring gently to simmering point and keep it at a low simmer for 1½–2 hours – the longer it is cooked, the thicker and darker the caramel will be. Make sure you keep the pan topped up with hot water. Remove from the heat and leave the tin in the saucepan until it is completely cold before opening.

It's worth preparing several tins at a time – to save on fuel. Once cooked, the unopened tins will keep for up to a year, but do remember to mark the cans so you know what they are.

Toppers

The topping, or the finishing touch on a cake, will turn any cake into something rather special and eye-catching. Just a simple dusting of icing sugar will do the trick in many cases, while a specially prepared icing will flatter and bring harmony to the cake. Do make sure the cake is completely cool before filling or topping it – a warm cake will soften the mix and it will drip and ooze all over the place. The exceptions are those cakes that are baked with their toppings already in place, for instance the Dundee cake and those with crumbly streusel-type toppings.

In addition to the velvety smooth icings used to coat the tops and sides of cakes, the true finishing touches are special adornments you choose to decorate the cake. These could be a boxful of coloured cake candles, lit to celebrate a birthday or anniversary. If you take a glance around the garden or hedgerow from springtime through to autumn, you will find edible flowers and other natural and earthy decorations to gather for free. Then again, a handful of whole or chopped nuts will give a lovely finish to many cakes.

Nonetheless, a few well-chosen shop-bought sugar cake decorations certainly won't go amiss, and will allow you to speedily pretty up freshly baked cakes and biscuits. I like the fair-trade chocolate drops and the vermicelli decorations from Steenbergs (see directory, p.244) and sugary flowers (particularly the violets) from Cakes, Cookies and Crafts (see directory, p.244).

Caster sugar

A simple sprinkling of caster sugar will give freshly baked biscuits and many cakes their finishing touch. In fact this free-flowing sugar is the classic topping for the ever-favourite Victoria sandwich.

Icing sugar

Dusted lightly over the top of a cake, this superfine sugar powder is often sufficient to give an attractive finish. Alternatively, paper doilies or homemade stencils can be used to create a simple or intricate pattern – just place the doily or stencil on top of the cake and dust with icing sugar. Remove the paper very carefully to reveal an instant work of art.

An equal mix of sifted cocoa powder and icing sugar can be used to give a lovely chocolatey finish.

FILLERS & TOPPERS 53

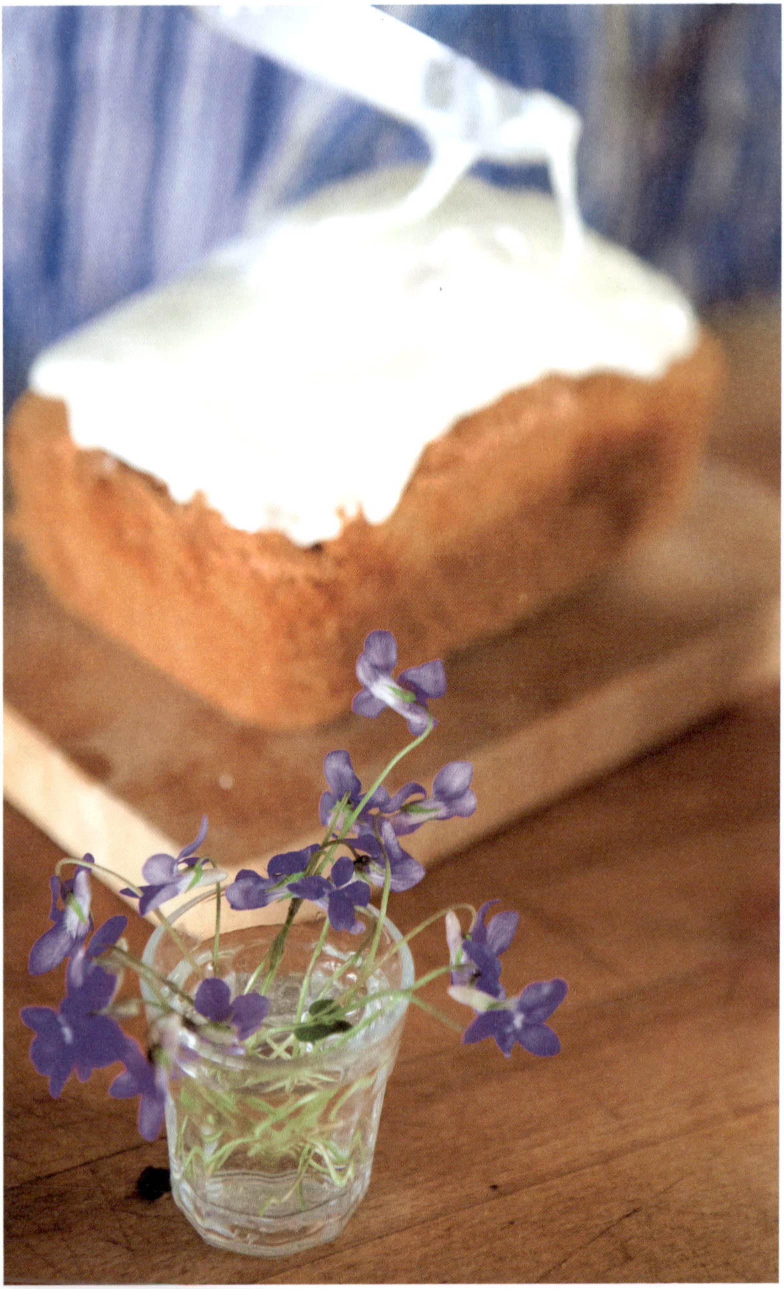

Glacé icing

This straightforward icing, also known as 'water icing', sets to form a crisp surface, but doesn't become hard. The trick is in getting this ever-so-simple icing 'just right'. Too thick, and the icing will not be glistening and glossy; too thin and it will run all over the place. Add less liquid than you think you need; you can always add more. Keep it pure and white, or dress it up with fresh fruit juice, coffee, chocolate, coconut – whatever takes your – or your cake's – fancy.

To top a 20cm round or 18cm square cake or 12 cup cakes
250g icing sugar
About 2 tbsp hot water or flavouring (see variations)

Sift the icing sugar into a mixing bowl. Add 1 tbsp of the liquid to start with and then a little at a time, beating until the mixture is smooth and glossy and thick enough to coat the back of the spoon. Adjust, if necessary, with a drop more water or a little more sifted icing sugar.

Variations
Citrus Use 2 tbsp freshly squeezed lemon, orange or lime juice.

Smooth berry Macerate 75g crushed ripe raspberries or strawberries with 1 tsp icing sugar. Leave until the juices begin to run, and then pass through a sieve to remove the pips.

Whole berry Simply crush or blend 75g berries of your choice to a purée, or use 2 tbsp fruit coulis.

Elderflower Replace 1 tbsp of the water with 1 tbsp elderflower cordial.

Rosehip Replace 1 tbsp of the water with 1 tbsp rosehip cordial.

Coffee Dissolve 1 tbsp instant coffee in 2 tbsp hot water, or use 2 tbsp very strong filter coffee.

Earl Grey or jasmine tea Infuse 1 tea bag in 50ml boiling water, using sufficient to mix to the required texture.

Caramel Simply use unrefined icing sugar.

Chocolate Replace 1 tbsp of the icing sugar with 2 tbsp drinking chocolate or 1 tbsp sifted cocoa powder.

Coconut Replace 1–2 tbsp of the icing sugar with desiccated coconut; this will give you a textured icing.

Feather icing

This is my party piece! It's incredibly simple, but very effective. You will need two different colours of glacé icing – one to coat the cake and another one to feather with. I generally keep the main icing white, then use a strong or vivid colour for the feathering bit. You can use natural food colouring, of course, but a drop or two of blackcurrant cordial or fresh raspberry juice works just as well. Now this is where enterprise comes into play by using, if you like, some fairly whacky colours to feather up your cake.

To cover a 20cm round cake
250g quantity of white Glacé icing (see p.55)
A little natural food colouring

First, take a good tablespoonful of the icing and colour with the food colouring. Place this in a small plastic bag, pushing it into one corner, and set aside. Then, smoothly coat the top of the cake with the white glacé icing. Next, snip off the very tip of the icing-filled point of the plastic bag. Pipe the feathering icing in thin lines across the cake. Now, using the tip of a knife or a skewer, score parallel lines across the piped lines from one side of the cake to the other, alternating directions to create a soft feather-like pattern.

Citrus frosting

A lively topping for plain sponges or cup cakes. The crunchy sugar stays on top while the citrus syrup soaks in. Try using a citrus liqueur in place of half or all the juice.

To top a 20cm round, 18cm square or 12cm x 25cm loaf cake
Juice of 1 lemon, small orange, lime or tangerine (about 50ml)
125g granulated sugar

Mix the citrus juice with the sugar and set aside for 10 minutes. Spoon over the slightly cooled cake before the sugar has fully dissolved.

Cream cheese topping

This is an all-time great for carrot cakes, banana cakes and muffins. Do use a full-fat cream cheese: low-fat ones result in a sloppy icing that runs off the cake.

To top a 20cm round cake or 10 large muffins
100g full-fat cream cheese
25g unsalted butter, softened and cut into small pieces
150–175g icing sugar, sifted
1 tsp vanilla extract or orange flower water, or
  the finely grated zest of 1 unwaxed orange or lemon

Beat the cream cheese and butter together until smooth. Add the icing sugar and any flavouring and beat until the mixture is very light and creamy. Cover and refrigerate for an hour or so to firm up before using.

Yoghurt and white chocolate topping

A soft, smooth covering for many cakes, including sponges, carrot cake, ginger cake and cup cakes.

To top a 20cm cake or 18–20 cup cakes
100g white chocolate, broken into small pieces
50–100ml full-fat plain yoghurt

Put the chocolate into a small heatproof bowl. Place over a pan of barely simmering water, without allowing the bowl to touch the water, and leave until the chocolate has just melted. Remove from the heat and beat in sufficient yoghurt to give a smooth, creamy topping. Rest in the fridge for 30 minutes before using.

Marzipan

This timeless nutty confection is somewhat exceptional because it fills and tops, as well as being used for making decorations. Homemade marzipan only takes a few minutes to prepare and it is a thousand times nicer than the bought stuff. It's traditionally made with ground almonds but there is no reason why cashews, hazelnuts or walnuts cannot be used – simply blitz whole skinned nuts (see p.32) in a food processor until they are finely ground.

Marzipan keeps well so you can prepare it in advance and have it to hand when you want to cover a Christmas cake, bake a stollen, sandwich it into a Simnel cake, wrap up a Battenberg or mould it into decorative shapes.

To thickly cover the top and sides of an 18cm round cake
1 medium egg
1 tbsp brandy, whisky or orange liqueur
125g caster sugar
125g icing sugar, sifted
250g ground almonds

Break the egg into a large bowl. Add the alcohol and whisk well together. Add the caster sugar, icing sugar and ground almonds and mix to a stiff paste. Sprinkle your work surface with a little icing sugar, then turn the almond paste out onto it. Knead until the marzipan is soft and smooth (your hands will be soft too). Seal the marzipan in a plastic bag and store in the fridge until required.

To marzipan a round or square cake To cover the top of the cake, take roughly half of the marzipan and place it on a sheet of greaseproof paper lightly dusted with icing sugar. Roll out the marzipan so that it is about 1cm thick and a little larger than the diameter of the cake. Lightly brush the top of the cake with either a little lightly beaten egg white or warmed sieved apricot jam. The easiest way to put the marzipan on the cake is to invert the cake onto the marzipan and give it a good thwack. Trim away the excess marzipan round the edge of the cake before re-inverting and placing on a cake board.

To cover the side of the cake, measure the depth and the circumference of the cake – a piece of string is a handy way to do this. Roll out the remaining marzipan to fit; you may find it easiest to do this in two sections. Brush the sides of the cake with egg white or warm sieved apricot jam and press the marzipan band(s) in place. Use either a straight-sided jam jar or drinking glass to run around the edge of the cake to smooth the sides and fix firmly in place.

Leave the cake in a cool, dry place for 2–3 days to allow the marzipan to dry before applying icing.

To toast marzipan on a rich fruit cake Either just top or completely cover the cake with marzipan (see above). Roll out any leftover marzipan to approximately a 5mm thickness. Use biscuit cutters to cut out shapes: snowflakes, hearts, stars, etc. Brush the cake with lightly beaten egg yolk, then position the marzipan shapes on the top. Brush these with egg yolk too. Place in the oven, preheated to 200°C/Gas mark 6, and bake for about 15 minutes to toast – don't forget it! For a cake only topped with marzipan, tie a band of double-thickness greaseproof paper around the side of the cake to protect it and prevent it from catching.

To colour marzipan Place it on a clean, dry surface dusted with icing sugar. Flatten the marzipan with a rolling pin, and dab a little of the required colouring in the centre. Fold it over a couple of times and roll out again. Repeat the process of folding and rolling until the colour is evenly distributed through the marzipan.

To make marzipan shapes Lightly dust the work surface with icing sugar and roll out the marzipan to approximately a 5mm thickness, then use biscuit cutters to cut out shapes. Alternatively, you can mould shapes, such as vegetables, fruits, flowers, etc., by hand. Just 50g of marzipan will make a bunch of carrots any grocer would be proud to sell. You can use everyday kitchen utensils and store-cupboard ingredients to add texture and finish. For instance, roll moulded oranges over a fine grater or simply use a sharp knife to score lines around the bodies of shapely carrots. Leave on a wire rack for 2–3 days to dry.

FILLERS & TOPPERS

Royal icing

As its name suggests, this icing is reserved for top-notch celebration cakes. It's traditionally spread so smoothly that the surface is like a coating of perfect virgin snow, or swirled and lifted to resemble snow peaks. I rarely use royal icing, except to whip up a chaotic snowy scene on my Christmas cake.

To thickly cover the top and sides of a 20cm round or 18cm square cake
2 egg whites
500g icing sugar, sifted
1 tsp lemon juice or orange flower water
1 tsp glycerine (optional, but stops the icing becoming brittle)

Place the egg whites in a large mixing bowl and whisk lightly. Incorporate the icing sugar a spoonful at a time until the mixture falls in a thick ribbon from a spoon. Stir in the flavouring and glycerine if using, then, using either a wooden spoon or a hand-held electric whisk, beat until the icing will stand up in soft peaks. Cover with a damp cloth and leave for roughly 15 minutes to allow any air bubbles to rise to the surface. Cover the top and the sides of the cake with the icing. For an ultra-smooth finish, dip a palette knife into a jug of very hot water to work over the cake, or do as I do and roughly swirl over and rough up with the blade of a knife or a fork.

Fondant icing

Although there are several good proprietary fondant icing sugars on the market (that include in the ingredients a little dried glucose), this really is a lovely icing to add to your repertoire. The lemon in this recipe cuts cleanly through the sweet icing, but by all means ring the changes by replacing both water and lemon juice with other fruity flavours: fresh orange juice, fruity squash or even blitzed summer berries.

To cover a 20cm round cake
2 tbsp glucose syrup (obtainable from chemists)
4 tbsp water
4 tbsp lemon juice
800–850g icing sugar

Have ready a pan of simmering water. Put the glucose syrup, water and lemon juice in a heatproof bowl that will fit snugly over the pan without touching the water. Sift in the icing sugar and beat with a balloon whisk until well combined. Sit the bowl on the pan and heat gently until the mixture is thick and glossy. Remove from the pan and let cool to roughly blood temperature (37°C). When ready to use, place the cake or cakes on a wire rack over a tray or a piece of baking parchment. Pour the icing onto the centre of the cake and allow it to spread over the top and down the sides. Any excess can be scraped from underneath, re-warmed and used again.

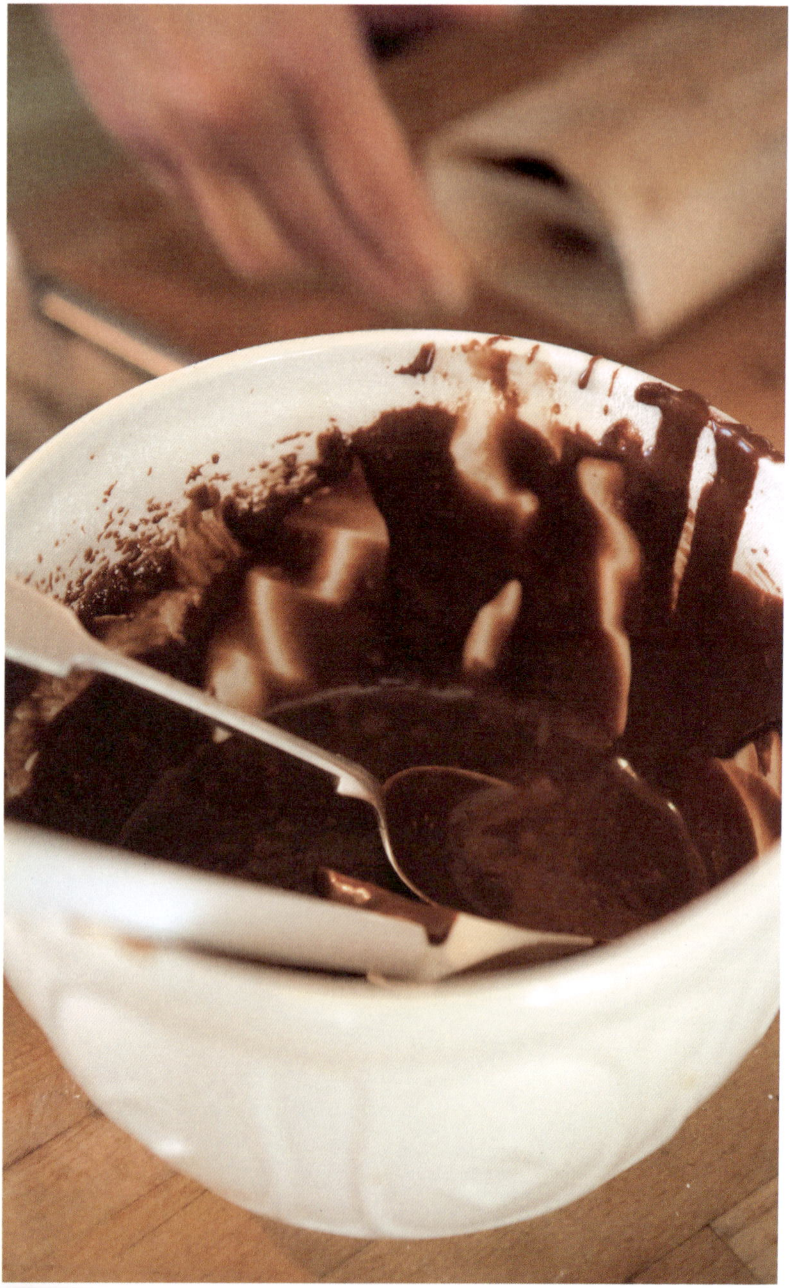

Chocolate icing

Smooth, rich and delicious, chocolate icing will dreamily top off any plain, chocolate or coffee cake. Melted chocolate on its own won't do – it sets into a brittle coating that will crack and splinter. A proportion of butter will keep it meltingly soft.

To top a 20cm cake
100g dark chocolate, broken into small pieces
50g unsalted butter, cut into small pieces

Have ready a small pan of simmering water. Place the chocolate in a small heatproof bowl, sit over the pan (make sure it doesn't touch the water) and allow the chocolate to almost completely melt. Just before the last pieces disappear, remove the bowl from the heat. It's important not to get the chocolate too hot, or overwork it; either can cause it to 'split' into grainy solids and a fatty liquid (when it won't be good for anything). Little by little, add the butter, beating until the mixture is smooth and glossy. Set aside for 5–10 minutes to thicken up before spreading over your cake.

Variations

Mocha Add 1 tsp coffee granules when melting the chocolate.

Boozy Fold in 1 tbsp Cointreau, Grand Marnier or brandy once the chocolate and butter are combined and have cooled a little.

Chocolate fudge icing

This soft, mousse-like filling is just the thing to turn a chocolate cake into perfection. Use it also to cover cup cakes or to fill and top a Victoria sandwich or coffee cake.

To fill and top a 20cm cake
150g plain or semi-sweet chocolate, broken into small pieces
75g unsalted butter, diced
2 tbsp milk
3 egg yolks
150g icing sugar, sifted

Put the chocolate, butter and milk into a medium heatproof bowl. Place over a pan of just-simmering water until the chocolate and butter have melted – the mixture should be warm but not hot. Remove from the heat and beat until smooth. Add the egg yolks, one at a time, beating until well combined. Add the sugar, a third at a time, beating to a thick, smooth spreading consistency. Use as required.

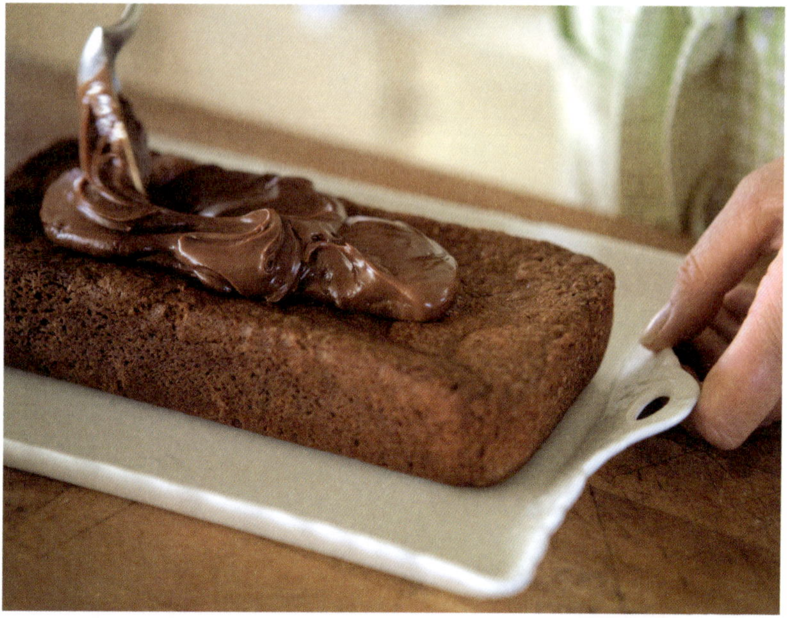

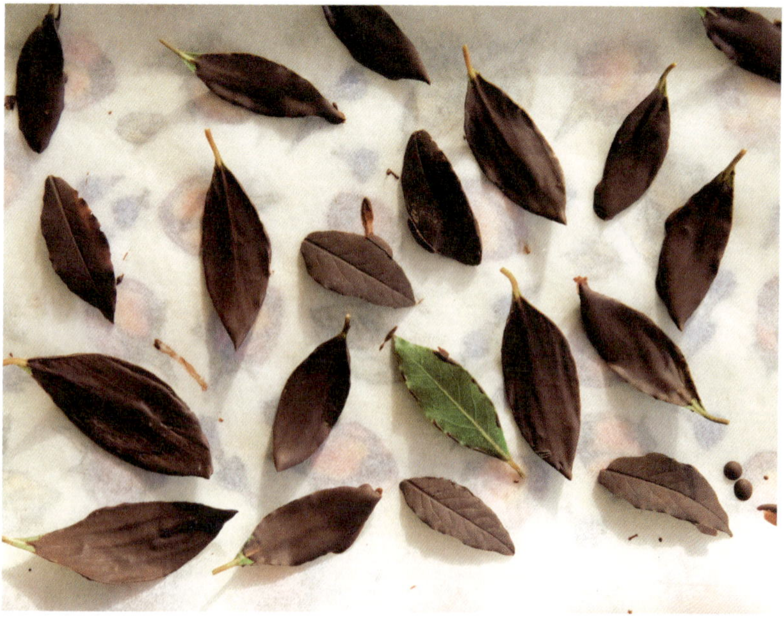

Chocolate ganache

Bitter, dark chocolate is normally used for this smooth, creamy classic, but it is also delicious made with a semi-sweet milk or even a creamy white chocolate.

To cover a 20cm cake
125ml double cream
125g dark chocolate, broken into small pieces

Place the cream in a small saucepan and heat very gently until very hot but not boiling. Add the broken chocolate pieces and beat with a wooden spoon until the chocolate has melted and the mixture is smooth. Pour into a clean bowl and set aside to cool. Use at room temperature to pour over a cake, or chill until cold and then whip for a silky chocolate cream to fill, top or smother all over the cake.

Variation
Chocolate crème fraîche (or yoghurt) topping In a similar vein, you can make a lovely chocolate topping by mixing cooled, melted chocolate or chocolate hazelnut spread into the same quantity of plain yoghurt or crème fraîche.

Chocolate leaves

Edible chocolate leaves, moulded from fresh leaves, will cheer up any number of cakes, big or small. Use robust non-toxic leaves with their stems attached – rose, blackberry and bay leaves all work well. Thickly coat the underside of the leaf with melted chocolate, making sure you do not get any on the top side (otherwise it will be difficult to remove). Place on baking parchment and allow to dry completely before peeling off the leaves to reveal perfect chocolate leaves.

Edible flowers

From shrinking violets found in April, nestling in sheltered corners, to late summer's bounty of sensuous garden lavender, many flowers can be snitched away to lavish upon iced or otherwise unadorned cakes. Do take care though, just because a flower is edible, it doesn't mean it tastes good. Camomile, for example, is lovely in tea but bitter on a cake. Stick to familiar faces such as primroses, roses, borage, jasmine, violas, nasturtiums, cornflowers, sage or tiny thyme flowers. I like honeysuckle blooms too – but please remember the berries are poisonous. If you are unsure about whether or not a flower is edible, then do check it out before using. The freshness and verve of these natural decorations will bring free spirit and joy to your cakes. And you can extend their lives by crystallising them in sugar (see overleaf). Store them away and they can bring new life to your baking, even in deep winter.

Crystallised flowers

For some, preparing these may seem a bit of a fiddle, but the time spent gathering and preparing the flowers pales into insignificance when you consider their lasting ethereal beauty. Primroses, violets, violas, apple blossom, rose petals and borage all respond well to the crystallising process. However, in all cases, success depends on both the flowers and the sugar being perfectly dry. Pick the flowers on a dry, sunny day when they are fully open. Remove the stalks.

Pour a lightly beaten (but not frothy) egg white into a saucer. Have another saucer of caster sugar beside it. Using tweezers, dip the flower heads or petals first into the egg white and then into the sugar. Use a fine paintbrush to tease the sugar into any crinkles and hollows within the flower. Shake off any excess sugar before laying the flowers on a sheet of baking parchment. Place in a warm, dry and airy spot to dry for 24–48 hours.

When fully dry, store the crystallised flowers carefully between layers of baking parchment or greaseproof paper in an airtight container.

Angelica

When candied, angelica is rather like a green goddess to the cake-maker. Its slender green stems can be slivered and sliced and used with stunning effect on simple iced cakes or festive glacé-fruit topped cakes. If you have access to young, fresh angelica stems (and angelica is an easy herb to grow), do have a go at candying some yourself. They will be far superior to their shop-bought alternative – less startling in colour, perhaps, but rich with angelica's unique aromatic, slightly astringent flavour. Also look out for the bright young leaves of alexanders, which flourish along roadsides during spring and early summer. The stems of these seaside-loving plants, as John Wright suggests in his *Edible Seashore* handbook, make a delicious addition to cakes. This is John's recipe to candy alexanders, which I've appropriated for angelica.

Choose young, tender springtime shoots and trim to roughly 10cm lengths. Place them in a saucepan with just enough water to cover and simmer until softened. Remove from the heat and allow to cool a little. Remove the angelica with a slotted spoon, reserving the water, and trim away any tough outer fibres. Weigh the stems, then add the same weight of sugar to the pan of cooking water. Dissolve over a medium heat and bring to the boil. Lay the angelica stems in a flat dish and pour over the sugar syrup. Cover and leave for a day.

Pour the syrup back into the pan and bring to the boil. Simmer for a few minutes to reduce slightly, then pour back over the angelica and leave for another day.

Repeat the process for another 2 days, then drain off the remaining syrup and lay the angelica stems on wire racks. Either dry them in a low oven at 40–50°C for 4 hours or in a warm, dry place over several days. Store, when completely dry, wrapped in greaseproof paper in a sealed jam jar or airtight container.

FILLERS & TOPPERS 67

Small Cakes & Bakes

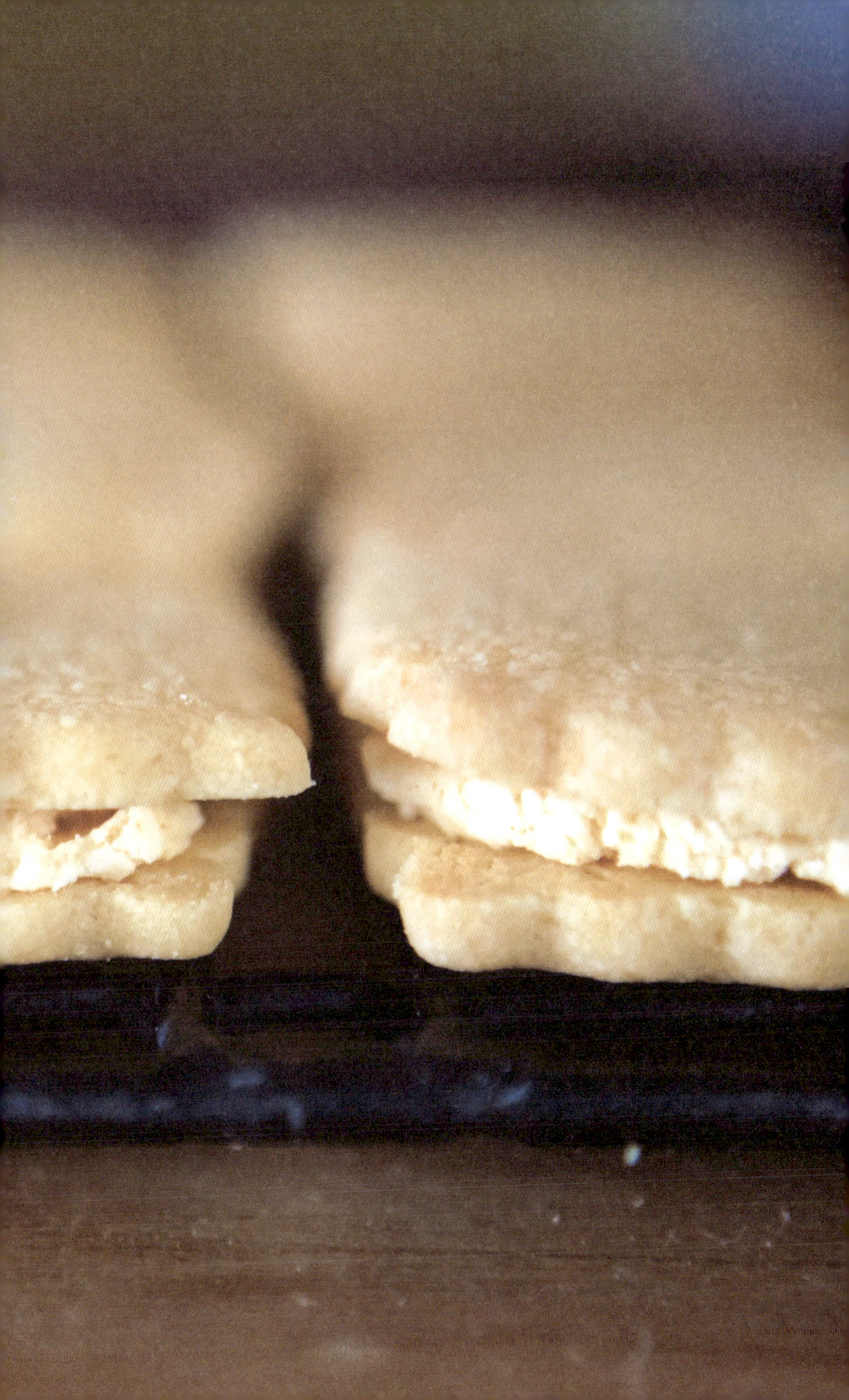

The little gems in this chapter break down into three categories. First there are the utilitarian ones, quick to fix and great hunger stoppers – the unleavened kind that are typical of the earliest of 'cakes'. These recipes are the sort you get to know by heart and can effortlessly knock up in a few minutes or so, brilliant to bake as your guests arrive at the door. They include the down-to-earth, swift-to-make Welsh cakes – cooked on a hot griddle in no more than 6 minutes – and the ever-popular energy-packed bars like flapjacks. Incidentally, the cakes King Alfred burnt were most likely the forerunners of Welsh cakes.

Then there are the everyday specials – crisp biscuits warmly flavoured with lively spices and soft-centred cookies to bake off whenever the desire arises. Not forgetting the timeless classic of the Scottish larder, shortbread – once perfected, this will give you a baking reputation second to none. However, here lies a word of warning from a voice of experience. If you enter the shortbread class at your local show, bear in mind that judging at these village affairs can be very subjective. If, for some reason, your entry does not win, graciously accept the miscarriage of justice and don't worry about it. Well, at least not until the following year.

The ultimates in this section are the heartbreakers, the adorables, the enticers – the little devils that destroy all your willpower by their persuasive sumptuousness: sweet chewy macaroons, salt caramel shortbread, the unctuous and universally popular chocolate brownie. The members of this elite and somewhat flamboyant set are unquestionably best reserved for special times when you will need to exercise a certain amount of restraint if you are to have just the one portion and no more. Even in their making, you'll be giddy with excitement and anticipation, knowing the best moment is yet to come.

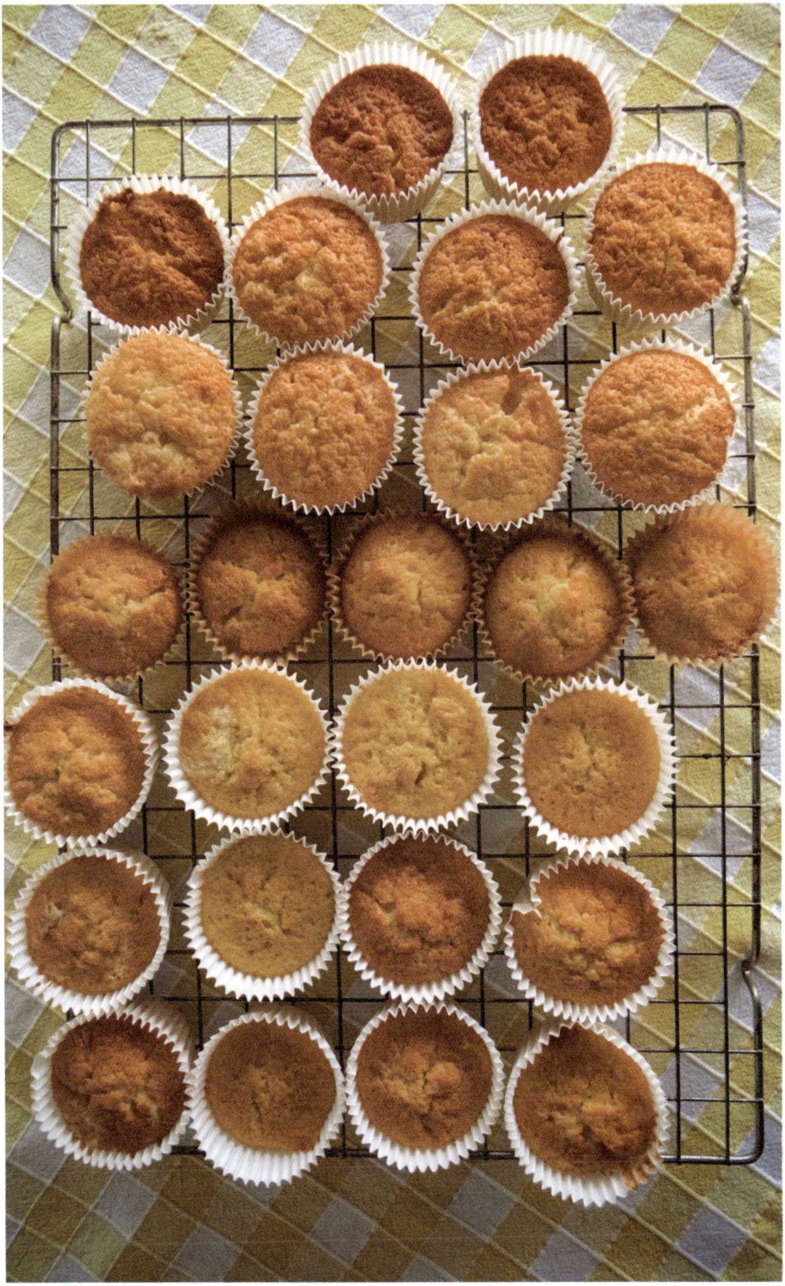

Welsh cakes

These little icons of the Welsh table – *Teisen lap* – are as symbolic of their country as the leek and daffodil. Similar to a scone, they are often referred to as 'bakestones', which harks back to times past when baking was done on a hot hearth or flagstone. These days, a good heavy-based frying pan will suffice. Welsh cakes are delicious just as they are, or spread with butter and perhaps a little jam. Then again, a couple of leeks and a little cheese will turn them into a savoury teatime treat.

Makes 12

250g self-raising flour
½ tsp sea salt
100g unsalted butter, cut into small cubes
100g caster sugar, plus 1 tbsp to finish
100g currants
1 egg, beaten
1 tbsp milk, plus a bit extra if needed

Sift the flour and salt into a large bowl. With your fingertips, lightly rub in the butter until the mixture resembles fine breadcrumbs, then add the caster sugar and currants. Mix in the beaten egg and bring the mixture together with a fork to form a soft dough, adding as much milk as you need to do so.

Turn onto a floured surface and use your palm or a rolling pin to pat or roll out to a 6–7mm thickness. Using a scone cutter or upturned glass, cut out 6–7cm circles.

Heat an ungreased griddle or frying pan over a medium heat. It needs to be hot, but not so hot that it will blacken the cakes. Drop the cakes onto the hot surface and cook one side before turning over to cook the other. The rule of thumb is to cook for about 3 minutes on each side until a lovely medium caramel colour. If they are browning more quickly than this, your griddle is probably too hot.

Transfer the cakes to a wire rack and leave to cool. Before serving, sprinkle with a little caster sugar.

Variations

Honey (*Teisen mel*) Replace the sugar with 2 level tbsp honey and add the grated zest of an unwaxed lemon or an orange.

Mincemeat (*Teisen briwgig*) Omit the milk and add 3–4 tbsp mincemeat to the mixture. Use a star cutter to shape festive cakes.

Leek and cheese (*Teisen cennin*) Soften 100g finely sliced leeks in a little butter, cool and add to the dough with 50g grated Cheddar or Caerphilly cheese.

SMALL CAKES & BAKES 73

Flapjacks

Soft and chewy or crisp and crunchy, as you prefer, flapjacks are one of the all-time greats – lunchtime or teatime, a good flapjack is difficult to beat. They are really easy to make; indeed they were the first things I ever baked as a child. This well-used recipe is easily adapted to make a flapjack to please everyone.

Now when it comes to your oats, perhaps surprisingly, biggest isn't the best. Medium-sized (normal) porridge oats stick together much better than jumbo oats.

Makes 12–16

175g unsalted butter, cut into cubes
1 tbsp golden syrup
150g demerara sugar
250g medium porridge oats
Pinch of sea salt
1 tbsp desiccated coconut (optional)

Equipment
25 x 20cm shallow baking tin, lightly greased and base-lined with baking parchment

Preheat the oven to 180°C/Gas mark 4. Place the butter, golden syrup and sugar in a large heavy-based saucepan. Heat gently, stirring often, until the butter has just melted and the sugar is still grainy. Remove from the heat and pour in the porridge oats, salt and desiccated coconut, if using. Mix together until evenly combined.

Turn the mixture into the prepared baking tray, spread evenly and firm down well with a fork or the back of a spoon. For a soft and chewy flapjack, bake for about 20 minutes until a light-medium golden colour. Give it a bit longer if you prefer a crispy, well-cooked flapjack.

Run a knife round the edge to release the flapjack, leave for 5 minutes, then mark into bars or squares. Leave in the tin until nearly cold before cutting into pieces and removing to a wire rack. The flapjacks will keep in an airtight tin for up to 10 days.

Variations

Raisin and honey Omit the coconut and golden syrup. Replace with 2 level tbsp honey (about 50g), 100g raisins and the grated zest of 1 unwaxed orange.

Muesli Replace the oats with 300g of your favourite muesli.

Cherry and coconut Add 50g desiccated coconut and 75g quartered glacé cherries.

Walnut and maple syrup Omit the desiccated coconut, replace the golden syrup with 1–2 tbsp maple syrup and add 75g chopped walnuts.

SMALL CAKES & BAKES 75

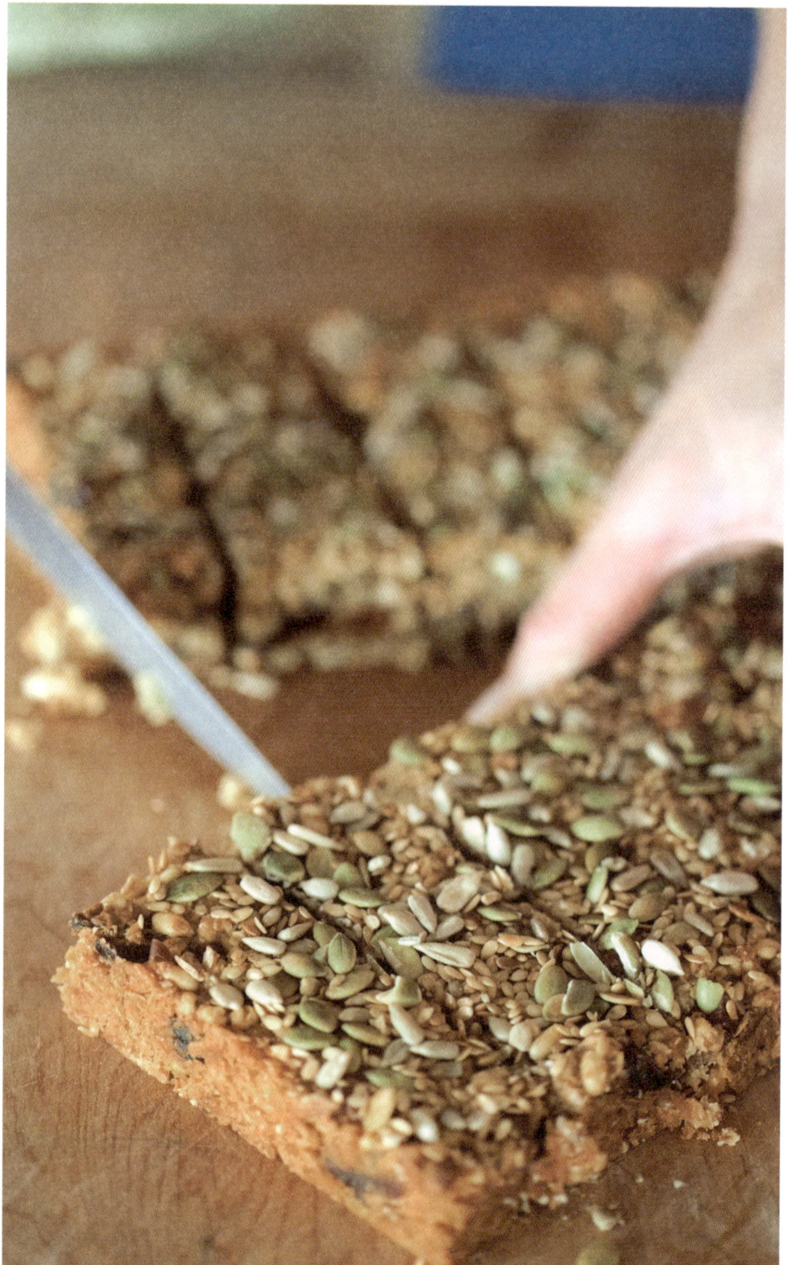

Fruit, nut and honey bars

Judging by the number of different 'energy bars' on the market these days, we all ought to be bursting with vitality and *joie de vivre*. You'll find these sweet snacks, breakfast bars and filler-uppers just about everywhere – at railway stations for munching on long lonely journeys and at health food shops and supermarkets. Many of them are tempting, but some are little more than sugar and additives. Nevertheless, the idea of an energy-dense, sustaining, compact mini meal that's easy to eat on the move is certainly a good one. This is my take on the theme: packed with loads of fruit, nuts and seeds, these natural snack bars are easy to make, nutritious and much cheaper than shop-bought alternatives.

Makes 15–16
125g unsalted butter, cut into cubes
100g light soft brown or demerara sugar
100g honey
150ml fresh apple or orange juice
Finely grated zest of 1 orange
200g porridge oats (or 150g oats plus 50g puffed rice or wheat flakes)
100g dried dates, chopped
100g dried apricots, chopped
50g chopped walnuts, hazelnuts or almonds
125g mixed seeds such as pumpkin, linseed, poppy, sunflower

Equipment
18 x 25cm or 20cm square shallow baking tin, lightly greased and base-lined with baking parchment

Preheat the oven to 180°C/Gas mark 4. Put the butter, sugar, honey, fruit juice and orange zest into a large saucepan over a low heat and stir from time to time until the butter has melted and the ingredients are blended together. Remove from the heat, add the oats, puffed rice or wheat if using, dried dates and apricots, nuts and 100g of the mixed seeds. Stir well.

Transfer the mixture to the prepared baking tin and level the surface with the back of the spoon. Sprinkle the remaining seeds evenly over the top. Bake in the oven for 25–30 minutes until golden brown on top.

Leave in the tin to cool before turning out and cutting into squares or fingers with a sharp knife. They will keep for 10 days stored in an airtight tin.

Rock cakes

Hard or soft, igneous or indigenous, rock cakes are archetypal of church fêtes and school bazaars. Often and unfairly outdone by the more louche and luscious-looking chocolate brownie, they're the plain Janes of the station buffet. But don't judge a book by its cover – freshly made rock cakes are quite delightful. Their name derives not from their texture but from their rather craggy appearance; they should not be *rock* hard, but soft and crumbly inside with a golden baked exterior. Using everyday store-cupboard ingredients, they are quick and easy to make, ideal for impromptu picnics and unexpected teatime visitors.

Makes 8
100g self-raising white flour
100g self-raising wholemeal flour
Pinch of sea salt
100g unsalted butter, cut into small pieces
75g light soft brown sugar

175g raisins
Finely grated zest of 1 unwaxed orange
1 large egg, beaten

Equipment
Large baking sheet, lightly greased

Preheat the oven to 190°C/Gas mark 5. Sift the flours and salt into a mixing bowl. Add the butter and lightly rub into the flour, using your fingertips, until the mixture resembles fine, even breadcrumbs. Mix in the brown sugar, raisins and orange zest, tossing together until evenly mixed.

Add the beaten egg and use a fork to bring the mix together into a soft, crumbly dough. It may be necessary to knead a little by hand but keep the dough light and open-textured so it can form some good outcrops.

Divide the mixture into 8 pieces, shape into irregular balls and place well apart on the greased baking sheet. Bake for 15–20 minutes, until golden and firm to the touch. Leave for 5–10 minutes before removing with a palette knife to a wire rack to cool.

Rock cakes will keep for up to 3 days in an airtight container but they are definitely best eaten fresh.

Variations

Currant and lemon Replace the raisins and orange with currants and lemon zest.

Spelt, date, apricot and ginger Replace the flours with spelt or wholemeal flour and the raisins with 75g chopped dates, 75g chopped apricots and 50g chopped preserved stem ginger, drained of its syrup.

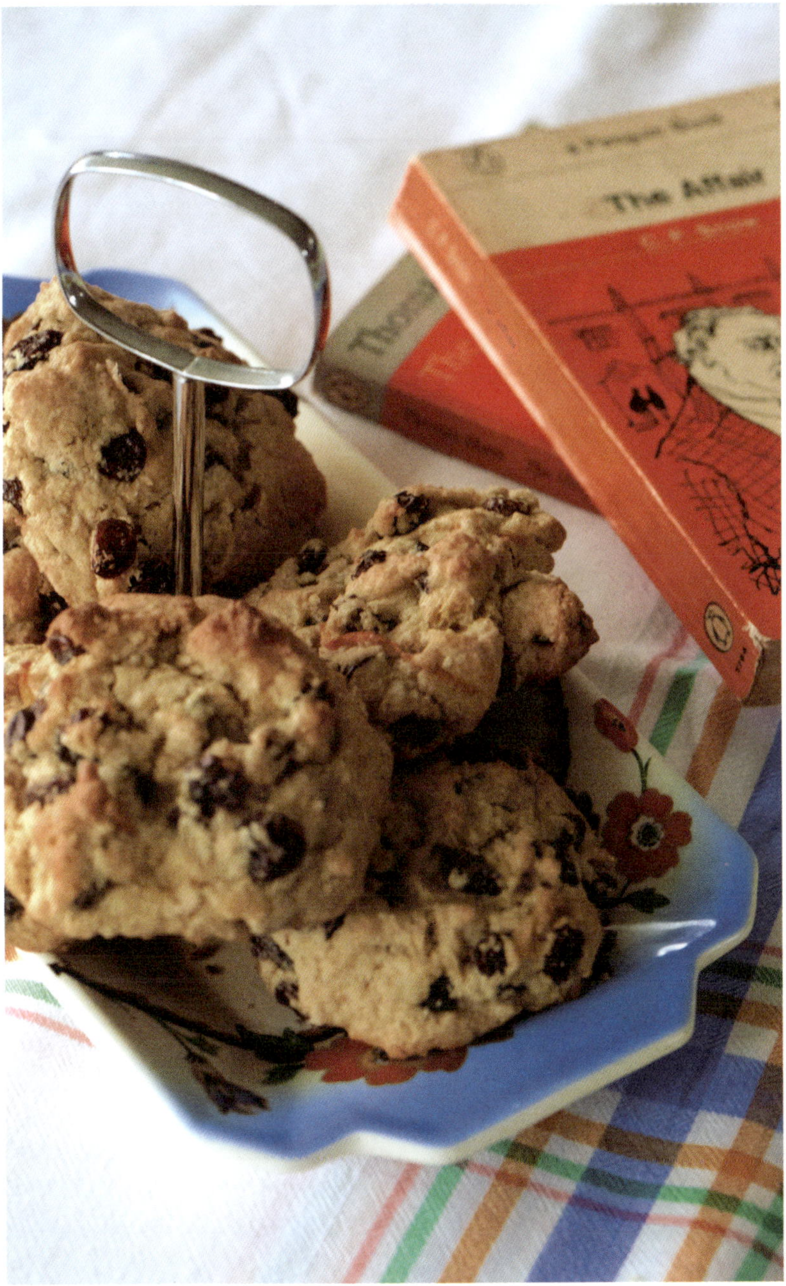
The Affair

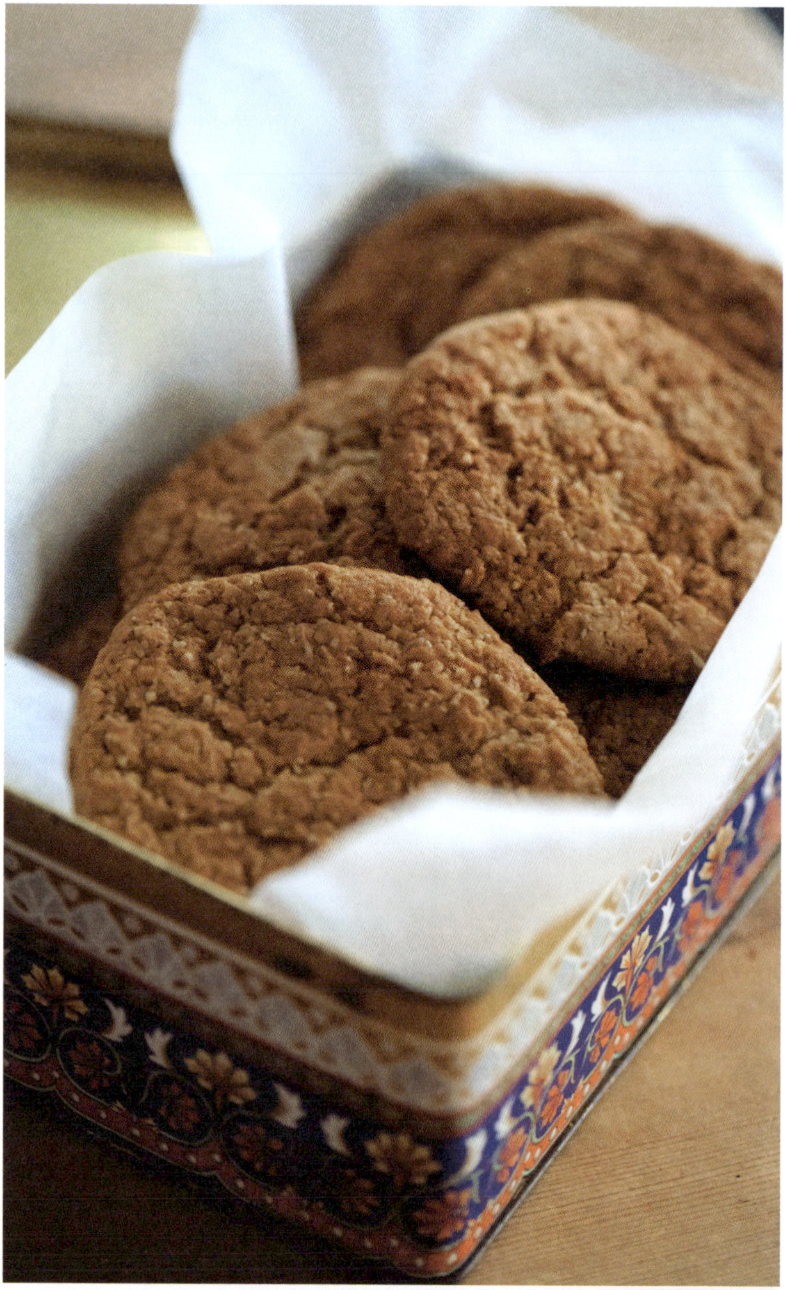

Anzac biscuits

This recipe from Down Under is a poignant reminder of the hardships the Forces endured during World War I. Wives, lovers and mothers would make these oaty biscuits to send to Anzac (Australian and New Zealand Army Corps) troops fighting thousands of miles away at Gallipoli in Turkey. There was no refrigeration on the ships, so the biscuits required a good shelf (or ship) life to ensure they didn't go off during the two-month voyage.

Makes 12
125g plain flour
100g medium oatmeal or porridge oats
100g light soft brown sugar
50g desiccated coconut
100g unsalted butter, cut into cubes
1 tbsp golden syrup or honey
½ tsp bicarbonate of soda
1 tbsp boiling water

Equipment
Large baking sheet, lightly greased or lined with baking parchment

Preheat the oven to 170°C/Gas mark 3. Sift the flour into a medium mixing bowl. Add the oatmeal, brown sugar and coconut and mix together thoroughly.

Put the butter and golden syrup or honey into a small saucepan. Place over a low heat until the butter has melted. Meanwhile, put the bicarbonate of soda into a cup and pour on the boiling water to dissolve.

Next, stir the bicarbonate of soda mix into the melted butter; be very careful – the mixture will rapidly fizz and foam up. Pour the frothing mixture into the dry ingredients. Using a wooden spoon, quickly mix together to form a thick batter.

Place generous tablespoonfuls of the mixture onto the prepared baking sheet, allowing room for spreading. Gently flatten the tops with the back of a fork. Bake for about 20 minutes until golden brown.

Leave the biscuits on the baking sheet for 10 minutes to firm up before transferring to a wire rack to cool. Stored in an airtight tin, they will keep for up to 3 months.

Variation
If you have any stale cornflakes that need using up, lightly crush 75g of these and use instead of the oatmeal.

Shortbread

Originally I thought that this would be a short recipe. However, the more I bake this member of the biscuit clan, the more I realise that to make tender melt-in-the-mouth shortbread, you need to understand a few hard-and-fast rules.

Shortbread relies on really good-quality unsalted butter for its flavour, so don't skimp on this and never use margarine! The high butter (or 'shortening') content helps to keep the gluten in the flour short and soft. But, for that delectable, friable texture, it's also important to keep a light hand. Overworking the mixture will make the dough oily; it will also develop the gluten in the flour and make the shortbread tough.

You need to choose your flour carefully. Most recipes call for a 2:1 mix of plain wheat flour and rice flour or cornflour, for a very soft texture, but you can also use semolina for a slightly crunchier result. Sifting in the flour is a valuable step that helps to keep the shortbread light and melting.

And the final crucial thing to remember is that shortbread must be only barely coloured, never browned. So, don't forget it's in the oven…

Makes about 15
150g unsalted butter, cut into small pieces, softened
75g caster sugar (I like to use vanilla sugar), plus extra for dredging
150g plain flour
75g rice flour

Equipment
2 baking sheets, lined with baking parchment, or a 20cm loose-based fluted flan tin or plain sandwich tin

Preheat the oven to 170°C/Gas mark 3. Put the softened butter into a bowl. Using a wooden spoon, gradually work in the sugar until it is well mixed and forms a soft paste. Sift in the flour and rice flour. Using a fork, bring together lightly to form a soft, crumbly dough. It's hands-on (or in) time now: bring the mix to a soft, pliable, crack-free dough by kneading it as lightly as possible.

For biscuits, place the dough between two sheets of lightly floured greaseproof paper. Using a rolling pin, roll out to a 5mm thickness. Remove the top paper and cut out biscuits using a 6–7cm fluted cutter or a shaped biscuit cutter (heart, star, leaf, etc.). Place the biscuits on the baking sheets and prick the surface with a fork.

For a shortbread round, lightly press the dough into the loose-based 20cm flan tin or sandwich tin, or shape into a round, about 2cm thick, by hand. To finish the edge, pinch into little flutes with your thumb and finger. Prick the surface with a fork.

Bake the shortbread in the oven until very lightly coloured; allow about 20 minutes for biscuits, 30–35 minutes for a shortbread round. Dredge with sugar and place on a wire rack to cool. Shortbread will keep for up to 4 weeks in an airtight tin.

Variations

Hazelnut shortbread Replace the caster with light soft brown sugar and the rice flour with 75g ground hazelnuts.

Lovers' shortbread Add 2–3 tsp rose water with the sifted flour. Use a heart-shaped biscuit cutter.

Thyme shortbread Add 1 tbsp finely chopped thyme. This is lovely with summer sorbets, ices and fruits.

Lancashire (Goosenargh) shortbread Add 1 tsp caraway seeds and ½ tsp ground coriander powder with the flour.

Chocolate-dipped shortbread Melt 100g chocolate in a bowl over a pan of hot water. Dip one half of each shortbread biscuit in the chocolate to partially coat. Place on baking parchment to dry.

Strawberry shortbread Cover a shortbread round with whipped double cream and top with fresh strawberries (or raspberries).

Jammy dodgers

Some might say that life is too short to bake homemade versions of biscuit tin favourites. However, I think you might find these homages to some of our favourite sweet treats will become the revered jewels of your tea table. They will delight everyone, bring a smile or two (because they normally come in packets) and turn a simple tea into a ritzy, classy occasion.

Makes 6 or 7

175g plain flour
Pinch of sea salt
75g unrefined icing sugar
125g unsalted butter, cut into small pieces
1 egg yolk
1 tsp vanilla extract
150g raspberry jam (or whatever flavour you like)

Equipment

2 large baking sheets, lined with baking parchment
6–7cm biscuit cutter, crinkle-edged or plain
2.5cm heart, square, round or animal biscuit cutter, crinkle-edged or plain

Sift the flour, salt and icing sugar into a large mixing bowl. Add the butter and lightly rub into the flour mix, using your fingertips, until the mixture resembles fine breadcrumbs.

In a small bowl, whisk the egg yolk and vanilla extract together. Make a well in the centre of the flour mix. Add the egg and vanilla mix and work together to form a soft, smooth dough. Alternatively, you can simply place everything in a food processor and bring to this stage. Seal the dough in a polythene bag and chill in the fridge for 25–30 minutes.

Preheat the oven to 170°C/Gas mark 3. Divide the dough into two equal portions. Place one portion between two pieces of lightly floured greaseproof paper and, using a rolling pin, roll the dough to approximately a 4mm thickness. Repeat with the second piece of dough. Remove the top paper.

With the larger biscuit cutter, cut the dough into discs (make sure you have an even number). Using the smaller cutter, cut out and remove the centre of half the biscuit discs; the cut-out pieces can either be kneaded back into the remaining dough or baked just as they are.

Place all the discs on the baking sheets. Bake for 15–20 minutes until just firm and barely coloured.

Remove from the oven and place a teaspoonful of jam in the centre of each whole biscuit round. Spread to 1.5cm from the edge. Place the cut-out rounds on top. Return to the oven and cook for a further 5–6 minutes by which time the biscuits will be evenly cooked and the jam sufficiently hot to stick the biscuits together.

Leave the biscuits to cool for 5 minutes before transferring to a wire cooling rack.

Variations

Custard creams Replace 50g of the flour with custard powder. Use a 5cm square biscuit cutter. Bake the biscuits for about 20 minutes until lightly coloured. Cool on a wire rack. To make the custard cream filling, simply cream together 75g softened unsalted butter, 75g icing sugar and 25g custard powder. To finish, sandwich the cooled biscuits together in pairs with a teaspoonful of the filling. *Makes 14*

Bourbon biscuits Replace 50g of the flour with drinking chocolate powder or, for a dark rich biscuit, use cocoa powder. Use an oblong biscuit cutter, about 6–7 x 2.5cm. With a fork, lightly prick the surface of the uncooked biscuits (just like the packet ones). Bake for approximately 20 minutes. To make the chocolate cream filling, cream together 75g softened unsalted butter, 75g icing sugar and 25g drinking chocolate or cocoa powder. To finish, sandwich the cooled biscuits together in pairs with a teaspoonful of the filling. *Makes 12*

Christmas tree biscuits

For me, one of the highlights in the lead-up to Christmas is a happy few hours spent at my friend Henriette's house, making biscuits for the festive season. It's an afternoon of free choice, when tree-shaped biscuits sometimes turn pink and sugared sheep can end up with multi-coloured fleeces. This is the recipe I always use – it produces lovely, crunchy, warmly spiced biscuits. They are by no means exclusively for Christmas, by the way. You can use the recipe to make 'run, run, as fast as you can' gingerbread men too (see overleaf).

Makes about 24 (depending on size of cutters)
275g plain flour
1 level tsp baking powder
1 tsp ground ginger
1 tsp ground cinnamon
100g soft brown sugar
75g unsalted butter, cut into small pieces
1 egg, lightly beaten
50g golden syrup

Equipment
2 baking sheets, lightly greased or lined with baking parchment
Christmas biscuit cutters (trees, stars, holly leaves, etc.)

To decorate
Glacé icing (see p.55)
2 or 3 natural food colourings (see p.56)
Cherries, angelica, currants, desiccated coconut, flaked almonds, walnuts, sesame seeds, chocolate or coloured sprinkles, sugar, etc.

Preheat the oven to 170°C/Gas mark 3. Sift the flour, baking powder and spices into a mixing bowl. Add the brown sugar and mix well. Add the butter and rub in with your fingertips until the mixture resembles fine breadcrumbs.

In another bowl, mix the egg and golden syrup together until smooth and well blended. Make a well in the centre of the rubbed-in mixture and pour in the egg and syrup. Using a wooden spoon, mix together to form a ball of dough.

Put the dough into a polythene bag and place in the fridge for 30 minutes to rest; this will make it much easier to roll out.

(continued overleaf)

SMALL CAKES & BAKES 87

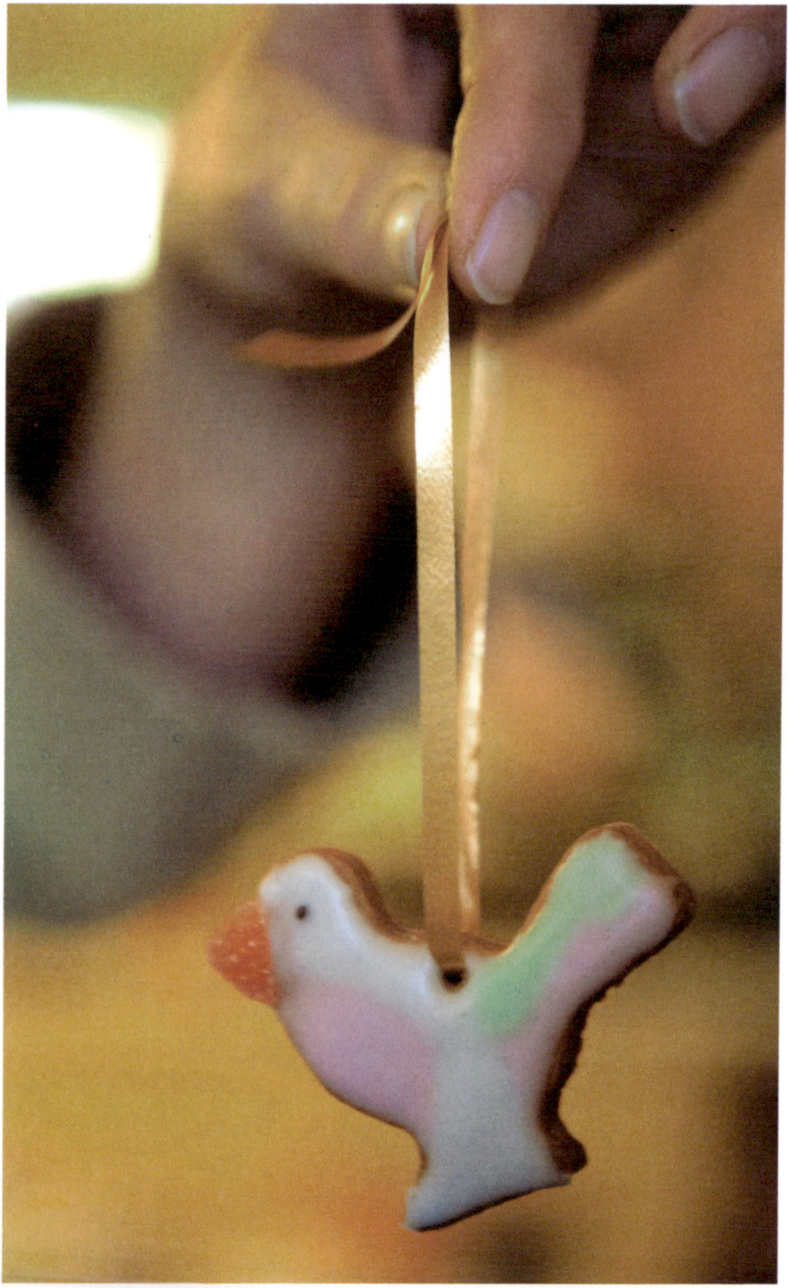

When you are ready to bake the biscuits, place the dough between two lightly floured sheets of greaseproof paper. Roll the dough out evenly until it is approximately 5mm thick, then remove the top paper. Cut out shapes from the dough with your chosen biscuit cutters.

Place the biscuits on the baking sheets, leaving space in between for them to spread a little. Use a knitting needle or skewer to make a hole near the top of each shape (this is to thread a hanging ribbon through).

Bake for 15–20 minutes until the biscuits are golden brown. They will still seem soft at this stage, but will firm up as they cool. If necessary, re-make the holes while they are still hot. Transfer to a wire rack to cool.

When ready to finish, divide the white glacé icing between three or four small bowls. Keep one bowl white and colour the others as desired. Using either the back of a spoon or a small round-ended knife, carefully spread plain or coloured glacé icing over one side of each biscuit (to get a really smooth finish, dip the spoon or knife in a jug of just-boiled water first). Add decorations of your choice. Lay the biscuits on a wire rack and leave until the icing has set.

Finally, thread the biscuits with ribbon or raffia and hang on the Christmas tree. For utmost effect, hang a few biscuits on the tree every couple of days. Alternatively, and to last for the full festive period, wrap the biscuits in cellophane before hanging.

These biscuits will keep un-iced for 3 months in an airtight tin.

Variation

Gingerbread men Use a traditional 'gingerbread man' biscuit cutter. To give the biscuits their endearing personalities, before baking add currants for eyes, sliced cherries for lips and dried cranberries/diced dried apricots for shirt buttons. For gingerbread girls, use a jumble of finely cut dried fruits to create skirts to skip in. Alternatively, leave the biscuits plain and then ice and titivate with coloured chocolate buttons, etc., after baking and cooling.

Dog bone biscuits

I do think it's important to keep everyone in the family happy. These are designed as very special treats for dogs, but there's nothing in them that would bar anyone else from taking a chew.

Makes about 24 large bones or 100 little ones

250g wholemeal flour
125g fine oatmeal
125g porridge oats
150ml sunflower or rapeseed oil
2 eggs, lightly beaten
200g carrots, trimmed and finely grated (only peel if dirty)
2 tsp caraway seeds
2 tbsp finely chopped parsley

Equipment
2 large baking sheets, lined with baking parchment
Dog bone biscuit cutter, about 12x3cm (or a smaller one)

Preheat the oven to 170°C/Gas mark 3. Sift the flour into a mixing bowl. Add the oatmeal and porridge oats and mix together. Make a well in the centre and pour in the oil, followed by the beaten eggs, carrots, caraway seeds and parsley. Mix with a wooden spoon until well blended and you have a fairly sticky dough.

Lightly dust the work surface with flour, then turn out the dough and knead for a few minutes until the mixture is smooth and pliable.

Place the dough between two sheets of lightly floured greaseproof paper. Using a rolling pin, roll the dough out to about a 5mm thickness and remove the top paper. Cut out biscuits using the bone cutter and place on the prepared baking sheets.

Bake in the oven for about 50 minutes or until the biscuits are crisp and lightly golden. Cool on a wire rack. These will keep for 2 months in an airtight container.

Variation

Courgette and ginger Replace the carrots with courgettes, the caraway seeds with ginger and the parsley with coriander.

P.S. For 'human' dog bone biscuits, use the recipe for Jammy dodgers (see p.84) or the one for Christmas tree biscuits (see p.86), but cut out with the bone cutter. Coat with Glacé icing (see p.55) and decorate with chocolate buttons, sugar sprinkles, glacé cherries or nuts, though you may find the family prefer the dog's bones!

SMALL CAKES & BAKES 91

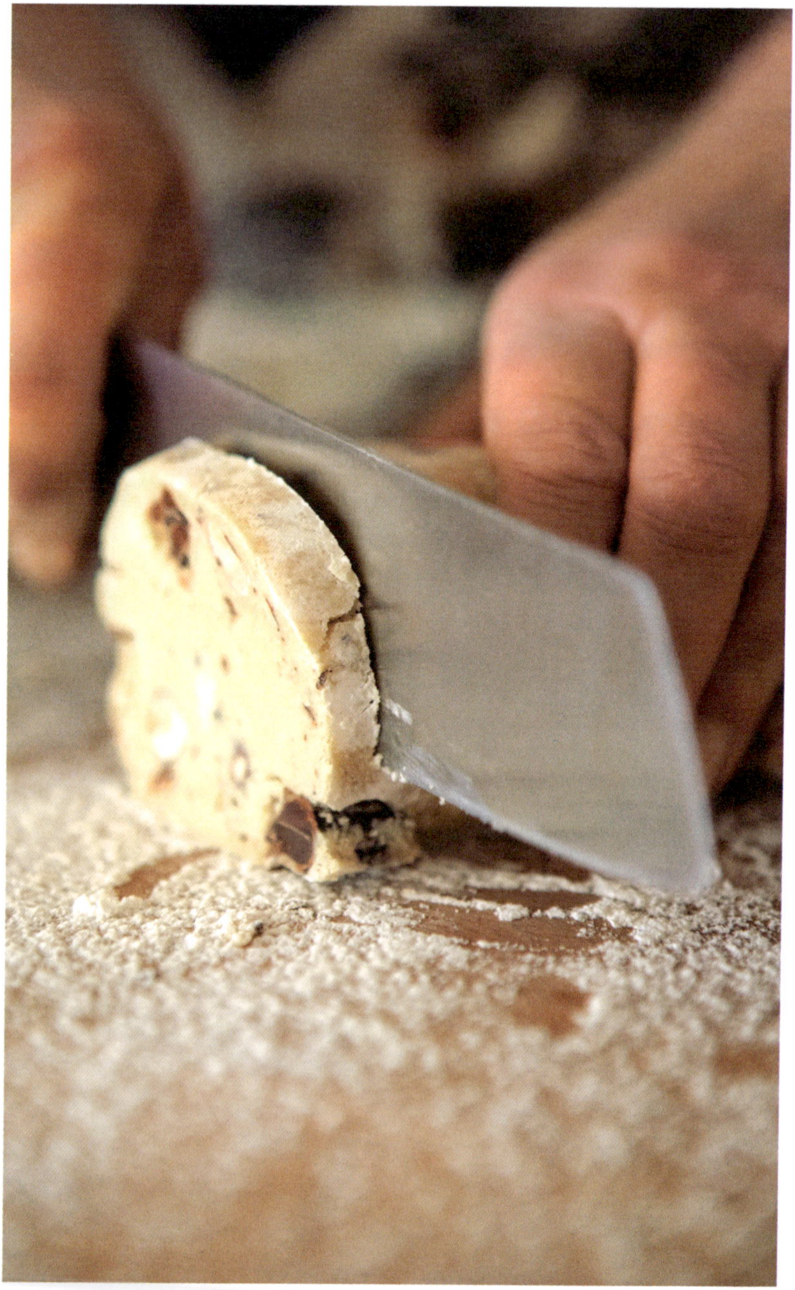

'Bake-off' cookies

Lightly crisp on the outside, meltingly soft inside, who doesn't love cookies straight from the oven? Keep a roll of cookie dough in the fridge (for up to a week), and you can enjoy these freshly baked treats any time. Alternatively, the dough can be sliced and frozen, allowing you to 'bake off' any number at a time. Freeze on a tray before packing into a sealed bag; allow to defrost for 15 minutes before baking.

Makes 18
225g unsalted butter, softened
225g caster sugar
1 egg yolk
250g plain flour
½ tsp baking powder
Pinch of sea salt

100g plain chocolate, roughly chopped into 1cm pieces
50g hazelnuts, roughly chopped

Equipment
2 baking sheets, lightly greased or lined with baking parchment

Beat the butter and sugar together in a mixing bowl until light and creamy, then mix in the egg yolk. Sift in the flour, baking powder and salt. Using a fork, bring together to a soft dough. Carefully mix in the chocolate and nuts until evenly distributed.

Lightly dust a piece of greaseproof paper with flour and turn the dough onto it. Shape into a cylinder, about 7cm in diameter and 20cm long, and wrap securely in the paper. Place in the fridge for about an hour to firm up.

When ready to cook, preheat the oven to 170°C/Gas mark 3. Remove the dough from the fridge and cut into slices, 1–1.5cm thick, using a sharp knife. Place on the baking sheets, leaving plenty of space for the cookies to spread.

Bake for 20–25 minutes until the cookies are just turning golden brown at the edges. Use a palette knife to transfer them to a wire rack and leave to cool.

These cookies will keep in an airtight container for up to 2 days.

Variations

Classic chocolate chip Omit the hazelnuts and increase the chocolate to 200g. (You can use plain, milk or white chocolate.)

Oatmeal and raisin Replace 100g of the flour with oatmeal or porridge oats. Omit the chocolate and nuts. Add 150g Lexia raisins and the zest of 1 unwaxed orange.

Ginger Replace the chocolate and nuts with 125g roughly chopped stem ginger.

Cornish fairings

A close cousin of the gingernut, the Cornish fairing is a spicy, crisp gingery biscuit, nutty brown in colour and deeply cracked. The name originates from early lively trading and festival fairs, where the biscuits were bought by visitors as gifts or 'fairings' to take home. This recipe, by far the best I've found, comes from Jo, one of our lady Cornish pilot gig rowers in Lyme Regis.

Makes 6 large fairings
125g plain flour
1 tsp baking powder
½ tsp bicarbonate of soda
1 good tsp ground ginger
1 tsp ground mixed spice
50g caster sugar
50g unsalted butter, cut into small pieces
2 tbsp golden syrup

Equipment
Baking sheet, lightly greased or lined with baking parchment

Preheat the oven to 200°C/Gas mark 6. Sift the first five ingredients into a large bowl and stir in the caster sugar. Add the butter and, using your fingertips, lightly rub it in until the mixture resembles fine breadcrumbs. Add the golden syrup and use a fork to bring the mixture together to a soft dough. Alternatively, simply place all the ingredients in a food processor and whiz until mixed to a smooth dough.

Divide the dough into 6 pieces. With floured hands, roll each into a ball about the size of a very large walnut. Place on the baking sheet, allowing plenty of room for spreading. Keeping them round, flatten slightly with the back of a fork.

Bake in the oven for 7–8 minutes, until nutty golden brown in colour and deeply cracked on the surface. Stay around and don't get too engrossed on the phone – a minute or two too long and you'll have half a dozen frisbees instead of fairings.

Leave to firm up on the baking sheet for a couple of minutes before transferring to a wire cooling rack. Once cool, these will keep for a week or so in an airtight tin.

P.S. Golden syrup is tricky to measure accurately. The easiest way is to place a metal measuring spoon in a cup of very hot water prior to measuring out the syrup. The heat makes the syrup slip off the spoon neatly and cleanly and should give you a fairly true measure.

SMALL CAKES & BAKES 95

Butterfly and fairy cakes

So simple to make, these feather-light party favourites will please young and old alike. A nick with a knife transforms the basic fairy cake into a fluttering butterfly cake. Straightforward iced cup cakes can be made from this recipe too: just flood the surface with plain or flavoured Glacé icing (see p.55) or Buttercream (see p.49) and titivate with decorations of your choice.

Makes 12 or 24 (depending on tray)
175g self-raising flour
1 tsp baking powder
125g caster sugar
125g unsalted butter, softened and cut into small pieces
2 eggs
1 tsp vanilla extract (optional)

Equipment
12-hole muffin tray, holes about 6.5cm in diameter and 2cm deep, lightly greased or lined with paper muffin cases, or 2 x 12-hole bun tins, lined with small paper cake cases

To finish
1 quantity Vanilla buttercream (see p.49)
Icing sugar to dredge

Preheat the oven to 190°C/Gas mark 5. Sift the flour and baking powder into a large mixing bowl. Add the sugar and beat for a few seconds until well blended. Add the butter, eggs, vanilla extract, if using, and 1 tbsp hot water. Using an electric whisk, beat until smooth; this should take no more than 1½–2 minutes.

Carefully spoon the mixture into the paper cases so they are about two-thirds full. Give the baking tray a couple of sharp taps on the work surface to level the mixture in the cases.

Bake in the oven until well risen and golden; allow 12–14 minutes for smaller cakes and an extra couple of minutes for bigger cakes. Leave in the trays for 5 minutes before moving to a wire rack and leaving to cool completely.

Once the cakes have cooled, you can simply top them with the vanilla buttercream to make fairy cakes.

Alternatively, to make butterfly cakes, use a small sharp knife to cut a circle from the top of each cake, leaving a border of about 1cm. Remove the cone-shaped centre, leaving a slight hollow. Cut the removed cones in half to make the butterfly wings and set aside (no nibbling, butterflies need two wings). Put 1 tsp buttercream into the hollow of each cake. Press the wings, cut side uppermost, into the icing and sift over a little icing sugar to finish. These will keep for 5 days in an airtight tin.

Variations

Change the look and taste of butterfly cakes by placing a fresh raspberry or strawberry between the wings or dropping a little jam in the centre before topping with the buttercream. Or use chocolate buttercream and top with chocolate buttons.

98 CAKES

'Veg patch' gnome cakes

These fab (and fatless) relatives of the fairy cake are a brilliant way to use up surplus produce from the veg patch. They are also perfect for enticing young reluctant veg eaters. Camouflaged in a sweet cake mix, you'll find grated pumpkin, parsnips, carrots and courgettes disappear without a murmur of dissent…

Makes 12 large cup cakes
200g self-raising flour
1 tsp baking powder
Pinch of sea salt
3 eggs
175g caster sugar
200g uncooked, finely grated pumpkin
Finely grated zest of 1 unwaxed orange

For the icing
1 quantity Cream cheese topping flavoured with orange zest (see p.57)

To decorate
Edible flowers (borage, marigolds, fennel), Marzipan vegetables (see p.59), or other decorations of your choice

Equipment
12-hole muffin tray, holes about 6.5cm in diameter and 2cm deep, lightly greased or lined with paper muffin cases, or 2 x 12-hole bun tins, lined with small paper cake cases

Preheat the oven to 180°C/Gas mark 4. Sift the flour with the baking powder and salt. Beat the eggs and sugar together in a large bowl with a hand-held electric whisk for 5–6 minutes until the mixture is thick, creamy and pale. Fold in the flour, half at a time, using a large metal spoon. Finally fold in the pumpkin and orange zest.

Carefully spoon the mixture into the paper cases so they are three-quarters full. Bake for about 20 minutes or until lightly golden and springy to the touch. Leave in the trays for about 5 minutes, then transfer to a wire rack to cool.

When cool, top with the cream cheese topping and add decorations of your choice. These will keep for 2–3 days in an airtight tin.

Variations

Carrot gnome Replace the pumpkin with carrot and the orange zest with lemon.

Parsnip gnome Replace the pumpkin with parsnip and the orange zest with lime.

Courgette gnome Replace the pumpkin with courgette, the orange zest with lemon and add ½ tsp freshly grated nutmeg.

Muffins (American-style)

Making voluminous, blowsy, puffed-up muffins – with bags more tops than bottoms – is simplicity itself. Once you've got the hang of it, you'll have great fun dreaming up your own variations, flavoured with perfectly partnered ingredients. Make your muffins sweet or savoury, for breakfast, lunch or tea. You'll also find them a thrifty way to use up odds and ends discovered during a fridge clear-out. There are a couple of rules for success but, once you've learnt them, you'll soon find yourself turning out batches of whopping big muffins in minutes.

I could practically fill a book with muffin recipes alone – the basic recipe is so endlessly adaptable. Before you begin experimenting with flavouring ingredients, you can play around with the main ones.

Flour Use a plain flour of your choice: either white, wholemeal, spelt or a 50/50 mix of any of these. Alternatively, you can make gluten-free muffins with a pre-mixed gluten-free self-raising cake flour, such as those made by Doves Farm or Bia Nua (see directory, p.244). Add ½ tsp each of baking powder and bicarbonate of soda per batch of muffins or 250g flour.

Sugar Caster is the classic choice, but you can switch it for soft brown or muscovado. Alternatively, sweeten your muffins with honey, golden syrup or molasses, replacing the caster sugar with about three-quarters of the amount. Add more, or less, to suit the muffin and please the palate.

Milk/yoghurt You can use full-fat or semi-skimmed milk. Try goat's milk as an alternative – or soya milk and soya yoghurt for dairy-free muffins. You can also replace the yoghurt with buttermilk or soured cream.

Fat/oil Butter, which needs to be melted then cooled, is most often used in muffins, but I also like to use sunflower or rapeseed oil or a mixture of both.

The golden rules of muffin-making:
Ingredients are divided into wet and dry. The dry ingredients (i.e. flour, raising agents, spices, etc.) are sifted into a mixing bowl, combined with the sugar and blended thoroughly. Ideally, and to save on the washing up, you can then put all the wet ingredients into a measuring jug (angled if possible), along with any herbs or essences, and beat until thoroughly combined.

The mixing method contrasts with many other cake-making techniques in that it does not involve vigorous beating or whisking. Instead, a large metal spoon or flexible spatula is used to mix the combined wet ingredients swiftly and lightly into the dry ones, forming a lumpy batter. *Do not* beat to a super-smooth batter or you will find yourself with dense, heavy muffins.

The batter can be put straight into the well-greased cups of a muffin tray, or paper muffin cases can be used to line the cups – for big muffin tops, use paper cases about 3cm high, rather than deep ones. But the way I like to cook my muffins is to line the cups with baking parchment squares, roughly 15cm square. Don't try to line the whole muffin tray before filling, just line as you fill. The squares are easiest to mould into the cups if they are first folded in half diagonally and opened as you fill. For full-blown muffin tops, three-quarter fill the cups with the muffin batter.

Bake the muffins in the centre of a fairly hot oven (200°C/Gas mark 6) for 20–25 minutes until very well risen and domed. They should spring back into shape when lightly touched with a finger. Leave in the tray for a few minutes, then transfer to a wire rack to cool a little before eating.

Muffins don't keep well and are best eaten fresh from the oven or within 24 hours of baking. However, they do freeze very well if frozen on the day of baking.

And now for the recipes:

I've given three types of muffin over the following pages: a substantial breakfast one; a delectable savoury affair; and a sweet, fruity muffin. In each case, I've suggested lots of variations and I hope you'll add your own...

Banana breakfast muffins

Generally, even the sparrows turn their beaks up at cold leftover porridge. But this resourceful recipe is a great way to use up the cup or so of glutinous stuff that often remains at the bottom of the porridge pan. Prepare the wet and dry ingredients the night before and you can quickly turn leftover porridge into a rather splendid way to start the following day.

Makes 10 large muffins
225g plain flour
2 tsp baking powder
½ tsp bicarbonate of soda
½ tsp sea salt
1–2 tsp ground cinnamon
100g light muscovado sugar, plus extra for sprinkling
100ml plain yoghurt
30–50ml milk
1 egg
100ml sunflower or rapeseed oil
150g cold cooked porridge
2 ripe bananas, 1 mashed to a purée, 1 sliced into 10 pieces

Equipment
12-hole muffin tray, holes about 6.5cm in diameter and 2cm deep, 10 lightly greased or lined with 10 paper muffin cases or 15cm baking parchment squares

Preheat the oven to 200°C/Gas mark 6. Sift the first five ingredients into a medium mixing bowl. Add the sugar and mix together evenly, either by mixing with a spoon or beating with an electric mixer for about 30 seconds on the lowest speed.

Next put the measured yoghurt, 30ml milk, egg, oil, porridge and the mashed banana into a large mixing jug or bowl. Beat together until well combined and the mixture is like a very thick batter, adding extra milk if it is too thick. Pour into the dry ingredients and stir very lightly, scraping the sides down, until *just* combined, with no clumps of dry flour lurking in the bottom of the mixing bowl.

Divide the mixture between the muffin cups, filling each to three-quarters full (this will be about one fully laden tablespoonful per cup). Pop a piece of banana in the centre of each and sprinkle with a little muscovado sugar.

Bake in the oven for 20–25 minutes until well risen and the tops are golden. The muffins should spring back into shape when lightly touched.

Breakfast muffin variations

Follow the simple method of combining the dry ingredients, combining the wet ingredients, then mixing lightly together.

Marmalade For the dry ingredients, use 250g plain flour, 2 tsp baking powder, ½ tsp bicarbonate of soda, ½ tsp sea salt, ½ tsp ground ginger or 1 tsp ground cardamom and 100g light muscovado sugar. For the wet ingredients, use 125ml milk, 125ml plain yoghurt, 1 egg, 100ml sunflower oil and 150g marmalade. Sprinkle with 1 tbsp muscovado sugar to finish.

Smoked salmon and eggs For the dry ingredients, use 250g plain flour, 2 tsp baking powder, ½ tsp bicarbonate of soda, ½ tsp sea salt and ½ tsp cayenne pepper. For the wet ingredients, use 125ml milk, 125ml soured cream, 2 eggs, 100ml sunflower oil, 125g smoked salmon pieces and 1 tbsp chopped chives.

Mopping-up muffins for bacon and egg breakfast juices For the dry ingredients, use 125g cornflour, 125g wholemeal flour, 75g light muscovado sugar, 2 tsp baking powder, ½ tsp bicarbonate of soda and ½ tsp sea salt. For the wet ingredients, use 125ml milk and 125ml plain yoghurt (or just 250ml milk), 1 egg and 100ml sunflower or rapeseed oil.

Wild garlic and cheese muffins

I have more fun dreaming up mouthwatering ideas for savoury muffins than any others. Baked for elevenses or lunchtime, these are a delight to make and utterly delicious to eat. Wild garlic appears from the middle of March until the second or third week of May. Its heady, yet sweet aroma combines beautifully with strong, flavoursome Cheddar to make moreishly good muffins. Replace the wild garlic with fresh garden herbs when the season is over, or use 1–2 tbsp pesto instead.

Makes 10 large muffins

250g plain flour
2 tsp baking powder
½ tsp bicarbonate of soda
½ tsp sea salt
1 tsp English mustard powder or ½ tsp cayenne powder (optional)
125ml milk
125ml plain yoghurt
1 egg
100ml sunflower or rapeseed oil
2 level tbsp finely chopped wild garlic leaves (about 20 leaves)

100–150g strong Cheddar cheese, finely grated
5 cherry tomatoes, halved

Equipment
12-hole muffin tray, holes about 6.5cm in diameter and 2cm deep, 10 lightly greased or lined with 10 paper muffin cases or 15cm baking parchment squares

Preheat the oven to 200°C/Gas mark 6. Sift the first five ingredients into a medium mixing bowl. Make sure they are evenly blended together by either mixing with a spoon or beating with an electric mixer for about 30 seconds on the lowest speed.

Next put the measured milk, yoghurt, egg, oil, chopped garlic leaves and three-quarters of the cheese into a large mixing jug or bowl. Beat together until well combined and the mixture is like a very thick batter. Pour into the dry ingredients and stir very lightly, scraping down the sides, until *just* combined, with no clumps of dry flour lurking in the bottom of the bowl.

Divide the mixture between the muffin cups, filling each to three-quarters full (this will be about one fully laden tablespoonful per cup). Place half a tomato, cut side uppermost, on the top of each muffin and sprinkle with the remaining cheese.

Bake in the oven for about 20 minutes until well risen and the tops are golden. The muffins should spring back into shape when lightly touched.

Savoury muffin variations

Follow the simple method of combining the dry ingredients, combining the wet ingredients, then mixing lightly together.

Cheese and Marmite This is my favourite! For the dry ingredients, use 250g plain flour, 2 tsp baking powder, ½ tsp bicarbonate of soda and 1 tsp English mustard powder. For the wet ingredients, use 125ml milk, 125ml plain yoghurt, 1 egg, 100ml sunflower oil, 125g grated mature Cheddar cheese and 2–3 tsp Marmite or other yeast extract. Finish with 5 cherry tomatoes, halved, and a sprinkling of grated cheese.

Blue cheese, apple and honey For the dry ingredients, use 250g spelt flour, 2 tsp baking powder and ½ tsp bicarbonate of soda. For the wet ingredients, use 125ml milk, 125ml plain yoghurt, 1 egg, 100ml rapeseed oil, 1 tbsp honey, 125g grated or finely crumbled blue cheese. Finish with 1 small apple, cored and finely sliced.

Anchovy and French dressing For the dry ingredients, use 250g plain flour, 2 tsp baking powder, ½ tsp bicarbonate of soda and 50g sunflower seeds. For the wet ingredients, use 125ml milk, 125ml plain yoghurt, 1 egg, 90ml French dressing and 2 tbsp anchovy essence. Finish with 5 cherry tomatoes, halved.

Blackberry and apple muffins

The beloved pairing of autumn blackberries and juicy apples makes the homeliest of muffins. Blackberries, those cherished gifts of the hedgerow, can be picked in season and frozen to use later in the year. For this recipe, you can use the blackberries straight from the freezer, but you will need to bake the muffins for 3–4 minutes longer.

Makes 10 large muffins

125g plain flour
125g wholemeal flour
2 tsp baking powder
½ tsp bicarbonate of soda
Pinch of sea salt
125ml milk
125ml plain yoghurt
1 egg
125g honey
100ml unsalted butter, melted and cooled
1 tsp vanilla extract

100–125g blackberries
1 medium dessert apple (100–125g), unpeeled, cored and finely diced
1 tbsp icing sugar, to finish

Equipment
12-hole muffin tray, holes about 6.5cm in diameter and 2cm deep, 10 lightly greased or lined with 10 paper muffin cases or 15cm baking parchment squares

Preheat the oven to 200°C/Gas mark 6. Sift the first five ingredients into a medium mixing bowl. Make sure they are evenly blended together by either mixing with a spoon or beating with an electric mixer for about 30 seconds on the lowest speed.

Next put the measured milk, yoghurt, egg, honey, butter and vanilla extract into a mixing jug or bowl. Beat together until well combined and the mixture is like a very thick batter. Pour into the dry ingredients and stir very lightly, scraping down the sides, until *just* combined, with no clumps of dry flour lurking in the bottom of the bowl. Add the blackberries and diced apples and mix through lightly.

Divide the mixture between the muffin cups, filling each to three-quarters full (this will be about one fully laden tablespoonful per cup). For lightly crisp, glazed tops, dust with sifted icing sugar before they go into the oven. (Alternatively, dust with icing sugar once baked.)

Bake in the oven for about 20 minutes until well risen and the tops are golden. The muffins should spring back into shape when lightly touched.

Sweet muffin variations

Follow the simple method of combining the dry ingredients, combining the wet ingredients, then mixing lightly together.

Fruity fresh Replace the blackberries with blueberries, raspberries, strawberries or black- or redcurrants. Replace the apple with a dessert pear.

Mincemeat For the dry ingredients, use 125g plain flour, 125g wholemeal flour, 2 tsp baking powder, ½ tsp bicarbonate of soda, pinch of sea salt, 1 tsp ground cinnamon and 100g soft brown sugar. For the wet ingredients, use 125ml milk, 125ml yoghurt, 1 egg, 100ml sunflower oil and 4 tbsp mincemeat. To finish, use ½ red-skinned dessert apple, finely sliced, or 1 tbsp flaked almonds, plus 1 tbsp soft brown sugar.

Poppy seed For the dry ingredients, use 125g plain flour, 125g wholemeal flour, 2 tsp baking powder, ½ tsp bicarbonate of soda, pinch of sea salt, 125g caster sugar and 50g poppy seeds. For the wet ingredients, use 250ml buttermilk, 1 egg, 100ml rapeseed oil and the finely grated zest of an unwaxed lemon. While still hot from the oven, drizzle with the juice of 1 lemon mixed with 50g caster sugar.

Gooseberry friands

These moist, light-as-air little cakes are a breeze to make. I love this fragrant, zesty orange and gooseberry combination, but you could use any fresh fruit you like – raspberries, strawberries, a string of redcurrants, it really doesn't matter. What does matter is the burst of mouthwatering fruitiness when you bite into them. They're traditionally baked in special oval tins, but a deep muffin tray will do just as well.

Makes 12
175g unsalted butter
225g icing sugar
100g plain flour
125g ground almonds
6 egg whites
12 large gooseberries (red dessert or green)

To finish
Finely pared zest of 1 unwaxed orange
2 tbsp fresh orange juice
100g caster sugar

Equipment
12-hole friand or muffin tray, well greased and lightly dusted with flour

Preheat the oven to 200°C/Gas mark 6. Melt the butter in a pan over a low heat and set aside to cool slightly. Sift the icing sugar and flour into a mixing bowl, add the ground almonds and mix together thoroughly, then make a well in the middle.

Place the egg whites in a clean bowl and lightly whisk with a fork for 20–30 seconds, until they are just broken and combined. Pour into the well, with the melted butter. Stir lightly, but don't overdo it; the mixture should be gooey, soft and elastic.

Spoon the mixture into the prepared tins, filling each cup three-quarters full. Lightly place a gooseberry in the centre of each. Bake in the oven for 20–25 minutes or until the friands are pale golden and springy to the touch.

Meanwhile, put the orange zest in a small pan with a little water to cover. Bring to a simmer and cook for 10 minutes to soften, then drain and leave to dry.

When you take the friands from the oven, leave them in their tins for a few minutes. To remove from the tins, slide a knife down one side and the cakes should pop out – crisp, clean and irresistible. Transfer to a rack to cool.

Make a frosting by mixing the orange juice and caster sugar together. Leave for 15 minutes to allow the sugar to partially dissolve. Drizzle the frosting over the cooled cakes and top with a pinch of orange zest. Eat on the day you make them.

SMALL CAKES & BAKES 109

My chocolate brownies

Not that I like to crow, but over the years, my brownies have built up something of a reputation. You could almost say they are my trademark. So what's the secret? It's difficult to pinpoint but there are three things I consider important. Firstly, the eggs and sugar need to be whisked vigorously so the mixture increases vastly in volume. Secondly, I use a good-quality chocolate with 60–70% cocoa solids. Thirdly, and perhaps most importantly, these brownies must be made with love. Until now this recipe has been a closely guarded family secret, so please value it and use with reverence! These brownies are a celebration of pure indulgence...

Makes 12–16, depending on size
185g plain chocolate (60–70% cocoa solids), broken into small pieces
185g unsalted butter
1 tsp instant coffee (optional)
3 large eggs
275g golden caster sugar
85g plain flour
40g cocoa powder

50g white chocolate, roughly chopped
50g milk chocolate, roughly chopped

Equipment
25 x 20cm shallow baking tin, lightly greased and base-lined with baking parchment

Preheat the oven to 180°C/Gas mark 4. Put the plain chocolate in a heatproof bowl with the butter and coffee, if using. Place over a pan of barely simmering water on a very low heat and leave until melted. Stir to blend together and take off the heat.

Meanwhile, whisk the eggs and sugar together, using either a free-standing mixer or a hand-held electric whisk, until thick, pale and quadrupled in volume. This will take 4–5 minutes in a free-standing mixer, 8–10 minutes with a hand-held whisk.

Fold the chocolate mixture into the mousse-like egg mixture. Sift in the flour and cocoa powder, then, using a large metal spoon, fold in very carefully so as not to lose the tiny air bubbles. Finally, fold in the chopped white and milk chocolate.

Pour the mixture into the prepared tin and bake in the oven for about 35 minutes, until the brownie no longer wobbles when softly shaken and the top is dark and shiny. Leave to cool in the tin.

When cold, carefully turn out onto a clean folded tea-towel to preserve the shiny top, then invert onto a board and cut into squares or triangles. These brownies can be stored for 4–5 days in an airtight tin, or for up to a week in a sealed container in the fridge.

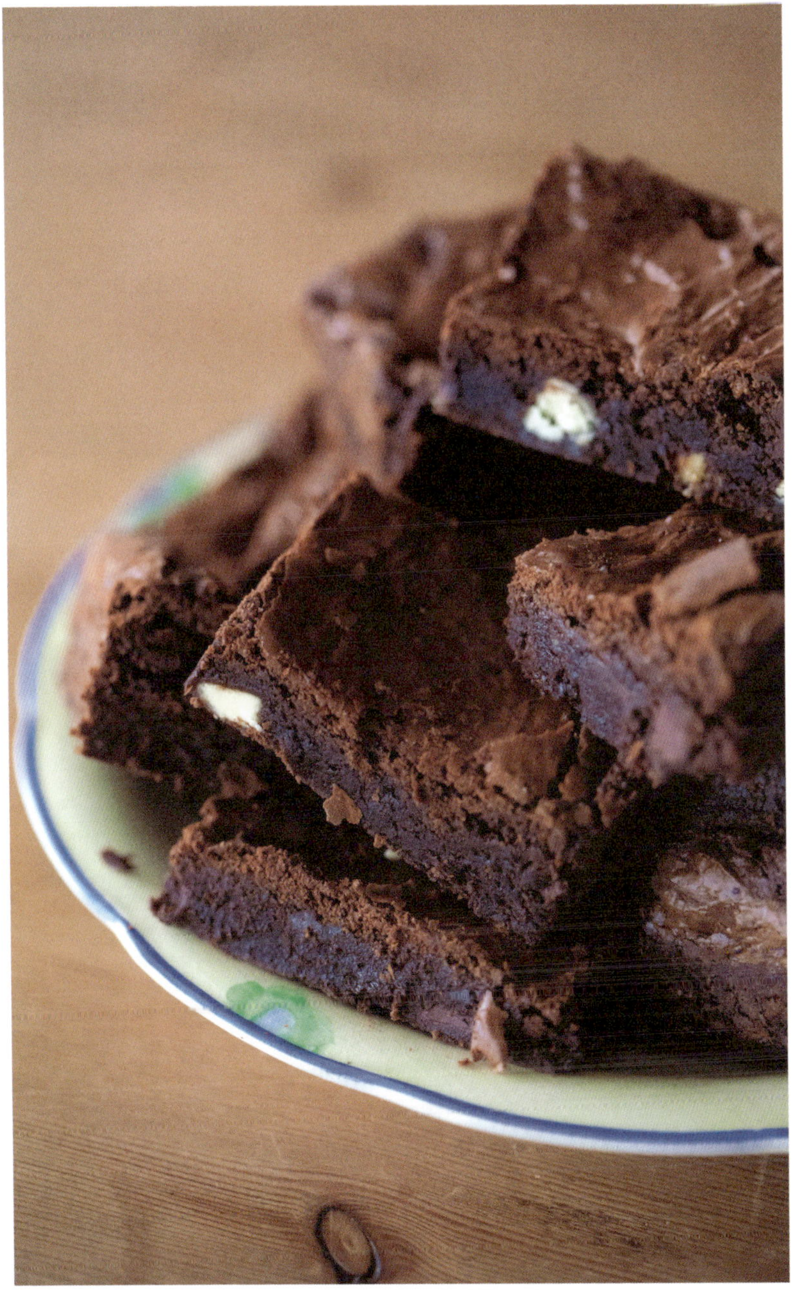

Meringues

There is something rather magical about meringues, with their crisp shells and light-as-air middles. They team up perfectly with fresh fruit and/or ice cream and are gorgeous sandwiched together with a blob of clotted cream.

They require only a couple of ingredients and are fairly easy to make, though there are a few 'meringue secrets' to keep in mind. Success depends on incorporating oodles of air into the egg whites. Any trace of grease will thwart the eggs' ability to whisk to maximum volume, so you must use a spotlessly clean, dry bowl (best to avoid using a plastic one). The eggs should be at room temperature and, ideally, several days old. The sugar needs to be fine-grained to ensure it will dissolve quickly. Caster sugar is the norm, but icing sugar, soft brown sugar or a combination can be used to produce melt-in-the-mouth meringues.

Makes 10–12
3 egg whites
150g caster sugar, sifted icing sugar or soft brown sugar

Equipment
2 large baking sheets, lined with baking parchment

For near white, crisp, dry meringues Preheat the oven to 110°C/Gas mark ¼. Put the egg whites into a large mixing bowl and whisk, using a hand-held electric whisk, until cotton wool-like and forming a stiff peak on the end of the whisk; do not over-whisk or the whites will become dry and break down. Next, add the sugar, 1 tbsp at a time, whisking on medium speed until the mixture is stiff, with a glossy sheen.

Place tablespoonfuls of the mixture on the prepared baking sheet. Bake in the oven for 2–2½ hours or until the meringues are crisp and dry and come away easily from the baking sheet. Transfer to a wire rack to cool. When cold, store in an airtight container – they will keep for several weeks.

For light-golden, gooey-centred meringues Preheat the oven to 150°C/ Gas mark 2. Put the egg whites into a large mixing bowl and whisk, using a hand-held electric whisk, until the eggs are cotton wool-like and form a stiff peak on the end of the whisk; be careful not to over-whisk. Next, add the sugar, 1 tbsp at a time, whisking on a medium speed until the mixture is stiff, with a glossy sheen.

Place tablespoonfuls on the prepared baking sheet. Bake for about 40 minutes, or until the meringues are slightly golden and come away easily from the baking sheet. Remove to a wire rack to cool. Once cold, store in an airtight container – they will keep for several weeks.

Variation

Coffee meringues Use soft brown sugar and whisk 2–3 tsp coffee essence or instant coffee powder into the meringue mix after all the sugar has been added. Top each mound with a walnut half before putting into the oven.

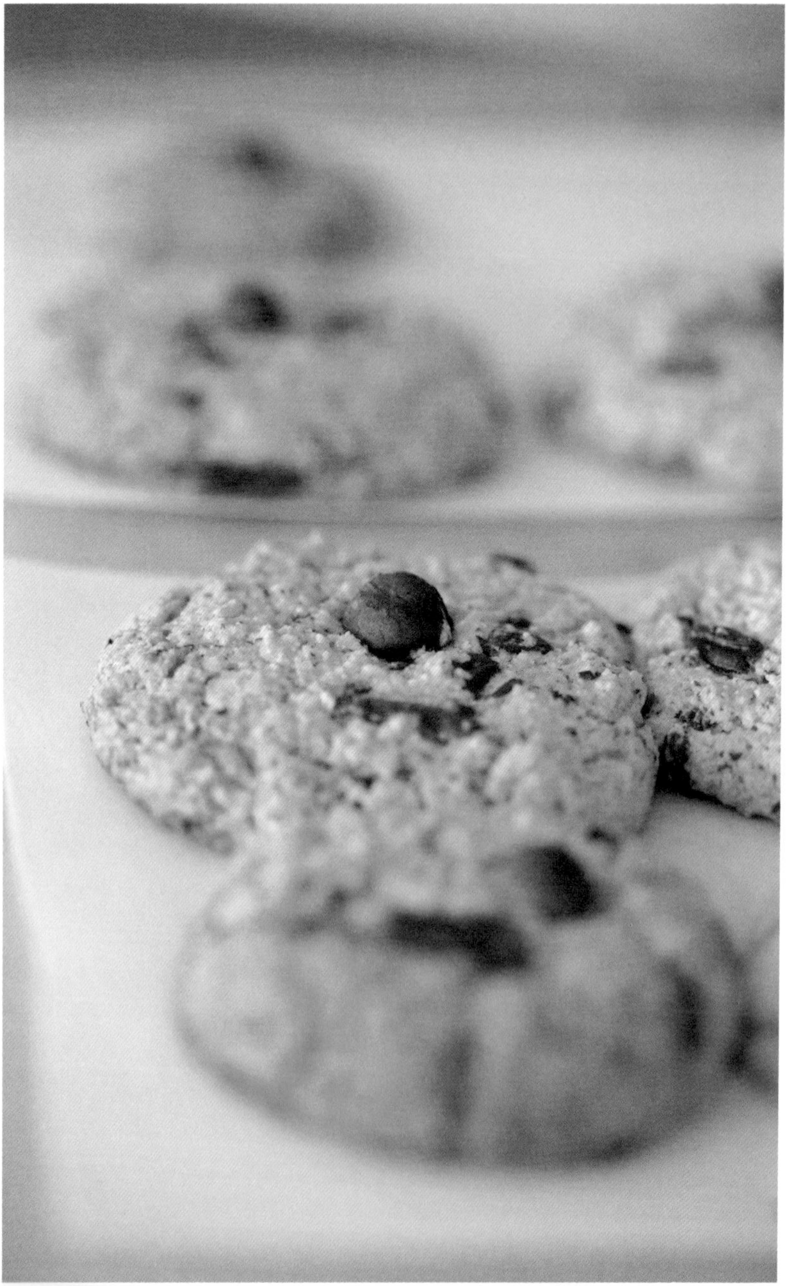

Pip's hazelnut macaroons

My elder daughter Pip is a real whiz at making macaroons, so I turned to her to discover the secret of these chewy, nutty sweet treats. The chocolate-studded recipe that she's come up with is a real winner. Pip favours ground hazelnuts over the customary almonds. They are not as commonly available as ground almonds, but you can easily prepare them yourself: lightly toast the hazelnuts, then remove their skins (see p.32) before blitzing the nuts in a food processor until finely ground.

Cooked on baking parchment, these macaroons release very easily. However, Pip is still charmed by the fun of eating paper, so always bakes hers on rice paper.

Makes 10 (or 24 petits fours)
125g ground hazelnuts
150g caster sugar
2 egg whites
1 tsp vanilla extract
50g plain chocolate, chopped roughly into 1cm pieces

Equipment
Large baking sheet lined with 2 or 3 sheets of rice paper or baking parchment

To finish
Whole hazelnuts

Preheat the oven to 180°C/Gas mark 4. In a medium mixing bowl, combine the ground hazelnuts and caster sugar.

In a separate bowl, lightly whisk the egg whites until white and frothy, but not stiff. Using a large metal spoon, lightly fold the egg whites into the nut and sugar mixture. When evenly combined, fold in the vanilla extract and chocolate pieces.

Place dessertspoonfuls of the mixture on the prepared baking sheet, leaving sufficient room in between for the macaroons to spread. (For petits fours macaroons, use a teaspoon instead.) Place a whole hazelnut in the centre of each biscuit.

Bake in the oven for 10–15 minutes until just firm and lightly coloured. Leave to cool on the baking sheet, then strip off the rice paper surrounding each one or simply use a palette knife to remove from the baking parchment.

Stored in an airtight tin, these macaroons will keep for 3–4 weeks.

Salt caramel shortbread

Gloriously self-indulgent and rather addictive, this lovely salty-sweet treat will wake up dull or sluggish taste buds. The sprinkle of sea salt brings out the creamy richness of the sweet caramel, while at the same time complementing the pure, smooth dark chocolate. Make sure you use a soft, sweet-tasting, unrefined natural salt – Maldon, Halen Môn or Cornish sea salt – and good-quality chocolate.

Makes 12

For the shortbread base
150g unsalted butter, softened
75g caster sugar
150g plain flour
75g semolina

For the caramel layer
½ tsp flaky sea salt
1 quantity Caramel cream (see p.51)

For the chocolate topping
150g plain chocolate, chopped
25g butter
1 tsp flaky sea salt

Equipment
20cm square, 5cm deep baking tin, lightly greased and base-lined with baking parchment

Preheat the oven to 170°C/Gas mark 3. Put the butter in a bowl and gradually work in the sugar, using a wooden spoon, until well mixed to a soft paste. Sift in the flour and semolina. Using a fork, bring together to form a soft, crumbly dough. Knead as lightly as possible, until you have a soft, pliable, crack-free dough. (Or put the butter, sugar, flour and semolina into an electric mixer and mix on low speed until the mix starts to come together, then increase the speed a little to knead lightly.)

Press this shortbread dough into the baking tin and lightly prick the surface with a fork. Bake in the oven for 30 minutes or until lightly coloured and firm to the touch. Leave in the tin until completely cool.

For the caramel layer, sprinkle the salt into the caramel cream and mix until well blended, then smooth over the shortbread base. Refrigerate for 30 minutes.

In the meantime, put the chocolate into a heatproof bowl with the butter and place over a pan of barely simmering water (making sure the bowl isn't touching the water) until just melted. Remove from the heat.

Pour the melted chocolate over the caramel-topped shortbread and immediately sprinkle with the 1 tsp sea salt. Leave (if you can) for at least a couple of hours to firm up. Cut as required into squares, fingers or sweet canapé bites. These shortbreads will keep for up to 2 weeks in an airtight tin.

SMALL CAKES & BAKES 117

Hazelnut Florentines

Florentines, bedecked and bejewelled with glacé fruit and nuts, are redolent of opulence and riches, and very high-ranking in the biscuit hierarchy. However, despite their overt flamboyancy, they are quick, easy and very satisfying to make. Appealing and rather special, half a dozen will delight any beneficiary lucky enough to receive them.

Makes 12

- 75g unsalted butter
- 75g light soft brown sugar
- 25g (about 1 tbsp) honey (runny or thick)
- 1 tbsp plain yoghurt
- 50g finely chopped preserved stem ginger (drained of its syrup)
- 100g dried pears, sliced into long strands
- 50g glacé cherries, quartered
- 50g hazelnuts, toasted and roughly chopped (see p.32)
- 40g plain flour – white, spelt or chestnut flour
- 125g chocolate – plain, milk or white, broken into small pieces

Equipment
2 large baking sheets, lined with baking parchment

Preheat the oven to 180°C/Gas mark 4. Put the butter, brown sugar and honey into a heavy-based saucepan. Heat very gently over a low heat, stirring, until the butter has melted and the mixture is absolutely smooth. Remove from the heat.

Stir the yoghurt into the mixture, then add the ginger, pears, glacé cherries and hazelnuts; mix well. Finally, sift in the flour and fold in with a large metal spoon.

Place generous dessertspoonfuls of the mixture onto the prepared baking sheets, spacing them about 5cm apart to allow room for a little spreading (like middle age). With the back of a spoon or fork, flatten each to a 5cm round.

Bake in the oven for about 20 minutes until lightly browned and slightly crisp around the edges, or allow a little longer if you prefer a very crisp biscuit.

Leave the Florentines on the baking sheet for 10–15 minutes to firm up. When cool and firm enough to handle, use a palette knife (or your fingers) to release them, flip them over and transfer to a wire rack to cool completely.

Put the chocolate into a heatproof bowl and place over a pan of hot water, making sure the basin isn't actually touching the water. Leave until the chocolate has just melted and is smooth and glossy.

Now you need to coat the smooth bottoms of the Florentines with the melted chocolate. The easiest way to do this is to spoon the chocolate onto the centre of the Florentine base, then spread it evenly with a flat-sided knife that has been dipped into a jug of very hot water.

Leave to set, chocolate side uppermost, on a wire rack. The Florentines will keep for up to 10 days stored in an airtight tin.

Variations

Replace the stem ginger with mixed candied peel, the pears with dried apricots, and/or the hazelnuts with flaked almonds.

Big Cakes

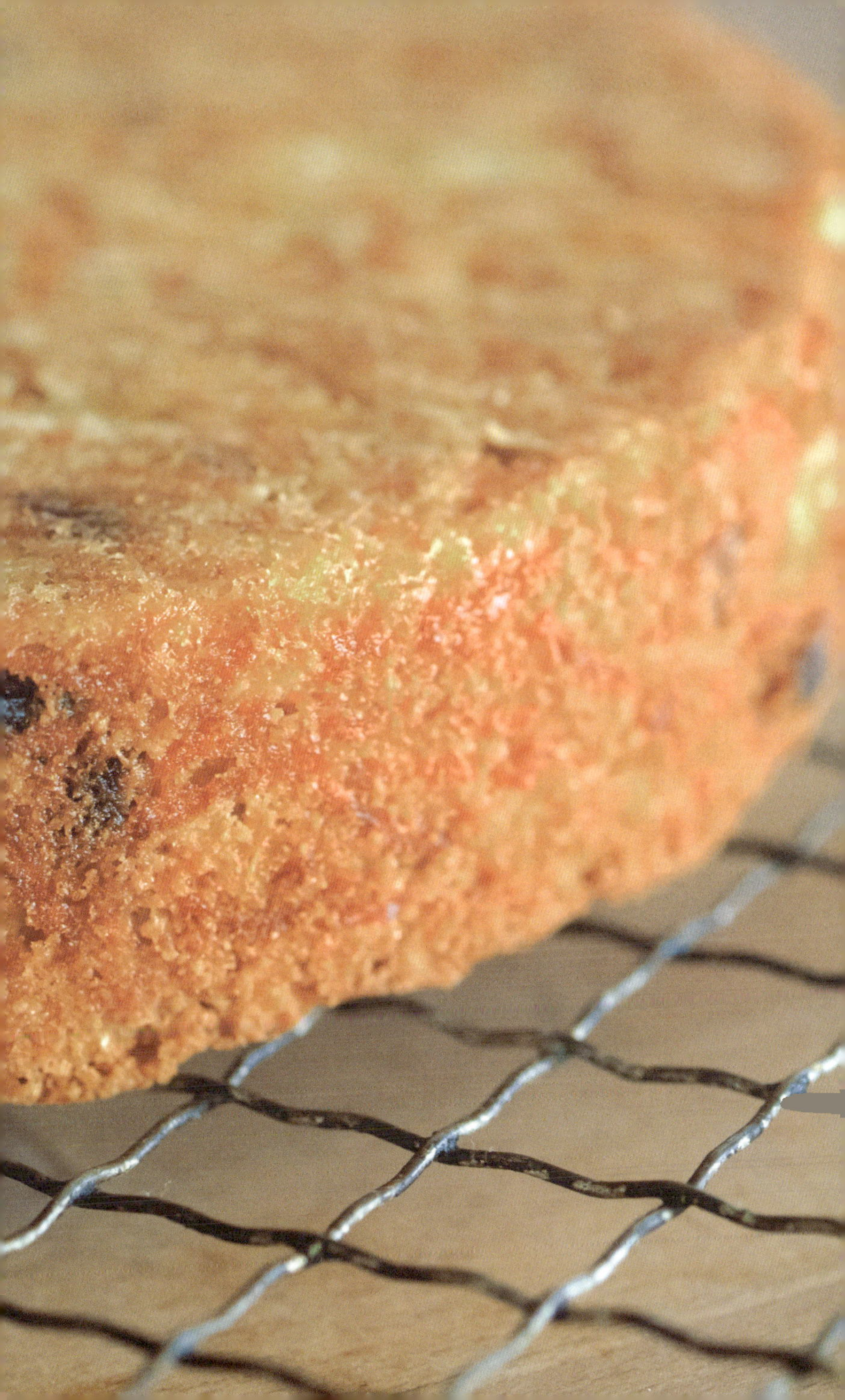

Bring back teatime

and tablecloths! This chapter features the darlings of the old-fashioned teatime cake trolley: Madeira cake, coffee cake, cherry cake, the indomitable Victoria sandwich. Their familiar and comforting names, unchanged for generations, are like badges of honour, signifying their faithful service as the great classics of the tea table.

Many of these great cakes share the same origin. They are descendants of the 'pound cake', a traditional recipe using equal weights of the four main ingredients – butter, sugar, flour and eggs – sometimes delicately flavoured with a hint of citrus or finished with a filling of jam. But this simple foundation can be embellished with more indulgent ingredients, such as cocoa, coffee, fruit or nuts, to create delectable wholesome cakes. These uncomplicated – somehow rather pure – cakes serve as a splendid base for rich icings and creamy fillings; they can also be infused with fresh-tasting or aromatic drizzles and syrups.

While the cakes in this chapter are particularly well suited to a proper sit-down high tea, the less rich examples will agreeably fit the bill at different times of the day. A chunk of homely Apple cake (see p.138) is totally justifiable mid-morning, for instance, while a little nibble of lightly spiced Cardamom cake (see p.159) is welcome whenever friends drop by.

There are also cakes here that lead double lives, by which I mean those that are overtly confident and adept at fitting into more than one occasion. Equally at home on the tea table or as the last course of a meal, these are what I call 'pudding cakes'. Frequently enriched with a little fresh fruit and yoghurt or cultured cream, they are neither too sweet nor too rich and therefore great to eat at any time of the day – or night for that matter.

I hope you will get great pleasure from baking the cakes in this chapter. Be adventurous and be prepared to improvise as well. If, for example, you find you only have two eggs when the recipe says three, improvise and make up the difference with a splash of milk. And, of course, you can adapt the flavourings or alter the finish of the cake as the fancy takes you.

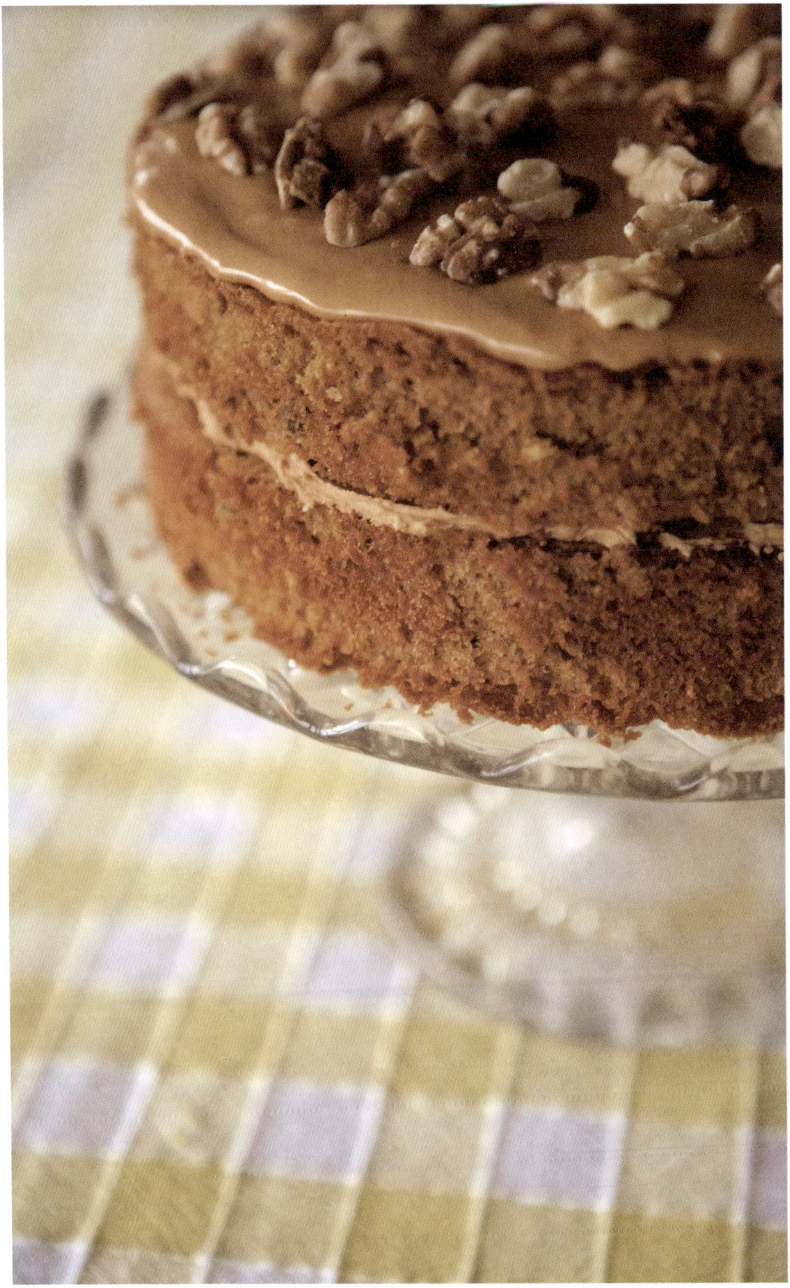

Victoria sandwich

If you only ever make one cake, let it be the glorious Victoria sandwich. The simple mix of equal quantities of eggs, butter, sugar and flour, sandwiched together with raspberry jam, is unquestionably the queen of British cakes. It has long reigned supreme at the tea table, the village fête and the garden party – indeed, a freshly baked Victoria sandwich will lend itself to almost any occasion.

Originally, to make a perfect cake, the eggs were first weighed in their shells and the exact equivalent weights of butter, sugar and flour were measured out. With the strict grading of eggs these days, it's not essential to do this, but I would stick to this rule if you're not sure precisely what size your eggs are – for instance, if you keep hens yourself. If you are buying eggs in a shop, I recommend using medium ones to equal the quantities of the other ingredients in this recipe.

Get to know this recipe if you can, not least because it forms the basis of all manner of other cakes. With the addition of a few well-chosen extra ingredients, the classic Victoria can swiftly be altered to almost any flavour you fancy (see variations overleaf). You can also use this recipe to make cup cakes.

Serves 8–10
175g self-raising flour
Pinch of sea salt
175g unsalted butter, cut into small pieces and softened
175g caster or vanilla sugar, plus extra to finish
3 medium eggs, lightly beaten
1 tsp vanilla extract
3–4 tbsp soft-set raspberry jam

Equipment
2 x 20cm sandwich tins or a 23cm round tin, lightly greased and base-lined with baking parchment

NOTE For total egg weight less than 175g use 2 x 18cm sandwich tins, or a 20cm round tin

Preheat the oven to 180°C/Gas mark 4. Sift the flour and salt together into a bowl and put aside.

In a large mixing bowl, using either a wooden spoon or a hand-held electric whisk, beat the butter to a cream.

Add the caster sugar and continue to beat until the mixture is very light and creamy (this will take about 5 minutes with a hand-held electric whisk and up to 10 minutes using a wooden spoon). The lighter and fluffier the butter and sugar mix is, the easier it will be to blend in the eggs, which in turn helps to prevent the mixture curdling (see p.42).

(continued overleaf)

BIG CAKES

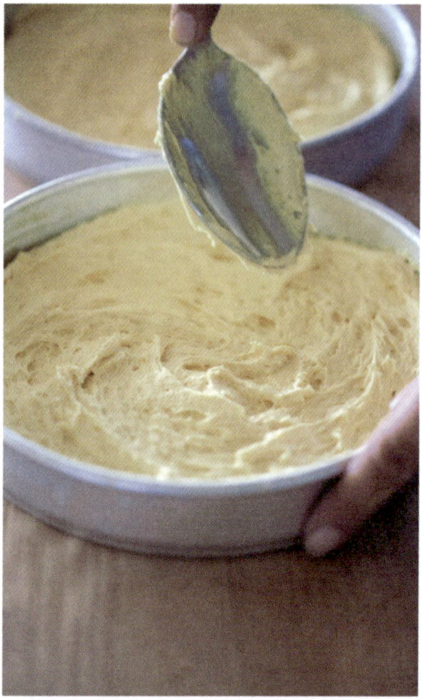
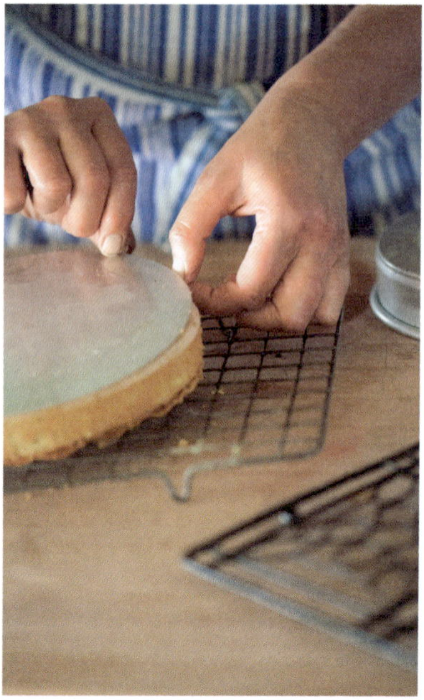
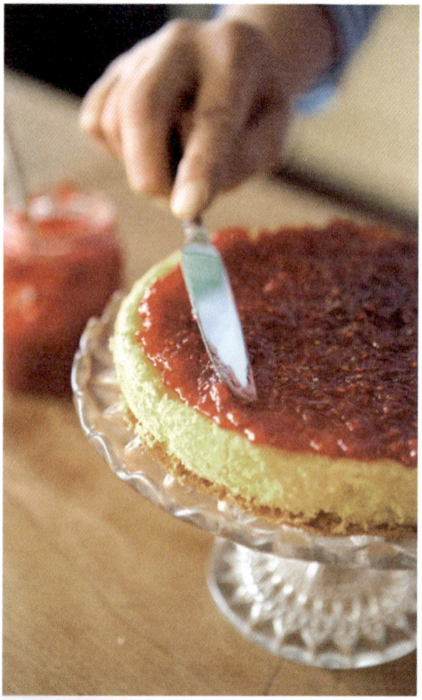
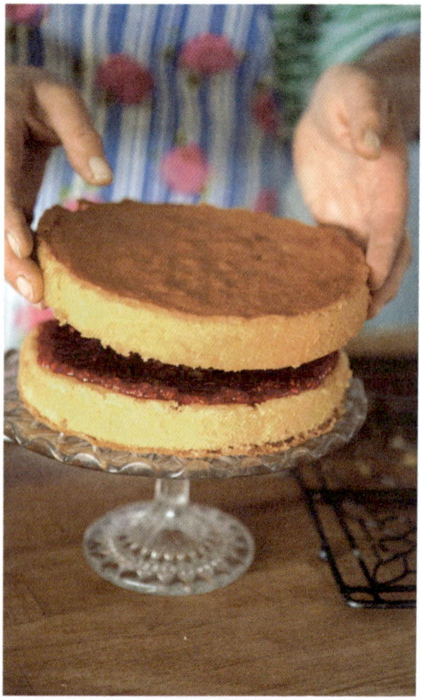

Add the eggs, about a quarter at a time, adding 1 tbsp of the weighed-out flour with each addition and beating thoroughly before adding the next. Beat in the vanilla extract with the last of the egg.

Sift in the rest of the flour, half at a time, and use a large metal spoon to carefully fold it in. The mixture should drop off the spoon easily when tapped against the side of the bowl. If it doesn't, then add a spoonful or two of hot water.

Divide the mixture equally between the prepared sandwich tins (or spoon it all into the larger cake tin if using), spreading it out lightly and evenly with the back of a spoon. Bake in the centre of the oven for about 25 minutes or until the cake(s) are lightly golden and spring back into shape when gently pressed with a finger.

Leave the cake(s) in the tin(s) for a couple of minutes before turning them out onto a wire rack to cool completely. (If you've baked a single cake, once cooled, cut it horizontally into two equal layers.)

When cold, spread one cake layer with the jam, place the second on top and dust lightly with caster sugar. The cake will keep for 5 days in an airtight tin.

Variations

Fillings and toppings Instead of raspberry jam, fill with any other favourite jam or homemade Lemon curd (see p.50), or fill and top with chocolate hazelnut spread. Instead of sprinkling with sugar, top with Glacé icing (see p.55). Or, in the summer, fill with strawberries or raspberries and whipped cream and dust with icing sugar.

Heavenly scented Place 3 or 4 deliciously scented geranium leaves, such as Mabel Grey or Attar of Roses, in the base of the lined tin. Remove when the cake is turned out to cool.

Chocolate Replace 25g of the flour with cocoa powder. Fill the cake with Chocolate buttercream (see p.49) and top with Chocolate glacé icing (see p.55), or fill and top with Chocolate crème fraîche topping (see p.65).

Coffee Omit the vanilla. Dissolve 1 tbsp instant coffee in 1 tbsp hot water and add to the mixture with the final egg. Fill and top with Coffee buttercream (see p.49).

Victoria cup cakes Bake the mixture in one or two well-greased or paper lined muffin trays; there should be enough to make 18 cup cakes. When cool, split in half and fill with jam and whipped cream.

Genoese sponge

The texture of a classic Genoese sponge – light yet pleasantly firm – lends itself to many uses. It's lovely cut into layers and sandwiched together with Buttercream (see p.49) and soft-set jam; or topped with whipped cream and a pile of fresh berries; or lightly drizzled with a fruit or liqueur syrup, dusted with icing sugar and served with a fresh fruit compote. It's also perfect for a traditional trifle.

Serves 12–14
125g plain flour
Pinch of sea salt
4 eggs
125g caster sugar
75g unsalted butter, melted and cooled

Equipment
23cm round or 20cm square tin, or 2 x 20cm deep sandwich tins, sides lightly greased and lightly dusted with flour, and base-lined with baking parchment

Preheat the oven to 180°C/Gas mark 4. Sift together the flour and salt twice and set aside. Have ready a large saucepan half full of simmering water, over which a heatproof mixing bowl will fit without touching the water.

Put the eggs and sugar in the heatproof bowl and place over the pan of simmering water. Using a hand-held electric whisk, beat at top speed for about 8 minutes until the mixture has at least tripled in size, is very pale and thick – it should hold a 'ribbon' on the surface when the whisk is lifted. Remove the bowl from the heat. (Or use a free-standing electric mixer; it will take about 5 minutes at its highest speed.)

Sift half the sifted flour over the mixture and use a large metal spoon to carefully fold it in. Repeat with the remaining flour. Dribble the melted butter over the surface a little at a time and then carefully but quickly fold it into the mixture, to minimise the loss of volume.

Pour the mixture into the prepared tin(s) and bake in the oven for 25–30 minutes, or until the cake is golden brown, firm and springs back into shape when lightly pressed. If you are using sandwich tins, the baking time will be barely 25 minutes. Leave in the tin(s) for 10 minutes before turning out onto a wire rack to cool.

When cold, the cake(s) will keep for a couple of days in an airtight tin, or they can be frozen for up to 6 weeks. Once filled, a Genoese sponge is best eaten on the day.

Variation
Chocolate Genoese Replace 25g of the flour with cocoa powder.

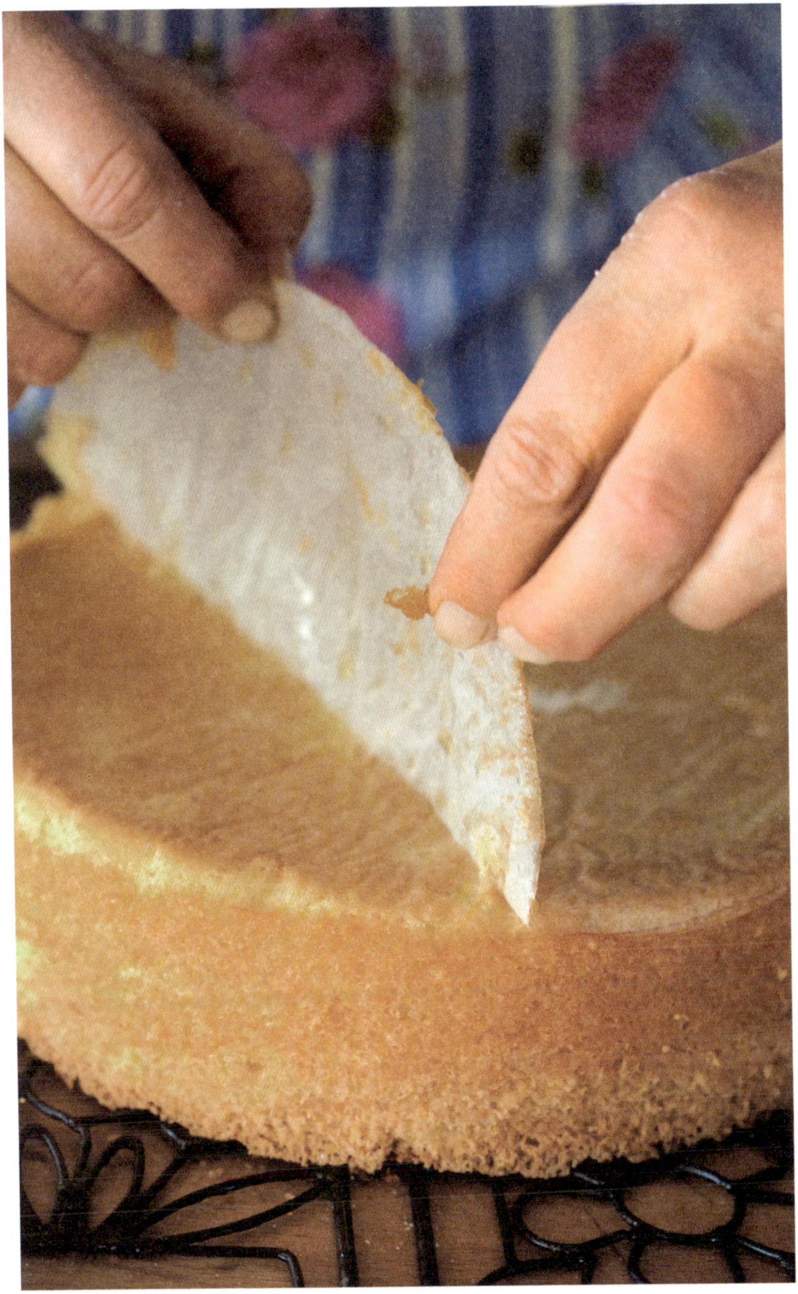

Zesty lemon Madeira cake

The name of this lovely light, buttery cake derives from the Victorian habit of enjoying a glass of Madeira alongside it. It's a shame we no longer do the same (though feel free). A classic English recipe, using classic cake ingredients, you'll find its homely aroma will fill the kitchen and beyond in the most pleasing way.

I like to top my Madeira cake with a zesty lemony icing. However, you can serve it un-iced, in which case I think it's nice to scatter some strips of candied citron peel (available from health food stores) over the cake before baking.

Serves 10

For the cake
200g plain flour
1 tsp baking powder
150g unsalted butter, cut into small pieces and softened
Finely grated zest of 2 unwaxed lemons, plus 2 tbsp juice
150g golden granulated sugar
4 eggs

For the topping
150g icing sugar
1½ tbsp lemon juice
Fresh, crystallised or sugared violets, or candied citron peel

Equipment
1 litre loaf tin, about 20x10cm lightly greased, base and long sides lined with baking parchment

Preheat the oven to 180°C/Gas mark 4. Sift the flour and baking powder together and set aside.

In a mixing bowl, beat the butter with the lemon zest, using either a wooden spoon or a hand-held electric whisk, to a cream. Add the sugar and continue to beat until the mixture is very light and creamy. Add the eggs one at a time, adding 1 tbsp of the flour with each and beating thoroughly before adding the next egg. Fold in the remaining flour, using a large metal spoon, then fold in the 2 tbsp lemon juice.

Spoon the mixture into the prepared tin and spread out lightly and evenly with the back of the spoon. Bake in the oven for about 50 minutes until the cake is well risen, springy to the touch and a skewer inserted in the centre comes out clean. Leave in the tin for 10 minutes before turning out onto a wire rack to cool.

Meanwhile, for the topping, sift the icing sugar into a bowl. Beat in the lemon juice, a little at a time, until the icing is glossy and fairly stiff. Spread thickly on top of the cake and decorate with violets or candied citron peel.

This cake will keep for 10 days in an airtight tin.

BIG CAKES 131

Coffee and walnut cake

This traditional cake never fails to please; its bitter-sweet flavours make it one of my all-time favourites. I like to use old-fashioned Camp coffee essence for the coffee bit. Still made in Scotland, this iconic dark brown syrup is a blend of chicory and coffee. It dates back to 1876 when it was used by the military as an easy-to-prepare hot drink for sustaining troops during foreign campaigns. However, you can use instant coffee or very strong freshly brewed coffee instead.

Serves 10

For the cake
200g plain flour
1½ tsp baking powder
200g unsalted butter, cut into small pieces and softened
100g light soft brown sugar
100g caster sugar
3 eggs
50ml coffee essence (or 1 tbsp instant coffee dissolved in 1 tbsp boiling water, or 3 tbsp very strong fresh coffee)
100g chopped walnuts
25–50ml milk

For the buttercream
60g unsalted butter, cut into small pieces and softened
125g icing sugar, sifted
10ml coffee essence (or 2 tsp instant coffee dissolved in 2 tsp boiling water or 1 tbsp strong fresh coffee)

For the topping
200g icing sugar
2 tsp coffee essence (or 2 tsp instant coffee dissolved in 2 tbsp boiling water, or 1 tbsp strong fresh coffee)
50g chopped walnuts

Equipment
2 x 20cm sandwich tins, lightly greased and base-lined with baking parchment

Preheat the oven to 180°C/Gas mark 4. Sift the flour and baking powder together and set aside.

In a large mixing bowl, using either a wooden spoon or a hand-held electric whisk, beat the butter to a cream. Add the brown and caster sugars and beat until light and creamy. Add the eggs, one at a time, adding 1 tbsp flour with each and beating thoroughly before adding the next. Stir in the coffee essence.

Now carefully fold in the remaining flour, half at a time, with a large metal spoon. Fold in the chopped walnuts and sufficient milk to give a soft dropping consistency.

Spoon the mixture into the prepared tins, spreading it out evenly with the back of the spoon. Bake in the oven for 25–30 minutes until the tops are a light golden brown and the cakes spring back into shape when gently pressed. Leave in the tins for 10 minutes before turning out to cool on a wire rack.

Meanwhile, prepare the buttercream. Beat the butter to a cream, add the icing sugar and the coffee essence and beat until light and creamy.

To make the glacé icing for the topping, sift the icing sugar into a bowl, add the coffee essence and 1–2 tbsp boiling water, and mix until thick.

Spread one of the cooled cakes with the buttercream. Sandwich together with the second cake and cover the top with glacé icing. Finish with the chopped walnuts. This cake will keep for a week in an airtight tin.

Variation

Streusel-topped coffee cake Spoon the cake mixture into one 23cm round tin. To make the streusel topping, mix together 125g light soft brown sugar, 50g plain flour, 1 tsp ground cinnamon, 125g chopped walnuts and 50g melted butter until evenly combined. Sprinkle over the surface of the cake mixture in the tin and bake for 40–45 minutes until golden brown on top.

Chocolate cake

Of all cakes, this is the one with the highest expectations, but fear not, I promise this recipe will meet the toughest standards. For the perfect dreamy chocolate experience, I recommend filling and topping the cake with my fudgy icing, but you might like to verge into Black Forest territory with the white choc-cherry variation. Either way, the cake is at its best a day or two after making, when cake and filling have subtly and deliciously become one.

Serves 12–16

For the cake
25g cocoa powder
25g drinking chocolate powder
200g plain flour
1 tsp baking powder
1 tsp bicarbonate of soda
Good pinch of sea salt
175g unsalted butter, cut into small pieces and softened
100g light soft brown sugar
100g caster sugar
4 eggs
150ml buttermilk (or 75ml whole milk mixed with 75ml plain yoghurt)
100g ground almonds

For the filling and topping
2 x quantity Chocolate fudge icing (see p.63)
50g plain chocolate, finely grated

Equipment
23cm round loose-bottomed cake tin or 2 x 20cm sandwich tins, 5cm deep, sides well greased and base-lined with baking parchment

Preheat the oven to 180°C/Gas mark 4. Put the cocoa powder and drinking chocolate into a small bowl. Add 50ml freshly boiled water, mix to a paste and set aside. Sift the flour, baking powder, bicarbonate of soda and salt together and set aside.

In a large mixing bowl, using either a wooden spoon or a hand-held electric whisk, beat the butter to a cream. Add both the sugars and the cocoa paste. Continue beating until light and very creamy. Add the eggs one at a time, adding 1 tbsp of the flour with each and beating thoroughly before adding the next. Then fold in the remaining flour with the buttermilk little by little – dry, wet, dry, wet – until you have a very soft, creamy mixture. Finally, carefully fold in the ground almonds.

Spoon the mixture into the prepared tin(s), spreading it out lightly and evenly with the back of the spoon. Bake in the oven, allowing 45–50 minutes for a cake in a 23cm tin and 35–40 minutes for cakes in 20cm deep sandwich tins.

Leave the cake(s) in the tin(s) for 10 minutes before turning out and placing on a wire rack to cool completely.

When cold, cut the 23cm cake into three layers, or each of the 20cm cakes into two layers. Sandwich the layers together with the chocolate fudge icing, saving sufficient to smother over the top. Finish the top with a sprinkling of grated chocolate. This cake will keep for 5–6 days in an airtight tin.

Variations

Black Forest Combine 200g warm cherry or damson jam with 200g melted white chocolate. Use to layer the cake together and top with Chocolate icing (see p.63) and Chocolate leaves (see p.65).

Triple-layer cake Halve the listed quantities and bake the cake in an 18cm round tin. Assemble as above.

Wholemeal orange cake
with Earl Grey icing

The bergamot orange is one of those slightly confused citrus fruits that doesn't quite know what it is. Its flavour lies somewhere between a sweet orange and a grapefruit, but it is yellow in colour and could be mistaken for a lemon, were it not for its slightly pear-like shape. Unquestionably, it is the bergamot's fragrant oil, used to flavour and scent Earl Grey tea, which gives this muddled fruit its status in the citrus world. The combination of a surprisingly light wholemeal orange cake and an aromatic Earl Grey icing is a firm favourite with my family.

Serves 8–10

For the cake
100g self-raising wholemeal flour
75g self-raising white flour
1 tsp baking powder
Pinch of sea salt
175g unsalted butter, cut into small pieces and softened
Finely grated zest of 1 unwaxed orange, plus the juice of ½ orange (50ml)
175g caster sugar
3 eggs

For the filling
1 quantity Cream cheese topping flavoured with orange zest (see p.57)

For the topping
1 Earl Grey tea bag
250g unrefined icing sugar
12 walnut halves

Equipment
2 x 20cm sandwich tins, lightly greased and base-lined with baking parchment

Preheat the oven to 180°C/Gas mark 4. Sift the wholemeal and self-raising flours together with the baking powder and salt; set aside.

In a large mixing bowl, beat the butter and orange zest to a cream, using either a wooden spoon or a hand-held electric whisk. Add the sugar and continue to beat until the mixture is very light and fluffy. Beat in the eggs one at a time, adding 1 tbsp flour with each. Using a large metal spoon, fold in the remaining flour. Finally fold in the orange juice.

Spoon the mixture into the prepared tins, spreading it out lightly and evenly with the back of the spoon. Bake in the oven for about 25 minutes until cooked and the centre springs back into shape when lightly touched with a finger.

Leave the cakes in the tins for 5–10 minutes before turning out and placing on a wire rack to cool. When cold, sandwich together with the cream cheese filling.

For the Earl Grey icing, infuse the tea bag in 2 tbsp boiling water for about 5 minutes, then remove. Sift the icing sugar into a bowl. Little by little, add the tea to the icing sugar, beating until thick and glossy. Using a palette knife, spread the icing evenly over the top of the cake. Decorate with the walnut halves.

This cake will keep for 3–4 days in an airtight tin.

Apple cake

You should be able to throw this homely country cake together easily, since it uses ingredients that we usually have in our kitchens. You can make it with cooking or dessert apples, whichever is to hand. To peel or not to peel? For new season's apples, I'd say leave the skins on, but older or waxy-skinned ones are best peeled.

Serves 10

For the cake
125g self-raising white flour
125g self-raising wholemeal flour
½ tsp bicarbonate of soda
2 tsp ground nutmeg
½ tsp ground cloves
Pinch of sea salt
125g unsalted butter, cut into small pieces
125g soft brown sugar
350g cored apples (prepared weight)
1 egg, beaten
50ml milk

For the topping
1 small eating apple (ideally red-skinned, cored but not peeled)
1 tbsp caster sugar

Equipment
23cm round loose-bottomed or springform tin, or a 20cm square loose-bottomed tin, greased and base-lined with baking parchment

Preheat the oven to 180°C/Gas mark 4. Sift the first six ingredients into a large bowl and mix well together. Add the butter and, using your fingertips, rub it into the flour until the mixture resembles medium breadcrumbs. Stir in the sugar. Cut the apples into 1cm dice and toss lightly in the rubbed-in mixture until evenly distributed. Add the egg and milk and bring the mix together with a wooden spoon to a sticky, lumpy dough. Spoon into the prepared tin and level with the back of the spoon.

For the topping, cut the apple across into 7 or 8 slices and poke out any residual pips embedded in the flesh. Lay the apple slices on top of the cake. Sprinkle the caster sugar evenly over the mixture and apples (to give the cake a lovely crisp topping).

Bake for 45–50 minutes until the top is golden brown, firm and crispy to the touch. Leave in the tin for 20–30 minutes before turning out onto a wire rack. This cake will keep for 2–3 days in an airtight tin in a cool place.

Variation

Special day apple cake Soak 125g sultanas in a little brandy and add to the mix with the chopped apple. Sprinkle 2 tbsp flaked almonds over the top before baking.

BIG CAKES 139

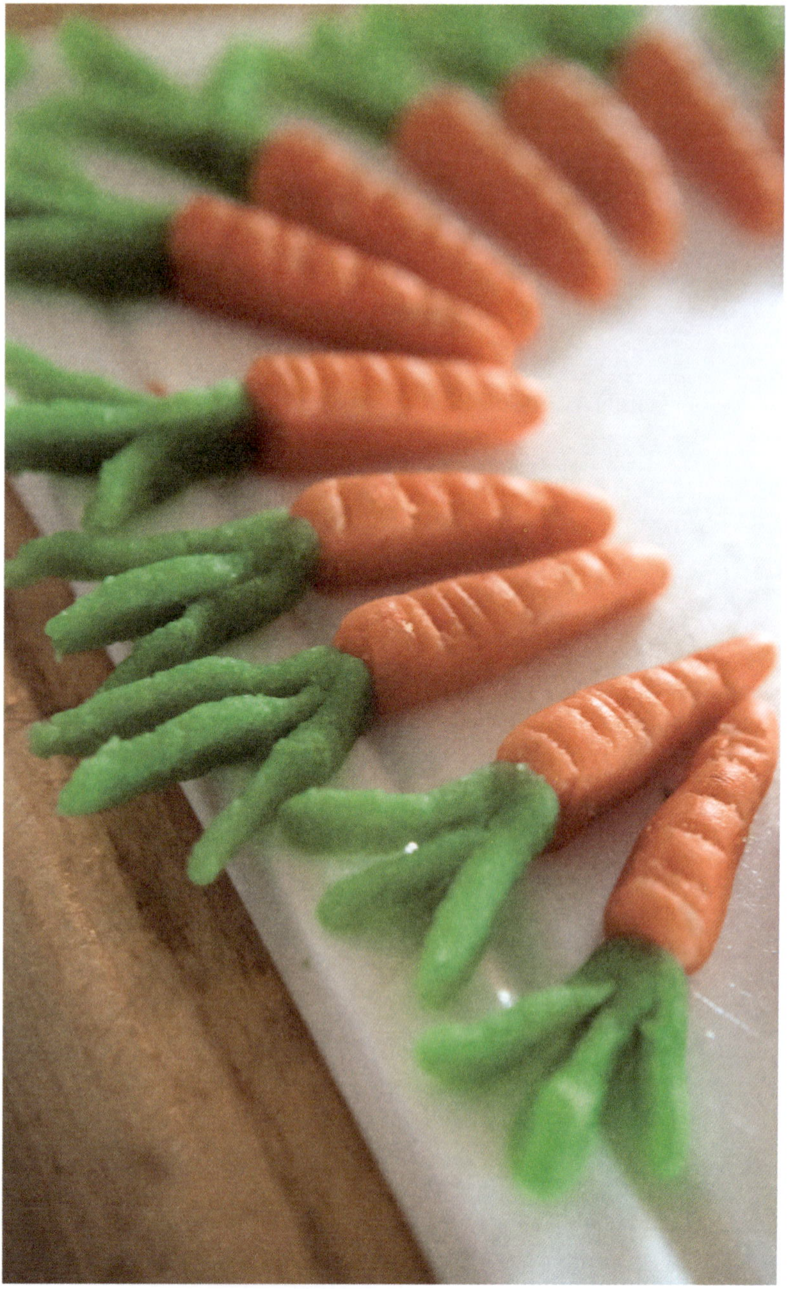

Carrot cake

High in natural sugars and full of juice, carrots have long been valued as ingredients in cakes and puddings. Carrot cake is also known as 'Passion cake', because it was once made as a cheaper alternative to a formal richly fruited wedding cake. All that love and fervour – no wonder carrot cake is such a perpetual favourite.

Serves 8–10

For the cake
125g self-raising wholemeal flour
1 tsp ground mixed spice
1 tsp baking powder
Pinch of sea salt
150g unsalted butter, cut into small pieces and softened
Finely grated zest of 1 orange
150g golden caster sugar
3 eggs
75g ground almonds
250g finely grated carrot
75g sultanas or raisins
75g flaked almonds or chopped walnuts

For the topping
1 quantity Cream cheese topping (see p.57)
75g Marzipan, shaped into carrots (see p.59), to decorate (optional)

Equipment
20cm round or 18cm square tin, lightly greased and base-lined with baking parchment

Preheat the oven to 180°C/Gas mark 4. Sift together the flour, mixed spice, baking powder and salt into a bowl and set aside.

In a large mixing bowl, beat the butter and orange zest to a cream, using either a wooden spoon or a hand-held electric whisk. Add the sugar and continue to beat until the mixture is light and fluffy.

Add the eggs, one at a time, adding 1 tbsp of the flour mix with each and beating thoroughly before adding the next. Using a large metal spoon, fold in the remaining flour mix, followed by the ground almonds, grated carrot, dried fruit and nuts.

Spoon the mixture into the prepared tin, smoothing it out gently with the back of the spoon. Bake in the oven for 45–50 minutes until the cake is evenly coloured and springs back into shape when lightly pressed with a finger. Leave in the tin for 10 minutes before turning out onto a wire rack to cool.

When the cake is cold, spread with the cream cheese topping. Finish with marzipan carrots, if using. This cake will keep for 3–4 days in an airtight tin in a cool place.

Old-fashioned cherry cake

The glacé cherry plays a supporting role in lots of recipes. It lends glamour to fruit cakes, crystal-like jewels to Florentines and very often it's the cherry on top of the cake! Allow it sovereignty and you will truly appreciate its flavour and texture. Undoubtedly one of my favourites, cherry cake is an absolute teatime classic.

Serves 10

For the cake
250g natural undyed glacé cherries
75g plain flour, plus ½ tbsp to dust cherries
100g self-raising flour
Pinch of sea salt
175g unsalted butter, cut into small pieces and softened
175g caster sugar
3 eggs
100g ground almonds
2 tsp vanilla extract
75ml milk, to mix

To finish
Glacé icing (see p.55)
3–4 glacé cherries, halved
3–4 pieces candied angelica (optional)

Equipment
2 litre loaf tin, about 25x13cm, lightly greased and lined with baking parchment, or a 20cm round or 18cm square tin lightly greased and base-lined with baking parchment

Preheat the oven to 180°C/Gas mark 4. Start by rinsing the sticky sugar syrup off the cherries. To do this, place them in a sieve and rinse with a little warm water. Dry thoroughly with a piece of kitchen paper, then cut the cherries in half and toss with ½ tbsp plain flour; set aside. Sift the flours and salt together.

In a large mixing bowl, using either a wooden spoon or hand-held electric whisk, beat the butter to a cream. Add the sugar and continue beating until the mixture is very light and fluffy. Add the eggs, one at a time, adding 1 tbsp of the flour with each and beating thoroughly before adding the next egg.

Fold in the remaining flour, ground almonds and the glacé cherries. Add the vanilla extract and incorporate sufficient milk to give a light dropping consistency.

Spoon the mixture into the prepared tin, smoothing over the surface with the back of the spoon. Bake in the oven for 55–60 minutes until evenly cooked and the centre springs back when lightly touched with a finger.

Leave the cake to cool in the tin for 10 minutes before turning out and placing on a wire rack to cool completely.

To finish, spread the glacé icing evenly over the surface of the cake. Decorate with glacé cherry halves and finely cut strips of angelica. This cake will keep for about a week in an airtight tin.

Variations

Cherry and chocolate Instead of glacé icing, top with bitter-sweet Chocolate crème fraîche topping (see p.65) and decorate as above.

Fresh cherry For a summertime special, use fresh rather than glacé cherries. Rinse the cherries, dry well and remove the stones before adding to the mixture.

Marble cake

The fun of the marble cake is that no piece is ever the same – each slice is a work of art in itself, which is why it has fascinated children for generations. The success of the marbling depends on how the uncooked mixture is spooned into the tin. Keep the spoonfuls irregular in size and not too big and hopefully your cake will be swirly and patterned throughout. Alternatively, this easy recipe can be baked unmarbled – either all chocolate or all vanilla – to make a lovely plain cake or to use as a base for other flavours or fruity drizzles.

Serves 10
300g self-raising flour
200g unsalted butter, cut into small pieces and softened
250g caster sugar
3 eggs
200ml soured cream
25g cocoa powder
2 tsp vanilla extract

Equipment
20cm round or 18cm square tin, lightly greased and base-lined with baking parchment

Preheat the oven to 180°C/Gas mark 4. Sift the flour into a bowl and set aside.

In a mixing bowl, using either a wooden spoon or a hand-held electric whisk, beat the butter to a cream. Add the sugar and continue to beat until the mixture is very light and creamy. Add the eggs, one at a time, adding 1 tbsp of the flour with each and beating thoroughly before adding the next. Beat in the soured cream until evenly combined. Using a large metal spoon, carefully fold in the remaining flour.

Divide the mixture between two bowls. Into one, sift the cocoa powder and carefully fold in. To the second, add the vanilla extract and gently blend in.

Without being too neat and tidy, drop dessertspoonfuls of each mixture alternately into the prepared tin. When they are all added, tap the tin sharply on the work top to level the surface, then lightly swirl a skewer through the mixture to give the cake its distinctive marbled look.

Bake in the oven for 45–50 minutes until the cake is evenly golden and springs back into shape when lightly pressed.

Leave in the tin for 10 minutes before turning out to cool on a wire rack. This cake will keep for up to a week in an airtight tin.

BIG CAKES 145

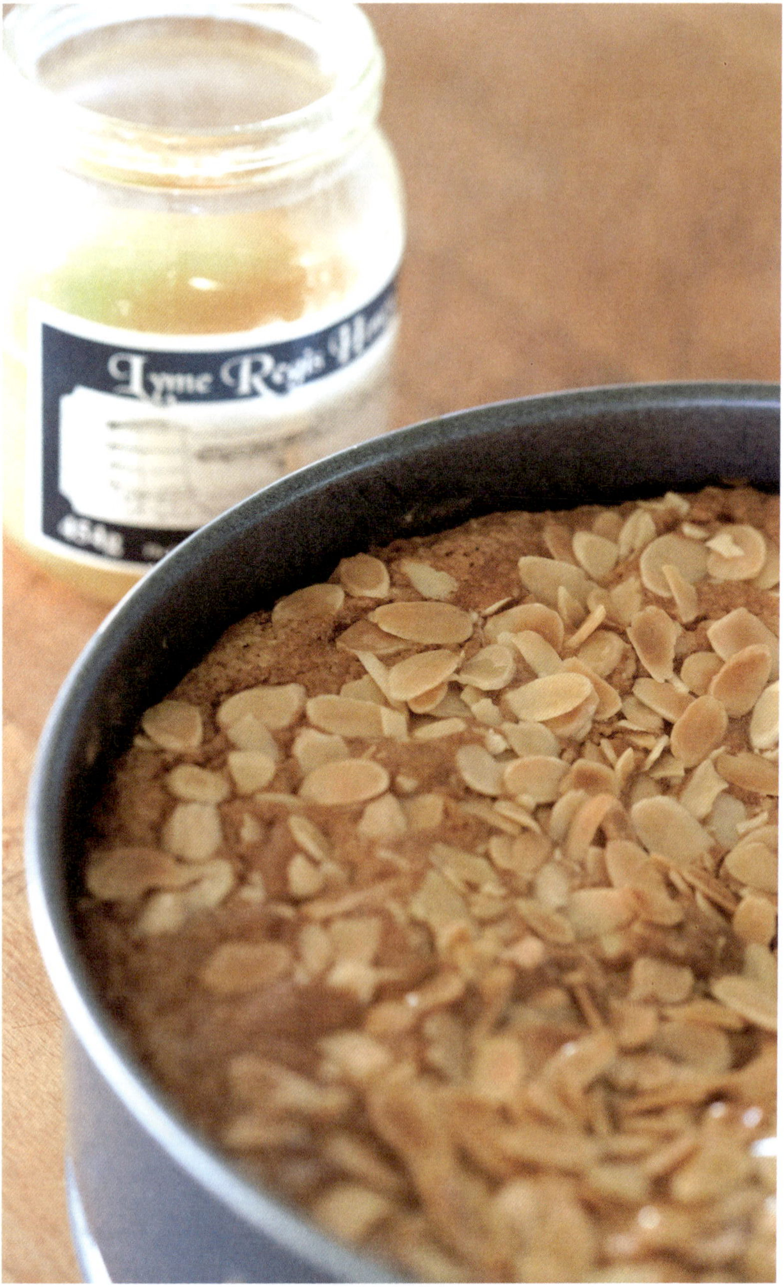
Lyme Regis

Gill's honey cake

This well-loved recipe comes from Gill Meller, head chef at River Cottage, and it is frequently served to guests at Park Farm. One of the lovely things about this cake is that the taste will vary depending on the honey you choose. Try, if you can, to use a local honey. Not only will this be uniquely flavoured by the flowers and blossoms of your region, it's better for the environment too – bee miles, unlike other air miles, don't count towards your carbon footprint!

Serves 10

300g unsalted butter, cut into small pieces and softened
250g caster sugar
4 eggs
150g self-raising wholemeal flour
1 tsp baking powder
150g ground almonds
50g flaked almonds
4 tbsp runny honey (or set honey, warmed sufficiently to trickle)

Equipment
23cm springform cake tin, or a 20cm square loose-bottomed tin, lightly greased and base-lined with baking parchment

Preheat the oven to 170°C/Gas mark 3. In a large mixing bowl, beat the butter to a cream. Add the sugar and beat thoroughly until very light and fluffy. Beat in the eggs, one at a time, adding a spoonful of the flour with each and beating thoroughly before adding the next.

Combine the remaining flour with the baking powder and sift into the bowl. Using a large metal spoon, carefully fold into the mixture. Stir in the ground almonds until evenly mixed.

Spoon the mixture into the prepared tin, spreading it evenly with the back of the spoon. Scatter over the flaked almonds. Stand the tin on a baking sheet (as the cake may leak a little butter during cooking). Bake in the oven for about 45 minutes, until springy to the touch and a skewer inserted into the centre comes out clean.

On removing from the oven, trickle the honey over the surface so that it soaks into the hot cake. Leave in the tin for half an hour or so before turning out and placing on a wire rack to cool completely.

This cake is best kept for a day or two before eating. It keeps well for at least a week, stored in an airtight tin.

Golden syrup cake

I'm not going to try and convince you that this is a 'healthy' cake, but it certainly is irresistible. Amber in colour with a sweet, honey-like flavour, the golden syrup gives it a unique and delicious savour, while breadcrumbs lend a lovely light texture. Fantastic with mid-morning coffee or packed in a lunch box, it also makes an easy pud – served warm with custard or ice cream.

Serves 8–10
250g golden syrup
100g unsalted butter, cut into cubes
150g self-raising flour
½ tsp bicarbonate of soda
½ tsp fine sea salt
50g fresh white breadcrumbs
Finely grated zest of ½ unwaxed lemon
1 egg
150ml plain yoghurt

Equipment
1 litre loaf tin, about 22x10cm, lightly greased, base and sides lined with baking parchment

Preheat the oven to 180°C/Gas mark 4. Put 200g of the golden syrup and the butter in a small saucepan, place over a low heat and stir until the butter has melted and combined with the syrup. Set aside to cool.

Meanwhile sift the flour, bicarbonate of soda and salt into a medium mixing bowl. Add the breadcrumbs and lemon zest and mix together until well combined. Make a well in the centre.

In another bowl, lightly beat the egg and mix in the yoghurt. Pour into the well in the dry ingredients and add the cooled syrup mixture. Using either a wooden spoon or a hand-held electric whisk on medium speed, beat until smooth and glossy.

Pour the mixture into the prepared tin and bake in the oven for about 40 minutes until the surface is evenly golden and the cake springs back when lightly touched. Shortly before the cake will be ready, mix the remaining golden syrup with 1 tbsp freshly boiled water.

As you take the cake from the oven, prick the surface deeply (but not right through to the bottom) all over with a skewer. Pour the warm syrup evenly over the surface. Leave the cake in the tin until cool before turning out.

This cake will keep for 5–6 days in an airtight tin.

'Men only' lemon drizzle

The village horticultural show throws up no end of emotions on show day: angst, resentment, joy, disbelief and elation, to name a few. A win turns you giddy with success, whereas a harsh comment from a judge can hurt and humiliate. There's always fierce competition in the 'Men only' class – daggers drawn and all that stuff. Rob Prosser kindly gave me the recipe for his winning lemon drizzle cake.

Serves 8

For the cake
175g self-raising flour, sifted
1 tsp baking powder
175g caster sugar
175g unsalted butter, cut into small pieces and softened
Finely grated zest of 2 unwaxed lemons
3 eggs

For the drizzle
Juice of 2 lemons
100g granulated sugar

Equipment
18cm round or 15cm square tin, greased and base-lined with baking parchment, or a 1 litre loaf tin, approx 20x10cm, greased, base and long sides lined with parchment

Preheat the oven to 180°C/Gas mark 4. Sift the flour and baking powder into a mixing bowl. Add all the other cake ingredients and, using a hand-held electric mixer, beat for about 1½ minutes, until you have a smooth, thick batter. Spoon the mixture into the prepared tin, levelling out the surface with the back of a spoon.

Bake for 40–45 minutes or until the surface is golden brown and a skewer inserted into the centre of the cake comes out clean. Leave in the tin for about 10 minutes before turning out and placing on a wire rack.

Meanwhile, prepare the drizzle. Mix the lemon juice with the granulated sugar; do not let the sugar dissolve. Prick the surface of the warm cake all over with a skewer and carefully trickle the drizzle over the surface, a spoonful at a time, ensuring each addition has soaked in before spooning over the next. Leave to cool completely.

This cake will keep for 5 days in an airtight tin.

Variation
Mincemeat cake Spoon half the cake mixture into the prepared tin, spread 3–4 tbsp mincemeat over the surface and top with the remaining cake mix. Sprinkle with 1–2 tbsp flaked almonds and bake as above. Omit the lemon drizzle.

Lime and coconut cake
(gluten free)

Creamy coconut and zesty lime team up perfectly to flavour this lovely gluten-free cake. Because the recipe uses rice flour rather than conventional wheat flour, it does have a tendency to sink a bit in the middle. This doesn't bother me in the least – in fact, I rather enjoy the dense centre. However, if you're concerned about it, you can prevent the cake sinking by adding a little xanthan gum, which acts as a substitute for the stretchy, bouncy gluten found in wheat flours and will bind the mixture together. Xanthan gum is available from health food stores and the baking section of larger supermarkets.

Serves 10–12

For the cake
125g rice flour
2 tsp gluten-free baking powder
1 tsp xanthan gum (optional)
175g unsalted butter, cut into small pieces and softened
Finely grated zest of 3–4 small limes
175g caster sugar
3 eggs
50g desiccated coconut

For the drizzle
75g caster sugar
100ml freshly squeezed lime juice (about 3–4 limes)

Equipment
1 litre loaf tin, approx 20x10cm, lightly greased, base and long sides lined with baking parchment, or a 20cm round or 18cm square tin, lightly greased and base-lined with baking parchment

Preheat the oven to 180°C/Gas mark 4. Sift together the rice flour, baking powder and xanthan gum, if using, into a bowl.

In a mixing bowl, beat the butter and lime zest to a cream, using either a wooden spoon or a hand-held electric whisk. Add the sugar and continue to beat until the mixture is light and creamy. Add the eggs, one at a time, adding 1 tbsp flour with each and beating thoroughly before adding the next. Carefully fold in the remaining flour with a large metal spoon, then fold in the desiccated coconut.

Spoon the mixture into the prepared tin, lightly smoothing over the surface with the back of a spoon. Bake in the oven for 40–45 minutes or until the surface is nicely golden and the cake feels springy to the touch. Shortly before the cake will be ready, prepare the drizzle by dissolving the sugar in the lime juice.

When the cake comes out of the oven, prick the surface deeply (but not to the very bottom) all over with a skewer. Spoon half the lime syrup over the surface and leave to cool for 10 minutes before spooning over the remainder. Make sure you pour plenty of drizzle down the sides of the tin. Leave in the tin until cool before turning out.

This cake will keep for 5 days in an airtight tin.

Variations

St Clement's cake Replace the limes with a mix of lemons and oranges.

Christmas cracker Replace the limes with tangerines. For the drizzle, replace 50ml of the juice with 50ml orange liqueur.

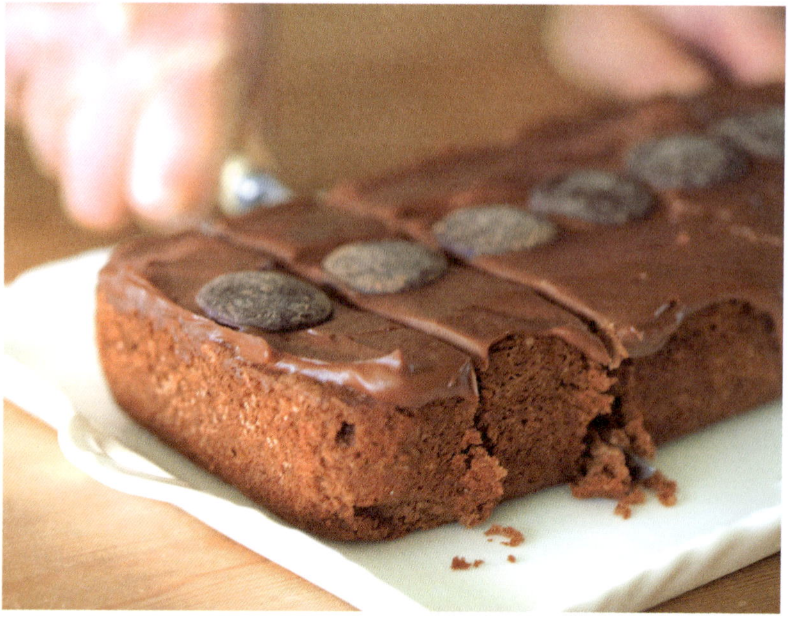

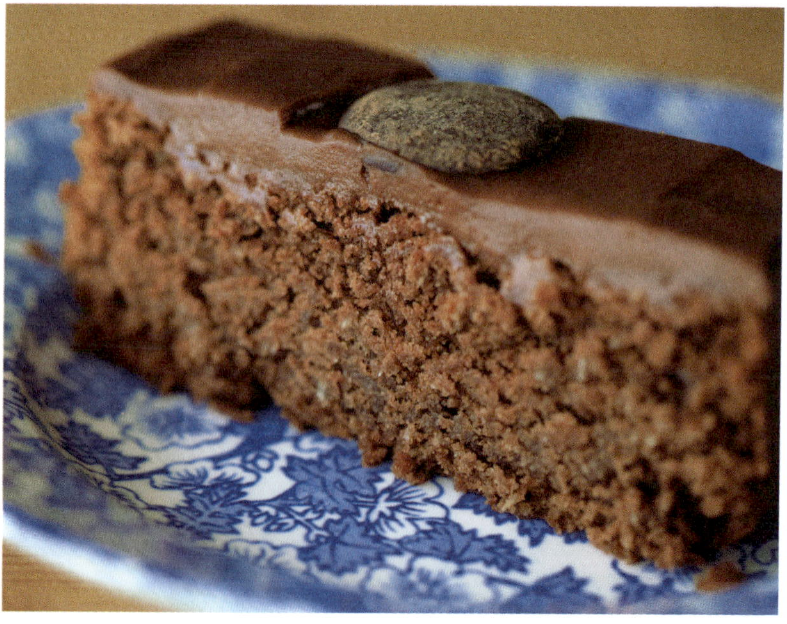

Bounty bar cake

Inspired by a well-known chocolate bar, this dense, chocolatey wonder is an adaptation of my mother's recipe for a moist coconut cake. The coconut needs to soak for a couple of hours, so remember to start well before you're planning to bake the cake.

Serves 10

For the cake
50g desiccated coconut
150ml full-fat or reduced-fat coconut milk (or you can use ordinary milk)
150g self-raising flour
25g cocoa powder
150g caster sugar
150g unsalted butter, cut into small pieces and softened
2 eggs

To finish
1 quantity Chocolate crème fraîche topping (see p.65)
Large chocolate buttons, to decorate

Equipment
1 litre loaf tin, approx 20 x 10cm, lightly greased, base and long sides lined with baking parchment, or a 20cm round tin, lightly greased

Preheat the oven to 180°C/Gas mark 4. Put the desiccated coconut into a bowl and pour on the coconut milk (or ordinary milk). Leave for a couple of hours to swell and rehydrate.

Sift the flour and cocoa powder into a mixing bowl. Add the sugar and mix until evenly distributed, then add the butter and eggs. Using a hand-held electric whisk, beat for about 1½ minutes until the mixture is light and creamy. Carefully stir in the coconut, along with any residual liquid, mixing until well combined.

Spoon the mixture into the prepared tin, levelling the surface with the back of the spoon. Bake in the centre of the oven, allowing about 40 minutes for a cake in a loaf tin, 25–30 minutes for a round cake. When done, the cake should spring back into shape when lightly pressed.

Leave to cool in the tin for 10 minutes before turning out and placing on a wire rack. Leave to cool completely.

To finish, spread the chocolate crème fraîche topping evenly over the top of the cake and decorate with chocolate buttons.

This cake will keep for 5 days in an airtight tin.

Caraway and orange cake

The joy of this cake is that you need only one bowl and one measure. Using a 150ml yoghurt pot (or any other 150ml measure), you'll be able to knock it up effortlessly wherever you are. You can leave it plain, or flavour it as you choose. I love to add caraway – to make a sweetly aromatic, old-fashioned seed cake – but I realise not everyone shares my passion for this feisty little seed. If you're not so keen, try one of my suggested variations (below).

Serves 8–10
1 tbsp caraway seeds
2 x 150ml pots plain full-fat or semi-skimmed yoghurt
½ x 150ml pot (75ml) rapeseed oil
2 eggs
2 x 150ml pots caster sugar
Finely grated zest of 1 unwaxed orange
3 x 150ml pots plain flour
¼ x 150ml pot flaked almonds

Equipment
2 litre loaf tin, about 25x13cm, or a 1 litre loaf tin, approx 20x10cm, for a deeper cake, lightly greased, base and long sides lined with baking parchment

Preheat the oven to 180°C/Gas mark 4. Heat a small frying pan over a medium heat for a couple of minutes, then add the caraway seeds and toast them gently for 2–3 minutes, stirring constantly, until they become fragrant. Pound the seeds lightly (they don't have to be reduced to a powder) to release their sweet, aromatic flavour.

Put the yoghurt, oil, eggs, sugar and orange zest into a large mixing bowl and beat with a wooden spoon to a smooth, creamy batter. Sift in the flour and beat lightly until well incorporated. Spoon into the prepared tin and sharply tap the tin on the work surface to level the mixture. Sprinkle the flaked almonds evenly over the top.

Bake in the oven for 45–50 minutes until golden brown and a skewer inserted in the centre of the cake comes out clean. Leave in the tin for 20 minutes or so before removing to a wire rack to cool. This cake will keep for a week in an airtight tin.

Variations

Plain Jane Omit the caraway seeds and flaked almonds.

Poppy seed and lemon Replace the caraway with poppy seeds and the orange with lemon zest. Mix the juice of 1 lemon with 100g granulated sugar and pour over the hot baked cake – the juice will sink in and the sugar will form a crunchy topping.

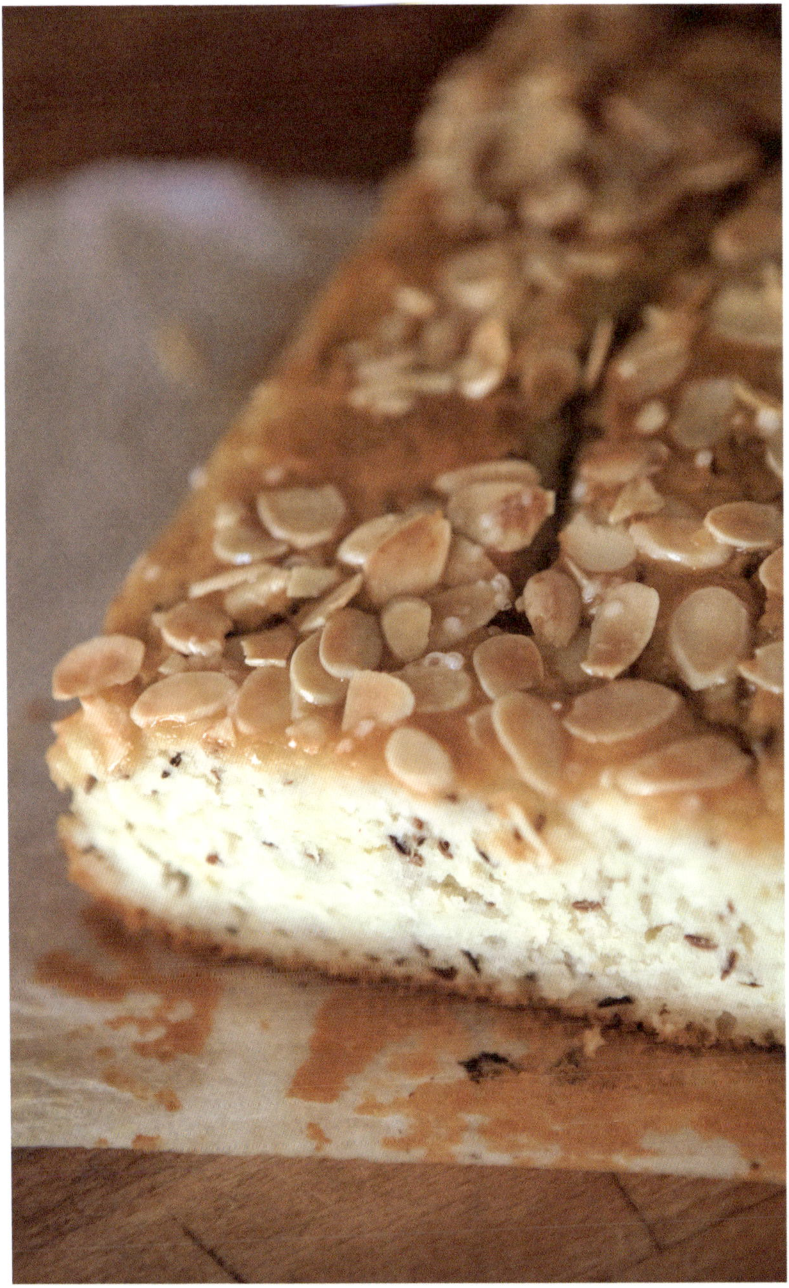

Swiss roll with poppy seeds and lemon curd filling

The Americans call this type of cake a 'jelly roll', while the French know it as *gâteau roulé*. No one is quite sure why we call this feather-light, rolled-up sponge a Swiss roll. It doesn't seem to have any particular link with Switzerland. In fact, this simple rolled cake – or something like it – is made the world over. You can easily alter the recipe by adding flavourings to the sponge or by tinkering with the all-important gluey filling. In this case, some delightfully sharp lemon curd sets off the sweet, nutty flavour of the poppy seeds in the sponge.

Serves 8

For the cake
75g plain flour
Pinch of sea salt
3 eggs
75g caster sugar
2 tbsp poppy seeds

For the filling
1 quantity Lemon curd (see p.50)

To finish
Caster sugar, for dusting
Icing sugar, for dusting (optional)

Equipment
20x35cm Swiss roll tin, base-lined with baking parchment, and sides and base lightly greased and dusted with flour

Preheat the oven to 190°C/Gas mark 5. Sift the flour and salt together into a bowl and set aside.

Place the eggs and sugar in a large mixing bowl. Using either a hand-held electric whisk or a free-standing electric mixer, whisk until the mixture has almost quadrupled in volume, is very light and fluffy, and holds its shape. This will take around 7–8 minutes with a hand-held whisk and 4–5 minutes in a free-standing electric mixer.

Add 1 tbsp warm water and fold in carefully. Sift half of the flour over the mixture and sprinkle in 1 tbsp of the poppy seeds. Using a large metal spoon, carefully fold them in before adding the remaining flour and poppy seeds in the same way. Scrape down the sides of the bowl well with a spatula.

Pour the mixture into the prepared tin and spread it out lightly and evenly, making sure it fills the corners of the tin.

Bake in the oven for 12–14 minutes until the sponge feels firm to the touch in the centre.

Have ready a piece of greaseproof paper 10cm larger all round than the Swiss roll tin. Lay the paper on your work surface and dust lightly with caster sugar.

As soon as the sponge comes out of the oven, turn it onto the sugared paper. Remove the tin and carefully peel away the baking parchment. Roll up the cake from the short side, rolling the sugared paper inside the cake as you go. Lift onto a wire rack and leave to cool.

When you are ready to fill the sponge, carefully unroll it. Spread the lemon curd over the sponge, leaving a 1cm margin free all around. Then, using the greaseproof paper as a guide, re-roll the cake. Place it, seam side down, on a wire rack or serving plate and dust with caster or icing sugar before serving.

This will keep for 3 days in an airtight tin but it is best eaten within a day or two.

Variations

Traditional Swiss roll Omit the poppy seeds. Add 1 tsp vanilla extract instead with the egg and sugar. Replace the lemon curd filling with your favourite jam.

Chocolate Swiss roll Replace 25g of the flour with cocoa powder. Blend 100ml plain yoghurt with 100g chocolate hazelnut spread and use for the filling.

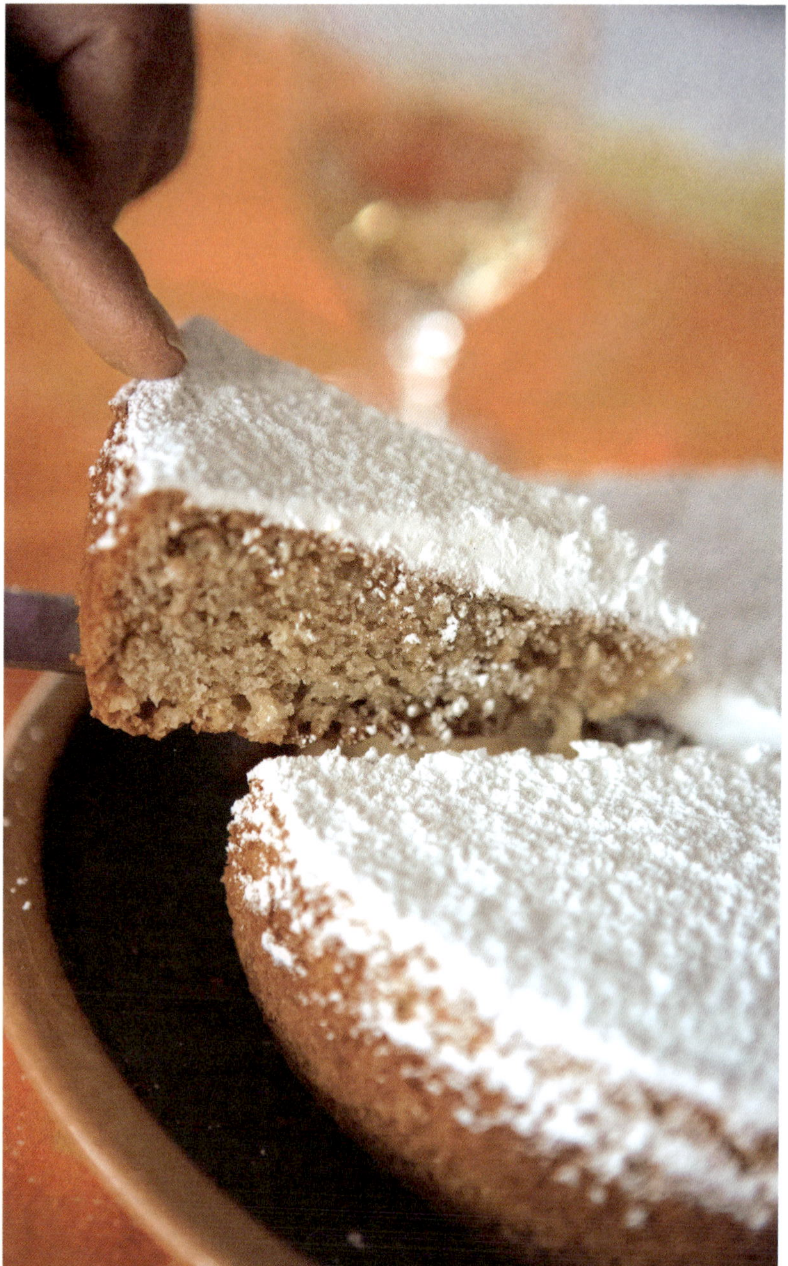

Cardamom cake

I love the smell of this cake: the mellow, warming fragrance of cardamom lingers enticingly long after the cake has been taken from the oven. And I love the fact that it's so simple to make: no vigorous beating or whisking and only one bowl to wash up. But most of all I love this cake because it's just so very good. Enjoy it with good coffee or even a glass of sweet Sauternes and you'll see what I mean.

It is a flat cake and sometimes it can sink a bit – but don't worry, just think of this as another of its charms. Incidentally, it's a useful recipe if you are catering for someone who can't eat eggs. Note that you need the lemony seeds from green cardamom pods, not the camphor-flavoured seeds of the black cardamom.

Serves 8–10

About 20 green cardamom pods
250g self-raising flour
Pinch of sea salt
½ tsp bicarbonate of soda
100g unsalted butter, cut into small pieces
200g caster sugar
300ml crème fraîche

To finish
Caster sugar or icing sugar, for dredging

Equipment
20cm round tin, greased and base-lined with baking parchment

Preheat the oven to 170°C/Gas mark 3. Split the green cardamom pods open, remove the seeds and grind with a pestle and mortar or spice grinder. Sift the flour, salt, bicarbonate of soda and ground seeds together into a bowl and set aside.

Warm the butter gently in a small pan until it has just melted; do not allow it to get too hot. Put the sugar in a large bowl. Add the butter and beat for a minute or so. Add the crème fraîche and beat until you have a thick creamy batter.

Incorporate the flour mix, a third at a time, folding it in carefully with a large metal spoon. The mixture will be quite sticky and dough-like. Spoon into the prepared tin, spreading it out evenly and gently with the back of the spoon.

Bake in the oven for 50–60 minutes until the top is golden brown and the cake springs back into shape when lightly touched. Allow to cool for 5–10 minutes before turning out onto a wire rack, bottom side up, to cool.

Now you have the choice of either dredging the top with caster sugar while the cake is hot or leaving it until it is cold and dusting liberally with icing sugar. This cake will keep for 5 days in an airtight tin.

Scent from heaven cake
(lemon verbena)

My garden is crowded with herbs and in early summer, when they are abundant and most fragrant, I instil their uplifting essence into my baking whenever I can. Often these self-effacing plants shy away from attention by producing insignificant flowers. But crush their shapely leaves and they release the most exquisite of perfumes. A few sprigs of an intensely aromatic herb can absolutely transform an otherwise simple cake. Lightly infuse the herb in water and the resulting liquor can be added to drizzles, icings and – in the case of this recipe – the cake itself.

Serves 10–12

For the cake
5–6 lemon verbena sprigs
100g plain flour
1 tsp baking powder
200g ground rice
200g unsalted butter, cut into small pieces and softened
150g caster sugar
3 eggs

To finish
100g icing sugar, sifted
4–5 lemon verbena leaves

Equipment
2 litre loaf tin, about 25 x 13cm, or an 18cm square tin, sides lightly greased and base-lined with baking parchment

Preheat the oven to 180°C/Gas mark 4. Strip the lemon verbena leaves off the stalks. Place 5 or 6 leaves on the lined base of the tin. Put the rest into a measuring jug and cover with 200ml freshly boiled water, making sure all the leaves are completely immersed to prevent them oxidising and discolouring. Set aside to cool.

Sift the flour and baking powder into a bowl, add the ground rice and mix well to combine; set aside.

In a large mixing bowl, using either a wooden spoon or a hand-held electric whisk, beat the butter to a cream. Add the sugar and beat until light and creamy. Incorporate the eggs one at a time, adding a spoonful of the flour mix with each one, and beating thoroughly before adding the next. Using a large metal spoon, carefully fold in the remaining flour mix.

Strain the verbena-infused water. Add 100ml to the cake mixture, reserving the rest, and gently fold it in, to give a very soft dropping consistency. Spoon the mixture into the prepared tin, smoothing it evenly and lightly with the back of the spoon.

Bake in the oven for about 50 minutes until the cake is lightly golden and springs back into shape when gently pressed. Just before it is done, prepare the drizzle by mixing the remaining 100ml verbena-infused water with the icing sugar and stirring until dissolved.

As the cake comes out of the oven, prick it all over deeply (but not to the bottom) with a skewer and spoon half the drizzle over the surface. Leave for 10 minutes, then spoon over the remainder, making sure you pour plenty down the sides of the tin.

Leave the cake in the tin until cool before turning out. Arrange the lemon verbena leaves on top to decorate. The cake will keep for 5 days in an airtight tin.

Variations

Rose-scented geranium Replace the lemon verbena with a few leaves of a scented geranium such as Mabel Grey or Attar of Roses.

Lavender with lemon Replace the lemon verbena with either 2 tbsp fresh lavender flowers or 1 tbsp dried ones. Prepare the drizzle by dissolving 100ml caster sugar in 100ml lemon juice.

Chocolate and peppermint Replace the lemon verbena with fresh peppermint leaves and 25g of the flour with cocoa powder.

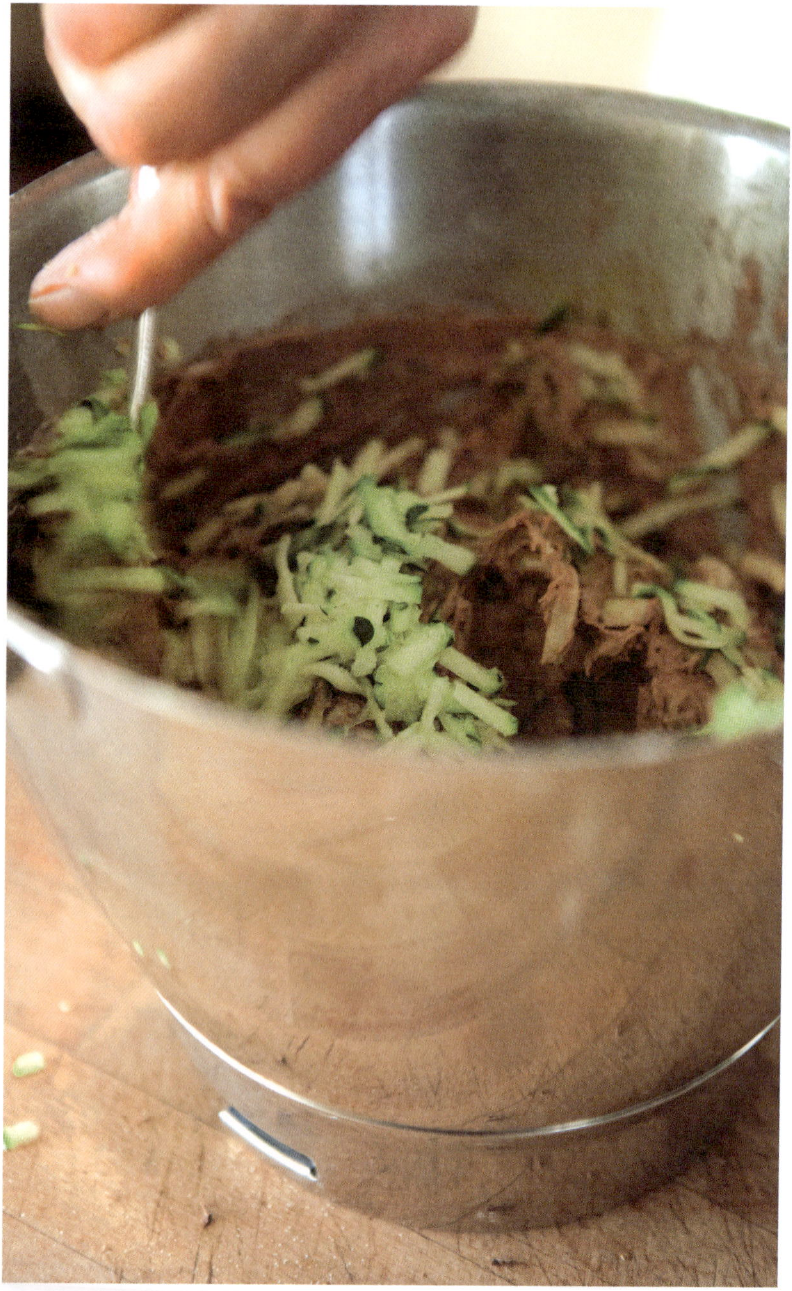

'Hebegebe' cake
(courgette and chocolate)

Hebe, the naughtiest dog we've ever had, is a retriever by name, but not by nature. Find a cake she certainly can, but retrieve it she will not. Instead, she'll scoff the lot. That is what she did the first time I made this lovely moist courgette cake. I took it as a resounding vote of confidence in the recipe and named the cake in Hebe's honour. Incidentally, this is a great way to use up some of those overgrown courgettes that seem to swell to monster proportions in the garden overnight.

Serves 12

175g unsalted butter, cut into small pieces and softened
175g golden granulated sugar
3 eggs, beaten
100ml plain yoghurt
1 tsp vanilla extract
250g plain flour, sifted
1½ tsp baking powder
3 tbsp cocoa powder
About 250g courgettes, unpeeled, finely grated
150g chocolate (plain, milk, white or a mix), roughly cut into 1.5cm chunks

Equipment
20cm square or 23cm round tin, lightly greased and base-lined with baking parchment

Preheat the oven to 180°C/Gas mark 4. In a mixing bowl, beat the butter to a cream. Add the sugar and, using either a wooden spoon or a hand-held electric whisk, beat until light and creamy. Gradually add the eggs, one at a time, beating well after each addition. Mix in the yoghurt and vanilla extract.

Combine the flour, baking powder and cocoa powder. Sift them into the mixture, one third at a time, using a large metal spoon to carefully fold them in. Stir in the grated courgettes and half of the chocolate. Pour into the prepared tin and sprinkle the remaining chocolate pieces over the top.

Bake for 45–50 minutes until the cake is firm but springy to the touch. Leave in the tin (out of dog reach) for 20 minutes before turning out and placing on a wire rack to finish cooling. This cake will keep for 3 days stored in an airtight tin. For longer keeping, store in the fridge.

Banana and chocolate cake

Black, blighted and limp they may be, but don't throw those overripe bananas away. This is a great recipe for using them up. In fact, really ripe fruits lend much more flavour to a cake than under-ripe ones. I pop overlooked bananas into the freezer until I have sufficient to make a cake. They go even blacker and I do get the odd sideways glance from anyone who comes across them. However, any dubious comments are withdrawn when a freshly baked banana cake is up for grabs.

Serves 10–12

225g self-raising flour
½ tsp bicarbonate of soda
125g unsalted butter, cut into small pieces and softened
125g soft brown sugar
2 large eggs
2–3 very ripe bananas (250–300g when peeled)
150ml plain yoghurt
2 tsp vanilla extract
100g plain or milk chocolate, roughly cut into 1.5cm chunks

Equipment
23cm garland or ring mould, well greased, or a 20cm round cake tin, lightly greased and base-lined with baking parchment

Preheat the oven to 180°C/Gas mark 4. Sift together the flour and the bicarbonate of soda into a bowl. Set aside.

In a large mixing bowl, beat the butter and sugar together, using a wooden spoon or a hand-held electric whisk, until the mixture is light and creamy. Beat in the eggs, one at a time, adding 1 tbsp of the flour with each.

Mash the bananas to a thick purée and beat into the mixture. Stir in the yoghurt and vanilla extract. Using a large metal spoon, fold in the remaining flour, followed by the chocolate pieces.

Spoon the mixture into the prepared tin, spreading it evenly with the back of the spoon. If using a ring mould, tap it firmly on the work surface to level the mixture. Bake in the oven for about 30 minutes, until the cake is well risen and will spring back into shape when lightly touched.

Leave in the tin for 5 minutes before turning out onto a wire rack to cool completely. Once cold, this cake will keep for 3–4 days in an airtight tin.

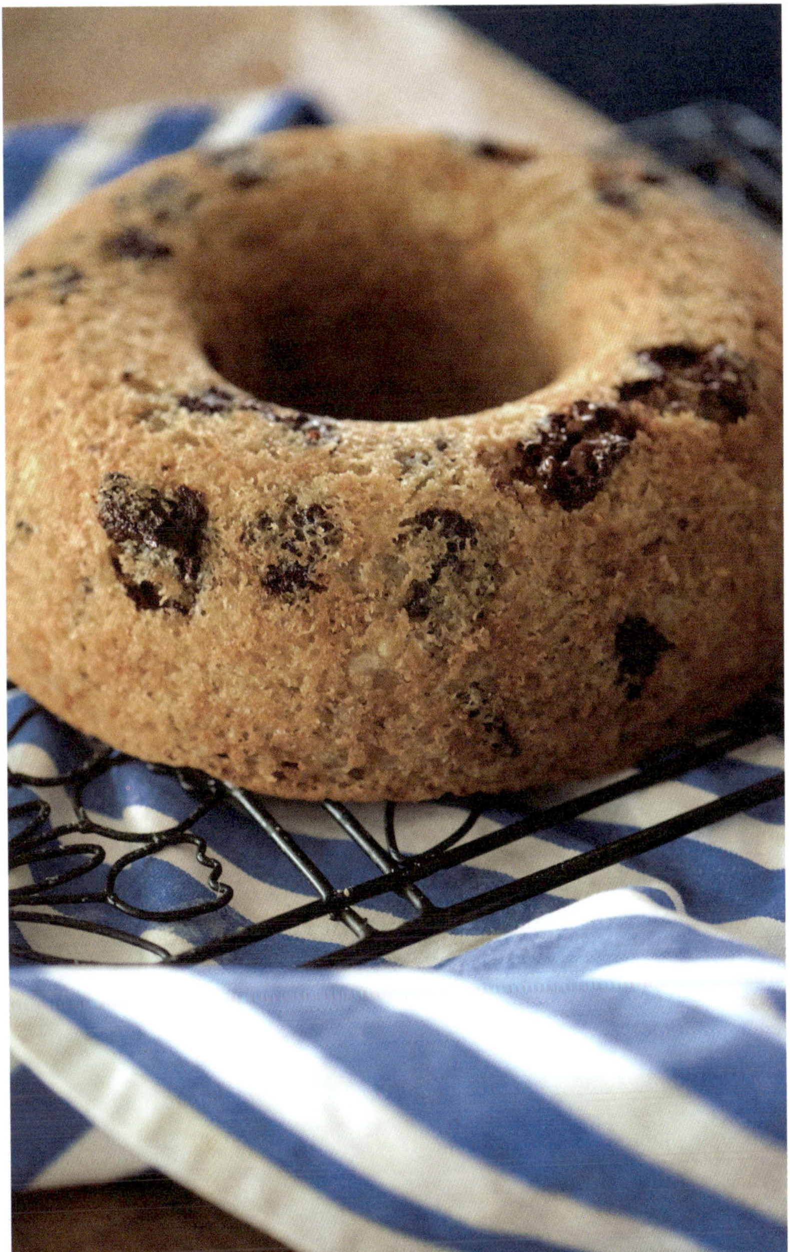

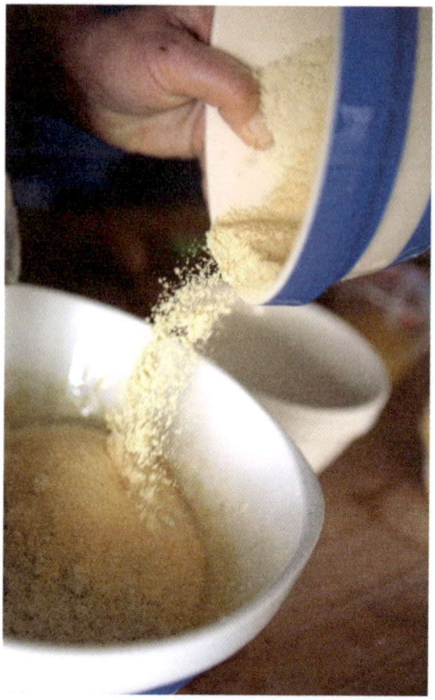
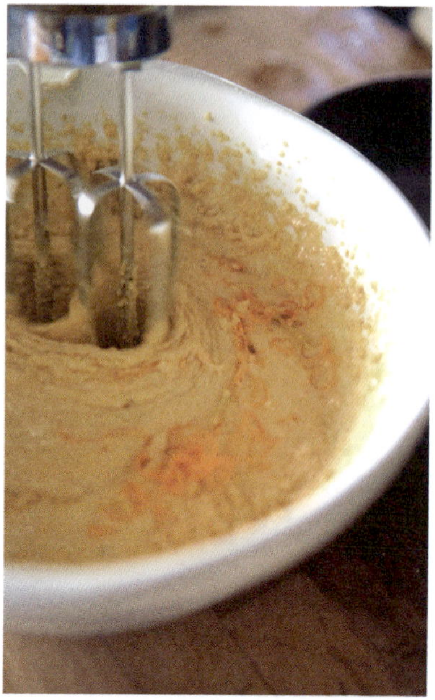
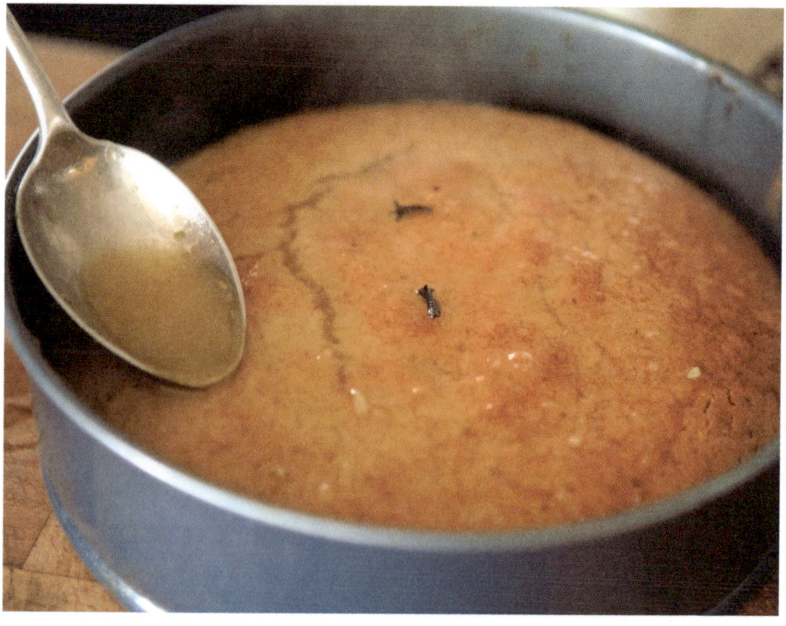

Seville orange polenta cake (gluten free)

The first of the Seville oranges arrive from Spain in January. Too bitter and acidic to be eaten raw, these citrus fruits are full of flavour and quintessential for marmalade-making. Their distinctive taste is also excellent in cakes, such as this lovely gluten-free cake, which is deliciously lightly spiced with warming cloves. When it's closed season for Sevilles, you can ring the citrus changes by using lemons, limes or sweet oranges instead.

Serves 12

For the cake
125g fine polenta
225g ground almonds
1 tsp baking powder
½ tsp ground cloves
225g unsalted butter, cut into small pieces and softened
200g caster sugar
Finely grated zest of 3 Seville oranges
3 eggs

For the drizzle
100ml Seville orange juice (2–3 oranges)
50g golden caster sugar
3 or 4 cloves

Equipment
23cm loose-bottomed or springform cake tin, well greased and base-lined with baking parchment

Preheat the oven to 170°C/Gas mark 3. Put the polenta, ground almonds, baking powder and ground cloves into a bowl and mix together well.

In another mixing bowl, beat the butter to a cream, using either a wooden spoon or a hand-held electric whisk. Add the sugar and half the orange zest and continue to beat until light and fluffy. Incorporate the eggs one at a time, beating well before adding the next. Using a large metal spoon, carefully fold in the polenta and almond mix. Spoon into the prepared tin, spreading evenly with the back of the spoon.

Bake in the oven for about 50 minutes until golden on top and springy to the touch. Shortly before the cake is done, prepare the orange drizzle by gently warming the orange juice, remaining orange zest, the sugar and whole cloves in a small pan until the sugar has dissolved, then simmer for a couple of minutes.

While the cake is still hot, prick the surface with a skewer or cocktail stick and spoon the orange syrup carefully over it. Leave to cool in the tin before turning out. Once cold, this cake will keep for 5–6 days in an airtight tin.

Somerset cider cake
with hazelnut topping

This moist yet light-textured cake, with its crumbly nutty topping, will be subtly different depending on the type of cider you use. With more than 400 different apple varieties growing throughout the West Country's ciderlands, there's plenty of choice, from 'Slack my Girdle' to 'Tremlett's Bitter'. A sweet cider will blush the cake pink, while a bitter-sharp brew will lend a lightly golden hue. A couple I like to use here are the fruity Somerset Redstreak and the aromatic Kingston Black.

Serves 10–12

For the cake
150g raisins
250ml sparkling cider
125g plain flour
125g plain wholemeal flour
Pinch of sea salt
1 tsp bicarbonate of soda
½ whole nutmeg, freshly grated
125g unsalted butter, cut into small pieces and softened
125g light soft brown sugar
3 eggs

For the topping
50g unsalted butter, cut into small pieces
75g soft light brown sugar
25g plain flour
½ tsp freshly grated nutmeg
75g hazelnuts, chopped

Equipment
20cm springform cake tin, lightly greased and base-lined with baking parchment

Preheat the oven to 180°C/Gas mark 4. Place the raisins in a small bowl and pour over 100ml of the cider. Leave in a warm place to plump up for a couple of hours or overnight, if you have time.

To make the nutty topping, put the butter into a small pan and warm over a gentle heat until it has just melted. Remove from the heat and add the rest of the topping ingredients. Lightly mix together until well combined. Set aside.

For the cake, sift the flours, salt and bicarbonate of soda together into a bowl. Add the grated nutmeg and set aside.

In a mixing bowl, beat the butter to a cream, using either a wooden spoon or a hand-held electric whisk. Add the sugar and continue to beat until the mixture is soft and creamy. Add the eggs, one at a time, adding 1 tbsp of the sifted flour with each and beating thoroughly before adding the next.

Sift in half of the remaining flour and use a large metal spoon to carefully fold it in. Add the rest of the cider to the mix and gently stir in (it will foam up enthusiastically). Sift in the remaining flour and lightly fold it in. Finally, incorporate the cider-soaked raisins, together with any liquor.

Spoon the mixture into the prepared tin, spreading it out evenly with the back of the spoon. Sprinkle the topping over the surface.

Bake in the oven for 45–50 minutes, until the cake is golden brown and a skewer inserted in the centre comes out clean. Leave in the tin for 30 minutes before turning out and transferring to a wire rack to cool completely.

The cake will keep for a week stored in an airtight tin.

Variations
Soak the raisins in cider brandy rather than cider. Use walnuts instead of hazelnuts.

Raspberry Battenberg cake

The Battenberg, sometimes called the 'church window cake', is such a pretty thing to create. Although it may look difficult, it's easy and fun to make and quite heavenly to eat. It's simply a cake of two flavours, stuck together with raspberry jam and wrapped up in soft, sweet almond marzipan. Using fresh raspberries to colour the pink bit means an escape from bottled food colouring, and also gives a fabulous fresh fruit flavour.

Once you've mastered this raspberry and vanilla combination, you'll dream up lots of other scrummy alternatives. You could even add a third flavour – chocolate works well – building a cake of six squares.

Serves 12

For the cake
- 100g raspberries (either fresh or frozen and defrosted)
- 175g caster sugar, plus 1 tsp for the raspberries
- 100g rice flour
- 1½ tsp baking powder
- 100g ground almonds
- 175g unsalted butter, cut into small pieces and softened
- 3 eggs
- ¼ tsp vanilla paste or ½ tsp vanilla extract

To finish
- 150g soft-set raspberry jam
- Icing sugar, for dusting
- 450g Marzipan (see p.58)

Equipment
- 2 x 1 litre loaf tins, approx 20 x 10cm, lined with baking parchment

Preheat the oven to 180°C/Gas mark 4. Start by making the pink colouring for the cake. Place the raspberries in a small bowl and mix in 1 tsp caster sugar. Leave until the juices begin to run, then use the back of a spoon to crush the fruit to a pulp. Sieve to remove the pips. Set aside.

Sift the rice flour and baking powder into a mixing bowl and mix thoroughly. Add the ground almonds, butter, sugar and eggs. Using either a wooden spoon or a hand-held electric whisk, beat for a couple of minutes until all the ingredients are well combined and the mixture is light and creamy.

Divide the mixture in half and place in two bowls. Add 2 tbsp of the raspberry purée to one portion and the vanilla to the other. Carefully mix the flavouring into each portion until well blended.

(continued overleaf)

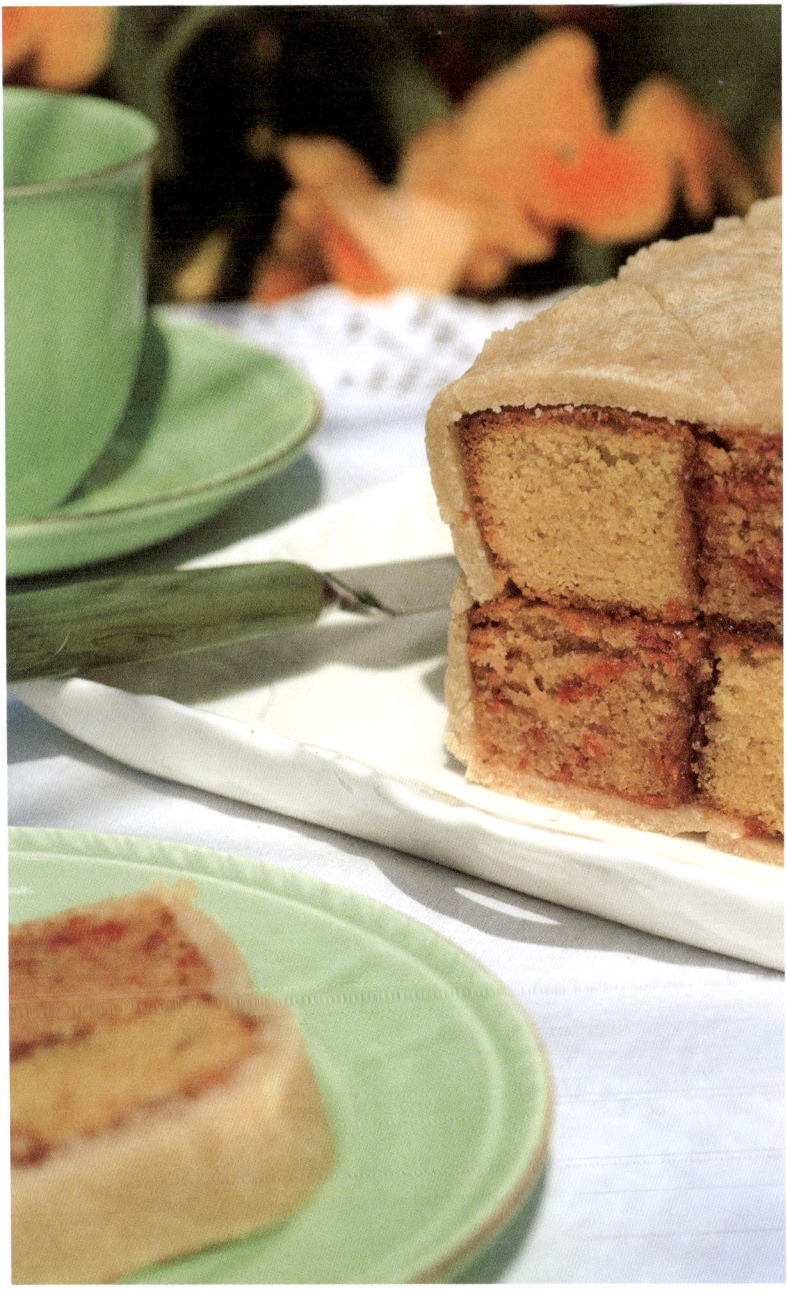

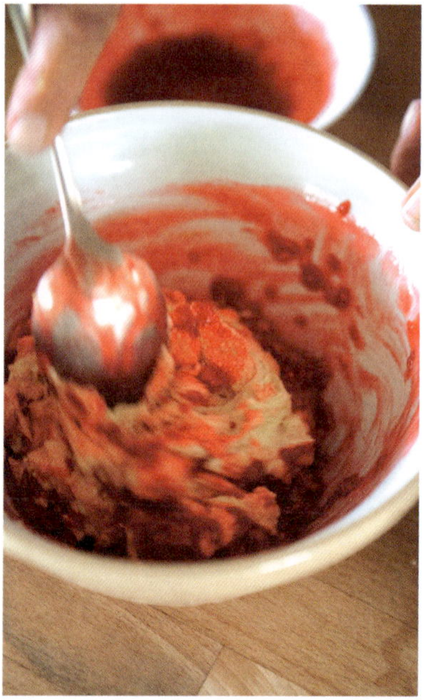
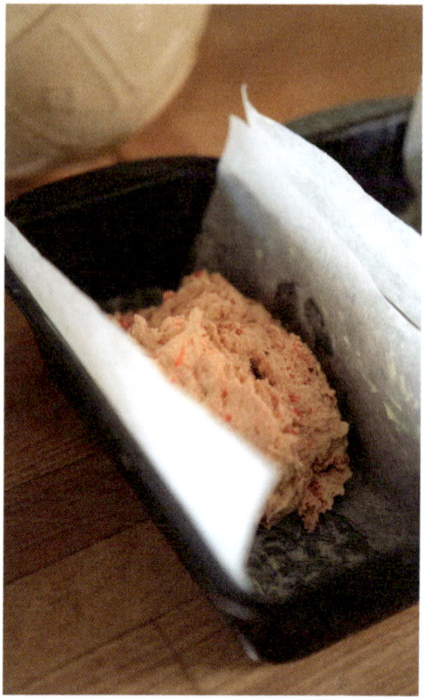
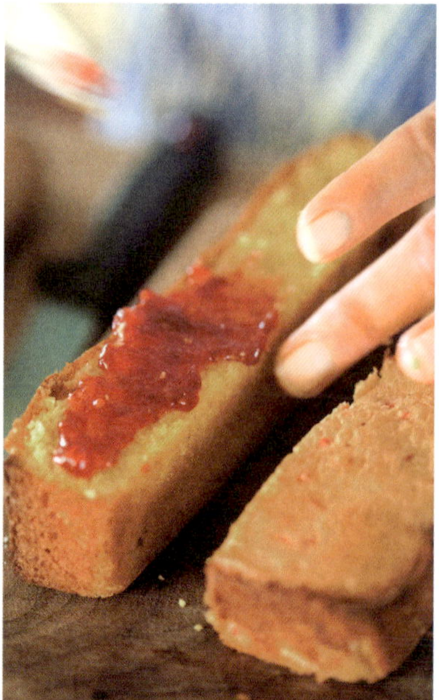
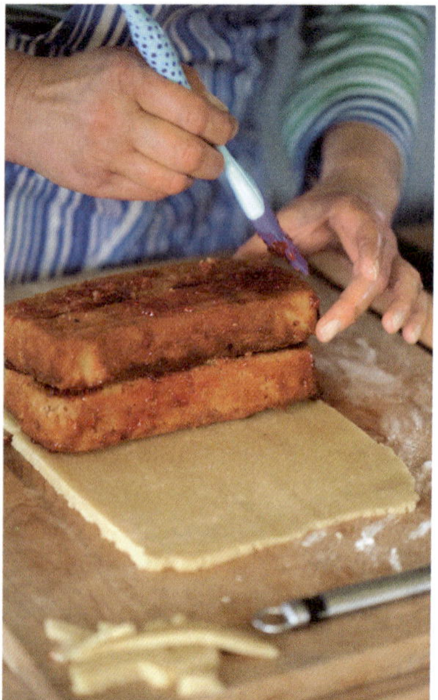

Spoon the raspberry mixture into one prepared loaf tin and the vanilla mixture into the other, smoothing them both evenly and lightly with the back of the spoon. Bake in the oven for 25–30 minutes until evenly coloured and firm to the touch. Leave the cakes in their tins for 5–10 minutes before removing and transferring to a wire rack to cool completely.

When cool, carefully trim off the ends of each cake, then slice each one lengthways in two, so you have four rectangles, exactly the same size. Brush the strips of cake with raspberry jam and sandwich them together, alternating the raspberry and vanilla strips, to create the characteristic chequered pattern.

Next dust your work surface with icing sugar and roll out the marzipan to a rectangle, about 20x32cm (or big enough to wrap around your cake). Brush the top of the cake with raspberry jam and invert the cake onto the centre of the marzipan. Brush the remaining three sides with raspberry jam. With jam-free fingers, wrap the marzipan round the remaining three sides of the cake and press the edges together to make a neat join. Carefully invert the cake, so the seam is underneath.

To finish, use your finger and thumb to crimp and decorate the top edges, then very lightly score the top of the cake with a knife to create a criss-cross pattern.

This cake will keep for a week stored in an airtight tin.

Variation

Chocolate and hazelnut Battenberg Replace the almonds with ground hazelnuts. Instead of using raspberries to colour one half of the cake pink, replace 25g of the rice flour with 25g cocoa powder. Use chocolate hazelnut spread to bond the cake pieces together, rather than raspberry jam.

Hugh's fresh cherry cake
with streusel topping

Available for only a few weeks of the year, delicious homegrown cherries are highly seasonal. What's more, these summer gems are as coveted by the blackbirds as they are by us. Anyone lucky enough to have a cropping cherry tree will have to pit themselves against these feathered foragers in order to gather in a harvest. Otherwise you'll need to keep a sharp eye out for them in farm shops, markets or your local greengrocer's. Bringing home even a small bag of these lovely cherries is worthwhile, though, as this gorgeous pudding cake from Hugh F-W shows. The crumbly, nutty streusel topping is a crunchy delight.

Serves 8

For the cake
125g unsalted butter, cut into small pieces and softened
125g caster sugar
2 eggs
75g self-raising white or wholemeal flour
75g ground almonds (ready-ground or whizzed in a food processor)
1 tsp almond extract (optional but lovely if you like that extra-almondy, frangipane taste)
300g fresh cherries, stoned and halved

For the topping
25g plain white or wholemeal flour
25g ground almonds
50g caster sugar
25g unsalted butter, cut into small pieces
50g blanched almonds, slivered (see p.32)

Equipment
20cm springform cake tin, lightly greased and base-lined with baking parchment

Preheat the oven to 180°C/Gas mark 4. Start by making the streusel topping. Sift the flour into a mixing bowl. Add the ground almonds and caster sugar and stir to combine. Rub in the butter, using your fingertips, until the mixture resembles coarse breadcrumbs. Set aside.

For the cake, in a mixing bowl, using either a wooden spoon or hand-held electric whisk, beat the butter to a cream. Add the caster sugar and continue to beat until the mixture is light and fluffy. Add the eggs one at a time, incorporating 1 tbsp of the flour with each, and beating until thoroughly combined before adding the next. Stir in the ground almonds and almond extract, if using. Sift in the remaining flour and fold in gently, using a large metal spoon.

Spoon the cake mixture into the prepared tin, smoothing it out evenly and gently with the back of the spoon. Lay the cherries over the top of the mixture. Sprinkle the streusel topping evenly over the cherries and then scatter the slivered almonds all over the top.

Bake in the oven for 45–50 minutes, until the almonds are lightly browned and a skewer inserted into the centre of the cake comes out clean. Leave for 10 minutes before releasing the tin and moving the cake to a wire rack to cool.

This cake is delicious warm or cold, with custard (if serving warm) or clotted cream or Greek yoghurt. It will keep for up to 3 days in an airtight tin.

Variations

Plum and walnut cake For the cake, replace the cherries with halved plums and the ground almonds with walnuts. For the topping, replace the ground almonds with porridge oats and the slivered almonds with chopped walnuts.

Apricot and almond cake For the cake, replace the cherries with halved apricots.

P.S. To help save the British cherry, visit www.foodloversbritain.com and look up their CherryAid campaign.

Toffee apple cake

Heavy with sweet apples and creamy caramel, this scrumptious cake is just the thing to use up the glut of orchard apples that a good cropping year provides.

Serves 8–10

For the cake
3–4 medium eating apples, such as Cox's or Russets
125g dark soft brown sugar
175g self-raising flour
1 tsp baking powder
½ tsp fine sea salt
175g golden caster sugar
175g unsalted butter, cut into small pieces and softened
3 eggs

For the filling
1 quantity Caramel cream (see p.51)

Equipment
2 x 20cm sandwich tins, lightly greased and base-lined with baking parchment

Preheat the oven to 180°C/Gas mark 4. Core, peel and quarter the apples. Slice each quarter into 4 or 5 thin slices. Place the brown sugar in a bowl, add the apple slices and toss until well covered. Starting from the outside and working inwards, arrange the apples over the base of each prepared tin, finishing with a ring in the centre.

Sift the flour, baking powder and salt into a large mixing bowl and mix thoroughly. Add the caster sugar, butter and eggs. Using either a wooden spoon or a hand-held electric whisk, beat together for a couple of minutes until the mixture is light, creamy and well blended.

Divide the mixture equally between the apple-lined tins, spreading it out evenly with the back of the spoon. Bake the cakes in the oven for about 25 minutes or until lightly golden and they spring back into shape when gently touched with a finger.

Leave the cakes in the tins for 10 minutes, before carefully turning out and placing on a wire rack. Remove the parchment to reveal the rich brown caramelised apples.

When completely cold, sandwich the two cakes together with a generous layer of caramel cream. This cake is best eaten within a couple of days.

Variation
Turn the apples in 3 or 4 tbsp of marmalade instead of the brown sugar. For the filling, use marmalade instead of caramel cream.

BIG CAKES 177

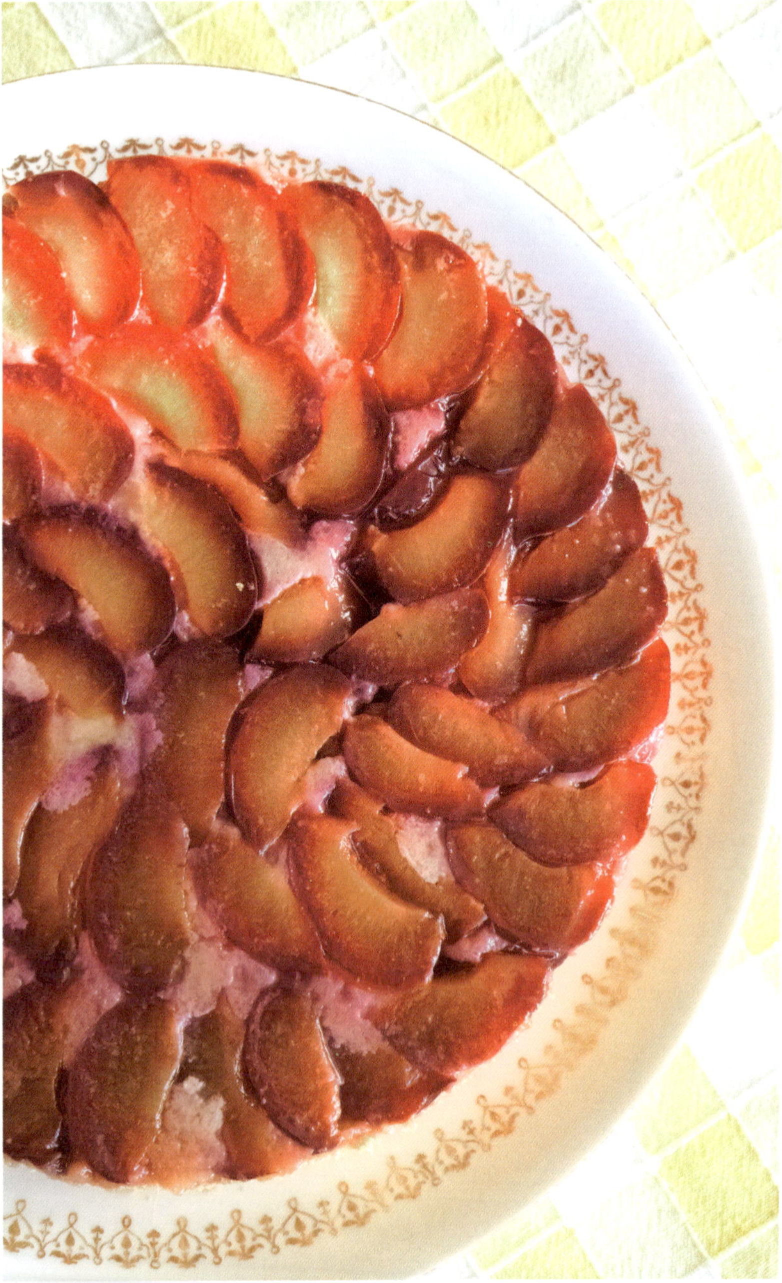

Plum upside-down cake

The plum season stretches from mid-July until October, starting with the small, blushing hedgerow cherry plums and ending with their dark-skinned cousins. This is a lovely recipe to use whatever variety comes your way. It can easily be adapted to use other stone fruits or blackberries, blueberries or gooseberries. I like to serve it slightly warm, with a dollop of fromage frais or clotted cream.

Serves 8–10

For the cake
200g self-raising flour
Pinch of sea salt
200ml buttermilk
2 tsp vanilla extract
100g unsalted butter, cut into
   small pieces and softened
125g caster sugar
2 eggs

For the upside-down top
About 500g plums (any variety)
100g runny honey (or set honey,
   slightly warmed)
2–3 tsp rose water

Equipment
23cm round loose-bottomed or
   springform cake tin, greased and
   base-lined with baking parchment

Preheat the oven to 180°C/Gas mark 4. First prepare the top of the cake. Halve the plums lengthways with a sharp knife. Twist them apart and remove the stone with the point of the knife. Use small cherry plums in halves, quarter larger Victoria-type plums or slice very large plums. Arrange the plums, cut side down, over the base of the tin. Trickle over the honey and sprinkle with the rose water. Set aside.

Sift the flour and salt together and set aside. Combine the buttermilk and vanilla extract in a jug; put to one side.

In a mixing bowl, beat the butter to a cream, using a wooden spoon or a hand-held electric whisk. Add the sugar and beat until light and creamy. Add the eggs, one at a time, adding 1 tbsp of the flour with each, and beating thoroughly before adding the next. Incorporate the remaining flour and the buttermilk little by little – dry, wet, dry, wet – until evenly combined and you have a soft dropping consistency.

Spoon the mixture over the plums, spreading it out evenly with the back of the spoon. Bake in the oven for 45–50 minutes until the cake is golden and the juices from the fruit are bubbling around the edge.

While the cake is still warm, place a flat plate on the tin and turn out. This cake is best eaten when freshly made but it will keep for a couple of days in a cool place.

Rhubarb pudding cake
with custard

Forced in warm, dark growing sheds (or under rhubarb bells), the tender blush-pink stalks of early rhubarb are our first homegrown crop of the year. This attractive pudding cake is a wonderful way to savour their fresh and exhilarating newness. Of course, later in the season, outdoor-grown, or 'field' rhubarb, can be used instead, but it is often a little more tart, and doesn't have the exquisite colour and tenderness of the early shoots. You can easily adapt this recipe using other homely comfort-pud combinations (see variations), any of which can be enjoyed as a pudding or as a teatime treat.

Serves 10

250g rhubarb (trimmed weight), sliced into 5mm pieces
200g self-raising flour, plus 1 tbsp for dusting
50g custard powder or cornflour
½ tsp bicarbonate of soda
125g unsalted butter, cut into small pieces and softened
175g golden caster sugar
3 eggs
150ml plain yoghurt
2 tsp vanilla extract
1 tbsp rose water (optional)
Custard or clotted cream, to serve

Equipment
23cm ring tin, well greased, or a 20cm loose-bottomed round tin, lightly greased and base-lined with greaseproof paper

Preheat the oven to 180°C/Gas mark 4. Put the rhubarb into a bowl, sprinkle with 1 scant tbsp self-raising flour and toss until the pieces are all covered. This floury coating will help to prevent the rhubarb sinking in the cake.

Sift the flour, custard powder or cornflour and bicarbonate of soda together into a bowl. Set aside.

In a large mixing bowl, using either a wooden spoon or a hand-held electric whisk, beat the butter to a cream. Add the sugar and beat together until very light and fluffy. Beat in the eggs, one at a time, adding 1 tbsp of the flour mix with each, and beating thoroughly before adding the next. Stir in the yoghurt, vanilla extract and rose water, if using. Fold in the remaining flour followed by the sliced rhubarb.

Spoon the mixture into the prepared tin, levelling the surface with the back of the spoon or giving the tin a good sharp tap on the work surface to level the mix.

Bake in the oven for 40–45 minutes until the cake is well risen and springs back into shape when lightly pressed. Leave in the tin for 10 minutes before turning out onto a wire rack to cool.

Serve the pudding cake either warm with custard, or cold just as it is or with a dollop of clotted cream. It keeps for a couple of days in an airtight tin. If you want to keep it for any longer, put it in the fridge.

Variations

Raspberry and rice cake Replace the rhubarb with raspberries and the custard powder with rice flour.

Blackberry and semolina cake Replace the rhubarb with blackberries and the custard powder with semolina.

Potato and apple cake

This traditional Irish recipe typifies how easy it is to take everyday ingredients and speedily turn them into something scrumptious. Peel a few extra spuds when making mash and you'll have enough for this cake. Of course you can glam it up a bit by adding a spoonful or two of rum-soaked raisins or a handful of hedgerow blackberries to the apples. Or for a savoury note, add a little grated Cheddar to the potato dough. However, I like it most of all made simply with the unassuming, but very worthy, cooking apple.

Serves 4–8 (depending on appetites)

For the cake
500g mashed potatoes
25g unsalted butter, melted
125g plain flour
1 tsp baking powder
1 tsp sea salt
400g cooking apples
Pinch of ground cloves

To finish
25g unsalted butter, cut into 4 slices
100g caster sugar

Equipment
Large baking sheet, lightly floured

Preheat the oven to 200°C/Gas mark 6. Place the mashed potatoes in a mixing bowl (if using freshly cooked potatoes allow them to dry off first). Add the melted butter and sift in the flour, baking powder and salt. Using a wooden spoon or your hand, bring together to form a soft, smooth dough. Divide the mixture in two.

On a floured surface, shape each portion of dough into a 20cm circle, then place one round on the baking sheet. Peel, core and finely slice the apples. Layer them on top of the dough to within 1cm of the edge and dust with the ground cloves. Dampen the edge of the dough with a little water. Place the second dough round on top. Seal the edges by lightly turning with the sides of your hands, moulding until the cake is neatly formed with a flat top and is about 3cm deep. Using a sharp knife, lightly score a cross on the surface and make a small hole in the centre.

Bake in the oven for 35–50 minutes until golden. Remove from the oven and, working quickly from the centre, lightly prise back each quarter and insert the butter slices and sugar, then replace the dough. Return to the oven for 5 minutes to allow the butter to melt.

This cake is best by far when eaten fresh from the oven, but any left over will not disappoint when cold.

BIG CAKES 183

Fruity Cakes
& Gingerbread

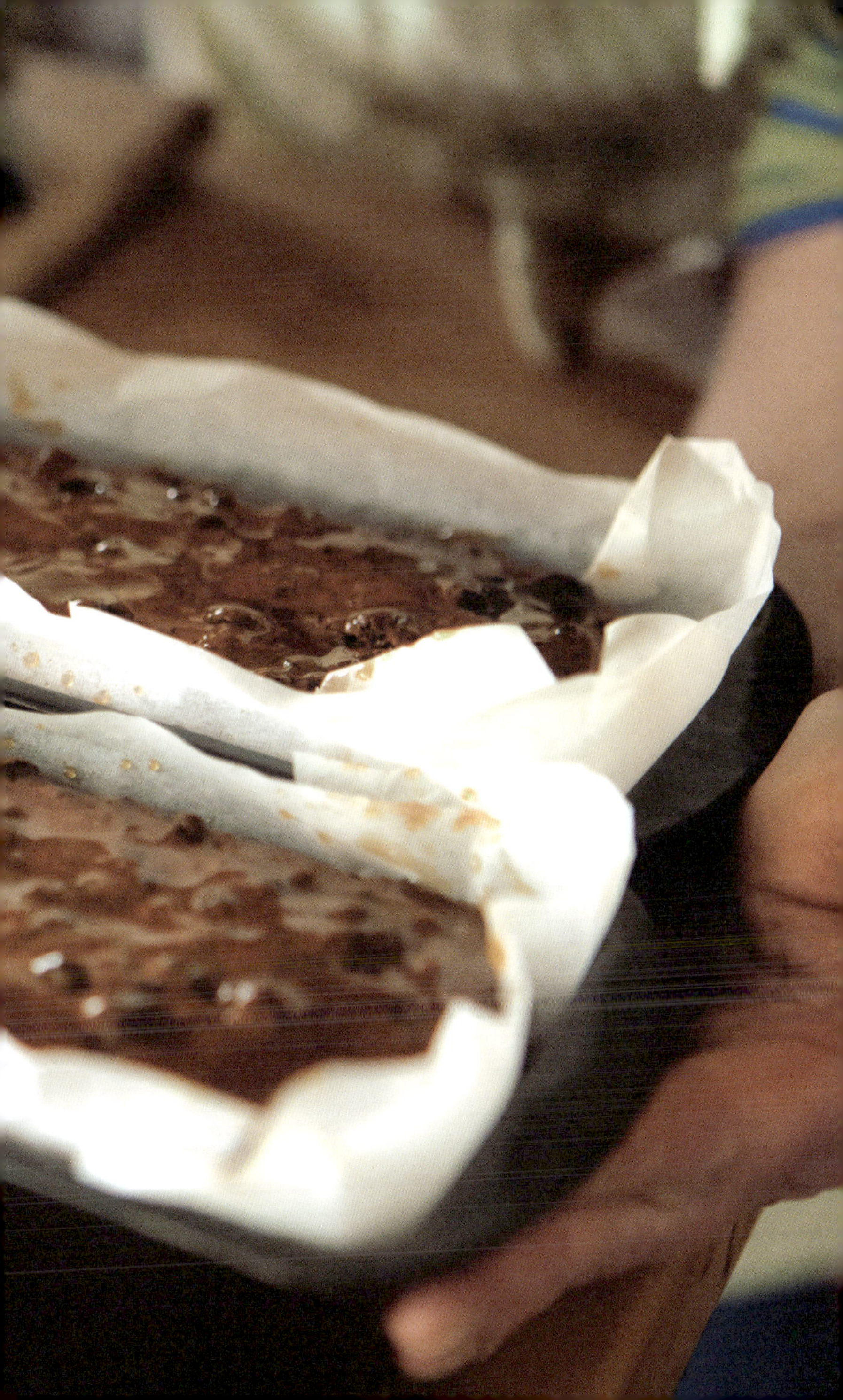

The proud descendants of the great cakes of old feature in this chapter, their ancestral roots stemming back to the sweet fancies of the medieval period. At that time, such treats were no more than a basic bread dough, enriched with added ingredients such as butter, honey, dried fruits and spices. The extra ingredients were scarce and costly, so bakers were banned from producing this type of confection for any occasion other than the festivities of the Christian calendar: Christmas, Easter, weddings, christenings and funerals.

Fruit cakes come from extensive families and include a good number of regional variations. Their outward appearance is understated, yet their insides are a sweet medley of aromatic and wholesome ingredients. More often than not, early fruit cakes were termed 'plum cakes', simply because of the inclusion of dried plums (prunes) in the recipes – a prudent and good use of the late-summer plum harvest. These days, the plums have been replaced by raisins, sultanas and currants in nearly all recipes. Favoured for their exceptional keeping quality, good fruit cakes are also delectably moreish.

Gingerbreads take their name from their sixteenth-century ancestors, which did in fact contain grated bread. These hard, flat gingerbreads – often made in the shape of men or numbers – were a combination of grated bread, ginger, aniseed, liquorice and pepper, sweetened with honey and mixed to a stiff paste with ale. In due course, flour, eggs and fat replaced the bread, and treacle took the place of the honey. Thick, moist gingerbreads, as we know them today, came about in the nineteenth century, when bicarbonate of soda was added to the list of ingredients, helping to leaven and lighten the dough.

Bastions of the cake tin, both gingerbreads and fruit cakes will, I hope, become firm favourites of your baking repertoire.

P.S. The expression 'baker's dozen' originates from the practice of medieval English bakers of including an extra loaf when selling a dozen, in order to avoid the harsh punishments for selling short weight. It's comparable to the application of the current-day euro 'e'. This little understood symbol, found next to the weight on commercially prepared foods, is a safety valve for producers to indicate that the weight has been taken as an average over a number of units.

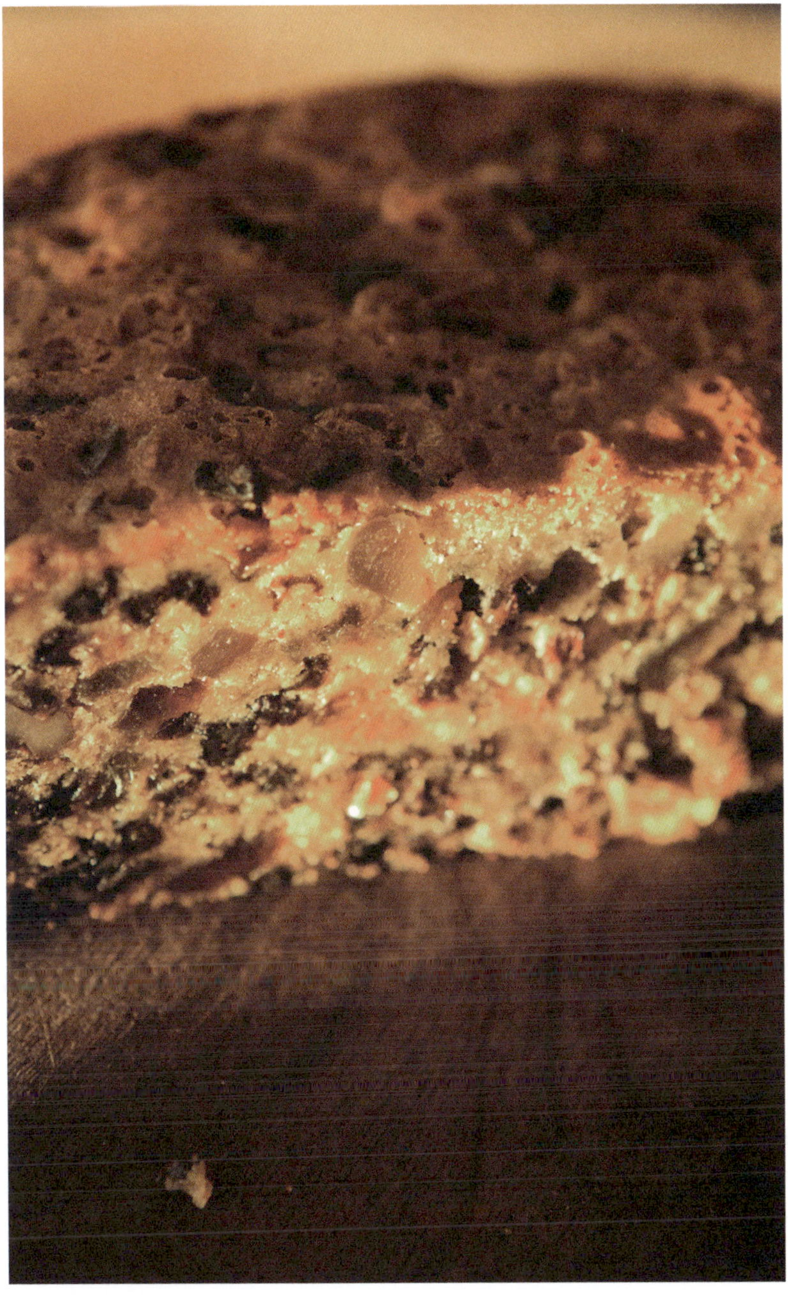

Banana bread

This fragrant, gently spiced tea bread is a true pick-me-up – perfect for ravenous children returning from school, or anyone in need of cheering up. Bananas become much sweeter and more deliciously scented as they mature, so make sure the ones you use are well ripened. They will be much easier to mash too.

Serve this tea bread thickly sliced – just as it is or with butter. After a few days, it's best lightly toasted and buttered.

Serves 8–10
250g self-raising flour
Good pinch of sea salt
1½ tsp ground cardamom
100g unsalted butter, cut into small pieces
125g light muscovado sugar
100g raisins
2 ripe bananas (about 250g, peeled weight)
1 egg, lightly beaten
1 tbsp demerara sugar

Equipment
1 litre loaf tin, approx 20 x 10cm, base and long sides lined with baking parchment, short ends well greased

Preheat the oven to 180°C/Gas mark 4. Sift the flour, salt and ground cardamom into a large mixing bowl. Add the butter and rub in, with your fingertips, until the mixture resembles medium breadcrumbs. Add the muscovado sugar and raisins and mix lightly until well distributed. Make a well in the centre.

In another bowl, mash the bananas to a soft and slightly lumpy purée. Add the egg and blend together, then pour into the well in the dry ingredients. Mix together with a wooden spoon and then beat until the mixture is thoroughly combined and has a soft dropping consistency.

Spoon the mixture into the prepared tin, levelling it out with the back of the spoon. Sprinkle the demerara sugar over the top. Bake for about 45 minutes until well risen and a skewer inserted into the centre comes out clean.

This cake will keep for 5 days in an airtight tin and freezes superbly.

Variations
Replace the raisins with dates or walnuts.

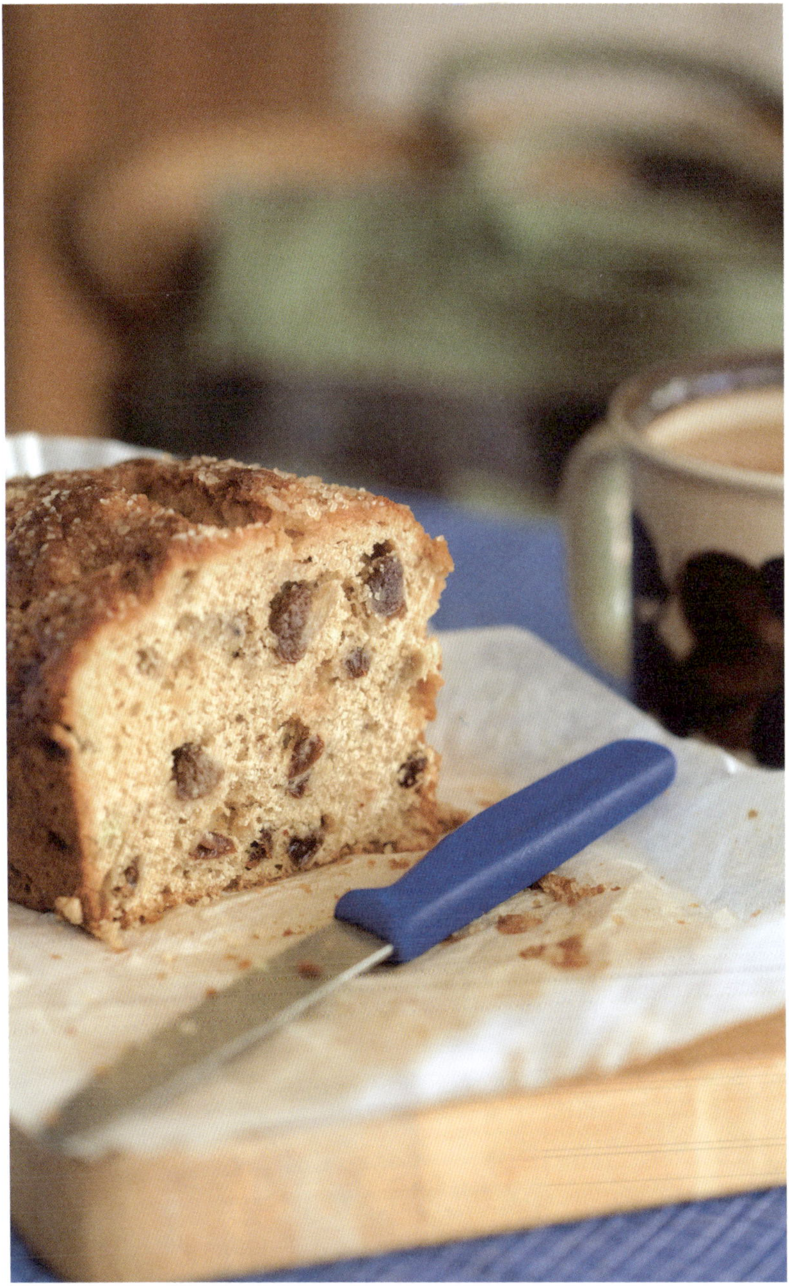

Bara brith

Bara brith or 'speckled bread' is a traditional Welsh tea bread. The vine fruits used in the recipe are first soaked in tea to give a beautifully moist result. In the Irish equivalent, tea brack, there is often a good drop of whiskey added too. It is easy to make, keeps well and, incidentally, doesn't contain any fat. You can serve it as it is, or spread it with butter. It's also lovely with a slice of Cheddar. This recipe has been in my family for years, but I can't resist sometimes making a few changes, such as varying the dried fruits, replacing the tea with apple or orange juice, or adding a tablespoonful of marmalade. And, as it's such a good keeper and freezes well, you'll find it's worth doubling up the quantities to make a couple at a time.

Serves 16
175ml strong, warm tea
225g mixed dried fruit, such as
    sultanas, currants or raisins
Finely grated zest and juice of
    1 unwaxed orange
150g light soft brown sugar
1 egg, lightly beaten
225g self-raising flour
Pinch of sea salt
1 tsp ground mixed spice

Equipment
1 litre loaf tin, approx 20x10cm,
    lightly greased, base and long sides
    lined with baking parchment

I usually use the remains of a pot of tea to steep the fruit. Otherwise, infuse a tea bag in 175ml boiling water for 5–10 minutes to create a good strong brew.

Place the dried fruit, orange zest and juice, sugar and tea in a mixing bowl large enough to hold everything. Cover and leave overnight for the fruit to plump up.

When you're ready to make the teabread, preheat the oven to 180°C/Gas mark 4. Add the egg to the fruit mix and stir in. Next, sift the flour, salt and mixed spice together over the mixture. Using a metal spoon, carefully mix together to a soft dough. Spoon into the prepared tin and give it a sharp tap to level the surface.

Bake in the oven for about 1 hour, until the top is golden brown and a skewer inserted into the centre of the tea bread comes out clean. Leave in the tin for 10 minutes before turning out to cool on a wire rack.

Once cold, wrap the tea bread in greaseproof paper, store in an airtight tin and leave to mature for several days before eating. It will keep for 2–3 weeks in the tin.

FRUITY CAKES & GINGERBREAD 191

Malted fruit loaf

Malt, which comes from germinating barley grains, has long been prized for its nutrients and soothing properties. Some take their malt in the form of beer, or even a shot of whisky, but I can assure you it is equally good in this well-loved fruited tea bread. It was an economical, but very flavoursome bake during the war and post-war rationing years and remains so – the nutty-sweet taste of the toasted barley corn concealing the lack of any butter or other fat.

Makes 16–18 slices

For the loaf
100g malt extract
100g golden syrup
100ml milk
75g dried dates, roughly chopped
75g sultanas
125g self-raising wholemeal flour
100g plain flour
½ tsp bicarbonate of soda
Pinch of sea salt
1 egg, lightly beaten

For the glaze
1 tbsp caster sugar
1 tbsp milk

Equipment
1 litre loaf tin, approx 20 x 10cm, greased, base and long sides lined with baking parchment

Preheat the oven to 180°C/Gas mark 4. Put the malt extract, golden syrup and milk into a medium saucepan. Stir over a gentle heat until the mixture is hot and all the ingredients are well combined. Remove from the heat and add the chopped dates and sultanas. Mix well and set aside to cool.

Meanwhile, sift the flours, bicarbonate of soda and salt into a mixing bowl and make a well in the centre. Pour in the malty fruit mixture and egg. Using a wooden spoon, beat well until the mixture forms a heavy, sticky dough.

Spoon the mixture into the prepared tin, spreading it out evenly with the back of the spoon. Bake in the oven for about 40 minutes, until the loaf is well risen and firm to the touch.

Meanwhile, to prepare the glaze, dissolve the sugar in 1 tbsp water in a small pan over a low heat. Add the milk, bring to the boil and boil for 1 minute.

Brush the glaze over the surface of the cake while it is still hot from the oven. Turn out of the tin and place on a wire rack to cool. Once cold, this cake will keep for 5 days stored in an airtight tin.

'Bird table' bread cake

Much as I love to watch the sparrows feeding in the garden, this dense pudding-cum-cake, based on an old wartime recipe, is a brilliant way to use up the end of a stale old loaf. I like to add a few nourishing seeds to give a little crunch.

Makes 10 big pieces

250g stale bread, sliced and crusts removed (to feed the birds…)
100g raisins
100g currants
1 tbsp linseeds
1 tbsp sunflower seeds
125g soft brown sugar
1–2 tsp ground mixed spice
Finely grated zest of 1 unwaxed lemon or orange
1 apple or firm pear, finely grated with skin on
75ml rapeseed oil, or 75g unsalted butter, melted and cooled
1 egg, lightly beaten
300ml milk
1 tbsp demerara sugar, to finish

Equipment
25 x 20cm baking tin, 6cm deep (or a tin with similar dimensions), lightly greased and base-lined with baking parchment

Cut the bread slices into quarters, place in a large mixing bowl and cover with about 500ml cold water. Leave to soak for an hour or so.

Preheat the oven to 180°C/Gas mark 4. With your hands, squeeze out as much water from the bread as you can. Return the bread pulp to the bowl. Mix in the dried fruit, linseeds, sunflower seeds, sugar, mixed spice, citrus zest and apple or pear.

Mix in the rapeseed oil or butter, followed by the egg and milk. Using a wooden spoon, beat everything together to form a wet, sloppy batter.

Pour into the prepared tin and bake in the oven for 1¼ –1½ hours or until the top is crisp and golden. While still hot, sprinkle the demerara sugar over the top.

Serve as a hot pudding, with custard, or leave in the tin to cool before slicing and serving as a cake. Once cool, it will keep for a couple of days in an airtight tin. For longer keeping, store in the fridge.

Variations

In summertime, replace the apple or pear with a handful of fresh berries or red- or blackcurrants. At other times, an overripe banana, well mashed, can be used as the fresh fruit element.

'Elevenses' lumberjack cake

As its name suggests, this favourite of the burly Canadian woodcutter, is a hearty cake, full of fruity goodness. It's just the thing to keep the wolf from the door when the hunger pangs kick in and lunchtime still seems hours away.

Feeds 8 hungry lumberjacks

For the cake
2 large eating apples (175–200g), such as Cox's or Russets
250g chopped dates
1 tsp bicarbonate of soda
125g unsalted butter, cut into small pieces and softened
175g light soft brown sugar
1 egg
150g plain flour
Pinch of salt
Pinch of ground cloves

For the topping
75g unsalted butter
75g soft brown sugar (light or dark)
60g desiccated coconut
75ml milk

Equipment
20cm round or 18cm square cake tin, lightly greased and base-lined with baking parchment

Preheat the oven to 180°C/Gas mark 4. Peel, core and coarsely grate the apples into a bowl. Add the chopped dates and bicarbonate of soda, cover with 250ml boiling water and stir together. Leave until warm.

Meanwhile, in a mixing bowl, beat the butter to a cream, using a wooden spoon or hand-held electric whisk. Add the sugar and continue to beat until light and fluffy. Beat in the egg until well combined. Stir in the apple and date mixture, including the liquid, and mix well. Sift the flour, salt and ground cloves over the mixture and fold in carefully. The mixture will seem quite sloppy, but this is how it should be.

Pour into the prepared tin and bake for about 40 minutes or until quite firm to the touch. While the cake is in the oven, prepare the topping. Place all the ingredients in a small saucepan and stir over a low heat until the butter has melted and the ingredients are well combined.

Take the cake out of the oven and spread the coconut mix over the top. Bake for a further 25–30 minutes until the topping is golden and the cake is cooked through.

Leave the cake in the tin until completely cool before turning out. Lumberjack cake will keep for 3 days in an airtight tin. If you wish to keep it any longer, because of its high moisture content, it will need to be stored in the fridge.

FRUITY CAKES & GINGERBREAD 195

Seasonal fresh fruit cake (no sugar)

Goodness, no sugar, eggs or baking powder! But this excellent fresh fruit cake is a brilliant way to make use of any type of fresh fruit in season. I've used plums here, but you could replace them with apples and pears, berries or bananas, peaches, nectarines or even pineapple. The fruit can be all one kind or a mixture, depending on what you have to hand. Likewise, the dried fruit and nut element can be varied.

Serves 12–16

500g plums, stones removed, or other fruit (see above)
100g desiccated coconut
150g porridge oats
½ tsp salt
150g dried apricots, roughly chopped into 1cm pieces, or 150g golden sultanas
100g hazelnuts, whole or roughly chopped
200ml sunflower oil
150g plain flour (approx)

Equipment
20x25cm baking tin, about 6cm deep (or a tin with similar dimensions), lightly greased and base-lined with baking parchment

Preheat the oven to 180°C/Gas mark 4. Roughly chop the plums or blitz them in a food processor. (If you are using strawberries, raspberries or other soft berries, simply crush with a potato masher. If you are using pears or apples, grate them straight into the mix.)

Put all the ingredients, except the flour, into a large mixing bowl and mix well together; the mixture will be quite sticky. Sift in enough flour to make a light, crumbly dough – you may need a little more than 150g if the fruit is very moist, or less if it's very dry.

Press the mixture into the prepared baking tray, firming it down with the back of a fork. Bake in the oven for 40–50 minutes until firm and lightly golden. Leave in the tin until cool before turning out.

This cake will keep for 4 days stored in an airtight tin in a cool larder.

Vinegar cake

This lovely, light, everyday fruit cake is easy to make, although it does involve some chemistry! Customarily baked when hens were 'off lay', this East Anglian speciality has no eggs. Instead, the cake is aerated and leavened by a mass of tiny carbon dioxide bubbles that erupt when bicarbonate of soda is mixed with vinegar.

Serves 18
250g plain flour
250g wholemeal flour
Good pinch of salt
200g unsalted butter, chilled and cut into small pieces
150g light soft brown sugar
250g raisins
250g sultanas
50g mixed peel (optional)
300ml whole milk, plus 1 tbsp
50ml cider vinegar
1 tsp bicarbonate of soda
2 tbsp golden syrup
1 generous tbsp demerara sugar

Equipment
28 x 22cm baking tin, about 6cm deep (or a small roasting tin with similar dimensions), lightly greased and base-lined with baking parchment, or for a deeper cake, a 23cm round or 20cm square tin, lightly greased and base-lined with parchment

Preheat the oven to 170°C/Gas mark 3. Sift both flours and the salt into a large mixing bowl. Add the butter and lightly rub in with your fingertips (or using a food processor) until the mixture resembles fine breadcrumbs. Add the sugar, raisins, sultanas and mixed peel, if using, and lightly mix together until evenly distributed.

Pour 300ml milk into a large mixing jug and add the vinegar. Dissolve the bicarbonate of soda in 1 tbsp milk. Now the fun begins: pour the bicarbonate of soda mix into the milk and vinegar and watch it rapidly froth up to nearly three times its original volume. Tip the foaming milk into the dried fruit mixture and add the golden syrup. Mix with a wooden spoon until thoroughly blended to a soft, lumpy batter.

Spoon into the prepared tin, spreading evenly with the back of the spoon. Lightly sprinkle with demerara sugar and bake for 1¼–1½ hours, until the top is golden and a skewer inserted into the centre comes out clean; allow up to 30 minutes longer for a deeper cake. Leave in the tin for 30 minutes, then remove to a wire rack to cool.

This cake will keep for up to 3 weeks in an airtight tin.

Boil and bait
fisherman's cake

A saucepan and a wooden spoon are the only pieces of equipment you will need to make this scrumptious moist fruit cake. Eaten with a good chunk of farmhouse Cheddar, creamy Caerphilly or crumbly Cheshire, this is an incredibly easy packed lunch, making it the perfect 'bite' for fishermen while waiting for a fish to bite… If you've not got any dried apricots or figs, simply replace these with currants or sultanas, or use a 500g pack of ready-mixed dried fruits to replace all of the dried fruits in the recipe, which makes it very straightforward.

Serves 10–12

125g unsalted butter or 125ml sunflower oil or rapeseed oil
125g light soft brown or muscovado sugar
1 good tbsp golden syrup or honey
125ml milk
200g raisins
150g dried apricots, each cut into 5 or 6 pieces
150g dried figs, each cut into 6 or 8 pieces
2 eggs, lightly beaten
250g self-raising flour

Equipment
18cm deep round or 15–16cm deep square tin, lightly greased and lined with baking parchment

Put the butter or oil, sugar, syrup or honey, milk and dried fruit into a saucepan with 125ml water. Stir over a gentle heat until the butter has melted and the ingredients are well combined. Simmer for about 15 minutes, until the mixture is slightly thickened and a soft caramel colour, stirring from time to time to prevent it sticking to the base. Remove from the heat and leave to cool for about 30 minutes.

Preheat the oven to 170°C/Gas mark 3. When the mixture is cool, stir in the beaten eggs and sift in the flour. Then, using a wooden spoon, beat together thoroughly until well combined.

Spoon the mixture into the prepared tin, levelling it out with the back of the spoon. Bake in the oven for 60–70 minutes until the top is evenly browned and a skewer inserted into the centre comes out very slightly sticky. Leave the cake in the tin until cold before turning out.

This is a cake that is better left for a few days before eating. It will keep for several weeks stored in an airtight tin.

FRUITY CAKES & GINGERBREAD 199

Cut and come again
(spelt and pear fruit cake)

Despite its lack of glamour (no cherries or exotic fruits), I put this pear cake in the 'cut-and-come-again' category because it's so good, you just can't help but have another slice. Dependable farmhouse cake recipes like this can be found all over the country. Buttermilk, the liquid left after butter-making, is often one of the ingredients – its acidity works with the bicarbonate of soda to make the cake rise.

Makes 15 pieces

500g plain white spelt flour
Pinch of salt
1 tsp bicarbonate of soda
2 tsp ground mixed spice
200g unsalted butter, chilled and cut into small pieces
250g soft brown sugar (light or dark)
175g raisins
175g sultanas
150g currants

2 eggs, lightly beaten
1 tbsp treacle or molasses
300ml buttermilk
2–3 firm medium pears (200–250g)

Equipment
23cm square or 25cm round tin, lightly greased and lined with baking parchment

Preheat the oven to 180°C/Gas mark 4. Sift the flour, salt, bicarbonate of soda and mixed spice into a roomy bowl, making sure they are well mixed. Add the butter and lightly rub in until the mixture resembles fine breadcrumbs. Add the sugar, followed by the dried fruit. Mix well until all the ingredients are evenly distributed.

Now add the eggs and the treacle to the buttermilk and beat until well combined. Pour the buttermilk mix into the dried fruit mixture. Grate in the pears (skins and all), then mix it all together to a soft dropping consistency.

Spoon the mixture into the prepared tin, smoothing the surface with the back of the spoon. Bake for 30 minutes, then reduce the temperature to 170°C/Gas mark 3 and bake for a further 1¼–1½ hours until the top is nutty brown and a skewer inserted in the centre comes out clean. Leave to cool in the tin before turning out.

Wrap the cake in greaseproof paper and store in an airtight tin. It keeps well for up to 3 weeks, but the chances are it won't be around that long!

P.S. If you can't get buttermilk, improvise by adding 1 tbsp vinegar or lemon juice to 300ml milk; leave for 10 minutes before using. Alternatively, use plain yoghurt.

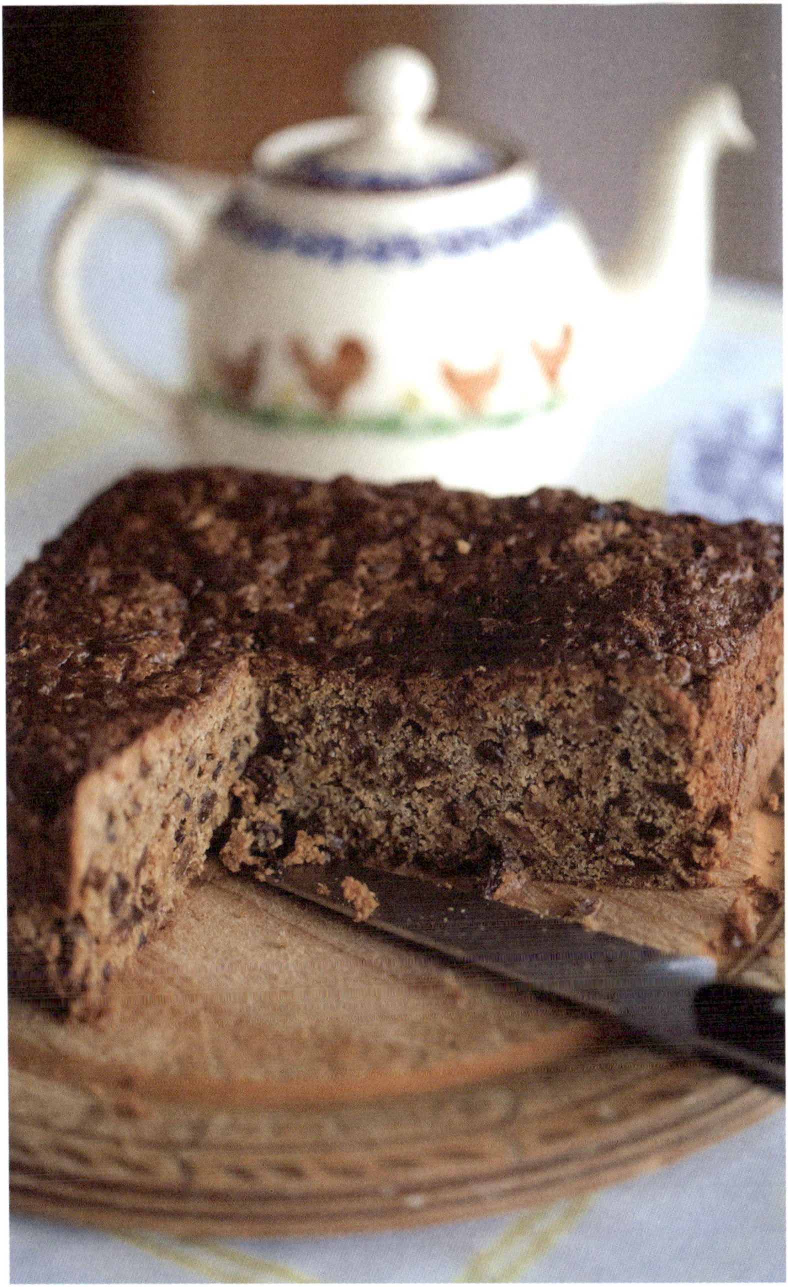

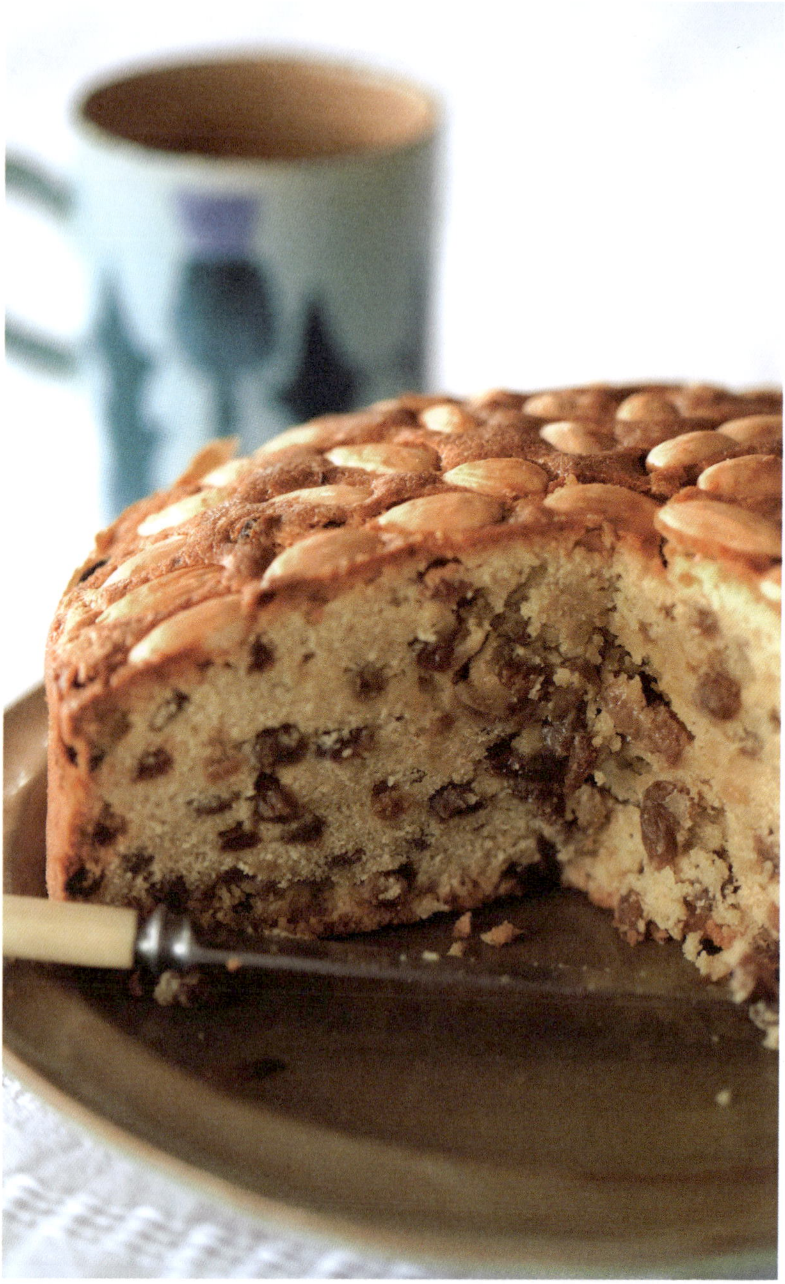

Dundee cake

The Dundee cake proudly bears a wreath of golden almonds, like an insignia, denoting its authority in the fruit cake world. Its origins are linked with the early Scottish marmalade industry. The Keiller family – pioneering and resourceful marmalade-makers – used factory downtime to make this legend of the Scottish tea table. The original recipe used only sultanas and lots of orange peel. These days, commercial recipes seem to favour a rich mix of vine fruits and cherries.

Serves 12
500g sultanas
75ml whisky
250g unsalted butter, cut into small pieces and softened
Grated zest of 2 unwaxed oranges (use Seville oranges if in season)
250g light soft brown sugar
5 eggs
275g plain flour
Pinch of sea salt

125g ground almonds
2 tbsp Seville orange marmalade or 50g chopped candied orange peel
50–75g whole blanched almonds (see p.32)

Equipment
20cm round tin, lightly greased and lined with baking parchment

Preheat the oven to 170°C/Gas mark 3. Bring the sultanas back to life by placing them in an ovenproof dish, pouring over the whisky and covering the dish with foil. Place in a very cool oven – say 130°C /Gas mark ½ – and leave for 30 minutes to allow the whisky to warm and moisten the fruit.

In a mixing bowl, beat the butter and orange zest to a cream. Add the sugar and beat thoroughly until light and creamy. Add the eggs, one at a time, adding 1 tbsp of the flour with each and beating thoroughly before adding the next. Sift the remaining flour and salt over the mixture and fold in, using a metal spoon. Finally fold in the ground almonds, whisky-soaked sultanas and the marmalade or peel.

Spoon the mixture into the prepared tin, spreading it out evenly with the back of the spoon. Lightly place the whole almonds on top of the cake, starting from the outside, and working towards the centre in ever-decreasing circles.

Bake in the oven for about 1½ hours until a skewer inserted in the centre comes out clean. Check after 1 hour and, if the surface is getting too brown, lay a piece of foil over the top. Leave to cool in the tin before removing.

Wrap in greaseproof paper and store in an airtight tin. It will keep for 6 weeks.

The 'Mother' fruit cake

This recipe makes for a jolly good rich fruit cake. Ideal as a classic Christmas cake, it can also be used to make a traditional Simnel cake or a superb wedding cake. The list of ingredients is not set in stone. For instance, if you don't care for glacé cherries, you can replace them with dried cranberries. Dried pears can be swapped for dried apricots or dried pineapple and if, for some reason, you prefer a booze-free cake, you can use fresh orange or apple juice instead of liqueur. Don't fret if you haven't managed to make the cake ahead of time either – it's still lovely when freshly baked.

The chart opposite will enable you to make a cake/cakes to suit most of your requirements. Apart from these sizes, I sometimes like to use a deep 10cm-diameter pork pie tin (this will take about 500g of cake mix) to make a mini cake – perfect topped with toasted marzipan (see p.59) to give as a small festive gift. The recipe method follows overleaf.

Ingredients	18cm round or 15cm square	20cm round or 18cm square	23cm round or 20cm square	25cm round or 23cm square
Currants	150g	225g	300g	375g
Sultanas	150g	225g	300g	375g
Raisins	150g	225g	300g	375g
Dried pears	100g	150g	200g	250g
Glacé cherries	75g	115g	150g	200g
Orange or lemon zest	½	1	1½	2
Brandy, rum or orange liqueur	1 tbsp, plus 1 tbsp to finish	2 tbsp, plus 2 tbsp to finish	3 tbsp, plus 3 tbsp to finish	4 tbsp, plus 4 tbsp to finish
Plain flour	125g	185g	250g	315g
Salt	Small pinch	Pinch	Good pinch	Big pinch
Ground mixed spice	½ tsp	¾ tsp	1 tsp	1¼ tsp
Nutmeg, freshly grated	½ tsp	¾ tsp	1 tsp	1¼ tsp
Ground ginger	Good pinch	2 good pinches	½ tsp	¾ tsp
Soft brown sugar	100g	150g	200g	250g
Unsalted butter, softened	125g	185g	250g	315g
Eggs, lightly beaten	3	4	6	8
Golden syrup or black treacle	½ tbsp	1 tbsp	1 good tbsp	1½ tbsp
Walnuts, chopped	50g	75g	100g	125g
Cooking apple, peeled, cored and finely grated	100g	150g	200g	250g
Approximate baking time	2–2½ hours	2½–3 hours	3–3½ hours	3½–4 hours
Approximate total weight	1.25 kg	2kg	2.75kg	3.5kg

Lightly grease the base and sides of your chosen tin and line with baking parchment. To prevent the outside edges of the cake drying out, tie a double band of brown paper, 3cm deeper than the depth of the tin, around the outside of the tin.

To get the best out of the fruit, put the first seven ingredients in a large ovenproof dish, mix well together and cover the dish with a piece of foil. Place in a very cool oven, about 130°C/Gas mark ½, and leave for about 30 minutes, to allow the fruit to warm and become a little sticky. As you remove the foil, the fruity aroma will give you a whiff of what is to come. Set aside to cool.

Preheat the oven to 145°C/Gas mark 1–2. Sift the flour, salt, mixed spice, nutmeg and ginger into a large mixing bowl, add the sugar and combine well together. Add the butter, three-quarters of the beaten egg and the golden syrup or treacle. Using either a hand-held electric whisk or a free-standing electric mixer, beat for about 1½ minutes until the mixture is light and creamy. Add the remaining egg and beat for a further 30 seconds.

Add the dried fruit, walnuts and grated apple. Use a large metal spoon to fold them in until everything is thoroughly mixed together.

Spoon the mixture into the prepared tin, smoothing it out lightly with the back of the spoon. Make a slight hollow in the centre of the cake – this will prevent the cake from rising in the centre. Place a piece of foil, with a hole (about 4cm wide) cut in the middle, over the cake tin.

Bake in the oven for roughly half the allotted cooking time. Remove the foil and continue to bake until the cake is golden in colour and a skewer inserted in the centre comes out clean. Trickle the remaining brandy over the top of the hot cake.

Allow to cool completely before turning out. Leave the baking parchment on the cake until you're ready to slice it.

The cake will mature nicely if kept wrapped in greaseproof paper in an airtight container. You can store it like this for up to 3 months.

Variation

Mojita Replace the brandy with rum, the orange zest with lime, the dried pears with dried pineapple and the walnuts with cashews.

FRUITY CAKES & GINGERBREAD 207

Family 'hun-ger' cake

A marvellous family filler, this 1950s recipe for a lightly gingered, not-too-sweet cake came from my friend Juliet, who remembers her mother making it as a beach and picnic cake. Assembled from everyday store-cupboard ingredients, its name is a play on two of the main ingredients – honey and ginger. It is very easy to put together, keeps well and is surprisingly moreish.

Feeds 12 hungry mouths
250g plain flour
1½ tsp bicarbonate of soda
½ tsp salt
1 tsp ground cinnamon
2 tsp ground ginger
Good pinch of ground cloves
125g unsalted butter, softened
125g light soft brown sugar
100–125g runny honey (or set honey, warmed sufficiently to trickle)
1 egg, lightly beaten
150ml plain yoghurt

Equipment
20cm square tin, or a 15x25cm baking tin (or a tin with similar dimensions), lightly greased and base-lined with baking parchment

Preheat the oven to 180°C/Gas mark 4. Sift the first 6 ingredients together into a bowl. Make sure they are evenly blended together by either mixing with a spoon or beating with an electric mixer for about 30 seconds on the lowest speed.

Put the butter, sugar and honey into another mixing bowl. Beat thoroughly until well blended and creamy. (It will not be as light and fluffy as a pure butter-and-sugar mix because of the honey.)

Add the egg and 1 tbsp of the flour mixture. Beat thoroughly until the mixture is well combined and like a soft cream. Stir in the yoghurt. Now use a large metal spoon to fold in the dry ingredients, a third at a time.

Spoon the mixture into the prepared tin, spreading it out evenly with the back of the spoon. Bake in the centre of the oven for about 40 minutes until the cake is golden brown and springs back into shape when lightly touched with a finger. Leave in the tin for 20 minutes before turning out onto a wire rack to cool.

'Hun-ger' cake keeps well for a couple of weeks wrapped in greaseproof paper and stored in an airtight tin.

FRUITY CAKES & GINGERBREAD 209

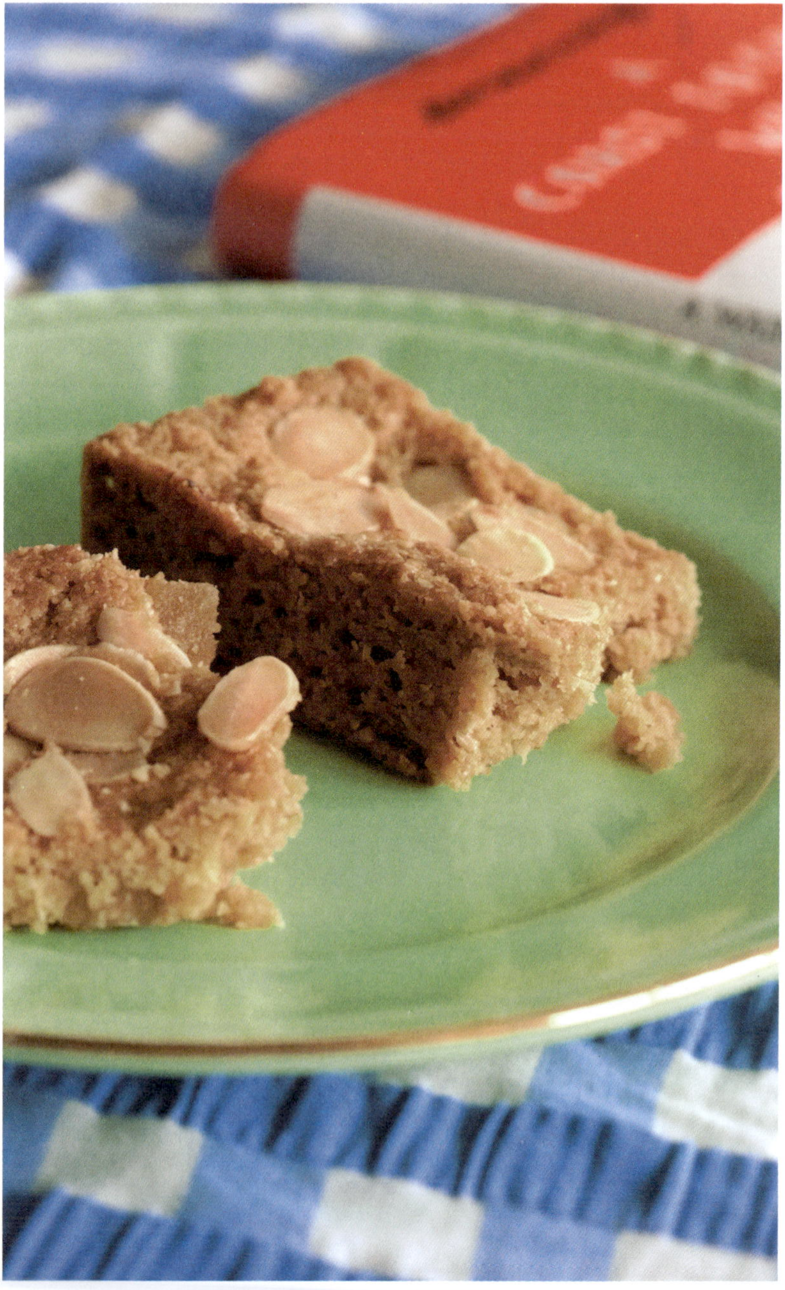

Grasmere gingerbread

This is more a chewy, gingery shortbread than the dark gooey cake we think of as gingerbread. A Lake District speciality, it has been made and sold in Grasmere since the mid-nineteenth century. The original recipe is a well-kept secret. I'm sure it didn't include lime or root ginger, or have almonds on top, but as I've yet to find two recipes the same, I've no qualms about presenting my own take on it. Jolly good it is too – the fruitiness of the lime balancing the fiery bite of the ginger.

Makes 12–16 pieces

125g plain flour
2 tsp ground ginger
½ tsp baking powder
125g fine or medium oatmeal
125g soft brown sugar
175g unsalted butter
50g fresh root ginger, grated, or
    50g glacé ginger, finely chopped
Finely grated zest and juice of 1 lime
2 tbsp flaked almonds

Equipment
20x25cm shallow baking tin (or a tin with similar dimensions), lightly greased and base-lined with baking parchment

Preheat the oven to 180°C/Gas mark 4. Sift the flour, ground ginger and baking powder together into a mixing bowl. Add the oatmeal and sugar and mix well.

Put the butter into a small saucepan and heat gently until completely melted. Pour into the dry ingredients, then add the ginger and the lime zest and juice. Using a wooden spoon, pound until the mixture forms a moist dough.

Press the mixture into the prepared tin. It may seem a bit skimpy, but don't worry, this is how it's meant to be – it will swell up in the oven. Sprinkle the flaked almonds over the surface and bake for about 30 minutes until slightly risen and lightly brown. Immediately mark into squares or fingers, then leave to cool in the tin.

Once cold, wrap the gingerbread in greaseproof paper and store in an airtight tin for up to 2 weeks.

P.S. Rum butter, another Lakeland speciality, is rather nice with this gingerbread. To make it, beat together 150g softened unsalted butter and 150g soft brown sugar (light or dark) until light and creamy. Gradually add 50ml dark rum, or to taste – do this slowly or the alcohol will 'split' the mixture and it will curdle. Rum butter is also great served with festive mince pies and Christmas pud.

Gillian's sticky gingerbread

Few things give me more pleasure than sitting in the corner of a cosy café with a cup of coffee and a slice of good cake. That's how I came across this gingerbread, at The Ceilidh Place in Ullapool. It's a deliciously moist, gingery creation, subtly flavoured with lemon zest, which nicely balances the rich sweetness of the cake.

Serves 10

For the gingerbread
100g golden syrup
100g black treacle
75g unsalted butter
75g light soft brown or muscovado sugar
150g plain flour
1 tsp ground ginger
½ tsp ground mixed spice
½ tsp ground cinnamon
1 egg, lightly beaten
75ml milk
Finely grated zest of 1 unwaxed lemon
½ tsp bicarbonate of soda
75–100g finely chopped preserved stem ginger in syrup (drained)

To finish (optional)
50g icing sugar, sifted
1 tbsp lemon juice or water
50g whole stem ginger (2 pieces)

Equipment
1 litre loaf tin, approx 20x10cm, lightly greased, base and long sides lined with baking parchment

Preheat the oven to 170°C/Gas mark 3. Put the golden syrup, treacle, butter and sugar into a small saucepan. Place over a gentle heat and stir until the butter has melted and the ingredients are evenly blended. Set aside to cool.

Sift the flour, ground ginger, mixed spice and cinnamon into a medium mixing bowl. Make a well in the centre and add the cooled treacle mixture, egg, milk and lemon zest. Using a wooden spoon, beat well until the mixture is smooth and glossy. Dissolve the bicarbonate of soda in 1 tbsp hot water. Add to the mixture with the chopped ginger and mix thoroughly to create a soft, pourable batter.

Pour into the prepared tin and bake in the oven for 50–60 minutes, or until the cake is firm to the touch and a skewer inserted into the centre comes out clean. Leave in the tin for 10 minutes before turning the cake out onto a wire rack to cool.

When cold, if you wish, mix the icing sugar with the lemon juice or water and drizzle over the cake, then top with slivers of stem ginger.

This cake is best stored for 3–4 days before eating. It keeps well for 2 weeks and freezes beautifully.

FRUITY CAKES & GINGERBREAD 213

Bonfire night parkin

A member of the gingerbread family, this treacly oatmeal cake is a speciality of Northern England, Yorkshire in particular. Inextricably linked with bonfire night, it is frequently enjoyed around a blazing fire with a burning effigy of Guy Fawkes, the Yorkshire traitor, on the top. Parkin improves with keeping and is best made ahead of time and left to mature for a couple of weeks. For a change, and to really set things on fire, pep up with a little finely chopped fresh chilli (see variation).

Makes 12 pieces
225g plain flour
3 tsp ground ginger
1 tsp freshly grated nutmeg
½ tsp bicarbonate of soda
Pinch of salt
125g medium oatmeal
Finely grated zest of 1 unwaxed orange
125g unsalted butter
125g light muscovado sugar

100g golden syrup
100g treacle or molasses
75ml milk
1 egg, beaten

Equipment
20cm square cake tin, base and sides greased and lined with baking parchment

Preheat the oven to 180°C/Gas mark 4. Sift the flour, ginger, nutmeg, bicarbonate of soda and salt into a large bowl. Stir in the oatmeal and orange zest.

Put the butter, sugar, golden syrup, treacle or molasses, and milk into a saucepan. Heat gently, stirring from time to time, until the butter has melted and the sugar dissolved. Remove from the heat and allow to cool before adding the beaten egg.

Make a well in the centre of the dry ingredients and pour in the buttery syrup mix. Blend together until the mixture is glossy and pourable. Pour into the prepared tin, making sure you've scraped all the gooey mix from the sides of the bowl. Give the tin a shake to make sure the mixture is evenly spread.

Cover with foil and bake in the oven for 35–40 minutes. Remove the foil and bake for a further 20 minutes until the cake is smooth and glossy on top and a skewer inserted in the middle comes out clean. Leave to cool in the tin.

When cool, turn out, wrap in greaseproof paper and store in an airtight tin. Leave to mature for at least a week before eating if possible. It will keep for 4 weeks.

Variation
For fiery hot parkin, add 1–2 tsp finely chopped fresh chilli.

FRUITY CAKES & GINGERBREAD 215

Party Cakes

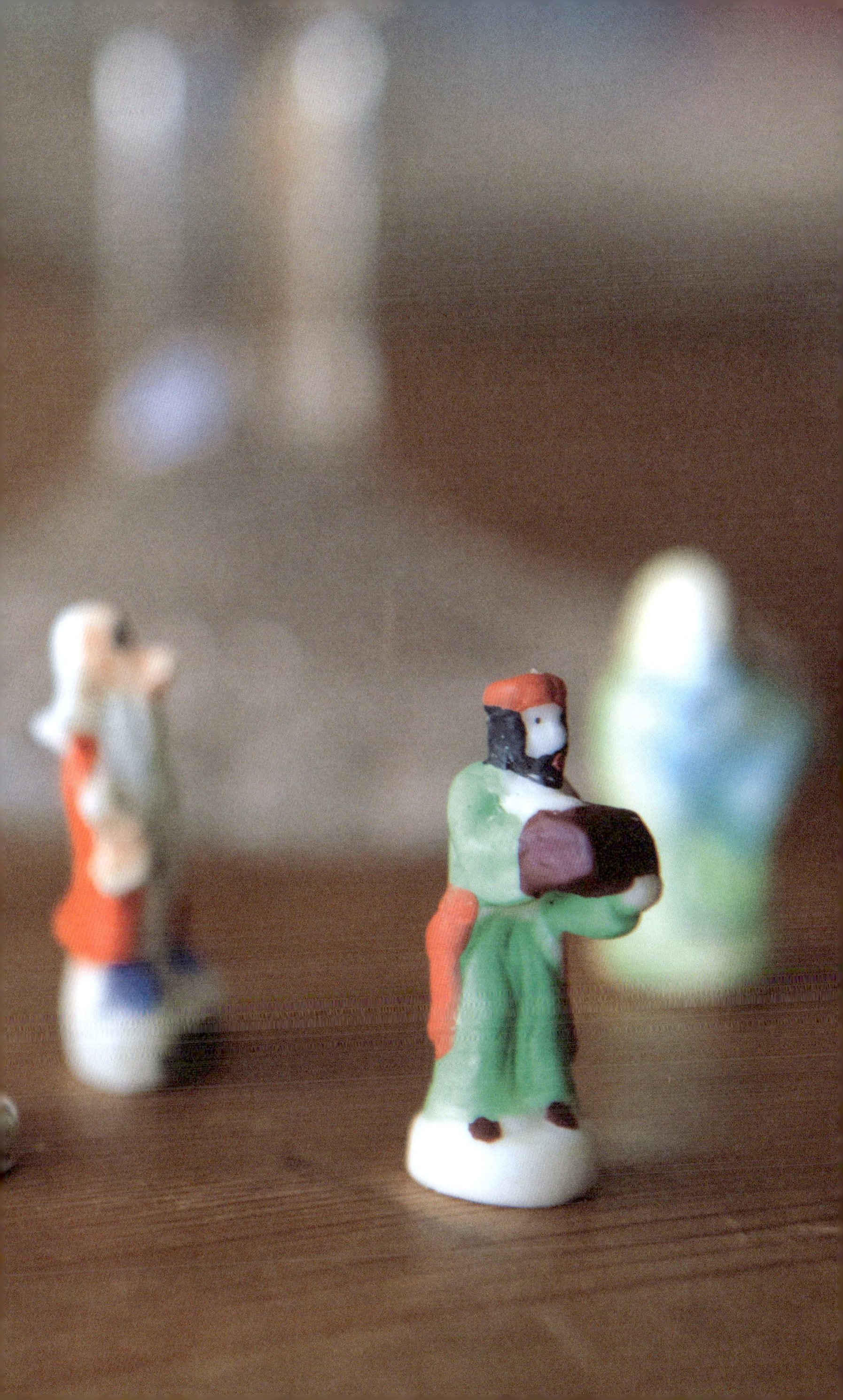

Place a candle on any cake

and you turn it into a cake to party with. A simple gesture, perhaps, but more often than not, that's what the archetypal party cake is all about: an effortless centrepiece, adorned with lit candles, enthusiastically presented and accompanied by a chorus of the proverbial 'Happy Birthday to you'. This somewhat *laissez-faire* approach allows you the freedom to choose the sort of cake to make or, perhaps more importantly, the type of cake the recipient truly likes. It needn't be elaborate in ingredients or decorations – a light fruity cake, a simple sponge or even a plate of muffins will do to celebrate the special event.

This aside, there are festivities where a certain type of cake has become associated with the occasion: a rich fruit cake, enrobed in soft, sweet marzipan and crisp royal icing is the classic for the merry Christmas season; it is also the foundation for the Easter Simnel cake and a traditional tiered wedding cake.

When it comes to birthday cakes for children, keep things easy: a glacé-iced jam-filled sponge or a chocolate sponge topped with chocolate icing will always please. The most important thing is that you have the right number of candles on the cake. In all probability, young children will be more interested in blowing out the candles than eating the cake, so expect to re-light them several times. Of course, for girls you can pretty the cake up with fresh flowers or ribbons; for boys, you could create a farmyard scene with model animals, or a football pitch with toy figures.

As time goes by, and your baking skills blossom, I hope you will create all sorts of cakes to celebrate special times and events throughout the year. 'What a swell party this is,' sang Frank Sinatra and Bing Crosby in Cole Porter's *High Society*. Remember, no party is complete without its centrepiece – the quintessential and wonderful cake.

PARTY CAKES 219

Vanilla cheesecake

Although perhaps considered more a dessert than a teatime cake, the baked cheesecake deserves a place amongst the great cakes of the world. I love to load my cheesecake with plenty of sweet aromatic vanilla, making it a perfect base to serve with fresh seasonal fruit or a thick fruity coulis. Use a young, soft cheese – curd cheese, such as Quark, or a simple cream cheese, but not cottage cheese.

Serves 12

For the base
30g unsalted butter
1 tbsp honey
200g digestive biscuits

For the cake
500g curd cheese or cream cheese
275ml soured cream
1–2 vanilla pods, seeds scraped out, or 2–3 tsp vanilla paste or extract
3 eggs, plus 1 egg yolk
175g caster sugar
30g cornflour, sifted

To finish
3–4 tbsp soured cream, plain yoghurt or fromage frais
250g fresh strawberries, raspberries or blueberries

Equipment
23cm springform cake tin, sides well greased and base-lined with baking parchment

Preheat the oven to 180°C/Gas mark 4. To make the base, put the butter and honey into a small saucepan and place over a gentle heat until the butter has melted. Stir to combine. Meanwhile, crush the biscuits by either placing them in a large plastic bag and whacking them with a rolling pin, or whizzing them in a food processor to crumbs. Mix with the butter and honey until evenly combined.

Press the crumb mixture into the prepared tin. Bake in the oven for 10 minutes, then remove. Turn the oven setting down to 170°C/Gas mark 3.

In a large mixing bowl, mix the soft cheese, soured cream, and vanilla seeds, paste or extract until well combined. In another large bowl, beat the eggs, egg yolk and sugar together using a hand-held electric whisk or balloon whisk, until fairly thick and creamy. Carefully fold into the cheese mixture with the cornflour.

Pour the cheesecake mix on top of the biscuit base and give the tin a gentle shake to level it. Bake for about 1 hour until it is lightly golden and feels firm when gently touched – the centre may still be a little soft but this will firm up as it cools down.

Remove from the oven and run a palette knife or spatula around the inside edge of the cake tin – this will help to prevent the top splitting as it cools down. Leave the cheesecake in the tin until cold.

To serve, carefully remove the cheesecake from the tin and place on a plate. Spread the soured cream, yoghurt or fromage frais on the top and cover with berries.

This cheesecake improves after a day, keeps for up to 5 days in the fridge and freezes (without the topping and fruit) beautifully.

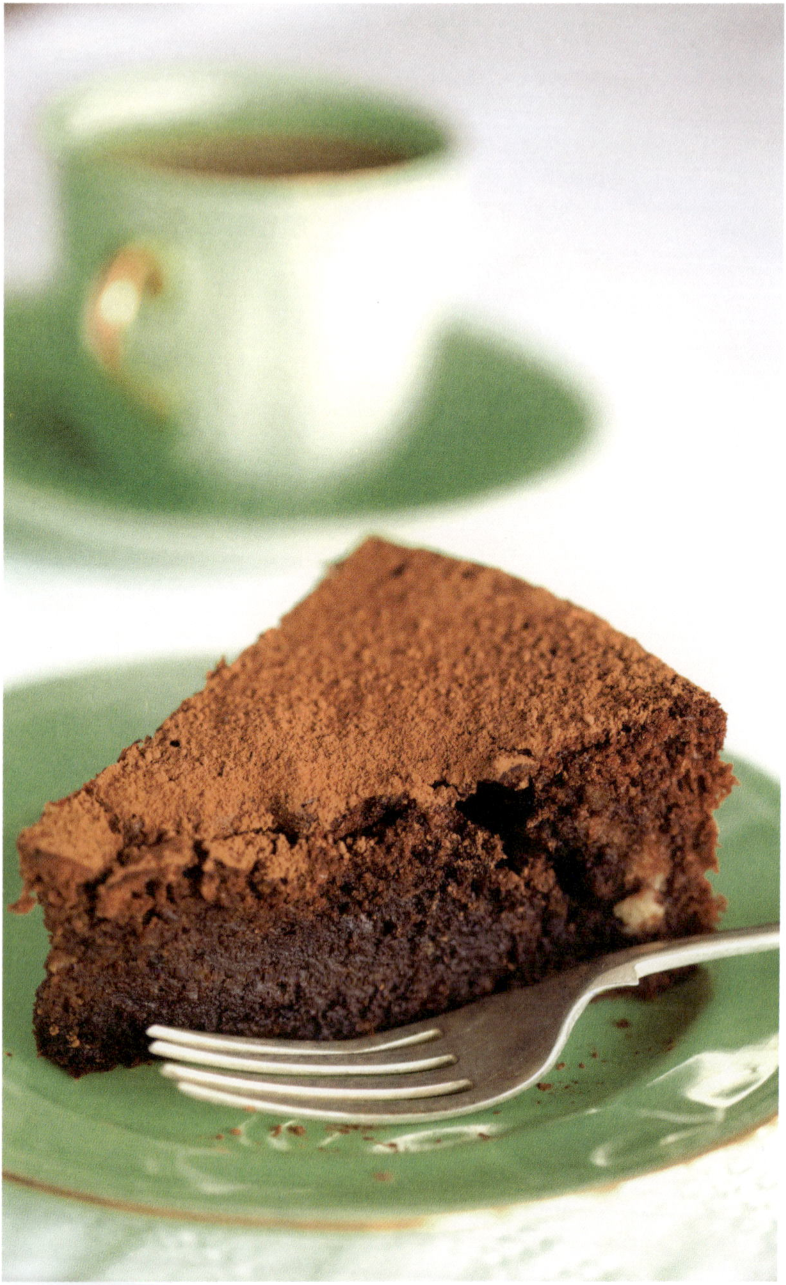

Mocha cake

This deliciously rich, moist cake, adapted from a recipe given to me by my friend Claire Love, will satisfy the most intense chocolate cravings. I love the combination of dark chocolate and coffee, but this recipe works exceedingly well without the coffee, or you can ring the changes by flavouring the mix with a little ground cardamom or very finely chopped chilli or finely grated orange zest instead. For a softer, sweeter approach, replace the plain with milk or semi-sweet chocolate.

Serves 10

200g unsalted butter, cut into small pieces
200g good-quality dark chocolate, broken into small pieces
2 tbsp strong filter coffee, or 1 tbsp instant coffee powder dissolved in 2 tbsp hot water
50g plain flour
50g ground almonds

5 eggs
75g light soft brown sugar
100g caster sugar
1 tbsp sifted cocoa powder, for dusting

Equipment
20cm springform cake tin, lightly greased and lined with baking parchment

Preheat the oven to 180°C/Gas mark 4. Have ready a saucepan of simmering water. Put the butter, chocolate and coffee into a smallish heatproof bowl and set over the pan, making sure the base is not touching the water. Leave until melted, but don't let the mixture get too hot. Remove from the heat and stir until well combined.

Meanwhile, sift the flour into a bowl and mix in the ground almonds; set aside.

Separate the eggs into two large bowls. Add the brown sugar to the egg yolks and beat, using a hand-held electric whisk, until thoroughly combined and creamy. Now carefully fold in the melted chocolate mix, making sure it is evenly combined – the chocolate has a tendency to sink to the bottom of the bowl, so dig down deep.

Whisk the egg whites and caster sugar together to soft peaks. Carefully fold the flour and almond mix into the chocolate mixture, followed by the egg whites and sugar.

Pour into the prepared tin and bake for about 40–45 minutes or until a skewer inserted in the middle comes out a little sticky. The aim is to slightly undercook the cake so it will be soft and a little sunken in the middle. Leave to cool in the tin.

Before serving, remove from the tin and dust with the cocoa. The cake is lovely eaten warm with a little cream. It will keep for 5 days in an airtight tin in a cool place.

Simnel cakelets

These little Easter cakes are inspired by Kerri Spong, an outstanding cake-maker from Axminster who supplies the River Cottage Canteen and stores with them at Easter. They make a lovely change from the classic marzipan-topped Simnel cake, and they're quick to bake, fun to decorate and scrumptious to eat. You can use ready-mixed dried fruit or mix up a medley of your choice.

Don't just make these little sweet treats for Easter; they adapt brilliantly to other festive occasions. And of course you can soak the fruit in something a little stronger than orange juice if you like!

Makes 12
250g mixed dried fruit
Finely grated zest and juice of
 1 large unwaxed orange
250g self-raising flour
1 tsp ground mixed spice
½ tsp freshly grated nutmeg
175g caster sugar
175g unsalted butter, cut into small
 pieces and softened
3 eggs
75ml milk

To fill and decorate
300g Marzipan (see p.58) (or
 150g if decorating the cakes with
 chocolate eggs)
250g Glacé icing (see p.55)
Chocolate eggs (optional)

Equipment
12-hole muffin tray, holes about
 6.5cm in diameter and 2cm deep,
 lined with paper muffin cases
Small (5–6cm) rabbit, chick or flower
 biscuit cutters (if decorating with
 marzipan shapes)

Put the dried fruit into a bowl with the orange zest and juice. Leave in a warm place for an hour or so to allow the fruit to plump up.

When ready to bake, preheat the oven to 180°C/Gas mark 4. Sift the flour, mixed spice and nutmeg into a large mixing bowl. Add the caster sugar and mix together.

Add the butter, eggs and milk to the flour and spice mixture. Using a hand-held electric whisk, beat for 1½–2 minutes until light and fluffy. Fold in the fruit and any residual orange juice.

Half fill the muffin cases with the mixture. Take 150g of the marzipan and divide it into 12 pieces. Flatten each piece into a disc and place on top of the mixture in the muffin cases. Spoon the remaining mixture over the top of the marzipan.

Bake in the oven for about 25 minutes until the cakes are nicely golden and spring back into shape when lightly pressed. Leave in the tray for about 10 minutes before moving to a wire rack to cool.

Meanwhile, roll out the remaining marzipan, if using, and cut it into Easter shapes with the biscuit cutters. Have the glacé icing ready.

When the cakes are completely cold, top with the glacé icing. Place either a marzipan shape or 2–3 chocolate eggs on top of each one to decorate.

These cakes can be stored in a single layer in an airtight tin for up to a week.

Variation

Christmas cakelets Top with marzipan holly leaves, stars and Christmas trees.

Hallowe'en pumpkin cake

The old Irish custom of making vegetable lanterns to ward off evil spirits has long been associated with Hallowe'en. Irish immigrants in America found pumpkins much easier to carve than the turnips and swedes of their homeland, and so the pumpkin lantern has become an enduring symbol of modern-day Hallowe'en. The carved-out pumpkin flesh is often used to make soup or sweet pies. This cake is another alternative: sweetly perfumed, light and crispy in texture, it's a wicked way to make sure nothing goes to waste.

Serves 12

150g unsalted butter, cut into small pieces and softened
300g caster sugar
3 eggs
340g self-raising flour
225g finely grated raw pumpkin flesh
150g amaretti or dry macaroons, lightly crushed
50ml whole or semi-skimmed milk

To finish (optional)
Orange Glacé icing (see p.55)
Hallowe'en sweets

Equipment
23cm garland or ring mould, well greased, or a 20cm round tin lightly greased and base-lined with baking parchment

Preheat the oven to 180°C/Gas mark 4. In a mixing bowl, beat the butter to a cream, using a wooden spoon or a hand-held electric whisk. Add the sugar and continue to beat until well creamed. (It won't be as light and fluffy as a classic sponge mix.)

Add the eggs, one at a time, adding 1 tbsp of the flour with each, and beating well before adding the next. Sift in half the remaining flour, then use a large metal spoon to carefully fold it in. Repeat with the other half. Fold in the grated pumpkin, crushed amaretti or macaroons, and the milk – to give a soft dropping consistency.

Spoon the mixture into the prepared tin and bake in the oven for 45 minutes, until the cake is lightly golden, springs back to shape when pressed with a finger and is beginning to pull away from the sides of the tin. Leave in the tin for 5 minutes before carefully turning out and placing on a wire rack to cool.

For children, trickle the cake with orange glacé icing and scatter with sweets. For adults, serve it plain with hot mulled cider punch. It will keep in a tin for 5 days.

Variation
Add 50g mini marshmallows along with the amaretti for a gooey Hallowe'en cake.

PARTY CAKES 227

Hedgelog
(Yule log)

This cake is a nod to the pagan ritual of burning a Yule log at the winter solstice, a ceremony intended to drive away the short dark days of winter. The tradition of making a chocolate log for the festive season originates from the practice. I can assure you I'm not in the habit of burning hedgehogs but, for fun, I have traded in the customary Yule log for this bright-eyed chocolatey 'Hedgelog'.

Serves 10

For the log
150g dark chocolate, broken into small pieces
4 eggs, separated
150g caster sugar
1 tbsp icing sugar mixed with 1 tsp cocoa powder, for dusting

For the filling and topping
200g tin sweetened chestnut purée
1 quantity whipped-up Chocolate ganache (see p.65)

To decorate
Large chocolate buttons
2 hazelnuts
1 glacé cherry

Equipment
20 x 35cm (approx) Swiss roll tin, sides greased and base-lined with baking parchment

Preheat the oven to 180°C/Gas mark 4. Have ready a small saucepan of simmering water. Put the chocolate into a small heatproof bowl that will sit snugly on the pan without the base touching the water. Set the bowl over the pan and leave until the chocolate has melted, making sure it doesn't get too hot. Remove from the heat and set aside.

Meanwhile, place the egg yolks and sugar in a mixing bowl and beat, using a hand-held electric whisk, for 5–6 minutes, until the mixture is pale lemon in colour. In another bowl, and using clean beaters, whip the eggs whites to firm peaks.

Add the melted chocolate to the beaten yolks and mix until evenly combined. Fold in the whisked egg whites, being careful not to lose too much of the incorporated air.

Spoon the mixture into the prepared tin and bake for 15–20 minutes or until the mixture is firm to the touch. Leave to cool for 5 minutes before covering with a slightly damp tea-towel (to prevent a crust from forming). Leave for several hours.

When ready to assemble, lay a piece of greaseproof paper on your work surface and dust with the icing sugar and cocoa mix. Remove the tea-towel from the cake and invert onto the paper. Remove the tin and baking parchment.

Spread about three-quarters of the chestnut purée onto the cake, leaving a clear margin of about 1.5cm along each edge. Using the paper as a guide, roll up the sponge like a Swiss roll. Place it, seam side down, on a cake board or plate. Shape one end of the cake to create a pointy hedgehog face.

Mix the remaining chestnut purée into the chocolate ganache and smother over the 'hedgelog'. Use the blade of a knife or a fork to prickle up the surface. Insert chocolate buttons for hedgehog spines, hazelnuts for eyes and the cherry for a shiny nose.

Variation

'Seventies' chocolate roulade Fill with whipped cream and dust with icing sugar.

Raisin and cherry stollen

This traditional sweet German Christmas bread is much simpler to make than it looks, so please don't be alarmed by the length of the recipe. The richness of the dough means you need to allow more time for proving than normal bread; the recipe should take about 4 hours from start to finish. You will find this stollen much nicer than the shop-bought alternatives and it doesn't need to be made at the last minute. In fact, it is best made well ahead to allow the marzipan time to relax into the fruit-packed dough.

Makes 2 loaves (18 slices each)

For the dough
200g raisins
100g glacé cherries, quartered
Finely grated zest of 1 large unwaxed orange
50ml dark rum
100g unsalted butter
175ml milk
3 tsp (15g) dried yeast
125g caster sugar
500g strong white bread flour
½ tsp salt
2 eggs, beaten
A little sunflower oil, for greasing
50g flaked almonds
Seeds from 6 cardamom pods, crushed

For the filling
250–300g Marzipan (see p.58)

To finish
25g unsalted butter, melted
Icing sugar for dredging

Equipment
1 floured baking sheet

Place the raisins, glacé cherries, orange zest and rum in a bowl and toss to mix. Cover and leave in a warm place to macerate and allow the raisins to plump up while you make the stollen dough.

Melt the butter in a small pan, then leave to cool down. Warm the milk until tepid (not hot), add the yeast and sugar and stir until dissolved. Set aside until the mixture has started to bubble.

Sift the flour and salt into a large mixing bowl. Make a well in the centre and pour in the yeast mixture, melted butter and beaten eggs. Mix first with a wooden spoon, then with your hands, until the mixture forms a dough that comes away cleanly from the bowl.

(continued overleaf)

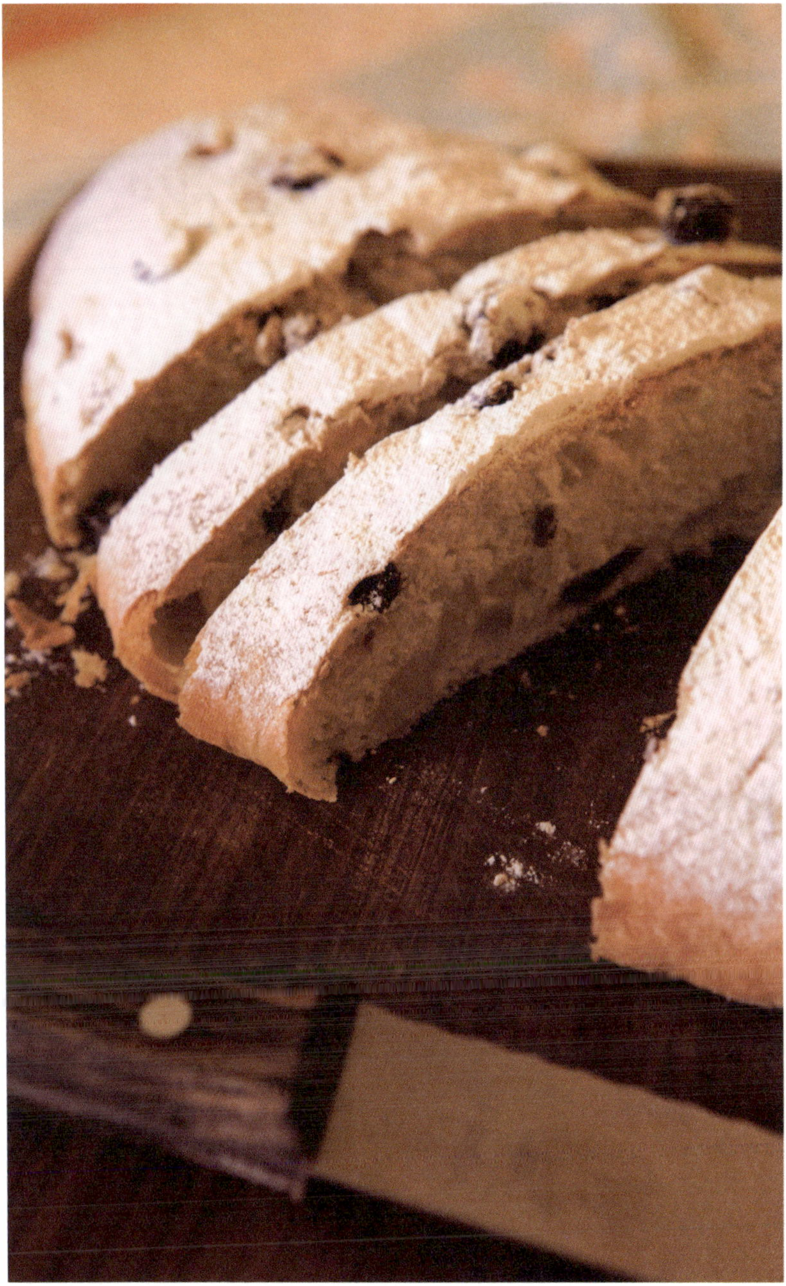

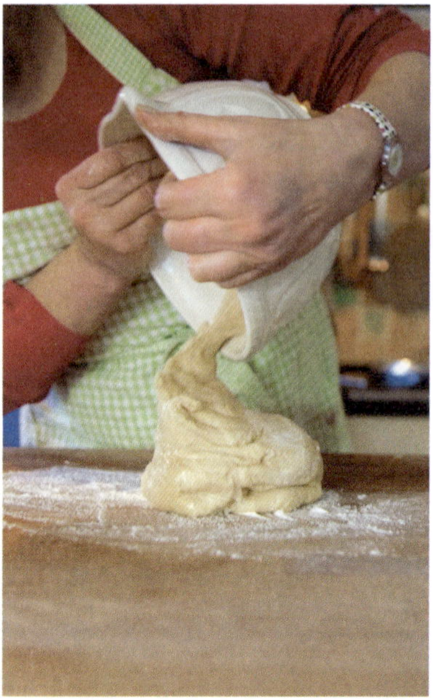
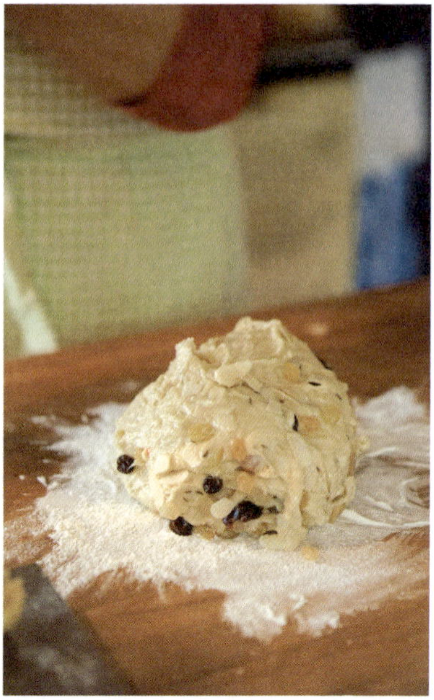
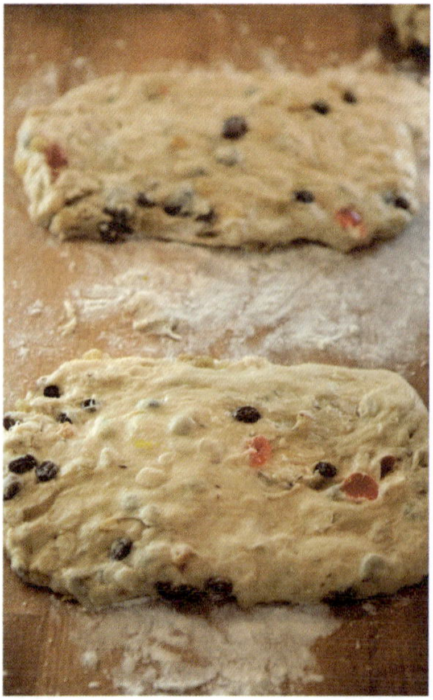
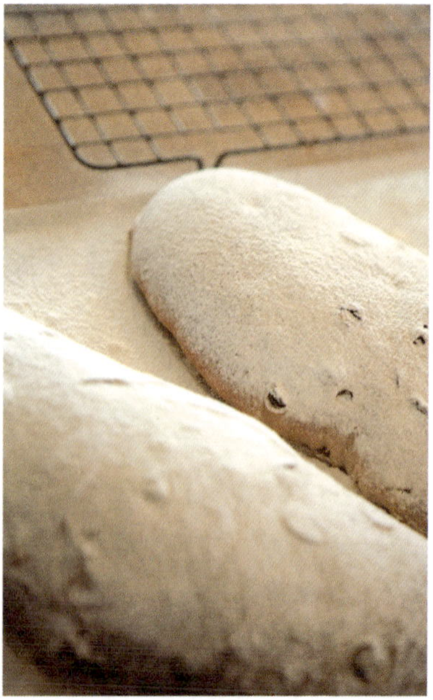

Turn the dough out onto a floured surface and knead until it is soft, elastic and no longer sticking to the surface. Alternatively, use a free-standing electric mixer fitted with the dough hook to bring the dough to this stage.

Lightly oil a large bowl, place the dough in it and turn the dough so that it is covered all over with a thin layer of oil. Cover the bowl with cling film and leave in a warm place for 1–2 hours or until the dough has doubled in size.

Turn the dough onto a lightly floured surface and knock back. Flatten the dough with the palm of your hand and sprinkle with half the rum-soaked fruit, flaked almonds and crushed cardamom seeds. Mix in by first folding the dough over the fruit, then lightly kneading until the fruit is evenly distributed. Repeat until all the fruit, plus any residual rum, has been worked in.

Divide the dough into two pieces. Flatten each to a rectangle about 25 x 15cm. Split the marzipan in two and roll each piece into a sausage shape the same length as the dough. Position a marzipan roll along each dough rectangle, slightly off centre. Fold the dough over the marzipan to make two long, loose loaves.

Place the loaves, seam side down, on a floured baking sheet. Cover with a tea-towel and leave in a warm place for 1–1½ hours until doubled in bulk. Meanwhile, preheat the oven to 180°C/Gas mark 4.

Bake the loaves for approximately 25 minutes, until pale golden. Immediately brush the stollen with the melted butter, then transfer to a wire rack to cool.

Once cold, dust freely with icing sugar. Wrap in greaseproof paper and store in an airtight tin for a week or so before eating. This stollen will keep for up to 3 weeks.

Variations

Prune and apricot stollen Replace the raisins with chopped prunes, the glacé cherries with dried apricots, the rum with brandy, and the cardamom with ½ freshly grated nutmeg. Work 100g finely diced dried apricots into the marzipan.

Harlequin stollen Omit the raisins and add 50g chopped angelica, 50g chopped candied citron or lemon peel and an extra 100g glacé cherries instead. Use gin in place of rum. Replace the flaked almonds with chopped toasted hazelnuts and the cardamom with 2 tsp fennel seeds.

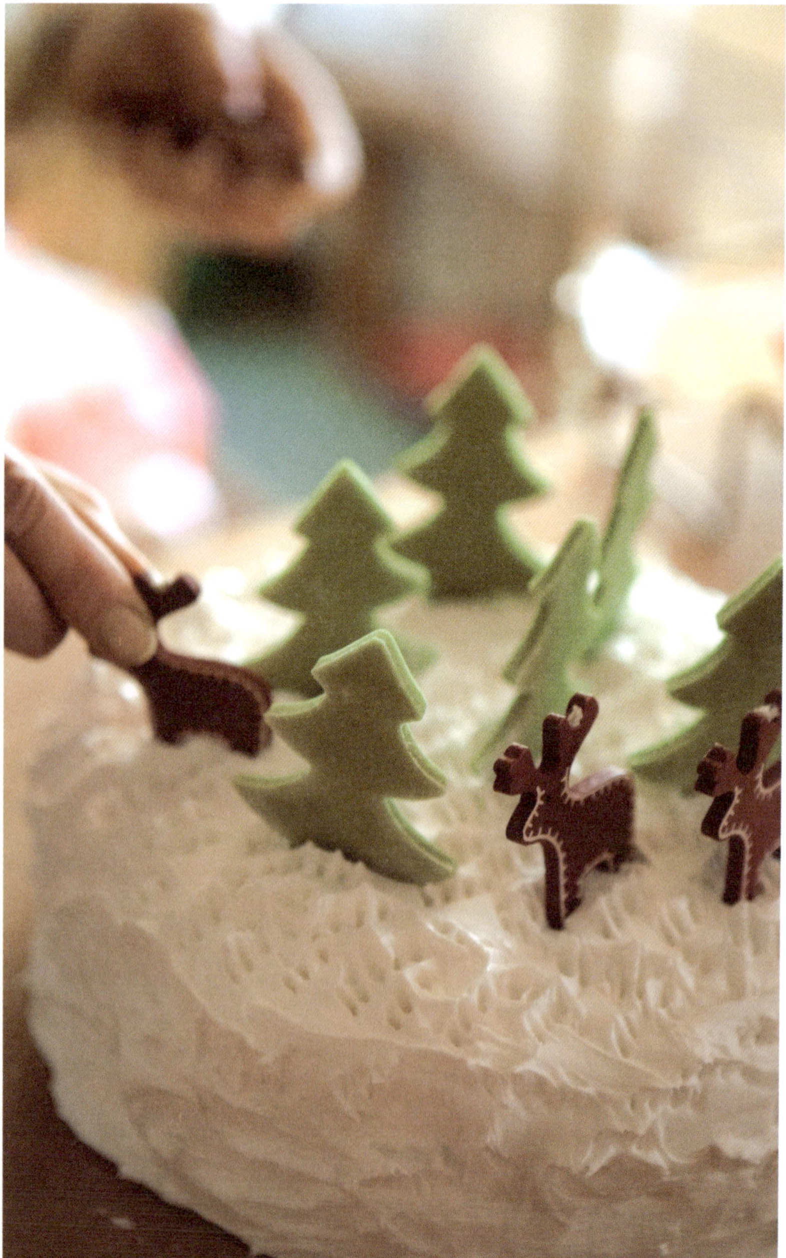

Snowy Christmas cake

Despite all good intentions, the decorating of our Christmas cake is usually a hurried affair, entrusted to anyone who is willing to take it on. I asked my daughters Pip and Maddy to do the job some years ago, when they were quite young. They spent days making a small forest of green marzipan Christmas trees, which I imagined would be stuck to the sides of the cake. Instead, the girls stood them upright on top, creating a rather magical three-dimensional snowy scene, a tradition we still keep today. To be able to create this look, the marzipan Christmas trees need to be prepared at least a week ahead to allow them time to dry and firm up enough to stand up.

Use the 'Mother' fruit cake recipe (on p.204) to make your cake. The chart below gives you the quantities of marzipan and royal icing you will need depending on the size of your cake. The recipes and directions for applying these to the cake are on pp.58 and 60 respectively.

I have allowed plenty of marzipan, enough for a 1cm covering with some left over for your Christmas trees, or reindeers, stockings, stars – whatever festive decoration takes your fancy. The marzipan trees are made by cutting out coloured marzipan with a tree-shaped biscuit cutter 5–6cm in length. You could make them smaller, but I wouldn't suggest them being any loftier.

Covering	18cm round or 15cm square	20cm round or 18cm square	23cm round or 20cm square	25cm round or 23cm square
Marzipan (see p.58)	500g	750g	1kg	1.25kg
Royal icing (see p.60)	600g	750g	900g	1kg

P.S. If you prefer not to go the whole hog with the royal icing, you can make a very impressive cake covered with marzipan alone. Follow the instructions to toast a marzipan cake on p.59. Decorated with Christmassy marzipan shapes, this makes a lovely alternative to a fully decked out Christmas cake.

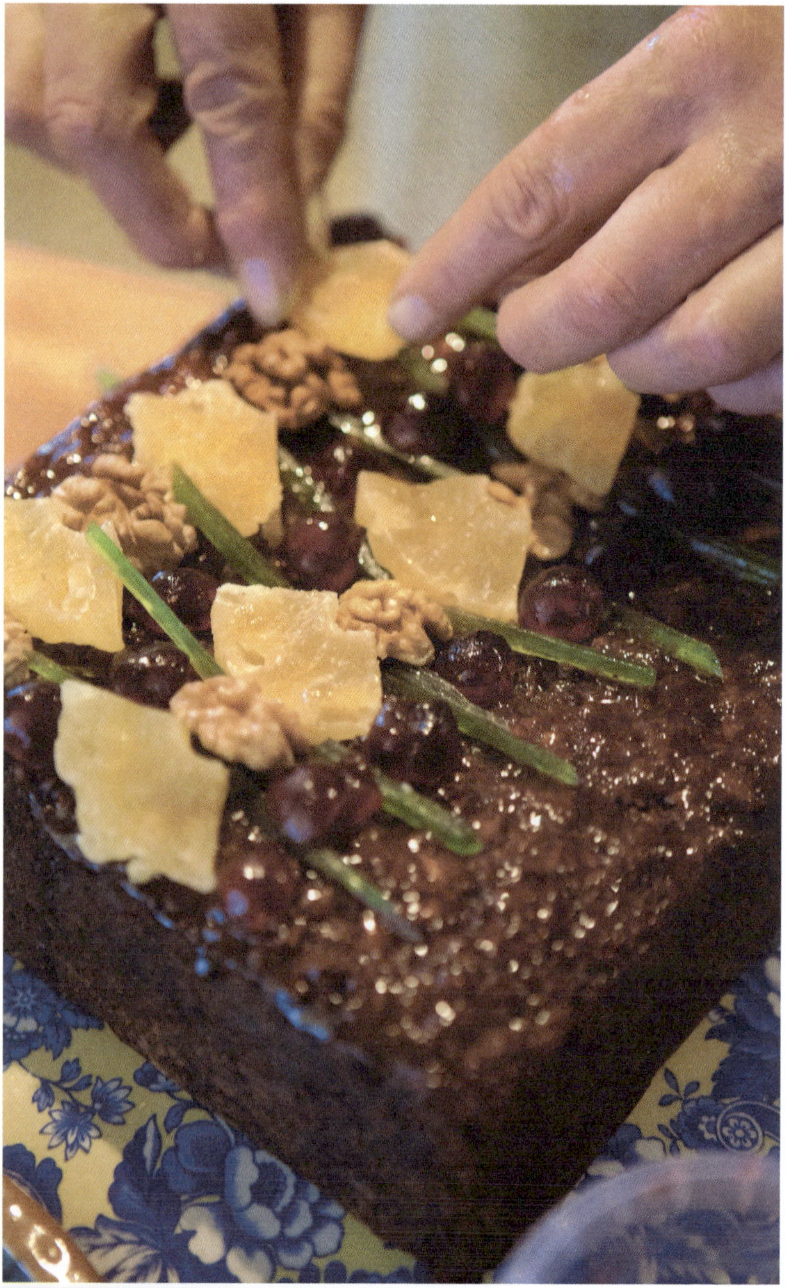

Certosino

Festooned with glacé fruits and nuts, this exquisite honey-sweetened Italian Christmas cake is jam-packed with fragrant and exotic things. This recipe, a little altered, comes from cakeophile Alison Finch's informative Brief History of the Christmas Cake. *Try replacing the cooking apple with fragrant quince, if you happen to have some (see variation, overleaf). Make this well ahead of time: it is a cake which, like so many of us, improves with keeping.*

Serves 24

100g raisins
50ml Marsala or brandy
250g runny honey
100g soft brown sugar
60g unsalted butter
350g plain flour
2 tsp bicarbonate of soda
½ tsp salt
2 tsp ground mixed spice
2 tsp fennel seeds, lightly crushed
250g cooking apples, cored, peeled and finely grated
50g pine nuts
100g almonds, blanched and slivered (see p.32)
100g walnuts, roughly chopped
100g dark chocolate, roughly chopped into 1cm pieces
50g crystallised ginger, finely chopped
100g mixed candied orange and lemon peel, roughly chopped into 1cm pieces

To decorate

About 4 tbsp apricot jam, sieved and warmed
A selection of glacé or crystallised fruits, such as cherries, angelica and pineapple
12–16 walnut halves

Equipment

24cm springform round or 22cm square loose-bottomed tin, lined with baking parchment

Preheat the oven to 170°C/Gas mark 3. Put the raisins and the Marsala or brandy into a small bowl and leave to soak for at least 30 minutes.

Put the honey, brown sugar, butter and 75ml water into a small saucepan and place over a gentle heat. Heat, stirring until the ingredients have softened and are well combined, without allowing it to boil. Set aside.

(continued overleaf)

238 CAKES

Sift the flour, bicarbonate of soda, salt and mixed spice into a large mixing bowl. Toss in the fennel seeds and the grated apple. Next, pour in the warm honey mixture and the soaked raisins and mix to a batter. Stir in the pine nuts, almonds, walnuts, chocolate, crystallised stem ginger and candied peel until evenly mixed.

Spoon the mixture into the prepared tin, spreading it out evenly with the back of the spoon. Bake for about 1¼ hours until just firm and a skewer inserted into the centre comes out clean. Leave in the tin until completely cold. Wrap in greaseproof paper and store in an airtight tin until ready to decorate.

Before serving, brush the top of the cake evenly with half the apricot jam. Arrange the glacé fruits and walnut halves decoratively on the top and brush over the remaining apricot jam. Leave to set before serving.

Stored in an airtight tin, this cake will keep for 10 weeks or even longer.

Variation
Certosino with quince Replace the grated apple with 250g quince purée. To prepare the purée, soften the peeled and cored quince by simmering in a little water, with the juice of ½ lemon added, until tender. Then either push through a sieve or purée in a blender or food processor until smooth. Allow to cool before adding to the cake mixture. A wonderful way to use quince.

King cake

This is my interpretation of the French *Galette des Rois*, a delicious almond-rich cake customarily made for Twelfth Night (6 January), when the three kings are said to have arrived in Bethlehem. Traditionally the cake is served topped with a cardboard crown and a small treasure, such as a cake charm or coin, hidden within it. As the cake is cut, the youngest person sits under the table and calls out the name of the guest who should receive each piece. Whoever finds the charm wears the crown, reigns supreme for the evening and is exempt from the washing up…

Serves 12
15–18 glacé cherries
75g plain flour
150g unsalted butter, softened
200g caster sugar
4 eggs
150g ground almonds
About 2 tbsp milk

To assemble
Cake charm or coin
icing sugar, for dusting
150–200g Marzipan (see p.58)

Equipment
20cm loose-bottomed or springform cake tin, lightly greased and base-lined with baking parchment

Preheat the oven to 180°C/Gas mark 4. Rinse the sticky sugar syrup off the cherries in a sieve with a little warm water. Dry thoroughly with kitchen paper. Cut the cherries in half and set aside. Sift the flour into a mixing bowl and set aside.

In a mixing bowl, beat the butter with a wooden spoon or hand-held electric whisk until very light and creamy. Add the sugar and beat until light and fluffy. Add the eggs, one at a time, adding 1 tbsp flour with each and beating thoroughly before adding the next. Carefully fold in the remaining flour, using a large metal spoon. Fold in the ground almonds and sufficient milk to give a soft dropping consistency.

Spoon the mixture into the prepared tin, levelling it out with the back of the spoon. Drop the cake charm or coin into the mix.

Dust the work surface with icing sugar and roll out the marzipan to a 5mm thickness. Cut into strips 20cm x 1.5cm. Arrange these in a lattice pattern on top of the cake and lightly balance a cherry half in the centre of each of the lattice squares.

Bake in the oven for about 45 minutes, until a skewer inserted into the centre comes out clean. Leave to cool in the tin before turning out. This cake will keep for 2 weeks stored in an airtight tin.

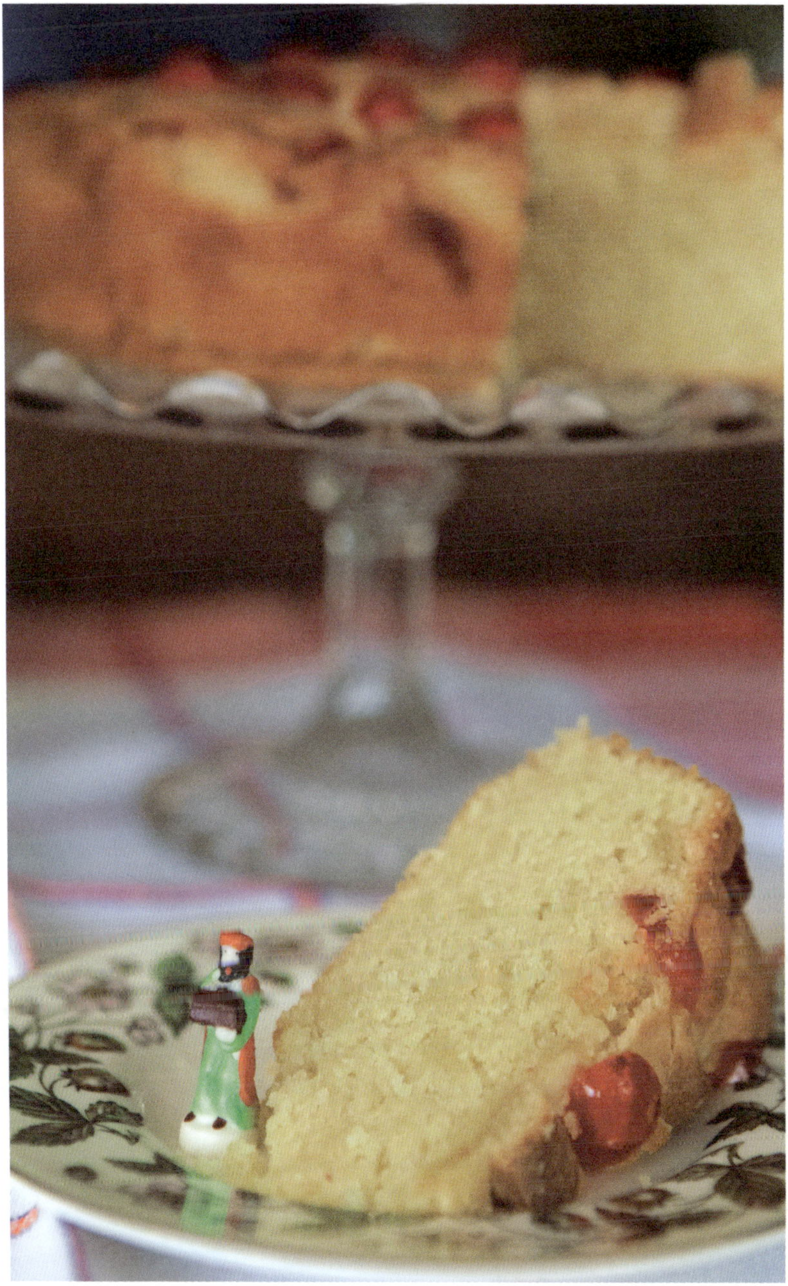

Useful Things

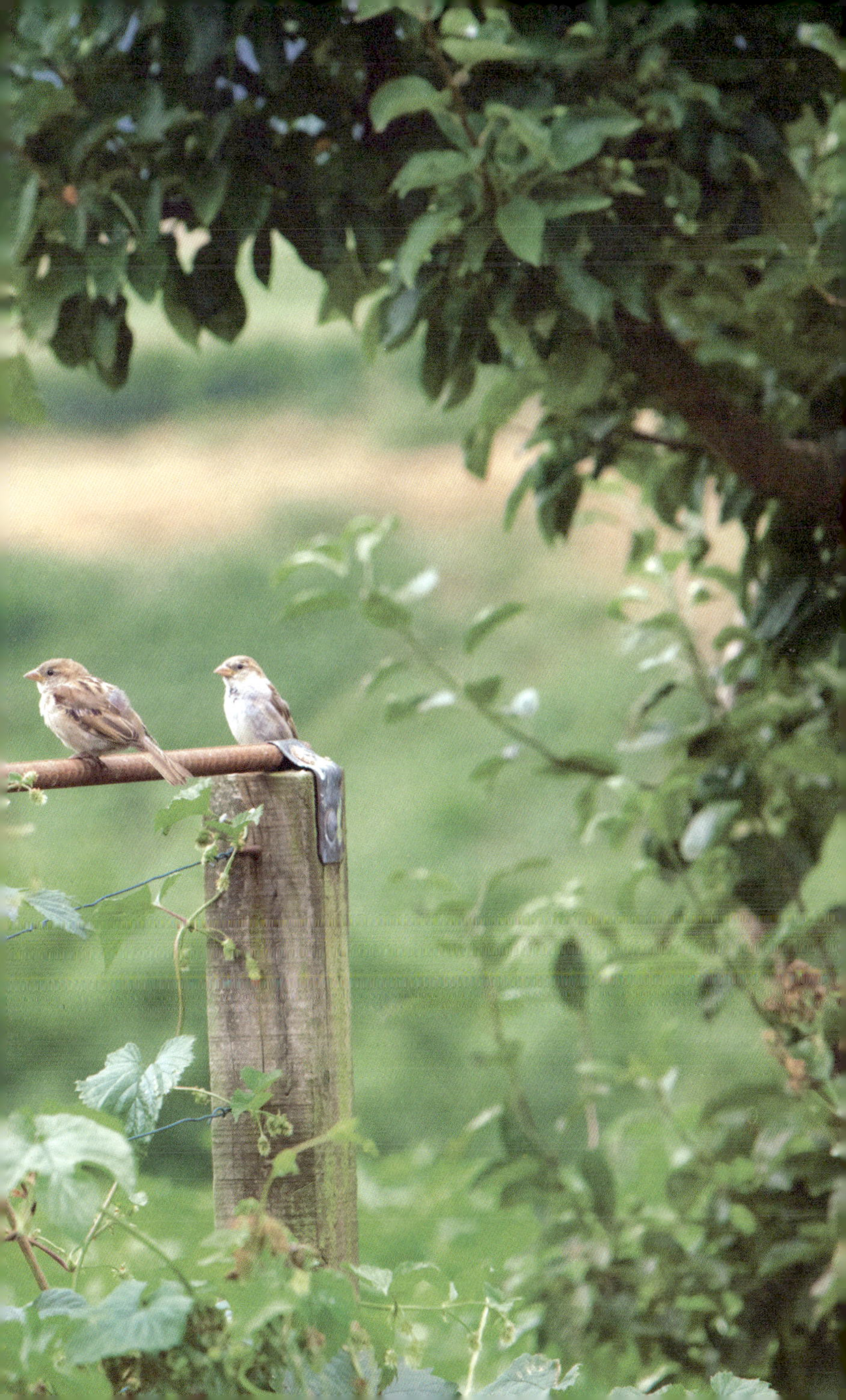

Directory

Bakeware and cooking equipment

Silverwood
www.alansilverwood.co.uk
0121 454 3571

Lakeland Ltd
www.lakeland.co.uk
01539 488100

Kitchen Craft
www.kitchencraft.co.uk
0121 604 6000

Specialist ingredients

Doves Farm
for specialist and organic flours
www.dovesfarm.co.uk
01488 684880

Marriage's
for fine wheat flour
www.marriagesmillers.co.uk
01245 354455

Sharpham Park
for British spelt flour
www.sharphampark.com
01458 844080

Bia Nua
for gluten-free cake flour
www.bianua.com
01460 298060

Billington's
for unrefined sugar
www.billingtons.co.uk
01733 422696

Steenbergs
for organic and fair-trade spices
and other baking ingredients
www.steenbergs.co.uk
01765 640088

Crazy Jack
for organic dried fruit
www.crazyjack.co.uk
01455 556878

Little Pod
for well-sourced vanilla extract/paste
www.littlepod.co.uk
01395 511243

Cocoa Loco
for organic chocolate
www.cocoaloco.co.uk
01403 865687

Green & Black's
for organic chocolate
www.greenandblacks.com
0800 8401000

The Somerset Cider Brandy Company
for English apple brandy
www.ciderbrandy.co.uk
01460 240782

Cakes, Cookies and Crafts
for cake cases and sugared decorations
www.cakescookiesandcraftsshop.co.uk
0845 61 71 810

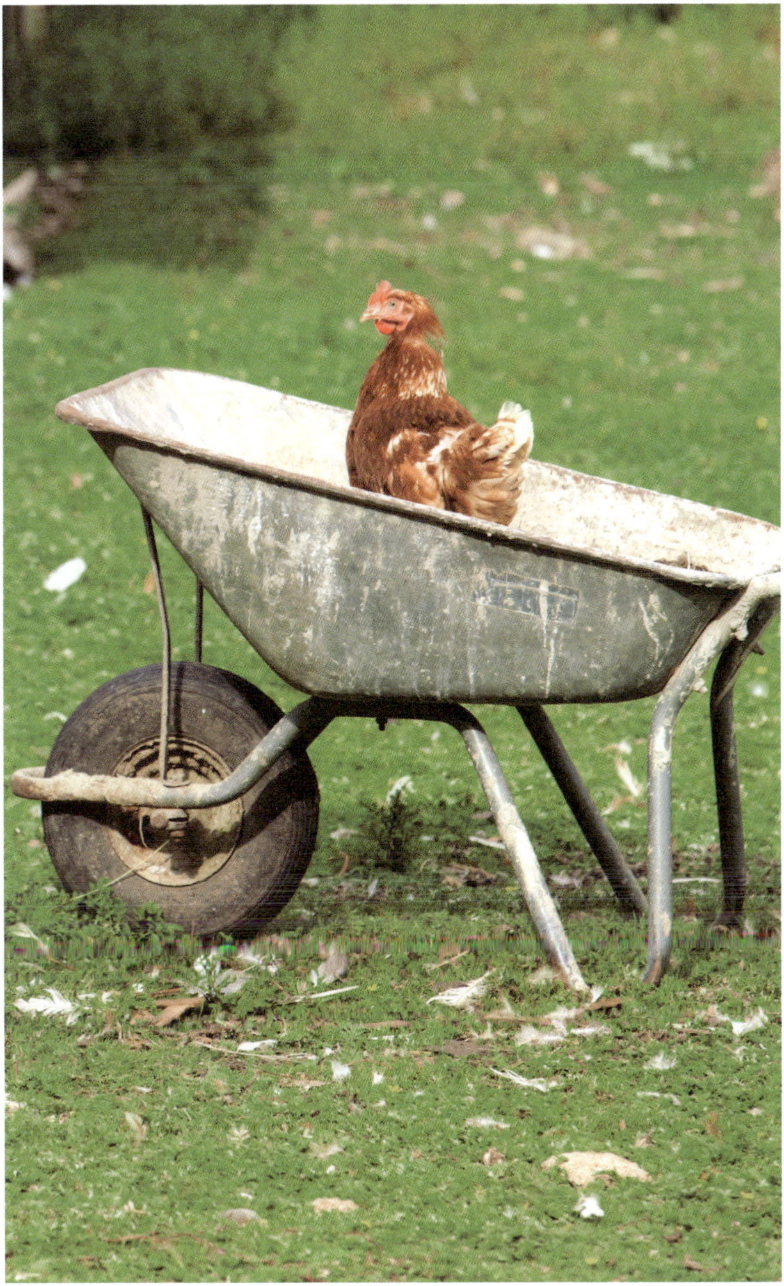

Conversion charts

Metric quantities are given in the recipes. Use the following conversions if you prefer to work in imperial measures.

Weight

Metric	Imperial
25g–30g	1oz
50g–60g	2oz
100g–125g	4oz
170g	6oz
200g	7oz
225g	8oz
275g	10oz
340g	12oz
400g	14oz
450g	1lb
500g	1lb 2oz
900g	2lb
1kg	2lb 4oz

Liquid/volume

Metric	Imperial
150ml	5fl oz (¼ pint)
300ml	10fl oz (½ pint)
600ml	20fl oz (1 pint)
1 litre	35fl oz (1¾ pints)

1 tsp (1 teaspoon) = 5ml
1 tbsp (1 tablespoon) = 15ml

What is a gill? This old-fashioned term often crops up in old recipe books and one gill is equivalent to 150ml or ¼ pint.

Liquid volume An average lemon will yield roughly 50ml lemon juice. Citrus fruits juice more easily if rolled by hand on a work surface for 2 or 3 minutes.

Oven temperatures

	°C	°F	Gas mark
Very cool	130	250	½
Very cool	140	275	1
Cool	150	300	2
Warm	160–170	325	3
Moderate	180	350	4
Fairly hot	190–200	375–400	5–6
Hot	210–220	425	7
Very Hot	230–240	450–475	8–9

For fan ovens, set the oven 10–20°C lower than indicated in the recipe.

Acknowledgements

I've always baked cakes, but it was only when John Wright (with three River Cottage handbooks under his belt), rather provokingly threw down the gauntlet and challenged me by saying, '*You can't write only one book in your life,*' that I was driven to thinking I could write a book about cakes. And what a joyful journey it's been, with many a happy hour spent in the kitchen, plus all those cakes to eat – thank you, John.

However, it goes without saying, the creation of this book has been far from me alone, but includes a rather wonderful collection of people who have contributed their professionalism – many have also taken on the vital role of 'honorary cake tasters'.

First of all, immense thanks to Gavin Kingcome – it's been simply brilliant to work with you again, Gavin, and your photography has truly illuminated my recipes. Huge thanks also to Nikki Duffy for her expertise, clear thinking and for ironing out any blunders.

Sincere thanks go to Bloomsbury literary experts Richard Atkinson and Natalie Hunt for their unflagging patience and encouragement. To Will Webb, for his inimitable style in bringing the book together. And to editor Janet Illsley for her warmth and absolute care in setting my mind at rest. Thanks also to Antony Topping for keeping a keen eye on the whole project.

A special thank you to Harcombe Farm hens for their constant supply of freshly laid golden-yolk eggs.

To family and friends who have generously given me tips, and those 'lovely hand-me-down recipes' to share with cake-makers the world over. To husband Hugh and daughters Pip and Maddy for never tiring of having to try *yet* another cake and for their obliging and much welcome kitchen porter skills. And again to Pip and also Trish Bye for valuable help on photo-shoot days.

I would like to thank Rob Love for his insight and commitment towards River Cottage.

And, finally, heartfelt thanks to Hugh FW – to you, Hugh, I owe so much for your boundless enthusiasm and inspiration – none of this could have happened without you.

Index

alexanders, candied 66
'all-in-one' method 39
almonds 32
  blanching 32
  caraway and orange cake 154
  certosino 237–9
  chocolate cake 134–5
  Dundee cake 203
  Gill's honey cake 147
  gooseberry friands 108
  Grasmere gingerbread 211
  Hugh's fresh cherry cake with streusel topping 174–5
  king cake 240
  marzipan 58–9
  old-fashioned cherry cake 142–3
  praline 33
  raspberry Battenberg cake 170–3
  Seville orange polenta cake 167
amaretti biscuits: Hallowe'en pumpkin cake 226
anchovy and French dressing muffins 105
angelica, candied 66
Anzac biscuits 81
apples 28
  apple cake 138
  'bird table' bread cake 193
  blackberry and apple muffins 106
  blue cheese, apple and honey muffins 105
  certosino 237–9
  'elevenses' lumberjack cake 194
  'mother' fruit cake 205–6
  potato and apple cake 182
  special day apple cake 138
  toffee apple cake 176
apricots, dried 31
  boil and bait fisherman's cake 198
  fruit, nut and honey bars 77
  prune and apricot stollen 233
  seasonal fresh fruit cake 196
  spelt, date, apricot and ginger rock cakes 78

Bake-O-Glide 16
'bake-off' cookies 93
'baker's dozen' 186
baking expressions 42–3
baking methods 37–9
baking papers 16
baking parchment 16, 40
baking powder 11, 21
baking tins 15–16
bananas: banana and chocolate cake 164
  banana bread 188
  banana breakfast muffins 102
bantam eggs 26
bara brith 190
Battenberg cake: chocolate and hazelnut Battenberg 173
  raspberry Battenberg cake 170–3
berries: glacé icing 55
  see also raspberries, strawberries, etc
bicarbonate of soda 11, 21
Bird, Alfred 11
'bird table' bread cake 193
birthday cakes 218
biscuits: Anzac biscuits 81
  'bake-off' cookies 93
  Bourbon biscuits 85
  Christmas tree biscuits 86–9
  Cornish fairings 94
  custard creams 85
  dog bone biscuits 90
  gingerbread men 89
  jammy dodgers 84–5
  Pip's hazelnut macaroons 115
  shortbread 82–3
Black Forest cake 135
blackberries: blackberry and apple muffins 106
  blackberry and semolina cake 181
blanching almonds 32
blitz method 39
blue cheese, apple and honey muffins 105
boil and bait fisherman's cake 198
bonfire night parkin 214
boozy icing 63
Bounty bar cake 163
Bourbon biscuits 85
bowls 12
brandy: boozy icing 63
  certosino 237–9
  special day apple cake 138
bread cake, 'bird table' 193
breakfast muffins 102–3
brown sugar 22, 23
brownies, my chocolate 110
butter 26–7
  baking methods 37
buttercream 48
  vanilla 49
butterfly cakes 96–7
buttermilk: chocolate cake 134–5
  cut and come again (spelt and pear fruit cake) 200
  plum upside-down cake 179

cake tins 45
  liners 16
candied angelica 66
candied peel 28
  certosino 237–9
caramel: caramel cream 51
  glacé icing 55

praline 33
  salt caramel shortbread 116
  toffee apple cake 176
caraway seeds 34
  caraway and orange cake 154
  Lancashire shortbread 83
cardamom cake 159
carrots 28
  carrot cake 141
  dog bone biscuits 90
  gnome cakes 99
caster sugar 22
  topping cakes with 52
certosino 237–9
cheese: blue cheese, apple and honey muffins 105
  cheese and Marmite muffins 105
  cream cheese topping 57
  leek and cheese Welsh cakes 72
cheesecake, vanilla 220–1
cherries: fresh cherry cake 143
  Hugh's fresh cherry cake with streusel topping 174–5
cherries, dried 31
cherries, glacé 31
  cherry and chocolate cake 143
  flapjacks 74
  hazelnut Florentines 118–19
  king cake 240
  old-fashioned cherry cake 142–3
  raisin and cherry stollen 230–3
chestnut flour 21
chestnut purée: hedgelog (Yule log) 228–9
chocolate 35
  'bake-off' cookies 93
  banana and chocolate cake 164
  Black Forest cake 135
  boozy icing 63
  Bounty bar cake 163
  Bourbon biscuits 85
  buttercream 49
  certosino 237–9
  cherry and chocolate cake 143
  chocolate and hazelnut Battenberg 173
  chocolate and peppermint cake 161
  chocolate cake 134–5
  chocolate-dipped shortbread 83
  chocolate fudge icing 63
  chocolate Swiss roll 157
  chocolate yoghurt topping 65
  classic chocolate chip cookies 93
  crème fraîche topping 65
  ganache 65
  Genoese sponge 128
  glacé icing 55
  hazelnut Florentines 118–19
  'Hebegebe' cake 163
  hedgelog (Yule log) 228–9
  icing 63
  leaves 48, 65
  marble cake 144
  mocha cake 223
  mocha icing 63
  my chocolate brownies 110
  Pip's hazelnut macaroons 115
  salt caramel shortbread 116
  'Seventies' chocolate roulade 229
  triple-layer smaller chocolate cake 135
  Victoria sandwich 127
  yoghurt and white chocolate topping 57
chopping nuts 32
Christmas: certosino 237–9
  Christmas cakelets 225
  Christmas cracker 151
  Christmas tree biscuits 86–9
  snowy Christmas cake 235
cider: Somerset cider cake with hazelnut topping 168–9
cider vinegar: vinegar cake 197
cinnamon 34
  cinnamon sugar 24
citrus fruits 27
  frosting 57
  glacé icing 55
  zesters 15
  see also lemon, oranges, etc
cocoa powder 35
  topping cakes with 52
  see also chocolate
coconut 31
  Anzac biscuits 81
  Bounty bar cake 163
  'elevenses' lumberjack cake 194
  glacé icing 55
  lime and coconut cake (gluten free) 150–1
  seasonal fresh fruit cake 196
coffee: buttercream 49
  coffee and walnut cake 132–3
  glacé icing 55
  meringues 113
  mocha cake 223
  mocha icing 63
  streusel-topped coffee cake 133
  Victoria sandwich 127
Cointreau: boozy icing 63
colouring marzipan 59
condensed milk: caramel cream 51
conversion charts 246–7
cookies, 'bake-off' 93
cooling racks 15
cornflakes: Anzac biscuits 81
cornflour 20
Cornish fairings 94

courgettes 28
   courgette and ginger dog bone biscuits 90
   gnome cakes 99
   'Hebegebe' cake 163
cranberries, dried 31
cream: caramel cream 51
   chocolate ganache 65
   meringutan 51
cream cheese topping 57
cream of tartar 21
creamed cakes 45
creaming method 37
crème fraîche: cardamom cake 159
   chocolate crème fraîche topping 65
crystallised flowers 66
cup cakes, Victoria 127
cupcake papers 16
curdling 42
currants 31
   'bird table' bread cake 193
   currant and lemon rock cakes 78
   Welsh cakes 72
   see also dried fruits
custard, rhubarb pudding cake with 180–1
custard creams 85
cut and come again (spelt and pear fruit cake) 200

dates 31
   'elevenses' lumberjack cake 194
   fruit, nut and honey bars 77
   malted fruit loaf 192
   spelt, date, apricot and ginger rock cakes 78
decorations 48
   chocolate leaves 65
   edible flowers 65–6
   marzipan shapes 59
demerara sugar 23
dog bone biscuits 90
doneness, testing for 44
dried fruits 31
   bara brith 190
   cut and come again (spelt and pear fruit cake) 200
   fruit, nut and honey bars 77
   'mother' fruit cake 205–6
   Simnel cakelets 224–5
   see also currants, raisins, *etc*
dripping 27
drizzles 48
dropping consistency 42
duck eggs 26
Dundee cake 203

Earl Grey tea: glacé icing 55
   wholemeal orange cake with Earl Grey icing 136–7
edible wafer paper 16
egg whites: folding in 42

   freezing 26
eggs 25–6
   curdling 42
   smoked salmon and egg breakfast muffins 103
   whisking method 37–9
elderflowers 35
   glacé icing 55
electric mixers 12
'elevenses' lumberjack cake 194
equipment 12–16

fairings, Cornish 94
fairy cake papers 16
fairy cakes 96–7
family 'hun-ger' cake 208
fatless sponges 45
fats 26–7
   muffins 100
feather icing 56
figs, dried 31
   boil and bait fisherman's cake 198
fillers 49–51
fisherman's cake 198
flapjacks 74
flavoured sugars 23–4
Florentines, hazelnut 118–19
flour 19–21
   dusting tins with 39
   folding in 42
   sifting 44
flowers 35, 48
   crystallised flowers 66
   as decorations 65–6
folding in 42
fondant icing 61
freezing: cakes 45
   egg whites 26
friands, gooseberry 108
frosting, citrus 57
fruit 28–31
   'bird table' bread cake 193
   citrus fruits 27
   fruity fresh muffins 107
   muffins 100
   see also apples, raspberries, *etc*
fruit cakes 45, 184–206
   boil and bait fisherman's cake 198
   cut and come again (spelt and pear fruit cake) 200
   Dundee cake 203
   'elevenses' lumberjack cake 194
   Mojita fruit cake 206
   'mother' fruit cake 205–6
   seasonal fresh fruit cake 196
   Simnel cakelets 224–5
   snowy Christmas cake 235
   Somerset cider cake with hazelnut topping 168–9

vinegar cake 197
see also tea breads
fruit, nut and honey bars 77
fudge icing, chocolate 63

ganache, chocolate 65
garland moulds 40
garlic *see* wild garlic
Genoese sponge 128
geranium leaves *see* rose-scented geranium leaves
gill 246
Gillian's sticky gingerbread 212
Gill's honey cake 147
ginger 35
 bonfire night parkin 214
 certosino 237–9
 Christmas tree biscuits 86–9
 Cornish fairings 94
 courgette and ginger dog bone biscuits 90
 family 'hun-ger' cake 208
 Gillian's sticky gingerbread 212
 ginger cookies 93
 gingerbread 186
 gingerbread men 89
 Grasmere gingerbread 211
 hazelnut Florentines 118–19
 spelt, date, apricot and ginger rock cakes 78
glacé cherries *see* cherries, glacé
glacé icing 55
 feather icing 56
gluten, in flour 19, 20
gluten-free flours 21
gnome cakes, 'veg patch' 99
golden syrup 23
 bonfire night parkin 214
 Gillian's sticky gingerbread 212
 golden syrup cake 148
 malted fruit loaf 192
 measuring 94
goose eggs 26
gooseberry friands 108
Goosnargh shortbread 83
granulated sugar 22
Grasmere gingerbread 211
graters 15
greaseproof paper 16
greasing tins 39
grinding nuts 33

Hallowe'en pumpkin cake 226
harlequin stollen 233
hazelnuts 32–3
 'bake-off' cookies 93
 chocolate and hazelnut Battenberg 173
 chocolate Swiss roll 157
 hazelnut Florentines 118–19

 Pip's hazelnut macaroons 115
 praline 33
 seasonal fresh fruit cake 196
 shortbread 83
 skinning 32–3
 Somerset cider cake with hazelnut topping 168–9
'Hebegebe' cake 163
hedgelog (Yule log) 228–9
herbs 35
honey 23
 blue cheese, apple and honey muffins 105
 buttercream 49
 certosino 237–9
 family 'hun-ger' cake 208
 fruit, nut and honey bars 77
 Gill's honey cake 147
 plum upside-down cake 179
 raisin and honey flapjacks 74
 Welsh cakes 72
Hugh's fresh cherry cake with streusel topping 174–5
'hun-ger' cake 208

icing sugar 24
 topping cakes with 52
icings 48
 boozy icing 63
 chocolate fudge icing 63
 chocolate ganache 65
 chocolate icing 63
 feather icing 56
 fondant icing 61
 glacé icing 55
 mocha icing 63
 royal icing 60
ingredients 19–35

jam: Black Forest cake 135
 filling cakes 49
 jammy dodgers 84–5
 raspberry Battenberg cake 170–3
 Victoria sandwich 124–7
jammy dodgers 84–5
jasmine tea: glacé icing 55
jugs, measuring 14

king cake 240

Lancashire shortbread 83
lavender: lavender sugar 24
 scent from heaven cake 161
leaves, chocolate 48, 65
 see also rose-scented geranium leaves
leek and cheese Welsh cakes 72
lemon: candied peel 28
 currant and lemon rock cakes 78
 frosting 57

glacé icing 55
lemon curd 50
lemon sugar 24
'men only' lemon drizzle 149
St Clement's cake 151
scent from heaven cake 161
Swiss roll with poppy seeds and lemon curd filling 156–7
zesty lemon Madeira cake 130
lemon verbena 35, 40
scent from heaven cake 160–1
limes: frosting 57
glacé icing 55
lime and coconut cake (gluten free) 150–1
lining papers 16
lining tins 39–40
linseeds: 'bird table' bread cake 193
loaf tins, lining 40
lovers' shortbread 83
lumberjack cake 194

macaroons, Pip's hazelnut 115
Madeira cake, zesty lemon 130
malted fruit loaf 192
maple syrup: walnut and maple syrup flapjacks 74
marble cake 144
margarine 27
marmalade: Dundee cake 203
marmalade breakfast muffins 103
Marmite: cheese and Marmite muffins 105
Marsala: certosino 237–9
marshmallows: Hallowe'en pumpkin cake 226
marzipan 58–9
colouring 59
king cake 240
raisin and cherry stollen 230–3
raspberry Battenberg cake 170–3
shapes 59
Simnel cakelets 224–5
snowy Christmas cake 235
toasting 59
measurements, conversion charts 246–7
measuring jugs 14
measuring spoons 14
Mellor, Gill 147
melting method 39
'men only' lemon drizzle 149
meringues 112–13
merringutan 51
metal spoons 14
milk: muffins 100
mincemeat: mincemeat cake 149
muffins 107
Welsh cakes 72
mint 35
chocolate and peppermint cake 161

mixed spice 34
mixers, electric 12
mixing bowls 12
mocha cake 223
mocha icing 63
Mojita fruit cake 206
molasses 23
mopping up muffins 103
'mother' fruit cake 205–6
muesli flapjacks 74
muffin papers 16
muffins 45, 100–7
banana breakfast muffins 102
blackberry and apple muffins 106
savoury muffins 104–5
wild garlic and cheese muffins 104
muscovado sugar 22, 23
my chocolate brownies 110

non-wheat flours 20–1
nutmeg 34
nuts 32–3
buttercream 49
chopping 32
fruit, nut and honey bars 77
grinding 33
see also almonds, walnuts, *etc*

oats 21
Anzac biscuits 81
bonfire night parkin 214
dog bone biscuits 90
flapjacks 74
fruit, nut and honey bars 77
Grasmere gingerbread 211
oatmeal and raisin cookies 93
seasonal fresh fruit cake 196
oils 27
for muffins 100
old-fashioned cherry cake 142–3
orange flower water 35
orange liqueur: Christmas cracker 151
oranges: candied peel 28
caraway and orange cake 154
frosting 57
glacé icing 55
orange sugar 24
St Clement's cake 151
Seville orange polenta cake 167
wholemeal orange cake with Earl Grey icing 136–7
ovens: temperatures 44, 247
thermometers 15

papers, lining 16
parkin, bonfire night 214

parsnips 28
  gnome cakes 99
party cakes 216–41
pears 28
  cut and come again (spelt and pear fruit cake) 200
  hazelnut Florentines 118–19
peel, candied 28
peppermint 35
  chocolate and peppermint cake 161
pineapple, dried: Mojita fruit cake 206
Pip's hazelnut macaroons 115
plain flour 19, 21
plums: plum upside-down cake 179
  seasonal fresh fruit cake 196
polenta 20
  Seville orange polenta cake 167
poppy seeds 34
  muffins 107
  Swiss roll with poppy seeds and lemon curd filling 156–7
potato and apple cake 182
potato starch flour 21
pound cake 122
praline 33
prunes 31
  prune and apricot stollen 233
pumpkin: Hallowe'en pumpkin cake 226
  'veg patch' gnome cakes 99

quince: certosino with quince 239

racks, cooling 15
raising agents 21
raisins 31
  banana bread 188
  'bird table' bread cake 193
  boil and bait fisherman's cake 198
  certosino 237–9
  oatmeal and raisin cookies 93
  raisin and cherry stollen 230–3
  raisin and honey flapjacks 74
  rock cakes 78
  Somerset cider cake with hazelnut topping 168–9
  vinegar cake 197
  see also dried fruits
rapeseed oil 27
raspberries: glacé icing 55
  raspberry and rice cake 181
  raspberry Battenberg cake 170–3
rhubarb 28
  rhubarb pudding cake with custard 180–1
ribbon consistency 43
rice flour 20
  raspberry and rice cake 181
rice, ground: scent from heaven cake 160–1
ring moulds 40

rock cakes 78
rose-scented geranium leaves 35, 40
  rose-scented geranium sugar 24
  scent from heaven cake 161
rose water 35
  lovers' shortbread 83
rosehips: glacé icing 55
roulade, 'Seventies' chocolate 229
round tins, lining 40
royal icing 60
  snowy Christmas cake 235
rubbing-in method 37
rum: raisin and cherry stollen 230–3

St Clement's cake 151
salt 35
  salt caramel shortbread 116
scales 12
scent from heaven cake 160–1
seasonal fresh fruit cake 196
seeds: 'bird table' bread cake 193
  fruit, nut and honey bars 77
self-raising flour 19, 21
semolina: blackberry and semolina cake 181
'Seventies' chocolate roulade 229
Seville orange polenta cake 167
shortbread 82–3
  salt caramel shortbread 116
sieves 14
sifting flour 44
silicone baking moulds 16
Simnel cakelets 224–5
skinning nuts 32–3
smoked salmon and egg breakfast muffins 103
snowy Christmas cake 235
soft brown sugar 22, 23
Somerset cider cake with hazelnut topping 168–9
soured cream: marble cake 144
  smoked salmon and egg breakfast muffins 103
spatulas 14
special day apple cake 138
spelt flour 20
  cut and come again (spelt and pear fruit cake) 200
  spelt, date, apricot and ginger rock cakes 78
spices 34–5
Spong, Kerri 224
sponge cakes: baking methods 37–9
  fatless sponges 45
  Genoese sponge 128
  Victoria sandwich 124–7
spoons 12, 14
springform tins 15
square tins, lining 40
stencils, icing sugar 52
stollen, raisin and cherry 230–3

storage: cakes 45
  flour 20
  spices 34
strawberries: glacé icing 55
  strawberry shortbread 83
  vanilla cheesecake 220–1
streusel: Hugh's fresh cherry cake with streusel topping 174–5
  streusel-topped coffee cake 133
sugar 22–4
  candied angelica 66
  creaming method 37
  crystallised flowers 66
  muffins 100
  whisking method 37–9
sultanas 31
  carrot cake 141
  Dundee cake 203
  malted fruit loaf 192
  special day apple cake 138
  vinegar cake 197
  see also dried fruits
sunflower oil 27
sunflower seeds: 'bird table' bread cake 193
sweeteners 22–4
Swiss roll: chocolate Swiss roll 157
  lining tins 40
  Swiss roll with poppy seeds and lemon curd filling 156–7
  traditional Swiss roll 157
syrups 23

tangerines: Christmas cracker 151
  frosting 57
tea: glacé icing 55
  wholemeal orange cake with Earl Grey icing 136–7
tea breads: banana bread 188
  bara brith 190
  malted fruit loaf 192
  see also fruit cakes
techniques 37–9
testing for doneness 44
thermometers, oven 15
thyme shortbread 83
tins: baking tins 15–16
  cake tins 45
  lining 39–40
toasting marzipan 59
toffee apple cake 176
toppers 52–66
treacle 23
  bonfire night parkin 214
  Gillian's sticky gingerbread 212
triple-layer smaller chocolate cake 135
turning out cakes 43

upside-down cake, plum 179

vanilla 34
  buttercream 49
  vanilla cheesecake 220–1
  vanilla sugar 23, 24
'veg patch' gnome cakes 99
vegetable oils 27
vegetables 28
Victoria cup cakes 127
Victoria sandwich 124–7
vinegar cake 197

wafer paper, edible 16
walnuts 33
  certosino 237–9
  coffee and walnut cake 132–3
  Somerset cider cake with hazelnut topping 168–9
  streusel-topped coffee cake 133
  walnut and maple syrup flapjacks 74
warming method 39
water icing 55
weights, conversion charts 246
Welsh cakes 72
wheat flour 19–20
wheat-free flours 21
whisking method 37–9
whisks, electric 12
whisky: Dundee cake 203
white chocolate 35
  yoghurt and white chocolate topping 57
white flour 20
wholemeal flour 19, 20
wholemeal orange cake with Earl Grey icing 136–7
wild garlic and cheese muffins 104
wire cooling racks 15
wooden spoons 12

xanthan gum 21
  lime and coconut cake 150–1

yoghurt: banana and chocolate cake 164
  caraway and orange cake 154
  chocolate yoghurt topping 65
  family 'hun-ger' cake 208
  golden syrup cake 148
  'Hebegebe' cake 163
  muffins 100
  rhubarb pudding cake with custard 180–1
  yoghurt and white chocolate topping 57
  yoghurt-topped flapjacks 74
Yule log 228–9

zest, citrus fruits 27
zesters 15
zesty lemon Madeira cake 130

INDEX 255

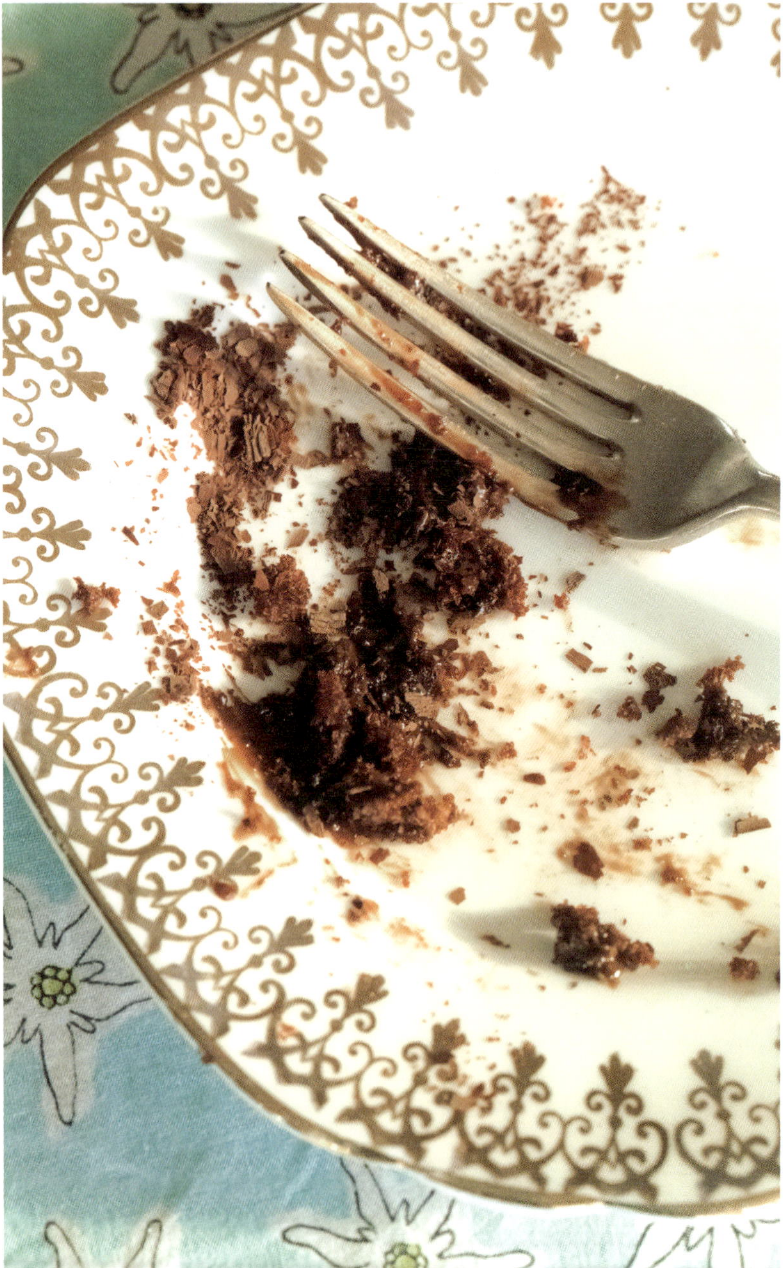

The River Cottage

Fruit Handbook

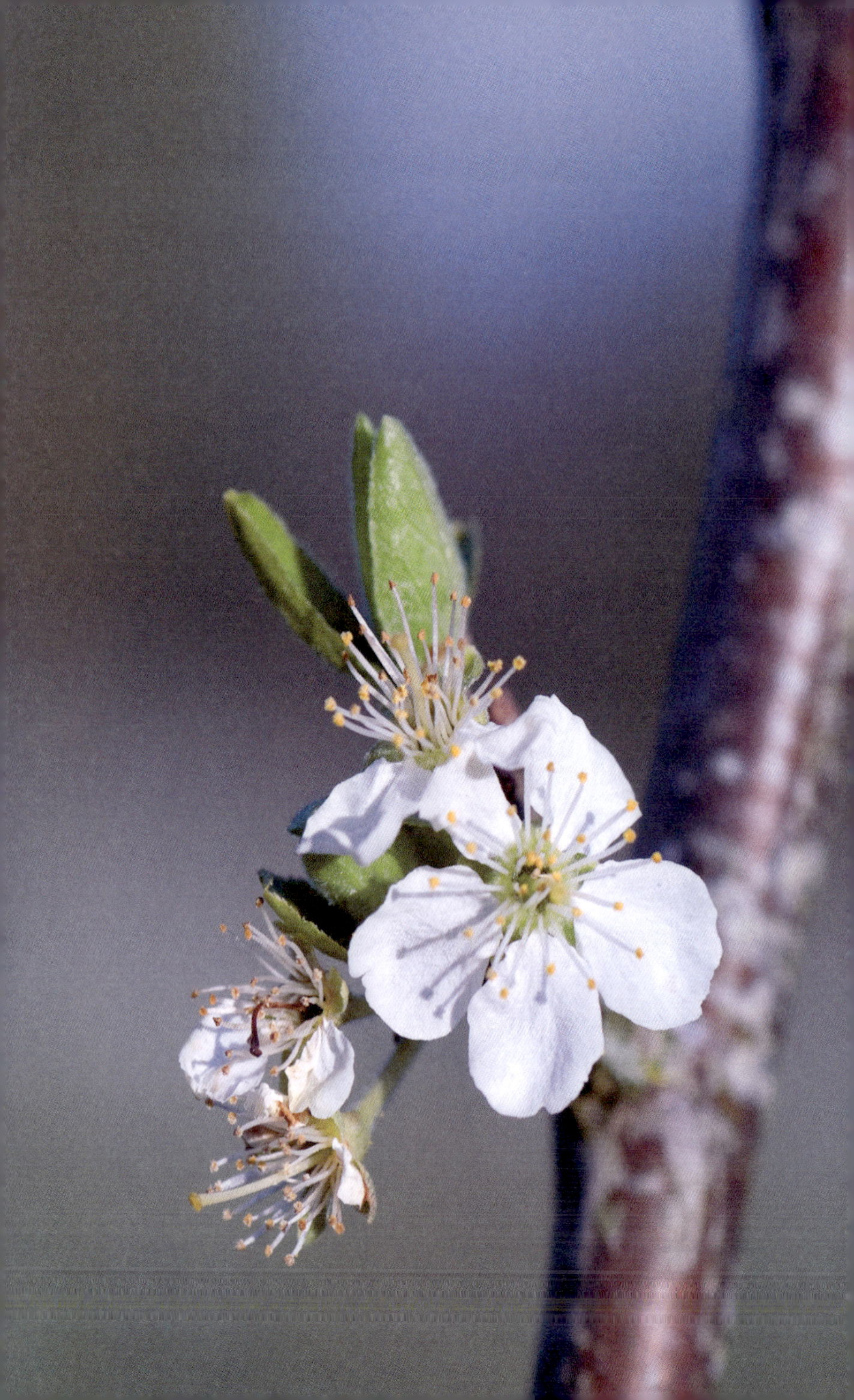

The River Cottage Fruit Handbook

by Mark Diacono

with an introduction by
Hugh Fearnley-Whittingstall

www.rivercottage.net

BLOOMSBURY
LONDON · NEW DELHI · NEW YORK · SYDNEY

For my mum

First published in Great Britain 2011
This paperback edition published 2012

Text and photography copyright © 2011 by Mark Diacono
Illustrations © 2011 by Toby Atkins

The moral right of the author has been asserted

Bloomsbury Publishing Plc, 50 Bedford Square, London WC1B 3DP
Bloomsbury Publishing, London, New Delhi, New York and Sydney

A CIP catalogue record for this book is available from the British Library

ISBN 978 1 4088 3613 2
10 9 8 7 6 5 4 3 2 1

Project Editor: Janet Illsley
Designer: Will Webb
Illustrator: Toby Atkins

Printed in China by C&C Offset Printing Co., Ltd.

MIX
Paper from responsible sources
FSC® C008047

While every effort has been made to ensure the accuracy of the information contained in this book, in no circumstances can the publisher or the author accept any legal responsibility or liability for any loss or damage (including damage to property and/or personal injury) arising from any error in or omission from the information contained in this book, or from the failure of the reader to properly and accurately follow any instructions contained in the book.

www.bloomsbury.com/rivercottage

Contents

Growing your own Fruit	8
Fruit A–Z	28
Sourcing & Creating your Plants	122
Planning, Preparation & Planting	136
Caring for your Plants	148
Growing in Containers & Under Cover	182
Recipes	192
Useful Things	246

It's no secret that I'm an absolute fruit fiend. I revel in the stuff, I am in awe of its utter deliciousness and its evolutionary neatness. If one food was designed, unambiguously, to be eaten, then surely it has to be fruit. We consume it, we spread the seed, more fruit grows, everyone's happy. It's in Nature's best interests to make it as enticing as possible and she's certainly done so. Fruit is a real treat that often needs no embellishment and is resoundingly, unequivocally good for us. Mark Diacono's first River Cottage handbook, *Veg Patch*, was a joy: a thorough, yet accessible guide to raising homegrown produce that has established Mark as one of the foremost thinkers and writers on the subject of growing what you eat. Now he's turned his attention to fruit and, as you're about to discover, has written another confidence-inspiring, anxiety-reducing little gem… or perhaps that should be little peach.

It's no mean feat, because getting people to grow their own fruit presents particular challenges. In many ways it's the last frontier of domestic horticulture. While there's been a revolution in the growing of vegetables and herbs in the UK in recent years, home fruit growing has lagged a little behind. I suspect this is because there's a certain air of mystery attached to growing fruit, a sense that specialist knowledge and hard-won skills must be acquired before one can make a go of it. Also, being that much more delicate and squashable than a celeriac or a carrot, a raspberry or a plum can appear to need rather more cosseting. In his gardening courses at River Cottage, I've seen Mark banish these myths and give people the confidence to start producing their own berries, apples, plums, melons and apricots. This book, I know, will do the same thing. As Mark explains, fruit wants to grow – you just have to let it – and he's here to show you how.

It's a common mantra – and how could I not endorse it – that we should all be eating fruit every day, ideally several times a day. It is one of the easiest ways to add goodness, sweetness, colour and flavour to our diets. More than any other food, it makes us feel good in body and soul. Yet so often our fruit hails from far afield, cling-wrapped and air-freighted from some tropical clime, or super-chilled in little plastic punnets and transported from the far end of the country. I'm not about to advocate that we all give up bananas and oranges, but there are so many fruits that can grow successfully in our own backyards, and I think we should give them precedence. Buying seasonal British fruit from a local farm shop, a pick-your-own farm or a good greengrocer is a very sound choice. But there is no more sustainable, and no more pleasing way to put fruit on the table than to grow it yourself.

I believe that everyone should have some fruit growing within their reach, for at least part of the year. You don't even need a garden to achieve this: a couple of blueberry bushes in a big pot on a patio, or a window box of alpine strawberries, is easy to maintain and delightful to plunder. If you have even a small garden, you can do much more: tiny plots can foster small, but very productive fruit trees, as well as compact currant bushes. Your location needn't hold you back either. In fact, as Mark points out, the urban or suburban gardener often has an advantage over the rural dweller when it comes to fruit growing. A sun-trap patio or roof garden can provide a microclimate where nectarines, apricots or greengages will flourish much more readily than they would in a windswept country acre. If you have anything approaching a regular-sized veg patch you can easily produce more fruit than you can immediately eat: a moderate garden can comfortably support a plum, a pear and an apple tree, plus several soft fruit bushes. Providing you get the hang of storing apples (not difficult, as Mark explains), and if you have a freezer, this can give you fruit from the end of May until well after Christmas.

In the first instance, I hope you will greedily peruse this book as one would a menu. Feast your eyes on the many different varieties of fruit that can be grown in this country and then think about the ones that appeal most to you. Mark's perennial advice, which I heartily second, is that you should only grow what you like to eat. But with that in mind, you may want to ask yourself: are you sure you know what you like to eat? Or, to put it another way, keep an open mind, and an open mouth! It's easy to dismiss a lot of fruit – even strawberries, plums and pears – if you've only ever tried one bland, under-ripe supermarket variety. But a sun-warmed 'Royal Sovereign' strawberry or a perfectly ripe 'Doyenne du Comice' pear could completely change your mind.

And if you think you don't like apples, I'd have to suggest that you simply haven't met the right apple for you yet. There are hundreds of varieties to choose from. I'm a bit of an apple fascist myself, favouring the crisp and the sharp – nothing soft, woolly or too sweet for me – so I grow the delectable 'Ashmead's Kernel' in my garden, as well as 'Orleans Reinette', 'Blenheim Orange' and 'Lord Lambourne'. I'm lucky to have the space to do that, but it's possible now, through the wonders of modern grafting techniques, to have an apple tree which produces up to four different varieties of apple. You could produce Cox's, Bramleys, Russets and, dare I say, 'Ashmead's Kernel', all on one bit of tailormade rootstock.

I reckon there's a latent fruit grower lurking in all of us, even if we don't know it yet. This book, shot through as it is with Mark's customary 'just do it' attitude, will surely release it. Never one to let the grass grow under his feet, or to beat around the (gooseberry) bush, Mark demonstrates that fruit growing is neither an arcane science or a hopeless fantasy, but an entirely do-able and unbelievably satisfying undertaking that will enrich your life, and your diet, in untold ways. So never mind the skin and pips – they're all part of the pleasure – just take a big bite of luscious, fruity flesh, and let the juice trickle down your chin.

Hugh Fearnley-Whittingstall, East Devon, May 2011

Growing your own Fruit

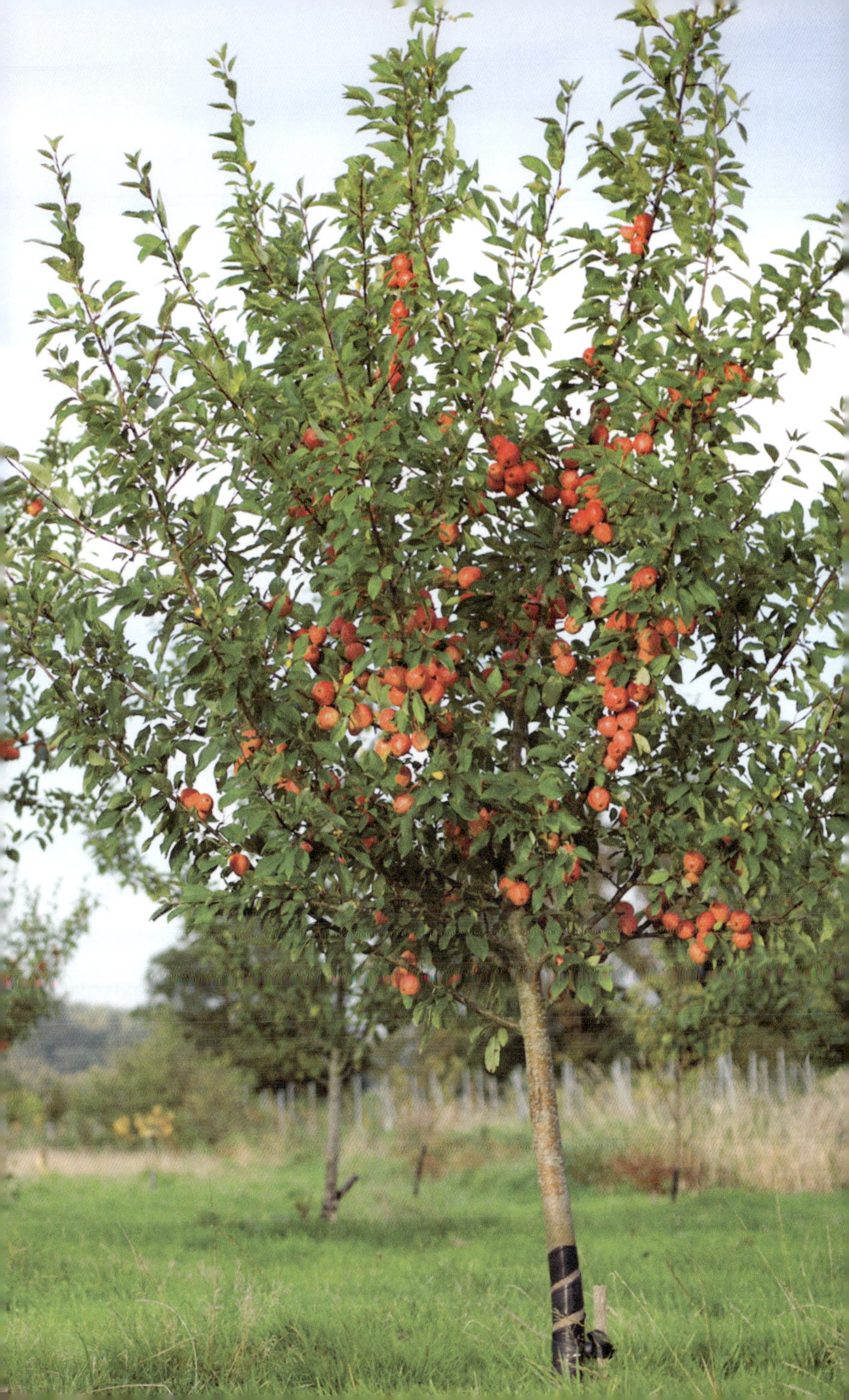

The taste of homegrown

juicy peaches, aromatic plums, crisp bright early apples and the sweet-sharp of the summer's strawberries are, I promise you, some of life's richest pleasures. The depth of flavour, scent and succulence that comes with your own fruit, enjoyed in the garden that grew it, is so far from the fruit you can buy that, once tasted, you'll be reluctant to go back.

You'll find yourself trying to squeeze in a currant here, a berry there or a fan-trained tree against a wall. Even a few pots of fruit can open a whole world of flavour that's exclusive to the home grower. Mulberries, Japanese wineberries, damsons and medlars are rarely, if ever, in the shops. Even apples, the commonest of the tree fruit, can be a revelation grown at home as you can take your pick from thousands of varieties to suit your taste buds and your location.

And if you get it right you can enjoy something different every month: forced rhubarb from March, stone fruit, berries and currants in the summertime, through to autumn with the late ripeners – grapes and figs among them – and into winter with quince, medlars and the stored-to-ripen apples and pears.

Add to that the pleasures of preserving some of those flavours in jams, chutneys, leathers, syrups, vodkas and vinegars and you'll be enjoying your own fruit for months, if not years ahead.

Flavour isn't the only reward. You may find that the fruit you pick isn't so much the whole point of growing it as one of a chain of pleasures that comes along the way. The medlar's lazy flowers, the house-filling perfume of ripening quince and the shock of cherry blossom across a tree in spring lift the soul as much as any ornamental plant.

Starting up can be more costly with fruit than it is for vegetables. There are trees and bushes that you may wish to buy, some tools too, but most fruit plants deliver for years and investment now will save you a fortune over time. After the initial outlay you'll be in for virtually free harvests year after year. Fruit is generally expensive to buy and growing your own insulates you against rising prices, while giving you the finest fruit there is.

Fruit is a longer game than veg, so take time to consider what you're planting. You can always drop vegetables after a summer of fun but with fruit it's marriage. Planting a bush or a tree makes a statement – it says I'm here and I intend to stay... or at the very least, I'm here and I care enough about those who follow to plant this tree. You choose, plant and care for something that could be with you for years, generations even.

It's not one-way traffic though. Grow some fruit and we are, of course, falling for the oldest trick in the book. Like most plants, a fruit plant produces seeds in the hope of succeeding in its one true aim – to replicate itself. If all those seeds fell in the shade of the parent's branches, the competition and lack of light would doom most to failure, so plants have developed strategies for getting the seeds

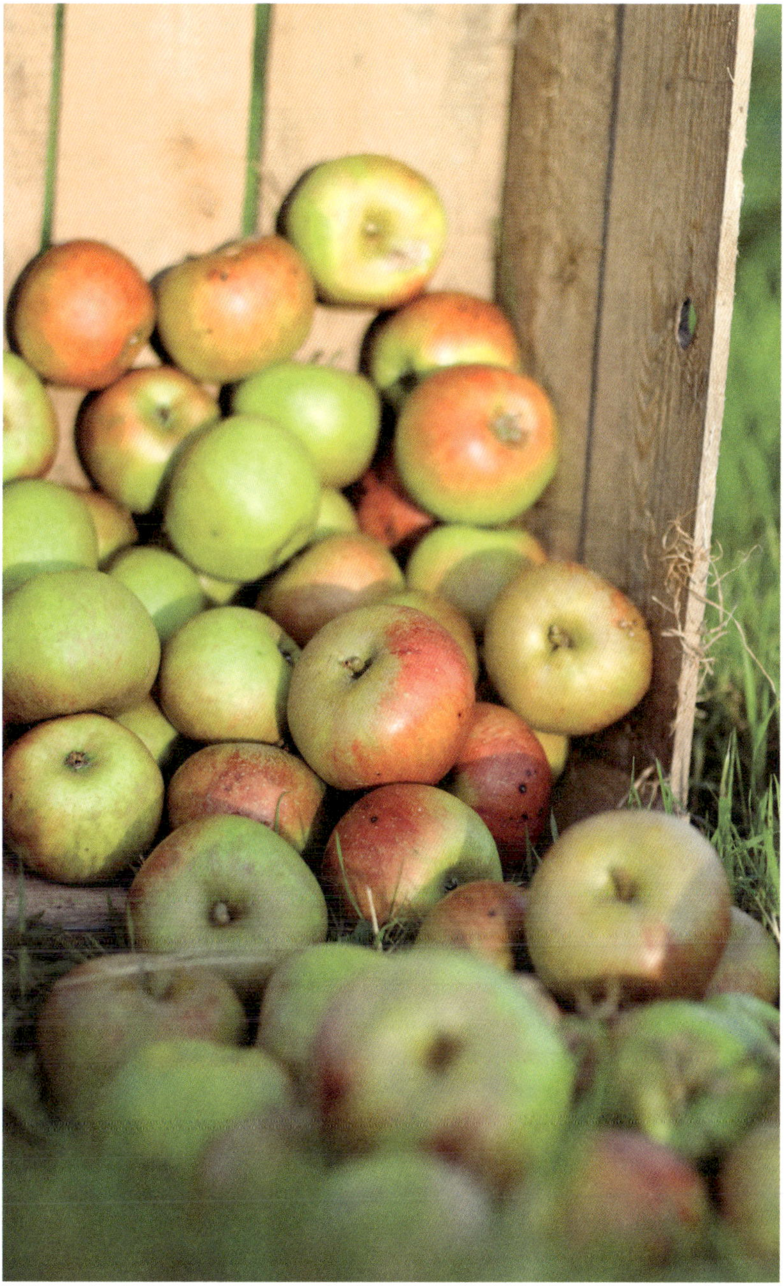

further afield. Some use the wind, others hitch a ride on the fur of passing animals, while many produce a delicious coating around the seed which entices wild animals and us humans to tuck in. We devour the fruit largely oblivious that it is at its peak of delicious ripeness precisely because the seed is in the ideal state for travel. We sink our teeth in and the discarded or excreted seeds make it beyond the umbrella of the plant. It is the perfect bribe and everybody wins.

Fruit is naturally low carbon. Almost all fruit plants are perennial – they grow and produce year after year rather than being sown afresh every spring as most vegetables are. There's no need to buy fresh seed nor cultivate the soil each year, and once the plant is established it has the engine room below ground and above to get on with growing quickly when the starter's gun fires in spring.

Where a veg patch needs constant input, most fruit gets by with minimal care. As a result, perennials are much more capable than annual plants of growing well without man-made fertilisers. This is an important point. Our reliance on fossil fuels is the major cause of climate change and the way we feed ourselves accounts for almost a third of our carbon footprint. So reliant are we on the man-made fertilisers (made with vast quantities of oil and water) and so extended is the supply chain from plot to plate that for every unit of energy we gain from our food, we use 10 units in growing it and getting it to our table.

Growing fruit also offers a more secure food supply. Ninety per cent of the fruit we eat in the UK is imported. If that doesn't shock you or you think that figure may be comprised mainly of exotic fruit that we are unable to grow for ourselves, bear in mind that three-quarters of our apples – a fruit perfectly suited to growing in our climate – come from overseas, while many of our orchards stand with their fruit unharvested. It's an extraordinary state of affairs and one that leaves us vulnerable to shortages and rising prices elsewhere, especially when most of the chemicals and energy we use to grow fruit in the UK is also imported.

Growing your own fruit may seem insignificant in the face of such global issues, but it is millions of tiny votes cast every day when we shop that has given us such a carbon-heavy food supply. Each time we grow a little it is a vote for a future which has a local, low-carbon diet at its heart. And local doesn't get any more local than homegrown.

'Local' even tastes better. Of the thousands of apple varieties we can feast on, we make do largely with a handful of long-life so-so favourites, such as Fuji, which can last for 6 months with refrigeration. Symmetrical and unblotched, they are visually seductive, they even taste ok, but when there are so many outstanding apples out there, why settle for ok? It's a similar story for pears, plums and many others. Local varieties suit local conditions and they tend to do well without chemical inputs, while adding biodiversity value and character to the landscape. It's a winner on every level.

Of course we can't hope to grow all the fruit we eat, but growing what best suits our soils and climate, while still trading for the lemons, oranges and other exotics that can't be grown (at least sustainably) in this country, has to be part of how we feed ourselves in the future. And you planting some fruit is a real step towards it.

This is a food book, driven by how we use fruit in the kitchen. It wasn't written in Pedants' Corner. You know what makes a fruit a fruit and a vegetable a vegetable – and tomatoes are most definitely not in this book. My aim is to help and encourage you to grow some fruit and to make the experience as trouble-free and delicious as possible. I could have happily written a book for each fruit but what you have in your hands is a guide to what you have to do, some of the important options and as much personal experience as it seems sensible to impart.

I have offered you a few ideas of what to do with each fruit to get the best out of them in the kitchen, plus some recipes which are happily adaptable to many other fruit. Do nose around on the internet, speak to allotmenters, gardeners and nursery owners, and follow a few bloggers who are out there doing it for themselves. Other people's experiences is well worth learning from but don't be afraid to go your own way and experiment if you feel the urge.

We are blessed with living in interesting if challenging times, and for many growing some of what we eat feels like a good thing to do. The wave of interest in doing just that in the last decade isn't just people looking for an antidote to city life, or a burst of nostalgia – these are people who find that growing some of what you eat enriches your life in many (often unexpected) ways. This is not a passing moment but an enduring movement, the early steps in a more sane and delicious way of eating. The next decades will see individuals, families and communities building on what the pioneers are doing now – allotments, edible back gardens, living roofs, forest gardens, Community Supported Agriculture, village orchards and city farms are just the beginning. And fruit is right at the heart of it.

Essential to life as it is, there is something luxurious about fruit, especially when grown for yourself. Fruit is satisfying to grow in a different way from vegetables, as Jane Grigson observed:

'This special feeling towards fruit, its glory and abundance, is I would say universal... we respond to strawberry fields or cherry orchards with a delight that a cabbage patch or even an elegant vegetable garden cannot provoke.'

Fruit plants lace the years together, growing along with you and your loved ones. They bring unexpected pleasures. Much as I love my veg patch, there's a different kind of happiness that comes with seeing the fruit trees I planted when my daughter was waiting to be born that she now plays beneath, picks and eats the fruit from and one day soon will be climbing in.

I hope you'll grow some.

Choosing what to grow

Deciding which fruit to invite into your garden, allotment or collection of pots is a big decision. The plants may be with you for years and take up a reasonable amount of space. Fruit plants are often costly – that's not to say expensive in the long term. When you look at likely harvests over the lifespan of the plant, the plant itself is often little short of a bargain, but there is still a substantial initial outlay. There may be a little wait while the plant gets up to full productivity, so you'll want to be looking forward to its fruit and not disappointed when it arrives. A wish list is vital.

Make a list of whichever fruit takes your fancy. Don't be hamstrung by practical considerations such as space or climate at this point; you may be surprised by what new varieties or dwarfing rootstocks can make possible. Write down your favourites first, discover some others you like the sound of by reading through the Fruit A–Z (pp.28–121), and whittle the list down based on practicalities if you have to.

There are a number of factors I'd suggest you consider when trying to come up with your fruity wish list.

Grow what you most like to eat

This should be a mantra that constantly sings in the back of your mind when planning what to grow. Grow some of your favourite food and you'll look forward to every harvest time, success will be delicious and any expense or effort along the way will feel worth it. Don't feel compelled to grow something you think only OK, simply because it's popular – if apples are 'fine' to you, try something else you love. That said...

Challenge your taste buds

Do look to open the larder door a little, to welcome a few new flavours into your kitchen. With vegetables I always suggest growing two things you dislike (as homegrown veg can be so very different from shop-bought) and two things you've not tasted (better still, never heard of) each year, but with fruit it's not so simple. It is more of a waste to dig up a plum tree when you've confirmed your dislike of them than it is to give your harvest of Brussels sprouts to a neighbour and vow never to grow them again. But the principle of trying new flavours, of seeing whether growing the best varieties for yourself can be so much superior to those you buy in the shops stands.

It's certainly worthwhile trying fruit that's new to you, or that you think you dislike, before you invest in a plant. Visit nurseries and allotments, nose around on the internet and seek advice from local groups and organisations to find the best locally grown fruit to try. Obviously the more money and land you have at your

'Peregrine' peach, fan-trained against a wall

Dittisham plums

disposal the more you can take a risk on an unknown or disliked fruit, but whatever your situation, do stay inquisitive about fruit.

Prioritise the unbuyables

A consideration I always let wander across my brain is whether I can buy a particular fruit locally or in the shops, and if so whether the best varieties are available. It doesn't mean I won't grow it if it's in the shops – a barrowful of homegrown Victoria plums is not hard to enjoy even if you can buy them in town – but there are often others as good that you can grow instead and still enjoy Victorias from the shops. It's how I came across the Dittisham plum, which has given me as much pleasure as any fruit I've grown. As with big maincrop potatoes, there are many apple varieties that are largely indistinguishable from those you can buy and I can see little reason for growing these varieties when there are other incredible cultivars out there screaming for your attention.

Similarly, you may be unfamiliar with quince, medlars or mulberries as they're rarely to be found for sale. This has nothing to do with their flavour; it's partly that they went out of fashion and partly because they don't suit the supermarket supply chain – mulberries, for example, should be picked when perfectly ripe, when they are devilishly delicate and far from robust enough to make the long journey to the supermarket shelves. All three are truly wonderful.

Complement the wild harvest

Even if you live in the city, you are likely to have some forageable fruit nearby – blackberries, apples and plums being among the most likely. If you do, consider whether you really need to grow more in your garden. You may even choose to grow fruit specifically to go with a hedgerow treat – gooseberries to go with foraged elderflowers for one. Please do lay your hands on John Wright's *Hedgerow* handbook to open the door to what may be on your doorstep – together with your garden's crop it'll give you the widest of fruity possibilities.

Grow the expensive fruit

Most fruit is costly, more so when it has a short season and labour-intensive production. Forced rhubarb comes early and sweet and is one of the great fruit treats of the year. Its price reflects a degree of palaver and a brief season of harvest, yet it is simple and cheap to grow this delight for yourself. Blueberries, quince, grapes and figs are also among the more expensive fruit: if you love any of them, then there's a strong claim to a place on your wish list on cost alone.

List the food you love to eat or would like to try and check it against your shopping receipts and online suppliers and consider whether to prioritise the most expensive ahead of some of the cheaper fruit.

Japanese plum in blossom

Consider diversity and succession

Look at your emerging wish list and ask yourself if you have a breadth of flavours. Some bright early apples, a few rich plums, sour gooseberries and some sharp yet sweet raspberries, for example. Or perhaps you'd rather go for a larger harvest of fewer fruit by having either more plants of one type or a spread of varieties of one fruit. Either way is fine, whichever suits you best, but do consciously consider the degree of diversity in your garden.

For each of the fruit on your wish list, use the chart on pp.32–3 to map out when you are likely to be picking your fruit. The only rule is that you are prepared for what's coming – gluts are no better or worse than a steadier supply, but you shouldn't be taken unawares. If the apples all seem to be coming at once and you'd like them more steadily, you may need to alter your choice of varieties.

Grow something beautiful

By 'beautiful' I don't just mean a plant that's pleasing to the eye – I mean create a space that you'd like to spend time in. If it's the place you're drawn to read the paper, have a picnic, a glass of wine or catch an afternoon snooze then you're likely to find it becoming a central part of your life.

It's also worth considering how your plants will look through the year. Most look appetising enough when in fruit, but check the variety descriptions and you may just get fabulous autumnal foliage or stunning flowers as an added bonus. And if you're unsure about whether to go for a Japanese wineberry or a blackberry, it may be the wineberry's furry red/pink winter canes that make the difference.

Consider degrees of risk

Almost all the fruit in this book will grow happily in any part of the UK, but there are a few which are more accustomed to long, hot summers in their natural home. Peaches, nectarines, apricots, figs and grapes are undoubtedly more risky the further north you live but with these less reliable fruit the importance of the microclimate cannot be understated. An apricot trained against a sunny, south-facing wall with shelter from winter and early spring winds grown in Lancashire is likely to have more chance of fruiting well than a freestanding tree exposed to harsh winds in Cornwall.

There are no mathematical formulae for success – just a few elements you have to ensure are favourable if you want to tackle any of the riskier fruit in a more northerly location or at a higher altitude. The rest is a matter for your sense of risk and whether you feel lucky.

One thing that is vital to success, especially in marginal locations, is your choice of variety. The Fruit A–Z (pp.28–121) includes those I think are best for each fruit, but some general principles apply, as follows.

Choosing varieties

Once you have your wish list in place, you'll need to consider which variety of each fruit you are going to plant. This is a critical step as it can guide what time of year you'll be eating your fruit, what that fruit tastes like, the shape of the plant and even the degree of trouble pests may give you. It is the single decision that will most determine how satisfied you will be with your produce. Spend as much time selecting a variety as you have choosing the type of fruit itself. Here are a few pointers to getting the best ones for you.

On the whole, commercial growers prioritise disease resistance, yield and consistency of appearance. All are fine characteristics, but I'd encourage you to put flavour above all. If you can get the other three to fall handily into line behind outstanding flavour then you have the ideal, but if you ask me, a smaller crop of delicious fruit trumps a skipful from a plain variety every time. Do read descriptions, seek advice from suppliers and, most importantly, talk to other growers before you go over your pencilled list in pen.

Many varieties of fruit require another nearby for pollination. Plenty of others do not. If you have room for only one tree, choose a self-fertile variety (i.e. a tree that can pollinate itself) if these are available. Otherwise you'll need to ensure that flowering at least partially overlaps. To help you with this, if you are planning to grow apples, varieties are organised into pollination groups and most good suppliers will indicate this in their catalogue, on their website and on their plant label. Whether this is done with letters (A–H) or numbers (1–8), the key is to choose varieties that coincide or are adjacent (for example, Pollination Group 3 will pollinate trees from Groups 2, 3 and 4). Even self-fertile varieties will usually give you a better harvest if cross-pollinated.

Consider varieties that ripen successionally. Planting three apple trees – one an early-, one a mid- and one a late-season apple – will keep you in fruit over a long, long period and help avoid huge gluts. Of course, if you want to eat or process bigger harvests, the opposite is true. Either way, take a few minutes to marry up how you want your food to be ready with your choice of varieties. The Fruit A–Z (pp.28–121) offers guidance for each of the fruits where relevant, and a good supplier will also be able to advise.

This brings me to my final piece of advice: make friends with good nurseries. There are some excellent nurseries, many of which are in the Directory (see p.248), but check locally too. The best nurseries will give you advice about the ideal rootstocks, varieties and combinations for your location and conditions. They care that you come back, that their plants give you pleasure and perform as they should. They should happily send you elsewhere if there is a plant that somebody else sells that suits you better than their own stock.

Redcurrant grown as a standard

Essential tools

There are many tools out there; some you will call on most weeks if not most days, others are very particular to specific tasks. The list below includes those you are most likely to consider.

When it comes to tools you have a choice: buy well once and enjoy your investment every time you use it, or go cheap and cheerless and regret the inadequacies every time it's in your hand.

If you are on a budget and not growing many plants you may decide to spend a little less on your tools. If so, then make every effort to do as you would with top-quality tools: keep blades sharp, joints oiled and everything clean – to get some proper service from them. Not only will they do a better job, making cleaner cuts that are less likely to invite disease, but the experience of using good tools adds to the pleasure rather than contributing to a chore.

There are, of course, various other garden tools you may find yourself calling on, depending what you choose to grow. A shredder, a hoe, a rake, a water butt, a rubber-ended mallet for knocking in stakes, tree ties, as well as tree guards against rabbits and deer spring to mind.

And don't forget a sharpening stone for keeping blades keen.

Secateurs A sort of heavy-duty pair of mini garden shears, secateurs are a vital tool as they are used for more plant cutting tasks than any other implement. They easily cut through branches up to 1cm across. I'm not supposed to have favourites but Felco's (see Directory, p.249) are the best by an absolute mile.

Loppers Effectively heavy-duty secateurs on long (often extendable) handles that give you extra reach and leverage when pruning in hard-to-access places. Some loppers come with a racheting action that allows you to prune your way through thicker branches more easily.

Penknife There are any number of garden-related knives available – designed specifically for grafting, pruning and other individual tasks. Buy the specialist ones if you find you are doing those tasks regularly; otherwise keep a well-made penknife – always sharp – in your pocket every time you go into your garden. As well as coming in handy for tidying up minor damage or untidy cuts, a knife can be quickly employed whenever you see a need for it, including minor pruning, taking cuttings and cutting string.

Pruning saw A pruning saw is required for cutting through branches of a larger diameter. These curved mini-saws are usually tapered to allow you to prune in tighter areas, and may have single or double-edged blades. Either is fine. You may use a pruning saw less frequently than secateurs but it is likely to be operating under considerable force when you do, so get the best you can afford – you'll be glad you did. Unless you have mature plants that need sawing already, you will be able to delay buying a saw for a few years until your trees have matured a little, so the expense needn't be at the beginning.

Fork The workhorse that takes the brunt of any soil turning or plant lifting. Excellent for turning compost and incorporating compost or manure into the soil. A good-quality fork is a sound investment.

Spade Used for digging, cutting straight edges and turning compost that is too fine to fork.

Trowel and hand fork An elementary set of tools for small-scale, in-close digging, soil turning and weeding.

Wheelbarrow, watering can and two buckets or trugs You'll use all of these for any number of tasks, especially at planting time.

Essential terms

As with many things, growing fruit comes with its share of jargon. It helps to be familiar with the terms that crop up fairly often.

Annual A plant that lives for one year only.

Anther The male part of a flower, which bears pollen.

Bare root A plant sold without soil (or with very little) around its roots.

Biennial bearing Where a plant produces fruit every 2 years.

Biological control A means of controlling pest numbers using their predators and/or parasites.

Bush trees Trees that have a short trunk, 90cm at most, from which branches spread to form a low canopy.

Cordon A tree or bush trained as a single stem (occasionally two or three,) against a wall and/or wire support.

Cultivar Shortened from 'cultivated variety', a term initially used to indicate a variety that had originated in cultivation rather than one found in the wild, but now used (as it is in this book) interchangeably with 'variety'.

Dwarf A fruit tree or bush kept to a smaller size, either by restricting its root space or by grafting it on the rootstock of a smaller species. Dwarf trees enable fruit to be grown in restricted spaces – in tubs on patios, for example.

Ericaceous compost Compost with a pH below 7, ideally suited to plants that thrive in acidic conditions (such as blueberries).

Espalier A tree or bush trained with a single vertical trunk and horizontal laterals – almost always using wire support, often against a wall.

Family tree A tree with more than one variety grafted onto the rootstock, which – if compatible varieties are chosen – can ensure that a single tree takes care of its own pollination, and gives harvests of more than one variety.

Fan A tree or bush trained with branches radiating from a short trunk.

Dwarf peach 'Bonanza' in blossom

Foliar feeding Applying a nourishing solution to a plant's leaves. High potassium feeds (such as seaweed feed and comfrey tea) are very effective when sprayed on the leaves of many fruiting plants from flowering onwards.

Forcing Accelerating a plant's growth, usually by excluding light and/or using heat. Rhubarb (see p.115) and chicory are the most commonly forced edible plants.

Graft The union (usually slightly swollen) on a plant where the scion and the rootstock have been joined. Also describes the act of joining a rootstock to a scion.

Half-standards Trees (and occasionally currant and gooseberry bushes) with a clear trunk (i.e. no branches) of around 1.5m.

June drop Some fruit plants (apple, pear and plum, for example) may shed some of their immature fruit in early summer. Whether this occurs depends on the variety, weather and the size of the potential crop. Losing some of that potential crop allows the plant to direct its resources to taking the remaining fruit to maturity.

Lateral A branch growing from the main stem.

Layering The practice of using a plant's tendency to grow roots when parts of the plant touch the ground to produce new plants.

Leader The central branch from which laterals will grow, it forms the main stem or trunk at the centre of the plant.

Maiden A tree in the first year after grafting. If it has branches it may be referred to as a 'feathered maiden', if not it may be referred to as a 'maiden whip'.

Minarettes These are essentially cordon trees, grown vertically and not usually attached to wires. They are also known as column, ballerina or leg trees. Minarettes can be planted closely together (perhaps 60cm apart, depending on variety).

Mulch A layer of material primarily used to suppress weeds and minimise water loss from the soil. There is a variety of materials to choose from: mulch mat works well around trees and other large plants as well as over large areas; a 5cm layer of well-rotted manure and/or compost gives a nourishing mulch that releases nutrients over time; and shredded bark, gravel and chippings work well in domestic settings.

Perennial A plant that lives for a number of years.

pH A measure of relative acidity/alkalinity, ranging from 1 (acidic) to 14 (alkaline). Plants may have very specific pH requirements to enable them to thrive.

Pollination Where pollen from the anther reaches the stigma, leading to fertilisation of the flowers and in turn to fruit.

Propagation Creating new plants using material from existing plants, usually by grafting, taking cuttings, layering, using runners, suckers or by dividing them.

Pyramid A tree grown in a pyramid shape (like a Christmas tree), tapering towards the top. A spindlebush is a shorter, squatter version.

Rootstock The lower part of a grafted tree, usually comprising the root system and a short section of the trunk. The rootstock controls the size the plant can grow to, and may be chosen to allow the variety grafted onto it to grow in soils it may otherwise be unable to thrive in.

Runners Stems that usually grow along the surface of the soil, which can root and produce child plants at their end.

Scion A length of fruit wood taken from a parent tree and grafted to a rootstock. It grows into the upper section of the tree and produces fruit of the same variety as the parent.

Self-fertile A plant that is able to pollinate itself.

Spur A short branch or group of branches which bear fruit buds and therefore the flowers and fruit.

Standard A tree with a single clear trunk up to 2m in height. Half-standards are shorter versions.

Stepover A short, trained T-shaped tree (usually a pear or apple), rarely more than 60cm high. In essence, a single-tiered espalier.

Stigma The female part of the flower which receives the pollen from the anther.

Sublateral A shoot growing from a lateral.

Sucker A shoot that grows from the root or rootstock.

//www.youtube.com/watch?v=...

Fruit A–Z

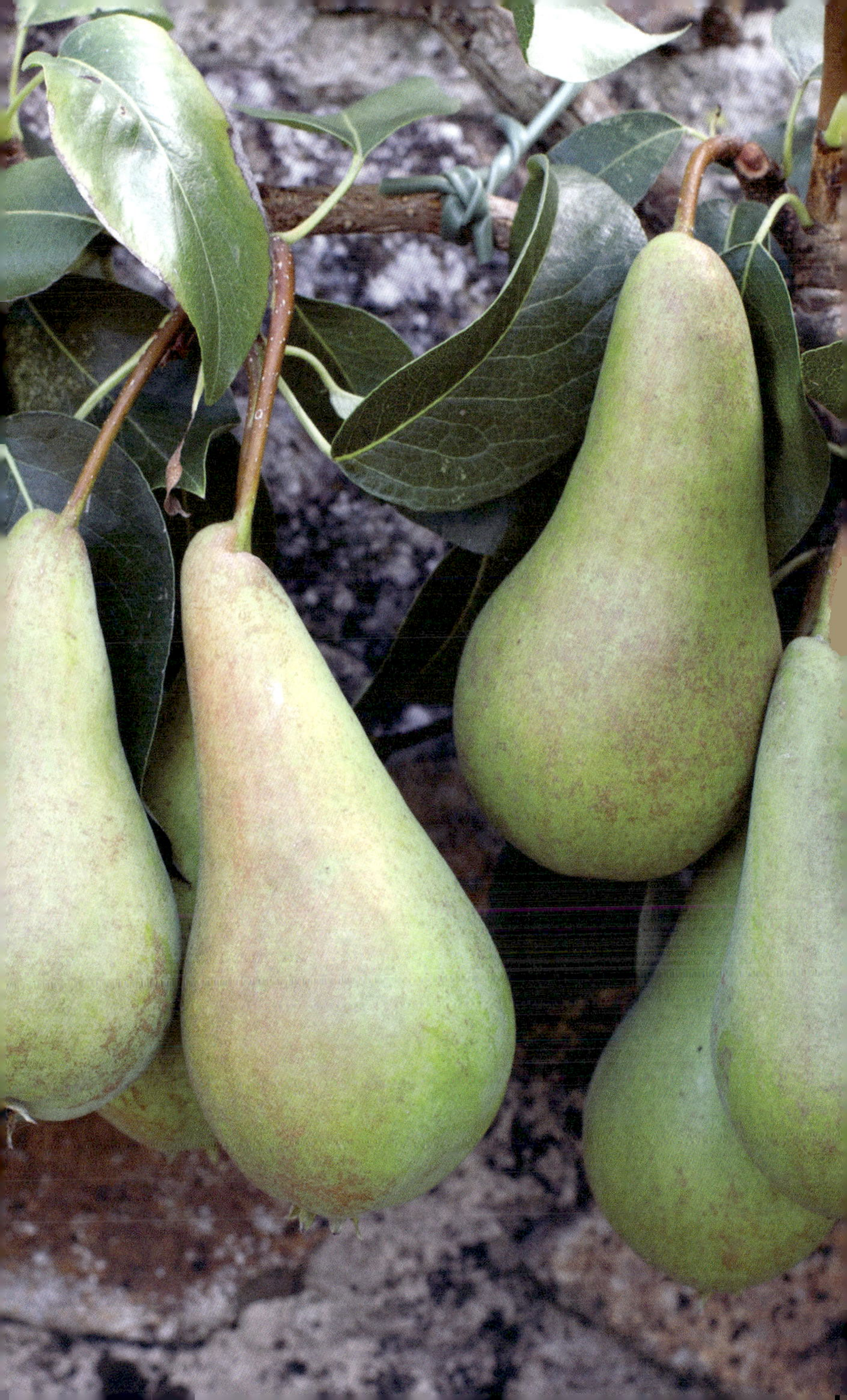

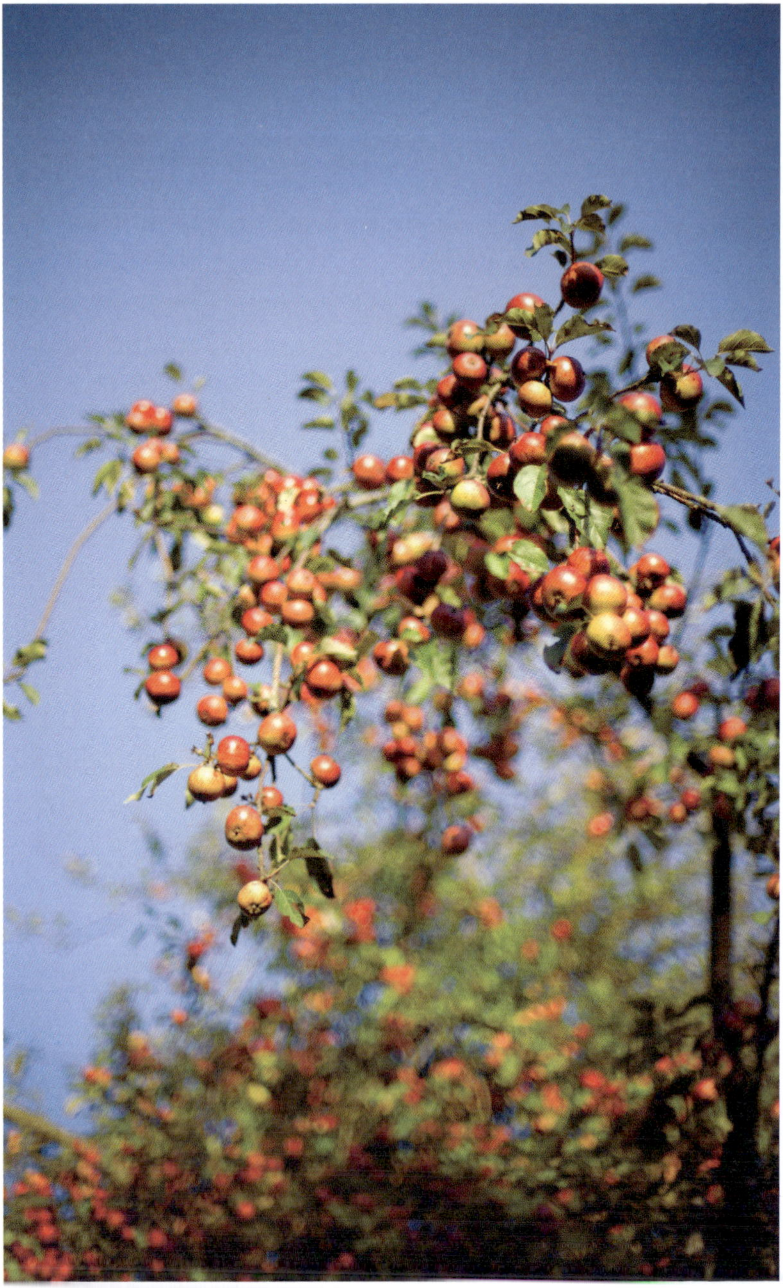

All of the well-known fruit that you can grow across most of the country is included in this A–Z. The usual suspects are here – such as pears, plums and apples – as well as a few personal favourites of lesser-known fruit, including Japanese wineberries, which I've included because they're just too good not to be shared.

I grow a lot of marginal fruit here in the Southwest, such as persimmons and pineapple guavas, as the climate is favourable, but for most parts of the country these are not an option so they are not included. Neither are citrus fruit, passion fruit, kiwis or cranberries, because they are unreliable for most, and there are equally delicious and/or more reliable alternatives. That said, I have included some fruit that are far from certainties to produce every year, notably peaches, nectarines and apricots, as they are incredibly satisfying to grow for yourself and in reality you are more likely to get fruit than not. Beyond these few favourites I have drawn a line.

The entries for the different fruit vary in length, but this is no reflection of their deliciousness, nor an indication of their trickiness to grow. Some have particular requirements and it is occasionally vital to give lengthy instructions. Don't be put off by these. You won't find them difficult or time-consuming to follow, it's just that accuracy results in a healthier plant and a bigger harvest.

For each fruit I've included the varieties that have done well for me, that I know to be outstanding or that suit particular requirements such as container growing. There may well be others that are equally delicious or that you may prefer, so be nosy and try to taste the variety you plant before you buy it. If not, trust my suggestions: they're all good.

Pests and diseases that may trouble you are mentioned, and there's a longer description of the main tediums on pp.176–181. Too many growing books start off telling you about the pests and diseases that may come your way – this is a little like the vicar telling you about the rows you will have on the day you get married. You are very likely to come across the odd pest or disease in your garden (as you are likely to have the odd 'frank exchange' with your partner) but it has to be better to celebrate the upside of your partnership rather than meditate on the down. And make no mistake, growing fruit is a partnership – with luck your plants will be with you for some time, so choose well.

Advice on specific growing requirements and harvesting is given under each entry and the chart overleaf provides a guide to overall pruning and harvesting times, so you can see when work needs to be done throughout the year and when you are likely to be gathering the fruit of your labours.

And from the very beginning, remember the point: delicious food to enrich the lives of you and your loved ones. Each fruit includes some ideas for enjoying it, with fuller recipes on pp.192–245.

Pruning and harvesting times

Times for most garden-related tasks vary with the weather, location and aspect, and the varieties you've chosen. Use the following as a guide, rather than a series of deadlines, especially when it comes to harvesting. If the cherries look good but you're unsure whether the timing is right, try one – your taste buds will tell you.

The time to prune is less open to interpretation. Stick with this guide, at least in terms of whether to prune in winter or not, as the timing can greatly influence the likelihood of disease occurring. Prune a plum in winter, for example, and you risk silver leaf far more than if the cuts are made when the sap is rising.

The table doesn't include planting times as there is a simple rule: if your plant is delivered or grown in a pot you can plant it out when you like; if it is bare-root it should be planted between November and March.

	JAN	FEB	MARCH	APRIL	MAY	JUNE	JULY	AUG	SEPT	OCT	NOV	DEC
APPLES												
Pruning	•	•									•	•
Harvest							•	•	•	•		
APRICOTS												
Pruning					•	•						
Harvest							•	•	•			
BLACKBERRIES & HYBRID BERRIES												
Pruning										•	•	•
Harvest							•	•	•			
BLACKCURRANTS												
Pruning	•							•	•	•	•	•
Harvest							•	•				
BLUEBERRIES												
Pruning	•										•	•
Harvest							•	•	•			
CHERRIES												
Pruning					•	•						
Harvest							•	•	•			
FIGS												
Pruning					•	•	•	•				
Harvest								•	•			
GOOSEBERRIES												
Pruning	•						•	•			•	•
Harvest						•	•	•				

	JAN	FEB	MARCH	APRIL	MAY	JUNE	JULY	AUG	SEPT	OCT	NOV	DEC
GRAPES												
Pruning	•					•	•				•	•
Harvest								•	•	•		
JAPANESE WINEBERRIES												
Pruning	•										•	•
Harvest								•	•			
MEDLARS												
Pruning	•										•	•
Harvest										•		
MELONS												
Sowing				•	•							
Harvest								•	•	•		
MULBERRIES												
Pruning				•	•							
Harvest								•	•			
PEACHES & NECTARINES												
Pruning						•	•					
Harvest							•	•	•			
PEARS												
Pruning	•	•									•	•
Harvest								•	•	•	•	
PLUMS, DAMSONS, GAGES ETC.												
Pruning						•	•					
Harvest							•	•	•	•		
QUINCE												
Pruning	•	•									•	•
Harvest										•		
RASPBERRIES												
Pruning		•	•						•	•	•	
Harvest							•	•	•	•	•	
REDCURRANTS & WHITE CURRANTS												
Pruning	•				•	•					•	•
Harvest							•	•				
RHUBARB												
Harvest			•	•	•	•	•					
STRAWBERRIES												
Harvest					•	•	•	•	•	•		

Apple 'Lord Lambourne'

Apples *Malus domestica*

PRUNE	November–February
HARVEST	July–October

Apple trees were probably the first trees grown intentionally for fruit, initially in Turkey, before spreading more widely as people selected better and more fruitful varieties. Tasty, refreshing, nourishing and plentiful at harvest, apples rarely attract birds or wasps and are happy to ripen without a glorious summer. It's easy to see why apples are the most popular fruit tree.

Ordinarily I'd be asking you to consider growing fruit less easy to find in the shops, but all apples are not born the same. There are endless delicious varieties from which to choose but I love the earlies in particular. Ready from midsummer onwards, the early harvested varieties have a fresh liveliness rare in later apples and they're perfect straight off the branch, without the period of storage many later varieties need after picking. 'Beauty of Bath', nipped off the tree in August, are simply astounding. They are at their best only for a short window after picking, which makes them less suitable for the shops. Like mulberries, grapes and the best strawberries, the finest early apples are the preserve of the home grower.

Varieties

With over 7000 varieties to choose from it would be easy to feel overwhelmed by the options and although you'll find only a fraction of those possibilities are easily available, your choice is still a wide one.

I have my own favourites and there are many that are commonly regarded as very fine indeed (see below), but to make the best choice you should ask yourself whether you want apples to eat, cook, make cider or more than one of those.

Cooking apples tend to be larger and more tart than eaters, cider apples are often too harsh for happy eating and dual-purpose varieties may be sharp earlier in the season, mellowing and becoming sweeter as the weeks pass.

Here are a few that I think are outstanding varieties to check out:
Eaters 'Orleans Reinette', 'Beauty of Bath', 'Blenheim Orange', 'Ashmead's Kernel', 'Cox's Orange Pippin' (self-fertile), 'Lord Lambourne', 'Old Somerset Russet'
Cookers 'Bramley', 'Annie Elizabeth'
Ciders 'Kingston Black', 'Browns'
Dual-purpose 'Veitch's Perfection'

If you have limited space to dedicate to growing apples, you should go for a variety that is self-fertile (i.e. it can pollinate itself) otherwise you should ensure that your chosen varieties have flowering periods that at least partially coincide (see p.20). Otherwise a family tree may be for you. These are trees which have two or more varieties grafted onto one main trunk, giving you the opportunity to have different apples on each of the main branches. Approach a fruit nursery direct and they may even be willing to graft the varieties of your choice ready to deliver the following year.

It's also worth considering local varieties as these are likely to flourish where you live. 'Veitch's Perfection' originated a few miles from my home and the trees in my apple orchard grow quickest, produce reliably well and are the healthiest, most round-flavoured apples of the whole orchard. Find yourself a good supplier who'll advise you about any local and delicious cultivars and you will give yourself every chance of fabulous apples and a healthy tree.

There is now an extensive range of rootstocks (see p.126) but the main ones you will find are coded – for example, M27 for a rootstock which produces a dwarfing tree, M106 for a medium-sized tree (around 3m in height) and M25 for a full standard tree. There are many options dependent on site and size, so check with your nursery to find the best for you.

Growing

Apples are as easy to grow as any fruit tree. Although they tend to be happiest as freestanding trees, they do take well to all manner of training – stopovers, cordons, espaliers and even arches – which makes them infinitely adaptable to even the smallest of spaces.

Spacing depends on rootstock and whether and how the tree is being trained (see p.128). For cordons, space your trees 50cm apart, espaliers and stopovers 2m or so apart, and for freestanding trees 3–9m apart (your supplier will give you guidance depending on your rootstock and local conditions).

Whatever the rootstock and whether training or not, plant your tree as outlined on p.146. Mulch around the base, water through extended dry periods in the early years and feed every spring with a good top dressing of well-rotted manure or similar. With a dwarfing rootstock you can grow apples in a large container but the importance of keeping up with feeding and watering greatly increases.

Once formative pruning has taken place (see pp.153–9 for your options), pruning should focus on removing diseased, dead and damaged wood, as well as crossing branches and any congestion in the centre if you're growing your tree as a bush. Prune unwanted branches back flush with the trunk or main branch, but if they're large and likely to leave a long ovate wound, leave them cut as short stubs as this minimises the risk of disease getting in. There are a few options with pruning but for an easy life I'd recommend doing all ongoing apple (and pear) pruning during the dormant winter period between late November and early March.

Spur-bearing

Tip-bearing

The detail of pruning for freestanding trees varies depending whether your variety produces fruit on spurs or the tips of shoots:

Spur-bearing Most apples and pears are of this type, bearing fruit in clusters on spurs (stubby branches) that are at least 2 years old. Cut each lateral back by a third every winter, and each sublateral to five buds to encourage more fruiting buds (and eventually spurs) to develop.

Tip-bearing These trees bear fruit on the tips of last year's growth, so most fruit will be at branch ends rather than along their length. Pruning of tip-bearers involves taking out a quarter of the oldest fruiting branches each year, thereby completely renewing the growth that comes from the main branches every 4 years. Avoid pruning sideshoots and new growth as most fruit will develop here.

Pruning also varies according to any style of training you use (see pp.156–9).

Harvesting and storage

Early apple varieties are ready from late July into September. Eat them immediately as (like early potatoes) they don't keep for long. Most other varieties are ready from October and may need a little storage after picking until they are really at their

Cordon apples

best. Many can be stored for anything up to 6 months. Taste-testing the readiness of these late varieties is tricky. At the right time there should be a few windfall apples at the base of the tree. Pick one from the tree itself and slice it in half – if it's ready the pips should be brown rather than white.

When it comes to picking, take any that give with a gentle, cupped, twisting motion – there should be no sense of pulling as this not only indicates the fruit needs the tree a little longer, but it can also damage fruiting spurs and reduce the following year's crop.

Any apples to be stored should be kept in a dry cool place (such as a garage). Store them in a single layer, not touching each other, ideally on slatted shelving for air circulation, otherwise on newspaper. They should keep for months (depending on seasonality) but check them regularly and remove any that are spoiling.

You can also cook them gently to a pulp and freeze, or cut your apples into rings and dry them in a dehydrator or on the lowest setting of your oven.

Pests and diseases

The legendary caterpillars of fairy tales and nursery rhymes are usually codling moth larvae – just cut out any you see before eating or cooking your apple. If you find them particularly upsetting or your tree appears to be inundated, you can use pheromone traps. These non-chemical traps work by attracting the males, which stick to the trap and hence the females go unmated, halting the life cycle before the caterpillar stage.

Scab (see p.180) can be a pain, and some varieties (such as 'Ashmead's Kernel' and 'Egremont Russet') offer a degree of resistance. Nectria canker (see p.179), a fungal disease, can also be a nuisance.

Eating

Apples combine beautifully with so many partners including black pudding, pork, cabbage and cheese on the savoury side. And most apple varieties take well to cooking, as well as eating raw. Cored whole apples are wonderful baked: stuff them with a cream made by beating equal amounts of butter and sugar together and flavouring with a little ground cinnamon; or try a mincemeat filling.

Peeled, cored and sliced, apples make a wonderful simple compote when slow-cooked with star anise and/or cinnamon, plus a little sugar. Delicious on its own or with yoghurt and granola, the compote can also be used as the fruity part of the cranachan, fool and mess recipes (p.218, p.213 and p.224 respectively).

Recipes Orchard ice cream with caramelised walnuts (p.195) and Blackberry apple compote (p.200). See also variations for fruit leather (p.234), crumble (p.239) and cake (p.232).

Apricot 'Flavourcot'

Apricots *Prunus armeniaca*

PRUNE	May–June
HARVEST	July–September

The Romans developed a taste for apricots after Alexander the Great brought them to Europe, but they didn't quite get to grips with the particularities of growing them in the UK. Others tried in the thirteenth and the sixteenth centuries before they became properly established in the grander homes of the nineteenth century. Until recently you'd rarely see apricots growing anywhere less regal, but they have become increasingly common in gardens and allotments.

The growing interest is at least partly down to the availability of new varieties. Although apricots originate from the warm climes of Armenia, they don't need a spectacular summer to do well here. The fruit are usually ripe by midsummer, even in the northern parts of the country, but the flowers are vulnerable in early spring. Apricots flower early, at the same time as blackthorn, before most of our other fruit blossom dares brave a look, and late frosts can kill off the flowers that would otherwise turn to fruit. New varieties (see below) have been bred to flower later, which, with climate change nudging the last frosts back earlier into the year, really ups your chances of homegrown apricots.

Like peaches, apricots are one of those delights that bear little resemblance to those you buy in shops. Although less luscious than peaches, homegrown apricots have a deeper, richer, muskier flavour than you might be used to. If you can get the flowers past the last frosts you'll find them little troubled by pests and diseases and there's no chance of catching the leaf curl that can deplete other stone fruit.

Varieties

Any of the more recent late-flowering varieties (many of which end in 'cot') are likely to give you the best chance of fresh apricots. 'Flavourcot' ripens just after 'Tomcot', so if you grow them together you'll enjoy a longer picking season.

If you've a sunny, sheltered spot (and are happy to use horticultural fleece to protect the blossom) then do try older varieties such as 'Bredase' and 'Alfred' as, to my mind, they may just pip the newer varieties for depth of flavour.

Apricot trees are usually grafted onto the semi-vigorous 'Torinel' or 'St Julien A' rootstocks, or the semi-dwarfing 'Pixy'.

Look out for new dwarf varieties. I grow 'Champion' which gets to around 1.3m in height and is wonderfully productive for its size.

Apricots are self-fertile so growing a single tree is fine.

Growing

Apricot trees are pretty low maintenance but they do need shelter from harsh winds, and a sunny frost-free spot with a well-drained soil. Neutral to slightly alkaline conditions are best, and avoid sandy or chalky sites.

Plant your tree as described on p.146 and allow at least 4.5m from its neighbour, depending on the rootstock. Apricot trees will happily grow as pyramids, bushes or trained as fans.

Hand pollination with a soft brush will really boost your harvests (see p.189), and even if you grow one of the newer late-flowering varieties it's worth fleecing against late spring frosts that may harm the blossom. Water your tree well through dry periods, especially in the first few years.

Some people thin the fruit, taking out cramped apricots as they develop so that those left on the tree are around 8cm apart, thinking it boosts the viability of the remaining fruit. I tend not to do so, unless the fruit is very obviously touching and overcrowded, as I find the tree naturally jettisons any excess. The choice is yours.

Formative pruning of freestanding apricots follows that of plums (see p.154) and should be done in late spring and summer when the sap is rising to minimise the risk of silver leaf disease (see p.180). Ongoing pruning should be limited to removing dead, diseased and overcrowded branches.

If you are growing your apricot tree as a fan, it should be pruned as described on pp.156–8.

Harvesting and storage

Depending on variety, location and the nature of the summer, apricots can be ready to eat by midsummer even in our unreliable British climate, or as late as early September. Unless you're drying or cooking them, don't try storing apricots. They can be dried in a dehydrator or by placing them in the oven on its lowest setting overnight until they reach the state you require, but they are so much better eaten sun-warm and fresh, straight from the tree, or cooked from fresh.

Pests and diseases

As far as diseases are concerned, bacterial canker (see p.176) and silver leaf (see p.180) are your two main worries.

Birds can wreak havoc with the ripening fruit, although they may not bother them at all – use netting at the first sign of any interest from the birds.

Eating

Fresh from the tree, apricots are a sweet aromatic pleasure and any not eaten in this way are too precious to mess around with too much. Although they make a wonderful jam, I'd avoid preserving too many unless you have a real glut. Enjoy them at their best as they are, or in smoothies or dipped in melted dark chocolate. Or to make a delectable compote, halve, stone and lightly stew apricots – with or without a little cardamom and/or cinnamon. This is delicious with yoghurt, rippled through a flapjack mixture, or used in the fool, cranachan or mess recipes (p.213, p.218 and p.224 respectively).

Recipes Apricots on toast (p.199) and Lamb and apricot tagine (p.196). See also variations for compote (p.200), cake (p.232) and fruit leather (p.234).

Dwarf apricot 'Champion'

Blackberry

Blackberries and hybrid berries
Rubus spp.

PRUNE	October–December
HARVEST	July–September

Whether garden-grown or foraged, blackberries are famously nutritious, being high in fibre, vitamins and minerals. Humans have eaten them for thousands of years, and during the First World War children in England collected blackberries during school time to be juiced and sent to the front line to maintain soldiers' health. Not only fabulous for you, blackberries are easy to grow and happily romp away in almost any soil. So, if you're a beginner, have a less than perfect site, or just fancy some easily acquired and mouthwatering fruit, a homegrown blackberry is definitely for you.

Before anyone gets up in arms, I'm not wanting to put an end to wandering around the hedgerows with a plastic container in search of free fruit – blackberrying is as much a part of summertime as sand castles and ice cream. But many of the domestic varieties are deliciously different to their wild relative and worth growing as well as – rather than instead of – the hedgerow favourites.

Cultivated varieties tend to have fruit that is larger, sweeter and more heavy-cropping than the fruit you forage for. This doesn't make them 'better' – tart can be as delicious as sweet – but where domestic varieties can have the edge is that many are thornless and grow naturally upright, which makes them both pleasant to handle and easier for training.

Of the blackberry hybrids available, tayberries with their gentle acidity to offset the sweetness, along with boysenberries and loganberries with their longer flavour and juiciness, are to my mind the best. Either are worthy of their own spot in the garden on flavour alone, but particularly so as neither fruit is commonly for sale.

Varieties

Of the newer thornless blackberry varieties I've tried, 'Adrienne', 'Helen' (early-fruiting and disease-resistant) and 'Oregon Thornless' are the tastiest. If you'd like to bring the taste of wild blackberries to your garden, then the heavy-cropping 'Ashton Cross' is the one for you.

As far as the hybrids are concerned, tayberries, boysenberries and loganberries are usually sold as generic varieties.

All blackberries and hybrids are self-fertile. Look for certified virus-free plants.

Growing

Blackberries may well be the easiest of all fruit to grow for yourself. They're vigorous and unfussy about site, doing perfectly happily in exposed or shady conditions, or even in heavy soils.

You can let them ramble about for a low-effort harvest or beautify them with support and allow the increased air and sun to give you more fruit into the bargain. If you fancy training them you can just tie them to wires fixed to walls or a shed, or grow them more formally as a fan.

When planting blackberries, cut the strongest stems back to around 30cm, removing any thin shoots to encourage strong shoots to grow. Train strong stems into a fan, tying them across horizontal wires. Snip the ends off when they get to 2m long (or a little less if you're pushed for space), as this encourages lateral shoots to form, which will in turn bear fruit.

Boysenberry

At the end of the harvest, any stems that have produced fruit should be cut right back to the base. This allows new canes to grow and be tied in to the wires, replacing the canes that have fruited.

As with most fruit, blackberries will establish better if you water them well through extended dry periods in the first summer, and if you mulch them around the base every spring with well-rotted organic matter. A watering with comfrey tea or seaweed feed (see p.161) from flowering will boost your crop.

Harvesting and storage

The fruit ripens gradually across the plant from midsummer onwards (depending on the variety) and the best way to test is to pull them gently. When they're ready they will separate easily from the plant, taking the plug with them (raspberries leave it behind when ready). Many of the best new varieties are highly productive – you may get up to 5kg from each plant in a good year. Pick them on a dry day, as wet berries quickly deteriorate. Harvest regularly, as they ripen, to ensure most for you and fewest for the birds.

Blackberries will keep in the fridge for a day or two and freeze very well.

Pests and diseases

Blackberries are fairly trouble-free, although raspberry beetle (see p.109) and birds can deplete your harvest so net them (at least from when the fruit starts to colour) if you can.

Eating

A classic 'one in the basket, one for me' fruit when picking. So deliciously versatile are blackberries you'll find you can adapt all manner of recipes to use them.

And do try blackberry whisky: put 1.5kg blackberries and 250g caster sugar into a large sterilised jar or bottle and pour over a bottle of whisky. The whisky needn't be expensive but it should be a minimum of 40 per cent strength to develop a full flavour. Seal the jar or bottle and, for a month or two, invert the bottle back and forth once a day (on as many days as you remember to). After 3 months, strain the flavoured alcohol into a sterilised bottle and allow the flavour to develop for a year if you can, longer if you have the patience. The result is hard to identify as either part blackberry or whisky, but it is quite superb.

Recipes Blackberry apple compote (p.200), Summer pudding (p.202) and Frozen summer berries and hot white chocolate sauce (p.201). See also variations for cranachan (p.218), mess (p.224), trifle (p.244), granita (p.243), crumble (p.239), clafoutis (p.209), tarts (p.214 and p.240), muffins (p.207), fruit leather (p.234), bottled fruit (p.236) and fruit vodka (p.233).

Blackcurrant 'Ben Hope'

Blackcurrants *Ribes nigrum*

PRUNE	August–January
HARVEST	July–August

Many of us have grown up drinking a rather famous brand of blackcurrant cordial and its popularity probably stems from the Second World War. With our usual overseas supplies of citrus fruit largely blocked by U-boats, the UK was in danger of being starved of vitamin C, so the government encouraged people to grow blackcurrants, which are incredibly high in that essential nutrient. For a few years, from 1942, most of the country's blackcurrants were made into cordial (by the originators of that famous brand) and distributed free as a simple, delicious way of getting vitamin C into the nation's children. And from that moment it's been a familiar part of our lives.

One of the endearing things about blackcurrants is that they are uncomplicated to look after – and you can combine your harvesting with the pruning. As the currants ripen to a deep black you can get in there with the secateurs and snip off the short trusses of fruit or better still chop out the oldest third of the plant right down to the crown with the trusses still attached to the branch. It's the perfect time to cut these branches to the ground to encourage new growth but in doing so you get a good portion of the fruit out without the fiddle. And you can always pick any remaining fruit off the branches.

Put the cut branches into a vase of water at home and you'll have a little longer to use the fruit – just snip or carefully pluck currants off the branch when you're ready to eat them. And don't ignore the leaves (see p.50).

Varieties

There are many blackcurrant varieties to choose from and the 'Ben' cultivars are well worth investigating. They've all been bred to resist frosts and a range of pests and diseases, as well as producing delicious harvests. 'Ben Hope', 'Ben Lomond' and 'Big Ben' (with double-sized berries) have all given hefty harvests of delicious berries for me. 'Ebony' is particularly sweet straight from the bush – and it arrives early, in the first half of July.

Jostaberries are a complicated cross between a gooseberry and a blackcurrant – of a size between the two and tasting more like gooseberries when picked early, and maturing more towards a blackberry flavour. They are delicious, and almost always sold as a generic variety.

Blackcurrants and their crosses are self-fertile.

Growing blackcurrants

Blackcurrants are pleasingly versatile. Happiest in a sunny, fertile location, they'll do perfectly well in a damper spot where most other fruit would complain. Most varieties get to around 1.5m in height and spread, so plant your bush a little more than that distance from its neighbour.

Although they will get by if ignored for a while, blackcurrants will be grateful for watering until they're established and a good mulch of well-rotted manure or compost in spring will be well rewarded. Blackcurrants are hungry and thirsty plants so keep them well fed and watered to get the best from them.

In the first spring after planting, chop the stems down to just above a bud (i.e. almost to the ground). Every year after, you want to chop out around a third of the plant – the oldest parts – to encourage new stems to grow through. You can do this in winter but I prefer to kill a few birds with one stone by doing it at harvest time (see above). Cut as close to the ground as you can.

Blackcurrants can be grown in containers of around 40cm diameter. You'll need to water and feed them very regularly and repot them every 3 years or so.

Harvesting and storage

Blackcurrants are ready to harvest in midsummer. Ripe perfection is quite tough to call – usually it's a little while after the currants turn the deep colour you're expecting. Leave them as long as you can and they'll get even sweeter.

Use a fork to strip the currants from the trusses.

Pests and diseases

Birds seem to know exactly when the fruit is perfectly ripe and will leave it entirely undisturbed until that moment. Having lulled you into a false sense of security, they can decimate your crop in no time, so do net your plants as they ripen.

Gall midge maggots and blister aphids love young blackcurrant leaves. Pick off and incinerate any leaves that discolour or distort.

Bud mites can inhabit the buds, making them fat and rounded instead of long and thin. It's easy to spot their effect in spring as growth begins. Cut off any affected stems.

Eating

Small, tart-sweet and intense blackcurrants are perhaps best used almost as herbs, where their flavour rather than their substance is what matters. Ice cream, granita, jam, curd, sauce and jelly are all wonderful vehicles for full-flavoured blackcurrants to shine.

And do try the leaves: not only do they make a refreshing tea (and I'm no fan of most fruit teas), but blackcurrant leaf sorbet is particularly fine. It is also comforting to have a recipe for the leaves if the birds have beaten you to any unnetted currants. Dissolve 140g caster sugar in 220ml boiling water. Throw in a generous handful of blackcurrant leaves and take off the heat. Once completely cool, strain and add the juice and finely grated zest of 2 lemons, then pour into a large, shallow plastic container. Freeze until almost firm, then scratch up thoroughly with a fork and incorporate a lightly beaten egg white. Freeze until solid.

Recipes Frozen summer berries and hot white chocolate sauce (p.201), Summer pudding (p.202) and Crème de cassis (p.204). See also variations for fruit leather (p.234), compote (p.200), granita (p.243), fool (p.213), muffins (p.207), clafoutis (p.209), tart (p.214) and cake (p.232).

Blueberry 'Bluecrop'

Blueberries *Vaccinium* spp.

PRUNE	November–January
HARVEST	July–September

If you like your fruit sweet with a little balancing sharpness, and perfect to eat when plucked straight from the plant, blueberries are for you. They look like a flashy blackcurrant – a little larger and dusted with icing sugar. Their flavour lives up to their looks and they're well worth the particular care they need.

Native to North America, blueberries came to the UK in 1949, imported by the Trehane family who still run the Dorset Blueberry Company, growing the fruit and selling excellent blueberry plants. There aren't endless blueberry farms dotted across the countryside for one main reason: blueberries need acidic soil, anything else just won't do. We don't produce many for the domestic market, yet demand is ever-increasing. It keeps the price of blueberries high in the shops, and gives you another fine reason to grow them.

They are as beautiful as they are tasty. Check out the base of the fruit where the blossom formed, away from the stem. This lazily lobed five-pointed star on each fruit was seen by some Native Americans as a sign that the Great Spirit had sent 'starberries' to ease hunger in times of famine. They are also famously nutritious, full of vitamins and minerals, and reputed to have beneficial effects on anything from heart disease to depression. Whether they are or not, they make a mighty fine muffin, so they get my vote.

Varieties

There are plenty of fabulous, prolific fruiters out there: 'Sunshine Blue', 'Bluecrop' and 'Chandler' are all excellent, but do go to a specialist provider to make sure you get the best plants. They are partially self-fertile, which in theory at least means one plant should produce some fruit but in practice they do poorly – I've found that three bushes or more will give me all the blueberries I need and ensure good pollination.

Look for certified disease-free plants, or propagate your own (using softwood cuttings, see p.131) from healthy plants.

Growing

It is very easy to coax a heavy, reliable harvest from blueberries if you give them the right conditions. They will only thrive in a rich acidic soil (ideally pH 5.5 or lower), which has good drainage. You'll need to water your plants with rainwater as tap

Blueberry 'General' in flower

water tends to be alkaline and ongoing watering will gradually neutralise the compost and productivity will slide. The same applies with mulching – use acidic material such as shredded bark or pine needles. Given their particular requirements, blueberries are the perfect candidates for container growing (using an ericaceous compost), where it tends to be easier to maintain the ideal pH.

Blueberries do like light and heat, so give them a sheltered spot with as much summer sun as you can. Plant them at least 1.5m or so from their neighbour.

Use a lime-free fertiliser to boost soil nutrient levels without compromising the pH.

Do your pruning in the winter, taking out any damaged or dead shoots and about a quarter of the dominant shoots. Also cut back by half any weaker shoots to encourage strong growth each year.

Harvesting and storage

With a spread of varieties you can be eating fresh blueberries from midsummer through to autumn. Blueberries fruit on wood that's up to 3 years old, ripening to their talcy-blue colour from midsummer onwards. The berries ripen gradually across the plant rather than all at once, so you need take only those that have reached perfect ripeness each time. Be patient and let them develop a deep indigo colour – as they do so their flavour is getting better and better.

Blueberries should keep for a couple of weeks in the fridge but the flavour can deteriorate fairly quickly. In practice you'll be lucky to get many as far as the kitchen, they taste so good straight off the bush, but any surplus can be frozen.

Pests and diseases

Blueberries are remarkably trouble-free, other than the birds, which can be netted against if they become a nuisance.

Eating

Much of the flavour of blueberries comes from their skin so they don't take as well to sauces and the like as blackcurrants. They're better kept whole rather than stewed, although cooking does bring out their flavour. Get them into anything that's baked and they shine – muffins, tarts, cakes, pancakes and puddings.

Recipes Blueberry muffins (p.207) and Frozen summer berries and hot white chocolate sauce (p.201). See also variations for cranachan (p.218), clafoutis (p.209), tart (p.214), summer pudding (p.202), fruity melons (p.223) and compote (p.200).

Cherry 'Morello'

Cherries *Prunus avium* and *Prunus cerasus*

PRUNE	May–June
HARVEST	July–September

The cherry matches the sublime flavour of its fruit with its looks for much of the year, more so than any other fruit tree. Littered with early blousy blossom in spring, hanging with juicy earrings through summer, followed by classic autumn leaves, cherries are as good value as you can get from a tree. We used to grow them in vast numbers in the UK but the manpower shortages during the world wars started a slide that was exacerbated by cheap imports, to such a degree that we've lost 95 per cent of our cherry orchards in 60 years. On the upside, over the last few decades plant breeders have succeeded in developing smaller self-fertile trees, ideal for either back gardens or commercial orchards, dispensing with the need for huge ladders and endlessly extending loppers.

There are sweet (*Prunus avium*) and sour or acid (*Prunus cerasus*) cherries, and I'd urge you to look as long and hard at the sour as the sweet when making your choice. The prince of the sour cherries is the 'Morello' – for 400 years it's had few contenders for its crown. Sours are twice as laden with vitamin C as sweet varieties and will happily fruit on a north- or east-facing wall.

If you fancy the sweet cherries, and why not, then you'll be battling with our feathered friends (*avium* means 'for the birds') so be prepared to net your trees, as they'll decimate them in the time it takes to load your blunderbuss.

Varieties

The 'Morello' is hard to rival if you're after a sour cherry, and the trees are self-fertile so growing just one is fine.

There are many fabulous sweet varieties to choose from, so I can do little more than recommend the ones I've found best, while steering you towards nurseries (such as Thornhayes, see Directory, p.248) who know their cherries and those that might suit your location well. 'Lapins', 'Stella' and 'Summer Sun' are as good as any of the newer self-fertile varieties, and if you fancy your chances of growing one without netting, then the white-cherried 'Vega' is the one for you.

You may still find the odd nursery selling trees that are crosses between sour and sweet cherries. These are known as 'Dukes', and their name often gives that away; 'May Duke' is one example.

Modern varieties on dwarfing rootstocks (like 'Gisela') can be kept to a couple of metres in height, but allow 3–4m if you want to train them into a fan.

If you are growing varieties which are not self-fertile, make sure that their pollination groups are compatible. These are usually numbered or lettered, as for apples and pears, and should be either the same or adjacent.

Most cherries are grafted onto 'Colt' (semi-vigorous, 4–5m height) or 'Gisela 5' (dwarfing, 2–3m height).

Growing

Sweet cherries love full sun, whereas sour cherries make a perfect choice for shady spots, especially north- or east-facing walls. The blossom tends to come early and can be susceptible to frost damage, so give them a sheltered position and keep horticultural fleece to hand as a nocturnal duvet – but do remove it early in the morning to allow pollination to occur.

Cherries need a good deep, fertile, well-drained soil. You should avoid a site that ever becomes waterlogged, but they do like a reasonable amount of water and their shallow roots make them susceptible to drying out fairly quickly. Water them well through dry periods, especially in the early years. A good ring of compost and slow-release fertiliser in late winter will help keep the upper layers of soil fertile for these shallow-rooting trees.

Very dwarfing rootstocks mean you can plant trees as close as 2.5m from each other, or over 6m for full-sized trees.

Cherries can be grown as bushes and pyramids but, given their delicate blossom and the attention of birds, training (as a minarette or fan) is an attractive option for cherries. That said, if you can give a freestanding cherry protection from harsh winds and frosts, little beats the sight of one in full blossom in spring.

Pruning and training freestanding sweet cherries is as for plums (see p.154). Ideally, you should choose a plant with a good goblet shape. And, because they fruit in clusters at the base of year-old stems and on older wood, limit pruning of freestanding cherries to taking out dead, diseased or crossing branches after harvesting. Silver leaf (see p.180) loves cherry trees and pruning cuts are the easiest way in for it, though this is minimised in the warmer months with the sap rising.

Freestanding sour cherries are pruned as for sweet varieties until the third year. Sour varieties crop along the length of stems that grew the previous year so, whether you're growing yours in a fan or freestanding, chop out a good amount of the older wood as this is unproductive, and removing it encourages new growth that will fruit the following year. If you're hoping to grow your cherry as a fan then I'd advise you to buy one already partially trained, otherwise follow the formative training as for plums (see pp.156–8).

Sweet cherry fans need ongoing pruning in early summer to maintain their shape. Any growth pointing towards the wall or outwards can be snipped off, as can some of the older unproductive growth where there are strong newer shoots to be tied in to replace it. Snip back new shoots to 8cm to direct energies to ripening fruit. Sour cherries grown as fans need more pruning than sweet varieties: in summer prune out older branches, tying in new growth which will then produce fruit the next year.

Cherries naturally thin their fruit, dropping any excess they feel incapable of taking to ripeness, so you won't need to do any thinning out early on.

Unless you're growing white cherries, have some netting to hand once the fruit begins to colour to deter birds, which are capable of decimating a crop in no time.

Cherries on dwarfing rootstocks can be grown in pots but you'll need to keep right on top of watering and feeding to stop them struggling.

Harvesting and storage

Most cherries will be ready to eat in the second half of summer. Pick them by the stalks in dry weather, taking care to avoid bruising the delicate fruit. Cherries may keep in the fridge for up to a fortnight but the flavour of sweet varieties may decline in the cold – it's best to eat these as soon as you can. Sour cherries are too harsh to eat raw unless you get them perfectly ripe, but cooked they are stupendous.

Pests and diseases

Bacterial canker (see p.176) and silver leaf (see p.180) are the main culprits, and you may find blackfly at the tips of new shoots, which can be wiped off quite easily. Blossom wilt (see p.176), phytophtera (see p.179) and shothole (see p.180) can trouble your cherry too.

Eating

Cherries are a precious crop. If you've managed to get them past the birds' attentions you'll want to enjoy each and every one. Sweet cherries are irresistible fresh from the tree. And they are excellent in salads with lively leaves such as rocket, and with goat's cheese and hazelnuts or walnuts.

Sour cherries are usually best cooked. A compote of sour cherries with hot smoked sea trout is one of my favourite of Hugh's recipes: gently cook the halved, stoned cherries in a pan with 1 tbsp water and around a fifth of the cherries' weight in light brown sugar. You can always add a little more sugar when the cherries have broken down to form a compote but they should still be a little tart.

Cherries and chocolate is one of the finest combinations – try finishing the clafoutis with a dusting of cocoa. The stones carry more than a hint of almond, so leave the stones in when cooking cherries if you want to enhance the flavour.

Recipes Clafoutis (p.209) and Fruity melons (p.223). See also variations for bottled fruit (p.236), pear and rocket salad (p.228), tart (p.214) and cake (p.232).

Fig 'White Marseilles'

Figs *Ficus carica*

PRUNE	April–July
HARVEST	August–September

Figs are one of those 'fruits' that's not really a fruit, as any resident of Pedants' Corner will rejoice in reminding us. Each of those delicious bulbous knobbles is an extraordinary capsule of tiny flowers, which somehow, in the absence of light, bloom and develop seeds while hidden away. Sink your teeth into that luscious sweet flesh and you're sucking up a soup of yesterday's flowers, and there are few fruity flavours to touch it.

Figs have a reputation for being tricky to care for and trickier to coax a harvest out of, but, as with many fruits, get a few things right and choose the best varieties and you'll give yourself every chance of success.

They need a cracking position with plenty of sun and shelter if you want to get a good harvest of well-ripened fruit – and full ripeness is critical to enjoying the full, deep, luscious flavour of a fig. At their peak, the aromatics tell you the fruit is ready. At this point figs may be very delicate and difficult to handle – far beyond being suitable for transporting to the supermarkets. They can be good if you buy them close to the place they were grown, but this is why nothing beats your own. The telltale sign is a sweet honey tear in the eye of the fig – when you see that, you're in.

Varieties

Although wild figs are pollinated by a wasp that enters the fruit, domestic cultivars are almost without exception self-fertile. Figs come in varieties that bear brown-purple fruit or white-green fruit, which is often given away in the variety name. 'Brown Turkey' is probably the most widely available of any and, although delicious and reliable, it can be a little ordinary in a less-than-sunny summer. 'Petite Nigra', as its name suggests, produces small dark figs which are as good as any for flavour. It's also the one that seems happiest growing in a pot.

'Rouge de Bordeaux', with its small purple fruits and ruby-coloured flesh, is a delicious variety that ripens reliably both under cover and in sheltered, sunny spots outside.

Although marginally less reliable than 'Brown Turkey', I prefer the flavourful sweetness of 'White Marseilles'. It can get rust on the leaves, which is usually only cosmetic, but the taste makes it worth a little occasional shabbiness. 'Excel' is another excellent new white fig.

Growing

Contrary to the common view, figs are easy, low-maintenance plants but they are very particular about a few things. If you're growing them outside they will do best against (or near) a south-facing wall to maximise the light and heat they receive. They need a fertile humus-rich, well-drained soil (or compost if grown in a pot) and some restriction placed on their root system.

If allowed to grow freely, the roots will spread and encourage green growth rather than fruiting so it's best to plant them in a large container (70cm or so in diameter) or restrict their root growth in the ground. You can buy root-restricting bags (from Reads or other suppliers, see Directory, pp.248–9) or create a box (70cm square and deep) with paving slabs or similar. This should reduce their spread from up to 3m high and wide to around half that.

An early spring mulch of composted horse manure or a slow-release organic fertiliser will give them a real boost, and fortnightly liquid feeds of comfrey or seaweed will encourage productivity. Avoid nitrogen-rich feeds (such as nettle tea) as these will encourage green growth over fruiting. Water figs regularly through the summer: this should be daily during dry periods or if you're growing your plant in a container.

Refresh the top 3–4cm of compost for any container-grown figs every spring, and pot them into a larger pot every 4 years or so, but not too often as they fruit particularly well when slightly pot-bound.

Figs can be grown as bushes, half-standards or trained into fans.

For freestanding trees, look for a tree with a well-established goblet framework of five or so branches from a central stem. Every spring prune out any dead, diseased or crossing branches and remove any branch that may be trying to form a new central leader. If there are a few long laterals that are fruiting only at their tips you can prune them back to a bud around 8cm from the trunk or branch to encourage new growth, but do bear in mind when pruning that new fruit will develop near the end of young shoots. In the summer, you can also prune off the growing tip of new shoots once six leaves have appeared – this directs energies to producing the second burst of young fruit.

If you intend to grow figs in a fan, I would recommend buying an established one, as this will save much early grief. Otherwise train your young plant initially as outlined on pp.156–8, spacing the branches well apart as the leaves are large and will shade the fruit if grown too closely together. Once established, aim to remove around a quarter of the oldest branches each spring to reduce congestion and stimulate new growth. In midsummer remove any buds or shoots that are growing into or out from the wall or fence, and prune out any growth that is shading the developing fruit. Tie in any new growth that will add to the main framework of the fan.

Do wear gloves when pruning as the sap can irritate your skin. It also helps to prune from low to high on the plant, to avoid being dripped on.

Plants can produce new young figs twice a year – once in spring and later in summer. This means the plants will often have fruit of different sizes as summer comes to a close: large almost-ripe figs, tiny fruit (pea-sized and smaller, some of which may be tucked into a joint between leaf and stem), and those in between. The large ones will soon be ready to eat, the small ones are next year's fruit and the ones in between should be removed. They won't ripen this year and are likely to toughen over winter, split and weaken the plant, which can impair the ripening of further fruit. Be ruthless: snip them off every November.

If your plant is in a pot, move it under cover for the winter if you can, otherwise insulating with horticultural fleece, bubble wrap and/or straw will do much to nurse your fig through the cold months.

Harvesting and storage

Figs are best eaten straight from the tree, in the late-summer sun. Most varieties ripen a handful every day over a period of a couple of weeks or so, the centre turning tacky and moist with the eye at the base opening a little. This eye may even weep a sugary tear – the perfect time to pick. The longer you can leave it before you pick, the sweeter your reward.

If (and it's a big if) you don't devour your figs sun-warm from the tree, you can preserve them by drying gently in a low oven (55°C) overnight, keeping the dried figs in the fridge until you eat them.

Pests and diseases

Coral spot (see p.178) is the only nuisance other than birds and wasps for outdoor figs, but you will need to watch for red spider mite (see p.179) and brown scale (see p.177) for those grown under cover.

Eating

Ripeness is the critical factor with figs – their perfume develops late and embellishes the flavour beautifully. For the most part it's best to keep it simple with figs – focusing on combinations that bring out their best. Saltiness and nuts are wonderful partners – blue cheese, prosciutto, walnuts and hazelnuts in particular.

Recipes Baked figs with honey and cardamom (p.210). See also variations for bottled fruit (p.236) and pear and rocket salad (p.228).

Gooseberries *Ribes uva-crispa*

PRUNE	July–August, November–January
HARVEST	May–July

Getting together once a year to see who's got the largest gooseberries may seem little more than a harmless, peculiarly male, British pastime, but for over 200 years this is exactly what's been happening every second Tuesday in August in Egton Bridge, Yorkshire. Thank goodness it has been. Once one of a hundred or more gooseberry shows, the Egton Bridge get-together has sown a 200-year thread from a time when gooseberries enjoyed huge popularity, through the leaner periods, to the current beginnings of a resurgence.

Dips in popularity were mainly due to our obsession with sweetness. A tax on sugar in the nineteenth century saw a huge decline in soft-fruit growing, especially those fruit on the sharper side. And in the latter part of the twentieth century, as our tastes became ever sweeter, they appeared less and less in allotments and back gardens. Now they're back on the up, as more of us have learnt to love their early-season sharpness and the fragrant sweetness of those harvested later in the summer. And for that we should be grateful to those who kept the candle burning.

Varieties

Gooseberries are self-fertile, so growing just one plant is fine. Although a slightly untidy division, gooseberries are usually sold as either cooking or dessert varieties. The latter is supposed to indicate that when fully ripe the berries are sweet enough to eat fresh from the bush, but in practice many of the cookers sweeten considerably if left on the plant to develop longer. 'Leveller' has been around for over 150 years and is the one I'd recommend for the half-and-half harvest, as it produces heavy crops of large golden-green berries. These are gorgeous taken sharp and early, leaving some to grow on into sweet, delicious late-season gooseberries.

'Hinnomaki Red' is one of my favourite sweeter varieties, producing a good crop of big, sweet deep-red/purple berries, while being pretty resistant to mildew.

Growing

Although very hardy, gooseberries love sun and shelter, and growing in a moist but well-drained fertile soil. It's best to avoid shallow sandy soils, which tend to be dry and encourage mildew. Gooseberries will still throw out a good (if reduced) harvest in a shady position, and are worth considering if you have a north-facing wall in need of trained fruit.

Gooseberry 'Hinnomaki Red'

Gooseberries are most commonly grown as bushes, pruned into an open goblet on a short trunk. They also take well to being grown with a taller trunk as a standard, or as a cordon. This last option involves growing the plant as a single tall, narrow stem. It produces excellent harvests for its size and is perfect for those with limited space. Gooseberries can also be fan-trained against a wall and/or wire supports. Position your plants around 90cm from each other, or half as much if grown as cordons.

Watering through dry periods will help good fruit development, and it is essential in the first year as the plant gets established. Gooseberries love potassium (comfrey or seaweed feed is a particularly good source) as it encourages healthy fruiting while reducing the likelihood of mildew. Spraying or watering every fortnight from mid-spring through summer is ideal.

Gooseberries appear on short spurs growing from laterals that are 2 or 3 years old. Older laterals produce very few, so the aim is to have a plant with laterals between 1 and 3 years old.

As soon as you plant your gooseberry, prune off any laterals lower than 20cm up the trunk; this gives a clear 'leg' of the goblet shape you are aiming for. Choose the six (at most) best, well-spaced laterals to form your main framework. Cut these back by half to an outward-facing bud and prune any other laterals off completely.

Next winter, prune back the new growth on the six laterals by half. Also prune back any new growth in the centre of the plant or towards the ground to just a single bud; this encourages fruiting spurs to develop.

In subsequent years, first do as you should with any pruning: clip out dead or diseased branches, and any shoots growing out of the main trunk. Any crossing branches or those in congested areas should be cut back to around 2cm long. Prune off old, unproductive laterals, shortening those that remain by a quarter to an inward-facing bud, to retain the upright shape of the plant. If what remains is still slightly overcrowded, then don't be afraid to thin out some of the new growth a little. Cutting out the old material keeps the plant lively and productive, while an open centre allows light and air to get in, keeping disease to a minimum and encouraging good fruiting. In early summer, brave the sharpness of the prickles and prune back the sublaterals to five leaves or so.

If you fancy growing a gooseberry as a cordon, immediately after planting choose one strong branch as your vertical leader and tie this to a cane. Cut off any shoots lower than 15cm above the ground and prune the rest down to one or two buds. The following summer, prune back new growth to five leaves or so and keep tying in the vertical leader. The following winter, shorten the leader by around a third, and snip back that year's growth to one or two buds. As ever, prune anything that's dead, diseased or damaged, and any congested areas should be thinned to allow light and air in.

Continue this cycle of pruning every year, keeping the leader snipped back to the desired height, and you'll have a healthy gooseberry harvest from virtually no ground space.

Harvesting and storage

I like to pick gooseberries in two main instalments: half when they're not fully ripe in late spring/early summer when the elderflower is still about, leaving the rest to ripen further for picking later in the summer, when they'll be much sweeter than the early tart fruit. Some varieties have the potential to become naturally sweeter than others (see above) and if the plant and the summer looks like it's going well, I occasionally leave the lot to develop.

Wear gloves – the thorns are unforgiving.

Pests and diseases

American mildew can form on young shoots, leaves and fruit, especially in crowded plants where air circulation is poor. Resistant varieties are available, although the likelihood of getting mildew is greatly reduced by hard pruning and good air circulation. If it turns up, wipe off the powdery bloom and prune any affected shoots once you've harvested the fruit.

Sawfly caterpillars are only 2cm long but can strip leaves in a very short time, wiping the plant out if left unchecked, so keep a close eye on the plants and pick off any caterpillars you spot immediately.

Birds can be a nuisance, especially with the sweeter berries, so do net your plants if you're not willing to share more than a few.

Eating

Gooseberries are as generous as it gets: prolific and offering an early sharp/sour harvest followed by a sweet picking later in summer. Although just topped and tailed they can star in tarts and crumbles, a gentle stewing gives you the base to create a sharp sauce that's wonderful with oily and/or smoked fish, or to use in dessert recipes.

Recipes Gooseberry fool with elderflower (p.213), Gooseberry curd (p.216) and Gooseberry tart (p.214). See also variations for crumble (p.239), cake (p.232), mess (p.224), cranachan (p.218), compote (p.200) and granita (p.243).

Grapes *Vitis vinifera*

PRUNE	June–July, November–January
HARVEST	August–October

Years ago I went grape picking in France and Switzerland. It was hard work, but the countryside was incredible, the air fresh and we were offered huge meals. Six times a day, starting at 9.30am (a couple of hours into the working day), we were offered chocolate and wine. The sense of celebration at the harvest stuck with me. We don't seem to have that so much in this country any more but now I've planted a small vineyard of my own I'm determined to recreate it. I hope you will too, even if you only plant one or two vines for making wine or for eating the grapes.

Few plants are so devoted to the sun. Every extra moment of sunshine that hits your grapes adds another degree of sweetness to their flavour, and many won't reach perfection until mid-autumn. Unfortunately this leaves your harvest a hostage to the weather. One year you may be snipping off huge, healthy bunches, the next cursing the late frosts or the lack of late summer sun. Take heart: there is a vineyard in Scotland, and with the right choice of varieties and the relative shelter of your garden or allotment, you should get fruit more summers than not. It's well worth it as grapes eaten fresh from your own vine (or turned into wine) are very special.

Even if you're short of space, grapes are one fruit you should still be able to find room for. Growing them vertically means they take up little ground space, and as long as you keep nutrients and water topped up they'll produce perfectly happily grown in large pots.

Varieties

'Solaris' and 'Phoenix' are two excellent white varieties to grow if you want to have grapes for both eating and wine-making.

'Muscat of Alexandria' has a wonderful muscat flavour and aroma, but its oval berries need a little protection to get them fully ripe.

'Regent' is a vigorous, disease-resistant variety producing very large, sweet, blue-black grapes. It is great for winemaking and eating fresh, and its beautiful red autumn foliage adds end-of-season colour to the garden. 'Black Hamburg' is another delicious black grape variety, often producing enormous bunches, but it does need the very sunniest site or to be grown under cover.

'Madeleine Angevine' is a sweet white grape, ideal for anyone wanting to make wine further up-country, as it flowers late, missing the frosts, and ripens early.

Grapes are self-fertile.

Grape 'Seyval Blanc'

Growing

Grapes love sun and warmth, so give them as much as you can. Plant them in a free-draining soil, shelter them from cold winds and late spring frosts and you'll have a good chance of healthy plentiful bunches.

It's hard to beat a south-facing wall, where the extra heat and shelter will tip the odds of ripe fruit in your favour. For support and to guide growth, you'll want a pair of horizontal galvanised wires at least 15cm from the wall, 35cm or so apart, with the lowest 40cm or so above the ground, fixed with vine eyes drilled into the wall or posts.

If you're growing vines in a row, align them north to south so that the sunlight reaches both sides of the plants equally.

However you're growing your vine, planting is the same. In late autumn or early spring dig down to at least 50cm to ensure you give your plant good drainage. Add well-rotted manure or compost and dig it into the base of the hole along with a few handfuls of grit or gravel. Plant the grape to the same depth as it was in the pot, backfilling with the soil you dug out.

Although grapes will usually be perfectly OK without, a good 10cm layer of well-rotted manure or compost around (but not touching) the base of the plant will act as a nourishing, weed-suppressing mulch. And from flowering through fruiting, a fortnightly feed with seaweed or comfrey liquid will give the plant extra potassium, which will boost the health and size of your crop.

Sunlight is the key to perfectly ripe grapes – tear off any leaves shading the bunches. Watering through extended dry periods will improve your chances of fruit. Keep a particular eye out if you are growing your vine near a wall as it is likely to dry out more quickly.

As long as you keep up with the watering and feeding, grapes can be grown perfectly well in containers with a minimum 30cm diameter. And there's the advantage that you can take them indoors through the coldest months.

Don't be intimidated by what can seem like a bit of a pruning palaver with grapes. There are endless methods for training vines formally along a line and the 'Double Guyot' is as good as any, but for most people, growing grapes under cover, in a container or small space or up and over a pergola are more likely options, and for this you should proceed as follows:

Fix three horizontal wires 45cm apart and with the lowest 45cm above the soil. After planting your vine, push a bamboo cane into the soil by the vine and tie it in to the wires vertically. As the shoots begin to grow, choose the strongest and train it up the cane, rubbing or pruning off the others, including any sideshoots that try to grow. The following winter cut the main stem down to just below the top wire.

The next spring/summer choose the strongest shoot at the top of the main stem to grow, pinching off any others. Choose three shoots along either side of the main

Training a grapevine

Second summer: Tie in laterals, prune at 30cm, and pinch off the top of the vertical shoot from the main stem.

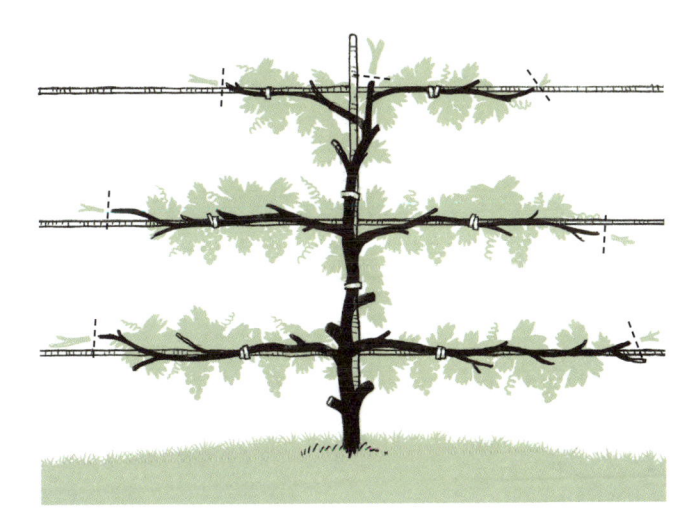

Third summer: Prune off lateral tips three leaves beyond the second bunch of grapes. Rub off shoots growing from the top of the main stem.

stem that are best placed to be trained along the three horizontal wires and tie them in loosely to the wires. Prune off any other sideshoots. When these sideshoots (known as laterals) reach 30cm or so, snip or pinch off the growing tips, and do the same with the vertical shoot from the main stem. You can let two or three bunches develop this year but no more – allow the plant to use most of its energy to establish itself. Remove any others that try to develop when they are tiny.

The following winter, prune back the main stem to just below the top wire and snip back the sideshoots to short spurs of three buds.

In spring/summer, these buds will start to grow. Choose the strongest new sideshoot from each spur, and as it grows tie it along the wire, pruning off any other sideshoots. These sideshoots will produce bunches of grapes – you should allow a maximum of two bunches per sideshoot. Pinch off the end of each sideshoot three leaves beyond its second bunch of grapes – this focuses the plant's energies on producing fruit rather than growing further outwards. Prune off any shoots trying to grow from the top of the main stem.

In subsequent years you can follow the same process as for this third year, although you should be able to allow three bunches per sideshoot.

If you are letting your grape ramble over a pergola or other object, just concentrate on training the main stem up to the required height, tying it in loosely to give it support. After a couple of years a woody framework will have formed and your vine will begin to produce flowers, and then grapes. You can adopt the system described above perfectly well for pergolas too. For a year or two it's worth pinching out the weakest bunches when they're small, leaving four bunches per vine. This isn't essential but it will allow the four to develop fully and means the plant gets enough resources to establish too. From mid-December and before the end of January, thin out overcrowded growth and prune back any areas that are outgrowing the space you have for it.

As with most fruit grown in containers, keep up with watering and ensure the nutrients are topped up with manure, compost and liquid feeds.

Harvesting and storage

Harvest timing varies with variety, the sunniness (or otherwise) of the summer and location, but you may be eating your grapes any time between mid-August and the end of October. Although most grapes approaching ripeness become softer (and in the case of white grapes, more glassy and opaque), tasting the odd grape is really the best way of ascertaining the right moment to pick. Leave the fruit to develop as long as you dare, and snip the whole bunch off when you pick.

Grapes will keep for up to a fortnight in the fridge, depending on the variety and ripeness.

Pests and diseases

Downy and powdery mildews (see pp.178 and 179) can be a problem in damp years. Ventilation and good air circulation is vital – a gentle wind is the best fungicide there is. But should either of these mildews become evident, a sulphur-based spray (see Directory for suppliers, pp.248–9) will help minimise damage.

Birds and wasps can be a nuisance to varying degrees from year to year. Netting and wasp traps are your best remedy.

Eating

You'll not find grapes in too many recipes – they tend not to take well to cooking. They are lovely with cheese, nuts and spicy leaves, such as mizuna and rocket, of course, but if you ask me, you may as well just revel in the pleasure of your own grapes eaten fresh from the vine.

Recipes Chicken Véronique (p.217) and Fruity melons (p.223).

Japanese wineberry

Japanese wineberries
Rubus phoenicolasius

PRUNE	November–January
HARVEST	August–September

Japanese wineberries are one of my very favourite fruit and an absolute must for even the smallest garden.

Although related to raspberries, Japanese wineberries are not a hybrid. They were brought to Europe and North America from their native China, Korea and Japan to cross with raspberries, but their taste stands up on its own. While there is a superficial similarity with raspberries, the flavour of wineberries is longer and has a winey depth like that of well-ripened grapes.

They'll be equally happy grown formally or left ramshackle: you can allow their long, hairy plum-red canes to clamber around as they like, or train them into a strict fan. These long canes throw out sideshoots with large clusters of small pale-pink flowers in early summer that turn into succulent, unbelievably sweet berries, which develop within a papery covering (the calyx). This protects the berries as they grow, peeling open only as the fruit nears maturity. Looking like small raspberries, they poke out green, before traffic-lighting through yellow, orange, and into ripe deep-red over a day or two. This gives the birds little warning and means you get the lot with almost no competition.

After picking, as the colder weather arrives, you get to enjoy the colour of their arching leafless canes as a reminder of the fruit that's gone and is to come.

Varieties
Japanese wineberries are almost always sold as a generic variety.

Growing
Japanese wineberries are self-fertile so having only one plant is fine. While you can grow them from seed, they're rarely available, so start with a plant and you'll also be that much nearer to delicious fruit. If you know someone who has a Japanese wineberry or you want to expand your numbers, you can take advantage of their ability to spread by rooting. All you need to do is encourage the tip of a wineberry cane into the ground and it will form roots. Cut this free from the main plant 30cm or so above the new roots once they are well formed and you have a new plant. You can take hardwood cuttings (see p.130) in late autumn too.

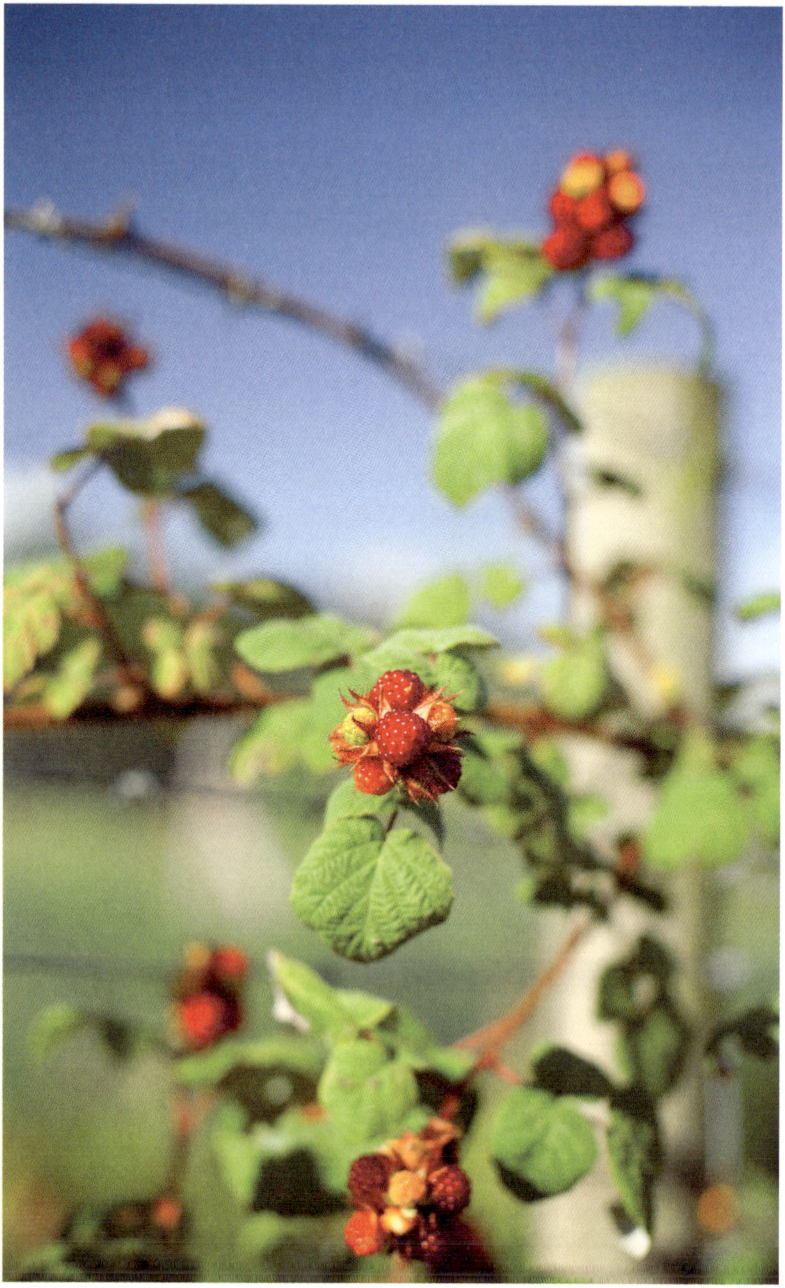

Japanese wineberries pretty much take care of themselves. They are equally at home in a shady spot or a sunny one, and will survive in most soils, but give them a sheltered position with a moist, well-drained soil and they'll fruit prolifically.

You can allow them to scramble about as they like, train them tightly into fans or somewhere in between. Mine are loosely tied to a wire fence, which gives them enough opportunity to ramble but with some sense of order. I have a walnut tree I'm thinking of growing one through too – they fruit equally happily however you grow them.

The furry canes often grow over 2m in length in the first year but grow no longer the following year. Instead, sideshoots with small leaves begin to pop out along the length of each cane, followed by flowers on the ends of the sideshoots in late spring/early summer. These form the fruit.

Pruning is simple. Snip out the canes that have fruited (the ones with old crusty calyxes) any time from autumn onwards but I leave it until late winter, so I can enjoy the fuzzy plum-coloured canes in the winter sunshine.

Harvesting and storage

Japanese wineberries' lack of thorns makes picking them a treat, and the timing of the harvest couldn't be better – filling the lull between the peak of the summer and autumn raspberries, so I get to keep eating Eton mess without a break.

The fruit ripens slowly across the plant rather than in one go, so you're likely to have at least a fortnight of gentle harvesting. Let them get deeply red before you pick, to allow the flavour to develop fully – it's worth the wait.

Pests and diseases

I've never known a wineberry suffer from any diseases, and their magical ability to cover their fruit until they're almost ready means the pests get little chance to get in before you.

Eating

Picked at perfect ripeness, Japanese wineberries are easily polished off way before they make it to your kitchen. If you decide to cook with them don't lose them in a mix of berries – let their individuality come through on its own.

Recipes Cranachan (p.218) and Frozen summer berries with hot white chocolate sauce (p.201). See also variations for mess (p.224), fool (p.213), compote (p.200), bottled fruit (p.236), vodka (p.233), granita (p.243) and fruit leather (p.234).

Medlar 'Nottingham'

Medlars *Mespilus germanica*

PRUNE	November–January
HARVEST	October

Cover your ears and eyes those of a delicate disposition, but you can't talk about medlars without saying (quietly perhaps) 'dog's arse'. Looking much like small, flattened russet apples, medlars have an open end away from the stem that looks unmistakably like a canine's behind. The similarity wasn't lost on the Victorians who christened them somewhat frankly, as did the French and many others, so you can blame them, not me, for any offence taken.

Thankfully the flavour is altogether more appealing – somewhere between an apple and a date. Its truly unique deep, musky and winey taste sits happily next to and within sweet and savoury dishes. The classic recipes of medlar jelly and medlar cheese, sweet as they may be, belong more to the savoury shelf with their affinity with almost any meat and cheese.

Medlars also make beautifully untamed trees, throwing out randomly twisting arms. They really aren't candidates for being trained and constrained to fit wires or flattened against a wall, but let them do their own thing and you'll be rewarded with one of the more characterful small trees you can have in your garden. It will give you rich autumn colours with its leaves, and once they've fallen the delectable fruit will be left hanging like Christmas decorations – perfect for picking after the first frosts.

Varieties

I've never had a bad medlar – every variety seems to be equally tasty. They are self-fertile too. 'Nottingham' is probably the most widely available and has grown and fruited happily for me. It's worth looking out for 'Royal' too – its larger fruit is a little quicker to deal with in the kitchen.

Growing

Growing food doesn't get much easier than a medlar. Plant it as outlined on p.146 and after any formative pruning to give a clear stem for a metre or so, allow it to ramble as it pleases. You may want to just control its spread if it tries to get too large for your site with a little careful pruning in winter.

The wild rose-like flowers appear on the tips of sideshoots and spurs, developing into the characteristic fruits. Take a few moments to enjoy them in spring – they're like lazy dog rose flowers.

Pull any suckers (shoots appearing from the base) as soon as you spot them: cutting can leave short stubs to regrow while pulling is more likely to remove any dormant buds that may throw out suckers the following year.

Harvesting and storage

Medlars are usually enjoyed after they've started to soften and bruise (known as bletting). To get them in this state you can either pick them in mid-autumn when they are still hard and allow them to blet indoors, or wait a few weeks until the frost hits them and race the wildlife to pick the soft fallen ones. You can also hasten the bletting process by giving firm medlars a night in the freezer. I usually pick some medlars early to blet a little indoors, as this is perfect for making jelly, whereas fully soft fruit is ideal for any other use.

Try to pick them on a dry day, to keep moisture on the fruit to a minimum.

Pests and diseases

Medlars are pretty untroubled by ailments, although hawthorn leaf spot can be a problem. It shows as multiple brown leaf spots, about 2mm in diameter, and there is no remedy other than collecting up and incinerating the leaves.

Eating

Medlars aren't for savouring fresh from the tree, they need cooking. Medlar jelly and jam are as fine as any. They also work well in mincemeat – especially paired with that other forgotten fruit, quince. I made a medlar version of the chestnut jam in Pam Corbin's *Preserves* handbook: runnier than most jams, it's more of a sauce and perfect with pancakes or drop scones.

Bake or quarter and gently stew a few handfuls of medlars, then sieve and sweeten to taste and you'll have a rich and datey purée that's a delicious change in creamy recipes such as the mess (p.224) and cranachan (p.218).

Recipes Medlar jelly (p.220).

Fallen medlars ready for picking

Melon 'Minnesota Midget'

Melons *Cucumis melo*

SOW	March–April
HARVEST	August–October

One of the few annual fruits, melons bring a welcome couple of weeks of the exotic to the garden. They look and taste like the slightly wayward children that a cucumber and a squash might come up with, although much, much sweeter and far more succulent than either.

Melons are reliant on getting the heat and sunshine they crave to ripen their fruit, but with the right varieties, a little care and a half-decent summer, the gamble is one worth taking. Growing them under cover, with a little help from a cloche, and/or near a sunny wall, will edge the odds strongly in your favour.

With luck you'll have melons that are far more luscious and aromatic than the ones you're used to buying because you can pick them at their just-ripe peak.

There are three main types of melon: honeydew, which usually have yellow flesh, a firm texture and keep well; musk, with skin that looks as if it's covered in netting, green or orange flesh and which are generally only fruitful under cover; and cantaloupe, usually with ribbed skin and orange flesh. Cantaloupe types need less heat and sun to ripen and are the best options for cooler parts of the country.

Varieties

Many new varieties are being developed which need fewer sunshine hours to ripen, and concentrate energies on fruit production rather than green growth. It's fair to say that these may be your most reliable route to ripe melons, but I think many of the older varieties have the edge on flavour.

'Blenheim Orange' is my favourite of the musk melons, 'Sweetheart' is a fine cantaloupe that's reliable indoors or out, and 'Rocky Ford Honey Dew' is as good as I've had of the honeydews.

Watermelons, although loosely considered as melons, belong to a different family (*Citrullus lanatus*). 'Sugar Baby' is delicious, but needs a lot of water and sunshine to ripen.

Growing

Melons are annuals – sown, grown and harvested within the year. Start them off in small pots in late March or early April on your windowsill, with up to four well-spaced seeds per pot. They tend to germinate well and grow strongly. Water them so that they're moist (but not wet) most of the time. Any extra warmth (from a heated propagator or on a windowsill near a radiator) will move things along well. When the roots have developed and three or four leaves have grown, pot them on into 10–12cm pots.

If you are growing melons outside, harden your plants off, by leaving them outside during the day, and bringing them back indoors at night, for about 2 weeks in early May. This will acclimatise them to outdoor conditions and temperature swings. From late May, plant them outside in a sunny, sheltered patch, under a cloche if you have one for speedier growth, or against a south-facing wall.

If you're growing melons under cover you can plant them without hardening off in mid-May.

Melons like a well-drained, humus-rich soil to grow in. Ensure the soil is loose at the bottom of the hole, so that the roots have an easy route down and out in search of much-needed water and nutrients.

Plant your seedlings just below the top of the root system – don't overdo this as planting too deep can lead to rotting. You can plant them on a small mound of soil, watering sparingly into a moat around the mound until the plant gets to a good size.

Allow 50cm or so distance from their neighbour if growing them up a cane, or twice that if allowing them to scramble willy-nilly.

Water the plants only a little at first to minimise the risk of rotting, increasing gradually as the plant grows. A comfrey feed (or similar, see p.161) every week or so from when flowering starts will really help productivity. Water and feed little and often (rather than deluge at lengthy intervals) as the fruit swells.

Melons are self-fertile, producing both male and female flowers on each plant. They're easy to tell apart – the female flowers have a round swelling at the base of the petals where the fruit will develop. When flowers appear, use a small, soft, dry paintbrush to lightly brush pollen from male flowers onto female flowers to promote good pollination. The best time to do this is in the middle of a hot, humid day.

Netting comes in useful with melons. They are vines that will naturally clamber up or scramble across netting, and keeping the plant largely off the ground helps to reduce the likelihood of disease and rotting.

Don't be tempted to pinch out sideshoots, as this is where flowers develop, but do snip off the growing tips a couple of leaves beyond any fruit. This diverts energies towards the fruit rather than unnecessary green growth.

Having run the gauntlet of researching melons at length on the internet, I've discovered that – rather fittingly – the support the fruit require once they reach tennis-ball size can be most ably provided by an old brassiere. Lacy is best, allowing more light and air through for even ripening. Tights will do equally, if not quite as poetically, well.

Harvesting and storage

Melons enjoy a long season of sun and most will be ready at the end of summer, perhaps even the start of autumn, depending on the variety and how the summer has been. The scent is the giveaway: it should be deep, rich and musky. The skin around the stalk may also start to split and soften, while the south pole of the melon (i.e. away from the stalk) should give a little to thumb pressure. Cut, rather than pull, the fruit from the plant.

Melons will be OK in the fridge for a few days, but do let them get to room temperature for a couple of hours before eating – they'll be better than those you can buy but they never quite recapture that just-picked loveliness.

Pests and diseases

Melons need water, but too much early on can lead to neck rot, where the roots rot away, killing the plant.

Powdery mildew can be a problem, so remove and burn any affected leaves as soon as they're spotted. Red spider mite (see p.179) and whitefly can be problematic to melons grown indoors. Whitefly suck the sap of many plants, encouraging moulds and weakening the plant. It thrives in hot conditions and is usually only a problem for plants grown under cover. Treat with biological control (see Directory, pp. 248–9 for suppliers). Slugs and snails are their usual tedious selves – take whichever measures you favour (see p.180).

Cucumber mosaic virus appears as a mosaic pattern on the leaves and in stunted growth. There is no cure, so burn infected plants immediately and wash your hands and any tools that have come into contact with affected plants to avoid passing it on.

To avoid diseases building up in the soil, don't grow melons in the same bed 2 years in a row.

Eating

One of the loveliest cool garden treats, melons are best treated simply. Their refreshing, grassy sweetness makes for wonderful chilled soups, sorbets and salads, especially in combination with a little mint. For a simple but delicious soup to serve 6, peel, deseed and cube 2 perfectly ripe melons and zap them in a blender with 3 tbsp honey and the juice of 2 lemons. Serve well chilled with a few finely chopped mint and/or basil leaves scattered over.

Recipes Fruity melons (p.223) and Melon salad with goat's cheese, mint and red onion (p.222).

Mulberry 'King James'

Mulberries *Morus* spp.

PRUNE	March–April
HARVEST	August–September

My favourite fruit of all. The first time I ate them was only ten or so years ago. Friends had an ancient tree in their garden and I happened to be staying at just the right time. I wasn't expecting anything too good – I still assumed that if something was tasty it would be widely available – but they were incredible. If you've yet to try them (they're rarely in the shops), look forward to a deeper, winier version of a raspberry with an edge of blackcurrant to it, and a gentle sherbertiness. Comparing their delightful flavour with that of other fruit (and confectionery) doesn't do them full justice – they are utterly delicious.

You won't need to worry about any frosts damaging your chances of fruit: mulberry leaves and flowers are shy of the cold and burst late, providing a reliable signal that spring is properly upon us and the frosts behind. Even with this late kick-off they get their fruit grown and ripened quickly, usually by late July/early August, which makes them a great choice for anyone in a colder area where some of the more frost-susceptible fruit is particularly marginal.

Like medlars, mulberries are beautifully individual in their growth, throwing entirely random shapes that defy any sense of order you might have for them. They're lazily charming, which along with their large pointing-heart leaves, makes mulberries almost as rewarding for their looks as their fruit.

Varieties

Mulberries come in black, white and red varieties – don't let this concern you too much as their fruit doesn't necessarily correlate in colour, so a red mulberry may have black fruit. It is choice of variety that is all important with mulberries. Many are delicious but most take time to start fruiting – often over 10 years. 'Illinois Everbearing', 'Carman', and 'Ivory' are a few of those that will get started after 3 years or so – and once you've tasted mulberries you won't want to wait too long for your own. Mulberries are self-fertile, so growing a single tree is fine.

Growing

Mulberries are easy to grow, needing almost no pruning and attracting few pests or diseases. Plant them as you would most trees (see p.146), in a sunny, sheltered position, avoiding chalky sites. Water in dry periods, especially when the tree is carrying fruit. Prune out any parts that die back after the winter cold.

Inside the canopy of a mulberry

Harvesting and storage

Mulberries ripen their fruit on older wood, during late summer, when the berries become sweet, soft and juicy. They are delicate, so while they can stain clothes, hand-picking is much better than anything too rough.

Perfectly ripe mulberries keep for a very short window (at least part of the reason why you'll very rarely see them for sale), so eat them quickly after harvesting, preferably as they are or treated simply.

Pests and diseases

Slugs love mulberry leaves and can cause serious damage, even killing a young tree, so do use slug pubs, organic pellets and/or go on slug hunts at dusk.

Eating

Please don't mess about with mulberries. Eat as many as you can as you pick them. Any left are fabulous in place of other berries in any of the recipes and the warming qualities of mulberry vodka are so great that it's worth having a cold winter to fully appreciate them. Follow the process for Quince vodka (see p.233) using 500g mulberries, 700ml vodka (or gin) and 160g sugar.

Recipes Mulberry mess (p.224). See also variations for crumble (p.239), clafoutis (p.209), tart (p.214), granita (p.243), trifle (p.244) and cranachan (p.218).

Peach 'Peregrine'

Peaches and nectarines
Prunus persica

PRUNE	May–June
HARVEST	July–September

I can think of no other homegrown food that is so unlike that which you buy in the shops than a peach or a nectarine. Warm from the tree, the fruit is an experience, rather than simply a revelation of flavour.

You'll need patience and considerable restraint to stop yourself picking the tempting fruit when it reaches visual perfection, so possibly handcuff yourself for a few days until your nose fills with the scent of intense peach. The fruit should almost fall into your hand at this point, with only the light touch of your fingers for encouragement.

Peaches and nectarines are far from certs to produce every year – you will need a sunny, well-drained, sheltered site, no late frosts, a reasonable summer and a willingness to employ a wrapping of nocturnal horticultural fleece around the flowers if the temperatures plummet. But if you can sidestep the late frosts, a peach or nectarine tree will reward you well.

And the difference between the two: a single gene which makes peaches gently furry and nectarines smooth.

Varieties

'Peregrine' has a reputation for being the most flavoursome variety, but I find 'Red Haven' and 'Rochester' equally delicious, while much more resistant to leaf curl. Don't believe the hype about 'Avalon Pride' being immune to leaf curl. Not only is it far from the finest-flavoured variety, the 40 trees I have grown at River Cottage and Otter Farm became riddled with leaf curl. As for nectarines, 'Pineapple' and the slightly more leaf-curl resistant 'Flavourtop' are the two choicest nectarines in my view.

Most peaches and nectarines are grafted onto 'St Julien A' rootstock (semi-vigorous, 5–6m height).

'Nectarella' nectarine and 'Bonanza' peach are dwarf varieties that grow slowly to only 1.3m or so, needing no pruning at all, and are the perfect choice for growing in a pot (minimum 50cm diameter).

Both peaches and nectarines are self-fertile, so you can grow a single tree, should you so wish.

Growing

Choose your site well, giving your tree shelter and sunshine. Plant as you would any fruit tree (see p.146), ensuring a good well-drained, fertile soil. Flowering time is the crucial period when you'll need to pay attention. Growing later-flowering varieties helps avoid the potential for frost damage, which would ruin any prospect of fruiting. But if you want to up your chances even more, get ready with some horticultural fleece to protect the blossom from cold night-time temperatures, making sure you get it off early in the morning so that pollination can take place. Hand pollinating (see p.189) with a soft, dry brush, every day through flowering if you can, will really increase the likelihood of fruit – especially in years where the blossom comes early and there are few pollinating insects around.

From the emergence of blossom, give the tree a good feed with comfrey liquid every fortnight to promote good fruit development.

Spacing depends on your chosen rootstock, but 6m is usual for larger trees. You can thin the growing fruit when they are small, or if any are wedged between branches or against a wall, so that the remaining fruit are 10cm or so apart. Those left on the tree should grow on more reliably to full-sized fruit.

Nectarines and peaches both take well to fan training (see pp.156–8), as well as being grown freestanding as a bush or pyramid.

The initial training of freestanding peaches and nectarines is as for plums (see p.154); you're after an open-centred bush or well-balanced pyramid. Once established, prune every summer and when doing so think of the next growing season. Peaches and nectarines fruit on branches and shoots grown the previous year so you'll want to snip out older wood to allow newer growth to develop and fruit. Cut back to a growth bud (these are pointed, while the fruit buds are fatter), to encourage new shoots which may bear fruit the next year. Remove any dead, diseased or damaged branches.

As with all stone fruit trees, pruning should take place on a dry, sunny day in late spring or summer to minimise the likelihood of silver leaf (see p.180) and bacterial canker (see p.176). Disinfect your secateurs after pruning each tree to avoid disease contamination.

Harvesting and storage

Depending on the variety, where you are in the country and the nature of the summer, your fruit should be ready from late July through August. Ripening occurs gradually over the tree, so you'll need to harvest daily once they get going.

Allow the fruit to develop its distinctive deep aroma – this can be a few days after you think it looks ready to eat, but be patient. Cup your hand around the fruit very gently (as if the peach was a cracked egg) and give a slow half-twist without any downward pull. When it's perfectly ready, the fruit will surrender.

Pests and diseases

While you can grow peaches and nectarines out in the open, if you train them against a sunny wall or grow dwarf varieties in pots it is much easier to protect them from their main enemy, leaf curl (see p.178), by covering or taking potted dwarf varieties indoors.

If you are growing your peaches and nectarines under cover, red spider mite (see p.179) can trouble them, as can brown scale (see p.177).

Eating

So fine are homegrown peaches and nectarines that it's almost inconceivable that you'll not eat them all fresh, beneath the tree. If the summer fades before all your peaches and nectarines are perfectly ripe then a gentle poaching in white wine with a few aromatic spices such as star anise, cloves and cinnamon is all they need to draw out the flavour and soften them beautifully.

Nectarines and peaches both have an affinity with cream, milk and yoghurt, so try them in smoothies too.

Recipes Peach (or nectarine) salsa (p.227) and Fruity melons (p.223). See also variations for apricots on toast (p.199), cranachan (p.218), fool (p.213) cake (p.232) and pear and rocket salad (p.228).

Immature nectarine fruit

Pears *Pyrus communis*

PRUNE	November–February
HARVEST	August–November

Pears, as Eddie Izzard noted, are 'gorgeous little beasts, but they're ripe for half an hour, and you're never there'. An exaggeration perhaps, but one that's not too far from the truth.

Pears are less of an instant pleasure than apples, most of which you can munch straight off the tree, but they are worth the gentle inconvenience. You pick them early and firm to ripen indoors, and while this delays the eating, it does mean few are troubled by pests or damaged while harvesting.

Pear trees can take a while to start fruiting properly and they don't take kindly to the cold or an imperfect supply of water. However, if you choose the most suitable varieties and eat them right at the ripe point, then you can expect a depth and complexity of flavour, as well as a succulence, that's of a different order entirely from those in the shops.

Varieties

'Conference' and 'Doyenne du Comice' are commonly grown in the UK and both are reliable and relatively easy to coax a good harvest out of. These varieties ripen in October–November.

Of the many other varieties, my favourites are: 'Beurre Giffard', which gives melting, winey early pears that are ready to eat in August; 'Fondante d'Automne' with its musky, lightly russeted fruit in September–October; 'Louise Bonne of Jersey' with its aromatic pears ready in October; and the late 'Glou Morceau', ready in time to see the New Year in.

A few new varieties are self-fertile and if you have room for only one pear then do make sure you choose one of these. That said, self-fertile varieties will crop better with a pollinating partner nearby. As with apples, the pollination group of your chosen varieties should be the same or from an adjacent group. Occasionally neighbours remain stubbornly incompatible (I know how they feel); for example 'Doyenne du Comice' and 'Onward' should, but won't pollinate each other. Check with your nursery.

Pears are usually grafted onto 'Quince A' (semi-vigorous, 4–6m height) or 'Quince C' (semi-dwarfing, 2.5–5m height) rootstocks.

A family tree (see p.24), where more than one variety is grafted onto a single stem, is also an option.

Pear 'Concorde'

Growing

Pears can be a little temperamental but so many of the best varieties aren't available in the shops that it makes the little effort required more than worthwhile. All but 'Conference', which can rough it a little, require a sheltered, sunny location with a fertile, well-drained soil, ideally neutral or slightly acidic. Avoid sandy soils.

Plant your tree as suggested on p.146, spaced 5m from its neighbour if on 'Quince A' rootstock, or 3.5m if on 'Quince C'.

Pears take well to espalier training (plant at least 2.5m apart), as well as single and double cordons (80cm and 1.5m apart respectively), and stepovers (see p.128).

Pear trees are pruned and trained as for apples (see p.153), and almost all are spur-bearers.

Water pear trees through any extended dry periods in summer and add well-rotted manure as a fertilising top dressing around (but not touching) the base in early spring. A good feed with compost or well-rotted manure every late winter or early spring can make all the difference to your harvest.

Harvesting and storage

There are three stages to bear in mind when harvesting pears: picking, storing and ripening.

You'll almost always pick pears while they're hard. They need time in a cool, dry, dark place (a garage is ideal) to mature. Judging the time for picking is the key. Firstly, ask your supplier (or look online) for the approximate time of picking for your variety, and then you'll need to be eagle-eyed for one or more of the following: the first windfalls; an often subtle lightening or flushing of the skin; and if, when you cup a pear and lift it upwards and gently twist, it separates from the tree with the stalk intact. It sounds like it might be a fuss but if you relax and check frequently one or more of those signs will show itself.

You can also try the taste test: the pears will be hard to the bite but when ready they should be sweet. This works for all except late-season pears, which are best cup-lift-twist tested.

Don't be tempted to leave pears too long on the tree. Left past the right point they can go 'sleepy' (grainy, soft and sometimes brown) in storage.

Store them in a single layer, not touching each other. Don't be tempted to bring them straight into the house to ripen – they usually either refuse to soften or go mealy. Regularly check pears while they're in storage and remove any showing signs of rot. Bring them into the main part of the house a few days before you want to eat them to allow them to ripen nicely.

Check ripening pears regularly. If you don't keep half an eye on them they'll take the opportunity to turn from stone to mush while you're out of the room making a cup of tea.

Pests and diseases
Pears can suffer from scab (see p.180) and fireblight (see p.178). Pear leaf blister mite causes blistering, and pear midges can cause leaves to roll up; in both cases, pull off and burn any affected leaves.

Eating
Wonderful in leafy or fruit salads, pears work exceptionally well with salty foods – blue and goat's cheeses and air-dried ham especially – as well as walnuts, pecans and hazelnuts.

If you're impatient, have a glut or are just looking for another way to treat pears, you can eat them early, poaching them to soften in white wine or sugar syrup with aromatic flavourings, such as bay, cloves, star anise, cinnamon and/or a vanilla pod.

Recipes Poached pears and chocolate sauce (p.231), Orchard ice cream with caramelised walnuts (p.195), Fruity melons (p.223) and Pear and rocket salad with Blue Vinny and walnuts (p.228). See also variations for melon salad (p.222), compote (p.200), clafoutis (p.209), cake (p.232) and vodka (p.233).

Pear 'Louise Bonne of Jersey' in storage

Plum 'Purple Pershore'

Plums, damsons, bullaces and gages *Prunus domestica* and *Prunus insititia*

PRUNE	May–June
HARVEST	July–October

Last summer I picked the first basket of Dittisham plums, eating a fair few while I was at it and on the walk back to the house. The rest went into a bowl. Within a couple of hours the house was filled with a heavy, sweet, invisible cloud of plum. A more perfect alternative to those hideous plug-in room fresheners I can't imagine.

The recipe for this house-filling perfume is a simple one. Find a fruit nursery that specialises in local varieties and tell them about your proposed site; buy two varieties for best pollination (and therefore fruiting); then wait a couple of years at most. Every summer thereafter you'll be able to enjoy the aroma – and the taste.

There is a rather fuzzy line between plums, damsons, bullaces and greengages. All plums and gages are varieties of *Prunus domestica*, with gages (sweet, green plums brought to the UK from France 300 years ago) tending to be sweeter and more spherical than plums. Damsons and bullaces are varieties of *Prunus insititia*, producing smaller fruits than their relatives, on small, hardy trees. Both fruits tend to be flavoursome but tart, excellent for cooking rather than eating fresh. You'll find damsons, bullaces and gages much less frequently in the shops, so do consider them for a space in your garden.

The markings on plum stones are unique to each variety, a fruity fingerprint of sorts. When Henry VIII's flagship, the *Mary Rose*, was raised after 450 years at the bottom of the sea, over 100 varieties of plum stone were found – a clue to the importance of plums in our diet at the time, and our appreciation of the range of flavours and textures plums and their relatives offer. You'll be lucky to find 50 tree varieties available now.

Varieties

Grow two if you can – even self-fertile varieties fruit more reliably with a compatible partner. Or if growing one tree, make it a self-fertile variety and use a soft brush to move pollen from one blossom to another. You can choose plums that will fruit in early, mid or late season but as with apples, you'll need to ensure your varieties belong to coinciding or adjacent pollination groups.

'Victoria' is a reliable, high-yielding, self-fertile cooker/eater and an excellent choice for a single tree, but there are finer-flavoured plums out there if you have room for two or more trees. 'Jefferson', 'Rivers' Early Prolific', 'Pershore Yellow Egg' and 'Kirke's Blue' are fabulous, but do look into your local and other vanishing varieties. There are some spectacularly tasty gems out there.

If you're after a later-ripening variety, 'Marjorie's Seedling' will give you plums as late as October some years.

'Blue Violet' (from the Lake District), 'Farleigh Damson' and 'Dittisham Damson' are my favourite of the damsons.

All the bullace varieties I've tried have been equally delicious, less fine for eating fresh but all good for making excellent preserves.

Do try gages. 'Oullin's Gage' (self-fertile) is great for cooking or eating fresh and its tendency to flower late gives the blossom a better chance of missing any late frosts. 'Coe's Golden Drop' and 'Golden Transparent' are wonderfully sweet too.

As with pears, some from the same or adjacent pollination groups refuse to pollinate each other: 'Rivers' Early Prolific' and 'Jefferson'; 'Cambridge Gage' and 'Old Green Gage', for example. Check with your supplier for incompatibilities.

Mirabelles, also known as cherry plums, are popularly grown in France but comparatively rare here, yet their apricot-sized fruit is delicious, ripening more quickly than plums. Mirabelles are also hardier than many plums, making them a great choice for growing in the UK. 'Golden Sphere' and 'Gypsy' are both good.

Most plums and their close relatives are grafted onto 'St Julien A' (semi-vigorous, 2.5–3m height) or 'Pixy' (semi-dwarfing, 2–2.2m height).

Growing

Plums and their near relatives enjoy a fertile, well-drained soil in a sunny, sheltered position. They are a little particular when it comes to water, as they like a reasonable amount of it through the warmer months but hate waterlogged soils at any time of the year. A heavyish but well-drained site is ideal. If your position doesn't quite match up to this, you can add plenty of organic matter to help retain water. Make sure you water the tree in the first year and through any extended dry spells. Mulching generously every spring particularly helps to retain precious water.

The trees themselves are generally very hardy but flowering is the crunch time. They usually blossom early and can be very susceptible to frosts killing off the flowers – and your chances of fruit. Avoid frost pockets or windy sites and (if you can be bothered) use horticultural fleece on cold nights once the flowers appear, removing it early in the morning so pollination isn't compromised.

Flowers are carried mainly at the base of year-old shoots and along the length of 2-year-old shoots, as well as any fruiting spurs.

Fruit is usually thinned as it develops, especially in the early years. This involves snipping out some when they're small and still green, leaving around 8cm between fruit. Those remaining will develop much more happily. Thinning also helps those varieties (such as 'Victoria') that are prone to one heavy harvest followed by a much lesser one to have a more consistent harvest. Branches are less likely to snap under the weight of developing fruit too. Don't be alarmed if the tree sheds some fruit; known as 'June drop', this is just its way of managing the crop it can handle.

Plums and their close relations are happily grown as bushes or pyramids, or trained as cordons, minarettes or fans (see p.128). It's easier if you buy them part trained. Once the initial pruning is done, keep pruning to an absolute minimum, as it invites diseases. Just take out dead, diseased, damaged or crossing branches from freestanding trees in summer and prune fans as described on pp.156–8.

With a dwarfing rootstock such as 'Pixy', plums can be grown in large pots but watering is critical as any drying out can stress the plant and reduce productivity.

Harvesting and storage

Depending on the variety, location and the type of summer, plums, damsons and gages can be ready to harvest between July and mid-October.

The first few fruits dropping of their own accord is the green light for picking. Colour is a reasonable indicator of readiness but not as accurate as aroma and the ease of separating the fruit from the tree. The fruit ripens gradually across the tree so you'll need to harvest in more than one visit. Pick carefully to avoid bruising the delicate fruit and, if possible, leave a short stalk to keep the fruit and next year's buds intact. The fruit should give up their grip with the gentlest of persuasion.

Pests and diseases

Silver leaf disease (see p.180) is the most likely nuisance and minimising pruning helps enormously in reducing the likelihood. Brown rot (see p.177), blossom wilt (see p.176), bacterial canker (see p.176) and rust (see p.179) can occur. Gummy spots of resin appearing on the bark is usually a sign of stress.

Aphids may appear in early spring but rarely do more than cosmetic damage, though it can be worth stringing up pheromone traps in mid-May to trap male plum moths and prevent their larvae decimating your ripening fruit.

Eating

Plums and their relations are among the most rewarding of fruits to grow. Available in sweet or sharper varieties, they offer endless culinary possibilities. Eaten fresh as they're picked, stewed into a compote to enjoy hot or cold, baked in a clafoutis, cake, crumble or tart, or even left in a jar with sugar and vodka, they are superb.

Recipes Plum and hazelnut cake (p.232). See also variations for apricots on toast (p.199), baked figs (p.211), compote (p.200), clafoutis (p.209), crumble (p.239), tart (p.214), cranachan (p.218), fool (p.213), granita (p.243) and vodka (p.233).

Quince 'Meeches Prolific'

Quince *Cydonia oblonga*

PRUNE	November–February
HARVEST	October

Quince are about deferred culinary pleasure. There is no luscious, succulent, aromatic loveliness to pick from the tree; you have to wait a little longer. You'll almost always pick quince hard, sharp and by all immediate culinary measures inedible. But once indoors quince will ripen gradually, and as the fruit sweetens and softens it releases a perfume that lifts the entire house.

Quince are now fairly uncommon in this country, but it wasn't always this way. King Edward I planted the first quince on these shores in the grounds of the Tower of London 800 years ago. They gained and retained popularity for all but the last century when we became keener on increasingly available and more 'immediate' exotic fruit. They are enjoying something of a resurgence, but you'll still rarely find quince for sale, so you may have to grow a tree to enjoy this marvellous fruit.

Varieties

'Meeches Prolific' and 'Vranja' both ripen early and are reliably heavy croppers, bearing large, delicious fruit. They fruit early in life and although all quince are self-fertile they will pollinate each other, meaning you get a larger crop. 'Leskovac' and 'Krymsk' are newer, similarly delicious varieties that show promise of ripening fully on the tree in good, long sunny summers.

Quince are one of the few trees usually grown on its own rootstock: 'Quince A' for a plant 4–4.5m high; 'Quince C' for one 3–3.5m.

Growing

Quince like the same conditions as most fruit trees: shelter, good sunshine and a good fertile soil. They will be happy in a moist (but not waterlogged) soil but don't try growing them in alkaline conditions as they like neutral to mildly acidic soils. Plant as outlined on p.146, allowing 5m or so from its neighbour, or 4m if you've chosen a tree on a 'Quince C' rootstock. Quince are low-maintenance trees, requiring only watering through dry periods. A good spring mulch is worth the trouble, keeping the roots cool and retaining precious water.

Flowers develop mainly at the end of year-old stems, with some also on short spurs. The fruit follows quickly but can be a little discouraging – sitting there, mostly unchanging for a few summer months until autumn approaches, when the small nuggets become plump.

Quince flowering

Give your quince a monthly comfrey tea or seaweed feed (see p.161), by leaf spraying or watering around the roots, from the start of flowering through to harvesting, and you're likely to have a larger crop.

Prune quince trees in winter to establish a goblet shape, but do remember that they are naturally erratic in shape and will throw random twists and arcs. Don't be too strict with them if you want to release their full charm. And bearing in mind they are predominantly tip-bearing, don't remove much in the way of year-old stems. Once established, prune out dead, diseased or congested growth only.

Harvesting and storage

Quince are usually picked unripe in early autumn, when they separate from the tree easily without twisting or yanking. Hard and sour before fully ripened, quince will ripen in storage or in a bowl in the house. You'll know when they've got there as you'll have a house full of their incredible scent. Don't pick them too soon – every extra day will be of benefit to the fruit – but do make sure you get them in before the first frosts.

You'll have plenty of time to enjoy your quince as they usually store well into (and occasionally through) winter. Keep quince separate from other fruits in storage – their perfume may taint them.

Pests and diseases

Quince are susceptible to powdery mildews (see p.179), brown rot (see p.177) and fireblight (see p.178). Quince leaf blight can be a nuisance too, showing itself as small brown dots on the leaves, which, although usually cosmetic only, can develop into serious infections that stress the tree considerably. Rake up any affected fallen leaves and burn them to reduce the likelihood of repetition the following year. If your tree has had a bad infection, consider spraying with Bordeaux mixture (a copper-based fungicide) as the leaves emerge the following spring.

Eating

As with pears, quince are rarely ready to eat straight from the tree. Once they reach their aromatic peak they are ready to core, stuff with butter and sugar and bake – to be eaten warm with yoghurt or ice cream, added sparingly to apple pies and tarts to give a hint of their lovely perfume and colour, or to be made into membrillo (quince cheese), a firm jelly that's incredible, especially with cheese.

Recipes Orchard ice cream with caramelised walnuts (p.195) and Quince vodka (p.233). See also variations for pear and rocket salad (p.228), tagine (p.196), poached pears (p.231), compote (p.200), crumble (p.239), granita (p.243), jelly (p.220) and fruit leather (p.234).

Raspberries *Rubus idaeus*

PRUNE	September–November, February–March
HARVEST	July–November

Everybody should grow raspberries, they are so easy and delicious. It should be the law. All that lovely sweet-sharpness for virtually no effort.

Greek myth has it that all raspberries were once white, until the nymph Ida, while picking wild raspberries for Jupiter, pricked her finger on the thorns, her blood staining the fruit from that moment on. You may struggle to find white raspberries, but yellow varieties are sold widely and tend to dodge the birds' attention more than red ones.

I'm not a great one for getting too deeply into the botanicals, but occasionally it's worthwhile, especially when it shines a light on something in the kitchen. Raspberries are a case in point. They aren't berries as such, but clusters of drupelets. Each of these individual bobbles of the 'berry' is a fruit in itself, enclosing its own seed, and attached to its neighbours by the fine threads that look like micro-hairs. This binding allows the cluster of drupelets to stay together, coming away from the core intact when picked. It gives them their characteristic hollow centre, which rather pleasingly scoops up cream.

Varieties

Raspberries are self-fertile and come in summer-fruiting and autumn-fruiting varieties that can be equally delicious, although they behave a little differently from each other and have a few differing requirements, as detailed below. If you have the space it's good to grow both to enjoy a long, tasty season. Of the summer varieties, I like 'Glen Moy' (spineless too), 'Glen Ample' and 'Glen Magna'. 'Autumn Bliss' and the yellow 'Allgold' are my favourite autumn-fruiters.

Growing

Raspberries are fairly tolerant of most situations, apart from alkaline soils. Neutral to slightly acidic soils, rich in organic matter, are ideal. Any mulching you can give your plants will help to retain the moisture raspberries need. Shelter and sun are vital for the largest crop.

Plant raspberries 45cm or so apart, with 2m between rows for summer varieties and 1m for autumn cultivars. Don't plant them with their roots spread wide, or too deeply as raspberries are shallow-rooting. Some people snip off the top of the cane after planting, to just above a bud, 25cm above ground level.

Raspberry 'Glen Ample'

Trained raspberries

Summer raspberries, harvested in the hottest months, produce fruit on canes that grew the year before, so you'll not get fruit in the first summer. Each cane fruits only once, so remove fruited canes after harvesting, leaving room for new canes to grow through. Tie canes to horizontal wires as they grow to stop them flailing around and the older shoots from snapping in the wind.

Autumn raspberries ripen their fruit on the current year's canes so after you've enjoyed the fruit from them they won't produce any more the next year. Wait until late winter then cut all the canes to the ground. As new shoots grow steadily in early summer thin them to avoid overcrowding, leaving 8cm or so between developing canes. You can support the growing shoots by tying them to horizontal wires. Alternatively, be lazy and just snip out overcrowded patches and let your raspberries grow as a hedge – they'll look less classically beautiful but be very productive.

Raspberries can spread sideways by growing suckers. If an expanding raspberry patch isn't something you want, do pull them up as they appear.

After 10 years or so, raspberry plants decline in productivity and often become more susceptible to diseases, so after 8 or 9 years it pays to replace them with new canes. You can take advantage of their suckering habit as a cheap way of replenishing your stocks (see p.135). Plant them in a different part of your plot to minimise the likelihood of diseases building up.

Raspberries will do reasonably well in containers, if a little lower in yield, and you'll need to water and feed them regularly. Autumn varieties, being smaller, suit container growing best. Three canes in a 30cm diameter pot is about right. Be prepared to support them as they grow if necessary.

Harvesting and storage

Summer-fruiting varieties are usually ready from mid-June to mid-August, while autumn raspberries ripen from August to October.

Raspberries are perfectly ripe when a gentle pull separates the fruit from the plant, leaving the plug clean and intact – usually a day or two after they look ready. Any that you may have let go beyond perfect ripeness should still be picked and composted. This stimulates new fruit to develop, whereas any decaying fruit left on the plant will encourage pests and diseases.

Raspberries freeze well. To stop them clumping together, freeze in a single layer on a tray, then tip into a bag or tub when frozen – in quantities to suit.

Pests and diseases

Raspberries are susceptible to a number of viruses, which usually appear first as mottling and yellow blotching of the leaves or, in the case of cane blight and cane spot, as purple spots or black bases on the canes. Your plants will be weakened and your harvest limited. It pays to buy certified virus-free plants to keep your troubles to a minimum. There's no cure for most viruses, although some varieties are more resistant than others, and thinning encourages air circulation, which helps reduce the likelihood of infections. If your plants are affected, dig up and incinerate them immediately.

Birds can be a complete nuisance or they may ignore your raspberries entirely. Net your plants if the former.

Raspberry beetle will indicate its presence through dried patches at the stalk end of the fruit, usually around July, and you'll find a maggot. There is no cure, so if you see the adults, which are brown and 5mm long, squash them immediately. Autumn-fruiting varieties are less affected.

Eating

Raspberries will take happily to many of the recipes in this book, though you may prefer to enjoy them just as they are, or simply with cream or crème fraîche.

Recipes Raspberry fruit leather (p.234), Fruity melons (p.223), Bottled raspberries (p.236), Frozen summer berries and hot white chocolate sauce (p.201) and Summer pudding (p.202). See also variations for mess (p.224), fool (p.213), granita (p.243), trifle (p.244), cranachan (p.218), tart (p.214), crumble (p.239) and vodka (p.233).

Redcurrant 'Red Lake'

Redcurrants and white currants *Ribes rubrum*

PRUNE	May–June, November–January
HARVEST	July–August

Alongside medlars, red- and white currants make the finest jelly – especially good with lamb, game and cheese. Given that these soft fruits are rarely available in the shops and expensive when they are, this is reason alone to grow them.

Although red- and white currants are usually sharp and so best enjoyed in the kitchen, if you can be patient and have your currants netted against birds you may get to eat them deliciously sweet as you pick them. Not that sweeter is necessarily better, but by protecting your ripening currants you open up the possibility of a double harvest (as with gooseberries).

Usually 5–10mm in diameter, these currants hang in tassels, known as racemes or strigs, that poke through the leaves like a nosy neighbour. Both are keenly snaffled by birds, who are happy to nip them off one at a time as they mature, so do net them if you can, or if you can't, use bird-scarers of one kind or another (CDs swinging on string are great).

Varieties

'Jonkheer van Tets', 'Red Lake' and 'Redstart' are excellent redcurrant varieties, that ripen one after the other. Of the white currant varieties, 'White Versailles' is a long-established favourite and hard to rival as a reliable, flavoursome choice. 'Rovada' is also good and ripens after 'White Versailles', giving you a longer season if you grow both.

Growing

Red- and white currants are self-fertile and like a sheltered, well-drained spot with a fertile soil. They are best positioned in sun for the sweetest fruit, but they will tolerate a little shade, making them good for training against a shady wall.

Plant them 1.3m apart or 60cm from each other if grown as double cordons (see p.128). Plant bare-root currants in late autumn ideally (but no later than the end of winter). If you've bought container-grown plants, they may be planted at any time. Mulch plants every spring and water through extended dry periods.

Red- and white currants fruit on buds that form at the base of last year's new shoots. Whether grown as open bushes, standards, cordons or fans, red- and white

Fan-trained white currant

currants should be pruned hard in winter to take out unproductive and crossing branches. Prune sublaterals back to one bud to encourage new spurs, which will develop flowers and fruit.

Cordons should also be pruned as summer arrives: cut new sublaterals back to five leaves. In winter, cut back the leader to just above one bud of last year's growth and prune all sublaterals to two buds to encourage new fruiting spurs.

Whichever form you grow your red- or white currants in, use canes and twine to tie the branches, as they will become heavy when in fruit. Netting against birds is crucial unless you're happy to share much of your crop.

Currants are shallow-rooting and therefore happy to be grown in containers (30cm minimum diameter is ideal).

Harvesting and storage

The fruit is ready mid to late summer. Redcurrants become a lively red, with white currants developing a richer, creamy ivory colour. But be patient with redcurrants – they need a little longer after reddening to develop sweetness. Pinch them from the plant as whole trusses, running a fork down the trusses to release the currants. They tend to spoil fairly quickly in the fridge but freeze well – spread out in a single layer on a tray and freeze, before bagging them up in quantities to suit you.

Pests and diseases

Redcurrant blister aphids cause red blisters on redcurrant leaves in summer, and yellow blistering to white and blackcurrants. Check the underside of leaves in late spring for yellow aphids and remove them – but don't reach for the chemicals as the effect is only cosmetic – you'll still be in for fruit. If you do want to do something about the impact, try pyrethrum – an organic treatment made from the white flowerheads of the pyrethrum plant. Also, in mid-June, cut back the sideshoots to a centimetre or two short of the first fruit to remove any blistered leaves and encourage good air circulation around the fruit.

If your plants are affected by sawfly larvae or coral spot (see p.178), cut any affected shoots back to good wood and burn the prunings.

Eating

Red- and white currants make a fabulous jelly to complement meat and cheese, but for the most part they are better in a supporting role, bringing their colour and sweet/sharp edge to any number of puds.

Recipes Frozen summer berries and hot white chocolate sauce (p.201) and Summer pudding (p.202). See also variations for jelly (p.220), tart (p.214), fool (p.213), cranachan (p.218) and bottled fruit (p.236).

Forced 'Timperley Early' rhubarb

Rhubarb *Rheum* x *hybridum*

HARVEST	March–July

I couldn't be without rhubarb. I love its sour sharpness but as with all the kitchen-garden essentials, timing is what turns something fabulous into a real must-have. Depending on the variety, you can be pulling stalks from mid-April through summer but if you've a forcing pot (or a large bucket) you can not only get yourself an early harvest, you'll get one of the great treats of the edible garden.

A few square miles of Yorkshire countryside has the perfect conditions for growing the very finest rhubarb. With the right level of rain, ideal soil and waste wool, ashes and soot from the local nineteenth-century industries, a flourishing community of forced-rhubarb producers sprang up. Competition for the earliest sales (and therefore the best prices) drove new methods for growing until the classic outdoor-indoor method was found.

The plants are grown in the field for 2 years to give them a good start, then brought indoors each winter after a period of cold induces dormancy. The sheds are warm to cause the plant to awaken but, with the light excluded, the plant uses its own reserves (glucose in its base) to feed the early growth of new stalks. This happens at such a rate that you can hear the creaks and cracks of expansion.

Without light the rhubarb grows a wonderful livid pink with yellow leaves, instantly distinguishable from maincrop rhubarb. It is also more succulent and sweeter than the unhurried version. Harvested by candlelight, as exposure to strong light halts this type of growth, the forced rhubarb ensures a steady crop until the outdoor harvest begins.

You can replicate these conditions by placing a rhubarb forcer or a large bucket over the crowns in late winter. If you can pile fresh manure around it all the better; it's not essential but the raised temperature will speed up the growth even more. Your reward will be stunning stalks a good 4 or 5 weeks ahead of the main harvest. You may not want to do this for all your plants though, as once the forced crop is over you should leave your plants to recover over the spring and summer, ready to produce the following year. After harvesting, remove the forcer or bucket.

Varieties

'Timperley Early', 'Raspberry Red' and 'Victoria' are as good as any varieties, with 'Victoria' fruiting a little later than the other two. 'Timperley Early' produces earlier than most varieties, but it does have a fairly high chilling requirement (i.e. it needs lots of winter cold) and so is particularly suited to colder areas.

Rhubarb forcers

Growing

Rhubarb is pretty simple to grow – it's the courgette of the fruit world. You can buy young crowns or divide established ones (see p.135) to multiply your stock. If you are buying young crowns, allow the plant to establish for a year in the ground before harvesting more than the odd stalk.

Give your plant a rich, well-manured position in full sun, water it through dry periods, and you'll be able to return every day or two to pull repeated harvests through its season. Allow at least 90cm between plants.

If flowers appear, cut them off, as they reduce the vigour of the leafy stalk growth which is the part you want to eat. In autumn, as the foliage withers, remove dead leaves and add well-rotted manure and a good mulch to give them the best start to the following growing season.

Harvesting and storage

Depending on the variety and the sunniness of the season, you can be harvesting rhubarb from March until the end of July, when you should stop picking to allow the plant to grow and store reserves for the following year. For the most flavoursome, tender stalks, choose stems with good colour, where the leaves have just unfolded fully. Don't cut the stems – there's a knack to harvesting: grasp the stem low on the plant, and give a sharp pull-and-twist to remove the stalk cleanly.

Chop off leaves and get them straight into the compost heap; they're poisonous to eat so there's no point bringing them into the kitchen.

Pests and diseases

Rhubarb is pretty immune from diseases. If you notice limp foliage, weak stems and new buds dying off during the growing season your plant may have a fungal disease, crown rot. There's no alternative to digging the plant up, incinerating and planting new crowns.

Eating

Stewed gently with a little sugar or sweet cicely, rhubarb makes a great sauce for oily fish or poultry.

Rhubarb is also fabulous roasted. Cut into short lengths, lay in an ovenproof dish and grate the zest of an orange and a 3–4cm piece of fresh ginger over it. Dust with sugar, cover loosely with foil and roast in the oven at 160°C/Gas mark 3 for about 40 minutes until tender.

Recipes Rhubarb crumble (p.239) and Rhubarb and strawberry tart (p.240). See also variations for fool (p.213), mess (p.224), cranachan (p.218), trifle (p.244), tart (p.214) and granita (p.243).

Strawberry 'Honeoye'

Strawberries *Fragaria* x *ananassa*

HARVEST	May–October

Until last summer I had always been a little sniffy about strawberries. I love them as any sane person should, but given a straight choice, I'd have taken raspberries every time. I'm not so sure now. Last summer I grew six varieties and gave them a little more attention than I have in the past and they were extraordinary. I was even out there with the tennis racket for any wasps that got a little crabby when I was picking. I don't mind sharing a bit, but there are limits.

The secret seems to be getting belting varieties and preparing the ground with well-rotted manure and/or keeping up with the liquid feed from flowering onwards. I was expecting pleasant enough strawberries but, as with many fruits, the telltale sign is in the scent. When they're on their way to full ripeness the aroma draws you in. The wasps are awake to the fragrance too, so do set up wasp traps – not much beats the old 'jam round the rim/water in the bottom of the jar' treatment.

I know they're synonymous with Wimbledon but plant a few varieties that ripen in succession and your promise of a cream tea will last way beyond... even until October with a good summer and the right selection.

Varieties

I've found my favourite varieties come from the newest and the oldest available. 'Honeoye' is a delicious early-season strawberry, seeing you all through June, handing over the baton to 'Cambridge Favourite', an oldie, that is perfect for late June (i.e. Wimbledon) and all of July, even a little longer some years. 'Mara des Bois' is a perpetual fruiter, which, while not exactly up there with the self-refilling pint, does offer a sweet, aromatic, steady harvest from the second half of August into autumn. But the winner for flavour may well be 'Royal Sovereign' – not as high yielding or as large as some new varieties, but wait until you taste it.

Do consider alpine strawberries too, especially the variety 'Mignonette'. Easy to sow from seed, these non-spreading strawberries grow as medium-sized domes – showered in fruit from May right through the summer. The berries are too small for all but the most patient to pick in huge amounts. Instead, throw a handful into muffins, eat them warm from the plant, or allow a few to dissolve in a glass of sparkling wine.

Strawberries are self-fertile so growing one variety is fine.

Look for certified virus-free plants from a good supplier and plant them out as soon as you can after they arrive.

Growing

The ideal time to plant young strawberry plants is in late summer/early autumn, as this allows the roots to establish easily in soil that still has a little warmth. Planting later in autumn or even in spring is fine but don't expect a sizeable crop in the first year. Do choose a spot in full sun, where you haven't grown any of the *Solanaceae* family (such as potatoes and tomatoes) or chrysanthemums. These are all susceptible to verticillium wilt (leaves turn brown and wilt), which can kill your strawberries.

Prepare the ground well (see p.142) and trim any long roots and brown leaves off your plants. Dig a trench or holes and spread the roots widely, ensuring that the crown is level with the surface of the soil. Backfill and water well and gently firm in. Water well over the coming weeks while your plants establish.

Allow 50cm between plants and 90cm between rows ideally, although you can squeeze this by a third if you have very fertile ground and/or are growing your strawberries in raised beds.

Strawberries are shallow-rooting and are likely to suffer in dry periods and from weed competition, so as the first fruits appear, lay straw between the plants and under the developing fruit to suppress weeds, retain water and prevent water splash on the berries, which can lead them to turn mouldy.

After you've harvested all the berries, snip off all old fruiting stems, runners and leaves, give your strawberry bed a good comfrey feed and add more well-rotted manure. This will give the plants a boost, encouraging them to throw out some new healthy growth, which will set them up for the following year's cropping.

Strawberry plants will produce well for 4 years or so, but after this you should replace them with new plants. By changing your plants in a staggered system (say around one third each year), you'll spread the expenditure and never leave yourself without fruit.

To create new plants, you can propagate runners from your existing strawberry plants (see p.135) if you wish.

Strawberries are perfectly happy in containers and raised beds, even grow bags and hanging baskets, but you'll need to keep particularly on top of watering and feeding to keep them moist but never waterlogged. Little and often is best.

Harvesting and storage

Depending on variety, you can harvest strawberries from May until October. Pick the berries when they are well coloured all over, preferably when the sun is hot, to really bring out the flavour and aroma of your fruit.

Strawberries don't freeze as well as other berries, but if you have a glut it's worth stashing some away for use in tarts, etc. Freeze them in a single layer on a tray so they don't stick together, tipping the fruit into a bag or container once frozen.

Pests and diseases

Birds can be a real pain and although scaring devices (like ribbons on a cane and spinning CDs) can help, netting is the only certain remedy.

Botrytis (see p.177) can affect strawberries, especially in a rainy summer. It's exacerbated by splashing the fruit as you water, so do take care. Keeping weeds down and ensuring that plants have plenty of air circulating around them is hugely helpful in minimising the likelihood of getting this tedious disease.

Blotchy and/or yellow leaves usually indicate strawberry virus especially if yields simultaneously decline. Once it arrives, pull up and incinerate any affected plants before it spreads.

Slugs and snails can be a nuisance, especially in wetter summers. Deal with them as you prefer (see p.180).

Eating

I rarely get too many strawberries into the house. If it's not me, then my wife or daughter will eat those that ripen each day in the sun. Strawberry jam is rightly popular, but I like to get the fresh berries into tarts and next to anything dairy.

Recipes Rhubarb and strawberry tart (p.240), Strawberry granita (p.243), Fruity melons (p.223) and Strawberry trifle (p.244). See also variations for cranachan (p.218), mess (p.224) and muffins (p.207).

Sourcing & Creating your Plants

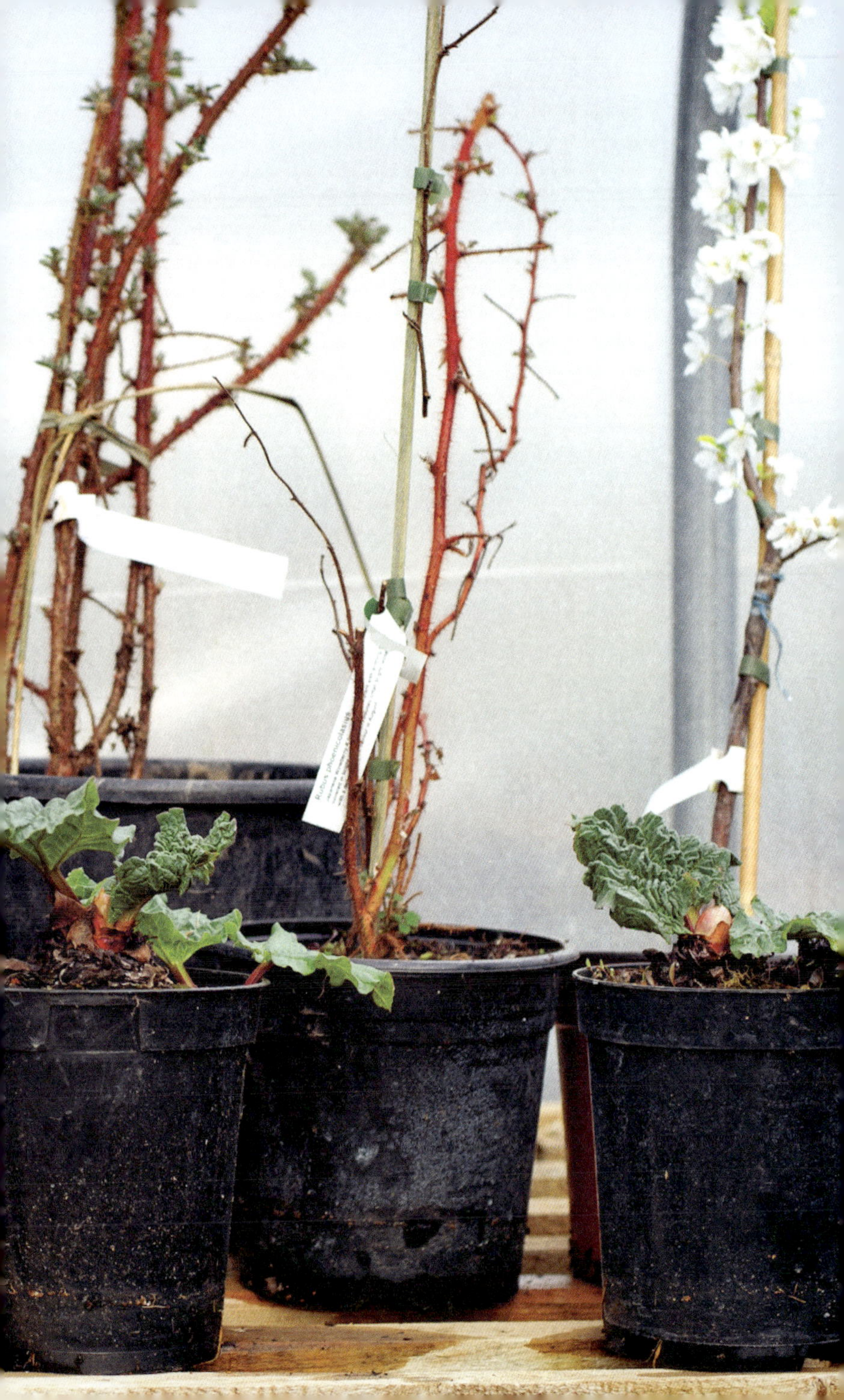
Rubus phoenicolasius

You can pick up a tree or bush for your garden from any
garden centre and the chances are it'll be just fine. Having got this far through the book though, I hope I've managed to dissuade you from settling for 'just fine'. With fruit this is crucial: if the varieties of potato you went for aren't too special, there's always next year's catalogues to peruse for alternatives, but most fruit will be with you far longer. Plant the wrong apple or quince tree and you and your ancestors may have a few hundred years to live with 'OK' fruit. It pays to get the choice right first off.

Sourcing plants

You wouldn't go into a plant nursery for light bulbs and door paint, so don't go to a home store for your plants. You're starting a long relationship with your plants, so show them a little love from the start and buy from people who raise them for a living. There are some wonderful nurseries and suppliers listed in the Directory (pp.248–9). I have used each of them over the years and they are all excellent. They know what they're doing, having built up expertise, knowledge and a reputation over many years. They care that your plants grow, and they hope you will come back for more.

Getting the best

For many fruits it pays to look nearby to find a nursery that specialises in local varieties. Apples, plums and pears are among the fruits that have endless varieties available and local cultivars are well worth considering, as a plant that has evolved in the soils, climate and with the seasonal variations you want to plant it in is very likely to grow happily and healthily. I'm fortunate to have Thornhayes a few miles away; I need go no further if I want an apple that originates from a pip-spitting distance away from my orchard. Look for a similar source near you, and if not go for one of the suppliers in the Directory (pp.248–9).

Of course, many types of fruit have only one (or just a few) available varieties, and some (like apricots) have a less busy history of cultivation in this country. However, there are usually some varieties of each that sit above the rest, and I have identified these in the Fruit A–Z (pp.28–121).

The less common varieties and the more unusual fruit are likely to be found with specialist nurseries. Check the Directory for these too.

If you possibly can, go to open days and Apple Day celebrations where you get the chance to try the fruit before you buy the plants. Check out the events at Brogdale (the home of the National Fruit Collection in Kent) as well as any venues closer to home.

Cordon gooseberries

Choosing rootstocks

Many fruit trees and some bushes are grown on roots from other plants. A young branch is taken from the parent plant of the variety you require (e.g. 'Ashmead's Kernel' apple) and grafted (i.e. joined) to a root system (known as a rootstock) specially grown for that purpose. The rootstock helps control the speed and extent of the plant's growth, and encourages many to fruit much earlier than they might otherwise. It also allows the plant to be grown in soils that the parent tree might not suit, and it can offer a degree of protection against some diseases.

Grafting plant material from a parent tree onto a rootstock will always result in a new plant of the same variety as the parent, so you always know what you are getting, whereas growing from seed can produce unpredictable results due to cross pollination. To avoid potential disappointment, I'd recommend going for grafted trees. It also means you get a tree that suits your taste and your available space.

Dwarfing rootstocks are increasingly available for fruit trees, often resulting in a tree no more than 1.3m in height and perfectly productive grown in a large pot.

Don't fret too much about the different types of rootstock. There's little need to remember the array of illogical letters and numbers that make up the names of most rootstocks. For the relevant fruit, I've outlined the commonest rootstocks but do let your nursery advise, based on your site and available space.

Choosing the shape: freestanding trees

Freestanding trees are, as the name implies, grown without support or a guiding structure. This usually means they are in a classic goblet, in order of increasing size: bush, half-standard or standard trees, and pyramid shape. Your choice of rootstock will guide the eventual size of each of these freestanding possibilities.

Bush trees These have a short trunk, 90cm at most, from which branches spread to form a low canopy.

Half-standard trees These are similar to bush trees, but with a taller trunk, usually about 1.5m, and consequently taller than most bushes, reaching 4–5m overall.

Standard trees The largest form, with 2m of main trunk and a large canopy. This form is suitable only for larger gardens and fields where you can access the crop.

Pyramid trees These are Christmas tree-shaped, tapering from short branches at the apex to wider spreading branches lower down. Sunlight can reach most of the tree, but it does take regular pruning to maintain the shape. Pyramids can also be grown (and maintained more easily) on dwarfing rootstocks. Spindlebushes are variations on pyramids, being shorter and often wider.

Freestanding tree shapes

Bush tree

Half-standard tree

Standard tree

Pyramid tree

Choosing the shape: trained forms

Trees can be grown in a range of shapes, from the classic tall pyramid to a 30cm-high single-branched stepover. Your choice of rootstock plays a role in determining the potential shapes open to you, but initial pruning is equally important. Many suppliers sell trees where this initial training has been either partially or fully carried out. With careful planning you'll be able to grow fruit trees even in a small space.

For many plants, there is the option of training them into a range of styles and shapes. I've identified these options for each fruit in the A–Z where this applies.

Some varieties are more suitable for training than others and spur-bearing varieties (see p.37) are usually best. Tip-bearers (those that produce fruit on the end of short sideshoots) would have their sideshoots pruned off if grown in most training styles. Most pears are suitable as they tend to be spur-bearers, while many apples are not. So, it pays to seek advice from a nursery as to the best varieties to suit your location and the training method you're considering.

Common trained options include:

Espaliers Grown flat against a wall and/or framework of wires, with three or four levels of evenly spaced horizontal branches growing either side of the vertical trunk. Apples and pears are particularly suited to being trained in this manner.

Fans Similar to espaliers, but the main trunk is short, with branches that radiate from the base of the plant rather than growing horizontally. This method suits many of the stone fruit and some currants and berries.

Stepovers Grown either as a low single cordon bent over to the horizontal or with a branch going both ways so that they resemble a low single-tiered espalier.

Cordons Most commonly single-stemmed trees grown at an angle of around 45°, usually against a wall and/or a wire supporting system. This is a particularly good method for squeezing a few trees into a small space. You may find double cordons for sale, where two main stems are trained into a U-shape or even a multiple cordon with three or four arms. Spur-fruiting varieties are needed (see p.37).

Minarettes are essentially cordon trees, grown vertically and not usually attached to wires. Also known as column, ballerina or leg trees, they can be planted close together (perhaps 60cm depending on variety).

If the idea of one of these trained shapes appeals, I'd recommend investing in a partially trained plant. Although more expensive than an untrained plant, buying one with the hard work done gets you off to a good start and nearer a harvest.

Trained tree shapes

Espalier

Fan

Stepover

Cordon

Creating your own plants

Creating your own plants is pretty straightforward, though it may seem intimidating at first. It usually means you'll be a little behind in harvesting than if you'd bought plants, but it's a good way of starting cheaply, or extending what you grow.

Cuttings

Taking cuttings can feel a little hit and miss but it is by far the simplest and most widely applicable way of creating new plants from old. Cuttings are usually taken using either hardwood at the end of the season's growth or soft new growth.

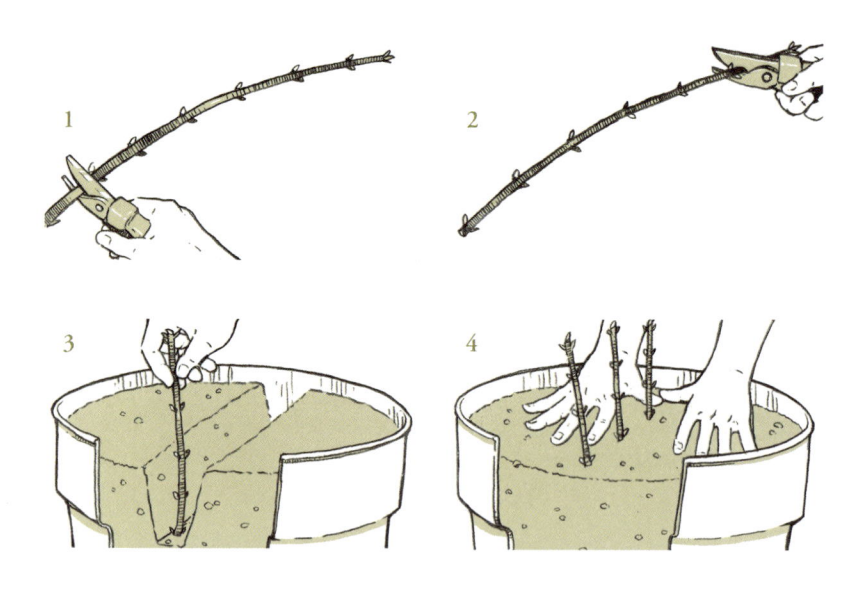

For hardwood cuttings In autumn or winter, prune at least half a dozen healthy 20cm lengths of this year's growth, cutting just below a leaf bud (1). Cut off any sideshoots. Using a sloping cut, snip off the top end of each cutting, just above a leaf bud (2). This ensures water and any leaking sap will drain away from the cut, and serves as a handy reminder of which way up the cutting is. Sink the cuttings into a pot filled with moist, well-drained compost (3) so that only one-third is above soil level. Firm cuttings in well (4), water and stand the pots in a light, sheltered, frost-free location over winter. It may be several months before hardwood cuttings take. Resist the temptation to pester them, and don't pot them on until new growth is well established.

For softwood cuttings Take several cuttings, about 10cm in length (1), early in the growing season as new growth appears. Using a sharp knife, cut just below a leaf joint at the base (2), slicing off all but two or three leaves at the top of the cutting, flush with the stem. Make holes in your compost around the rim of the container with a pencil and gently ease your cuttings in (3). Cover the cuttings with a clear plastic bag (food/freezer bags are ideal) using an elastic band or string to hold it in place (4) to keep the humidity up. Keep the pot in a bright spot but out of direct sunlight. Root development and subsequent growth are much faster than with hardwood cuttings but the delicate tissues are more liable to wilt.

Whichever type of cutting you are taking, a few rules are worth following:
- Whether using a knife or secateurs, the blade should be very sharp and clean.
- Take cuttings that have a minimum of two leaf nodes: the bottom one will form roots, the top one will form new growth.
- Unless taking cuttings from plants needing ericaceous conditions (such as blueberries), use special cutting compost mixed with grit for good drainage.
- Keep cuttings in a dry, sheltered, bright location but not in direct sunlight.
- Although the compost should be moist when you put the cuttings into it, you should keep watering to an absolute minimum (i.e. when the compost has dried out) until rooting has occurred.
- Using organic hormone rooting compounds can considerably increase your success rate.

Grafting

Grafting is a technique of joining the roots of one plant to a piece of wood of another (known as a scion) to produce a plant that will fruit true to the variety of the stem but tolerate the conditions and grow to the size imposed by the rootstock. It is an unreliable process as grafts can fail to take, some need extra heat and it's not without its fiddle but once you've grafted your first tree you may feel the urge to start your own nursery. It's as simple as choosing a new shoot and splicing it (in one of a few very particular ways) onto your chosen rootstock and sealing it until the graft has taken.

There are a few approaches but the simplest is the 'whip-and-tongue' method. For each tree you want, cut a length of the previous year's growth in December or January and store it in a fridge in a plastic bag to keep the wood dormant. This scion should be 5mm–1.5cm in diameter. Acquire a rootstock for each tree you require (see Directory, pp.248–9, for suppliers); the supplier can advise.

The graft should be made from February to April and must be done under cover, in a greenhouse, polytunnel or even your house. Take the scion with two to four buds and make a long diagonal cut away from you, through the scion, to create an exposed face 3–5cm long. The scion sloping cut is known as the 'whip'.

Then make a second cut starting a third of the way down the sloping cut: you are aiming for a cut almost parallel to the sloping cut, but not all the way through the wood, creating a 'tongue', so that a jagged 'Z' edge results. Make as near identical cuts as you can on the rootstock at a point where the diameter matches that of the scion, and join the two – they should slide snugly in together, held by the tongue of each.

This graft needs to be taped together to support it while the union takes. You can buy biodegradable grafting tape, although plastic tape or even masking tape

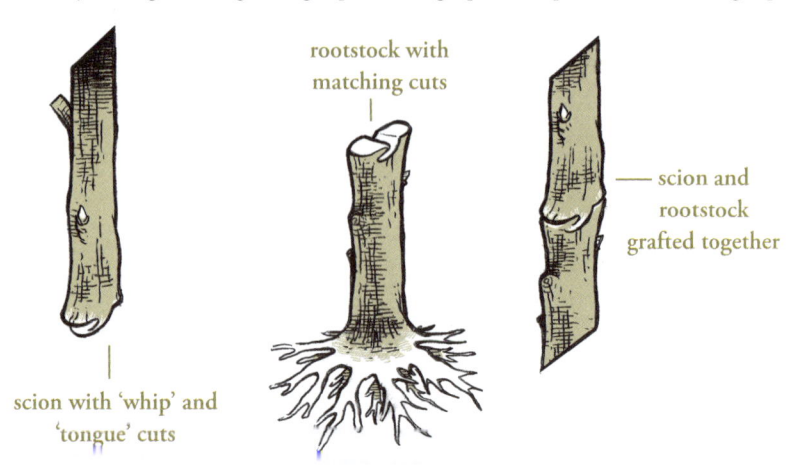

scion with 'whip' and 'tongue' cuts

rootstock with matching cuts

scion and rootstock grafted together

does a reasonable job, but you need to remember to cut the tape off in midsummer to avoid constricting growth.

Apples and pears are relatively easy to home-produce using grafting, but others (plums included) need additional warmth to succeed.

Layering

Many of the cane fruit, such as Japanese wineberries and blackberries, have evolved a marvellous strategy for colonising new ground: they produce new roots wherever their stems touch the soil. The enterprising grower can take advantage of this by simply organising this natural tendency to suit.

Choose a healthy shoot and strip off the leaves around 20cm from the shoot's tip (1). Bend the shoot to the ground and excavate a small groove in the soil where the bare part of the stem touches the ground. Make a small cut in the shoot's skin that will be in contact with the soil (in order to stimulate root growth), and use a bent piece of wire (or two) to hold the stem to the ground (2). Tie the rest of the stem with the growing tip to a short cane to keep it growing vertically (3). Bury the bald part of the stem in the groove and water well (4).

Once the plant has rooted, you can separate it from its parent with secateurs and pot on your new plant.

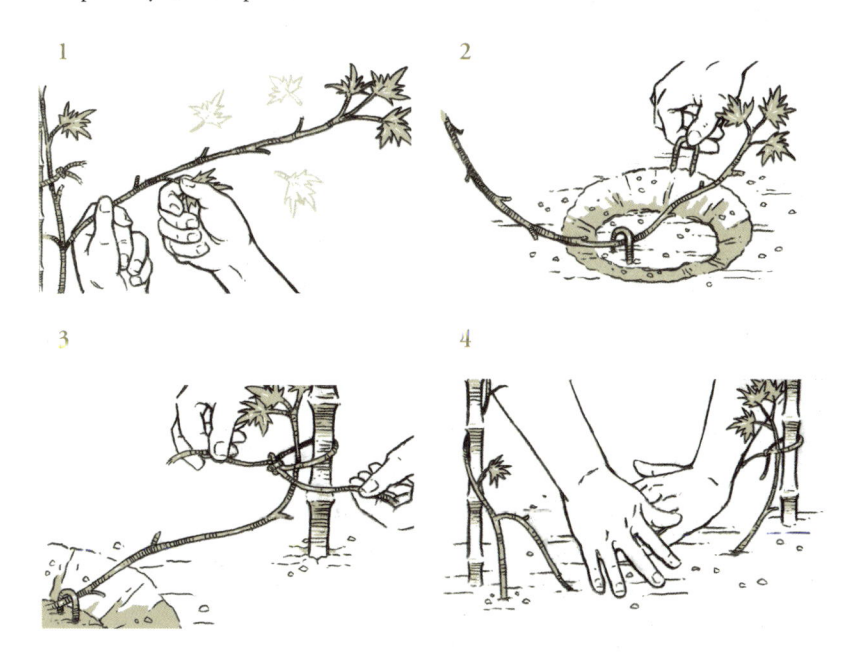

Divided, potted rhubarb plants

Division

Rhubarb can be divided to create new plants. As winter approaches you can split the core vertically into three of four pieces (depending on the size of the plant) using a spade, making sure each section has healthy roots and at least one dormant bud. You can be fairly forceful, if careful. Although this looks like a rather medieval approach, the established parent plant will be much happier afterwards. Pot each section up ready for planting out in early spring, or plant them out immediately.

Runners

Strawberries mainly spread laterally, throwing out long arms with mini-plants growing on them (1). Lift these up and you'll notice what look like short dry roots; these are merely waiting to come into contact with a suitable growing medium. All you have to do is to pin them with a piece of bent wire into a pot of compost (2) or against a bare patch of soil and wait. You can even sink this pot into the ground to help retain moisture. Within a month those roots should be growing happily, and you can separate the new plant from the parent in autumn, keeping it in the pot until planting out the following spring.

1

2

Suckers

Raspberries throw up stems from the base that can grow where you don't want them to, crowding out the other stems. These are known as suckers. If you carefully excavate around these and separate them from the base of the main plant, along with a reasonable amount of root system, you'll have a new plant to pot on or replant immediately.

Sowing

Compared to vegetables and herbs, not many fruits are best grown from seed. Melons and alpine strawberries are exceptions; refer to the A–Z entry on melons (p.83) for guidance on sowing and growing.

Planning, Preparation & Planting

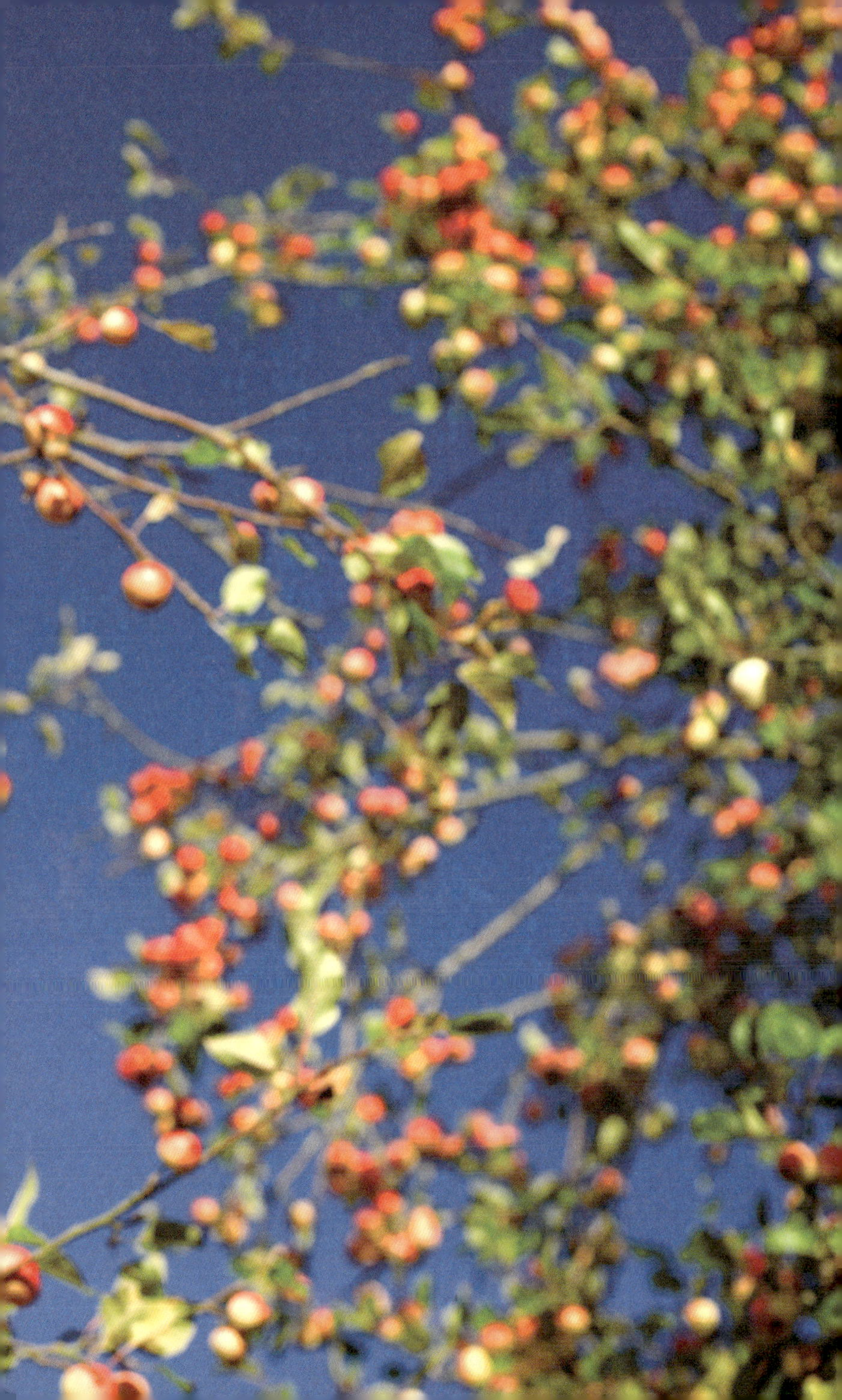

It can be very tempting to rush straight to the planting, digging a hole and getting your plants into their new homes as quickly as possible, but resist the urge. If you spend some time planning and preparing, the planting will be simpler and your garden is likely to be more fruitful.

Planning your space

Find a piece of paper and a pencil and sketch out your garden, allotment, balcony or patio. Gently shade areas that have the least sun and mark any areas you want to keep clear for access, for eating or whatever else your space is called upon to provide. Take a moment to consider whether you are being realistic. The space dedicated to paths and other access is almost always underestimated, so be on the generous side.

Make a list of opportunities and constraints – access to sunshine, water, shelter or the degree of shade, wind and potential drought are all key factors, as is any perceived lack of space. Think about what you're hoping for from your space too, and list it: are you after maximum productivity regardless of aesthetics; are you hoping to encourage wildlife to your space; must it be beautiful, etc. The questions and responses will be yours alone. And don't be discouraged by what seems like a negative point, such as limited sunlight. Such constraints are often just signposts to a delicious edible solution. For example, 'Morello' cherries are perfectly fruitful on a north-facing wall and raspberries will tolerate some shade.

Your wish list of what you would like to grow in an ideal world and the Fruit A–Z (pp.28–121) will help you select potential candidates for your space but do take your time at this stage. Consider the suggestions below for the ways you can grow your fruit, look into container growing (see p.184) if you think that may be for you, and be happy with your plan before you get your hands dirty.

Preparation is frequently overlooked and planting often undertaken in a hurry, both of which can hold your plants back. Do both steps well and your plants have every chance of establishing and growing healthily. And if they do that, you will have fruit much sooner.

Fruit in a small space

Everyone wants more space. Even if you have a field the chances are you'd like another, but if you're genuinely limited for space, fear not, you'll be able to grow most fruit plants.

Dwarfing rootstocks are available for most fruit trees (see A–Z entries) and there are any number of ways of training plants against walls and/or wires to get a considerable harvest from an almost-flat plant.

Vertical planting is another wonderful way of laying your hands on some fruit without taking up much ground space. Grapes will happily climb up and over a structure, and some fruit (apples and pears in particular) can be grown in a narrow shape, even fruiting from a single main stem (see cordons, p.128). Nurseries are always coming up with varieties to suit growing in small spaces – it's a huge market. For example, there are now strawberry varieties that suit either growing downwards from hanging baskets or being trained vertically to take up little room. Keep your eyes out for tasty-sounding newcomers.

Container growing is a great way to go and there are a number of options and considerations you should be aware of (see pp.184–7).

Planning an orchard

The secret to creating a good orchard is in choosing the right mix of trees. You should be led by the different fruit you'd like to eat, certainly, but you'll need to consider pollination and spacing too. Are your trees self-fertile or will you be looking to plant compatible varieties? The key to getting things right on the ground is to make a plan to scale on graph paper, then mark it out on the ground with canes. Don't be tempted to squeeze trees closer together than they should be. They may look like lonely teenagers at their first school dance, but only for a few years while they establish. They'll make an orchard soon enough.

Growing in a fruit cage

Growing in a fruit cage

If you've been cleared out of a summer's precious harvest of currants or berries by the birds even once, you'll have let the idea of a fruit cage cross your mind. A metal or wooden frame, usually at least 2m tall, supports a netting fine enough to exclude birds while allowing pollinating insects through unimpeded. I'm no fan of netting when it comes to vegetables as it excludes you from the plants, can accidentally trap birds and is usually plain ugly, but fruit cages are entirely different. They create a room in which the plants can grow without the nuisance and allow through everything that is beneficial: light, care and you included.

Fruit cages aren't cheap to buy but, like a polytunnel, once up, their framework will last for years with only the occasional replacement or repair to the covering.

Allotment and garden growing

Most people will grow their fruit in a garden or at their allotment where it's likely that some plants are already grown. This is perfectly fine but requires a little forethought, notably whether to keep your fruit in its own separate area or integrate it with the other plants. Growing fruit in dedicated beds makes for a simple start-up, allowing you to prepare the whole area well (see p.142), ensuring it is free from grass and weed competition from the start. Take time to make a paper plan, as for an orchard, and similarly don't be panicked if it all looks a little sparse after planting – it'll look that way for a short time followed by years of fully grown productivity. Planting closer may look less empty early on, but as your plants grow they'll begin to crowd each other and the shade and competition for nutrients and space will reduce your harvests and encourage disease.

One way of finding room for fruit (and vegetables) is to grow them alongside ornamentals in the garden. With allotment waiting lists not getting any shorter and food prices increasing, those who want to grow some of what they eat are planting trees, shrubs, vines and smaller fruit wherever they can find a space. Lawns are shrinking and ornamentals are being replaced with good-looking edibles to get the best of both worlds. Again, be aware of how big plants will eventually become. And remember that there are many edibles (mint, for example) as well as ornamentals that prefer to be in the shade of a tree or bush.

Forest gardens

If you want to take the idea of integrating plants together to another level then a forest garden may be for you. These multi-level gardens take the home gardens of Kerala, India as their inspiration, planting some or all of the layers found in a young forest to make a productive whole. Layers span from underground tubers, through the herb, fungi and ground cover layer, up through shrubs and smaller plants to smaller trees and potentially a canopy later at the top. Climbing plants may crawl between each layer. In Europe it is rare for a canopy layer to exist, as it can severely limit the light that reaches lower tiers, limiting productivity in the process. The idea works on any scale, from acres down to a corner of a garden: you just select the uppermost layer where plants are typically largest that makes sense for your space. It takes careful planning and preparation but the main advantage of going for a forest garden is that once established it functions as a balanced ecosystem with minimal intervention from you. You'll probably need to plant more than just fruit to create a functioning forest garden but if it tickles your fancy, see the Directory (pp.248–9) for additional sources of information.

The aspect

Whether you're planning for an orchard or a fruit cage, integrating fruit into your garden or intending to grow your fruit in a collection of containers, the degree of exposure to harsh winds, to sunshine and the slope of the land – collectively, the aspect – will significantly affect how happy and productive your plants will be.

Generally speaking, fruit enjoys shelter, sun and heat, so look for a space that offers these. With the odd exception, you should give your sunniest spot to fruit.

Shelter is often the critical factor when it comes to fruit. Any exposure to harsh winds when flowering is happening can severely impair pollination rates, fruit set and, in turn, your harvest. If you haven't a sheltered spot, then consider planting some windbreak hedging. It's nowhere near as exciting as planting a peach or a mulberry but it may be the difference between eating the fruit and not.

Preparing the ground

Unless you are growing your fruit in containers, you'll need to spend a little time ensuring the soil is ready for your plants. The ideal is a soil with a fine tilth (i.e. in small, crumbly particles rather than large clods) to a depth below the bottom of the root system of the plants you are putting in. It should be free from weeds and grass and have a good level of nutrients to get the plants off to a healthy start.

Clearing any grass is vital as it can compete strongly with establishing plants and compromise their growth. If you have a few months before planting you can lay thick cardboard directly on top of the grass, keeping it in place with bricks. Over the course of a few months the cardboard will kill the grass and any weeds underneath, leaving a clean patch to plant into. Otherwise, strip off the top 7–10cm with a spade, leaving the turf somewhere to break down as it's very nutrient rich.

Whichever route you take, or if your ground was grass- and weed-free to begin with, dig over the area well and add compost or composted horse manure if you can – to give the soil a nutrient and humus boost before you plant.

Getting to know your soil

Fruit grows best in a fertile, deep soil – one that retains moisture to a degree but also drains well. You will need to get to know your soil. If it's in an ideal state then happy days. If not, don't be deterred – there is much you can do to nudge it towards the conditions you want.

Getting a professional analysis of your soil is simply a matter of posting a couple of trowelfuls to someone who offers the service and waiting a few days to receive their report. You'll learn about the texture, pH and nutrient status of your soil – all of which play a huge part in the livelihood and the quality of your fruit harvest. The information is accurate, reasonably detailed and not expensive for what you get, and (if you request it) you may well be given advice about how to improve any deficiencies.

I have to confess I didn't bother with soil testing when I started growing veg but as soon as I thought about planting fruit I had a soil analysis done. Trees aren't cheap, they are with you a long time and the investment really is worth it. Don't let yourself be intimidated by a little science. Taking a sample and understanding the results is a straightforward business and getting to know your soil pays dividends year after year, harvest after harvest.

If you prefer, you can also take a rough and ready approach and analyse the soil yourself (see below). This is certainly perfectly adequate if you are planting only a small area.

Soil texture Heavier, more water-retentive soils contain a large proportion of clay whereas at the other end of the spectrum you'll find the free-draining sandy soils. Somewhere in the middle are the loamy soils with a reasonably equal amount of sand and clay, capable of retaining some moisture while freely letting excess drain. This is the perfection that blesses few of us, so to move the soil nearer the ideal we need to examine our soil texture.

Take a good handful of soil and assess it. If it feels gritty and will crumble easily through your fingers you have a sandy soil. Moisten it a little and although it may form a cracked golf-ball-sized sphere it will refuse to roll into a sausage. These soils drain freely, warm up very quickly in spring and are easy to work for most of the year. All good news, but the sandiness creates air spaces which let precious water drain away rapidly in times when it might be needed, often taking valuable nutrients with it. This can lead to a dry soil that becomes increasingly acidic as the calcium is leached out, which in turn can limit the availability of the nutrients that remain. The soil becomes 'hungry', dependent on regular watering and feeds.

Clay's small particle size limits air spaces, meaning clay soils drain less readily than others, holding on to moisture and making them harder to dig and grow in.

Compost

They also tend to be easy to compact and slower to warm up in the spring. Grab a handful, moisten it and it will form a sphere easily and be happy to extend into a thin sausage shape. The ease with which these soils compact means that any extended period without rain leaves them hard and dry. They tend to be rich in nutrients, but without the air spaces for water to move about, these nutrients are often locked up and unavailable to plants.

Loams take the middle ground. Neither too sandy or clayey, they enjoy some drainage thanks to the sand, balanced with the moisture-retaining quality of the clay. They also have good nutrient levels, which the air spaces make readily available to growing plants. This is the happy medium, and if you have it, crack open a bottle of your favourite tipple and celebrate.

Chalky soils usually display their chalky lumps fairly obviously when dug. They're alkaline (see below) and usually shallow, which together can limit the choice of plants that will do well.

Other soil types are comparatively rare and either less than suitable for growing (thin moorland soils, for example) or famously productive (such as peat). You are unlikely to have these soils but if you do, then seek professional advice.

In most cases your key to moving towards (or maintaining) the perfect loam is the same: organic matter. Adding organic matter in the form of compost, as well as top-dressing with more compost and/or well-rotted manure in subsequent years, adds essential fibre and air spaces to clay soils, body and water retention to sandy soils, and dilutes the chalk component of a chalky soil.

Soil pH This is a measure of the relative acidity or alkalinity of your soil. As with soil texture, the majority of plants do well in a reasonably neutral soil, near the middle of the scale. There are some fruits (such as blueberries) which prefer something a little more extreme, and where this is the case, it's covered in the specific entry in the Fruit A–Z (pp.28–121).

The pH influences the availability of nutrients in the soil and can, for various reasons, often to do with solubility, prevent your plants accessing nutrients that are present. The results of a professional soil test will include a pH analysis and may offer advice about any action to take.

Many garden centres and other suppliers will sell a home pH testing kit that serves reasonably well too. It is simple to use one of these: put some soil in the tube supplied, add a few drops of test solution, shake and leave it to settle. After a few minutes you compare the colour of the sample with the colour chart supplied and read the result.

Most soils, especially in domestic gardens, will be somewhere towards neutral, neither strongly acidic nor alkaline. This is ideal. If your result indicates a soil that is strongly acidic you can neutralise the acid by applying an alkali. Agricultural lime (naturally occurring calcium carbonate) is the cheapest, most widely available form of lime for the grower and it can be applied at any time of the year, although best in late winter. It's easy to use: just throw it over the area you want to affect at the rate suggested on the packet. The result isn't instant as it needs to be incorporated into the soil, but it is effective and relatively cheap. It's also easy to find in garden centres, countryside suppliers or through specialist suppliers, but do make sure the lime comes from a sustainable source.

Strongly alkaline soils are extremely rare. They can, in theory, be acidified using sulphates but this is costly and environmentally damaging. If you are one of the unlucky few it's much better to dilute the alkalinity by incorporating as much compost, topsoil and well-rotted manure as you can lay your hands on. Your other alternative is to grow fruit in containers (see p.184).

Get to know your soil, make a few adjustments to counter any extremes of soil texture and pH if necessary, but don't strive too hard for the (often unattainable) holy grail of the perfect neutralish loam across the whole of your garden. Unless you are growing only a few types of fruit that enjoy very specific requirements, you should find that as long as you're away from the harsh extremities of texture and pH your plants will do pretty well.

In any event, while many plants prefer the soil to be just so, they are reasonably productive across a range of soil conditions either side of the ideal. And you can always add a little localised lime to those that like their soil slightly alkaline, and a little ericaceous compost around the roots of those that prefer things a touch more acidic.

Planting a tree

Planting a tree well is about a little more than just digging a hole to make room for the root ball of your plant. Do it properly and your tree will romp away happily, do it less well and you'll put a halt to healthy establishment that can take the tree some time to get over.

You can plant bare-root trees any time in the dormant season, from November to March, and pot-grown plants can be planted at any time of year. November is the ideal time for either, as the soil is still warm, allowing roots to start to become established before the winter dormancy begins. This means that in the following spring the trees grow away quickly. Note that bare-root trees should be kept in shallow soil until you are ready to plant them, so they don't dry out.

There will always be some difference of opinion about how best to plant and stake a tree – here are some tips that have worked well for me.

- Give your tree's roots a good pre-planting soak in a bucket of water.
- If you are planting into grassland or lawn, remove any turf so that you have at least 1m^2 of bare ground, even if your plant is considerably smaller in spread.
- Dig a hole 10cm or so below the depth that you'll need to plant the tree.
- Place a cane across the top of the hole and put the tree into the hole to check that the graft (if the tree has one) is at least 10cm above ground level and that the whole of the root system is below. If the tree has no graft, plant it to the depth it was in the pot, or if supplied as a bare-root plant, ensure the roots are completely below the surface of the soil.
- Whether pot-grown or bare-rooted, you should be able to tell from the trunk how deep the tree was grown at the nursery – plant it at the same depth.
- After checking that the depth of the hole and the position of the tree are correct, put the tree back in the bucket of water to keep the roots moist.
- Probably the most important part of planting is to loosen the sides and the base of the hole. Doing this improves drainage and ensures the hole doesn't act like a box, ready to fill with water in rainy periods. It also gives the roots broken earth to grow into rather than a wall of soil. The heavier and more clayey your soil, the more beneficial this is.
- I plant trees and many other plants with mycorrhizal fungi. Available as a powder or gel, these fungi work in symbiosis with the root system, bringing nutrients to the plant as they establish in the ground in exchange for a few of the plant's carbohydrates. It benefits the tree and stimulates healthy growth.
- Crumble handfuls of soil between the roots – into and under the centre of the tree. Aim to fill the heart of the root system with small soil particles, leaving no large air pockets.

- Break up the turf you removed from the surface into small pieces and lay it, grass down, in the bottom of the hole around the tree, then backfill with loose soil, treading in well.
- Thoroughly water immediately.
- I don't add compost and fertiliser when planting as I feel it entices the roots to stay where they are, in a reservoir of nutrients. Without that reservoir the roots have an incentive to grow away in search of more.
- When you stake you are aiming to secure the roots rather than prevent the tree from moving at all. To achieve this you only need to use a short 70cm stake with 40cm knocked into the ground – the 30cm above ground is tied to the tree with a rubber figure-of-eight loop. This secures the base of the tree, preventing the root system from being forced up in strong winds, but leaves the top to move in the wind, developing its own strength.

A newly planted tree: staked, mulched and guarded

Caring for your Plants

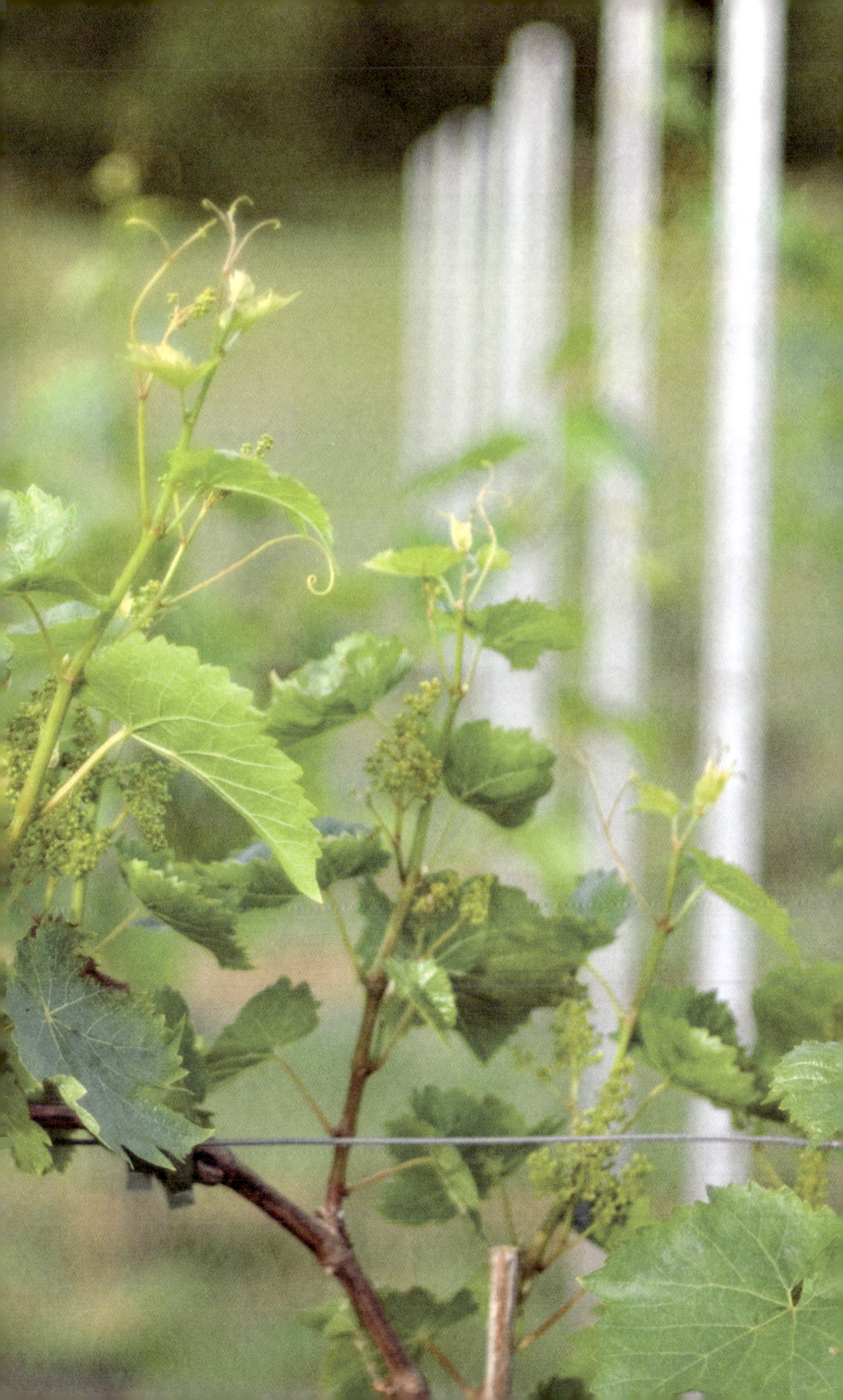

Fruit plants more or less take care of themselves.

Almost all are perennial and once established they tend to grow away early each spring and can be productive for many years. Left to their own devices, they will give you a harvest more often than not, but if you are prepared to do a little to help them on their way you'll not only encourage a healthier tree, you'll likely as not end up with a far larger crop to take to the kitchen.

The ongoing tasks are pruning, watering, feeding and weed control. As with most things in the garden or the allotment, good timing for those once-in-a-while tasks is vital and anything you need to do more frequently, such as watering, is best undertaken little and often.

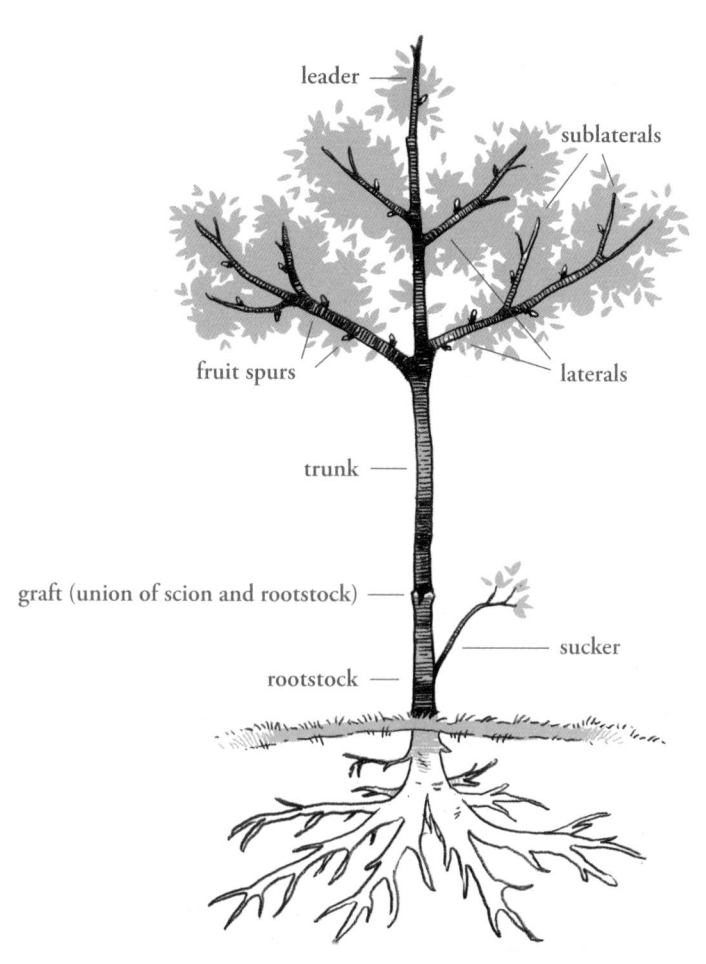

- leader
- sublaterals
- fruit spurs
- laterals
- trunk
- graft (union of scion and rootstock)
- sucker
- rootstock

Pruning

Pruning is the art of removing plant growth to help shape your plant, maximise your harvests and minimise the threat of disease. Unpruned, most fruit would survive reasonably well and produce something to eat, but to maintain a healthier, long-lived, more happily cropping plant you'll need to prune.

Pruning helps to guide the plant into a shape you want; to reduce, train or encourage growth and fruiting; and to remove dead, congested, damaged or diseased wood. If you leave them to develop of their own accord, many plants will grow too congested, with closing, rubbing or densely packed branches. This stops good air flow and light penetration, encouraging disease and damage. Pruning to remove affected branches opens up the centre of the plant to air and light, helps prevent disease getting in through damaged tissue, and encourages vitality and health for the whole plant.

Pruning also reduces the volume of top growth, meaning that the roots don't have to work so hard to service the leafy, woody growth. In effect, this leaves a surplus of energy which the plant can use to produce seeds and fruit. If, in taking off some of the top growth, you do it in such a way as to leave the growth that has the best chance of giving you fruit, you'll be killing two birds with one stone – and that's the essence of much good pruning.

If you're new to it you may find the idea of pruning a little daunting. I did when faced with my first fruit trees that I knew I had to tackle one way or another. You may even convince yourself out of it by telling yourself that plants aren't pruned in their natural habitat, they're allowed to grow as they wish. This may be true, but the plant you have for your garden is being grown to give you the healthiest, largest (hopefully) crop of delicious fruit. And it is likely to have been bred – or at the very least selected – for domesticated growing. Pruning is part of the cycle of interaction between you and the plant that ensures it pays its edible rent every year.

Pruning isn't difficult. It is particular though, and rather than all plants being pruned the same way, each has its preferred treatment. It's simply a matter of knowing what to do when. Rhubarb, melons and strawberries will excuse you with a tidy-up rather than pruning as such, but the rest need a little more attention. Read carefully and take this book with you to the trees.

Some plants should only be pruned if absolutely necessary, while others will quickly reduce their harvest if you don't get busy with the secateurs. Specific advice is given for each entry in the Fruit A–Z (pp.28–121), but there are some general principles it's worth familiarising yourself with.

That said, if you forget or miss a year of pruning the plant is unlikely to die but please do, at the very least, keep a watch for crossing, dead or damaged branches and snip these out as this will help minimise the likelihood of diseases.

Pruning tools

Secateurs are a must, a penknife desirable, and a pruning saw and loppers vital if you are growing trees and larger shrubs. Go for the best you can afford (see p.22).

When to prune

The ideal time to prune varies with each fruit. Most of the fruit we grow in the UK prefers to be pruned in the dormant period through winter, with some happier to be pruned in the hotter months: the A–Z explains the details for each fruit and the chart on pp.32–3 should help you plan when to do your pruning.

How to prune

Before you pick up your tools, take a piece of chalk and mark the branches you are thinking of removing or shortening. After every major cut, stand back and see if you are moving towards the desired shape. Next decide whether secateurs are comfortably up to the task (i.e. if the branch is 1cm across or less), if not use loppers or a saw. This ensures the best chance of a clean cut.

Place the branch or stem in the centre of the blades rather than close to the pivot or near the tip. Never twist the tool – it will tear the cut, leaving rough edges where disease can more easily take hold. If you're tempted to twist, it usually means you should use a larger tool for the job – so stop and use a larger tool for the job.

If you are cutting off part of a stem, you'll want to cut about 6–8mm above a bud. You do this for two reasons: growth hormones are concentrated around buds

Chalk-marked branches, ready for pruning

Pruning to an outward-facing bud

and these hormones encourage rapid healing as well as new growth. Cutting just above the bud gives the plant minimal exposure to disease and ensures that new growth from this bud takes over the main growth of this stem. The choice of bud is important. New growth occurs in the direction the bud faces, and usually you want to encourage new growth outwards, away from the heart of the plant. This avoids overcrowding and gives the stems a better chance of getting good light.

The angle at which you make your cut depends on how the plant produces its buds. If they are in pairs on opposite sides of the stem then cut straight across about 6mm above the pair of buds. If the buds are borne singly (usually spread along the stem) then make an angled cut of around 30° sloping back from the bud, as this minimises the likelihood of water or sap collecting on the cut surface, helping it heal more quickly. Whichever type of cut you make, use a tool with a sharp blade as a smooth cut heals well and lessens the opportunity for disease to get in.

Pruning a freestanding tree

A freestanding tree (as opposed to one that's been trained into an espalier, etc) is the most common form of tree. Most nurseries can supply a tree that will take perfectly happily to being grown as a freestanding tree but you may have to do a little early pruning, known as formative pruning, to guide it into shape. Once established, routine pruning is needed to keep your tree healthy and productive. Freestanding trees are grown as bushes, half-standards, standards and pyramids.

Bush, half-standard and standard trees These are pruned into a goblet shape, where a ring of branches defines an open centre, allowing light and air into the heart of the tree. This promotes good health, minimises disease and ensures that developing fruit have the conditions they like to grow well.

If you have bought a maiden whip (a one-year-old tree with a single long trunk and no side branches), you'll need to cut this to the height where you'd like the side branches to develop. You may be supplied a tree that's a year older where this first step has already been carried out. Whether bought at this latter stage or created from a maiden whip, the side branches (laterals) should be at a wide angle to the trunk and will form the core shape of your bush or standard tree. The next formative steps are simple.

For apples and pears the timings are as follows:
- First winter After planting your tree in winter, prune the central leader to a bud that's around 25cm above the highest lateral. Cut back the laterals by half, 6mm or so above an outward-facing bud. Remove any other branches that develop along the trunk. These are the most important cuts you'll make as this gives you the main structure from which your tree develops.

- Second winter Prune the laterals by one-third, each to just above an outward-facing bud, to encourage an open centre to the tree. Sublaterals will have grown from the laterals: choose three on each branch that aren't facing into the centre of the tree, as equally spaced as possible, and cut them back by a third. Shorten other sublaterals to three or four buds to encourage them to develop into fruiting spurs. Again, remove any shoots that have grown along the trunk.
- Third winter Choose further well-placed sublaterals to prune back by one-third to extend the network of branches, and prune back others to form short spurs of three or four buds as before. Remove any branches that are crossing or growing towards the centre of the tree.

Follow this process and your tree should have a good frame of laterals, each with a few sublaterals, and have formed a goblet shape. Pruning from this point follows a winter-only routine that is different for spur-bearing fruit and tip-bearing fruit.

Spur-bearing fruit This type of tree carries its fruit in clusters on short branches known as spurs. Fruiting spurs are at least 2 years old. Each winter cut back laterals by one-third, and prune sublaterals to leave four or five buds on each – this encourages new spurs to form, which will eventually fruit. Then prune off old, crowded or weak spurs, to leave at least 10cm or so between spurs.

Tip-bearing fruit This type of tree carries its fruit mainly on the ends of shoots produced the previous year. Each year you should prune out 25 per cent of the oldest branches and look to keep an open centre to the tree. Then prune back the tips on the remaining branches and snip out any shoots growing from the base. Over time, this method of pruning refreshes the whole top growth and ensures new productive fruiting branches.

For plum trees the timings are as follows:
- First spring Cut back the laterals by half, 6mm or so above an outward-facing bud. Remove any other branches that develop along the trunk, and cut back the central leader to just above the highest lateral. These are the most important cuts, giving you the main structure from which your tree develops.
- Second spring Sublaterals will have grown from the laterals. Choose three or four on each branch that are not facing into the centre of the tree, as equally spaced as possible, and cut them back by one-third. Remove any other sublaterals along with any shoots that have grown along the trunk.

The other stone fruit (cherries, peaches, nectarines and apricots) follow the process as for plums with any variations noted in their A–Z entry.

Pyramid trees These have the classic Christmas tree shape, with branches gradually shortening towards the top. The primary aim of pruning is to ensure space between fruiting branches so that light and air can get in and allow fruit to develop well. If your tree wasn't supplied already trained into a pyramid for you, make sure you buy a feathered maiden (see p.26) from which you can create a strong framework with the desired shape. It's very simple – although timing varies with different fruit (see relevant entries in the A–Z).

For apples and pears the timing is as follows:
- First winter Immediately after planting or during the first winter, shorten the leader to a strong bud around 75cm above the ground, and prune any good laterals by two-thirds to downward-facing buds. Prune off any weak or crowding laterals. You are aiming for a well-spaced network of branches.
- First summer Late in the summer new laterals will be apparent, mainly towards the top of the tree. Prune all of these new laterals back to five leaves.
- Second winter Cut back any of this year's growth to leave around 25cm of new growth.

With your pyramid shape established, routine winter pruning should aim to maintain the shape and healthy fruiting by pruning back the central leader to five new buds and thinning crowded spurs (leaving them no closer than 12cm apart). You can also cut out older branches and shoots to ensure good spacing and promote new growth. Each summer you should also prune back new laterals to around five leaves, and any sublaterals to three leaves, aiming to maintain the pyramid shape.

For pyramid plum trees the timings are as follows:
- First spring Starting with a feathered maiden, cut the central leader off at 1.5m or so with an angled cut. Remove any laterals lower than 0.5m and prune back the rest by half to an outward-facing bud.
- First summer Cut back main laterals to about 20cm of this year's growth, to a downward-facing bud.
- Second spring Prune back the central leader to a third of last year's growth.

In subsequent springs, cut back the central leader of your plum by two-thirds of last summer's growth until it reaches the required height. Each summer, once established, prune the leader back to 2–3cm of last summer's growth, and prune the upper branches to retain the Christmas tree shape. Remove any diseased, dead or damaged wood as well as any unproductive wood from congested areas.

The other stone fruit (cherries, peaches, nectarines and apricots) follow the process as for plums with any variations noted in their entry in the A–Z section.

Pruning trained fruit trees

Pruning trained fruit trees isn't tricky but it is very specific, so read carefully and if necessary take this book with you when you prune.

Espaliers These are essentially trees grown flat against a wall and/or framework of wires, with horizontal branches growing either side of the vertical trunk. Espalier training is particularly suited to apples and pears. It's usual for branches to be spaced around 40cm apart.

If you like the idea of an espalier tree then buy one already trained. It will be more expensive than an untrained tree but this reflects the time and effort taken in getting the tree to its initial shape and the amount of trouble it'll be saving you. If you want to do it for yourself, buy a maiden whip (i.e. an unbranching year-old tree). Set up your wire framework (either against a wall or freestanding) with the lowest wire 45cm or so from the ground and spacing further wires above 45cm or so apart. Plant your tree 5cm or so in front of the wires.

Prune your espalier tree as follows:
- First winter After planting your tree in winter, prune the central leader to just above the lowest wire.
- First spring In early spring, as new growth emerges, choose two good shoots under, but near the wire. These will grow into the first pair of horizontal branches.
- First summer Tie canes to these two growing shoots and tie them to the wires at an angle of 45°. Prune any sublaterals back to five leaves; remove any other shoots from the trunk. At the end of summer, untie the canes from the wires and laterals, bend the laterals down to the bottom wire and tie them to it.
- Second winter Prune the central leader to just above the second wire up, and prune the first pair of horizontals back by one-third to encourage good growth and fruiting spurs.
- Second summer Tie canes to two new growing shoots and follow the pruning advice for the first summer.

Repeat this process until your espalier has reached the desired height.

Ongoing routine pruning involves pruning sublaterals back to three leaves and any weaker growth to a single bud each summer, and thinning out spurs to 10cm or more between each.

Fans Fan-training suits many stone fruit, including peaches, apricots, cherries and some plums, as well as figs. It works best against a wall where these fruit benefit from the extra warmth and residual heat offered by the building. As with espaliers,

Fan-trained plum tree

fan-trained trees use horizontal wires (spaced 30cm or so apart) to support them but rather than grow horizontally, the branches themselves are trained across the wires into a fan shape, radiating roughly from the centre. The other key difference is that the initial branches (laterals) and some of the branches that come from them (sublaterals) both form the fan. Again, I'd suggest you buy trees that are at least partly trained as it takes around 4 years to train the tree into shape yourself. If you want to do this all for yourself, on the other hand, here are the steps to take.

- First spring After growth has commenced, prune off all but two shoots, which should be 30cm or so above the ground (where the first wire coincides with the trunk). Tie these two shoots outwards, either side of the centre at an angle of about 30° to the horizontal. Snip the leader down to the base of these two laterals. This is the core of your fan, from which all other branches will grow.
- First summer Select two sublaterals growing above and one below each lateral, and tie them to canes, which are in turn tied to the wire framework. Aim to establish a spreading hand of branches either side of the short trunk. Cut any other shoots back to one leaf.
- Second spring Prune the end of each branch (whether sublateral or lateral) by one-third to a bud facing the direction you want growth to continue in. This will encourage fruit-bearing spurs to develop. Remove any shoots growing into or out from the wire framework, along with any on the trunk below the laterals or crowding the centre.

Each year repeat the last two stages (first summer and second spring), adding canes and tying in new sublaterals until you have a well-balanced fan across the space you have available for it.

Once you have this structure in place, your pruning is very much more about encouraging new fruiting buds to develop. This involves stimulating new shoots to grow to replace old ones that have fruited. It is a simple process. Late in summer, prune off the shoots that have produced fruit and snip the shoots you have chosen to replace them back to three leaves to encourage new buds to develop, then tie them in. Keep up with this routine pruning or fruiting will slow dramatically.

Cordons Cordon trees are single-stemmed trees usually grown at an angle of around 45°, generally against a wall or a wire supporting system. This single main stem grows short fruiting spurs along its length, and growing at this angle allows you a greater harvest. You can grow them singly or (as many do) in greater numbers to get a hefty harvest from a relatively short space. Buy them with formative pruning already done for an easy life. Otherwise get a feathered maiden (see p.26), plant it at 45°, with the trunk attached to a cane.

That winter prune any laterals back to around four buds, just above an outward-facing bud. The following summer prune laterals back to three leaves and sublaterals to one leaf; fruiting spurs will result.

Ongoing routine pruning is simple. Each midsummer, prune laterals back to three leaves to form fruiting spurs and cut sublaterals back to just one leaf. This keeps a good balance of leaves while removing those not needed for good fruiting. Each winter, thin fruiting spurs to a minimum of 10cm from each other and prune back the leader in late spring.

Minarettes and stepovers These are pruned as for cordons.

Pruning soft fruit

Most soft fruit requires some pruning to maintain its health and productivity. As the method tends to vary for different fruit, this is covered in the A–Z entries.

Watering

Any plant is likely to get hungry and thirsty, even more so if it produces fruit. As plants get older, larger and more established, their developed root system can usually find plentiful water apart from during extended dry periods, but while a plant is getting established the level of care you give it can make the difference between surviving and thriving.

After planting, most fruit plants require frequent watering to help them through the establishment phase. How long and how much depends on the size of the plant but equally important is when it was planted. If you plant in autumn, as most nurseries recommend, almost all plants will be established by the time growth starts again in spring. Occasional watering during dry periods through the winter is the most you are likely to have to do.

Fruit planted in winter and spring (or later if pot-grown) will be trying to get its root system established while putting on new season's growth above ground in warming temperatures, so you will be required to give your hard-working plant water when the weather doesn't. Fruit planted in spring should ideally be watered throughout the first growing season when there is any period of dry weather.

Established trees rarely need watering other than in severe drought conditions. Strawberries have shallow roots and are particularly vulnerable to drying out, so do prioritise if you are growing them. Good mulching of strawberries is vital to help retain water and minimise the need for using the watering can. All other fruit will thank you for a soak once a week if it hasn't been raining, and more frequent drinks are a good idea for any plants near a wall or in containers.

Comfrey flowering

Maintaining health and fertility

A fruiting plant expends a vast amount of energy producing its fruit – or rather the seeds within it. Naturally, the typically large root system drives into the soil in search of nutrients, but you'll enjoy a heftier harvest if you make life a little easier for it. A combination of composted horse manure and/or compost around the base of the plant in the winter and potassium-rich feeds through the growing season will pay dividends when fruiting time arrives. You may well have to call on other sources of nutrients too.

Comfrey and liquid feeding

Once flowering begins it's also a good idea to keep topping up the nutrient bank. Many gardeners use seaweed and tomato feeds for their fruit – these are high in potassium, the essential nutrient required for healthy fruiting. Both are diluted in a watering can before use. Better still, you can make your own potassium-rich feed using comfrey.

You'll find comfrey, with its small pinky-white bell flowers and long, rough leaves, on many riverbanks. It looks very much like a borage plant that's enjoyed a good night out. Although far from unattractive, comfrey's real value lies in its capacity to accumulate minerals and nutrients. Deep-rooting, it scours the lower tiers of the soil horizon to bring precious potassium, phosphorus and nitrogen to the surface. It also grows rapidly. All you have to do is cut armfuls of leaves through the summer, which you can use in a variety of ways. Lay them, just cut and torn up, as a mulch around the base of your fruit plants and as they break down their nutrients will leach gently into the soil for the plants to take up as they need. Alternatively, you can incorporate them, torn up, into your compost bin where they act as an accelerator, driving compost-making rapidly onwards.

Both are fabulous ways of employing comfrey but I use almost all of mine as a liquid feed. Making your own is simple. Place torn-up leaves in an old onion net and suspend it in your water butt. Over the following weeks the leaves will decompose (the net stops sludgy bits blocking the tap) to create comfrey tea. You'll know when it's ready as it'll smell like an anchovy's plimsoll. Rough as it is, you will learn to love the stench, just a little, as it means a free boost to your fruiting plants, and more fruit for you. Just water it on or spray the leaves any time from when flowering begins. If you do not have a water butt or don't need very much, you can either use the same approach (with fewer leaves) in a watering can or chop the bottom off an upturned water bottle and fill it with leaves, using half a brick or similar to keep the leaves under pressure. Over the next 10 days or so a dark liquid will ooze from the leaves into the neck of the bottle. To use it, undo the lid and dilute the treacly liquid 15:1.

Comfrey leaves

Giving fruit plants a fortnightly feed is very effective in promoting health and good fruiting – better still to apply every other feed as a spray for the leaves. The leaves take in the nutrients quickly, not only making the leaves themselves healthier but also driving the nutrients rapidly into the plant's system with little waste. You will use less too.

Unless you have plenty of room to allow wild comfrey to grow, you'll want to source the Bocking 14 variety (see Directory, pp.248–9, for suppliers), as it's a sterile variety that doesn't set seed so you can easily control its spread. Expanding your comfrey bed is simple. Either divide the roots vertically with a spade, or dig the root up and chop across it to make slices like pound coins then grow these in pots until they're a good size to plant out.

You can follow the same method to make nettle tea, which is rich in nitrogen. This is ideal for stimulating green growth, so use it when that's what you want to encourage.

Making your own liquid feed like this saves money as well as the resources involved in creating bought feeds. Once you start growing a small patch of comfrey, you'll learn to love it as much as the fruit it feeds. It's an easy-to-grow, natural cut-and-come-again way of adding vital nutrients while you water that makes the fruit garden more self-reliant in nutrients. And those flowers provide the bees with a party venue, which means you have plenty around for the pollination your trees will require. And it's pretty much free.

Slow-release fertilisers

I'm not a fan of adding bought-in nutrients. I can live with adding composted horse manure, as it's usually locally available and puts a waste product to wonderful use, but I'm not one for throwing man-made/chemical fertilisers around. Most are made using fossil fuels, much water and even more energy, turning the simple energy-giving wonder of growing food into an energy- and carbon-heavy process. However, there are low-carbon alternatives.

Of the various options, I prefer organic pelleted chicken manure. High in the essential nutrients of nitrogen, potassium, phosphate and calcium, as well as many trace elements, the pellets are dried manure in an easy-to-use form that can be scattered around or dug into the growing medium. The pellets gently break down and dissolve, releasing their goodness for the plant to take up over an extended period. Follow the instructions on the packaging for frequency and amount to use. Look for a supplier using manure from chickens kept in free-range conditions (see Directory, p.249).

Compost

Compost is the secret of organic growing. Plant or sow something and chances are you'll have a reasonable first harvest, but without compost you're likely to see that fine start decline. Creating fruit is a hungry business for your plants and you'll need to put some of those nutrients into the equation if you don't want your soil to become depleted and the plants unproductive. Manure and liquid feeds are excellent sources, but compost has the added pleasure of turning waste that might otherwise make it to landfill into something that feeds the soil – and you and your family in turn. It closes a circle and makes it a cycle.

As an all-round plant fitness treatment, it's hard to beat compost. It replenishes nutrients, helps retain moisture, improves soil structure and makes a fine mulch. It is the cornerstone of organic growing and it's perfectly simple to make your own.

Making a compost bin While you don't need a bin to make compost (you can do it just in piles), it is far more practical to use one. Plastic bins are neat and easy to manage, but you can make your own. The most basic structure is a square of pallets lashed together, with the front able to be opened for access. It works well, especially to get you started. As your requirements grow, you can always replace it with more substantial bins. They're not expensive or time-consuming to make: you only need some wood, a saw, a hammer and nails. And they are more aesthetically pleasing.

Three adjacent bins are ideal. This is because turning the waste is the key to effective, rapid compost-making. Having bins next to each other makes turning easy and gives you the capacity to keep compost at different stages of decomposition separate from each other.

The process is simple: the first bin is the only one you add waste to. When it's full you turn it into the second bin and continue adding new waste to the first bin. Turning the compost in bin 2, watering each time, accelerates decomposition, so do it as often as you can. When bin 1 becomes full, turn the contents of bin 2 into bin 3, and bin 1 into the now-empty bin 2. Use the compost in bin 3 when ready; it will look and feel crumbly and (apart from a few twigs) be well broken down.

Pick a level, well-drained sunny spot for your bin(s), preferably on top of soil to allow excess water to drain, worms to get in, and the warmth of the sun to accelerate decomposition. If you can't site it on soil, add a base layer of soil or compost to ensure worms and beneficial organisms are present in the mix from the start.

At almost every course I run at River Cottage, someone tells me they can't make compost. They can. It's a perfectly natural process, but one that is often inadvertently halted by sealing the waste from the air. Throw on a binful of grass clippings and you won't have to wait long for it to turn to a slimy layer that will act like cling film, excluding air and halting decomposition. To make good compost all you have to do is avoid excluding the air and keep a reasonable balance of Greens to Browns (see below). There is nothing you need to do to force composting, it wants to happen anyway. Your job is to encourage the conditions for decomposition to happen efficiently. The secret lies in the mix of ingredients, and a little forethought really helps you get to grips with making fine compost.

Suitable materials for your compost bin:
Think of the ingredients as belonging to one of two groups: the Greens and the Browns. The Greens tend to be rich in nitrogen, and many are activators that nudge the Browns into quicker decomposition.

The main Greens include:
- Diluted urine (half a pint of urine to a gallon of water if you're asking)
- Grass cuttings
- Nettles
- Comfrey leaves

Other Greens that can be included:
- Raw vegetable peelings
- Tea bags and coffee grounds
- Young annual weeds (but avoid weeds with seeds at all costs)
- Unwoody prunings
- Animal manure (see p.167) from herbivores such as cows and horses (organic is ideal)
- Poultry manure and bedding

While often low in nutrients, Browns are rich in carbon. They decompose more slowly than Greens, but accelerate when composted with green activators.

The Browns include:
- Waste paper – shredded or torn
- Cardboard
- Bedding from omnivorous pets (such as rabbits)
- Tough hedge clippings
- Woody prunings – shredded or chopped
- Old bedding plants
- Sawdust and wood shavings
- Bracken
- Fallen leaves

Your compost bins will take much of what you and your garden have no need of but there are some waste products that you should very definitely leave out. Meat, fish, dairy and cooked food (including bread) are an invitation to pests, especially rats. Cat litter and dog faeces are a definite no-go. When it comes to perennial weeds and diseased plants, I generally incinerate them and add the ashes to the compost bin.

Wood shavings and shreddings are great as a weed-suppressing mulch but they can lock up valuable nitrogen, so it's best to keep them away from the base of your plants. You can put them into your compost but they can take longer to break down than many of the other ingredients in your bin, so add only in small quantities and with green activators, or let them break down for a year or two first. Avoid using any wood that has been treated with preservatives.

Even a thrown-together pile that has been lazily cared for will eventually decay, so it can be used as a fertiliser, but to make really good compost without an interminable wait there are some considerations.

Golden rules for making your own compost:
- Use more or less equal volumes of Greens and Browns but for your own mix take into account your site, the weather, the time you're able to put into it. Learn from your experiences, and remember...
- Greens and Browns regulate each other: if your compost is too wet, add more Browns; too dry, add some Greens.
- Don't use too thick a layer of either – the best compost is made when Greens and Browns are well integrated.
- Use green activators like grass cuttings to activate otherwise slow-rotting Browns.

- You can use the tougher Browns – in combination with the Greens they provide essential bulk and structure to your finished product. If you maximise their surface area by chopping or shredding you'll find the accelerating Greens will nudge tougher Browns along and you can always fish them out and put them into bin 1 again if you need to.
- Ideally, have three bins side by side and keep them turning and well watered.

Your compost should be ready to use after around 9 months but if you're feeling determined it can be yours in as little as 2 months. The principles are the same as for making any compost, but the key is in getting air and water into the mix and getting the waste in small pieces before you add it to the bin. Depending on the grade and volume of material you have to compost, use a chipper, shears or a mower to shred your material before adding it to the heap – this creates a greater surface area for decomposition to take place.

The more you mix your compost, the more air is incorporated. This generates heat as decomposition proceeds, which in turn speeds up the process. And as you turn your compost, water it well. Even better, pee on it... being careful of any nettles you may have added.

After a week or two the heap should be starting to warm up – plunge your hand into the centre to test. Warmth is good: it's telling you that decomposition is under way. Keep turning and peeing and it may get properly hot in the centre. Following on from a neighbour who successfully baked a jacket potato overnight in the centre of his compost bin, I 'hard-boiled' an egg in mine in a few hours this summer... I need to get out more.

If the compost starts to cool you'll need to turn it again, adding more water or urine if it's dry, or more material if it is too damp. Full-on warm composting will follow. You can repeat this a few times but eventually the heating effect will diminish. The heap can now be left to finish off by itself.

Whether you go for the speedy version or the more relaxed approach to compost-making, as the ingredients break down they will reduce in volume to produce a chocolate-coloured blend that's sweet-smelling and earthy. It may have more lumps and twiggy bits than garden-centre compost, but that's often the case. Bash up any larger lumps, and if there are any bigger twigs, snap them up and return them to bin 1 to compost some more.

Compost can be added to your garden or around the base of plants at any time of the year, but I tend to add most of mine in winter to ensure the plants are well set up for the growing season to come. Some like to incorporate their compost into the soil by digging it in during late winter or early spring but if you're a fan of the no-dig approach or prefer an easier life you can add compost as a mulch and allow the rain and earthworms to take the nutrients and organic matter into the soil.

Other sources of nutrients

With your own compost and comfrey to call on, your fruit plants should have a good bank of nutrients to keep them on top form. If you find that you need more, or that practical considerations make compost-making and comfrey tea impractical, there are other sources of organic matter you can add.

Horse or farmyard manure This is usually reasonably easy to source and is one of those pleasurable commodities which is a nuisance waste product to the owner and gold to the person taking it away. Everybody wins. High in essential nutrients and fibre, manure releases its goodness gradually into the soil as the winter rain and worm action take effect. Gently, over the whole year, the benefit of a layer of composted manure ringed around the roots (but not touching the trunk) will feed the tree and do much to give it the reserves to grow healthy, plentiful fruit. Make sure any horse manure you use has composted well – for a year is usually best. You should also ensure that the horses' bedding is straw; wood shavings may rob nutrients from the manure and the soil it is applied to as they break down.

Chicken manure Although very high in nutrients, this can be too harsh for your plants if applied neat, so it's best to add it to your compost to dilute it.

Seaweed This is very high in potassium. Small-scale harvesting (the odd carrier bagful) is a fantastic option if you live near the sea. All you need to do is rinse it clean of salt, before laying it on the ground around your plants or mixing into your compost bin.

Adding horse manure around rhubarb

Borage

Companion planting

This is the art of growing plants together, or in close proximity, so that one or both benefit from their relationship. It can take a number of forms:

- Attracting beneficial insects
- Repelling pests
- Accumulating minerals and/or fixing nitrogen for neighbouring or subsequent crops
- Disguising the scent of crops vulnerable to pests that navigate by their sense of smell
- Acting as a sacrificial plant; i.e. to attract pests away from the main crop and its fruit
- Providing physical help, such as shelter and support
- Acting as a natural fungicide

While nitrogen-fixing plants (see Green manures, p.171) are excellent ways of maintaining essential nutrient levels, companion planting may be more useful for fruit in attracting beneficial insects. For the organic fruit and vegetable grower, attracting insects that will help to keep potential pests in check makes an inexpensive, environmentally friendly and often beautiful first line of defence against trouble.

Flowers are the key. Early-flowering plants provide a picnic for the first bees and other pollinating insects, while others flowering through the growing season will not only keep pollination rates up, they'll attract a range of natural predators, such as ladybirds, that will feed on your aphids and other pests. Diversity of plants leads to diversity of insects and other organisms, promoting a natural balance that's more resilient to harm.

Some of the aromatic herbs – mint and lemon balm in particular – are thought to act as a natural fungicide by exuding essential oils. I'm unaware of any scientific proof of this, but many growers I know observe it working and underplant all their fruit trees. The choice is yours.

The principle of growing in tiers (see Forest gardens, p.141) allows you to use your fruit to both offer support to and receive support from other plants. Taking advantage of a tree (fruiting or not) to grow a grapevine through while planting shade-tolerant plants beneath is one example. In this way three harvests may be enjoyed from one location. While the grapes clamber through the fruit tree, lettuces may be grown beneath, with the shade preventing them from bolting (growing quickly to seed) in midsummer while still allowing them enough light to grow steadily. These partnerships are there for you to dream up and try, obviously within the limits of what the plant requires to thrive.

As well as some of the more general happy partnerships you can create for and with your fruit plants, there are some companionships that deliver very specific benefits for particular fruit. The following table includes some that I think work particularly well.

Companion	Companion for	Acts by
Basil	Apricots, nectarines and peaches	Releasing aromatic insect-repellent from its foliage
Umbellifer herbs, such as fennel, coriander, dill and parsley	Any fruit	Attracting natural predators, such as hoverflies and wasps (the nectar feeds them), which in turn prey on aphids, caterpillars and other pests
Mexican marigold (*Tagetes minuta*)	Woody fruit plants, such as Japanese wineberries	Suppressing weed germination
Lemon balm, oregano and mint	Most fruit, stone fruit especially	Releasing aromatic insect-repellent from its foliage
Comfrey	Any fruit	Deep-rooting mineral accumulator, high in potassium. Flowers early and loved by bees
Garlic	Raspberries	Repelling aphids
Borage	Strawberries	Increasing yields
Nasturtium	Apple	Climbing through the tree, repelling codling moth
Nasturtium	Melons	Attracting aphids away from the melons – a sacrificial crop
Alliums, i.e. onions, chives, garlic and leeks	Apple	Preventing apple scab (when established)
Hyssop	Grapes	Stimulating growth

Green manures

A group of plants that can greatly improve the health of your garden, allotment or even a group of pots. They achieve this by doing one or more of the following:

- Rooting deeply, aerating the soil and helping to break up heavy ground
- Taking nitrogen from the air, making it available in the soil to neighbouring plants. This is known as nitrogen fixing
- Covering the soil, minimising erosion, nutrient leaching and compaction
- Suppressing weeds
- Producing a mass of foliage that can be composted or dug in to improve soil structure and replenish soil nutrients
- Flowering early and/or lengthily through the growing season to bring beneficial insects to the garden

There's a big crossover between green manures and companion planting. In essence most green manures *are* companion plants, and this is particularly apparent in relation to fruit. They are a no-brainer for the organic grower – sow some green manures and while you enjoy the prospect of fruit, they set about quietly improving the soil structure, raising the nutrient status and attracting insects that pollinate your fruit plants and prey on potential pests.

You can use green manures across a whole field, in a small pot, or anywhere in between. Prepare the ground well, clearing it of all weeds and grass (see p.142). Sow evenly into a fine tilth before raking the seed in gently and shallowly. Water well.

The following table includes the green manures I think can work well with fruit, giving an idea of when to use them and the benefits they offer.

Green manure	Sow	Mow or dig in	Benefits
Alfalfa	May–July	Aug–Oct or overwinter	Nitrogen fixer. Very rich in main elements needed for good growth and draws up other trace elements from deep in the soil
Agricultural lupins	March–June	Sept–Nov	Flowers attract beneficial insects. Very deep-rooting, which helps to improve heavy soils and draw deep minerals to the surface. Nitrogen fixer; loves an acid soil
Buckwheat	April–Aug	July–Nov	Deep-rooting, attracts beneficial insects, good on poor ground (which it also improves)
Crimson clover	March–Aug	June–Nov or overwinter	Nitrogen fixer. If left to flower, will attract beneficial insects
Field beans	Sept–Nov	After winter	Nitrogen fixer. Excellent winter coverage for otherwise bare beds
Yellow trefoil	March–June	Sept–Nov	Nitrogen fixer. Low-growing with pretty small yellow flowers which bring bees to pollinate
Phacelia	March–Sept	June–Dec or overwinter in the South	Beautiful blue-purple flowers attract beneficial insects
Red clover	April–Aug	2 months after sowing or up to 2 years	Nitrogen fixer. Attracts beneficial insects
White clover	April–Aug	3 months or more after sowing	Nitrogen fixer. Low-growing plant. Attracts beneficial insects
Vetches	March–Oct	3 months after sowing but best overwintered	Nitrogen fixer. Likes a heavy soil

Controlling weeds

As with any plant you are cultivating domestically, you will need to keep on top of weeds. Nettles, docks and dandelions are a few of the plants that colonise ground quickly, often out-competing neighbouring plants to establish themselves in dense populations. You may find them unsightly but the primary downside of weeds is in robbing your fruit plants of precious resources – light, water and nutrients in particular.

Keep the competition to a minimum and your plants will establish more quickly; not only will they fruit sooner, they'll be better able to take care of themselves. With larger plants like trees and large shrubs, there will come a time when their size overcomes any competition weeds might offer, but in the early years of their life – and on an ongoing basis with smaller plants – weed control is really essential.

We have become lazy users of weedkiller, using a squirt or two of chemicals to kill off the nuisance weeds. Effective as this can be, weedkiller can also harm other plants and animals, unwittingly upsetting what is likely to be a perfectly happy, natural soil ecology in the process. There are a few organic, low-input methods of keeping the weeds at bay. And whether you spray or mulch (see p.175) or do neither, you'll find yourself having to manually remove any weeds that appear once in a while.

Manual weeding

With vegetables, a hoe is indispensable for slicing through the weeds that appear on the soil's surface, but many fruit plants, such as blackcurrants, have shallow roots that spread laterally from the plant and hoeing can cause damage. It's fine for very small weeds if the hoe's cutting action is kept shallow, but whereas vegetables are often grown in beds with relatively large, accessible lanes of bare soil separating the plants, fruit is often part of a more integrated garden and a hoe tends to be impractical.

The best way of tackling weed removal is to use a trowel – a narrow one is normally best, with sharp clean edges. You'll need to be diligent in digging down to the lowest of the roots if you want to be sure of getting rid of the weeds. This form of spot weeding may take a little time but it is very effective as you can be sure of removing all traces of the roots, which for perennial weeds such as docks is the only way of ensuring that they don't reappear. Do this as early as you can, when the plants are still young and small, and your work will be much, much quicker and easier. Whatever you do, don't let your weeds go to seed, get them early – if the wind gets hold of the seeds and spreads them through your garden, your battle will have multiplied enormously.

Strawberries grown through mulch mat

An even simpler method of controlling weeds is to smother them out before they have a chance to appear – using a mulch.

Mulching

A mulch is a layer of material on the surface of the soil that helps you and your crops by performing one or more of the following:

- Suppressing weeds
- Adding nutrients
- Retaining water in summer
- Reducing run-off in winter
- Improving soil structure
- Reducing temperature fluctuations
- Encouraging beneficial soil organisms
- Protecting edible crops that might otherwise touch the soil and rot (such as melons)

Mulches are pretty essential with most fruit plants, as weed competition – even for trees – can severely impede their development. With trees or large shrubs, or when planting in lines (such as a hedgerow), mulch mat provides an excellent long-term weed suppressant. You can buy it in 1m squares, as well as rolls of varying width and length.

Planting through mulch mat is simply a matter of making a small slit (if there isn't one in the mat already), planting through it, and turning the edges of the mat into the soil with the blade of a spade. Not only will the mat prevent weeds from draining the plant by competing with its roots, it will also help to retain moisture and keep the soil temperature up. Make sure you source mulch mat that is breathable and allows water through.

You can use manure or compost as a nourishing, as well as an effective mulch. Spread a 5–15cm deep layer of material around your plants to reap the benefits, having first watered the ground well to ensure that moisture is retained. Winter is an excellent time for applying a compost or manure mulch, as it allows nutrients to be incorporated into the soil before the new growing season.

If you can lay your hands on hay, straw, seaweed or spent mushroom compost, these are particularly good mulches. For larger expanses of otherwise bare soil, green manures (see p.171) or some of the companion herbs (see p.170) are your best options.

The same suppressing effect can be provided by gravel, tree bark, rubber chips and other bitty mulches. Choose whichever suits your garden, your sense of aesthetics and your pocket.

Pests and diseases

The best way of dealing with pests and diseases is through prevention. Maintaining a healthy soil, keeping up with pruning, growing green manures, companion planting and encouraging a diverse garden will all minimise the likelihood of pests and diseases, but once in a while they will appear. Knowing how to recognise and (if necessary) deal with them is vital, not only to the chances of getting a crop but potentially to the ongoing health of your plant.

The most common pests and diseases are covered in this section. If your chosen fruit is likely to be troubled by any of those listed, I have indicated the possibility in the Fruit A–Z (pp.28–121). A few problems that may affect only one or two fruit species are included in the relevant A–Z entries.

If you are troubled by larger creatures or birds, the main defence is obstruction. Rabbits and deer have to be fenced out of gardens, or for field-grown trees guarded against. Squirrels have to be trapped and dispatched, birds should be netted against, and/or scarers (such as CDs tied with string to flash in the sunlight) employed.

Aphids

Aphids affect many fruit, especially in early summer. In themselves they usually cause little damage, but they can harbour and transmit viruses, which may well impact more severely. Squash them when you see them and encourage predators such as ladybirds by planting a diverse garden.

Bacterial canker

Bacterial canker affects the *Prunus* family – cherries, almonds, peaches, plums, nectarines and apricots – and apples, revealing itself as small brown spots that turn into holes on the leaves. The following year the leaves may appear deformed, if at all, quickly discolouring and withering. Branches may begin to die back. This disease can potentially kill the tree. Cut back any affected areas and incinerate them as soon as you spot any trouble, and use a copper-based fungicide such as Bordeaux mixture in late summer, repeating at the start of autumn.

Birds

Birds are a somewhat random nuisance, wiping out a crop one year and totally ignoring it the next. Currants, cherries and berries are most susceptible. You can take the gamble, or you can net vulnerable plants as ripeness approaches.

Blossom wilt

Stone fruit, apples and pears are vulnerable to this disease, which shows itself by causing withered and rotting blossom. It can then continue into the plant through

Blossom wilt

Leaf curl (see p.178)

the foliage, causing considerable damage and weakening the plant, thereby making it susceptible to other attacks. Bordeaux mixture, sprayed just prior to flowering, is your best remedy. Cut out any affected areas and incinerate them immediately.

Botrytis

Botrytis is a grey, felty mould that can affect any part of the plant. It is most common in greenhouses and polytunnels when ventilation is poor and conditions are old and damp. It can also affect grapes as they approach ripeness. Maintaining good ventilation is the best preventative measure. Pick off any affected parts, as few effective fungicides are licensed for home use.

Brown rot

This fungal infection creates brown areas of rot in many kinds of fruit – apples, pears and many of the stone fruit in particular. The disease usually enters the plant through pest damage, so keep a good eye on your plants and ensure you prune with clean cuts. Remove and incinerate affected fruit immediately.

Brown scale

Sap-sucking insect, 2–4mm across, which causes leaves to turn yellow and die. Treat with an organic spray.

Codling moth
The larvae of this moth tunnels to the fruit's core to feed, not only spoiling some fruit but drilling a pilot hole for other pests such as wasps to take advantage of. Pheromone traps are available which attract and trap the males in late spring, leaving the females unmated.

Coral spot
This can affect many of the woody fruit, including figs, although the currants are particularly susceptible. Wet conditions encourage the disease; untidy pruning cuts do too. Orangy-pink spots appear on dead wood, which if not pruned out immediately, can spread down the plant. Act quickly, cutting out any affected areas and incinerating them.

Downy mildew
This appears as grey downy growth on the underside of leaves and yellow patches on the upper surface. It affects grapes and melons in particular. Ventilation, as with all mildews, is the key to reducing the likelihood of infection. Remove infected leaves and incinerate immediately. A sulphur-based spray (for suppliers, see Directory, pp.248–9) will help minimise damage.

Fireblight
A bacterial disease that blackens the leaves, shoots and flowers of apples, pears and quince. Affected areas look as if they've been burnt, hence the name. The bad news is it's incurable. So, you will need to prune off any affected area plus an extra 50cm or so of healthy growth and incinerate immediately. Disinfect secateurs after pruning each affected tree.

Fungal leaf spot
This can affect many fruit – berries and currants in particular – but it is very easy to identify, appearing on the leaves as purple-brown spots ringed with yellow. It can spread very quickly, weakening the plant considerably. Good ventilation, keeping humidity low, and removing and incinerating any affected leaves immediately is your best course of action.

Leaf curl
A fungal disease that affects peaches and nectarines, and almond trees, severely distorting the leaves (illustrated on p.177). Most trees drop affected leaves, leading to a loss of vigour and lack of fruit. Spring rains can encourage the disease; protecting trees during early spring can help, otherwise Bordeaux mixture may offer some remedy.

Mealy bugs

These small white insects, about 5mm across, may appear near the leaf axils and leaf midribs of grapes, figs and some citrus fruit. A sticky residue may be visible on the leaves, which often develop dark moulds. Biological controls are available for small or under-cover infestations. For outside remedies, use organic sprays.

Nectria canker

This tedious disease affects apples, making the bark crack and peel, causing sap leakage and dieback; it even kills off some trees. Prune out any affected areas, disinfecting your secateurs after dealing with each tree, and burning any diseased material. Bordeaux mixture sprayed in autumn offers a good degree of protection, and a quick spraying any time that you notice the infection may help arrest it.

Phytophtera

This is a fungus which can affect any woody fruit plant grown in a waterlogged area. It is easy to identify. After the plant has declined and died, the roots will often be orange in colour and smell sour. Don't replant in an area that has been affected and if you have only one alternative site with similar conditions, do improve the drainage before planting. There is no cure.

Powdery mildew

A fungal disease that affects leaves, which will look as if they are covered in a white powder. Affected leaves may turn yellow and deform. Good air circulation is vital in avoiding this disease. Powdery mildew can be a sign that the soil is too dry, so keep susceptible plants (like grapevines) from drying out. Remove any affected leaves and incinerate immediately.

Red spider mite

Infestations usually occur under cover where humidity levels are low, but they can also occur in dry conditions, such as where fruit is grown against a wall. You may notice dusty webs on the underside of leaves, along with yellowing and/or withering of leaves. Spraying the leaves and/or the floor of a polytunnel or greenhouse may help by raising the humidity levels. Biological controls and organic insecticides can remedy an infestation.

Rust

Plums and their close relations, pears and some of the berries are susceptible to rusts. Bright-orange blisters appear on the underside of leaves in summer, turning gradually brown. Plants can weaken considerably, so remove and incinerate any affected leaves.

Scab
Scab is apparent as brown or green spots on the leaves and shoots, and can lead to misshapen fruit. Some varieties offer a degree of resistance but if it appears then chemical sprays are your only redress.

Shothole
Stone fruit are vulnerable to this disease. As the name suggests, it appears as a peppering of small circular dots on the leaves, which turn to holes over summer. Shothole can indicate the presence of mildews and bacterial canker, so prune off badly affected leaves immediately.

Silver leaf
Silver leaf affects the *Prunus* family (apricots, cherries, peaches, nectarines, plums and damsons), giving leaves a silver sheen before they wither and die. Purply-brown fungal brackets can appear on the branches. Pruning in the summer when the sap is rising minimises the risk of your tree succumbing to silver leaf. If, however, it becomes affected, cut back the stem (you'll notice a brown stain running through the branch) to at least 15cm beyond any staining. There is no cure, but if you act early you may get lucky.

Slugs and snails
Slugs and snails are much less of a nuisance with fruit than they are with vegetables, but they can cause major problems for strawberries, melons and mulberries. Picking the creatures off at dusk is a good measure. You can also buy organic pellets, which curb their appetites rather than poison them, and slug pubs are particularly effective.

To make a slug pub, cut off the bottom 10–12cm of a plastic drinks bottle and sink it almost completely to soil level. Leaving 2cm or so above the soil ensures that beetles and other small animals don't fall in. Fill it with that awful 2 per cent beer. It attracts the molluscs, which fall in and expire. Tip them with the liquid onto the compost heap and refill. If you place a ridge roof tile over the slug pub it will keep the area dark and damp yet accessible – just how slugs and snails like it.

Viruses
There are any number of viruses that can affect fruit, most appearing as marbling, blotches or yellowing leaves. They can debilitate or even finish off your plant and for the most part they are incurable.

Source certified virus-free plants where possible, and keep greenfly under control as they can be effective carriers of many viruses. Incinerate any affected plants immediately.

Wasps

Wasps can be a complete nuisance. They love the easy pickings of raspberries and strawberries but will happily bore into apples, plums and pears amongst others, potentially causing huge damage to crops. Once they start on your fruit, their presence can make it tricky to harvest what's left. Wasp traps work well.

To make a wasp trap, dissolve a spoonful or two of jam in twice the amount of water, pour it into a jam jar and puncture a hole in the lid, large enough to allow wasps in but not too much larger. Empty every few days and keep redoing.

Winter moths

Caterpillars love to eat and can strip a plant of succulent leaves rapidly. Winter moth caterpillars can damage the leaves, buds and flowers of pears, cherries and plums in particular. If there's only the odd one, just keep an eye on things – birds will usually even things up naturally. If numbers increase or there are plenty of eggs, squish them sharpish. You can take preventative measures against some caterpillars by ringing the trunk with sticky strips from a horticultural supplier or even using a ring of Vaseline – the caterpillar can't work its way across either.

Woolly vine scale

Grapes and currants are most susceptible to this small flat brown insect, only about 5mm across. White woolly eggs covered in cottony threads laid in spring develop into the insect which feeds on the sap. Organic sprays are available.

Eyed hawk moth caterpillar

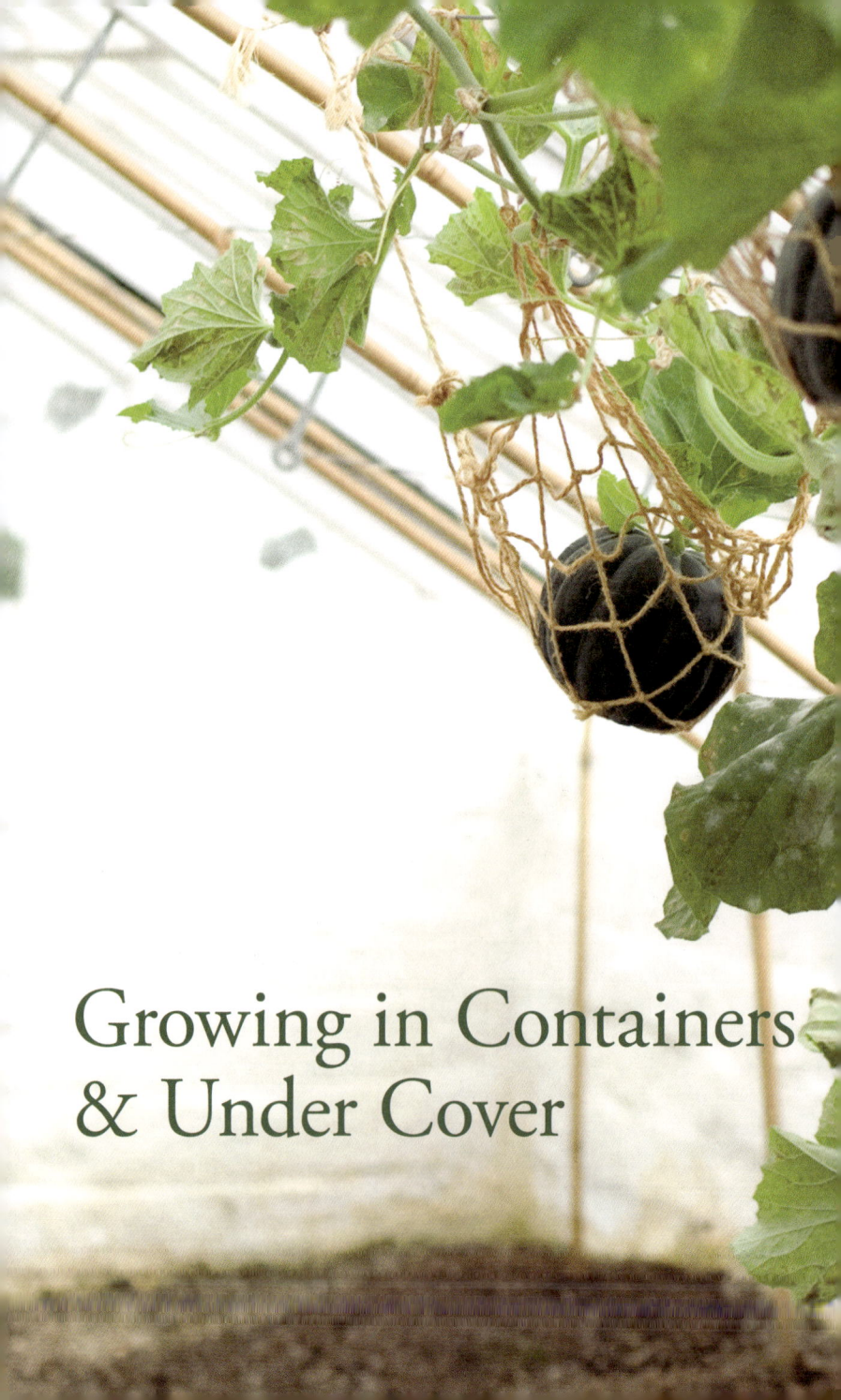

Growing in Containers
& Under Cover

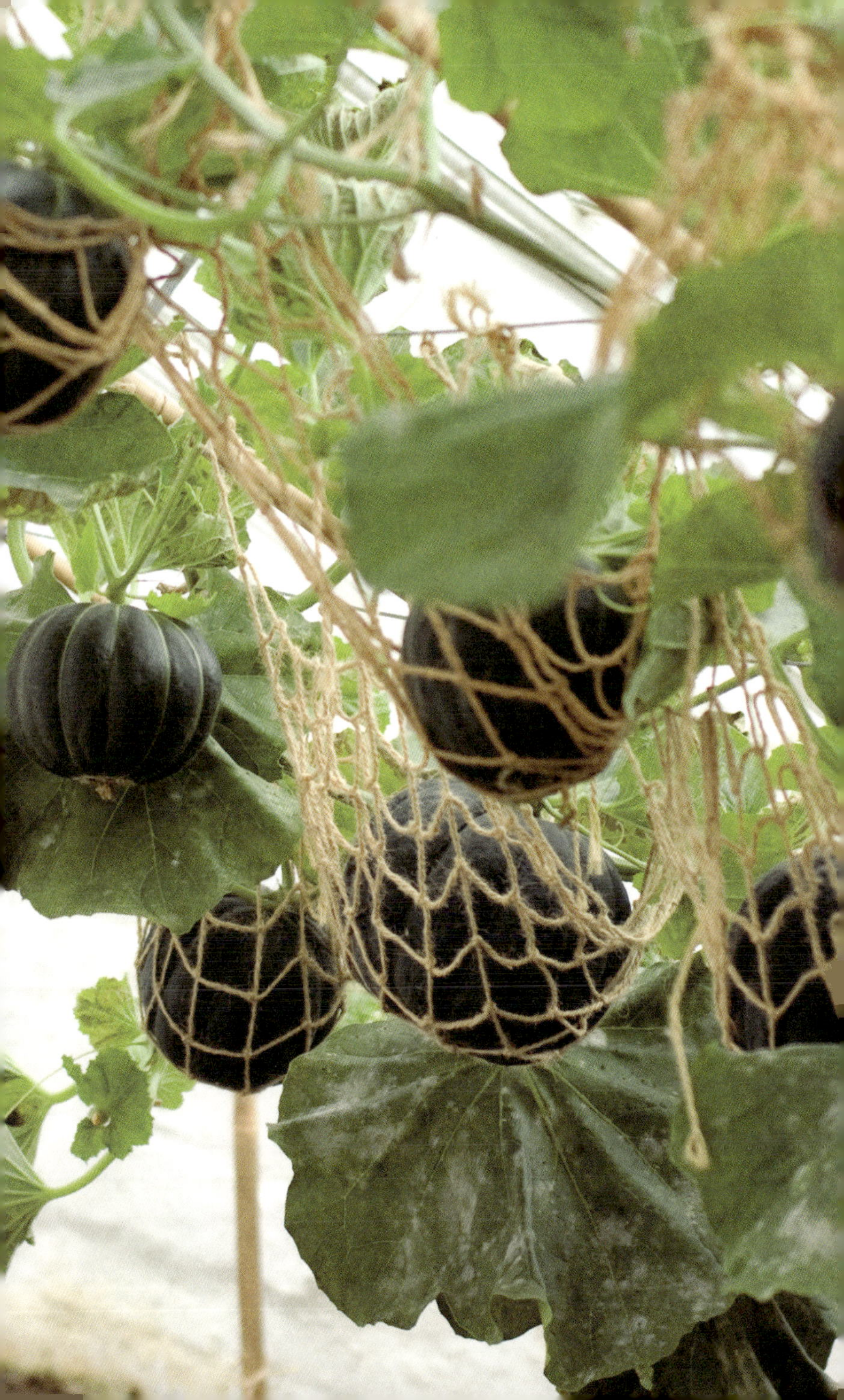

Growing in containers

or in a protected space, such as a greenhouse, can provide you with the opportunity of growing fruit where space or climatic limitations might not otherwise allow it. Some fruit take to container and under-cover growing better than others, but if you select the most suitable varieties and exercise a little care, both methods – growing fruit in containers and growing under cover – can produce great results.

Container growing

More and more people are growing fruit in pots, trugs, barrels and any other kind of container they can lay their hands on. And, happily, plant breeders are coming up with more varieties (including trees on dwarfing rootstocks) that are suitable for container growing.

While fruit tends to take very well to container growing, you may find that your plant does not produce the same yields as those grown in the ground. But if you haven't got the space, or you just prefer to keep your fruit in containers, you can still get a good, healthy harvest with a little care.

Container growing is also an excellent way (sometimes the only way) to overcome any limitations your soil may have. It also gives you the possibility of taking your plants indoors through the winter and even through early spring when some plants' flowers might be susceptible to frost damage.

There are some golden rules if you want to make container growing work for you. You'll need to start your plants off in ideal conditions, and then, equally importantly, keep up the love and attention.

Choosing containers

Trugs, wooden barrels, hanging baskets, old wellies, olive oil tins, raised beds and pots of terracotta, plastic, metal or wood: the list of containers in which you can grow fruit is as long as your imagination. Each has its own qualities, and you should really choose very much in line with your sense of what suits, what's around and any budget you may have. The only considerations you need to bear in mind are that your container should be large enough for the plant (see below), physically strong enough to cope with the combined weight of the plant(s) and moist compost, and have good drainage.

Put a plant into a sealed box and water will be unable to drain away. The compost will become waterlogged and the plant will decline and likely as not die rapidly. It's one of the critical balances of growing most plants. They will need a plentiful supply of water, but most prefer to sip regularly rather than drown in a bathful. Punch or drill holes into the base of your container if it has none.

Strawberries growing in a bucket

Don't try to squeeze a £20 plant into a 20p pot. Use a container that's large enough to accommodate your plant well. There should be some room for the roots to grow into, but don't make it too large. Over-potting does the plant no good at all. And keep it in mind that you'll need to move up a pot size at some stage. Allowing plants to outgrow their container and become pot-bound is the easiest and most common way of mistreating container plants. It slows them down, arrests development and productivity, and it can be tricky to get your plant to recover.

The rule of thumb is to plant your container fruit one or two pot sizes up from that which it was supplied in. If you've bought bare-root plants, make sure the roots have plenty of room – they shouldn't be cramped or squashed against the sides or base. Trees, bushes and energetic climbers need a pot with a minimum diameter of 38cm to start with, and may need potting on as the years pass into considerably larger containers, depending on type and rootstock.

Choosing compost

Start with good-quality potting compost. By 'good-quality' I mean peat-free, preferably organic, blended specifically for container growing, and sourced from a reputable supplier (see Directory, pp.248–9). This will give your plants the best growing environment they can have without contributing to the destruction of precious and declining peat habitats. You may want to add some grit for drainage. Some plants (such as blueberries) need a very specific growing medium; where this is the case, I've covered it in the Fruit A–Z (pp.28–121).

Planting in containers

Before you start piling in compost, put a layer of stones, gravel or broken pots into the bottom of your container to ensure water can drain away readily. Take your plant and just size it up in the pot. You'll want to plant it as deep in the compost as it was in the pot (or as deep as it was in the ground if it's a bare-root plant). You also want to leave 3–4cm between the top of the compost and the rim of the pot to allow for expansion when you water.

Scoop some compost into the container, but not too much – you are only trying to make a base for the plant to sit on to get it at the right height. Once that's accomplished, gently ease compost evenly around the plant, pushing it reasonably firmly in, to ensure no major air pockets, until the plant is happily snug.

Water well and, if you need to, add a little more compost if it has sunk around the sides of the plant. Once the water has been absorbed, you should still have that 3–4cm gap between the top of the compost and the rim of the container.

You can always add a layer of gravel, bark, or similar to the surface. This top dressing helps minimise weed growth, reduces evaporation and stops the surface of the compost solidifying in the sun.

Ongoing container care

A plant in a container is feeding off a limited well of resources. It should be perfectly happy, but only if you keep replenishing this well. Being awake to watering is essential. When your plant is in fruit you may need to water daily. You'll also need to be on top of feeding. Within a month or two most of the nutrients in your compost will have been exhausted, and you'll need to replace them. You have a few options when it comes to what you feed them with (see p.161) and, whatever you choose, fix a time to do it every week between April and the end of August. I say this because it's very easy to lose track of time and find your plants have been a few weeks without.

Apart from that, prune and care for your container plants as you would if they were growing in the soil.

Growing under cover

Our famously erratic climate can sometimes do with a little help to ripen the more marginal fruit. Grow your apricots in a greenhouse or polytunnel and your chances of fruit, and a hefty harvest thereof, are much increased. There is, however, a price to pay. You'll need to water more frequently, watch out for diseases, and as temperatures fluctuate over the year, you may need to move some plants into or out of your under-cover areas. But if you're prepared to do that you'll certainly open the door to a few otherwise uncertain harvests.

Advantages of growing under cover:
- Temperatures are raised under cover, meaning spring arrives earlier, winter comes later
- Summer temperatures are higher
- There is some degree of frost protection
- Some fruit that might otherwise be very unlikely becomes possible, and the marginal fruit more reliable
- Being grown under cover protects the plants that are susceptible to leaf curl from the spring rains that can encourage the disease
- Your structure not only protects the plants from the worst of the cold and rainy weather, it protects you – so you can carry on gardening
- Having a polytunnel or greenhouse allows you to grow container-grown plants outside during the summer and take them under cover for the colder months
- Watering using a sprinkler or drip-feed system is usually more practical to set up under cover

Drip irrigation

Things to bear in mind when growing under cover:
- Most plants will require more watering than if they were grown outside
- For most plants, good ventilation is vital to ensuring healthy development and keeping diseases to a minimum
- Summer temperatures can be too high for some plants

Preparation

Whether you are growing in containers or into the soil, preparation will be similar for growing under cover as outside. Take the same care over what you fill your container with (see p.186) and dig over and add organic matter to the soil as you would if you were planting out in the open. Think about how you plan on watering before you plant anything.

Watering and feeding under cover

If you think you're happy to water and feed your plants using watering cans, bear in mind you may need to do this at least once a day through the hottest part of the year. Overhead watering is an option but is much better suited to low-growing plants rather than leafy, tall trees, which will mostly deflect the spray away from the developing root zone. Seep hose has perforations along its length to gently release water at regular intervals and works reasonably well.

My preferred choice, however, is a drip system, where narrow pipes with small drop attachments junction off from the main water pipe and are held in place next to each plant by spikes. Keeping the water on a low pressure causes drops to pop out constantly from each narrow pipe and drip down the spike into the root zone. It's an efficient, low-cost system that takes the strain out of summer watering.

Do be mindful of different plants' watering requirements though. There are some (including most citrus) that prefer a drench once a week even if that leaves them dry between, whereas most other fruit prefer more consistent moisture.

However you water, but especially if you are using a watering can or overhead system, you'll need to increase feeding when growing fruit under cover. Extra watering takes the nutrients more rapidly out of the upper layers of the soil or potting compost. You'll need to liquid-feed every fortnight through the growing season and consider using a slow-release pelleted chicken feed or similar that will gently let its goodness out (see Directory, pp.248–9, for suppliers).

Hand pollination

Extending the growing season is one of the advantages of growing under cover. The protected conditions fool your plants into thinking spring has come a little earlier than it has outside. Growth starts early, as does flowering, and while being under cover gives the blossom protection, there are likely to be fewer pollinators

Aiding pollination with a soft brush

around as these flowers emerge. With limited pollination you are likely to get limited fruit – so you'll need to step in and help things along. A soft, small artist's brush is perfect for the job of gently brushing over the pollen-laden anthers of each blossom, gently transferring pollen from one flower to another as you go.

Dealing with too much heat

Greenhouses in particular can give you too much of a good thing – heat and light. While it helps your otherwise marginal fruit to mature more reliably, too much heat and harsh light can be stressful for your plants and provide ideal conditions for many pests. You can paint the glass of greenhouses with a shade paint, though this can be as tedious to remove as it is easy to apply. Shade netting works well although it is slightly fiddly to set up, but you'll still need to get doors and ventilation open early in the day. It's also well worth watering the floor – known as 'damping down' – as this increases humidity as the moisture evaporates in the heat, reducing the likelihood of numerous pests.

Polytunnels usually have a cloudier covering of semi-transparent plastic, which takes the edge off the heat without diminishing the light levels significantly.

Ongoing and winter care

With more heat and a longer growing season you are likely to have more plant growth, so you'll need to keep up with pruning to stop your plants becoming over-stretched and unproductive. You'll not need to do anything differently from what you'd do if the plants were growing outside, but you may have to get accustomed to taking more growth off when the time comes. With more vigorous growth, you may need to consider wires and/or canes, etc, to keep your plants supported.

When the heat has passed, you'll still have a few tasks to undertake. Most plants will lose their leaves through winter. Do keep on top of removing them, as they not only clutter the floor, they can also harbour disease that will affect your plants the following season. Add them to your compost heap or leaf-litter pile. Some plants (such as melons) that are annuals are grown just for one growing season and the whole spent plant will need removing once the fruit has been taken.

You may have to shuffle some plants around as the cold weather approaches. Move in any of your container-grown plants that would benefit from a warmer winter, protection through spring flowering, or keeping out of spring rains which can encourage leaf curl. You may also need to remove citrus plants if your greenhouse or polytunnel is unheated. These enjoy a minimum of 10°C, so you may have to bring them into the house or conservatory if you have one.

Towards the end of winter, top-dress containers with new compost along with slow-release natural fertiliser, and dig slow-release fertiliser and compost into the topsoil if you're growing fruit under cover in the ground.

Recipes

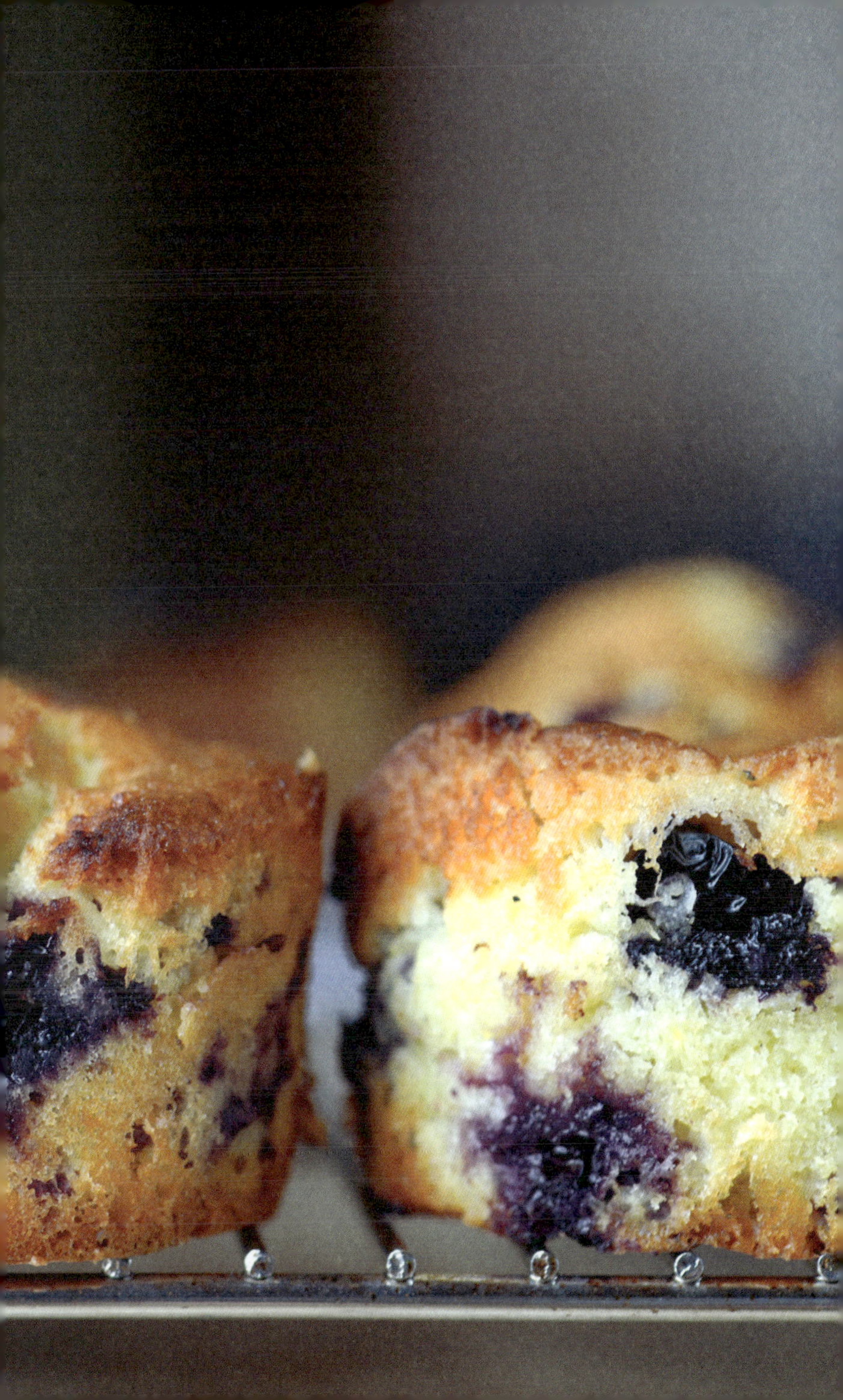

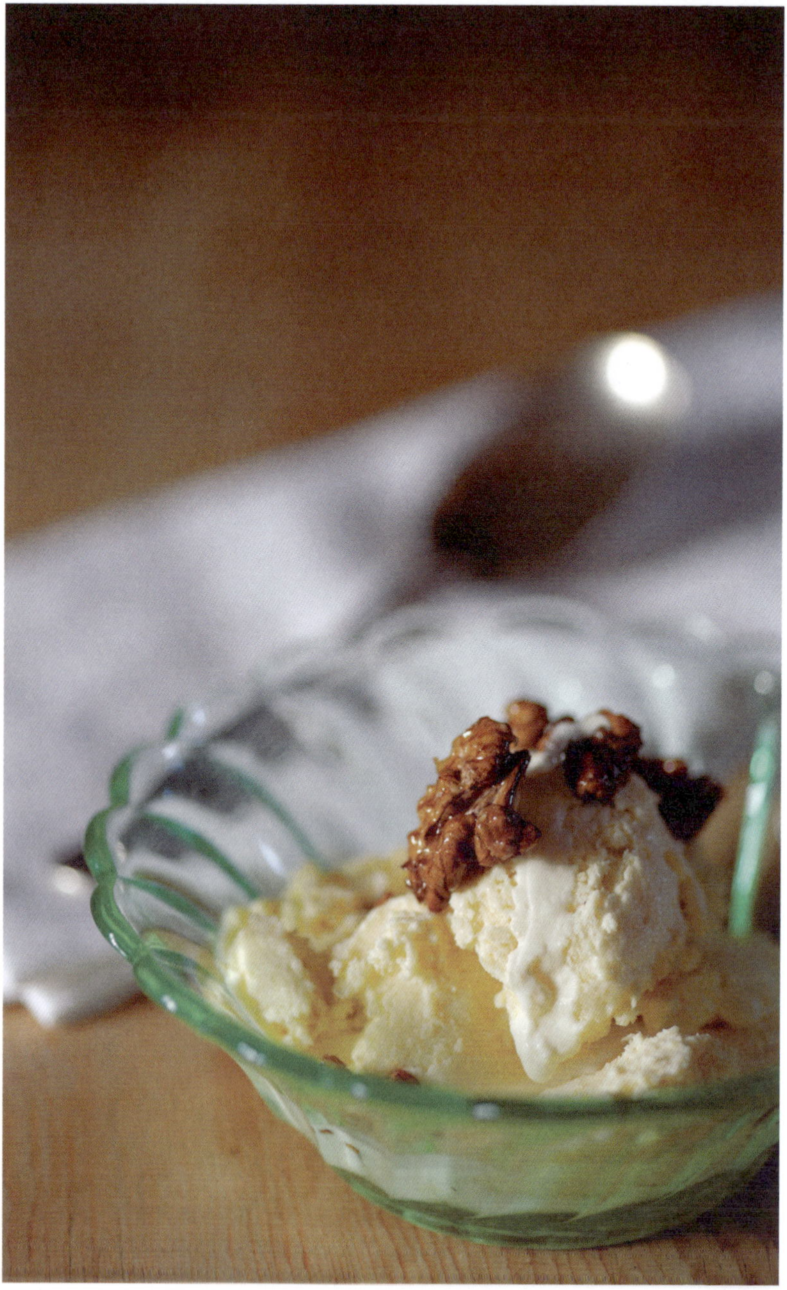

Orchard ice cream
with caramelised walnuts

Vary the combination of fruit according to taste and availability – my favourite is half apples, half quince – and try adding a little cinnamon before cooking. A touch of cream dribbled over the ice cream cuts the floral quince beautifully.

Serves 4–6

350g mixed apples, pears and/or quince (in any proportion), washed
60g unsalted butter
3 tbsp cider brandy (optional)
300ml double cream
1 vanilla pod, split lengthways
4 eggs yolks
140g caster sugar

For the caramelised walnuts
A couple of handfuls of shelled walnuts
2 tbsp honey
2 tbsp brown sugar
A good pinch of salt

Peel, core and chop the fruit. Put into a pan with the butter and 2 tbsp water. Cook gently, covered, until completely soft. Push the purée through a sieve if it appears too grainy (most likely if you've used a lot of quince). Add the brandy if using.

Pour the cream into a large saucepan, add the vanilla pod and bring to just below the boil, then take off the heat. Meanwhile, whisk the egg yolks and sugar in a bowl until creamy and thick. Remove the vanilla pod from the cream, then slowly pour onto the sugar/egg mixture, whisking as you do so. Return to the pan and cook gently, stirring constantly with a wooden spoon; don't let it boil. After 15–20 minutes the custard should have thickened enough to coat the back of the spoon.

Stir the custard into the fruit purée. Allow to cool completely, then chill. Churn in an ice-cream maker if you have one. (If not, freeze in a shallow lidded tub, beating with a fork every 45 minutes or so, for a smooth result.)

For the caramelised walnuts, preheat the oven to 180°C/Gas mark 4. Toast the nuts on a baking tray for 5–10 minutes; don't burn. Heat the honey and 2 tbsp water in a frying pan until bubbling, then add the walnuts, tossing to coat. Scatter over the sugar and salt. When the sugar has melted, toss the nuts again. Tip onto greaseproof paper, separating the nuts. Once cool, break apart any that are stuck together.

Before serving, soften the ice cream in the fridge for 30 minutes. Serve scattered with caramelised walnuts. Store the rest of them in a sealed tub for up to a week.

Lamb and apricot tagine

Don't be put off by the long list of ingredients: this is very simple to make. The many spices build up a lovely depth of flavour that brings out the best in the lamb and apricots. Avoiding browning the meat first is something I picked up from the wonderful Debora Robertson, who I worked with on *A Taste of the Unexpected*. Moroccans don't, and it makes for a straightforward, deliciously authentic dish.

As a variation, quince – quartered and poached for 30 minutes – work every bit as well as the apricots.

Serves 4–6

1kg shoulder of lamb, cut into 3cm chunks
1 cinnamon stick
2 tsp ground cumin
1 tsp sweet paprika
1 tsp hot paprika
1 tsp ground coriander
1 tsp ground turmeric
4 cardamom pods, lightly crushed
400g tin chopped tomatoes
2 onions, peeled and finely sliced
25g fresh ginger, peeled and grated
1 tsp saffron threads
1 tbsp tomato purée
2 tbsp olive oil
4 garlic cloves, peeled and finely chopped
500g fresh apricots, halved and stoned (or this quantity of dried apricots)
A little pared zest and the juice of 1 lemon
2–4 tbsp honey
Sea salt and freshly ground black pepper
A handful of coriander leaves, finely chopped, plus a few sprigs to garnish
A small handful of mint leaves, finely chopped
Lemon wedges, to serve

Put the lamb into a bowl, add all the dry spices and mix together well. Cover and leave to stand in a cool place for at least 3 hours.

Put the spiced lamb, tomatoes and onions into a large pot and add enough water to just cover. Bring to a simmer, then add the ginger, saffron, tomato purée, olive oil and garlic. Stir well, return to a simmer, then lower the heat. Cook very gently, with the lid partially on, for 2 hours.

Add the apricots, lemon zest and juice, and 2 tbsp honey. Cook gently for another 30 minutes, adding a little water if you think it is needed. Taste and season, adding a little more honey if you fancy. Stir in the chopped coriander and mint.

Serve garnished with coriander sprigs, with lemon wedges on the side. Accompany with Moroccan breads or rice.

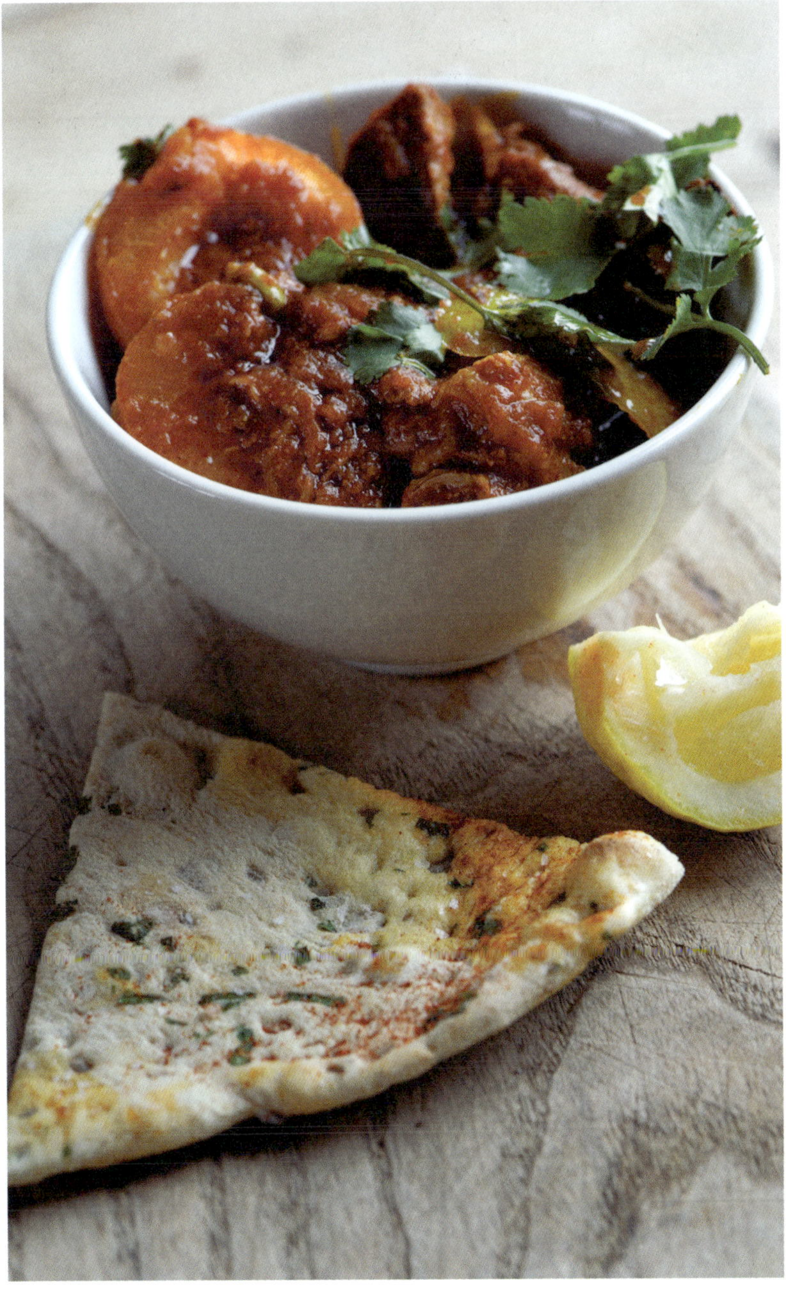

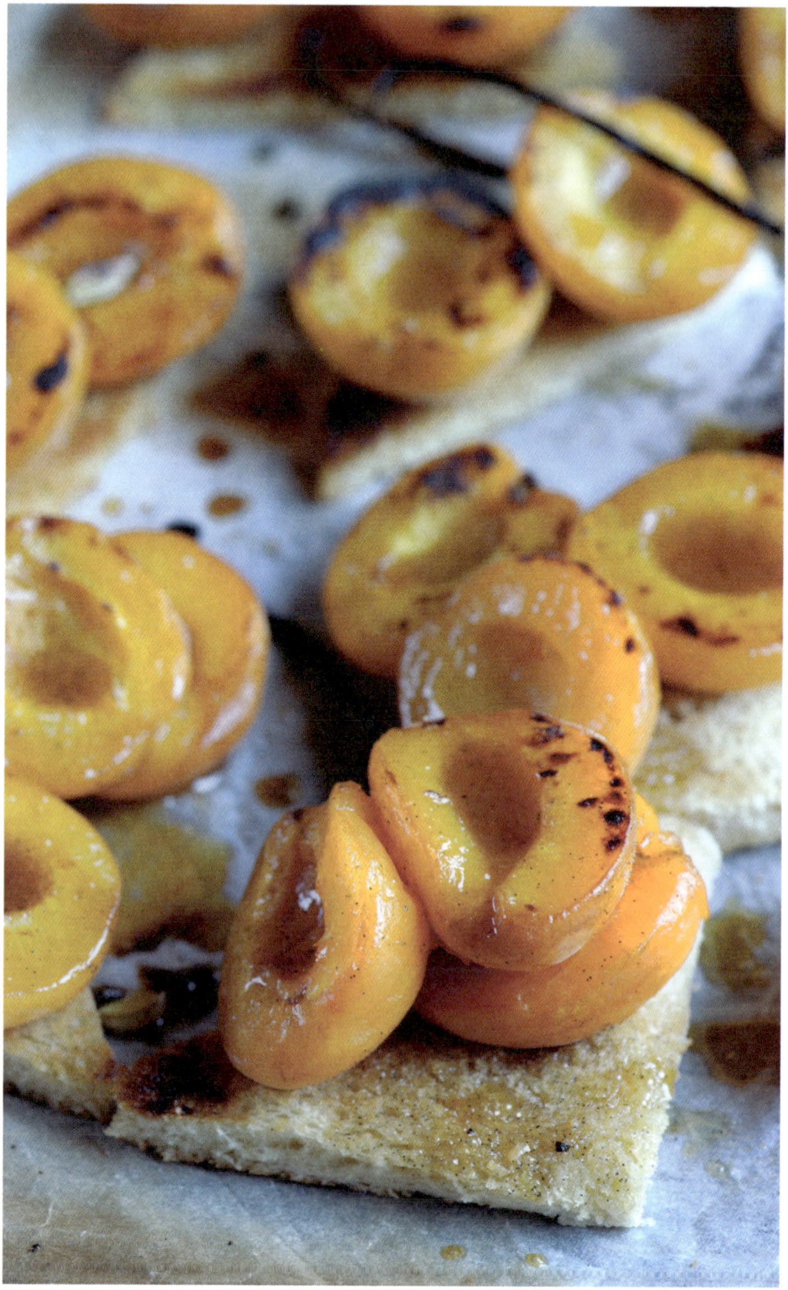

Apricots on toast

This gorgeous, spicy and sweet snack works equally well with nectarines or peaches in place of the apricots. If you want to make a bit more of it, leave out the toast and serve the fruit as a dessert with a simple, not-too-sweet fresh raspberry sauce (see variation).

Serves 4

4 slices of white bread, crusts removed, cut into triangles
100g unsalted butter
120g runny honey
1 vanilla pod, split lengthways
4–6 cardamom pods
16 firm apricots

Preheat the grill to high and toast each slice of bread on one side.

Melt the butter and honey together in a small saucepan. Scrape out the vanilla seeds from the pod and add them, along with the pod and the cardamom pods, to the honey and butter. Increase the heat, bring to the boil and boil for 30 seconds. Remove from the heat.

Halve the apricots and remove the stones. Place them, skin side up, on a baking sheet and grill for a minute or two until they start to colour. Remove the baking sheet from the grill.

Lay the half-done toast, uncooked side up, on another baking sheet. Use a spatula to turn the apricots, cut side up, over onto the toast, spoon the honey butter over and grill for 3–5 minutes until soft and cooked through. Serve straight away.

Variation

Rather than have the apricots on toast, serve them with a raspberry sauce: pulse 200g raspberries with 2 tbsp caster sugar and 2 tbsp water in a food processor and sieve before pouring over the apricots.

Blackberry apple compote

I can't seem to make enough of this really delicious, slightly addictive compote. Once a jar has been opened in our house, it tends to appear on the table every breakfast time until it's gone. The mix can become very thick if you overcook it – something I do frequently – but I'm starting to prefer it that way. Even when thick, it doesn't seem like a jam, as the low sugar content ensures it doesn't become cloying, though that means it won't keep as long as most jams.

Makes 4 x 220ml jars
250g caster sugar
6 finely pared strips of lemon zest
2 cinnamon sticks
2 star anise

500g cooking or dessert apples, peeled, cored and sliced
250g blackberries

Put the sugar into a large pan with 550ml water and stir over a moderate heat until the sugar has dissolved. Add the lemon zest, cinnamon and star anise, then turn up the heat and bring the liquid to the boil. Reduce to a simmer.

Add the apples to the pan and cook gently for 5 minutes. Now add the blackberries and simmer until you have a smooth, thick compote. Spoon into several sterilised jars, fishing out the star anise, cinnamon and lemon zest as you go.

Seal the jars and store in a cool, dry place. The compote will keep for a few months but will need to be refrigerated once opened. Serve with yoghurt, with pancakes or drop scones, or in any other way you fancy.

Variations
Most fruit will make a fine compote but the berries, blackcurrants, pears, plums and apricots are perhaps the best. Apple and quince compote is particularly good: use 600g apple and 150g quince.

Frozen summer berries
and hot white chocolate sauce

This wonderful, simple pudding, made famous by the Ivy restaurant in London, exploits the contrast between hot and cold, sweet and sharp. Use any mix of your favourite berries and fresh summer currants. Personally, I would avoid using solely sharp currants – but if you like them, why not?

To keep berries and currants from freezing together into a solid lump, freeze them first spread out on a tray, then tip them into a bag once frozen.

Serves 4
200g good white chocolate, broken into small pieces
200ml double cream
1 tsp white rum (optional)
500g mixed frozen berries (and currants if you like)

For the sauce, put the chocolate and cream into a heatproof bowl over a pan of very gently simmering water, making sure the bowl isn't actually touching the water. Heat *very* gently for 10–15 minutes, stirring occasionally as the chocolate melts; the mixture will thicken steadily. Stir in the rum, if using.

A few minutes before serving, distribute the frozen berries among individual dishes – a few minutes at room temperature takes the edge off their chill.

When you're ready to serve, pour the hot white chocolate sauce into a jug and let everyone help themselves.

Summer pudding

When I first heard about summer pudding many years ago I couldn't have been less excited about the prospect. White bread, fruit, sugar, and the pudding wasn't even cooked: how good could that be? As good as any other pudding, I was soon to discover. Use whichever mix of currants and berries takes your fancy; just keep the total weight of fruit the same. The key to making the very loveliest summer pudding is to heat the fruit only until the sugar dissolves and the juices start to run, no longer.

Serves 4–6

500g raspberries
250g redcurrants
150g blackcurrants or blackberries

200g caster sugar
10 thick slices of good white bread, crusts removed

Put all the fruit and the sugar into a large saucepan and cook over a gentle heat for 4 minutes or so – just until the juices begin to run and the sugar is dissolved. Remove from the heat.

Line an 850ml pudding basin with a double layer of cling film, leaving plenty overhanging the rim. Line the bottom and sides of the bowl with bread slices, overlapping them slightly to ensure there are no gaps and keeping one slice back for the lid.

Drain 100ml of the juice from the fruit into a small bowl, cover and refrigerate. Spoon the rest of the fruit and its juice into the pudding basin. Place a slice of bread on top and fold over the cling film to seal the pudding. Place a saucer or small plate, which just fits inside the bowl, on top of the pudding and add a weight such as a bag or two of sugar, or some tins of food. Refrigerate overnight.

When you are ready to serve the pudding, lift off the plate and peel back the cling film. Place a serving plate over the top of the pudding and invert the pudding and plate carefully. Lift off the bowl and remove the cling film. Spoon the extra chilled juices over the pudding and serve with thick double cream.

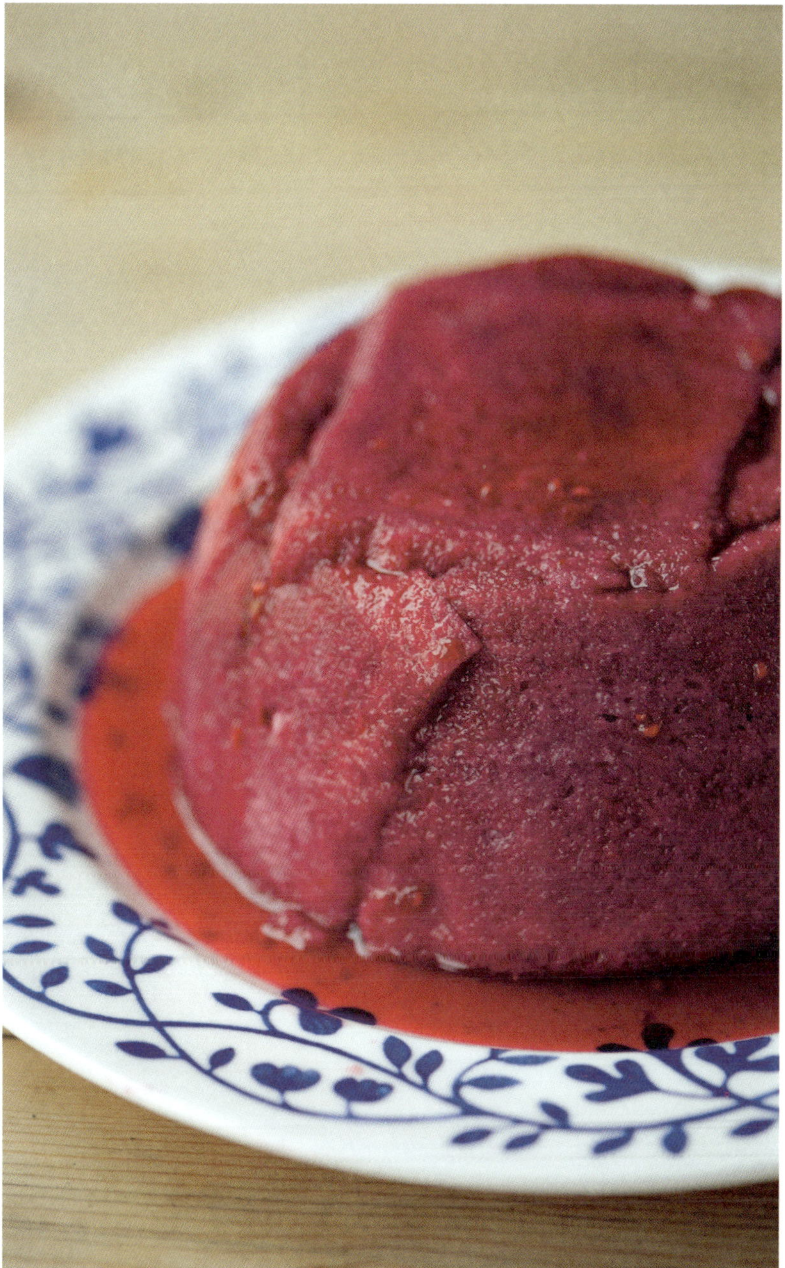

Crème de cassis

Blackcurrants are one of those fruits that seem to take us by surprise. We want them for the many months they aren't in season, then run out of ideas for what to do with them when harvest time arrives. This is an excellent way to preserve their inimitable flavour to enjoy whenever you like.

A little homemade crème de cassis (about 1cm) in a wine glass topped off with white wine gives you the perfect kir and it's fantastic dribbled over ice cream or whirled through a cake mix. The leaves add a greater depth of flavour than the currants alone and contribute a delicious, gently spicy edge.

Makes about 2 litres
1kg blackcurrants
20 blackcurrant leaves
1 litre gin
650g granulated sugar

Wash the blackcurrants and pinch off their stalks. Dry the fruit thoroughly and put it into a large glass jar with the blackcurrant leaves. Pour in the gin and leave for at least 4 months.

Strain the gin into a large jug, discard the leaves and purée the blackcurrants in a food processor. Strain the blackcurrant pulp through a muslin-lined sieve and mix with the gin.

In a saucepan over a gentle heat, dissolve the sugar in 140ml water. Increase the heat and simmer gently for 5 minutes until the sugar syrup thickens. Remove from the heat and allow to cool completely.

How much of the sugar syrup you add to the fruity alcohol to sweeten it is up to you – add it in instalments, stirring and tasting regularly. Once it is as you like it, pour into sterilised bottles and seal. Although the liqueur will be delicious immediately, it will improve with age and it keeps indefinitely.

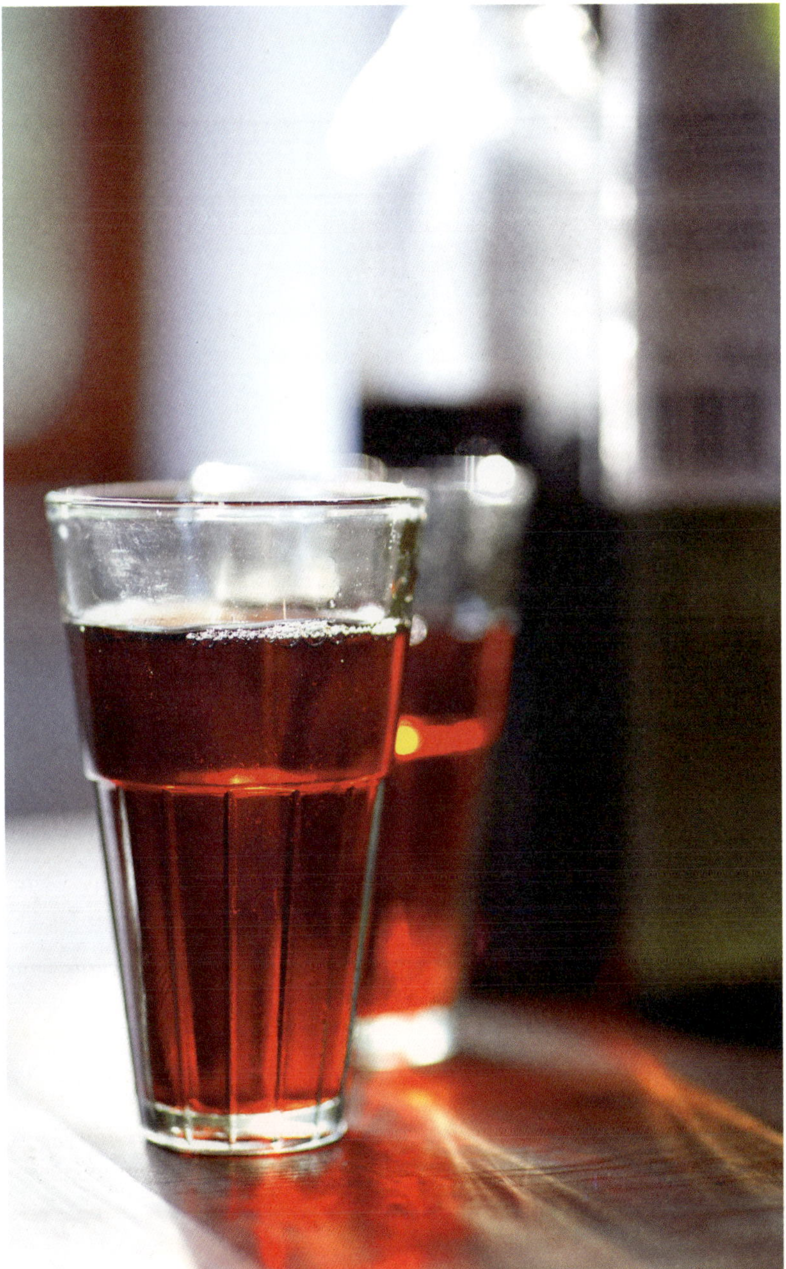

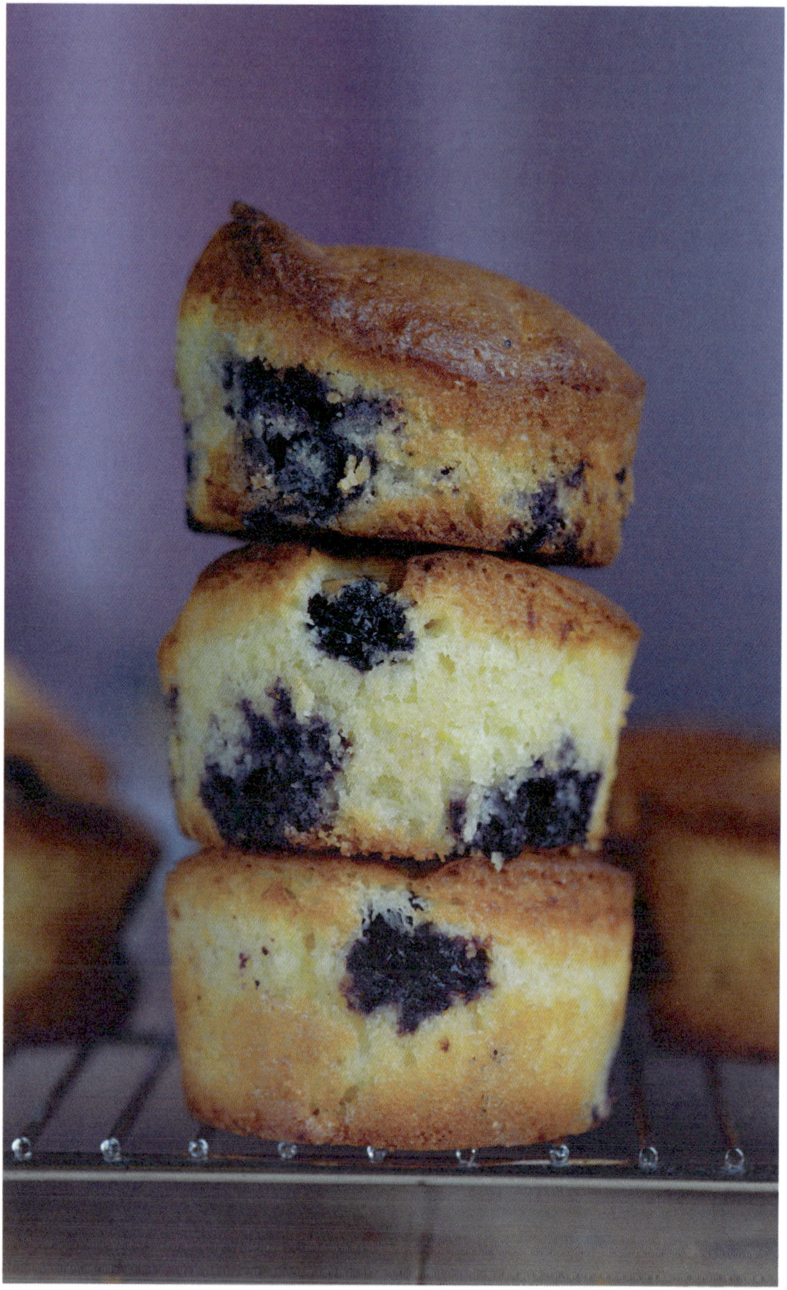

Blueberry muffins

This is a wonderful muffin recipe that also works deliciously with anything from alpine strawberries to currants. You can even throw in a few crushed nuts. The more adventurous should try adding half a teaspoonful of freshly ground coriander seeds when you add the blueberries – I know it sounds peculiar, but it works...

A few of these muffins, crumbled up, are perfect as the sponge element in a trifle (see p.244).

Makes 12
250g plain flour
2 tsp baking powder
½ tsp bicarbonate of soda
A good pinch of salt
120g unsalted butter, melted

120g caster sugar
2 eggs, lightly beaten
100ml full-fat milk
Finely grated zest and juice of 1 lemon
180g blueberries

Preheat the oven to 190°C/Gas mark 5 and line a 12-hole muffin tray with paper muffin cases. Sift the flour, baking powder, bicarbonate of soda and salt together.

In a separate bowl, beat together the butter, sugar, eggs, milk, lemon zest and juice until evenly combined. Gently fold in the flour mixture using a spatula, then fold in the blueberries; don't overmix.

Spoon the mixture into the muffin cases and bake for 16 minutes. To check, insert a cocktail stick into the middle of a muffin; if it comes out clean, they are ready, if not, give them another couple of minutes.

Transfer to a wire rack to cool. The muffins are best eaten the same day – ideally still slightly warm from the oven. Any that aren't devoured can be stored in an airtight container once they are completely cool and eaten the next day.

Variations
Blackcurrants, blackberries and alpine strawberries are all excellent substitutes for the blueberries in these muffins.

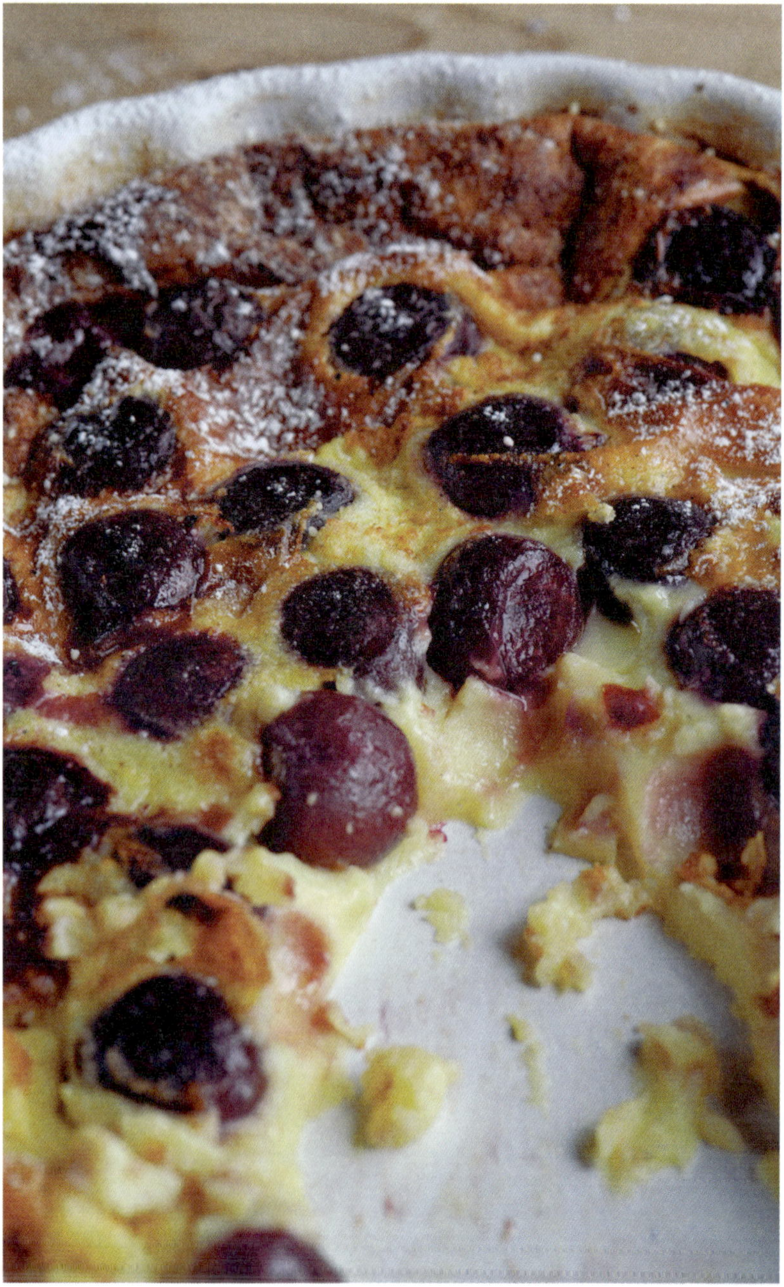

Cherry clafoutis

Clafoutis has long been one of my favourite puddings, but I was persuaded by Debora Robertson to cut back every gram of flour I possibly could to get the perfect combination of lightness, creamy centre and crisp top. As ever, she was right. This clafoutis is delicious with or without alcohol. Many liqueurs work well, but almonds and cherries were made for each other, so do give amaretto a try. The dusting of cocoa gives just a hint of chocolate that suits the cherries too.

Serves 6

- 20g unsalted butter, diced, plus extra for greasing the dish
- 75g plain flour, plus extra for dusting
- A pinch of salt
- ½ tsp vanilla extract or seeds from ½ vanilla pod
- 1 tbsp amaretto, crème de cassis (see p.204) or kirsch (optional)
- 350ml whole milk
- 2 large eggs
- 40g caster sugar
- 300g cherries
- 1 tbsp cocoa powder
- 1 tbsp icing sugar

Preheat the oven to 230°C/Gas mark 8. Butter a round baking dish, about 25cm in diameter, or a rectangular one, about 28 x 20cm. Dust lightly with flour.

Sift the flour and salt into a large bowl and add the vanilla extract (or seeds), the liqueur (if using) and half the milk. Whisk to a smooth batter. Add the eggs, one at a time, whisking quickly as you add them. Now whisk in the caster sugar and the rest of the milk until the batter is just smooth.

Spread the cherries out in the baking dish, pour in the batter and dot the cubes of butter over the top. Bake for 25 minutes or until the batter is plump and golden.

Let the pudding stand for 5 minutes or so, then dust the cocoa over the surface, followed by the icing sugar. Serve warm, with double cream.

Variations

Many other kinds of fruit can be used instead of cherries but mulberries, pears, blueberries and plums are my favourites.

Baked figs with honey
and cardamom

Figs are wonderful baked. A brief time in the oven brings out their succulence and sweetness and they don't need much to help them along. You can leave out any of the spices and herbs if you like.

Serves 4
16 large fresh figs
2–3 tsp ground cinnamon or
    2 cinnamon sticks
3 cardamom pods, lightly crushed
3 tbsp runny honey

3 tbsp Marsala, Madeira, port,
    or water
3 thyme sprigs (or use lemon thyme
    if you have it)

Preheat the oven to 190°C/Gas mark 5. Cut the figs vertically into quarters, leaving them attached at the base. Squeeze each fig at the base to open them out a little. Stand the figs in a fairly small baking dish lined with greaseproof paper to prevent them sticking; they should be quite closely packed.

Dust over the ground cinnamon or add the sticks (whole or broken up) and sprinkle on the cardamom. Drizzle over the honey and alcohol or water, making sure some goes into the cuts. Scrunch up the thyme sprigs and throw over the figs. Roast in the middle of the oven for 15–20 minutes, depending on the size of the figs.

Serve warm with vanilla ice cream, or cream.

Variation
Plums, with their stones removed, are superb in place of the figs.

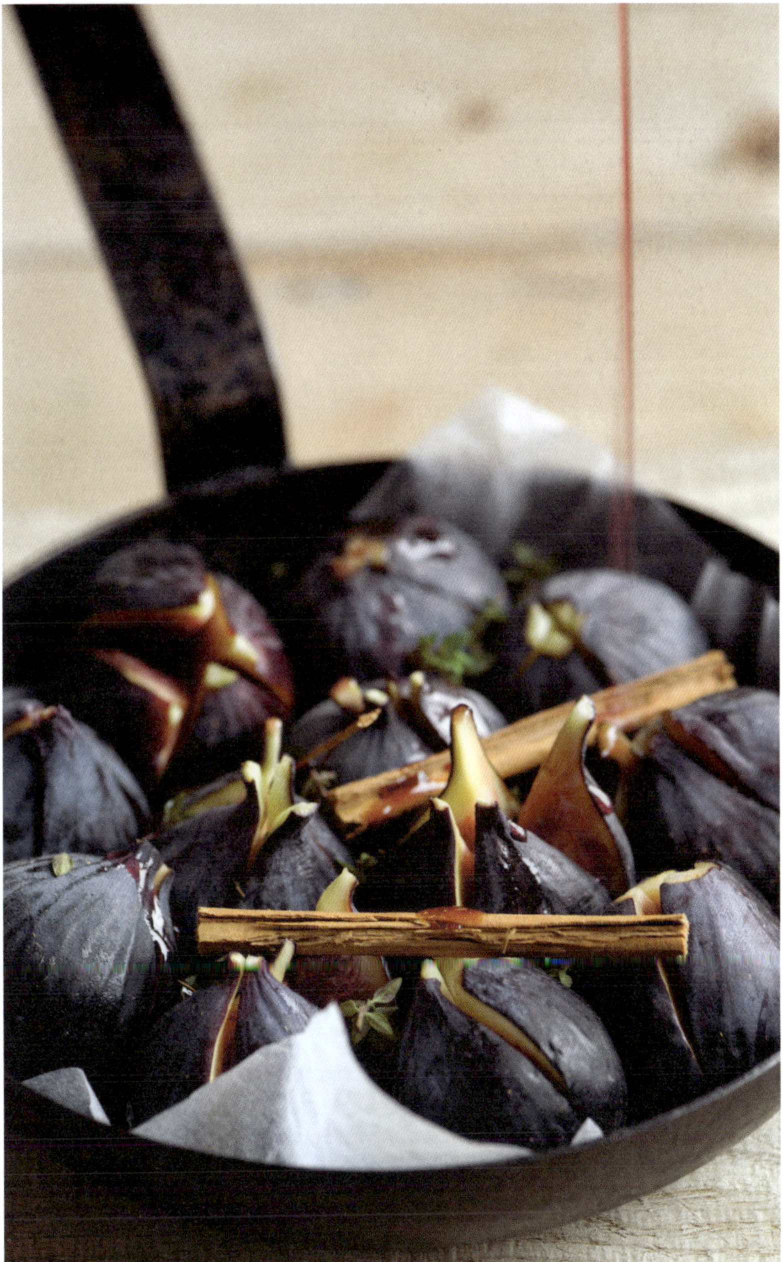

212 FRUIT

Gooseberry fool
with elderflower

A classic marriage of spring-into-summer flavours, as simple to make as it is delicious. You might like to top it off with a little cooked crumble mix (see p.239). Alternatively, serve it with almond tuiles, gingersnaps or shortbread.

Serves 4
500g gooseberries
4 tbsp caster sugar
2 finely pared strips of lemon zest
12 medium heads of elderflower, plus a few to decorate
300ml double cream

Put the gooseberries into a pan with the sugar, lemon zest and a few splashes of water and throw the elderflower heads on top. Heat gently until the gooseberries begin to break up, then simmer for 15 minutes or so, stirring occasionally. Push the pulpy mush through a sieve and leave to cool completely.

Whisk the cream until soft peaks form, then fold into the gooseberry purée – either leaving it as a ripple or combining evenly. Refrigerate for a couple of hours before serving.

Spoon the chilled fruit fool into serving glasses and top each with a sprig of elderflower to decorate.

Variations
The various berries and currants, as well as rhubarb, will happily take the place of gooseberries.

Gooseberry tart

This is a fantastic tart that can easily be adapted to most berries and currants, although you may want to leave off the demerara for sweeter fruit, and the elderflower cordial unless you're using strawberries, which it pairs with beautifully. It is equally good with green or purple gooseberries, although I think it looks best with purple ones. Early-season gooseberries may call for a little more sugar.

Serves 6–8

For the pastry
200g plain flour
50g icing sugar
A pinch of salt
100g cold, unsalted butter, cubed, plus an extra knob of butter, melted
2 egg yolks

For the filling
100ml crème fraîche
2 egg yolks
1 tsp balsamic vinegar
40–60g caster sugar (see above)
500g gooseberries, topped and tailed
A little elderflower cordial (optional)
A few tsp demerara sugar

For the pastry, put the flour, icing sugar and salt into a food processor and blitz briefly to combine, or sift together into a bowl. Add the cubed butter and pulse, or rub in with your fingertips until the mixture resembles breadcrumbs. Lightly beat 1 egg yolk and stir it into the pastry, adding a few teaspoons of iced water at a time until the dough forms a ball. Wrap in cling film and refrigerate for 20 minutes.

Preheat the oven to 180°C/Gas mark 4. Dust your work surface and rolling pin with flour and roll out the pastry to a thickness of around 3mm. Use to line a 26–28cm tart tin placed on a baking sheet. Gently press the pastry into the base and sides of the tin, leaving any excess overhanging the rim. Prick the pastry base a few times with a fork and bake for 10 minutes. Lightly beat the other egg yolk, brush over the pastry and bake for a further 10 minutes. Trim off any overhanging pastry.

For the filling, whisk the crème fraîche, egg yolks, balsamic vinegar and sugar together. Scatter the gooseberries evenly in the pastry case and drizzle on a few drops of elderflower cordial if you fancy. Pour in the custard and sprinkle the surface evenly with the demerara sugar. Bake for about 40 minutes until the custard is set. Let the tart rest for 5 minutes before serving. Double cream is all it needs.

Variations
Stoned cherries, the currants and berries, roasted rhubarb and halved or quartered plums can be used equally well in place of the gooseberries.

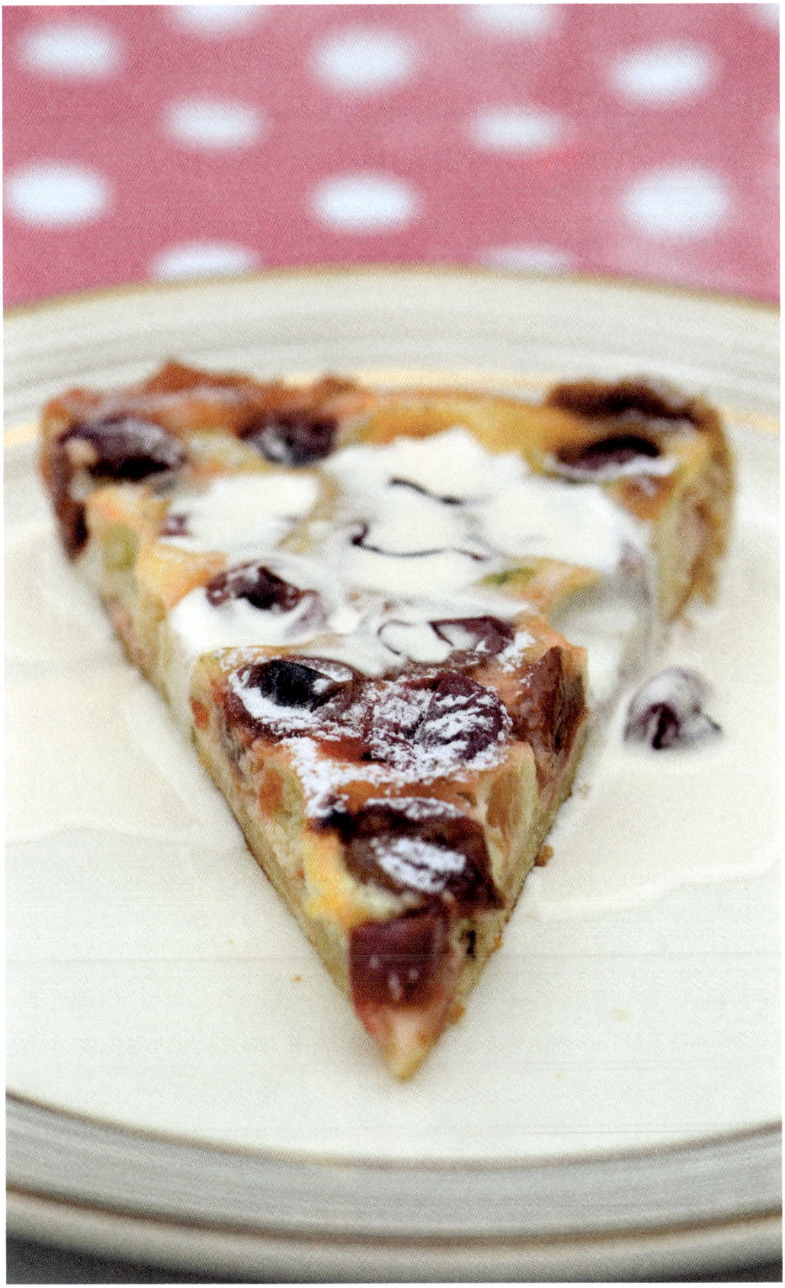

Gooseberry curd

This is a variation on Pam Corbin's fantastic curd recipe. I love making it with purple gooseberries. They produce a lovely bright pink-purple curd, but green/yellow varieties are just as delicious. The curd is also good with apples in place of the gooseberries. For lemon curd, leave out the gooseberries, double the lemon juice and use the zest of 3 lemons.

Makes 5 x 225g jars

450g gooseberries, topped and tailed
Finely grated zest and strained juice of 2 unwaxed lemons (you need 100ml strained juice)
125g unsalted butter, cut into cubes
450g granulated sugar
4–5 large eggs, well beaten (you need 200ml beaten egg)

Put the gooseberries and lemon zest in a pan with 100ml water and cook gently until soft and fluffy. Leave to cool slightly, then rub through a nylon sieve, using a wooden spoon.

Put the sieved purée into a heatproof bowl with the lemon juice, butter and sugar. Stand the bowl over a pan of simmering water on a low heat. Heat gently, stirring, until the mixture is hot and glossy, then whisk in the eggs using a balloon whisk. Don't allow the mixture to overheat, otherwise it will 'split' and curdle when the beaten egg is added. If you have a sugar thermometer, use it to check the mixture goes no higher than 60°C. If the mixture does split, take the pan off the heat and whisk vigorously until smooth.

Once the eggs are incorporated, stir the curd over a gentle heat for 10 minutes or so until it is thick and creamy, using a spatula to scrape down the sides of the bowl every few minutes.

Pour the curd into warm, sterilised jars and seal. It will keep unopened for a month. Once opened, keep in the fridge and use it up fairly quickly.

Chicken Véronique

Chicken, wine, garlic, herbs and cream... retro perhaps, but the combination is so good. The late addition of the grapes adds an edge and texture to complement the wine flavour. This is one of those dishes that's very fine the following day too.

Serves 6

20g unsalted butter
4 tsp olive oil
1 free-range chicken, about 1.7kg
2 medium onions, peeled and finely sliced
3 garlic cloves, peeled and finely chopped
A bunch of thyme and/or tarragon
Sea salt and freshly ground black pepper
350ml white wine
2 or 3 bay leaves
250g white grapes, halved or whole
130ml double cream
A knob of soft unsalted butter, mixed with 1 tbsp plain flour (if needed)

Heat half the butter and half the olive oil in a large frying pan over a medium heat and add the whole chicken. Cook, turning from time to time, until you've browned as much of the bird as you can.

Meanwhile, heat the remaining olive oil and butter in a heavy-bottomed cooking pot (large enough to take the chicken) over a medium heat. Add the onions and sauté for about 10 minutes. Throw in the garlic and sauté for a couple of minutes.

Put the thyme and/or tarragon into the chicken cavity, then lay the bird on top of the onions and garlic and season well with salt and pepper. Pour in the wine and add the bay leaves. Bring up to a simmer, turn the heat down slightly, then put a lid on the pan and simmer gently for 1¾ hours.

Add the grapes and cook, uncovered, for another 10 minutes. Take the pot off the heat and, holding the chicken's legs with a cloth, lift the bird out onto a warm plate. Cover loosely with foil and leave to rest while you finish the sauce.

Return the pot to the heat and stir in the cream. If the sauce seems too thin for your liking, you can thicken it with the paste of softened butter and flour (known as beurre manié). Add it in little nuggets to the sauce, whisking or stirring all the time and allowing a minute or two for each addition to thicken the sauce. You may not need all of it. Once you've achieved the consistency you like, simmer gently for a further 2 minutes to cook the flour through. Taste to check the seasoning.

Carve or portion the chicken and serve with the sauce, potatoes and some greens.

Cranachan
with Japanese wineberries

Cranachan is a fantastic Scottish pudding, somewhere between a trifle and a fool, usually with raspberries at its heart. However, any berry or currant works well and Japanese wineberries, in my view, make the best cranachan of all. This is a pud to experiment with: adjust the sugar as you like, and try other spirits, liqueurs or sherry in place of whisky. My favourite version uses an Islay whisky such as Laphroaig – the smokiness sets off the toasted oats beautifully. Pungent heather honey is traditional but not essential – try other honey varieties.

Serves 4
50g rolled or porridge oats
2–3 tbsp whisky
3 tbsp caster sugar
300ml double cream
2 tbsp runny honey
350g Japanese wineberries

Gently toast the oats in a dry frying pan over a medium heat until golden; keep an eye on them as they can burn easily. Tip the oats onto a plate and leave to cool.

Stir the whisky and sugar together in a bowl, add the cream and whisk to soft peaks. Gently fold in the oats, honey and wineberries, aiming for a rippled effect rather than a complete blend. Don't worry if the berries bruise and leak a little of their juice: this adds to the beauty of the cranachan. Spoon into glasses and serve immediately.

Variations

Any of the berries, apples, plums and rhubarb can stand in for the Japanese wineberries, with gooseberries, apples, plums and rhubarb best poached to soften and even puréed first.

RECIPES 219

Medlar jelly

Medlar jelly is a fine accompaniment to rich meats. This deep amber preserve has just the right mix of sharp and sweet, with a fruity edge that I love. Unbletted medlars (see p.80) have a higher pectin content, while bletted ones have a deeper flavour – a mix of both is ideal. Don't throw away the leftover pulp – it adds a lovely datey flavour to chutneys (remove the seeds before using), and can be frozen.

Makes 4 x 225g jars
1kg medlars – ideally around half bletted, half not
½–1 lemon

About 500g granulated sugar
1 vanilla pod, split lengthways (optional)

Cut the medlars in half, or into quarters if large. Put them in a large pan and pour in just enough water to cover. Add the lemon juice (use the whole lemon for a sharper flavour). Bring to the boil, lower the heat and simmer for 1 hour. Give it an occasional stir but don't squash the medlars as this will make your jelly cloudy.

Now you need to strain the soft fruit through a jelly bag into a bowl; I do this overnight. If you haven't got a jelly bag you can use an upturned chair on a table (with the seat resting on the tabletop and the legs in the air). Tie the corners of a large square of muslin to the legs of the chair so the muslin forms a bag and allow the pulp to strain through into a bowl placed underneath. Don't squeeze or press the pulp down as your jelly will go cloudy.

Chill a small plate in the fridge. Measure the juice and pour it into a clean pan. For every 500ml, add 375g sugar. Add the vanilla pod, if using. Warm gently, stirring, until the sugar is dissolved, then increase the heat and boil, without stirring, for 5 minutes. Turn off the heat and test for setting: spoon a few drops onto the cold plate, leave for a minute, then push with your finger. It should wrinkle; if not, give it another 5 minutes and test again. Be prepared to test a few times as the pectin varies considerably with the degree of bletting that has occurred.

Pour the jelly into warm, sterilised jars and seal. It will keep in a cool, dark place for at least a year. Once open, store the jar in the fridge – it should still last for several months.

Variations

Quince, redcurrants and white currants all make deliciously different variations on this jelly.

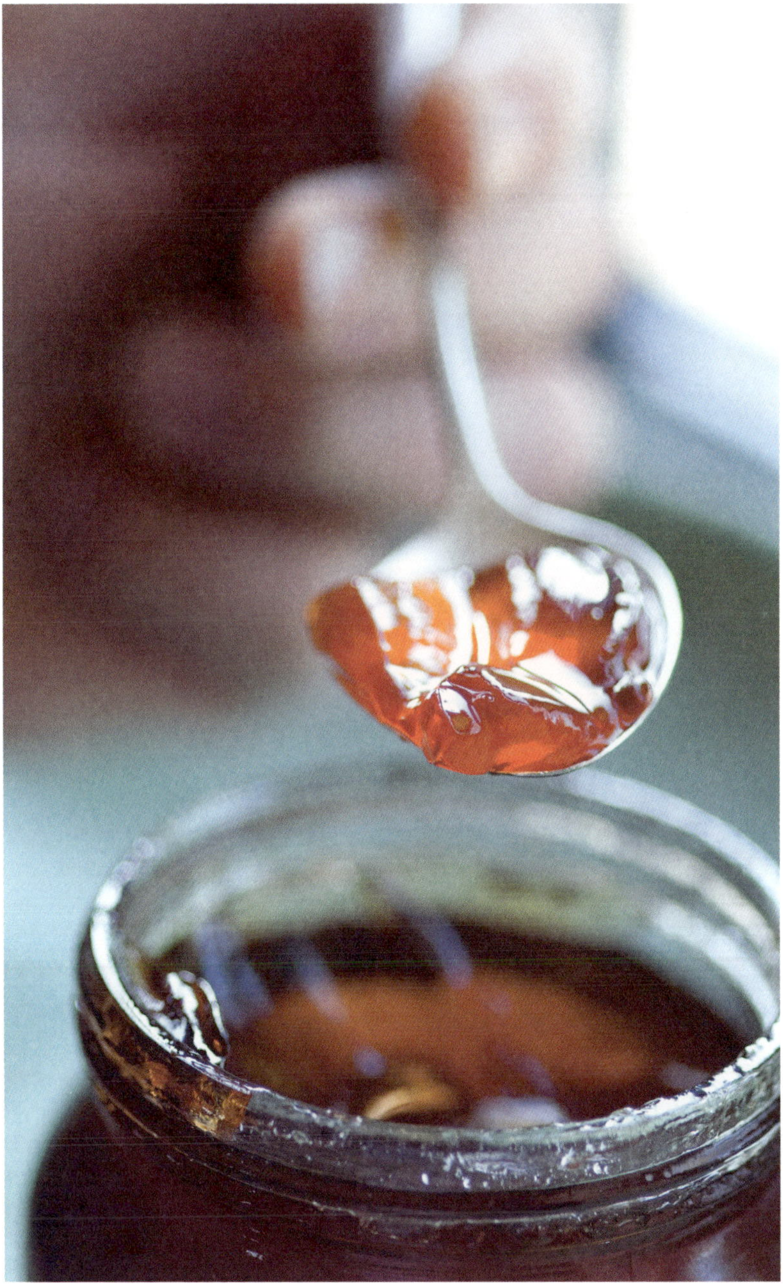

Melon salad
with goat's cheese, mint and red onion

A delightful, fresh salad that works equally (though differently) with melon or watermelon, this is very adaptable. Try Caerphilly rather than goat's cheese, for instance, basil instead of mint, spring onions instead of red onion or a sharp, mustardy dressing in place of the chilli oil. It goes with so many things – fish especially – and is perfect as a barbecue side dish.

Serves 4

800g melon (or watermelon)
300g hard goat's cheese, sliced or crumbled
10 mint leaves, torn or chopped
½ red onion, peeled and thinly sliced
Chilli oil (or olive oil and a little finely chopped chilli)

Remove the skin and seeds from the melon (or watermelon) and cut the flesh into thick chunks. Mix or organise the melon, cheese, mint and onion as you like on a large serving plate, then drizzle with a little chilli oil.

Variation
Pears, either poached or perfectly ripe, can replace the melon.

Fruity melons

For this easy dessert, the only essential ingredient is the melon. The other fruit is very much up to you, although soft and ripe is ideal. You are looking for around 300g extra fruit, depending on the size of your melons.

Serves 4

- 1 large melon (or 2 medium, or 4 small ones)
- 1 ripe peach or pear, peeled and cut into 1cm dice or half-slices
- A handful of grapes, deseeded, or cherries, stoned
- A handful of raspberries and/or halved strawberries
- 3 tbsp caster sugar
- 2 tbsp lime juice
- 3 tbsp cider brandy, rum, dessert wine or port

Cut the top off the melon(s) and remove the seeds. Using a melon baller or spoon, scoop out as much flesh as possible (in balls if you can, but chunks are fine) without getting close enough to the skin to bruise it.

Put the melon flesh into a large bowl with the other fruit and add the sugar, lime juice and alcohol. Toss together.

Spoon the mixture back into the melon(s), put the top(s) back on and refrigerate for a couple of hours before serving.

Variations

The melons can be filled with whatever combination of fruit you fancy.

Mulberry mess

A classic Eton mess – made with raspberries and/or strawberries – is divine, but throw mulberries into the mix instead and you have what I think is one of the most gorgeous of all puddings. It's also brilliant with a blackberry apple compote (p.200) in place of the berries.

Serves 4
500g mulberries
40g caster sugar
350ml double cream

For the meringue
2 medium egg whites
100g caster sugar

Preheat the oven to 120°C/Gas mark 1 and line a baking sheet with baking parchment.

To make the meringue, put the egg whites into a clean bowl and whisk until they form soft peaks. Add half the sugar and whisk until it is completely incorporated. Add the rest of the sugar gradually, whisking until the mixture is thick, glossy and forms stiff peaks.

Spoon the meringue into smallish mounds on the baking sheet, spacing them apart to allow room for expansion. Bake in the centre of the oven for 2 hours. The meringues should be crisp on the outside and lift off the paper easily. They should be squidgy in the centre but you'll have to wait until you eat them to find out for sure! Transfer the meringues to a wire rack and leave to cool completely.

While the meringues are in the oven, put the mulberries into a large bowl with the 40g sugar, cover and leave to macerate in the fridge.

Any time up to an hour before you want to serve the pudding, lightly whip the cream. Break the meringues into pieces and fold them into the cream. Now fold in the fruit but not too thoroughly – this should be a marbled 'mess' rather than a thorough blend. Spoon into glasses and you're ready to serve.

Variations
Any of the berries – or apples, plums or rhubarb – can replace the mulberries. Gooseberries, apples, plums and rhubarb are best softened or even puréed first.

RECIPES 225

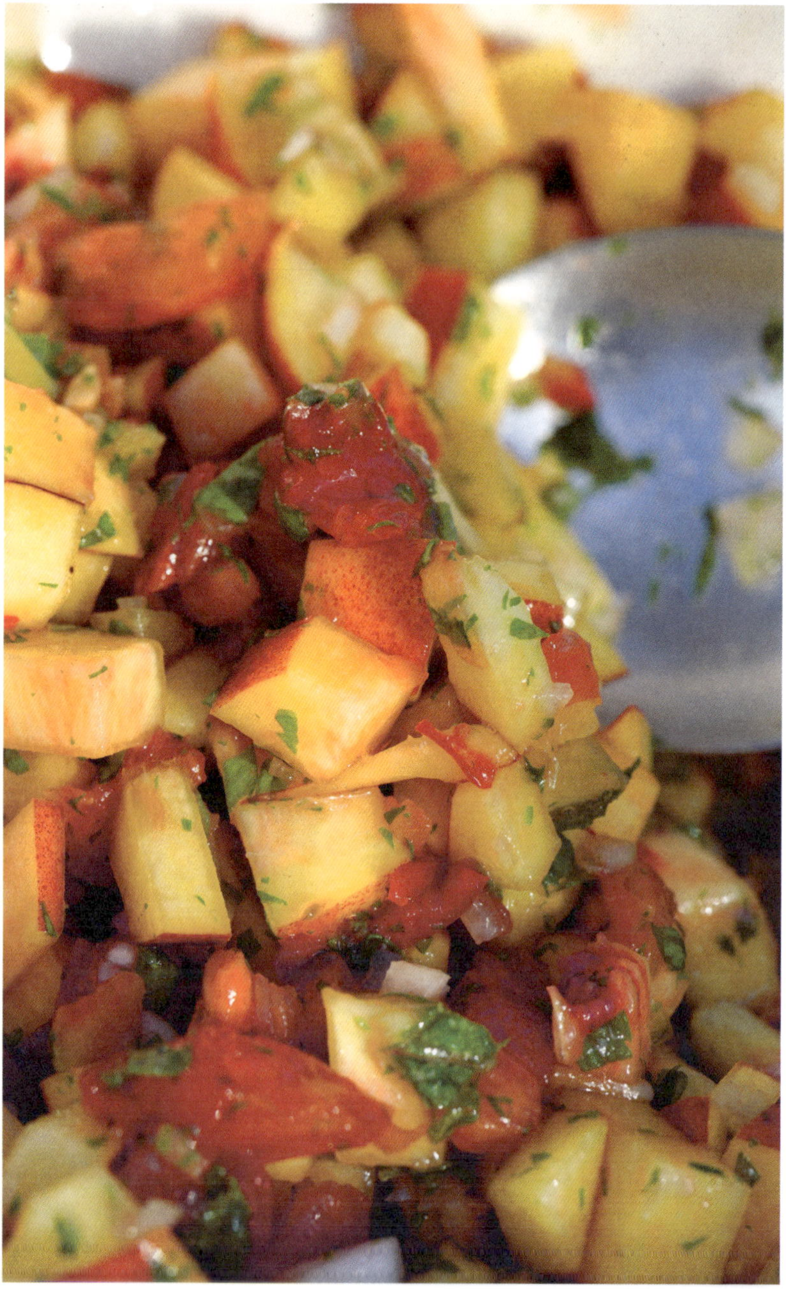

Peach salsa

This lively salsa is wonderful with fish, chicken or lamb, especially at a barbecue. It's beautifully adaptable too: the key thing is to include fruitiness, acidity, spicy punch and something aromatic. How you achieve this mix is up to you. The recipe works equally well with nectarines instead of peaches, for instance. You could also leave out the tomatoes, replace the spring onions with finely sliced red onion, or tinker with the herbs.

Serves 4–6

2 peaches (or nectarines), halved and stoned
1 ripe tomato, halved and deseeded
2 spring onions, trimmed and finely sliced
Juice of 1 lime
½ tsp caster sugar
1 small chilli (such as habañero), seeds and membrane removed, finely sliced
A small bunch of coriander, larger stalks removed, roughly chopped
5 mint sprigs, chopped
Sea salt and freshly ground black pepper

Cut the peaches and tomato into 5–7mm cubes. Simply toss together with all the other ingredients in a large bowl and season with a pinch or two of salt and plenty of pepper. The salsa is at its best if left for 10 minutes before serving.

Variation

Firm plums are a fine substitute for the peaches.

Pear and rocket salad
with Blue Vinny and walnuts

Each of the main ingredients here forms a happy partnership with any one of the others, so bringing the four together makes for a wonderfully harmonious whole. If I wanted to change this at all, I might consider adding a little extra edge with more mustard or some chopped chilli in the dressing. I've also used poached quince instead of pears, watercress in place of rocket, and hazelnuts rather than walnuts. You're not limited in your choice of blue cheese either – any good, salty one will work.

Serves 4

- A handful of shelled walnuts
- A few good handfuls of rocket (about 150g)
- 3 ripe pears
- 180g Blue Vinny or other blue cheese, crumbled
- A dozen or so mint leaves, finely sliced (**optional**)

For the dressing
- Juice of 1 lemon
- 1 tsp English grain mustard
- Sea salt and freshly ground black pepper
- 5 tbsp extra virgin olive oil

Toast the walnuts in a hot, dry frying pan until golden, shaking the pan regularly to ensure the nuts don't burn.

For the dressing, put the lemon juice, mustard and some seasoning into a small bowl. Whisk in the olive oil. Taste and add more seasoning if you like. Pour half of the dressing into a large serving bowl and add the rocket. Turn it through the dressing until a thin slick coats the leaves.

Peel the pears and, holding each one by its stem, slice thinly, discarding the middle slice with the core. Add to the rocket with the cheese and walnuts. Scatter the sliced mint, if using, over the lot. Drizzle with the remaining dressing and serve.

Variations
Cherries, perfectly ripe figs, peaches or nectarines, or poached quince can replace the pear.

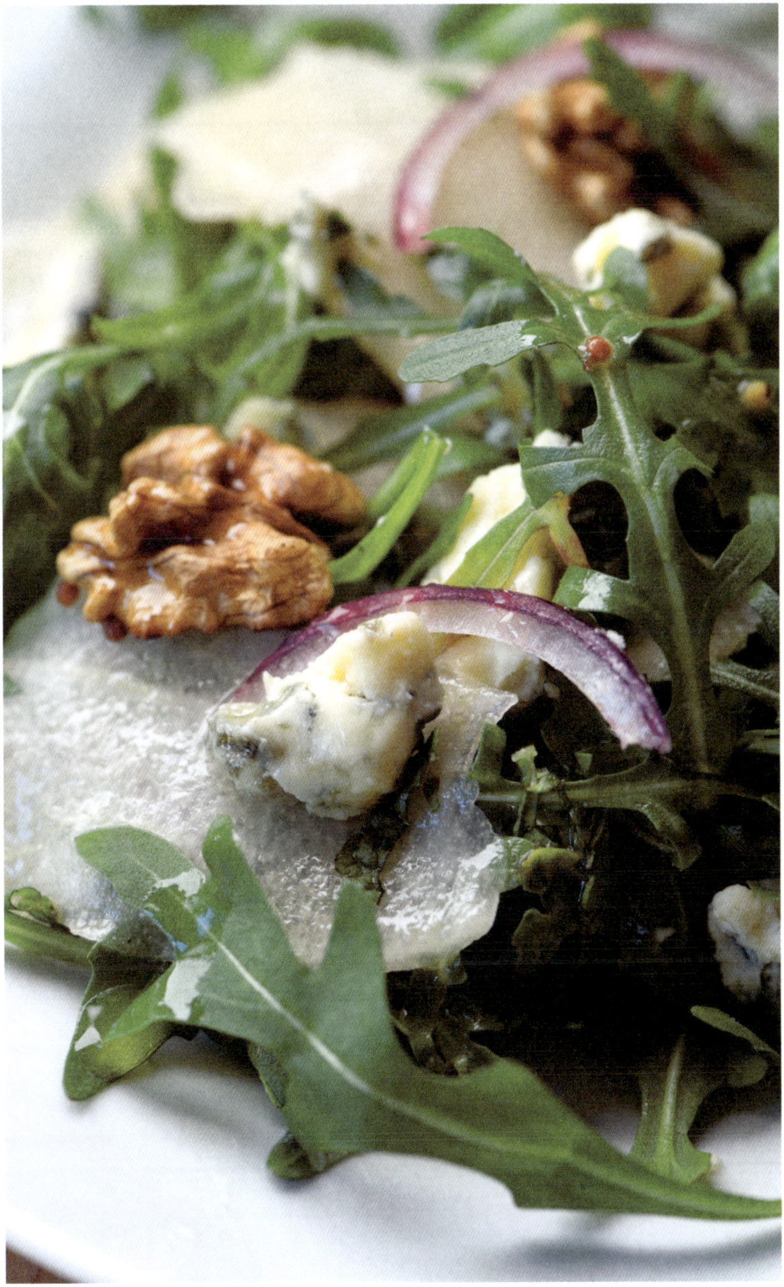

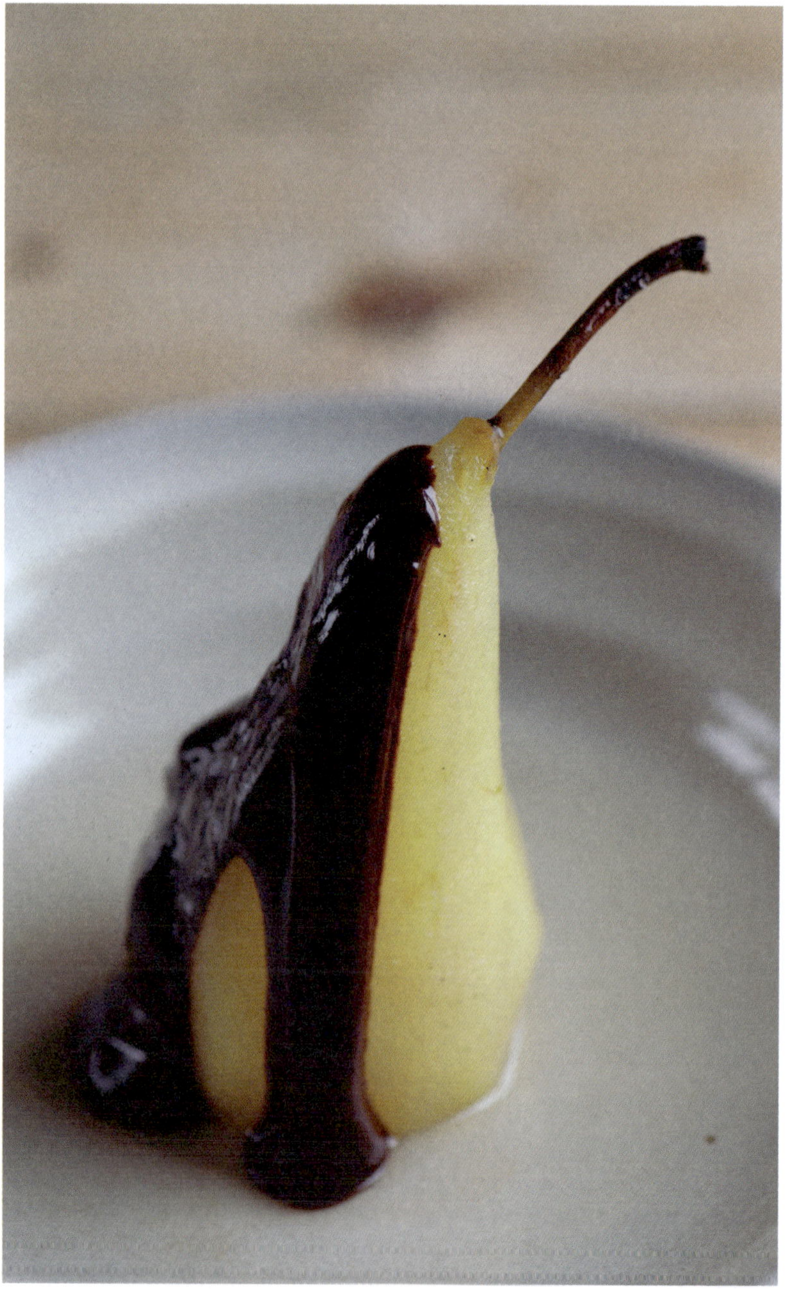

Poached pears
and chocolate sauce

This gorgeous dessert makes the most of under-ripe pears or cooking varieties. The spices are yours to alter, and you can poach the pears in half wine or cider and half water. The cooking time will vary depending on the variety of pear and degree of ripeness. Conference are ideal because they won't fall to pieces as softer varieties can. The pears will keep in their poaching liquor for up to 5 days in the fridge.

Serves 4

250g caster sugar
8 firm pears, peeled
1 cinnamon stick
½ tsp cloves
½ vanilla pod, split lengthways
½ tsp black peppercorns (optional)
½ lemon (optional)
2 star anise (optional)

For the chocolate sauce
170g dark chocolate, broken into
  small pieces
80g unsalted butter, cubed

Dissolve the sugar in 700ml water in a large saucepan over a medium heat. Add the pears and all the flavourings. The fruit must be completely submerged; add a little more water if needed. A 'cartouche' (a circle of baking parchment with a small hole cut in the centre) laid on the surface of the liquid will keep the pears submerged. Adjust the heat so the liquid is at a gentle simmer and cook for 15 minutes.

Meanwhile, make the chocolate sauce. Melt the chocolate and butter in a heatproof bowl set over a saucepan of simmering water, stirring occasionally. Once smooth, remove from the heat but leave the bowl over the water to keep the sauce warm.

Test the pears with a sharp knife – they should feel tender. If necessary, simmer for a few minutes longer. Once cooked, take the pan off the heat and allow the pears to cool a little in the liquid. If you prefer a sweeter, more intense syrup, transfer the pears to a warm bowl and reduce the liquid by boiling for a few minutes.

Serve the pears while still warm, bathed in a few spoonfuls of the aromatic syrup and the chocolate sauce. Clotted cream and/or shortbread are perfect on the side.

Variations
Try using quince. A combination of pear and quince is particularly special.

Plum and hazelnut cake

I love cakes that include ground almonds as well as flour. They have a fantastic fudginess and almondy background that is especially good paired with any of the stone fruit.

Serves 8

- 150g unsalted butter, softened, plus extra for greasing
- 150g caster sugar
- 3 eggs, lightly beaten
- 65g plain flour
- 1 tsp baking powder
- 110g ground almonds
- 60g hazelnuts, lightly toasted and crushed
- 16 plums, stoned and halved (quartered if very large)

Preheat the oven to 180°C/Gas mark 4. Lightly grease a 20cm round cake tin and line the base with baking parchment.

Beat the butter and sugar together until light, pale and creamy. Gradually work in the beaten eggs, adding a spoonful of flour at the same time to guard against curdling. Sift the remaining flour with the baking powder over the mixture and fold in lightly, using a large metal spoon. Now fold in the ground almonds, followed by the crushed hazelnuts.

Spoon the mixture into the prepared tin. Arrange the plums over the surface (you may have a few spare depending on the size of your plums); they will sink in a little as the cake cooks. Bake in the middle of the oven for 40 minutes, then test with a skewer – if it comes out clean, the cake is ready. If not, return to the oven for an extra 5 minutes or so.

When the cake comes out of the oven, allow it to rest for 10 minutes before removing from the tin. It's good cold but fabulous still warm, with clotted cream.

Variations

You could substitute peaches, cherries, gooseberries or even chunks of pear or apple for the plums, and replace the hazelnuts with walnuts.

Quince vodka

This is a wonderful way to enjoy quince months after the aroma of the ripening fruit has left the house. The basic recipe makes a lovely drink but one or more of the optional aromatics will give it a bit of a twist.

Makes about 800ml
2 large ripe quince
125g caster sugar
3 cinnamon sticks, 20 cloves and/or
    a few sprigs of fennel (optional)
700ml vodka

Wipe the quince, removing any fluffy down from the skin. Grate the fruit into a large, sterilised jar, picking out any pips. Add the sugar along with any of the aromatics you fancy. Pour over the vodka. Seal the jar and invert it a few times to mix the ingredients.

Leave the vodka for 2 months, inverting the jar every now and then when you remember. Taste and add a little more sugar if you like.

Leave it for another 2 months before straining it through a sieve, ideally through a funnel and back into the original vodka bottle. If you are impatient, you can drink it straight away but if you leave it a few months longer, a year if you can, the flavour will only improve.

Variations
Blackcurrants, the berries (apart from gooseberries), pears and plums all work well in place of the quince.

Raspberry fruit leather

This unusual preserve works well with almost any fruit. Don't be put off by the long cooking time. The method is as simple as it gets and the result is an intensely flavoured snack – one of the best ways I know to enjoy the flavour of a fruit long after the harvest.

Use this recipe as a template for other fruit leathers. Essentially, you just need to make a thick, smooth, gloopy purée of your chosen fruit and sugar and then dry it out very slowly in the oven until you have a pliable leather as clear and vivid as a stained glass window. Remember to add lemon juice if you are using fruit that is likely to discolour.

Makes 2 sheets, roughly 20 x 30cm
500g raspberries
500g peeled, cored and chopped cooking apples
Juice of 1 lemon
About 150g runny honey

Preheat the oven to 70°C/Gas mark ¼. Line two baking sheets (about 24 x 30cm) with baking parchment.

Put the raspberries, apples and lemon juice into a large pan. Bring to a low simmer then partially cover the pan and cook gently for about 20 minutes until pulpy. Allow the mixture to cool a little then push it through a sieve with the back of a spoon or pass it through a mouli. Weigh the purée. You should have about 750g. Add one-fifth of the weight of purée in honey and mix well.

Divide the purée between the two baking sheets, gently tipping the sheets to spread the mixture to the edges if it helps. Dry in the oven for 8–10 hours or until slightly tacky but not sticky, and easy to peel from the paper.

Leave the leather to cool completely, then tear it into pieces and store in a plastic tub, or roll it up in greaseproof paper or cling film and store in an airtight container. Either way, keep in a cool place and use within 3 months. The leather can also be frozen in a sealed container, for up to a year.

Variations
Most of the fruit in this book lends itself to leather (see above). The berries, apricots, peaches and nectarines work particularly well.

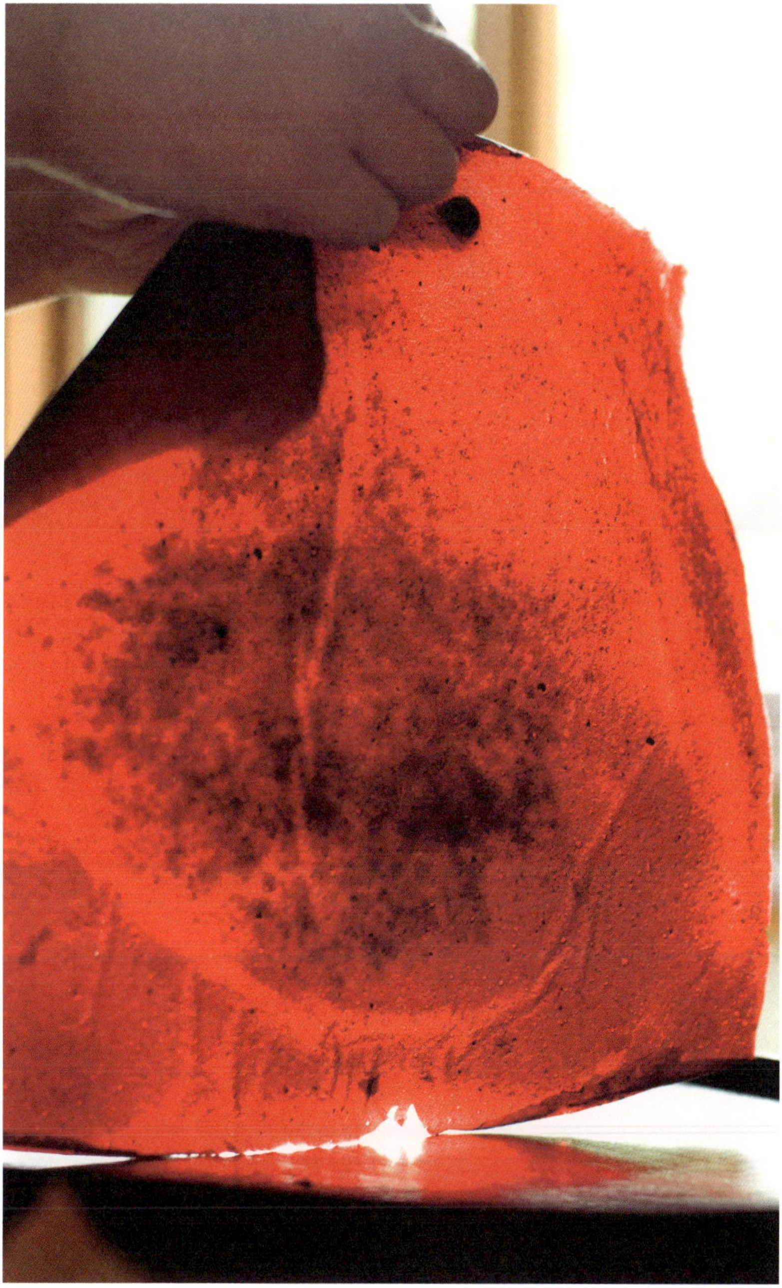

Bottled raspberries

Bottling is an old-fashioned way of preserving fruit – very simple, very good and much overlooked. It is essentially keeping fruit under liquid, such as a syrup made with sugar or honey. A little alcohol is a good addition too – brandy is lovely with raspberries. This is a variation on a recipe from Pam Corbin's *Preserves* handbook.

The following method works for most fruits, although you might want to use less sugar for sweet fruit, more for sharp or tightly packed fruit. You can also consider aromatics, such as cinnamon, cloves, sweet cicely and star anise. A few leaves of basil or mint add a lovely background note to these raspberries. And you can always combine fruits: half raspberries, half figs is a wonderful pairing.

Makes 6 x 225g jars
180g caster sugar
1kg raspberries (or 500g raspberries, 500g figs)
A few basil or mint leaves (optional)
150ml brandy (optional)

To make the syrup, put the sugar into a large pan with 700ml water and dissolve over a medium heat, stirring constantly.

Fill 6 sterilised screw-top or Kilner jars with the raspberries, handling the fruit carefully and making sure you don't compact it. Add the basil or mint and pour 25ml brandy into each jar, if using. Now pour in the hot syrup, filling the jars to the brim. If using screw-top jars, screw on the lids, then undo them half a turn – this allows steam to escape when they are in the pan. If you are using Kilner jars, rest the rubber seals and lids in place but don't fasten them down with the clips.

Stand the jars in a pan that is deeper than the jars and fill the pan with warm water, completely covering the jars. Bring the water up to simmering point very slowly, ideally over 30 minutes, and, once there, keep it simmering for 2 minutes. Remove from the heat. Once cooled a little, remove the jars and sit them on a folded tea towel to cool and dry completely. Tighten screw lids when they are cool enough to handle. The seal is critical, so if you're using Kilners, lift them carefully by the lid – if the whole jar lifts, the seal is tight and you can fasten the lids with the clips.

Store for up to a year in a cool, dark cupboard. Once opened, refrigerate and eat within a week.

Variations
Cherries, figs, plums, the berries and currants are all delicious bottled.

RECIPES 237

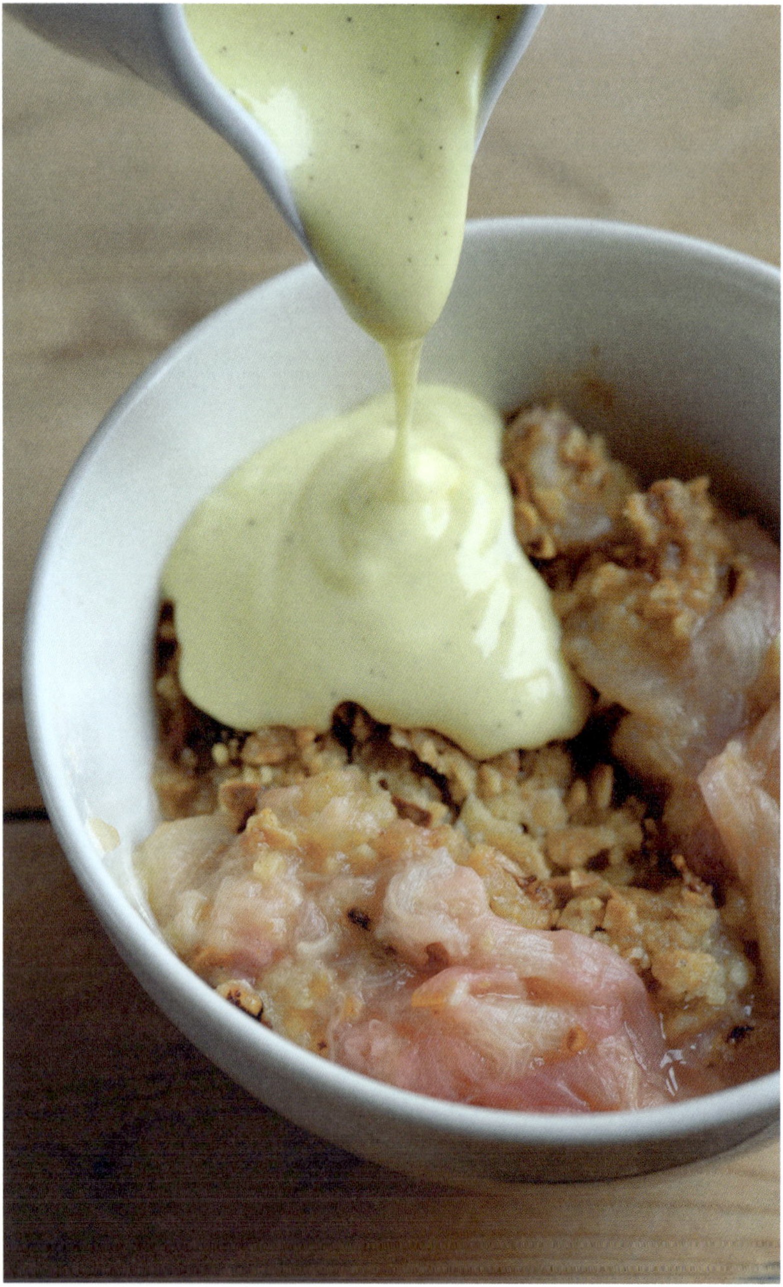

Rhubarb crumble

I love this almond crumble topping, with its shortbread-like fudginess. Putting the ginger into the topping rather than in with the rhubarb works a treat. If you're not familiar with sweet cicely, do give it a try; it's a herb that's very easy to grow. As well as adding a lovely aromatic edge to a dish, the aniseedy leaves make tart fruits seem sweeter, which means you can use less sugar.

Serves 4
750g rhubarb, trimmed
3 tbsp finely chopped sweet cicely leaves or 3 tbsp caster sugar

For the crumble topping
200g plain flour
A pinch of salt
140g caster sugar
2–4 tsp ground ginger, to taste
250g flaked almonds
200g cold, unsalted butter, cubed

Preheat the oven to 180°C/Gas mark 4. For the topping, put the flour, salt, sugar and ginger together into a food processor and blitz briefly to combine. Add the flaked almonds and process just enough to break them up but not turn them to dust. Add the butter and process until well mixed. The crumble should be in fudgy clods rather than in fine crumbs or, conversely, in one solid lump. Getting this right may take a little tweaking as the almonds can vary considerably. If the mix is too dry, add a little more butter; if it's in one or two lumps, add a little flour.

Cut the rhubarb into 5cm lengths, spread evenly in a baking dish and sprinkle with the sweet cicely or sugar. Scatter the clods of crumble mix fairly evenly over the fruit, letting them sit where they fall rather than pressing them down. Bake in the centre of the oven for 30 minutes or until the topping is golden with a few darker brown patches. Serve with cream or custard.

Variations

Apple crumble is the obvious variation on this recipe, and the pairing of apple with blackberries. But do also try apple in tandem with a few handfuls of raspberries or blueberries, or with a few slices of fragrant quince. Plums, mulberries, gooseberries and even apricots make lovely crumbles too.

Rhubarb and strawberry tart

The combination of strawberries, rhubarb and fresh ginger makes this one of the tastiest tarts I know, and the lack of a custard makes it one of the easiest.

Serves 6–8

For the pastry
200g plain flour
50g icing sugar
A pinch of salt
100g cold, unsalted butter, cubed, plus an extra knob, melted
2 egg yolks

For the filling
180g rhubarb, trimmed
200g strawberries, hulled and halved
40ml white wine
100g caster sugar
1 tbsp cornflour
1 tsp lemon juice
½ tsp grated fresh ginger

For the filling, cut the rhubarb into 3cm lengths and place in a large bowl with the strawberries, wine, sugar, cornflour, lemon juice and ginger. Toss to combine and leave to macerate while you make the pastry.

Put the flour, icing sugar and salt into a food processor and blitz briefly to combine, or sift together into a bowl. Add the cubed butter and pulse, or rub in with your fingertips, until the mixture resembles breadcrumbs. Lightly beat 1 egg yolk and stir into the pastry, adding a few teaspoons of iced water at a time until the dough forms a ball. Wrap the pastry in cling film and refrigerate for 20 minutes.

Preheat the oven to 180°C/Gas mark 4. Dust your work surface and rolling pin with flour and roll out the pastry to a thickness of around 3mm. Use to line a 26–28cm tart tin placed on a baking sheet. Gently press the pastry into the base and sides of the tin, leaving any excess overhanging the rim. Prick the base a few times with a fork and bake for 10 minutes. Lightly beat the other egg yolk, brush over the pastry and bake for a further 10 minutes. Trim off any overhanging pastry.

Using a slotted spoon, fill the tart with the fruit. Add 5–6 tbsp of the liquid too, but do not overfill. Stand the tin on a baking sheet and bake on a low oven shelf for 45 minutes–1 hour, until a golden crust forms and the liquid has set; it will thicken a little more as it cools. Let the tart cool before removing it from the tin. Serve with crème fraîche or double cream.

Variations

Any of the berries (apart from gooseberries) can replace the strawberries.

RECIPES 241

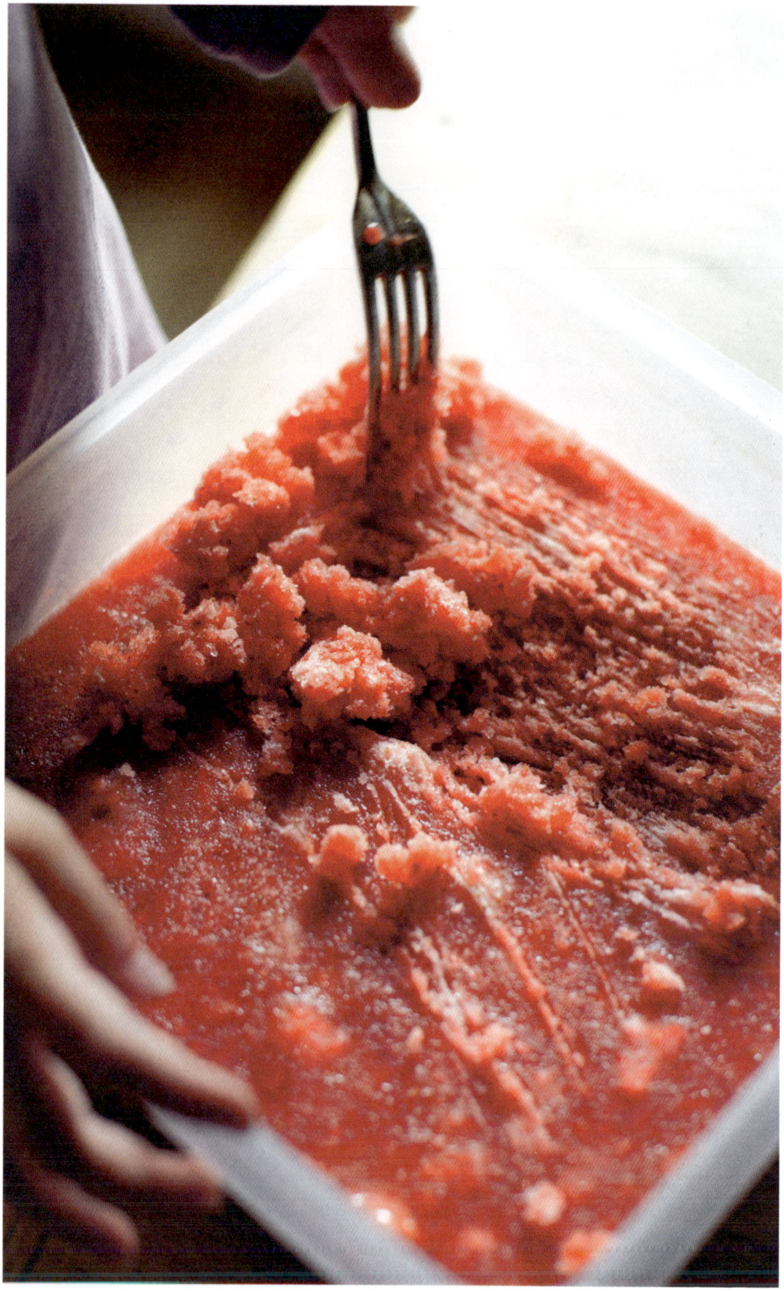

Strawberry granita

I've pinched the basics of this recipe from Hugh's *River Cottage Everyday* book. I love it mostly because it is so delicious but also because a granita is such a very simple and quick way to turn a glut of fruit into a fabulous frozen pudding without the need for an ice-cream maker. The texture is crunchy, the flavour sweet-tart and the experience deeply refreshing. You can try the recipe with any berries, stone fruit or even rhubarb, adjusting the sugar and lemon to suit.

Serves 8
1kg strawberries, hulled
200g icing sugar
Juice of 1–2 lemons

Put the strawberries in a large bowl and crush with your hands, then tip into a nylon sieve and rub them through to get rid of the seeds.

The amount of sugar and lemon juice you now add will vary depending on the variety of strawberries, their ripeness and your taste. I'd whisk in 140g sifted icing sugar and the juice of 1 lemon to start with, then taste and adjust. The key with most frozen puddings is to add more sugar and lemon juice than you think you need as both those tastes are muted on freezing. Pour the fruit purée into a plastic tub and freeze until solid.

Allow the granita to soften for approximately 20 minutes at room temperature, then take a strong fork to the surface, scratching and chipping it into a mass of shards and crystals. Pile your frosted scrapings into individual glass bowls and serve immediately.

Strawberry trifle

I couldn't write this book and not include a trifle recipe. This one brings together strawberries and elderflower, one of the loveliest fruity pairings. Any berries (except perhaps gooseberries), or currants, or even roasted rhubarb, can replace the strawberries. For a touch of luxury, finish with dark or white chocolate curls.

Serves 6

For the custard
4 egg yolks
1 heaped tbsp caster sugar
1 tbsp cornflour
350ml whole milk
1 vanilla pod, split lengthways

For the fruit
700g strawberries, halved if large
3 tbsp icing sugar

For the sponge base
4 muffins, plain or fruited (see p.207), or other cake, or sponge fingers
25ml strong elderflower cordial
125ml white wine or water

For the topping
440ml double cream, whipped, or half mascarpone/half double cream
A handful of toasted hazelnuts, roughly chopped

For the custard, mix the egg yolks, sugar and cornflour together in a bowl until smooth. Pour the milk into a heavy-based saucepan. Scrape the seeds from the vanilla pod with the tip of a knife into the milk and add the pod too. Bring to just below the boil. Take off the heat, discard the vanilla pod, then slowly pour the milk onto the egg mix, whisking constantly. Pour back into the pan. Cook gently, stirring constantly, for 5–10 minutes until thickened; do not allow to boil. Pour the custard into a bowl and cover the surface with cling film or greaseproof paper to prevent a skin forming. Leave to cool completely.

Put half the strawberries into a bowl, dust with the icing sugar and mash lightly.

Break the muffins or cake into big chunks and use to cover the base of a large glass bowl, placing the rest around the side. Dilute the elderflower cordial with the wine or water and drizzle over the sponge. Allow to stand for a few minutes.

Mix the lightly crushed strawberries with all but a dozen of the intact berries and tip them into the cup formed by the cake pieces. Spoon on the custard, levelling the surface. Whip the cream or whisk the mascarpone and cream together until smooth, then spoon on top of the custard. Dot with the remaining strawberries and scatter over the toasted hazelnuts. Refrigerate until ready to serve.

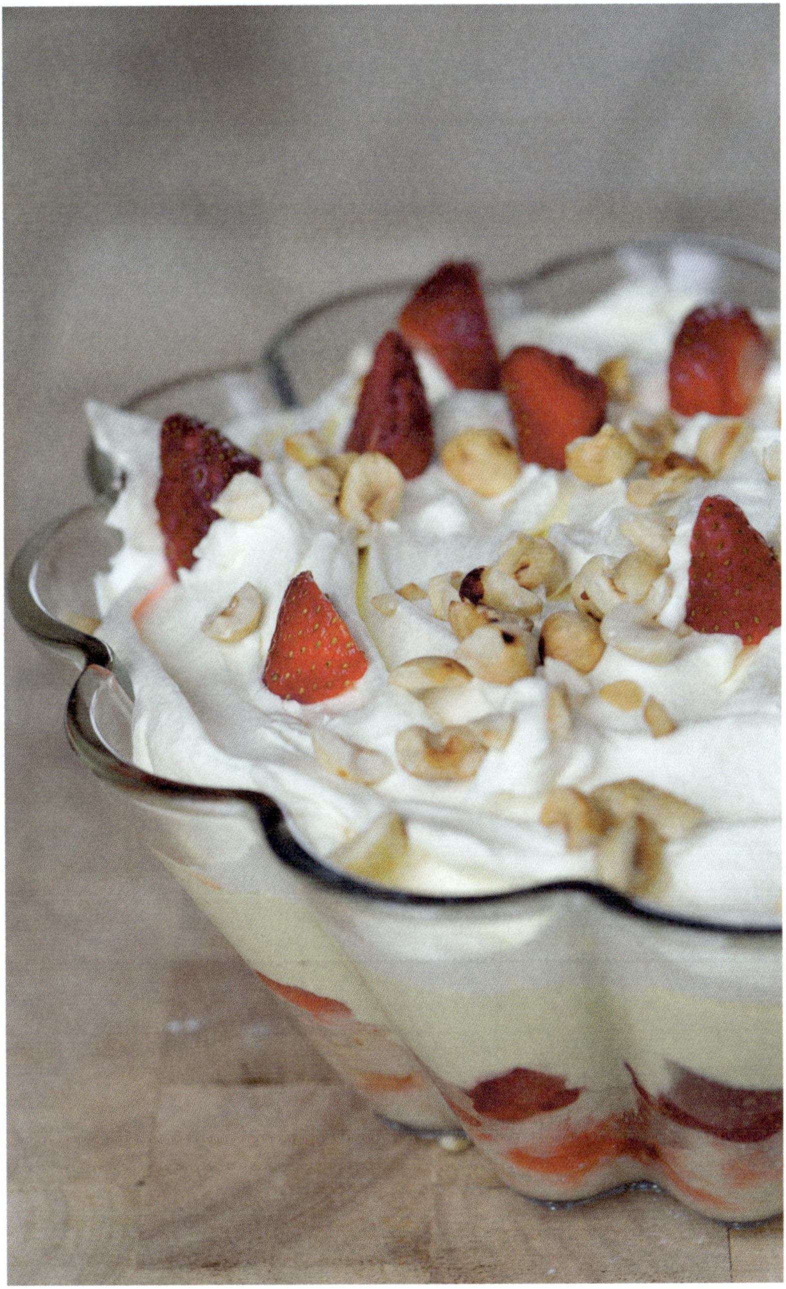

Useful Things

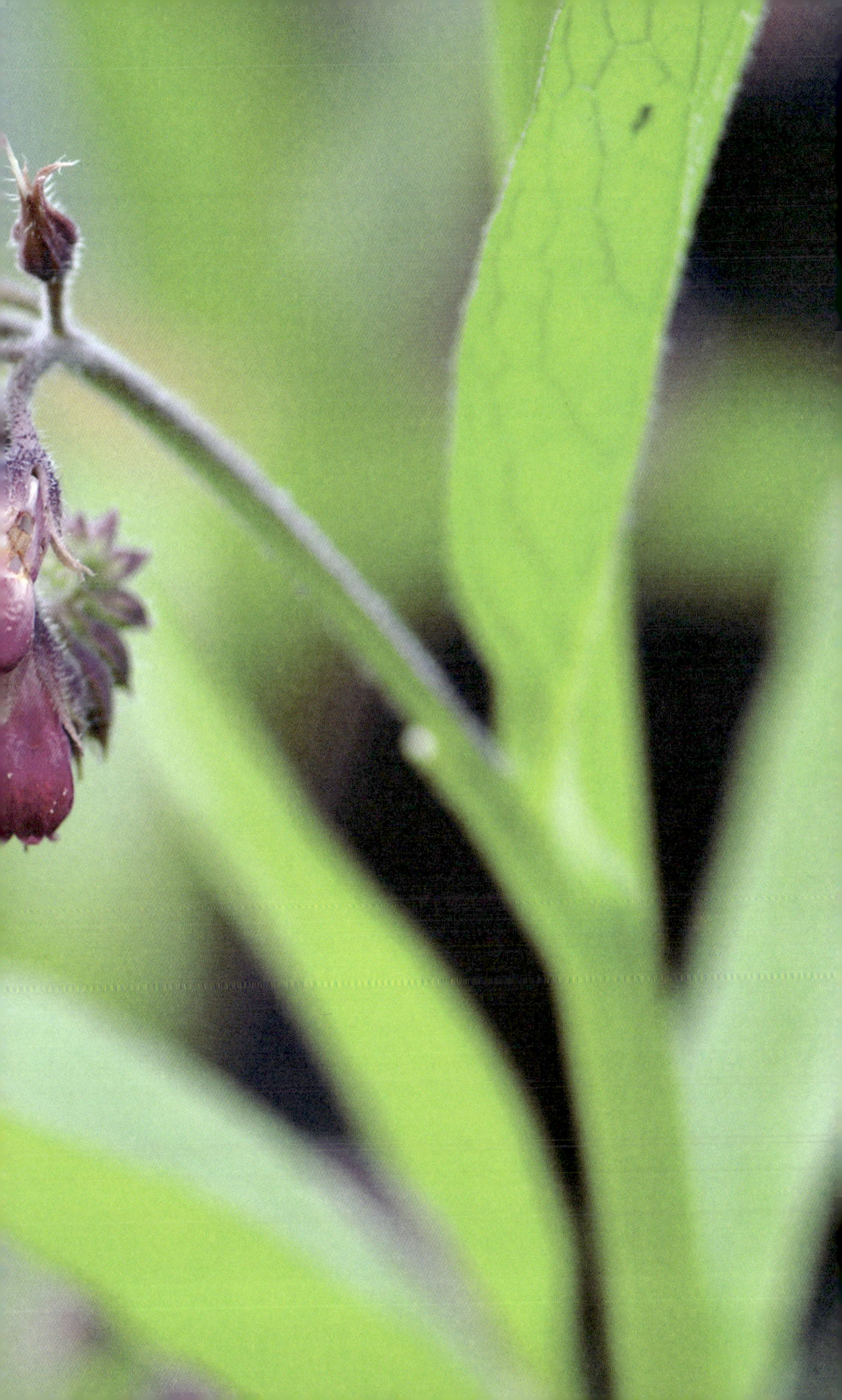

Directory

Plants and seeds

There are many good suppliers across the country. Those listed below are, for the most part, small to medium-sized businesses that I can recommend, having dealt with them personally.

Otter Farm Shop
www.otterfarmshop.co.uk
Modesty almost prevents me from telling you about this excellent range of fruit trees, bushes and seeds, including trained fruit and green manure seeds

Blackmoor Fruit Nursery
www.blackmoor.co.uk
01420 477978
Excellent range of fruit, including rootstocks

Reads Nursery
www.readsnursery.co.uk
01508 548 395
A wide range of fruit, including unusual varieties

Talaton Plants
www.talatonplants.co.uk
01404 841166
A wide range of fruit, with excellent varieties

Thornhayes Nursery
www.thornhayes-nursery.co.uk
01884 266746
Supplier of quality fruit trees, many uncommon varieties

Victoriana Nursery
www.victoriananursery.co.uk
01233 740529
Fine range of plants and seeds

Agroforestry Research Trust
www.agroforestry.co.uk
Diverse range of plants and seeds. Also courses

Other supplies

Fertile fibre
www.fertilefibre.com
01432 853111
Organically certified peat-free compost and more

Harrod Horticultural
www.harrodhorticultural.com
0845 402 5300
Wide range of fruit (and general garden) supplies, including excellent fruit cages

The Natural Gardener
www.thenaturalgardener.co.uk
01568 611729
Coir and biodegradable pots, compost and sustainable pest control

LBS Garden Warehouse
www.lbsgardenwarehouse.co.uk
01282 873370
General garden supplies, including mulch mat/ground cover and soil-testing kits

World of Felco
www.worldoffelco.co.uk
020 8829 8850
The best secateurs

Implementations
www.implementations.co.uk
0845 330 3148
Bronze/copper tools – hardwearing and beautiful

Green Gardener
www.greengardener.co.uk
01493 750061
Extensive range of biological pest control, plus general veg patch supplies

Rooster Pelleted Manure
www.rooster.uk.com
01325 339971
Pelleted manure (non-battery chickens)

Useful organisations

Garden Organic
www.gardenorganic.org.uk
024 7630 3517
Charity dedicated to organic growing. Join to get access to a wealth of advice. Also an excellent source for seeds and everything to do with growing

Slow Food
www.slowfood.org.uk
020 7099 1132
Promoting the locality, diversity and enjoyment of food

Royal Horticultural Society
www.rhs.org.uk
0845 062 1111
A great source of advice, with numerous excellent gardens to visit; also offers a soil analysis service

The National Fruit Collection
www.brogdalecollections.co.uk
01795 533225
Tours, events, courses and identification of varieties

Reference books

You should find all the information you need to grow your own fruit in this handbook. If you're looking to grow something a little more unusual then allow me to immodestly steer you towards *A Taste of the Unexpected*, by myself.

If you're looking for more ideas for what to do with your harvest, then Pam Corbin's River Cottage *Preserves* handbook is utterly indispensable.

For a wealth of wonderful fruit recipes, plus much more, try Jane Grigson's *Fruit Book*. And Niki Segnit's *The Flavour Thesaurus* is a beautifully written source of ideas for which flavours might work well together.

Acknowledgements

Writing a book about fruit – with all the growing, eating and drinking involved – is a pretty pleasurable way of spending your time. While I do that, everyone else tries to make what I've done look great. If only life was always like that.

Here's where I say thank you.

I am hugely grateful for the way Richard Atkinson and Natalie Hunt at Bloomsbury have dedicated themselves to making this book as good as it possibly can be. To Janet Illsley, for her sensitive and insightful editing. To Toby Atkins, for his excellent illustrations. To Nikki Duffy, for her thoughts on the recipes. And to Will Webb, a designer whose wonderful eye just gets finer. This book has been a collaboration with you all, so thank you for your vision and enthusiasm.

Enormous thanks also to my agent, Caroline Michel at PFD, whose energy and ideas make such a difference.

To everyone at RCHQ, thank you for making going to work such a pleasure. Particular thanks to Ali Thomson, Kate Colwell and Michelle Wheeler, who make up the finest garden team anyone could wish for. Thanks to the kitchen team, especially Neil Matthews, Nonie Dwyer, Piers Harrison and Head Chef Gill Meller, who make it impossible to walk through the kitchen without picking up ideas as well as an extra inch or two to the waist. Steven Lamb: you great fool. To Rob Love, some fruit to go fishing with. And, of course, huge thanks to Hugh who somehow made River Cottage happen.

Coming up with recipes for fruit isn't too tricky – if you involve cream and/or meringue something marvellous generally follows. Going further and exploring fruity preserves and booze is equally rewarding and I am lucky to have Pam Corbin and John Wright as colleagues and friends. Thank you.

Lastly and most importantly, Candida and Nell – thank you for giving me the time and freedom to write this, as well as the reason to be growing it all in the first place. And to my mum, dad and sis for those distant memories of blackberrying before I could ride a bike.

Index

Page numbers in *italic* refer to the illustrations

acid soils 143, 145
agricultural lupins 172
alfalfa 172
alkaline soils 144, 145
alliums 170
allotments 141
almonds
  plum and hazelnut cake 232
  rhubarb crumble *238*, 239
annuals 24
anthers 24
aphids 176
apples 10–12, *34*, 35–9, *37*, *38*
  blackberry apple compote 200
  buying plants 124
  calendar 32
  cordons *38*, 128
  eating 39
  growing 36–7
  harvesting and storage 37–9
  orchard ice cream with caramelised walnuts *194*, 195
  pests and diseases 39
  pruning 36–7, 153–4, *155*
  raspberry fruit leather 234, *235*
  successional ripening 20
  varieties 35–6
apricots 19, *40*, 41–3, *43*
  apricots on toast *198*, 199
  calendar 32
  eating 42–3
  growing 42
  harvesting and storage 42
  lamb and apricot tagine 196, *197*
  pests and diseases 42
  varieties 41
aspect 142

bacterial canker 176
bare-root plants 24
  planting trees 146
basil 170
bees 169
berries
  frozen summer berries and hot white chocolate sauce 201
  see also raspberries, strawberries *etc*
biennial bearing 24
biological controls 24
bird pests 176
blackberries *44*, 45–7
  blackberry apple compote 200
  calendar 32
  eating 47
  growing 46–7
  harvesting and storage 47
  pests and diseases 47
  varieties 45
blackcurrants *48*, 49–51, *51*
  calendar 32
  crème de cassis 204, *205*
  eating 50–1
  growing 50
  harvesting and storage 50
  pests and diseases 50
  summer pudding 202, *203*
  varieties 49
blossom wilt 176–7, *177*
blueberries 17, *52*, 53–5, *54*
  blueberry muffins *206*, 207
  calendar 32
  eating 55
  growing 53–5
  harvesting and storage 55
  pests and diseases 55
  varieties 53
borage *168*, 170
botrytis 177
boysenberries *46*
bread
  apricots on toast *198*, 199
  summer pudding 202, *203*
brown rot 177
brown scale 177
buckets 23
buckwheat 172
buds, and pruning 152–3
bullaces 99–101
bush trees 24, 126, *127*
  pruning 153–4
buying plants 124

cages *140*, 141
cake, plum and hazelnut 232
calcium 163
calcium carbonate 145
calendar 32–3
canker
  bacterial 176
  nectria 179
caramelised walnuts *194*, 195
cardamom, baked figs with honey and 210, *211*
cardboard mulches 142
chalky soils 144
cheese
  melon salad with goat's cheese, mint and red onion 222

INDEX   251

pear and rocket salad with Blue Vinny and
  walnuts 228, *229*
cherries *56*, 57–9
  calendar 32
  cherry clafoutis *208*, 209
  eating 59
  growing 58–9
  harvesting and storage 59
  pests and diseases 59
  varieties 57–8
chicken manure 163, 167
chicken Véronique 217
chives 170
chocolate
  frozen summer berries and hot white
    chocolate sauce 201
  poached pears and chocolate sauce *230*, 231
choosing fruit 14–19
choosing varieties 20
citrus plants 189, 191
clafoutis, cherry *208*, 209
clay soil 143–4
climate change 10
clover 172
codling moth 178
comfrey *160*, 162
  companion planting 170
  as liquid feed 161–2
companion planting 169–70, *171*
compost *144*, 161
  compost bins 163–4
  improving soil 142, 144
  mulches 175
  potting compost 186
  suitable materials for 164–6
container growing 184–7, *185*
  care of plants 187
  choosing containers 184–5
  compost for 186
  drainage 184
  planting in 186
  sizes 186
  small gardens 139
coral spot 178
cordons 24, *38*, 128, *129*
  pruning 158–9
coriander 170
cranachan with Japanese wineberries 218, *219*
cream
  cranachan with Japanese wineberries 218, *219*
  gooseberry fool with elderflower *212*, 213
  mulberry mess 224, *225*
  strawberry trifle 244, *245*
crème de cassis 204, *205*
crimson clover 172
crumble, rhubarb *238*, 239

cultivars 24
custard
  strawberry trifle 244, *245*
cuttings 130–1, *130–1*

'damping down', greenhouses 191
damsons 99–101
dill 170
diseases 176–81
  see also individual types of fruit
division *134*, 135
downy mildew 178
drainage, containers 186
drip systems, watering 189
dwarfing rootstocks 126, 138

elderflower, gooseberry fool with *212*, 213
equipment 22–3
  pruning tools 152
ericaceous compost 24
espaliers 24, 128, *129*
  pruning 156

family trees 24
fans 24, 128, *129*
  pruning 156–8, *157*
farmyard manure 167
feathered maidens 26, 158
fennel (herb) 170
fertilisers 10, 161–3
  comfrey liquid feed 161–2
  container growing 187
  growing under cover 189, 191
  slow-release fertilisers 163
field beans 172
figs 17, *60*, 61–3
  baked figs with honey and cardamom 210, *211*
  calendar 32
  eating 63
  growing 62–3
  harvesting and storage 63
  pests and diseases 63
  varieties 61
fireblight 178
foliar feeding 24, 162
fool, gooseberry with elderflower *212*, 213
foraging 17
forcing 26
  rhubarb *114*, 115, *116*
forest gardens 141–2, 169
forks 23
freestanding trees 126, *127*
  pruning 153–5
frozen summer berries and hot white
  chocolate sauce 201

252 FRUIT

fruit cages *140*, 141
fruit leather, raspberry 234, *235*
fruit spurs *150*
fungi
  fungal leaf spot 178
  mycorrhizal fungi 146

gages 99–101
garlic 170
gin
  crème de cassis 204, *205*
goat's cheese
  melon salad with goat's cheese, mint and red onion 222
gooseberries 64–7, *65*
  calendar 32
  eating 67
  gooseberry curd 216
  gooseberry fool with elderflower *212*, 213
  gooseberry tart 214, *215*
  growing 64–7
  harvesting and storage 67
  pests and diseases 67
  varieties 64
grafting 26, 126, 132–3, *132*, *150*
granita, strawberry *242*, 243
grapes 17, 68–73, *69*, *72*
  calendar 33
  chicken Véronique 217
  eating 73
  fruity melons 223
  growing 70–3
  harvesting and storage 73
  pests and diseases 73
  pruning 70–3, *71*
  varieties 68
green manures 171–2, 175
greenhouses 187–91
growth hormones 152–3

half-standard trees 26, 126, *127*
  pruning 153–4
hanging baskets, growing strawberries in 139
hardwood cuttings 130, *130–1*
harvesting 32–3
  see also individual types of fruit
hazelnuts
  plum and hazelnut cake 232
hedges 142
herbs, companion planting 169–70
hoeing weeds 173
honey
  baked figs with honey and cardamom 210, *211*
hormones, growth 152–3
horse manure 142, 161, 163, 167, *167*

hybrid berries 45–7
  calendar 32
  eating 47
  growing 46–7
  harvesting and storage 47
  pests and diseases 47
  varieties 45
hyssop 170

ice cream
  orchard ice cream with caramelised walnuts *194*, 195
insects, companion planting and 169–70

Japanese wineberries *74*, 75–7, *76*
  calendar 33
  cranachan with Japanese wineberries 218, *219*
  eating 77
  growing 75–7
  harvesting and storage 77
  pests and diseases 77
jelly, medlar 220, *221*
June drop 26

lamb and apricot tagine 196, *197*
laterals 26, *150*
layering 26, 133, *133*
leaders 26, *150*
leaf curl *177*, 178
leather, raspberry fruit 234, *235*
leeks 170
lemon balm 169, 170
lime 145
liquid feeding 161–2
loamy soil 143, 144
loganberries 45
loppers 22, 152
lupins, agricultural 172

maiden whips 26
maidens, feathered 26, 158
manure 163, 167, *167*
  chicken manure 167
  improving soil 142, 161
  mulches 175
marigolds 170
mealy bugs 179
medlars 17, *78*, 79–80, *81*
  calendar 33
  eating 80
  growing 79–80
  harvesting and storage 80
  medlar jelly 220, *221*
  pests and diseases 80
  varieties 79

melons *82*, 83–5
  calendar 33
  eating 85
  fruity melons 223
  growing 83–4
  harvesting and storage 85
  melon salad with goat's cheese, mint and red onion 222
  pests and diseases 85
  varieties 83
meringues
  mulberry mess 224, *225*
mildew 178, *179*
minarettes 26, 128
mint 169, 170
  melon salad with goat's cheese and 222
mirabelles 100
muffins, blueberry *206*, 207
mulberries 17, *86*, 87–9, *88*
  calendar 33
  eating 89
  growing 87
  harvesting and storage 89
  mulberry mess 224, *225*
  pests and diseases 89
  varieties 87
mulches 26, 173–5
  cardboard mulches 142
  containers 186
  manure as 175
  mulch mats *174*, 175
  strawberries 159, *174*
  wood shreddings 165
mycorrhizal fungi 146

nasturtiums 170
nectarines 91–3, *93*
  calendar 33
  eating 93
  growing 92
  harvesting and storage 92
  pests and diseases 93
  varieties 91
nectria canker 179
nettle tea 162
nitrogen
  chicken manure 163
  comfrey and 161
  green manures 171
  nettle tea 162
  wood shavings and 165
nurseries 20, 124
nutrients
  fertilisers 161–3
  soil pH and 145
  soil texture and 143, 144

oats
  cranachan with Japanese wineberries 218, *219*
onions 170
  melon salad with goat's cheese, mint and red onion 222
orchard ice cream with caramelised walnuts *194*, 195
orchards, planning 139
oregano 170
organic matter 144

parsley 170
peaches *15*, *90*, 91–3
  calendar 33
  eating 93
  fruity melons 223
  growing 92
  harvesting and storage 92
  peach salsa *226*, 227
  pests and diseases 93
  varieties 91
pears 94–7, *95*, *97*
  calendar 33
  eating 97
  growing 96
  harvesting and storage 96
  orchard ice cream with caramelised walnuts *194*, 195
  pear and rocket salad with Blue Vinny and walnuts 228, *229*
  pests and diseases 97
  poached pears and chocolate sauce *230*, 231
  pruning 153–4, *155*
  varieties 94
penknives 22
perennials 27
pests 176–81
  companion planting 169–70
  see also individual types of fruit
pH values, soil 26, 145
phacelia 172
phosphorus 161, 163
phytophtera 179
planning 138–9
planting
  in containers 186
  trees 146–7, *147*
plums *16*, 17, *18*, *98*, 99–101
  calendar 33
  eating 101
  growing 100–1
  harvesting and storage 101
  pests and diseases 101
  plum and hazelnut cake 232
  pruning 154, *155*
  varieties 99–100
pollination 27

choosing varieties 20
companion planting 169
hand pollination 189–91, *190*
planning an orchard 139
self-fertile plants 20, 27
polytunnels 187–91
potassium 161, 163, 167
potting compost 186
powdery mildew 179
propagation 27, 130–5
   cuttings 130–1, *130–1*
   division *134*, 135
   grafting 132–3, *132*
   layering 133, *133*
   runners 135, *135*
   sowing seeds 135, *135*
   suckers 135, *135*
   see also individual types of fruit
pruning 151–9
   calendar 32–3
   freestanding trees 153–5
   growing under cover 191
   tools 152
   trained forms 128, *129*, 156–9
   when to prune 152
   see also individual types of fruit
pruning saws 22–3, 152
pyramid trees 27, 126, *127*
   pruning 155

quince 17, *102*, 103–5, *104*
   calendar 33
   eating 105
   growing 103
   harvesting and storage 105
   orchard ice cream with caramelised walnuts *194*, 195
   pests and diseases 105
   quince vodka 233
   varieties 103

raspberries 106–9, *107*, *108*
   bottled raspberries 236, *236*
   calendar 33
   eating 109
   fruity melons 223
   growing 106–9
   harvesting and storage 109
   pests and diseases 109
   raspberry fruit leather 234, *235*
   suckers 135
   summer pudding 202, *203*
   varieties 106
red clover 172
red spider mite 179
redcurrants *21*, *110*, 111–13
   calendar 33
   eating 113
   growing 111–13
   harvesting and storage 113
   pests and diseases 113
   summer pudding 202, *203*
   varieties 111
rhubarb 17, 115–17, *167*
   calendar 33
   division *134*, 135
   eating 117
   forcing *114*, 115, *116*
   growing 117
   harvesting and storage 117
   pests and diseases 117
   rhubarb and strawberry tart 240, *241*
   rhubarb crumble *238*, 239
   varieties 115
ripening, successional 20
rocket
   pear and rocket salad with Blue Vinny and walnuts 228, *229*
roots
   and nutrients 161
   planting trees 146, *147*
rootstocks 27, *150*
   choosing 126
   dwarfing rootstocks 126, 138
   grafting 126, 132–3, *132*
runners 27, 135, *135*
rust 179

salad, pear and rocket with Blue Vinny and walnuts 228, *229*
salsa, peach *226*, 227
sandy soil 143
saws, pruning 22–3, 152
scab 180
scions, grafting 27, 132, *132*
seaweed 167, 175
secateurs 22, 152
seeds 12, 13, 135
self-fertile plants 20, 27
shade, greenhouses 191
shapes
   freestanding trees 126, *127*
   trained forms 128, *129*
shelter 142
shothole 180
silver leaf 180
sloping sites 142
slow-release fertilisers 163
slugs 180
small gardens 138–9
snails 180
soft fruit, pruning 159

softwood cuttings 130–1, 131
soil 142–5
  growing under cover 189, 191
  pH values 26, 145
  potting compost 186
  testing 143
  texture 143–4
sourcing plants 124
sowing seeds 135
spades 23
spur-bearing fruit 37, *37*, 154
spurs 27, *150*
staking trees 147, *147*
standard trees 27, 126, *127*
  pruning 153–4
stepovers 27, 128, *129*
stigma 27
storage *see individual types of fruit*
strawberries *118*, 119–21, *121*
  calendar 33
  container growing 139, *185*
  eating 121
  growing 120
  harvesting and storage 120
  mulches 159, *174*
  pests and diseases 121
  rhubarb and strawberry tart 240, *241*
  runners 135, *135*
  strawberry granita *242*, 243
  strawberry trifle 244, *245*
  varieties 119
  watering 159
sublaterals 27, *150*
successional ripening 20
suckers 27, 135, *150*
summer pudding 202, *203*
sunshine 142
supports
  growing under cover 191
  staking trees 147, *147*

tagine, lamb and apricot 196, *197*
tarts
  gooseberry tart 214, *215*
  rhubarb and strawberry tart 240, *241*
tayberries 45
terminology 24–7, *150*
tip-bearing fruit 37, *37*, 154
toast, apricots on *198*, 199
tomatoes
  lamb and apricot tagine 196, *197*
tools 22–3
  pruning 152
top-dressing containers 186, 191
trained fruit trees 128, *129*
  pruning 156–9

trees
  freestanding trees 126, *127*
  grafting 126, 132–3, *132*
  planning orchards 139
  planting 146–7, *147*
  pruning 151–9
  rootstocks 126, 138
  trained forms 128, *129*
  watering 159
trefoil, yellow 172
trifle, strawberry 244, *245*
trugs 23
trowels 23, *173*
trunk *150*

under-cover fruit 187–91

varieties, choosing 20
ventilation, greenhouses 191
vertical planting 139
vetches 172
virus diseases 180
vodka, quince 233

walnuts
  caramelised walnuts *194*, 195
  pear and rocket salad with Blue Vinny and walnuts 228, *229*
wasps 181
watering 159
  containers 186, 187
  growing under cover 189
watering cans 23
weeds 142, 173–5
wheelbarrows 23
'whip-and-tongue' grafting 132–3, *132*
whisky
  cranachan with Japanese wineberries 218, *219*
white clover 172
white currants 111–13, *112*
  calendar 33
  eating 113
  growing 111–13
  harvesting and storage 113
  pests and diseases 113
  varieties 111
white fly 85
windbreaks 142
winds 142
wineberries *see* Japanese wineberries
winter care, growing under cover 191
winter moths 181, *181*
wood shreddings 165
woolly vine scale 181

yellow trefoil 172

The River Cottage

Herb Handbook

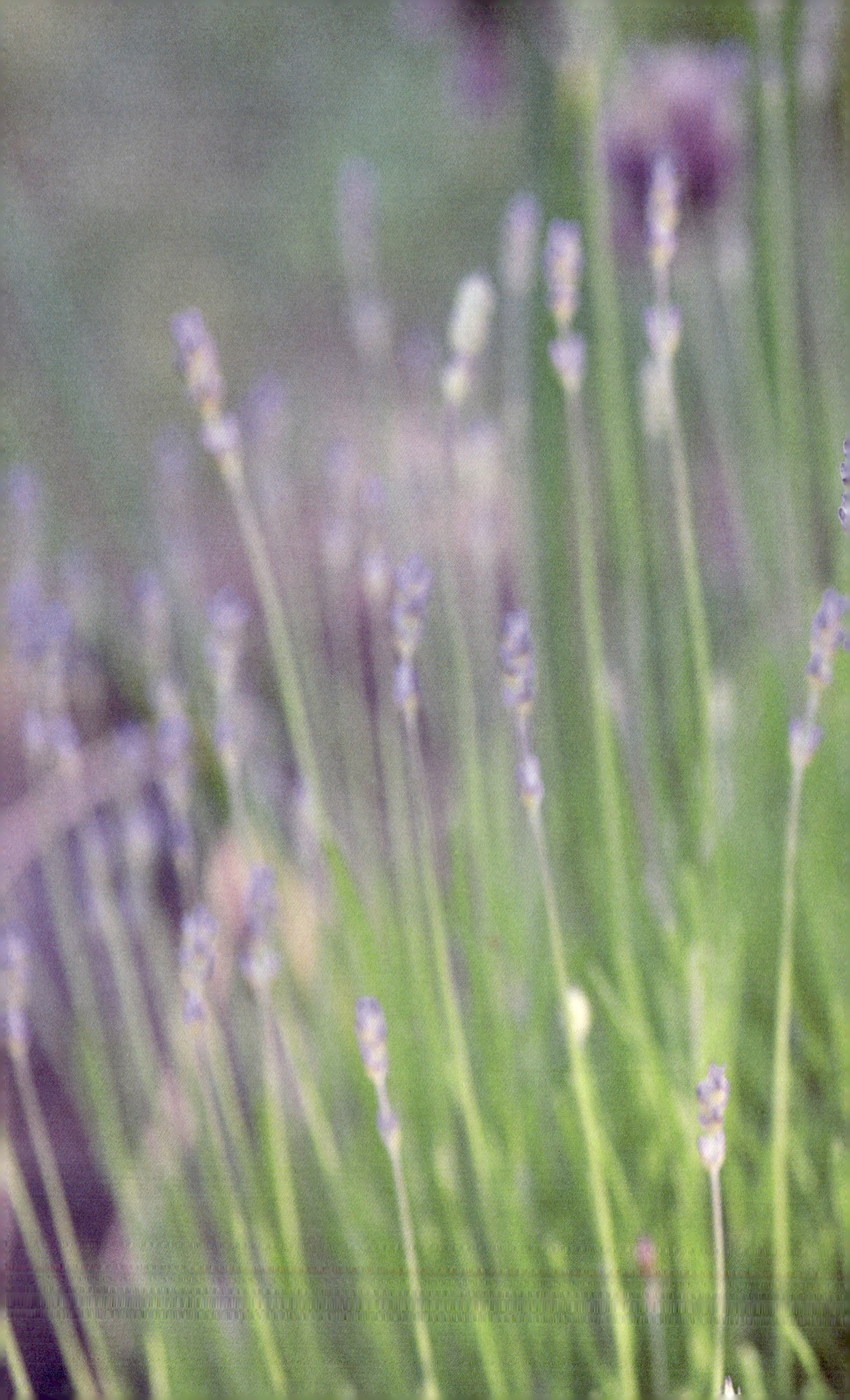

The River Cottage Herb Handbook

by Nikki Duffy

with an introduction by
Hugh Fearnley-Whittingstall

www.rivercottage.net

BLOOMSBURY
LONDON · NEW DELHI · NEW YORK · SYDNEY

In memory of all my grandparents

First published in Great Britain 2012
This paperback edition published 2012

Text © 2012 by Nikki Duffy
Photography © 2012 by Mark Diacono,
except p.46 © GAP Photos/FhF Greenmedia

The moral right of the author has been asserted

Bloomsbury Publishing Plc, 50 Bedford Square, London WC1B 3DP
Bloomsbury Publishing, London, New Delhi, New York and Sydney

A CIP catalogue record for this book is available from the British Library
ISBN 978 1 4088 3614 9
10 9 8 7 6 5 4 3 2 1

Project editor: Janet Illsley
Design: willwebb.co.uk
Printed in China by C&C Offset Printing Co., Ltd.

MIX
Paper from responsible sources
FSC® C008047

While every effort has been made to ensure the accuracy of the information contained in this book, in no circumstances can the publisher or the author accept any legal responsibility or liability for any loss or damage (including damage to property and/or personal injury) arising from any error in or omission from the information contained in this book, or from the failure of the reader to properly and accurately follow any instructions contained in the book.

www.bloomsbury.com/rivercottage

Contents

Making the Most of Herbs	8
Growing Herbs	22
Herb A–Z	38
Recipes	156
Useful Things	246

Herbs are central to the River Cottage way of cooking and eating. It's high time that a volume on these lovely ingredients was added to our other handbooks, and I'm delighted that Nikki has been the one to write it. She is as passionate as I am about the culinary properties of these wonderful plants. Like me, she is in thrall to their intoxicating scents and their gorgeous flowers, which are frequently at least as useful as their leaves.

Herbs are often real catalysts, both in the garden and the kitchen. They function in an immediate way, getting the juices flowing because they are so instantly enticing and appetite-piquing. But, in a broader sense, herbs can be the plants that make you into a gardener, even a very small-scale one, and the ingredients that turn you into a creative cook. They are so easy to grow and so simple to use that they form an irresistible first step on a road towards self-sufficiency.

That needn't be the end goal, of course; in fact it's really an endless and ever-life-enhancing journey. That journey, away from industrially produced, sterile food towards everything that is local, seasonal and exciting, is what River Cottage is, and has always been, about. And Nikki's book is now a vital part of that road map. It's a wonderfully useful guide that will introduce you to the satisfaction of growing and cooking some of your own food, if you don't already. If you do, you will find much in these pages to inspire you and take you further. There are plenty of classic recipes here, but also bags of new ideas that will have you using your homegrown herbs in ways you may never have considered before. Bay-infused ice cream, white chocolate truffles with basil, and lavender-scented lamb are just a few among a host of tempting aromatic recipes.

What I love about herbs is their easiness, the lack of effort they require from the cook. These ingredients don't ask you for any big commitment beyond the bid to make something even more delicious to eat. Preparation is usually minimal: pulling some leaves off a stem, maybe chopping them, maybe not. Quantities need not be precise. One herb can often be substituted for another. And while I'd be the first to try to persuade you to grow your own, you don't actually have to do so in order to get good, flavoursome specimens (see Nikki's list of the herbs most worth buying from shops on p.13). And yet, while they ask so little of you, herbs will give and give and give in terms of flavour, colour, texture and that indefinable ability they have to just 'make' a dish.

Herbs were among the first things I tackled when setting up my fledgling kitchen garden at the original River Cottage. I knew that these plants would instantly enliven my cooking, long before I could start lifting my own homegrown potatoes or cutting my first spears of asparagus. So I went and bought some pots of bay, rosemary, parsley and chives from a local nursery, planted them, and I was away. They were ready to cut almost immediately and, with a bit of undemanding maintenance work, they continued to provide me with an aromatic harvest right up to the day we moved out. Now, the altogether larger-scale kitchen plot at Park Farm is absolutely bursting with herbs. Nasturtiums shout from every corner, angelica lifts its long, elegant stems by the farmhouse, and there are beds bristling with chives, mint, parsley, rosemary, sage and lovage to satisfy the kitchen's considerable needs.

While it's not essential to grow your own herbs in order to enjoy them, I do think you're missing a bit of a trick if you don't. Most look and taste their absolute best when freshly cut, and their very presence on your windowsill or by the back door will encourage you to use them. You don't need a veg patch, greenhouse or polytunnel; you can grow herbs with no garden at all. Of course, the more space you have, the more possibilities suggest themselves, but a window box, sunny patio or even a doorstep with a few pots on will suffice.

If you think you know your herbs pretty well, then step outside the zone of what is already familiar to you. Treat yourself to a pot of intense Thai basil or a glowing purple-bronze perilla plant and see how you get on. I am certain you will be won over by these delicious aromatic plants. Browse through the pages of this book and see what else tickles your fancy. With Nikki's warm and wise text to guide you, there is very little to stand in the way of an ever-increasing exploration and enjoyment of the herbal world. Immerse yourself in it, breathe in deeply, and savour the sheer joy that it brings.

Hugh Fearnley-Whittingstall, East Devon, December 2011

Making the Most of Herbs

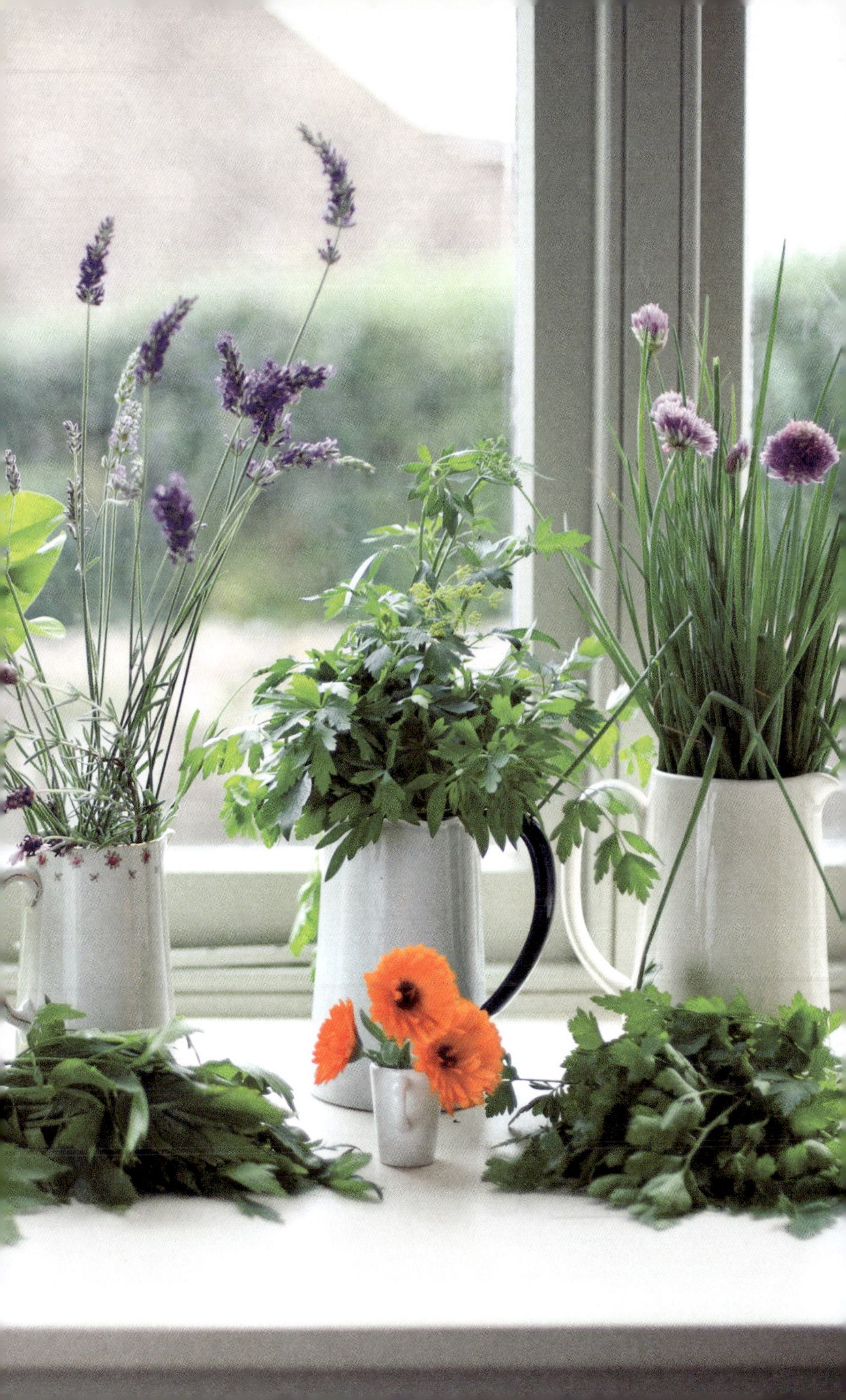

Herbs are beautiful, life-enhancing, seductive things. Whether you see them primarily as plants or as ingredients, they are enticing. I find it hard to believe that anyone could look at a lavender bush nodding in the sunshine, or sniff a torn bay leaf and not experience, at the very least, a flicker of pleasure. And herbs can give much more than that: their aromas, their flavours, their colours and shapes can make you feel positively joyful.

I think the appeal of herbs lies, first of all, in the incredibly strong response we tend to have to their scents. Those intense, penetrating aromas send messages directly to the limbic system, the part of our brain that deals with emotion and memory. One thread of scent can cause the mind to retrieve distinct images, but also more fugitive recollections and feelings that can completely alter our mood. A sniff of rosemary or a breath of thyme can awaken powerful associations with comfort, pleasure and satisfaction. Herbs bypass our thinking, analytical minds and go straight to our hungry souls.

You can enjoy herbs simply by being close to them – by having them in your garden, or in a jug on the windowsill. But if you go one step further and actually use them, you hold in your hands the power to tempt and delight other people (and yourself, of course). By doing something as simple as pouring a cup of mint tea or spooning out some fragrant pesto, you can tap into the deep, instinctive rush of good feeling that these plants evoke. What's more, herbs can enhance and define food in a unique way by adding that crucial aromatic element that gets the mouth watering even before you take the first bite. And the wonderful thing is, they deliver on their promise: they taste as good as they smell.

This is primarily a book about cooking with herbs, about the delicious ways they can flavour and perfume the food you serve. I hope it will encourage you to try herbs that you've not eaten before, and to experiment with new ways of using your old favourites. No one need feel unsure about cooking with these plants. They can be the most liberating and confidence-boosting of ingredients. They allow you to innovate and bring individuality to your cooking while, at the same time, anchoring you in sound culinary tradition because they are often responsible for those key flavours that 'make' a dish (the sage in the stuffing, the tarragon in the béarnaise, the bay in the béchamel).

Some herbs are very strong and can be overpowering in large quantities, but it's still hard to completely ruin a meal by adding too much, in the way you could by overdoing the salt or the chilli powder. Herbs invite experimentation, and rarely make you suffer for it.

This is also, however, a book about growing herbs. That's because, even if your focus is in the kitchen, your garden, greenhouse or windowsill can provide you with raw materials that may otherwise be very difficult to get hold of. Winter savory, scented geraniums and bergamot are rarely to be found for sale as cut herbs, but they can all be at your fingertips if you grow your own. You don't need to be any kind of horticultural whiz (I assure you, I'm no Percy Thrower). You don't even need to be a particularly keen gardener. If you do not have the time or inclination to raise plants from seed or prepare a dedicated herb bed, then you can easily source your herbs as young potted plants from specialist suppliers. Then all you need is some basic know-how on the best way to keep them producing their glorious, fragrant leaves.

I have not written about the medicinal properties of herbs. This is not because I don't have a lot of faith in their power to heal, soothe and relieve, but simply because I am no expert in this huge and complex subject.

There are hundreds, probably thousands, of edible plants that we would classify as herbs and of course I haven't included all of them here. Instead I have limited myself to the ones I know taste good, and which are easy to grow in this country. That is still a very big and very delicious mixed bag which, I hope, you are about to dip into and enjoy.

Buying herbs

It would be wonderful if we all had the time, space and motivation to grow great armfuls of different herbs in our own backyards, but for most of us that's far from realistic. I certainly don't grow all of the herbs I use. At least some of the time, you're likely to be buying herbs from a retailer. I like sourcing herbs from farm shops and farmers' markets as these often offer a wide choice, very fresh generous bunches, and some free information to boot. However, supermarkets are part of my supply chain too.

When you're looking for fresh herbs in a shop, I would think first and foremost about the variety itself. The more robust herbs, such as bay and rosemary, simply withstand packing and travelling better than their tender brethren. Very pungent herbs, like basil and mint, can also be fine from a packet if they are very fresh. Some of the more delicate, subtle herbs, such as chives and chervil, are nearly always disappointing when bought in packets.

As with any fresh produce, it makes sense to buy herbs within their natural season, where possible. In Britain, this is generally April to September, with a real peak in quality in June, July and August. There are plenty of herbs that a home-grower can produce in the autumn and winter, but the commercial herb season is more restricted. With the probable exception of bay, fresh herbs bought in the winter months will almost certainly be imported. In-season herbs, particularly if they are harvested locally, are likely to taste much better and be more pungent than those that have been transported great distances.

Flat-leaf parsley *Petroselinum crispum* var. *neapolitana*

Almost without exception, the more recently a herb has been picked, the better. So look carefully for signs of freshness including a bright colour, plump stems and perfect, unwilted leaves. If the herb is not wrapped in plastic, then smelling it, or crushing one leaf in your fingers to release its oils, will help you ascertain if it's bursting with flavour or not. If possible, find out when the herb was picked; this certainly may be possible at a farmers' market or in a small greengrocer's. If not, be guided by use-by dates.

Here's a list of the fresh herbs I think most worth shopping for, all of which have the potential, at least, to be flavourful and good when bought from a retailer. I nearly always buy packets or cut bunches. Those pots of 'growing' herbs often have the weediest texture and weakest flavour of all.

Bay I use this every day, more or less, so I'd always grow it but, if you can't, the fragrance and flavour survive very well when packaged. Dried bay is just about worth buying too – but fresh is better. (See Bay, p.49.)

Thyme/lemon thyme These hardy little herbs hang on to their flavour well, so a packet or bundle should stand you in good stead. (See Thyme/lemon thyme, p.147.)

Rosemary Another robust herb that travels pretty well. (See Rosemary, p.125.)

Garlic Growing your own is satisfying but if, like me, you use it in great quantity, you may struggle to grow enough to meet all your needs. (See Garlic, p.77.)

Horseradish Magnificent gnarled roots of horseradish are becoming easier to find in greengrocer's. It's a wonderful ingredient to use fresh and a well-wrapped root keeps for weeks in the fridge. (See Horseradish, p.82.)

Basil This is not the easiest of herbs to grow and it is often required in large amounts – a single pesto recipe could use your whole homegrown crop. I've found very fresh, fragrant bought basil to be absolutely fine. (See Basil, p.44.)

Flat-leaf parsley As with basil, it can be hard to keep up with the demand for this tender herb. I often buy large bunches and keep them in a jug of water. They rarely go to waste. (See Parsley, p.113.)

Marjoram/oregano If harvested at their peak, these are usually still very pungent and flavourful after a sojourn on the shop shelf. (See Marjoram/oregano p.101.)

Coriander Worth buying in bunches provided it's very fresh. (See Coriander, p.66.)

Picking herbs

If you are picking herbs from a garden, you can obviously have total confidence in their freshness. It's also worth knowing that most herbs reach a peak of aromatic flavour just before flowering – often when buds are forming, but not yet opening. This is the point in the plant's life cycle when it is generally at its strongest and its concentration of essential oils tends to be greatest. If you allow herbs to reach this state then cut them, and keep doing so, you will hold off the actual flowering and hopefully maximise your harvest of flavourful leaves.

Don't stop all your herbs from flowering altogether, though – often the flowers themselves make delicious and beautiful ingredients, and if you want a plant to set seed, it obviously needs to flower first.

Storing herbs

Once you have fresh herbs back in the kitchen, it pays to use them as soon as possible. However, if you don't need to use them straight away, or you have half a bunch left over, you can prolong their lives a little. I treat them like cut flowers and place them in jugs of water.

First trim the stem ends because these may have dried and formed a seal, rendering them unable to take up fresh water. Put the bunch of herbs into a jug of cool water and keep it away from direct sunlight or the heat from your oven or radiators. Check the herb regularly and change the water as soon as it starts to look murky or smell musty.

In hot, dry weather or, conversely, in the depths of winter when your kitchen may actually be rather warm, it's best to keep fresh herbs in the fridge, in an open plastic bag. This protects them while still allowing ethylene gas, released by the cut stalks, to escape (ethylene hastens decay).

If you are planning to store herbs in the fridge, make sure the leaves are dry, to inhibit rotting. Before putting the herbs in the bag, you can wrap them loosely in a piece of kitchen paper to absorb any vestiges of moisture. Woody herbs such as rosemary, bay and thyme can keep quite well like this for a week or so. For tender parsley, coriander, fennel and the like, you've only got a few days. Basil does not respond well to chilling, so keep it in a cool part of the kitchen rather than in the fridge.

Some herbs, such as chives, may look all right after a few days in the fridge, but their flavour will have all but disappeared.

With a couple of exceptions, discussed later on, I don't buy dried herbs. They just don't cut it in terms of flavour and have a very short shelf life.

Oregano *Origanum vulgare*

Drying and freezing herbs

There is something appealing about having dried herbs in your kitchen – a bunch or two of thyme hanging from the ceiling, perhaps, or some crumbled sage in a tiny jar – but in most cases there is little point in drying herbs in my view. Delicate grassy, feathery varieties, such as chervil, parsley, chives or coriander, cannot be dried successfully. It is very hard to capture and retain the inimitable scents and flavours they deliver when fresh, because the compounds that provide these evaporate along with the water from their leaves. With woodier herbs, such as thyme, rosemary, savory, myrtle, bay, lavender, and also with mint, marjoram and lovage, you will still get flavour from the dried leaves or flowers. In fact, it can be very concentrated. But it is never, to my taste, as good, clear, sweet and true as the flavour of the fresh herb.

As always, there are some exceptions. It's worth drying some fennel seeds for winter roasts, for instance, and maybe some lavender flowers for Christmas biscuits and cakes. If you are inclined to drying herbs, remember that the more delicate the flavour and texture of the herb, the less likely it is to dry successfully.

Gather herbs for drying when their flavour is at its peak, usually just before flowering. They must be completely dry – mid-morning on a warm, sunny day is a good time. Lay them on a rack and place in an airing cupboard or very low oven (maximum 30°C) with the door slightly open. Never try to dry them in the sun.

The drying process may take a few hours or a few days, depending on the variety and the conditions. Stop when the herbs are dry and brittle, but still green and fragrant. Try putting a sprig of the dried herb into a jam jar, closing the lid and leaving it for a few hours. If any moisture or condensation appears, the herb is not 'done'. Once dried, strip the leaves from the stems and transfer them to perfectly dry glass jars, preferably dark-coloured. Seal, label and store in a cool, dry, dark place. Use within a year.

Freezing is also reasonably successful in some cases, especially with those tender herbs that don't dry well at all, such as basil and parsley. Pick perfect, undamaged leaves, divide into the sort of quantities you think you'll be using, and wrap loosely but securely in foil or cling film before freezing. Once defrosted, you can add them to dishes as you would fresh herbs. The flavour should still be good but their texture and colour will have been altered. They'll have darkened and become limp, so they won't be much use for garnishing or salads.

Another way of freezing herbs is in ice. Chop the herb and pack into ice-cube trays, pouring over a little water before freezing them into solid herb blocks.

There are other methods of preserving herbal flavours which I do think are very worthwhile – namely herb butters and purées, such as pesto, which freeze well, and flavoured vinegars and jellies. You'll find recipes for these later in the book.

Flavour chemistry

I go into detail on methods of cooking individual herbs in the main body of this book. However, there are some basics which are worth understanding at the outset.

Herbs are imbued with various compounds which give flavour and aroma. The general idea, when cooking, is to release those compounds from the plant so you can smell and taste them while you're eating. Some herbal flavours are released so readily that it's best to simply eat the herb fresh, whole and raw so the flavours are set free in your mouth. As soon as you start chopping and heating and exposing to air, that fugitive flavour is lost. Other compounds are a little less ethereal and can be captured and held in a dish.

The various traditional ways of using herbs that have evolved over the centuries reflect accumulated knowledge on how best to control those all-important compounds. And every time you cook with herbs you, too, are making choices about how to manipulate those essential chemicals, even if you don't realise you're doing so.

It is often the more woody-stemmed herbs with their relatively robust leaves that have the most stable, long-lived flavour compounds. In many cases, these are plants which are natives of hot places – they have evolved to conserve water and they tend to retain their flavour with it. Imagine wild thyme or rosemary baking under a Mediterranean sun and you'll get a feeling for the way the flavour is held fast in their leaves, concentrated, pungent and penetrating.

With delicate thin-leaved herbs, the flavour compounds are usually more volatile and evaporate easily, which is why some herbs such as chives and basil almost completely lose their flavour when cooked.

There are also in-between herbs – parsley, lovage and fennel spring to mind – which can take a bit of heat. Their flavour may well change during light cooking, but they will still inform the dish. And often you can get very delicious results by adding the same herb both at the beginning and the end of cooking, creating a multi-layered experience of its flavour.

It's not just heat that helps to liberate flavour, damage to the plant's cell membranes has a similar effect. Whole sprigs or bouquets garnis added to slow-cooked dishes, with perhaps just a twist or a light whack with a rolling pin to help release the flavour, will have a relatively subtle, mellow influence. The same herbs, finely chopped, will give a much more pungent effect.

It's also worth knowing that these flavour compounds are usually more soluble in fat than in water and so can be drawn out by immersion in various plant oils and animal fats. If you stir rosemary into an oily dressing, or beat chopped parsley into butter, there will be a release of flavour. If you put sprigs of the same herbs in a jug of cold water, without first bruising or chopping them, not much would happen.

Chopping

To chop herbs finely, strip the leaves from the stems and place them on a large chopping board. It's much easier to chop herbs well if they are dry so, after washing, give them a whiz in a salad spinner or pat dry carefully with a clean tea towel.

Choose a large, reasonably heavy, sharp cook's knife. Holding the handle firmly in one hand, place the fingers of your other hand on top of the blade, at the pointed end. Use your fingers to anchor this end of the knife on the board, then work the handle end up and down, across the herb leaves, gradually reducing them to a finely chopped state. You'll need to stop and change direction a few times and perhaps scoop and redistribute the herbs on the board to achieve a nice even chop.

Shredding

Herbs with fairly large, thin leaves, such as mint or basil, can be very good when finely shredded. The technical term for these ribboned herbs is a 'chiffonade'. Stack several leaves on top of one another then roll them up tightly into a 'cigar'. Secure the cigar with one hand, keeping your fingers tucked in, then slice very thinly with a large, sharp knife.

Tying a bouquet garni

A bouquet garni is simply a bundle of herbs used to infuse flavour into soups, stews and stocks. There are no hard and fast rules as to what to include, except that bay is pretty much essential. I would always include thyme, too, and either a strip of leek or a length of celery stalk, plus a handful of parsley stalks. These are the classic fail-safe bouquet garni herbs, but you might like to branch out a bit with sprigs of rosemary or marjoram. Sage, winter savory and lovage can be used too, and these will contribute more distinctive flavours.

Keep the herbs you want to use in large sprigs. Cut a piece of cotton string and lay it on a board, then place the bundle of herbs on top. Bring the ends of the string up over the herbs and tie them tightly.

Alternatively, you can use a small piece of fine muslin to enclose the herbs. Lay the muslin over a tea cup, so it sinks to form a little bag. Put the herbs in the middle, bring the edges of the muslin up around them and secure with cotton string. This is an effective method if you want to include peppercorns or a whole garlic clove in your bouquet. It's also good with rosemary, which often tends to shed its leaves when cooked for a long time.

Preparing garlic

A garlic clove, with its paper-thin skin tightly hugging the crisp, juicy, pungent inner flesh, is a ticket to all sorts of delicious destinations. It is, therefore, well worth mastering a few simple techniques that will enable you to liberate its amazing flavour without faffing and frustration. You'll find more about this unbelievably versatile and delicious ingredient on pp.77–81.

Peeling This is one of those slightly fiddly jobs that can become irksome if you have to do it over and over. My preferred way is to put the garlic clove on a board then press down on it, slowly and firmly, with the flat blade of a large knife, just until I hear a little crack. This is the skin releasing its hold. Slice off the flat end of the clove and the skin should then be easy to remove.

Crushing There are various ways of doing this, just use whichever you find easiest. Garlic snobs eschew the proprietary garlic crusher; I'm not entirely sure why, although I do think they can be tricky to clean. I prefer to simply crush garlic on a board, with the flat of a knife.

Put a little pinch of salt on your board first, to help your knife get to grips with the garlic, and to draw out its juices. Put the peeled garlic clove on top and then the flat of the knife blade. Smash the clove to break it open then scrape the blade over it again and again until you have a sticky garlic purée.

A pestle and mortar is another useful tool for crushing garlic – again, much easier with a pinch of salt.

If you don't fancy crushing, then grating garlic on a fine grater is an easy way to achieve very similar results.

Chopping The easiest way to get a nice finely chopped bit of garlic is to apply a classic onion-chopping technique. Hold the clove on a board and slice it fairly thinly, but leave it intact at the root end. Turn the clove on its side and slice again, perpendicular to the first cuts, but still keeping it uncut at the far end. Then slice across the clove, so you're cutting fine dice. This gives you a medium-fine chop.

For a really fine or minced finish, use the basic chopping technique for leafy herbs (see p.18), working your knife backwards and forwards over the chopped garlic to reduce it to smaller and smaller pieces.

Crushing garlic

Chopping garlic

MAKING THE MOST OF HERBS

Growing Herbs

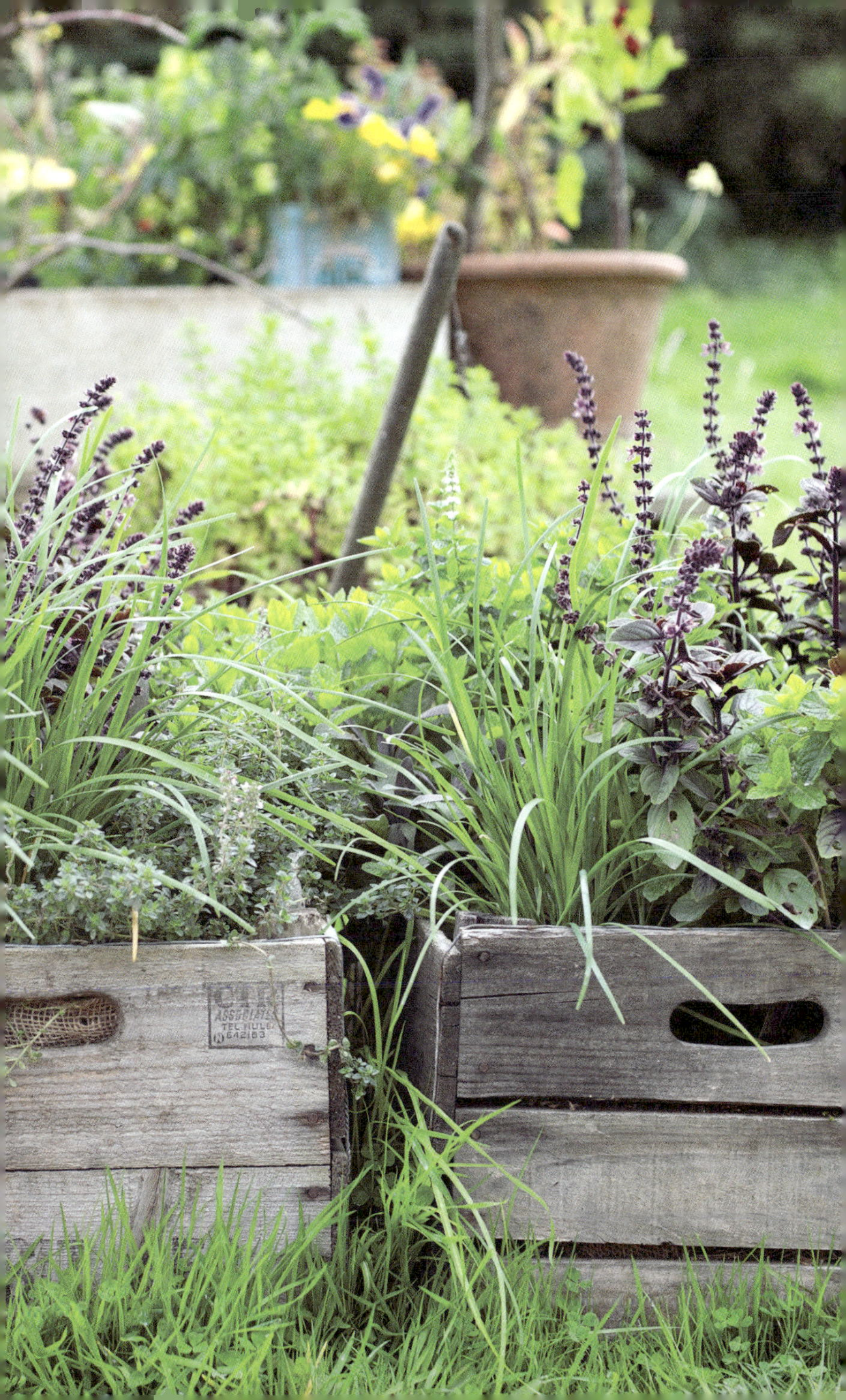

If you enjoy cooking with herbs and particularly if you want to expand your repertoire beyond the fabulous but familiar five – parsley, thyme, rosemary, sage and bay – I would wholeheartedly encourage you to grow some. Of course, it helps if you have a garden, or at least an outside space that will accommodate a few pots, but it is by no means essential.

Why grow herbs?

Quite simply, so that you can eat them. You can buy a reasonable range of the more commonly used herbs from retailers, but you will never get a true experience of the extraordinary range of scents, savours and textures that herbs can provide if you don't grow some of them yourself. A cook can get by with packets of parsley, coriander and thyme from the shops, but with some shrubby lemon verbena and hyssop, a glorious angelica plant and a few pots of savory, celery leaf and bergamot growing outside the back door, your culinary opportunities are vastly increased.

The freshness of homegrown herbs is always a boon. Quantity is another advantage. If you want to make mint tea every day, or a batch of chervil soup or sorrel sauce, then you need big handfuls of fresh herbs, which can be expensive to buy. The converse is also true: herbs such as lovage and sage are often best used in small quantities – buy even a diminutive bunch and you may well find a lot of it going to waste.

One final reason for growing these edible plants is their sheer beauty. Even if you never eat a single leaf, herbs will enhance any plot. Group a few together, whether in pots or your own little herb patch, and you'll be rewarded by a panoply of shades of green, a variety of forms, and many different and glorious flowers. You will bring bees and butterflies to your garden, and probably ward off unwanted insects too. And you will have the opportunity to crush a few aromatic leaves between your fingers whenever you feel like it, just for the sheer joy of their scent.

Preparing to grow

If you were to make a careful plan of the perfect garden for growing a big range of herbs, you'd need full sun, partial shade, dappled shade, sheltered spots, open spaces, rich soil, sandy soil, chalky soil, moist soil, poor soil, a big range of pots and a greenhouse. Well, I have only a few of these conditions in my garden, and I've still managed to grow nearly all the herbs in this book, so don't feel limited by the garden you've got. Most soils can be improved, most conditions can be created or mimicked, and a great many herbs can be grown in pots, which gives you the ability to change their environment easily. And, at the end of the day, most herbs are pretty forgiving. I constantly remind myself of an adage in *The River Cottage Cookbook*: 'The plants you put out really want to grow. You don't have to make them, you just have to let them.' That's as true with herbs as any other edible plant.

In addition, a herb can reward you so easily and so readily because in the vast majority of cases you're not waiting for it to fruit or produce a sizeable root, seed or other edible appendage. At the minimum, all you need is a few leaves, perhaps a flower or two. And with a bit of preparation and some simple maintenance, most herb plants will give you far more than that.

Sunlight

Once you've decided what you'd like to grow (see Herb A–Z, pp.38–155), the first thing to establish is whether your herb likes sun or shade. Once it is planted, the amount of sunlight it gets is the thing you have least control over. Most gardens have spots that receive plenty of sun, and others that are dappled or shady. The majority of the herbs in this book enjoy bright conditions, but some will thrive in shady conditions too.

Top five herbs to grow in shady places

Angelica	see p.40
Bergamot	see p.53
Sorrel	see p.138
Sweet cicely	see p.142
Wild garlic	see p.153

Soil type and drainage

Once you know which area to put your herb in, you can think about preparing the soil. You need to understand what kind of soil you've got. This is something you can do by digging up a few forkfuls, working it over in your hands, and having a good look at it. It might be light, dry and sandy; it might be heavy, wet, dense and clay-like; or it may be a lovely crumbly dark loam. The latter is particularly desirable, but any soil type can be worked with.

A 'rich' or 'good' soil is one that is full of decomposing organic matter and therefore nutrients. A lot of plants like such a soil, which is why, generally speaking, digging in some good well-rotted compost before planting – and then applying more from time to time as a 'mulch' (a layer on top) – will boost the growth of whatever you plant. For some herbs, a really rich soil is ideal and added nutrients in the form of well-rotted manure are helpful. However, others prefer what is termed a 'poor' soil, which is not very rich in nutrients at all. In this case, go easy on the compost, but don't leave it out altogether.

You will see that I suggest growing almost every herb in this book in well-drained soil. There may be some which like moist or damp conditions, but still drainage is important. I don't know of any herb that likes sitting in waterlogged earth, and wet conditions can lead to failure to thrive and all sorts of rotting and fungal problems, as well as outright death of the plant. So ensuring good drainage is one of the best preparatory steps you can take, whether you're looking at an expansive herb bed or a few little pots. You may be lucky enough to have a garden of lovely friable, lightly sandy loam already, i.e. the kind of soil that drains well naturally. If not, then adjusting drainage qualities is a straightforward though sometimes physically demanding task.

If you dig good well-rotted compost into your soil before planting, you will open up its structure as well as enriching it. The latest horticultural thinking tends to go against frequent digging in, which can potentially disturb a healthy soil ecology and certainly releases carbon. And, obviously, you can't do much digging in if you already have established plants growing. But it's still something worth doing initially, to prepare a plot or a specific small area, especially if you need to improve soil condition and drainage.

In a very dry sandy soil, compost will actually enhance the moisture-holding properties as well as adding nutrients, and you can boost the richness further with manure. In a heavy soil, compost will aid drainage. A soil that is naturally heavy and claggy will benefit further from the addition of sharp sand, of the kind you can buy from any DIY outlet. If you have a really dense clay-based soil, then some sand is pretty much essential. You might want to go one step further and add grit, which is also available from garden centres. Grit is almost always a good idea for herbs such as lavender and rosemary, which prefer dry conditions and a very free-draining soil.

Even with some preparation and improvement, it still makes sense to work with rather than against the soil you've got. If you have light, sandy, poor soil, then you are on to a winner with Mediterranean herbs such as thyme and rosemary. If you have a rich, moisture-retaining soil and shady patches, you should have no trouble with angelica and bergamot. But no herb is beyond your reach: garden soil itself is one thing, what you put in a pot is quite another.

Another factor is the pH value of your soil, which affects the availability of different nutrients. You can check this easily with an inexpensive tester kit from your local garden centre. Most herbs like a fairly neutral soil with a pH between 6.5 and 7 but don't panic unless your soil departs wildly from that in either direction. If it does, there are steps you can take: agricultural lime will raise the pH of a very acid soil, and good compost will help to correct a very alkaline one.

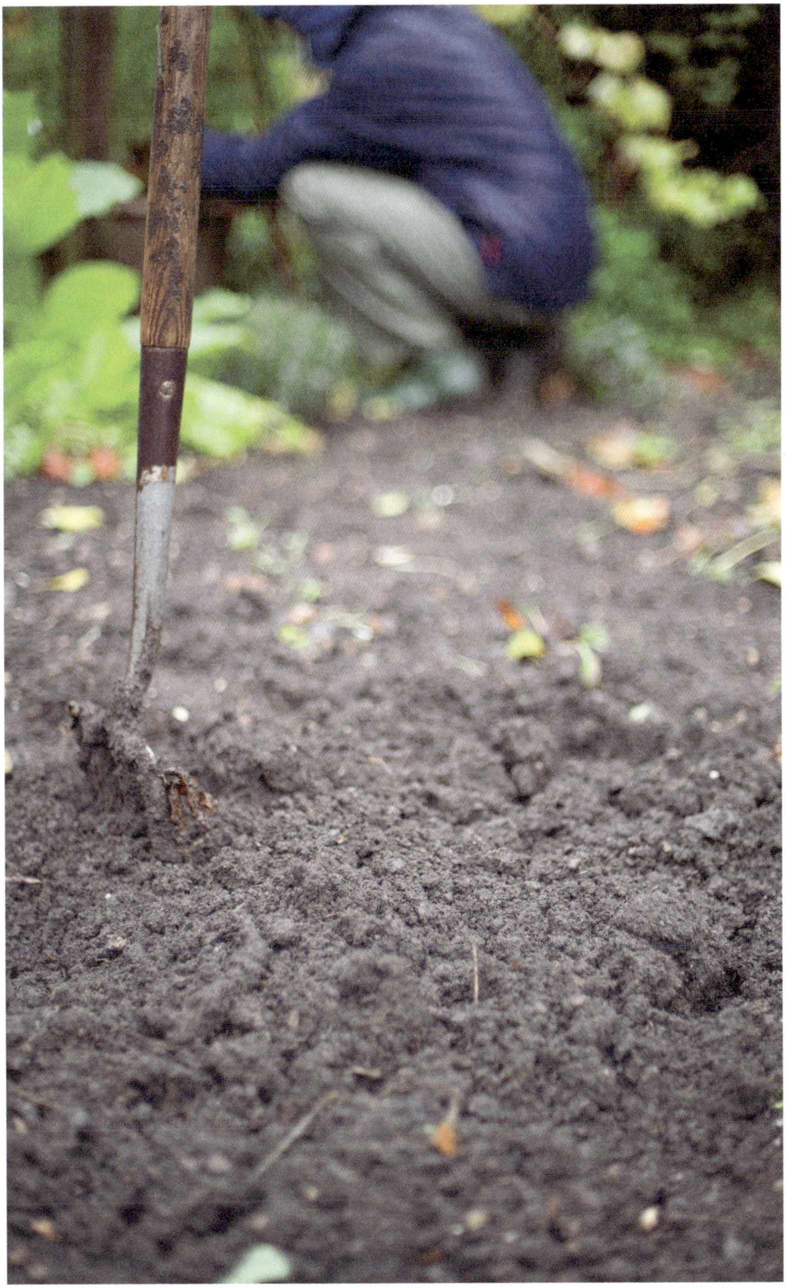

Container growing

If the soil you have seems hopelessly inappropriate for something you want to grow, or you've run out of soil space in a sunny corner, turn to container gardening, which gives you much more control. Even big, fast-growing perennial herbs such as mint can thrive in a container – if it's large and deep enough and you keep the plant watered and fed. Pots are great, of course, but consider half-barrels, old baths or sinks, buckets, fruit crates, even polystyrene boxes.

If you are planting herbs in pots or containers, drainage is still very important. Preparatory potting composts are designed to be free draining. If you are mixing your own, including some sand in the mix is helpful. And before you put anything into a pot at all, make sure it has a hole at the bottom for drainage. Standard plant pots will already have one but if you are improvising with containers such as welly boots, old buckets or crates, you must make a few small holes in the base.

Before you fill any pot or container with earth or compost, line the base with a shallow layer of 'crocks'. These are conventionally bits of broken pot but could be pebbles or small stones or even chunks of broken-up polystyrene – from a plant tray, perhaps. The idea is to provide a free-draining layer so the soil in the pot will never become waterlogged. All this free drainage does mean, of course, that you need to water pots regularly, especially in warm weather, to keep that moisture passing through.

If you have little or no garden space, there are lots of herbs which grow well in relatively small pots indoors or on a windowsill. Those which don't include plants which are naturally tall or large in stature, such as lovage, bergamot or fennel, and those with long, thick roots, such as angelica and horseradish.

Top choices for windowsill-growing

Basil (any variety)	see p.44
Chives	see p.63
Coriander	see p.66
Lemongrass	see p.94
Marigold	see p.98
Marjoram and oregano	see p.101
Nasturtium	see p.110
Parsley	see p.113
Rosemary	see p.125
Scented geranium	see p.135
Summer savory	see p.141

Compost

It is easy to make your own compost and a great way to recycle household waste if you have a garden with space for a compost bin. If you are looking to improve your soil right here, right now and you have no homemade compost to hand, then you can buy an organic soil improver (see Directory, p.249), which will do a similar job.

Making your own compost You will need a compost bin or a bespoke composting container of some kind to contain the compost, keep away unwelcome animals and allow you to mix and aerate the contents easily. This should be put on bare earth or grass to give worms and soil-borne bacteria easy access, as they help break down compost. A reasonably sunny site is ideal because warmth speeds decomposition.

Feed your bin with raw fruit, vegetable and herb trimmings, crushed eggshells, used tea bags and coffee grounds, grass clippings, prunings, young annual weeds that haven't formed seeds, dead leaves and torn-up newspaper or cardboard. To get the right chemical balance and texture, keep an even mix of wetter, quicker-to-decompose 'green' waste (grass and vegetable matter) and drier, tougher 'brown' waste (woody garden trimmings, egg shells, paper and cardboard). Compost needs air, so mix it from time to time with a garden fork, and don't compact it.

Once your bin is full, you need to leave the compost alone to give it time to break down into a crumbly dark brown mass, which can take up to a year. So, ideally you need two bins on the go: one that's full and rotting down, one that you're feeding.

For more information on home-composting, I recommend the *River Cottage Veg Patch Handbook*, as well as www.recyclenow.com/home_composting.

Potting composts If you are planting herbs in pots, you'll need to fill them with a 'growing medium'. You can simply scoop up earth from your garden, but it will come with its own cargo of weed seeds. The alternative is to use a potting compost.

Many proprietary potting composts contain extracted peat, which is an environmental no-no and goes against the principles of organic gardening, although there are some organic potting composts which use 'derived' peat, filtered from water that's run naturally from peat moors. However, it's easy to buy peat-free potting composts specifically designed for growing vegetables and herbs.

The other alternative is to mix up your own potting compost using fine, weed-free garden topsoil (mole hills are good, apparently), along with homemade compost that has rotted down to a fine, crumbly consistency, plus some sand and a moisture-retaining material such as vermiculite, perlite or composted bark. The relative amounts of each vary: there are many different recipes to be found. This is probably a project for devoted large-scale gardeners who have plenty of good topsoil to spare and a well-established composting system. Homemade potting compost will not be sterile and completely weed free, as a bought compost will.

Growing from seed

Growing herbs from seed is immensely satisfying and gives you a lot of control over what you're growing and how it is treated. You can buy almost any herb you might want to grow as a seed, if you look to specialist suppliers (see Directory, p.248), and you will invariably have seedlings aplenty to give away to your friends. However, seed-raising involves more work, more space and more care than simply buying young plants. In addition, some herbs are difficult to raise from seed and some varieties will not 'come true' if started in this way, which means new plants won't be exactly the same as their parents.

Unless you have a potting shed and plenty of time to devote to cosseting your seedlings, you might find it best to buy most of your herbs as young plants, growing just a select few from seed. I go for more unusual herbs as well as annuals that need to be raised afresh every year. Growing from seed is also more economical and effective with annual herbs which you might want to use in large quantities and/or those which run to seed fairly quickly. These can be sown successively, every few weeks in the spring and summer, so you always have a good crop coming through.

Top herbs to grow from seed

Basil	see p.44
Chervil	see p.60
Coriander	see p.66
Nasturtiums	see p.110
Perilla	see p.117
Summer savory	see p.141
Thai basil	see p.47

Growing most herbs from seed is pretty straightforward and I have given suggestions for the optimum techniques in each A–Z entry. But I am also wedded to the basic River Cottage principle of 'seed packet gardening', i.e. do what it says on the pack and you can't go far wrong.

When to sow

As a general rule, herb seeds should be sown in spring. There are a few exceptions: angelica and sweet cicely both need to be sown in autumn, for instance, because they will not germinate without a spell of cold weather. And there are others, such as parsley and rocket, that you can sow at pretty much any time of year. But spring is optimum in most cases.

Where to sow

Some seeds need a lot of warmth to germinate and should be sown indoors or in a greenhouse. Some must be sown outdoors due to temperature requirements, such as angelica and sweet cicely (see When to sow, left). Others, such as dill and coriander, need to go directly into their growing site – be it ground or container – because they don't like being disturbed and replanted. But many can be sown indoors or out. Generally, in early spring when the ground is still cold, say late February to early April, inside is good. As the year progresses, the ground warms and the days lengthen, outside sowing becomes feasible.

Observe when the weeds are starting to sprout in your garden and this will give you a clue as to when it's worth sowing outside. To quote gardening writer Sarah Raven: 'If nature's doing it, you do it too.' Dig, bash and rake the soil to as fine a consistency as possible, removing all weeds as you go. Water it before sowing so the seeds go into a moist environment.

Equipment

For indoor or greenhouse sowing, invest in plug trays, or module trays. These make it very easy to remove a seedling and move it to a pot or growing site. Open seed trays are less easy to use and you're more likely to damage your seedlings when removing them. Guttering is another good seed receptacle, see p.33.

Fill your plugs with a good seed compost. Special seed composts are fine-textured and have fewer nutrients in them than potting composts. This is because, initially, the germinating seed contains all the nutrients it needs within its case. Added extras aren't necessary; indeed some can actually damage the seed, and they'll also give an unwelcome boost to other competitive weeds or organisms. Some seed packets call for a 'soil-less' seed compost. This often means a peat-based compost, which isn't a good idea (see p.29). However, you can buy peat-free seed composts (see Directory, p.249).

Sowing herb seeds

Most seeds like darkness to germinate, i.e. they need to be covered with compost or soil, not lying on top of it. A light covering is usually enough. However, as soon as the shoots have started to appear, they need plenty of light so, if they're not already outdoors, they should be in a greenhouse or on a windowsill.

Most seeds need moisture to germinate but they should definitely not be kept wet. Give them a light sprinkling of water after the initial sowing – or spritz with a plant spray bottle. With very fine seeds in plugs, it's better to sit the plug trays in a tray of water so the compost can absorb moisture from the base up. Lift out the plug trays when the compost is moist. In all cases, keep a close eye on your seedlings and give just enough light watering to keep the compost moist.

Coriander seedlings growing in guttering

Transplanting or thinning out your seedlings

After germination, herb plants will first produce a pair of baby leaves which look similar on most plants. After that, 'true' leaves will form, which look like the ones you'll be harvesting. Once a seedling has several true leaves and looks robust, if it's in a plug, it's time to transplant it – roots need room to grow and seed compost will no longer provide enough nutrients. Transplant healthy-looking seedlings into pots filled with potting compost. Once these have developed into strong young plants, they can be moved again – either into larger containers, or into the garden itself.

If you are sowing seeds directly in the garden, you will need to 'thin out' the baby seedlings. This means removing some of the plants to leave the strongest ones growing with plenty of space around them. The space you should leave varies from plant to plant, so refer to the seed packet. If you don't thin out, individual plants will struggle to get enough light, air and nutrients from the soil.

Seedlings that have been started indoors will benefit from a period of 'hardening off' before being moved outside. This simply means breaking them in gently to outside temperatures and conditions by putting them outside in the day, then bringing them in at night. A week of this should be plenty for most herbs.

Protecting your seedlings

Seedlings outdoors will need protection from marauding gastropods, birds, rabbits and so on. For slugs and snails, try broken egg shells, beer traps, copper rings, plant collars or any other method of control available from organic gardening suppliers. A cover of fine horticultural mesh is a good barrier against larger predators, as well as many flying pests. Cloches or frames can be used to protect individual plants – you can get some very nifty self-supporting pop-up mesh 'tents' now too.

Seeds in guttering

Growing seeds in lengths of guttering is a clever technique, used by River Cottage head gardener Mark Diacono. When ready to transplant, you can simply ease the entire length of compost out of the end of the guttering into some prepared ground.

Guttering can also provide you with a harvest of tasty 'micro-leaves', which can be cut as little as 10 days after sowing – to scatter in salads or on soups. Herbs with quite delicate, fast-growing aromatic leaves, such as basil, coriander and chervil, are ideal. Fill a length of guttering – whatever you have room for – with seed compost. You can leave the ends open, letting the compost shelve off gently, or you can seal off the ends with gaffer tape. Sow the seeds fairly thickly down the middle and cover with another thin layer of compost. Water only very lightly – just enough to keep the compost moist – and keep in a warm, light place such as a greenhouse or on a windowsill. Your seeds should begin sprouting within a few days and micro-leaves will be ready to harvest in a couple of weeks, if not sooner.

Taking cuttings of perennial herbs

This is a good way to propagate woodier herbs, including rosemary and lavender, which do not always grow true and easy from seed. In the spring or early summer when the plant is sending out vigorous new growth, carefully pull away strong new offshoots of non-flowering stem. They should have a small 'heel', or strip of the main stem, still attached at the base. Remove the lower leaves and plant immediately in potting compost with extra sand mixed in. Cover the cutting loosely with a plastic bag, with a couple of little holes snipped in it, to create a humid environment. Put somewhere warm but out of bright sunlight. Keep the compost moist. Remove the bag after a few weeks. Let the plant develop plenty of roots before planting it in the garden or a larger pot during the following spring or summer.

Propagating rosemary cuttings

Buying plants

Shopping for herb plants is a delicious and exciting pastime. In a decent nursery, or even browsing the pages of an internet supplier, you can easily get carried away, purchasing more than you had initially intended. The beauty of buying herbs as young plants is that all the crucial work of germination and early nurturing has been done for you. With many plants, you can start harvesting straight away. They will at the very least be established and ready to plant in a larger pot, or the garden.

There are only two cons, as far as I can see. Firstly, it costs more to buy a couple of plants than a packet of seeds which could, potentially, give you tens of specimens. Secondly, you don't know how that herb has been nurtured and raised. A herb may have been treated with artificial fertilisers, chemical sprays and growth hormones which are absorbed into the leaves. I prefer to buy herb plants from specialist herb suppliers. Some are certified organic and even those who aren't will often be very willing to talk to you about how their plants are treated and raised. If you've bought perennial herbs from a source you're not sure about, you can plant them and wait for a year before using them, until a fresh cycle of growth has started. There should be little or no residue in the leaves by then.

Watering

All plants need water to thrive but the amount they need varies a great deal and very few plants respond well to over-watering. Large perennial herbs, once established in a particular spot, often need no more than rainfall. This is especially true of the Mediterranean herbs, such as lavender, thyme, rosemary and hyssop, which thrive in dry conditions. There are others, however – angelica springs to mind – which really like quite a moist soil all the time. And of course very dry weather can make even well-established plants suffer, so always keep a careful eye on them for signs of wilting and general failure to thrive.

Annual herbs, which will not have the time or inclination to put down such long, deep roots, need more attention, and any herb grown in a pot or container will need watering. As a general rule, keep the soil of pot herbs just damp. Water in the cooler parts of the day – early morning or evening – to minimise evaporation. Be aware, however, that basil is a herb that does not like to 'go to bed wet'.

It is generally better to use rainwater, collected in a water butt and applied with a watering can, than tap water from a hosepipe. Not only is collecting rainwater a good way of conserving this precious resource, but it will also be free of substances such as chlorine, which are routinely added to tap water. Artificially softened tap water is not good for plants as it contains a lot of salt.

Feeds and fertilisers

It is a central tenet of organic gardening, indeed of most traditional common-sense gardening, that the soil itself gives us everything we need, just as long as we look after it properly. So if you care for your soil, adding organic compost and perhaps manure regularly, you shouldn't need to worry about feeds and fertilisers. These only tend to feed the plant, rather than the soil itself, and they don't do anything to improve soil structure, which compost does. Feeds and fertilisers are also often designed to help a plant produce more fruit, which is not usually relevant for herbs.

However, most successful gardeners would agree that a bit of a boost every now and then can work wonders for some plants, and feeding is important for herbs grown in pots, where there is a much more limited supply of nutrients. Apply liquid feeds perhaps a few times during the growing season, particularly after cutting back. Always err on the side of under- rather than over-feeding. Herbs do not require feeding as much as vegetables or fruit do.

Organic chicken manure pellets A few of these can be added to pots early in the season and will slowly release nutrients, which means you don't have to remind yourself about applying fresh feed.

Organic liquid feeds I tend to use these as they're so easy to apply. They may be based on seaweed, fungi or on worm casts. If you have your own little wormery (see wigglywigglers.com), it will produce a rich and nutritious wormy liquid that makes an excellent feed.

Homemade comfrey or nettle 'teas' These are packed full of nutrients and can really give plants a boost. You can make them by simply soaking a good quantity of comfrey or nettle leaves in a tub full of rainwater for 3–5 weeks. The resulting brew (which will be really quite extraordinarily stinky) can then be diluted and used as a liquid feed.

Weeds

I know this might sound blooming obvious, but it's certainly something I need to remind myself of often enough: do try and keep your herb patch fairly weed free. One can get a bit blasé about weeds, but remember they are strong, hungry and competitive plants that will take some of the water, nutrients, light and space that you want to go to your beloved herbs.

My favourite herbs to grow

Any herb that you really enjoy eating is a good one for you to grow, but if you're not quite sure where to begin, these are the ones that I believe best reward the small-scale culinary gardener. I've given my reasons for loving each of them, but all are easy to maintain, beautiful to look at and extremely versatile in the kitchen.

My top ten herbs to grow at home

Bay	p.49	It is the most useful and versatile herb of all time.
Lovage	p.96	You rarely need more than a few leaves at a time – much easier to pick from your own plant.
Rosemary	p.125	It's always there, winter or summer, and it's an essential herb for roasts. It's also very beautiful and attracts the bees and the butterflies.
Lavender	p.86	It's an underrated culinary herb – and another favourite with the pollinating insects.
Mint	p.105	A cup of freshly brewed real mint tea is the most refreshing thing imaginable. Mint is also endlessly useful and versatile.
Chives	p.63	A fresh-cut chive is a thing of wonder – and a chive flower possibly even better – while one from a packet is emphatically not. A quintessential summer herb.
Tarragon	p.144	It just has the most incredible anise flavour that enhances so many foods.
Lemon verbena	p.92	It is so very pretty and so incredibly fragrant, a wonderful herb for sweets and puds.
Angelica	p.40	You certainly can't buy it fresh, and it's a magnificent plant. It is wonderful cooked with fruit.
Borage	p.54	It is so beautiful and the flowers are incredibly versatile for decorating all sorts of dishes and drinks.

Herb A–Z

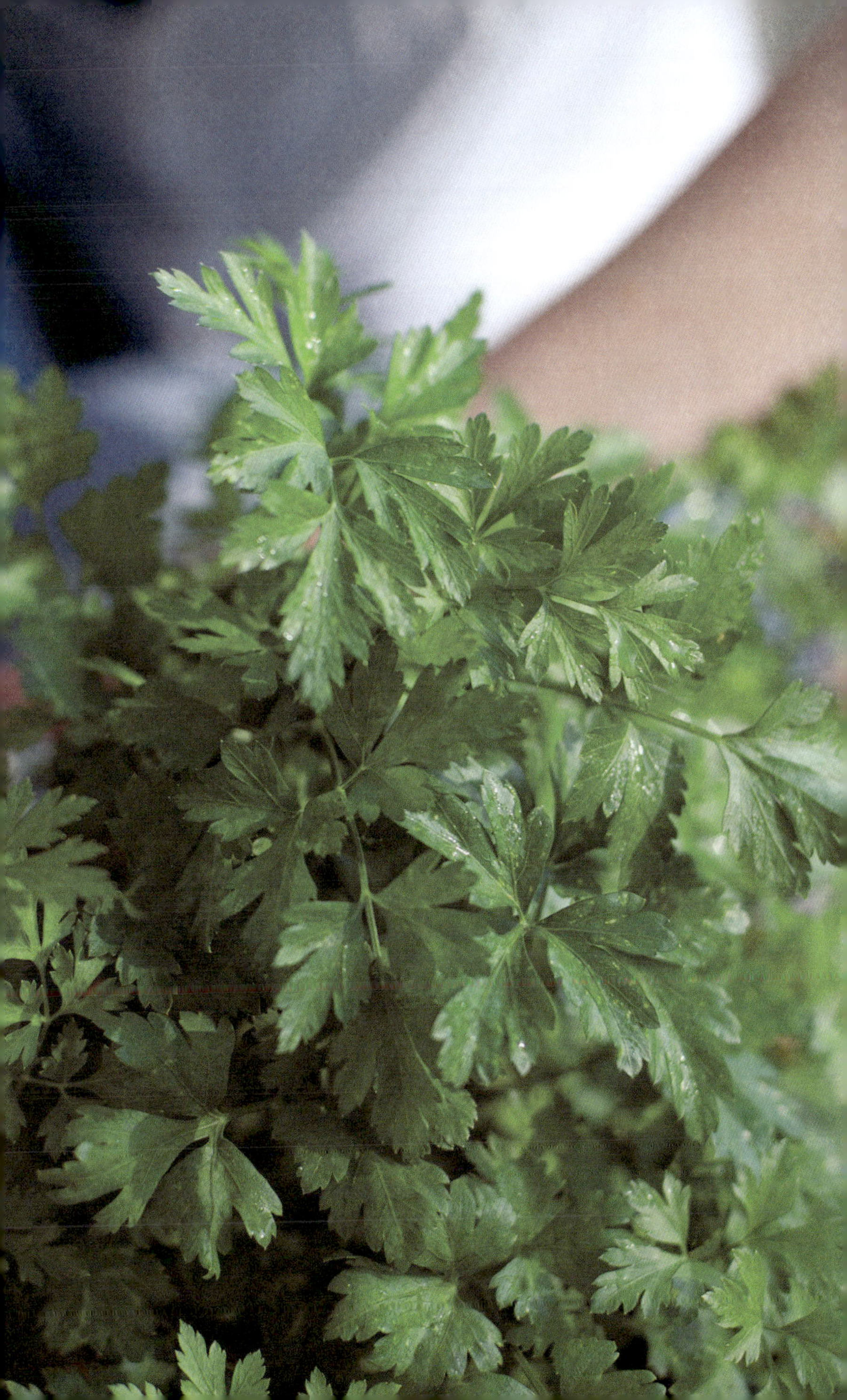

Angelica *Angelica archangelica*

PLANT GROUP	Hardy biennial
HARVEST	May–September

In its full glory, this is a lovely, generous plant with thick ridged stems, effulgent leaves and bouncing flowerheads. I would grow it for its looks alone, but it's a useful herb too. Angelica has some notes similar to juniper and, like that spice, is one of the classic flavourings for gin. If you're partial to the occasional refreshing 'G and T', you'll probably recognise angelica's astringent, slightly musky but fragrant flavour. There's also a sort of sherbety brightness to it, a tingle on the tongue, which makes it a winning companion to fruit.

In the kitchen

You can eat very tender young angelica leaves in salads (though I'd attach provisos to this, see below). It's also said that you can cook them lightly, like spinach, while the stems can be steamed like asparagus. I've tried these things and found the results unedifying – even quite young stems and leaves can be bitter and tough. However, angelica really shines when it is cooked with fruit and/or sugar. When you combine it with a tart fruit, such as rhubarb or gooseberries, something wonderful happens. The herb has an acidity-reducing, lightening effect on the flavour of the fruit, which means you can go a little easier on the sugar, and it contributes its own musky flavour too. I always find the stems more effective and flavourful than the leaves – but you can use a mix of the two. Candying angelica is also very definitely worth doing.

- Finely chopped angelica stems can be added to the fruit when making rhubarb, currant or gooseberry jam.
- The very first tender leaves of the year can be used in salads. However, they do have a distinct bitterness, so I would shred them finely and combine them with other herb leaves – try sorrel (p.138) and/or anise hyssop (p.43), as well as some more bland, sweet lettuce-type leaves.
- **Rhubarb crumble with angelica** (p.223)
- **Candied angelica**, plus angelica syrup (p.237)

How to grow

Because the seeds need to be sown fresh – within a few weeks of coming off the stem – it's a good idea to buy your first angelica as a little fledgling plant. (You can buy the seeds, but they will be dormant and need 'stratifying', which means subjecting to a period of artificial cold weather. This can be done by layering the seeds in damp kitchen paper and putting them in the fridge for several weeks.)

When choosing a site for your first angelica plant, it's important to remember that this stately creature can reach 2 metres in its second year. Once established, it doesn't like to be moved either – another reason to think carefully about where to put it. Its size and spread mean it's not ideal for containers.

Angelica likes a fairly shady situation and deep, fairly moist, but well-drained soil. Water it frequently until it's well established, and thereafter in dry spells.

Angelica won't produce flowers during the first year, but should grow fairly dramatically, giving you plenty of leaves and tender stems. It will then die back over the winter and emerge in spring for a second year, when it should produce bonny, blowsy flowerheads. Sometimes this doesn't happen until the third or even fourth year. You can often persuade the plant to live longer by cutting off the flowers before the seeds develop. Seed formation signifies the beginning of the end for that particular plant but you can gather the seeds to start the next cycle.

The plant is very hardy so you can simply sow the seeds in autumn, soon after harvesting, straight into the ground. Alternatively, let the plant self-seed and transplant the seedlings if necessary, when still very small.

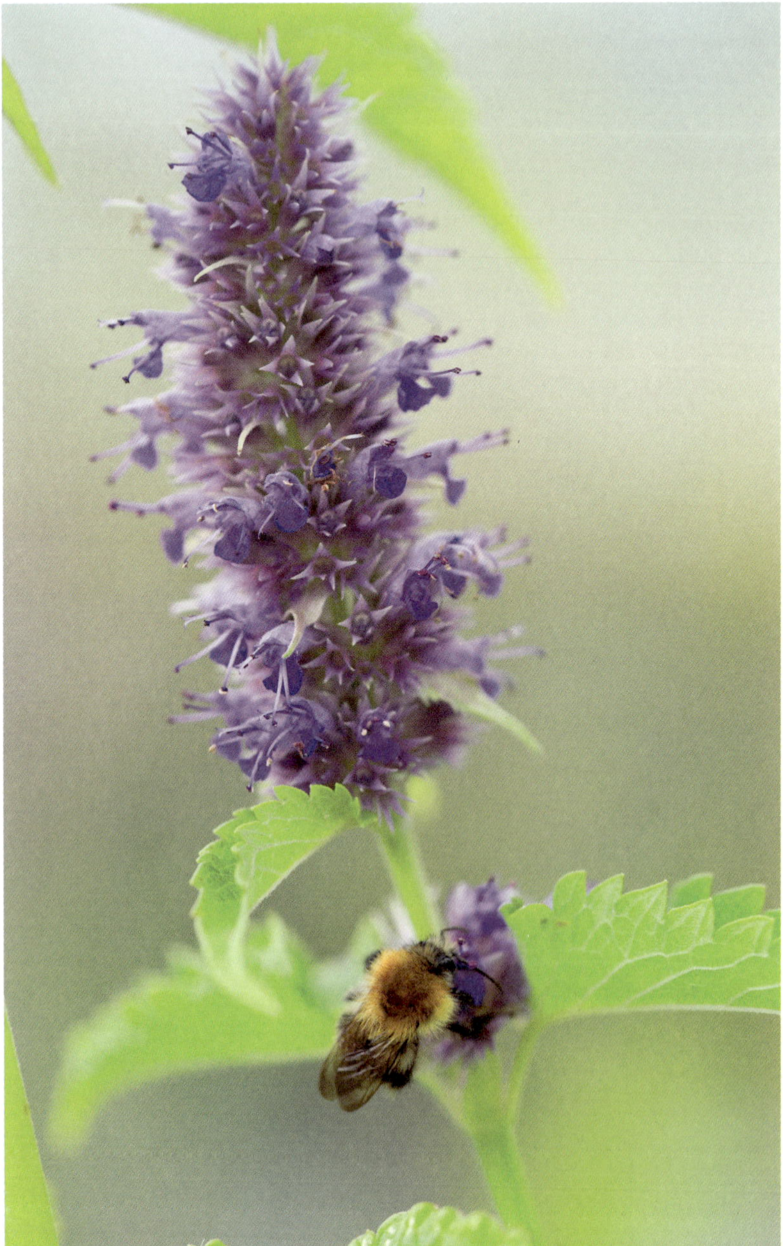

Anise hyssop *Agastache foeniculum*

PLANT GROUP	Hardy perennial
HARVEST	May–September

This statuesque herb has a sweet, fresh minty aniseed flavour. It is also called liquorice mint, which tells you pretty much all you need to know. It's lovely with shellfish and has a delicate seasoning effect on sweet foods, not dissimilar to mint.

In the kitchen
Anise hyssop is a herb to use fresh, rather than cooked. If you do cook it, do so only briefly. The leaves can be a little on the tough side, so always shred or chop them finely. You can use the blooms as well – pinch them into little flowerlets.

- Anise hyssop is really good chopped finely and combined with sliced strawberries and plenty of caster sugar. Try it sprinkled on peaches too.
- Try anise hyssop, finely chopped, sprinkled on seared scallops, cold cooked crab or prawns. Finish with a spritz of lemon juice.
- You can use it in place of mint in many recipes.
- Infuse a jar of warmed honey with anise hyssop leaves and flowers.
- Anise hyssop makes a delicate tea, very soothing after a meal.
- In small amounts, it's nice in mixed fresh herbs – in an omelette, for instance, or tossed with a knob of butter into just-cooked carrots or peas.

How to grow
This hardy perennial can be grown from seed but it needs warmth to germinate. Put your plug trays in a warm spot indoors, or sow outdoors in summer, using horticultural fleece or a cloche to protect seedlings in cold weather. Young plants for spring and summer planting are easy to buy from a specialist herb-grower.

Anise hyssop likes rich soil and full sun, where its waving brush-like flowers can soak up the light. It grows tall and upright so it looks great at the back of a bed, against a sunny wall or fence. It should produce its purple-blue blooms in mid to late summer. Pinch out the flowers to maintain good leaf production (they can be used in the kitchen), but leave some on in late summer to give the plant the chance to self-seed. Anise hyssop can be grown in a pot outdoors but you'll need a big one.

Relatives
Korean mint (*Agastache rugosa*) can be used in similar ways but it's more pungently pepperminty, so I'd be cautious about using it in delicate savoury dishes.

Basil *Ocimum basilicum*

PLANT GROUP	Half-hardy annual
HARVEST	June–September

Glorious basil, fragrant almost to a fault, has a unique honeyed, aniseedy pungency that becomes quite addictive. As long as you remember the golden rule – don't actually *cook* it – it's a fabulous herb in the kitchen. Basil has many gorgeous manifestations (see overleaf) but the classic green 'Sweet Genovese' variety is an absolute essential for so many good things: a simple caprese salad with tomato and mozzarella, a piquant pesto, the ultimate chicken sandwich and a thousand different pasta dishes, to name but a few. It's also exquisite in some sweet dishes, such as ice creams or truffles.

In the kitchen

Where shall I start? Basil can enhance so many things. The important point, as I've said, is to cook it very little or not at all. It's best torn or shredded and added raw, right at the end, just lightly stirred into a dish or simply scattered on top. Long cooking and intense heat will render it undetectable. There are rumours put about that you should only ever tear basil, not cut it. It certainly looks pretty when torn, but a finely sliced chiffonade (see p.18), or a processor-blitzed pesto should convince you that a knife blade will not somehow steal its flavour. I generally only use the leaves, but you can use the stalks to infuse flavour in a cream or a soup. They are a bit tough and slightly bitter for straight eating.

- Basil is lovely in salads, and particularly good with tomatoes, cucumber, grilled or sautéed courgettes or aubergine, peppers and mild salty cheeses such as halloumi or a firm goat's cheese.
- Basil works well with soft fruit too. Toss it with sliced, sugared strawberries or a fresh peach and blueberry salad.
- Add basil to any lemony dressing or sauce, including mayonnaise (p.159).
- This herb is delicious on soups – particularly pea or bean soups, gazpacho, or any kind of light chicken broth.
- I love to throw a handful of roughly chopped basil into veg and pasta combinations just before serving – such as broccoli, garlic and chilli.
- **Basil and parsley pesto** (p.166)
- **Herb noodle soup** (p.173)
- **Raspberry ripple basil ice cream** (p.219)
- **White chocolate truffles with basil** (p.229)

Basil *Ocimum basilicum* 'Sweet Genovese'

Thai basil *Ocimum basilicum* 'Horapha'

How to grow

Basil is not entirely without trial for the gardener. It's a bit fussy and it likes warmth – not surprisingly, since it came originally from Asia.

Generally, I'd say basil is a herb to raise from seed, with successional sowings, so you can produce lots of it, and to grow in a pot so you can more easily control its environment. You can also try the guttering approach (p.33).

This is very much a summer herb – to enjoy from around June to September. Sow in late spring, cosseting your basil in a greenhouse, a sunny conservatory or kitchen or a very warm, sheltered bit of garden. While it loves the sun, it does not like to dry out – in fact, it likes a humid environment and rich, moist soil.

Keep a daily check on your basil plants for any sign of wilting. Water them from the base, pouring water into the tray they're sitting in, to encourage roots downwards. Water early in the day, not the evening. If you do have your basil outside, bring it indoors if the weather is less than warm – say, 18°C or lower in the daytime. You should certainly bring it in if it drops to 5°C or lower at night. Pinch out the growing tips and flowers to encourage bushy, tender growth and the best flavour.

Varieties

Thai basil (*Ocimum basilicum* 'Horapha') Also just known as horapha, this tastes really very different to classic sweet basil, though it is related. I love it. Ridiculously aniseedy – almost liquorice-like – it's a wonderful pungent addition to curries, laksas and spicy soups (such as the one on p.173).

Greek basil or bush basil (*Ocimum basilicum* var. *minimum*) This has small leaves, which, perhaps due to their Latin name, seem to have an inferiority complex that they tackle by veritably yelling with flavour. This basil is great sprinkled liberally on top of stews or meaty soups at the last minute.

Purple basil (*Ocimum basilicum* var. *purpurascens*) This looks stunning, but doesn't have quite the same purity and pungency of flavour as good old green basil and is harder to grow.

Holy basil (*Ocimum basilicum sanctum*) This has an intense, slightly minty flavour and is often used in Thai cooking.

Then there's lemon basil, cinnamon basil, lime basil and tempting exotic spicy varieties such as 'Spicy Globe' and 'Siam Queen'. Most of these are hard to buy as fresh herbs, but you can easily source the seeds for a huge range of basils (see Directory, p.248). So, if you have a greenhouse or, at least, a capacious windowsill or two, experiment away.

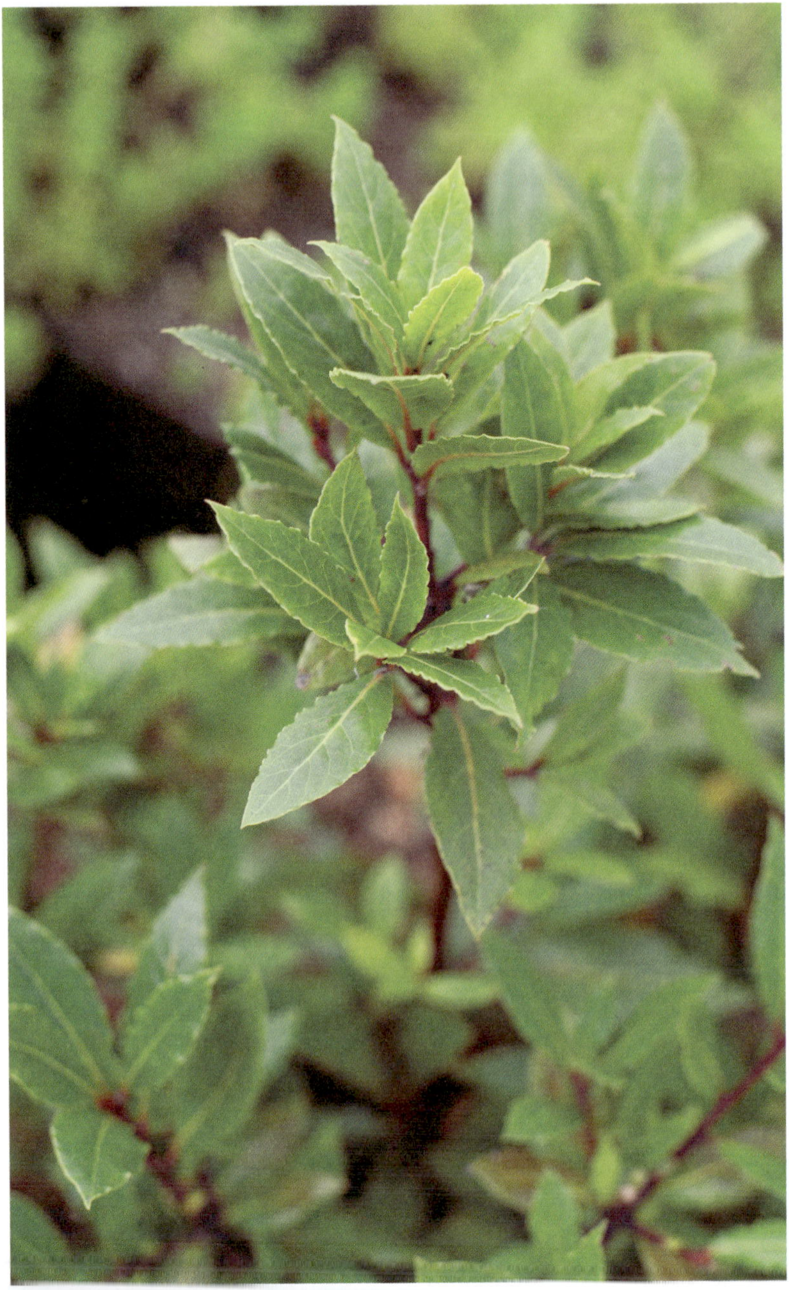

Bay *Laurus nobilis*

PLANT GROUP	Perennial evergreen
HARVEST	All year round

I love bay. Its scent – of lemon and new-split wood and smoke and roses – transports me to a place of safety. I use it almost every day and it would be my desert island herb because it is so deep and rich in flavour and so incredibly versatile. I associate bay with that culinary moment when a dish is assembled but not yet complete – the torn or twisted leaf, dropped into the stockpot, the roasting dish or the milk pan, is like a signal for the magic to begin.

In the kitchen

Bay ranks alongside salt, pepper and lemons as an essential everyday seasoning. It enhances and underlines, rather than dominates, and gives a warm, earthy base note to everything it's cooked with – a little citrusy, a little resinous. It can be just as lovely in a sweet dish as a savoury one. You have to unlock its flavour with heat and, usually, with infusion in a liquid – hence the success of simmering it in stews, stocks and sauces, soups, custards or syrups. Having said that, bay leaves simply added to the skewer for barbecue kebabs, or thrown into a pan before frying fish or a chunk of meat, will still give up their lovely perfume. However I use bay, I always tease the essential oils out a little by damaging the leaf in some way – a twist, a tear or a quick whack with a pestle. One or two leaves is usually enough in most dishes, but add more if you like. It's quite hard to overuse the herb because you don't eat the leaves themselves (they are tough and bitter) but rather capture their flavour in another medium.

- Bay is essential to the classic bouquet garni (see p.19), which gives flavour to many a stew. Tie a couple of leaves together with a good sprig of thyme and some parsley stalks, adding a strip of leek or celery for extra flavour.
- Add bay to oil-based marinades – try shredding the leaves finely first to maximise flavour transfer.
- There are very few soups that don't benefit from a bay leaf or two added before cooking, but do remember to remove them before puréeing or you'll have a soup full of tough little leaf scraps (obviously, I've never done this myself...)
- Bay is used in Indian cooking, typically added to hot oil with other spices in the early stages of a dish.
- Never make any kind of stock without at least one bay leaf. Just don't.

- Whenever you're heating milk for a béchamel or cheese sauce, add a bay leaf too. A halved onion and a few peppercorns further add to the subtle savoury flavour.
- Try using bay liberally with fish: stuff it inside a fish before baking, add it to the pan when frying, or make a bed of the leaves for the fish to bake on. Throw bay on to a barbecue before grilling fish too.
- Bay always adds something to a tomato sauce, and to tomato-based dishes such as bolognese or chilli.
- Add a twisted bay leaf to a rice pudding before baking, in place of the more usual vanilla pod.
- Use bay to scent a syrup for poaching fruit, such as pears.
- Tear the fleshy parts of a few bay leaves away from their central stalks. Using a pestle and mortar, pound and crush with either a measure of granulated sugar or flaky sea salt to a green powder. Add bay sugar to a fruit pie filling; use bay salt as part of a rub for meat before cooking.
- If you have plenty of bay to spare, try throwing a leafy twig or two on to barbecue coals to create a wonderfully fragrant smoke.
- **White beans with winter herbs** (p.204)
- **Herb ice cream** (p.219)

How to grow

It is possible to buy bay seeds but growing a productive bush from scratch would be a lengthy and possibly frustrating process. Much better to invest in a small bay shrub and plant it in a large pot or a sunny patch of garden. It should provide you with many years' continuous harvest.

Bay is a native of southern Europe so, although it is just about frost-hardy, it doesn't like the cold or the wet – young plants especially. Aim to give it warmth, free-draining gritty soil and as much shelter from wind and frost as you can manage. It will grow well in a large pot, and this tactic enables you to keep it protected from the worst of the weather, even bringing it inside during winter when the shrub is still young.

As the tree matures, it tends to become tougher and hardier, so you can plant it out. In the right conditions, if nothing gets in its way, it will simply keep growing – unchecked bay trees can be several metres high.

Infusing milk for a béchamel sauce with bay

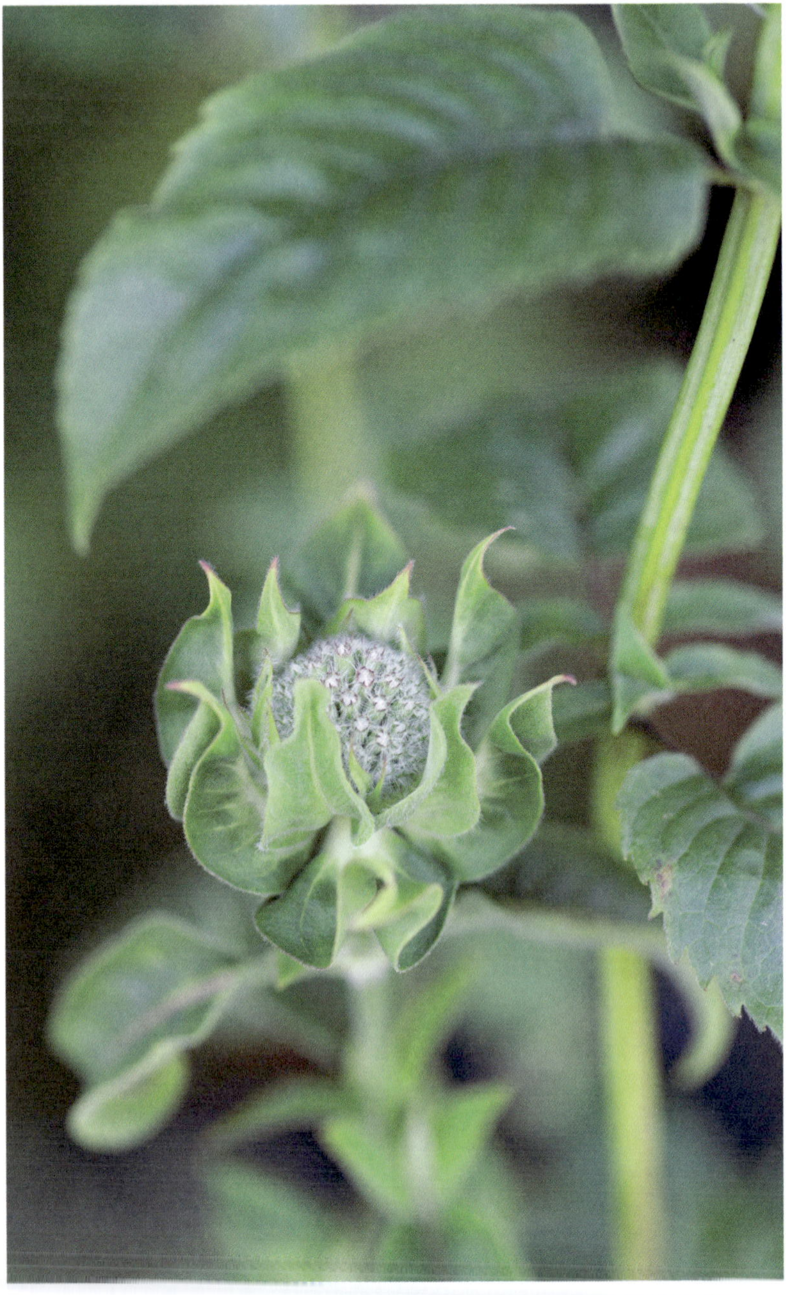

Bergamot *Monarda didyma*

PLANT GROUP	Hardy perennial
HARVEST	April–August

Spectacular as it grows, this lovely pungent herb is a member of the mint family, though with its strong citrusy flavour, it reminds me most of marjoram. Note that the herb is not related to the bergamot orange (*Citrus aurantium bergamia*), whose aromatic oil gives Earl Grey tea its distinctive fragrance. However, you can use the herb to make a very nice tea of its own (see p.244), or put a good sprig into black tea while it brews, for a refreshing, warming, slightly resinous extra layer of flavour.

In the kitchen
Bergamot ranks close to thyme, rosemary, marjoram and the savories as a punchy, aromatic all-rounder. As it's quite strong, start with a little and work your way up.

- Stir chopped bergamot into roasted squash as soon as it comes out of the oven, or blend into a roasted squash soup.
- Bergamot is a good addition when fresh mixed herbs are called for in a recipe – combine it with parsley, thyme or tarragon.
- Try substituting bergamot for oregano or marjoram in almost any recipe.
- **Bergamot scones** (p.215)

How to grow
Bergamot grows well from seed but it needs plenty of warmth to germinate and is best sown indoors. Or you can buy a few young plants for late-spring or summer planting. Bergamot is tall and slightly spindly so several plants together look best. It is not an obvious choice for containers, but should grow well in a large, deep one. The plants like sun or partial shade and rich, moist, but not wet, soil; don't let them dry out. The leaves will taste best before flowering in mid to late summer, but do let those flowers come because the plant will attract lots of bees.

Although this herb is a perennial and should give you little trouble once established, it's best to dig up the plant after 2 or 3 years and remove the centre, then replant the younger outer parts.

Relatives
Lemon bergamot (*Monarda citriodora*) is an annual which also has flamboyant blooms. The leaves have a strong lemon flavour. Wild bergamot (*Monarda fistulosa*) is very strong and more often used medicinally or as a tea than for eating.

Borage *Borago officinalis*

PLANT GROUP	Hardy annual
HARVEST	April–October

Borage, for me, is all about the flowers. Some greengrocers and supermarkets now sell it, but I would highly recommend growing this herb yourself so you can harvest plenty of its gorgeous, delicate and delicious blooms. They look beautiful scattered on puddings, cakes, or salads (sweet or savoury) and are lovely dropped into drinks. When you eat them, they pop in the mouth, releasing a little bead of refreshing, sweet, delicately cucumbery juice. Borage is a handsome plant, and easy to grow – what's not to like?

In the kitchen

Borage leaves are traditionally cooked as a vegetable or used as a herb in various European cultures. However, I find their thick, hairy, coarse texture off-putting, even when they are young. And their very mild cucumber taste doesn't do an awful lot for me. That said, I have found the finely chopped young leaves are a good way to flavour crème fraîche (see below).

Don't take my word for it, though – if you're growing borage for its flowers, you might as well try the leaves too. I would, however, strongly recommend chopping them up pretty finely.

- To make borage and smoked salmon canapés, stir a good 2 tbsp finely chopped young borage leaves into 200ml crème fraîche. Season lightly with salt and pepper. Put small dollops of the mixture on top of crostini or squares of brown toast, add a curl of smoked salmon, and garnish with a borage flower.
- Put borage flowers into ice-cube trays, top up with water and freeze. These ice cubes are beautiful in summer drinks (see p.240).
- Borage is, of course, a key ingredient in the classic Pimms cocktail – often replaced, but never bettered, by a bit of cucumber.
- I would scatter borage flowers on almost any kind of salad, but they are particularly good on strawberries or raspberries, and with savoury ingredients such as chicken and soft goat's cheeses that pair naturally well with cucumber.
- Use to finish off cucumber dishes, salads and soups in particular.
- **Simple herb salad** (p.175)
- **Sorrel wine cup** (p.243)

How to grow

This herb is very easy to raise from seed. Sow directly in the garden – try a couple of sowings through spring and summer for lots of flowers. You can also start borage off in plugs but it grows fast, so transplant before it gets too big. The plant can reach 1 metre in height and has a deep root. I wouldn't choose it as a container plant because of its fast-growing, expansive nature.

Borage isn't too fussy about where it grows, though it likes sun and open sandy free-draining soil if possible. It should give you blooms from early summer through to autumn. Deadhead it to prolong flowering, but leave some flowers late in the season if you want it to self-seed, which it will readily do – I've found it's happy to spread itself about the garden with no help from me.

Borago officinalis has blue flowers, and the plants sometimes produce random pink ones too. You can also buy *Borago officinalis* 'Alba', which blooms white and is equally pretty. The flowers are rich in nectar and bees absolutely love them – so much so that one fetching old name for this herb is 'bee bread'. Pale, delicate borage honey is well worth seeking out.

Borage is believed to be a friendly companion plant to tomatoes, legumes, brassicas and strawberries, luring away bugs and mysteriously improving the flavour of the fruit or vegetable.

Caraway *Carum carvi*

PLANT GROUP	Hardy biennial
HARVEST	Leaves: May–June
	Seeds: September–October of the second year

This delicious plant is really used more as a spice than a herb. You can eat caraway leaves – they have a pleasant, parsley-ish flavour – but they're not really anything to write home about. Caraway is best known for its seed, and understandably so. The long, gently curved brown seeds are packed with a distinctive warm, spicy, nutty-sweet flavour.

In the kitchen

Caraway seed is one of those flavours that works equally well in sweet and savoury applications. While my favourite way to enjoy it is in cakes and puddings, it goes incredibly well with cabbages, beans and other greens, as well as meats and cheeses. As with most seeds, the flavour is maximised if you use it relatively fresh, toast it very lightly in a dry frying pan, then crush, grind or pound it in a spice mill or with a pestle and mortar.

- Caraway enhances many a spice mix, including the North African merguez blend: toast equal quantities of caraway, cumin, fennel and coriander seeds and black peppercorns in a dry frying pan, then crush with a pestle and mortar. Use the blend in a stew, soup or tagine, stir into a hot chickpea salad with plenty of olive oil and lemon juice, or blend with crushed garlic, salt and oil to make a delicious rub for a joint of meat.
- Fiery harissa paste, also North African, needs caraway too. Recipes vary but usually include the four 'c's – chilli, cumin, coriander and caraway – blended with olive oil, garlic and sometimes tomatoes. A teaspoonful will transform bland rice or couscous dishes, or it can be thinned with a little more oil to make a delicious swirl on houmous or a vegetable soup.
- Caraway is the seed in good old-fashioned seed cake: simply add 2–3 tsp to any Victoria sponge, pound cake or Madeira cake recipe to enjoy the effect. It's also excellent in biscuits – try it in the recipe on p.225.
- Mix a little crushed caraway with cooking apples and sugar for a pie or crumble. Or stuff a pinch into the centre of an apple before baking, with some butter and brown sugar. It goes with plums, apricots and pears too.
- Toss lightly toasted caraway into steamed or stir-fried cabbage, kale, Brussels sprouts or other greens to lift and sweeten their earthy flavour.

How to grow

Raising caraway for your own seed harvest is, to some extent, a labour of love because you have to wait for its second year before the seed forms, and you would need several plants to yield more than a few tablespoonfuls of seed. However, caraway is not hard to grow and I do think that freshly harvested seeds – of this and other herbs with fragrant seeds, such as fennel, celery leaf and coriander – really have the edge on flavour.

Growing caraway from seed is straightforward and an economical way to grow lots of plants. It has a long tap root and is not ideal for containers. Instead, sow the seeds straight into weed-free ground, in a sheltered, sunny place. They really need warmth to germinate and grow, so late spring or early summer is the best time. You can also sow in late summer or early autumn. Thin out the seedlings once they are established to ensure a good healthy crop.

The plants will flower in their second summer and you can collect the seeds in late summer or early autumn once they are dry and look brown. Cut the seed heads in the middle of the day when there is no moisture on them. Keep the heads in a bowl or paper bag, in a dry place, for a week or two, then just pull or shake the seeds off. Store them in an airtight jar in a cool, dark cupboard.

Caraway seeds

Celery leaf *Apium graveolens*

PLANT GROUP	Hardy biennial
HARVEST	Leaves and stems: Any time in the first year Seeds: September–October of the second year

Also known as cutting celery, wild celery or, rather charmingly, smallage, this is the plant from which our familiar thick-stemmed salad celery was originally bred, and knobbly-rooted celeriac too. The herb has all the marvellous earthy, peppery savour of those vegetables, and can be used to add a deep note of flavour to dishes in much the same way. Indeed, if you grow celery leaf, you will probably find that you have far less call on conventional celery. Easy to grow and very pretty too, I'd put it in any herb patch.

In the kitchen

Celery leaf is quite pungent and slightly bitter so I'd suggest using it sparingly, adding more if you see fit. You can use the stems as well as the leaves. Added at the beginning of cooking, celery leaf will contribute a background note of savoury flavour. Keep it back until the last minute, or have it raw if you want a more defined peppery kick. The tiny, delicately ridged seeds have a delicious celery flavour too.

- Add a few roughly chopped leaves to a simple cheese sandwich, or combine with grated cheese for cheese on toast or a rarebit.
- Add a good sprig to any stock, or sweat down about 1 tbsp finely chopped leaves and stems with onions and garlic as the base for almost any soup.
- Celery leaf makes a very good addition to a pork and apple stuffing.
- Celery seeds have a strong nutty, slightly spicy flavour. They're so tiny that you can use them whole, or toast very lightly and roughly bash using a pestle and mortar to really maximise flavour. They're great added to a spice mix for a curry, pickle or chutney, delicious in breads (try in the recipe on p.211) and lend flavour to sweating onions for the base of a soup.
- **Celery leaf and lovage soup** (p.172)
- **Apple and celery leaf salad with Cheddar and walnuts** (p.175)

How to grow

You can grow celery leaf easily from seed, sowing it in plug trays in early spring, or straight into the ground a bit later on.

In the wild, celery leaf often grows in marshy ground. It's a plant that likes to be kept moist and it will wilt somewhat alarmingly if it doesn't get enough water.

Rich, well-fed soil in a not-too-sunny position is best. I have also grown celery leaf very successfully in large containers.

If kept in a reasonably sheltered spot, and assuming you don't experience sub-arctic temperatures, a first-year celery leaf plant should give you a harvest of fresh leaves and stems right through the winter. In its second summer, it will flower. Cut back the flowers straight away if you want to keep a crop of leaves going, but leave them if you want to harvest the seed. If you want to do both, grow more than one plant, perhaps planting one each year to maximise production.

When the flowers have faded and the green-yellow seeds have ripened and look dry and a light dun colour, snip the seed heads off the plant. Keep the heads in a bowl or paper bag, in a dry place, for a week or two. I find it easiest to simply pinch and rub the tiny seeds off the stalks, on to a large white plate. Any unwanted bits of plant matter can be picked out with your fingers and you should be left with a cache of perfect little seeds. You can put them in a fine sieve and shake it to get rid of little bits of husk and dust, but some of the smaller seeds may pass through too.

Keep your seeds in an airtight container in a cool, dark place and use within a year. You won't get a great volume of seed from each plant, but what you do get will taste wonderful.

Chervil *Anthriscus cerefolium*

PLANT GROUP	Hardy annual
HARVEST	All year round

Sweet, grassy, tender and delicately aniseedy, this is the most summery and salady of herbs, though it's possible to grow it right through the winter too. You can eat it raw by the forkful without feeling overpowered by it, and it subtly enhances all sorts of other flavours, particularly eggs, fish, green vegetables and chicken. Fine and feathery chervil is also one of the most beautiful edible leaves. It's lovely as a delicate garnish – just a couple of leaves floating on a soup, say.

As a herb though, it's one to use in quantity and as freshly picked as possible, so growing your own is a good idea. It grows easily from seed and, if you make successional sowings every few weeks from about March onwards, you should have a flourishing crop for most of the year. Chervil is also a herb that's fairly easy to buy, but it's hard to know whether the flavour will be good or not.

In the kitchen

Use chervil fresh, raw and generously. Think of it both as a delicate herb and a salad leaf. Add a few sprigs to almost any green salad for a light seasoning effect, or, for more of a chervil hit, make it the base of the dish, along with some mild leaves such as lamb's lettuce. Add one or two other ingredients – blanched green beans or broad beans, asparagus, new potatoes, tomatoes, oranges, cold chicken, hard-boiled eggs, a few toasted seeds – and dress lightly with a simple vinaigrette. If you are going to cook chervil, do so very briefly.

- Combined in roughly equal quantities with tarragon, parsley and chives, chervil is an essential part of *fines herbes*, the classic French blend which is so good in an omelette or stirred into a creamy sauce for chicken or fish.
- Chop chervil fairly finely and stir it into homemade mayonnaise (p.159), with a little grated lemon zest – lovely with crab or other seafood.
- Stir at the last minute into a bowl of just-boiled new potatoes.
- Add chervil to just-cooked carrots, along with a knob of unsalted butter, a squeeze of lemon and lots of pepper. Serve as they are or blitz into a buttery purée.
- Make a simple salad of cooked, dressed Puy lentils, crumbled goat's cheese and quartered cherry tomatoes. Toss lots of chervil through it, and finish off with a bit more on top.
- **Chervil soup** (p.170)

- **Chervil and lemon zest mayonnaise** (p.159)
- **Béarnaise sauce** (p.160)
- **Simple herb salad** (p.175)
- **Crab and broad bean salad** (p.176)
- **Herb omelette** (p.182)

How to grow

Given that there's not much point mucking about with chervil in piddly quantities, it's more economical to grow lots of it from seed, sowing two or three times through the year, than to buy loads of plants.

In early spring or autumn, sow chervil in plug trays or guttering (see p.33), then, once the seedlings look robust, transfer them to a bed or large pots in a lightly shaded spot outdoors. Rich, moisture-retaining soil is ideal. In warm weather, sow it straight into the ground – the seedlings prefer not to be moved.

To encourage constant new leafy growth, keep harvesting chervil, cutting any flowering stems right back, and watering well. Too much sun and too little water can make it flower quickly, then you lose the leaves. In a sheltered position, chervil should give leaves all through the winter.

Chives *Allium schoenoprasum* 'Corsican White'

Chives *Allium schoenoprasum*

PLANT GROUP	Hardy perennial
HARVEST	April–October

This is not a herb I would ever want to be without, and it's immeasurably better when freshly snipped. The true flavour of chives is really quite punchy, a deep allium hit – but it fades incredibly quickly, so doesn't survive well when packaged and chilled. A pot of chives on your windowsill will stand you in good stead for all manner of salady, sandwichy applications. But if you can stretch to a lovely wild-haired clump or two growing in the garden, you'll be even better off.

One of the great things about growing your own chives is having the opportunity to use the flowers (see below). I wouldn't want to eat a whole one – a strange and overpowering mouthful that would be. But if you pinch out the little flowerlets with your fingertips, you have a handful of tiny oniony taste-bombs.

In the kitchen

Harvest your chives by cropping them close to the earth. To chop them, use a very sharp, heavy knife or scissors (often easier), holding the chives together in a bundle on your chopping board (or in your hand if using scissors) and starting at the base. Chives are best used raw or very lightly cooked. I like them in an omelette or with scrambled eggs, but they really come into their own in salads. Combined with mayonnaise, oil or any kind of vinaigrette, they enliven and enhance lettuces and greens, potatoes, chicken, fish, eggs, beans, tomatoes, other alliums, squashes… the list goes on.

- Tiny pinched-out chive flowerlets are wonderful scattered on salads, savoury tarts or pizzas, in sandwich fillings, or used to finish a soup.
- For a lovely supper, bake some potatoes, then scoop out the soft flesh. Mash it with a knob of butter, some scraps of ham or cooked bacon and lots of snipped chives and/or chive flowers. Season with salt and pepper then pack back into the potato skins and return to the oven until crisp.
- For a delicious smoked mackerel and chive pâté, blitz 250g skinned, de-boned hot-smoked mackerel in a processor with 1 tsp English mustard, 2 tbsp crème fraîche, 2–3 tbsp snipped chives, some salt, pepper and lemon juice. Very good on oatcakes or brown toast.
- To make the simplest of chive sauces, just stir lots of the chopped herb into warmed crème fraîche. Season with salt, pepper and a squeeze of lemon and serve with fish or chicken and simply cooked veg.

Chives in flower

- **Chive mayonnaise** (p.159)
- **Simple herb salad** (p.175)
- **Herb omelette** (p.182)

How to grow

You will probably find it easiest to buy baby chive plants or divide established ones, but you can grow this herb from seed. It needs warmth to germinate so start it off in spring in plug trays on a warm windowsill or in a heated greenhouse.

Once planted out, chives aren't overly fussy but prefer a rich, moist soil and plenty of sun. It's a good idea to prepare the ground with compost or manure before planting.

Once chives begin to flower, the stems harden and their flavour diminishes so you need to remove the flowering stems to get optimum tender chivey growth. My approach is to cut flowering stems right down at the base, then use some of the flowers. Standard chives have purple flowers but you can get very pretty white and variegated varieties too. Once the flowers are coming thick and fast, or you've used up most of the clump, cut it right back, almost to the ground. Sprinkle a little earth over the plant, water it well and you should get a thriving second crop; repeat and you'll get a third or even fourth, taking you right through to autumn. Allow the last of the leaves to die back naturally – these will feed the bulbs underground. Chives grow well in pots but keep watering.

You get the best flavour from one- or two-year-old plants, so replace regularly. You can divide the roots of existing plants by carefully digging them up in spring or autumn, pulling the bulb cluster apart and replanting.

Chives are good companion plants. Their scent deters carrot fly and, like other alliums, they are a useful partner for roses, helping to protect them from both greenfly and fungal diseases.

Relatives

Garlic chives (*Allium tuberosum*) are delicious flat-leaved, white-flowered relatives of standard chives. You can use them in much the same way, and they contribute a subtly more garlicky savour. If you grow any, make sure you let at least some of them flower. They are larger and more statuesque than ordinary chives and their beautiful white blooms – lots of little ones clustered together into one gorgeous umbel – are absolutely fantastic to eat. If you can bear to remove them from the garden, scatter them on salads, just-cooked pizza or roasted red peppers, or use them in an omelette (see p.182).

Coriander *Coriandrum sativum*

PLANT GROUP	Hardy annual
HARVEST	Leaves: May–September Seeds: September–October

This pretty, delicate, lacy herb, which is also known as cilantro, has a unique character yet it's incredibly versatile and very widely used. That hard-to-define flavour is sweet, astringent, citrusy, cleansing and somehow perfumed, all at the same time. Cooks have been adding coriander to dishes for thousands of years and its dominion is broad. It is, as the wonderful vegetarian cookery writer Nadine Abensur writes, part of 'the joys of almost all cooking outside Europe'. You'll find it used widely in so many cuisines, including Indian, Thai, Chinese, Portuguese, North African, Middle Eastern and Mexican, and within these you'll discover how deliciously well it partners spices, garlic, ginger and, above all, chilli – the cooling, fragrant foil to the fire.

In the kitchen

Coriander is a deeply aromatic herb that can give enormous character to a dish. It's best used very fresh, and in quantity. Some recipes – most notably curries, where it is often added in huge handfuls – call for coriander to be added during cooking, but the flavour does dissipate. It is most often added at the end of cooking, or sprinkled on generously before serving. You can add the more tender parts of the stalks to dishes as well as the leaves, but they do need to be chopped finely.

If you are among those who really don't enjoy the flavour of coriander, then basil or mint, or a combination of the two, can be successful alternatives.

- **Chermoula** Based around coriander, chilli and garlic, this fabulous rich and spicy North African sauce is traditionally served with fish but it's also delicious with chicken, lamb and grilled or roasted vegetables. Or you can serve it as a side dip to a mezze-style spread of salads and breads, or add a swirl to a dish of houmous. Either serve it raw or add to a cooked dish. To make chermoula, finely chop 2 garlic cloves on a large board. Finely chop 1 deseeded green chilli and add to the garlic. Add the leaves from a large bunch of coriander and a slightly smaller bunch of flat-leaf parsley. Now chop together as finely as you can (see p.18). Transfer to a bowl and stir in 1 tsp sweet smoked paprika, 1 tsp ground cumin, the juice and zest of ½ lemon and enough olive oil to make a thick paste (around 150ml). Season with salt, pepper and a pinch of sugar.

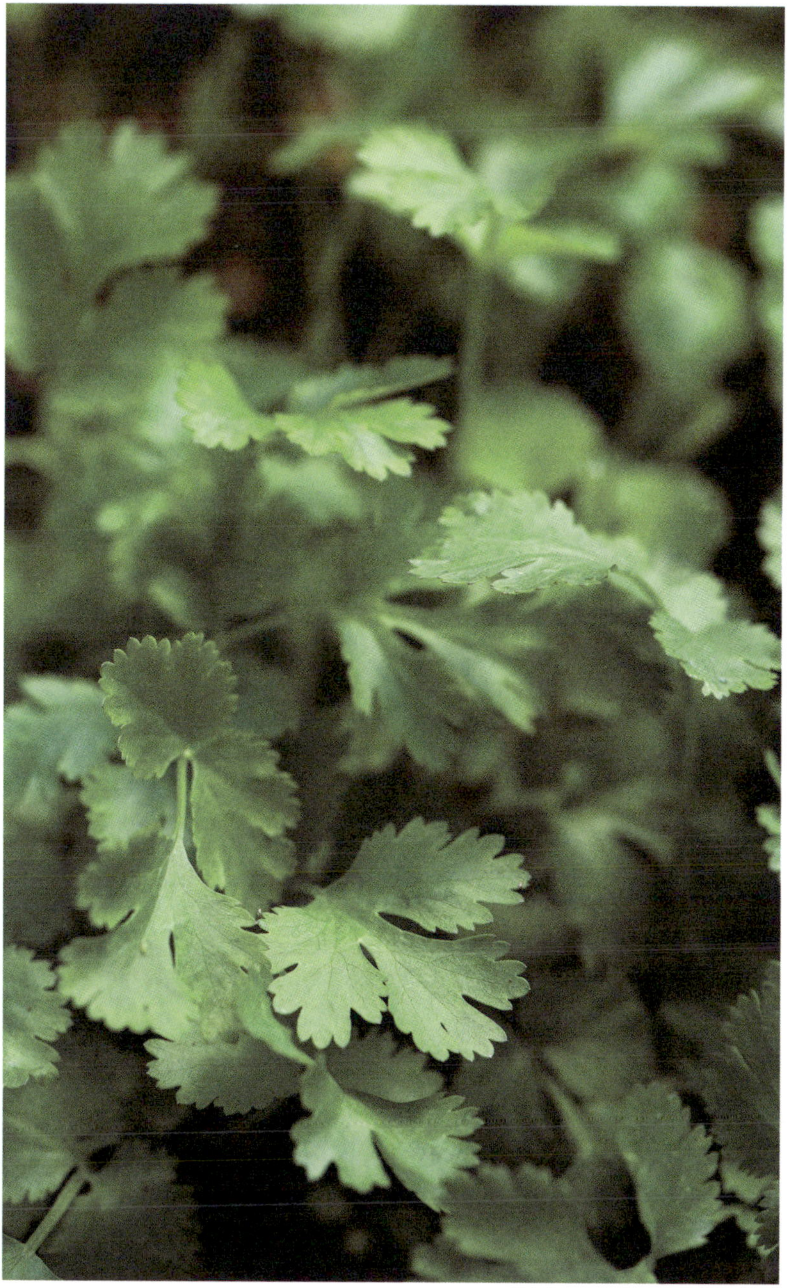

Coriander seedlings

- Add at the last minute to laksas and noodle soups – keep the leaves whole so they can float, flower-like, in the broth.
- Use coriander in homemade Thai curry pastes. Even if you 'cheat' and use a good ready-made curry paste (which I frequently do), a generous snowfall of fresh chopped coriander will finish the dish very nicely.
- Coriander is essential in guacamole.
- For a lovely simple salsa, chop about 250g tomatoes (green tomatoes or tomatilloes if you have them, though red are fine too). Toss lightly with a deseeded and finely chopped green chilli, a chopped large bunch of coriander, 1 tbsp olive oil, the juice and grated zest of ½ lime and a good pinch each of salt and sugar. This is also very good if you add snipped chives or little chive flowerlets. Delicious with burgers or alongside a chilli.
- Coriander is brilliant in rice or noodle salads with other big flavours, such as lime juice, garlic and toasted cumin seeds.
- Coriander seed has a wonderful warm spice flavour, quite different from the leaves. If you grow your own, you can use the seed when it is still green and fresh – roughly crush and add to curries, stews or dressings. The dried seed has countless uses, from curries and tagines to preserves and cakes. It is usually included in proprietary 'mixed spice' blends too.
- **Herby chicken noodle salad** (p.179)
- **Herb noodle soup** (p.173)

How to grow

As a fast grower that you're likely to want to use in quantity, this is a herb to raise from seed. Sow directly into the growing site as it dislikes being moved. It grows well in a container too, but choose a fairly deep one to accommodate the tap root.

Coriander can go from a mass of lush leaves to a leggy, flowery, seedy thing in an alarmingly short space of time. To keep it leafy and kitchen-friendly, let it see some sun but not too much – if grown in a heat-trap, it may seed quickly. Give it lightish, well-drained soil but plenty of water – don't let the soil dry out. And, most importantly, keep cutting the leaves. Even with these provisos, it will still run to seed relatively quickly. Sow successionally from April/May onwards to guarantee a good supply of this lovely herb all through summer and into the autumn.

Don't chuck away your seedy plants: the seeds are all part of coriander's appeal. When they are still just fat green berries, they have the most amazing fresh spice flavour. Alternatively, leave them on the plant until dry and beige, and they can be harvested and stored in the same way as other herb seeds, such as caraway (see p.57).

Coriander is one herb that responds very well to the 'micro-leafing' approach (see p.33) and this means you can enjoy its flavour without worrying about the whole bolting/going to seed issue.

Dill *Anethum graveolens*

PLANT GROUP	Hardy annual
HARVEST	Leaves: May–September Seeds: September–October

Pungent, fresh, aniseedy, this is an assertive herb but one that's easy to fall in love with. In looks, taste and application, it has something in common with fennel, but is by no means the same, being rather more penetrating and astringent.

In the kitchen

Dill doesn't respond well to long cooking but is fabulous raw and can stand up to really big flavours such as smoked fish, beetroot, mustard and onions. It's quite a deep, lingering taste and you don't necessarily need a huge amount of it, but, nevertheless, it can be effective if used in large quantities.

- Use scissors to snip dill over almost any fish dish before serving.
- Dill is lovely tossed with just-cooked broad beans or peas along with a snippet of unsalted butter.
- Stir lots of chopped dill into a mustardy mayonnaise (see p.159) to serve with green salads, beetroot, cucumber, eggs, fish or chicken.
- For a tasty canapé, mix 100g cream cheese or mild soft goat's cheese with 1 tbsp chopped dill, 2 tsp rinsed baby capers, a squeeze of lemon juice and plenty of pepper. Spread thickly on squares of rye bread and top with a curl of smoked trout. Or use the combination as a sandwich filling.
- For a cucumber salad, peel 1 large cucumber, halve lengthways, scoop out the seeds and slice thickly. Toss with 1 tsp cider vinegar, 1 tbsp rapeseed or olive oil, a pinch each of salt, sugar and pepper and 1 tbsp chopped dill.
- Dill seed has a warm anise-tinged flavour and is a traditional pickling spice.
- **Potato salad with dill and pickled red onion** (p.181)
- **Carrot soup with dill and mustard** (p.169)

How to grow

Dill is easy to grow from seed and is best sown directly into the ground or a pot as it doesn't like being moved. Sow several times during the spring and summer for a good supply. Site well away from any fennel plants as the two can cross-pollinate.

Dill favours a light, well-drained soil in sun or partial shade. Keep it well watered, remove any flower stems and keep cutting the leaves. Once the plant has gone to seed (it will, eventually), let the seeds ripen, then harvest as for caraway (see p.57).

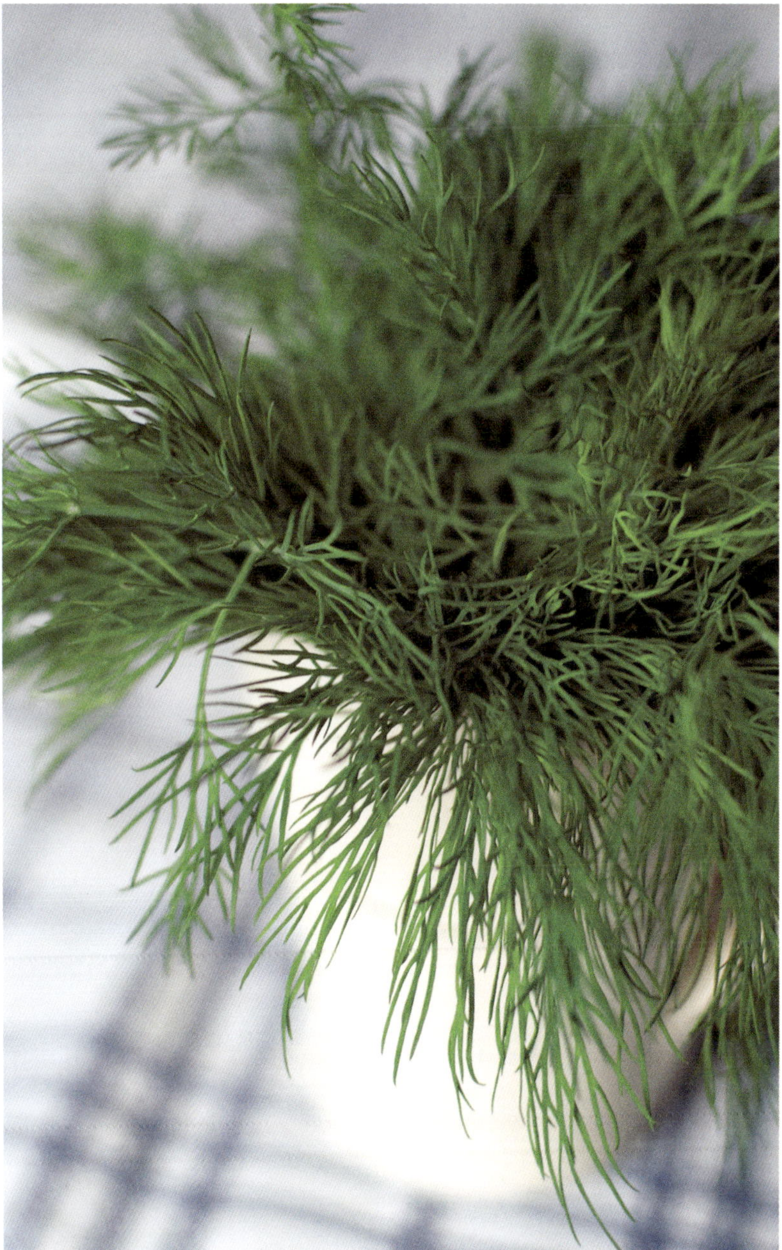

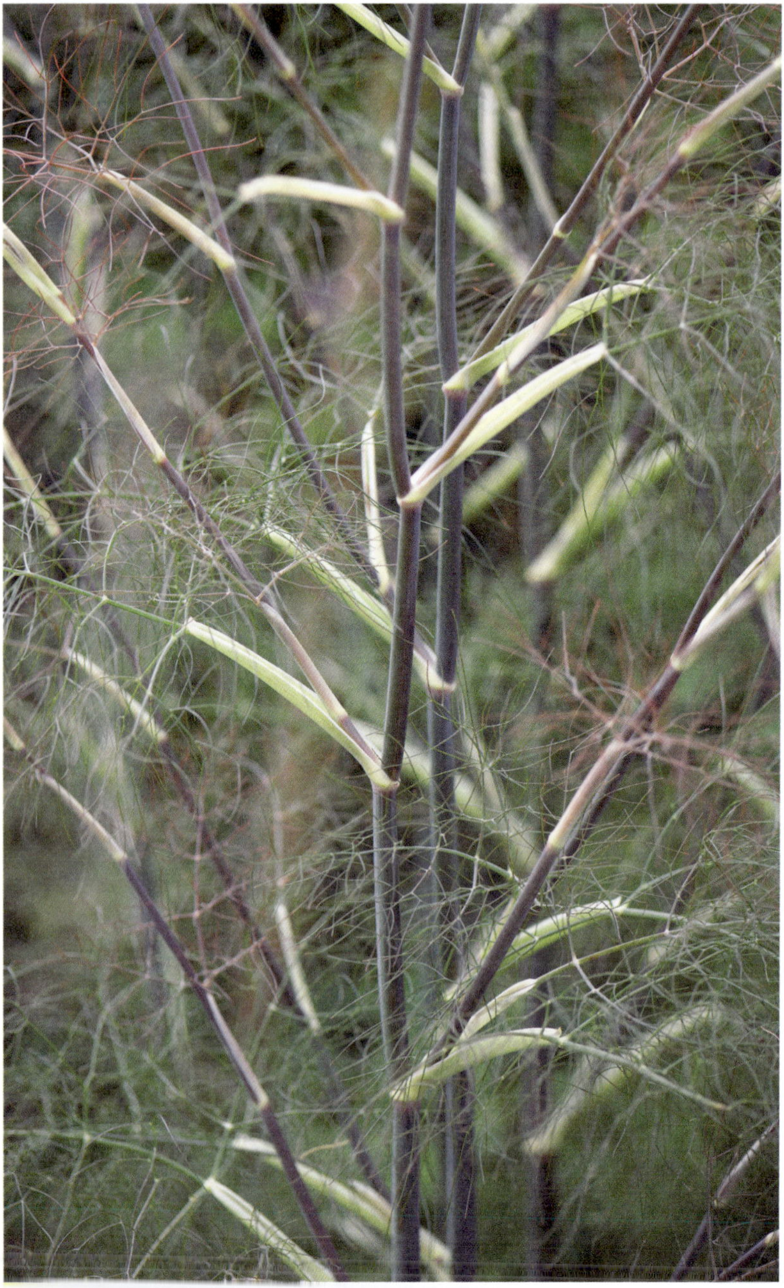

Fennel *Foeniculum vulgare*

PLANT GROUP	Hardy perennial
HARVEST	Leaves: May–September Seeds: September–October

Fennel herb, which is available in green and bronze varieties, is not the same as the tasty fat white bulb of the vegetable Florence fennel (*Foeniculum vulgare* var. *dulce*). You can grow Florence fennel and still take advantage of the leafy fronds – often if you buy a bulb it will have a few fronds still attached – but the flavour is not as punchy. The taste of a young, freshly picked frond of fennel herb is out of this world – intensely sweet and aniseedy, fragrant, almost floral.

Fennel seeds are also a delicious and unique seasoning, different from and more spicy than the leaves. They are easy to buy but, if you have a plant or two, you will be able to collect the ripe seeds yourself (see overleaf).

In the kitchen

The sharp, sweet aniseed tang of fennel is lovely with rich foods such as lamb, pork, creamy vegetable soups or oil-rich breads. Fennel fronds can take a bit of heat but not too much – raw or lightly cooked is best. I always think it's worth chopping fennel pretty fine. Eating a whole frond, with its almost hair-like texture, is vaguely disconcerting. I find the flavour of green fennel to be slightly better than that of the bronze variety.

Fennel seeds are a whole other ingredient – much stronger and more penetrating than the leaf. Whether fresh and green or mature and dried, they can be roughly crushed or completely ground and make a marvellous addition to all sorts of spice mixes, to sauces, soups and dressings, to breads and some sweet dishes too.

- It's almost a cliché to serve fennel with fish – but, like most clichés, it has become one for a very good reason. Stuff fennel fronds generously inside fish before baking or, if you've got some juices from frying or roasting fish, enrich them with a little cream or butter and stir in lots of finely chopped fennel. Add fennel to a homemade fish stock or court bouillon (a delicately flavoured liquid often used for poaching fish).
- Chopped fennel works very well with tomatoes, too, and in a potato and/or beetroot salad.
- Combine chopped fennel with soured cream or full-fat yoghurt, season well with salt and pepper and use alongside houmous and other dips, or mashed into a hot baked potato.

Fennel seeds

- Fennel herb always combines well with fennel bulb. Use the herb to enhance a salad of very finely sliced raw fennel bulb, dressed with olive oil, lemon juice, salt and pepper. Finish off with goat's cheese.
- For a lovely simple starter, cook some 'soft hard-boiled' eggs (7 minutes' boiling for a large egg at room temperature), peel and cut open while still warm. Pop a knob of butter on the yolks, add a grinding of pepper and scatter with lots of chopped fresh fennel and a few baby capers.
- **Double fennel braise** (p.207)
- **Fennel seed bread** (p.211)
- **Pasta with sardines and fennel** (p.187)
- **Pork with fennel and rosemary** (p.191)
- **Fennel fudge** (p.230)

How to grow

Fennel herb, whether green or bronze, is a tall, handsome plant that will give structure and height to any herb or veg patch. It grows readily from seed – sow in early spring indoors, or outside a bit later on. (Keep it away from dill as the two may cross-pollinate.) Because of its stature, fennel is not one for indoor growing, though I have raised it successfully in a large, deep pot. It likes sun and rich, well-drained soil.

As with all herbs, not allowing it to flower will encourage lots of leafy growth. However, since the seeds of fennel are one of its great attractions, do leave some flowers, or keep a plant or two just for seed production.

Around September time, the fennel flowers will have faded and been replaced by umbels of plump little green berries. You can eat the seeds when still young and juicy like this – just chewing a few fresh from the plant is a lovely way to freshen the breath. But if you want to gather and store the dry seeds, wait until they have faded on the plant from bright green berries to little delicately striped, dun-coloured pellets. Don't let them get to the point where they turn black. If you nibble one it should give you a real shot of fresh, pungent fennely flavour, without mustiness. Cut the seed heads in the middle of the day when there is no moisture on them. Keep the heads in a bowl or a paper bag, in a dry place, for a week or two, then just pull the seeds off. Store them in an airtight jar in a cool, dark cupboard.

Cut back the spent stalks of your fennel plants in the winter. The plant will die right down and then reappear in spring. It self-seeds enthusiastically. Replace plants after 3 or 4 years.

Garlic prepared for roasting

Garlic *Allium sativum*

PLANT GROUP	Hardy perennial grown as an annual
HARVEST	Green garlic: May–June Mature garlic: July–August

There must be very few cooks who don't use garlic regularly: it is an almost indispensable flavouring with impressive versatility. Depending on the way you prepare and cook it, garlic can be a subtle and almost undetectable seasoning, or a loud-and-proud shout of flavour that dominates a dish, and pretty much anything in between.

It's not just mature garlic cloves you can use in the kitchen. Garlic 'scapes' are slender, curling flower stems taken from the young growing plant. You only get them with slightly less common 'hardneck' types of garlic, and they are hard to find unless you grow your own. However, if you do, they're very good when lightly cooked or used in a dressing or pesto.

Immature bulbs, or 'green garlic', harvested in spring, also make good eating. Tender and plump, the cloves within them are small and mild and can be used whole – sliced up rather like an onion, skin and all. Sweat them down as you would onions or leeks. They are very good in soups.

Mature garlic bulbs, with firm cloves and thin, papery skin, are at their peak shortly after harvesting, following a brief period of drying. As garlic is now imported from all over the world, you can usually find it in this peak condition at most times of the year. Garlic grown in Britain tends to be at its best during late summer.

As garlic ages in storage, the cloves start to soften and shrink a little and soft green shoots begin to germinate at their hearts. Garlic like this is no longer at its best and is heading towards bitterness. You can discard any incipient baby shoots from the middle of the cloves and still use the rest of them, but garlic that is clearly shooting is not good for eating.

Storing garlic in the fridge isn't advised because chilling affects the flavour, making it less intense. In addition, garlic stored at very low temperatures may start shooting (it's cold weather that stimulates growth in the plant). Really, you want to store garlic in a cool, dry place, with some air circulation around the bulbs, so hanging it in a cool larder would be ideal. If you don't have these conditions, then brief storage in the fridge is probably preferable to a warm and/or humid kitchen.

In the kitchen

Your kitchen knife calls the shots when it comes to getting the right results from garlic. For basic peeling, crushing and chopping techniques, see p.20.

- **Crushed garlic** Crushing garlic breaks down the cell membranes and releases compounds that deliver garlicky flavour at its most intense and ferocious. Hot and strong it may be, but this is a wonderful flavouring ingredient. Use it to add piquancy to a mayonnaise or dressing, to beat into butter, or to add to any dish where you want a powerful and persistent garlic flavour.
- **Chopped garlic** Chop garlic finely and you'll get a significant garlicky flavour, without the heat and pungency of the crushed clove. Chopped garlic can be very good raw if it's used in small quantities and combined with other ingredients – gremolata (overleaf) is the perfect example – but it is most often cooked. I like to add finely chopped garlic to a pasta dish, stir-fry or soup right at the end of cooking, giving it only a minute or two's heating. This is just enough to take the sharp edge off the garlic without diminishing its penetrating flavour. Chopped garlic added at the beginning of cooking will lend a more gentle but nonetheless notable sweet pungent note to a dish.
- **Slivered garlic** Finely slivered garlic always seems to me a little more subtle than chopped. It's particularly good gently infused in hot oil before trickling on a pizza or freshly baked focaccia, or in a dish such as pasta aglio e olio (see overleaf).
- **Whole roasted garlic** Keep garlic cloves whole and unpeeled and roast them until soft, and you have a whole different flavour again: sweet, mellow and mild. To roast a bulb whole, cut off the tip of the bulb to just expose the cloves, then put it on a piece of foil, trickle with olive or rapeseed oil and seal the foil loosely. Bake at 190°C/Gas mark 5 for about 45 minutes, or until the cloves are really soft. Alternatively, release the cloves from the bulb and toss them with chopped veg before roasting. Soft roasted garlic is good smeared on bruschetta or blended into soups or just squeezed from its skin and smudged all over the veg or meat you've roasted it with.

Always remember that garlic, which is rich in sugars, burns very easily. Put it in a pan on too high a heat and you'll get a brown, bitter result in no time. You need to cook it gently and protect it. This can be done by adding salt to draw the juice out of the garlic, helping it sweat rather than sear, or by combining it with other ingredients, such as onions, cream or tomatoes, whose liquid will stop it burning.

There are a million and one recipes that use garlic as a crucial supporting player. There are rather fewer in which it is the star of the show but these include some real corkers – do try chicken with forty cloves of garlic (p.196). There are also everyday uses that I return to time and again.

Green garlic

- **Gremolata** This is simply finely chopped raw garlic, parsley and lemon zest, mixed together. Say, 1 clove of garlic, the zest of 1 lemon and 1 heaped tbsp chopped parsley. The mix is traditionally strewn over the Italian dish of osso bucco (braised veal shanks). However, it can be good on almost any rich meat dish, as well as risottos, pasta dishes, fish, soups and roasted vegetables.
- **Garlic butter** Combine 250g softened unsalted butter with 3 finely crushed garlic cloves, 1 heaped tbsp finely chopped parsley, the finely grated zest of 1 lemon, and some salt and pepper. This gives you enough butter to make garlic bread with 1 large baguette, or to stuff under the skin of a large chicken before roasting, with a bit left over. You can also freeze it in a log, wrapped in cling film, to slice into thick discs for melting on grilled fish, steak or mushrooms – I think it's best with at least a little cooking, however, to soften the garlic a touch.
- **Chapon** This is simply a stale chunk of bread, rubbed all over with a cut clove of garlic, then tossed into a green salad. It imparts a delicate garlicky savour to the leaves. You're not meant to eat the actual chapon.
- **Pasta aglio e olio** This is one of the best answers I've ever come across to the old it's-late-and-I'm-hungry-and-there's-no-food-in-the-house dilemma. Put some pasta on to boil (spaghetti or linguine is best). Very gently warm 2–3 tbsp good olive oil in a small pan. Add 1–2 finely slivered cloves of garlic and either some chopped fresh red chilli or a good pinch of dried chilli flakes. Warm through so the garlic cooks a little but doesn't go beyond the palest yellow colour. Drain the cooked pasta, toss it in this garlicky oil, add some salt and pepper and dust with grated Parmesan. Pure satisfaction.
- **Bruschetta** This is toast at its finest. Toast a thick slice of good sourdough or other robust country-style bread. Cut a clove of garlic in half and rub the cut sides all over the hot rough surface of the bread. Trickle generously with extra virgin olive oil and sprinkle with salt. On its own, this is a lovely breakfast or snack, but of course you can top it with anything from fresh tomatoes to wilted kale, a poached egg or shaved Parmesan, grilled sardines or a thousand other things.
- **Skordalia** (p.165)
- **Parsley mayonnaise** (p.159)
- **Basil and parsley pesto** (p.166)
- **Salmoriglio sauce** (p.165)
- **Baked chicken with forty cloves of garlic** (p.196)
- **Pork with fennel and rosemary** (p.191)
- **White beans with winter herbs** (p.204)

How to grow

Is it worth growing garlic when it's so readily available, and when most of us use it in large quantities? I'd say yes, if you've got a bit of room, and not least for the pure satisfaction of it. Growing your own enables you to try different varieties, to get your garlic very fresh, and gives you access to tender green garlic. And, if you choose a 'hardneck' variety, you'll be able to have tasty garlic scapes (see below).

In theory, you could simply take a few sprouting cloves from shop-bought garlic and plonk them in the soil. They would probably grow, but they would be prone to viruses. Varieties specifically bred for garden growing in our climate, such as 'Cristo', 'Albigensian Wight' or 'Solent Wight', will give you much better results. They prefer a sunny site and rich, well-drained soil; work in compost and also sand beforehand if you can. If you have an acid soil, below pH 6.5, you may have trouble growing garlic.

Most garlic is planted in autumn or early winter, although you can also find spring-planted varieties. After preparing your soil, press individual cloves, pointy end up, 5–10cm down into the soil, spacing them about 15cm apart. Garlic likes cold temperatures, and it actually needs several weeks below 10°C after planting if it is to produce lots of new cloves (if it doesn't get cold enough, you'll just get one clove). Keep away the weeds and water your garlic well, but don't let it sit in waterlogged soil.

You can grow garlic in containers if they are deep, and this is one way to ensure good drainage. I've had some success growing garlic in old chimney pots, placed directly on the soil and filled with organic compost and a little sand.

'Hardneck' garlic varieties produce a long, tender flower stalk called a scape ('softneck' varieties don't usually flower). The scape should be removed once it starts to curl round on itself and before the top starts to open, so the plant can direct all its energy into its bulb. Scapes are delicious lightly cooked.

The immature 'green garlic' bulbs can be harvested in spring or early summer when the leaves are still green. Mature garlic is ready to harvest in the summer once its leaves have turned yellow – usually July but later for spring-planted types. The garlic is ready to be used straight away or you can dry it, ideally just by leaving it outside for a few days in warm, sunny weather; it can then be stored for several months in a cool, dry, well-ventilated place.

Incidentally, garlic is an excellent companion plant for carrots as its scent helps to ward off carrot fly. It's also a traditional companion to roses because, according to legend, it is a sure-fire way to deter greenfly. Many anecdotal sources corroborate this, while the charming *Old Wives' Lore for Gardeners*, published in the 1970s, goes so far as to call garlic 'the systemic insecticide to end all others'.

Horseradish *Armoracia rusticana*

PLANT GROUP	Hardy perennial
HARVEST	From September of the first year onwards

Either you love the hot thwack of horseradish or you don't. If, like me, you do, it's worth finding a good source. Many greengrocers and farm shops now sell fat lengths of this gnarled root, usually in the colder months of the year, and it keeps well, tightly wrapped, in the fridge. It's then ready to use – either in quantity as the main player in a sauce or dressing, or in smaller pinches as a fiery seasoning. This magnificently foliated plant is easy to cultivate and grows readily in the wild – swathes of plumey horseradish can be seen populating roadsides and waste ground all over the country. It is easily recognisable from its glossy leaves, which are like giant ruffled dock leaves. To be extra sure, crush some of the leaf between your fingers and you will get a faint whiff of that horseradish scent. You should know that digging up the root of any wild plant is illegal, unless you have the permission of the landowner. Personally, I imagine few landowners would begrudge you a root or two of this prolific weed, as long as you don't damage anything else.

In the kitchen

When grated, horseradish releases pungent fumes which burn the nose and wet the eyes. As with chilli and pepper and mustard, that irritation and its accompanying endorphin high is fundamental to the delicious horseradish experience. The fumes (thiocyanites, if you want to know) are highly volatile, however, and soon lost. That's why freshly grated horseradish, mixed into an acidic stabilising medium, always tastes better than any that's been grated and stored. My basic preparation of horseradish is to peel a small section of root, grate it (I use a fine Microplane grater) and immediately combine it with enough lemon juice to make a damp (but not wet) mixture. You can also use vinegar to stabilise the grated root but I think lemon juice allows the horseradish flavour to shine a little more. Use straight away or keep, covered, in the fridge for a day or two.

- Blend a little freshly grated 'lemon-ed' horseradish root with crème fraîche and a pinch of sugar. Use this simple horseradish cream as a finishing touch to a soup – beetroot, carrot or pumpkin especially. It's also excellent as a dressing for, say, smoked mackerel and a heap of watercress.
- To make a dressing for coleslaw, add some grated horseradish to plain full-fat yoghurt, thin down with a little olive oil and season to taste. This is particularly nice with a mixture of shredded red cabbage and grated carrot.

- Stir some freshly grated horseradish root into softened unsalted butter with an extra squeeze of lemon juice, chopped parsley or chives and some seasoning. Use on baked or plain boiled potatoes.
- **Horseradish sauce** (p.161)

How to grow

Horseradish is generally propagated from the root, not seed. You can either buy a young specimen or replant a section of root from a mature plant.

Spring is the ideal time to plant, but pretty much any bit of horseradish root, once put in the ground and given some water, will grow into a new plant. It's not fussy, but to maximise your chances of a long, strong root, give it moist, deep, rich soil and some sun. If you want to put it in a container, it needs to be a deep one.

The flavour becomes stronger as it grows and is really eye-watering around midwinter of its first year but you should be able to find useful amounts of root on a first-year plant from early autumn onwards.

Horseradish is an invasive plant. Pull up what you don't need or want – and be prepared to do this often, once it's taken hold. If there's a significant amount of root attached, so much the better – a great gift for a culinary friend.

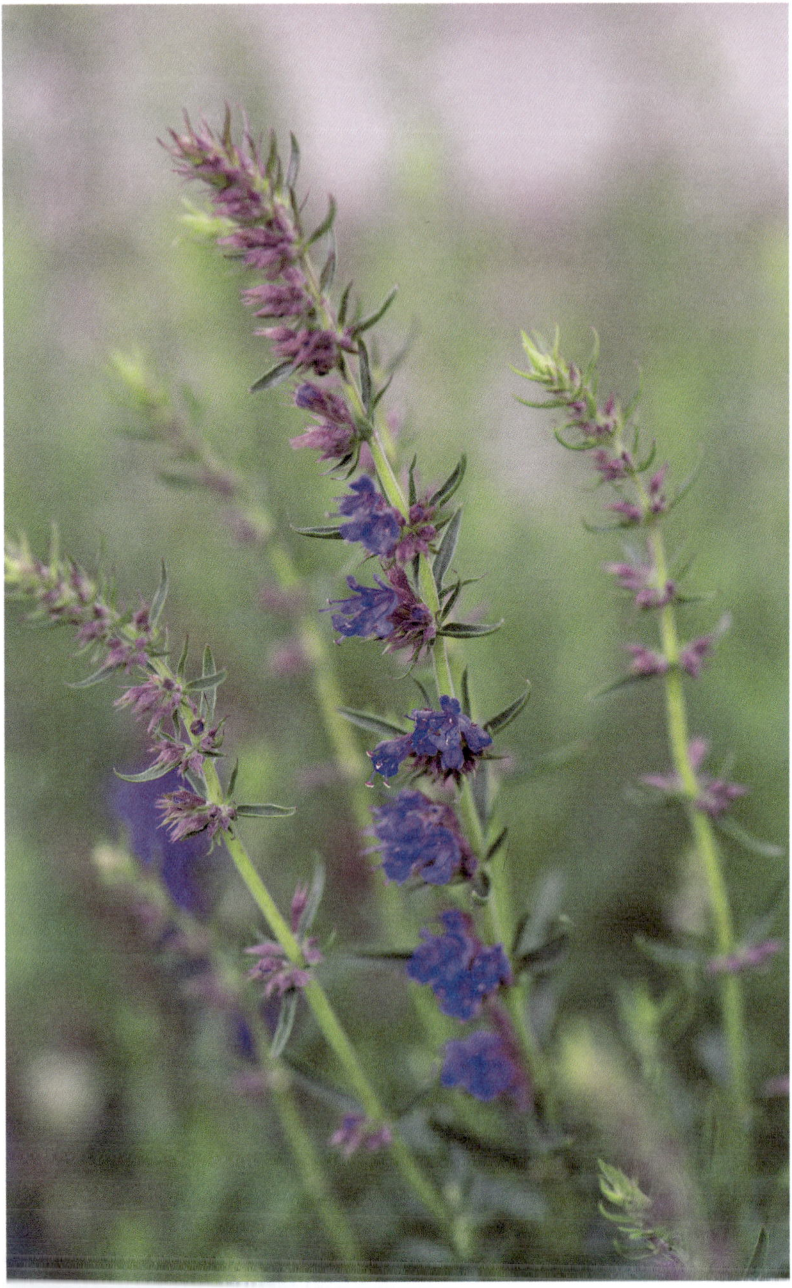

Hyssop *Hyssopus officinalis*

PLANT GROUP	Hardy perennial
HARVEST	All year round

This has become one of my favourite herbs. It's just so pretty in the garden, its narrow, dark green leaves complemented by either blue, white or pink flowers, to which you will often find a bee or two happily attached. The flavour comprises a sour, bitter lemonish tang over a deep rosemary-like resinousness. The result is quite bitter if you eat it neat, but this herb is incredibly delicious when mingled with creamy, rich or salty ingredients. Do not confuse it with anise hyssop (p.43), which is completely different.

In the kitchen

Use hyssop almost as you would lemon juice or black pepper, as a seasoning and a foil to rich, unctuous foods. Add it fairly sparingly and experiment with eating it raw and cooked.

- I love hyssop with cheese. Scatter it whole or coarsely chopped over fried halloumi or a mozzarella salad.
- A sprinkling of hyssop used to finish a buttery, garlicky mushroom pasta dish cuts the richness very nicely.
- Add the chopped leaves to rich meaty stews and soups. The technique of adding some at the beginning of cooking and some at the end is worthwhile to get the full benefit of its complex flavour.
- Hyssop is a natural choice for homemade burgers, sausages or stuffings – try substituting it for sage in a sage and onion stuffing (p.129).
- **Baked white fish with a hyssop and orange crust** (p.188)

How to grow

Hyssop is not difficult to grow from seed. It can be sown indoors from March, or straight into the ground in late spring. If you're impatient, like me, buy an established young plant. As a native of the Mediterranean, hyssop desires a sunny, well-drained location on light soil. Try it in a pot that can be moved to the garden's hottest spots or sited on a windowsill.

It should be cut back hard in the spring to promote new growth and the flowers deadheaded in the summer to encourage fresh leaves. When flowering, it's a good plant for bees. So far, mine has surprised me with its hardiness and vigour, still valiantly offering some snippets of leaf even in bitter winter weather.

Lavender *Lavandula*

PLANT GROUP	Hardy evergreen perennial (some varieties half-hardy)
HARVEST	May–July

One of my earliest memories is of my grandmother showing me how to crush purple lavender flowerheads in my small fist to release their deep, warm scent. To this day, I can't pass a lavender bush without reaching out to grasp a stem or two, and the sight of this elegant silver-stemmed plant, nodding in the breeze, is not something I'd want to be without in my garden. That beautiful scent attracts bees and butterflies, while a few cut stems brought into the house in a jug or jam jar always look incredibly pretty. But lavender is a valuable culinary herb too, with a warm, aromatic and subtly floral flavour.

Like many herbs, lavender contains camphor among its aromatic compounds. Camphor is not a particularly pleasant flavour so, for cooking, you want a lavender with low levels. To ensure this, choose a *Lavandula angustifolia* variety and harvest the leaves and flower buds in the spring and early summer when the flavour is more delicate. *Angustifolia* have a more fragrant, sweeter taste than some of the alternative species, such as the bract-topped French lavender (*Lavandula stoechas*), which can be harsh. 'Hidcote' is a classic, hardy and very widely available cultivar of *Lavandula angustifolia*, and you can't really go wrong with it, but there are many others, such as 'Munstead' and 'Alba', which has white flowers.

There is an exception to the *angustifolia* rule: the hybrid *Lavandula* x *intermedia* 'Provence' is rated by some as the best of all for cooking. You will need to go to a specialist grower to find it (see Directory, p.248). For myself, I'd say it certainly gives very good results, but it doesn't put *angustifolia* in the shade.

In the kitchen

Use lavender leaves for cooking, as well as flowers. Both can be dried but I always use fresh. Commercially dried flowers are available to use when lavender is out of season, but the flavour and scent are never as sweet and fragrant as fresh. Dried lavender is also pretty pungent, so halve the quantity. Ideally, cook with lavender during the spring and early summer, choosing tender leaves and flower buds which are developed and just tinged with colour, but not fully opened. I have used fresh lavender leaves well into the autumn, but the flavour is definitely a little less fine.

- Stir 1 tbsp chopped fresh lavender into a plain cake mixture. This is particularly nice used to make fairy cakes. Ice with a simple white glacé icing, then top with a few lavender buds, marigold petals or borage flowers.

Lavender *Lavandula angustifolia* 'Munstead'

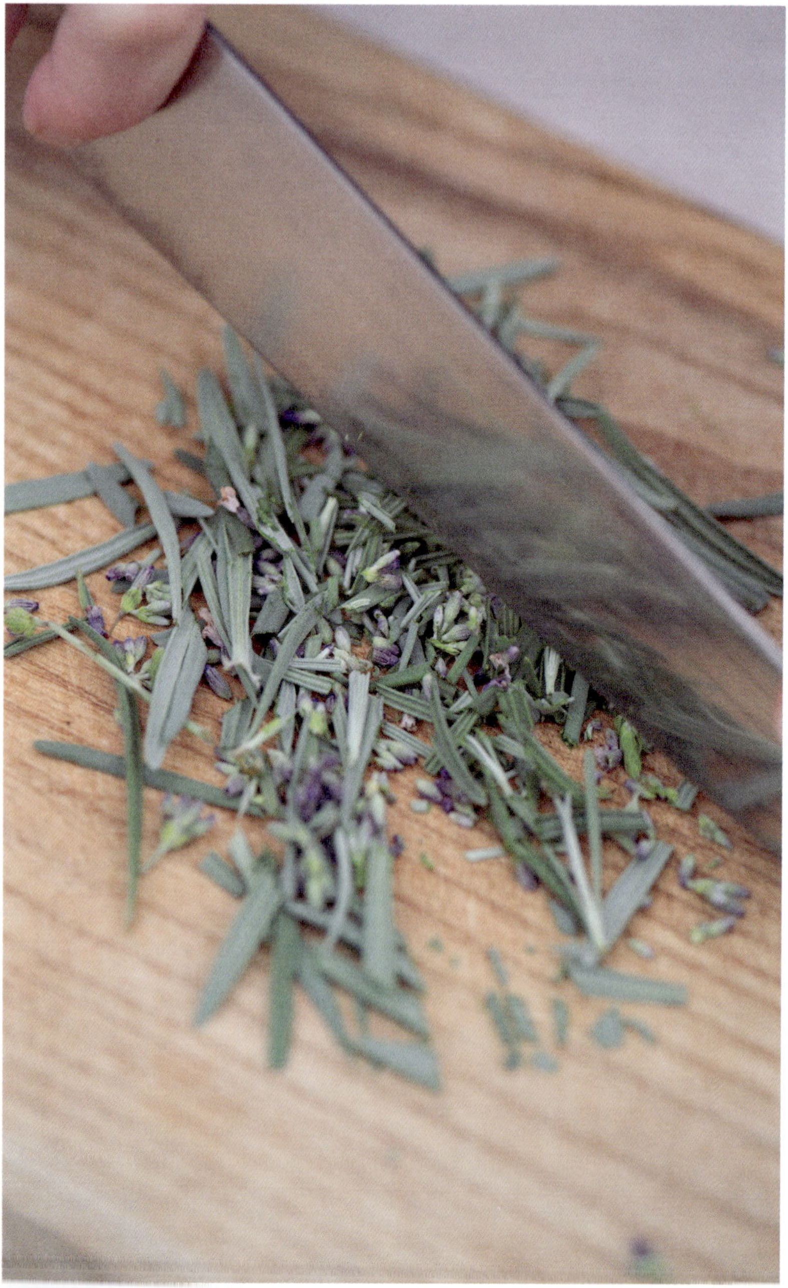

- To make a lavender-scented syrup, put 150g caster sugar and 150ml water in a saucepan. Heat gently, stirring often, until the sugar has dissolved, then increase the heat. Add 1–2 tbsp fresh lavender buds and/or chopped leaves. Once simmering, cook gently for 5 minutes. Remove from the heat, cool and strain before using. This scented syrup is lovely with peaches, raspberries or strawberries, or try a delicate trickle on vanilla ice cream. It will keep in the fridge for at least a week.
- I love a little sprig of lavender combined with mint in a fresh herb tea.
- **Loin of lamb with lavender and lemon thyme** (p.194)
- **Lemon and lavender biscuits** (p.225)
- **Herb ice cream or custard** (p.219)
- **Apple herb jelly** (p.232)

How to grow

There are many different species of lavender and they often do not 'come true' from seed, which means the new plant may not turn out to be the same as its parent. I would buy a young plant – ideally from a specialist grower (see Directory, p.248). You can also take cuttings from established lavenders (see p.34).

A native of the Mediterranean, lavender will thrive best in a sunny, open place, on light free-draining soil. Wet winters are bad news, as lavender tends not to do well in cold waterlogged soil. Making sure it is as well drained as possible is the best precaution, and digging sand or grit into your patch before planting is almost certainly a good idea unless you already have a very sandy soil. Lavender also grows well in a container.

To keep a lavender plant relatively neat and tidy, with plenty of new growth and not too much woodiness, it needs regular cutting. It's best to do this in spring and summer and if you're harvesting regularly, you'll effectively be trimming it anyway. Late in the summer, after flowering, give it a more wholesale cut-back, reducing the size of the plant by anything up to 50 per cent. Don't cut into the old wood and leave some green shoots on the plant, as it needs these to help it regenerate. You will find marvellous gnarled old lavender bushes in some gardens, their twisted woody stems bristling incongruously with the new year's green growth. But it's a good idea to replace the plant completely every 3–5 years, in order to give yourself plenty of fresh tender foliage and flowers.

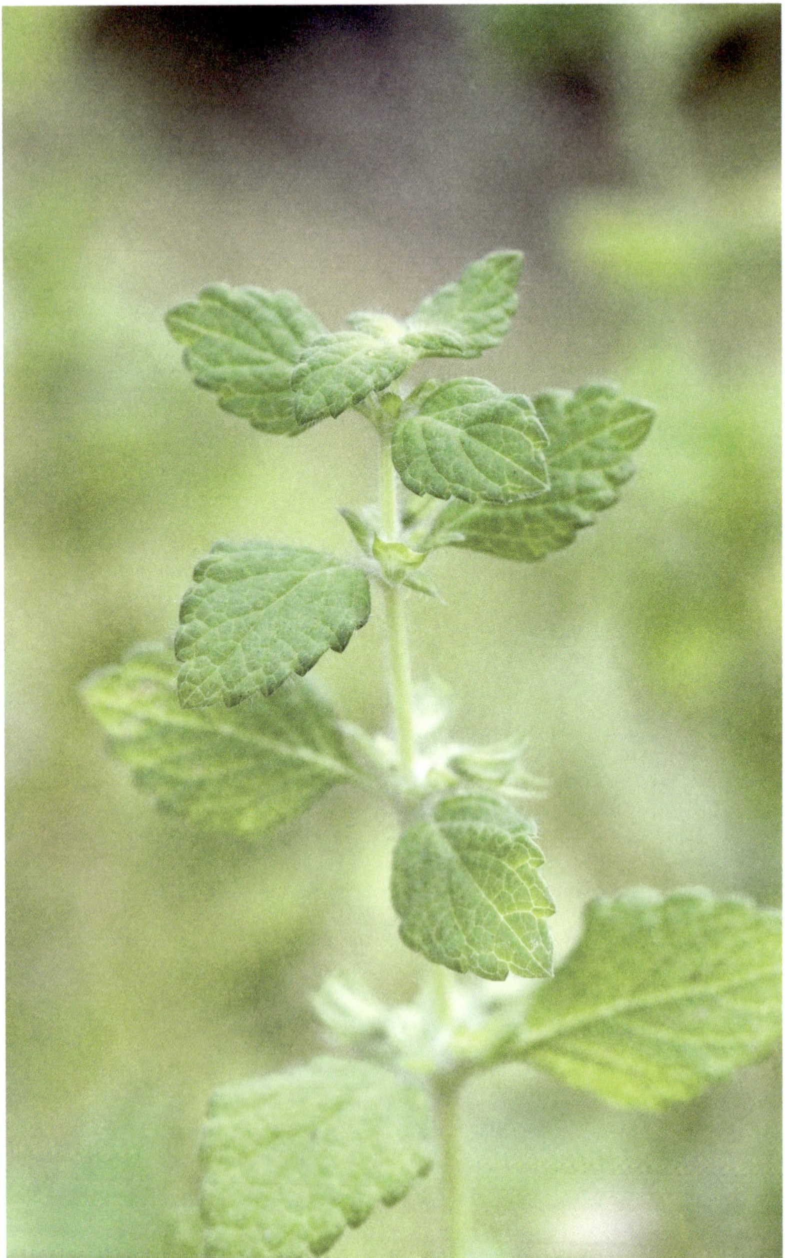

Lemon balm *Melissa officinalis*

PLANT GROUP	Hardy perennial
HARVEST	April–September

Also sometimes called melissa, this is one of the first herbs I ever grew and I always like to have some in the garden. It's such an easy, generous plant, sending up its gold-green leaves year after year, whether you tend it carefully or not, and offering a mild, sweet lemony flavour.

In the kitchen
This is a gently flavoured creature – much more delicate than other lemony herbs, such as lemon thyme or lemon verbena. I turn to it most often to perfume and lift a cup of tea – either on its own or combined with black tea – but you can add it to dishes as well. Using the herb raw or infused is the way to go, rather than subjecting it to direct heat.

- You can use lemon balm raw in salads – fruit or vegetable – finely shredded for a delicious hint of lemony flavour. The young leaf tips make a beautiful edible garnish.
- Chop lemon balm leaves with other fairly delicate herbs such as parsley and fennel to make a light summery mix for an omelette, or to finish a soup.
- Try adding a generous quantity of finely chopped lemon balm leaves to a sponge cake batter.

How to grow
Lemon balm grows easily and vigorously and is invasive. Plant it in a corner and, by next year, it will be coming up between your paving stones halfway across the garden. For this reason, it's a good herb to grow in a pot, but make it a large one, so the plant can stretch its legs and show off its lovely foliage.

You can start it from seed in plugs. Alternatively, dig up an established melissa in spring or autumn and divide the roots to form two or three new plants to be replanted. It doesn't need much except sun and water. Cut it regularly, removing flowerheads, to keep it bushy and lush through the summer. If you leave some flowers, however, it will attract plenty of bees. Lemon balm dies right back in winter but don't worry, it will return.

Lemon verbena *Aloysia triphylla*

PLANT GROUP	Half-hardy deciduous perennial
HARVEST	May–October

With its elegant elongated leaves, lemon verbena looks rather demure but, in fact, it packs an intense punch of fragrant citrus flavour. What's more, though it's hard to believe when you first see a tender little verbena plant, it will eventually grow into a gorgeously scented, beautiful shrub – a lovely thing to have in your garden.

In the kitchen

The flavour of this herb is incomparable: intensely lemony, floral, perfumed and slightly piney. The flavour comes predominantly from a compound called citral, which is also found in lemongrass. Lemon verbena is indeed a powerfully lemony ingredient, more pungent than lemon balm or lemon thyme and an absolute gift in sweet recipes. It also has savoury applications but do go gently with it – too much can actually make a dish taste rather synthetic. Always chop lemon verbena very finely if it's to be eaten, because the leaves are very slightly tough and waxy.

- Lemon verbena is a great flavouring for a custard or ice cream (see p.219).
- A verbena syrup, made in the same way as a lavender syrup (see p.89), is delicious trickled over cakes or fruit salads.
- For verbena sugar, pound 2–3 tbsp finely chopped young lemon verbena leaves with a roughly equivalent amount of golden caster sugar using a pestle and mortar until you have a fine, pale green sugar. Sprinkle over fruit or a cheesecake. Use the sugar up quickly as the flavour will fade.
- Lemon verbena makes a lovely tea – on its own or with mint (see p.244).
- **Lemon verbena layer with raspberries** (p.220)
- **Apple herb jelly** (p.232)

How to grow

A young verbena plant will grow beautifully in a pot or, if you want to let it develop its full shrubby potential, plant it in the ground in a well-drained, sunny, sheltered place – against a south-facing wall would be ideal. In very cold weather it's a good idea to mulch it (put a thick insulating layer of compost, hay or other mulching material around the roots). If it's in a pot, you can bring it inside. It loses its leaves in winter but should come back with a vengeance in late spring or early summer. Cut it back in the autumn to encourage fresh bushy growth.

Lemon verbena is difficult to raise from seeds or cuttings in our climate.

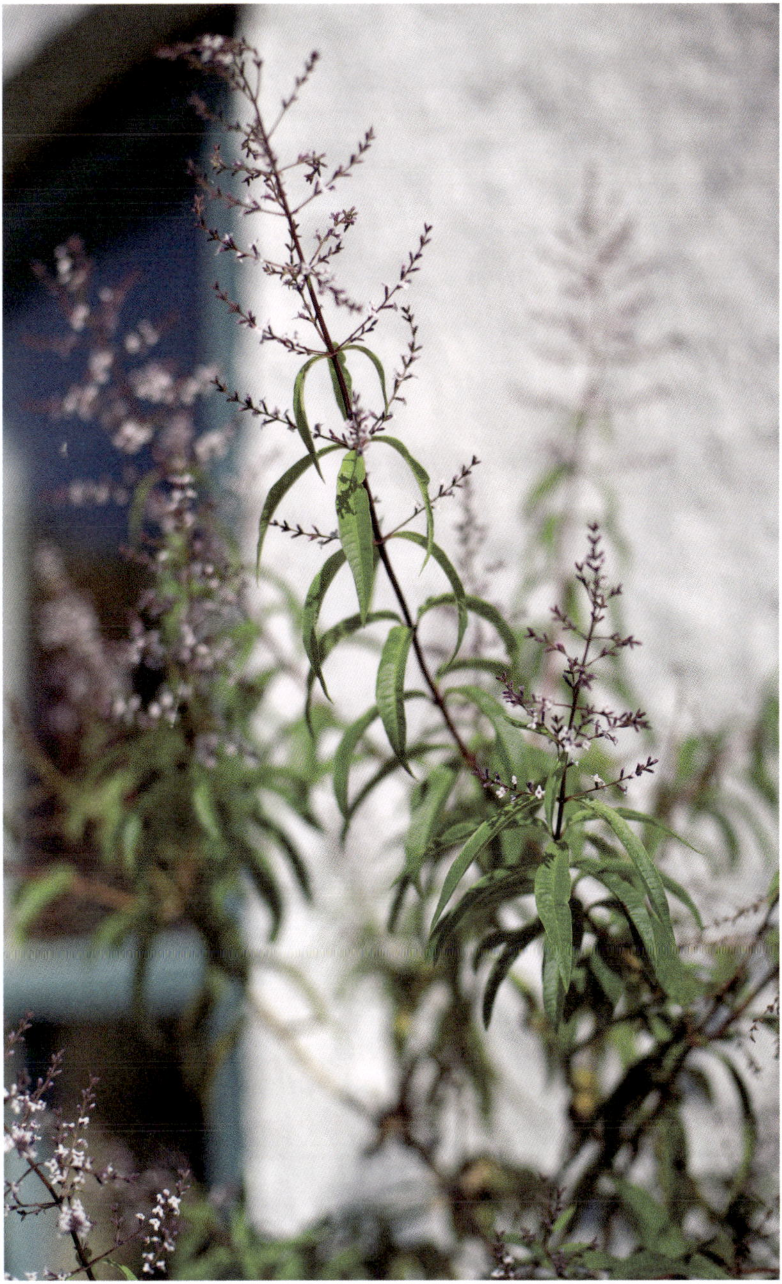

Lemongrass *Cymbopogon citrates*

PLANT GROUP	Tender perennial
HARVEST	May–October

Lemongrass is unlike any other herb – or, indeed, any other flavouring – in the sweet, pungent aromatic lift it contributes to a dish. We associate it primarily with the cooking of southeast Asia, and Thai curries in particular, but there's no reason not to exploit its perfumed lemonyness in other dishes, including soups and puddings. If you grow the herb yourself, you have the advantage of being able to use its long, slender leaves as well as its stem. The leaves are milder but share the same unique flavour and are great in a spicy soup or a tea.

In the kitchen

Finely sliced or chopped lemongrass is fantastic in curry pastes, soups and dips and it is a great companion to chilli, lime, garlic, ginger, coriander and mint. Lemongrass has a lovely tender centre, but a very tough, fibrous outer layer. To get nicely chopped lemongrass that won't stick in your teeth, you have to peel off at least three outer layers of the stem. These are too fibrous to eat, but you can add them to a soup, stock or syrup to infuse with a lemongrass flavour. Once you've got down to the heart of the stem, where it feels tender and easily sliceable, start chopping. Sometimes the yield from one stem is not very great and that's why I often use two stems when a recipe calls for one. Lemongrass stems freeze well.

- Lemongrass is a key ingredient – typically pounded with garlic, chillies, lime, ginger and coriander – in Thai curry pastes and laksa soups.
- Infusing a bashed lemongrass stem in a syrup (as for lavender syrup, see p.89) makes a fragrant drizzle for cakes or puddings, or a base for a sorbet.
- Immerse a bruised lemongrass stem in the liquid when poaching fruit such as pears.
- Try adding a bashed stem of lemongrass to rice while it's cooking.
- For a slightly more subtle flavour than you get with chopped lemongrass, you can put a whole stem, just lightly bruised to help release the flavour, into a simmering soup or curry.
- Lemongrass is great with fish. Try it in a marinade for scallops, or in crab or fish cakes.
- You can infuse lemongrass in drinks – use in herbal teas (see p.244) or in a scented lemonade (p.241).
- **Herb noodle soup** (p.173)

How to grow

Lemongrass is well worth growing because you can then exploit the leaves as well as the stem (you only get the stem if you buy it in the shops). It can be grown from seed in spring (it needs lots of warmth and takes some time to germinate – up to a month), or bought as a young plant.

However, you should be able to get a shop-bought cut stem to take root as well. Make sure there is a bit of woody base still on the stem then put it in a glass of water. Within a few weeks, it should have formed a ball of roots (see below). Plant it in a pot, keep it moist and warm and it will start to produce green leaves and new stems. Lemongrass eventually develops into a flamboyant multi-stemmed plant with a great crown of grassy leaves.

Unless you live somewhere near the Equator, this herb is best kept in a pot. It needs warmth – don't let it get below 7°C – and moisture during the spring to autumn growing season. Although lemongrass should be all right outside in high summer, growing it indoors, or in a warm greenhouse, is probably the best plan.

You can harvest both the leaves and the whole lemongrass stems, cutting them off at the base. In winter, the plant needs little water, but still plenty of warmth, and it should regenerate in spring. You can divide established clumps to create new plants.

Rooting lemongrass stems

Slicing peeled lemongrass stems

Lovage *Levisticum officinale*

PLANT GROUP	Hardy perennial
HARVEST	April–September

I love lovage and I am not alone: I know several herb-growers and cooks who rate it as one of their favourite herbs. It has the most amazing powerful, deeply savoury scent and flavour – akin to celery but more intense, more spicy, more complex. Its unique backnote can add great depth and strength to soups or stocks, and I also love it combined with eggs and cheese.

You can now buy lovage in some supermarkets as well as from more adventurous greengrocers' and farm shops. However, it's not as widely available as, say, parsley, rosemary and thyme, so you've everything to gain by raising your own. To that I must add that lovage is a vigorous grower. Over the period of a few years, it can reach over 2 metres in height and 1 metre in width, dwarfing other herbs and, indeed, you. So give it some space but enjoy its stature. You'll rarely need more than a few leaves of lovage at a time, so you can rely on even a smaller plant to provide structure and presence in your herb patch throughout the year.

In the kitchen

Lovage is often written about with a hint of warning – it certainly is very strong, and it will leave its tenacious scent on your fingers long after you've picked it. But it is a herb to be embraced, not feared. The key is to choose the younger, more tender leaves, and to use it in small amounts. Literally a couple of leaves or two added to a stock will give it weight and character, and a teaspoonful or two of chopped lovage stirred into a soup at the beginning of cooking lends an amazing depth – added at the end, it is akin to a spice.

- Very young, mild lovage leaves can be added straight to a salad.
- Finely chopped lovage adds a great flavour to a homemade burger mix.
- Wrap a wedge of Cheddar, Wensleydale or other firm, nutty cheese in a few lovage leaves, securing the package in greaseproof paper or cling film. After a few days the flavour will have subtly and deliciously permeated.
- Chopped lovage added to wilted greens, such as spinach or rocket, gives them body and richness.
- A whisper of lovage stirred into the beaten egg for an omelette or frittata is very good, especially when combined with waxy new potatoes.
- Another nice way to use lovage very subtly is to crush a few leaves and rub them around a bowl before pouring in almost any kind of veg-based soup.

- Lovage is good with parsley – use much more parsley than lovage. I really like this herb duo in an omelette (see p.182), or stirred into freshly cooked rice with sautéed onion and toasted pine nuts to make a simple sort of pilaf.
- Try finely chopped lovage in a cheese sandwich, or with cheese on toast.
- **Celery leaf and lovage soup** (p.172)
- **Beef stew with lovage** (p.192)

How to grow

You can sow lovage seeds in plugs – or directly into the garden – in the spring or summer. You can also dig up the roots of existing plants in spring, cut off pieces of root with growing shoots attached and replant these. Lovage is not overly fussy but prefers a sunny position on rich soil. Give it plenty of space as it grows quickly and expansively. You can also contain it in a reasonably sized pot.

The older the leaves, the more intense, even overpowering, the flavour. Therefore, for the cook, it's a good idea to cut the plant right back in the summer, in order to encourage new tender growth. Allow lovage to die back in the winter and it will start to send up shoots early in the spring.

Wrapping cheese in lovage leaves

Marigold *Calendula officinalis*

PLANT GROUP	Hardy annual
HARVEST	May–October

These pretty flowers are the bustling cherry-cheeked housewives of the herb garden. All good will and enthusiasm, they bring sunshine to any border or patch, offer one of the simplest and prettiest of all herb garnishes, and are hard-working companion plants to boot (see below). The name, so it goes, is a contraction of 'Mary's gold', an epithet that honours the Virgin.

You can eat both the leaves and the petals of the marigold. There's not much discernible flavour in the petals. They're pleasant enough to eat, with a delicate, sweet nuttiness when cooked, but, for me, they're all about the vibrant colour, and that's reason enough to add them to a dish. The young leaves, on the other hand, have a lovely taste – fresh and sweetish, with a peppery finish.

In the kitchen

Fresh marigold petals are just gorgeous as a garnish. Many sources will tell you that you can also infuse the petals in liquid or fat and use the golden colour to stain other foodstuffs – a sort of poor man's saffron, though without the pungent flavour. I have tried warming them in water, milk, butter and oil and can report zero success with this enterprise (although, lightly fried, they taste lovely). My petals stubbornly hang on to their colour.

- Pluck marigold petals from a freshly picked flowerhead and scatter them directly on to salads, cakes, fruity puddings – even pizzas or tarts, dips or summery soups.
- The leaves are very good in salads – go for the young, slender, tender ones.
- **Green and gold salad** (p.176)

How to grow

This is a very low-maintenance herb. Marigolds grow easily and prolifically and, though they are annuals, they will self-seed without encouragement. You can sow your own seed, of course – scattering it straight into a patch of well-drained soil in the spring. Marigolds like to soak up the sun, but aren't too fussy beyond that. Remove dead heads to prolong flowering (if you have a decent clump of marigolds, this will become an almost daily task by late summer). They make nice pot plants.

Marigolds are often used as companion plants – they deter asparagus beetle and attract predators such as hoverflies, which eat aphids. They are also attractive to blackfly, luring them away from other plants. This is unfortunate, of course, if it's the marigolds you want to use. The trick is to get rid of the blackfly before they take hold because as soon as a few take up residence they send out 'come on over, the party's started' signals to all their friends and relations. On hot, humid days, check your marigolds assiduously. Remove any blackfly you find by simply wiping them off. You can also cut away the affected part of the plant if it isn't too large. If the flies really are building up, you can spray the affected parts with a solution of horticultural soft soap (see Directory, p.249); this is not the same as detergent. The herb will still be safe to eat within a few days, as long as you wash it well first.

Relatives

Calendula officinalis is also widely known as pot marigold or common marigold. *Tagetes patula*, or French marigold, is a different species. It is not good to eat, but is prized as a companion plant, emitting a strong scent as well as a substance from the roots that deters unwelcome soil-bound creatures including nematodes and slugs. French marigolds are particularly valuable alongside potatoes and tomatoes but many gardeners rate them as one of the best all-round companions in the veg patch.

Marigold *Calendula officinalis*

Marjoram *Origanum majorana*

Marjoram and oregano
Origanum majorana; Origanum vulgare

PLANT GROUP	Half-hardy perennial; hardy perennial
HARVEST	May–October

What is the difference between marjoram and oregano? It's a question of intensity, really. Both are members of the *Origanum* genus and share similar warm, spicy flavour characteristics, but they are different species. If you buy a fresh herb labelled 'marjoram', it is likely to be *Origanum majorana*, or sweet marjoram, whereas something called 'oregano' is more likely to be *Origanum vulgare*, also called pot marjoram or wild marjoram. The former has a finer, sweeter flavour; the latter is more pungent and earthy.

Generally, marjoram is considered culinarily superior and would perhaps be the one to choose if you wanted to grow just one *Origanum* species. It's also the case that the flavour of oregano can vary a lot depending on the climate and its situation. When grown in hot, dry places, it tends to be much more intense and flavourful, hence its importance in both Mediterranean and South American cooking.

In the kitchen

Think of these as two siblings. The more tender and delicate marjoram needs a little mollycoddling and is best used raw or briefly cooked, with lighter flavours such as raw tomatoes, green vegetables, cheese, chicken or fish. Big, tough oregano can look after itself, so chuck it whole or chopped into a chilli, stews, soups and slow-cooked tomato sauces.

Oregano is one of the few herbs that dries really well and a good-quality bought version can be useful (and in some cases better than the fresh herb) for hearty winter cooking with tinned tomatoes, dried beans or red meat.

- For a lovely supper dish, try spaghetti squash with marjoram. Fry a sliced garlic clove extremely gently in 2 tbsp olive or rapeseed oil for a couple of minutes. Add the broken-up flesh of a cooked spaghetti squash (or any cooked squash or pumpkin for that matter) and toss in the oil to reheat. Stir in a knob of butter, a generous tbsp chopped marjoram and plenty of salt and pepper. Serve as it is, or tossed into pasta, with lots of finely grated Parmesan sprinkled on top.
- Try these herbs roughly chopped in any tomato sauce. Add oregano at the beginning of cooking and marjoram at the end – or do both!

- Scrunch a few marjoram or oregano leaves in your fingers and rub them into the surface of some just-toasted sourdough bread. Trickle with oil and sprinkle with salt and you have a fantastic bruschetta to be eaten just as it is or topped with raw tomatoes and slivers of Parmesan.
- Baby leaves of marjoram are fantastic sprinkled on a just-baked pizza.
- Oregano takes baked mushrooms to a whole new level. Choose big open-capped mushrooms, place stalk side up in an oven dish and scatter with chopped garlic, salt and pepper and lots of the finely chopped herb. Add a little knob of butter to each mushroom. Bake at 190°C/Gas mark 5 for 15–20 minutes until tender, juicy and bubbling. Serve as a starter or a side dish. These mushrooms are very nice simply with a jacket potato and a green salad.
- **Salmoriglio sauce** (p.165)
- **Herb omelette** (p.182)

How to grow

I always tend to buy the woodier perennial herbs like these as young plants, so that the work of getting them established has already been done, but you can grow them from seed if you want to. Oregano (*Origanum vulgare*) can be sown in plugs at any time, but marjoram (*Origanum majorana*) should be sown in early spring; both need warmth to germinate. Once established, *origanum* species like sunshine and dry conditions. Marjoram is only half-hardy and is often grown as an annual, even though it is technically a perennial. It likes a chalky soil. Oregano is a tougher customer and more likely to thrive year after year as long as it's grown in a sheltered, sunny, well-drained spot. Both are good grown in pots. They should be cut back after flowering and again in the autumn.

Relatives

Greek oregano (*Origanum vulgare* subsp. *hirtum* 'Greek') is very intense and pungent and an inimitable part of Greek cooking, though it may be hard to get it to realise its true flavour potential in our climate.

There are many other varieties of *Origanum* to choose from, including golden and variegated ones, many of which are very pretty. All are worth experimenting with but it is still probably good old *Origanum majorana* that will give you the greatest culinary satisfaction. I have found the flavour of the variegated 'Gold Tip' variety particularly disappointing.

Oregano *Origanum vulgare*

Spearmint *Mentha spicata*

Mint *Mentha*

PLANT GROUP	Hardy perennial
HARVEST	April–October

The clean, refreshing sweetness of mint is welcome in a multitude of dishes, sweet and savoury, making this surely one of the most useful of all culinary herbs. It's an easy herb to buy, but the quality can be hit and miss. You may well get a lovely aromatic bunch of leaves from a supermarket or greengrocer, but sometimes it will be disappointing. I like to grow mint (it's ridiculously easy to do) so a cup of mint tea, a pepped-up fruit salad or even a summery mint pesto are never far away.

There are numerous different types of mint, but the three main species are spearmint (*Mentha spicata*), peppermint (*Mentha* x *piperita*) and applemint (*Mentha suaveolens*). As a general rule, spearmint is sweeter, peppermint is sharper, fresher, more pungent and mentholly, and applemint is milder and more subtle.

Spearmint, also known as garden mint, is the best all-rounder and is what you'll get if you buy mint from a supermarket. If you grow your own, two varieties, Moroccan mint (*Mentha spicata crispa* 'Moroccan') and Tashkent mint (*Mentha spicata* 'Tashkent'), are particularly good for fresh mint tea (see p.244). However, there are those who swear that only a peppermint such as black peppermint (*Mentha* x *piperita* 'Black Peppermint') should be used for infusions.

Peppermints can be useful for cooking too, particularly in syrups or puddings where you want quite a penetrating mint flavour. *Mentha* x *piperita* 'Berries and Cream' is lovely in a fruit salad. If you're looking to grow your own mint, and you only have space for one, I'd try Moroccan mint. But if you can get some peppermint in too, even better. Applemint, with its furry leaves, is worth growing but will tend to lose its flavour when exposed to heat, so try it chopped raw into salads.

In the kitchen

Mint is delicious in so many things, just use it as fresh as possible. Although it will give up its flavour beautifully when infused in a hot liquid, you shouldn't actually cook it for any length of time. It's also worth investigating dried mint – a traditional ingredient in many Greek, Turkish and Arabic dishes. It adds an authentic, strong and, I think, almost smoky tea-like flavour to kebabs, stuffings, salads and soups.

- You'll know that adding a stem of fresh spearmint to simmering peas or new potatoes enhances their flavour beautifully. But you can do the same with almost any vegetable, as well as lentils and beans. Adding finely chopped mint and a knob of butter to the cooked veg takes things a step further.

- For a tabbouleh salad, mix cooked bulgar wheat (or couscous, pearled spelt or barley) with a vast quantity of finely chopped parsley and a slightly less vast quantity of spearmint. Add diced tomatoes, the very best olive oil you can afford, a spritz of lemon juice and plenty of salt and pepper.
- Shredded or roughly chopped mint is a good addition to a fruit salad. It's particularly complementary to strawberries and I also love it with mango.
- If you want to experiment with dried mint, try this simple dip/sauce. Whisk together 3 tbsp plain yoghurt, 1 tbsp olive oil, 1 tsp dried mint, a pinch of dried chilli flakes, a scrap of crushed garlic and some salt and pepper. Leave for at least 30 minutes for the flavours to develop, then serve with falafel, or as a sauce for kebabs or chicken, stuffed into pita breads.
- **Mint sauce** (p.163)
- **Minty chocolate fridge cake** (p.226)
- **Minty apple mojito** (p.243)
- **Minted red berry sorbet** (p.216)
- **Apple herb jelly** (p.232)

How to grow

Mint is rarely grown from seed, as there are no guarantees of exactly what you'll get. But plants are very easy to grow – your problem is more likely to be how to stop them. Mints like plenty of water, a rich soil and partial or full sun but, even in less than perfect conditions, these are rampant and invasive growers. They are best planted in large containers (I use an old half-barrel). If planting directly into a bed, limit spread by planting your mint within a large bucket or similar container with the bottom cut out, sunk into the soil.

Keep different varieties separate as they can cross-pollinate. Water them well and feed the soil (see p.36) a few times during the growing season. Cut back to the ground in winter, feed the soil with compost or manure and your mint should flourish again the following year. It's worth replacing plants every few years.

It's easy to propagate new from old. Just dig up a section of root and cut a piece which has a young growing shoot attached. Plant this and it will soon establish a new plant. Remove any flowering stems to keep the plant bushy and tender.

Relatives

Of the many varieties, special mention must go to two other much-loved species at River Cottage. Eastern mint (*Mentha longifolia* subsp. *schimperi*) doesn't look like a mint at all, with its long, pointed silvery leaves. It is very strong and pepperminty, and good in tea. Then there is Kentucky mint (*Mentha spicata* 'Kentucky Colonel'), a very sweet, fragrant herb, which is traditionally used in a mint julep cocktail but works equally well in other drinks, such as a mojito (p.243).

Peppermint *Mentha* x *piperita* 'Berries and Cream'

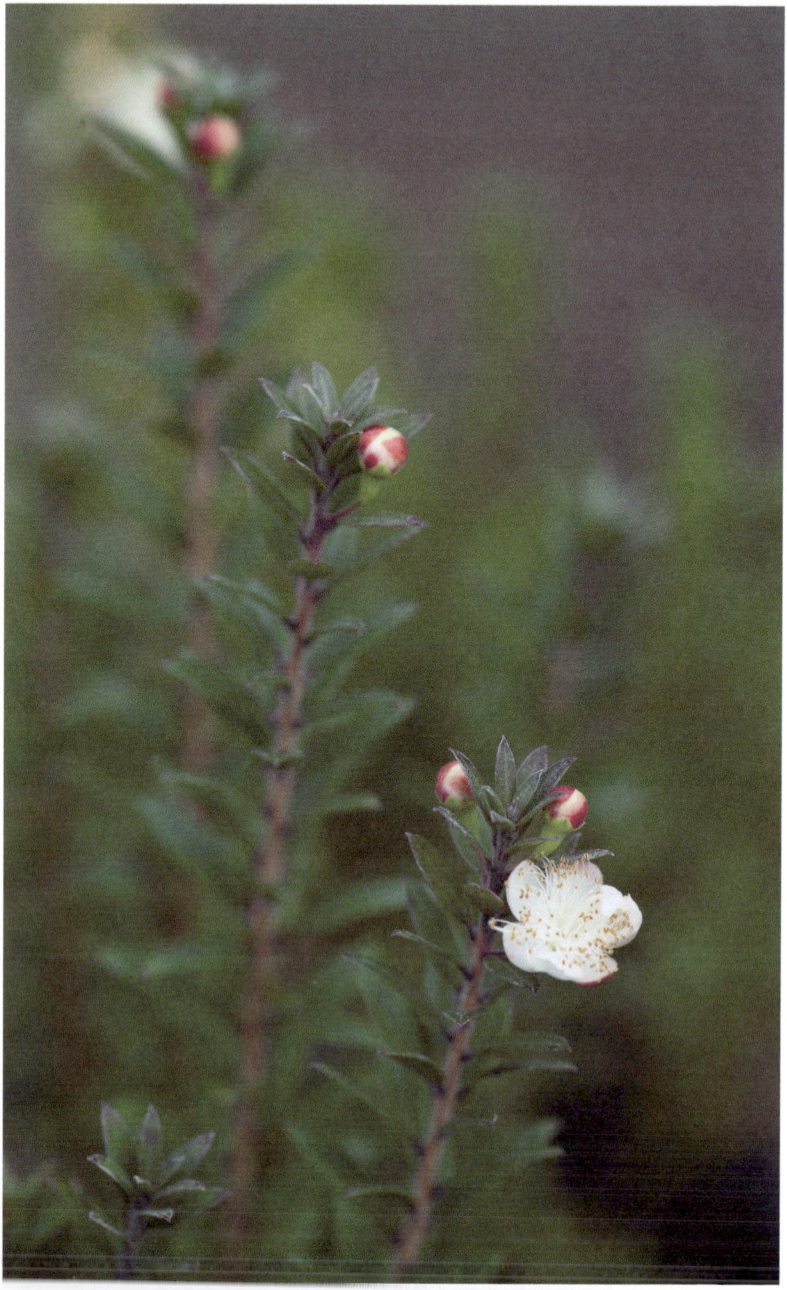

Myrtle *Myrtus communis*

PLANT GROUP	Half-hardy evergreen shrub
HARVEST	All year round

This slightly waxy-leaved herb is beautifully aromatic. Crush some leaves, take a sniff and you will find a sweet, almost orangey note which gives way to a fragrance reminiscent of both bay and juniper. The flavour has a bitter, astringent edge too. Myrtle has leaves all year round, so it's an ideal winter ingredient. It also produces berries which you can use as an alternative to juniper. In parts of the Mediterranean, branches of myrtle are traditionally thrown on cooking fires to flavour food, and you can put trimmings from the plant over barbecue coals to the same end.

Do not confuse this herb with lemon myrtle, which is a different thing altogether (an Australian tree with intensely lemony and aromatic leaves).

In the kitchen

You can use fresh myrtle leaves almost like miniature bay leaves, though the flavour is more subtle and more fugitive, so add towards the end of cooking. The leaves work well chopped or crushed too, and combined with other herbs or added to stews. The herb has a slight bitterness so err on the side of caution when using it.

- Stuff myrtle leaves into the cavity of a fish before baking, then press some more into slashes cut in the sides of the fish. You can also stuff the leaves into the cavity of a chicken or any game bird before roasting.
- Add a few chopped leaves to a beef or game stew at the end of cooking.
- The dried berries can be used in a similar way to juniper berries – lightly crushed and added to marinades for red meat.
- **Roast chicken with lemon and myrtle (p.198)**

How to grow

You have to be a little bit careful with myrtle. It really doesn't like to get too wet or too cold. Buy it as a young shrub and choose its position with care – a sheltered, sunny place is essential and free-draining soil. It can be finished off by winter rain or by heavy frost – if this is forecast, you can protect it with horticultural fleece.

Myrtle is a good herb to grow in a pot, so you can move it when necessary – though it can grow up to 3 metres given the chance.

Relatives

Myrtus communis subsp. *tarentina* is a particularly pretty small-leaved variety.

Nasturtium *Tropaeolum majus*

PLANT GROUP	Half-hardy annual
HARVEST	May–August

These are such wonderful edible plants, offering both stunning flowers that look fantastic in salads and intensely peppery green leaves to rival rocket or mizuna. You can even harvest and pickle the peppery little seed pods and eat them like capers, as Pam Corbin describes in her *River Cottage Preserves Handbook*. You can buy nasturtiums as a summer ingredient from some enterprising outlets, but they don't travel well and this is an easy plant to grow in a pot on a patio.

In the kitchen

Nasturtium leaves are very spicy and best used when young and tender, combined with something else. The flowers are a little sweeter and milder, but still peppery.

- Add the flowers at the last minute to a light salad of dressed lettuce, or scatter over more substantial salads – potato or cucumber or fennel, say.
- Toss young nasturtium leaves, shredded or torn, with sweeter salad leaves.
- You can also wilt the leaves down in a soup or even toss into a pasta dish.
- To make nasturtium leaf mayonnaise, stir 1 tbsp finely chopped nasturtium leaves (around 6 leaves) into about 150ml mayonnaise (p.159). This is great in chicken sandwiches or with cold fish.
- **Nasturtium flower dressing** (p.164)

How to grow

Nasturtiums are easy to raise from seed, in plugs or sown direct into the ground in spring. They are also sold as young plants by the trayful. Plant them in full sun – they're happy in most conditions but prefer a poor soil – and keep them well watered. They're a great choice for pots or hanging baskets, but also look lovely around the edges of a herb garden. Remove the dead heads as soon as the flowers wilt, but look out for the seed pods if you want to collect them.

There are lots of different nasturtium varieties to choose from, with all sorts of glorious colours, but I do not believe you will notice any great difference between them in terms of flavour.

The one drawback with growing nasturtiums is their tendency to attract blackfly. This makes them useful as companion plants, as they draw the little blighters away from your broad beans and cabbages, but it's pretty annoying if it's the nasturtiums themselves you want to eat. See my note on blackfly and marigolds (p.98).

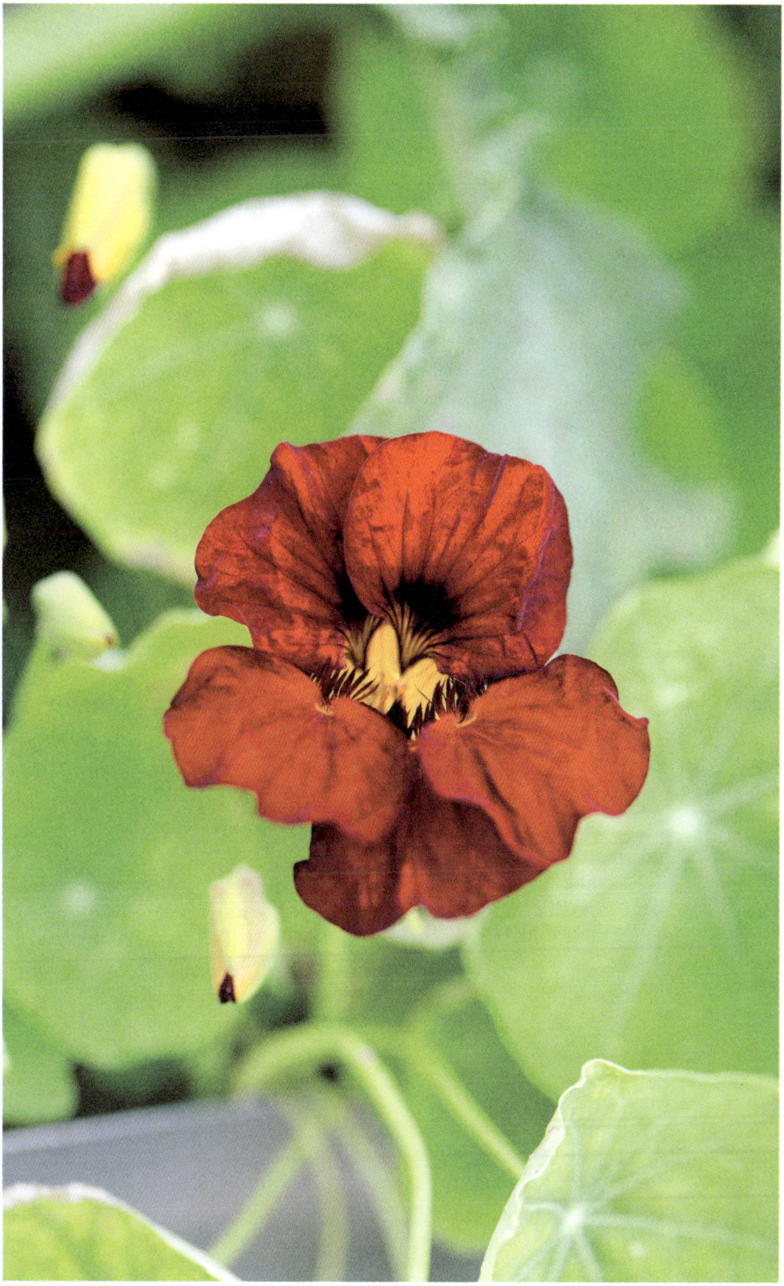

Flat-leaf parsley *Petroselinum crispum* var. *neapolitana*

Parsley, curly and flat-leaf

Petroselinum crispum; *P. crispum* var. *neapolitana*

| PLANT GROUP | Hardy biennials |
| HARVEST | All year round |

Ubiquitous and yet underrated, there's something of a paradox around parsley. It is so often used as the worst kind of garnish – one completely divorced from the dish it decorates and often uneatable. If it's not in the dish itself and you're not even going to eat it, what's the point? Parsley certainly can finish a dish beautifully, but it's much better added in such a way that it echoes or enhances the flavours, and can be consumed too. The fact is, though, this herb can be so much more than a finishing touch. It is a mild but aromatic and delicious leaf that should be used generously and broadly, one that subtly enhances everything from eggs and cheese to almost any kind of vegetable, via meat, fish and pulses. It rarely dominates a dish but pretty much always helps to define and deepen it.

In the kitchen

Flat-leaf, also known as French or Italian parsley, has a fuller, finer flavour than curly. It's the one I instinctively turn to most often, and it is far nicer to eat raw. In fact, when whole or only roughly chopped, the leaves are fantastic used in quantity in salads, or even cooked as a vegetable. I have no issue with using coarser-textured, slightly less characterful curly parsley, as long as it is well chopped. In either case, I always think of parsley as a 'cool' herb, whose subtle, grassy, clean character balances richer, sweeter flavours beautifully.

- Parsley goes brilliantly with garlic, and also lemon. Gremolata, a mix of finely chopped garlic, parsley and lemon zest, is one of my favourite finishing touches (see p.80). Leave out the lemon for a persillade – an equally handy mix that transforms simple things such as fried potatoes or lamb chops when added to the pan at the very last minute.
- Whole leaves of flat-leaf parsley combined with cold cooked white beans or Puy lentils make a fantastic salad. Dress with a vinaigrette and add something a little sharp, such as finely chopped shallot or spring onion. Tomatoes are another good addition.
- Combine chopped parsley with tarragon, chives and chervil to create the classic blend *fines herbes*, which is extremely good in omelettes (see p.182) and other egg dishes.

- Use the coarse stalks of parsley in bouquets garnis, or add to stocks.
- Flat-leaf parsley can be used as a cooked vegetable too. Use at least 50g per person and remove all but the finest stems. You can either steam it until wilted then roughly chop, or chop it first then heat a generous knob of butter with a splash of oil in a large frying pan over a medium heat and cook the parsley until dark, wilted and reduced. In either case, season with salt, pepper and a squeeze of lemon. Serve as an intensely flavoured side dish, or use to top bruschetta.
- The fresh, grassy taste of parsley is lovely with root vegetables, particularly the sweeter ones like carrots, parsnips or celeriac. Any soup, purée or salad of any of these roots is enhanced by parsley.
- You can make a very good parsley sauce by simply stirring lots of finely chopped parsley into a bay-and-onion-infused béchamel sauce. This is especially good with baked gammon.
- **Basil and parsley pesto** (p.166)

How to grow

This is a herb that's definitely worth growing, especially if you use as much of it as I do. The leaves you pick from the parsley plant in your backyard will be the freshest-tasting, most flavourful you'll ever eat. It isn't that I grow so much that I never need to buy any, but the just-picked stuff really is superb. Even a couple of good plants in a pot will provide you with abundant cutting leaves for salads. But if you put aside a good amount of space and sow your own two or three times during the year, you'll have a very decent crop.

Both types of parsley need plenty of warmth and moisture to germinate, so are best started inside. Germination is always slow. You can sow some in late summer and you should have parsley through the winter, though it may need protection with a cloche, cold frame or fleece if it's outside.

Parsley needs rich, moist soil and a mostly sunny position; you really shouldn't let the soil dry out. It also grows well in containers. As a biennial, parsley will naturally produce flowers and seeds and lose leaf quality in its second year, hence it is usually grown as an annual. Being part of the carrot family, it can attract carrot fly and it's worth planting it near onions or garlic to deter this pest.

Curly parsley *Petroselinum crispum*

Purple perilla *Perilla frutescens* var. *purpurascens*

Perilla *Perilla frutescens*

PLANT GROUP	Half-hardy annual
HARVEST	May–October

This is a 'new' herb, i.e. one not traditional in our culinary culture, but it deserves to become an old favourite. You can get green and purple varieties. I have grown the latter and loved it – its magnificent jagged purple leaves immediately draw the eye. The flavour of perilla is unique and very interesting – sweetly pungent with a distinct note of cumin.

Also known as shiso, perilla is a herb most associated with Chinese and Japanese cooking. The green variety is typically served with sushi and sashimi, as a garnish for tempura, or used in stir-fries. Purple perilla is a classic ingredient in pickled umeboshi plums.

In the kitchen

Perilla is related to basil and mint and can be used in similar ways. Green perilla has a particularly good flavour, whereas the purple variety looks fabulous. Neither variety will take well to long cooking. Instead, use the leaves raw or just wilted briefly, in generous quantities.

- Scatter shredded perilla on to noodle soups (see p.173).
- Add shredded to salads or wilt into fried vegetables.
- For a quick and delicious perilla prawn stir-fry, heat some sunflower oil in a wok over a high heat. Fry some thin strips of red pepper for a couple of minutes, then add some finely chopped garlic and chilli and fry for 30 seconds more. Throw in some peeled Atlantic prawns and stir-fry for a couple of minutes until cooked. Add 2–3 tbsp shredded perilla leaves and turn off the heat. Stir briefly until the perilla is wilted, season with salt and pepper and serve with rice or noodles.
- **Aubergines with perilla** (p.201)

How to grow

This annual herb likes sun or partial shade and rich soil. Sow it indoors in spring, or outside in early summer. Alternatively, buy young plants and site them in a reasonably sheltered, sunny spot, or put them in pots. Once the plants are established, pinching out the growing tips encourages lots of bushy leafy growth. If you keep attending to it, you should have plenty of leaves through to autumn and, with luck, it will self-seed.

Rocket, salad and wild

Eruca vesicaria subsp. *sativa*; *Diplotaxis muralis*

PLANT GROUP	Half-hardy annual; hardy perennial
HARVEST	All year round

Rocket, also known as roquette or arugula, has suffered from its own popularity. Now that it is so prevalent on menus and in supermarket salad bags, it's hardly the prized leaf it once was but forget that. It's a completely delicious and riotously peppery leaf that works equally well in small quantities as a herb or salad ingredient, or as the main player in a dish. There are two basic varieties: 'salad' rocket and the sharper-leaved, hotter-flavoured 'wild' rocket.

In the kitchen

Rocket is, undoubtedly, a fantastic salad ingredient. In a green salad to be served up as a dish in its own right, I think this peppery leaf is best combined with other leaves that offer varying tastes and textures – some crisp cos and lemony sorrel, perhaps, or a few soft, sweet butterhead lettuce leaves and some chervil or parsley. However, when rocket is accompanying something else – like a big, hearty warm salad of roasted squash and walnuts, or a garlicky aubergine parmigiana or moussaka – it needs no amelioration. In most cases, I lean towards wild rocket rather than salad rocket, simply because the flavour is hotter and richer, and the leaf more elegantly spear-like. Your own tastes may take you in the other direction.

- Rocket can be wilted down in a little oil and/or butter in the same way as spinach (and is considerably less watery). Just pop it straight into the pan on a medium-low heat and cook until it collapses. I love it cooked like this and combined with sautéed fennel or raw tomatoes and tossed into pasta.
- Wilted with a little garlic, then chopped and combined with soft goat's cheese and a touch of grated Parmesan, rocket makes a delicious filling for homemade ravioli.
- Rocket is a superb partner to bland, rich, creamy ingredients like avocado and mozzarella, to salty-sharp things such as air-dried ham or capers, and to bulky starches like potatoes, squashes or pulses. Keep these attributes in mind and you can see that the salad possibilities are endless. Try, for instance, a few curls of peppery wild rocket with sliced cold potatoes and a good trickle of extra virgin olive oil. Add some shreds of air-dried ham and finish off with a few rocket flowers.

- Add rocket to soups, instead of or as well as spinach leaves.
- Scatter rocket leaves over an omelette before folding (see p.182).
- Both types of rocket produce small, pretty flowers, which are very good to eat too. They are particularly delicious sprinkled on a pizza before serving.

How to grow

Rocket is easy to grow and if you sow your own every month or two from February to September you can create an almost year-round supply of fresh young leaves.

In early spring, start rocket seeds off in plugs. During warmer weather, choose a partly shaded spot and sow directly into the ground or a big pot. Cut the leaves as soon as they look big enough, as and when you want them, and the plants will grow more. After 2 or 3 months, the leaves will start to become tougher and more bitter and those plants can be pulled up and discarded.

In cold weather, salad rocket may need protection under a cold frame, cloche or fleece – or you can grow it in the greenhouse if you have one. Keep well watered in dry weather and cut the leaves often. Generally, the bigger and more mature rocket leaves are, the more peppery kick they have. Hot, dry conditions make the leaves more pungent too. Salad rocket has a tendency to bolt very quickly, especially in hot and dry weather, so is best for early spring or autumn sowing.

Wild rocket *Diplotaxis muralis*

Salad rocket *Eruca vesicaria sativa*

Climbing patio rose 'Nice Day'

Rose *Rosa*

PLANT GROUP	Perennial
HARVEST	June–July

The scent and flavour of roses is not to everyone's taste but don't be put off the idea of using them in your cooking just because you don't like Turkish delight. Rose petals can be used to add flavour and scent in a very subtle way and a homemade infusion or preserve will be considerably less overpowering than many commercially prepared rose waters.

Roses for use in cooking or preserving must be deeply, headily fragranced. There is a huge and frankly fairly confusing variety to choose from. I selected two hybrid tea roses: deep red 'Velvet Fragrance' and the peachy 'Chandos Beauty', simply because of their exquisite perfume. Also recommended for their fragrance are 'Falstaff' and 'Munstead Wood' (both 'English' roses) and various types of Damask rose (*Rosa damascena*) and Apothecary's rose (*Rosa gallica*). *Rosa rugosa* is another useful species – a fast-growing, low-maintenance rose with a wonderful heavy scent. When buying roses, it's worth thinking about hardiness and disease resistance as well as perfume. Some types of rose, particularly *gallica* and *rugosa* roses, tick both boxes.

The best thing, undoubtedly, is to go to a specialist rose retailer, ask their advice and then have a good sniff around. A deep colour in the petals is important if you want your rose infusion to be a pretty pink. A mixture of petals that includes just a few deep red ones should be enough to give an enticing rose shade, but pale blooms can still give exquisite scent even with a less exotic colour. My first batch of rose petal jelly, made from peach-hued roses, turned out a beautiful deep honey shade.

It's important that the roses you use for any culinary purposes are unsprayed. Finding an organic grower of roses is nigh-on impossible and, although modern varieties are generally far more disease resistant than many older ones, I think it's safe to assume that roses bought from any conventional retailer will almost certainly have been dosed with something. If you buy a rose in flower, wait for its original blooms to fade, then start harvesting the fresh unsprayed ones as they open. Alternatively, depending on when you buy your rose, you may have to wait until next year.

In the kitchen

To capture the fragrance of rose petals, you need a good number of them and you need to infuse them in hot liquid. Once heated, they will wilt into an unprepossessing brownish tangle, but do not worry – their magical perfume will pass from their collapsed cells into the surrounding solution. Strain them from their hot bath and press the spent petals hard with a wooden spoon to extract every last drop of flavour.

- Perfect rose petals make a lovely garnish on a cake or cream-topped trifle. You can use them just as they are or frost them by brushing them delicately with lightly beaten egg white, then dusting with caster sugar. Don't expect too much in the way of flavour though – petals eaten neat like this may not taste of much at all. The white 'heel', where the petal joins the plant, can be bitter.
- **Rose petal jelly** (p.234)
- **Rose elixir** (p.241), ideal for adding to drinks

How to grow

There is abundant specialist advice to be had about rose-growing and you should get good information from the grower you buy from. However, I think if you start off by looking at your rose bushes as being part of a lovely and varied herb garden, rather than as single specimens to be isolated and obsessed about, you are on the right track. Mixed planting and companion planting are at the heart of organic gardening and apply to roses as much as any other genus. This approach is one of the best ways to protect against disease.

Choose a well-drained sunny patch for your newly acquired rose plants and enrich the soil before planting with manure or compost. Early in the spring, prune them back hard. (The degree and style of pruning required depends on the type of rose, so ask when you buy.) Water roses in dry weather and be vigilant about watering if your roses are in containers. Feed them after pruning and again in the summer after their first flowering. Organic rose feeds and fertilisers are available. Deadhead regularly to encourage fresh flowers, cutting away old blooms cleanly with secateurs just above the next five-leafed stem.

Put in place a plan of defence against pests such as greenfly, with companion planting as the main plank of it. Good companion plants include garlic and other alliums that deter the dreaded aphids, and plants which attract hoverflies and insects that love to eat aphids – members of the Umbelliferae family, such as dill and fennel, as well as poppies, evening primroses and yarrow. If greenfly do appear, you can remove them by hand, though obviously this becomes an impossible task if your buds are really infested.

The fungus and moulds that sometimes attack roses are often a consequence of particular conditions – too much or too little rain, for instance. Concentrating on raising the healthiest plants you can – with an approach of mixed planting plus good pruning, watering and feeding – is the best precaution.

Rose *Rosa rugosa*

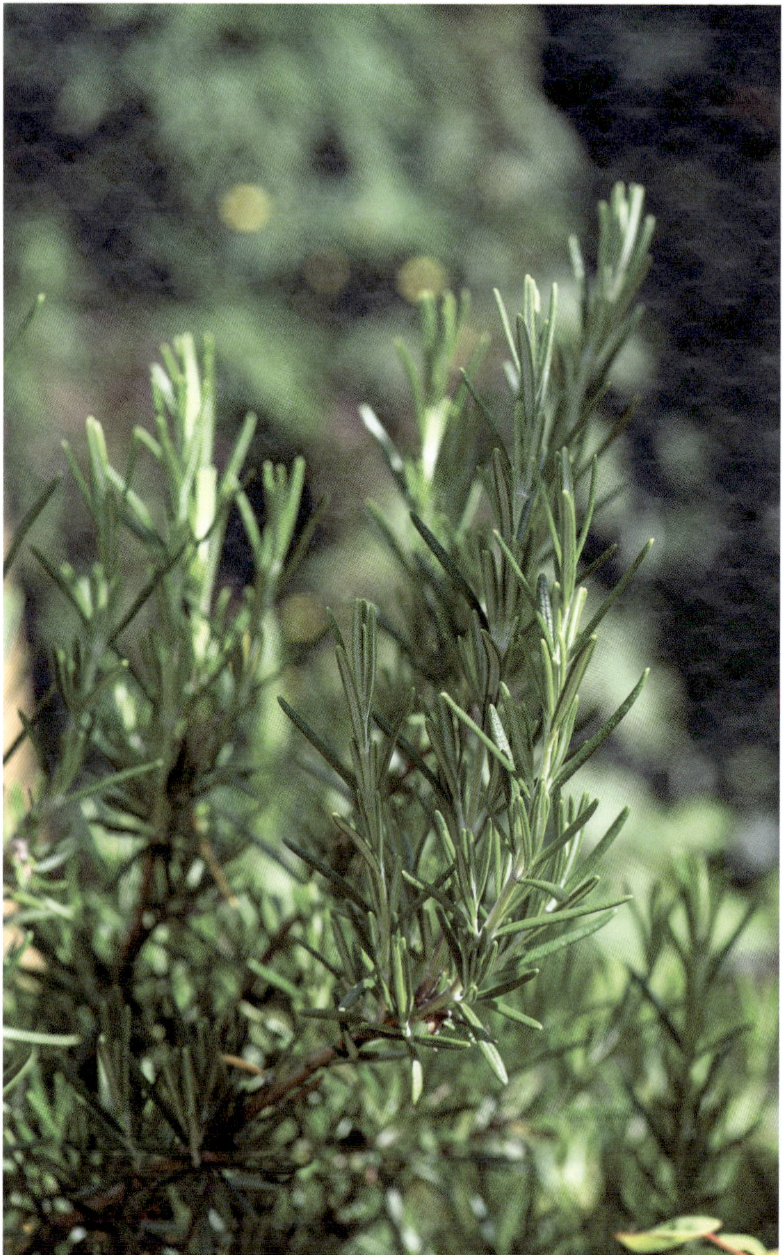

Rosemary *Rosmarinus officinalis*

PLANT GROUP	Hardy evergreen perennial
HARVEST	All year round

Rosemary, as Ophelia said, is for remembrance, and this surely is one of the most evocatively scented herbs of all. I defy anyone to take a good breath of it and not be transported to a very lovely place. Viewed by aromatherapists as stimulating and mind-clearing, the scent of rosemary is also warming, penetrating and, to my mind, healing. Burning cuttings of the herb – either on a barbecue or open fire – is one lovely way to release its scent.

Rosemary is a pretty vital culinary herb. Its warm, resinous, piney scent is enticing and the flavour more than fulfils that promise. Like bay, it is enormously versatile and complements a huge range of foods. Also like bay, it has such a powerful character that you don't need to actually eat it to get the benefit – simply infusing it in a liquid, or cooking it alongside other ingredients, can be enough.

In the kitchen

There are two basic ways to cook this herb. Firstly, as an infuser, whole sprigs can be tossed with roasting vegetables or immersed in a simmering stew or lightly crushed and added to a marinade. Secondly, you can use the flavour more directly by chopping the herb and adding it to a dish before or during cooking. The first method is obviously a little more subtle, but none the less effective. Take care with raw rosemary, as the leaves are relatively tough and there is a hint of bitterness to the herb, which is most noticeable when it is uncooked. However, when finely chopped and used judiciously, raw rosemary can be wonderful in a dressing; heating it very gently in oil is a good idea to get the flavour flowing.

- Tuck a few sprigs of rosemary inside and under a roasting chicken, or any joint of roasting meat. If you're stuffing a joint, add a stem or two to the middle before rolling up and tying.
- Stud a lamb joint with little sprigs of rosemary before roasting.
- Rosemary is also good with fish, particularly flaky white fish from the cod family. Trickle a gently infused rosemary and garlic oil over grilled or roast fillets, or add chopped rosemary to a breadcrumb crust for baked fish.
- Add large sprigs of rosemary to any tray of vegetables before roasting, particularly potatoes, pumpkin or parsnips.
- Infuse a lightly bruised stem or two of rosemary in a simmering soup, first tying it in a piece of muslin as the leaves have a tendency to break loose.

- Finely chopped rosemary is great in meaty stuffings. Here apple is a good complementary flavour, as are lemon and orange zests.
- **White beans with winter herbs (p.204)**
- **Soda bread with rosemary and sultanas (p.212)**
- **Rosemary focaccia (p.209)**
- **Rosemary and chilli oil (p.238)**
- **Pork with fennel and rosemary (p.191)**
- **Apple herb jelly (p.232)**

How to grow

Rosemary is not the easiest herb to raise from seed and cultivars will not 'come true' from seed. If you're looking to buy a rosemary plant, you can't go wrong with the basic *Rosmarinus officinalis*, which is full of that classic pungent, piney rosemary flavour. However, there are some good cultivars. 'Tuscan Blue' tends to be less woody and has a slightly more lemony, peppery tone than the standard herb. 'Miss Jessop's Upright' is a striking plant that sends its stems straight up to the sky. It's more woody than some and needs lots of cutting, but this is handy if you actually want rosemary wood – to scent your barbecue, for instance, or to form skewers for threading kebabs. It also has a quite gingery scent. 'Prostratus Group', as the name suggests, has a low-growing, almost creeping habit and is great for pots or for trailing over a wall.

Rosemary is a Mediterranean herb and all varieties like full sun, a light, sandy soil and dry conditions. Growing the plant against a south-facing wall or fence, where it can soak up the sun and is protected from wind and rain, is a good idea. However, it is a hardy evergreen and will tolerate frost, snow and cold as long as it is not sitting in waterlogged ground. You should be able to harvest rosemary right through the winter. It also grows well in containers.

Rosemary is very prone to woodiness. If left to its own devices it eventually becomes a sort of tree. It can live for 20 or 30 years and there's nothing wrong with that if you've got the space for it but you'll get more abundant and tender leaves from a young managed plant. To keep it compact, avoid woodiness and promote lots of tender new growth, you need to keep cutting back. Proceed with caution, however. Drastic cutting back can kill or damage a plant, especially if done in autumn or winter. It's best to prune little and often (which is what you will be doing, in effect, if you use it regularly in the kitchen), rather than let it get too large then slash it back in one fell swoop.

If you have an overgrown rosemary bush, try cutting it gradually during spring and summer, without going right back into the old wood, allowing fresh new growth to come through in stages. In spring, you can use tender young cuttings to start new plants (see p.34), while the woodier trimmings make a fragrant fuel.

HERB A–Z 127

Sage *Salvia officinalis*

Sage *Salvia officinalis*

PLANT GROUP	Hardy evergreen perennial
HARVEST	All year round

This pungent, spicy herb, with its slightly bitter camphorous quality, is a true stalwart. Not everyone loves it. Elizabeth David is among the many to have looked down her nose at it, and it is telling that it was used as a medicine rather than a foodstuff for centuries. But I think sage is definitely worth getting to grips with. It can be used all year round to give a deep savoury herbiness to rich and substantial dishes... it just needs to be added with a little care.

As with so many herbs, it's the mother species, the original model, that tends to give the best flavour. *Salvia officinalis*, with its velvety silver-green tongue-shaped leaves is a true friend in the kitchen, and my first choice for the garden. Variegated and fruit-scented sages, while pretty, are not so satisfactory for cooking, in my experience. You can find all sorts of 'exotics' – blackcurrant-, pineapple- or tangerine-scented sages, or species with purple, silver or red-splashed foliage. Among these, some have delicate heart-shaped leaves and, in many cases, the leaves have an astonishing scent – crush them between your fingers and you can drink in a burst of extraordinary fruity perfume. Their flowers are often gorgeous too – cerise or purple or scarlet. Any would make a wonderful addition to your garden but not necessarily to your kitchen patch.

In the kitchen

Sage is strong stuff. Eat a leaf neat and you'll find it powerful and probably unpalatable. However, when used in small quantities, cooked and combined with other strong flavours, sage really shines. You can happily add it to a dish that will be cooked for some time, knowing that its flavour will inform the whole thing.

- A simple sage and onion stuffing is fantastic with pork, duck or goose. Finely chop 2 large onions and sauté in 25g butter and a dash of oil until really soft and golden. Allow to cool, then stir in 3 tbsp chopped sage, 75g fresh white breadcrumbs and enough beaten egg (1–2 large eggs) to make a sticky mixture that will hold together in a ball. Season well then form into balls and bake at 180°C/Gas mark 4 for 20–25 minutes.
- A simple sage butter – just a few slivered leaves warmed gently in barely foaming unsalted butter – is delicious spooned over homemade ravioli or any other fresh pasta, or freshly cooked gnocchi. Add a little grated Parmesan to finish.

- Sage has an amazing affinity with squashes. Toss cubed or sliced pumpkin or squash with a few smashed garlic cloves, lots of sage leaves, some olive or rapeseed oil and plenty of salt and pepper, then roast at 190°C/Gas mark 5 for 40–60 minutes until tender and caramelised. The squash (and the crisp, almost burnt sage leaves) can be eaten just as they are, thrown into a warm salad, a risotto or pasta dish, or puréed into a soup with some stock.
- A little chopped sage is lovely in homemade burgers.
- I love a saltimbocca with sage. Get a rose veal escalope and whack it gently with a mallet or pestle until nice and thin. Wrap a slice of air-dried ham around it and use a cocktail stick to secure a couple of sage leaves to it. Season, then fry in oil and butter. Remove from the pan and deglaze with marsala or white wine. Absolutely delicious with sagey roast potatoes.
- Sage leaves, briefly fried in hot oil until crisp, make a great garnish for a soup or risotto.
- You can add sage to a bouquet garni (see p.19) for flavouring soups, stews and slow-cooked beans.
- **Apple sauce with sage** (p.163)
- **White beans with winter herbs** (p.204)
- **Apple herb jelly** (p.232)

How to grow

You can raise sage from spring-sown seed, take cuttings (see p.34) or buy young plants. Plant it out in a well-drained soil, in a sunny spot. It does well in a container, but you'll need a large one. As long as it's reasonably sheltered and the ground is not waterlogged, sage should be perfectly harvestable all year round. It's a great winter herb. My one caveat is that, in the winter, it can sometimes become overly camphorous in flavour. If this happens, wait for the new spring growth.

Sage will eventually become woody, and it's worth replacing plants every 4 or 5 years. To encourage bushy tender growth, cut it back hard in early spring, then keep cutting back the flowers through the growing season to maintain good leaf production (though it's worth letting it flower at least a little bit if you want to attract bees to your garden). Trim it back after flowering in late summer but before the cold weather.

Purple sage *Salvia officinalis* 'Purpurascens'

Salad burnet *Sanguisorba minor*

PLANT GROUP	Hardy evergreen perennial
HARVEST	All year round

This very attractive plant looks diminutive and even fragile, but is actually quite a tough customer that will stay green and give you leaves all through the winter. For that reason alone, it is a very useful addition to any herb garden. The delicate cucumber-like flavour of its small, serrated leaves also offers a nice counterpoint to the strong, piney flavours of many other perennial herbs. It becomes slightly more bitter as the leaves age and the year progresses, but pleasantly so. Whatever the time of year, a confetti fall of little burnet leaves will enliven and undeniably prettify all kinds of dishes.

In the kitchen
As the name suggests, this herb really is most at home tossed straight into a salad. I wouldn't cook it.

- Used raw and fresh, salad burnet will enhance any green salad, but is also good with sweet little cherry tomatoes, green beans or with cucumber.
- Add burnet to winter salads too; there are few flavours it will clash with. Try it with potatoes, aubergines, fennel or carrots.
- The leaves add a new dimension to sliced, lightly sugared strawberries.
- Salad burnet is also good added to cold drinks. Float some on a jug of Pimms, or use it in place of sorrel in the wine cup recipe on p.243.
- A few salad burnet leaves make a lovely garnish for a soup, whether it's a chilled summer broth or a hearty winter warmer.
- Combine salad burnet with parsley, chervil, chives and a little tarragon. Chop finely and stir into a warm white bean salad, with some rapeseed or extra virgin olive oil and a squeeze of lemon. This herb mix is also good stirred into cream cheese for sandwiches, or mayonnaise, or in an omelette.

How to grow
Sow seeds in spring into plugs, or dig up an established plant in spring or autumn and divide it to create new ones. Salad burnet's natural habitat is chalky soil, but it should grow well in any free-draining ground. It's also good in containers. It likes sun or partial shade. Salad burnet looks delicate but is in fact very hardy – just keep cutting back the flowers to encourage leafy growth, or leave some at the end of the season if you want the plant to self-seed.

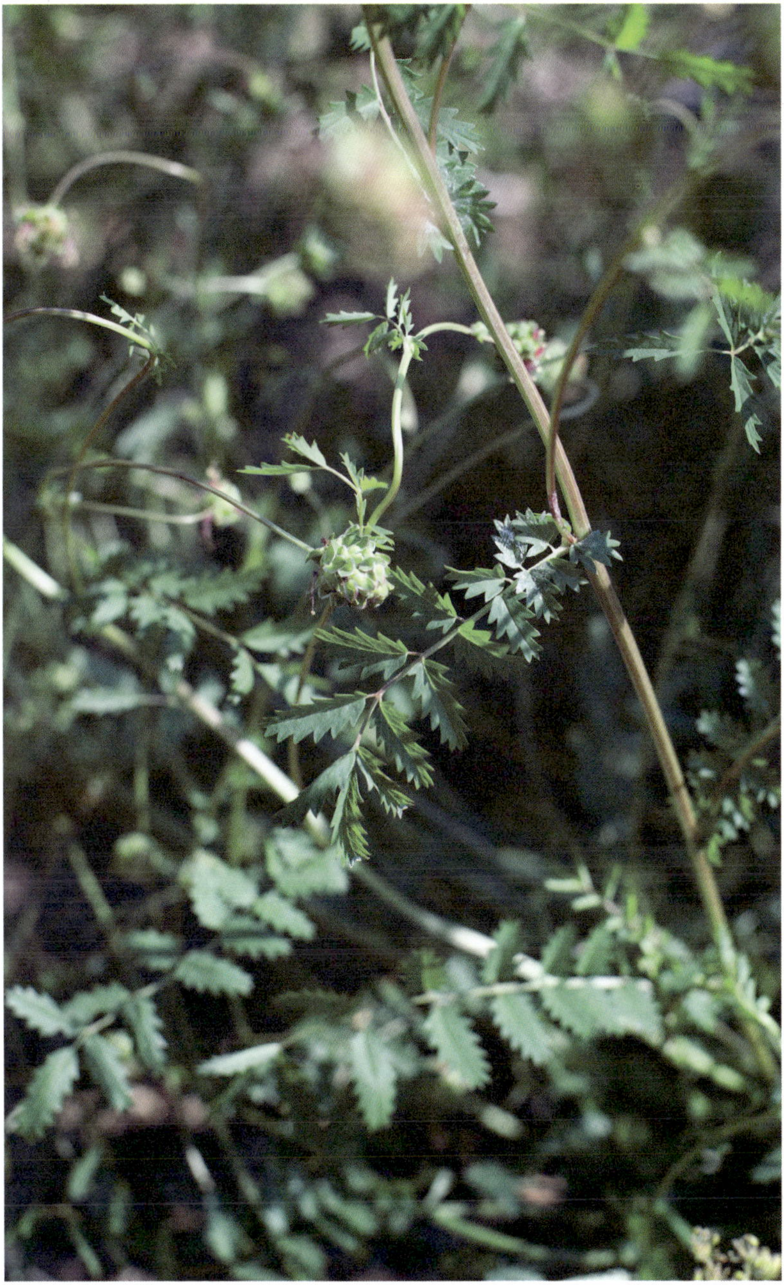

Scented geranium *Pelargonium graveolens*

Scented geranium *Pelargonium*

PLANT GROUP	Half-hardy evergreen perennial
HARVEST	All year round

I've never particularly liked the scent of conventional garden geraniums, though I love their glorious flowers. With scented geraniums, the opposite is true. Their blooms are fairly forgettable but the scent of their leaves is unbeatable. It can be used to perfume cakes, syrups, sauces and jams – almost anything where the leaf can be infused, in fact.

It's the rose- and lemon-scented geraniums which are most useful to the cook. These have particularly intense fragrances which permeate and infuse well. Good examples include 'Attar of Roses' (*Pelargonium capitatum* 'Attar of Roses') and the rosy-citrusy *Pelargonium graveolens*, as well as the very lemony 'Mabel Grey' and 'Lara Nomad' varieties. I have also found the fruity scent of 'Big Apple' to carry successfully. But you can also buy pelargoniums that smell of peaches, various spices, peppermint, oranges and even chocolate – and many with intoxicating mingled scents that encompass several of the above.

If you get the chance to see the plant before you buy, crush a leaf gently between your fingers. If you are rewarded with a deep scent that pleases you, give it a try. Even if they don't prove pungent enough for culinary purposes, there's pleasure in simply liberating the scents from their handsome leaves with your fingertips. Some suppliers will also send you batches of fresh-cut leaves for cooking, so you don't necessarily have to invest in a plant to begin with (see Directory, p.248).

In the kitchen

Scented geranium leaves should not actually be eaten: all of them are tough and not a little bitter, and some, such as the lemony *Pelargonium crispum* species, may cause stomach upsets if consumed in any quantity. Instead, the leaves are best infused into liquids.

Scented geraniums are particularly useful if you like the scent and flavour of roses in your cooking – roses themselves have only a short summer season, whereas a rose-tinged pelargonium will produce leaves all year.

- You may well have heard of the technique of using scented geranium leaves to line cake tins before baking, thereby giving a delicate perfume to the finished cake. I've done this but find the result is really too subtle. I prefer to use a scented geranium syrup (see overleaf) as a drizzle over the top of a freshly baked skewer-pierced cake.

Scented geranium 'Lara Nomad'

- For a scented geranium syrup, put 150g caster sugar and 150ml water into a saucepan. Heat gently, stirring often, until the sugar has dissolved, then increase the heat. Once simmering, cook the syrup for 5 minutes. Remove from the heat, add 2–3 large scented geranium leaves (or 5–6 small ones), giving them a bit of a twist and a crush in your hands first. Push the leaves down under the surface of the syrup. Leave to cool. This makes enough to drip and drizzle over one large plain cake. You can also use it on a fruit salad, or, diluted down a bit, for poaching fruit.
- A few lemon-scented leaves on the base of an apple, or apple and blackberry pie give a lovely new dimension to the fruit.
- **Sweet raspberry vinegar with scented geranium** (p.239)
- **Scented lemonade** (p.241)

How to grow

These plants do not grow readily from seed, so buy young plants or take cuttings from established ones. Cuttings should be taken in late summer and sliced off cleanly with a knife, rather than leaving a heel, then follow the procedure on p.34.

Scented geraniums are best grown in pots, so you can easily control their environment. They must have free drainage so use a peat-free potting compost with a little fine sand mixed in. They are quite delicate but should be fine outside in a sheltered, sunny spot during good weather. However, they must be brought in before there's a chance of frost. They also do well in greenhouses, conservatories and other warm, light, protected places. I keep mine on a windowsill.

The greatest mistake is to confine them in too small a pot. Scented geraniums are expansive creatures and can grow pretty quickly, so give them room. They also really thrive on plenty of light. If, like me, you are absolutely terrible at remembering to water pot plants, make a diary or calendar note to do it regularly, i.e. before they're wilting! Give them an occasional feed too – well-diluted organic tomato feed or a spot of nettle tea, perhaps (see p.36), though this isn't ideal if you're growing indoors due to its penetrating aroma!

Sorrel (broad-leaved) *Rumex acetosa*

PLANT GROUP	Hardy perennial
HARVEST	April–October

I never fail to be pleasantly shocked by just how sharp and lemony sorrel is. The name itself is derived from an old French word *surele*, meaning 'sour'. Small tender leaves are more gentle, while large mature leaves can almost overpower the taste buds. Although you can sometimes buy the fresh leaves, sorrel is a very easy and forgiving plant to grow, pushing up its leaves well into the colder weather, then obligingly reappearing in spring, whether you tend it carefully or not.

Sorrel is also a leaf that grows abundantly in the wild in Britain, in grassy places, hedgerows and on heathland. It makes a lovely wild harvest and is worth looking out for from March onwards, always bearing in mind good foraging etiquette – tread carefully, pick sparingly. Make sure you don't confuse it with Lords and Ladies, which has similar-looking leaves, and is poisonous. Take a good illustrated forager's guide with you, such as John Wright's *River Cottage Hedgerow Handbook* (see Directory, p.249).

In the kitchen

This tender arrow-shaped leaf is half herb, half salad, and deliciously refreshing however you use it. Combined with a few other herbs, baby sorrel leaves make a wonderful mini-salad – the sort of tiny tangle of green leaves that goes well alongside something rich. Or you can shred it into more substantial leafy salads with lettuces, spring onions, eggs and/or potatoes.

The flavour of grown-up sorrel is also robust enough for a bit of light cooking. Stir the shredded leaves into a risotto, soup or omelette for the last few minutes to transform the flavour. In all cases, exercise a little caution: taste the raw leaf first to ascertain how astringent it is. Different plants at different times of year can vary quite a bit, depending on the levels of oxalic acid they contain. This acid, also found in spinach, is responsible for the leaf's sharp sourness. In large quantities, it is actually poisonous – but you'd have to eat a lot to be affected (best not give it to your tortoise, though). Use sorrel as soon as you can after picking – it wilts quickly. When cooked, it collapses to a fraction of its former volume, and will also turn from bright green to dull khaki.

- For a tasty lentil and sorrel soup, simmer brown lentils in water until very soft, then purée. Reheat, adding plenty of chopped sorrel, some double cream and seasoning.

- Stir a couple of generous handfuls of shredded sorrel into freshly cooked hot new potatoes, along with some seasoning and a splosh of olive oil.
- **Simple herb salad** (p.175)
- **Sorrel sauce** (p.164)
- **Sorrel wine cup** (p.243)

How to grow

Sorrel is easily raised from seeds – just sow in plugs in the spring. It tends to grow abundantly in most situations but it prefers a rich, damp soil and partial shade. Cut back its tall flowering spikes to promote leafy growth and don't be worried about razing the whole lot to the ground during the season to stimulate the production of a new crop of baby leaves. Once established, sorrel will come back year after year, but it's worth replacing often as young plants have the best flavour.

Relatives

French or buckler-leaf sorrel (*Rumex scutatus*) has a shorter, rounder leaf. Its flavour is a little less astringent and powerful than the broad-leaved variety. Wood sorrel (*Oxalis acetosella*) is a tiny, delicate, trefoil-leaved plant found in woodland all over Britain. It has a similar lemon-sharp flavour to broad-leaved sorrel.

Sorrel *Rumex acetosa*

Shredding sorrel

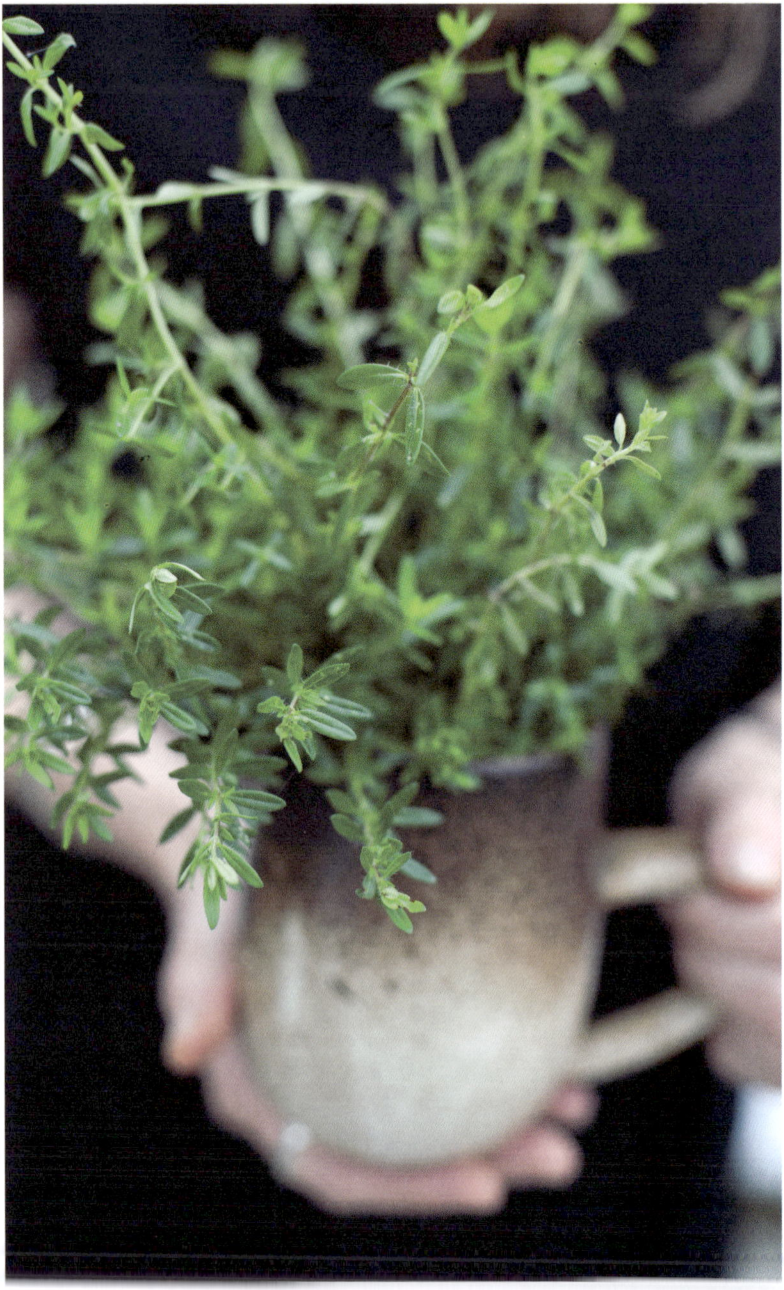

Summer savory *Satureja hortensis*

PLANT GROUP	Hardy annual
HARVEST	May–September

This is a very attractive herb, with slender upright stalks that bear pretty little flowers. The flavour is definitely in the 'woody' category: strongly aromatic, slightly peppery and piney, with hints of black tea. It is a native of hot places, including Greece, where it is said the satyrs grazed on it, hence the Latin name.

In the kitchen

Summer savory is rather like thyme in the flavours it complements – everything from green veg to chicken and fish, cheese and cream. However, savory can have a slightly piney edge that thyme does not, so I wouldn't use it in very delicate dishes such as salads or omelettes. Summer savory can be added during or after cooking. If you do both, you'll get layers of flavour. If you are adding late-season leaves to a dish at the end of cooking, chop them very finely as they can be a little tough.

- Add finely chopped summer savory to homemade sausages, burgers, pâtés, potted meats or meat stuffings. I particularly like it combined with some sautéed finely chopped onion and garlic and used to flavour lamb burgers.
- Try summer savory stirred into a tomato sauce or soup – add some at the beginning of cooking and a pinch more at the end.
- After frying pork chops, chicken breasts or veal escalopes, deglaze the pan with a little white wine, then add 1 tbsp chopped summer savory and a splosh of cream. Simmer briefly and season before pouring over the meat.
- The pungency of summer savory makes it a good foil to creamy and earthy flavours – try adding a chopped tablespoonful to the garlic-infused cream for a classic potato gratin.
- **Runner beans with summer savory (p.203)**

How to grow

I've not had any trouble raising summer savory from seed, sown in the spring into plugs. It prefers a sunny spot on light, well-drained soil. It's also great in a pot and can be grown on a windowsill. Extend its short life by pinching out flowering tips as soon as they appear.

Relatives

Winter savory, see p.155.

Sweet cicely *Myrrhis odorata*

PLANT GROUP	Hardy perennial
HARVEST	Leaves: March–October
	Seeds: June–September

In late spring, when its frothy white flowers are at their peak and the frondy leaves at their lush green best, sweet cicely is one of the prettiest things you can have in your herb garden. The leaves have a delicate honeyed anise quality. The large seeds, harvested green and juicy rather than dried, can be used in cooking too.

In the kitchen

Sweet cicely has much in common with chervil. The flavour is sweeter but it has the same subtle, aniseedy note and is similarly used in salads, mayonnaise and omelettes. It is also one of those herbs that reduces acidity in other ingredients, so is often cooked with gooseberries, rhubarb, cooking apples or blackcurrants, and means the dish needs less sugar. The green seeds work very well used in this way.

- I really like sweet cicely in a flavoured butter with some seasoning and lemon juice, tossed into freshly cooked vegetables, or smeared on chicken.
- For a gooseberry and sweet cicely compote, top and tail 500g gooseberries and put in a pan with 2 tbsp sugar, 2 tbsp water and 2 tbsp finely chopped sweet cicely (leaves and/or seed pods). Bring to a simmer and cook for a few minutes, until soft. Taste and add more sugar if you like (a lot depends on the variety of gooseberry). Well chilled, this is lovely with a spoonful of yoghurt or cream, or you can use it to make a crumble (serving 2–3).
- This herb's sweetness means it contributes something very pleasant to drinks. Try it in a wine cup (see p.243).
- **Rhubarb crumble with angelica** (p.223)

How to grow

Sweet cicely seeds must be sown outside in the autumn as they need several months of low temperatures before they will germinate. Choose a partially shaded site, with rich, moist but well-drained soil. This isn't a herb for container-growing as its long root needs plenty of depth. However, in a suitable bed it is a plant that will provide leaves for the greater part of the year. As with so many herbs, cutting it back after flowering will promote the growth of fresh new leaves. The flowers themselves are very pretty and, if left, will form elegant elongated seeds. These can be harvested and used fresh for flavouring. Any seed left on the plant will sow itself quite readily.

Sweet cicely seeds

Tarragon (French)
Artemesia dracunculus

PLANT GROUP	Half-hardy perennial
HARVEST	May–September

Cold chicken, cold new potatoes, mayonnaise, lots of chopped fresh tarragon… if there is a better summer lunch, I do not know of it. This feathery-leaved plant is queen of all the anise-scented herbs and an ingredient in many classic dishes with very good reason – the unique flavour is quite penetrating and tenacious but still manages to be delicate and refined. That anise quality acts as both flavour and seasoning. It rarely overpowers but enhances, defines and enlivens a dish.

In the kitchen

A little tarragon can sometimes go a long way but, at the same time, it's not a herb you necessarily need to hold back with. Adding an excessive quantity to something won't make it taste unpleasant, just very tarragony. This is a herb that can withstand a bit of cooking but in reality you are more likely to use tarragon in a raw or lightly cooked form.

- To make a lovely tarragon vinegar, fantastic in dressings, mayonnaises or sauces, just loosely pack a clean jam jar with tarragon leaves. Cover completely with white wine vinegar and leave at room temperature for 2 weeks before straining into a sterilised bottle and sealing.
- Tarragon is lovely with all sorts of green vegetables. I particularly like it with beans. Try adding sliced runner or green beans to a pan of soft sweated onions, along with a little water. Cook until the beans are just tender, then finish with salt and pepper, a squeeze of lemon and plenty of chopped tarragon.
- Combine tarragon with parsley, chives and chervil to create the classic blend *fines herbes* – exceptionally good in an omelette (see p.182).
- For a tasty supper, brown some chicken joints, then place in a roasting tin. Deglaze the browning pan with white wine and add to the tin. Season the chicken well and roast until golden and cooked through. Strew lots of roughly chopped tarragon over the chicken, leave for a few minutes so the flavours begin to release, then serve with bread or crushed new potatoes.
- Tarragon mayonnaise (p.159)
- Béarnaise sauce (p.160)

- **Creamed swiss chard** (p.208)
- **Tarragon eggs** (p.184)
- **Herb omelette** (p.182)

How to grow

French tarragon likes full sun and well-drained soil and does not thrive at all in cold, wet conditions. I have grown it successfully in pots, but it needs space and can easily become pot-bound.

Tarragon rarely produces seed, but propagates itself via underground runners. It's easy to start new plants from these runners yourself. Just dig up an established tarragon plant in the spring and you will see white growing shoots among the roots. Ease the roots apart and break off small sections with shoots attached. Replant the root/shoot sections, completely covering them with compost, and keep just moist. New green shoots should soon appear. This process is worth doing every few years because older tarragon plants lose their flavour.

Relatives

The similar-looking Russian tarragon (*Artemesia dracunculoides*) has an inferior flavour, as its nickname 'false tarragon' suggests.

Tarragon *Artemesia dracunculus*

Thyme *Thymus vulgaris*

Thyme and lemon thyme
Thymus vulgaris; Thymus x *citriodorus*

PLANT GROUP	Hardy evergreen perennial
HARVEST	All year round

Thyme is a precious ingredient, one whose fragrant woody, smoky taste pretty much epitomises the 'herby' flavour that we crave in some dishes. It has the same fundamental usefulness as bay in the way it infuses a lovely note into stocks, soups, stews, dressings, stuffings and a multitude of other dishes. But it's more versatile: you can eat it raw or cooked, add it finely chopped for a really thymey hit, or keep a sprig whole for a more subtle effect.

In the kitchen
You really can't go wrong with thyme: raw or cooked, generous or judicious, it's rarely going to do anything but enhance a dish. It's a fiddly one, though – removing the tiny leaves from the stems can be tricky. If you have very tender sprigs of thyme, you can finely chop the whole lot, stem and all, into a dish. If you have a woody sprig, pick off the leaves as best you can with your fingertips but accept that you may not get every one. Tougher stalks are really not nice to eat, but, even with most of the leaves removed, they are perfectly good for infusing in things.

- I always like to add a sprig of thyme to a simmering stock or a bouquet garni (see p.19).
- Put a few sprigs of thyme into the cavity of a chicken before roasting and flavour butter to stuff under the skin with chopped thyme (see p.198).
- Finely chopped thyme is fantastic added to savoury dumplings to go on top of a stew.
- Tiny whole fresh thyme leaves are delicious scattered over a tomato salad.
- Thyme is a must with roasted or braised root vegetables, especially pungent roots, such as swede, parsnip and celeriac, as well as beetroot and kohlrabi.
- Roughly crushed thyme leaves add a great deal of character to marinades and dressings.
- Thyme flowers are beautiful and the perfect edible garnish for a homemade pizza or bruschetta.
- **Soda bread with thyme, Cheddar and mustard** (p.212)
- **Apple herb jelly** (p.232)
- **Salmoriglio sauce** (p.165)
- **Loin of lamb with lavender and lemon thyme** (p.194)

How to grow

I have struggled a little with growing thyme. The plants always start off well but seem to become twiggy, unproductive and rather morose within a year or so. I think this is because, despite being a hardy perennial, it really hankers for the hot, dry thin-soiled hillsides of its native lands. It intensely resents our wet winters and it doesn't really like being cut too much. My approach now is to focus on young tender-stemmed plants, and not to expect too much of them in terms of longevity.

You can grow *Thymus vulgaris* from seed and this is one way to maintain a good supply, although the plants are slow to develop. Sow them indoors in plugs in the spring, in a warm place, and don't transplant them outside until the weather is warm and the plants seem robust – even if that isn't until the following spring. Make sure you harden them off (see p.33).

Thyme loves warmth and well-drained poor soil and hates prolonged contact with frost, rain and wind. Plant it in a sheltered but sunny position. Apart from when first planting, keep watering to a minimum. In the summer, cut it regularly but not too drastically and trim back after flowering to encourage new growth. However, keep cutting to a minimum in winter when you may find it stops growing almost completely.

Thyme grows well in containers, so having some in a pot on a windowsill is one way to help ensure fresh thyme through the winter.

Relatives

There are a huge number of thyme varieties, many of them very beautiful and fragrant. However, few species hit the culinary spot in the same way as the good old *Thymus vulgaris*. One notable exception is lemon thyme (*Thymus* x *citriodorus*). It is so intensely flavoured – pungently lemony, with that warm, woody thyme backnote – that it really functions as a completely different herb in its own right.

Lemon thyme is delicious but should be used fairly carefully because it is so strong. I love it in stuffings, or combined with soft sweated onions then mixed with wilted chopped spinach, but you can also use it to perfume a custard or cake batter. If you can't get hold of lemon thyme when a recipe calls for it, you can use ordinary thyme combined with finely grated lemon zest. The flavour will not be the same, but you'll be in the right ballpark.

I also like orange thyme (*Thymus fragrantissimus*). Crushing it in your hands releases the most wonderful dry, warm, spicy fragrance, which you can capture by infusing it in olive oil with some garlic (as for the rosemary and chilli oil on p.238), or by beating it into soft butter with orange zest, chilli and black pepper.

Lemon thyme *Thymus* x *citriodorus*

Welsh onion *Allium fistulosum*

PLANT GROUP	Hardy perennial
HARVEST	All year round

This handsome allium offers a lot: you can eat the young and the mature stems, as well as the flowers. It has real presence in the garden too, looking rather like a giant thick-shafted chive, and producing a similar flower from its second year onwards. It doesn't form an actual bulb but you can pull the whole stem out to use like a thick spring onion or, alternatively, cut the young stem tops like chives. You can eat the flowers too, separated into their little individual parts.

The name is slightly misleading as this allium has nothing in particular to do with Wales. 'Welsh' is believed to be a corruption of the German *walsch*, meaning foreign. In fact, the plant hails from Siberia. It is also known as the Japanese leek and the bunching onion.

In the kitchen

You can eat the stems of the Welsh onion raw, slicing them thinly and scattering into salads or over pizza. They have quite a strong oniony punch, which you may find delicious. I've never been much of a fan of raw onion, so I prefer them cooked. Sliced thinly and sautéed gently in butter with a pinch of salt and a dash of oil, you can use them in a hundred different ways.

Once the onion is flowering, the stalk will harden and become unpalatable, but the flower itself, pinched apart into little white flowerlets, makes a delicious and pretty oniony sprinkle that can be used much like chive flowers (see p.63). I particularly like them on vegetable risottos.

- Use sautéed Welsh onion as the first layer of a pizza topping. Try layering thinly sliced cooked new potatoes, thyme and a rich melting cheese, such as mozzarella or Stinking Bishop, on top.
- Blind bake a 25cm pastry crust and fill with as many sautéed Welsh onions as you can, or combine with other alliums such as shallots, spring onions or green garlic. Then add some grated flavoursome cheese and pour on a well-seasoned custard (200ml whole milk beaten with 200ml double cream, 2 whole eggs and 1 extra egg yolk). Bake at 180°C/Gas mark 4 for around 35 minutes until golden and just set.
- For a simple light onion soup, sauté Welsh onions until very soft, then add a splash of white wine and some well-flavoured chicken stock and simmer for another 30 minutes or so. Season and serve with croûtons.

- For a very simple and lovely supper, stir cooked Welsh onions into hot pasta with a splosh of cream and some chopped black olives.

How to grow

Sow Welsh onion seeds outside in March or April, directly into their growing site, which should have well-drained, rich soil and sun or partial shade. The Welsh onion is a hardy herb that you should be able to harvest even in the depths of winter, but bear in mind it needs to be well watered and weeded during the summer. It should then produce more and more stems year by year. Take care when pulling up the stems for eating, as you don't want to damage those left in the ground. Cut back spent stalks completely after flowering to allow new shoots to come through, and divide large clumps after a few years to promote vigorous fresh growth.

Relatives

The tree onion (*Allium cepa* Proliferum group) is a not dissimilar plant which has the distinction of producing bulbs at the top end of its stalk which grow crazily, sending their tendrils out into the air. Each of these baby bulbs, which you should get in the second year of growth, can be plucked and eaten, or planted to produce a new plant. You can eat the stems too.

Welsh onion *Allium fistulosum*

Welsh onion flowers

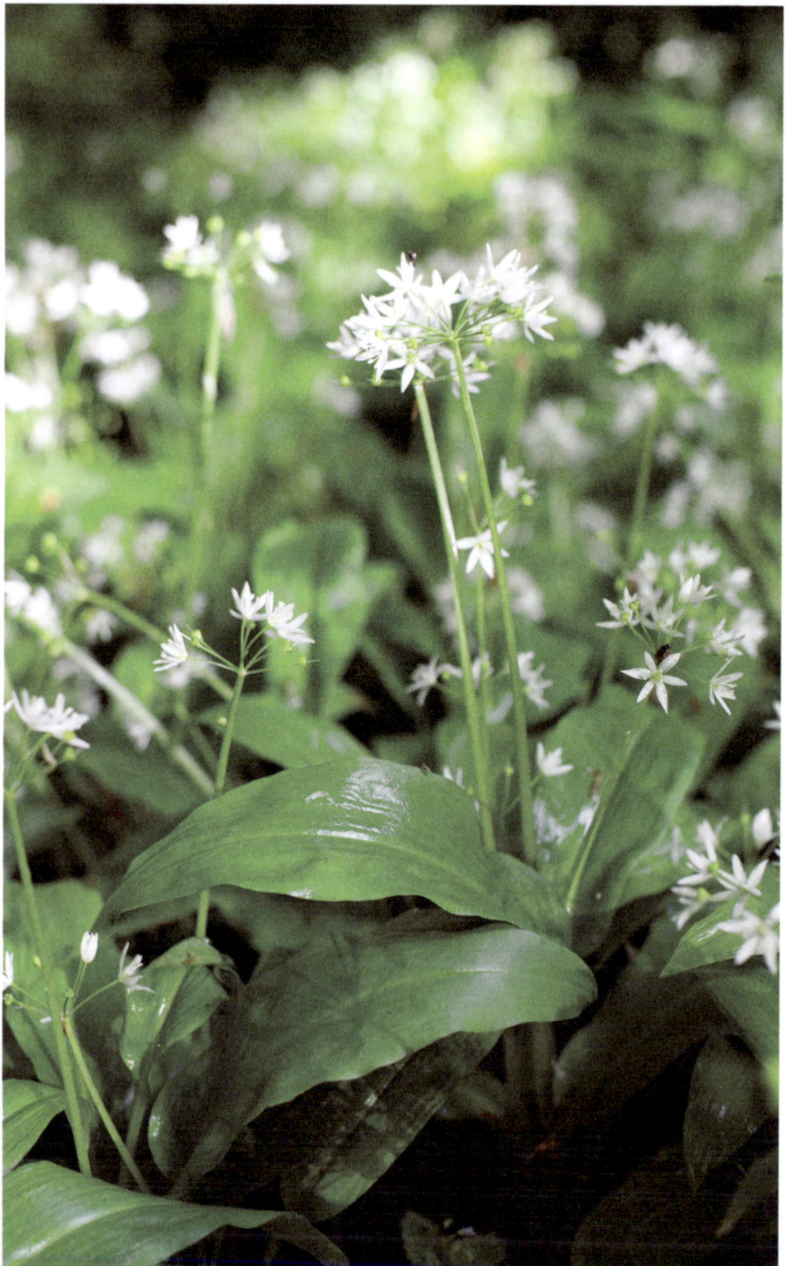

Wild garlic *Allium ursinum*

PLANT GROUP	Hardy perennial
HARVEST	March–May

From March to May this delicious wild food – also known as ramsons, bear garlic or wood garlic – appears in dense patches in damp, shady, wooded places. The powerful garlicky scent is unmistakable. Its elegant stems, delicate tulip-like leaves, bulbs and, later in the season, starry white flowers, are all edible, but if you're gathering this herb wild, it's best to leave the bulbs untouched for next year's crop. Wild garlic grows throughout Europe but is localised. However, once you've found a patch, you should be able to return year after year for a harvest.

In the kitchen

Quite pungent but subtly different to conventional garlic, wild garlic is more like a strong, garlicky chive. It quickly loses its flavour on cooking, so is best eaten raw or only lightly cooked. Roll up the leaves and slice them across into thin ribbons. Add to dishes at the end of cooking, or scatter on just before serving.

- For an easy soup, simmer potato and onion or leek in chicken or veg stock, adding shredded wild garlic at the end. Purée, finish with cream and season.
- Try stirring shredded wild garlic into a risotto at the last minute. This is particularly good with a chicken or mushroom risotto.
- Wild garlic flowers look really pretty on a salad or homemade pizza.
- Use wild garlic to replace chives or garlic chives in any recipe.
- **Spring pasta with wild garlic and purple sprouting broccoli** (p.199)
- **Herb omelette** (p.182)
- **Walnut and wild garlic pesto** (p.166)
- **Herb noodle soup** (p.173)

How to grow

Wild garlic is easy to cultivate but it's invasive so be cautious. Buy seeds or gather them from wild flowerheads, sow directly in a shady and slightly damp spot in the autumn and they should shoot up the following spring. You can also buy young plants. Once established, future work is more likely to be taming than encouraging.

Relatives

Three-cornered garlic (*Allium triquetrum*), with its distinctive triangular cross-section stem, is similarly delicious and can be used in much the same way.

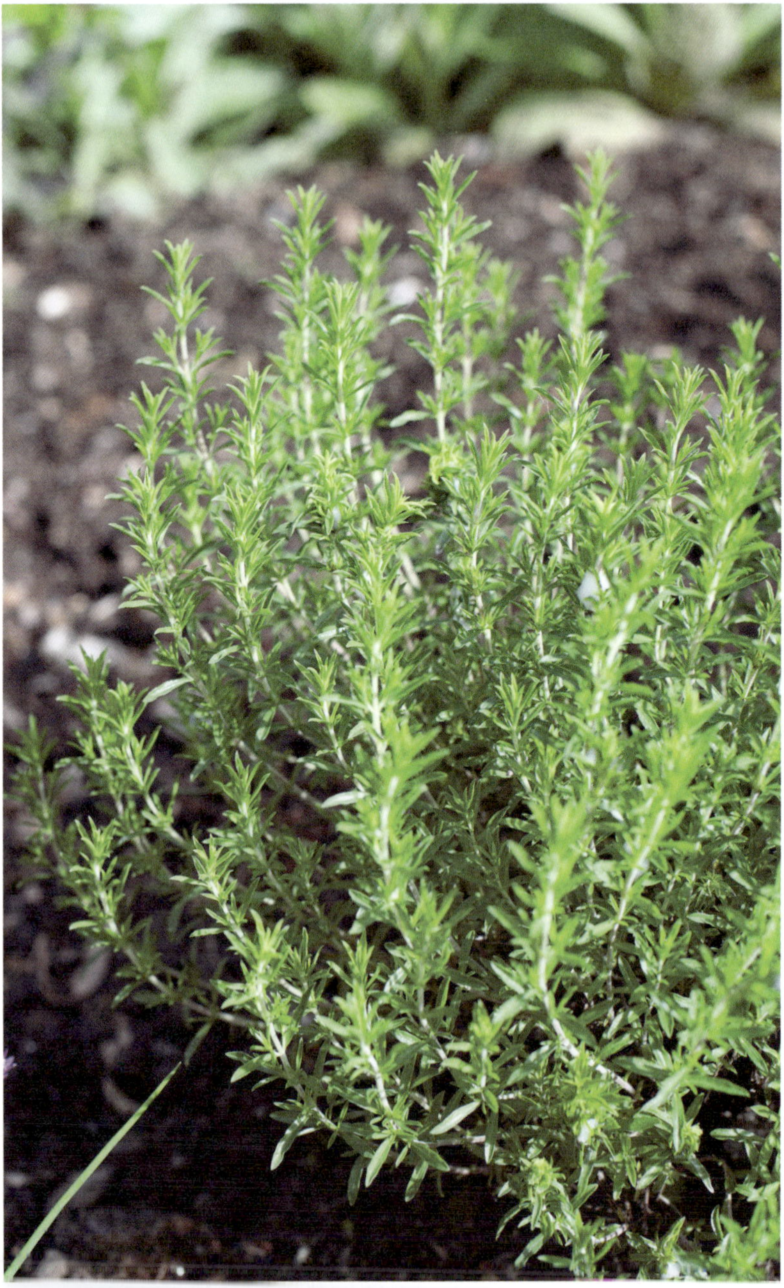

Winter savory *Satureja montana*

PLANT GROUP	Hardy evergreen perennial
HARVEST	All year round

Evergreen winter savory is a very attractive plant with dark, glossy needle-like leaves. Stronger and more pungent than its summer cousin, it is piney, a little like a combination of mint, pepper and thyme, with hints of menthol and a cleansing, almost tingling effect in the mouth if you sample it raw.

In the kitchen

The name says it all really: winter savory is definitely one for cold-weather cooking and comfort food. It's an excellent partner to red meats, dried pulses and winter vegetables. Chop the leaves fairly finely and add in small quantities, or use it as an infusing herb in a bouquet garni (see p.19).

- Add chopped winter savory to homemade sausages, burgers and pâtés.
- Finely chopped, this is a very good herb for meat stuffings.
- **Stuffed breast of lamb with dried apricots and winter savory** (p.193)
- **White beans with winter herbs** (p.204)

How to grow

If you want to grow this herb from seed, sow indoors in early spring and just press the seeds lightly into the compost but leave them uncovered, as they need light to germinate. The young plants will need hardening off before planting out (see p.33). You can also take spring cuttings of winter savory (see p.34)

Like its summer sibling, winter savory prefers a warm, sunny position on light, well-drained soil. I have grown it very successfully in a pot on the patio where it seems happy to keep going all year round as long as it doesn't get too dry and I keep cutting from it, little and often, but more cautiously in the winter.

Relatives

Summer savory, see p.141.

Recipes

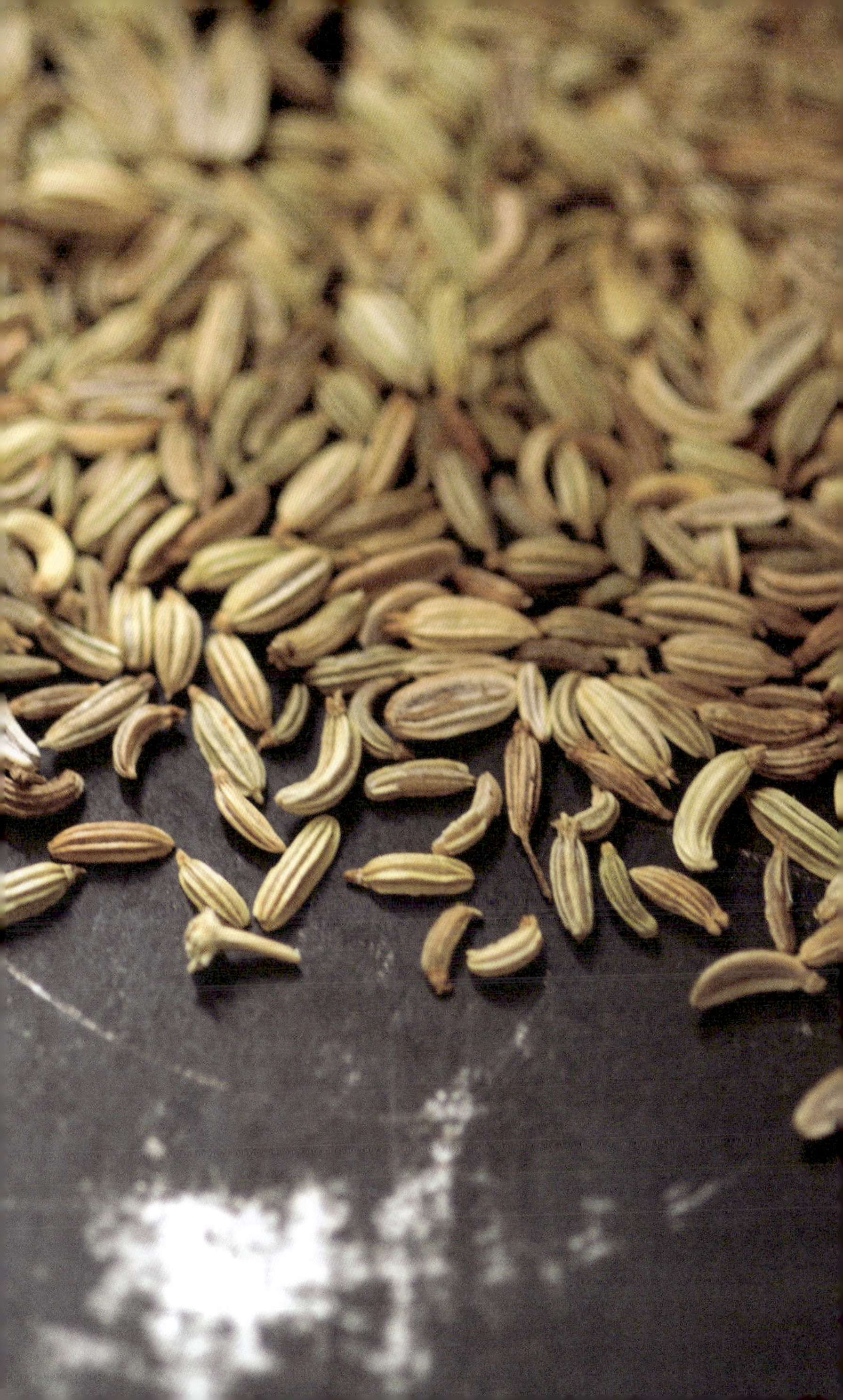

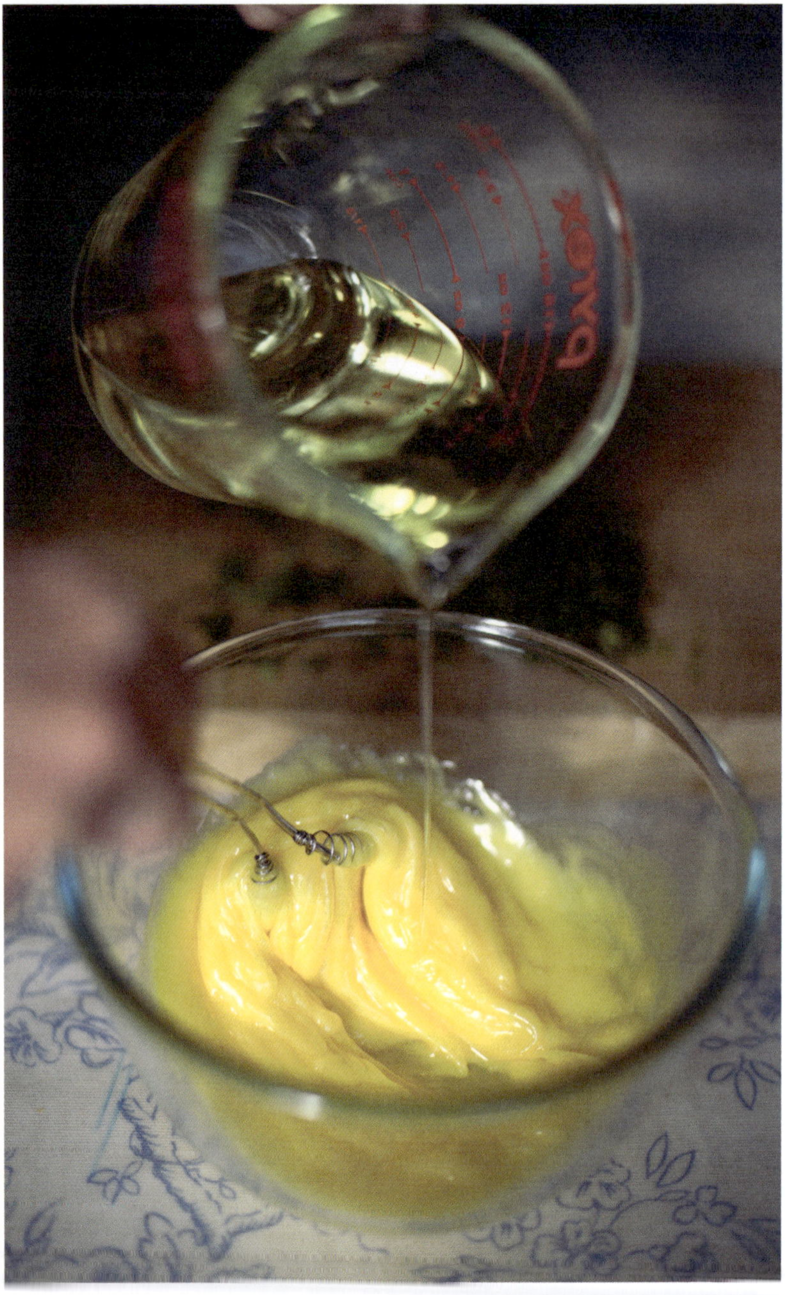

Mayonnaise

A good homemade mayonnaise recipe is a great thing to have in your repertoire. It's particularly useful for the summer months when you can lace it with herbs of your choice and serve it with all kinds of vegetables, salads, fish, eggs and meat.

Makes about 300ml, enough for 6–8

½ small garlic clove
2 large egg yolks
½ tsp English mustard
1 tsp white wine vinegar (or tarragon vinegar, see p.144)

About 250ml light olive oil, or 100ml extra virgin olive oil blended with 150ml sunflower oil
Sea salt and freshly ground black pepper

Crush the garlic with a good pinch of salt (see p.20). Scrape into a bowl and add the egg yolks, mustard, vinegar and some pepper.

Start whisking in the oil, a few drops at a time to start with, then in small dashes, whisking in each addition so it is fully amalgamated. Stop when you have a glossy, wobbly mayonnaise. Taste and add more salt, pepper and vinegar as required.

Variations

Flavour the basic mayonnaise generously with any of the following chopped herbs, adding at least a good 2 tbsp:

Chives Essential for a new potato salad.
Tarragon Lovely with eggs, chicken or potatoes.
Basil Fantastic with tomatoes or in sandwiches with cold chicken or ham.
Parsley A versatile mayonnaise to go with most things. For a garlic and parsley mayo, increase the garlic to a whole clove; this is good with shellfish or you can use it as the base for a tartare sauce.
Chervil and lemon zest Particularly good with green beans, asparagus, potatoes, cold chicken, fish or shellfish.

Béarnaise sauce

This classic velvety sauce is delicate but rich and fragrant with tarragon. Serve it with simply cooked steak, trout or chicken.

Serves 4

- 1 medium shallot, peeled and finely chopped
- A few black peppercorns
- 2 tbsp white wine vinegar
- 2 tbsp dry white wine
- 2 tbsp chopped tarragon
- 2 tsp chopped chervil (optional)
- 2 large egg yolks, at room temperature
- 150g unsalted butter, melted and slightly cooled
- A pinch of sugar
- Sea salt and freshly ground black pepper

Put the shallot, peppercorns, wine vinegar, wine, 1 tbsp of the chopped tarragon, and the chervil, if using, into a small saucepan. Bring to a simmer and cook for a few minutes until the liquid has reduced to 1 tbsp. Tip into a sieve over a bowl, pressing the shallot mixture to extract every last drop of juice. Leave to cool.

Add the egg yolks to the cooled liquor and whisk together. Now slowly whisk in the warm melted butter, little by little, to form a smooth emulsion, rather like a very loose mayonnaise. Stir in the remaining chopped tarragon and season to taste with salt and pepper, and a pinch of sugar if necessary.

Serve the sauce pretty much straight away (though you can keep it warm in a bowl over a saucepan of hot water for a little while).

Horseradish sauce

This is the basic River Cottage procedure for making fresh creamed horseradish, and it's hard to beat. There are, however, a few optional additions that work very well (see below). Horseradish sauce is marvellous, of course, with roast beef, but also with burgers, in meaty sandwiches, with smoked or oily fish, and with sweet roasted root vegetables too. There's little point in making up the sauce in large quantities, as it doesn't keep well and grating the root is fairly hard work.

Serves 4

1 tsp cider vinegar or lemon juice
½ tsp English mustard
50g fresh horseradish root
60g crème fraîche

A pinch of sugar, or to taste
Sea salt and freshly ground black pepper

Put the cider vinegar or lemon juice and mustard into a bowl and mix together. Peel the horseradish and grate it finely into the mixture, stirring it in once or twice as you work your way through the root. The acid in the vinegar or lemon helps to 'fix' the pungent, volatile oil of the root.

Stir in the crème fraîche, then season with salt, pepper and sugar (you don't want too much, but a hint of sweetness can transform the sauce). Serve straight away or refrigerate for up to 24 hours.

Variations

- For a slightly milder, sweeter version, add 1 peeled and grated cooking apple.
- For a great sauce to serve with a lamb burger, add 2–3 tbsp finely chopped mint leaves.
- To accompany beef or chicken, add 2–3 tbsp finely snipped chives.

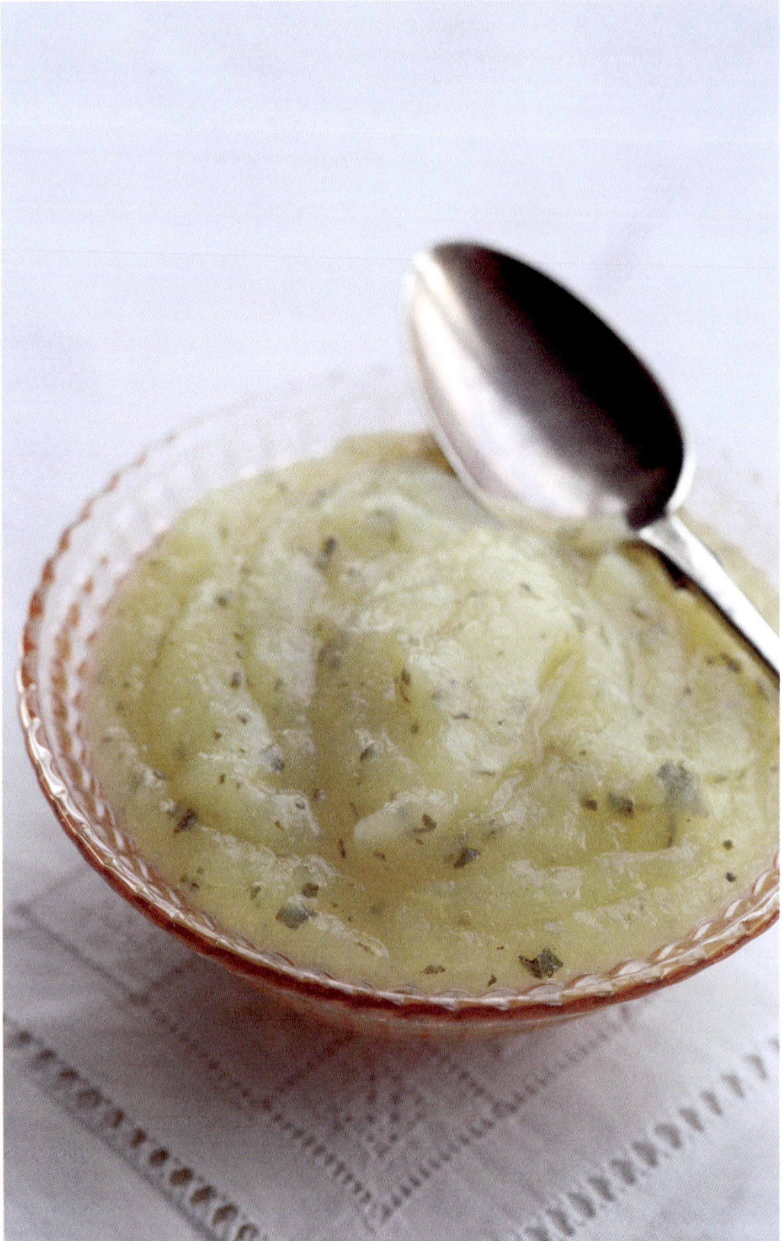

Apple sauce with sage

There's nothing wrong with a plain apple sauce, but adding a little chopped sage gives it an extra fragrant edge that really complements pork or goose.

Serves 4–6
3 cooking apples (about 750g)
1 tsp chopped sage
About 2 tsp caster sugar

Peel, core and slice the apples, dropping them straight into a bowl of water to prevent browning. Drain the apples and transfer them to a steaming basket. Steam over a pan of boiling water, stirring them carefully once or twice, until completely soft and fluffy; this will take 5–10 minutes.

Put the hot apples into a blender with the chopped sage and 2 tsp sugar and blitz until smooth. Transfer to a bowl and leave to cool, then taste and add a little more sugar if you like, but keep the sauce tart.

Mint sauce

This is a traditional 'wet' mint sauce – fragrant, slightly sweet-sour and very good with roast lamb, whether hot from the oven or sliced cold the next day. If you prefer something less runny, try a delicious apple mint jelly (p.232).

Serves 4
4 tbsp finely chopped spearmint
1 tsp caster sugar
A pinch of salt
Juice of ½ lemon
1 tbsp white wine vinegar
½ tsp Dijon mustard

Combine the chopped mint in a bowl with the sugar, salt, lemon juice and wine vinegar. Add the mustard and 1 tbsp just-boiled water and stir until the mustard is incorporated and the sugar dissolved. Serve the sauce straight away.

Sorrel sauce

This intense rich-but-sharp sauce is an absolute classic with plainly cooked fish. It's also good with grilled or roasted chicken – or try a spoonful on a poached egg on toast. Choose youngish, reasonably tender leaves of sorrel if you can.

Serves 2–3

About 100g bunch of sorrel, tough stalks removed
A large knob of unsalted butter
100g crème fraîche
1 egg yolk
A pinch of sugar
Sea salt and freshly ground black pepper

Stack several sorrel leaves on top of one another, roll them tightly into a 'cigar', then shred finely. Repeat with all the sorrel.

Heat the butter in a small pan over a low heat. When melted, add the sorrel and cook gently, turning it over from time to time, for a couple of minutes, or until completely wilted. Add the crème fraîche and stir until it softens and combines with the sorrel and is steaming hot but not boiling. Remove from the heat.

Let the sauce cool for a minute or so, then beat in the egg yolk. Season with salt, pepper and a pinch of sugar. Serve straight away.

Nasturtium flower dressing

For this recipe, I must thank the wonderful Cheryl Waller of the National Herb Society. It makes a lovely refreshing sauce that can be served with cold meat or fish, or used in a potato or pasta salad.

Serves 4

125ml mayonnaise (ideally (homemade, see p.159)
125ml plain full-fat yoghurt or fromage frais
About 15 nasturtium flowers
A pinch of sugar
Sea salt and freshly ground black pepper

Simply combine the mayonnaise, yoghurt or fromage frais, the flowers, sugar and some seasoning in a blender. Blitz until smooth. Check the seasoning and serve.

Salmoriglio sauce

I love the slightly bitter, smoky tang of oregano in this Sicilian-style sauce. You only need a little bit to deliciously dress a piece of barbecued fish or roast lamb.

Serves 4

2 tbsp finely chopped oregano
1 tbsp finely chopped thyme
Grated zest of ½ lemon, plus a squeeze of juice
1 small garlic clove, very finely chopped
1 tsp Dijon mustard
4 tbsp olive oil
A pinch of sugar
Sea salt and freshly ground black pepper

Put the oregano, thyme, lemon zest and garlic into a small bowl and mix well. Add a squeeze of lemon juice, the mustard, olive oil, sugar and some salt and pepper and mix well. Taste and add more salt, pepper and/or lemon juice as needed.

Skordalia

This Greek dip is ridiculously garlicky. Actually, this version uses less garlic than many, but it's still pretty powerful stuff and possibly not ideal before a big date! But I love its rich, oily, sweet, strong taste, especially with contrasting foods such as raw fennel or carrots. Other crudités work well too and it's traditionally served with roasted beetroot.

Serves 4–6 as an accompaniment

50g whole blanched almonds, lightly toasted and cooled
50g fresh white breadcrumbs
2 fat garlic cloves, peeled and crushed
2 tsp red wine vinegar
About 100ml extra virgin olive oil
Sea salt and freshly ground black pepper

Put the toasted almonds, breadcrumbs, garlic, wine vinegar and some salt and pepper into a food processor and whiz until the nuts are finely chopped. Transfer to a dish and gradually stir in the extra virgin olive oil until you have a thick, oily purée. Taste and adjust the seasoning, adding a little more vinegar if you like.

Basil and parsley pesto

The classic Italian *pesto alla Genovese* is made with basil and pine nuts, and extremely fine it is too. But the idea can be adapted to other herbs, and other nuts, as you'll see here. I particularly like the combination of basil and parsley, though you can use parsley alone. You can also use mint in a pesto, or stronger herbs, such as sage or thyme, though these are best combined with parsley so they don't overpower the sauce. As well as being excellent with pasta, pestos make a superb finishing touch to soups. They are also good with steak or chicken, delicious smeared over roasted vegetables and lovely as a simple dip with crudités.

Makes enough for pasta for 4

50g pine nuts, lightly toasted
30g bunch of basil, leaves only
30g bunch of flat-leaf parsley, leaves only
1 garlic clove, peeled and chopped
35g Parmesan, finely grated
Finely grated zest of ½ lemon
100–150ml extra virgin olive oil
A good squeeze of lemon juice
Sea salt and freshly ground black pepper

First toast the pine nuts: put them in a dry frying pan and toast over a medium heat for a few minutes, tossing frequently, until golden brown. Remove them from the pan immediately, so they don't burn, and leave to cool.

Put the toasted nuts into a food processor, along with the basil, parsley, garlic, Parmesan and lemon zest. Blitz to a paste. Then, with the motor running, slowly pour in the extra virgin olive oil until you have a thick, sloppy purée.

Scrape the pesto into a bowl. Season with salt and pepper and add a good squeeze of lemon juice to taste. This pesto will keep in a jar in the fridge for a few days.

Variation

Walnut and wild garlic pesto Replace the pine nuts with walnuts, lightly toasted in an oven preheated to 180°C/Gas mark 4 for 5–8 minutes. Replace the basil and parsley with roughly chopped wild garlic leaves and stems.

SAUCES, DRESSINGS & DIPS 167

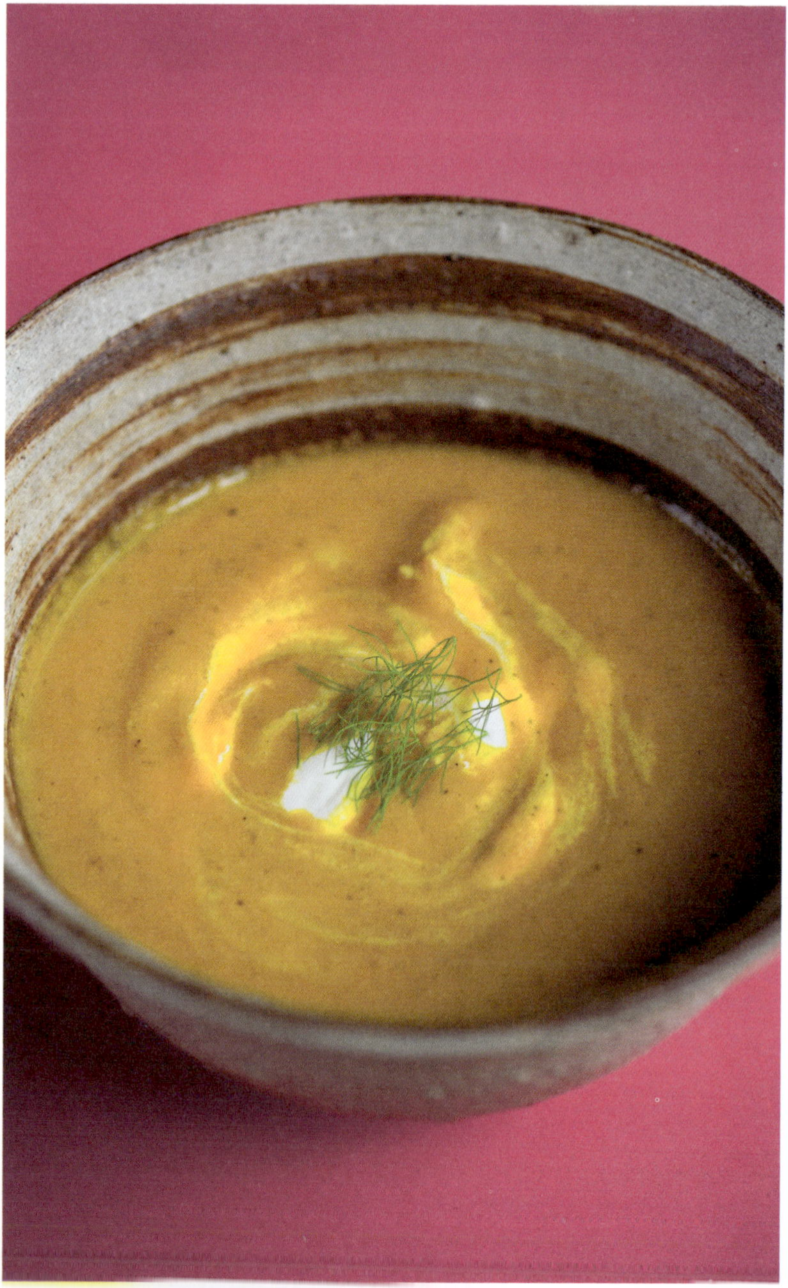

Carrot soup with dill
and mustard

Carrot and coriander soup is a ubiquitous dish with good reason, as it's very tasty. You certainly could use coriander here. However, the clean freshness of dill is lovely with the sweetness of carrots.

Serves 4–6

- 2 tbsp rapeseed or olive oil
- 1 onion, peeled and sliced
- 1 celery stick, sliced
- 500g carrots, peeled and sliced
- 800ml chicken or vegetable stock, or water, or a mixture
- 15–20g bunch of dill
- 1 heaped tsp Dijon mustard
- 2 heaped tbsp crème fraîche
- Sea salt and freshly ground black pepper

Heat the oil in a large saucepan over a medium heat. Add the onion, celery and carrots. Once they start to sizzle, reduce the heat, cover the pan and sweat the veg, stirring once or twice, for 10 minutes. Add the stock and/or water. Bring to a simmer and cook for 12–15 minutes, or until the carrots are tender.

Meanwhile, cut the top quarter off the bunch of dill and set aside for serving. Discard the stalks from the remaining dill, then roughly chop the frondy leaves.

Add the chopped dill to the soup and simmer for another 2 minutes only. Add the mustard, then purée the soup in a blender. Return to the pan and season well with salt and pepper. Reheat if necessary.

Serve the soup in warmed bowls, topped with the crème fraîche. Finish with the remaining dill and a good grinding of pepper.

Chervil soup

Rich, deeply coloured and intense, this is ideal to serve in small portions as a starter. And since chervil can be persuaded to grow all year round (see p.60), you can enjoy this as a summer or winter dish.

Serves 4 as a starter

50g unsalted butter
5 shallots, peeled and thinly sliced
1 inner celery stick, thinly sliced
500ml chicken or vegetable stock
150g bunch of chervil
2 egg yolks
50ml double cream, plus a little extra to finish
A squeeze of lemon juice
Sea salt and freshly ground black pepper

Melt the butter in a saucepan over a low heat. Add the shallots and celery and sweat, covered, for about 10 minutes. Add the stock, bring to the boil, then reduce the heat and simmer for about 10 minutes.

Separate out a small handful of the chervil and set aside. Roughly chop the rest, stalks and all, and add to the saucepan. Once the stock has returned to a simmer, cook for just 1–2 minutes, then remove from the heat. Transfer to a blender and purée until smooth. Return to a clean pan.

Whisk the egg yolks and cream together, then whisk into the soup. Reheat gently, stirring constantly, until just below a simmer; don't let it get to simmering point. The egg yolk will thicken the soup slightly. Season with salt, pepper and a squeeze of lemon juice to taste.

Pick the leaves from the reserved chervil and chop finely, or leave whole if you prefer. Serve the soup in warmed bowls, finished with the extra chervil and a little swirl of cream.

SOUPS 171

Celery leaf and lovage soup

This is a creamy, deeply flavoured soup – perfect for lunch on a cold day. Try it with a hunk of homemade soda bread, either plain or herby (see p.212). Alternatively, make the soup even more hearty with a scattering of croûtons or chopped ham.

Serves 4

- A knob of unsalted butter
- 2 tbsp rapeseed or olive oil
- 2 leeks, trimmed, well washed and sliced
- 1 garlic clove, peeled and sliced
- 3–4 slender stems of celery leaf, leaves separated, stems chopped
- 400g potato (1 large one), peeled and cut into large pieces
- 1 litre chicken stock
- 1 tbsp roughly chopped lovage
- 1 good tsp Dijon mustard
- 4–5 tbsp double cream
- Sea salt and freshly ground black pepper

Melt the butter with the oil in a pan over a medium heat. Add the leeks, garlic and the chopped celery leaf stems. Cover the pan, reduce the heat and sweat together for about 10 minutes, until soft. Add the potato and the stock. Bring to a simmer and cook, covered, for about 12 minutes, until the potato is soft. Scoop out the pieces of potato with a slotted spoon and set aside.

Roughly chop the celery leaves and combine with the chopped lovage. You should have 2–3 tbsp chopped herbs altogether. Add to the soup, along with a good pinch of salt and lots of freshly ground pepper. Purée, using a blender. Return the soup to the pan.

Put the potato through a ricer (or push through a sieve), back into the soup. Stir until incorporated. Reheat if necessary, then stir in the mustard and cream. Taste and adjust the seasoning, then serve.

Herb noodle soup

This is so simple and quick, and yet so satisfying. It's soothing comfort food, but actually quite light and delicate at the same time. You can use various different herbs, depending on what you have to hand. I've given the recipe in a one-person quantity as it's the sort of dish you might make for yourself when eating alone after a hard day. But just increase the quantities to scale it up for more people. If you want to make the dish vegetarian, replace the chicken stock with vegetable stock, and the chicken with tofu.

Herbs to use (alone or in combination)
Shredded wild garlic
Shredded basil or Thai basil
Finely chopped lemongrass leaves or stem
Shredded mint
Snipped chives or garlic chives
Chopped coriander
Shredded perilla

Serves 1

400ml good chicken stock
A little deseeded and finely sliced red chilli
1 small garlic clove, sliced
50g dried egg noodles
About 50g cold cooked chicken, shredded or cubed
About 3 tbsp chopped or shredded herbs (see above)
Optional seasonings: soy sauce, lemon or lime juice, toasted sesame oil
Sea salt and freshly ground black pepper

Put the stock, chilli and garlic into a saucepan and bring to a simmer. Season with salt and pepper to taste. Use your hands to break up the noodles as much as you can, dropping them into the simmering stock as you go. Once back up to a simmer, cook for about 3 minutes, stirring to break up the noodles.

Add the chicken and simmer for another minute, to heat it through, then add the herbs and immediately turn off the heat. Taste again and adjust the seasoning – you could add a dash of soy sauce if you like or perhaps a squeeze of lemon or lime juice, or a dash of toasted sesame oil.

Serve the soup straight away, piping hot, in a deep bowl. Slurping is unavoidable.

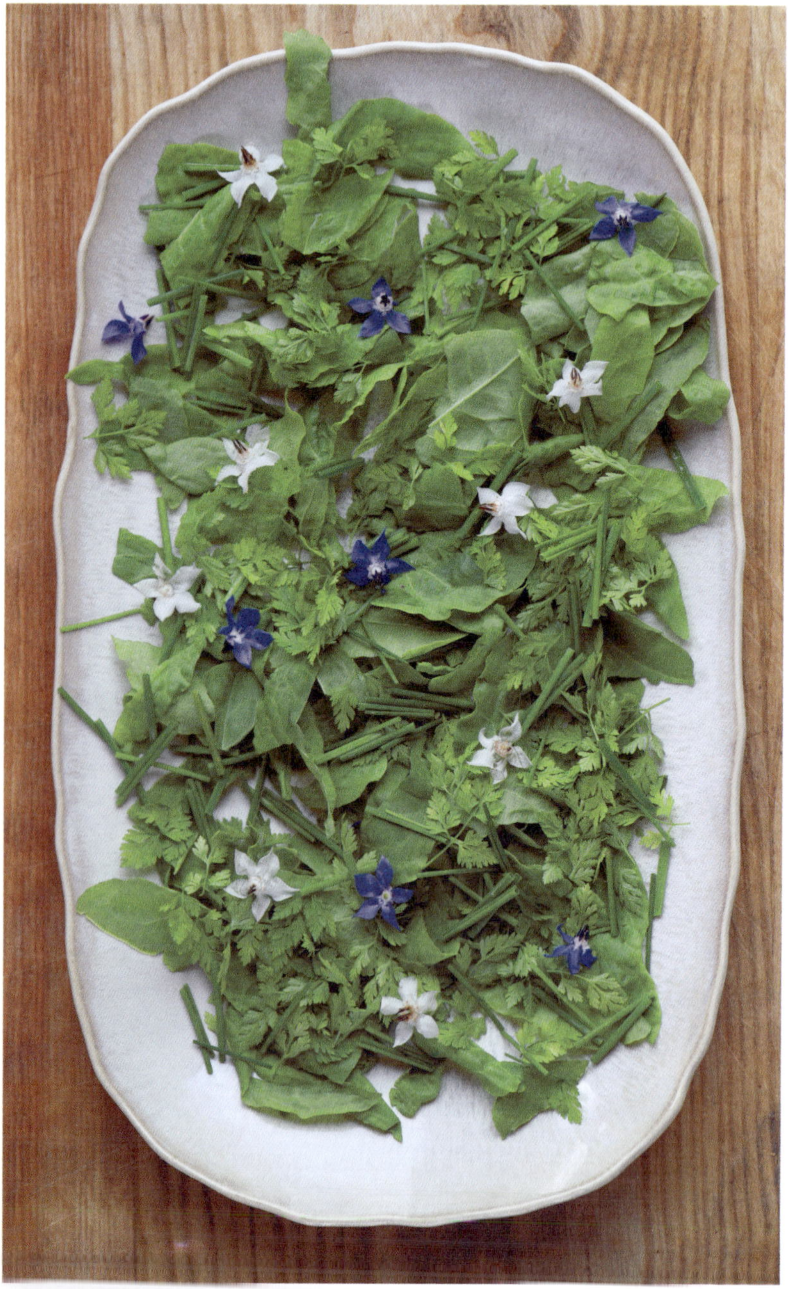

Simple herb salad

Although this looks rather summery, I actually came up with it in October, when all the ingredients were still going strong in my garden. It's a fresh and delicate little dish, ideal as a very simple starter or a palate-cleanser between richer courses.

Per person

A small handful of tender sorrel leaves, stalks removed
A few sprigs of chervil (leaves only)
3–4 chives, snipped into 2–3cm lengths
A little extra virgin olive or rapeseed oil
About 6 borage flowers

Arrange the sorrel leaves on each serving plate, or on a larger platter, then add the chervil and snipped chives. Sprinkle a little oil over the salad, then finish with the borage flowers.

Apple and celery leaf salad
with Cheddar and walnuts

This super-simple little salad relies on the wonderful affinity between apples and celery. A bit of nutty Cheddar finishes the whole thing nicely. I could easily polish off this quantity myself, but it would make a nice starter for two.

Serves 1–2

1 crisp, tart dessert apple, such as Cox
A squeeze of lemon or orange juice
1 tbsp finely chopped celery leaf and stem
About 50g strongish Cheddar, diced
A few walnuts, roughly chopped
Sea salt and freshly ground black pepper

Core and chop the apple (there's no need to peel it) and toss immediately with the lemon or orange juice to prevent browning. Stir in the chopped celery leaf and stem, the Cheddar, walnuts and a little salt and pepper to taste. Serve straight away with a chunk of well-buttered wholemeal bread on the side.

Green and gold salad

Try serving this as part of a spread of dips, breads and mezze or tapas. The orange flower water has a unique way of lifting and subtly perfuming the salad, but you could use a squeeze of orange juice instead.

Serves 4

- 2 tbsp olive oil
- ½ tsp orange flower water
- A squeeze of lemon juice
- 4 handfuls lamb's lettuce, or another mild, tender leaf, such as purslane
- About 50 small, young marigold leaves
- 4 marigold flowers
- Sea salt and freshly ground black pepper

Mix the olive oil, orange flower water, lemon juice and some seasoning together to make a dressing. Put the lamb's lettuce or other salad leaves and marigold leaves into a bowl and toss lightly with the dressing (you might not need it all). Arrange on a serving plate. Pull the petals from the flowers, scatter over the leaves and serve.

Crab and broad bean salad

This is lovely served as an elegant starter. It's delicious when made in the summer with freshly picked baby broad beans, but it's also successful with frozen ones.

Serves 2

- 200g podded broad beans (small ones if possible)
- About 100g fresh brown and white crabmeat (1 small crab should be about right)
- A handful of tender chervil sprigs
- A little extra virgin olive oil
- A squeeze of lemon juice
- Sea salt and freshly ground black pepper

Bring a pan of water to the boil. Add the broad beans and cook until tender – just a couple of minutes for fresh little ones. Drain and, when cool enough to handle, pop the beans out of their skins.

Arrange the broad beans and crabmeat in separate piles on individual plates. Add a little pile of chervil sprigs. Trickle the whole thing with some extra virgin olive oil, a good spritz of lemon and some salt and pepper, then serve.

SALADS 177

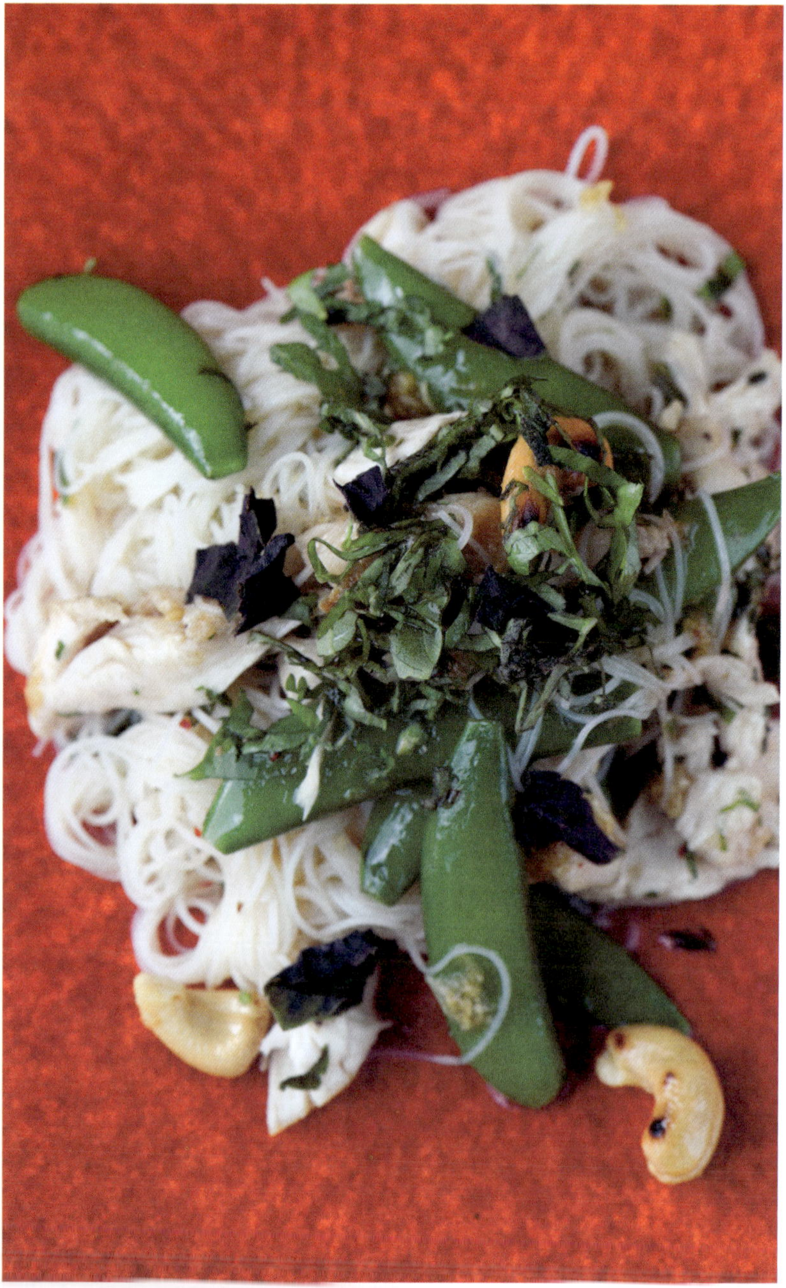

Herby chicken noodle salad

The pungent aromatic herbs used in this flavour-packed, generous salad are no mere garnish; they form a crucial part of the body of the dish so don't hold back. You could use even more than I suggest here.

Serves 4

200g rice noodles
150g mangetout, sugarsnap peas or green beans
200g cold cooked chicken, roughly shredded or chopped
3 tbsp shredded basil or, even better, Thai basil
3 tbsp roughly chopped coriander
3 tbsp shredded spearmint
75g cashew nuts, lightly toasted

For the dressing

1 tbsp soy sauce
2 tsp clear honey
1 garlic clove, peeled and grated
1 good tsp grated root ginger
1 red chilli, deseeded and very finely chopped
Juice of 1 lime
4 tbsp sunflower oil

For the dressing, put all the ingredients into a screw-topped jar, secure the lid and shake well to combine and emulsify.

Cook the rice noodles according to the pack instructions. Drain, rinse under cold water and drain well again, then transfer to a bowl and add the dressing. Toss well.

Steam or simmer the mangetout, sugarsnaps or beans very briefly, until just tender but still crunchy. Drain, refresh under cold water, drain again and toss with the rice noodles.

Toss the chicken and about two-thirds of the chopped herbs into the noodles and transfer to a large serving dish. Scatter over the toasted nuts, then the remaining herbs and serve.

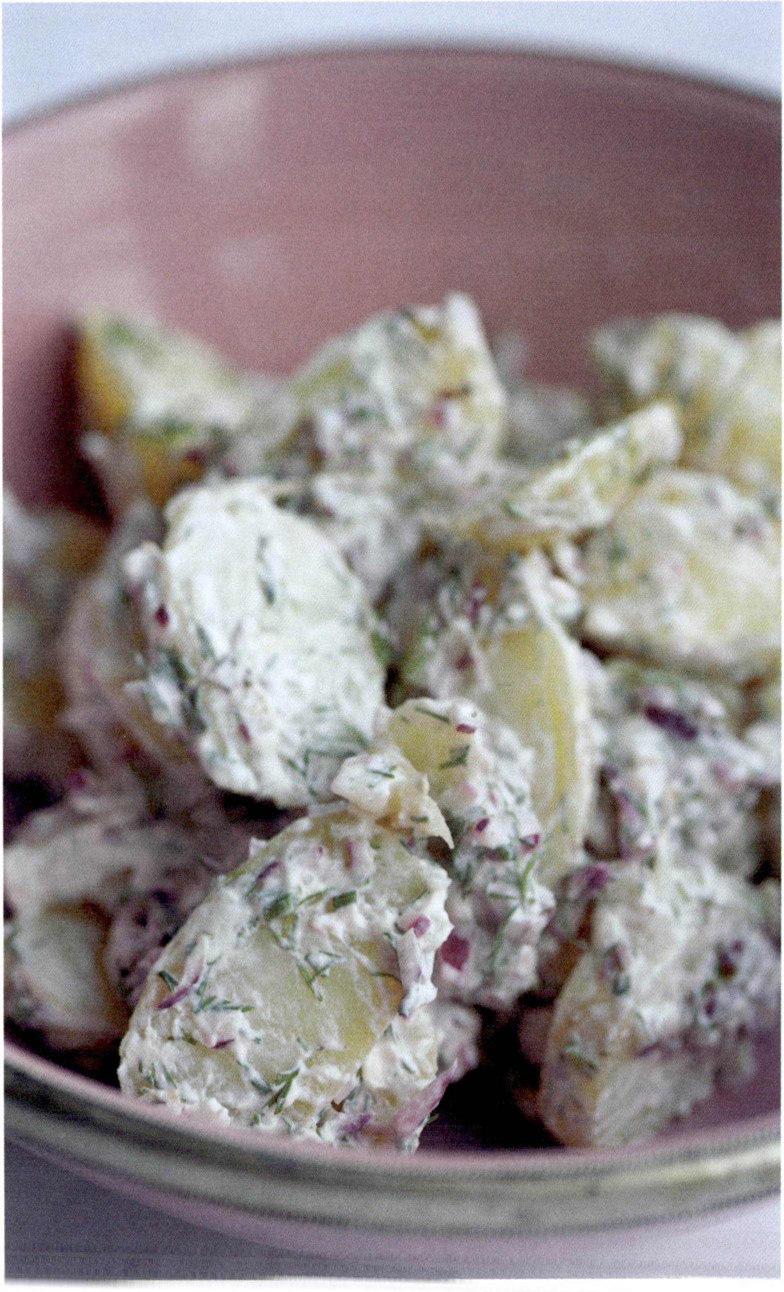

Potato salad with dill
and pickled red onion

This quick pickling treatment for onion comes from River Cottage Canteen chef, Tim Maddams. He does it with rosemary, but the light sugar-salt-vinegar cure really brings out the flavour of dill too. This creamy, moreish side dish is very good with salmon or trout, whether smoked or cooked and cooled. I also like it with a bit of salty ham.

Serves 4 as a side dish

½ fairly small red onion, peeled and finely chopped
A good pinch of caster sugar
2 tsp cider vinegar
2 heaped tbsp chopped dill
300g cold cooked new potatoes, thickly sliced
4 tbsp soured cream
Sea salt and freshly ground black pepper

Put the chopped onion into a bowl. Sprinkle over a good pinch each of salt and sugar and a grinding of pepper. Toss well and leave for 10 minutes to soften. If the onion releases a lot of liquid, drain it off.

Sprinkle over the cider vinegar and chopped dill, stir and then leave to stand for another 10 minutes. Fold in the potatoes and the soured cream, check the seasoning (it may well need a bit more salt) and serve.

Herb omelette

A simple omelette is not just an almost instant and very delicious lunch, it's also an ideal way to taste and savour any number of different herbs – the perfect quick recipe, in fact, if you're experimenting with something new.

Herbs to use
Chives and/or garlic chives
***Fines herbes* (a blend of tarragon, parsley, chervil and chives)**
Flat-leaf parsley with a tiny bit of lovage
Marjoram
Rocket
Sorrel
Wild garlic

Serves 1
2 eggs
Small knob of unsalted butter (about 5g)
About 1 tbsp chopped or shredded herbs (see above)
Sea salt and freshly ground black pepper

Lightly beat the eggs together with some salt and pepper. Heat a 15–20cm frying pan or omelette pan over a medium heat, then add the butter.

As soon as the butter is melted and bubbling, pour in the eggs. Use a fork to lift and push the sides of the omelette as it starts to set, so the liquid egg can run down on to the base of the pan.

After about a minute, scatter the herbs evenly over the omelette. Keep cooking for a minute or so longer, until done to your liking, then fold the omelette in half with a fork or spatula and slide on to a plate. Eat straight away.

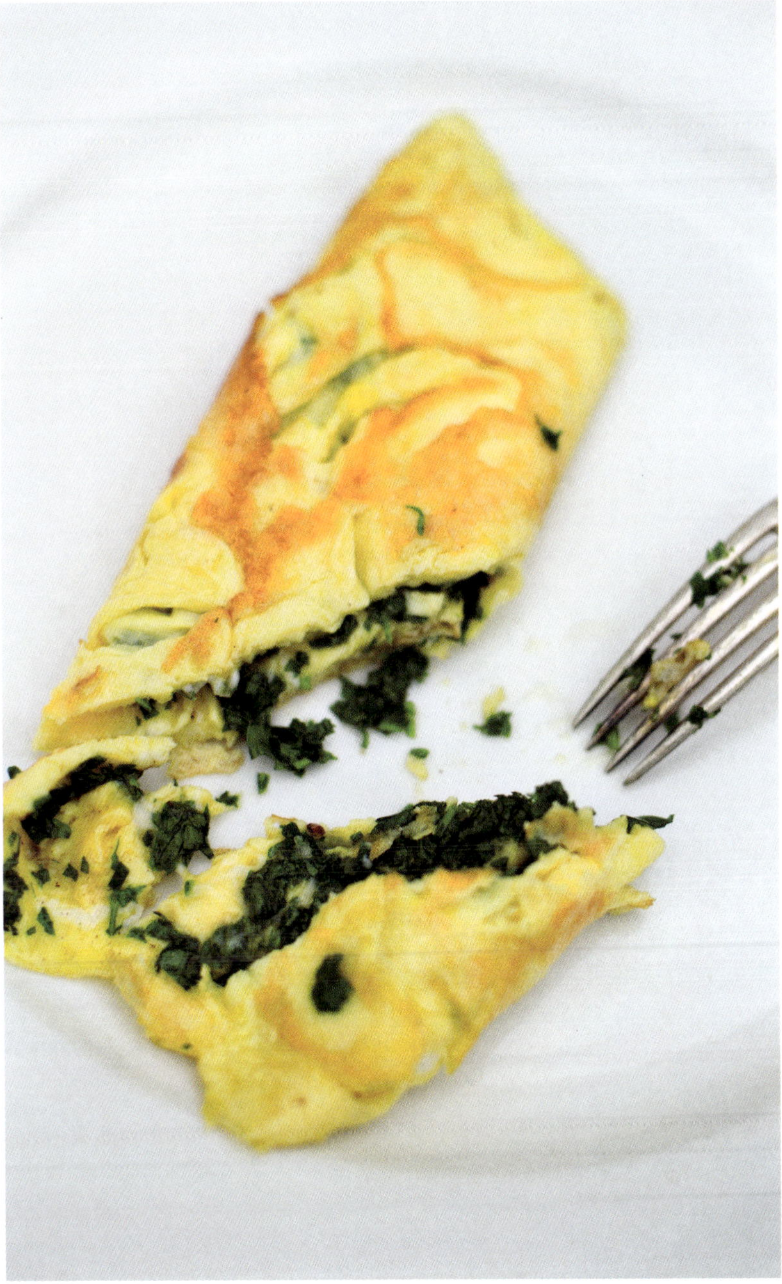

Tarragon eggs

This simple, slightly retro little dish makes a lovely starter. Tarragon is very good with eggs but, like the previous omelette recipe, this one is open to variation, as the egg and mayonnaise make an excellent vehicle for many different herbs. Try fennel, a pinch of lovage or very finely chopped young borage leaves, for instance.

Serves 4 as a starter

4 large eggs, at room temperature
3 tbsp mayonnaise (ideally homemade, see p.159)
4 tsp finely chopped tarragon
Little Gem or other sweet, crisp lettuce leaves
Sea salt and freshly ground black pepper (if needed)

Bring a pan of water to the boil. Add the eggs and simmer them for 9 minutes. Immediately drain and run the eggs under cold water to stop them cooking.

When cool enough to handle, peel the eggs. Halve them lengthways, scoop out the yolks and mash these in a bowl with the mayonnaise and tarragon (you shouldn't need to add seasoning if the mayonnaise is already well seasoned).

Carefully spoon the egg mayonnaise mixture back into the egg hollows. Serve with a few crisp lettuce leaves.

Variation

If you leave the boiled eggs whole and chop them, whites and all, before combining with the mayonnaise and herbs, you have a lovely topping for a crisp brown bread canapé, or a rather elegant sandwich filling.

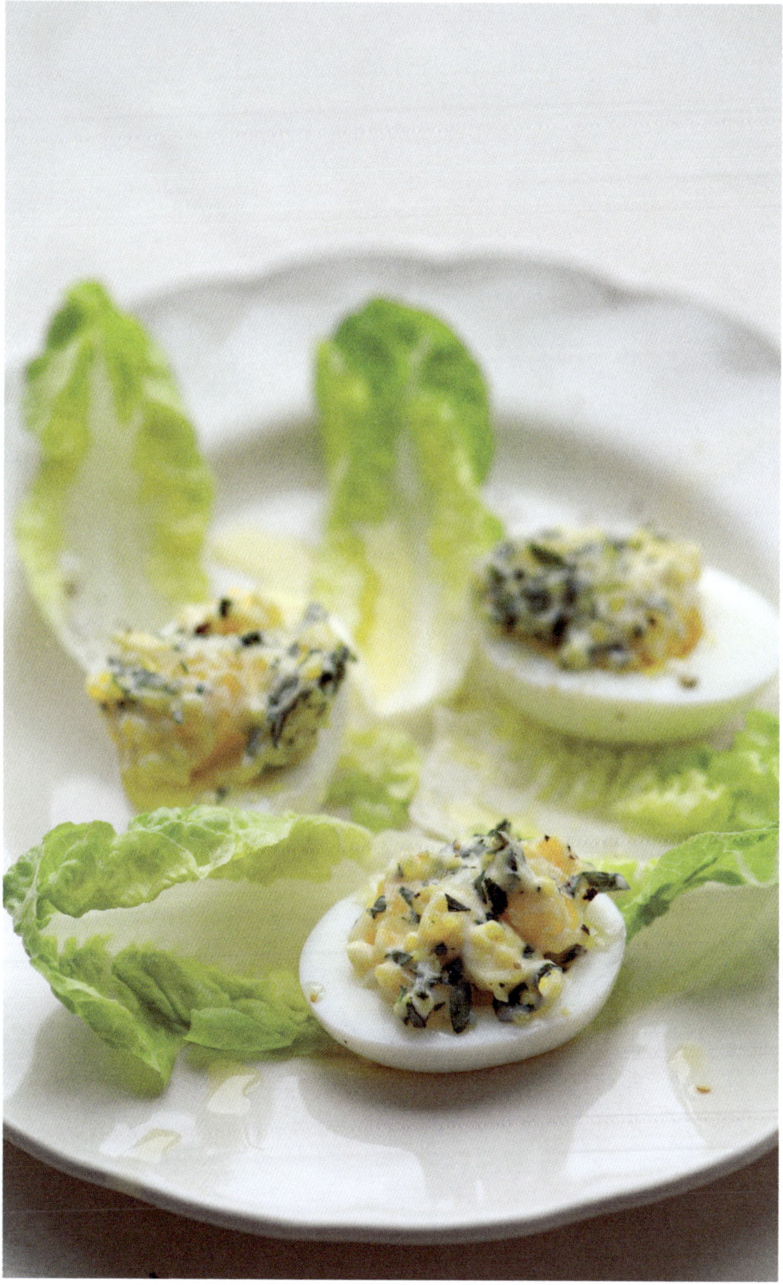

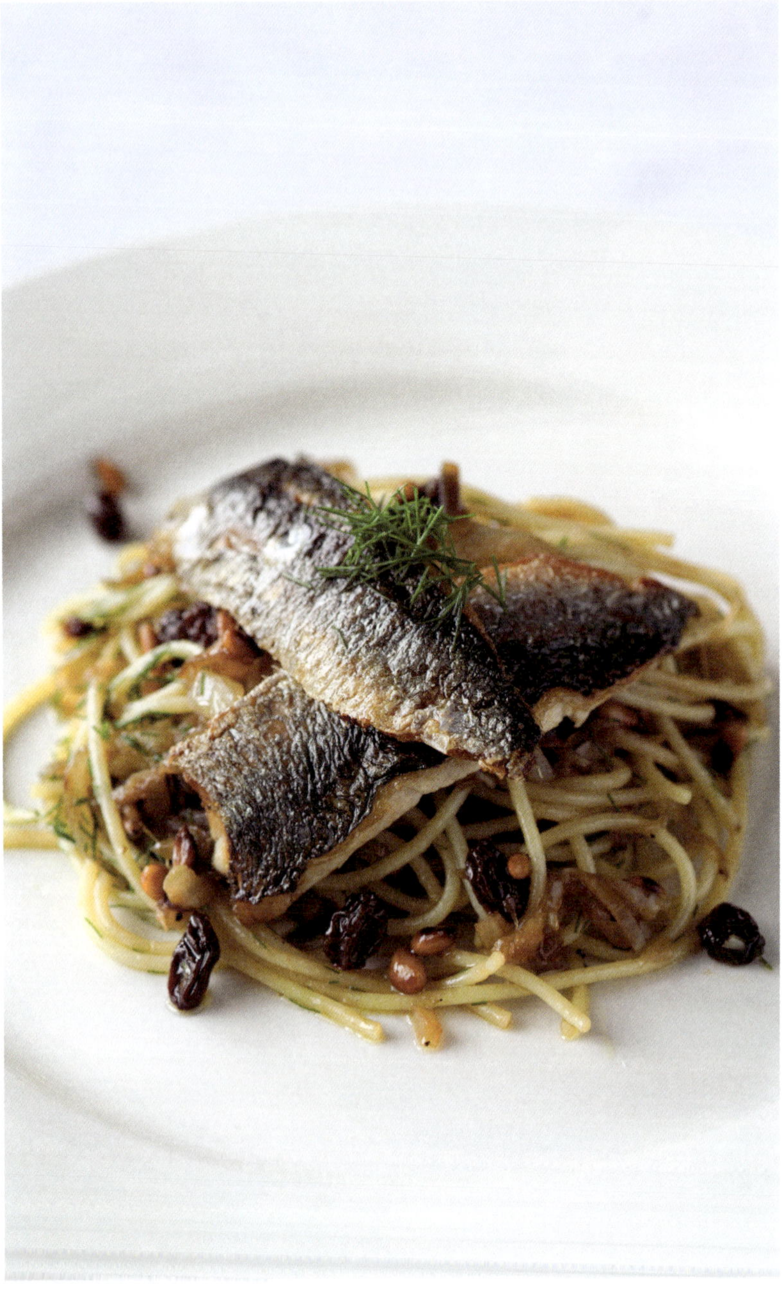

Pasta with sardines and fennel

This is my take on a traditional Sicilian dish. If you object to the tiny bones in sardine fillets, you could use mackerel instead.

Serves 4

- 300g linguine or spaghetti, or pasta shapes
- 4 tbsp olive oil
- 1 onion, peeled, quartered and finely sliced
- 1 garlic clove, peeled and cut into slivers
- 3–4 tbsp chopped fennel herb
- 50g sultanas or raisins
- 50g pine nuts, toasted
- 2 tsp balsamic vinegar
- A few squeezes of lemon juice
- 8 sardine fillets (or use 4 whole sardines, if you prefer)
- Sea salt and freshly ground black pepper

Bring a large pan of water to the boil, salt it well and then add the pasta. Cook until al dente, using the time suggested on the packet as a guide.

Meanwhile, heat 3 tbsp olive oil in a frying pan over a medium heat. Add the onion with a pinch each of salt and pepper and sweat for about 5 minutes, until soft and golden. Add the garlic, most of the fennel (reserve a little for finishing), the sultanas and pine nuts. Cook for another 2 minutes, then stir in the balsamic vinegar and turn off the heat.

Drain the pasta well and tip it into the frying pan with the onion mixture. Stir, then return the lot to the hot pasta pan, scraping in all the oil and flavourings. Add a squeeze of lemon juice and toss well. Check the seasoning, then cover the pan to keep everything warm.

Cook the sardines quickly: wipe out the frying pan, add another 1 tbsp oil and put over a medium heat. Season the flesh side of the sardine fillets well. Put them, skin side down, in the pan and cook for about 2 minutes, until the flesh is just about all opaque. Flip over and cook for another minute.

Heap the pasta into warmed dishes, top with the sardine fillets, give the whole lot a good squeeze of lemon juice and finish with a sprinkling of fennel.

Baked white fish
with a hyssop and orange crust

This is a quick and simple way to make a plain slab of white fish that much more delicious and enticing. I love the slight sourness of hyssop with the juicy sweetness of the fish flesh, but this recipe will also work well with rosemary or lemon thyme, and with lemon instead of orange zest.

Serves 4

4 fat fillets of white fish, such as pollack, coley or sustainably caught cod or haddock, about 175g each
A little olive oil
Sea salt and freshly ground black pepper

For the crust
200g fresh white breadcrumbs (from good robust bread such as sourdough)
1 tbsp finely chopped hyssop
1 large garlic clove, peeled and finely chopped
Finely grated zest of 1 large or 2 small oranges
2 tbsp olive oil

Preheat the oven to 220°C/Gas mark 7. Lightly oil a baking tray with a shallow lip (you want the fish to be exposed to the heat on all sides, but its juices need to be contained).

For the crust, mix all the ingredients together well and season with salt and pepper. Lightly oil and season the fish fillets and put them on the baking tray. Press the breadcrumb crust all over the fish in a thick, even layer.

Bake for 15 minutes until the crust is golden brown and the fish is cooked through, then serve straight away. This is very nice with roasted cherry tomatoes and roughly crushed potatoes, although green veg would work well too.

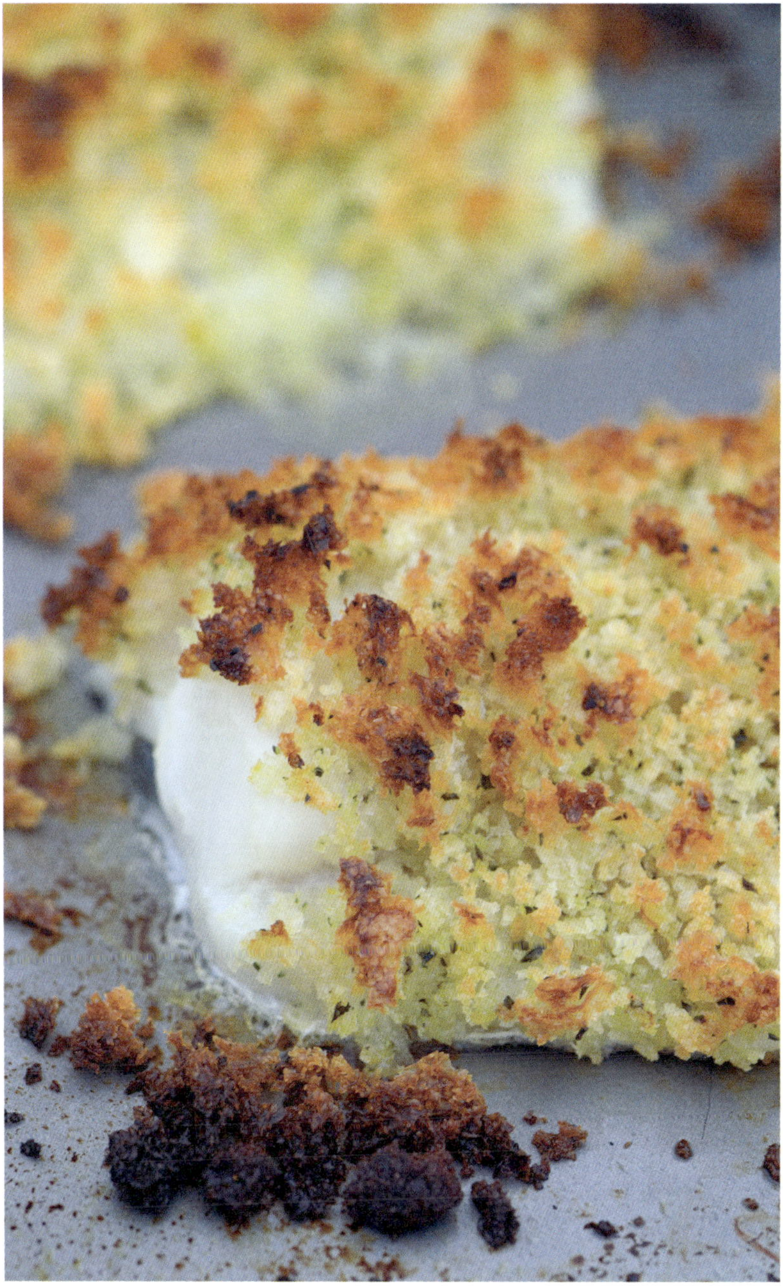

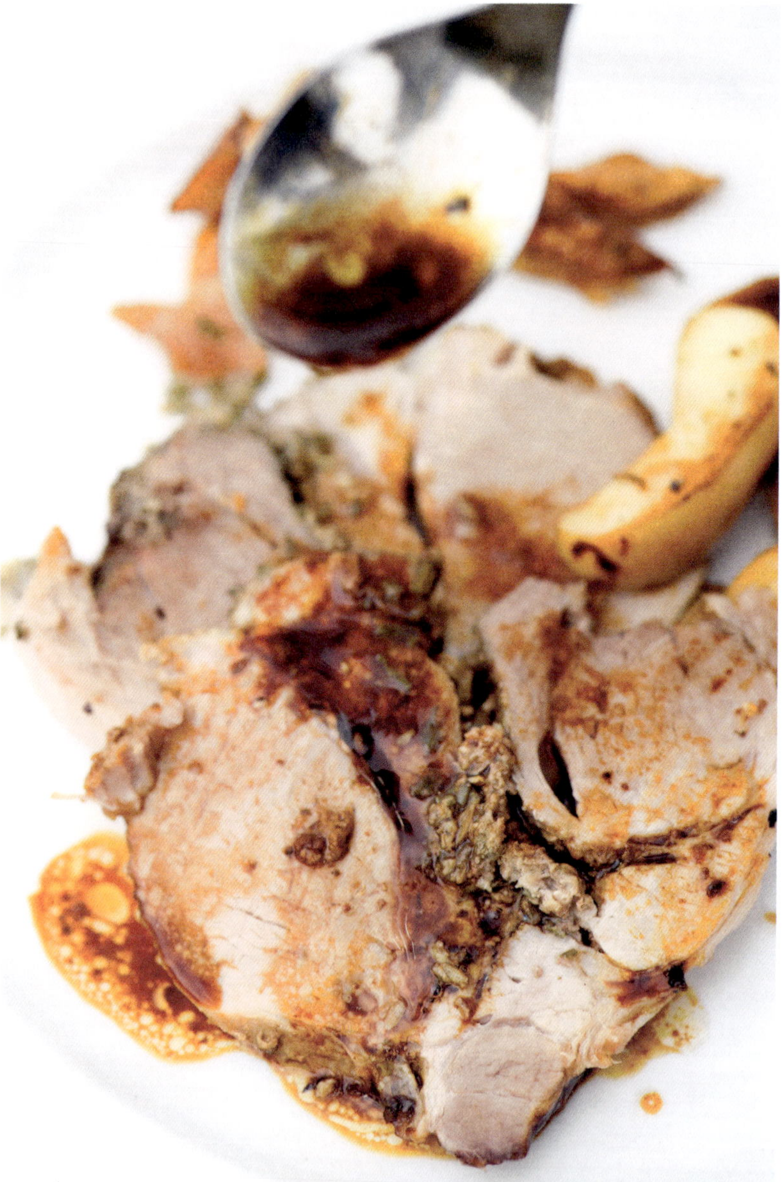

Pork with fennel and rosemary

This is inspired by the traditional Italian dish of *porchetta*, where a whole suckling pig is stuffed and roasted. Aromatic fennel and rosemary are often used to flavour the meat, and they work just as well on a smaller scale. If possible, store the pork uncovered in the fridge for at least 12 hours before cooking. This helps to dry out the rind, resulting in better crackling.

Serves 4–8

1–2kg piece of boned-out pork shoulder
2–4 dessert apples (depending on the size of your joint), cored and cut into 6–8 wedges each
About 300ml well-flavoured chicken or vegetable stock
Fine sea salt

For the flavouring paste
3 garlic cloves, peeled
2 tsp fennel seeds
2 tbsp chopped rosemary
Finely grated zest of 1 lemon
2–4 tbsp olive oil
Sea salt and freshly ground black pepper

Preheat the oven to 240°C/Gas mark 9. Score the pork rind if it isn't already scored.

For the paste, crush the garlic with a pinch of salt in a mortar. Add the fennel seeds and pound roughly, then work in the rosemary, lemon zest and some pepper. Bind together with the olive oil – just enough to make a coarse spreadable paste.

Open out the pork and lay it skin side down on a board. If it is mostly in one thick piece, use a sharp knife to open up the existing cavity or slice into the thicker parts to create a bigger surface area. Rub the herb paste all over the inside of the meat, working it into every crevice. Roll up the meat as best you can and tie tightly with string in 3 or 4 places. Place, skin side up, in a roasting tin. Wipe any excess oil or stuffing off the skin with kitchen paper. Sprinkle the rind generously with fine salt.

Roast for 20 minutes, then lower the setting to 180°C/Gas mark 4 and roast for a further 35 minutes per 500g, putting the apples around the meat about 30 minutes before the end of cooking. Check that the meat is cooked by piercing the thickest part and pressing the joint; there must be no trace of pink in the juices.

Leave the pork to rest in a warm place for 10–15 minutes before carving. Spoon the rich juices from the dish over the meat as you serve it. Or, to make more of a gravy, take the pork and apples out of the roasting tin, add about 300ml stock to the tin and let it bubble over a medium heat on the hob to reduce while you scrape up the caramelised bits, then pour into a jug. The pork is also very nice cold.

Beef stew with lovage

Lovage lends a good deep flavour to any stew or soup and in this hearty beef dish its delicately spicy side comes to the fore as well.

Serves 6–8

4 tbsp rapeseed or olive oil
2 medium onions, peeled and finely sliced
1kg braising steak or other stewing beef, cut into cubes
4 medium carrots, peeled and sliced
2 tbsp chopped lovage
150ml red wine
A couple of bay leaves or, even better, a bouquet garni (see p.19)
About 300ml beef or chicken stock, or water
About 500g potatoes, peeled and thickly sliced
Sea salt and freshly ground black pepper

Heat 2 tbsp oil in a large flameproof casserole. Add the onions and sweat down for 10 minutes or so.

Meanwhile, heat another 1 tbsp oil in a large frying pan over a fairly high heat. Season half the beef with salt and pepper and add to the hot frying pan. Fry, turning once or twice, until nicely browned all over, then add to the casserole with the onions. Repeat the process to brown the rest of the beef. Add to the casserole with the sliced carrots and half the chopped lovage.

Use the wine to deglaze the frying pan, stirring well to scrape up any caramelised bits, and letting it simmer for a few minutes to reduce a little. Add to the casserole.

Add the bay leaves or bouquet garni and enough stock or water to just barely cover the meat and veg. Bring to a simmer. Cover, turn the heat to very low and cook at a very gentle simmer for an hour.

Add the sliced potatoes, give the stew a stir and cook at a very low simmer for another hour. Stir in the remaining chopped lovage and some salt and pepper and serve with shredded greens and some rice or bread.

Stuffed breast of lamb
with dried apricots and winter savory

Breast of lamb is a strange-looking cut of meat, but so delicious and inexpensive. It's made for stuffing and rolling, and the pungent piney note of winter savory enhances it beautifully.

Serves 2–3

1 breast of lamb
Sea salt and freshly ground
   black pepper

For the stuffing

1 tbsp rapeseed or olive oil
1 small onion, peeled and chopped
1 garlic clove, peeled and chopped
50g breadcrumbs
3 dried apricots, chopped
2 tbsp chopped winter savory
1 small egg, beaten

Preheat the oven to 200°C/Gas mark 6.

For the stuffing, heat the oil in a frying pan over a medium heat. Add the onion and garlic and sauté gently for about 10 minutes, until soft. Leave to cool a little, then combine with the breadcrumbs, dried apricots, winter savory, beaten egg and some seasoning.

Unroll the breast of lamb, season the surface with salt and pepper, and spread the stuffing over it. Roll up again and secure with cocktail sticks or string. Roast for 30 minutes, then lower the oven setting to 150°C/Gas mark 2 and cook for a further 1½ hours.

Leave the lamb to rest in a warm place for 15 minutes, then slice it thickly. As this cut of lamb is rich and quite fatty, you only need some simply cooked vegetables with it – perhaps boiled or mashed potatoes and some steamed greens, sauced with a lick of the rich juices from the tin.

Loin of lamb with lavender
and lemon thyme

I'm certainly not the first person to think of roasting lamb with lavender, but this is my particular take on the idea. The lemon thyme seems to work so well, really enhancing the floral qualities of the lavender. If you don't have any, you could use ordinary thyme.

Serves 4

2 tbsp finely chopped lavender leaves
2 tsp finely chopped lemon thyme
Finely grated zest of 1 lemon
1 fat garlic clove, peeled and finely chopped
About 2 tbsp rapeseed or olive oil
500–600g piece of boned-out lamb loin
A little white wine or stock, for deglazing (optional)
Sea salt and freshly ground black pepper

Preheat the oven to 220°C/Gas mark 7.

Combine the lavender, lemon thyme, lemon zest and garlic in a small bowl. Add some seasoning and just enough oil to make a thick paste.

Lay the meat, skin side down, on a board and smear the herb mixture all over the inside surface, working it into all the cracks and crevices. Fold the meat over on itself and tie securely in several places with string. Smear any escaping oil over the outside and season with salt and pepper.

Place the meat in a roasting dish, with the 'open' edge uppermost to keep the flavouring mix inside. Roast for 15 minutes, then lower the oven setting to 170°C/Gas mark 3 and roast for a further 15 minutes for just-pink lamb.

Leave the lamb to rest in a warm place for 15 minutes before slicing. Deglaze the pan with a little white wine or stock, or even a splash of water, to create a few spoonfuls of flavoursome gravy.

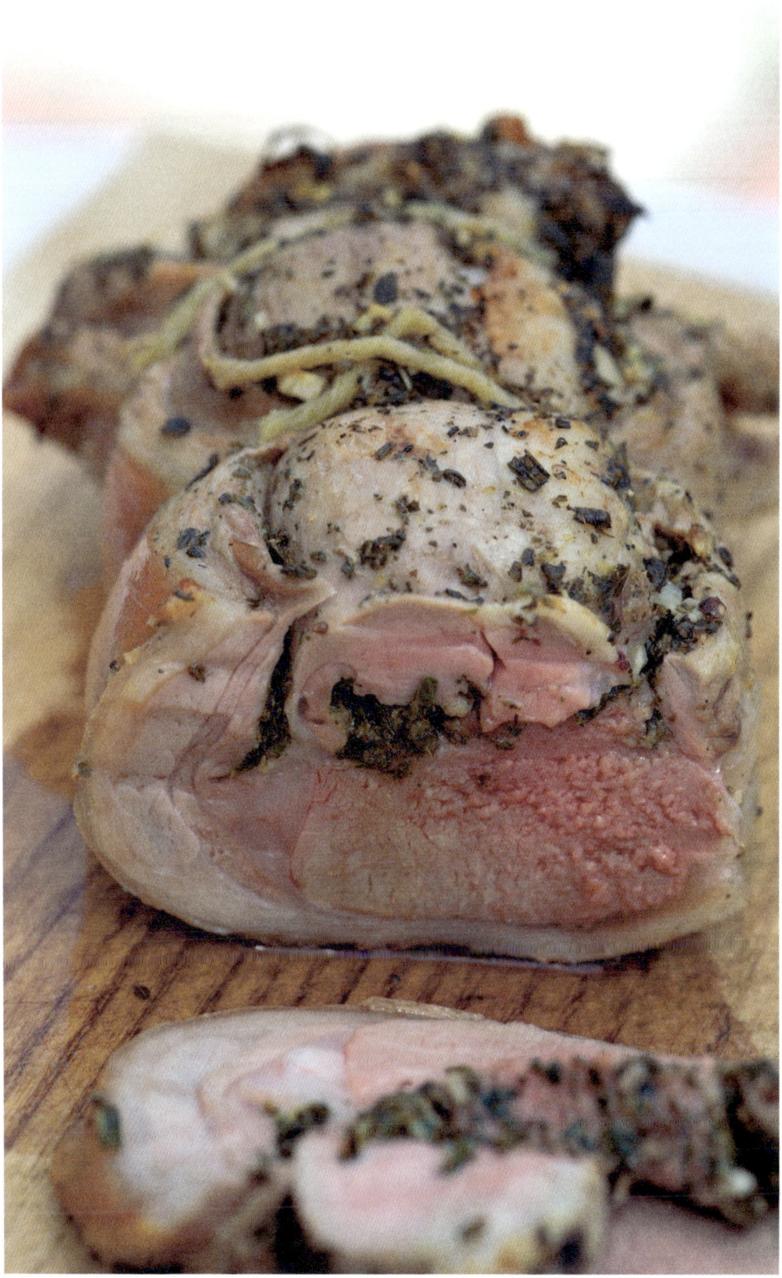

Baked chicken
with forty cloves of garlic

This is an incredibly simple and delicious dish. It's worth making it to feed three or four, then using the leftovers over the next few days. The garlic-infused chicken is wonderful cold in sandwiches, or chopped up and reheated in its rich oily juices then combined with waxy potatoes and peas or beans. Choose a good, but not too overpowering, olive oil – its flavour will be significant in the finished dish.

Serves 6–8

1 chicken, about 1.8kg, jointed into 8 pieces
100ml extra virgin olive oil
A few sprigs of rosemary
A couple of bay leaves
4 garlic bulbs, broken into individual cloves (unpeeled)
½ glass of white wine (optional)
Juice of ½ lemon
Sea salt and freshly ground black pepper

Preheat the oven to 180°C/Gas mark 4.

Season the chicken pieces well all over with salt and pepper. Heat 2–3 tbsp of the extra virgin olive oil in a large non-stick frying pan over a medium-high heat and sear the chicken all over. You'll probably have to do this in two batches. Transfer the chicken pieces to an oven dish, placing them skin side up.

Tuck the rosemary and bay leaves around the chicken pieces, then scatter over the unpeeled garlic cloves, pushing them down so they nestle low in the pan, between the chicken pieces.

Deglaze the browning pan with the wine (or use water), stirring well to scrape up any bits of caramelised chicken. Pour this into the tin (not over the chicken skin). Squeeze over the lemon juice, trickle over the remaining olive oil and scatter extra salt and pepper on the chicken skin.

Cover the dish with foil and bake for 30 minutes, then uncover, turn the oven up to 190°C/Gas mark 5 and bake for a further 20 minutes, or until the chicken pieces are well browned and cooked through.

Serve with something that will soak up the abundant oily juices – new potatoes, mash, rice or good bread – and a green vegetable or salad, such as watercress.

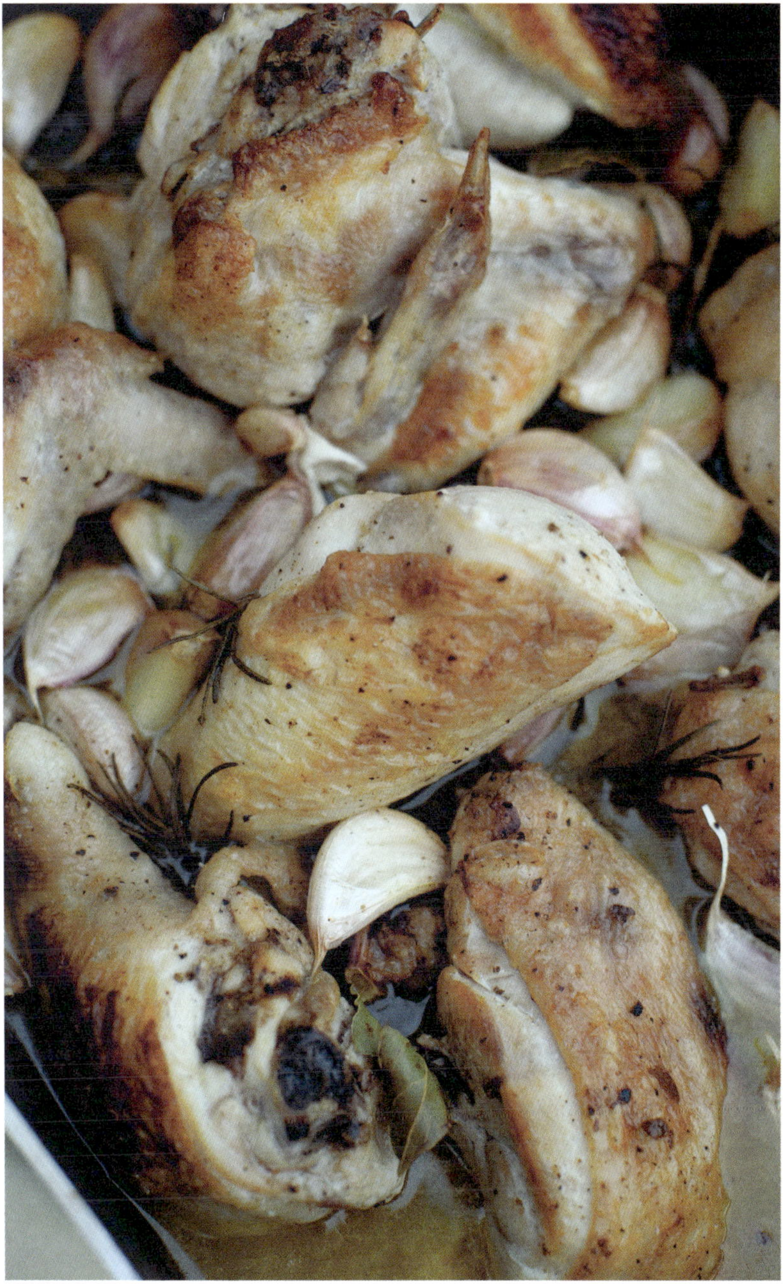

Roast chicken with
lemon and myrtle

The bay-and-orange scent of myrtle informs this dish in a wonderfully subtle way. You could replace it with another woody herb: thyme, rosemary, summer savory and marjoram all spring to mind, or a combination of two or three of these.

Serves 4, with leftovers

1 chicken, about 1.75–2kg
2 large sprigs of myrtle, each with 15–20 leaves
1 lemon
1 small garlic clove, peeled
100g unsalted butter, softened
A small glass of dry white wine (optional)
Sea salt and freshly ground black pepper

Take the chicken out of the fridge about an hour before cooking so it comes up to room temperature. Preheat the oven to 220°C/Gas mark 7.

Take the leaves from 1 myrtle sprig and chop them roughly. Put in a mortar. Grate the zest from the lemon and add this, with the garlic and a good pinch each of salt and pepper. Crush to a rough paste, then combine with the softened butter.

Untruss the chicken and put it in a roasting dish. Pull the legs away from the body slightly so hot air can circulate. Pack as much of the flavoured butter as you can under the skin of the breast, smoothing it along without tearing the skin. Smear any remaining butter over the outside of the bird. Put two quarters of the derinded lemon inside the bird. Bash the remaining myrtle sprig to crush the leaves a little and add to the cavity too. Season the skin and the cavity with more salt and pepper.

Roast the chicken for 20 minutes. Remove the roasting tin from the oven and pour the wine (or just use water) into the tin (not over the bird). Lower the oven setting to 180°C/Gas mark 4 and roast the chicken for a further 40 minutes.

Turn the oven off, prop the door open slightly and leave the chicken inside to rest and finish cooking for 15 minutes. Check that it is cooked by plunging a skewer into the thickest part of the meat, where the leg joins the body. Press with a spoon; the juices that run out should be clear. If they are pink, the chicken is not cooked.

Carve the chicken and serve with its delicious buttery juices – all the gravy you'll need. This requires nothing more than some bread and a crisp salad, but potatoes and other veg – particularly wilted shredded greens or kale – would be good too.

Spring pasta with wild garlic
and purple sprouting broccoli

If you're not lucky enough to have a source of wild garlic, you can use a freshly snipped bunch of chives or, even better, garlic chives here. Very finely sliced Welsh onion tops would be good too. And, of course, you could use ordinary broccoli instead of purple sprouting.

Serves 2

- 175g pasta shapes of your choice
- 150g purple sprouting broccoli (or ordinary broccoli), chopped into small pieces
- A knob of unsalted butter
- 50g soft rindless goat's cheese
- 4–6 wild garlic leaves, finely shredded
- A little extra virgin olive oil
- Sea salt and freshly ground black pepper
- Finely grated Parmesan or hard goat's cheese, to serve

Bring a large pan of water to the boil, salt it well and then add the pasta. Cook until al dente, using the time suggested on the packet as a guide, adding the broccoli to the pan about 5 minutes before the pasta will be done.

Drain the pasta and broccoli and, while still piping hot, add the butter and goat's cheese, letting them melt and coat the pasta and veg. Season with salt and pepper to taste, then fold in the wild garlic.

Serve straight away in warmed bowls. Top with a trickle of good extra virgin olive oil and a scattering of Parmesan or hard goat's cheese.

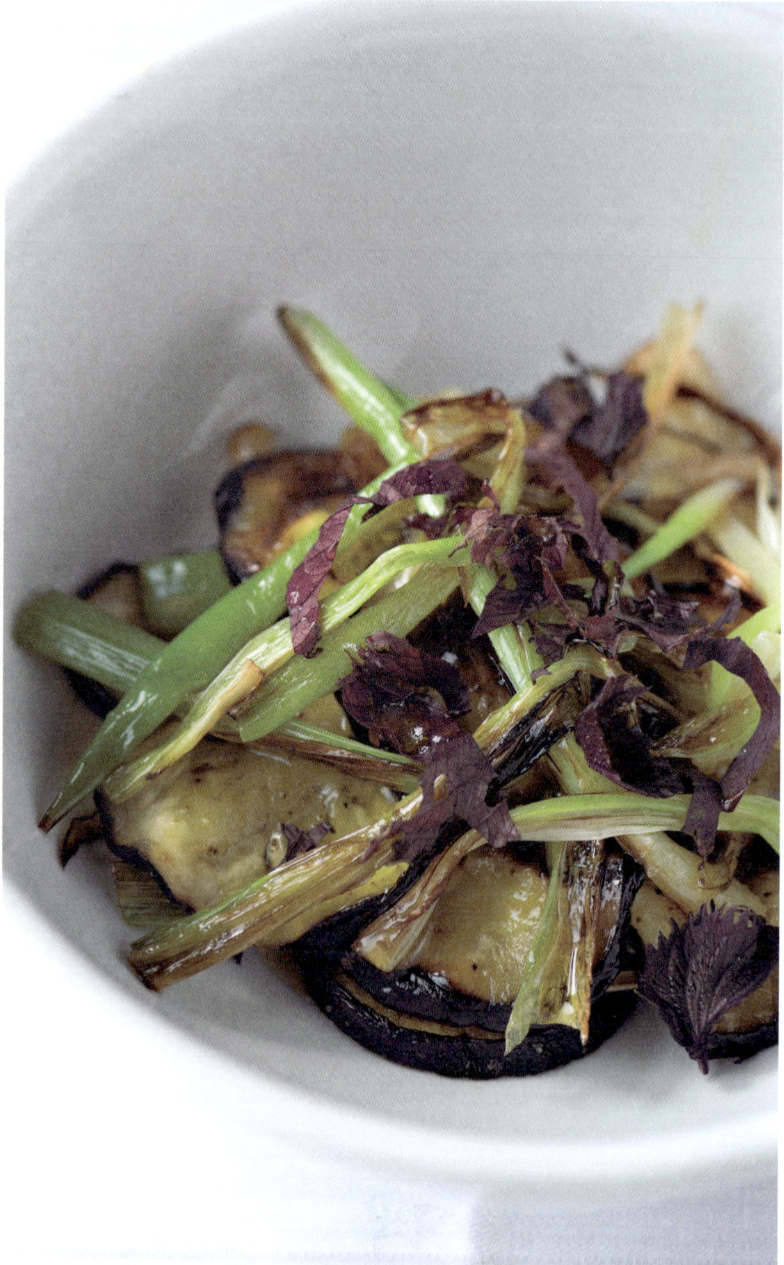

Aubergines with perilla

The slightly cumin-like flavour of perilla is lovely with aubergines. You could use the green or the purple variety here, though the purple looks particularly striking. This is delicious with some warm flatbreads and a scoop of soft goat's cheese or some garlicky yoghurt.

Serves 4 as a starter or side dish

2 medium aubergines, thinly sliced
Olive oil for brushing
12 spring onions, halved lengthways
About 12 perilla leaves, chopped
Sea salt and freshly ground
    black pepper

For the dressing
3 tbsp olive oil
A good squirt of lemon juice
½ tsp thin honey

Sprinkle the aubergine slices with salt and leave in a colander for 30 minutes or so to draw out the juices. Rinse the aubergines quickly and pat dry with kitchen paper.

For the dressing, mix the olive oil, lemon juice and honey together and season well with salt and pepper.

Brush the aubergines with olive oil and sear in a hot pan for a couple of minutes each side, until tender and golden. Do the same thing with the spring onions.

Layer the hot veg in a dish, trickling a little dressing and scattering some of the perilla over each layer. Leave until just warm, or completely cold, then serve.

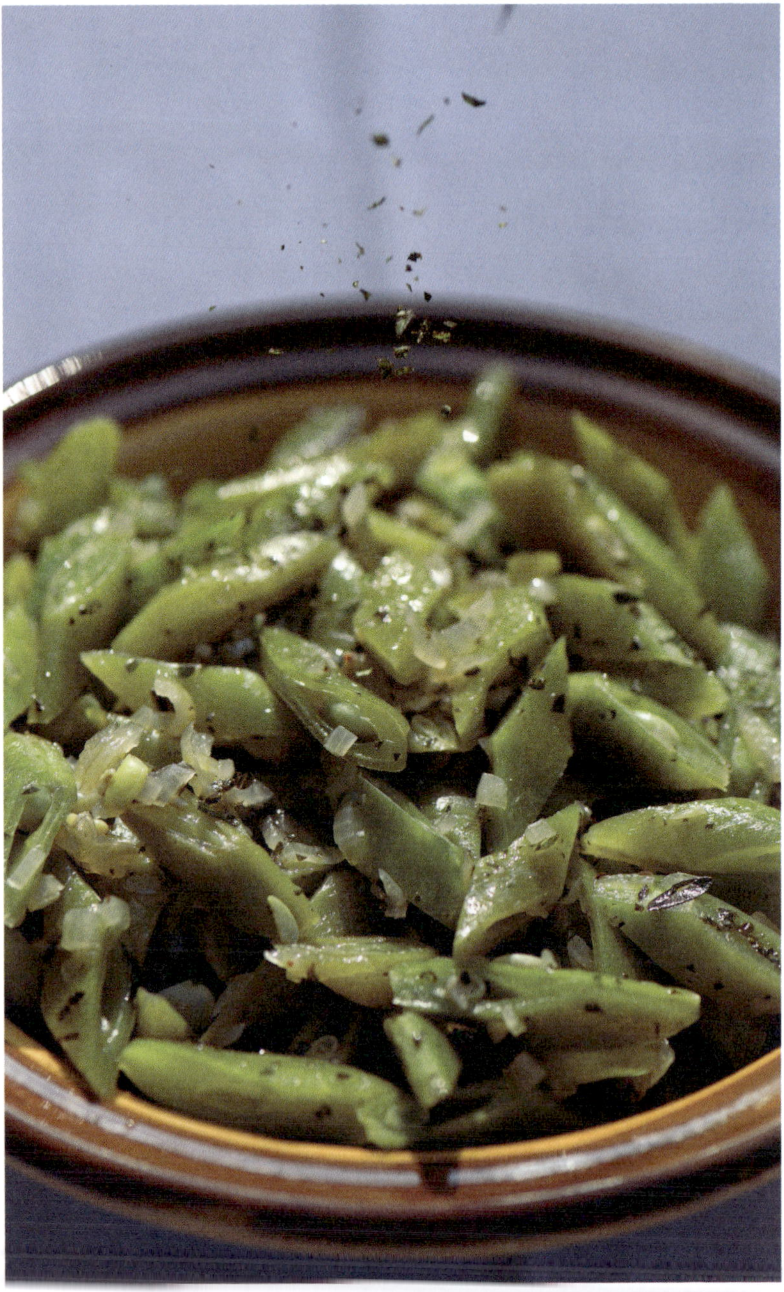

Runner beans
with summer savory

This is good served alongside anything from a simple potato and onion frittata to barbecued sausages. It works well with herbs other than summer savory – try tarragon, lemon thyme, marjoram or anise hyssop. You could use French beans too; these will need a little less cooking.

Serves 4 as a side dish

500g runner beans
2 tbsp rapeseed or olive oil
3–4 shallots or 1 small onion, peeled and finely chopped
1 small garlic clove, peeled and finely chopped
1 tbsp finely chopped summer savory
Sea salt and freshly ground black pepper

Use a potato peeler to remove the stringy fibres from the edges of the runner beans, top and tail them, then cut into 1–2cm pieces.

Heat the oil in a wide saucepan over a medium heat. Add the shallots or onion and sweat down for about 10 minutes, until soft. Add the garlic and beans. Cover the pan, lower the heat and sweat for another 10 minutes.

Add about 150ml water and continue to cook, uncovered, for a further 10–15 minutes, stirring from time to time. You want the beans to be just tender but still with a bit of crunch. Add the savory a couple of minutes before the end of cooking. Season with salt and pepper to taste and serve.

White beans with winter herbs

Baked beans, but not as you know them… This simple, pleasingly rustic dish is inspired by a Simon Hopkinson recipe. It is a doddle to do, very economical and fabulous comfort food.

Serves 4

250g dried white beans, such as cannellini, soaked for several hours in cold water
1–2 bay leaves, twisted
1 large sprig of rosemary
1 large sprig of winter savory or sage
2–3 garlic cloves (unpeeled), roughly squashed
500ml lamb or chicken stock
Sea salt and freshly ground black pepper

To finish
A little olive oil
100g diced pancetta or bacon lardons
1 garlic clove, peeled and finely chopped
1 tsp finely chopped rosemary
Extra virgin olive or rapeseed oil

Preheat your oven to 160°C/Gas mark 3.

Drain and rinse the soaked beans and put them into a casserole dish. Add the herbs, garlic cloves and stock. (I usually tie up the herbs in a square of muslin to stop the leaves straying throughout the dish, but this isn't essential.) Bring to the boil on the hob, then cover and transfer to the oven. Bake for 1–2 hours, until the beans are beautifully tender. Fish out the herbs and garlic.

To finish, heat a splash of olive oil in a frying pan and fry the bacon or pancetta for a few minutes, until just turning crisp. Add the chopped garlic and rosemary and immediately turn off the heat. Stir them into the bacon so the residual heat mellows the garlic, just a touch.

Season the beans with salt and pepper to taste. Ladle into deep dishes, scatter the bacon mixture over the top and finish with a swirl of virgin oil. Serve with bread.

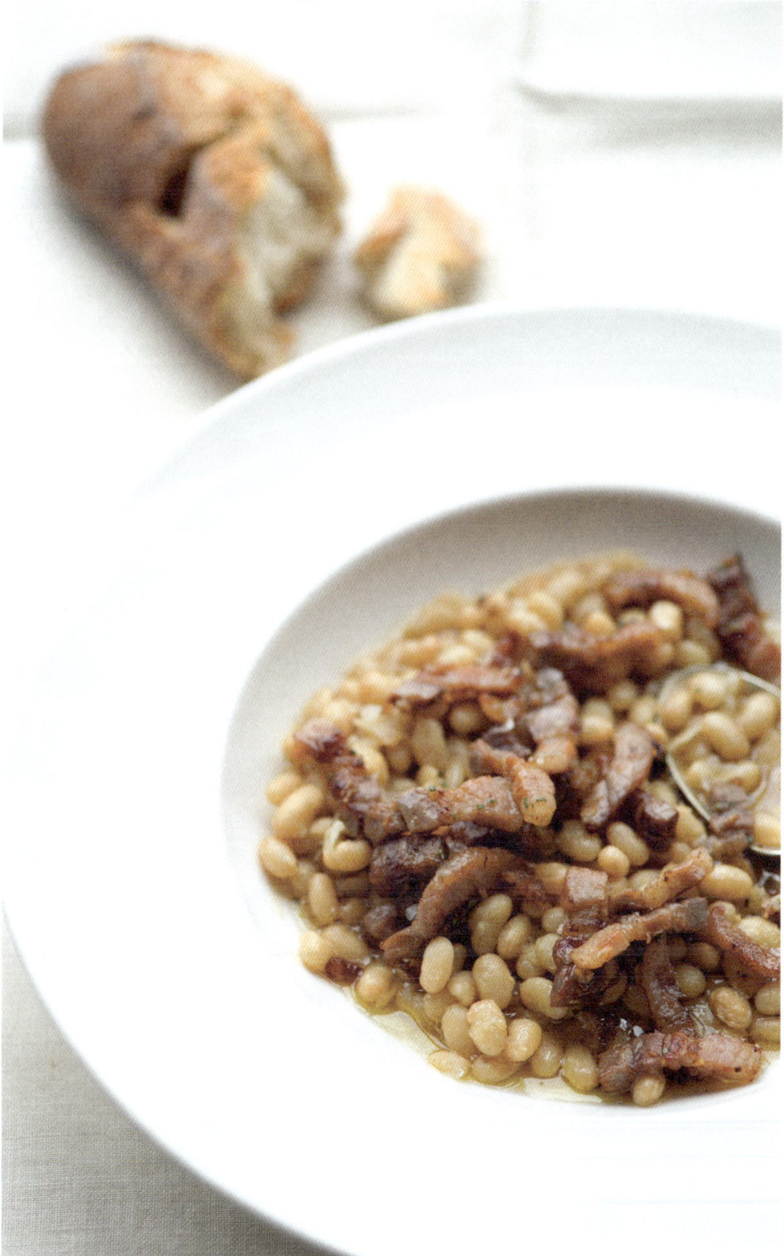

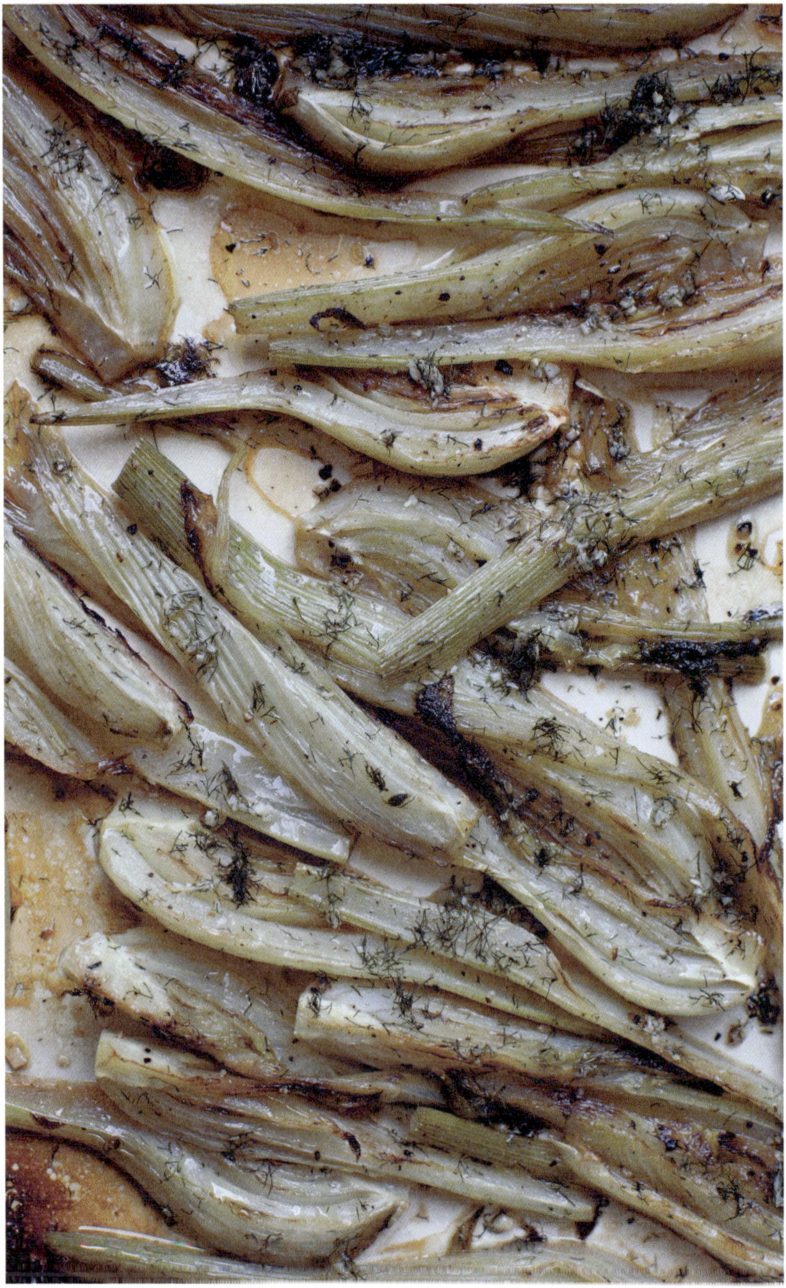

Double fennel braise

I have a passion for fennel – the herb and the vegetable – so I'm very fond of this dish. It makes a lovely accompaniment to fish but is also very good simply tossed into pasta and finished with some Parmesan.

Serves 4

1 tbsp olive or rapeseed oil
4 fat bulbs of Florence fennel, tough outer layers removed, cut into 8 wedges each, intact at the core
About 200ml chicken or vegetable stock
1 fat garlic clove
2 tbsp finely chopped fennel herb
Sea salt and freshly ground black pepper

Preheat the oven to 180°C/Gas mark 4.

Heat the oil in a large frying pan over a medium-high heat. Add the fennel wedges and sear for about 10 minutes, turning once or twice, until they are caramelised on both sides. Transfer to an oven dish.

Deglaze the frying pan with the stock, letting it fizz and simmer for a minute, then pour over the fennel in the dish. Add a good sprinkling of salt and pepper and transfer to the oven. Braise for 20 minutes, or until the fennel is tender.

Meanwhile, finely chop the garlic and combine with the chopped fennel herb. Once the braised fennel is ready, immediately stir in the herb mix, so the heat of the fennel just softens the raw garlic. Serve straight away.

Creamed Swiss chard

This recipe is closely based on one I came across in a lovely American cookbook, *With A Measure of Grace*, written by the owners of a Buddhist restaurant in Utah. It travels well. This is a rich and comforting side dish and a little goes a long way – try it with roast chicken, or simply cooked Puy lentils.

Serves 4–6

- A large knob of unsalted butter
- 1 onion, peeled and finely chopped
- 1 garlic clove, peeled and finely chopped
- 350g Swiss chard leaves, including the tender parts of the stems, shredded
- 250ml double cream
- 20g Parmesan, grated
- 35g fresh breadcrumbs
- 1 heaped tbsp finely chopped tarragon
- Sea salt and freshly ground black pepper

Heat the butter in a large saucepan over a medium-low heat. Add the onion and sweat down gently for about 10 minutes until softened. Add the garlic and cook for a few more minutes.

Add the shredded chard, cream, Parmesan, breadcrumbs, chopped tarragon and some salt and pepper. Keep the heat low and cook gently, stirring often, for about 10 minutes or until you have a rich, thick mixture. Check the seasoning and serve.

Rosemary focaccia

Serve this shallow Italian bread still warm and fragrant from the oven, ready to be torn into chunks and dipped into soup, stew or just a bit more olive oil. The dough is very loose and sticky. Persevere with it if you can: the wet consistency ensures the relaxed form and lovely open texture of a really good focaccia. If you're new to kneading, or you just don't feel very confident, you can either start off with a touch less water – try 325ml – or add generous amounts of flour while you knead. Your bread will still be good. Alternatively, use a mixer with a dough hook.

Serves 6–8

500g strong white bread flour
1 tsp easy-blend yeast
10g fine sea salt
3 tbsp extra virgin olive oil, plus extra to finish

1 tbsp chopped rosemary
Coarse sea salt, to finish

Put the flour, yeast and salt into a large bowl and mix well. Add the 3 tbsp extra virgin olive oil and 350ml warm water. Mix to a rough dough. Turn out on to a floured surface and knead for about 5 minutes, adding extra flour only if you need to. My technique is to slap the dough down, then use the heel of one hand to push it away from me, stretching it out, then scoop it back over itself and repeat. It will stick to your hands but it's worth it.

Oil your hands generously with more olive oil and scoop up the kneaded dough, oiling it all over as you do so. Put in a clean bowl, cover with cling film and leave to rise in a warm place until doubled in size (at least an hour, up to two).

Brush a shallow-sided baking tray, about 22 x 30cm, with olive oil. Tip the dough out on to a floured work surface. Without 'knocking it back' first, flatten into a rough rectangle, then transfer to the oiled baking tray. Push the dough out to fill the tray in an even layer. Cover again and leave until puffy and increased in size by about half (at least 30 minutes). Meanwhile, heat your oven to 220°C/Gas mark 7.

Use a fingertip to push deep dimples all over the dough. Scatter with the chopped rosemary and some coarse salt, then trickle generously with more olive oil. Bake for 10 minutes, then reduce the heat to 180°C/Gas mark 4 and bake for a further 10 minutes, until golden.

Allow to cool a little, but serve still warm. Focaccia is best eaten soon after baking. If it's gone cold, reheat it gently before serving.

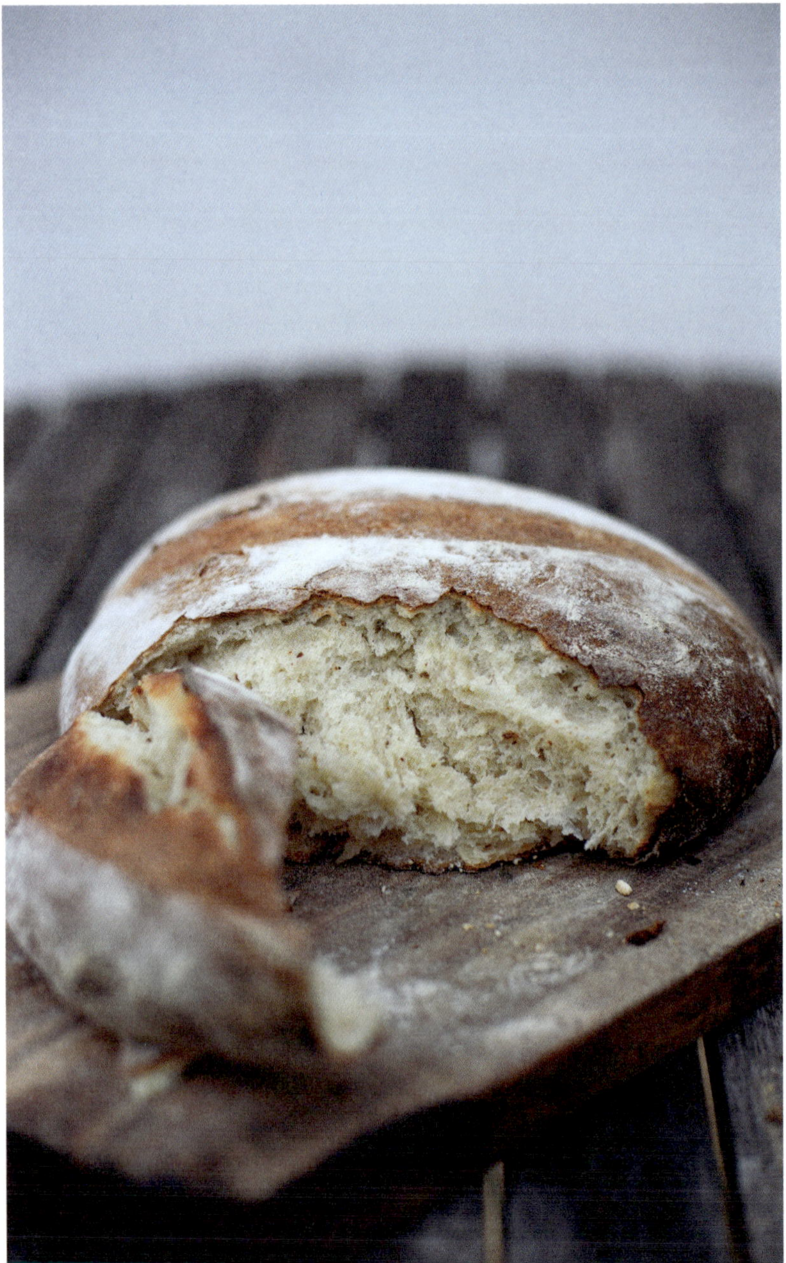

Fennel seed bread

This well-flavoured loaf is great with cheese or salty air-dried ham. You can replace some of the fennel seeds with celery seeds for a subtly different flavour.

Makes 1 loaf

2 tbsp fennel seeds
500g strong white flour
10g fine sea salt
1 tsp easy-blend yeast
2 tbsp thin honey
1 tbsp olive oil

Lightly toast the fennel seeds in a dry frying pan for a few minutes, until fragrant. Transfer to a mortar and roughly crush with the pestle.

Combine the crushed seeds with the flour, salt and yeast. Measure the honey into a measuring jug and make up to 325ml with warm water. Add to the flour with the olive oil and mix to a rough dough.

Turn out on to a clean surface and knead for 5–10 minutes. It will be quite a sticky dough, which is as it should be – you get better bread this way. You can add a little more flour to help you knead if you like, but don't overdo it. Alternatively, smear a little more olive oil on your work surface and hands to stop the dough sticking.

Shape the kneaded dough into a smooth round, coat with a little olive oil and place in a large clean bowl. Cover with cling film and leave to rise in a warm place until doubled in size – at least an hour, up to two.

Tip the risen dough out on to a lightly floured surface and deflate it with your fingertips. Shape again into a neat round, or a short, fat baguette if you prefer. Place on an oiled baking sheet. Alternatively, use a proving basket, if you have one. Cover lightly with a tea towel and leave until roughly doubled in size again (about an hour).

Preheat your oven to its highest setting. Cut a couple of slashes in the top of the loaf with a sharp knife or a baker's razor blade (a lame), or make deep snips with scissors. Bake at maximum temperature for 10 minutes, then reduce the setting to 180°C/Gas mark 4 and bake for a further 20 minutes, or until the loaf is golden brown and sounds hollow when tapped underneath. Transfer to a wire rack and leave to cool completely before slicing.

Soda bread with rosemary and sultanas

Soda bread is quick, easy and just as delicious as freshly baked yeasted bread. You can doctor your homemade soda breads with various additions, including fresh herbs – woody, pungent ones, such as thyme and rosemary, work best. This particular incarnation is a quick-to-make homage to the divine rosemary and raisin bread made at Sally Clarke's bakery in London. It's lovely with soup or a salad, or just spread with salty butter – as is the cheesy thyme variation below.

Makes 1 large loaf

500g plain white or refined spelt flour
1 tsp fine sea salt
1 tsp bicarbonate of soda
1 tbsp finely chopped rosemary
150g sultanas
300ml plain full-fat yoghurt
200ml whole milk

Preheat the oven to 200°C/Gas mark 6. Lightly oil a baking sheet or line one with baking parchment.

Sift the flour, salt and bicarbonate of soda together into a bowl. Stir in the chopped rosemary and sultanas. Make a well in the middle.

Whisk the yoghurt and milk together until smooth. Add to the dry ingredients and mix until just combined. This will give you a soft, sticky dough, which is how I like it, as it makes a nice moist loaf.

With floured hands, or a spatula, scrape the dough on to the prepared baking sheet and pat it into a rough round. Bake for 45 minutes until risen and golden brown.

Leave the bread to cool on a wire rack. Eat as it is within 24 hours or, if you've left it longer than that, toast the slices. The loaf freezes well too.

Variation

Soda bread with thyme, Cheddar and mustard Use 250g spelt or wholemeal flour mixed with 250g plain white flour. Replace the rosemary and sultanas with 100g grated strong Cheddar and 1 tbsp finely chopped thyme. Whisk 2 tsp English mustard into the yoghurt and milk before combining with the dry ingredients.

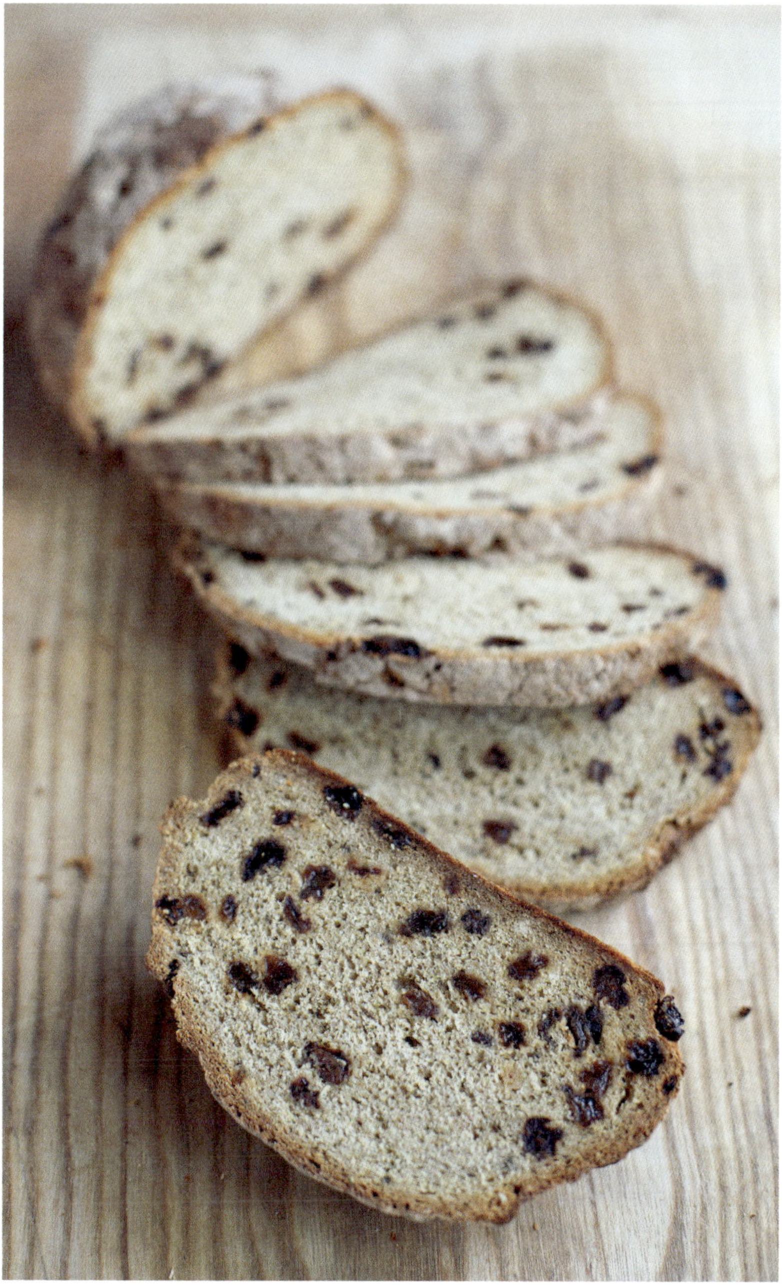

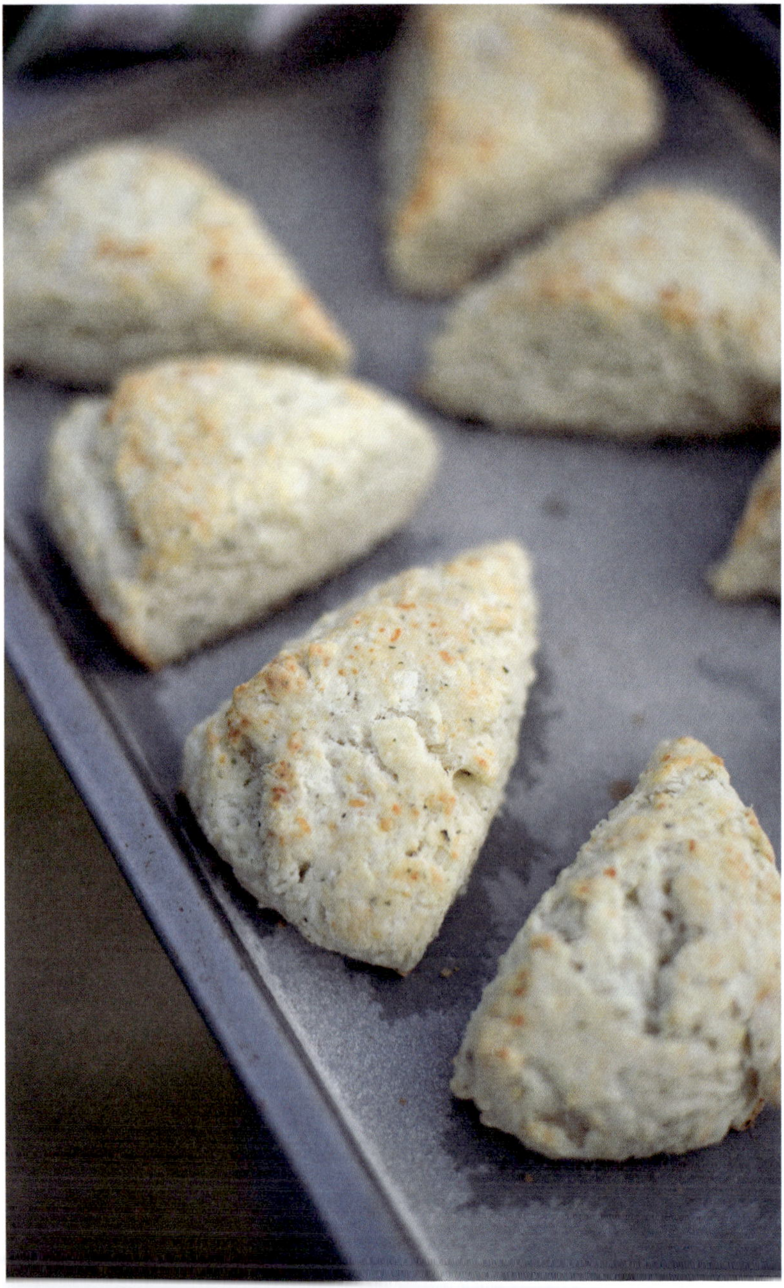

Bergamot scones

The subtle herby flavour of these savoury scones makes them delicious alongside a bowl of soup, but I like to eat them on their own too – warm from the oven, with just a smear of salty butter. They are also good made with thyme or marjoram.

Makes 8

250g self-raising white flour
¼ tsp salt
50g cold unsalted butter, diced
1 good tbsp finely chopped bergamot

35g Parmesan, finely grated
175ml whole milk, plus extra
  for glazing

Preheat the oven to 220°C/Gas mark 7 and grease a baking tray.

Sift the flour and salt into a bowl. Add the butter and rub in with your fingertips until thoroughly incorporated. Alternatively, do this in a food processor, then tip into a mixing bowl. Stir in the bergamot and Parmesan. Mix in the milk to form a soft, slightly sticky dough, but don't overwork it.

Tip the dough out on to a floured surface, knead lightly, then pat or roll to a rough circle 2.5–3cm thick. Cut into 8 triangles. Transfer to the baking sheet and brush each scone with milk. Bake for about 12 minutes, until risen and golden. Eat these scones on the day you make them, ideally still warm, or freeze.

Minted red berry sorbet

The mintiness of this gorgeous deep-pink sorbet makes it especially refreshing. Mint also has a seasoning effect on many fruits, and really enhances the raspberry and strawberry flavours here. Make sure you use spearmint rather than the more pungent peppermint (see p.105).

Serves 4

115g caster sugar
2 large leafy stems of spearmint,
 plus 2 tbsp finely chopped
 spearmint leaves to finish
500g mixed raspberries and
 strawberries, roughly half and half

Put the sugar into a saucepan with 200ml water. Heat gently, stirring often, until the sugar has dissolved. Increase the heat. Once simmering, cook the sugar syrup for 5 minutes. Turn off the heat. Roughly bruise the stems of mint and add these to the hot syrup, pushing them under the surface. Leave to cool completely.

Crush the berries roughly with your hands or a potato masher to get the juices flowing, then transfer to a blender and blitz to a purée. Work the purée through a sieve to remove all the pips.

Strain the cooled minty syrup into the berry purée, pressing the mint with a spoon to extract every last drop of flavour. Stir in the finely chopped mint leaves, then chill in the fridge.

Once cold, churn in an ice-cream maker until just set, then transfer to a suitable container and freeze until solid. (If you don't have an ice-cream maker, freeze in a shallow container, beating with a fork at hourly intervals until the sorbet is solid.)

Transfer the sorbet to the fridge 30 minutes or so before serving to soften. Serve scooped into small dishes.

PUDDINGS & SWEET TREATS

Raspberry ripple basil ice cream

Herb ice cream or custard

A classic custard, or *crème anglaise*, subtly infused with the scent and flavour of one well-chosen herb can be a heady delight. And, of course, it can form the base for a delectable homemade herb ice cream. A frozen custard, however, needs to be sweeter than a chilled one, so use 100g sugar if making ice cream rather than 50g.

If you're making the custard, serve it chilled with lightly sugared strawberries or raspberries, or baked sweetened rhubarb, poached pears, a gooseberry compote, or roasted peaches or plums.

Herbs to use
Bay leaves Use 4–6 leaves, each torn into 2–3 pieces
Lavender Use 2 tbsp chopped leaves and/or flowers
Lemon verbena Use 8–12 roughly chopped leaves
Basil Use 1 bunch (about 40g), stalks and leaves roughly torn or chopped

Makes about 600ml

200ml double cream
300ml whole milk
Your choice of herb (see above)
4 large egg yolks
50–100g caster sugar (see above)

Put the cream, milk and chosen herb into a saucepan. Bring to just below boiling point, then remove from the heat and set aside to infuse for about 1 hour.

Whisk the egg yolks and sugar together in a bowl (use 50g sugar for a custard, 100g for an ice cream). Strain the cream mixture into a jug, pressing the herbs with a spoon to extract all the flavour. Pour on to the yolks and sugar, whisking all the time. Pour the mixture into a clean saucepan. Heat gently, stirring all the time, until the custard thickens; don't let it boil, or it will curdle. Remove from the heat and cover the surface with cling film to stop a skin forming.

Once cool, your custard can be chilled, ready to serve. Alternatively, for a fragrant ice, churn the sweeter custard in an ice-cream maker, then put into the freezer.

Variation
Raspberry ripple basil ice cream For the ripple, put 300g raspberries, 30g caster sugar and 2 tbsp water into a pan. Bring to the boil and simmer for a few minutes. Press through a sieve back into the pan and boil for 5–10 minutes until thick. Cool and chill. Make a basil custard and churn until thick. Marble the raspberry sauce through the semi-set ice cream before putting in the freezer.

Lemon verbena layer
with raspberries

This is a very simple way to showcase the lovely citrus tang of lemon verbena, which goes perfectly with raspberries. You could use strawberries instead if you like, or a sweetened blackcurrant purée.

Serves 4

- 100g digestive or shortbread biscuits, crushed to rough crumbs
- 2 tsp finely chopped lemon verbena, plus 4 little sprigs, to garnish
- 50g caster sugar
- 100g full-fat fromage frais
- 100ml double cream
- 1 large egg white
- 300g raspberries
- Icing sugar, to serve

Divide the biscuit crumbs between 4 glass tumblers or sundae dishes.

Using a pestle and mortar, grind and pound the chopped lemon verbena with half the sugar until you have a fine, pale green sugar with no significant pieces of lemon verbena leaf visible.

Mix the verbena sugar with the fromage frais and cream in a large bowl. If the mixture is not already thick (this depends on the texture of the fromage frais to start with), beat until it forms soft peaks.

Beat the egg white until it holds stiff peaks. Add the remaining sugar and beat again until you have a glossy meringue that holds firm peaks. Fold this lightly into the fromage frais mixture. Spoon over the biscuits in the glasses.

Top with the raspberries and chill for an hour or so. Just before serving, add the sprigs of lemon verbena and a dusting of icing sugar.

PUDDINGS & SWEET TREATS 221

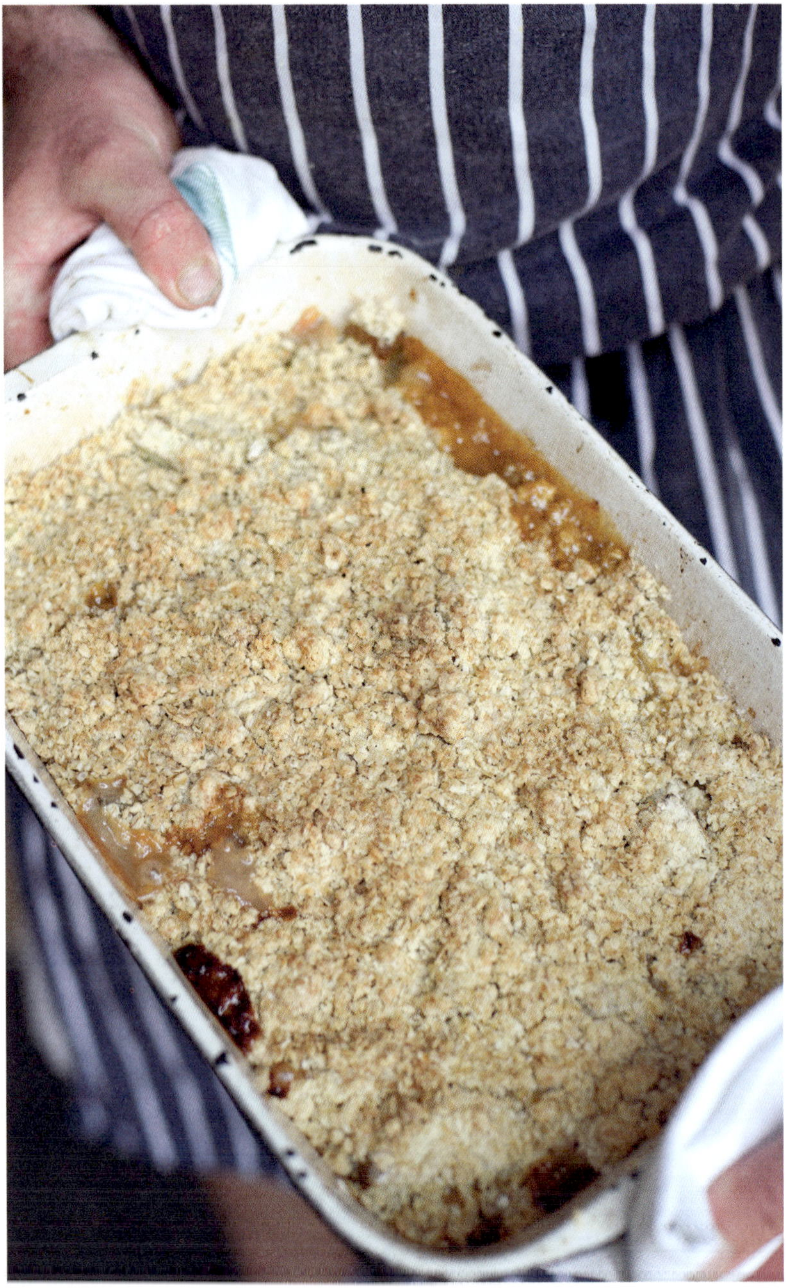

Rhubarb crumble
with angelica

Tender angelica stalk is just wonderful combined with rhubarb, lifting its flavour and softening its acidity. The fresh green seeds of sweet cicely have a very similar effect. You can use your favourite crumble topping here, or mine.

Serves 4–6

750g rhubarb, trimmed and chopped
50ml apple or orange juice
1 tbsp finely chopped young angelica stem (or finely chopped young green sweet cicely pods)
50g caster sugar

For the crumble topping
150g plain flour
150g fine oatmeal
A pinch of fine sea salt
125g cold unsalted butter, cubed
85g demerara sugar

Preheat the oven to 180°C/Gas mark 4.

To make the topping, put the flour, oatmeal and salt in a food processor. Add the butter and pulse just until combined. Tip the mixture out into a bowl and stir in the demerara sugar.

Put the rhubarb into a 20cm square oven dish (or similar). Sprinkle over the apple or orange juice and the angelica. Toss together lightly, then sprinkle the sugar evenly over. Put into the oven for about 20 minutes to soften the fruit.

Give the fruit a stir and pat it down into a fairly flat, even layer. Squeeze handfuls of the topping together in your hands, then crumble them over the fruit so you get a lumpy, crumbly mix. Bake for 30 minutes, until the crumble is golden brown and the fruit is bubbling underneath. Serve with cream or ice cream.

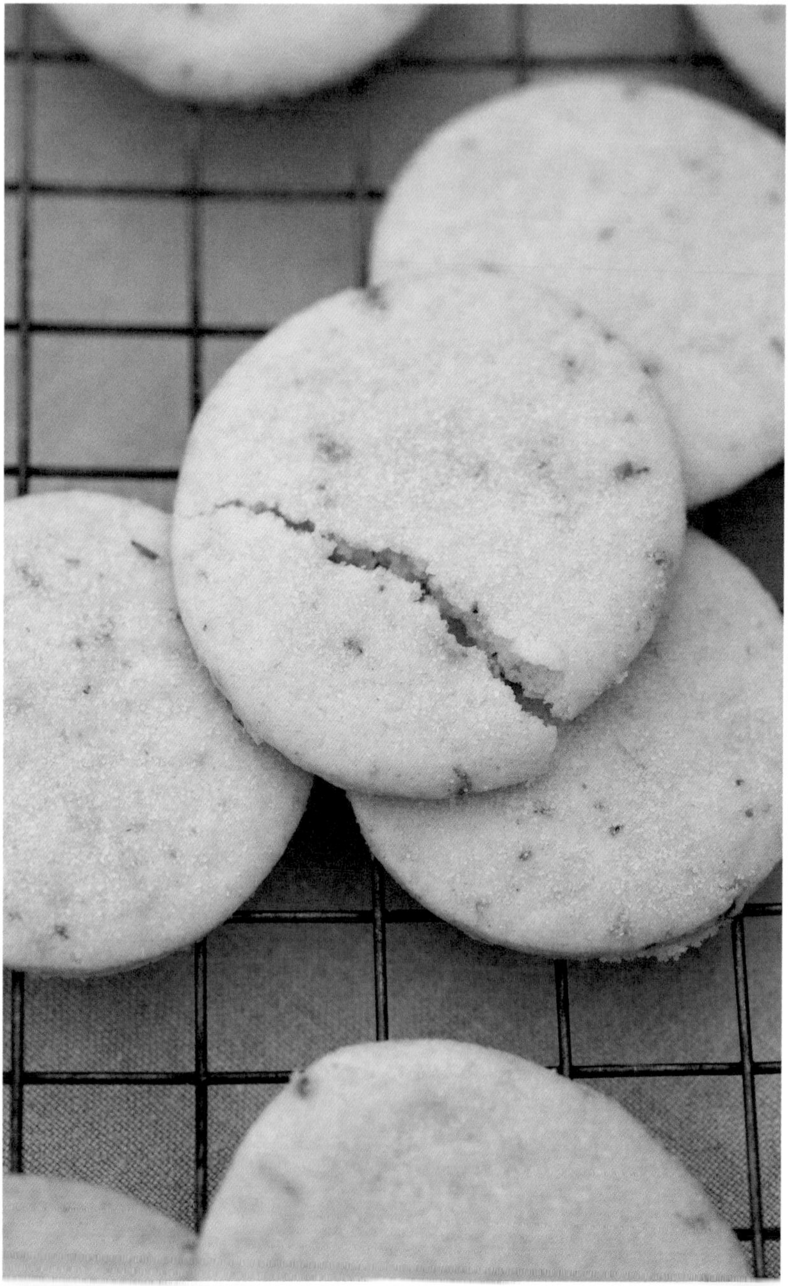

Lemon and lavender biscuits

These delicate buttery biscuits are perfect with an afternoon cup of tea (or some late-night ice cream). For a quite different result, replace the lavender with 1 tsp lightly toasted and roughly crushed caraway seeds.

Makes about 25

125g unsalted butter, softened
75g caster sugar, plus a little extra for dredging
1 tbsp finely chopped fresh lavender leaves and/or flowers
Finely grated zest of 1 lemon
100g plain flour
100g cornflour
A pinch of fine sea salt

Beat the butter, sugar, lavender and lemon zest together briefly in a large bowl, just until well combined. Sift the flour, cornflour and salt together over the butter and sugar mixture. Use a fork to bring the mixture together into a soft dough. Knead it very briefly in the bowl. Pat into a flat disc, wrap in cling film and refrigerate for 30 minutes.

Preheat the oven to 180°C/Gas mark 4. Line one or two baking sheets with baking parchment or a non-stick liner.

Roll out the dough to a 3–4mm thickness: it's a fairly sticky dough so flour the surface well, or you might find it easier to roll it out on a sheet of baking parchment. Cut out discs using a 6cm cookie cutter and place on the baking sheet(s). Gather the trimmings, re-roll and keep cutting until the dough is all used up.

Bake for about 10 minutes, or until the biscuits are just turning golden at the edges. If you have only one baking sheet, you'll need to bake them in batches.

Leave to cool a little to allow the biscuits to firm up slightly, then carefully transfer to a wire rack. Dredge with a little more caster sugar and leave to cool completely. Store in an airtight tin and eat within a few days.

Minty chocolate fridge cake

This is one of the nicest combinations of chocolate and mint I've ever tried – using fresh peppermint, rather than a bottled essence, seems to make the mix more fragrant and less pungent. You can cut it into smaller pieces than I suggest here if you like, for a very pleasing petit four.

Makes 12 pieces
100g unsalted butter
1 tbsp golden syrup
2 large stems of peppermint, roughly bruised, plus 1 tbsp finely chopped leaves
150g dark chocolate, broken into pieces
100g raisins
75g skinned hazelnuts
75g digestive, shortbread or oaty biscuits, broken into small chunks

Line a loaf tin, about 20 x 10cm, with baking parchment.

Put the butter, golden syrup and bruised peppermint stems into a small pan and heat gently until the butter melts, stirring and crushing the peppermint as you do so. Leave to infuse for half an hour or so, then reheat gently to re-melt the butter.

Put the chocolate into a bowl and strain the minty butter through a sieve on to it, pressing the mint with a spoon to extract every last drop of flavour. Put the bowl of chocolate and butter inside a larger bowl filled with just-boiled water and leave to melt, stirring from time to time.

Meanwhile, combine the raisins, hazelnuts, broken biscuits and chopped mint in a large bowl. When the chocolate and butter mixture is completely melted and smooth, pour it over the raisin mixture and mix thoroughly. Tip into the prepared tin and spread out as evenly as possible. Leave to cool, then refrigerate until firm.

Leave for at least 24 hours to allow the flavours to develop, then lift the cake out of the tin and cut into 12 pieces. Store in an airtight container in the fridge and eat within a week.

PUDDINGS & SWEET TREATS 227

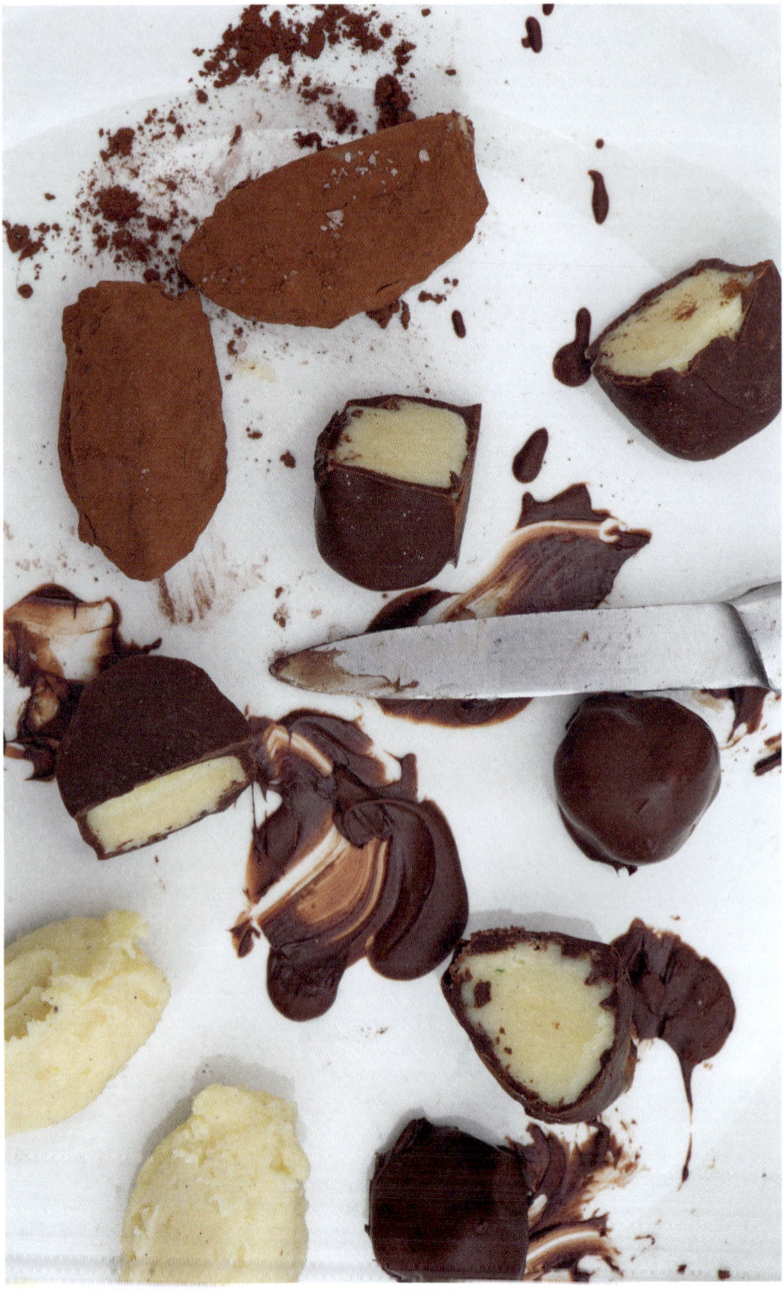

White chocolate truffles
with basil

These are fabulously indulgent and lovely with a cup of coffee. The sweet richness of white chocolate is nicely cut by basil's delicate aniseed flavour.

Makes about 15

100ml double cream
25g bunch of basil (stalks and leaves), roughly chopped
200g white chocolate, broken into small pieces

Cocoa powder for dusting
 OR 100g dark chocolate, broken into small pieces, for coating

Put the cream and basil into a small saucepan. Bring to just below boiling point, stirring and crushing the basil a little, then take off the heat and leave to infuse until cool.

Slowly melt the white chocolate in a bowl set inside a larger bowl filled with just-boiled water. Allow to cool slightly. Strain the basil-infused cream through a sieve on to the melted chocolate, pressing the basil leaves to extract every last drop of flavour. Stir until smooth; the mixture will thicken slightly and darken in colour. Leave to cool completely, then chill for several hours until set firm.

Scoop out teaspoonfuls of the chilled truffle mixture and roll quickly between the palms of your hands to form balls (it's a very sticky mix). You could also, if you're adept, use two teaspoons to form the mix into quenelles. You can now either roll the truffles in cocoa powder and return to the fridge, or coat them in chocolate.

For chocolate-coated truffles, put the truffles in the freezer while you melt the dark chocolate in a bowl set inside a larger bowl filled with just-boiled water. Leave the melted chocolate to cool until thickened and barely warm. Now use a spoon and fork to quickly coat the semi-frozen truffles in the chocolate. Drain each one briefly on the fork then place on a board lined with baking parchment to set before transferring to the fridge.

Keep the truffles in an airtight container in the fridge and eat within a few days.

Fennel fudge

This utterly moreish sweetmeat is delectably crumbly and melt-in-the-mouth. It can also be made with caraway seeds, although these are best given a good pounding with the pestle and mortar, or a whiz in a spice grinder to break them down a bit as they can be quite tough. Don't reduce them to a powder though – the fudge needs a bit of seedy texture.

Makes at least 25 pieces

A few drops of sunflower oil
300g caster sugar
1 tbsp golden syrup
100g unsalted butter, cut into chunks
100ml double cream
1 tbsp fennel seeds
A large pinch of fine sea salt

Put a few drops of sunflower oil on a piece of kitchen paper and use to lightly grease a baking dish, about 20cm square.

Put the sugar, golden syrup, butter and cream into a heavy-based, deep saucepan, making sure the pan is no more than one-third full, as the fudge mixture will bubble up. Heat gently, stirring often, until the butter is melted and the sugar has fully dissolved.

Stop stirring, put a sugar thermometer into the pan and turn up the heat. Bring to the boil and boil until the mixture registers 116°C on the thermometer. Take the pan off the heat and leave to stand for 10 minutes.

Meanwhile, roughly crush the fennel seeds, using a pestle and mortar. Add the fennel seeds to the fudge mixture with the salt and beat vigorously with a wooden spoon until it thickens, loses its gloss, becomes slightly grainy and starts to come away from the base of the pan. This should only take a minute or two of beating, but it can sometimes take longer.

Tip the hot fudge into the greased dish, smooth out and leave to set. Mark the fudge into squares with a small sharp knife as soon as it has set enough to hold the cut. Leave for 3–4 hours to set completely, then remove from the dish.

Store the fudge in an airtight container and use within a couple of weeks.

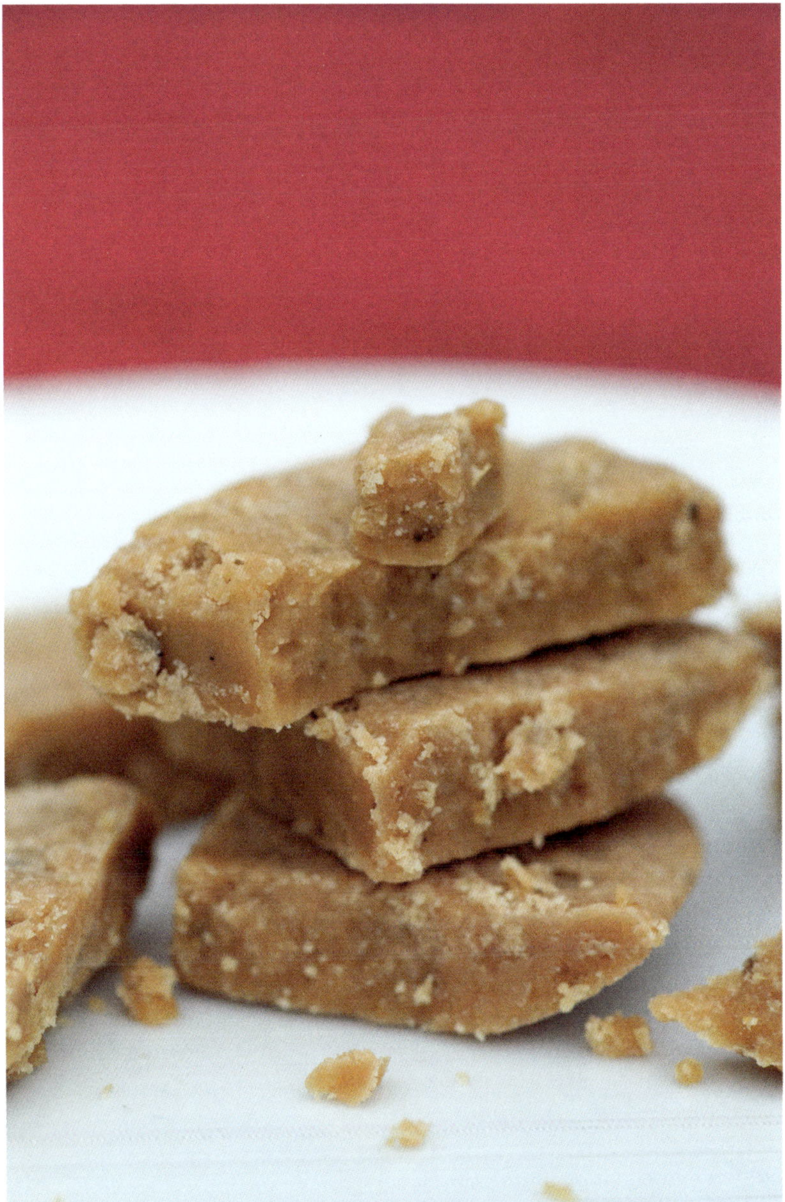

Apple herb jelly

You can use various herbs to produce pretty, fragrant jellies. For best results, choose from the more pungent, penetrating varieties, such as those listed below. If you use lemon juice to add the required acidity, the jelly will be relatively light and sweet, and you can use it rather like a fruit jam. If you use vinegar, you will get a slightly more assertive sweet-sour finish, which is ideal if you want to use the jelly alongside savoury dishes – sage jelly with pork, for instance, or mint jelly with lamb. In order to get the chopped herbs suspended evenly throughout the jelly, it's important to leave it to cool slightly before potting.

Herbs to use

Mint Use vinegar for acidity. Mint jelly is perfect with roast lamb, of course.
Sage Use vinegar for acidity. Sage jelly is great with pork.
Rosemary Use vinegar for a jelly that is good with almost any roast meat.
Thyme Use vinegar. Thyme jelly is lovely with goat's cheese and fresh bread.
Lemon verbena Use lemon juice for a nice sweet jelly.
Lavender Use lemon juice. Lavender jelly is lovely on scones with cream.

Makes 6–8 medium jam jars

2kg cooking apples, such as Bramley
3–4 large leafy stems of your chosen herb, plus about 4 tbsp finely chopped herb
About 1.5kg granulated sugar
About 4 lemons OR 200ml cider vinegar or white wine vinegar (see above)

Quarter the apples – cores, skin and all – and thickly slice each quarter. Put the apples into a preserving pan. Roughly bruise, twist or tear the whole stems of herb and add these too. Pour in enough water to just cover the apples. Bring to the boil, then lower the heat and simmer until the apples are completely soft – probably about 15 minutes, but it depends on the apples. You can give the fruit a stir, but avoid crushing or mashing it.

Ladle the apples, herb stems and juices into a jelly bag suspended over a large bowl and leave to drip overnight or at least for several hours. Don't squeeze the jelly bag.

Measure the strained juice. For every 500ml juice, you will need 390g sugar, the strained juice of 1 lemon or 50ml vinegar, and 1 tbsp chopped herbs.

Put a saucer in the fridge to chill. Put the apple juice, sugar and strained lemon juice or vinegar into the cleaned preserving pan. Heat, stirring often, until the sugar is completely dissolved, then bring to a rolling boil. Start checking for setting point after 8 minutes of boiling. Turn off the heat under the jelly while you do so.

To test for a set, drip a little of the jelly on to the cold saucer and return to the fridge for a minute. Push the jelly with your fingertip. If it has formed a significant skin that wrinkles with the push, setting point has been reached. If it hasn't, turn on the heat and boil the jelly for another 2–3 minutes before testing again. If you are unsure, always err on the side of caution here; a lightly set jelly is far nicer to use and eat than a solid one.

Once setting point is reached, turn off the heat and stir in the chopped herbs. Leave the jelly to cool for about 10 minutes, stirring once or twice to help distribute the herbs. Watch carefully and you will be able to observe the point when they are suspended throughout the hot jelly, rather than all floating on top. Pour the jelly slowly and carefully into hot sterilised jars. Seal straight away. Label when cool, then store in a cool, dark place and use within a year. Refrigerate after opening.

Rose petal jelly

For a pretty pink jelly, you need red rose petals, but this is worth making with any heavily fragranced petals, whatever their colour. Avoid petals that may have been sprayed (see p.121). This is lovely spooned delicately on to freshly baked scones.

Makes 3–4 medium jam jars

500ml loosely packed rose petals (about 6 blooms)
Juice of 1 lemon
500g jam sugar with pectin

Put the rose petals into a pan with 500ml water. Bring to a simmer and cook gently for 5 minutes. Leave to cool completely, then strain into a clean pan, crushing out every last drop from the petals with the back of a spoon.

Put a saucer into the fridge to chill. Add the lemon juice and sugar to the rose petal liquid. Heat slowly, stirring, until the sugar has dissolved, then bring to a rolling boil. Allow to boil steadily for 4 minutes, then turn off the heat under the jelly while you test for setting point.

Drip a little of the jelly on to the cold saucer and leave for a minute. Push the jelly with your fingertip. If it has formed a significant skin that wrinkles with the push, setting point has been reached. If it hasn't, turn on the heat and boil the jelly for another minute before testing again. If unsure, always err on the side of caution; a lightly set jelly is far nicer to use and eat than a tough, solid one.

Pour the hot jelly into hot sterilised jars and seal immediately. Label when the jars are completely cool. Store in a cool, dry place and use within a year. Once opened, store in the fridge.

PRESERVES & DRINKS 235

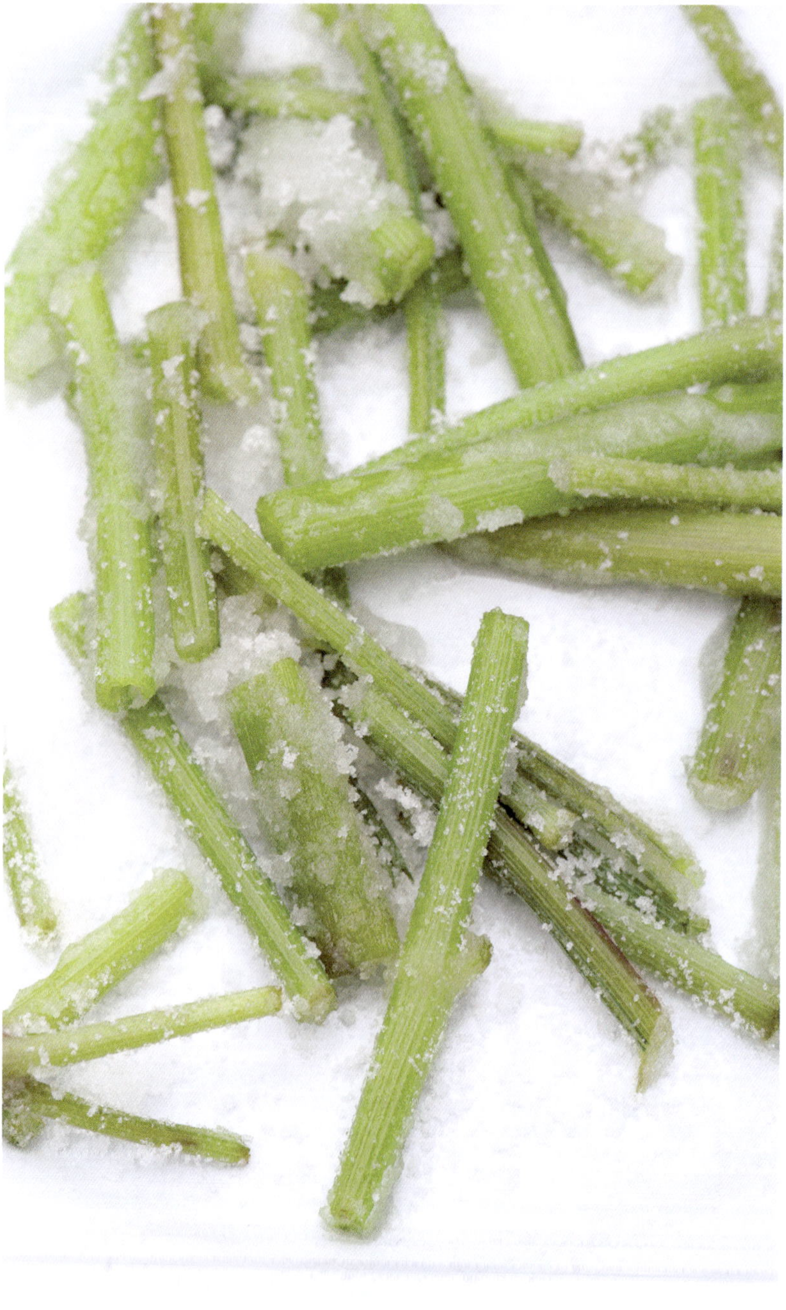

Candied angelica

These sweet, intensely flavoured fragments can be used as a decoration, but they are more interesting chopped and added to fruit cakes, or simply nibbled as a sweet treat after a meal. The candying process also gives you an angelica-flavoured syrup, which can be added to a fruit salad, or combined with fruit such as cooking apples or rhubarb before cooking. For candying, ideally you need angelica stems that are at least 2cm in diameter but still have a bit of bend in them. Hard, woody stems just won't work.

About 200g angelica stems
About 200g caster sugar

Cut the angelica stems into short lengths. Put them into a saucepan, cover with water and bring to the boil. Lower the heat and simmer until the stems are tender. This could take as little as 5 or as long as 20 minutes. Drain.

Use a small, sharp knife to peel away the tough fibres on the outside of each stem. Weigh the peeled angelica stems and put them into a container in which they will fit in one layer. Add the same weight of caster sugar and toss the lot together. Leave for 1–2 days until the sugar has formed a rich syrup.

Pour off the syrup into a pan, bring to the boil and simmer for 1 minute, then pour back over the angelica, turning the stems in the hot syrup. Leave for 24 hours, then repeat. Leave for 24 hours and then repeat again.

Drain off the syrup (saving it to use as suggested above). Lay the angelica stems on a rack lined with baking parchment and put into a very low oven (at about 50°C) until dry. This can take anywhere between 2 and 6 hours, depending on the thickness of the stems. The angelica should be dry to the touch, not sticky, but not brittle and desiccated.

Store the candied angelica in an airtight container in a cool, dark cupboard. It will keep for up to 1 year.

Rosemary and chilli oil

I don't make flavoured oils for long keeping because of the slight risk of botulism. The spores of the bacterium which causes botulism can be present on anything that grows in the earth – including herbs and garlic – and flourish in low-acidity conditions where oxygen is excluded, such as when covered in oil. If you do want to keep flavoured oils, store them in the fridge, where the temperature will inhibit bacterial growth.

Instead, I prefer to make oils like this gorgeous, peppy, fragrant one to be used straight away. It's delicious trickled on pizza or pasta, or over salads, and is the sort of magic ingredient that can turn a motley collection of leftovers (cold rice or potatoes, a few tomatoes, white beans and a scrap of Parmesan, say) into a lovely lunch or supper. You'll have enough here for 6 pasta or pizza servings.

Makes 150ml
1 large stem of rosemary, leaves only, roughly chopped
A good pinch of dried chilli flakes
1 garlic clove, peeled and cut into slivers (optional)
150ml extra virgin olive oil

Put all the ingredients into a small saucepan and heat gently, so the oil is just fizzing, for 3–5 minutes. Set aside until completely cool, then it is ready to use. You can strain out the flavourings, or not, as you please.

Keep any leftover oil in the fridge and use within a week. If it thickens and turns cloudy, just return to room temperature before using.

Sweet raspberry vinegar
with scented geranium

This is based on Pam Corbin's wonderful raspberry vinegar in her *River Cottage Preserves Handbook* (see Directory, p.249). The scented geranium adds another flavour dimension, making this a great addition to a vinaigrette.

Makes about 750ml
500g raspberries
4–6 scented geranium leaves
300ml white wine vinegar
About 225g granulated sugar

Put the raspberries into a bowl or large jug, along with the scented geranium leaves. Crush them together with the end of a rolling pin, or similar implement. Pour over the wine vinegar. Cover and leave the mixture in the fridge for 4 days, stirring every now and then.

Tip the raspberry mixture into a jelly bag suspended over a large bowl and leave to drip through overnight.

Measure the strained liquid and pour into a saucepan. Add 225g sugar for every 300ml liquid. Heat slowly, stirring, until the sugar has dissolved, then bring to the boil. Boil for about 8 minutes, skimming off any scum, then leave to cool. Bottle and seal when cold. Use within 12 months.

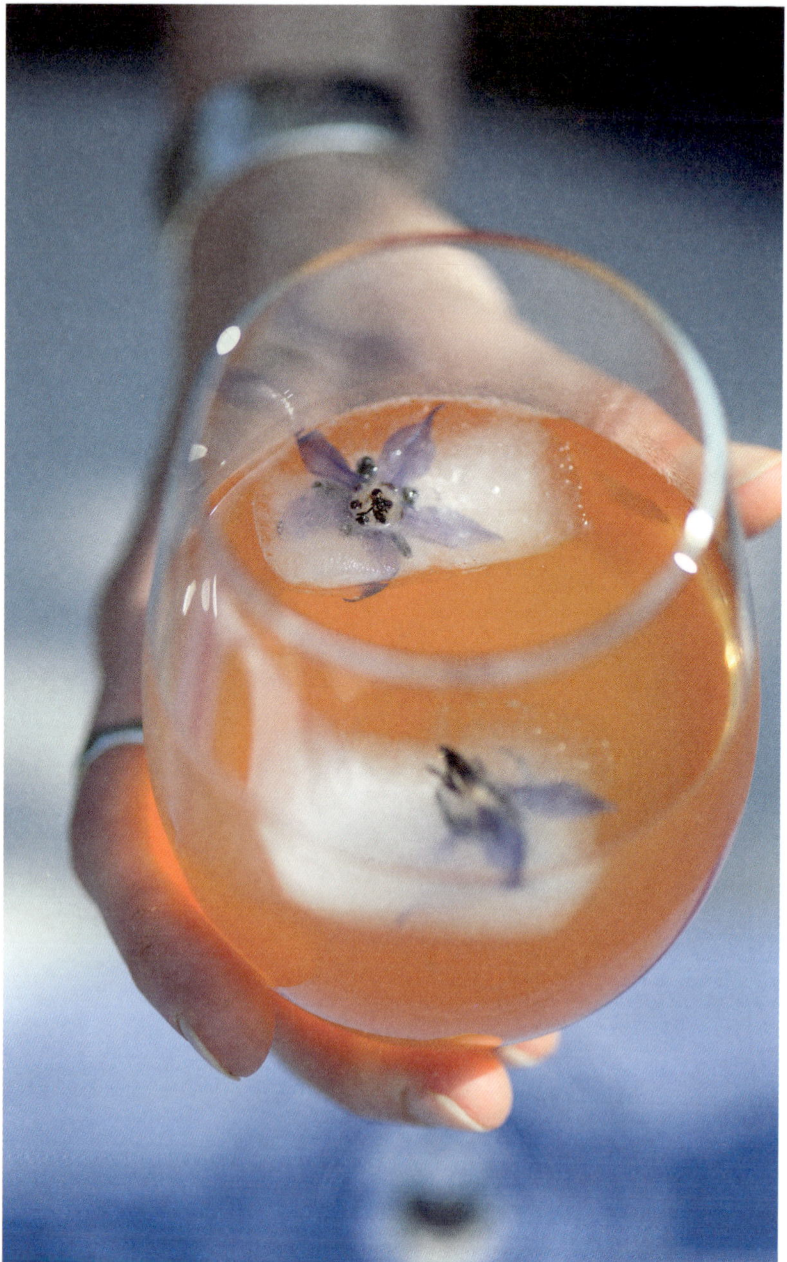

Rose elixir

This sweet, scented cordial is particularly special – a sort of homemade version of rose water without the overpowering perfumeyness. It's lovely added to drinks, alcoholic or otherwise. For a virgin cocktail, mix 1 part rose elixir to 4 parts chilled apple or pear juice. Serve with ice and a fresh rose petal garnish, or borage flower ice cubes (see p.54). The elixir can also be trickled on to fruit for an exotic salad.

Makes about 850ml

50g very fragrant rose petals
 (around 8 blooms)

Juice of 1 lemon
350g caster or granulated sugar

Put the rose petals into a deep bowl. Pour on 500ml just-boiled water and leave for about 8 hours to infuse. Strain into a pan, crushing out every drop of liquid with a spoon. Add the lemon juice and sugar. Heat gently, stirring, until the sugar has dissolved. Continue to heat until the liquid is steaming hot but not boiling. Pour immediately into warmed sterilised bottles (small ones, as the cordial won't keep well once opened), leaving a 1cm gap at the top, and seal tightly. Cool then store in a cool, dark place for up to 6 months. Once opened, use within a week or two.

Scented lemonade

This is a really refreshing drink for a hot summer's day. It looks lovely with borage flower ice cubes bobbing in it (see p.54). For a subtly different fragrance, replace the scented geranium leaves with a well-bashed stem of lemongrass.

Makes about 1.5 litres

5 lemons
About 8 large (10–15 small) lemon-scented
 geranium leaves, roughly twisted or crushed
75g caster sugar

Use a potato peeler or sharp knife to pare the zest in thick strips from one of the lemons. Put into a large container with the scented geranium leaves and sugar. Pour on 1.5 litres just-boiled water. Stir to help the sugar dissolve, then leave until completely cool. Squeeze the juice from the lemons and add to the infused liquid. Strain the whole lot into a clean jug and chill before serving, with ice.

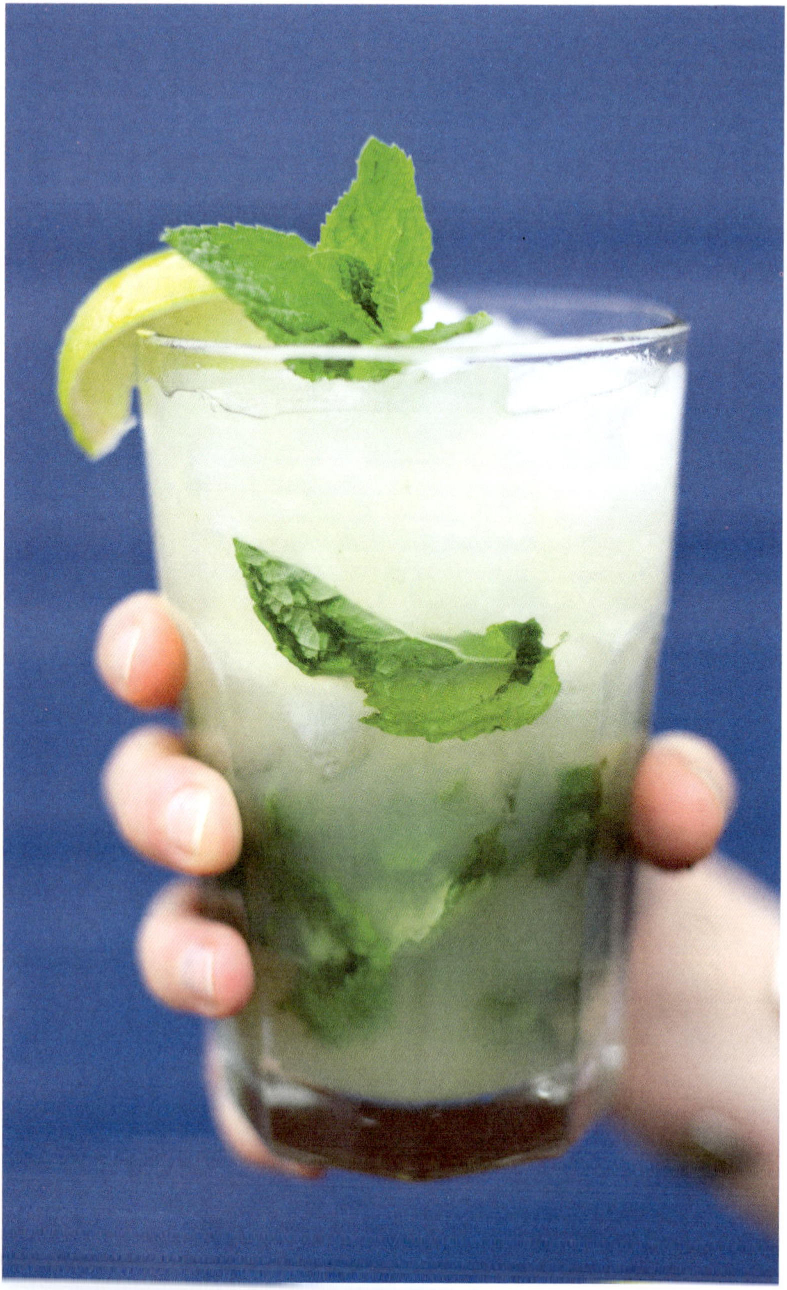

Minty apple mojito

I love a mojito, and with mint straight from the garden and some (inauthentic, but very nice) cloudy fresh apple juice, it's wonderfully refreshing. You can use the traditional soda water in place of the apple juice for a drier drink.

Per person

12 fresh spearmint leaves, plus extra to garnish
1 tsp caster sugar
Juice of 1 lime (a wedge of the squeezed lime reserved)
Crushed ice
50ml white rum
Chilled cloudy apple juice
Lime wedge, to serve

Put the mint, sugar, lime juice and squeezed lime wedge in a tall glass and 'muddle' or crush them together with the end of a wooden spoon or similar implement (a cocktail 'muddler' if you have one). Fill the glass with crushed ice, add the rum, then fill up with apple juice and stir. Finish with a sprig of mint and a lime wedge.

Sorrel wine cup

A very good use for rather overgrown, mature sorrel leaves, this is based on an old Constance Spry recipe. The sorrel infuses the drink with a subtle lemony acidity.

Serves 6

50g bunch of sorrel
3 tsp caster sugar
375ml sweet white wine, such as an inexpensive dessert wine
375ml fizzy water
Juice of 2 oranges
Borage flowers, to serve (optional)

Tear the sorrel leaves, stalks and all, and put in a plastic container or a jug that will fit in your fridge. Add the sugar and 'muddle' with the sorrel (i.e. crush together with the end of a wooden spoon or similar implement). Add the wine, water and orange juice and stir until the sugar has dissolved. Cover and refrigerate for about 6 hours. To serve, strain into a chilled jug and float a few borage flowers on top.

Variation

Use 50g salad burnet leaves or sweet cicely, roughly chopped, in place of the sorrel.

Herb teas

A cup of strongly minty tea, perhaps with just a pinch of sugar, is one of the most refreshing and reviving of drinks. Fantastic as a *digestif* after a meal, lovely as an afternoon cuppa, ideal at any time really if, like me, you sometimes find yourself relying a little too much on the great god caffeine. The mintiness seems to give a little buzz all of its own.

The trick is to be generous. Don't bother making mint tea with less than 3 large sprigs per cup, at least 10 if you're making a pot. Opinions vary as to the best types of mint for tea. Peppermints are more freshly, pungently minty; spearmints are sweeter (see p.105). On balance, I think I'm probably a spearmint girl, but I know others who swear peppermint is the only type for infusions.

Much as I enjoy a pure mint tea, I often use mint as the base, and then season it with a sprig or two of something more penetrating. As I write this, a steaming cup of mint, lemon thyme and lavender tea sits beside me. Lavender is wonderfully soothing in teas. You could also augment mint tea with a leaf or two of sage or lemon verbena, a sprig of lemon balm or the tip of a rosemary stem.

To make a herb tea (technically a tisane), all you need do is pluck your chosen herbs, wash them and check for insect life, then place in a pot or mug. Bring some freshly drawn water to the boil, then let it cool for about 1 minute before pouring on to the herbs, making sure they are completely covered. Water that is absolutely boiling can scald the herbs and damage the flavour. Leave to infuse for at least 5 minutes, or until cool enough to drink. I often like to add a pinch of sugar to enhance a herb tea, but that's purely a matter of taste.

You can also make a very delicious drink by combining garden herbs with standard black tea. I frequently add a generous sprig of lemon balm or bergamot to a brewing mug of afternoon tea. And I add milk too, although drinking it plain black or with a spritz of lemon would also be lovely.

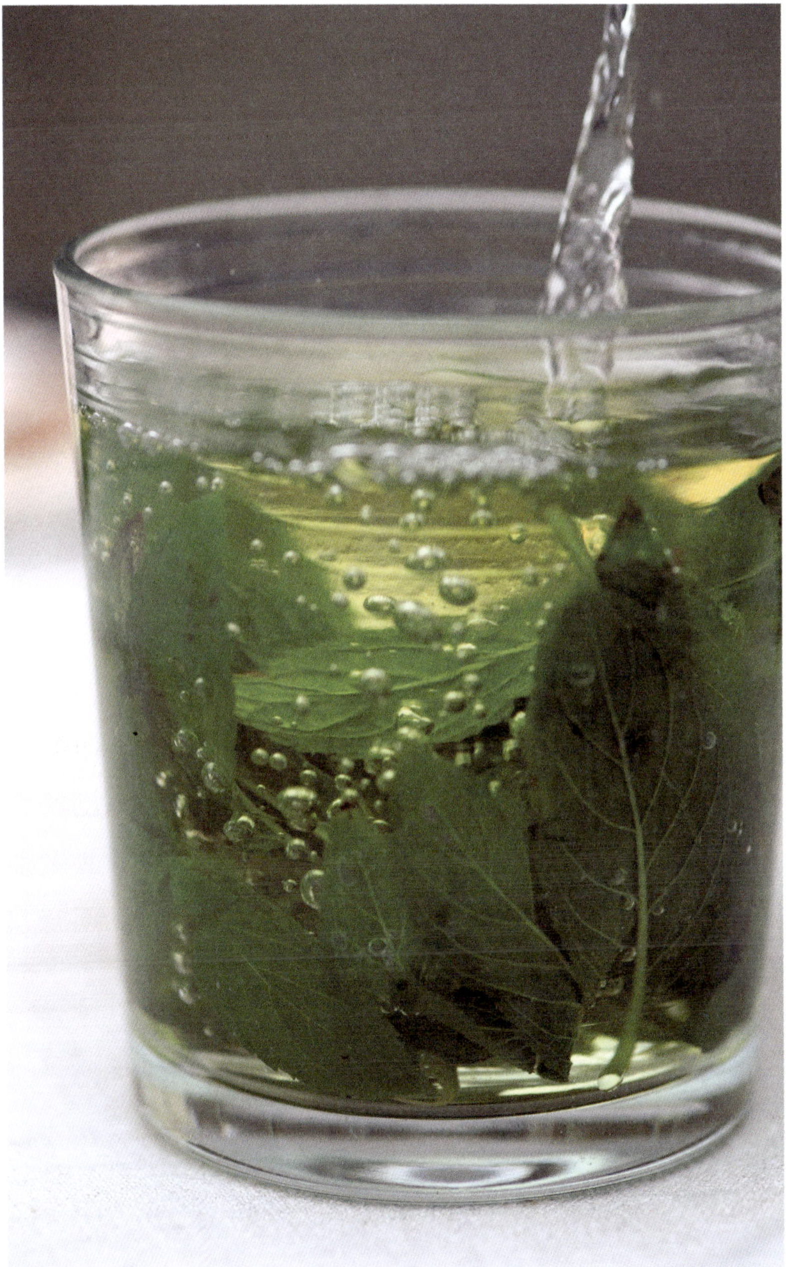

Useful Things

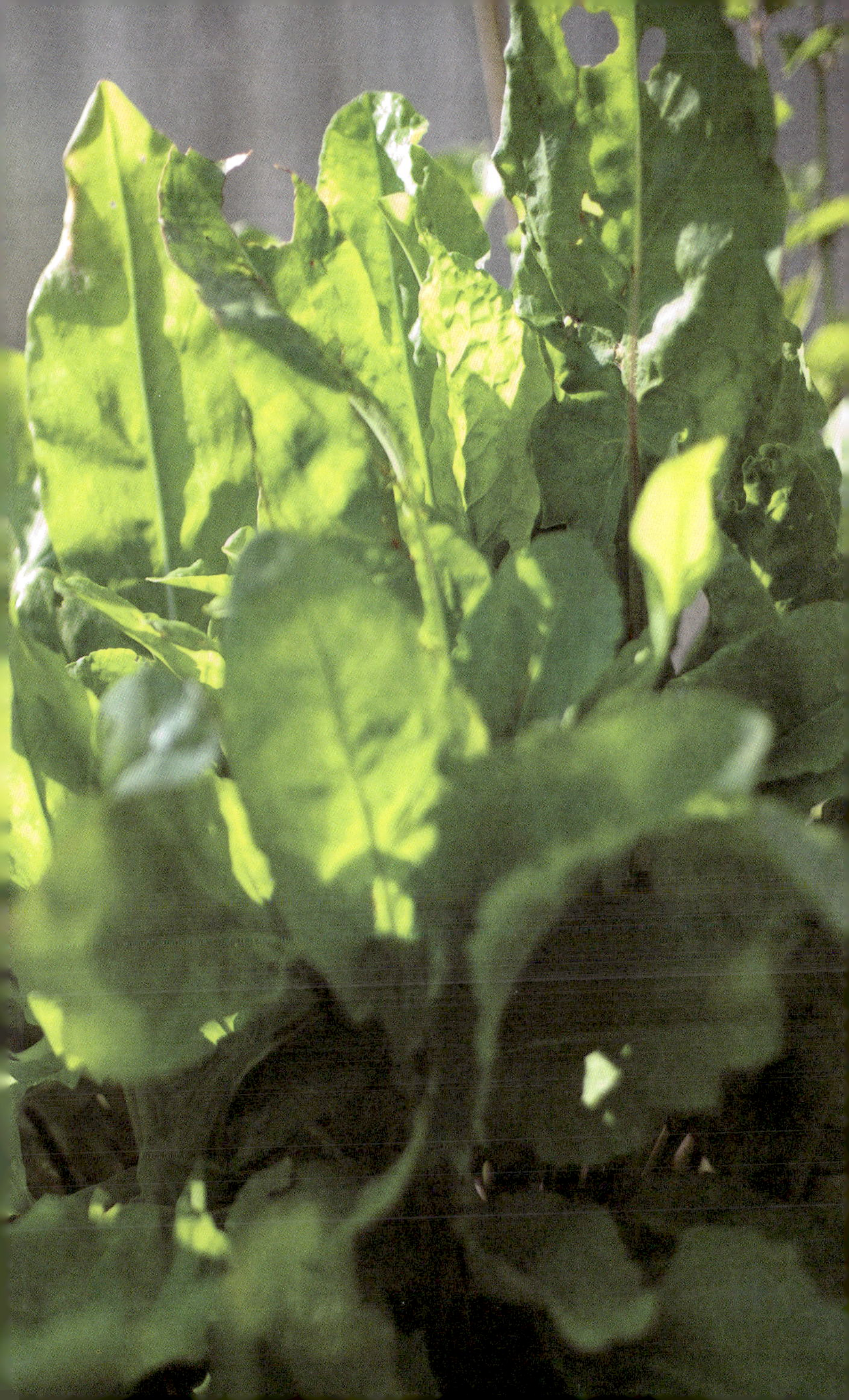

Directory

Plants and seeds

You can buy herb seeds or plants at any garden centre, but specialists will always offer you a far greater range, and usually better advice and information too.

Arne Herbs
www.arneherbs.co.uk
01275 333399
Bristol-based herb specialist.

Downderry Nursery
www.downderry-nursery.co.uk
01732 810081
Specialist in lavender and rosemary situated in Kent, offering a range of varieties by mail (including *lavandula* x *intermedia* 'Provence'). Website provides good info on planting and nurturing.

Edulis
www.edulis.co.uk
01635 578113
Berkshire-based grower of rare plants, including unusual herb varieties.

Green Garden Herbs
www.greengardenherbs.co.uk
01728 452597
Herb specialist based in Aldeburgh, Suffolk. Range includes many lavenders, sages, mints and basils.

Halsall's Herbs
01206 323158
Herb specialist based in Dedham, Suffolk. Sells herbs at farmers' markets and fairs, and by appointment.

Jekka's Herb Farm
www.jekkasherbfarm.com
01454 418878
Supplier of a huge range of organic herb plants and seeds by mail order.

Laurel Farm Herbs
www.laurelfarmherbs.co.uk
01728 668223
Suffolk-based supplier of herb plants by mail order.

Norfolk Lavender
www.norfolk-lavender.co.uk
01485 570384
Offers a large range of lavender plants by mail (including *lavandula* x *intermedia* 'Provence').

Otter Farm
www.otterfarm.co.uk
Devon-based organic farm run by Mark Diacono. Shop sells herb plants and seeds (free delivery on seed-only orders).

Roses UK
www.rosesuk.com
01243 389532
Website listing rose suppliers in the UK. Also gives useful information on many rose varieties.

Scented Geraniums
www.scentedgeraniums.co.uk
Specialist selling huge range of scented geraniums by mail order, also bags of loose leaves for immediate use. Good advice, growing tips and information too.

Suffolk Herbs
www.suffolkherbs.com
01376 572456
Supplier of extensive range of herb seeds, including many basils and mints.

Gardening equipment/supplies

Harrod Horticultural
www.harrodhorticultural.com
0845 402 5300
Supplier of gardening products, including organic feeds. Also organic herb seeds.

The Organic Gardening Catalogue
www.organiccatalogue.com
01932 253666
Range of supplies includes herb seeds, organic potting compost and soil improver, organic fertilisers and feeds.

Websites

The Herb Society
www.herbsociety.org.uk
0845 491 8699
Fantastic charity working to increase the understanding and use of herbs.

Garden Organic
www.gardenorganic.org.uk
024 7630 3517
National charity for organic growing, an encyclopedic source of information.

Recycle Now
www.recyclenow.com
Includes advice on home composting.

Books

The Complete Gardener, **Monty Don**
Some very good sections on the more commonly used herbs.

The Great Vegetable Plot, **Sarah Raven**
Excellent advice on growing many herbs.

Growing Herbs, **Jessica Houdret**
Herb Society booklet, summarising the basics for many popular herbs.

Herb and Spice, **Jill Norman**
Sound information on the culinary uses of herbs and spices, plus a recipe section.

Jekka's Complete Herb Book, **Jekka McVicar**
Comprehensive advice on growing herbs.

McGee on Food and Cooking, **Harold McGee**
Accessible work of kitchen science with a very good section on herbs and spices.

The River Cottage Hedgerow Handbook, **John Wright**
An in-depth look at gathering wild foods.

The River Cottage Preserves Handbook, **Pam Corbin**
Excellent guide to home preserving.

The River Cottage Veg Patch Handbook, **Mark Diacono**
Great advice on establishing your own thriving organic kitchen garden.

Acknowledgements

There are many people who have generously given their time and shared their wisdom with me during the writing of this handbook. I owe a huge debt of thanks to one colleague in particular, without whom this would be a lesser book. The incredibly talented Mark Diacono has not only brought my words to life with his fantastic photographs but, in his capacity as River Cottage head gardener and general horticultural oracle, has given advice and suggestions that have never failed to help and inspire me. Thank you so much, Mark.

Another fellow author and friend, Pam Corbin, has been as always so generous in sharing her knowledge and experience with me, not to mention a good quantity of her own homegrown herbs.

I must also thank Cheryl Waller of the National Herb Society, whose garden at Sulgrave Manor so inspired me. Also Andrea Halsall of Halsall's Herbs in Dedham, who has provided me with so many thriving herb plants and so much good advice. Andy Strachan, of Garden Organic, has shared some crucial insider info with me, and Peter Miller of King's Seeds (Suffolk Herbs) gave me some excellent information and some very good seeds early on.

Mat Prestwich of R & G Herbs has supplied me with many lush fresh-cut herbs for recipe testing and Trudy Carr at my local farm shop, Brookelynne at Beaumont-cum-Moze, has done the same. Thanks also to the lovely Wendy Sarton of The Fountain House restaurant in Dedham, for loading me up with angelica and good thoughts.

At Bloomsbury, I must thank my charming and enthusiastic editors Natalie Hunt and Richard Atkinson, my wonderful project editor Janet Illsley, and my talented and preternaturally youthful designer Will Webb.

My thanks as always to the River Cottage team, who make it possible for me to do a job I really love – particularly Rob Love and Hugh Fearnley-Whittingstall for giving me the chance to write this book in the first place, and Gill Meller and Oliver Gladwin who did such terrific work cooking for some of the photos.

My deepest love and thanks go to my gorgeous daughters, Tara and Edie, for their love and their faith in me. And last, but really most, I want to thank my parents – the finest anyone could wish for. They've helped with everything from photo shoots to recipe testing (not to mention childcare), and they support and encourage me every day in everything I do. Thanks, Mum and Dad.

Recipe index

Sauces, dressings & dips
Mayonnaise (p.159)
Béarnaise sauce (p.160)
Horseradish sauce (p.161)
Apple sauce with sage (p.163)
Mint sauce (p.163)
Sorrel sauce (p.164)
Nasturtium flower dressing (p.164)
Salmoriglio sauce (p.165)
Skordalia (p.165)
Basil and parsley pesto (p.166)

Soups
Carrot soup with dill and mustard (p.169)
Chervil soup (p.170)
Celery leaf and lovage soup (p.172)
Herb noodle soup (p.173)

Salads
Simple herb salad (p.175)
Apple and celery leaf salad (p.175)
Green and gold salad (p.176)
Crab and broad bean salad (p.176)
Herby chicken noodle salad (p.179)
Potato salad with dill and onion (p.181)

Eggs
Herb omelette (p.182)
Tarragon eggs (p.184)

Fish
Pasta with sardines and fennel (p.187)
Baked fish with a hyssop crust (p.188)

Meat
Pork with fennel and rosemary (p.191)
Beef stew with lovage (p.192)
Stuffed breast of lamb with savory (p.193)
Lamb with lavender and thyme (p.194)
Chicken with forty cloves of garlic (p.196)
Roast chicken with myrtle (p.198)

Vegetables
Spring pasta with wild garlic and purple sprouting broccoli (p.199)
Aubergines with perilla (p.201)
Runner beans with summer savory (p.203)
White beans with winter herbs (p.204)
Double fennel braise (p.207)
Creamed Swiss chard (p.208)

Breads & savoury scones
Rosemary focaccia (p.209)
Fennel seed bread (p.211)
Soda bread with rosemary (p.212)
Bergamot scones (p.215)

Puddings & sweet treats
Minted red berry sorbet (p.216)
Herb ice cream or custard (p.219)
Lemon verbena layer with berries (p.220)
Rhubarb crumble with angelica (p.223)
Lemon and lavender biscuits (p.225)
Minty chocolate fridge cake (p.226)
White chocolate truffles with basil (p.229)
Fennel fudge (p.230)

Preserves & drinks
Apple herb jelly (p.232)
Rose petal jelly (p.234)
Candied angelica (p.237)
Rosemary and chilli oil (p.238)
Raspberry vinegar (p.239)
Rose elixir (p.241)
Scented lemonade (p.241)
Minty apple mojito (p.243)
Sorrel wine cup (p.243)
Herb teas (p.244)

Index

Page numbers in *italic* refer to the illustrations

Agastache foeniculum 42, 43
Agastache rugosa 43
Allium cepa Proliferum group 151
   A. fistulosum 150–1, *151*
   A. sativum 76, 77–81, *79*
   A. schoenoprasum 62, 63–5, *64*
   A. triquetrum 153
   A. tuberosum 65
   A. ursinum 152, 153
almonds: skordalia 165
Aloysia triphylla 92, *93*
Anethum graveolens 70, *71*
angelica 37, 40–1, *41*
   candied angelica *236*, 237
   rhubarb crumble with angelica *222*, 223
Angelica archangelica 40–1, *41*
anise hyssop *42*, 43
Anthriscus cerefolium 60–1, *61*
Apium graveolens 58–9, *59*
Apothecary's rose 121
applemint 105
apples: apple and celery leaf salad 175
   apple herb jelly 232–3, *233*
   apple sauce with sage *162*, 163
   minty apple mojito *242*, 243
   pork with fennel and rosemary *190*, 191
apricots: stuffed breast of lamb with dried apricots and winter savory 193
Armoracia rusticana 82–3, *83*
Artemisia dracunculoides 145
Artemisia dracunculus 144–5, *145*
arugula *see* rocket
aubergines with perilla *200*, 201

basil 13, 44–7, *45*, *46*
   basil and parsley pesto 166, *167*
   basil mayonnaise 159
   raspberry ripple basil ice cream *218*, 219
   white chocolate truffles with basil *228*, 229
bay 13, 37, *48*, 49–50, *51*
   bay salt 50
   bay sugar 50
beans: white beans with winter herbs 204, *205*
bear garlic *see* wild garlic
béarnaise sauce 160
béchamel sauce 49
beef stew with lovage 192
bergamot *52*, 53
   bergamot scones *214*, 215
biscuits, lemon and lavender *224*, 225
blackfly 98–9, 110

borage 37, 54–5, *55*
   borage and smoked salmon canapés 54
Borago officinalis 54–5, *55*
bouquet garni 19, 49
bread: bruschetta 80
   chapon 80
   fennel seed bread *210*, 211
   rosemary focaccia 209
   soda bread with rosemary and sultanas 212, *213*
   soda bread with thyme, Cheddar and mustard 212
broad beans: crab and broad bean salad 176
broccoli: spring pasta with wild garlic and purple sprouting broccoli 199
bruschetta 80
buckler-leaf sorrel 139
bulgar wheat: tabbouleh salad 106
bush basil 47
butter: garlic butter 80
   sage butter 129
buying herbs 11–13
buying plants 35

cakes: minty chocolate fridge cake 226, *227*
   seed cake 56
Calendula officinalis 98–9, *99*
canapés: borage and smoked salmon canapés 54
   cream cheese and dill canapés 70
candied angelica *236*, 237
caraway 56–7, *57*
carrot soup with dill and mustard *168*, 169
celery leaf 58–9, *59*
   apple and celery leaf salad 175
   celery leaf and lovage soup 172
celery seeds 58, 59
chapon 80
cheese: apple and celery leaf salad 175
   basil and parsley pesto 166, *167*
   cheese sauce 49
   cream cheese and dill canapés 70
   soda bread with thyme, Cheddar and mustard 212
   Welsh onion tart 150
chermoula 66
chervil 60–1, *61*
   chervil and lemon zest mayonnaise 159
   chervil soup 170, *171*
   crab and broad bean salad 176
   simple herb salad *174*, 175
chicken: baked chicken with forty cloves of garlic 196, *197*
   chicken with tarragon 144
   herby chicken noodle salad *178*, 179
   roast chicken with lemon and myrtle 198
chiffonade 18
chillies: chermoula 66
   rosemary and chilli oil 238

chives 37, *62*, 63–5, *64*
　chive mayonnaise 159
　chive sauce 63
　smoked mackerel and chive pâté 63
chocolate: minty chocolate fridge cake 226, *227*
　white chocolate truffles with basil *228*, 229
chopping herbs 18
cilantro *see* coriander
comfrey 'tea' 36
compost 29
containers, growing herbs in 28
coriander 13, *32*, 66–9, *67*, *68*
　chermoula 66
　salsa 69
coriander seeds 69
Coriandrum sativum 66–9, *67*, *68*
crab and broad bean salad 176
crumble, rhubarb with angelica *222*, 223
cucumber salad 70
custard, herb 219
cuttings 34, *34*
Cymbopogon citrates 94–5, *95*

Damask rose 121
dill 70, *71*
　carrot soup with dill and mustard *168*, 169
　cream cheese and dill canapés 70
　cucumber salad 70
　potato salad with dill and pickled red onion *180*, 181
dill seeds 70
Diplotaxis muralis 118–19
dips: skordalia 165
drainage, growing herbs and 26, 28
drinks: minty apple mojito *242*, 243
　rose elixir *240*, 241
　scented lemonade 241
　sorrel wine cup 243
drying herbs 16

Eastern mint 106
eggs: béarnaise sauce 160
　herb ice cream or custard 219
　herb omelette 182, *183*
　lovage omelette or frittata 96
　mayonnaise 159
　'soft hard-boiled' eggs with fennel 75
　tarragon eggs 184, *185*
　Welsh onion tart 150
Eruca vesicaria subsp. *sativa* 118–19, *119*

fennel *72*, 73–5, *74*
　double fennel braise *206*, 207
　fennel fudge 230, *231*
　pasta with sardines and fennel *186*, 187
　pork with fennel and rosemary *190*, 191

fennel seeds 73, *74*, 75
　fennel seed bread *210*, 211
fertilisers 36
fines herbes 60, 113, 144
fish: baked white fish with a hyssop and orange crust 188, *189*
　borage and smoked salmon canapés 54
　fish baked or barbecued with bay leaves 50
　fish baked with fennel 73
　fish baked with myrtle 109
　fish baked or grilled with rosemary 125
　pasta with sardines and fennel *186*, 187
　smoked mackerel and chive pâté 63
flavour chemistry 17
focaccia, rosemary 209
Foeniculum vulgare 72, 73–5, *74*
freezing herbs 16
French marigold 99
French sorrel 139
French tarragon 144–5, *145*
fudge, fennel 230, *231*

garlic 13, *76*, 77–81, *79*
　baked chicken with forty cloves of garlic 196, *197*
　bruschetta 80
　chapon 80
　chermoula 66
　garlic butter 80
　gremolata 80, 113
　pasta aglio e olio 80
　preparation 20, *21*, 78
　skordalia 165
　whole roasted garlic 78
　see also wild garlic
garlic chives 65
geranium, scented *134*, 135–7, *136*
　scented geranium syrup 137
　scented lemonade 241
　sweet raspberry vinegar with scented geranium 239
gooseberry and sweet cicely compote 142
Greek basil 47
Greek oregano 102
green and gold salad 176, *177*
green garlic 77, *79*, 81
gremolata 80, 113
growing herbs 22–37
guttering, sowing seeds in *32*, 33

harissa paste 56
herb ice cream or custard 219
herb noodle soup 173
herb omelette 182, *183*
herb teas 244, *245*
holy basil 47
horseradish 13, 82–3, *83*
　horseradish sauce 161

INDEX   253

hyssop *84*, 85
   baked white fish with a hyssop and orange crust 188, *189*
Hyssopus officinalis 84, 85

ice cream: herb ice cream 219
   raspberry ripple basil ice cream *218*, 219

jelly: apple herb jelly 232–3, *233*
   rose petal jelly 234, *235*

Kentucky mint 106
Korean mint 43

lamb: loin of lamb with lavender and lemon thyme 194, *195*
   stuffed breast of lamb with dried apricots and winter savory 193
lamb's lettuce: green and gold salad 176, *177*
Laurus nobilis 48, 49–50, *51*
Lavandula angustifolia 86–9, *87*, *88*
   L. x *intermedia* 'Provence' 86
lavender 37, 86–9, *87*, *88*
   lavender-scented syrup 89
   lemon and lavender biscuits *224*, 225
   loin of lamb with lavender and lemon thyme 194, *195*
leeks: celery leaf and lovage soup 172
lentils: lentil and sorrel soup 138
lemon: gremolata 80, 113
   lemon and lavender biscuits *224*, 225
   roast chicken with lemon and myrtle 198
   scented lemonade 241
lemon balm *90*, 91
lemon bergamot 53
lemon thyme 13, 147, 148, *149*
   loin of lamb with lavender and lemon thyme 194, *195*
lemon verbena 37, 92, *93*
   lemon verbena layer with raspberries 220, *221*
   verbena sugar 92
lemongrass 94–5, *95*
   lemongrass syrup 94
Levisticum officinale 96–7, *97*
lovage 37, 96–7, *97*
   beef stew with lovage 192
   celery leaf and lovage soup 172

marigold 98–9, *99*
   green and gold salad 176, *177*
marjoram 13, *100*, 101–2
   spaghetti squash with marjoram 101
mayonnaise *158*, 159
   nasturtium flower dressing 164
   nasturtium leaf mayonnaise 110
Melissa officinalis 90, 91

Mentha 104, 105–6, *107*
   M. longifolia subsp. *schimperi* 106
   M. x *piperita* 105, *107*
   M. spicata 104, 105
   M. s. crispa 'Moroccan' 105
   M. s. 'Kentucky Colonel' 106
   M. s. 'Tashkent' 105
   M. suaveolens 105
merguez spice mix 56
'micro-leaves' 33
mint 28, 37, *104*, 105–6, *107*
   herb teas 244, *245*
   mint dip/sauce 106
   mint sauce 163
   minted red berry sorbet 216, *217*
   minty apple mojito *242*, 243
   minty chocolate fridge cake 226, *227*
   tabbouleh salad 106
module trays, sowing seeds in 31
mojito, minty apple *242*, 243
Monarda citriodora 53
Monarda didyma 52, 53
Monarda fistulosa 53
Moroccan mint 105
mushrooms with oregano 102
Myrrhis odorata 142, *143*
myrtle *108*, 109
   roast chicken with lemon and myrtle 198
Myrtus communis 108, 109

nasturtium 110, *111*
   nasturtium flower dressing 164
   nasturtium leaf mayonnaise 110
nettle 'tea' 36
noodles: herb noodle soup 173
   herby chicken noodle salad *178*, 179

Ocimum basilicum 44–7, *45*, *46*
   O. b. 'Horapha' 47
   O. b. var. *minimum* 47
   O. b. var. *purpurascens* 47
   O. b. sanctum 47
oil, rosemary and chilli 238
omelette, herb 182, *183*
onions: sage and onion stuffing 129
   see also Welsh onion
orange thyme 148
oranges: baked fish with a hyssop crust 188, *189*
   sorrel wine cup 243
oregano 13, 101–2, *103*
   mushrooms with oregano 102
   salmoriglio sauce 165
Origanum majorana 100, 101–2
Origanum vulgare 101–2, *103*
   O. v. subsp. *hirtum* 'Greek' 102
Oxalis acetosella 139

pancetta: white beans with winter herbs 204, *205*
parsley 13, *112*, 113–14, *115*
  basil and parsley pesto 166, *167*
  as a cooked vegetable 114
  gremolata 80, 113
  parsley mayonnaise 159
  parsley sauce 114
  persillade 113
  tabbouleh salad 106
pasta: pasta aglio e olio 80
  pasta with sardines and fennel *186*, 187
  spring pasta with wild garlic and purple sprouting broccoli 199
pâté, smoked mackerel and chive 63
Pelargonium 135–7, *136*
  P. capitatum 'Attar of Roses' 135
  P. crispum 135
  P. graveolens 134, 135
peppermint 105, *107*
  minty chocolate fridge cake 226, *227*
perilla *116*, 117
  aubergines with perilla *200*, 201
  perilla prawn stir-fry 117
Perilla frutescens 116, 117
persillade 113
pesto: basil and parsley pesto 166, *167*
  walnut and wild garlic pesto 166
Petroselinum crispum 113–14, *115*
  P. c. var. *neapolitana 112*, 113–14
pH values, soil 26
picking herbs 14
pine nuts: basil and parsley pesto 166, *167*
plug trays, sowing seeds in 31
pork with fennel and rosemary *190*, 191
potatoes: baked potatoes with chives 63
  baked potatoes with fennel 73
  celery leaf and lovage soup 172
  potato salad with dill and pickled red onion *180*, 181
potting composts 29
prawns: perilla prawn stir-fry 117
propagation 30–4
pumpkin, sage with 130
purple basil 47

raisins: minty chocolate fridge cake 226, *227*
ramsons *see* wild garlic
raspberries: lemon verbena layer with raspberries 220, *221*.
  minted red berry sorbet 216, *217*
  raspberry ripple basil ice cream *218*, 219
  sweet raspberry vinegar with scented geranium 239
rhubarb crumble with angelica *222*, 223
rice pudding 50
rocket 118–19, *119*

Rosa 120, 121–2, *123*
  R. damascena 121
  R. gallica 121
  R. rugosa 121
rose *120*, 121–2, *123*
  frosted petals 122
  rose elixir *240*, 241
  rose petal jelly 234, *235*
rosemary 13, 37, *124*, 125–6, *127*
  cuttings 34, *34*
  pork with fennel and rosemary *190*, 191
  rosemary and chilli oil 238
  rosemary focaccia 209
  soda bread with rosemary and sultanas 212, *213*
Rosmarinus officinalis 124, 125–6, *127*
Rumex acetosa 138–9, *139*
Rumex scutatus 139
runner beans: runner beans with summer savory *202*, 203
  runner beans with tarragon 144
Russian tarragon 145

sage *128*, 129–30, *131*
  apple sauce with sage *162*, 163
  sage and onion stuffing 129
  sage butter 129
  sage with pumpkin 130
  saltimbocca 130
salad burnet 132, *133*
salads: apple and celery leaf salad 175
  chapon 80
  crab and broad bean salad 176
  cucumber salad 70
  green and gold salad 176, *177*
  herby chicken noodle salad *178*, 179
  potato salad with dill and pickled red onion *180*, 181
  simple herb salad *174*, 175
  tabbouleh salad 106
salmoriglio sauce 165
salsa 69
salt, bay 50
saltimbocca 130
Salvia officinalis 128, 129–30, *131*
Sanguisorba minor 132, *133*
sardines, pasta with fennel and *186*, 187
Satureja hortensis 140, 141
Satureja montana 154, 155
sauces: apple sauce with sage *162*, 163
  basil and parsley pesto 166, *167*
  béarnaise sauce 160
  horseradish sauce 161
  mint sauce 163
  salmoriglio sauce 165
  sorrel sauce 164
  walnut and wild garlic pesto 166

savory *see* summer savory; winter savory
scented geranium *134*, 135–7, *136*
   scented geranium syrup 137
   scented lemonade 241
   sweet raspberry vinegar with scented geranium 239
scones, bergamot *214*, 215
seed cake 56
seedlings, growing herb *32*, 33
seeds, sowing 30–3
shade, growing herbs in 25
shiso *see* perilla
shredding herbs 18
skordalia 165
smallage *see* celery leaf
smoked mackerel and chive pâté 63
smoked salmon: borage and smoked salmon canapés 54
soda bread with rosemary and sultanas 212, *213*
soda bread with thyme, Cheddar and mustard 212
soil, growing herbs in 24–6
sorbet, minted red berry 216, *217*
sorrel 138–9, *139*
   simple herb salad *174*, 175
   sorrel sauce 164
   sorrel wine cup 243
soups: carrot soup with dill and mustard *168*, 169
   celery leaf and lovage soup 172
   chervil soup 170, *171*
   herb noodle soup 173
   Welsh onion soup 150
   wild garlic soup 153
sowing seeds 30–3
spaghetti squash with marjoram 101
spearmint *104*, 105
   mint sauce 163
   minted red berry sorbet 216, *217*
spice mixes: merguez blend 56
spring pasta with wild garlic and purple sprouting broccoli 199
squash: sage with squash 130
   spaghetti squash with marjoram 101
stews: beef stew with lovage 192
storing herbs 14–16
strawberries: minted red berry sorbet 216, *217*
stuffing, sage and onion 129
sugar: bay sugar 50
   verbena sugar 92
sultanas, soda bread with rosemary and 212, *213*
summer savory *140*, 141
   runner beans with summer savory *202*, 203
sweet cicely 142, *143*
   gooseberry and sweet cicely compote 142
sweet raspberry vinegar with scented geranium 239
Swiss chard, creamed 208, *208*
syrup: lavender scented syrup 89
   lemon verbena syrup 92

lemongrass syrup 94
scented geranium syrup 137

tabbouleh salad 106
Tagetes patula 99
tarragon 37, 144–5, *145*
   béarnaise sauce 160
   chicken with tarragon 144
   creamed Swiss chard 208, *208*
   runner beans with tarragon 144
   tarragon eggs 184, *185*
   tarragon mayonnaise 159
   tarragon vinegar 144
tart, Welsh onion 150
Tashkent mint 105
teas, herb 244, *245*
Thai basil 47
three-cornered garlic 153
thyme 13, *146*, 147–8
   soda bread with thyme, Cheddar and mustard 212
Thymus x *citriodorus* 147, 148, *149*
   T. fragrantissimus 148
   T. vulgaris 146, 147–8
tomatoes: salsa 69
   tomato sauce 50
transplanting seedlings 33
tree onion 151
Tropaeolum majus 110, *111*
truffles: white chocolate truffles with basil *228*, 229

veal: saltimbocca 130
vinegar: sweet raspberry vinegar with scented geranium 239
   tarragon vinegar 144

walnut and wild garlic pesto 166
watering herbs 35
weeds 36
Welsh onion 150–1, *151*
   Welsh onion soup 150
   Welsh onion tart 150
white beans with winter herbs 204, *205*
white chocolate truffles with basil *228*, 229
wild garlic *152*, 153
   spring pasta with wild garlic and purple sprouting broccoli 199
   walnut and wild garlic pesto 166
   wild garlic soup 153
wine: beef stew with lovage 192
   sorrel wine cup 243
winter savory *154*, 155
   stuffed breast of lamb with dried apricots and winter savory 193
wood garlic *see* wild garlic

yoghurt: mint dip/sauce 106